TUFF STUFF® 2003 Standard Catalog of®

BASKETBALL CARDS

6TH EDITION

PRICE GUIDE EDITORS OF
TUFF STUFF® MAGAZINE

Published by

krause publications
An F&W Publications Company

700 East State Street • Iola, WI 54990-0001
715-445-2214 • 888-457-2873
www.krause.com

Please call or write for our free catalog.
Our toll-free number to place an order or obtain a free catalog is 800-258-0929
or please use our regular business telephone 715-445-2214
for editorial comment and further information.

Library of Congress Catalog Number: 97-73043
ISBN: 0-87349-474-1

Printed in the United States of America

Online Tools For
Managing Your Collection
Over 1.5 Million
Cards Listed:
Baseball
Basketball
Football
Hockey
Racing
Golf
Boxing
Soccer
Wrestling
Transaction Free:
Auctions & Stores
Online:
Buy
Sell
Trade
Inventory
Reports
Discounts On:
Memorabilia &
Grading
Collectionmonster
By Card Collector Services Inc.
www.collectionmonster.com
www.ccs-cards.com

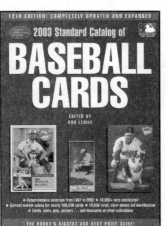

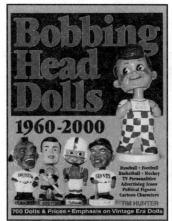

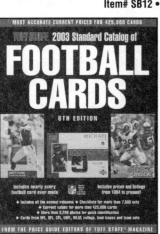

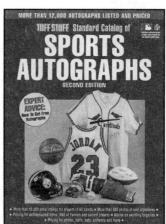

TABLE OF CONTENTS

A

B

C

D

E

F

G

H

I

J

K

L

M

N

O

P

Q

R

S

T

U

W

COLLEGE

TUFF STUFF® 2003 Standard Catalog of® BASKETBALL CARDS

ABOUT THE AUTHORS

Thank you for purchasing the sixth edition of *Tuff Stuff's Standard Catalog of Basketball Cards.*

This book is the most comprehensive annual basketball card price guide in the industry, complete with listings for more than 155,000 cards and checklists for more than 3,600 sets. The entire Krause Publications price guide staff contributed to this book, including coordinator Dan Loken and staff members Steve Bloedow, Joe Clemens and Bert Lehman.

Krause Publications' *Standard Catalog of Baseball Cards* has widely been accepted in the sports card hobby as the most comprehensive annual price guide, containing current values for nearly 500,000 cards and checklists of more than 10,000 sets. Authored each year by Bob Lemke, the *Standard Catalog of Baseball Cards* is a standard tool of trade for the serious baseball card dealer and collector.

Given the outstanding performance of the *Standard Catalog of Baseball Cards* and the rising popularity of the basketball card market, it was only natural for the price guide staff to extend the successful formula for its baseball catalog to the *Tuff Stuff's Standard Catalog of Basketball Cards.*

HOW TO USE THIS CATALOG

This catalog has been uniquely designed to serve the needs of beginning and advanced basketball card collectors. It provides a comprehensive guide to more than 70 years of sports card issues, arranged so that even the most novice collector can consult it with confidence and ease.

The following explanations summarize the general practices used in preparing this catalog's listings. However, because of specialized requirements which may vary from card set to card set, these must not be considered ironclad, but used as guidelines.

ARRANGEMENT

Because the most important feature in identifying, and pricing, a sports card is its set of origin, this catalog has been alphabetically arranged according to the name by which the set is most popularly known to collectors.

Those sets that were issued for more than one year are then listed chronologically, from earliest to most recent.

Within each set, the cards are listed by their designated card number, or in the absence of card numbers, alphabetically according to the last name of the player pictured.

IDENTIFICATION

While most modern sports cards are well identified on front, back or both, as to date and issue, such has not always been the case. In general, the back of the card is more useful in identifying the set of origin than the front. The issuer or sponsor's name will usually appear on the back since, after all, sports cards were first produced as a promotional item to stimulate sales of other products. More often than not, that issuer's name is the name by which the set is known to collectors and under which it will be found listed in this catalog.

In some difficult cases, identifying a sports card's general age, if not specific year of issue, can usually be fixed by studying the biological or statistical information on the back of the card. The last year mentioned in either the biography or stats is usually the year which preceded the year of issue.

PHOTOGRAPHS

A photograph of the front of at least one representative card from virtually every set listed in this catalog has been incorporated into the listings to aid in identification.

Photographs have been printed in reduced size. The actual size of cards in each set is given in the introductory text preceding its listing, unless the card is the standard size 2-1/2" by 3-1/2".

DATING

The dating of sports cards by year of issue on the front or back of the card itself is a relatively new phenomenon. In most cases, to accurately determine a date of issue for an unidentified card, it must be studied for clues. As mentioned, the biography, career summary or statistics on the back of the card are the best way to pinpoint a year of issue. In most cases, the year of issue will be the year after the last season mentioned on the card.

Luckily for today's collector, earlier generations have done much of the research in determining your year of issue for those cards which bear no clues. The painstaking task of matching players listed and/or pictured team against their career records often allowed an issue date to be determined.

In some cases, particular card sets were issued over a period of more than one calendar year, but since they are collected together as a single set, their specific year of issue is not important. Such sets will be listed with their complete known range of issue years.

NUMBERING

While many sports card issues as far back as the early 1900s have contained card numbers assigned by the issuer to facilitate the collecting of a complete set, the practice has by no means been universal. Even today, not every set bears card numbers.

Logically, those sports cards that were numbered by their manufacturer are presented in that numerical order within the listings of this catalog. The many unnumbered issues, however, have been assigned Tuff Stuff Card Price Guide numbers to facilitate their universal identification within the hobby, especially when buying and selling by mail.

In all cases, numbers which have been assigned or which otherwise do not appear on the card through error or by design, are shown in this catalog within parentheses. In virtually all cases, unless a more natural system suggested itself by the unique matter of a particular set, the assignment of Tuff Stuff Sports Card Price Guide numbers by the cataloging staff has been done by alphabetical arrangement of the players' last names or the card's principal title.

Significant collectible variations for any particular card are noted within the listings by the application of a suffix letter within parentheses. In instances of variations, the suffix "a" is assigned to the variation which was created first.

NAMES

The identification of a player by full name on the front of his sports card has been a common practice only since the 1940s. Prior to that, the player's name and team were the usual information found on the card front.

As a general practice, the listings in the Tuff Stuff Sports Card Price Guide present the player's name as it is more commonly known. If the player's name only appears on the back, rather than on the front of the card, the listing corresponds to that designation.

In cases where only the player's last name is given on the card, the cataloging staff has included the first name by which he was most often known for ease of identification.

Cards which contain misspelled first or last names, or even wrong initials, will have included in their listings the incorrect information, with a correction accompanying in parentheses. This extends, also, to cases where the name on the card does not correspond to the player actually pictured.

GRADING

The vast majority of cards in this book were issued between 1981 and 2002 and feature NBA players only. The term "card" is used rather loosely as in this context it is construed to include virtually any series of cardboard or paper product, of whatever size and/or shape, depicting basketball players. Further, "cards" printed on wood, metal, plastic and other materials are either by their association with other issues or by their compatibility in size with the current 2-1/2" x 3-1/2" card standard also listed here.

Because modern cards are generally not popularly collected in lower grades, cards in this section carry only a Mint (MT) value quote. In general, post-1980 cards which grade Near Mint (NM) will retail at about 75% of the Mint price, while Excellent (EX) condition cards bring 40%.

Here is a more detailed look at grading procedures:

Mint (MT): A perfect card. Well-centered, with parallel borders which appear equal to the naked eye. Four sharp, square corners. No creases, edge dents, surface scratches, paper flaws, loss of luster, yellowing or fading, regardless of age. No imperfectly printed card — out of register, badly cut or ink flawed — or card stained by contact with gum, wax or other substances can be considered truly Mint even if new out of the pack.

Near Mint (NR MT): A nearly perfect card. At first glance, a Near Mint card appears perfect; upon a closer examination, however, a minor flaw will be discovered. On well-centered cards, three of the four corners must be perfectly sharp; only one corner shows a minor imperfection upon close inspection. A slightly off-center card with one or more borders being noticeably unequal — but still present — would also fit this grade.

Excellent (EX): Corners are still fairly sharp with only moderate wear. Card borders may be off center. No creases. May have very minor gum, wax or product stains, front or back. Surfaces may show slight loss of luster from rubbing across other cards.

Very Good (VG): Shows obvious handling. Corners rounded and/or perhaps showing minor creases. Other minor creases may be visible. Surfaces may exhibit loss of luster, but all printing is intact. May show major gum, wax or other packaging stains. No major creases, tape marks or extraneous markings or writing. Exhibit honest wear.

Good (G — generally 50% of the VG price): A well-worn card, but exhibits no intentional damage or abuse. May have major or multiple creases. Corners rounded well beyond the border.

Fair (F — generally 50% of the Good price): Shows excessive wear, along with damage or abuse. Will show all the wear characteristics of a Good card, along with such damage as thumb tack holes in or near margins, evidence of having been taped or pasted, perhaps small tears around the edges, or creases so heavy as to break the cardboard. Backs may show minor added pen or pencil writing, or be missing small bits of paper. Still, basically a complete card.

Poor (P): A card that has been tortured to death. Corners or other areas may be torn off. Card may have been trimmed, show holes from a paper punch or have been used for BB gun practice. Front may have extraneous pen or pencil writing, or other defacement. Major portions of front or back design may be missing. In other words, not a pretty sight.

In addition to these terms, collectors may encounter intermediate grades, such as VG-EX or EX-MT. These cards usually have characteristics of both the lower and higher grades, and are generally priced midway between those two values.

VALUATIONS

Values quoted in this book represent the current retail market and are compiled from recommendations provided and verified through the authors' daily involvement in the publication of the hobby's leading advertising periodicals, as well as the input of specialized consultants.

It should be stressed, however, that this book is intended to serve only as an aid in evaluating cards; actual market conditions are constantly changing. This is especially true of the cards of current players, whose on-field performance during the course of a season can greatly affect the value of their cards — upwards or downward.

Publication of this book is not intended as a solicitation to buy or sell the listed cards by the editors, publishers or contributors.

Again, the values here are retail prices — what a collector can expect to pay when buying a card from a dealer. The wholesale price, that which a collector can expect to receive from a dealer when selling cards, will be significantly lower.

Most dealers operate on a 100 percent mark-up, generally paying about 50 percent of a card's retail value. On some high-demand cards, dealers will pay up to 75 percent or even 100 percent or more of retail value, anticipating continued price increases. Conversely, for many low-demand cards, such as common players' cards of recent years, dealers may pay 25 percent or even less of retail.

SETS

Collectors may note that the complete set prices for newer issues quoted in these listings are usually significantly lower than the total of the value of the individual cards which comprise the set. This reflects two factors in the sports card market. First, a seller is often willing to take a lower composite price for a complete set as a "volume discount" and to avoid inventorying a large number of common player or other lower-demand cards.

Second, to a degree, the value of common cards can be said to be inflated as a result of having a built-in overhead charge to justify the dealer's time in sorting cards, carrying them in stock and filling orders. This accounts for the fact that even brand new sports cards, which cost the dealer around 1 cent each when bought in bulk, carry individual price tags of 3 cents or higher.

ERRORS/VARIATIONS

It is often hard for the beginning collector to understand that an error on a sports card, in and of itself, does not usually add premium value to that card. It is usually only when the correcting of an error in the subsequent printing creates a variation that premium value attaches to an error.

Minor errors, such as wrong stats or personal data, create a variation that attaches to an error. Misspellings, inconsistencies, etc. — usually affecting the back of the card — are very common, especially in recent years. Unless a corrected variation was also printed, these errors are not noted in the listings of this book because they are not generally perceived by collectors to have premium value.

On the other hand, major effort had been expended to include the most complete listings ever for collectible variation cards. Many scarce and valuable variations are included in these listings because they are widely collected and often have significant premium value.

COUNTERFEITS/REPRINTS

As the value of sports cards has risen in the past 10-20 years, certain cards and sets have become too expensive for the average collector to obtain. This, along with changes in the technology of color printing, has given rise to increasing numbers of counterfeit and reprint cards.

While both terms describe essentially the same thing — a modern day copy which attempts to duplicate as closely as possible an original sports card — there are differences which are important to the collector.

Generally, a counterfeit is made with the intention of deceiving somebody into believing it is genuine, and thus paying large amounts of money for it. The counterfeiter takes every pain to try to make his fakes look as authentic as possible.

A reprint, on the other hand, while it may have been made to look as close as possible to an original card, is made with the intention of allowing collectors to buy them as substitutes for cards they may never be otherwise able to afford. The big difference is that a reprint is generally marked as such, usually on the back of the card.

In other cases, like the Topps 1952 baseball reprint set, the replicas are printed in a size markedly different from the originals. Collectors should be aware, however, that unscrupulous persons will sometimes cut off or otherwise obliterate the distinguishing word — "Reprint," "Copy," — or modern copyright date on the back of a reprint card in an attempt to pass it as genuine.

A collector's best defense against reprints and counterfeits is to acquire a knowledge of the look and feel of genuine sports cards of various eras and issues.

UNLISTED CARDS

Readers who have cards or sets which are not covered in this edition are invited to correspond with the editor for purposes of adding to the compilation of work now in progress. Address: Tuff Stuff's Standard Catalog of Basketball Cards, 700 E. State St., Iola, WI 54990. Contributors will be acknowledged in future editions.

COLLECTOR ISSUES

There exists within the hobby a great body of cards which do not fall under the scope of this catalog by virtue of their nature of having been issued solely for the collector market. Known as "collector issues," these cards and sets are distinguished from "legitimate" issues in not having been created as a sales promotional item for another product or service — bubble gum, soda, snack cakes, dog food, cigarettes, gasoline, etc.

By their nature, and principally because the person issuing them is always free to print and distribute more of the same if they should ever attain any real value, collector issues are generally regarded by collectors as having little or no premium value.

NEW ISSUES

Because new sports cards are being issued all the time, the cataloging of them remains an on-going challenge. The editor will attempt to keep abreast of new issues so that they may be added to future editions of this book. Readers are invited to submit news of new issues, especially limited-edition or regionally issued cards to the editors. Address: Tuss Stuff's Standard Catalog of Basketball Cards, 700 E. State St., Iola, WI 54990.

ACKNOWLEDGEMENTS

The editors wish to thank the many collectors, dealers and hobbyists who helped us compile, checklist and price the data contained in this edition.

HISTORY OF BASKETBALLCARDS

Bowman

In 1948, Bowman produced the first trading card set that was exclusively devoted to basketball players. Up to that point, many sets had been released, but they contained only a fraction of basketball players, usually in a mix of many other sports. The 72-card set is smaller than standard-sized cards but makes one of the larger impacts since it marked the beginning of the basketball card market. The key single in the set is clearly the rookie card of Hall of Famer George Mikan, which is one of the most important and valuable cards in the hobby.

The Bowman name returned in 1996 when Topps produced Bowman's Best Basketball, a chromium finished product that utilized Topps' Finest technology. The set included 80 cards in its base set, along with a Rookies and Throwbacks subset and four inserts.

Topps

Topps jumped into the basketball card market in 1957-58 with the second major issue set – an 80-card set that included rookie cards of all-time greats such as Bill Russell, Bob Cousy and Bob Pettit. This was followed by inactivity until 1969-70.

In 1969-70, Topps tipped off a 13-year run of basketball cards that would continue until 1981-82. The 1969-70 and 1970-71 Topps sets were oversized and difficult to store in plastic sheets or top loads. The 1969-70 set included Lew Alcindor (Kareem Abdul-Jabbar) and John Havlicek rookie cards, while the 1970-71 set featured Pete Maravich and Pat Riley's rookies as well as Lew Alcindor's second-year card.

Topps continued with basketball through the '70s and then, due to a decreasing market, produced 1980-81 Topps, which was made up of three-card panels. Although it was not a very popular set and was very difficult to collect, it did set the scene for one of the most popular cards ever in basketball – the Magic Johnson, Larry Bird and Julius Erving card that included Johnson's and Bird's rookie.

Topps ended its reign of the basketball market in 1981-82, which opened the door for Star Co. to begin filling the void for basketball collectors. The 1981-82 were releases issued as a 66-card national set and 43-card regional issues for the East, Midwest and West.

Topps reappeared in 1992-93, in the year that Shaquille O'Neal dominated the hobby. That year it produced not only its base Topps brand, but also a premium brand called Stadium Club. Both were very successful, largely due to the success of rookie Shaquille O'Neal, as well as other talented rookies including Alonzo Mourning, Latrell Sprewell, Christian Laettner, Tom Gugliotta, Clarence Weatherspoon, Robert Horry and Walt Williams.

In 1993-94, Topps unveiled its Finest brand in basketball. Finest featured chromium finished cards that first appeared in 1993 Finest Baseball and were a huge success. The Finest set was highlighted by cards of Anfernee Hardaway, Chris Webber and Vin Baker as well as the first Finest cards of Michael Jordan, Shaquille O'Neal and Larry Bird. Refractor versions of each card were also produced and soared in popularity to some of the most sought-after cards in the hobby.

Topps has also produced sets like Archives in 1992-93, Embossed in 1994-95, Gallery in 1996-97, NBA Topps Stars, which captured the NBA at 50 anniversary with the 50 greatest players of all-time in 1996, and Topps Chrome in 1996-97.

In recent years, Topps has created new sets like Heritage, Pristine, High Topps' and Xpectations. Heritage depicts classic sets from Topps past and Pristine originated the pack, within a pack, within a pack concept that collectors have proven to enjoy. These sets, as well as numerous others have brought variety to the new Topps basketball products. Topps has Shaquille O'Neal, Tim Duncan and recent draft choice Mike Dunleavy as its NBA spokesmen.

Fleer

Fleer's first shot at basketball cards came at the same time it was making its move in football and baseball cards, 1961. Fleer's premier 66-card set has a distinctive design featuring the team name in bold type in a huge box at the top of the card. Despite some design flaws, the set is one of the most popular sets ever, full of big-time rookie cards of Jerry West, Wilt Chamberlain, Elgin Baylor, Lenny Wilkens and Oscar Robertson, as well as the only cards of K.C. Jones and Sam Jones.

After 1961, Fleer took a break from basketball for the next 25 years, leaving the market to Topps and Star Co., which issued a series of scarce semi-national and regional team issues from 1982-85. Under pressure from the NBA, Star relinquished its contract, which passed to Fleer. Fleer then returned in 1986-87 with one of the most important basketball cards sets ever issued. Its 1986-87 set was complete at 132 cards and is loaded with top rookie cards, including Michael Jordan, Patrick Ewing, Isiah Thomas, Dominique Wilkins, Karl Malone, Hakeem Olajuwon and Charles Barkley. Of course, all those players were not actually rookies in that season, but since Star Co. cards were never recognized in the hobby as those players true rookie cards, Fleer's debut set contained the first cards of all of those players. Despite its relative scarcity, this set didn't pick up steam until the summer of 1989, and then it took off. It is now among the most sought-after sets of all sports sets issued in the '80s.

Fleer's second 132-card set in 1987-88 included rookie cards of Brad Daugherty, A.C. Green, Detlef Schrempf, Ron Harper, Terry Porter and Chuck Person, but is best known for its second-year card of Michael Jordan. The following year, Fleer produced its third straight 132-card set. The 1988-89 product included rookie cards of Scottie Pippen, Horace Grant, Dennis Rodman, Reggie Miller and John Stockton.

In 1992-93 Fleer produced its Ultra line of basketball cards, its first attempt at a premium set. The set contains 375 cards, which was issued in two separate series during Shaquille O'Neal's rookie season.

Fleer debuted its super premium Flair brand in 1993-94 to commemorate the USA Basketball Team. Its first regular-issue Flair product was in the 1994-95 season. It also produced the oversized Jam Session in 1993-94, and has since taken on brands such as Metal Universe and Flair Showcase, which debuted during 1996-97.

In 1996, Fleer bought SkyBox and became Fleer/SkyBox. Since the purchase, Fleer/SkyBox concentrated on consistency between its two sides, and differentiation between its Fleer and SkyBox sides.

The NBA lockout of 1998-99 stalled the use of rookies in new card issues since they hadn't signed NBA contracts. Once the lockout ended, instead of issuing Series II products for its traditional brands, Fleer/SkyBox used the opportunity to produce new brands such as SkyBox Molten Metal and Fleer Brilliants.

In 1999, Fleer became the exclusive licensee of the WNBA and has produced sets each year since. Fleer also has been the traditional sponsor of the NBA All-Star Jam Session. Jam Session is the premiere fan and collector event surrounding the NBA All-Star Weekend. In 2000, Fleer gained exclusive rights to Vince Carter making him the company's leading NBA spokesman.

Star Co.

After Topps gave up on the basketball card business in early 1983, the license to make and sell NBA cards passed to the Star Co. Star was at the time making the first of a long run of single-player baseball sets, but it entered the basketball card market at full speed, making a 276-card set that it sold in four series. Star packaged and sold its cards by series and by team.

Many of the teams in the first series are scarce because of production problems. Dallas Mavericks cards are the rarest of them all, with Celtics, Bucks, Lakers and 76ers not far behind. Although Star Co. cards carry lofty price tags, they are not actually considered rookie cards, and were the focus of many counterfeiters through the '90s, which has softened the market for Star cards.

The 1984-85 set had better production, more even distribution and a Michael Jordan card, making it one of the most expensive sets of the past decade.

Star Co. issued its final basketball set in 1985-96, but reappeared in 1990 with several player-oriented sets. Unfortunately, the Star Co. cards also reappeared during 1997 in one of the biggest scams of the decade. Claims were made that many different Star Co. sets that were never issued in the 1980s had been found in a warehouse, and were for sale. The cards were marketed heavy by such organizations as Shop at Home, but through ink testing, it was proven that the presses were actually turned back on and the cards had recently been produced with no license. This has heavily tainted the Star Co. name and made many of the cards that were in high demand unwanted by collectors.

In 2001, the grading and authenticating company, SCD Authentic, became the official source for grading and authenticating Star Co. cards. This should take out the skepticism of past years and put the value back into this product.

Upper Deck

Upper Deck's first venture into the basketball card market was in 1991-92. The company's popularity was on the rise since its debut into the sports card industry with 1989 Upper Deck Baseball. Its cards contained a hologram on the back, which made the cards impossible to counterfeit.

The 1991-92 set arrived in a high and low series containing 400 and 100 cards, respectively. The low series contained many of the top draft picks in posed pictures, such as Larry Johnson, Dikembe Mutombo, Steve Smith, Stacey Augmon and Terrell Brandon. The high series included many more rookies in action photos. Upper Deck also had a 10-card Hologram insert that was quite popular and the first hologram used in basketball.

In 1993-94 Upper Deck introduced a base brand called Collector's Choice, which retailed for a buck per pack and was tailored toward kids. In the same year, it released its first SP product in basketball. The super premium, hobby-only SP contained 165 cards and Holoview Collection inserts that also arrived in die-cut versions. In addition, Upper Deck sent SP Championship Basketball to retail locations.

In 1996-97 Upper Deck added UD Cubed to its basketball mix, then changed its Collector's Choice brand name to UD Choice in 1997-98 and added SP Authentic to its product line.

During the 1998-99 NBA lockout, Upper Deck used its relationship with Michael Jordan to produce MJx and MJ Living Legend products, which featured Jordan exclusively. In addition, throughout its remaining products, Upper Deck featured Jordan subsets and inserts in nearly every release for the 1998-99 year.

During the past few years, Upper Deck has released several new products including UD Graded, Ovation, NBA Legends, Black Diamond and several other new sets. UD Graded features the concept of adding one graded card per pack. Upper Deck continues to have Michael Jordan and Kobe Bryant as NBA spokesmen, and has recently added Jay Williams to this list of spokesmen.

Press Pass/SA•GE

Press Pass entered the basketball card market in 1996 and SA•GE in 1998. Both Press Pass and SA•GE have found a niche in the hobby with the production of first year cards of the top draft picks. The companies have gained popularity with collectors by including autograph and memorabilia cards of most if not all the top NBA draft choices for the year and releasing them well before most of the other major companies. Fans are able to get an early look at the top players, and many times the popularity of these early issues carry on into the rest of the releases.

A

1970-71 ABA All-Star 5x7 Picture Pack

This set consists of black-and-white photos of 12 ABA All-Stars. The cards measure 5" x 7", are unnumbered and have blank backs.

		NM
Complete Set (12):		60.00
Common Player:		5.00
1	Rick Barry	15.00
2	John Brisker	5.00
3	George Carter	5.00
4	Mack Calvin	5.00
5	Joe Caldwell	5.00
6	Warren Jabali	5.00
7	Larry Jones	5.00
8	George Lehmann	5.00
9	Jim McDaniel	5.00
10	Bill Melchionni	5.00
11	John Roche	5.00
12	George Thompson	5.00

1997 AT & T NBA PrePaid Phone Cards

These 29 phone cards were available through ads in AT&T and Chevron billing statements. The entire set could be purchased for $265.50 or cards could be bought individually. The twelve 15-minute cards cost $5.25 each, 30-minute cards sold for $10.50 and a sixty minute card cost $21. The cards have no expiration date. The card fronts feature two player photos against a blue background. The backs include the card information. The cards are unnumbered.

		MT
Complete Set (29):		350.00
Comp. 15 Minute Set (12):		50.00
Common 15 Minute:		5.00
Comp. 30 Minute Set (9):		100.00
Common 30 Minute:		10.00
Comp. 60 Minute Set (8):		200.00
Common 60 Minute:		20.00
1	Vin Baker 15 MIN	7.00
2	Shawn Bradley 15 MIN	5.00
3	Dale Ellis 15 MIN	5.00
4	Tom Gugliotta 15 MIN	7.00
5	Howard Juwan 15 MIN	8.00
6	Jim Jackson 15 MIN	5.00
7	Dikembe Mutombo 15 MIN	5.00
8	Bobby Phills 15 MIN	5.00
9	Dino Radja 15 MIN	5.00
10	Clifford Robinson 15 MIN	5.00
11	David Robinson 15 MIN	8.00
12	Latrell Sprewell 15 MIN	6.00
13	Greg Anthony 30 MIN	10.00
14	Brent Barry 30 MIN	10.00
15	Anfernee Hardaway 30 MIN	25.00
16	Kevin Johnson 30 MIN	12.00
17	Shawn Kemp 30 MIN	20.00
18	Karl Malone 30 MIN	15.00
19	Alonzo Mourning 30 MIN	15.00
20	Mitch Richmond 30 MIN	15.00
21	Clarence Weatherspoon 30 MIN	10.00
22	Clyde Drexler 60 MIN	30.00
23	Grant Hill 60 MIN	45.00
24	Eddie Jones 60 MIN	30.00
25	Toni Kukoc 60 MIN	25.00
26	Reggie Miller 60 MIN	25.00
27	Charles Oakley 60 MIN	20.00
28	Glen Rice 60 MIN	25.00
29	Damon Stoudamire 60 MIN	35.00

2001-02 AT & T Upper Deck L.A. Clippers Giveaway

		MT
Complete Set (9):		15.00
Common Player:		2.00
LAC1	Elton Brand	2.00
LAC2	Darius Miles	3.00
LAC3	Lamar Odom	3.00
LAC4	Corey Maggette	2.00
LAC5	Quentin Richardson	2.00
LAC6	Keyon Dooling	2.00
LAC7	Jeff McInnis	2.00
LAC8	Eric Piatkowski	2.00
LAC9	Michael Olowokandi	2.00

1990 Action Packed Promos

These unnumbered cards preview Action Packed's first card design, using its traditional gold foil stamping. Two Patrick Ewing versions exist - with a white border or a gold one. All the cards are standard size, with rounded corners, and have stats, biographical information, a color or mug shot and career highlights on the back. The card is stamped on the back as being a sample.

	MT
Complete Set (5):	400.00
Common Player:	40.00
Patrick Ewing (gold)	40.00
Patrick Ewing (white)	60.00
Magic Johnson	90.00
Michael Jordan	250.00
Sugar Ray Leonard	35.00

1993 Action Packed Hall of Fame

These card fronts feature sculptured images, gold foil and a full-bleed photo of a basketball Hall of Famer, plus the Hall of Fame's 25th Anniversary logo in gold foil. The backs feature career highlights, stats and the year of induction overlaid on the floor of a basketball court. The set has 37 Hall of Famers and a five-card Larry Bird subset. Subsets include the One-on-One cards, which feature dream matchups, and coaches cards, for enshrined coaches.

		MT
Complete Set (84):		30.00
Complete Series 1 (42):		15.00
Complete Series 2 (42):		15.00
Common Player:		.30
1	Walt Frazier	.75
2	Jerry West	1.25
3	Dave Bing	.30
4	Earl Monroe	.75
5	Willis Reed	.75
6	Dave Cowens	.60
7	Bill Bradley	.60
8	Elgin Baylor	.75
9	Elvin Hayes	.50
10	Nate Thurmond	.40
11	Red Auerbach CO	.50
12	John Wooden CO	.50
13	Red Holzman CO	.30
14	Lou Carnesecca CO	.30
15	Bob Knight CO	.50
16	Dean Smith CO	.50
17	Larry Bird	1.50
18	Larry Bird	1.50
19	Larry Bird	1.50
20	Larry Bird	1.50
21	Larry Bird	1.50
22	K.C. Jones	.30
23	Slater Martin	.30
24	Bob Wanzer	.30
25	Bob Davies	.30
26	Nate Archibald	.50
27	Bill Sharman	.40
28	Tom Gola	.30
29	Tom Heinsohn	.30
30	Clyde Lovellette	.30
31	Bob Pettit	.50
32	Dolph Schayes	.50
33	Jack Twyman	.30
34	Hal Greer	.40
35	Sam Jones	.50
36	Dave DeBusschere	.40
37	Connie Hawkins	.75
38	Jerry Lucas	.50
39	Pete Maravich	1.50
40	Oscar Robertson	1.00
41	Lenny Wilkens	.40
42	Bob Lanier	.40
43	Paul Arizin	.30
44	Harry Gallatin	.30
45	Frank Ramsey	.30
46	Ed Macauley	.30
47	Bob Kurland	.30
48	Rick Barry	.40
49	John Havlicek	.75
50	Hank Luisetti	.30
51	Wes Unseld	.40
52	Al McGuire	.50
53	Frank McGuire	.30
54	Ray Meyer	.30
55	Pete Newell	.30
56	Jack Ramsay	.30
57	Adolph Rupp	.40
58	Clarence Gaines	.30
59	Henry Iba	.50
60	Dan Issel	.40
61	Walt Bellamy	.30
62	Dick McGuire	.30
63	Calvin Murphy	.50
64	Uljana Semjonova	.30
65	Bill Walton	.60
66	Ann Meyers	.30
67	Julius Erving	1.00
68	Julius Erving	1.00
69	Julius Erving	1.00
70	Julius Erving	1.00
71	Julius Erving	1.00
72	Julius Erving	1.00
73	Larry O'Brien	.30
74	Bill Bradley	.60
75	Pete Maravich	1.50
76	Elvin Hayes	.75
77	Jerry West	1.25
78	Oscar Robertson	1.00
79	K.C. Jones	.30
80	Tom Heinsohn	.40
81	Billy Cunningham	.50
82	Red Holzman	.30
83	Bill Sharman	.40
84	Bill Sharman	.40
XXO	Oscar Robertson	4.00

1993 Action Packed Hall of Fame 24K Gold

	MT
Complete Set (84):	900.00
Complete Series 1 (42):	450.00
Complete Series 2 (42):	450.00
Common Player:	9.00
Gold Parallels:	15x-30x

1995 Action Packed Hall of Fame

This 40-card set is limited to a production run of 2,000 numbered cases and is considered a third series for the company's previous basketball effort. Each card front has a color photo which is ghosted into the background on the card back. The set logo and player's name also appear on the card front. The back is numbered and provides a player profile. Each card in the regular set is also featured as an autographed insert (one per box), except Pete Maravich's autograph appears to be short-printed. Bob Cousy and Bill Russell are not included in the regular set, but are contained in the autographed set.

		MT
Complete Set (38):		12.00
Common Player:		.30
1	Nate Archibald	.50
2	Dick McGuire	.30
3	Lou Carnesecca	.30
4	Red Holzman	.30
5	Rick Barry	.40
6	Billy Cunningham	.50
7	Connie Hawkins	.75
8	Dan Issel	.40
9	Walt Bellamy	.30
10	Elvin Hayes	.75
11	Calvin Murphy	.50
12	Bob Knight	.50
13	Al McGuire	.40
14	K.C. Jones	.30
15	Jack Ramsay	.30
16	John Wooden	.60
17	Ray Meyer	.30
18	Lenny Wilkens	.40
19	Dean Smith	.50
20	Ed Macauley	.30
21	Nate Thurmond	.40
22	Dolph Schayes	.60
23	Bill Sherman	.40
24	Jerry Lucas	.50
25	Frank Ramsey	.30
26	Pete Maravich	1.50
27	Bob Pettit	.50
28	Hal Greer	.40
29	Bill Walton	.60
30	Bill Bradley	.60
31	Tom Gola	.30
32	Carol Blazejowski	.30
33	Denny Crum	.30
34	Chuck Daly	.40
35	Buddy Jeanette	.30
36	Cesare Rubini	.30
37	Bill Bradley	.60
38	Bill Walton	.60

1995 Action Packed Hall of Fame Autographs

		MT
Common Player:		15.00
Inserted 1:box		
1	Nate Archibald	25.00
2	Dick McGuire	15.00
3	Lou Carnesecca	15.00
4	Red Holzman	15.00
5	Rick Barry	20.00
6	Billy Cunningham	25.00
7	Connie Hawkins	35.00
8	Dan Issel	20.00
9	Walt Bellamy	15.00
10	Elvin Hayes	35.00
11	Calvin Murphy	25.00
12	Bob Knight	25.00
13	Al McGuire	20.00
14	K.C. Jones	15.00
15	Jack Ramsay	15.00
16	John Wooden	30.00
17	Ray Meyer	15.00
18	Lenny Wilkens	20.00
19	Dean Smith	25.00
20	Ed Macauley	15.00
21	Nate Thurmond	20.00
22	Dolph Schayes	30.00
23	Bill Sherman	20.00
24	Jerry Lucas	25.00
25	Frank Ramsey	15.00
26	Pete Maravich	125.00
27	Bob Pettit	25.00
28	Hal Greer	20.00
29	Bill Walton	30.00
30	Bill Bradley	30.00
31	Tom Gola	15.00
32	Carol Blazejowski	15.00
33	Denny Crum	15.00
34	Chuck Daly	20.00
35	Buddy Jeanette	15.00
36	Cesare Rubini	15.00
37	Bill Bradley	30.00
38	Bill Walton	30.00
39	Bob Cousy	100.00
40	Bill Russell	400.00

1995 Action Packed Hall of Fame 24K Gold

	MT
Complete Set (38):	240.00
Common Player:	6.00
Gold Parallels:	10x-20x

1995-96 All-Star Jam Session D. Robinson

The four-card, standard-size set was distributed at the All-Star Weekend Jam Session Feb. 9-11 in San Antonio. Although the cards are from different manufacturers, each has "All-Star Weekend, San Antonio '96" printed. Production of each card was 10,500.

		MT
Complete Set (4):		25.00
Common Player:		7.00
1	David Robinson (Upper Deck)	7.00
2	David Robinson (Stadium Club)	7.00
3	David Robinson (Fleer)	7.00
4	David Robinson (SkyBox)	7.00

1996-97 All-Star Jam Session T. Brandon

This three-card set was available via wrapper redemption at the NBA All-Star Weekend Jam Session in Cleveland. The cards feature a special All-Star Weekend emblem. Only 6,200 sets were produced.

		MT
Complete Set (3):		6.00
Common Player:		2.00
1	Terrell Brandon (Ultra)	2.00
2	Terrell Brandon (SkyBox)	2.00
3	Terrell Brandon (Stadium Club)	2.00

2000 American Express Postcards

		MT
Complete Set (4):		10.00
Common Player:		1.00
1	Marcus Camby	1.00
2	Marcus Camby, Allan Houston	2.00
3	Walt Frazier	2.00
4	Shaquille O'Neal	8.00

1979 Arizona Sports Collectors Show

The 10-card, 3" x 5" set was sponsored by Scottsdale Dodge and Scottsdale Boys Club and was distributed at the 1979 Arizona Sports Collectors Show. The cards have black and white photos on the fronts with blank backs. The cards are unnumbered and feature eight baseball players and two basketball players.

	NM
Complete Set (10):	19.00
Common Player:	1.00
Jim Colborn	1.00
Jocko Conlan	3.00
Gary Gentry	1.00
Charlie Grimm	2.00
Gary Jestadt	1.00
Ken Rudolph	1.00
Mike Sadek	1.00
Dick Van Arsdale	3.50
Tom Van Arsdale	3.00
George Zuverink	1.00

1992 Australian Futera NBL

The 96-card, standard-size set, sponsored by Mitsubishi Motors, featured eight cards of each of the 12 teams. The card fronts feature the player's name along the left border with the team logo in the upper right corner. The cards are unnumbered and checklisted below alphabetically by team.

	MT
Complete Set (96):	40.00
Common Player:	.25
Mark Bradtke	1.50
Mike Corkeron	.25
Mark Davis	1.00
Jerry Dennard	.25
Butch Hays	.75
Graham Kubank	.25
Albert Leslie (ACO)	.25
Brett Maher	.25
Mike McKay	.25
Don Shipway (CO)	.25
Kym Taylor	.25
Brett Wheeler	.25
Adrian Branch	2.00
Lyndon Brieffies	.25
Greg Fox	.25
Luke Gribble	.25
Shane Heal	3.00
Brian Kerle (CO)	.25
Simon Kerle	.25
Leroy Loggins	1.50
Gordie McLeod (ACO)	.25
Andre Moore	.50
Paul Rees	.50
Blair Smith	.25
Lachlan Armfield	.50
Barry Barnes (CO)	.25
Simon Cottrell	.25
Ian Ellis (ACO)	.25
Steve Hood	1.00
Jamie Kennedy	.25
Herb McEachin	.25
Jason Reese	.25
Phil Smyth	.50
John Stelzer	.25
Matt Witkowski	.50
Mat Zauner	.25
Lanard Copeland	1.50
Andrew Gaze	2.50
Lindsay Gaze (CO)	.50
Warrick Giddey	.25
Ray Gordon	.25
Steven Lunardon	.25
Nigel Purchase	.25
Robert Sibley	.25
David Simmons	.75
Dean Vickerman	.25
Alan Westover (ACO)	.25
Steven Whitehead	.75
Glenn Binnes (ACO)	.25
Ray Borner	.50
Martin Clarke	.25
Scott Fisher	1.00
David Graham	.25
Rod Johnson	.25
Mark Leader	.25
Paul Maley	.75
Bruce Palmer (CO)	.25
Darryl Pearce	.25
Pat Reidy	.50
Andrew Simons	.25
Murray Arnold (CO)	.25
James Crawford	.75
Michael Ellis	.25
Ricky Grace	1.50
Dave Hancock (ACO)	.25
Peter Hansen	.25
Vince Hinchen	.40
Griffin Longley	.25
Tiny Pinder	3.00
Trevor Torrance	.25
Andrew Vlahov	1.00
Eric Watterson	.25
Lucas Agrums	.25
Bruce Bolden	1.00
John Dorge	.75
Brian Goorjian (CO)	.25
Andrew Howey	.25
Darren Lucas	.40
Milt Newton	1.50
Scott Ninnis	.50
Andrew Parkinson	.25
Darren Perry	.75
Tony Ronaldson	.25
Ian Stacker	.25
Jody Austin	.25
Brad Dalton	.25
Mark Dalton	.25
Tony De Ambrosis	.25
Peter Hill	.25
Damian Keogh	.50
Dwayne McClain	1.00
Ken McClary	.25
Tim Morrissey	.25
Cory Reader	.25
Bob Turner (CO)	.25
Dean Uthoff	2.00

1992 Australian Stops NBL

The 92-card, standard-size set features black-bordered glossy fronts with the player's name appearing in white letters along the top edge of the photo. The cards are numbered and grouped alphabetically by team.

		MT
Complete Set (92):		50.00
Common Player:		.50
1	Ken Watson (CO)	1.00
2	Mark Bradtke	2.00
3	Mark Davis	1.50
4	Butch Hays	1.00
5	Michael McKay	.50
6	Graham Kubank	.50
7	Leroy Loggins	1.50
8	Andre Moore	1.00
9	Shane Heal	3.00
10	Simon Kerle	.50
11	Greg Fox	.50
12	Adrian Branch	2.00
13	Jamie Kennedy	.50
14	Herb McEachin	.50
15	Phil Smyth	.50
16	Simon Cottrell	.50
17	Jason Reese (UER) (Card front says Canberra Cannons)	1.00
18	Steve Hood	1.50
19	Robert Locke	1.00
20	Cecil Exum	1.00
21	Matthew Alexander	1.00
22	Wayne Larkins	.50
23	Mike Mitchell	1.50
24	Larry Sengstock	.50
25	Andre LaFleur	1.25
26	Matthew Reece (UER) (Card front says Gold Coast Rollers)	.50
27	Ron Radliff	.50
28	Rodger Smith	.50
29	Cal Bruton (CO)	.50
30	Wayne McDaniel	1.00
31	Justin Cass	.50
32	Shane Froling	.50
33	David Stiff	.50
34	Lindsay Gaze (CO)	.75
35	Andrew Gaze	4.00
36	David Simmons	1.00
37	Stephen Whitehead	1.00
38	Warrick Giddey	.50
39	Lanard Copeland	2.00
40	Robert Sibley	.50
41	Terry Dozier	2.00
42	Michael Johnson	.50
43	Al Green	.50
44	Paul Kuiper	.50
45	Bruce Palmer (CO)	.50
46	Scott Fisher	1.25
47	Ray Borner	.50
48	Paul Maley	1.00
49	Pat Reidy	.75
50	Mark Leader	.50
51	Darryl Pearce (UER) (Card front says North Melbourne Giants)	.50
52	Murray Arnold (CO)	.50
53	Ricky Grace	2.00
54	Andrew Vlahov	1.00
55	Tiny Pinder (SP)	2.00
56	James Crawford	1.25
57	Mike Ellis	.50
58	Vince Hinchen (UER) (Card front says Perth Wilcats)	1.00
59	Perth Team Photo	.75
60	Justin Withers	.75
61	Greg Hubbard	.75
62	Chuck Harmison	1.25
63	Melvin Thomas	1.50
64	Doug Overton	3.00
65	Brian Goorjian (CO)	.50
66	Bruce Bolden	1.50
67	Darren Lucas	.50
68	Darren Perry	.75
69	John Dorge	.50
70	Andrew Parkinson	.75
71	Scott Ninnis	1.00
72	Bob Turner (CO)	.50
73	Dean Uthoff	2.00
74	Damian Keogh	1.00
75	Dwayne McClain	3.00
76	Ken McClary	1.00
77	Tim Morrissey	.50
78	Mark Dalton	.50
79	The Jester (Sydney Kings mascot)	.75
80	Balmy (Melbourne Tigers mascot)	.75
81	Eddie Crouch (REF)	.50
82	Jim Pappas (CO)	.50
83	Debbie Black	.50
84	Joanne Moyle	.50
85	Australian Women's Team	.75
86	Annie Burgess	.50
87	Dandenong Rangers Team Photo	.75
88	Ballarat Miners (Eric Cooks)	.50
89	Knox Raiders Team Photo	.75
90	Checklist	.50
91	Ricky Grace (SP) (Back to Back Champions)	2.00
92	Logo Card (SP)	2.00

1993 Australian Futera NBL

The 110-card, standard-size set features white borders on the glossy fronts with the backs containing player stats and career highlights in a gray box. The cards are numbered and listed alphabetically by team.

		MT
Complete Set (110):		30.00
Common Player:		.15
1	Chris Blakemore	.75
2	Brett Maher	.15
3	Phil Smyth	.40
4	Scott Ninnis	.40
5	Mark Davis	1.00

6 Mike McKay .15
7 Jerry Dennard .15
8 Nigel Purchase .15
9 Shane Heal 2.00
10 Larry Loggins 1.00
11 Dave Colbert .40
12 Andre Moore .50
13 Rodger Smith .15
14 Luke Gribble .15
15 Shane Froling .15
16 Lachlan Armfield .40
17 John Stelzer .15
18 Simon Cottrell .15
19 Rodney Monroe 1.50
20 Fred Herzog .50
21 Matt Witkowski .40
22 Adam Kendrick .15
23 Justin Withers .40
24 Michael Morrison .50
25 Cecil Exum .50
26 Ray Borner .25
27 Adrian Branch 1.50
28 Wayne Larkins .15
29 Alex Hetenyi .15
30 Vince Hinchen .25
31 Mike Mitchell 1.00
32 Andre LaFleur .75
33 Andrew Goodwin .15
34 Greg Fox .15
35 Matthew Reece .15
36 Peter Hill .15
37 Chuck Harmison 1.50
38 Butch Hays .50
39 Melvin Thomas .75
40 Chris Steele .15
41 Dene MacDonald .15
42 Mike Corkeron .15
43 Wayne McDaniel .50
44 Jim Havrilla .15
45 Donald Whiteside .40
46 David Close .15
47 Neil Turner .15
48 Anthony Stewart .25
49 Justin Cass .15
50 Andrew Svaldenis .15
51 Warrick Giddey .15
52 Andrew Gaze 2.00
53 Mark Bradtke 1.50
54 Lanard Copeland 1.50
55 Ray Gordon .15
56 Stephen Whitehead .15
57 Robert Sibley .15
58 David Simmons .50
59 Shawn Dennis .15
60 Michael Johnson .15
61 Everette Stephens 1.00
62 Al Green .15
63 Grant Kruger .15
64 Jason Joynes .15
65 Terry Dozier 1.50
66 Peter Harvey .15
67 Paul Kuiper .15
68 Terry Johnson .15
69 Darryl Pearce .15
70 Mark Leader .15
71 Larry Sengstock .15
72 Pat Reidy .15
73 Jason Reese .50
74 Rod Johnson .15
75 Paul Rees .30
76 Paul Maley .50
77 Scott Fisher .75
78 James Crawford .50
79 Andrew Vlahov 1.00
80 Eric Watterson .15
81 Ricky Grace 1.00
82 Chris Carroll .15
83 Trevor Torrance .15
84 Steve Davis .15
85 David Blades .15
86 Rimas Kurtinaitis .75
87 Ricky Jones .50
88 Lucas Agrums .15
89 Graham Kubank .15
90 Tonny Jensen .15
91 Paul Simpson .15
92 Darren Perry .50
93 Bruce Bolden .75
94 Robert Rose 1.00
95 Darren Lucas .25
96 Andrew Parkinson .15
97 Tony Ronaldson .40
98 Shane Bright .15
99 David Graham .15
100 Simon Kerle .15
101 Andre Lemamis UER (Misspelled Andrej on back) .15
102 John Dorge .50
103 Dwayne McClain .75
104 Damiam Keogh .40
105 Ken McClary .15
106 Tony De Ambrosis .15
107 Greg Hubbard .40
108 Tim Morrissey .15
109 Dean Uthoff 1.50
110 Mark Dalton .15
NNO Melbourne Magic 20.00
NNO Legends Card (Herb McEachin) 30.00

1993 Australian Futera Best of Both Worlds

Randomly inserted into foil packs, the insert set was a redemption offer for the four cards of NBL players who previously played in the NBA. Only 500 cards were produced and each redeemed card was accompanied by a certification card.

MT
Complete Set (8): 150.00
Common Player: 5.00
1 Terry Dozier 40.00
1R Redemption Card 5.00
2 Dwayne McClain 40.00
2R Redemption Card 5.00
3 Adrian Branch 40.00
3R Redemption Card 5.00
4 Doug Overton 40.00
4R Redemption Card 5.00

1993 Australian Futera Honours Awards

The 11-card set was randomly inserted into packs with the production of each card held at 1,000. The fronts have color action shots with the backs having a close-up with season highlights.

MT
Complete Set (11): 200.00
Common Player: 7.50
1 Scott Fisher MVP 20.00
2 Andrew Gaze MVP 25.00
3 Andrew Svaudenis MIP 7.50
4 Terry Dozier D-POY 20.00
5 Lachlan Armfield ROY 7.50
6 Brian Goorjian COY 7.50
7 Doug Overton 1st 20.00
8 Andrew Gaze 1st 30.00
9 Dwayne McClain 1st 20.00
10 Andrew Vlahov 1st 25.00
11 Scott Fisher 1st 20.00

1993 Australian Futera Super Gold

The 14-card, standard-size set was randomly inserted into Futera packs with production held at 1,000. "Super Gold Card" is printed along the top border with the horizontal backs season highlights and statistics.

MT
Complete Set (14): 120.00
Common Player: 7.50
1 John Dorge 7.50
2 Lanard Copeland 20.00
3 Pat Reidy 7.50
4 Cecil Exum 7.50
5 Melvin Thomas 15.00
6 Dean Uthoff 7.50
7 Terry Dozier 20.00
8 Mark Davis 20.00
9 Rimas Kurtinaitis 15.00
10 Shane Heal 28.00
11 Mike Mitchell 15.00
12 Justin Withers 7.50
13 Ricky Grace 30.00
14 Donald Whiteside 7.50

1993 Australian Stops NBL

The 92-card, standard-size set features white borders on the glossy front. The player's name appears along the top edge. The team name appears in black along the bottom edge next to "STOPS '92." The backs contained a player shot with bio information and the team logo.

MT
Complete Set (92): 50.00
Common Player: .50
1 Terry Dozier 1.00
2 Steve Hood SD 1.00
3 Shane Heal 1.75
4 Tim Morrissey .50
5 Cecil Exum .50
6 Andrew Svaldenis .50
7 Andrew Goodwin .50
8 Al Green .50
9 Wayne McDaniel .50
10 Couch REF, Mildenhall REF .50
11 Cal Bruton CO .50
12 American All-Stars 1.00
13 Craig Adams .50
14 Stephen Whitehead .50
15 Michael Johnson .50
16 Everette Stephens 2.00
17 Donald Whiteside .50
18 Michael McKay .50
19 Grant Kruger .50
20 James Crawford .75
21 Paul Maley .50
22 Pat Reidy .50
23 Australian Boomers .50
24 Trevor Torrance .50
25 Luc Longley 6.00
26 Chuck Harmison 1.00
27 Tony Ronaldson .50
28 Tony DeAmbosis .50
29 Mark Davis .50
30 Lanard Copeland SD 1.00
31 Darren Perry .75
32 Everette Stephens SD 1.00
33 Checklist .75
34 Andrew Parkinson .50
35 David Simmons .50
36 Warrick Giddey .50
37 Phil Smyth .50
38 Scott Ninnis .50
39 Leroy Loggins 1.50
40 Rodney Monroe 2.00
41 Lachlan Armfield .75
42 Michael Morrison .50
43 Ray Borner .50
44 Mike Mitchell 1.50
45 Andre LaFleur .75
46 Andrew Vlahov .75
47 Scott Fisher .75
48 Dean Uthoff 1.00
49 Bruce Bolden 1.00
50 Greg Hubbard .75
51 Damiam Keogh .75
52 Rimas Kurtinaitis 1.00
53 Adrian Branch 2.00
54 Vince Hinchen .50
55 Ricky Jones .50
56 Paris McCurdy 1.00
57 Brett Maher .50
58 Shane Froling .50
59 1992 Magic Champs .50
60 Andre Moore .50
61 Fred Herzog .50
62 Justin Withers .50
63 Graham Kubank .50
64 Wayne Larkins .50
65 Lucas Agrums .50
66 Matthew Reese .50
67 Jim Havrilla .75
68 Chris Steele .50
69 Ray Gordon .50
70 Mark Bradtke 1.00
71 Larry Sengstock .50
72 Darryl Pearce .50
73 Rod Johnson .50
74 Brett Brown CO .50
75 Jason Reese .50
76 Ricky Grace 1.50
77 Darren Lucas .50
78 Bruce Palmer CO .50
79 Tigerman .75
80 Robert Sibley .50
81 Robert Rose 1.00
82 David Graham .50
83 Ken McClary .50
84 Dwayne McClain 2.00
85 Brian Goorjian CO .50
86 Peter Hill .50
87 Butch Hays .50
88 Andrew Gaze 3.00
89 Tony Jensen .50
90 Melvin Thomas .50
91 Lanard Copeland 2.00
92 Checklist 1.00

1994 Australian Futera NBL Promos

The five-card, standard-size promo pack was given away at the 1994 National Convention in Houston. The player's name was printed in gold along the bottom front edge with the National logo appearing in the upper right corner. Set production was limited to 5,000 sets. Cards are numbered with an "RC" prefix.

MT
Complete Set (5): 6.00
Common Player: .75
1 Allan Border (Cricket) .75
2 Conan Hayes (Surfing) .75
3 David Nilsson (Baseball) 2.00
4 Mark Bosnich (Soccer) .75
5 Andrew Gaze (Basketball) 2.00

1994 Australian Futera NBL

The 220-card, standard-size set had two versions - U.S. and Australian - with the U.S. version having a silver-foil "World Export Edition" seal. The fronts have the player's name down the right edge with the backs featuring another color shot and a player profile.

MT
Complete Set (220): 45.00
Complete Series 1 (110): 23.00
Complete Series 2 (110): 23.00
Common Player (1-110): .15
Common Player (111-220): .15
1 Phil Smyth .25
2 Scott Ninnis .40
3 Brett Maher .15
4 Mike McKay .15
5 Mark Davis .40
6 David Robinson .15
7 Dave Colbert .25
8 Shane Froling .15
9 Rodger Smith .15
10 Leroy Loggins 1.00
11 Andre Moore .25
12 Shane Heal 1.50
13 Luke Gribble .15
14 Rodney Monroe 1.00
15 Justin Withers .25
16 Matt Witlowski .15
17 Fred Herzog .25
18 Lachlan Armfield .15
19 John Stelzer .15
20 Wayne Larkins .15
21 Adrian Branch 1.00
22 Cecil Exum .15
23 Ray Borner .25
24 Michael Morrison .15
25 Vince Hinchen .25
26 Andrew Goodwin .15
27 Andre LaFleur .40
28 John Szigetti .15
29 Matthew Reece .15
30 Mike Mitchell .75
31 Greg Fox .15
32 Justin Cass .15
33 David Close .15
34 Andrew Svaldenis .15
35 Donald Whiteside .25
36 Wayne McDaniel .25
37 Anthony Stewart .25
38 Butch Hays .15
39 Chris Steele .15
40 Melvin Thomas .40
41 Dene MacDonald .15
42 Chuck Harmison 1.25
43 Mike Corkeron .15
44 Lanard Copeland 1.00
45 Stephen Whitehead .15
46 Robert Sibley .15
47 Mark Bradtke 1.00
48 Andrew Gaze 1.50
49 David Simmons .40
50 Warrick Giddey .15
51 Michael Johnson .15
52 Al Green .15
53 Peter Harvey .15
54 Everette Stephens .50
55 Grant Kruger .15
56 Terry Dozier 1.00
57 Simon O'Donnell .15
58 Paul Maley .50
59 Darryl Pearce .15
60 Mark Leader .15
61 Jason Reese .40
62 Rod Johnson .15
63 Pat Reidy .25
64 Paul Rees [illegible]
65 Larry Sengstock .15
66 Trevor Torrance .15
67 Andrew Vlahov .75
68 James Crawford .40
69 Ricky Grace 1.00
70 Scott Fisher .50
71 Eric Watterson .15
72 Chris Carroll .15
73 Darren Lucas .25
74 Bruce Bolden .50
75 Robert Rose .75
76 John Dorge .40
77 Andrew Parkinson .15
78 David Graham .15
79 Darren Perry .40
80 Tony Ronaldson .40
81 Greg Hubbard .40
82 Dwayne McClain .75
83 Ken McClary .15
84 Tim Morrissey .15
85 Damian Keogh .25
86 Tony De Ambrosis .15
87 Dean Uthoff 1.25
88 Wayne Womack .40
89 David Blades .15
90 Ricky Jones .40
91 Rimas Kurtinaitis .15
92 Brian Andrews .15
93 Lucas Agrums .15
94 Tonny Jensen .15
95 Paul Simpson .15
96 Darrin Smith .15
97 MVP Award (Robert Rose) .40
98 Most Efficient Player (Andrew Gaze) 1.00
99 Top Point Scorer (Andrew Gaze) 1.00
100 Best Defensive Player (Terry Dozier) .50
101 Good Hands Award (Andre LaFleur) .25
102 Top Rebounder (Bruce Bolden) .25
103 Rookie of the Year (Chris Blakemore) .40
104 Most Improved Player (Scott Ninnis) .25
105 Int'l. POY (Andrew Vlahov) .40
106 Coach of the Year (Alan Black) .25
107 Checklist 1-37 .15
108 Checklist 38-80 .15
109 Checklist 81-110 .15
110 Checklist Specials .15
111 Robert Rose .75
112 Mark Davis .75
113 Chris Blakemore .50
114 Phil Smyth .25
115 Brett Maher .15
116 Mike McKay .15
117 David Colbert .15
118 Shane Heal 1.50
119 Leroy Loggins .75
120 Andre Moore .25
121 Robert Sibley .30
122 Jason Reese .15
123 Lachlan Armfield .30
124 Fred Herzog .30
125 Justin Withers .25
126 Adam Kendrick .15
127 Everette Stephens .50
128 Ray Borner .15
129 Cecil Exum .35
130 Simon Kerle .15
131 Mike Mitchell .50
132 Matthew Reece .15
133 Tony De Ambrosis .15
134 Andre LaFleur .40
135 Peter Hill .15
136 Calvin Talford 1.00
137 Darren Perry .25
138 Wayne McDaniel .25
139 Anthony Stewart .25
140 Keith Nelson .15
141 Butch Hays .50
142 Melvin Thomas .30
143 Chuck Harmison 1.25
144 Chris Steele .15
145 Dene MacDonald .15
146 Lanard Copeland .75
147 David Simmons .25
148 Mark Bradtke 1.25
149 Andrew Gaze 1.25
150 Warrick Giddey .15
151 Ray Gordon .15
152 Derek Rucker .75
153 Terry Dozier .75
154 Tonny Jensen .15
155 Grant Kruger .15
156 Paul Kuiper .15
157 Darryl McDonald 1.50
158 Paul Maley .50
159 Mark Leader .15
160 Larry Sengstock .15
161 Pat Reidy .25
162 Paul Rees .30
163 Ricky Grace 1.00
164 James Crawford .40
165 Andrew Vlahov .75
166 Scott Fisher .50
167 Martin Cattalini .15
168 Adonis Jordan 1.50
169 Darren Lucas .25
171 Andrew Parkinson .15
172 Tony Ronaldson .40
173 David Graham .15
174 Mario Donaldson .15
175 Leon Trimmingham 1.50
176 Tim Morrissey .15
177 Greg Hubbard .40
178 Dean Uthoff .75
179 Damian Keogh .75
180 Brendan LeGassick .15
181 Ricky Jones .50
182 Lucas Agrums .15
183 Graham Kubank .15
184 1993 Finals Series Perth Defeats Brisbane .15
185 1993 Finals Series Melbourne Defeats SE Melbourne .15
186 1993 Finals Series Melbourne Leads Perth .15
187 1993 Finals Series Perth Squares the Series .15
188 1993 Finals Series Melbourne Defeats Perth .15
189 1993 Finals Series Grand Final MVP .15
190 1993 Finals Series Victory At Last .15
191 Lanard Copeland, Andrew Gaze 1.00
192 Ricky Grace, James Crawford .60
193 Andre LaFleur, Mike Mitchell .50
194 Shane Heal, Leroy Loggins 1.00
195 Melvin Thomas, Butch Hays .75
196 Leon Trimmingham, Mario Donaldson .75
197 Patrick Reidy, Darryl McDonald .75
198 Sam MacKinnon 1.50
199 C.J. Bruton .50
200 Aaron Trahair 1.00
201 Brad Williams .15
202 Ryan Knights .15
203 Darrin Smith .15
204 Opals Header .15
204A Jenny Whittel .50
205 Annie Burgess .15
206 Sandy Brondello .15
207 Allison Cook .15
208 Michele Timms 5.00
209 Shelley Gorman .40
210 Robyn Maher .15
211 Trish Fallon .50
212 Rachael Sport .15
213 Karen Dalton .15
214 Michelle Brogan .75
215 Samantha Thornton .15
216 Tom Maher .15
217 Checklist 111-151 .15
218 Checklist 152-183 .15
219 Checklist 184-220 .15
220 Checklist Specials .15

1994 Australian Futera Best of Both Worlds

The insert set was randomly inserted into every 300 packs and featured players who previously had NBA experience. The cards were individually numbered out of 1,000 with each of the two series having redemption cards. The expiration date for the first series was December 31, 1994 with the second series at August 31, 1995.

MT
Complete Set (12): 425.00
Common Player: 30.00
BW1 Picture Card (Ricky Grace) 30.00
BW2 Picture Card (Lanard Copeland) 30.00
BW3 Picture Card (Andrew Gaze) 50.00
BW4 Picture Card (Adonis Jordan) 50.00
CC3 Certification Card (Andrew Gaze) 50.00
CC4 Certification Card (Adonis Jordan) 50.00
CD1 Certification Card (Ricky Grace) 30.00
CD2 Certification Card (Lanard Copeland) 30.00
RC3 Redemption Card (Andrew Gaze) 50.00
RC4 Redemption Card (Adonis Jordan) 50.00
RD1 Redemption Card (Ricky Grace) 30.00
RD2 Redemption Card (Lanard Copeland) 30.00

1994 Australian Futera Defensive Giants

Randomly inserted into Series II packs, the seven-card, standard-size insert set highlights the top defensive players of the league. Production was limited to 3,000 and each card is individually numbered with a "DG" prefix. The card fronts feature the player's name in gold foil while the backs have career summaries.

MT
Complete Set (7): 75.00
Common Player: 5.00
1 Terry Dozier 8.00
2 Robert Rose 15.00
3 Darren Lucas 5.00
4 Melvin Thomas 15.00
5 Derek Rucker 15.00
6 Mark Davis 15.00
7 Mark Bradtke 15.00

1994 Australian Futera Lords of the Ring

Randomly inserted into foil packs, the 12-card set focuses on the best dunkers in the league. The fronts show the players dunking while the backs contain player profiles. Cards are numbered with a "LR" prefix.

MT
Complete Set (12): 70.00
Common Player: 4.00
1 Robert Rose 8.00
2 Lanard Copeland 8.00
3 Ricky Jones 4.00
4 Mark Bradtke 8.00
5 David Simmons 5.00
6 Andrew Vlahov 10.00
7 James Crawford 10.00
8 Bruce Bolden 10.00
9 Mike Mitchell 8.00
10 Darryl McDonald 15.00
11 Paul Maley 8.00
12 Leon Trimmingham 15.00

1994 Australian Futera NBL Heroes

The 14-card, standard-size set highlights the careers of NBL legends Leroy Loggins (1-7, Series I) and Scott Fisher (8-14, Series II). Just 5,000 of each card was produced and each card is individually numbered with a "NH" prefix.

MT
Complete Set (14): 30.00
Common Player: 2.50
1 Leapin' Leroy Drawing (Leroy Loggins) 4.00
2 1989 (Leroy Loggins) 3.00
3 1990 (Leroy Loggins) 3.00
4 1991 (Leroy Loggins) 3.00
5 1992 (Leroy Loggins) 3.00
6 1993 (Leroy Loggins) 3.00
7 Olympic Career (Leroy Loggins) 3.00
8 Drawing (Scott Fisher) 4.00
9 1988 (Scott Fisher) 2.50
10 1989 (Scott Fisher) 2.50
11 1990 (Scott Fisher) 2.50
12 1991 (Scott Fisher) 2.50
13 1992 (Scott Fisher) 2.50
14 1993 (Scott Fisher) 2.50

1994 Australian Futera New Horizons

Randomly inserted into Series II packs, the six-card set focuses on the young stars of the league. The card fronts have a player action shot over that player's city skyline. Just 3,000 of the individually numbered cards were produced. Each card carries a "HZ" prefix.

MT
Complete Set (6): 50.00
Common Player: 5.00
1 Calvin Talford 7.50
2 Darryl McDonald 12.00
3 Leon Trimmingham 12.00
4 Mario Donaldson 5.00
5 Adonis Jordan 10.00
6 Keith Jordan 5.00

1994 Australian Futera Offensive Threats

Randomly inserted in Series I packs, the 14-card, standard-size set was limited to a production total of 5,000. The cards are individually numbered with an "OT" prefix, while the backs have career summaries on a green panel.

MT
Complete Set (14): 45.00
Common Player: 4.00
1 Andrew Gaze 10.00
2 Ricky Jones 4.00
3 Adrian Branch 6.00
4 Jason Reese 4.00
5 Melvin Thomas 4.00
6 Rodney Monroe 6.00
7 Dwayne McClain 6.00
8 Scott Fisher 6.00
9 Leroy Loggins 6.00
10 Mike Mitchell 6.00
11 Mark Davis 4.00
12 Bruce Bolden 6.00
13 Everette Stephens 6.00
14 Wayne McDaniel 4.00

1994 Australian Futera Signature Series

The seven-card, Second Series set features signed cards of some of the league's top players. Just 500 of each of the serially numbered cards were produced. They each carry a "SS" prefix.

MT
Complete Set (7): 375.00
Common Player: 20.00
1 Checklist 20.00
2 Calvin Talford 50.00
3 Darryl McDonald 100.00
4 Mario Donaldson 50.00
5 Leon Trimmingham 100.00
6 Andrew Vlahov 60.00
7 Bruce Bolden 50.00

1995 Australian Futera NBL

The 110-card, first-series release was issued in nine-card packs. The fronts have a player action shot with the player's name and team logo running along a side in a red stripe. The backs bio and stat information with season and career highlights.

MT
Complete Set (110): 24.00
Common Player: .15
1 Darryl McDonald 1.00
2 Ricky Grace .75
3 Fred Cofield 1.00
4 Brett Maher .15
5 Lanard Copeland .75
6 Dean Uthoff 1.00
7 Everette Stephens .50
8 Andre LaFleur .40
9 Graham Kubank .15
10 Luke Gribble .15
11 Darryl Johnson .15
12 Mike Corkeron .15
13 Keith Nelson .15
14 Greg Hubbard .15
15 Robert Rose .75
16 Andrew Vlahov .75
17 Paul Kuiper .15
18 Wayne McDaniel .25
19 Jason Reese .30
20 Justin Cass .15
21 Butch Hays .50
22 Paul Maley .50
23 Dave Simmons .15
24 Mike Mitchell .75
25 Bruce Bolden .40
26 David Colbert .15

27	Pat Reidy	.25
28	Mark Dalton	.15
29	Chris Blakemore	.50
30	Checklist 1-44	.15
31	Simon Kerle	.15
32	Chris Steele	.15
33	Paul Rees	.30
34	Warrick Giddey	.15
35	Doug Peacock	.15
36	Damian Keogh	.25
37	Michael Johnson	.15
38	Justin Withers	.25
39	Aaron Trahair	.50
40	Leroy Loggins	.75
41	Mark Leader	.15
42	Anthony Stewart	.25
43	Adonis Jordan	1.50
44	Scott Ninnis	.40
45	Leon Trimmingham	1.50
46	David Blades	.15
47	Grant Kruger	.15
48	Robert Sibley	.15
49	Vince Hinchen	.25
50	Chuck Harmison	1.00
51	Matthew Alexander	.15
52	Simon Cottrell	.15
53	Tony De Ambrosis	.15
54	Calvin Talford	1.00
55	Sam MacKinnon	.75
56	Martin Cattalini	.15
57	Mike McKay	.15
58	Larry Sengstock	.15
59	Andrew Gaze	2.00
60	Checklist 45-88	.15
61	Rodger Smith	.15
62	Melvin Thomas	.30
63	Peter Hill	.15
64	Mario Donaldson	.15
65	Darren Perry	.25
66	Matt Witkowski	.25
67	Derek Rucker	.75
68	Cecil Exum	.50
69	Lucas Agrums	.15
70	Darren Lucas	.25
71	Mark Bradtke	1.00
72	Mark Davis	.75
73	Peter Harvey	.15
74	Ray Borner	.25
75	Dene MacDonald	.15
76	John Dorge	.25
77	Ricky Jones	.30
78	Shane Heal	1.50
79	Terry Dozier	.75
80	Paul Crombie	.15
81	Stephen Whitehead	.15
82	Lachlan Armfield	.30
83	James Crawford	.40
84	Cameron Dickinson	.15
85	Tony Ronaldson	.40
86	Scott Fisher	.50
87	Andrew Parkinson	.15
88	Ray Gordon	.15
89	Checklist 89-110	.15
90	Giants vs Magic Semi-Finals	.15
91	Sixers vs Tigers Semi-Finals	.15
92	Sixers vs Giants Semi-Finals	.15
93	Giants vs Sixers Semi-Finals	.15
94	N Melbourne Giants Championship Team	.15
95	Paul Rees	.30
96	Shane Heal	1.50
97	Derek Rucker	.50
98	Shane Heal	1.50
99	Mark Bradtke	1.00
100	Keith Nelson	.30
101	Andrew Gaze	1.00
102	Darryl McDonald	.50
103	Sam MacKinnon	.50
104	Brett Brown	.30
105	Andrew Gaze	1.00
106	Darren Lucas	.30
107	Chris Blakemore	.50
108	Mark Bradtke	1.00
109	Checklist	.15
110	Checklist Specials	.15

1995 Australian Futera Airborne

The nine-card, standard-size insert set features players in the league with outstanding jumping ability. The card front has the player over a speckled background with the backs having descriptive narratives. Cards are numbered with a "NA" prefix.

		MT
Complete Set (9):		5.00
Common Player:		.50
1	Sam MacKinnon	1.50
2	Butch Hays	.75
3	Paul Maley	.75
4	Calvin Talford	.75
5	Mike Mitchell	1.00
6	Dave Simmons	.50
7	Ricky Jones	.50
8	Darryl McDonald	2.00
9	Checklist	.50

1995 Australian Futera Clutchmen

The 15-card, standard-size set highlights the "Clutchmen" of the league with the insert title running down the right border. The backs contain a player profile. Cards are numbered with a "CM" prefix.

		MT
Complete Set (15):		15.00
Common Player:		.50
1	Robert Rose	1.00
2	Leroy Loggins	2.00
3	Fred Cofield	.50
4	Cecil Exum	.50
5	Doug Peacock	.50
6	Darren Perry	.50
7	Butch Hays	.75
8	Andrew Gaze	2.00
9	Derek Rucker	2.00
10	Darryl McDonald	2.00
11	Ricky Grace	1.50
12	Tony Ronaldson	.50
13	Leon Trimmingham	.50
14	Cameron Dickinson	2.00
15	Checklist	.50

1995 Australian Futera Head to Head

Randomly inserted into Series I packs, the six die-cut, double-sided cards feature 12 NBL stars. The cards are individually numbered with a "H" prefix out of 5,000 5,000 and were inserted every 23 packs.

		MT
Complete Set (6):		100.00
Common Player:		10.00
1	Andrew Gaze, Darren Lucas	30.00
2	Leroy Loggins, Robert Rose	30.00
3	Leon Trimmingham, Ricky Jones	25.00
4	Melvin Thomas, Keith Nelson	15.00
5	Fred Cofield, Tony Jensen	10.00
6	Peter Hill, Simon Kerle	10.00

1995 Australian Futera Instant Impact

The six-card, standard-size highlights new players to the league and was numbered out of 2,500. The cards were inserted every 53 packs and feature gold foil on the front. Cards are numbered with an "II" prefix.

		MT
Complete Set (6):		100.00
Common Player:		10.00
1	Darryl McDonald	20.00
2	Sam MacKinnon	20.00
3	Leon Trimmingham	25.00
4	Chris Blakemore	10.00
5	Derek Rucker	20.00
6	Calvin Talford	10.00

1995 Australian Futera MVP/Rookie Redemption

Randomly inserted into foil packs, the three-card set featured 1994-95 MVP Andrew Gaze and Rookie of the Year Sam MacKinnon. The card was signed by both players and a redemption card for it was inserted every 3,200 packs. Cards are numbered with a "MR" prefix.

		MT
Complete Set (3):		275.00
Common Player:		25.00
1	Redemption Card	25.00
2	Andrew Gaze, Sam MacKinnon	225.00
3	Certification Card	25.00

1995 Australian Futera Star Challenge

The 10-card, standard-size set was inserted every 16 packs and highlights players from the 1994 All-Star Challenge in Sydney. The cards are individually numbered out of 5,000. They carry a "NBL" prefix.

		MT
Complete Set (10):		40.00
Common Player:		2.50
1	Tony Ronaldson	5.00
2	Paul Rees	2.50
3	Mark Bradtke	5.00
4	Andrew Gaze	10.00
5	Shane Neal	6.00
6	Derek Rucker	6.00
7	Butch Hays	5.00
8	Mario Donaldson	2.50
9	Leon Trimmingham	10.00
10	Lanard Copeland	6.00

1995 Australian Futera 300 Club

The 17-card insert set features players who have played in 300 or more NBL games. The cards depict a peel-away corner which reveals the number of games the player has played. Cards are numbered with a "GC" prefix.

		MT
Complete Set (17):		10.00
Common Player:		.50
1	Larry Sengstock	.50
2	Leroy Loggins	1.00
3	Damian Keogh	.50
4	Herb McEachin	.50
5	James Crawford	.75
6	Al Green	.50
7	Ray Borner	.50
8	Darryl Pearce	.50
9	Michael Johnson	.50
10	Phil Smyth	.50
11	Chuck Harmison	.50
12	Mike Ellis	.50
13	Tim Morrissey	.50
14	Simon Cottrell	.50
15	Eric Waterson	.50
16	Mike McKay	.50
17	Checklist	.50

1995 Australian Futera Abdul-Jabbar Adidas Promo

The four-card promo set was issued to promote the 1995 Adidas Streetball Challenge. The cards are individually numbered out of 5,000 and the fronts depict various action shots of Abdul-Jabbar. They carry a "K" prefix.

		MT
Complete Set (4):		40.00
Common Player:		10.00
1	Kareem Abdul-Jabbar (Blocking shot)	10.00
2	Kareem Abdul-Jabbar (Playing defense)	10.00
3	Kareem Abdul-Jabbar (Wearing road uniform)	10.00
4	Kareem Abdul-Jabbar (Sky-Hook)	10.00

1996 Australian Futera NBL

		MT
Complete Set (100):		20.00
Common Player:		.15
1	Mark Davis	.25
2	Brett Maher	.15
3	Chris Blakemore	.15
4	Scott Ninnis	.15
5	Robert Rose	.15
6	Mike McKay	.15
7	Leroy Loggins	1.00
8	Mike Mitchell	.25
9	Robert Sibley	.15
10	Andrew Goodwin	.15
11	Shane Heal	2.00
12	John Rillie	.15
13	Ray Borner	.15
14	Jamie Pearlman	.15
15	David Close	.15
16	Simon Dwight	.15
17	Lachlan Armfield	.15
18	Jervaughn Scales	.50
19	Andrew Svaldenis	.15
20	Cecil Exum	.15
21	Joey Wright	.15
22	Simon Kerle	.15
23	Greg Smith	.25
24	Justin Cass	.15
25	Trevor Torrance	.15
26	John Szigetti	.15
27	Peter Harvey	.15
28	Doug Peacock	.15
29	Tony De Ambrosis	.15
30	Steve Woodberry	.25
31	Darren Smith	.15
32	Mark Nash	.15
33	Darren Perry	.15
34	David Stiff	.15
35	Andre Moore	.15
36	Jerome Scott	.15
37	Chuck Harmison	.50
38	Terry Johnson	.15
39	Dene MacDonald	.15
40	Melvin Thomas	.15
41	Andre LaFleur	.15
42	Marc Brandon	.15
43	Andrew Gaze	4.00
44	Mark Bradtke	.15
45	Lanard Copeland	.75
46	Blair Smith	.15
47	Dave Simmons	.15
48	Stephen Whitehead	.15
49	Butch Hays	.15
50	Michael Johnson	.15
51	Tonny Jensen	.15
52	Grant Kruger	.15
53	Martin McClean	.15
54	Matthew Alexander	.15
55	Darryl McDonald	.15
56	Paul Rees	.15
57	Larry Sengstock	.15
58	Paul Maley	.15
59	Pat Reidy	.15
60	Rod Johnson	.15
61	Andrew Vlahov	.75
62	Aaron Trahair	.15
63	Anthony Stewart	.15
64	Ricky Grace	1.00
65	Scott Fisher	1.00
66	James Crawford	.50
67	John Dorge	.15
68	Darren Lucas	.15
69	Tony Ronaldson	.15
70	Chris Anstey	2.50
71	Andrew Parkinson	.15
72	Sam MacKinnon	.15
73	Bruce Bolden	.15
74	Leon Trimmingham	.15
75	Justin Withers	.15
76	Brad Williams	.15
77	Greg Hubbard	.15
78	Mark Dalton	.15
79	Derek Rucker	.15
80	Clarence Tyson	.15
81	Shane Froling	.15
82	Cameron Dickinson	.15
83	David Blades	.15
84	Jason Cameron	.15
85	Michele Timms	1.00
86	Allison Cook	.15
87	Trish Fallon	.15
88	Sandy Brondello	.15
89	Shelley Gorman	.15
90	Andrew Gaze MVP	1.00
91	John Rillie ROY	.50
92	Darren Lucas	.15
93	Reggie Smith	.15
94	Tonny Jensen	.15
95	Darryl McDonald	.15
96	Andrew Gaze	1.00
97	Alan Black, Tom Wisman CO	.15
98	Championship Team # Perth Wildcats	.15
99	Checklist 1	.15
100	Checklist 2	.15
TTP2	Andrew Gaze, Leroy Loggins	75.00

1996 Australian Futera NBL All-Stars

		MT
Complete Set (10):		60.00
Common Player:		5.00
ASN1	Shane Heal	15.00
ASN2	Derek Rucker	5.00
ASN3	Leroy Loggins	15.00
ASN4	Leon Trimmingham	5.00
ASN5	Clarence Tyson	5.00
ASS1	Andrew Gaze	25.00
ASS2	Darryl McDonald	5.00
ASS3	Mark Davis	5.00
ASS4	Andrew Vlahov	5.00
ASS5	John Dorge	5.00

1996 Australian Futera NBL Future Forces

		MT
Complete Set (10):		40.00
Common Player:		4.00
FFB1	Chris Blakemore	4.00
FFB2	David Stiff	4.00
FFB3	John Rillie	4.00
FFB4	Jason Smith	4.00
FFB5	Ruper Sapwell	4.00
FFC1	Brett Maher	4.00
FFC2	Chris Anstey	20.00
FFC3	Terry Johnson	4.00
FFC4	Brad Williams	4.00
FFC5	Martin Catallini	4.00

1996 Australian Futera NBL Outer Limits

		MT
Complete Set (8):		20.00
Common Player:		2.00
OL1	Shane Heal	6.00
OL2	Andrew Gaze	10.00
OL3	Aaron Trahair	2.00
OL4	Simon Kerle	2.00
OL5	Chris Jent	3.00
OL6	Derek Rucker	2.00
OL7	Terry Johnson	2.00
OL8	Andrew Parkinson	2.00

1993-94 Avia Clyde Drexler

The six-card, standard-size set was sponsored by Avia and G.I. Joe's. "Drexler" is printed in gold foil along the upper border with all team logos airbrushed off the cards. The card backs feature career highlights and are numbered as "of 6." The redemption card could be exchanged for three Drexler cards during a one-week window in early 1994.

		MT
Complete Set (6):		10.00
Common Player:		2.50
1	Clyde Drexler (15,000)	2.50
2	Clyde Drexler (College)	2.50
3	Clyde Drexler (All Star)	2.50
4	Clyde Drexler (Offense)	2.50
5	Clyde Drexler (Leader)	2.50
6	Clyde Drexler (Playoffs)	2.50
NNO	Redemption Card	1.25

B

1993 Charles Barkley Collector's Edition

		MT
Complete Set (14):		10.00
Common Player:		1.00
1	Charles Barkley	1.00
2	Charles Barkley	1.00
3	Charles Barkley	1.00
4	Charles Barkley	1.00
5	Charles Barkley	1.00
6	Charles Barkley	1.00
7	Charles Barkley	1.00
8	Charles Barkley	1.00
9	Charles Barkley	1.00
10	Charles Barkley	1.00
11	Charles Barkley	1.00
12	Charles Barkley	1.00
13	Charles Barkley	1.00
14	Charles Barkley	1.00

1994 Bleachers/ Classic 23K Promos

The seven-card, standard-size set was issued to promote Classic licensed sets produced by Bleachers. The cards feature 23K, all-golf sculptured design and were included in each gold-foil stamped box. Some of the cards have Classic logos while others have the Bleachers logo. The card backs feature a player profile and are unnumbered.

		MT
Complete Set (7):		20.00
Common Player:		2.00
1	Bleachers All-Gold (Alonzo Mourning) (Jumping center, Georgetown uniform)	2.50
2	Classic All-Gold (Shaquille O'Neal) (Squashing ball)	5.00
3	Classic All-Gold (Shaquille O'Neal) (Running down court, white LSU uniform)	5.00
4	Classic Gold Border (Shaquille O'Neal) (Running down court, purple LSU uniform)	5.00
5	Classic All-Gold (Shaquille O'Neal) (Wearing South all-star jersey)	5.00
6	Bleachers All-Gold (Chris Webber) (Dunking, Michigan uniform)	2.00
7	Class of '93 - Bleachers All-Gold (Chris Webber, Anfernee Hardaway, Jamal Mashburn)	2.00

1994-00 Bleachers 23 Karat Gold

		MT
Common Player:		10.00
1	Larry Bird Bleachers 10,000	25.00
2	Kobe Bryant E-X2000	50.00
3	Chicago Bulls Hoops Starting Five	25.00
4	Tim Duncan Score Board 1,997	40.00
5	Patrick Ewing 1986-87 Fleer	10.00
6	A. Hardaway Ultra Courtmasters 10,000	20.00
7	Grant Hill Classic 10,000	10.00
8	Grant Hill Flair Showcase	20.00
9	Grant Hill Ultra Courtmasters 10,000	20.00
10	Grant Hill, Jason Kidd Classic of 10,000	20.00
11	Michael Jordan UD Diamond Star 25,000	50.00
12	Michael Jordan 1986-87 Fleer Sticker	50.00
13	Michael Jordan 1996-97 Flair Showcase	50.00
14	Michael Jordan Ultra Courtmasters 10,000	50.00
15	Michael Jordan Ultra Starring Role	50.00
16	Michael Jordan Upper Deck 25,000	50.00
17	Michael Jordan Upper Deck 25,000	50.00
18	Michael Jordan Upper Deck 50,000	30.00
19	Michael Jordan Z-Force	50.00
20	Karl Malone Ultra Courtmasters 10,000	20.00
21	Alonzo Mourning Bleachers 10,000	10.00
22	Shaquille O'Neal Classic 10,000	30.00
23	Shaquille O'Neal Classic 10,000	30.00
24	Shaquille O'Neal Classic 24,900	30.00
25	Shaquille O'Neal Classic 25,000	30.00
26	Shaquille O'Neal Classic 10,000 - Jumbo	30.00
27	Shaquille O'Neal Classic 10,000/Lakers	30.00
28	Shaquille O'Neal Classic 10,000/Orlando	30.00
29	Shaquille O'Neal Score Board 10,000	30.00
30	Shaq. O'Neal Ultra Courtmasters 10,000	30.00
31	Scottie Pippen Classic 10,000	10.00
32	Scottie Pippen Classic 2,000	35.00
33	Scottie Pippen, Dennis Rodman Bleachers 10,000	20.00
34	Scottie Pippen Ultra Courtmasters 10,000	20.00
35	David Robinson Classic 10,000	10.00
36	Glenn Robinson Classic 4,996	25.00
37	D. Rodman Bleachers 10,000/Rainbow Hair	25.00
38	Rodman Bleachers 10,000/Green-Pink Hair	25.00
39	D. Rodman Bleachers 10,000/Diamond Star	25.00
40	Jerry Stackhouse Classic 25,000	10.00
41	John Stockton Ultra Courtmasters 10,000	15.00
42	Damon Stoudamire Classic 4,996	15.00
43	Chris Webber Bleachers 10,000	20.00

1997 Bleachers/Fleer Gold

		MT
Complete Set (12):		100.00
Common Player:		5.00
Production 10,000 sets		
Black Foil Cards:		2x
Holographic Foil Cards:		4x
1	Charles Barkley 1986-87	10.00
2	Clyde Drexler 1986-87	10.00
3	Patrick Ewing 1986-87	10.00
4	Anfernee Hardaway 1993-94	15.00
5	Grant Hill 1994-95	15.00
6	Michael Jordan 1986-87	25.00
7	Shawn Kemp 1990-91	5.00
8	Karl Malone 1986-87	10.00
9	Hakeem Olajuwon 1986-87	10.00
10	Shaquille O'Neal 1992-93	15.00
11	Scottie Pippen 1988-89	10.00
12	Dennis Rodman 1988-89	10.00
Promo1	Anfernee Hardaway	5.00
Promo2	Grant Hill	10.00

1996-97 Blockbuster NBA at 50 Postcards

This five postcard set was sold at Blockbuster with the purchase of NBA at 50 - A Musical Celebration tapes and CDs. The front features a player photo and the backs have an entry form. The cards could be mailed in for a chance to win a trip to the 1997 Conference Finals. The cards are unnumbered.

		MT
Complete Set (5):		10.00
Common Player:		2.50
1	Shareef Abdur-Rahim	3.00
2	Grant Hill	4.00
3	Hakeem Olajuwon	2.50
4	Scottie Pippen	3.00
5	Damon Stoudamire	2.50

1948 Bowman

Bowman's only major basketball set, a 72-card issue, was released in two series; the second is somewhat harder to find than the first. This is widely considered as the first major basketball set and the only major basketball set produced until 1957. Cards measure roughly 2" x 2-1/2". Rookies in this set include Bill Holzman, Joe Fulks, Jim Pollard and George Mikan. The set also includes a number of diagrammed play cards. There are variations in the set. Some of the Series II cards have been found without background color. These gray background cards are difficult to find.

		NM
Complete Set (72):		8300.
Common Player (1-36):		55.00
Common Player (37-72):		100.00
1	*Ernie Calverley*	220.00
2	Ralph Hamilton	50.00
3	Gale Bishop	50.00
4	*Fred Lewis*	50.00
5	Basketball Play (single cut off post)	50.00
6	*Bob Feerick*	50.00
7	John Hogan	50.00
8	Mel Riebe	50.00
9	*Andy Philip*	140.00
10	*Bob Davies*	150.00
11	Basketball Play (single cut with return pass to post)	50.00
12	*Ken Sailors*	50.00
13	Paul Armstrong	50.00
14	*Howard Dallmar*	50.00
15	*Bruce Hale*	50.00
17	Basketball Play (single cut)	50.00
19	Eddie Ehlers	50.00
20	Ellis (Gene) Vance	50.00
21	*Fuzzy Levane*	50.00
22	Earl Shannon	50.00
23	Basketball Play (double cut off post)	50.00
24	Leo (Crystal) Klier	50.00
25	George Senesky	50.00
26	Price Brookfield	50.00
27	John Norlander	50.00
28	Don Putman	50.00
29	Basketball Play (double post)	50.00
30	Jack Garfinkel	50.00
31	Chuck Gilmur	50.00
32	*Red Holzman*	425.00
33	Jack Smiley	50.00
34	*Joe Fulks*	425.00
35	Basketball Play (screen play)	50.00
36	Hal Tidrick	50.00
37	Don (Swede) Carlson	100.00
38	*Buddy Jeanette*	140.00
39	Ray Kuka	100.00

40	Stan Miasek	100.00
41	Basketball Play (double screen)	100.00
42	George Nostrand	100.00
43	*Chuck Halbert*	100.00
44	Arnie Johnson	100.00
45	Bob Doll	100.00
46	*Horace McKinney*	160.00
47	Basketball Play (out of bounds)	100.00
48	Ed Sadowski	100.00
49	Bob Kinney	100.00
50	Charles (Hawk) Black	100.00
51	Jack Dwan	100.00
52	*Cornelius Simmons*	100.00
53	Basketball Play (out of bounds)	100.00
54	*Bud Palmer*	140.00
55	*Max Zaslofsky*	300.00
56	Lee Roy Robbins	100.00
57	Arthur Spector	100.00
58	*Arnie Risen*	140.00
59	Basketball Play (out of bounds)	100.00
60	Ariel Maughan	100.00
61	Dick O'Keefe	100.00
62	Herman Schaefer	100.00
63	John Mahnken	100.00
64	Tommy Byrnes	100.00
65	Basketball Play (held ball)	100.00
66	*Jim Pollard*	400.00
67	Lee Mogus	100.00
68	Lee Knorek	100.00
69	*George Mikan*	4500.
70	Walter Budko	100.00
71	Baketball Play (guards play)	100.00
72	*Carl Braun*	500.00

1996-97 Bowman's Best

The debut set for Bowman's Best Basketball arrived with 125 cards in the base set. Regular-issue cards are numbered 1-80, with a 25-card Rookies subset and 20 Throwbacks that are considered part of the regular-issue set, but numbered as inserts. We have listed them separately. The cards are printed with chromium technology and include a thick border on the left side along with a double border across the bottom that includes the player's name. In addition to the Rookies and Throwbacks subsets, inserts include: Cuts, Shots, Picks and Honor Roll, along with Refractor and Atomic Refractor versions of the entire set and all the inserts.

	MT
Complete Set (125):	120.00
Common Player (1-80/TB1-20):	.25
Common Player (R1-25):	.75
Minor Stars:	.50
Pack (6):	10.00
Wax Box (24):	140.00

1	Scottie Pippen	2.00
2	Glen Rice	.50
3	Bryant Stith	.25
4	Dino Radja	.25
5	Horace Grant	.25
6	Mahmoud Abdul-Rauf	.25
7	Mookie Blaylock	.25
8	Clifford Robinson	.25
9	Vin Baker	.75
10	Grant Hill	4.00
11	Terrell Brandon	.50
12	P.J. Brown	.25
13	Kendall Gill	.25
14	Brent Barry	.25
15	Hakeem Olajuwon	1.50
16	Allan Houston	.50
17	Elden Campbell	.25
18	Latrell Sprewell	.50
19	Jerry Stackhouse	1.00
20	Robert Horry	.25
21	Mitch Richmond	.50
22	Gary Payton	.75
23	Rik Smits	.25
24	Jim Jackson	.25
25	Damon Stoudamire	1.50
26	Bobby Phills	.25
27	Chris Webber	1.00
28	Shawn Bradley	.25
29	Arvydas Sabonis	.25
30	John Stockton	.75
31	Anfernee Hardaway	3.00
32	Christian Laettner	.50
33	Juwan Howard	1.00
34	Anthony Mason	.25
35	Tom Gugliotta	.50
36	Avery Johnson	.25
37	Cedric Ceballos	.25
38	Patrick Ewing	.50
39	Joe Smith	1.00
40	Dennis Rodman	2.50
41	Alonzo Mourning	.50
42	Kevin Garnett	4.00
43	Antonio McDyess	.75
44	Detlef Schrempf	.25
45	Reggie Miller	.50
46	Charles Barkley	1.00
47	Derrick Coleman	.25
48	Brian Grant	.50
49	Kenny Anderson	.25
50	Otis Thorpe	.25
51	Rod Strickland	.25
52	Eric Williams	.25
53	Rony Seikaly	.25
54	Danny Manning	.25
55	Karl Malone	.75
56	B.J. Armstrong	.25
57	Greg Anthony	.25
58	Larry Johnson	.50
59	Loy Vaught	.25
60	Sean Elliott	.25
61	Dikembe Mutombo	.50
62	Clarence Weatherspoon	.25
63	Jamal Mashburn	.25
64	Bryant Reeves	.25
65	Vlade Divac	.25
66	Shawn Kemp	1.00
67	LaPhonso Ellis	.25
68	Tyrone Hill	.25
69	David Robinson	1.00
70	Shaquille O'Neal	3.00
71	Doug Christie	.25
72	Jayson Williams	.25
73	Michael Finley	.50
74	Tim Hardaway	.50
75	Clyde Drexler	.75
76	Joe Dumars	.25
77	Glenn Robinson	.50
78	Dana Barros	.25
79	Jason Kidd	1.50
80	Michael Jordan	10.00
R1	*Allen Iverson*	20.00
R2	*Stephon Marbury*	12.00
R3	*Shareef Abdur-Rahim*	10.00
R4	*Marcus Camby*	5.00
R5	*Ray Allen*	10.00
R6	*Antoine Walker*	3.00
R7	*Lorenzen Wright*	2.00
R8	*Kerry Kittles*	5.00
R9	*Samaki Walker*	2.00
R10	*Tony Delk*	2.00
R11	*Vitaly Potapenko*	1.00
R12	*Jerome Williams*	.75
R13	*Todd Fuller*	.75
R14	*Erick Dampier*	2.00
R15	*Derek Fisher*	2.50
R16	*Donald Whiteside*	.75
R17	*John Wallace*	3.00
R18	*Steve Nash*	3.00
R19	*Brian Evans*	.75
R20	*Jermaine O'Neal*	5.00
R21	*Roy Rogers*	.75
R22	*Priest Lauderdale*	.75
R23	*Kobe Bryant*	40.00
R24	*Martin Muursepp*	.75
R25	*Zydrunas Ilgauskas*	8.00
TB1	Avery Johnson	.25
TB2	Chris Webber	.50
TB3	Sean Elliott	.25
TB4	Joe Dumars	.25
TB5	Grant Hill	2.00
TB6	Gary Payton	.50
TB7	Shawn Kemp	.50
TB8	Shaquille O'Neal	1.50
TB9	Eddie Jones	.75
TB10	John Wallace	.50
TB11	Patrick Ewing	.50
TB12	Jerry Stackhouse	.50
TB13	Allen Iverson	3.00
TB14	Latrell Sprewell	.50
TB15	Dino Radja	.25
TB16	David Wesley	.25
TB17	Joe Smith	.50
TB18	Damon Stoudamire	.75
TB19	Marcus Camby	1.00
TB20	Juwan Howard	.50

1996-97 Bowman's Best Refractors

All 125 cards in Bowman's Best Basketball had parallel Refractor versions. They were inserted every 12 packs of Hobby and every 20 packs of Retail. The fronts feature a refractive foil, while the backs contain the word "Refractor" within the white card number box.

	MT
Refractors:	5x-10x
Refractor Rookies:	2x-4x

1996-97 Bowman's Best Atomic Refractors

All 125 cards in Bowman's Best Basketball also had Atomic Refractor parallel versions. They were inserted every 24 packs of Hobby and every 40 packs of Retail. Atomic Refractors featured a prismatic refractive foil on the card fronts and the words "Atomic Refractor" on the back within the white card number box.

	MT
Atomic Refractors:	15x-30x
Atomic Rookies:	6x-12x

1996-97 Bowman's Best Cuts

Bowman's Best Cuts is a 20-card insert that is numbered BC1-BC20. The cards are die-cut on the right side and featured a gold strip down that side with the player's name in it. The insert name is in the upper left corner, with the player's facsimile signature along the left side. Regular versions are seeded every 24 hobby and 40 retail packs; Refractors are seeded every 96 hobby and 160 retail packs; and Atomic Refractors are seeded every 192 hobby and 320 retail packs.

	MT
Complete Set (20):	180.00
Common Player:	4.00
Refractors:	2x
Atomic Refractors:	2x-4x

1	Karl Malone	5.00
2	Michael Jordan	45.00
3	Juwan Howard	6.00
4	Charles Barkley	6.00
5	Jerry Stackhouse	6.00
6	Anfernee Hardaway	18.00
7	Shaquille O'Neal	15.00
8	Alonzo Mourning	4.00
9	Shawn Kemp	6.00
10	Scottie Pippen	12.00
11	David Robinson	6.00
12	Kevin Garnett	25.00
13	Patrick Ewing	4.00
14	Hakeem Olajuwon	10.00
15	Damon Stoudamire	10.00
16	Grant Hill	25.00
17	Dennis Rodman	15.00
18	Chris Webber	8.00
19	Gary Payton	6.00
20	John Stockton	4.00

1996-97 Bowman's Best Shots

Bowman's Best Shots are printed on clear plastic with a green tint, with the insert name in the upper left corner and the player's name in the lower left. The insert consists of 10 cards and is numbered with a "BS" prefix. Regular versions are seeded every 12 hobby and 20 retail packs, while Refractor versions are seeded every 48 hobby and 80 retail packs and Atomic Refractors are found every 96 hobby and 160 retail packs.

	MT
Complete Set (10):	65.00
Common Player:	2.00
Refractors:	2x
Atomic Refractors:	2x-4x

1	Scottie Pippen	5.00
2	Gary Payton	2.00
3	Shaquille O'Neal	7.00
4	Hakeem Olajuwon	4.00
5	Kevin Garnett	10.00
6	Michael Jordan	20.00
7	Anfernee Hardaway	8.00
8	Grant Hill	10.00
9	Shawn Kemp	2.50
10	Dennis Rodman	6.00

1996-97 Bowman's Best Picks

This 10-card set is die-cut to resemble the Best Cuts insert; it has a die-cut on the right side at the bottom. The player's name appears in the silver strip on the right side, with the insert name in the upper left and a facsimile signature below it. Best Picks are numbered BP1-BP10, with regular versions seeded one per 24 hobby and one per 40 retail, Refractor versions every 96 hobby and 160 retail and Atomic Refractor versions seeded every 192 hobby and one per 320 retail.

	MT
Complete Set (10):	75.00
Common Player:	1.50
Refractors:	2x
Atomic Refractors:	3x-6x

1	Stephon Marbury	16.00
2	Marcus Camby	5.00
3	Lorenzen Wright	3.00
4	John Wallace	4.00
5	Ray Allen	6.00
6	Kerry Kittles	5.00
7	Shareef Abdur-Rahim	10.00
8	Todd Fuller	1.50
9	Allen Iverson	16.00
10	Kobe Bryant	30.00

1996-97 Bowman's Best Honor Roll

Honor Roll is a 10-card, double-sided insert that highlights 20 top NBA draft picks dating back to 1984. The cards feature a mostly silver border, with the top corners in black. The cards are numbered HR1-HR10. Regular versions are seeded one per 48 hobby and one per 80 retail; Refractors are seeded one per 192 hobby and one per 320 retail; and Atomic Refractors are seeded one per 384 hobby and one per 640 retail.

	MT
Complete Set (10):	180.00
Common Player:	8.00
Refractors:	2x-3x
Atomic Refractors:	3x-6x

1	Charles Barkley, John Stockton	10.00
2	Michael Jordan, Hakeem Olajuwon	60.00
3	Patrick Ewing, Karl Malone	8.00
4	Dennis Rodman, Arvydas Sabonis	14.00
5	Scottie Pippen, David Robinson	18.00
6	Glen Rice, Shawn Kemp	6.00
7	Shaquille O'Neal, Alonzo Mourning	20.00
8	Anfernee Hardaway, Chris Webber	30.00
9	Grant Hill, Juwan Howard	30.00
10	Kevin Garnett, Jerry Stackhouse	30.00

1997-98 Bowman's Best

Bowman's Best consisted of 125 cards including 90 current stars printed on a gold design, 25 draft picks printed on a silver design and 10 Bowman's Best Performers printed on gold, borderless cards. Card backs are horizontal with a closeup of the player on the left and stats on the right. Inserts include: Best Techniques, Best Cuts, Mirror Image and Best Picks. Every card in the regular set and inserts is available in both a Refractor and Atomic Refractor version.

	MT
Complete Set (125):	80.00
Common Player:	.20
Minor Stars:	.40
Pack:	5.00
Wax Box (24):	95.00

1	Scottie Pippen	1.50
2	Michael Finley	.40
3	David Wesley	.20
4	Brent Barry	.20
5	Gary Payton	.75
6	Christian Laettner	.40
7	Grant Hill	3.00
8	Glenn Robinson	.40
9	Reggie Miller	.40
10	Tyus Edney	.20
11	Jim Jackson	.20
12	John Stockton	.50
13	Karl Malone	.50
14	Samaki Walker	.20
15	Bryant Stith	.20
16	Clyde Drexler	.50
17	Danny Ferry	.20
18	Shawn Bradley	.20
19	Bryant Reeves	.20
20	John Starks	.20
21	Joe Dumars	.20
22	Latrell Sprewell	.40
23	Antonio McDyess	.50
24	Jeff Hornacek	.20
25	Terrell Brandon	.40
26	Kendall Gill	.20
27	LaPhonso Ellis	.20
28	Shaquille O'Neal	2.00
29	Mahmoud Abdul-Rauf	.20
30	Eric Williams	.20
31	Lorenzen Wright	.20
32	Shareef Abdur-Rahim	1.50
33	Avery Johnson	.20
34	Juwan Howard	.50
35	Vin Baker	.50
36	Dikembe Mutombo	.40
37	Patrick Ewing	.40
38	Allen Iverson	2.50
39	Alonzo Mourning	.40
40	Travis Knight	.20
41	Ray Allen	.75
42	Detlef Schrempf	.20
43	Kevin Johnson	.20
44	David Robinson	.75
45	Tim Hardaway	.40
46	Shawn Kemp	1.00
47	Marcus Camby	.50
48	Rony Seikaly	.20
49	Eddie Jones	.50
50	Rik Smits	.20
51	Jayson Williams	.20
52	Malik Sealy	.20
53	Chris Mullin	.20
54	Larry Johnson	.40
55	Isaiah Rider	.20
56	Dennis Rodman	1.75
57	Bob Sura	.20
58	Hakeem Olajuwon	1.00
59	Steve Smith	.20
60	Michael Jordan	6.00
61	Jerry Stackhouse	.50
62	Joe Smith	.50
63	Walt Williams	.20
64	Anthony Peeler	.20
65	Charles Barkley	.75
66	Erick Dampier	.40
67	Horace Grant	.20
68	Anthony Mason	.20
69	Anfernee Hardaway	2.00
70	Elden Campbell	.20
71	Cedric Ceballos	.20
72	Allan Houston	.20
73	Kerry Kittles	.50
74	Antoine Walker	1.50
75	Sean Elliott	.20
76	Jamal Mashburn	.40
77	Mitch Richmond	.40
78	Damon Stoudamire	.75
79	Tom Gugliotta	.20
80	Jason Kidd	1.00
81	Chris Webber	1.00
82	Glen Rice	.40
83	Loy Vaught	.20
84	Olden Polynice	.20
85	Kenny Anderson	.20
86	Stephon Marbury	2.50
87	Calbert Cheaney	.20
88	Kobe Bryant	4.00
89	Arvydas Sabonis	.20
90	Kevin Garnett	3.00
91	Grant Hill BP	1.50
92	Clyde Drexler BP	.20
93	Patrick Ewing BP	.20
94	Shawn Kemp BP	.50
95	Shaquille O'Neal BP	1.00
96	Michael Jordan BP	3.00
97	Karl Malone BP	.20
98	Allen Iverson BP	1.25
99	Shareef Abdur-Rahim BP	.75
100	Dikembe Mutombo BP	.20
101	*Bobby Jackson*	5.00
102	*Tony Battie*	3.00
103	*Keith Booth*	.40
104	*Keith Van Horn*	5.00
105	*Paul Grant*	1.00
106	*Tim Duncan*	25.00
107	*Scot Pollard*	.40
108	*Maurice Taylor*	3.00
109	*Antonio Daniels*	5.00
110	*Austin Croshere*	1.50
111	*Tracy McGrady*	8.00
112	*Charles O'Bannon*	.40
113	*Rodrick Rhodes*	2.00
114	*Johnny Taylor*	.40
115	*Danny Fortson*	1.00
116	*Chauncey Billups*	6.00
117	*Tim Thomas*	7.00
118	*Derek Anderson*	6.00
119	*Ed Gray*	.40
120	*Jacque Vaughn*	1.50
121	*Kelvin Cato*	1.00
122	*Tariq Abdul-Wahad*	1.50
123	*Ron Mercer*	10.00
124	*Brevin Knight*	6.00
125	*Adonal Foyle*	1.50

1997-98 Bowman's Best Refractors

Refractors versions of all 125 cards were produced and inserted one per 12 packs. Cards featured a holographic rainbow look to the card front and the word "Refractor" was typed on the back near the card number.

	MT
Refractor Stars:	6x-12x
Refractor Rookies:	2x-4x

1997-98 Bowman's Best Atomic Refractors

Atomic Refrators paralleled all 125 cards in Bowman's Best. These prismatic Refractors cards were inserted one per 24 packs and the words "Atomic Refractor" were typed on the back by the card number.

	MT
Atomic Refractor Stars:	15x-30x
Atomic Refractor Rookies:	5x-10x

1997-98 Bowman's Best Autographs

Five gold veterans and five silver rookies signed cards, along with a special Karl Malone MVP card were signed and inserted into Bowman's Best packs. Each card arrived with a Topps "Certified Autograph Issue" stamp, with regular versions seeded one per 373 packs, Refractors seeded one per 1,987 packs and Atomic Refractor versions seeded one per 5,961 packs.

	MT
Complete Set (11):	600.00
Common Player:	25.00
Inserted 1:373	
Refractors:	2x
Inserted 1:1,987	
Atomic Refractors:	3x
Inserted 1:5,961	

8	Glenn Robinson	50.00
13	Karl Malone	75.00
36	Dikembe Mutombo	25.00
59	Steve Smith	25.00
77	Mitch Richmond	50.00
102	Tony Battie	30.00
104	Keith Van Horn	60.00
116	Chauncey Billups	50.00
123	Ron Mercer	100.00
125	Adonal Foyle	25.00
KM	Karl Malone (MVP)	100.00

1997-98 Bowman's Best Cuts

Best Cuts was a 10-card insert set featuring intricate laser cutting and a psychadelic square pattern on the front. Backs were numbered with a "BC" prefix and were yellow with a similar square pattern. Regular versions were seeded one per 24 packs, Refractors were seeded every 48 packs and Atomic Refractors were inserted every 96 packs.

	MT
Complete Set (10):	50.00
Common Player:	1.00
Refractors:	1x-2x
Atomic Refractors:	2x-4x

1	Vin Baker	3.00
2	Patrick Ewing	1.00
3	Scottie Pippen	7.00
4	Karl Malone	3.00
5	Kevin Garnett	14.00
6	Anfernee Hardaway	10.00
7	Shawn Kemp	4.00
8	Charles Barkley	3.00
9	Stephon Marbury	14.00
10	Shaquille O'Neal	10.00

1997-98 Bowman's Best Picks

Best Picks are printd on a similar background as the Best Cuts with intricate laser-cutting and a psychedelic background. This 10-card insert set featured top picks from the 1997 NBA Draft and was numbered with a "BP" prefix.

		MT
Complete Set (10):		60.00
Common Player:		1.00
Refractors:		1x-2x
Atomic Refractors:		2x-4x
1	Adonal Foyle	1.00
2	Maurice Taylor	3.00
3	Austin Croshere	1.00
4	Tracy McGrady	7.00
5	Antonio Daniels	5.00
6	Tony Battie	3.00
7	Chauncey Billups	6.00
8	Tim Duncan	20.00
9	Ron Mercer	10.00
10	Keith Van Horn	10.00

1997-98 Bowman's Best Techniques

This 10-card insert set captured players over a spiral, foil background. The cards were numbered with a "T" prefix, with regular versions seeded one per 12 packs, Refractors every 48 packs and Atomic Refractors every 96 packs.

		MT
Complete Set (10):		60.00
Common Player:		2.50
Refractors:		1x-2x
Atomic Refractors:		2x-4x
1	Dikembe Mutombo	2.50
2	Michael Jordan	20.00
3	Grant Hill	10.00
4	Kobe Bryant	14.00
5	Gary Payton	3.00
6	Glen Rice	2.50
7	Dennis Rodman	7.00
8	Hakeem Olajuwon	4.00
9	Allen Iverson	8.00
10	John Stockton	2.50

1997-98 Bowman's Best Mirror Image

Mirror Image was a 10-card insert that showcased the top four players at each position, two from each conference all on one double-sided card. Fronts were split diagonally by a wide strip that included both players' names, while backs were numbered with a "M" prefix. Regular versions were seeded one per 48 packs, Refractors one per 96 and Atomic Refractors every 192 packs.

		MT
Complete Set (10):		150.00
Common Player:		5.00
Refractors:		1x-2x
Atomic Refractors:		2x-4x
1	Michael Jordan, Ron Mercer, Stephon Marbury, Gary Payton	50.00
2	Tim Thomas, Chris Webber, Shaquille O'Neal, Adonal Foyle	20.00
3	Tim Hardaway, Allen Iverson, Bobby Jackson, Jason Kidd	20.00
4	Scottie Pippen, Keith Van Horn, Kobe Bryant, Cedric Ceballos	30.00
5	Grant Hill, Tracy McGrady, Shareef Abdur-Rahim, Kevin Garnett	30.00
6	Shawn Kemp, Marcus Camby, Tim Duncan, David Robinson	10.00
7	Ray Allen, Steve Smith, Shandon Anderson, Sean Elliott	5.00
8	Chauncey Billups, Terrell Brandon, Antonio Daniels, Kevin Johnson	15.00
9	Kerry Kittles, Reggie Miller, Tony Battie, Hakeem Olajuwon	5.00
10	Larry Johnson, Antoine Walker, Maurice Taylor, Vin Baker	8.00

1998-99 Bowman's Best

This 125-card set included 100 veterans on gold foil and 25 rookies on silver foil seeded 1:4 packs. Refractor versions of each were sequentially numbered to 400 sets on the back, while Atomic Refractor versions were numbered to 100 and featured prismatic foil on the front. Inserts include: Refractors (1:25 packs), Atomic Refractors (1:100), Autographs, Mirror Image Fusion, Best Performers and Franchise Best.

		MT
Complete Set (125):		125.00
Common Player:		.20
Minor Stars:		.40
Common Rookie:		1.00
Inserted 1:4		
Pack (6):		5.00
Wax Box (24):		100.00
1	Jason Kidd	1.00
2	Dikembe Mutombo	.40
3	Chris Mullin	.40
4	Terrell Brandon	.40
5	Cedric Ceballos	.20
6	Rod Strickland	.40
7	Darrell Armstrong	.50
8	Anfernee Hardaway	1.50
9	Eddie Jones	.75
10	Allen Iverson	.75
11	Kenny Anderson	.40
12	Toni Kukoc	.60
13	Lawrence Funderburke	.20
14	P.J. Brown	.20
15	Jeff Hornacek	.20
16	Mookie Blaylock	.20
17	Avery Johnson	.20
18	Donyell Marshall	.20
19	Detlef Schrempf	.20
20	Joe Dumars	.40
21	Charles Barkley	.75
22	Maurice Taylor	.60
23	Chauncey Billups	.60
24	Lee Mayberry	.20
25	Glen Rice	.40
26	John Stockton	.40
27	Rik Smits	.20
28	LaPhonso Ellis	.40
29	Kerry Kittles	.40
30	Damon Stoudamire	.60
31	Kevin Garnett	2.50
32	Chris Mills	.20
33	Kendall Gill	.20
34	Tim Thomas	1.00
35	Derek Anderson	.50
36	Billy Owens	.20
37	Bobby Jackson	.50
38	Allan Houston	.40
39	Horace Grant	.20
40	Ray Allen	.50
41	Shawn Bradley	.20
42	Arvydas Sabonis	.20
43	Rex Chapman	.20
44	Larry Johnson	.40
45	Jayson Williams	.40
46	Joe Smith	.50
47	Ron Mercer	1.00
48	Rodney Rogers	.20
49	Corliss Williamson	.20
50	Tim Duncan	2.50
51	Rasheed Wallace	.40
52	Vin Baker	.50
53	Reggie Miller	.40
54	Patrick Ewing	.40
55	Michael Finley	.40
56	Bryant Reeves	.40
57	Glenn Robinson	.40
58	Walter McCarty	.20
59	Brent Barry	.20
60	John Starks	.20
61	Clarence Weatherspoon	.20
62	Calbert Cheaney	.20
63	Lamond Murray	.20
64	Zydrunas Ilgauskas	.40
65	Anthony Mason	.20
66	Bryon Russell	.20
67	Dean Garrett	.20
68	Tom Gugliotta	.40
69	Dennis Rodman	1.00
70	Keith Van Horn	1.00
71	Jamal Mashburn	.40
72	Steve Smith	.40
73	David Wesley	.20
74	Chris Webber	1.00
75	Isaiah Rider	.40
76	Stephon Marbury	1.50
77	Tim Hardaway	.60
78	Jerry Stackhouse	.40
79	John Wallace	.40
80	Karl Malone	.75
81	Juwan Howard	.40
82	Antonio McDyess	.60
83	David Robinson	.75
84	Bobby Phills	.20
85	Scottie Pippen	1.00
86	Brevin Knight	.60
87	Alan Henderson	.20
88	Kobe Bryant	3.00
89	Shawn Kemp	.60
90	Antoine Walker	1.00
91	Tracy McGrady	1.00
92	Hakeem Olajuwon	.75
93	Mark Jackson	.20
94	Bison Dele	.20
95	Gary Payton	.75
96	Ron Harper	.20
97	Shareef Abdur-Rahim	1.00
98	Alonzo Mourning	.40
99	Grant Hill	2.50
100	Shaquille O'Neal	1.50
101	*Michael Olowokandi*	3.00
102	*Mike Bibby*	6.00
103	*Raef LaFrentz*	5.00
104	*Antawn Jamison*	15.00
105	*Vince Carter*	40.00
106	*Robert Traylor*	2.00
107	*Jason Williams*	10.00
108	*Larry Hughes*	12.00
109	*Dirk Nowitzki*	15.00
110	*Paul Pierce*	12.00
111	*Bonzi Wells*	12.00
112	*Michael Doleac*	1.00
113	*Keon Clark*	3.00
114	*Michael Dickerson*	4.00
115	*Matt Harpring*	2.00
116	*Bryce Drew*	1.00
117	*Pat Garrity*	2.00
118	*Roshown McLeod*	2.00
119	*Ricky Davis*	4.00
120	*Brian Skinner*	1.00
121	*Tyronn Lue*	1.00
122	*Felipe Lopez*	2.00
123	*Al Harrington*	5.00
124	*Corey Benjamin*	1.00
125	*Nazr Mohammed*	1.00

1998-99 Bowman's Best Refractors

This 125-card set reprinted each card in Bowman's Best with a Refractor finish. Cards were inserted 1:25 packs and sequentially numbered to 400 sets. The cards were also distinguished by the word "Refractor" printed in small black letters below the card number.

		MT
Refractor Veterans:		8x-16x
Refractor Rookies:		3x-6x
Inserted 1:25		
Production 400 Sets		
1	Jason Kidd	1.00
2	Dikembe Mutombo	.40
3	Chris Mullin	.40
4	Terrell Brandon	.40
5	Cedric Ceballos	.20
6	Rod Strickland	.40
7	Darrell Armstrong	.50
8	Anfernee Hardaway	1.50
9	Eddie Jones	.75
10	Allen Iverson	2.00
11	Kenny Anderson	.40
12	Toni Kukoc	.60
13	Lawrence Funderburke	.20
14	P.J. Brown	.20
15	Jeff Hornacek	.20
16	Mookie Blaylock	.20
17	Avery Johnson	.20
18	Donyell Marshall	.20
19	Detlef Schrempf	.20
20	Joe Dumars	.40
21	Charles Barkley	.75
22	Maurice Taylor	.60
23	Chauncey Billups	.60
24	Lee Mayberry	.20
25	Glen Rice	.40
26	John Stockton	.40
27	Rik Smits	.20
28	LaPhonso Ellis	.40
29	Kerry Kittles	.40
30	Damon Stoudamire	.60
31	Kevin Garnett	2.50
32	Chris Mills	.20
33	Kendall Gill	.20
34	Tim Thomas	1.00
35	Derek Anderson	.50
36	Billy Owens	.20
37	Bobby Jackson	.50
38	Allan Houston	.40
39	Horace Grant	.20
40	Ray Allen	.50
41	Shawn Bradley	.20
42	Arvydas Sabonis	.20
43	Rex Chapman	.20
44	Larry Johnson	.40
45	Jayson Williams	.40
46	Joe Smith	.50
47	Ron Mercer	1.00
48	Rodney Rogers	.20
49	Corliss Williamson	.20
50	Tim Duncan	2.50
51	Rasheed Wallace	.40
52	Vin Baker	.50
53	Reggie Miller	.40
54	Patrick Ewing	.40
55	Michael Finley	.40
56	Bryant Reeves	.40
57	Glenn Robinson	.40
58	Walter McCarty	.20
59	Brent Barry	.20
60	John Starks	.20
61	Clarence Weatherspoon	.20
62	Calbert Cheaney	.20
63	Lamond Murray	.20
64	Zydrunas Ilgauskas	.40
65	Anthony Mason	.20
66	Bryon Russell	.20
67	Dean Garrett	.20
68	Tom Gugliotta	.40
69	Dennis Rodman	1.00
70	Keith Van Horn	1.00
71	Jamal Mashburn	.40
72	Steve Smith	.40
73	David Wesley	.20
74	Chris Webber	1.00
75	Isaiah Rider	.40
76	Stephon Marbury	1.50
77	Tim Hardaway	.60
78	Jerry Stackhouse	.40
79	John Wallace	.40
80	Karl Malone	.75
81	Juwan Howard	.40
82	Antonio McDyess	.60
83	David Robinson	.75
84	Bobby Phills	.20
85	Scottie Pippen	1.00
86	Brevin Knight	.60
87	Alan Henderson	.20
88	Kobe Bryant	3.00
89	Shawn Kemp	.50
90	Antoine Walker	1.00
91	Tracy McGrady	1.00
92	Hakeem Olajuwon	.75
93	Mark Jackson	.20
94	Bison Dele	.20
95	Gary Payton	.75
96	Ron Harper	.20
97	Shareef Abdur-Rahim	1.00
98	Alonzo Mourning	.40
99	Grant Hill	2.50
100	Shaquille O'Neal	1.50
101	*Michael Olowokandi*	6.00
102	*Mike Bibby*	10.00
103	*Raef LaFrentz*	6.00
104	*Antawn Jamison*	15.00
105	*Vince Carter*	35.00
106	*Robert Traylor*	6.00
107	*Jason Williams*	25.00
108	*Larry Hughes*	10.00
109	*Dirk Nowitzki*	3.00
110	*Paul Pierce*	20.00
111	*Bonzi Wells*	3.00
112	*Michael Doleac*	4.00
113	*Keon Clark*	4.00
114	*Michael Dickerson*	6.00
115	*Matt Harpring*	4.00
116	*Bryce Drew*	3.00
117	*Pat Garrity*	3.00
118	*Roshown McLeod*	3.00
119	*Ricky Davis*	4.00
120	*Brian Skinner*	2.00
121	*Tyronn Lue*	3.00
122	*Felipe Lopez*	5.00
123	*Al Harrington*	5.00
124	*Corey Benjamin*	2.00
125	*Nazr Mohammed*	2.00

1998-99 Bowman's Best Atomic Refractors

This 125-card parallel set reprinted each card in Bowman's Best with a prismatic Refractor front. Atomic Refractors were inserted 1:100 packs and sequentially numbered to 100 sets. The cards were also distinguished by the word "Atomic" above the card number and "Refractor" below the card number, both in small black print.

		MT
Atomic Ref. Veterans:		25x-50x
Atomic Ref. Rookies:		10x-20x
Inserted 1:100		
Production 100 Sets		
1	Jason Kidd	1.00
2	Dikembe Mutombo	.40
3	Chris Mullin	.40
4	Terrell Brandon	.40
5	Cedric Ceballos	.20
6	Rod Strickland	.40
7	Darrell Armstrong	.50
8	Anfernee Hardaway	1.50
9	Eddie Jones	.75
10	Allen Iverson	2.00
11	Kenny Anderson	.40
12	Toni Kukoc	.60
13	Lawrence Funderburke	.20
14	P.J. Brown	.20
15	Jeff Hornacek	.20
16	Mookie Blaylock	.20
17	Avery Johnson	.20
18	Donyell Marshall	.20
19	Detlef Schrempf	.20
20	Joe Dumars	.40
21	Charles Barkley	.75
22	Maurice Taylor	.60
23	Chauncey Billups	.60
24	Lee Mayberry	.20
25	Glen Rice	.40
26	John Stockton	.40
27	Rik Smits	.20
28	LaPhonso Ellis	.40
29	Kerry Kittles	.40
30	Damon Stoudamire	.60
31	Kevin Garnett	2.50
32	Chris Mills	.20
33	Kendall Gill	.20
34	Tim Thomas	1.00
35	Derek Anderson	.50
36	Billy Owens	.20
37	Bobby Jackson	.50
38	Allan Houston	.40
39	Horace Grant	.20
40	Ray Allen	.50
41	Shawn Bradley	.20
42	Arvydas Sabonis	.20
43	Rex Chapman	.20
44	Larry Johnson	.40
45	Jayson Williams	.40
46	Joe Smith	.50
47	Ron Mercer	1.00
48	Rodney Rogers	.20
49	Corliss Williamson	.20
50	Tim Duncan	2.50
51	Rasheed Wallace	.40
52	Vin Baker	.50
53	Reggie Miller	.40
54	Patrick Ewing	.40
55	Michael Finley	.40
56	Bryant Reeves	.40
57	Glenn Robinson	.40
58	Walter McCarty	.20
59	Brent Barry	.20
60	John Starks	.20
61	Clarence Weatherspoon	.20
62	Calbert Cheaney	.20
63	Lamond Murray	.20
64	Zydrunas Ilgauskas	.40
65	Anthony Mason	.20
66	Bryon Russell	.20
67	Dean Garrett	.20
68	Tom Gugliotta	.40
69	Dennis Rodman	1.00
70	Keith Van Horn	1.00
71	Jamal Mashburn	.40
72	Steve Smith	.40
73	David Wesley	.20
74	Chris Webber	1.00
75	Isaiah Rider	.40
76	Stephon Marbury	1.50
77	Tim Hardaway	.60
78	Jerry Stackhouse	.40
79	John Wallace	.40
80	Karl Malone	.75
81	Juwan Howard	.40
82	Antonio McDyess	.60
83	David Robinson	.75
84	Bobby Phills	.20
85	Scottie Pippen	1.00
86	Brevin Knight	.60
87	Alan Henderson	.20
88	Kobe Bryant	3.00
89	Shawn Kemp	1.00
90	Antoine Walker	1.00
91	Tracy McGrady	1.00
92	Hakeem Olajuwon	.75
93	Mark Jackson	.20
94	Bison Dele	.20
95	Gary Payton	.75
96	Ron Harper	.20
97	Shareef Abdur-Rahim	1.00
98	Alonzo Mourning	.40
99	Grant Hill	2.50
100	Shaquille O'Neal	1.50
101	*Michael Olowokandi*	6.00
102	*Mike Bibby*	10.00
103	*Raef LaFrentz*	6.00
104	*Antawn Jamison*	15.00
105	*Vince Carter*	35.00
106	*Robert Traylor*	6.00
107	*Jason Williams*	25.00
108	*Larry Hughes*	10.00
109	*Dirk Nowitzki*	3.00
110	*Paul Pierce*	20.00
111	*Bonzi Wells*	3.00
112	*Michael Doleac*	4.00
113	*Keon Clark*	4.00
114	*Michael Dickerson*	6.00
115	*Matt Harpring*	4.00
116	*Bryce Drew*	3.00
117	*Pat Garrity*	3.00
118	*Roshown McLeod*	3.00
119	*Ricky Davis*	4.00
120	*Brian Skinner*	2.00
121	*Tyronn Lue*	3.00
122	*Felipe Lopez*	5.00
123	*Al Harrington*	5.00
124	*Corey Benjamin*	2.00
125	*Nazr Mohammed*	2.00

1998-99 Bowman's Best Autograph Cards

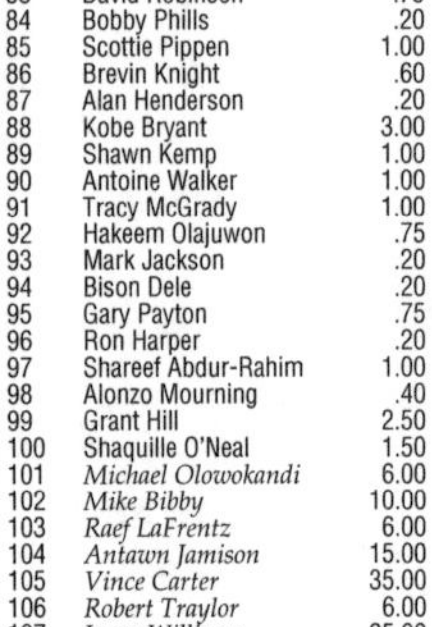

Five veteran and five rookie autographs were inserted into Bowman's Best. Each card arrived with a Topps "Certified Autograph Issue" stamp. Regular, Refractor and Atomic Refractor versions of each existed, with veterans seeded 1:628, 1:3,358 and 10,073 packs and rookies seeded 1:598, 1:4,172 and 1:12,515 packs, respectively.

		MT
Complete Set (9):		
Common Player:		15.00
Veterans Inserted 1:628		
Rookies Inserted 1:598		
Refractors:		2x
Veteran Refractors 1:3,358		
Rookie Refractors 1:4,172		
Atomic Refractors:		4x
Veteran Atomic Ref. 1:10,073		
Rookie Atomic Ref. 1:12,515		
Card No. 7 Does Not Exist		
1	Kobe Bryant	125.00
2	Tim Duncan	125.00
3	Eddie Jones	40.00
4	Gary Payton	40.00
5	Antoine Walker	15.00
6	Antawn Jamison	60.00
8	Mike Bibby	30.00
9	Vince Carter	300.00
10	Michael Doleac	15.00

1998-99 Bowman's Best Mirror Image Fusion

This insert featured the top eight players at each position with four veterans and four young stars from both conferences. Each double-sided die-cut card featured a tandem from either the Eastern or Western Conference. Regular Fusion cards were inserted 1:12 packs, Refractors sequentially numbered to 100 sets (1:628) and Atomic Refractors numbered to 25 sets (1:2,504).

		MT
Complete Set (20):		100.00
Common Player:		1.00
Inserted 1:12		
Refractor Cards:		3x-5x
Inserted 1:628		
Production 100 Sets		
Atomic Ref. Cards:		6x-12x
Inserted 1:2,504		
Production 25 Sets		
1	Tim Hardaway, Brevin Knight	3.00
2	Gary Payton, Damon Stoudamire	3.00
3	Anfernee Hardaway, Allen Iverson	12.00
4	John Stockton, Stephon Marbury	8.00
5	Ray Allen, Kerry Kittles	2.00
6	Eddie Jones, Kobe Bryant	12.00
7	Steve Smith, Ron Mercer	5.00
8	Isaiah Rider, Michael Finley	2.00
9	Latrell Sprewell, Antoine Walker	5.00
10	Detlef Schrempf, Shareef Abdur-Rahim	4.00
11	Grant Hill, Tim Thomas	12.00
12	Scottie Pippen, Kevin Garnett	12.00
13	Jayson Williams, Juwan Howard	2.00
14	Vin Baker, Antonio McDyess	3.00
15	Shawn Kemp, Keith Van Horn	3.00
16	Karl Malone, Tim Duncan	10.00
17	Alonzo Mourning, Zydrunas Ilgauskas	2.00
18	Shaquille O'Neal, Bryant Reeves	6.00
19	Dikembe Mutombo, Theo Ratliff	1.00
20	David Robinson, Greg Ostertag	2.00

1998-99 Bowman's Best Best Performers

This 10-card insert highlights five veterans and five rookies who have outstanding ability. Regular versions are seeded 1:12 packs, with Refractors 1:628 and numbered to 200 and Atomic Refractors numbered to 50 sets and seeded 1:2,504 packs. Best Performers are numbered with a "BP" prefix.

		MT
Complete Set (10):		50.00
Common Player:		1.00
Inserted 1:12		
Refractor Cards:		3x-6x
Inserted 1:628		
Production 200 Sets		
Atomic Ref. Cards:		10x-20x
Inserted 1:2,504		
Production 50 Sets		
1	Shaquille O'Neal	5.00
2	Kevin Garnett	10.00
3	Dikembe Mutombo	1.00
4	Grant Hill	10.00
5	Tim Duncan	10.00
6	Antawn Jamison	6.00
7	Raef LaFrentz	3.00
8	Mike Bibby	5.00
9	Paul Pierce	8.00
10	Jason Williams	10.00

1998-99 Bowman's Best Franchise Best

This 10-card insert was seeded 1:23 packs of Bowman's Best. Cards were printed on 26-point stock, featured a gold pin-striped background and were numbered with an "FB" prefix.

		MT
Complete Set (10):		90.00
Common Player:		3.00
Inserted 1:23		
1	Michael Jordan	30.00
2	Karl Malone	3.00
3	Antoine Walker	5.00
4	Grant Hill	15.00
5	Kevin Garnett	15.00
6	Shaquille O'Neal	8.00
7	Gary Payton	3.00
8	Keith Van Horn	5.00
9	Tim Duncan	15.00
10	Allen Iverson	10.00

1999-00 Bowman's Best

Bowman's Best consisted of 133 cards, with 90 veterans, 10 Best Performers (five veterans and five rookies) and 33 rookies, which were seeded one per pack. The veteran cards had a gold background, the Best Performers had a red background and the rookies had a silver background. The set was paralleled in both Refractors (400 numbered sets) and Atomic Refractors (100 numbered sets). Inserts included: Rookie Locker Room Collection Autographs and Game Jerseys, Bowman's Best Autographs, NBA Draft Lottery Class Photo, Franchise Favorites, World's Best, Franchise Foundations, Franchise Futures and Best Techniques.

		MT
Complete Set (133):		75.00
Common Player:		.20
Minor Stars:		.40
Common Rookie (101-133):		.75
Inserted 1:1		
Pack (6):		5.00
Wax Box (24):		75.00
1	Vince Carter	3.00
2	Dikembe Mutombo	.40
3	Steve Nash	.20
4	Matt Harpring	.40
5	Stephon Marbury	1.00
6	Chris Webber	1.50
7	Jason Kidd	1.25
8	Theo Ratliff	.20
9	Damon Stoudamire	.50
10	Shareef Abdur-Rahim	1.00
11	Rod Strickland	.40
12	Jeff Hornacek	.20
13	Vin Baker	.40
14	Joe Smith	.20
15	Alonzo Mourning	.50
16	Isaiah Rider	.40
17	Shaquille O'Neal	1.50
18	Chris Mullin	.20
19	Charles Barkley	.75
20	Grant Hill	2.50
21	Chris Mills	.20
22	Antonio McDyess	.50
23	Brevin Knight	.20
24	Toni Kukoc	.50
25	Antoine Walker	.60
26	Eddie Jones	.75
27	Tim Thomas	.75
28	Latrell Sprewell	.60
29	Larry Hughes	.75
30	Tim Duncan	2.50
31	Horace Grant	.20
32	John Stockton	.40
33	Mike Bibby	.60
34	Mitch Richmond	.40
35	Allan Houston	.40
36	Terrell Brandon	.40
37	Glenn Robinson	.40
38	Tyrone Nesby	.40
39	Glen Rice	.40
40	Hakeem Olajuwon	.74
41	Jerry Stackhouse	.50
42	Elden Campbell	.20
43	Ron Harper	.20
44	Kenny Anderson	.40
45	Michael Finley	.40
46	Scottie Pippen	1.25
47	Lindsey Hunter	.20
48	Michael Olowokandi	.50
49	P.J. Brown	.20
50	Keith Van Horn	.75
51	Michael Doleac	.40
52	Anfernee Hardaway	2.50
53	Rasheed Wallace	.40
54	Nick Anderson	.20
55	Gary Payton	.75
56	Tracy McGrady	1.25
57	Ray Allen	.50
58	Kobe Bryant	3.00
59	Ron Mercer	.75
60	Shawn Kemp	.50
61	Anthony Mason	.20
62	Tim Hardaway	.50
63	Antawn Jamison	1.00
64	Mark Jackson	.20
65	Tom Gugliotta	.40
66	Marcus Camby	.40
67	Kerry Kittles	.20
68	Vlade Divac	.20
69	Avery Johnson	.20
70	Karl Malone	.75
71	Juwan Howard	.40
72	Alan Henderson	.20
73	Hersey Hawkins	.20
74	Darrell Armstrong	.20
75	Allen Iverson	2.00
76	Maurice Taylor	.40
77	Gary Trent	.20
78	John Starks	.20
79	Paul Pierce	1.25
80	Kevin Garnett	2.50
81	Patrick Ewing	.40
82	Steve Smith	.40
83	Jason Williams	1.50
84	David Robinson	.75
85	Charles Oakley	.20
86	Bryant Reeves	.20
87	Nick Van Exel	.40
88	Reggie Miller	.40
89	Chris Gatling	.20
90	Brian Grant	.20
91	Allen Iverson	1.50
92	Tim Duncan	1.25
93	Keith Van Horn	.40
94	Kevin Garnett	1.25
95	Kobe Bryant	1.50
96	Elton Brand	3.00
97	Baron Davis	2.00
98	Lamar Odom	5.00
99	Wally Szczerbiak	2.50
100	Jason Terry	1.00
101	*Elton Brand*	5.00
102	*Steve Francis*	10.00
103	*Baron Davis*	4.00
104	*Lamar Odom*	6.00
105	*Jonathan Bender*	5.00
106	*Wally Szczerbiak*	3.00
107	*Richard Hamilton*	3.00
108	*Andre Miller*	4.00
109	*Shawn Marion*	5.00
110	*Jason Terry*	3.00
111	*Trajan Langdon*	2.00
112	*Aleksandar Radojevic*	.75
113	*Corey Maggette*	3.00
114	*William Avery*	1.50
115	*DeMarco Johnson*	.75
116	*Ron Artest*	2.00
117	*Cal Bowdler*	.75
118	*James Posey*	1.50
119	*Quincy Lewis*	1.25
120	*Dion Glover*	1.25
121	*Jeff Foster*	.75
122	*Kenny Thomas*	1.50
123	*Devean George*	1.50
124	*Tim James*	1.25
125	*Vonteego Cummings*	1.50
126	*Jumaine Jones*	1.25
127	*Scott Padgett*	1.25
128	*Anthony Carter*	2.00
129	*Chris Herren*	1.00
130	*Todd MacCullough*	1.00
131	*John Celestand*	1.00
132	*Adrian Griffin*	1.50
133	*Mursad Turkcan*	.75
CS1	Group shot of top 13 draft picks	12.00

1999-00 Bowman's Best Refractors

This 133-card set reprinted every card in Bowman's Best with a Refractor finish. Refractors are sequentially numbered to 400 sets and inserted 1:8 packs.

		MT
Common Player:		2.00
Refractor Cards:		5x-10x
Refractor Rookies:		2x-4x
Inserted 1:8		
Production 400 Sets		
1	Vince Carter	3.00
2	Dikembe Mutombo	.40
3	Steve Nash	.20
4	Matt Harpring	.40
5	Stephon Marbury	1.00
6	Chris Webber	1.50
7	Jason Kidd	1.25
8	Theo Ratliff	.20
9	Damon Stoudamire	.50
10	Shareef Abdur-Rahim	1.00
11	Rod Strickland	.40
12	Jeff Hornacek	.20
13	Vin Baker	.40
14	Joe Smith	.20
15	Alonzo Mourning	.50
16	Isaiah Rider	.40
17	Shaquille O'Neal	1.50
18	Chris Mullin	.20
19	Charles Barkley	.75
20	Grant Hill	2.50
21	Chris Mills	.20
22	Antonio McDyess	.50
23	Brevin Knight	.20
24	Toni Kukoc	.50
25	Antoine Walker	.60
26	Eddie Jones	.75
27	Tim Thomas	.75
28	Latrell Sprewell	.60
29	Larry Hughes	.75
30	Tim Duncan	2.50
31	Horace Grant	.20
32	John Stockton	.40
33	Mike Bibby	.60
34	Mitch Richmond	.40
35	Allan Houston	.40
36	Terrell Brandon	.40
37	Glenn Robinson	.40
38	Tyrone Nesby	.40
39	Glen Rice	.40
40	Hakeem Olajuwon	.74
41	Jerry Stackhouse	.50
42	Elden Campbell	.20
43	Ron Harper	.20
44	Kenny Anderson	.40
45	Michael Finley	.40
46	Scottie Pippen	1.25
47	Lindsey Hunter	.20
48	Michael Olowokandi	.50
49	P.J. Brown	.20
50	Keith Van Horn	.75
51	Michael Doleac	.40
52	Anfernee Hardaway	2.50
53	Rasheed Wallace	.40
54	Nick Anderson	.20
55	Gary Payton	.75
56	Tracy McGrady	1.25
57	Ray Allen	.50
58	Kobe Bryant	3.00
59	Ron Mercer	.75
60	Shawn Kemp	.50
61	Anthony Mason	.20
62	Tim Hardaway	.50
63	Antawn Jamison	1.00
64	Mark Jackson	.20
65	Tom Gugliotta	.40
66	Marcus Camby	.40
67	Kerry Kittles	.20
68	Vlade Divac	.20
69	Avery Johnson	.20
70	Karl Malone	.75
71	Juwan Howard	.40
72	Alan Henderson	.20
73	Hersey Hawkins	.20
74	Darrell Armstrong	.20
75	Allen Iverson	2.00
76	Maurice Taylor	.40
77	Gary Trent	.20
78	John Starks	.20
79	Paul Pierce	1.25
80	Kevin Garnett	2.50
81	Patrick Ewing	.40
82	Steve Smith	.40
83	Jason Williams	1.50
84	David Robinson	.75
85	Charles Oakley	.20
86	Bryant Reeves	.20
87	Nick Van Exel	.40
88	Reggie Miller	.40
89	Chris Gatling	.20
90	Brian Grant	.20
91	Allen Iverson	1.50
92	Tim Duncan	1.25
93	Keith Van Horn	.40
94	Kevin Garnett	1.25
95	Kobe Bryant	1.50
96	Elton Brand	3.00
97	Baron Davis	2.00
98	Lamar Odom	5.00
99	Wally Szczerbiak	2.50
100	Jason Terry	1.00
101	*Elton Brand*	15.00
102	*Steve Francis*	20.00
103	*Baron Davis*	8.00
104	*Lamar Odom*	20.00
105	*Jonathan Bender*	10.00
106	*Wally Szczerbiak*	10.00
107	*Richard Hamilton*	5.00
108	*Andre Miller*	8.00
109	*Shawn Marion*	5.00
110	*Jason Terry*	3.00
111	*Trajan Langdon*	2.50
112	*Aleksandar Radojevic*	1.00
113	*Corey Maggette*	10.00
114	*William Avery*	2.50
115	*DeMarco Johnson*	1.00
116	*Ron Artest*	5.00
117	*Cal Bowdler*	1.00
118	*James Posey*	2.50
119	*Quincy Lewis*	2.00
120	*Dion Glover*	1.25
121	*Jeff Foster*	1.00
122	*Kenny Thomas*	1.50
123	*Devean George*	1.50
124	*Tim James*	1.25
125	*Vonteego Cummings*	2.00
126	*Jumaine Jones*	1.25
127	*Scott Padgett*	1.50
128	*Anthony Carter*	1.25
129	*Chris Herren*	1.25
130	*Todd MacCullough*	1.25
131	*John Celestand*	1.25
132	*Adrian Griffin*	2.50
133	*Mursad Turkcan*	1.00
CS1	Group shot of top 13 draft picks	12.00

1999-00 Bowman's Best Atomic Refractor

This 133-card parallel set reprinted every card in Bowman's Best on an iridescent Refractor surface. Atomic Refrators were sequentially numbered to 100 and inserted 1:33 packs.

		MT
Common Player:		6.00
Refractor Cards:		15x-30x
Refractor Rookies:		8x-16x
Inserted 1:33		
Production 100 Sets		
1	Vince Carter	3.00
2	Dikembe Mutombo	.40
3	Steve Nash	.20
4	Matt Harpring	.40
5	Stephon Marbury	1.00
6	Chris Webber	1.50
7	Jason Kidd	1.25
8	Theo Ratliff	.20
9	Damon Stoudamire	.50
10	Shareef Abdur-Rahim	1.00
11	Rod Strickland	.40
12	Jeff Hornacek	.20
13	Vin Baker	.40
14	Joe Smith	.20
15	Alonzo Mourning	.50
16	Isaiah Rider	.40
17	Shaquille O'Neal	1.50
18	Chris Mullin	.20
19	Charles Barkley	.75
20	Grant Hill	2.50
21	Chris Mills	.20
22	Antonio McDyess	.50
23	Brevin Knight	.20
24	Toni Kukoc	.50
25	Antoine Walker	.60
26	Eddie Jones	.75
27	Tim Thomas	.75
28	Latrell Sprewell	.60
29	Larry Hughes	.75
30	Tim Duncan	2.50
31	Horace Grant	.20
32	John Stockton	.40
33	Mike Bibby	.60
34	Mitch Richmond	.40
35	Allan Houston	.40
36	Terrell Brandon	.40
37	Glenn Robinson	.40
38	Tyrone Nesby	.40
39	Glen Rice	.40
40	Hakeem Olajuwon	.74
41	Jerry Stackhouse	.50
42	Elden Campbell	.20
43	Ron Harper	.20
44	Kenny Anderson	.40
45	Michael Finley	.40
46	Scottie Pippen	1.25
47	Lindsey Hunter	.20
48	Michael Olowokandi	.50
49	P.J. Brown	.20
50	Keith Van Horn	.75
51	Michael Doleac	.40
52	Anfernee Hardaway	2.50
53	Rasheed Wallace	.40
54	Nick Anderson	.20
55	Gary Payton	.75
56	Tracy McGrady	1.25
57	Ray Allen	.50
58	Kobe Bryant	3.00
59	Ron Mercer	.75
60	Shawn Kemp	.50
61	Anthony Mason	.20
62	Tim Hardaway	.50
63	Antawn Jamison	1.00
64	Mark Jackson	.20
65	Tom Gugliotta	.40
66	Marcus Camby	.40
67	Kerry Kittles	.20
68	Vlade Divac	.20
69	Avery Johnson	.20
70	Karl Malone	.75
71	Juwan Howard	.40
72	Alan Henderson	.20
73	Hersey Hawkins	.20
74	Darrell Armstrong	.20
75	Allen Iverson	2.00
76	Maurice Taylor	.40
77	Gary Trent	.20
78	John Starks	.20
79	Paul Pierce	1.25
80	Kevin Garnett	2.50
81	Patrick Ewing	.40
82	Steve Smith	.40
83	Jason Williams	1.50
84	David Robinson	.75
85	Charles Oakley	.20
86	Bryant Reeves	.20
87	Nick Van Exel	.40
88	Reggie Miller	.40
89	Chris Gatling	.20
90	Brian Grant	.20
91	Allen Iverson	1.50
92	Tim Duncan	1.25
93	Keith Van Horn	.40
94	Kevin Garnett	1.25
95	Kobe Bryant	1.50
96	Elton Brand	3.00
97	Baron Davis	2.00
98	Lamar Odom	5.00
99	Wally Szczerbiak	2.50
100	Jason Terry	1.00
101	*Elton Brand*	15.00
102	*Steve Francis*	20.00
103	*Baron Davis*	8.00
104	*Lamar Odom*	20.00
105	*Jonathan Bender*	10.00
106	*Wally Szczerbiak*	10.00
107	*Richard Hamilton*	5.00
108	*Andre Miller*	8.00
109	*Shawn Marion*	5.00
110	*Jason Terry*	3.00
111	*Trajan Langdon*	2.50
112	*Aleksandar Radojevic*	1.00
113	*Corey Maggette*	10.00
114	*William Avery*	2.50
115	*DeMarco Johnson*	1.00
116	*Ron Artest*	5.00
117	*Cal Bowdler*	1.00
118	*James Posey*	2.50
119	*Quincy Lewis*	2.00
120	*Dion Glover*	1.25
121	*Jeff Foster*	1.00
122	*Kenny Thomas*	1.50
123	*Devean George*	1.50
124	*Tim James*	1.25
125	*Vonteego Cummings*	2.00
126	*Jumaine Jones*	1.25
127	*Scott Padgett*	1.50
128	*Anthony Carter*	1.25
129	*Chris Herren*	1.25
130	*Todd MacCullough*	1.25
131	*John Celestand*	1.25
132	*Adrian Griffin*	2.50
133	*Mursad Turkcan*	1.00
CS1	Group shot of top 13 draft picks	12.00

1999-00 Bowman's Best Autographs

This 11-card insert featured autographs from four veterans and seven rookies. Autographs were numbered with a "BBA" prefix and inserted 1:79 packs.

		MT
Complete Set (11):		275.00
Common Player:		15.00
Inserted 1:79		
BBA1	Mitch Richmond	15.00
BBA2	Damon Stoudamire	20.00
BBA3	Antoine Walker	15.00
BBA4	Antonio McDyess	20.00
BBA5	Trajan Langdon	20.00
BBA6	Jumaine Jones	15.00
BBA7	Andre Miller	35.00
BBA8	Richard Hamilton	25.00
BBA9	Jonathan Bender	35.00
BBA10	William Avery	20.00
BBA11	Shawn Marion	35.00

1999-00 Bowman's Best Franchise Favorites

This three-card set included former Spurs legend George Gervin, current Spurs star Tim Duncan and a third card with both players. Franchise Favorites were numbered with a "FR" prefix and an A, B or C prefix, and inserted 1:14 packs. Each also arrived in an autographed version, with Duncan autographs seeded 1:2,174, Gervin 1:966 and combination autographs 1:8,694 packs.

		MT
Complete Set (3):		15.00
Common Player:		3.00
Inserted 1:14		
Duncan Auto Inserted 1:2,174		
Gervin Auto Inserted 1:966		
Dual Auto Inserted 1:8,694		
FR1A	Tim Duncan	10.00
FR1A	Tim Duncan Auto	
FR2B	George Gervin	3.00
FR2B	George Gervin Auto	
FR3C	Tim Duncan, George Gervin	5.00
FR3C	Tim Duncan Auto, George Gervin Auto	

1999-00 Bowman's Best Franchise Foundations

This 13-card insert set showcases top young players on a a die-cut design, with all cards featuring a Refractor finish. Franchise Foundations are numbered with an "FF" prefix and seeded 1:21 packs.

		MT
Complete Set (13):		55.00
Common Player:		1.00
Inserted 1:21		
FF1	Allen Iverson	6.00
FF2	Tim Duncan	8.00
FF3	Kevin Garnett	8.00
FF4	Shareef Abdur-Rahim	2.50
FF5	Kobe Bryant	10.00
FF6	Grant Hill	8.00
FF7	Keith Van Horn	2.00
FF8	Vince Carter	10.00
FF9	Antoine Walker	1.50
FF10	Shaquille O'Neal	5.00
FF11	Jason Williams	5.00
FF12	Stephon Marbury	2.50
FF13	Antonio McDyess	1.00

1999-00 Bowman's Best Franchise Futures

This 10-card insert displays the top rookies from the 1999-2000 season on a perimeter die-cut card with a Refractor finish. Franchise Futures are numbered with an "FFT" prefix and inserted 1:27 packs.

		MT
Complete Set (10):		40.00
Common Player:		2.00
Inserted 1:27		
FFT1	Elton Brand	8.00
FFT2	Steve Francis	10.00
FFT3	Baron Davis	4.00
FFT4	Lamar Odom	10.00
FFT5	Jonathan Bender	5.00
FFT6	Wally Szczerbiak	5.00
FFT7	Richard Hamilton	3.00
FFT8	Andre Miller	3.00
FFT9	Shawn Marion	3.00
FFT10	Jason Terry	2.00

1999-00 Bowman's Best Rookie Locker Room Autographs

This five-card insert set featured autographs from five top rookies from the 1999-00 season on a horizontal design. These inserts were numbered with an "LCRA" prefix and inserted 1:174 packs. Redemption cards were issued for cards of Elton Brand and Steve Francis.

		MT
Complete Set (5):		425.00
Common Player:		50.00
Inserted 1:174		
LRCA1	Elton Brand	125.00
LRCA2	Steve Francis	150.00
LRCA3	Wally Szczerbiak	75.00
LRCA4	Baron Davis	50.00
LRCA5	Corey Maggette	60.00

1999-00 Bowman's Best Rookie Locker Room Jerseys

This four-card insert featured jersey swatches from four top rookies during the 1999-00 season on a horizontal design. The cards were numbered with an "LRCJ" prefix and inserted 1:197 packs. A redemption card was issued for Elton Brand's jersey card.

		MT
Complete Set (4):		350.00
Common Player:		50.00
Inserted 1:197		
LRCJ1	Elton Brand	125.00
LRCJ2	Steve Francis	150.00
LRCJ3	Wally Szczerbiak	75.00
LRCJ4	Baron Davis	50.00

1999-00 Bowman's Best Best Techniques

Best Techniques was a 13-card insert set which highlighted players who stand out with unique skills or techniques. The cards featured rounded corners, like a playing card, were numbered with a "BT" prefix and inserted 1:21 packs.

		MT
Complete Set (13):		35.00
Common Player:		1.00
Inserted 1:21		
BT1	Tim Duncan	8.00
BT2	Tim Hardaway	1.50
BT3	Shaquille O'Neal	5.00
BT4	Vince Carter	10.00
BT5	Dikembe Mutombo	1.00
BT6	Grant Hill	8.00
BT7	Gary Payton	1.00
BT8	Jason Williams	5.00
BT9	Stephon Marbury	2.50
BT10	Reggie Miller	1.00
BT11	Scottie Pippen	3.00
BT12	John Stockton	1.00
BT13	Karl Malone	2.00

1999-00 Bowman's Best World's Best

This nine-card insert set featured members of the Men's Team USA Basketball squad that will compete in the 2000 Summer Olympics. The cards feature a Refractor finish and arrive with Olympic colors in the background. World's Best inserts are numbered with a "WB" prefix and seeded 1:30 packs.

		MT
Complete Set (9):		25.00
Common Player:		1.00
Inserted 1:30		
WB1	Allan Houston	1.00
WB2	Kevin Garnett	10.00
WB3	Gary Payton	3.00
WB4	Steve Smith	1.00
WB5	Tim Hardaway	2.00
WB6	Tim Duncan	10.00
WB7	Jason Kidd	5.00
WB8	Tom Gugliotta	1.00
WB9	Vin Baker	1.00

2000-01 Bowman's Best Promos

		MT
Complete Set (6):		6.00
Common Player:		.50
1	Jason Kidd	2.00
2	Alonzo Mourning	.75
3	John Stockton	.50
4	Antoine Walker	.75
5	Scottie Pippen	2.00
6	Allan Houston	.75

2000-01 Bowman's Best

Bowman's Best arrived with 133 cards in the base set, including 100 veterans and 33 rookies. The rookies were all available in three different versions, with each version sequentially numbered to 499 sets. The product included no Refractor or Atomic Refractor versions of cards since all cards arrived with a Refractor-like finish. The insert lineup included Locker Room, Locker Room Autographs, Locker Room Jersey cards, Autographs, Jersey cards, Lottery Class Photo, Expressions and Elements of the Game.

		MT
Complete Set (133):		500.00
Common Player:		.15
Minor Stars:		.30
Common Rookie:		3.00
Three versions Numbered to 499		
Pack (6):		5.00
Box (24):		120.00
1	Allen Iverson	2.50
2	Darrell Armstrong	.15
3	Kendall Gill	.15
4	Marcus Camby	.30
5	Glen Rice	.30
6	Eddie Jones	.75
7	Wally Szczerbiak	.40
8	Antawn Jamison	1.00
9	Raef LaFrentz	.15
10	Steve Francis	2.50
11	Tracy McGrady	1.25
12	Brian Grant	.15
13	Vlade Divac	.15
14	Gary Payton	.60
15	Vince Carter	5.00
16	John Stockton	.30
17	Mike Bibby	.30
18	Derek Anderson	.30
19	Juwan Howard	.30
20	Allan Houston	.40
21	Kevin Garnett	2.50
22	Michael Olowokandi	.15
23	Maurice Taylor	.15
24	Jerry Stackhouse	.30
25	Nick Van Exel	.30
26	Andre Miller	.50
27	Michael Finley	.30
28	Jamal Mashburn	.30
29	Ron Mercer	.30
30	Jim Jackson	.15
31	Kenny Anderson	.30
32	Karl Malone	.60
33	Rod Strickland	.30
34	Shaquille O'Neal	2.00
35	Glenn Robinson	.30
36	Keith Van Horn	.50
37	Grant Hill	2.00
38	Eric Snow	.15
39	Anfernee Hardaway	1.25
40	Scottie Pippen	1.25
41	Jason Williams	.60
42	Elton Brand	1.25
43	Stephon Marbury	.75
44	David Robinson	.60
45	Antonio Davis	.15
46	Michael Dickerson	.15
47	Mitch Richmond	.30
48	Rashard Lewis	.60
49	Jermaine O'Neal	.40
50	Tim Duncan	2.00
51	Tom Gugliotta	.15
52	Theo Ratliff	.15
53	Joe Smith	.15
54	Tim Thomas	.40
55	Brevin Knight	.15
56	Dale Davis	.15
57	Cuttino Mobley	.30
58	Cedric Ceballos	.15
59	Christian Laettner	.15
60	Dirk Nowitzki	1.00
61	Paul Pierce	.60
62	Derrick Coleman	.15
63	Dikembe Mutombo	.15
64	Lamond Murray	.15
65	Antonio McDyess	.40
66	Reggie Miller	.30
67	Hakeem Olajuwon	.60
68	Corey Maggette	.50
69	Lamar Odom	1.25
70	Larry Hughes	.75
71	Anthony Mason	.15
72	Sam Cassell	.15
73	Terrell Brandon	.15
74	Latrell Sprewell	1.00
75	Kobe Bryant	4.00
76	Tim Hardaway	.40
77	Mark Jackson	.15
78	Vin Baker	.15
79	Jonathan Bender	.75
80	Chris Webber	2.00
81	Rasheed Wallace	.40
82	Shawn Marion	1.00
83	Toni Kukoc	.50
84	Patrick Ewing	.30
85	Ray Allen	.40
86	Isaiah Rider	.15
87	Danny Fortson	.15
88	Jerome Williams	.15
89	Shawn Kemp	.40
90	Ron Artest	.30
91	P.J. Brown	.15
92	Baron Davis	.50
93	Antoine Walker	.50
94	Jason Terry	.40
95	Jalen Rose	.40
96	Avery Johnson	.15
97	Shareef Abdur-Rahim	.60
98	Bryon Russell	.15
99	Richard Hamilton	.40
100	Jason Kidd	1.25
101	*Kenyon Martin*	30.00
102	*Stromile Swift*	40.00
103	*Darius Miles*	150.00
104	*Marcus Fizer*	20.00
105	*Mike Miller*	40.00
106	*DerMarr Johnson*	20.00
107	*Chris Mihm*	10.00
108	*Jamal Crawford*	20.00
109	*Joel Przybilla*	8.00
110	*Keyon Dooling*	20.00
111	*Jerome Moiso*	10.00
112	*Etan Thomas*	8.00
113	*Courtney Alexander*	20.00
114	*Mateen Cleaves*	12.00
115	*Jason Collier*	5.00
116	*Hidayet Turkoglu*	20.00
117	*Desmond Mason*	25.00
118	*Quentin Richardson*	25.00
119	*Jamaal Magloire*	10.00
120	*Craig "Speedy" Claxton*	8.00
121	*Morris Peterson*	30.00
122	*Donnell Harvey*	8.00
123	*DeShawn Stevenson*	30.00
124	*Dalibor Bagaric*	3.00
125	*Iakovos Tsakalidis*	3.00
126	*Mamadou N'diaye*	6.00
127	*Lavor Postell*	6.00
128	*Erick Barkley*	10.00
129	*Mark Madsen*	10.00
130	*Khalid El-Amin*	6.00
131	*A.J. Guyton*	6.00
132	*Stephen Jackson*	10.00
133	*Michael Redd*	6.00
LCP1	Draft Picks	40.00

2000-01 Bowman's Best Expression

Expressions pictured close-up head shots of 20 players, along with a smaller action shot in the lower left corner. Cards were numbered with an "E" prefix and seeded 1:8 packs.

		MT
Complete Set (20):		30.00
Common Player:		.60
Inserted 1:8		
1	Shaquille O'Neal	4.00
2	Kevin Garnett	5.00
3	Allen Iverson	5.00
4	Antonio McDyess	1.00
5	Rasheed Wallace	.75
6	Steve Francis	5.00
7	Kobe Bryant	6.00
8	Vince Carter	8.00
9	Chris Webber	3.00
10	Gary Payton	1.25
11	Latrell Sprewell	2.00
12	Tracy McGrady	2.50
13	Reggie Miller	.60
14	Antoine Walker	.60
15	Jason Williams	1.25
16	Michael Finley	.60
17	Patrick Ewing	.60
18	Karl Malone	1.25
19	Elton Brand	2.50
20	Lamar Odom	2.50

2000-01 Bowman's Best Elements of the Game

Elements of the Game featured 13 players over a background resembling an element table. Cards were numbered with an "EG" prefix and seeded 1:12 packs.

		MT
Complete Set (13):		25.00
Common Player:		1.00
Inserted 1:12		
1	Shaquille O'Neal	4.00
2	Allen Iverson	5.00
3	Vince Carter	10.00
4	Jason Kidd	2.50
5	Kevin Garnett	5.00
6	Tracy McGrady	2.50
7	Tim Duncan	4.00
8	Gary Payton	1.00
9	Larry Hughes	1.25
10	Lamar Odom	2.50
11	Jason Williams	1.00
12	Kobe Bryant	8.00
13	Karl Malone	1.00

2000-01 Bowman's Best Franchise Favorites

Franchise Favorites was a 10-card insert, with the first three featuring autographs and the final seven including dual Game Jersey cards of teammates. The autographed cards featured Shaquille O'Neal on one, Magic Johnson on the other and both on the third. O'Neal autographs were seeded 1,926 packs, Johnson autographs were seeded 1:852 packs, dual autographs were seeded 1:5,488 (overall odds were 1:320 packs) and numbered with an "FFA" prefix. Jersey cards were seeded 1:637 packs, sequentially numbered to 100 sets and numbered with an "FFJ" prefix.

		MT
Common Player:		30.00
Autos Inserted 1:320		
Jerseys Inserted 1:637		
Jersey Production 100 Sets		
A1	Shaquille O'Neal	125.00
A2	Magic Johnson	125.00
A3	Shaquille O'Neal, Magic Johnson	450.00
J1	Tracy McGrady, Grant Hill	150.00
J2	Antoine Walker, Paul Pierce	35.00
J3	Darius Miles, Keyon Dooling	125.00
J4	Stephon Marbury, Kenyon Martin	60.00
J5	Jason Kidd, Anfernee Hardaway	125.00
J6	Shareef Abdur-Rahim, Stromile Swift	60.00
J7	Juwon Howard, Rod Strickland	30.00

2000-01 Bowman's Best Locker Room Collection

Locker Room Collection featured 15 rookies on a horizontal design. Cards were numbered with an "LRC" prefix and seeded 1:4 packs. Parallel versions with either an autograph or jersey swatch of some were avaialable.

		MT
Complete Set (15):		20.00
Common Player:		.75
Inserted 1:4		
1	Kenyon Martin	4.00
2	Stromile Swift	4.00
3	Darius Miles	8.00
4	Marcus Fizer	2.50
5	Mike Miller	2.50
6	DerMarr Johnson	2.00
7	Chris Mihm	1.00
8	Jamal Crawford	2.00
9	Joel Przybilla	.75
10	Keyon Dooling	2.00
11	Jerome Moiso	1.00
12	Courtney Alexander	2.00
13	Mateen Cleaves	1.50
14	Craig "Speedy" Claxton	.75
15	DeShawn Stevenson	3.00

2000-01 Bowman's Best Locker Room Collection Autographs

This 14-card insert featured players, including some rookies, on a horizontal design with half containing the player image and the other half featuring an autograph. Cards were seeded 1:32 packs and numbered with an "LRCA" prefix. In addition, there were three Flashback cards, which included Steve Francis on one card, Elton Brand on another and both signatures on the third. The overall odds for the Flashback Autographs were 1:274 packs and these were numbered with an "LRCF" prefix.

		MT
Common Player:		8.00
Autos Inserted 1:32		
FB Autos Inserted 1:274		
1	Jamal Crawford	20.00
2	Courtney Alexander	20.00
3	Keyon Dooling	20.00
4	Mateen Cleaves	20.00
5	A.J. Guyton	10.00
6	Khalid El-Amin	12.00
7	Mike Bibby	8.00
8	Raef LaFrentz	5.00
9	Larry Hughes	15.00
10	Maurice Taylor	5.00
11	Tim Thomas	10.00
12	Antawn Jamison	15.00
13	Jonathan Bender	12.00
14	Baron Davis	12.00
1	Steve Francis	50.00
2	Elton Brand	25.00
3	Steve Francis, Elton Brand	100.00

2000-01 Bowman's Best Locker Room Collection Jersey Relics

This 25-card insert set featured rookies on a horizontal design, with half the card featuring the player's image and the other half featuring a jersey swatch. Cards were seeded 1:41 packs and numbered with an "LRCR" prefix.

A card number in parentheses ( ) indicates the set is unnumbered.

		MT
Common Player:		10.00
Inserted 1:14		
1	Kenyon Martin	40.00
2	Stromile Swift	40.00
3	Darius Miles	80.00
4	Marcus Fizer	30.00
5	Mike Miller	30.00
6	DerMarr Johnson	25.00
7	Chris Mihm	12.00
8	Mark Madsen	15.00
9	Joel Przybilla	10.00
10	Keyon Dooling	20.00
11	Jerome Moiso	15.00
12	Etan Thomas	10.00
13	Courtney Alexander	25.00
14	Mateen Cleaves	20.00
15	Jason Collier	10.00
16	Desmond Mason	25.00
17	Quentin Richardson	25.00
18	Jamaal Magloire	12.00
19	Craig "Speedy" Claxton	12.00
20	Morris Peterson	30.00
21	Donnell Harvey	12.00
22	DeShawn Stevenson	30.00
23	Mamadou N'diaye	10.00
24	Erick Barkley	15.00
25	Hidayet Turkoglu	20.00

1974-75 Braves Buffalo Linnett

The three-card, 8-1/2" x 11" set was sketched by sports artist Charles Linnett. The player's facsimile autograph appears across the card front and the backs are blank.

		NM
Complete Set (3):		16.00
Common Player:		5.00
1	Ernie DiGregorio	8.00
2	Garfield Heard	5.00
3	Jim McMillian	5.00

1950-51 Bread for Energy

The four-card, 2-3/4" x 2-3/4" set was found in bread loaf packages. The four NBA Bread For Energy cards were part of the movie, western and sports stars set issued in 1951.

		NM
Complete Set (4):		5500.
Common Player:		400.00
1	Bob Davies	600.00
2	Joe Fulks	800.00
3	Dick McGuire	400.00
4	George Mikan	4000.

1950 Bread For Health

These unnumbered cards were included as inserts for several bakeries, including Fisher's Bread and NBC Bread. The cards, which were used as bread end labels, feature NBA stars and have a B.E.B copyright label on the front, along with a colorful picture. Each card measures 2-3/4" x 2-3/4".

		NM
Complete Set (32):		11000.
Common Player:		220.00
	Walter Budko	200.00
	Paul (Bear) Hoffman	200.00
	Buddy Jeanette	275.00
	Bob Kinney	200.00
	Tony Lavelli	200.00
	Brady Walker	200.00
	Stan Miasek	200.00
	Andy Phillips	400.00
	Max Zaslofsky	400.00
	Paul Armstrong	200.00
	Fred Schaus	325.00
	Ralph Beard	200.00
	Alex Groza	275.00
	Bruce Hale	200.00
	Arnie Ferrin	200.00
	George Mikan	3500.
	Vince Boryla	200.00
	Harry Gallatan	375.00
	Cornelius Simmons	200.00
	Joe Fulks	500.00
	Ron Livingstone	200.00
	George Senesky	200.00
	Bob Davies	375.00
	Arnie Risen	275.00
	Al Cervi	200.00
	Dolph Schayes	700.00
	Paul Seymour	200.00
	Dwight Eddleman	200.00
	Ellis Vance	200.00
	Chuck Gilmur	200.00
	Horace McKinney	350.00
	Fred Scolari	200.00

1976 Buckman Discs

These unnumbered discs, featuring 20 NBA stars of the time, were distributed through Buckman's Ice Cream Village in Rochester, N.Y., which is indicated on the card backs. Each disc has a black-and-white drawing on the front, along with a facsimile autograph, and measures 3-3/8" in diameter. Biographical and statistical info runs along the card, too.

		NM
Complete Set (20):		60.00
Common Player:		1.00
	Nate Archibald	5.00
	Rick Barry	8.00
	Tom Boerwinkle	1.00
	Bill Bradley	8.00
	Dave Cowens	6.00
	Bob Dandridge	1.00
	Walt Frazier	5.00
	Gail Goodrich	4.00
	John Havlicek	8.00
	Connie Hawkins	5.00
	Lou Hudson	1.50
	Kareem Abdul-Jabbar	15.00
	Sam Lacey	1.00
	Bob Lanier	5.00
	Bob Love	2.00
	Bob McAdoo	4.00
	Earl Monroe	4.00
	Jerry Sloan	3.00
	Norm Van Lier	2.00
	Jo Jo White	2.00

1970-71 Bucks Team Issue

This set consists of 10 black and white, 5" x 7" photos. The cards are unnumbered and have blank backs.

		NM
Complete Set (10):		65.00
Common Player:		2.00
	Lew Alcindor	30.00
	Lucius Allen	5.00
	Bob Boozer	2.00
	Larry Costello CO	2.00
	Dick Cunningham	2.00
	Bob Dandridge	5.00
	Bob Greacen	2.00
	John McGlocklin	5.00
	Oscar Robertson	20.00
	Greg Smith	2.00

1971-72 Bucks Team Issue

This set consists of 12 black and white, 5" x 7" photos. The cards are unnumbered and have blank backs.

		NM
Complete Set (12):		50.00
Common Player:		2.00
	Kareem Abdul-Jabbar	25.00
	Lucius Allen	4.00
	John Block	2.00
	Larry Costello CO	2.00
	Bob Dandridge	4.00
	Toby Kimball	2.00
	John McGlocklin	2.00
	McCoy McLemore	2.00
	Barry Nelson	2.00
	Oscar Robertson	15.00
	Greg Smith	2.00
	Jeff Webb	2.00

1973-74 Bucks Linnett

The six-card, 8-1/2" x 11" set was sketched by sports artist Charles Linnett. The player's facsimile autograph is printed on the card front with the backs being blank. The set contains Oscar Robertson after his final NBA season.

		NM
Complete Set (6):		35.00
Common Player:		3.00
1	Lucius Allen	4.00
2	Kareem Abdul-Jabbar	20.00
3	Terry Driscoll	3.00
4	Russell Lee	3.00
5	Curtis Perry	3.00
6	Oscar Robertson	12.00

1974-75 Bucks Linnett

The ten-card, 8-1/2" x 11" set was sketched by sports artist Charles Linnett. Like the set from the previous year, the card fronts contain a player facsimile autograph and the backs are blank.

		NM
Complete Set (10):		30.00
Common Player:		2.00
1	Kareem Abdul-Jabbar	20.00
2	Gary Brokaw	3.00
3	Bob Dandridge	4.00
4	Mickey Davis	2.00
5	Steve Kuberski	3.00
6	Jon McGlocklin	4.00
7	Jim Price	2.00
8	Kevin Restani	3.00
9	George Thompson	2.00
10	Cornell Warner	2.00

1976-77 Bucks Playing Cards

This 55-card deck of playing cards has rounded corners and measures 2-1/4" x 3-1/2". The backs have the White Hen Pantry and Coca-Cola logos. The fronts feature a Bucks' player photo, basic player information and the cards suit and rank. Two coaches cards were included for use as jokers and a filler card has the Bucks and White Hen logos.

		NM
Complete Set (55):		50.00
Common Player:		.75
C1	Bucks Logo	1.00
C2	Brian Winters	1.00
C3	Lloyd Walton	.75
C4	Junior Bridgeman	1.50
C5	Alex English	8.00
C6	Quinn Buckner	3.00
C7	David Meyers	.75
C8	Swen Nater	1.50
C9	Scott Lloyd	.75
C10	Bob Dandridge	1.50
C11	Kevin Restani	.75
C12	Rowland Garrett	.75
C13	Fred Carter	1.50
D1	Bucks Logo	.75
D2	Fred Carter	1.50
D3	Rowland Garrett	.75
D4	Kevin Restani	.75
D5	Bob Dandridge	1.50
D6	Scott Lloyd	.75
D7	Swen Nater	1.50
D8	David Meyers	.75
D9	Quinn Buckner	3.00
D10	Alex English	8.00
D11	Junior Bridgeman	1.50
D12	Lloyd Walton	.75
D13	Brian Winters	1.00
H1	Bucks Logo	.75
H2	Fred Carter	1.50
H3	Rowland Garrett	.75
H4	Kevin Restani	.75
H5	Bob Dandridge	1.50
H6	Scott Lloyd	.75
H7	Swen Nater	1.50
H8	David Meyers	.75
H9	Quinn Buckner	3.00
H10	Alex English	8.00
H11	Junior Bridgeman	1.50
H12	Lloyd Walton	.75
H13	Brian Winters	1.00
S1	Bucks Logo	.75
S2	Brian Winters	1.00
S3	Lloyd Walton	.75
S4	Junior Bridgeman	2.00
S5	Alex English	8.00
S6	Quinn Buckner	3.00
S7	David Meyers	.75
S8	Swen Nater	1.50
S9	Scott Lloyd	.75
S10	Bob Dandridge	1.50
S11	Kevin Restani	.75
S12	Rowland Garrett	.75
S13	Fred Carter	1.50
NNO	Don Nelson CO	3.00
NNO	Bucks Logo (White Hen Pantry Ad)	.75
NNO	K.C. Jones ACO	2.50

1977-78 Bucks Action Photos

The 10-card, 5" x 7" set feature color action shots with the player's facsimile autograph. The backs of the thin-stock cards are blank.

		NM
Complete Set (10):		15.00
Common Player:		1.00
1	Kent Benson	2.00
2	Junior Bridgeman	2.00
3	Quinn Buckner	2.00
4	Alex English	8.00
5	John Gianelli	1.00
6	Ernie Grunfeld	1.50
7	Marques Johnson	3.00
8	Dave Meyers	2.00
9	Lloyd Walton	1.00
10	Brian Winters	2.00

1979 Bucks Open Pantry

The 12-card, 5" x 6" set featured representatives from Wisconsin's three sports teams: Milwaukee Brewers (1-5); Milwaukee Bucks (6-10) and Green Bay Packers (11-12). The cards are black and white with a red border and were sponsored by Open Pantry.

		NM
Complete Set (12):		30.00
Common Baseball (1-5):		2.00
Common Basketball (6-10):		4.00
Common Football (11-12):		2.00
1	Jerry Augustine	2.00
2	Sal Bando	3.00
3	Cecil Cooper	3.00
4	Larry Hisle	3.00
5	Larry Sorensen	2.00
6	Kent Benson	4.00
7	Junior Bridgeman	4.00
8	Quinn Buckner	5.00
9	Marques Johnson	5.00
10	Jon McGlocklin	4.00
11	Rich McGeorge	2.00
12	Steve Wagner	2.00

1979-80 Bucks Police/Spic'n Span

The 12-card, standard-size set features the Milwaukee Bucks and was sponsored by Spic 'n' Span. The cards were available one per cleaning order or as a set from the Wisconsin Sports Collectors Association for $2.25. The fronts feature a color photo with a Spic 'n' Span logo in the lower left corner and the horizontal backs feature bio and stat information.

		NM
Complete Set (13):		125.00
Common Player:		6.00
2	Junior Bridgeman	10.00
4	Sidney Moncrief	30.00
6	Pat Cummings	6.00
7	Dave Meyers	10.00
8	Marques Johnson	16.00
11	Lloyd Walton	6.00
21	Quinn Buckner	10.00
31	Richard Washington	7.50
32	Brian Winters	6.00
42	Harvey Catchings	6.00
54	Kent Benson	7.50
NNO	Don Nelson CO, John Killilea ACO	8.00
NNO	Coupon Card	35.00

1985 Bucks Card Night/Star

The 13-card, standard-size set was given away on Milwaukee Bucks "Card Night" on Jan. 21, 1985. The cards were produced by Star and have the logo in the upper right corner of the green border. Card No. 10 (Larry Micheaux) was pulled due to the player's free-agent signing immediately after the printing of the set.

		MT
Complete Set (13):		55.00
Common Player:		2.50
1	Don Nelson (CO)	4.00
2	Randy Breuer	2.50
3	Terry Cummings	5.00
4	Charlie Davis	2.50
5	Mike Dunleavy	5.00
6	Kenny Fields	2.50
7	Kevin Grevey	2.50
8	Craig Hodges	3.00
9	Alton Lister	2.50
10	Larry Micheaux (SP)	35.00
11	Paul Mokeski	2.50
12	Sidney Moncrief	5.00
13	Paul Pressey	3.00

1986 Bucks Lifebuoy/Star

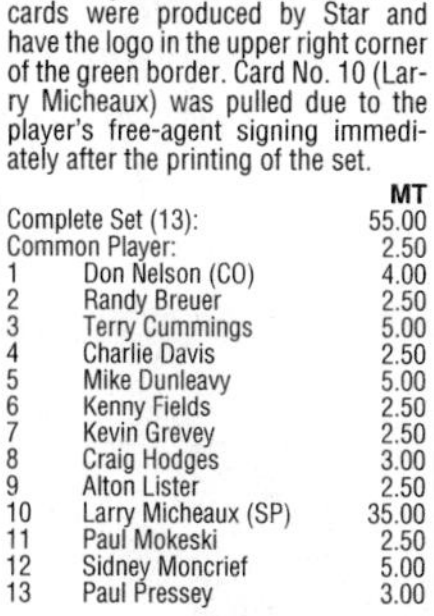

The 13-card, standard-size set features 12 Buck players and one coaches card. The set's design is identical to the base Star design, but with the Lifebuoy logo in the lower left corner of the card front.

		MT
Complete Set (13):		15.00
Common Player:		1.25
1	Don Nelson (CO)	2.00
2	Randy Breuer	1.25
3	Terry Cummings	3.00
4	Charlie Davis	1.25
5	Kenny Fields	1.25
6	Craig Hodges	1.50
7	Jeff Lamp	1.25
8	Alton Lister	1.25
9	Paul Mokeski	1.25
10	Sidney Moncrief	4.00
11	Ricky Pierce	2.00
12	Paul Pressey	1.50
13	Jerry Reynolds	1.25

1987-88 Bucks Polaroid

The 16-card, 2-3/4" x 4" set contains 14 player cards, one coaches card and a team title card. The front borders are green with the backs having bio information. The cards were distributed via perforated sheets.

		MT
Complete Set (16):		40.00
Common Player:		2.00
2	Junior Bridgeman	3.00
3	Pace Mannion	2.00
4	Sidney Moncrief	7.00
10	John Lucas	5.00
15	Craig Hodges	3.00
21	Conner Henry	2.00
25	Paul Pressey	3.00
34	Terry Cummings	5.00
35	Jerry Reynolds	2.00
42	Larry Krystkowiak	3.00
43	Jack Sikma	4.00
44	Paul Mokeski	2.00
45	Randy Breuer	2.00
54	John Stroeder	2.00
NNO	Bucks Coaches (Del Harris CO, Frank Hamblen ACO, Mack Calvin ACO, Mike Dunleavy ACO, Jeff Snedeker TR)	3.00
NNO	Title Card (discount offer detailed on back)	2.50

1988-89 Bucks Green Border

Measuring 2-3/4" x 4", the cards in this 16-card set were released in four four-card panels, with each card being perforated. One four-card strip was handed out to fans at four Bucks home games. The fronts are anchored by a color photo, which is bordered in green. The Bucks' logo is printed in the lower left, with the player's name in the lower right. The unnumbered card backs feature the Bucks' Bango the mascot logo in the upper left, along with the years, the player's name, number and bio.

		MT
Complete Set (16):		40.00
Common Player:		2.00
	Kareem Abdul-Jabbar	10.00
	Randy Breuer	2.00
	Terry Cummings	4.00
	Jeff Grayer	2.00
	Del Harris (CO)	3.00
	Tito Horford	2.00
	Jay Humphries	3.00
	Larry Krystkowiak	2.00
	Paul Mokeski	2.00
	Sidney Moncrief	5.00
	Ricky Pierce	3.00
	Paul Pressey	2.00
	Fred Roberts	2.00
	Jack Sikma	4.00
	The Bradley Center	2.00
	Coaching Staff (Del Harris CO, Frank Hamblen ACO, Mack Calvin ACO, Mike Dunleavy ACO, Jeff Snedeker TR)	2.50

1954-55 Bullets Gunther Beer

Measuring 2-5/8" x 3-5/8", the 11-card set, sponsored by Gunther Beer, showcased a black-and-white player photo on the front with "What's the good word?" printed at the top. "Gunther Beer" appears inside a bottle cap in the lower left. The player's name and his facsimile signature are printed in the lower right. The unnumbered card backs have "Follow the Bullets with" in the upper left, while "Gunther Beer" is printed inside a bottle cap in the upper right. The player's name, bio and write-up are printed in the center of the card. A black stripe at the bottom of the card back includes where a Bullets fan could listen to or watch the team's games.

		NM
Complete Set (11):		2000.
Common Player:		175.00
1	Leo Barnhorst	175.00
2	Clair Bee CO	500.00
3	Bill Bolger	175.00
4	Ray Felix	225.00
5	Jim Fritsche	175.00
6	Rollen Hans	175.00
7	Paul (Bear) Hoffman	225.00
8	Bob Houbregs	300.00
9	Ed Miller	175.00
10	Al Roges	175.00
11	Harold Uplinger	175.00

1969-70 Bullets Team Issue

This set consists of 12 black and white 8" x 10" photos. The photos feature a facsimile autograph. The backs are blank and the photos are unnumbered.

		NM
Complete Set (12):		50.00
Common Player:		2.00
1	Mike Davis	2.00
2	Fred Carter	5.00
3	Leroy Ellis	2.00
4	Gus Johnson	5.00
5	Kevin Loughery	5.00
6	Ed Manning	2.00
7	Jack Martin	2.00
8	Earl Monroe	14.00
9	Bob Quick	2.00
10	Ray Scott	2.00
11	Gene Shue	5.00
12	Wes Unseld	12.00

1973-74 Bullets Standups

Six players were featured on two 11-1/4" x 14" sheets, which were produced by Johnny Pro Enterprises. Each card measured 3-3/4" x 7-1/16" inches and were perforated. Johnny Pro printed 6,000 albums of cards that were distributed at a Bullets game in the Captial Centre. The player photos are die-cut, which allowed a collector to push the player photo out to form a stand-up card. A color photo anchors the front. The player's name is also printed on the front. The unnumbered cards are blank on the back. The set housed in the album carries a value two times what is listed here.

		NM
Complete Set (12):		40.00
Common Player:		2.50
	Phil Chenier	5.00
	Archie Clark	5.00
	Elvin Hayes	20.00
	Tom Kozelko	2.50
	Manny Leaks	2.50
	Louie Nelson	2.50
	Kevin Porter	4.00
	Mike Riordan	3.00
	Dave Stallworth	3.00
	Wes Unseld	10.00
	Nick Weatherspoon	3.00
	Walt Wesley	2.50

1975-76 Bullets Team Issue

		NM
Complete Set (11):		40.00
Common Player:		2.00
1	Dave Bing	8.00
2	Bernie Bickerstaff Asst. CO	6.00
3	Clem Haskins	3.00
4	Elvin Hayes	15.00
5	Jimmy Jones	2.00
6	K.C. Jones CO	4.00
7	Tom Kozelko	2.00
8	Mike Riordan	2.00
9	Leonard Robinson	2.00
10	Nick Weatherspoon	2.00
11	Wes Unseld	8.00

1976-77 Bullets Team Issue

This set consists of 15 black and white 5" x 7" photos. The player's name is printed below the photo on the front. The backs are blank and the photos are not numbered.

		NM
Complete Set (15):		40.00
Common Player:		1.50
1	Bernie Bickerstaff	2.00
2	Dave Bing	4.00
3	Phil Chenier	3.00
4	Leonard Gray	1.50
5	Kevin Grevey	3.00
6	Elvin Hayes	12.00
7	Jimmy Jones	1.50
8	Mitch Kupchak	4.00
9	Dick Motta CO	2.00
10	Joe Pace	1.50
11	Mike Riordan	2.00
12	Len Robinson	1.50
13	Wes Unseld	6.00
14	Bob Weiss	2.00
15	Larry Wright	1.50

1977-78 Bullets Standups

This unnumbered 11-card set was produced by Johnny Pro Enterprises and housed in a collectors album. Like the 1973-74 cards, these are die-cut for collectors to push out the player photo and display it as a stand-up card. The cards are blank-backed. The set housed in the album carries a value two times what is listed here.

		NM
Complete Set (11):		30.00
Common Player:		2.00
	Greg Ballard	2.00
	Phil Chenier	5.00
	Bob Dandridge	3.00
	Kevin Grevey	2.00
	Elvin Hayes	18.00
	Tom Henderson	2.00
	Mitch Kupchak	3.00
	Joe Pace	2.00
	Wes Unseld	12.00
	Phil Walker	2.00
	Larry Wright	2.00

1992-93 Bullets Crown/Topps

The nine-card set was sold in four-card strips at participating Crown Gasoline stations. Three player cards and one coupon card, which also served as a checklist, were featured on each vertical strip. Each card in the set, which is also known as "Great Bullets Past and Present," was the standard 2-1/2" x 3-1/2". The set was distributed as follows: 1-3, 4-6 and 7-9. The card design was the same as the 1992-93 Topps base series. The cards are numbered with a "WB" prefix on the backs.

		MT
Complete Set (12):		8.00
Common Player (1-9):		.50
Common Player (10-12):		.25
1	Tom Gugliotta	2.00
2	Rex Chapman	.75
3	Phil Chenier	.75
4	Pervis Ellison	.75
5	Brent Price	.50
6	Wes Unseld	1.50
7	Michael Adams	.50
8	Harvey Grant	.50
9	Elvin Hayes	2.50
NNO	Crown Gasoline Coupon (Checklist)	.25
NNO	Crown Gasoline Coupon (Checklist)	.25
NNO	Crown Gasoline Coupon (Checklist)	.25

1995-96 Bullets Police

The standard-sized seven-card set was a joint effort between the Bullets and the District of Columbia Metro Police Department. Children could receive the cards from a police officer. If the child completed the entire set, including the unnumbered mascot card, he/she could receive two tickets to a Bullets game. The fronts include a full-bleed photo, with the player's name and position inside a stripe and "Kids 'n cops presented by Nations Bank" included inside a red rectangle. The unnumbered card backs feature a headshot in the upper left, while the player's name and bio are in the upper right. His facsimile autograph, a safety tip and sponsors are listed.

		MT
Complete Set (6):		10.00
Common Player:		1.00
	Calbert Cheaney	1.25
	Juwan Howard	3.00
	Gheorghe Muresan	1.50
	Robert Pack	1.00
	Rasheed Wallace	3.00
	Chris Webber	3.00
	Hoops Mascot Card	1.00

1969-70 Bulls Pepsi

Measuring 8" x 10", the 13-card set is anchored by a large black-and-white photo on the front. The player's name and height are printed beneath the photo, along with the Bulls' and Pepsi logos. "You've got a lot to live. Pepsi's got a lot to give" appears at the bottom of the card. The cards are unnumbered and blank-backed.

		NM
Complete Set (13):		120.00
Common Player:		5.00
	Tom Boerwinkle	10.00
	Shaler Halimon	5.00
	Clem Haskins	10.00
	Bob Kauffman	5.00
	Bob Love	35.00
	Ed Manning	8.00
	Dick Motta (CO)	10.00
	Loy Petersen	5.00
	Jerry Sloan	25.00
	Al Tucker	5.00
	Chet Walker	25.00
	Bob Weiss	12.00
	Walt Wesley	5.00

1970-71 Bulls Hawthorne Milk

Measuring 3-1/4" x 3-3/8", the six-card set was included on the side panels of Hawthorne Milk cartons. A blue-toned photo is showcased inside a circle, with the player's facsimile signature beneath it. To add confusion to the set, there is a second Bob Weiss card that measures 4-11/16" x 2-7/8". Each card is bordered in red. The cards are unnumbered and blank-backed.

		NM
Complete Set (6):		900.00
Common Player:		100.00
	Bob Love	225.00
	Jerry Sloan (Photo in blue/gray with red border)	150.00
	Jerry Sloan (Photo in red tint with red border)	150.00
	Chet Walker	150.00
	Bob Weiss (Regular size)	100.00
	Bob Weiss (Large size)	125.00

1977-78 Bulls White Hen Pantry

Measuring 5" x 7", the seven-card set features a full-bleed action photo on the front, along with the player's facsimile autograph. Printed on thin paper stock, the cards are unnumbered and have blank backs.

		NM
	Complete Set (7):	10.00
	Common Player:	1.50
	Tom Boerwinkle	2.00
	Artis Gilmore	4.00
	Wilbur Holland	1.50
	Mickey Johnson	2.00
	Scott May	2.50
	John Mengelt	2.00
	Norm Van Lier	2.50

1979-80 Bulls Police

Measuring 2-5/8" x 4-1/8", the 16-card set showcase a photo on the front bordered in white. The photo includes a facsimile autograph. The player's number, name and bio are printed beneath the photo. The card backs have "Kiwanis Cue Cards" printed at the top. Inside a box is a basketball and a safety tip. The Kiwanis, La Margarita Restaurant, NBA and Aztech logos are printed at the bottom. The cards are numbered respectively with the player's uniform number. The cards are found with rounded or square corners. Reggie Theus and Coby Dietrick cards are the toughest to find.

		NM
	Complete Set (16):	100.00
	Common Player:	4.00
1	Delmer Beshore	4.00
13	Dwight Jones	5.00
15	John Mengelt	5.00
17	Scott May	7.50
20	Dennis Awtrey	5.00
24	Reggie Theus (SP)	30.00
26	Coby Dietrick (SP)	15.00
27	Ollie Johnson	4.00
28	Sam Smith	4.00
34	David Greenwood	7.50
40	Ricky Sobers	5.00
53	Artis Gilmore	15.00
54	Mark Landsberger	4.00
NNO	Jerry Sloan (CO)	10.00
NNO	Phil Johnson (ACO)	5.00
NNO	Luv-A-Bull	7.50

1985 Bulls Interlake

Measuring 5" x 7", the two-card set showcases a color action photo of either Michael Jordan or Orlando Woolridge on thin paper. The fronts are anchored with a large photo bordered in white. The Bulls' logo is printed at the top, with the Boy Scouts' and Interlake logos printed in circles in the two bottom corners. At the bottom center are the player's name, height and position. The cards are unnumbered and have blank backs. Be on the lookout, as the Jordan card has been counterfeited. The fake cards are glossier than the originals, printed on thin paper and are smaller than the originals.

		MT
	Complete Set (2):	90.00
	Common Player:	10.00
	Michael Jordan	85.00
	Orlando Woolridge	10.00

1985-86 Bulls Team Issue

This set consists of two 8" x 10" sheets. Each sheet features black-and-white headshots of eight members of the team. The backs are blank and the photos are unnumbered.

		MT
	Complete Set (2):	60.00
	Common Player:	10.00
1	Sidney Green, Michael Jordan, Kyle Macy, Billy McKinney, Charles Oakley, Jawann Oldham, Mike Smrek, Orlando Woolridge	50.00
2	Stan Albeck CO, Murray Arnold ACO, Gene Banks, Dave Corzine, George Gervin, Jerry Krause GM, Mike Thibault ACO, Tex Winter ACO	10.00

1987-88 Bulls Entenmann's

Measuring 2-5/8" x 4", the 12-card set is anchored by a large photo bordered in white. Beneath the photo are the player's jersey number, name, height, position and the Entenmann's logo. The entire set was a giveaway at a Bulls game that season. The cards are numbered according to the player's jersey number. The card backs are blank.

		MT
	Complete Set (12):	180.00
	Common Player:	2.00
2	Rory Sparrow	2.00
3	Sedale Threatt	4.00
5	John Paxson	6.00
6	Brad Sellers	2.00
17	Mike Brown	2.00
23	Michael Jordan	100.00
31	Granville Waiters	2.00
33	Scottie Pippen	60.00
34	Charles Oakley	6.00
40	Dave Corzine	2.00
54	Horace Grant	15.00
NNO	Doug Collins (CO)	6.00

1988-89 Bulls Entenmann's

Measuring 2-5/8" x 4", the 12-card set is anchored by a large photo on the front, with the player's jersey number, name, height, position and Entenmann's logo printed beneath the photo. The cards are numbered according to the player's jersey number. The backs are blank. The set was a freebie at a Bulls game that season.

		MT
	Complete Set (12):	125.00
	Common Player:	2.50
2	Brad Sellers	2.50
5	John Paxson	3.50
11	Sam Vincent	2.50
14	Craig Hodges	2.50
15	Jack Haley	2.50
22	Charles Davis	2.50
23	Michael Jordan	80.00
24	Bill Cartwright	2.50
32	Will Perdue	2.50
33	Scottie Pippen	35.00
40	Dave Corzine	2.50
54	Horace Grant	10.00

1989-90 Bulls Dairy Council

Measuring 4" x 8", the six-card set showcases a caricature of a Bulls player on the front, along with a "Grow like a pro" slogan. The bottom of each card front has a drawing of an apple, a glass of milk, a slice of bread and a steak. The backs promote the goodness of milk. The unnumbered cards are printed on thin stock and are sponsored by the Dairy Council of Wisconsin, Inc.

		MT
	Complete Set (6):	115.00
	Common Player:	2.00
	Bill Cartwright (Milk is Good for Snacks)	4.00
	Horace Grant (Milk is Good for Teeth)	10.00
	Michael Jordan (Milk is Good for Breakfast)	85.00
	Stacey King (Milk is Good for Skin)	2.00
	John Paxson (Milk is Good for Bones)	4.00
	Scottie Pippen (Milk is Good for Eyes)	30.00

1989-90 Bulls Equal

Measuring 3" x 4-1/4", the 12-card set is anchored by a full-bleed photo on the front, with the exception of a white stripe at the bottom that includes the player's jersey number, name, height, position and Equal Sweetener logo. The card backs have a trademark tag line. Reports say 10,000 sets were handed out to fans at a Bulls game that season. The cards are unnumbered.

		MT
	Complete Set (12):	50.00
	Common Player:	.75
	B.J. Armstrong	5.00
	Bill Cartwright	1.00
	Charles Davis	.75
	Horace Grant	4.00
	Craig Hodges	1.00
	Michael Jordan	30.00
	Stacey King	1.50
	Ed Nealy	.75
	John Paxson	2.00
	Will Perdue	1.00
	Scottie Pippen	12.00
	Jeff Sanders	.75

1990-91 Bulls Equal/Star

The standard-sized 16-card set commemorates the 25th anniversary of the Bulls. Produced in a quantity of 10,000, the set was printed by the Star Co. and handed out to fans at a game that season. Current Bulls players have color photos, while past players had blue-toned photos. The 25th anniversary banner logo appears in the upper left, while "The Silver Season" is printed in the upper right. The player's name appears in a stripe running diagonally near the bottom of the photo. The Equal logo is printed beneath the photo. The unnumbered card backs have the player's name and Star logo at the top, with his bio and stats below.

		MT
	Complete Set (16):	23.00
	Common Player:	.50
	Michael Jordan	10.00
	Tom Boerwinkle	.50
	Bob Boozer	.50
	Bill Cartwright	1.00
	Artis Gilmore	1.50
	Horace Grant	2.50
	Phil Jackson (CO)	1.50
	Johnny Kerr	1.50
	Bob Love	1.50
	Dick Motta (CO)	.75
	John Paxson	1.00
	Scottie Pippen	6.00
	Guy Rodgers	.50
	Jerry Sloan	1.50
	Norm Van Lier	1.00
	Chet Walker	1.00

C

1990 88's Calgary WBL

The 13-1/2" x 20-1/4" sheet featured 24 player cards and six discount coupons. If cut, the cards measure 2-1/2" x 3-1/2" and the fronts have a KFC logo in the upper right corner. The horizontal backs feature player bio information.

		MT
	Complete Set (24):	20.00
	Common Player:	1.00
1	David Boone	1.00
2	Scott Hicks	1.00
3	Dwayne McClain	2.00
4	Chip Engelland (Driving to loop)	1.00
5	Perry Young	1.00
6	Chip Engelland	1.00
7	Steve Smith	1.00
8	Jim Thomas (Setting up play)	1.00
9	George Jackson (Dunking)	1.00
10	George Jackson	1.00
11	Perry Young	1.00
12	Carlos Clark (Dribbling)	1.00
13	Dave Henderson (Shooting)	1.00
14	Carlos Clark	1.00
15	John Hegwood	1.00
16	Perry Young (Shooting)	1.00
17	Chip Engelland (Shooting)	1.00
18	Sean Chambers	1.00
19	Carlos Clark (Shooting)	1.00
20	1989 WBL Playoffs (Jim Thomas)	1.00
21	1989 WBL Playoffs (Final Standings on back)	1.00
22	Jim Thomas	1.00
23	Team Photo	1.00
24	Perry Young (Rebounding)	1.00

1975 Carvel Discs

These discs, similar to the 1976 Buckman Discs, measure 3-3/8" in diameter and have different colored borders for each player. The discs, unnumbered and blank backed, have black-and-white drawings on the front, plus biographical and statistical info. One of five different colors was used for the border. Some white border discs exist, too; they come in two versions - with or without Carvel at the top. These discs are scarcer than the regular colored ones. A poster was also produced to display all 36 discs.

		NM
	Complete Set (36):	135.00
	Common Player:	1.00
	Nate Archibald	6.00
	Bill Bradley	10.00
	Don Chaney	3.00
	Dave Cowens	6.00
	Bob Dandridge	1.50
	Ernie DiGregorio	2.50
	Walt Frazier	6.00
	John Gianelli	1.00
	Gail Goodrich	4.00
	Happy Hairston	1.50
	John Havlicek	12.00
	Spencer Haywood	2.00
	Garfield Heard	1.00
	Lou Hudson	2.00
	Kareem Abdul-Jabbar	25.00
	Phil Jackson	7.00
	Sam Lacey	1.00
	Bob Lanier	5.00
	Bob Love	2.00
	Bob McAdoo	4.00
	Jim McMillian	1.50
	Dean Meminger	1.00
	Earl Monroe	6.00
	Don Nelson	3.00
	Jim Price	1.00
	Clifford Ray	1.00
	Charlie Scott	1.50
	Paul Silas	3.00
	Jerry Sloan	4.00
	Randy Smith	2.50
	Dick Van Arsdale	2.00
	Norm Van Lier	2.00
	Chet Walker	2.50
	Paul Westphal	5.00
	Jo Jo White	2.50
	Hawthorne Wingo	4.00

1976 Cavaliers Royal Crown Cola Cans

		NM
	Complete Set (7):	30.00
	Common Player:	5.00
1	Jim Brewer	5.00
2	Austin Carr	10.00
3	Bill Fitch	8.00
4	Jim Chones	5.00
5	Jim Cleamons	5.00
6	Dick Snyder Auto	8.00
6A	Dick Snyder	5.00
7	Bingo Smith	5.00

1993-94 Cavaliers Nickles Bread

These 13 standard-size, unnumbered cards were inserted one per loaf of Nickles brand bread.

		MT
	Complete Set (13):	12.00
	Common Player:	.75
	John Battle	.75
	Terrell Brandon	2.00
	Brad Daugherty	1.00
	Danny Ferry	1.00
	Jay Guidinger	.75
	Tyrone Hill	1.00
	Gerald Madkins	.75
	Chris Mills	1.25
	Larry Nance	3.00
	Bobby Phills	1.00
	Mark Price	3.00
	Gerald Wilkins	.75
	John Williams	1.00

1974-75 Celtics Linnett

Measuring 8-1/2" x 11", the nine sketches are portraits of each player's head. Artist Charles Linnett drew the sketches. The Boston Celtics' logo and the player's facsimile signature are included on the front. The cards are unnumbered and have blank backs. Even though a 1969 NBA Properties copyright is printed on the card and a 1973 NBAPA copyright is printed on the package, the set is from 1974-75. The cards were sold in two-card packages.

		NM
	Complete Set (9):	75.00
	Common Player:	4.00
	Don Chaney	6.00
	Dave Cowens	15.00
	Steve Downing	4.00
	Henry Finkel	4.00
	Phil Hankinson	4.00
	John Havlicek	20.00
	Don Nelson	12.00
	Paul Silas	8.00
	Jo-Jo White	8.00

1975-76 Celtics Linnett Green Borders

Measuring 4" x 6", the three cards were also created by artist Charles Linnett. The fronts feature a sketch bordered in green and by athletes from different sports. The Celtics' logo is in the lower left, while the player's facsimile autograph is printed at the bottom of the sketch. The appropriate NBA logos are in the top two corners. The card backs are blank and unnumbered. The cards were sold in three-card packs.

		NM
	Complete Set (3):	20.00
	Common Player:	5.00
	Dave Cowens	10.00
	John Havlicek	15.00
	Jo-Jo White	5.00

1977-78 Celtics Citgo

Measuring 8-1/2" x 11", the 17 photos in the set showcase glossy full-bleed color action photos. The backs have the player's name, bio, stats and career summary, except card No. 5, which has a chart that tracks the Celtics vs. NBA opponents over the years 1946-77, and card No. 6, which includes the team's roster for the 1977-78 season. The Kermit Washington photo is the only posed shot in the set. A Citgo logo appears on the unnumbered card backs.

		NM
	Complete Set (17):	75.00
	Common Player:	3.00
	Dave Bing	8.00
	Tom Boswell	3.00
	Don Chaney	5.00
	Dave Cowens	10.00
	Dave Cowens (With John Havlicek and Curtis Rowe)	10.00
	Dave Cowens (With Charlie Scott)	8.00
	John Havlicek	15.00
	Sam Jones	7.50
	Cedric Maxwell	4.00
	Curtis Rowe	5.00
	Tom Sanders (CO)	4.00
	Fred Saunders	3.00
	Kevin Stacom	3.00
	Kermit Washington	3.00
	Jo-Jo White	6.00
	Sidney Wicks	6.00
	Ballboy Contest	3.00

1988-89 Celtics Citgo

Measuring 10-1/2" x 12-1/2", the color artwork is bordered in white. The bottom of the card front has a facsimile autograph and a player biography. The backs are unnumbered and blank. Printed on thin paper stock, the cards are sponsored by Citgo.

		MT
	Complete Set (7):	45.00
	Common Player:	3.00
	Danny Ainge	6.00
	Larry Bird	20.00
	Dennis Johnson	4.00
	Reggie Lewis	6.00
	Kevin McHale	8.00
	Robert Parish	6.00
	Team Picture	7.00

1989-90 Celtics Citgo Posters

Measuring 17" x 11", the six posters have color artwork anchoring the front, while the right border of the card features a sketch of the player, his name, bio and career highlights. The Citgo logo is in the lower right corner. The blank-backed posters are unnumbered.

		MT
	Complete Set (6):	30.00
	Common Player:	3.00
a	Bob Cousy	12.00
b	Dave Cowens	10.00
	Tom Heinsohn	8.00
	Sam Jones	6.00
	Tom Sanders	3.00
	Paul Silas	4.00

1994-95 Celtics Tribute

Measuring 8-1/2" x 11", the eight-card set features either a photo or artwork on the front. The white-bordered fronts have an "Honor the Tradition" logo in the lower left. The unnumbered card backs showcase the player's name at the top and the date the former player or coach was honored by the team. The player's career highlights and stats are also printed on the backs. Cellular One sponsored Larry Bird's photo. Each of the photos were printed on glossy thin paper stock.

		MT
	Complete Set (8):	19.00
	Common Player:	2.00
	Red Auerbach (CO)	2.00
	Larry Bird	8.00
	Bob Cousy	4.00
	Dave Cowens	3.00
	John Havlicek	4.00
	Tom Heinsohn	3.00
	K.C. Jones	2.00
	Kevin McHale	3.00

A player's name in *italic type* indicates a rookie

2001 Celtics/Topps

		MT
	Complete Set (10):	6.00
	Common Player:	.50
1	Antoine Walker	1.00
2	Paul Pierce	1.50
3	Kenny Anderson	.75
4	Bryant Stith	.50
5	Vitaly Potapenko	.50
6	Eric Williams	.50
7	Mark Blount	.50
8	Tony Battie	.75
9	Jerome Moiso	1.50
10	Randy Brown	.50

1992-93 Center Court

Artist Ron Lewis' work is featured in this set which includes NBA Hall of Fame players, coaches and referees. Each card is 3-1/2" x 5-1/2" and has a colorful posed drawing. The back, similar to a postcard, has the year of induction, the set number (out 10,000), Lewis' signature, the Hall of Fame logo, and the name of the producer (Forgotten Heroes). The set was available through the mail from the producer and was also sold at the Hall of Fame. It is updated annually.

		MT
	Complete Set (53):	80.00
	Complete Series 1 (26):	40.00
	Complete Series 2 (27):	40.00
	Common Player (1-26):	2.00
	Common Player (27-52):	2.00
1	George Mikan	6.00
2	Bill Bradley	5.00
3	Bob Wanzer	2.00
4	Ed McCauley	2.00
5	Harry Gallatan	2.00
6	Willie "Pop" Gates	3.00
7	Bobby Knight (CO)	6.00
8	Dolph Schayes	2.50
9	Bob Pettit	3.00
10	Walt Frazier	3.00
11	Elvin Hayes	3.00
12	Paul Arizin	2.00
13	Phogg Allen (CO)	2.50
14	Oscar Robertson	6.00
15	John Wooden (CO)	5.00
16	Red Holzman (CO)	2.50
17	Jack Twyman	2.00
18	Dean Smith (CO)	6.00
19	John Nucatola	2.00
20	Elgin Baylor	4.00
21	Dave Bing	3.00
22	Lester Harrison	2.00
23	Joe Lapchick	2.50
24	Rick Barry	3.00
25	Lou Carnesecca (CO)	2.50
26	Checklist	2.00
27	Red Auerbach	4.00
28	Dave DeBusschere	2.50
29	Clarence Gaines	3.00
30	Tom Gola	2.00
31	Hal Greer	2.00
32	Luisa-Harris Stewart	2.00
33	K.C. Jones	2.00
34	Sam Jones	2.00
35	Bob Davies	2.00
36	Harry Litwack	2.00
37	Clyde Lovelette	2.50
38	Slater Martin	2.00
39	Al McGuire	3.00
40	Ray Meyer	3.00
41	Earl Monroe	3.00
42	Andy Phillip	2.00
43	Jim Pollard	2.00
44	Bill Sharman	3.00
45	J. Dallas Shirley	2.50
46	Nate Thurmond	2.50
47	Stan Watts	3.00
48	Bobby McDermott	2.00
49	Clair F. Bee	2.50
50	Willis Reed	2.50
51	Larry O'Brien	3.00
52	Checklist	2.00
PD1	George Mikan	5.00

1992 Champion HOF Inductees

This 10-card set features black-and-white photos of the 1992 Basketball Hall of Fame inductees. The cards have white and gray borders with the set name at the top and the player or coach's name at the bottom. The backs have a horizontal layout with biography, career highlights and statistics.

		MT
	Complete Set (10):	75.00
	Common Player:	6.00
1	Bob Lanier	12.00
2	Sergei Belov	6.00
3	Lou Carnesecca CO	6.00
4	Connie Hawkins	15.00
5	Al McGuire CO	6.00
6	Jack Ramsay CO	6.00
7	Nera White	6.00
8	Phil Woolpert CO	6.00
9	Luisa Harris-Stewart	6.00
10	Title card	6.00

1991 Classic Draft Promos

The three regular-sized promo cards were issued to preview Classic's 50-card draft set in 1991. The backs have "For Promotional Purposes Only" printed.

		MT
Complete Set (3):		5.00
Common Player:		1.25
1	(Larry Johnson) (UNLV)	3.00
2	Dikembe Mutombo (Georgetown)	2.00
3	Billy Owens (Syracuse)	1.25

1991 Classic Draft

Released in August 1991, this issue came as a 50-card complete set which was numbered. There were 450,000 sets produced. The set includes 11 exclusively-signed players: Billy Owens, Dikembe Mutombo, Stanley Roberts, Brian Williams, Anderson Hunt, Victor Alexander, Isaac Austin, Greg Sutton, Damon Lopez, Thomas Jordan and Rodney Monroe. Three promo cards were also produced to preview the set; the photos on the fronts are the same as those in the regular set, but the back is blank, except for the notation "For Promotional Purposes Only." The unnumbered cards are 1) Larry Johnson, 2) Dikembe Mutombo, 3) Billy Owens. Classic also produced six certified autograph cards, which on the back say "Congratulations on receiving this limited edition autographed Classic Draft Pick Card." A serial number and production number (1,110 each) were also indicated.

		MT
Complete Set (50):		3.00
Common Player:		.04
1	Larry Johnson (UNLV)	1.00
2	Billy Owens (Syracuse)	.50
3	Dikembe Mutombo (Georgetown)	.75
4	Mark Macon (Temple)	.04
5	Brian Williams (Arizona)	.15
6	Greg Anthony	.60
7	Terrell Brandon	.60
8	Dale Davis (Clemson)	.30
9	Anthony Avent (Seton Hall)	.04
10	Chris Gatling (Old Dominion)	.20
11	Victor Alexander (Iowa State)	.15
12	Kevin Brooks (Southwest Louisiana)	.04
13	Eric Murdock (Providence)	.25
14	LeRon Ellis (Syracuse)	.04
15	Stanley Roberts (LSU)	.15
16	Rick Fox (North Carolina)	.25
17	Pete Chilcutt (North Carolina)	.15
18	Kevin Lynch (Minnesota)	.04
19	George Ackles (UNLV)	.04
20	Rodney Monroe (North Carolina State)	.04
21	Randy Brown (New Mexico State)	.04
22	Chad Gallagher (Creighton)	.04
23	Donald Hodge (Temple)	.04
24	Myron Brown (Slippery Rock)	.04
25	Mike Iuzzolino (St. Francis)	.04
26	Chris Corchiani (North Carolina State)	.04
27	Elliot Perry UER (Memphis State)	.25
28	Joe Wylie (Miami (FL))	.04
29	Jimmy Oliver (Purdue)	.04
30	Doug Overton (LaSalle)	.04
31	Sean Green (Iona)	.04
32	Steve Hood (James Madison)	.04
33	Lamont Strothers (Chris Newport)	.04
34	Alvaro Teheran (Houston)	.04
35	Bobby Phills (Southern)	.40
36	Richard Dumas (DNP (Spain/Okla.St.))	.04
37	Keith Hughes (Rutgers)	.04
38	Isaac Austin (Arizona State)	.04
39	Greg Sutton (Oral Roberts)	.04
40	Joey Wright (Texas)	.04
41	Anthony Jones (Oral Roberts)	.04
42	Von McDade (Milwaukee/Wisconsin)	.04
43	Marcus Kennedy (E. Michigan)	.04
44	Larry Johnson (UNLV Top Pick)	.50
45	Larry Johnson, Billy Owens (UNLV and Syracuse)	.30
46	Anderson Hunt (UNLV)	.04
47	Darrin Chancellor (S. Mississippi)	.04
48	Damon Lopez (Fordham)	.04
49	Thomas Jordan (DNP (Spain/Okla.St.))	.04
50	Tony Farmer (Nebraska)	.04

1991 Classic Draft Autographs

The six-card, standard-size set features the same design as the base cards, except for the autographs on the card fronts and the backs which announce to the collector that he or she has received a "limited edition autographed Classic Draft Pick Card." The cards are numbered as "x of 1,100."

		MT
Complete Set (6):		80.00
Common Player:		5.00
1	Victor Alexander (Iowa State)	7.50
2	Anderson Hunt (UNLV)	5.00
3	Dikembe Mutombo (Georgetown)	40.00
4	Billy Owens (Syracuse)	25.00
5	Stanley Roberts (LSU)	7.50
6	Brian Williams (Arizona)	12.50

1991 Classic Four-Sport

This 230-card multi-sport set combines the four Classic Draft Pick sets from that year and adds 30 additional cards. The cards have different photos than the original sets inside a blue-gray border. "1991 Classic Draft Picks" appears as a seal on the front. The color backs have biographical and statistical information. Autographed cards were inserted at least two per case. The LPs insert was also included in packs. This set was produced in English and bilingual versions.

		MT
Complete Set (230):		10.00
Common Player:		.05
French-Same Value		
1	Future Stars (Larry Johnson, Brien Taylor, Russell Maryland, Eric Lindros)	.50
2	Pat Falloon	.25
3	Scott Niedermayer	.25
4	Scott Lachance	.25
5	Peter Forsberg	1.50
6	Alex Stojanov	.05
7	Richard Matvichuk	.05
8	Patrick Poulin	.05
9	Martin Lapointe	.05
10	Tyler Wright	.05
11	Philippe Boucher	.05
12	Pat Peake	.25
13	Markus Naslund	.05
14	Brent Bilodeau	.05
15	Glen Murray	.05
16	Niklas Sundblad	.05
17	Martin Rucinsky	.05
18	Trevor Halverson	.05
19	Dean McAmmond	.05
20	Ray Whitney	.05
21	Rene Corbet	.05
22	Eric Lavigne	.05
23	Zigmund Palffy	.75
24	Steve Staios	.05
25	Jim Campbell	.25
26	Jassen Cullimore	.05
27	Martin Hamrlik	.05
28	Jamie Pushor	.05
29	Donevan Hextall	.05
30	Andrew Verner	.05
31	Jason Dawe	.25
32	Jeff Nelson	.05
33	Darcy Werenka	.05
34	Jozef Stumpel	.25
35	Francois Groleau	.05
36	Guy Leveque	.05
37	Jamie Matthews	.05
38	Dody Wood	.05
39	Yanic Perreault	.25
40	Jamie McLennan	.05
41	Yanick Dupre UER (Yanic misspelled on both sides)	.05
42	Sandy McCarthy	.05
43	Chris Osgood	1.00
44	Fredrik Lindquist	.05
45	Jason Young	.05
46	Steve Konowalchuk	.05
47	(Michael Nylander UER)	.05
48	Shane Peacock	.05
49	Yves Sarault	.05
50	Marcel Cousineau	.05
51	Brien Taylor	.05
52	Mike Kelly	.05
53	David McCarty	.05
54	Dmitri Young	.25
55	Joe Vitiello	.25
56	Mark Smith	.05
57	Tyler Green	.25
58	(Shawn Estes UER) (reversed negative)	.50
59	Doug Glanville	.15
60	Manny Ramirez	2.00
61	Cliff Floyd	.40
62	Tyrone Hill	.05
63	Eduardo Perez	.05
64	Al Shirley	.05
65	Benji Gil	.05
66	Calvin Reese	.25
67	Allen Watson	.05
68	Brian Barber	.05
69	Aaron Sele	.40
70	(Jon Farrell UER)	.05
71	Scott Ruffcorn	.05
72	Brent Gates	.25
73	Scott Stahoviak	.05
74	Tom McKinnon	.05
75	Shawn Livsey	.05
76	Jason Pruitt	.05
77	Greg Anthony (baseball)	.05
78	Justin Thompson	.75
79	Steve Whitaker	.05
80	Jorge Fabregas	.05
81	Jeff Ware	.05
82	Bobby Jones	.40
83	J.J. Johnson	.05
84	Mike Rossiter	.05
85	Dan Cholowsky	.05
86	Jimmy Gonzalez	.05
87	Trever Miller UER	.05
88	Scott Hatteberg	.05
89	Mike Groppuso	.05
90	Ryan Long	.05
91	Eddie Williams	.05
92	Mike Durant	.05
93	Buck McNabb	.05
94	Jimmy Lewis	.05
95	Eddie Ramos	.05
96	Terry Horn	.05
97	Jon Barnes	.05
98	Shawn Curran	.05
99	Tommy Adams	.05
100	Trevor Mallory	.05
101	Frank Rodriguez	.25
102	Rocket Ismail	.25
103	Russell Maryland	.25
104	Eric Turner	.25
105	Bruce Pickens	.05
106	Mike Croel	.25
107	Todd Lyght	.05
108	Eric Swann	.25
109	Antone Davis	.05
110	Stanley Richard	.05
111	Pat Harlow	.05
112	Alvin Harper	.25
113	Mike Pritchard	.25
114	Leonard Russell	.05
115	Dan McGwire	.05
116	Bobby Wilson	.05
117	Vinnie Clark	.05
118	Kelvin Pritchett	.05
119	Harvey Williams	.25
120	Stan Thomas	.05
121	Randal Hill	.25
122	Todd Marinovich	.05
123	Henry Jones	.25
124	Mike Dumas	.05
125	Ed King	.05
126	Reggie Johnson	.05
127	Roman Phifer	.25
128	Mike Jones	.05
129	Brett Favre	2.00
130	Browning Nagle	.05
131	Esera Tuaolo	.05
132	George Thornton	.05
133	Dixon Edwards	.05
134	Darryll Lewis	.05
135	Eric Bieniemy	.05
136	Shane Curry	.05
137	Jerome Henderson	.05
138	Wesley Carroll	.05
139	Nick Bell	.05
140	John Flannery	.05
141	Ricky Watters	.75
142	Jeff Graham	.40
143	Eric Moten	.05
144	Jesse Campbell	.05
145	Chris Zorich	.25
146	Doug Thomas	.05
147	Phil Hansen	.05
148	Reggie Barrett	.05
149	Larry Johnson	.50
150	Billy Owens	.25
151	Dikembe Mutombo	.50
152	Mark Macon	.05
153	Brian Williams	.05
154	Terrell Brandon	.25
155	Greg Anthony (basketball)	.05
156	Dale Davis	.25
157	Anthony Avent	.05
158	Chris Gatling	.25
159	Victor Alexander	.05
160	Kevin Brooks	.05
161	Eric Murdock	.25
162	LeRon Ellis	.05
163	Stanley Roberts	.05
164	Rick Fox	.05
165	Pete Chilcutt	.05
166	Kevin Lynch	.05
167	George Ackles	.05
168	Rodney Monroe	.05
169	Randy Brown	.05
170	Chad Gallagher	.05
171	Donald Hodge	.05
172	Myron Brown	.05
173	Mike Iuzzolino	.05
174	Chris Corchiani	.05
175	Elliott Perry	.25
176	Joe Wylie	.05
177	Jimmy Oliver	.05
178	Doug Overton	.05
179	Sean Green	.05
180	Steve Hood	.05
181	Lamont Strothers	.05
182	Alvaro Teheran	.05
183	Bobby Phills	.25
184	Richard Dumas	.05
185	Keith Hughes	.05
186	Isaac Austin	.25
187	Greg Sutton	.05
188	Joey Wright	.05
189	Anthony Jones	.05
190	Von McDade	.05
191	Marcus Kennedy	.05
192	(Larry Johnson) (Number One Pick)	.50
193	Classic One on One II	.05
194	Anderson Hunt	.05
195	Darrin Chancellor	.05
196	Damon Lopez	.05
197	Thomas Jordan	.05
198	Tony Farmer	.05
199	Billy Owens (Number Three Pick)	.05
200	Owens Takes 4-3 Lead (Billy Owens)	.05
201	Johnson Slams for 6-6 Tie (Larry Johnson)	.05
202	Score Tied with :49 Left	.05
203	Gary Brown	.25
204	Rob Carpenter	.05
205	Ricky Ervins	.05
206	Donald Hollas	.05
207	Greg Lewis	.05
208	Darren Lewis	.05
209	Anthony Morgan	.05
210	Chris Smith	.05
211	Perry Carter	.05
212	Melvin Cheatum	.05
213	Jerome Harmon	.05
214	Keith (Mister) Jennings	.05
215	Brian Shorter	.05
216	Dexter Davis	.05
217	Ed McCaffrey	.05
218	Joey Hamilton	.25
219	Marc Kroon	.05
220	Moe Gardner	.05
221	Jon Vaughn	.05
222	Lawrence Dawsey	.05
223	Michael Stonebreaker	.05
224	Shawn Moore	.05
225	Shawn Green	.50
226	Scott Pisciotta	.05
227	Checklist 1	.05
228	Checklist 2	.05
229	Checklist 3	.05
230	Checklist 4	.05

1991 Classic Four-Sport Autographs

Sixty-one players signed cards for this set. The cards are hand-numbered with a "A" suffix and were inserted at a rate of two or more per case.

		MT
Complete Set (61):		900.00
Common Autograph:		10.00
2	Pat Falloon/1100	20.00
3	Scott Niedermayer/1250	20.00
4	Scott Lachance/1100	20.00
6	Alek Stojanov/950	10.00
8	Patrick Poulin/1100	10.00
10	Tyler Wright/950	10.00
11	Philippe Boucher/1150	10.00
12	Pat Peake/1100	20.00
14	Brent Bilodeau/1000	10.00
15	Glen Murray/1100	10.00
16	Niklas Sundblad/900	10.00
17	Martin Rucinsky/1100	10.00
18	Trevor Halverson/1100	10.00
19	Dean McAmmond/1100	10.00
20	Ray Whitney/2600	10.00
21	Rene Corbet/950	10.00
22	Eric Lavigne/1100	10.00
24	Steve Staios/1100	10.00
25	Jim Campbell/1100	25.00
26	Jassen Cullimore/1000	10.00
28	Jamie Pushor/1050	20.00
29	Donevan Hextall/1100	10.00
30	Andrew Verner/1200	10.00
31	Jason Dawe/950	20.00
32	Jeff Nelson/1100	10.00
33	Darcy Werenka/1150	10.00
35	Francois Groleau/1150	10.00
36	Guy Leveque/1150	10.00
37	Jamie Matthews/1100	10.00
38	Dody Wood/1050	10.00
39	Yanic Perreault/1100	20.00
40	Jamie Matthews/1100	10.00
41	Yanick Dupre/1050	25.00
42	Sandy McCarthy/1150	10.00
43	Chris Osgood/1100	60.00
44	F. Lindquist/1100	10.00
45	Jason Young/1200	10.00
46	Steve Konowalchuk/1350	10.00
47	Michael Nylander/1100	10.00
48	Shane Peacock/1150	10.00
49	Yves Sarault/1150	10.00
50	Marcel Cousineau/1100	10.00
51	Brien Taylor/2600	10.00
52	Mike Kelly/2600	10.00
53	David McCarty/2450	10.00
54	Dmitri Young/2600	25.00
55	Joe Vitiello/1900	25.00
56	Mark Smith/1700	10.00
58	Shawn Estes/2000	30.00
59	Doug Glanville/2000	20.00
61	Cliff Floyd/2000	40.00
62	Tyrone Hill/1000	10.00
63	Eduardo Perez/950	10.00
101	Frank Rodriguez/1450	20.00
102	Rocket Ismail/2000	25.00
103	Russell Maryland/1000	25.00
150	Billy Owens/2500	25.00
151	Dikembe Mutombo/1000	40.00
153	Brian Williams/1500	10.00
163	Stanley Roberts/2000	10.00
218	Joey Hamilton/2000	25.00

1991 Classic Four-Sport LPs

This 10-card set was inserted in packs of 1991 Classic Draft Picks Collection. The cards can be distinguished from the base set by the silver or gold inner border on the front. The cards have a "LP" prefix.

		MT
Complete Set (10):		15.00
Common Player:		1.00
French: Same Value		
1	Rocket Lands in Canada	2.00
2	Rocket Surveys The Future	2.00
3	Rocket Launch	2.00
4	Track Star (Rocket Ismail)	2.00
5	Rocket Knows Classic	2.00
6	Larry Johnson's Guns	2.00
7	Brien Taylor	1.00
8	Classic Gold Card SP	5.00
9	The Final Shot (Larry Johnson, Billy Owens)	2.00
10	Russell Maryland (Number One Pick)	1.00

1992 Classic Draft Preview

These five cards, numbered #1 of 5, etc., were inserted into 1992 Classic foil packs to introduce the basketball set. The fronts have glossy action photos. 10,000 sets were made.

		MT
Complete Set (5):		125.00
Common Player:		5.00
1	Shaquille O'Neal	85.00
2	Alonzo Mourning	30.00
3	Don MacLean	5.00
4	Walt Williams	8.00
5	Christian Laettner	10.00

1992 Classic Draft Promos

The six-card, standard-size set was issued as a preview for the 1992 Classic Draft. The cards parallel the base set in design with "For Promotional Purposes Only" printed on the card backs.

		MT
Complete Set (6):		45.00
Common Player:		1.00
1	Shaquille O'Neal (LSU)	25.00
2	Alonzo Mourning (Georgetown)	12.00
3	Christian Laettner (Duke)	6.00
4	Walt Williams (Maryland)	4.00
5	Don MacLean (UCLA)	1.00
6	Jimmy Jackson (Ohio State)	8.00

1992 Classic Draft Gold Promo

The standard-size card parallels the base design with gold-foil stamping along the front bottom border. The card backs have "For Promotional Purposes Only" printed.

		MT
Complete Set (1):		12.00
Common Player:		12.00
2	Alonzo Mourning (Promotional Georgetown)	12.00

1992 Classic Draft

This 100-card glossy set features the draft picks from the June 1992 NBA draft. The 2-1/2" x 3-1/2" cards have color photos on the fronts. The backs do too, plus collegiate stats and a scouting report. Approximately one million sets were distributed through foil packs. Shaquille O'Neal is featured in the set. Classic also produced 8,500 sequentially numbered gold sets in their own walnut display cases. The cards have the same design format as the regular ones, but include the player's name, position and Classic Draft Picks Gold logo stamped in gold foil. These cards are generally worth three to six times more than their regular counterparts. Each set also included an autographed Shaquille O'Neal card. O'Neal is also featured on one of the six promo cards Classic made to preview its regular 1992 Classic Draft Picks set. In place of statistics on the card back, the back says "For Promotional Purposes Only."

		MT
Complete Set (100):		15.00
Common Player:		.05
Complete Gold Set (101):		260.00
Common Gold:		.30
Shaquille O'Neal Auto./8500		
1	Shaquille O'Neal	5.00
2	Walt Williams	.50
3	Lee Mayberry	.15
4	Tony Bennett	.05
5	Litterial Green	.05
6	Chris Smith	.05
7	Henry Williams	.05
8	Terrell Lowery	.05
9	Radenko Dobras	.05
10	Curtis Blair	.05
11	Randy Woods	.10
12	Todd Day	.25
13	Anthony Peeler	.10
14	Darin Archbold	.05
15	Benford Williams	.05
16	Torrence Lewis	.05
17	Jim McCoy	.05
18	Damon Patterson	.05
19	Bryant Stith	.25
20	Doug Christie	.10
21	Latrell Sprewell	1.00
22	Hubert Davis	.15
23	David Booth	.05
24	Dave Johnson	.05
25	Jon Barry	.10
26	Everick Sullivan	.05
27	Brian Davis	.05
28	C. Weatherspoon	.75
29	Malik Sealy	.25
30	Matt Geiger	.15
31	Jim Jackson	1.00
32	Matt Steigenga	.05
33	Robert Horry	.60
34	Marlon Maxey	.05
35	Reggie Slater	.05
36	Lucius Davis	.05
37	Chris King	.05
38	Dexter Cambridge	.05
39	Alonzo Jamison	.05
40	Anthony Tucker	.05
41	Tracy Murray	.10
42	Vernel Singleton	.05
43	Christian Laettner	.50
44	Don MacLean	.25
45	Adam Keefe	.10
46	Tom Gugliotta	.75
47	LaPhonso Ellis	.25
48	Byron Houston	.10
49	Oliver Miller	.20
50	Ron "Popeye" Jones	.25
51	P.J. Brown	.30
52	Eric Anderson	.05
53	Darren Morningstar	.05
54	Isaiah Morris	.05
55	Stephen Howard	.05
56	Reggie Smith	.05
57	Elmore Spencer	.05
58	Sean Rooks	.25
59	Robert Werdann	.05
60	Alonzo Mourning	1.00
61	Steve Rogers	.05
62	Tim Burroughs	.05
63	Ed Book	.05
64	Herb Jones	.05
65	Mik Kilgore	.05
66	Ken Leeks	.05
67	Sam Mack	.05
68	Sean Miller	.05
69	Craig Upchurch	.05
70	Van Usher	.05
71	Corey Williams	.05
72	Duane Cooper	.05
73	Brett Roberts	.05
74	Elmer Bennett	.05
75	Brent Price	.10
76	Daimon Sweet	.05
77	Darric Martin	.20
78	Gerald Madkins	.05
79	Jo Jo English	.05
80	Alex Blackwell	.05
81	Anthony Dade	.05
82	Matt Fish	.05
83	Byron Tucker	.05
84	Harold Miner	.10
85	Greg Dennis	.05
86	Jeff Roulston	.05
87	Keir Rogers	.05
88	Billy Law	.05
89	Geoff Lear	.05
90	Lambert Shell	.05
91	Elbert Rogers	.05
92	Ron Ellis	.05
93	Predrag Danilovic	.25
94	Calvin Talford	.05
95	Flashback #1 (Stacey Augmon)	.10
96	Flashback #2 (Steve Smith)	.10
97	Flashback #3 (Billy Owens)	.10
98	Flashback #4 (Dikembe Mutombo)	.10
99	Checklist #1	.05
100	Checklist #2	.05
NNO	Christian Laettner	1.00

1992 Classic Draft Gold

There were 8,500 numbered sets produced, with two sets per case. Each set is in a walnut display box and includes one autographed Shaquille O'Neal card. With the exception of a gold foil stamp on the player's name, the cards are identical to the regular Classic issue.

		MT
Complete Fact. Set (101):		300.00
Common Player:		.50
1	Shaquille O'Neal	75.00
2	Walt Williams	12.00
3	Lee Mayberry	2.00
4	Tony Bennett	1.00
5	Litterial Green	1.00
6	Chris Smith	.50
7	Henry Williams	.50
8	Terrell Lowery	.50
9	Radenko Dobras	.50
10	Curtis Blair	.50
11	Randy Woods	.50
12	Todd Day	9.00
13	Anthony Peeler	6.00
14	Darin Archbold	.50
15	Benford Williams	.50
16	Terrence Lewis	.50
17	Jim McCoy	.50
18	Damon Patterson	.50
19	Bryant Stith	5.00
20	Doug Christie	1.00
21	Latrell Sprewell	8.00
22	Hubert Davis	2.00
23	David Booth	.60
24	Dave Johnson	1.00
25	Jon Barry	1.00
26	Everick Sullivan	.50
27	Brian Davis	.50
28	C. Weatherspoon	8.00
29	Malik Sealy	2.00
30	Matt Geiger	.50
31	Jim Jackson	15.00
32	Matt Steigenga	.50
33	Robert Horry	8.00
34	Marlon Maxey	.50
35	Reggie Slater	.50
36	Lucius Davis	.50
37	Chris King	.50
38	Dexter Cambridge	.50
39	Alonzo Jamison	.50
40	Anthony Tucker	.50
41	Tracy Murray	1.00
42	Vernel Singleton	.50
43	Christian Laettner	15.00
44	Don MacLean	1.00
45	Adam Keefe	5.00
46	Tom Gugliotta	12.00
47	LaPhonso Ellis	8.50
48	Byron Houston	3.00

49	Oliver Miller	10.00
50	Ron "Popeye" Jones	.50
51	P.J. Brown	.50
52	Eric Anderson	.50
53	Darren Morningstar	.50
54	Isaiah Mooris	.50
55	Stephen Howard	.50
56	Reggie Smith	.50
57	Elmore Spencer	1.00
58	Sean Rooks	3.00
59	Robert Werdann	.50
60	Alonzo Mourning	75.00
61	Steve Rogers	.50
62	Tim Burroughs	.50
63	Ed Book	.50
64	Herb Jones	.50
65	Mik Kilgore	.50
66	Ken Leeks	.50
67	Sam Mack	.50
68	Sean Miller	.50
69	Craig Upchurch	.50
70	Van Usher	.50
71	Corey Williams	2.00
72	Duane Cooper	2.00
73	Brett Roberts	.50
74	Elmer Bennett	.50
75	Brent Price	1.00
76	Daimon Sweet	.50
77	Darrick Martin	.50
78	Gerald Madkins	.50
79	Jo Jo English	.50
80	Alex Blackwell	.50
81	Anthony Dade	.50
82	Matt Fish	.50
83	Byron Tucker	.50
84	Harold Miner	10.00
85	Greg Dennis	.50
86	Jeff Roulston	.50
87	Keir Rogers	.50
88	Billy Law	.50
89	Geoff Lear	.50
90	Lambert Shell	.50
91	Elbert Rogers	.50
92	Ron Ellis	.50
93	Predrag Danilovic	.50
94	Calvin Talford	.50
95	Stacey Augmon	1.00
96	Steve Smith	1.00
97	Billy Owens	1.00
98	Dikembe Mutombo	1.00
99	Checklist #1 (1-50)	.50
100	Checklist #2 (51-100)	.50
----	Shaquille O'Neal (Auto)	200.00

1992 Classic Draft LPs

These cards were randomly inserted in foil boxes, two per box. There were 56,000 glossy sets produced, so each card is foil stamped "1 of 56,000" etc. on the front. Fronts feature a color action photo and the player's name. The backs also have a color photo and tell when the player was picked in the 1992 NBA draft. Cards measure 2-1/2" x 3-1/2".

		MT
Complete Set (10):		75.00
Common Player:		1.00
1	Shaquille O'Neal	35.00
2	Alonzo Mourning	10.00
3	Christian Laettner	5.00
4	Jim Jackson	10.00
5	LaPhonso Ellis	3.00
6	Tom Gugliotta	6.00
7	Walt Williams	4.00
8	Todd Day	2.00
9	C. Weatherspoon	5.00
10	Adam Keefe	1.00

1992 Classic Draft Magicians

90,000 sets of this subset were made after Classic oversold foil cases of its regular 100-card draft pick set. As part of an agreement with distributors, Classic made a limited amount of cases in jumbo form, with 20 sets per case. Each foil pack contains a "Magician" card, which is identical to the regular draft pick set except it's numbered differently and is foil stamped "Magician" on the front and on the player's name.

		MT
Complete Set (20):		12.00
Common Player:		.25
1	Doug Christie	.50
2	Billy Owens (FB)	.25
3	Latrell Sprewell	3.00
4	Stacey Augmon (FB)	.25
5	Steve Smith (FB)	.25
6	Jon Barry	.25
7	Christian Laettner	1.50
8	Jim Jackson	3.00
9	Tracy Murray	.25
10	Walt Williams	.50
11	Todd Day	.50
12	Dave Johnson	.25
13	Byron Houston	.25
14	Robert Horry	.75
15	Harold Miner	.25
16	Bryant Stith	.50
17	Malik Sealy	.50
18	Randy Woods	.25
19	Anthony Peeler	.25
20	Lee Mayberry	.25

1992 Classic Four-Sport Previews

These five preview cards were inserted in baseball and hockey draft picks packs. The fronts have a full-bleed photo with the player's name and position in a black bar down the left side. The Classic logo and "Preview" appear in the upper left corner. The backs have "Preview" printed at the top and a congratulatory message. Only 10,000 of each card was produced. The cards have a "CC" prefix.

		MT
Complete Set (5):		50.00
Common Player:		1.50
1	Shaquille O'Neal	30.00
2	Desmond Howard	2.00
3	Roman Hamrlik	2.50
4	Phil Nevin	1.50
5	Alonzo Mourning	15.00

1992 Classic Four-Sport

Classic Four-Sport is a 325-card set that combines the four draft picks sets from 1992. The card fronts have a full-bleed photo with the player's name and position in a black bar on the left side. The backs have another photo, college statistics and a brief biography. Autographed cards, Bonus Cards and Limited Prints were randomly inserted in packs. A gold version of the set could be purchased as a boxed set with one Future Stars autograph per box.

		MT
Complete Set (325):		15.00
Common Player:		.05
Comp. Fact. Gold Set (326)		150.00
Common Gold		.40
Fut. Superstars AU/9500		75.00
One Fut. Stars Auto per Fact. Gold Set		
*Gold Stars:		6x
1	Shaquille O'Neal	3.00
2	Walt Williams	.25
3	Lee Mayberry	.05
4	Tony Bennett	.05
5	Litterial Green	.05
6	Chris Smith	.05
7	Henry Williams	.05
8	Terrell Lowery	.05
9	Curtis Blair	.05
10	Randy Woods	.05
11	Todd Day	.25
12	Anthony Peeler	.05
13	Darin Archibold	.05
14	Benford Williams	.05
15	Damon Patterson	.05
16	Bryant Stith	.25
17	Doug Christie	.25
18	Latrell Sprewell	.75
19	Hubert Davis	.25
20	David Booth	.05
21	Dave Johnson	.05
22	Jon Barry	.05
23	Everick Sullivan	.05
24	Brian Davis	.05
25	Clarence Weatherspoon	.25
26	Malik Sealy	.25
27	Matt Geiger	.05
28	Jimmy Jackson	.50
29	Matt Steigenga	.05
30	Robert Horry	.25
31	Marlon Maxey	.05
32	Chris King	.05
33	Dexter Cambridge	.05
34	Alonzo Jamison	.05
35	Anthony Tucker	.05
36	Tracy Murray	.25
37	Vernel Singleton	.05
38	Christian Laettner	.60
39	Don MacLean	.10
40	Adam Keefe	.25
41	Tom Gugliotta	.60
42	LaPhonso Ellis	.25
43	Byron Houston	.05
44	Oliver Miller	.05
45	Popeye Jones	.05
46	P.J. Brown	.05
47	Eric Anderson	.05
48	Darren Morningstar	.05
49	Isaiah Morris	.05
50	Stephen Howard	.05
51	Elmore Spencer	.05
52	Sean Rooks	.05
53	Robert Werdann	.05
54	Alonzo Mourning	1.00
55	Steve Rogers	.05
56	Tim Burroughs	.05
57	Herb Jones	.05
58	Sean Miller	.05
59	Corey Williams	.05
60	Duane Cooper	.05
61	Brett Roberts	.05
62	Elmer Bennett	.05
63	Brent Price	.15
64	Daimon Sweet	.05
65	Darrick Martin	.05
66	Gerald Madkins	.05
67	Jo Jo English	.05
68	Math Fish	.05
69	Harold Miner	.05
70	Greg Dennis	.05
71	Jeff Roulston	.05
72	Keir Rogers	.05
73	Geoff Lear	.05
74	Ron Ellis	.05
75	Predrag Danilovic	.05
76	Desmond Howard	.40
77	David Klingler	.05
78	Quentin Coryatt	.25
79	Bill Johnson	.05
80	Eugene Chung	.05
81	Derek Brown	.05
82	Carl Pickens	1.00
83	Chris Mims	.05
84	Charles Davenport	.05
85	Ray Roberts	.05
86	Chuck Smith	.10
87	Tony Smith RB	.05
88	Ken Swilling	.05
89	Greg Skrepenak	.05
90	Phillippi Sparks	.05
91	Alonzo Spellman	.05
92	Bernard Dafney	.05
93	Edgar Bennett	.50
94	Shane Dronett	.05
95	Jeremy Lincoln	.05
96	Dion Lambert	.05
97	Siran Stacy	.05
98	Tony Sacca	.05
99	Sean Lumpkin	.05
100	Tommy Vardell	.05
101	Keith Hamilton	.05
102	Sean Gilbert	.25
103	Casey Weldon	.05
104	Marc Boutte	.05
105	Arthur Marshall	.05
106	Santana Dotson	.05
107	Ronnie West	.05
108	Mike Pawlawski	.05
109	Dale Carter	.25
110	Carlos Snow	.05
111	Mark D'Onofrio	.05
112	Matt Blundin	.05
113	Patrick Rowe	.05
114	Joel Steed	.05
115	Erick Anderson	.05
116	Rodney Culver	.05
117	Chris Hakel	.05
118	Kevin Smith	.05
119	Robert Brooks	1.00
120	Bucky Richardson	.05
121	Steve Israel	.05
122	Marco Coleman	.25
123	Johnny Mitchell	.05
124	Scottie Graham	.05
125	Keith Goganious	.05
126	Tommy Maddox	.05
127	Terrell Buckley	.05
128	Dana Hall	.05
129	Ty Detmer	.40
130	Darryl Williams	.05
131	Jason Hanson	.25
132	Leon Searcy	.05
133	Will Furrer	.05
134	Darren Woodson	.40
135	Corey Widmer	.05
136	Larry Tharpe	.05
137	Lance Olberding	.05
138	Stacey Dillard	.05
139	Anthony Hamlet	.05
140	Mike Evans	.05
141	Chester McGlockton	.25
142	Marquez Pope	.05
143	Tyrone Legette	.05
144	Derrick Moore	.25
145	Calvin Holmes	.05
146	Eddie Robinson Jr.	.05
147	Robert Jones	.05
148	Ricardo McDonald	.05
149	Howard Dinkins	.05
150	Todd Collins	.05
151	Roman Hamrlik	.25
152	Alexei Yashin	.50
153	Mike Rathje	.05
154	Darius Kasparaitis	.25
155	Cory Stillman	.05
156	Robert Petrovicky	.05
157	Andrei Nazarov	.05
158	Jason Bowen	.05
159	Jason Smith	.05
160	David Wilkie	.05
161	Curtis Bowen	.05
162	Grant Marshall	.05
163	Valeri Bure	.25
164	Jeff Shantz	.05
165	Justin Hocking	.05
166	Mike Pecca	.05
167	Marc Hussey	.05
168	Sandy Allan	.05
169	Kirk Maltby	.25
170	Cale Hulse	.05
171	Sylvain Cloutier	.05
172	Martin Gendron	.05
173	Kevin Smyth	.05
174	Jason McBain	.05
175	Lee J. Leslie	.05
176	Ralph Intranuovo	.05
177	Martin Reichel	.20
178	Stefan Ustorf	.05
179	Jarkko Varvio	.05
180	Martin Straka	.25
181	Libor Polasek	.05
182	Jozef Cierny	.05
183	Sergei Krivokrasov	.25
184	Sergei Gonchar	.05
185	Boris Mironov	.05
186	Denis Metyluk	.05
187	Sergei Klimovich	.05
188	Sergei Brylin	.05
189	Andrei Nikolishin	.05
190	Alexander Cherbayev	.05
191	Vitali Tomilin	.05
192	Sandy Moger	.05
193	Darrin Madeley	.05
194	Denny Felsner	.05
195	Dwayne Norris	.05
196	Joby Messier	.05
197	Michael Stewart	.05
198	Scott Thomas	.05
199	Daniel Laperriere	.05
200	Martin Lacroix	.05
201	Scott LaGrand	.05
202	Scott Pellerin	.05
203	Jean-Yves Roy	.05
204	Rob Gaudreau	.05
205	Jeff McLean	.05
206	Dallas Drake	.05
207	Doug Zmolek	.05
208	Duane Derksen	.05
209	Jim Cummins	.05
210	Lonnie Loach	.05
211	Rob Zamuner	.05
212	Brad Werenka	.05
213	Brent Grieve	.05
214	Sean Hill	.05
215	Peter Ciavaglia	.05
216	Jason Ruff	.05
217	Shawn McCosh	.05
218	Dave Tretowicz	.05
219	Mike Vukonich	.05
220	Kevin Wortman	.05
221	Jason Muzzatti	.05
222	Dmitri Kvartalnov	.05
223	Ray Whitney	.05
224	Manon Rheaume	3.00
225	Viktor Kozlov	.40
226	Phil Nevin	.05
227	Paul Shuey	.05
228	B.J. Wallace	.05
229	Jeffrey Hammonds	.25
230	Chad Mottola	.05
231	Derek Jeter	4.00
232	Michael Tucker	.25
233	Derek Wallace	.05
234	Kenny Felder	.05
235	Chad McConnell	.05
236	Sean Lowe	.05
237	Ricky Greene	.05
238	Chris Roberts	.05
239	Shannon Stewart	.25
240	Benji Grigsby	.05
241	Jamie Arnold	.05
242	Rick Helling	.05
243	Jason Kendall	.50
244	Todd Steverson	.05
245	Dan Serafini	.05
246	Jeff Schmidt	.05
247	Sherard Clinkscales	.05
248	Ryan Luzinski	.05
249	Shon Walker	.05
250	Brandon Cromer	.05
251	Dave Landaker	.05
252	Michael Matthews	.05
253	Brian Sackinsky	.05
254	Jon Lieber	.05
255	Jim Rosenbohm	.05
256	DeShawn Warren	.05
257	Mike Buddie	.05
258	Chris Smith	.05
259	Dwain Bostic	.05
260	Bobby Hughes	.25
261	Rick Magdellano	.05
262	Bob Wolcott	.05
263	Mike Gulan	.05
264	Yuri Sanchez	.05
265	Tony Sheffield	.05
266	Dan Melandez	.05
267	Jason Giambi	.50
268	Ritchie Moody	.05
269	Trey Beamon	.05
270	Tim Crabtree	.05
271	Chad Roper	.05
272	Mark Thompson	.05
273	Marquis Riley	.05
274	Tom Knauss	.05
275	Chris Holt	.05
276	Jon Nunnally	.05
277	Everett Stull	.05
278	Billy Owens	.05
279	Todd Etler	.05
280	Benji Simonton	.05
281	Dwight Maness	.05
282	Chris Eddy	.05
283	Brant Brown	.40
284	Kurt Ehmann	.05
285	Chris Widger	.05
286	Steve Montgomery	.05
287	Chris Gomez	.05
288	Jared Baker	.05
289	Doug Hecker	.05
290	David Spykstra	.05
291	Scott Miller	.05
292	Carey Paige	.05
293	Dave Manning	.05
294	James Keefe	.05
295	Levon Largusa	.05
296	Roger Bailey	.05
297	Rich Ireland	.05
298	Matt Williams	.15
299	Scott Gentile	.05
300	Hut Smith	.05
301	Dave Brown	.25
302	Bobby Bonds Jr.	.05
303	Reggie Smith	.05
304	Preston Wilson	.05
305	John Burke	.05
306	Rodney Henderson	.05
307	Pete Janicki	.05
308	Brien Taylor FLB	.05
309	Mike Kelly FLB	.05
310	Rocket Ismail FLB	.05
311	Billy Owens FLB	.05
312	Dikembe Mutombo FLB	.25
313	Ty Detmer, Desmond Howard	.50
314	Jim Pittsley	.05
315	Christian Laettner JWA	.25
316	Harold Miner JWA	.05
317	Jimmy Jackson JWA	.40
318	Shaquille O'Neal JWA	1.50
319	Alonzo Mourning JWA	.40
320	Checklist 1	.05
321	Checklist 2	.05
322	Checklist 3	.05
323	Checklist 4	.05
324	Checklist 5	.05
325	Checklist 6 (Foil checklist includes LP's; jumbo checklist only list regular cards)	.05

1992 Classic Four-Sport Autographs

These autographed versions were randomly inserted into Four Sport packs, with 54 known cards available. Card fronts are similar to regular-issue cards, but have the player's autograph added to the front along with how many cards each player autographed. Backs included a "Congratulations. You have received a Classic Games Autograph Card." message. Jan Caloun and Jan Vopat were not included in the regular set and therefore are unnumbered.

		MT
Complete Set (54):		2500.
Common Player:		10.00
Listed by corresponding regular card beware O'Neal/Mourning counterfeits		
1A	Shaquille O'Neal/150	1500.
2A	Walt Williams/2550	25.00
3A	Lee Mayberry/2575	10.00
11A	Todd Day/1575	25.00
25A	Clarence Weatherspoon/1575	25.00
26A	Malik Sealy/1575	25.00
28A	Jimmy Jackson/1575	40.00
36A	Tracy Murray/1450	25.00
38A	Christian Laettner/725	50.00
39A	Don MacLean/2575	20.00
40A	Adam Keefe/1575	20.00
54A	Alonzo Mourning/975	80.00
69A	Harold Miner/1475	10.00
76A	Desmond Howard/975	25.00
77A	David Klingler/1125	10.00
78A	Quentin Coryatt/3500	20.00
82A	Carl Pickens/1475	50.00
87A	Tony Smith/3450	10.00
97A	Siran Stacy/4325	10.00
98A	Tony Sacca/1575	10.00
103A	Casey Weldon/4350	10.00
112A	Matt Blundin/1575	10.00
127A	Terrell Buckley/1475	10.00
129A	Ty Detmer/1475	25.00
144A	Derrick Moore/1575	25.00
151A	Roman Hamrlik/1550	20.00
153A	Mike Rathje/2075	10.00
155A	Cory Stillman/2125	10.00
158A	Jason Bowen/2075	10.00
159A	Jason Smith/2075	10.00
165A	Justin Hocking/2075	10.00
170A	Cale Hulse/1850	10.00
181A	Libor Polasek/1950	10.00
185A	Boris Mironov/2075	10.00
192A	Sandy Moger/1075	10.00
195A	Dwayne Norris/1075	10.00
196A	Joby Messier/1075	10.00
207A	Doug Zmolek/1075	10.00
226A	Phil Nevin/1475	10.00
227A	Paul Shuey/4050	10.00
229A	Jeffrey Hammonds/2950	20.00
231A	Derek Jeter/1125	80.00
233A	Derek Wallace/1475	10.00
241A	Jamie Arnold/1575	10.00
242A	Rick Helling/2875	10.00
245A	Dan Serafini/1475	10.00
248A	Ryan Luzinski/1575	10.00
253A	Brian Sackinsky/1575	10.00
259A	Dwain Bostic/2075	10.00
290A	David Spykstra/1575	10.00
301A	Dave Brown/1575	25.00
307A	Pete Janicki/1875	10.00
---	Jan Caloun/1975	10.00
---	Jan Vopat/1775	10.00

1992 Classic Four-Sport BCs

These 20 bonus cards were inserted one per jumbo pack of 1992 Classic Four-Sport. The cards are similar to the base set except they feature silver foil. The Future Superstars card is considered card #21 in this set. It features a player from each sport on the front. Only 10,000 cards were produced. The cards have a "BC" prefix.

		MT
Complete Set (20):		20.00
Common Player:		.25
1	Alonzo Mourning	2.50
2	Christian Laettner	.75
3	Jimmy Jackson	1.00
4	Tom Gugliotta	1.00
5	Walt Williams	.75
6	Harold Miner	.25
7	Roman Hamrlik	.75
8	Valeri Bure	.75
9	Dallas Drake	.25
10	Dmitri Kvartalnov	.25
11	Manon Rheaume	8.00
12	Viktor Kozlov	.75
13	Desmond Howard	.75
14	David Klingler	.25
15	Terrell Buckley	.25
16	Quentin Coryatt	.75
17	Carl Pickens	2.00
18	Phil Nevin	.25
19	Jeffrey Hammonds	.75
20	Michael Tucker	.75
FS1	Future Superstars (Phil Nevin, Shaquille O'Neal, Desmond Howard, Roman Hamrlik)	30.00

1992 Classic Four-Sport LPs

This 25-card set is similar to the 1992 Classic Four-Sport base set but features gold foil on both sides. "One of 46,080" appears in gold foil on the front. The cards have a "LP" prefix.

		MT
Complete Set (25):		50.00
Common Player:		.50
1	Desmond Howard	1.00
2	David Klingler	.50
3	Tommy Maddox	.50
4	Casey Weldon	.50
5	Tony Smith RB	.50
6	Terrell Buckley	.50
7	Carl Pickens	3.00
8	Shaquille O'Neal	20.00
9	Jimmy Jackson	4.00
10	Alonzo Mourning	6.00
11	Christian Laettner	2.00
12	Harold Miner	.50
13	Todd Day	1.00
14	The King and His Heir (Kareem Abdul-Jabbar, Shaquille O'Neal)	12.00
15	Future Superstars (Phil Nevin, Shaquille O'Neal, Roman Hamrlik)	12.00
16	Classic Quarterbacks (Matt Blundin, David Klingler, Tommy Maddox, Mike Pawlawski, Tony Sacca, Casey Weldon)	.50
17	Phil Nevin	.50
18	Jeffrey Hammonds	1.00
19	Paul Shuey	.50
20	Ryan Luzinski UER	.50
21	Brien Taylor	.50
22	Roman Hamrlik	1.00
23	Mike Rathje	.50
24	Valeri Bure	1.00
25	Alexei Yashin	1.00

1992 Classic Show Promos

The 20-card, standard-size set was released one card at a time at the various collectible shows where Classic had a manufacturer table. Each card back is numbered as "x of 20" and the fronts feature varying designs.

		MT
Complete Set (20):		80.00
Common Player:		1.00
1	Billy Owens (1992 Sports Spectacular)	2.00
2	Dikembe Mutombo (1992 SportsNet National) (Georgetown)	3.00
3	Brien Taylor (1992 SportsNet National) (New York Yankees)	1.00
4	David Klingler (1992 Sports Spectacular) (Houston)	1.00
5	Carl Lewis (July 1992 Arlington Marcus show)	2.00
6	Quentin Coryatt (July 1992 Arlington Marcus show)	2.00
7	Brien Taylor (1992 Atlanta National Convention) (New York Yankees)	1.00
8	Frankie Rodriguez (1992 Atlanta National Convention) (Boston Red Sox)	1.00
9	Jimmy Jackson (July 9-12, 1992, at Atlanta National)	5.00
10	Ken Griffey Jr. (July 9-12, 1992, at Atlanta National) (Seattle Mariners)	5.00
11	Shaquille O'Neal (July 9-12, 1992, at Atlanta National) (LSU)	20.00
12	Alonzo Mourning (July 9-12, 1992, at Atlanta National) (Georgetown)	16.00
13	Christian Laettner (1992 East Coast National) (Duke)	2.00
14	Nolan Ryan (1992 East Coast National) (Texas Rangers)	5.00
15	Roman Hamrlik (1992 Tri-Star St. Louis)	3.00
16	Phil Nevin (1992 Tri-Star St. Louis) (Cal-State Fullerton)	1.00
17	Shaquille O'Neal (1992 Tri-Star St. Louis)	20.00
18	David Klingler (1992 Tri-Star Houston) (Houston)	1.00
19	Phil Nevin (1992 Tri-Star Houston) (Cal-State Fullerton)	1.00
20	Harold Miner (1992 Tri-Star Houston) (USC)	1.00

1993 Classic Draft Promos

These unnumbered cards, previewing Classic's 1993 Draft Picks basketball set, were random inserts in the company's 1993 Classic Football Draft Picks and Pro Line Collection packs. Two cards appeared in each case; there were 17,500 of each preview card produced, as indicated on the red card back, which features a set logo.

	MT
Complete Set (4):	65.00
Common Player:	7.00
Chris Webber	18.00
Jamal Mashburn	20.00
Anfernee Hardaway	25.00
Allan Houston	7.00

1993 Classic Draft

Classic signed four of the top five 1993 NBA draft picks to exclusive contracts for this 110-card set - Chris Webber, Anfernee Hardaway, Jamal Mashburn and J.R. Rider. The set has 110 regular-print cards, 10 limited-print, gold foil-stamped cards and five 1993 Classic Hockey Draft Pick Preview cards. Classic produced a special insert set called "Draft Stars," - Webber, Hardaway, Mashburn, Rider and Rodney Rogers complete a panoramic image created by the visually integrated acetate plastic cards. Classic produced 32,500 cases of the draft pick issue, which were packaged 10 cards per pack, 36 packs per box and 10 boxes per case.

		MT
Complete Set (110):		8.00
Common Player:		.05
Comp. Gold Set (112):		75.00
Common Gold:		.25
Jamal Mashburn Auto./9500		25.00
Chris Webber Auto./9500		30.00
Gold Cards:		2x-4x
Wax Box:		
1	Chris Webber	1.50
2	Anfernee Hardaway	1.50
3	Jamal Mashburn	.50
4	Isaiah Rider	.50
5	Vin Baker	1.00
6	Rodney Rogers	.30
7	Lindsey Hunter	.30
8	Allan Houston	.50
9	George Lynch	.10
10	Toni Kukoc	.75
11	Ashraf Amaya	.05
12	Mark Bell	.05
13	John Best	.10
14	Corie Blount	.10
15	Dexter Boney	.05
16	Tim Brooks	.05
17	James Bryson	.05
18	Evers Burns	.05
19	Scott Burrell	.30
20	Sam Cassell	.50
21	Derrick Chandler	.05
22	Sam Crawford	.05
23	Ron Curry	.05
24	William Davis	.05
25	Rodney Dobard	.05
26	Tony Dunkin	.05
27	Spencer Dunkley	.05
28	Bill Edwards	.05
29	Bryan Edwards	.05
30	Doug Edwards	.10
31	Chuck Evans	.05
32	Terry Evans	.05
33	Will Flemons	.05
34	Alphonso Ford	.05
35	Brian Gilgeous	.05
36	Josh Grant	.05
37	Evric Gray	.05
38	Geert Hammink	.05
39	Lucious Harris	.05
40	Joe Harvell	.05
41	Antonio Harvey	.05
42	Scott Haskin	.05
43	Brian Hendrick	.05
44	Sascha Hupmann	.05
45	Stanley Jackson	.05
46	Ervin Johnson	.25
47	Adonis Jordan	.05
48	Warren Kidd	.05
49	Malcolm Mackey	.05
50	Rich Manning	.05
51	Chris McNeal	.05
52	Conrad McRae	.05
53	Lance Miller	.05
54	Chris Mills	.50
55	Matt Nover	.05
56	Charles "Bo" Outlaw	.05
57	Eric Pauley	.05
58	Mike Peplowski	.05
59	Stacey Poole	.05
60	Anthony Reed	.05
61	Eric Riley	.10
62	Darrin Robinson	.05
63	Jackie Robinson	.05
64	James Robinson	.20
65	Byron Russell	.25
66	Brent Scott	.05
67	Bennie Seltzer	.05
68	Ed Stokes	.10
69	Antoine Stoudamire	.05
70	Dirkk Surles	.05
71	Justus Thigpen	.05
72	Kevin Thompson	.05
73	Ray Thompson	.05
74	Gary Trost	.05
75	Nick Van Exel	1.00
76	Jerry Walker	.05
77	Rex Walters	.10
78	Leonard White	.05
79	Chris Whitney	.05
80	Steve Worthy	.05
81	Alex Wright	.05
82	Luther Wright	.10
83	Mark Buford	.05
84	Keith Bullock	.05
85	Mitchell Butler	.05
86	Brian Clifford	.05
87	Terry Dehere	.10
88	Acie Earl	.10
89	Greg Graham	.05
90	Angelo Hamilton	.05
91	Thomas Hill	.05
92	Alex Holcombe	.05
93	Khari Jaxon	.05
94	Darnell Mee	.05
95	Sherron Mills	.05
96	Gheorghe Muresan	.30
97	Marcelo Nicola	.05
98	Julius Nwosu	.05
99	Richard Petruska	.05
100	Bryan Sallier	.05
101	Harper Williams	.05
102	Ike Williams	.05
103	Byron Wilson	.05
104	Shaquille O'Neal	.50
105	Alonzo Mourning	.25
106	Christian Laettner	.10
107	Jim Jackson	.25
108	Harold Miner	.10
109	Checklist 1	.05
110	Checklist 2	.05

1993 Classic Draft Gold

The 112-card, standard-size set paralleled the base set, but with gold-foil highlights. Jamal Mashburn and Chris Webber autographed cards were also issued, limited to 9,500 each.

		MT
Complete Factory Set (112):		80.00
Common Player:		.25
Gold Stars:		2x-4x
AU	Jamal Mashburn AU (Kentucky) (Certified autograph, one of 9500)	30.00
AU	Chris Webber AU (Michigan) (Certified autograph, one of 9500)	20.00

1993 Classic Draft Acetate Stars

The five acetate cards were randomly inserted into foil packs and by interlocking the cards, the collector could create a "Draft Stars" panoramic image featuring Chris Webber, Anfernee Hardaway, Jamal Mashburn, J.R. Rider and Rodney Rogers. The cards are unnumbered with a "AD" prefix and were found three per 10-box case.

	MT
Complete Set (5):	30.00
Common Player:	4.00
Anfernee Hardaway (Memphis St.)	8.00
Jamal Mashburn (Kentucky)	7.00
J.R. Rider (UNLV)	5.00
Rodney Rogers (Wake Forest)	4.00
Chris Webber (Michigan)	8.00

1993 Classic Draft Chromium Stars

The 20-card, standard-size set were inserted one per jumbo pack and feature borderless metallic fronts. The cards are numbered with the "DS" prefix.

		MT
Complete Set (20):		15.00
Common Player:		.40
1	Vin Baker (Hartford)	3.00
2	Terry Dehere (Seton Hall)	.40
3	Sam Cassell (Florida State)	1.00
4	Doug Edwards (Florida State)	.40
5	Greg Graham (Indiana)	.40
6	Scott Haskin (Oregon State)	.40
27	Allan Houston (Tennessee)	1.00
28	Toni Kukoc (Benetton)	1.50
29	George Lynch (North Carolina)	.40
30	Jamal Mashburn (Kentucky)	2.00
31	Harold Miner	.40
32	Rex Walters (Kansas)	.40
33	James Robinson (Alabama)	.60
34	Rodney Rogers (Wake Forest)	.60
35	Luther Wright (Seton Hall)	.40
36	Alonzo Mourning	.75
37	Anfernee Hardaway (Memphis State)	3.00
38	Isaiah Rider (UNLV)	1.00
39	Lindsey Hunter (Jackson State)	.40
40	Chris Webber (Michigan)	3.00

1993 Classic Draft Draft Day

The 12-card, standard-size set was given away on the NBA Draft Day (June 30, 1993). The cards depict the top players expected to be drafted with the best-guess team that could draft them printed in the upper right corner. Production was limited to 19,930 of each. The sets were also sold via the QVC Shopping Network.

		MT
Complete Set (12):		40.00
Common Player:		1.00
1	Anfernee Hardaway	8.00
2	Anfernee Hardaway	8.00
3	Anfernee Hardaway	8.00
4	Jamal Mashburn	3.00
5	Jamal Mashburn	3.00
6	Jamal Mashburn	3.00
7	Shaquille O'Neal (1992 Overall Number One Draft Pick)	6.00
8	Rodney Rogers	1.00
9	Rodney Rogers	1.00
10	Chris Webber	3.00
11	Chris Webber	3.00
12	Chris Webber	3.00

1993 Classic Draft Illustrated

The three-card, standard-size set featured illustrations by sports artist Craig Hamilton. The cards were inserted three to every 10-box case with the player's name and position appearing in a white bar across the bottom on the card face. Cards are numbered with a "SS" prefix.

		MT
Complete Set (3):		20.00
Common Player:		5.00
1	Chris Webber (Michigan)	8.00
2	Jamal Mashburn (Kentucky)	5.00
3	Anfernee Hardaway (Memphis State)	8.00

1993 Classic Draft LPs

The 10-card, standard-size set was inserted twice in every box of 1993 Classic Basketball Draft Picks. Production was limited to 74,500. The cards are numbered on the back with the "LP" prefix.

		MT
Complete Set (10):		30.00
Common Player:		1.00
1	Chris Webber (Michigan)	6.00
2	Anfernee Hardaway (Memphis State)	6.00
3	Jamal Mashburn (Kentucky)	4.00
4	J.R. Rider (UNLV)	1.00
5	Vin Baker (Hartford)	6.00
6	Rodney Rogers (Wake Forest)	1.00
7	Lindsey Hunter (Jackson State)	1.00
8	Toni Kukoc (Italy)	4.00
9	Shaquille O'Neal FLB (LSU)	6.00
10	Alonzo Mourning FLB (Georgetown)	2.00

1993 Classic Draft Special Bonus

Issued one per jumbo sheet, the 20-card, standard-size set has borderless color action shots on the fronts with stats and bio information on the horizontal card backs. The cards are numbered with the "SB" prefix and the unnumbered Webber card was randomly inserted.

		MT
Complete Set (20):		20.00
Common Player:		.40
1	Chris Webber (Michigan)	3.00
2	Anfernee Hardaway (Memphis State)	5.00
3	Jamal Mashburn (Kentucky)	1.50
4	Isaiah Rider (UNLV)	1.00
5	Rodney Rogers (Wake Forrest)	.60
6	Vin Baker (Hartford)	3.00
7	Lindsey Hunter (Jackson State)	.40
8	Allan Houston (Tennessee)	1.25
9	Toni Kukoc (Benetton)	1.50
10	Acie Earl (Iowa)	.40
11	George Lynch (North Carolina)	.40
12	Terry Dehere (Seton Hall)	.60
13	Rex Walters (Kansas)	.40
14	Harold Miner	.40
15	Scott Haskin (Oregon State)	.40
16	Doug Edwards (Florida State)	.40
17	Greg Graham (Indiana)	.40
18	Christian Laettner	1.00
19	Alonzo Mourning	1.25
20	Shaquille O'Neal	3.00
NNO	Chris Webber Special (Michigan)	10.00

1993 Classic Futures

These Classic Futures cards are 1-1/4 inches taller than standard-size cards. Full-bleed shots, enhanced by foil stamping, are on both sides. Players featured are Anfernee Hardaway, Jamal Mashburn, Chris Webber, Toni Kukoc and J.R. Rider. All 4,500 20-box cases were reserved for hobby dealers and hobby stores only. One unnumbered promo card, featuring Isaiah Rider, was also produced. It is labeled on the back as being "For Promotional Purposes Only."

		MT
Complete Set (100):		12.00
Common Player:		.10
Wax Box:		24.00
1	Chris Webber	2.00
2	Bill Edwards	.10
3	Anfernee Hardaway	4.00
4	Bryan Edwards	.10
5	Jamal Mashburn	1.00
6	Doug Edwards	.10
7	Isaiah Rider	.50
8	Chuck Evans	.10
9	Vin Baker	1.75
10	Terry Evans	.10
11	Rodney Rogers	.50
12	Will Flemons	.10
13	Lindsey Hunter	.50
14	Alphonso Ford	.10
15	Allan Houston	.75
16	Josh Grant	.10
17	George Lynch	.20
18	Evric Gray	.10
19	Toni Kukoc	1.00
20	Geert Hammink	.10
21	Ashraf Amaya	.10
22	Lucious Harris	.10
23	Mark Bell	.10
24	Joe Harvell	.10
25	Corie Blount	.20
26	Antonio Harvey	.10
27	Dexter Boney	.10
28	Scott Haskin	.10
29	Tim Brooks	.10
30	Brian Hendrick	.10
31	James Bryson	.10
32	Sascha Hupmann	.10
33	Evers Burns	.10
34	Stanley Jackson	.10
35	Scott Burrell	.50
36	Ervin Johnson	.20
37	Sam Cassell	.75
38	Adonis Jordan	.10
39	Sam Crawford	.10
40	Warren Kidd	.10
41	Ron Curry	.10
42	Malcolm Mackey	.10
43	William Davis	.10
44	Rich Manning	.10
45	Rodney Dobard	.10
46	Chris McNeal	.10
47	Tony Dunkin	.10
48	Conrad McRae	.10
49	Spencer Dunkley	.10
50	Lance Miller	.10
51	Chris Mills	.50
52	Chris Whitney	.10
53	Matt Nover	.10
54	Steve Worthy	.10
55	Charles "Bo" Outlaw	.10
56	Luther Wright	.10
57	Eric Pauley	.10
58	Mark Buford	.10
59	Mike Peplowski	.10
60	Mitchell Butler	.10
61	Stacey Poole	.10
62	Brian Clifford	.10
63	Anthony Reed	.10
64	Terry Dehere	.10
65	Eric Riley	.10
66	Acie Earl	.20
67	Darrin Robinson	.10
68	Greg Graham	.10
69	James Robinson	.20
70	Angelo Hamilton	.10
71	Bryan Russell	.10
72	Thomas Hill	.10
73	Brent Scott	.10
74	Khari Jaxon	.10
75	Bennie Seltzer	.10
76	Darnell Mee	.10
77	Ed Stokes	.10
78	Sherron Mills	.10
79	Antoine Stoudamire	.10
80	Gheorghe Muresan	.50
81	Dirkk Surles	.10
82	Eddie Rivera	.10
83	Justus Thigpen	.10
84	Julius Nwosu	.10
85	Kevin Thompson	.10
86	Bryan Sallier	.10
87	Ray Thompson	.10
88	Bryan Sallier	.10
89	Gary Trost	.10
90	Harper Williams	.10
91	Nick Van Exel	1.00
92	Ike Williams	.10
93	Jerry Walker	.10
94	Byron Wilson	.10
95	Rex Walters	.10
96	Alex Holcombe	.10
97	Leonard White	.10
98	Alex Wright	.10
99	Checklist 1-50	.10
100	Checklist 51-100	.10
Promo	(JR Rider)	2.00

1993 Classic Futures LPs

These unnumbered cards feature full-bleed color action photos on the front, with the player's name and Classic logo in a white panel at the bottom. The back indicates the number of cards produced is 29,500, and includes collegiate stats, a career summary, biographical information and the player's name. The cards measure 2-1/2" x 4-3/4".

	MT
Complete Set (5):	20.00
Common Player:	2.50
Anfernee Hardaway	10.00
Toni Kukoc	3.50
Jamal Mashburn	3.00
Isaiah Rider	2.50
Chris Webber	6.00

1993 Classic Futures Team

These cards were randomly inserted in packs and are numbered using a "CFT" prefix. The card front has an oval with a player photo inside, against a white background. The player's name and position are stamped in gold foil at the bottom. The card back has another color photo, plus a career summary.

		MT
Complete Set (5):		25.00
Common Player:		3.00
1	Chris Webber	6.00
2	Anfernee Hardaway	10.00
3	Jamal Mashburn	4.00
4	Isaiah Rider	3.00
5	Toni Kukoc	4.00

1993 Classic Four-Sport Previews

These five preview cards were inserted in packs of 1993 Classic Hockey. The cards are similar in design to the 1993 Classic Four-Sport regular set. The backs feature a congratulatory message and are unnumbered.

	MT
Complete Set (5):	25.00
Common Player:	3.00
Alexandre Daigle	3.00
Jeff Granger	3.00
Rick Mirer	3.00
Chris Webber	15.00
Toni Kukoc	6.00

1993 Classic Four-Sport

This 325-card set features draft picks from the four major sports. The fronts have full-bleed photos with the player's name printed in green and gold foil vertically on the right side. The Classic Four-Sport logo is in gold foil at the bottom. The backs have another photo, statistics and biographical information. Insert sets include Acetates, Autographs, Chromium Draft Stars, LPs and Tri-Cards. Classic Four-Sport could also be purchased as a boxed set, with all 325 base cards and autographed cards of Jerome Bettis, Chris Gratton, Alonzo Mourning and Alex Rodriguez.

		MT
Complete Set (325):		15.00
Common Player:		.05
Comp. Fact. Gold Set (329):		250.00
Common Gold		.40
Jerome Bettis Au/3900:		40.00
Chris Gratton AU/3900:		20.00
Alonzo Mourning AU/3900:		40.00
Alex Rodriguez AU/3900:		60.00
All four autos in each Fact. Gold Set		
*Gold Stars:		6x
1	Chris Webber	1.00
2	Anfernee Hardaway	2.00
3	Jamal Mashburn	.50
4	Isaiah Rider	.25
5	Vin Baker	1.00
6	Rodney Rogers	.05
7	Lindsey Hunter	.25
8	Allan Houston	.25
9	George Lynch	.05
10	Toni Kukoc	.60
11	Ashraf Amaya	.05
12	Mark Bell	.05
13	Corie Blount	.05
14	Dexter Boney	.05
15	Tim Brooks	.05
16	James Bryson	.05
17	Evers Burns	.05
18	Scott Burrell	.25
19	Sam Cassell	.25
20	Sam Crawford	.05
21	Ron Curry	.05
22	William Davis	.05
23	Rodney Dobard	.05
24	Tony Dunkin	.05
25	Spencer Dunkley	.05
26	Bryan Edwards	.05
27	Doug Edwards	.05
28	Chuck Evans	.05
29	Terry Evans	.05
30	Will Flemons	.05
31	Alphonso Ford	.05
32	Josh Grant	.05
33	Eric Gray	.05
34	Geert Hammink	.05
35	Joe Harvell	.05
36	Scott Haskin	.05
37	Brian Hendrick	.05
38	Sascha Hupmann	.05
39	Stanley Jackson	.05
40	Ervin Johnson	.25
41	Adonis Jordan	.05
42	Malcolm Mackey	.05
43	Rich Manning	.05
44	Chris McNeal	.05
45	Conrad McRae	.05
46	Lance Miller	.05
47	Chris Mills	.25
48	Matt Nover	.05
49	Charles "Bo" Outlaw	.05
50	Eric Pauley	.05
51	Mike Peplowski	.05
52	Stacey Poole	.05
53	Anthony Reed	.05
54	Eric Riley	.05
55	Darrin Robinson	.05
56	James Robinson	.05
57	Bryon Russell	.25
58	Brent Scott	.05
59	Bennie Seltzer	.05
60	Ed Stokes	.05
61	Antoine Stoudamire	.05
62	Dirk Surles	.05
63	Justus Thigpen	.05
64	Kevin Thompson	.05
65	Ray Thompson	.05
66	Gary Trost	.05
67	Nick Van Exel	.50
68	Jerry Walker	.05
69	Rex Walters	.05
70	Chris Whitney	.05
71	Steve Worthy	.05
72	Luther Wright	.05
73	Mark Buford	.05
74	Mitchell Butler	.05
75	Brian Clifford	.05
76	Terry Dehere	.05
77	Acie Earl	.05
78	Greg Graham	.05
79	Angelo Hamilton	.05
80	Thomas Hill	.05
81	Khari Jaxon	.05
82	Darnell Mee	.05
83	Sherron Mills	.05
84	Gheorghe Muresan	.25
85	Eddie Rivera	.05
86	Richard Petruska	.05
87	Bryan Sallier	.05
88	Harper Williams	.05
89	Ike Williams	.05
90	Byron Wilson	.05
91	Drew Bledsoe	1.00
92	Rick Mirer	.25
93	Garrison Hearst	.40
94	Marvin Jones	.25
95	John Copeland	.05
96	Eric Curry	.05
97	Curtis Conway	.25
98	Willie Roaf	.25
99	Lincoln Kennedy	.05
100	Jerome Bettis	1.00
101	Mike Compton	.05
102	John Gerak	.05
103	Will Shields	.05
104	Ben Coleman	.05
105	Ernest Dye	.05
106	Lester Holmes	.05
107	Brad Hopkins	.05
108	Everett Lindsay	.05
109	Todd Rucci	.05
110	Lance Gunn	.05
111	Elvis Grbac	.75
112	Shane Matthews	.05
113	Rudy Harris	.05
114	Richie Anderson	.05
115	Derek Brown	.05
116	Roger Harper	.05
117	Terry Kirby	.25
118	Natrone Means	.75
119	Glyn Milburn	.05
120	Adrian Murrell	.60
121	Lorenzo Neal	.05
122	Roosevelt Potts	.25
123	Kevin Williams WR	.05
124	Fred Baxter	.05
125	Troy Drayton	.25
126	Chris Gedney	.05
127	Irv Smith	.05
128	Olanda Truitt	.05
129	Victor Bailey	.05
130	Horace Copeland	.05
131	Ron Dickerson Jr.	.05
132	Willie Harris	.05
133	Tyrone Hughes	.05
134	Qadry Ismail	.25
135	Reggie Brooks	.05
136	Sean LaChapelle	.05
137	O.J. McDuffie	.50
138	Kenny Shedd	.05
139	Brian Stablein	.05
140	Lamar Thomas	.05
141	Kevin Williams RB	.05
142	Othello Henderson	.05
143	Kevin Henry	.05
144	Todd Kelly	.05
145	Devon McDonald	.05
146	Michael Strahan	.25
147	Dan Williams	.05
148	Gilbert Brown	.25
149	Mark Caesar	.05
150	John Parrella	.05
151	Leonard Renfro	.05
152	Coleman Rudolph	.05
153	Ronnie Bradford	.05
154	Tom Carter	.25
155	Deon Figures	.25
156	Derrick Frazier	.05
157	Darrien Gordon	.05
158	Carlton Gray	.05
159	Adrian Hardy	.05
160	Mike Reid	.05
161	Thomas Smith	.05
162	Robert O'Neal	.05
163	Chad Brown	.25
164	Demetrius DuBose	.05
165	Reggie Givens	.05
166	Travis Hill	.05
167	Rich McKenzie	.05
168	Darrin Smith	.25
169	Steve Tovar	.05
170	Patrick Bates	.05
171	Dan Footman	.05
172	Ryan McNeil	.05
173	Danan Hughes	.05
174	Mark Brunell	1.50
175	Ron Moore	.05
176	Antonio London	.05
177	Steve Everitt	.05
178	Wayne Simmons	.05
179	Robert Smith	.25

180	Dana Stubblefield	.25
181	George Teague	.05
182	Carl Simpson	.05
183	Billy Joe Hobert	.05
184	Gino Torretta	.05
185	Alexandre Daigle	.05
186	Chris Pronger	.40
187	Chris Gratton	.25
188	Paul Kariya	1.25
189	Rob Niedermayer	.25
190	Viktor Kozlov	.25
191	Jason Arnott	.50
192	Niklas Sundstrom	.25
193	Todd Harvey	.25
194	Jocelyn Thibault	.25
195	Kenny Jonsson	.25
196	Denis Pederson	.05
197	Adam Deadmarsh	.25
198	Mats Lindgren	.05
199	Nick Stadjuhar	.05
200	Jason Allison	.40
201	Jesper Mattsson	.05
202	Saku Koivu	.75
203	Anders Eriksson	.05
204	Todd Bertuzzi	.05
205	Eric Lecompte	.05
206	Nikolai Tsulygin	.05
207	Janne Niinimaa	.25
208	Maxim Bets	.05
209	Rory Fitzpatrick	.05
210	Eric Manlow	.05
211	David Roche	.05
212	Vladimir Chebaturkin	.05
213	Bill McCauley	.05
214	Chad Lang	.05
215	Cosmo DuPaul	.05
216	Bob Wren	.05
217	Chris Simon	.05
218	Ryan Brown	.05
219	Mikhail Shtalenkov	.05
220	Vladimir Krechin	.05
221	Jason Saal	.05
222	Dion Darling	.05
223	Chris Helleher	.05
224	Antti Aalto	.05
225	Alain Nasreddine	.05
226	Paul Vincent	.05
227	Manny Legace	.05
228	Igor Chibirev	.05
229	Tom Noble	.05
230	Mike Bales	.05
231	Jozef Cierny	.05
232	Ivan Droppa	.05
233	Anatoli Fedotov	.05
234	Martin Gendron	.05
235	Daniel Guerard	.05
236	Corey Hirsch	.05
237	Steven King	.05
238	Sergei Krivokrasov	.25
239	Darrin Madeley	.05
240	Grant Marshall	.05
241	Sandy McCarthy	.05
242	Bill McDougall	.05
243	Dean Melanson	.05
244	Roman Oksiuta	.05
245	Robert Petrovicky	.05
246	Mike Rathje	.05
247	Eldon Reddick	.05
248	Andrei Trefilov	.05
249	Jiri Slegr	.05
250	Leonid Torpchenko	.05
251	Dody Wood	.05
252	Kevin Paden	.05
253	Manon Rheaume	1.50
254	Cammi Granato	.50
255	Patrick Charboneau	.05
256	Curtis Bowen	.05
257	Kevin Brown	.05
258	Valeri Bure	.25
259	Janne Laukkanen	.05
260	Alex Rodriguez	3.00
261	Darren Dreifort	.50
262	Matt Brunson	.05
263	Matt Drews	.05
264	Wayne Gomes	.05
265	Jeff Granger	.05
266	Steve Soderstrom	.05
267	Brooks Kieschnick	.40
268	Daron Kirkreit	.05
269	Billy Wagner	.25
270	Alan Benes	.25
271	Scott Christman	.05
272	Willie Adams	.05
273	Jermaine Allensworth	.25
274	Jason Baker	.05
275	Brian Banks	.05
276	Marc Barcelo	.05
277	Jeff D'Amico IF (Redmond high; see also card 306)	.25
278	Todd Dunn	.05
279	Dan Ehler	.05
280	Tony Fuduric	.05
281	Ryan Hancock	.05
282	Vee Hightower	.05
283	Andre King (See also card 288A)	.05
284	Brett King	.05
285	Derrek Lee	.50
286	Andrew Lorraine	.05
287	Eric Ludwick	.05
288A	Ryan McGuire ERR (Card misnumbered 283; should be 288)	.05
288B	Ryan McGuire COR (in jumbo packs)	.05
289	Anthony Medrano	.05
290	Joel Moore	.05
291	Dan Perkins	.05
292	Kevin Pickford	.05
293	Jon Ratliff	.05
294	Bryan Rekar	.05
295	Andy Rice	.05
296	Carl Schulz	.05
297	Chris Singleton	.05
298	Cameron Smith	.05
299	Marc Valdes	.05
300	Joe Wagner	.05
301	John Wasdin	.05
302	Pat Watkins	.05
303	Dax Winslett	.05
304	Jamey Wright	.05
305	Kelly Wunsch	.05
306A	Jeff D'Amico ERR (Northeast High; card misnumbered 277, should be 306)	.25
306B	Jeff D'Amico COR (in jumbo packs)	.25
307	Brian Anderson	.05
308	Trot Nixon	.05
309	Kirk Presley	.05
310	John Wooden CO	.25
311	Chris Webber JWA	.50
312	Jamal Mashburn JWA	.25
313	Anfernee Hardaway JWA	.50
314	Terry Dehere JWA	.05
315	Shaquille O'Neal ART	.50
316	Alonzo Mourning ART	.20
317	Christian Laettner ART	.25
318	Jimmy Jackson ART	.25
319	Harold Miner ART	.05
320	Checklist 1	.05
321	Checklist 2	.05
322	Checklist 3	.05
323	Checklist 4	.05
324	Checklist 5	.05
325	Checklist 6	.05
PR1	Gold Promo (Anfernee Hardaway)	5.00
---	Draft Star Mail-In (Jamal Mashburn)	2.50

1993 Classic Four-Sport Acetates

This 12-card set was inserted in packs of 1993 Classic Four-Sport and printed on plastic. The fronts have a color player photo on a background design featuring items from his sport. The backs have the player's name in a lower corner and career highlights.

		MT
Complete Set (12):		35.00
Common Player:		1.50
1	Chris Webber	5.00
2	Anfernee Hardaway	8.00
3	Jamal Mashburn	3.00
4	Isaiah Rider	2.00
5	Toni Kukoc	3.00
6	Drew Bledsoe	6.00
7	Rick Mirer	1.50
8	Garrison Hearst	3.00
9	Alex Rodriguez	10.00
10	Jeff Granger	1.50
11	Alexandre Daigle	1.50
12	Chris Pronger	1.50

1993 Classic Four-Sport Autographs

The design of this set is similar to the Classic Four-Sport base set. Twenty-six players signed and hand-numbered cards for this insert. The number of cards each person signed varies from 150 to 4,500. Cards have a "A" suffix.

		MT
Complete Set (26):		2200.
Common Autograph:		10.00
Listed by corresponding regular card:		
1	Chris Webber AU/550	150.00
3	Jamal Mashburn AU/800	80.00
4	Isaiah Rider AU/4100	20.00
6	Rodney Rogers AU/4000	20.00
77	Acie Earl AU/550	10.00
91	Drew Bledsoe AU/275	250.00
92	Rick Mirer AU/375	50.00
93	Garrison Hearst AU/650	50.00
94	Marvin Jones AU/3650	25.00
184	Gino Torretta AU/3200	10.00
189	Rob Niedermayer AU/4500	20.00
196	Denis Pederson AU/2050	10.00
197	Adam Deadmarsh AU/4250	25.00
218	Ryan Brown AU/900	10.00
222	Dion Darling AU/1500	10.00
253	Manon Rheaume AU/1250	100.00
260	Alex Rodriguez AU/4300	80.00
261	Darren Dreifort AU/3875	20.00
265	Jeff Granger AU/150	10.00
267	Brooks Kieschnick AU/450	40.00
268	Daron Kirkreit AU/275	10.00
310	John Wooden AU/150	400.00
315	Shaquille O'Neal AU/500	300.00
316	Alonzo Mourning AU/400	150.00
---	Jason Jennings AU/1475	10.00
---	Wade Klippenstein AU/800	10.00

1993 Classic Four-Sport Chromium Draft Stars

These 20 cards feature color photos on a metallic background. The player's name and the production number are printed in gold foil. The backs have another photo on the right and biographical information on the left. Inserted one per jumbo pack, each card was limited to 80,000. Cards have a "DS" prefix.

		MT
Complete Set (20):		18.00
Common Player:		.30
41	Chris Webber	2.00
42	Anfernee Hardaway	4.00
43	Jamal Mashburn	.75
44	Isaiah Rider	.30
45	Toni Kukoc	.75
46	Rodney Rogers	.30
47	Chris Mills	.30
48	Drew Bledsoe	2.50
49	Rick Mirer	.30
50	Garrison Hearst	.75
51	Jerome Bettis	2.00
52	Terry Kirby	.30
53	Glyn Milburn	.30
54	Reggie Brooks	.30
55	Alex Rodriguez	5.00
56	Brooks Kieschnick	.30
57	Jeff Granger	.30
58	Alexandre Daigle	.30
59	Chris Pronger	.30
60	Chris Gratton	.75

1993 Classic Four-Sport LPs

These 25 cards have a similar design to the Classic Four-Sport base set. The production number (1 of 63,400) is printed in gold foil on the front. The cards were randomly inserted in packs. They carry a "LP" prefix.

		MT
Complete Set (25):		35.00
Common Player:		.75
1	Four-in-One Card (Chris Webber, Drew Bledsoe, Alex Rodriguez, Alexandre Daigle)	4.00
2	Chris Webber	5.00
3	Anfernee Hardaway	8.00
4	Jamal Mashburn	1.50
5	Isaiah Rider	.75
6	Shaquille O'Neal	3.00
7	Toni Kukoc	2.00
8	Rodney Rogers	.75
9	Lindsey Hunter	1.50
10	Drew Bledsoe	6.00
11	Rick Mirer	.75
12	Garrison Hearst	1.50
13	Jerome Bettis	4.00
14	Marvin Jones	.75
15	Terry Kirby	.75
16	Glyn Milburn	.75
17	Reggie Brooks	.75
18	Alex Rodriguez	10.00
19	Darren Dreifort	1.00
20	Jeff Granger	.75
21	Brooks Kieschnick	.75
22	Alexandre Daigle	.75
23	Chris Pronger	.75
24	Chris Gratton	2.00
25	Paul Kariya	5.00

1993 Classic Four-Sport McDonald's

Classic produced this four-sport set for a McDonald's promotion in Pennsylvania, Delaware, New Jersey and Florida. Available in five-card packs, the base set features color photos on the front with the player's name and position printed in gold foil in a gray stripe on the right side. The backs have another photo, statistics and a brief biography. A five-card limited print subset was randomly inserted in packs, as were Chris Webber autographed cards and instant win cards for Score Board memorabilia.

		MT
Complete Set (35):		12.00
Common Player:		.10
1	Troy Aikman	2.00
2	Drew Bledsoe	1.50
3	Eric Curry	.20
4	Garrison Hearst	.75
5	Lester Holmes	.10
6	Marvin Jones	.20
7	O.J. McDuffie	.75
8	Rick Mirer	.75
9	Leonard Renfro	.10
10	Jerry Rice	1.50
11	Darren Daulton	.20
12	Vyacheslav Butsayev	.10
13	Kevin Dineen	.10
14	Andre Faust	.10
15	Roman Hamrlik	.25
16	Mark Recchi	.20
17	Manon Rheaume	1.50
18	Dominic Roussel	.10
19	Teemu Selanne	.75
20	Tommy Soderstrom	.20
21	Anfernee Hardaway	2.00
22	Jimmy Jackson	.50
23	Christian Laettner	.50
24	Jamal Mashburn	.40
25	Harold Miner	.10
26	Bull and Baby Bull (Greg Luzinski, Ryan Luzinski)	.10
27	Alonzo Mourning	.50
28	Shaquille O'Neal	1.50
29	Clarence Weatherspoon	.30
30	Chris Webber	1.00
31	Chad McConnell	.10
32	Phil Nevin	.10
33	Paul Shuey	.10
34	Derek Wallace	.10
35	Trench Warfare (Leonard Renfro, Lester Holmes)	.10

1993 Classic Four-Sport McDonald's LPs

This five-card set is identical to the 1993 Classic Four-Sport McDonald's base set except the bar on the right is in gold foil and the production number (1 of 16,750) is listed on the front. Chris Webber autographed 1,250 cards which are priced along with this set. They have a "LP" prefix.

		MT
Complete Set (5):		20.00
Common Player:		.75
1	Darren Daulton	1.00
2	Trench Warfare (Leonard Renfro, Lester Holmes)	.75
3	Alonzo Mourning	3.00
4	Manon Rheaume	12.00
5	Steve Young	4.00
---	Chris Webber AU/1250 (certified autograph)	100.00

1993 Classic Four-Sport Power Pick Bonus

Inserted one per jumbo pack, these 20 cards feature full-bleed photos with the player in color and the rest of the shot in black-and-white. The player's name and the production number (1 of 80,000) are printed in green foil at the bottom. The backs have another color player photo and biographical information. They have a "PP" prefix.

		MT
Complete Set (20):		15.00
Common Player:		.30
1	Chris Webber	2.00
2	Anfernee Hardaway	3.00
3	Jamal Mashburn	.75
4	Isaiah Rider	.30
5	Toni Kukoc	.75
6	Rodney Rogers	.30
7	Chris Mills	.30
8	Drew Bledsoe	2.50
9	Rick Mirer	.30
10	Garrison Hearst	.75
11	Jerome Bettis	2.00
12	Terry Kirby	.30
13	Glyn Milburn	.30
14	Reggie Brooks	.30
15	Alex Rodriguez	5.00
16	Brooks Kieschnick	.30
17	Jeff Granger	.30
18	Alexandre Daigle	.30
19	Chris Pronger	.30
20	Chris Gratton	.75
---	For in One Special	5.00

1993 Classic Four-Sport Tri-Cards

This five-card insert was randomly inserted in Four-Sport foil packs. Three players are featured on each card. The fronts have three separate color action photos and a horizontal layout. Each player's name is printed in green and gold foil at the bottom of their photo. The backs have individual player head shots on the left and biographical information on the right. They have a "TC" prefix.

		MT
Complete Set (5):		50.00
Common Panel:		5.00
1	Anfernee Hardaway, TC6 Shaquille O'Neal, TC11 Chris Webber	15.00
2	Drew Bledsoe, TC7 Rick Mirer, TC12 Garrison Hearst	10.00
3	Jeff Granger, TC8 Brooks Kieschnick, TC13 Alex Rodriguez	8.00
4	Alexandre Daigle, TC9 Chris Pronger, TC14 Chris Gratton	5.00
5	Drew Bledsoe, TC10 Chris Webber, TC15 Alex Rodriguez	20.00

1993 Classic C3 Promos

Members of the Classic Collectors Club received one standard-size card with each newsletter. The cards have a gold foil C3 stamp on the card front. Cards have a "PR" suffix. Production of each was limited to 25,000.

		MT
Complete Set (2):		15.00
Common Player:		5.00
1	Shaquille O'Neal (LSU)	10.00
2	Chris Webber (Michigan)	5.00

1993 Classic Deathwatch Jumbos

The three-card, 3-1/2" x 5" jumbo set was inserted into Classic Deathwatch comic card boxes. The fronts feature color action shots with simulated wood borders. The cards are numbered with the "SE" prefix and limited in production to 25,000 each.

		MT
Complete Set (3):		20.00
Common Player:		6.00
1	Chris Webber (Michigan)	8.00
2	Jamal Mashburn (Kentucky)	6.00
3	Anfernee Hardaway (Memphis State)	15.00

1993 Classic Tri-Star Promos

These two promo cards were issued by Classic for Tri-Star Productions in 1993. The card backs state the promo information with the Classic logo along the bottom border. The cards are both 2-1/2" x 3-1/2" and unnumbered.

		MT
Complete Set (2):		4.00
Common Player:		2.00
	Chris Webber	4.00
	Jamal Mashburn	2.00

1994 Classic Draft Previews

The five standard-size cards were randomly inserted into packs of 1994 Classic Football and Pro Line Football releases. The complete set was also available via a redemption card insert. Cards are numbered using a "BP" prefix.

		MT
Complete Set (5):		25.00
Common Player:		3.00
1	Eric Montross (North Carolina)	3.00
2	Jason Kidd (California)	12.00
3	Yinka Dare (George Washington)	3.00
4	Glenn Robinson (Purdue)	10.00
5	Clifford Rozier (Louisville)	3.00

1994 Classic Draft

For the fourth consecutive year, Classic produced its Basketball Draft Picks set. Shaquille O'Neal personally autographed 500 cards and commentator Dick Vitale wrote the card backs. The set contained 105 cards, including a five-card All-Rookie Team subset, five Centers of Attention cards and five draft pick art cards. Many random insert sets are also included in packs. Among them are: Dicky V's PTP'ers, Rookie of the Year Sweepstakes, Hockey Previews and Classic Picks. They also have two parallel sets, which include a gold card of each regular-issue card and a very limited, Printer's Proof card of all 105 cards in the set.

		MT
Complete Set (105):		10.00
Common Player:		.05
Comp. Gold Set (105):		40.00
Gold Cards:		2x-4x
Comp. Prin. Proof Set (105):		400.00
Printer's Proof Cards:		20x-40x
Wax Box:		30.00
1	Glenn Robinson	1.00
2	Jason Kidd	1.00
3	Charlie Ward	.25
4	Grant Hill	3.00
5	Juwan Howard	1.00
6	Eric Montross	.40
7	Carlos Rogers	.25
8	Wesley Person	.30
9	Anthony Miller	.10
10	Dwayne Morton	.10
11	Chris Mills	.10
12	Jamal Mashburn	.15
13	Chris Webber	.20
14	Anfernee Hardaway	.20
15	Isaiah Rider	.10
16	Billy McCaffrey	.05
17	Steve Woodberry	.05
18	Damon Bailey	.10
19	Deon Thomas	.10
20	Dontonio Wingfield	.05
21	Albert Burditt	.05
22	Aaron McKie	.20
23	Stevin Smith	.05
24	Tony Dumas	.20
25	Adrian Autry	.05
26	Monty Williams	.05
27	Askia Jones	.05
28	Howard Eisley	.20
29	Brian Grant	.50
30	Eddie Jones	1.50
31	Dickey Simpkins	.15
32	Michael Smith	.20
33	Clifford Rozier	.10
34	Travis Ford	.05
35	Jervaughn Scales	.05
36	Tracy Webster	.05
37	Brooks Thompson	.05
38	Jim McIlvaine	.05
39	Eric Piatkowski	.10
40	Arturas Karnishovas	.05
41	Rodney Dent	.05
42	Robert Shannon	.05
43	Derrick Phelps	.05
44	Brian Reese	.05
45	Kevin Salvadori	.05
46	Shon Tarver	.05
47	Anthony Goldwire	.15
48	Jamie Watson	.05
49	Damon Key	.05
50	Kevin Rankin	.05
51	Khalid Reeves	.40
52	Doremus Bennerman	.05
53	Sharone Wright	.30
54	Melvin Simon	.05
55	Andrei Fetisov	.05
56	Barry Brown	.05
57	B.J. Tyler	.05
58	Lawrence Funderburke	.05
59	Darrin Hancock	.05
60	Gaylon Nickerson	.05
61	Jeff Webster	.05
62	Derrick Alston	.05
63	Kendrick Warren	.05
64	Yinka Dare	.10
65	Shawnelle Scott	.05
66	Patrick Ewing	.10
67	Dikembe Mutombo	.10
68	Alonzo Mourning	.10
69	Shaquille O'Neal	.25
70	Hakeem Olajuwon	.10
71	Thomas Hamilton	.05
72	Joey Brown	.05
73	Voshon Lenard	.30
74	Donyell Marshall	.20
75	Abdul Fox	.05
76	Checklist 1	.05
77	Checklist 2	.05
78	Jalen Rose	.20
79	Trevor Ruffin	.05
80	Sam Mitchell	.05
81	Dick Vitale	.25
82	Charlie Ward	.20
83	Cornell Parker	.05
84	Clayton Ritter	.05
85	Carl Ray Harris	.05
86	Randy Blocker	.05
87	Chuck Graham	.05
88	Greg Minor	.10
89	Bill Curley	.10
90	Harry Moore	.05
91	Melvin Booker	.05
92	Gary Collier	.05
93	Myron Walker	.05
94	Jamie Brandon	.05
95	Eric Mobley	.05
96	Byron Starks	.05
97	Antonio Lang	.05
98	Jevon Crudup	.05
99	Robert Churchwell	.05
100	Aaron Swinson	.05
101	Glenn Robinson	.75
102	Jason Kidd	.75
103	Juwan Howard	.75
104	Charlie Ward	.25
105	Eric Montross	.30
AU1	Shaquille O'Neal AU/500	400.00
NNO	Shaquille O'Neal Chrome	20.00

1994 Classic Draft Gold

The 105-card, standard-size set paralleled the base set and was inserted in every foil or jumbo pack. The player's name and position are stamped in gold foil near the bottom border.

		MT
Complete Set (105):		40.00
Common Player:		.15
Stars:		2x-4x

1994 Classic Draft Printer's Proofs

The 105-card, standard-size set was randomly inserted in hobby boxes and are virtually identical to the base cards except for a "Printer's Proof" stamp and "1 of 975" on the card front.

	MT
Complete Set (105):	400.00
Common Player:	2.00
Stars:	20x-40x

1994 Classic Draft BCs

The 25-card set was randomly inserted into periodical packs and features color player images on metallic fronts. The player's biography appears in the lower right corner of the card back in a ghosted triangle. The set is numbered with the "BC" prefix.

		MT
Complete Set (25):		12.00
Common Player:		.25
1	Glenn Robinson (Purdue)	2.00
2	Jason Kidd (California)	2.00
3	Grant Hill (Duke)	5.00
4	Donyell Marshall (Connecticut)	.25
5	Juwan Howard (Michigan)	2.50
6	Sharone Wright (Clemson)	.60
7	Brian Grant (Xavier)	1.00
8	Eric Montross (North Carolina)	.50
9	Eddie Jones (Temple)	4.00
10	Carlos Rogers (Tennessee State)	.25
11	Khalid Reeves (Arizona)	.25
12	Jalen Rose (Michigan)	.60
13	Yinka Dare (George Washington)	.25
14	Eric Piatkowski (Nebraska)	.25
15	Clifford Rozier (Louisville)	.25
16	Aaron McKie (Temple)	.25
17	Eric Mobley (Pittsburgh)	.25
18	Tony Dumas (Missouri-KC)	.25
19	B.J. Tyler (Texas)	.25
20	Dickey Simpkins (Providence)	.25
21	Bill Curley (Boston College)	.25
22	Wesley Person (Auburn)	.75
23	Monty Williams (Notre Dame)	.25
24	Greg Minor (Louisville)	.25
25	Charlie Ward (Florida State)	.40
NNO	Jason Kidd Chrome	12.00

1994 Classic Draft Game Cards

The five-card set was inserted one per jumbo pack and the set was redeemable for a gold sheet. The card backs feature instructions on how to play and scratch the cards for the gold sheet prize. Cards are numbered with a "GC" prefix.

		MT
Complete Set (5):		5.00
Common Player:		.50
Prize Box Scratched: Half Value		
1	Glenn Robinson	1.00
2	Jason Kidd	1.00
3	Juwan Howard	1.50
4	Donyell Marshall	.50
5	Sharone Wright	.50

1994 Classic Draft Phone Cards $2

Inserted every seven 12-card jumbo packs, the cards included $2 of pre-paid Sprint phone time. The packs were available at retail outlets such as WalMart, Bookland and Sam's and the usage expired June 30, 1995. The Score Board logo appears in the upper right corner with a Sprint logo found in the upper left corner. The insertion marks the first time Classic included Sprint phone cards.

		MT
Complete Set (6):		15.00
Common Player:		2.00
1	Yinka Dare	2.00
2	Jason Kidd	8.00
3	Donyell Marshall	2.00
4	Eric Montross	3.00
5	Glenn Robinson	8.00
6	Jalen Rose	3.00

1994 Classic Draft Picks

Classic Pics features five of the top picks in the draft. These were inserted at a rate of five per case into foil packs of Classic 1994 Draft Picks.

		MT
Complete Set (5):		30.00
Common Player:		3.00
6	Glenn Robinson	6.00
7	Jason Kidd	6.00
8	Grant Hill	15.00
9	Eric Montross	3.00
10	Juwan Howard	8.00

1994 Classic Draft ROY Sweepstakes

Only 6,225 of each Rookie of the Year card were made. This 20-card set contains most of the candidates for Rookie of the Year. If the player featured on the insert had won the ROY, it could be redeemed for an uncut sheet of Dickey V's PTP'ers and a special commemorative card of the 1994-95 Rookie of the Year. Only five of these cards were inserted into each case.

		MT
Complete Set (20):		100.00
Common Player:		2.00
1	Glenn Robinson	15.00
2	Jason Kidd	15.00
3	Grant Hill	40.00
4	Sharone Wright	6.00
5	Juwan Howard	15.00
6	Monty Williams	5.00
7	Khalid Reeves	6.00
8	Eddie Jones	20.00
9	Clifford Rozier	6.00
10	Aaron McKie	6.00
11	Eric Montross	8.00
12	Askia Jones	2.00
13	Yinka Dare	4.00
14	Dontonio Wingfield	2.00
15	Carlos Rogers	4.00
16	Eric Piatkowski	4.00
17	Charlie Ward	5.00
18	Deon Thomas	2.00
19	Dickey Simpkins	3.00
20	Field Card	4.00

1994 Classic Draft Vitale's PTPers

Dicky V's PTP'ers is a 15-card, chrome-finished set, showcasing most of the 1994 draft picks. These were inserted at a rate of 1.5 per box.

		MT
Complete Set (15):		45.00
Common Player:		1.00
1	Glenn Robinson	6.00
2	Jason Kidd	6.00
3	Grant Hill	14.00
4	Sharone Wright	2.00
5	Juwan Howard	8.00
6	Billy McCaffrey	1.00
7	Khalid Reeves	3.00
8	Eddie Jones	10.00
9	Clifford Rozier	2.00
10	Charlie Ward	4.00
11	Eric Montross	4.00
12	Wesley Person	4.00
13	Yinka Dare	2.00
14	Dontonio Wingfield	1.00
15	Carlos Rogers	1.00

1994 Classic Assets

This 100-card set features players from the five major sports. The card fronts have a color photo with the player's name printed in silver at the bottom and the Assets logo at the top. The backs have another photo inset on the left with biographical and statistical information also featured.

		MT
Complete Set (100):		20.00
Common Player:		.10
Series 1 Wax Box:		85.00
Series 2 Wax Box:		85.00
1	Shaquille O'Neal	1.00
2	Hakeem Olajuwon	.40
3	Troy Aikman	.50
4	Nolan Ryan	.75
5	Dale Earnhardt	1.00
6	Glenn Robinson	1.50
7	Marshall Faulk	1.50
8	Ed Jovanovski	.30
9	Drew Bledsoe	1.00
10	Alonzo Mourning	.25
11	Steve Young	.50
12	Dan Wilkinson	.10
13	Paul Wilson	.40
14	Jason Kidd	1.50
15	Charlie Garner	.20
16	Derrick Alexander	.20
17	Donyell Marshall	.35
18	Ben Grieve	.75
19	Eric Montross	.25
20	Radek Bonk	.25
21	Manon Rheaume	1.00
22	Jalen Rose	.30
23	Antonio Langham	.15
24	Greg Hill	.20
25	Checklist 1	.10
26	Shaquille O'Neal	1.00
27	Hakeem Olajuwon	.40
28	Troy Aikman	.50
29	Nolan Ryan	.75
30	Dale Earnhardt	1.00
31	Glenn Robinson	1.00
32	Marshall Faulk	1.00
33	Ed Jovanovski	.30
34	Drew Bledsoe	1.00
35	Alonzo Mourning	.25
36	Steve Young	.50
37	Dan Wilkinson	.10
38	Paul Wilson	.50
39	Jason Kidd	1.50
40	Charlie Garner	.20
41	Derrick Alexander	.20
42	Donyell Marshall	.35
43	Ben Grieve	.75
44	Eric Montross	.25
45	Radek Bonk	.25
46	Manon Rheaume	1.00
47	Jalen Rose	.40
48	Antonio Langham	.15
49	Greg Hill	.20
50	Checklist 2	.10
51	Dikembe Mutombo	.10
52	Rashaan Salaam	1.00
53	Anfernee Hardaway	.75
54	Isaiah Rider	.30
55	Emmitt Smith	1.00
56	Juwan Howard	.75
57	Jeff O'Neill	.30
58	Jamal Mashburn	.60
59	Byron Morris	.25
60	Petr Sykora	.60
61	Errict Rhett	.75
62	Eric Fichaud	.30
63	Heath Shuler	.40
64	Doug Million	.20
65	Barry Bonds	.50
66	William Floyd	.25
67	Willie McGinest	.15
68	Jeff Gordon	1.00
69	Eddie Jones	.35
70	Steve McNair	.50
71	Ki-Jana Carter	.50
72	Manon Rheaume	1.00
73	Shaquille O'Neal	1.00
74	Drew Bledsoe	1.00
75	Checklist #1	.10
76	Dikembe Mutombo	.10
77	Rashaan Salaam	.75
78	Anfernee Hardaway	.75
79	Isaiah Rider	.30
80	Emmitt Smith	1.00
81	Juwan Howard	.75
82	Jeff O'Neill	.25
83	Jamal Mashburn	.50
84	Byron Morris	.25
85	Petr Sykora	.60
86	Errict Rhett	.75
87	Eric Fichaud	.30
88	Heath Shuler	.40
89	Doug Million	.15
90	Barry Bonds	.50
91	William Floyd	.25
92	Willie McGinest	.10
93	Jeff Gordon	1.00
94	Eddie Jones	.35
95	Steve McNair	.50
96	Ki-Jana Carter	.50
97	Manon Rheaume	1.00
98	Shaquille O'Neal	1.00
99	Drew Bledsoe	1.00
100	Checklist #2	.10

1994 Classic Assets Die-Cut Cards

This 25-card insert has the same design on the front as the Assets base cards. The cards are cut around the player photo enabling it to be popped out of the otherwise standard-size card. The backs of the pop-out have basic player information. Cards are numbered with a "DC" prefix.

		MT
Complete Set (25):		150.00
Complete Series 1 (10):		60.00
Complete Series 2 (15):		90.00
Common Player:		2.50
1	Shaquille O'Neal	12.00
2	Hakeem Olajuwon	4.00
3	Troy Aikman	6.00
4	Nolan Ryan	10.00
5	Dale Earnhardt	12.00
6	Glenn Robinson	10.00
7	Marshall Faulk	12.00
8	Steve Young	6.00
9	Ed Jovanovski	4.00
10	Manon Rheaume	10.00
11	Grant Hill	15.00
12	Jason Kidd	12.00
13	Eddie Jones	6.00
14	Heath Shuler	5.00
15	Nomar Garciaparra	4.00
16	Byron Morris	4.00
17	Barry Bonds	2.50
18	Paul Wilson	5.00
19	Jeff Gordon	12.00
20	Isaiah Rider	2.50
21	Steve McNair	6.00
22	Donyell Marshall	5.00
23	Errict Rhett	8.00
24	Eric Fichaud	4.00
25	Emmitt Smith	10.00

1994 Classic Assets Images Previews

This five-card set was inserted one per 24 packs of 1994-95 Assets Series Two. The cards have the same design as the regular 1995 Images set. The backs are numbered "1 of 5,000" with an "IP" prefix.

		MT
Complete Set (5):		50.00
Common Player:		10.00
1	Grant Hill	15.00
2	Shaquille O'Neal	12.00
3	Marshall Faulk	15.00
4	Manon Rheaume	12.00
5	Emmitt Smith	15.00

1994 Classic Assets 1 Minute and $2 Foncards

These 48 cards measure 2" x 3-1/4" and have rounded corners. The cards have a similar design to the base set but have the Sprint logo at the top and the amount of time the card is good for printed vertically in large script letters. The backs have instructions on how to use the cards.

		MT
Complete Set (48):		95.00
Common Player:		1.00
$2 Foncards:		2.5x
1	Alonzo Mourning	2.00
2	Ben Grieve	2.00
3	Antonio Langham	1.00
4	Charlie Garner	1.00
5	Dale Earnhardt	5.00
6	Dan Wilkinson	1.00
7	Derrick Alexander	1.00
8	Donyell Marshall	1.50
9	Drew Bledsoe	2.50
10	Ed Jovanovski	1.50
11	Eric Montross	1.00
12	Glenn Robinson	2.00
13	Greg Hill	1.00
14	Hakeem Olajuwon	2.00
15	Jalen Rose	1.50
16	Marshall Faulk	5.00
17	Jason Kidd	5.00
18	Nolan Ryan	3.50
19	Manon Rheaume	5.00
20	Paul Wilson	3.00
21	Radek Bonk	1.50
22	Shaquille O'Neal	3.50
23	Steve Young	2.00
24	Troy Aikman	2.00
25	Dikembe Mutombo	1.00
26	Rashaan Salaam	5.00
27	Anfernee Hardaway	4.00
28	Isaiah Rider	1.00
29	Emmitt Smith	5.00
30	Juwan Howard	4.00
31	Jeff O'Neill	1.50
32	Jamal Mashburn	1.50
33	Byron Morris	1.00
34	Petr Sykora	2.00
35	Errict Rhett	2.00
36	Eric Fichaud	1.50
37	Heath Shuler	1.50
38	Doug Million	1.00
39	Barry Bonds	1.50
40	William Floyd	1.50
41	Willie McGinest	1.50
42	Jeff Gordon	5.00
43	Eddie Jones	1.50
44	Steve McNair	4.00
45	Ki-Jana Carter	2.00
46	Manon Rheaume	5.00
47	Shaquille O'Neal	3.50
48	Drew Bledsoe	2.50

1994 Classic Assets $5 Foncards

This 15-card set measures 2" x 3-1/4" and has rounded corners. The card fronts are the similar to the base set but feature the Sprint logo and have "Five Dollars" printed vertically in large script. The backs have instructions on how to use the card. The cards expired in 1995.

		MT
Complete Set (15):		200.00
Common Player:		8.00
1	Jason Kidd	20.00
2	Drew Bledsoe	15.00
3	Hakeem Olajuwon	15.00
4	Nolan Ryan	20.00
5	Troy Aikman	10.00
6	Rashaan Salaam	20.00
7	Ki-Jana Carter	10.00
8	Jeff Gordon	15.00
9	Drew Bledsoe	15.00
10	Jason Kidd	20.00
11	Glenn Robinson	15.00
12	Manon Rheaume	20.00
13	Barry Bonds	6.00
14	Emmitt Smith	20.00
15	Byron Morris	10.00

1994 Classic Assets $25 Bonus

		MT
Complete Set (2):		75.00
Common Player:		40.00
1	Troy Aikman, Steve Young	50.00
2	Shaquille O'Neal, Glenn Robinson	50.00

1994 Classic Assets $25 Foncards

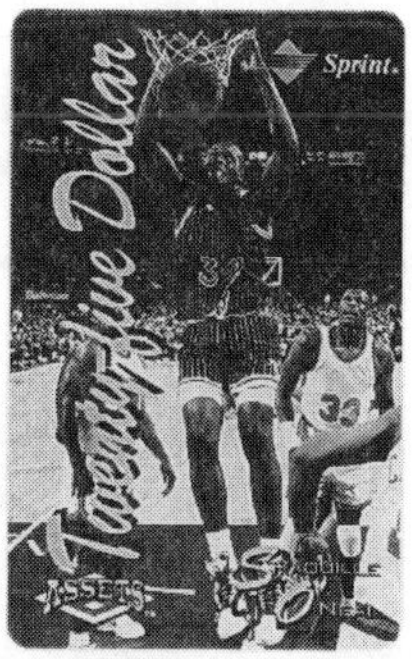

Measuring 2" x 3-1/4", these five phone cards were inserted in Series One packs. The cards have rounded corners. The fronts feature a player photo with "Twenty-five Dollars" written on the left side. The backs have instructions on how to use the cards. Two special cards featuring two players each were available to dealers who made large purchases.

		MT
Complete Set (5):		3000.
Common Player:		50.00
1	Dale Earnhardt	70.00
2	Glenn Robinson	60.00
3	Marshall Faulk	70.00
4	Manon Rheaume	70.00
5	Shaquille O'Neal	70.00

1994 Classic Assets $50 Foncards

Measuring 2" x 3-1/4", these five phone cards were inserted in Series Two packs. The cards have rounded corners. The fronts feature a player photo with "Fifty Dollars" written on the left side. The backs have instructions on how to use the cards.

		MT
Complete Set (5):		475.00
Common Player:		75.00
1	Shaquille O'Neal	120.00
2	Steve Young	100.00
3	Emmitt Smith	120.00
4	Marshall Faulk	120.00
5	Anfernee Hardaway	100.00

1994 Classic Assets $100 Foncards

Measuring 2" x 3-1/4", these five phone cards were inserted in Series Ones packs. The cards have rounded corners. The fronts feature a player photo with "One Hundred Dollars" written on the left side. The backs have instructions on how to use the cards.

		MT
Complete Set (5):		700.00
Common Player:		100.00
1	Drew Bledsoe	150.00
2	Hakeem Olajuwon	125.00
3	Jason Kidd	175.00
4	Nolan Ryan	175.00
5	Troy Aikman	140.00

1994 Classic Assets $200 Foncards

Measuring 2" x 3-1/4", these five phone cards were inserted in Series Two packs. The cards have rounded corners. The fronts feature a player photo with "Two Hundred Dollars" written on the left side. The backs have instructions on how to use the cards.

		MT
Complete Set (5):		1050.
Common Player:		200.00
1	Rashaan Salaam	250.00
2	Ki-Jana Carter	200.00
3	Barry Bonds	200.00
4	Drew Bledsoe	250.00
5	Jason Kidd	250.00

1994 Classic Assets $1,000 Foncards

Measuring 2" x 3-1/4", these five phone cards were installed in Series One packs. The cards have rounded corners. The fronts feature a player photo with "$1,000" written on the left side. The backs have instructions on how to use the cards. A Shaquille O'Neal promo card was issued. The front has "Sample" stamped across it with a set description on the back.

		MT
Complete Set (5):		6000.
Common Player:		1000.
1	Dale Earnhardt	1400.
2	Glenn Robinson	1200.
3	Marshall Faulk	1400.
4	Manon Rheaume	1200.
5	Shaquille O'Neal	1400.

1994 Classic Assets $2,000 Foncards

Measuring 2" x 3-1/4", these five phone cards were inserted in Series Two packs. The cards have rounded corners. The fronts feature a player photo with "2,000" written on the left side. The backs have instructions on how to use the cards.

		MT
Complete Set (5):		10000.
Common Player:		2000.
1	Shaquille O'Neal	2400.
2	Steve Young	2400.
3	Emmitt Smith	2400.
4	Marshall Faulk	2400.
5	Manon Rheaume	2200.

1994 Classic Four-Sport Previews

Inserted three per case of 1994-95 Classic hockey, these five preview cards feature full-bleed color photos. The player's name and "4-Sport Preview" are stamped in gold foil on the front. The backs have a close-up photo with statistics and biography at the bottom. The cards carry a "P" prefix.

		MT
Complete Set (5):		50.00
Common Player:		5.00
1	Jeff O'Neill	5.00
2	Marshall Faulk	10.00
3	Grant Hill	20.00
4	Jason Kidd	8.00
5	Ben Grieve	12.00

1994 Classic Four Sport

Classic Four-Sport consists of a 200-card base set. The cards have a full-bleed photo on the front with the player's name in gold foil at the bottom. The backs have another full-bleed photo with stats and biographical information in a shadow box at the bottom. One hundred Glenn Robinson Instant Winner Cards were inserted in packs. They could be redeemed for a complete set of the Autographs insert. Also inserted were 4,695 hand-numbered 4-in-1 cards featuring the top pick from each league. Collectors could redeem wrappers for special cards based on how many wrappers they redeemed. A special Player of the Year set and autographed cards were among the redemption prizes.

		MT
Complete Set (200):		15.00
Common Player:		.05
Printer's Proofs		25x to 40x
Gold		1.5 to 3x
Wax Box:		25.00
1	Glenn Robinson	.75
2	Jason Kidd	1.25
3	Grant Hill	2.00
4	Donyell Marshall	.25
5	Juwan Howard	1.00
6	Sharone Wright	.15
7	Billy McCaffrey	.05
8	Brian Grant	.25
9	Eric Montross	.15
10	Eddie Jones	1.00
11	Carlos Rogers	.10
12	Khalid Reeves	.15
13	Jalen Rose	.40
14	Yinka Dare	.15
15	Eric Piatkowski	.15
16	Clifford Rozier	.15
17	Aaron McKie	.15
18	Eric Mobley	.15
19	Tony Dumas	.10
20	B.J. Tyler	.15
21	Dickey Simpkins	.15
22	Bill Curley	.08
23	Wesley Person	.25
24	Monty Williams	.10
25	Greg Minor	.10
26	Charlie Ward	.25
27	Brooks Thompson	.10
28	Deon Thomas	.10
29	Antonio Lang	.10
30	Howard Eisley	.05
31	Rodney Dent	.05
32	Jim McIlvaine	.10
33	Derrick Alston	.05
34	Gaylon Nickerson	.05
35	Michael Smith	.10
36	Andrei Fetisov	.05
37	Dontonio Wingfield	.10
38	Darrin Hancock	.05
39	Anthony Miller	.05
40	Jeff Webster	.05
41	Arturas Karnishovas	.05
42	Gary Collier	.10
43	Shawnelle Scott	.10
44	Damon Bailey	.10
45	Dwayne Morton	.10
46	Jamie Watson	.05
47	Jevon Crudup	.05
48	Melvin Booker	.05
49	Brian Reese	.05
50	Lawrence Funderburke	.10
51	Dan Wilkinson	.10
52	Marshall Faulk	.50
53	Heath Shuler	.25
54	Willie McGinest	.15
55	Trev Alberts	.10
56	Trent Dilfer	.25
57	Bryant Young	.35
58	Sam Adams	.05
59	Antonio Langham	.15
60	Jamir Miller	.10
61	John Thierry	.10
62	Aaron Glenn	.10
63	Joe Johnson	.05
64	Bernard Williams	.05
65	Wayne Gandy	.05
66	Aaron Taylor	.10
67	Charles Johnson	.20
68	Dewayne Washington	.05
69	Todd Steussie	.05
70	Tim Bowens	.05
71	Johnnie Morton	.25
72	Rob Fredrickson	.05
73	Shante Carver	.05
74	Thomas Lewis	.10
75	Calvin Jones	.05
76	Henry Ford	.05
77	Jeff Burris	.05
78	William Floyd	.25
79	Derrick Alexander	.20
80	Darnay Scott	.15
81	Tre Johnson	.05
82	Eric Mahlum	.05
83	Errict Rhett	.15
84	Kevin Lee	.05
85	Andre Coleman	.05
86	Corey Sawyer	.05
87	Chuck Levy	.10
88	Greg Hill	.15
89	David Palmer	.15
90	Ryan Yarborough	.05
91	Charlie Garner	.15
92	Mario Bates	.20
93	Bert Emanuel	.20
94	Thomas Randolph	.05
95	Bucky Brooks	.20
96	Rob Waldrop	.05
97	Charlie Ward	.15
98	Winfred Tubbs	.05
99	James Folston	.05
100	Kevin Mitchell	.05
101	Aubrey Beavers	.05
102	Fernando Smith	.05
103	Jim Miller	.05
104	Bam Bam Morris	.25
105	Donnell Bennett	.05
106	Jason Sehorn	.05
107	Glenn Foley	.05
108	Lonnie Johnson	.05
109	Tyronne Drakeford	.05
110	Vaughn Parker	.05
111	Doug Nussmeier	.05
112	Perry Klein	.05
113	Jason Gildon	.05
114	Lake Dawson	.15
115	Ed Jovanovski	.15
116	Oleg Tverdovsky	.15
117	Radek Bonk	.15
118	Jason Bonsignore	.10
119	Jeff O'Neill	.15
120	Ryan Smyth	.10
121	Jamie Storr	.25
122	Jason Wiemer	.15
123	Evgeni Ryabchikov	.05
124	Nolan Baumgartner	.10
125	Jeff Friesen	.15
126	Wade Belak	.05
127	Maxim Bets	.05
128	Ethan Moreau	.10
129	Alexander Kharlamov	.05
130	Eric Fichaud	.20
131	Wayne Primeau	.10
132	Brad Brown	.05
133	Chris Dingman	.05
134	Craig Darby	.05
135	Darby Hendrickson	.05
136	Yan Golubovsky	.05
137	Chris Wells	.05
138	Vadim Sharifjanov	.05
139	Dan Cloutier	.15
140	Todd Marchant	.15
141	David Roberts	.05
142	Brian Rolston	.10
143	Garth Snow	.05
144	Cory Stillman	.10
145	Chad Penney	.05
146	Jeff Nelson	.05
147	Michael Stewart	.05
148	Mike Dunham	.05
149	Joe Frederick	.10
150	Mark DeSantis	.05
151	David Cooper	.10
152	Andrei Buschan	.05
153	Mike Greenlay	.05
154	Geoff Sarjeant	.05
155	Pauli Jaks	.05
156	Greg Andrusak	.05
157	Denis Metlyuk	.05
158	Mike Fountain	.05
159	Brent Gretzky	.15
160	Jason Allison	.25
161	Paul Wilson	.25
162	Ben Grieve	1.00
163	Doug Million	.15
164	C.J. Nitkowski	.15
165	Tommy Davis	.05
166	Dustin Hermanson	.10
167	Travis Miller	.05
168	McKay Christiansen	.05
169	Victor Rodriguez	.05
170	Jacob Cruz	.25
171	Rick Heiserman	.05
172	Mark Farris	.10
173	Nomar Garciaparra	2.00
174	Paul Konerko	.50
175	Trey Moore	.05
176	Brian Stephenson	.10
177	Matt Smith	.05
178	Kevin Brown	.10
179	Cade Gaspar	.05
180	Bret Wagner	.20
181	Mike Thurman	.05
182	Doug Webb	.05
183	Ryan Nye	.05
184	Brian Buchanan	.10
185	Scott Elarton	.05
186	Mark Johnson	.15
187	Jacob Shumate	.05
188	Kevin Witt	.10
189	Glenn Robinson	.50
190	Jason Kidd	.50
191	Grant Hill	.75
192	Donyell Marshall	.25
193	Eric Montross	.15
194	Khalid Reeves	.10
195	Jalen Rose	.25
196	Clifford Rozier	.15
197	Damon Bailey	.10
198	Checklist #1	.05
199	Checklist #2	.05
200	Checklist #3	.05

1994 Classic Four-Sport Autographs

These 82 cards have an identical design to the 1994 Classic Four-Sport base set. The fronts feature the player's autograph and are hand-numbered. The back has a congratulatory message and the cards are unnumbered.

		MT
Complete Set (82):		1000.
Common Player:		10.00
1A	Glenn Robinson AU/1000	50.00
2A	Jason Kidd AU/1300	60.00
5A	Juwan Howard AU/940	60.00
9A	Eric Montross AU/1000	10.00
11A	Carlos Rogers AU/660	10.00
13A	Jalen Rose AU/970	25.00
15A	Eric Piatkowski AU/1090	10.00
16A	Clifford Rozier AU/900	10.00
22A	Bill Curley AU/1120	10.00
23A	Wesley Person AU/1000	20.00
24A	Monty Williams AU/1000	10.00
28A	Deon Thomas AU/1090	10.00
30A	Howard Eisley AU/970	20.00
32A	Jim McIlvaine AU/965	10.00
33A	Derrick Alston AU/1050	10.00
36A	Andrei Fetisov AU/1080	10.00
39A	Anthony Miller AU/1000	10.00
40A	Jeff Webster AU/1070	10.00
41A	Arturas Karnishovas AU/980	10.00
42A	Gary Collier AU/1000	10.00
44A	Damon Bailey AU/1050	10.00
45A	Dwayne Morton AU/1000	10.00
46A	Jamie Watson AU/1080	10.00
47A	Jevon Crudup AU/1180	10.00
49A	Brian Reese AU/960	10.00
53A	Heath Shuler AU/1330	25.00
55A	Trev Alberts AU/2520	10.00
56A	Trent Dilfer AU/1495	25.00
81A	Tre Johnson AU/1000	10.00
82A	Eric Mahlum AU/1090	10.00
90A	Ryan Yarborough AU/1020	10.00
93A	Bert Emanuel AU/1100	20.00
96A	Rob Waldrop AU/1095	10.00
97A	Charlie Ward AU/1520	20.00
99A	James Folston AU/1100	10.00
100A	Kevin Mitchell AU/1090	10.00
103A	Jim Miller AU/1030	10.00
108A	Lonnie Johnson AU/1050	10.00
110A	Vaughn Parker AU/750	10.00
115A	Ed Jovanovski AU/1180	30.00
119A	Jeff O'Neill AU/3000	20.00
124A	Nolan Baumgartner AU/2900	10.00
134A	Craig Darby AU/2990	10.00
139A	Dan Cloutier AU/2980	10.00
140A	Todd Marchant AU/3100	10.00
143A	Garth Snow AU/3050	10.00
144A	Cory Stillman AU/3000	10.00
148A	Mike Dunham AU/2960	10.00
149A	Joe Frederick AU/3000	10.00
150A	Mark DeSantis AU/3000	10.00
154A	Geoff Sarjeant AU/3000	10.00
156A	Greg Andrusak AU/2970	10.00
157A	Denis Metlyuk AU/2960	10.00
158A	Mike Fountain AU/3000	10.00
161A	Paul Wilson AU/2400	20.00
162A	Ben Grieve AU/2500	50.00
163A	Doug Million AU/1020	10.00
164A	C.J. Nitkowski AU/970	10.00
165A	Tommy Davis AU/960	10.00
166A	Dustin Hermanson AU/1020	20.00
167A	Travis Miller AU/760	10.00
169A	Victor Rodriguez AU/1000	10.00
170A	Jacob Cruz AU/990	20.00
171A	Rick Heiseman AU/600	10.00
172A	Mark Farris AU/1090	10.00
173A	Nomar Garciaparra AU/1020	100.00
174A	Paul Konerko AU/970	40.00
176A	Brian Stephenson AU/1100	10.00
177A	Matt Smith AU/1090	10.00
178A	Kevin Brown AU/1090	10.00
179A	Cade Gaspar AU/1090	10.00
180A	Bret Wagner AU/970	10.00
181A	Mike Thurman AU/990	10.00
183A	Ryan Nye AU/1015	10.00
184A	Brian Buchanan AU/950	10.00
186A	Mark Johnson AU/1000	10.00
187A	Jacob Shumate AU/980	10.00
188A	Kevin Witt AU/970	10.00

1994 Classic Four-Sport BCs

This 20-card set was inserted one per jumbo pack of 1994 Classic Four-Sport. The fronts have color photos and the backs have biographical information. Cards are numbered with a "BC" prefix.

		MT
Complete Set (20):		20.00
Common Player:		.25
1	Marshall Faulk	2.00
2	Heath Shuler	.25
3	Antonio Langham	.25
4	Derrick Alexander	.75
5	Byron "Bam" Morris	.25
6	Glenn Robinson	1.00
7	Jason Kidd	1.25
8	Grant Hill	4.00
9	Jalen Rose	.75
10	Donyell Marshall	.25
11	Juwan Howard	2.00
12	Khalid Reeves	.25
13	Paul Wilson	.75
14	Ben Grieve	2.00
15	Doug Million	.25
16	Nomar Garciaparra	3.00
17	Ed Jovanovski	.50
18	Radek Bonk	.25
19	Jeff O'Neill	.50
20	Ethan Moreau	.25

1994 Classic Four Sport CHL Previews

		MT
Complete Set (6):		15.00
Common Player:		2.00
1	Wayne Primeau	3.00
2	Eric Fichaud	5.00
3	Wade Redden	6.00
4	Jason Doig	4.00
5	Vitali Yachmeneu	2.00
6	Nolan Baumgartner	2.00

1994 Classic Four Sport High Voltage

The card fronts in this 20-card set feature a color photo with lightning in the background. The cards are printed on holographic foil board. The backs have a player closeup at the top with biographical information on the left and a lightning design on the right. The even-numbered cards are sequentially-numbered to 2,995 and the odd-numbered cards are numbered to 5,495.

		MT
Complete Set (20):		250.00
Common Player:		5.00
1	Dan Wilkinson	5.00
2	Glenn Robinson	25.00
3	Paul Wilson	8.00
4	Ed Jovanovski	8.00
5	Marshall Faulk	15.00
6	Jason Kidd	30.00
7	Ben Grieve	20.00
8	Oleg Tverdovski	5.00
9	Heath Shuler	10.00
10	Grant Hill	60.00
11	Dustin Hermanson	8.00
12	Radek Bonk	5.00
13	Trent Dilfer	12.00
14	Donyell Marshall	8.00
15	Doug Million	5.00
16	Jason Bonsignore	5.00
17	Willie McGinest	5.00
18	Juwan Howard	30.00
19	Jeff O'Neill	5.00
20	Nomar Garciaparra	40.00

1994 Classic Four Sport Phonecards

This eight-card set was printed on plastic and each card measures 2-1/8" x 3-3/8" with rounded corners. The fronts have full-bleed photos with the player's name printed vertically on the right in red. The dollar value and Sprint logo appear in the upper right corner. The backs have instructions on how to use the cards. The cards are unnumbered. They expired November 30, 1995.

	MT
Complete Set (8):	30.00
Common Player:	1.00
Paul Wilson	5.00
Ben Grieve	2.00
Glenn Robinson	6.00
Jason Kidd	9.00
Ed Jovanovski	3.00
Jeff O'Neill	2.00
Trent Dilfer	1.00
Marshall Faulk	10.00

1994 Classic Four-Sport Picks

This 10-card set was randomly inserted in packs of Classic Four-Sport. The fronts have color photos and the backs have a smaller photo on the right side ghosted over a larger version of the same photo. The backs also have biographical information.

		MT
Complete Set (10):		40.00
Common Player:		3.00
16	Paul Wilson	4.00
17	Ben Grieve	10.00
18	Trey Moore	3.00
19	Nomar Garciaparra	12.00
20	Doug Million	3.00
21	Dan Wilkinson	3.00
22	Willie McGinest	4.00
23	Khalid Reeves	3.00
24	Grant Hill	15.00
25	Ethan Moreau	3.00

1994 Classic Four Sport Shaq-Fu Tip Cards

This 25-card insert featured characters and special moves from the Shaq-Fu video game. Cards 1-12 are character cards, with a biography on the back. Cards 13-24 each detail a special maneuver for one of the characters from the game and card 25 has a secret game tip. The cards were seeded one per 18 packs.

		MT
Complete Set (25):		15.00
Common Shaq-Fu:		.75
2	Kaori	.75
3	Voodoo	.75
4	Rajah	.75
5	Mephis	.75
6	Beast	.75
7	Sett Ra	.75
8	Nezu	.75
9	Leotsu	.75
10	Colonel X	.75
11	Aurok	.75
12	Diesel	.75
13	Shaq-uriken	.75
14	Teleport Kick	.75
15	Voodoo Doll Stab	.75
16	Sword Toss	.75
17	Summon Lightning	.75
18	Auto Three Hit Combo	.75
19	Earth Rap Attack	.75
20	Eno Bomb	.75
21	Thunder Kai	.75
22	Micro Missile	.75
23	European Fist	.75
24	Knuckle Dash	.75
25	Secret Tip	.75

1994 Classic Four Sport Tricards

These five cards each feature three players. The fronts have a horizontal layout with each player appearing in a seperate photo. The backs give information on why the players were grouped together. The cards are sequentially numbered to 2,695.

		MT
Complete Set (5):		40.00
Common Player:		4.00
1	Faulk, Jones, Rhett	18.00
2	McGinest, Alberts, Miller	4.00
3	Rose, Kidd, Reeves	14.00
4	Bonk, Wells, O'Neill	8.00
5	Wilson, Million, Gaspar	8.00

1994 Classic Images

This 150-card set has full-bleed color photos with the backgrounds out of focus. The player's name, position and the Classic Images logo are printed in gold foil on the front. The backs have a color photo on the right and statistics and a biography on the left. Inserts included Acetates, Chrome, Marshall Faulk and Sudden Impact. A redemption card good for a set of basketball draft preview cards was inserted one per case.

		MT
Complete Set (150):		15.00
Common Player:		.05
1	Drew Bledsoe	1.25
2	Chris Webber	.50
3	Alex Rodriguez	3.00
4	Alexandre Daigle	.05
5	Rick Mirer	.05
6	Anfernee Hardaway	1.50
7	Jeff D'Amico	.25
8	Chris Pronger	.25
9	Robert Smith	.25
10	Sherron Mills	.05
11	Alan Benes	.25
12	Warren Kidd	.05
13	Bryon Russell	.25
14	Mike Peplowski	.05
15	Jeff Granger	.05
16	Jim Montgomery	.05
17	Todd Marchant	.50
18	Doug Edwards	.05
19	Daron Kirkreit	.05
20	Mike Dunham	.05
21	Garth Snow	.25
22	Darnell Mee	.05
23	Billy Wagner	.25
24	Barry Richter	.05
25	Lincoln Kennedy	.05
26	Jerome Bettis	.50
27	Corie Blount	.05
28	Matt Martin	.05
29	Deon Figures	.25
30	Rob Niedermayer	.25
31	Brian Anderson	.05
32	Jesse Belanger	.05
33	George Teague	.05
34	Chris Schwab	.05
35	Peter Ferraro	.05
36	Shaquille O'Neal Rap	1.00
37	Matt Brunson	.05
38	Ted Drury	.05
39	Glyn Milburn	.05
40	George Lynch	.05
41	Gheorghe Muresan	.25
42	Kirk Presley	.05
43	Derek Plante	.25
44	Gino Torretta	.05
45	Roger Harper	.05
46	Jim Campbell	.50
47	Chris Carpenter	.05
48	Victor Bailey	.05
49	Kelly Wunsch	.05
50	Isaiah Rider	.25
51	Jon Ratliff	.05
52	Wayne Gomes	.05
53	Thomas Smith	.05
54	Trot Nixon	.25
55	Andre King	.05
56	Chris Osgood	.50
57	Reggie Brooks	.05
58	Ron Moore	.05
59	Vin Baker	.50
60	Rodney Rogers	.05
61	Dan Footman	.05
62	Jason Arnott	.50
63	Darren Dreifort	.25
64	Tom Carter	.25
65	Qadry Ismail	.25
66	Josh Grant	.05
67	Luther Wright	.05
68	Allan Houston	.25
69	Brooks Kieschnick	.05
70	Marvin Jones	.25
71	Garrison Hearst	.50
72	John Copeland	.05
73	Darrien Gordon	.05
74	Jocelyn Thibault	.25
75	Lindsey Hunter	.25
76	Scott Burrell	.25
77	Torii Hunter	.05
78	Chad Brown	.25
79	Sam Cassell	.25
80	Steve Soderstrom	.05
81	Jimmy Jackson	.50
82	Irv Smith	.05
83	Troy Drayton	.25
84	Chris Mills	.25
85	Derrek Lee	.50
86	Chris Gratton	.25
87	Carlton Gray	.05

88	Billy Joe Hobert	.05
89	Acie Earl	.05
90	Terry Dehere	.05
91	Carl Simpson	.05
92	Mike Rathje	.05
93	Jay Powell	.05
94	James Robinson	.05
95	Roosevelt Potts	.25
96	Jamal Mashburn	.50
97	Derek Brown RB	.05
98	Ed Stokes	.05
99	Ervin Johnson	.25
100	Nick Van Exel	.50
101	Martin Brodeur	.50
102	Curtis Conway	.25
103	Lamar Thomas	.05
104	Willie Roaf	.25
105	Matt Drews	.05
106	Paul Kariya	1.00
107	Eric Curry	.05
108	Todd Kelly	.05
109	Rex Walters	.05
110	Chris Whitney	.05
111	Manon Rheaume	1.50
112	Alonzo Mourning	.25
113	Lucious Harris	.05
114	Horace Copeland	.05
115	Scott Christman	.05
116	Terry Kirby	.25
117	Demetrius DuBose	.05
118	Will Shields	.05
119	Natrone Means	.50
120	O.J. McDuffie	.25
121	Felix Potvin	.40
122	Dino Radja	.25
123	Harold Miner	.05
124	Greg Graham	.05
125	Alexei Yashin	.40
126	Kevin Williams WR	.05
127	Lorenzo Neal	.05
128	Shaquille O'Neal B/W	.50
129	Drew Bledsoe B/W	.50
130	Alexei Yashin B/W	.25
131	Kirk Presley B/W	.05
132	Chris Webber B/W	.25
133	Rick Mirer B/W	.05
134	Anfernee Hardaway B/W	.60
135	Chris Pronger B/W	.15
136	Alonzo Mourning B/W	.25
137	Jerome Bettis B/W	.25
138	Chris Gratton B/W	.25
139	Trot Nixon B/W	.05
140	Terry Kirby BW	.05
141	Jamal Mashburn B/W	.25
142	Jason Arnott B/W	.25
143	Alex Rodriguez B/W	1.50
144	Derek Brown RB BW	.05
145	Isaiah Rider B/W	.05
146	Harold Miner BW	.05
147	Manon Rheaume B/W	1.50
148	Checklist 1	.05
149	Checklist 2	.05
150	Checklist 3	.05
---	BK Preview Redemption	.50

1994 Classic Images Acetates

These four cards are printed on clear plastic. The front has a color player cut-out which is also visible on the back. The player's name is printed vertically in a black bar. Career highlights are listed on the back. The cards were inserted four per case and limited to 6,500 each.

		MT
Complete Set (4):		25.00
Common Player:		7.00
1	Chris Webber	10.00
2	Jerome Bettis	10.00
3	Steve Young	8.00
4	Hakeem Olajuwon	8.00

1994 Classic Images Chrome

Randomly inserted in packs of 1994 Classic Images, these 20 cards were limited to 9,750. The fronts have full-bleed action photos with a metallic finish. The Images logo is in the background and at the bottom with the player's name at the top. The backs have a close-up photo and career highlights. The set could be obtained as an uncut sheet for the Marshall Faulk M5 redemption card. Cards have a "CC" prefix.

		MT
Complete Set (20):		90.00
Common Player:		2.50
Comp. Uncut Sheet:		75.00
1	Chris Webber	8.00
2	Anfernee Hardaway	12.00
3	Jimmy Jackson	3.00
4	Nick Van Exel	4.00
5	Jamal Mashburn	4.00
6	Isaiah Rider	3.00
7	Drew Bledsoe	10.00
8	Jerome Bettis	6.00
9	Terry Kirby	3.00
10	Dana Stubblefield	3.00
11	Rick Mirer	2.50
12	Cammi Granato	5.00
13	Alexei Yashin	4.00
14	Alexandre Daigle	2.50
15	Manon Rheaume	10.00
16	Radek Bonk	2.50
17	Alex Rodriguez	15.00
18	Kirk Presley	2.50
19	Trot Nixon	2.50
20	Brooks Kieschnick	2.50

1994 Classic Images Sudden Impact

This 20-card set was inserted one per pack. The cards were printed on gold foil-board and feature full-bleed photos in front of an out-of-focus background. The backs have another photo at the top with career highlights at the bottom. Cards have a "SI" prefix.

		MT
Complete Set (20):		10.00
Common Player:		.10
1	Carlos Delgado	.25
2	Vin Baker	.50
3	Derek Jeter	1.50
4	Alex Rodriguez	3.00
5	Alexandre Daigle	.10
6	Rob Niedermayer	.25
7	Jocelyn Thibault	.25
8	Derek Plante	.10
9	Shaquille O'Neal	1.00
10	Alonzo Mourning	.25
11	Harold Miner	.10
12	Chris Webber	.50
13	Anfernee Hardaway	2.00
14	Jamal Mashburn	.50
15	Drew Bledsoe	1.25
16	Rick Mirer	.10
17	Derek Brown RB	.10
18	Ron Moore	.10
19	Jerome Bettis	.50
20	Dino Radja	.25

1994 Classic National Promos

These cards were distributed to promote the 15th National Convention in Houston. The fronts have full-bleed photos with the player's name printed in red in a black bar at the bottom. The backs have the National logo printed in gold foil. The cards are unnumbered.

	MT
Complete Set (5):	15.00
Common Player:	2.00
Jason Arnott	2.00
Grant Hill (Duke)	5.00
Jason Kidd (California)	3.00
Heath Shuler	2.00
Emmitt Smith	5.00

1994 Classic National Party Autographs

The three, standard-size cards were issued at the 15th National Collectors Convention in Houston. Attendees were entitled to have one card signed by one of three athletes present.

		MT
Complete Set (3):		50.00
Common Player:		10.00
1	Michigan (Juwan Howard AU) (Congratulations)	30.00
2	Connecticut (Donyell Marshall AU) (Congratulations)	10.00
3	Michigan (Jalen Rose AU) (Congratulations)	20.00

1995 Classic Draft Previews

The five-card, standard-size set was inserted one per box of Classic Assets Gold and NFL Pro Line. The set was also available via a redemption program in 1995 Images packs. The hobby version has an aqua Printer's Proof logo while the retail version has the player's name along the bottom border in silver foil script. The cards are prefixed "RP" for the retail and "HP" for the hobby versions.

		MT
Complete Set (5):		20.00
Common Player:		2.50
Hobby/Retail Version: Same value		
1	Ed O'Bannon	2.50
2	Corliss Williamson	2.50
3	Joe Smith	6.00
4	Rasheed Wallace	3.00
5	Damon Stoudamire	8.00

1995 Classic Draft

Classic Basketball Rookies features all the top draft picks, including Joe Smith, Antonio McDyess, Jerry Stackhouse, Rasheed Wallace and former prep phenom Kevin Garnett. The 120-card set includes 11 Wooden Award Contenders, five Classic All-Rookies, four Centers of Attention and 10 Snap Shots. Each card front has a full-bleed color photo on it, with "Rookies" and a ball and hoop in the upper right corner. The player's name is between a stripe at the bottom. The horizontal back has a photo on the left, with a green box on the right which contains a recap of the player's collegiate accomplishments against a ghosted image of a hoop. A black rectangle at the top has the player's name in it, with his position underneath. An adjacent red box has the card number in it. Below the recap is a black band which contains biographical information. Then, a red box follows which contains the player's statistics. Two parallel sets were also made. Silver series cards appear one per every pack, while Printer's Proofs cards are at a rate of two per every box. Production of these proof cards was limited to 949 sets. Insert sets include: Center Stage, Rookie of the Year redemption cards, Autographed cards (one per box), Classic Clear Cuts and Pro Line Series II preview $2 and $5 phone cards. Also, every pack in a specially-marked hot box contains an insert card, plus a five-card Classic Clear Cut sequentially-numbered die-cut acetate set exclusive to Hot Boxes. There's an average of one Hot Box per every six cases.

		MT
Complete Set (120):		12.00
Common Player:		.05
Comp. Prin. Proofs Set (12):		300.00
Common PP Card:		1.00
Prin. Proof Cards:		10x-20x
Comp. Silver Set (120):		40.00
Common Silver Card:		.10
Silver Stars:		1x-3x
Comp. Silv. Sig. Set (120):		160.00
Common Silv. Sig.		.50
Silv. Sig. Stars:		5x-10x
1	Joe Smith	1.25
2	Antonio McDyess	.75
3	Jerry Stackhouse	1.25
4	Rasheed Wallace	.50
5	Kevin Garnett	2.50
6	Damon Stoudamire	1.75
7	Shawn Respert	.15
8	Ed O'Bannon	.30
9	Kurt Thomas	.30
10	Gary Trent	.30
11	Cherokee Parks	.30
12	Corliss Williamson	.20
13	Eric Williams	.40
14	Brent Barry	.40
15	Bob Sura	.40
16	Theo Ratliff	.30
17	Randolph Childress	.30
18	Jason Caffey	.30
19	Michael Finley	.60
20	George Zidek	.20
21	Travis Best	.20
22	Loren Meyer	.15
23	David Vaughn	.15
24	Sherell Ford	.15
25	Mario Bennett	.15
26	Greg Ostertag	.15
27	Cory Alexander	.15
28	Lou Roe	.15
29	Dragan Tarlac	.10
30	Terrence Rencher	.10
31	Junior Burrough	.15
32	Andrew DeClercq	.15
33	Jimmy King	.15
34	Lawrence Moten	.10
35	Frankie King	.10
36	Rashard Griffith	.10
37	Donny Marshall	.15
38	Julius Michalik	.05
39	Erik Meek	.10
40	Donnie Boyce	.10
41	Eric Snow	.10
42	Anthony Pelle	.10
43	Troy Brown	.10
44	George Banks	.10
45	Tyus Edney	.50
46	Mark Davis	.10
47	Jerome Allen	.10
48	Fred Hoiberg	.10
49	Constantin Popa	.10
50	Erwin Claggett	.05
51	Michael McDonald	.10
52	Andre Riddick	.05
53	Cuonzo Martin	.10
54	Don Reid	.10
55	James Forrest	.10
56	Glen Whisby	.05
57	Dwight Stewart	.05
58	Jamal Faulkner	.05
59	Tom Kleinschmidt	.10
60	Donald Williams	.05
61	Dan Cross	.05
62	Rick Brunson	.05
63	Corey Beck	.10
64	Lance Hughes	.05
65	Bernard Blunt	.05
66	Clint McDaniel	.05
67	John Amaechi	.05
68	Lorenzo Orr	.05
69	Randy Rutherford	.10
70	Ray Jackson	.10
71	Reggie Jackson	.05
72	Russell Larson	.05
73	Carlin Warley	.05
74	James Scott	.05
75	Roderick Anderson	.05
76	Antoine Gillespie	.05
77	Gerard King	.05
78	Petey Sessoms	.05
79	Steve Payne	.05
80	William Gates	.10
81	Arthur Agee	.10
82	Rebecca Lobo	.75
83	Devin Gray	.05
84	Scotty Thurman	.10
85	Matt Maloney	.50
86	Michael Evans	.05
87	LaZelle Durden	.05
88	Ronnie McMahan	.05
89	Ed O'Bannon	.20
90	Mario Bennett	.10
91	Randolph Childress	.10
92	Rasheed Wallace	.25
93	Lawrence Moten	.10
94	Shawn Respert	.10
95	Lou Roe	.10
96	Damon Stoudamire	1.00
97	Gary Trent	.10
98	Corliss Williamson	.20
99	Jerry Stackhouse	.50
100	Glenn Robinson	.30
101	Jason Kidd	.30
102	Juwan Howard	.30
103	Brian Grant	.10
104	Eddie Jones	.50
105	Shaquille O'Neal	.50
106	Dikembe Mutombo	.10
107	Alonzo Mourning	.10
108	Hakeem Olajuwon	.15
109	Cherokee Parks	.10
110	Corliss Williamson	.10
111	Shawn Respert	.10
112	Bob Sura	.10
113	Michael Finley	.20
114	Greg Ostertag	.10
115	Lou Roe	.10
116	Loren Meyer	.10
117	Mario Bennett	.10
118	Cuonzo Martin	.05
119	Checklist 1	.30
120	Checklist 2	.40

1995 Classic Draft Printer's Proofs

The 120-card, standard-size set is virtually identical to the base Classic Rookies, but with the words, "Printer's Proof, 1 of 949" across the top. The cards were inserted every 18 packs.

	MT
Complete Set (120):	300.00
Common Player:	1.25
Stars:	10x-20x

1995 Classic Draft Silver Signatures

The 120-card, standard-size set parallels the base Classic Rookies set, but with a metallic sheen and a silver signature.

	MT
Complete Set (120):	175.00
Common Player:	.50
Stars:	6x-12x

1995 Classic Draft Autographs

The 80-card, standard-size set was randomly inserted in boxes of Classic Rookies at a rate of one per box. The players are listed with the total number of cards signed. The backs have a congratulatory message.

		MT
Complete Set (80):		1200.
Common Player:		5.00
Auto. Edition Set (63):		500.00
Classic Autograph Edition:		1x
Auto. Edition AU/200:		3x
1	Joe Smith (1230)	50.00
2	Antonio McDyess (1270)	40.00
3	Jerry Stackhouse (2370)	60.00
4	Rasheed Wallace (1275)	30.00
6	Damon Stoudamire (1255)	70.00
7	Shawn Respert (1275)	8.00
8A	Ed O'Bannon	12.00
9	Kurt Thomas (3420)	10.00
10	Gary Trent (3420)	10.00
11	Cherokee Parks (2630)	8.00
12	Corliss Williamson (3355)	12.00
13	Eric Williams (2435)	12.00
14	Brent Barry (2690)	12.00
15	Bob Sura (2690)	12.00
16	Theo Ratliff (3310)	8.00
17	Randolph Childress (1260)	8.00
18	Jason Caffey (2500)	8.00
19	Michael Finley (3695)	25.00
20	George Zidek (2650)	10.00
21	Travis Best (1990)	8.00
22	Loren Meyer (2920)	10.00
23	David Vaughn (3320)	5.00
24	Sherell Ford (3635)	5.00
25	Mario Bennett (2620)	5.00
26	Greg Ostertag (2600)	8.00
27	Cory Alexander (3335)	5.00
28	Lou Roe (2845)	5.00
30	Terrence Rencher (3275)	5.00
31	Junior Burrough (3220)	5.00
32	Andrew DeClerq (4080)	5.00
33	Jimmy King (3740)	8.00
37	Donny Marshall (4000)	5.00
45	Tyus Edney (3600)	10.00
46	Mark Davis (3475)	5.00
54	Don Reid (2700)	5.00
80	William Gates (3290)	10.00
81	Arthur Agee (3285)	10.00
101	Jason Kidd (300)	200.00
102	Juwan Howard (285)	200.00
105	Shaquille O'Neal (400)	350.00
107	Alonzo Mourning (2550)	60.00

1995 Classic Draft Center Stage

These cards, numbered on the back using a "CS" prefix, were random inserts in 1995 Classic Basketball Rookies packs, one per every six boxes. The set features the most dynamic draft picks on a specially-designed card with foil stamping. These cards are limited to a maximum of 1,995 and will be sequentially numbered. The metallic-like card front has a full-bleed color action photo, with the player's name and set logo at the top and the set icon in the lower right corner. The card back has a vertical band on the left which has the player's name and card number in it; a set icon is below the band. The right side has a photo at the top, with a recap of the player's collegiate accomplishments below.

		MT
Complete Set (10):		100.00
Common Player:		7.00
1	Joe Smith	15.00
2	Antonio McDyess	10.00
3	Rasheed Wallace	7.00
4	Kevin Garnett	40.00
5	Damon Stoudamire	25.00
6	Ed O'Bannon	8.00
7	Gary Trent	7.00
8	Corliss Williamson	7.00
9	Jerry Stackhouse	15.00
10	Randolph Childress	7.00

1995 Classic Draft Clear Cuts

These Classic Clear Cuts were seeded at a ratio of four per every 1995 Classic Basketball Rookies Hot Box. The cards combine two different technologies - die-cutting and acetate. Each card is sequentially numbered to a maximum of 595. The card front has the player's name running vertically down the left side between two lines. The right side is die-cut, with a color action photo of the player against a shaded, ghosted image of a hoop. The back side has a panel along the right which contains a card number at the top (using a "CCH" prefix), the brand logo and the sequential number. The die-cut side shows the backside of the image from the front. H cards are in hobby packs, R cards are in retail packs.

		MT
Complete Set (10):		500.00
Common Player:		30.00
CCH1	Shaquille O'Neal	100.00
CCH2	Joe Smith	75.00
CCH3	Rasheed Wallace	50.00
CCH4	Kevin Garnett	150.00
CCH5	Corliss Williamson	30.00
CCR1	Jason Kidd	70.00
CCR2	Ed O'Bannon	30.00
CCR3	Antonio McDyess	50.00
CCR4	Damon Stoudamire	125.00
CCR5	Shawn Respert	30.00

1995 Classic Draft Draft Day

The 14-card, standard-size set was randomly inserted into retail jumbo packs. The fronts have color action photos with the backs having player information.

		MT
Complete Set (14):		15.00
Common Player:		.30
1	Joe Smith (Maryland)	3.00
2	Joe Smith (Golden State)	3.00
3	Joe Smith	1.50
4	Rasheed Wallace (North Carolina)	1.25
5	Rasheed Wallace	.60
6	Rasheed Wallace (Washington)	1.25
7	Ed O'Bannon (UCLA)	.30
8	Ed O'Bannon	.30
9	Ed O'Bannon	.30
10	Corliss Williamson (Arkansas)	.30
11	Corliss Williamson	.30
12	Corliss Williamson	.30
13	Jason Kidd, Grant Hill (ROY)	4.00
14	Checklist	.30

1995 Classic Draft Instant Energy

The 20-card, standard-size set was inserted once per retail jumbo pack. The fronts feature a player cut out on a metallic background while the backs have another cutout over a lightning background. Cards are numbered with a "IE" prefix.

		MT
Complete Set (20):		25.00
Common Player:		.30
1	Joe Smith	3.00
2	Antonio McDyess	2.00
3	Jerry Stackhouse	3.00
4	Rasheed Wallace	1.50
5	Kevin Garnett	6.00
6	Damon Stoudamire	4.50
7	Shawn Respert	.30
8	Ed O'Bannon	.50
9	Kurt Thomas	.50
10	Gary Trent	.50
11	Cherokee Parks	.30
12	Corliss Williamson	.30
13	Eric Williams	.75
14	Brent Barry	.75
15	Bob Sura	.75
16	Theo Ratliff	.30
17	Randolph Childress	.30
18	Jason Caffey	.30
19	Michael Finley	1.00
20	George Zidek	.50

1995 Classic Draft Rookie of the Year

Collectors were given the chance to win prizes if they found a Rookie of the Year redemption card in 1995 Classic Basketball Rookies packs. The set consists of 19 player cards and a field card; they were seeded one per every six boxes. Cards numbered 1-100 depicting the 1995-96 Rookie of the Year could be redeemed for a $25 phone card of the player and a complete set of Printer's Proofs cards. Cards depicting the 1995-96 ROY that are stamped "1 of 3,999" are redeemable for a special bonus card.

		MT
Complete Set (20):		100.00
Common Player:		2.50
1	Joe Smith	15.00
2	Rasheed Wallace	8.00
3	Ed O'Bannon	5.00
4	Antonio McDyess	10.00
5	Shawn Respert	2.50
6	Mario Bennett	2.50
7	Jerry Stackhouse	15.00

8	Cherokee Parks	2.50
9	Damon Stoudamire	25.00
10	Kurt Thomas	5.00
11	Randolph Childress	2.50
12	Brent Barry	6.00
13	Corliss Williamson	2.50
14	Gary Trent	2.50
15	Bob Sura	5.00
16	David Vaughn	2.50
17	Michael Finley	8.00
18	Rashard Griffith	2.50
19	Lou Roe	2.50
20	Field Card	2.50

1995 Classic Draft Showtime

The 20-card, standard-size set was randomly inserted into retail packs. The cards feature a metallic background with color streaks resembling spotlights. The cards are numbered with an "S" prefix.

		MT
Complete Set (20):		75.00
Common Player:		2.50
Card #S4 K. Garnett Does Not Exist.		
1	Joe Smith	15.00
2	Antonio McDyess	8.00
3	Rasheed Wallace	6.00
5	Shawn Respert	4.00
6	Kurt Thomas	6.00
7	Gary Trent	6.00
8	Cherokee Parks	4.00
9	Eric Williams	8.00
10	Jerry Stackhouse	25.00
11	Travis Best	2.50
12	Michael Finley	10.00
13	George Zidek	6.00
14	David Vaughn	3.00
15	Mario Bennett	3.00
16	Greg Ostertag	2.50
17	Bob Sura	6.00
18	Lou Roe	4.00
19	Tyus Edney	6.00
20	Jimmy King	4.00

1995 Classic Draft Spotlight

The 10-card, standard-size set was randomly inserted into auto edition packs. The fronts display a color action photo with a blurred background. The card backs have a single photo with a career summary. The cards have the "RS" prefix.

		MT
Complete Set (10):		30.00
Common Player:		1.25
1	Joe Smith	5.00
2	Antonio McDyess	3.00
3	Jason Kidd	2.00
4	Rasheed Wallace	2.50
5	Kevin Garnett	12.00
6	Damon Stoudamire	10.00
7	Ed O'Bannon	2.00
8	Shawn Respert	1.25
9	Kurt Thomas	1.25
10	Randolph Childress	1.25

1995 Classic Assets Gold

Assets Gold is a 50-card set. The card front has a full-bleed photo with the player's name printed in gold at the bottom. The backs have another photo with statistics and a biography. Inserts include Silver Die-Cuts and five different values of Phone Cards.

		MT
Complete Set (50):		18.00
Common Player:		.15
Printer's Proof Set (50):		350.00
Common Printer's Proofs:		2.00
Printer's Proofs:		15x to 20x
Complete Silver Signature Set:		120.00
Common Silver Signatures:		.75
Silver Signatures:		4x to 6x
1	Dale Earnhardt	1.50
2	Jeff O'Neill	.30
3	Jeff Friesen	.40
4	Aki-Petteri Berg	.60
5	Todd Marchant	.15
6	Blaine Lacher	.30
7	Petr Sykora	.60
8	David Oliver	.25
9	Manon Rheaume	1.00
10	Ed Jovanovski	.40
11	Nolan Ryan	1.00
12	Barry Bonds	.40
13	Ben Grieve	.75
14	Dustin Hermanson	.20
15	Rashaan Salaam	1.00
16	Kyle Brady	.35
17	J.J. Stokes	.75
18	Michael Stewart	.25
19	Michael Westbrook	.75
20	Ki-Jana Carter	.60
21	Steve McNair	.75
22	Kerry Collins	1.50
23	Byron Morris	.25
24	Errict Rhett	1.00
25	William Floyd	.25
26	Drew Bledsoe	1.00
27	Marshall Faulk	2.00
28	Troy Aikman	.75
29	Steve Young	.75
30	Trent Dilfer	.40
31	Emmitt Smith	1.00
32	Rasheed Wallace	.50
33	Corliss Williamson	.30
34	Tyus Edney	.35
35	Ed O'Bannon	.40
36	Damon Stoudamire	2.50
37	Eddie Jones	.50
38	Khalid Reeves	.30
39	Jason Kidd	1.50
40	Glenn Robinson	1.25
41	Juwan Howard	1.00
42	Jamal Mashburn	.50
43	Shaquille O'Neal	1.00
44	Alonzo Mourning	.30
45	Donyell Marshall	.35
46	Jalen Rose	.35
47	Wesley Person	.35
48	Grant Hill	2.50
49	Rasheed Wallace (Checklist)	.25
50	Ki-Jana Carter (Checklist)	.25

1995 Classic Assets Gold and Silver Die-Cuts

This 20-card set was inserted one per 18 packs. The cards are die-cut around the Assets Gold logo at the top. The front features a color action photo and the backs have career highlights. Die-Cuts Gold versions were inserted 1:72. Cards are numbered with a "GDC" prefix.

		MT
Complete Silver Set (20):		150.00
Common Player:		5.00
Gold Die-Cuts:		3x
1	Ben Grieve	5.00
2	Shaquille O'Neal	10.00
3	Kyle Brady	6.00
4	Glenn Robinson	9.00
5	Marshall Faulk	12.00
6	Grant Hill	14.00
7	Rasheed Wallace	8.00
8	Ed O'Bannon	8.00
9	Barry Bonds	5.00
10	Dale Earnhardt	10.00
11	Ki-Jana Carter	8.00
12	Rashaan Salaam	10.00
13	Manon Rheaume	7.50
14	Jason Kidd	9.00
15	Emmitt Smith	10.00
16	Drew Bledsoe	10.00
17	Kerry Collins	8.00
18	Nolan Ryan	7.50
19	Michael Westbrook	8.00
20	Heath Shuler	5.00

1995 Classic Assets Gold $2 Foncards

The cards in this 47-card set measure 2-1/8" x 3-3/8". The fronts have full-bleed color photos with the Sprint logo in the upper right, the player's name in the lower right and "Two Dollars" printed on the left side. The backs have instructions on how to use the card.

		MT
Complete Set (47):		120.00
Common Player:		2.00
1	Dale Earnhardt	5.00
2	Jeff O'Neill	2.50
3	Jeff Friesen	2.00
4	Aki-Petteri Berg	3.00
5	Todd Marchant	2.00
6	Blaine Lacher	2.00
7	Petr Sykora	3.50
8	David Oliver	2.00
9	Manon Rheaume	6.00
10	Ed Jovanovski	3.00
11	Nolan Ryan	6.00
12	Barry Bonds	2.00
13	Ben Grieve	3.00
14	Dustin Hermanson	2.00
15	Rashaan Salaam	5.00
16	Kyle Brady	2.50
17	J.J. Stokes	5.00
18	James Stewart	2.50
19	Michael Westbrook	4.00
20	Ki-Jana Carter	3.00
21	Steve McNair	3.50
22	Kerry Collins	6.00
23	Byron Morris	2.00
24	Errict Rhett	3.00
25	William Floyd	2.00
26	Drew Bledsoe	4.00
27	Marshall Faulk	5.00
28	Troy Aikman	4.00
29	Steve Young	4.00
30	Trent Dilfer	2.00
31	Emmitt Smith	5.00
32	Rasheed Wallace	3.00
33	Corliss Williamson	2.50
34	Tyus Edney	2.50
35	Ed O'Bannon	2.50
36	Damon Stoudamire	6.00
37	Eddie Jones	2.00
38	Khalid Reeves	2.00
39	Jason Kidd	5.00
40	Glenn Robinson	4.00
41	Juwan Howard	4.00
42	Jamal Mashburn	3.00
43	Shaquille O'Neal	4.00
44	Alonzo Mourning	2.50
45	Donyell Marshall	2.00
46	Jalen Rose	2.00
47	Wesley Person	2.00

1995 Classic Assets Gold $5 Foncards

The cards in this 16-card set measure 2-1/8" x 3-3/8". The fronts have full-bleed color photos with the Sprint logo in the upper right, the player's name in the lower right and "Five Dollars" printed on the left side. The backs have instructions on how to use the card.

		MT
Complete Set (16):		200.00
Common Player:		8.00
1	J.J. Stokes	15.00
2	Michael Westbrook	12.00
3	Marshall Faulk	20.00
4	Damon Stoudamire	20.00
5	Manon Rheaume	14.00
6	Nolan Ryan	15.00
7	Emmitt Smith	20.00
8	Drew Bledsoe	15.00
9	Ki-Jana Carter	12.00
10	Ed O'Bannon	10.00
11	Dale Earnhardt	20.00
12	Glenn Robinson	20.00
13	Barry Bonds	6.00
14	Shaquille O'Neal	20.00
15	Troy Aikman	10.00
16	Jason Kidd	18.00

1995 Classic Assets Gold $25 Foncards

This five-card set was randomly inserted. The fronts feature two players, with their names in gold below the photo. The calling value is printed vertically separating the two players. The cards, unnumbered, have instructions on the back.

		MT
Complete Set (5):		300.00
Common Player:		50.00
1	Ed O'Bannon, Corliss Williamson	70.00
2	Ki-Jana Carter, Marshall Faulk	85.00
3	Steve McNair, Kerry Collins	80.00
4	Nolan Ryan, Barry Bonds	60.00
5	Rasheed Wallace, Glenn Robinson	65.00

1995 Classic Assets Gold $100 Foncards

The fronts of the five-card set contain color photos, with the player's name below. The calling value is printed vertically down the left side. The card expired 7/31/96.

		MT
Complete Set (5):		550.00
Common Player:		100.00
1	Rasheed Wallace	125.00
2	Kerry Collins	160.00
3	Emmitt Smith	175.00
4	Jason Kidd	175.00
5	Steve Young	140.00

1995 Classic Assets Gold $1000 Foncards

The five-card set have fronts with color action photos of the players, with the name below. The calling value is printed on the left. The cards, unnumbered, expired 7/31/96, with instructions on the back.

		MT
Complete Set (5):		6000.
Common Player:		1000.
1	Shaquille O'Neal	1500.
2	Marshall Faulk	1200.
3	Dale Earnhardt	1400.
4	Drew Bledsoe	1200.
5	Nolan Ryan	1500.

1995 Classic Visions

This premium 105-card set from Classic features pro basketball's top players, both rookies and veterans, on high-quality 24-point stock with double foil stamping and an embossed Classic logo. There are 65 regular cards in the set, plus three subsets: Shaquille O'Neal one-on-one (Shaq talks about himself and his foes), Jason Kidd one-on-one (he discusses the NBA's top backcourt players), and Clipboard cards (analyze the strong points of the league's top newcomers and veterans). Each card is also reprinted in a parallel set, called Vision Effects (one per 10 packs), which features holographic foil. Two insert sets, Hardcourt Skills and LaserArt, were also produced.

		MT
Complete Set (100):		35.00
Common Player:		.10
Wax Box:		55.00
1	Joe Smith	1.50
2	Antonio McDyess	.75
3	Jerry Stackhouse	1.50
4	Rasheed Wallace	.60
5	Kevin Garnett	3.00
6	Damon Stoudamire	2.00
7	Shawn Respert	.20
8	Ed O'Bannon	.20
9	Kurt Thomas	.20
10	Gary Trent	.20
11	Cherokee Parks	.20
12	Corliss Williamson	.20
13	Eric Williams	.50
14	Brent Barry	.50
15	Bob Sura	.50
16	Theo Ratliff	.30
17	Randolph Childress	.20
18	Jason Caffey	.40
19	Michael Finley	.75
20	George Zidek	.25
21	Travis Best	.25
22	Loren Meyer	.20
23	David Vaughn	.20
24	Sherell Ford	.20
25	Mario Bennett	.20
26	Greg Ostertag	.25
27	Cory Alexander	.20
28	Lou Roe	.20
29	Dragan Tarlac	.10
30	Terrence Rencher	.10
31	Junior Burrough	.10
32	Andrew DeClercq	.10
33	Jimmy King	.15
34	Lawrence Moten	.10
35	Frankie King	.10
36	Rashard Griffith	.10
37	Donny Marshall	.20
38	John Amaechi	.10
39	Erik Meek	.10
40	Donnie Boyce	.10
41	Eric Snow	.10
42	Anthony Pelle	.10
43	Troy Brown	.10
44	George Banks	.10
45	Tyus Edney	.25
46	Mark Davis	.10
47	Jerome Allen	.10
48	Fred Holberg	.10
49	Constantin Popa	.10
50	Michael McDonald	.10
51	Chris Carr	.10
52	Cuonzo Martin	.10
53	Don Reid	.10
54	Shaquille O'Neal	.50
55	Hakeem Olajuwon	.25
56	Alonzo Mourning	.25
57	Dikembe Mutombo	.25
58	Jason Kidd	.30
59	Glenn Robinson	.30
60	Juwan Howard	.30
61	Brian Grant	.20
62	Eddie Jones	.50
63	Rebecca Lobo	.75
64	Clint McDaniel	.10
65	Scotty Thurman	.10
66	Joe Smith	1.00
67	Jerry Stackhouse	1.00
68	Rasheed Wallace	.50
69	Kevin Garnett	2.50
70	Ed O'Bannon	.25
71	Gary Trent	.25
72	Corliss Williamson	.25
73	Brent Barry	.25
74	Shaquille O'Neal	.30
75	Hakeem Olajuwon	.20
76	Jason Kidd	.25
77	Eddie Jones	.50
78	Glenn Robinson	.25
79	Brian Grant	.20
80	Rebecca Lobo	.75
81	Jerry Stackhouse	1.00
82	Damon Stoudamire	1.50
83	Shawn Respert	.10
84	Gary Trent	.10
85	Ed O'Bannon	.20
86	Glenn Robinson	.30
87	Randolph Childress	.20
88	Travis Best	.20
89	Eddie Jones	.50
90	Tyus Edney	.20
91	Joe Smith	1.00
92	Antonio McDyess	.50
93	Rasheed Wallace	.50
94	Kevin Garnett	2.50
95	Alonzo Mourning	.20
96	Kurt Thomas	.20
97	Cherokee Parks	.20
98	Corliss Williamson	.20
99	Hakeem Olajuwon	.20
100	Shaquille O'Neal	.40

1995 Classic Visions Effects

The 100-card, standard-size set parallels the Visions set and was inserted every 10 packs. The words, "Visions Effects" run vertically down the right side with the player image on a dimensional holographic background.

	MT
Complete Set (100):	200.00
Common Player:	.50
Stars:	2x-4x

1995 Classic Visions Hardcourt Skills

These 15 cards, printed on an actual grained-wood stock, assess the strong points of basketball's biggest names. Printed on 24-point stock, the cards are also foil-stamped. The card front has a color photo in the middle, with a set icon in the lower left corner. The player's name is along the bottom. The back is numbered using an "HC" prefix. Cards were seeded one per every box of 1995 Classic Basketball Visions product.

		MT
Complete Set (15):		175.00
Common Player:		3.00
1	Joe Smith	25.00
2	Antonio McDyess	15.00
3	Jerry Stackhouse	35.00
4	Rasheed Wallace	8.00
5	Damon Stoudamire	35.00
6	Shawn Respert	3.00
7	Ed O'Bannon	8.00
8	Jimmy King	3.00
9	Randolph Childress	3.00
10	Shaquille O'Neal	25.00
11	Hakeem Olajuwon	10.00
12	Jason Kidd	15.00
13	Alonzo Mourning	8.00
14	Scottie Pippen	10.00
15	Glenn Robinson	12.00

1995 Classic Visions Laser Art

These 10 1995 Classic Basketball Visions insert cards feature players such as Alonzo Mourning and Ed O'Bannon on an innovative laser diecut duplexed "fabric" card stock. The cards, seeded one per every 145 packs, are numbered with an "LA" prefix.

		MT
Complete Set (10):		275.00
Common Player:		10.00
1	Shaquille O'Neal	40.00
2	Jason Kidd	25.00
3	Alonzo Mourning	15.00
4	Damon Stoudamire	60.00
5	Glenn Robinson	20.00
6	Joe Smith	35.00
7	Jerry Stackhouse	60.00
8	Kevin Garnett	35.00
9	Ed O'Bannon	10.00
10	Rebecca Lobo	15.00

1995 Classic Five-Sport Previews

This set was randomly issued in classic hockey packs and contained five cards. This set features the leaders and up- and-coming rookies of five sports. The fronts have a color photo with a gold foil stamp of "preview" and the player's name, school and position printed on the right side. The back has another color shot, with statistics. The cards are numbered with a "SP" prefix.

		MT
Complete Set (5):		30.00
Common Player:		5.00
1	Dale Earnhardt	8.00
2	Joe Smith	8.00
3	Michael Westbrook	5.00
4	Bryan Berard	5.00
5	Paul Wilson	5.00

1995 Classic Five-Sport

First issued in one series of 200 standard-size cards, this set was issued in 10-card packs with an SRP of $1.99. One autographed card was included in each pack, with one certified autographed card in each box. Memorabilia redemption cards were also one per box. Along with photos of the player on the front, balls of the sports run vertically down the right side with the player's name and position.

		MT
Complete Set (200):		15.00
Common Player:		.05
Comp. Silver Die Cut (200):		75.00
Common Silver Die Cut:		.15
Stars:		5x
Comp. Red Die Cut (200):		200.00
Common Red Die Cut:		.50
Stars:		15x
Comp. Print Proof Set (200):		300.00
Common Printer's Proof:		1.00
Stars:		20x
1	Joe Smith	.75
2	Antonio McDyess	.60
3	Jerry Stackhouse	.60
4	Rasheed Wallace	.05
5	Kevin Garnett	2.00
6	Damon Stoudamire	1.50
7	Shawn Respert	.05
8	Ed O'Bannon	.05
9	Kurt Thomas	.05
10	Gary Trent	.05
11	Cherokee Parks	.05
12	Corliss Williamson	.25
13	Eric Williams	.05
14	Brent Barry	.05
15	Bob Sura	.05
16	Theo Ratliff	.05
17	Randolph Childress	.05
18	Jason Caffey	.05
19	Michael Finley	.40
20	George Zidek	.05
21	Travis Best	.25
22	Loren Meyer	.05
23	David Vaughn	.05
24	Sherell Ford	.05
25	Mario Bennett	.05
26	Greg Ostertag	.05
27	Cory Alexander	.05
28	Lou Roe	.05
29	Dragan Tarlac	.05
30	Terrence Rencher	.05
31	Junior Burrough	.05
32	Andrew DeClercq	.05
33	Jimmy King	.05
34	Lawrence Moten	.05
35	Donny Marshall	.05
36	Eric Snow	.05
37	Anthony Pelle	.05
38	Tyus Edney	.25
39	Jerome Allen	.05
40	Fred Hoiberg	.05
41	Constantin Popa	.05
42	Rebecca Lobo	.50
43	Ki-Jana Carter	.25
44	Tony Boselli	.05
45	Steve McNair	1.00
46	Michael Westbrook	.25
47	Kerry Collins	1.00
48	Kevin Carter	.05
49	Mike Mamula	.05
50	Joey Galloway	.75
51	Kyle Brady	.05
52	J.J. Stokes	.05
53	Derrick Alexander	.15
54	Warren Sapp	.25
55	Mark Fields	.05
56	Ruben Brown	.05
57	Ellis Johnson	.05
58	Hugh Douglas	.05
59	Tyrone Wheatley	.05
60	Napoleon Kaufman	.25
61	James O. Stewart	.05
62	Luther Ellis	.05
63	Rashaan Salaam	.25
64	Tyrone Poole	.05
65	Ty Law	.05
66	Korey Stringer	.05
67	Devin Bush	.05
68	Mark Bruener	.05
69	Derrick Brooks	.15
70	Craig Powell	.05
71	Craig Newsome	.25
72	Anthony Cook	.05
73	Ray Zellars	.25
74	Todd Collins	.05
75	Sherman Williams	.25
76	Frank Sanders	.50
77	Corey Fuller	.05
78	Kordell Stewart	1.50
79	Curtis Martin	1.50
80	Lorenzo Styles	.05
81	Chris T. Jones	.25
82	Zack Crockett	.05
83	Stoney Case	.05
84	Eric Zeier	.05
85	Jimmy Hitchcock	.05
86	Rodney Thomas	.05
87	Rob Johnson	.40
88	Tyrone Davis	.05
89	Chad May	.05
90	Ed Hervey	.05
91	Terrell Davis	2.00
92	John Walsh	.05
93	Ben Grieve	1.00
94	Roger Cedeno	.05
95	Michael Barrett	.40
96	Ben Davis	.05
97	Paul Wilson	.05
98	Calvin Reese	.05
99	Jermaine Dye	.05
100	Alvie Shepherd	.05
101	Ryan Jaroncyk	.05
102	Mark Farris	.10
103	Karim Garcia	.05
104	Rey Ordonez	.05
105	Jay Payton	.40

106	Dustin Hermanson	.05
107	Tommy Davis	.05
108	C.J. Nitkowski	.05
109	Todd Greene	.05
110	Billy Wagner	.05
111	Mark Redman	.10
112	Brooks Kieschnick	.05
113	Paul Konerko	1.00
114	Brad Fullmer	.05
115	Vladimir Guerrero	1.50
116	Bartolo Colon	.50
117	Doug Million	.05
118	Steve Gibralter	.05
119	Tony McKnight	.20
120	Derrek Lee	.25
121	Nomar Garciaparra	1.50
122	Chad Hermansen	.75
123	Bryan Berard	.25
124	Wade Redden	.05
125	Aki-Petteri Berg	.05
126	Nolan Baumgartner	.05
127	Jason Bonsignore	.05
128	Steve Kelly	.05
129	George Breen	.05
130	Terry Ryan	.05
131	Greg Bullock	.05
132	Jarome Iginla	.75
133	Petr Buzek	.05
134	Brad Church	.05
135	Jay McKee	.05
136	Jan Hlavac	.05
137	Petr Sykora	.05
138	Ed Jovanovski	.25
139	Chris Kenady	.05
140	Marc Moro	.05
141	Kaj Linna	.05
142	Aaron MacDonald	.05
143	Chad Kilger	.05
144	Tyler Moss	.05
145	Christian Laflamme	.05
146	Brian Mueller	.05
147	Daymond Langkow	.05
148	Brent Peterson	.05
149	Chad Quenneville	.05
150	Chris Van Dyk	.05
151	Kent Fearns	.05
152	Adam Wiesel	.05
153	Marc Chouinard	.05
154	Jason Doig	.05
155	Denis Smith	.05
156	Radek Dvorak	.05
157	Donald MacLean	.05
158	Shane Kenny	.05
159	Brian Holzinger	.05
160	Eric Flinton	.05
161	Dale Earnhardt	1.00
162	John Andretti	.05
163	Derrike Cope	.05
164	Richard Childress	.05
165	Rusty Wallace	.50
166	Bobby Labonte	.25
167	Brett Bodine	.05
168	Michael Waltrip	.25
169	Sterling Marlin	.25
170	Kyle Petty	.05
171	Ricky Rudd	.25
172	Jeff Burton	.05
173	Dick Trickle	.05
174	Ernie Irvan	.50
175	Dale Jarrett	.50
176	Darrell Waltrip	.25
177	Geoff Bodine	.05
178	Ted Musgrave	.05
179	Morgan Shepherd	.05
180	Todd Bodine	.05
181	Jerry Stackhouse, Jimmy Hitchcock	.05
182	Antonio McDyess, Sherman Williams	.25
183	Nomar Garciaparra, Travis Best	.75
184	Andrew DeClercq, Ki-Jana Carter	.05
185	Tyrone Wheatley, Jimmy King	.05
186	J.J. Stokes, Ed O'Bannon	.05
187	Warren Sapp, Constantin Popa	.05
188	Paul Wilson, Derrick Brooks	.05
189	Eric Williams, George Breen	.05
190	Bob Sura, Derrick Alexander	.05
191	Steve Young	.25
192	Hakeem Olajuwon	.25
193	Barry Bonds	.25
194	Marshall Faulk	.25
195	Troy Aikman	.50
196	Drew Bledsoe	.50
197	Emmitt Smith	.75
198	Jason Kidd	.25
199	Shaquille O'Neal	.75
200	Alonzo Mourning	.25

1995 Classic Five-Sport Autographs

The same as the base set, except it conatins autographed cards. Randomly inserted into packs, the backs have the message "Congratulations" to identify it as a autograph card.

		MT
Complete Set (110):		1200.
Common Autograph (1-200):		5.00
Common Racing AU/225:		20.00
Signings AU/225:		3x
1	Joe Smith	50.00
2A	Antonio McDyess SP	60.00
2B	Antonio McDyess/225	150.00
4A	Rasheed Wallace SP	30.00
4B	Rasheed Wallace/225	75.00
6A	Damon Stoudamire SP	120.00
6B	Damon Stoudamire/225	300.00
8	Ed O'Bannon	5.00
9	Kurt Thomas	5.00
11	Cherokee Parks	5.00
14A	Brent Barry SP	18.00
14B	Brent Barry/225	40.00
15	Bob Sura	8.00
16	Theo Ratliff	8.00
17	Randolph Childress SP	8.00
19	Michael Finley	30.00
20	George Zidek	5.00
24	Sherrell Ford	5.00
27	Cory Alexander	5.00
30	Terrence Rencher	5.00
32	Andrew DeClercq SP	8.00
35	Donny Marshall	5.00
36	Eric Snow	5.00
37	Anthony Pelle	5.00
38	Tyus Edney	10.00
39	Jerome Allen	5.00
40	Fred Hoiberg	5.00
41	Constantin Popa	5.00
45	Steve McNair	40.00
47	Kerry Collins	50.00
49	Mike Mamula	5.00
50	Joey Galloway	40.00
51	Kyle Brady	5.00
55	Mark Fields	5.00
58	Hugh Douglas	8.00
60A	Napoleon Kaufman SP	60.00
60B	Napoleon Kaufman/225	120.00
64	Tyrone Poole	5.00
77	Corey Fuller	5.00
84	Eric Zeier	5.00
87	Rob Johnson	20.00
89	Chad May	5.00
92	John Walsh	5.00
93	Ben Grieve	40.00
94	Roger Cedeno SP	8.00
95	Michael Barrett	10.00
96	Ben Davis	5.00
97	Paul Wilson	8.00
98	Calvin Reese	5.00
99	Jermaine Dye	8.00
100	Alvie Shepherd	5.00
101	Ryan Jaroncyk	5.00
102	Mark Farris	5.00
103	Karim Garcia	20.00
104	Rey Ordonez	20.00
105	Jay Payton	10.00
106	Dustin Hermanson	5.00
109	Todd Greene	10.00
110	Billy Wagner	10.00
111	Mark Redman	5.00
112	Brooks Kieschnick	8.00
113	Paul Konerko	40.00
114	Brad Fullmer	20.00
115	Vladimir Guerrero	40.00
116	Bartolo Colon	25.00
117	Doug Million	5.00
118	Steve Gibralter	5.00
119	Tony McKnight	6.00
120	Derrek Lee	15.00
121	Nomar Garciaparra	50.00
122	Chad Hermansen	25.00
126	Nolan Baumgartner	5.00
127	Jason Bonsignore	8.00
128	Steve Kelly	5.00
129	George Breen	5.00
131	Greg Bullock	5.00
132	Jarome Iginla	15.00
135	Jay McKee	5.00
137A	Petr Sykora SP	20.00
137B	Petr Sykora/225	50.00
138	Ed Jovanovski	15.00
139	Chris Kenady	5.00
140	Marc Moro	5.00
142	Aaron MacDonald	5.00
144	Tyler Moss	5.00
145	Christian Laflamme	5.00
146	Brian Mueller	5.00
148	Brent Peterson	5.00
149	Chad Quenneville	5.00
150	Chris Van Dyk SP	8.00
151	Kent Ferns	5.00
153	Marc Chouinard SP	8.00
154	Jason Doig	5.00
155	Denis Smith	5.00
156	Radek Dvorak	8.00
157	Don MacLean	5.00
158	Shane Kenny	5.00
161A	Dale Earnhardt	100.00
161B	Dale Earnhardt/225	250.00
164	Richard Childress/225	15.00
166	Bobby Labonte/225	15.00
167	Brett Bodine/225	15.00
169	Sterling Marlin/225	25.00
170	Kyle Petty/225	15.00
171	Ricky Rudd/225	25.00
173	Dick Trickle/225	15.00
174	Ernie Irvan	75.00
175	Dale Jarrett/225	25.00
176	Darrell Waltrip/225	15.00
177	Geoff Bodine/225	15.00
178	Ted Musgrave/225	15.00
179	Morgan Shepherd/225	25.00
180	Todd Bodine/225	15.00
191	Steve Young/225	250.00
192A	Hakeem Olajuwon	90.00
192B	Hakeem Olajuwon/225	150.00
193A	Barry Bonds	75.00
193B	Barry Bonds/225	125.00
196	Drew Bledsoe/225	200.00
198A	Jason Kidd SP	70.00
198B	Jason Kidd/225	150.00
199A	Shaquille O'Neal	250.00
199B	Shaquille O'Neal/225	500.00
200	Alonzo Mourning	60.00

1995 Classic Five-Sport Hot Box Autographs

The set contains six cards, that were randomly inserted in Hobby Hot boxes. The cards are the same as the regular Hot box inserts, but these grace a player's signature on the front.

		MT
Complete Set (6):		650.00
Common Auto.:		50.00
Inserts in Hobby Hot Boxes		
1	Barry Bonds	75.00
2	Kerry Collins	75.00
3	Dale Earnhardt	100.00
4	Jason Kidd	125.00
5	Steve McNair	75.00
6	Shaquille O'Neal	175.00

1995 Classic Five-Sport Fast Track

This 20-card set was randomly inserted, featuring rising stars of various sports. The fronts are borderless, with a color photo of the athlete. The backs also have a color shot in a box with a player profile beneath it. Cards are numbered with a "FT" prefix.

		MT
Complete Set (20):		150.00
Common Player:		2.50
1	Joe Smith	12.00
2	Michael Westbrook	5.00
3	Jeff Gordon	8.00
4	Kyle Brady	2.50
5	Bryan Berard	5.00
6	Jerry Stackhouse	12.00
7	Shawn Respert	3.00
8	Napoleon Kaufman	10.00
9	Rasheed Wallace	6.00
10	Ed O'Bannon	5.00
11	J.J. Stokes	5.00
12	Kevin Garnett	35.00
13	Ben Grieve	10.00
14	Petr Sykora	5.00
15	Tyrone Wheatley	3.00
16	Antonio McDyess	6.00
17	Rashaan Salaam	5.00
18	Damon Stoudamire	25.00
19	Steve McNair	12.00
20	Corliss Williamson	5.00

1995 Classic Five-Sport $3 Foncards

Issued at 1:72, this five-card set has a color action shot on the front, with a $3 emblem in the upper right corner. The Sprint logo is at the bottom, with directions on the back.

		MT
Complete Set (5):		30.00
Common Player:		4.00
1	Dale Earnhardt	9.00
2	Brian Holzinger	4.00
3	C.J. Nitkowski	4.00
4	Rashaan Salaam	9.00
5	Joe Smith	10.00

1995 Classic Five-Sport Phone Cards $4

Found in one of every 72 packs, this five-card set featured five top prospects in various sports. The sprint logo and $4 is printed along the top.

		MT
Complete Set (5):		25.00
Common Player:		5.00
1	Sterling Marlin	8.00
2	Nomar Garciaparra	10.00
3	Wade Redden	5.00
4	Jerry Stackhouse	8.00
5	Michael Westbrook	5.00

1995 Classic Five-Sport NFL Experience Previews

The five-card set was randomly inserted into Hot packs, and feature the NFL's elite with color photos and text. Cards are numbered with a "EP" prefix.

		MT
Complete Set (5):		25.00
Common Player:		5.00
1	Emmitt Smith	10.00
2	Drew Bledsoe	8.00
3	Steve Young	8.00
4	Rashaan Salaam	5.00
5	Marshall Faulk	5.00

1995 Classic Five-Sport On Fire

Of the 20 cards in this set, 10 were released in Hobby Hot packs, with the other 10 released in retail Hot packs. The fronts have a full-color cutout against a flame background, with an On Fire logo at the bottom. The player's name is printed vertically, in white, on the left side.

		MT
Complete Set (20):		200.00
Common Player:		8.00
H1	Drew Bledsoe	15.00
H2	Joe Smith	10.00
H3	Dale Earnhardt	15.00
H4	Ki-Jana Carter	8.00
H5	Michael Westbrook	8.00
H6	Rasheed Wallace	8.00
H7	Jerry Stackhouse	8.00
H8	Tyrone Wheatley	8.00
H9	Kevin Garnett	40.00
H10	Rebecca Lobo	12.00
R1	Jason Kidd	15.00
R2	Antonio McDyess	10.00
R3	Jeff Gordon	12.00
R4	Steve McNair	18.00
R5	Rashaan Salaam	8.00
R6	Ed O'Bannon	8.00
R7	J.J. Stokes	10.00
R8	Kyle Brady	8.00
R9	Bryan Berard	10.00
R10	Napoleon Kaufman	12.00

1995 Classic Five-Sport Record Setters

Inserted in retail packs, this 10-card set contains the stars and rookies of five sports. Full-bleed color action shots grace the fronts, with the title "Record Setters" along the bottom. The cards are numbered on the back with a "RS" prefix.

		MT
Complete Set (10):		90.00
Common Player:		5.00
1	Kerry Collins	12.00
2	Bryan Berard	8.00
3	Ed O'Bannon	5.00
4	Dale Earnhardt	12.00
5	Joe Smith	10.00
6	Jerry Stackhouse	12.00
7	Paul Wilson	5.00
8	Rashaan Salaam	5.00
9	Kevin Garnett	30.00
10	Shaquille O'Neal	12.00

1995 Classic Five-Sport Classic Standouts

Randomly inserted into packs at a rate of 1:216, the 10-card set features young and old stars of five sports. The fronts have color cutouts of the athlete against a black and gold background. The back has another another photo with career highlights on the bottom. Cards have a "CS" prefix.

		MT
Complete Set (10):		35.00
Common Player:		3.00
1	Joe Smith	4.00
2	Rebecca Lobo	3.00
3	Dale Earnhardt	6.00
4	Rashaan Salaam	3.00
5	Bryan Berard	5.00
6	Jerry Stackhouse	5.00
7	Kerry Collins	5.00
8	Rasheed Wallace	3.00
9	Michael Westbrook	3.00
10	Emmitt Smith	8.00

1995 Classic Five-Sport Strive For Five

This set contains 65 cards and was used for an interactive game. Collectors aimed to get a full suit of cards to be redeemed for prizes. Odds of finding such a card is 1:10. The fronts have a full-color photo, with the card numbered on the top and bottom. The back has a green background with the game rules.

		MT
Complete Set (65):		160.00
Common Player:		2.50
BA1	Paul Wilson	2.50
BA2	Billy Wagner	2.50
BA3	Ben Grieve	6.00
BA4	Bartolo Colon	4.00
BA5	Tommy Davis	2.50
BA6	C.J. Nitkowski	2.50
BA7	Mark Redman	3.50
BA8	Todd Greene	2.50
BA9	Jay Payton	3.00
BA10	Nomar Garciaparra	12.00
BA11	Ben Davis	2.50
BA12	Doug Million	2.50
BA13	Dustin Hermanson	2.50
BK1	Joe Smith	5.00
BK2	Gary Trent	2.50
BK3	Kurt Thomas	2.50
BK4	Ed O'Bannon	2.50
BK5	Shawn Respert	2.50
BK6	Damon Stoudamire	12.00
BK7	Kevin Garnett	20.00
BK8	Rasheed Wallace	2.50
BK9	Antonio McDyess	5.00
BK10	Hakeem Olajuwon	3.00
BK11	Jason Kidd	3.00
BK12	Rebecca Lobo	5.00
BK13	Jerry Stackhouse	5.00
FB1	Ki-Jana Carter	3.00
FB2	Rashaan Salaam	2.50
FB3	Napoleon Kaufman	3.00
FB4	Tyrone Wheatley	2.50
FB5	J.J. Stokes	2.50
FB6	Joey Galloway	6.00
FB7	Kerry Collins	10.00
FB8	Michael Westbrook	2.50
FB9	Steve McNair	8.00
FB10	Drew Bledsoe	7.00
FB11	Marshall Faulk	3.00
FB12	Troy Aikman	4.00
FB13	Steve Young	4.00
HK1	Wade Redden	2.50
HK2	Jan Hlavac	2.50
HK3	Brad Church	2.50
HK4	Steve Kelly	2.50
HK5	Radek Dvorak	2.50
HK6	Jason Bonsignore	2.50
HK7	Petr Sykora	2.50
HK8	Daymond Langkow	2.50
HK9	Chad Kilger	2.50
HK10	Nolan Baumgartner	2.50
HK11	Brian Holzinger	2.50
HK12	Aki-Petteri Berg	2.50
HK13	Ed Jovanovski	3.00
RC1	John Andretti	2.50
RC2	Dick Trickle	2.50
RC3	Kyle Petty	2.50
RC4	Bobby Labonte	3.00
RC5	Ricky Rudd	3.00
RC6	Darrell Waltrip	3.00
RC7	Dale Jarrett	4.00
RC8	Brett Bodine	2.50
RC9	Geoff Bodine	2.50
RC10	Ernie Irvan	4.00
RC11	Jeff Burton	2.50
RC12	Sterling Marlin	3.00
RC13	Rusty Wallace	4.00

1995 Classic Images Previews

Inserted 1:24 in second series '94-95 Assets packs, the set contained five cards. Only 5,000 of each card was produced, with the backs showing the player's identification and a note saying it's a limited edition card. Cards are numbered with a "IP" prefix.

		MT
Complete Set (5):		50.00
Common Player:		10.00
1	Grant Hill	20.00
2	Shaquille O'Neal	15.00
3	Marshall Faulk	10.00
4	Manon Rheaume	12.00
5	Emmitt Smith	15.00

1995 Classic Images

This 120-card set was printed on 18-point micro-lined foil board. The set features the top draft picks of the four major sports, and was produced in 1,995 sequentially- numbered 16-box hobby cases. The series also featured a "Hot Box" in every four cases, with each pack including at least one card from five insert sets, along with the Clear Excitement chase cards. That makes a grand total of 24 inserts per Hot Box. A promotional card of Grant Hill, numbered HP1, was also made.

		MT
Complete Set (120):		25.00
Common Player:		.10
1	Glenn Robinson	1.00
2	Jason Kidd	1.50
3	Grant Hill	4.00
4	Donyell Marshall	.40
5	Juwan Howard	1.50
6	Sharone Wright	.25
7	Brian Grant	.40
8	Eric Montross	.40
9	Eddie Jones	2.00
10	Carlos Rogers	.20
11	Khalid Reeves	.25
12	Jalen Rose	.60
13	Yinka Dare	.10
14	Eric Piatkowski	.10
15	Clifford Rozier	.20
16	Aaron McKie	.10
17	Eric Mobley	.15
18	B.J. Tyler	.10
19	Dickey Simpkins	.15
20	Bill Curley	.10
21	Wesley Person	.60
22	Monty Williams	.20
23	Antonio Lang	.10
24	Darrin Hancock	.10
25	Michael Smith	.25
26	Rodney Dent	.10
27	Charlie Ward	.25
28	Jim McIlvaine	.15
29	Brooks Thompson	.10
30	Gaylon Nickerson	.10
31	Jamie Watson	.10
32	Damon Bailey	.15
33	Dontonio Wingfield	.10
34	Trevor Ruffin	.10
35	Greg Minor	.10
36	Dwayne Morton	.10
37	Shaquille O'Neal	1.00
38	Dan Wilkinson	.10
39	Marshall Faulk	.50
40	Heath Shuler	.25
41	Willie McGinest	.20
42	Trev Alberts	.10
43	Trent Dilfer	.50
44	Bryant Young	.40
45	Sam Adams	.10
46	Antonio Langham	.15
47	Jamir Miller	.10
48	Aaron Glenn	.10
49	Bernard Williams	.10
50	Charles Johnson	.25
51	Dewayne Washington	.10
52	Tim Bowens	.25
53	Johnnie Morton	.50
54	Rob Fredrickson	.25
55	Shante Carver	.10
56	Henry Ford	.10
57	Jeff Burris	.10
58	William Floyd	.25
59	Derrick Alexander	.25
60	Darnay Scott	.25
61	Errict Rhett	.40
62	Greg Hill	.25
63	David Palmer	.10
64	Charlie Garner	.40
65	Mario Bates	.25
66	Bert Emanuel	.40
67	Thomas Randolph	.10
68	Aubrey Beavers	.10
69	Byron Morris	.40
70	Lake Dawson	.40
71	Todd Steussie	.10
72	Aaron Taylor	.20
73	Corey Sawyer	.10
74	Kevin Mitchell	.10
75	Emmitt Smith	1.00
76	Paul Wilson	.40
77	Ben Grieve	2.00
78	Doug Million	.25
79	Bret Wagner	.25
80	Dustin Hermanson	.40
81	Doug Webb	.10
82	Brian Stephenson	.10
83	Jacob Cruz	1.00
84	Cade Gaspar	.15
85	Nomar Garciaparra	3.00
86	Mike Thurman	.20
87	Brian Buchanan	.15
88	Mark Johnson	.20
89	Jacob Shumate	.20
90	Kevin Witt	.25
91	Victor Rodriguez	.15
92	Trey Moore	.10
93	Barry Bonds	.50
94	Ed Jovanovski	.25
95	Oleg Tverdovsky	.25
96	Radek Bonk	.25
97	Jason Bonsignore	.20
98	Jeff O'Neill	.25
99	Ryan Smyth	.25
100	Jamie Storr	.50
101	Jason Wiemer	.25
102	Nolan Baumgartner	.20
103	Jeff Friesen	.25
104	Wade Belak	.10
105	Ethan Moreau	.15
106	Alexander Kharlamov	.20
107	Eric Fichaud	.40
108	Wayne Primeau	.20
109	Brad Brown	.10
110	Chris Dingman	.10
111	Chris Wells	.10
112	Vadim Sharifjanov	.20
113	Dan Cloutier	.20
114	Jason Allison	.20
115	Todd Marchant	.20
116	Brent Gretzky	.20
117	Petr Sykora	.40
118	Manon Rheaume	1.50
119	Checklist #1 (Hill)	1.00
120	Checklist #2 (Faulk)	.25

1995 Classic Images Classic Performances

Inserted at 1:12, this 20-card set looks back at 20 former stars. Each card is numbered out of 4,495, with the fronts featuring the player against a gold background. The cards are numbered with a "CP" prefix.

		MT
Complete Set (20):		140.00
Common Player:		4.00
1	Glenn Robinson	12.00
2	Grant Hill	30.00
3	Jason Kidd	12.00
4	Juwan Howard	15.00
5	Shaquille O'Neal	12.00
6	Alonzo Mourning	6.00
7	Jamal Mashburn	6.00
8	Steve Young	10.00
9	Marshall Faulk	10.00
10	Derrick Alexander	4.00
11	William Floyd	4.00
12	Errict Rhett	4.00
13	Byron Morris	4.00
14	Heath Shuler	6.00
15	Emmitt Smith	10.00
16	Paul Wilson	6.00
17	Barry Bonds	4.00
18	Nolan Ryan	12.00
19	Ed Jovanovski	4.00
20	Eric Fichaud	4.00

1995 Classic Images Clear Excitement

The two five-card acetate sets were randomly inserted at a rate of 1:24, featuring five stars from different sports. Cards with the prefix "E" were inserted in hobby hot boxes, while those with the prefix "C" were in retail hot boxes. Cards are numbered out of 300.

		MT
Complete Set (10):		900.00
Common Player:		75.00
C1	Shaquille O'Neal	125.00
C2	Emmitt Smith	125.00
C3	Troy Aikman	100.00
C4	Steve Young	75.00
C5	Nolan Ryan	175.00
E1	Grant Hill	125.00
E2	Marshall Faulk	75.00
E3	Drew Bledsoe	125.00
E4	Hakeem Olajuwon	75.00
E5	Manon Rheaume	75.00

1995 Classic Images Draft Challenge Acetates

Featuring a color action image on the front, the set contains five cards which is obtained through a mail-in wrapper offer.

		MT
Complete Set (5):		20.00
Common Player:		3.00
Autographs:		25x
1	Rashaan Salaam	3.00
2	Ki-Jana Carter	4.00
3	John Walsh	3.00
4	Steve McNair	8.00
5	Kerry Collins	6.00

1995 Classic Images Flashbacks

The 10-card, standard-size set was inserted into every 24 retail packs. The card fronts feature a color action photo with "Flashbacks" printed along the card face top border. The backs contain another action shot and player information. Cards are numbered with a "TF" prefix.

		MT
Complete Set (10):		125.00
Common Player:		3.00
1	Glenn Robinson (Purdue)	20.00
2	Jason Kidd (California)	25.00
3	Grant Hill (Duke)	30.00
4	Donyell Marshall (Connecticut)	3.00
5	Jamal Mashburn (Kentucky)	6.00
6	Eric Montross (North Carolina)	4.00
7	Eddie Jones (Temple)	20.00
8	Alonzo Mourning (Georgetown)	7.00
9	Jalen Rose (Michigan)	3.00
10	Shaquille O'Neal (LSU)	20.00

1995 Classic Images NFL Draft Challenge

Inserted at 1:24, the 25-card set contains previews of expected stars in the NFL. Five players are featured in four different uniforms, and a field card. Only 3,195 cards were produced. Redemption options included receiving a five-cards acetate set, and a single acetate card. One could also receive a five-card autographed set. The redemption program ran until October 31, 1995. Cards are numbered with a "DC" prefix.

		MT
Complete Set (25):		75.00
Common Player:		1.00
1	Rashaan Salaam	1.00
2	Rashaan Salaam	1.00
3	Rashaan Salaam	3.00
4	Rashaan Salaam	1.00
5	Rashaan Salaam	1.00
6	Ki-Jana Carter	2.00
7	Ki-Jana Carter	2.00
8	Ki-Jana Carter	2.00
9	Ki-Jana Carter	5.00
10	Ki-Jana Carter	2.00
11	John Walsh	1.00
12	John Walsh	1.00
13	John Walsh	1.00
14	John Walsh	1.00
15	John Walsh	1.00
16	Steve McNair	3.00
17	Steve McNair	3.00
18	Steve McNair	18.00
19	Steve McNair	3.00
20	Steve McNair	3.00
21	Kerry Collins	3.00
22	Kerry Collins	3.00
23	Kerry Collins	3.00
24	Kerry Collins	3.00
25	Kerry Collins	12.00

1995 Classic Images Player of the Year

A four-card set obtained through a mail-in wrapper offer, was also available as one set per retail box. The fronts are borderless, with a color action image on a metallic background. The back has a headshot, with another photo along the side. The cards are numbered with a "POY" prefix.

		MT
Complete Set (4):		12.00
Common Player:		2.00
1	Steve Young	2.00
2	Emmitt Smith	3.00
3	Grant Hill	6.00
4	Shaquille O'Neal	4.00

1995 Classic Images Update

		MT
Complete Set (10):		50.00
Common Player:		2.50
126	Emmitt Smith	12.00
127	Troy Aikman	8.00
128	Steve Young	8.00
129	Deion Sanders	4.00
130	Ben Coates	2.50
131	Natrone Means	5.00
132	Drew Bledsoe	20.00
133	Cris Carter	4.00
134	Marshall Faulk	6.00
135	Errict Rhett	2.50

1996 Classic Assets

Assets was issued in one set of 50 cards, featuring top stars. The cards contain action photos and statistics. Hot Print cards are parallel cards randomly inserted into Hot Packs.

		MT
Complete Set (50):		20.00
Common Player:		.10
1	Troy Aikman	.50
2	Drew Bledsoe	.50
3	Todd Bodine	.10
4	Barry Bonds	.50
5	Isaac Bruce	.25
6	Kerry Collins	1.50
7	Trent Dilfer	.10
8	Radek Dvorak	.30
9	Dale Earnhardt	1.00
10	Marshall Faulk	1.00
11	William Floyd	.10
12	Joey Galloway	1.50
13	Kevin Garnett	1.25
14	Brian Holzinger	.20
15	Juwan Howard	.50
16	Eddie Jones	.40
17	Ed Jovanovski	.25
18	Jason Kendall	.10
19	Jason Kidd	1.00
20	Rebecca Lobo	.25
21	Sterling Marlin	.20
22	Mark Martin	.50
23	Antonio McDyess	1.00
24	Steve McNair	1.00
25	Byron Morris	.20
26	Alonzo Mourning	.25
27	Ted Musgrave	.10
28	Dikembe Mutombo	.10
29	Ed O'Bannon	.40
30	Shaquille O'Neal	.75
31	Hakeem Olajuwon	.50
32	Cherokee Parks	.25
33	Jay Payton	.50
34	Scottie Pippen	.25
35	Errict Rhett	.50
36	Ruben Rivera	.75
37	Glenn Robinson	1.00
38	Jalen Rose	.20
39	Nolan Ryan	.40
40	Darnay Scott	.25
41	Emmitt Smith	1.25
42	Joe Smith	1.00
43	Jerry Stackhouse	2.00
44	Damon Stoudamire	1.50
45	Petr Sykora	.50
46	Rasheed Wallace	.60
47	Corliss Williamson	.40
48	Paul Wilson	.40
49	Steve Young	.40
50	Eric Zeier	.40

1996 Classic Assets A Cut Above

The 20-card set was inserted at 1:8, comprising of 10 phone cards and 10 trading cards. The cards have rounded corners, except for one. The fronts have a player cutout superimposed over a gray background with the words "cut above" printed throughout. The backs have a player summary. Cards are numbered with a "CA" prefix.

		MT
Complete Set (20):		120.00
Common Player:		4.00
1	Keyshawn Johnson	12.00
2	Troy Aikman	10.00
3	Shaquille O'Neal	15.00
4	Brian Holzinger	4.00
5	Scottie Pippen	8.00
6	Mark Martin	8.00
7	Kevin Hardy	4.00
8	Emmitt Smith	12.00
9	Jerry Stackhouse	6.00
10	Barry Bonds	6.00
11	Marshall Faulk	6.00
12	Rasheed Wallace	4.00
13	Drew Bledsoe	12.00
14	Joe Smith	6.00
15	Kevin Garnett	20.00
16	Jason Kidd	8.00
17	Sterling Marlin	6.00
18	Rebecca Lobo	6.00
19	Kerry Collins	6.00
20	Glenn Robinson	6.00

1996 Classic Assets A Cut Above Phone Cards

The 10-card set has rounded corners, except for one which is straight. The front has a player cutout superimposed over a gray background, with the words "cut above" printed throughout. The card expired 1/31/97.

		MT
Complete Set (10):		125.00
Common Player:		8.00
Expiration: 1-31-97		
1	Dale Earnhardt	15.00
2	Shaquille O'Neal	20.00
3	Scottie Pippen	12.00
4	Cal Ripken Jr.	20.00
5	Jerry Stackhouse	20.00
6	Marshall Faulk	15.00
7	Drew Bledsoe	15.00
8	Kevin Garnett	15.00
9	Ed O'Bannon	8.00
10	Kerry Collins	18.00

1996 Classic Assets $5 Crystals

		MT
Complete Set (10):		150.00
Common Player:		10.00
1	Troy Aikman	15.00
2	Drew Bledsoe	15.00
3	Dale Earnhardt	15.00
4	Marshall Faulk	15.00
5	Shaquille O'Neal	20.00
6	Scottie Pippen	10.00
7	Cal Ripken Jr.	20.00
8	Jason Kidd	15.00
9	Joe Smith	15.00
10	Jerry Stackhouse	25.00

1996 Classic Assets $20 Crystals

Inserted at a rate of 1:250, the 10-card insert set featured clear holographic phone cards worth five minutes of long- distance calling. The fronts have rounded corners and portray a double vision of the player, with his name along the right side. The card expired 1/31/97.

		MT
Complete Set (10):		340.00
Common Player:		25.00
1	Troy Aikman	35.00
2	Drew Bledsoe	30.00
3	Dale Earnhardt	30.00
4	Marshall Faulk	35.00
5	Shaquille O'Neal	45.00
6	Scottie Pippen	25.00
7	Cal Ripken Jr.	45.00
8	Jason Kidd	30.00
9	Joe Smith	45.00
10	Jerry Stackhouse	60.00

1996 Classic Assets $2 Phone Cards

The 30-card set was inserted at 1:1, with a minimum value of $2. The cards have rounded corners, with a color action photo, and the players name in a red bar underneath. Hot Print cards were inserted in Hot Packs.

		MT
Complete Set (30):		90.00
Common Player:		2.50
1	Troy Aikman	5.00
2	Drew Bledsoe	4.00
3	Barry Bonds	2.50
4	Isaac Bruce	2.50
5	Kerry Collins	5.00
6	Dale Earnhardt	4.00
7	Marshall Faulk	4.00
8	William Floyd	2.50
9	Kevin Garnett	5.00
10	Eddie Jones	2.50
11	Jason Kidd	4.00
12	Sterling Marlin	2.00
13	Mark Martin	2.50
14	Antonio McDyess	5.00
15	Steve McNair	4.00
16	Alonzo Mourning	2.50
17	Ed O'Bannon	3.00
18	Shaquille O'Neal	6.00
19	Hakeem Olajuwon	4.00
20	Scottie Pippen	3.00
21	Cal Ripken Jr.	6.00
22	Glenn Robinson	4.00
23	Nolan Ryan	5.00
24	Joe Smith	5.00
25	Jerry Stackhouse	7.50
26	Damon Stoudamire	6.00
27	Petr Sykora	3.50
28	Rasheed Wallace	4.00
29	Corliss Williamson	3.00
30	Steve Young	3.50

1996 Classic Assets $5 Phone Cards

Measuring 2-1/8" x 3-3/8", these 20 phone cards have rounded corners, with full-bleed color photos on the front. The player's name is at the bottom along with the Assets logo. The backs have the value of the card and instructions on how to use it.

		MT
Complete Set (20):		175.00
Common Player:		8.00
1	Troy Aikman	12.00
2	Drew Bledsoe	10.00
3	Barry Bonds	6.00
4	Isaac Bruce	8.00
5	Kerry Collins	12.00
6	Dale Earnhardt	10.00
7	Marshall Faulk	12.00
8	Kevin Garnett	12.00
9	Jason Kidd	10.00
10	Mark Martin	8.00
11	Shaquille O'Neal	15.00
12	Hakeem Olajuwon	10.00
13	Scottie Pippen	8.00
14	Cal Ripken Jr.	15.00
15	Nolan Ryan	12.00
16	Emmitt Smith	15.00
17	Joe Smith	12.00
18	Jerry Stackhouse	18.00
19	Rasheed Wallace	10.00
20	Steve Young	10.00

1996 Classic Assets $10 Phone Cards

Measuring 2-1/8" x 3-3/8", these 10 phone cards have rounded corners, with full-bleed color photos on the front. The player's name is at the bottom along with the Assets logo. The backs have the value of the card and instructions on how to use it. An unnumbered Jackie Robinson Phone Card was also created.

		MT
Complete Set (10):		25.00
Common Player:		2.00
1	Troy Aikman	3.00
2	Drew Bledsoe	3.00
3	Dale Earnhardt	3.00
4	Marshall Faulk	3.00
5	Shaquille O'Neal	5.00
6	Scottie Pippen	4.00
7	Cal Ripken Jr.	6.00
8	Isaac Bruce	2.00
9	Joe Smith	2.00
10	Jerry Stackhouse	2.00

1996 Classic Assets $100 Phone Cards

Measuring 2-1/8" x 3-3/8", these five phone cards have rounded corners, with full-bleed color photos on the front. The player's name is at the bottom along with the Assets logo. The backs have the value of the card and instructions on how to use it.

		MT
Complete Set (5):		225.00
Common Player:		30.00
1	Dale Earnhardt	40.00
2	Scottie Pippen	40.00
3	Marshall Faulk	30.00
4	Cal Ripken Jr.	60.00
5	Shaquille O'Neal	50.00

1996 Classic Assets Silksations

This 10-card insert was printed on cloth stock. The fronts have a color photo, the Assets logo in the upper right and the player's name at the bottom. The backs have a headshot and career summary. Silksations cards were inserted 1:100. Cards are numbered with a "S" prefix.

		MT
Complete Set (10):		375.00
Common Player:		20.00
1	Barry Bonds	15.00
2	Kerry Collins	40.00
3	Dale Earnhardt	30.00
4	Marshall Faulk	35.00
5	Jason Kidd	35.00
6	Shaquille O'Neal	60.00
7	Scottie Pippen	25.00
8	Emmitt Smith	60.00
9	Joe Smith	60.00
10	Jerry Stackhouse	80.00

1996 Classic Clear Assets

This multi-sport set consists of 70 clear acetate cards. The cards have a color player photo on the front, with the player's name at the bottom, the Clear Assets logo in the upper right and the player's sport printed in the background. The inserts include Phone Cards and 3X.

		MT
Complete Set (70):		20.00
Common Player:		.10
1	Shaquille O'Neal	1.00
2	Hakeem Olajuwon	.25
3	Scottie Pippen	.25
4	Alonzo Mourning	.25
5	Damon Stoudamire	.25
6	Jerry Stackhouse	.25
7	Joe Smith	.25
8	Antonio McDyess	.25
9	Rasheed Wallace	.25
10	Kevin Garnett	3.00
11	Shawn Respert	.10
12	Ed O'Bannon	.10
13	Kurt Thomas	.10
14	Gary Trent	.10
15	Cherokee Parks	.10
16	Corliss Williamson	.10
17	Eric Williams	.10
18	Brent Barry	.10
19	Bob Sura	.10
20	Michael Finley	.25
21	Jimmy King	.10
22	Jason Kidd	.25
23	Dikembe Mutombo	.10
24	Greg Ostertag	.25
25	Cory Alexander	.20
26	Glenn Robinson	.25
27	Tyus Edney	.10
28	Rebecca Lobo	.30
29	Emmitt Smith	1.00
30	Jeff Lewis	.10
31	Joey Galloway	.25
32	Steve McNair	.25
33	Eric Moulds	.25
34	Steve Young	.25
35	Mike Alstott	.25
36	Marshall Faulk	.25
37	Kerry Collins	.10
38	Kyle Brady	.10
39	Drew Bledsoe	.25
40	Troy Aikman	.25
41	Duane Clemons	.10
42	Napoleon Kaufman	.25
43	Stanley Pritchett	.10
44	Marcus Coleman	.10
45	Amani Toomer	.10
46	Richard Huntley	.10
47	Tony Banks	.10
48	Keyshawn Johnson	.25
49	Kevin Hardy	.10
50	Karim Abdul-Jabbar	.10
51	Manon Rheaume	1.00
52	Barry Bonds	.50
53	Chad Hermansen	.10
54	Ben Davis	.10
55	Jay Payton	.10
56	Bryan Berard	.10
57	Petr Sykora	.10
58	Ed Jovanovski	.10
59	Radek Dvorak	.10
60	Ricky Rudd	.10
61	Bobby Hamilton	.10
62	Dale Jarrett	.25
63	Brett Bodine	.10
64	Dale Earnhardt	1.00
65	Sterling Marlin	.25
66	Mark Martin	.25
67	Ted Musgrave	.10
68	Bobby Labonte	.25
69	Ricky Craven	.10
70	Kyle Petty	.25

1996 Classic Clear Assets $2 Phone Cards

This 30-card set of acetate phone cards was inserted one per pack. The cards have a color photo on the front, with the player's name at the bottom and the card's value at the top. The backs have instructions on how to use the card.

		MT
Complete Set (30):		
Common Player:		
1	Shaquille O'Neal	4.00
2	Marshall Faulk	3.00
3	Jerry Stackhouse	2.00
4	Mark Martin	2.00
5	Wade Redden	2.00
6	Barry Bonds	4.00
7	Troy Aikman	2.00
8	Nolan Ryan	4.00
9	Jason Kidd	3.00
10	Jeff Lewis	2.00
11	Manon Rheaume	3.00
12	Drew Bledsoe	2.00
13	Joe Smith	2.00
14	Eric Moulds	2.00
15	Damon Stoudamire	2.00
16	Cal Ripken Jr.	4.00
17	Hakeem Olajuwon	2.00
18	Joey Galloway	2.00
19	Dale Earnhardt	5.00
20	Dikembe Mutombo	2.00
21	Kerry Collins	2.00
22	Petr Sykora	2.00
23	Mike Alstott	2.00
24	Duane Clemons	2.00
25	Alonzo Mourning	2.00
26	Stanley Pritchett	2.00
27	Steve Young	2.00
28	Rasheed Wallace	2.00
29	Ed O'Bannon	2.00
30	Michael Finley	2.00

1996 Classic Clear Assets $5 Phone Cards

This 20-card set of acetate phone cards was inserted one per 10 packs. The cards have a color photo on the front, with the player's name at the bottom and the card's value at the top. The backs have instructions on how to use the card.

		MT
Complete Set (20):		
Common Player:		
1	Shaquille O'Neal	10.00
2	Emmitt Smith	10.00
3	Jerry Stackhouse	5.00
4	Dale Earnhardt	15.00
5	Barry Bonds	10.00
6	Troy Aikman	10.00
7	Keyshawn Johnson	5.00
8	Jason Kidd	10.00
9	Brent Barry	5.00
10	Drew Bledsoe	5.00
11	Joe Smith	5.00
12	Cal Ripken Jr.	10.00
13	Hakeem Olajuwon	5.00
14	Dikembe Mutombo	5.00
15	Kerry Collins	5.00
16	Petr Sykora	5.00
17	Mike Alstott	5.00
18	Alonzo Mourning	5.00
19	Steve Young	5.00
20	Marshall Faulk	5.00

1996 Classic Clear Assets $10 Phone Cards

This 10-card set of acetate phone cards was inserted 1:30. The cards have a color photo on the front, with the player's name at the bottom and the card's value at the top. The backs have instructions on how to use the card.

		MT
Complete Set (10):		
Common Player:		

1	Shaquille O'Neal	15.00
2	Troy Aikman	15.00
3	Dale Earnhardt	20.00
4	Keyshawn Johnson	10.00
5	Cal Ripken Jr.	15.00
6	Joe Smith	10.00
7	Napoleon Kaufman	10.00
8	Mark Martin	10.00
9	Scottie Pippen	10.00
10	Jason Kidd	15.00

1996 Classic Clear Assets $1,000 Phone Cards

This five-card set of acetate phone cards was inserted one per 8,640 packs. The cards have a color photo on the front, with the player's name at the bottom and the card's value at the top. The backs have instructions on how to use the card.

		MT
Complete Set (5):		1500.
Common Player:		100.00
1	Shaquille O'Neal	500.00
2	Troy Aikman	300.00
3	Kerry Collins	100.00
4	Keyshawn Johnson	200.00
5	Cal Ripken Jr.	600.00

1996 Classic Clear Assets 3x

This 10-card set was inserted 1:100. The acetate cards feature a color player cut-out on the front with a large X in the background. The X is clear, but the rest of the card is opaque. The back has a brief biography.

		MT
Complete Set (10):		450.00
Common Player:		25.00
1	Mark Martin	25.00
2	Rasheed Wallace	25.00
3	Rebecca Lobo	25.00
4	Barry Bonds	20.00
5	Emmitt Smith	75.00
6	Joe Smith	60.00
7	Damon Stoudamire	90.00
8	Keyshawn Johnson	90.00
9	Jerry Stackhouse	75.00
10	Troy Aikman	40.00

1996 Classic Signings

This 100-card set features silver foil facsimile autographs on the card fronts. The color player photo has a border of basketballs on one side. The backs have another color photo and a brief biography. Three parallels of the base set were created - die-cut, blue signature and red signature - and randomly inserted in packs. Inserts included Etched in Stone and Freshly Inked.

		MT
Complete Set (100):		35.00
Common Player:		.10
1	Joe Smith	2.00
2	Antonio McDyess	1.25
3	Jerry Stackhouse	3.00
4	Rasheed Wallace	.75
5	Kevin Garnett	2.00
6	Damon Stoudamire	3.00
7	Shawn Respert	.20
8	Ed O'Bannon	.50
9	Kurt Thomas	.50
10	Gary Trent	.40
11	Cherokee Parks	.30
12	Corliss Williamson	.40
13	Eric Williams	.50
14	Brent Barry	.50
15	Bob Sura	.40
16	Randolph Childress	.25
17	Michael Finley	1.00
18	George Zidek	.40
19	Travis Best	.20
20	David Vaughn	.10
21	Mario Bennett	.10
22	Greg Ostertag	.10
23	Lou Roe	.10
24	Junior Burrough	.10
25	Andrew DeClercq	.10
26	Lawrence Moten	.20
27	Donny Marshall	.10
28	Tyus Edney	.75
29	Jimmy King	.20
30	Rebecca Lobo	.50
31	Ki-Jana Carter	.50
32	Tony Boselli	.25
33	Steve McNair	.75
34	Michael Westbrook	1.00
35	Kerry Collins	1.50
36	Kevin Carter	.20
37	Mike Mamula	.40
38	Joey Galloway	1.50
39	Kyle Brady	.25
40	J.J. Stokes	1.25
41	Derrick Alexander	.25
42	Warren Sapp	.25
43	Hugh Douglas	.50
44	Tyrone Wheatley	.60
45	Napoleon Kaufman	1.00
46	James Stewart	.40
47	Rashaan Salaam	1.25
48	Ty Law	.10
49	Mark Bruener	.25
50	Derrick Brooks	.35
51	Curtis Martin	2.50
52	Todd Collins	.20
53	Sherman Williams	.35
54	Frank Sanders	.60
55	Eric Zeier	.50
56	Rob Johnson	.10
57	Chad May	.10
58	Terrell Davis	1.25
59	[illegible]	.10
60	Ben Grieve	.40
61	Paul Wilson	.60
62	Calvin Reese	.25
63	Karim Garcia	.50
64	Mark Farris	.25
65	Jay Payton	.75
66	Dustin Hermanson	.20
67	Michael Barnett	.30
68	Ryan Jaroncyk	.25
69	Ben Davis	.50
70	Bryan Berard	.50
71	Wade Redden	.30
72	Aki-Petteri Berg	.30
73	Nolan Baumgartner	.10
74	Jason Bonsignore	.10
75	Ed Jovanovski	.30
76	Radek Dvorak	.50
77	Brian Holzinger	.10
78	Brad Church	.20
79	Dale Earnhardt	1.25
80	John Andretti	.10
81	Rusty Wallace	.40
82	Bobby Labonte	.10
83	Michael Waltrip	.10
84	Sterling Marlin	.25
85	Brett Bodine	.10
86	Kyle Petty	.15
87	Ricky Rudd	.10
88	Ernie Irvan	.35
89	Darrell Waltrip	.10
90	Geoff Bodine	.10
91	Steve Young	.75
92	Hakeem Olajuwon	.50
93	Barry Bonds	.50
94	Marshall Faulk	1.00
95	Troy Aikman	.75
96	Drew Bledsoe	.75
97	Emmitt Smith	1.25
98	Jason Kidd	1.00
99	Shaquille O'Neal	1.00
100	Alonzo Mourning	.40

1996 Classic Signings Etched in Stone

This 10-card set could only be found in Hot Boxes, which were inserted once every five cases.

		MT
Complete Set (10):		125.00
Common Player:		5.00
1	Shaquille O'Neal	30.00
2	Jason Kidd	15.00
3	Scottie Pippen	15.00
4	Alonzo Mourning	10.00
5	Emmitt Smith	30.00
6	Troy Aikman	10.00
7	Steve Young	10.00
8	Barry Bonds	10.00
9	Mark Martin	5.00
10	Hakeem Olajuwon	10.00

1996 Classic Signings Freshly Inked

This 30-card set featured full-bleed color photos on the front with the player's name printed in gold foil. The backs have an artist's drawing of the player with career highlights listed below.

		MT
Complete Set (30):		220.00
Common Player:		2.50
1	Joe Smith	15.00
2	Antonio McDyess	12.00
3	George Zidek	4.00
4	Ed O'Bannon	5.00
5	Damon Stoudamire	25.00
6	Jerry Stackhouse	25.00
7	Cherokee Parks	2.50
8	Bob Sura	4.00
9	Rasheed Wallace	7.00
10	Shawn Respert	2.50
11	Hugh Douglas	4.00
12	Curtis Martin	20.00
13	Michael Westbrook	14.00
14	Kerry Collins	16.00
15	Kevin Carter	2.50
16	Joey Galloway	16.00
17	Eric Zeier	7.50
18	Terrell Davis	16.00
19	Napoleon Kaufman	8.00
20	Rashaan Salaam	10.00
21	Paul Wilson	12.00
22	Nomar Garciaparra	12.00
23	Brian Holzinger	4.00
24	Radek Dvorak	5.00
25	Petr Sykora	10.00
26	Daymond Langkow	4.00
27	John Andretti	2.50
28	Derrick Cope	2.50
29	Todd Bodine	2.50
30	Jeff Burton	2.50

1996 Classic Visions

This 150-card set featured players from baseball, football, hockey and basketball on full-bleed color photos. The player's name and position are presented in blue foil, with logos printed in gold foil. Card backs feature another color shot of the player along with college statistics and biographical information.

		MT
Complete Set (150):		40.00
Common Player:		.10
1	Shaquille O'Neal	1.00
2	Scottie Pippen	.40
3	Jason Kidd	1.00
4	Hakeem Olajuwon	.50
5	Juwan Howard	.75
6	Alonzo Mourning	.50
7	Glenn Robinson	.75
8	Rasheed Wallace	.60
9	Ed O'Bannon	.50
10	Joe Smith	2.00
11	Jerry Stackhouse	3.00
12	Damon Stoudamire	3.00
13	Cherokee Parks	.20
14	Gary Trent	.40
15	Shawn Respert	.10
16	Kevin Garnett	2.00
17	Kurt Thomas	.40
18	Jalen Rose	.10
19	Michael Finley	1.00
20	Jason Caffey	.10
21	Randolph Childress	.10
22	Tyus Edney	.75
23	George Zidek	.50
24	Antonio McDyess	1.00
25	Corliss Williamson	.40
26	Theo Ratliff	.25
27	Eric Williams	.50
28	Dikembe Mutombo	.10
29	Lawrence Moten	.15
30	Jimmy King	.15
31	Donyell Marshall	.10
32	Brian Grant	.20
33	Sharone Wright	.10
34	Eddie Jones	.35
35	Greg Ostertag	.10
36	Terrence Rencher	.10
37	David Vaughn	.10
38	Rebecca Lobo	.50
39	Troy Aikman	.75
40	Emmitt Smith	1.00
41	Marshall Faulk	1.00
42	Kerry Collins	1.50
43	Michael Westbrook	1.00
44	Steve Young	.60
45	Mike Mamula	.30
46	Joey Galloway	1.25
47	Kyle Brady	.20
48	J.J. Stokes	1.00
49	Steve McNair	.75
50	Kordell Stewart	1.25
51	Drew Bledsoe	.75
52	Hugh Douglas	.40
53	Curtis Martin	2.50
54	Ki-Jana Carter	.60
55	Tyrone Wheatley	.60
56	Napoleon Kaufman	.75
57	James Stewart	.40
58	Rashaan Salaam	1.50
59	Eric Zeier	.50
60	Bobby Taylor	.30
61	Ty Law	.10
62	Mark Bruener	.25
63	Devin Bush	.10
64	Frank Sanders	.75
65	Derrick Brooks	.25
66	Craig Powell	.10
67	Craig Newsome	.20
68	Trent Dilfer	.10
69	Sherman Williams	.40
70	Chris T. Jones	.10
71	Corey Fuller	.20
72	Luther Elliss	.20
73	Warren Sapp	.40
74	Isaac Bruce	.40
75	Tamarick Vanover	.40
76	Terrell Davis	1.25
77	Byron Morris	.15
78	Rodney Thomas	.50
79	Errict Rhett	.75
80	Kevin Carter	.25
81	Darnay Scott	.10
82	Bryan Berard	.50
83	Jeff Friesen	.25
84	Petr Buzek	.10
85	Nolan Baumgartner	.10
86	Jason Bonsignore	.10
87	Jan Hlavac	.10
88	Ethan Moreau	.10
89	Radek Dvorak	.40
90	Brian Holzinger	.20
91	Petr Sykora	.60
92	Ed Jovanovski	.35
93	Jeff O'Neill	.30
94	Manon Rheaume	.75
95	Barry Bonds	.40
96	Nolan Ryan	1.00
97	Ben Grieve	.50
98	Ben Davis	.50
99	Paul Wilson	.75
100	C.J. Nitkowski	.10
101	Chad Hermansen	.75
102	Jason Kendall	.10
103	Todd Greene	.20
104	Dustin Hermanson	.10
105	Karim Garcia	.40
106	Doug Million	.10
107	Jay Payton	.75
108	#3 GM Goodwrench Car	.10
109	Dale Jarrett	.30
110	Mark Martin	.35
111	Ernie Irvan	.35
112	Ricky Rudd	.10
113	Bobby Labonte	.10
114	#2 MGD Car	.10
115	Michael Waltrip	.10
116	Sterling Marlin	.20
117	Dick Trickle	.10
118	John Andretti	.10
119	Darrell Waltrip	.10
120	Kyle Petty	.10
121	Shaquille O'Neal (Legendary Futures)	1.00
122	Troy Aikman (Legendary Futures)	.75
123	Petr Sykora (Legendary Futures)	.60
124	Dale Earnhardt (Legendary Futures)	1.00
125	Scottie Pippen (Legendary Futures)	.40
126	Emmitt Smith (Legendary Futures)	1.00
127	Mark Martin (Legendary Futures)	.30
128	Jason Kidd (Legendary Futures)	1.00
129	Marshall Faulk (Legendary Futures)	1.00
130	Nolan Ryan (Legendary Futures)	1.00
131	Joe Smith (Freshman Futures)	2.00
132	Rasheed Wallace (Freshman Futures)	.50
133	Ed O'Bannon (Freshman Futures)	.50
134	Michael Finley (Freshman Futures)	1.00
135	Jerry Stackhouse (Freshman Futures)	3.00
136	Tyus Edney (Freshman Futures)	.60
137	Damon Stoudamire (Freshman Futures)	3.00
138	Antonio McDyess (Freshman Futures)	1.00
139	Kevin Garnett (Freshman Futures)	2.00
140	Corliss Williamson (Freshman Futures)	.40
141	Joey Galloway (Freshman Futures)	1.00
142	Kerry Collins (Freshman Futures)	1.50
143	Michael Westbrook (Freshman Futures)	1.00
144	Terrell Davis (Freshman Futures)	1.25
145	Kyle Brady (Freshman Futures)	.20
146	Kordell Stewart (Freshman Futures)	1.25
147	Curtis Martin (Freshman Futures)	2.50
148	Tyrone Wheatley (Freshman Futures)	.75
149	Napoleon Kaufman (Freshman Futures)	1.00
150	Rashaan Salaam (Freshman Futures)	1.50

1996 Classic Visions Update

The 10-card set was intially intended to update the 1995 Visions basketball draft picks 100-card set, but were used only as inserts in 1996 Visions multisport packs. The cards were numbered with a "BV" prefix and were inserted at 1:40.

		MT
Complete Set (10):		100.00
Common Player:		2.00
1	Shaquille O'Neal	20.00
2	Jason Kidd	10.00
3	Alonzo Mourning	10.00
4	Damon Stoudamire	5.00
5	Glenn Robinson	10.00
6	Joe Smith	5.00
7	Jerry Stackhouse	5.00
8	Kevin Garnett	30.00
9	Ed O'Bannon	2.00
10	Rebecca Lobo	10.00

1996 Classic Visions Signings

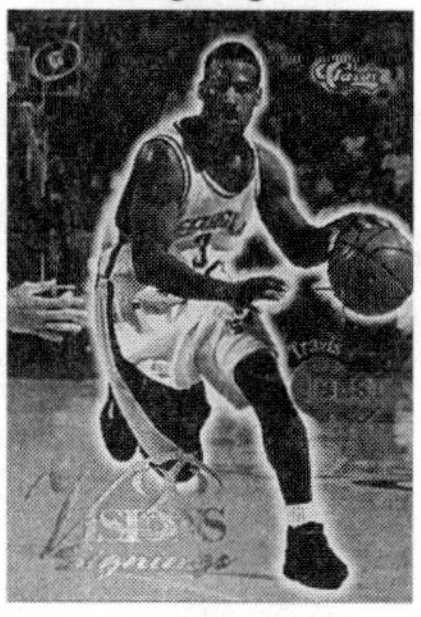

One-hundred standard-sized cards make up this set. The fronts have full-colored action shots, with the player's name, and Classic logo also on the front. Five sports are included, and were released in six-card packs in June of 1996. Autographed memorabilia redemption cards were inserted 1:10.

		MT
Complete Set (100):		40.00
Common Player:		.10
1	Shaquille O'Neal	1.00
2	Scottie Pippen	.75
3	Jason Kidd	.75
4	Hakeem Olajuwon	.40
5	Alonzo Mourning	.40
6	Glenn Robinson	.40
7	Rasheed Wallace	.40
8	Ed O'Bannon	.10
9	Joe Smith	.75
10	Damon Stoudamire	2.00
11	Cherokee Parks	.10
12	Gary Trent	.10
13	Shawn Respert	.10
14	Kurt Thomas	.10
15	Michael Finley	.50
16	Jason Caffey	.10
17	Randolph Childress	.10
18	Tyus Edney	.50
19	George Zidek	.10
20	Antonio McDyess	.40
21	Corliss Williamson	.40
22	Theo Ratliff	.40
23	Eric Williams	.40
24	Brent Barry	.40
25	Lawrence Moten	.40
26	Bob Sura	.40
27	Travis Best	.40
28	Terrance Rencher	.10
29	Troy Aikman	.75
30	Emmitt Smith	1.00
31	Marshall Faulk	.40
32	Kerry Collins	.75
33	Steve Young	.50
34	Drew Bledsoe	.75
35	Kyle Brady	.10
36	Steve McNair	.50
37	Napoleon Kaufman	.50
38	Karim Abdul-Jabbar	1.00
39	Mike Alstott	.75
40	Tim Biakabutuka	.50
41	Duane Clemons	.10
42	Daryl Gardener	.10
43	Joey Galloway	.40
44	Eddie George	3.00
45	Terry Glenn	2.00
46	Kevin Hardy	.10
47	Bobby Hoying	.40
48	Keyshawn Johnson	1.25
49	Derrick Mayes	.40
50	Eric Moulds	.10
51	Jonathan Ogden	.10
52	Simeon Rice	.40
53	Orpheus Roye	.10
54	Amani Toomer	.10
55	Chris Doering	.10
56	Jevon Langford	.10
57	Jeff Lewis	.10
58	Jamain Stephens	.10
59	Steve Taneyhill	.10
60	Alex Van Dyke	.10
61	Boyd Devereaux	.10
62	Alexandre Volchkov	.10
63	Trevor Wasyluk	.10
64	Luke Curtin	.10
65	Richard Jackman	.10
66	Jon Zukiwsky	.10
67	Geoff Peters	.10
68	Daniel Briere	.75
69	Chris Allen	.10
70	Jason Sweitezer	.10
71	Steve Nimigon	.10
72	Jay McKee	.10
73	Henry Kuster	.10
74	Jonathan Aitken	.10
75	Ed Jovanovski	.25
76	Petr Sykora	.10
77	Bryan Berard	.40
78	Manon Rheaume	1.00
79	Radek Dvorak	.10
80	Barry Bonds	.40
81	Nolan Ryan	1.00
82	Ben Davis	.25
83	Chad Hermansen	1.00
84	Jason Kendall	.40
85	Todd Greene	.25
86	Karim Garcia	.25
87	Jay Payton	.25
88	Dale Jarrett	.75
89	Mark Martin	.75
90	Ernie Irvan	.75
91	Ricky Rudd	.75
92	Bobby Labonte	.40
93	Michael Waltrip	.25
94	Sterling Marlin	.25
95	Dick Trickle	.40
96	Darrell Waltrip	.25
97	Kyle Petty	.25
98	John Andretti	.25
99	Miller Car	.25
100	Goodwrench Car	.75

1996 Classic Visions Signings Artistry

A 10-card set printed on 24-point stock, the cards were inserted at 1:60.

		MT
Complete Set (10):		200.00
Common Player:		10.00
1	Damon Stoudamire	25.00
2	Emmitt Smith	50.00
3	Dale Earnhardt	50.00
4	Joe Smith	20.00
5	Joey Galloway	20.00
6	Petr Sykora	10.00
7	Jerry Stackhouse	20.00
8	Kordell Stewart	40.00
9	Mark Martin	15.00
10	Rashaan Salaam	10.00

1996 Classic Visions Signings Autographs Gold

This set was inserted in Visions Signings packs at a rate of 1:12. Both silver and gold cards were signed, with gold cards being signed at a much higher rate.

		MT
Complete Set (69):		500.00
Common Player:		5.00
5A	Alonzo Mourning	40.00
9A	Joe Smith	40.00
15A	Michael Finley	20.00
17A	Randolph Childress	5.00
18A	Tyus Edney	10.00
19A	George Zidek	5.00
22A	Theo Ratliff	8.00
24A	Brent Barry	8.00
25A	Lawrence Moten	5.00
26A	Bob Sura	5.00
38A	Karim Abdul-Jabbar	40.00
39A	Mike Alstott	20.00
40A	Tim Biakabutuka	15.00
53A	Orpheus Roye	5.00
55A	Chris Doering	5.00
57A	Jeff Lewis	5.00
58A	Jamain Stephens	5.00
59A	Steve Taneyhill	5.00
60A	Alex Van Dyke	5.00
61A	Boyd Devereaux	5.00
62A	Alexandre Volchkov	5.00
63A	Trevor Wasyluk	5.00
64A	Luke Curtin	5.00
65A	Richard Jackman	5.00
66A	Jon Zukiwsky	5.00
67A	Geoff Peters	5.00
68A	Daniel Briere	12.00
69A	Chris Allen	5.00
70A	Jason Sweitzer	5.00
71A	Steve Nimigon	5.00
72A	Jay McKee	5.00
73A	Henry Kuster	5.00
74A	Jonathan Aitken	5.00
75A	Ed Jovanovski	8.00
82A	Ben Davis	15.00
85A	Todd Greene	15.00
86A	Karim Garcia	25.00
87A	Jay Payton	10.00
BK1	Cory Alexander	5.00
BK2	Junior Burrough	5.00
BK3	Fred Hoiberg	5.00
BK4	Constantin Popa	5.00
FB1	Jerod Cherry	5.00
FB2	Sedric Clark	5.00
FB3	Marcus Coleman	5.00
FB4	Chris Darkins	5.00
FB5	Donnie Edwards	5.00
FB6	Ray Farmer	5.00
FB7	Randall Godfrey	5.00
FB8	Scott Greene	5.00
FB9	Jeff Hartings	5.00
FB10	Jimmy Herndon	5.00
FB11	Richard Huntley	5.00
FB12	Dietrich Jells	5.00
FB13	Ray Mickens	5.00
FB14	Lawyer Milloy	5.00
FB15	Bryant Mix	5.00
FB16	Alex Molden	5.00
FB17	Jason Odom	5.00
FB18	Jason Ritchey	5.00
FB19	Brian Roche	5.00
FB20	Jon Runyan	5.00
FB21	Scott Slutzker	5.00
FB22	Matt Stevens	5.00
FB23	Zach Thomas	8.00
FB24	Kyle Wacholtz	5.00
FB25	Stepfret Williams	5.00
FB26	Jerome Woods	5.00
FB27	Dusty Zeigler	5.00

1996 Classic Visions Signings Autographs Silver

These were inserted at a rate of 1:12 in Visions Signings packs. Silver and gold cards were signed, with silver cards being individually numbered. The quantity is listed after the player's name.

		MT
Complete Set (83):		4000.
Common Player:		10.00
1A	Shaquille O'Neal/190	500.00
3A	Jason Kidd/145	225.00
4A	Hakeem Olajuwon/270	200.00
5A	Alonzo Mourning/405	125.00
9A	Joe Smith/390	100.00
15A	Michael Finley/190	100.00
17A	Randolph Childress/320	10.00
18A	Tyus Edney/375	20.00
19A	George Zidek/365	10.00
22A	Theo Ratliff/375	20.00
24A	Brent Barry/395	20.00
25A	Lawrence Moten/170	10.00
26A	Bob Sura/385	10.00
29A	Troy Aikman/190	250.00
30A	Emmitt Smith/90	700.00
31A	Marshall Faulk/185	150.00
33A	Steve Young/95	500.00
34A	Drew Bledsoe/110	300.00
38A	Karim Abdul-Jabbar/365	100.00
39A	Mike Alstott/345	60.00
40A	Tim Biakabutuka/390	40.00
53A	Orpheus Roye/350	10.00
55A	Chris Doering/390	10.00
57A	Jeff Lewis/385	20.00
58A	Jamain Stephens/380	10.00
59A	Steve Taneyhill/420	10.00
60A	Alex Van Dyke/385	20.00
61A	Boyd Devereaux/350	10.00
62A	Alexandre Volchkov/375	10.00
63A	Trevor Wasyluk/365	10.00
64A	Luke Curtin/370	10.00
65A	Richard Jackman/400	10.00
66A	Jon Zukiwsky/375	10.00
67A	Geoff Peters/390	10.00
68A	Daniel Briere/390	20.00
69A	Chris Allen/385	10.00
70A	Jason Sweitzer/355	10.00
71A	Steve Nimigon/380	10.00
72A	Jay McKee/385	10.00
73A	Henry Kuster/415	10.00
74A	Jonathan Aitken/360	10.00
75A	Ed Jovanovski/405	20.00
80A	Barry Bonds/240	150.00
82A	Ben Davis/360	20.00
85A	Todd Greene/385	20.00
86A	Karim Garcia/370	40.00
87A	Jay Payton/365	25.00
89A	Mark Martin/315	75.00
90A	Ernie Irvan/265	50.00
91A	Ricky Rudd/285	40.00
93A	Michael Waltrip/285	40.00
95A	Dick Trickle/285	20.00
BK1	Cory Alexander/375	10.00
BK2	Junior Burrough/395	10.00
BK3	Fred Hoiberg/395	10.00
BK4	Constantin Popa/355	10.00
FB1	Jerod Cherry/355	10.00
FB2	Sedric Clark/410	10.00
FB3	Marcus Coleman/395	10.00
FB4	Chris Darkins/395	10.00
FB5	Donnie Edwards/395	10.00
FB6	Ray Farmer/395	10.00
FB7	Randall Godfrey/380	10.00
FB8	Scott Greene/395	10.00
FB9	Jeff Hartings/380	10.00
FB10	Jimmy Herndon/380	10.00
FB11	Richard Huntley/380	10.00
FB12	Dietrich Jells/350	10.00
FB13	Ray Mickens/390	10.00
FB14	Lawyer Milloy/365	10.00
FB15	Bryant Mix/390	10.00
FB16	Alex Molden/365	10.00
FB17	Jason Odom/390	10.00
FB18	Jason Ritchey/360	10.00
FB19	Brian Roche/395	10.00
FB20	Jon Runyan/430	10.00
FB21	Scott Slutzker/385	10.00
FB22	Matt Stevens/390	10.00
FB23	Zach Thomas/390	20.00
FB24	Kyle Wacholtz/385	10.00
FB25	Stepfret Williams/385	10.00
FB26	Jerome Woods/430	10.00
FB27	Dusty Zeigler/395	10.00

1996 Classic Visions Signings Rookies Redemption

The five-card set featured the top five players taken in the 1996 NBA draft. The set was distributed exclusively through a redemption card inserted in Hot boxes. Cards were numbered with a "VBR" prefix.

		MT
Complete Set (5):		50.00
Common Player:		10.00
1	Allen Iverson	15.00
2	Marcus Camby	10.00
3	Shareef Abdur-Rahim	10.00
4	Antoine Walker	5.00
5	Stephon Marbury	12.00

1996 Classic Legends of the Final Four

The 32-card set, sponsored by Sears, highlighted players and coaches who have competed in the NCAA Final Four. Each seven-card pack contained six player cards and one "Coaches vs. Cancer" card. "Legends of the Final Four" is stamped in gold foil across the bottom. The set is divided into four subsets: Female players (1-10), male players (11-20), male coaches (MC1-MC5) and female coaches (WC1-WC5). The wrappers were a coupon, giving collectors 10% off Craftsman tools.

		MT
Complete Set (32):		12.00
Common Player (1-20):		.10
Common Coach (MC1-MC5):		.50
Common Coach (WC1-WC5):		.10
1	Sheryl Swoopes	.75
2	Cheryl Miller	.40
3	Rebecca Lobo	.75
4	Jennifer Azzi	.50
5	Dawn Staley	.50
6	Charlotte Smith	.20
7	Bridgette Gordon	.15
8	Erica Westbrooks	.10
9	Tracy Claxton	.10
10	Clarissa Davis	.15
11	Kareem Abdul-Jabbar	.75
12	Hakeem Olajuwon	.75
13	Bill Walton	.75
14	James Worthy	.40
15	Isiah Thomas	.75
16	Darrell Griffith	.15
17	Bobby Hurley	.15
18	Glen Rice	.40
19	Ed Pinckney	.10
20	Danny Manning	.40
MC1	John Wooden	1.00
MC2	Dean Smith	.75
MC3	Nolen Richardson	.50
MC4	Mike Krzyzewski	.50
MC5	John Thompson	.50
WC1	Tara Vanderveer	.25
WC2	Pat Summitt	.25
WC3	Marianne Stanley	.10
WC4	Sylvia Hatchell	.15
WC5	Geno Auriemma	.25
NNO	Checklist (Sears Trophy)	.10
NNO	Coaches vs. Cancer (DP)	.10

1991 Cleo Michael Jordan Valentines

These 11 Valentine cards were packaged in 32- and 38-card packages. The fronts of the cards showcase action photos or posed shots of Michael Jordan. Card Nos. 2-5, 7 and 11 measure 2-1/2" x 3-1/4" inches, while Nos. 1, 6, 8-10 measure 2-1/4" x 5". The cards are perforated. The bottom of the box includes three bonus cutout cards that were the same as Nos. 7, 10 and 11, with the exception that they were produced on gray cardboard. Each of the cards are unnumbered and have a Valentine's saying included in a red heart.

	MT
Complete Set (11):	6.00
Common Player:	1.00
Happy Valentine's Day, Champ	1.00
Have a high-flying day	1.00
Have a jammin' day	1.00
I like your style	1.00
Lookin' fine	1.00
No one could fill YOUR shoes	1.00
Time out for fun	1.00
You give me a lift	1.00
You're a winner	1.00
You're A Winner, Teacher	1.00
You're cool	1.00

1978-79 Clippers Handyman

Measuring 2" x 4-1/4", the nine-card set has a lenticular photo on the front, with a coupon attached to the bottom of the card. The card backs feature the Clippers' logo in the upper left, with the player's name and bio to the right of it. His career highlights and stats are printed below. The unnumbered Gene Shue card was not distributed with the other eight cards in the set because it was the grand prize winner of the contest that ran along with this card promotion. A signature version of the Lloyd Free card was also released.

		NM
Complete Set (9):		45.00
Common Player:		3.00
1	Randy Smith - 9	6.00
2	Nick Weatherspoon - 12	4.00
3	Freeman Williams - 20	4.00
4	Sidney Wicks - 21	7.00
5A	Lloyd Free - 24	6.00
5B	Lloyd Free - 24 (Signature variation)	18.00
6	Swen Nater - 31	5.00
7	Jerome Whitehead - 33	3.00
8	Kermit Washington - 42	4.00
9	Kevin Kunnert - 44	20.00
NNO	Gene Shue (CO SP)	1600.

1990-91 Clippers Star

The standard-sized cards were produced by the Star Co. The photo on the front is bordered in a red that goes from light in the middle to dark at the top and bottom. The Star logo is printed in the upper right, while the player's name is in the lower left and his team and position are located in the lower right. The unnumbered card backs have the player's name, along with the Kudos' and Clippers' logos at the top. His bio and stats fill out the rest of the card back.

	MT
Complete Set (12):	4.00
Common Player:	.25
Ken Bannister	.25
Winston Garland	.25
Tom Garrick	.25
Gary Grant	.25
Ron Harper	.75
Bo Kimble	.25
Danny Manning	1.50
Jeff Martin	.25
Ken Norman	.50
Mike Schuler (CO)	.25
Charles Smith	.50
Loy Vaught	1.50

2001 Clippers/Topps

		MT
Complete Set (10):		15.00
Common Player:		.50
1	Lamar Odom	2.50
2	Michael Olowokandi	.75
3	Corey Maggette	1.50
4	Alvin Gentry CO	.50
5	Header Card	.50
6	Eric Piatkowski	.50
7	Brian Skinner	.50
8	Darius Miles	8.00
9	Keyon Dooling	2.50
10	Quentin Richardson	3.00

1995 Collect-A-Card

The 100-card, standard-size set features the player's name on the card front down the right border while the horizontal backs have bio and stat information, along with career highlights.

		MT
Complete Set (100):		20.00
Common Player:		.05
1	Cory Alexander	.05
2	Mario Bennett	.15
3	Travis Best	.20
4	Jason Caffey	.05
5	Randolph Childress	.05
6	Michael Finley	.75
7	Sherell Ford	.15
8	Kevin Garnett	3.00
9	Alan Henderson	.40
10	Antonio McDyess	.75
11	Loren Meyer	.25
12	Ed O'Bannon	.40
13	Greg Ostertag	.15
14	Cherokee Parks	.20
15	Theo Ratliff	.25
16	Bryant Reeves	.75
17	Shawn Respert	.15
18	Joe Smith	2.00
19	Jerry Stackhouse	2.00
20	Damon Stoudamire	2.00
21	Bob Sura	.30
22	Kurt Thomas	.50
23	Gary Trent	.30
24	Rasheed Wallace	.50
25	Eric Williams	.40
26	Corliss Williamson	.40
27	George Zidek	.30
28	Alan Henderson	.40
29	Donnie Boyce	.05
30	Cuonzo Martin	.05
31	Eric Williams	.40
32	Junior Burrough	.05
33	Bob Sura	.30
34	Donny Marshall	.15
35	George Zidek	.40
36	Jason Caffey	.05
37	Cherokee Parks	.20
38	Loren Meyer	.25
39	Anthony Pelle	.05
40	Theo Ratliff	.25
41	Randolph Childress	.05
42	Lou Roe	.15
43	Andrew DeClerq	.05
44	Michael McDonald	.05
45	Travis Best	.05
46	Fred Hoiberg	.05
47	Antonio McDyess	.75
48	Constantin Popa	.05
49	Kurt Thomas	.50
50	Gary Trent	.30
51	Eric Snow	.05
52	Kevin Garnett	3.00
53	Larry Sykes	.05
54	Jerome Allen	.15
55	Ed O'Bannon	.40
56	Jerry Stackhouse	2.00
57	Michael Finley	.75
58	Mario Bennett	.15
59	Shawn Respert	.05
60	Corliss Williamson	.40
61	Tyus Edney	.60
62	Cory Alexander	.05
63	Sherell Ford	.15
64	Damon Stoudamire	2.00
65	Jimmy King	.15
66	Greg Ostertag	.15
67	Bryant Reeves	.75
68	Lawrence Moten	.05
69	Terrence Rencher	.05
70	Corey Beck	.05
71	Bryan Collins	.05
72	Dan Cross	.05
73	Joe Smith	2.00
74	Michael Hawkins	.05
75	Scott Highmark	.05
76	Ray Jackson	.05
77	Tom Kleinschmidt	.05
78	Matt Maloney	.05
79	Clint McDaniel	.05
80	Julius Michalik	.05
81	Paul O'Liney	.05
82	Randy Rutherford	.05
83	James Scott	.05
84	Dwight Stewart	.05
85	Scotty Thurman	.05
86	Rasheed Wallace	.50
87	John Amaechi	.05
88	Jamal Faulkner	.05
89	Jerry Stackhouse, Rasheed Wallace	.75
90	Scotty Thurman, Corey Beck, Clint McDaniel	.05
91	Loren Meyer, Julius Michalik, Fred Hoiberg	.05
92	Ed O'Bannon, Tyus Edney	.40
93	Cory Alexander, Junior Burrough	.05
94	Antonio McDyess, Jason Caffey	.25
95	Bryant Reeves, Randy Rutherford	.25
96	Matt Maloney, Jerome Allen	.05
97	Ray Jackson, Jimmy King	.05
98	Shawn Respert, Eric Snow	.05
99	Andrew DeClerq, Dan Cross	.05
100	Checklist	.05

1995 Collect-A-Card Ignition

The 15-card set was inserted every five packs of 1995 Collect-A-Card. The card fronts have a player photo cutout on a metallic marble background with the player's name printed vertically in a gold border on one side. The cards are numbered with the "I" prefix.

		MT
Complete Set (15):		15.00
Common Player:		.40
1	Travis Best	.40
2	Randolph Childress	.40
3	Michael Finley	1.00
4	Sherell Ford	.40
5	Alan Henderson	1.00
6	Shawn Respert	.40
7	Jerry Stackhouse	4.00
8	Damon Stoudamire	5.00
9	Bob Sura	.75
10	Gary Trent	.75
11	Kevin Garnett	7.00
12	Cory Alexander	.40
13	Tyus Edney	.75
14	Fred Hoiberg	.40
15	Jerome Allen	.40

1995 Collect-A-Card Liftoff

The 15-card set was inserted every five packs and features a player cutout on a silver background with the school logo on the front. The cards are numbered with the "L" prefix.

		MT
Complete Set (15):		12.00
Common Player:		.40
1	Lou Roe	.40
2	Mario Bennett	.40
3	Joe Smith	3.00
4	Constantin Popa	.40
5	Antonio McDyess	2.00
6	Loren Meyer	.60
7	Ed O'Bannon	1.00
8	Greg Ostertag	.40
9	Cherokee Parks	.40
10	Theo Ratliff	.60
11	Bryant Reeves	2.00
12	Kurt Thomas	.60
13	Eric Williams	1.00
14	Corliss Williamson	.60
15	Rasheed Wallace	1.25

1995-96 Collect-A-Card Stackhouse

The five-card Jerry Stackhouse set was inserted randomly into packs and feature a short highlight from the UNC star's career. The cards are numbered with the "J" prefix.

		MT
Complete Set (5):		20.00
Common Player:		4.00
1	Jerry Stackhouse	4.00
2	Jerry Stackhouse	4.00
3	Jerry Stackhouse	4.00
4	Jerry Stackhouse	4.00
5	Jerry Stackhouse	4.00

1995 Collect-A-Card 2 on 1

The 10-card, standard-size set was inserted every 21 packs of 1995 Collect-A-Card. The card insert name is printed down the right side. The cards are numbered with a "T" prefix.

		MT
Complete Set (10):		15.00
Common Player:		.40
1	Antonio McDyess, Kurt Thomas	3.00
2	Jerry Stackhouse, Kevin Garnett	5.00
3	Ed O'Bannon, Corliss Williamson	1.50
4	Michael Finley, Mario Bennett	1.25
5	Tyus Edney, Damon Stoudamire	2.00
6	Joe Smith, Rasheed Wallace	3.00
7	Cherokee Parks, Bryant Reeves	1.25
8	Greg Ostertag, George Zidek	.75
9	Shawn Respert, Jerome Allen	.40
10	Sherrell Ford, Randolph Childress	.40

1996 Collector's Edge Rookie Rage

Collector's Edge Rookie Rage Basketball Draft Picks has 48 different cards in the base set, plus two checklists. Each card front has a color action photo of the player in his collegiate uniform, against a metallic background with an orange basketball in the lower left corner. "Rookie Rage" and the player's name is stamped in silver foil along the sides of the card, which has a Collector's Edge logo in the lower right corner. The card back has a close-up shot of the player at the top, with his name above in an arch and his NBA team's city below. Biographical information and 1995-96 and career stats follow underneath. A basketball icon is in the lower right corner, with a Collector's Edge logo inside. A card number is in the lower left corner. Two parallel versions were also made, in silver and gold. Three insert sets, each with parallel versions, were also made - Key Kraze (normal and holofoil); Time Warp (normal, holofoil and gold); and Radical Recruits (normal and mosaic prism). A Scratch n' Win redemption card is also found in each pack. Prizes include an Ice Sculpture card (1:18), an uncut Rookie Rage sheet (1:36), an uncut Key Kraze sheet (1:72) and an uncut Time Warp sheet (1:108). Collectors can also send in for an 8" x 10" version of a Time Warp card by sending in 24 Rookie Rage wrappers and $3.95 for shipping and handling. An autographed version signed by an NBA legend may be found by including an upgrade card found in packs.

		MT
Complete Set (50):		10.00
Common Player:		.05
Minor Stars:		.10
1	Shareef Abdur-Rahim	1.00
2	Ray Allen	1.00
3	Drew Barry	.05
4	Terrell Bell	.05
5	Joseph Blair	.05
6	Kobe Bryant	2.00
7	Marcus Camby	1.75
8	Erick Dampier	.30
9	Ben Davis	.05
10	Tony Delk	.50
11	Brian Evans	.10
12	Jamie Feick	.05
13	Dereck Fisher	.05
14	Todd Fuller	.10
15	Steve Hamer	.05
16	Othella Harrington	.10
17	Mark Hendrickson	.05
18	Reggie Geary	.05
19	Allen Iverson	2.50
20	Dontae Jones	.25
21	Kerry Kittles	.75
22	Travis Knight	.10
23	Priest Lauderdale	.05
24	Randy Livingston	.10
25	Marcus Mann	.05
26	Stephon Marbury	1.25
27	Walter McCarty	.50
28	Amal McCaskill	.05
29	Jeff McInnis	.05
30	Ryan Minor	.10
31	Darnell Robinson	.05
32	Steve Nash	.40
33	Moochie Norris	.05
34	Jermaine O'Neal	.50
35	Mark Pope	.05
36	Vitaly Potapenko	.15
37	Shandon Anderson	.05
38	Ron Riley	.05
39	Roy Rogers	.10
40	Malik Rose	.05
41	Jason Sasser	.05
42	Doron Sheffer	.05
43	Ronnie Henderson	.05
44	Antoine Walker	.40
45	Samaki Walker	.75
46	John Wallace	.40
47	Jerome Williams	.10
48	Lorenzen Wright	.40
49	Checklist	.05
50	Checklist	.05

1996 Collector's Edge Rookie Rage Key Kraze

Two versions of this 1996 Collector's Edge Rookie Rage were made - normal versions (seeded one every 56 packs) and holofoil versions (seeded one every 90 packs). The regular versions were limited to 3,200 sets; holofoils were limited to 2,000 sets. The basic card design has a color photo of the player in his college uniform, against a silver foiled, swirled pattern which has a ghosted image of the player in the background. "Key Kraze" is written along the left side of the card in silver foil, with the player's name at the top. An Edge logo is in the lower left corner. The card back has an artist's version of the photo from the front, with a square next to it containing a head shot. Biographical information and a recap of the player's collegiate accomplishments are written over the card. A card number is in the upper right corner; the serial number, out of 3,200, is along the lower right side.

		MT
Complete Set (25):		200.00
Common Player:		3.00
Comp. Holofoil Set (25):		600.00
Holofoil Cards:		1.5x-3x
1	Shareef Abdur-Rahim	20.00
2	Ray Allen	16.00
3	Kobe Bryant	20.00
4	Marcus Camby	25.00
5	Erick Dampier	7.00
6	Tony Delk	10.00
7	Todd Fuller	3.00
8	Reggie Geary	3.00
9	Allen Iverson	30.00
10	Dontae Jones	3.00
11	Kerry Kittles	10.00
12	Stephon Marbury	20.00
13	Walter McCarty	10.00
14	Darnell Robinson	3.00
15	Steve Nash	8.00
16	Ben Davis	3.00
17	Mark Pope	3.00
18	Roy Rogers	3.00
19	Ronnie Henderson	3.00
20	Antoine Walker	5.00
21	Samaki Walker	10.00
22	John Wallace	8.00
23	Jerome Williams	3.00
24	Lorenzen Wright	3.00
25	Checklist	3.00

1996 Collector's Edge Rookie Rage Key Kraze Holofoil

This 25-card insert reprinted the Key Kraze insert with a holofoil finish and individually numbered up to 2,000. Holofoil Key Kraze versions were inserted every 90 packs of Rookie Rage.

	MT
Complete Set (25):	600.00
Holofoil Cards:	1.5x-3x

1996 Collector's Edge Rookie Rage Radical Recruits

Twenty-four top draft picks are showcased in this 1996 insert set. Normal versions are seeded one every 14 packs and are limited to 6,750, while mosaic prism versions are limited to 2,500 and are seeded one every 72 packs. The basic card front has a color photo against a basketball going through a net. The player's name is along the left side; Radical Recruits and Edge logos are in the bottom corners. The card back has a ghosted image of the player as a background, with a recap of the player's collegiate achievements and biographical information on it. A color photo is in the lower left corner. The player's name is at the top, with a card number in the upper right corner. A serial number (out of 6,750) is along the right side.

		MT
Complete Set (25):		100.00
Common Player:		2.00
Comp. Holofoil Set (25):		300.00
Holofoil Cards:		1.5x-3x
1	Shareef Abdur-Rahim	10.00
2	Ray Allen	8.00
3	Kobe Bryant	10.00
4	Marcus Camby	12.00
5	Erick Dampier	4.00
6	Tony Delk	5.00
7	Todd Fuller	2.00
8	Allen Iverson	15.00
9	Dontae Jones	2.00
10	Kerry Kittles	5.00
11	Darnell Robinson	2.00
12	Stephon Marbury	10.00
13	Walter McCarty	4.00
14	Steve Nash	4.00
15	Ben Davis	2.00
16	Reggie Geary	2.00
17	Mark Pope	2.00
18	Roy Rogers	2.00
19	Ronnie Henderson	2.00
20	Antoine Walker	2.50
21	Samaki Walker	5.00
22	John Wallace	3.00
23	Jerome Williams	2.00
24	Lorenzen Wright	2.00
25	Checklist	2.00

1996 Collector's Edge R.R. Radical Recruits Holofoil

This 25-card insert paralleled the Radical Recruits insert, but featured prismatic foil on the front, as well as individual hand-numbering. The back was also individually numbered to 2,500. Holofoil versions were inserted every 72 packs.

	MT
Complete Set (25):	300.00
Holofoil Cards:	1.5x-3x

1996 Collector's Edge Rookie Rage TimeWarp

These 1996 Collector's Edge Rookie Rage inserts pair an NBA legend with a 1996 draft pick. The background of the front is a blurred image of the same photo used for the draft pick. The players' two last names are in the bottom corners. The horizontal back has a hardwood court pattern, with photos of each player, plus biographical information and a comparison of the players' talents. A card number, using a "TW" prefix, is in the upper right corner. A serial number, out of 12,000, is also given along the bottom. One of these inserts was seeded in every eighth pack, but two parallel versions also exist. Holofoil TimeWarps are found every 72 packs and are limited to 2,500 each; gold foil-stamped cards are limited to 1,000 and are seeded one per every 180 packs.

		MT
Complete Set (12):		40.00
Common Player:		1.50
Comp. Holofoil Set (12):		160.00
Holofoil Cards:		2x-4x
1	Shareef Abdur-Rahim, David Robinson	4.00
2	Ray Allen, Alex English	4.00
3	Kobe Bryant, Alex English	6.00
4	Marcus Camby, Moses Malone	6.00
5	Erick Dampier, George Gervin	1.50
6	Allen Iverson, Isiah Thomas	8.00
7	Kerry Kittles, Isiah Thomas	4.00
8	Stephon Marbury, David Thompson	5.00
9	Antoine Walker, Moses Malone	1.50
10	Samaki Walker, Walter Frazier	3.00
11	John Wallace, George Gervin	3.00
12	Lorenzen Wright, Walter Frazier	1.50

1996 Collector's Edge Rookie Rage TimeWarp Gold

This 12-card insert paralleled the TimeWarp insert, but was gold foil stamped on the front and individually numbered to 1,000. Gold foil stamped versions were inserted every 180 packs of Rookie Rage.

	MT
Complete Set (12):	160.00
Gold Cards:	2x-4x

1996 Collector's Edge Rookie Rage TimeWarp Holofoil

This 12-card insert reprinted each card in the TimeWarp insert, but was printed with a holofoil finish on the front and individually numbered to 2,500. This parallel version was seeded one per 72 packs.

	MT
Complete Set (12):	160.00
Holofoil Cards:	2x-4x

1997 Collector's Edge Promos

This six-card set was distributed to promote Collector's Edge Impulse Basketball in 1997. The cards similar to the base cards, but are numbered "of 6" with the word "Promo" printed above it.

		MT
Complete Set (6):		10.00
Common Player:		.50
1	Tim Duncan	3.00
2	Scottie Pippen	1.00
3	Ron Mercer	1.00
4	Keith Van Horn	1.00
5	Antonio Daniels	.50
6	Kobe Bryant	3.00

1997 Collector's Edge Impulse

The 45-card set appeared in three versions, including base cards, Die-Cut Parallel (1:1 pack) and Impulse Metal Parallel (1:1). The base cards have a full-bleed photo on the front, with a gold-foil pulse line at the top. The Edge Impulse "award" logo is in the lower left. The player's name is printed inside a gold-foil banner in the lower right. The backs have the player's name and bio printed vertically in the upper left. The card number is printed inside a red diamond in the upper right, while his stats and highlights are printed at the bottom. All the information is printed over a full-bleed photo of the player. The Die-Cut Parallel has the photo superimposed over a basketball at the top and a purple and white "groovy" mixture of colors beneath it. The player's name and draft pick status are printed inside a silver foil banner at the bottom of the front. The backs include the player's photo inside a basketball at the top, along with his name. His bio, stats and highlights are printed inside a rectangle at the bottom of the card back. The Metal Parallel has a player photo superimposed over a foil background of a basketball. The player's name and draft status are printed inside a gold-foil banner at the bottom. The card backs are identical to the base card's.

		MT
Complete Set (45):		15.00
Common Player:		.10
Minor Stars:		.20
Die-Cut Cards:		1.5x
Metal Cards:		1.5x
Wax Box:		60.00
1	Tim Duncan	3.00
2	Keith Van Horn	1.00
3	Kebu Stewart	.20
4	Antonio Daniels	1.00
5	Tony Battie	1.25
6	Ron Mercer	1.50
7	Tim Thomas	.75
8	Adonal Foyle	.75
9	Chauncey Billups	1.25
10	Danny Fortson	.75
11	Austin Croshere	.50
12	Derek Anderson	.75
13	Antoine Walker	.40
14	Kobe Bryant	1.00
15	Shareef Abdur-Rahim	.50
16	Stephon Marbury	.75
17	Scottie Pippen	.30
18	Kelvin Cato	.75
19	Scot Pollard	.20
20	Paul Grant	.10
21	Anthony Parker	.10
22	Ed Gray	.10
23	Bobby Jackson	.50
24	John Thomas	.10
25	Charles Smith	.20
26	Jacque Vaughn	.50
27	Keith Booth	.10
28	Charles O'Bannon	.50
29	James Collins	.10
30	Marc Jackson	.10
31	Anthony Johnson	.10
32	Jason Lawson	.10
33	Alvin Williams	.10
34	DeJuan Wheat	.10
35	Nate Erdmann	.10
36	Olivier Saint-Jean	1.00
37	Serge Zwikker	.10
38	Antoine Walker	.40
39	Kobe Bryant	1.00
40	Shareef Abdur-Rahim	.50
41	Stephon Marbury	.75
42	Scottie Pippen	.30
43	Checklist 1	.10
44	Checklist 2	.10
45	Checklist 3	.10

1997 Collector's Edge Air Apparent

Inserted 1:72 packs, the 15-card set features two players on both the front and back of the cards. "Air Apparent" is printed at the top, while the player's name appears vertically along the left border. Both photos are superimposed over a basketball background. The card number is printed in the upper left inside a red diamond.

		MT
Complete Set (16):		150.00
Common Player:		8.00
1	Duncan, Pippen	40.00
2	Van Horn, Bryant	30.00
3	Saint-Jean, Abdur-Rahim	8.00
4	Daniels, Marbury	15.00
5	Battie, Pippen	10.00
6	Mercer, Marbury	15.00
7	T. Thomas, Bryant	15.00
8	Foyle, Abdur-Rahim	8.00
9	Billups, Marbury	15.00
10	Fortson, Pippen	10.00
11	Walker, A. Walker	8.00
12	Anderson, Bryant	15.00
13	Cato, Abdur-Rahim	8.00
14	A. Walker, A. Walker	8.00
15	A. Walker, Walker	8.00
NNO	Checklist	8.00

1997 Collector's Edge Energy

Inserted 1:12 packs, the 25-card set features a player photo superimposed over a motion background of a backboard being shattered by a basketball. The player's name is printed inside a yellow stripe at the bottom of the front. The backs have the card number in the upper right. The player photo dominates the back, with his name and bio printed in the lower left. "Edge Energy" appears in the lower right.

		MT
Complete Set (13):		30.00
Common Player:		.50
1	Antonio Daniels	4.00
2	Austin Croshere	3.00
3	Charles O'Bannon	.50
4	Scot Pollard	.50
5	Paul Grant	.50
6	Danny Fortson	2.00
7	Keith Van Horn	3.00
8	Kelvin Cato	2.00
9	Ron Mercer	5.00
10	Tim Duncan	8.00
11	Tim Thomas	3.00
12	Chauncey Billups	3.00
NNO	Checklist	.50

1997 Collector's Edge Extra

Inserted 1:48 packs, the 12-card set has a photo of the player "coming out" of a newspaper design background on the front. The player's name and his draft status are printed beneath the player photo in the lower left. The backs have "Edge Sports" printed at the top, with a photo, the player's name, bio, highlights and card number rounding out the back.

		MT
Complete Set (13):		100.00
Common Player:		1.50
1	Tim Duncan	25.00
2	Keith Van Horn	10.00
3	Olivier Saint-Jean	6.00
4	Antonio Daniels	12.00
5	Tony Battie	8.00
6	Ron Mercer	15.00
7	Tim Thomas	8.00
8	Antoine Walker	1.00
9	Kobe Bryant	15.00
10	Shareef Abdur-Rahim	1.50
11	Stephon Marbury	10.00
12	Scottie Pippen	8.00
NNO	Checklist	1.50

1997 Collector's Edge Game-Used Ball

Inserted 1:36 packs, the five-card set boasts a circular piece of a game-used basketball on the front. The player photo is printed over a basketball floor background. "Authentic game-used ball" is printed at the top. The player's name is printed at the bottom center below a pulse line.

		MT
Complete Set (5):		90.00
Common Player:		15.00
1	Antoine Walker	10.00
2	Kobe Bryant	30.00
3	Shareef Abdur-Rahim	15.00
4	Stephon Marbury	25.00
5	Scottie Pippen	20.00

1997 Collector's Edge Hardcourt Force

Inserted 1:36 packs, the 25-card set features a player photo superimposed over a parquet floor background. "Hard Court Force" is printed vertically along the left border. The player's name, position and draft status are printed at the bottom center inside a basketball floor design. The card back has a player photo inside a basketball at the top center of the back. The card number is inside a red diamond in the upper right. The player's name and bio are printed at the bottom center of the backs.

		MT
Complete Set (25):		200.00
Common Player:		2.00
1	Chauncey Billups	15.00
2	Tony Battie	15.00
3	Tim Duncan	30.00
4	Paul Grant	2.00
5	John Thomas	2.00
6	Scottie Pippen	8.00
7	Scot Pollard	2.00
8	Ron Mercer	20.00
9	Tim Thomas	10.00
10	Kobe Bryant	15.00
11	Antonio Daniels	10.00
12	Kelvin Cato	10.00
13	Danny Fortson	8.00
14	Ed Gray	2.00
15	Derek Anderson	10.00
16	Bobby Jackson	8.00
17	Antoine Walker	5.00
18	Anthony Parker	2.00
19	Shareef Abdur-Rahim	10.00
20	Olivier Saint-Jean	6.00
21	Stephon Marbury	12.00
22	Keith Van Horn	12.00
23	Austin Croshere	6.00
24	Adonal Foyle	6.00
25	Serge Zwikker	2.00

1997 Collector's Edge Swoosh

Inserted 1:24 packs, the 12-card set features a player photo superimposed over a background of basketballs on the front of the acetate cards. "Swoosh" is printed vertically along the left border of the front. The player's name appears at the bottom center of the front. The backs have the card number in the upper left inside a red diamond. The player's name and bio is printed at the bottom center of the backs.

		MT
Complete Set (13):		50.00
Common Player:		.75
1	Adonal Foyle	.75
2	Keith Booth	.75
3	Danny Fortson	3.00
4	Derek Anderson	4.00
5	Jacque Vaughn	3.00
6	Keith Van Horn	6.00
7	Kelvin Cato	4.00
8	Ron Mercer	8.00
9	Tim Duncan	15.00
10	Tony Battie	5.00
11	Chauncey Billups	6.00
12	Charles O'Bannon	2.00
13	Checklist	.75

1998 Collector's Edge Impulse

This 100-card set featured top players eligible for the 1998 NBA Draft. Card fronts have a borderless design with the logo in the top right corner and the player's name across the bottom in gold foil. The set was paralled once and packs contained five different inserts, including: KB8, Pro Signatures Authentic, Memorable Moments, Swoosh and T3.

		MT
Complete Set (100):		20.00
Common Player:		.10
Minor Stars:		.20
Wax Box:		70.00
1	Michael Olowokandi	1.50
2	Antawn Jamison	2.00
3	Vince Carter	5.00
4	Robert Traylor	1.50
5	Jason Williams	2.00
6	Paul Pierce	2.50
7	Bonzi Wells	.50
8	Keon Clark	.50
9	Radoslav Nesterovic	.10
10	Pat Garrity	.20
11	Ricky Davis	.20
12	Tyrron Lue	.10
13	Felipe Lopez	.50
14	Al Harrington	.50
15	Corey Benjamin	.10
16	Rashard Lewis	.75
17	Jelani McCoy	.20
18	Shammond Williams	.50
19	DeMarco Johnson	.20
20	Korleone Young	.20
21	Miles Simon	.20
22	Toby Bailey	.20
23	J.R. Henderson	.20
24	Charles Jones	.10
25	Jeff Sheppard	.10
26	Kobe Bryant	2.00
27	Stephon Marbury	.50
28	Tracy McGrady	.20
29	Scottie Pippen	.40
30	Tim Thomas	.20
31	Checklist (Michael Olowokandi)	1.25
32	Checklist (Antawn Jamison)	1.00
33	Michael Olowokandi	1.25
34	Antawn Jamison	1.00
35	Vince Carter	.75
36	Robert Traylor	.75
37	Jason Williams	.25
38	Paul Pierce	.50
39	Bonzi Wells	.10
40	Keon Clark	.10
41	Radoslav Nesterovic	.10
42	Pat Garrity	.10
43	Michael Olowokandi	1.25
44	Antawn Jamison	1.00
45	Vince Carter	.50
46	Robert Traylor	.50
47	Jason Williams	.20
48	Paul Pierce	.50
49	Bonzi Wells	.10
50	Keon Clark	.10
51	Paul Pierce, Kobe Bryant	.75
52	Paul Pierce, Scottie Pippen	.50
53	Antawn Jamison, Stephon Marbury	.50
54	Antawn Jamison, Tracy McGrady	.50
55	Michael Olowokandi, Tim Thomas	.50
56	Michael Olowokandi, Kobe Bryant	1.25
57	Keon Clark, Scottie Pippen	.20
58	Keon Clark, Stephon Marbury	.20
59	Pat Garrity, Tracy McGrady	.20

60 Pat Garrity, Tim Thomas .20
61 Corey Benjamin, Kobe Bryant .75
62 Corey Benjamin, Scottie Pippen .20
63 Robert Traylor, Stephon Marbury .20
64 Robert Traylor, Tracy McGrady .20
65 Rashard Lewis, Tim Thomas .40
66 Rashard Lewis, Kobe Bryant .75
67 Bonzi Wells, Scottie Pippen .20
68 Bonzi Wells, Stephon Marbury .20
69 J.R. Henderson, Tracy McGrady .20
70 J.R. Henderson, Tim Thomas .20
71 Toby Bailey, Kobe Bryant .75
72 Toby Bailey, Scottie Pippen .20
73 Tyrron Lue, Stephon Marbury .20
74 Tyrron Lue, Tracy McGrady .20
75 Radisav Nesterovic, Tim Thomas .20
76 Radisav Nesterovic, Kobe Bryant .75
77 Miles Simon, Scottie Pippen .20
78 Miles Simon, Stephon Marbury .20
79 Jeff Sheppard, Tracy McGrady .20
80 Jeff Sheppard, Tim Thomas .20
81 Felipe Lopez, Kobe Bryant .75
82 Felipe Lopez, Scottie Pippen .20
83 Shammond Williams, Stephon Marbury .20
84 Shammond Williams, Tracy McGrady .20
85 Charles Jones, Tim Thomas .20
86 Charles Jones, Kobe Bryant .75
87 Jason Williams, Scottie Pippen .20
88 Jason Williams, Stephon Marbury .20
89 Ricky Davis, Tracy McGrady .20
90 Ricky Davis, Tim Thomas .20
91 Korleone Young, Kobe Bryant .75
92 Korleone Young, Scottie Pippen .20
93 Vince Carter, Stephon Marbury .20
94 Vince Carter, Tracy McGrady .20
95 Al Harrington, Tim Thomas .20
96 Al Harrington, Kobe Bryant .75
97 Jelani McCoy, Scottie Pippen .20
98 Jelani McCoy, Stephon Marbury .20
99 DeMarco Johnson, Tracy McGrady .20
100 DeMarco Johnson, Tim Thomas .20
NNO Memorable Moments Exchange 50.00

1998 Collector's Edge Impulse

This 100-card parallel reprinted each card on a thicker stock than used on the base cards. These were inserted one per pack.

MT
Complete Set (100): 40.00
Parallel Cards: 2x
Inserted 1:1

1998 Collector's Edge Impluse KB8

This five-card insert features Lakers star Kobe Bryant and arrives in four different versions. Bronze cards are seeded 1:36, Silvers are 1:54, Golds are 1:72 and Holofoil versions are found one per 90 packs.

MT
Complete Bronze Set (5): 30.00
Common Bronze Player: 8.00
Inserted 1:36
Complete Silver Set (5): 50.00
Silver Cards: 1.5x
Inserted 1:54
Complete Gold Set (5): 60.00
Gold Cards: 2x
Inserted 1:72
Complete Holofoil Set (5):
Holofoil Cards: 2.5x
Inserted 1:90
1 Kobe Bryant 6.00
2 Kobe Bryant 6.00
3 Kobe Bryant 6.00
4 Kobe Bryant 6.00
5 Kobe Bryant 6.00

1998 Collector's Edge Impulse Memorable Moments

This five-card set was available for exchange cards inserted into packs at a rate of one per 360 packs. Once redeemed, the cards featured pieces of game-used ball on the front.

MT
Complete Set (5):
Common Player:
1 Kobe Bryant 150.00
2 Stephon Marbury 40.00
3 Tracy McGrady 70.00
4 Scottie Pippen 30.00
5 Tim Thomas 30.00

1998 Collector's Edge Impulse Pro Signatures

This 30-card set featured authentic signatures from 25 rookies and five veterans. Fourteen of these inserts were available exclusively through redempion cards, while three others were partially available through redemptions. Pro Signatures were seeded one per 18 packs.

MT
Common Player: 5.00
Inserted 1:18
Toby Bailey 5.00
Corey Benjamin 5.00
Kobe Bryant 200.00
Vince Carter 100.00
Keon Clark 10.00
Ricky Davis 10.00
Pat Garrity 10.00
Zendon Hamilton 5.00
Al Harrington 15.00
J.R. Henderson 5.00
Antawn Jamison 40.00
DeMarco Johnson 5.00
Rashard Lewis 15.00
Felipe Lopez 15.00
Tyrron Lue 10.00
Stephon Marbury 100.00
Jelani McCoy 10.00
Tracy McGrady 75.00
Michael Olowokandi 30.00
Paul Pierce 60.00
Scottie Pippen 175.00
Jeff Sheppard 5.00
Miles Simon 5.00
Tim Thomas 75.00
Robert Traylor 30.00
Bonzi Wells 10.00
Jason Williams 75.00
Shammond Williams 5.00
Korleone Young 10.00

1998 Collector's Edge Impulse Swoosh

Swoosh included 24 cards in total, with 12 different pairs of left and right cards that fit together. Printed on an acetate stock, these were inserted one per 72 packs.

MT
Complete Set (26): 230.00
Common Player: 5.00
Inserted 1:72
1 Michael Olowokandi 20.00
2 Antawn Jamison 20.00
3 Vince Carter 40.00
4 Robert Traylor 20.00
5 Jason Williams 20.00
6 Paul Pierce 25.00
7 Bonzi Wells 5.00
8 Keon Clark 5.00
9 Radisav Nesterovic 5.00
10 Pat Garrity 5.00
11 Ricky Davis 8.00
12 Tyrron Lue 5.00
13 Felipe Lopez 8.00
14 Al Harrington 8.00
15 Corey Benjamin 5.00
16 Rashard Lewis 5.00
17 Jelani McCoy 5.00
18 Shammond Williams 8.00
19 DeMarco Johnson 5.00
20 Korleone Young 5.00
21 Miles Simon 5.00
22 Kobe Bryant 30.00
23 Stephon Marbury 15.00
24 Tracy McGrady 10.00
25 Scottie Pippen 12.00
26 Tim Thomas 10.00

1998 Collector's Edge Impulse T3

This 15-card insert included 10 rookies and five veterans. Cards included a "T3" logo in the top right corner and arrived in three different versions. Bronze versions were seeded 1:12, Silver versions were seeded 1:18 and Gold versions were seeded 1:36 packs.

MT
Complete Set (15): 50.00
Common Gold Player (1-5): 5.00
Inserted 1:36
Common Silver Player (6-10): 2.00
Inserted 1:18
Common Bronze Player (11-15): 1.00
Inserted 1:12
1 Michael Olowokandi G 8.00
2 Antawn Jamison G 8.00
3 Kobe Bryant G 15.00
4 Scottie Pippen G 8.00
5 Robert Traylor G 5.00
6 Stephon Marbury S 5.00
7 Paul Pierce S 10.00
8 Vince Carter S 15.00
9 Shammond Williams S 2.00
10 Tim Thomas S 2.00
11 Bonzi Wells B 1.00
12 Tracy McGrady B 2.00
13 Rashard Lewis B 1.50
14 Keon Clark B 1.00
15 Corey Benjamin B 1.00

1999 Collector's Edge Rookie Rage

MT
Complete Set (50): 12.00
Common Player: .10
Minor Stars: .20
1 Ron Artest .50
2 William Avery .40
3 Michael Batiste .10
4 Jonathan Bender 1.25
5 Roberto Bergersen .10
6 Calvin Booth .40
7 Cal Bowdler .20
8 A.J. Bramlett .10
9 Rodney Buford .20
10 John Celestand .10
11 Kris Clack .10
12 Lonnie Cooper .10
13 Vonteego Cummings .40
14 Baron Davis 1.00
15 Evan Eschmeyer .20
16 Jeff Foster .20
17 Jelani Gardner .10
18 Devean George .60
19 Dion Glover .20
20 Richard Hamilton .75
21 Richard Hamilton .10
22 Rico Hill .10
23 Tim James .20
24 Jumaine Jones .20
25 J.R. Koch .10
26 Trajan Langdon .50
27 Bobby Lazor .10
28 Melvin Levett .20
29 Quincy Lewis .30
30 Corey Maggette 1.00
31 Shawn Marion 2.00
32 B.J. McKie .10
33 Andre Miller 1.50
34 Lee Nailon .20
35 Ademola Okulaja .10
36 Scott Padgett .20
37 James Posey .60
38 Aleksandar Radojevic .10
39 Michael Ruffin .20
40 Leon Smith .20
41 Jason Terry .75
42 Kenny Thomas .40
43 Tyrone Washington .10
44 Frederic Weis .10
45 Alvin Young .10
46 Kobe Bryant 1.50
47 Vince Carter 1.50
48 Antawn Jamison .50
49 Paul Pierce .40
50 Jason Williams .40

1999 Collector's Edge Rookie Rage Gold

MT
Complete Set (50): 18.00
Common Player: .15
Minor Stars: .30
Gold Cards: 1.5x
1 Ron Artest .50
2 William Avery .40
3 Michael Batiste .10
4 Jonathan Bender 1.25
5 Roberto Bergersen .10
6 Calvin Booth .40
7 Cal Bowdler .20
8 A.J. Bramlett .10
9 Rodney Buford .20
10 John Celestand .10
11 Kris Clack .10
12 Lonnie Cooper .10
13 Vonteego Cummings .40
14 Baron Davis 1.00
15 Evan Eschmeyer .20
16 Jeff Foster .20
17 Jelani Gardner .10
18 Devean George .60
19 Dion Glover .20
20 Richard Hamilton .75
21 Richard Hamilton .10
22 Rico Hill .10
23 Tim James .20
24 Jumaine Jones .20
25 J.R. Koch .10
26 Trajan Langdon .50
27 Bobby Lazor .10
28 Melvin Levett .20
29 Quincy Lewis .30
30 Corey Maggette 1.00
31 Shawn Marion 2.00
32 B.J. McKie .10
33 Andre Miller 1.50
34 Lee Nailon .20
35 Ademola Okulaja .10
36 Scott Padgett .20
37 James Posey .60
38 Aleksandar Radojevic .10
39 Michael Ruffin .20
40 Leon Smith .20
41 Jason Terry .75
42 Kenny Thomas .40
43 Tyrone Washington .10
44 Frederic Weis .10
45 Alvin Young .10
46 Kobe Bryant 1.50
47 Vince Carter 1.50
48 Antawn Jamison .50
49 Paul Pierce .40
50 Jason Williams .40

1999 Collector's Edge Rookie Rage Holo Gold

MT
Common Player: 4.00
Holo Gold Cards: 20x-40x
Production 50 sets.
1 Ron Artest .50
2 William Avery .40
3 Michael Batiste .10
4 Jonathan Bender 1.25
5 Roberto Bergersen .10
6 Calvin Booth .40
7 Cal Bowdler .20
8 A.J. Bramlett .10
9 Rodney Buford .20
10 John Celestand .10
11 Kris Clack .10
12 Lonnie Cooper .10
13 Vonteego Cummings .40
14 Baron Davis 1.00
15 Evan Eschmeyer .20
16 Jeff Foster .20
17 Jelani Gardner .10
18 Devean George .60
19 Dion Glover .20
20 Richard Hamilton .75
21 Richard Hamilton .10
22 Rico Hill .10
23 Tim James .20
24 Jumaine Jones .20
25 J.R. Koch .10
26 Trajan Langdon .50
27 Bobby Lazor .10
28 Melvin Levett .20
29 Quincy Lewis .30
30 Corey Maggette 1.00
31 Shawn Marion 2.00
32 B.J. McKie .10
33 Andre Miller 1.50
34 Lee Nailon .20
35 Ademola Okulaja .10
36 Scott Padgett .20
37 James Posey .60
38 Aleksandar Radojevic .10
39 Michael Ruffin .20
40 Leon Smith .20
41 Jason Terry .75
42 Kenny Thomas .40
43 Tyrone Washington .10
44 Frederic Weis .10
45 Alvin Young .10
46 Kobe Bryant 1.50
47 Vince Carter 1.50
48 Antawn Jamison .50
49 Paul Pierce .40
50 Jason Williams .40

1999 Collector's Edge Rookie Rage Future Legends

MT
Complete Set (10): 8.00
Common Player: .20
Inserted 1:8
1 Ron Artest .75
2 William Avery .50
3 Jonathan Bender 1.50
4 Baron Davis 1.25
5 Richard Hamilton 1.00
6 Trajan Langdon .60
7 Corey Maggette 1.25
8 Andre Miller 1.50
9 Jason Terry 1.00
10 Frederic Weis .15

1999 Collector's Edge Rookie Rage Game Ball

MT
Complete Set (5): 100.00
Common Player: 15.00
Inserted 1:72
1 Kobe Bryant 50.00
2 Vince Carter 50.00
3 Antawn Jamison 18.00
4 Paul Pierce 15.00
5 Jason Williams 15.00

1999 Collector's Edge Rookie Rage Livin' Large

MT
Complete Set (5): 10.00
Common Player: 1.00
Inserted 1:16
1 Kobe Bryant 5.00
2 Vince Carter 5.00
3 Antawn Jamison 1.50
4 Paul Pierce 1.00
5 Jason Williams 1.00

1999 Collector's Edge Rookie Rage Loud and Proud

MT
Complete Set (5): 10.00
Common Player: 1.00
Inserted 1:16
1 Kobe Bryant 5.00
2 Vince Carter 5.00
3 Antawn Jamison 1.50
4 Paul Pierce 1.00
5 Jason Williams 1.00

1999 Collector's Edge Rookie Rage Pro Signatures

MT
Common Player: 2.00
Minor Stars: 3.00
Inserted 1:12
1 Ron Artest 5.00
2 William Avery 3.00
3 Michael Batiste 2.00
4 Jonathan Bender 15.00
5 Roberto Bergersen 2.00
6 Calvin Booth 2.00
7 Cal Bowdler 2.00
8 A.J. Bramlett 2.00
9 Rodney Buford 3.00
10 John Celestand 3.00
11 Kris Clack 2.00
12 Lonnie Cooper 2.00
13 Vonteego Cummings 4.00
14 Baron Davis 10.00
15 Evan Eschmeyer 2.00
16 Jeff Foster 2.00
17 Jelani Gardner 2.00
18 Devean George 5.00
19 Dion Glover 3.00
20 Richard Hamilton 6.00
21 Venson Hamilton 2.00
22 Rico Hill 2.00
23 Tim James 3.00
24 Jumaine Jones 3.00
25 J.R. Koch 2.00
26 Trajan Langdon 5.00
27 Bobby Lazor 2.00
28 Melvin Levett 2.00
29 Quincy Lewis 3.00
30 Corey Maggette 15.00
31 Shawn Marion 15.00
32 B.J. McKie 2.00
33 Andre Miller 10.00
34 Lee Nailon 2.00
35 Ademola Okulaja 2.00
36 Scott Padgett 3.00
37 James Posey 5.00
38 Aleksandar Radojevic 2.00
39 Michael Ruffin 2.00
40 Leon Smith 3.00
41 Jason Terry 6.00
42 Kenny Thomas 3.00
43 Tyrone Washington 2.00
44 Frederic Weis 2.00
45 Alvin Young 2.00
46 Kobe Bryant/39 200.00
47 Vince Carter 100.00
48 Antawn Jamison 12.00
49 Paul Pierce 10.00
50 Jason Williams 10.00

1999 Collector's Edge Rookie Rage Successors

MT
Complete Set (10):
Common Player: .20
Inserted 1:8
1 Ron Artest .75
2 William Avery .50
3 Jonathan Bender 1.50
4 Baron Davis 1.25
5 Richard Hamilton 1.00
6 Trajan Langdon .60
7 Corey Maggette 1.25
8 Andre Miller 1.50
9 Jason Terry 1.00
10 Frederic Weis .15

1971 Colonels Marathon Oil

Measuring 7-1/2" x 9-7/8", this 11-card set boasts color artwork on the front consisting of a headshot and action artwork over the black background. The player's facsimile autograph is printed in white at the bottom of the front. The bottom of each portrait had a postcard measuring 7-1/2" x 4" after perforation. The backs of each portrait offer memorabilia like posters, tumblers and a photo album. The cards were unnumbered.

NM
Complete Set (11): 75.00
Common Player: 5.00
Darrell Carrier 6.00
Bobby Croft 5.00
Louie Dampier 12.00
Les Hunter 6.00
Dan Issel 30.00
Jim Ligon 5.00
Cincy Powell 8.00
Mike Pratt 6.00
Walt Simon 5.00
Sam Smith 6.00
Howard Wright 5.00

1972-73 COMSPEC

NM
Complete Set (35): 1000.
Common Player:
1 Kareem Abdul-Jabbar 150.00
2 Rick Adelman 10.00
3 Nate Archibald 40.00
4 Rick Barry 40.00
5 Walt Bellamy 20.00
6 Dave Bing 35.00
7 Austin Carr 20.00
8 Wilt Chamberlain 150.00
9 Dave Cowens 50.00
10 Walt Frazier 40.00
11 Gail Goodrich 30.00
12 John Havlicek 70.00
13 Connie Hawkins 40.00
14 Elvin Hayes 40.00
15 Spencer Haywood 15.00
16 John Hummer 6.00
17 Don Kojis 8.00
18 Bob Lanier 35.00
19 Kevin Loughery 15.00
20 Jerry Lucas 40.00
21 Pete Maravich 200.00
22 Jack Marin 12.00
23 Calvin Murphy 30.00
24 Geoff Petrie 12.00
25 Willis Reed 40.00
26 Oscar Robertson 80.00
27 Cazzie Russell 10.00
28 Elmore Smith 8.00
29 Dick Snyder 8.00
30 Wes Unseld 35.00
31 Dick Van Arsdale 10.00
32 Tom Van Arsdale 10.00
33 Norm Van Lier 12.00
34 Chet Walker 15.00
35 Jerry West 90.00
36 Lenny Wilkens 40.00

1971-72 Condors Pittsburgh ABA

Measuring 5-1/2" x 7", this 11-photo set pictured players from the Pittsburgh ABA team. Anchoring the front are posed black-and-white photos bordered in white. The player's name and team name are located in the white border beneath the photo. The unnumbered photos have blank backs.

NM
Complete Set (11): 60.00
Common Player: 6.00
John Brisker 8.00
George Carter 6.00
Mickey Davis 6.00
Stew Johnson 6.00
Arvesta Kelly 6.00
Dave Lattin 10.00
Mike Lewis 6.00
Jimmy O'Brien 6.00
Paul Ruffner 6.00
Skeeter Swift 6.00
George Thompson 8.00

1969 Converse Staff Shoes

This 10-card set promotes Converse's line of athletic shoes. Each card is 2-1/4" x 2-3/4" and features a portrait shot of a former star, plus biographical information about him. A basketball tip is also included on the front. The cards are unnumbered and have blank backs.

NM
Complete Set (10): 75.00
Common Player: 7.00
Bob Davies 10.00
Joe Dean 7.50
Gib Ford 7.50
Bob Houbregs 10.00
Rod Hundley 10.00
Stu Inman 7.00
Bunny Levitt 10.00
Earl Lloyd 7.00
John Norlander 7.00
Phil Rollins 7.00

1989 Converse

This set features color photos of NBA players who endorse Converse shoes. The set, officially licensed by the NBA, was produced by Sports Marketing, which made 50,000 sets. The 2-1/2" x 3-1/2" cards are unnumbered and include career highlights and an anti-drug message on the back.

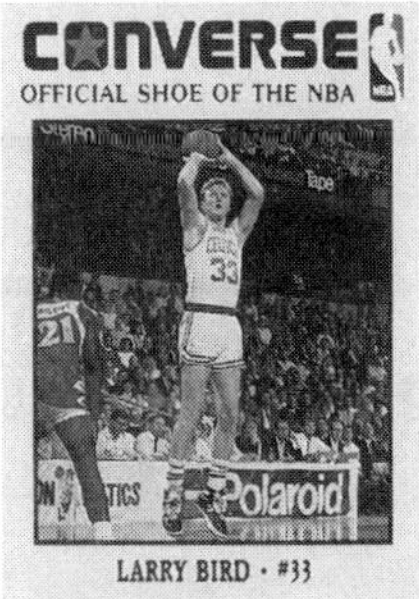

		MT
Complete Set (14):		15.00
Common Player:		.75
	Checklist	.75
	Mark Aguirre	.75
	Larry Bird	6.00
	Rolando Blackman	.75
	Tyrone Bogues	1.00
	Rex Chapman	.75
	Magic Johnson	4.00
	Bernard King	.75
	Bill Laimbeer	.75
	Karl Malone	3.00
	Kevin McHale	2.00
	Mark Price	1.50
	Jack Sikma	.75
	Reggie Theus	.75

1992 Courtside Flashback Promo Sheet

The sheet features four players in their collegiate uniforms and when cut, are the standard 2-1/2" x 3-1/2" size. Production was limited to 5,000.

		MT
Complete Set (1):		3.00
Common Player:		3.00
1	Courtside Promo Sheet (Chris Mullin - St. John's, Kareem Abdul-Jabbar - UCLA, David Robinson - Navy, Rick Barry)	3.00

1991 Courtside Bk

This first set from the Burlingame, Calif., company featured 1991 basketball prospects. Cards were released in August and were issued as complete sets. A total of 198,000 sets were issued; about one out of seven was randomly packed with an autographed card. There were 50 complete autographed sets distributed. Cards were printed on pearlescent paper with metallic ink. The set includes two special cards of Larry Johnson, the first pick in the 1991 draft.

		MT
Complete Set (45):		5.00
Common Player:		.05
Common Autograph:		10.00
Star Autographs:		25x-50x
1	Larry Johnson (FDP)	.50
2	Kenny Anderson	.75
3	Greg Anthony	.15
4	Anthony Avent	.10
5	Terrell Brandon	.40
6	Kevin Brooks	.05
7	Marc Brown	.05
8	Myron Brown	.05
9	Randy Brown	.10
10	Darrin Chancellor	.05
11	Pete Chilcutt	.05
12	Chris Corchiani	.05
13	John Crotty	.05
14	Dale Davis	.25
15	Marty Dow	.05
16	Patrick Eddie	.05
17	Richard Dumas	.10
18	Tony Farmer	.05
19	Tony Fisher	.05
20	Rick Fox	.20
21	Chad Gallagher	.05
22	Chris Gatling	.10
23	Sean Green	.05
24	Reggie Hanson	.05
25	Donald Hodge	.05
26	Steve Hood	.05
27	Keith Hughes	.05
28	Mike Iuzzolino	.05
29	Keith Jennings	.10
30	Larry Johnson	[illegible]
31	Treg Lee	.05
32	Cedric Lewis	.05
33	Kevin Lynch	.05
34	Mark Macon	.10
35	Jason Matthews	.05
36	Eric Murdock	.20
37	Jimmy Oliver	.10
38	Doug Overton	.05
39	Elliot Perry	.25
40	Brian Chorter	.05
41	Alvaro Teheran	.05
42	Joey Wright	.05
43	Joe Wylie	.05
----	Larry Johnson (POY)	.40
----	Larry Johnson (#1 draft pick)	3.00

1991 Courtside Flashback

This glossy flashback set features cards of former college coaches and players, who are pictured in action wearing their collegiate uniforms. The backs include career highlights and another color action photo. There were 199,000 boxed sets produced. More than 10,000 autographed cards were also randomly inserted.

		MT
Complete Set (45):		9.00
Common Player:		.05
1	Tommy Amaker	.05
2	Charles Barkley	.75
3	Rick Barry	.75
4	Larry Bird	1.00
5	Larry Brown (C)	.10
6	Quinn Buckner	.10
7	Tom Burleson	.10
8	Austin Carr	.20
9	Phil Ford	.20
10	Andrew Gaze	.05
11	Artis Gilmore	.25
12	Jack Givens	.10
13	Gail Goodrich	.20
14	Kevin Grevey	.10
15	Ernie Grunfeld	.05
16	Elvin Hayes	.35
17	Walt Hazzard	.10
18	Kareem Abdul-Jabbar	1.00
19	Marques Johnson	.15
20	John Lucas	.10
21	Kyly Macy	.10
22	Rollie Massimino (C)	.10
23	Cedric Maxwell	.05
24	Bob McAdoo	.20
25	Al McGuire (C)	.10
26	George Mikan	1.00
27	Sidney Moncrief	.25
28	Chris Mullin	.50
29	Calvin Murphy	.20
30	Sam Perkins	.25
31	David Robinson	.75
32	Curis Rowe	.05
33	Cazzie Russell	.10
34	Charlie Scott	.10
35	Dean Smith (C)	.10
36	Jerry Tarkanian (C)	.10
37	David Thompson	.25
38	Nate Thurmond	.20
39	Monte Towe	.05
40	Jim Valvano (C)	.10
41	Bill Walton	.75
42	Paul Westphal	.15
43	Derek Whittenburg	.05
44	Sidney Wicks	.15
45	John Wooden (C)	.15

1991 Courtside Hologram

Card fronts for this three-card set feature action hologram photos which say Draft Pix on the bottom right. Backs include collegiate stats and a summary. There were 98,000 sets made.

		MT
Complete Set (3):		4.00
1	Greg Anthony	.75
2	Larry Johnson	3.00
3	Mark Macon	.50

1991 Cousy Collection Preview

The five standard-sized cards previewed the Bob Cousy set. The card front showcase a black-and-white photo that is bordered in black. Cousy's name is printed in white and green at the top, while "Preview Edition" is printed beneath the photo. The backs are numbered in a circle on the upper left side. A bio and career highlights, along with the card's serial number, highlight the back.

		MT
Complete Set (5):		5.00
Common Player:		1.50
1	Rookie Card	[illegible]
2	High School 1945-46	1.50
3	1940-50 Senior Year Holy Cross	1.50
4	1962-63 Season	1.50
5	Coaching Boston College	1.50

1991 Cousy Card Collection

This 25-card set devoted to Boston Celtics great Bob Cousy was produced by Milton Kahn in Santa Barbara, Calif. The fronts feature black-and-white photos framed by green and black borders. Card backs have information about the front; the cards are checklisted from that information. The sets are numbered; approximately 10,000 sets were made. There was also a five-card prototype set issued which has identical photos to the regular set, but the backs are different. They can be distinguished by a "No. C" on them. Cards from both sets are 2-1/2" x 3-1/2".

		MT
Complete Set (25):		12.00
Common Player:		1.00
1	Rookie Card	3.00
2	"First Year" card 1929	1.25
3	The Playground 1944-45	1.00
4	High School 1945-46	1.25
5	MCAA Kings 1946-47	1.00
6	Holy Cross Senior Year 1949-50	1.00
7	"Double Trouble" 1951-52	1.50
8	Star of the Stars 1954	1.00
9	"Stan the Man" 1955	3.50
10	Timely Idea 1955	1.50
11	"Star" Again 1957	1.25
12	The MVP 1957	1.00
13	The Deal 1959	1.00
14	"Four" Plan 1958-59	1.75
15	At Home 1960	1.00
16	Victory Watch 1961-62	1.50
17	Visit with J.F.K. 1962-62	1.50
18	Master and Mentor 1963	1.00
19	His "Day" 1963	1.00
20	A Career 1963	1.00
21	Author 1965	1.00
22	"Podnuhs" 1965	1.00
23	Coaching Boston College 1968-69	1.00
24	Coaching Cincinnati Royals 1969-70	1.00
25	Made for TV 1990-91	1.00

1976 Crane Discs

These cards, issued by Crane Potato Chips, have a picture of the company logo on the front to distinguish it from similar discs which have been made. The fronts have a posed photo of the player, a biography, statistics and an NBA license logo. Backs have a picture of the Crane logo and say Crane Potato Chips. Cards are unnumbered and measure about 3-1/2" in diameter.

		NM
Complete Set (20):		300.00
Common Player:		10.00
	Nate Archibald	20.00
	Rick Barry	25.00
	Tom Boerwinkle	10.00
	Bill Bradley	25.00
	Dave Cowens	20.00
	Bob Dandridge	10.00
	Walt Frazier	20.00
	Gail Goodrich	20.00
	John Havlicek	30.00
	Connie Hawkins	20.00
	Lou Hudson	10.00
	Kareem Abdul-Jabbar	35.00
	Sam Lacey (spelled Lacy)	10.00
	Bob Lanier	15.00
	Bob Love	12.00
	Bob McAdoo	20.00
	Earl Monroe	20.00
	Jerry Sloan	15.00
	Norm Van Lier	12.00
	Jo Jo White	15.00

D

1970 Dayton Daily News

These 3-3/8" x 3-3/4" cards were included in issues of the Dayton Daily News in 1970-71. Card fronts have a black-and-white photo, a caption which says "Today's Hero," biographical and statistical information, and a card number. The cards are also labeled as bubble-gumless cards. The backs are blank.

		NM
Complete Set (8):		60.00
Common Player:		5.00
83	John Havlicek	15.00
218	Johnny Green	5.00
225	Norm Van Lier	6.00
247	Walt Bellamy	6.00
249	Hal Greer	12.00
251	Jerry West	20.00
252	Tom Van Arsdale	6.00
254	Donny May	5.00

1977 Dell Flipbooks

These 24-page booklets feature color action photos of the players which simulate motion when they are rifled through. Each shows a player demonstrating a basketball technique and includes player statistics. The booklets are 4" x 3-3/16" and were produced by Pocket Money Basketball Co.

		NM
Complete Set (6):		100.00
Common Player:		18.00
1	Kareem Abdul-Jabbar	30.00
2	Dave Cowens	18.00
3	Julius Erving	30.00
4	Pete Maravich	35.00
5	David Thompson	18.00
6	Bill Walton	25.00

1970 Detroit Free Press

		NM
Complete Set (6):		45.00
Common Player:		3.75
1	Dave Bing	3.75
2	Howard Komives	3.75
3	Eddie Miles	3.75
4	Ralph Simpson	3.75
5	Rudy Tomjanovich	3.75
6	Jimmy Walker	3.75

E

1994-95 E-Motion

Each of the cards in SkyBox's 1994-95 E-Motion set is printed on 24-point stock enhanced with film lamination and foil stamping. Each front has an "emotion" action shot of an NBA star, with a descriptive phrase given to convey the passion of the player. The E-Motion logo, player's last name and brand logo are stamped in gold foil on each card front, also. The back side has a montage of photos, plus a few lines of text describing the player. In addition to the two 10-card subsets which were made - Masters and Rookies - two insert sets were produced. They are X-Cited and N-Tense cards.

		MT
Complete Set (121):		50.00
Common Player:		.25
Minor Stars:		.50
Pack (8):		4.00
Wax Box (36):		125.00
1	Stacey Augmon	.25
2	Mookie Blaylock	.25
3	Steve Smith	.25
4	Greg Minor	.50
5	Eric Montross	.50
6	Dino Radja	.50
7	Dominique Wilkins	.50
8	Muggsy Bogues	.25
9	Larry Johnson	1.00
10	Alonzo Mourning	1.00
11	B.J. Armstrong	.50
12	Toni Kukoc	.50
13	Scottie Pippen	1.50
14	Dickey Simpkins	.50
15	Tyrone Hill	.25
16	Chris Mills	.25
17	Mark Price	.50
18	Tony Dumas	1.00
19	Jim Jackson	1.00
20	*Jason Kidd*	8.00
21	Jamal Mashburn	.50
22	LaPhonso Ellis	.50
23	Dikembe Mutombo	.75
24	Rodney Rogers	.25
25	*Jalen Rose*	4.00
26	Bill Curley	.50
27	Joe Dumars	.50
28	*Grant Hill*	10.00
29	Tim Hardaway	.50
30	Donyell Marshall	.50
31	Chris Mullin	.50
32	Carlos Rogers	.50
33	Clifford Rozier	.50
34	Latrell Sprewell	.50
35	Sam Cassell	.50
36	Clyde Drexler	1.50
37	Robert Horry	.50
38	Hakeem Olajuwon	[illegible]
39	Mark Jackson	.25
40	Reggie Miller	1.00
41	Rik Smits	.50
42	Lamond Murray	.50
43	Eric Piatkowski	.50
44	Loy Vaught	.25
45	Cedric Ceballos	.25
46	*Eddie Jones*	4.00
47	George Lynch	.25
48	Nick Van Exel	.75
49	Harold Miner	.25
50	Khalid Reeves	.50
51	Glen Rice	.50
52	Kevin Willis	.50
53	Vin Baker	1.00
54	Eric Mobley	.25
55	Eric Murdock	.25
56	*Glenn Robinson*	4.00
57	Tom Gugliotta	.25
58	Christian Laettner	.25
59	Isaiah Rider	.50
60	Kenny Anderson	.50
61	Derrick Coleman	.50
62	Yinka Dare	.50
63	Patrick Ewing	1.00
64	John Starks	.50
65	Charlie Ward	.50
66	Monty Williams	.25
67	Nick Anderson	.50
68	Horace Grant	.50
69	Anfernee Hardaway	4.00
70	Shaquille O'Neal	5.00
71	Brooks Thompson	.50
72	Dana Barros	.50
73	Shawn Bradley	.50
74	B.J. Tyler	.50
75	Clarence Weatherspoon	.50
76	Sharone Wright	1.00
77	Charles Barkley	1.00
78	Kevin Johnson	.50
79	Dan Majerle	.50
80	Danny Manning	.50
81	Wesley Person	.50
82	Aaron McKie	.50
83	Cliff Robinson	.50
84	Rod Strickland	.25
85	*Brian Grant*	2.00
86	Bobby Hurley	.25
87	Mitch Richmond	.50
88	Sean Elliott	.25
89	David Robinson	2.00
90	Dennis Rodman	2.00
91	Shawn Kemp	1.00
92	Gary Payton	.75
93	Dontonio Wingfield	.50
94	Jeff Hornacek	.25
95	Karl Malone	1.00
96	John Stockton	1.00
97	Calbert Cheaney	.50
98	*Juwan Howard*	4.00
99	Chris Webber	1.50
100	Michael Jordan	13.00
101	Brian Grant	.75
102	Grant Hill	4.00
103	Juwan Howard	1.00
104	Eddie Jones	.75
105	Jason Kidd	2.00
106	Eric Montross	.50
107	Lamond Murray	.50
108	Wesley Person	.50
109	Glenn Robinson	1.00
110	Sharone Wright	.50
111	Anfernee Hardaway	2.50
112	Shawn Kemp	.50
113	Karl Malone	.75
114	Alonzo Mourning	.75
115	Shaquille O'Neal	2.00
116	Hakeem Olajuwon	1.00
117	Scottie Pippen	.50
118	David Robinson	1.00
119	Latrell Sprewell	.75
120	Chris Webber	.75
121	Checklist	.25
NNO	G. Hill Skymotion	50.00

1994-95 E-Motion N-Tense

These 1994-95 SkyBox E-Motion insert cards, featuring NBA "interior" players who attack on the inside, were seeded one per every 18 packs. The card front has a color action shot, with a gold metallic background. The player's last name is stamped in foil along the left side; foil stamping is also used for the brand and insert set logos on the front. The back has a full-bleed action shot, with the player's last name written near the bottom of the card. Cards are numbered using an "N" prefix.

		MT
Complete Set (10):		100.00
Common Player:		5.00
1	Charles Barkley	8.00
2	Patrick Ewing	5.00
3	Michael Jordan	50.00
4	Shawn Kemp	5.00
5	Karl Malone	5.00
6	Alonzo Mourning	5.00
7	Shaquille O'Neal	20.00
8	Hakeem Olajuwon	8.00
9	David Robinson	8.00
10	Glenn Robinson	6.00

1994-95 E-Motion X-Cited

These 20 cards feature NBA players who dominate the perimeter. Cards were randomly inserted into 1994-95 SkyBox packs, one every fourth pack. The metallic front has the player's last name spelled out across the top; gold foil stamping is used for the insert set and brand logos. The back is numbered using an "X" prefix.

		MT
Complete Set (20):		70.00
Common Player:		1.00
Minor Stars:		2.00
1	Kenny Anderson	2.00
2	Anfernee Hardaway	12.00
3	Tim Hardaway	2.00
4	Grant Hill	15.00
5	Jimmy Jackson	3.00
6	Eddie Jones	7.00
7	Jason Kidd	10.00
8	Dan Majerle	1.00
9	Jamal Mashburn	3.00
10	Lamond Murray	2.00
11	Gary Payton	3.00
12	Wesley Person	2.00
13	Scottie Pippen	7.00
14	Mark Price	2.00
15	Mitch Richmond	1.00
16	Isaiah Rider	2.00
17	Latrell Sprewell	2.00
18	John Stockton	3.00
19	Rod Strickland	1.00
20	Nick Van Exel	3.00

1995-96 E-XL

In what is considered by Fleer/SkyBox to be an "evolution of E-Motion," this 100-card set includes 73 veterans, 17 rookies, nine Untouchables subset cards and a checklist. Regular player cards feature silhouetted action photos over a multi-colored background framed in one of five different die-cut window designs. The black borders around the card are printed on non-coated stock, which gives each card a unique look and feel. The card back has a player action photo, stats, the player's name, a card number and a brief player profile. Four insert sets were made - Unstoppable, No Boundaries, Natural Born Thrillers and A Cut Above.

		MT
Complete Set (100):		50.00
Common Player:		.20
Minor Stars:		.40
Comp. Blue Set (100):		100.00
Blue Cards:		2x
Pack (7):		2.50
Wax Box (24):		50.00
1	Stacey Augmon	.20
2	Mookie Blaylock	.20
3	Christian Laettner	.20
4	Dana Barros	.20
5	Dino Radja	.20
6	*Eric Williams*	.75
7	Kenny Anderson	.20
8	Larry Johnson	.75
9	Glen Rice	.20
10	Michael Jordan	10.00
11	Toni Kukoc	.20
12	Scottie Pippen	2.00
13	Dennis Rodman	3.00
14	Terrell Brandon	.20
15	Bobby Phills	.20
16	*Bob Sura*	.40
17	Jim Jackson	.50
18	Jason Kidd	2.00
19	Jamal Mashburn	.50
20	Mahmoud Abdul-Rauf	.20
21	*Antonio McDyess*	4.00
22	Dikembe Mutombo	.40
23	Joe Dumars	.20
24	Grant Hill	3.00
25	Allan Houston	.20
26	*Joe Smith*	2.00

27	Latrell Sprewell	.40
28	Kevin Willis	.20
29	Sam Cassell	.20
30	Clyde Drexler	1.00
31	Robert Horry	.20
32	Hakeem Olajuwon	2.00
33	Derrick McKey	.20
34	Reggie Miller	1.00
35	Rik Smits	.20
36	*Brent Barry*	1.00
37	Loy Vaught	.20
38	Brian Williams	.20
39	Cedric Ceballos	.50
40	Magic Johnson	3.00
41	Nick Van Exel	.50
42	Tim Hardaway	.40
43	Alonzo Mourning	.75
44	*Kurt Thomas*	.75
45	Walt Williams	.20
46	Vin Baker	.75
47	*Shawn Respert*	.50
48	Glenn Robinson	1.25
49	*Kevin Garnett*	12.00
50	Tom Gugliotta	.20
51	Isaiah Rider	.20
52	Shawn Bradley	.20
53	Chris Childs	.20
54	*Ed O'Bannon*	.40
55	Patrick Ewing	.75
56	Anthony Mason	.20
57	Charles Oakley	.20
58	Horace Grant	.40
59	Anfernee Hardaway	5.00
60	Shaquille O'Neal	4.00
61	Derrick Coleman	.20
62	*Jerry Stackhouse*	5.00
63	Clarence Weatherspoon	.20
64	Charles Barkley	1.25
65	*Michael Finley*	4.00
66	Kevin Johnson	.40
67	Clifford Robinson	.20
68	*Arvydas Sabonis*	2.00
69	Rod Strickland	.20
70	*Tyus Edney*	.40
71	Billy Owens	.20
72	Mitch Richmond	.40
73	Sean Elliot	.20
74	Avery Johnson	.20
75	David Robinson	1.50
76	Shawn Kemp	1.00
77	Gary Payton	.60
78	Detlef Schrempf	.20
79	Tracy Murray	.20
80	*Damon Stoudamire*	2.00
81	Sharone Wright	.20
82	Jeff Hornacek	.20
83	Karl Malone	.75
84	John Stockton	.75
85	Greg Anthony	.20
86	*Bryant Reeves*	1.50
87	Byron Scott	.20
88	Juwan Howard	1.50
89	Gheorghe Muresan	.20
90	*Rasheed Wallace*	4.00
91	Steve Smith	.20
92	Dikembe Mutombo	.20
93	Brent Barry	.40
94	Glenn Robinson	.40
95	Armon Gilliam	.20
96	Nick Anderson	.20
97	Gary Trent	.20
98	Brian Grant	.20
99	Bryant Reeves	.40
100	Checklist	.20

1995-96 E-XL Blue

This insert paralleled the black bordered, or regular- issue cards, but were inserted one or more per pack. The cards featured a dark blue border instead of the black border on regular-issue cards. Blues carry a slight premium in pricing.

	MT
Complete Set (100):	100.00
Blue Cards:	2x

1995-96 E-XL A Cut Above

These are the most difficult inserts to find in SkyBox's 1995-96 E-XL basketball product; cards are seeded one per every 130 packs. Cards from this 10-card set are constructed on three different layers. The first layer contains an action photo on a UV-coated background, the second layer has a die-cut photo mounted in the foreground, while the third layer presents a navy blue non-coated frame that is embossed and foil stamped.

		MT
Complete Set (10):		150.00
Common Player:		10.00
Inserted 1:130		
1	Scottie Pippen	25.00
2	Jason Kidd	25.00
3	Grant Hill	40.00
4	Joe Smith	8.00
5	Hakeem Olajuwon	12.00
6	Magic Johnson	18.00
7	Shaquille O'Neal	40.00
8	Jerry Stackhouse	10.00
9	Charles Barkley	12.00
10	David Robinson	12.00

1995-96 E-XL Natural Born Thrillers

Ten of the NBA's top crowd pleasers are showcased in this 1995-96 SkyBox E-XL insert set. The cards use a die-cut look similar to SkyBox's SkyView inserts. Each player's image is partly on the card and partly off, due to the image being over a die-cut window. "Natural Born Thrillers" is written at the bottom of the card; "Born" is in gold foil, as is the player's name and SkyBox logo. The card back is black, with gold foil used for the icons at the bottom, plus the brief player profile and card number (1 of 10, etc.). A pencil-like etching of the player is also on the back. Cards were seeded one per every 48 packs.

		MT
Complete Set (10):		200.00
Common Player:		10.00
Inserted 1:48		
1	Michael Jordan	100.00
2	Antonio McDyess	12.00
3	Grant Hill	30.00
4	Clyde Drexler	10.00
5	Kevin Garnett	45.00
6	Anfernee Hardaway	20.00
7	Jerry Stackhouse	12.00
8	Michael Finley	12.00
9	Shawn Kemp	5.00
10	Damon Stoudamire	10.00

1995-96 E-XL No Boundaries

These 1995-96 SkyBox E-XL inserts were exclusive to hobby packs only, one per every 18 packs. The cards feature 10 players who are the heart and soul of their team. The front has a color action photo against a metallic background. The brand logo, set icon and player's name are stamped in gold foil and are located in three corners. The card back is printed on white card stock with a die-cut set of brackets around a player profile. A die-cut area also has a circular mug shot photo inside it. The card number is in the upper right corner (1 of 10, etc.).

		MT
Complete Set (10):		75.00
Common Player:		3.00
Inserted 1:18 Hobby		
1	Michael Jordan	40.00
2	Antonio McDyess	8.00
3	Hakeem Olajuwon	5.00
4	Magic Johnson	10.00
5	Vin Baker	3.00
6	Patrick Ewing	3.00
7	Anfernee Hardaway	10.00
8	Jerry Stackhouse	5.00
9	Gary Payton	8.00
10	Damon Stoudamire	5.00

1995-96 E-XL Unstoppable

These were the most common 1995-96 SkyBox E-XL insert cards produced; they were seeded one per every six packs. The cards feature 20 players who can take over a game. Each card front has a color action photo, with a black circle in the background which has "Unstoppable" written in gold foil along the arc. Gold foil is also used for the player's name along the bottom, and the brand logo in the upper left corner. The card back is dominated by a close-up shot of the player. A brief description of why the player is considered unstoppable is beneath the player photo. "Unstoppable" is written along the left side of the card; a card number, 1 of 20, etc., is in the upper right corner.

		MT
Complete Set (20):		50.00
Common Player:		1.00
Inserted 1:6		
1	Alan Henderson	1.00
2	Glen Rice	1.00
3	Scottie Pippen	8.00
4	Dennis Rodman	5.00
5	Terrell Brandon	1.00
6	Jason Kidd	8.00
7	Grant Hill	12.00
8	Joe Smith	4.00
9	Sam Cassell	1.00
10	Reggie Miller	3.00
11	Alonzo Mourning	2.00
12	Shaquille O'Neal	12.00
13	Charles Barkley	4.00
14	Clifford Robinson	1.00
15	Sean Elliot	1.00
16	David Robinson	4.00
17	Shawn Kemp	2.00
18	Karl Malone	4.00
19	John Stockton	2.00
20	Juwan Howard	1.00

1996-97 E-X2000

E-X2000 Basketball was an 80-card set featuring SkyView technology that had previously been used in 1995-96 NBA Hoops Series II SkyView inserts. The technology utilized a die-cut holofoil border and the player silhouetted in front of a transparent window featuring a variety of sky patterns. Inserts include: Star Date 2000, Net Assets, Autographs, A Cut Above and the parallel Credentials insert. E-X2000 arrived in two-card packs and carried exclusive Autographics inserts of Damon Stoudamire, Antoine Walker and Kerry Kittles.

		MT
Complete Set (80):		400.00
Common Player:		.75
Minor Stars:		1.50
Pack (2):		20.00
Wax Box (24):		400.00
1	Christian Laettner	.75
2	Dikembe Mutombo	.75
3	Steve Smith	.75
4	*Antoine Walker*	8.00
5	David Wesley	.75
6	*Tony Delk*	3.00
7	Anthony Mason	.75
8	Glen Rice	1.50
9	Michael Jordan	15.00
10	Scottie Pippen	4.00
11	Dennis Rodman	5.00
12	Terrell Brandon	.75
13	Chris Mills	.75
14	Shawn Bradley	.75
15	Michael Finley	.75
16	Dale Ellis	.75
17	Antonio McDyess	2.00
18	Joe Dumars	.75
19	Grant Hill	8.00
20	Chris Mullin	.75
21	Joe Smith	2.00
22	Latrell Sprewell	1.50
23	Charles Barkley	2.00
24	Clyde Drexler	1.50
25	Hakeem Olajuwon	4.00
26	*Erick Dampier*	3.00
27	Reggie Miller	1.50
28	Loy Vaught	.75
29	*Lorenzen Wright*	5.00
30	*Kobe Bryant*	125.00
31	Eddie Jones	3.00
32	Shaquille O'Neal	5.00
33	Nick Van Exel	.75
34	Tim Hardaway	.75
35	Jamal Mashburn	.75
36	Alonzo Mourning	1.50
37	*Ray Allen*	25.00
38	Vin Baker	1.50
39	Glenn Robinson	1.50
40	Kevin Garnett	8.00
41	Tom Gugliotta	.75
42	*Stephon Marbury*	25.00
43	Kendall Gill	.75
44	*Kerry Kittles*	10.00
45	Jim Jackson	.75
46	Patrick Ewing	1.50
47	Larry Johnson	.75
48	*John Wallace*	5.00
49	Nick Anderson	.75
50	Horace Grant	.75
51	Anfernee Hardaway	5.00
52	Derrick Coleman	.75
53	*Allen Iverson*	50.00
54	Jerry Stackhouse	1.00
55	Cedric Ceballos	.75
56	Kevin Johnson	.75
57	Jason Kidd	2.00
58	Clifford Robinson	.75
59	Arvydas Sabonis	.75
60	Rasheed Wallace	.75
61	Mahmoud Abdul-Rauf	.75
62	Brian Grant	.75
63	Mitch Richmond	1.50
64	Sean Elliott	.75
65	David Robinson	2.00
66	Dominique Wilkins	.75
67	Shawn Kemp	2.00
68	Gary Payton	2.00
69	Detlef Schrempf	.75
70	*Marcus Camby*	15.00
71	Damon Stoudamire	3.00
72	Walt Williams	.75
73	Shandon Anderson	.75
74	Karl Malone	2.00
75	John Stockton	2.00
76	*Shareef Abdur-Rahim*	20.00
77	Bryant Reeves	.75
78	Roy Rogers	.75
79	Juwan Howard	2.00
80	Chris Webber	2.00
81	Checklist	.75
82	Checklist	.75

1996-97 E-X2000 Credentials

Credentials paralleled all 80 cards in the 1996-97 E-X2000 basketball set. These inserts are printed on holographic silver foil and sequentially numbered up to 499. The word "Credentials" is printed across the top of the card on these one-per-50-pack inserts.

	MT
Credential Rookies:	6x-12x
Credential Stars:	12x-24x

1996-97 E-X2000 A Cut Above

This 10-card insert featured color shots of the player over a holographic foil saw blade, which was die-cut on the top in the saw blade shape. The words "Cut Above" and the player's name appears in the lower left corner and is slightly embossed. A Cut Above inserts were seeded every 288 packs of E-X2000.

		MT
Complete Set (10):		700.00
Common Player:		20.00
1	Allen Iverson	90.00
2	Anfernee Hardaway	60.00
3	Dennis Rodman	60.00
4	Glenn Robinson	20.00
5	Grant Hill	100.00
6	Hakeem Olajuwon	30.00
7	Kevin Garnett	90.00
8	Michael Jordan	225.00
9	Shaquille O'Neal	60.00
10	Shawn Kemp	20.00

1996-97 E-X2000 Net Assets

Net Assets featured 20 cards die-cut in the shape of a basketball net, with the ball going through it. Sections of the net and the insert name, which runs across the top in yellow letters, are all die-cut. One per 20 packs included this insert, which was numbered "of 20".

		MT
Complete Set (20):		220.00
Common Player:		2.00
1	Ray Allen	10.00
2	Charles Barkley	6.00
3	Patrick Ewing	2.00
4	Kevin Garnett	25.00
5	Anfernee Hardaway	15.00
6	Grant Hill	30.00
7	Allen Iverson	25.00
8	Michael Jordan	50.00
9	Jason Kidd	2.00
10	Kerry Kittles	8.00
11	Karl Malone	4.00
12	Alonzo Mourning	4.00
13	Shaquille O'Neal	20.00
14	Gary Payton	4.00
15	Bryant Reeves	2.00
16	David Robinson	6.00
17	Dennis Rodman	20.00
18	Joe Smith	6.00
19	Damon Stoudamire	8.00
20	Chris Webber	6.00

1996-97 E-X2000 Star Date 2000

Star Date 2000 showcased 15 top rookies from the 1996-97 season on an outer space background. The insert name, player's name and team appeared in the lower left corner. Star Date 2000 inserts were found in every nine packs of E-X2000.

		MT
Complete Set (15):		100.00
Common Player:		1.50
1	Shareef Abdur-Rahim	12.00
2	Ray Allen	8.00
3	Kobe Bryant	25.00
4	Marcus Camby	12.00
5	Erick Dampier	1.50
6	Juwan Howard	5.00
7	Allen Iverson	20.00
8	Jason Kidd	3.00
9	Kerry Kittles	6.00
10	Stephon Marbury	16.00
11	Jamal Mashburn	1.50
12	Antonio McDyess	3.00
13	Joe Smith	5.00
14	Damon Stoudamire	7.00
15	Antoine Walker	8.00

1997-98 E-X2001

E-X2001 was an 80-card, super-premium set that was available to hobby stores only. The base cards arrived two per pack and were two layered, with one layer containing a die-cut image of the player over a prismatic background, with the other layer consisting of thick plastic that is clear on the right side, but in team colors as it fades behind the player. E-X2001 arrived with an Essential Credentials Now and Future parallel sets, as well as Stardate 2001, Gravity Denied, Jam-Balaya and Autographics inserts.

		MT
Complete Set (80):		125.00
Common Player:		.50
Minor Stars:		1.00
Pack (2):		5.00
Wax Box:		120.00
1	Grant Hill	6.00
2	Kevin Garnett	6.00
3	Allen Iverson	5.00
4	Anfernee Hardaway	4.00
5	Dennis Rodman	4.00
6	Shawn Kemp	1.50
7	Shaquille O'Neal	4.00
8	Kobe Bryant	10.00
9	Michael Jordan	15.00
10	Marcus Camby	1.00
11	Scottie Pippen	3.00
12	Antoine Walker	3.00
13	Stephon Marbury	5.00
14	Shareef Abdur-Rahim	3.00
15	Jerry Stackhouse	1.00
16	Eddie Jones	2.00
17	Charles Barkley	1.50
18	David Robinson	1.50
19	Karl Malone	1.25
20	Damon Stoudamire	2.00
21	Patrick Ewing	1.00
22	Kerry Kittles	1.00
23	Gary Payton	1.25
24	Glenn Robinson	1.00
25	Hakeem Olajuwon	2.00
26	John Starks	.50
27	John Stockton	1.00
28	Vin Baker	1.50
29	Reggie Miller	1.00
30	Clyde Drexler	1.25
31	Alonzo Mourning	1.00
32	Juwan Howard	1.25
33	Ray Allen	1.25
34	Christian Laettner	1.00
35	Terrell Brandon	1.00
36	Sean Elliott	.50
37	Rod Strickland	1.00
38	Rodney Rogers	.50
39	Donyell Marshall	.50
40	David Wesley	.50
41	Sam Cassell	.50
42	Cedric Ceballos	.50
43	Mahmoud Abdul-Rauf	.50
44	Rik Smits	.50
45	Lindsey Hunter	.50
46	Michael Finley	1.00
47	Steve Smith	.50
48	Larry Johnson	1.00
49	Dikembe Mutombo	.50
50	Tom Gugliotta	1.00
51	Joe Dumars	.50
52	Glen Rice	1.00
53	Bryant Reeves	.50
54	Tim Hardaway	1.00
55	Isaiah Rider	.50
56	Rasheed Wallace	.50
57	Jason Kidd	1.50
58	Joe Smith	1.00
59	Chris Webber	2.00
60	Mitch Richmond	1.00
61	Antonio McDyess	1.00
62	*Bobby Jackson*	5.00
63	*Derek Anderson*	5.00
64	*Kelvin Cato*	1.50
65	*Jacque Vaughn*	1.50
66	*Tariq Abdul-Wahad*	1.00
67	*Johnny Taylor*	1.00
68	*Chris Anstey*	1.00
69	*Maurice Taylor*	4.00
70	*Antonio Daniels*	4.00
71	*Chauncey Billups*	5.00
72	*Austin Croshere*	1.50
73	*Brevin Knight*	5.00
74	*Keith Van Horn*	8.00
75	*Tim Duncan*	30.00
76	*Danny Fortson*	2.00
77	*Tim Thomas*	10.00
78	*Tony Battie*	2.00
79	*Tracy McGrady*	30.00
80	*Ron Mercer*	15.00
	Grant Hill Sample	6.00
	Grant Hill Hawaii	20.00

1997-98 E-X2001 Essential Credentials Future

Essential Credentials Future cards were parallel to the 80-card E-X2001 set. The cards were printed on a pinkish red color plastic, with a holographic cardboard strip on the left side and the parallels name in small letters above his number on the plastic part. Cards were sequentially numbered to 81 minus the card number. For example, Shareef Abdur-Rahim is card No. 14 so his Future card is numbered to 67 (81-14). Together with the Now parallel, the total number of cards equal 81. The set is called Future because the rookies in the set, numbers 62-80 are the shortest printed cards.

		MT
Common Player:		50.00
Unable To Price #70-80		
1	Grant Hill	450.00
2	Kevin Garnett	450.00
3	Allen Iverson	350.00
4	Anfernee Hardaway	250.00
5	Dennis Rodman	250.00
6	Shawn Kemp	100.00
7	Shaquille O'Neal	250.00
8	Kobe Bryant	700.00
9	Michael Jordan	1000.
10	Marcus Camby	50.00
11	Scottie Pippen	200.00
12	Antoine Walker	125.00
13	Stephon Marbury	300.00
14	Shareef Abdur-Rahim	225.00
15	Jerry Stackhouse	75.00
16	Eddie Jones	125.00
17	Charles Barkley	100.00
18	David Robinson	100.00
19	Karl Malone	100.00
20	Damon Stoudamire	120.00
21	Patrick Ewing	75.00
22	Kerry Kittles	75.00
23	Gary Payton	100.00
24	Glenn Robinson	75.00
25	Hakeem Olajuwon	150.00
26	John Starks	50.00
27	John Stockton	75.00
28	Vin Baker	100.00
29	Reggie Miller	75.00
30	Clyde Drexler	100.00
31	Alonzo Mourning	75.00
32	Juwan Howard	75.00
33	Ray Allen	75.00
34	Christian Laettner	50.00
35	Terrell Brandon	50.00
36	Sean Elliott	50.00
37	Rod Strickland	50.00
38	Rodney Rogers	50.00
39	Donyell Marshall	50.00
40	David Wesley	50.00
41	Sam Cassell	50.00
42	Cedric Ceballos	50.00
43	Mahmoud Abdul-Rauf	50.00
44	Rik Smits	50.00
45	Lindsey Hunter	50.00
46	Michael Finley	100.00
47	Steve Smith	75.00
48	Larry Johnson	75.00
49	Dikembe Mutombo	75.00
50	Tom Gugliotta	75.00
51	Joe Dumars	75.00
52	Glen Rice	100.00
53	Bryant Reeves	75.00
54	Tim Hardaway	150.00
55	Isaiah Rider	75.00
56	Rasheed Wallace	75.00
57	Jason Kidd	300.00
58	Joe Smith	100.00
59	Chris Webber	300.00
60	Mitch Richmond	125.00
61	Antonio McDyess	150.00
62	*Bobby Jackson*	100.00
63	*Derek Anderson*	225.00
64	*Kelvin Cato*	100.00
65	*Jacque Vaughn*	120.00
66	*Tariq Abdul-Wahad*	100.00
67	*Johnny Taylor*	120.00
68	*Chris Anstey*	120.00
69	*Maurice Taylor*	250.00
70	*Antonio Daniels*	300.00

1997-98 E-X2001 Essential Credentials Now

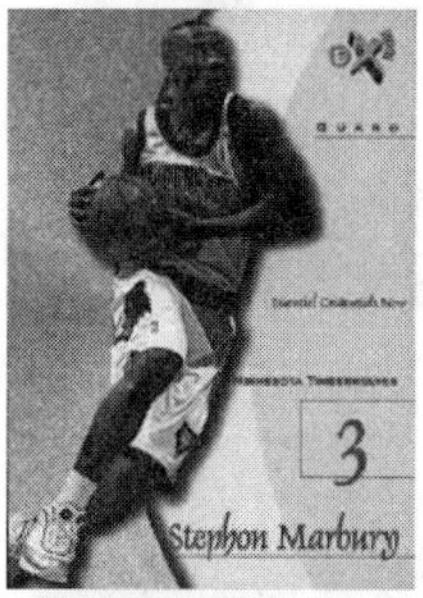

Essential Credentials Now was a parallel set that reprinted all 80 cards on a greenish yellow plastic stock. The cards also had a holographic cardboard strip up the left side and the insert name printed in small letters above his number. Cards were sequentially numbered to the player's card number in the set. For example, Shareef Abdur-Rahim is card No. 14, so he would have 14 Now cards. Together with the Future parallel, the total parallel cards for each player added up to 81.

		MT
Common Player:		50.00
Unable To Price #1-10		
11	Scottie Pippen	600.00
12	Antoine Walker	500.00
13	Stephon Marbury	800.00
14	Shareef Abdur-Rahim	600.00
15	Jerry Stackhouse	175.00
16	Eddie Jones	400.00
17	Charles Barkley	300.00
18	David Robinson	300.00
19	Karl Malone	300.00
20	Damon Stoudamire	250.00
21	Patrick Ewing	175.00
22	Kerry Kittles	150.00
23	Gary Payton	175.00
24	Glenn Robinson	100.00
25	Hakeem Olajuwon	225.00
26	John Starks	50.00
27	John Stockton	175.00
28	Vin Baker	200.00
29	Reggie Miller	200.00
30	Clyde Drexler	175.00
31	Alonzo Mourning	100.00
32	Juwan Howard	100.00
33	Ray Allen	100.00
34	Christian Laettner	50.00
35	Terrell Brandon	75.00
36	Sean Elliott	50.00
37	Rod Strickland	50.00
38	Rodney Rogers	50.00
39	Donyell Marshall	50.00
40	David Wesley	50.00
41	Sam Cassell	50.00
42	Cedric Ceballos	50.00
43	Mahmoud Abdul-Rauf	50.00
44	Rik Smits	50.00
45	Lindsey Hunter	50.00
46	Michael Finley	75.00
47	Steve Smith	50.00
48	Larry Johnson	75.00
49	Dikembe Mutombo	75.00
50	Tom Gugliotta	75.00
51	Joe Dumars	50.00
52	Glen Rice	75.00
53	Bryant Reeves	50.00
54	Tim Hardaway	100.00
55	Isaiah Rider	50.00
56	Rasheed Wallace	50.00
57	Jason Kidd	125.00
58	Joe Smith	75.00
59	Chris Webber	175.00
60	Mitch Richmond	75.00
61	Antonio McDyess	75.00
62	*Bobby Jackson*	75.00
63	*Derek Anderson*	100.00
64	*Kelvin Cato*	50.00
65	*Jacque Vaughn*	50.00
66	*Tariq Abdul-Wahad*	50.00
67	*Johnny Taylor*	50.00
68	*Chris Anstey*	50.00
69	*Maurice Taylor*	100.00
70	*Antonio Daniels*	100.00
71	*Chauncey Billups*	100.00
72	*Austin Croshere*	50.00
73	*Brevin Knight*	100.00
74	*Keith Van Horn*	125.00
75	*Tim Duncan*	400.00
76	*Danny Fortson*	50.00
77	*Tim Thomas*	100.00
78	*Tony Battie*	75.00
79	*Tracy McGrady*	275.00
80	*Ron Mercer*	150.00

1997-98 E-X2001 Gravity Denied

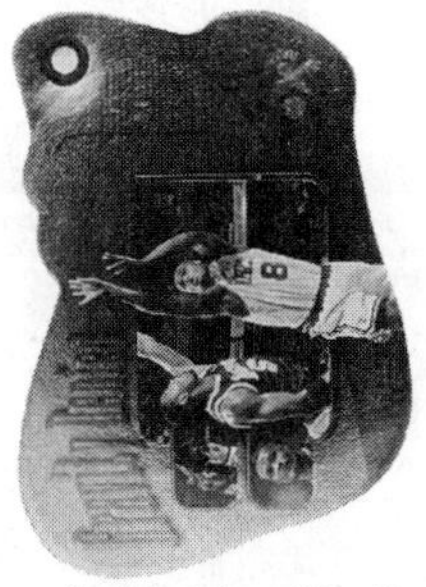

Gravity Denied was a 20-card insert set that was inserted one per 24 packs of E-X2001. It featured a clear plastic layer with a color image of the player that was hinged over a silver foil card. When the two cards were moved over each other, the pictures lined up with each other. An actual metal hinge was placed in the top right corner, while card backs were numbered with a "GD" suffix.

		MT
Complete Set (20):		275.00
Common Player:		3.00
1	Vin Baker	8.00
2	Charles Barkley	8.00
3	Tony Battie	6.00
4	Kobe Bryant	45.00
5	Patrick Ewing	3.00
6	Kevin Garnett	35.00
7	Anfernee Hardaway	25.00
8	Grant Hill	35.00
9	Michael Jordan	70.00
10	Shawn Kemp	10.00
11	Kerry Kittles	3.00
12	Karl Malone	6.00
13	Tracy McGrady	12.00
14	Hakeem Olajuwon	12.00
15	Shaquille O'Neal	20.00
16	Scottie Pippen	20.00
17	Jerry Stackhouse	6.00
18	Tim Thomas	12.00
19	Antoine Walker	15.00
20	Chris Webber	10.00

1997-98 E-X2001 Jam-Balaya

Jam-Balaya was a 15-card die-cut insert set that was limited to only one per 720 packs of E-X2001. Each card was die-cut with a prismatic, three-dimensional background to it and the insert's name written up the middle. Fronts and backs had a black border around the perimeter and was numbered with a "JB" suffix.

		MT
Complete Set (15):		1600.
Common Player:		40.00
1	Allen Iverson	225.00
2	Anfernee Hardaway	125.00
3	Dennis Rodman	125.00
4	Grant Hill	200.00
5	Kevin Garnett	200.00
6	Michael Jordan	600.00
7	Shaquille O'Neal	175.00
8	Tim Duncan	200.00
9	Keith Van Horn	80.00
10	Stephon Marbury	150.00
11	Shareef Abdur-Rahim	100.00
12	Kobe Bryant	400.00
13	Damon Stoudamire	40.00
14	Scottie Pippen	100.00
15	Eddie Jones	75.00

1997-98 E-X2001 Star Date 2001

This 15-card insert set captured the top rookies from the 1997 NBA Draft and was inserted one per 12 packs. Each card was die-cut with the player's image over a space background and the insert's name across the bottom. A closer image of the player was pictured on the back and the card was numbered with a "SD" suffix.

		MT
Complete Set (15):		100.00
Common Player:		2.00
1	Shareef Abdur-Rahim	8.00
2	Tony Battie	4.00
3	Kobe Bryant	20.00
4	Antonio Daniels	6.00
5	Tim Duncan	20.00
6	Adonal Foyle	4.00
7	Allen Iverson	12.00
8	Matt Maloney	2.00
9	Stephon Marbury	12.00
10	Tracy McGrady	8.00
11	Ron Mercer	10.00
12	Tim Thomas	8.00
13	Keith Van Horn	8.00
14	Jacque Vaughn	2.00
15	Antoine Walker	6.00

1998-99 SkyBox E-X Century

E-X Century continued the SkyBox brand that started in 1994-95 as E-Motion. The 90-card set included 60 veterans and 30 rookies seeded 1:1.5 packs. Cards were printed on thick plastic, with a cut-out player's image and team color strip over the top of it. The player's name runs down the right side in holographic letters. Inserts include: Generation E-X, Dunk 'N' Go Nuts, Authen-Kicks and Autographics. All 90 cards are also paralleled in Essential Credentials Now (numbered to the player's card number) and Essential Credentials Future (numbered to the number that combined with Essential Credentials Now equals 91).

		MT
Complete Set (90):		150.00
Common Player:		.25
Minor Stars:		.50
Pack (3):		90.00
Wax Box (18):		
1	Keith Van Horn	1.25
2	Scottie Pippen	1.50
3	Tim Thomas	1.00
4	Stephon Marbury	2.00
5	Allen Iverson	3.00
6	Grant Hill	5.00
7	Tim Duncan	5.00
8	Latrell Sprewell	.50
9	Ron Mercer	1.00
10	Kobe Bryant	6.00
11	Antoine Walker	1.00
12	Reggie Miller	.50
13	Kevin Garnett	5.00
14	Shaquille O'Neal	2.00
15	Karl Malone	.75
16	Dennis Rodman	1.00
17	Tracy McGrady	1.50
18	Anfernee Hardaway	2.00
19	Shareef Abdur-Rahim	1.00
20	Marcus Camby	.75
21	Eddie Jones	.75
22	Vin Baker	.50
23	Charles Barkley	.75
24	Patrick Ewing	.50
25	Jason Kidd	1.50
26	Mitch Richmond	.50
27	Tim Hardaway	.60
28	Glen Rice	.50
29	Shawn Kemp	.50
30	John Stockton	.50
31	Ray Allen	.60
32	Brevin Knight	.50
33	David Robinson	.75
34	Juwan Howard	.50
35	Alonzo Mourning	.60
36	Hakeem Olajuwon	.75
37	Gary Payton	.75
38	Damon Stoudamire	.60
39	Steve Smith	.50
40	Chris Webber	1.50
41	Michael Finley	.60
42	Jayson Williams	.50
43	Maurice Taylor	.75
44	Jalen Rose	.25
45	Sam Cassell	.25
46	Jerry Stackhouse	.25
47	Toni Kukoc	.60
48	Charles Oakley	.25
49	Jim Jackson	.25
50	Dikembe Mutombo	.25
51	Wesley Person	.25
52	Antonio Daniels	.25
53	Isaiah Rider	.25
54	Tom Gugliotta	.50
55	Antonio McDyess	.75
56	Jeff Hornacek	.25
57	Joe Dumars	.50
58	Jamal Mashburn	.50
59	Donyell Marshall	.25
60	Glenn Robinson	.50
61	*Jelani McCoy*	3.00
62	*Predrag Stojakovic*	10.00
63	*Randell Jackson*	1.00
64	*Brad Miller*	2.00
65	*Corey Benjamin*	2.00
66	*Toby Bailey*	1.00
67	*Nazr Mohammed*	1.00
68	*Dirk Nowitzki*	25.00
69	*Andrae Patterson*	1.00
70	*Michael Dickerson*	5.00
71	*Cory Carr*	1.00
72	*Brian Skinner*	2.00
73	*Pat Garrity*	2.00
74	*Ricky Davis*	5.00
75	*Roshown McLeod*	3.00
76	*Matt Harpring*	3.00
77	*Jason Williams*	10.00
78	*Keon Clark*	6.00
79	*Al Harrington*	6.00
80	*Felipe Lopez*	3.00
81	*Michael Doleac*	2.00
82	*Paul Pierce*	15.00
83	*Robert Traylor*	3.00
84	*Raef LaFrentz*	6.00
85	*Michael Olowokandi*	4.00
86	*Mike Bibby*	8.00
87	*Antawn Jamison*	20.00
88	*Bonzi Wells*	12.00
89	*Vince Carter*	50.00
90	*Larry Hughes*	12.00

1998-99 SkyBox E-X Century Essential Credentials Future

This 90-card parallel set was sequentially numbered to a number that, when combined with "Now", equals total production of 91 cards. This parallel features gold color vs. the clear plastic used in regular-issue cards.

		MT
Common Player:		20.00
Minor Stars:		30.00
Cards 82-90 Unable to Price		
1	Keith Van Horn	75.00
2	Scottie Pippen	100.00
3	Tim Thomas	75.00
4	Stephon Marbury	100.00
5	Allen Iverson	125.00
6	Grant Hill	200.00
7	Tim Duncan	200.00
8	Latrell Sprewell	30.00
9	Ron Mercer	75.00
10	Kobe Bryant	300.00
11	Antoine Walker	50.00
12	Reggie Miller	30.00
13	Kevin Garnett	200.00
14	Shaquille O'Neal	120.00
15	Karl Malone	50.00
16	Dennis Rodman	100.00
17	Tracy McGrady	125.00
18	Anfernee Hardaway	175.00
19	Shareef Abdur-Rahim	125.00
20	Marcus Camby	65.00
21	Eddie Jones	75.00
22	Vin Baker	60.00
23	Charles Barkley	75.00
24	Patrick Ewing	50.00
25	Jason Kidd	125.00
26	Mitch Richmond	50.00
27	Tim Hardaway	60.00
28	Glen Rice	40.00
29	Shawn Kemp	50.00
30	John Stockton	40.00
31	Ray Allen	75.00
32	Brevin Knight	30.00
33	David Robinson	100.00
34	Juwan Howard	40.00
35	Alonzo Mourning	60.00
36	Hakeem Olajuwon	100.00
37	Gary Payton	100.00
38	Damon Stoudamire	60.00
39	Steve Smith	40.00
40	Chris Webber	150.00
41	Michael Finley	60.00
42	Jayson Williams	40.00
43	Maurice Taylor	75.00
44	Jalen Rose	30.00
45	Sam Cassell	30.00
46	Jerry Stackhouse	40.00
47	Toni Kukoc	125.00
48	Charles Oakley	20.00
49	Jim Jackson	20.00
50	Dikembe Mutombo	30.00
51	Wesley Person	20.00
52	Antonio Daniels	60.00
53	Isaiah Rider	40.00
54	Tom Gugliotta	40.00
55	Antonio McDyess	100.00
56	Jeff Hornacek	20.00
57	Joe Dumars	50.00
58	Jamal Mashburn	50.00
59	Donyell Marshall	20.00
60	Glenn Robinson	75.00
61	*Jelani McCoy*	40.00
62	*Predrag Stojakovic*	40.00
63	*Randell Jackson*	30.00
64	*Brad Miller*	30.00
65	*Corey Benjamin*	40.00
66	*Toby Bailey*	30.00
67	*Nazr Mohammed*	40.00
68	*Dirk Nowitzki*	50.00
69	*Andrae Patterson*	40.00
70	*Michael Dickerson*	100.00
71	*Cory Carr*	40.00
72	*Brian Skinner*	60.00
73	*Pat Garrity*	50.00
74	*Ricky Davis*	100.00
75	*Roshown McLeod*	50.00
76	*Matt Harpring*	150.00
77	*Jason Williams*	500.00
78	*Keon Clark*	100.00
79	*Al Harrington*	200.00
80	*Felipe Lopez*	150.00
81	*Michael Doleac*	100.00

1998-99 SkyBox E-X Century Essential Credentials Now

This 90-card parallel set was sequentially numbered to that player's card number on the back of the regular- issue card. Cards featured a silver foil finish vs. the clear plastic of the regular-issue cards.

		MT
Common Player:		20.00
Minor Stars:		30.00
Cards 1-9 Unable to Price		
10	Kobe Bryant	750.00
11	Antoine Walker	250.00
12	Reggie Miller	125.00
13	Kevin Garnett	600.00
14	Shaquille O'Neal	500.00
15	Karl Malone	250.00
16	Dennis Rodman	300.00
17	Tracy McGrady	350.00
18	Anfernee Hardaway	500.00
19	Shareef Abdur-Rahim	300.00
20	Marcus Camby	200.00
21	Eddie Jones	150.00
22	Vin Baker	100.00
23	Charles Barkley	150.00
24	Patrick Ewing	100.00
25	Jason Kidd	250.00
26	Mitch Richmond	100.00
27	Tim Hardaway	125.00
28	Glen Rice	100.00
29	Shawn Kemp	100.00
30	John Stockton	100.00
31	Ray Allen	100.00
32	Brevin Knight	60.00
33	David Robinson	150.00
34	Juwan Howard	60.00
35	Alonzo Mourning	100.00
36	Hakeem Olajuwon	150.00
37	Gary Payton	150.00
38	Damon Stoudamire	75.00
39	Steve Smith	50.00
40	Chris Webber	200.00
41	Michael Finley	75.00
42	Jayson Williams	50.00
43	Maurice Taylor	100.00
44	Jalen Rose	30.00
45	Sam Cassell	30.00
46	Jerry Stackhouse	40.00
47	Toni Kukoc	125.00
48	Charles Oakley	30.00
49	Jim Jackson	30.00
50	Dikembe Mutombo	30.00
51	Wesley Person	20.00
52	Antonio Daniels	50.00
53	Isaiah Rider	30.00
54	Tom Gugliotta	40.00
55	Antonio McDyess	75.00
56	Jeff Hornacek	20.00
57	Joe Dumars	30.00
58	Jamal Mashburn	30.00
59	Donyell Marshall	20.00
60	Glenn Robinson	50.00
61	*Jelani McCoy*	30.00
62	*Predrag Stojakovic*	30.00
63	*Randell Jackson*	20.00
64	*Brad Miller*	20.00
65	*Corey Benjamin*	30.00
66	*Toby Bailey*	20.00
67	*Nazr Mohammed*	20.00
68	*Dirk Nowitzki*	30.00
69	*Andrae Patterson*	20.00
70	*Michael Dickerson*	50.00
71	*Cory Carr*	20.00
72	*Brian Skinner*	30.00
73	*Pat Garrity*	30.00
74	*Ricky Davis*	40.00
75	*Roshown McLeod*	30.00
76	*Matt Harpring*	40.00
77	*Jason Williams*	200.00
78	*Keon Clark*	40.00
79	*Al Harrington*	50.00
80	*Felipe Lopez*	40.00
81	*Michael Doleac*	30.00
82	*Paul Pierce*	150.00
83	*Robert Traylor*	50.00
84	*Raef LaFrentz*	50.00
85	*Michael Olowokandi*	50.00
86	*Mike Bibby*	75.00
87	*Antawn Jamison*	100.00
88	*Bonzi Wells*	30.00
89	*Vince Carter*	300.00
90	*Larry Hughes*	75.00

1998-99 SkyBox E-X Century Authen-Kicks

Authen-Kicks was Fleer/SkyBox's first mainstream game-used material on a card insert. It included game-worn sneaker swatches from 12 top young players, with one version including a leather swatch and the other version offering a piece of shoe lace. Cards were thick and horizontal in the format, with each card hand-numbered on the front. Quantities varied between players depending on how many cards could be made from the player's shoe, and are listed next to the player's name below.

		MT
Complete Set (12):		1250.
Common Player:		75.00
1	Antawn Jamison (285)	150.00
2	Tracy McGrady (225)	125.00
3	Ron Mercer (180)	90.00
4	Antoine Walker (125)	125.00
5	Mike Bibby (165)	100.00
6	Michael Dickerson (230)	75.00
7	Larry Hughes (115)	150.00
8	Raef LaFrentz (160)	75.00
9	Keith Van Horn (125)	100.00
9A	Keith Van Horn Auto (44)	400.00
10	Tim Thomas (215)	75.00
11	Allen Iverson (165)	300.00
12	Robert Traylor (215)	75.00

Post-1980 cards in Near Mint condition will generally sell for about 75% of the quoted Mint value. Excellent-condition cards bring no more than 40%.

1998-99 SkyBox E-X Century Dunk N'Go Nuts

This 20-card insert featured top athletes on thick plastic cards with the insert name, player's name and product logo printed in holographic letters in the background. Cards were inserted 1:36 packs and numbered with a "DG" suffix.

		MT
Complete Set (20):		225.00
Common Player:		3.00
Inserted 1:36		
1	Tim Thomas	8.00
2	Grant Hill	20.00
3	Shareef Abdur-Rahim	8.00
4	Tim Duncan	20.00
5	Allen Iverson	12.00
6	Kobe Bryant	30.00
7	Antoine Walker	5.00
8	Kevin Garnett	20.00
9	Shaquille O'Neal	12.00
10	Tracy McGrady	8.00
11	Antawn Jamison	12.00
12	Vince Carter	25.00
13	Robert Traylor	5.00
14	Scottie Pippen	10.00
15	Michael Jordan	50.00
16	Michael Olowokandi	5.00
17	Anfernee Hardaway	12.00
18	Michael Dickerson	3.00
19	Ron Mercer	8.00
20	Felipe Lopez	3.00

1998-99 SkyBox E-X Century Generation E-X

This 15-card insert was composed of players with three or less years of NBA experience. Each card featured an interior die-cut of the player's image surrounded by a black border. Generation E-X cards were inserted 1:18 packs and numbered with a "GE" suffix.

		MT
Complete Set (15):		90.00
Common Player:		2.00
Inserted 1:18		
1	Larry Hughes	8.00
2	Michael Olowokandi	6.00
3	Tim Duncan	12.00
4	Vince Carter	25.00
5	Antawn Jamison	10.00
6	Kevin Garnett	12.00
7	Al Harrington	2.00
8	Mike Bibby	8.00
9	Raef LaFrentz	6.00
10	Ron Mercer	5.00
11	Tracy McGrady	5.00
12	Kobe Bryant	15.00
13	Keith Van Horn	4.00
14	Stephon Marbury	8.00
15	Allen Iverson	10.00

1999-00 E-X

This 90-card set included 60 veterans and 30 rookies, which were numbered to 3,499. E-X shortened its name in 1999-00 after years of changing from things like E-XL, E-X2000, E-X2001 and E-X Century, and also went to a single-layer card instead of the double-layered plastic cards used for the past two years. The set was paralleled twice - Essential Credentials Now and Essential Credentials Future. Inserts included: E-Xceptional Red, Green and Blue, E-Xciting, E-Xplosive, E-Xplosive Autographs, Generation E-X and Genuine Coverage.

		MT
Complete Set (90):		200.00
Common Player:		.25
Minor Stars:		.40
Common Rookie:		5.00
Production 3,499 Sets		
Pack (9):		6.00
Wax Box (36):		70.00
1	Stephon Marbury	1.00
2	Antawn Jamison	1.25
3	Patrick Ewing	.40
4	Nick Anderson	.25
5	Charles Barkley	.75
6	Marcus Camby	.60
7	Ron Mercer	.75
8	Avery Johnson	.25
9	Maurice Taylor	.25
10	Isaiah Rider	.25
11	Dirk Nowitzki	1.00
12	Damon Stoudamire	.50
13	Alonzo Mourning	.50
14	Jason Kidd	1.50
15	Juwan Howard	.40
16	Vince Carter	4.00
17	Tim Duncan	3.00
18	Paul Pierce	1.50
19	Tim Hardaway	.60
20	Grant Hill	3.00
21	Keith Van Horn	.75
22	Shaquille O'Neal	2.00
23	Jason Williams	1.50
24	Shareef Abdur-Rahim	1.00
25	Kobe Bryant	4.00
26	David Robinson	.75
27	Anfernee Hardaway	1.50
28	Vin Baker	.40
29	Hakeem Olajuwon	.75
30	Michael Olowokandi	.50
31	Mike Bibby	.50
32	Tracy McGrady	1.50
33	Antoine Walker	.60
34	Larry Hughes	.75
35	Chris Webber	1.50
36	Ray Allen	.50
37	Danny Fortson	.25
38	Shawn Kemp	.40
39	Michael Doleac	.40
40	Gary Payton	.75
41	Toni Kukoc	.50
42	Kevin Garnett	3.00
43	Steve Smith	.40
44	Scottie Pippen	1.50
45	Allen Iverson	2.00
46	Latrell Sprewell	.60
47	Matt Harpring	.40
48	Lindsey Hunter	.25
49	Karl Malone	.75
50	Michael Finley	.40
51	Jerry Stackhouse	.60
52	Cedric Ceballos	.25
53	Brent Barry	.25
54	Elden Campbell	.25
55	Glenn Robinson	.40
56	Eddie Jones	.75
57	Reggie Miller	.40
58	Mitch Richmond	.40
59	Raef LaFrentz	.60
60	John Starks	.25
61	*Elton Brand*	25.00
62	*William Avery*	8.00
63	*Cal Bowdler*	3.00
64	*Dion Glover*	5.00
65	*Lamar Odom*	35.00
66	*Richard Hamilton*	15.00
67	*Kenny Thomas*	8.00
68	*Shawn Marion*	25.00
69	*Baron Davis*	20.00
70	*Wally Szczerbiak*	15.00
71	*Scott Padgett*	5.00
72	*Jason Terry*	12.00
73	*Trajan Langdon*	10.00
74	*Andre Miller*	20.00
75	*Jeff Foster*	5.00
76	*Tim James*	5.00
77	*Alek Radojevic*	5.00
78	*Quincy Lewis*	6.00
79	*James Posey*	10.00
80	*Steve Francis*	50.00
81	*Jonathan Bender*	25.00
82	*Corey Maggette*	20.00
83	*Obinna Ekezie*	5.00
84	*Laron Profit*	6.00
85	*Devean George*	10.00
86	*Ron Artest*	12.00
87	*Rafer Alston*	6.00
88	*Vonteego Cummings*	8.00
89	*Evan Eschmeyer*	5.00
90	*Jumaine Jones*	6.00

1999-00 E-X Essential Credentials Future

This 90-card parallel set reprinted every card in E-X on plastic with a metallized background. Each card was sequentially numbered, with veterans numbered 60-1 and rookies numbered 30-1. For example, Lamar Odom is card No. 65, which means his Future card was sequentially numbered to 26, while Now cards were numbered to just 5. In this parallel, the total of Future and Now cards for veterans is 61 each and 31 each for rookies.

		MT
Common Player:		25.00
Minor Stars:		30.00
Veterans numbered 60-1		
Cards 51-60 Unpriced		
Rookies numbered 30-1		
Cards 81-90 Unpriced		
1	Stephon Marbury	75.00
2	Antawn Jamison	100.00
3	Patrick Ewing	30.00
4	Nick Anderson	25.00
5	Charles Barkley	75.00
6	Marcus Camby	30.00
7	Ron Mercer	50.00
8	Avery Johnson	25.00
9	Maurice Taylor	25.00
10	Isaiah Rider	25.00
11	Dirk Nowitzki	100.00
12	Damon Stoudamire	30.00
13	Alonzo Mourning	40.00
14	Jason Kidd	150.00
15	Juwan Howard	30.00
16	Vince Carter	500.00
17	Tim Duncan	300.00
18	Paul Pierce	100.00
19	Tim Hardaway	50.00
20	Grant Hill	300.00
21	Keith Van Horn	60.00
22	Shaquille O'Neal	300.00
23	Jason Williams	150.00
24	Shareef Abdur-Rahim	125.00
25	Kobe Bryant	500.00
26	David Robinson	75.00
27	Anfernee Hardaway	200.00
28	Vin Baker	25.00
29	Hakeem Olajuwon	75.00
30	Michael Olowokandi	40.00
31	Mike Bibby	75.00
32	Tracy McGrady	250.00
33	Antoine Walker	100.00
34	Larry Hughes	200.00
35	Chris Webber	250.00
36	Ray Allen	100.00
37	Danny Fortson	25.00
38	Shawn Kemp	50.00
39	Michael Doleac	25.00
40	Gary Payton	125.00
41	Toni Kukoc	150.00
42	Kevin Garnett	600.00
43	Steve Smith	40.00
44	Scottie Pippen	300.00
45	Allen Iverson	400.00
46	Latrell Sprewell	250.00
47	Matt Harpring	50.00
48	Lindsey Hunter	25.00
49	Karl Malone	200.00
50	Michael Finley	125.00
51	Jerry Stackhouse	
52	Cedric Ceballos	
53	Brent Barry	
54	Elden Campbell	
55	Glenn Robinson	
56	Eddie Jones	
57	Reggie Miller	
58	Mitch Richmond	
59	Raef LaFrentz	
60	John Starks	
61	*Elton Brand*	400.00
62	*William Avery*	60.00
63	*Cal Bowdler*	25.00
64	*Dion Glover*	40.00
65	*Lamar Odom*	400.00
66	*Richard Hamilton*	100.00
67	*Kenny Thomas*	75.00
68	*Shawn Marion*	150.00
69	*Baron Davis*	125.00
70	*Wally Szczerbiak*	150.00
71	*Scott Padgett*	40.00
72	*Jason Terry*	75.00
73	*Trajan Langdon*	75.00
74	*Andre Miller*	150.00
75	*Jeff Foster*	25.00
76	*Tim James*	40.00
77	*Alek Radojevic*	25.00
78	*Quincy Lewis*	50.00
79	*James Posey*	75.00
80	*Steve Francis*	750.00
81	*Jonathan Bender*	
82	*Corey Maggette*	
83	*Obinna Ekezie*	
84	*Laron Profit*	
85	*Devean George*	
86	*Ron Artest*	
87	*Rafer Alston*	
88	*Vonteego Cummings*	
89	*Evan Eschmeyer*	
90	*Jumaine Jones*	

1999-00 E-X Essential Credentials Now

This 90-card parallel set reprinted every card in E-X on plastic with a metallized background. Each card was sequentially numbered, with veterans numbered 1-60 and rookies numbered 1-30. For example, Lamar Odom is card No. 65, which means his Future card was sequentially numbered to 26, while Now cards were numbered to just 5. In this parallel, the total of Future and Now cards for veterans is 61 each and 31 each for rookies.

		MT
Common Player:		25.00
Minor Stars:		30.00
Veterans numbered 1-60		
Cards 1-10 Unpriced		
Rookies numbered 1-30		
Cards 61-70 Unpriced		
1	Stephon Marbury	
2	Antawn Jamison	
3	Patrick Ewing	
4	Nick Anderson	
5	Charles Barkley	
6	Marcus Camby	
7	Ron Mercer	
8	Avery Johnson	
9	Maurice Taylor	
10	Isaiah Rider	
11	Dirk Nowitzki	200.00
12	Damon Stoudamire	50.00
13	Alonzo Mourning	75.00
14	Jason Kidd	300.00
15	Juwan Howard	50.00
16	Vince Carter	1000.
17	Tim Duncan	500.00
18	Paul Pierce	175.00
19	Tim Hardaway	100.00
20	Grant Hill	500.00
21	Keith Van Horn	80.00
22	Shaquille O'Neal	400.00
23	Jason Williams	200.00
24	Shareef Abdur-Rahim	150.00
25	Kobe Bryant	600.00
26	David Robinson	125.00
27	Anfernee Hardaway	250.00
28	Vin Baker	40.00
29	Hakeem Olajuwon	125.00
30	Michael Olowokandi	40.00
31	Mike Bibby	75.00
32	Tracy McGrady	200.00
33	Antoine Walker	75.00
34	Larry Hughes	150.00
35	Chris Webber	200.00
36	Ray Allen	75.00
37	Danny Fortson	25.00
38	Shawn Kemp	40.00
39	Michael Doleac	25.00
40	Gary Payton	75.00
41	Toni Kukoc	75.00
42	Kevin Garnett	300.00
43	Steve Smith	30.00
44	Scottie Pippen	150.00
45	Allen Iverson	200.00
46	Latrell Sprewell	100.00
47	Matt Harpring	30.00
48	Lindsey Hunter	25.00
49	Karl Malone	75.00
50	Michael Finley	40.00
51	Jerry Stackhouse	40.00
52	Cedric Ceballos	25.00
53	Brent Barry	25.00
54	Elden Campbell	25.00
55	Glenn Robinson	30.00
56	Eddie Jones	100.00
57	Reggie Miller	30.00
58	Mitch Richmond	30.00
59	Raef LaFrentz	40.00
60	John Starks	25.00
61	*Elton Brand*	
62	*William Avery*	
63	*Cal Bowdler*	
64	*Dion Glover*	
65	*Lamar Odom*	
66	*Richard Hamilton*	
67	*Kenny Thomas*	
68	*Shawn Marion*	
69	*Baron Davis*	
70	*Wally Szczerbiak*	
71	*Scott Padgett*	50.00
72	*Jason Terry*	75.00
73	*Trajan Langdon*	75.00
74	*Andre Miller*	200.00
75	*Jeff Foster*	40.00
76	*Tim James*	50.00
77	*Alek Radojevic*	25.00
78	*Quincy Lewis*	60.00
79	*James Posey*	75.00
80	*Steve Francis*	600.00
81	*Jonathan Bender*	250.00
82	*Corey Maggette*	150.00
83	*Obinna Ekezie*	25.00
84	*Laron Profit*	40.00
85	*Devean George*	60.00
86	*Ron Artest*	125.00
87	*Rafer Alston*	50.00
88	*Vonteego Cummings*	75.00
89	*Evan Eschmeyer*	30.00
90	*Jumaine Jones*	30.00

1999-00 E-X E-Xceptional

This 15-card set featured top stars on a die-cut, Warp Tek design. Cards were numbered with an "XC" suffix and inserted 1:16 packs. Basic versions of this insert featured a red background, while the parallel sets were distinguished by a different color background - Green (numbered to 500) and Blue (numbered to 250).

		MT
Complete Set (15):		75.00
Common Player:		2.00
Inserted 1:16		
Green Parallel Cards:		2x
Production 500 Sets		
Blue Parallel Cards:		4x
Production 250 Sets		
XC1	Jason Williams	5.00
XC2	Kevin Garnett	8.00
XC3	Allen Iverson	5.00
XC4	Paul Pierce	3.00
XC5	Keith Van Horn	1.50
XC6	Grant Hill	8.00
XC7	Scottie Pippen	3.00
XC8	Stephon Marbury	2.00
XC9	Tim Duncan	8.00
XC10	Kobe Bryant	10.00
XC11	Vince Carter	10.00
XC12	Shaquille O'Neal	5.00
XC13	Steve Francis	10.00
XC14	Elton Brand	8.00
XC15	Lamar Odom	8.00

1999-00 E-X E-Xceptional Blue

This 15-card parallel was the rarest of three levels of E-Xceptional inserts. Cards featured a Blue Warp Tek design in the background and were numbered to 250.

		MT
Complete Set (15):		70.00
Common Player:		2.00
Inserted 1:16		
Green Parallel Cards:		2x
Production 500 Sets		
Blue Parallel Cards:		4x
Production 250 Sets		
1	Jason Williams	5.00
2	Kevin Garnett	8.00
3	Allen Iverson	5.00
4	Paul Pierce	3.00
5	Keith Van Horn	1.50
6	Grant Hill	8.00
7	Scottie Pippen	3.00
8	Stephon Marbury	2.00
9	Tim Duncan	8.00
10	Kobe Bryant	10.00
11	Vince Carter	10.00
12	Shaquille O'Neal	5.00
13	Steve Francis	8.00
14	Elton Brand	5.00
15	Lamar Odom	8.00

1999-00 E-X E-Xceptional Green

This 15-card parallel set was the middle tier of three levels of E-Xceptional inserts. Cards featured a Green Warp Tek design in the background and were numbered to 500.

		MT
Complete Set (15):		70.00
Common Player:		2.00
Inserted 1:16		
Green Parallel Cards:		2x
Production 500 Sets		
Blue Parallel Cards:		4x
Production 250 Sets		
1	Jason Williams	5.00
2	Kevin Garnett	8.00
3	Allen Iverson	5.00
4	Paul Pierce	3.00
5	Keith Van Horn	1.50
6	Grant Hill	8.00
7	Scottie Pippen	3.00
8	Stephon Marbury	2.00
9	Tim Duncan	8.00
10	Kobe Bryant	10.00
11	Vince Carter	10.00
12	Shaquille O'Neal	5.00
13	Steve Francis	8.00
14	Elton Brand	5.00
15	Lamar Odom	8.00

1999-00 E-X E-Xciting

This 10-card insert was die-cut in the shape of a jersey and contained the featured player in front of his team's jersey. E-Xciting inserts were numbered with an "XCT" suffix and inserted 1:24 packs.

		MT
Complete Set (10):		75.00
Common Player:		2.00
Inserted 1:24		
XCT1	Jason Williams	8.00
XCT2	Vince Carter	15.00
XCT3	Allen Iverson	8.00
XCT4	Kevin Garnett	12.00
XCT5	Shaquille O'Neal	8.00
XCT6	Larry Hughes	2.00
XCT7	Tim Duncan	12.00
XCT8	Kobe Bryant	15.00
XCT9	Grant Hill	12.00
XCT10	Paul Pierce	5.00

1999-00 E-X E-Xplosive

This 10-card insert set featured top rookies from the 1999-00 season on a plastic card with an exploding background. E-Xplosive cards were numbered with an "XP" suffix and sequentially numbered to 1,999 sets. In addition, there are 99 sequentially numbered autographed versions of each card. These are not the first 99 cards as was first stated when the product released, but a separate 99 cards produced specifically for autographs.

		MT
Complete Set (10):		
Common Player:		2.00
Common Autographs:		15.00
XP1	William Avery	2.00
XP1a	William Avery AU	15.00
XP2	Baron Davis	2.00
XP2a	Baron Davis AU	35.00
XP3	Richard Hamilton	2.00
XP3a	Richard Hamilton AU	35.00
XP4	Trajan Langdon	2.00
XP4a	Trajan Langdon AU	25.00
XP5	Wally Szczerbiak	3.00
XP5a	Wally Szczerbiak AU	35.00
XP6	Jason Terry	2.00
XP6a	Jason Terry AU	35.00
XP7	Shawn Marion	4.00
XP7a	Shawn Marion AU	60.00
XP8	James Posey	2.00
XP8a	James Posey AU	25.00
XP9	Lamar Odom	2.00
XP9a	Lamar Odom AU	25.00
XP10	Quincy Lewis	2.00
XP10a	Quincy Lewis AU	15.00

1999-00 E-X Generation E-X

This 15-card insert featured top young players over a space-like background. Generation E-X cards were numbered with a "GX" suffix and inserted 1:8 packs.

		MT
Complete Set (15):		25.00
Common Player:		.50
Inserted 1:8		
GX1	Michael Olowokandi	.50
GX2	Kobe Bryant	5.00
GX3	Allen Iverson	2.00
GX4	Tim Duncan	3.00
GX5	Vince Carter	5.00
GX6	Paul Pierce	1.50
GX7	Jason Williams	2.00
GX8	Steve Francis	4.00
GX9	Lamar Odom	3.00
GX10	Elton Brand	3.00
GX11	Larry Hughes	1.00
GX12	Antawn Jamison	1.50
GX13	Mike Bibby	.75
GX14	Keith Van Horn	.75
GX15	Raef LaFrentz	.75

1999-00 E-X Genuine Coverage

This 20-card insert featured player-worn jersey swatches on a horizontal design. Genuine Coverage cards were numbered with a "GC" suffix and inserted 1:72 packs.

		MT
Complete Set (20):		1300.
Common Player:		30.00
Inserted 1:72		
GC1	Shaquille O'Neal	175.00
GC2	Vince Carter	300.00
GC3	Jason Kidd	100.00
GC4	Karl Malone	60.00
GC5	Joe Smith	30.00
GC6	Terrell Brandon	30.00
GC7	John Stockton	60.00
GC8	Lamar Odom	175.00
GC9	Shareef Abdur-Rahim	60.00
GC10	David Robinson	80.00
GC11	Larry Hughes	60.00
GC12	Michael Olowokandi	30.00
GC13	Antonio McDyess	40.00
GC14	Mike Bibby	40.00
GC15	Stephon Marbury	60.00
GC16	Michael Finley	40.00
GC17	Gary Payton	80.00
GC18	Keith Van Horn	30.00
GC19	Jamal Mashburn	30.00
GC20	Grant Hill	100.00

2000-01 Fleer E-X

		MT
Complete Set (130):		300.00
Common Player:		.25
Minor Stars:		.40
Common Rookie:		3.00
Cards 101-110 Production 1,000 Sets		
Cards 111-120 Production 1,250 Sets		
Cards 121-130 Production 1,500 Sets		
Pack (5):		5.00
Box (24):		100.00
1	Dikembe Mutombo	.25
2	Jim Jackson	.25
3	Jason Terry	.40
4	Kenny Anderson	.40
5	Antoine Walker	.50
6	Paul Pierce	.75
7	Jamal Mashburn	.40
8	Baron Davis	.60
9	Derrick Coleman	.25
10	Elton Brand	1.50
11	Ron Artest	.40
12	Andre Miller	.75
13	Brevin Knight	.25
14	Trajan Langdon	.25
15	Lamond Murray	.25
16	Dirk Nowitzki	1.25
17	Michael Finley	.40
18	Nick Van Exel	.40
19	Antonio McDyess	.50
20	Raef LaFrentz	.25
21	Tariq Abdul-Wahad	.25
22	Cedric Ceballos	.25
23	Jerry Stackhouse	.40
24	Jerome Williams	.25
25	Larry Hughes	1.00
26	Antawn Jamison	1.25
27	Mookie Blaylock	.25
28	Steve Francis	3.00
29	Hakeem Olajuwon	.75
30	Maurice Taylor	.25
31	Jonathan Bender	1.00
32	Reggie Miller	.40
33	Austin Croshere	.25
34	Travis Best	.25
35	Jalen Rose	.50
36	Lamar Odom	1.50
37	Corey Maggette	.60
38	Shaquille O'Neal	2.50
39	Kobe Bryant	5.00
40	Horace Grant	.25
41	Isaiah Rider	.25
42	Brian Grant	.25
43	Eddie Jones	1.00
44	Tim Hardaway	.50
45	Anthony Mason	.25
46	Glenn Robinson	.40
47	Ray Allen	.50
48	Sam Cassell	.25
49	Tim Thomas	.50
50	Kevin Garnett	3.00
51	Terrell Brandon	.25
52	Joe Smith	.25
53	Wally Szczerbiak	.50
54	Chauncey Billups	.25
55	Stephon Marbury	1.00
56	Keith Van Horn	.60
57	Kerry Kittles	.25
58	Allan Houston	.50
59	Latrell Sprewell	1.25
60	Larry Johnson	.25
61	Glen Rice	.40
62	Grant Hill	2.50
63	Tracy McGrady	1.50
64	Darrell Armstrong	.25
65	Allen Iverson	3.00
66	Toni Kukoc	[illegible]
67	Theo Ratliff	.25
68	Jason Kidd	1.50
69	Anfernee Hardaway	1.50
70	Tom Gugliotta	.25
71	Clifford Robinson	.25
72	Shawn Kemp	.40
73	Scottie Pippen	1.50
74	Rasheed Wallace	.60
75	Steve Smith	.40
76	Chris Webber	2.00
77	Jason Williams	.75
78	Predrag Stojakovic	.50
79	Tim Duncan	2.50
80	David Robinson	.75
81	Sean Elliott	.25
82	Derek Anderson	.40
83	Vin Baker	.40
84	Rashard Lewis	.75
85	Gary Payton	.75
86	Patrick Ewing	.40
87	Vince Carter	6.00
88	Mark Jackson	.25
89	Antonio Davis	.25
90	Karl Malone	.75
91	John Stockton	.40
92	Bryon Russell	.25
93	Donyell Marshall	.25
94	Shareef Abdur-Rahim	.75
95	Mike Bibby	.50
96	Michael Dickerson	.25
97	Mitch Richmond	.40
98	Juwan Howard	.40
99	Richard Hamilton	.50
100	Rod Strickland	.40
101	*DerMarr Johnson*	20.00
101B	*DerMarr Johnson GJ/275*	40.00
102	*Kenyon Martin*	30.00
102B	*Kenyon Martin GJ/275*	100.00
102B		.25
103	*Marcus Fizer*	20.00
103B	*Marcus Fizer Ball/275*	50.00
103B		.25
104	*Courtney Alexander*	20.00
104B	*Courtney Alexander AU/500*	30.00
105	*Stromile Swift*	40.00
105B	*Stromile Swift GJ/275*	100.00
106	*Darius Miles*	100.00
106B	*Darius Miles GJ/275*	200.00
107	*Mike Miller*	40.00
107B	*Mike Miller GJ/275*	75.00
108	*Jamal Crawford*	20.00
108B	*Jamal Crawford AU/250*	40.00
109	*Craig "Speedy" Claxton*	6.00
109B	*Speedy Claxton GJ/275*	20.00
110	*Quentin Richardson*	25.00
110B	*Quentin Richardson GJ/275*	50.00
111	*Keyon Dooling*	15.00
111B	*Keyon Dooling AU/250*	40.00
112	*Desmond Mason*	20.00
112B	*Desmond Mason AU/500*	40.00
113	*Mateen Cleaves*	10.00
113B	*Mateen Cleaves AU/500*	30.00
114	*Morris Peterson*	20.00
114B	*Morris Peterson GJ/275*	75.00
115	*Hidayet Turkoglu*	12.00
115B	*Hidayet Turkoglu AU/250*	40.00
116	*Donnell Harvey*	6.00
116B	*Donnell Harvey AU/250*	15.00
117	*Jerome Moiso*	8.00
117B	*Jerome Moiso GJ/275*	25.00
118	*Jason Collier*	4.00
118B	*Jason Collier AU/250*	12.00
119	*Jamaal Magloire*	6.00
120	*Erick Barkley*	8.00
120B	*Erick Barkley AU/250*	15.00
121	*Etan Thomas*	5.00
121B	*Etan Thomas GJ/275*	20.00
122	*DeShawn Stevenson*	25.00
122B	*DeShawn Stevenson GJ/275*	75.00
123	*Dan Langhi*	3.00
123B	*Dan Langhi AU/500*	12.00
124	*Mark Madsen*	5.00
125	*Khalid El-Amin*	6.00
125B	*Khalid El-Amin AU/500*	20.00
126	*Lavor Postell*	4.00
126B	*Lavor Postell AU/500*	12.00
127	*Eddie House*	6.00
127B	*Eddie House AU/500*	25.00
128	*Michael Redd*	4.00
128B	*Michael Redd AU/500*	15.00
129	*Chris Porter*	12.00
129B	*Chris Porter AU/500*	30.00
130	*Mike Smith*	3.00
130B	*Mike Smith AU/500*	10.00

2000-01 Fleer E-X Credentials

		MT
Common Player:		2.00
Credentials:		4x-8x
Production 201 Sets		
Common Rookie:		20.00
Production 21 Sets		
1	Dikembe Mutombo	.25
2	Jim Jackson	.25
3	Jason Terry	.40
4	Kenny Anderson	.40
5	Antoine Walker	.50
6	Paul Pierce	.75
7	Jamal Mashburn	.40
8	Baron Davis	.60
9	Derrick Coleman	.25
10	Elton Brand	1.50
11	Ron Artest	.40
12	Andre Miller	.75
13	Brevin Knight	.25
14	Trajan Langdon	.25
15	Lamond Murray	.25
16	Dirk Nowitzki	1.25
17	Michael Finley	.40
18	Nick Van Exel	.40
19	Antonio McDyess	.50
20	Raef LaFrentz	.25
21	Tariq Abdul-Wahad	.25
22	Cedric Ceballos	.25
23	Jerry Stackhouse	.40
24	Jerome Williams	.25
25	Larry Hughes	1.00
26	Antawn Jamison	1.25
27	Mookie Blaylock	.25
28	Steve Francis	3.00
29	Hakeem Olajuwon	.75
30	Maurice Taylor	.25
31	Jonathan Bender	1.00
32	Reggie Miller	.40
33	Austin Croshere	.25
34	Travis Best	.25
35	Jalen Rose	.50
36	Lamar Odom	1.50
37	Corey Maggette	.60
38	Shaquille O'Neal	2.50
39	Kobe Bryant	5.00
40	Horace Grant	.25
41	Isaiah Rider	.25
42	Brian Grant	.25
43	Eddie Jones	1.00
44	Tim Hardaway	.50
45	Anthony Mason	.25
46	Glenn Robinson	.40
47	Ray Allen	.50
48	Sam Cassell	.25
49	Tim Thomas	.50
50	Kevin Garnett	3.00
51	Terrell Brandon	.25
52	Joe Smith	.25
53	Wally Szczerbiak	.50
54	Chauncey Billups	.25
55	Stephon Marbury	1.00
56	Keith Van Horn	.60
57	Kerry Kittles	.25
58	Allan Houston	.50
59	Latrell Sprewell	1.25
60	Larry Johnson	.25
61	Glen Rice	.40
62	Grant Hill	2.50
63	Tracy McGrady	1.50
64	Darrell Armstrong	.25
65	Allen Iverson	3.00
66	Toni Kukoc	.60
67	Theo Ratliff	.25
68	Jason Kidd	1.50
69	Anfernee Hardaway	1.50
70	Tom Gugliotta	.25
71	Clifford Robinson	.25
72	Shawn Kemp	.40
73	Scottie Pippen	1.50
74	Rasheed Wallace	.60
75	Steve Smith	.40
76	Chris Webber	2.00
77	Jason Williams	.75
78	Predrag Stojakovic	.50
79	Tim Duncan	2.50
80	David Robinson	.75
81	Sean Elliott	.25
82	Derek Anderson	.40
83	Vin Baker	.40
84	Rashard Lewis	.75
85	Gary Payton	.75
86	Patrick Ewing	.40
87	Vince Carter	6.00
88	Mark Jackson	.25
89	Antonio Davis	.25
90	Karl Malone	.75
91	John Stockton	.40
92	Bryon Russell	.25
93	Donyell Marshall	.25
94	Shareef Abdur-Rahim	.75
95	Mike Bibby	.50
96	Michael Dickerson	.25
97	Mitch Richmond	.40
98	Juwan Howard	.40
99	Richard Hamilton	.50
100	Rod Strickland	.40
101	DerMarr Johnson	75.00
102	Kenyon Martin	100.00
102B		.25
103	Marcus Fizer	60.00
103B		.25
104	Courtney Alexander	100.00
105	Stromile Swift	125.00
106	Darius Miles	400.00
107	Mike Miller	150.00
108	Jamal Crawford	60.00
109	Craig "Speedy" Claxton	30.00
110	Quentin Richardson	75.00
111	Keyon Dooling	60.00
112	Desmond Mason	75.00
113	Mateen Cleaves	40.00
114	Morris Peterson	125.00
115	Hidayet Turkoglu	75.00
116	Donnell Harvey	25.00
117	Jerome Moiso	30.00
118	Jason Collier	20.00
119	Jamaal Magloire	30.00
120	Erick Barkley	30.00
121	Etan Thomas	25.00
122	DeShawn Stevenson	125.00
123	Dan Langhi	15.00
124	Mark Madsen	30.00
125	Khalid El-Amin	[illegible]
126	Lavor Postell	25.00
127	Eddie House	50.00
128	Michael Redd	25.00
129	Chris Porter	60.00
130	Mike Smith	15.00

2000-01 Fleer E-X Generation E-X

		MT
Complete Set (21):		60.00
Common Player:		1.00
Inserted 1:24		
1	Vince Carter	10.00
2	Grant Hill	5.00
3	Lamar Odom	3.00
4	Allen Iverson	6.00
5	Keith Van Horn	1.00
6	Shareef Abdur-Rahim	1.50
7	Dirk Nowitzki	2.50
8	Morris Peterson	3.00
9	Mike Miller	3.00
10	Darius Miles	10.00
11	Craig "Speedy" Claxton	1.00
12	Kenyon Martin	5.00
13	Stromile Swift	5.00
14	Courtney Alexander	2.00
15	Vince Carter, Morris Peterson	10.00
16	Grant Hill, Mike Miller	8.00
17	Lamar Odom, Darius Miles	12.00
18	Allen Iverson, Craig Claxton	5.00
19	Keith Van Horn, Kenyon Martin	4.00
20	Shareef Abdur-Rahim, Stromile Swift	6.00
21	Dirk Nowitzki, Courtney Alexander	4.00

2000-01 Fleer E-X Generation E-X Game Jerseys

		MT
Common Player:		20.00
Inserted 1:85		
Production 600 Sets		
1	Vince Carter	125.00
2	Grant Hill	50.00
3	Lamar Odom	30.00
4	Allen Iverson	60.00
5	Keith Van Horn	20.00
6	Shareef Abdur-Rahim	20.00
7	Dirk Nowitzki	50.00
8	Morris Peterson	50.00
9	Mike Miller	40.00
10	Darius Miles	100.00
11	Craig "Speedy" Claxton	20.00
12	Kenyon Martin	50.00
13	Stromile Swift	50.00
14	Courtney Alexander	25.00
15	Vince Carter, Morris Peterson	200.00
16	Grant Hill, Mike Miller	75.00
17	Lamar Odom, Darius Miles	150.00
18	Allen Iverson, Craig Claxton	75.00
19	Keith Van Horn, Kenyon Martin	75.00
20	Shareef Abdur-Rahim, Stromile Swift	60.00
21	Dirk Nowitzki, Courtney Alexander	4.00

2000-01 Fleer E-X Gravity Denied

		MT
Complete Set (10):		50.00
Common Player:		3.00
Inserted 1:48		
1	Vince Carter	20.00
2	Jason Kidd	5.00
3	Eddie Jones	3.00
4	Tracy McGrady	5.00
5	Kobe Bryant	[illegible]
6	Grant Hill	8.00
7	Lamar Odom	5.00
8	Steve Francis	10.00
9	Kevin Garnett	10.00
10	Allen Iverson	10.00

2000-01 Fleer E-X NBA Debut Postmarks

		MT
Complete Set (11):		150.00
Common Player:		10.00
Inserted 1:288		
1	Kenyon Martin	30.00
3	Darius Miles	75.00
4	Marcus Fizer	25.00
5	Mike Miller	30.00
6	DerMarr Johnson	20.00
7	Jamal Crawford	20.00
8	Jerome Moiso	10.00
9	Courtney Alexander	20.00
11	Hidayet Turkoglu	15.00
13	Jamaal Magloire	10.00
14	Keyon Dooling	20.00

2000-01 Fleer E-X Net Assets

		MT
Complete Set (20):		30.00
Common Player:		.75
Inserted 1:8		
1	Vince Carter	10.00
2	Reggie Miller	.75
3	Karl Malone	1.00
4	Ray Allen	.75
5	Dirk Nowitzki	1.50
6	Scottie Pippen	2.50
7	Tracy McGrady	2.50
8	Kobe Bryant	8.00
9	Larry Hughes	1.25
10	Shareef Abdur-Rahim	1.00
11	Tim Duncan	4.00
12	Gary Payton	1.00
13	Eddie Jones	1.50
14	Steve Francis	5.00
15	Antoine Walker	.75
16	Kevin Garnett	5.00
17	Chris Webber	3.00
18	Shaquille O'Neal	4.00
19	Jason Kidd	2.50
20	Elton Brand	2.50

2000-01 Fleer E-X No Boundaries

		MT
Complete Set (10):		25.00
Common Player:		1.00
Inserted 1:12'		
1	Vince Carter	8.00
2	Shareef Abdur-Rahim	1.00
3	Elton Brand	2.50
4	Shaquille O'Neal	4.00
5	Kobe Bryant	6.00
6	Allen Iverson	5.00
7	Tim Duncan	4.00
8	Steve Francis	5.00
9	Kevin Garnett	5.00
10	Grant Hill	4.00

2001-02 Fleer E-X

		MT
Complete Set (100):		375.00
Common Player:		.30
Minor Stars:		.60
Common Rookie (101-130):		4.00
Pack (4):		4.00
Box (24):		85.00
1	Shareef Abdur-Rahim	.75
2	DerMarr Johnson	.60
3	Jason Terry	.60
4	Paul Pierce	1.00
5	Antoine Walker	1.00
6	Baron Davis	1.00
7	Jamal Mashburn	.60
8	Chris Mihm	.30
9	Andre Miller	.60
10	Dirk Nowitzki	1.25
11	Michael Finley	.75
12	Raef LaFrentz	.30
13	Antonio McDyess	.60
14	Jerry Stackhouse	1.00
15	Antawn Jamison	1.25
16	Steve Francis	2.00
17	Jalen Rose	.60
18	Elton Brand	1.25
19	Darius Miles	4.00
20	Lamar Odom	1.25
21	Mitch Richmond	.30
22	Michael Dickerson	.30
23	Stromile Swift	.60
24	Alonzo Mourning	.60
25	Courtney Alexander	.60
26	Ray Allen	1.00
27	Glenn Robinson	.75
28	Terrell Brandon	.60
29	Wally Szczerbiak	.75
30	Joe Smith	.30
31	Jason Kidd	1.50
32	Kenyon Martin	.60
33	Keith Van Horn	.60
34	Grant Hill	1.25
35	Tracy McGrady	2.50
36	Mike Miller	2.00
37	Allen Iverson	3.00
38	Speedy Claxton	.60
39	Dikembe Mutombo	.60
40	Tom Gugliotta	.30
41	Anfernee Hardaway	.60
42	Stephon Marbury	1.00
43	Shawn Marion	1.25
44	Rasheed Wallace	.75
45	Predrag Stojakovic	.75
46	Mike Bibby	.60
47	Chris Webber	2.00
48	David Robinson	.75
49	Vin Baker	.60
50	Rashard Lewis	.60
51	Desmond Mason	.60
52	Gary Payton	1.00
53	Vince Carter	5.00
54	Antonio Davis	.30
55	Hakeem Olajuwon	.75
56	Morris Peterson	.60
57	Karl Malone	1.25
58	DeShawn Stevenson	.60
59	John Stockton	1.00
60	Richard Hamilton	.60
61	Corey Maggette	.60
62	Steve Smith	.60
63	Tim Thomas	.60
64	Lindsey Hunter	.30
65	Jermaine O'Neal	.75
66	Cuttino Mobley	.60
67	Nick Van Exel	.75
68	Juwan Howard	.60
69	James Posey	.30
70	David Wesley	.30
71	Marcus Fizer	.60
72	Jumaine Jones	.30
73	Tim Hardaway	.60
74	Danny Fortson	.30
75	Jonathan Bender	.60
76	Quentin Richardson	.60
77	Eddie House	.30
78	Kurt Thomas	.30
79	Anthony Mason	.30
80	Theo Ratliff	.30
81	Allan Houston	.60
82	Latrell Sprewell	1.25
83	Jason Williams	.60
84	Eddie Jones	.75
85	Damon Stoudamire	.30
86	Sam Cassell	.60
87	Clifford Robinson	.60
88	Patrick Ewing	.60
89	Tim Duncan	2.00
90	Marcus Camby	.30
91	Brian Grant	.30
92	Kobe Bryant	5.00
93	Ron Mercer	.60
94	Reggie Miller	1.00
95	Shaquille O'Neal	2.50
96	Kevin Garnett	3.00
97	Scottie Pippen	1.25
98	Michael Jordan	12.00
99	Steve Nash	.60
100	Derek Anderson	.60
101	*Kedrick Brown/1750*	6.00
102	*Joseph Forte/1750*	10.00
103	*Joe Johnson/1250*	15.00
104	*Kirk Haston/1750*	8.00
105	*Tyson Chandler/750*	25.00
106	*Eddy Curry/1250*	15.00
107	*DeSagana Diop/1750*	5.00
108	*Trenton Hassell/1250*	8.00
109	*Zeljko Rebraca/1250*	6.00
110	*Rodney White/1750*	8.00
111	*Troy Murphy/1250*	8.00
112	*Jason Richardson/750*	50.00
113	*Eddie Griffin/750*	25.00
114	*Terence Morris/1750*	4.00
115	*Oscar Torres/1250*	5.00
116	*Jamaal Tinsley/750*	25.00
117	*Pau Gasol/750*	35.00
118	*Shane Battier/750*	40.00
119	*Brandon Armstrong/1250*	6.00
120	*Richard Jefferson/750*	15.00
121	*Steven Hunter/1250*	5.00
122	*Samuel Dalembert/1750*	4.00
123	*Zach Randolph/1250*	10.00
124	*Gerald Wallace/1750*	12.00
125	*Tony Parker/750*	35.00
126	*Vladimir Radmanovic/1250*	[illegible]
127	*Michael Bradley/1750*	4.00
128	*Jarron Collins/1750*	4.00
129	*Andrei Kirilenko/750*	15.00
130	*Kwame Brown/750*	25.00

2001-02 Fleer E-X Behind The Numbers

		MT
Common Player:		20.00
Inserted 1:288		
1BN	Larry Bird	100.00
2BN	Allen Iverson	50.00
3BN	David Robinson	20.00
4BN	Karl Malone	25.00
5BN	Tracy McGrady	40.00
6BN	Steve Francis	40.00
7BN	Jason Terry	20.00
8BN	Antoine Walker	20.00
9BN	Grant Hill	20.00
10BN	Michael Finley	20.00
11BN	Jason Kidd	30.00
12BN	Alonzo Mourning	20.00
13BN	Darius Miles	35.00
14BN	Ray Allen	20.00
15BN	Vince Carter	60.00
Only GU	Dirk Nowitzki	
Only GU	Gary Payton	
Only GU	Kenyon Martin	
Only GU	Paul Pierce	
Only GU	Baron Davis	

2001-02 Fleer E-X Box Office Draws

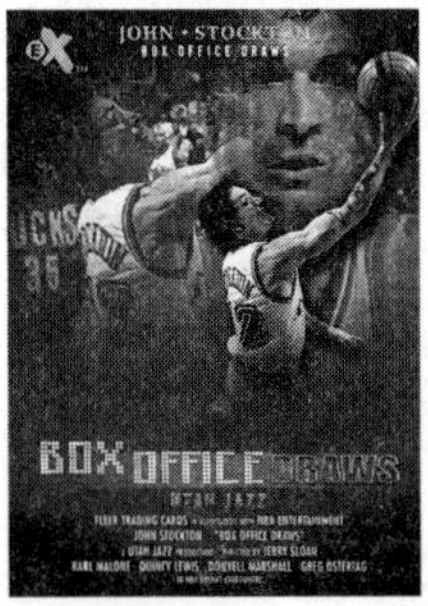

		MT
Complete Set (20):		60.00
Common Player:		2.00
Inserted 1:24		
1BD	Shareef Abdur-Rahim	2.00
2BD	John Stockton	3.00
3BD	Predrag Stojakovic	3.00
4BD	Elton Brand	4.00
5BD	Stephon Marbury	3.00
6BD	Eddie Jones	2.00
7BD	Baron Davis	3.00
8BD	Keith Van Horn	2.00
9BD	Paul Pierce	3.00
10BD	Gary Payton	3.00
11BD	Grant Hill	3.00
12BD	Chris Webber	6.00
13BD	Latrell Sprewell	4.00
14BD	Jerry Stackhouse	3.00
15BD	Vince Carter	15.00
16BD	Allen Iverson	10.00
17BD	Dirk Nowitzki	4.00
18BD	Shawn Marion	4.00
19BD	Steve Francis	6.00
20BD	Richard Hamilton	2.00
Only GU	Lamar Odom	
Only GU	Michael Finley	
Only GU	Tracy McGrady	

2001-02 Fleer E-X Net Assets

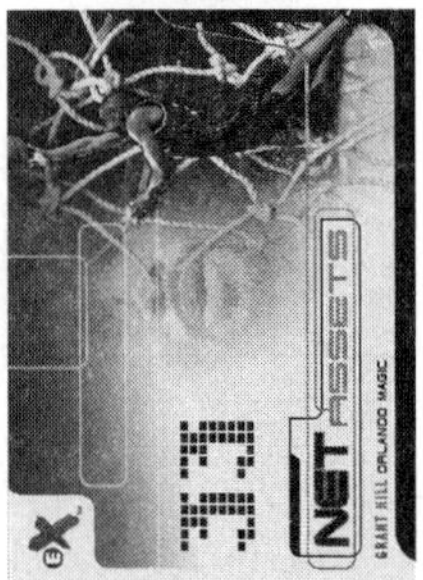

		MT
Complete Set (15):		75.00
Common Player:		3.00
Inserted 1:12		
1NA	Kobe Bryant	12.00
2NA	Kwame Brown	8.00
3NA	Kevin Garnett	8.00
4NA	Eddie Griffin	8.00
5NA	Shaquille O'Neal	6.00
6NA	Tim Duncan	5.00
7NA	Tyson Chandler	8.00
8NA	Allen Iverson	8.00
9NA	Grant Hill	3.00
10NA	Michael Jordan	20.00
11NA	Ray Allen	3.00
12NA	Jason Richardson	12.00
13NA	Eddy Curry	6.00
14NA	Dirk Nowitzki	3.00
15NA	Vince Carter	12.00

1948-49 Exhibits Sports Champions

Measuring 3-1/4" x 5-3/8", the multi-sport, 50-card set boasts a black-and-white photo on the front. Near the bottom of the card front is a facsimile autograph and a career highlight. The cards are unnumbered and have blank backs. The cards released in 1949 are more difficult to find than the 1948 cards. Variations of the Button and Scott cards were released with different highlights. The cards were sold in penny arcade machines. An assortment of 1949 cards honor Summer Olympic champions and offer a second card of Scott and Button. The George Mikan card is the anchor of this set.

	NM
Complete Set (50):	3200.
Common Football:	25.00
Common Hockey:	40.00
Common Boxer:	25.00
Common Basketball:	60.00
Common Other Sports:	10.00
Ted Allen (49) (Horseshoe Pitching Champion)	50.00
Sammy Baugh (Football Washington Redskins)	80.00
Doug Bentley, Max Bentley (Hockey)	75.00
Buddy Bomar (Bowling)	10.00
Richard Button (Figure Skating) (Dark coat, signature in black)	20.00
Richard Button (Figure Skating) (White coat, signature in white, 49)	25.00
Citation (49) (Racehorse) (No agate type line)	25.00
John Cobb (Auto racing)	35.00
Roy Conacher (Hockey (49) Chicago Blackhawks)	75.00
Bob "Tarmac" Cook (Basketball Wisconsin)	60.00
Ann Curtis (Swimming Free Style)	10.00
Ned Day (49) (All Events Champion)	20.00
Jack Dempsey (Boxing)	60.00
Harrison Dillard (Track 49)	30.00
Glenn Dobbs (Football 49 Los Angeles Dons)	75.00
Gil Dodds (Track Indoor Mile)	10.00
Bill Durnan (Hockey Montreal Canadiens)	60.00
Bump Elliott (Football)	30.00
Joe Fulks (Basketball 49)	350.00
Edward Gauden (49 Track Broad Jump)	20.00
Lucien Goudin (Fencing 49)	15.00
Otto Graham (Football Cleveland Browns)	80.00
Pat Harder (Football Chicago Cardinals)	25.00
Sonja Heine (Figure Skating)	15.00
Ben Hogan (Golf 49 US Open Champion)	120.00
Willie Hoppe (Billards)	10.00
Jack Jacobs (Football Green Bay Packers)	25.00
Jack Kramer (Tennis)	15.00
Gus Lewis (Handball Champion 49)	20.00
Guy Lombardo (Boat Racing 49)	35.00
Joe Louis (Boxing Heavyweight Champion)	80.00
Sid Luckman (Football Chicago Bears)	60.00
Johnny Lujack (Football Notre Dame/Chicago Bears)	60.00
Man O'War (American's Greatest Racehorse)	30.00
Bob Mathias (Track Decathion 49)	40.00
Bobby McDermott (Basketball)	75.00
Gretchen Merrill (Figure Skating)	10.00
George Mikan (Basketball)	600.00
Dick Miles (Table Tennis)	10.00
Marion Motley (Football 49 Cleveland Browns)	75.00
Charley Paddock (49 Track Olympic Champion)	50.00
Andy Phillip (Basketball)	275.00
Bobby Riggs (Tennis)	30.00
Barbara Ann Scott (Figure Skating) (Looking straight, signature in black)	15.00
Barbara Ann Scott (Figure Skating) (49, looking to side, signature in white)	30.00
Ben Sklar (Marble Shooting)	10.00
Clyde "Bulldog" Turner (Football Chicago Bears)	35.00
Steve Van Buren (Football Philadelphia Eagles)	35.00
Andy Veripapa (Bowling)	20.00
Bob Waterfield (Football 49 Los Angeles Rams)	75.00
Murray Weir (Basketball 49)	180.00
Claude Buddy Young (Hands on knees, Football, New York Yankees)	30.00

1973 Equitable

This set, sponsored by the Equitable Life Assurance Society of the United States, features the black-and-white artwork of two artists - George Loh and Robert Ringer. Each of Loh's cards (#s 1-5) show two action shots and a portrait of the player. Riger's sketches (#s 6-9) have one action shot of the player, plus a drawing of Riger himself as a child. The blank-backed cards are unnumbered and measure 8" x 10". They are listed below alphabetically. A second Bob Pettit card, 4a, was used as an advertisement in a March 1965 issue of Sports Illustrated.

		NM
Complete Set (10):		150.00
Common Player:		10.00
1	Elgin Baylor	15.00
2	Hal Greer	10.00
3	Jerry Lucas	10.00
4	Bob Pettit	15.00
4a	Bob Pettit (ad)	25.00
5	Willis Reed	15.00
6	Wilt Chamberlain	20.00
7	Bob Cousy	20.00
8	George Mikan	30.00
9	Bill Russell	20.00

F

1993 FCA

The Fellowship of Christian Athletes sponsored this 50-card, multi-sport set. The fronts have a color photo with a blue and white border. The FCA logo is in the upper left corner, with the player's sport on the left side and his name under the picture. The backs have a head shot, biography and the player's testimony.

		MT
Complete Set (50):		10.00
Common Player:		.10
1	Title Card	.10
2	Zenon Andrusyshyn	.10
3	Bobby Bowden	1.50
4	Eric Boyles	.10
5	John Brandes	.10
6	Dan Britton	.10
7	Brian Cabral	.10
8	Bobby Clampett	.10
9	Paul Coffman	.10
10	Jeff Coston	.10
11	Tanya Crevier	.10
12	Doug Dawson	.10
13	Donnie Dee	.10
14	Denise DeWalt	.10
15	Mitch Donahue	.10
16	Curtis Duncan	.10
17	Mike Gartner	.50
18	Brian Harper	.10
19	Janice Harrer	.10
20	Ed Hearn	.10
21	Bobby Hebert	.25
22	Julie Hermann	.10
23	David Dean	.10
24	Steve Jones	.25
25	Brian Kinchen	.25
26	Todd Kinchen	.25
27	Jerry Kindall	.10
28	Betsy King	.35
29	Tom Lehman	1.25
30	Neil Lomax	.35
31	LaVonna Martin-Floreal	.10
32	Dan Meers	.10
33	Mike Merriweather	.25
34	Ken Norton Jr.	.35
35	Greg Olson	.10
36	Tim Peddie	.10
37	Rob Pelinka	.10
38	Steve Pelluer	.25
39	Brent Price	.25
40	Jan Ripple	.10
41	Kyle Rote Jr.	.25
42	Ted Schulz	.10
43	Scott Simpson	.35
44	R.C. Slocum	.25
45	Grant Teaff	.25
46	Pat Tilley	.25
47	Bill Wegman	.10
48	Wendy White	.10
49	Charlton Young	.10
50	Kay Yow	.10

1993 FCA Final Four

The Fellowship of Christian Athletes handed out this seven-card set at Final Four viewing parties. The color photos are bordered with a pink line, while the card borders go from purple to white from top to bottom. A cross is located at the top left, with "FCA" printed inside a banner below it. The player's name and position are printed in the lower right corner. The card backs have a head shot in the upper left, with the player's name, bio, position and card number listed to the right of the photo. The player's religious beliefs are printed in the center of the card backs. The bottom of the card backs feature the toll-free FCA telephone number.

		MT
Complete Set (7):		6.00
Common Player:		.50
1	Steve Alford	1.00
2	John Wooden CO	3.00
3	Bobby Jones	1.50
4	Rod Foster	1.00
5	Keith Erickson	1.00
NNO	Cover Card	.50
NNO	Order Form	.50

1991 Farley's Fruit Snacks

This set of four packages of fruit snacks measures 4-1/2" x 2-3/4" and lists the complete set of questions on the outside of the box. The set was sponsored by Farley's Candy Co. (Chicago) and features a different red, orange or brown drawing of Jordan with each group of four questions (16 total).

		MT
Complete Set (4):		10.00
Common Player:		2.50
1	Michael Jordan (Dribbling up court)	2.50
2	Michael Jordan (Tossing Ball)	2.50
3	Michael Jordan (Shooting ball)	2.50
4	Michael Jordan (Resting posture)	2.50

1993 Fax Pax World of Sport

The set was issued in Great Britain, with 40 cards in all. The set highlights athletes who are recognized world-wide, with an Olympic subset included. Photos in the front are both action and still shots, with the player's country's flag in the nameplate along the bottom. The back has the player's sport and position, along with biographical information.

		MT
Complete Set (40):		12.00
Common Player:		1.00
1	Roger Clemens (Baseball)	1.00
2	Ken Griffey Jr. (Baseball)	3.00
3	John Olerud (Baseball)	.25
4	Nolan Ryan (Baseball)	2.50
5	Charles Barkley (Basketball)	1.00
6	Patrick Ewing (Basketball)	.50
7	Michael Jordan (Basketball)	4.00
8	Shaquille O'Neal (Basketball)	1.50
9	Riddick Bowe (Boxing)	.40
10	Julio Cesar Chavez (Boxing)	.50
11	Lennox Lewis (Boxing)	.40
12	Allan Border (Cricket)	.10
13	Ian Botham (Cricket)	.10
14	Vic Richards (Cricket)	.10
15	Dan Marino (Football)	3.00
16	Joe Montana (Football)	2.00
17	Emmitt Smith (Football)	2.00
18	Paul Gascoigne (Soccer)	.10
19	John Harkes (Soccer)	.20
20	Gary Lineker (Soccer)	.10
21	Diego Maradona (Soccer)	.50
22	Seve Ballesteros (Golf)	.25
23	John Daly (Golf)	.50
24	Jack Nicklaus (Golf)	2.00
25	Wayne Gretzky (Hockey)	3.00
26	Brett Hull (Hockey)	.50
27	Eric Lindros (Hockey)	1.50
28	Linford Christie (Track and Field)	.25
29	Oscar De La Hoya (Boxing)	1.00
30	Sally Gunnell (Track and Field)	.10
31	Jackie Joyner-Kersee (Track and Field)	.25
32	Toni Kukoc (Basketball)	.50
33	Carl Lewis (Track and Field)	.50
34	Katarina Witt (Figure Skating)	.50
35	Nigel Mansell (Racing)	.25
36	Richard Petty (Racing)	1.00
37	Will Carling (Rugby)	.10
38	Boris Becker (Tennis)	.50
39	Steffi Graf (Tennis)	.75
40	John McEnroe (Tennis)	.75

1993-94 Finest

This set features cards which have rainbow-colored metallic card fronts featuring color action shots against a marble background. The player's name is in a blue bar in the upper left corner. The card back also has a marble background with white borders and includes another color photo. The player's biography, statistics and player profile are also on the card. His name and position are in the upper right corner in a gold bar. Cards are numbered on the back. A 40-card subset was made; it features 10 of the best players in each of the four divisions (cards 90-129). A refractor version was also made for each of 220 cards in the set; odds were 1 in 9 packs of finding one. Main Attraction insert cards were made and randomly included in jumbo packs; each of the 27 NBA teams is represented by one player.

		MT
Complete Set (220):		130.00
Common Player:		.25
Minor Stars:		.50
Pack (7):		12.00
Wax Box (24):		250.00
1	Michael Jordan	20.00
2	Larry Bird	5.00
3	Shaquille O'Neal	9.00
4	Benoit Benjamin	.25
5	Ricky Pierce	.25
6	Ken Norman	.25
7	Victor Alexander	.25
8	Mark Jackson	.25
9	Mark West	.25
10	Don MacLean	.50
11	Reggie Miller	2.00
12	Sarunas Marciulionis	.25
13	Craig Ehlo	.25
14	*Toni Kukoc*	7.00
15	Glen Rice	.50
16	Otis Thorpe	.25
17	Reggie Williams	.25
18	Charles Smith	.25
19	Micheal Williams	.25
20	Tom Chambers	.25
21	David Robinson	4.00
22	*Jamal Mashburn*	7.00
23	Cliff Robinson	.25
24	*Acie Earl*	.50
25	Danny Ferry	.25
26	*Bobby Hurley*	.50
27	Eddie Johnson	.25
28	Detlef Schrempf	.25
29	Mike Brown	.25
30	Latrell Sprewell	1.50
31	Derek Harper	.25
32	Stacey Augmon	.25
33	Pooh Richardson	.25
34	Larry Krystkowiak	.25
35	Pervis Ellison	.25
36	Jeff Malone	.25
37	Sean Elliott	.25
38	John Paxson	.25
39	Robert Parish	.25
40	Mark Aguirre	.25
41	Danny Ainge	.25
42	Brian Shaw	.25
43	LaPhonso Ellis	.50
44	Carl Herrera	.25
45	Terry Cummings	.25
46	Chris Dudley	.25
47	Anthony Mason	.25
48	Chris Morris	.25
49	Todd Day	.25
50	*Nick Van Exel*	10.00
51	Larry Nance	.25
52	Derrick McKey	.25
53	Muggsy Bogues	.25
54	Andrew Lang	.25
55	Chuck Person	.25
56	Michael Adams	.25
57	Spud Webb	.25
58	Scott Skiles	.25
59	A.C. Green	.25
60	Terry Mills	.25
61	Xavier McDaniel	.25
62	B.J. Armstrong	.50
63	Donald Hodge	.25
64	Gary Grant	.25
65	Billy Owens	.25
66	Greg Anthony	.25
67	Jay Humphries	.25
68	Lionel Simmons	.25
69	Dana Barros	.25
70	Steve Smith	.25
71	*Ervin Johnson*	.50
72	Sleepy Floyd	.25
73	Blue Edwards	.25
74	Clyde Drexler	2.00
75	Elden Campbell	.25
76	Hakeem Olajuwon	5.00
77	C. Weatherspoon	.50
78	Kevin Willis	.25
79	*Isaiah Rider*	3.00
80	Derrick Coleman	.50
81	Nick Anderson	.50
82	Bryant Stith	.25
83	Johnny Newman	.25
84	*Calbert Cheaney*	1.00
85	Oliver Miller	.25
86	Loy Vaught	.25
87	Isiah Thomas	1.00
88	Dee Brown	.25
89	Horace Grant	1.00
90	Patrick Ewing (AF)	1.00
91	C. Weatherspoon (AF)	.50
92	Ron Seikaly (AF)	.25
93	Dino Radja (AF)	.25
94	Kenny Anderson (AF)	.50
95	John Starks (AF)	.25
96	Tom Gugliotta (AF)	.25
97	Steve Smith (AF)	.25
98	Derrick Coleman (AF)	.50
99	Shaquille O'Neal (AF)	6.00
100	Brad Daugherty (CF)	.25
101	Horace Grant (CF)	.50
102	Dominique Wilkins (CF)	.50
103	Joe Dumars (CF)	.50
104	Alonzo Mourning (CF)	2.00
105	Scottie Pippen (CF)	2.00
106	Reggie Miller (CF)	.50
107	Mark Price (CF)	.25
108	Ken Norman (CF)	.25
109	Larry Johnson (CF)	1.00
110	Jamal Mashburn (MF)	1.00
111	Christian Laettner (MF)	.25
112	Karl Malone (MF)	2.00
113	Dennis Rodman (MF)	2.00
114	Mahmoud Abdul-Rauf (MF)	.25
115	Hakeem Olajuwon (MF)	2.00
116	Jim Jackson (MF)	.50
117	John Stockton (MF)	1.00
118	David Robinson (MF)	2.00
119	Dikembe Mutombo (MF)	.50
120	Vlade Divac (PF)	.25
121	Dan Majerle (PF)	.25
122	Chris Mullin (PF)	.50
123	Shawn Kemp (PF)	1.00
124	Danny Manning (PF)	.25
125	Charles Barkley (PF)	2.00
126	Mitch Richmond (PF)	.25
127	Tim Hardaway (PF)	.25
128	Detlef Schrempf (PF)	.25
129	Clyde Drexler (PF)	1.00
130	Christian Laettner	.50
131	*Rodney Rogers*	1.00
132	Rik Smits	.50
133	*Chris Mills*	1.50
134	Corie Blount	.50
135	Mookie Blaylock	.25
136	Jim Jackson	3.00
137	Tom Gugliotta	.50
138	Dennis Scott	.25
139	*Vin Baker*	7.00
140	Gary Payton	2.00
141	Sedale Threatt	.25
142	Orlando Woolridge	.25
143	Avery Johnson	.25
144	Charles Oakley	.25
145	Harvey Grant	.25
146	Bimbo Coles	.25
147	Vernon Maxwell	.25
148	Danny Manning	.50
149	Hersey Hawkins	.25
150	Kevin Gamble	.25
151	Johnny Dawkins	.25
152	Olden Polynice	.25
153	Kevin Edwards	.25
154	Willie Anderson	.25
155	Wayman Tisdale	.25
156	*Popeye Jones*	1.00
157	Dan Majerle	.25
158	Rex Chapman	.25
159	Shawn Kemp	1.50
160	Eric Murdock	.25
161	Randy White	.25
162	Larry Johnson	2.00
163	Dominique Wilkins	.50
164	Dikembe Mutombo	.50
165	Patrick Ewing	2.00
166	Jerome Kersey	.25
167	Dale Davis	.25
168	Ron Harper	.25
169	*Sam Cassell*	7.00
170	Bill Cartwright	.25
171	John Williams	.25
172	*Dino Radja*	1.00
173	Dennis Rodman	5.00
174	Kenny Anderson	.50
175	Robert Horry	1.00
176	Chris Mullin	.50
177	John Salley	.25
178	*Scott Burrell*	1.00
179	Mitch Richmond	1.00
180	Lee Mayberry	.25
181	James Worthy	.25
182	Rick Fox	.25
183	Kevin Johnson	1.00
184	*Lindsey Hunter*	3.00
185	Marlon Maxey	.25
186	Sam Perkins	.25
187	Kevin Duckworth	.25
188	Jeff Hornacek	.25
189	*Anfernee Hardaway*	25.00
190	*Rex Walters*	.50
191	Mahmoud Abdul-Rauf	.25
192	*Terry Dehere*	.50
193	Brad Daugherty	.25
194	John Starks	.25
195	Rod Strickland	.25
196	*Luther Wright*	.50
197	Vlade Divac	.25
198	Tim Hardaway	.50
199	Joe Dumars	1.00
200	Charles Barkley	3.00
201	Alonzo Mourning	3.00
202	Doug West	.25
203	Anthony Avent	.25
204	Lloyd Daniels	.25
205	Mark Price	.25
206	Rumeal Robinson	.25
207	Kendall Gill	.25
208	Scottie Pippen	4.00
209	Kenny Smith	.25
210	Walt Williams	.25
211	Hubert Davis	.25
212	*Chris Webber*	50.00
213	Rony Seikaly	.25
214	Sam Bowie	.25
215	Karl Malone	2.00
216	Malik Sealy	.25
217	Dale Ellis	.25
218	Harold Miner	.25
219	John Stockton	2.00
220	*Shawn Bradley*	4.00

1993-94 Finest Refractors

This parallel of the 220-card Finest set features refracting foil that gives the cards a glossy look. This was the first year for basketball refractors. The cards were inserted one per nine packs.

MT
Complete Set (220): 2500.
Common Player: 4.00
Minor Stars: 8.00
1 Michael Jordan 300.00
2 Larry Bird 45.00
3 Shaquille O'Neal 160.00
4 Benoit Benjamin 4.00
5 Ricky Pierce 4.00
6 Ken Norman 4.00
7 Victor Alexander 15.00
8 Mark Jackson 4.00
9 Mark West 4.00
10 Don MacLean 10.00
11 Reggie Miller 45.00
12 Sarunas Marciulionis 40.00
13 Craig Ehlo 4.00
14 *Toni Kukoc* 40.00
15 Glen Rice 20.00
16 Otis Thorpe 4.00
17 Reggie Williams 4.00
18 Charles Smith 4.00
19 Micheal Williams 4.00
20 Tom Chambers 4.00
21 David Robinson 40.00
22 *Jamal Mashburn* 50.00
23 Cliff Robinson 4.00
24 *Acie Earl* 4.00
25 Danny Ferry 4.00
26 *Bobby Hurley* 10.00
27 Eddie Johnson 4.00
28 Detlef Schrempf 10.00
29 Mike Brown 4.00
30 Latrell Sprewell 25.00
31 Derek Harper 4.00
32 Stacey Augmon 4.00
33 Pooh Richardson 15.00
34 Larry Krystkowiak 4.00
35 Pervis Ellison 10.00
36 Jeff Malone 15.00
37 Sean Elliott 8.00
38 John Paxson 4.00
39 Robert Parish 8.00
40 Mark Aguirre 10.00
41 Danny Ainge 15.00
42 Brian Shaw 4.00
43 LaPhonso Ellis 8.00
44 Carl Herrera 4.00
45 Terry Cummings 8.00
46 Chris Dudley 4.00
47 Anthony Mason 15.00
48 Chris Morris 25.00
49 Todd Day 10.00
50 *Nick Van Exel* 60.00
51 Larry Nance 4.00
52 Derrick McKey 4.00
53 Muggsy Bogues 10.00
54 Andrew Lang 4.00
55 Chuck Person 10.00
56 Michael Adams 10.00
57 Spud Webb 10.00
58 Scott Skiles 4.00
59 A.C. Green 4.00
60 Terry Mills 4.00
61 Xavier McDaniel 4.00
62 B.J. Armstrong 4.00
63 Donald Hodge 4.00
64 Gary Grant 30.00
65 Billy Owens 4.00
66 Greg Anthony 15.00
67 Jay Humphries 4.00
68 Lionel Simmons 4.00
69 Dana Barros 4.00
70 Steve Smith 8.00
71 *Ervin Johnson* 8.00
72 Sleepy Floyd 4.00
73 Blue Edwards 4.00
74 Clyde Drexler 45.00
75 Elden Campbell 4.00
76 Hakeem Olajuwon 50.00
77 C. Weatherspoon 10.00
78 Kevin Willis 15.00
79 *Isaiah Rider* 25.00
80 Derrick Coleman 10.00
81 Nick Anderson 8.00
82 Bryant Stith 4.00
83 Johnny Newman 4.00
84 *Calbert Cheaney* 50.00
85 Oliver Miller 4.00
86 Loy Vaught 4.00
87 Isiah Thomas 10.00
88 Dee Brown 4.00
89 Horace Grant 15.00
90 Patrick Ewing (AF) 8.00
91 C. Weatherspoon (AF) 15.00
92 Ron Seikaly (AF) 4.00
93 Dino Radja (AF) 4.00
94 Kenny Anderson (AF) 8.00
95 John Starks (AF) 4.00
96 Tom Gugliotta (AF) 4.00
97 Steve Smith (AF) 4.00
98 Derrick Coleman (AF) 4.00
99 Shaquille O'Neal (AF) 60.00
100 Brad Daugherty (CF) 4.00
101 Horace Grant (CF) 4.00
102 Dominique Wilkins (CF) 8.00
103 Joe Dumars (CF) 4.00
104 Alonzo Mourning (CF) 20.00
105 Scottie Pippen (CF) 60.00
106 Reggie Miller (CF) 30.00
107 Mark Price (CF) 10.00
108 Ken Norman (CF) 4.00
109 Larry Johnson (CF) 8.00
110 Jamal Mashburn (MF) 15.00
111 Christian Laettner (MF) 4.00
112 Karl Malone (MF) 8.00
113 Dennis Rodman (MF) 100.00
114 Mahmoud Abdul-Rauf (MF) 4.00
115 Hakeem Olajuwon (MF) 30.00
116 Jim Jackson (MF) 15.00
117 John Stockton (MF) 8.00
118 David Robinson (MF) 50.00
119 Dikembe Mutombo (MF) 8.00
120 Vlade Divac (PF) 4.00
121 Dan Majerle (PF) 4.00
122 Chris Mullin (PF) 4.00
123 Shawn Kemp (PF) 20.00
124 Danny Manning (PF) 4.00
125 Charles Barkley (PF) 20.00
126 Mitch Richmond (PF) 8.00
127 Tim Hardaway (PF) 8.00
128 Detlef Schrempf (PF) 15.00
129 Clyde Drexler (PF) 15.00
130 Christian Laettner 20.00
131 *Rodney Rogers* 8.00
132 Rik Smits 8.00
133 *Chris Mills* 70.00
134 Corie Blount 4.00
135 Mookie Blaylock 8.00
136 Jim Jackson 25.00
137 Tom Gugliotta 25.00
138 Dennis Scott 4.00
139 *Vin Baker* 75.00
140 Gary Payton 75.00
141 Sedale Threatt 4.00
142 Orlando Woolridge 15.00
143 Avery Johnson 8.00
144 Charles Oakley 4.00
145 Harvey Grant 4.00
146 Bimbo Coles 4.00
147 Vernon Maxwell 15.00
148 Danny Manning 8.00
149 Hersey Hawkins 4.00
150 Kevin Gamble 4.00
151 Johnny Dawkins 4.00
152 Olden Polynice 4.00
153 Kevin Edwards 4.00
154 Willie Anderson 4.00
155 Wayman Tisdale 15.00
156 *Popeye Jones* 8.00
157 Dan Majerle 8.00
158 Rex Chapman 4.00
159 Shawn Kemp 40.00
160 Eric Murdock 4.00
161 Randy White 4.00
162 Larry Johnson 20.00
163 Dominique Wilkins 10.00
164 Dikembe Mutombo 10.00
165 Patrick Ewing 40.00
166 Jerome Kersey 4.00
167 Dale Davis 4.00
168 Ron Harper 4.00
169 *Sam Cassell* 35.00
170 Bill Cartwright 25.00
171 John Williams 4.00
172 *Dino Radja* 15.00
173 Dennis Rodman 100.00
174 Kenny Anderson 15.00
175 Robert Horry 10.00
176 Chris Mullin 8.00
177 John Salley 4.00
178 *Scott Burrell* 8.00
179 Mitch Richmond 30.00
180 Lee Mayberry 15.00
181 James Worthy 8.00
182 Rick Fox 30.00
183 Kevin Johnson 10.00
184 *Lindsey Hunter* 20.00
185 Marlon Maxey 4.00
186 Sam Perkins 4.00
187 Kevin Duckworth 4.00
188 Jeff Hornacek 4.00
189 *Anfernee Hardaway* 200.00
190 *Rex Walters* 10.00
191 Mahmoud Abdul-Rauf 8.00
192 *Terry Dehere* 4.00
193 Brad Daugherty 4.00
194 John Starks 8.00
195 Rod Strickland 15.00
196 *Luther Wright* 4.00
197 Vlade Divac 8.00
198 Tim Hardaway 25.00
199 Joe Dumars 8.00
200 Charles Barkley 40.00
201 Alonzo Mourning 40.00
202 Doug West 4.00
203 Anthony Avent 4.00
204 Lloyd Daniels 10.00
205 Mark Price 8.00
206 Rumeal Robinson 4.00
207 Kendall Gill 8.00
208 Scottie Pippen 100.00
209 Kenny Smith 8.00
210 Walt Williams 8.00
211 Hubert Davis 15.00
212 *Chris Webber* 200.00
213 Rony Seikaly 8.00
214 Sam Bowie 4.00
215 Karl Malone 25.00
216 Malik Sealy 4.00
217 Dale Ellis 15.00
218 Harold Miner 10.00
219 John Stockton 25.00
220 *Shawn Bradley* 25.00

1993-94 Finest Main Attraction

These cards, randomly inserted in 14-card 1993-94 Finest packs, have a player from each NBA team represented. The card front uses metallic backgrounds and a semi-embossed color action shot. The player's name is in an orange bar at the bottom, next to the Topps logo. The back has a brick pattern for a background and includes an action photo, player's name and position along the left side, plus a career summary and statistics. The cards are numbered 1 of 27, etc.

MT
Complete Set (27): 100.00
Common Player: 1.00
Minor Stars: 2.00
1 Dominique Wilkins 2.00
2 Dino Radja 3.00
3 Larry Johnson 5.00
4 Scottie Pippen 10.00
5 Mark Price 2.00
6 Jamal Mashburn 7.00
7 Mahmoud Abdul-Rauf 1.00
8 Joe Dumars 2.00
9 Chris Webber 20.00
10 Hakeem Olajuwon 10.00
11 Reggie Miller 4.00
12 Danny Manning 2.00
13 Doug Christie 1.00
14 Steve Smith 1.00
15 Eric Murdock 1.00
16 Isaiah Rider 4.00
17 Derrick Coleman 2.00
18 Patrick Ewing 4.00
19 Shaquille O'Neal 30.00
20 Shawn Bradley 3.50
21 Charles Barkley 7.00
22 Clyde Drexler 5.00
23 Mitch Richmond 2.00
24 David Robinson 8.00
25 Shawn Kemp 6.00
26 Karl Malone 4.00
27 Tom Gugliotta 2.00

1994-95 Finest

Topps Finest Basketball marks the first product to utilize the Topps Finest Protector, a peel-off laminate that insures each card is untouched by human hands until the coating is removed. The protective cover guards against scratching and improves the card's color, intensity and brightness. The cards feature Topps chromium technology, a multi-color metalization technology, which gives the card depth and dimension. The main set has one subset - Finest City Legend - and six insert sets. The insert sets include: Refractors, Marathon Men, Iron Men, Cornerstone, Lottery Prize and Rack Pack. The Refractors are a parallel set to the main set; each card is done with more intense colors. they are in every ninth pack.

MT
Complete Set (331): 350.00
Complete Series 1 (165): 125.00
Complete Series 2 (166): 225.00
Common Player: .50
Minor Stars: 1.00
Prices Are For Unpeeled Cards
Series 1 Pack (7): 7.50
Series 1 Wax Box (24): 170.00
Series 2 Pack (7): 15.00
Series 2 Wax Box (24): 300.00
1 Chris Mullin 1.00
2 Anthony Mason .50
3 John Salley .50
4 Jamal Mashburn 2.00
5 Mark Jackson .50
6 Mario Elie .50
7 Kenny Anderson 1.00
8 Rod Strickland .50
9 Kenny Smith .50
10 Olden Polynice .50
11 Derek Harper .50
12 Danny Ainge .50
13 Dino Radja .75
14 Eric Murdock .50
15 Sean Rooks .50
16 Dell Curry .50
17 Victor Alexander .50
18 Rodney Rogers .50
19 John Salley .50
20 Brad Daugherty .50
21 Elmore Spencer .50
22 Mitch Richmond 1.00
23 Rex Walters .50
24 Antonio Davis .50
25 B.J. Armstrong .50
26 Andrew Lang .50
27 Carl Herrera .50
28 Kevin Edwards .50
29 Micheal Williams .50
30 Clyde Drexler 2.00
31 Dana Barros .50
32 Shaquille O'Neal 10.00
33 Patrick Ewing 2.00
34 Charles Barkley 4.00
35 J.R. Reid .50
36 Lindsey Hunter .50
37 Jeff Malone .50
38 Rik Smits .75
39 Brian Williams .50
40 Shawn Kemp 4.00
41 Terry Porter .50
42 James Worthy .50
43 Rex Chapman .50
44 Stanley Roberts .50
45 Chris Smith .50
46 Dee Brown .50
47 Chris Gatling .50
48 Donald Hodge .50
49 Bimbo Coles .50
50 Derrick Coleman 1.00
51 Muggsy Bogues .50
52 Reggie Williams .50
53 David Wingate .50
54 Sam Cassell .75
55 Sherman Douglas .50
56 Keith Jennings .50
57 Kenny Gattison .50
58 Brent Price .50
59 Luc Longley .50
60 Jamal Mashburn 3.00
61 Doug West .50
62 Walt Williams .50
63 Tracy Murray .50
64 Robert Pack .50
65 Johnny Dawkins .50
66 Vin Baker 4.00
67 Sam Cassell .75
68 Dale Davis .50
69 Terrell Brandon .50
70 Billy Owens .50
71 Ervin Johnson .50
72 Allan Houston 2.00
73 Craig Ehlo .50
74 Loy Vaught .50
75 Scottie Pippen 7.00
76 Sam Bowie .50
77 Anthony Mason .50
78 Felton Spencer .50
79 P.J. Brown .50
80 Christian Laettner .50
81 Todd Day .50
82 Sean Elliott .50
83 Grant Long .50
84 Xavier McDaniel .50
85 David Benoit .50
86 Larry Stewart .50
87 Donald Royal .50
88 Duane Causwell .50
89 Vlade Divac .50
90 Derrick McKay .50
91 Kevin Johnson 1.00
92 LaPhonso Ellis .50
93 Jerome Kersey .50
94 Muggsy Bogues .50
95 Tom Gugliotta 2.00
96 Jeff Hornacek .50
97 Kevin Willis .50
98 Chris Mills .50
99 Sam Perkins .50
100 Alonzo Mourning 2.50
101 Derrick Coleman .75
102 Glen Rice .50
103 Kevin Willis .50
104 Chris Webber 3.00
105 Terry Mills .50
106 Tim Hardaway .75
107 Nick Anderson .50
108 Terry Cummings .50
109 Hersey Hawkins .50
110 Ken Norman .50
111 Nick Anderson .50
112 Tim Perry .50
113 Terry Dehare .50
114 Chris Morris .50
115 John Williams .50
116 Jon Barry .50
117 Rony Seikaly .50
118 Detlef Schrempf .75
119 Terry Cummings .50
120 Chris Webber 6.00
121 David Wingate .50
122 Popeye Jones .50
123 Sherman Douglas .50
124 Greg Anthony .50
125 Mookie Blaylock .50
126 Don MacLean .50
127 Lionel Simmons .50
128 Scott Brooks .50
129 Jeff Turner .50
130 Bryant Stith .50
131 Shawn Bradley .75
132 Byron Scott .50
133 Doug Christie .50
134 Dennis Rodman 8.00
135 Dan Majerle .50
136 Gary Grant .50
137 Byron Russell .50
138 Will Perdue .50
139 Gheorghe Muresan .50
140 Kendall Gill .50
141 Isaiah Rider 1.00
142 Terry Mills .50
143 Willie Anderson .50
144 Hubert Davis .50
145 Lucious Harris .50
146 Spud Webb .50
147 Glen Rice 3.00
148 Dennis Scott .50
149 Robert Horry 1.00
150 John Stockton 2.00
151 Stacey Augmon .50
152 Chris Mills .50
153 Elden Campbell .50
154 Jay Humphries .50
155 Reggie Miller 1.00
156 George Lynch .50
157 Tyrone Hill .50
158 Lee Mayberry .50
159 Jon Koncak .50
160 Joe Dumars 1.00
161 Vernon Maxwell .50
162 Joe Kleine .50
163 Acie Earl .50
164 Steve Kerr .50
165 Rod Strickland .50
166 *Glenn Robinson* 12.00
167 Anfernee Hardaway 5.00
168 Latrell Sprewell 2.00
169 Sergei Bazarevich .50
170 Hakeem Olajuwon 3.00
171 Nick Van Exel 2.00
172 Buck Williams .50
173 Antoine Carr .50
174 Corie Blount .50
175 Dominique Wilkins 1.00
176 *Yinka Dare* .75
177 Byron Houston .50
178 LaSalle Thompson .50
179 Doug Smith .50
180 David Robinson 2.00
181 *Eric Piatkowski* .75
182 Scott Skiles .50
183 Scott Burrell .50
184 Mark West .50
185 Billy Owens .50
186 *Brian Grant* 7.00
187 Scott Williams .50
188 Gerald Madkins .50
189 Reggie Williams .50
190 Danny Manning 1.00
191 Mike Brown .50
192 Charles Smith .50
193 Elden Campbell .50
194 Ricky Pierce .50
195 Karl Malone 2.00
196 Brooks Thompson .75
197 Alaa Abdelnaby .50
198 Tyrone Corbin .50
199 Johnny Newman .50
200 Grant Hill FB 10.00
201 Kenny Anderson .75
202 Olden Polynice .50
203 Horace Grant .50
204 Muggsy Bogues .50
205 Mark Price .50
206 Tom Gugliotta .50
207 Christian Laettner .50
208 Eric Montross 1.00
209 Sam Cassell .75
210 Charles Oakley .50
211 Harold Ellis .50
212 Nate McMillan .50
213 Chuck Person .50
214 Harold Miner .50
215 Clarence Weatherspoon .75
216 Robert Parish 1.00
217 Michael Cage .50
218 Kenny Smith .50
219 Larry Krystkowiak .50
220 Dikembe Mutombo 1.00
221 Wayman Tisdale .50
222 Kevin Duckworth .50
223 Vern Fleming .50
224 *Eric Mobley* .75
225 Patrick Ewing 1.00
226 Cliff Robinson .50
227 Eric Murdock .50
228 Derrick Coleman .50
229 Otis Thorpe .50
230 Alonzo Mourning 1.00
231 Donyell Marshall 1.00
232 Dikembe Mutombo .50
233 Rony Seikaly .50
234 Chris Mullin .75
235 Reggie Miller 2.00
236 Benoit Benjamin .50
237 Sean Rooks .50
238 Terry Davis .50
239 Anthony Avent .50
240 *Grant Hill* 40.00
241 Randy Woods .50
242 Tom Chambers .50
243 Michael Adams .50
244 *Monty Williams* .75
245 Chris Mullin .75
246 Bill Wennington .50
247 Mark Jackson .50
248 Blue Edwards .50
249 *Jalen Rose* 15.00
250 Glenn Robinson 2.00
251 Kevin Willis .50
252 B.J. Armstrong .50
253 Jim Jackson 1.00
254 Steve Smith .50
255 Chris Webber 1.00
256 Glen Rice .50
257 Derek Harper .50
258 Jalen Rose .50
259 Juwan Howard FB 3.00
260 Kenny Anderson 1.00
261 Calbert Cheaney .50
262 Bill Cartwright .50
263 Mario Elie .50
264 Chris Dudley .50
265 Jim Jackson 2.00
266 Antonio Harvey .50
267 *Bill Curley* .75
268 Moses Malone .50
269 A.C. Green .50
270 Larry Johnson 1.50
271 Marty Conlon .50
272 Greg Graham .50
273 *Eric Montross* 1.00
274 Stacey King .50
275 Charles Barkley 2.00
276 Chris Morris .50
277 Robert Horry .50
278 Dominique Wilkins .75
279 Latrell Sprewell 1.00
280 Shaquille O'Neal 3.00
281 Wesley Person 1.00
282 Mahmoud Abdul-Rauf .50
283 Jamal Mashburn 2.00
284 Dale Ellis .50
285 Gary Payton 1.00
286 *Jason Kidd* 40.00
287 Ken Norman .50
288 *Juwan Howard* 10.00
289 *Lamond Murray* 4.00
290 Cliff Robinson .50
291 Frank Brickowski .50
292 Adam Keefe .50
293 Ron Harper .50
294 Tom Hammonds .50
295 Otis Thorpe .50
296 Rick Mahorn .50
297 Alton Lister .50
298 Vinny Del Negro .50
299 Danny Ferry .50
300 John Starks .50
301 Duane Ferrell .50
302 Hersey Hawkins .50
303 *Khalid Reeves* 1.00
304 Anthony Peeler .50
305 Tim Hardaway 1.00
306 Rick Fox .50
307 Jay Humphries .50
308 Brian Shaw .50
309 Dan Schayes .50
310 Stacey Augmon .50
311 Oliver Miller .50
312 Pooh Richardson .50
313 *Donyell Marshall* 4.00
314 *Aaron McKie* 3.00
315 Mark Price .50
316 *B.J. Tyler* .75
317 Olden Polynice .50
318 Avery Johnson .50
319 Derek Strong .50
320 Toni Kukoc 1.00
321 *Charlie Ward* 3.00
322 *Wesley Person* 4.00
323 *Eddie Jones* 20.00
324 Horace Grant 1.00
325 Mahmoud Abdul-Rauf .50
326 *Sharone Wright* 2.00
327 Kevin Gamble .50
328 Sarunas Marciulionis .50
329 Harvey Grant .50
330 Bobby Hurley .50
331 Michael Jordan 25.00

1994-95 Finest Refractors

Refractors are a parallel of the 331-card Finest base set. The cards have a refractive foil finish to give them a glossy appearance. Each Refractor had the Finest Protector to prevent the front of the card from damage or scratches. Refractors were inserted 1:12 packs.

MT
Complete Set (331): 6000.
Complete Series 1 (165): 2500.
Complete Series 2 (166): 3500.
Common Player: 6.00
Minor Stars: 12.00
Prices Are For Unpeeled Cards
1 Chris Mullin CY 25.00
2 Anthony Mason CY 20.00
3 John Salley CY 6.00
4 Jamal Mashburn CY 25.00
5 Mark Jackson 6.00
6 Mario Elie 6.00
7 Kenny Anderson 12.00
8 Rod Strickland 12.00
9 Kenny Smith 6.00
10 Olden Polynice 6.00
11 Derek Harper 6.00
12 Danny Ainge 6.00
13 Dino Radja 6.00
14 Eric Murdock 6.00
15 Sean Rooks 6.00
16 Dell Curry 6.00
17 Victor Alexander 6.00
18 Rodney Rogers 25.00
19 John Salley 6.00
20 Brad Daugherty 6.00
21 Elmore Spencer 6.00
22 Mitch Richmond 45.00
23 Rex Walters 6.00
24 Antonio Davis 6.00
25 B.J. Armstrong 6.00
26 Andrew Lang 6.00
27 Carl Herrera 20.00
28 Kevin Edwards 6.00
29 Micheal Williams 6.00
30 Clyde Drexler 50.00
31 Dana Barros 6.00
32 Shaquille O'Neal 150.00
33 Patrick Ewing 35.00
34 Charles Barkley 70.00
35 J.R. Reid 6.00
36 Lindsey Hunter 12.00
37 Jeff Malone 6.00
38 Rik Smits 20.00
39 Brian Williams 20.00
40 Shawn Kemp 60.00
41 Terry Porter 6.00
42 James Worthy 6.00
43 Rex Chapman 6.00
44 Stanley Roberts 6.00
45 Chris Smith 6.00
46 Dee Brown 6.00
47 Chris Gatling 6.00
48 Donald Hodge 6.00
49 Bimbo Coles 6.00
50 Derrick Coleman 12.00
51 Muggsy Bogues 6.00
52 Reggie Williams 6.00
53 David Wingate 6.00
54 Sam Cassell 12.00
55 Sherman Douglas 6.00
56 Keith Jennings 6.00
57 Kenny Gattison 6.00
58 Brent Price 6.00
59 Luc Longley 6.00
60 Jamal Mashburn 35.00
61 Doug West 6.00
62 Walt Williams 12.00
63 Tracy Murray 6.00
64 Robert Pack 6.00
65 Johnny Dawkins 6.00
66 Vin Baker 60.00
67 Sam Cassell 12.00
68 Dale Davis 6.00
69 Terrell Brandon 30.00
70 Billy Owens 6.00
71 Ervin Johnson 6.00
72 Allan Houston 60.00
73 Craig Ehlo 6.00
74 Loy Vaught 6.00
75 Scottie Pippen 125.00
76 Sam Bowie 6.00
77 Anthony Mason 15.00
78 Felton Spencer 6.00
79 P.J. Brown 12.00
80 Christian Laettner 20.00
81 Todd Day 6.00
82 Sean Elliott 6.00
83 Grant Long 6.00
84 Xavier McDaniel 6.00
85 David Benoit 6.00

86	Larry Stewart	6.00
87	Donald Royal	6.00
88	Duane Causwell	6.00
89	Vlade Divac	12.00
90	Derrick McKey	6.00
91	Kevin Johnson	12.00
92	LaPhonso Ellis	12.00
93	Jerome Kersey	6.00
94	Muggsy Bogues	6.00
95	Tom Gugliotta	35.00
96	Jeff Hornacek	6.00
97	Kevin Willis	6.00
98	Chris Mills	6.00
99	Sam Perkins	6.00
100	Alonzo Mourning	45.00
101	Derrick Coleman	12.00
102	Glen Rice CY	120.00
103	Kevin Willis	6.00
104	Chris Webber CY	100.00
105	Terry Mills	6.00
106	Tim Hardaway CY	30.00
107	Nick Anderson	6.00
108	Terry Cummings	6.00
109	Hersey Hawkins	6.00
110	Ken Norman	6.00
111	Nick Anderson	6.00
112	Tim Perry	6.00
113	Terry Dehare	6.00
114	Chris Morris	6.00
115	John Williams	6.00
116	Jon Barry	6.00
117	Rony Seikaly	12.00
118	Detlef Schrempf	12.00
119	Terry Cummings	6.00
120	Chris Webber	200.00
121	David Wingate	6.00
122	Popeye Jones	6.00
123	Sherman Douglas	6.00
124	Greg Anthony	6.00
125	Mookie Blaylock	12.00
126	Don MacLean	6.00
127	Lionel Simmons	6.00
128	Scott Brooks	6.00
129	Jeff Turner	6.00
130	Bryant Stith	6.00
131	Shawn Bradley	15.00
132	Byron Scott	6.00
133	Doug Christie	6.00
134	Dennis Rodman	150.00
135	Dan Majerle	20.00
136	Gary Grant	6.00
137	Byron Russell	6.00
138	Will Perdue	15.00
139	Gheorghe Muresan	25.00
140	Kendall Gill	25.00
141	Isaiah Rider	12.00
142	Terry Mills	6.00
143	Willie Anderson	15.00
144	Hubert Davis	6.00
145	Lucious Harris	6.00
146	Spud Webb	6.00
147	Glen Rice	60.00
148	Dennis Scott	6.00
149	Robert Horry	20.00
150	John Stockton	70.00
151	Stacey Augmon	6.00
152	Chris Mills	6.00
153	Elden Campbell CY	25.00
154	Jay Humphries	6.00
155	Reggie Miller CY	50.00
156	George Lynch	15.00
157	Tyrone Hill	6.00
158	Lee Mayberry	6.00
159	Jon Koncak	6.00
160	Joe Dumars	12.00
161	Vernon Maxwell	6.00
162	Joe Kleine	25.00
163	Acie Earl	6.00
164	Steve Kerr	20.00
165	Rod Strickland	20.00
166	Glenn Robinson	120.00
167	Anfernee Hardaway	300.00
168	Latrell Sprewell	30.00
169	Sergei Bazarevich	6.00
170	Hakeem Olajuwon	60.00
171	Nick Van Exel	45.00
172	Buck Williams	6.00
173	Antoine Carr	6.00
174	Corie Blount	6.00
175	Dominique Wilkins	12.00
176	*Yinka Dare*	6.00
177	Byron Houston	6.00
178	LaSalle Thompson	6.00
179	Doug Smith	6.00
180	David Robinson	40.00
181	*Eric Piatkowski*	6.00
182	Scott Skiles	6.00
183	Scott Burrell	6.00
184	Mark West	6.00
185	Billy Owens	6.00
186	Brian Grant	40.00
187	Scott Williams	6.00
188	Gerald Madkins	6.00
189	Reggie Williams	6.00
190	Danny Manning	12.00
191	Mike Brown	6.00
192	Charles Smith	6.00
193	Elden Campbell	6.00
194	Ricky Pierce	6.00
195	Karl Malone	40.00
196	Brooks Thompson	6.00
197	Alaa Abdelnaby	6.00
198	Tyrone Corbin	6.00
199	Johnny Newman	6.00
200	Grant Hill CB	150.00
201	Kenny Anderson	12.00
202	Olden Polynice	6.00
203	Horace Grant	6.00
204	Muggsy Bogues	6.00
205	Mark Price	6.00
206	Tom Gugliotta CB	15.00
207	Christian Laettner	12.00
208	Eric Montross	6.00
209	Sam Cassell	12.00
210	Charles Oakley	6.00
211	Harold Ellis	6.00
212	Nate McMillan	6.00
213	Chuck Person	6.00
214	Harold Miner	6.00
215	Clarence Weatherspoon	12.00
216	Robert Parish	12.00
217	Michael Cage	6.00
218	Kenny Smith	6.00
219	Larry Krystkowiak	6.00
220	Dikembe Mutombo	15.00
221	Wayman Tisdale	6.00
222	Kevin Duckworth	6.00
223	Vern Fleming	6.00
224	Eric Mobley	6.00
225	Patrick Ewing CB	15.00
226	Cliff Robinson	6.00
227	Eric Murdock	6.00
228	Derrick Coleman	12.00
229	Otis Thorpe	6.00
230	Alonzo Mourning CB	20.00
231	Donyell Marshall	12.00
232	Dikembe Mutombo	12.00
233	Rony Seikaly	12.00
234	Chris Mullin	12.00
235	Reggie Miller	40.00
236	Benoit Benjamin	6.00
237	Sean Rooks	6.00
238	Terry Davis	6.00
239	Anthony Avent	6.00
240	Grant Hill	500.00
241	Randy Woods	6.00
242	Tom Chambers	6.00
243	Michael Adams	6.00
244	Monty Williams	6.00
245	Chris Mullin	12.00
246	Bill Wennington	6.00
247	Mark Jackson	6.00
248	Blue Edwards	6.00
249	Jalen Rose	15.00
250	Glenn Robinson CB	35.00
251	Kevin Willis	6.00
252	B.J. Armstrong	6.00
253	Jim Jackson	12.00
254	Steve Smith	6.00
255	Chris Webber CB	60.00
256	Glen Rice CB	25.00
257	Derek Harper	6.00
258	Jalen Rose	6.00
259	Juwan Howard CB	60.00
260	Kenny Anderson	15.00
261	Calbert Cheaney	6.00
262	Bill Cartwright	6.00
263	Mario Elie	6.00
264	Chris Dudley	6.00
265	Jim Jackson	20.00
266	Antonio Harvey	6.00
267	Bill Curley	6.00
268	Moses Malone	6.00
269	A.C. Green	6.00
270	Larry Johnson	25.00
271	Marty Conlon	6.00
272	Greg Graham	6.00
273	Eric Montross	6.00
274	Stacey King	6.00
275	Charles Barkley CB	20.00
276	Chris Morris	6.00
277	Robert Horry	12.00
278	Dominique Wilkins	12.00
279	Latrell Sprewell CB	30.00
280	Shaquille O'Neal CB	50.00
281	Wesley Person	12.00
282	Mahmoud Abdul-Rauf	6.00
283	Jamal Mashburn CB	20.00
284	Dale Ellis	6.00
285	Gary Payton	75.00
286	Jason Kidd	170.00
287	Ken Norman	6.00
288	Juwan Howard	100.00
289	Lamond Murray	6.00
290	Cliff Robinson	6.00
291	Frank Brickowski	6.00
292	Adam Keefe	6.00
293	Ron Harper	6.00
294	Tom Hammonds	6.00
295	Otis Thorpe	6.00
296	Rick Mahorn	6.00
297	Alton Lister	6.00
298	Vinny Del Negro	6.00
299	Danny Ferry	6.00
300	John Starks	12.00
301	Duane Ferrell	6.00
302	Hersey Hawkins	6.00
303	Khalid Reeves	12.00
304	Anthony Peeler	6.00
305	Tim Hardaway	40.00
306	Rick Fox	6.00
307	Jay Humphries	6.00
308	Brian Shaw	6.00
309	Dan Schayes	6.00
310	Stacey Augmon	6.00
311	Oliver Miller	6.00
312	Pooh Richardson	6.00
313	Donyell Marshall	15.00
314	Aaron McKie	6.00
315	Mark Price	6.00
316	B.J. Tyler	6.00
317	Olden Polynice	6.00
318	Avery Johnson	6.00
319	Derek Strong	6.00
320	Toni Kukoc	45.00
321	Charlie Ward	12.00
322	Wesley Person	20.00
323	Eddie Jones	175.00
324	Horace Grant	6.00
325	Mahmoud Abdul-Rauf	6.00
326	Sharone Wright	6.00
327	Kevin Gamble	6.00
328	Sarunas Marciulionis	6.00
329	Harvey Grant	6.00
330	Bobby Hurley	6.00
331	Michael Jordan	41.00

1994-95 Finest Cornerstone

These 1994-95 Topps Finest Series II inserts feature 15 men who are the heart and soul of their teams - the foundation that the roster is built on. The cards were available one in every 24 packs.

		MT
	Complete Set (15):	150.00
	Common Player:	3.00
	Prices Are For Unpeeled Cards	
1	Shaquille O'Neal	35.00
2	Alonzo Mourning	10.00
3	Patrick Ewing	7.00
4	Karl Malone	7.00
5	Kenny Anderson	3.00
6	Latrell Sprewell	10.00
7	Dikembe Mutombo	3.00
8	Charles Barkley	12.00
9	John Stockton	7.00
10	Reggie Miller	7.00
11	Jamal Mashburn	5.00
12	Anfernee Hardaway	35.00
13	Jim Jackson	3.00
14	David Robinson	10.00
15	Hakeem Olajuwon	15.00

1994-95 Finest Iron Men

These 1994-95 Topps Finest Series I inserts feature 10 players who played more than 3,000 minutes last season. The cards were included one per every 24 packs.

		MT
	Complete Set (10):	60.00
	Common Player:	2.00
	Prices Are For Unpeeled Cards	
1	Shaquille O'Neal	20.00
2	Kenny Anderson	2.00
3	Jim Jackson	4.00
4	Clarence Weatherspoon	2.00
5	Karl Malone	4.00
6	Dan Majerle	2.00
7	Anfernee Hardaway	25.00
8	David Robinson	8.00
9	Latrell Sprewell	3.00
10	Hakeem Olajuwon	8.00

1994-95 Finest Lottery Prize

These insert cards, available in 1994-95 Topps Finest Series II packs, feature 22 lottery draft picks who have emerged as impact players for their teams. The cards could be found one in every six packs.

		MT
	Complete Set (22):	60.00
	Common Player:	1.00
	Minor Stars:	2.00
	Prices Are For Unpeeled Cards	
1	Patrick Ewing	3.00
2	Chris Mullin	1.00
3	David Robinson	7.00
4	Scottie Pippen	7.00
5	Kevin Johnson	2.00
6	Danny Manning	1.00
7	Mitch Richmond	1.00
8	Derrick Coleman	2.00
9	Gary Payton	3.00
10	Mahmoud Abdul-Rauf	1.00
11	Larry Johnson	3.00
12	Kenny Anderson	2.00
13	Dikembe Mutombo	2.00
14	Stacey Augmon	1.00
15	Shaquille O'Neal	16.00
16	Alonzo Mourning	5.00
17	Clarence Weatherspoon	1.00
18	Robert Horry	1.00
19	Chris Webber	7.00
20	Anfernee Hardaway	20.00
21	Jamal Mashburn	3.00
22	Vin Baker	3.00

1994-95 Finest Marathon Men

This set salutes 20 players who played in all 82 games during the last season. The cards were random inserts in 1994-95 Topps Finest Series I packs, one per every 12 packs.

		MT
	Complete Set (20):	50.00
	Common Player:	2.00
	Minor Stars:	4.00
	Prices Are For Unpeeled Cards	
1	Latrell Sprewell	8.00
2	Gary Payton	8.00
3	Kenny Anderson	4.00
4	Jim Jackson	6.00
5	Lindsey Hunter	2.00
6	Rod Strickland	2.00
7	Hersey Hawkins	2.00
8	Gerald Wilkins	2.00
9	B.J. Armstrong	3.00
10	Anfernee Hardaway	30.00
11	Stacey Augmon	2.00
12	Eric Murdock	2.00
13	Clarence Weatherspoon	4.00
14	Karl Malone	6.00
15	Charles Oakley	2.00
16	Rick Fox	2.00
17	Otis Thorpe	2.00
18	Dikembe Mutombo	6.00
19	Mike Brown	2.00
20	A.C. Green	2.00

1994-95 Finest Rack Pack

These cards were random inserts in 1994-95 Topps Finest Series II packs, one per every 72 packs, making them the scarcest of the Finest insert cards. The cards feature seven rookies who are destined to become the future of the NBA.

		MT
	Complete Set (7):	125.00
	Common Player:	3.00
	Prices Are For Unpeeled Cards	
1	Grant Hill	60.00
2	Wesley Person	5.00
3	Juwan Howard	15.00
4	Lamond Murray	3.00
5	Glenn Robinson	20.00
6	Donyell Marshall	3.00
7	Jason Kidd	30.00

1995-96 Finest

Topps released its 1995-96 Finest set in two series. The first series contains 140 cards, including a 29-card Draft Picks subset and a checklist. The regular cards feature the Finest players on one of five innovative designs as each card highlights a player's position - point guard, shooting guard, small forward, power forward and center. Series II has 110 cards and includes all the stars which weren't in the first series. Each card in both series is reprinted as part of a parallel Refractors set; cards are seeded one per every 12 packs. Inserts in Series I are Dish and Swish, Hot Stuff, Mystery Finest and Mystery Finest Refractors. Series II also has Mystery Finest and Mystery Finest Refractors, plus Rack Pack and Veteran/Rookie inserts.

		MT
	Complete Set (251):	250.00
	Comp. Series 1 (140):	210.00
	Comp. Series 2 (111):	40.00
	Common Player:	.20
	Minor Stars:	.40
	Series 1 Pack (6):	20.00
	Series 1 Wax Box (24):	425.00
	Series 2 Pack (6):	8.00
	Series 2 Wax Box (24):	160.00
1	Hakeem Olajuwon	2.00
2	Stacey Augmon	.20
3	John Starks	.20
4	Sharone Wright	.40
5	Jason Kidd	2.50
6	Lamond Murray	.40
7	Kenny Anderson	.40
8	James Robinson	.20
9	Wesley Person	.20
10	Latrell Sprewell	1.50
11	Sean Elliott	.20
12	Greg Anthony	.20
13	Kendall Gill	.20
14	Mark Jackson	.20
15	John Stockton	1.00
16	Steve Smith	.20
17	Bobby Hurley	.20
18	Ervin Johnson	.20
19	Elden Campbell	.20
20	Vin Baker	.75
21	Michael Williams	.20
22	Steve Kerr	.20
23	Kevin Duckworth	.20
24	Willie Anderson	.20
25	Joe Dumars	.40
26	Dale Ellis	.20
27	Bimbo Coles	.20
28	Nick Anderson	.40
29	Dee Brown	.20
30	Tyrone Hill	.20
31	Reggie Miller	1.00
32	Shaquille O'Neal	5.00
33	Brian Grant	.40
34	Charles Barkley	2.00
35	Cedric Ceballos	.75
36	Rex Walters	.20
37	Kenny Smith	.20
38	Popeye Jones	.20
39	Harvey Grant	.20
40	Gary Payton	1.50
41	John Williams	.20
42	Sherman Douglas	.20
43	Oliver Miller	.20
44	Kevin Willis	.20
45	Isaiah Rider	.40
46	Gheorghe Muresan	.40
47	Blue Edwards	.20
48	Jeff Hornacek	.20
49	J.R. Reid	.20
50	Glenn Robinson	1.00
51	Dell Curry	.20
52	Greg Graham	.20
53	Ron Harper	.20
54	Derek Harper	.20
55	Dikembe Mutombo	.75
56	Terry Mills	.20
57	Victor Alexander	.20
58	Malik Sealy	.20
59	Vincent Askew	.20
60	Mitch Richmond	.40
61	Duane Ferrell	.20
62	Dickey Simpkins	.20
63	Pooh Richardson	.20
64	Khalid Reeves	.40
65	Dino Radja	.40
66	Lee Mayberry	.20
67	Kenny Gattison	.20
68	Joe Kleine	.20
69	Tony Dumas	.20
70	Nick Van Exel	1.00
71	Armon Gilliam	.20
72	Craig Ehlo	.20
73	Adam Keefe	.20
74	Chris Dudley	.20
75	Clyde Drexler	1.50
76	Jeff Turner	.20
77	Calbert Cheaney	.20
78	Vinny Del Negro	.20
79	Tim Perry	.20
80	Tim Hardaway	.75
81	B.J. Armstrong	.20
82	Muggsy Bogues	.20
83	Mark Macon	.20
84	Doug West	.20
85	Jalen Rose	.20
86	Chris Mills	.20
87	Charles Oakley	.20
88	Andrew Lang	.20
89	Olden Polynice	.20
90	Sam Cassell	.20
91	Todd Day	.20
92	P.J. Brown	.20
93	Benoit Benjamin	.20
94	Sam Perkins	.20
95	Eddie Jones	3.00
96	Robert Parish	.20
97	Avery Johnson	.20
98	Lindsey Hunter	.20
99	Billy Owens	.20
100	Shawn Bradley	.20
101	Dale Davis	.20
102	Terry Dehere	.20
103	A.C. Green	.20
104	Christian Laettner	.20
105	Horace Grant	.40
106	Rony Seikaly	.20
107	Reggie Williams	.20
108	Toni Kukoc	.20
109	Terrell Brandon	.20
110	Clifford Robinson	.40
111	*Joe Smith*	5.00
112	*Antonio McDyess*	20.00
113	*Jerry Stackhouse*	25.00
114	*Rasheed Wallace*	25.00
115	*Kevin Garnett*	125.00
116	*Bryant Reeves*	3.00
117	*Damon Stoudamire*	6.00
118	*Shawn Respert*	.75
119	*Ed O'Bannon*	.50
120	*Kurt Thomas*	1.00
121	*Gary Trent*	3.00
122	*Cherokee Parks*	1.50
123	*Corliss Williamson*	3.00
124	*Eric Williams*	2.00
125	*Brent Barry*	2.00
126	*Alan Henderson*	3.00
127	*Bob Sura*	3.00
128	*Theo Ratliff*	5.00
129	*Randolph Childress*	.75
130	*Jason Caffey*	2.00
131	*Michael Finley*	20.00
132	*George Zidek*	.75
133	*Travis Best*	4.00
134	*Loren Meyer*	.75
135	*David Vaughn*	.75
136	*Sherell Ford*	.75
137	*Mario Bennett*	.75
138	*Greg Ostertag*	1.00
139	*Cory Alexander*	1.00
140	Checklist	.20
141	Chucky Brown	.20
142	Eric Mobley	.20
143	Tom Hammonds	.20
144	Chris Webber	1.50
145	Carlos Rogers	.20
146	Chuck Person	.20
147	Brian Williams	.20
148	Kevin Gamble	.20
149	Dennis Rodman	7.00
150	Pervis Ellison	.20
151	Jayson Williams	.20
152	Buck Williams	.20
153	Allan Houston	.40
154	Tom Gugliotta	.20
155	Charles Smith	.20
156	Chris Gatling	.20
157	Darrin Hancock	.20
158	Blue Edwards	.20
159	Shawn Kemp	1.50
160	Michael Cage	.20
161	Sedale Threatt	.20
162	Byron Scott	.20
163	Elliot Perry	.20
164	Jim Jackson	.50
165	Wayman Tisdale	.20
166	Vernon Maxwell	.20
167	Brian Shaw	.20
168	Haywoode Workman	.20
169	Mookie Blaylock	.20
170	Donald Royal	.20
171	Lorenzo Williams	.20
172	Eric Piatkowski	.20
173	Sarunas Marciulionis	.20
174	Otis Thorpe	.20
175	Rex Chapman	.20
176	Felton Spencer	.20
177	John Salley	.20
178	Pete Chilcutt	.20
179	Scottie Pippen	4.00
180	Robert Pack	.20
181	Dana Barros	.20
182	Mahmoud Abdul-Rauf	.20
183	Eric Murdock	.20
184	Anthony Mason	.20
185	Will Perdue	.20
186	Jeff Malone	.20
187	Anthony Peeler	.20
188	Chris Childs	.20
189	Glen Rice	.20
190	Grant Hill	7.00
191	Michael Smith	.20
192	Sean Rooks	.20
193	Clifford Rozier	.20
194	Rik Smits	.20
195	Spud Webb	.20
196	Aaron McKie	.20
197	Nate McMillan	.20
198	Bobby Phills	.20
199	Dennis Scott	.20
200	Mark West	.20
201	George McCloud	.20
202	B.J. Tyler	.20
203	Lionel Simmons	.20
204	Loy Vaught	.20
205	Kevin Edwards	.20
206	Eric Montross	.20
207	Kenny Gattison	.20
208	Mario Elie	.20
209	Karl Malone	1.00
210	Ken Norman	.20
211	Antonio Davis	.20
212	Doc Rivers	.20
213	Hubert Davis	.20
214	Jamal Mashburn	.75
215	Donyell Marshall	.20
216	*Sasha Danilovic*	1.00
217	Danny Manning	.20
218	Scott Burrell	.20
219	Vlade Divac	.20
220	Marty Conlon	.20
221	Clarence Weatherspoon	.20
222	Terry Porter	.20
223	Luc Longley	.20
224	Juwan Howard	2.00
225	Danny Ferry	.20
226	Rod Strickland	.20
227	Bryant Stith	.20
228	Derrick McKey	.20
229	Michael Jordan	20.00
230	Jamie Watson	.20
231	Rick Fox	.20
232	Scott Williams	.20
233	Larry Johnson	1.00
234	Anfernee Hardaway	6.00
235	Hersey Hawkins	.20
236	Robert Horry	.40
237	Kevin Johnson	.40
238	Rodney Rogers	.20
239	Detlef Schrempf	.20
240	Derrick Coleman	.40
241	Walt Williams	.20
242	LaPhonso Ellis	.20
243	Patrick Ewing	.75
244	Grant Long	.20
245	David Robinson	2.00
246	Chris Mullin	.20
247	Alonzo Mourning	1.00
248	Dan Majerle	.20
249	Johnny Newman	.20
250	Chris Morris	.20
252	Magic Johnson	4.00

1995-96 Finest Refractors

These cards, available in both series of 1995-96 Topps Finest product, are a parallel set to the regular issue. There were 110 cards from the first series reprinted using this technique; 111 from Series II are done this way. Refractors were seeded one per every 12 packs.

		MT
Complete Set (221):		1400.
Comp. Series 1 (110):		500.00
Comp. Series 2 (111):		900.00
Common Player:		4.00
Minor Stars:		8.00
Inserted 1:12		
1	Hakeem Olajuwon	20.00
2	Stacey Augmon	4.00
3	John Starks	4.00
4	Sharone Wright	4.00
5	Jason Kidd	30.00
6	Lamond Murray	4.00
7	Kenny Anderson	8.00
8	James Robinson	4.00
9	Wesley Person	4.00
10	Latrell Sprewell	15.00
11	Sean Elliott	4.00
12	Greg Anthony	4.00
13	Kendall Gill	4.00
14	Mark Jackson	4.00
15	John Stockton	10.00
16	Steve Smith	4.00
17	Bobby Hurley	4.00
18	Ervin Johnson	4.00
19	Elden Campbell	4.00
20	Vin Baker	8.00
21	Michael Williams	4.00
22	Steve Kerr	4.00
23	Kevin Duckworth	4.00
24	Willie Anderson	4.00
25	Joe Dumars	8.00
26	Dale Ellis	4.00
27	Bimbo Coles	4.00
28	Nick Anderson	4.00
29	Dee Brown	4.00
30	Tyrone Hill	4.00
31	Reggie Miller	10.00
32	Shaquille O'Neal	50.00
33	Brian Grant	4.00
34	Charles Barkley	20.00
35	Cedric Ceballos	4.00
36	Rex Walters	4.00
37	Kenny Smith	4.00
38	Popeye Jones	4.00
39	Harvey Grant	4.00
40	Gary Payton	20.00
41	John Williams	4.00
42	Sherman Douglas	4.00
43	Oliver Miller	4.00
44	Kevin Willis	4.00
45	Isaiah Rider	4.00
46	Gheorghe Muresan	4.00
47	Blue Edwards	4.00
48	Jeff Hornacek	4.00
49	J.R. Reid	4.00
50	Glenn Robinson	8.00
51	Dell Curry	4.00
52	Greg Graham	4.00
53	Ron Harper	4.00
54	Derek Harper	4.00
55	Dikembe Mutombo	8.00
56	Terry Mills	4.00
57	Victor Alexander	4.00
58	Malik Sealy	4.00
59	Vincent Askew	4.00
60	Mitch Richmond	8.00
61	Duane Ferrell	4.00
62	Dickey Simpkins	4.00
63	Pooh Richardson	4.00
64	Khalid Reeves	4.00
65	Dino Radja	4.00
66	Lee Mayberry	4.00
67	Kenny Gattison	4.00
68	Joe Kleine	4.00
69	Tony Dumas	4.00
70	Nick Van Exel	8.00
71	Armon Gilliam	4.00
72	Craig Ehlo	4.00
73	Adam Keefe	4.00
74	Chris Dudley	4.00
75	Clyde Drexler	12.00
76	Jeff Turner	4.00
77	Calbert Cheaney	4.00
78	Vinny Del Negro	4.00
79	Tim Perry	4.00
80	Tim Hardaway	8.00
81	B.J. Armstrong	4.00
82	Muggsy Bogues	4.00
83	Mark Macon	4.00
84	Doug West	4.00
85	Jalen Rose	4.00
86	Chris Mills	4.00
87	Charles Oakley	4.00
88	Andrew Lang	4.00
89	Olden Polynice	4.00
90	Sam Cassell	4.00
91	Todd Day	4.00
92	P.J. Brown	4.00
93	Benoit Benjamin	4.00
94	Sam Perkins	4.00
95	Eddie Jones	35.00
96	Robert Parish	4.00
97	Avery Johnson	4.00
98	Lindsey Hunter	4.00
99	Billy Owens	4.00
100	Shawn Bradley	4.00
101	Dale Davis	4.00
102	Terry Dehere	4.00
103	A.C. Green	4.00
104	Christian Laettner	4.00
105	Horace Grant	4.00
106	Rony Seikaly	4.00
107	Reggie Williams	4.00
108	Toni Kukoc	15.00
109	Terrell Brandon	8.00
110	Clifford Robinson	4.00
141	Chucky Brown	4.00
142	Eric Mobley	4.00
143	Tom Hammonds	4.00
144	Chris Webber	30.00
145	Carlos Rogers	4.00
146	Chuck Person	4.00
147	Brian Williams	4.00
148	Kevin Gamble	4.00
149	Dennis Rodman	25.00
150	Pervis Ellison	4.00
151	Jayson Williams	4.00
152	Buck Williams	4.00
153	Allan Houston	15.00
154	Tom Gugliotta	8.00
155	Charles Smith	4.00
156	Chris Gatling	4.00
157	Darrin Hancock	4.00
158	Blue Edwards	4.00
159	Shawn Kemp	8.00
160	Michael Cage	4.00
161	Sedale Threatt	4.00
162	Byron Scott	4.00
163	Elliot Perry	4.00
164	Jim Jackson	4.00
165	Wayman Tisdale	4.00
166	Vernon Maxwell	4.00
167	Brian Shaw	4.00
168	Haywoode Workman	4.00
169	Mookie Blaylock	4.00
170	Donald Royal	4.00
171	Lorenzo Williams	4.00
172	Eric Piatkowski	4.00
173	Sarunas Marciulionis	4.00
174	Otis Thorpe	4.00
175	Rex Chapman	4.00
176	Felton Spencer	4.00
177	John Salley	4.00
178	Pete Chilcutt	4.00
179	Scottie Pippen	40.00
180	Robert Pack	4.00
181	Dana Barros	4.00
182	Mahmoud Abdul-Rauf	4.00
183	Eric Murdock	4.00
184	Anthony Mason	4.00
185	Will Perdue	4.00
186	Jeff Malone	4.00
187	Anthony Peeler	4.00
188	Chris Childs	4.00
189	Glen Rice	12.00
190	Grant Hill	75.00
191	Michael Smith	4.00
192	Sean Rooks	4.00
193	Clifford Rozier	4.00
194	Rik Smits	4.00
195	Spud Webb	4.00
196	Aaron McKie	4.00
197	Nate McMillan	4.00
198	Bobby Phills	4.00
199	Dennis Scott	4.00
200	Mark West	4.00
201	George McCloud	4.00
202	B.J. Tyler	4.00
203	Lionel Simmons	4.00
204	Loy Vaught	4.00
205	Kevin Edwards	4.00
206	Eric Montross	4.00
207	Kenny Gattison	4.00
208	Mario Elie	4.00
209	Karl Malone	15.00
210	Ken Norman	4.00
211	Antonio Davis	4.00
212	Doc Rivers	4.00
213	Hubert Davis	4.00
214	Jamal Mashburn	8.00
215	Donyell Marshall	4.00
216	Predrag Danilovic	4.00
217	Danny Manning	4.00
218	Scott Burrell	4.00
219	Vlade Divac	4.00
220	Marty Conlon	4.00
221	Clarence Weatherspoon	4.00
222	Terry Porter	4.00
223	Luc Longley	4.00
224	Juwan Howard	15.00
225	Danny Ferry	4.00
226	Rod Strickland	4.00
227	Bryant Stith	4.00
228	Derrick McKey	4.00
229	Michael Jordan	300.00
230	Jamie Watson	4.00
231	Rick Fox	4.00
232	Scott Williams	4.00
233	Larry Johnson	8.00
234	Anfernee Hardaway	75.00
235	Hersey Hawkins	4.00
236	Robert Horry	4.00
237	Kevin Johnson	4.00
238	Rodney Rogers	4.00
239	Detlef Schrempf	4.00
240	Derrick Coleman	8.00
241	Walt Williams	4.00
242	LaPhonso Ellis	4.00
243	Patrick Ewing	12.00
244	Grant Long	4.00
245	David Robinson	12.00
246	Chris Mullin	8.00
247	Alonzo Mourning	12.00
248	Dan Majerle	4.00
249	Johnny Newman	4.00
250	Chris Morris	4.00
252	Magic Johnson	25.00

1995-96 Finest Dish and Swish

These double-sided Finest cards make their debut in this 29-card 1995-96 Topps Series I insert set. Two players are featured on these cards. One side highlights a player known for passing and the other showcases the highest scoring finisher who converts those passes into points. Cards are numbered with a "DS" prefix.

		MT
Complete Set (29):		200.00
Common Player:		2.00
Inserted 1:24 Series I		
1	Mookie Blaylock, Steve Smith	2.00
2	Sherman Douglas, Dino Radja	2.00
3	Muggsy Bogues, Larry Johnson	3.00
4	Scottie Pippen, Michael Jordan	70.00
5	Mark Price, Chris Mills	2.00
6	Jason Kidd, Jamal Mashburn	15.00
7	Mahmoud Abdul-Rauf, Dikembe Mutombo	2.00
8	Joe Dumars, Grant Hill	25.00
9	Tim Hardaway, Chris Mullin	2.00
10	Clyde Drexler, Hakeem Olajuwon	10.00
11	Mark Jackson, Reggie Miller	5.00
12	Pooh Richardson, Lamond Murray	2.00
13	Nick Van Exel, Cedric Ceballos	3.00
14	Khalid Reeves, Glen Rice	2.00
15	Eric Murdock, Glenn Robinson	3.00
16	Tom Gugliotta, Christian Laettner	2.00
17	Kenny Anderson, Derrick Coleman	2.00
18	Derek Harper, Patrick Ewing	3.00
19	Anfernee Hardaway, Shaquille O'Neal	30.00
20	Dana Barros, Clarence Weatherspoon	2.00
21	Kevin Johnson, Charles Barkley	8.00
22	Rod Strickland, Clifford Robinson	2.00
23	Walt Williams, Mitch Richmond	2.00
24	Avery Johnson, David Robinson	8.00
25	Gary Payton, Shawn Kemp	8.00
26	B.J. Armstrong, Oliver Miller	2.00
27	John Stockton, Karl Malone	10.00
28	Greg Anthony, Byron Scott	2.00
29	Chris Webber, Juwan Howard	15.00

1995-96 Finest Hot Stuff

These 15 cards, printed on a silver foil background, focus on NBA players who are known for their slam-ming and jamming. The cards were seeded one per every eight packs of 1995-96 Topps Finest Series I products. The front has a color action photo on it, with the player's name running vertically along the left side. A team logo and a "Hot Stuff" logo are at the bottom of the card. The Topps Finest logo is at the top. The card back has a mug shot and a ghosted action shot as a background. The player's team name is along the top, with his name and position underneath in white letters. A card number is also given, using an "HS" prefix. A shaded box toward the bottom of the card has brief statistical tidbits.

		MT
Complete Set (15):		70.00
Common Player:		1.00
1	Michael Jordan	25.00
2	Grant Hill	10.00
3	Clyde Drexler	3.00
4	Anfernee Hardaway	14.00
5	Sean Elliott	1.00
6	Latrell Sprewell	1.50
7	Larry Johnson	2.00
8	Eddie Jones	4.00
9	Karl Malone	2.00
10	John Starks	1.00
11	Scottie Pippen	6.00
12	Shawn Kemp	3.00
13	Chris Webber	4.00
14	Isaiah Rider	1.00
15	Robert Horry	1.00

1995-96 Finest Mystery

Mystery Finest cards appear in three different forms in the 1995-96 Topps Finest set - bordered (one in every pack), borderless (one every 24 packs) and borderless Refractors (one every 96 packs). The players are the same for each form, but collectors must peel off the opaque protector to see the player and type of card they have. Series II cards changed the format from Series I; these cards come in gold (one in every 96 packs), silver (one in 24) and bronze (one per pack). Each box contains either a gold or silver version. Cards are numbered with an "M" prefix.

		MT
Complete Set (44):		50.00
Comp. Border Ser. 1 (22):		30.00
Common Border Player:		.50
Comp. Borderless Ser. 1 (22):		225.00
Borderless Cards:		3x-6x
Refractors:		10x-20x
Comp. Bronze Ser. 2 (22):		20.00
Common Bronze Player:		.50
Comp. Silver Ser. 2 (22):		100.00
Silver Cards:		3x-6x
Gold Cards:		10x-20x
1	Michael Jordan	15.00
2	Grant Hill	5.00
3	Anfernee Hardaway	3.00
4	Shawn Kemp	1.00
5	Kenny Anderson	.50
6	Charles Barkley	2.00
7	Latrell Sprewell	2.00
8	Chris Webber	3.00
9	Jason Kidd	3.00
10	Glenn Robinson	1.00
11	David Robinson	2.00
12	Karl Malone	2.00
13	Larry Johnson	1.00
14	Reggie Miller	1.00
15	Scottie Pippen	3.00
16	Patrick Ewing	1.00
17	Mitch Richmond	.50
18	Glen Rice	.50
19	Jamal Mashburn	1.00
20	Juwan Howard	.50
21	Hakeem Olajuwon	2.00
22	Shaquille O'Neal	5.00
23	Alonzo Mourning	1.00
24	Dennis Rodman	2.00
25	Joe Dumars	.50
26	Tim Hardaway	.50
27	Clyde Drexler	1.00
28	Jerry Stackhouse	2.00
29	John Stockton	1.00
30	Derrick Coleman	.50
31	Michael Finley	3.00
32	Glen Rice	.50
33	Mahmoud Abdul-Rauf	.50
34	Anthony Mason	.50
35	Nick Van Exel	1.00
36	Vin Baker	.50
37	Horace Grant	.50
38	John Starks	.50
39	Clarence Weatherspoon	.50
40	Kevin Johnson	.50
41	Joe Smith	2.00
42	Dikembe Mutombo	.50
43	Damon Stoudamire	3.00
44	Antonio McDyess	3.00

1995-96 Finest Mystery Bronze

		MT
Complete Bronze Set (22):		30.00
Common Bronze:		.50
Silver Cards:		3x-6x
Gold Cards:		15x-30x
23	Alonzo Mourning	.50
24	Dennis Rodman	4.00
25	Joe Dumars	.50
26	Tim Hardaway	.50
27	Clyde Drexler	1.00
28	Jerry Stackhouse	5.00
29	John Stockton	1.00
30	Derrick Coleman	.50
31	Michael Finley	3.00
32	Glen Rice	.50
33	Mahmoud Abdul-Rauf	.50
34	Anthony Mason	.50
35	Nick Van Exel	1.00
36	Vin Baker	.50
37	Horace Grant	.50
38	John Starks	.50
39	Clarence Weatherspoon	.50
40	Kevin Johnson	.50
41	Joe Smith	5.00
42	Dikembe Mutombo	1.00
43	Damon Stoudamire	8.00
44	Antonio McDyess	3.00

1995-96 Finest Rack Pack

The NBA's best young stars are featured on these 1995-96 Topps Finest insert cards. The cards, numbered using an "RP" prefix, are seeded one per every 72 packs. The card front has a color action photo, with "Rack Pack" written around the photo. The Topps Finest brand logo is at the top of the card, with the player's name and a team logo underneath toward the upper right corner.

		MT
Complete Set (7):		75.00
Common Player:		5.00
Inserted 1:72 H; 1:96 R		
1	Jerry Stackhouse	15.00
2	Brent Barry	5.00
3	Damon Stoudamire	12.00
4	Joe Smith	10.00
5	Michael Finley	15.00
6	Antonio McDyess	18.00
7	Rasheed Wallace	15.00

1995-96 Finest Veteran/Rookie

These double-sided Finest cards were randomly seeded one per every 24 packs of 1995-96 Topps Finest Series II packs. Each card pairs a top 1995 rookie with one of his team's best veteran players. Cards are numbered with an "RV" prefix.

		MT
Complete Set (29):		250.00
Common Player:		2.00
Inserted 1:24 H; 1:18 R		
1	Joe Smith, Latrell Sprewell	20.00
2	Antonio McDyess, Dikembe Mutombo	15.00
3	Jerry Stackhouse, Clarence Weatherspoon	12.00
4	Rasheed Wallace, Chris Webber	30.00
5	Kevin Garnett, Tom Gugliotta	40.00
6	Bryant Reeves, Greg Anthony	2.00
7	Damon Stoudamire, Willie Anderson	8.00
8	Shawn Respert, Vin Baker	2.00
9	Ed O'Bannon, Armon Gilliam	2.00
10	Kurt Thomas, Alonzo Mourning	3.00
11	Gary Trent, Rod Strickland	2.00
12	Cherokee Parks, Jamal Mashburn	3.00
13	Corliss Williamson, Mitch Richmond	2.00
14	Eric Williams, Dino Radja	2.00
15	Brent Barry, Loy Vaught	2.00
16	Alan Henderson, Mookie Blaylock	2.00
17	Bob Sura, Terrell Brandon	2.00
18	Theo Ratliff, Grant Hill	25.00
19	Randolph Childress, Rod Strickland	2.00
20	Jason Caffey, Michael Jordan	50.00
21	Michael Finley, Kevin Johnson	12.00
22	George Zidek, Larry Johnson	5.00
23	Travis Best, Reggie Miller	3.00
24	Loren Meyer, Jason Kidd	15.00
25	David Vaughn, Shaquille O'Neal	25.00
26	Sherell Ford, Shawn Kemp	4.00
27	Mario Bennett, Charles Barkley	10.00
28	Greg Ostertag, Karl Malone	10.00
29	Cory Alexander, David Robinson	8.00

1996-97 Finest

Finest Basketball consisted of 291 cards and was issued in two series, with Series I containing 146 cards and Series II containing 145 cards. Series I was broken into four subsets - Gladiators, Maestros, Apprentices and Sterling, while Series II was broken down into Heirs, Foundations, Mainstays and Sterling. Both series were also broken down into Bronze (common), Silver (uncommon) and Gold (rare). Both included 100 Bronze and 27 Silver while Series I had 19 Golds and Series II had 18. The cards are easily identified by the bronze, silver or gold border surrounding the card, as well as the large subset heading in the top center. The backs include a small box in the lower right corner with the overall card number, subset number and common, uncommon or rare distinction. Bronze are considered the base cards, while Silvers are seeded one per four packs and Golds are seeded one per 24 packs. The only insert in either series is a parallel Refractor version of each card, which is also identified in the number box on the back.

		MT
Complete Set (291):		1400.
Complete Bronze 1 (100):		190.00
Complete Bronze 2 (100):		30.00
Common Bronze Player:		.50
Complete Silver 1 (27):		75.00
Complete Silver 2 (27):		120.00
Common Silver Player:		1.00
Complete Gold 1 (19):		500.00
Complete Gold 2 (18):		600.00
Common Gold Player:		7.00
Series 1 Pack (6):		22.00
Series 1 Wax Box (24):		300.00
Series 2 Pack (6):		6.00
Series 2 Wax Box (24):		100.00
1	Scottie Pippen	3.00
2	Tim Legler	.50
3	Rex Walters	.50
4	Calbert Cheaney	.50
5	Dennis Rodman	3.00
6	Tyrone Hill	.50
7	Christian Laettner #136	.50
8	Dell Curry	.50
9	Olden Polynice	.50
10	*John Wallace*	5.00
11	*Martin Muursepp*	.50
12	Chuck Person	.50
13	Grant Hill	4.00
14	Shawn Kemp	1.50
15	B.J. Armstrong	.50
16	Gary Trent	.50
17	Scott Williams	.50
18	Dino Radja	.50
19	*Roy Rogers*	1.00
20	*Tony Delk*	3.00
21	Clifford Robinson	.50
22	*Ray Allen*	15.00
23	Clyde Drexler	1.00
24	Elliott Perry	.50
25	Gary Payton	1.00
26	Dale Davis	.50
27	Horace Grant	.50
28	*Brian Evans*	1.00
29	Joe Smith	1.00
30	Reggie Miller	1.00
31	*Jermaine O'Neal*	12.00
32	Avery Johnson	.50
33	Ed O'Bannon	.50
34	Cedric Ceballos	.50
35	Jamal Mashburn	.50
36	Michael Williams	.50
37	Detlef Schrempf	.50
38	Damon Stoudamire	2.00
39	Jason Kidd	1.50
40	Tom Gugliotta	.50
41	Arvydas Sabonis	.50
42	*Samaki Walker*	2.00
43	*Derek Fisher*	4.00
44	Patrick Ewing	1.00
45	Bryant Reeves	.50
46	Mookie Blaylock	.50
47	George Zidek	.50
48	Jerry Stackhouse	2.00
49	Vin Baker	1.00
50	Michael Jordan	12.00
51	Terrell Brandon	.50
52	Karl Malone	1.00
53	*Lorenzen Wright*	3.00
54	*Shareef Abdur-Rahim*	18.00
55	Kurt Thomas	.50
56	Glen Rice	.50
57	Shawn Bradley	.50
58	*Todd Fuller*	.50
59	Dale Ellis	.50
60	David Robinson	1.00
61	Doug Christie	.50
62	*Stephon Marbury*	25.00
63	Hakeem Olajuwon	2.00
64	Lindsey Hunter	.50
65	Anfernee Hardaway	5.00
66	Kevin Garnett	5.00
67	Kendall Gill	.50
68	Sean Elliott	.50
69	*Allen Iverson*	35.00

70 *Erick Dampier* 3.00
71 *Jerome Williams* 1.00
72 Charles Jones .50
73 Danny Manning .50
74 *Kobe Bryant* 80.00
75 *Steve Nash* 6.00
76 Sam Perkins .50
77 Horace Grant .50
78 Alonzo Mourning 1.00
79 *Kerry Kittles* 8.00
80 LaPhonso Ellis .50
81 Michael Finley 1.00
82 *Marcus Camby* 10.00
83 Antonio McDyess 1.00
84 *Antoine Walker* 6.00
85 Juwan Howard 1.00
86 Bryon Russell .50
87 *Walter McCarty* 4.00
88 *Priest Lauderdale* .50
89 Clarence Weatherspoon .50
90 John Stockton 1.00
91 Mitch Richmond 1.00
92 *Dontae Jones* 1.00
93 Michael Smith .50
94 Brent Barry .50
95 Chris Mills .50
96 Dee Brown .50
97 Terry Dehere .50
98 Danny Ferry .50
99 Gheorghe Muresan .50
100 Checklist .50
101 Jim Jackson (S) 2.00
102 Cedric Ceballos (S) 1.00
103 Glen Rice (S) 2.00
104 Tom Gugliotta (S) 2.00
105 Mario Elie (S) 1.00
106 Nick Anderson (S) 1.00
107 Glenn Robinson (S) 3.00
108 Terrell Brandon (S) 2.00
109 Tim Hardaway (S) 2.00
110 John Stockton (S) 3.00
111 Brent Barry (S) 1.00
112 Mookie Blaylock (S) 1.00
113 Tyus Edney (S) 1.00
114 Gary Payton (S) 4.00
115 Joe Smith (S) 3.00
116 Karl Malone (S) 3.00
117 Dino Radja (S) 1.00
118 Alonzo Mourning (S) 2.00
119 Bryant Stith (S) 1.00
120 Derrick McKey (S) 1.00
121 Clyde Drexler (S) 3.00
122 Michael Finley (S) 3.00
123 Sean Elliott (S) 1.00
124 Hakeem Olajuwon (S) 5.00
125 Joe Dumars (S) 1.00
126 Shawn Bradley (S) 1.00
127 Michael Jordan (S) 30.00
128 Latrell Sprewell (G) 14.00
129 Anfernee Hardaway (G) 50.00
130 Grant Hill (G) 60.00
131 Damon Stoudamire (G) 25.00
132 David Robinson (G) 20.00
133 Scottie Pippen (G) 30.00
134 Patrick Ewing (#136) (G) 14.00
135 Jason Kidd (G) 14.00
136 Jeff Hornacek (G) 7.00
137 Jerry Stackhouse (G) 20.00
138 Kevin Garnett (G) 60.00
139 Mitch Richmond (G) 14.00
140 Juwan Howard (G) 20.00
141 Reggie Miller (G) 14.00
142 Christian Laettner (G) 14.00
143 Vin Baker (G) 14.00
144 Shawn Kemp (G) 15.00
145 Dennis Rodman (G) 45.00
146 Shaquille O'Neal (G) 45.00
147 Mookie Blaylock .50
148 Derek Harper .50
149 Gerald Wilkins .50
150 Adam Keefe .50
151 Billy Owens .50
152 Terrell Brandon .50
153 Antonio Davis .50
154 Muggsy Bogues .50
155 Cherokee Parks .50
156 Rasheed Wallace .50
157 Lee Mayberry .50
158 Craig Ehlo .50
159 Todd Fuller .50
160 Charles Barkley 1.00
161 Glenn Robinson .75
162 Charles Oakley .50
163 Chris Webber 1.25
164 Frank Brickowski .50
165 Mark Jackson .50
166 Jayson Williams .50
167 Clarence Weatherspoon .50
168 Toni Kukoc .50
169 Alan Henderson .50
170 Tony Delk .75
171 Jamal Mashburn .50
172 Vinny Del Negro .50
173 Greg Ostertag .50
174 Shawn Bradley .50
175 Gheorghe Muresan .50
176 Brent Price .50
177 Rick Fox .50
178 Stacey Augmon .50
179 P.J. Brown .50
180 Jim Jackson .50
181 Hersey Hawkins .50
182 Danny Manning .50
183 Dennis Scott .50
184 Tom Gugliotta .50
185 Tyrone Hill .50
186 Malik Sealy .50
187 John Starks .50
188 Mark Price .50
189 Elden Campbell .50
190 Mahmoud Abdul-Rauf .50
191 Will Perdue .50
192 Nate McMillan .50
193 Robert Horry .50
194 Dino Radja .50
195 Loy Vaught .50
196 Dikembe Mutombo .50
197 Eric Montross .50
198 Sasha Danilovic .50
199 Kenny Anderson .50
200 Sean Elliott .50
201 Mark West .50
202 Vlade Divac .50
203 Joe Dumars .50
204 Allan Houston .50
205 Kevin Garnett 5.00
206 Rod Strickland .50
207 Robert Parish .50
208 Jalen Rose .50
209 Armon Gilliam .50
210 Kerry Kittles 3.00
211 Derrick Coleman .50
212 Greg Anthony .50
213 Joe Smith 1.00
214 Steve Smith .50
215 Tim Hardaway .50
216 Tyus Edney .50
217 Steve Nash .50
218 Anthony Mason .50
219 Otis Thorpe .50
220 Eddie Jones 1.00
221 Rik Smits .50
222 Isaiah Rider .50
223 Bobby Phills .50
224 Antoine Walker 3.00
225 Rod Strickland .50
226 Hubert Davis .50
227 Eric Williams .50
228 Danny Manning .50
229 Dominique Wilkins .50
230 Brian Shaw .50
231 Larry Johnson .50
232 Kevin Willis .50
233 Bryant Stith .50
234 Blue Edwards .50
235 Robert Pack .50
236 Brian Grant .50
237 Latrell Sprewell .75
238 Glen Rice .75
239 Jerome Williams .50
240 Allen Iverson 5.00
241 Popeye Jones .50
242 Clifford Robinson .50
243 Shaquille O'Neal 4.00
244 *Vitaly Potapenko* 1.00
245 Ervin Johnson .50
246 Checklist .50
247 Scottie Pippen (S) 6.00
248 Jason Kidd (S) 3.00
249 Antonio McDyess (S) 3.00
250 Latrell Sprewell (S) 2.00
251 Lorenzen Wright (S) 1.00
252 Ray Allen (S) 4.00
253 Stephon Marbury (S) 14.00
254 Patrick Ewing (S) 2.00
255 Anfernee Hardaway (S) 12.00
256 Kenny Anderson (S) 1.00
257 David Robinson (S) 4.00
258 Marcus Camby (S) 4.00
259 Shareef Abdur-Rahim (S) 12.00
260 Dennis Rodman (S) 8.00
261 Juwan Howard (S) 3.00
262 Damon Stoudamire (S) 3.00
263 Shawn Kemp (S) 3.00
264 Mitch Richmond (S) 2.00
265 Jerry Stackhouse (S) 2.00
266 Horace Grant (S) 1.00
267 Kerry Kittles (S) 3.00
268 Vin Baker (S) 3.00
269 Kobe Bryant (G) 120.00
270 Reggie Miller (S) 3.00
271 Grant Hill (S) 14.00
272 Oliver Miller (S) 1.00
273 Chris Webber (S) 4.00
274 Dikembe Mutombo (G) 7.00
275 Antonio McDyess (G) 14.00
276 Clyde Drexler (G) 20.00
277 Brent Barry (G) 7.00
278 Tim Hardaway (G) 14.00
279 Glenn Robinson (G) 16.00
280 Allen Iverson (G) 60.00
281 Hakeem Olajuwon (G) 25.00
282 Marcus Camby (G) 20.00
283 John Stockton (G) 14.00
284 Shareef Abdur-Rahim (G) 35.00
285 Karl Malone (G) 16.00
286 Gary Payton (G) 16.00
287 Stephon Marbury (G) 60.00
288 Alonzo Mourning (G) 14.00
289 Shaquille O'Neal (S) 14.00
290 Charles Barkley (G) 20.00
291 Michael Jordan (G) 125.00

1996-97 Finest Refractors

Each card in the 291-card Finest Basketball set has a parallel Refractor version. Common Refractors were seeded every 12 packs, with Silvers every 48 packs and Gold Refractors every 288 packs. The fronts contain the familiar Refractor finish, while the backs have the word Refractor written in the number box in the lower right corner.

MT
Complete Bronze 1 (100): 2200.
Complete Bronze 2 (100): 700.00
Common Bronze Player: 5.00
Complete Silver 1 (27): 600.00
Complete Silver 2 (27): 900.00
Common Silver Player: 10.00
Complete Gold 1 (19): 1700.
Complete Gold 2 (18): 3000.
Common Gold Player: 20.00
1 Scottie Pippen 50.00
2 Tim Legler 5.00
3 Rex Walters 5.00
4 Calbert Cheaney 5.00
5 Dennis Rodman 80.00
6 Tyrone Hill 5.00
7 Christian Laettner #136 10.00
8 Dell Curry 5.00
9 Olden Polynice 5.00
10 John Wallace 20.00
11 Martin Muursepp 5.00
12 Chuck Person 5.00
13 Grant Hill 80.00
14 Shawn Kemp 30.00
15 B.J. Armstrong 5.00
16 Gary Trent 5.00
17 Scott Williams 5.00
18 Dino Radja 5.00
19 Roy Rogers 5.00
20 Tony Delk 20.00
21 Clifford Robinson 5.00
22 Ray Allen 60.00
23 Clyde Drexler 20.00
24 Elliott Perry 5.00
25 Gary Payton 25.00
26 Dale Davis 5.00
27 Horace Grant 5.00
28 Brian Evans 5.00
29 Joe Smith 35.00
30 Reggie Miller 20.00
31 Jermaine O'Neal 40.00
32 Avery Johnson 5.00
33 Ed O'Bannon 5.00
34 Cedric Ceballos 5.00
35 Jamal Mashburn 10.00
36 Michael Williams 5.00
37 Detlef Schrempf 5.00
38 Damon Stoudamire 50.00
39 Jason Kidd 25.00
40 Tom Gugliotta 5.00
41 Arvydas Sabonis 10.00
42 Samaki Walker 12.00
43 Derek Fisher 20.00
44 Patrick Ewing 20.00
45 Bryant Reeves 10.00
46 Mookie Blaylock 5.00
47 George Zidek 5.00
48 Jerry Stackhouse 20.00
49 Vin Baker 10.00
50 Michael Jordan 150.00
51 Terrell Brandon 5.00
52 Karl Malone 20.00
53 Lorenzen Wright 12.00
54 Shareef Abdur-Rahim 100.00
55 Kurt Thomas 5.00
56 Glen Rice 10.00
57 Shawn Bradley 5.00
58 Todd Fuller 5.00
59 Dale Ellis 5.00
60 David Robinson 25.00
61 Doug Christie 5.00
62 Stephon Marbury 150.00
63 Hakeem Olajuwon 40.00
64 Lindsey Hunter 5.00
65 Anfernee Hardaway 90.00
66 Kevin Garnett 80.00
67 Kendall Gill 5.00
68 Sean Elliott 5.00
69 Allen Iverson 150.00
70 Erick Dampier 12.00
71 Jerome Williams 5.00
72 Charles Jones 5.00
73 Danny Manning 5.00
74 Kobe Bryant 300.00
75 Steve Nash 20.00
76 Sam Perkins 5.00
77 Horace Grant 5.00
78 Alonzo Mourning 20.00
79 Kerry Kittles 40.00
80 LaPhonso Ellis 5.00
81 Michael Finley 20.00
82 Marcus Camby 40.00
83 Antonio McDyess 25.00
84 Antoine Walker 40.00
85 Juwan Howard 20.00
86 Bryon Russell 5.00
87 Walter McCarty 20.00
88 Priest Lauderdale 5.00
89 Clarence Weatherspoon 5.00
90 John Stockton 20.00
91 Mitch Richmond 10.00
92 Dontae Jones 10.00
93 Michael Smith 5.00
94 Brent Barry 5.00
95 Chris Mills 5.00
96 Dee Brown 5.00
97 Terry Dehere 5.00
98 Danny Ferry 5.00
99 Gheorghe Muresan 5.00
100 Checklist 5.00
101 Jim Jackson (S) 25.00
102 Cedric Ceballos (S) 10.00
103 Glen Rice (S) 15.00
104 Tom Gugliotta (S) 15.00
105 Mario Elie (S) 10.00
106 Nick Anderson (S) 10.00
107 Glenn Robinson (S) 20.00
108 Terrell Brandon (S) 15.00
109 Tim Hardaway (S) 15.00
110 John Stockton (S) 20.00
111 Brent Barry (S) 10.00
112 Mookie Blaylock (S) 10.00
113 Tyus Edney (S) 10.00
114 Gary Payton (S) 45.00
115 Joe Smith (S) 50.00
116 Karl Malone (S) 20.00
117 Dino Radja (S) 10.00
118 Alonzo Mourning (S) 20.00
119 Bryant Stith (S) 10.00
120 Derrick McKey (S) 10.00
121 Clyde Drexler (S) 40.00
122 Michael Finley (S) 20.00
123 Sean Elliott (S) 10.00
124 Hakeem Olajuwon (S) 60.00
125 Joe Dumars (S) 15.00
126 Shawn Bradley (S) 15.00
127 Michael Jordan (S) 200.00
128 Latrell Sprewell (G) 50.00
129 Anfernee Hardaway (G) 400.00
130 Grant Hill (G) 275.00
131 Damon Stoudamire (G) 175.00
132 David Robinson (G) 125.00
133 Scottie Pippen (G) 250.00
134 Patrick Ewing (#136) (G) 100.00
135 Jason Kidd (G) 100.00
136 Jeff Hornacek (G) 20.00
137 Jerry Stackhouse (G) 75.00
138 Kevin Garnett (G) 275.00
139 Mitch Richmond (G) 50.00
140 Juwan Howard (G) 125.00
141 Reggie Miller (G) 75.00
142 Christian Laettner (G) 50.00
143 Vin Baker (G) 50.00
144 Shawn Kemp (G) 150.00
145 Dennis Rodman (G) 325.00
146 Shaquille O'Neal (G) 350.00
147 Mookie Blaylock 5.00
148 Derek Harper 5.00
149 Gerald Wilkins 5.00
150 Adam Keefe 5.00
151 Billy Owens 5.00
152 Terrell Brandon 5.00
153 Antonio Davis 5.00
154 Muggsy Bogues 5.00
155 Cherokee Parks 5.00
156 Rasheed Wallace 5.00
157 Lee Mayberry 5.00
158 Craig Ehlo 5.00
159 Todd Fuller 5.00
160 Charles Barkley 25.00
161 Glenn Robinson 20.00
162 Charles Oakley 20.00
163 Chris Webber 20.00
164 Frank Brickowski 5.00
165 Mark Jackson 5.00
166 Jayson Williams 5.00
167 Clarence Weatherspoon 5.00
168 Toni Kukoc 5.00
169 Alan Henderson 5.00
170 Tony Delk 10.00
171 Jamal Mashburn 5.00
172 Vinny Del Negro 5.00
173 Greg Ostertag 5.00
174 Shawn Bradley 5.00
175 Gheorghe Muresan 5.00
176 Brent Price 5.00
177 Rick Fox 5.00
178 Stacey Augmon 5.00
179 P.J. Brown 5.00
180 Jim Jackson 5.00
181 Hersey Hawkins 5.00
182 Danny Manning 5.00
183 Dennis Scott 5.00
184 Tom Gugliotta 5.00
185 Tyrone Hill 5.00
186 Malik Sealy 5.00
187 John Starks 5.00
188 Mark Price 5.00
189 Elden Campbell 5.00
190 Mahmoud Abdul-Rauf 5.00
191 Will Perdue 5.00
192 Nate McMillan 5.00
193 Robert Horry 5.00
194 Dino Radja 5.00
195 Loy Vaught 5.00
196 Dikembe Mutombo 5.00
197 Eric Montross 5.00
198 Sasha Danilovic 5.00
199 Kenny Anderson 5.00
200 Sean Elliott 5.00
201 Mark West 5.00
202 Vlade Divac 5.00
203 Joe Dumars 5.00
204 Allan Houston 5.00
205 Kevin Garnett 80.00
206 Rod Strickland 5.00
207 Robert Parish 5.00
208 Jalen Rose 5.00
209 Armon Gilliam 5.00
210 Kerry Kittles 25.00
211 Derrick Coleman 5.00
212 Greg Anthony 5.00
213 Joe Smith 25.00
214 Steve Smith 5.00
215 Tim Hardaway 5.00
216 Tyus Edney 5.00
217 Steve Nash 5.00
218 Anthony Mason 5.00
219 Otis Thorpe 5.00
220 Eddie Jones 20.00
221 Rik Smits 5.00
222 Isaiah Rider 5.00
223 Bobby Phills 5.00
224 Antoine Walker 20.00
225 Rod Strickland 5.00
226 Hubert Davis 5.00
227 Eric Williams 5.00
228 Danny Manning 5.00
229 Dominique Wilkins 5.00
230 Brian Shaw 5.00
231 Larry Johnson 5.00
232 Kevin Willis 5.00
233 Bryant Stith 5.00
234 Blue Edwards 5.00
235 Robert Pack 5.00
236 Brian Grant 5.00
237 Latrell Sprewell 20.00
238 Glen Rice 20.00
239 Jerome Williams 5.00
240 Allen Iverson 75.00
241 Popeye Jones 5.00
242 Clifford Robinson 5.00
243 Shaquille O'Neal 75.00
244 Vitaly Potapenko 5.00
245 Ervin Johnson 5.00
246 Checklist 5.00
247 Scottie Pippen (S) 70.00
248 Jason Kidd (S) 25.00
249 Antonio McDyess (S) 15.00
250 Latrell Sprewell (S) 20.00
251 Lorenzen Wright (S) 15.00
252 Ray Allen (S) 25.00
253 Stephon Marbury (S) 75.00
254 Patrick Ewing (S) 25.00
255 Anfernee Hardaway (S) 120.00
256 Kenny Anderson (S) 10.00
257 David Robinson (S) 20.00
258 Marcus Camby (S) 20.00
259 Shareef Abdur-Rahim (S) 60.00
260 Dennis Rodman (S) 80.00
261 Juwan Howard (S) 20.00
262 Damon Stoudamire (S) 50.00
263 Shawn Kemp (S) 30.00
264 Mitch Richmond (S) 25.00
265 Jerry Stackhouse (S) 40.00
266 Horace Grant (S) 10.00
267 Kerry Kittles (S) 20.00
268 Vin Baker (S) 25.00
269 Kobe Bryant (G) 550.00
270 Reggie Miller (S) 25.00
271 Grant Hill (S) 100.00
272 Oliver Miller (S) 10.00
273 Chris Webber (S) 45.00
274 Dikembe Mutombo (G) 20.00
275 Antonio McDyess (G) 75.00
276 Clyde Drexler (G) 100.00
277 Brent Barry (G) 50.00
278 Tim Hardaway (G) 60.00
279 Glenn Robinson (G) 80.00
280 Allen Iverson (G) 300.00
281 Hakeem Olajuwon (G) 175.00
282 Marcus Camby (G) 75.00
283 John Stockton (G) 80.00
284 Shareef Abdur-Rahim (G) 200.00
285 Karl Malone (G) 100.00
286 Gary Payton (G) 120.00
287 Stephon Marbury (G) 300.00
288 Alonzo Mourning (G) 60.00
289 Shaquille O'Neal (S) 100.00
290 Charles Barkley (G) 150.00
291 Michael Jordan (G) 900.00

1997-98 Finest Promos

This six-card set was issued to dealers and members of the media to promote the 1997-98 Finest set. The cards were exactly like regular-issue cards except the words "Promotional Sample Not For Resale" printed in red letters across the back.

MT
Complete Set (6): 8.00
Common Player: 1.00
27 Chris Webber 2.00
45 Vin Baker 1.00
57 Allen Iverson 4.00
67 Eddie Jones 1.00
68 Joe Smith 1.00
80 Gary Payton 1.00

1997-98 Finest

Finest Basketball was released in two series and contained 326 cards in 1997-98. The first series had 173 cards, with commons 1-120 (101-120 was a 1997 NBA Draft Picks subset), 121-153 uncommons (1:4 packs) and 154-173 rare (1:24 packs). Themed subsets included Debuts, BallHawks, Catalysts, Finishers, Force and Masters. Series II had 153 cards, with 174-273 commons, 274-306 uncommons (1:4) and 307-326 rares (1:24). Themed subsets in Series II included Showstoppers, Masters, Creators, Defenders and Arrivals. While commons were only paralleled in Refractor versions, all uncommons were paralleled in both Refractors and embossed versions, while rares were paralleled in both Refractors and die-cut embossed versions. Cards are numbered within the set and within each theme.

MT
Complete Set (326): 975.00
Complete Bronze 1 (120): 120.00
Complete Bronze 2 (100): 40.00
Common Bronze Player: .25
Minor Bronze Stars: .50
Complete Silver 1 (33): 100.00
Complete Silver 2 (33): 100.00
Common Silver Player: 1.00
Minor Silver Stars: 2.00
Embossed Silvers: 2x
Complete Gold 1 (20): 225.00
Complete Gold 2 (20): 400.00
Common Gold Player: 5.00
Minor Gold Stars: 10.00
Embossed Die-Cut Golds: 2x
Series 1 Pack (6): 10.00
Series 1 Wax Box (24): 210.00
Series 2 Pack (6): 7.00
Series 2 Wax Box (24): 110.00
1 Scottie Pippen 2.00
2 Tim Hardaway .50
3 Charles Outlaw .25
4 Rik Smits .25
5 Dale Ellis .25
6 Clyde Drexler .75
7 Steve Smith .25
8 Nick Anderson .25
9 Juwan Howard 1.00
10 Cedric Ceballos .25
11 Shawn Bradley .50
12 Loy Vaught .25
13 Todd Day .25
14 Glen Rice .50
15 Bryant Stith .25
16 Bob Sura .25
17 Derrick McKey .25
18 Ray Allen 1.00
19 Stephon Marbury 3.00
20 David Robinson 1.00
21 Anthony Peeler .25
22 Isaiah Rider .25
23 Mookie Blaylock .25
24 Damon Stoudamire 1.00
25 Rod Strickland .25
26 Glenn Robinson .75
27 Chris Webber 1.25
28 Christian Laettner .50
29 Joe Dumars .25
30 Mark Price .25
31 Jamal Mashburn .50
32 Danny Manning .25
33 John Stockton .75
34 Detlef Schrempf .25
35 Tyus Edney .25
36 Chris Childs .25
37 Dana Barros .25
38 Bobby Phills .25
39 Michael Jordan 8.00
40 Grant Hill 4.00
41 Brent Barry .50
42 Rony Seikaly .25
43 Shareef Abdur-Rahim 2.00
44 Dominique Wilkins .25
45 Vin Baker .75
46 Kendall Gill .25
47 Muggsy Bogues .25
48 Hakeem Olajuwon 1.50
49 Reggie Miller .75
50 Shaquille O'Neal 3.00
51 Antonio McDyess .50
52 Michael Finley .50
53 Jerry Stackhouse .75
54 Brian Grant .25
55 Greg Anthony .25
56 Patrick Ewing .75
57 Allen Iverson 3.00
58 Rasheed Wallace .25
59 Shawn Kemp 1.00
60 Bryant Reeves .50
61 Kevin Garnett 4.00
62 Allan Houston .50
63 Stacey Augmon .25
64 Rick Fox .25
65 Derek Harper .25
66 Lindsey Hunter .25
67 Eddie Jones 1.25
68 Joe Smith .75
69 Alonzo Mourning .50
70 LaPhonso Ellis .25
71 Tyrone Hill .25
72 Charles Barkley 1.00
73 Malik Sealy .25
74 Shandon Anderson .25
75 Arvydas Sabonis .25
76 Tom Gugliotta .50
77 Anfernee Hardaway 3.00
78 Sean Elliott .25
79 Marcus Camby 1.75
80 Gary Payton 1.00
81 Kerry Kittles 1.00
82 Dikembe Mutombo .50
83 Antoine Walker 1.50
84 Terrell Brandon .50
85 Otis Thorpe .25
86 Mark Jackson .25
87 A.C. Green .25
88 John Starks .25
89 Kenny Anderson .25
90 Karl Malone 1.00
91 Mitch Richmond .50
92 Derrick Coleman .25
93 Horace Grant .25
94 John Williams .25
95 Jason Kidd 1.00
96 Mahmoud Abdul-Rauf .25
97 Walt Williams .25
98 Anthony Mason .25
99 Latrell Sprewell .50
100 Checklist .25
101 *Tim Duncan* 20.00
102 *Keith Van Horn* 8.00
103 *Chauncey Billups* 3.00
104 *Antonio Daniels* 4.00
105 *Tony Battie* 2.00
106 *Tim Thomas* 8.00
107 *Tracy McGrady* 20.00
108 *Adonal Foyle* 2.00
109 *Maurice Taylor* 3.00
110 *Austin Croshere* 2.00
111 *Bobby Jackson* 2.00
112 *Olivier Saint-Jean* 2.00
113 *John Thomas* 1.00
114 *Derek Anderson* 5.00
115 *Brevin Knight* 1.00
116 *Charles Smith* 1.00
117 *Johnny Taylor* 1.00
118 *Jacque Vaughn* 2.00
119 *Anthony Parker* 1.00
120 *Paul Grant* 1.00
121 Stephon Marbury S 12.00
122 Terrell Brandon S 2.00
123 Dikembe Mutombo S 1.00
124 Patrick Ewing S 2.00
125 Scottie Pippen S 6.00
126 Antoine Walker S 6.00
127 Karl Malone S 2.00
128 Sean Elliott S 1.00
129 Chris Webber S 4.00
130 Shawn Kemp S 3.00
131 Hakeem Olajuwon S 4.00
132 Tim Hardaway S 2.00
133 Glen Rice S 2.00
134 Vin Baker S 3.00
135 Jim Jackson S 1.00
136 Kevin Garnett S 12.00
137 Kobe Bryant S 20.00
138 Damon Stoudamire S 3.00
139 Larry Johnson S 2.00
140 Latrell Sprewell S 2.00
141 Lorenzen Wright S 1.00
142 Toni Kukoc S 2.00
143 Allen Iverson S 12.00
144 Elden Campbell S 1.00
145 Tom Gugliotta S 2.00
146 David Robinson S 3.00
147 Jayson Williams S 1.00
148 Shaquille O'Neal S 8.00
149 Grant Hill S 14.00
150 Reggie Miller S 2.00
151 Clyde Drexler S 3.00
152 Ray Allen S 4.00
153 Eddie Jones S 4.00
154 Michael Jordan G 90.00
155 Dominique Wilkins G 5.00
156 Charles Barkley G 15.00
157 Jerry Stackhouse G 10.00
158 Juwan Howard G 12.00
159 Marcus Camby G 12.00
160 Christian Laettner G 5.00
161 Anthony Mason G 5.00
162 Joe Smith G 10.00
163 Kerry Kittles G 10.00
164 Mitch Richmond G 10.00
165 Shareef Abdur-Rahim G 25.00
166 Alonzo Mourning G 10.00
167 Dennis Rodman G 30.00
168 Antonio McDyess G 10.00
169 Shawn Bradley G 5.00
170 Anfernee Hardaway G 30.00
171 Jason Kidd G 12.00
172 Gary Payton G 12.00
173 John Stockton G 10.00
174 Allan Houston .50
175 Bob Sura .25
176 Clyde Drexler .75
177 Glenn Robinson .75
178 Joe Smith .75
179 Larry Johnson .50

180 Mitch Richmond .50
181 Rony Seikaly .25
182 Tyrone Hill .25
183 Allen Iverson 2.50
184 Brent Barry .25
185 Damon Stoudamire 1.00
186 Grant Hill 3.00
187 John Stockton .75
188 Latrell Sprewell .50
189 Mookie Blaylock .25
190 Samaki Walker .25
191 Vin Baker .75
192 Alonzo Mourning .75
193 Brevin Knight 2.00
194 Danny Manning .25
195 Hakeem Olajuwon 1.25
196 Johnny Taylor .25
197 Lorenzen Wright .25
198 Olden Polynice .25
199 Scottie Pippen 1.50
200 Lindsey Hunter .25
201 Anfernee Hardaway 2.50
202 Greg Anthony .25
203 David Robinson .75
204 Horace Grant .25
205 Calbert Cheaney .25
206 Loy Vaught .25
207 Tariq Abdul-Wahad .75
208 Sean Elliott .25
209 Rodney Rogers .25
210 Anthony Mason .25
211 Bryant Reeves .25
212 David Wesley .25
213 Isaiah Rider .25
214 Karl Malone .75
215 Mahmoud Abdul-Rauf .25
216 Patrick Ewing .50
217 Shaquille O'Neal 2.00
218 Antoine Walker 1.50
219 Charles Barkley .75
220 Dennis Rodman 2.00
221 Jamal Mashburn .50
222 Kendall Gill .25
223 Malik Sealy .25
224 Rasheed Wallace .25
225 Shareef Abdur-Rahim 1.50
226 Antonio Daniels 1.50
227 Charles Oakley .25
228 Derek Anderson 2.00
229 Jason Kidd .75
230 Kenny Anderson .25
231 Marcus Camby .75
232 Ray Allen .75
233 Shawn Bradley .25
234 Antonio McDyess .75
235 Chauncey Billups 2.00
236 Detlef Schrempf .25
237 Jayson Williams .25
238 Kerry Kittles .75
239 Jalen Rose .25
240 Reggie Miller .50
241 Shawn Kemp .75
242 Arvydas Sabonis .25
243 Tom Gugliotta .50
244 Dikembe Mutombo .50
245 Jeff Hornacek .25
246 Kevin Garnett 3.00
247 Matt Maloney .25
248 Rex Chapman .25
249 Stephon Marbury 2.50
250 Austin Croshere .75
251 Chris Childs .25
252 Eddie Jones .75
253 Jerry Stackhouse .75
254 Kevin Johnson .50
255 Maurice Taylor 1.00
256 Chris Mullin .50
257 Terrell Brandon .50
258 Avery Johnson .25
259 Chris Webber 1.00
260 Gary Payton .75
261 Jim Jackson .50
262 Kobe Bryant 4.00
263 Michael Finley .50
264 Rod Strickland .25
265 Tim Hardaway .50
266 B.J. Armstrong .25
267 Christian Laettner .50
268 Glen Rice .50
269 Joe Dumars .25
270 LaPhonso Ellis .25
271 Michael Jordan 6.00
272 *Ron Mercer* 5.00
273 Checklist .25
274 Anfernee Hardaway S 8.00
275 Dennis Rodman S 8.00
276 Gary Payton S 3.00
277 Jamal Mashburn S 2.00
278 Shareef Abdur-Rahim S 8.00
279 Steve Smith S 1.00
280 Tony Battie S 3.00
281 Alonzo Mourning S 2.00
282 Bobby Jackson S 3.00
283 Christian Laettner S 2.00
284 Jerry Stackhouse S 2.00
285 Terrell Brandon S 2.00
286 Chauncey Billups S 5.00
287 Michael Jordan S 25.00
288 Glenn Robinson S 3.00
289 Jason Kidd S 3.00
290 Joe Smith S 2.00
291 Michael Finley S 2.00
292 Rod Strickland S 1.00
293 Ron Mercer S 10.00
294 Tracy McGrady S 8.00
295 Adonal Foyle S 3.00
296 Marcus Camby S 3.00
297 John Stockton S 3.00
298 Kerry Kittles S 3.00
299 Mitch Richmond S 2.00
300 Shawn Bradley S 1.00
301 Anthony Mason S 1.00
302 Antonio Daniels S 4.00
303 Antonio McDyess S 3.00
304 Charles Barkley S 3.00
305 Keith Van Horn S 6.00
306 Tim Duncan S 16.00
307 Dikembe Mutombo G 5.00
308 Grant Hill G 50.00
309 Shaquille O'Neal G 30.00
310 Keith Van Horn G 20.00
311 Shawn Kemp G 10.00
312 Antoine Walker G 20.00
313 Hakeem Olajuwon G 15.00
314 Vin Baker G 12.00
315 Patrick Ewing G 10.00
316 Tracy McGrady G 25.00
317 Glen Rice G 12.00
318 Reggie Miller G 12.00
319 Kevin Garnett G 50.00
320 Allen Iverson G 35.00
321 Karl Malone G 12.00
322 Scottie Pippen G 20.00
323 Kobe Bryant G 70.00
324 Stephon Marbury G 35.00
325 Tim Duncan G 50.00
326 Chris Webber G 15.00

1997-98 Finest Refractors

Refractor versions were made for all 326 cards in Finest Basketball. Common Refractors were seeded one per 12 packs, uncommon Refractors were seeded 1:48 packs and rare Refractors were seeded 1:288 packs. Uncommon embossed Refractors were seeded 1:192 packs and rare embossed die-cut Refactors were inserted 1:1,152 packs. Regular uncommon Refractors were sequentially numbered to 1,090, uncommon embossed Refractors were numbered to 192, rare Refractors were numbered to 289 and rare embossed die-cut Refractors were numbered to 74 sets. All Refractors are labeled on the card back near the number.

	MT
Comp. Bronze 1 (120):	1500.
Comp. Bronze 2 (100):	800.00
Common Bronze Player:	3.00
Minor Bronze Stars:	6.00
Complete Silver 1 (33):	400.00
Complete Silver 2 (33):	400.00
Common Silver Player:	4.00
Minor Silver Stars:	8.00
Embossed Silvers:	2x
Complete Gold 1 (20):	1700.
Complete Gold 2 (20):	2500.
Common Gold Player:	30.00
Embossed Die-Cut Golds:	2x

1 Scottie Pippen 25.00
2 Tim Hardaway 6.00
3 Charles Outlaw 3.00
4 Rik Smits 3.00
5 Dale Ellis 3.00
6 Clyde Drexler 8.00
7 Steve Smith 3.00
8 Nick Anderson 3.00
9 Juwan Howard 8.00
10 Cedric Ceballos 3.00
11 Shawn Bradley 6.00
12 Loy Vaught 3.00
13 Todd Day 3.00
14 Glen Rice 8.00
15 Bryant Stith 3.00
16 Bob Sura 3.00
17 Derrick McKey 3.00
18 Ray Allen 10.00
19 Stephon Marbury 35.00
20 David Robinson 10.00
21 Anthony Peeler 3.00
22 Isaiah Rider 3.00
23 Mookie Blaylock 3.00
24 Damon Stoudamire 12.00
25 Rod Strickland 3.00
26 Glenn Robinson 6.00
27 Chris Webber 12.00
28 Christian Laettner 6.00
29 Joe Dumars 3.00
30 Mark Price 3.00
31 Jamal Mashburn 6.00
32 Danny Manning 3.00
33 John Stockton 8.00
34 Detlef Schrempf 3.00
35 Tyus Edney 3.00
36 Chris Childs 3.00
37 Dana Barros 3.00
38 Bobby Phills 3.00
39 Michael Jordan 90.00
40 Grant Hill 45.00
41 Brent Barry 6.00
42 Rony Seikaly 3.00
43 Shareef Abdur-Rahim 25.00
44 Dominique Wilkins 3.00
45 Vin Baker 10.00
46 Kendall Gill 3.00
47 Muggsy Bogues 3.00
48 Hakeem Olajuwon 15.00
49 Reggie Miller 8.00
50 Shaquille O'Neal 30.00
51 Antonio McDyess 8.00
52 Michael Finley 6.00
53 Jerry Stackhouse 6.00
54 Brian Grant 3.00
55 Greg Anthony 3.00
56 Patrick Ewing 8.00
57 Allen Iverson 35.00
58 Rasheed Wallace 3.00
59 Shawn Kemp 15.00
60 Bryant Reeves 6.00
61 Kevin Garnett 45.00
62 Allan Houston 6.00
63 Stacey Augmon 3.00
64 Rick Fox 3.00
65 Derek Harper 3.00
66 Lindsey Hunter 3.00
67 Eddie Jones 12.00
68 Joe Smith 6.00
69 Alonzo Mourning 6.00
70 LaPhonso Ellis 3.00
71 Tyrone Hill 3.00
72 Charles Barkley 10.00
73 Malik Sealy 3.00
74 Shandon Anderson 3.00
75 Arvydas Sabonis 3.00
76 Tom Gugliotta 6.00
77 Anfernee Hardaway 30.00
78 Sean Elliott 3.00
79 Marcus Camby 8.00
80 Gary Payton 10.00
81 Kerry Kittles 8.00
82 Dikembe Mutombo 6.00
83 Antoine Walker 20.00
84 Terrell Brandon 6.00
85 Otis Thorpe 3.00
86 Mark Jackson 3.00
87 A.C. Green 3.00
88 John Starks 3.00
89 Kenny Anderson 3.00
90 Karl Malone 8.00
91 Mitch Richmond [illegible]
92 Derrick Coleman 3.00
93 Horace Grant 3.00
94 John Williams 3.00
95 Jason Kidd 12.00
96 Mahmoud Abdul-Rauf 3.00
97 Walt Williams 3.00
98 Anthony Mason 3.00
99 Latrell Sprewell 6.00
100 Checklist 3.00
101 Tim Duncan 220.00
102 Keith Van Horn 60.00
103 Chauncey Billups 70.00
104 Antonio Daniels 45.00
105 Tony Battie 35.00
106 Tim Thomas 75.00
107 Tracy McGrady 80.00
108 Adonal Foyle 20.00
109 Maurice Taylor 60.00
110 Austin Croshere 15.00
111 Bobby Jackson 50.00
112 Olivier Saint-Jean 20.00
113 John Thomas 10.00
114 Derek Anderson 60.00
115 Brevin Knight 60.00
116 Charles Smith 10.00
117 Johnny Taylor 10.00
118 Jacque Vaughn 15.00
119 Anthony Parker 10.00
120 Paul Grant 10.00
121 Stephon Marbury S 45.00
122 Terrell Brandon S 8.00
123 Dikembe Mutombo S 8.00
124 Patrick Ewing S 8.00
125 Scottie Pippen S 30.00
126 Antoine Walker S 25.00
127 Karl Malone S 10.00
128 Sean Elliott S 4.00
129 Chris Webber S 15.00
130 Shawn Kemp S 15.00
131 Hakeem Olajuwon S 20.00
132 Tim Hardaway S 10.00
133 Glen Rice S 10.00
134 Vin Baker S 15.00
135 Jim Jackson S 8.00
136 Kevin Garnett S 60.00
137 Kobe Bryant S 70.00
138 Damon Stoudamire S 15.00
139 Larry Johnson S 8.00
140 Latrell Sprewell S 8.00
141 Lorenzen Wright S 4.00
142 Toni Kukoc S 8.00
143 Allen Iverson S 45.00
144 Elden Campbell S 4.00
145 Tom Gugliotta S 8.00
146 David Robinson S 12.00
147 Jayson Williams S 4.00
148 Shaquille O'Neal S 35.00
149 Grant Hill S 60.00
150 Reggie Miller S 8.00
151 Clyde Drexler S 10.00
152 Ray Allen S 10.00
153 Eddie Jones S 15.00
154 Michael Jordan G 700.00
155 Dominique Wilkins G 30.00
156 Charles Barkley G 60.00
157 Jerry Stackhouse G 30.00
158 Juwan Howard G 40.00
159 Marcus Camby G 40.00
160 Christian Laettner G 30.00
161 Anthony Mason G 30.00
162 Joe Smith G 40.00
163 Kerry Kittles G 40.00
164 Mitch Richmond G 40.00
165 Shareef Abdur-Rahim G 130.00
166 Alonzo Mourning G 40.00
167 Dennis Rodman G 150.00
168 Antonio McDyess G 40.00
169 Shawn Bradley G 30.00
170 Anfernee Hardaway G 160.00
171 Jason Kidd G 75.00
172 Gary Payton G 50.00
173 John Stockton G 40.00
174 Allan Houston 6.00
175 Bob Sura 3.00
176 Clyde Drexler 8.00
177 Glenn Robinson 6.00
178 Joe Smith 6.00
179 Larry Johnson 6.00
180 Mitch Richmond 6.00
181 Rony Seikaly 3.00
182 Tyrone Hill 3.00
183 Allen Iverson 35.00
184 Brent Barry 3.00
185 Damon Stoudamire 12.00
186 Grant Hill 45.00
187 John Stockton 6.00
188 Latrell Sprewell 6.00
189 Mookie Blaylock 3.00
190 Samaki Walker 3.00
191 Vin Baker 10.00
192 Alonzo Mourning 6.00
193 Brevin Knight 15.00
194 Danny Manning 3.00
195 Hakeem Olajuwon 15.00
196 Johnny Taylor 3.00
197 Lorenzen Wright 3.00
198 Olden Polynice 3.00
199 Scottie Pippen 20.00
200 Lindsey Hunter 3.00
201 Anfernee Hardaway 30.00
202 Greg Anthony 3.00
203 David Robinson 10.00
204 Horace Grant 3.00
205 Calbert Cheaney 3.00
206 Loy Vaught 3.00
207 Tariq Abdul-Wahad 8.00
208 Sean Elliott 3.00
209 Rodney Rogers 3.00
210 Anthony Mason 3.00
211 Bryant Reeves 3.00
212 David Wesley 3.00
213 Isaiah Rider 3.00
214 Karl Malone 8.00
215 Mahmoud Abdul-Rauf 3.00
216 Patrick Ewing 8.00
217 Shaquille O'Neal 30.00
218 Antoine Walker 20.00
219 Charles Barkley 10.00
220 Dennis Rodman 30.00
221 Jamal Mashburn 6.00
222 Kendall Gill 3.00
223 Malik Sealy 3.00
224 Rasheed Wallace 3.00
225 Shareef Abdur-Rahim 20.00
226 Antonio Daniels 10.00
227 Charles Oakley 3.00
228 Derek Anderson 15.00
229 Jason Kidd 12.00
230 Kenny Anderson 3.00
231 Marcus Camby 8.00
232 Ray Allen [illegible]
233 Shawn Bradley 3.00
234 Antonio McDyess 8.00
235 Chauncey Billups 12.00
236 Detlef Schrempf 3.00
237 Jayson Williams 3.00
238 Kerry Kittles 8.00
239 Jalen Rose 3.00
240 Reggie Miller 8.00
241 Shawn Kemp 10.00
242 Arvydas Sabonis 3.00
243 Tom Gugliotta 6.00
244 Dikembe Mutombo 6.00
245 Jeff Hornacek 3.00
246 Kevin Garnett 45.00
247 Matt Maloney 3.00
248 Rex Chapman 3.00
249 Stephon Marbury 35.00
250 Austin Croshere 6.00
251 Chris Childs 3.00
252 Eddie Jones 12.00
253 Jerry Stackhouse 6.00
254 Kevin Johnson 6.00
255 Maurice Taylor 18.00
256 Chris Mullin 6.00
257 Terrell Brandon 6.00
258 Avery Johnson 3.00
259 Chris Webber 12.00
260 Gary Payton 8.00
261 Jim Jackson 6.00
262 Kobe Bryant 70.00
263 Michael Finley 6.00
264 Rod Strickland 3.00
265 Tim Hardaway 6.00
266 B.J. Armstrong 3.00
267 Christian Laettner 6.00
268 Glen Rice 6.00
269 Joe Dumars 3.00
270 LaPhonso Ellis 3.00
271 Michael Jordan 90.00
272 Ron Mercer 120.00
273 Checklist 3.00
274 Anfernee Hardaway S 35.00
275 Dennis Rodman S 35.00
276 Gary Payton S 10.00
277 Jamal Mashburn S 8.00
278 Shareef Abdur-Rahim S 30.00
279 Steve Smith S 4.00
280 Tony Battie S 8.00
281 Alonzo Mourning S 8.00
282 Bobby Jackson S 10.00
283 Christian Laettner S 8.00
284 Jerry Stackhouse S 8.00
285 Terrell Brandon S 8.00
286 Chauncey Billups S 15.00
287 Michael Jordan S 100.00
288 Glenn Robinson S 8.00
289 Jason Kidd S 14.00
290 Joe Smith S 8.00
291 Michael Finley S 8.00
292 Rod Strickland S 4.00
293 Ron Mercer S 30.00
294 Tracy McGrady S 30.00
295 Adonal Foyle S 8.00
296 Marcus Camby S 8.00
297 John Stockton S 8.00
298 Kerry Kittles S 8.00
299 Mitch Richmond S 8.00
300 Shawn Bradley S 4.00
301 Anthony Mason S 4.00
302 Antonio Daniels S 10.00
303 Antonio McDyess S 10.00
304 Charles Barkley S 12.00
305 Keith Van Horn S 25.00
306 Tim Duncan S 60.00
307 Dikembe Mutombo G 30.00
308 Grant Hill G 275.00
309 Shaquille O'Neal G 175.00
310 Keith Van Horn G 100.00
311 Shawn Kemp G 75.00
312 Antoine Walker G 80.00
313 Hakeem Olajuwon G 100.00
314 Vin Baker G 70.00
315 Patrick Ewing G 40.00
316 Tracy McGrady G 125.00
317 Glen Rice G 40.00
318 Reggie Miller G 40.00
319 Kevin Garnett G 275.00
320 Allen Iverson G 220.00
321 Karl Malone G 50.00
322 Scottie Pippen G 125.00
323 Kobe Bryant G 325.00
324 Stephon Marbury G 220.00
325 Tim Duncan G 250.00
326 Chris Webber G 100.00

1997-98 Finest Embossed Silvers

Embossed Silver or uncommons were available in both series, with cards 121-153 in Series I and 274-306 in Series II. This 66-card set featured embossed versions of each silver card and was inserted one per 16 packs, while Refractor versions were seeded one per 192 packs and sequentially numbered to 263. Only Silver versions arrived in an embossed only verions - Embossed Gold cards were all die-cut.

	MT
Silver Cards:	2x
Silver Refractors:	4x-8x

1997-98 Finest Embossed Golds

The rare cards from both Series I and II were also available in embossed/die-cut versions. In Series I, the rare cards were 154-173, while in Series II they were numbered 307-326. Only these rare or gold versions were avalable in this format, with regular embossed/die-cut versions seeded one per 96 packs, while Refractor versions were seeded one per 1,152 packs. Series II embossed/die-cut cards were sequentially numbered to 74 on the back.

	MT
Gold Cards:	2x
Gold Refractors:	5x-10x

1998-99 Finest Promos

This six-card promotional set was distributed to dealers and members of the media to promote the 1998-99 Finest product. The cards were identical to the regular-issue cards except they were numbered PP1-PP6 on the back.

		MT
Complete Set (6):		4.00
Common Player:		.25
1	Dikembe Mutombo	.25
2	Antoine Walker	1.50
3	Reggie Miller	.50
4	John Stockton	.50
5	Eddie Jones	.75
6	Gary Payton	.75

1998-99 Finest

Finest was released in two 125-card series in 1998-99. Each card in the 250-card set was available in four versions - regular (with protective peel), No-Protector (1:4), Refractors (with protective peel, 1:12) and No-Protector Refractors (1:24). No-Protectors featured a foil-darkened background, while No-Protector Refractors featured the Refractor finish on both sides. Inserts in Series I included: Centurions, Hardwood Heroes, Mystery Finest and Oversized Finest. Inserts in Series II included: Mystery Finest, Arena Stars, Court Control and Oversized Finest.

	MT
Complete Set (250):	150.00
Complete Series 1 (125):	25.00
Complete Series 2 (125):	125.00
Common Player:	.25
Minor Stars:	.50
Common Rookie:	2.00
Pack (6):	5.00
Wax Box (24):	90.00

1 Chris Mills .25
2 Matt Maloney .50
3 Sam Mitchell .25
4 Corliss Williamson .25
5 Bryant Reeves .50
6 Juwan Howard .50
7 Eddie Jones 1.25
8 Ray Allen .50
9 Larry Johnson .50
10 Travis Best .25
11 Isaiah Rider .25
12 Hakeem Olajuwon 1.00
13 Gary Trent .25
14 Kevin Garnett 3.00
15 Dikembe Mutombo .50
16 Brevin Knight .75
17 Keith Van Horn 1.50
18 Theo Ratliff .25
19 Tim Hardaway .75
20 Blue Edwards .25
21 David Wesley .25
22 Jaren Jackson .25
23 Nick Anderson .25
24 Rodney Rogers .25
25 Antonio Davis .25
26 Clarence Weatherspoon .25
27 Kelvin Cato .25
28 Tracy McGrady 1.50
29 Mookie Blaylock .25
30 Ron Harper .25
31 Allan Houston .50
32 Brian Williams .25
33 John Stockton .50
34 Hersey Hawkins .25
35 Donyell Marshall .25
36 Mark Strickland .25
37 Rod Strickland .25
38 Cedric Ceballos .25
39 Danny Fortson .25
40 Shaquille O'Neal 2.00
41 Kendall Gill .25
42 Allen Iverson 1.50
43 Travis Knight .25
44 Cedric Henderson .50
45 Steve Kerr .25
46 Antonio McDyess .50
47 Darrick Martin .25
48 Shandon Anderson .25
49 Shareef Abdur-Rahim 1.25
50 Antoine Carr .25
51 Jason Kidd 1.00
52 Calbert Cheaney .25
53 Antoine Walker 1.50
54 Greg Anthony .25
55 Jeff Hornacek .25
56 Reggie Miller .50
57 Lawrence Funderburke .25
58 Derek Strong .25
59 Robert Horry .25
60 Shawn Bradley .25
61 Matt Bullard .25
62 Terrell Brandon .50
63 Dan Majerle .25
64 Jim Jackson .25
65 Anthony Peeler .25
66 Charles Outlaw .25
67 Khalid Reeves .25
68 Toni Kukoc .50
69 Mario Elie .25
70 Derek Anderson .75
71 Jalen Rose .25
72 Tyrone Corbin .25
73 Anthony Mason .50
74 Lamond Murray .25
75 Tom Gugliotta .50
76 Arvydas Sabonis .25
77 Brian Shaw .25
78 Rick Fox .25
79 Danny Manning .25
80 Lindsey Hunter .25
81 Michael Jordan 6.00
82 LaPhonso Ellis .25
83 David Robinson .75
84 Christian Laettner .50
85 Armon Gilliam .25
86 Sherman Douglas .25
87 Charlie Ward .25
88 Shawn Kemp .75
89 Gary Payton .75
90 Doug Christie .25
91 Voshon Lenard .25
92 Detlef Schrempf .25
93 Walter McCarty .25
94 Sam Cassell .25
95 Jerry Stackhouse .50
96 Billy Owens .25
97 Matt Geiger .25
98 Avery Johnson .25
99 Bobby Jackson .50
100 Rex Chapman .25
101 Andrew DeClercq .25
102 Vlade Divac .25
103 Erick Strickland .25
104 Dean Garrett .25
105 Grant Long .25
106 Adonal Foyle .25
107 Isaac Austin .25
108 Michael Curry .25
109 Darrell Armstrong .25
110 Aaron McKie .25
111 Stacey Augmon .25
112 Anthony Johnson .25
113 Vinny Del Negro .25
114 Reggie Slater .25
115 Lee Mayberry .25
116 Tracy Murray .25
117 Scottie Pippen 1.50
118 Sam Perkins .25
119 Derek Fisher .25
120 Mark Bryant .25
121 Dale Davis .25
122 B.J. Armstrong .25
123 Charles Barkley .75
124 Horace Grant .25
125 Checklist .25
126 Alonzo Mourning .50
127 Kerry Kittles .50
128 Eldridge Recasner .25
129 Dell Curry .25
130 Jamal Mashburn .50
131 Eric Piatkowski .25
132 Othella Harrington .25
133 Pete Chilcutt .25
134 Corie Blount .25
135 Patrick Ewing .50
136 Danny Schayes .25
137 John Williams .25
138 Joe Smith .50
139 Tariq Abdul-Wahad .25
140 Vin Baker 1.00
141 Elden Campbell .25
142 Chris Carr .25
143 John Starks .25
144 Felton Spencer .25
145 Mark Jackson .25
146 Dana Barros .25
147 Eric Williams .25
148 Wesley Person .25
149 Joe Dumars .50
150 Steve Smith .50
151 Randy Brown .25
152 A.C. Green .25
153 Dee Brown .25
154 Brian Grant .25
155 Tim Thomas 1.50
156 Howard Eisley .25
157 Malik Sealy .25
158 Maurice Taylor .75
159 Tyrone Hill .25
160 Chris Gatling .25
161 Rodrick Rhodes .25
162 Muggsy Bogues .25
163 Kenny Anderson .50
164 Zydrunas Ilgauskas .75
165 Grant Hill 3.00
166 Lorenzen Wright .25
167 Tony Battie .50
168 Bobby Phills .25
169 Michael Finley .75
170 Anfernee Hardaway 2.00
171 Terry Porter .25
172 P.J. Brown .25
173 Clifford Robinson .25
174 Olden Polynice .25
175 Kobe Bryant 5.00
176 Sean Elliott .25
177 Latrell Sprewell .50
178 Rik Smits .25
179 Darrell Armstrong .50
180 Stephon Marbury 2.00
181 Brent Price .25
182 Danny Fortson .25
183 Vitaly Potapenko .25
184 Anthony Parker .25
185 Glenn Robinson .50
186 Erick Dampier .25
187 George McCloud .25
188 Rasheed Wallace .50
189 Aaron Williams .25
190 Tim Duncan 3.00
191 Chauncey Billups .75

192 Jim McIlvaine .25
193 Chris Mullin .25
194 George Lynch .25
195 Damon Stoudamire .75
196 Bryon Russell .25
197 Luc Longley .25
198 Ron Mercer 1.50
199 Alan Henderson .25
200 Jayson Williams .50
201 Ben Wallace .25
202 Elliot Perry .25
203 Walt Williams .25
204 Cherokee Parks .25
205 Brent Barry .25
206 Hubert Davis .25
207 Terry Davis .25
208 Loy Vaught .25
209 Adam Keefe .25
210 Karl Malone 1.00
211 Chuck Person .25
212 Chris Childs .25
213 Rony Seikaly .25
214 Ervin Johnson .25
215 Derrick McKey .25
216 Jerome Williams .25
217 Glen Rice .50
218 Steve Nash .25
219 Nick Van Exel .50
220 Chris Webber 1.50
221 Marcus Camby .75
222 Antonio Daniels .25
223 Mitch Richmond .50
224 Otis Thorpe .25
225 Charles Oakley .25
226 *Michael Olowokandi* 3.00
227 *Mike Bibby* 5.00
228 *Raef LaFrentz* 3.00
229 *Antawn Jamison* 10.00
230 *Vince Carter* 40.00
231 *Robert Traylor* 2.00
232 *Jason Williams* 8.00
233 *Larry Hughes* 8.00
234 *Dirk Nowitzki* 10.00
235 *Paul Pierce* 8.00
236 *Bonzi Wells* 8.00
237 *Michael Doleac* 2.00
238 *Keon Clark* 3.00
239 *Michael Dickerson* 4.00
240 *Matt Harpring* 3.00
241 *Bryce Drew* 2.00
242 *Pat Garrity* 2.00
243 *Roshown McLeod* 2.00
244 *Ricky Davis* 4.00
245 *Brian Skinner* 2.00
246 *Tyronn Lue* 2.00
247 *Felipe Lopez* 3.00
248 *Sam Jacobson* 2.00
249 *Corey Benjamin* 2.00
250 *Nazr Mohammed* 2.00

1998-99 Finest No Protector

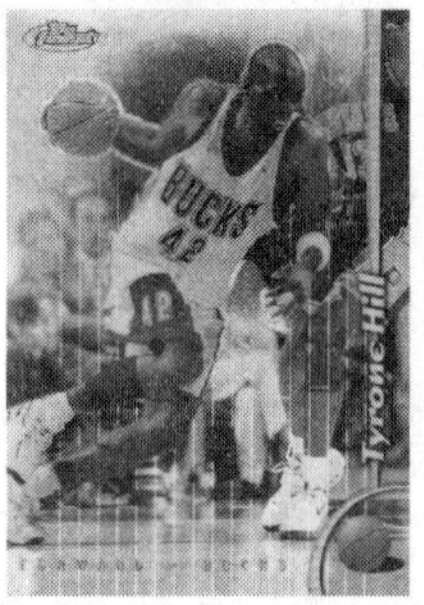

This 250-card parallel set reprinted each card from Finest I and II with the absence of a Finest protector. Card fronts and backs featured a darkened, silver tint. No-Protector cards were inserted 1:4 packs.

MT
Complete Set (250): 300.00
Complete Series 1 (125): 75.00
Complete Series 2 (125): 225.00
No Protector Cards: 3x
No Protector Rooies: 2x
Inserted 1:4
1 Chris Mills .25
2 Matt Maloney .50
3 Sam Mitchell .25
4 Corliss Williamson .25
5 Bryant Reeves .50
6 Juwan Howard .50
7 Eddie Jones 1.25
8 Ray Allen .50
9 Larry Johnson .50
10 Travis Best .25
11 Isaiah Rider .25
12 Hakeem Olajuwon 1.00
13 Gary Trent .25
14 Kevin Garnett 3.00
15 Dikembe Mutombo .50
16 Brevin Knight .75
17 Keith Van Horn 1.50
18 Theo Ratliff .25
19 Tim Hardaway .75
20 Blue Edwards .25
21 David Wesley .25
22 Jaren Jackson .25
23 Nick Anderson .25
24 Rodney Rogers .25
25 Antonio Davis .25
26 Clarence Weatherspoon .25
27 Kelvin Cato .25
28 Tracy McGrady 1.50
29 Mookie Blaylock .25
30 Ron Harper .25
31 Allan Houston .50
32 Brian Williams .25
33 John Stockton .50
34 Hersey Hawkins .25
35 Donyell Marshall .25
36 Mark Strickland .25
37 Rod Strickland .25
38 Cedric Ceballos .25
39 Danny Fortson .25
40 Shaquille O'Neal 2.00
41 Kendall Gill .25
42 Allen Iverson 1.50
43 Travis Knight .25
44 Cedric Henderson .50
45 Steve Kerr .25
46 Antonio McDyess .50
47 Darrick Martin .25
48 Shandon Anderson .25
49 Shareef Abdur-Rahim 1.25
50 Antoine Carr .25
51 Jason Kidd 1.00
52 Calbert Cheaney .25
53 Antoine Walker 1.50
54 Greg Anthony .25
55 Jeff Hornacek .25
56 Reggie Miller .50
57 Lawrence Funderburke .25
58 Derek Strong .25
59 Robert Horry .25
60 Shawn Bradley .25
61 Matt Bullard .25
62 Terrell Brandon .50
63 Dan Majerle .25
64 Jim Jackson .25
65 Anthony Peeler .25
66 Charles Outlaw .25
67 Khalid Reeves .25
68 Toni Kukoc .50
69 Mario Elie .25
70 Derek Anderson .75
71 Jalen Rose .25
72 Tyrone Corbin .25
73 Anthony Mason .50
74 Lamond Murray .25
75 Tom Gugliotta .50
76 Arvydas Sabonis .25
77 Brian Shaw .25
78 Rick Fox .25
79 Danny Manning .25
80 Lindsey Hunter .25
81 Michael Jordan 6.00
82 LaPhonso Ellis .25
83 David Robinson .75
84 Christian Laettner .50
85 Armon Gilliam .25
86 Sherman Douglas .25
87 Charlie Ward .25
88 Shawn Kemp .75
89 Gary Payton .75
90 Doug Christie .25
91 Voshon Lenard .25
92 Detlef Schrempf .25
93 Walter McCarty .25
94 Sam Cassell .25
95 Jerry Stackhouse .50
96 Billy Owens .25
97 Matt Geiger .25
98 Avery Johnson .25
99 Bobby Jackson .50
100 Rex Chapman .25
101 Andrew DeClercq .25
102 Vlade Divac .25
103 Erick Strickland .25
104 Dean Garrett .25
105 Grant Long .25
106 Adonal Foyle .25
107 Isaac Austin .25
108 Michael Curry .25
109 Darrell Armstrong .25
110 Aaron McKie .25
111 Stacey Augmon .25
112 Anthony Johnson .25
113 Vinny Del Negro .25
114 Reggie Slater .25
115 Lee Mayberry .25
116 Tracy Murray .25
117 Scottie Pippen 1.50
118 Sam Perkins .25
119 Derek Fisher .25
120 Mark Bryant .25
121 Dale Davis .25
122 B.J. Armstrong .25
123 Charles Barkley .75
124 Horace Grant .25
125 Checklist .25
126 Alonzo Mourning .50
127 Kerry Kittles .50
128 Eldridge Recasner .25
129 Dell Curry .25
130 Jamal Mashburn .50
131 Eric Piatkowski .25
132 Othella Harrington .25
133 Pete Chilcutt .25
134 Corie Blount .25
135 Patrick Ewing .50
136 Danny Schayes .25
137 John Williams .25
138 Joe Smith .50
139 Tariq Abdul-Wahad .25
140 Vin Baker 1.00
141 Elden Campbell .25
142 Chris Carr .25
143 John Starks .25
144 Felton Spencer .25
145 Mark Jackson .25
146 Dana Barros .25
147 Eric Williams .25
148 Wesley Person .25
149 Joe Dumars .50
150 Steve Smith .50
151 Randy Brown .25
152 A.C. Green .25
153 Dee Brown .25
154 Brian Grant .25
155 Tim Thomas 1.50
156 Howard Eisley .25
157 Malik Sealy .25
158 Maurice Taylor .75
159 Tyrone Hill .25
160 Chris Gatling .25
161 Rodrick Rhodes .25
162 Muggsy Bogues .25
163 Kenny Anderson .50
164 Zydrunas Ilgauskas .75
165 Grant Hill 3.00
166 Lorenzen Wright .25
167 Tony Battie .50
168 Bobby Phills .25
169 Michael Finley .75
170 Anfernee Hardaway 2.00
171 Terry Porter .25
172 P.J. Brown .25
173 Clifford Robinson .25
174 Olden Polynice .25
175 Kobe Bryant 5.00
176 Sean Elliott .25
177 Latrell Sprewell .50
178 Rik Smits .25
179 Darrell Armstrong .25
180 Stephon Marbury 2.00
181 Brent Price .25
182 Danny Fortson .25
183 Vitaly Potapenko .25
184 Anthony Parker .25
185 Glenn Robinson .50
186 Erick Dampier .25
187 George McCloud .25
188 Rasheed Wallace .50
189 Aaron Williams .25
190 Tim Duncan 3.00
191 Chauncey Billups .75
192 Jim McIlvaine .25
193 Chris Mullin .25
194 George Lynch .25
195 Damon Stoudamire .75
196 Bryon Russell .25
197 Luc Longley .25
198 Ron Mercer 1.50
199 Alan Henderson .25
200 Jayson Williams .50
201 Ben Wallace .25
202 Elliot Perry .25
203 Walt Williams .25
204 Cherokee Parks .25
205 Brent Barry .25
206 Hubert Davis .25
207 Terry Davis .25
208 Loy Vaught .25
209 Adam Keefe .25
210 Karl Malone 1.00
211 Chuck Person .25
212 Chris Childs .25
213 Rony Seikaly .25
214 Ervin Johnson .25
215 Derrick McKey .25
216 Jerome Williams .25
217 Glen Rice .50
218 Steve Nash .25
219 Nick Van Exel .50
220 Chris Webber 1.50
221 Marcus Camby .75
222 Antonio Daniels .25
223 Mitch Richmond .50
224 Otis Thorpe .25
225 Charles Oakley .25
226 *Michael Olowokandi* 8.00
227 *Mike Bibby* 10.00
228 *Raef LaFrentz* 8.00
229 *Antawn Jamison* 12.00
230 *Vince Carter* 30.00
231 *Robert Traylor* 8.00
232 *Jason Williams* 20.00
233 *Larry Hughes* 10.00
234 *Dirk Nowitzki* 4.00
235 *Paul Pierce* 20.00
236 *Bonzi Wells* 3.00
237 *Michael Doleac* 4.00
238 *Keon Clark* 4.00
239 *Michael Dickerson* 8.00
240 *Matt Harpring* 5.00
241 *Bryce Drew* 2.00
242 *Pat Garrity* 2.00
243 *Roshown McLeod* 3.00
244 *Ricky Davis* 3.00
245 *Brian Skinner* 2.00
246 *Tyronn Lue* 3.00
247 *Felipe Lopez* 4.00
248 *Sam Jacobson* 2.00
249 *Corey Benjamin* 2.00
250 *Nazr Mohammed* 2.00

1998-99 Finest No-Protector Refractors

This 250-card parallel set reprinted every card from Finest Series I and II, but added a Refractor finish to both the front and back. The word "Refractor" was also printed in small black letters below the card number. No-Protector Refractors were seeded 1:24 packs.

MT
Complete Set (250): 1900.
Complete Series 1 (125): 500.00
Complete Series 2 (125): 1400.
NP Refractor Cards: 10x-20x
NP Refractor Rookies: 3x-6x
Inserted 1:24
1 Chris Mills .25
2 Matt Maloney .50
3 Sam Mitchell .25
4 Corliss Williamson .25
5 Bryant Reeves .50
6 Juwan Howard .50
7 Eddie Jones 1.25
8 Ray Allen .50
9 Larry Johnson .50
10 Travis Best .25
11 Isaiah Rider .25
12 Hakeem Olajuwon 1.00
13 Gary Trent .25
14 Kevin Garnett 3.00
15 Dikembe Mutombo .50
16 Brevin Knight .75
17 Keith Van Horn 1.50
18 Theo Ratliff .25
19 Tim Hardaway .75
20 Blue Edwards .25
21 David Wesley .25
22 Jaren Jackson .25
23 Nick Anderson .25
24 Rodney Rogers .25
25 Antonio Davis .25
26 Clarence Weatherspoon .25
27 Kelvin Cato .25
28 Tracy McGrady 1.50
29 Mookie Blaylock .25
30 Ron Harper .25
31 Allan Houston .50
32 Brian Williams .25
33 John Stockton .50
34 Hersey Hawkins .25
35 Donyell Marshall .25
36 Mark Strickland .25
37 Rod Strickland .25
38 Cedric Ceballos .25
39 Danny Fortson .25
40 Shaquille O'Neal 2.00
41 Kendall Gill .25
42 Allen Iverson 1.50
43 Travis Knight .25
44 Cedric Henderson .50
45 Steve Kerr .25
46 Antonio McDyess .50
47 Darrick Martin .25
48 Shandon Anderson .25
49 Shareef Abdur-Rahim 1.25
50 Antoine Carr .25
51 Jason Kidd 1.00
52 Calbert Cheaney .25
53 Antoine Walker 1.50
54 Greg Anthony .25
55 Jeff Hornacek .25
56 Reggie Miller .50
57 Lawrence Funderburke .25
58 Derek Strong .25
59 Robert Horry .25
60 Shawn Bradley .25
61 Matt Bullard .25
62 Terrell Brandon .50
63 Dan Majerle .25
64 Jim Jackson .25
65 Anthony Peeler .25
66 Charles Outlaw .25
67 Khalid Reeves .25
68 Toni Kukoc .50
69 Mario Elie .25
70 Derek Anderson .75
71 Jalen Rose .25
72 Tyrone Corbin .25
73 Anthony Mason .50
74 Lamond Murray .25
75 Tom Gugliotta .50
76 Arvydas Sabonis .25
77 Brian Shaw .25
78 Rick Fox .25
79 Danny Manning .25
80 Lindsey Hunter .25
81 Michael Jordan 6.00
82 LaPhonso Ellis .25
83 David Robinson .75
84 Christian Laettner .50
85 Armon Gilliam .25
86 Sherman Douglas .25
87 Charlie Ward .25
88 Shawn Kemp .75
89 Gary Payton .75
90 Doug Christie .25
91 Voshon Lenard .25
92 Detlef Schrempf .25
93 Walter McCarty .25
94 Sam Cassell .25
95 Jerry Stackhouse .50
96 Billy Owens .25
97 Matt Geiger .25
98 Avery Johnson .25
99 Bobby Jackson .50
100 Rex Chapman .25
101 Andrew DeClercq .25
102 Vlade Divac .25
103 Erick Strickland .25
104 Dean Garrett .25
105 Grant Long .25
106 Adonal Foyle .25
107 Isaac Austin .25
108 Michael Curry .25
109 Darrell Armstrong .25
110 Aaron McKie .25
111 Stacey Augmon .25
112 Anthony Johnson .25
113 Vinny Del Negro .25
114 Reggie Slater .25
115 Lee Mayberry .25
116 Tracy Murray .25
117 Scottie Pippen 1.50
118 Sam Perkins .25
119 Derek Fisher .25
120 Mark Bryant .25
121 Dale Davis .25
122 B.J. Armstrong .25
123 Charles Barkley .75
124 Horace Grant .25
125 Checklist .25
126 Alonzo Mourning .50
127 Kerry Kittles .50
128 Eldridge Recasner .25
129 Dell Curry .25
130 Jamal Mashburn .50
131 Eric Piatkowski .25
132 Othella Harrington .25
133 Pete Chilcutt .25
134 Corie Blount .25
135 Patrick Ewing .50
136 Danny Schayes .25
137 John Williams .25
138 Joe Smith .50
139 Tariq Abdul-Wahad .25
140 Vin Baker 1.00
141 Elden Campbell .25
142 Chris Carr .25
143 John Starks .25
144 Felton Spencer .25
145 Mark Jackson .25
146 Dana Barros .25
147 Eric Williams .25
148 Wesley Person .25
149 Joe Dumars .50
150 Steve Smith .50
151 Randy Brown .25
152 A.C. Green .25
153 Dee Brown .25
154 Brian Grant .25
155 Tim Thomas 1.50
156 Howard Eisley .25
157 Malik Sealy .25
158 Maurice Taylor .75
159 Tyrone Hill .25
160 Chris Gatling .25
161 Rodrick Rhodes .25
162 Muggsy Bogues .25
163 Kenny Anderson .50
164 Zydrunas Ilgauskas .75
165 Grant Hill 3.00
166 Lorenzen Wright .25
167 Tony Battie .50
168 Bobby Phills .25
169 Michael Finley .75
170 Anfernee Hardaway 2.00
171 Terry Porter .25
172 P.J. Brown .25
173 Clifford Robinson .25
174 Olden Polynice .25
175 Kobe Bryant 5.00
176 Sean Elliott .25
177 Latrell Sprewell .50
178 Rik Smits .25
179 Darrell Armstrong .50
180 Stephon Marbury 2.00
181 Brent Price .25
182 Danny Fortson .25
183 Vitaly Potapenko .25
184 Anthony Parker .25
185 Glenn Robinson .50
186 Erick Dampier .25
187 George McCloud .25
188 Rasheed Wallace .50
189 Aaron Williams .25
190 Tim Duncan 3.00
191 Chauncey Billups .75
192 Jim McIlvaine .25
193 Chris Mullin .25
194 George Lynch .25
195 Damon Stoudamire .75
196 Bryon Russell .25
197 Luc Longley .25
198 Ron Mercer 1.50
199 Alan Henderson .25
200 Jayson Williams .50
201 Ben Wallace .25
202 Elliot Perry .25
203 Walt Williams .25
204 Cherokee Parks .25
205 Brent Barry .25
206 Hubert Davis .25
207 Terry Davis .25
208 Loy Vaught .25
209 Adam Keefe .25
210 Karl Malone 1.00
211 Chuck Person .25
212 Chris Childs .25
213 Rony Seikaly .25
214 Ervin Johnson .25
215 Derrick McKey .25
216 Jerome Williams .25
217 Glen Rice .50
218 Steve Nash .25
219 Nick Van Exel .50
220 Chris Webber 1.50
221 Marcus Camby .75
222 Antonio Daniels .25
223 Mitch Richmond .50
224 Otis Thorpe .25
225 Charles Oakley .25
226 *Michael Olowokandi* 8.00
227 *Mike Bibby* 10.00
228 *Raef LaFrentz* 8.00
229 *Antawn Jamison* 12.00
230 *Vince Carter* 30.00
231 *Robert Traylor* 8.00
232 *Jason Williams* 20.00
233 *Larry Hughes* 10.00
234 *Dirk Nowitzki* 4.00
235 *Paul Pierce* 20.00
236 *Bonzi Wells* 3.00
237 *Michael Doleac* 4.00
238 *Keon Clark* 4.00
239 *Michael Dickerson* 8.00
240 *Matt Harpring* 5.00
241 *Bryce Drew* 2.00
242 *Pat Garrity* 2.00
243 *Roshown McLeod* 3.00
244 *Ricky Davis* 3.00
245 *Brian Skinner* 2.00
246 *Tyronn Lue* 3.00
247 *Felipe Lopez* 4.00
248 *Sam Jacobson* 2.00
249 *Corey Benjamin* 2.00
250 *Nazr Mohammed* 2.00

1998-99 Finest Refractor

This 250-card parallel set reprinted each card from Finest I and II, but added a Refractor finish to the card front. Cards arrived with a protective peel and were inserted 1:12 packs. The word "Refractor" was printed in small black letters below the card number on the back.

MT
Complete Set (250): 1150.
Complete Series 1 (125): 250.00
Complete Series 2 (125): 900.00
Refractor Cards: 5x-10x
Refractor Rookies: 2x-4x
Inserted 1:12
1 Chris Mills .25
2 Matt Maloney .50
3 Sam Mitchell .25
4 Corliss Williamson .25
5 Bryant Reeves .50
6 Juwan Howard .50
7 Eddie Jones 1.25
8 Ray Allen .50
9 Larry Johnson .50
10 Travis Best .25
11 Isaiah Rider .25
12 Hakeem Olajuwon 1.00
13 Gary Trent .25
14 Kevin Garnett 3.00
15 Dikembe Mutombo .50
16 Brevin Knight .75
17 Keith Van Horn 1.50
18 Theo Ratliff .25
19 Tim Hardaway .75
20 Blue Edwards .25
21 David Wesley .25
22 Jaren Jackson .25
23 Nick Anderson .25
24 Rodney Rogers .25
25 Antonio Davis .25
26 Clarence Weatherspoon .25
27 Kelvin Cato .25
28 Tracy McGrady 1.50
29 Mookie Blaylock .25
30 Ron Harper .25
31 Allan Houston .50
32 Brian Williams .25
33 John Stockton .50
34 Hersey Hawkins .25
35 Donyell Marshall .25
36 Mark Strickland .25
37 Rod Strickland .25
38 Cedric Ceballos .25
39 Danny Fortson .25
40 Shaquille O'Neal 2.00
41 Kendall Gill .25
42 Allen Iverson 1.50
43 Travis Knight .25
44 Cedric Henderson .50
45 Steve Kerr .25
46 Antonio McDyess .50
47 Darrick Martin .25
48 Shandon Anderson .25
49 Shareef Abdur-Rahim 1.25
50 Antoine Carr .25
51 Jason Kidd 1.00
52 Calbert Cheaney .25
53 Antoine Walker 1.50
54 Greg Anthony .25
55 Jeff Hornacek .25
56 Reggie Miller .50
57 Lawrence Funderburke .25
58 Derek Strong .25
59 Robert Horry .25
60 Shawn Bradley .25
61 Matt Bullard .25
62 Terrell Brandon .50
63 Dan Majerle .25
64 Jim Jackson .25
65 Anthony Peeler .25
66 Charles Outlaw .25
67 Khalid Reeves .25
68 Toni Kukoc .50
69 Mario Elie .25
70 Derek Anderson .75
71 Jalen Rose .25
72 Tyrone Corbin .25
73 Anthony Mason .50
74 Lamond Murray .25
75 Tom Gugliotta .50
76 Arvydas Sabonis .25
77 Brian Shaw .25
78 Rick Fox .25
79 Danny Manning .25
80 Lindsey Hunter .25
81 Michael Jordan 6.00
82 LaPhonso Ellis .25
83 David Robinson .75
84 Christian Laettner .50
85 Armon Gilliam .25
86 Sherman Douglas .25
87 Charlie Ward .25
88 Shawn Kemp .75
89 Gary Payton .75
90 Doug Christie .25
91 Voshon Lenard .25
92 Detlef Schrempf .25
93 Walter McCarty .25
94 Sam Cassell .25
95 Jerry Stackhouse .50
96 Billy Owens .25
97 Matt Geiger .25
98 Avery Johnson .25
99 Bobby Jackson .50
100 Rex Chapman .25
101 Andrew DeClercq .25
102 Vlade Divac .25
103 Erick Strickland .25
104 Dean Garrett .25
105 Grant Long .25
106 Adonal Foyle .25
107 Isaac Austin .25
108 Michael Curry .25
109 Darrell Armstrong .25
110 Aaron McKie .25
111 Stacey Augmon .25
112 Anthony Johnson .25
113 Vinny Del Negro .25
114 Reggie Slater .25
115 Lee Mayberry .25
116 Tracy Murray .25
117 Scottie Pippen 1.50
118 Sam Perkins .25
119 Derek Fisher .25
120 Mark Bryant .25
121 Dale Davis .25
122 B.J. Armstrong .25
123 Charles Barkley .75
124 Horace Grant .25
125 Checklist .25
126 Alonzo Mourning .50
127 Kerry Kittles .50
128 Eldridge Recasner .25
129 Dell Curry .25
130 Jamal Mashburn .50
131 Eric Piatkowski .25
132 Othella Harrington .25
133 Pete Chilcutt .25
134 Corie Blount .25
135 Patrick Ewing .50
136 Danny Schayes .25
137 John Williams .25
138 Joe Smith .50
139 Tariq Abdul-Wahad .25
140 Vin Baker 1.00
141 Elden Campbell .25
142 Chris Carr .25
143 John Starks .25
144 Felton Spencer .25
145 Mark Jackson .25
146 Dana Barros .25
147 Eric Williams .25
148 Wesley Person .25
149 Joe Dumars .50
150 Steve Smith .50
151 Randy Brown .25
152 A.C. Green .25

153	Dee Brown	.25
154	Brian Grant	.25
155	Tim Thomas	1.50
156	Howard Eisley	.25
157	Malik Sealy	.25
158	Maurice Taylor	.75
159	Tyrone Hill	.25
160	Chris Gatling	.25
161	Rodrick Rhodes	.25
162	Muggsy Bogues	.25
163	Kenny Anderson	.50
164	Zydrunas Ilgauskas	.75
165	Grant Hill	3.00
166	Lorenzen Wright	.25
167	Tony Battie	.50
168	Bobby Phills	.25
169	Michael Finley	.75
170	Anfernee Hardaway	2.00
171	Terry Porter	.25
172	P.J. Brown	.25
173	Clifford Robinson	.25
174	Olden Polynice	.25
175	Kobe Bryant	5.00
176	Sean Elliott	.25
177	Latrell Sprewell	.50
178	Rik Smits	.25
179	Darrell Armstrong	.50
180	Stephon Marbury	2.00
181	Brent Price	.25
182	Danny Fortson	.25
183	Vitaly Potapenko	.25
184	Anthony Parker	.25
185	Glenn Robinson	.50
186	Erick Dampier	.25
187	George McCloud	.25
188	Rasheed Wallace	.50
189	Aaron Williams	.25
190	Tim Duncan	3.00
191	Chauncey Billups	.75
192	Jim McIlvaine	.25
193	Chris Mullin	.25
194	George Lynch	.25
195	Damon Stoudamire	.75
196	Bryon Russell	.25
197	Luc Longley	.25
198	Ron Mercer	1.50
199	Alan Henderson	.25
200	Jayson Williams	.50
201	Ben Wallace	.25
202	Elliot Perry	.25
203	Walt Williams	.25
204	Cherokee Parks	.25
205	Brent Barry	.25
206	Hubert Davis	.25
207	Terry Davis	.25
208	Loy Vaught	.25
209	Adam Keefe	.25
210	Karl Malone	1.00
211	Chuck Person	.25
212	Chris Childs	.25
213	Rony Seikaly	.25
214	Ervin Johnson	.25
215	Derrick McKey	.25
216	Jerome Williams	.25
217	Glen Rice	.50
218	Steve Nash	.25
219	Nick Van Exel	.50
220	Chris Webber	1.50
221	Marcus Camby	.75
222	Antonio Daniels	.25
223	Mitch Richmond	.50
224	Otis Thorpe	.25
225	Charles Oakley	.25
226	*Michael Olowokandi*	8.00
227	*Mike Bibby*	10.00
228	*Raef LaFrentz*	8.00
229	*Antawn Jamison*	12.00
230	*Vince Carter*	30.00
231	*Robert Traylor*	8.00
232	*Jason Williams*	20.00
233	*Larry Hughes*	10.00
234	*Dirk Nowitzki*	4.00
235	*Paul Pierce*	20.00
236	*Bonzi Wells*	3.00
237	*Michael Doleac*	4.00
238	*Keon Clark*	4.00
239	*Michael Dickerson*	8.00
240	*Matt Harpring*	5.00
241	*Bryce Drew*	2.00
242	*Pat Garrity*	2.00
243	*Roshown McLeod*	3.00
244	*Ricky Davis*	3.00
245	*Brian Skinner*	2.00
246	*Tyronn Lue*	3.00
247	*Felipe Lopez*	4.00
248	*Sam Jacobson*	2.00
249	*Corey Benjamin*	2.00
250	*Nazr Mohammed*	2.00

1998-99 Finest Arena Stars

Arena Stars was a 20-card insert exclusive to Series II Finest packs. They featured holo-foil printing on Finest technology with stars in the background. Cards were numbered with an "AS" prefix and were inserted 1:48 hobby packs and 1:20 HTA Collectors packs.

		MT
Complete Set (20):		[illegible]
Common Player:		3.00
Inserted 1:48 Series 2		
1	Shaquille O'Neal	15.00
2	Stephon Marbury	15.00
3	Allen Iverson	20.00
4	John Stockton	3.00
5	Kobe Bryant	35.00
6	Alonzo Mourning	3.00
7	Damon Stoudamire	6.00
8	Scottie Pippen	12.00
9	Tim Hardaway	4.00
10	Karl Malone	5.00
11	Tim Duncan	30.00
12	Gary Payton	6.00
13	Antoine Walker	8.00
14	Keith Van Horn	8.00
15	Juwan Howard	3.00
16	David Robinson	5.00
17	Michael Finley	3.00
18	Shareef Abdur-Rahim	12.00
19	Michael Jordan	60.00
20	Vin Baker	6.00

1998-99 Finest Centurions

Centurions featured 20 players that will lead the NBA into the millennium. Regular versions were numbered to 500 sets and inserted 1:91 packs, while Refractor versions were numbered to 75 and inserted 1:609 packs. Centurions were numbered with a "C" prefix and exclusive to Series I packs.

		MT
Complete Set (20):		450.00
Common Player:		10.00
Inserted 1:91 Series 1		
Production 500 Sets		
Refractor Cards:		2x-3x
Inserted 1:609 Series 1		
Production 75 Sets		
1	Grant Hill	60.00
2	Tim Thomas	20.00
3	Eddie Jones	20.00
4	Michael Finley	10.00
5	Shaquille O'Neal	35.00
6	Kobe Bryant	75.00
7	Keith Van Horn	25.00
8	Tim Duncan	60.00
9	Antoine Walker	20.00
10	Shareef Abdur-Rahim	25.00
11	Stephon Marbury	40.00
12	Kevin Garnett	60.00
13	Ray Allen	10.00
14	Kerry Kittles	10.00
15	Allen Iverson	30.00
16	Damon Stoudamire	10.00
17	Brevin Knight	15.00
18	Bryant Reeves	10.00
19	Ron Mercer	30.00
20	Zydrunas Ilgauskas	10.00

1998-99 Finest Centurions Refractors

This 20-card parallel set reprinted each Centurions insert in Refractor version. Cards were sequentially numbered to 75 and inserted 1:609 Series I packs.

		MT
Complete Set (20):		1200.
Refractor Cards:		2x-3x
Inserted 1:609 Series 1		
Production 75 Sets		
C1	Grant Hill	60.00
C2	Tim Thomas	20.00
C3	Eddie Jones	20.00
C4	Michael Finley	10.00
C5	Shaquille O'Neal	35.00
C6	Kobe Bryant	75.00
C7	Keith Van Horn	25.00
C8	Tim Duncan	60.00
C9	Antoine Walker	20.00
C10	Shareef Abdur-Rahim	25.00
C11	Stephon Marbury	40.00
C12	Kevin Garnett	60.00
C13	Ray Allen	10.00
C14	Kerry Kittles	10.00
C15	Allen Iverson	30.00
C16	Damon Stoudamire	10.00
C17	Brevin Knight	15.00
C18	Bryant Reeves	10.00
C19	Ron Mercer	30.00
C20	Zydrunas Ilgauskas	10.00

1998-99 Finest Court Control

Court Control was a 20-card insert that showcased top players over a basketball court background with a blue border on the right side featuring the insert name. Regular versions were inserted 1:76 hobby packs and 1:35 HTA Collector packs and numbered to 750 sets. Refractors were seeded 1:379 packs (1:175 HTA) and numbered to 150 sets. Court Control inserts were exclusive to Series II packs and numbered with a "CC" prefix.

		MT
Complete Set (20):		350.00
Common Player:		5.00
Inserted 1:76 Series 2		
Production 750 Sets		
Refractors		2x
Inserted 1:379 Series 2		
Production 150 Sets		
1	Shareef Abdur-Rahim	15.00
2	Keith Van Horn	10.00
3	Tim Duncan	35.00
4	Antoine Walker	10.00
5	Stephon Marbury	20.00
6	Kevin Garnett	35.00
7	Grant Hill	35.00
8	Michael Finley	5.00
9	Ron Mercer	15.00
10	Damon Stoudamire	10.00
11	Michael Olowokandi	15.00
12	Mike Bibby	20.00
13	Antawn Jamison	20.00
14	Vince Carter	40.00
15	Jason Williams	30.00
16	Larry Hughes	20.00
17	Paul Pierce	25.00
18	Michael Dickerson	12.00
19	Bryce Drew	5.00
20	Felipe Lopez	8.00

1998-99 Finest Court Control Refractors

This 20-card parallel set reprinted every card from the Court Control insert in a Refractor version. Cards were sequentially numbered to 150 sets and inserted 1:379 packs of Series II.

		MT
Complete Set (20):		900.00
Refractors:		2x-3x
Inserted 1:379 Series 2		
Production 150 Sets		
CC1	Shareef Abdur-Rahim	15.00
CC2	Keith Van Horn	10.00
CC3	Tim Duncan	35.00
CC4	Antoine Walker	10.00
CC5	Stephon Marbury	20.00
CC6	Kevin Garnett	35.00
CC7	Grant Hill	35.00
CC8	Michael Finley	5.00
CC9	Ron Mercer	15.00
CC10	Damon Stoudamire	10.00
CC11	Michael Olowokandi	15.00
CC12	Mike Bibby	20.00
CC13	Antawn Jamison	20.00
CC14	Vince Carter	40.00
CC15	Jason Williams	30.00
CC16	Larry Hughes	20.00
CC17	Paul Pierce	25.00
CC18	Michael Dickerson	12.00
CC19	Bryce Drew	5.00
CC20	Felipe Lopez	8.00

1998-99 Finest Hardwood Honors

Hardwood Heroes showcased 20 players who won awards during the 1997-98 season. Cards featured holo-foil printing on Finest technology and had basketballs in the background. Cards were exclusive to Series I packs, numbered with an "H" prefix and inserted 1:33 packs.

		MT
Complete Set (20):		130.00
Common Player:		5.00
Inserted 1:33 Series 1		
1	Michael Jordan	50.00
2	Shaquille O'Neal	15.00
3	Karl Malone	7.00
[illegible]	[illegible]	[illegible]
5	Dikembe Mutombo	5.00
6	Wesley Person	5.00
7	Glen Rice	5.00
8	David Robinson	8.00
9	Rik Smits	5.00
10	Steve Smith	5.00
11	Allen Iverson	12.00
12	Jayson Williams	5.00
13	Nick Anderson	5.00
14	Tim Duncan	25.00
15	Jason Kidd	10.00
16	Alonzo Mourning	5.00
17	Sam Cassell	5.00
18	Alan Henderson	5.00
19	Gary Payton	8.00
20	Scottie Pippen	12.00

1998-99 Finest Jumbo

This 14-card insert reprinted seven cards from each series on a 3-1/2" x 5" version. Jumbos were inserted as box toppers at a rate of one per box. Refractor versions were also available and seeded 1:12 packs (1:6 HTA).

		MT
Complete Set (14):		100.00
Complete Series 1 (7):		50.00
Complete Series 2 (7):		50.00
Common Player:		2.00
Inserted 1:3 Series 1/2 Boxes		
Refractor Cards:		2x
Inserted 1:12 Series 1/2 Boxes		
1	Kevin Garnett	15.00
2	Keith Van Horn	6.00
3	Shaquille O'Neal	10.00
4	Shareef Abdur-Rahim	5.00
5	Antoine Walker	4.00
6	Gary Payton	2.00
7	Scottie Pippen	8.00
8	Alonzo Mourning	2.00
9	Kerry Kittles	2.00
10	Kobe Bryant	20.00
11	Stephon Marbury	10.00
12	Tim Duncan	15.00
13	Ron Mercer	5.00
14	Karl Malone	2.00

1998-99 Finest Jumbo Refractors

		MT
Complete Set (14):		200.00
Complete Series 1 (7):		100.00
Complete Series 2 (7):		100.00
Common Player:		4.00
Refractor Cards:		2x
Inserted 1:12 Series 1/2 Boxes		
1	Kevin Garnett	15.00
2	Keith Van Horn	6.00
3	Shaquille O'Neal	10.00
4	Shareef Abdur-Rahim	5.00
5	Antoine Walker	4.00
6	Gary Payton	2.00
7	Scottie Pippen	8.00
8	Alonzo Mourning	2.00
9	Kerry Kittles	2.00
10	Kobe Bryant	20.00
11	Stephon Marbury	10.00
12	Tim Duncan	15.00
13	Ron Mercer	5.00
14	Karl Malone	2.00

1998-99 Finest Mystery Finest

20 Mystery Finest inserts were inserted into both series of Finest. This 40-card set featured double-sided Finest cards, with two stars matched up back-to-back. These were numbered with an "M" prefix and inserted 1:33 packs of Series I and 1:36 packs of Series II, while Refractor versions were seeded 1:133 Series I packs and 1:144 Series II packs. All Mystery Finest inserts arrived with a black opaque protector over both [illegible] veal which players were on the card.

		MT
Complete Set (40):		500.00
Complete Series 1 (20):		250.00
Complete Series 2 (20):		250.00
Common Player:		5.00
Inserted 1:33 Series 1		
Inserted 1:36 Series 2		
Refractor Cards:		2x-4x
Inserted 1:133 Series 1		
Inserted 1:144 Series 2		
1	Michael Jordan, Kobe Bryant	50.00
2	Kobe Bryant, Shaquille O'Neal	30.00
3	Shaquille O'Neal, David Robinson	15.00
4	David Robinson, Tim Duncan	20.00
5	Tim Duncan, Keith Van Horn	15.00
6	Keith Van Horn, Scottie Pippen	10.00
7	Scottie Pippen, Shareef Abdur-Rahim	12.00
8	Shareef Abdur-Rahim, Grant Hill	20.00
9	Grant Hill, Kevin Garnett	25.00
10	Kevin Garnett, Stephon Marbury	20.00
11	Stephon Marbury, Gary Payton	15.00
12	Gary Payton, Vin Baker	5.00
13	Vin Baker, Karl Malone	5.00
14	Karl Malone, Shawn Kemp	5.00
15	Shawn Kemp, Tim Thomas	5.00
16	Tim Thomas, Antoine Walker	8.00
17	Antoine Walker, Ron Mercer	8.00
18	Ron Mercer, Kerry Kittles	10.00
19	Kerry Kittles, Eddie Jones	5.00
20	Eddie Jones, Michael Jordan	40.00
21	Alonzo Mourning, Scottie Pippen	10.00
22	Scottie Pippen, Antoine Walker	8.00
23	Antoine Walker, Shareef Abdur-Rahim	6.00
24	Shareef Abdur-Rahim, Kevin Garnett	18.00
25	Kevin Garnett, Keith Van Horn	15.00
26	Keith Van Horn, Tim Thomas	8.00
27	Tim Thomas, Grant Hill	15.00
28	Grant Hill, Anfernee Hardaway	20.00
29	Anfernee Hardaway, Kerry Kittles	10.00
30	Kerry Kittles, Jayson Williams	5.00
31	Jayson Williams, Karl Malone	6.00
32	Karl Malone, John Stockton	6.00
33	John Stockton, Gary Payton	6.00
34	Gary Payton, Ron Mercer	10.00
35	Ron Mercer, Stephon Marbury	20.00
36	Stephon Marbury, Allen Iverson	20.00
37	Allen Iverson, Kobe Bryant	30.00
38	Kobe Bryant, Tim Duncan	40.00
39	Tim Duncan, Shaquille O'Neal	25.00
40	Shaquille O'Neal, Alonzo Mourning	10.00

1998-99 Finest Mystery Finest Refractors

		MT
Complete Set (40):		1500.
Common Player:		10.00
Refractor Cards:		2x-4x
Inserted 1:133 Series 1		
Inserted 1:144 Series 2		
M1	Michael Jordan, Kobe Bryant	50.00
M2	Kobe Bryant, Shaquille O'Neal	30.00
M3	Shaquille O'Neal, David Robinson	15.00
M4	David Robinson, Tim Duncan	20.00
M5	Tim Duncan, Keith Van Horn	15.00
M6	Keith Van Horn, Scottie Pippen	8.00
M7	Scottie Pippen, Shareef Abdur-Rahim	12.00
M8	Shareef Abdur-Rahim, Grant Hill	20.00
M9	Grant Hill, Kevin Garnett	25.00
M10	Kevin Garnett, Stephon Marbury	20.00
M11	Stephon Marbury, Gary Payton	15.00
M12	Gary Payton, Vin Baker	5.00
M13	Vin Baker, Karl Malone	5.00
M14	Karl Malone, Shawn Kemp	5.00
M15	Shawn Kemp, Tim Thomas	5.00
M16	Tim Thomas, Antoine Walker	8.00
M17	Antoine Walker, Ron Mercer	8.00
M18	Ron Mercer, Kerry Kittles	10.00
M19	Kerry Kittles, Eddie Jones	5.00
M20	Eddie Jones, Michael Jordan	40.00
[illegible]	[illegible] Scottie Pippen	[illegible]
M22	Scottie Pippen, Antoine Walker	8.00
M23	Antoine Walker, Shareef Abdur-Rahim	5.00
M24	Shareef Abdur-Rahim, Kevin Garnett	18.00
M25	Kevin Garnett, Keith Van Horn	15.00
M26	Keith Van Horn, Tim Thomas	8.00
M27	Tim Thomas, Grant Hill	15.00
M28	Grant Hill, Anfernee Hardaway	20.00
M29	Anfernee Hardaway, Kerry Kittles	10.00
M30	Kerry Kittles, Jayson Williams	5.00
M31	Jayson Williams, Karl Malone	6.00
M32	Karl Malone, John Stockton	6.00
M33	John Stockton, Gary Payton	6.00
M34	Gary Payton, Ron Mercer	10.00
M35	Ron Mercer, Stephon Marbury	20.00
M36	Stephon Marbury, Allen Iverson	20.00
M37	Allen Iverson, Kobe Bryant	30.00
M38	Kobe Bryant, Tim Duncan	40.00
M39	Tim Duncan, Shaquille O'Neal	25.00
M40	Shaquille O'Neal, Alonzo Mourning	10.00

1999-00 Finest

Finest consisted of 266 cards in 1999-00 and was issued in two, 133-card series. Each series had 100 base cards and 33 subset cards that were seeded one per pack. In Series I, the subsets were 15 Rookies, nine Gems and nine Sensations, while in Series II the subsets were 15 Rookies, nine Catalysts and nine Edge cards. Every card in the set was paralleled in a Refractor and Gold Refractor version. Inserts in Series I included: Dunk Masters, New Millennium, Producers, Future's Finest, Double Feature, Team Finest, Leading Indicators and Finest Salute. Inserts in Series II included: Heirs to Air, Double Double, Next Generation, Box Office Draws, 24-Karat Touch, Team Finest and Finest Salute.

		MT
Complete Set (266):		350.00
Complete Series I Set (133):		100.00
Complete Series II Set (133):		250.00
Common Player:		.25
Minor Stars:		.50
Common Rookie (110-124):		2.00
Common Rookie (252-266):		3.00
Production 2,000 Sets		
Series 1 Pack (6):		5.00
Series 2 Pack (6):		6.00
Series 1 Wax Box (24):		70.00
Series 2 Wax Box (24):		90.00
1	Shareef Abdur-Rahim	1.50
2	Kevin Willis	.25
3	Sean Elliott	.25
4	Vlade Divac	.25
5	Tom Gugliotta	.50
6	Matt Harpring	.50
7	Kerry Kittles	.25
8	Joe Smith	.50
9	Jamal Mashburn	.50
10	Tyrone Nesby	.50
11	Alan Henderson	.25
12	Vitaly Potapenko	.25
13	Dickey Simpkins	.25
14	Michael Finley	.50
15	Lindsey Hunter	.25
16	Antawn Jamison	1.50
17	Reggie Miller	.50
18	Maurice Taylor	.60
19	Clarence Weatherspoon	.25
20	Sam Mitchell	.25
21	Latrell Sprewell	.50
22	Michael Doleac	.50
23	Rex Chapman	.25
24	Predrag Stojakovic	.50
25	Vladimir Stepania	.25
26	Tracy McGrady	1.25
27	Cherokee Parks	.25
28	LaPhonso Ellis	.25
29	Hakeem Olajuwon	.75
30	Adonal Foyle	.25
31	Bryant Stith	.25
32	Andrew DeClercq	.25
33	Toni Kukoc	.60
34	Kenny Anderson	.50
35	Mike Bibby	1.00
36	Glen Rice	.50
37	Avery Johnson	.25
38	Arvydas Sabonis	.25
39	Kornel David	.25
40	Hubert Davis	.25
41	Grant Hill	3.00
42	Donyell Marshall	.25
43	Jalen Rose	.50
44	Derrick Coleman	.50
45	P.J. Brown	.25
46	Vin Baker	.50

47 Clifford Robinson .25
48 Allan Houston .50
49 Kendall Gill .25
50 Matt Geiger .25
51 Larry Hughes 1.00
52 Corliss Williamson .25
53 Darrell Armstrong .50
54 Bobby Jackson .25
55 Bryon Russell .25
56 Juwan Howard .50
57 Dikembe Mutombo .50
58 Eddie Jones .75
59 Randy Brown .25
60 Dirk Nowitzki 1.00
61 Jerome Williams .25
62 Scottie Pippen 1.50
63 Dale Davis .25
64 Kobe Bryant 4.00
65 Robert Traylor .75
66 Tim Hardaway .60
67 Michael Olowokandi .75
68 Walter McCarty .25
69 Damon Stoudamire .60
70 Othella Harrington .25
71 Chauncey Billups .25
72 John Starks .25
73 Ricky Davis .50
74 Glenn Robinson .50
75 Dean Garrett .25
76 Chris Childs .25
77 Shawn Kemp .75
78 Allen Iverson 2.50
79 Brian Grant .25
80 David Robinson .75
81 Tracy Murray .25
82 Howard Eisley .25
83 Doug Christie .25
84 Gary Payton .75
85 John Stockton .50
86 Rod Strickland .50
87 Tyrone Corbin .25
88 Antonio Daniels .25
89 Dee Brown .25
90 Antoine Walker 1.00
91 Theo Ratliff .25
92 Larry Johnson .25
93 Stephon Marbury 1.50
94 Brevin Knight .25
95 Antonio McDyess .60
96 Bison Dele .25
97 Cuttino Mobley .50
98 Haywood Workman .25
99 J.R. Reid .25
100 Travis Best .25
101 Chris Webber 2.00
102 Grant Hill 4.00
103 Kevin Garnett 4.00
104 Jason Kidd 2.00
105 Gary Payton 1.50
106 Shaquille O'Neal 3.00
107 Alonzo Mourning 1.00
108 Karl Malone 1.50
109 John Stockton 1.00
110 *Elton Brand* 10.00
111 *Baron Davis* 8.00
112 *Aleksandar Radojevic* 2.00
113 *Cal Bowdler* 2.00
114 *Jumanie Jones* 2.50
115 *Jason Terry* 5.00
116 *Trajan Langdon* 5.00
117 *Dion Glover* 2.50
118 *Jeff Foster* 2.00
119 *Lamar Odom* 15.00
120 *Wally Szczerbiak* 6.00
121 *Shawn Marion* 10.00
122 *Kenny Thomas* 3.00
123 *Devean George* 5.00
124 *Scott Padgett* 3.00
125 Tim Duncan 4.00
126 Jason Williams 3.00
127 Paul Pierce 3.00
128 Kobe Bryant 5.00
129 Keith Van Horn 1.50
130 Vince Carter 5.00
131 Matt Harpring 1.00
132 Antawn Jamison 2.00
133 Tracy McGrady 2.00
134 Tim Duncan 3.00
135 Tariq Abdul-Wahad .25
136 Luc Longley .25
137 Steve Smith .40
138 Alonzo Mourning .50
139 Kevin Garnett 3.00
140 Christian Laettner .25
141 Rik Smits .25
142 Cedric Henderson .25
143 Jim Jackson .25
144 Dan Majerle .25
145 Bryant Reeves .25
146 Antonio Davis .25
147 Michael Smith .25
148 Charlie Ward .25
149 Chris Mullin .25
150 Danny Manning .25
151 Eric Williams .25
152 Hersey Hawkins .25
153 Isaiah Rider .25
154 Shandon Anderson .25
155 Jason Kidd 1.50
156 Chris Whitney .25
157 Brent Barry .25
158 Patrick Ewing .40
159 George Lynch .25
160 Dickey Simpkins .25
161 Derek Anderson .40
162 Ron Mercer .75
163 David Wesley .25
164 Mookie Blaylock .25
165 Terrell Brandon .40
166 Detlef Schrempf .25
167 Olden Polynice .25
168 Jayson Williams .25
169 Eric Piatkowski .25
170 A.C. Green .25
171 Chris Mills .25
172 Chris Webber 1.50
173 Jeff Hornacek .25
174 Calbert Cheaney .25
175 Wesley Person .25
176 Corey Benjamin .40
177 Loy Vaught .25
178 Keith Closs .25
179 Charles Outlaw .25
180 Mitch Richmond .40
181 Charles Oakley .25
182 Felipe Lopez .40
183 Eric Snow .25
184 Paul Pierce 1.25
185 Elden Campbell .25
186 Shaquille O'Neal 2.00
187 Charles Barkley .75
188 Mark Jackson .25
189 Scott Burrell .25
190 Anfernee Hardaway 2.00
191 Samaki Walker .25
192 Karl Malone .75
193 Jermaine O'Neal .25
194 Mario Elie .25
195 Malik Sealy .25
196 Voshon Lenard .25
197 Chris Gatling .25
198 Walt Williams .25
199 Nick Van Exel .40
200 Bimbo Coles .25
201 John Wallace .25
202 Anthony Mason .25
203 Steve Nash .25
204 Erick Dampier .25
205 Cedric Ceballos .25
206 Derek Fisher .25
207 Marcus Camby .50
208 Tyrone Hill .25
209 Nick Anderson .25
210 Sam Cassell .40
211 Raef LaFrentz .60
212 Ruben Patterson .40
213 Rick Fox .25
214 Jason Williams 1.50
215 Vince Carter 5.00
216 Michael Dickerson .40
217 Steve Kerr .25
218 Rasheed Wallace .40
219 Keith Van Horn .75
220 Bob Sura .25
221 Ray Allen .50
222 Jerry Stackhouse .50
223 Shawn Bradley .25
224 Horace Grant .25
225 Tim Duncan 5.00
226 Kevin Garnett 5.00
227 Jason Kidd 3.00
228 Steve Smith .40
229 Allan Houston .40
230 Tom Gugliotta .40
231 Gary Payton 1.50
232 Tim Hardaway .75
233 Vin Baker .40
234 Karl Malone 1.50
235 Vince Carter 8.00
236 Jason Williams 3.00
237 Alonzo Mourning .75
238 Anfernee Hardaway 4.00
239 Mitch Richmond .40
240 Steve Smith .40
241 Charles Barkley 1.50
242 Ron Mercer 1.50
243 Shaquille O'Neal 4.00
244 Jason Kidd 3.00
245 Kevin Garnett 5.00
246 Tim Duncan 5.00
247 Ray Allen .75
248 Chris Webber 3.00
249 Jerry Stackhouse 1.00
250 Keith Van Horn 1.00
251 Patrick Ewing .40
252 *Steve Francis* 125.00
253 *Jonathan Bender* 40.00
254 *Richard Hamilton* 25.00
255 *Andre Miller* 30.00
256 *Corey Maggette* 30.00
257 *William Avery* 10.00
258 *Ron Artest* 15.00
259 *James Posey* 12.00
260 *Quincy Lewis* 6.00
261 *Tim James* 5.00
262 *Vonteego Cummings* 8.00
263 *Anthony Carter* 12.00
264 *Mirsad Turkcan* 3.00
265 *Adrian Griffin* 8.00
266 *Ryan Robertson* 3.00

1999-00 Finest Refractors

This 266-card parallel set reprinted each card in Finest Series I and II with a Refractor finish. Cards 1-251 were inserted 1:12 packs, while the Series II Rookies (252-266) were seeded 1:138 (1:64 HTA) packs and sequentially numbered to 200 sets.

MT
Refractor Cards: 5x-10x
Refractor Subset Cards: 3x-6x
Series I Rookies: 2x-4x
Inserted 1:12
Series II Rookies: 1.5x
Production 200 Sets

1 Shareef Abdur-Rahim 1.50
2 Kevin Willis .25
3 Sean Elliott .25
4 Vlade Divac .25
5 Tom Gugliotta .50
6 Matt Harpring .50
7 Kerry Kittles .25
8 Joe Smith .50
9 Jamal Mashburn .50
10 Tyrone Nesby .50
11 Alan Henderson .25
12 Vitaly Potapenko .25
13 Dickey Simpkins .25
14 Michael Finley .50
15 Lindsey Hunter .25
16 Antawn Jamison 1.50
17 Reggie Miller .50
18 Maurice Taylor .60
19 Clarence Weatherspoon .25
20 Sam Mitchell .25
21 Latrell Sprewell .50
22 Michael Doleac .50
23 Rex Chapman .25
24 Predrag Stojakovic .50
25 Vladimir Stepania .25
26 Tracy McGrady 1.25
27 Cherokee Parks .25
28 LaPhonso Ellis .25
29 Hakeem Olajuwon .75
30 Adonal Foyle .25
31 Bryant Stith .25
32 Andrew DeClercq .25
33 Toni Kukoc .60
34 Kenny Anderson .50
35 Mike Bibby 1.00
36 Glen Rice .50
37 Avery Johnson .25
38 Arvydas Sabonis .25
39 Kornel David .25
40 Hubert Davis .25
41 Grant Hill 3.00
42 Donyell Marshall .25
43 Jalen Rose .50
44 Derrick Coleman .50
45 P.J. Brown .25
46 Vin Baker .50
47 Clifford Robinson .25
48 Allan Houston .50
49 Kendall Gill .25
50 Matt Geiger .25
51 Larry Hughes 1.00
52 Corliss Williamson .25
53 Darrell Armstrong .50
54 Bobby Jackson .25
55 Bryon Russell .25
56 Juwan Howard .50
57 Dikembe Mutombo .50
58 Eddie Jones .75
59 Randy Brown .25
60 Dirk Nowitzki .50
61 Jerome Williams .25
62 Scottie Pippen 1.50
63 Dale Davis .25
64 Kobe Bryant 4.00
65 Robert Traylor .75
66 Tim Hardaway .60
67 Michael Olowokandi .75
68 Walter McCarty .25
69 Damon Stoudamire .60
70 Othella Harrington .25
71 Chauncey Billups .25
72 John Starks .25
73 Ricky Davis .50
74 Glenn Robinson .50
75 Dean Garrett .25
76 Chris Childs .25
77 Shawn Kemp .75
78 Allen Iverson 2.00
79 Brian Grant .25
80 David Robinson .75
81 Tracy Murray .25
82 Howard Eisley .25
83 Doug Christie .25
84 Gary Payton .75
85 John Stockton .50
86 Rod Strickland .50
87 Tyrone Corbin .25
88 Antonio Daniels .25
89 Dee Brown .25
90 Antoine Walker 1.00
91 Theo Ratliff .25
92 Larry Johnson .25
93 Stephon Marbury 1.50
94 Brevin Knight .25
95 Antonio McDyess .60
96 Bison Dele .25
97 Cuttino Mobley .50
98 Haywood Workman .25
99 J.R. Reid .25
100 Travis Best .25
101 Chris Webber 2.00
102 Grant Hill 4.00
103 Kevin Garnett 4.00
104 Jason Kidd 2.00
105 Gary Payton 1.50
106 Shaquille O'Neal 3.00
107 Alonzo Mourning 1.00
108 Karl Malone 1.50
109 John Stockton 1.00
110 *Elton Brand* 12.00
111 *Baron Davis* 10.00
112 *Aleksandar Radojevic* 2.00
113 *Cal Bowdler* 2.00
114 *Jumanie Jones* 3.00
115 *Jason Terry* 5.00
116 *Trajan Langdon* 6.00
117 *Dion Glover* 2.00
118 *Jeff Foster* 2.00
119 *Lamar Odom* 20.00
120 *Wally Szczerbiak* 15.00
121 *Shawn Marion* 8.00
122 *Kenny Thomas* 2.00
123 *Devean George* 3.00
124 *Scott Padgett* 3.00
125 Tim Duncan 4.00
126 Jason Williams 3.00
127 Paul Pierce 3.00
128 Kobe Bryant 5.00
129 Keith Van Horn 1.50
130 Vince Carter 4.00
131 Matt Harpring 1.00
132 Antawn Jamison 2.00
133 Tracy McGrady 2.00
134 Tim Duncan 3.00
135 Tariq Abdul-Wahad .25
136 Luc Longley .25
137 Steve Smith .40
138 Alonzo Mourning .50
139 Kevin Garnett 3.00
140 Christian Laettner .25
141 Rik Smits .25
142 Cedric Henderson .25
143 Jim Jackson .25
144 Dan Majerle .25
145 Bryant Reeves .25
146 Antonio Davis .25
147 Michael Smith .25
148 Charlie Ward .25
149 Chris Mullin .25
150 Danny Manning .25
151 Eric Williams .25
152 Hersey Hawkins .25
153 Isaiah Rider .25
154 Shandon Anderson .25
155 Jason Kidd 1.50
156 Chris Whitney .25
157 Brent Barry .25
158 Patrick Ewing .40
159 George Lynch .25
160 Dickey Simpkins .25
161 Derek Anderson .40
162 Ron Mercer .75
163 David Wesley .25
164 Mookie Blaylock .25
165 Terrell Brandon .40
166 Detlef Schrempf .25
167 Olden Polynice .25
168 Jayson Williams .25
169 Eric Piatkowski .25
170 A.C. Green .25
171 Chris Mills .25
172 Chris Webber 1.50
173 Jeff Hornacek .25
174 Calbert Cheaney .25
175 Wesley Person .25
176 Corey Benjamin .40
177 Loy Vaught .25
178 Keith Closs .25
179 Charles Outlaw .25
180 Mitch Richmond .40
181 Charles Oakley .25
182 Felipe Lopez .40
183 Eric Snow .25
184 Paul Pierce 1.25
185 Elden Campbell .25
186 Shaquille O'Neal 2.00
187 Charles Barkley .75
188 Mark Jackson .25
189 Scott Burrell .25
190 Anfernee Hardaway 2.00
191 Samaki Walker .25
192 Karl Malone .75
193 Jermaine O'Neal .25
194 Mario Elie .25
195 Malik Sealy .25
196 Voshon Lenard .25
197 Chris Gatling .25
198 Walt Williams .25
199 Nick Van Exel .40
200 Bimbo Coles .25
201 John Wallace .25
202 Anthony Mason .25
203 Steve Nash .25
204 Erick Dampier .25
205 Cedric Ceballos .25
206 Derek Fisher .25
207 Marcus Camby .50
208 Tyrone Hill .25
209 Nick Anderson .25
210 Sam Cassell .40
211 Raef LaFrentz .60
212 Ruben Patterson .40
213 Rick Fox .25
214 Jason Williams 1.50
215 Vince Carter 5.00
216 Michael Dickerson .40
217 Steve Kerr .25
218 Rasheed Wallace .40
219 Keith Van Horn .75
220 Bob Sura .25
221 Ray Allen .50
222 Jerry Stackhouse .50
223 Shawn Bradley .25
224 Horace Grant .25
225 Tim Duncan 5.00
226 Kevin Garnett 5.00
227 Jason Kidd 3.00
228 Steve Smith .40
229 Allan Houston .40
230 Tom Gugliotta .40
231 Gary Payton 1.50
232 Tim Hardaway .75
233 Vin Baker .40
234 Karl Malone 1.50
235 Vince Carter 8.00
236 Jason Williams 3.00
237 Alonzo Mourning .75
238 Anfernee Hardaway 4.00
239 Mitch Richmond .40
240 Steve Smith .40
241 Charles Barkley 1.50
242 Ron Mercer 1.50
243 Shaquille O'Neal 4.00
244 Jason Kidd 3.00
245 Kevin Garnett 5.00
246 Tim Duncan 5.00
247 Ray Allen .75
248 Chris Webber 3.00
249 Jerry Stackhouse 1.00
250 Keith Van Horn 1.00
251 Patrick Ewing .40
252 Steve Francis 200.00
253 Jonathan Bender 50.00
254 Richard Hamilton 25.00
255 Andre Miller 30.00
256 Corey Maggette 50.00
257 William Avery 15.00
258 Ron Artest 30.00
259 James Posey 20.00
260 Quincy Lewis 12.00
261 Tim James 12.00
262 Vonteego Cummings 20.00
263 Anthony Carter 15.00
264 Mirsad Turkcan 5.00
265 Adrian Griffin 15.00
266 Ryan Robertson 5.00

1999-00 Finest Gold Refractors

This 266-card parallel set reprinted each card in Finest Series I and II, but added a gold Refractor finish to the front along with postage stamp-like die-cutting around the edges. Gold Refractors were inserted in Series I at a rate of 1:62 (1:28 HTA) packs, and in Series II packs at a rate of 1:31 (1:14 HTA) packs. All Gold Refractors were sequentially numbered to 100 sets.

MT
Refractor Cards: 15x-30x
Refractor Gems/Sensations: 10x-20x
Series I Rookies: 5x-10x
Inserted 1:62
Series II Rookies: 2x
Inserted 1:31
Production 100 Sets

1 Shareef Abdur-Rahim 1.50
2 Kevin Willis .25
3 Sean Elliott .25
4 Vlade Divac .25
5 Tom Gugliotta .50
6 Matt Harpring .50
7 Kerry Kittles .25
8 Joe Smith .50
9 Jamal Mashburn .50
10 Tyrone Nesby .50
11 Alan Henderson .25
12 Vitaly Potapenko .25
13 Dickey Simpkins .25
14 Michael Finley .50
15 Lindsey Hunter .25
16 Antawn Jamison 1.50
17 Reggie Miller .50
18 Maurice Taylor .60
19 Clarence Weatherspoon .25
20 Sam Mitchell .25
21 Latrell Sprewell .50
22 Michael Doleac .50
23 Rex Chapman .25
24 Predrag Stojakovic .50
25 Vladimir Stepania .25
26 Tracy McGrady 1.25
27 Cherokee Parks .25
28 LaPhonso Ellis .25
29 Hakeem Olajuwon .75
30 Adonal Foyle .25
31 Bryant Stith .25
32 Andrew DeClercq .25
33 Toni Kukoc .60
34 Kenny Anderson .50
35 Mike Bibby 1.00
36 Glen Rice .50
37 Avery Johnson .25
38 Arvydas Sabonis .25
39 Kornel David .25
40 Hubert Davis .25
41 Grant Hill 3.00
42 Donyell Marshall .25
43 Jalen Rose .50
44 Derrick Coleman .50
45 P.J. Brown .25
46 Vin Baker .50
47 Clifford Robinson .25
48 Allan Houston .50
49 Kendall Gill .25
50 Matt Geiger .25
51 Larry Hughes 1.00
52 Corliss Williamson .25
53 Darrell Armstrong .50
54 Bobby Jackson .25
55 Bryon Russell .25
56 Juwan Howard .50
57 Dikembe Mutombo .50
58 Eddie Jones .75
59 Randy Brown .25
60 Dirk Nowitzki .50
61 Jerome Williams .25
62 Scottie Pippen 1.50
63 Dale Davis .25
64 Kobe Bryant 4.00
65 Robert Traylor .75
66 Tim Hardaway .60
67 Michael Olowokandi .75
68 Walter McCarty .25
69 Damon Stoudamire .60
70 Othella Harrington .25
71 Chauncey Billups .25
72 John Starks .25
73 Ricky Davis .50
74 Glenn Robinson .50
75 Dean Garrett .25
76 Chris Childs .25
77 Shawn Kemp .75
78 Allen Iverson 2.00
79 Brian Grant .25
80 David Robinson .75
81 Tracy Murray .25
82 Howard Eisley .25
83 Doug Christie .25
84 Gary Payton .75
85 John Stockton .50
86 Rod Strickland .50
87 Tyrone Corbin .25
88 Antonio Daniels .25
89 Dee Brown .25
90 Antoine Walker 1.00
91 Theo Ratliff .25
92 Larry Johnson .25
93 Stephon Marbury 1.50
94 Brevin Knight .25
95 Antonio McDyess .60
96 Bison Dele .25
97 Cuttino Mobley .50
98 Haywood Workman .25
99 J.R. Reid .25
100 Travis Best .25
101 Chris Webber 2.00
102 Grant Hill 4.00
103 Kevin Garnett 4.00
104 Jason Kidd 2.00
105 Gary Payton 1.50
106 Shaquille O'Neal 3.00
107 Alonzo Mourning 1.00
108 Karl Malone 1.50
109 John Stockton 1.00
110 *Elton Brand* 12.00
111 *Baron Davis* 10.00
112 *Aleksandar Radojevic* 2.00
113 *Cal Bowdler* 2.00
114 *Jumanie Jones* 3.00
115 *Jason Terry* 5.00
116 *Trajan Langdon* 6.00
117 *Dion Glover* 2.00
118 *Jeff Foster* 2.00
119 *Lamar Odom* 20.00
120 *Wally Szczerbiak* 15.00
121 *Shawn Marion* 8.00
122 *Kenny Thomas* 2.00
123 *Devean George* 3.00
124 *Scott Padgett* 3.00
125 Tim Duncan 4.00
126 Jason Williams 3.00
127 Paul Pierce 3.00
128 Kobe Bryant 5.00
129 Keith Van Horn 1.50
130 Vince Carter 4.00
131 Matt Harpring 1.00
132 Antawn Jamison 2.00
133 Tracy McGrady 2.00
134 Tim Duncan 3.00
135 Tariq Abdul-Wahad .25
136 Luc Longley .25
137 Steve Smith .40
138 Alonzo Mourning .50
139 Kevin Garnett 3.00
140 Christian Laettner .25
141 Rik Smits .25
142 Cedric Henderson .25
143 Jim Jackson .25
144 Dan Majerle .25
145 Bryant Reeves .25
146 Antonio Davis .25
147 Michael Smith .25
148 Charlie Ward .25
149 Chris Mullin .25
150 Danny Manning .25
151 Eric Williams .25
152 Hersey Hawkins .25
153 Isaiah Rider .25
154 Shandon Anderson .25
155 Jason Kidd 1.50
156 Chris Whitney .25
157 Brent Barry .25
158 Patrick Ewing .40
159 George Lynch .25
160 Dickey Simpkins .25
161 Derek Anderson .40
162 Ron Mercer .75
163 David Wesley .25
164 Mookie Blaylock .25
165 Terrell Brandon .40
166 Detlef Schrempf .25
167 Olden Polynice .25
168 Jayson Williams .25
169 Eric Piatkowski .25
170 A.C. Green .25
171 Chris Mills .25
172 Chris Webber 1.50
173 Jeff Hornacek .25
174 Calbert Cheaney .25
175 Wesley Person .25
176 Corey Benjamin .40
177 Loy Vaught .25
178 Keith Closs .25
179 Charles Outlaw .25
180 Mitch Richmond .40
181 Charles Oakley .25
182 Felipe Lopez .40
183 Eric Snow .25
184 Paul Pierce 1.25
185 Elden Campbell .25
186 Shaquille O'Neal 2.00
187 Charles Barkley .75
188 Mark Jackson .25
189 Scott Burrell .25
190 Anfernee Hardaway 2.00
191 Samaki Walker .25
192 Karl Malone .75
193 Jermaine O'Neal .25
194 Mario Elie .25
195 Malik Sealy .25
196 Voshon Lenard .25
197 Chris Gatling .25
198 Walt Williams .25
199 Nick Van Exel .40
200 Bimbo Coles .25
201 John Wallace .25
202 Anthony Mason .25
203 Steve Nash .25
204 Erick Dampier .25
205 Cedric Ceballos .25
206 Derek Fisher .25
207 Marcus Camby .50
208 Tyrone Hill .25
209 Nick Anderson .25
210 Sam Cassell .40
211 Raef LaFrentz .60
212 Ruben Patterson .40
213 Rick Fox .25
214 Jason Williams 1.50
215 Vince Carter 5.00
216 Michael Dickerson .40
217 Steve Kerr .25
218 Rasheed Wallace .40
219 Keith Van Horn .75
220 Bob Sura .25
221 Ray Allen .50
222 Jerry Stackhouse .50
223 Shawn Bradley .25
224 Horace Grant .25
225 Tim Duncan 5.00
226 Kevin Garnett 5.00
227 Jason Kidd 3.00
228 Steve Smith .40
229 Allan Houston .40
230 Tom Gugliotta .40
231 Gary Payton 1.50
232 Tim Hardaway .75
233 Vin Baker .40
234 Karl Malone 1.50
235 Vince Carter 8.00
236 Jason Williams 3.00
237 Alonzo Mourning .75
238 Anfernee Hardaway 4.00
239 Mitch Richmond .40
240 Steve Smith .40
241 Charles Barkley 1.50
242 Ron Mercer 1.50
243 Shaquille O'Neal 4.00
244 Jason Kidd 3.00
245 Kevin Garnett 5.00
246 Tim Duncan 5.00
247 Ray Allen .75
248 Chris Webber 3.00
249 Jerry Stackhouse 1.00
250 Keith Van Horn 1.00
251 Patrick Ewing .40
252 Steve Francis 200.00
253 Jonathan Bender 50.00
254 Richard Hamilton 25.00
255 Andre Miller 30.00
256 Corey Maggette 50.00
257 William Avery 15.00
258 Ron Artest 30.00
259 James Posey 20.00
260 Quincy Lewis 12.00
261 Tim James 12.00
262 Vonteego Cummings 20.00

263	Anthony Carter	15.00
264	Mirsad Turkcan	5.00
265	Adrian Griffin	15.00
266	Ryan Robertson	5.00

1999-00 Finest 24 Karat Touch

This 10-card Series II insert set featured some of the game's top sharpshooters on a golden patterned background. 24-Karat Touch cards were numbered with a "KT" prefix and inserted 1:30 (1:15 HTA) packs. Refractor versions of each card also existed and were seeded 1:300 (1:150 HTA) packs.

		MT
Complete Set (10):		10.00
Common Player:		.50
Inserted 1:30 Series II		
Refractors:		2x-4x
Inserted 1:300		
KT1	Reggie Miller	.75
KT2	Keith Van Horn	2.00
KT3	Allan Houston	.50
KT4	Patrick Ewing	.75
KT5	Anfernee Hardaway	5.00
KT6	Steve Smith	.50
KT7	Glen Rice	.50
KT8	Ray Allen	1.00
KT9	Charles Barkley	2.00
KT10	Mitch Richmond	.50

1999-00 Finest 24 Karat Touch Refractor

This 10-card parallel set reprinted every 24-Karat Touch insert with a Refractor finish. Refractors were seeded 1:300 (1:150 HTA) packs.

		MT
Complete Set (10):		10.00
Common Player:		.50
Inserted 1:30 Series II		
Refractors:		2x-4x
Inserted 1:300		
1	Reggie Miller	.75
2	Keith Van Horn	2.00
3	Allan Houston	.50
4	Patrick Ewing	.75
5	Anfernee Hardaway	5.00
6	Steve Smith	.50
7	Glen Rice	.50
8	Ray Allen	1.00
9	Charles Barkley	2.00
10	Mitch Richmond	.50

1999-00 Finest Box Office Draws

This 10-card insert Series II set pictures top players over a movie theater-like background. Box Office Draws inserts were numbered with a "BOD" prefix and inserted 1:30 (1:15 HTA) packs. Refractor versions also existed and were seeded 1:300 (1:150 HTA) packs.

		MT
Complete Set (10):		30.00
Common Player:		1.00
Inserted 1:30 Series II		
Refractors:		2x-4x
Inserted 1:300		
BOD1	Shaquille O'Neal	6.00
BOD2	Patrick Ewing	1.00
BOD3	Karl Malone	2.00
BOD4	Jason Williams	5.00
BOD5	Charles Barkley	2.00
BOD6	Tim Duncan	10.00
BOD7	Kevin Garnett	10.00
BOD8	Alonzo Mourning	1.50
BOD9	Mitch Richmond	1.00
BOD10	Elton Brand	6.00

1999-00 Finest Box Office Draws Refractors

This 10-card parallel set was inserted 1:300 (1:150 HTA) packs and were marked "Refractor" on the back by the card number.

		MT
Complete Set (10):		30.00
Common Player:		1.00
Inserted 1:30 Series II		
Refractors:		2x-4x
Inserted 1:300		
1	Shaquille O'Neal	6.00
2	Patrick Ewing	1.00
3	Karl Malone	2.00
4	Jason Williams	5.00
5	Charles Barkley	2.00
6	Tim Duncan	10.00
7	Kevin Garnett	10.00
8	Alonzo Mourning	1.50
9	Mitch Richmond	1.00
10	Elton Brand	6.00

1999-00 Finest Double Double

This 15-card Series II insert showcased top double-double statistical performers and was split from top to bottom with two different photos. Double Double cards were numbered with a "D" prefix and seeded 1:20 (1:15 HTA) packs. Refractor versions also existed and were seeded 1:200 (1:150 HTA) packs.

		MT
Complete Set (15):		50.00
Common Player:		1.00
Inserted 1:20 Series II		
Refractors:		2x-4x
Inserted 1:200		
D1	Jason Kidd	5.00
D2	Kobe Bryant	12.00
D3	Antoine Walker	1.50
D4	Chris Webber	5.00
D5	Anfernee Hardaway	6.00
D6	Shawn Kemp	2.00
D7	Tim Duncan	10.00
D8	Antonio McDyess	1.50
D9	Grant Hill	10.00
D10	Karl Malone	2.50
D11	Shaquille O'Neal	6.00
D12	Allen Iverson	6.00
D13	Jayson Williams	1.00
D14	Keith Van Horn	2.00
D15	Gary Payton	2.50

1999-00 Finest Double Double Refractors

This 15-card parallel set reprinted each Double Double card with a Refractor finish. Refractor versions were seeded 1:200 (1:150 HTA) packs and marked on the back by the card number.

		MT
Complete Set (15):		50.00
Common Player:		1.00
Inserted 1:20 Series II		
Refractors:		2x-4x
Inserted 1:200		
1	Jason Kidd	5.00
2	Kobe Bryant	10.00
3	Antoine Walker	1.50
4	Chris Webber	5.00
5	Anfernee Hardaway	6.00
6	Shawn Kemp	1.50
7	Tim Duncan	10.00
8	Antonio McDyess	1.50
9	Grant Hill	10.00
10	Karl Malone	2.50
11	Shaquille O'Neal	6.00
12	Allen Iverson	6.00
13	Jayson Williams	1.00
14	Keith Van Horn	2.00
15	Gary Payton	2.50

1999-00 Finest Double Feature

This 14-card insert featured two teammates on a split, horizontal card, with the insert name running up the middle. Double Feature cards were numbered with a "DF" prefix and seeded 1:26 (1:12 HTA) packs of Series I. Base versions featured a Refractor finish on either the right or left side, with either side variations carrying the same value. Cards with both sides of the front in Refractor finish also existed and were inserted 1:78 (1:36 HTA) packs.

		MT
Complete Set (14):		75.00
Common Player:		3.00
Inserted 1:26 Series 1		
Dual Refractors:		2x
Inserted 1:78 Series 1		
DF1	Hakeem Olajuwon, Scottie Pippen	5.00
DF2	Paul Pierce, Antoine Walker	6.00
DF3	Shareef Abdur-Rahim, Mike Bibby	6.00
DF4	Alonzo Mourning, Tim Hardaway	3.00
DF5	Glenn Robinson, Ray Allen	3.00
DF6	Kevin Garnett, Joe Smith	12.00
DF7	Keith Van Horn, Stephon Marbury	4.00
DF8	Chris Webber, Jason Williams	10.00
DF9	Tim Duncan, David Robinson	12.00
DF10	Gary Payton, Vin Baker	3.00
DF11	Karl Malone, John Stockton	4.00
DF12	Jason Kidd, Tom Gugliotta	5.00
DF13	Mitch Richmond, Juwan Howard	3.00
DF14	Kobe Bryant, Shaquille O'Neal	15.00

1999-00 Finest Double Feature Dual Refractors

This 14-card parallel set reprinted the Double Feature insert set, but featured a Refractor finish on both sides vs. either the left or right side of base versions.

		MT
Dual Refractors:		
Inserted 1:78 Series 1		
1	Hakeem Olajuwon, Scottie Pippen	5.00
2	Paul Pierce, Antoine Walker	5.00
3	Shareef Abdur-Rahim, Mike Bibby	6.00
4	Alonzo Mourning, Tim Hardaway	3.00
5	Glenn Robinson, Ray Allen	3.00
6	Kevin Garnett, Joe Smith	12.00
7	Keith Van Horn, Stephon Marbury	4.00
8	Chris Webber, Jason Williams	10.00
9	Tim Duncan, David Robinson	12.00
10	Gary Payton, Vin Baker	3.00
11	Karl Malone, John Stockton	4.00
12	Jason Kidd, Tom Gugliotta	5.00
13	Mitch Richmond, Juwan Howard	3.00
14	Kobe Bryant, Shaquille O'Neal	15.00

1999-00 Finest Dunk Masters

This 15-card Series I insert set featured top dunkers with a color action shot in the foreground and a black-and-white closeup shot in the background. Dunk Masters were numbered with a "DM" prefix, seeded 1:73 (1:34 HTA) packs and sequentially numbered to 750 sets. Refractor versions were seeded 1:364 (1:168 HTA) packs and sequentially numbered to 150 sets.

		MT
Complete Set (15):		200.00
Common Player:		5.00
Inserted 1:73 Series 1		
Production 750 Sets		
Refractors:		2x
Inserted 1:364 Series 1		
Production 150 Sets		
DM1	Kobe Bryant	35.00
DM2	Shaquille O'Neal	20.00
DM3	Chris Webber	12.00
DM4	Antonio McDyess	8.00
DM5	Michael Finley	5.00
DM6	Shawn Kemp	6.00
DM7	Tracy McGrady	12.00
DM8	Antoine Walker	8.00
DM9	Alonzo Mourning	5.00
DM10	Ray Allen	5.00
DM11	Kevin Garnett	30.00
DM12	Allen Iverson	20.00
DM13	Vince Carter	30.00
DM14	Tim Duncan	30.00
DM15	Scottie Pippen	12.00

1999-00 Finest Dunk Masters Refractors

This 15-card parallel set reprinted each Dunk Masters card with a Refractor finish. Cards were 1:364 (1:168 HTA) packs and sequentially numbered to 150 sets.

		MT
Refractors:		2x
Inserted 1:364 Series 1		
Production 150 Sets		
1	Kobe Bryant	35.00
2	Shaquille O'Neal	20.00
3	Chris Webber	12.00
4	Antonio McDyess	8.00
5	Michael Finley	5.00
6	Shawn Kemp	6.00
7	Tracy McGrady	12.00
8	Antoine Walker	8.00
9	Alonzo Mourning	5.00
10	Ray Allen	5.00
11	Kevin Garnett	30.00
12	Allen Iverson	20.00
13	Vince Carter	30.00
14	Tim Duncan	30.00
15	Scottie Pippen	12.00

1999-00 Finest Future's Finest

This 15-card Series I insert set featured rookies from the class of 1999-00. Future's Finest cards were numbered with an "FF" prefix, seeded 1:73 (1:34 HTA) packs and sequentially numbered to 750 sets. Refractor versions for each card also existed, and were seeded 1:364 (1:168 HTA) packs and sequentially numbered to 150 sets.

		MT
Complete Set (15):		100.00
Common Player:		1.50
Inserted 1:73 Series 1		
Production 750 Sets		
Refractors:		2x
Inserted 1:364 Series 1		
Production 150 Sets		
FF1	Elton Brand	20.00
FF2	Steve Francis	25.00
FF3	Baron Davis	6.00
FF4	Lamar Odom	20.00
FF5	Jonathan Bender	10.00
FF6	Wally Szczerbiak	10.00
FF7	Richard Hamilton	5.00
FF8	Andre Miller	6.00
FF9	Shawn Marion	6.00
FF10	Jason Terry	3.00
FF11	Trajan Langdon	2.00
FF12	Aleksandar Radojevic	1.50
FF13	Corey Maggette	10.00
FF14	William Avery	2.00
FF15	Ron Artest	6.00

1999-00 Finest Future's Finest Refractors

This 15-card parallel insert set reprinted each Future's Finest insert with a Refractor finish. Refractor versions were seeded 1:364 (1:168 HTA) packs and sequentially numbered to 150.

		MT
Refractors:		2x
Inserted 1:364 Series 1		
Production 150 Sets		
1	Elton Brand	20.00
2	Steve Francis	25.00
3	Baron Davis	18.00
4	Lamar Odom	30.00
5	Jonathan Bender	15.00
6	Wally Szczerbiak	25.00
7	Richard Hamilton	12.00
8	Andre Miller	10.00
9	Shawn Marion	12.00
10	Jason Terry	8.00
11	Trajan Langdon	10.00
12	Aleksandar Radojevic	5.00
13	Corey Maggette	15.00
14	William Avery	6.00
15	Ron Artest	6.00

1999-00 Finest Heirs to Air

This 10-card Series II insert set features the game's top leapers on clear plastic. Heirs to Air cards were numbered with an "HA" prefix and seeded 1:36 (1:16 HLA) packs.

		MT
Complete Set (10):		50.00
Common Player:		1.00
Inserted 1:36 Series II		
HA1	Michael Finley	1.50
HA2	Brent Barry	1.00
HA3	Corey Maggette	5.00
HA4	Ron Mercer	3.00
HA5	Eddie Jones	3.00
HA6	Tracy McGrady	5.00
HA7	Vince Carter	20.00
HA8	Jerry Stackhouse	2.00
HA9	Ray Allen	2.00
HA10	Kobe Bryant	15.00

1999-00 Finest Leading Indicators

This 10-card Series I insert featured heat-sensitive, thermal ink technology that collectors could touch and statistics would appear. Leading Indicators were numbered with an "L" prefix and inserted 1:30 (1:14 HTA) packs.

		MT
Complete Set (10):		50.00
Common Player:		2.00
Inserted 1:30		
L1	Stephon Marbury	6.00
L2	Paul Pierce	8.00
L3	Jason Kidd	5.00
L4	Gary Payton	3.00
L5	Keith Van Horn	3.00
L6	Reggie Miller	2.00
L7	Jason Williams	8.00
L8	Vince Carter	12.00
L9	Ray Allen	2.00
L10	Kobe Bryant	15.00

1999-00 Finest New Millennium

This 10-card Series I insert set featured six rookies and four veterans who will carry the game into the next century. New Millennium inserts were numbered with a "NM" prefix, sequentially numbered to 1,500 sets and seeded 1:55 (1:25 HTA) packs. Refractor versions of each card also existed and were seeded 1:273 (1:126 HTA) packs and sequentially numbered to 300 sets.

		MT
Complete Set (10):		75.00
Common Player:		3.00
Inserted 1:55 Series 1		
Production 1,500 Sets		
Refractors:		2x
Inserted 1:273 Series 1		
Production 300 Sets		
NM1	Jason Williams	10.00
NM2	Vince Carter	15.00
NM3	Paul Pierce	10.00
NM4	Mike Bibby	3.00
NM5	Elton Brand	10.00
NM6	Steve Francis	12.00
NM7	Baron Davis	8.00
NM8	Lamar Odom	15.00
NM9	Jonathan Bender	5.00
NM10	Wally Szczerbiak	12.00

1999-00 Finest New Millennium Refractors

This 10-card parallel set reprinted each card in the New Millennium insert set with a Refractor finish. Refractors were seeded 1:273 (1:126 HTA) packs and sequentially numbered to 300 sets.

		MT
Refractors:		2x
Inserted 1:273 Series 1		
Production 300 Sets		
1	Jason Williams	10.00
2	Vince Carter	15.00
3	Paul Pierce	10.00
4	Mike Bibby	3.00
5	Elton Brand	10.00
6	Steve Francis	12.00
7	Baron Davis	8.00
8	Lamar Odom	15.00
9	Jonathan Bender	5.00
10	Wally Szczerbiak	12.00

1999-00 Finest Next Generation

This 15-card Series II insert set featured top rookies from the 1999 NBA Draft. Next Generation cards were numbered with an "NG" prefix and inserted 1:20 (1:10 HTA) packs. Refractor versions of each card were also existed and were seeded 1:200 (1:100 HTA) packs.

		MT
Complete Set (15):		35.00
Common Player:		
Inserted 1:20 Series II		
Refractors:		2x-4x
Inserted 1:200		
NG1	Steve Francis	10.00
NG2	Jonathan Bender	5.00
NG3	Richard Hamilton	3.00
NG4	Andre Miller	3.00
NG5	Corey Maggette	5.00
NG6	William Avery	1.50
NG7	Ron Artest	3.00
NG8	Wally Szczerbiak	5.00
NG9	Quincy Lewis	1.00
NG10	Devean George	1.00
NG11	Vonteego Cummings	2.00
NG12	Lamar Odom	8.00
NG13	Shawn Marion	3.00
NG14	Elton Brand	8.00
NG15	Baron Davis	3.00

1999-00 Finest Next Generation Refractors

This 15-card parallel set reprinted each card in the Next Generation insert set with a Refractor finish. Refractors were inserted 1:200 (1:100 HTA) packs.

		MT
Complete Set (15):		35.00
Common Player:		
Inserted 1:20 Series II		
Refractors:		2x-4x
Inserted 1:200		
1	Steve Francis	10.00
2	Jonathan Bender	5.00
3	Richard Hamilton	3.00
4	Andre Miller	3.00
5	Corey Maggette	5.00
6	William Avery	1.50
7	Ron Artest	3.00
8	Wally Szczerbiak	5.00
9	Quincy Lewis	1.00
10	Devean George	1.00
11	Vonteego Cummings	2.00
12	Lamar Odom	8.00
13	Shawn Marion	3.00
14	Elton Brand	8.00
15	Baron Davis	3.00

1999-00 Finest Producers

This 10-card Series I insert set featured top statistical performers. Producers were numbered with an "FP" prefix and seeded 1:22 (1:10 HTA) packs. Refractor versions also existed and were seeded 1:109 (1:50 HTA) packs.

		MT
Complete Set (10):		35.00
Common Player:		2.00
Inserted 1:22 Series 1		
Refractors:		2x
Inserted 1:109 Series 1		
FP1	Shaquille O'Neal	6.00
FP2	Chris Webber	4.00
FP3	Karl Malone	2.00
FP4	Allen Iverson	6.00
FP5	Kevin Garnett	10.00
FP6	Jason Kidd	4.00
FP7	Grant Hill	10.00
FP8	Shareef Abdur-Rahim	4.00
FP9	Gary Payton	2.00
FP10	Charles Barkley	2.00

1999-00 Finest Producers Refractors

This 10-card parallel set reprinted the entire Producers insert set with a Refractor finish. Refractor versions were seeded 1:109 (1:50 HTA) packs.

		MT
Refractors:		2x
Inserted 1:109 Series 1		
1	Shaquille O'Neal	6.00
2	Chris Webber	4.00
3	Karl Malone	2.00
4	Allen Iverson	6.00
5	Kevin Garnett	10.00
6	Jason Kidd	4.00
7	Grant Hill	10.00
8	Shareef Abdur-Rahim	4.00
9	Gary Payton	2.00
10	Charles Barkley	2.00

1999-00 Finest Finest Salute

This two-card insert set was distributed with one card in Series I featuring Tim Duncan, Vince Carter and Allen Iverson, and one card in Series II featuring the top six picks in the 1999 NBA Draft. The Series I card was seeded 1:108 (1:50 HTA) packs, while the Series II card was seeded 1:100 (1:50 HTA) packs. Refractor and Gold Refractor versions were also available for each with the following odds: Series I Refractor 1:5,305 (1:2,333 HTA), Series I Gold Refractor 1:16,992 (1:7,423 HTA), Series II Refractor 1:4,616 (1:2,194 HTA) and Gold Refractor 1:8,539 (1:3,790 HTA) packs.

		MT
Complete Set (2):		20.00
Inserted 1:108 Series I		
Inserted 1:100 Series II		
Refractors:		5x
Inserted 1:5,054 Series I		
Inserted 1:4,616 Series II		
Gold Refractors:		15x
Inserted 1:16,992 Series I		
Inserted 1:8,539 Series II		
Production 100 Sets		
FS1	Tim Duncan, Allen Iverson, Vince Carter	15.00
FS2	Elton Brand, Steve Francis, Baron Davis, Lamar Odom, Jonathan Bender, Wally Szczerbiak	10.00

1999-00 Finest Team Finest Blue

This 20-card insert set had 10 cards in Series I and 10 in Series II and arrived in six different versions. Base versions were Blue and numbered to 1,500 (1:55/1:25 HTA Series I; 1:28/1:13 HTA Series II) and Blue Refractors were numbered to 150 (1:546/1:252 HTA Series I; 1:276/1:127 HTA Series II). Red and Gold versions were exclusive to HTA packs at the following odds: Red cards were numbered to 500 (1:18 Series I, 1:9 Series II), Red Refractors were numbered to 50 (1:175 Series I, 1:89 Series II), Gold cards were numbered to 250 (1:35 Series I, 1:18 Series II) and Gold Refractors were numbered to 25 (1:352 Series I, 1:180 Series II). All Team Finest inserts were numbered with a "TF" prefix.

		MT
Complete Set (20):		140.00
Complete Series I (10):		60.00
Complete Series II (10):		80.00
Common Player:		3.00
Production 1,500 Sets		
Blue Refractors:		4x
Production 150 Sets		
Gold Cards:		2x
Production 500 Sets		
Gold Refractors:		4x-8x
Production 50 Sets		
Gold Cards:		3x
Inserted: 1:35 Series 1 HTA		
Production 250 Sets		
Gold Refractors:		8x-16x
Inserted 1:352 Series 1 HTA		
Production 25 Sets		
TF1	Shareef Abdur-Rahim	6.00
TF2	Stephon Marbury	8.00
TF3	Shawn Kemp	2.50
TF4	Allen Iverson	10.00
TF5	Antoine Walker	5.00
TF6	Hakeem Olajuwon	3.00
TF7	Tim Duncan	15.00
TF8	Karl Malone	3.00
TF9	Grant Hill	15.00
TF10	Keith Van Horn	4.00
TF11	Alonzo Mourning	3.00
TF12	Jason Kidd	8.00
TF13	Chris Webber	8.00
TF14	Shaquille O'Neal	10.00
TF15	Gary Payton	4.00
TF16	Kevin Garnett	15.00
TF17	Antonio McDyess	3.00
TF18	Kobe Bryant	20.00
TF19	Scottie Pippen	8.00
TF20	Vince Carter	25.00

1999-00 Finest Team Finest Blue Refractors

This 20-card parallel set was issued with 10 cards in Series I and 10 in Series II, with each featuring a Refractor finish. Blue Refractors were seeded 1:546 (1:252 HTA) packs of Series I and 1:276 (1:127 HTA) packs of Series II. They were also sequentially numbered to 150 sets on the back.

		MT
Complete Set (20):		140.00
Complete Series I (10):		60.00
Complete Series II (10):		80.00
Common Player:		3.00
Production 1,500 Sets		
Blue Refractors:		4x
Production 150 Sets		
Gold Cards:		2x
Production 500 Sets		
Gold Refractors:		4x-8x
Production 50 Sets		
Gold Cards:		3x
Inserted: 1:35 Series 1 HTA		
Production 250 Sets		
Gold Refractors:		8x-16x
Inserted 1:352 Series 1 HTA		
Production 25 Sets		
1	Shareef Abdur-Rahim	6.00
2	Stephon Marbury	8.00
3	Shawn Kemp	3.00
4	Allen Iverson	10.00
5	Antoine Walker	4.00
6	Hakeem Olajuwon	3.00
7	Tim Duncan	15.00
8	Karl Malone	3.00
9	Grant Hill	15.00
10	Keith Van Horn	4.00
11	Alonzo Mourning	3.00
12	Jason Kidd	8.00
13	Chris Webber	8.00
14	Shaquille O'Neal	10.00
15	Gary Payton	4.00
16	Kevin Garnett	15.00
17	Antonio McDyess	3.00
18	Kobe Bryant	20.00
19	Scottie Pippen	8.00
20	Vince Carter	25.00

1999-00 Finest Team Finest Gold

This 20-card parallel set was issued with 10 cards in Series I and 10 cards in Series II, and featured a gold background on both the front and back. Gold Team Finest cards were exclusive to HTA packs and inserted 1:35 Series I and 1:18 Series II. Gold Team Finest cards were also sequentially numbered to 250 sets.

		MT
Complete Set (20):		140.00
Complete Series I (10):		60.00
Complete Series II (10):		80.00
Common Player:		3.00
Production 1,500 Sets		
Blue Refractors:		4x
Production 150 Sets		
Gold Cards:		2x
Production 500 Sets		
Gold Refractors:		4x-8x
Production 50 Sets		
Gold Cards:		3x
Inserted: 1:35 Series 1 HTA		
Production 250 Sets		
Gold Refractors:		8x-16x
Inserted 1:352 Series 1 HTA		
Production 25 Sets		
1	Shareef Abdur-Rahim	6.00
2	Stephon Marbury	8.00
3	Shawn Kemp	3.00
4	Allen Iverson	10.00
5	Antoine Walker	4.00
6	Hakeem Olajuwon	3.00
7	Tim Duncan	15.00
8	Karl Malone	3.00
9	Grant Hill	15.00
10	Keith Van Horn	4.00
11	Alonzo Mourning	3.00
12	Jason Kidd	8.00
13	Chris Webber	8.00
14	Shaquille O'Neal	10.00
15	Gary Payton	4.00
16	Kevin Garnett	15.00
17	Antonio McDyess	3.00
18	Kobe Bryant	20.00
19	Scottie Pippen	8.00
20	Vince Carter	25.00

1999-00 Finest Team Finest Gold Refractors

This 20-card parallel set was issued with 10 cards in Series I and 10 in Series II and featured a Refractor finish. Gold Team Finest Refractors were exclusive to HTA packs and inserted 1:35 Series I and 1:18 Series II. Gold Team Finest Refractors were also sequentially numbered to 25 sets.

		MT
Complete Set (20):		140.00
Complete Series I (10):		60.00
Complete Series II (10):		80.00
Common Player:		3.00
Production 1,500 Sets		
Blue Refractors:		4x
Production 150 Sets		
Gold Cards:		2x
Production 500 Sets		
Gold Refractors:		4x-8x
Production 50 Sets		
Gold Cards:		3x
Inserted: 1:35 Series 1 HTA		
Production 250 Sets		
Gold Refractors:		8x-16x
Inserted 1:352 Series 1 HTA		
Production 25 Sets		
1	Shareef Abdur-Rahim	6.00
2	Stephon Marbury	8.00
3	Shawn Kemp	3.00
4	Allen Iverson	10.00
5	Antoine Walker	4.00
6	Hakeem Olajuwon	3.00
7	Tim Duncan	15.00
8	Karl Malone	3.00
9	Grant Hill	15.00
10	Keith Van Horn	4.00
11	Alonzo Mourning	3.00
12	Jason Kidd	8.00
13	Chris Webber	8.00
14	Shaquille O'Neal	10.00
15	Gary Payton	4.00
16	Kevin Garnett	15.00
17	Antonio McDyess	3.00
18	Kobe Bryant	20.00
19	Scottie Pippen	8.00
20	Vince Carter	25.00

1999-00 Finest Team Finest Red

This 20-card parallel set was issued with 10 cards in Series I and 10 in Series II and featured a red background on both the front and back. Red Team Finest cards were exclusive to HTA packs and were inserted 1:18 Series I and 1:9 Series II packs. Red Team Finest cards were also sequentially numbered to 500 sets.

		MT
Complete Set (20):		140.00
Complete Series I (10):		60.00
Complete Series II (10):		80.00
Common Player:		3.00
Production 1,500 Sets		
Blue Refractors:		4x
Production 150 Sets		
Red Cards:		2x
Production 500 Sets		
Red Refractors:		4x-8x
Production 50 Sets		
Gold Cards:		3x
Inserted: 1:35 Series 1 HTA		
Production 250 Sets		
Gold Refractors:		8x-16x
Inserted 1:352 Series 1 HTA		
Production 25 Sets		
1	Shareef Abdur-Rahim	6.00
2	Stephon Marbury	8.00
3	Shawn Kemp	3.00
4	Allen Iverson	10.00
5	Antoine Walker	4.00
6	Hakeem Olajuwon	3.00
7	Tim Duncan	15.00
8	Karl Malone	3.00
9	Grant Hill	15.00
10	Keith Van Horn	4.00
11	Alonzo Mourning	3.00
12	Jason Kidd	8.00
13	Chris Webber	8.00
14	Shaquille O'Neal	10.00
15	Gary Payton	4.00
16	Kevin Garnett	15.00
17	Antonio McDyess	3.00
18	Kobe Bryant	20.00
19	Scottie Pippen	8.00
20	Vince Carter	25.00

1999-00 Finest Team Finest Red Refractor

This 20-card parallel set was issued with 10 cards in Series I and 10 in Series II and featured the red background and a Refractor finish. Red Refractors were exclusive to HTA packs and inserted 1:175 Series I packs and 1:89 Series II. They were also sequentially numbered to 50 sets.

		MT
Complete Set (20):		140.00
Complete Series I (10):		60.00
Complete Series II (10):		80.00
Common Player:		3.00
Production 1,500 Sets		
Blue Refractors:		4x
Production 150 Sets		
Gold Cards:		2x
Production 500 Sets		
Gold Refractors:		4x-8x
Production 50 Sets		
Gold Cards:		3x
Inserted: 1:35 Series 1 HTA		
Production 250 Sets		
Gold Refractors:		8x-16x
Inserted 1:352 Series 1 HTA		
Production 25 Sets		
1	Shareef Abdur-Rahim	6.00
2	Stephon Marbury	8.00
3	Shawn Kemp	3.00
4	Allen Iverson	10.00
5	Antoine Walker	4.00
6	Hakeem Olajuwon	3.00
7	Tim Duncan	15.00
8	Karl Malone	3.00
9	Grant Hill	15.00
10	Keith Van Horn	4.00
11	Alonzo Mourning	3.00
12	Jason Kidd	8.00
13	Chris Webber	8.00
14	Shaquille O'Neal	10.00
15	Gary Payton	4.00
16	Kevin Garnett	15.00
17	Antonio McDyess	3.00
18	Kobe Bryant	20.00
19	Scottie Pippen	8.00
20	Vince Carter	25.00

2000-01 Finest

		MT
Complete Set (173):		500.00
Common Player:		.25
Minor Stars:		.40
Common Rookies (126-150):		5.00
Production 1,599 Sets		
Common OTM (151-163):		1.00
Inserted 1:8		
Common Gems (164-173):		2.00
Inserted 1:24		
Pack (6):		5.00
Box (24):		70.00
1	Shaquille O'Neal	2.50
2	P.J. Brown	.25
3	Joe Smith	.25
4	Kendall Gill	.25
5	Corey Maggette	.75
6	Marcus Camby	.40
7	Toni Kukoc	.50
8	Kobe Bryant	4.00
9	David Robinson	.75
10	Ruben Patterson	.25
11	Allen Iverson	2.50
12	Glenn Robinson	.40
13	Anthony Carter	.40
14	Jonathan Bender	1.25
15	Vince Carter	5.00
16	Jerry Stackhouse	.40
17	Raef LaFrentz	.25
18	Dikembe Mutombo	.25
19	Baron Davis	.60
20	Kenny Anderson	.40
21	Corey Benjamin	.25
22	Andre Miller	.60
23	Cedric Ceballos	.25
24	Christian Laettner	.25
25	Shandon Anderson	.25
26	Rik Smits	.25
27	Michael Olowokandi	.25
28	Sam Cassell	.40
29	Tom Gugliotta	.40
30	Jason Williams	.75
31	Avery Johnson	.25
32	Karl Malone	.75
33	Grant Hill	2.50
34	Paul Pierce	.75
35	Antonio Davis	.25
36	Nick Anderson	.25
37	Alan Henderson	.25
38	Eddie Jones	1.00
39	Ron Artest	.50
40	Brevin Knight	.25
41	Keon Clark	.25
42	Elton Brand	1.50
43	Reggie Miller	.40
44	Steve Francis	2.50
45	Derek Anderson	.40
46	Alonzo Mourning	.50
47	Terrell Brandon	.40
48	Larry Johnson	.40
49	Keith Van Horn	.75
50	Jason Kidd	1.50
51	Scottie Pippen	1.50
52	Gary Payton	.75
53	Robert Pack	.25
54	Adrian Griffin	.25
55	Jim Jackson	.25
56	Lamond Murray	.25
57	Larry Hughes	1.00
58	Dirk Nowitzki	.75
59	Vonteego Cummings	.40
60	Jalen Rose	.40
61	Arvydas Sabonis	.25
62	Kerry Kittles	.25
63	Kevin Garnett	3.00
64	Latrell Sprewell	1.00
65	Shawn Marion	1.00
66	Darrell Armstrong	.25
67	Ron Mercer	.40
68	Damon Stoudamire	.40
69	Tracy McGrady	1.50
70	Theo Ratliff	.25
71	Lamar Odom	1.50
72	Charlie Ward	.25
73	John Amaechi	.25
74	Quincy Lewis	.40
75	Othella Harrington	.25
76	Doug Christie	.25
77	Richard Hamilton	.50
78	Donyell Marshall	.25
79	Vlade Divac	.25
80	Clifford Robinson	.25
81	Sean Elliott	.25
82	Rashard Lewis	.75
83	Wally Szczerbiak	.50
84	Dale Davis	.25
85	Kelvin Cato	.25
86	Cuttino Mobley	.25
87	Travis Best	.25
88	Robert Horry	.25
89	Maurice Taylor	.40
90	Jamal Mashburn	.40
91	Tim Thomas	.50
92	Stephon Marbury	1.25
93	Patrick Ewing	.40
94	Eric Snow	.25
95	Anfernee Hardaway	1.50
96	Steve Smith	.40
97	Chris Webber	1.50
98	Rodney Rogers	.25
99	John Stockton	.40
100	Tim Duncan	2.50
101	Ray Allen	.50
102	Glen Rice	.40
103	Bryon Russell	.25
104	Tim Hardaway	.50
105	Allan Houston	.50
106	Rasheed Wallace	.60
107	Vin Baker	.40
108	Michael Dickerson	.25
109	Juwan Howard	.40
110	Hakeem Olajuwon	.75
111	Shareef Abdur-Rahim	.75
112	Rod Strickland	.40
113	Hersey Hawkins	.25
114	Jason Terry	.40
115	Anthony Mason	.25
116	Mike Bibby	.40
117	Shawn Kemp	.30
118	Derrick Coleman	.40
119	Antoine Walker	.60
120	Antawn Jamison	.75
121	Michael Finley	.40
122	Antonio McDyess	.50
123	Nick Van Exel	.25
124	Mitch Richmond	.40
125	Lindsey Hunter	.25
126	*Kenyon Martin*	30.00
127	*Stromile Swift*	40.00
128	*Darius Miles*	100.00
129	*Marcus Fizer*	20.00
130	*Mike Miller*	40.00
131	*DerMarr Johnson*	20.00
132	*Chris Mihm*	10.00
133	*Jamal Crawford*	20.00
134	*Joel Przybilla*	8.00
135	*Keyon Dooling*	20.00
136	*Jerome Moiso*	10.00
137	*Etan Thomas*	8.00
138	*Courtney Alexander*	20.00
139	*Mateen Cleaves*	15.00
140	*Jason Collier*	5.00
141	*Desmond Mason*	25.00
142	*Quentin Richardson*	25.00
143	*Jamaal Magloire*	8.00
144	*Craig Claxton*	8.00
145	*Morris Peterson*	30.00
146	*Donnell Harvey*	8.00
147	*DeShawn Stevenson*	30.00
148	*Mamadou N'diaye*	5.00
149	*Erick Barkley*	10.00
150	*Mark Madsen*	8.00
151	Allen Iverson, Stephon Marbury	5.00
152	Vince Carter, Kobe Bryant	8.00
153	Kevin Garnett, Shareef Abdur-Rahim	4.00
154	Scottie Pippen, Tracy McGrady	3.00
155	Tim Duncan, Elton Brand	5.00
156	Steve Francis, Gary Payton	4.00
157	Karl Malone, Chris Webber	2.00
158	Alonzo Mourning, Patrick Ewing	1.00
159	Latrell Sprewell, Eddie Jones	2.00
160	Jason Kidd, John Stockton	1.50
161	Reggie Miller, Allan Houston	1.00
162	Rasheed Wallace, Antoine Walker	1.00
163	Jerry Stackhouse, Jalen Rose	1.00
164	Shaquille O'Neal	5.00
165	Kobe Bryant	8.00
166	Vince Carter	10.00
167	Kevin Garnett	6.00
168	Jason Williams	2.00
169	Tracy McGrady	3.00
170	Steve Francis	6.00
171	Tim Duncan	5.00
172	Elton Brand	3.00
173	Grant Hill	5.00

2000-01 Finest Gold Die-cut Refractors

		MT
Common Player:		5.00
Minor Stars:		8.00
Common Rookies (126-150):		10.00
Production 100 Sets		
Veterans:		10x-20x

OTM Cards:		8x-15x
Gems Cards:		4x-8x
1	Shaquille O'Neal	2.50
2	P.J. Brown	.25
3	Joe Smith	.25
4	Kendall Gill	.25
5	Corey Maggette	.75
6	Marcus Camby	.40
7	Toni Kukoc	.50
8	Kobe Bryant	4.00
9	David Robinson	.75
10	Ruben Patterson	.25
11	Allen Iverson	2.00
12	Glenn Robinson	.40
13	Anthony Carter	.40
14	Jonathan Bender	1.25
15	Vince Carter	5.00
16	Jerry Stackhouse	.40
17	Raef LaFrentz	.25
18	Dikembe Mutombo	.25
19	Baron Davis	.60
20	Kenny Anderson	.40
21	Corey Benjamin	.25
22	Andre Miller	.60
23	Cedric Ceballos	.25
24	Christian Laettner	.25
25	Shandon Anderson	.25
26	Rik Smits	.25
27	Michael Olowokandi	.25
28	Sam Cassell	.40
29	Tom Gugliotta	.40
30	Jason Williams	.75
31	Avery Johnson	.25
32	Karl Malone	.75
33	Grant Hill	2.50
34	Paul Pierce	.75
35	Antonio Davis	.25
36	Nick Anderson	.25
37	Alan Henderson	.25
38	Eddie Jones	1.00
39	Ron Artest	.50
40	Brevin Knight	.25
41	Keon Clark	.25
42	Elton Brand	1.50
43	Reggie Miller	.40
44	Steve Francis	2.50
45	Derek Anderson	.40
46	Alonzo Mourning	.50
47	Terrell Brandon	.40
48	Larry Johnson	.40
49	Keith Van Horn	.75
50	Jason Kidd	1.50
51	Scottie Pippen	1.50
52	Gary Payton	.75
53	Robert Pack	.25
54	Adrian Griffin	.25
55	Jim Jackson	.25
56	Lamond Murray	.25
57	Larry Hughes	1.00
58	Dirk Nowitzki	.50
59	Vonteego Cummings	.40
60	Jalen Rose	.40
61	Arvydas Sabonis	.25
62	Kerry Kittles	.25
63	Kevin Garnett	3.00
64	Latrell Sprewell	1.00
65	Shawn Marion	1.00
66	Darrell Armstrong	.25
67	Ron Mercer	.40
68	Damon Stoudamire	.40
69	Tracy McGrady	1.50
70	Theo Ratliff	.25
71	Lamar Odom	1.50
72	Charlie Ward	.25
73	John Amaechi	.25
74	Quincy Lewis	.40
75	Othella Harrington	.25
76	Doug Christie	.25
77	Richard Hamilton	.50
78	Donyell Marshall	.25
79	Vlade Divac	.25
80	Clifford Robinson	.25
81	Sean Elliott	.25
82	Rashard Lewis	.75
83	Wally Szczerbiak	.50
84	Dale Davis	.25
85	Kelvin Cato	.25
86	Cuttino Mobley	.25
87	Travis Best	.25
88	Robert Horry	.25
89	Maurice Taylor	.40
90	Jamal Mashburn	.40
91	Tim Thomas	.50
92	Stephon Marbury	1.25
93	Patrick Ewing	.40
94	Eric Snow	.25
95	Anfernee Hardaway	1.50
96	Steve Smith	.40
97	Chris Webber	1.50
98	Rodney Rogers	.25
99	John Stockton	.40
100	Tim Duncan	2.50
101	Ray Allen	.50
102	Glen Rice	.40
103	Bryon Russell	.25
104	Tim Hardaway	.50
105	Allan Houston	.50
106	Rasheed Wallace	.60
107	Vin Baker	.40
108	Michael Dickerson	.25
109	Juwan Howard	.40
110	Hakeem Olajuwon	.75
111	Shareef Abdur-Rahim	.75
112	Rod Strickland	.40
113	Hersey Hawkins	.25
114	Jason Terry	.40
115	Anthony Mason	.25
116	Mike Bibby	.40
117	Shawn Kemp	.30
118	Derrick Coleman	.40
119	Antoine Walker	.60
120	Antawn Jamison	.75
121	Michael Finley	.40
122	Antonio McDyess	.50
123	Nick Van Exel	.25
124	Mitch Richmond	.40
125	Lindsey Hunter	.25
126	*Kenyon Martin*	150.00
127	*Stromile Swift*	100.00
128	*Darius Miles*	300.00
129	*Marcus Fizer*	75.00
130	*Mike Miller*	75.00
131	*DerMarr Johnson*	50.00
132	*Chris Mihm*	25.00
133	*Jamal Crawford*	50.00
134	*Joel Przybilla*	20.00
135	*Keyon Dooling*	40.00
136	*Jerome Moiso*	25.00
137	*Etan Thomas*	20.00
138	*Courtney Alexander*	50.00
139	*Mateen Cleaves*	40.00
140	*Jason Collier*	10.00
141	*Desmond Mason*	50.00
142	*Quentin Richardson*	60.00
143	*Jamaal Magloire*	20.00
144	*Craig Claxton*	25.00
145	*Morris Peterson*	60.00
146	Donnell Harvey	20.00
147	*DeShawn Stevenson*	75.00
148	*Mamadou N'diaye*	10.00
149	*Erick Barkley*	30.00
150	*Mark Madsen*	15.00
151	Allen Iverson, Stephon Marbury	4.00
152	Vince Carter, Kobe Bryant	8.00
153	Kevin Garnett, Shareef Abdur-Rahim	4.00
154	Scottie Pippen, Tracy McGrady	3.00
155	Tim Duncan, Elton Brand	5.00
156	Steve Francis, Gary Payton	4.00
157	Karl Malone, Chris Webber	2.00
158	Alonzo Mourning, Patrick Ewing	1.00
159	Latrell Sprewell, Eddie Jones	2.00
160	Jason Kidd, John Stockton	1.50
161	Reggie Miller, Allan Houston	1.00
162	Rasheed Wallace, Antoine Walker	1.00
163	Jerry Stackhouse, Jalen Rose	1.00
164	Shaquille O'Neal	5.00
165	Kobe Bryant	8.00
166	Vince Carter	10.00
167	Kevin Garnett	6.00
168	Jason Williams	2.00
169	Tracy McGrady	3.00
170	Steve Francis	6.00
171	Tim Duncan	5.00
172	Elton Brand	3.00
173	Grant Hill	5.00

2000-01 Finest Finest Moments

		MT
Complete Set (20):		20.00
Common Player:		.50
Inserted 1:14		
Refractors:		2x
Inserted 1:24		
FMEB	Elton Brand	3.00
FMAC	Anthony Carter	.75
FMMC	Mateen Cleaves	2.00
FMTD	Tim Duncan	5.00
FMSE	Sean Elliott	.50
FMSF	Steve Francis	6.00
FMTH	Tim Hardaway	1.00
FMAH	Allan Houston	1.00
FMAI	Allen Iverson	5.00
FMLJ	Larry Johnson	.50
FMMJ	Magic Johnson	10.00
FMJK	Jason Kidd	3.00
FMTK	Toni Kukoc	1.25
FMKM	Karl Malone	1.50
FMTM	Tracy McGrady	3.00
FMSO	Shaquille O'Neal	5.00
FMGP	Gary Payton	1.50
FMGR	Glen Rice	.60
FMJR	Jalen Rose	1.00
FMJS	John Starks	.50

2000-01 Finest Finest Moments Refractor Autographs

		MT
Common Player:		10.00
Inserted 1:90 Hobby		
Inserted 1:41 HTA		
FMEB	Elton Brand	40.00
FMMC	Mateen Cleaves	20.00
FMTD	Tim Duncan	100.00
FMSE	Sean Elliott	10.00
FMSF	Steve Francis	75.00
FMAH	Allan Houston	20.00
FMLH	Larry Hughes	30.00
FMAI	Allen Iverson	70.00
FMLJ	Larry Johnson	15.00
FMMJ	Magic Johnson	200.00
FMEJ	Eddie Jones	30.00
FMTM	Tracy McGrady	50.00
FMSO	Shaquille O'Neal	200.00
FMGP	Gary Payton	30.00
FMGR	Glen Rice	10.00
FMMR	Mitch Richmond	10.00
FMJR	Jalen Rose	40.00
FMJS	John Starks	15.00

2000-01 Finest Finest Moments Relics

		MT
Complete Set (12):		250.00
Common Player:		20.00
Inserted 1:48		
FMR1	Vin Baker	20.00
FMR2	Antonio McDyess	30.00
FMR3	Jason Kidd	60.00
FMR4	Tim Hardaway	30.00
FMR5	Allan Houston	30.00
FMR6	Steve Smith	20.00
FMR7	Alonzo Mourning	25.00
FMR8	Gary Payton	40.00
FMR9	Ray Allen	35.00
FMR10	Shareef Abdur-Rahim	35.00
FMR11	Vince Carter/1000	60.00

2000-01 Finest Man to Man

		MT
Complete Set (10):		25.00
Common Brand:		2.50
Common Duncan:		5.00
Inserted 1:25		
1A	Tim Duncan	5.00
1B	Elton Brand	2.50
2A	Tim Duncan	5.00
2B	Elton Brand	2.50
3A	Tim Duncan	5.00
3B	Elton Brand	2.50
4A	Tim Duncan	5.00
4B	Elton Brand	2.50
5A	Tim Duncan	5.00
5B	Elton Brand	2.50

2000-01 Finest Showmen

		MT
Complete Set (10):		10.00
Common Player:		.50
Inserted 1:13		
S1	Chris Webber	2.00
S2	Elton Brand	2.00
S3	Tim Duncan	4.00
S4	Shareef Abdur-Rahim	1.00
S5	Jason Williams	1.00
S6	Grant Hill	4.00
S7	Lamar Odom	2.00
S8	Larry Hughes	1.50
S9	Michael Finley	.50
S10	Latrell Sprewell	1.50

Classic Doubles features seven pairs of NBA stars. Two figures are packaged together with a full-color collectable card for each player.

2000-01 Finest Title Quest

		MT
Complete Set (10):		40.00
Common Player:		2.00
Inserted 1:54		
APT1	Reggie Miller	2.00
APT2	Alonzo Mourning	2.00
APT3	Allen Iverson	10.00
APT4	Latrell Sprewell	4.00
APT5	Jalen Rose	2.00
APT6	Scottie Pippen	6.00
APT7	Shaquille O'Neal	12.00
APT8	Kobe Bryant	20.00
APT9	Chris Webber	6.00
APT10	Rasheed Wallace	2.00

2000-01 Finest World's Finest

		MT
Complete Set (15):		60.00
Common Player:		1.50
Inserted 1:36		
WF1	Tim Duncan	10.00
WF2	Vince Carter	20.00
WF3	Grant Hill	10.00
WF4	Kevin Garnett	12.00
WF5	Scottie Pippen	6.00
WF6	Karl Malone	3.00
WF7	Patrick Ewing	2.00
WF8	Tim Hardaway	2.00
WF9	Anfernee Hardaway	6.00
WF10	Reggie Miller	2.00
WF11	John Stockton	2.00
WF12	Ray Allen	2.00
WF13	Hakeem Olajuwon	3.00
WF14	David Robinson	3.00
WF15	Steve Smith	1.50

1994-95 Flair

Fleer printed its Flair cards on 30-point stock, with polyester laminate and gold foil stamping on both sides. The set was issued in two series; Series II features several celebrated rookies, traded veterans and free agents in their new uniforms. Inserts within the set include: Center Spotlight, Scoring Power, Hot Numbers, Wave of the Future, Playmakers and Rejectors.

		MT
Complete Set (326):		75.00
Complete Series 1 (175):		30.00
Complete Series 2 (151):		45.00
Common Player:		.20
Minor Stars:		.40
Series 1 Pack (10):		2.00
Series 1 Wax Box (24):		40.00
Series 2 Pack (10):		4.00
Series 2 Wax Box (24):		55.00
1	Stacey Augmon	.20
2	Mookie Blaylock	.20
3	Craig Ehlo	.20
4	Jon Koncak	.20
5	Andrew Lang	.20
6	Dee Brown	.20
7	Sherman Douglas	.20
8	Acie Earl	.20
9	Rick Fox	.20
10	Kevin Gamble	.20
11	Xavier McDaniel	.20
12	Dino Radja	.40
13	Tony Bennett	.20
14	Dell Curry	.20
15	Kenny Gattison	.20
16	Hersey Hawkins	.20
17	Larry Johnson	1.00
18	Alonzo Mourning	1.50
19	David Wingate	.20
20	B.J. Armstrong	.20
21	Steve Kerr	.20
22	Toni Kukoc	.75
23	Pete Myers	.20
24	Scottie Pippen	2.00
25	Bill Wennington	.20
26	Terrell Brandon	.20
27	Brad Daugherty	.20
28	Tyrone Hill	.20
29	Bobby Phills	.20
30	Mark Price	.30
31	Gerald Wilkins	.20
32	John Williams	.20
33	Lucious Harris	.20
34	Jim Jackson	1.00
35	Jamal Mashburn	1.00
36	Sean Rooks	.20
37	Doug Smith	.20
38	Mahmoud Abdul-Rauf	.20
39	LaPhonso Ellis	.20
40	Dikembe Mutombo	.75
41	Robert Pack	.20
42	Rodney Rogers	.20
43	Brian Williams	.20
44	Reggie Williams	.20
45	Joe Dumars	.50
46	Allan Houston	.30
47	Lindsey Hunter	.20
48	Terry Mills	.20
49	Victor Alexander	.20
50	Chris Gatling	.20
51	Billy Owens	.20
52	Latrell Sprewell	.50
53	Chris Webber	1.00
54	Sam Cassell	.50
55	Carl Herrera	.20
56	Robert Horry	.20
57	Hakeem Olajuwon	3.00
58	Kenny Smith	.20
59	Otis Thorpe	.20
60	Antonio Davis	.20
61	Dale Davis	.20
62	Reggie Miller	1.00
63	Byron Scott	.20
64	Rik Smits	.40
65	Haywoode Workman	.20
66	Terry Dehere	.20
67	Harold Ellis	.20
68	Gary Grant	.20
69	Elmore Spencer	.20
70	Loy Vaught	.20
71	Elden Campbell	.20
72	Doug Christie	.20
73	Vlade Divac	.20
74	George Lynch	.20
75	Anthony Peeler	.20
76	Nick Van Exel	1.00
77	James Worthy	.20
78	Bimbo Coles	.20
79	Harold Miner	.20
80	John Salley	.20
81	Rony Seikaly	.20
82	Steve Smith	.20
83	Vin Baker	1.00
84	Jon Barry	.20
85	Todd Day	.20
86	Lee Mayberry	.20
87	Eric Murdock	.20
88	Mike Brown	.20
89	Christian Laettner	.20
90	Isaiah Rider	.40
91	Doug West	.20
92	Michael Williams	.20
93	Kenny Anderson	.40
94	Benoit Benjamin	.20
95	PJ Brown	.20
96	Derrick Coleman	.40
97	Kevin Edwards	.20
98	Hubert Davis	.20
99	Patrick Ewing	1.25
100	Derek Harper	.20
101	Anthony Mason	.20
102	Charles Oakley	.20
103	Charles Smith	.20
104	John Starks	.20
105	Nick Anderson	.20
106	Anfernee Hardaway	6.00
107	Shaquille O'Neal	6.00
108	Dennis Scott	.20
109	Jeff Turner	.20
110	Dana Barros	.20
111	Shawn Bradley	.25
112	Jeff Malone	.20
113	Tim Perry	.20
114	C. Weatherspoon	.30
115	Danny Ainge	.20
116	Charles Barkley	1.50
117	A.C. Green	.20
118	Kevin Johnson	.40
119	Dan Majerle	.20
120	Clyde Drexler	1.00
121	Harvey Grant	.20
122	Jerome Kersey	.20
123	Clifford Robinson	.20
124	Rod Strickland	.20
125	Buck Williams	.20
126	Randy Brown	.20
127	Olden Polynice	.20
128	Mitch Richmond	.40
129	Lionel Simmons	.20
130	Spud Webb	.20
131	Walt Williams	.20
132	Willie Anderson	.20
133	Vinny Del Negro	.20
134	Sean Elliott	.20
135	Avery Johnson	.20
136	JR Reid	.20
137	David Robinson	2.00
138	Dennis Rodman	3.00
139	Kendall Gill	.20
140	Ervin Johnson	.20
141	Shawn Kemp	1.50
142	Nate McMillan	.20
143	Gary Payton	1.00
144	Sam Perkins	.20
145	David Benoit	.20
146	Jeff Hornacek	.20
147	Jay Humphries	.20
148	Karl Malone	1.00
149	Bryon Russell	.20
150	Felton Spencer	.20
151	John Stockton	1.00
152	Rex Chapman	.20
153	Calbert Cheaney	.20
154	Tom Gugliotta	.20
155	Don MacLean	.20
156	Gheorghe Muresan	.20
157	Doug Overton	.20
158	Brent Price	.20
159	Derrick Coleman	.30
160	Joe Dumars	.30
161	Tim Hardaway	.30
162	Kevin Johnson	.30
163	Larry Johnson	.40
164	Shawn Kemp	.50
165	Dan Majerle	.20
166	Reggie Miller	.30
167	Alonzo Mourning	.50
168	Shaquille O'Neal	2.50
169	Mark Price	.20
170	Steve Smith	.20
171	Isiah Thomas	.30
172	Dominique Wilkins	.20
173	Checklist	.20
174	Checklist	.20
175	Checklist	.20
176	Tyrone Corbin	.20
177	Grant Long	.20
178	Ken Norman	.20
179	Steve Smith	.20
180	Blue Edwards	.20
181	Pervis Ellison	.20
182	*Greg Minor*	.30
183	*Eric Montross*	.40
184	Derek Strong	.20
185	David Wesley	.20
186	Dominique Wilkins	.40
187	Michael Adams	.20
188	Muggsy Bogues	.20
189	Scott Burrell	.20
190	*Darrin Hancock*	.30
191	Robert Parish	.30
192	Jud Buechler	.20
193	Ron Harper	.20
194	Larry Krystkowiak	.20
195	Will Perdue	.20
196	*Dickey Simpkins*	.40
197	Michael Cage	.20
198	Tony Campbell	.20
199	Danny Ferry	.20
200	Chris Mills	.20
201	Popeye Jones	.20
202	*Jason Kidd*	10.00
203	Roy Tarpley	.20
204	Lorenzo Williams	.20
205	Dale Ellis	.20
206	Tom Hammonds	.20
207	*Jalen Rose*	4.00
208	*Reggie Slater*	.20
209	Bryant Stith	.20
210	Rafael Addison	.20
211	*Bill Curley*	.30
212	Johnny Dawkins	.20
213	*Grant Hill*	15.00
214	Mark Macon	.20
215	Oliver Miller	.20
216	*Ivano Newbill*	.20
217	Mark West	.20
218	Tom Gugliotta	.20
219	Tim Hardaway	.40
220	Keith Jennings	.20
221	*Dwayne Morton*	.20
222	Chris Mullin	.40
223	Ricky Pierce	.20
224	*Carlos Rogers*	.40
225	*Clifford Rozier*	.40
226	Rony Seikaly	.20
227	*Tim Breaux*	.20
228	Scott Brooks	.20
229	Mario Elie	.20
230	Vernon Maxwell	.20
231	*Zan Tabak*	.20
232	Mark Jackson	.20
233	Derrick McKey	.20
234	Tony Massenburg	.20
235	*Lamond Murray*	.40
236	Charles Outlaw	.20
237	*Eric Piatkowski*	.40
238	Pooh Richardson	.20
239	Malik Sealy	.20
240	Cedric Ceballos	.20
241	*Eddie Jones*	4.00
242	*Anthony Miller*	.20
243	Tony Smith	.20
244	Sedale Threatt	.20
245	Ledell Eackles	.20
246	Kevin Gamble	.20
247	Matt Geiger	.20
248	Brad Lohaus	.20
249	Billy Owens	.20
250	*Khalid Reeves*	.40
251	Glen Rice	.40
252	Kevin Willis	.20
253	Marty Conlon	.20
254	*Eric Mobley*	.40
255	Johnny Newman	.20
256	Ed Pinckney	.20
257	*Glenn Robinson*	5.00
258	Pat Durham	.20
259	*Howard Eisley*	.20
260	Winston Garland	.20
261	Stacey King	.20
262	*Donyell Marshall*	.40
263	Sean Rooks	.20
264	Chris Smith	.20
265	*Chris Childs*	1.00
266	Sleepy Floyd	.20
267	Armon Gilliam	.20
268	Sean Higgins	.20
269	Rex Walters	.20
270	Greg Anthony	.20
271	*Charlie Ward*	.40
272	Herb Williams	.20
273	*Monty Williams*	.30
274	Anthony Avent	.20
275	Anthony Bowie	.20
276	Horace Grant	.40
277	Donald Royal	.20
278	Brian Shaw	.20
279	*Brooks Thompson*	.30
280	*Derrick Alston*	.20
281	Willie Burton	.20
282	Greg Graham	.20
283	*B.J. Tyler*	.30
284	Scott Williams	.20
285	*Sharone Wright*	.40
286	Joe Kleine	.20
287	Danny Manning	.30

288	Elliot Perry	.20
289	*Wesley Person*	1.00
290	*Trevor Ruffin*	.30
291	Wayman Tisdale	.20
292	Mark Bryant	.20
293	Chris Dudley	.20
294	*Aaron McKie*	1.00
295	Tracy Murray	.20
296	Terry Porter	.20
297	James Robinson	.20
298	Alaa Abdelnaby	.20
299	Duane Causwell	.20
300	*Brian Grant*	3.00
301	Bobby Hurley	.20
302	*Michael Smith*	.50
303	Terry Cummings	.20
304	Moses Malone	.20
305	*Julius Nwosu*	.20
306	Chuck Person	.20
307	Doc Rivers	.20
308	Vincent Askew	.20
309	Sarunas Marciulionis	.20
310	Detlef Schrempf	.20
311	*Dontonio Wingfield*	.20
312	Antoine Carr	.20
313	Tom Chambers	.20
314	John Crotty	.20
315	Adam Keefe	.20
316	*Jamie Watson*	.30
317	Mitchell Butler	.20
318	Kevin Duckworth	.20
319	*Juwan Howard*	3.00
320	*Jim McIlvaine*	.20
321	Scott Skiles	.20
322	*Anthony Tucker*	.30
323	Chris Webber	1.00
324	Checklist	.20
325	Checklist	.20
326	Michael Jordan	15.00

1994-95 Flair Center Spotlight

These inserts, randomly included in 1994-95 Fleer Flair Series I packs, showcase six of the NBA's top centers. The cards use a 100-percent foil-etched background which features each center on a solid white background, with the player casting two colored shadows against the background. The player's name, set name and Fleer Flair logo are also on the card front in gold foil. Each card back has the set name and player's name in gold foil too, along with a color photo of the player casting colorful shadows against a white background. A brief player profile and card number (1 of 6, etc.) are also included.

		MT
Complete Set (6):		60.00
Common Player:		5.00
1	Patrick Ewing	5.00
2	Alonzo Mourning	7.00
3	Hakeem Olajuwon	10.00
4	Shaquille O'Neal	30.00
5	David Robinson	10.00
6	Chris Webber	10.00

1994-95 Flair Hot Numbers

These 1994-95 Fleer Flair Series I inserts show a player on a colored background with the words "Hot Numbers" in bold. The players are those who consistently put up impressive numbers. The "Hot Numbers" logo and the player's uniform number are also on the card front, stamped in gold foil. The card back has the player's name, set name and card number (1 of 20, etc.) stamped in gold foil, along with a color photo and player profile. The card's overall color pattern on both sides fits the player's team colors.

		MT
Complete Set (20):		65.00
Common Player:		1.00
1	Vin Baker	3.00
2	Sam Cassell	1.50
3	Patrick Ewing	2.50
4	Anfernee Hardaway	18.00
5	Robert Horry	2.00
6	Shawn Kemp	4.00
7	Toni Kukoc	3.00
8	Jamal Mashburn	3.00
9	Reggie Miller	3.00
10	Dikembe Mutombo	1.50
11	Hakeem Olajuwon	8.00
12	Shaquille O'Neal	13.00
13	Scottie Pippen	7.00
14	Isaiah Rider	2.50
15	David Robinson	5.00
16	Latrell Sprewell	2.00
17	John Starks	1.00
18	John Stockton	2.50
19	Nick Van Exel	3.00
20	Chris Webber	3.00

1994-95 Flair Playmakers

This 10-card insert set features NBA stars who are known for their play-making ability. The card front has a full-color action photo, against a background utilizing a basketball court motif in its design. The set's logo and player's name are foil stamped into the card. Cards were random inserts in 1994-95 Fleer Flair Series II packs.

		MT
Complete Set (10):		15.00
Common Player:		1.00
1	Kenny Anderson	1.50
2	Mookie Blaylock	1.00
3	Sam Cassell	1.50
4	Anfernee Hardaway	9.00
5	Robert Pack	1.00
6	Scottie Pippen	3.00
7	Mark Price	1.00
8	Mitch Richmond	1.00
9	John Stockton	2.00
10	Nick Van Exel	2.00

1994-95 Flair Rejectors

This six-card set spotlights some of the NBA's NBA's top defensive standouts. The cards, which are numbered on the back (1 of 6, etc.), have foil stamping on the front for the player's name and set logo. The cards were random inserts in 1994-95 Fleer Flair Series II packs and are the scarcest of the inserts. Each card is printed on 100 percent etched foil.

		MT
Complete Set (6):		70.00
Common Player:		5.00
1	Patrick Ewing	5.00
2	Alonzo Mourning	8.00
3	Dikembe Mutombo	5.00
4	Hakeem Olajuwon	14.00
5	Shaquille O'Neal	30.00
6	David Robinson	10.00

1994-95 Flair Scoring Power

This 1994-95 Fleer Flair Series I insert set features 10 contenders for the league scoring title. Each card front has the words "Scoring Power" printed in large bold letters on the background. Two shots of the player are cast over the words, with one shot a closeup and the other an action photo. The card back has the player's name and card number (1 of 10, etc.) in gold foil, along with another photo and player profile. The set's title is also printed on the card's background.

		MT
Complete Set (10):		40.00
Common Player:		1.00
1	Charles Barkley	5.00
2	Patrick Ewing	2.50
3	Karl Malone	3.00
4	Hakeem Olajuwon	8.00
5	Shaquille O'Neal	12.00
6	Scottie Pippen	7.00
7	Mitch Richmond	1.00
8	David Robinson	5.00
9	Latrell Sprewell	2.00
10	Dominique Wilkins	1.00

1994-95 Flair Wave of the Future

This 10-card set showcases some of the season's impressive rookie crop. The cards, numbered on the back, (1 of 10, etc.), use foil stamping on the front for the player's name and set logo. The cards were random inserts in 1994-95 Fleer Flair Series II packs.

		MT
Complete Set (10):		50.00
Common Player:		1.00
1	Brian Grant	3.00
2	Grant Hill	20.00
3	Juwan Howard	10.00
4	Eddie Jones	10.00
5	Jason Kidd	10.00
6	Donyell Marshall	1.00
7	Eric Montross	1.00
8	Lamond Murray	1.00
9	Wesley Person	1.00
10	Glenn Robinson	8.00

1994 Flair USA Basketball

The United State's men's Olympic basketball "Dream Team II" is honored in this 120-card set from Fleer. The cards are standard size, but use thicker stock. Each card front has a color photo, and the player's name is stamped in gold foil at the bottom. The back has another photo, statistics and silver foil lettering. A card number is also included. Each player has several cards in the set devoted to him; legends of the USA Basketball Women's team are also represented in a six-card subset (#s 113-118). Cards were sold in packs of 10 and generally feature the players in their Olympic uniform or with a red-white-and-blue USA theme.

		MT
Complete Set (120):		25.00
Common Player:		.10
Minor Stars:		.20
1	Don Chaney (1-2)	.10
3	Pete Gillen (3-4)	.10
5	Rick Majerus (5-6)	.10
7	Don Nelson (7-8)	.10
9	Derrick Coleman (9-15)	.20
16	Joe Dumars (16-24)	.25
25	Tim Hardaway (25-32)	.15
33	Larry Johnson (33-40)	.40
41	Shawn Kemp (41-48)	.75
49	Dan Majerle (49-56)	.10
57	Reggie Miller (57-64)	.50
65	Alonzo Mourning (65-72)	.50
73	Shaquille O'Neal (73-80)	2.00
81	Mark Price (81-88)	.10
89	Steve Smith (89-96)	.10
97	Isiah Thomas (97-104)	.25
105	Dominique Wilkins (105-112)	.25
113	Women (113-120)	.10

1994 Flair USA Kevin Johnson

This 10-card set was available through a wrapper redemption offer on packs of 1994 Flair USA. The first eight cards feature Johnson, while the final two are checklists that are updated to include him along with the team photo. The redemption card allowed the collector to send in $4 to Fleer and it expired October 31, 1994.

		MT
Complete Set (10):		10.00
Common Player:		1.25
M1	Strong Suit	1.25
M2	Career Highlights	1.25
M3	Golden Moment	1.25
M4	Biography	1.25
M5	Rookie Year	1.25
M6	Weights and Measures	1.25
M7	Personal Note	1.25
M8	Dreamscapes	1.25
119	Team Checklist	2.00
120	Team Checklist	2.00

1995-96 Flair

Fleer released its 1995-96 basketball line, featuring extra thick card stock, in two series. Cards fronts are 100 percent foil-etched, with two photos of the player in action. His name and initials are at the bottom of the card, in silver and gold foil. The horizontal card back has another action photo, with the player's statistics listed. A team logo, the player's name and a card number are stamped in gold in the upper right corner. Series I inserts include: Class of '95, Perimeter Power, Center Spotlight, and Hot Numbers. Series II, which includes 42 updated players not in Series I, plus six expansion team players, 30 rookies, two checklists and 20 Style subset cards, has 180 cards. Series II inserts include: Anticipation, Stackhouse's Scrapbook, New Heights, Play Makers and Wave of the Future.

		MT
Complete Set (250):		100.00
Complete Series 1 (150):		45.00
Complete Series 2 (100):		55.00
Common Player:		.25
Minor Stars:		.50
Series 1 Pack (9):		3.50
Series 1 Wax Box (36):		90.00
Series 2 Pack (9):		3.00
Series 2 Wax Box (36):		65.00
1	Stacey Augmon	.25
2	Mookie Blaylock	.25
3	Grant Long	.25
4	Steve Smith	.25
5	Dee Brown	.25
6	Sherman Douglas	.25
7	Eric Montross	.25
8	Dino Radja	.25
9	David Wesley	.25
10	Muggsy Bogues	.25
11	Scott Burrell	.25
12	Dell Curry	.25
13	Larry Johnson	1.00
14	Alonzo Mourning	1.00
15	Michael Jordan	12.00
16	Steve Kerr	.25
17	Toni Kukoc	.25
18	Scottie Pippen	2.00
19	Terrell Brandon	.25
20	Tyrone Hill	.25
21	Chris Mills	.25
22	Bobby Phills	.25
23	Mark Price	.25
24	John Williams	.25
25	Jim Jackson	1.00
26	Popeye Jones	.25
27	Jason Kidd	3.00
28	Jamal Mashburn	1.00
29	Lorenzo Williams	.25
30	Mahmoud Abdul-Rauf	.50
31	Dikembe Mutombo	.50
32	Robert Pack	.25
33	Jalen Rose	.25
34	Bryant Stith	.25
35	Reggie Williams	.25
36	Joe Dumars	.50
37	Grant Hill	5.00
38	Allan Houston	.25
39	Lindsey Hunter	.25
40	Terry Mills	.25
41	Chris Gatling	.25
42	Tim Hardaway	.50
43	Donyell Marshall	.25
44	Chris Mullin	.50
45	Carlos Rogers	.25
46	Clifford Rozier	.25
47	Latrell Sprewell	.75
48	Sam Cassell	.25
49	Clyde Drexler	1.00
50	Mario Elie	.25
51	Robert Horry	.50
52	Hakeem Olajuwon	2.00
53	Kenny Smith	.25
54	Antonio Davis	.25
55	Dale Davis	.25
56	Mark Jackson	.25
57	Derrick McKey	.25
58	Reggie Miller	1.00
59	Rik Smits	.25
60	Lamond Murray	.25
61	Pooh Richardson	.25
62	Malik Sealy	.25
63	Loy Vaught	.25
64	Elden Campbell	.25
65	Cedric Ceballos	.50
66	Vlade Divac	.25
67	Eddie Jones	1.50
68	Nick Van Exel	1.00
69	Bimbo Coles	.25
70	Billy Owens	.25
71	Khalid Reeves	.25
72	Glen Rice	.50
73	Kevin Willis	.25
74	Vin Baker	.50
75	Todd Day	.25
76	Eric Murdock	.25
77	Glenn Robinson	1.50
78	Tom Gugliotta	.25
79	Christian Laettner	.25
80	Isaiah Rider	.25
81	Doug West	.25
82	Kenny Anderson	.25
83	P.J. Brown	.25
84	Derrick Coleman	.25
85	Armon Gilliam	.25
86	Chris Morris	.25
87	Hubert Davis	.25
88	Patrick Ewing	.75
89	Derek Harper	.25
90	Anthony Mason	.25
91	Charles Oakley	.25
92	Charles Smith	.25
93	John Starks	.25
94	Nick Anderson	.25
95	Horace Grant	.50
96	Anfernee Hardaway	5.00
97	Shaquille O'Neal	4.00
98	Dennis Scott	.25
99	Brian Shaw	.25
100	Dana Barros	.25
101	Shawn Bradley	.25
102	Clarence Weatherspoon	.25
103	Sharone Wright	.25
104	Charles Barkley	2.00
105	A.C. Green	.25
106	Kevin Johnson	.50
107	Dan Majerle	.25
108	Danny Manning	.25
109	Elliot Perry	.25
110	Wesley Person	.25
111	Terry Porter	.25
112	Clifford Robinson	.25
113	Rod Strickland	.25
114	Otis Thorpe	.25
115	Buck Williams	.25
116	Brian Grant	.50
117	Bobby Hurley	.25
118	Olden Polynice	.25
119	Mitch Richmond	.50
120	Walt Williams	.25
121	Vinny Del Negro	.25
122	Sean Elliott	.25
123	Avery Johnson	.25
124	David Robinson	2.00
125	Dennis Rodman	3.00
126	Shawn Kemp	1.50
127	Nate McMillan	.25
128	Gary Payton	1.00
129	Sam Perkins	.25
130	Detlef Schrempf	.25
131	B.J. Armstrong	.25
132	Jerome Kersey	.25
133	Oliver Miller	.25
134	John Salley	.25
135	David Benoit	.25
136	Antoine Carr	.25
137	Jeff Hornacek	.25
138	Karl Malone	1.00
139	John Stockton	1.00
140	Greg Anthony	.25
141	Benoit Benjamin	.25
142	Blue Edwards	.25
143	Byron Scott	.25
144	Calbert Cheaney	.25
145	Juwan Howard	1.50
146	Gheorghe Muresan	.25
147	Scott Skiles	.25
148	Chris Webber	2.00
149	Checklist	.25
150	Checklist	.25
151	Stacey Augmon	.25
152	Mookie Blaylock	.25
153	Andrew Lang	.25
154	Steve Smith	.25
155	Dana Barros	.25
156	Rick Fox	.25
157	Kendall Gill	.25
158	Khalid Reeves	.25
159	Glen Rice	.25
160	Dennis Rodman	3.00
161	Dan Majerle	.25
162	Tony Dumas	.50
163	Dale Ellis	.25
164	Otis Thorpe	.25
165	Rony Seikaly	.25
166	Sam Cassell	.25
167	Clyde Drexler	1.00
168	Robert Horry	.25
169	Hakeem Olajuwon	2.00
170	Ricky Pierce	.25
171	Rodney Rogers	.25
172	Brian Williams	.25
173	Magic Johnson	3.00
174	Alonzo Mourning	1.00
175	Lee Mayberry	.25
176	Terry Porter	.25
177	Shawn Bradley	.50
178	Jayson Williams	.25
179	Gary Grant	.25
180	Jon Koncak	.25
181	Derrick Coleman	.25
182	Vernon Maxwell	.25
183	John Williams	.25
184	Aaron McKie	.25
185	Michael Smith	.25
186	Chuck Person	.25
187	Hersey Hawkins	.25
188	Shawn Kemp	1.00
189	Gary Payton	.50
190	Detlef Schrempf	.25
191	Chris Morris	.25
192	Robert Pack	.25
193	Willie Anderson	.25
194	Oliver Miller	.25
195	Alvin Robertson	.25
196	Greg Anthony	.25
197	Blue Edwards	.25
198	Byron Scott	.25
199	*Cory Alexander*	.25
200	*Brent Barry*	1.00
201	*Travis Best*	1.00
202	*Jason Caffey*	.50
203	*Sasha Danilovic*	.50
204	*Tyus Edney*	.50
205	*Michael Finley*	5.00
206	*Kevin Garnett*	12.00
207	*Alan Henderson*	.50
208	*Antonio McDyess*	5.00
209	*Loren Meyer*	.25
210	*Lawrence Moten*	.25
211	*Ed O'Bannon*	.50
212	*Greg Ostertag*	.25
213	*Cherokee Parks*	.50
214	*Theo Ratliff*	2.00
215	*Bryant Reeves*	1.00
216	*Shawn Respert*	.50
217	*Arvydas Sabonis*	2.00
218	*Joe Smith*	2.00
219	*Jerry Stackhouse*	6.00
220	*Damon Stoudamire*	2.00
221	*Bob Sura*	.50
222	*Kurt Thomas*	.50
223	*Gary Trent*	.50
224	*David Vaughn*	.25
225	*Rasheed Wallace*	5.00
226	*Eric Williams*	.50
227	*Corliss Williamson*	.50
228	*George Zidek*	.50
229	Vin Baker (Style)	.25
230	Charles Barkley (Style)	.75
231	Patrick Ewing (Style)	.50
232	Anfernee Hardaway (Style)	2.50
233	Grant Hill (Style)	1.00
234	Larry Johnson (Style)	.50
235	Michael Jordan (Style)	5.00
236	Jason Kidd (Style)	1.25
237	Karl Malone (Style)	.50
238	Jamal Mashburn (Style)	.50
239	Reggie Miller (Style)	.50
240	Shaquille O'Neal (Style)	2.00
241	Scottie Pippen (Style)	.75
242	Mitch Richmond (Style)	.25
243	Clifford Robinson (Style)	.25
244	David Robinson (Style)	.50
245	Glenn Robinson (Style)	.50
246	John Stockton (Style)	.50
247	Nick Van Exel (Style)	.50
248	Chris Webber (Style)	.50
249	Checklist	.25
250	Checklist	.25

1995-96 Flair Anticipation

These 1995 Fleer Flair Series II inserts were seeded one per every 36 packs. The cards feature an embossed design on the front, against a ghosted, strobe-like background. The set name runs along the left side of the card; the player's name runs along the bottom, stamped in gold. The card back has another color action photo, plus a summary of the player's skills. A card number (1 of 10, etc.) is also given.

		MT
Complete Set (10):		100.00
Common Player:		5.00
Inserted 1:36 Series II		
1	Grant Hill	20.00
2	Michael Jordan	60.00
3	Shawn Kemp	4.00
4	Jason Kidd	15.00
5	Alonzo Mourning	5.00
6	Hakeem Olajuwon	8.00
7	Shaquille O'Neal	20.00
8	Glenn Robinson	5.00
9	Joe Smith	5.00
10	Jerry Stackhouse	8.00

1995-96 Flair Center Spotlight

Six of the NBA's top centers are featured on these 1995-96 Fleer Flair Series I inserts, available one per every 18 packs. The cards are plastic, with a color action photo on them. Gold foil stamping is used for the player's name and set name along the bottom. A brand logo is in the upper right.

		MT
Complete Set (6):		35.00
Common Player:		2.00
1	Vlade Divac	2.00
2	Patrick Ewing	4.00
3	Alonzo Mourning	5.00
4	Hakeem Olajuwon	10.00
5	Shaquille O'Neal	18.00
6	David Robinson	8.00

1995-96 Flair Class of '95

This set features 15 of the top picks from the 1995 NBA Draft. The card front has a foil-etched background of a basketball, with a color photo of the player. "Class of '95" is written in silver in the lower left corner, along with the player's name and team name, which are in gold. The horizontal back has another action photo of the player, plus a recap of the skills the player showed in college which enabled him to be drafted. His name and a card number, using an "R" prefix, are given in gold foil in the upper right corner.

		MT
Complete Set (15):		35.00
Common Player:		1.00
1	Brent Barry	2.00
2	Kevin Garnett	15.00
3	Antonio McDyess	5.00
4	Ed O'Bannon	1.00
5	Cherokee Parks	1.00
6	Bryant Reeves	3.00
7	Shawn Respert	1.00
8	Joe Smith	7.00
9	Jerry Stackhouse	5.00
10	Damon Stoudamire	8.00
11	Kurt Thomas	2.00
12	Gary Trent	3.00
13	Rasheed Wallace	4.00
14	Eric Williams	1.00
15	Corliss Williamson	1.00

1995-96 Flair Hot Numbers

These 1995-96 Fleer Flair Series I inserts showcase 15 top stars on a 3-D lenticular design. The cards, therefore, have a wax coating. In the background of each card front is a collage of the key statistical numbers he put up in the previous season. These numbers are used for the back of the card, too, which has a number in the lower right corner (1 of 15, etc.). A recap of all the key numbers is given, along with a color action photo. Cards were seeded one per every 36 packs.

		MT
Complete Set (15):		200.00
Common Player:		5.00
1	Charles Barkley	10.00
2	Grant Hill	40.00
3	Eddie Jones	15.00
4	Michael Jordan	80.00
5	Shawn Kemp	10.00
6	Jason Kidd	15.00
7	Karl Malone	8.00
8	Alonzo Mourning	8.00
9	Dikembe Mutombo	5.00
10	Hakeem Olajuwon	20.00
11	Shaquille O'Neal	30.00
12	Glenn Robinson	10.00
13	Dennis Rodman	20.00
14	Latrell Sprewell	5.00
15	Chris Webber	10.00

1995-96 Flair New Heights

These 10 inserts, exclusive to 1995-96 Fleer Flair Series II hobby packs, are seeded one per every 18 packs. The card front has a collage of the same photo in different sizes, against a metallic background. The brand name logo, player's name and "New Heights" are stamped in foil on the front. The card back is numbered (1 of 10, etc.).

		MT
Complete Set (10):		80.00
Common Player:		5.00
1	Anfernee Hardaway	15.00
2	Grant Hill	20.00
3	Larry Johnson	5.00
4	Michael Jordan	50.00
5	Shawn Kemp	6.00
6	Karl Malone	5.00
7	Hakeem Olajuwon	10.00
8	David Robinson	8.00
9	Glenn Robinson	6.00
10	Chris Webber	5.00

1995-96 Flair Perimeter Power

These 1995-96 Fleer Flair Series I inserts, featuring 15 of the NBA's top shooters from the outside, were seeded one per every six packs. A color action photo appears on the front, against a swirled background with silver foil used for a compass-like pattern, along with the player's name and brand name and insert set name. The white back repeats the pattern used for the front's background, and includes a color photo, silver foil stamping (for the player's name and set logo), 1994-95 season recap and number (1 of 15, etc.).

		MT
Complete Set (15):		20.00
Common Player:		1.00
1	Dana Barros	1.00
2	Clyde Drexler	4.00
3	Anfernee Hardaway	8.00
4	Tim Hardaway	1.50
5	Dan Majerle	1.00
6	Jamal Mashburn	2.00
7	Reggie Miller	3.00
8	Gary Payton	2.00
9	Scottie Pippen	7.00
10	Glen Rice	1.50
11	Mitch Richmond	1.50
12	Steve Smith	1.00
13	John Starks	1.00
14	John Stockton	3.00
15	Nick Van Exel	3.00

1995-96 Flair Play Makers

These cards, featuring 10 of the league's top players who make things happen, were the rarest of all 1995-96 Fleer Flair Series II inserts. Cards, numbered on the back, (1 of 10, etc.), were seeded one per every 54 packs. The card design uses Fleer's 3-D lenticular format.

		MT
Complete Set (10):		200.00
Common Player:		12.00
1	Clyde Drexler	30.00
2	Anfernee Hardaway	60.00
3	Jamal Mashburn	20.00
4	Reggie Miller	30.00
5	Gary Payton	15.00
6	Scottie Pippen	45.00
7	Mitch Richmond	12.00
8	David Robinson	35.00
9	Jerry Stackhouse	20.00
10	Nick Van Exel	25.00

1995-96 Flair Stackhouse's Scrapbook

These two cards are part of the card set which chronicles the NBA career of Philadelphia 76ers' rookie Jerry Stackhouse. The cards were available in 1995-96 Fleer Flair Series II packs, one per every 24 packs.

		MT
Complete Set (2):		16.00
Common Player:		8.00
1	Jerry Stackhouse	8.00
2	Jerry Stackhouse	8.00

1995-96 Flair Wave of the Future

These 10 cards, randomly inserted one per every 12 packs of 1995-96 Fleer Flair Series II packs, feature 10 top NBA rookies. Cards are numbered (1 of 10, etc.).

		MT
Complete Set (10):		50.00
Common Player:		2.00
1	Tyus Edney	2.00
2	Michael Finley	4.00
3	Kevin Garnett	18.00
4	Antonio McDyess	10.00
5	Ed O'Bannon	2.00
6	Arvydas Sabonis	5.00
7	Joe Smith	8.00
8	Jerry Stackhouse	7.00
9	Damon Stoudamire	8.00
10	Rasheed Wallace	4.00

1996-97 Flair Showcase Promo Sheet

This three-card sheet was used to promote the release of Flair Showcase Basketball. Jerry Stackhouse was featured in a Style, Grace and Showcase front to preview each of the three different fronts used in the set.

		MT
Complete Set (3):		3.00
Common Player:		1.00
16	Jerry Stackhouse (Style - Row 0)	1.00
16	Jerry Stackhouse (Grace - Row 1)	1.00
16	Jerry Stackhouse (Showcase - Row 2)	1.00

1996-97 Flair Showcase Row 2

All 90 players in the Flair Showcase set were featured in a Row 2, or Style front design, with 30 cards in each of the three back designs. Cards with a Style front and a Showtime back were inserted one per pack, Style/ Showstoppers were inserted one per 1.5 packs and Style/ Showpiece versions were inserted one per two packs. Style fronts have a large closeup of the player on the right three-quarters of the card, with an action shot on the left side.

		MT
Complete Set (90):		70.00
Common Player:		.25
Minor Stars:		.50
Pack (5):		15.00
Wax Box (24):		325.00
1	Anfernee Hardaway	4.00
2	Mitch Richmond	.50
3	*Allen Iverson*	10.00
4	Charles Barkley	1.00
5	Juwan Howard	1.00
6	David Robinson	1.00
7	Gary Payton	.75
8	*Kerry Kittles*	2.00
9	Dennis Rodman	2.50
10	Shaquille O'Neal	2.50
11	*Stephon Marbury*	8.00
12	John Stockton	.50
13	Glenn Robinson	.50
14	Hakeem Olajuwon	1.75
15	Jason Kidd	1.00
16	Jerry Stackhouse	1.00
17	Joe Smith	1.00
18	Reggie Miller	.50
19	Grant Hill	5.00
20	Damon Stoudamire	1.50
21	Kevin Garnett	5.00
22	Clyde Drexler	1.00
23	Michael Jordan	10.00
24	Antonio McDyess	.75
25	Chris Webber	1.50
26	*Antoine Walker*	5.00
27	Scottie Pippen	2.00
28	Karl Malone	1.00
29	*Shareef Abdur-Rahim*	5.00
30	Shawn Kemp	1.00
31	*Kobe Bryant*	20.00
32	Derrick Coleman	.50
33	Alonzo Mourning	.50
34	Anthony Mason	.25
35	*Ray Allen*	6.00
36	Arvydas Sabonis	.25
37	Brian Grant	.25
38	Bryant Reeves	.25
39	Christian Laettner	.25
40	Tom Gugliotta	.25
41	Latrell Sprewell	.25
42	*Erick Dampier*	1.00
43	Gheorghe Muresan	.25
44	Glen Rice	.50
45	Patrick Ewing	.50
46	Jim Jackson	.25
47	Michael Finley	.25
48	Toni Kukoc	.50
49	*Marcus Camby*	2.50
50	Kenny Anderson	.25
51	Mark Price	.25
52	Tim Hardaway	.75
53	Mookie Blaylock	.25
54	Steve Smith	.25
55	Terrell Brandon	.25
56	*Lorenzen Wright*	1.00
57	Sasha Danilovic	.25
58	Jeff Hornacek	.25
59	Eddie Jones	1.25
60	Vin Baker	1.00
61	Chris Childs	.25
62	Clifford Robinson	.25
63	Anthony Peeler	.25
64	Dino Radja	.25
65	Joe Dumars	.25
66	Loy Vaught	.25
67	Rony Seikaly	.25
68	*Vitaly Potapenko*	.50
69	Chris Gatling	.25
70	Dale Ellis	.25
71	Allan Houston	.50
72	Doug Christie	.25
73	LaPhonso Ellis	.25
74	Kendall Gill	.25
75	Rik Smits	.25
76	Bobby Phills	.25
77	Malik Sealy	.25
78	Sean Elliott	.25
79	Vlade Divac	.25
80	David Wesley	.25
81	Dominique Wilkins	.25
82	Danny Manning	.25
83	Detlef Schrempf	.25
84	Hersey Hawkins	.25
85	Lindsey Hunter	.25
86	Mahmoud Abdul-Rauf	.25
87	Shawn Bradley	.25
88	Horace Grant	.25
89	Cedric Ceballos	.25
90	Jamal Mashburn	.25

1996-97 Flair Showcase Row 1

All 90 players in Flair Showcase were available in a Row 1, or Grace front, with 30 cards in each of the three back designs. Cards with a Grace front and a Showtime back were inserted one per two packs, Grace/ Showstoppers inserted one per 2.5 packs and Grace/ Showpiece inserted one per 3.5 packs.

		MT
Complete Set (90):		140.00
Common Player:		.50
Minor Stars:		1.00
1	Anfernee Hardaway	6.00
2	Mitch Richmond	1.00
3	Allen Iverson	12.00
4	Charles Barkley	1.50
5	Juwan Howard	1.50
6	David Robinson	1.50
7	Gary Payton	1.25
8	Kerry Kittles	3.00
9	Dennis Rodman	3.75
10	Shaquille O'Neal	3.75
11	Stephon Marbury	12.00
12	John Stockton	1.00
13	Glenn Robinson	1.00
14	Hakeem Olajuwon	2.50
15	Jason Kidd	2.00
16	Jerry Stackhouse	1.50
17	Joe Smith	1.50
18	Reggie Miller	1.00
19	Grant Hill	7.50
20	Damon Stoudamire	2.25
21	Kevin Garnett	7.50
22	Clyde Drexler	1.50
23	Michael Jordan	15.00
24	Antonio McDyess	1.25
25	Chris Webber	2.25
26	Antoine Walker	8.00
27	Scottie Pippen	3.00
28	Karl Malone	1.50
29	Shareef Abdur-Rahim	7.50
30	Shawn Kemp	1.50
31	Kobe Bryant	30.00
32	Derrick Coleman	.50
33	Alonzo Mourning	1.00
34	Anthony Mason	.50
35	Ray Allen	3.75
36	Arvydas Sabonis	.50
37	Brian Grant	.50
38	Bryant Reeves	.50
39	Christian Laettner	.50
40	Tom Gugliotta	1.00
41	Latrell Sprewell	1.00
42	Erick Dampier	1.50
43	Gheorghe Muresan	.50
44	Glen Rice	1.00
45	Patrick Ewing	1.00
46	Jim Jackson	.50
47	Michael Finley	1.00
48	Toni Kukoc	1.00
49	Marcus Camby	3.75
50	Kenny Anderson	.50
51	Mark Price	.50
52	Tim Hardaway	1.25
53	Mookie Blaylock	.50
54	Steve Smith	.50
55	Terrell Brandon	1.00
56	Lorenzen Wright	1.50
57	Sasha Danilovic	.50
58	Jeff Hornacek	.50
59	Eddie Jones	1.75
60	Vin Baker	1.50
61	Chris Childs	.50
62	Clifford Robinson	.50
63	Anthony Peeler	.50
64	Dino Radja	.50
65	Joe Dumars	.50
66	Loy Vaught	.50
67	Rony Seikaly	.50
68	Vitaly Potapenko	1.00
69	Chris Gatling	.50
70	Dale Ellis	.50
71	Allan Houston	1.00
72	Doug Christie	.50
73	LaPhonso Ellis	.50
74	Kendall Gill	.50
75	Rik Smits	.50
76	Bobby Phills	.50
77	Malik Sealy	.50
78	Sean Elliott	.50
79	Vlade Divac	.50
80	David Wesley	.50
81	Dominique Wilkins	.50
82	Danny Manning	.50
83	Detlef Schrempf	.50
84	Hersey Hawkins	.50
85	Lindsey Hunter	.50
86	Mahmoud Abdul-Rauf	.50
87	Shawn Bradley	.50
88	Horace Grant	.50
89	Cedric Ceballos	.50
90	Jamal Mashburn	1.00

1996-97 Flair Showcase Row 0

This 90-card set featured each player in the Flair Showcase set and was the most difficult of the three frontal designs to get. Row 0, or Showcase fronts displayed an action shot of the player on a gold, sparkling background, with a closeup shot in the bottom right. Showcase fronts with a Showtime back were inserted one per five packs, Showcase/Showstoppers were one per 10 packs and Showcase/Showpiece were one per 24. The 90-card set had 30 cards with each type of card back.

		MT
Complete Set (90):		1200.
Common Player (1-30):		10.00
Common Player (31-60):		2.00
Minor Stars (31-60):		4.00
Common Player (61-90):		.50
Minor Stars (61-90):		1.00
1	Anfernee Hardaway	50.00
2	Mitch Richmond	10.00
3	Allen Iverson	70.00
4	Charles Barkley	20.00
5	Juwan Howard	20.00
6	David Robinson	20.00
7	Gary Payton	20.00
8	Kerry Kittles	15.00
9	Dennis Rodman	40.00
10	Shaquille O'Neal	50.00
11	Stephon Marbury	60.00
12	John Stockton	10.00
13	Glenn Robinson	10.00
14	Hakeem Olajuwon	30.00
15	Jason Kidd	20.00
16	Jerry Stackhouse	20.00
17	Joe Smith	20.00
18	Reggie Miller	10.00
19	Grant Hill	60.00
20	Damon Stoudamire	25.00
21	Kevin Garnett	80.00
22	Clyde Drexler	20.00
23	Michael Jordan	150.00
24	Antonio McDyess	15.00
25	Chris Webber	30.00
26	Antoine Walker	30.00
27	Scottie Pippen	30.00
28	Karl Malone	20.00
29	Shareef Abdur-Rahim	40.00
30	Shawn Kemp	15.00
31	Kobe Bryant	100.00
32	Derrick Coleman	4.00
33	Alonzo Mourning	6.00
34	Anthony Mason	2.00
35	Ray Allen	12.00
36	Arvydas Sabonis	2.00
37	Brian Grant	2.00
38	Bryant Reeves	2.00
39	Christian Laettner	4.00
40	Tom Gugliotta	4.00
41	Latrell Sprewell	4.00
42	Erick Dampier	5.00
43	Gheorghe Muresan	2.00
44	Glen Rice	4.00
45	Patrick Ewing	4.00
46	Jim Jackson	2.00
47	Michael Finley	4.00
48	Toni Kukoc	4.00
49	Marcus Camby	12.00
50	Kenny Anderson	2.00
51	Mark Price	2.00
52	Tim Hardaway	10.00
53	Mookie Blaylock	2.00
54	Steve Smith	2.00
55	Terrell Brandon	4.00
56	Lorenzen Wright	5.00
57	Sasha Danilovic	2.00
58	Jeff Hornacek	2.00
59	Eddie Jones	20.00
60	Vin Baker	10.00
61	Chris Childs	.50
62	Clifford Robinson	.50
63	Anthony Peeler	.50
64	Dino Radja	.50
65	Joe Dumars	1.00
66	Loy Vaught	.50
67	Rony Seikaly	.50
68	Vitaly Potapenko	2.00
69	Chris Gatling	.50
70	Dale Ellis	.50
71	Allan Houston	1.00
72	Doug Christie	.50
73	LaPhonso Ellis	.50
74	Kendall Gill	.50
75	Rik Smits	.50
76	Bobby Phills	.50
77	Malik Sealy	.50
78	Sean Elliott	.50

79	Vlade Divac	.50
80	David Wesley	.50
81	Dominique Wilkins	.50
82	Danny Manning	.50
83	Detlef Schrempf	.50
84	Hersey Hawkins	.50
85	Lindsey Hunter	1.00
86	Mahmoud Abdul-Rauf	.50
87	Shawn Bradley	1.00
88	Horace Grant	.50
89	Cedric Ceballos	.50
90	Jamal Mashburn	1.00

1996-97 Flair Showcase Legacy

All 270 cards were included in the Legacy parallel set, with three different versions for each player. Fronts were stamped in blue foil instead of the gold used on base cards, while glossy finish was removed from the backs. Backs contained a matte finish and were serial numbered to 150 sets.

		MT
Common Player:		10.00
Minor Stars:		20.00
Each Player Has Three Different Cards.		
1	Anfernee Hardaway	250.00
2	Mitch Richmond	40.00
3	Allen Iverson	300.00
4	Charles Barkley	60.00
5	Juwan Howard	60.00
6	David Robinson	60.00
7	Gary Payton	60.00
8	Kerry Kittles	70.00
9	Dennis Rodman	200.00
10	Shaquille O'Neal	250.00
11	Stephon Marbury	250.00
12	John Stockton	40.00
13	Glenn Robinson	40.00
14	Hakeem Olajuwon	100.00
15	Jason Kidd	80.00
16	Jerry Stackhouse	60.00
17	Joe Smith	60.00
18	Reggie Miller	40.00
19	Grant Hill	275.00
20	Damon Stoudamire	90.00
21	Kevin Garnett	300.00
22	Clyde Drexler	50.00
23	Michael Jordan	600.00
24	Antonio McDyess	50.00
25	Chris Webber	100.00
26	Antoine Walker	100.00
27	Scottie Pippen	125.00
28	Karl Malone	50.00
29	Shareef Abdur-Rahim	160.00
30	Shawn Kemp	60.00
31	Kobe Bryant	700.00
32	Derrick Coleman	20.00
33	Alonzo Mourning	40.00
34	Anthony Mason	10.00
35	Ray Allen	75.00
36	Arvydas Sabonis	10.00
37	Brian Grant	10.00
38	Bryant Reeves	10.00
39	Christian Laettner	20.00
40	Tom Gugliotta	20.00
41	Latrell Sprewell	50.00
42	Erick Dampier	20.00
43	Gheorghe Muresan	10.00
44	Glen Rice	40.00
45	Patrick Ewing	40.00
46	Jim Jackson	20.00
47	Michael Finley	30.00
48	Toni Kukoc	30.00
49	Marcus Camby	70.00
50	Kenny Anderson	20.00
51	Mark Price	10.00
52	Tim Hardaway	30.00
53	Mookie Blaylock	10.00
54	Steve Smith	10.00
55	Terrell Brandon	30.00
56	Lorenzen Wright	20.00
57	Sasha Danilovic	10.00
58	Jeff Hornacek	10.00
59	Eddie Jones	100.00
60	Vin Baker	50.00
61	Chris Childs	10.00
62	Clifford Robinson	10.00
63	Anthony Peeler	10.00
64	Dino Radja	10.00
65	Joe Dumars	20.00
66	Loy Vaught	10.00
67	Rony Seikaly	10.00
68	Vitaly Potapenko	20.00
69	Chris Gatling	10.00
70	Dale Ellis	10.00
71	Allan Houston	20.00
72	Doug Christie	10.00
73	LaPhonso Ellis	10.00
74	Kendall Gill	10.00
75	Rik Smits	10.00
76	Bobby Phills	10.00
77	Malik Sealy	10.00
78	Sean Elliott	10.00
79	Vlade Divac	10.00
80	David Wesley	10.00
81	Dominique Wilkins	10.00
82	Danny Manning	10.00
83	Detlef Schrempf	10.00
84	Hersey Hawkins	10.00
85	Lindsey Hunter	10.00
86	Mahmoud Abdul-Rauf	10.00
87	Shawn Bradley	10.00
88	Horace Grant	10.00
89	Cedric Ceballos	10.00
90	Jamal Mashburn	20.00

1996-97 Flair Showcase Class of '96

This 20-card insert set features top players from the 1996 NBA Draft on a white background, with the words "Class of Ninety-six" written in script up the left side. Cards were inserted in one per five packs.

		MT
Complete Set (20):		70.00
Common Player:		1.50
1	Shareef Abdur-Rahim	6.00
2	Ray Allen	10.00
3	Shandon Anderson	1.50
4	Kobe Bryant	40.00
5	Marcus Camby	3.00
6	Erick Dampier	3.00
7	Derek Fisher	2.00
8	Todd Fuller	1.50
9	Othella Harrington	1.50
10	Allen Iverson	20.00
11	Kerry Kittles	5.00
12	Travis Knight	2.00
13	Matt Maloney	3.00
14	Stephon Marbury	8.00
15	Steve Nash	4.00
16	Jermaine O'Neal	4.00
17	Vitaly Potapenko	1.50
18	Roy Rogers	1.50
19	Antoine Walker	3.00
20	Lorenzen Wright	3.00

1996-97 Flair Showcase Hot Shots

This 20-card insert features some of the top players in the NBA on a die-cut in the shape of flames design. The player is pictured over a basketball, with orange and red flames throughout the background. Hot Shots were inserted one per 90 packs.

		MT
Complete Set (20):		700.00
Common Player:		12.00
1	Michael Jordan	175.00
2	Kevin Garnett	80.00
3	Damon Stoudamire	30.00
4	Anfernee Hardaway	60.00
5	Shaquille O'Neal	60.00
6	Grant Hill	75.00
7	Dennis Rodman	50.00
8	Shawn Kemp	20.00
9	Scottie Pippen	40.00
10	Juwan Howard	20.00
11	Jason Kidd	20.00
12	Hakeem Olajuwon	30.00
13	Karl Malone	12.00
14	Joe Smith	20.00
15	David Robinson	20.00
16	Jerry Stackhouse	20.00
17	Antonio McDyess	20.00
18	Clyde Drexler	12.00
19	Gary Payton	20.00
20	Eddie Jones	25.00

1997-98 Flair Showcase Promo Sheet

This four-card promo sheet pictured Grant Hill on four different Flair Showcase cards, including one from each of the four different rows. The sheet was issued to promote the 1997-98 set.

		MT
Complete Set (4):		4.00
Common Player:		1.00
2	Grant Hill (Flair - Row 0)	1.00
2	Grant Hill (Style - Row 1)	1.00
2	Grant Hill (Grace - Row 2)	1.00
2	Grant Hill (Showcase - Row 3)	1.00

1997-98 Flair Showcase Row 3

All 80 cards in Flair Showcase arrived in a Flair, or Row 3 front, with one of four different backs. Flair fronts with Showtime backs were inserted slightly less than one per pack, Flair/Showstopper one per 1.1, Flair/ Showdown 1:1.5 and Flair Showpiece one per two packs. Flair fronts have a very close shot of the player on the left, with an action shot over it and a silver foil background.

		MT
Complete Set (80):		70.00
Common Player:		.25
Minor Stars:		.50
Pack (5):		10.00
Wax Box (24):		225.00
1	Michael Jordan	10.00
2	Grant Hill	5.00
3	Allen Iverson	4.00
4	Kevin Garnett	5.00
5	*Tim Duncan*	20.00
6	Shawn Kemp	1.00
7	Shaquille O'Neal	3.00
8	Antoine Walker	3.00
9	Shareef Abdur-Rahim	2.50
10	Damon Stoudamire	1.50
11	Anfernee Hardaway	3.00
12	*Keith Van Horn*	8.00
13	Dennis Rodman	3.00
14	*Ron Mercer*	10.00
15	Stephon Marbury	5.00
16	Scottie Pippen	2.50
17	Kerry Kittles	.75
18	Kobe Bryant	7.00
19	Marcus Camby	.75
20	*Chauncey Billups*	5.00
21	*Tracy McGrady*	12.00
22	Joe Smith	.50
23	*Brevin Knight*	5.00
24	*Danny Fortson*	2.00
25	*Tim Thomas*	8.00
26	Gary Payton	1.00
27	David Robinson	1.00
28	Hakeem Olajuwon	1.50
29	*Antonio Daniels*	3.00
30	Antonio McDyess	.75
31	Eddie Jones	1.00
32	*Adonal Foyle*	.50
33	Glenn Robinson	.50
34	Charles Barkley	1.00
35	Vin Baker	1.00
36	Jerry Stackhouse	.50
37	Ray Allen	.75
38	*Derek Anderson*	5.00
39	Isaac Austin	.25
40	*Tony Battie*	2.00
41	*Tariq Abdul-Wahad*	1.50
42	Dikembe Mutombo	.50
43	Clyde Drexler	.75
44	Chris Mullin	.50
45	Tim Hardaway	.75
46	Terrell Brandon	.50
47	John Stockton	.50
48	Patrick Ewing	.50
49	Horace Grant	.25
50	Tom Gugliotta	.50
51	Mookie Blaylock	.25
52	Mitch Richmond	.50
53	Anthony Mason	.25
54	Michael Finley	.50
55	Jason Kidd	1.00
56	Karl Malone	1.00
57	Reggie Miller	.50
58	Steve Smith	.25
59	Glen Rice	.50
60	Bryant Stith	.25
61	Loy Vaught	.25
62	Brian Grant	.25
63	Joe Dumars	.25
64	Juwan Howard	.75
65	Rik Smits	.25
66	Alonzo Mourning	.50
67	Allan Houston	.50
68	Chris Webber	1.00
69	Kendall Gill	.25
70	Rony Seikaly	.25
71	Kenny Anderson	.25
72	John Wallace	.25
73	Bryant Reeves	.25
74	Brian Williams	.25
75	Larry Johnson	.50
76	Shawn Bradley	.25
77	Kevin Johnson	.25
78	Rod Strickland	.25
79	Rodney Rogers	.25
80	Rasheed Wallace	.25

1997-98 Flair Showcase Row 2

All 80 cards in Flair Showcase arrived in Row 2, or Style fronts, with four different backs to match. Style fronts with a Showtime back were inserted one per 2.5 packs, Style/Showstopper one per three, Style/Showdown one per 3.5 and Style/Showpiece cards were inserted one per four packs. The Row 2 fronts feature two shots of the player on a darkened, glossy background.

		MT
Complete Set (80):		175.00
Common Player:		.50
Minor Stars:		1.00
1	Michael Jordan	15.00
2	Grant Hill	7.50
3	Allen Iverson	6.00
4	Kevin Garnett	7.50
5	Tim Duncan	30.00
6	Shawn Kemp	1.50
7	Shaquille O'Neal	4.50
8	Antoine Walker	4.00
9	Shareef Abdur-Rahim	4.00
10	Damon Stoudamire	2.00
11	Anfernee Hardaway	4.50
12	Keith Van Horn	12.00
13	Dennis Rodman	4.50
14	Ron Mercer	15.00
15	Stephon Marbury	7.50
16	Scottie Pippen	4.00
17	Kerry Kittles	1.25
18	Kobe Bryant	10.00
19	Marcus Camby	1.25
20	Chauncey Billups	7.50
21	Tracy McGrady	12.00
22	Joe Smith	1.00
23	Brevin Knight	7.50
24	Danny Fortson	3.00
25	Tim Thomas	12.00
26	Gary Payton	1.50
27	David Robinson	1.50
28	Hakeem Olajuwon	2.50
29	Antonio Daniels	4.50
30	Antonio McDyess	1.25
31	Eddie Jones	1.50
32	Adonal Foyle	1.00
33	Glenn Robinson	1.00
34	Charles Barkley	1.50
35	Vin Baker	1.50
36	Jerry Stackhouse	1.00
37	Ray Allen	1.25
38	Derek Anderson	7.50
39	Isaac Austin	.50
40	Tony Battie	3.00
41	Tariq Abdul-Wahad	2.50
42	Dikembe Mutombo	1.00
43	Clyde Drexler	1.25
44	Chris Mullin	1.00
45	Tim Hardaway	1.25
46	Terrell Brandon	1.00
47	John Stockton	1.00
48	Patrick Ewing	1.00
49	Horace Grant	.50
50	Tom Gugliotta	1.00
51	Mookie Blaylock	.50
52	Mitch Richmond	1.00
53	Anthony Mason	.50
54	Michael Finley	1.00
55	Jason Kidd	1.50
56	Karl Malone	1.50
57	Reggie Miller	1.00
58	Steve Smith	.50
59	Glen Rice	1.00
60	Bryant Stith	.50
61	Loy Vaught	.50
62	Brian Grant	.50
63	Joe Dumars	.50
64	Juwan Howard	1.25
65	Rik Smits	.50
66	Alonzo Mourning	1.00
67	Allan Houston	1.00
68	Chris Webber	1.50
69	Kendall Gill	.50
70	Rony Seikaly	.50
71	Kenny Anderson	.50
72	John Wallace	.50
73	Bryant Reeves	.50
74	Brian Williams	.50
75	Larry Johnson	1.00
76	Shawn Bradley	.50
77	Kevin Johnson	.50
78	Rod Strickland	.50
79	Rodney Rogers	.50
80	Rasheed Wallace	.50

1997-98 Flair Showcase Row 1

All 80 cards in Flair Showcase arrived in Grace, or Row 1 versions, with four different backs to match. Grace fronts with Showtime backs were inserted one per six packs, Grace/Showstopper were seeded one per 10, Grace/ Showdown one per 16 and Grace/Showpiece were seeded one per 24 packs. The Row 1 cards have a prismatic foil background and feature two shots of the player.

		MT
Complete Set (80):		800.00
Common Player (1-20):		5.00
Minor Stars (1-20):		10.00
Common Player (21-40):		10.00
Common Player (41-60):		.50
Minor Stars (41-60):		1.00
Common Player (61-80):		2.00
Minor Stars (61-80):		4.00
1	Michael Jordan	80.00
2	Grant Hill	40.00
3	Allen Iverson	30.00
4	Kevin Garnett	40.00
5	Tim Duncan	60.00
6	Shawn Kemp	8.00
7	Shaquille O'Neal	25.00
8	Antoine Walker	20.00
9	Shareef Abdur-Rahim	20.00
10	Damon Stoudamire	12.00
11	Anfernee Hardaway	25.00
12	Keith Van Horn	25.00
13	Dennis Rodman	25.00
14	Ron Mercer	30.00
15	Stephon Marbury	40.00
16	Scottie Pippen	20.00
17	Kerry Kittles	10.00
18	Kobe Bryant	50.00
19	Marcus Camby	10.00
20	Chauncey Billups	15.00
21	Tracy McGrady	50.00
22	Joe Smith	10.00
23	Brevin Knight	35.00
24	Danny Fortson	15.00
25	Tim Thomas	55.00
26	Gary Payton	15.00
27	David Robinson	15.00
28	Hakeem Olajuwon	22.00
29	Antonio Daniels	20.00
30	Antonio McDyess	12.00
31	Eddie Jones	15.00
32	Adonal Foyle	10.00
33	Glenn Robinson	10.00
34	Charles Barkley	15.00
35	Vin Baker	15.00
36	Jerry Stackhouse	10.00
37	Ray Allen	12.00
38	Derek Anderson	35.00
39	Isaac Austin	10.00
40	Tony Battie	15.00
41	Tariq Abdul-Wahad	3.00
42	Dikembe Mutombo	1.00
43	Clyde Drexler	1.50
44	Chris Mullin	1.00
45	Tim Hardaway	1.50
46	Terrell Brandon	1.00
47	John Stockton	1.00
48	Patrick Ewing	1.00
49	Horace Grant	.50
50	Tom Gugliotta	1.00
51	Mookie Blaylock	.50
52	Mitch Richmond	1.00
53	Anthony Mason	.50
54	Michael Finley	1.00
55	Jason Kidd	3.00
56	Karl Malone	3.00
57	Reggie Miller	1.00
58	Steve Smith	.50
59	Glen Rice	1.00
60	Bryant Stith	.50
61	Loy Vaught	2.00
62	Brian Grant	2.00
63	Joe Dumars	2.00
64	Juwan Howard	5.00
65	Rik Smits	2.00
66	Alonzo Mourning	4.00
67	Allan Houston	4.00
68	Chris Webber	6.00
69	Kendall Gill	2.00
70	Rony Seikaly	2.00
71	Kenny Anderson	2.00
72	John Wallace	2.00
73	Bryant Reeves	2.00
74	Brian Williams	2.00
75	Larry Johnson	4.00
76	Shawn Bradley	2.00
77	Kevin Johnson	2.00
78	Rod Strickland	2.00
79	Rodney Rogers	2.00
80	Rasheed Wallace	2.00

1997-98 Flair Showcase Row 0

All 80 players in Flair Showcase horizontal, prismatic foil verions called Row 0. Each card in Row 0 was sequentially numbered, with cards 1-20 numbered to 250, 21-40 numbered to 500, cards 41-60 numbered to 1,000 and cards 61-80 numbered to 2,000. Parallel Legacy Collection versions of each also exist, but are distinguished by blue foil and numbering to 100 on the back.

		MT
Common Player (1-20):		25.00
Production 250 Sets		
Common Player (21-40):		5.00
Minor Stars (21-40):		10.00
Production 500 Sets		1.00
Common Player (41-60):		4.00
Minor Stars (41-60):		8.00
Production 1,000 Sets		
Common Player (61-80):		3.00
Minor Stars (61-80):		6.00
Production 2,000 Sets		
1	Michael Jordan	300.00
2	Grant Hill	150.00
3	Allen Iverson	100.00
4	Kevin Garnett	150.00
5	Tim Duncan	150.00
6	Shawn Kemp	40.00
7	Shaquille O'Neal	100.00
8	Antoine Walker	60.00
9	Shareef Abdur-Rahim	75.00
10	Damon Stoudamire	50.00
11	Anfernee Hardaway	100.00
12	Keith Van Horn	50.00
13	Dennis Rodman	100.00
14	Ron Mercer	100.00
15	Stephon Marbury	125.00
16	Scottie Pippen	75.00
17	Kerry Kittles	25.00
18	Kobe Bryant	200.00
19	Marcus Camby	25.00
20	Chauncey Billups	50.00
21	Tracy McGrady	50.00
22	Joe Smith	10.00
23	Brevin Knight	25.00
24	Danny Fortson	10.00
25	Tim Thomas	50.00
26	Gary Payton	25.00
27	David Robinson	25.00
28	Hakeem Olajuwon	30.00
29	Antonio Daniels	20.00
30	Antonio McDyess	15.00
31	Eddie Jones	35.00
32	Adonal Foyle	10.00
33	Glenn Robinson	10.00
34	Charles Barkley	25.00
35	Vin Baker	25.00
36	Jerry Stackhouse	10.00
37	Ray Allen	20.00
38	Derek Anderson	25.00
39	Isaac Austin	5.00
40	Tony Battie	10.00
41	Tariq Abdul-Wahad	4.00
42	Dikembe Mutombo	8.00
43	Clyde Drexler	12.00
44	Chris Mullin	8.00
45	Tim Hardaway	12.00
46	Terrell Brandon	8.00
47	John Stockton	8.00
48	Patrick Ewing	8.00
49	Horace Grant	4.00
50	Tom Gugliotta	8.00
51	Mookie Blaylock	4.00
52	Mitch Richmond	8.00
53	Anthony Mason	4.00
54	Michael Finley	8.00
55	Jason Kidd	20.00
56	Karl Malone	15.00
57	Reggie Miller	8.00
58	Steve Smith	4.00
59	Glen Rice	8.00
60	Bryant Stith	4.00
61	Loy Vaught	3.00
62	Brian Grant	3.00
63	Joe Dumars	6.00
64	Juwan Howard	6.00
65	Rik Smits	3.00
66	Alonzo Mourning	6.00
67	Allan Houston	6.00
68	Chris Webber	12.00
69	Kendall Gill	3.00
70	Rony Seikaly	3.00
71	Kenny Anderson	3.00
72	John Wallace	3.00
73	Bryant Reeves	3.00
74	Brian Williams	3.00
75	Larry Johnson	6.00
76	Shawn Bradley	3.00
77	Kevin Johnson	3.00
78	Rod Strickland	3.00
79	Rodney Rogers	3.00
80	Rasheed Wallace	3.00

1997-98 Flair Showcase Legacy

Legacy was a 320-card parallel that reprinted each card in all versions of Flair Showcase. A blue foil was added to the front, while the glossy finish was taken away from the back. The matte finish on the back was sequentially numbered to 100 sets. Rarer versions, called Legacy Masterpieces, were also produced and limited to only one set. Masterpieces used a purple foil versus the blue used in Legacy.

		MT
Common Player:		10.00
Minor Stars:		20.00
Each Player Has Four Different Cards.		
1	Michael Jordan	600.00
2	Grant Hill	250.00
3	Allen Iverson	200.00
4	Kevin Garnett	250.00
5	Tim Duncan	350.00
6	Shawn Kemp	50.00
7	Shaquille O'Neal	175.00
8	Antoine Walker	75.00
9	Shareef Abdur-Rahim	125.00
10	Damon Stoudamire	75.00
11	Anfernee Hardaway	175.00
12	Keith Van Horn	150.00
13	Dennis Rodman	175.00
14	Ron Mercer	175.00
15	Stephon Marbury	200.00
16	Scottie Pippen	125.00
17	Kerry Kittles	35.00
18	Kobe Bryant	325.00
19	Marcus Camby	35.00
20	Chauncey Billups	100.00
21	Tracy McGrady	150.00
22	Joe Smith	35.00
23	Brevin Knight	100.00
24	Danny Fortson	50.00
25	Tim Thomas	150.00
26	Gary Payton	75.00
27	David Robinson	75.00
28	Hakeem Olajuwon	90.00
29	Antonio Daniels	70.00
30	Antonio McDyess	50.00
31	Eddie Jones	80.00
32	Adonal Foyle	35.00
33	Glenn Robinson	40.00
34	Charles Barkley	75.00
35	Vin Baker	80.00
36	Jerry Stackhouse	35.00
37	Ray Allen	35.00
38	Derek Anderson	100.00
39	Isaac Austin	10.00
40	Tony Battie	50.00
41	Tariq Abdul-Wahad	40.00
42	Dikembe Mutombo	20.00
43	Clyde Drexler	50.00
44	Chris Mullin	20.00
45	Tim Hardaway	40.00
46	Terrell Brandon	20.00
47	John Stockton	40.00
48	Patrick Ewing	40.00
49	Horace Grant	10.00
50	Tom Gugliotta	20.00
51	Mookie Blaylock	10.00
52	Mitch Richmond	40.00
53	Anthony Mason	10.00
54	Michael Finley	20.00
55	Jason Kidd	80.00
56	Karl Malone	50.00
57	Reggie Miller	40.00
58	Steve Smith	10.00
59	Glen Rice	40.00
60	Bryant Stith	10.00
61	Loy Vaught	10.00
62	Brian Grant	10.00
63	Joe Dumars	10.00
64	Juwan Howard	50.00
65	Rik Smits	10.00
66	Alonzo Mourning	40.00
67	Allan Houston	20.00
68	Chris Webber	90.00
69	Kendall Gill	10.00
70	Rony Seikaly	10.00
71	Kenny Anderson	10.00
72	John Wallace	10.00
73	Bryant Reeves	10.00
74	Brian Williams	10.00
75	Larry Johnson	20.00
76	Shawn Bradley	10.00
77	Kevin Johnson	10.00
78	Rod Strickland	10.00
79	Rodney Rogers	10.00
80	Rasheed Wallace	10.00

1997-98 Flair Showcase Wave of the Future

Wave of the Future inserts showcases 12 different rookies not included in the set. The cards feature one cardboard card in plastic inside another outer coating of plastic, with the inner area filled with an oil substance and glitter. Backs are numbered with a "WF" prefix and the cards were inserted one per 20 packs.

		MT
Complete Set (12):		30.00
Common Player:		2.50
WF1	Corey Beck	2.50
WF2	Maurice Taylor	10.00
WF3	Chris Antsey	5.00
WF4	Keith Booth	2.50
WF5	Anthony Parker	2.50
WF6	Austin Croshere	5.00
WF7	Jacque Vaughn	5.00
WF8	God Shammgod	2.50
WF9	Bobby Jackson	6.00
WF10	Johnny Taylor	2.50
WF11	Ed Gray	5.00
WF12	Kelvin Cato	5.00

1998-99 Flair Showcase Promos

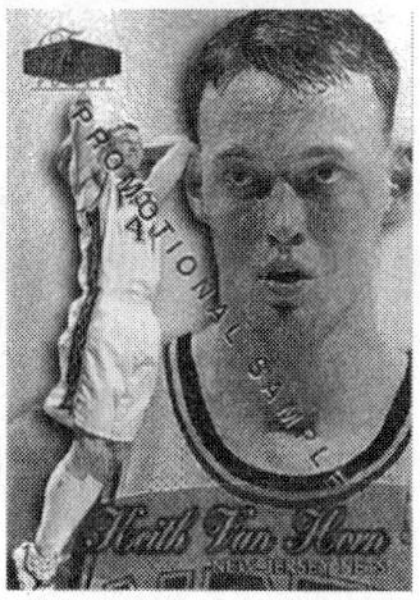

		MT
Complete Set (3):		3.00
Common Player:		1.00
1	Keith Van Horn Class 3	1.00
2	Keith Van Horn Class 2	1.00
3	Keith Van Horn Class 1	1.00

1998-99 Flair Showcase Row 3

Row 3, or Power, included all 90 players in Flair Showcase and was the easiest version to obtain from packs. Fronts featured a larger close-up shot and a smaller action shot of the player over silver background. Showtime cards (1-30) were inserted 1:.82 packs, Showdown cards (31-60) were inserted 1:1 pack and Showpiece cards (61-90) were inserted 1:1.2 packs.

		MT
Complete Set (90):		60.00
Common Player:		.25
Minor Stars:		.50
Common Rookie:		.75
1-30 Inserted 1:.08		
31-60 Inserted 1:1		
61-90 Inserted 1:1.2		
Pack (4):		3.00
Wax Box (24):		60.00
1	Keith Van Horn	1.00
2	Kobe Bryant	3.00
3	Tim Duncan	2.50
4	Kevin Garnett	2.50
5	Grant Hill	2.50
6	Allen Iverson	2.00
7	Shaquille O'Neal	1.50
8	Antoine Walker	1.00
9	Shareef Abdur-Rahim	1.00
10	Stephon Marbury	1.50
11	Ray Allen	.60
12	Shawn Kemp	.60
13	Tim Thomas	1.00
14	Scottie Pippen	1.00
15	Latrell Sprewell	.50
16	*Dirk Nowitzki*	8.00
17	*Antawn Jamison*	6.00
18	Anfernee Hardaway	1.25
19	*Larry Hughes*	6.00
20	*Robert Traylor*	1.00
21	Kerry Kittles	.50
22	Ron Mercer	1.00
23	*Michael Olowokandi*	2.00
24	Jason Kidd	1.00
25	*Vince Carter*	25.00
26	Charles Barkley	.75
27	Antonio McDyess	.75
28	*Mike Bibby*	3.00
29	*Paul Pierce*	6.00
30	*Raef LaFrentz*	2.50
31	Reggie Miller	.50
32	Michael Finley	.50
33	Eddie Jones	.60
34	Tim Hardaway	.60
35	Glenn Robinson	.60
36	Brevin Knight	.60
37	Gary Payton	.75
38	David Robinson	.75
39	Karl Malone	.75
40	Derek Anderson	.50
41	Patrick Ewing	.50
42	Juwan Howard	.50
43	Jayson Williams	.50
44	Terrell Brandon	.50
45	Hakeem Olajuwon	.75
46	Isaac Austin	.25
47	Glen Rice	.50
48	Maurice Taylor	.60
49	Damon Stoudamire	.60
50	*Brian Skinner*	1.00
51	*Nazr Mohammed*	1.00
52	Tom Gugliotta	.50
53	*Al Harrington*	3.00
54	*Pat Garrity*	1.00
55	*Jason Williams*	5.00
56	Tracy McGrady	1.00
57	*Keon Clark*	1.50
58	Vin Baker	.60
59	*Bonzi Wells*	5.00
60	John Stockton	.50
61	Isaiah Rider	.50
62	Alonzo Mourning	.50
63	Allan Houston	.50
64	Dennis Rodman	1.00
65	*Felipe Lopez*	1.50
66	Joe Smith	.50
67	Chris Webber	1.00
68	Mitch Richmond	.50
69	Brent Barry	.25
70	Mookie Blaylock	.25
71	Donyell Marshall	.25
72	Anthony Mason	.25
73	Rod Strickland	.25
74	*Roshown McLeod*	1.50
75	*Matt Harpring*	1.50
76	Detlef Schrempf	.25
77	*Michael Dickerson*	2.00
78	*Michael Doleac*	1.00
79	John Starks	.25
80	*Ricky Davis*	2.00
81	Steve Smith	.50
82	Voshon Lenard	.50
83	Toni Kukoc	.60
84	Steve Nash	.50
85	Vlade Divac	.25
86	Rasheed Wallace	.50
87	Bryon Russell	.25
88	Antonio Daniels	.50
89	Rik Smits	.25
90	Joe Dumars	.50

1998-99 Flair Showcase Row 2

Row 2, or Passion, included all 90 cards in Flair Showcase and were identified by the player's uniform number shown prominently in the background. Showdown cards (1-30) were inserted 1:3 packs, Showpiece cards (31-60) were seeded 1:1.3 packs and Showtime cards (61-90) were inserted 1:2 packs.

	MT
Complete Set (90):	100.00
Common Player:	.50
Minor Stars:	1.00
Common Rookie:	1.50
Row 2 Cards:	1x-2x Row 3
1-30 Inserted 1:3	
31-60 Inserted 1:2	
61-90 Inserted 1:1.3	

1998-99 Flair Showcase Row 1

Row 1 featured all 90 players included in Flair Showcase on a horizontal format, with two close-up images divided by an action shot over the player's uniform number. Row 1 also included sequential numbering on the front in the upper left corner. Cards 1-30 were numbered to 1,500, cards 31-60 were numbered to 3,000 and cards 61-90 were numbered to 6,000.

		MT
Complete Set (90):		
1-30 Common:		3.00
1-30 Rookie:		3.00
1-30 Numbered to 1,500		
31-60 Common:		1.00
31-60 Rookie:		2.00
31-60 Numbered to 3,000		
61-90 Common:		.75
61-90 Rookie:		2.50
61-90 Numbered to 6,000		
1	Keith Van Horn	6.00
2	Kobe Bryant	25.00
3	Tim Duncan	20.00
4	Kevin Garnett	20.00
5	Grant Hill	20.00
6	Allen Iverson	15.00
7	Shaquille O'Neal	10.00
8	Antoine Walker	6.00
9	Shareef Abdur-Rahim	6.00
10	Stephon Marbury	10.00
11	Ray Allen	4.00
12	Shawn Kemp	3.00
13	Tim Thomas	6.00
14	Scottie Pippen	6.00
15	Latrell Sprewell	3.00
16	*Dirk Nowitzki*	10.00
17	*Antawn Jamison*	15.00
18	Anfernee Hardaway	8.00
19	*Larry Hughes*	12.00
20	*Robert Traylor*	8.00
21	Kerry Kittles	3.00
22	Ron Mercer	6.00
23	*Michael Olowokandi*	8.00
24	Jason Kidd	6.00
25	*Vince Carter*	40.00
26	Charles Barkley	5.00
27	Antonio McDyess	5.00
28	*Mike Bibby*	12.00
29	*Paul Pierce*	20.00
30	*Raef LaFrentz*	8.00
31	Reggie Miller	2.00
32	Michael Finley	2.00
33	Eddie Jones	2.50
34	Tim Hardaway	2.50
35	Glenn Robinson	2.00
36	Brevin Knight	2.50
37	Gary Payton	3.00
38	David Robinson	3.00
39	Karl Malone	3.00
40	Derek Anderson	2.00
41	Patrick Ewing	2.00
42	Juwan Howard	2.00
43	Jayson Williams	2.00
44	Terrell Brandon	2.00
45	Hakeem Olajuwon	3.00
46	Isaac Austin	1.00
47	Glen Rice	2.00
48	Maurice Taylor	2.50
49	Damon Stoudamire	2.50
50	*Brian Skinner*	2.00
51	*Nazr Mohammed*	2.00
52	Tom Gugliotta	2.00
53	*Al Harrington*	5.00
54	*Pat Garrity*	2.50
55	*Jason Williams*	25.00
56	Tracy McGrady	5.00
57	*Keon Clark*	3.00
58	Vin Baker	2.50
59	*Bonzi Wells*	2.50
60	John Stockton	1.50
61	Isaiah Rider	1.50
62	Alonzo Mourning	1.50
63	Allan Houston	1.50
64	Dennis Rodman	4.00
65	*Felipe Lopez*	3.00
66	Joe Smith	1.50
67	Chris Webber	4.00
68	Mitch Richmond	1.50
69	Brent Barry	.75
70	Mookie Blaylock	.75
71	Donyell Marshall	.75
72	Anthony Mason	.75
73	Rod Strickland	1.50
74	*Roshown McLeod*	2.50
75	*Matt Harpring*	3.00
76	Detlef Schrempf	.75
77	*Michael Dickerson*	5.00
78	*Michael Doleac*	2.50
79	John Starks	.75
80	*Ricky Davis*	2.50
81	Steve Smith	1.50
82	Voshon Lenard	.75
83	Toni Kukoc	2.00
84	Steve Nash	1.50
85	Vlade Divac	.75
86	Rasheed Wallace	1.50
87	Bryon Russell	.75
88	Antonio Daniels	1.50
89	Rik Smits	.75
90	Joe Dumars	1.50

1998-99 Flair Showcase Legacy Collection

Legacy Collection featured all 270 cards from Flair Showcase in a parallel version that added blue foil stamping and was sequentially numbered to 99 sets. All 90 cards from Row 1, Row 2 and Row 3 were paralleled so that each player had three Legacy Collection cards.

		MT
Common Player:		5.00
Common Rookie:		10.00
Stars:		10x-20x
Rookies:		10x-15x
Production 99 sets		
Each player had 3 different cards.		
1	Keith Van Horn	40.00
2	Kobe Bryant	150.00
3	Tim Duncan	125.00
4	Kevin Garnett	125.00
5	Grant Hill	125.00
6	Allen Iverson	100.00
7	Shaquille O'Neal	75.00
8	Antoine Walker	50.00
9	Shareef Abdur-Rahim	50.00
10	Stephon Marbury	75.00
11	Ray Allen	25.00
12	Shawn Kemp	30.00
13	Tim Thomas	50.00
14	Scottie Pippen	50.00
15	Latrell Sprewell	20.00
16	*Dirk Nowitzki*	60.00
17	*Antawn Jamison*	120.00
18	Anfernee Hardaway	60.00
19	*Larry Hughes*	80.00
20	*Robert Traylor*	50.00
21	Kerry Kittles	20.00
22	Ron Mercer	50.00
23	*Michael Olowokandi*	50.00
24	Jason Kidd	50.00
25	*Vince Carter*	250.00
26	Charles Barkley	30.00
27	Antonio McDyess	30.00
28	*Mike Bibby*	75.00
29	*Paul Pierce*	150.00
30	*Raef LaFrentz*	50.00
31	Reggie Miller	20.00
32	Michael Finley	20.00
33	Eddie Jones	25.00
34	Tim Hardaway	25.00
35	Glenn Robinson	20.00
36	Brevin Knight	25.00
37	Gary Payton	30.00
38	David Robinson	30.00
39	Karl Malone	30.00
40	Derek Anderson	20.00
41	Patrick Ewing	20.00
42	Juwan Howard	20.00
43	Jayson Williams	20.00
44	Terrell Brandon	20.00
45	Hakeem Olajuwon	30.00
46	Isaac Austin	10.00
47	Glen Rice	20.00
48	Maurice Taylor	25.00
49	Damon Stoudamire	25.00
50	*Brian Skinner*	20.00
51	*Nazr Mohammed*	20.00
52	Tom Gugliotta	20.00
53	*Al Harrington*	40.00
54	*Pat Garrity*	20.00
55	*Jason Williams*	200.00
56	Tracy McGrady	50.00
57	*Keon Clark*	30.00
58	Vin Baker	25.00
59	*Bonzi Wells*	20.00
60	John Stockton	20.00
61	Isaiah Rider	20.00
62	Alonzo Mourning	20.00
63	Allan Houston	20.00
64	Dennis Rodman	50.00
65	*Felipe Lopez*	40.00
66	Joe Smith	20.00
67	Chris Webber	50.00
68	Mitch Richmond	20.00
69	Brent Barry	10.00
70	Mookie Blaylock	10.00
71	Donyell Marshall	10.00
72	Anthony Mason	10.00
73	Rod Strickland	20.00
74	*Roshown McLeod*	30.00
75	*Matt Harpring*	40.00
76	Detlef Schrempf	10.00
77	*Michael Dickerson*	60.00
78	*Michael Doleac*	30.00
79	John Starks	10.00
80	*Ricky Davis*	30.00
81	Steve Smith	20.00
82	Voshon Lenard	10.00
83	Toni Kukoc	25.00
84	Steve Nash	20.00
85	Vlade Divac	10.00
86	Rasheed Wallace	20.00
87	Bryon Russell	10.00
88	Antonio Daniels	20.00
89	Rik Smits	10.00
90	Joe Dumars	20.00

1998-99 Flair Showcase Class of '98

This 15-card insert featured the top rookies from the 1998 NBA Draft. Cards were sequentially numbered to 500 sets and featured full holofoil fronts with a sculptured embossed logo and player image. Class of '98 inserts were numbered with a "C" suffix.

		MT
Complete Set (15):		200.00
Commmon Player:		5.00
Production 500 Sets		
1	Michael Olowokandi	10.00
2	Mike Bibby	12.00
3	Raef LaFrentz	12.00
4	Antawn Jamison	25.00
5	Vince Carter	100.00
6	Robert Traylor	6.00
7	Jason Williams	30.00
8	Larry Hughes	20.00
9	Dirk Nowitzki	25.00
10	Paul Pierce	25.00
11	Bonzi Wells	8.00
12	Michael Doleac	5.00
13	Michael Dickerson	6.00
14	Pat Garrity	4.00
15	Al Harrington	6.00

1998-99 Flair Showcase takeit2.net

takeit2.net was a 15-card insert set in Flair Showcase. Top veterans were included on cards sequentially numbered to 1,000 sets. Card fronts featured multiple foils and a laser die-cut resembling a computer circuit board. takeit2.net cards were numbered with a "TN" suffix.

		MT
Complete Set (15):		300.00
Common Player:		10.00
Production 1,000 Sets		
1	Scottie Pippen	10.00
2	Tim Duncan	30.00
3	Keith Van Horn	12.00
4	Grant Hill	30.00
5	Kobe Bryant	35.00
6	Antoine Walker	10.00
7	Kevin Garnett	30.00
8	Allen Iverson	25.00
9	Shareef Abdur-Rahim	12.00
10	Anfernee Hardaway	18.00
11	Stephon Marbury	20.00
12	Ron Mercer	12.00
13	Michael Jordan	75.00
14	Shaquille O'Neal	20.00
15	Shawn Kemp	6.00

1999-00 Flair Showcase

Flair Showcase consisted of 130 cards, including 100 veterans and 30 rookies, which are sequentially numbered to 2,000 sets. The base cards feature full-color photography merged with holographic foil and gold foil player and team name. The image of the featured player is in color, while the background is black-and-white. Rookie cards feature a black-and-white close-up shot in the background with a color shot in front. Each card is paralleled by th a Legacy and Masterpiece (one of one) set. Inserts include: Next, Ball of Fame, ConVINCEing, Guaranteed Fresh, License to Skill, Elevators, Fresh Ink, Fresh Ink Rock Steady, Feel the Game and Rookie Showcase Firsts.

		MT
Complete Set (130):		450.00
Common Player:		.25
Minor Stars:		.40
Common Rookie (101-130):		5.00
Production 2,000 Sets		
Pack (5):		5.00
Wax Box (24):		60.00
1	Vince Carter	5.00
2	Anfernee Hardaway	1.50
3	Nick Van Exel	.40
4	Kerry Kittles	.25
5	Michael Doleac	.40
6	Sean Elliott	.25
7	Shaquille O'Neal	2.50
8	Avery Johnson	.25
9	Brian Grant	.25
10	Jerome Williams	.25
11	Larry Hughes	1.25
12	Jerry Stackhouse	.40
13	Alonzo Mourning	.50
14	Antonio McDyess	.50
15	Jason Kidd	1.50

16	Bryon Russell	.25
17	Hakeem Olajuwon	.75
18	Juwan Howard	.40
19	Paul Pierce	1.25
20	Vin Baker	.40
21	Larry Johnson	.40
22	Gary Trent	.25
23	Jayson Williams	.25
24	Tim Hardaway	.60
25	Dirk Nowitzki	1.00
26	Jamal Mashburn	.40
27	Glenn Robinson	.40
28	Shawn Bradley	.25
29	Tom Gugliotta	.40
30	Vlade Divac	.25
31	David Robinson	.75
32	Matt Geiger	.25
33	Grant Hill	3.00
34	Maurice Taylor	.40
35	Toni Kukoc	.60
36	Cedric Ceballos	.25
37	Patrick Ewing	.40
38	Ray Allen	.50
39	Michael Finley	.40
40	Robert Traylor	.40
41	Brevin Knight	.25
42	Marcus Camby	.50
43	Sam Cassell	.40
44	Antawn Jamison	1.25
45	Steve Smith	.40
46	Darrell Armstrong	.25
47	Mookie Blaylock	.25
48	Derek Anderson	.40
49	Hersey Hawkins	.25
50	Kobe Bryant	4.00
51	Shawn Kemp	.40
52	Scottie Pippen	1.50
53	Chris Webber	1.50
54	Damon Stoudamire	.50
55	Donyell Marshall	.25
56	Isaiah Rider	.40
57	Karl Malone	.75
58	Kevin Garnett	3.00
59	Mario Elie	.25
60	Michael Dickerson	.40
61	Jahidi White	.25
62	Joe Smith	.25
63	Kenny Anderson	.40
64	Reggie Miller	.40
65	Ruben Patterson	.40
66	Shareef Abdur-Rahim	1.00
67	Allen Iverson	2.50
68	Glen Rice	.40
69	Nick Anderson	.25
70	Rex Chapman	.25
71	Ron Mercer	.75
72	Tim Duncan	3.00
73	Al Harrington	.50
74	Brent Barry	.25
75	Eddie Jones	.75
76	Mike Bibby	.60
77	Anthony Mason	.25
78	Michael Olowokandi	.50
79	Matt Harpring	.40
80	Stephon Marbury	1.00
81	Tracy McGrady	1.50
82	Allan Houston	.40
83	Lindsey Hunter	.25
84	Tariq Abdul-Wahad	.25
85	Antoine Walker	.60
86	Charles Barkley	.75
87	Gary Payton	.75
88	John Stockton	.40
89	Mitch Richmond	.40
90	Terrell Brandon	.40
91	Charles Oakley	.25
92	Bryant Reeves	.25
93	Dikembe Mutombo	.40
94	Elden Campbell	.25
95	Jalen Rose	.40
96	Jason Williams	1.50
97	Keith Van Horn	.75
98	Latrell Sprewell	.75
99	Raef LaFrentz	.60
100	Rasheed Wallace	.40
101	*Cal Bowdler*	5.00
102	*Dion Glover*	6.00
103	*Jason Terry*	12.00
104	*Adrian Griffin*	6.00
105	*Baron Davis*	25.00
106	*Michael Ruffin*	5.00
107	*Elton Brand*	35.00
108	*Ron Artest*	12.00
109	*Andre Miller*	25.00
110	*Trajan Langdon*	10.00
111	*James Posey*	10.00
112	*Vonteego Cummings*	8.00
113	*Kenny Thomas*	6.00
114	*Steve Francis*	100.00
115	*Jonathan Bender*	35.00
116	*Lamar Odom*	50.00
117	*Devean George*	10.00
118	*Tim James*	6.00
119	*Anthony Carter*	10.00
120	*Wally Szczerbiak*	20.00
121	*William Avery*	8.00
122	*Evan Eschmeyer*	6.00
123	*Corey Maggette*	25.00
124	*Jumaine Jones*	6.00
125	*Shawn Marion*	40.00
126	*Ryan Robertson*	5.00
127	*Aleksandar Radojevic*	5.00
128	*Quincy Lewis*	6.00
129	*Scott Padgett*	6.00
130	*Richard Hamilton*	20.00

Values quoted in this guide reflect the retail price of a card — the price a collector can expect to pay when buying a card from a dealer. The wholesale price — that which a collector can expect to receive from a dealer when selling cards — will be significantly lower, depending on desirability and condition.

1999-00 Flair Showcase Legacy 2000

This 130-card parallel reprinted each card in the base set, but used silver foil on the front versus the gold foil used on base cards. Legacy 2000 cards were sequentially numbered to 20 sets on the back.

		MT
Common Player:		30.00
Minor Stars:		40.00
Legacy 2000 Cards:		100x-150x
Common Rookie (101-130):		25.00
Legacy 2000 Rookies:		3x-5x
Production 20 Sets		
1	Vince Carter	5.00
2	Anfernee Hardaway	1.50
3	Nick Van Exel	.40
4	Kerry Kittles	.25
5	Michael Doleac	.40
6	Sean Elliott	.25
7	Shaquille O'Neal	2.50
8	Avery Johnson	.25
9	Brian Grant	.25
10	Jerome Williams	.25
11	Larry Hughes	1.25
12	Jerry Stackhouse	.40
13	Alonzo Mourning	.50
14	Antonio McDyess	.50
15	Jason Kidd	1.50
16	Bryon Russell	.25
17	Hakeem Olajuwon	.75
18	Juwan Howard	.40
19	Paul Pierce	1.25
20	Vin Baker	.40
21	Larry Johnson	.40
22	Gary Trent	.25
23	Jayson Williams	.25
24	Tim Hardaway	.60
25	Dirk Nowitzki	1.00
26	Jamal Mashburn	.40
27	Glenn Robinson	.40
28	Shawn Bradley	.25
29	Tom Gugliotta	.40
30	Vlade Divac	.25
31	David Robinson	.75
32	Matt Geiger	.25
33	Grant Hill	3.00
34	Maurice Taylor	.40
35	Toni Kukoc	.60
36	Cedric Ceballos	.25
37	Patrick Ewing	.40
38	Ray Allen	.50
39	Michael Finley	.40
40	Robert Traylor	.40
41	Brevin Knight	.25
42	Marcus Camby	.50
43	Sam Cassell	.40
44	Antawn Jamison	1.25
45	Steve Smith	.40
46	Darrell Armstrong	.25
47	Mookie Blaylock	.25
48	Derek Anderson	.40
49	Hersey Hawkins	.25
50	Kobe Bryant	4.00
51	Shawn Kemp	.40
52	Scottie Pippen	1.50
53	Chris Webber	1.50
54	Damon Stoudamire	.50
55	Donyell Marshall	.25
56	Isaiah Rider	.40
57	Karl Malone	.75
58	Kevin Garnett	3.00
59	Mario Elie	.25
60	Michael Dickerson	.40
61	Jahidi White	.25
62	Joe Smith	.25
63	Kenny Anderson	.40
64	Reggie Miller	.40
65	Ruben Patterson	.40
66	Shareef Abdur-Rahim	1.00
67	Allen Iverson	2.50
68	Glen Rice	.40
69	Nick Anderson	.25
70	Rex Chapman	.25
71	Ron Mercer	.75
72	Tim Duncan	3.00
73	Al Harrington	.50
74	Brent Barry	.25
75	Eddie Jones	.75
76	Mike Bibby	.60
77	Anthony Mason	.25
78	Michael Olowokandi	.50
79	Matt Harpring	.40
80	Stephon Marbury	1.00
81	Tracy McGrady	1.50
82	Allan Houston	.40
83	Lindsey Hunter	.25
84	Tariq Abdul-Wahad	.25
85	Antoine Walker	.75
86	Charles Barkley	.75
87	Gary Payton	.75
88	John Stockton	.40
89	Mitch Richmond	.40
90	Terrell Brandon	.40
91	Charles Oakley	.25
92	Bryant Reeves	.25
93	Dikembe Mutombo	.40
94	Elden Campbell	.25
95	Jalen Rose	.40
96	Jason Williams	1.50
97	Keith Van Horn	.75
98	Latrell Sprewell	.75
99	Raef LaFrentz	.60
100	Rasheed Wallace	.40
101	*Cal Bowdler*	5.00
102	*Dion Glover*	8.00
103	*Jason Terry*	15.00
104	*Adrian Griffin*	10.00
105	*Baron Davis*	25.00
106	*Michael Ruffin*	5.00
107	*Elton Brand*	90.00
108	*Ron Artest*	25.00
109	*Andre Miller*	25.00
110	*Trajan Langdon*	15.00
111	*James Posey*	15.00
112	*Vonteego Cummings*	12.00
113	*Kenny Thomas*	12.00
114	*Steve Francis*	125.00
115	*Jonathan Bender*	40.00
116	*Lamar Odom*	75.00
117	*Devean George*	10.00
118	*Tim James*	8.00
119	*Anthony Carter*	12.00
120	*Wally Szczerbiak*	40.00
121	*William Avery*	12.00
122	*Evan Eschmeyer*	8.00
123	*Corey Maggette*	40.00
124	*Jumaine Jones*	8.00
125	*Shawn Marion*	25.00
126	*Ryan Robertson*	5.00
127	*Aleksandar Radojevic*	5.00
128	*Quincy Lewis*	10.00
129	*Scott Padgett*	8.00
130	*Richard Hamilton*	20.00

1999-00 Flair Showcase Ball of Fame

This 15-card insert set showcased the top rookies from the 1999-00 season within a large pile of basketballs from the NBA Rookie Photo Shoot. Ball of Fame cards are numbered with a "BF" suffix and seeded 1:5 packs.

		MT
Complete Set (15):		15.00
Common Player:		.40
Inserted 1:5		
BF1	Lamar Odom	4.00
BF2	Steve Francis	5.00
BF3	Elton Brand	4.00
BF4	Wally Szczerbiak	2.00
BF5	Shawn Marion	1.50
BF6	Jason Terry	1.00
BF7	Richard Hamilton	1.25
BF8	Andre Miller	1.50
BF9	Corey Maggette	2.00
BF10	Baron Davis	1.50
BF11	Vonteego Cummings	.75
BF12	Kenny Thomas	.75
BF13	Jumaine Jones	.40
BF14	Trajan Langdon	1.00
BF15	Jonathan Bender	2.00

1999-00 Flair Showcase ConVINCEing

This 10-card insert is devoted to Vince Carter and highlights top dunks in black-and-white on a horizontal format. ConVINCEing inserts are numbered with a "C" suffix and seeded 1:10 packs.

		MT
Complete Set (10):		25.00
Common Player:		3.00
Inserted 1:10		
C1	Vince Carter	3.00
C2	Vince Carter	3.00
C3	Vince Carter	3.00
C4	Vince Carter	3.00
C5	Vince Carter	3.00
C6	Vince Carter	3.00
C7	Vince Carter	3.00
C8	Vince Carter	3.00
C9	Vince Carter	3.00
C10	Vince Carter	3.00

1999-00 Flair Showcase Elevators

This 10-card insert set features some of the best leapers in the game on a prismatic, blue and silver foil background. Elevators are numbered with an "E" suffix and seeded 1:20 packs.

		MT
Complete Set (10):		45.00
Common Player:		2.00
Inserted 1:20		
E1	Vince Carter	12.00
E2	Lamar Odom	5.00
E3	Allen Iverson	5.00
E4	Kobe Bryant	10.00
E5	Grant Hill	8.00
E6	Eddie Jones	2.00
E7	Scottie Pippen	3.00
E8	Kevin Garnett	8.00
E9	Steve Francis	8.00
E10	Keith Van Horn	1.50

1999-00 Flair Showcase Feel the Game

This 15-card insert features a piece of player-worn uniform on a horizontal format. Feel the Game cards are unnumbered and listed below alphabetically, and are seeded 1:120 packs.

		MT
Complete Set (15):		900.00
Common Player:		30.00
Inserted 1:120		
1	Kenny Thomas	30.00
2	Shawn Marion	75.00
3	Vonteego Cummings	30.00
4	Karl Malone	75.00
5	Alonzo Mourning	50.00
6	Paul Pierce	50.00
7	Damon Stoudamire	40.00
8	Antoine Walker	30.00
9	Patrick Ewing	50.00
10	Brian Grant	40.00
11	David Robinson	75.00
12	Shaquille O'Neal	125.00
13	William Avery	30.00
14	Vince Carter	250.00
15	Lamar Odom	100.00

1999-00 Flair Showcase Fresh Ink

This 32-card insert set featured autographs from various NBA players. The cards feature a framed shot of the player with the autograph below. The cards are unnumbered and seeded 1:39 packs. There is also a parallel Rock Steady version of seven of the cards, which are hand-numbered to 25 sets.

		MT
Complete Set (32):		
Common Player:		5.00
1	Tariq Abdul-Wahad	5.00
2	Ron Artest	10.00
3	William Avery	5.00
4	Tony Battie	5.00
5	Vince Carter	100.00
6	Dion Glover	5.00
7	Chris Herren	5.00
8	Juwan Howard	10.00
9	Eddie Jones	10.00
10	Brevin Knight	5.00
11	Toni Kukoc	5.00
12	Trajan Langdon	10.00
13	Corey Maggette	10.00
14	Stephon Marbury	25.00
15	Tracy McGrady	50.00
16	Ron Mercer	10.00
17	Andre Miller	20.00
18	Lamar Odom	10.00
19	Hakeem Olajuwon	20.00
20	Scottie Pippen	15.00
21	James Posey	5.00
22	Glen Rice	10.00
23	Wally Szczerbiak	20.00
24	Jason Terry	10.00
25	Keith Van Horn	20.00
26	Jerome Williams	5.00
27	Quincy Lewis	5.00
28	Scott Padgett	5.00
29	Aleksandar Radojevic	10.00
30	Kenny Thomas	5.00
31	Cal Bowdler	5.00
32	Jumaine Jones	5.00

1999-00 Flair Showcase Fresh Ink Rock Steady

This seven-card insert set was an extension of Fresh Ink, but featured different designs, and cards were hand-numbered to 25 sets. The cards are numbered with an "RS" suffix on the back, and feature the player photo on the right side of the card.

		MT
Complete Set (7):		
Common Player:		50.00
1	Ron Mercer	100.00
2	Scottie Pippen	300.00
3	Kenny Thomas	50.00
4	Vince Carter	500.00
5	Lamar Odom	100.00
6	Chris Herren	50.00
7	Aleksandar Radojevic	75.00

1999-00 Flair Showcase Guaranteed Fresh

This 10-card insert set displayed the league's top young players on a water-color-looking background. Guaranteed Fresh cards were numbered with a "GF" suffix and seeded 1:10 packs.

		MT
Complete Set (10):		18.00
Common Player:		1.00
Inserted 1:10		
GF1	Vince Carter	6.00
GF2	Shaquille O'Neal	3.00
GF3	Kevin Garnett	4.00
GF4	Kobe Bryant	5.00
GF5	Paul Pierce	1.50
GF6	Jason Williams	2.00
GF7	Stephon Marbury	1.00
GF8	Lamar Odom	3.00
GF9	Keith Van Horn	.75
GF10	Wally Szczerbiak	1.50

1999-00 Flair Showcase License to Skill

This 10-card insert set pictures top players over an orange and black, spherical background. License to Skill cards were numbered with an "LS" suffix and seeded 1:20 packs.

		MT
Complete Set (10):		45.00
Common Player:		1.00
Inserted 1:20		
LS1	Vince Carter	12.00
LS2	Shaquille O'Neal	5.00
LS3	Tim Duncan	8.00
LS4	Keith Van Horn	1.50
LS5	Grant Hill	8.00
LS6	Allen Iverson	5.00
LS7	Antoine Walker	.75
LS8	Scottie Pippen	3.00
LS9	Kobe Bryant	10.00
LS10	Lamar Odom	5.00

1999-00 Flair Showcase Next

This 20-card insert set featured top rookies from the 1999-00 season on a silver foil background. Next cards were numbered with an "N" suffix and seeded 1:3 packs.

		MT
Complete Set (20):		12.00
Common Player:		.25
Inserted 1:3		
N1	Vince Carter	5.00
N2	James Posey	.50
N3	Jonathan Bender	1.00
N4	Corey Maggette	1.00
N5	Devean George	.40
N6	Trajan Langdon	.50
N7	Shawn Marion	.75
N8	William Avery	.40
N9	Adrian Griffin	.40
N10	Quincy Lewis	.40
N11	Kenny Thomas	.40
N12	Lamar Odom	2.50
N13	Dion Glover	.25
N14	Elton Brand	2.50
N15	Andre Miller	.75
N16	Jason Terry	.50
N17	Richard Hamilton	.60
N18	Steve Francis	3.00
N19	Baron Davis	.75
N20	Wally Szczerbiak	1.00

1999-00 Flair Showcase Rookie Showcase

This 30-card insert set featured all 30 rookies from the base set. The cards were in the same order as the base and feattured the same photos, but on a horizontal format with the photos side by side (action shot on the left, close-up shot on the right). Card backs were also similar, but were sequentially numbered to 500 sets and numbered "x of 30".

		MT
Complete Set (30):		500.00
Common Player:		3.00
Production 500 Sets		
1	Cal Bowdler	3.00
2	Dion Glover	5.00
3	Jason Terry	12.00
4	Adrian Griffin	8.00
5	Baron Davis	20.00
6	Michael Ruffin	3.00
7	Elton Brand	75.00
8	Ron Artest	20.00
9	Andre Miller	20.00
10	Trajan Langdon	12.00
11	James Posey	12.00
12	Vonteego Cummings	10.00
13	Kenny Thomas	10.00
14	Steve Francis	100.00
15	Jonathan Bender	30.00
16	Lamar Odom	60.00
17	Devean George	8.00
18	Tim James	5.00
19	Anthony Carter	10.00
20	Wally Szczerbiak	30.00
21	William Avery	10.00
22	Evan Eschmeyer	5.00
23	Corey Maggette	30.00
24	Jumaine Jones	5.00
25	Shawn Marion	20.00
26	Ryan Robertson	3.00
27	Aleksandar Radojevic	3.00
28	Quincy Lewis	8.00
29	Scott Padgett	5.00
30	Richard Hamilton	15.00

2001-02 Fleer Flair

		MT
Complete Set (121):		325.00
Common Player:		.30
Minor Stars:		.60
Common Rookie:		4.00
Production 1500 Sets		
Pack (5):		5.00
Box (20):		165.00
1	Tracy McGrady	2.50
2	Derek Fisher	.30
3	Allen Iverson	3.00
4	Chris Webber	2.00
5	Jalen Rose	.75
6	Kenyon Martin	.60
7	Jermaine O'Neal	1.00
8	Kobe Bryant	5.00
9	Bryon Russell	.30
10	Wally Szczerbiak	.60
11	Damon Stoudamire	.30
12	John Stockton	1.00
13	Glenn Robinson	.60
14	Steve Francis	2.00
15	Vince Carter	5.00
16	Predrag Stojakovic	1.00
17	Rick Fox	.30
18	Allan Houston	.60
19	Danny Fortson	.30
20	Gary Payton	.75
21	Darius Miles	4.00
22	Kevin Garnett	3.00
23	Marcus Camby	.60
24	Desmond Mason	.60

25 Tim Duncan 2.00
26 Jamal Mashburn .60
27 Andre Miller .60
28 Antonio McDyess .75
29 Morris Peterson .75
30 Rasheed Wallace .75
31 Shawn Marion 1.25
32 Karl Malone 1.25
33 Grant Hill 1.50
34 Shaquille O'Neal 2.50
35 Hakeem Olajuwon .75
36 Corliss Williamson .30
37 Paul Pierce 1.00
38 Antonio Davis .30
39 Antonio Daniels .30
40 Ray Allen 1.00
41 Dirk Nowitzki 1.25
42 Jerry Stackhouse .75
43 Donyell Marshall .30
44 Brian Grant .30
45 Raef LaFrentz .30
46 Corey Maggette .60
47 Mike Miller 2.00
48 Jason Williams .60
49 Jahidi White .30
50 David Robinson .75
51 Shareef Abdur-Rahim .75
52 Anfernee Hardaway .75
53 Baron Davis 1.00
54 DerMarr Johnson .60
55 Dikembe Mutombo .60
56 David Wesley .30
57 Chris Mihm .30
58 Michael Finley 1.00
59 Eddie House .60
60 Stromile Swift .60
61 Courtney Alexander .75
62 Ron Mercer .60
63 Cuttino Mobley .60
64 Tim Thomas .60
65 Eddie Jones .75
66 Lamar Odom 1.25
67 Terrell Brandon .60
68 Rashard Lewis .60
69 Antoine Walker 1.00
70 Latrell Sprewell 1.25
71 Sam Cassell .60
72 Mike Bibby .60
73 Speedy Claxton .60
74 Steve Nash .60
75 Mark Jackson .30
76 Ron Artest .30
77 Matt Harpring .30
78 Zhizhi Wang 1.50
79 Nazr Mohammed .30
80 Jason Terry .60
81 Nick Van Exel .75
82 Reggie Miller .75
83 Joe Smith .30
84 Jason Kidd 1.50
85 Richard Hamilton .60
86 Antawn Jamison 1.25
87 Alonzo Mourning .60
88 Stephon Marbury 1.00
89 Scottie Pippen 1.25
90 Elton Brand 1.25
91 *Kwame Brown* 20.00
92 *Eddie Griffin* 20.00
93 *Tyson Chandler* 20.00
94 *Omar Cook* 4.00
95 *Loren Woods* 10.00
96 *Alton Ford* 3.00
97 *Shane Battier* 30.00
98 *Joe Johnson* 15.00
99 *Rodney White* 10.00
100 *Pau Gasol* 25.00
101 *Zach Randolph* 12.00
102 *Vladimir Radmanovic* 6.00
103 *Brendan Haywood* 12.00
104 *Michael Bradley* 4.00
105 *Tony Parker* 20.00
106 *Jason Richardson* 30.00
107 *Gerald Wallace* 10.00
108 *Damone Brown* 4.00
109 *Richard Jefferson* 12.00
110 *Eddy Curry* 20.00
111 *DeSagana Diop* 6.00
112 *Brandon Armstrong* 4.00
113 *Troy Murphy* 8.00
114 *Kedrick Brown* 6.00
115 *Kirk Haston* 8.00
116 *Gilbert Arenas* 5.00
117 *Jeryl Sasser* 5.00
118 *Jamaal Tinsley* 25.00
119 *Terence Morris* 4.00
120 *Michael Wright* 4.00
121 Michael Jordan 10.00

2001-02 Fleer Flair Courting Greatness

MT
Common Player: 12.00
Inserted 1:23
1 Vince Carter 40.00
2 Dirk Nowitzki 20.00
3 Allen Iverson 25.00
4 Tracy McGrady 20.00
5 Karl Malone 15.00
6 Antawn Jamison 15.00
7 Predrag Stojakovic 15.00
8 Eddie Jones 12.00
9 Jason Williams 12.00
10 Hakeem Olajuwon 12.00
11 Antoine Walker 12.00
12 Jerry Stackhouse 15.00
13 Chris Webber 20.00
14 Latrell Sprewell 15.00
15 David Robinson 12.00
16 Stephon Marbury 15.00
17 Grant Hill 15.00
18 Shareef Abdur-Rahim 12.00
19 Jason Kidd 20.00
20 Scottie Pippen 15.00

2001-02 Fleer Flair Courting Greatness (Ball/court)

MT
Common Player: 25.00
Production 250 Sets
1 Vince Carter 100.00
2 Dirk Nowitzki 40.00
3 Allen Iverson 75.00
4 Tracy McGrady 50.00
5 Karl Malone 40.00
6 Antawn Jamison 30.00
7 Predrag Stojakovic 30.00
8 Eddie Jones 25.00
9 Jason Williams 25.00
10 Hakeem Olajuwon 25.00
11 Antoine Walker 25.00
12 Jerry Stackhouse 30.00
13 Chris Webber 50.00
14 Latrell Sprewell 40.00
15 David Robinson 25.00
16 Stephon Marbury 30.00
17 Grant Hill 30.00
18 Shareef Abdur-Rahim 25.00
19 Jason Kidd 40.00
20 Scottie Pippen 30.00

2001-02 Fleer Flair Jersey Heights

MT
Common Player: 12.00
Inserted 1:22
1 Darius Miles 30.00
2 Mike Miller 15.00
3 Tracy McGrady 25.00
4 Ray Allen 20.00
5 Baron Davis 15.00
6 Dikembe Mutombo 12.00
7 Kenyon Martin 12.00
8 Steve Francis 20.00
9 Patrick Ewing 15.00
10 Jason Kidd 20.00
11 Jerome Moiso 12.00
12 Richard Hamilton 15.00
13 Vince Carter 40.00
14 John Stockton 15.00
15 Mike Bibby 12.00
16 Reggie Miller 15.00
17 Jason Terry 12.00
18 Stephon Marbury 12.00
19 Chris Webber 25.00
20 Mitch Richmond 12.00

2001-02 Fleer Flair Hot Numbers

MT
Common Player: 25.00
Production 100 Sets
1 Darius Miles 75.00
2 Mike Miller 40.00
3 Tracy McGrady 75.00
4 Ray Allen 60.00
5 Baron Davis 40.00
6 Dikembe Mutombo 30.00
7 Kenyon Martin 30.00
8 Steve Francis 60.00
9 Patrick Ewing 40.00
10 Jason Kidd 60.00
11 Jerome Moiso 25.00
12 Richard Hamilton 30.00
13 Vince Carter 150.00
14 John Stockton 50.00
15 Mike Bibby 30.00
16 Reggie Miller 50.00
17 Jason Terry 30.00
18 Stephon Marbury 40.00
19 Chris Webber 75.00
20 Mitch Richmond 30.00

2001-02 Fleer Flair Sweet Shots

MT
Complete Set (25):
Common Player:
1JSY Ray Allen 60.00
2JSY Vince Carter 150.00
3JSY Baron Davis 30.00
4JSY Michael Dickerson 20.00
5JSY Steve Francis 75.00
6JSY Marc Jackson 20.00
7JSY Antawn Jamison 40.00
8JSY Rashard Lewis 25.00
9JSY Karl Malone 40.00
10JSY Shawn Marion 40.00
11JSY Kenyon Martin 25.00
12JSY Antonio McDyess 25.00
13JSY Tracy McGrady 75.00
14JSY Darius Miles 75.00
15JSY Mike Miller 50.00
16JSY Lamar Odom 40.00
17JSY Gary Payton 40.00
18JSY Morris Peterson 30.00
19JSY David Robinson 30.00
20JSY John Stockton 40.00
21JSY Predrag Stojakovic 40.00
22JSY Jason Terry 20.00
23JSY Antoine Walker 30.00
24JSY Chris Webber 60.00
25JSY Allen Iverson 100.00
26 Kwame Brown Auto/297 75.00
27 Eddy Curry Auto/368 50.00
28 Michael Bradley Auto/433 20.00
29 Brendan Haywood Auto/345 30.00
30 Jason Collins Auto/390 20.00
31 Richard Jefferson Auto/330 30.00
32 Kedrick Brown Auto/342 20.00
33 Vince Carter Auto/245 200.00

2001-02 Fleer Flair Warming Up

MT
Common Player: 12.00
Inserted 1:27
1 Jason Terry 12.00
2 Shareef Abdur-Rahim 12.00
3 Antoine Walker 15.00
4 Paul Pierce 15.00
5 Andre Miller 12.00
6 Steve Francis 20.00
7 Lamar Odom 20.00
8 Corey Maggette 12.00
9 Kenyon Martin 12.00
10 Grant Hill 20.00
11 Allen Iverson 35.00
12 Dikembe Mutombo 12.00
13 Stephon Marbury 15.00
14 Mike Bibby 12.00
15 Morris Peterson 15.00
16 Vince Carter 50.00
17 Karl Malone 20.00
18 John Stockton 15.00
19 Keith Van Horn 12.00
20 DerMarr Johnson 12.00

2001-02 Fleer Flair Warming Up Dual

MT
Common Player: 25.00
Inserted 1:80
1 Jason Terry, Shareef Abdur-Rahim 25.00
2 Antoine Walker, Paul Pierce 30.00
3 Andre Miller, Steve Francis 30.00
4 Lamar Odom, Corey Maggette 30.00
5 Kenyon Martin, Keith Van Horn 25.00
6 Allen Iverson, Dikembe Mutombo 40.00
7 Stephon Marbury, Mike Bibby 25.00
8 Morris Peterson, Vince Carter 60.00
9 Karl Malone, John Stockton 40.00
10 Grant Hill, DerMarr Johnson 30.00

1961-62 Fleer

Fleer entered the basketball card market for the first time in 1961, producing a 66-card set. The standard-size cards have the team name in bold type in a box at the top (the box is roughly a quarter of the size of the card). One of the most popular basketball sets ever, this issue has rookie cards for Jerry West, Wilt Chamberlain, Elgin Baylor, Len Wilkens and Oscar Robertson, as well as the only cards of K.C. Jones and Sam Jones and the final regular-issue cards of Bob Pettit, Bill Russell and Bob Cousy. AP means action pose.

NM
Complete Set (66): 4500.
Common Player: 20.00
Pack (6): 700.00
Wax Box (24): 12500.
1 *Al Attles* 100.00
2 Paul Arizin 45.00
3 *Elgin Baylor* 325.00
4 *Walt Bellamy* 50.00
5 Arlen Bockhorn 20.00
6 Bob Boozer 20.00
7 Carl Braun 20.00
8 *Wilt Chamberlain* 1300.
9 Larry Costello 20.00
10 Bob Cousy 220.00
11 Walter Dukes 20.00
12 *Wayne Embry* 30.00
13 Dave Gambee 20.00
14 Tom Gola 45.00
15 *Sihugo Green* 20.00
16 *Hal Greer* 80.00
17 *Richie Guerin* 40.00
18 Cliff Hagan 45.00
19 Tom Heinsohn 75.00
20 *Bailey Howell* 35.00
21 Rod Hundley 35.00
22 *K.C. Jones* 100.00
23 *Sam Jones* 100.00
24 Phil Jordan 20.00
25 John Kerr 45.00
26 *Rudy LaRusso* 30.00
27 George Lee 20.00
28 Bob Leonard 20.00
29 Clyde Lovellette 45.00
30 John McCarthy 20.00
31 Tom Meschery 20.00
32 Willie Naulls 25.00
33 *Don Ohl* 20.00
34 Bob Pettit 75.00
35 Frank Ramsey 40.00
36 *Oscar Robertson* 500.00
37 *Guy Rodgers* 25.00
38 Bill Russell 500.00
39 Dolph Schayes 45.00
40 Frank Selvy 20.00
41 Gene Shue 25.00
42 Jack Twyman 40.00
43 *Jerry West* 700.00
44 *Len Wilkens* 150.00
45 Paul Arizin (AP) 25.00
46 Elgin Baylor (AP) 135.00
47 Wilt Chamberlain 400.00
48 Larry Costello (AP) 20.00
49 Bob Cousy (AP) 110.00
50 Walter Dukes (AP) 20.00
51 Tom Gola (AP) 25.00
52 Richie Guerin (AP) 20.00
53 Cliff Hagan 25.00
54 Tom Heinsohn (AP) 40.00
55 Bailey Howell (AP) 20.00
56 John Kerr (AP) [illegible]
57 Rudy LaRusso (AP) 20.00
58 Clyde Lovellette (AP) 30.00
59 Bob Pettit (AP) 40.00
60 Frank Ramsey (AP) 25.00
61 Oscar Robertson 160.00
62 Bill Russell (AP) 240.00
63 Dolph Schayes (AP) 30.00
64 Gene Shue (AP) 20.00
65 Jack Twyman (AP) 25.00
66 Jerry West (AP) 280.00

1973-74 Fleer "The Shots"

This 21-card set was inserted into packs with one Shots card, two team logo cloth patches and a stick of gum. The cards were illustrated by artist R. G. Laughlin for Fleer and measure 2-1/2" x 4" with numbers on the back.

NM
Complete Set (21): 50.00
Common Player: 3.00
1 Two-Hand Set 4.00
2 Overhead Set 3.00
3 One-Hand Set 3.00
4 Two-Hand Jumper 3.00
5 One-Hand Jumper 3.00
6 Twisting Jumper 3.00
7 Hook Shot 3.00
8 Driving Hook 3.00
9 Layup 3.00
10 Reverse Layup 3.00
11 Underhand Layup 3.00
12 Pivot Shots 3.00
13 Step-Away 3.00
14 Running One-Hander 3.00
15 Stuff or Dunk 5.00
16 Tap-In 3.00
17 Bank Shot 3.00
18 Free Throw 3.00
19 Desperation Shot 3.00
20 Blocked Shot 3.00
21 The "Good" Shot 4.00

1974 Fleer Team Patches/Stickers

A cloth patch and sticker were produced for all 18 teams and were sold in wax packs. The cloth patches carry the team name in a color bar across the top of the patch with the logo printed on a brown basketball under the words "Property of." The stickers also carry the team name with the logo beneath it. Since both are unnumbered, the checklist below includes both in alphabetical order, with patches first and stickers following.

NM
Complete Set (38): 80.00
Common Patch (1-19): 2.00
Common Sticker (20-38): 2.50
NBA Logo 2.50
Atlanta Hawks 2.00
Boston Celtics 2.50
Buffalo Braves 2.50
Chicago Bulls 2.00
Cleveland Cavaliers 2.00
Detroit Pistons 2.00
Golden State Warriors 2.50
Houston Rockets 2.00
Kansas City Kings 2.00
Los Angeles Lakers 2.50
Milwaukee Bucks 2.00
New Orleans Jazz 2.50
New York Knicks 2.50
Philadelphia 76ers 2.00
Phoenix Suns 2.00
Portland Trail Blazers 2.00
Seattle Supersonics 2.00
Washington Bullets 2.00
NBA Logo 3.00
Atlanta Hawks 2.50
Boston Celtics 3.00
Buffalo Braves 3.00
Chicago Bulls 2.50
Cleveland Cavaliers 2.50
Detroit Pistons 2.50
Golden State Warriors 2.50
Houston Rockets 2.50
Kansas City Kings 3.00
Los Angeles Lakers 3.00
Milwaukee Bucks 2.50
New Orleans Jazz 3.00
New York Knicks 3.00
Philadelphia 76ers 2.50
Phoenix Suns 2.50
Portland Trail Blazers 2.50
Seattle Supersonics 2.50
Washington Bullets 2.50

1977-78 Fleer Team Stickers

This 22-card set included all NBA teams on 2-1/2" x 3-1/4" stickers. The stickers contained a color strip across the top with an NBA logo and the words "New 'All Pro' Hi-Gloss Stickers." The sticker itself contains the team name and the team's logo. All stickers were unnumbered with blank backs and included many different color variations.

NM
Complete Set (22): 10.00
Common Player: .60
Atlanta Hawks .60
Boston Celtics .75
Buffalo Braves .75
Chicago Bulls .60
Cleveland Cavaliers .60
Denver Nuggets .60
Detroit Pistons .60
Golden State Warriors .60
Houston Rockets .60
Indiana Pacers .60
Kansas City Kings .75
Los Angeles Lakers .75
Milwaukee Bucks [illegible]
New Jersey Nets .60
New Orleans Jazz .75
New York Knicks .75
Philadelphia 76ers .60
Phoenix Suns .60
Portland Trail Blazers .60
San Antonio Spurs .60
Seattle Supersonics .60
Washington Bullets .60

1986-87 Fleer

Fleer's first set since 1961 is one of the most important basketball sets issued. When Topps discontinued its basketball line after the 1981-82 season, only the tiny Star Co. issued sets - some regional, some national, but mostly the sets were hard to find. Fleer apparently made a bid for basketball cards in 1986, and Star reluctantly discontinued its line. Fleer's initial basketball effort of 132 cards showed players in alphabetical order on white cardboard stock with action photos on front and statistics on the back. More importantly, cards received a wider distribution than Star (though not as wide as NBA Hoops cards would be three years later). Fleer, however, apparently didn't have an expanded print run as it would with later basketball issues. Despite its relative scarcity, this set didn't pick up steam until the summer of 1989. This set includes possibly the largest amount of potential Hall of Fame rookies in any basketball set. Michael Jordan, Patrick Ewing, Isiah Thomas, Dominique Wilkins, Karl Malone, Akeem Olajuwon, and Charles Barkley are among them. There is one error in the set: Card #55, Steve Johnson, actually shows David Greenwood.

MT
Complete Set (132): 2000.
Common Player: 2.00
Minor Stars: 3.00
Pack (13): 450.00
Box (36): 14500.
1 Kareem Abdul-Jabbar 10.00
2 Alvan Adams 2.00
3 *Mark Aguirre* 3.00
4 *Danny Ainge* 10.00
5 *John Bagley* 2.00
6 *Thurl Bailey* 2.00
7 *Charles Barkley* 75.00
8 *Benoit Benjamin* 3.00
9 Larry Bird 45.00
10 Otis Birdsong 2.00
11 *Rolando Blackman* 3.00
12 *Manute Bol* 3.00
13 *Sam Bowie* 3.00
14 Joe Barry Carroll 2.00
15 *Tom Chambers* 5.00
16 Maurice Cheeks 3.00
17 Michael Cooper 3.00
18 Wayne Cooper 2.00
19 Pat Cummings 2.00
20 *Terry Cummings* 5.00
21 Adrian Dantley 2.00
22 Brad Davis 2.00
23 Walter Davis 2.00
24 Darryl Dawkins 3.00
25 Larry Drew 2.00
26 *Clyde Drexler* 70.00
27 *Joe Dumars* 30.00
28 *Mark Eaton* 3.00
29 James Edwards 2.00
30 Alex English 3.00
31 Julius Erving 25.00
32 *Patrick Ewing* 60.00
33 *Vern Fleming* 3.00
34 *Sleepy Floyd* 3.00
35 World B. Free 2.00
36 George Gervin 5.00
37 Artis Gilmore 3.00
38 Mike Gminski 2.00
39 Rickey Green 2.00
40 Sidney Green 2.00
41 David Greenwood 2.00
42 Darrell Griffith 2.00
43 Bill Hanzlik 2.00
44 *Derek Harper* 5.00
45 Gerald Henderson 2.00
46 Roy Hinson 2.00
47 *Craig Hodges* 3.00
48 Phil Hubbard 2.00
49 *Jay Humphries* 3.00
50 Dennis Johnson 3.00
51 *Eddie Johnson* 3.00
52 *Frank Johnson* 3.00
53 Magic Johnson 30.00
54 Marques Johnson 2.00
55 Steve Johnson 2.00
56 Vinnie Johnson 2.00
57 *Michael Jordan* 1200.
58 *Clark Kellogg* 2.00
59 Albert King 2.00
60 Bernard King 3.00
61 Bill Laimbeer 3.00
62 Allen Leavell 2.00
63 *Lafayette Lever* 2.00
64 Alton Lister 2.00
65 Lewis Lloyd 2.00
66 Maurice Lucas 2.00
67 *Jeff Malone* 5.00
68 *Karl Malone* 80.00
69 Moses Malone 5.00
70 Cedric Maxwell 2.00
71 *Rodney McCray* 2.00
72 *Xavier McDaniel* 5.00
73 Kevin McHale 4.00
74 Mike Mitchell 2.00
75 Sidney Moncrief 3.00
76 Johnny Moore 2.00
77 *Chris Mullin* 30.00
78 *Larry Nance* 5.00
79 Calvin Natt 2.00
80 Norm Nixon 2.00
81 *Charles Oakley* 8.00
82 *Hakeem Olajuwon* 70.00
83 Louis Orr 2.00
84 Robert Parish 4.00
85 Chuck Person 3.00
86 *Sam Perkins* 5.00
87 *Ricky Pierce* 3.00
88 *Paul Pressey* 2.00
89 *Kurt Rambis* 3.00
90 Robert Reid 2.00
91 *Doc Rivers* 7.00
92 *Alvin Robertson* 3.00
93 Clifford Robinson 2.00
94 Tree Rollins 2.00
95 Dan Roundfield 2.00
96 Jeff Ruland 2.00
97 *Ralph Sampson* 3.00
98 *Danny Schayes* 2.00
99 *Byron Scott* 6.00
100 Purvis Short 2.00
101 Jerry Sichting 2.00
102 Jack Sikma 3.00
103 Derek Smith 2.00
104 Larry Smith 2.00
105 Rory Sparrow 2.00
106 Steve Stipanovich 2.00
107 Terry Teagle 2.00
108 Reggie Theus 2.00
109 *Isiah Thomas* 30.00
110 *LaSalle Thompson* 2.00
111 Mychal Thompson 2.00
112 *Sedale Threatt* 3.00
113 *Wayman Tisdale* 5.00
114 Andrew Toney 2.00
115 Kelly Tripucka 2.00
116 Mel Turpin 2.00
117 *Kiki Vandeweghe* 3.00
118 Jay Vincent 2.00
119 Bill Walton 5.00
120 *Spud Webb* 6.00
121 *Dominique Wilkins* 45.00
122 *Gerald Wilkins* 3.00
123 *Buck Williams* 6.00
124 Gus Williams 2.00
125 *Herb Williams* 2.00
126 *Kevin Willis* 5.00
127 Randy Wittman 2.00
128 Al Wood 2.00
129 Mike Woodson 2.00
130 *Orlando Woolridge* 3.00
131 *James Worthy* 30.00
132 Checklist 18.00

1986-87 Fleer Stickers

These stickers were put one per pack in the Fleer basketball packs. The front shows an action photo; red, white and blue backs have information about the player's career. Stickers are listed in alphabetical order and are standard size.

MT
Complete Set (11): 450.00
Common Player: 2.00
1 Kareem Abdul Jabbar 5.00
2 Larry Bird 17.00
3 Adrian Dantley 2.00
4 Alex English 2.00
5 Julius Erving 7.00
6 Patrick Ewing 10.00
7 Magic Johnson 12.00
8 Michael Jordan 250.00
9 Hakeem Olajuwon 20.00
10 Isiah Thomas 5.00
11 Dominique Wilkins 5.00

1987-88 Fleer

Fleer's second set of 132 cards was, for the final time, arranged in alphabetical order by player name only. Rookie cards in this set include Terry

Catledge, Brad Daugherty, Johnny Dawkins, Dale Ellis, A.C. Green, Ron Harper, Chuck Person, Terry Porter, Darrell Walker and both John Williamses. The second-year cards in this set include that great crop of last year's official "rookie cards" - Michael Jordan, Patrick Ewing, Karl Malone, Isiah Thomas, Akeem Olajuwon, Charles Barkley and Dominique Wilkins. This set also has the final regular-issue cards of Julius Erving, Artis Gilmore and Cornbread Maxwell. Two errors exist in the set: the negatives were reversed on #6, Thurl Bailey, and #41, Mike Gminski.

		MT
Complete Set (132):		350.00
Common Player:		1.00
Minor Stars:		2.00
Pack (13):		69.00
Wax Box (36):		2200.
1	Kareem Abdul-Jabbar	12.00
2	Alvan Adams	1.00
3	Mark Aguirre	1.00
4	Danny Ainge	2.00
5	John Bagley	1.00
6	Thurl Bailey	1.00
7	Greg Ballard	1.00
8	Gene Banks	1.00
9	Charles Barkley	22.00
10	Benoit Benjamin	1.00
11	Larry Bird	30.00
12	Rolando Blackman	1.00
13	Manute Bol	1.00
14	Tony Brown	1.00
15	*Michael Cage*	1.00
16	Joe Barry Caroll	1.00
17	Bill Cartwright	1.00
18	*Terry Catledge*	1.00
19	Tom Chambers	2.00
20	Maurice Cheeks	1.00
21	Michael Cooper	1.00
22	Dave Corzine	1.00
23	Terry Cummings	2.00
24	Adrian Dantley	1.00
25	*Brad Daugherty*	3.00
26	Walter Davis	1.00
27	*Johnny Dawkins*	2.00
28	James Donaldson	1.00
29	Larry Drew	1.00
30	Clyde Drexler	15.00
31	Joe Dumars	7.00
32	Mark Eaton	1.00
33	*Dale Ellis*	3.00
34	Alex English	2.00
35	Julius Erving	12.00
36	Mike Evans	1.00
37	Patrick Ewing	15.00
38	Vern Fleming	1.00
39	Sleepy Floyd	1.00
40	Artis Gilmore	1.00
41	Mike Gminski	1.00
42	*A.C. Green*	6.00
43	Rickey Green	1.00
44	Sidney Green	1.00
45	David Greenwood	1.00
46	Darrell Griffith	1.00
47	Bill Hanzlik	1.00
48	Derek Harper	2.00
49	*Ron Harper*	12.00
50	Gerald Henderson	1.00
51	Roy Hinson	1.00
52	Craig Hodges	1.00
53	Phil Hubbard	1.00
54	Dennis Johnson	1.00
55	Eddie Johnson	1.00
56	Magic Johnson	20.00
57	Steve Johnson	1.00
58	Vinnie Johnson	1.00
59	Michael Jordan	160.00
60	*Jerome Kersey*	2.00
61	Bill Laimbeer	1.00
62	Lafayette Lever	1.00
63	*Cliff Levingston*	1.00
64	Alton Lister	1.00
65	John Long	1.00
66	John Lucas	1.00
67	Jeff Malone	1.00
68	Karl Malone	15.00
69	Moses Malone	3.00
70	Cedric Maxwell	1.00
71	Tim McCormick	1.00
72	Rodney McCray	1.00
73	Xavier McDaniel	2.00
74	Kevin McHale	3.00
75	*Nate McMillan*	3.00
76	Sidney Moncrief	1.00
77	Chris Mullin	4.00
78	Larry Nance	2.00
79	Charles Oakley	2.00
80	Hakeem Olajuwon	20.00
81	Robert Parish	3.00
82	Jim Paxson	1.00
83	*John Paxson*	3.00
84	Sam Perkins	2.00
85	*Chuck Person*	4.00
86	Jim Peterson	1.00
87	Ricky Pierce	1.00
88	*Ed Pinckney*	1.00
89	*Terry Porter*	3.00
90	Paul Pressey	1.00
91	Robert Reid	1.00
92	Doc Rivers	1.00
93	Alvin Robertson	1.00
94	Tree Rollins	1.00
95	Ralph Sampson	1.00
96	Mike Sanders	1.00
97	*Detlef Schrempf*	12.00
98	Byron Scott	2.00
99	Jerry Sichting	1.00
100	Jack Sikma	1.00
101	Larry Smith	1.00
102	Rory Sparrow	1.00
103	Steve Stipanovich	1.00
104	Jon Sundvold	1.00
105	Reggie Theus	1.00
106	Isiah Thomas	8.00
107	LaSalle Thompson	1.00
108	Mychal Thompson	1.00
109	*Otis Thorpe*	5.00
110	Sedale Threatt	1.00
111	Wayman Tisdale	1.00
112	Kelly Tripucka	1.00
113	*Trent Tucker*	1.00
114	Terry Tyler	1.00
115	Darnell Valentine	1.00
116	Kiki Vandeweghe	1.00
117	*Darrell Walker*	1.00
118	Dominique Wilkins	6.00
119	Gerald Wilkins	1.00
120	Buck Williams	1.00
121	Herb Williams	1.00
122	*John Williams*	1.00
123	*Hot Rod Williams*	4.00
124	Kevin Willis	2.00
125	*David Wingate*	1.00
126	Randy Wittman	1.00
127	Leon Wood	1.00
128	Mike Woodson	1.00
129	Orlando Woolridge	1.00
130	James Worthy	3.00
131	*Danny Young*	1.00
132	Checklist	3.00

1987-88 Fleer Stickers

Fleer's 11-card insert stickers were once again included one per pack of basketball cards. Stickers, attached to heavy white cardboard stock, show an action photo on the front and text of each player on the back. The NBA's superstars are once again featured. Fronts are red, white, blue and yellow; backs are red, white and blue. Stickers are standard size and are numbered (1 of 11, etc.).

		MT
Complete Set (11):		100.00
Common Player:		1.00
1	Magic Johnson	7.00
2	Michael Jordan	60.00
3	Hakeem Olajuwon	8.00
4	Larry Bird	8.00
5	Kevin McHale	1.00
6	Charles Barkley	8.00
7	Dominique Wilkins	3.00
8	Kareem Abdul-Jabbar	3.00
9	Mark Aguirre	1.00
10	Chuck Person	1.00
11	Alex English	1.00

1988-89 Fleer

Fleer's third and last set of 132 cards was arranged in alphabetical order by city name and by player. As it had the previous year, the quality of Fleer's photographs in this issue seemed to improve, as more action shots and fewer grainy photos were in the set. Rookies in this issue include Muggsy Bogues, Horace Grant, Scottie Pippen, Mark Price, Roy Tarpley, Dennis Rodman, John Salley, Kenny Smith and Reggie Miller. Second-year cards include Spud Webb, Brad Daugherty, Ron Harper, A.C. Green, Terry Porter and Dale Ellis. This set also contains the last regular-issue card of Kareem Abdul-Jabbar. AS means All-Star.

		MT
Complete Set (132):		225.00
Common Player:		.25
Minor Stars:		.50
Pack (13):		30.00
Wax Box (36):		1000.
1	*Antoine Carr*	1.00
2	Cliff Levingston	.25
3	Doc Rivers	.25
4	Spud Webb	.50
5	Dominique Wilkins	1.50
6	Kevin Willis	.50
7	Randy Whittman	.25
8	Danny Ainge	.50
9	Larry Bird	10.00
10	Dennis Johnson	.25
11	Kevin McHale	1.00
12	Robert Parish	1.00
13	*Tyrone Bogues*	3.00
14	*Dell Curry*	3.00
15	Dave Corzine	.25
16	*Horace Grant*	8.00
17	Michael Jordan	55.00
18	Charles Oakley	.25
19	Jim Paxson	.25
20	*Scottie Pippen*	50.00
21	*Brad Sellers*	.25
22	Brad Daugherty	.25
23	Ron Harper	.25
24	Larry Nance	.25
25	*Mark Price*	2.00
26	Hot Rod Williams	.25
27	Mark Aguirre	.25
28	Rolando Blackman	.25
29	James Donaldson	.25
30	Derek Harper	.25
31	Sam Perkins	.25
32	*Roy Tarpley*	1.00
33	*Michael Adams*	1.00
34	Alex English	.25
35	Lafayette Lever	.25
36	*Blair Rasmussen*	.25
37	Danny Schayes	.25
38	Jay Vincent	.25
39	Adrian Dantley	.25
40	Joe Dumars	2.00
41	Vinnie Johnson	.25
42	Bill Laimbeer	.25
43	*Dennis Rodman*	25.00
44	*John Salley*	.50
45	Isiah Thomas	2.00
46	*Winston Garland*	.25
47	Rod Higgins	.25
48	Chris Mullin	1.00
49	Ralph Sampson	.50
50	Joe Barry Carroll	.25
51	Sleepy Floyd	.25
52	Rodney McCray	.25
53	Hakeem Olajuwon	8.00
54	Purvis Short	.25
55	Vern Fleming	.25
56	John Long	.25
57	*Reggie Miller*	35.00
58	Chuck Person	.50
59	Steve Stipanovich	.25
60	Wayman Tisdale	.25
61	Benoit Benjamin	.25
62	Michael Cage	.25
63	Mike Woodson	.25
64	Kareem Abdul-Jabbar	3.00
65	Michael Cooper	.25
66	A.C. Green	1.00
67	Magic Johnson	8.00
68	Byron Scott	.50
69	Mychal Thompson	.25
70	James Worthy	.75
71	Duane Washington	.25
72	Kevin Williams	.25
73	*Randy Breuer*	.25
74	Terry Cummings	.25
75	Paul Pressey	.25
76	Jack Sikma	.25
77	John Bagley	.25
78	Roy Hinson	.25
79	Buck Williams	.25
80	Patrick Ewing	3.00
81	Sidney Green	.25
82	*Mark Jackson*	3.50
83	*Kenny Walker*	.25
84	Gerald Wilkins	.25
85	Charles Barkley	5.00
86	Maurice Cheeks	.25
87	Mike Gminski	.25
88	Clifford Robinson	.25
89	*Armon Gilliam*	2.00
90	Eddie Johnson	.25
91	*Mark West*	.50
92	Clyde Drexler	3.00
93	*Kevin Duckworth*	.25
94	Steve Johnson	.25
95	Jerome Kersey	.25
96	Terry Porter	.25
97	*Joe Kleine*	.75
98	Reggie Theus	.25
99	Otis Thorpe	.75
100	*Kenny Smith*	2.00
101	*Greg Anderson*	.25
102	*Walter Berry*	.25
103	*Frank Brickowski*	.25
104	Johnny Dawkins	.25
105	Alvin Robertson	.25
106	Tom Chambers	.25
107	Dale Ellis	.25
108	Xavier McDaniel	.25
109	*Derrick McKey*	2.00
110	Nate McMillan	.25
111	Thurl Bailey	.25
112	Mark Eaton	.25
113	Bobby Hansen	.25
114	Karl Malone	5.00
115	*John Stockton*	30.00
116	Bernard King	.25
117	Jeff Malone	.25
118	Moses Malone	1.00
119	John Williams	.25
120	Michael Jordan (AS)	20.00
121	Mark Jackson (AS)	.50
122	Byron Scott (AS)	.25
123	Magic Johnson (AS)	3.00
124	Larry Bird (AS)	4.00
125	Dominique Wilkins (AS)	1.00
126	Hakeem Olajuwon (AS)	4.00
127	John Stockton (AS)	5.00
128	Alvin Robertson (AS)	.25
129	Charles Barkley (AS)	4.00
130	Patrick Ewing (AS)	2.00
131	Mark Eaton (AS)	.25
132	Checklist	.50

1988-89 Fleer Stickers

These stickers are on heavy white cardboard stock with a color action photo of the player. Backs contain personal career data. Fronts are baby blue, red and white; the backs are pink and blue. The standard size stickers were issued one per pack of Fleer cards. Cards are numbered (1 of 11, etc.).

		MT
Complete Set (11):		35.00
Common Player:		.50
1	Mark Aguirre	.50
2	Larry Bird	4.00
3	Clyde Drexler	2.00
4	Alex English	.50
5	Patrick Ewing	2.00
6	Magic Johnson	3.00
7	Michael Jordan	30.00
8	Karl Malone	1.50
9	Kevin McHale	.75
10	Isiah Thomas	1.00
11	Dominique Wilkins	1.00

1989-90 Fleer

The cards in Fleer's fourth straight set were issued in early October. The set size increased from 132 to 168 cards. A new subset was included, featuring teammates in the 1989 NBA All-Star Game. Fleer also included special designations in its set: "Scoring Average Leader," "Free Throw Percentage Leader" and "Rookie Sensation." These designations were not on separate cards. Cards are again arranged alphabetically by player and by city name. Again, no factory sets were issued. Rookies in this set include Gary Grant, Rik Smits, Danny Manning, Charles Smith, Chris Morris and Kevin Johnson. Second-year cards include Scottie Pippen, Mark Price, Dennis Rodman and Reggie Miller. AS means All-Star.

		MT
Complete Set (168):		30.00
Common Player:		.10
Minor Stars:		.20
Pack (16):		5.50
Wax Box (36):		125.00
1	*John Battle*	.10
2	*Jon Koncak*	.10
3	Cliff Levingston	.10
4	Moses Malone	.20
5	Glenn Rivers	.10
6	Spud Webb	.10
7	Dominique Wilkins	.50
8	Larry Bird	3.00
9	Dennis Johnson	.10
10	*Reggie Lewis*	1.00
11	Kevin McHale	.20
12	Robert Parish	.20
13	Ed Pinckney	.10
14	*Brian Shaw*	.50
15	*Rex Chapman*	1.00
16	Kurt Rambis	.10
17	Robert Reid	.10
18	Kelly Tripucka	.10
19	Bill Cartwright	.10
20	Horace Grant	1.50
21	Michael Jordan	12.00
22	John Paxson	.10
23	Scottie Pippen	4.00
24	Brad Sellers	.10
25	Brad Daugherty	.20
26	*Craig Ehlo*	.20
27	Ron Harper	.10
28	Larry Nance	.10
29	Mark Price	.50
30	Mike Sanders	.10
31	Hot Rod Williams (Cavaliers)	.10
31A	Hot Rod Williams (Bullets back)	.10
32	Rolando Blackman	.10
33	Adrian Dantley	.10
34	James Donaldson	.10
35	Derek Harper	.10
36	Sam Perkins	.10
37	Herb Williams	.10
38	Michael Adams	.10
39	Walter Davis	.10
40	Alex English	.10
41	Lafayette Lever	.10
42	Blair Rasmussen	.10
43	Dan Schayes	.10
44	Mark Aguirre	.10
45	Joe Dumars	.50
46	James Edwards	.10
47	Vinnie Johnson	.10
48	Bill Laimbeer	.20
49	Dennis Rodman	3.00
50	Isiah Thomas	.50
51	John Salley	.10
52	Manute Bol	.10
53	Winston Garland	.10
54	Rod Higgins	.10
55	Chris Mullin	.30
56	*Mitch Richmond*	4.00
57	Terry Teagle	.10
58	Derrick Chievous	.10
59	Eric Floyd	.10
60	Tim McCormick	.10
61	Hakeem Olajuwon	2.00
62	Otis Thorpe	.10
63	Mike Woodson	.10
64	Vern Fleming	.10
65	Reggie Miller	2.00
66	Chuck Person	.10
67	Detlef Schrempf	.50
68	*Rik Smits*	1.50
69	Benoit Benjamin	.10
70	*Gary Grant*	.30
71	*Danny Manning*	1.00
72	*Ken Norman*	.50
73	*Charles Smith*	.50
74	*Reggie Williams*	.50
75	Michael Cooper	.10
76	A.C. Green	.20
77	Magic Johnson	2.00
78	Byron Scott	.10
79	Mychal Thompson	.10
80	James Worthy	.20
81	*Kevin Edwards*	.50
82	*Grant Long*	.50
83	*Rony Seikaly*	.50
84	Rory Sparrow	.10
85	Greg Anderson	.10
86	Jay Humphries	.10
87	*Larry Krystkowiak*	.20
88	Ricky Pierce	.10
89	Paul Pressey	.10
90	Alvin Robertson	.10
91	Jack Sikma	.10
92	Steve Johnson	.10
93	Rick Mahorn	.10
94	David Rivers	.10
95	Joe Barry Carroll	.10
96	Lester Conner	.10
97	Roy Hinson	.10
98	Mike McGee	.10
99	*Chris Morris*	.50
100	Patrick Ewing	1.00
101	Mark Jackson	.20
102	*Johnny Newman*	.20
103	Charles Oakley	.10
104	*Rod Strickland*	1.00
105	Trent Tucker	.10
106	Kiki Vandeweghe	.10
107	Gerald Wilkins	.10
108	Terry Catledge	.10
109	Dave Corzine	.10
110	*Scott Skiles*	.50
111	Reggie Theus	.10
112	*Ron Anderson*	.10
113	Charles Barkley	2.00
114	*Scott Brooks*	.20
115	Maurice Cheeks	.10
116	Mike Gminski	.10
117	*Hersey Hawkins*	1.00
118	Chris Welp	.10
119	Tom Chambers	.20
120	Armon Gilliam	.10
121	*Jeff Hornacek*	1.00
122	Eddie Johnson	.10
123	*Kevin Johnson*	1.50
124	*Dan Majerle*	1.00
125	Mark West	.10
126	Richard Anderson	.10
127	Mark Bryant	.10
128	Clyde Drexler	1.50
129	Kevin Duckworth	.10
130	Jerome Kersey	.10
131	Terry Porter	.10
132	Buck Williams	.10
133	Danny Ainge	.10
134	Ricky Berry	.10
135	Rodney McCray	.10
136	Jim Petersen	.10
137	Harold Pressley	.10
138	Kenny Smith	.10
139	Wayman Tisdale	.10
140	*Willie Anderson*	.30
141	Frank Brikowski	.10
142	Terry Cummings	.10
143	Johnny Dawkins	.10
144	*Vernon Maxwell*	.50
145	Michael Cage	.10
146	Dale Ellis	.10
147	Alton Lister	.10
148	Xavier McDaniel	.10
149	Derrick McKey	.10
150	Nate McMillen	.10
151	Thurl Bailey	.10
152	Mark Eaton	.10
153	Darrell Griffith	.10
154	Eric Leckner	.10
155	Karl Malone	1.50
156	John Stockton	2.00
157	Mark Alarie	.10
159	Bernard King	.10
160	Jeff Malone	.10
161	Darrell Walker	.10
162	John Williams (Bullets)	.10
162A	John Williams (Cleveland back)	.10
163	Karl Malone, Mark Eaton, John Stockton (AS)	.50
164	Hakeem Olajuwon, Clyde Drexler (AS)	.75
165	Dominique Wilkins, Karl Malone (AS)	.20
166	Brad Daugherty, Mark Price, Larry Nance (AS)	.10
167	Mark Jackson, Patrick Ewing (AS)	.20
168	Checklist	.10

1989-90 Fleer Stickers

With 11 stickers in all, these All-Star stickers were inserted one per pack in 1989-90 Fleer wax packs. Fronts show action shots of the players, surrounded by a blue and purple star design, plus "Fleer '89 All-Stars." This design is also used for the card backs, which are numbered.

		MT
Complete Set (11):		25.00
Common Player:		.20
1	Karl Malone	.50
2	Hakeem Olajuwon	1.00
3	Michael Jordan	20.00
4	Charles Barkley	1.00
5	Magic Johnson	1.00
6	Isiah Thomas	.30
7	Patrick Ewing	.40
8	Dale Ellis	.20
9	Chris Mullin	.30
10	Larry Bird	1.50
11	Tom Chambers	.20

1990-91 Fleer

Fleer's fifth consecutive set of NBA players expanded to 196 players (plus two checklists). Two subsets were mixed into the series: "All-Star" players and 10 different "Rookie Sensations." Five "League Leader" cards were also part of the basic set. This set includes the first Fleer David Robinson card plus the rookie card of Danny Ferry.

		MT
Complete Set (198):		12.00
Common Player:		.05
Minor Stars:		.10
Pack (15):		2.00
Wax Box (36):		38.00
1	John Battle	.05
2	Cliff Levingston	.05
3	Moses Malone	.05
4	Kenny Smith	.05
5	Spud Webb	.05
6	Dominique Wilkins	.15
7	Kevin Willis	.05
8	Larry Bird	.50
9	Dennis Johnson	.05
10	Joe Kleine	.05
11	Reggie Lewis	.10
12	Kevin McHale	.10
13	Robert Parish	.10
14	Jim Paxson	.05
15	Ed Pinckney	.05
16	Tyrone Bogues	.05
17	Rex Chapman	.05
18	Dell Curry	.05
19	Armon Gilliam	.05
20	*J.R. Reid*	.10
21	Kelly Tripucka	.05
22	*B.J. Armstrong*	.25
23	Bill Cartwright	.05
24	Horace Grant	.10
25	Craig Hodges	.05
26	Michael Jordan	6.00
27	*Stacey King*	.10
28	John Paxson	.05
29	Will Perdue	.05
30	Scottie Pippen	.40
31	Brad Daugherty	.05
32	Craig Ehlo	.05
33	*Danny Ferry*	.15
34	Steve Kerr	.05
35	Larry Nance	.05
36	Mark Price	.10
37	John Williams	.05
38	Rolando Blackman	.05
39	Adrian Dantley	.05
40	Brad Davis	.05
41	James Donaldson	.05
42	Derek Harper	.05
43	Sam Perkins	.05
44	Randy White	.05
45	Herb Williams	.05
46	Michael Adams	.05
47	Walter Davis	.05
48	Alex English	.05
49	Bill Hanzlik	.05
50	Lafayette Lever	.05
51	*Todd Lichti*	.05
52	Blair Rasmussen	.05
53	Dan Schayes	.05
54	Mark Aguirre	.05
55	Joe Dumars	.15
56	James Edwards	.05
57	Vinnie Johnson	.05
58	Bill Laimbeer	.05
59	Dennis Rodman	.40
60	John Salley	.05
61	Isiah Thomas	.20
62	Manute Bol	.05
63	*Tim Hardaway*	.50
64	Rod Higgins	.05
65	*Sarunas Marciulionis*	.10
66	Chris Mullin	.10
67	Mitch Richmond	.15
68	Terry Teagle	.05
69	*Anthony Bowie*	.05
70	Eric Floyd	.05
71	Buck Johnson	.05
72	Vernon Maxwell	.05
73	Hakeem Olajuwon	.50
74	Otis Thorpe	.05
75	Mitchell Wiggins	.05
76	Vern Fleming	.05
77	*George McCloud*	.25
78	Reggie Miller	.25
79	Chuck Person	.05
80	Mike Sanders	.05
81	Detlef Schrempf	.10
82	Rik Smits	.10
83	LaSalle Thompson	.05
84	Benoit Benjamin	.05
85	Winston Garland	.05
86	Ron Harper	.05
87	Danny Manning	.10
88	Ken Norman	.05
89	Charles Smith	.05
90	Michael Cooper	.05
91	*Vlade Divac*	.40
92	A.C. Green	.05
93	Magic Johnson	.50
94	Byron Scott	.05
95	Mychal Thompson	.05
96	Orlando Woolridge	.05
97	James Worthy	.05
98	*Sherman Douglas*	.20
99	Kevin Edwards	.05

100	Grant Long	.05
101	*Glen Rice*	.50
102	Rony Seikaly	.10
103	Billy Thompson	.05
104	*Jeff Grayer*	.05
105	Jay Humphries	.05
106	Ricky Pierce	.05
107	Paul Pressey	.05
108	Fred Roberts	.05
109	Alvin Robertson	.05
110	Jack Sikma	.05
111	Randy Breuer	.05
112	Tony Campbell	.05
113	Tyrone Corbin	.05
114	*Sam Mitchell*	.05
115	Tod Murphy	.05
116	*Pooh Richardson*	.10
117	*Mookie Blaylock*	.30
118	Sam Bowie	.05
119	Lester Conner	.05
120	Dennis Hopson	.05
121	Chris Morris	.05
122	Charles Shackleford	.05
123	Purvis Short	.05
124	Maurice Cheeks	.05
125	Patrick Ewing	.20
126	Mark Jackson	.05
127	Johnny Newman (J. on back)	.05
127A	Johnny Newman (Jr. on back)	.05
128	Charles Oakley	.05
129	Trent Tucker	.05
130	Kenny Walker	.05
131	Gerald Wilkins	.05
132	*Nick Anderson*	.30
133	Terry Catledge	.05
135	Otis Smith	.05
136	Reggie Theus	.05
137	Sam Vincent	.05
138	Ron Anderson	.05
139	Charles Barkley	.40
140	Scott Brooks	.05
141	Johnny Dawkins	.05
142	Mike Gminski	.05
143	Hersey Hawkins	.05
144	Rick Mahorn	.05
145	Derek Smith	.05
146	Tom Chambers	.05
147	Jeff Hornacek	.05
148	Eddie Johnson	.05
149	Kevin Johnson	.10
150	Dan Majerle	.10
151	Tim Perry	.05
152	Kurt Rambis	.05
153	Mark West	.05
154	Clyde Drexler	.25
155	Kevin Duckworth	.05
156	Byron Irvin	.05
157	Jerome Kersey	.05
158	Terry Porter	.05
159	*Cliff Robinson*	.40
160	Buck Williams	.05
161	Danny Young	.05
162	Danny Ainge	.05
163	Antoine Carr	.05
164	*Pervis Ellison*	.10
165	Rodney McCray	.05
166	Harold Pressley	.05
167	Wayman Tisdale	.05
168	Willie Anderson	.05
169	Frank Brickowski	.05
170	Terry Cummings	.05
171	*Sean Elliott*	.30
172	David Robinson	1.00
173	Rod Strickland	.05
174	David Wingate	.05
175	*Dana Barros*	.25
176	Michael Cage	.05
177	Dale Ellis	.05
178	*Shawn Kemp*	.75
179	Xavier McDaniel	.05
180	Derrick McKey	.05
181	Nate McMillan	.05
182	Thurl Bailey	.05
183	Mike Brown	.05
184	Mark Eaton	.05
185	*Blue Edwards*	.10
186	Robert Hansen	.05
187	Eric Leckner	.05
188	Karl Malone	.25
189	John Stockton	.25
190	Mark Alarie	.05
191	Ledell Eackles	.05
192	Harvey Grant (white letters)	.05
192A	Harvey Grant (black letters)	.05
193	*Tom Hammonds*	.05
194	Bernard King	.05
195	Jeff Malone	.05
196	Darrell Walker	.05
197	Checklist	.05
198	Checklist	.05

1990-91 Fleer All-Stars

These cards, which feature the top NBA stars, were inserted into 1990-91 wax packs, one every 5th pack. The fronts feature action shots against a hoop/net aqua-colored background. The card backs have a career summary with a pink and blue background and white borders. Cards are numbered (1 of 12, etc.).

		MT
Complete Set (12):		15.00
Common Player:		.25
1	Charles Barkley	1.00
2	Larry Bird	1.25
3	Hakeem Olajuwon	1.25
4	Magic Johnson	1.25
5	Michael Jordan	10.00
6	Isiah Thomas	.50
7	Karl Malone	1.00
8	Tom Chambers	.25
9	John Stockton	.75
10	David Robinson	1.50
11	Clyde Drexler	.75
12	Patrick Ewing	.50

1990-91 Fleer Rookie Sensations

Top rookies from the 1989-90 season are featured in this set. The cards were random inserts in 1990-91 Fleer cello packs, one per every six cello packs. The "Rookie Sensations" logo is on the front in yellow letters. Card backs, printed in red and black against a grey background, are numbered (1 of 10, etc.).

		MT
Complete Set (10):		40.00
Common Player:		1.50
1	David Robinson	25.00
2	Sean Elliott	4.00
3	Glen Rice	8.00
4	J.R. Reid	1.50
5	Stacey King	1.50
6	Pooh Richardson	1.50
7	Nick Anderson	5.00
8	Tim Hardaway	8.00
9	Vlade Divac	5.00
10	Sherman Douglas	1.50

1990-91 Fleer Update

Issued in mid-March, cards were released in a boxed set to hobby shops. Unlike Hoops and SkyBox, the set included all the top 1990 draft picks, not just the lottery picks. Cards were arranged alphabetically by team.

		MT
Complete Set (100):		5.00
Common Player:		.05
Minor Stars:		.10
1	John Koncak	.05
2	Tim McCormick	.05
3	Glenn Rivers	.05
4	*Rumeal Robinson*	.10
5	Trevor Wilson	.05
6	*Dee Brown*	.25
7	Dave Popson	.05
8	Kevin Gamble	.10
9	Brian Shaw	.10
10	Michael Smith	.05
11	*Kendall Gill*	.50
12	Johnny Newman	.05
13	Steve Scheffler	.05
14	Dennis Hopson	.05
15	Cliff Levingston	.05
16	*Chucky Brown*	.10
17	John Morton	.05
18	*Gerald Paddio*	.05
21	Rodney McCray	.05
22	Roy Tarpley	.05
23	*Randy White*	.10
24	*Anthony Cook*	.10
25	*Mahmoud Abdul-Rauf*	.30
26	*Marcus Liberty*	.10
27	Orlando Woolridge	.05
28	*William Bedford*	.10
29	*Lance Blanks*	.10
30	Scott Hastings	.05
31	*Tyrone Hill*	.40
32	*Les Jepsen*	.05
33	Steve Johnson	.05
34	*Kevin Pritchard*	.10
35	*Dave Jamerson*	.05
36	Kenny Smith	.05
37	*Greg Dreiling*	.05
38	*Ken Williams*	.05
39	*Michael Williams*	.10
40	Gary Grant	.05
41	*Bo Kimble*	.10
42	*Loy Vaught*	.40
43	*Elden Campbell*	.75
44	Sam Perkins	.10
45	*Tony Smith*	.10
46	Terry Teagle	.05
47	*Willie Burton*	.20
48	*Bimbo Coles*	.10
49	*Terry Davis*	.10
50	*Alec Kessler*	.10
51	Greg Anderson	.05
52	Frank Brickowski	.05
53	*Steve Henson*	.05
54	Brad Lohaus	.05
55	Dan Schayes	.05
56	*Gerald Glass*	.05
57	*Felton Spencer*	.20
58	*Doug West*	.20
59	Jud Buechler	.05
60	*Derrick Coleman*	.75
61	*Tate George*	.10
62	Reggie Theus	.05
63	*Greg Grant*	.10
64	*Jerrod Mustaf*	.10
65	*Eddie Lee Wilkins*	.10
66	Michael Ansley	.05
67	Jerry Reynolds	.05
68	*Dennis Scott*	.50
69	Manute Bol	.05
70	Armon Gilliam	.05
71	Brian Oliver	.10
72	*Kenny Payne*	.10
73	*Jayson Williams*	.75
74	*Kenny Battle*	.10
75	*Cedric Ceballos*	.40
76	*Negele Knight*	.10
77	Xavier McDaniel	.05
78	*Alaa Abdelnaby*	.10
79	Danny Ainge	.05
80	Mark Bryant	.05
81	*Drazen Petrovic*	.20
82	*Anthony Bonner*	.10
83	*Duane Causwell*	.10
84	Bobby Hansen	.05
85	Eric Leckner	.05
86	*Travis Mays*	.10
87	*Lionel Simmons*	.10
88	Sidney Green	.05
89	Tony Massenburg	.05
90	Paul Pressey	.05
91	*Dwayne Schintzius*	.10
92	*Gary Payton*	4.00
93	Olden Polynice	.05
94	Jeff Malone	.05
95	Walter Palmer	.05
96	Delaney Rudd	.05
97	Pervis Ellison	.05
98	*A.J. English*	.05
99	Greg Foster	.05
100	Checklist	.05

1991-92 Fleer

Fleer's sixth straight set was issued in late August. Expanded to 240 cards, the set has new subsets including Slam Dunk participants, coaches and All-Star game action. Fleer also produced full-color backs for the first time. LL means League Leader; SD means Slam Dunk; C means coach; AS means All-Star. Update cards, available in wax packs, continue where the regular Fleer set left off, starting with #241.

		MT
Complete Set (400):		8.00
Complete Series 1 (240):		4.00
Complete Series 2 (160):		4.00
Common Player:		.05
Minor Stars:		.10
Series 1 Pack (14):		.65
Series 1 Wax Box (36):		11.50
Series 2 Pack (14):		.60
Series 2 Wax Box (36):		10.50
1	John Battle	.05
2	Jon Koncak	.05
3	Rumeal Robinson	.05
4	Spud Webb	.05
5	Bob Weiss (C)	.05
6	Dominique Wilkins	.10
7	Kevin Willis	.05
8	Larry Bird	.50
9	Dee Brown	.05
10	Chris Ford (C)	.05
11	Kevin Gamble	.05
12	Reggie Lewis	.05
13	Kevin McHale	.10
14	Robert Parish	.10
15	Ed Pinckney	.05
16	Brian Shaw	.05
17	Tyrone Bogues	.05
18	Rex Chapman	.05
19	Dell Curry	.05
20	Kendall Gill	.05
21	Eric Leckner	.05
22	Gene Littles (C)	.05
23	Johnny Newman	.05
24	J.R. Reid	.05
25	B.J. Armstrong	.05
26	Bill Cartwright	.05
27	Horace Grant	.15
28	Phil Jackson (C)	.05
29	Michael Jordan	2.00
30	Cliff Levingston	.05
31	John Paxson	.05
32	Will Perdue	.05
33	Scottie Pippen	.50
34	Brad Daugherty	.05
35	Craig Ehlo	.05
36	Danny Ferry	.05
37	Larry Nance	.05
38	Mark Price	.05
39	Darnell Valentine	.05
40	John Williams	.05
41	Lenny Wilkens (C)	.05
42	Richie Adubato (C)	.05
43	Rolando Blackman	.05
44	James Donaldson	.05
45	Derek Harper	.05
46	Rodney McCray	.05
47	Randy White	.05
48	Herb Williams	.05
49	Mahmoud Abdul-Rauf	.10
50	Marcus Liberty	.05
51	Todd Lichti	.05
52	Blair Rasmussen	.05
53	Paul Westhead (C)	.05
54	Reggie Williams	.05
55	Joe Wolf	.05
56	Orlando Woolridge	.05
57	Mark Aguirre	.05
58	Chuck Daly (C)	.05
59	Joe Dumars	.10
60	James Edwards	.05
61	Vinnie Johnson	.05
62	Bill Laimbeer	.05
63	Dennis Rodman	.50
64	Isiah Thomas	.15
65	Tim Hardaway	.20
66	Rod Higgins	.05
67	Tyrone Hill	.05
68	Sarunas Marciulionis	.05
69	Chris Mullin	.10
70	Don Nelson (C)	.05
71	Mitch Richmond	.15
72	Tom Tolbert	.05
73	Don Chaney (C)	.05
74	Eric Floyd	.05
75	Buck Johnson	.05
76	Vernon Maxwell	.05
77	Hakeem Olajuwon	.50
78	Kenny Smith	.05
79	Larry Smith	.05
80	Otis Thorpe	.05
81	Vern Fleming	.05
82	Bob Hill (C)	.05
83	Reggie Miller	.15
84	Chuck Person	.05
85	Detlef Schrempf	.05
86	Rik Smits	.10
87	LaSalle Thompson	.05
88	Michael Williams	.05
89	Gary Grant	.05
90	Ron Harper	.05
91	Bo Kimble	.05
92	Danny Manning	.05
93	Ken Norman	.05
94	Olden Polynice	.05
95	Mike Schuler (C)	.05
96	Charles Smith	.05
97	Vlade Divac	.05
98	Mike Dunleavy (C)	.05
99	A.C. Green	.05
100	Magic Johnson	.50
101	Sam Perkins	.05
102	Byron Scott	.05
103	Terry Teagle	.05
104	James Worthy	.05
105	Willie Burton	.05
106	Vernell Coles	.05
107	Sherman Douglas	.05
108	Kevin Edwards	.05
109	Grant Long	.05
110	Kevin Loughery (C)	.05
111	Glen Rice	.10
112	Rony Seikaly	.05
113	Frank Brickowski	.05
114	Dale Ellis	.05
115	Del Harris (C)	.05
116	Jay Humphries	.05
117	Fred Roberts	.05
118	Alvin Robertson	.05
119	Dan Schayes	.05
120	Jack Sikma	.05
121	Tony Campbell	.05
122	Tyrone Corbin	.05
123	Sam Mitchell	.05
124	Tod Murphy	.05
125	Jerome Richardson	.05
126	Jim Rodgers (C)	.05
127	Felton Spencer	.05
128	Mookie Blaylock	.05
129	Sam Bowie	.05
130	Derrick Coleman	.10
131	Chris Dudley	.05
132	Bill Fitch (C)	.05
133	Chris Morris	.05
134	Drazen Petrovic	.05
135	Maurice Cheeks	.05
136	Patrick Ewing	.15
137	Mark Jackson	.05
138	Charles Oakley	.05
139	Pat Riley (C)	.05
140	Trent Tucker	.05
141	Kiki Vandeweghe	.05
142	Gerald Wilkins	.05
143	Nick Anderson	.10
144	Terry Catledge	.05
145	Matt Guokas (C)	.05
146	Jerry Reynolds	.05
147	Dennis Scott	.10
148	Scott Skiles	.05
149	Otis Smith	.05
150	Ron Anderson	.05
151	Charles Barkley	.30
152	Johnny Dawkins	.05
153	Armon Gilliam	.10
154	Hersey Hawkins	.05
155	Jim Lynam (C)	.05
156	Rick Mahorn	.05
157	Brian Oliver	.05
158	Tom Chambers	.05
159	Cotton Fitzsimmons (C)	.05
160	Jeff Hornacek	.05
161	Kevin Johnson	.10
162	Negele Knight	.05
163	Dan Majerle	.05
164	Xavier McDaniel	.05
165	Mark West	.05
166	Rick Adelman (C)	.05
167	Danny Ainge	.05
168	Clyde Drexler	.20
169	Kevin Duckworth	.05
170	Jerome Kersey	.05
171	Terry Porter	.05
172	Cliff Robinson	.10
173	Buck Williams	.05
174	Antoine Carr	.05
175	Duane Causell	.05
176	*Jim Les*	.05
177	Travis Mays	.05
178	Dick Motta (C)	.05
179	Lionel Simmons	.05
180	Rory Sparrow	.05
181	Wayman Tisdale	.05
182	Willie Anderson	.05
183	Larry Brown (C)	.05
184	Terry Cummings	.05
185	Sean Elliott	.05
186	Paul Pressey	.05
187	David Robinson	.40
188	Rod Strickland	.05
189	Benoit Benjamin	.05
190	Eddie Johnson	.05
191	K.C. Jones (C)	.05
192	Shawn Kemp	.50
193	Derrick McKey	.05
194	Gary Payton	.15
195	Ricky Pierce	.05
196	Sedale Threatt	.05
197	Thurl Bailey	.05
198	Mark Eaton	.05
199	Blue Edwards	.05
200	Jeff Malone	.05
201	Karl Malone	.15
202	Jerry Sloan (C)	.05
203	John Stockton	.15
204	Ledell Eackles	.05
205	Pervis Ellison	.05
206	A.J. English	.05
207	Harvey Grant	.05
208	Bernard King	.05
209	Wes Unseld (C)	.05
210	Kevin Johnson (AS)	.05
211	Michael Jordan (AS)	1.00
212	Dominique Wilkins (AS)	.05
213	Charles Barkley (AS)	.15
214	Hakeem Olajuwon (AS)	.20
215	Patrick Ewing (AS)	.05
216	Tim Hardaway (AS)	.05
217	John Stockton (AS)	.10
218	Chris Mullin (AS)	.05
219	Karl Malone (AS)	.10
220	Michael Jordan (LL)	1.00
221	John Stockton (LL)	.10
222	Alvin Robertson (LL)	.05
223	Hakeem Olajuwon (LL)	.20
224	Buck Williams (LL)	.05
225	David Robinson (LL)	.20
226	Reggie Miller (LL)	.10
227	Blue Edwards (SD)	.05
228	Dee Brown (SD)	.05
229	Rex Chapman (SD)	.05
230	Kenny Smith (SD)	.05
231	Shawn Kemp (SD)	.20
232	Kendall Gill (SD)	.05
233	AS game action	.40
234	AS game action	.05
235	AS game action	.05
236	AS game action	.05
237	AS game action	.05
238	AS game action	.40
239	Checklist	.05
240	Checklist	.05
241	*Stacey Augmon*	.25
242	Maurice Cheeks	.05
243	*Paul Graham*	.05
244	*Rodney Monroe*	.10
245	Blair Rasmussen	.05
246	Alexander Volkov	.05
247	John Bagley	.05
248	*Rick Fox*	.15
249	Rickey Green	.05
250	Joe Kleine	.05
251	Stojko Vrankovic	.05
252	Allan Bristow (C)	.05
253	Kenny Gattison	.05
254	Mike Gminski	.05
255	*Larry Johnson*	1.00
256	Bobby Hansen	.05
257	Craig Hodges	.05
258	Stacey King	.05
259	*Scott Williams*	.10
260	John Battle	.05
261	Winston Bennett	.05
262	*Terrell Brandon*	.50
263	Henry James	.05
264	Steve Kerr	.05
265	*Jimmy Oliver*	.05
266	Brad Davis	.05
267	Terry Davis	.05
268	*Donald Hodge*	.05
269	*Mike Iuzzolino*	.05
270	Fat Lever	.05
271	*Doug Smith*	.10
272	Greg Anderson	.05
273	*Kevin Brooks*	.05
274	Walter Davis	.05
275	Winston Garland	.05
276	*Mark Macon*	.10
277	*Dikembe Mutombo*	.75
278	William Bedford	.05
279	Lance Blanks	.05
280	John Salley	.05
281	Charles Thomas	.05
282	Darrell Walker	.05
283	Orlando Woolridge	.05
284	*Victor Alexander*	.10
285	*Vincent Askew*	.10
286	*Mario Elie*	.20
287	Alton Lister	.05
288	*Billy Owens*	.25
289	*Matt Bullard*	.05
290	*Carl Herrera*	.10
291	Tree Rollins	.05
292	John Turner	.05
293	*Dale Davis*	.25
294	*Sean Green*	.05
295	Ken Williams	.05
296	James Edwards	.05
297	*LeRon Ellis*	.05
298	Doc Rivers	.05
299	Loy Vaught	.05
300	Elden Campbell	.05
301	Jack Haley	.05
302	Keith Owens	.05
303	Tony Smith	.05
304	Sedale Threatt	.05
305	*Keith Askins*	.15
306	Alec Kessler	.05
307	John Morton	.05
308	Alan Ogg	.05
309	*Steve Smith*	.30
310	Lester Conner	.05
311	Jeff Grayer	.05
312	Frank Hamblen (C)	.05
313	Steve Henson	.05
314	Larry Krystkowiak	.05
315	Moses Malone	.10
316	Thurl Bailey	.05
317	Randy Breuer	.05
318	Scott Brooks	.05
319	Gerald Glass	.05
320	*Luc Longley*	.20
321	Doug West	.05
322	*Kenny Anderson*	.40
323	Tate George	.05
324	*Terry Mills*	.15
325	*Greg Anthony*	.15
326	*Anthony Mason*	.30
327	Tim McCormick	.05
328	Xavier McDaniel	.05
329	Brian Quinnett	.05
330	*John Starks*	.30
331	*Stanley Roberts*	.10
332	Jeff Turner	.05
333	Sam Vincent	.05
334	*Brian Williams*	.20
335	Manute Bol	.05
336	Kenny Payne	.05
337	Charles Shackleford	.05
338	Jayson Williams	.05
339	Cedric Ceballos	.15
340	Andrew Lang	.05
341	Jerrod Mustaf	.05
342	Tim Perry	.05
343	Kurt Rambis	.05
344	Alaa Abdelnaby	.05
345	*Robert Pack*	.20
346	Danny Young	.05
347	Anthony Bonner	.05
348	*Pete Chilcutt*	.05
349	Rex Hughes (C)	.05
350	Mitch Richmond	.10
351	Dwayne Schintzius	.05
352	Spud Webb	.05
353	Antoine Carr	.05
354	Sidney Green	.05
355	Vinnie Johnson	.05
356	Greg Sutton	.05
357	Dana Barros	.05
358	Michael Cage	.05
359	*Marty Conlon*	.10
360	*Rich King*	.10
361	Nate McMillan	.05
362	*David Benoit*	.15
363	Mike Brown	.05
364	Tyrone Corbin	.05
365	*Eric Murdock*	.10
366	Delaney Rudd	.05
367	Michael Adams	.05
368	Tom Hammonds	.05
369	*Larry Stewart*	.10
370	Andre Turner	.05
371	David Wingate	.05
372	Dominique Wilkins	.10
373	Larry Bird (TL)	.30
374	Rex Chapman (TL)	.05
375	Michael Jordan (TL)	1.00
376	Brad Daugherty (TL)	.05
377	Derek Harper (TL)	.05
378	Dikembe Mutombo	.15
379	Joe Dumars (TL)	.05
380	Chris Mullin (TL)	.05
381	Hakeem Olajuwon	.20
382	Chuck Person (TL)	.05
383	Charles Smith (TL)	.05
384	James Worthy (TL)	.05
385	Glen Rice (TL)	.05
386	Alvin Robertson (TL)	.05
387	Tony Campbell (TL)	.05
388	Derrick Coleman (TL)	.05
389	Patrick Ewing (TL)	.10
390	Scott Skiles (TL)	.05
391	Charles Barkley (TL)	.15
392	Kevin Johnson (TL)	.05
393	Clyde Drexler (TL)	.10
394	Lionel Simmons (TL)	.05
395	David Robinson (TL)	.20
396	Ricky Pierce (TL)	.05
397	John Stockton (TL)	.10
398	Michael Adams (TL)	.05
399	Checklist	.05
400	Checklist	.05

1991-92 Fleer Dikembe Mutombo

These cards, devoted to Dikembe Mutombo, were random inserts in 1991-92 Fleer Update wax packs, every sixth pack. The fronts have color action photos, against a ghosted background. The borders are dark red; lettering is mustard yellow. Card backs have a mug shot and career summary. They are numbered (1 of 12, etc.). A promo card featuring Mutombo, Jeff Massien (vice president of Fleer) and Dominique Wilkins was also produced to preview the limited edition sets for Wilkins and Mutombo. The unnumbered card back has text promoting the sets.

	MT
Complete Set (12):	5.00
Common Mutombo:	.50
Mutombo Auto:	75.00
Childhood in Zaire (Dikembe Mutombo)	.50
Georgetown Start (Dikembe Mutombo)	.50

	Arrival on College Scene (Dikembe Mutombo)	.50
	Capping College Career (Dikembe Mutombo)	.50
	NBA Draft (Dikembe Mutombo)	.50
	First NBA Games (Dikembe Mutombo)	.50
	Offensive Skills (Dikembe Mutombo)	.50
	What He Has Meant To Nuggets (Dikembe Mutombo)	.50
	Work Habits (Dikembe Mutombo)	.50
	Charmed Denver (Dikembe Mutombo)	.50
	The Future (Dikembe Mutombo)	.50
	The Mutombo Legend (Dikembe Mutombo)	.50

1991-92 Fleer Pro Visions

As in baseball and football, artist Terry Smith rendered some of the game's top players on these art cards. Pro Visions cards were random inserts in Fleer Series I 12-card plastic-wrap packs. Card backs are numbered (1 of 6, etc.).

		MT
Complete Set (6):		5.00
Common Player:		.25
1	David Robinson	.75
2	Michael Jordan	3.00
3	Charles Barkley	.75
4	Patrick Ewing	.25
5	Karl Malone	.50
6	Magic Johnson	.75

1991-92 Fleer Rookie Sensations

An idea carried over from the previous year, this subset featured the top rookies (as chosen by Fleer) from 1990-91. Cards were randomly packed in pre-priced cello packs, one every two packs. Fronts and backs have magenta borders, while the set logo appears on the front. A card number (1 of 10, etc.), appears on the card back.

		MT
Complete Set (10):		10.00
Common Player:		.50
Minor Stars:		1.00
1	Lionel Simmons	.50
2	Dennis Scott	1.50
3	Derrick Coleman	2.00
4	Kendall Gill	1.50
5	Travis Mays	.50
6	Felton Spencer	.50
7	Willie Burton	1.00
8	Mahmoud Abdul-Rauf	2.00
9	Gary Payton	5.00
10	Dee Brown	1.50

1991-92 Fleer Schoolyard

These cards, using a completely different design on the front, featured top players on the fronts with tips on playing basketball on the back. Cards were randomly inserted in Fleer rack packs, one per pack. Card backs are numbered (1 of 6, etc.).

		MT
Complete Set (6):		8.00
Common Player:		.75
1	Chris Mullin	1.50
2	Isiah Thomas	2.50
3	Kevin McHale	1.50
4	Kevin Johnson	2.00
5	Karl Malone	3.00
6	Alvin Robertson	.75

1991-92 Fleer Dominique Wilkins

These cards, randomly inserted into every sixth 1991-92 Fleer Update pack, give pictoral highlights of Dominique Wilkins' career. The design is similar to the Mutombo set. A promo card featuring Wilkins, Jeff Massien (vice president of Fleer) and Dikembe Mutombo was also produced to preview the limited edition sets for Wilkins and Mutombo. The unnumbered card back has text promoting the sets.

		MT
Complete Set (12):		5.00
Common Wilkins:		.50
Wilkins Auto:		75.00
	Overview (Dominique Wilkins)	.50
	College (Dominique Wilkins)	.50
	Early Years (Dominique Wilkins)	.50
	Early Career (Dominique Wilkins)	.50
	Dominique Emerges (Dominique Wilkins)	.50
	Another Milestone (Dominique Wilkins)	.50
	Wilkins Continues To Shine (Dominique Wilkins)	.50
	Best All Around Season (Dominique Wilkins)	.50
	Charitable Causes (Dominique Wilkins)	.50
	Durability (Dominique Wilkins)	.50
	Career Numbers (Dominique Wilkins)	.50
	Future (Dominique Wilkins)	.50

1991-92 Fleer Mutombo/Wilkins Promo

This promo card was used to introduce the inclusion of Dominique Wilkins and Dikembe Mutombo insert sets in 1991-92 Fleer Basketball. The card featured the two players in a posed shot with Fleer vice president Jeff Massien. It was available to direct dealers of Fleer and various media.

		MT
Complete Set (1):		10.00
Common Player:		10.00
1	Dikembe Mutombo, Dominique Wilkins (With Jeff Massien, VP of Fleer)	10.00

1991-92 Fleer Tony's Pizza

This 120-card set was issued in three-card packs inside specially marked Tony's Frozen Pizza during March and April. The cards are the same as regular-issue Fleer cards except for an "S" prefix on the card back number. Near the end of the promotion, there were apparently a limited number of cards inserted without the "S" prefix.

		MT
Complete Set (120):		200.00
Common Player:		1.00
1	Terry Teagle	1.00
2	Karl Malone	12.00
3	Patrick Ewing	8.00
4	Alvin Robertson	1.00
5	Scott Skiles	1.25
6	Frank Brickowski	1.00
7	Mookie Blaylock	2.00
8	Ricky Pierce	1.25
9	Gary Payton	8.00
10	Dennis Scott	1.00
11	Derrick McKey	1.00
12	Mark West	1.00
13	Mark Jackson	1.75
14	Glen Rice	3.00
15	Charles Barkley	12.00
16	David Robinson	12.00
17	Sam Bowie	1.25
18	Ron Harper	1.50
19	Reggie Miller	8.00
20	Lionel Simmons	1.00
21	Jerome Kersey	1.25
22	Rod Strickland	1.00
23	Charles Oakley	1.50
24	Rony Seikaly	1.00
25	Johnny Dawkins	1.00
26	Fred Roberts	1.00
27	Derrick Coleman	1.00
28	Bo Kimble	1.00
29	Chuck Person	1.25
30	Kiki Vandeweghe	1.25
31	Jeff Malone	1.00
32	Vlade Divac	1.50
33	Michael Jordan	45.00
34	Gerald Wilkins	1.00
35	Sarunas Marciulionis	1.00
36	Pooh Richardson	1.00
37	Hakeem Olajuwon	12.00
38	Rodney McCray	1.00
39	Larry Nance	2.00
40	Wayman Tisdale	1.00
41	Tom Chambers	2.00
42	A.C. Green	2.00
43	Bernard King	2.00
44	Reggie Williams	1.00
45	Chris Mullin	2.00
46	Bill Laimbeer	1.50
47	Kenny Smith	1.50
48	Harvey Grant	1.00
49	Mark Price	2.00
50	Olden Polynice	1.00
51	Isiah Thomas	6.00
52	Magic Johnson	17.00
53	John Paxson	1.50
54	Muggsy Bogues	2.00
55	Mitch Richmond	6.00
56	Dennis Rodman	10.00
57	Otis Thorpe	1.00
58	Larry Bird	20.00
59	Hot Rod Williams	1.00
60	Hersey Hawkins	1.50
61	Brian Shaw	1.00
62	Detlef Schrempf	1.25
63	Danny Manning	1.25
64	Thurl Bailey	1.00
65	Benoit Benjamin	1.00
66	Nick Anderson	1.50
67	Rex Chapman	1.50
68	Danny Ainge	3.00
69	Dee Brown	1.00
70	Chris Dudley	1.00
71	Kevin McHale	3.50
72	Dell Curry	1.00
73	Ken Norman	1.00
74	Mark Eaton	1.00
75	Shawn Kemp	9.00
76	Bill Cartwright	1.25
77	Terry Cummings	1.50
78	Clyde Drexler	9.00
79	Kevin Johnson	3.00
80	Dale Ellis	1.25
81	Tod Murphy	1.00
82	Brad Daugherty	1.25
83	Charles Smith	1.00
84	Horace Grant	2.00
85	Vernon Maxwell	1.00
86	Todd Lichti	1.00
87	Sean Elliott	1.50
88	Kevin Duckworth	1.00
89	Dan Majerle	2.00
90	James Worthy	3.00
91	Mark Aguirre	1.50
92	Kevin Willis	1.25
93	Reggie Lewis	1.50
94	Rumeal Robinson	1.00
95	Terry Porter	1.50
96	Rolando Blackman	1.50
97	Tony Campbell	1.00
98	Sam Perkins	1.50
99	Willie Burton	1.00
100	Joe Dumars	3.00
101	Felton Spencer	1.00
102	Danny Ferry	1.00
103	James Donaldson	1.00
104	Craig Ehlo	1.25
105	Cliff Robinson	2.00
106	Pervis Ellison	1.00
107	Tyrone Corbin	1.00
108	Byron Scott	1.50
109	Sherman Douglas	1.00
110	Tim Hardaway	4.00
111	Kendall Gill	1.00
112	J.R. Reid	1.00
113	Robert Parish	2.00
114	Dominique Wilkins	2.50
115	Buck Williams	1.50
116	Scottie Pippen	12.00
117	Sam Mitchell	1.00
118	John Stockton	10.00
119	Derek Harper	1.50
120	Chris Jackson	1.00

1991-92 Fleer Wheaties Sheets

Eight different nine-card panels were printed on the back of over four million Wheaties boxes during this promotion. The sheet contained eight regular-issue cards and one special card from subsets including All-Stars, League Leaders, Pro Visions, Rookie Sensations, Slam Dunk and Schoolyard. The cards are the same as regular-issue cards on the front, but are identified by their grey backs. They are not perforated and are identified by the eight different boxes they were contained on.

		MT
Complete Set (8):		120.00
Common Player:		6.00
1	Wheaties Box 1 (Terry Cummings, Felton Spencer RS, Mookie Blaylock, Joe Dumars, Charles Barkley PV, Rex Chapman, Reggie Miller LL, Horace Grant, Shawn Kemp)	5.00
2	Wheaties Box 2 (Chris Jackson RS, Sam Perkins, Sean Elliott, Tim Hardaway, Karl Malone PV, J.R. Reid, Wayman Tisdale, Chris Mullin SY, Rolando Blackman)	10.00
3	Wheaties Box 3 (Alvin Robertson, Robert Parish, Mark Aguirre, Tyrone Hill, Patrick Ewing PV, Brad Daugherty, Lionel Simmons RS, Terry Porter, Bimbo Coles)	9.00
4	Wheaties Box 4 (Blue Edwards SD, Bill Cartwright, Rony Seikaly, Vernon Maxwell, David Robinson PV, Sam Bowie, Hersey Hawkins, A.C. Green, Dee Brown RS)	10.00
5	Wheaties Box 5 (B.J. Armstrong, Jay Humphries, Isiah Thomas SY, Reggie Lewis, Kevin Johnson AS, Pooh Richardson, Dennis Scott RS, Kevin Duckworth, Otis Thorpe)	7.00
6	Wheaties Box 6 (Byron Scott, Kevin McHale SY, Muggsy Bogues, Detlef Schrempf, Michael Jordan PV, Willie Anderson, Johnny Dawkins, Kendall Gill RS, Glen Rice)	25.00
7	Wheaties Box 7 (Charles Smith, Derrick Coleman RS, Dennis Rodman, Gerald Wilkins, Hakeem Olajuwon AS, James Worthy, Tom Chambers, Buck Williams LL, Larry Bird)	18.00
8	Wheaties Box 8 (Kenny Smith SD, Scottie Pippen, Clyde Drexler, John Stockton, Dominique Wilkins AS, Derek Harper, Brian Shaw, Mark Price, Willie Burton RS)	18.00

1992-93 Fleer

These cards are 2-1/2" x 3-1/2" with color action photos on the front. The backs have color action shots and stats. Subsets within the main set include Coaches cards, League Leaders, Award Winners, Pro Visions, Schoolyard Stars, Slam Dunks, and checklists. A Larry Johnson card was also made as a promo for the set. Johnson is featured on the card front with Paul Mullan, chairman of Fleer. The card has a gold metallic border for the front, which also has a '92 Commemorative Card logo in the lower right corner. The back has a basketball-like texture pattern for the background and details the 1992-93 Fleer set and Johnson's 12-card set. It is unnumbered and worth $8.

		MT
Complete Set (444):		30.00
Complete Series 1 (264):		15.00
Complete Series 2 (180):		15.00
Common Player:		.05
Minor Stars:		.10
Series 1 Pack (15):		2.00
Series 1 Wax Box (36):		60.00
Series 2 Pack (15):		1.50
Series 2 Wax Box (36):		40.00
1	Stacey Augmon	.05
2	Duane Ferrell	.05
3	Paul Graham	.05
4	Jon Koncak	.05
5	Blair Rasmussen	.05
6	Rumeal Robinson	.05
7	Bob Weiss (Co.)	.05
8	Dominique Wilkins	.10
9	Kevin Willis	.05
10	John Bagley	.05
11	Larry Bird	1.00
12	Dee Brown	.10
13	Chris Ford (Co.)	.05
14	Rick Fox	.05
15	Kevin Gamble	.05
16	Reggie Lewis	.05
17	Kevin McHale	.10
18	Robert Parish	.10
19	Ed Pinckney	.05
20	Muggsy Bogues	.05
21	Allan Bristow (Co.)	.05
22	Dell Curry	.05
23	Kenny Gattison	.05
24	Kendall Gill	.05
25	Larry Johnson	.50
26	Johnny Newman	.05
27	J.R. Reid	.05
28	B.J. Armstrong	.05
29	Bill Cartwright	.05
30	Horace Grant	.15
31	Phil Jackson (Co.)	.05
32	Michael Jordan	2.50
33	Stacey King	.05
34	Cliff Levingston	.05
35	John Paxson	.05
36	Scottie Pippen	.50
37	Scott Williams	.05
38	John Battle	.05
39	Terrell Brandon	.10
40	Brad Daugherty	.05
41	Craig Ehlo	.05
42	Larry Nance	.05
43	Mark Price	.05
44	Mike Sanders	.05
45	Len Wilkens (Co.)	.05
46	John Williams	.05
47	Richie Adubato (Co.)	.05
48	Terry Davis	.05
49	Derek Harper	.05
50	Donald Hodge	.05
51	Mike Iuzzolino	.05
52	Rodney McCray	.05
53	Doug Smith	.05
54	Greg Anderson	.05
55	Winston Garland	.05
56	Dan Issel (Co.)	.05
57	Mahmoud Abdul-Rauf	.10
58	Marcus Liberty	.05
59	Mark Macon	.05
60	Dikembe Mutombo	.25
61	Reggie Williams	.05
62	Mark Aguirre	.05
63	Joe Dumars	.10
64	Bill Laimbeer	.05
65	Olden Polynice	.05
66	Dennis Rodman	.75
67	Ron Rothstein (Co.)	.05
68	John Salley	.05
69	Isiah Thomas	.20
70	Darrell Walker	.05
71	Orlando Woolridge	.05
72	Victor Alexander	.05
73	Mario Elie	.05
74	Tim Hardaway	.10
75	Tyrone Hill	.10
76	Sarunas Marciulionis	.05
77	Chris Mullin	.10
78	Don Nelson (Co.)	.05
79	Billy Owens	.10
80	Avery Johnson	.10
81	Sleepy Floyd	.05
82	Buck Johnson	.05
83	Vernon Maxwell	.05
84	Hakeem Olajuwon	.75
85	Kenny Smith	.05
86	Otis Thorpe	.05
87	Rudy Tomjanovich (Co.)	.05
88	Dale Davis	.10
89	Vern Fleming	.05
90	Bob Hill (Co.)	.05
91	Reggie Miller	.25
92	Chuck Person	.05
93	Detlef Schrempf	.05
94	Rik Smits	.10
95	LaSalle Thompson	.05
96	Michael Williams	.05
97	Larry Brown (Co.)	.05
98	James Edwards	.05
99	Gary Grant	.05
100	Ron Harper	.05
101	Danny Manning	.10
102	Ken Norman	.05
103	Doc Rivers	.05
104	Charles Smith	.05
105	Loy Vaught	.05
106	Elden Campbell	.05
107	Vlade Divac	.05
108	A.C. Green	.05
109	Sam Perkins	.05
110	Randy Pfund (Co.)	.05
111	Byron Scott	.05
112	Terry Teagle	.05
113	Sedale Threatt	.05
114	James Worthy	.05
115	Willie Burton	.05
116	Bimbo Coles	.05
117	Kevin Edwards	.05
118	Grant Long	.05
119	Kevin Loughery (Co.)	.05
120	Glen Rice	.10
121	Rony Seikaly	.05
122	Brian Shaw	.05
123	Steve Smith	.10
124	Frank Brickowski	.05
125	Mike Dunleavy (Co.)	.05
126	Blue Edwards	.05
127	Moses Malone	.10
128	Eric Murdock	.10
129	Fred Roberts	.05
130	Alvin Robertson	.05
131	Thurl Bailey	.05
132	Tony Campbell	.05
133	Gerald Glass	.05
134	Luc Longley	.05
135	Sam Mitchell	.05
136	Pooh Richardson	.05
137	Jimmy Rodgers	.05
138	Felton Spencer	.05
139	Doug West	.05
140	Kenny Anderson	.10
141	Mookie Blaylock	.05
142	Sam Bowie	.05
143	Derrick Coleman	.10
144	Chuck Daly (Co.)	.05
145	Terry Mills	.05
146	Chris Morris	.05
147	Drazen Petrovic	.05
148	Greg Anthony	.10
149	Rolando Blackman	.05
150	Patrick Ewing	.30
151	Mark Jackson	.05
152	Anthony Mason	.05
153	Xavier McDaniel	.05
154	Charles Oakley	.05
155	Pat Riley (Co.)	.05
156	John Starks	.10
157	Gerald Wilkins	.05
158	Nick Anderson	.10
159	Anthony Bowie	.05
160	Terry Catledge	.05
161	Matt Guokas (Co.)	.05
162	Stanley Roberts	.05
163	Dennis Scott	.10
164	Scott Skiles	.05
165	Brian Williams	.05
166	Ron Anderson	.05
167	Manute Bol	.05
168	Johnny Dawkins	.05
169	Armon Gilliam	.05
170	Hersey Hawkins	.05
171	Jeff Hornacek	.05
172	Andrew Lang	.05
173	Doug Moe (Co.)	.05
174	Tim Perry	.05
175	Jeff Ruland	.05
176	Charles Shackleford	.05
177	Danny Ainge	.05
178	Charles Barkley	.50
179	Cedric Ceballos	.15
180	Tom Chambers	.05
181	Kevin Johnson	.10
182	Dan Majerle	.05
183	Mark West	.05
184	Paul Westphal (Co.)	.05
185	Rick Adelman (Co.)	.05
186	Clyde Drexler	.25
187	Kevin Duckworth	.05
188	Jerome Kersey	.05
189	Robert Pack	.10
190	Terry Porter	.05
191	Cliff Robinson	.10
192	Rod Strickland	.05
193	Buck Williams	.05
194	Anthony Bonner	.05
195	Duane Causwell	.05
196	Mitch Richmond	.15
197	Gary St. Jean (Co.)	.05
198	Lionel Simmons	.05
199	Wayman Tisdale	.05
200	Spud Webb	.05
201	Willie Anderson	.05
202	Antoine Carr	.05
203	Terry Cummings	.05
204	Sean Elliott	.05
205	Dale Ellis	.05
206	Vinnie Johnson	.05
207	David Robinson	.50
208	Jerry Tarkanian (Co.)	.10
209	Benoit Benjamin	.05
210	Michael Cage	.05
211	Eddie Johnson	.05
212	George Karl (Co.)	.05
213	Shawn Kemp	.50
214	Derrick McKey	.05
215	Nate McMillan	.05
216	Gary Payton	.15
217	Ricky Pierce	.05
218	David Benoit	.05
219	Mike Brown	.05
220	Tyrone Corbin	.05
221	Mark Eaton	.05
222	Jay Humphries	.05
223	Larry Krystowiak	.05
224	Jeff Malone	.05
225	Karl Malone	.25
226	Jerry Sloan (Co.)	.05
227	John Stockton	.25
228	Michael Adams	.05
229	Rex Chapman	.05
230	Ledell Eackles	.05
231	Pervis Ellison	.05
232	A.J. English	.05
233	Harvey Grant	.05
234	LaBradford Smith	.05
235	Larry Stewart	.05
236	Wes Unseld (Co.)	.05
237	David Wingate	.05
238	Michael Jordan (LL)	1.25
239	Dennis Rodman (LL)	.30
240	John Stockton (LL)	.10
241	Buck Williams (LL)	.05
242	Mark Price (LL)	.05
243	Dana Barros (LL)	.05
244	David Robinson (LL)	.20
245	Chris Mullin (LL)	.05
246	Michael Jordan (MVP)	1.25
247	Larry Johnson (ROY)	.20
248	David Robinson (POY) (Defensive Player of the Year)	.20
249	Detlef Schrempf (Sixth Man of the Year)	.05
250	Clyde Drexler (PV)	.15
251	Tim Hardaway (PV)	.05
252	Kevin Johnson (PV)	.05
253	Larry Johnson (PV)	.20
254	Scottie Pippen (PV)	.20
255	Isiah Thomas (PV)	.10
256	Larry Bird (SY)	.50
257	Brad Daugherty (SY)	.05
258	Kevin Johnson (SY)	.05
259	Larry Johnson (SY)	.20
260	Scottie Pippen (SY)	.20
261	Dennis Rodman (SY)	.20
262	Checklist	.05
263	Checklist	.05
264	Checklist	.05
265	Charles Barkley (SD)	.25
266	Shawn Kemp (SD)	.20
267	Dan Majerle (SD)	.05
268	Karl Malone (SD)	.10
269	Buck Williams	.05
270	Clyde Drexler (SD)	.10
271	Sean Elliott	.05
272	Ron Harper	.05
273	Michael Jordan (SD)	1.25
274	James Worthy (SD)	.05
275	Cedric Ceballos	.05
276	Larry Nance	.05
277	Kenny Walker	.05
278	Spud Webb	.05
279	Dominique Wilkins	.10
280	Terrell Brandon	.05
281	Dee Brown	.05
282	Kevin Johnson (SD)	.05
283	Doc Rivers	.05

284	Byron Scott	.05
285	Manute Bol	.05
286	Dikembe Mutombo	.10
287	Robert Parish	.05
288	David Robinson (SD)	.20
289	Dennis Rodman (SD)	.20
290	Blue Edwards	.05
291	Patrick Ewing (SD)	.10
292	Larry Johnson (SD)	.25
293	Jerome Kersey	.05
294	Hakeem Olajuwon (SD)	.25
295	Stacey Augmon	.05
296	Derrick Coleman (SD)	.05
297	Kendall Gill (SD)	.05
298	Shaquille O'Neal (SD)	2.00
299	Scottie Pippen (SD)	.20
300	Darryl Dawkins	.05
301	Mookie Blaylock	.05
302	*Adam Keefe*	.10
303	Travis Mays	.05
304	Morlon Wiley	.05
305	Sherman Douglas	.05
306	Joe Kleine	.05
307	Xavier McDaniel	.05
308	*Tony Bennett*	.10
309	Tom Hammonds	.05
310	Kevin Lynch	.05
311	*Alonzo Mourning*	2.00
312	David Wingate	.05
313	Rodney McCray	.05
314	Will Perdue	.05
315	Trent Tucker	.05
316	*Corey Williams*	.10
317	Danny Ferry	.05
318	Jay Guidinger	.05
319	Jerome Lane	.05
320	Gerald Wilkins	.05
321	*Stephen Bardo*	.10
322	*Walter Bond*	.10
323	*Brian Howard*	.10
324	*Tracy Moore*	.10
325	*Sean Rooks*	.10
326	Randy White	.05
327	Kevin Brooks	.05
328	*LaPhonso Ellis*	.20
329	Scott Hastings	.05
330	Todd Lichti	.05
331	Robert Pack	.05
332	*Bryant Stith*	.25
333	Gerald Glass	.05
334	Terry Mills	.05
335	Isaiah Morris	.05
336	Mark Randall	.05
337	Danny Young	.05
338	Chris Gatling	.05
339	Jeff Grayer	.05
340	*Byron Houston*	.10
341	*Keith Jennings*	.10
342	Alton Lister	.05
343	*Latrell Sprewell*	1.25
344	Scott Brooks	.05
345	Matt Bullard	.05
346	Carl Herrera	.05
347	*Robert Horry*	.75
348	Tree Rollins	.05
349	Greg Dreiling	.05
350	George McCloud	.05
351	Sam Mitchell	.05
352	Pooh Richardson	.05
353	*Malik Sealy*	.15
354	Kenny Williams	.05
355	*Jaren Jackson*	.10
356	Mark Jackson	.05
357	*Stanley Roberts*	.10
358	Elmore Spencer	.05
359	Kiki Vandeweghe	.05
360	John Williams	.05
361	*Randy Woods*	.10
362	*Duane Cooper*	.10
363	James Edwards	.05
364	*Anthony Peeler*	.15
365	Tony Smith	.05
366	Keith Askins	.05
367	*Matt Geiger*	.20
368	Alec Kessler	.05
369	*Harold Miner*	.15
370	John Salley	.05
371	*Anthony Avent*	.10
372	*Todd Day*	.20
373	Blue Edwards	.05
374	Brad Lohaus	.05
375	*Lee Mayberry*	.10
376	Eric Murdock	.05
377	Dan Schayes	.05
378	Lance Blanks	.05
379	*Christian Laettner*	.50
380	Bob McCann	.05
381	Chuck Person	.05
382	Brad Sellers	.05
383	*Chris Smith*	.10
384	Michael Williams	.05
385	Rafael Addison	.05
386	Chucky Brown	.05
387	Chris Dudley	.05
388	Tate George	.05
389	Rick Mahorn	.05
390	Rumeal Robinson	.05
391	Jayson Williams	.05
392	*Eric Anderson*	.10
393	Rolando Blackman	.05
394	Tony Campbell	.05
395	*Hubert Davis*	.15
396	Doc Rivers	.05
397	Charles Smith	.05
398	Herb Williams	.05
399	*Litterial Green*	.10
400	Greg Kite	.05
401	*Shaquille O'Neal*	8.00
402	Jerry Reynolds	.05
403	Jeff Turner	.05
404	Greg Grant	.05
405	Jeff Hornacek	.05
406	Andrew Lang	.05
407	Kenny Payne	.05
408	Tim Perry	.05
409	*C. Weatherspoon*	.50
410	Danny Ainge	.05
411	Charles Barkley	.50
412	Negele Knight	.05
413	*Oliver Miller*	.20
414	Jerrod Mustaf	.05
415	Mark Bryant	.05
416	Mario Elie	.05
417	*Dave Johnson*	.10
418	*Tracy Murray*	.15
419	Reggie Smith	.05
420	Rod Strickland	[illegible]
421	Randy Brown	.05
422	Pete Chilcutt	.05
423	Jim Les	.05
424	*Walt Williams*	.50
425	*Lloyd Daniels*	.10
426	Vinny Del Negro	.05
427	Dale Ellis	.05
428	Sidney Green	.05
429	Avery Johnson	.05
430	Dana Barros	.05
431	Rich King	.05
432	*Isaac Austin*	.10
433	*John Crotty*	.10
434	*Stephen Howard*	.10
435	Jay Humphries	.05
436	Larry Krystkowiak	.05
437	*Tom Gugliotta*	.75
438	Buck Johnson	.05
439	Charles Jones	.05
440	*Don MacLean*	.10
441	Doug Overton	.05
442	*Brent Price*	.10
443	Checklist	.05
444	Checklist	.05
SD266	Shawn Kemp Auto.	100.00
SD277	Kenny Walker Auto.	15.00
SD300	Darryl Dawkins Auto.	30.00

1992-93 Fleer All-Stars

These gold foil-stamped, UV-coated cards are designed horizontally. The front has a posed and an action photo. The back has the player's career highlights. The cards were inserts in Fleer 17-card Series I packs.

		MT
Complete Set (24):		125.00
Common Player:		2.00
Minor Stars:		3.00
1	Michael Adams	2.00
2	Charles Barkley	7.00
3	Brad Daugherty	2.00
4	Joe Dumars	3.00
5	Patrick Ewing	5.00
6	Michael Jordan	50.00
7	Reggie Lewis	2.00
8	Scottie Pippen	15.00
9	Mark Price	3.00
10	Dennis Rodman	15.00
11	Isiah Thomas	3.00
12	Kevin Willis	2.00
13	Clyde Drexler	7.00
14	Tim Hardaway	3.00
15	Jeff Hornacek	2.00
16	Dan Majerle	2.00
17	Karl Malone	6.00
18	Chris Mullin	3.00
19	Dikembe Mutombo	3.00
20	Hakeem Olajuwon	12.00
21	David Robinson	7.00
22	John Stockton	5.00
23	Otis Thorpe	2.00
24	James Worthy	2.00

1992-93 Fleer Larry Johnson Promo

This standard-sized card announced Larry Johnson's insert set in 1992-93 Fleer Basketball. The card features Johnson in a posed photo with Paul Mullan, chairman and CEO of Fleer. The card features the front design of a 1992-93 Fleer card and contains a 1992 Commemorative Card logo in the lower right corner.

		MT
Complete Set (1):		10.00
Common Player:		10.00
NNO	Larry Johnson (With Paul Mullan, CEO of Fleer)	10.00

1992-93 Fleer Larry Johnson

This glossy set offers highlights from Larry Johnson's career. The color fronts use posed and action photo framed by orange and blue borders. Each card says "Larry Johnson NBA Rookie of the Year" at the top. Comments about Johnson are on the back. No specific title is given to each card, so they are listed according to the topic on the back. Cards were random inserts in Fleer Series I packs, but cards #13-15 were available only by a mail-in offer for $1 and 10 Fleer wrappers. The set price doesn't include these three cards.

		MT
Complete Set (12):		12.00
Common Johnson:		1.00
Johnson Auto:		100.00
Mail-In Johnson (13-15):		3.00
1	Hornet Uniform (Larry Johnson)	1.00
2	Friends Comments (Larry Johnson)	1.00
3	Growing Up (Larry Johnson)	1.00
4	Skyline High (Larry Johnson)	1.00
5	High School Past (Larry Johnson)	1.00
6	Odessa Junior College (Larry Johnson)	1.00
7	Transfer to UNLV (Larry Johnson)	1.00
8	UNLV (Larry Johnson)	1.00
9	Playing for Charlotte (Larry Johnson)	1.00
10	Bird, Drexler, Bristow Comments (Larry Johnson)	1.00
11	Rookie Season (Larry Johnson)	1.00
12	Player Comments (Larry Johnson)	1.00
13	Johnson's Comments (Larry Johnson)	3.00
14	Other Player's Comments (Larry Johnson)	3.00
15	Growing Up in Dallas (Larry Johnson)	3.00

1992-93 Fleer Rookie Sensations

These UV-coated, gold foil-stamped cards were random inserts in Fleer Series I cello packs. Each card shows a player standing on his team's name. Backs offer a synopsis of the player's career highlights.

		MT
Complete Set (12):		35.00
Common Player:		1.00
Minor Stars:		2.00
1	Greg Anthony	2.00
2	Stacey Augmon	2.00
3	Terrell Brandon	8.00
4	Rick Fox	1.00
5	Larry Johnson	15.00
6	Mark Macon	1.00
7	Dikembe Mutombo	7.00
8	Billy Owens	4.00
9	Stanley Roberts	1.00
10	Doug Smith	1.00
11	Steve Smith	4.00
12	Larry Stewart	1.00

1992-93 Fleer Sharpshooters

This 18-card insert set features the top shooters in the NBA. Cards were randomly inserted into 1992-93 Fleer Series II wax packs, one per every three to five packs. The card front has a color photo with a purple background and silver borders. The set's logo is stamped in the upper right corner in gold foil; gold foil is also used for the player's name, which appears at the bottom of the card. The back has a summary of the player's career, plus a mug shot. The borders are blue. A card number (1 of 18, etc.) is also given.

		MT
Complete Set (18):		18.00
Common Player:		.50
Minor Stars:		1.00
1	Reggie Miller	3.00
2	Dana Barros	1.00
3	Jeff Hornacek	.50
4	Drazen Petrovic	.50
5	Glen Rice	2.00
6	Terry Porter	.50
7	Mark Price	1.00
8	Michael Adams	.50
9	Hersey Hawkins	1.00
10	Chuck Person	.50
11	John Stockton	3.00
12	Dale Ellis	.50
13	Clyde Drexler	4.00
14	Mitch Richmond	2.00
15	Craig Ehlo	.50
16	Dell Curry	.50
17	Chris Mullin	1.00
18	Rolando Blackman	.50

1992-93 Fleer Team Leaders

These cards were available in Series I rack packs, with one team leader card or a Larry Johnson Signature Series card per pack. The player's name is foil-stamped at the bottom of the card, which features a glossy action color photo. The back also has a photo and career highlights.

		MT
Complete Set (27):		325.00
Common Player:		3.00
Minor Stars:		5.00
1	Dominique Wilkins	5.00
2	Reggie Lewis	3.00
3	Larry Johnson	16.00
4	Michael Jordan	175.00
5	Mark Price	5.00
6	Terry Davis	3.00
7	Dikembe Mutombo	10.00
8	Isiah Thomas	5.00
9	Chris Mullin	5.00
10	Hakeem Olajuwon	40.00
11	Reggie Miller	16.00
12	Danny Manning	5.00
13	James Worthy	3.00
14	Glen Rice	5.00
15	Alvin Robertson	3.00
16	Tony Campbell	3.00
17	Derrick Coleman	5.00
18	Patrick Ewing	12.00
19	Scott Skiles	3.00
20	Hersey Hawkins	3.00
21	Kevin Johnson	5.00
22	Clyde Drexler	16.00
23	Mitch Richmond	8.00
24	David Robinson	30.00
25	Ricky Pierce	3.00
26	Karl Malone	14.00
27	Pervis Ellison	3.00

1992-93 Fleer Total D

This set features 15 of the NBA's top defensive players. Cards were random inserts in 1992-93 Series II cello packs, one per every five packs. The UV-coated card front has a color action photo with black borders. The set's logo is in the lower left corner; the player's name is stamped in gold foil next to the set logo. The back has a color mug shot, card number (1 of 15, etc.), and career summary which concentrates on the player's defensive prowess.

		MT
Complete Set (15):		150.00
Common Player:		2.00
Minor Stars:		4.00
1	David Robinson	10.00
2	Dennis Rodman	[illegible]
3	Scottie Pippen	20.00
4	Joe Dumars	4.00
5	Michael Jordan	75.00
6	John Stockton	6.00
7	Patrick Ewing	6.00
8	Michael Williams	2.00
9	Larry Nance	2.00
10	Buck Williams	2.00
11	Alvin Robertson	2.00
12	Dikembe Mutombo	4.00
13	Mookie Blaylock	2.00
14	Hakeem Olajuwon	12.00
15	Rony Seikaly	2.00

1992-93 Fleer Drake's

These cards were inserts in specially-marked Drake's Bakery products, four per cello pack. The cards are numbered on the back and are standard size, utilizing the card design used for Fleer's regular 1992-93 set. The card number is the only difference on the cards; the photos, design and information are the same.

		MT
Complete Set (55):		110.00
Common Player:		.35
1	Dominique Wilkins	2.00
2	Mookie Blaylock	2.00
3	Reggie Lewis	.75
4	Dee Brown	.25
5	Alonzo Mourning	12.00
6	Larry Johnson	3.00
7	Michael Jordan	40.00
8	Scottie Pippen	5.00
9	Mark Price	1.00
10	Brad Daugherty	.50
11	Derek Harper	.50
12	Sean Rooks	.25
13	Dikembe Mutombo	2.00
14	Chris Jackson	.25
15	Isiah Thomas	2.00
16	Joe Dumars	2.00
17	Chris Mullin	2.00
18	Tim Hardaway	2.00
19	Hakeem Olajuwon	6.00
20	Kenny Smith	.50
21	Reggie Miller	4.00
22	Detlef Schrempf	1.00
23	Danny Manning	.75
24	Mark Jackson	1.00
25	Sedale Threatt	.25
26	James Worthy	2.00
27	Glen Rice	1.50
28	Rony Seikaly	.25
29	Blue Edwards	.25
30	Eric Murdock	.25
31	Christian Laettner	2.00
32	Micheal Williams	.25
33	Drazen Petrovic	1.00
34	Derrick Coleman	1.00
35	Patrick Ewing	5.00
36	John Starks	1.50
37	Shaquille O'Neal	25.00
38	Scott Skiles	1.00
39	Jeff Hornacek	1.00
40	Clarence Weatherspoon	1.00
41	Charles Barkley	5.00
42	Dan Majerle	1.50
43	Clyde Drexler	5.00
44	Terry Porter	.75
45	Mitch Richmond	2.00
46	Lionel Simmons	.25
47	David Robinson	6.00
48	Sean Elliott	.75
49	Shawn Kemp	4.00
50	Gary Payton	5.00
51	John Stockton	6.00
52	Karl Malone	7.00
53	Pervis Ellison	.25
54	Tom Gugliotta	1.25
NNO	Checklist	.50

1992-93 Fleer/Spalding Schoolyard Stars

Specially-marked Spalding basketballs included these Fleer cards, wrapped in cello. The card front has a color action photo against a gold background with black borders. The player's name is in the upper left corner, with "NBA Schoolyard Stars" running underneath along the left side in white and yellow letters. The back has the look of a basketball, with a blue box in the middle which describes an aspect of the player's game. The unnumbered card back also offers a few schoolyard tips.

		MT
Complete Set (5):		10.00
Common Player:		.50
(1)	Larry Bird (Pregame Preparation)	5.00
(2)	Kevin Johnson (Decision Making)	1.00
(3)	Larry Johnson (Offensive Rebounding)	2.00
(4)	Scottie Pippen (All-Around Play)	3.00
(5)	Title card	.50

1992-93 Fleer Team Night Sheets

Fleer Team Night Sheets included spots for 12 cards on a perforated sheet, although some displayed only 10 or 11 with the remaining spots filled with advertising. The Bulls sheet was available at Shell gas stations for 99 cents with an eight-gallon purchase. The Mavs sheet was handed out at a Mavs/Timberwolves game and featured the first card of Jim Jackson due to his late signing. The cards are identified by their perforated edge and no card number on the back.

		MT
Complete Set (9):		60.00
Common Player:		5.00
(1)	Boston Celtics (John Bagley, Dee Brown, Sherman Douglas, Rick Fox, Kevin Gamble, Joe Kleine, Reggie Lewis, Xavier McDaniel, Kevin McHale, Robert Parish, Ed Pinckney) (UNO Pizzeria) (Ad card)	7.00
(2)	Charlotte Hornets (Tony Bennett, Muggsy Bogues, Dell Curry, Kenny Gattison, Kendall Gill, Mike Gminski, Larry Johnson, Alonzo Mourning, Johnny Newman, David Wingate) (Hugo - Mascot Belk) (Ad card)	8.00
(3)	Chicago Bulls (B.J. Armstrong, Bill Cartwright, Horace Grant, Michael Jordan, Stacey King, Rodney McCray, John Paxson, Will Perdue, Scottie Pippen, Trent Tucker, Corey Williams, Scott Williams) (Back 2 Back) (Shell)	10.00
(4)	Dallas Mavericks (Walter Bond, Dexter Cambridge, Terry Davis, Derek Harper, Donald Hodge, Mike Iuzzolino, Jim Jackson, Sean Rooks, Doug Smith, Randy White, Morlon Wiley) (Lay's Potato Chips) (Ad card)	6.00
(5)	Indiana Pacers (Dale Davis, Vern Fleming, Bob Hill CO, George McCloud, Reggie Miller, Sam Mitchell, Pooh Richardson, Detlef Schrempf, Malik Sealy, Rik Smits, LaSalle Thompson) (Pacers Gift Shop) (Ad card)	5.00
(6)	Los Angeles Lakers (Elden Campbell, Duane Cooper, Vlade Divac, James Edwards, A.C. Green, Anthony Peeler, Sam Perkins, Byron Scott, Sedale Threatt, James Worthy) (Toyota) (Two ad cards)	6.00
(7)	Miami Heat (Keith Askins, Willie Burton, Vernell Coles, Kevin Edwards, Alec Kessler, Grant Long, Harold Miner, Glen Rice, John Salley, Ron Seikaly, Brian Shaw, Steve Smith)	5.00
(8)	Milwaukee Bucks (Anthony Avent, Frank Brickowski, Todd Day, Mike Dunleavy CO, Blue Edwards, Brad Lohaus, Moses Malone, Lee Mayberry, Eric Murdock, Fred Roberts, Alvin Robertson, Dan Schayes)	5.00
(9)	Orlando Magic (Nick Anderson, Anthony Bowie, Terry Catledge, Steve Kerr, Greg Kite, Shaquille O'Neal, Jerry Reynolds, Dennis Scott, Scott Skiles, Jeff Turner, Brian Williams) (Goodings) (Ad card)	12.00

1992-93 Fleer Tony's Pizza

More than eight million cards were inserted into Tony's Frozen Pizza packages between March and April of 1992, three per pack. The fronts and backs are identical to the regular issue Fleer cards, but this set is numbered differently and uses the prefix "S". There were no offers to get a complete set, so completing it is difficult.

		MT
Complete Set (108):		80.00
Common Player (1-72):		.25
Common Player (73-108):		.50
1	Michael Adams	.25
2	Kenny Anderson	.75
3	Willie Anderson	.25
4	Greg Anthony	.50
5	B.J. Armstrong	.25
6	Thurl Bailey	.25
7	Benoit Benjamin	[illegible]
8	Muggsy Bogues	.75
9	Sam Bowie	.25
10	Frank Brickowski	.25
11	Michael Cage	.25
12	Antoine Carr	.25

13	Duane Causwell	.25
14	Rex Chapman	.50
15	Tyrone Corbin	.25
16	Brad Daugherty	.50
17	Terry Davis	.25
18	Johnny Dawkins	.25
19	Vlade Divac	1.00
20	Joe Dumars	1.00
21	Craig Ehlo	.25
22	Pervis Ellison	.25
23	Duane Ferrell	.25
24	Vern Fleming	.25
25	Winston Garland	.25
26	Horace Grant	.75
27	Tim Hardaway	2.00
28	Derek Harper	.75
29	Hersey Hawkins	.75
30	Chris Jackson	.25
31	Reggie Lewis	1.00
32	Jeff Malone	.25
33	Moses Malone	1.00
34	Danny Manning	.50
35	Sarunas Marciulionis	.25
36	Vernon Maxwell	.25
37	Kevin McHale	1.25
38	Reggie Miller	2.50
39	Chris Mullin	1.00
40	Ken Norman	.25
41	Charles Oakley	.50
42	Billy Owens	.50
43	Drazen Petrovic	.50
44	Ricky Pierce	.25
45	J.R. Reid	.25
46	Glen Rice	1.50
47	Mitch Richmond	2.00
48	Alvin Robertson	.25
49	Clifford Robinson	1.00
50	Rumeal Robinson	.25
51	Detlef Schrempf	.75
52	Dennis Scott	.25
53	Rony Seikaly	.25
54	Charles Shackleford	.25
55	Brian Shaw	.25
56	Scott Skiles	.50
57	Doug Smith	.25
58	Kenny Smith	.50
59	Steve Smith	1.00
60	Felton Spencer	.25
61	John Stockton	3.50
62	Isiah Thomas	2.00
63	Otis Thorpe	.50
64	Sedale Threatt	.25
65	Wayman Tisdale	.25
66	Loy Vaught	.50
67	Doug West	.25
68	Brian Williams	.50
69	Micheal Williams	.25
70	Reggie Williams	.25
71	Scott Williams	.25
72	Orlando Woolridge	.25
73	Stacey Augmon SD	1.00
74	Charles Barkley SD	3.00
75	Manute Bol SD	.50
76	Terrell Brandon SD	2.00
77	Dee Brown SD	.50
78	Cedric Ceballos SD	.75
79	Derrick Coleman SD	1.00
80	Darryl Dawkins SD	1.00
81	Clyde Drexler SD	3.00
82	Blue Edwards SD	.50
83	Sean Elliott SD	.50
84	Patrick Ewing SD	2.50
85	Kendall Gill SD	.50
86	Ron Harper SD	.75
87	Kevin Johnson SD	1.00
88	Larry Johnson SD	2.00
89	Michael Jordan SD	25.00
90	Shawn Kemp SD	3.50
91	Jerome Kersey SD	.50
92	Dan Majerle SD	1.00
93	Karl Malone SD	3.50
94	Dikembe Mutombo SD	1.00
95	Larry Nance SD	.75
96	Hakeem Olajuwon SD	4.00
97	Shaquille O'Neal SD	20.00
98	Robert Parish SD	1.00
99	Scottie Pippen SD	5.00
100	Doc Rivers SD	.75
101	David Robinson SD	5.00
102	Dennis Rodman SD	4.00
103	Byron Scott SD	.75
104	Kenny Walker SD	.50
105	Spud Webb SD	.50
106	Dominique Wilkins SD	1.00
107	Buck Williams SD	.50
108	James Worthy SD	1.25
XX	Coupon Card	.50

1993-94 Fleer Promo Sheet

This page of cards was issued to promote the 1993-94 Fleer Basketball set and was distributed to dealers along with sales materials. The sheet included eight perforated cards showing the design of the set, with a "Fleer Basketball - A game in every pack" card in the middle.

		MT
Complete Set (1):		3.00
32	Scottie Pippen	1.00
67	Tim Hardaway	.50
93	Danny Manning	.25
133	Derrick Coleman	.25
144	Doc Rivers	.25
162	Danny Ainge	.25
199	Shawn Kemp	.50
213	Michael Adams	.25

1993-94 Fleer

Fleer's 1993-94 cards feature day-glow graphics bordered in white. The card fronts have color-enhanced action photos and are color coded by team. Backs have biographical information, stats and an action photo superimposed over the player's name along the left side of the card. Subsets include League Leaders, Award Winners and Pro Visions cards. Insert sets include All-Stars, Rookie Sensations, NBA Internationals, Clyde Drexler, First-Year Phenoms, Sharpshooters, NBA Superstars, Living Legends and Towers of Power.

		MT
Complete Set (400):		20.00
Complete Series 1 (240):		10.00
Complete Series 2 (160):		10.00
Common Player:		.05
Minor Stars:		.10
Ser. 1 or 2 Pack (15):		.75
Ser. 1 or 2 Wax Box (36):		25.00
1	Stacey Augmon	.05
2	Mookie Blaylock	.05
3	Duane Ferrell	.05
4	Paul Graham	.05
5	Adam Keefe	.05
6	Jon Koncak	.05
7	Dominique Wilkins	.15
8	Kevin Willis	.05
9	Alaa Abdelnaby	.05
10	Dee Brown	.05
11	Sherman Douglas	.05
12	Rick Fox	.05
13	Kevin Gamble	.05
14	Reggie Lewis	.05
15	Xavier McDaniel	.05
16	Robert Parish	.10
17	Muggsy Bogues	.05
18	Dell Curry	.05
19	Kenny Gattison	.05
20	Kendall Gill	.05
21	Larry Johnson	.25
22	Alonzo Mourning	.50
23	Johnny Newman	.05
24	David Wingate	.05
25	B.J. Armstrong	.05
26	Bill Cartwright	.05
27	Horace Grant	.10
28	Michael Jordan	2.50
29	Stacey King	.05
30	John Paxson	.05
31	Will Perdue	.05
32	Scottie Pippen	.75
33	Scott Williams	.05
34	Terrell Brandon	.05
35	Brad Daugherty	.05
36	Craig Ehlo	.05
37	Danny Ferry	.05
38	Larry Nance	.05
39	Mark Price	.10
40	Mike Sanders	.05
41	Gerald Wilkins	.05
42	John Williams	.05
43	Terry Davis	.05
44	Derek Harper	.05
45	Mike Iuzzolino	.05
46	Jim Jackson	.50
47	Sean Rooks	.10
48	Doug Smith	.05
49	Randy White	.05
50	Mahmoud Abdul-Rauf	.05
51	LaPhonso Ellis	.10
52	Marcus Liberty	.05
53	Mark Macon	.05
54	Dikembe Mutombo	.20
55	Robert Pack	.05
56	Bryant Stith	.05
57	Reggie Williams	.05
58	Mark Aguirre	.05
59	Joe Dumars	.10
60	Bill Laimbeer	.05
61	Terry Mills	.05
62	Olden Polynice	.05
63	Alvin Robertson	.05
64	Dennis Rodman	.75
65	Isiah Thomas	.15
66	Victor Alexander	.05
67	Tim Hardaway	.10
68	Tyrone Hill	.05
69	Byron Houston	.05
70	Sarunas Marciulionis	.05
71	Chris Mullin	.10
72	Billy Owens	.05
73	Latrell Sprewell	.40
74	Scott Brooks	.05
75	Matt Bullard	.05
76	Carl Herrera	.05
77	Robert Horry	.10
78	Vernon Maxwell	.05
79	Hakeem Olajuwon	.60
80	Kenny Smith	.05
81	Otis Thorpe	.05
82	Dale Davis	.05
83	Vern Fleming	.05
84	George McCloud	.05
85	Reggie Miller	.25
86	Sam Mitchell	.05
87	Pooh Richardson	.05
88	Detlef Schrempf	.05
89	Rik Smits	.10
90	Gary Grant	.05
91	Ron Harper	.05
92	Mark Jackson	.05
93	Danny Manning	.10
94	Ken Norman	.05
95	Stanley Roberts	.05
96	Loy Vaught	.05
97	John Williams	.05
98	Elden Campbell	.05
99	Doug Christie	.05
100	Duane Cooper	.05
101	Vlade Divac	.05
102	A.C. Green	.05
103	Anthony Peeler	.05
104	Sedale Threatt	.05
105	James Worthy	.05
106	Bimbo Coles	.05
107	Grant Long	.05
108	Harold Miner	.05
109	Glen Rice	.10
110	John Salley	.05
111	Rony Seikaly	.05
112	Brian Shaw	.05
113	Steve Smith	.05
114	Anthony Avent	.05
115	Jon Barry	.05
116	Frank Brickowski	.05
117	Todd Day	.05
118	Blue Edwards	.05
119	Brad Lohaus	.05
120	Lee Mayberry	.05
121	Eric Murdock	.05
122	Thurl Bailey	.05
123	Christian Laettner	.10
124	Luc Longley	.05
125	Chuck Person	.05
126	Felton Spencer	.05
127	Doug West	.05
128	Michael Williams	.05
129	Rafael Addison	.05
130	Kenny Anderson	.10
131	Sam Bowie	.05
132	Chucky Brown	.05
133	Derrick Coleman	.10
134	Chris Dudley	.05
135	Chris Morris	.05
136	Rumeal Robinson	.05
137	Greg Anthony	.05
138	Rolando Blackman	.05
139	Tony Campbell	.05
140	Hubert Davis	.05
141	Patrick Ewing	.25
142	Anthony Mason	.05
143	Charles Oakley	.05
144	Doc Rivers	.05
145	Charles Smith	.05
146	John Starks	.10
147	Nick Anderson	.05
148	Anthony Bowie	.05
149	Shaquille O'Neal	1.50
150	Donald Royal	.05
151	Dennis Scott	.05
152	Scott Skiles	.05
153	Tom Tolbert	.05
154	Jeff Turner	.05
155	Ron Anderson	.05
156	Johnny Dawkins	.05
157	Hersey Hawkins	.05
158	Jeff Hornacek	.05
159	Andrew Lang	.05
160	Tim Perry	.05
161	C. Weatherspoon	.10
162	Danny Ainge	.05
163	Charles Barkley	.40
164	Cedric Ceballos	.05
165	Tom Chambers	.05
166	Richard Dumas	.05
167	Kevin Johnson	.10
168	Negele Knight	.05
169	Dan Majerle	.05
170	Oliver Miller	.05
171	Mark West	.05
172	Mark Bryant	.05
173	Clyde Drexler	.20
175	Mario Elie	.05
176	Jerome Kersey	.05
177	Terry Porter	.05
178	Cliff Robinson	.05
179	Rod Strickland	.05
180	Buck Williams	.05
181	Anthony Bonner	.05
182	Duane Causwell	.05
183	Mitch Richmond	.10
184	Lionel Simmons	.05
185	Wayman Tisdale	.05
186	Spud Webb	.05
187	Walt Williams	.10
188	Antoine Carr	.05
189	Terry Cummings	.05
190	Lloyd Daniels	.05
191	Vinny Del Negro	.05
192	Sean Elliott	.05
193	Dale Ellis	.05
194	Avery Johnson	.05
195	J.R. Reid	.05
196	David Robinson	.40
197	Michael Cage	.05
198	Eddie Johnson	.05
199	Shawn Kemp	.20
200	Derrick McKey	.05
201	Nate McMillan	.05
202	Gary Payton	.15
203	Sam Perkins	.05
204	Ricky Pierce	.05
205	David Benoit	.05
206	Tyrone Corbin	.05
207	Mark Eaton	.05
208	Jay Humphries	.05
209	Larry Krystkowiak	.05
210	Jeff Malone	.05
211	Karl Malone	.25
212	John Stockton	.25
213	Michael Adams	.05
214	Rex Chapman	.05
215	Pervis Ellison	.05
216	Harvey Grant	.05
217	Tom Gugliotta	.10
218	Buck Johnson	.05
219	LaBradford Smith	.05
220	Larry Stewart	.05
221	B.J. Armstrong (LL)	.05
222	Cedric Ceballos (LL)	.05
223	Larry Johnson (LL)	.10
224	Michael Jordan (LL)	1.00
225	Hakeem Olajuwon (LL)	.25
226	Mark Price (LL)	.05
227	Dennis Rodman (LL)	.25
228	John Stockton (LL)	.10
229	Charles Barkley (AW)	.20
230	Hakeem Olajuwon (AW)	.25
231	Shaquille O'Neal (AW)	1.00
232	Cliff Robinson (AW)	.05
233	Shawn Kemp (PV)	.10
234	Alonzo Mourning (PV)	.25
235	Hakeem Olajuwon (PV)	.25
236	John Stockton (PV)	.10
237	Dominique Wilkins (PV)	.10
238	Checklist	.05
239	Checklist	.05
240	Checklist	.05
241	*Doug Edwards*	.10
242	Craig Ehlo	.05
243	Andrew Lang	.05
244	Ennis Whatley	.05
245	Chris Corchiani	.05
246	*Acie Earl*	.10
247	Jimmy Oliver	.05
248	Ed Pinckney	.05
249	*Dino Radja*	.25
250	Matt Wenstrom	.05
251	Tony Bennett	.05
252	*Scott Burrell*	.25
253	LeRon Ellis	.05
254	Hersey Hawkins	.05
255	Eddie Johnson	.05
256	*Corie Blount*	.10
257	Jo Jo English	.05
258	Dave Johnson	.05
259	Steve Kerr	.05
260	*Toni Kukoc*	1.00
261	Pete Myers	.05
262	Bill Wennington	.05
263	John Battle	.05
264	Tyrone Hill	.05
265	Gerald Madkins	.05
266	*Chris Mills*	.25
267	Bobby Phills	.05
268	Greg Dreiling	.05
269	*Lucious Harris*	.10
270	Donald Hodge	.05
271	*Popeye Jones*	.25
272	Tim Legler	.05
273	Fat Lever	.05
274	*Jamal Mashburn*	.75
275	Darren Morningstar	.05
276	Tom Hammonds	.05
277	*Darnell Mee*	.10
278	*Rodney Rogers*	.25
279	Brian Williams	.05
280	Greg Anderson	.05
281	Sean Elliott	.05
282	*Allan Houston*	1.50
283	*Lindsey Hunter*	.10
284	Marcus Liberty	.05
285	Mark Macon	.05
286	David Wood	.05
287	Jud Buechler	.05
288	Chris Gatling	.05
289	*Josh Grant*	.10
290	Jeff Grayer	.05
291	Avery Johnson	.05
292	*Chris Webber*	3.00
293	*Sam Cassell*	.50
294	Mario Elie	.05
295	*Richard Petruska*	.10
296	*Eric Riley*	.10
297	*Antonio Davis*	.10
298	*Scott Haskin*	.10
299	Derrick McKey	.05
300	Byron Scott	.05
301	Malik Sealy	.05
302	LaSalle Thompson	.05
303	Kenny Williams	.05
304	Haywoode Workman	.05
305	Mark Aguirre	.05
306	*Terry Dehere*	.10
307	Bob Martin	.05
308	Elmore Spencer	.05
309	Tom Tolbert	.05
310	Randy Woods	.05
311	Sam Bowie	.05
312	James Edwards	.05
313	*Antonio Harvey*	.10
314	*George Lynch*	.10
315	Tony Smith	.05
316	*Nick Van Exel*	1.00
317	Manute Bol	.05
318	Willie Burton	.05
319	Matt Geiger	.05
320	Alec Kessler	.05
321	*Vin Baker*	1.00
322	Ken Norman	.05
323	Dan Schayes	.05
324	Derek Strong	.05
325	Mike Brown	.05
326	Brian Davis	.05
327	Tellis Frank	.05
328	Marlon Maxey	.05
329	*Isaiah Rider*	.50
330	Chris Smith	.05
331	Benoit Benjamin	.05
332	P.J. Brown	.05
333	Kevin Edwards	.05
334	Armon Gilliam	.05
335	Rick Mahorn	.05
336	Dwayne Schintzius	.05
337	*Rex Walters*	.10
338	*David Wesley*	.20
339	Jayson Williams	.05
340	Anthony Bonner	.05
341	Herb Williams	.05
342	Litterial Green	.05
343	*Anfernee Hardaway*	5.00
344	Greg Kite	.05
345	Larry Krystkowiak	.05
346	Todd Lichti	.05
347	Keith Tower	.05
348	Dana Barros	.05
349	*Shawn Bradley*	.40
350	Michael Curry	.05
351	*Greg Graham*	.10
352	*Warren Kidd*	.10
353	Moses Malone	.05
354	Orlando Woolridge	.05
355	Duane Cooper	.05
356	Joe Courtney	.05
357	A.C. Green	.05
358	Frank Johnson	.05
359	Joe Kleine	.05
360	*Malcolm Mackey*	.10
361	Jerrod Mustaf	.05
362	Chris Dudley	.05
363	Harvey Grant	.05
364	Tracy Murray	.05
365	*James Robinson*	.15
366	Reggie Smith	.05
367	*Kevin Thompson*	.10
368	Randy Breuer	.05
369	Randy Brown	.05
370	*Evers Burns*	.10
371	Pete Chilcutt	.05
372	*Bobby Hurley*	.15
373	Jim Les	.05
374	*Mike Peplowski*	.15
375	Willie Anderson	.05
376	Sleepy Floyd	.05
377	Negele Knight	.05
378	Dennis Rodman	.50
379	*Chris Whitney*	.10
380	Vincent Askew	.05
381	Kendall Gill	.05
382	*Ervin Johnson*	.10
383	Chris King	.05
384	Rich King	.05
385	Steve Scheffler	.05
386	Detlef Schrempf	.05
387	Tom Chambers	.05
388	John Crotty	.05
389	*Byron Russell*	.10
390	Felton Spencer	.05
391	*Luther Wright*	.10
392	*Mitchell Butler*	.10
393	*Calbert Cheaney*	.40
394	Kevin Duckworth	.05
395	Don MacLean	.05
396	*Gheorghe Muresan*	.25
397	Doug Overton	.05
398	Brent Price	.05
399	Checklist	.05
400	Checklist	.05

1993-94 Fleer All-Stars

Cards from this limited-edition set were random inserts in 1993-94 Fleer Series I wax and rack packs, one every 10 packs. Twenty-four All-Stars, 12 from each conference, are featured. The card fronts are UV coated and have purple borders around an action photo. The player's name is stamped in gold foil at the bottom, where an NBA All-Star logo also appears. The card back, numbered 1 of 24, etc., has a color action photo and a recap of the player's previous season.

		MT
Complete Set (24):		100.00
Common Player:		1.00
1	Brad Daugherty	1.00
2	Joe Dumars	1.00
3	Patrick Ewing	3.00
4	Larry Johnson	4.00
5	Michael Jordan	40.00
6	Larry Nance	1.00
7	Shaquille O'Neal	25.00
8	Scottie Pippen	10.00
9	Mark Price	1.00
10	Detlef Schrempf	1.00
11	Isiah Thomas	2.00
12	Dominique Wilkins	3.00
13	Charles Barkley	5.00
14	Clyde Drexler	3.00
15	Sean Elliott	1.00
16	Tim Hardaway	1.00
17	Shawn Kemp	4.00
18	Dan Majerle	1.00
19	Karl Malone	3.00
20	Danny Manning	1.00
21	Hakeem Olajuwon	8.00
22	Terry Porter	1.00
23	David Robinson	5.00
24	John Stockton	3.00

1993-94 Fleer Clyde Drexler

This 12-card set is devoted to Portland Trailblazers' star Clyde Drexler. Cards were randomly put in all types of 1993-94 Fleer packs. Drexler autographed a limited number of the cards.

		MT
Complete Set (12):		6.00
Common Drexler:		.50
Drexler Send-Off (13-15):		2.00
Drexler Auto:		120.00
1	Clyde Drexler	.50
2	Clyde Drexler	.50
3	Clyde Drexler	.50
4	Clyde Drexler	.50
5	Clyde Drexler	.50
6	Clyde Drexler	.50
7	Clyde Drexler	.50
8	Clyde Drexler	.50
9	Clyde Drexler	.50
10	Clyde Drexler	.50
11	Clyde Drexler	.50
12	Clyde Drexler	.50

1993-94 Fleer First Year Phenoms

These 10 cards feature first-round NBA draft choices who have been successful in their first NBA season. The cards were random inserts in all 1993 Fleer Series II packs, one per every four packs. Fronts have a neon-colored court as a background, plus the "First Year Phenoms" logo in gold foil. The player's name is stamped in gold foil also, and runs vertically along the left side of the card. The horizontal back is also in neon and includes a player profile shot, a career summary and a card number (1 of 10, etc.).

		MT
Complete Set (10):		10.00
Common Player:		.25
1	Shawn Bradley	.50
2	Anfernee Hardaway	4.00
3	Lindsey Hunter	.25
4	Bobby Hurley	.25
5	Toni Kukoc	.50
6	Jamal Mashburn	1.00
7	Dino Radja	.50
8	Isaiah Rider	.75
9	Nick Van Exel	1.00
10	Chris Webber	2.00

1993-94 Fleer Internationals

These 12 cards, featuring NBA stars from foreign countries, were randomly included in all 1993-94 Fleer Series I packs, one every 10 packs. The fronts are UV coated and feature a color photo of the player, with a map of his native country used as a background. The player's name is stamped in gold foil at the top of the card. The backs, numbered 1 of 12, etc., have another color photo of the player, plus a brief summary of his career.

		MT
Complete Set (12):		5.00
Common Player:		.50
1	Alaa Abdelnaby	.50
2	Vlade Divac	.75
3	Patrick Ewing	1.50
4	Carl Herrera	.50
5	Luc Longley	.50
6	Sarunas Marciulionis	.50
7	Dikembe Mutombo	1.00
8	Rumeal Robinson	.50
9	Detlef Schrempf	.75
10	Rony Seikaly	.50
11	Rik Smits	1.00
12	Dominique Wilkins	1.00

1993-94 Fleer Living Legends

These cards feature six of the game's best players ever. The cards were random inserts in all types of Fleer 1993 Series II packs, one per every 37 packs. Fronts have two photos of the player against a metallic background. The set logo and player's name are stamped in gold foil at the bottom. The back is numbered 1 of 6, etc., and is horizontally designed. The player's name, team name, set logo, career summary and color player profile shot are included on the back.

		MT
Complete Set (6):		25.00
Common Player:		.50
1	Charles Barkley	3.00
2	Larry Bird	6.00
3	Patrick Ewing	1.25
4	Michael Jordan	14.00
5	Hakeem Olajuwon	4.00
6	Dominique Wilkins	.50

1993-94 Fleer Lottery Exchange

1993 collegiate draft picks who signed with their NBA teams before Nov. 1, 1993, are featured in this 11-card insert set. Draft Exchange Cards were randomly inserted in Fleer packs; finders could send the exchange card in for the set. The cards have the same design as Fleer's regular set, except a "Lottery Pick" logo is in the lower right corner. Card backs include a photo, biographical information, a team logo, stats and a card number (1 of 11, etc.).

		MT
Complete Set (11):		20.00
Common Player:		.50
1	Chris Webber	5.00
2	Shawn Bradley	1.00
3	Anfernee Hardaway	12.00
4	Jamal Mashburn	3.00
5	Isaiah Rider	1.00
6	Calbert Cheaney	1.00
7	Bobby Hurley	.50
8	Vin Baker	4.00
9	Rodney Rogers	1.00
10	Lindsey Hunter	.50
11	Allan Houston	2.50

1993-94 Fleer NBA Superstars

These cards feature 20 players who are on top of their game. The cards were random inserts in 1993 Fleer Series II 15-card packs, one per every three packs. Fronts have three photos, plus the player's last name on the left side in a team color-coded panel, which also has the set's logo stamped in gold foil. The horizontal back, numbered 1 of 10, etc., features another color closeup photo, the set logo and a career summary.

		MT
Complete Set (20):		18.00
Common Player:		.25
1	Mahmoud Abdul-Rauf	.25
2	Charles Barkley	1.00
3	Derrick Coleman	.50
4	Clyde Drexler	.75
5	Joe Dumars	.50
6	Patrick Ewing	.75
7	Michael Jordan	8.00
8	Shawn Kemp	1.00
9	Christian Laettner	.50
10	Karl Malone	.75
11	Danny Manning	.25
12	Reggie Miller	.50
13	Alonzo Mourning	1.00
14	Chris Mullin	.25
15	Hakeem Olajuwon	2.00
16	Shaquille O'Neal	5.00
17	Mark Price	.25
18	Mitch Richmond	.25
19	David Robinson	1.00
20	Dominique Wilkins	.75

1993-94 Fleer Rookie Sensations

These cards, randomly inserted into 1993-94 Fleer Series I pre-priced jumbo packs, feature top rookies from the 1992-93 season. The UV-coated card front features a player standing on a basketball with spotlights shining from it against a blue background. The player's name and set logo are stamped in silver in the lower left corner. The cards are numbered on the back (1 of 24, etc.) and have the player's name stamped in silver foil at the top. A recap of the player's rookie season and a color player profile shot are also included.

		MT
Complete Set (24):		50.00
Common Player:		1.00
Minor Stars:		2.00
1	Anthony Avent	1.00
2	Doug Christie	1.00
3	Lloyd Daniels	1.00
4	Hubert Davis	2.00
5	Todd Day	2.00
6	Richard Dumas	1.00
7	LaPhonso Ellis	2.00
8	Tom Gugliotta	4.00
9	Robert Horry	2.00
10	Byron Houston	1.00
11	Jim Jackson	4.00
12	Adam Keefe	1.00
13	Christian Laettner	2.00
14	Lee Mayberry	1.00
15	Oliver Miller	1.00
16	Harold Miner	2.00
17	Alonzo Mourning	7.00
18	Shaquille O'Neal	25.00
19	Anthony Peeler	1.00
20	Sean Rooks	2.00
21	Latrell Sprewell	6.00
22	Bryant Stith	2.00
23	C. Weatherspoon	2.00
24	Walt Williams	2.00

1993-94 Fleer Sharpshooters

These cards feature 10 of the game's top outside shooters. Cards were random inserts in 1993 Fleer Series II 15-card packs, one per every 11 packs. Fronts have two shots of the player, his name in gold foil, and the "Sharpshooters" logo. The horizontal back has a card number (1 of 10, etc.), career highlights, a player profile shot and the set's logo.

		MT
Complete Set (10):		25.00
Common Player:		1.00
1	Tom Gugliotta	1.00
2	Jim Jackson	2.00
3	Michael Jordan	20.00
4	Dan Majerle	1.00
5	Mark Price	1.00
6	Glen Rice	1.00
7	Mitch Richmond	1.00
8	Latrell Sprewell	4.00
9	John Starks	1.00
10	Dominique Wilkins	1.00

1993-94 Fleer Towers of Power

This set features 30 of the game's top big men. Cards were random inserts in 1993 Fleer Series II 21-card packs, one per every 12 packs. The fronts have the player pictured against a background of skyscrapers. His name is stamped in gold foil at the bottom; the set logo is stamped in gold foil at the top. The back also has a player photo on one half superimposed against a skyline background. Each is numbered (1 of 30, etc.) and includes a career summary on the other half.

		MT
Complete Set (30):		55.00
Common Player:		1.00
1	Charles Barkley	5.00
2	Shawn Bradley	3.00
3	Derrick Coleman	2.00
4	Brad Daugherty	1.00
5	Dale Davis	1.00
6	Vlade Divac	1.00
7	Patrick Ewing	3.00
8	Horace Grant	2.00
9	Tom Gugliotta	2.00
10	Larry Johnson	4.00
11	Shawn Kemp	3.00
12	Christian Laettner	1.00
13	Karl Malone	3.00
14	Danny Manning	1.00
15	Jamal Mashburn	6.00
16	Oliver Miller	1.00
17	Alonzo Mourning	5.00
18	Dikembe Mutombo	2.00
19	Ken Norman	1.00
20	Hakeem Olajuwon	7.00
21	Shaquille O'Neal	20.00
22	Robert Parish	1.00
23	Olden Polynice	1.00
24	Cliff Robinson	1.00
25	David Robinson	5.00
26	Dennis Rodman	10.00
27	Rony Seikaly	1.00
28	Wayman Tisdale	1.00
29	Chris Webber	10.00
30	Dominique Wilkins	3.00

1993-94 Jam Session

This 240-card set features the hobby's tallest cards since the 1969-70 Topps set. Cards, which have full-bleed photos and UV coating, are 2-1/2" x 4-3/4". Backs have biographical information, stats, a career summary and an action photo which takes up half of the card. Each 12-card pack contains one of four different types of insert cards - Second Year Stars, Slam Dunk Heroes, GameBreakers and Rookie Standouts - complete with gold foil stamping.

		MT
Complete Set (240):		25.00
Common Player:		.10
Minor Stars:		.20
Wax Box:		45.00
1	Stacey Augmon	.10
2	Mookie Blaylock	.10
3	*Doug Edwards*	.10
4	Duane Ferrell	.10
5	Paul Graham	.10
6	Adam Keefe	.10
7	Jon Koncak	.10
8	Dominique Wilkins	.20
9	Kevin Willis	.10
10	Alaa Abdelnaby	.10
11	Dee Brown	.10
12	Sherman Douglas	.10
13	Rick Fox	.10
14	Kevin Gamble	.10
15	Xavier Mcdaniel	.10
16	Robert Parish	.15
17	Muggsy Bogues	.10
18	*Scott Burrell*	.40
19	Dell Curry	.10
20	Kenny Gattison	.10
21	Hersey Hawkins	.10
22	Eddie Johnson	.10
23	Larry Johnson	.50
24	Alonzo Mourning	1.00
25	Johnny Newman	.10
26	David Wingate	.10
27	B.J. Armstrong	.15
28	*Corie Blount*	.20
29	Bill Cartwright	.10
30	Horace Grant	.20
31	Stacey King	.10
32	John Paxson	.10
33	Michael Jordan	5.00
34	Scottie Pippen	1.50
35	Scott Williams	.10
36	Terrell Brandon	.10
37	Brad Daugherty	.10
38	Danny Ferry	.10
39	Tyrone Hill	.10
40	*Chris Mills*	.50
41	Larry Nance	.10
42	Mark Price	.15
43	Gerald Wilkins	.10
44	John Williams	.10
45	Terry Davis	.10
46	Derek Harper	.10
47	Donald Hodge	.10
48	Jim Jackson	1.00
49	*Jamal Mashburn*	1.00
50	Sean Rooks	.10
51	Doug Smith	.10
52	Mahmoud Abdul-Rauf	.10
53	Kevin Brooks	.10
54	LaPhonso Ellis	.10
55	Mark Macon	.10
56	Dikembe Mutombo	.30
57	*Rodney Rogers*	.50
58	Bryant Stith	.10
59	Reggie Williams	.10
60	Joe Dumars	.20
61	Sean Elliott	.10
62	Bill Laimbeer	.10
63	Terry Mills	.10
64	Olden Polynice	.10
65	Alvin Robertson	.10
66	Isiah Thomas	.25
67	Victor Alexander	.10
68	Chris Gatling	.10
69	Tim Hardaway	.15
70	Byron Houston	.10
71	Sarunas Marciulionis	.10
72	Chris Mullin	.20
73	Billy Owens	.10
74	Latrell Sprewell	.75
75	*Chris Webber*	3.00
76	Scott Brooks	.10
77	Matt Bullard	.10
78	*Sam Cassell*	.75
79	Mario Elie	.10
80	Carl Herrera	.10
81	Robert Horry	.50
82	Vernon Maxwell	.10
83	Hakeem Olajuwon	1.00
84	Kenny Smith	.10
85	Otis Thorpe	.10
86	Dale Davis	.10
87	Vern Fleming	.10
88	Scott Haskin	.10
89	Reggie Miller	.40
90	Sam Mitchell	.10
91	Pooh Richardson	.10
92	Detlef Schrempf	.10
93	Malik Sealy	.10
94	Rik Smits	.15
95	*Terry Dehere*	.10
96	Ron Harper	.10
97	Mark Jackson	.10
98	Danny Manning	.15
99	Stanley Roberts	.10
100	Loy Vaught	.10
101	John Williams	.10
102	Sam Bowie	.10
103	Elden Campbell	.10
104	Doug Christie	.10
105	Vlade Divac	.10
106	James Edwards	.10
107	*George Lynch*	.10
108	Anthony Peeler	.10
109	Sedale Threatt	.10
110	James Worthy	.10
111	Bimbo Coles	.10
112	Grant Long	.10
113	Harold Miner	.10
114	Glen Rice	.15
115	John Salley	.10
116	Rony Seikaly	.10
117	Brian Shaw	.10
118	Steve Smith	.10
119	Anthony Avent	.10
120	*Vin Baker*	1.50
121	Jon Barry	.10
122	Frank Brickowski	.10
123	Todd Day	.10
124	Blue Edwards	.10
125	Brad Lohaus	.10
126	Lee Mayberry	.10
127	Eric Murdock	.10
128	Ken Norman	.10
129	Thurl Bailey	.10
130	Mike Brown	.10
131	Christian Laettner	.15
132	Luc Longley	.10
133	Chuck Person	.10
134	Chris Smith	.10
135	Doug West	.10
136	Michael Williams	.10
137	Kenny Anderson	.20
138	Benoit Benjamin	.10
139	Derrick Coleman	.20
140	Armon Gilliam	.10
141	Rick Mahorn	.10
142	Chris Morris	.10
143	Rumeal Robinson	.10
144	*Rex Walters*	.15
145	Greg Anthony	.10
146	Rolando Blackman	.10
147	Tony Campbell	.10
148	Hubert Davis	.10
149	Patrick Ewing	.40
150	Anthony Mason	.10
151	Charles Oakley	.10
152	Doc Rivers	.10
153	Charles Smith	.10
154	John Starks	.15
155	Herb Williams	.10
156	Nick Anderson	.10
157	Anthony Bowie	.10
158	Litterial Green	.10
159	*Anfernee Hardaway*	7.00
160	Shaquille O'Neal	3.50
161	Donald Royal	.10
162	Dennis Scott	.10
163	Scott Skiles	.10
164	Jeff Turner	.10
165	Dana Barros	.10
166	*Shawn Bradley*	.50
167	Johnny Dawkins	.10
168	*Greg Graham*	.10
169	Jeff Hornacek	.10
170	Moses Malone	.10
171	Tim Perry	.10
172	C. Weatherspoon	.20
173	Danny Ainge	.10
174	Charles Barkley	.75
175	Cedric Ceballos	.10
176	A.C. Green	.10
177	Frank Johnson	.10
178	Kevin Johnson	.25
179	Negele Knight	.10
180	Malcolm Mackey	.10
181	Dan Majerle	.15
182	Oliver Miller	.10
183	Mark West	.10
184	Clyde Drexler	.50
185	Chris Dudley	.10
186	Harvey Grant	.10
187	Jerome Kersey	.10
188	Terry Porter	.10
189	Cliff Robinson	.10
190	*James Robinson*	.25
191	Rod Strickland	.10
192	Buck Williams	.10
193	Randy Brown	.10
194	Duane Causwell	.10
195	*Bobby Hurley*	.25
196	Mitch Richmond	.20
197	Lionel Simmons	.10
198	Wayman Tisdale	.10
199	Spud Webb	.10
200	Walt Williams	.10
201	Willie Anderson	.10
202	Antoine Carr	.10
203	Terry Cummings	.10
204	Lloyd Daniels	.10
205	Vinny Del Negro	.10
206	Sleepy Floyd	.10
207	Avery Johnson	.10
208	J.R. Reid	.10
209	David Robinson	.75
210	Dennis Rodman	2.00
211	Michael Cage	.10
212	Kendall Gill	.10
213	*Ervin Johnson*	.10
214	Shawn Kemp	.60
215	Derrick McKey	.10
216	Nate McMillan	.10
217	Gary Payton	.40
218	Sam Perkins	.10
219	Ricky Pierce	.10
220	*Isaac Austin*	.10
221	David Benoit	.10
222	Tom Chambers	.10
223	Tyrone Corbin	.10
224	Mark Eaton	.10
225	Jay Humphries	.10
226	Jeff Malone	.10
227	Karl Malone	.40
228	John Stockton	.40
229	*Luther Wright*	.10
230	Michael Adams	.10
231	*Calbert Cheaney*	.75
232	Kevin Duckworth	.10
233	Pervis Ellison	.10
234	Tom Gugliotta	.10
235	Buck Johnson	.10
236	Doug Overton	.10
237	LaBradford Smith	.10
238	Larry Stewart	.10
239	Checklist	.10
240	Checklist	.10

1993-94 Jam Session GameBreakers

Eight of the NBA's top scorers are featured in this insert set. Cards, 2-1/2" x 4-3/4", have a color action photo on the front, with grid lines at the top and bottom of the card. The player's name and set logo are stamped in gold foil at the bottom. The card back has a close-up shot of the player, plus a career summary and a card number (1 of 8, etc.). Cards were random inserts in 1993-94 Fleer Jam Session packs.

		MT
Complete Set (8):		5.00
Common Player:		.25
1	Charles Barkley	1.25
2	Tim Hardaway	.25
3	Kevin Johnson	.50
4	Dan Majerle	.25
5	Scottie Pippen	2.00
6	Mark Price	.25
7	John Starks	.25
8	Dominique Wilkins	.50

1993-94 Jam Session Rookie Standouts

This set pictures top rookie prospects entering the 1993-94 NBA season. Cards, 2-1/2" x 4-3/4", were random inserts in Fleer's 1993-94 Jam Session packs. The card front has a color action photo, along with the player's name stamped in gold foil at the bottom of the card, next to a foil-stamped set logo. The card back has a career summary, player profile shot and card number 1 of 8, etc.

		MT
Complete Set (8):		20.00
Common Player:		.50
1	Vin Baker	2.00
2	Shawn Bradley	1.00
3	Calbert Cheaney	1.00
4	Anfernee Hardaway	14.00
5	Bobby Hurley	.50
6	Jamal Mashburn	3.00
7	Rodney Rogers	.50
8	Chris Webber	5.00

1993-94 Jam Session Second Year Stars

This set features eight of the NBA's top sophomores from the 1993-94 season. Cards, measuring 2-1/2" x 4-3/4", were random inserts in Fleer's 1993 Jam Session packs. The card front has a color action photo against a rainbow-colored background. The player's name is stamped in gold foil in the lower right corner; the set logo is adjacent to his name. The back also has a rainbow-colored background which features a close-up shot of the player and career highlights. A card number, 1 of 8, etc., is also given.

		MT
Complete Set (8):		8.00
Common Player:		.25
Minor Stars:		.50
1	Tom Gugliotta	.25
2	Jim Jackson	1.50
3	Christian Laettner	.25
4	Oliver Miller	.25
5	Harold Miner	.25
6	Alonzo Mourning	1.50
7	Shaquille O'Neal	5.00
8	Walt Williams	.25

1993-94 Jam Session Slam Dunk Heroes

Eight of the NBA's top slam dunkers are featured in this insert set. Cards, 2-1/2" x 4-3/4", were random inserts in Fleer's 1993 Jam Session packs. The card front has a color action photo, with the player's name stamped in gold foil at the bottom, near a foil-stamped set logo. The back has a close-up photo of the player at the top, with a career recap underneath. A card number, 1 of 8, etc., also appears on the card.

		MT
Complete Set (8):		10.00
Common Player:		.75

1	Patrick Ewing	1.00
2	Larry Johnson	1.00
3	Shawn Kemp	1.00
4	Karl Malone	.75
5	Alonzo Mourning	1.50
6	Hakeem Olajuwon	2.00
7	Shaquille O'Neal	5.00
8	David Robinson	1.50

1993-94 Jam Session Team Night Sheets

These cards are virtually identical to the standard-issue Jam Session cards, except that they are unnumbered. The cards measure 2-1/2" x 4-3/4" when perforated and were available on nine- or 12-card sheets at varying NBA games.

		MT
Complete Set (9):		30.00
Common Player:		4.00
(1)	Boston Celtics Sony - Ad card (Alaa Abdelnaby, Dee Brown, Sherman Douglas, Rick Fox, Kevin Gamble, Xavier McDaniel, Robert Parish CO)	4.00
(2)	Dallas Mavericks Doritos - Ad card (Quinn Buckner CO, Terry Davis, Lucious Harris, Donald Hodge, Jim Jackson, Popeye Jones, Tim Legler, Fat Lever, Jamal Mashburn, Sean Rooks, Doug Smith)	6.00
(3)	Chicago Bulls Rust-oleum - Ad card (B.J. Armstrong, Corie Blount, Bill Cartwright, Horace Grant, Phil Jackson CO, Stacey King, Toni Kukoc, John Paxson, Will Perdue, Scottie Pippen, Scott Williams)	6.00
(4)	Detroit Pistons Pistons Logo LCI International - Ad card (Joe Dumars, Sean Elliott, Bill Laimbeer, Terry Mills, Olden Polynice, Isiah Thomas)	4.00
(5)	Indiana Pacers Combos Snacks - Ad card (Larry Brown CO, Antonio Davis, Dale Davis, Vern Fleming, Scott Haskin, Derrick McKey, Reggie Miller, Sam Mitchell, Pooh Richardson, Malik Sealy, Rik Smits)	4.00
(6)	Los Angeles Clippers Snickers/Kudos - Ad card (Mark Aguirre, Terry Dehere, Gary Grant, Ron Harper, Mark Jackson, Danny Manning, Stanley Roberts, Elmore Spencer, Tom Tolbert, Loy Vaught, Bob Weiss CO)	4.00
(7)	Los Angeles Lakers Team Logo (Sam Bowie, Elden Campbell, Doug Christie, Vlade Divac, James Edwards, George Lynch, Anthony Peeler, Tony Smith, Sedale Threatt, Nick Van Exel)	6.00
(8)	Milwaukee Bucks Usinger's - Ad card (Vin Baker, Jon Barry, Frank Brickowski, Todd Day, Blue Edwards, Brad Lohaus, Lee Mayberry, Eric Murdock, Ken Norman, Dan Schayes, Derek Strong)	6.00
(9)	New York Knicks WIZ - Two ad cards (Greg Anthony, Rolando Blackman, Hubert Davis, Patrick Ewing, Derek Harper, Anthony Mason, Charles Oakley, Charles Smith, John Starks, Herb Williams)	4.00

1994-95 Fleer Promo Sheet

This cardboard sheet was distributed with sales material to promote the Fleer's 1994-95 Basketball set. It featured 10 cards on each side along with the NBA Jam Session logo. It consisted of one solid panel of cards and no perforation.

		MT
Complete Set (1):		4.00
NNO	John Starks, Dennis Rodman, Reggie Miller, Mookie Blaylock, Hakeem Olajuwon, Chris Mullin, Karl Malone, Mitch Richmond, Kevin Johnson, Larry Johnson, Dino Radja, Scottie Pippen, Gary Payton, Christian Laettner, Shawn Bradley, Derrick Coleman,,	4.00

1994-95 Fleer

Fleer's 1994 basketball set features a splashy new design and several different insert sets. The insert cards are seeded one per pack, collectors can also search for "Fleer Hot Packs," which are randomly inserted packs filled with nothing but inserts. The Hot Packs show up about one in every other box. Fleer's Series I cards are available in both 15 and 21-card packs. Every card features a "splash" of foil stamping on the front in one of six team-coded colors, plus UV coating on both sides of the card. The back design includes a vertical photo, stats and a different background design for each NBA team. Each insert set has a different design, although all have a borderless format and foil stamping. The roster includes: Pro Visions art cards, which form one large painting when put together in a nine-pocket sleeve; Triple Threat (10); Career Achievement Awards (6), with cards featuring a high-tech metallized design; Rookie Sensations (25); NBA All-Stars (26); League Leaders (8); Award Winners (4); and NBA All-Defensive Teams (10). In addition, collectors will find randomly inserted NBA Draft Lottery exchange cards, which can be redeemed through the mail for up to 11 first-round draft picks.

		MT
Complete Set (390):		25.00
Complete Series 1 (240):		10.00
Complete Series 2 (150):		15.00
Common Player:		.05
Minor Stars:		.10
Ser. 1 or 2 Pack (15):		1.25
Ser. 1 or 2 Wax Box (36):		35.00
1	Stacey Augmon	.05
2	Mookie Blaylock	.05
3	Craig Ehlo	.05
4	Duane Ferrell	.05
5	Adam Keefe	.05
6	Jon Koncak	.05
7	Andrew Lang	.05
8	Danny Manning	.10
9	Kevin Willis	.05
10	Dee Brown	.05
11	Sherman Douglas	.05
12	Acie Earl	.05
13	Rick Fox	.05
14	Kevin Gamble	.05
15	Xavier McDaniel	.05
16	Robert Parish	.10
17	Ed Pinckney	.05
18	Dino Radja	.10
19	Muggsy Bogues	.05
20	Frank Brickowski	.05
21	Scott Burrell	.05
22	Dell Curry	.05
23	Kenny Gattison	.05
24	Hersey Hawkins	.05
25	Eddie Johnson	.05
26	Larry Johnson	.20
27	Alonzo Mourning	.30
28	David Wingate	.05
29	B.J. Armstrong	.05
30	Horace Grant	.15
31	Steve Kerr	.05
32	Toni Kukoc	.10
33	Luc Longley	.05
34	Pete Myers	.05
35	Scottie Pippen	.50
36	Bill Wennington	.05
37	Scott Williams	.05
38	Terrell Brandon	.05
39	Brad Daugherty	.05
40	Tyrone Hill	.05
41	Chris Mills	.05
42	Larry Nance	.05
43	Bobby Phills	.05
44	Mark Price	.10
45	Gerald Wilkins	.05
46	John Williams	.05
47	Lucious Harris	.05
48	Donald Hodge	.05
49	Jim Jackson	.20
50	Popeye Jones	.05
51	Tim Legler	.05
52	Fat Lever	.05
53	Jamal Mashburn	.25
54	Sean Rooks	.05
55	Doug Smith	.05
56	Mahmoud Abdul-Rauf	.05
57	LaPhonso Ellis	.05
58	Dikembe Mutombo	.20
59	Robert Pack	.05
60	Rodney Rogers	.10
61	Bryant Stith	.05
62	Brian Williams	.05
63	Reggie Williams	.05
64	Greg Anderson	.05
65	Joe Dumars	.15
66	Sean Elliott	.05
67	Allan Houston	.10
68	Lindsey Hunter	.05
69	Terry Mills	.05
70	Victor Alexander	.05
71	Chris Gatling	.05
72	Tim Hardaway	.10
73	Keith Jennings	.05
74	Avery Johnson	.05
75	Chris Mullin	.10
76	Billy Owens	.05
77	Latrell Sprewell	.20
78	Chris Webber	.25
79	Scott Brooks	.05
80	Sam Cassell	.10
81	Mario Elie	.05
82	Carl Herrera	.05
83	Robert Horry	.05
84	Vernon Maxwell	.05
85	Hakeem Olajuwon	.60
86	Kenny Smith	.05
87	Otis Thorpe	.05
88	Antonio Davis	.05
89	Dale Davis	.05
90	Vern Fleming	.05
91	Derrick McKey	.05
92	Reggie Miller	.20
93	Pooh Richardson	.05
94	Byron Scott	.05
95	Rik Smits	.10
96	Haywoode Workman	.05
97	Terry Dehere	.05
98	Harold Ellis	.05
99	Gary Grant	.05
100	Ron Harper	.05
101	Mark Jackson	.05
102	Stanley Roberts	.05
103	Elmore Spencer	.05
104	Loy Vaught	.05
105	Dominique Wilkins	.15
106	Elden Campbell	.05
107	Doug Christie	.05
108	Vlade Divac	.05
109	George Lynch	.05
110	Anthony Peeler	.05
111	Tony Smith	.05
112	Sedale Threatt	.05
113	Nick Van Exel	.50
114	James Worthy	.05
115	Bimbo Coles	.05
116	Grant Long	.05
117	Harold Miner	.05
118	Glen Rice	.10
119	John Salley	.05
120	Rony Seikaly	.05
121	Brian Shaw	.05
122	Steve Smith	.05
123	Vin Baker	.20
124	Jon Barry	.05
125	Todd Day	.05
126	Blue Edwards	.05
127	Lee Mayberry	.05
128	Eric Murdock	.05
129	Ken Norman	.05
130	Derek Strong	.05
131	Thurl Bailey	.05
132	Stacey King	.05
133	Christian Laettner	.05
134	Chuck Person	.05
135	Isaiah Rider	.15
136	Chris Smith	.05
137	Doug West	.05
138	Michael Williams	.05
139	Kenny Anderson	.10
140	Benoit Benjamin	.05
141	P.J. Brown	.05
142	Derrick Coleman	.10
143	Kevin Edwards	.05
144	Armon Gilliam	.05
145	Chris Morris	.05
146	Johnny Newman	.05
147	Greg Anthony	.05
148	Anthony Bonner	.05
149	Hubert Davis	.05
150	Patrick Ewing	.20
151	Derek Harper	.05
152	Anthony Mason	.05
153	Charles Oakley	.05
154	Doc Rivers	.05
155	Charles Smith	.05
156	John Starks	.05
157	Nick Anderson	.05
158	Anthony Avent	.05
159	Anfernee Hardaway	1.25
160	Shaquille O'Neal	1.00
161	Donald Royal	.05
162	Dennis Scott	.05
163	Scott Skiles	.05
164	Jeff Turner	.05
165	Dana Barros	.05
166	Shawn Bradley	.10
167	Greg Graham	.05
168	Eric Leckner	.05
169	Jeff Malone	.05
170	Moses Malone	.05
171	Tim Perry	.05
172	Clarence Weatherspoon	.05
173	Orlando Woolridge	.05
174	Danny Ainge	.05
175	Charles Barkley	.30
176	Cedric Ceballos	.05
177	A.C. Green	.05
178	Kevin Johnson	.10
179	Joe Kleine	.05
180	Dan Majerle	.05
181	Oliver Miller	.05
182	Mark West	.05
183	Clyde Drexler	.25
184	Harvey Grant	.05
185	Jerome Kersey	.05
186	Tracy Murray	.05
187	Terry Porter	.05
188	Cliff Robinson	.05
189	James Robinson	.05
190	Rod Strickland	.05
191	Buck Williams	.05
192	Duane Causwell	.05
193	Bobby Hurley	.05
194	Olden Polynice	.05
195	Mitch Richmond	.10
196	Lionel Simmons	.05
197	Wayman Tisdale	.05
198	Spud Webb	.05
199	Walt Williams	.05
200	Trevor Wilson	.05
201	Willie Anderson	.05
202	Antoine Carr	.05
203	Terry Cummings	.05
204	Vinny Del Negro	.05
205	Dale Ellis	.05
206	Negele Knight	.05
207	J.R. Reid	.05
208	David Robinson	.30
209	Dennis Rodman	.75
210	Vincent Askew	.05
211	Michael Cage	.05
212	Kendall Gill	.05
213	Shawn Kemp	.40
214	Nate McMillan	.05
215	Gary Payton	.10
216	Sam Perkins	.05
217	Ricky Pierce	.05
218	Detlef Schrempf	.05
219	David Benoit	.05
220	Tom Chambers	.05
221	Tyrone Corbin	.05
222	Jeff Hornacek	.05
223	Jay Humphries	.05
224	Karl Malone	.20
225	Byron Russell	.05
226	Felton Spencer	.05
227	John Stockton	.20
228	Michael Adams	.05
229	Rex Chapman	.05
230	Calbert Cheaney	.05
231	Kevin Duckworth	.05
232	Pervis Ellison	.05
233	Tom Gugliotta	.05
234	Don McLean	.05
235	Gheorghe Muresan	.05
236	Brent Price	.05
237	Toronto Raptors	.05
238	Checklist	.05
239	Checklist	.05
240	Checklist	.05
241	*Sergei Bazarevich*	.05
242	Tyrone Corbin	.05
243	Grant Long	.05
244	Ken Norman	.05
245	Steve Smith	.05
246	Fred Vinson	.05
247	*Blue Edwards*	.05
248	*Greg Minor*	.10
249	*Eric Montross*	.30
250	Derek Strong	.05
251	David Wesley	.05
252	Dominique Wilkins	.15
253	Michael Adams	.05
254	Tony Bennett	.05
255	*Darrin Hancock*	.05
256	Robert Parish	.05
257	Corie Blount	.05
258	Jud Buechler	.05
259	Greg Foster	.05
260	Ron Harper	.05
261	Larry Krystkowiak	.05
262	Will Perdue	.05
263	*Dickey Simpkins*	.15
264	Michael Cage	.05
265	Tony Campbell	.05
266	Terry Davis	.05
267	*Tony Dumas*	.25
268	*Jason Kidd*	2.00
269	Roy Tarpley	.05
270	Morlon Wiley	.05
271	Lorenzo Williams	.05
272	Dale Ellis	.05
273	Tom Hammonds	.05
274	Cliff Levingston	.05
275	Darnell Mee	.05
276	*Jalen Rose*	2.00
277	*Reggie Slater*.	.10
278	*Bill Curley*	.15
279	Johnny Dawkins	.05
280	*Grant Hill*	3.00
281	Eric Leckner	.05
282	Mark Macon	.05
283	Oliver Miller	.05
284	Mark West	.05
285	Manute Bol	.05
286	Tom Gugliotta	.05
287	Ricky Pierce	.05
288	*Carlos Rogers*	.15
289	*Clifford Rozier*	.15
290	Rony Seikaly	.05
291	*Tim Breaux*	.05
292	Chris Jent	.05
293	Eric Riley	.05
294	*Zan Tabak*	.05
295	Duane Ferrell	.05
296	Mark Jackson	.05
297	John Williams	.05
298	*Matt Fish*	.05
299	Tony Massenburg	.05
300	*Lamond Murray*	.30
301	Charles Outlaw	.05
302	*Eric Piatkowski*	.20
303	Pooh Richardson	.05
304	Randy Woods	.05
305	Sam Bowie	.05
306	Cedric Ceballos	.05
307	Antonio Harvey	.05
308	*Eddie Jones*	2.00
309	*Anthony Miller*	.05
310	Ledell Eackles	.05
311	Kevin Gamble	.05
312	Brad Lohaus	.05
313	Billy Owens	.05
314	*Khalid Reeves*	.30
315	Kevin Willis	.05
316	Marty Conlon	.05
317	*Eric Mobley*	.15
318	Johnny Newman	.05
319	Ed Pinckney	.05
320	*Glenn Robinson*	1.00
321	Mike Brown	.05
322	Pat Durham	.05
323	*Howard Eisley*	.05
324	Andres Guibert	.05
325	*Donyell Marshall*	.50
326	Sean Rooks	.05
327	*Yinka Dare*	.10
328	Sleepy Floyd	.05
329	Sean Higgins	.05
330	Rick Mahorn	.05
331	Rex Walters	.05
332	Jayson Williams	.05
333	*Charlie Ward*	.15
334	Herb Williams	.05
335	*Monty Williams*	.15
336	Anthony Bowie	.05
337	Horace Grant	.15
338	Geert Hammink	.05
339	Tree Rollins	.05
340	Brian Shaw	.05
341	*Brooks Thompson*	.15
342	*Derrick Alston*	.05
343	Willie Burton	.05
344	Jaren Jackson	.05
345	*B.J. Tyler*	.10
346	Scott Williams	.05
347	*Sharone Wright*	.30
348	*Antonio Lang*	.05
349	Danny Manning	.10
350	Elliot Perry	.05
351	*Wesley Person*	.40
352	*Trevor Ruffin*	.10
353	Dan Schayes	.05
354	*Aaron Swinson*	.05
355	Wayman Tisdale	.05
356	Mark Bryant	.05
357	Chris Dudley	.05
358	James Edwards	.05
359	*Aaron McKie*	.50
360	Alaa Abdelnaby	.05
361	Frank Brickowski	.05
362	Randy Brown	.05
363	*Brian Grant*	.75
364	*Michael Smith*	.20
365	Henry Turner	.05
366	Sean Elliott	.05
367	Avery Johnson	.05
368	Moses Malone	.05
369	*Julius Nwosu*	.05
370	Chuck Person	.05
371	Chris Whitney	.05
372	Bill Cartwright	.05
373	Byron Houston	.05
374	Ervin Johnson	.05
375	Sarunas Marciulionis	.05
376	Antoine Carr	.05
377	John Crotty	.05
378	Adam Keefe	.05
379	*Jamie Watson*	.15
380	Mitchell Butler	.05
381	*Juwan Howard*	1.50
382	*Jim McIlvaine*	.10
383	Doug Overton	.05
384	Scott Skiles	.05
385	Larry Stewart	.05
386	Kenny Walker	.05
387	Chris Webber	.25
388	Vancouver Grizzlies	.05
389	Checklist	.05
390	Checklist	.05

1994-95 Fleer All-Defensive

The league's top 10 defensive players from 1993-94 are feautured on these insert cards, randomly included in all types of Fleer's 1994-95 Series I packs. The cards feature UV coating, full-bleed photos, foil stamping and are numbered 1 of 10, etc.

		MT
Complete Set (10):		8.00
Common Player:		.25
1	Mookie Blaylock	.25
2	Charles Oakley	.25
3	Hakeem Olajuwon	2.00
4	Gary Payton	.50
5	Scottie Pippen	2.00
6	Horace Grant	.50
7	Nate McMillan	.25
8	David Robinson	1.50
9	Dennis Rodman	2.00
10	Latrell Sprewell	.75

1994-95 Fleer All-Stars

This 26-card insert set features 13 All-Stars from each of the NBA's Western and Eastern conferences. Cards are numbered 1 of 26, etc., and feature foil stamping, UV coating and a borderless photo format. Cards were random inserts in Fleer's 1994-95 Series I packs and feature an orange dot pattern on the fronts, giving the card the feel of a basketball.

		MT
Complete Set (26):		30.00
Common Player:		.50
1	Kenny Anderson	.50
2	B.J. Armstrong	.50
3	Mookie Blaylock	.50
4	Derrick Coleman	.50
5	Patrick Ewing	1.50
6	Horace Grant	.75
7	Alonzo Mourning	1.75
8	Charles Oakley	.50
9	Shaquille O'Neal	7.00
10	Scottie Pippen	4.00
11	Mark Price	.50
12	John Starks	.50
13	Dominique Wilkins	.50
14	Charles Barkley	3.00
15	Clyde Drexler	1.50
16	Kevin Johnson	.75
17	Shawn Kemp	2.00
18	Karl Malone	1.25
19	Danny Manning	.50
20	Hakeem Olajuwon	3.00
21	Gary Payton	1.25
22	Mitch Richmond	.75
23	Clifford Robinson	.50
24	David Robinson	3.00
25	Latrell Sprewell	1.00
26	John Stockton	1.25

1994-95 Fleer Award Winners

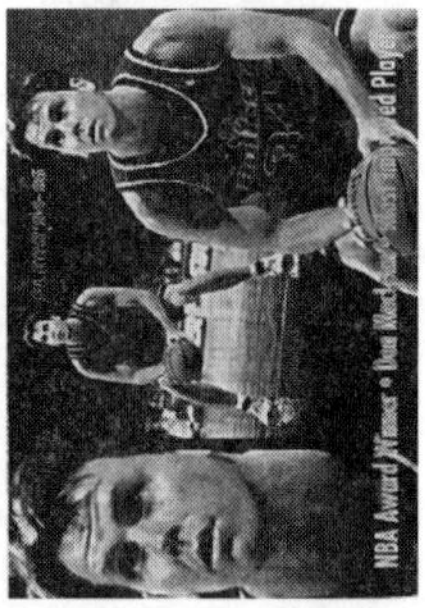

These four cards, randomly inserted in all types of Fleer's 1994-95 Series I packs, feature players who won awards after the 1993-94 NBA season. The UV coated cards use full-bleed photos with foil stamping on the fronts and are numbered on the backs 1 of 4, etc.

		MT
Complete Set (4):		4.00
Common Player:		.25
1	Dell Curry	.25
2	Don MacLean	.25
3	Hakeem Olajuwon	2.00
4	Chris Webber	1.50

1994-95 Fleer Career Achievement

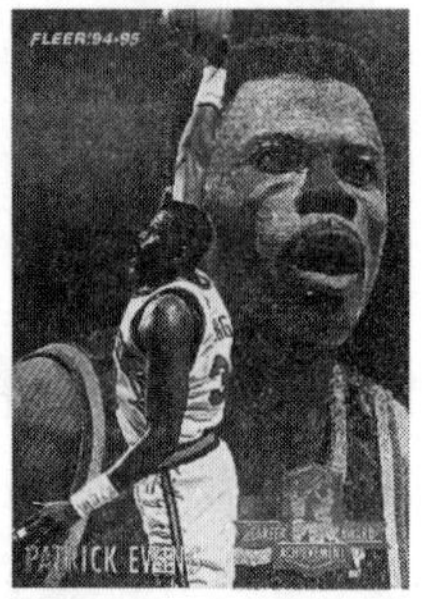

These six cards feature players who have accomplished career milestones. The cards, random inserts in all types of Fleer's 1994-95 Series I packs, feature a high-tech metalized design. UV coating, foil stamping and a borderless format are also used. Cards are numbered 1 of 6, etc.

		MT
Complete Set (6):		20.00
Common Player:		2.00
1	Patrick Ewing	4.00
2	Karl Malone	4.00
3	Hakeem Olajuwon	7.00
4	Robert Parish	2.00
5	Scottie Pippen	8.00
6	Dominique Wilkins	2.00

1994-95 Fleer First Year Phenoms

These 1994-95 Fleer Series II inserts feature 10 of the NBA's most promising rookies for the season, those who were slated to be a major impact on their new teams. The card front uses gold foil stamping on it and shows the player breaking out of the card, with a smaller version of the player featured in each of the four corners of the card. The cards were inserted into every fifth pack and are numbered 1 of 10, etc.. The back has another color photo of the player, against a ghosted background of the four smaller pictures from the front.

		MT
Complete Set (10):		20.00
Common Player:		1.00
1	Grant Hill	8.00
2	Jason Kidd	5.00
3	Donyell Marshall	1.00
4	Eric Montross	1.00
5	Lamond Murray	1.00
6	Wesley Person	1.25
7	Khalid Reeves	1.00
8	Glenn Robinson	3.00
9	Jalen Rose	1.00
10	Sharone Wright	1.00

1994-95 Fleer League Leaders

Statistical leaders in eight NBA categories are featured in this insert set. The UV coated cards, numbered 1 of 8, etc., feature foil stamping and have full-bleed photos. Cards were randomly included in 1994-95 Fleer Series I packs. The front features the player and his team's logo against a hardwood basketball court.

		MT
Complete Set (8):		10.00
Common Player:		.25
1	Mahmoud Abdul-Rauf	.25
2	Nate McMillan	.25
3	Tracy Murray	.25
4	Dikembe Mutombo	.75
5	Shaquille O'Neal	5.00
6	David Robinson	2.00
7	Dennis Rodman	2.00
8	John Stockton	1.25

1994-95 Fleer Lottery Exchange

This 11-card set was available by redeeming the Fleer Lottery Exchange card found in packs of Series I at a rate of one per 175. Card designs are very similar to those of regular-issue cards except for the Lottery Pick logo and the backs capture a head shot of the player with text under it and the number in the top right.

		MT
Complete Set (11):		25.00
Common Player:		.40
1	Glenn Robinson	4.00
2	Jason Kidd	6.00
3	Grant Hill	10.00
4	Donyell Marshall	.40
5	Juwan Howard	3.00
6	Sharone Wright	.75
7	Lamond Murray	.40
8	Brian Grant	1.25
9	Eric Montross	.75
10	Eddie Jones	2.50
NNO	Lottery Exchange Card	1.50

1994-95 Fleer Pro-Visions

These cards, which form one large painting when put together in a nine-pocket sleeve, were random inserts in all types of Fleer's 1994-95 Series I packs. The fronts feature artistic drawings of the players; backs are numbered 1 of 9, etc. The UV coated cards use a borderless format and foil stamping. The illustration's theme is reiterated on the back by the card's title, and a summary of the player's career and talents.

		MT
Complete Set (9):		5.00
Common Player:		.25
Minor Stars:		.50
1	Jamal Mashburn	.50
2	John Starks	.25
3	Toni Kukoc	.50
4	Derrick Coleman	.50
5	Chris Webber	.75
6	Dennis Rodman	1.00
7	Gary Payton	.50
8	Anfernee Hardaway	2.00
9	Dan Majerle	.25

1994-95 Fleer Rookie Sensations

These cards, which are UV coated and feature foil stamping, are devoted to 25 second-year players who excelled in their rookie NBA season in 1993-94. Cards were random inserts in 1994-95 Fleer Series I packs and are numbered 1 of 15, etc.

		MT
Complete Set (25):		30.00
Common Player:		.75
1	Vin Baker	3.00
2	Shawn Bradley	1.50
3	P.J. Brown	.75
4	Sam Cassell	1.50
5	Calbert Cheaney	.75
6	Antonio Davis	.75
7	Acie Earl	.75
8	Harold Ellis	.75
9	Anfernee Hardaway	12.00
10	Allan Houston	2.00
11	Lindsey Hunter	.75
12	Bobby Hurley	.75
13	Popeye Jones	.75
14	Toni Kukoc	2.00
15	George Lynch	.75
16	Jamal Mashburn	2.00
17	Chris Mills	.75
18	Gheorghe Muresan	.75
19	Dino Radja	1.50
20	Isaiah Rider	1.00
21	James Robinson	.75
22	Rodney Rogers	.75
23	Byron Russell	.75
24	Nick Van Exel	3.00
25	Chris Webber	3.00

1994-95 Fleer Sharpshooters

These 10 cards, random inserts in 1994-95 Fleer Series II 12-card retail packs, feature the NBA's top three-point shooters. The card front uses gold foil stamping and shows the player shooting, against a background of a net with a ball going through it.

		MT
Complete Set (10):		15.00
Common Player:		1.00
1	Dell Curry	1.00
2	Joe Dumars	1.50
3	Dale Ellis	1.00
4	Dan Majerle	1.00
5	Reggie Miller	3.00
6	Mark Price	1.00
7	Glen Rice	1.50
8	Mitch Richmond	1.50
9	Dennis Scott	1.00
10	Latrell Sprewell	2.00

1994-95 Fleer Superstars

These 1994-95 Fleer Series II inserts, utilizing 100 percent etched foil for the fronts, feature NBA veterans with true Hall of Fame potential. Only one in every 37 packs was slated to have a Superstars insert card. The card back, numbered 1 of 6, etc., has another color photo, plus a player profile.

		MT
Complete Set (6):		25.00
Common Player:		2.00
1	Charles Barkley	6.00
2	Patrick Ewing	3.00
3	Hakeem Olajuwon	8.00
4	Robert Parish	2.00
5	Scottie Pippen	10.00
6	Dominique Wilkins	2.00

1994-95 Fleer Team Leaders

Three star players from different NBA teams are featured on each of these nine insert cards. The cards, which have gold foil stamping on the front, were random inserts in 1994-95 Fleer Series II packs, one every third pack. The back has a profile of each player, plus a mug shot of each. Cards are numbered 1 of 9, etc.

		MT
Complete Set (9):		5.00
Common Player:		.25
1	Mookie Blaylock, Dominique Wilkins, Alonzo Mourning	.50
2	Scottie Pippen, Mark Price, Jamal Mashburn	1.00
3	Dikembe Mutombo, Joe Dumars, Latrell Sprewell	.50
4	Hakeem Olajuwon, Reggie Miller, Loy Vaught	1.00
5	Vlade Divac, Glen Rice, Vin Baker	.25
6	Isaiah Rider, Kenny Anderson, Patrick Ewing	.50
7	Shaquille O'Neal, Clarence Weatherspoon, Charles Barkley	2.00
8	Rod Strickland, Mitch Richmond, David Robinson	1.00
9	Shawn Kemp, John Stockton, Rex Chapman	.60

1994-95 Fleer Total D

These horizontally-designed insert cards were randomly included in 1994-95 Fleer Series II packs, one per every seven 12-card hobby packs. The top defenders in the league are showcased. The card front has a color photo of the player, against a background which has "Total D" written on it several times. The player's name and team are stamped in gold foil at the bottom of the card. The card back has a closeup shot of the player, plus a summary of the player's skills. Cards are numbered 1 of 10, etc.

		MT
Complete Set (10):		10.00
Common Player:		.50
1	Mookie Blaylock	.50
2	Nate McMillan	.50
3	Dikembe Mutombo	1.00
4	Charles Oakley	.50
5	Hakeem Olajuwon	4.00
6	Gary Payton	1.00
7	Scottie Pippen	3.00
8	David Robinson	3.00
9	Latrell Sprewell	1.00
10	John Stockton	1.00

1994-95 Fleer Towers of Power

These 1994-95 Fleer Series II cards were randomly included in 18-card jumbo packs, one every five packs. The set features the league's most dominant power forwards and centers. The card front has a photo of the player crashing the boards. Foil stamping is also used on the front.

		MT
Complete Set (10):		35.00
Common Player:		1.00
1	Charles Barkley	5.00
2	Patrick Ewing	2.00
3	Shawn Kemp	2.00
4	Karl Malone	2.00
5	Alonzo Mourning	3.00
6	Dikembe Mutombo	1.00
7	Hakeem Olajuwon	7.00
8	Shaquille O'Neal	12.00
9	David Robinson	4.00
10	Chris Webber	3.00

1994-95 Fleer Triple Threats

These 10 cards, random inserts in all types of Fleer's 1994-95 Series I packs, feature players who can shoot the three pointer. The front shows three identical images of the player, but in different sizes, against a background of basketball courts with the three point line. Cards, numbered 1 of 10, etc., have UV coating, full-bleed photos and foil stamping.

		MT
Complete Set (10):		8.00
Common Player:		.25
1	Mookie Blaylock	.25
2	Patrick Ewing	.50
3	Shawn Kemp	1.00
4	Karl Malone	.50
5	Reggie Miller	.50
6	Hakeem Olajuwon	1.50
7	Shaquille O'Neal	3.00
8	Scottie Pippen	1.00
9	David Robinson	1.00
10	Latrell Sprewell	.50

1994-95 Fleer Young Lions

These 1994-95 Fleer Series II inserts feature some of the game's top younger players. The card front uses gold foil stamping for the set's logo, which incorporates a lion into the design. The player is shown in action against a background which features a head shot of a lion. The back has a ghosted image of the lion, which has a player profile written over it. A second color photo and card number (1 of 6, etc.) also appear on the back. Cards were inserted into every fifth pack.

		MT
Complete Set (6):		10.00
Common Player:		1.00
1	Vin Baker	1.00
2	Anfernee Hardaway	5.00
3	Larry Johnson	1.00
4	Alonzo Mourning	1.00
5	Shaquille O'Neal	5.00
6	Chris Webber	1.50

1994 Jam Session Ticket Stubs

During the All-Star Game weekend in 1994, these ticket stub cards were given away to the public without the stubs attached (2-1/2" x 4-3/4"). One card was given away during each of the four days of the event: Thursday - Barkley, Friday - Pippen, Saturday - O'Neal and Sunday - Drexler/Robinson. The full-bleed fronts have a Fleer stripe along the bottom border below the NBA Jam Session logo. The card backs inform the ticket holder of the conditions governing the use of the ticket. Cards found with the stub still intact are valued at five times the prices given.

		MT
Complete Set (4):		15.00
Common Player:		2.50
1	Charles Barkley	4.00
2	Danny Manning, David Robinson	4.00
3	Shaquille O'Neal, Karl Malone	8.00
4	Scottie Pippen	3.00

1994-95 Jam Session

As are the previous Jam Session cards, these 1994-95 cards are 35 percent larger than a standard-size card. Each front has a color action photo, with a background that is color-coded by team. The player's name is printed in four horizontal bars, with a Jam Session logo underneath. The card back is numbered and features a color photo of the player against a basketball background. Statistics run up the right side; biographical information and a player profile are also included. All cards are UV coated. Inserts include Second Year Stars, Slam Dunk Heroes, GameBreakers and Flashing Stars.

		MT
Complete Set (200):		25.00
Common Player:		.10
Minor Stars:		.20
Wax Box:		45.00
1	Stacey Augmon	.10
2	Mookie Blaylock	.10
3	Tyrone Corbin	.10
4	Craig Ehlo	.10
5	Ken Norman	.10
6	Kevin Willis	.10
7	Dee Brown	.10
8	Sherman Douglas	.10
9	Acie Earl	.10
10	Blue Edwards	.10
11	Pervis Ellison	.10
12	Rick Fox	.10
13	Xavier McDaniel	.10
14	*Eric Montross*	.50
15	Dino Radja	.20
16	Dominique Wilkins	.25
17	Michael Adams	.10
18	Muggsy Bogues	.10
19	Dell Curry	.10
20	Kenny Gattison	.10
21	Hersey Hawkins	.10
22	Larry Johnson	.40
23	Alonzo Mourning	.60
24	Robert Parish	.15
25	B.J. Armstrong	.10
26	Ron Harper	.10
27	Steve Kerr	.10
28	Toni Kukoc	.20
29	Pete Myers	.10
30	Will Perdue	.10
31	Scottie Pippen	1.00
32	Terrell Brandon	.10
33	Michael Cage	.10
34	Brad Daugherty	.10
35	Chris Mills	.10
36	Bobby Phills	.10
37	Mark Price	.15
38	Gerald Wilkins	.10
39	John Williams	.10
40	Jim Jackson	.50
41	*Jason Kidd*	3.00
42	Jamal Mashburn	.75
43	Sean Rooks	.10
44	Doug Smith	.10
45	Mahmoud Abdul-Rauf	.10
46	LaPhonso Ellis	.10
47	Dikembe Mutombo	.25
48	Robert Pack	.10
49	Rodney Rogers	.15
50	*Jalen Rose*	.50
51	Bryant Stith	.10
52	Reggie Williams	.10
53	*Bill Curley*	.20
54	Joe Dumars	.20
55	*Grant Hill*	7.00
56	Allan Houston	.15
57	Lindsey Hunter	.10
58	Oliver Miller	.10
59	Terry Mills	.10
60	Mark West	.10
61	Chris Gatling	.10
62	Tim Hardaway	.15
63	Chris Mullin	.20
64	Billy Owens	.10
65	Ricky Pierce	.10
66	Latrell Sprewell	.50
67	Chris Webber	1.00
68	Sam Cassell	.20
69	Mario Elie	.10
70	Carl Herrera	.10
71	Robert Horry	.15
72	Vernon Maxwell	.10
73	Hakeem Olajuwon	1.00
74	Kenny Smith	.10
75	Otis Thorpe	.10
76	Antonio Davis	.10
77	Dale Davis	.10
78	Mark Jackson	.10
79	Derrick McKey	.10
80	Reggie Miller	.50
81	Byron Scott	.10
82	Rik Smits	.20
83	Haywoode Workman	.10
84	Gary Grant	.10
85	Pooh Richardson	.10
86	Stanley Roberts	.10
87	Elmore Spencer	.10
88	Loy Vaught	.10
89	Elden Campbell	.10
90	Cedric Ceballos	.10
91	Doug Christie	.10
92	Vlade Divac	.10
93	*Eddie Jones*	2.00
94	George Lynch	.10
95	Anthony Peeler	.10
96	Nick Van Exel	.50
97	James Worthy	.10
98	Grant Long	.10
99	Harold Miner	.10
100	Glen Rice	.20
101	John Salley	.10
102	Rony Seikaly	.10
103	Steve Smith	.10
104	Vin Baker	.50
105	Jon Barry	.10
106	Todd Day	.10
107	Lee Mayberry	.10
108	Eric Murdock	.10
109	Stacey King	.10
110	Christian Laettner	.10
111	*Donyell Marshall*	.50
112	Isaiah Rider	.40
113	Doug West	.10
114	Michael Williams	.10
115	Kenny Anderson	.20
116	P.J. Brown	.10
117	Derrick Coleman	.20
118	*Yinka Dare*	.15
119	Kevin Edwards	.10
120	Armon Gilliam	.10
121	Chris Morris	.10
122	Anthony Bonner	.10
123	Hubert Davis	.10
124	Patrick Ewing	.50
125	Derek Harper	.10
126	Anthony Mason	.10
127	Charles Oakley	.10
128	Doc Rivers	.10
129	Charles Smith	.10
130	John Starks	.10
131	*Charlie Ward*	.50
132	Nick Anderson	.10
133	Anthony Bowie	.10
134	Horace Grant	.20
135	Anfernee Hardaway	3.00
136	Shaquille O'Neal	2.50
137	Dennis Scott	.10
138	Jeff Turner	.10
139	Dana Barros	.10
140	Shawn Bradley	.15
141	Johnny Dawkins	.10
142	Jeff Malone	.10
143	Tim Perry	.10
144	Clarence Weatherspoon	.15
145	Scott Williams	.10
146	Danny Ainge	.10
147	Charles Barkley	1.00
148	A.C. Green	.10
149	Kevin Johnson	.20
150	Joe Kleine	.10
151	*Antonio Lang*	.15
152	Dan Majerle	.10
153	Danny Manning	.20
154	Wayman Tisdale	.10
155	Clyde Drexler	.50
156	Harvey Grant	.10
157	Tracy Murray	.10
158	Terry Porter	.10
159	Clifford Robinson	.10
160	Rod Strickland	.10
161	Buck Williams	.10
162	Bobby Hurley	.10
163	Olden Polynice	.10
164	Mitch Richmond	.15
165	Lionel Simmons	.10
166	Spud Webb	.10
167	Walt Williams	.10
168	Willie Anderson	.10
169	Terry Cummings	.10
170	Vinny Del Negro	.10
171	Sean Elliott	.10
172	Avery Johnson	.10
173	Chuck Person	.10
174	J.R. Reid	.10
175	David Robinson	1.00
176	Dennis Rodman	1.50
177	Bill Cartwright	.10
178	Kendall Gill	.10
179	Shawn Kemp	.50
180	Nate McMillan	.10
181	Gary Payton	.20
182	Sam Perkins	.10
183	Detlef Schrempf	.10
184	David Benoit	.10
185	Jeff Hornacek	.10
186	Jay Humphries	.10
187	Karl Malone	.50
188	Bryon Russell	.10
189	Felton Spencer	.10

190	John Stockton	.50
191	Mitchell Butler	.10
192	Rex Chapman	.10
193	Calbert Cheaney	.15
194	Tom Gugliotta	.10
195	Don MacLean	.10
196	Gheorghe Muresan	.10
197	Scott Skiles	.10
198	Checklist	.10
199	Checklist	.10
200	Checklist	.10

1994-95 Jam Session Flashing Stars

This 1994-95 Jam Session insert set exhibits players with real style on the court. Each card front has a full-color action photo of the player, against a background of neon-like orbs. The player's name and set name are stamped in gold foil at the bottom of the card. The back has a color photo of the player, and a brief description on why the player is a "Flashing Star." They are numbered 1 of 8, etc.

		MT
Complete Set (8):		8.00
Common Player:		.25
1	Anfernee Hardaway	5.00
2	Robert Horry	.25
3	Dan Majerle	.25
4	Reggie Miller	1.00
5	Mitch Richmond	.25
6	Isaiah Rider	.75
7	Latrell Sprewell	.50
8	Dominique Wilkins	.25

1994-95 Jam Session GameBreakers

These Fleer Jam Session insert cards feature eight of the NBA's top players. The Jam Session logo and "GameBreaker" are included on the card front, which features a "3D" color photo of the player. The card back, numbered 1 of 8, etc., has another color photo of the player, with a brief summary on why he's a Game Breaker in the NBA.

		MT
Complete Set (8):		12.00
Common Player:		1.00
1	Charles Barkley	2.00
2	Patrick Ewing	1.00
3	Karl Malone	1.00
4	Alonzo Mourning	1.00
5	Hakeem Olajuwon	2.00
6	Shaquille O'Neal	5.00
7	Scottie Pippen	2.00
8	David Robinson	2.00

1994-95 Jam Session Rookie Standouts

The 20-card, 2-1/2" x 4-3/4" set only issued through the mail. Information on obtaining the set was printed on the pack wrapper with the cost of the set at $3.95. The offer expired June 30, 1995. The fronts have full-bleed photos with a painted background. The NBA Jam Session logo is superimposed in the left corner.

		MT
Complete Set (20):		15.00
Common Player:		.25
1	Brian Grant	.50
2	Grant Hill	6.00
3	Juwan Howard	4.00
4	Eddie Jones	4.00
5	Jason Kidd	4.00
6	Donyell Marshall	.25
7	Eric Montross	.50
8	Lamond Murray	.25
9	Wesley Person	.50
10	Khalid Reeves	.25
11	Glenn Robinson	3.00
12	Carlos Rogers	.25
13	Jalen Rose	.50
14	Clifford Rozier	.25
15	Dickey Simpkins	.25
16	Michael Smith	.25
17	Anthony Tucker	.25
18	Charlie Ward	.50
19	Monty Williams	.25
20	Sharone Wright	.50

1994-95 Jam Session Second Year Stars

This eight-card insert set features the top sophomores in the NBA. Cards were random inserts in Jam Session packs. Each card front is horizontal and presents a fly's eye viewpoint; the main image is pictured repeatedly within a checkerboard pattern, with a medium-sized and large size version on the front, too. The back has a similar format, with the main larger image and several, smaller ghosted images incorporated into the background. Cards are numbered 1 of 8, etc. Gold foil stamping is used on the front.

		MT
Complete Set (8):		8.00
Common Player:		.50
1	Vin Baker	1.00
2	Anfernee Hardaway	5.00
3	Lindsey Hunter	.50
4	Toni Kukoc	.50
5	Jamal Mashburn	1.00
6	Dino Radja	.75
7	Isaiah Rider	.50
8	Chris Webber	1.00

1994-95 Jam Session Slam Dunk Heroes

These eight insert cards were randomly inserted into 1994-95 Jam Session packs. Each card is printed on 100 percent etched foil, used as a background for a full-color action photo which appears on the front. The player's name and set's logo are stamped in gold foil at the bottom of the card. The card back, numbered 1 of 8, etc., has another color photo and a player profile.

		MT
Complete Set (8):		80.00
Common Player:		4.00
1	Charles Barkley	10.00
2	Larry Johnson	6.00
3	Shawn Kemp	8.00
4	Jamal Mashburn	7.00
5	Dikembe Mutombo	4.00
6	Hakeem Olajuwon	15.00
7	Shaquille O'Neal	35.00
8	Chris Webber	10.00

1995 Fleer European

The 270-card, standard-size set was issued by Fleer for the French, German, Italian and Spanish card markets. The cards were distributed in eight-card packs and parallels the 1994-95 U.S. set. The wrappers and boxes contained multi-lingual text, but the cards only have English text. Since the numbering is the same as the U.S. set, the only difference is the small trademark on the card backs. The U.S. version has "1994 Fleer Corp." while the European cards have "1995 Fleer Corp."

		MT
Complete Set (270):		40.00
Common Player:		.10
1	Stacey Augmon	.25
2	Sergei Bazarevich	.10
3	Mookie Blaylock	.25
4	Tyrone Corbin	.10
5	Craig Ehlo	.10
6	Andrew Lang	.10
7	Grant Long	.10
8	Ken Norman	.10
9	Steve Smith	.25
10	Dee Brown	.10
11	Sherman Douglas	.10
12	Acie Earl	.10
13	Blue Edwards	.10
14	Rick Fox	.10
15	Xavier McDaniel	.10
16	Greg Minor	.40
17	Eric Montross	.75
18	Dino Radja	.40
19	Dominique Wilkins	.40
20	Michael Adams	.10
21	Muggsy Bogues	.25
22	Scott Burrell	.10
23	Dell Curry	.10
24	Kenny Gattison	.10
25	Hersey Hawkins	.25
26	Larry Johnson	.50
27	Alonzo Mourning	.75
28	Robert Parish	.40
29	David Wingate	.10
30	B.J. Armstrong	.25
31	Corie Blount	.10
32	Steve Kerr	.10
33	Larry Krystkowiak	.10
34	Toni Kukoc	.40
35	Luc Longley	.10
36	Will Perdue	.10
37	Scottie Pippen	1.50
38	Dickey Simpkins	.10
39	Terrell Brandon	.25
40	Brad Daugherty	.25
41	Tyrone Hill	.10
42	Chris Mills	.40
43	Bobby Phills	.10
44	Mark Price	.25
45	Gerald Wilkins	.10
46	John Williams	.25
47	Tony Dumas	.50
48	Jim Jackson	.75
49	Popeye Jones	.10
50	Jason Kidd	4.00
51	Jamal Mashburn	1.00
52	Doug Smith	.10
53	Roy Tarpley	.10
54	Mahmoud Abdul-Rauf	.25
55	Dale Ellis	.25
56	LaPhonso Ellis	.10
57	Dikembe Mutombo	.40
58	Robert Pack	.10
59	Rodney Rogers	.10
60	Jalen Rose	.75
61	Bryant Stith	.10
62	Brian Williams	.10
63	Reggie Williams	.10
64	Bill Curley	.25
65	Johnny Dawkins	.25
66	Joe Dumars	.40
67	Grant Hill	6.00
68	Allan Houston	.25
69	Lindsey Hunter	.10
70	Oliver Miller	.10
71	Terry Mills	.10
72	Mark West	.10
73	Victor Alexander	.10
74	Manute Bol	.10
75	Chris Gatling	.10
76	Tim Hardaway	.40
77	Chris Mullin	.40
78	Ricky Pierce	.10
79	Clifford Rozier	.25
80	Rony Seikaly	.10
81	Latrell Sprewell	.50
82	Chris Webber (Traded to Washington Bullets)	1.00
83	Scott Brooks	.10
84	Sam Cassell	.40
85	Mario Elie	.10
86	Carl Herrera	.10
87	Robert Horry	.50
88	Vernon Maxwell	.10
89	Hakeem Olajuwon	2.00
90	Kenny Smith	.10
91	Otis Thorpe	.25
92	Antonio Davis	.10
93	Dale Davis	.10
94	Vern Fleming	.10
95	Mark Jackson	.10
96	Derrick McKey	.10
97	Reggie Miller	1.00
98	Byron Scott	.25
99	Rik Smits	.40
100	John Williams	.10
101	Haywoode Workman	.10
102	Terry Dehere	.10
103	Gary Grant	.10
104	Lamond Murray	.50
105	Eric Piatkowski	.10
106	Pooh Richardson	.10
107	Malik Sealy	.10
108	Elmore Spencer	.10
109	Loy Vaught	.25
110	Elden Campbell	.10
111	Cedric Ceballos	.50
112	Vlade Divac	.25
113	Eddie Jones	2.00
114	George Lynch	.10
115	Anthony Peeler	.10
116	Tony Smith	.10
117	Sedale Threatt	.10
118	Nick Van Exel	.75
119	Bimbo Coles	.10
120	Kevin Gamble	.10
121	Harold Miner	.10
122	Billy Owens	.25
123	Khalid Reeves	.25
124	Glen Rice	.40
125	John Salley	.10
126	Kevin Willis	.25
127	Vin Baker	.75
128	Jon Barry	.10
129	Todd Day	.10
130	Lee Mayberry	.10
131	Eric Mobley	.10
132	Eric Murdock	.10
133	Johnny Newman	.10
134	Glenn Robinson	3.00
135	Mike Brown	.10
136	Stacey King	.10
137	Christian Laettner	.40
138	Donyell Marshall	.25
139	Isaiah Rider	.40
140	Sean Rooks	.10
141	Doug West	.10
142	Micheal Williams	.10
143	Kenny Anderson	.25
144	Benoit Benjamin	.10
145	P.J. Brown	.10
146	Derrick Coleman	.25
147	Yinka Dare	.25
148	Kevin Edwards	.10
149	Sleepy Floyd	.10
150	Armon Gilliam	.25
151	Chris Morris	.10
152	Greg Anthony	.10
153	Hubert Davis	.10
154	Patrick Ewing	1.00
155	Derek Harper	.25
156	Anthony Mason	.25
157	Charles Oakley	.25
158	Doc Rivers	.10
159	Charles Smith	.10
160	John Starks	.25
161	Charlie Ward	.40
162	Monty Williams	.10
163	Nick Anderson	.25
164	Anthony Avent	.10
165	Horace Grant	.40
166	Anfernee Hardaway	3.00
167	Shaquille O'Neal	3.00
168	Donald Royal	.10
169	Dennis Scott	.25
170	Brooks Thompson	.10
171	Jeff Turner	.10
172	Dana Barros	.25
173	Shawn Bradley	.40
174	Jeff Malone	.25
175	Tim Perry	.10
176	B.J. Tyler	.10
177	Clarence Weatherspoon	.25
178	Sharone Wright	.50
179	Danny Ainge	.25
180	Charles Barkley	2.00
181	A.C. Green	.25
182	Kevin Johnson	.40
183	Joe Kleine	.10
184	Dan Majerle	.25
185	Danny Manning	.40
186	Wesley Person	.50
187	Wayman Tisdale	.25
188	Clyde Drexler	1.00
189	Harvey Grant	.10
190	Jerome Kersey	.10
191	Aaron McKie	.40
192	Tracy Murray	.10
193	Terry Porter	.10
194	Clifford Robinson	.40
195	Rod Strickland	.25
196	Buck Williams	.25
197	Brian Grant	.75
198	Bobby Hurley	.25
199	Olden Polynice	.10
200	Mitch Richmond	.50
201	Lionel Simmons	.10
202	Spud Webb	.25
203	Walt Williams	.25
204	Trevor Wilson	.10
205	Willie Anderson	.10
206	Terry Cummings	.25
207	Vinny Del Negro	.10
208	Sean Elliott	.40
209	Avery Johnson	.25
210	Moses Malone	.50
211	J.R. Reid	.10
212	David Robinson	2.00
213	Dennis Rodman	2.50
214	Bill Cartwright	.10
215	Kendall Gill	.10
216	Ervin Johnson	.10
217	Shawn Kemp	1.00
218	Sarunas Marciulionis	.10
219	Nate McMillan	.10
220	Gary Payton	.40
221	Sam Perkins	.25
222	Detlef Schrempf	.40
223	David Benoit	.10
224	Jeff Hornacek	.10
225	Jay Humphries	.10
226	Karl Malone	1.00
227	Bryon Russell	.10
228	Felton Spencer	.10
229	John Stockton	1.00
230	Mitchell Butler	.10
231	Rex Chapman	.10
232	Calbert Cheaney	.25
233	Kevin Duckworth	.10
234	Tom Gugliotta (Traded to Golden State Warriors)	.25
235	Don MacLean	.10
236	Gheorghe Muresan	.40
237	Scott Skiles	.10
238	Atlanta Hawks	.10
239	Boston Celtics	.10
240	Charlotte Hornets	.10
241	Chicago Bulls	.10
242	Cleveland Cavaliers	.10
243	Dallas Mavericks	.10
244	Denver Nuggets	.10
245	Detroit Pitsons	.10
246	Golden State Warriors	.10
247	Houston Rockets	.10
248	Indiana Pacers	.10
249	Los Angeles Clippers	.10
250	Los Angeles Lakers	.10
251	Miami Heat	.10
252	Milwaukee Bucks	.10
253	Minnesota Timberwolves	.10
254	New Jersey Nets	.10
255	New York Knicks	.10
256	Orlando Magic	.10
257	Philadelphia 76ers	.10
258	Phoenix Suns	.10
259	Portland Trail Blazers	.10
260	Saramento Kings	.10
261	San Antonio Spurs	.10
262	Seattle Supersonics	.10
263	Utah Jazz	.10
264	Washington Bullets	.10
265	Toronto Raptors	.10
266	Vancouver Grizzlies	.10
267	MBA Logo	.10
268	Checklist 1-103	.10
269	Checklist 104-204	.10
270	Checklist 205-270 (Checklist Insert Sets)	.10

1995 Fleer European All-Defensive

The five-card set was inserted every six packs and features first- and second-team All-NBA defensive players. The cards are unnumbered and checklisted in alphabetical order.

		MT
Complete Set (5):		5.00
Common Player:		.75
(1)	Mookie Blaylock, Scottie Pippen	2.00
(2)	Horace Grant, Gary Payton	.75
(3)	Nate McMillan, Dennis Rodman	2.00
(4)	Charles Oakley, David Robinson	1.50
(5)	Hakeem Olajuwon, Latrell Sprewell	3.00

1995 Fleer European Award Winners

Randomly inserted every 12 packs, the two standard-size, double-sided cards highlight four NBA award winners from the 1993-94 season. The player's name and his award appears in gold foil.

		MT
Complete Set (2):		2.00
Common Player:		.75
1	Dell Curry, Chris Webber	.75
2	Don MacLean, Hakeem Olajuwon	1.50

1995 Fleer European Career Achievement Awards

Randomly inserted in Fleer's European packs at one in 12, the standard-size, double-sided cards highlight six of the top veteran superstars in the league. The player's name appears in gold foil in the lower corner.

		MT
Complete Set (3):		6.00
Common Player:		1.00
1	Patrick Ewing, Karl Malone	2.50
2	Hakeem Olajuwon, Scottie Pippen	4.00
3	Robert Parish, Dominique Wilkins	1.00

1995 Fleer European League Leaders

Randomly inserted into European packs at a rate of one in five, the four standard-size, double-sided cards highlight eight NBA league leaders. The cards are unnumbered and checklisted below alphabetically.

		MT
Complete Set (4):		4.00
Common Player:		.25
(1)	Mahmoud Abdul-Rauf, Dennis Rodman	1.00
(2)	Tracy Murray, Dikembe Mutombo	.25
(3)	Shaquille O'Neal, David Robinson	3.00
(4)	John Stockton, Nate McMillan	.50

1995 Fleer European Triple Threats

Randomly inserted in every five Fleer European packs, the five standard-size, double-sided cards highlight 10 of the top versatile NBA stars. The cards are borderless with multiple player images over a basketball court design.

		MT
Complete Set (5):		8.00
Common Player:		1.00
1	Mookie Blaylock, Reggie Miller	1.00
2	Patrick Ewing, Shaquille O'Neal	3.00
3	Shawn Kemp, David Robinson	1.50
4	Karl Malone, Latrell Sprewell	1.50
5	Hakeem Olajuwon, Scottie Pippen	3.00

Post-1980 cards in Near Mint condition will generally sell for about 75% of the quoted Mint value. Excellent-condition cards bring no more than 40%.

1995-96 Fleer

Fleer released its 1995-96 350-card basketball set in two series, each using the company's "Different By Design" concept. Four different designs are used for the regular cards, one for each division. Foil stamping is incorporated into the design. The cards in Series I are numbered alphabetically by team, then by players within each team subset. Series II's 150 cards include four subsets (40 Rookies, 20 Expansion Teams, 59 Updated Players and 29 Firm Foundation). Inserts in Series I include Total D, Rookie Sensations, Double Doubles, Franchise Futures, NBA All-Stars and Flair Hardwood Leaders. Series II inserts include End to End, Class Encounters, Towers of Power, Rookie Phenoms, Stackhouse Scrapbook and Total O. Two types of Hot Packs accompany Series II product. A 10-card parallel set of Rookie Phenoms, with special markings, plus a response card redeemable for a third Stackhouse Scrapbook card, are found in hobby Hot Packs. A 10-card parallel set of Total O, with special markings, plus a response card for a third Stackhouse Scrapbook card, are found in retail Hot Packs.

		MT
Complete Set (350):		27.00
Comp. Series 1 (200):		12.00
Comp. Series 2 (150):		15.00
Common Player:		.05
Minor Stars:		.10
Ser. 1 or 2 Pack (11):		1.50
Ser. 1 or 2 Wax Box (36):		44.00
1	Stacey Augmon	.05
2	Mookie Blaylock	.05
3	Craig Ehlo	.05
4	Andrew Lang	.05
5	Grant Long	.05
6	Ken Norman	.05
7	Steve Smith	.05
8	Dee Brown	.05
9	Sherman Douglas	.05
10	Eric Montross	.05
11	Dino Radja	.05
12	David Wesley	.05
13	Dominique Wilkins	.10
14	Muggsy Bogues	.05
15	Scott Burrell	.05
16	Dell Curry	.05
17	Hersey Hawkins	.05
18	Larry Johnson	.20
19	Alonzo Mourning	.20
20	Robert Parish	.05
21	B.J. Armstrong	.05
22	Michael Jordan	2.00
23	Steve Kerr	.05
24	Toni Kukoc	.05
25	Will Perdue	.05
26	Scottie Pippen	.50
27	Terrell Brandon	.05
28	Tyrone Hill	.05
29	Chris Mills	.05
30	Bobby Phills	.05
31	Mark Price	.05
32	John Williams	.05
33	Lucious Harris	.05
34	Jim Jackson	.20
35	Popeye Jones	.05
36	Jason Kidd	.75
37	Jamal Mashburn	.20
38	George McCloud	.05
39	Roy Tarpley	.05
40	Lorenzo Williams	.05
41	Mahmoud Abdul-Rauf	.05
42	Dale Ellis	.05
43	LaPhonso Ellis	.05
44	Dikembe Mutombo	.10
45	Robert Pack	.05
46	Rodney Rogers	.05
47	Jalen Rose	.10
48	Bryant Stith	.05
49	Reggie Williams	.05
50	Joe Dumars	.10
51	Grant Hill	1.00
52	Allan Houston	.10
53	Lindsey Hunter	.05
54	Oliver Miller	.05
55	Terry Mills	.05
56	Mark West	.05
57	Chris Gatling	.05
58	Tim Hardaway	.10
59	Donyell Marshall	.15
60	Chris Mullin	.10
61	Carlos Rogers	.05
62	Clifford Rozier	.05
63	Rony Seikaly	.05
64	Latrell Sprewell	.20
65	Sam Cassell	.10
66	Clyde Drexler	.20
67	Mario Elie	.05
68	Carl Herrera	.05
69	Robert Horry	.10
70	Vernon Maxwell	.05
71	Hakeem Olajuwon	.40
72	Kenny Smith	.05
73	Dale Davis	.05
74	Mark Jackson	.05

75	Derrick McKey	.05
76	Reggie Miller	.20
77	Sam Mitchell	.05
78	Byron Scott	.05
79	Rik Smits	.10
80	Terry Dehere	.05
81	Tony Massenburg	.05
82	Lamond Murray	.10
83	Pooh Richardson	.05
84	Malik Sealy	.05
85	Loy Vaught	.05
86	Elden Campbell	.05
87	Cedric Ceballos	.05
88	Vlade Divac	.05
89	Eddie Jones	.40
90	Anthony Peeler	.05
91	Sedale Threatt	.05
92	Nick Van Exel	.30
93	Bimbo Coles	.05
94	Matt Geiger	.05
95	Billy Owens	.05
96	Khalid Reeves	.10
97	Glen Rice	.10
98	John Salley	.05
99	Kevin Willis	.05
100	Vin Baker	.10
101	Marty Conlon	.05
102	Todd Day	.05
103	Lee Mayberry	.05
104	Eric Murdock	.05
105	Glenn Robinson	.30
106	Winston Garland	.05
107	Tom Gugliotta	.05
108	Christian Laettner	.05
109	Isaiah Rider	.10
110	Sean Rooks	.05
111	Doug West	.05
112	Kenny Anderson	.10
113	Benoit Benjamin	.05
114	P.J. Brown	.05
115	Derrick Coleman	.10
116	Armon Gilliam	.05
117	Chris Morris	.05
118	Rex Walters	.05
119	Hubert Davis	.05
120	Patrick Ewing	.15
121	Derek Harper	.05
122	Anthony Mason	.05
123	Charles Oakley	.05
124	Charles Smith	.05
125	John Starks	.05
126	Nick Anderson	.05
127	Anthony Bowie	.05
128	Horace Grant	.10
129	Anfernee Hardaway	1.50
130	Shaquille O'Neal	1.00
131	Donald Royal	.05
132	Dennis Scott	.05
133	Brian Shaw	.05
134	Derrick Alston	.05
135	Dana Barros	.05
136	Shawn Bradley	.10
137	Willie Burton	.05
138	Clarence Weatherspoon	.10
139	Scott Williams	.05
140	Sharone Wright	.10
141	Danny Ainge	.05
142	Charles Barkley	.30
143	A.C. Green	.05
144	Kevin Johnson	.10
145	Dan Majerle	.05
146	Danny Manning	.05
147	Elliott Perry	.05
148	Wesley Person	.10
149	Wayman Tisdale	.05
150	Chris Dudley	.05
151	Jerome Kersey	.05
152	Aaron McKie	.05
153	Terry Porter	.05
154	Cliff Robinson	.05
155	James Robinson	.05
156	Rod Strickland	.05
157	Otis Thorpe	.05
158	Buck Williams	.05
159	Brian Grant	.15
160	Bobby Hurley	.05
161	Olden Polynice	.05
162	Mitch Richmond	.10
163	Michael Smith	.05
164	Spud Webb	.05
165	Walt Williams	.05
166	Terry Cummings	.05
167	Vinny Del Negro	.05
168	Sean Elliott	.05
169	Avery Johnson	.05
170	Chuck Person	.05
171	J.R. Reid	.05
172	Doc Rivers	.05
173	David Robinson	.30
174	Dennis Rodman	.75
175	Vincent Askew	.05
176	Kendall Gill	.05
177	Shawn Kemp	.40
178	Sarunas Marciulionis	.05
179	Nate McMillan	.05
180	Gary Payton	.10
181	Sam Perkins	.05
182	Detlef Schrempf	.05
183	David Benoit	.05
184	Antoine Carr	.05
185	Blue Edwards	.05
186	Jeff Hornacek	.05
187	Adam Keefe	.05
188	Karl Malone	.20
189	Felton Spencer	.05
190	John Stockton	.20
191	Rex Chapman	.05
192	Calbert Cheaney	.05
193	Juwan Howard	.40
194	Don MacLean	.05
195	Gheorghe Muresan	.05
196	Scott Skiles	.05
197	Chris Webber	.15
198	Checklist	.05
199	Checklist	.05
200	Checklist	.05
201	Stacey Augmon	.05
202	Mookie Blaylock	.05
203	Grant Long	.05
204	Ken Norman	.05
205	Steve Smith	.05
206	Spud Webb	.05
207	Dana Barros	.05
208	Rick Fox	.05
209	Kendall Gill	.05
210	Khalid Reeves	.10
211	Glen Rice	.10
212	Luc Longley	.05
213	Dennis Rodman	1.00
214	Dan Majerle	.05
215	Tony Dumas	.05
216	Tom Hammonds	.05
217	Elmore Spencer	.05
218	Otis Thorpe	.05
219	B.J. Armstrong	.05
220	Sam Cassell	.05
221	Clyde Drexler	.20
222	Mario Elie	.05
223	Robert Horry	.10
224	Hakeem Olajuwon	.40
225	Kenny Smith	.05
226	Antonio Davis	.05
227	Eddie Johnson	.05
228	Ricky Pierce	.05
229	Eric Piatkowski	.05
230	Rodney Rogers	.05
231	Brian Williams	.05
232	Corie Blount	.05
233	George Lynch	.05
234	Kevin Gamble	.05
235	Alonzo Mourning	.20
236	Eric Mobley	.05
237	Terry Porter	.05
238	Michael Williams	.05
239	Kevin Edwards	.05
240	Vern Fleming	.05
241	Charlie Ward	.05
242	Jon Koncak	.05
243	Richard Dumas	.05
244	Jeff Malone	.05
245	Vernon Maxwell	.05
246	John Williams	.05
247	Harvey Grant	.05
248	Dontonio Wingfield	.05
249	Tyrone Corbin	.05
250	Sarunas Marciulionis	.05
251	Will Perdue	.05
252	Hersey Hawkins	.05
253	Ervin Johnson	.05
254	Shawn Kemp	.30
255	Gary Payton	.10
256	Sam Perkins	.05
257	Detlef Schrempf	.05
258	Chris Morris	.05
259	Robert Pack	.05
260	Willie Anderson	.05
261	Jimmy King	.05
262	Oliver Miller	.05
263	Tracy Murray	.05
264	Ed Pinckney	.05
265	Alvin Robertson	.05
266	Carlos Rogers	.05
267	John Salley	.05
268	Damon Stoudamire	1.00
269	Zan Tabak	.05
270	Ashraf Amaya	.05
271	Greg Anthony	.05
272	Benoit Benjamin	.05
273	Blue Edwards	.05
274	Kenny Gattison	.05
275	Antonio Harvey	.05
276	Chris King	.05
277	Lawrence Moten	.05
278	Bryant Reeves	.30
279	Byron Scott	.05
280	*Cory Alexander*	.10
281	*Jerome Allen*	.05
282	*Brent Barry*	.50
283	*Mario Bennett*	.10
284	*Travis Best*	.75
285	*Junior Burrough*	.10
286	*Jason Caffey*	.15
287	*Randolph Childress*	.15
288	*Sasha Danilovic*	.15
289	*Mark Davis*	.05
290	*Tyus Edney*	.10
291	*Michael Finley*	2.00
292	*Sherrell Ford*	.15
293	*Kevin Garnett*	4.00
294	*Alan Henderson*	.20
295	*Frankie King*	.10
296	*Jimmy King*	.10
297	*Donny Marshall*	.10
298	*Antonio McDyess*	2.00
299	*Loren Meyer*	.10
300	*Lawrence Moten*	.10
301	*Ed O'Bannon*	.10
302	*Greg Ostertag*	.10
303	*Cherokee Parks*	.20
304	*Theo Ratliff*	.75
305	*Bryant Reeves*	.75
306	*Shawn Respert*	.15
307	*Lou Roe*	.10
308	*Arvydas Sabonis*	.75
309	*Joe Smith*	1.00
310	*Jerry Stackhouse*	2.50
311	*Damon Stoudamire*	1.00
312	*Bob Sura*	.20
313	*Kurt Thomas*	.40
314	*Gary Trent*	.50
315	*David Vaughn*	.10
316	*Rasheed Wallace*	1.00
317	*Eric Williams*	.15
318	*Corliss Williamson*	.20
319	*George Zidek*	.15
320	Mookie Blaylock	.05
321	Dino Radja	.05
322	Larry Johnson	.10
323	Michael Jordan	1.00
324	Tyrone Hill	.05
325	Jason Kidd	.40
326	Dikembe Mutombo	.05
327	Grant Hill	.50
328	Joe Smith	.75
329	Hakeem Olajuwon	.20
330	Reggie Miller	.10
331	Loy Vaught	.05
332	Nick Van Exel	.10
333	Alonzo Mourning	.10
334	Glenn Robinson	.20
335	Kevin Garnett	1.00
336	Kenny Anderson	.05
337	Patrick Ewing	.05
338	Shaquille O'Neal	.50
339	Jerry Stackhouse	1.00
340	Charles Barkley	.20
341	Clifford Robinson	.05
342	Mitch Richmond	.05
343	David Robinson	.20
344	Shawn Kemp	.20
345	Damon Stoudamire	1.00
346	Karl Malone	.10
347	Bryant Reeves	.20
348	Chris Webber	.10
349	Checklist	.05
350	Checklist	.05

1995-96 Fleer All-Stars

These insert cards, featuring an NBA All-Star on each side, were randomly seeded one per every three packs of 1995 Fleer Series I basketball. Each side has a color action photo against a ghosted background of the crowd; a player from both conferences is represented on each card. Gold foil stamping is used for the brand name, player's name, card number and conference. An All-Star game logo is also on both sides; the players are wearing their respective conference's uniform. The card number (1 of 9, etc.) is on one side only.

		MT
Complete Set (13):		5.00
Common Player:		.25
1	Grant Hill, Charles Barkley	1.00
2	Scottie Pippen, Shawn Kemp	.60
3	Shaquille O'Neal, Hakeem Olajuwon	2.00
4	Anfernee Hardaway, Dan Majerle	1.00
5	Reggie Miller, Latrell Sprewell	.50
6	Vin Baker, Cedric Ceballos	.25
7	Tyrone Hill, Karl Malone	.25
8	Larry Johnson, Detlef Schrempf	.25
9	Patrick Ewing, David Robinson	.50
10	Alonzo Mourning, Dikembe Mutombo	.40
11	Dana Barros, Gary Payton	.25
12	Joe Dumars, John Stockton	.25
13	Mitch Richmond (Most Valuable Player)	.25

1995-96 Fleer Class Encounters

These 40 cards were random inserts in 1995 Fleer Series II packs, one per every two packs. The card front has gold foil stamping, and shows an action photo of the player on the left side of the card. The right side has three different sizes of the same photo, increasingly cropping tighter as head shots. The back also has a mug shot, along with a brief career summary. Cards are numbered 1 of 40, etc.

		MT
Complete Set (40):		17.00
Common Player:		.15
1	Derrick Alsted	.15
2	Brian Grant	.15
3	Grant Hill	2.00
4	Juwan Howard	1.00
5	Eddie Jones	.50
6	Jason Kidd	1.50
7	Donyell Marshall	.15
8	Anthony Mason	.15
9	Eric Mobley	.15
10	Eric Montross	.15
11	Lamond Murray	.15
12	Wesley Person	.15
13	Eric Piatkowski	.15
14	Khalid Reeves	.15
15	Glenn Robinson	1.00
16	Carlos Rogers	.15
17	Jalen Rose	.15
18	Clifford Rozier	.15
19	Michael Smith	.15
20	Sharone Wright	.15
21	Brent Barry	1.00
22	Jason Caffey	.15
23	Randolph Childress	.15
24	Kevin Garnett	7.00
25	Alan Henderson	.30
26	Antonio McDyess	2.00
27	Ed O'Bannon	.15
28	Cherokee Parks	.30
29	Theo Ratliff	.15
30	Bryant Reeves	.75
31	Shawn Respert	.30
32	Joe Smith	3.00
33	Jerry Stackhouse	4.00
34	Damon Stoudamire	5.00
35	Bob Sura	.15
36	Kurt Thomas	.50
37	Gary Trent	.30
38	Rasheed Wallace	1.00
39	Eric Williams	.25
40	Corliss Williamson	.30

1995-96 Fleer Double Doubles

These 1995 Fleer Series I basketball inserts feature 12 of the NBA's top leaders in Double Double statistical categories. The card front has two photos of the player, divided by a gold foil band which has his name stamped in gold running through it. "Double Double" is also written across the middle. The card back has a player photo also with a panel on the right superimposed over the photo to include a brief recap of the player's statistical averages. Cards are numbered 1 of 12, etc.

		MT
Complete Set (12):		7.00
Common Player:		.20
Minor Stars:		.40
1	Vin Baker	.40
2	Vlade Divac	.20
3	Patrick Ewing	.50
4	Tyrone Hill	.20
5	Popeye Jones	.20
6	Shawn Kemp	.60
7	Karl Malone	.50
8	Dikembe Mutombo	.50
9	Hakeem Olajuwon	1.50
10	Shaquille O'Neal	2.50
11	David Robinson	1.00
12	John Stockton	.50

1995-96 Fleer Flair Hardwood Leaders

These 1995 Fleer Basketball Series I inserts preview the Flair brand's extra-thick cardboard stock. Cards, randomly seeded one per pack, use gold foil stamping for the front (player name, team logo and base brand logo). A color action photo is in the center of the card, which has a court design for the background, with "Hardwood" and "Leader" written along the sides. The card back, numbered 1 of 27, etc., has another color photo, plus a recap of his 1994-95 accomplishments. His name is in gold foil at the top. The card's background has a court floor motif.

		MT
Complete Set (27):		17.00
Common Player:		.20
Minor Stars:		.40
1	Mookie Blaylock	.20
2	Dominique Wilkins	.40
3	Alonzo Mourning	.60
4	Michael Jordan	8.00
5	Mark Price	.20
6	Jim Jackson	.60
7	Dikembe Mutombo	.40
8	Grant Hill	3.00
9	Tim Hardaway	.20
10	Hakeem Olajuwon	1.50
11	Reggie Miller	.50
12	Loy Vaught	.20
13	Cedric Ceballos	.20
14	Glen Rice	.20
15	Glenn Robinson	.15
16	Christian Laettner	.20
17	Derrick Coleman	.20
18	Patrick Ewing	.50
19	Shaquille O'Neal	3.00
20	Dana Barros	.20
21	Charles Barkley	1.00
22	Cliff Robinson	.20
23	Mitch Richmond	.40
24	David Robinson	1.00
25	Gary Payton	.40
26	Karl Malone	.50
27	Chris Webber	.50

1995-96 Fleer End to End

These cards feature 20 players who have complete games on both ends of the court. Cards, using a horizontal format for the front, were random inserts, one every four 1995 Fleer Series II packs. The right side of the card has a team color-coded background with the End 2 End logo in it. The logo is also foil stamped in the upper right corner; the player's name and "Fleer 1995-96" are stamped in foil in the lower left corner. The left side of the card has an action photo on it. The center has a photo which overlaps each half of the card. The card back, numbered 1 of 20, etc., is also horizontal. The left side has a blurred image of the same photo from the front. The center has a new photo, while the right side has a card number and career summary.

		MT
Complete Set (20):		25.00
Common Player:		.25
Minor Stars:		.50
1	Mookie Blaylock	.25
2	Vlade Divac	.25
3	Clyde Drexler	1.25
4	Patrick Ewing	1.00
5	Horace Grant	.50
6	Anfernee Hardaway	5.00
7	Grant Hill	4.00
8	Eddie Jones	.50
9	Michael Jordan	10.00
10	Jason Kidd	3.00
11	Alonzo Mourning	1.00
12	Dikembe Mutombo	.50
13	Hakeem Olajuwon	2.50
14	Shaquille O'Neal	5.00
15	Gary Payton	.50
16	Scottie Pippen	2.00
17	David Robinson	2.00
18	Latrell Sprewell	.50
19	John Stockton	1.00
20	Rod Strickland	.25

1995-96 Fleer Franchise Futures

These nine cards feature players considered as being the foundations to build their teams around. The cards were seeded one in every 37 packs of Fleer 1995 Series I packs. The front has a foil-etched design, with the player's name and set name running along the right side. A metallic basketball and flames comprise the background, which has a color action photo in the foreground. The card back has a color photo in a panel on the left; a brief player profile is featured on a panel on the right. The backgrond is a repeated version of the front. Cards are numbered 1 of 9, etc.

		MT
Complete Set (9):		40.00
Common Player:		2.00
1	Vin Baker	3.00
2	Anfernee Hardaway	15.00
3	Jim Jackson	3.00
4	Jamal Mashburn	2.00
5	Alonzo Mourning	3.00
6	Dikembe Mutombo	2.00
7	Shaquille O'Neal	15.00
8	Nick Van Exel	2.00
9	Chris Webber	2.00

1995-96 Fleer Rookie Phenoms

These 1995 Fleer Basketball Series II inserts could be found in every 24th hobby pack. Gold foil stamping is used for the player's name, set logo and base brand logo. A 10-card parallel set was also created for Rookie Phenoms cards; each of these cards is stamped "Hot Packs" because they could only be found in hobby Hot Packs. The card front has an action photo of the player against a metallic spotlight which includes his team's name. The card back, numbered 1 of 10, etc., has an action photo on one half, with a summary of the player's accomplishments on the other. A team logo is also on the back.

		MT
Complete Set (10):		60.00
Common Player:		1.50
Hot Packs Stamp Half Price.		
1	Kevin Garnett	25.00
2	Antonio McDyess	15.00
3	Ed O'Bannon	1.50
4	Bryant Reeves	4.00
5	Shawn Respert	1.50
6	Joe Smith	10.00
7	Jerry Stackhouse	8.00
8	Damon Stoudamire	10.00
9	Gary Trent	3.00
10	Rasheed Wallace	4.00

1995-96 Fleer Rookie Phenoms Hot Packs

This 10-card insert was parallel to the Rookie Phenoms insert but included a red foil Hot Packs logo. Rookie Phenoms Hot Packs inserts were found in hobby Hot Packs that included the entire set, plus a special response card redeemable for a third Stackhouse Scrapbook. Hot Packs sets were seeded one per 72 hobby packs.

	MT
Complete Set (10):	
Hot Pack Cards:	.5x

1995-96 Fleer Rookie Sensations

These 15 cards feature top rookies from the 1994-95 NBA season. Cards were random inserts, one every 15 pre-priced packs of 1995 Fleer Series I basketball product.

		MT
Complete Set (15):		25.00
Common Player:		1.00
1	Brian Grant	1.00
2	Grant Hill	12.00

3	Juwan Howard	5.00
4	Eddie Jones	4.00
5	Jason Kidd	5.00
6	Donyell Marshall	1.00
7	Eric Montross	2.00
8	Lamond Murray	2.00
9	Wesley Person	2.00
10	Khalid Reeves	2.00
11	Glenn Robinson	4.00
12	Jalen Rose	1.00
13	Clifford Rozier	1.00
14	Michael Smith	1.00
15	Sharone Wright	2.00

1995-96 Fleer Stackhouse's Scrapbook

These two cards, featuring the third pick in the 1996 draft, are part of a set which chronicles Jerry Stackhouse's progress to the NBA. The cards, which have the insert set logo stamped in gold foil on the front, were random inserts in 1995 Fleer Series II packs, one every 24 packs. The card front and back has a ghosted image of Stackhouse as its background. The back, numbered S-1, etc., has a quote and/or summary of Stackhouse's accomplishments. A response card for a third Stackhouse card was also made; these cards are found in retail Hot Packs, one every 72 packs.

		MT
Complete Set (2):		6.00
Common Player:		3.00
S1	Jerry Stackhouse (Stackhouse-Third in NBA Draft)	3.00
S2	Jerry Stackhouse (Stackhouse Signs with 76ers)	3.00

1995-96 Fleer Total D

Ten of the NBA's best defensive players are featured on these 1995 Fleer basketball Series I inserts. Cards were seeded one per every five retail and hobby packs. The card front has a horizontal design, with a full-bleed action photo comprising most of it. The player's name is etched in foil along the left side, along with the set name. The back is also horizontal and has a card number (1 of 12, etc.) in the lower right corner. A player photo is on the left side; a career summary is on the right.

		MT
Complete Set (12):		18.00
Common Player:		.50
1	Mookie Blaylock	.50
2	Patrick Ewing	.50
3	Michael Jordan	10.00
4	Alonzo Mourning	.75
5	Dikembe Mutombo	.50
6	Hakeem Olajuwon	2.00
7	Shaquille O'Neal	4.00
8	Gary Payton	.50
9	Scottie Pippen	2.00
10	David Robinson	1.50
11	Dennis Rodman	2.00
12	John Stockton	.75

1995-96 Fleer Total O

These 10 cards could be found only in 1995 Fleer basketball retail packs (one per every 12 packs); they feature some of the top scorers in the NBA. The card front has a color photo of the player against a background of a pair of hands shooting a basketball. Two foil circles encircle the ball. "Total O" is written on the basketball. The card back has an action photo on one half, opposite a player photo. Cards are numbered 1 of 10, etc. A 10-card parallel set of Total O cards was also made; these cards have "Hot Packs" stamped in foil on them.

Complete Set (10):		40.00
Common Player:		2.00
Hot Packs Stamp Half Price		
1	Grant Hill	10.00
2	Michael Jordan	20.00
3	Jamal Mashburn	2.00
4	Reggie Miller	2.00
5	Hakeem Olajuwon	6.00
6	Shaquille O'Neal	10.00
7	Mitch Richmond	2.00
8	David Robinson	5.00
9	Glenn Robinson	3.00
10	Jerry Stackhouse	8.00

1995-96 Fleer Total O Hot Packs

This 10-card set paralleled the Total O insert, but included a red foil Hot Packs logo to identify it. One per 72 retail packs was considered a hot packs, meaning it included the full Total O Hot Packs insert, plus a special response card redeemable for a third Stackhouse Scrapbook insert.

	MT
Complete Set (10):	20.00
Hot Pack Cards:	.5x

1995-96 Fleer Towers of Power

These 1995 Fleer Series II basketball insert cards feature 10 of the NBA's top big men. Cards were random inserts, one per every 54 packs. The card front has an action photo of the player, with a ghosted image of him against a metallic, foil-like background. His name is on the left side of the card; the set logo is in the upper left corner. The card back has a number (1 of 10, etc.), photo and career summary.

		MT
Complete Set (10):		100.00
Common Player:		5.00
1	Shawn Kemp	8.00
2	Karl Malone	7.00
3	Antonio McDyess	10.00
4	Alonzo Mourning	7.00
5	Hakeem Olajuwon	15.00
6	Shaquille O'Neal	30.00
7	David Robinson	12.00
8	Glenn Robinson	8.00
9	Joe Smith	20.00
10	Chris Webber	5.00

1995-96 Jam Session

Once again, Fleer's 1995-96 version of Jam Session features oversize cards (4-11/16" x 2-1/2") in a variety of designs, die cuts and inserts. Included in the series are 78 standard player cards and a 40-card Connection Collection, which spotlights players that form a unique tandem, such as Dee Brown and Isaiah Rider (slam dunk competition winners). For all 118 regular cards there is also a parallel die-cut version, seeded one every pack. Insert sets include Rookies, Show Stoppers, Fuel Injectors, Pop-Ups and Bonus Pop-Ups. NBA Jam Session Pack Attack cards were also included in each pack; the game cards teach collectors how to play Pack Attack with their cards.

		MT
Complete Set (120):		20.00
Common Player:		.10
Minor Stars:		.20
Comp. Die Cut Set (120):		60.00
Die Cut Cards:		3x
Wax Box:		40.00
1	Stacey Augmon	.10
2	Mookie Blaylock	.10
3	Grant Long	.10
4	Steve Smith	.10
5	Dee Brown	.10
6	Sherman Douglas	.10
7	Eric Montross	.10
8	Dino Radja	.10
9	Muggsy Bogues	.10
10	Scott Burrell	.10
11	Larry Johnson	.30
12	Alonzo Mourning	.30
13	Michael Jordan	3.00
14	Steve Kerr	.10
15	Toni Kukoc	.10
16	Scottie Pippen	1.00
17	Terrell Brandon	.10
18	Tyrone Hill	.10
19	Mark Price	.10
20	John Williams	.10
21	Jim Jackson	.25
22	Popeye Jones	.10
23	Jason Kidd	.75
24	Jamal Mashburn	.40
25	Mahmoud Abdul-Rauf	.10
26	Dikembe Mutombo	.20
27	Robert Pack	.10
28	Jalen Rose	.10
29	Joe Dumars	.20
30	Grant Hill	1.25
31	Allan Houston	.10
32	Terry Mills	.10
33	Chris Gatling	.10
34	Tim Hardaway	.10
35	Donyell Marshall	.10
36	Chris Mullin	.10
37	Latrell Sprewell	.25
38	Sam Cassell	.10
39	Clyde Drexler	.40
40	Robert Horry	.20
41	Hakeem Olajuwon	.75
42	Kenny Smith	.10
43	Dale Davis	.10
44	Mark Jackson	.10
45	Reggie Miller	.30
46	Rik Smits	.10
47	Lamond Murray	.10
48	Pooh Richardson	.10
49	Malik Sealy	.10
50	Loy Vaught	.10
51	Cedric Ceballos	.10
52	Vlade Divac	.25
53	Eddie Jones	.40
54	Nick Van Exel	.40
55	Billy Owens	.10
56	Khalid Reeves	.10
57	Glen Rice	.10
58	Kevin Willis	.10
59	Vin Baker	.25
60	Todd Day	.10
61	Eric Murdock	.10
62	Glenn Robinson	.75
63	Tom Gugliotta	.10
64	Christian Laettner	.10
65	Isaiah Rider	.20
66	Doug West	.10
67	Kenny Anderson	.20
68	P.J. Brown	.10
69	Derrick Coleman	.20
70	Armon Gilliam	.10
71	Patrick Ewing	.25
72	Derek Harper	.10
73	Charles Oakley	.10
74	John Starks	.10
75	Horace Grant	.20
76	Anfernee Hardaway	2.00
77	Shaquille O'Neal	1.50
78	Dennis Scott	.10
79	Dana Barros	.10
80	Shawn Bradley	.10
81	Clarence Weatherspoon	.10
82	Sharone Wright	.10
83	Charles Barkley	.50
84	Kevin Johnson	.20
85	Dan Majerle	.10
86	Wesley Person	.10
87	Harvey Grant	.10
88	Clifford Robinson	.10
89	Rod Strickland	.10
90	Buck Williams	.10
91	Brian Grant	.25
92	Olden Polynice	.10
93	Mitch Richmond	.20
94	Walt Williams	.10
95	Sean Elliot	.10
96	Avery Johnson	.10
97	David Robinson	.50
98	Dennis Rodman	1.00
99	Shawn Kemp	.50
100	Nate McMillan	.10
101	Gary Payton	.20
102	Detlef Schrempf	.10
103	Willie Anderson	.10
104	Jerome Kersey	.10
105	Oliver Miller	.10
106	Ed Pinckney	.10
107	David Benoit	.10
108	Jeff Hornacek	.10
109	Karl Malone	.30
110	John Stockton	.30
111	Greg Anthony	.10
112	Benoit Benjamin	.10
113	Blue Edwards	.10
114	Kenny Gattison	.10
115	Calbert Cheaney	.10
116	Juwan Howard	.50
117	Gheorghe Muresan	.10
118	Chris Webber	.25
119	Checklist	.10
120	Checklist	.10
NNO	Grant Hill Foil Tribute	45.00

1995-96 Jam Session Die-Cuts

The 120-card set parallels the base 1995-96 Jam Session set. One of these die-cut cards was inserted into each foil pack. The Die-Cut inserts are prefixed with a "D" and only differ from the base set with the different die-cut styles.

	MT
Complete Set (120):	60.00
Die-Cut Cards:	3x

1995-96 Jam Session Fuel Injectors

These 1995-96 Fleer Jam Session inserts feature nine NBA stars of the 1990s. The cards, using gold foil stamping for the player's name on the front, were seeded one per 36 packs. The front has an action photo of the player, with a ghosted, blurred action shot background. The back has a photo of the player on the left, with biographical and NBA career statistical information on the right. Cards are numbered using an "F" prefix.

		MT
Complete Set (9):		65.00
Common Player:		3.00
1	Grant Hill	15.00
2	Larry Johnson	5.00
3	Eddie Jones	6.00
4	Jason Kidd	8.00
5	Hakeem Olajuwon	10.00
6	Shaquille O'Neal	20.00
7	Scottie Pippen	12.00
8	Glenn Robinson	8.00
9	Latrell Sprewell	3.00

1995-96 Jam Session Pop-Ups

These cards, random inserts in 1995-96 Fleer NBA Jam Session packs, were designed to pop-up, or stand, on a desktop or shelf. The front features a photo which is perforated; when the directions on the back are followed, the card pops up. The player's name is given in a panel at the top and bottom of the card; his team name and brand logo are in opposite upper and lower corners. Cards, numbered 1 of 25, etc., were seeded one per every 24 packs.

		MT
Complete Set (25):		10.00
Common Player:		.20
1	Kenny Anderson	.20
2	Charles Barkley	1.00
3	Mookie Blaylock	.20
4	Muggsy Bogues	.20
5	Shawn Bradley	.30
6	Sam Cassell	.30
7	Clyde Drexler	.75
8	Brian Grant	.40
9	Horace Grant	.30
10	Tim Hardaway	.20
11	Grant Hill	2.50
12	Jim Jackson	.50
13	Shawn Kemp	1.00
14	Christian Laettner	.20
15	Dan Majerle	.20
16	Eric Montross	.20
17	Alonzo Mourning	.50
18	Gheorghe Muresan	.20
19	Lamond Murray	.20
20	Dikembe Mutombo	.30
21	Charles Oakley	.20
22	Scottie Pippen	2.00
23	Mark Price	.20
24	Glen Rice	.20
25	Cliff Robinson	.20

1995-96 Jam Session Bonus Pop-Ups

These cards were random inserts in 1995-96 NBA Jam Session packs as a bonus. The Pop-Up cards can be distinguished from their regular counterparts by the numbering on the back; the bonus Pop-Ups are numbered 1 of 5, etc., unlike the regular cards, which are numbered 1 of 25, etc. The cards also use gold foil stamping for the player's first name on the front; his name is in panels at the top and bottom. The card is designed to stand up on a desk or shelf after it has been punched out and folded according to the directions on the back.

		MT
Complete Set (5):		25.00
Common Player:		2.00
1	Patrick Ewing	2.00
2	Grant Hill	10.00
3	Glenn Robinson	4.00
4	Jason Kidd	6.00
5	Jerry Stackhouse	17.00

1995-96 Jam Session Rookies

Ten top NBA rookies are featured in their new NBA uniforms on these 1995-96 Fleer NBA Jam Session inserts. The rookies are seeded one per every six packs. The card front has a photo of the player, with a swirl of stars around him and the word "rookie" written in the card's background. The player's name is at the bottom of the card; the brand logo is at the top. The back, numbered using an "R" prefix, has a second photo of the player in his NBA uniform, with his last name written above the photo. He is standing on a star, against a background which has "rookie" repeatedly written in it.

		MT
Complete Set (10):		20.00
Common Player:		.50
1	Joe Smith	5.00
2	Antonio McDyess	3.00
3	Jerry Stackhouse	8.00
4	Rasheed Wallace	2.00
5	Bryant Reeves	1.50
6	Shawn Respert	1.00
7	Cherokee Parks	1.00
8	Alan Henderson	1.00
9	George Zidek	.50
10	Sherell Ford	.50

1995-96 Jam Session Show Stoppers

These foil-stamped cards feature nine of the NBA's top stars against a metallic-like background. The player's name is at the bottom of the card, stamped in gold. The brand logo is at the top. The back has a ghosted image of the player on the left side; a second, smaller colored photo is on the right. NBA totals, biographical information and a brief recap of the player's previous season are provided on the back, which is numbered using an "S" prefix.

		MT
Complete Set (9):		200.00
Common Player:		6.00
1	Anfernee Hardaway	50.00
2	Grant Hill	30.00
3	Michael Jordan	120.00
4	Karl Malone	10.00
5	Jamal Mashburn	6.00
6	Reggie Miller	10.00
7	David Robinson	10.00
8	John Stockton	10.00
9	Chris Webber	12.00

1996 Fleer Australian Sprite

		MT
Complete Set (40):		60.00
Common Player:		.50
1	Kenny Anderson	1.00
2	Chris Mills	.50
3	Antonio McDyess	3.00
4	Joe Smith	1.00
5	Vin Baker	.75
6	Ed O'Bannon	.50
7	Anfernee Hardaway	5.00
8	Kevin Johnson	1.00
9	Mitch Richmond	1.00
10	Detlef Schrempf	1.00
11	John Stockton	2.00
12	Glen Rice	1.50
13	Clyde Drexler	1.50
14	Vlade Divac	1.00
15	Derek Harper	.50
16	Charles Barkley	3.00
17	Hersey Hawkins	.50
18	Karl Malone	3.00
19	Chris Webber	10.00
20	Alonzo Mourning	2.00
21	Clarence Weatherspoon	.50
22	Dino Radja	.50
23	Scottie Pippen	6.00
24	Jason Kidd	6.00
25	Grant Hill	10.00
26	Sam Cassell	1.00
27	Brian Williams	.50
28	Tom Gugliotta	1.00
29	John Starks	.50
30	Clifford Robinson	.50
31	David Robinson	3.00
32	Damon Stoudamire	1.00
33	Greg Anthony	.50
34	Toni Kukoc	1.50
35	Christian Laettner	1.00
36	Rik Smits	.50
37	Tim Hardaway	1.50
38	Nick Anderson	.50
39	Sean Elliott	.50
40	Juwan Howard	1.00

1996 Fleer French Kellogg's Frosties

		MT
Complete Set (30):		60.00
Common Player:		1.00
1	Kenny Anderson	2.00
2	Mookie Blaylock	1.00
3	Muggsy Bogues	1.00
4	Sam Cassell	2.00
5	Clyde Drexler	3.00
6	Brian Grant	2.00
7	Horace Grant	2.00
8	Tim Hardaway	3.00
9	Grant Hill	15.00
10	Kevin Johnson	2.00
11	Jim Jackson	1.00
12	Jason Kidd	12.00
13	Christian Laettner	2.00
14	Dan Majerle	1.00
15	Vernon Maxwell	1.00
16	Oliver Miller	1.00

17	Eric Montross	1.00
18	Gheorghe Muresan	1.00
19	Lamond Murray	1.00
20	Dikembe Mutombo	2.00
21	Charles Oakley	1.00
22	Hakeem Olajuwon	4.00
23	Scottie Pippen	10.00
24	Glen Rice	2.00
25	Clifford Robinson	1.00
26	Glenn Robinson	5.00
27	Byron Scott	1.00
28	Rik Smits	1.00
29	John Stockton	3.00
30	Tony the Tiger	1.00

1996 Fleer/Mountain Dew Stackhouse

This five-card set featuring Jerry Stackhouse was inserted in Mountain Dew products in the Philadelphia area. Each card has the Mountain Dew logo on the back.

		MT
Complete Set (5):		8.00
Common Player:		2.00
1	95-96 Fleer (Jerry Stackhouse)	2.00
2	95-96 Ultra (Jerry Stackhouse)	2.00
3	Jerry Stackhouse	2.00
4	95-96 SkyBox (Jerry Stackhouse)	2.00
5	95-96 Metal (Jerry Stackhouse)	2.00

1996-97 Fleer

Fleer's 1996-97 basketball set was issued in two 150-card series. Card fronts featured full-bleed photos with the player's name in the lower left corner and the Fleer 1996-97 logo in the top right. Backs were horizontal and included another shot of the player and statistics over a basketball-like background that includes the player's team logo. Series I had 119 regular-issue cards, 29 Hardwood Leaders and two checklists, while Series II had 118 regular cards, 20 All-Star Retro, 10 Crystal Ball and two checklists. Inserts in Series I include: Stackhouse's All-Fleer, Rookie Rewind, Lucky 13, Stackhouse's Scrapbook, Decade of Excellence, Franchise Futures and GameBreakers. Inserts in Series II include: Swing Shift, Towers of Power, Rookie Sensations, Decade of Excellence, Thrill Seekers and Total O.

		MT
Complete Set (300):		30.00
Complete Series 1 (150):		15.00
Complete Series 2 (150):		15.00
Common Player:		.05
Minor Stars:		.10
Series 1 or 2 Pack (11):		1.25
Series 1 or 2 Wax Box (24):		30.00
1	Stacey Augmon	.05
2	Mookie Blaylock	.05
3	Christian Laettner	.05
4	Grant Long	.05
5	Steve Smith	.05
6	Rick Fox	.05
7	Dino Radja	.05
8	Eric Williams	.10
9	Kenny Anderson	.05
10	Dell Curry	.05
11	Larry Johnson	.20
12	Glen Rice	.05
13	Michael Jordan	2.50
14	Toni Kukoc	.10
15	Scottie Pippen	.75
16	Dennis Rodman	.75
17	Terrell Brandon	.05
18	Chris Mills	.05
19	Bobby Phills	.05
20	Bob Sura	.05
21	Jim Jackson	.10
22	Jason Kidd	.75
23	Jamal Mashburn	.10
24	George McCloud	.05
25	Mahmoud Abdul-Rauf	.05
26	Antonio McDyess	.30
27	Dikembe Mutombo	.05
28	Jalen Rose	.05
29	Bryant Stith	.05
30	Joe Dumars	.05
31	Grant Hill	1.00
32	Allan Houston	.05
33	Theo Ratliff	.05
34	Otis Thorpe	.05
35	Chris Mullin	.05
36	Joe Smith	.50
37	Latrell Sprewell	.10
38	Kevin Willis	.05
39	Sam Cassell	.05
40	Clyde Drexler	.25
41	Robert Horry	.05
42	Hakeem Olajuwon	.50
43	Dale Davis	.05
44	Mark Jackson	.05
45	Derrick McKey	.05
46	Reggie Miller	.25
47	Rik Smits	.05
48	Brent Barry	.15
49	Malik Sealy	.05
50	Loy Vaught	.05
51	Brian Williams	.05
52	Elden Campbell	.05
53	Cedric Ceballos	.05
54	Vlade Divac	.05
55	Eddie Jones	.10
56	Nick Van Exel	.15
57	Tim Hardaway	.05
58	Alonzo Mourning	.20
59	Kurt Thomas	.05
60	Walt Williams	.05
61	Vin Baker	.15
62	Sherman Douglas	.05
63	Glenn Robinson	.25
64	Kevin Garnett	1.00
65	Tom Gugliotta	.05
66	Isaiah Rider	.05
67	Shawn Bradley	.05
68	Chris Childs	.05
69	Armon Gilliam	.05
70	Ed O'Bannon	.05
71	Patrick Ewing	.15
72	Derek Harper	.05
73	Anthony Mason	.05
74	Charles Oakley	.05
75	John Starks	.05
76	Nick Anderson	.05
77	Horace Grant	.05
78	Anfernee Hardaway	1.25
79	Shaquille O'Neal	1.00
80	Dennis Scott	.05
81	Derrick Coleman	.05
82	Vernon Maxwell	.05
83	Jerry Stackhouse	.75
84	Clarence Weatherspoon	.05
85	Charles Barkley	.30
86	Michael Finley	.50
87	Kevin Johnson	.05
88	Wesley Person	.05
89	Clifford Robinson	.05
90	Arvydas Sabonis	.20
91	Rod Strickland	.05
92	Gary Trent	.05
93	Tyus Edney	.10
94	Brian Grant	.05
95	Billy Owens	.05
96	Mitch Richmond	.05
97	Vinny Del Negro	.05
98	Sean Elliott	.05
99	Avery Johnson	.05
100	David Robinson	.40
101	Hersey Hawkins	.05
102	Shawn Kemp	.40
103	Gary Payton	.20
104	Detlef Schrempf	.05
105	Oliver Miller	.05
106	Tracy Murray	.05
107	Damon Stoudamire	.75
108	Sharone Wright	.05
109	Jeff Hornacek	.05
110	Karl Malone	.20
111	John Stockton	.20
112	Greg Anthony	.05
113	Bryant Reeves	.20
114	Byron Scott	.05
115	Calbert Cheaney	.05
116	Juwan Howard	.40
117	Gheorghe Muresan	.05
118	Rasheed Wallace	.15
119	Chris Webber	.15
120	Mookie Blaylock	.05
121	Dino Radja	.05
122	Larry Johnson	.10
123	Michael Jordan	1.25
124	Terrell Brandon	.05
125	Jason Kidd	.25
126	Antonio McDyess	.15
127	Grant Hill	.50
128	Latrell Sprewell	.05
129	Hakeem Olajuwon	.25
130	Reggie Miller	.10
131	Loy Vaught	.05
132	Cedric Ceballos	.25
133	Alonzo Mourning	.10
134	Vin Baker	.05
135	Isaiah Rider	.05
136	Armon Gilliam	.05
137	Patrick Ewing	.05
138	Shaquille O'Neal	.50
139	Jerry Stackhouse	.40
140	Charles Barkley	.15
141	Clifford Robinson	.05
142	Mitch Richmond	.05
143	David Robinson	.20
144	Shawn Kemp	.20
145	Damon Stoudamire	.50
146	Karl Malone	.10
147	Bryant Reeves	.10
148	Juwan Howard	.20
149	Checklist	.05
150	Checklist	.05
151	Alan Henderson	.05
152	*Priest Lauderdale*	.05
153	Dikembe Mutombo	.10
154	Dana Barros	.05
155	Todd Day	.05
156	*Brett Szabo*	.05
157	*Antoine Walker*	1.50
158	Scott Burrell	.05
159	*Tony Delk*	.25
160	Vlade Divac	.05
161	Matt Geiger	.05
162	Anthony Mason	.05
163	*Malik Rose*	.05
164	Ron Harper	.05
165	Steve Kerr	.05
166	Luc Longley	.05
167	Danny Ferry	.05
168	Tyrone Hill	.05
169	*Vitaly Potapenko*	.20
170	Tony Dumas	.05
171	Chris Gatling	.05
172	Oliver Miller	.05
173	Eric Montross	.05
174	*Samaki Walker*	.25
175	*Darvin Ham*	.05
176	Mark Jackson	.05
177	Ervin Johnson	.05
178	Stacey Augmon	.05
179	Joe Dumars	.05
180	Grant Hill	1.00
181	Grant Long	.05
182	Terry Mills	.05
183	Otis Thorpe	.05
184	*Jerome Williams*	.05
185	B.J. Armstrong	.05
186	*Todd Fuller*	.20
187	*Ray Owes*	.05
188	Mark Price	.05
189	Felton Spencer	.05
190	Charles Barkley	.40
191	Mario Elie	.05
192	*Othella Harrington*	.05
193	*Matt Maloney*	.50
194	Brent Price	.05
195	Kevin Willis	.05
196	Travis Best	.05
197	*Erick Dampier*	.25
198	Antonio Davis	.05
199	Jalen Rose	.05
200	Pooh Richardson	.05
201	Rodney Rogers	.05
202	*Lorenzen Wright*	.25
203	*Kobe Bryant*	10.00
204	*Derek Fisher*	.30
205	*Travis Knight*	.25
206	Shaquille O'Neal	1.25
207	Byron Scott	.05
208	P.J. Brown	.05
209	Sasha Danilovic	.05
210	Dan Majerle	.05
211	*Martin Muursepp*	.05
212	*Ray Allen*	2.00
213	Armon Gilliam	.05
214	Andrew Lang	.05
215	*Moochie Norris*	.05
216	Kevin Garnett	1.25
217	Tom Gugliotta	.05
218	*Shane Heal*	.05
219	*Stephon Marbury*	2.00
220	Stojko Vrankovic	.05
221	*Kerry Kittles*	1.25
222	Robert Pack	.05
223	Jayson Williams	.05
224	Allan Houston	.05
225	Larry Johnson	.10
226	*Dantae Jones*	.20
227	*Walter McCarty*	.05
228	*John Wallace*	.40
229	Charlie Ward	.05
230	*Brian Evans*	.05
231	*Amal McCaskill*	.05
232	Brian Shaw	.05
233	Mark Davis	.05
234	Lucious Harris	.05
235	*Allen Iverson*	3.50
236	Sam Cassell	.05
237	Robert Horry	.05
238	Danny Manning	.05
239	*Steve Nash*	.40
240	Kenny Anderson	.05
241	*Aleksandar Djordjevic*	.05
242	*Jermaine O'Neal*	.75
243	Isaiah Rider	.05
244	Rasheed Wallace	.05
245	Mahmoud Abdul-Rauf	.05
246	Michael Smith	.05
247	Corliss Williamson	.05
248	Vernon Maxwell	.05
249	Charles Smith	.05
250	Dominique Wilkins	.05
251	Craig Ehlo	.05
252	Jim McIlvaine	.05
253	Sam Perkins	.05
254	*Marcus Camby*	2.00
255	Popeye Jones	.05
256	*Donald Whiteside*	.05
257	Walt Williams	.05
258	Jeff Hornacek	.05
259	Karl Malone	.25
260	Bryon Russell	.05
261	John Stockton	.25
262	*Shareef Abdur-Rahim*	2.00
263	Anthony Peeler	.05
264	*Roy Rogers*	.20
265	Tim Legler	.05
266	Tracy Murray	.05
267	Rod Strickland	.05
268	*Ben Wallace*	.05
269	Kevin Garnett (Crystal Ball)	.60
270	Allan Houston (Crystal Ball)	.05
271	Eddie Jones (Crystal Ball)	.05
272	Jamal Mashburn (Crystal Ball)	.05
273	Antonio McDyess (Crystal Ball)	.05
274	Glenn Robinson (Crystal Ball)	.05
275	Joe Smith (Crystal Ball)	.20
276	Steve Smith (Crystal Ball)	.05
277	Jerry Stackhouse (Crystal Ball)	.30
278	Damon Stoudamire (Crystal Ball)	.40
279	Hakeem Olajuwon (All-Star Retro)	.30
280	Charles Barkley (All-Star Retro)	.20
281	Patrick Ewing (All-Star Retro)	.10
282	Michael Jordan (All-Star Retro)	1.50
283	Clyde Drexler (All-Star Retro)	.15
284	Karl Malone (All-Star Retro)	.10
285	John Stockton (All-Star Retro)	.10
286	David Robinson (All-Star Retro)	.20
287	Scottie Pippen (All-Star Retro)	.35
288	Shawn Kemp (All-Star Retro)	.20
289	Shaquille O'Neal (All-Star Retro)	.60
290	Mitch Richmond (All-Star Retro)	.05
291	Reggie Miller (All-Star Retro)	.05
292	Alonzo Mourning (All-Star Retro)	.05
293	Gary Payton (All-Star Retro)	.05
294	Anfernee Hardaway (All-Star Retro)	.75
295	Grant Hill (All-Star Retro)	.50
296	Dennis Rodman (All-Star Retro)	.60
297	Juwan Howard (All-Star Retro)	.05
298	Jason Kidd (All-Star Retro)	.25
299	Checklist	.05
300	Checklist	.05

1996-97 Fleer Decade of Excellence

These 20 cards feature reprints of active players' cards from Fleer's popular 1986-87 inaugural basketball set. The set was issued with 10 cards in Series I and 10 in Series II, with both carrying a one in 72 hobby pack insertion ratio. The cards are identified by a gold foil stamp in the lower left corner that reads "Fleer Decade of Excellence 1986-96." Cards are numbered with a "U" prefix.

		MT
Complete Set (20):		200.00
Complete Series 1 (10):		120.00
Complete Series 2 (10):		80.00
Common Player:		6.00
1	Clyde Drexler	18.00
2	Joe Dumars	8.00
3	Derek Harper	6.00
4	Michael Jordan	100.00
5	Karl Malone	18.00
6	Chris Mullin	8.00
7	Charles Oakley	6.00
8	Sam Perkins	6.00
9	Ricky Pierce	6.00
10	Buck Williams	6.00
11	Charles Barkley	20.00
12	Patrick Ewing	16.00
13	Eddie Johnson	6.00
14	Hakeem Olajuwon	30.00
15	Robert Parish	6.00
16	Byron Scott	6.00
17	Wayman Tisdale	6.00
18	Gerald Wilkins	6.00
19	Herb Williams	6.00
20	Kevin Willis	6.00

1996-97 Fleer Franchise Futures

Franchise Futures cards were seeded one per every 54 hobby packs of 1996-97 Fleer basketball product. Each embossed card front has a raised color action photo on it, with "Franchise Future" written in silver foil along the left side. The player's name is also in silver foil along the bottom; the Fleer logo is in silver in the upper right corner. The back has a color photo on one side, with a summary of why the player is a "Franchise Future." His name is written along the left side of the card in white letters; a card number (1 of 10, etc., also in white), is in the lower left corner. The card's background on both sides incorporates the team's primary colors into it.

		MT
Complete Set (10):		30.00
Common Player:		1.00
1	Kevin Garnett	10.00
2	Anfernee Hardaway	7.00
3	Grant Hill	10.00
4	Juwan Howard	3.00
5	Jason Kidd	2.50
6	Antonio McDyess	2.00
7	Glenn Robinson	1.00
8	Joe Smith	2.00
9	Jerry Stackhouse	2.00
10	Damon Stoudamire	3.00

1996-97 Fleer Game Breakers

These plastic cards feature two key members of a team who are "Game Breakers." Each card front is split in half, with each side showing an action photo of a player. "Game Breakers" is written in gold foil along the bottom of the card, just above the players' last names. The Fleer logo is in the upper left corner. The back side shows shadowed images of the photos of the front, and includes a description of how the player can take over a game. The card number is in the lower right corner (1 of 15) etc. Cards were random inserts in 1996-97 Fleer basketball packs, one per 54 hobby packs.

		MT
Complete Set (15):		250.00
Common Player:		5.00
1	Michael Jordan, Scottie Pippen	100.00
2	Jim Jackson, Jason Kidd	10.00
3	Grant Hill, Allan Houston	25.00
4	Joe Smith, Latrell Sprewell	10.00
5	Clyde Drexler, Hakeem Olajuwon	15.00
6	Cedric Ceballos, Nick Van Exel	5.00
7	Tim Hardaway, Alonzo Mourning	5.00
8	Vin Baker, Glenn Robinson	8.00
9	Kevin Garnett, Isaiah Rider	25.00
10	Anfernee Hardaway, Shaquille O'Neal	35.00
11	Jerry Stackhouse, Clarence Weatherspoon	10.00
12	Charles Barkley, Michael Finley	12.00
13	Sean Elliott, David Robinson	10.00
14	Shawn Kemp, Gary Payton	10.00
15	Karl Malone, John Stockton	7.00

1996-97 Fleer Lucky 13

This 13-card set was inserted into Series One packs at a rate of 1:30. Each card featured a number from 1-13 on the front and was redeemable for a card of the player chosen at that position in the 1996 NBA Draft. The redemption program expired on April 1, 1997.

		MT
Complete Set (13):		150.00
Common Player:		1.00
1	Allen Iverson	50.00
2	Marcus Camby	5.00
3	Shareef Abdur-Rahim	12.00
4	Stephon Marbury	20.00
5	Ray Allen	10.00
6	Antoine Walker	8.00
7	Lorenzen Wright	2.00
8	Kerry Kittles	3.00
9	Samaki Walker	1.50
10	Erick Dampier	1.50
11	Todd Fuller	1.00
12	Vitaly Potapenko	1.50
13	Kobe Bryant	125.00
NNO	Expired Trade Cards	.50

1996-97 Fleer Rookie Rewind

These cards recap the seasons of some of the top rookies from the previous NBA season who are likely to avoid a "sophomore jinx." Each card front has a color action photo on it, against a game action background. The player's last name and "Rookie Rewind" are written in gold foil along the bottom. The Fleer logo is in the upper right corner. The back, numbered 1 of 15, etc., has another photo of the player, with a recap of the player's first season in a parallelogram. Cards were seeded one per every 24 packs of 1996-97 Fleer basketball.

		MT
Complete Set (15):		30.00
Common Player:		1.00
1	Brent Barry	2.00
2	Tyus Edney	1.00
3	Michael Finley	3.00
4	Kevin Garnett	15.00
5	Antonio McDyess	3.00
6	Bryant Reeves	2.00
7	Arvydas Sabonis	2.00
8	Joe Smith	4.00
9	Jerry Stackhouse	4.00
10	Damon Stoudamire	8.00
11	Bob Sura	1.00
12	Kurt Thomas	1.00
13	Gary Trent	1.00
14	Rasheed Wallace	2.00
15	Eric Williams	1.00

1996-97 Fleer Rookie Sensations

This 15-card set highlighted the top rookies from the 1996-97 season, and were inserted one per 90 packs. The player's embossed image was cast over a copper foil background with silver foil around the border. In addition, the cards feature a Rookie Sensations logo in the lower right corner.

		MT
Complete Set (15):		200.00
Common Player:		3.00
1	Shareef Abdur-Rahim	30.00
2	Ray Allen	20.00
3	Kobe Bryant	45.00
4	Marcus Camby	30.00
5	Erick Dampier	3.00
6	Tony Delk	3.00
7	Allen Iverson	45.00
8	Kerry Kittles	18.00
9	Stephon Marbury	35.00
10	Steve Nash	6.00
11	Roy Rogers	3.00
12	Antoine Walker	12.00
13	Samaki Walker	3.00
14	John Wallace	8.00
15	Lorenzen Wright	3.00

1996-97 Fleer Stackhouse's All-Fleer

"Stackhouse's All-Fleer" and the name of the player he recaps are written in gold foil along the left side of the card front on each of these 1996-97 Fleer basketball insert cards. The Fleer logo is also on the front in gold, in the upper left corner. A color photo of the player 76ers' star Jerry Stackhouse reviews is also on the front. The back provides Stackhouse's analysis of the player, along with another color photo of the player and a card number (1 of 12, etc.). Cards were seeded one per every 12 packs of 1996- 97 Fleer basketball product.

		MT
Complete Set (12):		40.00
Common Player:		1.00
1	Charles Barkley	2.00
2	Anfernee Hardaway	7.00
3	Grant Hill	6.00
4	Michael Jordan	14.00
5	Shawn Kemp	2.00
6	Jason Kidd	3.00
7	Karl Malone	1.00
8	Hakeem Olajuwon	2.00
9	Shaquille O'Neal	5.00
10	Gary Payton	1.50
11	Scottie Pippen	3.00
12	David Robinson	2.00

1996-97 Fleer Stackhouse's Scrapbook

These two cards mark the final installment in Fleer's Jerry Stackhouse Scrapbook series. The cards, which recap Stackhouse's rookie season with the Philadelphia 76ers, were random inserts in 1996-97 Fleer basketball packs, one per every 24 packs.

		MT
Complete Set (2):		8.00
Common Player:		4.00
9	Jerry Stackhouse	4.00
10	Jerry Stackhouse	4.00

1996-97 Fleer Swing Shift

This 15-card set was inserted into Series II packs at a rate of one per six packs. The cards feature a color shot of the player over the words "Swing Shift" that appear all over the background. The backs are white and include another color shot of the player.

		MT
Complete Set (15):		18.00
Common Player:		.50
1	Ray Allen	1.75
2	Charles Barkley	1.00
3	Michael Finley	.50
4	Anfernee Hardaway	5.00
5	Grant Hill	5.00
6	Jim Jackson	.50
7	Eddie Jones	.50
8	Kerry Kittles	1.75
9	Reggie Miller	.75
10	Gary Payton	.75
11	Scottie Pippen	2.50
12	Mitch Richmond	.50
13	Steve Smith	.50
14	Latrell Sprewell	.75
15	Jerry Stackhouse	1.25

1996-97 Fleer Thrill Seekers

Thrill Seekers included 15 cards on lenticular technology. This insert was found in every 240 hobby packs of Series II, and attempts to provide a three-dimensional look around the featured player.

		MT
Complete Set (15):		500.00
Common Player:		10.00
1	Shareef Abdur-Rahim	50.00
2	Charles Barkley	20.00
3	Anfernee Hardaway	60.00
4	Grant Hill	90.00
5	Allen Iverson	80.00
6	Michael Jordan	175.00
7	Shawn Kemp	20.00
8	Jason Kidd	15.00
9	Stephon Marbury	70.00
10	Antonio McDyess	10.00
11	Reggie Miller	10.00
12	Alonzo Mourning	10.00
13	Shaquille O'Neal	60.00
14	David Robinson	20.00
15	Damon Stoudamire	40.00

1996-97 Fleer Total O

This 10-card insert was found only in Series II retail packs, at a rate of one per 44 packs. The cards are printed on plastic with a large basketball in the background and the "Total O" logo in the upper left corner.

Complete Set (10):		125.00
Common Player:		3.00
1	Anfernee Hardaway	20.00
2	Grant Hill	25.00
3	Juwan Howard	5.00
4	Michael Jordan	50.00
5	Shawn Kemp	6.00
6	Karl Malone	3.00
7	Alonzo Mourning	3.00
8	Hakeem Olajuwon	8.00
9	Shaquille O'Neal	20.00
10	Jerry Stackhouse	6.00

1996-97 Fleer Towers of Power

Towers of Power displays 10 of the NBA top big men on a foil etched background. Inserted in one per 30 packs of Series II, these cards have a rough painting of a city skyline in the background with the insert name running up the left side. The backs are horizontal and include another shot of the player along with text in white print.

		MT
Complete Set (10):		45.00
Common Player:		2.00
1	Shareef Abdur-Rahim	6.00
2	Marcus Camby	3.00
3	Patrick Ewing	2.00
4	Kevin Garnett	12.00
5	Shawn Kemp	3.00
6	Hakeem Olajuwon	5.00
7	Shaquille O'Neal	8.00
8	David Robinson	3.00
9	Dennis Rodman	8.00
10	Joe Smith	3.00

1996-97 Fleer European

This 330-card set was issued by Fleer for French, Spanish, Italian, Portugese, German, Japanese and Chinese markets. It's made up of two, 150-card series, with the 30-card translation set featuring team logos and inserted into both series. The cards were distributed by Panini and contain no foreign text on them, while some cards have different card numbers. The wrappers and the translation set feature foreign text. Stackhouse's All-Fleer, Rookie Rewind and Swing Shift inserts were available in Fleer European, but are identical to the regular Fleer inserts so they are not listed separately.

		MT
Complete Set (330):		80.00
Complete Series 1 (150):		25.00
Complete Series 2 (150):		50.00
Complete Translation Set (30):		5.00
Common Player:		.10
1	Stacey Augmon	.20
2	Mookie Blaylock	.10
3	Christian Laettner	.20
4	Grant Long	.10
5	Steve Smith	.20
6	Rick Fox	.10
7	Dino Radja	.10
8	Eric Williams	.10
9	Kenny Anderson	.20
10	Dell Curry	.10
11	Larry Johnson	.20
12	Glen Rice	.20
13	Michael Jordan	5.00
14	Toni Kukoc	.30
15	Scottie Pippen	1.00
16	Dennis Rodman	.50
17	Terrell Brandon	.20
18	Chris Mills	.10
19	Bobby Phills	.10
20	Bob Sura	.10
21	Jim Jackson	.10
22	Jason Kidd	1.00
23	Jamal Mashburn	.20
24	George McCloud	.10
25	Mahmoud Abdul-Rauf	.10
26	Antonio McDyess	.50
27	Dikembe Mutombo	.20
28	Jalen Rose	.40
29	Bryant Stith	.10
30	Joe Dumars	.20
31	Grant Hill	1.50
32	Allan Houston	.30
33	Theo Ratliff	.20
34	Otis Thorpe	.10
35	Chris Mullin	.20
36	Joe Smith	.20
37	Latrell Sprewell	.75
38	Kevin Willis	.10
39	Sam Cassell	.20
40	Clyde Drexler	.40
41	Robert Horry	.10
42	Hakeem Olajuwon	.50
43	Dale Davis	.10
44	Mark Jackson	.10
45	Derrick McKey	.10
46	Reggie Miller	.30
47	Rik Smits	.10
48	Brent Barry	.10
49	Malik Sealy	.10
50	Loy Vaught	.10
51	Brian Williams	.10
52	Elden Campbell	.10
53	Cedric Ceballos	.10
54	Vlade Divac	.20
55	Eddie Jones	.60
56	Nick Van Exel	.20
57	Tim Hardaway	.30
58	Alonzo Mourning	.30
59	Kurt Thomas	.10
60	Walt Williams	.10
61	Vin Baker	.20
62	Sherman Douglas	.10
63	Glenn Robinson	.20
64	Kevin Garnett	2.50
65	Tom Gugliotta	.20
66	Isaiah Rider	.20
67	Shawn Bradley	.10
68	Chris Childs	.10
69	Armon Gilliam	.10
70	Ed O'Bannon	.10
71	Patrick Ewing	.20
72	Derek Harper	.10
73	Anthony Mason	.20
74	Charles Oakley	.10
75	John Starks	.10
76	Nick Anderson	.10
77	Horace Grant	.20
78	Anfernee Hardaway	1.00
79	Shaquille O'Neal	1.50
80	Dennis Scott	.10
81	Derrick Coleman	.10
82	Vernon Maxwell	.10
83	Jerry Stackhouse	.30
84	Clarence Weatherspoon	.10
85	Charles Barkley	.50
86	Michael Finley	.30
87	Kevin Johnson	.20
88	Wesley Person	.10
89	Clifford Robinson	.20
90	Arvydas Sabonis	.20
91	Rod Strickland	.20
92	Gary Trent	.10
93	Tyus Edney	.10
94	Brian Grant	.20
95	Billy Owens	.10
96	Mitch Richmond	.20
97	Vinny Del Negro	.10
98	Sean Elliott	.10
99	Avery Johnson	.10
100	David Robinson	.50
101	Hersey Hawkins	.10
102	Shawn Kemp	.30
103	Gary Payton	.50
104	Detlef Schrempf	.20
105	Oliver Miller	.10
106	Tracy Murray	.10
107	Damon Stoudamire	.30
108	Sharone Wright	.10
109	Jeff Hornacek	.20
110	Karl Malone	.50
111	John Stockton	.30
112	Greg Anthony	.10
113	Bryant Reeves	.10
114	Byron Scott	.10
115	Calbert Cheaney	.10
116	Juwan Howard	.20
117	Gheorghe Muresan	.10
118	Rasheed Wallace	.50
119	Chris Webber	1.00
120	Mookie Blaylock HL	.10
121	Dino Radja HL	.10
122	Larry Johnson HL	.10
123	Michael Jordan HL	2.50
124	Terrell Brandon HL	.10
125	Jason Kidd HL	.50
126	Antonio McDyess HL	.20
127	Grant Hill HL	.75
128	Latrell Sprewell HL	.30
129	Hakeem Olajuwon HL	.25
130	Reggie Miller HL	.20
131	Loy Vaught HL	.10
132	Cedric Ceballos HL	.10
133	Alonzo Mourning HL	.20
134	Vin Baker HL	.10
135	Isaiah Rider HL	.10
136	Armon Gilliam HL	.10
137	Patrick Ewing HL	.20
138	Shaquille O'Neal HL	.75
139	Jerry Stackhouse HL	.20
140	Charles Barkley HL	.25
141	Clifford Robinson HL	.10
142	Mitch Richmond HL	.10
143	David Robinson HL	.25
144	Shawn Kemp HL	.20
145	Damon Stoudamire HL	.20
146	Karl Malone HL	.25
147	Bryant Reeves HL	.10
148	Juwan Howard HL	.10
149	Checklist	.10
150	Checklist	.10
151	Atlanta Hawks	.10
152	Boston Celtics	.10
153	Charlotte Hornets	.10
154	Chicago Bulls	.10
155	Cleveland Cavaliers	.10
156	Dallas Mavericks	.10
157	Denver Nuggets	.10
158	Detroit Pistons	.10
159	Golden State Warriors	.10
160	Houston Rockets	.10
161	Indiana Pacers	.10
162	Los Angeles Clippers	.10
163	Los Angeles Lakers	.10
164	Miami Heat	.10
165	Milwaukee Bucks	.10
166	Minnesota Timberwolves	.10
167	New Jersey Nets	.10
168	New York Knicks	.10
169	Orlando Magic	.10
170	Philadelphia 76ers	.10
171	Phoenix Suns	.10
172	Portland Trailblazers	.10
173	Sacramento Kings	.10
174	San Antonio Spurs	.10
175	Seattle Supersonics	.10
176	Toronto Raptors	.10
177	Utah Jazz	.10
178	Vancouver Grizzlies	.10
179	Washington Bullets	.10
181	Alan Henderson	.10
182	Priest Lauderdale	.10
183	Dikembe Mutombo	.20
184	Dana Barros	.10
185	Todd Day	.10
186	Brett Szabo	.10
187	Antoine Walker	2.00
188	Scott Burrell	.10
189	Tony Delk	.20
190	Vlade Divac	.20
191	Matt Geiger	.10
192	Anthony Mason	.20
193	Malik Rose	.10
194	Ron Harper	.10
195	Steve Kerr	.20
196	Luc Longley	.10
197	Danny Ferry	.10
198	Tyrone Hill	.10
199	Vitaly Potapenko	.10
200	Tony Dumas	.10
201	Chris Gatling	.10
202	Oliver Miller	.10
203	Eric Montross	.10
204	Samaki Walker	.20
205	Darvin Ham	.10
206	Mark Jackson	.10
207	Ervin Johnson	.10
208	Stacey Augmon	.10
209	Joe Dumars	.20
210	Grant Hill	1.50
211	Grant Long	.10
212	Terry Mills	.10
213	Otis Thorpe	.10
214	Jerome Williams	.50
215	B.J. Armstrong	.10
216	Todd Fuller	.10
217	Ray Owes	.10
218	Mark Price	.10
219	Felton Spencer	.10
220	Charles Barkley	.50
221	Mario Elie	.10
222	Othella Harrington	.30
223	Matt Maloney	.10
224	Brent Price	.10
225	Kevin Willis	.10
226	Travis Best	.20
227	Erick Dampier	.10
228	Antonio Davis	.10
229	Jalen Rose	.30
230	Pooh Richardson	.10
231	Rodney Rogers	.10
232	Lorenzen Wright	.20
233	Kobe Bryant	20.00
234	Derek Fisher	.75
235	Travis Knight	.10
236	Shaquille O'Neal	1.50
237	Byron Scott	.10
238	P.J. Brown	.10
239	Sasha Danilovic	.10
240	Dan Majerle	.20
241	Martin Muursepp	.10
242	Ray Allen	5.00
243	Armon Gilliam	.10
244	Andrew Lang	.10
245	Moochie Norris	.10
246	Kevin Garnett	2.50
247	Tom Gugliotta	.10
248	Shane Heal	.10
249	Stephon Marbury	5.00
250	Stojko Vrankovic	.10
251	Kerry Kittles	.75
252	Robert Pack	.10
253	Jayson Williams	.20
254	Allan Houston	.40
255	Larry Johnson	.20
256	Dontae Jones	.10
257	Walter McCarty	.10
258	John Wallace	.20
259	Charlie Ward	.10
260	Brian Evans	.10
261	Amal McCaskill	.10
262	Brian Shaw	.10
263	Mark Davis	.10
264	Lucious Harris	.10
265	Allen Iverson	10.00
266	Sam Cassell	.20
267	Robert Horry	.10
268	Danny Manning	.10
269	Steve Nash	.50
270	Kenny Anderson	.20
271	Aleksandar Djordjevic	.10
272	Jermaine O'Neal	2.00
273	Isaiah Rider	.20
274	Rasheed Wallace	.40
275	Mahmoud Abdul-Rauf	.10
276	Michael Smith	.10
277	Corliss Williamson	.10
278	Vernon Maxwell	.10
279	Charles Smith	.10
280	Dominique Wilkins	.30
281	Craig Ehlo	.10
282	Jim McIlvaine	.10
283	Sam Perkins	.10
284	Marcus Camby	2.00
285	Popeye Jones	.10
286	Donald Whiteside	.10
287	Walt Williams	.10
288	Jeff Hornacek	.20
289	Karl Malone	.50
290	Bryon Russell	.10
291	John Stockton	.30
292	Shareef Abdur-Rahim	4.00
293	Anthony Peeler	.10
294	Roy Rogers	.10
295	Tim Legler	.10
296	Tracy Murray	.10
297	Rod Strickland	.20
298	Ben Wallace	.10
299	Kevin Garnett CB	1.25
300	Allan Houston CB	.20
301	Eddie Jones CB	.30
302	Jamal Mashburn CB	.10
303	Antonio McDyess CB	.20
304	Glenn Robinson CB	.20
305	Joe Smith CB	.10
306	Steve Smith CB	.10
307	Jerry Stackhouse CB	.20
308	Damon Stoudamire CB	.20
309	Hakeem Olajuwon AS	.25
310	Charles Barkley AS	.25
311	Patrick Ewing AS	.20
312	Michael Jordan AS	2.50
313	Clyde Drexler AS	.20
314	Karl Malone AS	.25
315	John Stockton AS	.20
316	David Robinson AS	.25
317	Scottie Pippen AS	.50
318	Shawn Kemp AS	.20
319	Shaquille O'Neal AS	.75
320	Mitch Richmond AS	.20
321	Reggie Miller AS	.20
322	Alonzo Mourning AS	.20
323	Gary Payton AS	.25
324	Anfernee Hardaway AS	.50
325	Grant Hill AS	.75
326	Dennis Rodman AS	.20
327	Juwan Howard AS	.20
328	Jason Kidd AS	.50
329	Checklist	.10
330	Checklist	.10

1996-97 Fleer Sprite

This 40-card set is identical in design to the 1996-97 Fleer set, except the gold foil text is yellow. Customers who purchased Sprite at participating 7-Eleven stores received a four-card pack (three players and a checklist) and a $0.25 coupon for any Fleer or SkyBox product. A 10-card Grant Hill tribute set was randomly inserted in packs.

		MT
Complete Set (40):		30.00
Common Player:		.15
1	Dikembe Mutombo	.30
2	Steve Smith	.50
3	Antoine Walker	2.00
4	Anthony Mason	.30
5	Toni Kukoc	.30
6	Terrell Brandon	.30
7	Jim Jackson	.30
8	Jason Kidd	.75
9	Oliver Miller	.15
10	Antonio McDyess	1.00
11	Grant Hill	2.50
12	Joe Smith	.75
13	Charles Barkley	.75
14	Clyde Drexler	.75
15	Reggie Miller	.50
16	Brent Barry	.25
17	Kobe Bryant	7.00
18	Nick Van Exel	.30
19	Alonzo Mourning	.50
20	Ray Allen	2.50
21	Vin Baker	.50
22	Kevin Garnett	2.50
23	Stephon Marbury	4.00
24	Kerry Kittles	1.25
25	Patrick Ewing	.50
26	Larry Johnson	.30
27	Anfernee Hardaway	1.50
28	Allen Iverson	6.00
29	Arvydas Sabonis	.25
30	Mitch Richmond	.50
31	Vinny Del Negro	.15
32	Gary Payton	.75
33	Detlef Schrempf	.30
34	Marcus Camby	2.00
35	Damon Stoudamire	1.00
36	Karl Malone	1.00
37	John Stockton	1.00
38	Shareef Abdur-Rahim	3.50
39	Juwan Howard	.50
40	Chris Webber	1.50
NNO	Grant Hill Checklist	.15

1996-97 Fleer Sprite Grant Hill

This 10-card insert was randomly seeded in Fleer Sprite packs. The Fleer/SkyBox, Sprite and NBA logos appear on the front. The backs read "Grant Hill Special Issue" at the top and have biographical information.

		MT
Complete Set (10):		8.00
Common Player:		1.00
1	Senior Season (Grant Hill)	1.00
2	Collegiate Career (Grant Hill)	1.00
3	Born to Win (Grant Hill)	1.00
4	ROY (Grant Hill)	1.00
5	No Sophmore Jinx (Grant Hill)	1.00
6	Grant Hill	1.00
7	Up Close (Grant Hill)	1.00
8	Smooth as Silk (Grant Hill)	1.00
9	NBA Superstar (Grant Hill)	1.00
10	Mr. Popularity (Grant Hill)	1.00

1996 Fleer USA

Fleer uses its 3D lenticular technology for this set devoted to the United States' Olympic men's basketball team. Each pack contained two regular-issue cards on 20-point stock and one lenticular card. The set is divided into five subsets, each containing 10 cards. Non-lenticular subsets include By the Numbers and Masters of the Game; lenticular subsets include Around the World, In the Beginning and Defining Moment. In addition, hobby packs contain Heroes die-cut insert cards, which are seeded one per every 18 packs. Fleer/SkyBox also made it possible for collectors to complete their team sets by sending in 15 Fleer USAB wrappers (plus postage and handling fees) to receive three lenticular, two regular-issue and one insert card for both Charles Barkley and Mitch Richmond (12 cards total).

Complete Set (52):		100.00
Common Player:		.50
1	Anfernee Hardaway (In the Beginning)	9.00
2	Grant Hill (In the Beginning)	6.00
3	Karl Malone (In the Beginning)	1.50
4	Reggie Miller (In the Beginning)	1.50
5	Hakeem Olajuwon (In the Beginning)	4.00
6	Shaquille O'Neal (In the Beginning)	8.00
7	Scottie Pippen (In the Beginning)	4.00
8	David Robinson (In the Beginning)	3.00
9	Glenn Robinson (In the Beginning)	1.50
10	John Stockton (In the Beginning)	1.50
11	Anfernee Hardaway (By the Numbers)	3.00
12	Grant Hill (By the Numbers)	2.00
13	Karl Malone (By the Numbers)	.50
14	Reggie Miller (By the Numbers)	.50
15	Hakeem Olajuwon (By the Numbers)	1.25
16	Shaquille O'Neal (By the Numbers)	2.50
17	Scottie Pippen (By the Numbers)	1.25
18	David Robinson (By the Numbers)	1.00
19	Glenn Robinson (By the Numbers)	.50
20	John Stockton (By the Numbers)	.50
21	Anfernee Hardaway (Defining Moment)	9.00
22	Grant Hill (Defining Moment)	6.00
23	Karl Malone (Defining Moment)	1.50
24	Reggie Miller (Defining Moment)	1.50
25	Hakeem Olajuwon (Defining Moment)	4.00
26	Shaquille O'Neal (Defining Moment)	8.00
27	Scottie Pippen (Defining Moment)	4.00
28	David Robinson (Defining Moment)	3.00
29	Glenn Robinson (Defining Moment)	1.50
30	John Stockton (Defining Moment)	1.50
31	Anfernee Hardaway (Masters of the Game)	3.00
32	Grant Hill (Masters of the Game)	2.00
33	Karl Malone (Masters of the Game)	.50
34	Reggie Miller (Masters of the Game)	.50
35	Hakeem Olajuwon (Masters of the Game)	1.25
36	Shaquille O'Neal (Masters of the Game)	2.50
37	Scottie Pippen (Masters of the Game)	1.25
38	David Robinson (Masters of the Game)	1.00
39	Glenn Robinson (Masters of the Game)	.50
40	John Stockton (Masters of the Game)	.50
41	Anfernee Hardaway (Around the World)	9.00
42	Grant Hill (Around the World)	6.00
43	Karl Malone (Around the World)	1.50
44	Reggie Miller (Around the World)	1.50
45	Hakeem Olajuwon (Around the World)	4.00
46	Shaquille O'Neal (Around the World)	8.00
47	Scottie Pippen (Around the World)	4.00
48	David Robinson (Around the World)	3.00
49	Glenn Robinson (Around the World)	1.50
50	John Stockton (Around the World)	1.50
51	Checklist	2.00
52	Checklist	2.00

1996 Fleer USA Heroes

Hobby packs of Fleer's special 1996 USA Basketball contain cards from a Heroes insert set. These cards are die-cut with the top of the card clipped as the player is silhouetted across an American flag. The cards were seeded one per every 18 packs.

Complete Set (10):		140.00
Common Player:		8.00
1	Anfernee Hardaway	40.00
2	Grant Hill	25.00
3	Karl Malone	8.00
4	Reggie Miller	12.00
5	Hakeem Olajuwon	20.00
6	Shaquille O'Neal	30.00
7	Scottie Pippen	20.00
8	David Robinson	15.00
9	Glenn Robinson	8.00
10	John Stockton	8.00

1996 Fleer USA Wrapper Exchange

Collectors could redeem 15 Fleer USA wrappers for this 12-card set which featured the late additions to the 1996 Olympic "Dream Team" - Charles Barkley and Mitch Richmond. Each player has six cards. The first five correspond to the five subsets from 1996 Fleer USA and the sixth is a Heroes card. Cards are numbered with the "M" prefix.

		MT
Complete Set (12):		12.00
1	IB (Charles Barkley)	1.50
2	IB (Mitch Richmond)	1.00
3	BN (Charles Barkley)	.75
4	BN (Mitch Richmond)	.50
5	AW (Charles Barkley)	1.50
6	AW (Mitch Richmond)	1.00
7	MAS (Charles Barkley)	.75
8	MAS (Mitch Richmond)	.50
9	DM (Charles Barkley)	1.50
10	DM (Mitch Richmond)	1.00
11	Heroes (Charles Barkley)	2.00
12	Heroes (Mitch Richmond)	1.25

1997-98 Fleer

Fleer's 1997-98 set contained 350 cards, with 200 in Series I and 150 in Series II. Every base card was printed on matte finish. The fronts have full-bleed photos with the player's name, team and position printed in gold foil across the bottom and the Fleer logo in the upper right corner. Backs are white with a color photo at the top and statistics filling up the remainder. Inserts in Series I include: Fleer NBA Million Dollar Moments, Key Ingredients, Rookie Rewind, Flair Hardwood Legends, Decade of Excellence, Franchise Futures and Game Breakers, as well as two parallel sets called Tiffany Collection and Crystal Collection. Inserts in Series II include: Soaring Stars, Goudey Greats, Rookie Sensations, Total "O", Towers of Power, High Flying Soaring Stars, Zone, Thrill Seekers, Million Dollar Moments, Diamond Ink and Crystal and Tiffany Collection parallels.

		MT
Complete Set (350):		40.00
Complete Series 1 (200):		20.00
Complete Series 2 (150):		20.00
Common Player:		.05
Minor Stars:		.10
Crystal Stars:		3x-6x
Crystal Rookies:		2x-4x
Tiffany Stars:		25x-50x
Tiffany Rookies:		12x-24x
Ser. 1 or 2 Pack (10):		1.50
Ser. 1 or 2 Wax Box (36):		40.00
1	Anfernee Hardaway	1.25
2	Mitch Richmond	.15
3	Allen Iverson	1.25
4	Chris Webber	.30
5	Sasha Danilovic	.05
6	Avery Johnson	.05
7	Kenny Anderson	.05
8	Antoine Walker	.75
9	Nick Van Exel	.10
10	Mookie Blaylock	.05
11	Wesley Person	.05
12	Vlade Divac	.05
13	Glenn Robinson	.15
14	Chris Mills	.05
15	Latrell Sprewell	.20
16	Jayson Williams	.05
17	Travis Best	.05
18	Charlie Ward	.05
19	Theo Ratliff	.05
20	Gary Payton	.20
21	Marcus Camby	.50
22	Clyde Drexler	.20
23	Michael Jordan	3.00
24	Antonio McDyess	.15
25	Stephon Marbury	1.00
26	Isaac Austin	.05
27	Shareef Abdur-Rahim	.75
28	Malik Sealy	.05
29	Arvydas Sabonis	.05
30	Kerry Kittles	.30
31	Reggie Miller	.20
32	Karl Malone	.25
33	Grant Hill	1.50
34	Hakeem Olajuwon	.50
35	Danny Ferry	.05
36	Dominique Wilkins	.05
37	Armon Gilliam	.05
38	Danny Manning	.05
39	Larry Johnson	.10
40	Dino Radja	.05
41	Jason Caffey	.05
42	Jerry Stackhouse	.30
43	Alonzo Mourning	.20
44	Shawn Bradley	.05
45	Bo Outlaw	.05
46	Bryon Russell	.05
47	Doug West	.05
48	Lawrence Moten	.05
49	Dale Ellis	.05
50	Kobe Bryant	2.00
51	Carlos Rogers	.05
52	Todd Fuller	.05
53	Tyus Edney	.05
54	Horace Grant	.05
55	Dikembe Mutombo	.05
56	Jim McIlvaine	.05
57	Harvey Grant	.05
58	Dean Garrett	.05
59	Samaki Walker	.05
60	Johnny Newman	.05
61	Antonio Davis	.05
62	Jamal Mashburn	.10
63	Muggsy Bogues	.05
64	Rod Strickland	.05
65	Craig Ehlo	.05
66	Rex Walters	.05
67	Bob Sura	.05
68	Travis Knight	.05
69	Toni Kukoc	.05
70	Antoine Carr	.05
71	Mario Elie	.05
72	Popeye Jones	.05
73	David Wesley	.05
74	John Wallace	.10
75	Calbert Cheaney	.05
76	Grant Long	.05
77	Will Perdue	.05
78	Rasheed Wallace	.05
79	Chris Gatling	.05
80	Corliss Williamson	.05
81	B.J. Armstrong	.05
82	Brian Shaw	.05
83	Darrick Martin	.05
84	Vinny Del Negro	.05
85	Tony Delk	.05
86	Greg Anthony	.05
87	Mark Davis	.05
88	Anthony Goldwire	.05
89	Rex Chapman	.05
90	Stojko Vrankovic	.05
91	Dennis Rodman	.75
92	Detlef Schrempf	.05
93	Henry James	.05
94	Tracy Murray	.05
95	Voshon Lenard	.05
96	Sharone Wright	.05
97	Ed O'Bannon	.05
98	Gerald Wilkins	.05
99	Kevin Willis	.05
100	Shaquille O'Neal	1.00
101	Jim Jackson	.10
102	Mark Price	.05
103	Patrick Ewing	.20
104	Lorenzen Wright	.15
105	Tyrone Hill	.05
106	Ray Allen	.30
107	Jermaine O'Neal	.20
108	Anthony Mason	.05
109	Mahmoud Abdul-Rauf	.05
110	Terry Mills	.05
111	Gheorghe Muresan	.05
112	Mark Jackson	.05
113	Greg Ostertag	.05
114	Kevin Johnson	.05
115	Anthony Peeler	.05
116	Rony Seikaly	.05
117	Keith Askins	.05
118	Todd Day	.05
119	Chris Childs	.05
120	Chris Carr	.05
121	Erick Strickland	.05
122	Elden Campbell	.05
123	Elliott Perry	.05
124	Pooh Richardson	.05
125	Juwan Howard	.25
126	Ervin Johnson	.05
127	Eric Montross	.05
128	Otis Thorpe	.05
129	Hersey Hawkins	.05
130	Bimbo Coles	.05
131	Olden Polynice	.05
132	Christian Laettner	.05
133	Sean Elliott	.05
134	Othella Harrington	.05
135	Erick Dampier	.05
136	Vitaly Potapenko	.05
137	Doug Christie	.05
138	Luc Longley	.05
139	Clarence Weatherspoon	.05
140	Gary Trent	.05
141	Shandon Anderson	.05
142	Sam Perkins	.05
143	Derek Harper	.05
144	Robert Horry	.05
145	Roy Rogers	.05
146	John Starks	.05
147	Tyrone Corbin	.05
148	Andrew Lang	.05
149	Derek Strong	.05
150	Joe Smith	.30
151	Ron Harper	.05
152	Sam Cassell	.05
153	Brent Barry	.05
154	LaPhonso Ellis	.05
155	Matt Geiger	.05
156	Steve Nash	.05
157	Michael Smith	.05
158	Eric Williams	.05
159	Tom Gugliotta	.05
160	Monty Williams	.05
161	Lindsey Hunter	.05
162	Oliver Miller	.05
163	Brent Price	.05
164	Derrick McKey	.05
165	Robert Pack	.05
166	Derrick Coleman	.05
167	Isaiah Rider	.05
168	Dan Majerle	.05
169	Jeff Hornacek	.05
170	Terrell Brandon	.05
171	Nate McMillan	.05
172	Cedric Ceballos	.05
173	Derek Fisher	.05
174	Rodney Rogers	.05
175	Blue Edwards	.05
176	Brooks Thompson	.05
177	Sherman Douglas	.05
178	Sam Mitchell	.05
179	Charles Oakley	.05
180	Greg Minor	.05
181	Chris Mullin	.05
182	P.J. Brown	.05
183	Stacey Augmon	.05
184	Don MacLean	.05
185	Aaron McKie	.05
186	Dale Davis	.05
187	Vernon Maxwell	.05
188	Dell Curry	.05
189	Kendall Gill	.05
190	Billy Owens	.05
191	Steve Kerr	.05
192	Matt Maloney	.10
193	Dennis Scott	.05
194	A.C. Green	.05
195	George McCloud	.05
196	Walt Williams	.05
197	Eldridge Recasner	.05
198	Checklist	.05
199	Checklist	.05
200	Checklist	.05
201	*Tim Duncan*	3.00
202	*Tim Thomas*	1.00
203	Clifford Rozier	.05
204	Bryant Reeves	.05
205	Glen Rice	.20
206	Darrell Armstrong	.05
207	Juwan Howard	.30
208	John Stockton	.30
209	Antonio McDyess	.30
210	*James Cotton*	.10
211	Brian Grant	.05
212	Chris Whitney	.05
213	Antonio Davis	.05
214	Kendall Gill	.05
215	*Adonal Foyle*	.50
216	Dean Garrett	.05
217	Dennis Scott	.05
218	Zydrunas Ilgauskas	.40
219	*Antonio Daniels*	1.00
220	Derek Harper	.05
221	Travis Knight	.05
222	Bobby Hurley	.05
223	Greg Anderson	.05
224	Rod Strickland	.05
225	David Benoit	.05
226	*Tracy McGrady*	1.00
227	Brian Williams	.05
228	James Robinson	.05
229	Randy Brown	.05
230	Greg Foster	.05
231	Reggie Miller	.25
232	Eric Montross	.05
233	Malik Rose	.05
234	Charles Barkley	.30
235	*Tony Battie*	1.00
236	Terry Mills	.05
237	*Jerald Honeycutt*	.10
238	*Bubba Wells*	.10
239	John Wallace	.10
240	Jason Kidd	.30
241	Mark Price	.05
242	*Ron Mercer*	1.50
243	Derrick Coleman	.10
244	Fred Hoiberg	.05
245	Wesley Person	.05
246	Eddie Jones	.40
247	Allan Houston	.10
248	*Keith Van Horn*	1.50
249	Johnny Newman	.05
250	Kevin Garnett	1.50
251	Latrell Sprewell	.20
252	Tracy Murray	.05
253	Charles O'Bannon	.05
254	Lamond Murray	.05
255	Jerry Stackhouse	.30
256	Rik Smits	.05
257	Alan Henderson	.05
258	*Tariq Abdul-Wahad*	.20
259	Nick Anderson	.05
260	Calbert Cheaney	.05
261	Scottie Pippen	.75
262	*Rodrick Rhodes*	.75
263	*Derek Anderson*	1.00
264	Dana Barros	.05
265	Todd Day	.05
266	Michael Finley	.20
267	Kevin Edwards	.05
268	Terrell Brandon	.10
269	Bobby Phills	.05
270	*Kelvin Cato*	.20
271	Vin Baker	.30
272	*Eric Washington*	.10
273	Jim Jackson	.05
274	Joe Dumars	.05
275	David Robinson	.30
276	Jayson Williams	.05
277	Travis Best	.05
278	Kurt Thomas	.05
279	Otis Thorpe	.05
280	Damon Stoudamire	.40
281	John Williams	.05
282	Loy Vaught	.05
283	Charles Outlaw	.05
284	Todd Fuller	.05
285	Terry Dehere	.05
286	Clarence Weatherspoon	.05
287	*Danny Fortson*	.50
288	Howard Eisley	.05
289	Steve Smith	.05
290	Chris Webber	.50
291	Shawn Kemp	.50
292	Sam Cassell	.05
293	Rick Fox	.05
294	Walter McCarty	.05
295	Mark Jackson	.05
296	Chris Mills	.05
297	*Jacque Vaughn*	.50
298	Shawn Respert	.05
299	Scott Burrell	.05
300	Allen Iverson	1.25
301	*Charles Smith*	.05
302	Ervin Johnson	.05
303	*Hubert Davis*	.05
304	*Eddie Johnson*	.05
305	Erick Dampier	.05
306	Eric Williams	.05
307	*Anthony Johnson*	.10
308	David Wesley	.05
309	Eric Piatkowski	.05
310	*Austin Croshere*	.50
311	Malik Sealy	.05
312	George McCloud	.05
313	*Anthony Parker*	.10
314	*Cedric Henderson*	.40
315	*John Thomas*	.10
316	Cory Alexander	.05
317	*Johnny Taylor*	.10
318	Chris Mullin	.10
319	J.R. Reid	.05
320	George Lynch	.05
321	*Lawrence Funderburke*	.10
322	*God Shammgod*	.10
323	*Bobby Jackson*	1.00
324	Khalid Reeves	.05
325	Zan Tabak	.05
326	Chris Gatling	.05
327	*Alvin Williams*	.10
328	*Scot Pollard*	.10
329	Kerry Kittles	.30
330	Tim Hardaway	.10
331	*Maurice Taylor*	.75
332	*Keith Booth*	.10
333	Chris Morris	.05
334	Bryant Stith	.05
335	Terry Cummings	.05
336	*Ed Gray*	.10
337	Eric Snow	.05
338	Clifford Robinson	.05
339	Chris Dudley	.05
340	*Chauncey Billups*	1.50
341	*Paul Grant*	.10
342	Tyrone Hill	.05
343	Joe Smith	.30
344	Sean Rooks	.05
345	Harvey Grant	.05
346	Dale Davis	.05
347	*Brevin Knight*	1.25
348	*Serge Zwikker*	.10
349	Checklist	.05
350	Checklist	.05

1997-98 Fleer Crystal

Crystal Collection paralleled the regular-issue Fleer set, and was inserted every two hobby packs. Crystal Collection contains silver foil printing and a small logo that reads "Traditions Crystal" in the upper right corner. The set includes 345 cards, which is minus the five checklists from the 350-card Fleer set.

	MT
Complete Set (200):	120.00
Crystal Cards:	3x-6x

1997-98 Fleer Tiffany

This parallel set of Fleer was inserted at a rate of one per 20 hobby packs and contains each regular-issue card printed in holographic silver foil. The cards are identified by a Traditions Tiffany logo in the upper right corner. The set contained 345 of the 350 cards in the Fleer set minus five checklist cards.

	MT
Complete Set (200):	1000.
Tiffany Cards:	25x-50x

1997-98 Fleer Decade of Excellence

This 10-card insert set features designs from the 1987-88 Fleer set and includes players that have been active for 10 years in the NBA. Decade of Excellence inserts were found in one per 36 hobby packs. Rare Traditions versions of these also exist with a special foil treatment.

		MT
Complete Set (12):		100.00
Common Player:		3.00
1	Charles Barkley	12.00
2	Clyde Drexler	8.00
3	Patrick Ewing	6.00
4	Kevin Johnson	3.00
5	Michael Jordan	50.00
6	Karl Malone	8.00
7	Reggie Miller	6.00
8	Hakeem Olajuwon	15.00
9	Scottie Pippen	25.00
10	Dennis Rodman	25.00
11	John Stockton	8.00
12	Dominique Wilkins	3.00

1997-98 Fleer Decade of Excellence Rare Traditions

Decade of Excellence inserts arrived in two different versions, regular and Rare Traditions. Rare Traditions versions featured a special foil treatment and were inserted every 360 hobby packs.

	MT
Complete Set (12):	300.00
Rare Tradition Cards:	1.5x-3x

1997-98 Fleer Diamond Ink

Diamond Ink cards were inserted at a rate of one per pack in various Fleer Basketball products throughout the 1997-98 season. Fleer II, Ultra II and Flair Showcase all contained these cards which held either one, five or 10 points. When a prescribed point total was reached, collectors could redeem the points for an autographed mini-basketball from a group of around 10 players.

	MT
Common Player:	.10
Kobe Bryant	.75
Grant Hill	1.00
Kevin Garnett	.40
Joe Smith	.10
Antoine Walker	.20
Antonio McDyess	.10
Danny Fortson	.10
Tim Thomas	.10
Tracy McGrady	.15
Tony Battie	.10
Stephon Marbury	.30
Chauncey Billups	.20

1997-98 Fleer Flair Hardwood Leaders

Hardwood Leaders features one player from each of the 29 teams on a Flair-type card. The top and bottom of the card, as well as the border, give the appearance of wood grain, while the player's image is printed over a cloud background. The horizontal card back featured another shot of the player with text printed over the player's team logo and the border in a simulated wood grain style.

		MT
Complete Set (29):		55.00
Common Player:		.75
Minor Stars:		1.50
1	Christian Laettner	.75
2	Antoine Walker	3.00
3	Glen Rice	1.50
4	Michael Jordan	15.00
5	Terrell Brandon	.75
6	Michael Finley	1.50
7	Antonio McDyess	1.50
8	Grant Hill	8.00
9	Latrell Sprewell	2.00
10	Hakeem Olajuwon	3.00
11	Reggie Miller	1.50
12	Loy Vaught	.75
13	Shaquille O'Neal	6.00
14	Alonzo Mourning	1.50
15	Vin Baker	1.50
16	Kevin Garnett	8.00
17	Kerry Kittles	2.00
18	Patrick Ewing	1.50
19	Anfernee Hardaway	8.00
20	Jerry Stackhouse	2.00
21	Jason Kidd	1.50
22	Kenny Anderson	.75
23	Mitch Richmond	1.50
24	David Robinson	2.00
25	Shawn Kemp	2.00
26	Damon Stoudamire	2.50
27	Karl Malone	1.50
28	Shareef Abdur-Rahim	5.00
29	Chris Webber	2.00

1997-98 Fleer Franchise Futures

Franchise Futures was a 10-card insert that was found exclusively in retail packs at a rate of one per 36. The insert contained players who had less than three years of NBA experience and appeared to be the future of their teams.

		MT
Complete Set (10):		100.00
Common Player:		3.00
1	Shareef Abdur-Rahim	10.00
2	Ray Allen	3.00
3	Kobe Bryant	25.00
4	Kevin Garnett	20.00
5	Grant Hill	20.00
6	Juwan Howard	3.00
7	Allen Iverson	20.00
8	Kerry Kittles	3.00
9	Joe Smith	3.00
10	Damon Stoudamire	5.00

1997-98 Fleer Game Breakers

Inserted at one per 288 packs of Series I, Game Breakers included some of the NBA's most potent duos. Game Breakers featured embossed images of two players over a basketball background.

		MT
Complete Set (12):		600.00
Common Player:		15.00
1	Michael Jordan, Dennis Rodman	150.00
2	Joe Dumars, Grant Hill	80.00
3	Joe Smith, Latrell Sprewell	15.00
4	Charles Barkley, Hakeem Olajuwon	30.00
5	Eddie Jones, Shaquille O'Neal	60.00
6	Kevin Garnett, Stephon Marbury	80.00
7	Nick Anderson, Anfernee Hardaway	70.00
8	Allen Iverson, Jerry Stackhouse	60.00
9	Shawn Kemp, Gary Payton	25.00
10	Marcus Camby, Damon Stoudamire	40.00
11	Karl Malone, John Stockton	15.00
12	Juwan Howard, Chris Webber	25.00

1997-98 Fleer Goudey Greats

Goudey Greats was a 15-card set utilizing the design from 1934 Goudey, including the famous Goudey "Says" spotlighting Hall of Fame point guard Nate "Tiny" Archibald's analysis of today's players. These mini cards were inserted every four packs. Card fronts feature an old-time look, with the player's image larger and the bottom portion featuring Archibald. The back also resembles the 1934 Goudey look and is numbered "x of 15GG." These were found in Series II packs only.

		MT
Complete Set (15):		20.00
Common Player:		.50
Minor Stars:		1.00
1	Ray Allen	1.00
2	Clyde Drexler	1.50
3	Patrick Ewing	.50
4	Anfernee Hardaway	5.00
5	Grant Hill	6.00
6	Stephon Marbury	5.00
7	Alonzo Mourning	1.00
8	Shaquille O'Neal	4.00
9	Gary Payton	2.00
10	Scottie Pippen	2.50
11	David Robinson	1.50
12	Joe Smith	1.00
13	John Stockton	1.00
14	Damon Stoudamire	1.50
15	Antoine Walker	2.00

1997-98 Fleer Key Ingredients

This 15-card insert featured players who are the "key ingredients" to their NBA teams. These inserts were found every two retail packs of Series I.

Complete Set (15):		10.00
Common Player:		.25
Gold Cards:		4x-8x
1	Charles Barkley	.50
2	Marcus Camby	1.00
3	Anfernee Hardaway	1.75
4	Juwan Howard	.50
5	Shawn Kemp	.75
6	Karl Malone	.50
7	Stephon Marbury	1.50
8	Alonzo Mourning	.25
9	Shaquille O'Neal	1.50
10	Scottie Pippen	1.00
11	Mitch Richmond	.25
12	David Robinson	.50
13	Joe Smith	.50
14	Jerry Stackhouse	.50
15	Antoine Walker	1.00

1997-98 Fleer Key Ingredients Gold

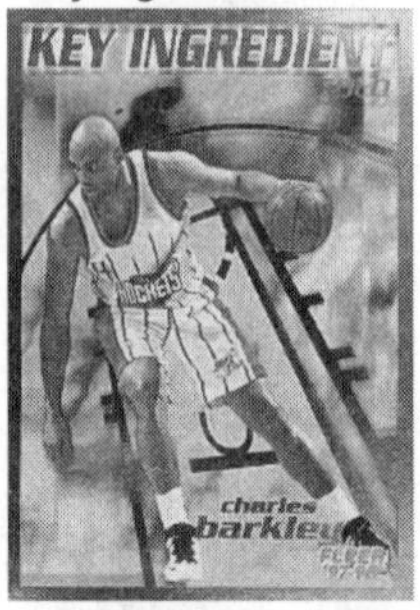

This 15-card, retail-only set paralleled the Key Ingredients set and was inserted one per 18 packs. Gold versions were printed on plastic and contained a thick gold foil border.

		MT
Complete Set (15):		10.00
Common Player:		.25
Gold Cards:		4x-8x
1	Charles Barkley	.50
2	Marcus Camby	1.00
3	Anfernee Hardaway	1.75
4	Juwan Howard	.50
5	Shawn Kemp	.50
6	Karl Malone	.50
7	Stephon Marbury	1.50
8	Alonzo Mourning	.25
9	Shaquille O'Neal	1.50
10	Scottie Pippen	1.00
11	Mitch Richmond	.25
12	David Robinson	.50
13	Joe Smith	.50
14	Jerry Stackhouse	.50
15	Antoine Walker	1.00

1997-98 Fleer Million Dollar Moments

This 50-card set was inserted one per pack of 1997-98 Fleer basketball products. Cards 46-50 were tougher to find. A collector who completed the 50-card set had a chance to win $1,000,000. The game ended August 31, 1998.

		MT
Complete Set (45):		6.00
Common Player:		.05
1	Checklist	.05
2	Mark Jackson	.05
3	Charles Barkley	.25
4	Terrell Brandon	.15
5	Wayman Tisdale	.05
6	Clyde Drexler	.20
7	Patrick Ewing	.15
8	Kevin Garnett	1.00
9	Tom Gugliotta	.15
10	Anfernee Hardaway	.75
11	Tim Hardaway	.15
12	Grant Hill	1.00
13	Allen Iverson	1.00
14	Shawn Kemp	.30
15	Jason Kidd	.15
16	Charles Oakley	.10
17	Karl Malone	.20
18	Alonzo Mourning	.15
19	Shaquille O'Neal	.75
20	Hakeem Olajuwon	.40
21	Chris Webber	.40
22	Scottie Pippen	.50
23	Glen Rice	.15
24	Mitch Richmond	.15
25	David Robinson	.25
26	Dennis Rodman	.75
27	Jerry Stackhouse	.20
28	John Stockton	.15
29	Mookie Blaylock	.10
30	Muggsy Bogues	.10
31	Kobe Bryant	2.00
32	Rex Chapman	.05
33	Joe Dumars	.15
34	Dale Ellis	.05
35	Horace Grant	.10
36	Jeff Hornacek	.10
37	Damon Stoudamire	.30
38	Kevin Johnson	.15
39	Larry Johnson	.15
40	Toni Kukoc	.10
41	Danny Manning	.10
42	Stephon Marbury	.75
43	Reggie Miller	.15
44	Chris Mullin	.10
45	Dikembe Mutombo	.15

1997-98 Fleer Rookie Rewind

This 10-card insert was inserted every four packs of Series I and contained the top rookies of the 1996 NBA Draft. The cards featured a color shot of the player, with the words "Rookie Rewind" in silver foil in a circular fashion.

		MT
Complete Set (10):		15.00
Common Player:		.50
1	Shareef Abdur-Rahim	2.50
2	Ray Allen	1.00
3	Kobe Bryant	8.00
4	Marcus Camby	2.00
5	Allen Iverson	4.00
6	Kerry Kittles	1.00
7	Matt Maloney	1.00
8	Stephon Marbury	3.00
9	Roy Rogers	.50
10	Antoine Walker	3.00

1997-98 Fleer Rookie Sensations

This 10-card insert set was seeded one per eight packs of Fleer Series II. The set included some of the top players chosen in the 1997 NBA Draft.

		MT
Complete Set (10):		30.00
Common Player:		.75
1	Derek Anderson	3.00
2	Tony Battie	2.00
3	Chauncey Billups	5.00
4	Austin Croshere	.75
5	Antonio Daniels	4.00
6	Tim Duncan	10.00
7	Tracy McGrady	5.00
8	Ron Mercer	5.00
9	Tim Thomas	3.00
10	Keith Van Horn	5.00

1997-98 Fleer Soaring Stars

This 20-card insert was found exclusively in Series II retail packs at a rate of one per two packs. Fronts had the words "Soaring Stars" down the left side outlined in red. The cards are numbered on the back with an "SS" suffix. High Flying versions were also made and contain silver foil instead of the red outlined letters.

		MT
Complete Set (20):		12.00
Common Player:		.25
Minor Stars:		.50
Soaring Stars:		4x-8x
1	Shareef Abdur-Rahim	1.25
2	Ray Allen	.50
3	Charles Barkley	.75
4	Kobe Bryant	3.00
5	Marcus Camby	.50
6	Kevin Garnett	2.00
7	Tim Hardaway	.25
8	Eddie Jones	.75
9	Michael Jordan	4.00
10	Shawn Kemp	.50
11	Jason Kidd	.50
12	Kerry Kittles	.50
13	Karl Malone	.50
14	Antonio McDyess	.25
15	Glen Rice	.25
16	Mitch Richmond	.25
17	Latrell Sprewell	.50
18	Jerry Stackhouse	.50
19	Antoine Walker	1.00
20	Chris Webber	.75

1997-98 Fleer High Flying Soaring Stars

High Flying Soaring Stars are similar to regular Soaring Stars versions, except they add silver foil to the insert name down the left side and the word "High Flying" is printed on the far left side. The backs are done in blue versus the red of regular versions, and the cards are numbered with an "HFSS" suffix. This 20-card set was inserted one per 24 packs into Fleer Series II packs.

		MT
Complete Set (20):		90.00
Common Player:		2.00
1	Shareef Abdur-Rahim	10.00
2	Ray Allen	4.00
3	Charles Barkley	6.00
4	Kobe Bryant	25.00
5	Marcus Camby	4.00
6	Kevin Garnett	20.00
7	Tim Hardaway	2.00
8	Eddie Jones	6.00
9	Michael Jordan	35.00
10	Shawn Kemp	4.00
11	Jason Kidd	4.00
12	Kerry Kittles	2.00
13	Karl Malone	4.00
14	Antonio McDyess	2.00
15	Glen Rice	2.00
16	Mitch Richmond	2.00
17	Latrell Sprewell	2.00
18	Jerry Stackhouse	2.00
19	Antoine Walker	6.00
20	Chris Webber	6.00

1997-98 Fleer Thrill Seekers

This 10-card insert set was found in one per 288 packs of Series II. Cards featured a framed look, with prismatic foil in the background in back of the player's cut-out image. Cards were numbered with a "TS" suffix.

Complete Set (10):		425.00
Common Player:		12.00
1	Shareef Abdur-Rahim	30.00
2	Kobe Bryant	80.00
3	Tim Duncan	60.00
4	Anfernee Hardaway	50.00
5	Grant Hill	60.00
6	Allen Iverson	60.00
7	Michael Jordan	120.00
8	Stephon Marbury	50.00
9	Dennis Rodman	35.00
10	Joe Smith	12.00

1997-98 Fleer Total O

Total "O" was found exclusively in retail packs at a rate of one per 18. Card fronts pictured a top offensive star over the free-throw lane of a basketball court. Card backs included a closeup and were numbered with a "TO" suffix. This insert included 10 cards.

		MT
Complete Set (10):		70.00
Common Player:		1.00
1	Anfernee Hardaway	10.00
2	Grant Hill	15.00
3	Juwan Howard	1.00
4	Allen Iverson	12.00
5	Michael Jordan	30.00
6	Karl Malone	1.00
7	Stephon Marbury	10.00
8	Hakeem Olajuwon	6.00
9	Shaquille O'Neal	10.00
10	Damon Stoudamire	4.00

1997-98 Fleer Towers of Power

Towers of Power was a unique, 12-card insert that featured a die-cut front and back and opened up into a 10-inch shot of the player. Inserted one per 18 packs, each card had the insert name on the front (closed card) and across the bottom when the card was opened, and carried a "TP" suffix on the card number on back.

		MT
Complete Set (12):		60.00
Common Player:		1.50
Minor Stars:		3.00
1	Shareef Abdur-Rahim	8.00
2	Marcus Camby	1.50
3	Patrick Ewing	1.50
4	Kevin Garnett	15.00
5	Shawn Kemp	4.00
6	Karl Malone	3.00
7	Hakeem Olajuwon	6.00
8	Shaquille O'Neal	10.00
9	Dennis Rodman	10.00
10	Joe Smith	3.00
11	Antoine Walker	5.00
12	Chris Webber	4.00

1997-98 Fleer Zone

Zone featured 15 NBA stars over a holographic green patterned background, with the name printed within circles in the top right corner. Backs were numbered with a "Z" suffix, with cards inserted every 36 hobby packs.

		MT
Complete Set (15):		130.00
Common Player:		1.50
1	Shareef Abdur-Rahim	8.00
2	Kobe Bryant	20.00
3	Marcus Camby	1.50
4	Tim Duncan	15.00
5	Kevin Garnett	15.00
6	Anfernee Hardaway	12.00
7	Grant Hill	15.00
8	Juwan Howard	1.50
9	Allen Iverson	15.00
10	Michael Jordan	30.00
11	Hakeem Olajuwon	6.00
12	Gary Payton	4.00
13	Scottie Pippen	8.00
14	Glen Rice	1.50
15	Keith Van Horn	10.00

1997 Fleer NBA Jam Session Commemorative Sheet

This sheet was issued at the 1997 NBA Jam Session in Cleveland. It was available through a wrapper redemption. The sheet featured six cards from the Fresh Faces insert that appeared in 1996-97 Fleer Series One and six cards from the All-Star subset in 1996-97 Fleer Series Two.

		MT
Complete Set (1):		10.00
1	Shareef Abdur-Rahim FF, Ray Allen FF, Kobe Bryant FF, Marcus Camby FF, Kerry Kittles FF, Stephon Marbury FF, Charles Barkley AS, Patrick Ewing AS, John Stockton AS, Alonzo Mourning AS, Grant Hill AS, Jason Kidd AS	10.00

1998-99 Fleer

Fleer Tradition Series I contained 150 cards, with 147 player cards and three checklists. This year's set featured players on a borderless design with the player's name, team and position stamped across the bottom in gold foil. There were two hobby-only parallels: Vintage '61 and Classic '61, which featured the first 147 players on a 1961-62 card design. Insert sets in Series I include: Timeless Memories, Great Expectations, Rookie Rewind, Electrifying, Lucky 13 and Playmakers Theatre.

		MT
Complete Set (150):		20.00
Common Player:		.10
Minor Stars:		.20
Pack (11):		2.00
Wax Box (36):		65.00
1	Kobe Bryant	2.00
2	Corliss Williamson	.10
3	Allen Iverson	1.00
4	Michael Finley	.20
5	Juwan Howard	.20
6	Marcus Camby	.20
7	Toni Kukoc	.20
8	Antoine Walker	.75
9	Stephon Marbury	1.00
10	Tim Hardaway	.25
11	Zydrunas Ilgauskas	.10
12	John Stockton	.25
13	Glenn Robinson	.20
14	Isaiah Rider	.10

15	Danny Fortson	.20
16	Donyell Marshall	.10
17	Chris Mullin	.10
18	Shareef Abdur-Rahim	.50
19	Bobby Phills	.10
20	Gary Payton	.30
21	Derrick Coleman	.10
22	Larry Johnson	.20
23	Michael Jordan	3.00
24	Danny Manning	.10
25	Nick Anderson	.10
26	Chris Gatling	.10
27	Steve Smith	.10
28	Chris Whitney	.10
29	Terrell Brandon	.20
30	Rasheed Wallace	.10
31	Reggie Miller	.25
32	Karl Malone	.25
33	Grant Hill	1.50
34	Hakeem Olajuwon	.50
35	Erick Dampier	.10
36	Vin Baker	.40
37	Tim Thomas	.75
38	Mark Price	.10
39	Shawn Bradley	.10
40	Calbert Cheaney	.10
41	Glen Rice	.20
42	Kevin Willis	.10
43	Chris Carr	.10
44	Keith Van Horn	.75
45	Jamal Mashburn	.10
46	Eddie Jones	.40
47	Brevin Knight	.30
48	Olden Polynice	.10
49	Bobby Jackson	.20
50	David Robinson	.40
51	Patrick Ewing	.25
52	Samaki Walker	.10
53	Antonio Daniels	.20
54	Rodney Rogers	.10
55	Dikembe Mutombo	.20
56	Tracy McGrady	.75
57	Walt Williams	.10
58	Walter McCarty	.10
59	Detlef Schrempf	.10
60	Ervin Johnson	.10
61	Michael Smith	.10
62	Clifford Robinson	.10
63	Brian Williams	.10
64	Shandon Anderson	.10
65	P.J. Brown	.10
66	Scottie Pippen	.75
67	Anthony Peeler	.10
68	Tony Delk	.10
69	David Wesley	.10
70	John Starks	.10
71	Nick Van Exel	.20
72	Kerry Kittles	.20
73	Tony Battie	.20
74	Lamond Murray	.10
75	Anfernee Hardaway	1.00
76	Jalen Rose	.10
77	Derek Anderson	.30
78	Avery Johnson	.10
79	Michael Stewart	.10
80	Brian Shaw	.10
81	Chauncey Billups	.30
82	Kenny Anderson	.10
83	Bryon Russell	.10
84	Jason Kidd	.40
85	Tyrone Hill	.10
86	Jim McIlvaine	.10
87	Brian Grant	.10
88	Bryant Stith	.10
89	Brent Price	.10
90	John Wallace	.10
91	Dennis Rodman	1.00
92	Alonzo Mourning	.20
93	Bimbo Coles	.10
94	Chris Anstey	.10
95	Lindsey Hunter	.10
96	Ed Gray	.10
97	Chris Mills	.10
98	Rick Fox	.10
99	Lorenzen Wright	.10
100	Kevin Garnett	1.50
101	Shawn Kemp	.50
102	Mark Jackson	.10
103	Sam Cassell	.10
104	Monty Williams	.10
105	Ron Mercer	1.00
106	Bryant Reeves	.10
107	Tracy Murray	.10
108	Ray Allen	.25
109	Maurice Taylor	.25
110	Jerome Williams	.10
111	Horace Grant	.10
112	Tariq Abdul-Wahad	.10
113	Travis Knight	.10
114	Kendall Gill	.10
115	Aaron McKie	.10
116	Dean Garrett	.10
117	Jeff Hornacek	.10
118	Todd Fuller	.10
119	Arvydas Sabonis	.10
120	Voshon Lenard	.10
121	Steve Nash	.10
122	Cedric Henderson	.10
123	Rodrick Rhodes	.10
124	Mookie Blaylock	.10
125	Hersey Hawkins	.10
126	Doug Christie	.10
127	Eric Piatkowski	.10
128	Sean Elliott	.10
129	Anthony Mason	.10
130	Allan Houston	.10
131	Antonio Davis	.10
132	Hubert Davis	.10
133	Rod Strickland	.10
134	Jason Kidd	.20
135	Mark Jackson	.10
136	Marcus Camby	.10
137	Dikembe Mutombo	.10
138	Shawn Bradley	.10
139	Dennis Rodman	.50
140	Jayson Williams	.10
141	Tim Duncan	.75
142	Michael Jordan	1.50
143	Shaquille O'Neal	.50
144	Karl Malone	.10
145	Mookie Blaylock	.10
146	Brevin Knight	.10
147	Doug Christie	.10
148	Checklist	.10
149	Checklist	.10
150	Checklist	.10

1998-99 Fleer Vintage 61

Vintage 61 paralleled the first 147 cards (checklists not included) on 1961-62 Fleer card designs. These were exclusive to hobby packs and seeded one per hobby pack. Rarer Classic 61 versions exist and are sequentially numbered to 61.

	MT
Vintage 61 Cards:	2x-4x
Inserted 1:2	

1998-99 Fleer Classic 61

	MT
Classic 61 Cards:	100x-200x
Production 61 Sets	

1998-99 Fleer Electrifying

This 10-card set features players over a gold prismatic foil background with embossing. These are numbered with an "E" suffix and inserted one per 72 Series I packs.

		MT
Complete Set (10):		200.00
Common Player:		7.00
Inserted 1:72		
1	Kobe Bryant	45.00
2	Kevin Garnett	30.00
3	Anfernee Hardaway	20.00
4	Grant Hill	30.00
5	Allen Iverson	20.00
6	Michael Jordan	60.00
7	Shawn Kemp	8.00
8	Stephon Marbury	20.00
9	Gary Payton	7.00
10	Dennis Rodman	20.00

1998-99 Fleer Great Expectations

Great Expectations was a 10-card insert that featured top players on a leather-like embossed card printed with team colors. These were numbered with a "GE" suffix and inserted one per 20 Series I packs.

		MT
Complete Set (10):		45.00
Common Player:		1.50
Inserted 1:20		
1	Shareef Abdur-Rahim	4.00
2	Ray Allen	1.50
3	Kobe Bryant	12.00
4	Tim Duncan	10.00
5	Kevin Garnett	10.00
6	Grant Hill	10.00
7	Allen Iverson	5.00
8	Stephon Marbury	6.00
9	Keith Van Horn	4.00
10	Antoine Walker	3.00

1998-99 Fleer Lucky 13

Lucky 13 was a draft redemption set that consisted of 13 different cards with a single digit 1-13. Each individual card was redeemable for the corresponding 1998 draft pick. These were seeded one per 96 Series I packs.

Complete Set (13):		800.00
Common Player:		5.00
Inserted 1:96		
1	Michael Olowokandi	15.00
2	Mike Bibby	25.00
3	Raef Lafrentz	20.00
4	Antawn Jamison	125.00
5	Vince Carter	600.00
6	Robert Traylor	10.00
7	Jason Williams	50.00
8	Larry Hughes	60.00
9	Dirk Nowitzki	125.00
10	Paul Pierce	60.00
11	Bonzi Wells	60.00
12	Michael Doleac	10.00
13	Keon Clark	10.00

1998-99 Fleer Playmakers Theatre

This insert included 15 players on gold holofoil stock with sculpted, debossed curtain-like backgrounds. The cards were numbered with a "PT" suffix, sequentially numbered to 100 on the back and only in Series I.

		MT
Complete Set (15):		2000.
Common Player:		25.00
Production 100 Sets		
1	Shareef Abdur-Rahim	75.00
2	Ray Allen	25.00
3	Kobe Bryant	250.00
4	Tim Duncan	200.00
5	Kevin Garnett	200.00
6	Anfernee Hardaway	120.00
7	Grant Hill	200.00
8	Allen Iverson	100.00
9	Michael Jordan	500.00
10	Karl Malone	50.00
11	Stephon Marbury	120.00
12	Shaquille O'Neal	120.00
13	Scottie Pippen	100.00
14	Keith Van Horn	75.00
15	Antoine Walker	60.00

1998-99 Fleer Rookie Rewind

Rookie Rewind featured the 1997-98 NBA All-Rookie Team on silver holofoil with accents and embossing. Cards are numbered with a "RR" suffix and inserted one per 36 Series I packs.

		MT
Complete Set (10):		45.00
Common Player:		1.50
Inserted 1:36		
1	Derek Anderson	3.00
2	Tim Duncan	15.00
3	Cedric Henderson	1.50
4	Zydrunas Ilgauskas	1.50
5	Bobby Jackson	2.00
6	Brevin Knight	3.00
7	Ron Mercer	10.00
8	Maurice Taylor	3.00
9	Tim Thomas	7.00
10	Keith Van Horn	6.00

1998-99 Fleer Timeless Memories

Timeless Memories was a 10-card insert featuring a large clock in the background with the player's face inside it. There is also an action shot of the player in the foreground. These inserts are numbered with a "TM" suffix and inserted one per 12 Series I packs.

		MT
Complete Set (10):		15.00
Common Player:		.75
Inserted 1:12		
1	Shareef Abdur-Rahim	2.00
2	Ray Allen	.75
3	Vin Baker	1.25
4	Anfernee Hardaway	3.00
5	Tim Hardaway	1.25
6	Shaquille O'Neal	3.00
7	Scottie Pippen	2.00
8	David Robinson	1.25
9	Dennis Rodman	3.00
10	Antoine Walker	1.50

1998-99 Fleer Brilliants

Fleer Brilliants contained 125 cards, included a 25-card Rookies subset that was seeded 1:2 packs. Brilliants cards featured a radial-etched mirror foil laminate background and were printed on 24-point styrene card stock. Three parallel versions of each card were also printed. First, Brilliant Blue veterans (1-100) were seeded 1:3 packs, with Rookies every six packs. Next, all 125 cards were printed in Brilliant Gold versions numbered to 99 sets. Third, all 125 cards had 24-karat Gold versions numbered to 24 sets and featuring an actual 24-karat gold logo. Three insert sets were included in Brilliants: Illuminators, Shining Stars and Pulsars, which was a parallel to Shining Stars.

		MT
Complete Set (125):		100.00
Common Player:		.15
Minor Stars:		.30
Common Rookie:		1.50
Inserted 1:2		
Pack (5):		5.50
Wax Box (24):		110.00
1	Tim Duncan	6.00
2	Dikembe Mutombo	.30
3	Steve Nash	.15
4	Charles Barkley	1.00
5	Eddie Jones	1.50
6	Ray Allen	.50
7	Stephon Marbury	4.00
8	Anfernee Hardaway	4.00
9	Gary Payton	1.00
10	Ron Mercer	4.00
11	Nick Van Exel	.30
12	Brent Barry	.15
13	Allan Houston	.30
14	Avery Johnson	.15
15	Shareef Abdur-Rahim	2.00
16	Rod Strickland	.30
17	Vin Baker	1.50
18	Patrick Ewing	.50
19	Maurice Taylor	.50
20	Shawn Kemp	1.00
21	Michael Finley	.50
22	Reggie Miller	.30
23	Joe Smith	.50
24	Toni Kukoc	.30
25	Blue Edwards	.15
26	Joe Dumars	.30
27	Tom Gugliotta	.30
28	Terrell Brandon	.30
29	Erick Dampier	.15
30	Antonio McDyess	.75
31	Donyell Marshall	.15
32	Jeff Hornacek	.15
33	David Wesley	.15
34	Derek Anderson	.50
35	Ron Harper	.15
36	John Starks	.15
37	Kenny Anderson	.30
38	Anthony Mason	.15
39	Brevin Knight	.50
40	Antoine Walker	2.00
41	Mookie Blaylock	.30
42	LaPhonso Ellis	.30
43	Tim Hardaway	.50
44	Jim Jackson	.15
45	Matt Maloney	.15
46	Lamond Murray	.15
47	Voshon Lenard	.15
48	Isaiah Rider	.30
49	Tracy Murray	.15
50	Grant Hill	6.00
51	Vlade Divac	.30
52	Glenn Robinson	.30
53	Tony Battie	.30
54	Bobby Jackson	.15
55	Jayson Williams	.30
56	Doug Christie	.15
57	Glen Rice	.30
58	Tim Thomas	2.00
59	Lindsey Hunter	.15
60	Scottie Pippen	3.00
61	Marcus Camby	.50
62	Clifford Robinson	.15
63	John Wallace	.30
64	Larry Johnson	.30
65	Bryon Russell	.15
66	Isaac Austin	.15
67	Sam Cassell	.30
68	Allen Iverson	4.00
69	Chauncey Billups	.50
70	Kobe Bryant	8.00
71	Kevin Willis	.15
72	Jason Kidd	2.00
73	Chris Webber	2.00
74	Rasheed Wallace	.15
75	Karl Malone	1.00
76	Shawn Bradley	.15
77	Kerry Kittles	.30
78	Mitch Richmond	.30
79	Antonio Daniels	.15
80	Kevin Garnett	6.00
81	Nick Anderson	.15
82	David Robinson	1.00
83	Jamal Mashburn	.30
84	Rodney Rogers	.15
85	Michael Stewart	.15
86	Rik Smits	.30
87	Billy Owens	.15
88	Damon Stoudamire	.75
89	Theo Ratliff	.30
90	Keith Van Horn	2.00
91	Hakeem Olajuwon	1.50
92	Alonzo Mourning	.50
93	Steve Smith	.30
94	Mark Jackson	.15
95	Cedric Ceballos	.15
96	Bryant Reeves	.30
97	Juwan Howard	.30
98	Detlef Schrempf	.15
99	John Stockton	.30
100	Shaquille O'Neal	4.00
101	*Michael Olowokandi*	2.00
102	*Mike Bibby*	4.00
103	*Raef LaFrentz*	2.50
104	*Antawn Jamison*	8.00
105	*Vince Carter*	30.00
106	*Robert Traylor*	2.00
107	*Jason Williams*	6.00
108	*Larry Hughes*	8.00
109	*Dirk Nowitzki*	8.00
110	*Paul Pierce*	6.00
111	*Bonzi Wells*	6.00
112	*Michael Doleac*	1.50
113	*Keon Clark*	2.00
114	*Michael Dickerson*	3.00
115	*Matt Harpring*	2.00
116	*Bryce Drew*	1.50
117	*Pat Garrity*	2.00
118	*Roshown McLeod*	1.50
119	*Ricky Davis*	3.00
120	*Rashard Lewis*	6.00
121	*Tyronn Lue*	1.50
122	*Al Harrington*	3.00
123	*Corey Benjamin*	2.00
124	*Felipe Lopez*	3.00
125	*Korleone Young*	2.00

1998-99 Fleer Brilliants 24-Karat Gold

Each card in the 125-card Fleer Brilliants set was reprinted in a 24-Karat Gold version. Cards featured gold foil fronts and were sequentially numbered to just 24 sets.

	MT
24-Karat Gold Cards:	40x-80x
24-Karat Gold Rookies:	5x-10x
Production 24 Sets	

1998-99 Fleer Brilliants Blue

All 125 cards in Fleer Brilliants were reprinted in this Brilliant Blue parallel. Cards featured blue foil on the front and were numbered on the back with a "B" suffix. Brilliant Blue veterans (1-100) were inserted 1:3 packs, while Rookies (101-125) were inserted 1:6 packs.

	MT
Complete Set (125):	300.00
Blue Veterans:	2x-3x
Inserted 1:3	
Blue Rookies:	1.5x
Inserted 1:6	

1998-99 Fleer Brilliants Gold

All 125 cards in Fleer Brilliants were reprinted in this Brilliant Gold parallel, which featured gold foil on the front. Cards were sequentially numbered to 99 sets and numbered with a "G" suffix on the back.

	MT
Brilliant Gold Cards:	20x-40x
Brilliant Gold Rookies:	3x-5x
Production 99 Sets	

1998-99 Fleer Brilliants Illuminators

Illuminators was a 15-card insert set that was seeded 1:10 packs. This insert featured 15 top rookies on a starburst background, with the insert name printed in larger letters across the top and the player's name across the bottom. Cards were numbered with an "I" suffix.

		MT
Complete Set (15):		80.00
Common Player:		1.50
Minor Stars:		3.00
Inserted 1:10		
1	Michael Olowokandi	8.00
2	Mike Bibby	10.00
3	Antawn Jamison	8.00
4	Vince Carter	15.00
5	Robert Traylor	6.00
6	Larry Hughes	6.00
7	Paul Pierce	12.00
8	Raef LaFrentz	6.00
9	Dirk Nowitzki	4.00
10	Corey Benjamin	1.50
11	Michael Dickerson	5.00
12	Roshown McLeod	3.00
13	Ricky Davis	3.00
14	Tyronn Lue	3.00
15	Al Harrington	3.00

1998-99 Fleer Brilliants Shining Stars

Shining Stars was a 15-card insert that featured top NBA players on a mirror-foil background. The insert name ran up the left side, while backs were numbered with an "SS" suffix. Cards from this insert were seeded 1:20 packs.

		MT
Complete Set (15):		150.00
Common Player:		8.00
Inserted 1:20		
Pulsar Cards:		5x-10x
Inserted 1:400		
1	Tim Thomas	8.00
2	Antoine Walker	6.00
3	Tim Duncan	20.00
4	Keith Van Horn	6.00
5	Grant Hill	20.00
6	Shaquille O'Neal	12.00
7	Kevin Garnett	20.00
8	Allen Iverson	12.00
9	Shareef Abdur-Rahim	8.00
10	Shawn Kemp	4.00
11	Anfernee Hardaway	12.00
12	Scottie Pippen	10.00
13	Stephon Marbury	12.00
14	Kobe Bryant	25.00
15	Ron Mercer	12.00

Post-1980 cards in Near Mint condition will generally sell for about 75% of the quoted Mint value. Excellent-condition cards bring no more than 40%.

1998-99 Fleer Brilliants Shining Stars Pulsars

Pulsars reprinted the 15-card Shining Stars insert, but added stars and a holographic finish to the background. These were inserted 1:400 packs.

MT
Complete Set (15): 800.00
Pulsar Cards: 3x-6x
Inserted 1:400
1 Tim Thomas 8.00
2 Antoine Walker 6.00
3 Tim Duncan 20.00
4 Keith Van Horn 10.00
5 Grant Hill 20.00
6 Shaquille O'Neal 12.00
7 Kevin Garnett 20.00
8 Allen Iverson 12.00
9 Shareef Abdur-Rahim 8.00
10 Shawn Kemp 4.00
11 Anfernee Hardaway 12.00
12 Scottie Pippen 10.00
13 Stephon Marbury 12.00
14 Kobe Bryant 25.00
15 Ron Mercer 12.00

1999 Fleer Dunkography

This oversized card featured Fleer spokesmen Vince Carter and Lamar Odom dunking against a sky background. The cards were sequentially numbered to 3,000, unnumbered on the back and were sent to hobby dealers.

MT
Common Player: 30.00
Vince Carter 30.00
Lamar Odom 30.00

1999-00 Fleer Tradition

Tradition contained 200 veterans and 20 rookies from the 1999 NBA Draft. Players from the Eastern Conference had blue foil stamping, while players from the Western Conference had red foil stamping and rookies had gold foil stamping. The set was paralleled twice - retail-only Roundball Collection and hobby-only Supreme Court Collection. Inserts included: Rookie Sensations, Masters of the Hardwood, Net Effect, Game Breakers and Fresh Ink.

MT
Complete Set (220): 40.00
Common Player: .10
Minor Stars: .20
Pack (10): 2.50
Wax Box (36): 40.00
1 Vince Carter 2.00
2 Kobe Bryant 2.00
3 Keith Van Horn .60
4 Tim Duncan 1.50
5 Grant Hill 1.50
6 Kevin Garnett 1.50
7 Anfernee Hardaway 1.00
8 Jason Williams 1.00
9 Paul Pierce .75
10 Mookie Blaylock .10
11 Shawn Bradley .10
12 Kenny Anderson .20
13 Chauncey Billups .20
14 Elden Campbell .10
15 Jason Caffey .10
16 Brent Barry .10
17 Charles Barkley .40
18 Derek Anderson .30
19 Darrick Martin .10
20 Bison Dele .10
21 Rick Fox .10
22 Antonio Davis .10
23 Terrell Brandon .20
24 P.J. Brown .10
25 Toby Bailey .20
26 Ray Allen .25
27 Brian Grant .20
28 Scott Burrell .10
29 Tariq Abdul-Wahad .10
30 Marcus Camby .25
31 John Stockton .20
32 Nick Anderson .20
33 Antonio Daniels .20
34 Matt Geiger .10
35 Vin Baker .20
36 Dee Brown .10
37 Shandon Anderson .10
38 Calbert Cheaney .10
39 Shareef Abdur-Rahim .50
40 LaPhonso Ellis .20
41 Cedric Ceballos .10
42 Tony Battie .20
43 Keon Clark .20
44 Derrick Coleman .20
45 Erick Dampier .10
46 Corey Benjamin .20
47 Michael Dickerson .30
48 Cedric Henderson .10
49 Lamond Murray .10
50 Joe Dumars .20
51 Shaquille O'Neal 1.00
52 Dale Davis .10
53 Dean Garrett .10
54 Tim Hardaway .30
55 Gerald Brown .10
56 Sam Cassell .20
57 Jim Jackson .10
58 Kendall Gill .10
59 Eric Williams .10
60 Chris Childs .10
61 Vlade Divac .20
62 Darrell Armstrong .20
63 Mario Elie .10
64 Tyrone Hill .10
65 Dale Ellis .10
66 Doug Christie .10
67 Howard Eisley .10
68 Juwan Howard .20
69 Mike Bibby .50
70 Alan Henderson .10
71 Michael Finley .25
72 Dana Barros .10
73 Danny Fortson .10
74 Ricky Davis .20
75 Adonal Foyle .10
76 Cory Carr .20
77 Bryce Drew .20
78 Shawn Kemp .30
79 Tyrone Nesby .20
80 Lindsey Hunter .10
81 Ruben Patterson .20
82 Al Harrington .30
83 Bobby Jackson .10
84 Dan Majerle .10
85 Rex Chapman .10
86 Dell Curry .10
87 Walt Williams .10
88 Kerry Kittles .10
89 Isaiah Rider .20
90 Patrick Ewing .20
91 Lawrence Funderburke .10
92 Isaac Austin .10
93 Sean Elliott .10
94 Larry Hughes .40
95 Hersey Hawkins .10
96 Tracy McGrady .60
97 Jeff Hornacek .10
98 Randell Jackson .10
99 J.R. Henderson .10
100 Roshown McLeod .20
101 Steve Nash .10
102 Ron Mercer .50
103 Raef LaFrentz .40
104 Eddie Jones .30
105 Antawn Jamison .60
106 Kornel David .10
107 Othella Harrington .10
108 Brevin Knight .10
109 Michael Olowokandi .40
110 Christian Laettner .10
111 J.R. Reid .10
112 Reggie Miller .20
113 Andrae Patterson .10
114 Jamal Mashburn .20
115 Glenn Robinson .20
116 Pat Garrity .20
117 Stephon Marbury 1.00
118 Arvydas Sabonis .10
119 Allan Houston .20
120 Predrag Stojakovic .10
121 Michael Doleac .20
122 Avery Johnson .10
123 Allen Iverson 1.50
124 Rashard Lewis .25
125 Charles Oakley .10
126 Karl Malone .40
127 Tracy Murray .10
128 Felipe Lopez .30
129 Dikembe Mutombo .20
130 Dirk Nowitzki .30
131 Vitaly Potapenko .10
132 Antonio McDyess .40
133 Anthony Mason .20
134 Donyell Marshall .10
135 Ron Harper .10
136 Cuttino Mobley .20
137 Wesley Person .10
138 Rodney Rogers .10
139 Jerry Stackhouse .20
140 Glen Rice .20
141 Chris Mullin .20
142 Anthony Peeler .10
143 Alonzo Mourning .30
144 Tom Gugliotta .20
145 Tim Thomas .50
146 Damon Stoudamire .30
147 Jason Williams .20
148 Larry Johnson .20
149 Chris Webber .60
150 Matt Harpring .20
151 David Robinson .40
152 George Lynch .10
153 Gary Payton .40
154 John Wallace .10
155 Greg Ostertag .10
156 Mitch Richmond .20
157 Cherokee Parks .10
158 Steve Smith .20
159 Gary Trent .20
160 Antoine Walker .60
161 Johnny Taylor .10
162 Brad Miller .10
163 Chris Mills .10
164 Charles R. Jones .10
165 Hakeem Olajuwon .40
166 Bob Sura .10
167 Brian Skinner .20
168 Korleone Young .20
169 Dennis Rodman .50
170 Jalen Rose .20
171 Joe Smith .20
172 Clarence Weatherspoon .10
173 Jason Kidd .60
174 Robert Traylor .40
175 Rasheed Wallace .20
176 Latrell Sprewell .20
177 Corliss Williamson .10
178 Charles Outlaw .10
179 Malik Rose .10
180 Nazr Mohammed .20
181 Olden Polynice .10
182 Kevin Willis .10
183 Bryon Russell .10
184 Bryant Reeves .20
185 Rod Strickland .20
186 Samaki Walker .10
187 Nick Van Exel .20
188 David Wesley .10
189 John Starks .10
190 Toni Kukoc .30
191 Scottie Pippen .60
192 Zydrunas Ilgauskas .20
193 Maurice Taylor .30
194 Rik Smits .10
195 Clifford Robinson .10
196 Bonzi Wells .20
197 Charlie Ward .10
198 Detlef Schrempf .20
199 Theo Ratliff .20
200 Rodrick Rhodes .10
201 *Ron Artest* 1.00
202 *William Avery* .50
203 *Elton Brand* 2.00
204 *Baron Davis* 1.50
205 *Jumanie Jones* .40
206 *Andre Miller* 1.50
207 *Lee Nailon* .40
208 *James Posey* .75
209 *Jason Terry* .75
210 *Kenny Thomas* .50
211 *Steve Francis* 5.00
212 *Wally Szczerbiak* 1.00
213 *Richard Hamilton* 1.00
214 *Jonathan Bender* 2.00
215 *Shawn Marion* 2.00
216 *Aleksandar Radojevic* .25
217 *Tim James* .40
218 *Trajan Langdon* .60
219 *Lamar Odom* 3.00
220 *Corey Meggette* 1.50

1999-00 Fleer Tradition Roundball Collection

Roundball Collection was a 220-card parallel set to Fleer Tradition. The cards were identified by silver foil stamping on the front, and they were seeded one per retail pack.

MT
Complete Set (220): 75.00
Roundball Cards: 2x-4x
Roundball Rookies: 1x-2x
Inserted 1:1 Retail

1999-00 Fleer Tradition Supreme Court Collection

Supreme Court Collection was a hobby-exclusive parallel set to all 220 cards in Fleer Tradition. The cards were identified by green foil stamping on the front and were sequentially numbered to 20 sets.

MT
Supreme Court Cards: 30x-60x
Supreme Court Rookies: 12x-24x
Production 20 Hobby Sets

1999-00 Fleer Tradition Fresh Ink

Fresh Ink featured autographs from 15 different players from the 1998 NBA Draft. These cards featured a color shot of the player, with a white space across the middle for the player's signature. Fresh Ink inserts were unnumbered on the back and hand-numbered to 400 sets.

MT
Common Player: 15.00
Production 400 Sets
Corey Benjamin 20.00
Mike Bibby 60.00
Michael Dickerson 40.00
Michael Doleac 30.00
Byrce Drew 25.00
Pat Garrity 25.00
Matt Harpring 35.00
Larry Hughes 60.00
Antawn Jamison 80.00
Raef LaFrentz 50.00
Felipe Lopez 35.00
Jelani McCoy 20.00
Brad Miller 15.00
Michael Olowokandi 50.00
Robert Traylor 50.00

1999-00 Fleer Tradition Game Breakers

Game Breakers featured 15 top players on a die-cut design. Cards were numbered with a "GB" suffix on the back and were sequentially numbered to just 100 sets.

MT
Complete Set (15): 2000.
Common Player: 75.00
Production 100 Sets
1 Shareef Abdur-Rahim 75.00
2 Kobe Bryant 250.00
3 Vince Carter 200.00
4 Tim Duncan 200.00
5 Kevin Garnett 200.00
6 Anfernee Hardaway 150.00
7 Grant Hill 200.00
8 Allen Iverson 175.00
9 Shawn Kemp 40.00
10 Stephon Marbury 125.00
11 Ron Mercer 75.00
12 Shaquille O'Neal 150.00
13 Keith Van Horn 40.00
14 Antoine Walker 60.00
15 Jason Williams 150.00

1999-00 Fleer Tradition Masters of the Hardwood

Masters of the Hardwood displayed 15 top players against a simulated wood background. Cards were numbered with an "MH" suffix and inserted 1:18 packs.

MT
Complete Set (15): 55.00
Common Player: 2.00
Inserted 1:18
1 Shareef Abdur-Rahim 3.00
2 Mike Bibby 2.00
3 Kobe Bryant 10.00
4 Tim Duncan 8.00
5 Kevin Garnett 8.00
6 Anfernee Hardaway 5.00
7 Grant Hill 8.00
8 Allen Iverson 6.00
9 Karl Malone 2.00
10 Stephon Marbury 4.00
11 Tracy McGrady 3.00
12 Ron Mercer 3.00
13 Scottie Pippen 3.00
14 Antoine Walker 2.00
15 Jason Williams 5.00

1999-00 Fleer Tradition Net Effect

This 10-card insert featured players on a die-cut design printed on opaque plastic. Cards were numbered with an "NE" suffix on the back and inserted 1:96 packs.

MT
Complete Set (10): 225.00
Common Player: 15.00
Inserted 1:96
1 Kobe Bryant 40.00
2 Vince Carter 30.00
3 Tim Duncan 30.00
4 Kevin Garnett 30.00
5 Grant Hill 30.00
6 Allen Iverson 25.00
7 Shaquille O'Neal 20.00
8 Paul Pierce 20.00
9 Scottie Pippen 15.00
10 Keith Van Horn 10.00

1999-00 Fleer Tradition Rookie Sensations

Rookie Sensations highlighted 20 rookies from the 1998-99 season over a white and gold foil background. This insert was numbered with an "RS" suffix and inserted 1:6 packs.

MT
Complete Set (20): 20.00
Common Player: .50
Inserted 1:6
1 Mike Bibby 1.50
2 Vince Carter 5.00
3 Ricky Davis .75
4 Michael Dickerson .75
5 Michael Doleac .50
6 Matt Harpring .75
7 Larry Hughes 1.25
8 Randell Jackson .50
9 Antawn Jamison 2.00
10 Raef LaFrentz 1.00
11 Felipe Lopez .75
12 Roshown McLeod .50
13 Brad Miller .50
14 Cuttino Mobley .60
15 Dirk Nowitzki 1.00
16 Michael Olowokandi 1.00
17 Paul Pierce 3.00
18 Predrag Stojakovic .50
19 Robert Traylor 1.00
20 Jason Williams 3.00

1999-00 Fleer Focus

Focus debuted in basketball with a 150 card set that included 100 veterans and 50 rookies. The rookies were sequentially numbered to 3,999, with the first 999 featuring a portrait shot and the last 3,000 featuring an action shot. The cards pictured a color or action shot surrounded surrounded by a white border. The set was paralleled twice - first in a green foil Masterpiece Mania parallel (300 numbered sets) and in a Masterpiece (one of one) set. Inserts included: Soar Subjects, Soar Subjects Vivid, Ray of Light, Focus Pocus, Fresh Ink and Feel the Game. The Toni Kukoc card was given out on Toni Kukoc Night and is not part of the regular-issue set.

Complete Set (150): 275.00
Common Player: .20
Minor Stars: .40
Common Rookies (101-150): 2.00
Production 3,999 Sets
Rookie Portrait Shot Cards: 2x
Portrait RC - First 999 of 3,999
Action RC - Last 3,000 of 3,999
Pack (8): 4.00
Wax Box (24): 50.00
1 Anfernee Hardaway 2.00
2 Derek Anderson .20
3 Jayson Williams .20
4 Ron Mercer .75
5 Jerry Stackhouse .50
6 Tariq Abdul-Wahad .20
7 Sean Elliott .20
8 Lindsey Hunter .20
9 Larry Johnson .40
10 Steve Smith .40
11 Raef LaFrentz .60
12 Jalen Rose .40
13 Stephon Marbury 1.00
14 Detlef Schrempf .20
15 Rod Strickland .40
16 Paul Pierce 1.50
17 Maurice Taylor .20
18 Allen Iverson 2.00
19 Mitch Richmond .40
20 Gary Trent .20
21 Reggie Miller .40
22 Kerry Kittles .20
23 Rasheed Wallace .40
24 Steve Nash .20
25 Scottie Pippen 1.50
26 Joe Smith .20
27 Jason Williams 2.00
28 Michael Finley .40
29 Hakeem Olajuwon .75
30 Kevin Garnett 3.00
31 Darrell Armstrong .20
32 David Robinson .75
33 Anthony Mason .20
34 Jamal Mashburn .40
35 Gary Payton .75
36 Byron Russell .20
37 Cedric Ceballos .20
38 Michael Dickerson .40
39 Robert Traylor .50
40 Vin Baker .40
41 Shawn Kemp .40
42 Charles Barkley .75
43 Glenn Robinson .40
44 Vince Carter 4.00
45 Zydrunas Ilgauskas .20
46 Sam Cassell .40
47 Tracy McGrady 1.50
48 Chris Mills .20
49 Antawn Jamison 1.00
50 Nick Anderson .20
51 Avery Johnson .20
52 Brent Barry .20
53 Alonzo Mourning .50
54 Karl Malone .75
55 Toni Kukoc .50
56 Ray Allen .50
57 Charles Oakley .20
58 Cuttino Mobley .40
59 Kenny Anderson .40
60 Tom Gugliotta .40
61 Antoine Walker .60
62 Kobe Bryant 4.00
63 Larry Hughes .75
64 Vlade Divac .20
65 Juwan Howard .40
66 Isaiah Rider .40
67 Antonio McDyess .50
68 Rik Smits .20
69 Keith Van Horn .60
70 Doug Christie .20
71 Elden Campbell .20
72 Shaquille O'Neal 2.00
73 Matt Geiger .20
74 Chris Webber 1.50
75 Troy Hudson .20
76 Eddie Jones .75
77 Tim Hardaway .60
78 Hersey Hawkins .20
79 Shareef Abdur-Rahim 1.00
80 Christian Laettner .20
81 Latrell Sprewell .50
82 Damon Stoudamire .50
83 Jason Caffey .20
84 Michael Olowokandi .60
85 Horace Grant .20
86 Grant Hill 3.00
87 Patrick Ewing .40
88 Clifford Robinson .20
89 Ricky Davis .40
90 Glen Rice .40
91 Matt Harpring .40
92 Mike Bibby .60
93 Dikembe Mutombo .40
94 Chris Mullin .20
95 Marcus Camby .40
96 Jason Kidd 1.50
97 John Starks .20
98 Terrell Brandon .40
99 Tim Duncan 3.00
100 John Stockton .40
101 *Ron Artest* 6.00
102 *William Avery* 3.00
103 *Jonathan Bender* 20.00
104 *Cal Bowdler* 2.00
105 *Elton Brand* 20.00
106 *Vonteego Cummings* 4.00
107 *Baron Davis* 12.00
108 *Jeff Foster* 2.00
109 *Steve Francis* 40.00
110 *Devean George* 5.00
111 *Dion Glover* 4.00
112 *Richard Hamilton* 10.00
113 *Tim James* 2.50
114 *Trajan Langdon* 5.00
115 *Quincy Lewis* 3.00
116 *Corey Maggette* 12.00
117 *Shawn Marion* 15.00
118 *Andre Miller* 12.00
119 *Lamar Odom* 25.00
120 *Scott Padgett* 2.00
121 *James Posey* 5.00
122 *Aleksandar Radojevic* 2.00
123 *Wally Szczerbiak* 10.00
124 *Jason Terry* 6.00
125 *Kenny Thomas* 3.00
126 *Jumanie Jones* 2.50
127 *Rick Hughes* 2.00
128 *John Celestand* 2.50
129 *Adrian Griffin* 3.00
130 *Michael Ruffin* 2.00
131 *Chris Herren* 3.00
132 *Evan Eschmeyer* 2.50
133 *Tim Young* 2.00
134 *Obinna Ekezie* 2.00
135 *Laron Profit* 3.00
136 *A.J. Bramlett* 2.00
137 *Eddie Robinson* 5.00
138 *Ryan Bowen* 2.00
139 *Chucky Atkins* 4.00
140 *Ryan Robertson* 2.00
141 *Derrick Dial* 2.00
142 *Todd MacCulloch* 2.50
143 *DeMarco Johnson* 2.00
144 *Anthony Carter* 5.00
145 *Lazaro Borrell* 2.50
146 *Rafer Alston* 3.00
147 *Nikita Morgunov* 2.00
148 *Rodney Buford* 3.00
149 *Milt Palacio* 2.00
150 *Jermaine Jackson* 2.00
NNO Toni Kukoc Night 5.00

1999-00 Fleer Focus Masterpiece Mania

This 150-card parallel set reprinted each card from Focus, but was printed with green foil. The cards used the action shots of the rookies (instead of the posed shot). The cards were numbered with an "R" suffix and sequentially numbered to 300.

MT
Common Player: 2.00
Mania Veterans: 5x-10x
Mania Rookies: 2x
Production 300 Sets
1 Anfernee Hardaway 2.00
2 Derek Anderson .20
3 Jayson Williams .20
4 Ron Mercer .75
5 Jerry Stackhouse .50
6 Tariq Abdul-Wahad .20
7 Sean Elliott .20
8 Lindsey Hunter .20
9 Larry Johnson .40
10 Steve Smith .40
11 Raef LaFrentz .60
12 Jalen Rose .40
13 Stephon Marbury 1.00
14 Detlef Schrempf .20
15 Rod Strickland .40
16 Paul Pierce 1.50
17 Maurice Taylor .20
18 Allen Iverson 2.00
19 Mitch Richmond .40
20 Gary Trent .20
21 Reggie Miller .40
22 Kerry Kittles .20
23 Rasheed Wallace .40
24 Steve Nash .20
25 Scottie Pippen 1.50
26 Joe Smith .20
27 Jason Williams 2.00
28 Michael Finley .40
29 Hakeem Olajuwon .75
30 Kevin Garnett 3.00
31 Darrell Armstrong .20
32 David Robinson .75
33 Anthony Mason .20
34 Jamal Mashburn .40
35 Gary Payton .75
36 Byron Russell .20
37 Cedric Ceballos .20
38 Michael Dickerson .40
39 Robert Traylor .50
40 Vin Baker .40
41 Shawn Kemp .40
42 Charles Barkley .75
43 Glenn Robinson .40
44 Vince Carter 4.00
45 Zydrunas Ilgauskas .20
46 Sam Cassell .40
47 Tracy McGrady 1.50
48 Chris Mills .20
49 Antawn Jamison 1.00

50	Nick Anderson	.20
51	Avery Johnson	.20
52	Brent Barry	.20
53	Alonzo Mourning	.50
54	Karl Malone	.75
55	Toni Kukoc	.50
56	Ray Allen	.50
57	Charles Oakley	.20
58	Cuttino Mobley	.40
59	Kenny Anderson	.40
60	Tom Gugliotta	.40
61	Antoine Walker	.60
62	Kobe Bryant	4.00
63	Larry Hughes	.75
64	Vlade Divac	.20
65	Juwan Howard	.40
66	Isaiah Rider	.40
67	Antonio McDyess	.50
68	Rik Smits	.20
69	Keith Van Horn	.60
70	Doug Christie	.20
71	Elden Campbell	.20
72	Shaquille O'Neal	2.00
73	Matt Geiger	.20
74	Chris Webber	1.50
75	Troy Hudson	.20
76	Eddie Jones	.75
77	Tim Hardaway	.60
78	Hersey Hawkins	.20
79	Shareef Abdur-Rahim	1.00
80	Christian Laettner	.20
81	Latrell Sprewell	.50
82	Damon Stoudamire	.50
83	Jason Caffey	.20
84	Michael Olowokandi	.60
85	Horace Grant	.20
86	Grant Hill	3.00
87	Patrick Ewing	.40
88	Clifford Robinson	.20
89	Ricky Davis	.40
90	Glen Rice	.40
91	Matt Harpring	.40
92	Mike Bibby	.60
93	Dikembe Mutombo	.40
94	Chris Mullin	.20
95	Marcus Camby	.40
96	Jason Kidd	1.50
97	John Starks	.20
98	Terrell Brandon	.40
99	Tim Duncan	3.00
100	John Stockton	.40
101	*Ron Artest*	10.00
102	*William Avery*	5.00
103	*Jonathan Bender*	15.00
104	*Cal Bowdler*	2.00
105	*Elton Brand*	30.00
106	*Vonteego Cummings*	4.00
107	*Baron Davis*	12.00
108	*Jeff Foster*	2.00
109	*Steve Francis*	35.00
110	*Devean George*	3.00
111	*Dion Glover*	2.50
112	*Richard Hamilton*	10.00
113	*Tim James*	2.50
114	*Trajan Langdon*	5.00
115	*Quincy Lewis*	4.00
116	*Corey Maggette*	12.00
117	*Shawn Marion*	10.00
118	*Andre Miller*	10.00
119	*Lamar Odom*	35.00
120	*Scott Padgett*	3.00
121	*James Posey*	5.00
122	*Aleksandar Radojevic*	2.00
123	*Wally Szczerbiak*	15.00
124	*Jason Terry*	6.00
125	*Kenny Thomas*	3.00
126	*Jumaine Jones*	2.50
127	*Rick Hughes*	2.00
128	*John Celestand*	2.50
129	*Adrian Griffin*	5.00
130	*Michael Ruffin*	2.50
131	*Chris Herren*	2.50
132	*Evan Eschmeyer*	2.50
133	*Tim Young*	2.00
134	*Obinna Ekezie*	2.00
135	*Laron Profit*	2.00
136	*A.J. Bramlett*	2.00
137	*Eddie Robinson*	4.00
138	*Ryan Bowen*	2.00
139	*Chucky Atkins*	3.00
140	*Ryan Robertson*	2.00
141	*Derrick Dial*	2.00
142	*Todd MacCulloch*	2.50
143	*DeMarco Johnson*	2.00
144	*Anthony Carter*	3.00
145	*Lazaro Borrell*	2.50
146	*Rafer Alston*	2.50
147	*Nikita Morgunov*	2.00
148	*Rodney Buford*	2.50
149	*Milt Palacio*	2.00
150	*Jermaine Jackson*	2.00

1999-00 Fleer Focus Feel The Game

This 10-card insert set featured swatches of player-worn jersey embedded in the card. Feel the Game inserts were vertical in format and inserted 1:288 packs.

		MT
Complete Set (10):		900.00
Common Player:		30.00
Inserted 1:288		
	Vin Baker	60.00
	Vince Carter	300.00
	Kevin Garnett	150.00
	Tim Hardaway	60.00
	Grant Hill	150.00
	Paul Pierce	100.00
	Bryant Reeves	30.00
	Bryon Russell	50.00
	Keith Van Horn	35.00
	Jayson Williams	50.00

1999-00 Fleer Focus Focus Pocus

This 10-card insert set featured top players on silver and patterned holofoil. Focus Pocus cards were numbered with an "FP" suffix and seeded 1:20 packs.

		MT
Complete Set (10):		50.00
Common Player:		2.00
Inserted 1:20		
FP1	Vince Carter	10.00
FP2	Tim Duncan	8.00
FP3	Shaquille O'Neal	5.00
FP4	Paul Pierce	2.00
FP5	Kobe Bryant	10.00
FP6	Kevin Garnett	8.00
FP7	Keith Van Horn	1.00
FP8	Jason Williams	5.00
FP9	Grant Hill	8.00
FP10	Allen Iverson	5.00

1999-00 Fleer Focus Fresh Ink

		MT
Common Player:		3.00
1	Charles Barkley	125.00
2	Vince Carter	150.00
3	Obinna Ekezie	3.00
4	Jeff Foster	3.00
5	Devean George	8.00
6	Tim Hardaway	12.00
7	Matt Harpring	6.00
8	Al Harrington	15.00
9	Juwan Howard	12.00
10	Eddie Jones	20.00
11	Shawn Kemp	12.00
12	Brevin Knight	8.00
13	Trajan Langdon	10.00
14	Stephon Marbury	30.00
15	Shawn Marion	25.00
16	Tracy McGrady	50.00
17	Roshown McLeod	6.00
18	Brad Miller	3.00
19	Alonzo Mourning	40.00
20	Shaquille O'Neal	200.00
21	Scott Padgett	3.00
22	Michael Ruffin	3.00
23	Damon Stoudamire	12.00
24	Wally Szczerbiak	20.00
25	Jason Terry	10.00
26	Keith Van Horn	20.00
27	Chris Webber	75.00

1999-00 Fleer Focus Ray of Light

This 15-card insert set featured rookies on a horizontal design and a black background. The facsimile signature of the player appears on the right side of the card, while a close-up shot is on the left. Ray of Light cards are numbered with an "RL" suffix and seeded 1:20 packs.

		MT
Complete Set (15):		45.00
Common Player:		.75
Inserted 1:20		
RL1	Andre Miller	3.00
RL2	Baron Davis	4.00
RL3	Corey Maggette	4.00
RL4	Dion Glover	.75
RL5	Elton Brand	8.00
RL6	Jason Terry	2.00
RL7	Jonathan Bender	5.00
RL8	Lamar Odom	10.00
RL9	Richard Hamilton	3.00
RL10	Shawn Marion	3.00
RL11	Steve Francis	10.00
RL12	Tim James	.75
RL13	Trajan Langdon	1.50
RL14	Wally Szczerbiak	5.00
RL15	William Avery	1.50

1999-00 Fleer Focus Soar Subjects

This 15-card insert set featured top players over a multi-colored foil background with silver and holofoil stamps. Soar Subjects are numbered with an "SS" suffix and seeded 1:6 packs.

		MT
Complete Set (15):		30.00
Common Player:		.75
Inserted 1:6		
Vivid Cards:		20x-40x
Production 50 Hobby Sets		
SS1	Allen Iverson	2.50
SS2	Anfernee Hardaway	2.50
SS3	Paul Pierce	1.00
SS4	Antoine Walker	.60
SS5	Grant Hill	4.00
SS6	Keith Van Horn	1.00
SS7	Kevin Garnett	4.00
SS8	Kobe Bryant	5.00
SS9	Larry Hughes	.75
SS10	Jason Williams	2.50
SS11	Scottie Pippen	2.00
SS12	Shaquille O'Neal	2.50
SS13	Vince Carter	5.00
SS14	Stephon Marbury	2.00
SS15	Tim Duncan	4.00

1999-00 Fleer Focus Soar Subjects Vivid

This 15-card insert paralleled Soar Subjects, but was hobby exclusive, die-cut and sequentially numbered to just 50 sets.

		MT
Vivid Cards:		15x-30x
Production 50 Hobby Sets		
1	Allen Iverson	2.50
2	Anfernee Hardaway	2.50
3	Paul Pierce	1.00
4	Antoine Walker	.60
5	Grant Hill	4.00
6	Keith Van Horn	1.00
7	Kevin Garnett	4.00
8	Kobe Bryant	5.00
9	Larry Hughes	.75
10	Jason Williams	2.50
11	Scottie Pippen	2.00
12	Shaquille O'Neal	2.50
13	Vince Carter	5.00
14	Stephon Marbury	2.00
15	Tim Duncan	4.00

1999-00 Fleer Focus Sean Elliott Night

		MT
Complete Set (1):		4.00
1	Sean Elliott	4.00

1999-00 Fleer Focus Toni Kukoc Night

		MT
Complete Set (1):		5.00
1	Toni Kukoc	5.00

1999-00 Fleer Force

Fleer Force mirrored Fleer Tradition Basketball, but added a metallic foil look to each card. The set consists of 200 veterans and 35 rookies, which were sequentially numbered to 1,600 sets. Each card was paralleled in a Forcefield set, while insert sets included: Attack Force, Special Forces, Mission Accomplished, Operation Invasion, Air Force One Five and Forcefield. Each insert set was also paralleled by a Forcefield version. Fleer Force also included a Sgt. Carter Feel the Force player-worn Army fatigues card (1:300 packs), as well as autographed versions (numbered to 300), which are listed at the end of the base set.

		MT
Complete Set (235):		400.00
Common Player:		.15
Minor Stars:		.30
Common Rookie (201-235):		5.00
Production 1,600 Sets		
Pack (5):		3.00
Wax Box (24):		50.00
1	Vince Carter	4.00
2	Kobe Bryant	3.00
3	Keith Van Horn	.60
4	Tim Duncan	2.50
5	Grant Hill	2.50
6	Kevin Garnett	2.50
7	Anfernee Hardaway	1.50
8	Jason Williams	1.50
9	Paul Pierce	1.00
10	Mookie Blaylock	.15
11	Shawn Bradley	.15
12	Kenny Anderson	.30
13	Chauncey Billups	.15
14	Elden Campbell	.15
15	Jason Caffey	.15
16	Brent Barry	.15
17	Charles Barkley	.60
18	Derek Anderson	.30
19	Darrick Martin	.15
20	Michael Curry	.15
21	Rick Fox	.15
22	Antonio Davis	.15
23	Terrell Brandon	.15
24	P.J. Brown	.15
25	Toby Bailey	.15
26	Ray Allen	.40
27	Brian Grant	.15
28	Scott Burrell	.15
29	Tariq Abdul-Wahad	.15
30	Marcus Camby	.40
31	John Stockton	.30
32	Nick Anderson	.15
33	Jamie Feick	.15
34	Matt Geiger	.15
35	Vin Baker	.30
36	Dee Brown	.15
37	Shandon Anderson	.15
38	Vernon Maxwell	.15
39	Shareef Abdur-Rahim	.75
40	LaPhonso Ellis	.15
41	Cedric Ceballos	.15
42	Tony Battie	.15
43	Keon Clark	.30
44	Derrick Coleman	.30
45	Erick Dampier	.15
46	Corey Benjamin	.15
47	Michael Dickerson	.40
48	Cedric Henderson	.15
49	Lamond Murray	.15
50	Jerome Williams	.15
51	Shaquille O'Neal	2.00
52	Dale Davis	.15
53	Dean Garrett	.15
54	Tim Hardaway	.50
55	Dennis Rodman	.75
56	Sam Cassell	.30
57	Jim Jackson	.15
58	Kendall Gill	.15
59	Eric Williams	.15
60	Chris Childs	.15
61	Vlade Divac	.15
62	Darrell Armstrong	.15
63	Mario Elie	.15
64	Jaren Jackson	.15
65	Dale Ellis	.15
66	Doug Christie	.15
67	Howard Eisley	.15
68	Juwan Howard	.30
69	Mike Bibby	.50
70	Alan Henderson	.15
71	Michael Finley	.30
72	Dana Barros	.15
73	Troy Hudson	.15
74	Ricky Davis	.30
75	*John Amaechi*	.50
76	Erick Strickland	.15
77	Bryce Drew	.15
78	Shawn Kemp	.50
79	Tyrone Nesby	.15
80	Lindsey Hunter	.15
81	Ruben Patterson	.30
82	Al Harrington	.40
83	Bobby Jackson	.15
84	Dan Majerle	.15
85	Rex Chapman	.15
86	Dell Curry	.15
87	Robert Pack	.15
88	Kerry Kittles	.15
89	Isaiah Rider	.30
90	Patrick Ewing	.30
91	Lawrence Funderburke	.15
92	Isaac Austin	.15
93	Sean Elliott	.15
94	Larry Hughes	1.00
95	Jelani McCoy	.15
96	Tracy McGrady	1.50
97	Jeff Hornacek	.15
98	Jahidi White	.15
99	Danny Manning	.15
100	Roshown McLeod	.15
101	Steve Nash	.15
102	Ron Mercer	.60
103	Raef LaFrentz	.40
104	Eddie Jones	.60
105	Antawn Jamison	1.00
106	*Chucky Atkins*	.75
107	Othella Harrington	.15
108	Brevin Knight	.15
109	Michael Olowokandi	.40
110	Christian Laettner	.15
111	J.R. Reid	.15
112	Reggie Miller	.30
113	*Lazaro Borrell*	.40
114	Jamal Mashburn	.30
115	Glenn Robinson	.30
116	Pat Garrity	.15
117	Stephon Marbury	.75
118	Arvydas Sabonis	.15
119	Allan Houston	.30
120	Predrag Stojakovic	.30
121	Michael Doleac	.15
122	Avery Johnson	.15
123	Allen Iverson	2.50
124	Rashard Lewis	.60
125	Charles Oakley	.15
126	Karl Malone	.60
127	Tracy Murray	.15
128	Felipe Lopez	.30
129	Dikembe Mutombo	.30
130	Dirk Nowitzki	.60
131	Vitaly Potapenko	.15
132	Antonio McDyess	.40
133	Anthony Mason	.15
134	Donyell Marshall	.15
135	Dickey Simpkins	.15
136	Cuttino Mobley	.30
137	Wesley Person	.15
138	Rodney Rogers	.15
139	Jerry Stackhouse	.30
140	Glen Rice	.30
141	Chris Mullin	.15
142	Anthony Peeler	.15
143	Alonzo Mourning	.40
144	Tom Gugliotta	.30
145	Tim Thomas	.50
146	Damon Stoudamire	.40
147	Jayson Williams	.15
148	Larry Johnson	.30
149	Chris Webber	1.50
150	Matt Harpring	.30
151	David Robinson	.60
152	George Lynch	.15
153	Gary Payton	.60
154	John Wallace	.15
155	Greg Ostertag	.15
156	Mitch Richmond	.30
157	Cherokee Parks	.15
158	Steve Smith	.30
159	Gary Trent	.15
160	Antoine Walker	.50
161	*Chris Herren*	.60
162	Ron Harper	.15
163	Chris Mills	.15
164	Fred Hoiberg	.15
165	Hakeem Olajuwon	.60
166	Bob Sura	.15
167	Brian Skinner	.15
168	Loy Vaught	.15
169	A.C. Green	.15
170	Jalen Rose	.30
171	Joe Smith	.15
172	Clarence Weatherspoon	.15
173	Jason Kidd	1.50
174	Robert Traylor	.30
175	Rasheed Wallace	.30
176	Latrell Sprewell	.60
177	Corliss Williamson	.15
178	Charles Outlaw	.15
179	Malik Rose	.15
180	Nazr Mohammed	.15
181	Eric Murdock	.15
182	Kevin Willis	.15
183	Bryon Russell	.15
184	Bryant Reeves	.15
185	Rod Strickland	.30
186	Samaki Walker	.15
187	Nick Van Exel	.30
188	David Wesley	.15
189	John Starks	.15
190	Toni Kukoc	.50
191	Scottie Pippen	1.50
192	Johnny Newman	.15
193	Maurice Taylor	.30
194	Rik Smits	.15
195	Clifford Robinson	.15
196	Bonzi Wells	.40
197	Charlie Ward	.15
198	Detlef Schrempf	.15
199	Theo Ratliff	.15
200	Kelvin Cato	.15
201	*Ron Artest*	12.00
202	*William Avery*	8.00
203	*Elton Brand*	50.00
204	*Baron Davis*	25.00
205	*Jumaine Jones*	5.00
206	*Andre Miller*	25.00
207	*Eddie Robinson*	10.00
208	*James Posey*	10.00
209	*Jason Terry*	12.00
210	*Kenny Thomas*	8.00
211	*Steve Francis*	100.00
212	*Wally Szczerbiak*	20.00
213	*Richard Hamilton*	20.00
214	*Jonathan Bender*	40.00
215	*Shawn Marion*	40.00
216	*Aleksandar Radojevic*	5.00
217	*Tim James*	5.00
218	*Trajan Langdon*	10.00
219	*Lamar Odom*	60.00
220	*Corey Maggette*	25.00
221	*Dion Glover*	6.00
222	*Cal Bowdler*	5.00
223	*Vonteego Cummings*	8.00
224	*Devean George*	10.00
225	*Anthony Carter*	10.00
226	*Laron Profit*	6.00
227	*Quincy Lewis*	6.00
228	*John Celestand*	5.00
229	*Obinna Ekezie*	5.00
230	*Scott Padgett*	5.00
231	*Michael Ruffin*	5.00
232	*Jeff Foster*	5.00
233	*Jermaine Jackson*	5.00
234	*Adrian Griffin*	6.00
235	*Todd MacCulloch*	6.00
	Vince Carter Sgt.	100.00
	Vince Carter Sgt. AU	300.00

1999-00 Fleer Force Forcefield

This 235-card parallel set reprinted every card in Fleer Force, but added a holographic finish to the front. The cards were labeled "Forcefield" on the back and veterans were inserted 1:12, while Rookies were sequentially numbered to 100 sets.

	MT
Forcefield Veterans (1-200):	2x-4x
Inserted 1:12	
Forcefield Rookies (201-235):	.5x-1.5x
Production 100 Sets	

1999-00 Fleer Force Air Force One Five

This 15-card insert set was devoted to Vince Carter and featured the Raptors star on an embossed, foil card. Air Force One Five, which is a play on words since Carter wears uniform number 15, cards were numbered with an "AF" suffix and seeded 1:24 packs. Forcefield parallel versions featured a holographic front, were marked on the back and sequentially numbered to 150 sets.

		MT
Complete Set (15):		60.00
Common Player:		5.00
Inserted 1:24		
Common Forcefield:		100.00
Production 150 Sets		
AF1	Vince Carter	5.00
AF2	Vince Carter	5.00
AF3	Vince Carter	5.00
AF4	Vince Carter	5.00
AF5	Vince Carter	5.00
AF6	Vince Carter	5.00
AF7	Vince Carter	5.00
AF8	Vince Carter	5.00
AF9	Vince Carter	5.00
AF10	Vince Carter	5.00
AF11	Vince Carter	5.00
AF12	Vince Carter	5.00
AF13	Vince Carter	5.00
AF14	Vince Carter	5.00
AF15	Vince Carter	5.00

1999-00 Fleer Force Air Force One Five Forcefield

This 15-card parallel set reprinted each card in the set with a holographic finish on the front. The cards were labeled "Forcefield" on the back and sequentially numbered to 150 sets.

	MT
Inserted 1:24	
Common Forcefield:	100.00
Production 150 Sets	

1999-00 Fleer Force Attack Force

This 20-card insert set featured a mix of stars and rookies over a team-color background, with the player's uniform number in large letters. Attack Force cards were numbered with an "A" suffix and seeded 1:6 packs. Forcefield parallel versions featured a holographic finish on the front, were labeled on the back and inserted 1:24 packs.

Complete Set (20):	25.00
Common Player:	.50
Inserted 1:6	
Complete Forcefield Set (20):	50.00
Forcefield Cards:	2x
Inserted 1:24	

A1	Vince Carter	6.00
A2	Lamar Odom	4.00
A3	Stephon Marbury	1.00
A4	Jason Terry	.75
A5	Richard Hamilton	1.00
A6	Steve Francis	5.00
A7	Wally Szczerbiak	2.00
A8	Tracy McGrady	2.00
A9	Michael Finley	.50
A10	Baron Davis	1.50
A11	Shawn Marion	1.50
A12	Jonathan Bender	2.00
A13	Elton Brand	4.00
A14	Shareef Abdur-Rahim	1.00
A15	Keith Van Horn	.75
A16	Jerry Stackhouse	.50
A17	Antonio McDyess	.60
A18	Antoine Walker	.60
A19	Steve Smith	.50
A20	Ron Artest	1.50

1999-00 Fleer Force Attack Force Forcefield

This 20-card parallel set reprinted each card in the Attack Force insert set with a holographic finish on the front. The cards were labeled "Forcefield" on the back and seeded 1:24 packs.

	MT
Complete Forcefield Set (20):	50.00
Forcefield Cards:	2x
Inserted 1:24	

1999-00 Fleer Force Forceful

This 15-card insert set featured players over a silver foil background with a black border on three sides. Forceful cards were numbered with an "F" suffix and seeded 1:36 packs. Forcefield versions also existed and included a holographic front, labeling on the back and were inserted 1:144 packs.

	MT
Complete Set (15):	90.00
Common Player:	1.50
Inserted 1:36	
Complete Forcefield Set (15):	175.00
Forcefield Cards:	2x
Inserted 1:144	

F1	Vince Carter	20.00
F2	Lamar Odom	10.00
F3	Shaquille O'Neal	8.00
F4	Alonzo Mourning	1.50
F5	Kevin Garnett	12.00
F6	Tim Duncan	12.00
F7	Kobe Bryant	15.00
F8	Allen Iverson	8.00
F9	Jason Williams	5.00
F10	Paul Pierce	4.00
F11	Shareef Abdur-Rahim	4.00
F12	Stephon Marbury	4.00
F13	Grant Hill	12.00
F14	Keith Van Horn	3.00
F15	Karl Malone	2.00

1999-00 Fleer Force Forceful Forcefield

This 15-card insert set reprinted each card in the Forceful insert, but added a holographic finish to the front. Cards were labeled "Forcefield" on the back and seeded 1:144 packs.

	MT
Complete Forcefield Set (15):	175.00
Forcefield Cards:	2x
Inserted 1:144	

1999-00 Fleer Force Mission Accomplished

This 15-card insert set showcased players who had already achieved major accomplishments in their careers over a multi-colored background. Mission Accomplished cards were numbered with an "MA" suffix and seeded 1:48 packs. A Forcefield parallel version also existed, which featured a holographic front, a gold foil "Forcefield" stamp on the back and was inserted 1:48 packs.

	MT
Complete Set (15):	35.00
Common Player:	1.00
Inserted 1:12	
Complete Forcefield Set (15):	70.00
Forcefield Cards:	2x
Inserted 1:48	

MA1	Vince Carter	8.00
MA2	Lamar Odom	4.00
MA3	Allen Iverson	3.00
MA4	Tim Duncan	5.00
MA5	Charles Barkley	1.00
MA6	Jason Kidd	2.00
MA7	Steve Francis	5.00
MA8	Elton Brand	4.00
MA9	Kevin Garnett	5.00
MA10	Baron Davis	1.50
MA11	Paul Pierce	1.50
MA12	Scottie Pippen	2.00
MA13	Chris Webber	2.00
MA14	Anfernee Hardaway	2.00
MA15	David Robinson	1.00

1999-00 Fleer Force Mission Accomplished Forcefield

This 15-card parallel set reprinted each card in the Mission Accomplished insert, but added a holographic finish to the front. Cards were labeled "Forcefield" in gold foil on the back and inserted 1:48 packs.

	MT
Inserted 1:12	
Complete Forcefield Set (15):	70.00
Forcefield Cards:	2x
Inserted 1:48	

1999-00 Fleer Force Operation Invasion

This 15-card insert set displayed the league's top scorers on a gold foil card that is die-cut around both the top and bottom. Operation Invasion cards are numbered with an "OI" suffix seeded 1:24 packs. A parallel Forcefield version also exists and arrives with a holographic front, die-cut around the bottom only and seeded 1:96 packs.

	MT
Complete Set (15):	60.00
Common Player:	1.00
Inserted 1:24	
Complete Forcefield Set (15):	120.00
Forcefield Cards:	2x
Inserted 1:96	

OI1	Vince Carter	12.00
OI2	Lamar Odom	6.00
OI3	Kobe Bryant	10.00
OI4	Tim Duncan	8.00
OI5	Paul Pierce	2.50
OI6	Kevin Garnett	8.00
OI7	Grant Hill	8.00
OI8	Allen Iverson	5.00
OI9	Jason Williams	3.00
OI10	Ron Mercer	1.50
OI11	Shaquille O'Neal	5.00
OI12	Keith Van Horn	1.50
OI13	Shareef Abdur-Rahim	2.00
OI14	Alonzo Mourning	1.00
OI15	Stephon Marbury	2.00

1999-00 Fleer Force Operation Invasion Forcefield

This 15-card parallel set reprinted each card in the Operation Invasion insert, but adds a holographic finish to the front and is die-cut around the bottom only. The cards are labeled "Forcefield" on the back in gold foil and are inserted 1:96 packs.

	MT
Complete Forcefield Set (15):	120.00
Forcefield Cards:	2x
Inserted 1:96	

Values quoted in this guide reflect the retail price of a card — the price a collector can expect to pay when buying a card from a dealer. The wholesale price — that which a collector can expect to receive from a dealer when selling cards — will be significantly lower, depending on desirability and condition.

1999-00 Fleer Force Special Forces

This 15-card insert set displays top NBA players on a horizontal, red-foil card. Special Forces inserts were numbered with an "SF" suffix and seeded 1:12 packs. A parallel Forcefield version also existed and featured a holographic front and was seeded 1:48 packs.

	MT
Complete Set (15):	30.00
Common Player:	.60
Inserted 1:12	
Complete Forcefield Set (15):	60.00
Forcefield Cards:	2x
Inserted 1:48	

SF1	Vince Carter	8.00
SF2	Lamar Odom	4.00
SF3	Keith Van Horn	1.00
SF4	Stephon Marbury	1.50
SF5	Scottie Pippen	2.00
SF6	Ray Allen	.75
SF7	Chris Webber	2.00
SF8	Jason Williams	2.00
SF9	Karl Malone	1.00
SF10	Patrick Ewing	.60
SF11	Elton Brand	4.00
SF12	Grant Hill	5.00
SF13	Eddie Jones	1.00
SF14	Shaquille O'Neal	3.00
SF15	Kobe Bryant	6.00

1999-00 Fleer Force Special Forces Forcefield

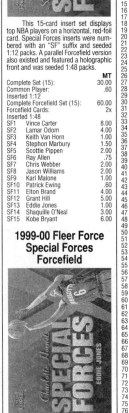

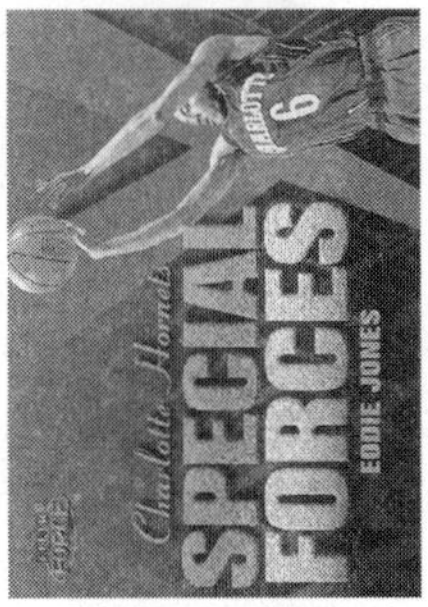

This 15-card parallel set reprinted each card in the Special Forces insert, but added a holographic finish to the card front. Cards were labeled "Forcefield" in gold foil on the back and were seeded 1:48 packs.

	MT
Complete Forcefield Set (15):	60.00
Forcefield Cards:	2x
Inserted 1:48	

1999-00 Fleer Mystique

Mystique consisted of 150 cards, including 40 Rookies sequentially numbered to 2,999 and 10 Stars sequentially numbered to 2,500. Each pack contained one "peel" card, which may or may not be a numbered card. Base cards featured a high-gloss finish, with the player's name in a silver foil, rounded area near the bottom and the word "Mystique" in large letters across the background in the middle. The first 100 cards in the set were paralleled in a Gold version, while inserts included: Feel the Game, Fresh Ink, Point Perfect, Raise the Roof and Slamboree.

		MT
Complete Set (150):		350.00
Common Player:		.25
Minor Stars:		.40
Common Rookie (101-140):		2.00
Production 2,999 Sets		
Common STAR (141-150):		2.00
Production 2,500 Sets		
Pack (5):		5.00
Wax Box (24):		40.00
1	Allen Iverson	2.50
2	Grant Hill	3.00
3	Antawn Jamison	1.25
4	Glenn Robinson	.40
5	Kenny Anderson	.40
6	Dikembe Mutombo	.40
7	Gary Trent	.25
8	Brevin Knight	.25
9	Chucky Brown	.25
10	Derek Anderson	.40
11	Ricky Davis	.40
12	Chris Webber	1.50
13	Jalen Rose	.40
14	Antoine Walker	.60
15	Michael Dickerson	.50
16	Tim Hardaway	.60
17	Toni Kukoc	.50
18	Raef LaFrentz	.50
19	Anthony Mason	.25
20	John Stockton	.40
21	Hakeem Olajuwon	1.00
22	Shaquille O'Neal	2.50
23	Scottie Pippen	1.50
24	Maurice Taylor	.25
25	Tariq Abdul-Wahad	.25
26	Tracy McGrady	1.50
27	Joe Smith	.25
28	Rod Strickland	.40
29	Ruben Patterson	.40
30	Tom Gugliotta	.40
31	Ray Allen	.50
32	Elden Campbell	.25
33	Lindsey Hunter	.25
34	Larry Johnson	.25
35	Michael Olowokandi	.40
36	Mario Elie	.25
37	Anfernee Hardaway	2.00
38	Juwan Howard	.40
39	Karl Malone	1.00
40	Alonzo Mourning	.50
41	Billy Owens	.25
42	Mitch Richmond	.40
43	Darrell Armstrong	.25
44	Jason Williams	2.00
45	Mookie Blaylock	.25
46	Gary Payton	1.00
47	Brian Grant	.25
48	Paul Pierce	1.50
49	Michael Finley	.40
50	Reggie Miller	.40
51	Corliss Williamson	.25
52	Shandon Anderson	.25
53	Stephon Marbury	1.25
54	Sam Cassell	.40
55	Bryon Russell	.25
56	Rasheed Wallace	.40
57	Jayson Williams	.25
58	Damon Stoudamire	.50
59	Terrell Brandon	.40
60	Loy Vaught	.25
61	Kobe Bryant	4.00
62	Vlade Divac	.25
63	Derek Fisher	.25
64	Isaiah Rider	.40
65	Eddie Jones	1.00
66	Kevin Garnett	3.00
67	David Robinson	1.00
68	Marcus Camby	.40
69	Glen Rice	.40
70	Mike Bibby	.50
71	Patrick Ewing	.40
72	Robert Traylor	.40
73	Tim Duncan	3.00
74	Michael Doleac	.25
75	Steve Smith	.40
76	Allan Houston	.40
77	Jamal Mashburn	.40
78	Brent Barry	.25
79	Charles Barkley	1.00
80	Ron Mercer	1.00
81	Jerry Stackhouse	.75
82	Keith Van Horn	.75
83	Hersey Hawkins	.25
84	Avery Johnson	.25
85	Cedric Ceballos	.25
86	P.J. Brown	.25
87	Doug Christie	.25
88	Shawn Kemp	.50
89	Dirk Nowitzki	.75
90	Erick Dampier	.25
91	Antonio McDyess	.50
92	Mark Jackson	.25
93	Clifford Robinson	.25
94	Vince Carter	5.00
95	Shareef Abdur-Rahim	1.25
96	Vin Baker	.40
97	Larry Hughes	1.25
98	Jason Kidd	1.50
99	Kerry Kittles	.25
100	Latrell Sprewell	.75
101	*Lamar Odom*	30.00
102	*Elton Brand*	20.00
103	*Baron Davis*	15.00
104	*Jason Terry*	10.00
105	*Corey Maggette*	15.00
106	*Wally Szczerbiak*	12.00
107	*Richard Hamilton*	12.00
108	*Milt Palacio*	2.00
109	*Ron Artest*	10.00
110	*Eddie Robinson*	8.00
111	*Jumaine Jones*	3.00
112	*Andre Miller*	15.00
113	*Chucky Atkins*	5.00
114	*Kenny Thomas*	6.00
115	*Scott Padgett*	3.00
116	*Devean George*	8.00
117	*Tim Young*	2.00
118	*Tim James*	3.00
119	*Quincy Lewis*	5.00
120	*James Posey*	8.00
121	*Shawn Marion*	20.00
122	*Aleksandar Radojevic*	2.00
123	*Trajan Langdon*	8.00
124	*Laron Profit*	5.00
125	*Jonathan Bender*	20.00
126	*William Avery*	6.00
127	*Cal Bowdler*	2.00
128	*Dion Glover*	4.00
129	*Jeff Foster*	2.00
130	*Steve Francis*	50.00
131	*Adrian Griffin*	4.00
132	*Vonteego Cummings*	6.00
133	*Rafer Alston*	5.00
134	*Michael Ruffin*	3.00
135	*Chris Herren*	5.00
136	*Jermaine Jackson*	2.00
137	*Lazaro Borrell*	2.00
138	*Obinna Ekezie*	2.00
139	*Rick Hughes*	2.00
140	*Todd MacCulloch*	3.00
141	Kobe Bryant STAR	15.00
142	Vince Carter STAR	20.00
143	Tim Duncan STAR	12.00
144	Kevin Garnett STAR	12.00
145	Allen Iverson STAR	8.00
146	Keith Van Horn STAR	2.00
147	Grant Hill STAR	12.00
148	Stephon Marbury STAR	4.00
149	Antoine Walker STAR	1.50
150	Shaquille O'Neal STAR	8.00

1999-00 Fleer Mystique Gold

This 100-card set was a partial parallel and included only the non-sequentially numbered singles from the base set, which means no Rookies or Stars subset cards. Gold versions are distinguished by the use of gold foil on the front and in the player's name area, which was silver foil on the base cards. These parallel versions were seeded 1:4 packs.

	MT
Gold Parallel Cards:	3x-6x

1999-00 Fleer Mystique Feel the Game Memorabilia

This 11-card insert set featured pieces of player-worn jerseys on a horizontal design. Feel the Game cards were unnumbered and are listed below in alphabetical order and seeded 1:120 packs.

		MT
Complete Set (11):		1000.
Common Player:		40.00
Inserted 1:96		
1	Vince Carter	350.00
2	Shaquille O'Neal	200.00
3	Karl Malone	75.00
4	David Robinson	75.00
5	Brian Grant	40.00
6	Joe Smith	40.00
7	Gary Payton	75.00
8	Raef LaFrentz	40.00
9	Alonzo Mourning	50.00
10	John Stockton	75.00
11	Glenn Robinson	40.00

1999-00 Fleer Mystique Fresh Ink

This 43-card insert set included autographs from various NBA players. Fresh Ink cards were inserted 1:40 packs. The back of each Fresh Ink card is a letter of authenticity stating the player's name and facsimile signed by Fleer senior vice president Lloyd Pawlak.

		MT
Common Player:		5.00
Inserted 1:40		
1	Ray Allen	25.00
2	Ron Artest	20.00
3	William Avery	8.00
4	Jonathan Bender	35.00
5	Mike Bibby	10.00
6	Cal Bowdler	5.00
7	Vince Carter	250.00
8	John Celestand	5.00
9	Vonteego Cummings	10.00
10	Baron Davis	20.00
11	Michael Dickerson	10.00
12	Michael Doleac	5.00
13	Evan Eschmeyer	5.00
14	Michael Finley	15.00
15	Steve Francis	125.00
16	Pat Garrity	8.00
17	Dion Glover	8.00
18	Brian Grant	8.00
19	Richard Hamilton	15.00
20	Tim Hardaway	12.00
21	Jumaine Jones	5.00
22	Shawn Kemp	12.00
23	Raef LaFrentz	10.00
24	Quincy Lewis	8.00
25	Stephon Marbury	30.00
26	Antonio McDyess	15.00
27	Andre Miller	20.00
28	Cuttino Mobley	10.00
29	Alonzo Mourning	40.00
30	Shaquille O'Neal	200.00
31	Lamar Odom	75.00
32	Hakeem Olajuwon	40.00
33	Michael Olowokandi	8.00

34	James Posey	12.00
35	Aleksandar Radojevic	5.00
36	Kenny Thomas	10.00
37	Robert Traylor	5.00
38	Keith Van Horn	15.00

1999-00 Fleer Mystique Point Perfect

This 10-card insert set showcased the league's top point guards on a double-foil card. Point Perfect cards were numbered with a "PP" suffix and sequentially numbered to 1,999 sets.

		MT
Complete Set (10):		50.00
Common Player:		2.00
Production 1,999 Sets		
PP1	Mike Bibby	2.00
PP2	Stephon Marbury	6.00
PP3	Jason Williams	10.00
PP4	Jason Kidd	10.00
PP5	William Avery	2.00
PP6	Allen Iverson	12.00
PP7	Andre Miller	5.00
PP8	Baron Davis	5.00
PP9	Steve Francis	15.00
PP10	Jason Terry	3.00

1999-00 Fleer Mystique Raise the Roof

This 10-card insert set highlighted the league's top players on a sky-like background with several other faint, identical images of the same player. The cards were numbered with an "RR" suffix and sequentially numbered to 100 sets.

		MT
Complete Set (10):		750.00
Common Player:		25.00
Production 100 Sets		
RR1	Grant Hill	100.00
RR2	Keith Van Horn	15.00
RR3	Tim Duncan	100.00
RR4	Kobe Bryant	125.00
RR5	Vince Carter	150.00
RR6	Allen Iverson	75.00
RR7	Kevin Garnett	100.00
RR8	Shaquille O'Neal	75.00
RR9	Paul Pierce	40.00
RR10	Anfernee Hardaway	50.00

1999-00 Fleer Mystique Slamboree

This 10-card insert features top dunkers over a colorful, multi-colored foil background with silver foil and full holofoil. Slamboree inserts are numbered with an "S" suffix and sequentially numbered to 999 sets.

		MT
Complete Set (10):		110.00
Common Player:		
Production 999 Sets		
S1	Antoine Walker	3.00
S2	Shareef Abdur-Rahim	10.00
S3	Antawn Jamison	10.00
S4	Tracy McGrady	15.00
S5	Larry Hughes	10.00
S6	Wally Szczerbiak	10.00
S7	Corey Maggette	10.00
S8	Lamar Odom	25.00
S9	Elton Brand	25.00
S10	Stephon Marbury	10.00

2000 Fleer Focus Jam Session Sheet

This eight-card set was available through a wrapper exchange program at the Fleer booth at NBA Jam Session in Oakland. The cards carry the Fleer Focus design and are unnumbered on the back. The sheet is perforated and carries the Jam Session logo.

		MT
Complete Set (1):		6.00
NNO	Vince Carter, Lamar Odom, Stephon Marbury, Keith Van Horn, Antawn Jamison, Allen Iverson, Grant Hill, Jason Williams	6.00

2000-01 Fleer

		MT
Complete Set (300):		60.00
Common Player:		.10
Minor Stars:		.20
Common Rookie:		.25
Pack (10):		1.50
Box (36):		40.00
1	Lamar Odom	.75
2	Christian Laettner	.10
3	Michael Olowokandi	.10
4	Anthony Carter	.10
5	Steve Francis	1.50
6	Darvin Ham	.10
7	Mitch Richmond	.20
8	Corliss Williamson	.10
9	Jason Terry	.25
10	Brian Grant	.10
11	Predrag Stojakovic	.20
12	Rick Fox	.10
13	Tyrone Hill	.10
14	Chauncey Billups	.10
15	Otis Thorpe	.10
16	Richard Hamilton	.25
17	Ervin Johnson	.10
18	Jim Jackson	.10
19	Theo Ratliff	.10
20	Doug Christie	.10
21	Jalen Rose	.25
22	John Wallace	.10
23	Ruben Patterson	.10
24	Steve Nash	.10
25	Toni Kukoc	.25
26	Anthony Peeler	.10
27	Ray Allen	.30
28	Adonal Foyle	.10
29	Chris Whitney	.10
30	Nick Van Exel	.20
31	Sean Elliott	.10
32	Erick Strickland	.10
33	Jerry Stackhouse	.20
34	Antawn Jamison	.60
35	Grant Hill	1.25
36	Antonio Daniels	.10
37	Karl Malone	.40
38	Keith Van Horn	.30
39	Ron Harper	.10
40	Stephon Marbury	.50
41	Bryon Russell	.10
42	Corey Maggette	.30
43	Hersey Hawkins	.10
44	Vince Carter	2.50
45	Paul Pierce	.40
46	Mikki Moore	.10
47	Othella Harrington	.10
48	Erick Dampier	.10
49	Jerome Williams	.10
50	Nick Anderson	.10
51	Tim Hardaway	.25
52	Allan Houston	.25
53	Tyrone Nesby	.10
54	Brevin Knight	.10
55	Chris Mills	.10
56	Ron Artest	.25
57	Walt Williams	.10
58	Duane Causwell	.10
59	Bonzi Wells	.30
60	Rasheed Wallace	.30
61	Dikembe Mutombo	.20
62	Jahidi White	.10
63	Chris Webber	.75
64	Tony Battie	.10
65	Mahmoud Abdul-Rauf	.10
66	Monty Williams	.10
67	Charlie Ward	.10
68	David Robinson	.40
69	Eric Snow	.10
70	Jermaine O'Neal	.30
71	Kurt Thomas	.10
72	James Posey	.10
73	Travis Best	.10
74	Jonathan Bender	.50
75	John Stockton	.20
76	Jacque Vaughn	.10
77	Ron Mercer	.25
78	Shawn Marion	.60
79	Larry Johnson	.10
80	Maurice Taylor	.10
81	Clifford Robinson	.10
82	Scot Pollard	.10
83	Patrick Ewing	.20
84	Terrell Brandon	.20
85	Horace Grant	.10
86	Vin Baker	.20
87	Al Harrington	.25
88	Larry Hughes	.50
89	David Wesley	.10
90	Wally Szczerbiak	.30
91	Charles Oakley	.10
92	Tim Thomas	.25
93	Mookie Blaylock	.10
94	Jamal Mashburn	.20
95	Roshown McLeod	.10
96	John Starks	.10
97	Rodney Rogers	.10
98	Juwan Howard	.20
99	Isaiah Rider	.20
100	Rashard Lewis	.40
101	Dion Glover	.10
102	Johnny Newman	.10
103	Avery Johnson	.10
104	Darrell Armstrong	.10
105	Eric Williams	.10
106	Gary Payton	.40
107	Antonio Davis	.10
108	Dirk Nowitzki	.60
109	Trajan Langdon	.10
110	Michael Dickerson	.20
111	Joe Smith	.10
112	Rod Strickland	.20
113	Shawn Kemp	.20
114	Voshon Lenard	.10
115	Marcus Camby	.20
116	Matt Harpring	.10
117	Isaac Austin	.10
118	Malik Rose	.10
119	Pat Garrity	.10
120	Kenny Thomas	.10
121	LaPhonso Ellis	.10
122	Danny Fortson	.10
123	Elton Brand	.75
124	Jason Williams	.40
125	Kobe Bryant	2.00
126	Tariq Abdul-Wahad	.10
127	Tracy McGrady	.75
128	Matt Geiger	.10
129	Antoine Walker	.30
130	Michael Finley	.20
131	Andre Miller	.30
132	Robert Horry	.10
133	Donyell Marshall	.10
134	Shareef Abdur-Rahim	.40
135	Vonteego Cummings	.10
136	Anthony Mason	.10
137	Mike Bibby	.30
138	Raef LaFrentz	.20
139	Glen Rice	.20
140	Chris Gatling	.10
141	Latrell Sprewell	.60
142	Austin Croshere	.10
143	Kenny Anderson	.20
144	Elden Campbell	.10
145	Jason Kidd	.75
146	Michael Doleac	.10
147	Muggsy Bogues	.10
148	Tim Duncan	1.25
149	Samaki Walker	.10
150	Gary Trent	.10
151	Kevin Garnett	1.50
152	Allen Iverson	1.25
153	Anfernee Hardaway	.75
154	Robert Traylor	.10
155	Scottie Pippen	.75
156	Shaquille O'Neal	1.25
157	Vlade Divac	.10
158	Lucious Harris	.10
159	Keon Clark	.10
160	Charles Outlaw	.10
161	P.J. Brown	.10
162	Derrick Coleman	.20
163	Mark Jackson	.10
164	Lamond Murray	.10
165	Dan Majerle	.10
166	Eddie Jones	.60
167	Cedric Ceballos	.10
168	Kendall Gill	.10
169	Tom Gugliotta	.10
170	Jeff McInnis	.10
171	Steve Smith	.20
172	Kevin Willis	.10
173	Lindsey Hunter	.10
174	Derek Anderson	.20
175	Shandon Anderson	.10
176	Adrian Griffin	.10
177	Baron Davis	.30
178	Radoslav Nesterovic	.10
179	Glenn Robinson	.20
180	Sam Cassell	.20
181	Chucky Atkins	.10
182	Arvydas Sabonis	.10
183	Damon Stoudamire	.20
184	Antonio McDyess	.30
185	Derek Fisher	.10
186	Bryant Reeves	.10
187	Hakeem Olajuwon	.40
188	Kerry Kittles	.10
189	Alan Henderson	.10
190	Sam Perkins	.10
191	Felipe Lopez	.10
192	Tracy Murray	.10
193	Shammond Williams	.10
194	Vitaly Potapenko	.10
195	John Amaechi	.10
196	Quincy Lewis	.10
197	Reggie Miller	.20
198	Cuttino Mobley	.20
199	Rex Chapman	.10
200	Dale Davis	.10
201	Andrew DeClercq	.10
202	Kelvin Cato	.10
203	Jon Barry	.10
204	Greg Anthony	.10
205	Brent Barry	.10
206	Derrick McKey	.10
207	Vince Carter	1.25
208	David Robinson	.20
209	Eric Snow	.10
210	Ray Allen	.10
211	Lamar Odom	.40
212	Dikembe Mutombo	.10
213	Brevin Knight	.10
214	Vin Baker	.10
215	Antoine Walker	.10
216	Mitch Richmond	.10
217	Elton Brand	.40
218	Jerome Williams	.10
219	Keith Van Horn	.10
220	Nick Van Exel	.10
221	Shaquille O'Neal	.60
222	Allan Houston	.10
223	Shareef Abdur-Rahim	.20
224	Karl Malone	.20
225	Terrell Brandon	.10
226	Eddie Jones	.30
227	*Stromile Swift*	4.00
228	*Dalibor Bagaric*	.40
229	*Erick Barkley*	.75
230	*Mike Miller*	4.00
231	*Kenyon Martin*	3.00
232	*Michael Redd*	.40
233	*Darius Miles*	8.00
234	*Chris Mihm*	.75
235	*Brian Cardinal*	.25
236	*Khalid El-Amin*	.60
237	*Hanno Mottola*	.50
238	*Jamaal Magloire*	.60
239	*Courtney Alexander*	1.50
240	*Mamadou N'diaye*	.40
241	*Chris Porter*	1.00
242	*Quentin Richardson*	2.00
243	*Eddie House*	.50
244	*Joel Przybilla*	.60
245	*Soumaila Samake*	.25
246	*Craig "Speedy" Claxton*	.60
247	*Desmond Mason*	2.00
248	*Mike Smith*	.25
249	*Lavor Postell*	.40
250	*Ruben Garces*	.25
251	*DeShawn Stevenson*	2.50
252	*Hidayet Turkoglu*	2.00
253	*Keyon Dooling*	1.50
254	*Dan Langhi*	.40
255	*Mateen Cleaves*	1.00
256	*Donnell Harvey*	.60
257	*DerMarr Johnson*	1.50
258	*Jason Collier*	.40
259	*Jake Voskuhl*	.25
260	*Mark Madsen*	.60
261	*Pepe Sanchez*	.40
262	*Morris Peterson*	2.00
263	*Daniel Santiago*	.50
264	*Etan Thomas*	.60
265	*A.J. Guyton*	.50
266	*Marcus Fizer*	2.00
267	*Jamal Crawford*	1.50
268	*Jerome Moiso*	.75
269	*Olumide Oyedji*	.25
270	*Paul McPherson*	.50
271	*Eduardo Najera*	.60
272	Dallas Mavericks	.10
273	Denver Nuggets	.10
274	Houston Rockets	.30
275	Minnesota Timberwolves	.30
276	San Antonio Spurs	.30
277	Utah Jazz	.20
278	Vancouver Grizzlies	.10
279	Golden State Warriors	.10
280	Los Angeles Clippers	.40
281	Los Angeles Lakers	.50
282	Phoenix Suns	.20
283	Portland Trail Blazers	.10
284	Sacramento Kings	.20
285	Seattle SuperSonics	.10
286	Boston Celtics	.10
287	Miami Heat	.10
288	New Jersey Nets	.10
289	New York Knicks	.10
290	Orlando Magic	.30
291	Philadelphia 76ers	.20
292	Washington Wizards	.10
293	Atlanta Hawks	.10
294	Charlotte Hornets	.10
295	Chicago Bulls	.10
296	Cleveland Cavaliers	.10
297	Detroit Pistons	.10
298	Indiana Pacers	.10
299	Milwaukee Bucks	.10
300	Toronto Raptors	.30
	Vince Carter Sticker	10.00
	Vince Carter 1986	40.00
	Vince Carter Auto/15	

2000-01 Fleer Autographics

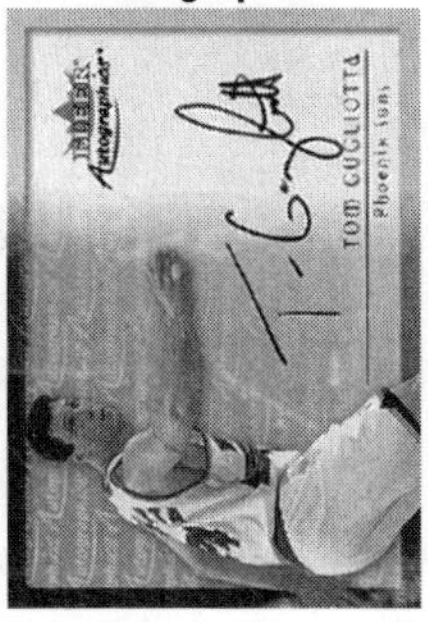

		MT
Common Player:		5.00
Inserted 1:288 Fleer Premium		
Inserted 1:48 Focus		
Inserted 1:23 Genuine		
Inserted 1:72 Hoops		
Inserted 1:48 Mystique		
Inserted 1:48 Ultra		
Inserted 1:287 Game Time		
1	Ray Allen	
2	Darrell Armstrong	6.00
3	Chucky Atkins	5.00
4	Vin Baker	
5	Travis Best	6.00
6	Mike Bibby	8.00
7	Muggsy Bogues	6.00
8	P.J. Brown	5.00
9	Elden Campbell	6.00
10	Vince Carter	150.00
11	Jason Collier	6.00
12	Baron Davis	12.00
13	Andrew DeClercq	5.00
14	Michael Dickerson	5.00
15	Vlade Divac	8.00
16	Michael Doleac	5.00
17	Dion Glover	5.00
18	Brian Grant	8.00
19	Adrian Griffin	5.00
20	Tom Gugliotta	6.00
21	A.J. Guyton	
22	Richard Hamilton	10.00
23	Al Harrington	10.00
24	Othella Harrington	6.00
25	Jason Hart	6.00
26	Shaheen Holloway	
27	Lindsey Hunter	
28	Allen Iverson	100.00
29	Antawn Jamison	15.00
30	Brevin Knight	5.00
31	Toni Kukoc	15.00
32	Raef LaFrentz	6.00
33	Voshon Lenard	5.00
34	Quincy Lewis	5.00
35	Rashard Lewis	
36	George Lynch	5.00
37	Corey Maggette	10.00
38	Jamaal Magloire	
39	Stephon Marbury	20.00
40	Shawn Marion	25.00
41	Donyell Marshall	5.00
42	Jamal Mashburn	12.00
43	Desmond Mason	
44	Antonio McDyess	
45	Tracy McGrady	35.00
46	Ron Mercer	10.00
47	Andre Miller	10.00
48	Reggie Miller	
49	Alonzo Mourning	50.00
50	Mamadou N'diaye	
51	Dirk Nowitzki	50.00
52	Lamar Odom	30.00
53	Hakeem Olajuwon	30.00
54	Jermaine O'Neal	20.00
55	Ruben Patterson	8.00
56	Scot Pollard	6.00
57	Theo Ratliff	8.00
58	Michael Redd	8.00
59	Mitch Richmond	10.00
60	Eddie Robinson	10.00
61	Glenn Robinson	12.00
62	Jalen Rose	
63	Bryon Russell	
64	Steve Smith	10.00
65	Jerry Stackhouse	15.00
66	Jason Terry	10.00
67	Kenny Thomas	6.00
68	Keith Van Horn	12.00
69	Antoine Walker	12.00

2000-01 Fleer Stickers

		MT
Common Player:		2.00
Stickers:		10x-20x
Rookies:		3x-6x
Inserted 1:36		
1	Andrew DeClercq	2.00
2	Kelvin Cato	2.00
3	Jon Barry	2.00
4	Greg Anthony	2.00
5	Brent Barry	2.00
6	Derrick McKey	2.00
7	Vince Carter UH	15.00
8	David Robinson UH	2.50
9	Eric Snow UH	2.00
10	Ray Allen UH	2.50
11	Lamar Odom UH	5.00
12	Dikembe Mutombo UH	2.00
13	Brevin Knight UH	2.00
14	Vin Baker UH	2.00
15	Antoine Walker UH	2.25
16	Mitch Richmond UH	2.25
17	Elton Brand UH	5.00
18	Jerome Williams UH	2.00
19	Keith Van Horn UH	2.50
20	Nick Van Exel UH	2.25
21	Shaquille O'Neal UH	8.00
22	Allan Houston UH	2.50
23	Shareef Abdur-Rahim UH	3.00
24	Karl Malone UH	3.00
25	Terrell Brandon UH	2.00
26	Eddie Jones UH	4.00
27	Stromile Swift	20.00
28	Dalibor Bagaric	3.00
29	Erick Barkley	6.00
30	Mike Miller	20.00
31	Kenyon Martin	15.00
32	Michael Redd	4.00
33	Darius Miles	40.00
34	Chris Mihm	5.00
35	Brian Cardinal	3.00
36	Khalid El-Amin	3.00
37	Hanno Mottola	3.00
38	Jamaal Magloire	6.00
39	Courtney Alexander	12.00
40	Mamadou N'diaye	3.00
41	Chris Porter	8.00
42	Quentin Richardson	10.00
43	Eddie House	8.00
44	Joel Przybilla	5.00
45	Soumaila Samake	3.00
46	Craig "Speedy" Claxton	5.00
47	Desmond Mason	12.00
48	Mike Smith	3.00
49	Lavor Postell	4.00
50	Ruben Garces	3.00
51	DeShawn Stevenson	15.00
52	Hidayet Turkoglu	10.00
53	Keyon Dooling	10.00
54	Dan Langhi	3.00
55	Mateen Cleaves	8.00
56	Donnell Harvey	5.00
57	DerMarr Johnson	10.00
58	Jason Collier	3.00
59	Jake Voskuhl	3.00
60	Mark Madsen	6.00
61	Pepe Sanchez	3.00
62	Morris Peterson	15.00
63	Daniel Santiago	3.00
64	Etan Thomas	5.00
65	A.J. Guyton	4.00
66	Marcus Fizer	8.00
67	Jamal Crawford	10.00
68	Jerome Moiso	6.00
69	Olumide Oyedji	3.00
70	Paul McPherson	4.00
71	Eduardo Najera	4.00
72	Dallas Mavericks CL	3.00
73	Denver Nuggets CL	2.00
74	Houston Rockets CL	3.00
75	Minnesota Timberwolves CL	3.00
76	San Antonio Spurs CL	4.00
77	Utah Jazz CL	3.00
78	Vancouver Grizzlies CL	2.00
79	Golden State Warriors CL	2.00
80	Los Angeles Clippers CL	3.00
81	Los Angeles Lakers CL	5.00
82	Phoenix Suns CL	3.00
83	Portland Trail Blazers CL	3.00
84	Sacramento Kings CL	4.00
85	Seattle Supersonics CL	3.00
86	Boston Celtics CL	2.00
87	Miami Heat CL	3.00
88	New Jersey Nets CL	2.00
89	New York Knicks CL	4.00
90	Orlando Magic CL	3.00
91	Philadelphia 76ers CL	3.00
92	Washington Wizards CL	2.00
93	Atlanta Hawks CL	2.00
94	Charlotte Hornets CL	3.00
95	Chicago Bulls CL	2.00
96	Cleveland Cavaliers CL	2.00
97	Detroit Pistons CL	2.00
98	Indiana Pacers CL	3.00
99	Milwaukee Bucks CL	3.00
100	Toronto Raptors CL	4.00

2000-01 Fleer Courting History

		MT
Complete Set (10):		20.00
Common Player:		2.00
Inserted 1:18		
CH1	Vince Carter	8.00
CH2	Shaquille O'Neal	3.00
CH3	Grant Hill	3.00
CH4	Kobe Bryant	6.00
CH5	Tim Duncan	3.00
CH6	Jason Kidd	2.00
CH7	Kevin Garnett	4.00
CH8	Allen Iverson	2.50
CH9	Steve Francis	4.00
CH10	Elton Brand	2.00

2000-01 Fleer Feel the Game

	MT
Common Player:	10.00
Inserted 1:48 Fleer Focus	
Inserted 1:56 Fleer Premium	
Inserted 1:48 Mystique	
Inserted 1:48 Ultra	
Shareef Abdur-Rahim	25.00
Mike Bibby	20.00
Terrell Brandon	15.00
Vince Carter	125.00
Sam Cassell	15.00
Baron Davis	25.00
Michael Finley	25.00
Robert Horry	15.00
Allan Houston	30.00
Allen Iverson	70.00
Eddie Jones	30.00
Jason Kidd	40.00
Quincy Lewis	10.00
Tyronn Lue	10.00
George Lynch	10.00
Corey Maggette	20.00
Karl Malone	30.00
Stephon Marbury	30.00
Shawn Marion	40.00
Tracy McGrady	50.00
Reggie Miller	50.00
Alonzo Mourning	30.00
Lamar Odom	40.00
Hakeem Olajuwon	30.00
Michael Olowokandi	10.00
Shaquille O'Neal	75.00
Scott Padgett	10.00
Gary Payton	40.00
Glenn Robinson	20.00
Joe Smith	15.00
John Stockton	40.00
Jason Terry	15.00
Keith Van Horn	20.00
Antoine Walker	20.00
Jason Williams	40.00

2000-01 Fleer Genuine Coverage Nostalgic

	MT
Common Player:	12.00
Inserted 1:144	
Courtney Alexander	30.00
Erick Barkley	20.00
Craig Claxton	20.00
Mateen Cleaves	25.00
Donnell Harvey	15.00
DerMarr Johnson	30.00
Mark Madsen	15.00
Kenyon Martin	60.00
Desmond Mason	40.00
Mike Miller	40.00
Jerome Moiso	15.00
Joel Pryzbilla	12.00
DeShawn Stevenson	60.00
Stromile Swift	60.00
Etan Thomas	12.00
Hidayet Turkoglu	25.00

2000-01 Fleer Hardcourt Classics

		MT
Complete Set (15):		20.00
Common Player:		.75
Inserted 1:9		
HC1	Vince Carter	5.00
HC2	Karl Malone	.75
HC3	Kobe Bryant	4.00
HC4	Tim Duncan	2.50
HC5	Lamar Odom	1.50
HC6	Jason Williams	.75
HC7	Kevin Garnett	3.00
HC8	Jason Kidd	1.50
HC9	Shaquille O'Neal	2.50
HC10	Chris Webber	1.50
HC11	Allen Iverson	2.50
HC12	Scottie Pippen	1.50
HC13	Grant Hill	2.50
HC14	Elton Brand	1.50
HC15	Tracy McGrady	1.50

2000-01 Fleer Rookie Retro

		MT
Complete Set (20):		75.00
Common Player:		2.00
Inserted 1:36		
RR1	Morris Peterson	6.00
RR2	DerMarr Johnson	5.00
RR3	Jerome Moiso	2.50
RR4	Darius Miles	20.00
RR5	Marcus Fizer	8.00
RR6	Hidayet Turkoglu	4.00
RR7	Mateen Cleaves	3.00
RR8	Kenyon Martin	12.00
RR9	Jamaal Magloire	2.00
RR10	Keyon Dooling	5.00
RR11	DeShawn Stevenson	8.00
RR12	Quentin Richardson	6.00
RR13	Courtney Alexander	5.00
RR14	Mark Madsen	2.00
RR15	Mike Miller	8.00
RR16	Desmond Mason	6.00
RR17	Stromile Swift	12.00
RR18	Craig "Speedy" Claxton	2.00
RR19	Etan Thomas	2.00
RR20	Chris Mihm	2.50

2000-01 Fleer Sharpshooters

		MT
Complete Set (20):		18.00
Common Player:		.50
Inserted 1:6		
SS1	Vince Carter	5.00
SS2	Wally Szczerbiak	.50
SS3	Kobe Bryant	4.00
SS4	Eddie Jones	1.00
SS5	John Stockton	.50
SS6	Ray Allen	.50
SS7	Tracy McGrady	1.50
SS8	Shareef Abdur-Rahim	.75
SS9	Antoine Walker	.60
SS10	Tim Duncan	2.50
SS11	Larry Hughes	1.00
SS12	Gary Payton	.75
SS13	Dirk Nowitzki	1.00
SS14	Grant Hill	2.50
SS15	Scottie Pippen	1.50
SS16	Chris Webber	1.50
SS17	Stephon Marbury	1.00
SS18	Anfernee Hardaway	1.50
SS19	Reggie Miller	.50
SS20	Steve Francis	3.00

2000-01 Fleer Focus

		MT
Complete Set (236):		200.00
Common Player:		.15
Minor Stars:		.30
Common Rookie:		1.00
Pack (10):		3.00
Box (24):		55.00
1	Vince Carter	4.00
2	Shawn Marion	1.00
3	Muggsy Bogues	.15
4	Dikembe Mutombo	.15
5	Stephon Marbury	.75
6	Michael Dickerson	.15
7	Andre Miller	.50
8	Toni Kukoc	.40
9	Nick Van Exel	.30
10	Aaron Williams	.15
11	Derrick Coleman	.30
12	Wally Szczerbiak	.40
13	Rodney Rogers	.15
14	Tom Gugliotta	.30
15	Vonteego Cummings	.15
16	Cedric Ceballos	.15
17	Malik Rose	.15
18	Vernon Maxwell	.15
19	Shandon Anderson	.15
20	Jacque Vaughn	.15
21	Jamie Feick	.15
22	Shawn Kemp	.40
23	Monty Williams	.15
24	Allan Houston	.40
25	Chauncey Billups	.15
26	Vlade Divac	.15
27	Othella Harrington	.15
28	Dale Davis	.15
29	Charlie Ward	.15
30	Hakeem Olajuwon	.60
31	Ray Allen	.30
32	Lamar Odom	1.25
33	Shaquille O'Neal	2.00
34	Chris Childs	.15
35	Nick Anderson	.15
36	Keon Clark	.15
37	Danny Fortson	.15
38	Sam Mitchell	.15
39	Travis Best	.15
40	Chris Webber	1.25
41	Brent Barry	.15
42	Scottie Pippen	1.25
43	Reggie Miller	.30
44	Bryant Reeves	.15
45	Bobby Jackson	.15
46	Antonio McDyess	.40
47	Elden Campbell	.15
48	Kenny Anderson	.30
49	Christian Laettner	.15
50	Darrell Armstrong	.15
51	Vinny Del Negro	.15
52	Quincy Lewis	.15
53	Predrag Stojakovic	.30
54	Matt Geiger	.15
55	Larry Hughes	1.00
56	Tracy McGrady	1.25
57	Tim Hardaway	.40
58	Brevin Knight	.15
59	Michael Finley	.30
60	Jason Kidd	1.25
61	Matt Harpring	.15
62	Antawn Jamison	1.00
63	Wesley Person	.15
64	Antonio Davis	.15
65	Roshown McLeod	.15
66	Anthony Peeler	.15
67	Grant Hill	2.00
68	Michael Olowokandi	.15
69	Kerry Kittles	.15
70	Elton Brand	1.25
71	Tariq Abdul-Wahad	.15
72	Aaron McKie	.15
73	Andrew DeClercq	.15
74	Anfernee Hardaway	1.25
75	Bimbo Coles	.15
76	Terrell Brandon	.30
77	Jalen Rose	.40
78	Radoslav Nesterovic	.15
79	Howard Eisley	.15
80	Steve Smith	.30
81	Rik Smits	.15
82	Jim Jackson	.15
83	Corey Maggette	.50
84	James Posey	.30
85	LaPhonso Ellis	.15
86	Eric Snow	.15
87	Mikki Moore	.15
88	Baron Davis	.50
89	Jason Williams	.60
90	Mike Bibby	.30
91	Marcus Camby	.30
92	Bryon Russell	.15
93	Steve Francis	2.50
94	Sam Cassell	.50
95	Rasheed Wallace	.50
96	Keith Van Horn	.60
97	Eddie Jones	1.00
98	Corliss Williamson	.15
99	Ron Mercer	.30
100	Sean Elliott	.15
101	Shareef Abdur-Rahim	.60
102	Glen Rice	.30
103	Patrick Ewing	.30
104	Adrian Griffin	.15
105	David Robinson	.60
106	Isaac Austin	.15
107	Anthony Mason	.15
108	P.J. Brown	.15
109	Kendall Gill	.15
110	Tyrone Nesby	.15
111	Damon Stoudamire	.30
112	Latrell Sprewell	1.00
113	Tim Duncan	2.50
114	Glenn Robinson	.30
115	John Wallace	.15
116	Erick Strickland	.15
117	Doug Christie	.15
118	Juwan Howard	.30
119	Tim Thomas	.40
120	Tyrone Hill	.15
121	Avery Johnson	.15
122	Jerome Williams	.15
123	Mitch Richmond	.30
124	Hersey Hawkins	.15
125	Donyell Marshall	.15
126	Derek Anderson	.30
127	Jamal Mashburn	.30
128	Richard Hamilton	.40
129	Alonzo Mourning	.40
130	Kelvin Cato	.15
131	Lamond Murray	.15
132	Charles Outlaw	.15
133	Chris Carr	.15
134	Jonathan Bender	.75
135	Paul Pierce	.60
136	Dan Majerle	.15
137	Ron Artest	.40
138	Jermaine O'Neal	.40
139	Chris Whitney	.15
140	Anthony Carter	.30
141	Gary Payton	.60
142	Kevin Garnett	2.50
143	Kevin Willis	.15
144	Charles Oakley	.15
145	Larry Johnson	.15
146	Bonzi Wells	.40
147	Clifford Robinson	.15
148	Chucky Atkins	.15
149	Brian Grant	.30
150	Voshon Lenard	.15
151	Antoine Walker	.50
152	Cuttino Mobley	.30
153	Robert Horry	.15
154	Tracy Murray	.15
155	Kobe Bryant	3.00
156	Joe Smith	.15
157	Jaren Jackson	.15
158	Scott Williams	.15
159	Allen Iverson	2.00
160	Rashard Lewis	.60
161	Chris Mills	.15
162	Karl Malone	.60
163	John Amaechi	.15
164	Jason Terry	.30
165	Ruben Patterson	.30
166	Austin Croshere	.30
167	Maurice Taylor	.15
168	Rod Strickland	.30
169	Clarence Weatherspoon	.15
170	Lindsey Hunter	.15
171	David Wesley	.15
172	Jerry Stackhouse	.30
173	Scott Burrell	.15
174	John Stockton	.30
175	Vitaly Potapenko	.15
176	Dirk Nowitzki	.75
177	Vin Baker	.30
178	Rick Fox	.15
179	Mookie Blaylock	.15
180	Dennis Scott	.15
181	*Chris Mihm*	4.00
182	*Mamadou N'diaye*	1.00
183	*Joel Przybilla*	3.00
184	*Jamaal Magloire*	2.00
185	*Iakovos Tsakalidis*	1.00
186	*Etan Thomas*	1.50
187	*Mark Madsen*	2.00
188	*Hanno Mottola*	1.50
189	*Donnell Harvey*	2.00
190	*Jason Collier*	1.00
191	*Eduardo Najera*	1.50
192	*Jerome Moiso*	2.00
193	*Mateen Cleaves*	4.00
194	*Keyon Dooling*	5.00
195	*Craig "Speedy" Claxton*	2.00
196	*Erick Barkley*	3.00
197	*A.J. Guyton*	2.00
198	*Jamal Crawford*	6.00
199	*Dan Langhi*	2.00
200	*Desmond Mason*	10.00
201	*Chris Porter*	8.00
202	*Cory Hightower*	1.50
203	*Morris Peterson*	12.00
204	*Mark Karcher*	1.00
205	*Courtney Alexander*	10.00
206	*Quentin Richardson*	10.00
207	*DeShawn Stevenson*	12.00
208	*Michael Redd*	2.00
209	*Chris Carrawell*	1.00
210	*Hidayet Turkoglu*	8.00
211	*Kenyon Martin*	15.00
212	*Marcus Fizer*	10.00
213	*Darius Miles*	40.00
214	*Mike Miller*	15.00
215	*DerMarr Johnson*	10.00
216	*Stromile Swift*	20.00
217	Shaquille O'Neal	1.00
218	Allen Iverson	1.00
219	Grant Hill	1.00
220	Vince Carter	2.00
221	Karl Malone	.30
222	Chris Webber	.60
223	Gary Payton	.30
224	Jerry Stackhouse	.15
225	Tim Duncan	1.00
226	Kevin Garnett	1.25
227	Michael Finley	.15
228	Kobe Bryant	1.50
229	Stephon Marbury	.40
230	Ray Allen	.15
231	Alonzo Mourning	.15
232	Glenn Robinson	.15
233	Antoine Walker	.15
234	Shareef Abdur-Rahim	.30
235	Elton Brand	.60
236	Eddie Jones	.50

2000-01 Fleer Focus Draft Position

	MT
Common Player:	1.50
Draft Position/100:	15x-30x
Draft Position/200:	10x-20x
Draft Position/300:	5x-10x

2000-01 Fleer Focus Arena Vision

		MT
Complete Set (15):		25.00
Common Player:		.75
Inserted 1:12		
AV1	Vince Carter	6.00
AV2	Eddie Jones	1.50
AV3	Tim Duncan	3.00
AV4	Kevin Garnett	4.00
AV5	Steve Francis	4.00
AV6	Jason Williams	1.00
AV7	Grant Hill	3.00
AV8	Elton Brand	2.00
AV9	Allen Iverson	3.00
AV10	Lamar Odom	2.00
AV11	Kobe Bryant	5.00
AV12	Jalen Rose	.75
AV13	Paul Pierce	1.00
AV14	Shaquille O'Neal	3.00
AV15	Stephon Marbury	1.00

2000-01 Fleer Focus Planet Hardwood

		MT
Complete Set (10):		35.00
Common Player:		3.00
Inserted 1:24		
VIP Editions:		3x-6x
Production 50 Sets		
PH1	Vince Carter	10.00
PH2	Tim Duncan	5.00
PH3	Kevin Garnett	6.00
PH4	Kobe Bryant	8.00
PH5	Lamar Odom	3.00
PH6	Steve Francis	6.00
PH7	Shaquille O'Neal	5.00
PH8	Tracy McGrady	3.00
PH9	Grant Hill	5.00
PH10	Allen Iverson	5.00

2000-01 Fleer Focus Planet Hardwood VIP Edition

	MT
VIP Editions:	3x-6x
Production 50 Sets	

2000-01 Fleer Focus Welcome to the NBA

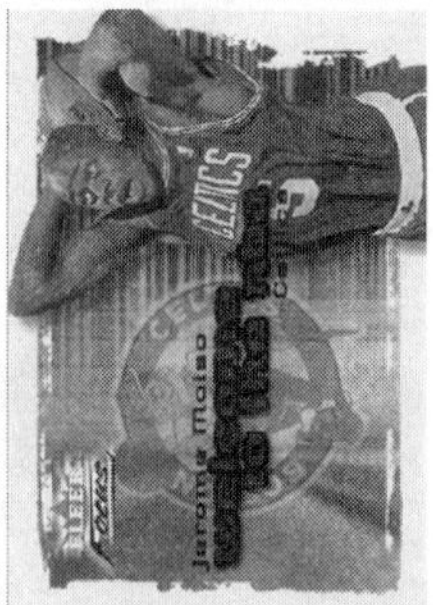

		MT
Complete Set (15):		18.00
Common Player:		.50
Inserted 1:6		
WN1	Kenyon Martin	3.50
WN2	Stromile Swift	3.00
WN3	Darius Miles	5.00
WN4	Marcus Fizer	2.00
WN5	Mike Miller	2.00
WN6	DerMarr Johnson	1.50
WN7	Chris Mihm	1.00
WN8	Jamal Crawford	1.50
WN9	Keyon Dooling	1.25
WN10	Jerome Moiso	1.00
WN11	Etan Thomas	.60
WN12	Courtney Alexander	1.50
WN13	Mateen Cleaves	1.00
WN14	Jason Collier	.50
WN15	Desmond Mason	1.50

2000-01 Fleer Futures

		MT
Complete Set (250):		90.00
Common Player:		.10
Minor Stars:		.20
Common Rookie:		.25
Odd Rookies Inserted 1:7		
Even Rookies Inserted 1:2		
Pack (10):		2.00
Box (24):		40.00
1	Vince Carter	3.00
2	Dan Majerle	.10
3	George McCloud	.10
4	Radoslav Nesterovic	.10
5	Corey Maggette	.40
6	Derek Anderson	.20
7	Ray Allen	.30
8	Greg Ostertag	.10
9	Cedric Ceballos	.10
10	Danny Fortson	.10
11	Roshown McLeod	.10
12	Christian Laettner	.10
13	Avery Johnson	.10
14	Clarence Weatherspoon	.10
15	Michael Curry	.10
16	Chris Whitney	.10
17	Anthony Mason	.10
18	Antonio McDyess	.30
19	Vitaly Potapenko	.10
20	Shaquille O'Neal	1.50
21	David Robinson	.50
22	Tyrone Hill	.10
23	Otis Thorpe	.10
24	Reggie Miller	.20
25	Kevin Garnett	2.00
26	Michael Dickerson	.10
27	John Amaechi	.10
28	Jason Kidd	1.00
29	Ron Artest	.20
30	Muggsy Bogues	.10
31	Antawn Jamison	.75
32	Brian Grant	.10
33	Stephon Marbury	.60
34	William Avery	.10
35	Paul Pierce	.50
36	Marcus Camby	.30
37	Kevin Willis	.10
38	Dikembe Mutombo	.10
39	Rashard Lewis	.50
40	Allan Houston	.30
41	Hakeem Olajuwon	.50
42	Rod Strickland	.20
43	Derrick Coleman	.10
44	Tariq Abdul-Wahad	.10
45	Terrell Brandon	.10
46	Michael Olowokandi	.10
47	Robert Horry	.10
48	Kelvin Cato	.10
49	Eric Williams	.10
50	Glen Rice	.20
51	Carlos Rogers	.10
52	Allen Iverson	2.00
53	P.J. Brown	.10
54	Jalen Rose	.30
55	Damon Stoudamire	.20
56	Damon Jones	.10
57	Darrell Armstrong	.10
58	Samaki Walker	.10
59	John Stockton	.20
60	Chucky Atkins	.10
61	Rasheed Wallace	.30
62	Jason Terry	.20
63	Aaron Williams	.10
64	Steve Nash	.10
65	Antoine Walker	.40
66	Patrick Ewing	.20
67	Cuttino Mobley	.20
68	Aaron McKie	.10
69	Jamal Mashburn	.20
70	Scottie Pippen	.50
71	Bryant Reeves	.10
72	Isaiah Rider	.10
73	Jaren Jackson	.10
74	Lindsey Hunter	.10
75	Jacque Vaughn	.10
76	Travis Best	.10
77	Vinny Del Negro	.10
78	Othella Harrington	.10
79	Michael Finley	.20
80	Brent Barry	.10
81	Brevin Knight	.10
82	Kurt Thomas	.10
83	Mark Jackson	.10
84	Richard Hamilton	.30
85	Anthony Carter	.20
86	Matt Harpring	.10
87	Bobby Jackson	.10
88	Jerome Williams	.10
89	Jahidi White	.10
90	Lorenzen Wright	.10
91	Kerry Kittles	.10
92	Anthony Peeler	.10
93	Kenny Anderson	.10
94	Latrell Sprewell	.75
95	Maurice Taylor	.10
96	Toni Kukoc	.30
97	Eddie Robinson	.20
98	Voshon Lenard	.10
99	Sam Mitchell	.10
100	Isaac Austin	.10
101	Michael Doleac	.10
102	Andre Miller	.40
103	Jason Williams	.50
104	Charles Oakley	.10
105	Mitch Richmond	.20
106	Bruce Bowen	.10
107	Keith Van Horn	.40
108	Wally Szczerbiak	.30
109	Tony Battie	.10
110	Larry Johnson	.10
111	Shandon Anderson	.10
112	Sam Cassell	.10
113	David Wesley	.10
114	James Posey	.10
115	Bonzi Wells	.40
116	Mike Bibby	.30
117	Andrew DeClercq	.10
118	Clifford Robinson	.10
119	Corliss Williamson	.10
120	Antonio Davis	.10
121	Eddie Jones	.60
122	Jamie Feick	.10
123	Anfernee Hardaway	1.00
124	Adrian Griffin	.10
125	Erick Strickland	.10
126	Doug Christie	.10
127	Scot Pollard	.10
128	Sam Perkins	.10
129	Raef LaFrentz	.10
130	Dale Davis	.10
131	Tyrone Nesby	.10
132	Rick Fox	.10
133	Tom Gugliotta	.10
134	Glenn Robinson	.20
135	Quincy Lewis	.10
136	Austin Croshere	.10
137	Shawn Kemp	.30
138	Lamar Odom	1.00
139	Tim Duncan	1.50
140	Tim Thomas	.40
141	Bryon Russell	.10
142	Jermaine O'Neal	.40
143	Erick Dampier	.10
144	Shareef Abdur-Rahim	.50
145	Bo Outlaw	.10
146	Gary Payton	.50
147	Chris Gatling	.10
148	Vlade Divac	.10
149	Ben Wallace	.10
150	Larry Hughes	.60
151	Ron Mercer	.20
152	Karl Malone	.50
153	Jonathan Bender	.60
154	Mookie Blaylock	.10
155	Jim Jackson	.10
156	Chris Crawford	.10
157	Vin Baker	.10
158	Lamond Murray	.10
159	Charlie Ward	.10
160	Steve Francis	2.00
161	Cherokee Parks	.10
162	Baron Davis	.40
163	Keon Clark	.10
164	Ruben Patterson	.10
165	Tracy McGrady	1.00
166	Antonio Daniels	.10
167	Scott Williams	.10
168	John Starks	.10
169	Jerry Stackhouse	.20
170	Vonteego Cummings	.10
171	LaPhonso Ellis	.10
172	Dirk Nowitzki	.75
173	Horace Grant	.10
174	Wesley Person	.10
175	Predrag Stojakovic	.20
176	Eric Snow	.10
177	Juwan Howard	.10
178	Tim Hardaway	.30
179	Kendall Gill	.10
180	Chauncey Billups	.10
181	Kobe Bryant	2.50
182	Sean Elliott	.10
183	Donyell Marshall	.10
184	Al Harrington	.30
185	Arvydas Sabonis	.10
186	Grant Hill	1.50
187	Malik Rose	.10
188	Nazr Mohammed	.10
189	Elden Campbell	.10
190	Nick Van Exel	.20
191	Steve Smith	.20
192	Sean Rooks	.10
193	Monty Williams	.10
194	Elton Brand	1.00
195	Chris Webber	1.25
196	Mikki Moore	.10
197	Chris Mills	.10
198	Alan Henderson	.10
199	Shawn Bradley	.10
200	Shawn Marion	.75
201	*Hidayet Turkoglu*	4.00
202	*Iakovos Tsakalidis*	.25
203	*Kenyon Martin*	5.00
204	*Mamadou N'diaye*	.40
205	*Stromile Swift*	8.00
206	*Pepe Sanchez*	.40
207	*Chris Mihm*	2.00
208	*Lavor Postell*	.50
209	*Marcus Fizer*	4.00
210	*Ruben Garces*	.25
211	*Courtney Alexander*	4.00
212	*A.J. Guyton*	.50
213	*Darius Miles*	15.00
214	*Ademola Okulaja*	.25
215	*Jerome Moiso*	2.00
216	*Khalid El-Amin*	1.00
217	*Joel Przybilla*	1.25
218	*Mike Smith*	.25
219	*DerMarr Johnson*	4.00
220	*Soumaila Samake*	.20
221	*Mike Miller*	8.00
222	*Eddie House*	1.00
223	*Quentin Richardson*	4.00
224	*Eduardo Najera*	.60
225	*Morris Peterson*	5.00
226	*Hanno Mottola*	.40
227	*Craig "Speedy" Claxton*	1.50
228	*Ruben Wolkowyski*	.25
229	*Keyon Dooling*	4.00
230	*Olumide Oyedji*	.25
231	*Mark Madsen*	1.50
232	*Mike Penberthy*	.75
233	*Mateen Cleaves*	3.00
234	*Brian Cardinal*	.25
235	*Etan Thomas*	1.50
236	*Garth Joseph*	.25
237	*Jason Collier*	1.00
238	*Paul McPherson*	.75
239	*Erick Barkley*	2.00
240	*Stephen Jackson*	1.00
241	*Desmond Mason*	4.00
242	*Jason Hart*	.40
243	*Jamal Crawford*	4.00
244	*Daniel Santiago*	.60
245	*DeShawn Stevenson*	5.00

246 *Stanislav Medvedenko* .25
247 *Donnell Harvey* 1.50
248 *Chris Porter* 3.00
249 *Jamaal Magloire* 1.50
250 *Dalibor Bagaric* .25

2000-01 Fleer Futures Black Gold

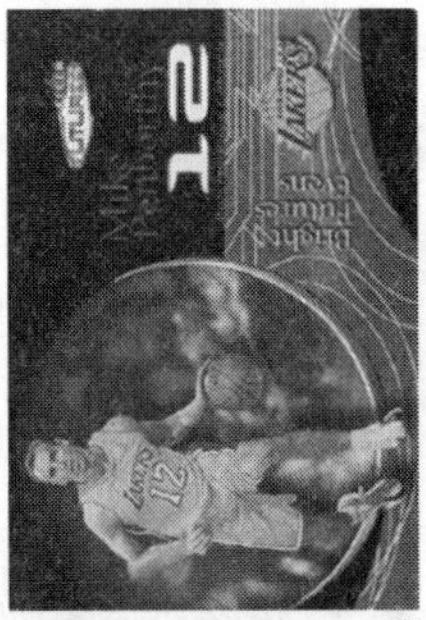

	MT
Black Gold Evens:	.5-1x
Black Gold Odds:	1.5x-3x.25
Production 500 Sets	

2000-01 Fleer Futures Copper

	MT
Common Player (1-200):	.60
Copper Cards:	3x-6x
Production 750 Sets	

2000-01 Fleer Futures Autographics On Location

		MT
Common Player:		15.00
Inserted 1:403		
1	Shareef Abdur-Rahim	30.00
2	Travis Best	20.00
3	Vince Carter/240	250.00
4	Austin Croshere	20.00
5	Baron Bavis	15.00
6	Rashard Lewis	35.00
7	Dan Majerle	40.00
8	Dirk Nowitzki	50.00
9	Lamar Odom/240	35.00
10	Mitch Richmond	25.00
11	Jalen Rose	30.00
12	Jerry Stackhouse/240	20.00

2000-01 Fleer Futures Characteristics

		MT
Complete Set (10):		30.00
Common Player:		1.50
Inserted 1:28		
1	Vince Carter	10.00
2	Kobe Bryant	8.00
3	Lamar Odom	3.00
4	Kevin Garnett	6.00
5	Allen Iverson	6.00
6	Grant Hill	5.00
7	Tim Duncan	5.00
8	Steve Francis	6.00
9	Jason Williams	1.50
10	Shaquille O'Neal	5.00

2000-01 Fleer Futures Hot Commodities

		MT
Complete Set (10):		35.00
Common Player:		3.00
Inserted 1:28		
1	Vince Carter	10.00
2	Kobe Bryant	8.00
3	Kevin Garnett	6.00
4	Allen Iverson	6.00
5	Shaquille O'Neal	5.00
6	Steve Francis	6.00
7	Grant Hill	5.00
8	Tim Duncan	5.00
9	Lamar Odom	3.00
10	Tracy McGrady	3.00

2000-01 Fleer Futures Question Air

		MT
Complete Set (15):		30.00
Common Player:		1.00
Inserted 1:14		
1	Kenyon Martin	5.00
2	Stromile Swift	5.00
3	Chris Mihm	1.50
4	Marcus Fizer	4.00
5	Courtney Alexander	3.00
6	Darius Miles	10.00
7	Jerome Moiso	1.50
8	Desmond Mason	3.00
9	DerMarr Johnson	3.00
10	Mike Miller	4.00
11	Quentin Richardson	3.00
12	Morris Peterson	4.00
13	Etan Thomas	1.00
14	Keyon Dooling	3.00
15	Mateen Cleaves	2.50

2000-01 Fleer Futures Rookie Game Jerseys

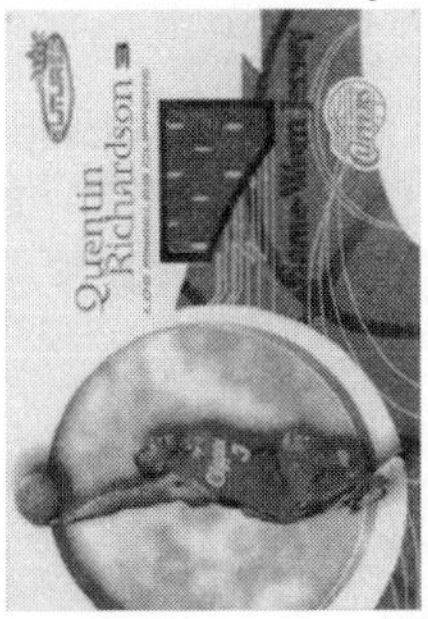

		MT
Common Player:		15.00
Production 300 Hobby Sets		
203	Kenyon Martin	60.00
207	Chris Mihm	20.00
213	Darius Miles	150.00
219	DerMarr Johnson	30.00
221	Mike Miller	40.00
223	Quentin Richardson	30.00
226	Hanno Mottola	15.00
227	Craig Claxton	20.00
229	Keyon Dooling	30.00
241	Desmond Mason	40.00

2000-01 Fleer Game Time

		MT
Complete Set (120):		150.00
Common Player:		.15
Minor Stars:		.30
Common Rookie:		1.50
Production 2,500 Sets		
Pack (5):		4.00
Box (24):		70.00
1	Vince Carter	4.00
2	Raef LaFrentz	.15
3	Kobe Bryant	3.00
4	Toni Kukoc	.40
5	Bonzi Wells	.40
6	Rashard Lewis	.60
7	Karl Malone	.60
8	Juwan Howard	.30
9	Lindsey Hunter	.15
10	Alonzo Mourning	.40
11	Larry Hughes	.75
12	Austin Croshere	.15
13	Charles Oakley	.15
14	Patrick Ewing	.30
15	Vlade Divac	.15
16	Michael Finley	.30
17	Tim Hardaway	.40
18	Jason Kidd	1.25
19	Cal Bowdler	.15
20	Dirk Nowitzki	1.00
21	Terrell Brandon	.15
22	Allan Houston	.40
23	Theo Ratliff	.15
24	Chris Webber	1.25
25	Shawn Kemp	.40
26	Jalen Rose	.40
27	Bryon Russell	.15
28	Jahidi White	.15
29	Trajan Langdon	.15
30	Baron Davis	.50
31	Cuttino Mobley	.30
32	Wally Szczerbiak	.40
33	Michael Dickerson	.15
34	Andre Miller	.50
35	Michael Olowokandi	.15
36	Ray Allen	.40
37	Latrell Sprewell	1.00
38	Jason Williams	.60
39	Mikki Moore	.15
40	Shawn Marion	1.00
41	Joe Smith	.15
42	Ron Artest	.30
43	Vonteego Cummings	.15
44	Anfernee Hardaway	1.25
45	Jerome Williams	.15
46	John Stockton	.30
47	Antawn Jamison	1.00
48	Grant Hill	2.00
49	Elden Campbell	.15
50	Steve Francis	2.50
51	Jamie Feick	.15
52	Gary Payton	.60
53	Elton Brand	1.25
54	Eddie Jones	.75
55	Tom Gugliotta	.15
56	Richard Hamilton	.40
57	Dion Glover	.15
58	Shaquille O'Neal	2.00
59	Kevin Garnett	2.50
60	Paul Pierce	.60
61	Brian Grant	.15
62	Tim Thomas	.40
63	Tracy McGrady	1.25
64	Jonathan Bender	1.00
65	Adrian Griffin	.15
66	Lamar Odom	1.25
67	Rasheed Wallace	.40
68	Mike Bibby	.30
69	Glenn Robinson	.30
70	Eddie Robinson	.15
71	Robert Horry	.15
72	Jerry Stackhouse	.30
73	Stephon Marbury	.75
74	Marcus Camby	.30
75	Scottie Pippen	1.25
76	David Robinson	.60
77	Jason Terry	.30
78	Reggie Miller	.30
79	Larry Johnson	.15
80	Antonio Daniels	.15
81	Shareef Abdur-Rahim	.60
82	Ruben Patterson	.15
83	Nick Van Exel	.30
84	Keith Van Horn	.50
85	Antonio Davis	.15
86	Antoine Walker	.50
87	Allen Iverson	2.00
88	Antonio McDyess	.40
89	Tim Duncan	2.50
90	Hakeem Olajuwon	.60
91	*Jamaal Magloire*	3.00
92	*DerMarr Johnson*	6.00
93	*Jerome Moiso*	3.00
94	*Marcus Fizer*	6.00
95	*Jamal Crawford*	6.00
96	*Chris Mihm*	3.00
97	*Donnell Harvey*	2.50
98	*Courtney Alexander*	6.00
99	*Etan Thomas*	2.50
100	*Mamadou N'diaye*	1.50
101	*Mateen Cleaves*	5.00
102	*Chris Porter*	5.00
103	*Jason Collier*	1.50
104	*Keyon Dooling*	6.00
105	*Darius Miles*	25.00
106	*Mark Madsen*	3.00
107	*Eddie House*	4.00
108	*Joel Przybilla*	2.00
109	*Kenyon Martin*	10.00
110	*Mike Miller*	12.00
111	*Craig "Speedy" Claxton*	2.50
112	*Iakovos Tsakalidis*	1.50
113	*Erick Barkley*	3.00
114	*Hidayet Turkoglu*	6.00
115	*Eduardo Najera*	2.00
116	*Desmond Mason*	6.00
117	*Morris Peterson*	10.00
118	*DeShawn Stevenson*	10.00
119	*Stromile Swift*	12.00
120	*Mike Smith*	1.50

2000-01 Fleer Game Time Extra

	MT
Common Player:	.60
Extra Veterans:	2x-4x
Inserted 1:8	
Common Rookie:	4.00
Extra Rookies:	1x-2x
Production 250 Sets	

2000-01 Fleer Game Time Attack the Rack

		MT
Complete Set (20):		20.00
Common Player:		.50
Inserted 1:4		
AR1	Vince Carter	5.00
AR2	Lamar Odom	1.50
AR3	Kobe Bryant	4.00
AR4	Shareef Abdur-Rahim	.75
AR5	Allen Iverson	2.50
AR6	Jason Williams	.75
AR7	Kevin Garnett	3.00
AR8	Tim Duncan	2.50
AR9	Latrell Sprewell	1.00
AR10	Shaquille O'Neal	2.50
AR11	Jalen Rose	.50
AR12	Antawn Jamison	1.00
AR13	Paul Pierce	.75
AR14	Grant Hill	2.50
AR15	Eddie Jones	1.00
AR16	Karl Malone	.75
AR17	Elton Brand	1.50
AR18	Tracy McGrady	1.50
AR19	Michael Finley	.50
AR20	Steve Francis	3.00

2000-01 Fleer Game Time Change the Game

		MT
Complete Set (15):		60.00
Common Player:		2.00
Inserted 1:24		
CG1	Vince Carter	15.00
CG2	Lamar Odom	5.00
CG3	Kobe Bryant	12.00
CG4	Allen Iverson	8.00
CG5	Jason Kidd	5.00
CG6	Grant Hill	8.00
CG7	Tim Duncan	8.00
CG8	Shaquille O'Neal	8.00
CG9	Kevin Garnett	10.00
CG10	Elton Brand	5.00
CG11	Stephon Marbury	3.00
CG12	Jason Williams	2.00
CG13	Keith Van Horn	2.00
CG14	Steve Francis	10.00
CG15	Gary Payton	2.50

2000-01 Fleer Game Time Uniformity

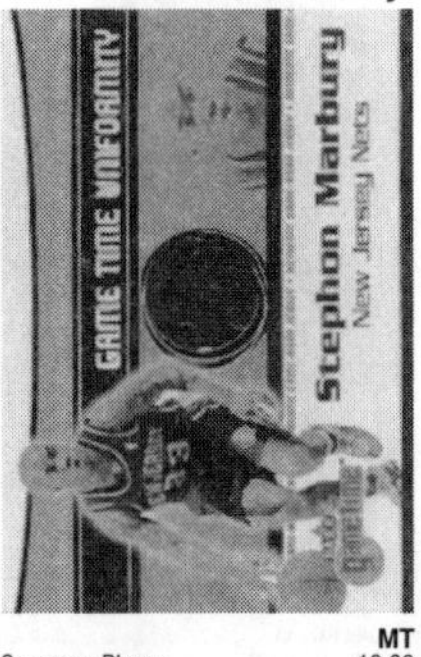

	MT
Common Player:	10.00
Inserted 1:24	
Shareef Abdur-Rahim	15.00
Mike Bibby	10.00
Vince Carter	100.00
Vince Carter Auto/150	250.00
Baron Davis	25.00
Sean Elliot	10.00
Allen Iverson	50.00
Toni Kukoc	25.00
Karl Malone	25.00
Stephon Marbury	25.00
Shawn Marion	25.00
Alonzo Mourning	20.00
Lamar Odom	30.00
Shaquille O'Neal Gold	60.00
Shaquille O'Neal Purple	60.00
Gary Payton	25.00
Scot Pollard	10.00
Jalen Rose	25.00
John Stockton	30.00
Wally Sczcerbiak	15.00
Jason Terry	15.00
Keith Van Horn	15.00
Antoine Walker	20.00
David Wesley	10.00

2000-01 Fleer Game Time Vince & the Revolution

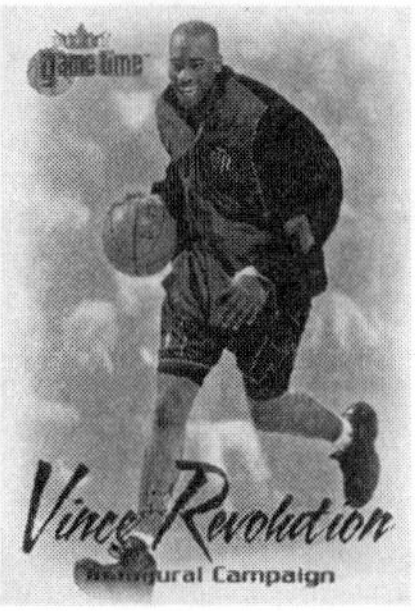

		MT
Complete Set (15):		75.00
Common Player (1-5):		2.00
Inserted 1:9		
Common Player (6-10):		8.00
Inserted 1:24		
Common Player (11-15):		15.00
Inserted 1:144		
VR1	Vince Carter	2.00
VR2	Vince Carter	2.00
VR3	Vince Carter	2.00
VR4	Vince Carter	2.00
VR5	Vince Carter	2.00
VR6	Vince Carter	8.00
VR7	Vince Carter	8.00
VR8	Vince Carter	8.00
VR9	Vince Carter	8.00
VR10	Vince Carter	8.00
VR11	Vince Carter	15.00
VR12	Vince Carter	15.00
VR13	Vince Carter	15.00
VR14	Vince Carter	15.00
VR15	Vince Carter	15.00

2000-01 Fleer Genuine

		MT
Complete Set (130):		300.00
Common Player:		.25
Minor Stars:		.40
Common Rookie:		4.00
Production 1,500 Sets		
Pack (5):		6.00
Box (24):		70.00
1	Vince Carter	5.00
2	Glenn Robinson	.40
3	Rasheed Wallace	.60
4	Michael Dickerson	.25
5	Mikki Moore	.25
6	Wally Szczerbiak	.50
7	Shawn Marion	1.25
8	Dan Majerle	.25
9	Trajan Langdon	.25
10	Joe Smith	.25
11	Jason Kidd	1.50
12	Derrick Coleman	.40
13	Jason Terry	.40
14	Eddie Jones	1.00
15	Scottie Pippen	1.50
16	Mike Bibby	.40
17	Ron Mercer	.40
18	Hakeem Olajuwon	.75
19	Patrick Ewing	.40
20	Ruben Patterson	.25
21	Kenny Anderson	.40
22	Alonzo Mourning	.50
23	Steve Smith	.40
24	Juwan Howard	.40
25	Antoine Walker	.50
26	Kobe Bryant	4.00
27	Chris Webber	1.50
28	Mitch Richmond	.40
29	Paul Pierce	.75
30	Shaquille O'Neal	2.50
31	Jason Williams	.60
32	Richard Hamilton	.50
33	Michael Finley	.40
34	Jalen Rose	.50
35	Grant Hill	2.50
36	John Stockton	.40
37	Vitaly Potapenko	.25
38	Glen Rice	.40
39	Vlade Divac	.25
40	Jahidi White	.25
41	Baron Davis	.60
42	Michael Olowokandi	.25
43	Tim Duncan	2.50
44	Rod Strickland	.25
45	Jamal Mashburn	.40
46	Lamar Odom	.40
47	David Robinson	1.50
48	Travis Best	.75
49	Raef LaFrentz	.25
50	Keith Van Horn	.75
51	Vonteego Cummings	.25
52	Jerome Williams	.25
53	Kevin Garnett	3.00
54	Anfernee Hardaway	1.50
55	Antonio McDyess	.50
56	Reggie Miller	.40
57	Tracy McGrady	1.50
58	Bryon Russell	.25
59	Nick Van Exel	.40
60	Allen Iverson	2.50
61	Karl Malone	.75
62	David Wesley	.25
63	Bob Sura	.25
64	Stephon Marbury	1.00
65	Antonio Daniels	.25
66	Shawn Kemp	.30
67	Cuttino Mobley	.40
68	Marcus Camby	.40
69	Gary Payton	.75
70	Dikembe Mutombo	.40
71	Tim Hardaway	.50
72	Bonzi Wells	.50
73	Shareef Abdur-Rahim	.75
74	Brevin Knight	.25
75	Steve Francis	3.00
76	Allan Houston	.40
77	Dion Glover	.25
78	Dirk Nowitzki	1.00
79	Jonathan Bender	1.00
80	Darrell Armstrong	.25
81	Antonio Davis	.25
82	Jerry Stackhouse	.40
83	Terrell Brandon	.40
84	Tom Gugliotta	.25
85	Sean Elliott	.25
86	Elton Brand	1.50
87	Larry Hughes	1.00
88	Kerry Kittles	.25
89	Vin Baker	.40
90	Donyell Marshall	.25
91	Tim Thomas	.50
92	Toni Kukoc	.50
93	Charles Oakley	.25
94	Andre Miller	.60
95	Austin Croshere	.25
96	Latrell Sprewell	1.00
97	Mark Jackson	.25
98	Antawn Jamison	1.00
99	Ray Allen	.50
100	Theo Ratliff	.25
101	*Chris Mihm*	6.00
102	*Mateen Cleaves*	10.00
103	*Etan Thomas*	5.00
104	*Morris Peterson*	20.00
105	*Jamal Crawford*	15.00
106	*Darius Miles*	50.00
107	*Desmond Mason*	15.00
108	*Joel Przybilla*	5.00
109	*Mike Miller*	25.00
110	*Quentin Richardson*	15.00
111	*Jason Collier*	4.00
112	*Keyon Dooling*	15.00
113	*Courtney Alexander*	15.00
114	*Eddie House*	8.00
115	*DerMarr Johnson*	15.00
116	*Michael Redd*	4.00
117	*Mark Madsen*	6.00
118	*Stromile Swift*	25.00
119	*Mamadou N'diaye*	4.00
120	*DeShawn Stevenson*	20.00
121	*Hidayet Turkoglu*	15.00
122	*Stephen Jackson*	6.00
123	*Marcus Fizer*	15.00
124	*Khalid El-Amin*	4.00
125	*Craig "Speedy" Claxton*	5.00
126	*Hanno Mottola*	4.00
127	*Jerome Moiso*	6.00
128	*Jamaal Magloire*	6.00
129	*Donnell Harvey*	5.00
130	*Kenyon Martin*	20.00
NNO	Vince Carter Main Man (150)	150.00
NNO	Vince Carter Main Man Auto (15)	

2000-01 Fleer Genuine Formidable

MT
Complete Set (15): 65.00
Common Player: 2.00
Inserted 1:23

F1	Vince Carter	15.00
F2	Lamar Odom	5.00
F3	Tracy McGrady	5.00
F4	Jason Williams	2.00
F5	Jason Kidd	5.00
F6	Chris Webber	5.00
F7	Elton Brand	5.00
F8	Steve Francis	10.00
F9	Grant Hill	8.00
F10	Shaquille O'Neal	8.00
F11	Allen Iverson	8.00
F12	Kobe Bryant	12.00
F13	Tim Duncan	8.00
F14	Kevin Garnett	10.00
F15	Latrell Sprewell	3.00

2000-01 Fleer Genuine Genuine Coverage PLUS

MT
Complete Set (8): 500.00
Common Player: 40.00
Production 150 Sets

1	Vince Carter	200.00
2	Lamar Odom	75.00
3	Karl Malone	60.00
4	Paul Pierce	50.00
5	Shawn Marion	60.00
6	Antoine Walker	40.00
7	Shaquille O'Neal	100.00
8	David Robinson	60.00

2000-01 Fleer Genuine Northern Flights

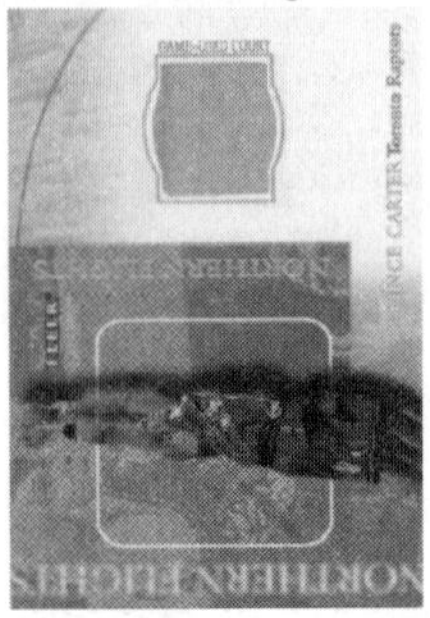

MT
Complete Set (5): 125.00
Common Player: 30.00
Inserted 1:22
Carter Autographs: 250.00
Production 150 Cards

2000-01 Fleer Genuine Smooth Operators

MT
Complete Set (15): 50.00
Common Player: 1.00
Inserted 1:23

SO1	Vince Carter	15.00
SO2	Lamar Odom	5.00
SO3	Allen Iverson	8.00
SO4	Kobe Bryant	12.00
SO5	Kevin Garnett	10.00
SO6	Tim Duncan	8.00
SO7	Antawn Jamison	3.00
SO8	Michael Finley	1.00
SO9	Ray Allen	1.50
SO10	Paul Pierce	2.00
SO11	Karl Malone	2.00
SO12	Shaquille O'Neal	8.00
SO13	Elton Brand	5.00
SO14	Jason Williams	2.00
SO15	Jalen Rose	1.50

2000-01 Fleer Genuine YES! Men

MT
Complete Set (10): 25.00
Common Player: 1.00
Inserted 1:23

Y1	Vince Carter	10.00
Y2	Lamar Odom	3.00
Y3	Kobe Bryant	8.00
Y4	Kevin Garnett	6.00
Y5	Tim Duncan	5.00
Y6	Eddie Jones	2.00
Y7	Allan Houston	1.00
Y8	Grant Hill	5.00
Y9	Elton Brand	3.00
Y10	Steve Francis	6.00

2000-01 Fleer Glossy

MT
Complete Set (251): 250.00
Common Player: .10
Minor Stars: .20
Common Rookie: 1.00
Pack (8): 3.00
Box (24): 60.00

1	Lamar Odom	1.00
2	Christian Laettner	.10
3	Michael Olowokandi	.10
4	Anthony Carter	.10
5	Steve Francis	2.00
6	Darvin Ham	.10
7	Mitch Richmond	.20
8	Corliss Williamson	.10
9	Jason Terry	.20
10	Brian Grant	.10
11	Predrag Stojakovic	.20
12	Rick Fox	.10
13	Tyrone Hill	.10
14	Chauncey Billups	.10
15	Otis Thorpe	.10
16	Richard Hamilton	.30
17	Ervin Johnson	.10
18	Jim Jackson	.10
19	Theo Ratliff	.10
20	Doug Christie	.10
21	Jalen Rose	.20
22	John Wallace	.10
23	Ruben Patterson	.10
24	Steve Nash	.10
25	Toni Kukoc	.30
26	Anthony Peeler	.10
27	Ray Allen	.30
28	Adonal Foyle	.10
29	Chris Whitney	.10
30	Nick Van Exel	.20
31	Sean Elliott	.10
32	Erick Strickland	.10
33	Jerry Stackhouse	.20
34	Antawn Jamison	.75
35	Grant Hill	1.50
36	Antonio Daniels	.10
37	Karl Malone	.50
38	Keith Van Horn	.40
39	Ron Harper	.10
40	Stephon Marbury	.60
41	Bryon Russell	.10
42	Corey Maggette	.40
43	Hersey Hawkins	.10
44	Vince Carter	4.00
45	Paul Pierce	.50
46	Mikki Moore	.10
47	Othella Harrington	.10
48	Erick Dampier	.10
49	Jerome Williams	.10
50	Nick Anderson	.10
51	Tim Hardaway	.30
52	Allan Houston	.30
53	Tyrone Nesby	.10
54	Brevin Knight	.10
55	Chris Mills	.10
56	Ron Artest	.20
57	Walt Williams	.10
58	Duane Causwell	.10
59	Bonzi Wells	.30
60	Rasheed Wallace	.40
61	Dikembe Mutombo	.10
62	Jahidi White	.10
63	Chris Webber	1.25
64	Tony Battie	.10
65	Mahmoud Abdul-Rauf	.10
66	Monty Williams	.10
67	Charlie Ward	.10
68	David Robinson	.50
69	Eric Snow	.10
70	Jermaine O'Neal	.40
71	Kurt Thomas	.10
72	James Posey	.10
73	Travis Best	.10
74	Jonathan Bender	.50
75	John Stockton	.20
76	Jacque Vaughn	.10
77	Ron Mercer	.20
78	Shawn Marion	.75
79	Larry Johnson	.10
80	Maurice Taylor	.10
81	Clifford Robinson	.10
82	Scot Pollard	.10
83	Patrick Ewing	.20
84	Terrell Brandon	.20
85	Horace Grant	.10
86	Vin Baker	.20
87	Al Harrington	.30
88	Larry Hughes	.50
89	David Wesley	.10
90	Wally Szczerbiak	.30
91	Charles Oakley	.10
92	Tim Thomas	.10
93	Mookie Blaylock	.10
94	Jamal Mashburn	.20
95	Roshown McLeod	.10
96	John Starks	.10
97	Rodney Rogers	.10
98	Juwan Howard	.20
99	Isaiah Rider	.20
100	Rashard Lewis	.40
101	Dion Glover	.10
102	Johnny Newman	.10
103	Avery Johnson	.10
104	Darrell Armstrong	.10
105	Eric Williams	.10
106	Gary Payton	.50
107	Antonio Davis	.10
108	Dirk Nowitzki	.75
109	Trajan Langdon	.10
110	Michael Dickerson	.20
111	Joe Smith	.10
112	Rod Strickland	.20
113	Shawn Kemp	.30
114	Voshon Lenard	.10
115	Marcus Camby	.30
116	Matt Harpring	.10
117	Isaac Austin	.10
118	Malik Rose	.10
119	Pat Garrity	.10
120	Kenny Thomas	.10
121	LaPhonso Ellis	.10
122	Danny Fortson	.10
123	Elton Brand	1.00
124	Jason Williams	.50
125	Kobe Bryant	3.00
126	Tariq Abdul-Wahad	.10
127	Tracy McGrady	1.00
128	Matt Geiger	.10
129	Antoine Walker	.30
130	Michael Finley	.30
131	Andre Miller	.40
132	Robert Horry	.10
133	Donyell Marshall	.10
134	Shareef Abdur-Rahim	.50
135	Vonteego Cummings	.10
136	Anthony Mason	.10
137	Mike Bibby	.20
138	Raef LaFrentz	.10
139	Glen Rice	.20
140	Chris Gatling	.10
141	Latrell Sprewell	.75
142	Austin Croshere	.10
143	Kenny Anderson	.20
144	Elden Campbell	.10
145	Jason Kidd	1.00
146	Michael Doleac	.10
147	Muggsy Bogues	.10
148	Tim Duncan	1.50
149	Samaki Walker	.10
150	Gary Trent	.10
151	Kevin Garnett	2.00
152	Allen Iverson	1.50
153	Anfernee Hardaway	1.00
154	Robert Traylor	.10
155	Scottie Pippen	1.00
156	Shaquille O'Neal	1.50
157	Vlade Divac	.10
158	Lucious Harris	.10
159	Keon Clark	.10
160	Bo Outlaw	.10
161	P.J. Brown	.10
162	Derrick Coleman	.10
163	Mark Jackson	.10
164	Lamond Murray	.10
165	Dan Majerle	.10
166	Eddie Jones	.60
167	Cedric Ceballos	.10
168	Kendall Gill	.10
169	Tom Gugliotta	.10
170	Jeff McInnis	.10
171	Steve Smith	.20
172	Kevin Willis	.10
173	Lindsey Hunter	.10
174	Derek Anderson	.20
175	Shandon Anderson	.10
176	Adrian Griffin	.10
177	Baron Davis	.40
178	Radoslav Nesterovic	.10
179	Glenn Robinson	.20
180	Sam Cassell	.20
181	Chucky Atkins	.10
182	Arvydas Sabonis	.10
183	Damon Stoudamire	.20
184	Antonio McDyess	.40
185	Derek Fisher	.10
186	Bryant Reeves	.10
187	Hakeem Olajuwon	.50
188	Kerry Kittles	.10
189	Alan Henderson	.10
190	Sam Perkins	.10
191	Felipe Lopez	.10
192	Tracy Murray	.10
193	Shammond Williams	.10
194	Vitaly Potapenko	.10
195	John Amaechi	.10
196	Quincy Lewis	.10
197	Reggie Miller	.20
198	Cuttino Mobley	.20
199	Rex Chapman	.10
200	Dale Davis	.10
201	*Stromile Swift 1000*	25.00
202	*Stephen Jackson 1000*	5.00
203	*Erick Barkley 1000*	5.00
204	*Mike Miller 1000*	25.00
205	*Kenyon Martin 1000*	15.00
206	*Michael Redd 1000*	3.00
207	*Darius Miles 1000*	50.00
208	*Chris Mihm 1000*	5.00
209	*Brian Cardinal 1000*	2.00
210	*Khalid El-Amin 1000*	3.00
211	*Hanno Mottola 1500*	2.00
212	*Jamaal Magloire 1500*	4.00
213	*Courtney Alexander 1500*	8.00
214	*Mamadou N'diaye 1500*	1.50
215	*Chris Porter 1500*	6.00
216	*Quentin Richardson 1500*	10.00
217	*Eddie House 1500*	6.00
218	*Joel Przybilla 1500*	3.00
219	*Soumaila Samake 1500*	1.00
220	*Craig "Speedy" Claxton 1500*	3.00
221	*Desmond Mason 1500*	10.00
222	*Mike Smith 1500*	1.00
223	*Lavor Postell 1500*	2.00
224	*Pepe Sanchez 1500*	2.00
225	*DeShawn Stevenson 1500*	12.00
226	*Hidayet Turkoglu 1500*	8.00
227	*Keyon Dooling 1500*	8.00
228	*Dan Langhi 1500*	2.00
229	*Mateen Cleaves 1500*	6.00
230	*Donnell Harvey 1500*	3.00
231	*DerMarr Johnson 1500*	8.00
232	*Jason Collier 1500*	2.00
233	*Jake Voskuhl 1500*	1.00
234	*Mark Madsen 1500*	4.00
235	*Jabari Smith 1250*	1.50
236	*Morris Peterson 1250*	12.00
237	*Daniel Santiago 1250*	1.50
238	*Etan Thomas 1250*	3.00
239	*A.J. Guyton 1250*	2.50
240	*Marcus Fizer 1250*	8.00
241	*Jamal Crawford 1250*	8.00
242	*Jerome Moiso 1250*	4.00
243	*Olumide Oyedji 1250*	1.50
244	*Paul McPherson 1250*	2.00
245	*Eduardo Najera 1250*	2.50
246	*Marc Jackson Auto/500*	50.00
247	*Mike Penberthy Auto/500*	15.00
248	*Dragan Tarlac Auto/500*	10.00
249	*Ruben Wolkowyski Auto/500*	10.00
250	*Iakovos Tsakalidis Auto/500*	10.00
251	*Ruben Garces Auto/500*	10.00

2000-01 Fleer Glossy Class Acts

MT
Complete Set (25): 125.00
Common Player: 1.50
Inserted 1:72

1	Hakeem Olajuwon	5.00
2	Karl Malone	5.00
3	Patrick Ewing	2.00
4	Ron Harper	1.50
5	David Robinson	5.00
6	Scottie Pippen	8.00
7	Mitch Richmond	2.00
8	Tim Hardaway	3.00
9	Gary Payton	5.00
10	Larry Johnson	1.50
11	Shaquille O'Neal	12.00
12	Allan Houston	3.00
13	Chris Webber	10.00
14	Jason Kidd	8.00
15	Grant Hill	12.00
16	Kevin Garnett	15.00
17	Allen Iverson	12.00
18	Kobe Bryant	20.00
19	Tracy McGrady	8.00
20	Tim Duncan	12.00
21	Dirk Nowitzki	6.00
22	Larry Hughes	5.00
23	Vince Carter	25.00
24	Elton Brand	8.00
25	Steve Francis	15.00

2000-01 Fleer Glossy Coach's Corner

MT
Common Player: 10.00
Inserted 1:108

1	Pat Riley	50.00
2	Doc Rivers	20.00
3	Paul Silas	10.00
4	Isiah Thomas	35.00
5	Rudy Tomjanovich	20.00
6	Jeff Van Gundy	20.00
7	Lenny Wilkens	20.00

2000-01 Fleer Glossy Game Breakers

MT
Complete Set (10): 40.00
Common Player: 4.00
Inserted 1:24

1	Allen Iverson	6.00
2	Elton Brand	4.00
3	Grant Hill	6.00
4	Jason Kidd	4.00
5	Kevin Garnett	8.00
6	Kobe Bryant	10.00
7	Shaquille O'Neal	6.00
8	Steve Francis	8.00
9	Tim Duncan	6.00
10	Vince Carter	12.00

2000-01 Fleer Glossy Hardwood Leaders

MT
Complete Set (20): 30.00
Common Player: 1.50
Inserted 1:12

1	Allen Iverson	4.00
2	Jason Williams	1.50
3	Vince Carter	8.00
4	Scottie Pippen	2.50
5	Kevin Garnett	5.00
6	Karl Malone	1.50
7	Grant Hill	4.00
8	Jason Kidd	2.00
9	Kobe Bryant	6.00
10	Elton Brand	2.50
11	Shaquille O'Neal	4.00
12	Tim Duncan	4.00
13	Tracy McGrady	2.50
14	Chris Webber	3.00
15	Lamar Odom	2.50

2000-01 Fleer Glossy Rookie Sensations

MT
Complete Set (25): 25.00
Common Player: .60
Inserted 1:6

1	Jamaal Magloire	1.00
2	Etan Thomas	1.00
3	Chris Mihm	1.00
4	Joel Przybilla	.75
5	Mamadou N'diaye	.60
6	Jason Collier	.60
7	DerMarr Johnson	2.00
8	Jerome Moiso	1.00
9	Darius Miles	8.00
10	Marcus Fizer	2.00
11	Kenyon Martin	3.00
12	Mark Madsen	1.00
13	Mike Miller	4.00
14	Desmond Mason	2.50
15	Morris Peterson	3.00
16	Hidayet Turkoglu	2.00
17	Mateen Cleaves	1.50
18	Keyon Dooling	2.00
19	DeShawn Stevenson	3.00
20	Quentin Richardson	2.50
21	Courtney Alexander	2.00
22	Stromile Swift	4.00
23	Stephen Jackson	1.00
24	Erick Barkley	1.00
25	Khalid El-Amin	.75

2000-01 Fleer Glossy Traditional Threads

MT
Common Player: 10.00
Inserted 1:63

1	Vince Carter	75.00
2	Baron Davis	20.00
3	Trajan Langdon	10.00
4	Grant Hill	35.00
5	Allen Iverson	50.00
6	Jason Kidd	30.00
7	Karl Malone	20.00
8	Stephon Marbury	20.00
9	Shawn Marion	25.00
10	Tracy McGrady	50.00
11	Andre Miller	15.00
12	Dikembe Mutombo	15.00
13	Lamar Odom	30.00
14	Shaquille O'Neal	50.00
15	Gary Payton	20.00
16	Jason Terry	15.00
17	John Stockton	25.00
18	Anfernee Hardaway	30.00
19	Jason Williams	25.00
20	Darius Miles	75.00
21	Chris Mihm	10.00
22	Desmond Mason	20.00
23	Keyon Dooling	15.00
24	DerMarr Johnson	15.00
25	Craig "Speedy" Claxton	10.00
26	Kenyon Martin	25.00
27	Hanno Mottola	10.00
28	Mike Miller	30.00
29	Quentin Richardson	20.00

2000-01 Fleer Mystique

MT
Complete Set (136): 450.00
Common Player: .25
Minor Stars: .40
Common Rookie: 1.00
Cards 101-106 Numbered to 750
Cards 107-112 Numbered to 1000
Cards 113-118 Numbered to 2000
Cards 119-124 Numbered to 3000
Cards 125-130 Numbered to 4000
Cards 131-136 Numbered to 5000
Pack (5): 5.00
Box (24): 60.00

1	Shaquille O'Neal	2.50
2	Gary Payton	.75
3	Nick Van Exel	.40
4	Alonzo Mourning	.50
5	Shawn Marion	1.00
6	Rod Strickland	.40
7	Mookie Blaylock	.25
8	Terrell Brandon	.40
9	Bryon Russell	.25
10	Jerry Stackhouse	.40
11	Glenn Robinson	.40
12	Rasheed Wallace	.60
13	Tracy McGrady	1.50
14	Raef LaFrentz	.25
15	P.J. Brown	.25
16	Anfernee Hardaway	1.50
17	Mike Bibby	.40
18	Elden Campbell	.25
19	Steve Francis	3.00
20	Keith Van Horn	.75
21	Karl Malone	.75
22	Dirk Nowitzki	.75
23	Glen Rice	.40
24	Tom Gugliotta	.25
25	Avery Johnson	.25
26	Michael Finley	.40
27	Theo Ratliff	.25
28	Juwan Howard	.40
29	Anthony Carter	.40
30	Kobe Bryant	4.00
31	Toni Kukoc	.50
32	Jason Terry	.40
33	Elton Brand	1.50
34	Reggie Miller	.40
35	Latrell Sprewell	1.00
36	Adrian Griffin	.25
37	Cuttino Mobley	.25
38	Maurice Taylor	.40
39	Allen Iverson	2.50
40	Tim Duncan	2.50
41	Andre Miller	.60
42	Antonio Davis	.25
43	Howard Eisley	.25
44	Vlade Divac	.25
45	Brevin Knight	.25
46	Lamar Odom	1.50
47	Ron Mercer	.40
48	Jason Williams	.75
49	Antawn Jamison	.75
50	Wally Szczerbiak	.50
51	Chris Webber	1.50
52	Larry Hughes	1.00
53	Kevin Garnett	3.00
54	Michael Dickerson	.25
55	Chucky Atkins	.25
56	Jalen Rose	.50
57	John Amaechi	.25
58	Shareef Abdur-Rahim	.75
59	Shawn Kemp	.40
60	Derek Anderson	.40
61	Darrell Armstrong	.25
62	Vin Baker	.40
63	Paul Pierce	.60
64	Donyell Marshall	.25
65	Jamie Feick	.25
66	Travis Best	.25
67	Baron Davis	.60
68	Hakeem Olajuwon	.75
69	Joe Smith	.25
70	Ruben Patterson	.25
71	Antonio McDyess	.60
72	Jamal Mashburn	.40
73	Jason Kidd	1.50

74	Eddie Jones	1.00
75	Kenny Thomas	.25
76	Marcus Camby	.40
77	Doug Christie	.25
78	Ron Artest	.50
79	Mark Jackson	.25
80	Allan Houston	.50
81	John Stockton	.40
82	Jerome Williams	.25
83	Tim Thomas	.60
84	Alan Henderson	.25
85	Antoine Walker	.75
86	Robert Horry	.25
87	Stephon Marbury	1.00
88	David Robinson	.75
89	Lindsey Hunter	.25
90	Richard Hamilton	.50
91	Damon Stoudamire	.40
92	Dikembe Mutombo	.40
93	Anthony Mason	.25
94	Austin Croshere	.25
95	Patrick Ewing	.40
96	Mitch Richmond	.40
97	Grant Hill	2.50
98	Ray Allen	.50
99	Scottie Pippen	1.50
100	Vince Carter	5.00
101	*Kenyon Martin*	40.00
102	*Stromile Swift*	60.00
103	*Darius Miles*	125.00
104	*Marcus Fizer*	30.00
105	*Mike Miller*	60.00
106	*DerMarr Johnson*	30.00
107	*Chris Mihm*	8.00
108	*Jamal Crawford*	20.00
109	*Joel Przybilla*	6.00
110	*Keyon Dooling*	15.00
111	*Jerome Moiso*	8.00
112	*Etan Thomas*	6.00
113	*Courtney Alexander*	15.00
114	*Mateen Cleaves*	12.00
115	*Jason Collier*	5.00
116	*Hidayet Turkoglu*	15.00
117	*Desmond Mason*	20.00
118	*Quentin Richardson*	20.00
119	*Jamaal Magloire*	5.00
120	*Craig Claxton*	4.00
121	*(Morris Peterson)*	15.00
122	*Donnell Harvey*	4.00
123	*DeShawn Stevenson*	15.00
124	*Mark Karcher*	2.00
125	*Mamadou N'diaye*	2.00
126	*Erick Barkley*	3.00
127	*Mark Madsen*	3.00
128	*Cory Hightower*	2.00
129	*Dan McClintock*	1.50
130	*Soumaila Samake*	1.50
131	*Hanno Mottola*	1.50
132	*Chris Carrawell*	1.50
133	*Olumide Oyedji*	1.00
134	*Michael Redd*	2.00
135	*Chris Porter*	6.00
136	*Jabari Smith*	1.50

2000-01 Fleer Mystique Gold

	MT
Gold Cards:	5x-10x
Common Rookie:	2.00
Inserted 1:20	

2000-01 Fleer Mystique Dial 1

		MT
Complete Set (10):		10.00
Common Player:		.60
Inserted 1:10		
DO1	Jason Kidd	2.00
DO2	Stephon Marbury	1.50
DO3	Allen Iverson	2.50
DO4	Jason Williams	1.00
DO5	Allan Houston	.60
DO6	Eddie Jones	1.25
DO7	Ray Allen	.60
DO8	Jalen Rose	.60
DO9	Anfernee Hardaway	2.00
DO10	Vince Carter	6.00

2000-01 Fleer Mystique Film at Eleven

		MT
Complete Set (10):		60.00
Common Player:		3.00
Inserted 1:40		
FE1	Vince Carter	20.00
FE2	Kobe Bryant	15.00
FE3	Allen Iverson	8.00
FE4	Kevin Garnett	12.00
FE5	Tim Duncan	10.00
FE6	Steve Francis	12.00
FE7	Lamar Odom	6.00
FE8	Elton Brand	6.00
FE9	Tracy McGrady	6.00
FE10	Jason Williams	3.00

2000-01 Fleer Mystique Middle Men

		MT
Complete Set (10):		12.00
Common Player:		1.00
Inserted 1:10		
MM1	Shaquille O'Neal	3.00
MM2	Vince Carter	6.00
MM3	Paul Pierce	1.00
MM4	Tim Duncan	3.00
MM5	Grant Hill	3.00
MM6	David Robinson	1.00
MM7	Tracy McGrady	2.00
MM8	Jason Williams	1.00
MM9	Elton Brand	2.00
MM10	Lamar Odom	2.00

2000-01 Fleer Mystique NBAwesome

		MT
Complete Set (10):		30.00
Common Player:		1.50
Inserted 1:20		
NA1	Grant Hill	5.00
NA2	Steve Francis	6.00
NA3	Kobe Bryant	8.00
NA4	Elton Brand	3.00
NA5	Vince Carter	10.00
NA6	Lamar Odom	3.00
NA7	Kevin Garnett	6.00
NA8	Allen Iverson	4.00
NA9	Shareef Abdur-Rahim	1.50
NA10	Shaquille O'Neal	5.00

Post-1980 cards in Near Mint condition will generally sell for about 75% of the quoted Mint value. Excellent-condition cards bring no more than 40%.

2000-01 Fleer Mystique Player of the Week

		MT
Complete Set (15):		15.00
Common Player:		.25
Inserted 1:5		
PW1	Sam Cassell	.25
PW2	Kevin Garnett	3.00
PW3	Vince Carter	5.00
PW4	Tim Duncan	2.50
PW5	Shaquille O'Neal	2.50
PW6	Alonzo Mourning	.50
PW7	Jason Kidd	1.50
PW8	Chris Webber	1.50
PW9	Grant Hill	2.50
PW10	Steve Francis	3.00
PW11	Dikembe Mutombo	.25
PW12	Michael Finley	.40
PW13	Karl Malone	.75
PW14	Jalen Rose	.50
PW15	Kobe Bryant	4.00

2000-01 Fleer Premium

		MT
Complete Set (241):		250.00
Common Player:		.15
Minor Stars:		.30
Common Rookie (201-241):		2.00
Production 1999 Sets		
Game Ball Rookies:		3x
Production: First 250 Sets		
Pack (8):		4.00
Box (24):		45.00
1	Vince Carter	4.00
2	Kobe Bryant	3.00
3	Jermaine Jackson	.15
4	Lamar Odom	1.25
5	Robert Traylor	.15
6	Jason Kidd	1.25
7	Rashard Lewis	.75
8	Ron Artest	.40
9	Grant Hill	2.00
10	Kenny Thomas	.30
11	Anthony Carter	.30
12	Kerry Kittles	.15
13	Pat Garrity	.15
14	David Robinson	.60
15	Bryant Reeves	.15
16	Fred Hoiberg	.15
17	Jerry Stackhouse	.30
18	Donyell Marshall	.15
19	Ron Harper	.15
20	Scott Burrell	.15
21	Ron Mercer	.30
22	Avery Johnson	.15
23	Jacque Vaughn	.15
24	Adrian Griffin	.15
25	Antonio McDyess	.40
26	Adonal Foyle	.15
27	Derek Fisher	.15
28	Terrell Brandon	.30
29	Matt Harpring	.15
30	Nazr Mohammed	.15
31	Tom Gugliotta	.30
32	Scott Padgett	.15
33	Detlef Schrempf	.15
34	Dirk Nowitzki	.50
35	Mookie Blaylock	.15
36	James Posey	.30
37	Latrell Sprewell	.50
38	Michael Doleac	.15
39	Damon Stoudamire	.30
40	Tim Duncan	2.00
41	John Stockton	.30
42	Danny Fortson	.15
43	Raef LaFrentz	.15
44	Steve Francis	2.50
45	Travis Knight	.15
46	Kevin Garnett	2.50
47	Mitch Richmond	.30
48	Olden Polynice	.15
49	Derrick Coleman	.30
50	Ervin Johnson	.15
51	Shandon Anderson	.15
52	Jamal Mashburn	.30
53	Joe Smith	.15
54	Charles Outlaw	.15
55	Clifford Robinson	.15
56	Scottie Pippen	1.25
57	Chris Webber	1.25
58	Doug Christie	.15
59	Michael Dickerson	.15
60	Anthony Mason	.15
61	Shawn Bradley	.15
62	Reggie Miller	.30
63	P.J. Brown	.15
64	Wally Szczerbiak	.40
65	Keon Clark	.15
66	Anthony Peeler	.15
67	Doug West	.15
68	Antoine Walker	.60
69	Trajan Langdon	.30
70	Mark Jackson	.15
71	Sam Cassell	.30
72	Kurt Thomas	.15
73	Ruben Patterson	.15
74	Alvin Williams	.15
75	Juwan Howard	.30
76	Baron Davis	.50
77	Otis Thorpe	.15
78	Austin Croshere	.15
79	Tony Delk	.15
80	William Avery	.15
81	Matt Geiger	.15
82	Richard Hamilton	.40
83	Ricky Davis	.15
84	Hubert Davis	.15
85	Jalen Rose	.50
86	Theo Ratliff	.15
87	Bobby Jackson	.15
88	Glenn Robinson	.30
89	Kendall Gill	.15
90	Laron Profit	.15
91	Brad Miller	.15
92	Cedric Ceballos	.15
93	Arvydas Sabonis	.15
94	Vitaly Potapenko	.15
95	Rod Strickland	.30
96	Erick Dampier	.15
97	Ryan Bowen	.15
98	Dale Davis	.15
99	Larry Johnson	.30
100	John Thomas	.15
101	Rodney Rogers	.15
102	Ray Allen	.40
103	Isaac Austin	.15
104	Radoslav Nesterovic	.15
105	Tariq Abdul-Wahad	.15
106	Jonathan Bender	1.00
107	Tim Hardaway	.40
108	Jamie Feick	.15
109	Toni Kukoc	.40
110	Tyrone Corbin	.15
111	Aleksandar Radojevic	.15
112	Tony Battie	.15
113	Andre Miller	.50
114	Derek Anderson	.30
115	Tim Thomas	.40
116	Corey Maggette	.60
117	Rasheed Wallace	.50
118	Shammond Williams	.15
119	Charlie Ward	.15
120	Paul Pierce	.40
121	Shawn Kemp	.30
122	Darrell Armstrong	.15
123	Fred Vinson	.15
124	Jim Jackson	.15
125	Steve Nash	.15
126	Michael Stewart	.15
127	Maurice Taylor	.30
128	Michael Ruffin	.15
129	Vlade Divac	.15
130	LaPhonso Ellis	.15
131	Eddie Jones	.75
132	Hakeem Olajuwon	.60
133	Rick Fox	.15
134	Patrick Ewing	.30
135	Brian Grant	.15
136	Jaren Jackson	.15
137	Christian Laettner	.15
138	Greg Ostertag	.15
139	Anfernee Hardaway	1.25
140	Nick Van Exel	.30
141	Jason Caffey	.15
142	Michael Olowokandi	.15
143	Darvin Ham	.15
144	Calbert Cheaney	.15
145	Steve Smith	.30
146	Jason Williams	.60
147	Jelani McCoy	.15
148	Karl Malone	.60
149	Dikembe Mutombo	.30
150	Wesley Person	.15
151	Kelvin Cato	.15
152	Alonzo Mourning	.40
153	Terry Mills	.15
154	Allen Iverson	2.00
155	Bonzi Wells	.30
156	Antonio Daniels	.15
157	Shareef Abdur-Rahim	.75
158	Randy Brown	.15
159	Mike Bibby	.40
160	Travis Best	.15
161	Dan Majerle	.15
162	Aaron McKie	.15
163	Jason Terry	.30
164	Michael Finley	.30
165	Antonio Davis	.15
166	Lindsey Hunter	.15
167	Cuttino Mobley	.15
168	Glen Rice	.30
169	Stephon Marbury	1.00
170	Sean Elliott	.15
171	Cedric Henderson	.15
172	Eric Snow	.15
173	Othella Harrington	.15
174	Vonteego Cummings	.30
175	John Amaechi	.15
176	Allan Houston	.40
177	Shawn Marion	.75
178	Scot Pollard	.15
179	Elton Brand	1.25
180	Loy Vaught	.15
181	Larry Hughes	.75
182	Shaquille O'Neal	2.00
183	Keith Van Horn	.60
184	Terry Porter	.15
185	Quincy Lewis	.30
186	Alan Henderson	.15
187	Brevin Knight	.15
188	Walt Williams	.15
189	Clarence Weatherspoon	.15
190	Marcus Camby	.30
191	Corliss Williamson	.15
192	Gary Payton	.60
193	Felipe Lopez	.15
194	Elden Campbell	.15
195	Jerome Williams	.15
196	Antawn Jamison	.50
197	Gerard King	.15
198	Andrae Patterson	.15
199	Vin Baker	.30
200	Tracy McGrady	1.25
201	*Chris Carrawell*	2.00
202	*Eduardo Najera*	3.00
203	*Olumide Oyedji*	2.00
204	*Hanno Mottola*	2.00
205	*Daniel McClintock*	2.00
206	*Jaquay Walls*	2.00
207	*Cory Hightower*	2.00
208	*Jamal Crawford*	10.00
209	*Soumaila Samake*	2.00
210	*Michael Redd*	3.00
211	*Jason Hart*	2.00
212	*Mark Karcher*	2.00
213	*Chris Porter*	8.00
214	*Eddie House*	6.00
215	*Jabari Smith*	2.00
216	*Dan Langhi*	3.00
217	*Desmond Mason*	12.00
218	*Darius Miles*	40.00
219	*Donnell Harvey*	4.00
220	*DeShawn Stevenson*	15.00
221	*Kenyon Martin*	15.00
222	*Joel Przybilla*	4.00
223	*Keyon Dooling*	10.00
224	*Craig Claxton*	4.00
225	*Jerome Moiso*	5.00
226	*Hidayet Turkoglu*	10.00
227	*Mark Madsen*	5.00
228	*Morris Peterson*	15.00
229	*Courtney Alexander*	10.00
230	*Etan Thomas*	4.00
231	*Mateen Cleaves*	8.00
232	*Stromile Swift*	20.00
233	*Marcus Fizer*	10.00
234	*Quentin Richardson*	12.00
235	*Jason Collier*	2.00
236	*Jamaal Magloire*	5.00
237	*Erick Barkley*	5.00
238	*DerMarr Johnson*	10.00
239	*Chris Mihm*	5.00
240	*Mamadou N'diaye*	2.00
241	*Mike Miller*	20.00

2000-01 Fleer Premium 10th Anni-VINCE-ry

		MT
Complete Set (10):		75.00
Common Player:		8.00
Inserted 1:24		
Common Premium Collection		150.00
Production 15 Sets		
AV1	Vince Carter	8.00
AV2	Vince Carter	8.00
AV3	Vince Carter	8.00
AV4	Vince Carter	8.00
AV5	Vince Carter	8.00
AV6	Vince Carter	8.00
AV7	Vince Carter	8.00
AV8	Vince Carter	8.00
AV9	Vince Carter	8.00
AV10	Vince Carter	8.00

2000-01 Fleer Premium Name Game

		MT
Complete Set (15):		60.00
Common Player:		1.00
Inserted 1:24		
NG1	Vince Carter	15.00
NG2	Allen Iverson	6.00
NG3	Shaquille O'Neal	8.00
NG4	Jason Kidd	5.00
NG5	Jason Williams	3.00
NG6	Glenn Robinson	1.00
NG7	Karl Malone	3.00
NG8	Reggie Miller	1.50
NG9	Hakeem Olajuwon	3.00
NG10	Lamar Odom	5.00
NG11	Tim Duncan	8.00
NG12	Grant Hill	8.00
NG13	Kobe Bryant	12.00
NG14	Tracy McGrady	5.00
NG15	Kevin Garnett	10.00

2000-01 Fleer Premium Name Game Premium

		MT
Common Player:		75.00
Production 50 Sets		
Cards Contain Game Jersey Patch		
NG1	Vince Carter	400.00
NG2	Allen Iverson	150.00
NG3	Shaquille O'Neal	200.00
NG4	Jason Kidd	200.00
NG5	Jason Williams	150.00
NG6	Glenn Robinson	75.00
NG7	Karl Malone	150.00
NG8	Reggie Miller	150.00
NG9	Hakeem Olajuwon	125.00
NG10	Lamar Odom	150.00

2000-01 Fleer Premium Rookie Remnants

	MT
Common Floor:	200.00
Prod: 100 Cards in Each Release	
Common Floor/GJ:	1000.
Prod: 15 Cards in Each Release	

2000-01 Fleer Premium Skilled Artists

		MT
Complete Set (15):		20.00
Common Player:		.75
Inserted 1:12		
SA1	Vince Carter	6.00
SA2	Steve Francis	4.00
SA3	Paul Pierce	1.00
SA4	Gary Payton	1.00
SA5	Jason Williams	1.00
SA6	Larry Hughes	1.25
SA7	Tim Duncan	3.00
SA8	Kobe Bryant	5.00
SA9	Chris Webber	2.00
SA10	Tracy McGrady	2.00
SA11	Dirk Nowitzki	1.50
SA12	Elton Brand	2.00
SA13	Andre Miller	1.00
SA14	Ray Allen	.75
SA15	Shareef Abdur-Rahim	1.00

2000-01 Fleer Premium Skilled Artists Premium

		MT
Common Player:		50.00
Production 100 Sets		
Cards Contain Game Jersey Swatch		
SA1	Vince Carter	300.00
SA2	Steve Francis	150.00
SA3	Paul Pierce	50.00
SA4	Gary Payton	50.00
SA5	Jason Williams	75.00
SA6	Chris Webber	100.00

2000-01 Fleer Premium Skylines

		MT
Complete Set (10):		100.00
Common Player:		40100.
Inserted 1:144		
SL1	Vince Carter	30.00
SL2	Allen Iverson	12.00
SL3	Kobe Bryant	25.00
SL4	Latrell Sprewell	8.00
SL5	Elton Brand	10.00
SL6	Grant Hill	15.00
SL7	Steve Francis	20.00
SL8	Richard Hamilton	4.00
SL9	Gary Payton	6.00
SL10	David Robinson	6.00

2000-01 Fleer Premium Sole Train

		MT
Complete Set (15):		15.00
Common Player:		.25
Inserted 1:6		
ST1	Vince Carter	5.00
ST2	Marcus Camby	.25
ST3	Wally Szczerbiak	.60
ST4	Lamar Odom	1.50
ST5	Shaquille O'Neal	2.50
ST6	Antoine Walker	.50
ST7	Eddie Jones	1.00
ST8	Larry Hughes	1.00
ST9	Baron Davis	.75
ST10	Mike Bibby	.50
ST11	Elton Brand	1.50
ST12	Kevin Garnett	3.00
ST13	Allen Iverson	2.00
ST14	Tim Duncan	2.50
ST15	Grant Hill	2.50

2000-01 Fleer Premium Sole Train Premium

		MT
Common Player:		50.00
Production 100 Sets		
Cards Contain Sneaker Swatch		
ST1	Vince Carter	300.00
ST2	Marcus Camby	60.00

ST3 Wally Szczerbiak 75.00
ST4 Lamar Odom 100.00
ST5 Shaquille O'Neal 150.00
ST6 Antoine Walker 60.00
ST7 Eddie Jones 75.00
ST8 Larry Hughes 75.00
ST9 Baron Davis 75.00
ST10 Mike Bibby 50.00

2000-01 Fleer Showcase

MT
Complete Set (121): 400.00
Common Player: .25
Minor Stars: .40
Common Rookie: 1.00
Rookies 91-100/121 Production 500 Sets
Rookies 101-110 Production 1,500 Sets
Rookies 111-120 Production 2,500 Sets
Pack (5): 5.00
Box (24): 60.00

1 Vince Carter 5.00
2 Lamar Odom 1.50
3 Larry Hughes 1.00
4 Brian Grant .25
5 Bryon Russell .25
6 Allan Houston .50
7 Juwan Howard .40
8 Cuttino Mobley .40
9 Keith Van Horn .60
10 Mike Bibby .40
11 Jerome Williams .25
12 Ray Allen .50
13 Antonio Davis .25
14 Adrian Griffin .25
15 Dan Majerle .25
16 Rasheed Wallace .60
17 Antonio McDyess .60
18 Tim Thomas .60
19 Theo Ratliff .25
20 Charles Oakley .25
21 Nick Van Exel .40
22 Glenn Robinson .40
23 Cal Bowdler .25
24 Raef LaFrentz .25
25 Terrell Brandon .25
26 Allen Iverson 2.50
27 Patrick Ewing .40
28 Ron Artest .40
29 Michael Olowokandi .25
30 Derek Anderson .40
31 Dirk Nowitzki 1.25
32 Wally Szczerbiak .50
33 Gary Payton .75
34 Michael Finley .40
35 Chauncey Billups .25
36 Jason Kidd 1.50
37 Rashard Lewis .60
38 Andre Miller .60
39 Kevin Garnett 3.00
40 Tim Duncan 2.50
41 Jalen Rose .50
42 Marcus Camby .40
43 Richard Hamilton .40
44 Austin Croshere .25
45 Latrell Sprewell 1.25
46 Shawn Marion 1.25
47 Jahidi White .25
48 Elton Brand 1.50
49 Reggie Miller .40
50 David Robinson .75
51 Trajan Langdon .25
52 Jonathan Bender .75
53 Antonio Daniels .25
54 Jason Terry .40
55 Eddie Jones 1.00
56 Mitch Richmond .40
57 Antoine Walker .50
58 Robert Horry .25
59 Tracy McGrady 1.50
60 Scottie Pippen 1.50
61 Jerry Stackhouse .40
62 Zydrunas Ilgauskas .25
63 Toni Kukoc .50
64 Karl Malone .75
65 Baron Davis .60
66 Shaquille O'Neal 2.50
67 Vlade Divac .25
68 Eddie Robinson .25
69 Dion Glover .25
70 Jason Williams .75
71 Steve Francis 3.00
72 Glen Rice .40
73 Clifford Robinson .25
74 Shareef Abdur-Rahim .75
75 Hakeem Olajuwon .75
76 Paul Pierce .75
77 Tim Hardaway .50
78 Darrell Armstrong .25
79 Bonzi Wells .50
80 Antawn Jamison 1.25
81 Stephon Marbury 1.00
82 Tony Delk .25
83 Michael Dickerson .25
84 Jamal Mashburn .40
85 Kobe Bryant 4.00
86 Grant Hill 2.50
87 Chris Webber 2.00
88 Vonteego Cummings .25
89 Jamie Feick .25
90 John Stockton .40
91 *Kenyon Martin* 40.00
92 *Stromile Swift* 50.00
93 *Darius Miles* 100.00
94 *Marcus Fizer* 25.00
95 *Mike Miller* 60.00
96 *DerMarr Johnson* 25.00
97 *Chris Mihm* 12.00
98 *Jamal Crawford* 25.00
99 *Joel Przybilla* 10.00
100 *Keyon Dooling* 20.00
101 *Jerome Moiso* 6.00
102 *Etan Thomas* 5.00
103 *Courtney Alexander* 10.00
104 *Mateen Cleaves* 8.00
105 *Jason Collier* 3.00
106 *Hidayet Turkoglu* 10.00
107 *Desmond Mason* 12.00
108 *Quentin Richardson* 12.00
109 *Jamaal Magloire* 5.00
110 *Craig "Speedy" Claxton* 5.00
111 *Morris Peterson* 12.00
112 *Donnell Harvey* 3.00
113 *DeShawn Stevenson* 12.00
114 *Dalibor Bagaric* 1.00
115 *Mamadou N'diaye* 2.00
116 *Erick Barkley* 4.00
117 *Mark Madsen* 4.00
118 *Chris Porter* 8.00
119 *Brian Cardinal* 1.00
120 *Iakovos Tsakalidis* 1.00
121 *Marc Jackson* 30.00

2000-01 Fleer Showcase Legacy Collection

MT
Common Player: 10.00
Minor Stars: 16.00
Veteran Legacy Cards: 20x-40x
Legacy Cards 91-100/121: 1x-1.5x
Legacy Cards 101-110: 2x-4x
Legacy Cards 111-120: 2x-5x
Production 50 Sets

2000-01 Fleer Showcase Avant Card

MT
Complete Set (20): 700.00
Common Player: 20.00
Production 201 Sets

1 Vince Carter 150.00
2 Lamar Odom 40.00
3 Kobe Bryant 125.00
4 Kevin Garnett 50.00
5 Steve Francis 50.00
6 Jason Williams 30.00
7 Eddie Jones 25.00
8 Grant Hill 40.00
9 Elton Brand 40.00
10 Shaquille O'Neal 50.00
11 Allen Iverson 50.00
12 Tim Duncan 40.00
13 Jason Kidd 30.00
14 Kenyon Martin 40.00
15 Stromile Swift 50.00
16 Darius Miles 75.00
17 Marcus Fizer 25.00
18 Mike Miller 40.00
19 Jamal Crawford 25.00
20 Mateen Cleaves 20.00

2000-01 Fleer Showcase ELEMENTary

MT
Complete Set (10): 50.00
Common Player: 2.00
Inserted 1:48

1 Vince Carter 15.00
2 Lamar Odom 5.00
3 Kevin Garnett 10.00
4 Steve Francis 10.00
5 Grant Hill 8.00
6 Eddie Jones 3.00
7 Jason Williams 2.00
8 Kobe Bryant 12.00
9 Allen Iverson 8.00
10 Shaquille O'Neal 8.00

2000-01 Fleer Showcase HIStory

MT
Complete Set (10): 30.00
Common Player: 1.00
Inserted 1:24

1 Vince Carter 10.00
2 Lamar Odom 3.00
3 Kobe Bryant 8.00
4 Shaquille O'Neal 5.00
5 Kevin Garnett 6.00
6 Allen Iverson 5.00
7 Steve Francis 6.00
8 Eddie Jones 2.00
9 Jason Williams 1.50
10 Michael Finley 1.00

2000-01 Fleer Showcase In the Paint

MT
Complete Set (26): 300.00
Common Player: 10.00
Inserted 1:110

1 Kenyon Martin 25.00
2 Stromile Swift 25.00
3 Darius Miles 60.00
4 Marcus Fizer 20.00
5 Mike Miller 25.00
6 DerMarr Johnson 20.00
7 Chris Mihm 12.00
8 Joel Przybilla 10.00
9 Keyon Dooling 20.00
10 Jerome Moiso 12.00
11 Etan Thomas 12.00
12 Courtney Alexander 20.00
13 Mateen Cleaves 15.00
14 Jason Collier 10.00
15 Hidayet Turkoglu 20.00
16 Desmond Mason 25.00
17 Quentin Richardson 25.00
18 Jamaal Magloire 15.00
19 Craig "Speedy" Claxton 15.00
20 Morris Peterson 25.00
21 Donnell Harvey 12.00
22 DeShawn Stevenson 25.00
23 Dalibor Bagaric 10.00
24 Mamadou N'diaye 10.00
25 Erick Barkley 15.00
26 Mark Madsen 15.00

2000-01 Fleer Showcase Showstoppers

MT
Complete Set (20): 15.00
Common Player: .50
Inserted 1:6

1 Vince Carter 5.00
2 Lamar Odom 1.50
3 Tracy McGrady 1.50
4 Karl Malone .75
5 Scottie Pippen 1.50
6 Antawn Jamison 1.25
7 Chris Webber 2.00
8 Allan Houston .50
9 Baron Davis .60
10 Rashard Lewis .60
11 Jerry Stackhouse .50
12 Ray Allen .50
13 Keith Van Horn .60
14 Tim Duncan 2.50
15 Shareef Abdur-Rahim .75
16 Jalen Rose .50
17 Gary Payton .75
18 Andre Miller .60
19 Paul Pierce .75
20 Antonio McDyess .60

A player's name in *italic type* indicates a rookie

2000-01 Fleer Showcase To Air is Human

MT
Complete Set (15): 20.00
Common Player: .75
Inserted 1:12

1 Vince Carter 8.00
2 Lamar Odom 2.50
3 Grant Hill 4.00
4 Shareef Abdur-Rahim 1.00
5 Michael Finley .75
6 Larry Hughes 1.50
7 Latrell Sprewell 2.00
8 Tracy McGrady 2.50
9 Ray Allen .75
10 Desmond Mason 1.50
11 Kenyon Martin 2.50
12 Morris Peterson 2.00
13 Stromile Swift 3.00
14 DerMarr Johnson 1.50
15 Mike Miller 2.50

2000-01 Fleer Triple Crown

MT
Complete Set (240): 75.00
Common Player: .10
Minor Stars: .20
Common Rookie: .75
Inserted 1:4
Pack (10): 2.50
Box (24): 45.00

1 *Quentin Richardson* 3.00
2 *Khalid El-Amin* 1.00
3 *Courtney Alexander* 3.00
4 *Mike Penberthy* 1.00
5 *DerMarr Johnson* 2.50
6 *A.J. Guyton* 1.00
7 *Erick Barkley* 1.50
8 *Jamal Crawford* 2.50
9 *Hidayet Turkoglu* 2.50
10 *Michael Redd* 1.00
11 *Stromile Swift* 5.00
12 *Eddie House* 2.00
13 *Keyon Dooling* 2.50
14 *Lavor Postell* 1.00
15 *Mateen Cleaves* 2.00
16 *Morris Peterson* 4.00
17 *DeShawn Stevenson* 4.00
18 *Darius Miles* 10.00
19 *Hanno Mottola* .75
20 *Jerome Moiso* 1.50
21 *Desmond Mason* 3.00
22 *Jason Collier* 1.00
23 *Ruben Wolkowyski* .75
24 *Eduardo Najera* 1.50
25 *Kenyon Martin* 4.00
26 *Marcus Fizer* 3.00
27 *Etan Thomas* 1.00
28 *Mark Madsen* 1.00
29 *Pepe Sanchez* .75
30 *Brian Cardinal* .75
31 *Chris Porter* 2.50
32 *Dan Langhi* .75
33 *Mike Miller* 5.00
34 *Chris Mihm* 1.50
35 *Mamadou N'diaye* 1.00
36 *Dragan Tarlac* .75
37 *Iakovos Tsakalidis* .75
38 *Stephen Jackson* 1.50
39 *Jamaal Magloire* 1.50
40 *Joel Przybilla* 1.00
41 Adrian Griffin .10
42 Allan Houston .30
43 Mahmoud Abdul-Rauf .10
44 Avery Johnson .10
45 Damon Stoudamire .20
46 Jim Jackson .10
47 Jason Williams .50
48 Jason Kidd 1.00
49 Ray Allen .30
50 Baron Davis .40
51 Mark Jackson .10
52 Darrick Martin .10
53 Derek Fisher .10
54 Anthony Peeler .10
55 Vince Carter 3.00
56 Tim Hardaway .30
57 Richard Hamilton .30
58 Malik Rose .10
59 Antonio Daniels .10
60 Lindsey Hunter .10
61 William Avery .10
62 Reggie Miller .30
63 Shareef Abdur-Rahim .50
64 Travis Best .10
65 John Stockton .20
66 Kenny Anderson .10
67 Trajan Langdon .10
68 Sam Cassell .10
69 Chucky Atkins .10
70 Laron Profit .10
71 Andre Miller .40
72 Erick Strickland .10
73 Ron Artest .20
74 Kobe Bryant 2.50
75 Ricky Davis .10
76 Allen Iverson 1.50
77 Steve Smith .20
78 Alvin Williams .10
79 Randy Brown .10
80 Michael Dickerson .10
81 Tyronn Lue .10
82 Bonzi Wells .30
83 Felipe Lopez .10
84 Steve Francis 2.00
85 Jaren Jackson .10
86 Anthony Carter .10
87 Mitch Richmond .20
88 Sherman Douglas .10
89 Cuttino Mobley .20
90 Mario Elie .10
91 Tariq Abdul-Wahad .10
92 Ron Mercer .20
93 Jalen Rose .30
94 Mike Bibby .20
95 Voshon Lenard .10
96 Derek Anderson .20
97 Kendall Gill .10
98 Muggsy Bogues .10
99 Eddie Jones .60
100 Larry Hughes .60
101 Latrell Sprewell .75
102 Stephon Marbury .60
103 Eric Piatkowski .10
104 Brevin Knight .10
105 Isaiah Rider .20
106 Wesley Person .10
107 Nick Van Exel .20
108 Dell Curry .10
109 Tony Delk .10
110 Glen Rice .20
111 Bobby Jackson .10
112 Kerry Kittles .10
113 John Starks .10
114 Gary Payton .50
115 Mookie Blaylock .10
116 David Wesley .10
117 Rod Strickland .20
118 Terrell Brandon .10
119 Steve Nash .10
120 Moochie Norris .10
121 Eric Snow .10
122 Chauncey Billups .10
123 Darrell Armstrong .10
124 Ron Harper .10
125 Dion Glover .10
126 Vin Baker .20
127 Terry Mills .10
128 Joe Smith .10
129 Kurt Thomas .10
130 Dirk Nowitzki .75
131 Sean Elliott .10
132 Jerome Williams .10
133 Larry Johnson .10
134 LaPhonso Ellis .10
135 Pat Garrity .10
136 Lawrence Funderburke .10
137 Elton Brand 1.00
138 Rashard Lewis .40
139 Shawn Kemp .20
140 Elden Campbell .10
141 Christian Laettner .10
142 Al Harrington .30
143 Billy Owens .10
144 Wally Szczerbiak .30
145 Jonathan Bender .50
146 Karl Malone .50
147 Andrew DeClercq .10
148 Danny Manning .10
149 Antoine Walker .30
150 Jason Caffey .10
151 P.J. Brown .10
152 Matt Harpring .10
153 Mark Strickland .10
154 Theo Ratliff .10
155 Ruben Patterson .10
156 Tom Gugliotta .10
157 Derrick Coleman .10
158 Lorenzen Wright .10
159 Tracy McGrady 1.00
160 Quincy Lewis .10
161 Tony Battie .10
162 Keith Van Horn .40
163 Paul Pierce .50
164 Glenn Robinson .20
165 John Wallace .10
166 Popeye Jones .10
167 Kevin Garnett 2.00
168 Donyell Marshall .10
169 Michael Finley .20
170 Nick Anderson .10
171 Danny Fortson .10
172 Keon Clark .10
173 Juwan Howard .20
174 Brian Grant .10
175 Marcus Camby .30
176 Scottie Pippen 1.00
177 Shawn Marion .75
178 Lamar Odom 1.00
179 Charles Oakley .10
180 Tim James .10
181 Eric Williams .10
182 Tim Duncan 1.50
183 Andrae Patterson .10
184 Toni Kukoc .30
185 Chris Mullin .10
186 Alan Henderson .10
187 Mark Taylor .10
188 Chris Webber 1.25
189 Jamal Mashburn .20
190 Rodney Rogers .10
191 Loy Vaught .10
192 Carlos Rogers .10
193 Grant Hill 1.50
194 George Lynch .10
195 Antonio McDyess .40
196 Tim Thomas .30
197 Roshown McLeod .10
198 Antawn Jamison .75
199 Clifford Robinson .10
200 Corey Maggette .40
201 Horace Grant .10
202 David Benoit .10
203 Cedric Ceballos .10
204 Antonio Davis .10
205 Lamond Murray .10
206 Jerry Stackhouse .30
207 Jermaine O'Neal .40
208 Anthony Mason .10
209 Cedric Henderson .10
210 Corliss Williamson .10
211 Austin Croshere .10
212 Radoslav Nesterovic .10
213 Hakeem Olajuwon .50
214 Nazr Mohammed .10
215 David Robinson .50
216 Jeff McInnis .10
217 Brad Miller .10
218 Evan Eschmeyer .10
219 Jelani McCoy .10
220 Sean Rooks .10
221 Dikembe Mutombo .10
222 Othella Harrington .10
223 John Amaechi .10
224 Erick Dampier .10
225 Calvin Booth .10
226 Adonal Foyle .10
227 Michael Doleac .10
228 Michael Olowokandi .10
229 Matt Geiger .10
230 Vlade Divac .10
231 Bryant Reeves .10
232 Shaquille O'Neal 1.50
233 Todd Fuller .10
234 Arvydas Sabonis .10
235 Jim McIlvaine .10
236 Isaac Austin .10
237 Raef LaFrentz .10
238 Rasheed Wallace .40
239 Kelvin Cato .10
240 Patrick Ewing .20

2000-01 Fleer Triple Crown Crown Jewels

MT
Complete Set (15): 125.00
Common Player: 5.00
Inserted 1:84

1 Kevin Garnett 15.00
2 Lamar Odom 8.00
3 Allen Iverson 12.00
4 Marcus Fizer 5.00
5 Shaquille O'Neal 12.00
6 Steve Francis 15.00
7 Paul Pierce 5.00
8 Elton Brand 8.00
9 Chris Webber 10.00
10 Tim Duncan 12.00
11 Kobe Bryant 25.00
12 Grant Hill 12.00
13 Kenyon Martin 8.00
14 Darius Miles 20.00
15 Vince Carter 30.00

2000-01 Fleer Triple Crown Heir Force 01

MT
Complete Set (15): 25.00
Common Player: .75
Inserted 1:10

1 Kenyon Martin 2.00
2 Stromile Swift 2.50
3 Darius Miles 5.00
4 Courtney Alexander 1.50
5 Marcus Fizer 1.50
6 Keyon Dooling 1.25
7 Steve Francis 4.00
8 Elton Brand 2.00
9 Lamar Odom 2.00
10 Wally Szczerbiak .75
11 Vince Carter 6.00
12 Antawn Jamison 1.50
13 Jason Williams 1.00
14 Tim Duncan 3.00
15 Kobe Bryant 5.00

2000-01 Fleer Triple Crown Scoring Kings

MT
Common Player: 20.00
Production 100 Sets

1 Vince Carter
2 Shaquille O'Neal 50.00
3 Allen Iverson 75.00
4 Grant Hill 75.00
5 Chris Webber 40.00
6 Glenn Robinson 20.00
7 Lamar Odom 30.00
8 Gary Payton 25.00
9 Eddie Jones 25.00
10 Latrell Sprewell

2000-01 Fleer Triple Crown Scoring Menance

MT
Complete Set (10): 20.00
Common Player: .50
Inserted 1:24
1 Vince Carter 10.00
2 Shaquille O'Neal 5.00
3 Allen Iverson 5.00
4 Grant Hill 5.00
5 Chris Webber 4.00
6 Glenn Robinson .50
7 Lamar Odom 3.00
8 Gary Payton 1.50
9 Eddie Jones 2.00
10 Latrell Sprewell 2.50

2000-01 Fleer Triple Crown Shoot Arounds

MT
Common Player: 10.00
Inserted 1:72
1 Vince Carter 100.00
2 Quentin Richardson 20.00
3 Hanno Mottola 10.00
4 Grant Hill 60.00
5 Desmond Mason 25.00
6 Keyon Dooling 20.00
7 Jason Kidd 40.00
8 Chris Mihm 12.00
9 Shawn Marion 25.00
10 Mike Miller 30.00
11 Darius Miles 60.00
12 Tracy McGrady 30.00
13 Allen Iverson 60.00
14 Andre Miller 15.00
15 John Stockton 30.00
16 Lamar Odom 25.00

2000-01 Fleer Triple Crown Triple Threats

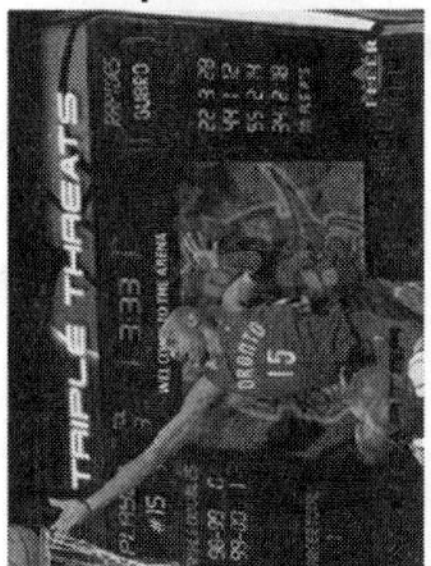

MT
Complete Set (15): 12.00
Common Player: .50
Inserted 1:5
1 Vince Carter 4.00
2 Jason Kidd 1.25
3 Gary Payton .60
4 Scottie Pippen 1.25
5 Hakeem Olajuwon .60
6 Kevin Garnett 2.50
7 Steve Francis 2.50
8 Antoine Walker .50
9 Andre Miller .50
10 Chris Webber 1.50
11 Lamar Odom 1.25
12 Tim Duncan 2.00
13 Grant Hill 2.00
14 David Robinson .50
15 Michael Finley .50

2001 Fleer NBA Jam Session Sheet

MT
Complete Sheet (8): 12.00
Common Player: 1.00
1 Vince Carter 4.00
2 Shaquille O'Neal 2.00
3 Allen Iverson 2.00
4 Tim Duncan 2.00
5 Kobe Bryant 3.00
6 Jason Kidd 1.00
7 Kevin Garnett 2.00
8 Chris Webber 1.50

2001-02 Fleer Authentix

MT
Complete Set (135): 350.00
Common Player: .25
Minor Stars: .50
Common Rookie: 4.00
Production 1,250 Sets
Pack (5): 4.00
Box (24): 70.00
1 Vince Carter 4.00
2 Terrell Brandon .50
3 Raef LaFrentz .25
4 Iakovos Tsakalidis .25
5 Elton Brand 1.00
6 David Robinson .60
7 Lamar Odom 1.00
8 Larry Hughes .50
9 Gary Payton .60
10 Rick Fox .25
11 Jamal Mashburn .50
12 Brian Grant .25
13 David Wesley .25
14 Steve Smith .50
15 Corey Maggette .50
16 Michael Jordan 8.00
17 Wally Szczerbiak .50
18 Antoine Walker .60
19 Marcus Camby .50
20 Rasheed Wallace .60
21 Travis Best .25
22 Theo Ratliff .50
23 LaPhonso Ellis .25
24 Dirk Nowitzki 1.00
25 Kurt Thomas .25
26 Steve Francis 1.50
27 Tim Duncan 1.50
28 Eddie House .50
29 Ron Mercer .50
30 Allan Houston .50
31 Trajan Langdon .25
32 Karl Malone 1.00
33 Glenn Robinson .60
34 Wang Zhizhi 1.25
35 Jason Kidd 1.25
36 Maurice Taylor .25
37 Chris Webber 1.50
38 Michael Dickerson .25
39 Paul Pierce .75
40 Bonzi Wells .50
41 Antawn Jamison 1.00
42 Rashard Lewis .50
43 Reggie Miller .60
44 Patrick Ewing .60
45 Marcus Fizer .50
46 Aaron McKie .25
47 Marc Jackson .25
48 Desmond Mason .50
49 Jermaine O'Neal .75
50 DeShawn Stevenson .50
51 John Stockton .75
52 Tim Thomas .50
53 Andre Miller .50
54 Jumaine Jones .25
55 Nick Van Exel .60
56 Damon Stoudamire .25
57 Stephon Marbury .75
58 Clifford Robinson .25
59 Hidayet Turkoglu .50
60 Kobe Bryant 4.00
61 Richard Hamilton .50
62 Stromile Swift .50
63 Chris Mihm .25
64 Tracy McGrady 2.00
65 Jalen Rose .60
66 Morris Peterson .60
67 Alonzo Mourning .50
68 Courtney Alexander .60
69 Michael Finley .75
70 Shawn Marion 1.00
71 Darius Miles 3.00
72 Antonio Davis .25
73 Ray Allen .75
74 Shareef Abdur-Rahim .60
75 Kevin Garnett 2.50
76 Latrell Sprewell 1.00
77 Antonio McDyess .60
78 Derek Anderson .50
79 Derek Fisher .25
80 Jason Terry .50
81 Eddie Jones .60
82 Hakeem Olajuwon .60
83 Toni Kukoc .50
84 Sam Cassell .50
85 Jamal Crawford .50
86 Allen Iverson 2.50
87 Steve Nash .50
88 Dikembe Mutombo .50
89 Shaquille O'Neal 2.00
90 Jerome Moiso .25
91 Kenyon Martin .50
92 Chucky Atkins .25
93 Grant Hill 1.25
94 Jerry Stackhouse .60
95 Jason Williams .50
96 Baron Davis .75
97 Mike Miller 1.50
98 Joe Smith .25
99 Predrag Stojakovic .75
100 Cuttino Mobley .50
101 *Kwame Brown* 20.00
102 *Jason Collins* 6.00
103 *Willie Solomon* 4.00
104 *Brendan Haywood* 10.00
105 *Jeff Trepagnier* 5.00
106 *Eddie Griffin* 20.00
107 *Joseph Forte* 12.00
108 *Rodney White* 10.00
109 *Jeryl Sasser* 5.00
110 *Samuel Dalembert* 5.00
111 *Shane Battier* 30.00
112 *Tony Parker* 20.00
113 *DeSagana Diop* 6.00
114 *Steven Hunter* 5.00
115 *Trenton Hassell* 8.00
116 *Michael Bradley* 6.00
117 *Brian Scalabrine* 5.00
118 *Troy Murphy* 10.00
119 *Brandon Armstrong* 5.00
120 *Pau Gasol* 25.00
121 *Gerald Wallace* 10.00
122 *Jason Richardson* 30.00
123 *Joe Johnson* 15.00
124 *Loren Woods* 10.00
125 *Vladimir Radmanovic* 8.00
126 *Jamaal Tinsley* 25.00
127 *Omar Cook* 5.00
128 *Kedrick Brown* 6.00
129 *Terence Morris* 4.00
130 *Richard Jefferson* 12.00
131 *Gilbert Arenas* 5.00
132 *Tyson Chandler* 20.00
133 *Kirk Haston* 8.00
134 *Eddy Curry* 20.00
135 *Zach Randolph* 12.00

Post-1980 cards in Near Mint condition will generally sell for about 75% of the quoted Mint value. Excellent-condition cards bring no more than 40%.

2001-02 Fleer Authentix Front Row

MT
Front Row Stars: 10x-20x
Front Row Rookies: 2x-4x
Production 100 Sets

2001-02 Fleer Authentix Second Row

MT
Second Row Stars: 6x-12x
Second Row Rookies: 1x-2x
Production 200 Sets

2001-02 Fleer Authentix Autographed Authentix

MT
Complete Set (3):
Common Player: 50.00
1AAR Kwame Brown 50.00
2AAR Eddy Curry 50.00
3AAR Vince Carter 100.00

2001-02 Fleer Authentix Auto. Jersey Authentix

MT
Complete Set (1)
Common Player:
1AJAR Vince Carter 550.00

2001-02 Fleer Authentix Courtside Classics

MT
Complete Set (15): 50.00
Common Player: 1.50
Inserted 1:22
1CC Steve Francis 4.00
2CC Mike Miller 4.00
3CC Kenyon Martin 1.50
4CC Vince Carter 10.00
5CC Alonzo Mourning 1.50
6CC Penny Hardaway 1.50
7CC Dikembe Mutombo 1.50
8CC Chris Webber 4.00
9CC Glenn Robinson 1.50
10CC Jerry Stackhouse 2.00
11CC Kobe Bryant 10.00
12CC Kevin Garnett 6.00
13CC Tim Duncan 4.00
14CC Shaquille O'Neal 5.00
15CC Michael Jordan 15.00

2001-02 Fleer Authentix Jersey Authentix Ripped

MT
Common Player: 10.00
Inserted 1:33
1JAR Allen Iverson 30.00
2JAR Darius Miles 25.00
3JAR Tracy McGrady 25.00
4JAR Glenn Robinson 10.00
5JAR Rashard Lewis 10.00
6JAR Elton Brand 15.00
7JAR Andre Miller 10.00
8JAR Jason Terry 10.00
9JAR Vince Carter 40.00
10JAR Karl Malone 15.00
11JAR David Robinson 15.00
12JAR Lamar Odom 15.00
13JAR Antoine Walker 12.00
14JAR Shareef Abdur-Rahim 12.00
15JAR Jamal Mashburn 10.00

2001-02 Fleer Authentix Sweet Selections

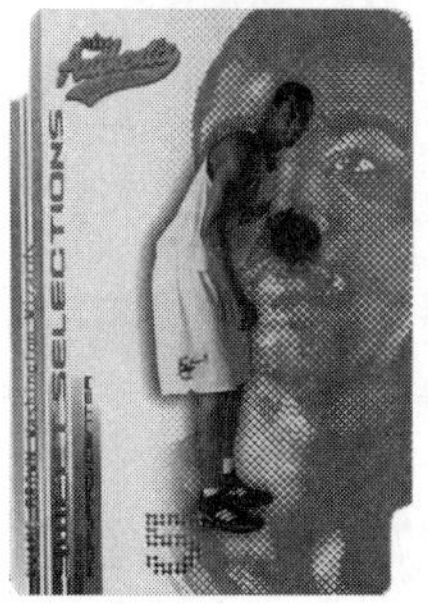

MT
Complete Set (15): 50.00
Common Player: 2.00
Inserted 1:11
1SS Kwame Brown 6.00
2SS Tyson Chandler 6.00
3SS Pau Gasol 8.00
4SS Eddy Curry 6.00
5SS Jason Richardson 10.00
6SS Shane Battier 10.00
7SS Eddie Griffin 6.00
8SS DeSagana Diop 2.00
9SS Rodney White 3.00
10SS Joe Johnson 5.00
11SS Kedrick Brown 2.00
12SS Vladimir Radmanovic 2.00
13SS Richard Jefferson 4.00
14SS Troy Murphy 3.00
15SS Steven Hunter 2.00

2001-02 Fleer Exclusive

MT
Complete Set (149): 750.00
Common Player: .30
Minor Stars: .60
Common Rookie (121-149): 12.00
Inserted 1:24
Pack (5): 4.00
Box (24): 80.00
1 Vince Carter 5.00
2 Tracy McGrady 2.50
3 Dikembe Mutombo .60
4 Kobe Bryant 5.00
5 Baron Davis .60
6 Alonzo Mourning .60
7 Allan Houston .60
8 Paul Pierce 1.00
9 Jason Williams .75
10 Marcus Camby .60
11 Jason Terry .60
12 Anfernee Hardaway .60
13 Cuttino Mobley .60
14 Kenyon Martin .60
15 Rashard Lewis .60
16 Darius Miles 4.00
17 Jamal Mashburn .60
18 Derek Fisher .60
19 Sam Cassell .60
20 Antonio McDyess .75
21 John Stockton 1.00
22 Andre Miller .75
23 Shawn Marion 1.25
24 Steve Nash .60
25 Kevin Garnett 3.00
26 Predrag Stojakovic .75
27 Dirk Nowitzki 1.25
28 Chris Webber 2.00
29 Shaquille O'Neal 2.50
30 Stephon Marbury 1.00
31 Eddie Jones .75
32 Raef LaFrentz .60
33 Wally Szczerbiak .60
34 Richard Hamilton .60
35 Michael Finley .60
36 Jason Kidd 1.50
37 Courtney Alexander .60
38 Glenn Robinson .75
39 Tim Duncan 2.00
40 Steve Francis 2.00
41 Stromile Swift .60
42 Desmond Mason .60
43 Shareef Abdur-Rahim .60
44 Terrell Brandon .60
45 Antawn Jamison 1.25
46 Latrell Sprewell 1.25
47 Mateen Cleaves .60
48 Karl Malone 1.25
49 Lamar Odom 1.25
50 Grant Hill 1.50
51 Reggie Miller .75
52 Ray Allen 1.00
53 David Robinson .75
54 Elton Brand 1.25
55 Jerry Stackhouse 1.00
56 Brian Grant .60
57 Hakeem Olajuwon .75
58 Jalen Rose .60
59 Allen Iverson 3.00
60 Darrell Armstrong .60
61 Joe Smith .60
62 Anthony Mason .60
63 Mike Bibby .60
64 Gary Payton 1.00
65 Glen Rice .60
66 Shandon Anderson .30
67 Antoine Walker .75
68 Tim Thomas .60
69 Patrick Ewing .60
70 Ben Wallace .30
71 Corey Maggette .60
72 Larry Hughes .60
73 Scottie Pippen 1.25
74 Michael Doleac .30
75 Clifford Robinson .30
76 Aaron McKie .60
77 Marc Jackson .30
78 Tom Gugliotta .30
79 James Posey .30
80 Moochie Norris .30
81 Speedy Claxton .60
82 Michael Redd .60
83 Rasheed Wallace .75
84 Juwan Howard .60
85 Nick Van Exel .60
86 Toni Kukoc .60
87 Jamaal Magloire .30
88 Jermaine O'Neal .75
89 Anthony Peeler .30
90 Marcus Fizer .60
91 Jumaine Jones .30
92 Kendall Gill .30
93 Antonio Daniels .30
94 DerMarr Johnson .60
95 Mitch Richmond .60
96 Antonio Davis .30
97 Ron Mercer .60
98 Keyon Dooling .60
99 Morris Peterson .75
100 Derek Anderson .60
101 Allen Iverson 2.50
102 Glenn Robinson .60
103 Tim Duncan 1.50
104 Shaquille O'Neal 2.00
105 Vince Carter 4.00
106 Tracy McGrady 2.00
107 Jason Kidd 1.25
108 Karl Malone 1.00
109 Michael Jordan 10.00
110 Shareef Abdur-Rahim .60
111 Grant Hill 1.25
112 Stephon Marbury .75
113 Michael Finley .60
114 Antoine Walker .60
115 Kobe Bryant 4.00
116 Dirk Nowitzki 1.00
117 Alonzo Mourning .60
118 John Stockton .75
119 Kevin Garnett 2.50
120 Eddie Jones .60
121 *Steven Hunter* 12.00
122 *Tony Parker* 50.00
123 *Zach Randolph* 30.00
124 *Richard Jefferson* 30.00
125 *Kedrick Brown* 25.00
126 *Kwame Brown* 50.00
127 *Brandon Armstrong* 12.00
128 *Pau Gasol* 60.00
129 *Troy Murphy* 20.00
130 *Rodney White* 20.00
131 *Jamaal Tinsley* 50.00
132 *Jeryl Sasser* 12.00
133 *Eddie Griffin* 40.00
134 *Michael Bradley* 12.00
135 *Vladimir Radmanovic* 20.00
136 *Jason Richardson* 80.00
137 *Shane Battier* 60.00
138 *Joe Johnson* 40.00
139 *Andrei Kirilenko* 40.00
140 *Kirk Haston* 20.00
141 *Jason Collins* 12.00
142 *Tyson Chandler* 50.00
143 *DeSagana Diop* 15.00
144 *Gerald Wallace* 25.00
145 *Joseph Forte* 20.00
146 *Brendan Haywood* 25.00
147 *Samuel Dalembert* 12.00
148 *Eddy Curry* 40.00
149 *Primoz Brezec* 12.00

2001-02 Fleer Exclusive Game Exclusive

MT
Common Player: 20.00
Production 100 Sets
1GE Vince Carter 80.00
2GE Allen Iverson 60.00
3GE Alonzo Mourning 25.00
4GE Karl Malone 30.00
5GE Darius Miles 50.00
6GE Antonio McDyess 20.00
7GE Ray Allen 40.00
8GE Steve Francis 40.00
9GE Lamar Odom 30.00
10GE Kenyon Martin 20.00
11GE Andre Miller 20.00
12GE Rashard Lewis 20.00
13GE Stromile Swift 20.00
14GE Antonio Davis 20.00
15GE Latrell Sprewell 30.00
16GE Tracy McGrady 40.00
17GE Jamal Mashburn 20.00
18GE Dikembe Mutombo 20.00
19GE Morris Peterson 20.00

2001-02 Fleer Exclusive Letter Perfect JV

MT
Common Player: 20.00
Production 100 Sets
1LP Vince Carter 80.00
2LP Allen Iverson 60.00
3LP Alonzo Mourning 25.00
4LP Karl Malone 30.00
5LP Darius Miles 50.00
6LP Antonio McDyess 20.00
7LP Ray Allen 40.00
8LP Steve Francis 40.00
9LP Lamar Odom 30.00
10LP Kenyon Martin 20.00
11LP Andre Miller 20.00
12LP Rashard Lewis 20.00
13LP Stromile Swift 20.00
14LP Antonio Davis 20.00
15LP Latrell Sprewell 30.00
16LP Keith Van Horn 20.00
17LP Tracy McGrady 40.00
18LP Desmond Mason 20.00
19LP Jason Terry 20.00
20LP Jamal Mashburn 20.00
21LP Paul Pierce 25.00
22LP Morris Peterson 20.00
23LP Baron Davis 25.00
24LP Antoine Walker 25.00

2001-02 Fleer Exclusive Team Fleer Dual

MT
Complete Set (1):
Common Player:
1TFT Vince Carter, Larry Bird 100.00

2001-02 Fleer Exclusive Vinsanity Collection

MT
Common Player: 40.00
Inserted 1:70
1VC Vince Carter 40.00
2VC Vince Carter 40.00
3VC Vince Carter 40.00
4VC Vince Carter 40.00
5VC Vince Carter 40.00

2001-02 Fleer Focus

		MT
Complete Set (130):		300.00
Common Player:		.25
Minor Stars:		.50
Common Rookie (101-130):		4.00
Production 1,850 Sets		
Pack (7):		3.00
Box (24):		70.00
1	Vince Carter	4.00
2	Steve Nash	.50
3	Anthony Mason	.50
4	Avery Johnson	.25
5	Predrag Stojakovic	.75
6	Shaquille O'Neal	2.00
7	Jason Kidd	1.25
8	Steve Smith	.50
9	Kobe Bryant	4.00
10	Eddie Robinson	.50
11	Allan Houston	.50
12	Larry Hughes	.50
13	Gary Payton	.75
14	Alonzo Mourning	.60
15	Baron Davis	.75
16	Craig "Speedy" Claxton	.50
17	Hakeem Olajuwon	.60
18	Anthony Carter	.25
19	Raef LaFrentz	.25
20	Dikembe Mutombo	.50
21	Moochie Norris	.25
22	Karl Malone	1.00
23	Darrell Armstrong	.25
24	Allen Iverson	2.50
25	Danny Fortson	.25
26	Antonio Davis	.50
27	Eddie Jones	.60
28	Patrick Ewing	.50
29	Stephon Marbury	.75
30	Cuttino Mobley	.50
31	Morris Peterson	.60
32	Glenn Robinson	.75
33	Paul Pierce	.75
34	Shawn Marion	1.00
35	Jermaine O'Neal	.60
36	Donyell Marshall	.25
37	Chauncey Billups	.25
38	Tracy McGrady	2.00
39	Vlade Divac	.50
40	Lamar Odom	1.00
41	Chris Mihm	.25
42	Kenyon Martin	.50
43	Antonio McDyess	.60
44	Mike Bibby	.50
45	Darius Miles	3.00
46	Wesley Person	.25
47	Mark Jackson	.25
48	Nick Van Exel	.50
49	Tim Duncan	1.50
50	Sam Cassell	.50
51	Jason Terry	.50
52	Bonzi Wells	.50
53	Al Harrington	.50
54	Richard Hamilton	.50
55	Wally Szczerbiak	.50
56	Toni Kukoc	.50
57	Rasheed Wallace	.60
58	Reggie Miller	.75
59	Courtney Alexander	.50
60	Terrell Brandon	.50
61	Dirk Nowitzki	1.00
62	Chris Webber	1.50
63	Lindsey Hunter	.25
64	Andre Miller	.50
65	Clifford Robinson	.50
66	David Robinson	.60
67	Stromile Swift	.50
68	Nazr Mohammed	.25
69	Kurt Thomas	.25
70	Corliss Williamson	.25
71	Rashard Lewis	.50
72	Lorenzen Wright	.25
73	David Wesley	.25
74	Derrick Coleman	.50
75	Jerry Stackhouse	.75
76	Antonio Daniels	.25
77	Mitch Richmond	.50
78	Ron Mercer	.50
79	Latrell Sprewell	1.00
80	Antawn Jamison	1.00
81	Desmond Mason	.50
82	Jason Williams	.50
83	Jamal Mashburn	.50
84	Grant Hill	1.25
85	Elton Brand	1.00
86	Brian Grant	.50
87	Antoine Walker	.75
88	Anfernee Hardaway	.50
89	Steve Francis	1.50
90	John Stockton	.75
91	Ray Allen	.75
92	Tim Hardaway	.50
93	Derek Anderson	.50
94	Jalen Rose	.50
95	Michael Jordan	10.00
96	Kevin Garnett	2.50
97	Shareef Abdur-Rahim	.60
98	Tony Delk	.25
99	Quentin Richardson	.50
100	Michael Finley	.60
101	*Jamaal Tinsley*	15.00
102	*Zach Randolph*	10.00
103	*Kedrick Brown*	6.00
104	*Kirk Haston*	6.00
105	*Tyson Chandler*	15.00
106	*Shane Battier*	20.00
107	*Richard Jefferson*	10.00
108	*Gerald Wallace*	10.00
109	*DeSagana Diop*	6.00
110	*Ruben Boumtje-Boumtje*	4.00
111	*Rodney White*	8.00
112	*Eddie Griffin*	15.00
113	*Pau Gasol*	20.00
114	*Tony Parker*	15.00
115	*Kwame Brown*	15.00
116	*Vladimir Radmanovic*	8.00
117	*Troy Murphy*	8.00
118	*Loren Woods*	8.00
119	*Joe Johnson*	12.00
120	*Brandon Armstrong*	5.00
121	*Trenton Hassell*	8.00
122	*Andrei Kirilenko*	12.00
123	*Jason Richardson*	25.00
124	*Jason Collins*	4.00
125	*Jeryl Sasser*	4.00
126	*Michael Bradley*	5.00
127	*Eddy Curry*	12.00
128	*Joseph Forte*	10.00
129	*Brendan Haywood*	10.00
130	*Zeljko Rebraca*	6.00

2001-02 Fleer Focus Materialistic

		MT
Common Player:		20.00
Inserted 1:26		
Home Versions:		2x-4x
Production 50 Sets		
1M	Kobe Bryant	50.00
2M	Shaquille O'Neal	30.00
3M	Kevin Garnett	30.00
4M	Tim Duncan	25.00
5M	Michael Jordan	80.00
6M	Allen Iverson	40.00
7M	Dirk Nowitzki	30.00
8M	Kwame Brown	25.00
9M	Tyson Chandler	20.00
10M	Eddie Griffin	20.00
11M	Shane Battier	25.00
12M	Tracy McGrady	25.00
13M	Steve Francis	20.00
14M	Chris Webber	20.00
15M	Vince Carter	50.00
15A	Vince Carter Auto	200.00
16M	Jamaal Tinsley	20.00
17M	Grant Hill	15.00
18M	Jason Kidd	20.00
19M	Karl Malone	20.00
20M	Ray Allen	20.00

2001-02 Fleer Focus ROY Collection

		MT
Complete Set (15):		100.00
Common Player:		2.00
Inserted 1:22		
1ROY	Vince Carter	15.00
2ROY	Allen Iverson	10.00
3ROY	Chris Webber	6.00
4ROY	David Robinson	3.00
5ROY	Steve Francis	6.00
6ROY	Patrick Ewing	3.00
7ROY	Damon Stoudamire	2.00
8ROY	Jason Kidd	5.00
9ROY	Mike Miller	6.00
10ROY	Larry Bird	20.00
11ROY	Grant Hill	5.00
12ROY	Michael Jordan	25.00
13ROY	Shaquille O'Neal	8.00
14ROY	Elton Brand	4.00
15ROY	Tim Duncan	6.00

2001-02 Fleer Focus ROY Collection Jersey

		MT
Common Player:		20.00
Inserted 1:55		
1ROY	Vince Carter	75.00
2ROY	Allen Iverson	50.00
3ROY	Chris Webber	30.00
4ROY	David Robinson	30.00
5ROY	Steve Francis	20.00
6ROY	Patrick Ewing	25.00
7ROY	Damon Stoudamire	20.00
8ROY	Jason Kidd	30.00
9ROY	Mike Miller	30.00
10ROY	Larry Bird	100.00
11ROY	Grant Hill	25.00
12ROY	Michael Jordan	20.00
13ROY	Shaquille O'Neal	20.00
14ROY	Elton Brand	20.00
15ROY	Tim Duncan	20.00

2001-02 Fleer Focus ROY Collection Patch

		MT
Patches:		2x-4x
Production 99 Sets		

2001-02 Fleer Focus Trading Places

		MT
Complete Set (15):		50.00
Common Player:		2.00
Inserted 1:12		
1TP	Vince Carter	10.00
2TP	Patrick Ewing	2.00
3TP	Mike Bibby	2.00
4TP	Jason Kidd	3.00
5TP	Stephon Marbury	2.00
6TP	Corey Maggette	2.00
7TP	Elton Brand	2.50
8TP	Hakeem Olajuwon	2.00
9TP	Dikembe Mutombo	2.00
10TP	Eddie Jones	2.00
11TP	Michael Jordan	20.00
12TP	Grant Hill	3.00
13TP	Chris Webber	4.00
14TP	Shaquille O'Neal	5.00
15TP	Tracy McGrady	5.00

2001-02 Fleer Force

		MT
Complete Set (180):		300.00
Common Player:		.25
Minor Stars:		.50
Common Rookie:		5.00
Production 999 Sets		
First 300 Rookie Sets Are Postmarks		
Pack (7):		3.00
Box (24):		60.00
1	Vince Carter	4.00
2	Allan Houston	.60
3	Steve Francis	1.50
4	Karl Malone	1.00
5	Joe Smith	.50
6	Raef LaFrentz	.50
7	David Robinson	.60
8	Tim Thomas	.50
9	Antonio McDyess	.60
10	Steve Smith	.50
11	Eddie Jones	.60
12	Jumaine Jones	.25
13	Derek Anderson	.50
14	Shaquille O'Neal	2.00
15	Eddie Robinson	.50
16	Stephon Marbury	.75
17	Darius Miles	3.00
18	Toni Kukoc	.50
19	Latrell Sprewell	1.00
20	Wang Zhizhi	1.25
21	Tim Duncan	1.50
22	Eddie House	.50
23	Chris Mihm	.25
24	Rasheed Wallace	.60
25	Kobe Bryant	4.00
26	Kenny Thomas	.25
27	John Stockton	.75
28	Mike Bibby	.50
29	Larry Hughes	.50
30	Antonio Davis	.50
31	Ray Allen	.75
32	Corliss Williamson	.25
33	Desmond Mason	.50
34	Sam Cassell	.50
35	Dirk Nowitzki	1.00
36	Chris Webber	1.50
37	Michael Dickerson	.25
38	Ron Mercer	.50
39	Iakovos Tsakalidis	.25
40	Derek Fisher	.50
41	Baron Davis	.75
42	Allen Iverson	2.50
43	Avery Johnson	.25
44	Courtney Alexander	.50
45	Alonzo Mourning	.60
46	Steve Nash	.60
47	Hidayet Turkoglu	.60
48	Jason Williams	.50
49	David Wesley	.25
50	Dikembe Mutombo	.50
51	LaPhonso Ellis	.25
52	Trajan Langdon	.25
53	Damon Stoudamire	.50
54	Rick Fox	.25
55	Paul Pierce	.75
56	Tracy McGrady	2.00
57	Lamar Odom	1.00
58	Antoine Walker	.75
59	Mike Miller	1.50
60	Jermaine O'Neal	.75
61	Michael Jordan	10.00
62	Jason Kidd	1.25
63	Marc Jackson	.50
64	Hakeem Olajuwon	.60
65	Kevin Garnett	2.50
66	Nick Van Exel	.50
67	Rashard Lewis	.50
68	Brian Grant	.50
69	Keith Van Horn	.50
70	Grant Hill	1.25
71	Reggie Miller	.75
72	Richard Hamilton	.60
73	Marcus Camby	.50
74	Clifford Robinson	.50
75	Gary Payton	.75
76	Andre Miller	.60
77	Bonzi Wells	.50
78	Stromile Swift	.50
79	Marcus Fizer	.50
80	Shawn Marion	1.00
81	Elton Brand	1.00
82	Jamal Mashburn	.50
83	Aaron McKie	.50
84	Corey Maggette	.50
85	Jason Terry	.50
86	Anfernee Hardaway	.50
87	Antawn Jamison	1.00
88	Morris Peterson	.60
89	Wally Szczerbiak	.60
90	Jerry Stackhouse	.75
91	Shareef Abdur-Rahim	.60
92	Glenn Robinson	.60
93	Michael Finley	.60
94	Predrag Stojakovic	.75
95	Jalen Rose	.50
96	Theo Ratliff	.50
97	Kurt Thomas	.25
98	Cuttino Mobley	.50
99	DeShawn Stevenson	.50
100	Terrell Brandon	.50
101	*Kwame Brown*	15.00
102	*Tyson Chandler*	15.00
103	*Pau Gasol*	20.00
104	*Eddy Curry*	15.00
105	*Jason Richardson*	30.00
106	*Shane Battier*	25.00
107	*Eddie Griffin*	15.00
108	*DeSagana Diop*	6.00
109	*Rodney White*	8.00
110	*Joe Johnson*	15.00
111	*Kedrick Brown*	6.00
112	*Vladimir Radmanovic*	6.00
113	*Richard Jefferson*	12.00
114	*Troy Murphy*	8.00
115	*Steven Hunter*	5.00
116	*Kirk Haston*	6.00
117	*Michael Bradley*	6.00
118	*Jason Collins*	5.00
119	*Zach Randolph*	12.00
120	*Brendan Haywood*	10.00
121	*Joseph Forte*	10.00
122	*Jeryl Sasser*	5.00
123	*Brandon Armstrong*	6.00
124	*Andrei Kirilenko*	12.00
125	*Gerald Wallace*	10.00
126	*Samuel Dalembert*	5.00
127	*Jamaal Tinsley*	20.00
128	*Tony Parker*	15.00
129	*Loren Woods*	8.00
130	*Primoz Brezec*	5.00
131	Dion Glover	.25
132	Moochie Norris	.25
133	Mark Jackson	.25
134	Bryon Russell	.25
135	Danny Fortson	.25
136	Kenyon Martin	.50
137	Alvin Williams	.25
138	Erick Dampier	.25
139	Clarence Weatherspoon	.25
140	Brent Barry	.25
141	Lamond Murray	.25
142	Lindsey Hunter	.25
143	Speedy Claxton	.50
144	James Posey	.50
145	Anthony Mason	.25
146	Mateen Cleaves	.25
147	Kenny Anderson	.50
148	Travis Best	.25
149	Patrick Ewing	.50
150	Dana Barros	.25
151	Lorenzen Wright	.25
152	Rodney Rogers	.25
153	Brad Miller	.25
154	Anthony Peeler	.25
155	Antonio Daniels	.25
156	Tim Hardaway	.50
157	Quentin Richardson	.60
158	Darrell Armstrong	.50
159	Nazr Muhammad	.25
160	Todd MacCulloch	.25
161	Ruben Patterson	.25
162	Wesley Person	.25
163	Jeff McInnis	.25
164	Vin Baker	.25
165	George McCloud	.25
166	Chris Gatling	.25
167	Derrick Coleman	.50
168	Elden Campbell	.50
169	Glen Rice	.50
170	Donyell Marshall	.50
171	Juwan Howard	.50
172	Mitch Richmond	.50
173	Tom Gugliotta	.25
174	Chucky Atkins	.25
175	Michael Redd	.50
176	Malik Rose	.25
177	Lee Nailon	.25
178	Al Harrington	.50
179	Matt Harpring	.25
180	Tyronn Lue	.25

2001-02 Fleer Force Emblematic

		MT
Common Player:		5.00
Production 399 Sets		
1E	Vince Carter	30.00
2E	Dikembe Mutombo	5.00
3E	Tracy McGrady	15.00
4E	Lamar Odom	8.00
5E	Jason Kidd	10.00
6E	Ray Allen	6.00
7E	John Stockton	6.00
8E	Paul Pierce	6.00
9E	Baron Davis	6.00
10E	Kenyon Martin	5.00
11E	Richard Hamilton	5.00
12E	Grant Hill	8.00
13E	Morris Peterson	6.00
14E	Shareef Abdur-Rahim	6.00
15E	Predrag Stojakovic	6.00
16E	Gary Payton	6.00
17E	Karl Malone	8.00
18E	Keith Van Horn	5.00
19E	Darius Miles	25.00
20E	Allen Iverson	20.00
21E	Michael Jordan	60.00
22E	Kobe Bryant	30.00
23E	Kevin Garnett	20.00
24E	Shaquille O'Neal	15.00
25E	Tim Duncan	12.00

2001-02 Fleer Force Inside the Game

		MT
Common Player:		3.00
Production 699 Sets		
1IG	Karl Malone	5.00
2IG	Keith Van Horn	3.00
3IG	Darius Miles	15.00
4IG	John Stockton	4.00
5IG	Allen Iverson	12.00
6IG	Alonzo Mourning	3.00
7IG	Dikembe Mutombo	3.00
8IG	Tracy McGrady	10.00
9IG	Lamar Odom	5.00
10IG	Baron Davis	4.00
11IG	Michael Jordan	40.00
12IG	Kobe Bryant	20.00
13IG	Kevin Garnett	12.00
14IG	Shaquille O'Neal	10.00
15IG	Tim Duncan	8.00
16IG	Vince Carter	20.00
17IG	Steve Francis	8.00
18IG	Dirk Nowitzki	5.00
19IG	Chris Webber	8.00
20IG	Predrag Stojakovic	4.00
NNO	Vince Carter Auto/275	150.00

2001-02 Fleer Force Inside the Game Jerseys

		MT
Common Player:		
Production 399 Sets		
1	Karl Malone	20.00
2	Keith Van Horn	12.00
3	Darius Miles	30.00
4	John Stockton	20.00
5	Allen Iverson	40.00
6	Alonzo Mourning	15.00
7	Dikembe Mutombo	12.00
8	Tracy McGrady	25.00
9	Lamar Odom	20.00
10	Baron Davis	15.00

2001-02 Fleer Force Inside the Game Numbers

		MT
Common Player:		
Production 99 Sets		
1	Karl Malone	60.00
2	Keith Van Horn	30.00
3	Darius Miles	100.00
4	John Stockton	60.00
5	Allen Iverson	125.00
6	Alonzo Mourning	50.00
7	Dikembe Mutombo	30.00
8	Tracy McGrady	80.00
9	Lamar Odom	60.00
10	Baron Davis	50.00

2001-02 Fleer Force Rookie Postmarks

		MT
Postmarks:		1x-2x
Production First 300 Sets		

2001-02 Fleer Force Special Forces

		MT
Veterans (1-100):		5x-10x
Production 250 Sets		
Rookies (101-130):		3x-6x
Production 50 Sets		

2001-02 Fleer Force True Colors

		MT
Common Player:		12.00
Production 400 Sets		
Two Colors:		1x-2x
Production 200 Sets		
Three Colors:		1.5x-3x
Production 100 Sets		
Four Colors:		2x-4x
Production 50 Sets		
1TC	Vince Carter	50.00
2TC	Kenyon Martin	12.00
3TC	Baron Davis	12.00
4TC	Tracy McGrady	30.00
5TC	Mike Miller	25.00
6TC	Aaron McKie	15.00
7TC	Darius Miles	40.00
8TC	Lamar Odom	25.00
9TC	Glenn Robinson	15.00
10TC	Karl Malone	20.00
11TC	John Stockton	20.00
12TC	Paul Pierce	20.00
13TC	Alonzo Mourning	20.00
14TC	Gary Payton	15.00
15TC	Stephon Marbury	15.00
16TC	Dikembe Mutombo	15.00
17TC	Shawn Marion	20.00
18TC	Richard Hamilton	15.00
19TC	Stromile Swift	12.00
20TC	Reggie Miller	20.00
21TC	Keith Van Horn	15.00
22TC	Steve Francis	30.00
23TC	Morris Peterson	20.00
24TC	Andre Miller	15.00
25TC	Quentin Richardson	15.00
26TC	Antonio McDyess	15.00
27TC	Anfernee Hardaway	15.00
28TC	Jason Williams	15.00
29TC	Grant Hill	20.00
30TC	Jason Terry	12.00

2001-02 Fleer Genuine

		MT
Complete Set (150):		325.00
Common Player:		.30
Minor Stars:		.60
Common Rookie:		4.00
Production 1,000 Sets		
Pack (5):		3.00
Box (24):		60.00
1	Larry Hughes	.60
2	Wally Szczerbiak	.60
3	Jahidi White	.30
4	Aaron McKie	.60
5	Antonio McDyess	.75
6	Tom Gugliotta	.30
7	Elton Brand	1.25
8	Lamar Odom	1.25
9	Chris Webber	2.00
10	Ron Artest	.30
11	Gary Payton	.75
12	Brian Grant	.30
13	Steve Nash	.60
14	DerMarr Johnson	.60
15	Vince Carter	5.00
16	Kurt Thomas	.30
17	Cuttino Mobley	.60
18	Marc Jackson	.30
19	Stromile Swift	.60
20	Grant Hill	1.50
21	Raef LaFrentz	.30
22	Marcus Fizer	.60
23	Antonio Davis	.30
24	John Starks	.30
25	Trajan Langdon	.30
26	Jason Williams	.60
27	Toni Kukoc	.30
28	Morris Peterson	.75
29	Allen Iverson	3.00
30	Andre Miller	.60
31	Larry Johnson	.30
32	Vitaly Potapenko	.30
33	Tim Thomas	.60
34	Eddie House	.60
35	Juwan Howard	.60
36	Joel Przybilla	.60
37	John Stockton	1.00
38	Michael Finley	1.00
39	Hidayet Turkoglu	.60
40	Keith Van Horn	.75
41	Shawn Marion	1.25
42	Derek Fisher	.30
43	Terrell Brandon	.60
44	Jamal Mashburn	.60
45	Shareef Abdur-Rahim	.75
46	Brevin Knight	.30
47	Antoine Walker	1.00
48	Mateen Cleaves	.30
49	Alonzo Mourning	.60
50	Jermaine O'Neal	1.00
51	Kenyon Martin	.60
52	Steve Smith	.60
53	Jerry Stackhouse	.75
54	Mike Bibby	.60
55	Latrell Sprewell	1.25
56	Iakovos Tsakalidis	.30
57	Sam Cassell	.60
58	Michael Dickerson	.30
59	Alan Henderson	.30
60	Allan Houston	.60
61	Patrick Ewing	.60
62	Joe Smith	.30
63	Rick Fox	.30
64	Tracy McGrady	2.50
65	Scottie Pippen	1.25
66	Chauncey Billups	.30
67	Voshon Lenard	.30
68	Jalen Rose	.75
69	Derrick Coleman	.30
70	Shaquille O'Neal	2.50
71	Anfernee Hardaway	.75
72	Derek Anderson	.60
73	Travis Best	.30
74	Darius Miles	4.00
75	Glenn Robinson	.75
76	Darrell Armstrong	.30
77	Dirk Nowitzki	1.25
78	Stephon Marbury	1.00
79	Tyronn Lue	.30
80	Bonzi Wells	.60
81	Mike Miller	2.00
82	Tim Duncan	2.00
83	Tim Hardaway	.60
84	Desmond Mason	.60
85	Ray Allen	1.00
86	Sean Elliott	.30
87	David Wesley	.30
88	Rasheed Wallace	.75
89	Kevin Garnett	3.00
90	Dikembe Mutombo	.60
91	Baron Davis	1.00
92	Donyell Marshall	.30
93	Eddie Jones	.75
94	Vin Baker	.60
95	Predrag Stojakovic	1.00
96	Antawn Jamison	1.25
97	Maurice Taylor	.30
98	Courtney Alexander	.75
99	Steve Francis	2.00
100	Chris Mihm	.30
101	Kobe Bryant	5.00
102	Hakeem Olajuwon	.75
103	Richard Hamilton	.60

104	Karl Malone	1.25
105	Chucky Atkins	.30
106	Eric Snow	.30
107	Ruben Patterson	.30
108	David Robinson	.75
109	Bryon Russell	.30
110	Jason Terry	.60
111	Jason Kidd	1.50
112	Charles Oakley	.30
113	Zhizhi Wang	1.50
114	Quentin Richardson	.60
115	Clarence Weatherspoon	.30
116	Nick Van Exel	.75
117	Reggie Miller	.75
118	Marcus Camby	.60
119	Corey Maggette	.60
120	Paul Pierce	1.00
121	*Kwame Brown*	20.00
122	*Eddie Griffin*	20.00
123	*Eddy Curry*	20.00
124	*Jamaal Tinsley*	25.00
125	*Jason Richardson*	35.00
126	*Shane Battier*	30.00
127	*Troy Murphy*	10.00
128	*Richard Jefferson*	12.00
129	*DeSagana Diop*	8.00
130	*Tyson Chandler*	20.00
131	*Joe Johnson*	15.00
132	*Zach Randolph*	12.00
133	*Gerald Wallace*	10.00
134	*Loren Woods*	10.00
135	*Jason Collins*	6.00
136	*Rodney White*	10.00
137	*Jeryl Sasser*	6.00
138	*Kirk Haston*	8.00
139	*Pau Gasol*	25.00
140	*Kedrick Brown*	6.00
141	*Steven Hunter*	4.00
142	*Michael Bradley*	5.00
143	*Joseph Forte*	12.00
144	*Brandon Armstrong*	5.00
145	*Samuel Dalembert*	4.00
146	*Trenton Hassell*	8.00
147	*Gilbert Arenas*	8.00
148	*Omar Cook*	4.00
149	*Tony Parker*	20.00
150	*Terence Morris*	4.00

2001-02 Fleer Genuine At Large

		MT
Complete Set (15):		40.00
Common Player:		1.50
Inserted 1:23		
1AL	Vince Carter	10.00
2AL	Dirk Nowitzki	20.00
3AL	Courtney Alexander	1.50
4AL	Jason Williams	1.50
5AL	Reggie Miller	2.00
6AL	Chris Webber	4.00
7AL	Elton Brand	2.50
8AL	Predrag Stojakovic	2.00
9AL	Ray Allen	2.00
10AL	Shaquille O'Neal	5.00
11AL	Kevin Garnett	6.00
12AL	Kobe Bryant	10.00
13AL	Tim Duncan	4.00
14AL	Antawn Jamison	2.50
15AL	Latrell Sprewell	2.50

2001-02 Fleer Genuine Final Cut

	MT
Common Player:	12.00
Inserted 1:24	
Shareef Abdur-Rahim	15.00
Vince Carter	75.00
Baron Davis	15.00
Sean Elliott	12.00
Patrick Ewing	15.00
Michael Finley	15.00
Anfernee Hardaway	15.00
Grant Hill	20.00
Allan Houston	15.00
Allen Iverson	50.00
Jason Kidd	25.00
Tyronn Lue	12.00
Karl Malone	20.00
Stephon Marbury	15.00
Shawn Marion	25.00
Kenyon Martin	15.00
Desmond Mason	12.00
Tracy McGrady	25.00
Andre Miller	15.00
Mike Miller	25.00
Alonzo Mourning	15.00
Lamar Odom	20.00
Gary Payton	15.00
Paul Pierce	15.00
Quentin Richardson	15.00
David Robinson	15.00
Glenn Robinson	15.00
John Stockton	20.00
Stromile Swift	15.00
Wally Szczerbiak	15.00
Jason Terry	15.00
Keith Van Horn	15.00
Antoine Walker	20.00
David Wesley	12.00
Jason Williams	20.00

2001-02 Fleer Genuine Genuine Coverage Plus

		MT
Common Player:		10.00
Inserted 1:24		
1	Shareef Abdur-Rahim	12.00
2	Darrell Armstrong	10.00
3	Mike Bibby	10.00
4	Vince Carter	40.00
5	Vince Carter warmup	40.00
6	Michael Dickerson	10.00
7	Patrick Ewing	12.00
8	Steve Francis	20.00
9	Richard Hamilton	12.00
10	Anfernee Hardaway	12.00
11	Grant Hill	15.00
12	DerMarr Johnson	10.00
13	Jason Kidd	15.00
14	Rashard Lewis	10.00
15	Corey Maggette	10.00
16	Stephon Marbury	12.00
17	Shawn Marion	15.00
18	Kenyon Martin	10.00
19	Tracy McGrady	20.00
20	Mike Miller	15.00
21	Lamar Odom	15.00
22	Quentin Richardson	10.00
23	Jerry Stackhouse	12.00
24	Keith Van Horn	12.00

2001-02 Fleer Genuine Names of the Game

		MT
Common Player:		12.00
Inserted 1:24		
1	Shareef Abdur-Rahim	10.00
2	Vince Carter	40.00
3	Steve Francis	20.00
4	Anfernee Hardaway	12.00
5	Allen Iverson	30.00
6	Jason Kidd	15.00
7	Karl Malone	15.00
8	Tracy McGrady	20.00
9	Dikembe Mutombo	10.00
10	Hakeem Olajuwon	12.00
11	Gary Payton	12.00
12	Morris Peterson	12.00
13	David Robinson	12.00
14	Glenn Robinson	12.00
15	Chris Webber	20.00

2001-02 Fleer Genuine Skywalkers

		MT
Complete Set (15):		35.00
Common Player:		1.50
Inserted 1:23		
1SW	Vince Carter	10.00
2SW	Lamar Odom	2.50
3SW	Shawn Marion	2.50
4SW	Kobe Bryant	10.00
5SW	Kevin Garnett	6.00
6SW	Tim Duncan	4.00
7SW	Antawn Jamison	2.50
8SW	Michael Finley	1.50
9SW	Ray Allen	2.00
10SW	Paul Pierce	2.00
11SW	Baron Davis	2.00
12SW	Antoine Walker	1.50
13SW	Desmond Mason	1.50
14SW	Jason Williams	1.50
15SW	Darius Miles	8.00

2001-02 Fleer Genuine Unstoppable

		MT
Complete Set (10):		30.00
Common Player:		2.00
Inserted 1:23		
1US	Vince Carter	10.00
2US	Darius Miles	8.00
3US	Shaquille O'Neal	5.00
4US	Jerry Stackhouse	2.00
5US	Tim Duncan	4.00
6US	Eddie Jones	2.00
7US	Jason Kidd	3.00
8US	Glenn Robinson	2.00
9US	Elton Brand	2.50
10US	Dirk Nowitzki	2.50

2001 Fleer Greats of the Game

		MT
Complete Set (84):		50.00
Common Player:		.75
Minor Stars:		1.25
Pack (4):		3.00
Box (20):		50.00
1	Adolph Rupp	.75
2	Alonzo Mourning	.75
3	Antawn Jamison	1.50
4	Antoine Walker	1.25
5	Bill Walton	1.50
6	Bob Cousy	1.50
7	Bob Lanier	1.50
8	Bobby Cremins	.75
9	Bobby Hurley	1.25
10	Bobby Knight	2.00
11	Cazzie Russell	.75
12	Charlie Ward	.75
13	Christian Laettner	1.50
14	Clyde Drexler	2.00
15	Danny Ainge	.75
16	Danny Ferry	1.25
17	Danny Manning	1.50
18	Darrell Griffith	.75
19	Dave Cowens	1.25
20	David Robinson	1.50
21	David Thompson	1.50
22	Dean Smith	1.50
23	Don Haskins	.75
24	Eddie Jones	1.25
25	Elvin Hayes	1.25
26	Gene Keady	.75
27	George Mikan	1.50
28	Glen Rice	1.25
29	Hakeem Olajuwon	1.50
30	Isiah Thomas	2.00
31	Jalen Rose	1.25
32	Jamal Mashburn	.75
33	James Worthy	1.50
34	Jerry Stackhouse	1.50
35	Jerry Lucas	.75
36	Jerry Tarkanian	.75
37	Jerry West	2.00
38	Jim Valvano	2.00
39	Joe Smith	.75
40	John Thompson	.75
41	John Havlicek	1.50
42	John Wooden	1.50
43	John Lucas	.75
44	Kareem Abdul-Jabbar	3.00
45	Keith Van Horn	1.25
46	Kent Benson	.75
47	Kerry Kittles	.75
48	Lamar Odom	1.50
49	Larry Bird	5.00
50	Larry Johnson	.75
51	Lefty Driesell	1.50
52	Lenny Wilkens	1.25
53	Lou Carnesecca	.75
54	Marques Johnson	.75
55	Mateen Cleaves	.75
56	Mike Bibby	1.25
57	Mike Krzyzewski	2.00
58	Mychal Thompson	.75
59	Nate Archibald	1.25
60	Pat Riley	1.50
61	Paul Arizin	1.25
62	Pete Maravich	2.00
63	Phil Ford	1.25
64	Ralph Sampson	1.25
65	Ray Meyer	.75
66	Rick Pitino	2.00
67	Rick Barry	1.50
68	Rollie Massimino	.75
69	Sam Jones	.75
70	Sidney Moncrief	.75
71	Spud Webb	.75
72	Steve Alford	1.25
73	Vince Carter	4.00
74	Walt Frazier	1.50
75	Wilt Chamberlain	2.00
76	Carol Blazejowski	2.00
77	Cynthia Cooper	2.00
78	Chamique Holdsclaw	3.00
79	Lisa Leslie	2.00
80	Nancy Lieberman-Cline	2.00
81	Rebecca Lobo	2.00
82	Cheryl Miller	2.00
83	Sheryl Swoopes	3.00
84	Marcus Camby	.75

Post-1980 cards in Near Mint condition will generally sell for about 75% of the quoted Mint value. Excellent-condition cards bring no more than 40%.

2001 Fleer Greats of Game All-American Collection

		MT
Complete Set (14):		30.00
Common Player:		2.00
Inserted 1:6		
1AAC	Hakeem Olajuwon	2.00
2AAC	Vince Carter	6.00
3AAC	James Worthy	2.00
4AAC	David Thompson	2.00
5AAC	Paul Arizin	2.00
6AAC	George Mikan	2.00
7AAC	Bob Cousy	3.00
8AAC	Steve Alford	3.00
9AAC	Kent Benson	2.00
10AAC	Isiah Thomas	3.00
11AAC	Wilt Chamberlain	4.00
12AAC	Marques Johnson	2.00
13AAC	Bill Walton	3.00
14AAC	Jerry West	3.00

2001 Fleer Greats of the Game Autographs

		MT
Common Player:		12.00
Inserted 1:12		
1	Kareem Abdul-Jabbar	75.00
2	Danny Ainge	25.00
3	Steve Alford	20.00
4	Nate Archibald	15.00
5	Paul Arizin	15.00
6	Rick Barry	15.00
7	Kent Benson	12.00
8	Mike Bibby	12.00
9	Larry Bird/200	400.00
10	Carol Blazejowski	30.00
11	Vince Carter	150.00
12	Mateen Cleaves	12.00
13	Cynthia Cooper	75.00
14	Bob Cousy	40.00
15	Dave Cowens	15.00
16	Clyde Drexler	25.00
17	Danny Ferry	15.00
18	Phil Ford	20.00
19	Walt Frazier	20.00
20	Darrell Griffith	15.00
21	John Havlicek/200	75.00
22	Elvin Hayes	15.00
23	Chamique Holdsclaw	75.00
24	Bobby Hurley	25.00
25	Antawn Jamison	20.00
26	Larry Johnson	15.00
27	Marques Johnson	15.00
28	Eddie Jones	15.00
29	Sam Jones	15.00
30	Kerry Kittles	12.00
31	Bobby Knight	75.00
32	Christian Laettner	20.00
33	Bob Lanier	15.00
34	Lisa Leslie	50.00
35	Nancy Lieberman-Cline	40.00
36	Jerry Lucas	15.00
37	John Lucas	15.00
38	Danny Manning	20.00
39	Jamal Mashburn	20.00
40	George Mikan/300	150.00
41	Cheryl Miller	75.00
42	Sidney Moncrief	15.00
43	Alonzo Mourning	25.00
44	Lamar Odom	20.00
45	Hakeem Olajuwon	25.00
46	Rick Pitino	35.00
47	Glen Rice	12.00
48	Pat Riley/150	75.00
49	David Robinson	100.00
50	Jalen Rose	15.00
51	Cazzie Russell	20.00
52	Ralph Sampson	20.00
53	Joe Smith	12.00
54	Jerry Stackhouse	15.00
55	Sheryl Swoopes	60.00
56	Isiah Thomas/219	50.00
57	David Thompson	15.00
58	Mychal Thompson	15.00
59	Keith Van Horn	15.00
60	Antoine Walker	20.00
61	Bill Walton	25.00
62	Charlie Ward	12.00
63	Spud Webb	15.00
64	Jerry West	30.00
65	Lenny Wilkens	15.00
66	John Wooden/300	60.00
67	James Worthy	40.00

A player's name in *italic type* indicates a rookie card.

2001 Fleer Greats of Game Coach's Corner

		MT
Complete Set (16):		75.00
Common Player:		4.00
Inserted 1:10		
1CC	Lou Carnesecca	4.00
2CC	Bobby Cremins	4.00
3CC	Lefty Driesell	6.00
4CC	Don Haskins	4.00
5CC	Mike Krzyzewski	8.00
6CC	Rollie Massimino	4.00
7CC	Ray Meyer	4.00
8CC	Rick Pitino	6.00
9CC	Adolph Rupp	6.00
10CC	Dean Smith	6.00
11CC	Jerry Tarkanian	4.00
12CC	John Thompson	4.00
13CC	Bobby Knight	4.00
14CC	John Wooden	6.00
15CC	Jim Valvano	6.00
16CC	Gene Keady	4.00

2001 Fleer Greats of the Game Coach's Corner Autographs

		MT
CC2	Bobby Cremins	25.00
CC3	Lefty Driesell	40.00
CC4	Don Haskins	25.00
CC5	Mike Krzyzewski	60.00
CC6	Rollie Massimino	25.00
CC7	Ray Meyer	40.00
CC8	Rick Pitino	40.00
CC10	Dean Smith	100.00
CC11	Jerry Tarkanian	40.00
CC12	John Thompson	50.00
CC13	Bobby Knight	75.00
CC14	John Wooden	60.00

2001 Fleer Greats of Game Feel The Game Classics

		MT
Complete Set (10):		
Common Player:		
1FTGC	Bob Knight	25.00
2FTGC	Bill Walton	15.00
3FTGC	Larry Johnson	10.00
4FTGC	Lou Carnesecca	15.00
5FTGC	Rick Barry	20.00
6FTGC	Larry Bird	75.00
7FTGC	J.R. Rider	10.00
8FTGC	Pete Maravich	125.00
9FTGC	Bob Cousy	200.00
10FTGC	Vince Carter	150.00

2001 Fleer Greats of Game Hardwood Greats

		MT
Complete Set (20):		
Common Player:		10.00
1HG	Vince Carter	20.00
2HG	Antawn Jamison	10.00
3HG	Dean Smith	10.00
4HG	James Worthy	15.00
5HG	Phil Ford	10.00
6HG	Mike Krzyzewski	15.00
7HG	Bobby Cremins	10.00
8HG	John Lucas	10.00
9HG	Bob Knight	15.00
10HG	Steve Alford	10.00
11HG	Glen Rice	10.00
12HG	Jalen Rose	10.00
13HG	Mateen Cleaves	10.00
14HG	Gene Keady	10.00
15HG	Antoine Walker	15.00
16HG	Marcus Camby	10.00
17HG	Danny Manning	10.00
18HG	Charlie Ward	10.00
19HG	Larry Johnson	10.00
20HG	Sheryl Swoopes	25.00

A card number in parentheses ( ) indicates the set is unnumbered.

2001 Fleer Greats of Game Player of Year

		MT
Complete Set (10):		50.00
Common Player:		4.00
Inserted 1:24		
1POY	Christian Laettner	6.00
2POY	Elvin Hayes	4.00
3POY	Larry Bird	15.00
4POY	Joe Smith	4.00
5POY	Cazzie Russell	5.00
6POY	Antawn Jamison	6.00
7POY	Danny Manning	6.00
8POY	David Robinson	6.00
9POY	Jerry Lucas	4.00
10POY	Kareem Abdul-Jabbar	8.00

2001-02 Fleer Hoops Hot Prospects

		MT
Complete Set (108):		650.00
Common Player:		.30
Minor Stars:		.60
Common Rookie:		10.00
Production 1,000 Sets		
Pack (5):		8.00
Box (15):		120.00
1	Vince Carter	5.00
2	John Stockton	1.00
3	Steve Smith	.30
4	Kevin Garnett	3.00
5	Larry Hughes	.60
6	Ron Mercer	.60
7	Marcus Fizer	.60
8	Rashard Lewis	.60
9	Mike Miller	2.00
10	Darius Miles	4.00
11	Michael Finley	.75
12	Marcus Camby	.60
13	Morris Peterson	.75
14	Shawn Marion	1.25
15	Alonzo Mourning	.60
16	Jamal Mashburn	.60
17	Michael Jordan	10.00
18	Jason Williams	.60
19	Latrell Sprewell	1.25
20	Reggie Miller	1.00
21	Glenn Robinson	.75
22	Steve Francis	2.00
23	Antoine Walker	.75
24	Stromile Swift	.60
25	Damon Stoudamire	.30
26	Allan Houston	.60
27	Kobe Bryant	5.00
28	Dirk Nowitzki	1.25
29	Iakovos Tsakalidis	.30
30	Gary Payton	1.00
31	Allen Iverson	3.00
32	Eddie Jones	1.00
33	Mateen Cleaves	.30
34	Nick Van Exel	.60
35	Terrell Brandon	.60
36	Wally Szczerbiak	.60
37	Jalen Rose	.75
38	Elton Brand	1.25
39	DerMarr Johnson	.60
40	Predrag Stojakovic	1.00
41	Jason Kidd	1.50
42	Sam Cassell	.60
43	Cuttino Mobley	.60
44	Toni Kukoc	.30
45	DeShawn Stevenson	.60
46	David Robinson	.75
47	Grant Hill	1.50
48	Shaquille O'Neal	2.50
49	Andre Miller	.60
50	Corey Maggette	.60
51	Jason Terry	.60
52	Aaron McKie	.60
53	Eddie House	.60
54	Steve Nash	.60
55	Clifford Robinson	.30
56	Chris Webber	2.00
57	Kenyon Martin	.60
58	Jermaine O'Neal	1.00
59	Baron Davis	1.00
60	Mitch Richmond	.60
61	Antawn Jamison	1.25
62	Paul Pierce	1.00
63	Shareef Abdur-Rahim	.75
64	Rasheed Wallace	.75
65	Ray Allen	1.00
66	Lamar Odom	1.25
67	Chris Mihm	.30
68	Raef LaFrentz	.30
69	Patrick Ewing	.60
70	Tracy McGrady	2.50
71	Derek Fisher	.30
72	Jerry Stackhouse	.75
73	Antonio McDyess	.75
74	Karl Malone	1.25
75	Dikembe Mutombo	.60
76	Hakeem Olajuwon	.75
77	David Wesley	.30
78	Courtney Alexander	.75
79	Tim Duncan	2.00
80	Stephon Marbury	1.00
81	*Kwame Brown*	40.00
82	*Tyson Chandler*	30.00
83	*Pau Gasol*	40.00
84	*Eddy Curry*	30.00
85	*Jason Richardson/300*	80.00

86	*Shane Battier*	50.00
87	*Eddie Griffin/300*	50.00
88	*DeSagana Diop*	12.00
89	*Rodney White*	15.00
90	*Joe Johnson/300*	50.00
91	*Kedrick Brown/300*	25.00
92	*Vladimir Radmanovic*	12.00
93	*Richard Jefferson*	20.00
94	*Troy Murphy*	15.00
95	*Steven Hunter*	10.00
96	*Kirk Haston*	12.00
97	*Michael Bradley*	10.00
98	*Jason Collins*	10.00
99	*Zach Randolph*	20.00
100	*Brendan Haywood*	15.00
101	*Joseph Forte*	20.00
102	*Jeryl Sasser*	10.00
103	*Brandon Armstrong*	25.00
104	*Andrei Kirilenko*	30.00
105	*Primoz Brezec*	10.00
106	*Samuel Dalembert/300*	20.00
107	*Jamaal Tinsley*	40.00
108	*Tony Parker*	40.00

2001-02 Fleer Hoops Hot Prospects Certified Cuts

		MT
Common Player:		15.00
Inserted 1:64		
1CC	Kwame Brown	60.00
2CC	Eddy Curry	30.00
3CC	Kedrick Brown	20.00
4CC	DeSagana Diop	15.00
5CC	Joe Johnson	50.00
6CC	Steven Hunter	15.00
7CC	Jamaal Tinsley	15.00
8CC	Loren Woods	15.00
9CC	Zach Randolph	15.00
10CC	Michael Bradley	15.00
11CC	Pau Gasol	15.00
12CC	Troy Murphy	15.00
13CC	Richard Jefferson	30.00
14CC	Brendan Haywood	25.00
15CC	Gilbert Arenas	15.00
16CC	Kirk Haston	20.00
17CC	Omar Cook	15.00
18CC	Vince Carter	200.00
19CC	Larry Bird	15.00

2001-02 Fleer Hoops Hot Prospects Hoops Hot Materials

		MT
Common Player:		8.00
Inserted 1:8		
1HM	Vince Carter	40.00
2HM	Darius Miles	30.00
3HM	Stephon Marbury	12.00
4HM	John Stockton	12.00
5HM	Steve Francis	15.00
6HM	Tracy McGrady	15.00
7HM	Lamar Odom	12.00
8HM	Corey Maggette	8.00
9HM	Stromile Swift	8.00
10HM	Morris Peterson	10.00
11HM	Jason Kidd	12.00
12HM	Karl Malone	12.00
13HM	Baron Davis	10.00
14HM	Gary Payton	10.00
15HM	Paul Pierce	15.00
16HM	Desmond Mason	8.00
17HM	Dikembe Mutombo	8.00
18HM	Mike Miller	15.00
19HM	Craig "Speedy" Claxton	8.00
20HM	Antoine Walker	10.00
21HM	Allen Iverson	30.00
22HM	Reggie Miller	15.00
23HM	Chris Webber	15.00
24HM	Shawn Marion	12.00
25HM	Allan Houston	10.00
26HM	Kenyon Martin	12.00
27HM	Alonzo Mourning	10.00
28HM	Grant Hill	12.00
29HM	Kwame Brown	25.00
30HM	Tyson Chandler	20.00
31HM	Eddy Curry	20.00
32HM	Shane Battier	30.00
33HM	Eddie Griffin	20.00
34HM	Rodney White	12.00
35HM	Pau Gasol	25.00
36HM	Jason Richardson	25.00
37HM	DeSagana Diop	10.00
38HM	Joe Johnson	8.00
39HM	Kedrick Brown	8.00
40HM	Vladimir Radmanovic	12.00
41HM	Richard Jefferson	15.00
42HM	Troy Murphy	8.00
43HM	Steven Hunter	10.00
44HM	Kirk Haston	10.00
45HM	Michael Bradley	10.00
46HM	Michael Bradley	10.00
47HM	Zach Randolph	12.00
48HM	Brendan Haywood	12.00

2001-02 Fleer Hoops Hot Prospects Hoops Hot Tandems

		MT
Common Player:		25.00
Production 100 Sets		
1HT	Vince Carter, Tracy McGrady	75.00
2HT	Kwame Brown, Eddy Curry	30.00
3HT	Karl Malone, John Stockton	40.00
4HT	DeSagana Diop, Stromile Swift	25.00
5HT	Shane Battier, Stromile Swift	40.00
6HT	Paul Pierce, Antoine Walker	30.00
7HT	Eddie Griffin, Jason Kidd	30.00
8HT	Rodney White, Steve Francis	30.00
9HT	Mike Miller, Michael Bradley	25.00
10HT	Tyson Chandler, Darius Miles	40.00
11HT	Stephon Marbury, Jason Kidd	30.00
12HT	Allen Iverson, Vince Carter	100.00
13HT	Allen Iverson, Darius Miles	60.00
14HT	Reggie Miller, Baron Davis	25.00
15HT	Chris Webber, Karl Malone	50.00
16HT	Alonzo Mourning, Dikembe Mutombo	30.00
17HT	Kenyon Martin, Lamar Odom	30.00
18HT	Allan Houston, Reggie Miller	25.00
19HT	Grant Hill, Tracy McGrady	40.00
20HT	Pau Gasol, Chris Webber	50.00
21HT	Dikembe Mutombo, Craig "Speedy" Claxton	25.00
22HT	Grant Hill, Steve Francis	40.00
23HT	Jason Richardson, Gary Payton	50.00
24HT	Gary Payton, Stephon Marbury	30.00
25HT	Joe Johnson, Antoine Walker	30.00
26HT	Kedrick Brown, Paul Pierce	30.00
27HT	Vladimir Radmanovic, Desmond Mason	25.00
28HT	Shawn Marion, Desmond Mason	25.00
29HT	Richard Jefferson, Kenyon Martin	25.00
30HT	Troy Murphy, Mike Miller	30.00
31HT	Kirk Haston, Baron Davis	25.00
32HT	Vince Carter, Morris Peterson	50.00
33HT	Vince Carter, Lamar Odom	40.00
34HT	Vince Carter, Darius Miles	75.00
35HT	Vince Carter, Kwame Brown	60.00
36HT	Vince Carter, Chris Webber	60.00
37HT	Allen Iverson, Stephon Marbury	40.00
38HT	Allen Iverson, Jason Kidd	50.00
39HT	Eddie Griffin, Darius Miles	40.00
40HT	Eddy Curry, Eddie Griffin	30.00
41HT	Eddie Griffin, Kwame Brown	40.00
42HT	Allen Iverson, Craig "Speedy" Claxton	40.00
43HT	Tyson Chandler, Eddy Curry	30.00
44HT	Tyson Chandler, Kwame Brown	40.00
45HT	Jason Richardson, Zach Randolph	40.00
46HT	Shane Battier, Tyson Chandler	40.00
47HT	Shane Battier, Kwame Brown	50.00
48HT	Shane Battier, Eddy Curry	40.00
49HT	Grant Hill, Reggie Miller	40.00
50HT	Chris Webber, Darius Miles	50.00

2001-02 Fleer Hoops Hot Prospects Inside Vince Carter

		MT
Complete Set (10):		
Common Player:		
1vc	Vince Carter/1000	50.00
2vc	Vince Carter/900	50.00
3vc	Vince Carter/800	50.00
4vc	Vince Carter/700	50.00
5vc	Vince Carter/600	50.00
6vc	Vince Carter/500	75.00
7vc	Vince Carter/400	75.00
8vc	Vince Carter/300	75.00
9vc	Vince Carter/200	75.00
10vc	Vince Carter/100	150.00

2001-02 Fleer Marquee

		MT
Complete Set (125):		
Common Player:		.15
Rookies numbered to 1500		
Dual Rookies numbered to 2500		
1	DerMarr Johnson	.15
2	Darius Miles	2.00
3	Michael Jordan	10.00
4	Craig "Speedy" Claxton	.15
5	Stromile Swift	.15
6	Michael Finley	.50
7	Kurt Thomas	.15
8	Tim Duncan	1.00
9	Kenyon Martin	.50
10	Jermaine O'Neal	.50
11	Elton Brand	.50
12	Jamal Mashburn	.15
13	Jumaine Jones	.15
14	Stephon Marbury	.15
15	Eddie Jones	.15
16	Antonio McDyess	.15
17	Tim Thomas	.15
18	Gary Payton	.50
19	Latrell Sprewell	.15
20	Grant Hill	.75
21	Jason Terry	.15
22	Marcus Fizer	.15
23	Anthony Mason	.15
24	Bonzi Wells	.15
25	Sam Cassell	.15
26	Jerry Stackhouse	.15
27	Hidayet Turkoglu	.50
28	Morris Peterson	.50
29	John Stockton	.75
30	Dikembe Mutombo	.50
31	Mitch Richmond	.15
32	Andre Miller	.75
33	Joe Smith	.15
34	Mike Bibby	.50
35	Wally Szczerbiak	.50
36	Steve Francis	1.00
37	Nazr Mohammed	.15
38	Antoine Walker	1.00
39	Courtney Alexander	.50
40	Shawn Marion	.15
41	Jason Williams	.15
42	Steve Nash	.50
43	Antonio Davis	.15
44	Steve Smith	.15
45	Jason Kidd	1.00
46	Reggie Miller	.50
47	Quentin Richardson	.15
48	Baron Davis	.50
49	Juwan Howard	.15
50	Rasheed Wallace	.15
51	Brian Grant	.15
52	Nick Van Exel	.15
53	Donyell Marshall	.15
54	Vin Baker	.15
55	Allan Houston	.15
56	Mike Miller	1.00
57	Shaquille O'Neal	3.00
58	Ron Mercer	.15
59	Lindsey Hunter	.15
60	Predrag Stojakovic	.75
61	Ray Allen	1.00
62	Antawn Jamison	.15
63	Theo Ratliff	.15
64	Vince Carter	3.00
65	DeShawn Stevenson	.15
66	Allen Iverson	3.00
67	Derek Fisher	.15
68	Dirk Nowitzki	1.00
69	Keith Van Horn	.15
70	David Robinson	.50
71	Terrell Brandon	.15
72	Cuttino Mobley	.15
73	Shareef Abdur-Rahim	.15
74	Paul Pierce	1.00
75	Elden Campbell	.15
76	Anfernee Hardaway	.15
77	Alonzo Mourning	.50
78	Raef LaFrentz	.15
79	Richard Hamilton	.75
80	Rashard Lewis	.15
81	Marcus Camby	.15
82	Jalen Rose	.15
83	Lamar Odom	.75
84	David Wesley	.15
85	James Posey	.15
86	Derek Anderson	.15
87	Glenn Robinson	.50
88	Clifford Robinson	.15
89	Kerry Kittles	.15
90	Hakeem Olajuwon	.50
91	Patrick Ewing	.50
92	Tracy McGrady	1.50
93	Kobe Bryant	4.00
94	Chris Mihm	.15
95	Lorenzen Wright	.15
96	Chris Webber	1.00
97	Kevin Garnett	1.00
98	Larry Hughes	.15
99	Keyon Dooling	.50
100	Karl Malone	.75
101	*Joe Johnson*	10.00
102	*Tyson Chandler*	10.00
103	*Eddy Curry*	10.00
104	*Jason Richardson*	25.00
105	*Troy Murphy*	10.00
106	*Eddie Griffin*	10.00
107	*Jamaal Tinsley*	12.00
108	*Pau Gasol*	25.00
109	*Shane Battier*	25.00
110	*Richard Jefferson*	15.00
111	*Steven Hunter*	10.00
112	*Tony Parker*	25.00
113	*Vladimir Radmanovic*	10.00
114	*Andrei Kirilenko*	10.00
115	*Kwame Brown*	20.00
126	*Mengke Bateer*	10.00
116	*Samuel Dalembert,Damone Brown*	8.00
117	*Joseph Forte,Kedrick Brown*	8.00
118	*Zach Randolph,Ruben Boumtje-Boumtje*	8.00
119	*Oscar Torres,Terence Morris*	8.00
120	*Alton Ford,Kenny Satterfield*	8.00
121	*Rodney White,Zeljko Rebraca*	8.00
122	*Trenton Hassell,Earl Watson*	8.00
123	*DeSagana Diop,Primoz Brezec*	8.00
124	*Ernest Brown,Gerald Wallace*	8.00
125	*Loren Woods,Brendan Haywood*	8.00

Post-1980 cards in Near Mint condition will generally sell for about 75% of the quoted Mint value. Excellent-condition cards bring no more than 40%.

2001-02 Fleer Marquee Banner Season

		MT
Complete Set (20):		
Common Player:		2.00
Inserted 1:20		
1BS	Vince Carter	8.00
2BS	Shaquille O'Neal	6.00
3BS	Allen Iverson	8.00
4BS	Kevin Garnett	4.00
5BS	Dirk Nowitzki	4.00
6BS	Tim Duncan	4.00
7BS	Michael Jordan	20.00
8BS	Steve Francis	4.00
9BS	Grant Hill	2.00
10BS	Kobe Bryant	12.00
11BS	Kenyon Martin	2.00
12BS	Shareef Abdur-Rahim	2.00
13BS	Ray Allen	2.00
14BS	Tracy McGrady	5.00
15BS	Baron Davis	2.00
16BS	Chris Webber	5.00
17BS	Jason Kidd	5.00
18BS	Darius Miles	6.00
19BS	Paul Pierce	4.00
20BS	Karl Malone	3.00

2001-02 Fleer Marquee Banner Season GW

		MT
Complete Set (15):		
Common Player:		10.00
Inserted 1:15		
	Shareef Abdur-Rahim	10.00
	Ray Allen	10.00
	Vince Carter	25.00
	Baron Davis	10.00
	Steve Francis	15.00
	Grant Hill	15.00
	Allen Iverson	25.00
	Jason Kidd	20.00
	Karl Malone	15.00
	Kenyon Martin	10.00
	Tracy McGrady	20.00
	Darius Miles	20.00
	Dirk Nowitzki	15.00
	Paul Pierce	15.00
	Chris Webber	15.00

2001-02 Fleer Marquee Co Stars

		MT
Complete Set (10):		
Common Player:		3.00
Inserted 1:10		
1CS	Michael Jordan, Kwame Brown	12.00
2CS	Steve Francis, Eddie Griffin	3.00
3CS	Tracy McGrady, Steven Hunter	5.00
4CS	Karl Malone, Andrei Kirilenko	3.00
5CS	Reggie Miller, Jamaal Tinsley	5.00
6CS	David Robinson, Tony Parker	10.00
7CS	Shane Battier, Pau Gasol	10.00
8CS	Jason Kidd, Richard Jefferson	10.00
9CS	Antawn Jamison, Jason Richardson	10.00
10CS	Ron Mercer, Eddy Curry	5.00

2001-02 Fleer Marquee Feature Presentation Autograph

		MT
Complete Set (1):		100.00
1	Vince Carter	100.00

2001-02 Fleer Marquee Feature Presentation Game-Worn

		MT
Complete Set (10):		
Common Player:		20.00
#'d to between 135 and 500		
1	Vince Carter	40.00
2	Darius Miles	30.00
3	Jason Kidd	30.00
4	Grant Hill	20.00
5	Chris Webber	30.00
6	Dirk Nowitzki	30.00
7	Allen Iverson	40.00
8	Tracy McGrady	30.00
9	Steve Francis	25.00
10	Karl Malone	20.00

2001-02 Fleer Marquee Feature Presentation Single

		MT
Complete Set (14):		
Common Player:		10.00
#'d to between 135 and 500		
1SS	Vince Carter	20.00
2SS	Darius Miles	15.00
3SS	Jason Kidd	15.00
4SS	Grant Hill	10.00
5SS	Chris Webber	10.00
6SS	Dirk Nowitzki	10.00
7SS	Allen Iverson	20.00
8SS	Tracy McGrady	15.00
9SS	Steve Francis	10.00
10SS	Karl Malone	10.00
11SS	Kevin Garnett	15.00
12SS	Kobe Bryant	25.00
13SS	Tim Duncan	15.00
14SS	Shaquille O'Neal	20.00

2001-02 Fleer Marquee Feature Presentation Triple

		MT
Complete Set (14):		
Common Player:		20.00
#'d to 135		
1TS	Vince Carter	45.00
2TS	Darius Miles	35.00
3TS	Jason Kidd	35.00
4TS	Grant Hill	20.00
5TS	Chris Webber	25.00
6TS	Dirk Nowitzki	25.00
7TS	Allen Iverson	45.00
8TS	Tracy McGrady	35.00
9TS	Steve Francis	20.00
10TS	Karl Malone	20.00
11TS	Kevin Garnett	20.00
12TS	Kobe Bryant	75.00
13TS	Tim Duncan	35.00
14TS	Shaquille O'Neal	45.00

2001-02 Fleer Marquee Lucky 13

		MT
Complete Set (1):		100.00
Numbered to 113		
	Vince Carter	

2001-02 Fleer Marquee We're No. One

		MT
Complete Set (11):		
Common Player:		5.00
Inserted 1:240		
1WO	Hakeem Olajuwon	5.00
2WO	David Robinson	5.00
3WO	Shaquille O'Neal	12.00
4WO	Chris Webber	10.00
5WO	Allen Iverson	15.00
6WO	Tim Duncan	10.00
7WO	Elton Brand	8.00
8WO	Kenyon Martin	5.00
9WO	Kwame Brown	15.00
10WO	Vince Carter	20.00
11WO	Larry Bird	40.00

2001-02 Fleer Marquee We're No. One Auto

		MT
Complete Set (5):		
Common Player:		20.00
Inserted 1:32		
	Larry Bird	250.00
	Kwame Brown	50.00
	Vince Carter	100.00
	Hakeem Olajuwon	20.00
	David Robinson	20.00

2001-02 Fleer Marquee We're No. One GW

		MT
Complete Set (8):		
Common Player:		12.00
Inserted 1:32		
	Larry Bird	75.00
	Elton Brand	12.00
	Kwame Brown	25.00
	Vince Carter	45.00
	Allen Iverson	45.00
	Kenyon Martin	15.00
	Hakeem Olajuwon	15.00
	David Robinson	15.00

2001-02 Fleer Maximum

		MT
Complete Set (220):		300.00
Common Player:		.20
Minor Stars:		.40
Common Rookie (181-220):		4.00
Production 1,000 Sets		
Pack (15):		5.00
Box (15):		60.00
1	Ray Allen, Grant Hill	.40
2	Elton Brand, Ray Allen	.60
3	Grant Hill, Allen Iverson	1.00
4	Tracy McGrady, Elton Brand	1.00
5	Chris Webber, Baron Davis	.60
6	Latrell Sprewell, Jason Terry	.40
7	Paul Pierce, Mike Bibby	.50
8	Jason Kidd, David Robinson	.50
9	Shaquille O'Neal, Paul Pierce	.75
10	Stephon Marbury, Dirk Nowitzki	.50
11	Steve Francis, Jerry Stackhouse	.60
12	Vince Carter, Shawn Marion	1.50
13	Allen Iverson, Tracy McGrady	1.50
14	Kevin Garnett, Anfernee Hardaway	.75
15	Eddie Jones, Vince Carter	1.50
16	Antoine Walker	.60
17	Kobe Bryant	3.00
18	Avery Johnson	.20
19	Damon Stoudamire	.20
20	Kurt Thomas	.20
21	Aaron McKie	.40
22	Chris Whitney	.20
23	David Robinson	.50
24	Erick Dampier	.20
25	Jumaine Jones	.20
26	Radoslav Nesterovic	.20
27	Robert Horry	.40
28	Ben Wallace	.40
29	Christian Laettner	.20
30	Eddie Robinson	.40
31	Alvin Williams	.20
32	Matt Harpring	.20
33	Terrell Brandon	.40
34	Tim Duncan	1.25
35	Bonzi Wells	.40
36	Clarence Weatherspoon	.20
37	George McCloud	.20
38	Jermaine O'Neal	.50
39	Al Harrington	.40
40	Antawn Jamison	.75
41	John Amaechi	.20
42	Rod Strickland	.40
43	Stacey Augmon	.20
44	Dion Glover	.20
45	Michael Dickerson	.20
46	Anfernee Hardaway	.50
47	Rashard Lewis	.50
48	Shawn Bradley	.20
49	Todd MacCulloch	.20
50	Antonio McDyess	.50
51	Darrell Armstrong	.40
52	Jalen Rose	.50
53	Mike Bibby	.40
54	P.J. Brown	.20
55	Quincy Lewis	.20
56	Doug Christie	.20
57	Elden Campbell	.40
58	James Posey	.20
59	Karl Malone	.75
60	Patrick Ewing	.40
61	Sam Cassell	.40
62	Baron Davis	.60
63	Corey Maggette	.40
64	Donyell Marshall	.20
65	Ervin Johnson	.20
66	Horace Grant	.20
67	Nick Van Exel	.50
68	Vlade Divac	.40
69	Allan Houston	.40
70	Antonio Davis	.40
71	Dale Davis	.20
72	Eduardo Najera	.20
73	Kenny Anderson	.40
74	Kevin Willis	.20
75	LaPhonso Ellis	.20
76	Anthony Mason	.40

77 Greg Ostertag .20
78 Jamal Mashburn .40
79 Jeff McInnis .20
80 Peja Stojakovic .50
81 Scott Williams .20
82 Bryon Russell .20
83 Chucky Atkins .20
84 Darius Miles 2.00
85 David Wesley .20
86 Hidayet Turkoglu .40
87 Mark Pope .20
88 Dana Barros .20
89 Glenn Robinson .50
90 John Stockton .60
91 Lamar Odom .75
92 Mike Miller 1.25
93 Ron Artest .20
94 Adonal Foyle .20
95 Andre Miller .40
96 Eric Snow .40
97 Stanislav Medvedenko .20
98 Steve Smith .40
99 Wally Szczerbiak .50
100 Chris Mihm .20
101 Danny Fortson .20
102 Dikembe Mutombo .40
103 Joe Smith .40
104 Lindsey Hunter .20
105 Malik Rose .20
106 Austin Croshere .20
107 Chris Gatling .20
108 Hakeem Olajuwon .50
109 Mark Jackson .20
110 Milt Palacio .20
111 Ruben Patterson .20
112 Steve Nash .40
113 Brian Grant .40
114 Dirk Nowitzki .75
115 Jeff Foster .20
116 Morris Peterson .40
117 Scottie Pippen .75
118 Lamond Murray .20
119 Larry Hughes .40
120 Shareef Abdur-Rahim .60
121 Tony Delk .20
122 Vin Baker .40
123 Art Long .20
124 Kenyon Martin .40
125 Michael Finley .50
126 Stromile Swift .40
127 Toni Kukoc .40
128 Alonzo Mourning .50
129 Charlie Ward .20
130 Eric Williams .20
131 Jerome Williams .20
132 Raef LaFrentz .40
133 Rasheed Wallace .50
134 Reggie Miller .60
135 Cuttino Mobley .40
136 Desmond Mason .20
137 Jason Williams .40
138 Keith Van Horn .40
139 Nazr Mohammed .20
140 Shawn Marion .75
141 Tim Hardaway .40
142 Anthony Carter .20
143 Danny Manning .20
144 Derek Anderson .40
145 Jason Terry .40
146 Kenny Thomas .20
147 Othella Harrington .20
148 Corliss Williamson .20
149 Derek Fisher .40
150 Ricky Davis .40
151 Stephen Jackson .20
152 Tyrone Nesby .20
153 Calvin Booth .20
154 Emanual Davis .20
155 Kerry Kittles .20
156 Marc Jackson .20
157 Samaki Walker .20
158 Tom Gugliotta .20
159 Wesley Person .20
160 Antonio Daniels .20
161 Charles Oakley .20
162 Chauncey Billups .20
163 Derrick Coleman .40
164 Jerry Stackhouse .60
165 Michael Jordan 8.00
166 Quentin Richardson .40
167 Gary Payton .75
168 Iakovos Tsakalidis .20
169 Juwan Howard .40
170 Lorenzen Wright .20
171 Marcus Camby .40
172 Maurice Taylor .20
173 Jacque Vaughn .20
174 Bruce Bowen .20
175 Clifford Robinson .40
176 Michael Olowokandi .20
177 Richard Hamilton .40
178 Ron Mercer .40
179 Craig "Speedy" Claxton .40
180 Tim Thomas .40
181 *Joe Johnson* 10.00
182 *Pau Gasol* 15.00
183 *Kwame Brown* 12.00
184 *Zach Randolph* 8.00
185 *Jason Richardson* 20.00
186 *Jamaal Tinsley* 12.00
187 *Oscar Torres* 3.00
188 *Rodney White* 6.00
189 *Kedrick Brown* 4.00
190 *Tony Parker* 15.00
191 *Samuel Dalembert* 3.00
192 *Shane Battier* 20.00
193 *Loren Woods* 6.00
194 *Richard Jefferson* 10.00
195 *Jeff Trepagnier* 3.00
196 *Terence Morris* 3.00
197 *Eddie Griffin* 12.00
198 *Primoz Brezec* 3.00
199 *Vladimir Radmanovic* 4.00
200 *Gerald Wallace* 8.00
201 *Alton Ford* 3.00
202 *Steven Hunter* 3.00
203 *Michael Bradley* 4.00
204 *Brandon Armstrong* 4.00
205 *Jamaal Tinsley* 12.00
206 *Bobby Simmons* 3.00
207 *Zeljko Rebraca* 4.00
208 *Tony Parker* 15.00
209 *Troy Murphy* 6.00
210 *Kwame Brown* 12.00
211 *Andrei Kirilenko* 10.00
212 *Trenton Hassell* 6.00
213 *Pau Gasol* 15.00
214 *Tang Hamilton* 0.00
215 *Joseph Forte* 6.00
216 *Eddy Curry* 12.00
217 *DeSagana Diop* 5.00
218 *Joe Johnson* 10.00
219 *Tyson Chandler* 12.00
220 *Jason Collins* 4.00

2001-02 Fleer Maximum Big Shots

MT
Complete Set (15): 25.00
Common Player: 1.00
Inserted 1:8
1 Grant Hill 2.00
2 Ray Allen 1.50
3 Allen Iverson 5.00
4 Elton Brand 2.00
5 Baron Davis 1.50
6 Jason Terry 1.00
7 Mike Bibby 1.00
8 David Robinson 1.00
9 Paul Pierce 1.50
10 Dirk Nowitzki 2.00
11 Jerry Stackhouse 1.50
12 Shawn Marion 2.00
13 Tracy McGrady 4.00
14 Anfernee Hardaway 1.00
15 Vince Carter 8.00

2001-02 Fleer Maximum Big Shots Jerseys

MT
Common Player: 15.00
Inserted 1:20
1 Grant Hill 15.00
2 Allen Iverson 30.00
3 Elton Brand 20.00
4 Jason Terry 12.00
5 Mike Bibby 12.00
6 David Robinson 15.00
7 Paul Pierce 20.00
8 Shawn Marion 20.00
9 Tracy McGrady 25.00
10 Anfernee Hardaway 15.00
11 Vince Carter 40.00

2001-02 Fleer Maximum Floor Score

MT
Complete Set (15): 40.00
Common Player: 1.00
Inserted 1:8
1FS Jason Kidd 3.00
2FS Lamar Odom 2.00
3FS Baron Davis 1.50
4FS Dirk Nowitzki 2.00
5FS Ray Allen 1.50
6FS Anfernee Hardaway 1.00
7FS Latrell Sprewell 2.00
8FS Chris Webber 3.00
9FS Grant Hill 2.00
10FS Vince Carter 8.00
11FS Shaquille O'Neal 4.00
12FS Michael Jordan 12.00
13FS Kobe Bryant 8.00
14FS Kevin Garnett 5.00
15FS Tim Duncan 3.00

2001-02 Fleer Maximum Floor Score Court

MT
Common Player: 12.00
Inserted 1:40
1 Jason Kidd 20.00
2 Lamar Odom 15.00
3 Baron Davis 12.00
4 Dirk Nowitzki 20.00
5 Ray Allen 15.00
6 Anfernee Hardaway 12.00
7 Latrell Sprewell 15.00
8 Chris Webber 15.00
9 Grant Hill 12.00
10 Vince Carter 30.00

2001-02 Fleer Maximum Maximum Performance

MT
Common Player:
Production 100 Sets
1MPF Vince Carter 60.00
2MPF Tracy McGrady 30.00
3MPF Kobe Bryant 60.00
4MPF Michael Jordan 120.00
5MPF Shaquille O'Neal 30.00
6MPF Allen Iverson 40.00
7MPF Grant Hill 20.00
8MPF Kevin Garnett 40.00
9MPF Steve Francis 25.00
10MPF Tim Duncan 25.00

2001-02 Fleer Maximum Maximum Power

MT
Complete Set (25): 50.00
Common Player: 2.00
Inserted 1:16
1MP Kobe Bryant 10.00
2MP Michael Jordan 15.00
3MP Shaquille O'Neal 5.00
4MP Kevin Garnett 6.00
5MP Tim Duncan 4.00
6MP Jason Kidd 3.50
7MP Richard Hamilton 2.00
8MP Vince Carter 10.00
9MP Alonzo Mourning 2.00
10MP John Stockton 2.50
11MP Elton Brand 3.00
12MP Steve Francis 4.00
13MP Keith Van Horn 2.00
14MP Stephon Marbury 2.50
15MP Darius Miles 8.00

2001-02 Fleer Maximum Maximum Power Warm-ups

MT
Common Player: 12.00
Inserted 1:20
1 Jason Kidd 25.00
2 Richard Hamilton 15.00
3 Vince Carter 40.00
4 Alonzo Mourning 15.00
5 John Stockton 20.00
6 Elton Brand 20.00
7 Steve Francis 25.00
8 Keith Van Horn 12.00
9 Stephon Marbury 15.00
10 Darius Miles 25.00

2001-02 Fleer Platinum

MT
Complete Set (250): 200.00
Common Player: .25
Minor Stars: .50
Common HL (201-220): 1.50
Inserted 1:6
Common Rookie (221-250): 3.00
Inserted 1:6
Pack (10): 2.50
Box (24): 50.00
1 Tyrone Hill .25
2 Sam Cassell .50
3 Elton Brand 1.00
4 Andre Miller .50
5 Vitaly Potapenko .25
6 Lamar Odom 1.00
7 Mike Bibby .50
8 Alan Henderson .25
9 Dan Majerle .25
10 Donyell Marshall .25
11 Jason Williams .50
12 Glen Rice .60
13 Kobe Bryant 4.00
14 Pat Garrity .25
15 Shawn Bradley .25
16 Aaron Williams .25
17 Antonio McDyess .60
18 Jonathan Bender .50
19 Ben Wallace .25
20 Vince Carter 4.00
21 Maurice Taylor .25
22 Antonio Daniels .25
23 Rodney Rogers .25
24 Patrick Ewing .50
25 Chauncey Billups .25
26 Steve Smith .50
27 Antawn Jamison 1.00
28 Mitch Richmond .50
29 Jumaine Jones .25
30 Glenn Robinson .60
31 Ron Mercer .50
32 Jelani McCoy .25
33 Paul Pierce .75
34 Jeff McInnis .25
35 Michael Dickerson .25
36 Toni Kukoc .50
37 Anthony Mason .50
38 Jamal Mashburn .50
39 John Stockton .75
40 Predrag Stojakovic .75
41 Charlie Ward .25
42 Donnell Harvey .25
43 Darrell Armstrong .50
44 Michael Finley .60
45 Kerry Kittles .25
46 Voshon Lenard .25
47 Reggie Miller .60
48 Joe Smith .50
49 Antonio Davis .50
50 Hakeem Olajuwon .60
51 David Robinson .60
52 Tony Delk .25
53 Gary Payton .75
54 Kevin Garnett 2.50
55 Arvydas Sabonis .25
56 Larry Hughes .50
57 Richard Hamilton .50
58 Aaron McKie .50
59 Tim Thomas .50
60 Ron Artest .25
61 Matt Harpring .25
62 Kenny Anderson .50
63 Quentin Richardson .50
64 Damon Jones .25
65 Theo Ratliff .50
66 Brian Grant .50
67 Eddie Robinson .50
68 Karl Malone 1.00
69 Bobby Jackson .25
70 Larry Johnson .25
71 Shareef Abdur-Rahim .60
72 Grant Hill 1.25
73 Eduardo Najera .25
74 Keith Van Horn .50
75 Nick Van Exel .50
76 Jalen Rose .50
77 Jerry Stackhouse .75
78 Jerome Williams .25
79 Cuttino Mobley .50
80 Derek Anderson .50
81 Anfernee Hardaway .50
82 Rashard Lewis .50
83 Terrell Brandon .50
84 Scottie Pippen 1.00
85 Danny Fortson .25
86 Jahidi White .25
87 Eric Snow .50
88 Ervin Johnson .25
89 Marcus Fizer .50
90 Lamond Murray .25
91 Antoine Walker .75
92 Keyon Dooling .50
93 Bryant Reeves .25
94 Hanno Mottola .25
95 Tim Hardaway .50
96 David Wesley .25
97 John Starks .25
98 Hidayet Turkoglu .50
99 Allan Houston .50
100 Rick Fox .25
101 Charles Outlaw .25
102 Juwan Howard .50
103 Kendall Gill .25
104 Raef LaFrentz .25
105 Austin Croshere .25
106 Chucky Atkins .25
107 Morris Peterson .60
108 Shandon Anderson .25
109 Sean Elliott .25
110 Wally Szczerbiak .50
111 Vin Baker .50
112 Wally Szczerbiak .50
113 Rasheed Wallace .60
114 Vonteego Cummings .25
115 Christian Laettner .25
116 Dikembe Mutombo .50
117 Lindsey Hunter .25
118 Jamal Crawford .50
119 Jim Jackson .25
120 Bryant Stith .25
121 Corey Maggette .50
122 Mahmoud Abdul-Rauf .60
123 Lorenzen Wright .25
124 Alonzo Mourning .50
125 Jamaal Magloire .25
126 Bryon Russell .25
127 Vlade Divac .50
128 Marcus Camby .50
129 Derek Fisher .50
130 Mike Miller 1.50
131 Steve Nash .50
132 Kenyon Martin .50
133 James Posey .50
134 Travis Best .25
135 Corliss Williamson .25
136 Alvin Williams .25
137 Walt Williams .25
138 Malik Rose .25
139 Clifford Robinson .50
140 Ruben Patterson .25
141 LaPhonso Ellis .25
142 Rod Strickland .50
143 Marc Jackson .25
144 Hubert Davis .25
145 Speedy Claxton .50
146 Scott Williams .25
147 Tyronn Lue .25
148 Chris Mihm .25
149 George Lynch .25
150 Michael Olowokandi .25
151 Nazr Mohammed .25
152 Eddie House .25
153 Elden Campbell .50
154 DeShawn Stevenson .50
155 Doug Christie .25
156 Kurt Thomas .50
157 Robert Horry .25
158 Radoslav Nesterovic .25
159 Zhizhi Wang .25
160 Stephen Jackson .25
161 George McCloud .25
162 Jermaine O'Neal .25
163 Mateen Cleaves .25
164 Charles Oakley .25
165 Kenny Thomas .25
166 Terry Porter .25
167 Iakovos Tsakalidis .25
168 Shammond Williams .25
169 Anthony Peeler .25
170 Damon Stoudamire .25
171 Chris Porter .25
172 Chris Whitney .25
173 *Raja Bell* 1.00
174 Darvin Ham .25
175 A.J. Guyton .25
176 Trajan Langdon .25
177 Jerome Moiso .25
178 Anthony Carter .25
179 P.J. Brown .25
180 Danny Manning .25
181 Scot Pollard .25
182 Mark Jackson .25
183 Mark Madsen .25
184 Michael Doleac .25
185 Calvin Booth .25
186 Kevin Willis .25
187 Al Harrington .50
188 Mikki Moore .25
189 Keon Clark .50
190 Moochie Norris .25
191 Ron Harper .25
192 Danny Ferry .25
193 Jacque Vaughn .25
194 Derrick Coleman .25
195 Brent Barry .25
196 Dion Glover .25
197 Felipe Lopez .25
198 Shawn Kemp .50
199 Mookie Blaylock .25
200 Bonzi Wells .50
201 Vince Carter 10.00
202 Ray Allen 2.00
203 Darius Miles 8.00
204 Shaquille O'Neal 5.00
205 Stromile Swift 1.50
206 DerMarr Johnson 1.50
207 Eddie Jones 1.50
208 Chris Webber 4.00
209 Latrell Sprewell 2.00
210 Tracy McGrady 5.00
211 Dirk Nowitzki 2.00
212 Stephon Marbury 2.00
213 Steve Francis 4.00
214 Tim Duncan 4.00
215 Jason Kidd 3.00
216 Shawn Marion 2.00
217 Desmond Mason 1.50
218 Courtney Alexander 1.50
219 Baron Davis 2.00
220 Allen Iverson 6.00
221 *Joe Johnson* 10.00
222 *Kedrick Brown* 5.00
223 *Joseph Forte* 6.00
224 *Kirk Haston* 6.00
225 *TBD* 6.00
226 *Eddy Curry* 10.00
227 *DeSagana Diop* 5.00
228 *Jeff Trepagnier* 4.00
229 *TBD* 6.00
230 *Rodney White* 6.00
231 *Jason Richardson* 20.00
232 *Troy Murphy* 5.00
233 *TBD* 6.00
234 *Jamaal Tinsley* 12.00
235 *Pau Gasol* 15.00
236 *Shane Battier* 20.00
237 *Richard Jefferson* 8.00
238 *Jason Collins* 4.00
239 *Brendan Haywood* 6.00
240 *Steven Hunter* 4.00
241 *Zach Randolph* 8.00
242 *Gerald Wallace* 8.00
243 *TBD* 6.00
244 *Vladimir Radmanovic* 6.00
245 *Michael Bradley* 6.00
246 *Andrei Kirilenko* 8.00
247 *Kwame Brown* 12.00
248 *Alton Ford* 3.00
249 *TBD* 6.00
250 *TBD* 6.00

2001-02 Fleer Platinum Classic Combinations

MT
Common Player: 3.00
1CC John Stockton, Karl Malone 5.00
2CC Allen Iverson, Dikembe Mutombo 6.00
3CC Jason Kidd, Grant Hill 5.00
4CC Steve Francis, Elton Brand 6.00
5CC Vince Carter, Antawn Jamison 10.00
6CC Hakeem Olajuwon, Patrick Ewing 3.00
7CC Vince Carter, Tracy McGrady 15.00
8CC Kobe Bryant, Shaquille O'Neal 15.00
9CC Tim Duncan, David Robinson 6.00
10CC Kevin Garnett, Darius Miles 12.00
11CC Dirk Nowitzki, Michael Finley 4.00
12CC Antoine Walker, Paul Pierce 3.00
13CC Ray Allen, Glenn Robinson 3.00
14CC Latrell Sprewell, Allan Houston 3.00
15CC Patrick Ewing, Alonzo Mourning 3.00

A player's name in *italic type* indicates a rookie

2001-02 Fleer Platinum 15th Anniversary Reprints

MT
Complete Set (25): 150.00
Common Player: 4.00
Inserted 1:12
1AR Michael Jordan 30.00
2AR Karl Malone 5.00
3AR Hakeem Olajuwon 4.00
4AR Patrick Ewing 4.00
5AR Reggie Miller 4.00
6AR John Stockton 4.00
7AR Scottie Pippen 5.00
8AR David Robinson 4.00
9AR Shaquille O'Neal 10.00
10AR Alonzo Mourning 4.00
11AR Chris Webber 8.00
12AR Grant Hill 6.00
13AR Jason Kidd 6.00
14AR Eddie Jones 4.00
15AR Kevin Garnett 12.00
16AR Kobe Bryant 20.00
17AR Allen Iverson 12.00
18AR Shareef Abdur-Rahim 4.00
19AR Tim Duncan 8.00
20AR Tracy McGrady 10.00
21AR Vince Carter 20.00
22AR Dirk Nowitzki 5.00
23AR Steve Francis 8.00
24AR Darius Miles 15.00
25AR Mike Miller 8.00

2001-02 Fleer Platinum Lucky 13

MT
Common Player: 25.00
Production 500 Sets
1 Kwame Brown 75.00
2 Tyson Chandler 60.00
3 Pau Gasol 100.00
4 Eddy Curry 60.00
5 Jason Richardson 125.00
6 Shane Battier 125.00
7 Eddie Griffin 75.00
8 DeSagana Diop 30.00
9 Rodney White 30.00
10 Joe Johnson 50.00
11 Kedrick Brown 25.00
12 Vladimir Radmanovic 25.00
13 Richard Jefferson 40.00

2001-02 Fleer Platinum Name Plates

MT
Common Player: 25.00
Inserted 1:12 jumbo
1NP Alonzo Mourning 30.00
2NP Hakeem Olajuwon 30.00
3NP Allen Iverson 100.00
4NP Stephon Marbury 40.00
5NP Gary Payton 40.00
6NP Glenn Robinson 25.00
7NP Shareef Abdur-Rahim 25.00
8NP Keith Van Horn 25.00
9NP John Stockton 60.00
10NP Antoine Walker 40.00
11NP David Robinson 50.00
12NP Michael Finley 30.00
13NP Vince Carter 150.00

2001-02 Fleer Platinum National Patch Time

MT
Common Player: 10.00
Inserted 1:24
1NPT Tom Gugliotta 10.00
2NPT Shawn Marion 15.00
3NPT Darius Miles 30.00
4NPT Mike Miller 25.00
5NPT Jason Terry 12.00
6NPT Stromile Swift 10.00
7NPT Keith Van Horn 10.00
8NPT Ray Allen 25.00
9NPT Baron Davis 15.00
10NPT Shareef Abdur-Rahim 12.00

11NPT	Stephon Marbury	15.00
12NPT	Jason Kidd	25.00
13NPT	Mike Bibby	12.00
14NPT	Jerome Moiso	10.00
15NPT	Richard Hamilton	12.00
16NPT	Paul Pierce	25.00
17NPT	Dikembe Mutombo	12.00
18NPT	Gary Payton	20.00
19NPT	Patrick Ewing	20.00
20NPT	Vince Carter	50.00
21NPT	Corey Maggette	12.00
22NPT	Jacque Vaughn	10.00
23NPT	Darrell Armstrong	10.00
24NPT	Mitch Richmond	10.00
25NPT	Allen Iverson	40.00
26NPT	Desmond Mason	10.00

2001-02 Fleer Platinum Platinum Edition

	MT
Cards 1-200:	6x-12x
Production 201 Sets	
Cards 201-250:	
Production 21 Sets	

2001-02 Fleer Platinum Stadium Standouts

		MT
Complete Set (15):		100.00
Common Player:		5.00
Inserted 1:18		
1SS	Vince Carter	20.00
2SS	Grant Hill	6.00
3SS	Kobe Bryant	20.00
4SS	Steve Francis	8.00
5SS	Tracy McGrady	10.00
6SS	Elton Brand	5.00
7SS	Kevin Garnett	12.00
8SS	Allen Iverson	12.00
9SS	Dirk Nowitzki	5.00
10SS	Shaquille O'Neal	10.00
11SS	Tim Duncan	8.00
12SS	Jason Kidd	6.00
13SS	Darius Miles	15.00
14SS	Chris Webber	8.00
15SS	Ray Allen	5.00

2001-02 Fleer Premium

		MT
Complete Set (185):		250.00
Common Player:		.25
Minor Stars:		.50
Common Rookie:		3.00
Production 1,500 Sets		
Pack (8):		3.00
Box (24):		50.00
1	Shareef Abdur-Rahim	.75
2	Charlie Ward	.25
3	Anfernee Hardaway	.75
4	Robert Horry	.25
5	Michael Jordan	10.00
6	Trajan Langdon	.25
7	Dan Majerle	.25
8	Tracy McGrady	2.00
9	Alonzo Mourning	.50
10	Gary Payton	.75
11	Erick Barkley	.25
12	Jerry Stackhouse	.75
13	Vince Carter	4.00
14	Speedy Claxton	.50
15	DerMarr Johnson	.50
16	Bryon Russell	.25
17	Derrick Coleman	.25
18	Kevin Willis	.25
19	Dirk Nowitzki	1.00
20	Derek Anderson	.25
21	Tim Hardaway	.50
22	Avery Johnson	.25
23	Quincy Lewis	.25
24	Shawn Marion	1.00
25	Joe Smith	.25
26	Tim Thomas	.50
27	Bonzi Wells	.50
28	Ron Artest	.25
29	Elton Brand	1.00
30	Mateen Cleaves	.25
31	Marcus Fizer	.50
32	Ervin Johnson	.25
33	Mark Madsen	.25
34	Andre Miller	.60
35	Nazr Mohammed	.25
36	Dikembe Mutombo	.50
37	Ben Wallace	.25
38	Scottie Pippen	1.00
39	Theo Ratliff	.25
40	Hidayet Turkoglu	.50
41	Alvin Williams	.25
42	Corey Maggette	.50
43	Steve Francis	2.00
44	Dean Garrett	.25
45	Wally Szczerbiak	.60
46	Brent Barry	.25
47	Vlade Divac	.25
48	LaPhonso Ellis	.25
49	Tyrone Hill	.25
50	Toni Kukoc	.25
51	George Lynch	.25
52	Antonio McDyess	.50
53	Paul Pierce	.75
54	Mitch Richmond	.50
55	Latrell Sprewell	1.00
56	Otis Thorpe	.25
57	Ray Allen	.75
58	Mike Bibby	.50
59	P.J. Brown	.25
60	Allan Houston	.50
61	Stephon Marbury	.75
62	Aaron McKie	.25
63	Reggie Miller	.50
64	Eduardo Najera	.25
65	Eddie Robinson	.25
66	John Stockton	.75
67	Chris Webber	1.50
68	Kenny Anderson	.25
69	Alan Henderson	.25
70	Dan Langhi	.25
71	Rashard Lewis	.50
72	Donyell Marshall	.25
73	Charles Oakley	.25
74	Stephen Jackson	.25
75	Clarence Weatherspoon	.25
76	David Wesley	.25
77	Kobe Bryant	4.00
78	Tom Gugliotta	.25
79	Darius Miles	3.50
80	Cuttino Mobley	.50
81	Jason Terry	.50
82	Shandon Anderson	.25
83	Antonio Daniels	.25
84	Larry Hughes	.50
85	Raef LaFrentz	.25
86	Kenyon Martin	.60
87	Lamar Odom	1.00
88	Jermaine O'Neal	.75
89	Glenn Robinson	.75
90	Damon Stoudamire	.25
91	Eddie House	.25
92	Antonio Davis	.25
93	Rick Fox	.25
94	Allen Iverson	2.50
95	Chris Mihm	.25
96	Hakeem Olajuwon	.75
97	Clifford Robinson	.25
98	Derek Fisher	.25
99	Joel Przybilla	.25
100	Sean Rooks	.25
101	Jason Kidd	1.25
102	Antoine Walker	.75
103	Jason Williams	.60
104	Jamal Mashburn	.50
105	Courtney Alexander	.60
106	Vin Baker	.50
107	Chauncey Billups	.25
108	Marcus Camby	.50
109	Kevin Garnett	2.50
110	Juwan Howard	.25
111	Marc Jackson	.25
112	Karl Malone	1.00
113	Ricky Davis	.25
114	Desmond Mason	.50
115	Jerome Moiso	.25
116	Steve Nash	.50
117	Quentin Richardson	.60
118	Predrag Stojakovic	.75
119	Rasheed Wallace	.75
120	Travis Best	.25
121	Terrell Brandon	.25
122	Austin Croshere	.25
123	Tony Delk	.25
124	Anthony Mason	.25
125	Patrick Ewing	.50
126	Brian Grant	.25
127	Bobby Jackson	.25
128	Eddie Jones	.75
129	Popeye Jones	.25
130	Brevin Knight	.25
131	Mike Miller	1.50
132	Shaquille O'Neal	2.00
133	Morris Peterson	.75
134	Mookie Blaylock	.25
135	David Robinson	.75
136	John Starks	.25
137	Stromile Swift	.60
138	Nick Van Exel	.50
139	Keith Van Horn	.50
140	Antawn Jamison	.75
141	Kurt Thomas	.25
142	Sam Cassell	.50
143	Tim Duncan	1.50
144	Baron Davis	.75
145	Jerome Williams	.25
146	Michael Finley	.75
147	Richard Hamilton	.60
148	Grant Hill	1.25
149	Jalen Rose	.75
150	Steve Smith	.25
151	*Kwame Brown*	12.00
152	*Jeryl Sasser*	3.00
153	*Shane Battier*	20.00
154	*Gilbert Arenas*	3.00
155	*Jarron Collins*	3.00
156	*Jamaal Tinsley*	15.00
157	*Brandon Armstrong*	3.00
158	*Michael Bradley*	4.00
159	*Tyson Chandler*	12.00
160	*Joseph Forte*	8.00
161	*Brendan Haywood*	8.00
162	*Joe Johnson*	10.00
163	*Vladimir Radmanovic*	5.00
164	*Gerald Wallace*	6.00
165	*Steven Hunter*	4.00
166	*Richard Jefferson*	8.00
167	*DeSagana Diop*	5.00
168	*Terence Morris*	3.00
169	*Jason Richardson*	20.00
170	*Jeff Trepagnier*	3.00
171	*Kirk Haston*	5.00
172	*Eddy Curry*	12.00
173	*Eddie Griffin*	12.00
174	*Omar Cook*	3.00
175	*Pau Gasol*	15.00
176	*Troy Murphy*	6.00
177	*Trenton Hassell*	5.00
178	*Kedrick Brown*	4.00
179	*Zeljko Rebraca*	4.00
180	*Tony Parker*	12.00
181	*Rodney White*	6.00
182	*Jason Collins*	4.00
183	*Samuel Dalembert*	3.00
184	*Zach Randolph*	8.00
185	*Willie Solomon*	3.00

2001-02 Fleer Premium Commanding Respect

		MT
Complete Set (25):		75.00
Common Player:		1.00
Inserted 1:20		
1CR	Shaquille O'Neal	6.00
2CR	Tim Duncan	5.00
3CR	Marc Jackson	1.00
4CR	Kevin Garnett	8.00
5CR	Kobe Bryant	12.00
6CR	Chris Webber	5.00
7CR	Michael Jordan	15.00
8CR	Dirk Nowitzki	3.00
9CR	Ray Allen	2.50
10CR	Courtney Alexander	2.00
11CR	David Robinson	2.00
12CR	Darius Miles	10.00
13CR	Baron Davis	2.50
14CR	Tracy McGrady	6.00
15CR	Vince Carter	12.00
16CR	Antawn Jamison	3.00
17CR	Jerry Stackhouse	2.00
18CR	Allen Iverson	8.00
19CR	Jason Kidd	4.00
20CR	Antoine Walker	2.00
21CR	Karl Malone	3.00
22CR	Grant Hill	4.00
23CR	Rasheed Wallace	2.00
24CR	Anfernee Hardaway	2.00
25CR	Steve Francis	5.00

2001-02 Fleer Premium Rookie Revolution

		MT
Complete Set (10):		30.00
Common Player:		2.00
Inserted 1:10		
1RR	Kwame Brown	6.00
2RR	Eddy Curry	6.00
3RR	Tyson Chandler	6.00
4RR	Pau Gasol	8.00
5RR	Joe Johnson	5.00
6RR	Michael Bradley	2.00
7RR	Jason Richardson	8.00
8RR	DeSagana Diop	3.00
9RR	Troy Murphy	3.00
10RR	Jamaal Tinsley	8.00

2001-02 Fleer Premium Solid Performers

		MT
Complete Set (30):		60.00
Common Player:		1.50
Inserted 1:20		
1SP	Tracy McGrady	6.00
2SP	John Stockton	2.50
3SP	Dirk Nowitzki	3.00
4SP	Antawn Jamison	3.00
5SP	Scottie Pippen	3.00
6SP	Morris Peterson	2.00
7SP	Ray Allen	2.50
8SP	Antoine Walker	2.00
9SP	Anfernee Hardaway	2.00
10SP	Michael Jordan	15.00
11SP	Jerry Stackhouse	2.00
12SP	Karl Malone	3.00
13SP	Jason Kidd	4.00
14SP	Chris Webber	5.00
15SP	Vince Carter	12.00
16SP	Allen Iverson	8.00
17SP	Courtney Alexander	2.00
18SP	Darius Miles	10.00
19SP	Steve Francis	5.00
20SP	Grant Hill	4.00
21SP	Rasheed Wallace	2.00
22SP	Kenyon Martin	1.50
23SP	Shawn Marion	3.00
24SP	Elton Brand	3.00
25SP	Jason Terry	1.50
26SP	Kobe Bryant	12.00
27SP	Tim Duncan	5.00
28SP	Kevin Garnett	8.00
29SP	Reggie Miller	2.00
30SP	Shaquille O'Neal	6.00

2001-02 Fleer Premium Star Ruby

	MT
Ruby Cards:	10x-20x
Production 100 Sets	
Ruby Rookies:	
Production 50 Sets	

2001-02 Fleer Premium Vertical Heights

		MT
Complete Set (25):		40.00
Common Player:		.75
Inserted 1:10		
1VH	Darius Miles	5.00
2VH	Tracy McGrady	3.00
3VH	Allen Iverson	4.00
4VH	Baron Davis	1.50
5VH	Desmond Mason	.75
6VH	Antoine Walker	1.00
7VH	Jerry Stackhouse	1.00
8VH	Michael Finley	1.00
9VH	Eddie Jones	1.00
10VH	Steve Francis	2.50
11VH	David Robinson	1.00
12VH	Antawn Jamison	2.00
13VH	Karl Malone	2.00
14VH	Michael Jordan	8.00
15VH	Vince Carter	6.00
16VH	Chris Webber	2.50
17VH	Latrell Sprewell	2.00
18VH	Ray Allen	1.50
19VH	Grant Hill	2.00
20VH	Dirk Nowitzki	2.00
21VH	Kobe Bryant	6.00
22VH	Shaquille O'Neal	3.00
23VH	Kevin Garnett	4.00
24VH	Tim Duncan	2.50
25VH	Stephon Marbury	1.50

2001-02 Fleer Shoebox Collection

		MT
Complete Set (180):		200.00
Common Player:		.25
Minor Stars:		.50
Common Rookie (151-180):		3.00
Production 2,500 Sets		
Pack (8):		3.00
Box (24):		70.00
1	Tariq Abdul-Wahad	.25
2	Glen Rice	.50
3	Derek Anderson	.50
4	Desmond Mason	.50
5	Al Harrington	.50
6	Mitch Richmond	.50
7	Felipe Lopez	.25
8	Andre Miller	.60
9	Jerry Stackhouse	.75
10	Jalen Rose	.60
11	Lindsey Hunter	.25
12	Tim Thomas	.50
13	Wally Szczerbiak	.60
14	Vince Carter	4.00
15	Nick Van Exel	.60
16	Jon Barry	.25
17	Aaron McKie	.50
18	Iakovos Tsakalidis	.25
19	Chris Webber	1.50
20	Karl Malone	1.00
21	Shareef Abdur-Rahim	.60
22	Baron Davis	.75
23	Michael Doleac	.25
24	Jermaine O'Neal	.60
25	Elton Brand	1.00
26	Glenn Robinson	.75
27	Tracy McGrady	2.00
28	Allen Iverson	2.50
29	Anfernee Hardaway	.60
30	Scot Pollard	.25
31	David Robinson	.60
32	John Stockton	.75
33	Jason Williams	.50
34	Voshon Lenard	.25
35	Shaquille O'Neal	2.00
36	Grant Hill	1.25
37	Shawn Marion	1.00
38	Vin Baker	.50
39	Raef LaFrentz	.25
40	Steve Francis	1.50
41	Michael Dickerson	.25
42	Hidayet Turkoglu	.50
43	Patrick Ewing	.50
44	Dirk Nowitzki	1.00
45	Keyon Dooling	.50
46	Marcus Camby	.50
47	Bonzi Wells	.50
48	Tim Duncan	1.50
49	Jamal Magloire	.25
50	Rick Fox	.25
51	Kendall Gill	.25
52	Michael Redd	.50
53	Keith Van Horn	.50
54	Eric Snow	.50
55	Theo Ratliff	.50
56	Clifford Robinson	.50
57	Moochie Norris	.25
58	Alonzo Mourning	.60
59	Joe Smith	.50
60	Brent Barry	.25
61	Alvin Williams	.25
62	Antoine Walker	.75
63	Antonio McDyess	.60
64	Derek Fisher	.50
65	Ron Mercer	.50
66	Hakeem Olajuwon	.60
67	Jamal Crawford	.50
68	Chris Mihm	.25
69	Ben Wallace	.25
70	Brian Grant	.50
71	Kevin Garnett	2.50
72	Shandon Anderson	.25
73	Shawn Bradley	.25
74	Danny Fortson	.25
75	Jeff McInnis	.25
76	LaPhonso Ellis	.25
77	Sam Cassell	.50
78	Rasheed Wallace	.60
79	Malik Rose	.25
80	Jahidi White	.25
81	Milt Palacio	.25
82	Tim Hardaway	.50
83	Antonio Daniels	.25
84	Tyronn Lue	.25
85	Cuttino Mobley	.50
86	DerMarr Johnson	.50
87	Lamond Murray	.25
88	Larry Hughes	.50
89	Reggie Miller	.60
90	Lorenzen Wright	.25
91	Eddie Jones	.60
92	Anthony Mason	.50
93	Todd MacCulloch	.25
94	Craig "Speedy" Claxton	.50
95	Mateen Cleaves	.50
96	Gary Payton	.75
97	Morris Peterson	.60
98	Mike Miller	1.50
99	Hanno Mottola	.25
100	Steve Nash	.50
101	Stromile Swift	.50
102	Ray Allen	.75
103	Mark Jackson	.25
104	Stephon Marbury	.75
105	Mike Bibby	.50
106	Rashard Lewis	.50
107	Jason Kidd	1.25
108	P.J. Brown	.25
109	Kobe Bryant	3.00
110	Tom Gugliotta	.25
111	Richard Hamilton	.50
112	Antawn Jamison	1.00
113	Lamar Odom	1.00
114	Kurt Thomas	.25
115	Robert Horry	.25
116	Dikembe Mutombo	.50
117	Tony Delk	.25
118	Predrag Stojakovic	.75
119	Donyell Marshall	.25
120	Paul Pierce	.75
121	Michael Finley	.60
122	Quentin Richardson	.50
123	Kenyon Martin	.50
124	Allan Houston	.50
125	Scottie Pippen	1.00
126	Steve Smith	.50
127	Bryon Russell	.25
128	James Posey	.50
129	Terrell Brandon	.50
130	Toni Kukoc	.50
131	Stephen Jackson	.25
132	Marc Jackson	.25
133	Kelvin Cato	.25
134	Travis Best	.25
135	David Wesley	.25
136	Anthony Carter	.25
137	Michael Jordan	10.00
138	Darrell Armstrong	.50
139	Matt Harpring	.25
140	Antonio Davis	.50
141	Courtney Alexander	.50
142	Jamal Mashburn	.50
143	Jason Terry	.50
144	Marcus Fizer	.50
145	Juwan Howard	.50
146	Darius Miles	3.00
147	Latrell Sprewell	1.00
148	Damon Stoudamire	.25
149	John Starks	.25
150	Jumaine Jones	.25
151	*Kedrick Brown*	4.00
152	*Trenton Hassell*	5.00
153	*Kwame Brown*	10.00
154	*Terence Morris*	3.00
155	*Richard Jefferson*	6.00
156	*Vladimir Radmanovic*	4.00
157	*Brandon Armstrong*	3.00
158	*Kirk Haston*	4.00
159	*Eddie Griffin*	10.00
160	*Steven Hunter*	3.00
161	*Troy Murphy*	4.00
162	*Andrei Kirilenko*	6.00
163	*Jeryl Sasser*	3.00
164	*Michael Bradley*	3.00
165	*Rodney White*	4.00
166	*Loren Woods*	5.00
167	*Zach Randolph*	6.00
168	*Joe Johnson*	8.00
169	*Eddy Curry*	8.00
170	*Jason Richardson*	15.00
171	*DeSagana Diop*	4.00
172	*Jamaal Tinsley*	10.00
173	*Pau Gasol*	12.00
174	*Jason Collins*	3.00
175	*Zeljko Rebraca*	3.00
176	*Shane Battier*	12.00
177	*Gerald Wallace*	6.00
178	*Joseph Forte*	5.00
179	*Tyson Chandler*	10.00
180	*Tony Parker*	10.00

2001-02 Fleer Shoebox Collection Footprints

	MT
Veterans:	6x-12x
Rookies:	3x-6x
Production 150 Sets	

2001-02 Fleer Shoebox Collection NBA Flight School

		MT
Complete Set (20):		70.00
Common Player:		2.00
Inserted 1:12		
1NFS	Richard Hamilton	2.00
2NFS	Kobe Bryant	10.00
3NFS	Michael Jordan	15.00
4NFS	Desmond Mason	2.00
5NFS	Antoine Walker	2.00
6NFS	Baron Davis	2.00
7NFS	Steve Francis	4.00
8NFS	Elton Brand	3.00
9NFS	Lamar Odom	3.00
10NFS	Kevin Garnett	6.00
11NFS	Latrell Sprewell	3.00
12NFS	Tracy McGrady	5.00
13NFS	Shawn Marion	3.00
14NFS	Chris Webber	4.00
15NFS	Vince Carter	10.00
16NFS	Tim Duncan	4.00
17NFS	Morris Peterson	2.00
18NFS	Karl Malone	3.00
19NFS	Jerry Stackhouse	2.00
20NFS	Darius Miles	8.00

2001-02 Fleer Shoebox Collection NBA Flight School Cadet

		MT
Common Player:		12.00
Inserted 1:63		
Captain Cards:		2x-4x
Production 75 Sets		
1	Richard Hamilton	12.00
2	Desmond Mason	12.00
3	Antoine Walker	15.00
4	Baron Davis	12.00
5	Steve Francis	25.00
6	Elton Brand	20.00
7	Lamar Odom	20.00
8	Tracy McGrady	30.00
9	Shawn Marion	20.00
10	Chris Webber	25.00
11	Vince Carter	50.00
12	Morris Peterson	12.00
13	Karl Malone	20.00
14	Jerry Stackhouse	15.00
15	Darius Miles	30.00

2001-02 Fleer Shoebox Collection Sole of the Game

		MT
Common Player:		4.00
Inserted 1:144		
1SOG	Karl Malone	5.00
2SOG	Dirk Nowitzki	5.00
3SOG	Ray Allen	4.00
4SOG	Shaquille O'Neal	10.00
5SOG	Antoine Walker	4.00
6SOG	Grant Hill	6.00
7SOG	Steve Francis	8.00
8SOG	Kobe Bryant	20.00
9SOG	Michael Jordan	40.00
10SOG	Larry Bird	30.00
11SOG	Darius Miles	15.00
12SOG	Chris Webber	8.00
13SOG	Allen Iverson	12.00
14SOG	Rasheed Wallace	4.00
15SOG	Vince Carter	20.00

2001-02 Fleer Shoebox Collection Sole of the Game Ball

MT
Common Player: 15.00
Production 300 Sets
1 Ray Allen 20.00
2 Vince Carter 50.00
3 Steve Francis 25.00
4 Grant Hill 20.00
5 Allen Iverson 40.00
6 Karl Malone 20.00
7 Darius Miles 30.00
8 Dirk Nowitzki 25.00
9 Antoine Walker 15.00
10 Rasheed Wallace 15.00
11 Chris Webber 25.00

2001-02 Fleer Shoebox Collection Sole of the Game Jersey

MT
Common Player:
Production 200 Sets
1 Ray Allen 25.00
2 Vince Carter 75.00
3 Steve Francis 30.00
4 Grant Hill 25.00
5 Allen Iverson 50.00
6 Karl Malone 25.00
7 Darius Miles 40.00
8 Dirk Nowitzki 30.00
9 Antoine Walker 20.00
10 Rasheed Wallace 20.00
11 Chris Webber

2001-02 Fleer Shoebox Collection Tougher than Leather

MT
Complete Set (20): 70.00
Common Player: 2.00
Inserted 1:36
1THL Alonzo Mourning 3.00
2THL Antonio McDyess 3.00
3THL Paul Pierce 4.00
4THL Predrag Stojakovic 4.00
5THL Dirk Nowitzki 5.00
6THL Allen Iverson 10.00
7THL Marcus Camby 3.00
8THL Tracy McGrady 8.00
9THL Kenyon Martin 3.00
10THL Dikembe Mutombo 3.00
11THL Rasheed Wallace 3.00
12THL David Robinson 3.00
13THL Shareef Abdur-Rahim 3.00
14THL Glenn Robinson 4.00
15THL Vince Carter 15.00
16THL Antoine Walker 4.00
17THL Trajan Langdon 2.00
18THL Scottie Pippen 5.00
19THL Eddie Jones 3.00
20THL Lamar Odom 5.00

2001-02 Fleer Shoebox Collec. Tougher than Leather Shoes

MT
Common Player: 25.00
Production 100 Sets
1THLS Alonzo Mourning 25.00
2THLS Antonio McDyess 25.00
3THLS Eddie Jones 25.00
4THLS Paul Pierce 30.00
5THLS Dirk Nowitzki 40.00
6THLS Marcus Camby 25.00
7THLS Tracy McGrady 50.00
8THLS Kenyon Martin 25.00
9THLS Dikembe Mutombo 25.00
10THLSRasheed Wallace 30.00
11THLSDavid Robinson 30.00
12THLSShareef Abdur-Rahim 30.00
13THLSGlenn Robinson 25.00
14THLSVince Carter 80.00
14aTHLSVince Carter Auto 200.00
15THLSAntoine Walker 30.00
16THLSAllen Iverson 60.00
17THLSScottie Pippen 30.00
18THLSPredrag Stojakovic 40.00
19THLSTrajan Langdon 25.00
20THLSLamar Odom 30.00

Classic Doubles features seven pairs of NBA stars. Two figures are packaged together with a full-color collectable card for each player.

2001-02 Fleer Showcase

MT
Complete Set (123): 500.00
Common Player: .30
Minor Stars: .60
87-97/123 Production 500 Sets
98-112 Production 1,000 Sets
113-123 Production 1,500 Sets
Pack (5): 4.00
Box (24): 75.00
1 Grant Hill 1.50
2 Elton Brand 1.25
3 Sam Cassell .60
4 John Stockton 1.00
5 James Posey .60
6 Eddie Jones .75
7 Damon Stoudamire .30
8 Nick Van Exel .75
9 Brian Grant .60
10 Mike Miller 2.00
11 Steve Smith .60
12 Michael Finley 1.00
13 Pedrag Stojakovic 1.00
14 DerMarr Johnson .60
15 Reggie Miller 1.00
16 Quentin Richardson .75
17 Latrell Sprewell 1.25
18 Richard Hamilton .75
19 Michael Doleac .30
20 Derek Fisher .60
21 Marcus Camby .60
22 Stephon Marbury 1.00
23 Bryon Russell .30
24 Jumaine Jones .30
25 Anfernee Hardaway .60
26 P.J. Brown .30
27 Marc Jackson .30
28 Dikembe Mutombo .60
29 Andre Miller .75
30 Robert Horry .60
31 Tom Gugliotta .30
32 David Robinson .75
33 Ron Mercer .60
34 Shawn Marion 1.25
35 Ron Artest .60
36 Jason Williams .75
37 Scottie Pippen 1.25
38 Jerry Stackhouse 1.00
39 Stromile Swift .60
40 Rasheed Wallace .75
41 Alonzo Mourning .75
42 Eddie Robinson .60
43 Shareef Abdur-Rahim .75
44 Wally Szczerbiak .75
45 Antonio Davis .60
46 Glen Rice .60
47 Jason Kidd 1.50
48 Gary Payton 1.00
49 Steve Nash .60
50 Lamar Odom 1.25
51 Glenn Robinson .75
52 Mike Bibby .60
53 Hakeem Olajuwon .75
54 Theo Ratliff .60
55 Kenyon Martin .60
56 Jamal Mashburn .60
57 Larry Hughes .60
58 Speedy Claxton .60
59 Rashard Lewis .75
60 Raef LaFrentz .60
61 Antonio Daniels .30
62 Jason Terry .60
63 Jalen Rose .60
64 Terrell Brandon .60
65 Karl Malone 1.25
66 Antonio McDyess .75
67 Anthony Carter .30
68 Tim Hardaway .60
69 Antoine Walker 1.00
70 Cuttino Mobley .60
71 Allan Houston .75
72 Desmond Mason .60
73 Kurt Thomas .30
74 Juwan Howard .60
75 Tim Thomas .60
76 Tracy McGrady 2.50
77 Dirk Nowitzki 1.25
78 Tim Duncan 2.00
79 Chris Webber 2.00
80 Steve Francis 2.00
81 Paul Pierce 1.00
82 Darius Miles 4.00
83 Ray Allen 1.00
84 Baron Davis 1.00
85 Antawn Jamison 1.25
86 Michael Jordan 30.00
87 Vince Carter 10.00
87A Vince Carter Auto/150 250.00
88 Kobe Bryant 30.00
89 Allen Iverson 15.00
90 Kevin Garnett 15.00
91 Shaquille O'Neal 15.00
92 *Kwame Brown* 30.00
93 *Eddie Griffin* 30.00
94 *Eddy Curry* 30.00
95 *Shane Battier* 50.00
96 *Joe Johnson* 25.00
97 *Tyson Chandler* 30.00
98 *Jason Richardson* 30.00
99 *Zach Randolph* 15.00
100 *Rodney White* 10.00
101 *Pau Gasol* 25.00
102 *Jamaal Tinsley* 20.00
103 *Troy Murphy* 10.00
104 *Richard Jefferson* 15.00
105 *DeSagana Diop* 8.00
106 *Joseph Forte* 12.00
107 *Gerald Wallace* 12.00
108 *Loren Woods* 10.00
109 *Jason Collins* 6.00
110 *Jeryl Sasser* 6.00
111 *Zeljko Rebraca* 8.00
112 *Kirk Haston* 10.00
113 *Kedrick Brown* 8.00
114 *Steven Hunter* 4.00
115 *Michael Bradley* 6.00
116 *Brandon Armstrong* 6.00
117 *Samuel Dalembert* 4.00
118 *Primoz Brezec* 4.00
119 *Andrei Kirilenko* 15.00
120 *Vladimir Radmanovic* 8.00
121 *Ratko Varda* 4.00
122 *Brendan Haywood* 10.00
123 *Wang Zhizhi* 15.00

2001-02 Fleer Showcase Beasts of the East

MT
Common Player: 12.00
Inserted 1:25
1BE Vince Carter 40.00
1A Vince Carter Auto/225 200.00
2BE Allen Iverson 30.00
3BE Alonzo Mourning 15.00
4BE Paul Pierce 20.00
5BE Tracy McGrady 30.00
6BE Keith Van Horn 12.00
7BE Antoine Walker 15.00
8BE Richard Hamilton 12.00
9BE Andre Miller 12.00
10BE Dikembe Mutombo 12.00
11BE Mike Miller 15.00
12BE Kenyon Martin 12.00
13BE Baron Davis 15.00
14BE Ray Allen 20.00

2001-02 Fleer Showcase Best of the West

MT
Common Player: 10.00
Inserted 1:25
1BW Terrell Brandon 10.00
2BW Karl Malone 20.00
3BW Lamar Odom 20.00
4BW Darius Miles 30.00
5BW David Robinson 15.00
6BW Chris Webber 25.00
7BW Gary Payton 15.00
8BW Steve Francis 25.00
9BW Desmond Mason 12.00
10BW Elton Brandon 20.00
11BW Shawn Marion 20.00
12BW John Stockton 20.00
13BW Antawn Jamison 15.00
14BW Antonio McDyess 12.00
15BW Jason Williams 15.00

2001-02 Fleer Showcase Legacy Collection

MT
Veterans: 20x-40x
Avant Cards: 2x-4x
Rookies: 3x-6x
Production 50 Sets

2001-02 Fleer Showcase Rival Revival

MT
Common Player: 30.00
Production 100 Sets
1RR Vince Carter, Tracy McGrady 75.00
2RR Vince Carter, Antawn Jamison 50.00
3RR Vince Carter, Allen Iverson 100.00
4RR David Robinson, Dikembe Mutombo 30.00
5RR Darius Miles, Kenyon Martin 40.00

2001 Fleer Tradition WNBA

MT
Complete Set (165): 30.00
Common Player: .15
Minor Stars: .25
Common Rookie: .75
Pack (10): 2.00
Box (36): 60.00
1 Lisa Leslie 2.00
2 Andrea Stinson .75
3 Tammy Jackson .15
4 *Nicky McCrimmon* .75
5 Vickie Johnson .25
6 Maria Stepanova .15
7 Michelle Edwards .50
8 Tausha Mills .15
9 Edwina Brown .25
10 Jurgita Streimikyte .15
11 *Keitha Dickerson* .75
12 Taj McWilliams .25
13 DeMya Walker .15
14 Adrienne Goodson .25
15 Eva Nemcova .60
16 *Danielle McCulley* .75
17 Shannon Johnson .40
18 Margo Dydek .15
19 Mery Andrade .15
20 Marlies Askamp .15
21 Adrian Williams .15
22 Sonja Henning .50
23 Astou Ndiaye-Diatta .15
24 Latasha Byears .25
25 *Kate Paye* .75
26 Yolanda Griffith 1.25
27 Kate Starbird .40
28 Jennifer Rizzotti .50
29 Umeki Webb .25
30 Tari Phillips .40
31 *Tully Bevilaqua* .75
32 Murriel Page .15
33 Tricia Bader Binford .15
34 Sheryl Swoopes 3.00
35 Debbie Black .15
36 Teresa Weatherspoon 1.50
37 Alisa Burras .15
38 *Stacey Lovelace* .75
39 Helen Darling .25
40 Tina Thompson 1.00
41 Katrina Colleton .15
42 Tamika Whitmore .15
43 Sylvia Crawley .15
44 *Jamie Redd* .75
45 Tracy Reid .15
46 Janeth Arcain .15
47 *Stacy Frese* .75
48 Grace Daley .25
49 Bridget Pettis .15
50 Katy Steding .15
51 Beth Cunningham .15
52 *Vickie Hall* .75
53 Amaya Valdemoro Madariaga .15
54 Milena Flores .25
55 Sue Wicks .25
56 Michelle Marciniak .25
57 Tracy Henderson .15
58 Kisha Ford .15
59 Jannon Roland .15
60 *Vanessa Nygaard* .75
61 *Pollyanna Johns* .75
62 Gordana Grubin .15
63 Shanta Owens .15
64 Cintia dos Santos .25
65 Lynn Pride .25
66 *Robin Threatt* .75
67 Claudia Maria das Neves .15
68 Chantel Tremitiere .15
69 Betty Lennox 1.25
70 Ruthie Bolton-Holifield 1.50
71 Korie Hlede .15
72 Dominique Canty .40
73 Alicia Thompson .15
74 Kristin Folkl .25
75 Elaine Powell .15
76 Cindy Blodgett .15
77 Charlotte Smith .25
78 Mwadi Mabika .15
79 *Marina Ferragut* .75
80 Brandy Reed .50
81 Quacy Barnes .15
82 Chamique Holdsclaw 3.00
83 Dawn Staley 1.00
84 *Nekeshia Henderson* .75
85 Rhonda Mapp .15
86 Becky Hammon 1.00
87 Edna Campbell .40
88 Nikki McCray 1.00
89 Anna DeForge .15
90 Rita Williams .15
91 Andrea Lloyd Curry .15
92 Nykesha Sales .40
93 *Stacy Clinesmith* .75
94 LaTonya Johnson .15
95 Markita Aldridge .15
96 Shalonda Enis .15
97 Wendy Palmer .75
98 Tamecka Dixon .25
99 Katie Smith 1.00
100 Tonya Edwards .50
101 Lady Hardmon .15
102 Dalma Ivanyi .15
103 *Tiffany Travis* .75
104 *Tiffani Johnson* .75
105 DeLisha Milton .25
106 Rebecca Lobo 1.50
107 Michele Timms 1.25
108 *Andrea Garner* .75
109 Andrea Nagy .25
110 Summer Erb .50
111 Ukari Figgs .25
112 Jennifer Gillom .75
113 Kendra Holland-Corn .25
114 Natalie Williams 1.50
115 Clarisse Machanguana .15
116 *E.C. Hill* .75
117 Lisa Harrison .15
118 Tangela Smith .15
119 Vicky Bullett .25
120 Ann Wauters .50
121 *Marla Brumfield* .75
122 Carla McGhee .15
123 Sophia Witherspoon .40
124 Tamicha Jackson .25
125 Kara Wolters .50
126 Maylana Martin .25
127 *Tiffany McCain* .75
128 Naomi Mulitauaopele .15
129 Chasity Melvin .25
130 Stephanie McCarty .60
131 Sheri Sam .40
132 Adrienne Johnson .15
133 Jennifer Azzi 1.00
134 Allison Feaster .15
135 *Elena Tornikidou* .75
136 Sonja Tate .15
137 *Michelle Brogan* .75
138 Ticha Penicheiro .75
139 Keisha Anderson .15
140 Merlakia Jones .40
141 Monica Maxwell .15
142 *Kristen Rasmussen* .75
143 Stacey Thomas .15
144 Kamila Vodichkova .25
145 Angie Braziel .15
146 Olympia Scott-Richardson .15
147 *Vedrana Grgin* .75
148 Shanele Stires .75
149 Coquese Washington .15
150 Crystal Robinson .40
151 Texlin Quinney .15
152 *Michelle Cleary* .75
153 La'Keshia Frett .15
154 Jessie Hicks .15
155 Katrina Hibbert .25
156 Cass Bauer .15
157 Jessica Bibby .25
158 *Shea Mahoney* .75
159 Charmin Smith .15
160 Oksana Zakaluzhnaya .15
161 Tonya Washington .15
162 Rushia Brown .15
163 *Amy Herrig* .75
164 Tara Williams .15
165 Sandy Brondello .75
Charlotte Sting 15.00
Cleveland Rockers 10.00
Detroit Shock 15.00
Houston Comets 20.00
Indiana Fever 40.00
Los Angeles Sparks 25.00
Miami Sol 25.00
Minnesota Lynx 25.00
New York Liberty 15.00
Orlando Miracle 25.00
Phoenix Mercury 20.00
Portland Fire 100.00
Sacramento Monarchs 15.00
Seattle Storm 40.00
Utah Starzz 20.00
Washington Mystics 25.00

2001 Fleer Tradition WNBA Autographics

MT
Common Player: 40.00
Inserted 1:144
1 Jennifer Azzi 50.00
2 Betty Lennox 40.00
3 Lisa Leslie 75.00
4 Katie Smith 50.00
5 Natalie Williams 50.00

2001 Fleer Tradition WNBA Autographics EXTRA

MT
Common Player: 75.00
Production 50 Sets
1 Jennifer Azzi 75.00
2 Betty Lennox 75.00
3 Lisa Leslie 100.00
4 Katie Smith 75.00
5 Natalie Williams 75.00

2001 Fleer Tradition WNBA Autographics PLUS

MT
Complete Set (5):
Common Player:
1AP Jennifer Azzi 40.00
2AP Cynthia Cooper 75.00
3AP Yolanda Griffith 40.00
4AP Chamique Holdsclaw 75.00
5AP Lisa Leslie 75.00

2001 Fleer Tradition WNBA Award Winners

MT
Complete Set (10): 35.00
Common Player: 1.00
Inserted 1:30
1AW Sheryl Swoopes 10.00
2AW Natalie Williams 5.00
3AW Lisa Leslie 6.00
4AW Ticha Penicheiro 2.00
5AW Tina Thompson 2.50
6AW Katie Smith 2.50
7AW Yolanda Griffith 4.00
8AW Teresa Weatherspoon 5.00
9AW Betty Lennox 3.00
10AW Tari Phillips 1.00

2001 Fleer Tradition WNBA Global Game

MT
Complete Set (20): 25.00
Common Player: .50
Inserted 1:6
1GG Janeth Arcain .50
2GG Marlies Askamp .50
3GG Mery Andrade .50
4GG Tully Bevilaqua 2.00
5GG Margo Dydek .50
6GG Gordana Grubin .50
7GG Mwadi Mabika .50
8GG Andrea Nagy .50
9GG Astou Ndiaye-Diatta .50
10GG Eva Nemcova 1.50
11GG Ticha Penicheiro 2.00
12GG Maria Stepanova .50
13GG Michele Timms 3.00
14GG Kamila Vodichkova .50
15GG Ann Wauters 1.00
16GG Yolanda Griffith 4.00
17GG Chamique Holdsclaw 10.00
18GG Katie Smith 2.50
19GG Nikki McCray 2.50
20GG Natalie Williams 4.00

2001 Fleer Tradition WNBA Starting Five

MT
Complete Set (15): 40.00
Common Player: .50
Inserted 1:12
1SF Vicky Bullett 1.00
2SF Andrea Stinson 2.00
3SF Merlakia Jones 1.50
4SF Eva Nemcova 2.00
5SF Janeth Arcain .50
6SF Sheryl Swoopes 12.00
7SF Tina Thompson 3.00
8SF Lisa Leslie 8.00
9SF Mwadi Mabika .50
10SF Rebecca Lobo 4.00
11SF Sue Wicks 1.00
12SF Teresa Weatherspoon 6.00
13SF Michele Timms 5.00
14SF Marlies Askamp .50
15SF Ruthie Bolton-Holifield 5.00

2001 Fleer Tradition WNBA Supreme Court

MT
Complete Set (10): 35.00
Common Player: 2.00
Inserted 1:18
1SC Chamique Holdsclaw 10.00
2SC Natalie Williams 5.00
3SC Betty Lennox 4.00
4SC Yolanda Griffith 4.00
5SC Sheryl Swoopes 10.00
6SC Tina Thompson 3.00
7SC Lisa Leslie 6.00
8SC Jennifer Gillom 2.00
9SC Ticha Penicheiro 2.00
10SC Michele Timms 4.00

2001 Fleer Ultra WNBA

MT
Complete Set (150): 250.00
Common Player: .25
Minor Stars: .50
Common Coach (110-123): 1.00
Pack (10): 3.00
Box (24): 70.00
1 Betty Lennox 2.00
2 Ukari Figgs .50
3 Tangela Smith .25
4 Sue Wicks .50
5 *Marla Brumfield* 1.00
6 Maria Stepanova .25
7 Murriel Page .25
8 Michele Timms 2.00
9 Janeth Arcain .25
10 Lisa Harrison .25
11 Tausha Mills .25
12 Sheri Sam .60
13 Sonja Henning .60

14	Adrienne Johnson	.25
15	Mwadi Mabika	.25
16	Chasity Melvin	.50
17	Allison Feaster	.25
18	Monica Maxwell	.25
19	Katie Smith	1.50
20	Stacey Thomas	.25
21	*Robin Threatt-Elliott*	1.00
22	Jennifer Azzi	1.50
23	Shannon Johnson	.50
24	Rhonda Mapp	.25
25	Eva Nemcova	.75
26	Edwina Brown	.50
27	Margo Dydek	.25
28	Ann Wauters	.50
29	*Nicky McCrimmon*	1.00
30	Dominique Canty	.75
31	Adrienne Goodson	.50
32	Taj McWilliams-Franklin	.50
33	DeLisha Milton	.50
34	Mery Andrade	.50
35	Yolanda Griffith	2.00
36	Tari Phillips	.60
37	Rita Williams	.25
38	Marlies Askamp	.25
39	Korie Hlede	.25
40	Tamicha Jackson	.50
41	Elaine Powell	.25
42	Elena Baranova	1.00
43	Astou Ndiaye-Diatta	.25
44	Nykesha Sales	.75
45	Natalie Williams	2.00
46	Debbie Black	.25
47	Vicky Bullett	.50
48	*Michelle Cleary*	1.00
49	Wendy Palmer	1.00
50	*Tully Bevilaqua*	1.00
51	Helen Darling	.50
52	Katy Steding	.25
53	Sheryl Swoopes	5.00
54	Kristin Folkl	.50
55	Lady Hardmon	.25
56	Jennifer Rizzotti	.75
57	Adrian Williams	.25
58	Tricia Bader Binford	.25
59	Kendra Holland-Corn	.50
60	Crystal Robinson	.25
61	Kara Wolters	.75
62	Rushia Brown	.25
63	Tamecka Dixon	.50
64	Ticha Penicheiro	1.25
65	Teresa Weatherspoon	2.50
66	Edna Campbell	.60
67	Sylvia Crawley	.25
68	Shalonda Enis	.25
69	Andrea Lloyd Curry	.25
70	Tina Thompson	1.50
71	Michelle Edwards	.75
72	Stephanie McCarty	1.00
73	Shanta Owens	.25
74	Shanele Stires	.25
75	DeMya Walker	.25
76	Quacy Barnes	.25
77	Cintia dos Santos	.50
78	Merlakia Jones	.60
79	Lisa Leslie	3.00
80	Grace Daley	.50
81	*Jamie Redd*	1.00
82	Charlotte Smith	.50
83	Jurgita Streimikyte	.25
84	Sophia Witherspoon	.60
85	Ruthie Bolton-Holifield	2.00
86	Vickie Johnson	.50
87	Andrea Stinson	1.25
88	Texlin Quinney	.25
89	Tammy Jackson	.25
90	Andrea Nagy	.50
91	Brandy Reed	.60
92	Umeki Webb	.25
93	Andrea Garner	.25
94	Maylana Martin	.50
95	Vanessa Nygaard	1.00
96	Kamila Vodichkova	.25
97	Coquese Washington	.25
98	Jennifer Gillom	1.25
99	Nikki McCray	1.25
100	Tracy Reid	.25
101	*Elena Tornikidou*	1.00
102	Becky Hammon	1.50
103	Dawn Staley	1.50
104	Alicia Thompson	.25
105	*Tiffany Travis*	1.00
106	Sandy Brondello	1.25
107	Tonya Edwards	.75
108	Chamique Holdsclaw	5.00
109	Olympia Scott-Richardson	.25
110	Anne Donovan	1.00
111	Brian Alger	1.00
112	Lin Dunn	1.00
113	Van Chancellor	1.00
114	Nell Fortner	1.00
115	Michael Cooper	1.00
116	Ron Rothstein	1.00
117	Richie Adubato	1.00
118	Cynthia Cooper	5.00
119	Linda Hargrove	1.00
120	Fred Williams	1.00
121	Dan Hughes	1.00
122	Carolyn Peck	1.00
123	Sonny Allen	1.00
124	*Brooke Wyckoff*	25.00
125	*Jackie Stiles*	125.00
126	*Svetlana Abrosimova*	8.00
127	*Tamika Catchings*	10.00
128	*Katie Douglas*	10.00
129	*Lauren Jackson*	80.00
130	*Shea Ralph*	6.00
131	*Ruth Riley*	10.00
132	*Kelly Miller*	6.00
133	*Marie Ferdinand*	6.00
134	*Tammy Sutton-Brown*	6.00
135	*Camille Cooper*	6.00
136	*Janell Burse*	4.00
137	*LaQuanda Barksdale*	6.00
138	*Niele Ivey*	6.00
139	*Coco Miller*	6.00
140	*Deanna Nolan*	6.00
141	*Penny Taylor*	6.00
142	*Kristen Veal*	6.00
143	*Kelly Schumacher*	6.00
144	*Amanda Lassiter*	6.00
145	*Semeka Randall*	6.00
146	*Jenny Mowe*	4.00
147	*Georgia Schweitzer*	4.00
148	*Jae Kingi*	4.00
149	*Erin Buescher*	6.00
150	*Michaela Pavlickova*	4.00
NNO	Cynthia Cooper Auto/350	100.00

2001 Fleer Ultra WNBA Feel the Game

		MT
	Common Player:	12.00
	Inserted 1:6	
1FG	Jennifer Azzi	12.00
2FG	Cynthia Cooper	25.00
3FG	Yolanda Griffith	15.00
4FG	Chamique Holdsclaw	25.00
5FG	Lisa Leslie	20.00
6FG	Natalie Williams	12.00

1971-72 McDonald's Floridians

This nine-card set of ABA Miami Floridians measures 2-1/2" x 4" including a tear-off tab at the bottom. The set was sponsored by McDonald's and includes an offer to receive an ABA basketball in exchange for the set of 10 different Floridian tickets. Cards from this set are unnumbered and are listed below in alphabetical order.

	NM
Complete Set (9):	750.00
Common Player:	75.00
Warren Armstrong	100.00
Mack Calvin	160.00
Ron Franz	75.00
Ira Harge	75.00
Larry Jones	75.00
Willie Long	75.00
Sam Robinson	75.00
George Tinsley	75.00
Lonnie Wright	75.00

1988 Foot Locker Slam Fest

Foot Locker produced this set in conjunction with its Slam Fest competition which aired on ESPN in May. The cards are standard size and feature color photos of the participants. They are unnumbered and were given away at participating Foot Locker shoe stores in May. The front borders are purple and blue. "Foot Locker" appears above the photo in a banner. A referee is drawn in the lower left corner. Each back uses blue ink and promotes the Slam Fest and special winner's card which entitled holders to receive a free pair of Wilson athletic shoes and 50 percent off any purchase. Mike Conley's card was designated as a winner's card.

	MT
Complete Set (9):	25.00
Common Player:	1.50
Carl Banks (football)	1.50
Mike Conley (track and field)	7.50
Thomas Hearns (boxing)	2.50
Bo Jackson (baseball/football)	10.00
Keith Jackson (football)	5.00
Karch Kiraly (volleyball)	3.00
Ricky Sanders (football)	1.50
Dwight Stones (track and field)	1.50
Devon White (baseball)	2.50

1989 Foot Locker Slam Fest

These Foot Locker Slam Fest cards were in cellophane packs which included a stick of gum. Participating Foot Locker stores gave them away to customers who asked for them. The participants in the Foot Locker's Slam Fest competition in March were featured in the set. Each card front has a color photo of the athlete, plus the Foot Locker banner at the top of the card. The back is unnumbered and includes the Foot Locker referee logo.

	MT
Complete Set (10):	8.00
Common Player:	.50
Mike Conley (track and field)	.50
Keith Jackson (football)	1.00
Vince Coleman (baseball)	.50
Eric Dickerson (football)	1.25
Steve Timmons (volleyball)	1.00
Matt Biondi (swimming)	1.00
Carl Lewis (track and field)	1.50
Mike Quick (football)	.50
Mike Powell (track and field)	1.00
Checklist	.50

1991 Foot Locker Slam Fest

These 10 cards were issued in three series to commemorate Foot Locker's 1991 Slam Fest competition. The Foot Locker banner appears arched above the player's photo on the front. The player's name and "Limited Edition" are written at the bottom of the card. The back has a card number and a summary of the player's career accomplishments.

	MT
Complete Set (30):	6.00
Common Player:	.15
Ken Griffey Jr. (baseball)	1.50
Delino DeShields (baseball)	.35
Barry Bonds (baseball)	.75
Jack Armstrong (baseball)	.15
Dave Justice (baseball)	.50
Deion Sanders (baseball/football)	.75
Michael Dean Perry (football)	.20
Tim Brown (football)	.35
Mike Conley (track and field)	.25
Mike Powell (track and field)	.25
Wilt Chamberlain (basketball)	.50
Cal Ramsey (basketball)	.15
Bobby Jones (basketball)	.25
John Havlicek (basketball)	.35
Calvin Murphy (basketball)	.25
Nate Thurmond (basketball)	.25
John Havlicek (basketball)	.35
The Dunkers (Series 1 checklist)	.15
The Judges (Series 2 checklist)	.15
Fest Moments (Series 3 checklist)	.15
Jerry Lucas (basketball)	.25
Bo Jackson (baseball/football)	.50
Elvin Hayes (basketball)	.25
Thomas Hearns (boxing)	.25
Matt Biondi (swimming)	.20
Earl Monroe (basketball)	.25
Eric Dickerson (football)	.35
Carl Lewis (track and field)	.35
Wilt Chamberlain (basketball)	.50
TV Slam Fest schedule	.15

1985 Fournier Ases del Baloncesto

The 33-card, playing-card set was produced in Spain and features mostly Spanish players in a game similar to "Go Fish." Jimmy Wright and David Russell are the to Americans featured in the set. The fronts have color action photos with an orange and white pattern on the back.

		MT
	Complete Set (33):	85.00
	Common Player:	3.00
1a	Juan A. Corbalan	3.00
1b	Fernando Martin	3.00
1c	Fernando Romay	3.00
1d	Lopez Iturriaga	3.00
2a	Jordi Freixanet	3.00
2b	Joaquin Costa	3.00
2c	Miguel Angel Pou	3.00
2d	Inaki Garayalde	3.00
3a	Pedro Rodriquez	3.00
3b	David Russell	8.00
3c	Fco. Javier Lafuente	3.00
3d	Alberto Ortega	3.00
4a	Oscar Pena	3.00
4b	Jose A. Alonso	3.00
4c	Joaquin Salvo	3.00
4d	Albert Illa	3.00
5a	Francisco J. Zapata	3.00
5b	Claude Riley	3.00
5c	Jose Luis Diaz	3.00
5d	Herminio San Epifanio	3.00
6a	Manuel Sanchez	3.00
6b	Jimmy Wright	5.00
6c	Suso Fernandez	3.00
6d	Pepe Collins	3.00
7a	Jose Maria Margall	3.00
7b	Jordi Villacampa	3.00
7c	Jose A. Montero	3.00
7d	Andres Jimenez	3.00
8a	J.A. San Epifanio	3.00
8b	Chico Sibilio	3.00
8c	Ignacio Solozabal	3.00
8d	Arturo S. Seara	3.00
NNO	Title Card	5.00

1988 Fournier NBA Estrellas

The 32-card set was issued in Spain by Fournier and features the top players of the NBA. The 2-1/8" x 3-7/16 set has the card number in the upper right corner of the front with the NBA logo taking up the entire back.

		MT
	Complete Set (33):	65.00
	Common Player:	.25
1	Larry Bird	5.00
2	Robert Parish	1.00
3	Kevin McHale	2.00
4	Magic Johnson	4.00
5	Kareem Abdul-Jabbar	3.00
6	Byron Scott	.50
7	Isiah Thomas	1.50
8	Adrian Dantley	.50
9	Dominique Wilkins	1.50
10	Spud Webb	.50
11	Clyde Drexler	2.00
12	Terry Porter	.50
13	Mark Aguirre	.50
14	Muggsy Bogues	1.50
15	Patrick Ewing	2.50
16	Karl Malone	4.00
17	Charles Barkley	2.50
18	Ron Harper	1.00
19	Alex English	1.00
20	Xavier McDaniel	.25
21	Jeff Malone	.50
22	Michael Jordan	30.00
23	Hakeem Olajuwon	3.00
24	Ralph Sampson	.50
25	Buck Williams	.50
26	Chuck Person	.50
27	Alvin Robertson	.25
28	Tom Chambers	.75
29	Paul Pressey	.25
30	Danny Manning	1.25
31	LaSalle Thompson	.25
32	John Stockton	4.00
xx	Jordan "Rules"	20.00

1988 Fournier NBA Estrellas Stickers

The 10-sticker set was issued in Spain by Fournier as a random insert with its regular-issue sets. The stickers (1" x 1-1/4") each picture a player headshot and are unnumbered. The Larry Bird, Magic Johnson and Michael Jordan stickers are double printed.

		MT
	Complete Set (10):	300.00
	Common Player:	20.00
(1)	Kareem Abdul-Jabbar	35.00
(2)	Mark Aquirre	20.00
(3)	Larry Bird DP	20.00
(4)	Magic Johnson DP	20.00
(5)	Michael Jordan DP	125.00
(6)	Moses Malone	25.00
(7)	Kevin McHale	30.00
(8)	Robert Parish	25.00
(9)	Isiah Thomas	25.00
(10)	James Worthy	25.00

1991 Front Row Draft

These cards feature action photos of players selected in the 1991 NBA draft. The backs also have color photos and collegiate stats. HL is a highlight card. There were 145,000 sets produced. Each card in the set also had Gold and Silver cards which were randomly inserted into wax packs. There were 5,000 Silver and 1,000 Gold sets made.

		MT
	Complete Set (50):	5.00
	Common Player:	.05
	Silver: 2x	
	Gold: 4x	
1	Larry Johnson	1.50
2	Kenny Anderson	.75
3	Rick Fox	.20
4	Pete Chilcutt	.05
5	George Ackles	.05
6	Mark Macon	.10
7	Greg Anthony	.20
8	Mike Iuzzolino	.05
9	Anthony Avent	.10
10	Terrell Brandon	.25
11	Kevin Brooks	.05
12	Myron Brown	.05
13	Chris Corchiani	.05
14	Chris Gatling	.10
15	Marcus Kennedy	.05
16	Eric Murdock	.25
17	Tony Farmer	.05
18	Keith Hughes	.05
19	Kevin Lynch	.05
20	Chad Gallagher	.05
21	Darrin Chancellor	.05
22	Jimmy Oliver	.05
23	Von McDade	.05
24	Donald Hodge	.05
25	Randy Brown	.10
26	Doug Overton	.05
27	LeRon Ellis	.05
28	Sean Green	.05
29	Elliott Perry	.30
30	Richard Dumas	.10
31	Dale Davis	.30
32	Lamont Strothers	.05
33	Steve Hood	.05
34	Joey Wright	.05
35	Patrick Eddie	.05
36	Joe Wylie	.05
37	Bobby Phills	.25
38	Alvaro Teheran	.05
39	Dale Davis (HL)	.10
40	Rick Fox (HL)	.10
41	Terrell Brandon (HI)	.10
42	Greg Anthony (HL)	.10
43	Mark Macon (HL)	.10
44	Larry Johnson (Career HL)	.30
45	Larry Johnson (Accomp.)	.30
46	Larry Johnson (Power)	.30
47	Larry Johnson (A Class Act)	.30
48	Larry Johnson (Flashback)	.30
49	Larry Johnson (Up Close & Personal)	.30
50	Marty Conlon	.05

1991 Front Row Draft All-Rookie Team

This 10-card set is devoted to the first 10 players selected in the 1991 NBA draft. The fronts feature color action photos. The backs also have a photo and stats. There were 75,000 sets produced.

		MT
	Complete Set (10):	20.00
1	Larry Johnson	5.00
2	Kenny Anderson	2.00
3	Billy Owens	3.00
4	Dikembe Mutombo	3.00
5	Steve Smith	2.00
6	Doug Smith	1.00
7	Luc Longley	.50
8	Mark Macon	.75
9	Stacey Augmon	2.00
10	Brian Williams	1.50

1991 Front Row Draft Update

There were 50,000 glossy sets produced; card numbering continues from the American and Japanese Draft Pick sets at #51. "Update 92" is on the front at the bottom left. Backs have a photo, biography, stats and achievements. There were also Gold and Silver foil-stamped cards of five different players randomly inserted. They are listed at the end of the checklist.

		MT
	Complete Set (50):	3.00
	Common Player:	.05
	Gold Cards	8x-10x
	Silver Cards	5x-6x
51	Billy Owens	.50
52	Dikembe Mutombo	.75
53	Steve Smith	.50
54	Luc Longley	.15
55	Doug Smith	.15
56	Stacey Augmon	.50
57	Brian Williams	.15
58	Stanley Roberts	.10
59	Rodney Monroe	.07
60	Isaac Austin	.05
61	Rich King	.05
62	Victor Alexander	.15
63	LaBradford Smith	.07
64	Greg Sutton	.05
65	John Turner	.05
66	Joao Viana	.05
67	Charles Thomas	.05
68	Carl Thomas	.05
69	Tharon Mayes	.05
70	David Benoit	.20
71	Corey Crowder	.05
72	Larry Stewart	.10
73	Steve Bardo	.05
74	Paris McCurdy	.05
75	Robert Pack	.25
76	Doug Lee	.05
77	Thomas Copa	.05
78	Keith Owens	.05
79	Mike Goodson	.05
80	John Crotty	.10
81	Sean Muto	.05
82	Chancellor Nichols	.05
83	Stevie Thompson	.05
84	Demetrius Calip	.05
85	Clifford Martin	.05
86	Andy Kennedy	.05
87	Oliver Taylor	.05
88	Gary Waites	.05
89	Matt Roe	.05
90	Cedric Lewis	.05
91	Emmanual Davis	.05
92	Jackie Jones	.05
93	Clifford Scales	.05
94	Cameron Burns	.05
95	Clinton Venable	.05
96	Ken Redfield	.05
97	Melvin Newburn	.05
98	Chris Harris	.05
99	Bonus Card	.50
100A	Checklist	.05
100B	Shawn Van Diver	.05

1991 Front Row Draft LE Stacey Augmon

Each of these 25,000 numbered sets devoted to Stacey Augmon comes with a certificate of authenticity. The front says the set is a "Limited Edition." The cards are checklisted according to the corresponding information presented on the backs.

		MT
	Complete Set (7):	3.00
1	Biography (Stacey Augmon)	.50
2	Accomplishments (Stacey Augmon)	.50
3	Career Highs (Stacey Augmon)	.50
4	Tarkanian on Augmon (Stacey Augmon)	.50
5	Defensive Player of the Year (Stacey Augmon)	.50
6	Statistics (Stacey Augmon)	.50
7	Style (Stacey Augmon)	.50

1991 Front Row Draft LE Larry Johnson

There were 50,000 10-card sets produced and devoted to Larry Johnson. The cards are listed by the information presented on the backs, which are in a horizontal format with a superimposed photo of Johnson in the background.

		MT
	Complete Set (10):	7.50
1	Accomplishments (Larry Johnson)	1.00
2	Career Highlights (Larry Johnson)	1.00
3	High School Highlights (Larry Johnson)	1.00
4	Stats-Odessa Jr. College (Larry Johnson)	1.00
5	Statistics-UNLV (Larry Johnson)	1.00
6	Personal Biography (Larry Johnson)	1.00
7	Vital Statistics (Larry Johnson)	1.00
8	Shark's Rebel (Larry Johnson)	1.00
9	Scouting Report (Larry Johnson)	1.00
10	Olympic Hopeful (Larry Johnson)	1.00

1991 Front Row Draft LE Dikembe Mutombo

Each of these 50,000 numbered sets devoted to Dikembe Mutombo includes a certificate of authenticity. The card fronts have white borders and indicate the set is a limited edition. The cards are titled according to the corresponding information given on the backs.

		MT
Complete Set (7):		4.00
1	Biography (Dikembe Mutombo)	.50
2	Accomplishments (Dikembe Mutombo)	.50
3	Career Highs (Dikembe Mutombo)	.50
4	The Experts on Mutombo (Dikembe Mutombo)	.50
5	Admirable Hoya (Dikembe Mutombo)	.50
6	Statistics (Dikembe Mutombo)	.50
7	Name (Dikembe Mutombo)	.50

1991 Front Row Draft LE Billy Owens

Each of the 25,000 numbered sets devoted to Billy Owens includes a certificate of authenticity. The fronts have white borders. The cards are listed according to information on the backs. "Limited Edition" is on the fronts.

		MT
Complete Set (7):		3.00
1	Biography (Billy Owens)	.50
2	Accomplishments (Billy Owens)	.50
3	Career Highs (Billy Owens)	.50
4	The Experts on Owens (Billy Owens)	.50
5	High School (Billy Owens)	.50
6	Statistics (Billy Owens)	.50
7	Career Highlights (Billy Owens)	.50

1991 Front Row Draft LE Steve Smith

Each of the 25,000 sets devoted to Steve Smith includes a letter of authenticity. Cards are checklisted according to the information on the back. Fronts indicate the set is a limited edition.

		MT
Complete Set (7):		3.00
1	Biography (Steve Smith)	.50
2	Accomplishments (Steve Smith)	.50
3	Career Highlights (Steve Smith)	.50
4	What's in a Nickname (Steve Smith)	.50
5	Dr. Heckle & Mr. Jive (Steve Smith)	.50
6	Statistics (Steve Smith)	.50
7	The Magic is Back (Steve Smith)	.50

1991 Front Row Draft Italian Promos

This set is the American version of the 1991 Front Row Draft pick set, which contains 50 cards. Included is a bonus card that can be redeemed for two Italian promo cards. The promo set consists of 10 cards. The cards are bordered in white with the player's name appearing in a red stripe beneath the picture.

		MT
Complete Set (10):		3.00
Common Player:		.25
1	Steve Bardo (Illinois)	.25
2	Corey Crowder (Kentucky Wesleyan)	.25
3	Danny Ferry (Duke)	.75
4	Doug Lee (Purdue)	.25
5	Tharon Mayes (Florida State)	.25
6	Robert Pack (USC)	1.00
7	Brian Shaw (UC Santa Barbara)	.50
8	Larry Stewart (Coppin State)	.25
9	Carl Thomas (Eastern Michigan)	.25
10	Charles Thomas (Eastern Michigan)	.25

1991 Front Row Draft Italian

About one-third of the 30,000 sets produced were distributed in Europe. The cards are bilingual, written in English and Italian. The colored fronts have action photos, UV coating and "Draft Pick '91" in the bottom left corner. Bilingual backs have career highlights and a small color photo. A Larry Johnson subset (7) was also created, as were Gold and Silver cards for each player in the set. These cards were random inserts. A 10-card Italian promo set was also produced; bonus cards were offered as a mail-in from American versions of the 1991 Front Row Draft Picks. Each bonus card was good for two promo cards.

		MT
Complete Set (100):		6.00
Common Player:		.05
1	Larry Johnson	2.00
2	Kenny Anderson	.75
3	Rick Fox	.30
4	Pete Chilcutt	.15
5	George Ackles	.07
6	Mark Macon	.10
7	Greg Anthony	.15
8	Mike Iuzzolino	.05
9	Anthony Avent	.10
10	Terrell Brandon	.20
11	Kevin Brooks	.07
12	Myron Brown	.07
13	Chris Corchiani	.10
14	Chris Gatling	.15
15	Marcus Kennedy	.05
16	Eric Murdock	.35
17	Tony Farmer	.05
18	Keith Hughes	.05
19	Kevin Lynch	.07
20	Chad Gallagher	.05
21	Darrin Chancellor	.05
22	Jimmy Oliver	.05
23	Von McDade	.05
24	Donald Hodge	.05
25	Randy Brown	.07
26	Doug Overton	.10
27	LeRon Ellis	.10
28	Sean Green	.07
29	Elliott Perry	.07
30	Richard Dumas	.07
31	Dale Davis	.45
32	Lamont Strothers	.07
33	Steve Hood	.05
34	Joey Wright	.05
35	Patrick Eddie	.05
36	Joe Wylie	.05
37	Bobby Phills	.10
38	Alvaro Teheran	.25
39	Dale Davis (HL)	.05
40	Rick Fox (HL)	.15
41	Terrell Brandon (HL)	.10
42	Greg Anthony (HL)	.10
43	Mark Macon (HL)	.10
44	Larry Johnson (Career HL)	.50
45	Larry Johnson (Accomp.)	.50
46	Larry Johnson (Power)	.50
47	Larry Johnson (A Class Act)	.50
48	Larry Johnson (Flashback)	.50
49	Larry Johnson (Up Close & Personal)	.50
50	Marty Conlon	.10
51	Mike Goodson	.05
52	Drexel Deveaux	.05
53	Sean Muto	.05
54	Keith Owens	.05
55	Joao Viana	.05
56	Chancellor Nichols	.05
57	Charles Thomas	.05
58	Carl Thomas	.05
59	Anthony Blakely	.05
60	Demetrius Calip	.05
61	Dale Turnquist	.05
62	Carlos Funchess	.05
63	Tharon Mayes	.05
64	Andy Kennedy	.05
65	Oliver Taylor	.05
66	David Benoit	.15
67	Gary Waites	.05
68	Corey Crowder	.05
69	Sydney Grider	.05
70	Derek Strong	.07
71	Larry Stewart	.10
72	Matt Roe	.05
73	Cedric Lewis	.05
74	Anthony Houston	.05
75	Steve Bardo	.05
76	Marc Brown	.05
77	Michael Cutright	.05
78	Emmanuel Davis	.05
79	Paris McCurdy	.05
80	Jackie Jones	.05
81	Mark Peterson	.05
82	Clifford Scales	.05
83	Robert Pack	.20
84	Doug Lee	.05
85	Cameron Burns	.05
86	Thomas Copa	.05
87	Clinton Venable	.05
88	Ken Redfield	.05
89	Melvin Newburn	.05
90	Darren Henrie	.05
91	Chris Harris	.05
92	John Crotty	.10
93	Paul Graham	.10
94	Stevie Thompson	.05
95	Clifford Martin	.05
96	Brian Shaw	.10
97	Danny Ferry	.10
98	Doug Loescher	.05
99	Checklist	.05
100A	Bonus Card	.50
100B	Robert Pack	.50

1991 Front Row Draft Japanese

This set is similar to the Italian version, except 60,000 sets were produced. Gold and Silver cards were randomly inserted in wax packs. There is a gold and silver card for every card in the set; 2,000 silver sets and 500 gold sets were produced.

		MT
Complete Set (50):		5.00
Common Player:		.04
1	Larry Johnson	2.00
2	Kenny Anderson	1.00
3	Rick Fox	.30
4	Pete Chilcutt	.05
5	George Ackles	.07
6	Mark Macon	.20
7	Greg Anthony	.15
8	Mike Iuzzolino	.10
9	Anthony Avent	.07
10	Terrell Brandon	.15
11	Kevin Brooks	.07
12	Myron Brown	.04
13	Chris Corchiani	.10
14	Chris Gatling	.20
15	Marcus Kennedy	.04
16	Eric Murdock	.25
17	Tony Farmer	.04
18	Keith Hughes	.04
19	Kevin Lynch	.07
20	Chad Gallagher	.04
21	Darrin Chancellor	.04
22	Jimmy Oliver	.04
23	Von McDade	.04
24	Donald Hodge	.10
25	Randy Brown	.07
26	Doug Overton	.07
27	LeRon Ellis	.04
28	Sean Green	.04
29	Elliott Perry	.04
30	Richard Dumas	.04
31	Dale Davis	.30
32	Lamont Strothers	.04
33	Steve Hood	.04
34	Joey Wright	.04
35	Patrick Eddie	.04
36	Joe Wylie	.04
37	Bobby Phills	.04
38	Alvaro Teheran	.04
39	Dale Davis (HL)	.10
40	Rick Fox (HL)	.10
41	Terrell Brandon (HL)	.10
42	Greg Anthony (HL)	.10
43	Mark Macan (HL)	.10
44	Larry Johnson (Car. Highlights)	.50
45	Larry Johnson (Accmplshmnts)	.50
46	Larry Johnson (Power)	.50
47	Larry Johnson (A Class Act)	.50
48	Larry Johnson (Flashback)	.50
49	Larry Johnson (Up Close and Personal)	.50
50A	Bonus Card	.40
50B	Marty Conlon	.50

1991-92 Front Row Draft Premier

This set contains all of the players selected in the 1991 NBA draft. There were 90,000 sets produced. Fronts have light blue borders. There were also gold foil-stamped cards and one silver foil-stamped card, of Larry Johnson, randomly inserted. There were 10,000 of the 10-card gold sets produced. They are listed at the end of the checklist. Cards marked HL are highlights cards.

		MT
Complete Set (120):		7.50
Common Player:		.05
Gold Cards:		20.00
1	Rich King	.07
2	Kenny Anderson	.75
3	Billy Owens (ACC)	.20
4	Ken Redfield	.05
5	Robert Pack	.25
6	Clinton Venable	.05
7	Tom Copa	.05
8	Rick Fox (HL)	.10
9	Cameron Burns	.05
10	Doug Lee	.05
11	LaBradford Smith	.07
12	Clifford Scales	.05
13	Mark Peterson	.05
14	Jackie Jones	.05
15	Paris McCurdy	.05
16	Dikembe Mutombo	.25
17	Emanuel Davis	.05
18	Michael Cutright	.05
19	Marc Brown	.05
20	Steve Bardo	.05
21	John Turner	.05
22	Anthony Houston	.05
23	Cedric Lewis	.05
24	Matt Roe	.05
25	Larry Stewart	.10
26	Derek Strong	.05
27	Sydney Grider	.05
28	Corey Crowder	.05
29	Gary Waites	.05
30	David Benoit	.15
31	Larry Johnson (ACC)	.50
32	Oliver Taylor (Corchiani back)	.05
33	Andy Kennedy	.05
34	Tharon Mayes	.05
35	Carlos Funchess	.05
36	Dale Turnquist	.05
37	Luc Longley	.15
38	Demetrius Calip	.05
39	Anthony Blakely	.05
40	Carl Thomas	.05
41	Charles Thomas	.05
42	Chancellor Nichols	.05
43	Joao Viana	.05
44	Keith Owens	.05
45	Sean Muto	.05
46	Drexel Duveaux	.05
47	Stacey Augmon	.20
48	Mike Goodson	.05
49	Marty Conlon	.05
50	Mark Macon	.10
51	Greg Anthony	.10
52	Dale Davis	.35
53	Isaac Austin	.05
54	Alvaro Teheran	.05
55	Bobby Phills	.05
56	Joe Wylie	.05
57	Patrick Eddie	.05
58	Joey Wright	.05
59	Steve Hood	.05
60	Lamont Strothers	.07
61	Victor Alexander	.15
62	Richard Dumas	.10
63	Elliot Perry	.07
64	Sean Green	.05
65	Rick Fox	.20
66	LeRon Ellis	.05
67	Doug Overton	.10
68	Randy Brown	.10
69	Donald Hodge	.07
70	Von McDade	.05
71	Greg Sutton	.05
72	Jimmy Oliver	.05
73	Terrell Brandon (HL)	.10
74	Darrin Chancellor	.05
75	Chad Gallagher	.05
76	Kevin Lynch	.07
77	Keith Hughes	.05
78	Tony Farmer	.05
79	Eric Murdock	.25
80	Marcus Kennedy	.05
81	Larry Johnson	2.00
82	Stacey Augmon	.50
83	Dikembe Mutombo	.75
84	Steve Smith	.50
85	Billy Owens (HL)	.50
86	Bonus Card	.05
86B	Stanley Roberts	.15
87	Brian Shaw	.07
88	Bonus Card	.05
88B	Rodney Monroe	.10
89	LaBradford Smith (HL)	.07
90	Bonus Card	.05
90B	Mark Randall	.10
91	Bonus Card	.05
91B	Brian Williams	.10
92	Danny Ferry	.07
93	Bonus Card	.05
93B	Shawn VanDiver	.10
94	Doug Smith (HL)	.07
95	Luc Longley (HL)	.10
96	Billy Owens (HL)	.15
97	Steve Smith (HL)	.20
98	Dikembe Mutombo (HL)	.25
99	Stacey Augmon (HL)	.15
100	Larry Johnson (HL)	.50
101	Chris Gatling	.15
102	Chris Corchiani	.10
103	Myron Brown	.05
104	Kevin Brooks	.05
105	Anthony Avent	.10
106	Steve Smith (ACC)	.20
107	Mike Iuzzolino	.07
108	George Ackles	.07
109	Melvin Newbern	.05
110	Robert Pack (HL)	.15
111	Darren Henrie	.05
112	Chris Harris	.05
113	John Grotty	.05
114	Terrell Brandon	.15
115	Paul Graham	.05
116	Stevie Thompson	.05
117	Clifford Martin	.05
118	Doug Smith	.15
119	Pete Chilcutt	.15
120	Checklist	.05

1992 Front Row Draft

This set features several 1992 NBA Draft picks. The glossy fronts have dark borders at the top and light blue ones at the bottom. The backs have stats and career highlights, plus the set's name in an orange banner. There were 150,000 sets produced.

		MT
Complete Set (100):		8.00
Common Player:		.05
Silver:		2x
Gold:		4x
1	Eric Anderson	.05
2	Darin Archbold	.05
3	Woody Austin	.05
4	Mark Baker	.05
5	Jon Barry	.10
6	Elmer Bennett	.05
7	Tony Bennett	.05
8	Alex Blackwell	.05
9	Curtis Blair	.05
10	Ed Book	.05
11	Marques Bragg	.05
12	P.J. Brown	.05
13	Anthony Buford	.05
14	Dexter Cambridge	.05
15	Brian Davis	.05
16	Lucius Davis	.05
17	Todd Day	.25
18	Greg Dennis	.05
19	Randenko Dobras	.05
20	Harold Ellis	.05
21	Chris King	.05
22	Jo Jo English	.05
23	Deron Feldhaus	.05
24	Matt Geiger	.10
25	Lewis Geter	.05
26	George Gilmore	.05
27	Litterial Green	.05
28	Tom Gugliotta	.75
29	Jim Havrilla	.05
30	Robert Horry	1.00
31	Stephen Howard	.05
32	Alonzo Jamison	.05
33	Dave Johnson	.05
34	Herb Jones	.05
35	Popeye Jones	.25
36	Adam Keefe	.10
37	Dan Cyrulik	.05
38	Ken Leeks	.05
39	Ricardo Leonard	.05
40	Gerald Madkins	.05
41	Eric Manuel	.05
42	Marlon Maxey	.05
43	Jim McCoy	.05
44	Oliver Miller	.10
45	Sean Miller	.05
46	Darren Morningstar	.05
47	Isiah Morris	.05
48	James Moses	.05
49	Doug Christie	.10
50	Damon Patterson	.05
51	John Pelphrey	.05
52	Brent Price	.10
53	Brett Roberts	.05
54	Steve Rogers	.05
55	Sean Rooks	.10
56	Malik Sealy	.25
57	Tom Schurfranz	.05
58	David Scott	.05
59	Rod Sellers	.05
60	Vernel Singleton	.05
61	Reggie Slater	.05
62	Elmore Spencer	.10
63	Chris Smith	.05
64	Latrell Sprewell	1.00
65	Matt Steigenga	.05
66	Bryant Stith	.25
67	Daimon Sweet	.05
68	Craig Upchurch	.05
69	Van Usher	.05
70	Tony Watts	.05
71	C. Weatherspoon	.60
72	Robert Werdann	.05
73	Benford Williams	.05
74	Corey Williams	.05
75	Henry Williams	.05
76	Tim Burroughs	.05
77	Eric Wilson	.05
78	Randy Woods	.10
79	Kendall Youngblood	.05
80	Terry Boyd	.05
81	Tracy Murray	.10
82	Reggie Smith	.10
83	Lee Mayberry	.10
84	Matthew Fish	.05
85	Hubert Davis	.10
86	Duane Cooper	.10
87	Anthony Peeler	.10
88	Harold Miner	.10
89	Harold Miner (Spec)	.10
90	Harold Miner (Spec)	.10
91	Christian Laettner	.50
92	Christian Laettner	.20
93	Christian Laettner	.20
94	Walt Williams	.50
95	Walt Williams (Spec)	.15
96	Walt Williams	.15
97	LaPhonso Ellis	.25
98	LaPhonso Ellis	.10
99	LaPhonso Ellis	.10
100	Checklist	.05

1992 Front Row Draft Dream Picks

This set, which includes 1991 and 1992 NBA draft picks, contains 20 players, each featured in a five-card set. Fronts have purple borders, with the player's name in a yellow block at the top. Backs have a yellow background, with the set's name, "Dream Picks," on an orange background going vertically across the card. There were 180,000 sets made, plus 5,000 numbered silver sets made from each card in the regular set. One silver card appears in every five regular foil packs. A gold card was also made for each numbered card in the set, and could be found in one of every 15 regular packs. There were 2,000 numbered gold sets produced.

		MT
Complete Set (100):		7.50
Common Player:		.05
1	Larry Johnson (1-5)	.50
2	Career Highlights (Larry Johnson)	.40
3	NBA All-Rookie Team (Larry Johnson)	.40
4	NBA Rookie of the Year (Larry Johnson)	.40
5	Larry Johnson	.40
6	Dikembe Mutombo (6-10)	.25
7	Career Highlights (Dikembe Mutombo)	.25
8	NBA All-Rookie Team (Dikembe Mutombo)	.25
9	NBA All-Star (Dikembe Mutombo)	.25
10	Dikembe Mutombo	.25
11	Stacey Augmon (11-15)	.10
12	Career Highlights (Stacey Augmon)	.10
13	NBA All-Rookie Team (Stacey Augmon)	.10
14	Defensive Specialist (Stacey Augmon)	.10
15	Stacey Augmon	.10
16	Billy Owens (16-20)	.15
17	Career Highlights (Billy Owens)	.15
18	NBA All-Rookie Team (Billy Owens)	.15
19	A Proven Winner (Billy Owens)	.15
20	Billy Owens	.15
21	C. Weatherspoon (21-25)	.25
22	Career Highlights (Clarence Weatherspoon)	.25
23	NBA Scouting Report (Clarence Weatherspoon)	.25
24	Flexible Golden Eagle (Clarence Weatherspoon)	.25
25	Clarence Weatherspoon	.25
26	Steve Smith (26-30)	.15
27	Career Highlights (Steve Smith)	.15
28	NBA All-Rookie Team (Steve Smith)	.15
29	Withstanding the Heat (Steve Smith)	.15
30	Steve Smith	.15
31	College Stats (Larry Stewart)	.05
32	Career Highlights (Larry Stewart)	.05
33	NBA All-Rookie Team (Larry Stewart)	.05
34	Against the Odds (Larry Stewart)	.05
35	Larry Stewart	.05
36	College Stats (Rick Fox)	.07
37	Career Highlights (Rick Fox)	.07
38	NBA All-Rookie Team (Rick Fox)	.07
39	Divine Intervention (Rick Fox)	.07
40	Rick Fox	.07
41	Christian Laettner (41-45)	.25
42	Career Highlights (Christian Laettner)	.25
43	NBA Scouting Report (Christian Laettner)	.25
44	Championship Season (Christian Laettner)	.25
45	Christian Laettner	.25
46	College Stats (Bryant Stith)	.07
47	Career Highlights (Bryant Stith)	.07
48	NBA Scouting Report (Bryant Stith)	.07
49	A Change of Perspective (Bryant Stith)	.07
50	Bryant Stith	.07
51	Harold Miner (51-55)	.15
52	Career Highlights (Harold Miner)	.15
53	NBA Scouting Report (Harold Miner)	.15
54	An Encounter with Michael (Harold Miner)	.15
55	Harold Miner	.15
56	College Stats (Mark Macon)	.05
57	Career Highlights (Mark Macon)	.05
58	NBA All-Rookie Team (Mark Macon)	.05
59	Stealing the Show (Mark Macon)	.05
60	Mark Macon	.05
61	College Stats (Adam Keefe)	.05
62	Career Highlights (Adam Keefe)	.05

63	NBA Scouting Report (Adam Keefe)	.05
64	Premier Big Man (Adam Keefe)	.05
65	Adam Keefe	.05
66	Tom Gugliotta (66-70)	.25
67	Career Highligts (Tom Gugliotta)	.25
68	NBA Scouting Report (Tom Gugliotta)	.25
69	Most Improved (Tom Gugliotta)	.25
70	Tom Gugliotta	.25
71	Todd Day (71-75)	.10
72	Career Highlights (Todd Day)	.10
73	NBA Scouting Report (Todd Day)	.10
74	One Bright Day (Todd Day)	.10
75	Todd Day	.10
76	Walt Williams (76-80)	.10
77	Career Highlights (Walt Williams)	.10
78	NBA Scouting Report (Walt Williams)	.10
79	The Nations (Walt Williams)	.10
80	Walt Williams	.10
81	College Stats (Malik Sealy)	.07
82	Career Highlights (Malik Sealy)	.07
83	NBA Scouting Report (Malik Sealy)	.07
84	Malik Wear (Malik Sealy)	.07
85	Malik Sealy	.07
86	College Stats (Stanley Roberts)	.05
87	Career Highlights (Stanley Roberts)	.05
88	NBA All-Rookie Team (Stanley Roberts)	.05
89	The Spanish League (Stanley Roberts)	.05
90	Stanley Roberts	.05
91	LaPhonso Ellis (91-95)	.20
92	College Stats (LaPhonso Ellis)	.20
93	Career Highlights (LaPhonso Ellis)	.20
94	Dream Come True? (LaPhonso Ellis)	.20
95	LaPhonso Ellis	.20
96	College Stats (Terrell Brandon)	.07
97	Career Highlights (Terrell Brandon)	.07
98	NBA All-Rookie Team (Terrell Brandon)	.07
99	Quickest in the League? (Terrell Brandon)	.07
100	Terrell Brandon	.30

1992 Front Row Draft Holograms

These cards feature a holographic design on the front. The blue backs have a colored action photo and a summary of the player's career achievements. There were 50,000 numbered sets produced, each with a letter of authenticity.

		MT
Complete Set (3):		4.00
1	Larry Johnson	2.50
2	Billy Owens	1.00
3	Dikembe Mutombo	1.50

1992 Front Row Christian Laettner

		MT
Complete Set (4):		3.00
Common Player:		1.00
1	Christian Laettner	1.00
2	Christian Laettner	1.00
3	Christian Laettner	1.00
4	Christian Laettner	1.00

1992 Front Row Draft LJ Pure Gold

This three-card gold-bordered set features Larry Johnson. His name is at the bottom in white on a red background. The back has a small color photo and an informational summary. There were 20,000 sets produced. A three-card uncut panel is also available.

		MT
Complete Set (3):		15.00
1	High School Highlights (Larry Johnson)	6.00
2	Stats and Achievements (Larry Johnson)	6.00
3	Accomplishments (Larry Johnson)	6.00

1993 Front Row Draft Grand MaMa

This glossy set, sponsored by Converse, features Larry Johnson dressed up like Grand MaMa. The card backs provide comments about the card title, superimposed over a picture of Grand MaMa. There were 100,000 sets produced. Front Row also produced 5,000 gold Grand MaMa sets featuring borderless color photos on the card front, with "The Gold Collection" stamped in gold foil along the left side. "Grand MaMa" is also stamped in gold at the bottom of the card. The card back is numbered 1 of 10, etc., and has a color photo and quote from Grand MaMa. The Converse logo is also on the card back.

		MT
Complete Set (7):		5.00
1G	Grand MaMa's New Shoes (Larry Johnson)	1.00
2G	My Grand MaMa Wears Converse (Larry Johnson)	1.00
3G	Confessions of Larry (Larry Johnson)	1.00
4G	Grand MaMa Reminisces (Larry Johnson)	1.00
5G	Grand MaMa: A Prophet? (Larry Johnson)	1.00
6G	Not a Typical Granny (Larry Johnson)	1.00
7G	Larry Johnson (No Card Title)	1.00

1993 Front Row LJ Grandmama Gold

		MT
Complete Set (10):		8.00
Common Player:		1.00
1	Larry Johnson	1.00
2	Larry Johnson	1.00
3	Larry Johnson	1.00
4	Larry Johnson	1.00
5	Larry Johnson	1.00
6	Larry Johnson	1.00
7	Larry Johnson	1.00
8	Larry Johnson	1.00
9	Larry Johnson	1.00
10	Larry Johnson	1.00

G

1997 Genuine Article

The 27-card set comes in seven-card packs, in 12-pack boxes. Produced by General Article Inc., the set consists of 27 cards. Each pack contains an autographed and insert card. On each card, "Hardwood Signature Series" is written in gold foil.

		MT
Complete Set (27):		10.00
Common Player:		.10
1	Derek Anderson UER	.75
2	Keith Booth	.25
3	Bobby Jackson	.75
4	Antonio Daniels	.75
5	Harold Deane	.10
6	Ya-Ya Dia	.10
7	Lee Wilson	.10
8	Kebu Stewart	.10
9	Adonal Foyle	.50
10	Othella Harrington	.10
11	Alvin Sims	.10
12	Brevin Knight	.75
13	Walter McCarty	.25
14	Victor Page	.25
15	Lorenzen Wright	.10
16	Scot Pollard	.25
17	Vitaly Potapenko	.10
18	Jamal Robinson	.10
19	Roy Rogers	.25
20	Shea Seals	.25
21	Carmelo Travieso	.25
22	Jacque Vaughn	.75
23	DeJuan Wheat	.25
24	Allen Iverson	1.00
25	Damon Stoudamire	.75
26	Ron Mercer	1.25
27	Keith Van Horn	1.00

1997 Genuine Article Autographs

This set is a parallel of the base set, with each player autographing 7,500 hand-numbered cards, with Ron Mercer and Keith Van Horn signing 200. The autographs are inserted one per pack.

		MT
Complete Set (27):		275.00
Common Player:		2.50
Each card numbered out of 7500		
1	Derek Anderson UER	12.00
2	Keith Booth	2.50
3	Bobby Jackson	10.00
4	Antonio Daniels	12.00
5	Harold Deane	2.50
6	Ya-Ya Dia	2.50
7	Lee Wilson	2.50
8	Kebu Stewart	2.50
9	Adonal Foyle	10.00
10	Othella Harrington	2.50
11	Alvin Sims	2.50
12	Brevin Knight	12.00
13	Walter McCarty	2.50
14	Victor Page	2.50
15	Lorenzen Wright	2.50
16	Scot Pollard	2.50
17	Vitaly Potapenko	2.50
18	Jamal Robinson	2.50
19	Roy Rogers	2.50
20	Shea Seals	2.50
21	Carmelo Travieso	2.50
22	Jacque Vaughn	10.00
23	DeJuan Wheat	2.50
24	Allen Iverson	25.00
25	Damon Stoudamire	20.00
26	Ron Mercer	60.00
27	Keith Van Horn	50.00

1997 Genuine Article Double Cards

This three-card set is randomly inserted and contains pros in their college uniforms.

		MT
Complete Set (3):		10.00
Common Player:		4.00
1	Antoine Walker, Ron Mercer, Derek Anderson	3.00
2	Allen Iverson, Damon Stoudamire	4.00
3	Ron Mercer, Keith Van Horn	3.00

1997 Genuine Article Double Cards Autographs

This set is an exact parallel to the insert set, with the cards now being autographed by the three players. The set is five cards and randomly inserted.

		MT
Complete Set (3):		325.00
Common Player:		35.00
1	Antoine Walker, Ron Mercer, Derek Anderson AU/200	100.00
2	Damon Stoudamire AU/200	35.00
2	Allen Iverson AU/200	80.00
3	Keith Van Horn AU/200	40.00
3	Ron Mercer AU/200	50.00

1997 Genuine Article Duo-Sport Preview

The five-card set portrays five football players in their college uniforms, and are numbered with a "DS" prefix.

		MT
Complete Set (5):		12.00
Common Player:		2.00
1	Eddie George	5.00
2	Karim Abdul-Jabbar	3.00
3	Jim Druckenmiller	4.00
4	Orlando Pace	2.00
5	Yatil Green	2.50

1997 Genuine Article Hometown Heroes

The set features eight players in the 15-card set. The fronts have a photo of a player with a background map indicating where they played, in college or in the pros. Cards are numbered with a "HH" prefix.

		MT
Complete Set (13):		20.00
Common Player:		1.00
1	Ray Allen	2.00
2	Ray Allen	2.00
3	Allen Iverson	3.00
4	Kerry Kittles	2.00
5	Kerry Kittles	2.00
6	Bryant Reeves	1.50
7	Glen Rice	2.50
8	Damon Stoudamire	2.00
9	Damon Stoudamire	2.00
10	Antoine Walker	2.00
11	Antoine Walker	2.00
12	Lorenzen Wright	1.00
13	Lorenzen Wright	1.00

1997 Genuine Article Hometown Heroes Autographs

This set is the same at the original Hometown Heroes set except the cards are autographed. Cards are numbered with a "HH" prefix.

		MT
Complete Set (13):		250.00
Common Player:		10.00
1	Ray Allen	20.00
2	Ray Allen	20.00
3	Allen Iverson	50.00
4	Kerry Kittles	20.00
5	Kerry Kittles	20.00
6	Bryant Reeves	20.00
7	Glen Rice	40.00
8	Damon Stoudamire	30.00
9	Damon Stoudamire	30.00
10	Antoine Walker	25.00
11	Antoine Walker	25.00
12	Lorenzen Wright	10.00
13	Lorenzen Wright	10.00

1997 Genuine Article Lottery Connection

The five-card set features five NBA players in the uniforms. The player's last name only is used in gold foil. Cards are numbered with a "LC" prefix.

		MT
Complete Set (5):		8.00
Common Player:		1.00
1	Derek Anderson	2.00
2	Bobby Jackson	2.00
3	Brevin Knight	3.00
4	Jacque Vaughn	2.00
5	Lorenzen Wright	1.00

1997 Genuine Article Lottery Connection Autographs

The set is the same as the base Lottery Connection set, only the cards are now autographed on the front. Cards are numbered with a "LC" prefix.

		MT
Complete Set (5):		80.00
Common Player:		12.00
1	Derek Anderson	25.00
2	Bobby Jackson	20.00
3	Brevin Knight	25.00
4	Jacque Vaughn	20.00
5	Lorenzen Wright	12.00

1997 Genuine Article Lottery Gems

The five-card set contains five of the top picks in the 1997 draft. The player's name is in gold foil on the bottom. Cards are numbered with a "LG" prefix.

		MT
Complete Set (5):		12.00
Common Player:		2.50
1	Antonio Daniels	2.50
2	Adonal Foyle	2.50
3	Danny Fortson	2.50
4	Ron Mercer	4.00
5	Keith Van Horn	3.00

1997 Genuine Article Lottery Gems Autographs

The same as the base set Lottery Gems, except the cards are autographed on the front. Cards are numbered with a "LG" prefix.

		MT
Complete Set (5):		125.00
Common Player:		25.00
1	Antonio Daniels	25.00
2	Adonal Foyle	25.00
3	Danny Fortson	25.00
4	Ron Mercer	40.00
5	Keith Van Horn	25.00

1997 Genuine Article Previews

		MT
Complete Set (5):		4.00
Common Player:		.25
BK1	Ray Allen	1.00
BK2	Allen Iverson	3.00
BK3	Kerry Kittles	.25
BK4	Antoine Walker	.50
BK5	Lorenzen Wright	.25

1998 GE David Robinson Phone Cards

		MT
Complete Set (5):		100.00
Common Player:		10.00
1	David Robinson (30 units)	10.00
2	David Robinson (60 units)	20.00
3	David Robinson (75 units)	25.00
4	David Robinson (90 units)	30.00
5	David Robinson (120 units)	40.00

1971 Harlem Globetrotters Cocoa Puffs

Fleer produced these 28 cards for General Mills to randomly insert in Cocoa Puffs cereal boxes, four cards per box. Fronts have action photos and a facsimile autograph, while backs have card numbers and information about the player or team. "Cocoa Puffs" is also written on the card back. Cards are 2-1/2" x 3-1/2".

		NM
Complete Set (28):		165.00
Common Player:		5.00
1	Ausbie & Neal	10.00
2	Neal & Meadowlark	8.00
3	Meadowlark is Safe	8.00
4	Meadowlark-Neal-Ausbie	8.00
5	Mel Davis, Bill Meggett	5.00
6	Ausbie-Meadowlark-Neal	8.00
7	Ausbie-Meadowlark-Neal	8.00
8	Mel Davis, Curly Neal	6.00
9	Meadowlark-Neal-Ausbie	8.00
10	Curly-Meadowlark-Mel	8.00
11	Football Routine	5.00
12	1970-71 Highlights	5.00
13	Pabs Robertson	5.00
14	Bobby Joe Mason	5.00
15	Pabs Robertson	5.00
16	Clarence Smith	5.00
17	Clarence Smith	5.00
18	Hubert "Geese" Ausbie	6.00
19	Hubert "Geese" Ausbie	6.00
20	Bobby Hunter	5.00
21	Bobby Hunter	5.00
22	Meadowlark Lemon	8.00
23	Meadowlark Lemon	8.00
24	Freddie "Curly" Neal	8.00
25	Freddie "Curly" Neal	8.00
26	Meadowlark Lemon	8.00
27	Mel Davis	5.00
28	Freddie "Curly" Neal	10.00

1972 Harlem Globetrotters

These cards feature color action photos on the fronts and biographical information on the back. Fleer produced the cards, which were issued in wax boxes. Cards are the standard 2-1/2" x 3-1/2" and are easier to find than their 1971 Cocoa Puffs counterparts.

		NM
Complete Set (84):		200.00
Common Player:		2.00
1	Bob "Showboat" Hall	12.00
2	Bob "Showboat" Hall	2.00
3	Bob "Showboat" Hall	2.00
4	Pablo "Pabs" Robertson	3.00
5	Pablo "Pabs" Robertson	2.00
6	Pablo "Pabs" Robertson	2.00
7	Pablo "Pabs" Robertson	2.00
8	Pablo "Pabs" Robertson	2.00
9	Meadowlark Lemon	6.00
10	Meadowlark Lemon	6.00
11	Meadowlark Lemon	6.00
12	Meadowlark Lemon	6.00
13	Meadowlark Lemon	6.00
14	Meadowlark Lemon	6.00
15	Meadowlark Lemon	6.00
16	Meadowlark Lemon	6.00
17	Meadowlark Lemon	6.00
18	Curly, Meadowlark, & Mel	6.00
19	Football Play	6.00
20	Meadowlark Lemon	6.00
21	Hubert "Geese" Ausbie	3.50
22	Hubert "Geese" Ausbie	3.50
23	Hubert "Geese" Ausbie	3.50
24	Hubert "Geese" Ausbie	3.50
25	Hubert "Geese" Ausbie	3.50
26	Ausbie and Neal	5.00
27	Freddie "Curly" Neal	6.00
28	Freddie "Curly" Neal	6.00
29	Freddie "Curly" Neal	6.00
30	Mel Davis & "Curly"	5.00
31	Freddie "Curly" Neal	6.00
32	Freddie "Curly" Neal	6.00
33	Mel Davis	2.00
34	Mel Davis	2.00
35	Mel Davis	2.00
36	Mel Davis	2.00
37	Mel Davis, Bill Meggett	2.00
38	Mel Davis	2.00
39	Bobby Joe Mason	2.00
40	Bobby Joe Mason	2.00
41	Bobby Joe Mason	2.00
42	Mason & Stephens	2.00
43	Bobby Joe Mason	2.00
44	Bobby Joe Mason	2.00
45	Clarence Smith	2.00
46	Clarence Smith	2.00
47	Clarence Smith	2.00
48	Clarence Smith	2.00
49	Jerry Venable	2.00
50	Frank Stephens	2.00
51	Frank Stephens	2.00
52	Frank Stephens	2.00
53	Frank Stephens	2.00
54	Theodis Ray Lee	2.00
55	Theodis Ray Lee	2.00
56	Jerry Venable	2.00
57	Doug Hines	2.00
58	Doug Hines	2.00
59	Bill Meggett	2.00
60	Bill Meggett	2.00
61	Vincent White	2.00
62	Vincent White	2.00
63	Pable & "Showboat"	2.00
64	Ausbie, Meadowlark & Neal	6.00
65	Curly, Neal, Quarterback	7.00
66	Ausbie, Meadowlark, & Neal	7.00
67	Neal and Meadowlark	7.00
68	Football Routine	3.00
69	Meadowlark, Neal, Ausbie	7.00
70	Meadowlark-Safe At Plate	7.00
71	1970-71 Highlights	3.00
72	1970-71 Highlights	6.00
73	Bobby Hunter	2.00
74	Bobby Hunter	2.00
75	Bobby Hunter	2.00
76	Bobby Hunter	2.00
77	Bobby Hunter	2.00
78	Jackie Jackson	3.00
79	Jackie Jackson	3.00
80	Jackie Jackson	3.00
81	Jackie Jackson	3.00
82	The Globetrotters	3.00
83	The Globetrotters	3.00
84	Dallas Thornton	6.00

A player's name in *italic type* indicates a rookie

1971-72 Globetrotters Phoenix Candy

The eight-card set, measuring 4-7/8" x 2-1/2", was issued on the backs of Phoenix Candy boxes. The cards are unnumbered and complete boxes are valued at 1.5 times the card prices.

NM
Complete Set (8): 300.00
Common Player: 30.00
J.C. Gipson 30.00
Bob "Showboat" Hall 30.00
Leon Hillard 30.00
Meadowlark Lemon 100.00
Freddie "Curly" Neal 75.00
Pablo "Pabs" Robertson 30.00
National Unit (team picture) 40.00
International Unit (team picture) 40.00

1974 Globetrotters Wonder Bread

Of the 25 cards inserted in loaves of Wonder Bread, six feature members of the Harlem Globetrotters. The card fronts depict a cartoon with the backs explaining how to do a magic trick. The cards are numbered as "x in a series of 25."

NM
Complete Set (6): 45.00
Common Player: 5.00
3 Curly Neal, Bobby Joe Mason 18.00
4 Curly Neal, Geese Ausbie 18.00
5 J.C. Gipson 5.00
14 Pablo "Pabs" Robertson 5.00
16 Meadowlark Lemon and Granny 12.00
20 J.C. Gipson and Granny 5.00

1985 Harlem Globetrotters

This 11-card set features members of the Harlem Globetrotters in posed color photos. The player's uniform number and pertinent information are on the back. Cards are 2-1/2" x 3-1/2".

MT
Complete Set (11): 120.00
Common Player: 6.00
1 Geese Ausbie 20.00
2 Clyde Austin 6.00
3 Jimmy Blaylock 6.00
4 Ovie Dotson 6.00
5 Sweet Lou Dunbar 12.00
6 Billy Ray Hobley 6.00
7 Harold Hubbard 6.00
8 Osborne Lockhart 6.00
9 Curly Neal 25.00
10 Robert Paige 6.00
11 Gator Rivers 8.00

1992 Globetrotters

The six-card promo set previews the 1992 90-card set. The cards are the standard 3-1/2" x 2-1/2" and each front has a metallic silver prism effect. The backs are similar to the base set with "Trotters Trivia" featured. Cards are numbered with a "P" prefix.

MT
Complete Set (6): 15.00
Common Player: 3.00
1 All-Tim Greats Sixty-Fifth Anniversary 3.00
2 Globetrotting (Freddie "Curly" Neal, Alan Alda) 4.00
3 Famous Feats (Freddie "Curly" Neal) 4.00
4 Media Darlings (Mickey Mouse, Freddie "Curly" Neal) 5.00
5 Honoraries - Team Photo 3.00
6 First City (Goldie Hawn) 4.00

1992 Harlem Globetrotters

Comic Images produced approximately 450,000 sets of these cards devoted to the Harlem Globetrotters. The card fronts feature full-bleed color, or black-and-white photos; backs describe the fronts or present Globetrotter trivia. Cards measure 2-1/2" x 3-1/3" and were available in wax packs. Six prism cards were also produced and were randomly inserted in wax boxes, three per box. Approximately 68,000 prism sets were made. The six, numbered with a "P" prefix on the back, are: P1) All-Time Greats; P2) Globetrotting; 3) Famous Feats; 4) Media Darlings; 5) Honoraries; 6) First City.

MT
Complete Set (90): 10.00
Common Player: .10
1 Abe Saperstein .35
2 In the Beginning .10
3 Hinckley, Ohio .10
4 What's In A Name .10
5 Uniforms .10
6 International Competition .10
7 A Tie?! .10
8 Hard Times .10
9 Black & White .15
10 "Courting" Success .10
11 First Tournament .10
12 World Champions .10
13 Tricks & Treats .40
14 Individual Talents .10
15 For The Boys .10
16 Globetrotting .10
17 The Big Screen .10
18 The Small Screen .10
19 Goodwill Ambassadors .10
20 Leaving their Mark .15
21 Traveling Troubles .10
22 Have Court, Will Travel .10
23 The NBA .25
24 Magic Powere .10
25 Almost Perfect .10
26 The End Of An Era .10
27 Celluloid Heroes .10
28 Star Power .10
29 Sweet Georgia Brown .15
30 The Year Of The Woman .30
31 Quotable Curly .30
32 Honorary Globie Speaks .10
33 "Whoopi" For The 'Trotter! .30
34 Globie Recollections .10
35 A B'Ball Oscar? .40
36 Singing Their Praises .10
37 Hurray For Hollywood .20
38 The Early Signs .10
39 Fast Forward .10
40 A Losing Streak .10
41 Pioneering Prankster .10
42 Changing Of The Guard .10
43 Breaking In .10
44 Trickster In Training .30
45 Wearing Many Hats .10
46 Beating The Odds .10
47 Double Take .10
48 "Sweetwater" .10
49 Founding Father .15
50 Fanciful First .10
51 Ernest Aughburns .20
52 Clyde Austin .10
53 J.B. Brown .10
54 Michael Douglas .10
55 Sherwin Durham .10
56 Billy Ray Hobley .10
57 Curley Johnson .10
58 Jolette Law .10
59 Derick Polk .10
60 James "Twiggy" Sanders .10
61 Donald "Clyde" Sinclair .10
62 Antoine Scott .10
63 "Sweet Lou" Dunbar .30
64 Osborne Lockhart .10
65 Lifelong Dream .30
66 A Real Show-Off .20
67 Competition .10
68 A Blend of Old and New .10
69 Globie Spirit .10
70 Carrying The Torch .35
71 Geese Ausbie .20
72 Fred "Curly" Neal .35
73 Go, Curly Go! .35
74 Larry "Gator" Rivers .10
75 Off-Season .10
76 Sore Losers? .10
77 Ovie Dotson .10
78 Come On In! .10
79 Practice Makes Perfect .10
80 Trotter' 1st Trip .10
81 Winningest Team .10
82 City Slickers .15
83 You Win Some .10
84 From Russia, With Love .10
85 Hold Your Fire .10
86 What A Crowd .15
87 Destined For Greatness .10
88 A Fantastic First .10
89 A Higher Calling .30
90 Checklist .10

1995-96 Grizzlies/Topps

Topps produced this nine-card set to commemorate the Grizzlies first NBA season. The cards are identical to the 1995-96 Topps set except for a gold-foil expansion logo on the front of the cards.

MT
Complete Set (9): 8.00
Common Player: 1.00
10 Numbered 175 (Byron Scott UER) 1.00
11 Numbered 177 (Blue Edwards UER) 1.00
12 Numbered 236 (Antonio Harvey UER) 1.00
13 Numbered 180 (Kenny Gattison UER) 1.00
14 Numbered 174 (Gerald Wilkins UER) 1.00
15 Numbered 178 (Greg Anthony UER) 1.00
16 Numbered 231 (Lawrence Moten UER) 1.00
17 Numbered 202 (Bryant Reeves UER) 5.00
18 Checklist 1.00

2001 Grizzlies/Topps

MT
Complete Set (10): 10.00
Common Player: .50
1 Shareef Abdur-Rahim 1.50
2 Mike Bibby 1.00
3 Michael Dickerson 1.00
4 Othella Harrington .75
5 Bryant Reeves .50
6 Damon Jones .50
7 Isaac Austin .50
8 Stromile Swift 4.00
9 Tony Massenburg .50
10 Grant Long .50

H

1968 Hall Of Fame Electees Pack

The Basketball Hall of Fame sold these cards in its book store. The unnumbered cards, printed on a thin paper stock, feature blue-tinted head shots on the front, along with a career summary at the bottom. Each card is 2-7/16" x 6-7/16" and is blank backed. Most cards in this set, also known as the Bookmark or Induction set, were issued in 1968.

NM
Complete Set (53): 45.00
Common Player: .50
Forrest C. Allen .50
Arnold J. Auerbach 1.50
Clair F. Bee .75
Bernhard Borgmann .50
Walter A. Brown .50
John W. Burn .50
Howard G. Cann .50
H. Clifford Carlson .50
Bernard Carnevale 3.00
Robert J. Cousy 7.00
Robert E. Davies 4.00
Everett S. Dean .50
Forrest S. Debernardi .50
Harold G. Dehnert .50
Harold E. Foster .50
Armory T. Gill .50
Victor A. Hanson .40
Edward J. Hickox .50
Paul D. Hinkle .50
Howard A. Hobson .75
Nat Holman .50
Charles D. Hyatt .50
Henry P. Iba .50
Edward S. Irish .65
Alvin F. Julian .25
Matthew P. Kennedy .75
Robert A. Kurland .50
Ward L. Lambert .70
Joe Lapchick .50
Kennith D. Loeffler .50
Angelo Luisetti 4.00
Edward C. Macauley .50
Branch McCracken .50
George L. Mikan 2.00
William G. Mokray .50
Charles C. Murphy .40
James Naismith 2.00
Robert C. Pettit 4.00
Andy Phillip .50
John S. Rousma 1.00
Adolph F. Rupp 1.00
John D. Russell .40
William F. Russell 10.00
Abraham M. Saperstein 3.00
Arthur A. Schabinger .50
Adolph S. Schayes 3.00
Amos Alonzo Stagg 1.00
Charles H. Taylor .50
John A. Thompson .50
David Tobey .50
Oswald Tower .50
David H. Walsh .50
John R. Wooden 2.00

1986 Hall Of Fame/Metallic

These cards feature reproductions of the players' busts from the Basketball Hall of Fame. The blank-backed cards are silver-toned anodized aluminun cards. The cards were produced in sets of eight, only 999 of each set was produced. As new players are inducted, new sets are expected to be made.

MT
Complete Set (192): 625.00
Common Player: 2.00
James Naismith 15.00
Frank Morgenweck 2.00
Edward Macauley 4.00
Jack NcCracken 3.00
James Pollard 5.00
Ernest Schmidt 2.00
Ken Loeffler 2.50
Adolph Rupp 8.00
Forrest Allen 2.00
Lynn St. John 2.00
Victor Hanson 2.00
H.O. Page 2.00
Robert Pettit 10.00
Charles Cooper 3.00
Henry Iba 8.00
Bruce Drake 2.00
Edward Hickox 2.00
Ned Irish 2.00
First Team 2.00
Forrest Debernardi 3.00
Robert Cousy 15.00
Joseph Brennan 2.00
Ward Lambert 2.00
Arthur Lonborg 2.00
Amos Stagg 3.00
David Walsh 3.00
Charles Murphy 2.00
Barney Sedran 2.00
Joe Lapchick 12.00
Robert Davies 6.00
Howard Hobson 2.00
Everett Case 2.00
Oswald Tower 3.00
Paul Hinkle 2.00
William Sharman 5.00
Branch McCracken 4.00
John Thompson 2.00
Edward Krause 2.00
Everett Dean 8.00
Edgar Hickey 2.00
Harold Olsen 2.50
John Bunn 2.00
John Nucatola 2.00
Original Celtics 6.00
Robert Kurland 3.00
Harold Greer 6.00
Ernest Blood 2.50
Edgar Diddle 3.00
Ralph Morgan 2.00
R. William Jones 2.50
David Tobey 2.00
John Wooden 9.00
John Roosma 2.00
Joseph Fulks 9.00
George Keogan 2.00
Justin Barry 2.00
Luther Gulick 2.00
Walter Brown 3.00
James Enright 3.00
Bennie Borgman 2.00
John Russell 2.50
Elgin Baylor 15.00
Frank Keaney 2.00
Ben Carnevale 2.00
Arthur Trester 2.50
Matthew Kennedy 2.00
Buffalo Germans 3.00
Andy Phillip 6.00
Paul Endacott 2.00
Oscar Robertson 15.00
Leonard Sachs 2.00
Harry Litwack 2.00
John O'Brien 2.50
George Hepbron 2.00
Charles Hyatt 2.00
Thomas Barlow 2.50
Robert Gruenig 2.00
Bill Russell 20.00
Howard Cann 2.00
Red Auerbach 10.00
H.V. Porter 2.00
Senda Abbott 3.00
Renaissance 3.00
John Schommer 2.00
Nat Holman 3.00
Wilt Chamberlain 20.00
Amory Gill 2.00
Everett Shelton 2.00
William Reid 2.00
Clair Bee 10.00
George Hoyt 2.00
George Mikan 15.00
Christian Steinmetz 2.00
Adolph Schayes 4.00
H. Clifford Carlson 2.00
L. Margaret Wade 2.00
Arthur Schabinger 2.00
Bertha Teague 2.00
Jerry West 15.00
Angelo Luisetti 4.00
Edward Wachter 2.00
Slater Martin 2.50
Walter Meanwell 2.00
Alvin Julian 2.00
Ferenc Hepp 2.00
William Mokray 2.75
J. Dallas Shirley 2.00
Robert Vandivier 2.00
Frank Ramsey 5.00
Thomas Gola 4.00
John Wooden 12.00
Marv Harshman 2.00
Lester Harrison 2.00
Elmer Ripley 2.50
Charles Taylor 2.00
Lloyd Leith 2.00
Willis Reed 5.00
Thomas Heinsohn 7.00
Dean Smith 5.00
James Gardner 2.00
Edward Gottlieb 2.00
Abe Saperstein 5.00
Edward Steitz 2.50
Zigmund Mihalik 2.00
Henry Dehnert 2.00
Robert Wanzer 3.00
John Havlicek 15.00
Frank McGuire 4.00
Clifford Fagan 2.00
Maurice Podoloff 3.00
Robert Houbregs 2.00
Nate Thurmond 3.00
Lauren Gale 3.00
Bill Bradley 12.00
Raymond Meyer 2.00
Clarence Gaines 2.50
Harry Fisher 2.00
John McLendon 2.00
Clifford Wells 3.00
Clifford Hagan 4.00
William Johnson 2.00
Walt Frazier 10.00
Arad McCutchan 2.00
Bill Holzman 10.00
Al Duer 2.00
Emil Liston 2.00
Jack Twyman 6.00
Jerry Lucas 8.00
John Beckman 2.00
Rick Barry 12.00
Stanley Watts 2.00
W. Harold Anderson 2.00
Robert Douglas 2.00
J. Walter Kennedy 3.00
Peter Newell 2.00
Lou Wilke 2.00
Sam Jones 9.00
Harold Foster 2.00
Pete Maravich 25.00
Fred Taylor 2.00
Ernest Quigley 2.00
Paul Airzin 3.00
Al Cervi 2.00
K.C. Jones 6.00
Clyde Lovellette 3.00
Bobby McDermott 3.00
Earl Monroe 6.00
Elvin Hayes 12.00
Dave DeBusschere 6.00
Billy Cunningham 5.00
Ralph Miller 2.00
Lenny Wilkens 5.00
Wes Unseld 4.00
Dave Bing 4.00
Neil Johnston 2.00
Bill Gates 2.00
Robert Knight 4.00
Lawrence O'Brien 2.00
Nate Archibald 4.00
Dave Cowens 8.00
Harry Gallatin 3.00
Lawrence Fleisher 3.00
Max Friedman 2.00
Borislav Stankovic 2.50
Sergei Belov 2.00
Lou Carnesecca 5.00
Luisa Harris-Stewart 2.00
Connie Hawkins 4.00
Bob Lanier 5.00
Al McGuire 4.00
Jack Ramsay 3.00
Nera White 2.50

1992 Hall Of Fame Enshrinement

Champions U.S.A. sponsored this set featuring 10 new Hall of Famers. Only those attending the 25th Annual Enshrinement Dinner on May 11, 1992, were able to obtain one of the 2,000 sets made. Cards, which measure 2-1/2" x 3-1/2", feature black-and-white action photos. The Hall of Fame logo is in the lower left corner. Card backs have a career summary and stats.

MT
Complete Set (10): 80.00
Common Player: 3.00
1 Bob Lanier 20.00
2 Sergei Belov 8.00
3 Lou Carnesecca 15.00
4 Connie Hawkins 20.00
5 Al McGuire 12.00
6 Jack Ramsay 10.00
7 Nera White 8.00
8 Phil Woolpert 6.00
9 Luisa Harris-Stewart 8.00
10 Checklist 3.00

1959-60 Hawks Busch Bavarian

The black-and-white set depicts five members of the St. Louis Hawks with each card having a facsimile autograph. The cards measure 4" x 5" and were sponsored by Busch Bavarian Beer.

NM
Complete Set (5): 800.00
Common Player: 100.00
1 Sihugo Green SP 225.00
2 Cliff Hagan 150.00
3 Clyde Lovellette 200.00
4 John McCarthy 100.00
5 Bob Pettit 250.00

1961 Hawks Essex Meats

The 13-card, 2-1/2" x 3-1/2" set features members of the St. Louis Hawks in black and white. Distributed by Bonnie Brands, the card backs contain bio information and are unnumbered. The key card is Bob Pettit.

NM
Complete Set (13): 275.00
Common Player: 14.00
Barney Cable 14.00
Al Ferrari 14.00
Larry Foust 18.00
Cliff Hagan 50.00
Vern Hatton 15.00
Cleo Hill 14.00
Fred LaCour 14.00
Fuzzy Levane CO 14.00
Clyde Lovellette 50.00
John McCarthy 14.00
Shellie McMillion 14.00
Bob Pettit 100.00
Bobby Sims 14.00

1969-70 Hawks Team Issue

The Hawks produced and distributed this 10-photo set to the media for the 1969-70 season. The black-and-white 8" x 10" photos had the player's name and "Atlanta Hawks" listed below. They are blank-backed and unnumbered.

NM
Complete Set (10): 30.00
Common Player: 2.25
1 Butch Beard 2.25
2 Bill Bridges 2.25
3 Joe Caldwell 2.25
4 Jim Davis 2.25
5 Gary Gregor 2.25
6 Richie Guerin CO 2.25
7 Walt Hazzard 2.25
8 Lou Hudson 2.25
9 Don Ohl 2.25
10 Grady O'Malley 2.25

1978-79 Hawks Coke/WPLO

The 3" x 4-1/4", 14-card set was sponsored by V-103/WPLO and Coca-Cola and were distributed at 7-Eleven stores. The fronts feature a bust drawing of the player with the backs containing the player's career summary.

NM
Complete Set (14): 50.00
Common Player: 3.00
1 Hubie Brown CO 6.00
2 Charlie Criss 5.00
3 John Drew 5.00
4 Mike Fratello CO 6.00
5 Jack Givens 6.00
6 Steve Hawes 3.00
7 Armond Hill 4.00
8 Eddie Johnson 5.00
9 Frank Layden CO 6.00
10 Butch Lee 3.00
11 Tom McMillen 6.00
12 Tree Rollins 6.00
13 Dan Roundfield 4.00
14 Rick Wilson 3.00

1979-80 Hawks Majik Market

The 15-card, 3" x 4-1/4" set are similar to the 1978-79 Coke/WPLO set in that the card fronts depict the player in a bust drawing. V-103/WP-LO also sponsored this set, along with Majik Market.

NM
Complete Set (15): 50.00
Common Player: 3.00
1 Hubie Brown CO 6.00
2 John Brown 3.00
3 Charlie Criss 5.00
4 John Drew 5.00
5 Mike Fratello ACO 6.00
6 Jack Givens 6.00
7 Steve Hawes 3.00
8 Armond Hill 4.00
9 Eddie Johnson 5.00
10 Jimmy McElroy 3.00
11 Tom McMillen 6.00
12 Sam Pellom 3.00
13 Tree Rollins 6.00
14 Dan Roundfield 4.00
15 Brendan Suhr ACO 3.00

1986-87 Hawks Pizza Hut

The 18-card set was distributed at a Hawks' game in 1987 on three 8-1/4" x 11" sheets. After perforating, the cards measure 2-1/4" x 3-3/4" and feature the sponsor's (Pizza Hut) logo on the card front. The card backs contain career statistics and are unnumbered. Uncut, full boxes carry a 25 percent premium.

MT
Complete Set (18): 35.00
Common Player: 1.00
Mike Fratello CO 2.00
Willis Reed ACO 4.00
Brendan Suhr ACO 1.00
Brian Hill ACO 2.50
Joe O'Toole TR 1.00
John Battle 1.50
Antoine Carr 2.00
Scott Hastings 1.00
Jon Koncak 2.00
Cliff Levingston 2.00
Mike McGee 1.00
Doc Rivers 5.00
Tree Rollins 1.50
Spud Webb 5.00
Dominique Wilkins 15.00
Gus Williams 2.00
Kevin Willis 5.00
Randy Wittman 1.00

1987-88 Hawks Pizza Hut

The 1987-88 17-card set was distributed at a home game in 1988 and contains the key card of Dominique Wilkins. As with the 1986-87 Pizza Hut set, these cards were made available on three sheets with each card measuring 2-3/16" x 3-3/4" after perforation. The fronts depict the Pizza Hut logo in the lower left corner with career stats contained on the backs. Uncut, full boxes carry a 25 percent premium.

MT
Complete Set (17): 40.00
Common Player: 1.00
1 Mike Fratello CO 2.00
2 Brendan Suhr ASST 1.00
3 Brian Hill ACO 1.50
4 Don Chaney ASST 1.50
5 Joe O'Toole TR 1.00
6 John Battle 1.50
7 Antoine Carr 2.00

8	Scott Hastings	1.00
9	Jon Koncak	2.00
10	Cliff Levingston	2.00
11	Doc Rivers	5.00
12	Tree Rollins	1.50
13	Chris Washburn	4.00
14	Spud Webb	4.00
15	Dominique Wilkins	15.00
16	Kevin Willis	5.00
17	Randy Wittman	1.00

2001 Hawks/Topps

		MT
Complete Set (14):		8.00
Common Player:		.50
1	Dikembe Mutombo	.75
2	Hanno Mottola	.75
3	Jim Jackson	.50
4	Alan Henderson	.75
5	Header Card	.50
6	Anthony Johnson	.50
7	Chris Crawford	.50
8	Logo Card	.50
9	Roshown McCleod	1.00
10	DerMarr Johnson	2.50
11	Cal Bowdler	.50
12	Lorenzen Wright	.75
13	Dion Glover	.75
14	Jason Terry	1.00

1989-90 Heat Publix

The 15-card set was distributed by Publix stores in the Miami area. The cards measure 2" x 3-1/2" and feature a color action photo on the front with statistical and biographical information contained on the back. An early card of Glen Rice is the top card in the set.

		MT
Complete Set (15):		100.00
Common Player:		4.00
1	Terry Davis	6.00
2	Sherman Douglas	10.00
3	Kevin Edwards	8.00
4	Tony Florentino CO	4.00
5	Tellis Frank	4.00
6	Scott Haffner	4.00
7	Grant Long	10.00
8	Heat Mascot	4.00
9	Glen Rice	45.00
10	Ron Rothstein CO	4.00
11	Rony Seikaly	14.00
12	Rory Sparrow	4.00
13	Jon Sundvold	4.00
14	Billy Thompson	4.00
15	Dave Wohl CO	4.00

1990-91 Heat Publix

The 16-card set was sponsored by Bumble Bee Tuna, Domino's Pizza and Dixie. The cards were issued on sheets with coupons and after perforation, measured 2-1/2" x 3-1/2". The fronts contain color photos with the unnumbered backs having bio and stat information.

	MT
Complete Set (16):	25.00
Common Player:	1.00
Keith Askins	1.50
Willie Burton	1.50
Bimbo Coles	2.00
Terry Davis	1.50
Sherman Douglas	3.00
Kevin Edwards	2.00
Alec Kessler	1.00
Grant Long	3.00
Alan Ogg	1.00
Glen Rice	14.00
Rony Seikaly	3.00
Jon Sundvold	1.00
Billy Thompson	1.00
Ron Rothstein CO	1.00
Dave Wohl CO	1.00
Tony Florentino CO	1.00

1993-94 Heat Bookmarks

The four-card, 2-1/2" x 8" bookmark set were sponsored by the Miami Herald. The bookmark fronts feature a color action shot with logos and slogans (Join the winning team - Read) with the backs containing tips for reading with children.

		MT
Complete Set (4):		5.00
Common Player:		1.00
1	Grant Long	1.00
2	Harold Miner	1.00
3	Rony Seikaly	1.00
4	Steve Smith	3.00

1997 Highland Mint Legends

This seven-card set was produced by Highland Mint, with Bronze and Silver versions produced for all three cards, and Gold versions for those that sold out of Bronze and Silver. The SRPs were $50 for Bronze, $235 for Silver and $500 for Gold. Cards arrived in a lucite display case in an album with a certificate of authenticity.

		MT
Complete Set (7):		1300.
Common Player:		50.00
1	Kareem Abdul-Jabbar Silver/1000	200.00
2	Kareem Abdul-Jabbar Bronze/1000	50.00
3	Larry Bird Gold/500	650.00
4	Larry Bird Silver/1000	300.00
5	Larry Bird Bronze/5000	75.00
6	Jerry West Silver/500	250.00
7	Jerry West Bronze/2500	50.00

1997 Highland Mint Magnum Series Medallions

This two-medallion set featured Michael Jordan and measured 2-1/2-inches in diameter. They arrived in a 6-x-5-inch velvet box.

		MT
Complete Set (2):		300.00
1	Michael Jordan Silver/750	250.00
2	Michael Jordan Bronze/3000	100.00

1997 Highland Mint Minis

Each card in this four-card set was individually numbered, includes a certificate of authenticity and packaged in a leather display box. The SRPs for the minis were $65 for Bronze and $150 for Silver.

		MT
Complete Set (4):		500.00
1	Grant Hill, Jason Kidd Silver/1000	150.00
2	Grant Hill, Jason Kidd Bronze/500	60.00
3	Michael Jordan, Michael Jordan Silver/1000	250.00
4	Michael Jordan, Michael Jordan Bronze/5000	100.00

1997 Highland Mint Fleer/Hoops/UD

This 19-card set is made up of replicas of previously issue Fleer, Hoops and Upper Deck cards. Each card arrives in a numbered album and a three-piece lucite display with a certificate of authenticity. SRPs for the cards were $50 for Bronze, $235 and for Silver.

		MT
Complete Set (19):		3000.
Common Player:		50.00
1	Charles Barkley 86-87 Silver 1000	235.00
2	Charles Barkley 86-87 Bronze 5000	50.00
3	Anfernee Hardaway 93-94 UD Silver 500	235.00
4	Anfernee Hardaway 93-94 UD Bronze 2500	50.00
5	Anfernee Hardaway 93-94 UDSE Silver 500	235.00
6	Anfernee Hardaway 93-94 UDSE Bronze 2500	50.00
7	Magic Johnson 90-91 Silver 1000	250.00
8	Magic Johnson 90-91 Bronze 5000	60.00
9	Michael Jordan 91-92 Gold 500	600.00
10	Michael Jordan 91-92 Silver 1000	300.00
11	Michael Jordan 91-92 Bronze 5000	125.00
12	Hakeem Olajuwon 86-87 Silver 250	235.00
13	Hakeem Olajuwon 86-87 Bronze 1500	50.00
14	David Robinson 89-90 Silver 1000	235.00
15	David Robinson 89-90 Bronze 5000	50.00
16	Jerry Stackhouse 95-96 Silver 500	235.00
17	Jerry Stackhouse 95-96 Bronze 2500	50.00
18	Damon Stoudamire 95-96 Silver 500	235.00
19	Damon Stoudamire 95-96 Bronze 2500	50.00

1997 Highland Mint Coins

This 31-medallion set features the player's likeness and are checklisted alphabetically. Bronze, Silver and Gold designations are listed below along with the mintage figure.

		MT
Complete Set (31):		2000.
Common Player:		
1	Larry Bird Silver 7500	25.00
2	Chicago Bulls 70 Wins Silver 2500	30.00
3	Chicago Bulls Division Silver 1000	30.00
4	Chicago Bulls Conference Silver 5000	25.00
5	Chicago Bulls Finals Silver 7500	20.00
6	Chicago Bulls Finals Gold 1500	75.00
7	Chicago Bulls/Seattle Sonics Silver 500	25.00
8	Kevin Garnett Silver 7500	30.00
9	Anfernee Hardaway Gold 1500	75.00
10	Anfernee Hardaway Silver 7500	30.00
11	Anfernee Hardaway Bronze 2500	10.00
12	Allen Iverson Silver 3000	25.00
13	Larry Johnson Silver 7500	15.00
14	Michael Jordan Gold 100	1200.
15	Michael Jordan Gold 1000	100.00
16	Michael Jordan Silver 7500	50.00
17	Michael Jordan Bronze 2500	20.00
18	Shawn Kemp Silver 7500	15.00
19	Orlando Magic Silver 5000	25.00
20	Orlando Magic Silver 1000	20.00
21	Scottie Pippen Silver 7500	25.00
22	Mitch Richmond Gold 1000	40.00
23	Dennis Rodman Silver 7500	30.00
24	Dennis Rodman Green Hair Bronze 12500	15.00
25	Dennis Rodman Yellow Hair Bronze 12500	15.00
26	Dennis Rodman 3-coin set Bronze 2500	75.00
27	San Antonio Spurs Silver 1000	20.00
28	Seattle Supersonics Silver 1000	20.00
29	Seattle Supersonics Silver 5000	15.00
30	John Stockton Silver 7500	20.00
31	Nick Van Exel Silver 7500	15.00

1994-95 Hoop Magazine/Mother's Cookies

The 27-card set features players on 8-1/2" x 11" cards and was distributed in Hoop game programs. Sponsored by Mother's Cookies, one standout player from each of the teams at the time was produced. The backs feature an ad for Mother's Cookies or other advertisers and are numbered as "No. x/27."

		MT
Complete Set (27):		100.00
Common Player:		2.50
1	Mookie Blaylock	3.00
2	Dee Brown	2.50
3	Alonzo Mourning	6.00
4	B.J. Armstrong	2.50
5	Mark Price	3.50
6	Jason Kidd	10.00
7	Dikembe Mutombo	3.00
8	Joe Dumars	3.50
9	Latrell Sprewell	3.00
10	Hakeem Olajuwon	8.00
11	Reggie Miller	5.00
12	Loy Vaught	2.50
13	Vlade Divac	2.50
14	Glen Rice	4.00
15	Vin Baker	5.00
16	Isaiah Rider	2.50
17	Kenny Anderson	2.50
18	Patrick Ewing	7.00
19	Shaquille O'Neal	14.00
20	Clarence Weatherspoon	2.50
21	Charles Barkley	8.00
22	Clyde Drexler	8.00
23	Mitch Richmond	4.00
24	David Robinson	8.00
25	Gary Payton	6.00
26	John Stockton	8.00
27	Calbert Cheaney	2.50

1995-96 Hoop Magazine/Mother's Cookies

Nearly identical to the 1994-95 set, the 8-1/2" x 11" cards were distributed in Hoop game programs and sponsored by Mother's Cookies. The set features 29 players (one from each team) with the card backs containing an ad for Mother's Cookies and numbered as "x/29."

		MT
Complete Set (29):		100.00
Common Player:		2.00
1	Craig Ehlo	2.00
2	Eric Montross	2.00
3	Larry Johnson	8.00
4	Michael Jordan	25.00
5	Terrell Brandon	3.00
6	Jim Jackson	3.00
7	Mahmoud Abdul-Rauf	2.00
8	Allan Houston	4.00
9	Tim Hardaway	3.00
10	Clyde Drexler	6.00
11	Rik Smits	2.00
12	Lamond Murray	2.00
13	Vlade Divac	2.00
14	Glen Rice	3.00
15	Glenn Robinson	5.00
16	Tom Gugliotta	3.00
17	Ed O'Bannon	3.00
18	Patrick Ewing	5.00
19	Anfernee Hardaway	6.00
20	Jerry Stackhouse	7.00
21	Kevin Johnson	3.00
22	Rod Strickland	2.00
23	Mitch Richmond	3.00
24	Avery Johnson	2.00
25	Detlef Schrempf	2.00
26	Damon Stoudamire	10.00
27	Karl Malone	6.00
28	Greg Anthony	2.00
29	Juwan Howard	4.00

1995-96 Hoop Magazine/Mother's Cookies Award Winners

The 7-card, over-sized set was distributed in issues of Hoop Magazine. Each card represents a different Award Winner from the 1994-95 campaign.

		MT
Complete Set (7):		20.00
Common Player:		2.00
1	David Robinson	7.00
2	Jason Kidd	7.00
3	Grant Hill	9.00
4	Dana Barros	2.00
5	Anthony Mason	2.00
6	Del Harris	2.00
7	Dikembe Mutombo	3.00

1989-90 Hoops

NBA Hoops released its premier set of 300 basketball cards in late October of 1989. A second series of 53 updates - including cards of the expansion Orlando Magic and Minnesota Timberwolves players, an action card of rookie David Robinson, traded players, and a Detroit Pistons championship card - was released January 1990. Cards were issued in packs only; no factory sets were issued. To make room for Series II cards, 52 cards from the first series were replaced with the update cards on NBA Hoops sheets. The "short-printed" cards that were pulled are marked with an (SP) notation. The Pistons card, which was in every 75th wax pack and was extremely short-printed, was presumably printed on a separate sheet. Wax packs of updated cards say "Look for Orlando & Minnesota Expansion Team Plus Trades" in yellow in the lower right corner. NBA Hoops issued a new Pistons card, #353, showing the Pistons logo on the front with the same information on the back. They were available from the company via a mail-in offer. Rookies include David Robinson, Danny Manning, Rex Chapman, Hersey Hawkins, Willie Anderson and Mitch Richmond. Second-year cards include Mark Price, Reggie Miller and Kevin Duckworth. The second series has players from the NBA expansion teams, the Magic and the Timberwolves, plus traded and other players. AS means All-Star, C means coach.

		MT
Complete Set (352):		25.00
Complete Series 1 (300):		20.00
Complete Series 2 (52):		5.00
Common Player:		.05
Common Player (SP):		.15
Minor Stars:		.10
Minor Stars (SP):		.25
Series 1 Wax Box:		40.00
Series 2 Wax Box:		15.00
1	Joe Dumars	.15
2	Wayne Rollins	.05
3	Kenny Walker	.05
4	Mychal Thompson	.05
5	Alvin Robertson (SP)	.15
6	*Vinny Del Negro*	.20
7	Greg Anderson (SP)	.15
8	*Rod Strickland*	.50
9	Ed Pinckney	.05
10	Dale Ellis	.05
11	*Chuck Daley* (CO)	.20
12	Eric Leckner	.05
13	Charles Davis	.05
14	Cotton Fitzsimmons	.05
15	Byron Scott	.05
16	Derrick Chievous	.05
17	*Reggie Lewis*	.30
18	Jim Paxson	.05
19	*Tony Campbell*	.10
20	Rolando Blackman	.05
21	Michael Jordan (AS)	1.50
22	Cliff Levingston	.05
23	Roy Tarpley	.05
24	Harold Pressley	.05
25	Larry Nance	.10
26	*Chris Morris*	.10
27	Bob Hansen	.05
28	Mark Price (AS)	.10
29	Reggie Miller	.50
30	Karl Malone	.25
31	Sidney Lowe (SP)	.15
32	Ron Anderson	.05
33	Mike Gminski	.05
34	*Scott Brooks*	.10
35	*Kevin Johnson*	.75
36	Mark Bryant	.05
37	*Rik Smits*	.75
38	*Tim Perry*	.10
39	Ralph Sampson	.05
40	*Danny Manning*	.50
41	*Kevin Edwards*	.10
42	Paul Mokeski	.05
43	Dale Ellis (AS)	.05
44	Walter Berry	.05
45	Chuck Person	.10
46	Rick Mahorn (SP)	.15
47	Joe Kleine	.05
48	Brad Daugherty (AS)	.05
49	Mike Woodson	.05
50	Brad Daugherty	.05
51	Shelton Jones (SP)	.15
52	Michael Adams	.05
53	Wes Unseld	.05
54	*Rex Chapman*	.20
55	Kelly Tripucka	.05
56	Rickey Green	.05
57	Frank Johnson (SP)	.15
58	*Johnny Newman*	.10
59	Billy Thompson	.05
60	Stu Jackson	.05
61	Walter Davis	.05
62	*Brian Shaw* (SP)	.50
63	Gerald Wilkins	.05
64	Armon Gilliam	.05
65	Maurice Cheeks (SP)	.15
66	Jack Sikma	.05
67	*Harvey Grant*	.20
68	Jim Lynam	.05
69	Clyde Drexler (AS)	.15
70	Xavier McDaniel	.05
71	Danny Young	.05
72	Fennis Dembo	.05
73	Mark Acres (SP)	.15
74	*Brad Lohaus* (SP)	.15
75	Manute Bol	.05
76	Purvis Short	.05
77	Allen Leavell	.05
78	Johnny Dawkins (SP)	.15
79	Paul Pressey	.05
80	Patrick Ewing	.25
81	Bill Wennington	.05
82	Dan Schayes	.05
83	Derek Smith	.05
84	Moses Malone (AS)	.05
85	Jeff Malone	.05
86	*Otis Smith* (SP)	.15
87	Trent Tucker	.05
88	Robert Reid	.05
89	John Paxson	.05
90	Chris Mullin	.10
91	Tom Garrick	.05
92	Willis Reed (SP CO)	.15
93	Dave Corzine (SP)	.15
94	Mark Alarie	.05
95	Mark Aguirre	.05
96	Charles Barkley (AS)	.25
97	Sidney Green (SP)	.15
98	Kevin Willis	.05
99	Dave Hoppen	.05
100	Terry Cummings (SP)	.15
101	Dwayne Washington (SP)	.15
102	Larry Brown (C)	.05
103	Kevin Duckworth	.05
104	Uwe Blab	.05
105	Terry Porter	.05
106	*Craig Ehlo*	.10
107	Don Casey	.05
108	Pat Riley	.05
109	John Salley	.05
110	Charles Barkley	.50
111	Sam Bowie (SP)	.15
112	Earl Cureton	.05
113	Craig Hodges	.05
114	Benoit Benjamin	.05
115	Spud Webb (1985)	.10
115A	Spud Webb (1989)	.10
116	Karl Malone (AS)	.15
117	Eric Floyd	.05
118	John Williams	.05
119	Michael Holton	.05
120	Alex English	.05
121	Dennis Johnson	.05
122	Wayne Cooper (SP)	.15
123	Don Chaney (C, no line on back)	.10
123A	Don Chaney (C, line on back)	.10
124	A.C. Green	.05
125	Adrian Dantley	.05
126	Del Harris	.05
127	Dick Harter	.05
128	*Reggie Williams*	.20
129	Bill Hanzlik	.05
130	Dominique Wilkins	.20
131	Herb Williams	.05
132	Steve Johnson (SP)	.15
133	Alex English (AS)	.05
134	Darrell Walker	.05
135	Bill Laimbeer	.05
136	*Fred Roberts*	.05
137	*Hersey Hawkins*	.25
138	*David Robinson* (SP)	10.00
139	Brad Sellers (SP)	.15
140	John Stockton	.50
141	*Grant Long*	.10
142	Marc Iavaroni (SP)	.15
143	Steve Alford (SP)	.15
144	Jeff Lamp (SP)	.15
145	Buck Williams (SP)	.15
146	Mark Jackson (AS)	.05
147	Jim Petersen	.05
148	Steve Stipanovich (SP)	.15
149	*Sam Vincent* (SP)	.15
150	Larry Bird	1.00
151	Jon Koncak	.05
152	*Olden Polynice*	.10
153	Randy Breuer	.05
154	John Battle	.05
155	Mark Eaton	.05
156	Kevin McHale (AS)	.05
157	Jerry Sichting (SP)	.15
158	Pat Cummings (SP)	.15
159	Patrick Ewing (AS)	.15
160	Mark Price	.20
161	Jerry Reynolds (SP)	.15
162	*Ken Norman*	.10
163	John Bagley (SP)	.15
164	Christian Welp (SP)	.15
165	Reggie Theus (SP)	.15
166	Magic Johnson (AS)	.30
167	John Long	.05
168	Larry Smith (SP)	.15
169	*Charles Shackleford*	.10
170	Tom Chambers	.05
171	John MacLeod (C, NBA logo on back)	.10
171A	John MacLeod (C, no NBA logo on back)	.10
172	Ron Rothstein (C)	.05
173	Joe Wolf	.05
174	Mark Eaton (AS)	.05
175	Jon Sundvold	.05
176	Scott Hastings (SP)	.15
177	Isiah Thomas (AS)	.10
178	Hakeem Olajuwon	.30
179	Michael Fratello	.05
180	Hakeem Olajuwon	.50
181	Randolph Keys	.05
182	Richard Anderson	.05
183	*Dan Majerle*	.50
184	Derek Harper	.05
185	Robert Parish	.10
186	Ricky Berry (SP)	.15
187	Michael Cooper	.05
188	Vinnie Johnson	.05
189	James Donaldson	.05
190	Clyde Drexler	.30
191	Jay Vincent (SP)	.15
192	Nate McMillan	.05
193	Kevin Duckworth (AS)	.05
194	*Ledell Eackles*	.10
195	Eddie Johnson	.05
196	Terry Teagle	.05
197	Tom Chambers (AS)	.05
198	Joe Barry Carroll	.05
199	Dennis Hopson	.05
200	Michael Jordan	3.00
201	*Jerome Lane*	.10
202	Greg Kite	.05
203	David Rivers (SP)	.15
204	Sylvester Gray	.05
205	Ron Harper	.05
206	Frank Brickowski	.05
207	Rory Sparrow	.05
208	Gerald Henderson	.05
209	Rod Higgins	.05
210	James Worthy	.05
211	Dennis Rodman	1.25
212	Ricky Pierce	.05
213	Charles Oakley	.05
214	Steve Colter	.05
215	Danny Ainge	.05
216	Lenny Wilkens (C)	.05
217	Larry Nance (AS)	.05
218	Tyrone Bogues	.05
219	James Worthy (AS)	.05
220	Lafayette Lever	.05
221	Quintin Dailey (SP)	.15
222	Lester Conner	.05
223	Jose Ortiz	.05
224	*Michael Williams* (SP)	.25
225	Wayman Tisdale	.05
226	Mike Sanders (SP)	.15
227	Jim Farmer (SP)	.15
228	Mark West	.05
229	*Jeff Hornacek*	.25
230	Chris Mullin (AS)	.10
231	Vern Fleming	.05
232	Kenny Smith	.05
233	Derrick McKey	.05
234	Dominique Wilkins	.10
235	*Willie Andersen*	.10
236	Keith Lee (SP)	.15
237	*Buck Johnson*	.10
238	Randy Wittman	.05
239	Terry Catledge (SP)	.15
240	Bernard King	.05
241	Darrell Griffith	.05
242	Horace Grant	.30
243	*Rony Seikaly*	.25
244	Scottie Pippen	1.00
245	Michael Cage	.05
246	Kurt Rambis	.05
247	*Morlon Wiley* (SP)	.15
248	Ronnie Grandison	.05
249	*Scott Skiles* (SP)	.75
250	Isiah Thomas	.20
251	Thurl Bailey	.05
252	Glenn Rivers	.05
253	Stuart Gray (SP)	.15
254	John Williams (W)	.05
255	Bill Cartwright	.05
256	Terry Cummings (AS)	.05
257	Rodney McCray	.05
258	*Larry Krystkowiak*	.10
259	*Will Perdue*	.15
260	*Mitch Richmond*	3.00
261	Blair Rasmussen	.05
262	*Charles Smith*	.15
263	*Tyrone Corbin* (SP)	.25
264	Kelvin Upshaw	.05
265	Otis Thorpe	.05
266	Phil Jackson	.05
267	Jerry Sloan	.05
268	John Shasky	.05
269	Bernie Bickerstaff (C, Feb. 11 birthdate)	.10
269A	Bernie Bickerstaff (C, Nov. 2 birthdate)	.10
270	Magic Johnson	.50
271	*Vernon Maxwell*	.15
272	Tim McCormick	.05
273	Don Nelson	.05
274	*Gary Grant*	.15

275	Sidney Moncrief (SP)	.25
276	Roy Hinson	.05
277	Jimmy Rodgers	.05
278	Antoine Carr	.05
279	Orlando Woolridge (no trademark by logo)	.10
279A	Orlando Woolridge (trademark by logo)	.15
280	Kevin McHale	.10
281	LaSalle Thompson	.05
282	Detlef Schrempf	.05
283	Doug Moe	.05
284	James Edwards (line by number)	.10
284A	James Edwards (no line by number)	.10
285	Jerome Kersey	.05
286	Sam Perkins	.05
287	Sedale Threatt	.05
288	Tim Kempton (SP)	.15
289	Mark McNamara	.05
290	Moses Malone	.10
291	Rick Adelman	.05
292	Dick Versace	.05
293	Alton Lister (SP)	.15
294	Winston Garland	.05
295	Kiki Vandeweghe	.05
296	Brad Davis	.05
297	John Stockton (AS)	.30
298	Jay Humphries	.05
299	Dell Curry	.05
300	Mark Jackson	.10
301	Morlon Wiley	.05
302	Reggie Theus	.05
303	Otis Smith	.05
304	Tod Murphy	.05
305	Sidney Green	.05
306	Shelton Jones	.05
307	Mark Acres	.05
308	Terry Catledge	.05
309	Larry Smith	.05
310	David Robinson (IA)	2.00
311	Johnny Dawkins	.05
312	Terry Cummings	.05
313	Sidney Lowe	.05
314	Bill Musselman	.05
315	Buck Williams	.05
316	Mel Turpin	.05
317	Scott Hastings	.05
318	Scott Skiles	.10
319	Tyrone Corbin	.05
320	Maurice Cheeks	.05
321	Mattie Guokas	.05
322	Jeff Turner	.05
323	David Wingate	.05
324	Steve Johnson	.05
325	Alton Lister	.05
326	Ken Bannister	.05
327	Bill Fitch	.05
328	Sam Vincent	.05
329	Larry Drew	.05
330	Rick Mahorn	.05
331	Christian Web	.05
332	Brad Lohaus	.05
333	Frank Johnson	.05
334	Jim Farmer	.05
335	Wayne Cooper	.05
336	*Mike Brown*	.10
337	Sam Bowie	.05
338	*Kevin Gamble*	.10
339	*Jerry Reynolds*	.05
340	Mike Sanders	.05
341	Bill Jones	.05
342	Greg Anderson	.05
343	Dave Corzine	.05
344	Michael Williams	.05
345	Jay Vincent	.05
346	David Rivers	.05
347	Caldwell Jones	.05
348	Brad Sellers	.05
350	Alvin Robertson	.05
351	*Steve Kerr*	.50
352	Stuart Gray	.05
353	Pistons Champions (SP)	4.00
353A	Pistons Champions	.50

1989-90 Hoops Checklists

The two-booklet checklist, measuring 2-1/2" x 3-1/2" when folded, was distributed by Hoops primarily via phone requests.

		MT
Complete Set (2):		4.00
Common Player:		2.00
CL1	Checklist 1-300	3.00
CL2	Checklist 1-353	2.00

1989-90 Hoops All-Star Panels

Limited to a production of 15,000 sets, the 21 card set was inserted in the All-Star Game program via four six-card panels. When perforated, the cards measure 2-1/2" x 3-1/2" with a color action photo of the player bordered by a red arch. The cards are identical to the All-Star cards from the base set and feature the same base-set numbering.

		MT
Complete Set (4):		20.00
Common Player:		5.00
Series 1 Poly Pack (15):		1.75
Series 1 Poly Wax Box (36):		35.00
Series 2 Poly Pack (15):		.95
Series 2 Poly Wax Box (36):		17.00
1	Panel 1 (Tom Chambers, Moses Malone, Chris Mullin, Larry Nance, John Stockton, Dominique Wilkins)	5.00
2	Panel 2 (Brad Daugherty, Kevin Duckworth, Alex English, Mark Jackson, Magic Johnson, Isiah Thomas)	5.00
3	Panel 3 (Terry Cummings, Dale Ellis, Kevin Malone, Kevin McHale, Hakeem Olajuwon, Mark Price)	5.00
4	Panel 4 (Charles Barkley, Clyde Drexler, Mark Eaton, Patrick Ewing, Michael Jordan, James Worthy)	10.00

1989-90 Hoops Announcers

Pro basketball announcers were given these cards to use as business cards; approximately 200 to 1,000 of each announcer was made. The cards have the same design format as NBA Hoops' regular 1989-90 issue, except cards for the TNT broadcasters (#s 2, 3, 4 and 7) have silver borders. The card backs are unnumbered and include an announcer profile.

	MT
Complete Set (7):	300.00
Common Player:	25.00
John Andarise	25.00
Rick Barry	150.00
Skip Caray	40.00
Jack Givens	40.00
Steve Jones	25.00
Pat Lafferty	25.00
Craig Sager	25.00

1990 Hoops Action Photos

These 8" x 10" glossy cards were issued in February 1990. The first 22 cards were available nationally and locally. The rest were available locally in each NBA city, five per team. Card backs are unnumbered and contain player stats. The local players are listed alphabetically by team after the 22 national cards.

	MT
Complete Set (136):	75.00
Common Player:	.60
Larry Bird	2.50
Charles Barkley	1.00
Tom Chambers	.60
Clyde Drexler	1.00
Joe Dumars	1.00
Dale Ellis	.60
Patrick Ewing	1.00
Magic Johnson	2.50
Kevin Johnson	.60
Michael Jordan	4.00
Karl Malone	1.50
Moses Malone	.75
Kevin McHale	.75
Chris Mullin	1.00
Akeem Olajuwon	1.50
Scottie Pippen	2.00
Mark Price	.60
David Robinson	1.50
John Stockton	1.00
Isiah Thomas	1.00
Dominique Wilkins	1.00
James Worthy	1.50
Doc Rivers	.60
Spud Webb	.60
Kevin Willis	.60
Reggie Lewis	.60
Robert Parish	1.00
Brian Shaw	.60
Muggsy Bogues	.60
Rex Chapman	.60
Dell Curry	.75
J.R. Reid	.60
Kelly Tripucka	.60
Bill Cartwright	.60
Horace Grant	.75
Stacey King	.60
Chucky Brown	.60
Brad Daugherty	.75
Craig Ehlo	.60
Larry Nance	.75
Rolando Blackman	.75
Brad Davis	.60
James Donaldson	.60
Derek Harper	.60
Roy Tapley	.75
Michael Adams	.60
Walter Davis	.75
Bill Hanzlik	.60
Todd Lichti	.60
Blair Rasmussen	.60
Bill Laimbeer	.60
Dennis Rodman	1.50
John Salley	.60
Tim Hardaway	1.00
Rod Higgins	.60
Sarunas Marciulionis	.60
Mitch Richmond	1.00
Sleepy Floyd	.60
Buck Johnson	.60
Vernon Maxwell	.60
Otis Thorpe	.60
Vern Fleming	.60
Reggie Miller	1.00
Chuck Person	.60
Rik Smits	.60
LaSalle Thompson	.60
Benoit Benjamin	.60
Gary Grant	.60
Danny Manning	.75
Ken Norman	.60
Charles Smith	.60
A.C. Green	.60
Byron Scott	.75
Vlade Divac	.75
Sherman Douglas	.75
Kevin Edwards	.60
Glen Rice	1.00
Rony Seikaly	.75
Billy Thompson	.60
Jay Humphries	.60
Brad Lohaus	.60
Ricky Pierce	.75
Alvin Robertson	.75
Jack Sikma	.75
Randy Breuer	.60
Tony Campbell	.60
Tyrone Corbin	.60
Sam Mitchell	.60
Pooh Richardson	.60
Mookie Blaylock	.60
Sam Bowie	.60
Lester Conner	.60
Roy Hinson	.60
Chris Morris	.60
Maurice Cheeks	.75
Mark Jackson	.75
Charles Oakley	.75
Gerald Wilkins	.60
Nick Anderson	.75
Michael Ansley	.60
Terry Catledge	.60
Sidney Green	.60
Sam Vincent	.60
Ron Anderson	.60
Mike Gminski	.60
Hersey Hawkins	.75
Rick Mahorn	.60
Jeff Hornacek	.60
Eddie Johnson	.60
Mark West	.60
Kevin Duckworth	.60
Jerome Kersey	.75
Terry Porter	.75
Buck Williams	.60
Antoine Carr	.60
Eric Leckner	.60
Ralph Sampson	1.00
Lionel Simmons	.60
Wayman Tisdale	.75
Willie Anderson	.60
Terry Cummings	1.00
Sean Elliott	.75
Rod Strickland	.75
Michael Cage	.60
Shawn Kemp	1.50
Xavier McDaniel	.60
Derrick McKey	.60
Thurl Bailey	.60
Mark Eaton	.60
Blue Edwards	.60
Harvey Grant	.75
Charles Jones	.50
Bernard King	1.00
Darrell Walker	.60
John Williams	.60
Checklist	.75

1990 Hoops Superstars

This yellow-bordered set, exactly like the 1989-90 Hoops cards, was available only through the Sears catalog. Approximately 30,000 sets were produced. The David Robinson card is his Hoops II rookie.

		MT
Complete Set (100):		15.00
Common Player:		.08
1	Doc Rivers	.50
2	Dominique Wilkins	.75
3	Spud Webb	.25
4	Moses Malone	.20
5	Reggie Lewis	.25
6	Larry Bird	2.50
7	Kevin McHale	.75
8	Robert Parish	.50
9	Tyrone Bogues	.75
10	Rex Chapman	.25
11	Kelly Tripucka	.08
12	Michael Jordan	5.00
13	Scottie Pippen	1.50
14	John Paxson	.10
15	Bill Cartwright	.10
16	Mark Price	.50
17	Larry Nance	.50
18	John Williams (Clev.)	.10
19	Brad Daugherty	.15
20	Derek Harper	.10
21	Rolando Blackman	.25
22	Sam Perkins	.25
23	James Donaldson	.08
24	Michael Adams	.10
25	Lafayette Lever	.08
26	Alex English	.10
27	Isiah Thomas	.50
28	Joe Dumars	.50
29	Bill Laimbeer	.10
30	Dennis Rodman	1.00
31	*Mitch Richmond*	1.75
32	Chris Mullin	.50
33	Manute Bol	.08
34	Rod Higgins	.08
35	Eric Floyd	.08
36	Otis Thorpe	.10
37	Buck Johnson	.08
38	Akeem Olajuwon	1.00
39	Vern Fleming	.08
40	Reggie Miller	1.00
41	Chuck Person	.10
42	*Rik Smits*	.75
43	Benoit Benjamin	.08
44	Charles Smith	.20
45	Gary Grant	.10
46	*Danny Manning*	1.00
47	Earvin Johnson	2.00
48	Byron Scott	.40
49	A.C. Green	.40
50	James Worthy	.75
51	Kevin Edwards	.10
52	Rory Sparrow	.08
53	Rony Seikaly	.25
54	Jay Humphries	.08
55	Alvin Robertson	.08
56	Ricky Pierce	.10
57	Jack Sikma	.10
58	Tyrone Corbin	.08
59	Sidney Lowe	.08
60	Steve Johnson	.08
61	Dennis Hoppen	.08
62	Chris Morris	.10
63	Roy Hinson	.08
64	Mark Jackson	.40
65	Gerald Wilkins	.08
66	Charles Oakley	.20
67	Patrick Ewing	.75
68	Reggie Theus	.10
69	Sam Vincent	.08
70	Terry Catledge	.10
71	*Hersey Hawkins*	1.00
72	Johnny Dawkins	.08
73	Charles Barkley	1.00
74	Mike Giminski	.08
75	*Kevin Johnson*	1.50
76	*Jeff Hornacek*	1.00
77	Tom Chambers	.20
78	Eddie Johnson	.08
79	Terry Porter	.15
80	Clyde Drexler	1.00
81	Jerome Kersey	.08
82	Kevin Duckworth	.08
83	Danny Ainge	.50
84	Rodney McCray	.08
85	Wayman Tisdale	.10
86	Willie Anderson	.20
87	Terry Cummings	.10
88	David Robinson	4.00
89	Dale Ellis	.08
90	Derrick McKey	.10
91	Xavier McDaniel	.10
92	Michael Cage	.08
93	John Stockton	2.00
94	Karl Malone	2.00
95	Thurl Bailey	.08
96	Mark Eaton	.08
97	Jeff Malone	.10
98	Darrell Walker	.08
99	Bernard King	.15
100	John Williams (Wash.)	.08

1990 Hoops Barcelona Knicks

These cards measure 2-1/2" x 3-1/2" when separated from a 10" x 14" perforated sheet. The sheet was distributed at a kids clinic conducted by Julius Erving in Barcelona, Spain, on Oct. 12, 1990. Cards, including the card numbers, are identical to 1990-91 cards, but #206, Johnny Newman, was omitted due to a trade. Coca-Cola sponsored the set to commemorate the Knicks' participation in the McDonald's Open. There were 20,000 sets produced.

		MT
Complete Set (12):		175.00
202	Maurice Cheeks	10.00
203	Patrick Ewing	50.00
204	Stuart Gray	7.50
205	Mark Jackson	15.00
207	Charles Oakley	25.00
208	Trent Tucker	10.00
209	Kiki Vandeweghe	15.00
210	Kenny Walker	10.00
211	Eddie Lee Wilkins	7.50
212	Gerald Wilkins	10.00
(1)	Coca-Cola Hoop Card	2.50
(2)	Coca-Cola Ad Card	2.50

1990-91 Hoops

Hoops returned with an even larger first series than the year before (300 cards in 1989 compared to 336 in 1990). The basic design - a basketball key - remained the same, as did the All-Star subset. Included in this year were checklists and a Danny Ferry rookie card. Cards were again issued in wax packs only. The second series of 104 cards included six playoff cards, 12 coaches cards, 11 lottery players, updates and team art cards. As was the case the previous year, cards were pulled from Series I to make room for these additional cards. AS means All-Star, FL means Flashback, AC means Art Card.

		MT
Complete Set (440):		15.00
Complete Series 1 (336):		10.00
Complete Series 2 (104):		5.00
Common Player:		.05
Minor Stars:		.10
Series 1 or 2 Wax Box:		10.00
1	(Charles Barkley) (AS) (SP)	.25
2	Larry Bird (AS) (SP)	.50
2A	Larry Bird (AS) (SP) (no "T" in TM on back)	1.00
3	Joe Dumars (AS) (SP)	.10
4	Patrick Ewing (AS) (SP)	.20
5	Michael Jordan (AS) (SP)	2.50
6	Kevin McHale (AS) (SP)	.10
6A	Kevin McHale (AS) (SP) (no "T" in TM on back)	.10
7	Reggie Miller (AS) (SP)	.25
8	Robert Parish (AS) (SP)	.10
8A	Robert Parish (AS) (SP) (no "T" in TM on back)	.10
9	Scottie Pippen (AS) (SP)	.50
10	Dennis Rodman (AS) (SP)	.50
11	Isiah Thomas (AS) (SP)	.20
12	Dominique Wilkins (AS) (SP)	.10
13	All-Star Checklist (Riley, Daly) (AS) (SP) (no number)	.10
13A	All-Star Checklist (Riley, Daly) (AS) (SP) (with number)	.10
14	Rolando Blackman (AS) (SP)	.10
15	Tom Chambers (AS) (SP)	.10
16	Clyde Drexler (AS) (SP)	.25
17	A.C. Green (AS) (SP)	.10
18	Magic Johnson (AS) (SP)	.50
19	Kevin Johnson (AS) (SP)	.10
20	Lafayette Lever (AS) (SP)	.10
21	Karl Malone (AS) (SP)	.25
22	Chris Mullin (AS) (SP)	.10
23	Hakeem Olajuwon (AS) (SP)	.50
24	David Robinson (AS) (SP)	.75
25	John Stockton (AS) (SP)	.20
26	James Worthy (AS) (SP)	.10
27	John Battle	.05
28	Jon Koncak	.05
29	Cliff Levinston (SP)	.10
30	John Long (SP)	.10
31	Moses Malone	.10
32	Glenn Rivers	.05
33	Kenny Smith (SP)	.10
34	Alexander Volkov	.05
35	Spud Webb	.05
36	Dominique Wilkins	.10
37	Kevin Willis	.05
38	John Bagley	.05
39	Larry Bird	.75
40	Kevin Gamble	.05
41	Dennis Johnson (SP)	.10
42	Joe Kleine	.05
43	Reggie Lewis	.05
44	Kevin McHale	.10
45	Robert Parish	.10
46	Jim Paxson (SP)	.10
47	Ed Pinckney	.05
48	Brian Shaw	.05
49	Richard Anderson (SP)	.10
50	Tyrone Bogues	.05
51	Rex Chapman	.05
52	Dell Curry	.05
53	*Kenny Gattison*	.10
54	Armon Gilliam	.05
55	Dave Hoppen	.05
56	Randolph Keys	.05
57	*J.R. Reid*	.10
58	Robert Reid (SP)	.10
59	Kelly Tripucka	.05
60	*B.J. Armstrong*	.15
61	Bill Cartwright	.05
62	Charles Davis (SP)	.10
63	Horace Grant	.20
64	Craig Hodges	.05
65	Michael Jordan	2.50
66	*Stacy King*	.10
67	John Paxson	.05
68	Will Perdue	.05
69	Scottie Pippen	.50
70	Winston Bennett	.05
71	*Chucky Brown*	.15
72	Derrick Chievous	.05
73	Brad Daugherty	.05
74	Craig Ehlo	.05
75	Steve Kerr	.05
76	Paul Mokeski (SP)	.10
77	John Morton	.05
78	Larry Nance	.05
79	Mark Price	.05
80	John Williams	.05
81	Steve Alford	.05
82	Rolando Blackman	.05
83	Adrian Dantley (SP)	.10
84	Brad Davis	.05
85	James Donaldson	.05
86	Derek Harper	.05
87	Sam Perkins (SP)	.10
88	Roy Tarpley	.05
89	Bill Wennington (SP)	.10
90	Herb Williams	.05
91	Michael Adams	.05
92	Joe Barry Carroll (SP)	.10
93	Walter Davis	.05
94	Alex English (SP)	.10
95	Bill Hanzlik	.05
96	Jerome Lane	.05
97	Lafayette Lever (SP)	.10
98	*Todd Lichti*	.10
99	Blair Rasmussen	.05
100	Dan Schayes (SP)	.10
101	Mark Aguirre	.05
102	*William Bedford*	.10
103	Joe Dumars	.10
104	James Edwards	.05
105	Scott Hastings	.05
106	Gerald Henderson (SP)	.10
107	Vinnie Johnson	.05
108	Bill Laimbeer	.05
109	Dennis Rodman	.50
110	John Salley	.05
111	Isiah Thomas	.20
112	Manute Bol (SP)	.10
113	*Tim Hardaway*	.50
114	Rod Higgins	.05
115	*Sarunas Marciulionis*	.10
116	Chris Mullin	.10
117	Jim Petersen	.05
118	Mitch Richmond	.20
119	Mike Smrek	.05
120	Terry Teagle (SP)	.10
121	Tom Tolbert	.05
122	Christian Welp (SP)	.10
123	Byron Dinkins (SP)	.10
124	Eric Floyd	.05
125	Buck Johnson	.05
126	Vernon Maxwell	.05
127	Hakeem Olajuwon	.50
128	Larry Smith	.05
129	Otis Thorpe	.05
130	Mitchell Wiggins (SP)	.10
131	Mike Woodson	.05
132	Greg Dreiling	.05
133	Vern Fleming	.05
134	Rickey Green (SP)	.10
135	Reggie Miller	.25
136	Chuck Person	.05
137	Mike Sanders	.05
138	Detlef Schrempf	.05
139	Rik Smits	.10
140	LaSalle Thompson	.05
141	Randy Wittman	.05
142	Benoit Benjamin	.05
143	Winston Garland	.05
144	Tom Garrick	.05
145	Gary Grant	.05
146	Ron Harper	.05
147	Danny Manning	.10
148	Jeff Martin	.05
149	Ken Norman	.05
150	David Rivers (SP)	.10
151	Charles Smith	.05
152	Joe Wolf (SP)	.10
153	Michael Cooper	.05
154	*Vlade Divac*	.40
155	Larry Drew	.05
156	A.C. Green	.05
157	Magic Johnson	.50
158	Mark McNamara (SP)	.10
159	Byron Scott	.05
160	Mychal Thompson	.05
161	Jay Vincent (SP)	.10
162	Orlando Woolridge (SP)	.10
163	James Worthy	.05
164	*Sherman Douglas*	.10
165	Kevin Edwards	.05
166	Tellis Frank (SP)	.10
167	Grant Long	.05
168	*Glen Rice*	.50
169	Rony Seikaly	.10
170	Rory Sparrow (SP)	.10
171A	Jon Sundvold	.05
171B	Billy Thompson (SP) (error)	.10
172A	Billy Thompson (SP)	.10
172B	Jon Sundvold (SP) (error)	.10
173	Greg Anderson	.05
174	Jeff Grayer	.05
175	Jay Humphries	.05
176	Frank Kornet	.05
177	Larry Krystkowiak	.05
178	Brad Lohaus	.05
179	Ricky Pierce	.05
180	Paul Pressey (SP)	.10
181	Fred Roberts	.05
182	Alvin Robertson	.05
183	Jack Sikma	.05
184	Randy Breuer	.05
185	Tony Campbell	.05
186	Tyrone Corbin	.05
187	Sidney Lowe (SP)	.10
188	Sam Mitchell	.05
189	Tod Murphy	.05
190	*Pooh Richardson*	.10
191	Scott Roth (SP)	.10
192	Brad Seller (SP)	.10
193	*Mookie Blaylock*	.50
194	Sam Bowie	.05
195	Lester Conner	.05
196	Derrick Gervin	.05
197	Jack Haley	.05
198	Roy Hinson	.05
199	Dennis Hopson (SP)	.10
200	Chris Morris	.05
201	Purvis Short (SP)	.10
202	Maurice Cheeks	.05
203	Patrick Ewing	.20
204	Stuart Gray	.05
205	Mark Jackson	.05
206	Johnny Newman (SP)	.10
207	Charles Oakley	.05
208	Trent Tucker	.05
209	Kiki Vandeweghe	.05
210	Kenny Walker	.05
211	Eddie Lee Wilkins	.05
212	Gerald Wilkins	.05
213	Mark Acres	.05
214	*Nick Anderson*	.50
215	Michael Ansley	.05
216	Terry Catledge	.05
217	Dave Corzine (SP)	.10
218	Sidney Green (SP)	.10
219	Jerry Reynolds	.05
220	Scott Skiles	.05
221	Otis Smith	.05
222	Reggie Theus (SP)	.10
223	Sam Vincent w/Jordan (SP) (Jordan wearing #12)	1.00
223A	Sam Vincent (solo, Series II)	.10
224	Ron Anderson	.05
225	Charles Barkley	.40
226	Scott Brooks (SP)	.10
227	Johnny Dawkins	.05

228	Mike Gminski	.05
229	Hersey Hawkins	.05
230	Rick Mahorn	.05
231	Derek Smith (SP)	.10
232	Bob Thornton	.05
233	Kenny Battle	.05
234	Tom Chambers (guard)	.05
234A	Tom Chambers (forward)	.05
235	*Greg Grant* (SP)	.10
236	Jeff Hornacek	.05
237	Eddie Johnson	.05
238	Kevin Johnson (guard)	.10
238A	Kevin Johnson (forward)	.10
239	Dan Majerle	.05
240	Tim Perry	.05
241	Kurt Rambis	.05
242	Mark West	.05
243	Mark Bryant	.05
244	Wayne Cooper	.05
245	Clyde Drexler	.30
246	Kevin Duckworth	.05
247	Jerome Kersey	.05
248	*Drazen Petrovic*	.15
249	Terry Porter	.05
250	*Cliff Robinson*	.75
251	Buck Williams	.05
252	Danny Young	.05
253	Danny Ainge (SP)	.10
254	Randy Allen (SP)	.10
255	Antoine Carr	.05
256	Vinny Del Negro (SP)	.10
257	*Pervis Ellison* (SP)	.15
258	Greg Kite (SP)	.10
259	Rodney McCray (SP)	.10
260	Harold Pressley (SP)	.10
261	Ralph Sampson	.05
262	Wayman Tisdale	.05
263	Willie Anderson	.05
264	Uwe Blab (SP)	.10
265	Frank Brickowski (SP)	.10
266	Terry Cummings	.05
267	*Sean Elliott*	.50
268	Caldwell Jones (SP)	.10
269	Johnny Moore (SP)	.10
270	David Robinson	1.00
271	Rod Strickland	.05
272	Reggie Williams	.05
273	David Wingate (SP)	.10
274	*Dana Barros*	.25
275	Michael Cage	.05
276	Quintin Dailey	.05
277	Dale Ellis	.05
278	Steve Johnson (SP)	.10
279	*Shawn Kemp*	1.50
280	Xavier McDaniel	.05
281	Derrick McKey	.05
282	Nate McMillian	.05
283	Olden Polynice	.05
284	Sedale Threatt	.05
285	Thurl Bailey	.05
286	Mike Brown	.05
287	Mark Eaton	.05
288	*Blue Edwards*	.10
289	Darrell Griffith	.05
290	Robert Hansen (SP)	.10
291	Eric Leckner (SP)	.10
292	Karl Malone	.25
293	Delaney Rudd	.05
294	John Stockton	.25
295	Mark Alarie	.05
296	Ledell Eackles (SP)	.10
297	Harvey Grant	.05
298	Tom Hammonds (with "Rookie")	.05
298A	Tom Hammonds (without "Rookie")	.05
299	Charles Jones	.05
300	Bernard King	.05
301	Jeff Malone (SP)	.10
302	Mel Turpin (SP)	.10
303	Darrell Walker	.05
304	John Williams	.05
305	Bob Weiss (C)	.05
306	Chris Ford (C)	.05
307	Gene Littles (C)	.05
308	Phil Jackson (C)	.05
309	Lenny Wilkens (C)	.05
310	Richie Adubato (C)	.05
311	Doug Moe (C-SP)	.05
312	Chuck Daly (C)	.05
313	Don Nelson (C)	.05
314	Don Chaney (C)	.05
315	Dick Versace (C)	.05
316	Mike Schuler (C)	.05
317	Pat Riley (C-SP)	.05
318	Ron Rothsten (C)	.05
319	Del Harris (C)	.05
320	Bill Musselman (C)	.05
321	Bill Fitch (C)	.05
322	Stu Jackson (C)	.05
323	Matt Guokas (C)	.05
324	Jim Lynam (C)	.05
325	Cotton Fitzsimmons (C)	.05
326	Rick Adelman (C)	.05
327	Dick Motta (C)	.05
328	Larry Brown (C)	.05
329	K.C. Jones (C)	.05
330	Jerry Sloan (C)	.05
331	Wes Unseld (C)	.05
332	Checklist 1 (SP)	.05
333	Checklist 2 (SP)	.05
334	Checklist 3 (SP)	.05
335	Checklist 4 (SP)	.05
336	*Danny Ferry* (SP)	.20
337	NBA Finals Game 1	.05
338	NBA Finals Game 2	.05
339	NBA Finals Game 3	.05
340	NBA Finals Game 4	.05
341	Detroit Championship (no "Sports" on back)	.05
341A	Detroit Championship (corrected)	.05
342	Championship	.05
343	K.C. Jones (FL)	.05
344	Wes Unseld (FL)	.05
345	Don Nelson (FL)	.05
346	Bob Weiss (FL)	.05
347	Chris Ford (FL)	.05
348	Phil Jackson	.05
349	Lenny Wilkens (FL)	.05
350	Don Chaney (FL)	.05
351	Mike Dunleavy (FL)	.05
352	Matt Guokas (FL)	.05
353	Rick Adelman (FL)	.05
354	Jerry Sloan (FL)	.05
355	Dominique Wilkins	.10
356	Larry Bird (TC)	.40
357	Rex Chapman (TC)	.05
358	Michael Jordan (TC)	1.25
359	Mark Price (TC)	.05
360	Rolando Blackman (TC)	.05
361	Michael Adams (TC)	.05
362	Joe Dumars (TC)	.05
363	Chris Mullin (TC)	.05
364	Hakeem Olajuwon (TC)	.25
365	Reggie Miller (TC)	.10
366	Danny Manning (TC)	.05
367	Magic Johnson (TC)	.25
368	Rony Seikaly (TC)	.05
369	Alvin Robertson (TC)	.05
370	Pooh Richardson (TC)	.05
371	Chris Morris (TC)	.05
372	Patrick Ewing (TC)	.10
373	Nick Anderson (TC)	.05
374	Charles Barkley (TC)	.20
375	Kevin Johnson (TC)	.10
376	Clyde Drexler (TC)	.15
377	Wayman Tisdale (TC)	.05
378	David Robinson (TC (half basketball))	.40
378A	David Robinson (TC (full basketball))	.40
379	Xavier McDaniel (TC)	.05
380	Karl Malone (TC)	.10
381	Bernard King (TC)	.05
382	Michael Jordan (Playground)	1.25
383	Lights, Camera, NBA Action (Karl Malone)	.05
384	European Imports (Vlade Divac, Sarunas Marciulionis)	.05
385	Magic Johnson, Michael Jordan	1.00
386	Stay In School (Johnny Newman)	.05
387	Stay In School (Dell Curry)	.05
388	Patrick Ewing (DFO)	.05
389	Don't Foul Out (Isiah Thomas)	.05
390	*Derrick Coleman*	.50
391	*Gary Payton*	.75
392	*Mahmoud Abdul-Rauf*	.50
393	*Dennis Scott*	.50
394	*Kendall Gill*	.25
395	*Felton Spencer*	.10
396	*Lionel Simmons*	.10
397	*Bo Kimble*	.10
398	*Willie Burton*	.10
399	*Rumeal Robinson*	.10
400	*Tyrone Hill*	.30
401	Tim McCormick	.05
402	Sidney Moncrief	.05
403	Johnny Newman	.05
404	Dennis Hopson	.05
405	Clif Levingston	.05
406	Danny Ferry	.05
407	Alex English	.05
408	Lafayette Lever	.05
409	Rodney McCray	.05
410	Mike Dunleavy (C)	.05
411	Orlando Woolridge	.05
412	Joe Wolf	.05
413	Tree Rollins	.05
414	Kenny Smith	.05
415	Sam Perkins	.05
416	Terry Teagle	.05
417	Frank Brickowski	.05
418	Danny Schayes	.05
419	Scott Brooks	.05
420	Reggie Theus	.05
421	Greg Grant	.05
422	Paul Westhead (C)	.05
423	Greg Kite	.05
424	Manute Bol	.05
425	Rickey Green	.05
426	Ed Nealy	.05
427	Danny Ainge	.05
428	Bobby Hansen	.05
429	Eric Leckner	.05
430	Rory Sparrow	.05
431	Bill Wennington	.05
432	Paul Pressey	.05
433	David Greenwood	.05
434	Mark McNamara	.05
435	Sidney Green	.05
436	Dave Corzine	.05
437	Jeff Malone	.05
438	Pervis Ellison	.05
439	Checklist	.05
440	Checklist	.05
1	David Robinson	1.50
2	Vlade Divac	1.50
3	Tim Hardaway	1.50
4	Pooh Richardson	1.50
5	Sherman Douglas	1.50

1990-91 Hoops All-Star Panels

The four panels, each one consisting of six 2-1/2" x 3-1/2" cards, were distributed one per game program at the 1991 All-Star Game. Cards with players from the East squad have a blue star and stripe on the front while West All-Star card fronts have a red star and border. The card backs feature stats and bio information and are unnumbered.

		MT
Complete Set (5):		25.00
Common Player:		4.00
Series 1 Poly Pack (15):		1.00
Series 1 Poly Wax Box (36):		19.00
Series 2 Poly Pack (15):		.85
Series 2 Poly Wax Box (36):		15.00
(1)	Panel 1 (Michael Jordan, James Worthy, Isiah Thomas, A.C. Green, Reggie Miller, Hakeem Olajuwon)	10.00
(2)	Panel 2 (Karl Malone, Magic Johnson, Patrick Ewing, David Robinson, Michael Jordan, Charles Barkley)	10.00
(3)	Panel 3 (Kevin McHale, Fat Lever, Joe Dumars, Rolando Blackman, Robert Parish, Kevin Johnson)	4.00
(4)	Panel 4 (Dominique Wilkins, David Robinson, Dennis Rodman, Chris Mullin, Scottie Pippen, Tom Chambers)	7.00
(5)	Patrick Ewing, Magic Johnson, Larry Bird, John Stockton, Charles Barkley, Clyde Drexler	9.00

1990-91 Hoops Announcers

The 57-card set features announcers from various radio and television stations and production of each card was limited between 250 and 1,000. The cards were given to the announcers to act as business cards. The card fronts feature a silver border and the backs contain the broadcaster's bio information.

		MT
Complete Set (58):		1600.
Common Player:		30.00
1	NBC MSG Network (Marv Albert)	60.00
2	KPIX (Steve Albert)	30.00
3	MSG (John Andarise)	30.00
4	WXIN-TV (Jerry Baker)	30.00
5	KPIX-TV (Jim Barnett)	40.00
6	Prism (Jim Barniak)	30.00
7	TBS (Rick Barry)	125.00
8	KSTU (Ron Boone)	40.00
9	WNDE (Mark Boyle)	30.00
10	TNT Sports (Hubie Brown)	40.00
11	KJR (Kevin Calabro)	30.00
12	WKCF (Harry Caray)	40.00
13	TBS Superstation (Skip Caray)	40.00
14	TNT Sports (Doug Collins)	50.00
15	PIA NBA Radio (Chet Coppock)	40.00
16	NBC (Bob Costas)	80.00
17	WGN (Jim Durham)	30.00
18	NBC (Dick Enberg)	40.00
19	KTRH (Jim Foley)	30.00
20	NBC, KTLA (Mike Fratello)	40.00
21	KFBK (Gary Gerould)	30.00
22	TNT Sports (Jack Givens)	40.00
23	SportsChannel (Mike Gorman)	30.00
24	T-Wolves TV (Tom Hanneman)	30.00
25	WDGY (Kevin Harlan)	30.00
26	WKBD (Dick Harter)	30.00
27	TNT (Fred Hickman)	50.00
28	WGST (Steve Holman)	30.00
29	WOAI (Jay Howard)	30.00
30	WTMJ (Jim Irwin)	30.00
31	KWGN (Dan Issel)	100.00
32	TNT Sports (Ernie Johnson)	40.00
33	NBC, Blazer Broadcasting (Steve Jones)	40.00
34	WGN (Johnny Kerr)	50.00
35	KOA (Jeff Kingery)	30.00
36	KLTA (Ralph Lawler)	30.00
37	PIA (Joe McConnell)	30.00
38	KTAR (L. Allen McCoy)	30.00
39	NBC Sports (Jonathan Miller)	30.00
40	TNT Sports (Bob Neal)	40.00
41	WEEI (Glenn Ordway)	30.00
42	HTS (Michael Proctor)	30.00
43	SportsChannel (Ed Randall)	30.00
44	KEX (Mike Rice)	30.00
45	NBC (Pat Riley)	80.00
46	NBC Sports (Andrew Rosenberg)	30.00
47	NBC Sports (Tommy Roy)	30.00
48	KFBK (Tim Roye)	30.00
49	TNT Sports (Play-by play, Craig Sager)	40.00
50	TNT Sports (Biography, Craig Sager)	40.00
51	KEX (Bill Schonely)	30.00
52	WTOP (Charles Slowes)	30.00
53	WWNZ (David Steele)	30.00
54	TNT (Hannah Storm)	50.00
55	TNT Sports (Ron Thulin)	30.00
56	WCCB-TV (Gerry Vaillancourt)	30.00
57	TNT Sports (Pete Wieren)	30.00
58	HSE (William Worrell)	30.00

1990-91 Hoops CollectABooks

The mini books (2-1/2" x 3-3/8") were issued in four different boxes with each box containing 12 different player books. Each book has eight pages with different color photos and bio and stat information. The Detroit Pistons booklet was available to collectors through an offer in the second series of 1990-91 Hoops packs.

		MT
Complete Sets (48):		12.00
Common Player:		.10
1	Sam Bowie	.15
2	Tom Chambers	.15
3	Clyde Drexler	1.00
4	Michael Jordan	4.00
5	Karl Malone	2.00
6	Kevin McHale	.40
7	Reggie Miller	.75
8	Mark Price	.15
9	Mitch Richmond	.60
10	Doc Rivers	.10
11	Rony Seikaly	.10
12	Wayman Tisdale	.15
13	Charles Barkley	1.25
14	Terry Cummings	.15
15	Patrick Ewing	.75
16	Terry Porter	.10
17	Danny Manning	.25
18	Larry Nance	.15
19	Robert Parish	.25
20	Chuck Person	.15
21	Ricky Pierce	.10
22	John Stockton	1.50
23	Isiah Thomas	.40
24	Spud Webb	.15
25	Michael Adams	.10
26	Muggsy Bogues	.25
27	Joe Dumars	.25
28	Hersey Hawkins	.15
29	Magic Johnson	1.25
30	Bernard King	.25
31	Chris Mullin	.50
32	Charles Oakley	.15
33	Alvin Robertson	.10
34	David Robinson	1.25
35	Dominique Wilkins	.75
36	Buck Williams	.15
37	Larry Bird	2.00
38	Rolando Blackman	.15
39	Mark Eaton	.10
40	Kevin Johnson	.40
41	J.R. Reid	.10
42	Xavier McDaniel	.10
43	Hakeem Olajuwon	1.25
44	Scottie Pippen	1.25
45	Pooh Richardson	.10
46	Dennis Rodman	1.25
47	Charles Smith	.10
48	James Worthy	.25
XX	Detroit Pistons	.25

1990-91 Hoops Team Night Sheets

The team sheets and cards were distributed by Hoops in early 1991 and each team set was individually sponsored. Fans and collectors attending NBA Hoops Nights received either a 12- card perforated sheet or the cut individual cards (Utah Jazz). The only team not participating in the giveaway was the Sacramento Kings. The cards parallel the design and format of the base set, except for the players listed with an asterisk.

		MT
Complete Set (26):		400.00
Common Player:		3.00
1	Atlanta Hawks - Del Taco (John Battle, Jon Koncak, Moses Malone, Tim McCormick, Sidney Moncrief, Doc Rivers, Rumeal Robinson, Spud Webb, Dominique Wilkins, Kevin Willis)	6.00
2	Boston Celtics - no sponsor (Larry Bird, Chris Ford CO, Kevin Gamble, Joe Kleine, Reggie Lewis, Kevin McHale, Robert Parish, Ed Pinckney, Brian Shaw)	10.00
3	Charlotte Hornets - Pizza Hut (Muggsy Bogues, Rex Chapman, Dell Curry, Kenny Gattison, Mike Gminski, Randolph Keys, Gene Littles CO, Johnny Newman, Robert Reid, Kelly Tripucka)	6.00
4	Chicago Bulls - Kodak/Osco Drugs 25th Anniversary (B.J. Armstrong, Bill Cartwright, Horace Grant, Horace Grant, Scottie Pippen, Dennis Hopson, Michael Jordan, Stacey King, Cliff Levingston, John Paxson, Will Perdue, Scottie	12.00
5	Cleveland Cavaliers - Coca Cola (Winston Bennett, Chucky Brown, Brad Daugherty, Craig Ehlo, Danny Ferry, Steve Kerr, Larry Nance, Mark Price, Len Wilkens CO, Hot Rod Williams)	6.00
6	Dallas Mavericks - Combos (Richie Adubato CO, Alex English, Rolando Blackman, Brad Davis, James Donaldson, Derek Harper, Fat Lever, Rodney McCray, Roy Tarpley, Randy White, Herb Williams)	10.00
7	Denver Nuggets - Pepsi/Pizza Hut (Michael Adams, Walter Davis, Bill Hanzlik, Chris Jackson, Jerome Lane, Todd Lichti, Blair Rasmussen, Paul Westhead CO, Joe Wolf, Orlando Woolridge)	6.00
8	Detroit Pistons - F and M Foods (Mark Aguirre, William Bedford, Chuck Daly CO, Joe Dumars, James Edwards, Scott Hastings, Vinnie Johnson, Bill Laimbeer, Dennis Rodman, John Salley, Isiah Thomas)	10.00
9	Golden State Warriors - Round Table Pizza (Tim Hardaway, Rod Higgins, Tyrone Hill, Sarunas Marciulionis, Chris Mullin, Don Nelson CO, Jim Petersen, Mitch Richmond, Mike Smrek, Tom Tolbert)	6.00
10	Houston Rockets - Coke/Phar-Mor (Don Chaney CO, Sleepy Floyd, Buck Johnson, Vernon Maxwell, Hakeem Olajuwon, Kenny Smith, Larry Smith, Otis Thorpe)	8.00
11	Indiana Pacers - Combos (Greg Dreiling, Vern Fleming, George McCloud, Reggie Miller, Chuck Person, Mike Sanders, Detlef Schrempf, Rik Smits, LaSalle Thompson, Randy Wittman)	6.00
12	Los Angeles Clippers - Combos (Benoit Benjamin, Winston Garland, Tom Garrick, Gary Grant, Ron Harper, Bo Kimble, Danny Manning, Jeff Martin, Ken Norman, Mike Schuler CO, Charles Smith)	5.00
13	Los Angeles Lakers - Taco Bell (Vlade Divac S2, Mike Dunleavy CO S3, A.C. Green S2, Magic Johnson S3, Sam Perkins S2, Byron Scott S1, Terry Teagle S1, Mychal Thompson S3, James Worthy S1)	7.00
14	Miami Heat - Stay in School (Willie Burton, Sherman Douglas, Kevin Edwards, Grant Long, Glen Rice, Ron Rothstein CO, Rony Seikaly, Jon Sundvold, Billy Thompson)	6.00
15	Milwaukee Bucks (Greg Anderson, Frank Brickowski, Jeff Grayer, Del Harris, Jay Humphries, Frank Kornet, Brad Lohaus, Ricky Pierce, Fred Roberts, Alvin Robertson, Dan Schayes, Jack Sikma)	6.00
16	Minnesota Timberwolves - Burger King (Randy Breuer S3, Scott Brooks S4, Tony Campbell S3, Tyrone Corbin S4, Sam Mitchell S2, Tod Murphy S2, Bill Musselman CO S1, Pooh Richardson S1)	5.00
17	New Jersey Nets - Charles Chips (Mookie Blaylock, Sam Bowie, Derrick Coleman, Lester Conner, Bill Fitch CO, Derrick Gervin, Jack Haley, Roy Hinson, Chris Morris, Reggie Theus)	6.00
18A	New York Knicks - Coca-Cola (Maurice Cheeks, Patrick Ewing, Stuart Gray, Mark Jackson, Charles Oakley, Trent Tucker, Kiki Vandeweghe, Kenny Walker, Eddie Lee Wilkins, Gerald Wilkins)	18.00
18B	New York Knicks - Coca-Cola (Maurice Cheeks, Patrick Ewing, Mark Jackson, Charles Oakley, Brian Quinnett, John Starks, Trent Tucker, Kiki Vandeweghe, Kenny Walker, Eddie Lee Wilkins, Gerald Wilkins)	8.00
19	Orlando Magic - Gooding's (Mark Acres, Nick Anderson, Michael Ansley, Terry Catledge, Matt Guokas CO, Greg Kite, Jerry Reynolds, Dennis Scott, Scott Skiles, Otis Smith, Sam Vincent)	7.00
20	Philadelphia 76ers - Kodak (Ron Anderson, Charles Barkley, Manute Bol, Johnny Dawkins, Armon Gilliam, Hersey Hawkins, Jim Lynam, Rick Mahorn)	7.00
21	Phoenix Suns - Diet Pepsi (Kenny Battle, Tom Chambers, Cotton Fitzsimmons CO, Jeff Hornacek, Kevin Johnson, Dan Majerle, Ed Nealy, Tim Perry, Kurt Rambis, Mark West)	6.00
22	Portland Trail Blazers - No sponsor (Rick Adelman CO, Danny Ainge, Mark Bryant, Wayne Cooper, Clyde Drexler, Kevin Duckworth, Jerome Kersey, Drazen Petrovic, Terry Porter, Cliff Robinson, Buck Williams, Danny Young)	25.00
23	San Antonio Spurs - Church's Chicken 89-90 Midwest Div. Champs (Willie Anderson, Larry Brown CO, Terry Cummings, Sean Elliott, David Greenwood, Paul Pressey, David Robinson, Rod Strickland, The Coyote - Mascot, Brad Townsend,	8.00
24A	Seattle Supersonics - Coke (Dana Barros, Michael Cage, Quintin Dailey, Dale Ellis, Eddie Johnson, Shawn Kemp, Derrick McKey, Nate McMillan, Gary Payton, Olden Polynice, Sedale Threatt)	6.00
24B	Seattle Supersonics - Combos (Dana Barros, Michael Cage, Quintin Dailey, Dale Ellis, Eddie Johnson, Shawn Kemp, Derrick McKey, Nate McMillan, Gary Payton, Olden Polynice, Sedale Threatt)	6.00
24C	Seattle Supersonics - Coke (Dana Barros, Benoit Benjamin, Michael Cage, Quintin Dailey, Eddie Johnson, Shawn Kemp, Derrick McKey, Nate McMillan, Gary Payton, Ricky Pierce, Sedale Threatt)	6.00
24D	Seattle Supersonics - Combos (Dana Barros, Benoit Benjamin, Michael Cage, Quintin Dailey, Eddie Johnson, Shawn Kemp, Derrick McKey, Nate McMillan, Gary Payton, Ricky Pierce, Sedale Threatt)	6.00
25	Utah Jazz - Colgate (Thurl Bailey, Mike Brown, Mark Eaton, Blue Edwards, Darrell Griffith, Jeff Malone, Karl Malone, Delaney Rudd, Jerry Sloan, John Stockton)	10.00
26	Washington Bullets (Mark Alarie, Pervis Ellison, Harvey Grant, Tom Hammonds, Charles Jones, Bernard King, Wes Unseld CO, Darrell Walker, John Williams)	7.00

1991 Hoops Superstars

This is the second straight set NBA Hoops made available through the Sears catalog. It's identical to the 1990-91 regular set except the card numbers are different, the card backs are white (not yellow) and the color on the front is gold (not silver).

		MT
Complete Set (100):		35.00
Common Player:		.05
1	Moses Malone	.50
2	Doc Rivers	.50
3	Spud Webb	.50
4	Dominique Wilkins	1.50
5	Larry Bird	6.00
6	Reggie Lewis	.50

7	Kevin McHale	1.50
8	Robert Parish	1.00
9	Brian Shaw	.25
10	Muggsy Bogues	.75
11	Johnny Newman	.15
12	Horace Grant	1.00
13	Michael Jordan	12.00
14	Scottie Pippen	3.50
15	Brad Daugherty	.15
16	Craig Ehlo	.25
17	Larry Nance	.75
18	Mark Price	.75
19	John Williams	.10
20	Rolando Blackman	.50
21	James Donaldson	.15
22	Derek Harper	.40
23	Fat Lever	.15
24	Roy Tarpley	.10
25	Michael Adams	.15
26	Orlando Woolridge	.15
27	Joe Dumars	1.00
28	Bill Laimbeer	.75
29	Vinnie Johnson	.15
30	Dennis Rodman	2.00
31	Isiah Thomas	1.50
32	Chris Mullin	1.25
33	Tim Hardaway	1.25
34	Mitch Richmond	1.25
35	Eric Floyd	.15
36	Akeem Olajuwon	3.00
37	Kenny Smith	.50
38	Otis Thorpe	.15
39	Reggie Miller	1.50
40	Chuck Person	.10
41	Detlef Schrempf	.75
42	Danny Manning	.50
43	Ken Norman	.15
44	Ron Harper	.50
45	Charles Smith	.10
46	Vlade Divac	.50
47	A.C. Green	.75
48	Magic Johnson	5.00
49	Byron Scott	.50
50	James Worthy	1.50
51	Sam Perkins	.50
52	Rony Seikaly	.20
53	Sherman Douglas	.20
54	Glen Rice	1.50
55	Jay Humphries	.15
56	Alvin Robertson	.15
57	Jack Sikma	.10
58	Tony Campbell	.15
59	Tyrone Corbin	.15
60	Pooh Richardson	.10
61	Roy Hinson	.15
62	Chris Morris	.15
63	Reggie Theus	.50
64	Maurice Cheeks	.50
65	Patrick Ewing	3.00
66	Mark Jackson	.50
67	Charles Oakley	.50
68	Nick Anderson	.15
69	Terry Catledge	.15
70	Scott Skiles	.30
71	Charles Barkley	3.00
72	Johnny Dawkins	.15
73	Hersey Hawkins	.20
74	Rick Mahorn	.15
75	Tom Chambers	.50
76	Jeff Hornacek	.50
77	Kevin Johnson	.50
78	Dan Majerle	.50
79	Mark West	.15
80	Clyde Drexler	3.00
81	Terry Porter	.50
82	Jerome Kersey	.50
83	Buck Williams	.50
84	Antoine Carr	.15
85	Wayman Tisdale	.10
86	Willie Anderson	.15
87	Terry Cummings	.50
88	Paul Pressey	.15
89	David Robinson	3.00
90	Rod Strickland	.50
91	Michael Cage	.15
92	Shawn Kemp	1.50
93	Derrick McKey	.15
94	Thurl Bailey	.15
95	Jeff Malone	.10
96	Karl Malone	4.00
97	John Stockton	4.00
98	Harvey Grant	.15
99	Bernard King	.50
100	Darrell Walker	.15

1991 Hoops Larry Bird Video

The 2-1/2" x 3-1/2" card came with the "Larry Bird - Basketball Legend" video and featured the former Indiana star shooting the ball on the front with a parquet-floor border. The back shows an outline of the state of Indiana with bio information.

		MT
Complete Set (1):		15.00
Common Player:		15.00
NNO	Larry Bird	15.00

1991 Hoops Prototypes

These prototypes, stamped as such on the card back, preview NBA Hoops' 1991-92 regular basketball set. They use the same design format as the regular set, and the card numbers are the same.

		MT
Complete Set (10):		40.00
Common Player:		4.00
3	Sidney Moncrief	5.00
9	Larry Bird	20.00
18	Tyrone Bogues	5.00
120	Alvin Robertson	4.00
135	Chris Dudley	4.00
142	Charles Oakley	5.00
150	Jerry Reynolds	4.00
155	Armon Gilliam	4.00
204	Sedale Threatt	4.00
210	Jeff Malone	5.00

1991 Hoops Prototypes 00

These prototypes can be distinguished from the other 1991 promo cards by the different numbering system on the card backs. The cards are the same design style as the regular 1991-92 NBA Hoops cards and promos, except the numbers have a "00" prefix. They are labeled on the backs as being prototypes.

		MT
Complete Set (10):		200.00
Common Player:		20.00
001	Clyde Drexler	15.00
002	Patrick Ewing	15.00
003	Magic Johnson	20.00
004	Michael Jordan	60.00
005	Karl Malone	20.00
006	Hakeem Olajuwon	20.00
007	Charles Barkley (AS)	35.00
008	Magic Johnson (AS)	45.00
009	Karl Malone (AS)	25.00
0010	Dominique Wilkins (AS)	20.00

1991-92 Hoops

Card fronts feature color action photos with the team logo in the team's color. Backs have a head shot plus collegiate and professional stats. Just over one million sets were made. Several subsets were also produced: Inside Stuff (IS), Milestones (M) and NBA Yearbook (YB). An unnumbered James Naismith card (CC1) and a Centennial Quiz card were available as send-aways and are listed at the end of the checklist. Series II had Olympic Dream Team cards and an unnumbered mail-in card, Head of the Class (10,000 were made, individually numbered.) An unnumbered USA Basketball gold-bordered card was also inserted into wax packs. A special Collectors Tin set, which contained both series and two unnumbered US Olympic Dream Team cards, was also made. The Tin set had subsets - Supreme Court (SC), Active Leaders (AL), Art cards (Art) and Stay in School (SS).

		MT
Complete Set (590):		25.00
Complete Series 1 (330):		10.00
Complete Series 2 (260):		15.00
Common Player:		.05
Minor Stars:		.10
Series 1 Pack (15):		.40
Series 1 Wax Box (36):		10.00
Series 2 Pack (15):		.50
Series 2 Wax Box (36):		15.00
1	John Battle	.05
2	Moses Malone	.10
3	Sidney Moncrief	.05
4	Glenn Rivers	.05
5	Rumeal Robinson	.05
6	Spud Webb	.05
7	Dominique Wilkins	.10
8	Kevin Willis	.05
9	Larry Bird	.75
10	*Dee Brown*	.15
11	Kevin Gamble	.05
12	Joe Kleine	.05
13	Reggie Lewis	.05
14	Kevin McHale	.10
15	Robert Parish	.10
16	Ed Pinckney	.05
17	Brian Shaw	.05
18	Muggsy Bogues	.05
19	Rex Chapman	.05
20	Dell Curry	.05
21	Kendall Gill	.10
22	Mike Gminski	.05
23	Johnny Newman	.05
24	J.R. Reid	.05
25	Kelly Tripucka	.05
26	B.J. Armstrong	.10
27	Bill Cartwright	.05
28	Horace Grant	.20
29	Craig Hodges	.05
30	Michael Jordan	2.50
31	Stacey King	.05
32	Cliff Levingston	.05
33	John Paxson	.05
34	Scottie Pippen	.50
35	Chucky Brown	.05
36	Brad Daugherty	.05
37	Craig Ehlo	.05
38	Danny Ferry	.05
39	Larry Nance	.05
40	Mark Price	.10
41	Darnell Valentine	.05
42	John Williams	.05
43	Rolando Blackman	.05
44	Brad Davis	.05
45	James Donaldson	.05
46	Derek Harper	.05
47	Fat Lever	.05
48	Rodney McCray	.05
49	Roy Tarpley	.05
50	Herb Williams	.05
51	Michael Adams	.05
52	Mahmoud Abdul-Rauf	.15
53	Jerome Lane	.05
54	Todd Lichti	.05
55	Blair Rasmussen	.05
56	Reggie Williams	.05
57	Joe Wolf	.05
58	Orlando Woolridge	.05
59	Mark Aguirre	.05
60	Joe Dumars	.10
61	James Edwards	.05
62	Vinnie Johnson	.05
63	Bill Laimbeer	.05
64	Dennis Rodman	.75
65	John Salley	.05
66	Isiah Thomas	.20
67	Tim Hardaway	.10
68	Rod Higgins	.05
69	Tyrone Hill	.10
70	Alton Lister	.05
71	Sarunas Marciulionis	.05
72	Chris Mullin	.10
73	Mitch Richmond	.15
74	Tom Tolbert	.05
75	Eric Floyd	.05
76	Buck Johnson	.05
77	Vernon Maxwell	.05
78	Hakeem Olajuwon	.50
79	Kenny Smith	.05
80	Larry Smith	.05
81	Otis Thorpe	.05
82	David Wood	.05
83	Vern Fleming	.05
84	Reggie Miller	.20
85	Chuck Person	.05
86	Mike Sanders	.05
87	Detlef Schrempf	.05
88	Rik Smits	.10
89	LaSalle Thompson	.05
90	Michael Williams	.05
91	Winston Garland	.05
92	Gary Grant	.05
93	Ron Harper	.05
94	Danny Manning	.10
95	Jeff Martin	.05
96	Ken Norman	.05
97	Olden Polynice	.05
98	Charles Smith	.05
99	Vlade Divac	.10
100	A.C. Green	.05
101	Magic Johnson	.50
102	Sam Perkins	.05
103	Byron Scott	.05
104	Terry Teagle	.05
105	Mychal Thompson	.05
106	James Worthy	.05
107	Willie Burton	.05
108	Bimbo Coles	.05
109	Terry Davis	.05
110	Sherman Douglas	.05
111	Kevin Edwards	.05
112	Alec Kessler	.05
113	Glen Rice	.10
114	Rony Seikaly	.05
115	Frank Brickowski	.05
116	Dale Ellis	.05
117	Jay Humphries	.05
118	Brad Lohaus	.05
119	Fred Roberts	.05
120	Alvin Robertson	.05
121	Dan Schayes	.05
122	Jack Sikma	.05
123	Randy Breuer	.05
124	Tony Campbell	.05
125	Tyrone Corbin	.05
126	Gerald Glass	.05
127	Sam Mitchell	.05
128	Tod Murphy	.05
129	Pooh Richardson	.05
130	Felton Spencer	.05
131	Mookie Blaylock	.05
132	Sam Bowie	.05
133	Jud Buechler	.05
134	Derrick Coleman	.10
135	Chris Dudley	.05
136	Chris Morris	.05
137	Drazen Petrovic	.05
138	Reggie Theus	.05
139	Maurice Cheeks	.05
140	Patrick Ewing	.25
141	Mark Jackson	.05
142	Charles Oakley	.05
143	Trent Tucker	.05
144	Kiki Vandeweghe	.05
145	Kenny Walker	.05
146	Gerald Wilkins	.05
147	Nick Anderson	.10
148	Michael Ansley	.05
149	Terry Catledge	.05
150	Jerry Reynolds	.05
151	Dennis Scott	.10
152	Scott Skiles	.05
153	Otis Smith	.05
154	Sam Vincent	.05
155	Ron Anderson	.05
156	Charles Barkley	.50
157	Manute Bol	.05
158	Johnny Dawkins	.05
159	Armon Gilliam	.05
160	Rickey Green	.05
161	Hersey Hawkins	.05
162	Rick Mahorn	.05
163	Tom Chambers	.05
164	Jeff Hornacek	.05
165	Kevin Johnson	.10
166	Andrew Lang	.05
167	Dan Majerle	.05
168	Xavier McDaniel	.05
169	Kurt Rambis	.05
170	Mark West	.05
171	Danny Ainge	.05
172	Mark Bryant	.05
173	Walter Davis	.05
174	Clyde Drexler	.25
175	Kevin Duckworth	.05
176	Jerome Kersey	.05
177	Terry Porter	.05
178	Cliff Robinson	.10
179	Buck Williams	.05
180	Anthony Bonner	.05
181	Antoine Carr	.05
182	Duane Causwell	.05
183	Bobby Hansen	.05
184	Travis Mays	.05
185	Lionel Simmons	.05
186	Rory Sparrow	.05
187	Wayman Tisdale	.05
188	Willie Anderson	.05
189	Terry Cummings	.05
190	Sean Elliott	.05
191	Sidney Green	.05
192	David Greenwood	.05
193	Paul Pressey	.05
194	David Robinson	.50
195	Dwayne Schintzius	.05
196	Rod Strickland	.05
197	Benoit Benjamin	.05
198	Michael Cage	.05
199	Eddie Johnson	.05
200	Shawn Kemp	.75
201	Derrick McKey	.05
202	Gary Payton	.25
203	Ricky Pierce	.05
204	Sedale Threatt	.05
205	Thurl Bailey	.05
206	Mike Brown	.05
207	Mark Eaton	.05
208	Blue Edwards	.05
209	Darrell Griffith	.05
210	Jeff Malone	.05
211	Karl Malone	.25
212	John Stockton	.25
213	Ledell Eackles	.05
214	Pervis Ellison	.05
215	A.J. English	.05
216	Harvey Grant	.05
217	Charles Jones	.05
218	Bernard King	.05
219	Darrell Walker	.05
220	John Williams	.05
221	Bob Weiss	.05
222	Chris Ford	.05
223	Gene Littles	.05
224	Phil Jackson	.05
225	Lenny Wilkens	.05
226	Richie Adubato	.05
227	Paul Westhead	.05
228	Chuck Daly	.05
229	Don Nelson	.05
230	Don Chaney	.05
231	Bob Hill	.05
232	Mike Schuler	.05
233	Mike Dunleavy	.05
234	Kevin Loughery	.05
235	Del Harris	.05
236	Jimmy Rodgers	.05
237	Bill Fitch	.05
238	Pat Riley	.05
239	Matt Guokas	.05
240	Jim Lynam	.05
241	Cotton Fitzsimmons	.05
242	Rick Adelman	.05
243	Dick Motta	.05
244	Larry Brown	.05
245	K.C. Jones	.05
246	Jerry Sloan	.05
247	Wes Unseld	.05
248	Charles Barkley (AS)	.25
249	Brad Daugherty (AS)	.05
250	Joe Dumars (AS)	.05
251	Patrick Ewing (AS)	.10
252	Hersey Hawkins (AS)	.05
253	Michael Jordan (AS)	1.25
254	Bernard King (AS)	.05
255	Kevin McHale (AS)	.05
256	Robert Parish (AS)	.05
257	Ricky Pierce (AS)	.05
258	Alvin Robertson (AS)	.05
259	Dominique Wilkins	.10
260	Coach (Chris Ford) (AS)	.05
261	Tom Chambers (AS)	.05
262	Clyde Drexler (AS)	.10
263	Kevin Duckworth (AS)	.05
264	Tim Hardaway (AS)	.05
265	Kevin Johnson (AS)	.05
266	Magic Johnson (AS)	.25
267	Karl Malone (AS)	.10
268	Chris Mullin (AS)	.05
269	Terry Porter (AS)	.05
270	David Robinson (AS)	.25
271	John Stockton (AS)	.10
272	James Worthy (AS)	.05
273	Coach (Rick Adelman) (AS)	.05
274	Atlanta	.05
275	Boston	.05
276	Charlotte	.05
277	Chicago	.05
278	Cleveland	.05
279	Dallas	.05
280	Denver	.05
281	Detroit	.05
282	Golden State	.05
283	Houston	.05
284	Indiana	.05
285	LA Clippers	.05
286	LA Lakers	.05
288	Milwaukee	.05
289	Minnesota	.05
290	New Jersey	.05
291	New York	.05
292	Orlando	.05
293	Philadelphia	.05
294	Phoenix	.05
295	Portland	.05
296	Sacramento	.05
297	San Antonio	.05
298	Seattle	.05
299	Utah	.05
300	Washington	.05
301	Centennial	.05
302	Kevin Johnson (IS)	.05
303	Reggie Miller (IS)	.10
304	Hakeem Olajuwon (IS)	.05
305	Robert Parish (IS)	.05
306	Scoring Leaders (Michael Jordan, Karl Malone)	1.00
307	3-Point Field Goal Percentage (Jim Les, Trent Tucker)	.05
308	Free Throw Percentage (Reggie Miller, Jeff Malone)	.10
309	Blocks (David Robinson, Hakeem Olajuwon)	.40
310	Steals (Alvin Robertson, John Stockton)	.10
311	Rebounds (David Robinson, Dennis Rodman)	.50
312	Assists (Magic Johnson, John Stockton)	.25
313	Field Goal Percentage (Robert Parish, Buck Williams)	.05
314	Larry Bird (MS)	.40
315	Alex English, Moses Malone (MS M)	.05
316	Magic Johnson (MS)	.25
317	Michael Jordan (MS)	1.25
318	Moses Malone (M)	.05
319	Larry Bird (YB)	.40
320	Maurice Cheeks (YB)	.05
321	Magic Johnson (YB)	.25
322	Bernard King (YB)	.05
323	Moses Malone (YB)	.05
324	Robert Parish (YB)	.05
325	All-Star Jam	.05
326	All-Star Jam	.05
327	David Robinson	.30
328	Checklist #1	.05
329	Checklist #2	.05
330	Checklist #3	.05
331	Maurice Cheeks	.05
332	Duane Ferrell	.05
333	Jon Koncak	.05
334	Gary Leonard	.05
335	Travis Mays	.05
336	Blair Rasmussen	.05
337	Alexander Volkov	.05
338	John Bagley	.05
339	Rickey Green	.05
340	Derek Smith	.05
341	Stojko Vrankovic	.05
342	Anthony Frederick	.05
343	Kenny Gattison	.05
344	Eric Leckner	.05
345	Will Perdue	.05
346	*Scott Williams*	.10
347	John Battle	.05
348	Winston Bennett	.05
349	Henry James	.05
350	Steve Kerr	.05
351	John Morton	.05
352	Terry Davis	.05
353	Randy White	.05
354	Greg Anderson	.05
355	Anthony Cook	.05
356	Walter Davis	.05
357	Winston Garland	.05
358	Scott Hastings	.05
359	Marcus Liberty	.05
360	William Bedford	.05
361	Lance Blanks	.05
362	Brad Sellers	.05
363	Darrell Walker	.05
364	Orlando Woolridge	.05
365	*Vincent Askew*	.10
366	*Mario Elie*	.25
367	Jim Petersen	.05
368	*Matt Bullard*	.10
369	Gerald Henderson	.05
370	Dave Jamerson	.05
371	Wayne Rollins	.05
372	Greg Dreiling	.05
373	George McCloud	.15
374	Ken Williams	.05
375	Randy Wittman	.05
376	Tony Brown	.05
377	Lanard Copeland	.05
378	James Edwards	.05
379	Bo Kimble	.05
380	Glenn Rivers	.05
381	Loy Vaught	.05
382	*Elden Campbell*	.15
383	Jack Haley	.05
384	Tony Smith	.05
385	Sedale Threatt	.05
386	*Keith Askins*	.15
387	Grant Long	.05
388	Alan Ogg	.05
389	Jon Sundvold	.05
390	Lester Conner	.05
391	Jeff Grayer	.05
392	Steve Henson	.05
393	Larry Krystkowiak	.05
394	Moses Malone	.10
395	Scott Brooks	.05
396	Tellis Frank	.05
397	Doug West	.05
398	*Rafael Addison*	.10
399	Dave Feitl	.05
400	Tate George	.05
401	*Terry Mills*	.20
402	Tim McCormick	.05
403	Xavier McDaniel	.05
404	*Anthony Mason*	.50
405	Brian Quinnett	.05
406	*John Starks*	.50
407	Mark Acres	.05
408	Greg Kite	.05
409	Jeff Turner	.05
410	Morlon Wiley	.05
411	Dave Hoppen	.05
412	Brian Oliver	.05
413	Kenny Payne	.05
414	Charles Shackleford	.05
415	Mitchell Wiggins	.05
416	Jayson Williams	.05
417	Cedric Ceballos	.30
418	*Negele Knight*	.10
419	Andrew Lang	.05
420	Jerrod Mustaf	.05
421	Ed Nealy	.05
422	Tim Perry	.05
423	Alaa Abdelnaby	.05
424	Wayne Cooper	.05
425	Danny Young	.05
426	Dennis Hopson	.05
427	Les Jepsen	.05
428	Jim Les	.05
429	Mitch Richmond	.15
430	Dwayne Schintzius	.05
431	Spud Webb	.05
432	Jud Buechler	.05
433	Antoine Carr	.05
434	Tom Garrick	.05
435	*Sean Higgins*	.10
436	Avery Johnson	.05
437	Tony Massenburg	.05
438	Dana Barros	.05
439	Quintin Dailey	.05
440	Bart Kofoed	.05
441	Nate McMillan	.05
442	Delaney Rudd	.05
443	Michael Adams	.05
444	Mark Alarie	.05
445	Greg Foster	.05
446	Tom Hammonds	.05
447	Andre Turner	.05
448	David Wingate	.05
449	Dominique Wilkins	.10
450	Kevin Willis (SC)	.05
451	Larry Bird (SC)	.40
452	Robert Parish (SC)	.05
453	Rex Chapman (SC)	.05
454	Kendall Gill (SC)	.05
455	Michael Jordan (SC)	1.25
456	Scottie Pippen (SC)	.25
457	Brad Daugherty (SC)	.05
458	Larry Nance (SC)	.05
459	Rolando Blackman (SC)	.05
460	Derek Harper (SC)	.05
461	Mahmoud Abdul-Rauf (SC)	.10
462	Todd Lichti (SC)	.05
463	Joe Dumars (SC)	.10
464	Isiah Thomas (SC)	.10
465	Tim Hardaway (SC)	.05
466	Chris Mullin (SC)	.05
467	Hakeem Olajuwon	.25
468	Otis Thorpe (SC)	.05
469	Reggie Miller (SC)	.10
470	Detlef Schrempf (SC)	.05
471	Ron Harper (SC)	.05
472	Charles Smith (SC)	.05
473	Magic Johnson (SC)	.25
474	James Worthy (SC)	.05
475	Sherman Douglas (SC)	.05
476	Rony Seikaly (SC)	.05
477	Jay Humphries (SC)	.05
478	Alvin Robertson (SC)	.05
479	Tyrone Corbin (SC)	.05
480	Pooh Richardson (SC)	.05
481	Sam Bowie (SC)	.05
482	Derrick Coleman (SC)	.05
483	Patrick Ewing (SC)	.10
484	Charles Oakley (SC)	.05
485	Dennis Scott (SC)	.05
486	Scott Skiles (SC)	.05
487	Charles Barkley (SC)	.25
488	Hersey Hawkins (SC)	.05
489	Tom Chambers (SC)	.05
490	Kevin Johnson (SC)	.05
491	Clyde Drexler (SC)	.10
492	Terry Porter (SC)	.05
493	Lionel Simmons (SC)	.05
494	Wayman Tisdale (SC)	.05
495	Terry Cummings (SC)	.05
496	David Robinson (SC)	.30
497	Shawn Kemp (SC)	.40
498	Ricky Pierce (SC)	.05
499	Karl Malone (SC)	.10
500	John Stockton (SC)	.10
501	Harvey Grant (SC)	.05
502	Bernard King (SC)	.05
503	Travis Mays (ART)	.05
504	Kevin McHale (ART)	.05
505	Muggsy Bogues (ART)	.05
506	Scottie Pippen (TC)	.25
507	Brad Daugherty (TC)	.05
508	Derek Harper (TC)	.05
509	Mahmoud Abdul-Rauf (TC)	.05
510	Isiah Thomas (TC)	.10
511	Tim Hardaway (TC)	.10
512	Otis Thorpe (TC)	.05
513	Chuck Person (TC)	.05
514	Ron Harper (TC)	.05
515	James Worthy (TC)	.05
516	Sherman Douglas (ART)	.05
517	Dale Ellis (ART)	.05
518	Tony Campbell (ART)	.05
519	Derrick Coleman (TC)	.10
520	Gerald Wilkins (TC)	.05
521	Scott Skiles (TC)	.05
522	Manute Bol (TC)	.05
523	Tom Chambers (TC)	.05
524	Terry Porter (TC)	.05
525	Lionel Simmons (TC)	.05
526	Sean Elliott (TC)	.05
527	Shawn Kemp (TC)	.40
528	John Stockton (TC)	.10
529	Harvey Grant (TC)	.05
530	Michael Adams (AL)	.05
531	Charles Barkley (AL)	.25
532	Larry Bird (AL)	.40
533	Maurice Cheeks (AL)	.05
534	Mark Eaton (AL)	.05
535	Magic Johnson (AL)	.25
536	Michael Jordan (AL)	1.25
537	Moses Malone (AL)	.05
538	NBA Finals Game 1	.05
539	NBA Finals Game 2	.25
540	NBA Finals Game 3	.05
541	NBA Finals Game 4	.05
542	Finals Game 5	1.25
543	Championship Card	1.25
544	Otis Smith (SS)	.05
545	Jeff Turner (SS)	.05
546	*Larry Johnson*	1.50
547	*Kenny Anderson*	.75
548	*Billy Owens*	.50
549	*Dikembe Mutombo*	1.00
550	*Steve Smith*	.50
551	*Doug Smith*	.15
552	*Luc Longley*	.25
553	*Mark Macon*	.10
554	*Stacey Augmon*	.25
555	*Brian Williams*	.25
556	*Terrell Brandon*	1.00
557	Walter Davis	.05
558	Vern Fleming	.05
559	Joe Kleine	.05
560	Jon Koncak	.05
561	Sam Perkins	.05
562	Alvin Robertson	.05
563	Wayman Tisdale	.05
564	Jeff Turner	.05
565	Willie Anderson	.05
566	Stacey Augmon (USA)	.10
567	Bimbo Coles (USA)	.10
568	Jeff Grayer (USA)	.10
569	Hersey Hawkins (USA)	.10

570	Dan Majerle (USA)	.10
571	Danny Manning (USA)	.10
572	J.R. Reid (USA)	.10
573	Mitch Richmond (USA)	.15
574	Charles Smith (USA)	.10
575	Charles Barkley (USA)	1.00
576	Larry Bird (USA)	1.75
577	Patrick Ewing (USA)	.50
578	Magic Johnson	1.25
579	Michael Jordan (USA)	5.00
580	Karl Malone (USA)	.50
581	Chris Mullin (USA)	.10
582	Scottie Pippen (USA)	1.50
583	David Robinson (USA)	1.00
584	John Stockton (USA)	.50
585	Chuck Daly	.10
586	Lenny Wilkens	.05
587	P.J. Carlesimo (USA CO)	.05
588	Mike Krzyzewski	.50
589	Checklist	.05
590	Checklist	.05
NNO	Centennial (Mail-In Offer)	.50
NNO	Head of the Class	25.00
NNO	Team USA	1.00
CC1	James Naismith	1.00
1CC	James Naismith	3.00
(2)	Centennial (Mail-In Offer)	.50
(1)	Team USA (NNO)	3.00
(2)	Head of the Class	30.00
(1)	Kept The World Spinning	5.00
(2)	In 1992 The US Baskt. Team	5.00

1991-92 Hoops MVP All-Stars

This subset is a continuation of the 1991-92 NBA Hoops Series I Slam Dunk set and was available only in Series II rack packs. NBA All-Star Game MVPs from 1986-91 are honored in this set. The player and an MVP trophy are on the card front. The backs show the player in action during the All-Star Game. Cards are numbered in Roman numerals.

		MT
Complete Set (6):		25.00
Common Player:		.50
7	Isiah Thomas	1.00
8	Tom Chambers	.50
9	Michael Jordan	20.00
10	Karl Malone	2.00
11	Magic Johnson	3.00
12	Charles Barkley	3.00

1991-92 Hoops Slam Dunk

This set features winners of the NBA All-Star Weekend slam dunk contest over the last six years. Two cards were in each 1991-92 NBA Hoops I rack pack. Card fronts feature photos of the players dunking. Backs, which are numbered with Roman numerals, describe the players' dunking abilities.

		MT
Complete Set (6):		25.00
Common Player:		.50
1	Larry Nance	.50
2	Dominique Wilkins	1.00
3	Spud Webb	.50
4	Michael Jordan	20.00
5	Kenny Walker	.50
6	Dee Brown	.75

1991 Hoops McDonald's

These cards were distributed at 4,600 participating McDonald's restaurants in all 27 NBA markets between Feb. 7 and March 11, 1992. Four-card packs, at 49 cents each, were available with Value Meals. Although the designs are the same, the photos are different from the regular NBA Hoops issues. There were 20,000 instant-win coupons inserted into packs, allowing winners to obtain a 70-card set. Cards #63-70 were distributed in the Chicago area only, making them more valuable. There were approximately 1.35 million of the 62-card sets, and 300,000 of the eight-card (63-70) sets, produced. Thus, there can not be more than 300,000 70-card sets.

		MT
Complete Set (70):		17.50
Common Player:		.05
1	Dominique Wilkins	.50
2	Larry Bird	1.25
3	Kevin McHale	.20
4	Robert Parish	.20
5	Michael Jordan	3.00
6	John Paxson	.10
7	Scottie Pippen	1.00
8	Brad Daugherty	.20
9	Rolando Blackman	.10
10	Derek Harper	.10
11	Joe Dumars	.25
12	Bill Laimbeer	.05
13	Isiah Thomas	.25
14	Tim Hardaway	.30
15	Chris Mullin	.30
16	Hakeem Olajuwon	1.00
17	Reggie Miller	.50
18	Chuck Person	.10
19	Charles Smith	.05
20	Vlade Divac	.10
21	James Worthy	.15
22	Rony Seikaly	.10
23	Alvin Robertson	.05
24	Pooh Richardson	.05
25	Derrick Coleman	.50
26	Patrick Ewing	.75
27	Xavier McDaniel	.05
28	Dennis Scott	.10
29	Scott Skiles	.05
30	Charles Barkley	1.00
31	Hersey Hawkins	.10
32	Tom Chambers	.10
33	Kevin Johnson	.30
34	Clyde Drexler	.30
35	Terry Porter	.10
36	Buck Williams	.05
37	Mitch Richmond	.15
38	Lionel Simmons	.10
39	Terry Cummings	.10
40	Sean Elliott	.15
41	David Robinson	1.00
42	Shawn Kemp	1.00
43	Ricky Pierce	.05
44	Karl Malone	.75
45	John Stockton	.50
46	Bernard King	.15
47	Larry Johnson	1.50
48	Dikembe Mutombo	1.00
49	Billy Owens	.75
50	Kenny Anderson	.50
51	Charles Barkley (US)	.75
52	Larry Bird (US)	1.00
53	Patrick Ewing (US)	.50
54	Magic Johnson (US)	1.00
55	Michael Jordan (US)	2.00
56	Karl Malone (US)	.50
57	Chris Mullin (US)	.25
58	Scottie Pippen (US)	.50
59	David Robinson (US)	.75
60	John Stockton (US)	.25
61	Chuck Daly (US)	.10
62	USA Team	.50
63	B.J. Armstrong	1.00
64	Bill Cartwright	.75
65	Horace Grant	2.00
66	Craig Hodges	.75
67	Stacey King	.75
68	Cliff Levingston	.75
69	Will Perdue	.75
70	Scott Williams	.75

1991-92 Hoops Team Night Sheets

The 12-card perforated sheets feature the cards (2-1/2" x 3-1/2") of players from each team with individual sponsors. The cards are unnumbered and certain sheets contained a coupon in the perforated card space.

		MT
Complete Set (27):		225.00
Common Sheet:		3.00
(1)	Atlanta Hawks - Del Taco/Minute Maid (Stacey Augmon, Maurice Cheeks, Jon Koncak, Blair Rasmussen, Rumeal Robinson, Alexander Volkov, Bob Weiss CO, Dominique Wilkins, Kevin Willis)	6.00
(2)	Boston Celtics - Osco Drug (John Bagley, Larry Bird, Dee Brown, Kevin Gamble, Joe Kleine, Reggie Lewis, Kevin McHale, Robert Parish, Ed Pinckney)	10.00
(3)	Charlotte Hornets - Coca-Cola (Muggsy Bogues, Rex Chapman, Dell Curry, Kenny Gattison, Kendall Gill, Mike Gminski, Larry Johnson, Eric Leckner, Johnny Newman, J.R. Reid) (Hugo - Mascot)	6.00
(4A)	Chicago Bulls - Kodak/Osco Drugs/Jewel (B.J. Armstrong, Bill Cartwright, Horace Grant, Bobby Hansen, Craig Hodges, Michael Jordan, Stacey King, Cliff Levingston, John Paxson, Will Perdue, Scottie Pippen, Scott Williams)	10.00
(4B)	Chicago Bulls - Kodak/Osco Drugs - SportsChannel (B.J. Armstrong, Bill Cartwright, Horace Grant, Bobby Hansen *, Craig Hodges, Michael Jordan, Stacey King, Cliff Levingston, John Paxson, Will Perdue, Scottie Pippen, Mark)	10.00
(5)	Cleveland Cavaliers (John Battle, Winston Bennett, Terrell Brandon, Brad Daugherty, Craig Ehlo, Danny Ferry, Henry James, Steve Kerr, Larry Nance, Mark Price, Len Wilkens CO, John Williams) (No sponsor)	8.00
(6)	Dallas Mavericks (Richie Adubato CO, Rolando Blackman, Brad Davis, Terry Davis, James Donaldson, Derek Harper, Fat Lever, Rodney McCray, Doug Smith, Randy White, Herb Williams)	6.00
(7)	Denver Nuggets - Safeway/Tropicana Twister (Cadillac Anderson, Walter Davis, Winston Garland, Chris Jackson, Marcus Liberty, Todd Lichti, Mark Macon, Dikembe Mutombo, Paul Westhead CO, Reggie William)	6.00
(8)	Detroit Pistons - Health Plus (Mark Aguirre, William Bedford, Chuck Daly CO, Joe Dumars, Bill Laimbeer, Dennis Rodman, John Salley, Brad Sellers, Isiah Thomas, Darrell Walker, Orlando Woolridge)	8.00
(9)	Golden State Warriors - Pizza Hut (Vincent Askew, Mario Elie, Tim Hardaway, Rod Higgins, Tyrone Hill, Alton Lister, Sarunas Marciulionis, Chris Mullin, Don Nelson CO, Jim Petersen, Tom Tolbert)	6.00
(10)	Houston Rockets - Whataburger (Don Chaney CO, Eric Floyd, Dave Jamerson, Buck Johnson, Vernon Maxwell, Hakeem Olajuwon, Kenny Smith, Larry Smith, Otis Thorpe)	8.00
(11)	Indiana Pacers - Combos (Greg Dreiling, Vern Fleming, George McCloud, Reggie Miller, Chuck Person, Detlef Schrempf, Rik Smits, LaSalle Thompson, Michael Williams, Randy Wittman)	6.00
(12)	Los Angeles Clippers - Combos (James Edwards, Gary Grant, Ron Harper, Bo Kimble, Danny Manning, Ken Norman, Olden Polynice, Doc Rivers, Mike Schuler CO, Charles Smith, Loy Vaught)	7.00
(13)	Los Angeles Lakers - Taco Bell (Elden Campbell, Vlade Divac, A.C. Green, Jack Haley, Sam Perkins, Byron Scott, Tony Smith, Sedale Threatt, James Worthy)	8.00
(14)	Miami Heat - Domino's Pizza - Diet Coke (Keith Askins, Willie Burton, Bimbo Coles, Kevin Edwards, Alec Kessler, Grant Long, Glen Rice, Rony Seikaly, Brian Shaw, Steve Smith)	6.00
(15)	Milwaukee Bucks - M&M/Mars (Frank Brickowski, Dale Ellis, Jeff Grayer, Jay Humphries, Larry Krystkowiak, Brad Lohaus, Moses Malone, Fred Roberts, Alvin Robertson, Dan Schayes) (Snickers USA Olympic Team 1992 with Steve Henson	6.00
(16)	Minnesota Timberwolves - Kodak/Target (Randy Breuer, Scott Brooks, Tony Campbell, Luc Longley, Sam Mitchell, Pooh Richardson, Felton Spencer, Doug West)	6.00
(17)	New Jersey Nets - Charles Chips (Rafael Addison, Kenny Anderson, Mookie Blaylock, Sam Bowie, Derrick Coleman, Chris Dudley, Tate George, Terry Mills, Chris Morris, Drazen Petrovic)	6.00
(18)	New York Knicks - Carvel Ice Cream (Greg Anthony, Anthony Mason, Patrick Ewing, Mark Jackson, Tim McCormick, Xavier McDaniel, Charles Oakley, Brian Quinnett, John Starks, Kiki Vandeweghe, Gerald Wilkins)	8.00
(19)	Orlando Magic - Gooding's (Mark Acres, Nick Anderson, Terry Catledge, Greg Kite, Jerry Reynolds, Dennis Scott, Scott Skiles, Otis Smith, Jeff Turner, Sam Vincent, Brian Williams)	6.00
(20)	Philadelphia 76ers - Kodak (Ron Anderson, Charles Barkley, Manute Bol, Johnny Dawkins, Armon Gilliam, Hersey Hawkins, Jim Lynam CO, Charles Shackleford)	7.00
(21)	Phoenix Suns - Checker Auto Parts (Cedric Ceballos, Tom Chambers, Cotton Fitzsimmons CO, Jeff Hornacek, Kevin Johnson, Negele Knight, Andrew Lang, Dan Majerle, Tim Perry)	8.00
(22)	Portland Trail Blazers - No sponsor (Alaa Abdelnaby, Danny Ainge, Mark Bryant, Wayne Cooper, Clyde Drexler, Kevin Duckworth, Jerome Kersey, Terry Porter, Cliff Robinson, Buck Williams, Danny Young)	10.00
(23)	Sacramento Kings - Safeway (Anthony Bonner, Randy Brown, Duane Causwell, Pete Chilcutt, Dennis Hopson, Les Jepsen, Jim Les, Mitch Richmond, Dwayne Schintzius, Lionel Simmons, Wayman Tisdale, Spud Webb)	6.00
(24)	San Antonio Spurs (Willie Anderson, Antoine Carr, Terry Cummings, Coby Dietrick, Dave Barnett ANN, Sean Elliott, Sidney Green, Paul Pressey, David Robinson, David Robinson (Portrait), Rod Strickland, Greg Sutton)	8.00
(25)	Seattle Supersonics - Combos (Dana Barros, Benoit Benjamin, Michael Cage, Marty Conlon, Eddie Johnson, Shawn Kemp, Rich King, Derrick McKey, Nate McMillan, Gary Payton, Ricky Pierce)	8.00
(26)	Utah Jazz - Combos (David Benoit, Mike Brown, Tyrone Corbin, Mark Eaton, Blue Edwards, Jeff Malone, Karl Malone, Eric Murdock, Delaney Rudd, Jerry Sloan CO, John Stockton)	9.00
(27)	Washington Bullets - Shoe City/Shoe City Sports (Michael Adams, Mark Alarie, Ledell Eackles, Pervis Ellison, A.J. English, Greg Foster, Harvey Grant, Tom Hammonds, Charles Jones, Bernard King, Wes Unseld CO)	6.00

1992 Hoops 100 Superstars

The 100-card, standard-size set was a partial reproduction of the 1991-92 Hoops base set, but was available through the Sears catalog. The cards are numbered on the back and grouped alphabetically by the team's city name.

		MT
Complete Set (100):		60.00
Common Player:		.35
1	Rumeal Robinson	.35
2	Dominique Wilkins	1.00
3	Kevin Willis	.50
4	Larry Bird	10.00
5	Dee Brown	.50
6	Kevin Gamble	.35
7	Kevin McHale	2.00
8	Robert Parish	1.00
9	Dell Curry	.35
10	Muggsy Bogues	1.00
11	Kendall Gill	.50
12	Johnny Newman	.35
13	Horace Grant	1.00
14	Michael Jordan	25.00
15	John Paxson	.50
16	Scottie Pippen	6.00
17	Brad Daugherty	.50
18	Larry Nance	1.00
19	Mark Price	1.00
20	Hot Rod Williams	.50
21	Rolando Blackman	.50
22	Derek Harper	.50
23	Rodney McCray	.35
24	Chris Jackson	.50
25	Todd Lichti	.35
26	Orlando Woolridge	.35
27	Joe Dumars	1.25
28	Bill Laimbeer	.75
29	Dennis Rodman	5.00
30	Isiah Thomas	3.00
31	Tim Hardaway	1.50
32	Sarunas Marciulionis	.35
33	Chris Mullin	1.25
34	Hakeem Olajuwon	5.00
35	Kenny Smith	.35
36	Otis Thorpe	.50
37	Reggie Miller	3.00
38	Chuck Person	.50
39	Detlef Schrempf	1.00
40	Ron Harper	.75
41	Danny Manning	.75
42	Ken Norman	.35
43	Charles Smith	.35
44	Vlade Divac	.50
45	A.C. Green	1.00
46	Magic Johnson	8.00
47	Sam Perkins	.75
48	Byron Scott	.75
49	James Worthy	1.50
50	Kevin Edwards	.35
51	Glen Rice	1.50
52	Rony Seikaly	.35
53	Dale Ellis	.50
54	Jay Humphries	.35
55	Moses Malone	.75
56	Alvin Robertson	.35
57	Tony Campbell	.35
58	Sam Mitchell	.35
59	Pooh Richardson	.35
60	Felton Spencer	.35
61	Mookie Blaylock	1.00
62	Sam Bowie	.50
63	Derrick Coleman	.50
64	Patrick Ewing	3.00
65	Xavier McDaniel	.35
66	Charles Oakley	1.00
67	Kiki Vandeweghe	.75
68	Gerald Wilkins	.35
69	Terry Catledge	.35
70	Dennis Scott	.50
71	Scott Skiles	.50
72	Charles Barkley	5.00
73	Johnny Dawkins	.50
74	Armon Gilliam	.50
75	Hersey Hawkins	.75
76	Tom Chambers	.75
77	Jeff Hornacek	.75
78	Kevin Johnson	1.00
79	Clyde Drexler	3.50
80	Jerome Kersey	.50
81	Terry Porter	.50
82	Mitch Richmond	2.00
83	Lionel Simmons	.35
84	Wayman Tisdale	.50
85	Spud Webb	.75
86	Antoine Carr	.35
87	Sean Elliott	.75
88	David Robinson	5.00
89	Rod Strickland	.50
90	Shawn Kemp	3.00
91	Gary Payton	4.00
92	Ricky Pierce	.35
93	Blue Edwards	.35
94	Jeff Malone	.50
95	Karl Malone	6.00
96	John Stockton	6.00
97	Michael Adams	.35
98	Pervis Ellison	.35
99	Harvey Grant	.35
100	Bernard King	.75

1992 Hoops Prototypes

These cards preview NBA Hoops' regular 1992-93 set. The player cards are similar to their regular counterparts on both sides, but the card backs are unnumbered. One non-player card, listed fourth in the checklist, was also produced and contains advertising for the regular set. The four cards were wrapped together in a cello pack. A mail-in offer allowed collectors to obtain extra packs.

		MT
Complete Set (4):		6.00
Common Player:		.50
(1)	Patrick Ewing	4.00
(2)	Magic Johnson	2.00
(3)	John Stockton	1.00
(4)	Cover card	.50

1992-93 Hoops

Approximately 617,000 1992-93 NBA Hopps sets were made, plus several unnumbered insert cards, which were randomly put in foil packs. Insert cards included 25,000 plastic USA Archer Olympic cards; 300,000 Ewing, Magic gold foil-stamped and USA team cards; and 25,000 lottery exchange cards, which could be used to obtain NBA draft lottery picks. The second series of cards, which features rookies and traded players, starts where the first series ended, with card #351. About 369,000 sets were available through foil packs. Rookie cards have a metallic gold seal. Limited-edition insert cards in the second series include AC (Art Card, 517,000 made); U (Ultimate Game, 117,000); and TR (Bulls Championship).

		MT
Complete Set (490):		40.00
Complete Series 1 (350):		15.00
Complete Series 2 (140):		25.00
Common Player:		.05
Minor Stars:		.10
Series 1 Pack (12):		.50
Series 1 Wax Box (36):		20.00
Series 2 Pack (12):		4.00
Series 2 Wax Box (36):		90.00
1	Stacey Augmon	.05
2	Maurice Cheeks	.05
3	Duane Ferrell	.05
4	Paul Graham	.05
5	Jon Koncak	.05
6	Blair Rasmussen	.05
7	Rumeal Robinson	.05
8	Dominique Wilkins	.10
9	Kevin Willis	.05
10	Larry Bird	1.00
11	Dee Brown	.10
12	Sherman Douglas	.05
13	Rick Fox	.10
14	Kevin Gamble	.05
15	Reggie Lewis	.05
16	Kevin McHale	.10
17	Robert Parish	.10
18	Ed Pinckney	.05
19	Muggsy Bogues	.05
20	Dell Curry	.05
21	Kenny Gattison	.05
22	Kendall Gill	.05
23	Mike Gminski	.05
24	Larry Johnson	.50
25	Johnny Newman	.05
26	J.R. Reid	.05
27	B.J. Armstrong	.05
28	Bill Cartwright	.05
29	Horace Grant	.15
30	Michael Jordan	3.00
31	Stacey King	.05
32	John Paxson	.05
33	Will Perdue	.05
34	Scottie Pippen	.75
35	Scott Williams	.05
36	John Battle	.05
37	Terrell Brandon	.05
38	Brad Daugherty	.05
39	Craig Ehlo	.05
40	Danny Ferry	.05
41	Henry James	.05
42	Larry Nance	.05
43	Mark Price	.10
44	John Williams	.05
45	Rolando Blackman	.05
46	Terry Davis	.05
47	Derek Harper	.05
48	Mike Iuzzolino	.05
49	Fat Lever	.05
50	Rodney McCray	.05
51	Doug Smith	.05
52	Randy White	.05
53	Herb Williams	.05
54	Cadillac Anderson	.05
55	Winston Garland	.05
56	Mahmoud Abdul-Rauf	.10
57	Marcus Liberty	.05
58	Todd Lichti	.05
59	Mark Macon	.05
60	Dikembe Mutombo	.30
61	Reggie Williams	.05
62	Mark Aguirre	.05
63	William Bedford	.05
64	Joe Dumars	.10
65	Bill Laimbeer	.05
66	Dennis Rodman	.75
67	John Salley	.05
68	Isiah Thomas	.15
69	Darrell Walker	.05
70	Orlando Woolridge	.05
71	Victor Alexander	.05
72	Mario Elie	.05
73	Chris Gatling	.05
74	Tim Hardaway	.10
75	Tyrone Hill	.10
76	Alton Lister	.05
77	Sarunas Marciulionis	.05
78	Chris Mullin	.10
79	Billy Owens	.05
80	Matt Bullard	.05
81	Eric Floyd	.05
82	Avery Johnson	.10
83	Buck Johnson	.05
84	Vernon Maxwell	.05
85	Hakeem Olajuwon	.50
86	Kenny Smith	.05
87	Larry Smith	.05
88	Otis Thorpe	.05
89	Dale Davis	.05
90	Vern Fleming	.05
91	George McCloud	.05
92	Reggie Miller	.30
93	Chuck Person	.05
94	Detlef Schrempf	.05
95	Rik Smits	.10
96	LaSalle Thompson	.05
97	Michael Williams	.05
98	James Edwards	.05
99	Gary Grant	.05
100	Ron Harper	.05
101	Danny Manning	.10
102	Ken Norman	.05
103	Olden Polynice	.05
104	Doc Rivers	.05
105	Charles Smith	.05
106	Loy Vaught	.05
107	Elden Campbell	.05
108	Vlade Divac	.05
109	A.C. Green	.05
110	Sam Perkins	.05
111	Byron Scott	.05
112	Tony Smith	.05
113	Terry Teagle	.05

114	Sedale Threatt	.05
115	James Worthy	.05
116	Willie Burton	.05
117	Bimbo Coles	.05
118	Kevin Edwards	.05
119	Alec Kessler	.05
120	Grant Long	.05
121	Glen Rice	.10
122	Rony Seikaly	.05
123	Brian Shaw	.05
124	Steve Smith	.10
125	Frank Brickowski	.05
126	Dale Ellis	.05
127	Jeff Grayer	.05
128	Jay Humphries	.05
129	Larry Krystkowiak	.05
130	Moses Malone	.10
131	Fred Roberts	.05
132	Alvin Robertson	.05
133	Dan Schayes	.05
134	Thurl Bailey	.05
135	Scott Brooks	.05
136	Tony Campbell	.05
137	Gerald Glass	.05
138	Luc Longley	.05
139	Sam Mitchell	.05
140	Pooh Richardson	.05
141	Felton Spencer	.05
142	Doug West	.05
143	Rafael Addison	.05
144	Kenny Anderson	.10
145	Mookie Blaylock	.05
146	Sam Bowie	.05
147	Derrick Coleman	.10
148	Chris Dudley	.05
149	Terry Mills	.05
150	Chris Morris	.05
151	Drazen Petrovic	.05
152	Greg Anthony	.05
153	Patrick Ewing	.25
154	Mark Jackson	.05
155	Anthony Mason	.05
156	Xavier McDaniel	.05
157	Charles Oakley	.05
158	John Starks	.05
159	Gerald Wilkins	.05
160	Nick Anderson	.10
161	Terry Catledge	.05
162	Jerry Reynolds	.05
163	Stanley Roberts	.05
164	Dennis Scott	.10
165	Scott Skiles	.05
166	Jeff Turner	.05
167	Sam Vincent	.05
168	Brian Williams	.05
169	Ron Anderson	.05
170	Charles Barkley	.40
171	Manute Bol	.05
172	Johnny Dawkins	.05
173	Armon Gilliam	.05
174	Hersey Hawkins	.05
175	Brian Oliver	.05
176	Charles Shackleford	.05
177	Jayson Williams	.05
178	Cedric Ceballos	.15
179	Tom Chambers	.05
180	Jeff Hornacek	.05
181	Kevin Johnson	.10
182	Negele Knight	.05
183	Andrew Lang	.05
184	Dan Majerle	.05
185	Tim Perry	.05
186	Mark West	.05
187	Alaa Abdelnaby	.05
188	Danny Ainge	.05
189	Clyde Drexler	.25
190	Kevin Duckworth	.05
191	Jerome Kersey	.05
192	Robert Pack	.05
193	Terry Porter	.05
194	Cliff Robinson	.05
195	Buck Williams	.05
196	Anthony Bonner	.05
197	Duane Causwell	.05
198	Pete Chilcutt	.05
199	Dennis Hopson	.05
200	Mitch Richmond	.15
201	Lionel Simmons	.05
202	Wayman Tisdale	.05
203	Spud Webb	.05
204	Willie Anderson	.05
205	Antoine Carr	.05
206	Terry Cummings	.05
207	Sean Elliott	.05
208	Sidney Green	.05
209	David Robinson	.40
210	Rod Strickland	.05
211	Greg Sutton	.05
212	Dana Barros	.05
213	Benoit Benjamin	.05
214	Michael Cage	.05
215	Eddie Johnson	.05
216	Shawn Kemp	.40
217	Derrick McKey	.05
218	Nate McMillan	.05
219	Gary Payton	.20
220	Ricky Pierce	.05
221	David Benoit	.05
222	Mike Brown	.05
223	Tyrone Corbin	.05
224	Mark Eaton	.05
225	Blue Edwards	.05
226	Jeff Malone	.05
227	Karl Malone	.25
228	Eric Murdock	.05
229	John Stockton	.25
230	Michael Adams	.05
231	Rex Chapman	.05
232	Ledell Eackles	.05
233	Pervis Ellison	.05
234	Mark Eaton	.05
235	Harvey Grant	.05
236	Charles Jones	.05
237	LaBradford Smith	.05
238	Larry Stewart	.05
239	Bob Weiss	.05
240	Chris Ford	.05
241	Allan Bristow	.05
242	Phil Jackson	.05
243	Lenny Wilkens	.05
244	Richie Adubato	.05
245	Dan Issel	.05
246	Ron Rothstein	.05
247	Don Nelson	.05
248	Rudy Tomjanovich	.05
249	Bob Hill	.05
250	Larry Brown	.05
252	Kevin Loughery	.05
253	Mike Dunleavy	.05
254	Jimmy Rodgers	.05
255	Chuck Daly	.05
256	Pat Riley	.05
257	Matt Guokas	.05
258	Doug Moe	.05
259	Paul Westphal	.05
260	Rick Adelman	.05
261	Garry St. Jean	.05
262	Jerry Tarkanian	.10
263	George Karl	.05
264	Jerry Sloan	.05
265	Wes Unseld	.05
266	Atlanta	.05
267	Boston	.05
268	Charlotte	.05
269	Chicago	.05
270	Cleveland	.05
271	Dallas	.05
272	Denver	.05
273	Detroit	.05
274	Golden State	.05
275	Houston	.05
276	Indiana	.05
277	LA Clippers	.05
278	LA Lakers	.05
279	Miami	.05
280	Milwaukee	.05
281	Minnesota	.05
282	New Jersey	.05
283	New York	.05
284	Orlando	.05
285	Philadelphia	.05
286	Phoenix	.05
287	Portland	.05
288	Sacramento	.05
289	San Antonio	.05
290	Seattle	.05
291	Utah	.05
292	Washington	.05
293	Michael Adams (AS)	.05
294	Charles Barkley (AS)	.20
295	Brad Daugherty (AS)	.05
296	Joe Dumars (AS)	.05
297	Patrick Ewing (AS)	.10
298	Michael Jordan (AS)	1.50
299	Reggie Lewis (AS)	.05
300	Scottie Pippen (AS)	.20
301	Mark Price (AS)	.05
302	Dennis Rodman (AS)	.20
303	Isiah Thomas (AS)	.10
304	Kevin Willis (AS)	.05
305	Coach (Phil Jackson) (AS)	.05
306	Clyde Drexler (AS)	.10
307	Tim Hardaway (AS)	.05
308	Jeff Hornacek (AS)	.05
309	Magic Johnson (AS)	.25
310	Dan Majerle (AS)	.05
311	Karl Malone (AS)	.10
312	Chris Mullin (AS)	.10
313	Dikembe Mutombo (AS)	.15
314	Hakeem Olajuwon (AS)	.25
315	David Robinson (AS)	.20
316	John Stockton (AS)	.10
317	Otis Thorpe (AS)	.05
318	James Worthy (AS)	.05
319	Coach (Don Nelson) (AS)	.05
320	Scoring (Michael Jordan, Karl Malone)	.75
321	3-Point Field Goal Pct. (Dana Barros, Drazen Petrovic)	.05
322	Free Throw Percent (Larry Bird, Mark Price)	.25
323	Blocks (David Robinson, Hakeem Olajuwon)	.30
324	Steals (John Stockton, Michael Williams)	.05
325	Rebounds (Dennis Rodman, Kevin Willis)	.05
326	Assists (Kevin Johnson, John Stockton)	.10
327	Field Goal Percentage (Buck Williams, Otis Thorpe)	.05
328	Magic Moments 1980	.10
329	Magic Moments 1985	.10
330	Magic Moments 1987, 1988	.05
331	Magic Numbers	.10
332	Drazen Petrovic (Inside Stuff)	.05
333	Patrick Ewing (IS)	.10
334	David Robinson (Stay)	.25
335	Kevin Johnson (Stay)	.05
336	Charles Barkley (USA)	.20
337	Larry Bird (USA)	.40
338	Clyde Drexler (USA)	.10
339	Patrick Ewing (USA)	.05
340	Magic Johnson (USA)	.30
341	Michael Jordan (USA)	1.50
342	*Christian Laettner*	.50
343	Karl Malone (USA)	.10
344	Chris Mullin (USA)	.05
345	Scottie Pippen (USA)	.20
346	David Robinson (USA)	.20
347	John Stockton (USA)	.10
348	Checklist #1	.05
349	Checklist #2	.05
350	Checklist #3	.05
351	Mookie Blaylock	.05
352	*Adam Keefe*	.15
353	Travis Mays	.05
354	Morlon Wiley	.05
355	Joe Kleine	.05
356	Bart Kofoed	.05
357	Xavier McDaniel	.05
358	*Tony Bennett*	.10
359	Tom Hammonds	.05
360	Kevin Lynch	.05
361	*Alonzo Mourning*	2.00
362	Rodney McCray	.05
363	Trent Tucker	.05
364	*Corey Williams*	.10
365	Steve Kerr	.05
366	Jerome Lane	.05
367	*Bobby Phills*	.40
368	Mike Sanders	.05
369	Gerald Wilkins	.05
370	Donald Hodge	.05
371	*Brian Howard*	.10
372	*Tracy Moore*	.10
373	*Sean Rooks*	.10
374	Kevin Brooks	.05
375	*LaPhonso Ellis*	.25
376	Scott Hastings	.05
377	Robert Pack	.05
378	*Bryant Stith*	.50
379	Robert Werdann	.05
380	Lance Blanks	.05
381	Terry Mills	.05
382	*Isaiah Morris*	.10
383	Olden Polynice	.05
384	Brad Sellers	.05
385	Jud Buechler	.05
386	Jeff Grayer	.05
387	*Byron Houston*	.10
388	*Keith Jennings*	.10
389	*Latrell Sprewell*	2.00
390	Scott Brooks	.05
391	Carl Herrera	.05
392	*Robert Horry*	1.00
393	Tree Rollins	.05
394	Kennard Winchester	.05
395	Greg Dreiling	.05
396	Sean Green	.05
397	Sam Mitchell	.05
398	Pooh Richardson	.05
399	*Malik Sealy*	.25
400	Kenny Williams	.05
401	*Jaren Jackson*	.10
402	Mark Jackson	.05
403	Stanley Roberts	.05
404	*Elmore Spencer*	.10
405	Kiki Vandeweghe	.05
406	John Williams	.05
407	*Randy Woods*	.10
408	Alex Blackwell	.05
409	*Duane Cooper*	.10
410	*Anthony Peeler*	.20
411	Keith Askins	.05
412	*Matt Geiger*	.20
413	*Harold Miner*	.20
414	John Salley	.05
415	Alaa Abdelnaby	.05
416	*Todd Day*	.30
417	Blue Edwards	.05
418	Brad Lohaus	.05
419	*Lee Mayberry*	.15
420	Eric Murdock	.05
421	Christian Laettner	.75
422	*Bob McCann*	.10
423	Chuck Person	.05
424	*Chris Smith*	.10
425	*Gundars Vetra*	.10
426	Michael Williams	.05
427	Chucky Brown	.05
428	Tate George	.05
429	Rick Mahorn	.05
430	Rumeal Robinson	.05
431	Jayson Williams	.05
432	*Eric Anderson*	.10
433	Rolando Blackman	.05
434	Tony Campbell	.05
435	*Hubert Davis*	.15
436	Bo Kimble	.05
437	Doc Rivers	.05
438	Charles Smith	.05
439	Anthony Bowie	.05
440	*Litterial Green*	.10
441	Greg Kite	.05
442	*Shaquille O'Neal*	10.00
443	Donald Royal	.05
444	Greg Grant	.05
445	Jeff Hornacek	.05
446	Andrew Lang	.05
447	Kenny Payne	.05
448	Tim Perry	.05
449	*C. Weatherspoon*	.50
450	Danny Ainge	.05
451	Charles Barkley	.75
452	Tim Kempton	.05
453	*Oliver Miller*	.40
454	Mark Bryant	.05
455	Mario Elie	.05
456	*Dave Johnson*	.10
457	*Tracy Murray*	.10
458	Rod Strickland	.05
459	Vincent Askew	.05
460	Randy Brown	.05
461	Marty Conlon	.05
462	Jim Les	.05
463	*Walt Williams*	.50
464	William Bedford	.05
465	*Lloyd Daniels*	.10
466	Vinny Del Negro	.05
467	Dale Ellis	.05
468	Larry Smith	.05
469	David Wood	.05
470	Rich King	.05
471	*Isaac Austin*	.10
472	John Crotty	.05
473	Stephen Howard	.05
474	Jay Humphries	.05
475	Larry Krystowiak	.05
476	*Tom Gugliotta*	1.00
477	Buck Johnson	.05
478	*Don MacLean*	.15
479	Doug Overton	.05
480	*Brent Price*	.10
481	David Robinson (TRV)	.40
482	Magic Johnson (TRV)	.40
483	John Stockton (TRV)	.25
484	Patrick Ewing (TRV)	.25
485	Trivia Answer Card	.25
486	NBA Stay in School	.25
487	NBA Inside Stuff	.05
488	Rookie Checklist	.05
489	Checklist #1	.05
490	Checklist #2	.05
NNO	Team USA	1.50
NNO	Patrick Ewing Game	.50
TR1	Bulls Champs	2.00
SU1	John Stockton Game	2.00
NNO	Magic Johnson Comm.	1.50
NNO	Barcelona Plastic	30.00
AC1	Patrick Ewing Art	.75

1992-93 Hoops Draft Redemption

This glossy set, featuring top picks from the 1992 NBA draft, could be obtained in exchange for a Hoops I lottery exchange card. Card fronts, which are borderless and feature posed, color photos, indicate with a big letter what order the player was drafted. The backs, which are numbered alphabetically, feature a small head shot, career highlights and stats. Production has been estimated at between 10,000 and 20,000 sets. This set contains the first pro card of Shaquille O'Neal.

		MT
Complete Set (10):		60.00
Common Player:		2.00
1A	Shaquille O'Neal	40.00
2B	Alonzo Mourning	10.00
3C	Christian Laettner	6.00
4D	LaPhonso Ellis	4.00
5E	Tom Gugliotta	8.00
6F	Walt Williams	3.00
7G	Todd Day	2.00
8H	C. Weatherspoon	3.00
9I	Adam Keefe	2.00
10J	Robert Horry	3.00
NNO	Redemption card	2.00
NNO	Redemption Card Stamped	2.00

1992-93 Hoops Magic's All-Rookie Team

These glossy cards were randomly inserted into Series II packs. Fronts have color action photos and the player's name and team stamped in gold foil. Magic's All-Rookie Team is written at the bottom of the card. Card backs, numbered 1 of 10, etc., have a comment from Magic about the player. There were 25,000 or less sets produced.

		MT
Complete Set (10):		120.00
Common Player:		3.00
1	Shaquille O'Neal	75.00
2	Alonzo Mourning	25.00
3	Christian Laettner	8.00
4	LaPhonso Ellis	6.00
5	Tom Gugliotta	10.00
6	Walt Williams	5.00
7	Todd Day	3.00
8	C. Weatherspoon	6.00
9	Robert Horry	8.00
10	Harold Miner	3.00

1992-93 Hoops More Magic

These cards were randomly inserted in 1992-93 NBA Series II wax packs, one per every 195 packs. 15,000 sets were produced. The cards commemorate Johnson's return to the team before the season and feature color photos with white borders. A team color-coded star appears in the lower left corner, with the words "More Magic" written in it. The card back has a number (MM1-MM3) and a ghosted image of the photo pictured on the card front. An explanation of Johnson's decision to return to the NBA, and subsquent decision to retire again, are presented on the backs.

		MT
Complete Set (3):		60.00
Common Magic:		20.00
1MM	Training Camp	20.00
2MM	L.A. vs. 76ers	20.00
3MM	Last Game	20.00

1992-93 Hoops Supreme Court

These cards were randomly put in Series II wax packs, about three cards per pack. Approximately 90,000 sets were made. The player's name is gold stamped on the card front. The backs have a photo and comments about the player. Both the back and the front say "The Fans' Choice."

		MT
Complete Set (10):		35.00
Common Player:		1.00
1SC	Michael Jordan	20.00
2SC	Scottie Pippen	4.00
3SC	David Robinson	4.00
4SC	Patrick Ewing	2.00
5SC	Clyde Drexler	2.00
6SC	Karl Malone	2.00
7SC	Charles Barkley	4.00
8SC	John Stockton	2.00
9SC	Chris Mullin	1.00
10SC	Magic Johnson	4.00

1993-94 Hoops Promo Panel

This nine-card perforated sheet was issued to promote the 1993-94 Hoops' set. The cards are identical to the regular series except they are unnumbered.

		MT
Complete Set (1):		5.00
Common Panel:		5.00
NNO	Hoops Panel (Joe Dumars, Patrick Ewing, Tim Hardaway, Dan Majerle, Jeff Malone, Xavier McDaniel, Reggie Miller, David Robinson)	5.00

1993-94 Hoops Prototypes

These cards were produced to preview NBA Hoops' 1993-94 cards. The cards feature the same design formats as the regular cards, but the card backs are unnumbered. A cover card was also produced for the set.

	MT
Complete Set (7):	8.00
Common Player:	1.00
Jimmy Jackson	1.50
Larry Johnson	1.50
Karl Malone	1.50
Harold Miner	1.50
Dikembe Mutombo	2.00
Shaquille O'Neal	3.50
Cover card	1.00

1993-94 Hoops

NBA Hoops' 1993-94 cards include four subsets: Hoops Scoops, All-Stars, League Leaders and Hoops Tribune, which are cards that recap events from the past season. Cards also say whether the player was traded or signed with another team during the off season. Rookies are also designated on the fronts. Collectors should be aware of a mistake in the numbering of the final 29 cards in the regular issue. Although numbering ends at #421, a Magic & Bird Commemorative card and the Hoops Scoops cards should have been numbered as part of the regular set. They are not inserts, and appear with the same frequency as cards 1-421. The mistake will not be corrected. In the checklist below, the number that appears on the card is listed, along with the corresponding set number. Inserts are BlackGold, Supreme Court, Magic's All-Rookie Team and Admiral's Choice. A David Robinson rookie card was also put in one of every 18 packs. A limited number of exchange cards were also made for the Robinson card, allowing finders to send them to SkyBox International for an autographed version. The same idea was used for the Magic & Bird commemorative card. Exchange cards were randomly inserted in Series II packs. As a parallel set to the regular set, NBA Hoops produced a set labled as its "Fifth Anniversary" set; these cards are the same as their counterparts in the main set, but have a Fifth Anniversary gold foil logo stamped on the front. The player's name is framed by gold stripes, too. The cards were inserted one per every 13-card pack, or two per jumbo pack. Stars are two to four times more valuable than their regular counterparts.

		MT
Complete Set (421):		20.00
Complete Series 1 (300):		12.00
Complete Series 2 (121):		8.00
Common Player:		.05
Complete Gold Set (421):		60.00
Complete Gold Series 1 (300):		35.00
Complete Gold Series 2 (121):		25.00
Common Gold Player:		.10
Unlisted Gold Stars:		1x-3x
Series 1 Pack (14):		1.00
Series 1 Wax Box (36):		26.00
Series 2 Pack (13):		1.00
Series 2 Wax Box (36):		25.00
1	Stacey Augmon	.05
2	Mookie Blaylock	.05
3	Duane Ferrell	.05
4	Paul Graham	.05
5	Adam Keefe	.05
6	Blair Rasmussen	.05
7	Dominique Wilkins	.15
8	Kevin Willis	.05
9	Alaa Abdelnaby	.05
10	Dee Brown	.05
11	Sherman Douglas	.05
12	Rick Fox	.05
13	Kevin Gamble	.05
14	Joe Kleine	.05
15	Xavier McDaniel	.05
16	Robert Parish	.05
17	Tony Bennett	.05
18	Muggsy Bogues	.05
19	Dell Curry	.05
20	Kenny Gattison	.05
21	Kendall Gill	.05
22	Larry Johnson	.25
23	Alonzo Mourning	.50
24	Johnny Newman	.05
25	B.J. Armstrong	.05
26	Bill Cartwright	.05
27	Horace Grant	.10
28	Michael Jordan	2.00
29	Stacey King	.05
30	John Paxson	.05
31	Will Perdue	.05
32	Scottie Pippen	.50
33	Scott Williams	.05
34	Moses Malone	.05
35	John Battle	.05
36	Terrell Brandon	.05
37	Brad Daugherty	.05
38	Craig Ehlo (S)	.05
39	Danny Ferry	.05
40	Larry Nance	.05
41	Mark Price	.10
42	Gerald Wilkins	.05
43	John Williams	.05
44	Terry Davis	.05
45	Derek Harper	.05
46	Donald Hodge	.05
47	Mike Iuzzolino	.05
48	Jim Jackson	.50
49	Sean Rooks	.05
50	Doug Smith	.05
51	Randy White	.05
52	Mahmoud Abdul-Rauf	.05
53	LaPhonso Ellis	.05
54	Marcus Liberty	.05
55	Mark Macon	.05
56	Dikembe Mutombo	.20
57	Robert Pack	.05
58	Bryant Stith	.05
59	Reggie Williams	.05
60	Mark Aguirre	.05
61	Joe Dumars	.15
62	Bill Laimbeer	.05
63	Terry Mills	.05
64	Olden Polynice	.05
65	Alvin Robertson	.05
66	Dennis Rodman	.75

67	Isiah Thomas	.15
68	Victor Alexander	.05
69	Tim Hardaway	.10
70	Tyrone Hill (T)	.05
71	Byron Houston	.05
72	Sarunas Marciulionis	.05
73	Chris Mullin	.10
74	Billy Owens	.05
75	Latrell Sprewell	.25
76	Scott Brooks	.05
77	Matt Bullard	.05
78	Carl Herrera	.05
79	Robert Horry	.10
80	Vernon Maxwell	.05
81	Hakeem Olajuwon	.50
82	Kenny Smith	.05
83	Otis Thorpe	.05
84	Dale Davis	.05
85	Vern Fleming	.05
86	George McCloud	.05
87	Reggie Miller	.20
88	Sam Mitchell	.05
89	Pooh Richardson	.05
90	Detlef Schrempf	.05
91	Malik Sealy	.05
92	Rik Smits	.05
93	Gary Grant	.05
94	Ron Harper	.05
95	Mark Jackson	.05
96	Danny Manning	.10
97	Ken Norman (S)	.05
98	Stanley Roberts	.05
99	Elmore Spencer	.05
100	Loy Vaught	.05
101	John Williams	.05
102	Randy Woods	.05
103	Benoit Benjamin (T)	.05
104	Elden Campbell	.05
105	Doug Christie	.05
106	Vlade Divac	.05
107	Anthony Peeler	.05
108	Tony Smith	.05
109	Sedale Threatt	.05
110	James Worthy	.05
111	Bimbo Coles	.05
112	Grant Long	.05
113	Harold Miner	.05
114	Glen Rice	.10
115	John Salley	.05
116	Rony Seikaly	.05
117	Brian Shaw	.05
118	Steve Smith	.05
119	Anthony Avent	.05
120	Jon Barry	.05
121	Frank Brickowski	.05
122	Todd Day	.05
123	Blue Edwards	.05
124	Brad Lohaus	.05
125	Lee Mayberry	.05
126	Eric Murdock	.05
127	*Derek Strong*	.05
128	Thurl Bailey	.05
129	Christian Laettner	.10
130	Luc Longley	.05
131	Marion Maxey	.05
132	Chuck Person	.05
133	Chris Smith	.05
134	Doug West	.05
135	Michael Williams	.05
136	Rafael Addison	.05
137	Kenny Anderson	.10
138	Sam Bowie (R)	.05
139	Chucky Brown	.05
140	Derrick Coleman	.10
141	Chris Morris	.05
142	Rumeal Robinson	.05
143	Greg Anthony	.05
144	Rolando Blackman	.05
145	Hubert Davis	.05
146	Patrick Ewing	.20
147	Anthony Mason	.05
148	Charles Oakley	.05
149	Doc Rivers	.05
150	Charles Smith	.05
151	John Starks	.10
152	Nick Anderson	.05
153	Anthony Bowie	.05
154	Lillerial Green	.05
155	Shaquille O'Neal	2.00
156	Donald Royal	.05
157	Dennis Scott	.05
158	Scott Skiles	.05
159	Tom Tolbert	.05
160	Jeff Turner	.05
161	Ron Anderson	.05
162	Johnny Dawkins	.05
163	Hersey Hawkins	.05
164	Jeff Hornacek	.05
165	Andrew Lang	.05
166	Tim Perry	.05
167	C. Weatherspoon	.10
168	Danny Ainge	.05
169	Charles Barkley	.40
170	Cedric Ceballos	.05
171	Richard Dumas	.05
172	Kevin Johnson	.10
173	Dan Majerle	.05
174	Oliver Miller	.05
175	Mark West	.05
176	Clyde Drexler	.20
177	Kevin Duckworth (T)	.05
178	Mario Elie (T)	.05
179	Dave Johnson	.05
180	Jerome Kersey	.05
181	Tracy Murray	.05
182	Terry Porter	.05
183	Cliff Robinson	.05
184	Rod Strickland	.05
185	Buck Williams	.05
186	Anthony Bonner	.05
187	Randy Brown	.05
188	Duane Causwell	.05
189	Pete Chilcutt	.05
190	Mitch Richmond	.10
191	Lionel Simmons	.05
192	Wayman Tisdale	.05
193	Spud Webb	.05
194	Walt Williams	.05
195	Willie Anderson	.05
196	Antoine Carr	.05
197	Terry Cummings	.05
198	Lloyd Daniels	.05
199	Sean Elliott	.05
200	Dale Ellis	.05
201	Avery Johnson	.05
202	J.R. Reid	.05
203	David Robinson	.40
204	Dana Barros	.05
205	Michael Cage	.05
206	Eddie Johnson	.05
207	Shawn Kemp	.25
208	Derrick McKey	.05
209	Nate McMillan	.05
210	Gary Payton	.15
211	Sam Perkins	.05
212	Ricky Pierce	.05
213	David Benoit	.05
214	Tyrone Corbin	.05
215	Mark Eaton	.05
216	Jay Humphries	.05
217	Jeff Malone	.05
218	Karl Malone	.25
219	John Stockton	.25
220	Michael Adams	.05
221	Rex Chapman	.05
222	Pervis Ellison	.05
223	Harvey Grant (T)	.05
224	Tom Gugliotta	.05
225	Don MacLean	.05
226	Doug Overton	.05
227	Brent Price	.05
228	LaBradford Smith	.05
229	Larry Stewart	.05
230	Lenny Wilkens (C)	.05
231	Chris Ford (C)	.05
232	Allan Bristow (C)	.05
233	Phil Jackson (C)	.05
234	Mike Fratello (C)	.05
235	Quinn Buckner (C)	.05
236	Dan Issel (C)	.05
237	Don Chaney (C)	.05
238	Don Nelson (C)	.05
239	Rudy Tomjanovich (C)	.05
240	Larry Brown (C)	.05
241	Bob Weiss (C)	.05
242	Randy Pfund (C)	.05
243	Kevin Loughery (C)	.05
244	Mike Dunleavy (C)	.05
245	Sidney Lowe (C)	.05
246	Chuck Daly (C)	.05
247	Pat Riley (C)	.05
248	Brian Hill (C)	.05
249	Fred Carter (C)	.05
250	Paul Westphal (C)	.05
251	Rick Adelman (C)	.05
252	Garry St. Jean (C)	.05
253	John Lucas (C)	.05
254	George Karl (C)	.05
255	Jerry Sloan (C)	.05
256	Wes Unseld (C)	.05
257	Michael Jordan (AS)	1.00
258	Isiah Thomas (AS)	.10
259	Scottie Pippen (AS)	.30
260	Larry Johnson (AS)	.15
261	Dominique Wilkins (AS)	.10
262	Joe Dumars (AS)	.10
263	Mark Price (AS)	.10
264	Shaquille O'Neal (AS)	1.00
265	Patrick Ewing (AS)	.10
266	Larry Nance (AS)	.05
267	Detlef Schrempf (AS)	.05
268	Brad Daugherty (AS)	.05
269	Charles Barkley (AS)	.15
270	Clyde Drexler (AS)	.15
271	Sean Elliott (AS)	.05
272	Tim Hardaway (AS)	.10
273	Shawn Kemp (AS)	.10
274	Dan Majerle (AS)	.05
275	Karl Malone (AS)	.15
276	Danny Manning (AS)	.05
277	Hakeem Olajuwon (AS)	.20
278	Terry Porter (AS)	.05
279	David Robinson (AS)	.15
280	John Stockton (AS)	.15
281	East team photo	.05
282	West team photo	.05
283	Scoring (Michael Jordan, Karl Malone, Dominique Wilkins)	.50
284	Rebounding (Shaquille O'Neal, Dennis Rodman, Dikembe Mutombo)	.40
285	Field Goal Percentage (Cedric Ceballos, Brad Daugherty, Dale Davis)	.05
286	Assists (John Stockton, Tim Hardaway, Scott Skiles)	.10
287	Free Throw Percentage (Eddie Johnson, Mark Price, Mahmoud Abdul-Rauf)	.10
288	3pt Field Goal Percentage (B.J. Armstrong, Chris Mullin, Kenny Smith)	.05
289	Steals (Michael Jordan, John Stockton, Mookie Blaylock)	.50
290	Blocks (Shaquille O'Neal, Hakeem Olajuwon, Dikembe Mutombo)	.50
291	Boys and Girls Club (David Robinson)	.15
292	Tribune 1 (B.J. Armstrong)	.05
293	Tribune 2 (Scottie Pippen)	.10
294	Tribune 3 (Kevin Johnson)	.05
295	Tribune 4 (Charles Barkley)	.25
296	Tribune 5 (Richard Dumas)	.05
297	Tribune 6 (Horace Grant)	.10
298	Checklist 1 (David Robinson)	.05
299	Checklist 2 (David Robinson)	.05
300	Checklist 3 (David Robinson)	.05
301	Craig Ehlo	.05
302	Jon Koncak	.05
303	Andrew Lang	.05
304	Chris Corchiani	.05
305	*Acie Earl*	.10
306	*Dino Radja*	.25
307	*Scott Burrell*	.25
308	Hersey Hawkins	.05
309	Eddie Johnson	.05
310	David Wingate	.05
311	*Corie Blount*	.10
312	Steve Kerr	.05
313	*Toni Kukoc*	.50
314	Pete Myers	.05
315	Jay Guidinger	.05
316	Tyrone Hill	.05
317	Gerald Madkins	.05
318	*Chris Mills*	.25
319	Bobby Phills	.05
320	*Lucious Harris*	.10
321	*Popeye Jones*	.25
322	Fat Lever	.05
323	*Jamal Mashburn*	1.25
324	Darren Morningstar	.05
325	Kevin Brooks	.05
326	Tom Hammonds	.05
327	*Darnell Mee*	.05
328	*Rodney Rodgers*	.25
329	Brian Williams	.05
330	Greg Anderson	.05
331	Sean Elliott	.05
332	*Allan Houston*	1.50
333	*Lindsey Hunter*	.15
334	David Wood	.05
335	Jud Buechler	.05
336	Chris Gatling	.05
337	*Josh Grant*	.05
338	Jeff Grayer	.05
339	Keith Jennings	.05
340	Avery Johnson	.05
341	*Chris Webber*	5.00
342	*Sam Cassell*	1.25
343	Mario Elie	.05
344	Eric Riley	.05
345	*Antonio Davis*	.10
346	Scott Haskin	.05
347	Gerald Paddio	.05
348	LaSalle Thompson	.05
349	Ken Williams	.05
350	Mark Aguirre	.05
351	*Terry Dehere*	.10
352	Henry James	.05
353	Sam Bowie	.05
354	*George Lynch*	.05
355	Kurt Rambis	.05
356	*Nick Van Exel*	1.00
357	Trevor Wilson	.05
358	Keith Askins	.05
359	Manute Bol	.05
360	Willie Burton	.05
361	Matt Geiger	.05
362	Alec Kessler	.05
363	*Vin Baker*	1.50
364	Ken Norman	.05
365	Dan Schayes	.05
366	Mike Brown	.05
367	*Isaiah Rider*	.50
368	Benoit Benjamin	.05
369	P.J. Brown	.05
370	Kevin Edwards	.05
371	Armon Gilliam	.05
372	Rick Mahorn	.05
373	Dwayne Schintzius	.05
374	*Rex Walters*	.05
375	Jayson Williams	.05
376	Eric Anderson	.05
377	Anthony Bonner	.05
378	Tony Campbell	.05
379	Herb Williams	.05
380	*Anfernee Hardaway*	4.00
381	Greg Kite	.05
382	Larry Krystkowiak	.05
383	Todd Lichti	.05
384	Dana Barros	.05
385	*Shawn Bradley*	.25
386	*Greg Graham*	.10
387	*Warren Kidd*	.10
388	Eric Leckner	.05
389	Moses Malone	.05
390	A.C. Green	.05
391	Frank Johnson	.05
392	Joe Kleine	.05
393	*Malcolm Mackey*	.10
394	Jerrod Mustaf	.05
395	Mark Bryant	.05
396	Chris Dudley	.05
397	Harvey Grant	.05
398	*James Robinson*	.20
399	Reggie Smith	.05
400	Randy Brown	.05
401	*Bobby Hurley*	.15
402	Jim Les	.05
403	Vinny Del Negro	.05
404	Sleepy Floyd	.05
405	Dennis Rodman	.75
406	*Chris Whitney*	.10
407	Vincent Askew	.05
408	Kendall Gill	.05
409	*Ervin Johnson*	.10
410	Rich King	.05
411	Detlef Schrempf	.05
412	Tom Chambers	.05
413	John Crotty	.05
414	Felton Spencer	.05
415	*Luther Wright*	.10
416	*Calbert Cheaney*	.30
417	Kevin Duckworth	.05
418	*Gheorghe Muresan*	.20
419	Checklist 1	.05
420	Checklist 2	.05
421	Rookie Checklist	.05
DR1	David Robinson (Com.)	.50
MB1	Commemorative (Magic Johnson, Larry Bird)	.50

1993-94 Hoops Gold

The 421-parallel set was inserted once in every 13-card pack and two per every 26-card jumbo pack. The only difference between the gold cards and the base 1993-94 cards is the Fifth Anniversary embossed gold-foil stamp and the gold-foil stripes highlighting the players' names on the front. Also, the gold cards are UV coated.

	MT
Complete Set (421):	60.00
Complete Series 1 (300):	35.00
Complete Series 2 (121):	25.00
Common Player:	.10
Semistars:	.20
Stars:	1.25x to 2.5x
Rookies:	1x to 2x

1993-94 Hoops Admiral's Choice

David Robinson, aka "The Admiral," has selected five impact players for this set - one player who entered the league in each of Robinson's first five seasons in the NBA. Fronts have the player's name in gold foil, plus an "Admiral's Choice" logo. Backs have a picture of the player, plus a summary of why Robinson selected him. Cards are numbered AC1-AC5.

		MT
	Complete Set (5):	5.00
	Common Player:	.25
1	Shawn Kemp	.75
2	Derrick Coleman	.25
3	Kenny Anderson	.25
4	Shaquille O'Neal	2.00
5	Chris Webber	2.00

1993-94 Hoops David's Best

This 1993-94 NBA Hoops Series I insert set, numbered DB1-DB5, highlights David Robinson's career with the San Antonio Spurs. They are random inserts. Each card commemorates one of Robinson's most memorable NBA games.

		MT
	Complete Set (5):	3.00
	Common Player:	.75
1	David Robinson (vs. Lakers)	.75
2	David Robinson (vs. Magic)	.75
3	David Robinson (vs. Trail Blazers)	.75
4	David Robinson (vs. Warriors)	.75
5	David Robinson (vs. Hornets)	.75

1993-94 Hoops David Robinson Commemorative

This 1994 NBA Hoops David Robinson Commemorative rookie card features the same front design as the original (1989-90), with UV coating, plus teal and gold-foil lettering added in the design. The back of the card has a montage of Robinson's cards from the past four seasons. The cards, numbered DR1, were random inserts in 1993-94 NBA Hoops Series II packs, one per every 18 packs. A limited number of autographed cards were also made and were available through randomly-inserted exchange cards.

		MT
	Complete Set:	2.00
	Common Robinson:	2.00
1	David Robinson (commemorative rookie)	2.00

1993-94 Hoops Draft Redemption

1993-94 NBA Hoops Series I packs had a redemption card randomly inserted in them allowing finders to send in for this 11-card set. The set features a full-color photo of the player taken during the draft. The player's name is in gold foil at the top of the card, along with a number representing what draft pick he was. The backs are in a horizontal format, with statistics and a player biography on the right and a mug shot on the left. The cards are numbered with an "LP" prefix.

		MT
	Complete Set (11):	50.00
	Common Player:	1.00
1	Chris Webber	15.00
2	Shawn Bradley	3.00
3	Anfernee Hardaway	20.00
4	Jamal Mashburn	6.00
5	Isaiah Rider	2.00
6	Calbert Cheaney	2.00
7	Bobby Hurley	1.00
8	Vin Baker	8.00
9	Rodney Rogers	1.50
10	Lindsey Hunter	1.00
11	Allan Houston	2.00

1993-94 Hoops Face to Face

This 12-card set features 1992-93's top rookies in dream match-ups against seasoned NBA stars. The cards, which were random inserts in 1993-94 NBA Hoops Series I packs, feature one player on the front and the other on the back.

		MT
	Complete Set (12):	45.00
	Common Player:	1.00
1	Shaquille O'Neal, David Robinson	10.00
2	Alonzo Mourning, Patrick Ewing	4.00
3	Christian Laettner, Shawn Kemp	2.00
4	Jim Jackson, Clyde Drexler	5.00
5	LaPhonso Ellis, Larry Johnson	3.00
6	Clarence Weatherspoon, Charles Barkley	4.00
7	Tom Gugliotta, Karl Malone	2.00
8	Walt Williams, Magic Johnson	4.00
9	Robert Horry, Scottie Pippen	3.00
10	Harold Miner, Michael Jordan	12.00
11	Todd Day, Chris Mullin	1.00
12	Richard Dumas, Dominique Wilkins	1.00

1993-94 Hoops Magic's All-Rookies

Ten standout rookies appear in this limited-edition insert set. Cards were available in 1993-94 NBA Hoops Series II packs, one per every 30 packs. Cards have a "Magic's All-Rookie Team" logo on the front. The backs, numbered 1 of 10, etc., have a quote from Johnson about the player represented on the card. An image of Johnson is ghosted in the background on the back.

		MT
	Complete Set (10):	70.00
	Common Player:	2.00
1	Chris Webber	15.00
2	Shawn Bradley	3.00
3	Anfernee Hardaway	20.00
4	Jamal Mashburn	7.00
5	Isaiah Rider	3.00
6	Calbert Cheaney	3.00
7	Bobby Hurley	2.00
8	Vin Baker	8.00
9	Lindsey Hunter	2.00
10	Toni Kukoc	5.00

1993-94 Hoops Scoops

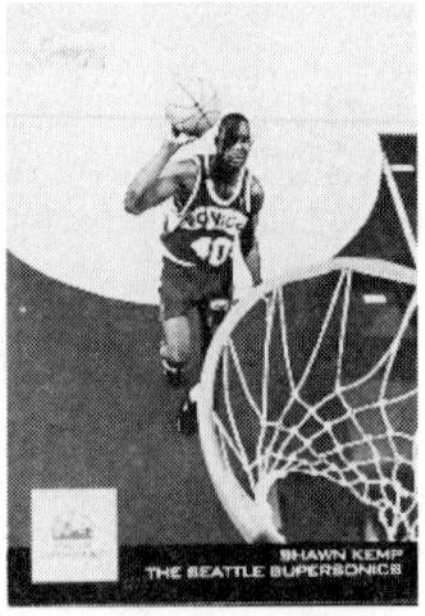

These cards were random inserts in 1993-94 NBA Hoops Series II packs and are numbered on the back using an "HS" prefix. Each NBA team is represented by a card; the player is shown from a camera angle looking down on the rim. His name, team name and team logo are in a black panel at the bottom of the card. The Hoops Scoops logo is at the top. The card back has several questions/answers about team history. A parallel gold foil-stamped set was also produced; these cards were random inserts in Series II packs. They are identical to the Hoops Scoops cards, except they also are UV coated. The stars are generally two to four times more valuable than their regular Hoops Scoops counterparts.

		MT
	Complete Set (28):	1.50
	Common Player:	.05
1	Dominique Wilkins	.15
2	Robert Parish	.07
3	Alonzo Mourning	.25
4	Scottie Pippen	.20
5	Larry Nance	.05
6	Derek Harper	.05
7	Reggie Williams	.05
8	Bill Laimbeer	.07
9	Tim Hardaway	.10
10	Hakeem Olajuwon	.25
11	LaSalle Thompson	.05
12	Danny Manning	.07
13	James Worthy	.10
14	Grant Long	.05
15	Blue Edwards	.05
16	Christian Laettner	.10
17	Derrick Coleman	.10
18	Patrick Ewing	.15
19	Nick Anderson	.07
20	Clarence Weatherspoon	.07
21	Charles Barkely	.25
22	Cliff Robinson	.07
23	Lionel Simmons	.05
24	David Robinson	.25
25	Shawn Kemp	.15
26	Karl Malone	.15
27	Rex Chapman	.05
28	Answer card	.05

1993-94 Hoops Scoops Fifth Anniversary Gold

Inserted randomly in 1993-94 Hoops Series Two foil packs, this 28-card set parallels the Hoops Scoops insert. The cards have a gold foil Fifth Anniversary logo and UV coating.

		MT
Complete Set (28):		3.00
Common Player:		.10
*Stars:		2x

1993-94 Hoops Supreme Court

This limited-edition insert set features 11 players chosen by several hundred members of the hobby media. A card of Michael Jordan, who retired before the 1993-94 season began, is also included. Cards were randomly inserted in 1993-94 NBA Hoops Series II packs, one per every 11 packs. Fronts have the player's name and "Supreme Court" stamped in silver foil; backs have a picture of the player, plus a summary of why the hobbyist selected the player. Cards are numbered SC1-SC11.

		MT
Complete Set (11):		10.00
Common Player:		.50
1	Charles Barkley	1.00
2	David Robinson	1.00
3	Patrick Ewing	.75
4	Shaquille O'Neal	4.00
5	Larry Johnson	.75
6	Karl Malone	.50
7	Alonzo Mourning	1.00
8	John Stockton	.50
9	Hakeem Olajuwon	1.50
10	Scottie Pippen	2.00
11	Michael Jordan	5.00

1993-94 Hoops Gold Medal Bread

The 49-card, standard-size set was produced by Hoops for Gold Medal bread and distributed in loaves. The card design is nearly identical to the 1993-94 set. The cards are unnumbered.

		MT
Complete Set (49):		60.00
Common Player:		1.00
(1)	B.J. Armstrong	1.50
(2)	Thurl Bailey	1.00
(3)	Rolando Blackman	1.50
(4)	Mookie Blaylock	1.50
(5)	Tyrone Bogues	2.00
(6)	Anthony Bowie	1.00
(7)	Chucky Brown	1.00
(8)	Dee Brown	1.00
(9)	Duane Causwell	1.00
(10)	Cedric Ceballos	3.00
(11)	Rex Chapman	1.50
(12)	Bimbo Coles	1.00
(13)	Tyrone Corbin	1.00
(14)	Terry Cummings	1.50
(15)	Todd Day	1.00
(16)	Joe Dumars	2.00
(17)	Mark Eaton	1.00
(18)	Vern Fleming	1.00
(19)	Kevin Gamble	1.00
(20)	Kendall Gill	1.00
(21)	Tom Gugliotta	2.00
(22)	Derek Harper	1.00
(23)	Ron Harper	1.50
(24)	Hersey Hawkins	1.00
(25)	Tyrone Hill	1.00
(26)	Adam Keefe	1.00
(27)	Shawn Kemp	12.00
(28)	Jerome Kersey	1.00
(29)	Stacey King	1.00
(30)	Luc Longley	1.00
(31)	Moses Malone	2.00
(32)	Anthony Mason	1.50
(33)	Vernon Maxwell	1.00
(34)	Xavier McDaniel	1.00
(35)	Oliver Miller	1.00
(36)	Sam Mitchell	1.00
(37)	Chris Morris	1.00
(38)	Dikembe Mutombo	3.00
(39)	Billy Owens	1.00
(40)	Robert Parish	2.50
(41)	Sam Perkins	1.50
(42)	Olden Polynice	1.00
(43)	Terry Porter	1.00
(44)	J.R. Reid	1.00
(45)	Rony Seikaly	1.00
(46)	Lionel Simmons	1.00
(47)	Scott Skiles	1.00
(48)	Sedale Threatt	1.00
(49)	Loy Vaught	1.00

1993-94 Hoops Sheets

The six-sheet set features players from the Chicago Bulls, Detroit Pistons, New Jersey Nets, New York Knicks, Phoenix Suns and Orlando Magic. Each team sheet has an individual sponsor and the card design is virtually identical to the 1993-94 Hoops base set. The cards are unnumbered.

		MT
Complete Set (6):		20.00
Common Player:		3.00
(1)	Chicago Bulls - Colonial Bakery - Iron Kids Bread (B.J. Armstrong, Bill Cartwright, Horace Grant, Phil Jackson, Stacy King, John Paxson, Will Perdue, Scottie Pippen, Scott Williams)	10.00
(2)	Detroit Pistons - Farmer Jack (Greg Anderson, Don Chaney CO, Joe Dumars, Sean Elliott, Allan Houston, Lindsey Hunter, Terry Mills, Olden Polynice, Isiah Thomas, David Wood)	3.00
(3)	New Jersey Nets - McCain/Ellio's Pizza (Kenny Anderson, Derrick Coleman, Chris Morris, Chuck Daly CO, Rick Mahorn, Jayson Williams, Kevin Edwards, Armon Gilliam, Dwayne Schintzius, Chucky Brown, Benoit Benjamin, Rex Walter	3.00
(4)	New York Knicks - Castrol (Greg Anthony, Patrick Ewing, Charles Oakley, Charles Smith, John Starks)	3.00
(5)	Phoenix Suns - Phelphs Dodge Corp. - Arizona Public Service Co. (Danny Ainge, Charles Barkley, Cedric Ceballos, A.C. Green, Kevin Johnson, Dan Majerle, Oliver Miller, Mark West, Paul Westphal CO)	4.00
(6)	Orlando Magic - Pepsi (Nick Anderson, Anthony Bowie, Shaquille O'Neal, Donald Royal, Scott Skiles, Jeff Turner)	5.00

1994-95 Hoops Promo Sheet

This 7" x 10-1/2" perforated sheet features six promo cards for the 1994-95 Hoops Series Two set. The cards are identical to the regular set except they are unnumbered.

		MT
Complete Set (6):		2.00
Common Player:		.15
1	Jason Kidd	1.00
2	Donyell Marshall	.15
3	Eric Montross, Rodney Rogers	.15
4	Alonzo Mourning	.30
5	John Starks	.15
6	Dennis Rodman	1.00

1994-95 Hoops Preview

The standard-size preview card of Spurs' center David Robinson shows the design of the 1994-95 Hoops card set. The card is unnumbered.

		MT
Complete Set (1):		2.00
Common Player:		2.00
NNO	David Robinson	2.00

1994-95 Hoops

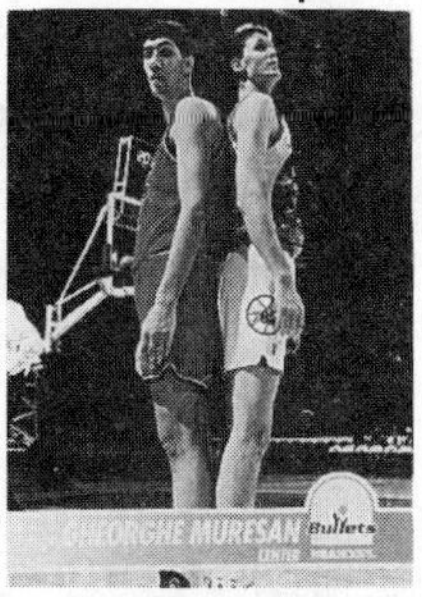

The SkyBox 1994-95 NBA Hoops basketball set features 300 cards, including 221 player cards, with the remainder made up of coaches, NBA All-Stars, league leaders, a Tribune set recapping the finals and a Magic Johnson commemorative coaching card. The front of each card has a borderless design with full UV-coating, along with each player's position and team logo. The backs feature a player head shot and expanded statistics. Hoops, once again, included an NBA Draft Lottery Pick Exchange card, along with Supreme Court and Big Number insert sets. An unnumbered David Robinson promo card was also produced to preview the regular set's design. The card is worth $2.50.

		MT
Complete Set (450):		25.00
Complete Series 1 (300):		10.00
Complete Series 2 (150):		15.00
Common Player:		.05
Minor Stars:		.10
Series 1 Pack (12):		.75
Series 1 Wax Box (36):		18.00
Series 2 Retail Pack (12):		1.25
Series 2 Retail Wax Box (36):		35.00
Series 2 Hobby Pack (12):		1.25
Series 2 Hobby Wax Box (36):		40.00
1	Stacey Augmon	.05
2	Mookie Blaylock	.05
3	Doug Edwards	.05
4	Craig Ehlo	.05
5	Jon Koncak	.05
6	Danny Manning	.10
7	Kevin Willis	.05
8	Dee Brown	.05
9	Sherman Douglas	.05
10	Acie Earl	.05
11	Kevin Gamble	.05
12	Xavier McDaniel	.05
13	Robert Parish	.05
14	Dino Radja	.10
15	Tony Bennett	.05
16	Muggsy Bogues	.05
17	Scott Burrell	.05
18	Dell Curry	.05
19	Hersey Hawkins	.05
20	Eddie Johnson	.05
21	Larry Johnson	.25
22	Alonzo Mourning	.25
23	B.J. Armstrong	.05
24	Corie Blount	.05
25	Bill Cartwright	.05
26	Horace Grant	.10
27	Toni Kukoc	.10
28	Luc Longley	.05
29	Pete Myers	.05
30	Scottie Pippen	.50
31	Scott Williams	.05
32	Terrell Brandon	.05
33	Brad Daugherty	.05
34	Tyrone Hill	.05
35	Chris Mills	.05
36	Larry Nance	.05
37	Bobby Phills	.05
38	Mark Price	.10
39	Gerald Wilkins	.05
40	John Williams	.05
41	Terry Davis	.05
42	Lucious Harris	.05
43	Jim Jackson	.25
44	Popeye Jones	.05
45	Tim Legler	.05
46	Jamal Mashburn	.30
47	Sean Rooks	.05
48	Mahmoud Abdul-Rauf	.05
49	LaPhonso Ellis	.05
50	Dikembe Mutombo	.10
51	Robert Pack	.05
52	Rodney Rogers	.05
53	Bryant Stith	.05
54	Brian Williams	.05
55	Reggie Williams	.05
56	Cadillac Anderson, Jeff Turner	.05
57	Joe Dumars	.10
58	Sean Elliott	.05
59	Allan Houston	.10
60	Lindsey Hunter	.05
61	Mark Macon	.05
62	Terry Mills	.05
63	Victor Alexander	.05
64	Chris Gatling	.05
65	Tim Hardaway	.10
66	Avery Johnson	.05
67	Sarunas Marciulionis	.05
68	Chris Mullin	.10
69	Billy Owens	.05
70	Latrell Sprewell	.25
71	Chris Webber	.30
72	Matt Bullard	.05
73	Sam Cassell	.10
74	Mario Elie	.05
75	Carl Herrera	.05
76	Robert Horry	.05
77	Vernon Maxwell	.05
78	Hakeem Olajuwon	.50
79	Kenny Smith	.05
80	Otis Thorpe	.05
81	Antonio Davis	.05
82	Dale Davis	.05
83	Vern Fleming	.05
84	Scott Haskin	.05
85	Derrick McKey	.05
86	Reggie Miller	.20
87	Byron Scott	.05
88	Rik Smits	.10
89	Haywoode Workman	.05
90	Terry Dehere	.05
91	Harold Ellis	.05
92	Gary Grant	.05
93	Ron Harper	.05
94	Mark Jackson	.05
95	Stanley Roberts	.05
96	Loy Vaught	.05
97	Dominique Wilkins	.15
98	Elden Campbell, Kendall Gill	.05
99	Doug Christie	.05
100	Vlade Divac	.05
101	Reggie Jordan	.05
102	George Lynch	.05
103	Anthony Peeler	.05
104	Sedale Threatt	.05
105	Nick Van Exel	.50
106	James Worthy	.05
107	Bimbo Coles	.05
108	Matt Geiger	.05
109	Grant Long	.05
110	Harold Miner	.05
111	Glen Rice	.10
112	John Salley	.05
113	Rony Seikaly	.05
114	Brian Shaw	.05
115	Steve Smith	.05
116	Vin Baker	.20
117	Jon Barry	.05
118	Todd Day	.05
119	Lee Mayberry	.05
120	Eric Murdock	.05
121	Ken Norman	.05
122	Mike Brown	.05
123	Stacey King	.05
124	Christian Laettner	.05
125	Chuck Person	.05
126	Isaiah Rider	.15
127	Chris Smith	.05
128	Doug West	.05
130	Kenny Anderson	.10
131	Benoit Benjamin	.05
132	P.J. Brown	.05
133	Derrick Coleman	.10
134	Kevin Edwards	.05
135	Armon Gilliam	.05
136	Chris Morris	.05
137	Rex Walters	.05
138	David Wesley	.05
139	Greg Anthony	.05
140	Anthony Bonner	.05
141	Hubert Davis	.05
142	Patrick Ewing	.20
143	Derek Harper	.05
144	Anthony Mason	.05
145	Charles Oakley	.05
146	Charles Smith	.05
147	John Starks	.05
148	Nick Anderson	.05
149	Anthony Avent	.05
150	Anthony Bowie	.05
151	Anfernee Hardaway	1.25
152	Shaquille O'Neal	1.00
153	Donald Royal	.05
154	Dennis Scott	.05
155	Scott Skiles	.05
157	Dana Barros	.05
158	Shawn Bradley	.10
159	Greg Graham	.05
160	Warren Kidd	.05
161	Eric Leckner	.05
162	Jeff Malone	.05
163	Tim Perry	.05
164	Clarence Weatherspoon	.05
165	Danny Ainge	.05
166	Charles Barkley	.40
167	Cedric Ceballos	.05
168	A.C. Green	.05
169	Kevin Johnson	.10
171	Dan Majerle	.05
172	Oliver Miller	.05
173	Mark West	.05
174	Clyde Drexler	.20
175	Chris Dudley	.05
176	Harvey Grant	.05
177	Tracy Murray	.05
178	Terry Porter	.05
179	Clifford Robinson	.05
180	James Robinson	.05
181	Rod Strickland	.05
182	Buck Williams	.05
183	Duane Causwell	.05
184	Bobby Hurley	.05
185	Olden Polynice	.05
186	Mitch Richmond	.05
187	Lionel Simmons	.05
188	Wayman Tisdale	.05
189	Spud Webb	.05
190	Walt Williams	.05
191	Willie Anderson	.05
192	Lloyd Daniels	.05
193	Vinny Del Negro	.05
194	Dale Ellis	.05
195	J.R. Reid	.05
196	David Robinson	.40
197	Dennis Rodman	.50
199	Ervin Johnson	.05
200	Shawn Kemp	.25
201	Chris King	.05
202	Nate McMillan	.05
203	Gary Payton	.10
204	Sam Perkins	.05
205	Ricky Pierce	.05
206	Detlef Schrempf	.05
207	David Benoit	.05
208	Tom Chambers	.05
209	Tyrone Corbin	.05
210	Jeff Hornacek	.05
211	Karl Malone	.25
212	Bryon Russell	.05
213	Felton Spencer	.05
214	John Stockton	.20
215	Luther Wright	.05
216	Michael Adams	.05
217	Mitchell Butler	.05
218	Rex Chapman	.05
219	Calbert Cheaney	.10
220	Pervis Ellison	.05
221	Tom Gugliotta	.05
222	Don MacLean	.05
223	Gheorghe Muresan	.05
224	Kenny Anderson	.10
225	B.J. Armstrong	.05
226	Mookie Blaylock	.05
227	Derrick Coleman	.10
228	Patrick Ewing	.10
229	Horace Grant	.10
230	Alonzo Mourning	.15
231	Shaquille O'Neal	.50
232	Charles Oakley	.05
233	Scottie Pippen	.25
234	Mark Price	.05
235	John Starks	.05
236	Dominique Wilkins	.05
237	East Team	.05
238	Charles Barkley	.20
239	Clyde Drexler	.10
240	Kevin Johnson	.05
241	Shawn Kemp	.15
242	Karl Malone	.10
243	Danny Manning	.05
244	Hakeem Olajuwon	.25
245	Gary Payton	.05
246	Mitch Richmond	.05
247	Clifford Robinson	.05
248	David Robinson	.20
249	Latrell Sprewell	.15
250	John Stockton	.10
251	West Team	.05
252	3-Point Goal	.05
253	Assists	.05
254	Blocks	.05
255	Free Throw	.05
256	Rebounds	.25
257	Scoring Leaders	.20
258	Steals	.05
259	Chris Webber (ROY)	.15
260	Hakeem Olajuwon	.25
261	Hakeem Olajuwon	.25
262	1993-94 NBA Sixth Man Award	.05
263	1994 NBA All-Star Game MVP	.25
264	Anfernee Hardaway	.50
265	1993-94 NBA Most Improved Player	.05
266	Game 1	.25
267	Game 2	.05
268	Game 3	.05
269	Game 4	.25
270	Game 5	.05
271	Game 6	.05
272	Game 7	.05
273	Champion Card	.25
274	Lenny Wilkens	.05
275	Chris Ford	.05
276	Allan Bristow	.05
277	Phil Jackson	.05
278	Mike Fratello	.05
279	Dick Motta	.05
280	Dan Issel	.05
281	Don Chaney	.05
282	Don Nelson	.05
283	Rudy Tomjanovich	.05
284	Larry Brown	.05
285	Del Harris	.05
286	Kevin Loughery	.05
287	Mike Dunleavy	.05
288	Sidney Lowe	.05
289	Pat Riley	.05
290	Brian Hill	.05
291	John Lucas	.05
292	Paul Westphal	.05
293	Garry St. Jean	.05
294	George Karl	.05
295	Jerry Sloan	.05
296	Magic Comm Card	.40
297	Boys and Girls Club	.10
298	Checklist 1	.05
299	Checklist 2	.05
300	Checklist 3	.05
301	*Sergei Bazarevich*	.05
302	Tyrone Corbin	.05
303	Grant Long	.05
304	Ken Norman	.05
305	Steve Smith	.05
306	Blue Edwards	.05
307	*Greg Minor*	.10
308	*Eric Montross*	.30
309	Dominique Wilkins	.10
310	Michael Adams	.05
311	*Darrin Hancock*	.05
312	Robert Parish	.05
313	Ron Harper	.05
314	*Dickey Simpkins*	.15
315	Michael Cage	.05
316	*Tony Dumas*	.25
317	*Jason Kidd*	2.00
318	Roy Tarpley	.05
319	Dale Ellis	.05
320	*Jalen Rose*	1.50
321	*Bill Curley*	.15
322	*Grant Hill*	3.00
323	Oliver Miller	.05
324	Mark West	.05
325	Tom Gugliotta	.05
326	Ricky Pierce	.05
327	*Carlos Rogers*	.20
328	*Clifford Rozier*	.20
329	Rony Seikaly	.05
330	*Tim Breaux*	.05
331	Duane Ferrell	.05
332	Mark Jackson	.05
333	*Lamond Murray*	.30
334	*Charles Outlaw*	.10
335	*Eric Piatkowski*	.20
336	Pooh Richardson	.05
337	Malik Sealy	.05
338	Cedric Ceballos	.05
339	*Eddie Jones*	2.00
340	*Anthony Miller*	.05
341	Kevin Gamble	.05
342	Brad Lohaus	.05
343	Billy Owens	.05
344	*Khalid Reeves*	.40
345	Kevin Willis	.05
346	*Eric Mobley*	.10
347	Johnny Newman	.05
348	Ed Pinckney	.05
349	*Glenn Robinson*	1.50
350	*Howard Eisley*	.05
351	*Donyell Marshall*	.25
352	*Yinka Dare*	.10
353	*Charlie Ward*	.15
354	*Monty Williams*	.15
355	Horace Grant	.10
356	Brian Shaw	.05
357	*Brooks Thompson*	.15
358	*Derick Alston*	.05
359	*B.J. Tyler*	.15
360	Scott Williams	.05
361	*Sharone Wright*	.40
362	*Tony Lang*	.05
363	Danny Manning	.10
364	*Wesley Person*	.50
365	Wayman Tisdale	.05
366	*Trevor Ruffin*	.15
367	*Aaron McKie*	.50
368	*Brian Grant*	.75
369	*Michael Smith*	.15
370	Sean Elliott	.05
371	Avery Johnson	.05
372	Chuck Person	.05
373	Bill Cartwright	.05
374	Sarunas Marciulionis	.05
375	*Dontonio Wingfield*	.05
376	Antoine Carr	.05
377	*Jamie Watson*	.15
378	*Juwan Howard*	1.00
379	*Jim McIlvaine*	.05
380	Scott Skiles	.05
381	*Anthony Tucker*	.10
382	Chris Webber	.30
383	Bill Fitch	.05
384	Bill Blair	.05
385	Butch Beard	.05
386	P.J. Carlesimo	.05
387	Bob Hill	.05
388	Jim Lynam	.05
389	Checklist 4	.05
390	Checklist 5	.05
391	Atlanta Hawks	.05
392	Boston Celtics	.05
393	Charlotte Hornets	.05
394	Chicago Bulls	.05
395	Cleveland Cavaliers	.05
396	Dallas Mavericks	.05
397	Denver Nuggets	.05
398	Detroit Pistons	.05
399	Golden State Warriors	.05
400	Houston Rockets	.05
401	Indiana Pacers	.05
402	L.A. Clippers	.05
403	L.A. Lakers	.05
404	Miami Heat	.05
405	Milwaukee Bucks	.05
406	Minnesota Timberwolves	.05
407	New Jersey Nets	.05
408	New York Knicks	.05
409	Orlando Magic	.05
410	Philadelphia 76ers	.05
411	Phoenix Suns	.05
412	Portland Trail Blazers	.05
413	Sacramento Kings	.05
414	San Antonio Spurs	.05
415	Seattle Supersonics	.05
416	Utah Jazz	.05
417	Washington Bullets	.05
418	Toronto Raptors	.05
419	Vancouver Grizzlies	.05
420	NBA Logo Card	.05
421	Glenn Robinson, Chris Webber	.25
422	Jason Kidd, Shawn Bradley	.75
423	Grant Hill, Anfernee Hardaway	1.00
424	Donyell Marshall, Jamal Mashburn	.25
425	Juwan Howard, Isaiah Rider	.25
426	Sharone Wright, Calbert Cheaney	.15
427	Tracy Murray, Bobby Hurley	.15
428	Horace Grant, Vin Baker	.15
429	Eric Montross, Rodney Rogers	.15
430	Eddie Jones, Lindsey Hunter	.25
431	Craig Ehlo	.05
432	Dino Radja	.05
433	Toni Kukoc	.05
434	Mark Price	.05
435	Latrell Sprewell	.15
436	Sam Cassell	.05
437	Vernon Maxwell	.05
438	Haywoode Workman	.05
439	Harold Ellis	.05
440	Cedric Ceballos	.05
441	Vlade Divac	.05
442	Nick Van Exel	.10
443	John Starks	.05
444	Scott Williams	.05
445	Clifford Robinson	.05
446	Spud Webb	.05
447	Avery Johnson	.05
448	Dennis Rodman	.25
449	Sarunas Marciulionis	.05
450	Nate McMillan	.05

1994-95 Hoops Big Numbers

Big Numbers was a 12-card set, randomly inserted into Hoops packs at a ratio of one every 30 packs. The cards are horizontal in design and present a player photo standing alongside his big number in the 1994-95 season.

		MT
Complete Set (12):		70.00
Common Player:		2.00
Comp. Rainbow Set (12):		70.00
Common Rainbow:		2.00
1	David Robinson	8.00
2	Jamal Mashburn	4.00
3	Hakeem Olajuwon	10.00

4	Patrick Ewing	5.00
5	Shaquille O'Neal	16.00
6	Latrell Sprewell	3.00
7	Chris Webber	5.00
8	Anfernee Hardaway	15.00
9	Scottie Pippen	10.00
10	Isaiah Rider	2.00
11	Alonzo Mourning	5.00
12	Charles Barkley	6.00

1994-95 Hoops Draft Redemption

As it has done in previous years, NBA Hoops offered a redemption card in its 1994-95 Series I packs; finders were entitled to a 10-card NBA Draft set if they mailed the card in. The cards were randomly seeded one per every 360 packs. The draft set cards show the players with their NBA teams.

		MT
Complete Set (10):		30.00
Common Player:		.50
1	Glenn Robinson	4.00
2	Jason Kidd	5.00
3	Grant Hill	10.00
4	Donyell Marshall	.50
5	Juwan Howard	7.00
6	Sharone Wright	1.00
7	Lamond Murray	1.00
8	Brian Grant	2.00
9	Eric Montross	1.00
10	Eddie Jones	6.00

1994-95 Hoops Magic's All-Rookies

This insert set, issued for the third straight year, has two versions - a normal version done with a reddish-orange background, or a FoilTech version printed on a foil background. The cards feature Magic Johnson's selections of the top 10 rookies entering the season. The normal card has a color action photo on the front, with All-Rookie printed in an arc on the front. The card back, numbered with an "AR" prefix, shows Johnson holding the card, and offers his thoughts about the player. Cards were random inserts in 1994-95 NBA Hoops Series II packs, one every 12th pack.

		MT
Complete Set (10):		25.00
Common Player:		1.00
Complete Jumbo Set (10):		50.00
Jumbo Cards:		1x-2x
Foil Cards:		2x
1	Glenn Robinson	3.00
2	Jason Kidd	4.00
3	Grant Hill	8.00
4	Donyell Marshall	1.00
5	Juwan Howard	4.00
6	Sharone Wright	1.00
7	Brian Grant	2.00
8	Eddie Jones	4.00
9	Jalen Rose	1.00
10	Wesley Person	1.00

1994-95 Hoops Power Ratings

Each 1994-95 NBA Hoops Series II pack contained one of 54 Power Ratings insert cards. The card front has an orange-lettered Hoops Power stamp on it, with the player's name in holographic foil at the bottom. The player is shown on a black and blue swirled background, with five orange, scratch-like lines running diagonally across the length of the card from upper left to lower right. The card back, numbered with a "PR" prefix, has a bar graph showing the player's statistics from the previous season. A photo is also given.

		MT
Complete Set (54):		10.00
Common Player:		.10
Minor Stars:		.25
1	Mookie Blaylock	.10
2	Stacey Augmon	.10
3	Dino Radja	.25
4	Dominique Wilkins	.25
5	Larry Johnson	.50
6	Alonzo Mourning	.50
7	Toni Kukoc	.25
8	Scottie Pippen	1.00
9	John Williams	.10
10	Mark Price	.25
11	Jim Jackson	.50
12	Jamal Mashburn	.50
13	Dale Ellis	.10
14	LaPhonso Ellis	.10
15	Joe Dumars	.25
16	Lindsey Hunter	.10
17	Latrell Sprewell	.50
18	Chris Mullin	.25
19	Vernon Maxwell	.10
20	Hakeem Olajuwon	1.00
21	Mark Jackson	.10
22	Reggie Miller	.50
23	Pooh Richardson	.10
24	Loy Vaught	.10
25	Vlade Divac	.10
26	Nick Van Exel	.50
27	Glen Rice	.25
28	Billy Owens	.10
29	Vin Baker	.40
30	Eric Murdock	.10
31	Christian Laettner	.10
32	Isaiah Rider	.40
33	Kenny Anderson	.25
34	Derrick Coleman	.25
35	Patrick Ewing	.50
36	John Starks	.10
37	Nick Anderson	.10
38	Anfernee Hardaway	2.00
39	Shawn Bradley	.25
40	Clarence Weatherspoon	.25
41	Charles Barkley	1.00
42	Kevin Johnson	.25
43	Clyde Drexler	.50
44	Cliff Robinson	.10
45	Mitch Richmond	.25
46	Olden Polynice	.10
47	Sean Elliott	.10
48	Chuck Person	.10
49	Shawn Kemp	.60
50	Gary Payton	.25
51	Jeff Hornacek	.10
52	Karl Malone	.50
53	Rex Chapman	.10
54	Don MacLean	.10

1994-95 Hoops Predators

These 1994-95 NBA Hoops Series II inserts are similar in appearance to the Hoops Power cards, except the word "Predator" is in green foil under the Hoops Power logo. The player's name is also in green foil. The card back uses a bar graph to show the player's statistics from the previous season. A second photo is also included. Cards are numbered using a "P" prefix and could be found in every 12th pack.

		MT
Complete Set (8):		5.00
Common Player:		.25
1	Mahmoud Abdul-Rauf	.25
2	Dikembe Mutombo	.50
3	Shaquille O'Neal	4.00
4	Tracy Murray	.25
5	David Robinson	1.00
6	Dennis Rodman	2.00
7	Nate McMillan	.25
8	John Stockton	.75

1994-95 Hoops Supreme Court

Supreme Court cards were randomly inserted into every four packs of Hoops. This 50-card set displays top pros with an enhanced photo and a gold embossed NBA Hoops Supreme Court logo on the front.

		MT
Complete Set (50):		20.00
Common Player:		.25
Minor Stars:		.50
1	Mookie Blaylock	.25
2	Danny Manning	.25
3	Dino Radja	.50
4	Larry Johnson	.75
5	Alonzo Mourning	1.00
6	B.J. Armstrong	.25
7	Horace Grant	.50
8	Toni Kukoc	.50
9	Brad Daugherty	.25
10	Mark Price	.25
11	Jim Jackson	1.00
12	Jamal Mashburn	1.00
13	Dikembe Mutombo	.50
14	Joe Dumars	.50
15	Lindsey Hunter	.25
16	Tim Hardaway	.50
17	Chris Mullin	.50
18	Sam Cassell	.50
19	Hakeem Olajuwon	2.00
20	Reggie Miller	.75
21	Dominique Wilkins	.50
22	Nick Van Exel	1.00
23	Harold Miner	.25
24	Steve Smith	.25
25	Vin Baker	1.00
26	Christian Laettner	.50
27	Isaiah Rider	.50
28	Kenny Anderson	.50
29	Derrick Coleman	.50
30	Patrick Ewing	.75
31	John Starks	.25
32	Anfernee Hardaway	4.00
33	Shaquille O'Neal	4.00
34	Shawn Bradley	.50
35	Clarence Weatherspoon	.50
36	Charles Barkley	1.50
37	Kevin Johnson	.50
38	Oliver Miller	.25
39	Clyde Drexler	.75
40	Cliff Robinson	.25
41	Mitch Richmond	.25
42	Bobby Hurley	.25
43	David Robinson	1.50
44	Dennis Rodman	2.00
45	Gary Payton	.75
46	Shawn Kemp	1.50
47	John Stockton	.75
48	Karl Malone	.75
49	Calbert Cheaney	.25
50	Tom Gugliotta	.25

1994-95 Hoops Schick

Part of a promotion by Schick Shaving Products, the 30-card set features 29 top rookies and a checklist card. Three cards were available in each specially marked package of Tracer 5 and 10 pack refills. The package also included a special mail-in offer card whereby the collector could receive the complete set by sending in three proof of purchase seals plus $2.50 P/H. The offer expired 12/31/95. The cards have the same design as the base-set cards, except the word rookie and the player's name on the front are in gold (rather than gold-foil) lettering. The cards are unnumbered.

	MT
Complete Set (30):	20.00
Common Player:	.25
Sergei Bazarevich	.25
Bill Curley	.25
Tony Dumas	.40
Brian Grant	3.00
Darrin Hancock	.25
Grant Hill	7.00
Eddie Jones	5.00
Jason Kidd	6.00
Aaron McKie	1.00
Donyell Marshall	.75
Anthony Miller	.25
Greg Minor	.40
Eric Mobley	.25
Eric Montross	.40
Lamond Murray	.50
Eric Piatkowski	.75
Wesley Person	.50
Khalid Reeves	.25
Glenn Robinson	4.00
Carlos Rogers	.25
Jalen Rose	4.00
Clifford Rozier	.25
Dickey Simpkins	.25
Brooks Thompson	.25
Anthony Tucker	.25
B.J. Tyler	.25
Charlie Ward	.75
Monty Williams	.25
Sharone Wright	.40
Checklist Card (Donyell Marshall) (Shaving)	.40

1994-95 Hoops Sheets

The nine- or 12-card sheets were given to fans at various NBA arenas and each sheet features varying sponsors. The cards are unnumbered and are virtually identical to the 1994-95 Hoops base set.

		MT
Complete Set (18):		40.00
Common Player:		3.00
(1)	Atlanta Hawks - Oscar Mayer (Stacey Augmon, Mookie Blaylock, Tyrone Corbin, Craig Ehlo, Jon Koncak, Andrew Lang, Ken Norman, Steve Smith, Len Wilkens CO)	3.00
(2)	Charlotte Hornets - Bojangle's Famous Chicken'n Biscuits (Michael Adams, Tony Bennett, Muggsy Bogues, Scott Burrell, Dell Curry, Kenny Gattison, Darrin Hancock, Hersey Hawkins, Larry Johnson, Alonzo Mourning, Robert Parish),	3.00
(3)	Charlotte Hornets - Southern Bell Yellow Pages (Muggsy Bogues, Dell Curry, Hersey Hawkins, Larry Johnson, Alonzo Mourning)	3.00
(4)	Charlotte Hornets - Belk/Reebok/WBTV 3 (Michael Adams, Tony Bennett, Muggsy Bogues, Scott Burrell, Dell Curry, Kenny Gattison, Hersey Hawkins, Larry Johnson, Alonzo Mourning, Robert Parish, David Wingate)	3.00
(5)	Chicago Bulls - Jewel/Nabisco (B.J. Armstrong, Corie Blount, Phil Jackson, Steve Kerr, Toni Kukoc, Luc Longley, Scottie Pippen, Bill Wennington)	5.00
(6)	Dallas Mavericks - Doritos (Terry Davis, Tony Dumas, Lucious Harris, Jim Jackson, Popeye Jones, Jason Kidd, Jamal Mashburn, Dick Motta CO)	4.00
(7)	Denver Nuggets - Blimpie/9 News/KYBG Sportstalk (Mahmoud Abdul-Rauf, LaPhonso Ellis, Dan Issel CO, Dikembe Mutombo, Robert Pack, Rodney Rogers, Bryant Stith, Brian Williams, Reggie Williams)	3.00
(8)	Detroit Pistons - Kmart/Castrol (Don Chaney CO, Bill Curley, Joe Dumars, Grant Hill, Allan Houston, Lindsey Hunter, Mark Macon, Oliver Miller, Terry Mills, Mark West)	5.00
(9)	Minnesota Timberwolves - Make-A-Wish Foundation (Bill Blair CO, Mike Brown, Stacey King, Christian Laettner, Donyell Marshall, Isaiah Rider, Doug West, Michael Williams)	3.00
(10)	New York Knicks - Nobody Beats the Wiz (Greg Anthony, Anthony Bonner, Hubert Davis, Patrick Ewing, Derek Harper, Anthony Mason, Charles Oakley, Charles Smith, John Starks, Herb Williams)	3.00
(11)	Orlando Magic - Gooding's Sporting Goods (Nick Anderson, Anthony Bowie, Horace Grant, Anfernee Hardaway, Shaquille O'Neal, Tree Rollins, Donald Royal, Dennis Scott, Brian Shaw, Brooks Thompson, Jeff Turner)	5.00
(12)	Phoenix Suns - Smith's Food, Drug Center (Danny Ainge, Charles Barkley, A.C. Green, Kevin Johnson, Joe Kleine, Dan Majerle, Danny Manning, Elliot Perry, Wesley Person, Wayman Tisdale)	4.00
(13)	Portland Trailblazers (P.J. Carlesimo CO, Clyde Drexler, Chris Dudley, Harvey Grant, Jerome Kersey, Tracy Murray, Terry Porter, Clifford Robinson, James Robinson)	3.00
(14)	Seattle Supersonics - Al's Auto Supply/Castrol (Vincent Askew, Bill Cartwright, Ervin Johnson, George Karl CO, Shawn Kemp, Sarunas Marciulionis, Nate McMillan, Gary Payton, Sam Perkins, Detlef Schrempf, Dontonio Wingfield)	4.00
(15)	Utah Jazz - Cache Valley Premium Cheese (David Benoit, Tom Chambers, John Crotty, Jeff Hornacek, Karl Malone, Byron Russell, Jerry Sloan CO, Felton Spencer, John Stockton)	3.00
(16)	Washington Bullets - Goodyear Tires Team Card (Mitchell Butler, Rex Chapman, Calbert Cheaney, Don MacLean, Gheorghe Muresan, Scott Skiles, Chris Webber)	3.00
(17)	Washington Bullets - HBO Saturday Nights (Mitchell Butler, Rex Chapman, Calbert Cheaney, Kevin Duckworth, Juwan Howard, Don MacLean, Jim McIlvaine, Gheorghe Muresan, Scott Skiles, Kenny Walker, Chris Webber)	3.00
(18)	Washington Bullets - Deer Park (Mitchell Butler, Rex Chapman, Calbert Cheaney, Kevin Duckworth, Juwan Howard, Don MacLean, Jim McIlvaine, Gheorghe Muresan, Scott Skiles, Kenny Walker, Chris Webber)	3.00

1995-96 Hoops National Promos

The seven-card promo release was issued to collectors at the SkyBox booth at the National Sports Collectors Convention in St. Louis. The set contains two regular-issue cards and four subset cards. The cards are identical to the eventual base release, except they are not numbered.

		MT
Complete Set (7):		4.00
Common Player:		.05
(1)	Kenny Anderson	.15
(2)	Vin Baker	1.00
(3)	A.C. Green	.05
(4)	Jason Kidd	2.00
(5)	Glen Rice	.75
(6)	Rony Seikaly	.20
(7)	Title Card	.05

1995-96 Hoops Promo Sheet 1

This six-card perforated sheet was distributed with sales material to promote Hoops 1995-96 Series I release. The sheet had examples of regular-issue cards along with subsets and several insert sets.

	MT
Complete Set (1):	5.00
Eddie Jones, Detlef Schrempf, Dan Majerle, Juwan Howard, Larry Johnson, Scott Burrell	

1995-96 Hoops Promo Sheet 2

This 7" x 10-1/2" perforated sheet features six promo cards for 1995-96 Hoops Series Two. The cards are identical to the regular set except they are unnumbered.

	MT
Complete Set (6):	6.00
Common Player:	.15
Anfernee Hardaway	3.00
John Stockton	.60
Antonio McDyess	2.00
Charles Barkley	1.00
John Salley	.15
Glenn Robinson	.75

1995-96 Hoops

NBA Hoops released its 1995-96 set in two series - 250 cards in the first, and 150 in the second. Each regular card has a full-bleed color action photo on the front, with a brand logo in the lower left corner. The player's name is stamped in gold foil along the left in a team-colored panel which includes a team logo. The card back has a color photo on the left, with collegiate and NBA career stats on the right. Six subsets are included in Series I: NBA Hoops Milestones, Sizzlin' Sophs, Class Act, Buzzer Beater, Triple Threat and Pipeline. Series II subsets feature Rookies, Expansion players, Earth Shakers, Rock the House and Wicked Dishes. Hoops packs each contained at least one insert card. Series I inserts, which adds a 3-D effect to the cards, include: Number Crunchers, Block Party, All-Time Rookie Team Remembered, Grant Hill Dunks and Grant Hill Slams. The cards could be seen with the aid of a special pair of Grant Hill 3-D glasses, available through a mail-in offer on the wrapper. The cards, however, are still clear without the glasses. Series II insert sets include: SkyView, Grant Hill's All-Rookie Team, Hot List, Power Palette, Slamland and HoopStars. A special Grant Hill tribute card was also produced. They were seeded one per every 360 packs.

		MT
Complete Set (400):		27.00
Comp. Series 1 (250):		12.00
Comp. Series 2 (150):		15.00
Common Player:		.05
Minor Stars:		.10
Wax Box:		40.00
1	Stacey Augmon	.05
2	Mookie Blaylock	.05
3	Craig Ehlo	.05
4	Andrew Lang	.05
5	Grant Long	.05
6	Ken Norman	.05
7	Steve Smith	.05
8	Dee Brown	.05
9	Sherman Douglas	.05
10	Pervis Ellison	.05
11	Eric Montross	.10
12	Dino Radja	.10
13	Dominique Wilkins	.10
14	Muggsy Bogues	.05
15	Scott Burrell	.05
16	Dell Curry	.05
17	Hersey Hawkins	.05
18	Larry Johnson	.20
19	Alonzo Mourning	.20
20	B.J. Armstrong	.05
21	Michael Jordan	2.00
22	Toni Kukoc	.05
23	Will Perdue	.05
24	Scottie Pippen	.50
25	Dickey Simpkins	.05
26	Terrell Brandon	.05
27	Tyrone Hill	.05

28	Chris Mills	.05
29	Bobby Phills	.05
30	Mark Price	.10
31	John Williams	.05
32	Tony Dumas	.05
33	Jim Jackson	.20
34	Popeye Jones	.05
35	Jason Kidd	.75
36	Jamal Mashburn	.20
37	Roy Tarpley	.05
38	Mahmoud Abdul-Rauf	.05
39	LaPhonso Ellis	.05
40	Dikembe Mutombo	.10
41	Robert Pack	.05
42	Rodney Rogers	.05
43	Jalen Rose	.10
44	Bryant Stith	.05
45	Joe Dumars	.10
46	Grant Hill	1.00
47	Allan Houston	.10
48	Lindsey Hunter	.05
49	Oliver Miller	.05
50	Terry Mills	.05
51	Chris Gatling	.05
52	Tim Hardaway	.10
53	Donyell Marshall	.15
54	Chris Mullin	.10
55	Carlos Rogers	.05
56	Clifford Rozier	.05
57	Rony Seikaly	.05
58	Latrell Sprewell	.20
59	Sam Cassell	.05
60	Clyde Drexler	.20
61	Robert Horry	.05
62	Vernon Maxwell	.05
63	Hakeem Olajuwon	.40
64	Kenny Smith	.05
65	Dale Davis	.05
66	Mark Jackson	.05
67	Derrick McKey	.05
68	Reggie Miller	.20
69	Byron Scott	.05
70	Rik Smits	.10
71	Terry Dehere	.05
72	Lamond Murray	.10
73	Eric Piatkowski	.05
74	Pooh Richardson	.05
75	Malik Sealy	.05
76	Loy Vaught	.05
77	Elden Campbell	.05
78	Cedric Ceballos	.05
79	Vlade Divac	.05
80	Eddie Jones	.40
81	Sedale Threatt	.05
82	Nick Van Exel	.30
83	Bimbo Coles	.05
84	Harold Miner	.05
85	Billy Owens	.05
86	Khalid Reeves	.05
87	Glen Rice	.10
88	Kevin Willis	.05
89	Vin Baker	.10
90	Marty Conlon	.05
91	Todd Day	.05
92	Eric Mobley	.05
93	Eric Murdock	.05
94	Glenn Robinson	.30
95	Winston Garland	.05
96	Tom Gugliotta	.05
97	Christian Laettner	.05
98	Isaiah Rider	.10
99	Sean Rooks	.05
100	Doug West	.05
101	Kenny Anderson	.10
102	Benoit Benjamin	.05
103	Derrick Coleman	.10
104	Kevin Edwards	.05
105	Armon Gilliam	.05
106	Chris Morris	.05
107	Patrick Ewing	.15
108	Derek Harper	.05
109	Anthony Mason	.05
110	Charles Oakley	.05
111	Charles Smith	.05
112	John Starks	.05
113	Monty Williams	.05
114	Nick Anderson	.05
115	Horace Grant	.10
116	Anfernee Hardaway	1.50
117	Shaquille O'Neal	1.00
118	Dennis Scott	.05
119	Brian Shaw	.05
120	Dana Barros	.05
121	Shawn Bradley	.05
122	Willie Burton	.05
123	Jeff Malone	.05
124	Clarence Weatherspoon	.10
125	Sharone Wright	.10
126	Charles Barkley	.30
127	A.C. Green	.05
128	Kevin Johnson	.10
129	Dan Majerle	.05
130	Danny Manning	.10
131	Elliot Perry	.05
132	Wesley Person	.10
133	Chris Dudley	.05
134	Cliff Robinson	.05
135	James Robinson	.05
136	Rod Strickland	.05
137	Otis Thorpe	.05
138	Buck Williams	.05
139	Brian Grant	.15
140	Olden Polynice	.05
141	Mitch Richmond	.10
142	Michael Smith	.05
143	Spud Webb	.05
144	Walt Williams	.05
145	Vinny Del Negro	.05
146	Sean Elliott	.05
147	Avery Johnson	.05
148	Chuck Person	.05
149	David Robinson	.30
150	Dennis Rodman	.75
151	Kendall Gill	.05
152	Ervin Johnson	.05
153	Shawn Kemp	.30
154	Nate McMillan	.05
155	Gary Payton	.10
156	Detlef Schrempf	.05
157	Dontonio Wingfield	.05
158	David Benoit	.05
159	Jeff Hornacek	.05
160	Karl Malone	.20
161	Felton Spencer	.05
162	John Stockton	.20
163	Jamie Watson	.05
164	Rex Chapman	.05
165	Calbert Cheaney	.05
166	Juwan Howard	.20
167	Don MacLean	.05
168	Gheorghe Muresan	.05
169	Scott Skiles	.05
170	Chris Webber	.15
171	Len Wilkens	.05
172	Alan Bristow	.05
173	Phil Jackson	.05
174	Mike Fratello	.05
175	Dick Motta	.05
176	Bernie Bickerstaff	.05
177	Doug Collins	.05
178	Rick Adelman	.05
179	Rudy Tomjanovich	.05
180	Larry Brown	.05
181	Bill Fitch	.05
182	Del Harris	.05
183	Mike Dunleavy	.05
184	Bill Blair	.05
185	Butch Beard	.05
186	Pat Riley	.05
187	Brian Hill	.05
188	John Lucas	.05
189	Paul Westphal	.05
190	P.J. Carlesimo	.05
191	Garry St. Jean	.05
192	Bob Hill	.05
193	George Karl	.05
194	Brendan Malone	.05
195	Jerry Sloan	.05
196	Kevin Pritchard	.05
197	Jim Lynam	.05
198	Brian Grant (Sizzlin' Sophs)	.05
199	Grant Hill (Sizzlin' Sophs)	.40
200	Juwan Howard (Sizzlin' Sophs)	.10
201	Eddie Jones (Sizzlin' Sophs)	.10
202	Jason Kidd (Sizzlin' Sophs)	.50
203	Donyell Marshall (Sizzlin' Sophs)	.05
204	Eric Montross (Sizzlin' Sophs)	.05
205	Glenn Robinson (Sizzlin' Sophs)	.25
206	Jalen Rose (Sizzlin' Sophs)	.05
207	Sharone Wright (Sizzlin' Sophs)	.05
208	Dana Barros (Milestones)	.05
209	Joe Dumars (Milestones)	.05
210	A.C. Green (Milestones)	.05
211	Grant Hill (Milestones)	.40
212	Karl Malone (Milestones)	.10
213	Reggie Miller (Milestones)	.10
214	Glen Rice (Milestones)	.05
215	John Stockton (Milestones)	.10
216	Len Wilkens (Milestones)	.05
217	Dominique Wilkins (Milestones)	.05
218	Kenny Anderson (Buzzer Beaters)	.05
219	Mookie Blaylock (Buzzer Beaters)	.05
220	Larry Johnson (Buzzer Beaters)	.10
221	Shawn Kemp (Buzzer Beaters)	.10
222	Toni Kukoc (Buzzer Beaters)	.05
223	Jamal Mashburn (Buzzer Beaters)	.10
224	Glen Rice (Buzzer Beaters)	.05
225	Mitch Richmond (Buzzer Beaters)	.05
226	Latrell Sprewell (Buzzer Beaters)	.10
227	Rod Strickland (Buzzer Beaters)	.05
228	Michael Adams, Darrick Martin (Pipeline)	.05
229	Craig Ehlo, Jerome Harmon (Pipeline)	.05
230	Mario Elie, George McCloud (Pipeline)	.05
231	Anthony Mason, Chucky Brown (Pipeline)	.05
232	John Starks, Tim Legler (Pipeline)	.05
233	Muggsy Bogues (Class Acts)	.05
234	Joe Dumars (Class Acts)	.05
235	LaPhonso Ellis (Class Acts)	.05
236	Patrick Ewing (Class Acts)	.05
237	Grant Hill (Class Acts)	.40
238	Kevin Johnson (Class Acts)	.05
239	Dan Majerle (Class Acts)	.05
240	Karl Malone (Class Acts)	.10
241	Hakeem Olajuwon (Class Acts)	.20
242	David Robinson (Class Acts)	.15
243	Dana Barros (Triple Threats)	.05
244	Scott Burrell (Triple Threats)	.05
245	Reggie Miller (Triple Threats)	.10
246	Glen Rice (Triple Threats)	.05
247	John Stockton (Triple Threats)	.10
248	Checklist #1	.05
249	Checklist #2	.05
250	Checklist #3	.05
251	*Alan Henderson*	.20
252	*Junior Burrough*	.05
253	*Eric Williams*	.20
254	*George Zidek*	.20
255	*Jason Caffey*	.05
256	*Donny Marshall*	.05
257	*Bob Sura*	.20
258	*Loren Meyer*	.20
259	*Cherokee Parks*	.30
260	*Antonio McDyess*	1.50
261	*Theo Ratliff*	.75
262	*Lou Roe*	.05
263	*Andrew DeClercq*	.05
264	*Joe Smith*	1.00
265	*Travis Best*	.05
266	*Brent Barry*	.40
267	*Frankie King*	.05
268	*Sasha Danilovic*	.20
269	*Kurt Thomas*	.30
270	*Shawn Respert*	.20
271	*Jerome Allen*	.05
272	*Kevin Garnett*	4.00
273	*Ed O'Bannon*	.20
274	*David Vaughn*	.05
275	*Jerry Stackhouse*	2.00
276	*Mario Bennett*	.05
277	*Michael Finley*	1.50
278	*Randolph Childress*	.05
279	*Arvydas Sabonis*	.75
280	*Gary Trent*	.20
281	*Tyus Edney*	.20
282	*Corliss Williamson*	.20
283	*Cory Alexander*	.05
284	*Sherell Ford*	.05
285	*Jimmy King*	.05
286	*Damon Stoudamire*	1.00
287	*Greg Ostertag*	.05
288	*Lawrence Moten*	.05
289	*Bryant Reeves*	.75
290	*Rasheed Wallace*	1.50
291	Spud Webb	.05
292	Dana Barros	.05
293	Rick Fox	.05
294	Kendall Gill	.05
295	Khalid Reeves	.05
296	Glen Rice	.05
297	Luc Longley	.05
298	Dennis Rodman	1.25
299	Dan Majerle	.05
300	Lorenzo Williams	.05
301	Dale Ellis	.05
302	Reggie Williams	.05
303	Otis Thorpe	.05
304	B.J. Armstrong	.05
305	Pete Chilcutt	.05
306	Mario Ellie	.05
307	Antonio Davis	.05
308	Ricky Pierce	.05
309	Rodney Rogers	.05
310	Brian Williams	.05
311	Corie Blount	.05
312	George Lynch	.05
313	Alonzo Mourning	.20
314	Lee Mayberry	.05
315	Terry Porter	.05
316	P.J. Brown	.05
317	Hubert Davis	.05
318	Charlie Ward	.05
319	Jon Koncak	.05
320	Derrick Coleman	.05
321	Richard Dumas	.05
322	Vernon Maxwell	.05
323	Wayman Tisdale	.05
324	Dontonio Wingfield	.05
325	Tyrone Corbin	.05
326	Bobby Hurley	.05
327	Will Perdue	.05
328	J.R. Reid	.05
329	Hersey Hawkins	.05
330	Sam Perkins	.05
331	Adam Keefe	.05
332	Chris Morris	.05
333	Robert Pack	.05
334	M.L. Carr	.05
335	Pat Riley	.05
336	Don Nelson	.05
337	Brian Winters	.05
338	Willie Anderson	.05
339	Acie Earl	.05
340	Jimmy King	.05
341	Oliver Miller	.05
342	Tracy Murray	.05
343	Ed Pinckney	.05
344	Alvin Robertson	.05
345	Carlos Rodgers	.05
346	John Salley	.05
347	Damon Stoudamire	1.00
348	Zan Tabak	.05
349	Greg Anthony	.05
350	Blue Edwards	.05
351	Kenny Gattison	.05
352	Antonio Harvey	.05
353	Chris King	.05
354	Darrick Martin	.05
355	Lawrence Moten	.05
356	Bryant Reeves	.20
357	Byron Scott	.05
358	Michael Jordan (Earthshakers)	1.00
359	Dikembe Mutombo (Earthshakers)	.05
360	Grant Hill (Earthshakers)	.50
361	Robert Horry (Earthshakers)	.05
362	Alonzo Mourning (Earthshakers)	.10
363	Vin Baker (Earthshakers)	.05
364	Isaiah Rider (Earthshakers)	.05
365	Charles Oakley (Earthshakers)	.05
366	Shaquille O'Neal (Earthshakers)	.50
367	Jerry Stackhouse (Earthshakers)	1.00
368	Clarence Weatherspoon (Earthshakers)	.05
369	Charles Barkley (Earthshakers)	.20
370	Sean Elliot (Earthshakers)	.05
371	Shawn Kemp (Earthshakers)	.15
372	Chris Webber (Earthshakers)	.05
373	Spud Webb (Rock/House)	.05
374	Muggsy Bogues (Rock/House)	.05
375	Toni Kukoc (Rock/House)	.05
376	Dennis Rodman (Rock/House)	.40
377	Jamal Mashburn (Rock/House)	.10
378	Jalen Rose (Rock/House)	.05
379	Clyde Drexler (Rock/House)	.15
380	Mark Jackson (Rock/House)	.05
381	Cedric Ceballos (Rock/House)	.05
382	Nick Van Exel (Rock/House)	.10
383	John Starks (Rock/House)	.05
384	Vernon Maxwell (Rock/House)	.05
385	Shawn Kemp (Rock/House)	.15
386	Gary Payton (Rock/House)	.05
387	Karl Malone (Rock/House)	.10
388	Mookie Blaylock (Wicked Dishes)	.05
389	Muggsy Bogues (Wicked Dishes)	.05
390	Jason Kidd (Wicked Dishes)	.50
391	Tim Hardaway (Wicked Dishes)	.05
392	Nick Van Exel (Wicked Dishes)	.10
393	Kenny Anderson (Wicked Dishes)	.05
394	Anfernee Hardaway (Wicked Dishes)	.50
395	Rod Strickland (Wicked Dishes)	.05
396	Avery Johnson (Wicked Dishes)	.05
397	John Stockton (Wicked Dishes)	.10
398	Grant Hill (Boys and Girls Club with Grant Hill)	.50
399	Checklist #1	.05
400	Checklist #2	.05
NNO	(Grant Hill TRIB.)	40.00
NNO	Grant Hill Co-ROY	20.00

1995-96 Hoops Block Party

These cards, available at a rate of one per every two packs of 1995-96 NBA Hoops Series I product, feature some of the NBA's top shot blockers. Each card front has "Block Party" stamped in gold foil at the top; the player's name is in gold foil at the bottom. An action photo dominates the card front. The back, numbered 1 of 25, etc., has a color photo on the left, with "Block Party" written along the side. The right half of the card has a brief player profile, with the player's name above. The player's stats from the previous season are also included.

		MT
Complete Set (25):		5.00
Common Player:		.10
1	Oliver Miller	.10
2	Dennis Rodman	1.00
3	Scottie Pippen	1.00
4	Dikembe Mutombo	.20
5	Vlade Divac	.10
6	Brian Grant	.30
7	Alonzo Mourning	.30
8	Hakeem Olajuwon	.75
9	Patrick Ewing	.30
10	Shawn Kemp	.50
11	Vin Baker	.30
12	Horace Grant	.15
13	Dale Davis	.10
14	Juwan Howard	.40
15	Eddie Jones	.50
16	Eric Montross	.15
17	Tyrone Hill	.10
18	Tom Gugliotta	.10
19	Shawn Bradley	.10
20	Dan Majerle	.10
21	Loy Vaught	.10
22	Donyell Marshall	.25
23	Chris Webber	.30
24	Derrick Coleman	.10
25	Walt Williams	.10

1995-96 Hoops Grant Hill Dunks

These five cards feature Detroit Pistons' star Grant Hill, capturing one moment in time from five different angles. The cards were random inserts in 1995-96 NBA Hoops Series I hobby packs (1 in 36). Each card front shows the same play, except the angle is different from the other four cards. The background has a letter (D, U, N, K or !) incorporated into it. Gold foil stamping is used for the player's name along the bottom of the card; a circle in the lower left corner has a number inside it (D1, etc.). The horizontal back has Dunk written along the top, with a card number (D1, etc.) in the upper right corner. An action photo is also included on the back, as is information about the player.

		MT
Complete Set (5):		25.00
Common Player:		5.00
1	D-Card	5.00
2	U-Card	5.00
3	N-Card	5.00
4	K-Card	5.00
5	!!-Card	5.00

1995-96 Hoops Grant Hill Slams

These five cards present one moment in time from five different angles. The cards, which feature Pistons' star Grant Hill, were seeded one per every 36 Series I retail packs of 1995-96 NBA Hoops. The cards spell out SLAM!; the front's background has one of those five characters incorporated into it. A card number (S1, etc.) is also included on the card front in a bullseye, using red foil. Hill's first name is also stamped in red foil at the top. The horizontal card back has SLAM! written along the top, with Hill's name in the upper left corner. An action photo is also on the back, along with information about Hill, plus a card number.

		MT
Complete Set (5):		25.00
Common Player:		5.00
1	S-Card	5.00
2	L-Card	5.00
3	A-Card	5.00
4	M-Card	5.00
5	!!-Card	5.00

1995-96 Hoops Grant's All-Rookies

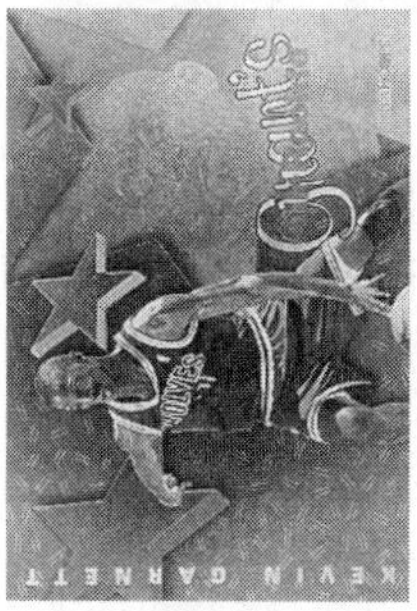

These cards were randomly inserted into 1995-96 NBA Hoops Series II packs, one per every 64 packs. The cards, which have a horizontal format, are Grant Hill's selections of the top rookies in the NBA. Cards are numbered using an "AR" prefix.

		MT
Complete Set (10):		70.00
Common Player:		2.00
1	Cherokee Parks	4.00
2	Antonio McDyess	12.00
3	Theo Ratliff	4.00
4	Joe Smith	12.00
5	Shawn Respert	2.00
6	Kevin Garnett	30.00
7	Ed O'Bannon	2.00
8	Jerry Stackhouse	12.00
9	Damon Stoudamire	20.00
10	Rasheed Wallace	6.00

1995-96 Hoops HoopStars

These 12 cards were randomly inserted into 1995-96 NBA Hoops Series II packs, one per every 16 packs. The cards have an action photo on the front, with a basketball rim as a background. Gold foil stamping is used for the bullets which run down the left side of the card, plus "Hoopstars," which is written along the bottom of the card. The player's name is included in a black bar along the bottom; his last name also uses gold foil. The horizontal card back has a color action photo on the left side, with a similar background as was used for the front. "Hoopstars" runs vertically in the middle of the card, next to a brief line of text which recaps the player's career, and his career totals. A card number, using an "HS" prefix, is in the upper left corner.

		MT
Complete Set (12):		25.00
Common Player:		1.00
1	Scottie Pippen	3.00
2	Jim Jackson	1.00
3	Antonio McDyess	3.00
4	Clyde Drexler	2.00
5	Alonzo Mourning	2.00
6	Glenn Robinson	2.00
7	Patrick Ewing	1.00
8	Anfernee Hardaway	8.00
9	Shawn Kemp	2.00
10	Karl Malone	2.00
11	Juwan Howard	2.00
12	Rasheed Wallace	3.00

1995-96 Hoops Hot List

These 10 cards were exclusive to 1995-96 NBA Hoops hobby packs only, one per every 32 packs. The card front has a color action photo against a fiery metallic background which has "HOT" spelled out in the background. The player photo penetrates the O in "HOT." Green foil stamping is used to spell the player's name out along the left side of the card; foil-stamped lines run perpendicular to the letters in his name. The card back, numbered 1 of 10, etc., has a similar design format for the back, except the player's name is spelled out along the perimeter of the O in "HOT." A color panel along the bottom of the card contains a brief player profile and a line for career stats.

		MT
Complete Set (10):		60.00
Common Player:		1.50
1	Michael Jordan	30.00
2	Jason Kidd	4.00
3	Jamal Mashburn	1.50
4	Grant Hill	12.00
5	Joe Smith	6.00
6	Hakeem Olajuwon	6.00
7	Glenn Robinson	4.00
8	Shaquille O'Neal	10.00
9	Jerry Stackhouse	6.00
10	David Robinson	4.00

1995-96 Hoops Number Crunchers

Several NBA offensive superstars are featured in this 1995-96 NBA Hoops Series I insert set. The cards, seeded one in every two packs, have a color action photo on the front. The background has a number in it, plus a pair of globes and a tic-tac-toe grid with the letters of Crunchers spelled out within it. The player's name is stamped in gold foil at the top in a black panel. The back has a card number (1 of 25, etc.) and color photo on part of it, plus a black box which includes the player's name, previous season's stats, and a recap of his season.

		MT
Complete Set (25):		10.00
Common Player:		.15
1	Michael Jordan	5.00
2	Shaquille O'Neal	2.00
3	Grant Hill	2.00
4	Detlef Schrempf	.15
5	Kenny Anderson	.15
6	Anfernee Hardaway	2.00
7	Latrell Sprewell	.30
8	Jamal Mashburn	.30
9	Nick Van Exel	.50
10	Charles Barkley	.75
11	Mitch Richmond	.30
12	David Robinson	.75
13	Gary Payton	.30
14	Rod Strickland	.15
15	Glenn Robinson	.75
16	Reggie Miller	.40
17	Karl Malone	.40
18	Jim Jackson	.40
19	Clyde Drexler	.40
20	Glen Rice	.15
21	Isaiah Rider	.30
22	Cedric Ceballos	.15
23	John Stockton	.40
24	Jason Kidd	1.25
25	Mookie Blaylock	.15

1995-96 Hoops Power Palette

These 10 cards are exclusive to 1995-96 NBA Hoops retail packs only; they are seeded one per every 36 packs. The card front has a player action photo against a square rainbow prism in the center. A metallic plum-colored border frames the card. The player's first name is written in gold-foiled script at the bottom of the card, with a gold line separating it from his last name, which is in regular type. Power Palette is written along the top of the card, with a scope in the upper left corner. The card back, numbered in the upper right 1 of 10, etc., has the player's name at the top, along with the scope in the upper left corner. Except for a different card color, the design is the same as the front's, with a reversed image of the photo from the front.

		MT
Complete Set (10):		70.00
Common Player:		3.00
1	Michael Jordan	30.00
2	Jason Kidd	5.00
3	Grant Hill	12.00
4	Joe Smith	7.00
5	Hakeem Olajuwon	7.00
6	Glenn Robinson	5.00
7	Anfernee Hardaway	12.00
8	Shaquille O'Neal	10.00
9	Jerry Stackhouse	7.00
10	Charles Barkley	3.00

1995-96 Hoops SkyView

These 10 extra-thick insert cards replace two cards in one per every 480 1995-96 NBA Hoops Series II packs. The cards have a die-cut photo over a multi-color window on the front; the card design is similar to the Power Palette inserts. The player's first name is written in gold foil script at the bottom of the card, with a gold line separating it from his last name, which is in regular type. Skyview is written along the top of the card, with a scope in the upper left corner. The back is numbered using an "SV" prefix.

		MT
Complete Set (10):		130.00
Common Player:		5.00
1	Michael Jordan	70.00
2	Jason Kidd	10.00
3	Grant Hill	20.00
4	Joe Smith	12.00
5	Hakeem Olajuwon	12.00
6	Glenn Robinson	5.00
7	Anfernee Hardaway	30.00
8	Shaquille O'Neal	25.00
9	Jerry Stackhouse	12.00
10	Charles Barkley	5.00

1995-96 Hoops Slamland

Each pack of 1995-96 NBA Hoops Series II cards contains one of these inserts. The cards feature 50 NBA players; each is shown dunking. Gold foil stamping is used for the card front for the insert set icon at the top, and the player's name in the lower right corner. The card back, numbered using an "SL" prefix, has an action photo plus numbers for 1994-95 NBA game averages.

		MT
Complete Set (50):		12.00
Common Player:		.10
1	Stacey Augmon	.10
2	Steve Smith	.10
3	Eric Montross	.10
4	Dino Radja	.10
5	Dell Curry	.10
6	Larry Johnson	.30
7	Scottie Pippen	1.00
8	Dennis Rodman	2.00
9	Tyrone Hill	.10
10	Jim Jackson	.25
11	Jamal Mashburn	.25
12	Dikembe Mutombo	.10
13	Joe Dumars	.10
14	Grant Hill	1.50
15	Allan Houston	.10
16	Donyell Marshall	.10
17	Latrell Sprewell	.10
18	Sam Cassell	.10
19	Hakeem Olajuwon	.75
20	Reggie Miller	.40
21	Loy Vaught	.10
22	Vlade Divac	.10
23	Eddie Jones	.30
24	Alonzo Mourning	.25
25	Kevin Willis	.10
26	Vin Baker	.20
27	Glenn Robinson	.75
28	Tom Gugliotta	.10
29	Kenny Anderson	.10
30	Derrick Coleman	.10
31	Patrick Ewing	.25
32	John Starks	.10
33	Dennis Scott	.10
34	Jerry Stackhouse	3.00
35	Charles Barkley	.50
36	Kevin Johnson	.10
37	Danny Manning	.10
38	Clifford Robinson	.10
39	Brian Grant	.10
40	Mitch Richmond	.10
41	Walt Williams	.10
42	David Robinson	.50
43	Gary Payton	.10
44	Detlef Schrempf	.10
45	Damon Stoudamire	3.00
46	Karl Malone	.25
47	John Stockton	.25
48	Bryant Reeves	.75
49	Juwan Howard	.50
50	Chris Webber	.25

1995-96 Hoops Top Ten

This set looks back at 10 top NBA rookies from the past decade, players who are on their way to, or have already reached, greatness. The horizontal card front has the insert set icon on the left side; a player photo is on the right. A 10 is stamped in gold foil in the O in the word Top. Gold foil is also used for the player's name in the upper right corner. The vertical back has the set logo along the left side, with a color action photo dominating the back. The player's name is in the upper right corner, along with a card number, which uses an "AR" prefix. A brief player profile is also given. Cards were seeded one per every 12 packs of 1995-96 NBA Hoops Series I product.

		MT
Complete Set (10):		45.00
Common Player:		2.00
1	Shaquille O'Neal	8.00
2	Grant Hill	10.00
3	Chris Webber	2.00
4	Jamal Mashburn	2.00
5	Anfernee Hardaway	10.00
6	Alonzo Mourning	2.00
7	Michael Jordan	20.00
8	Charles Barkley	4.00
9	Glenn Robinson	3.00
10	Jason Kidd	3.00

1995-96 Hoops Sheets

These team sheets carry similar designs to the 1995-96 Hoops regular-issue cards, but arrive on a perforated sheet. The cards are unnumbered and checklisted alphabetically.

		MT
Complete Set (13):		40.00
1	Atlanta Hawks - Oscar Mayer (Lenny Wilkens CO, Stacey Augmon, Mookie Blaylock, Craig Ehlo, Alan Henderson, Andrew Lang, Grant Long, Ken Norman, Steve Smith, Spud Webb)	3.00
2	Charlotte Hornets - Byran (Muggsy Bogues, Kendall Gill, Glen Rice, Scott Burrell, Larry Johnson, Dell Curry, George Zidek, Khalid Reeves)	3.00
3	Chicago Bulls - Jewel/Nabisco (Phil Jackson CO, Jason Caffey, Michael Jordan, Toni Kukoc, Luc Longley, Scottie Pippen, Dennis Rodman, Dickey Simpkins)	10.00
4	Detroit Pistons - Staples/Snickers Kudos/Farmer Jack - K-Mart/Castrol (Grant Hill, Joe Dumars, Terry Mills, Allan Houston, Lindsey Hunter, Theo Ratliff, Otis Thorpe, Doug Collins CO)	5.00
5	Los Angeles Lakers - Oscar Mayer (Sedale Threatt, Frankie King, Nick Van Exel, Vlade Divac, Cedric Ceballos, Eddie Jones, George Lynch, Elden Campbell, Corie Blount, Del Harris CO)	5.00
6	New Jersey Nets (Shawn Bradley, Kevin Edwards, Rick Mahorn, Kendall Gill, P.J. Brown, Butch Beard CO, Armon Gilliam, Ed O'Bannon, Chris Childs, Yinka Dare, Jayson Williams)	3.00
7	New York Knicks - Wiz (Patrick Ewing, Charles Oakley, John Starks, Anthony Mason, Don Nelson CO, Derek Harper, Charles Smith, Herb Williams, Hubert Davis)	5.00
8	Orlando Magic - Gooding's (Nick Anderson, Anthony Bowie, Horace Grant, Anfernee Hardaway, John Koncak, Shaquille O'Neal, Donald Royal, Dennis Scott, Brian Shaw, Jeff Turner, David Vaughn)	6.00
9	Phoenix Suns - Holsum (Elliot Perry, A.C. Green, Wayman Tisdale, Mario Bennett, Charles Barkley, Danny Manning, Wesley Person, Michael Finley, Kevin Johnson)	5.00
10	Portland Trail Blazers (Clifford Robinson, Rod Strickland, Chris Dudley, Arvydas Sabonis, Buck Williams, James Robinson, P.J. Carlesimo CO, Randolph Childress, Gary Trent, Dontonio Wingfield)	3.00
11	Sacramento Kings - Kellogg's (Mitch Richmond, Olden Polynice, Brian Grant, Michael Smith, Michael Smith, Tyus Edney, Bobby Hurley, Corliss Williamson, Garry St. Jean CO)	3.00
12	Utah Jazz - New Era/Pro Image (David Benoit, Jeff Hornacek, Karl Malone, Felton Spencer, John Stockton, Adam Keefe, Jerry Sloan CO)	5.00
13	Washington Bullets-Nationwide Insurance (Mitchell Butler, Calbert Cheaney, Juwan Howard, Tim Legler, Jim McIlvaine, Gheorghe Muresan, Robert Pack, Brent Price, Mark Price, Rasheed Wallace, Chris Webber)	8.00

1996-97 Hoops

NBA Hoops' 1996-97 was released in two series, with Series I containing 200 cards and Series II having 150 cards. Card fronts featured a full-bleed action shot of the player, with the bottom right corner colored in team colors with the team logo inside it. The player's name was stamped above it in gold foil, with a Hoops logo in the top left. Series I had 174 regular cards, 15 The Big Finish, nine Grant's Playback and two checklists, while Series II had 48 player updates, 40 rookies, 29 coaches, 10 Slam Talk, 20 Career Best Games, one Stackhouse Boys & Girls Clubs and two checklists. Inserts in Series I include: Hipnotized, Head to Head, Autographics, 10 Rookie Headliners and Superfeats. Inserts in Series II include: Autographics, 1996-97 Rookies, Starting Five, Hot List, Fly With and Grant's All-Rookie Team.

		MT
Complete Set (350):		30.00
Complete Series 1 (200):		15.00
Complete Series 2 (150):		15.00
Common Player:		.05
Minor Stars:		.10
Series 1 Pack (8):		1.50
Series 1 Wax Box (24):		25.00
Series 2 Pack (9):		1.25
Series 2 Wax Box (36):		30.00
1	Stacey Augmon	.05
2	Mookie Blaylock	.05
3	Alan Henderson	.05
4	Christian Laettner	.05
5	Grant Long	.05
6	Steve Smith	.05
7	Dana Barros	.05
8	Todd Day	.05
9	Rick Fox	.05
10	Eric Montross	.05
11	Dino Radja	.05
12	Eric Williams	.05
13	Kenny Anderson	.05
14	Scott Burrell	.05
15	Dell Curry	.05
16	Matt Geiger	.05
17	Larry Johnson	.20
18	Glen Rice	.05
19	Ron Harper	.05
20	Michael Jordan	3.00
21	Steve Kerr	.05
22	Toni Kukoc	.05
23	Luc Longley	.05
24	Scottie Pippen	.75
25	Dennis Rodman	.75
26	Terrell Brandon	.05
27	Danny Ferry	.05
28	Tyrone Hill	.05
29	Chris Mills	.05
30	Bobby Phills	.05
31	Bob Sura	.05
32	Tony Dumas	.05
33	Jim Jackson	.15
34	Popeye Jones	.05
35	Jason Kidd	.50
36	Jamal Mashburn	.15
37	George McCloud	.05
38	Cherokee Parks	.05
39	Mahmoud Abdul-Rauf	.05
40	LaPhonso Ellis	.05
41	Antonio McDyess	.30
42	Dikembe Mutombo	.05
43	Jalen Rose	.05
44	Bryant Stith	.05
45	Joe Dumars	.05
46	Grant Hill	1.00
47	Allan Houston	.05
48	Lindsey Hunter	.05
49	Terry Mills	.05
50	Theo Ratliff	.05
51	Otis Thorpe	.05
52	B.J. Armstrong	.05
53	Donyell Marshall	.05
54	Chris Mullin	.05
55	Joe Smith	.50
56	Rony Seikaly	.05
57	Latrell Sprewell	.10
58	Mark Bryant	.05
59	Sam Cassell	.05
60	Clyde Drexler	.25
61	Mario Elie	.05
62	Robert Horry	.05
63	Hakeem Olajuwon	.50
64	Travis Best	.05
65	Antonio Davis	.05
66	Mark Jackson	.05
67	Derrick McKey	.05
68	Reggie Miller	.25
69	Rik Smits	.05
70	Brent Barry	.05
71	Terry Dehere	.05
72	Pooh Richardson	.05
73	Rodney Rodgers	.05
74	Loy Vaught	.05
75	Brian Williams	.05
76	Elden Campbell	.05
77	Cedric Ceballos	.05
78	Vlade Divac	.05
79	Eddie Jones	.05
80	Anthony Peeler	.05
81	Nick Van Exel	.20
82	Predrag Danilovic	.05
83	Tim Hardaway	.05
84	Alonzo Mourning	.20
85	Kurt Thomas	.05
86	Walt Williams	.05
87	Vin Baker	.20
88	Sherman Douglas	.05
89	Johnny Newman	.05
90	Shawn Respert	.05
91	Glenn Robinson	.25
92	Kevin Garnett	1.00
93	Tom Gugliotta	.05
94	Andrew Lang	.05
95	Sam Mitchell	.05
96	Isaiah Rider	.05
97	Shawn Bradley	.05
98	P.J. Brown	.05
99	Chris Childs	.05
100	Armon Gilliam	.05
101	Ed O'Bannon	.10
102	Jayson Williams	.05
103	Hubert Davis	.05
104	Patrick Ewing	.20
105	Anthony Mason	.05
106	Charles Oakley	.05
107	John Starks	.05
108	Charlie Ward	.05
109	Nick Anderson	.05
110	Horace Grant	.05
111	Anfernee Hardaway	1.50
112	Shaquille O'Neal	1.00
113	Dennis Scott	.05
114	Brian Shaw	.05
115	Derrick Coleman	.05
116	Vernon Maxwell	.05
117	Trevor Ruffin	.05
118	Jerry Stackhouse	.75
119	Clarence Weatherspoon	.05
120	Charles Barkley	.30
121	Michael Finley	.50
122	A.C. Green	.05
123	Kevin Johnson	.10
124	Danny Manning	.05
125	Wesley Person	.05
126	John Williams	.05
127	Harvey Grant	.05
128	Aaron McKie	.05
129	Clifford Robinson	.05
130	Arvydas Sabonis	.25
131	Rod Strickland	.05
132	Gary Trent	.05
133	Tyus Edney	.10
134	Brian Grant	.05
135	Billy Owens	.05
136	Olden Polynice	.05
137	Mitch Richmond	.10
138	Corliss Williamson	.05
139	Vinny Del Negro	.05
140	Sean Elliot	.05
141	Avery Johnson	.05
142	Chuck Person	.05
143	David Robinson	.40
144	Charles Smith	.05
145	Sherell Ford	.05
146	Hersey Hawkins	.05
147	Shawn Kemp	.40
148	Nate McMillan	.05
149	Gary Payton	.20
150	Detlef Schrempf	.05
151	Oliver Miller	.05
152	Tracy Murray	.05
153	Carlos Rogers	.05
154	Damon Stoudamire	.75
155	Zan Tabak	.05
156	Sharone Wright	.05
157	Antoine Carr	.05
158	Jeff Hornacek	.05
159	Adam Keefe	.05
160	Karl Malone	.20
161	Chris Morris	.05
162	John Stockton	.20
163	Greg Anthony	.05
164	Blue Edwards	.05
165	Chris King	.05
166	Lawrence Moten	.05
167	Bryant Reeves	.20
168	Byron Scott	.05
169	Calbert Cheaney	.05
170	Juwan Howard	.40
171	Tim Legler	.05
172	Gheorghe Muresan	.05
173	Rasheed Wallace	.10
174	Chris Webber	.15
175	Steve Smith	.05
176	Michael Jordan	1.25
177	Scottie Pippen	.30
178	Dennis Rodman	.40
179	Allan Houston	.05
180	Hakeem Olajuwon	.20
181	Patrick Ewing	.05
182	Anfernee Hardaway	.75
183	Shaquille O'Neal	.50
184	Charles Barkley	.15
185	Arvydas Sabonis	.05
186	David Robinson	.20
187	Shawn Kemp	.20
188	Gary Payton	.05
189	Karl Malone	.05
190	Kenny Anderson	.05
191	Toni Kukoc	.05
192	Brent Barry	.05
193	Cedric Ceballos	.05
194	Shawn Bradley	.05
195	Charles Oakley	.05
196	Dennis Scott	.05
197	Clifford Robinson	.05
198	Mitch Richmond	.05
199	Checklist One	.05
200	Checklist Two	.05
201	Dikembe Mutombo	.10
202	Dee Brown	.05
203	David Wesley	.05
204	Vlade Divac	.05
205	Anthony Mason	.05
206	Chris Gatling	.05
207	Eric Montross	.05
208	Ervin Johnson	.05
209	Stacey Augmon	.05
210	Joe Dumars	.05
211	Grant Hill	1.00
212	Charles Barkley	.30
213	Jalen Rose	.05
214	Lamond Murray	.05
215	Shaquille O'Neal	1.25
216	P.J. Brown	.05
217	Dan Majerle	.05
218	Armon Gilliam	.05
219	Andrew Lang	.05
220	Kevin Garnett	1.00
221	Tom Gugliotta	.05
222	Cherokee Parks	.05
223	Doug West	.05
224	Kendall Gill	.05
225	Robert Pack	.05
226	Allan Houston	.05
227	Larry Johnson	.05
228	Rony Seikaly	.05
229	Gerald Wilkins	.05
230	Michael Cage	.05
231	Lucious Harris	.05
232	Sam Cassell	.05
233	Robert Horry	.05
234	Kenny Anderson	.05
235	Isaiah Rider	.05
236	Rasheed Wallace	.05
237	Mahmoud Abdul-Rauf	.05
238	Vernon Maxwell	.05
239	Dominique Wilkins	.05
240	Jim McIlvaine	.05
241	Hubert Davis	.05
242	Popeye Jones	.05
243	Walt Williams	.05
244	Karl Malone	.20
245	John Stockton	.20
246	Anthony Peeler	.05
247	Tracy Murray	.05
248	Rod Strickland	.05
249	Len Wilkens	.05
250	M.L. Carr	.05
251	Dave Cowens	.05
252	Phil Jackson	.05
253	Mike Fratello	.05
254	Jim Cleamons	.05
255	Dick Motta	.05
256	Doug Collins	.05
257	Rick Adelman	.05
258	Rudy Tomjanovich	.05
259	Larry Brown	.05
260	Bill Fitch	.05
261	Del Harris	.05
262	Pat Riley	.05
263	Chris Ford	.05
264	Flip Saunders	.05
265	John Calipari	.05
266	Jeff Van Gundy	.05
267	Brian Hill	.05
268	Johnny Davis	.05
269	Danny Ainge	.05
270	P.J. Carlesimo	.05
271	Garry St. Jean	.05
272	Bob Hill	.05
273	George Karl	.05
274	Darrell Walker	.05
275	Jerry Sloan	.05
276	Brian Winters	.05
277	Jim Lynam	.05
278	*Shareef Abdur-Rahim*	2.00
279	*Ray Allen*	2.00
280	*Shandon Anderson*	.10
281	*Kobe Bryant*	10.00
282	*Marcus Camby*	2.00
283	*Erick Dampier*	.25
284	*Emanuel Davis*	.05
285	*Tony Delk*	.25
286	*Brian Evans*	.05
287	*Derek Fisher*	.30
288	*Todd Fuller*	.20
289	*Dean Garrett*	.20
290	*Reggie Geary*	.05
291	*Darvin Ham*	.25
292	*Othella Harrington*	.20
293	*Shane Heal*	.05
294	*Mark Hendrickson*	.05
295	*Allen Iverson*	4.00
296	*Dontae Jones*	.20
297	*Kerry Kittles*	1.25
298	*Priest Lauderdale*	.05
299	*Matt Maloney*	.50
300	*Stephon Marbury*	2.00
301	*Walter McCarty*	.05
302	*Jeff McInnis*	.05
303	*Martin Muursepp*	.05
304	*Steve Nash*	.40
305	*Moochie Norris*	.05
306	*Jermaine O'Neal*	.60
307	*Vitaly Potapenko*	.20
308	*Virginius Praskevicius*	.05
309	*Roy Rogers*	.20
310	*Malik Rose*	.05
311	*James Scott*	.05
312	*Antoine Walker*	1.50
313	*Samaki Walker*	.25
314	*Ben Wallace*	.05
315	*John Wallace*	.40
316	*Jerome Williams*	.05
317	*Lorenzen Wright*	.25
318	Charles Barkley	.15
319	Derrick Coleman	.05
320	Michael Finley	.05
321	Stephon Marbury	.75
322	Reggie Miller	.10
323	Alonzo Mourning	.05
324	Shaquille O'Neal	.50
325	Gary Payton	.10
326	Dennis Rodman	.50
327	Damon Stoudamire	.25
328	Vin Baker	.10
329	Clyde Drexler	.15
330	Patrick Ewing	.10
331	Anfernee Hardaway	.75
332	Grant Hill	.50
333	Juwan Howard	.20
334	Larry Johnson	.05
335	Michael Jordan	1.25
336	Shawn Kemp	.20
337	Jason Kidd	.05
338	Karl Malone	.10
339	Reggie Miller	.10
340	Hakeem Olajuwon	.30
341	Scottie Pippen	.30
342	Mitch Richmond	.05
343	David Robinson	.20
344	Dennis Rodman	.50
345	Joe Smith	.20
346	Jerry Stackhouse	.20
347	John Stockton	.10
348	Jerry Stackhouse	.10
349	Checklist	.05
350	Checklist	.05

1996-97 Hoops Silver

This 98-card set features silver foil on the front and carries and insertion rate of one per retail pack.

	MT
Complete Set (98):	50.00
Common Silver:	.25
Silver Cards:	3x

1996-97 Hoops Fly With

This 10-card insert was found exclusively in Series II retail packs at a rate of one per 24. The cards are printed on plastic with the words "Fly With" appearing in large letters across the top half, with the entire background providing a sky-like appearance with clouds. The player's image is cast over the top of the background, with his name and team, along with the insert name, printed in gold foil in the lower left corner.

		MT
	Complete Set (10):	45.00
	Common Player:	3.00
1	Charles Barkley	5.00
2	Juwan Howard	5.00
3	Jason Kidd	4.00
4	Alonzo Mourning	3.00
5	Gary Payton	4.00
6	David Robinson	5.00
7	Dennis Rodman	12.00
8	Joe Smith	5.00
9	Jerry Stackhouse	5.00
10	Damon Stoudamire	7.00

1996-97 Hoops Grant's All-Rookies

Grant's All-Rookie Team features SkyView technology on 11 cards with individual numbering up to 1,996. Inserted only in packs of Series II, these two-layered cards feature a cut-out image of the selected rookie, with a plastic background that includes a head shot of Grant Hill. The mostly black border lists other members of the All-Rookie Team. The final card in the insert is of SkyBox spokesman Grant Hill, who the set is named for.

		MT
	Complete Set (11):	500.00
	Common Player:	10.00
1	Shareef Abdur-Rahim	45.00
2	Ray Allen	30.00
3	Kobe Bryant	300.00
4	Marcus Camby	20.00
5	Grant Hill	40.00
6	Allen Iverson	75.00
7	Kerry Kittles	20.00
8	Stephon Marbury	50.00
9	Antoine Walker	25.00
10	Samaki Walker	10.00
11	Lorenzen Wright	10.00

1996-97 Hoops Head to Head

Two NBA stars who have something in common based on stats are featured on these 1996-97 NBA Hoops I inserts. The cards are seeded one per every 24 packs. Each card front shows the two players, with their first names stamped in gold glitter, along with "Head 2 Head," in a gold banner at the bottom. The NBA Hoops logo is in an upper corner. The card back, numbered using an "HH" prefix, is divided into two halves, each with a color photo and corresponding player profile write-up.

		MT
	Complete Set (10):	50.00
	Common Player:	2.00
1	Larry Johnson, Glen Rice	2.00
2	Michael Jordan, Scottie Pippen	25.00
3	Jason Kidd, Grant Hill	10.00
4	Clyde Drexler, Hakeem Olajuwon	5.00
5	Vin Baker, Glenn Robinson	4.00
6	Anfernee Hardaway, Shaquille O'Neal	15.00
7	Antonio McDyess, Jerry Stackhouse	5.00
8	Sean Elliot, David Robinson	3.00
9	Joe Smith, Damon Stoudamire	6.00
10	Karl Malone, John Stockton	3.00

1996-97 Hoops HiPnotized

This 1996-97 NBA Hoops insert set highlights players who are difficult to stop one-on-one. Each UV-coated card front has a full-bleed color action photo on it, with a swirled image of the same photo in the background. "Hipnotized" and the player's last name are stamped in gold foil along the bottom. The NBA Hoops logo is in an upper corner. The horizontal card back, numbered using an "H" prefix, has a color photo on one side, with a swirled image as the background. The other side has a brief player profile, biographical information and statistics. Cards were seeded one per every four Series I packs.

		MT
	Complete Set (20):	20.00
	Common Player:	.25
	Minor Stars:	.50
1	Steve Smith	.25
2	Dana Barros	.25
3	Larry Johnson	1.00
4	Dennis Rodman	5.00
5	Terrell Brandon	.25
6	Jason Kidd	3.00
7	Grant Hill	4.00
8	Clyde Drexler	2.00
9	Reggie Miller	2.00
10	Alonzo Mourning	1.00
11	Glenn Robinson	1.50
12	Patrick Ewing	.50
13	Shaquille O'Neal	6.00
14	Jerry Stackhouse	3.00
15	Charles Barkley	2.00
16	Clifford Robinson	.25
17	Mitch Richmond	.25
18	David Robinson	2.00
19	Gary Payton	.50
20	Juwan Howard	1.50

1996-97 Hoops Hot List

This 20-card insert is printed on clear plastic with rolling flames covering the left side, while the right side is clear and the player's image lies on top. The words "Hot List" run down the left side in the flames. Hot List inserts were seeded one per 48 Series II hobby packs.

		MT
	Complete Set (20):	225.00
	Common Player:	3.00
1	Vin Baker	6.00
2	Patrick Ewing	6.00
3	Michael Finley	3.00
4	Kevin Garnett	30.00
5	Anfernee Hardaway	30.00
6	Grant Hill	30.00
7	Allan Houston	3.00
8	Michael Jordan	60.00
9	Shawn Kemp	8.00
10	Christian Laettner	3.00
11	Karl Malone	6.00
12	Antonio McDyess	3.00
13	Reggie Miller	6.00
14	Hakeem Olajuwon	15.00
15	Shaquille O'Neal	25.00
16	Scottie Pippen	15.00
17	Mitch Richmond	6.00
18	Isaiah Rider	3.00
19	Rod Strickland	3.00
20	Chris Webber	8.00

1996-97 Hoops Rookie Headliners

These cards are exclusive to 1996-97 NBA Hoops I hobby packs only; they are seeded one per every 72 packs. The cards feature some of the top rookies from the previous season. Each card front has a color photo in the middle, with a free throw circle stamped in gold on each end. The player's last name is stamped in gold. The right and left borders are stamped in gold, with "Rookie Headliners" written inside. The card back has a sepia-toned photo in the middle, with the player's name and card number (1 of 10, etc.) at the top. A recap of the player's rookie season accomplishments is also given. The left side of the card shows his statistics; the right side has copyright information.

		MT
	Complete Set (10):	80.00
	Common Player:	3.00
1	Antonio McDyess	7.00
2	Joe Smith	10.00
3	Brent Barry	3.00
4	Kevin Garnett	30.00
5	Jerry Stackhouse	10.00
6	Michael Finley	8.00
7	Arvydas Sabonis	3.00
8	Tyus Edney	3.00
9	Damon Stoudamire	15.00
10	Bryant Reeves	3.00

1996-97 Hoops Rookies

This 30-card set captured the top rookies during the 1996-97 season on a gold foil background. The word "rookie" runs down the left side, with a silver stamped logo in the bottom right corner. 1996-97 Rookies were found every six packs of Hoops Series II.

		MT
	Complete Set (30):	45.00
	Common Player:	.50
1	Shareef Abdur-Rahim	6.00
2	Ray Allen	4.00
3	Kobe Bryant	12.00
4	Marcus Camby	6.00
5	Erick Dampier	.50
6	Emanuel Davis	.50
7	Tony Delk	1.00
8	Brian Evans	.50
9	Derek Fisher	1.00
10	Todd Fuller	.50
11	Othella Harrington	.50
12	Allen Iverson	10.00
13	Dontae Jones	.50
14	Kerry Kittles	3.00
15	Priest Lauderdale	.50
16	Matt Maloney	2.00
17	Stephon Marbury	8.00
18	Walter McCarty	.50
19	Jeff McInnis	.50
20	Martin Muursepp	.50
21	Steve Nash	1.00
22	Moochie Norris	.50
23	Jermaine O'Neal	2.00
24	Vitaly Potapenko	.50
25	Roy Rogers	1.00
26	Antoine Walker	3.00
27	Samaki Walker	1.00
28	John Wallace	2.00
29	Jerome Williams	.50
30	Lorenzen Wright	.50

1996-97 Hoops Starting Five

Starting Five was a 29-card insert that captured each NBA team's starting lineup. The star player was cast over the team's logo for the majority of the card, with the other four players appearing in boxes across the bottom. This insert was seeded every 12 packs of Hoops II.

		MT
	Complete Set (29):	80.00
	Common Player:	1.00
1	Atlanta Hawks (Mookie Blaylock)	1.00
2	Boston Celtics (Dino Radja)	1.00
3	Charlotte Hornets (Glen Rice)	1.00
4	Chicago Bulls (Michael Jordan)	15.00
5	Cleveland Cavaliers (Tyrone Hill)	1.00
6	Dallas Mavericks (Jason Kidd)	1.00
7	Denver Nuggets (Antonio McDyess)	1.00
8	Detroit Pistons (Grant Hill)	10.00
9	Golden State Warriors (Joe Smith)	1.00
10	Houston Rockets (Hakeem Olajuwon)	4.00
11	Indiana Pacers (Reggie Miller)	1.00
12	Los Angeles Clippers (Rodney Rogers)	1.00
13	Los Angeles Lakers (Shaquille O'Neal)	10.00
14	Miami Heat (Alonzo Mourning)	1.00
15	Milwaukee Bucks (Ray Allen)	1.00
16	Minnesota Timberwolves (Kevin Garnett)	8.00
17	New Jersey Nets (Jayson Williams)	1.00
18	New York Knicks (Patrick Ewing)	1.00
19	Orlando Magic (Anfernee Hardaway)	10.00
20	Philadelphia 76ers (Jerry Stackhouse)	5.00
21	Phoenix Suns (Danny Manning)	1.00
22	Portland Trail Blazers (Isaiah Rider)	1.00
23	Sacramento Kings (Mitch Richmond)	1.00
24	San Antonio Spurs (David Robinson)	1.00
25	Seattle Supersonics (Shawn Kemp)	2.00
26	Toronto Raptors (Damon Stoudamire)	6.00
27	Utah Jazz (Karl Malone)	1.00
28	Vancouver Grizzlies (Bryant Reeves)	5.00
29	Washington Bullets (Juwan Howard)	1.00

1996-97 Hoops Superfeats

Last season's top statistical achievements are highlighted on these 1996-97 NBA Hoops I inserts, seeded one per every 36 retail packs only. Each card front has a full-bleed color action photo on it, with the player's name stamped inside a gold banner running down the right side. "Superfeats" and its logo are stamped in gold foil in the lower left corner. The NBA Hoops logo is in an upper corner. The card back has a color action photo to against a background which has the set's logo in it. The player's name and team name are below the photo, with a short recap of the players accomplishments underneath. A card number, 1 of 10, etc., is in a black circle in the upper right corner.

		MT
	Complete Set (10):	125.00
	Common Player:	2.00
1	Michael Jordan	60.00
2	Jason Kidd	8.00
3	Grant Hill	20.00
4	Hakeem Olajuwon	8.00
5	Alonzo Mourning	2.00
6	Anthony Mason	2.00
7	Anfernee Hardaway	15.00
8	Jerry Stackhouse	6.00
9	Shawn Kemp	6.00
10	Damon Stoudamire	10.00
	John A. Thompson	

1997-98 Hoops

Hoops was issued in two, 165-card series in 1997-98. The first series had 155 base cards, eight League Leaders and two checklists, while the Series II had 125 veterans and 40 Rookies. Series I marked the first release for the second season of Autographics. Cards had a white border, with the player shown over a large team logo. Backs had another large shot of the player, with stats on the right side over a white background. Inserts in Series I included: Talkin' Hoops, Dish N Swish, Chill with Hill, Frequent Flyer Club, Rookie Headliners, Autographics and Hooperstars. Inserts in Series II included: Great Shots, Chairmen of the Boards, Rock the House, High Voltage, Top of the World, 9-1-1, Autographics and High Voltage 500 Volts.

		MT
	Complete Set (330):	32.00
	Complete Series 1 (165):	14.00
	Complete Series 2 (165):	18.00
	Common Player:	.05
	Minor Stars:	.10
	Chill with Hill (10):	20.00
	Chill with Hill Cards:	2.00
	Ser. 1 or 2 Pack (10):	1.00
	Ser. 1 or 2 Wax Box (36):	30.00
1	Michael Jordan (league leader scoring)	1.50
2	Dennis Rodman (league leader rebounding)	.50
3	Mark Jackson (league leader assists)	.05
4	Shawn Bradley (league leader blocked shots)	.05
5	Glen Rice (league leader 3-pt shooting)	.05
6	Mookie Blaylock (league leader steals)	.05
7	Gheorghe Muresan (league leader FG%)	.05
8	Mark Price (league leader FT%)	.05
9	Tyrone Corbin	.05
10	Christian Laettner	.10
11	Priest Lauderdale	.05
12	Dikembe Mutombo	.10
13	Steve Smith	.05
14	Todd Day	.05
15	Rick Fox	.05
16	Brett Szabo	.05
17	Antoine Walker	.75
18	David Wesley	.05
19	Muggsy Bogues	.05
20	Dell Curry	.05
21	Tony Delk	.05
22	Anthony Mason	.05
23	Glen Rice	.15
24	Malik Rose	.05
25	Steve Kerr	.05
26	Toni Kukoc	.10
27	Luc Longley	.05
28	Robert Parish	.05
29	Scottie Pippen	.75
30	Dennis Rodman	1.00
31	Terrell Brandon	.10
32	Danny Ferry	.05
33	Tyrone Hill	.05
34	Bobby Phills	.05
35	Vitaly Potapenko	.05
36	Shawn Bradley	.05
37	Sasha Danilovic	.05
38	Derek Harper	.05
39	Martin Muursepp	.05
40	Robert Pack	.05
41	Khalid Reeves	.05
42	Vincent Askew	.05
43	Dale Ellis	.05
44	LaPhonso Ellis	.05
45	Ervin Johnson	.05
46	Antonio McDyess	.25
47	Joe Dumars	.05
48	Grant Hill	1.50
49	Lindsey Hunter	.05
50	Aaron McKie	.05
51	Theo Ratliff	.05
52	Scott Burrell	.05
53	Todd Fuller	.05
54	Chris Mullin	.05
55	Mark Price	.05
56	Joe Smith	.30
57	Latrell Sprewell	.20
58	Clyde Drexler	.25
59	Mario Elie	.05
60	Othella Harrington	.05
61	Matt Maloney	.15
62	Hakeem Olajuwon	.50
63	Kevin Willis	.05
64	Travis Best	.05
65	Antonio Davis	.05
66	Dale Davis	.05
67	Erick Dampier	.10
68	Mark Jackson	.05
69	Reggie Miller	.20
70	Brent Barry	.05
71	Darrick Martin	.05
72	Charles Outlaw	.05
73	Loy Vaught	.05
74	Lorenzen Wright	.05
75	Kobe Bryant	2.00
76	Derek Fisher	.05
77	Robert Horry	.05
78	Eddie Jones	.30
79	Travis Knight	.05
80	George McCloud	.05
81	Shaquille O'Neal	1.00
82	P.J. Brown	.05
83	Tim Hardaway	.10
84	Voshon Lenard	.05
85	Alonzo Mourning	.15
86	Jamal Mashburn	.05
87	Ray Allen	.25
88	Vin Baker	.20
89	Sherman Douglas	.05
90	Armon Gilliam	.05
91	Glenn Robinson	.05
92	Kevin Garnett	1.25
93	Dean Garrett	.05
94	Tom Gugliotta	.05
95	Stephon Marbury	.75
96	Stojko Vrankovic	.05
97	Chris Gatling	.05
98	Kendall Gill	.05
99	Jim Jackson	.10
100	Kerry Kittles	.25
101	Eric Montross	.05
102	Chris Childs	.05
103	Patrick Ewing	.20
104	Allan Houston	.05
105	Larry Johnson	.05
106	John Starks	.05
107	John Wallace	.15
108	Nick Anderson	.05
109	Horace Grant	.05
110	Anfernee Hardaway	1.25
111	Derek Strong	.05
112	Rony Seikaly	.05
113	Derrick Coleman	.05
114	Allen Iverson	1.00
115	Don MacLean	.05
116	Jerry Stackhouse	.15
117	Rex Walters	.05
118	Cedric Ceballos	.05
119	Kevin Johnson	.10
120	Jason Kidd	.10
121	Steve Nash	.05
122	Wesley Person	.05
123	Kenny Anderson	.05
124	Jermaine O'Neal	.20
125	Isaiah Rider	.05
126	Arvydas Sabonis	.05
127	Gary Trent	.05
128	Tyus Edney	.05
129	Brian Grant	.05
130	Olden Polynice	.05
131	Mitch Richmond	.15
132	Corliss Williamson	.05
133	Vinny Del Negro	.05
134	Sean Elliott	.05
135	Avery Johnson	.05
136	Will Perdue	.05
137	Dominique Wilkins	.05
138	Craig Ehlo	.05
139	Hersey Hawkins	.05
140	Shawn Kemp	.40
141	Jim McIlvaine	.05
142	Sam Perkins	.05
143	Detlef Schrempf	.05
144	Marcus Camby	.50
145	Doug Christie	.05
146	Popeye Jones	.05
147	Damon Stoudamire	.50
148	Walt Williams	.05
149	Jeff Hornacek	.05
150	Karl Malone	.25
151	Greg Ostertag	.05
152	Bryon Russell	.05

153	John Stockton	.25
154	Shareef Abdur-Rahim	.75
155	Greg Anthony	.05
156	Anthony Peeler	.05
157	Bryant Reeves	.05
158	Roy Rogers	.05
159	Calbert Cheaney	.05
160	Juwan Howard	.30
161	Gheorghe Muresan	.05
162	Rod Strickland	.05
163	Chris Webber	.30
164	Checklist	.05
165	Checklist	.05
166	*Tim Duncan*	3.00
167	*Chauncey Billups*	1.50
168	*Keith Van Horn*	1.50
169	*Tracy McGrady*	1.50
170	*John Thomas*	.05
171	*Tim Thomas*	1.25
172	*Ron Mercer*	1.50
173	*Scot Pollard*	.05
174	*Jason Lawson*	.05
175	*Keith Booth*	.05
176	*Adonal Foyle*	.50
177	*Bubba Wells*	.05
178	*Derek Anderson*	1.00
179	*Rodrick Rhodes*	.50
180	*Kelvin Cato*	.25
181	*Serge Zwikker*	.05
182	*Ed Gray*	.25
183	*Brevin Knight*	1.00
184	*Alvin Williams*	.05
185	*Paul Grant*	.05
186	*Austin Croshere*	.30
187	*Chris Crawford*	.05
188	*Anthony Johnson*	.05
189	*James Cotton*	.05
190	*James Collins*	.05
191	*Tony Battie*	.75
192	*Tariq Abdul-Wahad*	.50
193	*Danny Fortson*	.50
194	*Maurice Taylor*	.75
195	*Bobby Jackson*	1.00
196	*Charles Smith*	.05
197	*Johnny Taylor*	.05
198	*Jerald Honeycutt*	.05
199	*Marko Milic*	.10
200	*Anthony Parker*	.05
201	*Jacque Vaughn*	.50
202	*Antonio Daniels*	1.25
203	*Charles O'Bannon*	.10
204	*God Shammgod*	.10
205	*Kebu Stewart*	.10
206	Mookie Blaylock	.05
207	Chucky Brown	.05
208	Alan Henderson	.05
209	Dana Barros	.05
210	Tyus Edney	.05
211	Travis Knight	.05
212	Walter McCarty	.05
213	Vlade Divac	.05
214	Matt Geiger	.05
215	Bobby Phills	.05
216	J.R. Reid	.05
217	David Wesley	.05
218	Scott Burrell	.05
219	Ron Harper	.05
220	Michael Jordan	3.00
221	Bill Wennington	.05
222	Mitchell Butler	.05
223	Zydrunas Ilgauskas	.50
224	Shawn Kemp	.40
225	Wesley Person	.05
226	Shawnelle Scott	.05
227	Bob Sura	.05
228	Hubert Davis	.05
229	Michael Finley	.10
230	Dennis Scott	.05
231	Erick Strickland	.05
232	Samaki Walker	.05
233	Dean Garrett	.05
234	Priest Lauderdale	.05
235	Eric Williams	.05
236	Grant Long	.05
237	Malik Sealy	.05
238	Brian Williams	.05
239	Muggsy Bogues	.05
240	Bimbo Coles	.05
241	Brian Shaw	.05
242	Joe Smith	.25
243	Donyell Marshall	.05
244	Charles Barkley	.30
245	Emanuel Davis	.05
246	Brent Price	.05
247	Reggie Miller	.25
248	Chris Mullin	.10
249	Jalen Rose	.05
250	Rik Smits	.05
251	Mark West	.05
252	Lamond Murray	.05
253	Pooh Richardson	.05
254	Rodney Rogers	.05
255	Stojko Vrankovic	.05
256	Jon Barry	.05
257	Corie Blount	.05
258	Elden Campbell	.05
259	Rick Fox	.05
260	Nick Van Exel	.20
261	Isaac Austin	.05
262	Dan Majerle	.05
263	Terry Mills	.05
264	Mark Strickland	.05
265	Terrell Brandon	.10
266	Tyrone Hill	.05
267	Ervin Johnson	.05
268	Andrew Lang	.05
269	Elliot Perry	.05
270	Chris Carr	.05
271	Reggie Jordan	.05
272	Sam Mitchell	.05
273	Stanley Roberts	.05
274	Michael Cage	.05
275	Sam Cassell	.05
276	Lucious Harris	.05
277	Kerry Kittles	.25
278	Don MacLean	.05
279	Chris Dudley	.05
280	Chris Mills	.05
281	Charlie Ward	.05
282	Buck Williams	.05
283	Herb Williams	.05
284	Derek Harper	.05
285	Mark Price	.05
286	Gerald Wilkins	.05
287	Allen Iverson	1.25
288	Jim Jackson	.05
289	Eric Montross	.05
290	Jerry Stackhouse	.25
291	Clarence Weatherspoon	.05
292	Tom Chambers	.05
293	Rex Chapman	.05
294	Danny Manning	.05
295	Antonio McDyess	.25
296	Clifford Robinson	.05
297	Stacey Augmon	.05
298	Brian Grant	.05
299	Rasheed Wallace	.05
300	Mahmoud Abdul-Rauf	.05
301	Terry Dehere	.05
302	Billy Owens	.05
303	Michael Smith	.05
304	Cory Alexander	.05
305	Chuck Person	.05
306	David Robinson	.30
307	Charles Smith	.05
308	Monty Williams	.05
309	Vin Baker	.20
310	Jerome Kersey	.05
311	Nate McMillan	.05
312	Gary Payton	.30
313	Eric Snow	.05
314	Carlos Rogers	.05
315	Zan Tabak	.05
316	John Wallace	.05
317	Sharone Wright	.05
318	Shandon Anderson	.05
319	Antoine Carr	.05
320	Howard Eisley	.05
321	Chris Morris	.05
322	Pete Chilcutt	.05
323	George Lynch	.05
324	Chris Robinson	.05
325	Otis Thorpe	.05
326	Harvey Grant	.05
327	Darvin Ham	.05
328	Juwan Howard	.25
329	Ben Wallace	.05
330	Chris Webber	.50

1997-98 Hoops Chairman of the Boards

Chairmen of the Boards was a 10-card set that highlighted the league's top rebounders over a foil background that highlighted that player's various rebounding achievements. These cards were inserted in one per nine Series II packs and were numbered with a "CB" suffix.

		MT
Complete Set (10):		30.00
Common Player:		.75
Minor Stars:		1.50
1	Shaquille O'Neal	8.00
2	Dikembe Mutombo	.75
3	Dennis Rodman	5.00
4	Patrick Ewing	1.50
5	Charles Barkley	2.50
6	Karl Malone	2.00
7	Rasheed Wallace	.75
8	Chris Webber	4.00
9	Tim Duncan	10.00
10	Kevin Garnett	10.00

1997-98 Hoops Dish N Swish

This 10-card retail only insert was found in every 18 packs of Series I Hoops. It featured players who excel at scoring and assists, and contained the insert name in silver running up the left side. Cards are numbered with a "DS" prefix.

		MT
Complete Set (10):		50.00
Common Player:		1.00
1	Mookie Blaylock	1.00
2	Terrell Brandon	1.00
3	Anfernee Hardaway	10.00
4	Allen Iverson	10.00
5	Michael Jordan	20.00
6	Jason Kidd	2.00
7	Stephon Marbury	8.00
8	Gary Payton	2.00
9	John Stockton	2.00
10	Damon Stoudamire	3.00

1997-98 Hoops Frequent Flyer Club

Frequent Flyer inserts were seeded every 36 hobby packs in Hoops Series I. This 20-card insert was printed on a horizontal, credit card-type design with the player's image on the left and a Hoops Airlines logo on the right side with the words "Frequent Flyer" across the bottom in gold foil. A rarer Upgrade version, which is printed on plastic is also available in one per 360 hobby packs. Cards are numbered with a "FF" prefix.

		MT
Complete Set (20):		150.00
Common Player:		2.00
First Class Upgrades:		2x-4x
1	Christian Laettner	2.00
2	Antoine Walker	6.00
3	Glen Rice	2.00
4	Michael Jordan	40.00
5	Dennis Rodman	15.00
6	Grant Hill	20.00
7	Latrell Sprewell	2.00
8	Charles Barkley	6.00
9	Kobe Bryant	25.00
10	Shaquille O'Neal	15.00
11	Ray Allen	5.00
12	Kevin Garnett	20.00
13	Kerry Kittles	5.00
14	Anfernee Hardaway	15.00
15	Jerry Stackhouse	4.00
16	Cedric Ceballos	2.00
17	Shawn Kemp	5.00
18	Marcus Camby	10.00
19	Juwan Howard	6.00
20	Chris Webber	6.00

1997-98 Hoops Frequent Flyer Club Upgrade

Frequent Flyer Upgrades parallel the regular Frequent Flyer Club insert, but are printed on plastic instead of cardboard. The cards are also identified by a large "Upgrade" stamp across the bottom right side. Upgrade versions are seeded one per 360 hobby packs.

		MT
Complete Set (20):		600.00
Upgrade Cards:		2x-4x

1997-98 Hoops Great Shots

Great Shots highlighted 30 different players on 5"x 7" mini-posters. These inserts were seeded one per pack in Series II Hoops and featured a full-color shot on one side and a plain white back.

		MT
Complete Set (30):		15.00
Common Player:		.10
Minor Stars:		.20
1	Dikembe Mutombo	.10
2	Antoine Walker	1.00
3	Glen Rice	.30
4	Dennis Rodman	1.00
5	Anderson, Knight	.75
6	Michael Finley	.20
7	Fortson, Battie, Jackson	.50
8	Grant Hill	2.00
9	Joe Smith	.30
10	Charles Barkley	.40
11	Reggie Miller	.30
12	Lamond Murray	.10
13	Kobe Bryant	2.50
14	Alonzo Mourning	.30
15	Ray Allen	.75
16	Kevin Garnett	2.00
17	Stephon Marbury	1.25
18	Kerry Kittles	.30
19	Patrick Ewing	.30
20	Anfernee Hardaway	1.25
21	Allen Iverson	1.50
22	Jason Kidd	.40
23	Rasheed Wallace	.10
24	Mitch Richmond	.25
25	David Robinson	.40
26	Gary Payton	.40
27	Damon Stoudamire	.50
28	John Stockton	.30
29	Shareef Abdur-Rahim	1.00
30	Chris Webber	.75

1997-98 Hoops High Voltage

This 20-card insert was exclusive to Series II hobby packs. Card fronts featured an all-foil backgroud with black and silver bullseye stripes. Inserted at a rate of one per 36 packs, this insert is numbered with a "HV" suffix. Parallel 500 Voltage versions of each card were also produced and numbered sequentially to 500.

		MT
Complete Set (20):		150.00
Common Player:		1.50
Minor Stars:		3.00
Inserted 1:36		
Voltage 500 Cards:		5x
Production 500 Sets		
1	Kobe Bryant	20.00
2	Eddie Jones	5.00
3	Ray Allen	3.00
4	Anfernee Hardaway	12.00
5	Grant Hill	15.00
6	Shareef Abdur-Rahim	8.00
7	Marcus Camby	3.00
8	Allen Iverson	12.00
9	Kerry Kittles	1.50
10	Kevin Garnett	15.00
11	Stephon Marbury	12.00
12	Chris Webber	5.00
13	Antoine Walker	6.00
14	Michael Jordan	30.00
15	Tim Duncan	15.00
16	Dennis Rodman	10.00
17	Scottie Pippen	7.50
18	Shawn Kemp	3.00
19	Hakeem Olajuwon	5.00
20	Karl Malone	3.00

1997-98 Hoops HOOPerstars

This 10-card insert was seeded one per 288 packs of Hoops Series I, and features the player's name and the words "HOOPerstars" both printed in holographic silver foil on a die-cut design. Cards are numbered with a "H" prefix.

		MT
Complete Set (10):		300.00
Common Player:		6.00
1	Michael Jordan	100.00
2	Grant Hill	50.00
3	Shaquille O'Neal	30.00
4	Ray Allen	6.00
5	Stephon Marbury	40.00
6	Anfernee Hardaway	40.00
7	Allen Iverson	50.00
8	Shawn Kemp	15.00
9	Marcus Camby	25.00
10	Shareef Abdur-Rahim	25.00

1997-98 Hoops Rock the House

Rock the House was a 10-card, one per 18 retail exclusive insert found in Series II packs. Fronts captured the player over a foil background of rocks, with the insert name printed across the top. Backs were numbered with a "RTH" suffix.

		MT
Complete Set (10):		70.00
Common Player:		1.25
1	Anfernee Hardaway	12.00
2	Stephon Marbury	10.00
3	Grant Hill	15.00
4	Shaquille O'Neal	10.00
5	Kerry Kittles	1.25
6	Michael Jordan	30.00
7	Ray Allen	5.00
8	Damon Stoudamire	3.00
9	Kevin Garnett	15.00
10	Shawn Kemp	4.00

1997-98 Hoops Rookie Headliners

Rookie Headliners featured 10 top rookies from the 1996-97 season with a made-up newspaper background with that player dominating the headlines. This insert was found in packs of Hoops I at a one per 48 rate. Cards are numbered with a "RH" prefix.

		MT
Complete Set (10):		70.00
Common Player:		1.50
1	Antoine Walker	8.00
2	Matt Maloney	1.50
3	Kobe Bryant	25.00
4	Ray Allen	4.00
5	Stephon Marbury	15.00
6	Kerry Kittles	3.00
7	John Wallace	1.50
8	Allen Iverson	15.00
9	Marcus Camby	3.00
10	Shareef Abdur-Rahim	10.00

1997-98 Hoops Talkin' Hoops

Each pack of Hoops I contained one of 30 different Talkin' Hoops inserts featuring ex-NBA star Bill Walton. The cards were printed on silver foilboard, with the words "Talkin' Hoops" running up the left side in a black box and Bill Walton's close-up in the lower right corner. Cards are numbered with a "TH" prefix.

		MT
Complete Set (30):		10.00
Common Player:		.10
Minor Stars:		.20
1	Christian Laettner	.20
2	Antoine Walker	1.00
3	Glen Rice	.20
4	Dennis Rodman	2.00
5	Scottie Pippen	1.50
6	Terrell Brandon	.20
7	Michael Finley	.10
8	Grant Hill	3.00
9	Joe Smith	.30
10	Charles Barkley	.40
11	Hakeem Olajuwon	.75
12	Reggie Miller	.30
13	Loy Vaught	.10
14	Shaquille O'Neal	2.00
15	Kobe Bryant	3.50
16	Kevin Garnett	2.00
17	Tom Gugliotta	.10
18	Kerry Kittles	.50
19	John Wallace	.20
20	Patrick Ewing	.20
21	Jerry Stackhouse	.50
22	David Robinson	.50
23	Gary Payton	.50
24	Shawn Kemp	.75
25	Damon Stoudamire	.75
26	John Stockton	.30
27	Karl Malone	.30
28	Shareef Abdur-Rahim	1.50
29	Juwan Howard	.50
30	Chris Webber	.75

1997-98 Hoops Team Sheets

These nine-card perforated sheets were produced for different NBA teams and either handed out to fans at the team's arena during a give-away night or were given away through promotions by the sponsor during the regular season. Cards are identical to the regular-issue card of each players from either Series I or II and are usually numbered with the same number as in the set, although some are unnumbered. In addition, each of the sheets, except the Nuggets, includes the sponsor's logo as the ninth card on the sheet. It is unclear at press time whether all the teams had sheets or not so the checklist below may be a partial.

		MT
Complete Set (9):		30.00
Common Sheet:		3.00
CLEVELAND		4.00
32	Danny Ferry	
35	Vitaly Potapenko	
178	Derek Anderson	
183	Brevin Knight	
223	Zydrunas Ilgauskas	
224	Shawn Kemp	
225	Wesley Person	
227	Bob Sura	
---	Foot Locker/Reebok logo card	
CHICAGO		5.00
25	Steve Kerr	
26	Toni Kukoc	
27	Luc Longley	
29	Scottie Pippen	
30	Dennis Rodman	
219	Ron Harper	
220	Michael Jordan	
221	Bill Wennington	
---	Nabisco/Jewel logo card	
DENVER		3.00
---	Coach Bill Hanzlik	
44	LaPhonso Ellis	
46	Bryant Stith	
195	Bobby Jackson	
---	Eric Washington	
191	Tony Battie	
193	Danny Fortson	
233	Dean Garrett	
234	Priest Lauderdale	
MINNESOTA		6.00
---	Terry Porter	
1	Stanley Roberts	
---	Cherokee Parks	
92	Kevin Garnett	
94	Tom Gugliotta	
95	Stephon Marbury	
270	Chris Carr	
272	Sam Mitchell	
---	Pepsi logo card	
NEW JERSEY		4.00
---	Jayson Williams	
168	Keith Van Horn	
274	Michael Cage	
275	Sam Cassell	
276	Coach John Calipari	
277	Kerry Kittles	
---	Chris Gatling	
---	Kendall Gill	
---	Sunoco logo card	
ORLANDO		5.00
108	Nick Anderson	
109	Horace Grant	
110	Anfernee Hardaway	
111	Rony Seikaly	
112	Derek Strong	
285	Mark Price	
---	Charles Outlaw	
---	Darrell Armstrong	
---	Gooding's logo card	
SACRAMENTO		3.00
---	Michael Stewart	
130	Olden Polynice	
132	Corliss Williamson	
188	Anthony Johnson	
---	Lawrence Funderburke	
---	Bobby Hurley	
303	Michael Smith	
---	Coach Eddie Jordan	
---	Eggo/Lender's Bagels logo card	

SEATTLE		4.00
139	Hersey Hawkins	
141	Jim McIlvaine	
142	Sam Perkins	
143	Detlef Schrempf	
309	Vin Baker	
312	Gary Payton	
---	Dale Ellis	
---	Coach George Karl	
---	Castrol logo card	
UTAH		4.00
149	Jeff Hornacek	
150	Karl Malone	
151	Greg Ostertag	
152	Bryon Russell	
153	John Stockton	
201	Jacque Vaughn	
318	Shandon Anderson	
320	Howard Eisley	
---	Smith's logo card	

1997-98 Hoops Top of the World

This 15-card insert set was seeded one per 48 packs of Series II. Each player is photographed and superimposed on a globe background, while cards are numbered with a "TW" suffix.

		MT
Complete Set (15):		85.00
Common Player:		1.50
Minor Stars:		3.00
1	Tim Duncan	25.00
2	Tim Thomas	8.00
3	Tony Battie	6.00
4	Keith Van Horn	15.00
5	Antonio Daniels	8.00
6	Derek Anderson	6.00
7	Chauncey Billups	12.00
8	Tracy McGrady	12.00
9	Danny Fortson	3.00
10	Austin Croshere	3.00
11	Tariq Abdul-Wahad	3.00
12	Adonal Foyle	3.00
13	Rodrick Rhodes	3.00
14	Ron Mercer	12.00
15	Charles Smith	1.50

1997-98 Hoops 911

This 10-card insert set featured a card within a sleeve that could be pulled out to reveal the player. Each sleeve was laser engraved "9-1-1," and was fitted around the inner card. These cards were seeded one per 288 packs of Series II and numbered with a "N" suffix.

		MT
Complete Set (10):		400.00
Common Player:		12.00
1	Michael Jordan	125.00
2	Grant Hill	60.00
3	Shawn Kemp	15.00
4	Stephon Marbury	50.00
5	Damon Stoudamire	12.00
6	Shaquille O'Neal	45.00
7	Shareef Abdur-Rahim	30.00
8	Allen Iverson	50.00
9	Antoine Walker	25.00
10	Anfernee Hardaway	50.00

1998-99 Hoops

Hoops Series I featured 155 basic cards and 10 Steppin' Out subsets cards. Base cards featured an action shot of the player on the left, with a close-up shot of his face during the action shot in the background. This design faded into a white border around the card. The set was paralleled in a Starting Five set that was numbered to only five sets. Inserts sets in Series I included: Shout Outs, Pump Up the Jam, Rejectors, Freshman Flashback, Prime Twine, Bams, Slam Bams and Autographics.

		MT
Complete Set (165):		20.00
Common Player:		.10
Minor Stars:		.20
Pack (12):		38.00
Wax Box (36):		
1	Kobe Bryant	2.00
2	Glenn Robinson	.20
3	Derek Anderson	.30
4	Terry Dehere	.10
5	Jalen Rose	.10
6	Zydrunas Ilgauskas	.10
7	Scott Williams	.10
8	Toni Kukoc	.20
9	John Stockton	.30
10	Kevin Garnett	1.50
11	Jerome Williams	.10
12	Anthony Mason	.10
13	Harvey Grant	.10
14	Mookie Blaylock	.10
15	Tyrone Hill	.10
16	Dale Davis	.10
17	Eric Washington	.10
18	Aaron McKie	.10
19	Jermaine O'Neal	.10
20	Anfernee Hardaway	1.00
21	Derrick Coleman	.10
22	Allan Houston	.20
23	Michael Jordan	3.00
24	Jason Kidd	.40
25	Tyrone Corbin	.10
26	Jacque Vaughn	.10
27	Bobby Jackson	.20
28	Chris Anstey	.10
29	Brent Barry	.10
30	Shareef Abdur-Rahim	.50
31	Jeff Hornacek	.10
32	Ed Gray	.10
33	Grant Hill	1.50
34	Steve Smith	.10
35	Rony Seikaly	.10
36	Mark Jackson	.10
37	Shawn Bradley	.10
38	Corie Blount	.10
39	Erick Dampier	.10
40	Kerry Kittles	.20
41	David Wesley	.10
42	Horace Grant	.10
43	Bobby Hurley	.10
44	Tariq Abdul-Wahad	.10
45	Brian Williams	.10
46	Ray Allen	.20
47	Kenny Anderson	.10
48	Rodrick Rhodes	.10
49	Greg Foster	.10
50	Tim Duncan	1.50
51	Steve Nash	.10
52	Kelvin Cato	.10
53	Donyell Marshall	.10
54	Marcus Camby	.20
55	Kevin Willis	.10
56	Michael Finley	.20
57	Muggsy Bogues	.10
58	Mark Price	.10
59	Larry Johnson	.20
60	Karl Malone	.30
61	Greg Ostertag	.10
62	Sean Elliott	.10
63	Johnny Taylor	.10
64	Howard Eisley	.10
65	Chris Childs	.10
66	Walt Williams	.10
67	Tracy Murray	.10
68	Patrick Ewing	.20
69	Olden Polynice	.10
70	Allen Iverson	1.00
71	David Robinson	.30
72	Calbert Cheaney	.10
73	Lamond Murray	.10
74	Scot Pollard	.10
75	Alonzo Mourning	.20
76	Tracy McGrady	.75
77	Jim McIlvaine	.10
78	Bob Sura	.10
79	Anthony Peeler	.10
80	Keith Van Horn	.75
81	Maurice Taylor	.20
82	Charles Smith	.10
83	Dikembe Mutombo	.20
84	Nick Anderson	.10
85	Austin Croshere	.10
86	Armon Gilliam	.10
87	Eddie Jones	.50
88	Glen Rice	.20
89	Sam Cassell	.10
90	Stephon Marbury	1.00
91	Elliot Perry	.10
92	Jamal Mashburn	.20
93	Adonal Foyle	.10
94	Avery Johnson	.10
95	Michael Williams	.10
96	Danny Fortson	.10
97	Brevin Knight	.30
98	Ron Harper	.10
99	Chauncey Billups	.30
100	Shaquille O'Neal	1.00
101	Brent Price	.10
102	Tim Thomas	.75
103	Khalid Reeves	.10
104	Chris Gatling	.10
105	Terry Cummings	.10
106	Vin Baker	.30
107	Bryant Reeves	.10
108	John Starks	.10
109	Juwan Howard	.20
110	Antoine Walker	.75
111	Rodney Rogers	.10
112	Nick Van Exel	.20
113	Chris Whitney	.10
114	Bobby Phills	.10
115	Travis Knight	.10
116	Robert Horry	.10
117	Erick Strickland	.10
118	Dontae Jones	.10
119	Tony Battie	.20
120	Lindsey Hunter	.10
121	Reggie Miller	.20
122	John Wallace	.10
123	Ron Mercer	1.00
124	Antonio Daniels	.20
125	Paul Grant	.10
126	Voshon Lenard	.10
127	Shawn Kemp	.40
128	Antonio Davis	.10
129	Hakeem Olajuwon	.50
130	Danny Manning	.10
131	Bimbo Coles	.10
132	Tim Hardaway	.30
133	Lorenzo Williams	.10
134	Dan Majerle	.10
135	Bryant Stith	.10
136	Randy Brown	.10
137	Hubert Davis	.10
138	Gary Payton	.30
139	Rasheed Wallace	.10
140	Chris Robinson	.10
141	Doug Christie	.10
142	Brian Grant	.10
143	Isaiah Rider	.10
144	Kendall Gill	.10
145	Lorenzen Wright	.10
146	Ervin Johnson	.10
147	Monty Williams	.10
148	Keith Closs	.10
149	Tony Delk	.10
150	Hersey Hawkins	.10
151	Dean Garrett	.10
152	Cedric Henderson	.10
153	Detlef Schrempf	.10
154	Dana Barros	.10
155	Dee Brown	.10
156	Jayson Williams	.10
157	Charles Barkley	.20
158	Damon Stoudamire	.10
159	Scottie Pippen	.40
160	Joe Smith	.10
161	Antonio McDyess	.10
162	Jerry Stackhouse	.10
163	Dennis Rodman	.50
164	Shaquille O'Neal	.50
165	Grant Hill	.75

1998-99 Hoops Bams

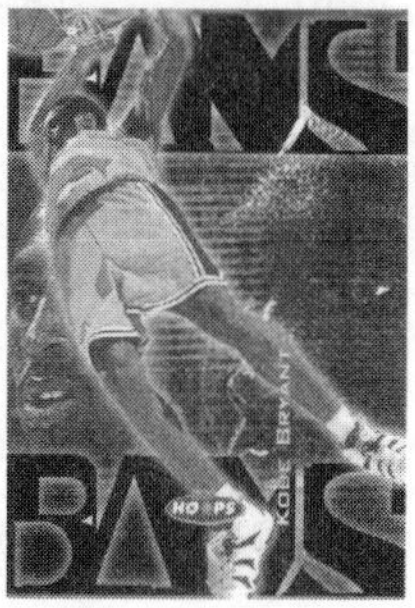

Bams displays 10 of the game's top dunkers on silver holofoil designs. These inserts are numbered with a "B" suffix, sequentially numbered to 250 sets and found in packs of Series I.

		MT
Complete Set (10):		850.00
Common Player:		40.00
Production 250 Sets		
Slam Bams:		2x
Production 100 Sets		
1	Michael Jordan	300.00
2	Kobe Bryant	200.00
3	Allen Iverson	100.00
4	Shaquille O'Neal	100.00
5	Tim Duncan	150.00
6	Shareef Abdur-Rahim	40.00
7	Keith Van Horn	60.00
8	Grant Hill	150.00
9	Anfernee Hardaway	100.00
10	Kevin Garnett	150.00

1998-99 Hoops Freshman Flashback

Freshman Flashback features some of the top newcomers in 1997-98. Cards show a close-up shot of the player on in a black-and-white format with a bronze tint over it. This 10-card set was sequentially numbered to 1,000 sets, numbered with a "FF" suffix and inserted in Series I.

		MT
Complete Set (10):		275.00
Common Player:		10.00
Production 1,000 Sets		
1	Tim Duncan	80.00
2	Keith Van Horn	35.00
3	Tim Thomas	40.00
4	Antonio Daniels	15.00
5	Brevin Knight	25.00
6	Danny Fortson	10.00
7	Maurice Taylor	15.00
8	Chauncey Billups	25.00
9	Bobby Jackson	15.00
10	Derek Anderson	25.00

1998-99 Hoops Prime Twine

Prime Twine captures 10 top players on cards die-cut inside and outside and printed on gold foil. Cards are numbered with a "PT" suffix, sequentially numbered to 500 sets and inserted in Series I packs.

		MT
Complete Set (10):		375.00
Common Player:		20.00
Production 500 Sets		
1	Dennis Rodman	70.00
2	Allen Iverson	80.00
3	Karl Malone	30.00
4	Antonio McDyess	20.00
5	Damon Stoudamire	20.00
6	Eddie Jones	40.00
7	Scottie Pippen	60.00
8	Shawn Kemp	30.00
9	Antoine Walker	40.00
10	Stephon Marbury	80.00

1998-99 Hoops Promo Sheet

This six-card promo sheet was distributed with sales material previous to the release of Series I. Cards are perforated with set information across the top of the sheet.

		MT
Complete Panel (6):		8.00
Common Player:		.50
1	Grant Hill	2.00
2	Kevin Garnett	3.00
3	Tim Duncan	2.00
4	Allen Iverson	2.00
5	Keith Van Horn	.50
6	Shaquille O'Neal	2.00

1998-99 Hoops Pump Up The Jam

This 10-card insert was seeded every four packs of Series I. Cards show a closeup of the player on the right side, with an action shot on the left, all over a black background. Card backs are numbered with a "P" suffix.

		MT
Complete Set (10):		25.00
Common Player:		.50
Inserted 1:4		
1	Stephon Marbury	3.00
2	Allen Iverson	3.00
3	Grant Hill	4.00
4	Kobe Bryant	6.00
5	Michael Jordan	8.00
6	Antoine Walker	1.50
7	Shareef Abdur-Rahim	2.00
8	Shawn Kemp	1.25
9	Anfernee Hardaway	2.50
10	Antonio McDyess	.50

1998-99 Hoops Rejectors

Rejectors was a 10-card insert that featured top shot blockers on a horizontal format. Cards were numbered with a "R" suffix, sequentially numbered to 2,500 and inserted in Series I.

		MT
Complete Set (10):		100.00
Common Player:		3.00
Production 2,500 Sets		
1	Dikembe Mutombo	3.00
2	Marcus Camby	6.00
3	Shaquille O'Neal	20.00
4	Tim Duncan	30.00
5	Shawn Bradley	3.00
6	Chris Webber	10.00
7	Patrick Ewing	3.00
8	Kevin Garnett	30.00
9	David Robinson	8.00
10	Michael Stewart	3.00

1998-99 Hoops Shout Outs

Thirty Shout Outs inserts were inserted at a rate of one per pack in Series I. It showed emotional shots of the player and was numbered with a "SO" suffix.

		MT
Complete Set (30):		8.00
Common Player:		.10
Minor Stars:		.20
Inserted 1:1		
1	Shareef Abdur-Rahim	.50
2	Chauncey Billups	.20
3	Terrell Brandon	.10
4	Patrick Ewing	.20
5	Michael Finley	.20
6	Adonal Foyle	.10
7	Kevin Garnett	1.00
8	Anfernee Hardaway	.60
9	Tim Hardaway	.25
10	Grant Hill	1.00
11	Tim Thomas	.50
12	Bobby Jackson	.10
13	Michael Jordan	2.00
14	Shawn Kemp	.30
15	Jason Kidd	.25
16	Karl Malone	.20
17	Stephon Marbury	.75
18	Anthony Mason	.10
19	Reggie Miller	.20
20	Dikembe Mutombo	.10
21	Kobe Bryant	1.25
22	Hakeem Olajuwon	.30
23	Gary Payton	.25
24	Michael Stewart	.10
25	David Robinson	.25
26	Maurice Taylor	.20
27	Keith Van Horn	.60
28	Antoine Walker	.60
29	Rasheed Wallace	.10
30	Juwan Howard	.20

1998-99 Hoops Slam Bams

Slam Bams was a parallel set to the Bams insert, but was sequentially numbered to only 100 and found only in Series I hobby packs.

	MT
Slam Bam Cards:	2x
Production 100 Sets	

1999-00 Hoops

Hoops arrived in 1999-2000 with a 185-card single-series release that included 117 basic cards, 48 Sophomore Sensations and 20 Future Phenoms. Each card featured a full color front with a rough white border. The set was paralleled in a Starting Five insert, while insert sets included Name Plates, Calling Card, Y2K Corps, The Dunk Mob, Pure Players, 100% Pure Players, Build Your Own Card and Autographics.

		MT
Complete Set (185):		30.00
Common Player:		.10
Minor Stars:		.20
Pack (12):		1.50
Wax Box (36):		40.00
1	Paul Pierce	1.00
2	Ray Allen	.20
3	Jason Williams	1.00
4	Sean Elliott	.10
5	Al Harrington	.30
6	Bobby Phills	.10
7	Tyronn Lue	.25
8	James Cotton	.10
9	Anthony Peeler	.10
10	LaPhonso Ellis	.20
11	Voshon Lenard	.10
12	Kornel David	.20
13	Michael Finley	.30
14	Danny Fortson	.10
15	Antawn Jamison	.75
16	Reggie Miller	.20
17	Shaquille O'Neal	1.00
18	P.J. Brown	.10
19	Roshown McLeod	.20
20	Larry Johnson	.20
21	Rashard Lewis	.30
22	Tracy McGrady	.75
23	Predrag Stojakovic	.10
24	Tracy Murray	.10
25	Gary Payton	.50
26	Ricky Davis	.25
27	Kobe Bryant	2.00
28	Avery Johnson	.10
29	Kevin Garnett	1.50
30	Charles R. Jones	.20
31	Brevin Knight	.10
32	Lindsey Hunter	.10
33	Felipe Lopez	.30
34	Rik Smits	.10
35	Maurice Taylor	.30
36	Corey Benjamin	.20
37	Ervin Johnson	.10
38	Steve Smith	.20
39	Austin Croshere	.10
40	Matt Geiger	.10
41	Tom Gugliotta	.20
42	Radoslav Nesterovic	.20
43	Juwan Howard	.20
44	Keon Clark	.25
45	Latrell Sprewell	.20
46	George Lynch	.10
47	Greg Ostertag	.10
48	J.R. Henderson	.20
49	Kerry Kittles	.20
50	Matt Harpring	.25
51	Duane Causwell	.10
52	Andrae Patterson	.20
53	Jerry Stackhouse	.20
54	Adonal Foyle	.10
55	Bryce Drew	.20
56	Chris Childs	.10
57	Charles Smith	.10
58	Rony Seikaly	.10
59	Chauncey Billups	.20
60	Grant Hill	1.50
61	Marlon Garnett	.20
62	Tim Hardaway	.40
63	Vlade Divac	.20
64	Chris Gatling	.10
65	Glenn Robinson	.20
66	Michael Olowokandi	.40
67	Elliot Perry	.10
68	Howard Eisley	.10
69	Glen Rice	.20
70	Marcus Camby	.30
71	Theo Ratliff	.20
72	Brian Skinner	.20
73	Kenny Anderson	.20
74	Jamal Mashburn	.20
75	Vladimir Stepania	.20
76	Jayson Williams	.20
77	Brian Grant	.20
78	Raef LaFrentz	.40
79	John Starks	.10
80	Mike Bibby	.60
81	Stephon Marbury	1.00
82	Armen Gilliam	.10
83	Sam Jacobson	.20
84	Derrick Coleman	.20
85	Allan Houston	.20
86	Miles Simon	.20
87	Allen Iverson	1.50
88	Derek Anderson	.20
89	Chris Anstey	.10
90	Larry Hughes	.50
91	Vitaly Potapenko	.10
92	Cherokee Parks	.10
93	Donyell Marshall	.10
94	Danny Manning	.10
95	Bryon Russell	.10
96	Randell Jackson	.20
97	Antoine Walker	.75
98	Dirk Nowitzki	.40
99	Karl Malone	.50
100	Vince Carter	2.00
101	Eddie Jones	.30
102	Bryant Stith	.10
103	Korleone Young	.20
104	Tim Duncan	1.50
105	Jerome Kersey	.10
106	Bonzi Wells	.20
107	Wesley Person	.10
108	Steve Nash	.10
109	Tyrone Nesby	.20

110	Doug Christie	.10
111	David Robinson	.50
112	Ruben Patterson	.20
113	Dikembe Mutombo	.20
114	Ron Mercer	.75
115	Elden Campbell	.10
116	Kevin Willis	.10
117	Hakeem Olajuwon	.50
118	Shawn Kemp	.40
119	Eric Montross	.10
120	Shareef Abdur-Rahim	.75
121	Bob Sura	.10
122	James Robinson	.10
123	Shawn Bradley	.10
124	Robert Traylor	.40
125	Dean Garrett	.10
126	Keith Van Horn	.60
127	Patrick Ewing	.20
128	Isaac Austin	.10
129	Jason Kidd	.75
130	Isaiah Rider	.20
131	Jerome James	.20
132	John Stockton	.20
133	Jason Caffey	.10
134	Bryant Reeves	.10
135	Michael Dickerson	.30
136	Chris Mullin	.20
137	Rasheed Wallace	.20
138	Cuttino Mobley	.20
139	Antonio McDyess	.40
140	Chris Webber	.75
141	Jelani McCoy	.20
142	Damon Stoudamire	.30
143	Gerald Brown	.20
144	Cory Carr	.20
145	Brent Barry	.10
146	Alan Henderson	.10
147	Nazr Mohammed	.20
148	Bison Dele	.10
149	Scottie Pippen	.75
150	Michael Doleac	.25
151	Nick Anderson	.20
152	Alonzo Mourning	.30
153	Jahidi White	.20
154	Jalen Rose	.20
155	Brad Miller	.20
156	Andrew DeClercq	.10
157	Erick Strickland	.10
158	Toni Kukoc	.30
159	Pat Garrity	.25
160	Bobby Jackson	.10
161	Steve Kerr	.10
162	Toby Bailey	.20
163	Charles Oakley	.10
164	Rod Strickland	.20
165	Rodrick Rhodes	.10
166	*Ron Artest*	.60
167	*William Avery*	.50
168	*Elton Brand*	2.00
169	*Baron Davis*	1.25
170	*John Celestand*	.40
171	*Jumanie Jones*	.40
172	*Andre Miller*	1.25
173	*Lee Nailon*	.40
174	*James Posey*	.60
175	*Jason Terry*	.75
176	*Kenny Thomas*	.50
177	*Steve Francis*	5.00
178	*Wally Szczerbiak*	1.00
179	*Richard Hamilton*	1.00
180	*Jonathan Bender*	2.00
181	*Shawn Marion*	2.00
182	*Aleksandar Radojevic*	.25
183	*Tim James*	.40
184	*Trajan Langdon*	.60
185	*Corey Maggette*	1.25

1999-00 Hoops Build Your Own Card

Build Your Own Card offer sheets were seeded 1:4 packs of Hoops. The offers opened like a book with a front displaying the player's name, the inside explaining the rules and showing the different front and back (three of each were available), and the back was a form to be filled out and sent in. Collectors could select the front and back of their choice, with six total versions available, each hand-numbered to 250. The requests were to be accompanied by a money order for $9.95. Ten different players were available in the set and the redemption cards were numbered with a "BC" suffix, while the offer sheets were unnumbered.

	MT
Complete Set (10):	10.00
Common Player:	.50
Inserted 1:4	
Tim Duncan	2.00
Keith Van Horn	.40
Vince Carter	2.00
Grant Hill	2.00
Shaquille O'Neal	1.00
Kevin Garnett	2.00
Allen Iverson	1.50
Jason Williams	1.00
Kobe Bryant	2.50
Paul Pierce	1.00

1999-00 Hoops Calling Card

This 15-card insert highlighted players' top moves on a die-cut card that resembled a calling card. The signature move of the player was written up the right side of the card. Calling Card inserts were numbered with a "CC" suffix and inserted 1:8 packs.

		MT
Complete Set (15):		25.00
Common Player:		.50
Inserted 1:8		
1	Kobe Bryant	5.00
2	Kevin Garnett	4.00
3	Tim Hardaway	.75
4	Grant Hill	4.00
5	Allen Iverson	3.00
6	Karl Malone	1.00
7	Shawn Kemp	1.00
8	Stephon Marbury	2.00
9	Shaquille O'Neal	2.50
10	Hakeem Olajuwon	1.00
11	Ray Allen	.50
12	Damon Stoudamire	.75
13	Jason Williams	2.50
14	Keith Van Horn	1.00
15	Dikembe Mutombo	.50

1999-00 Hoops Dunk Mob

This 10-card insert captures top dunkers over a silver rainbow holofoil background. The insert name appears in both a graffiti-like background and in the lower right corner of each card. Dunk Mob inserts were numbered with a "DM" suffix and inserted 1:144 packs.

		MT
Complete Set (10):		150.00
Common Player:		5.00
Inserted 1:144		
1	Shaquille O'Neal	25.00
2	Stephon Marbury	25.00
3	Paul Pierce	25.00
4	Antawn Jamison	15.00
5	Michael Olowokandi	5.00
6	Scottie Pippen	15.00
7	Antonio McDyess	5.00
8	Vince Carter	35.00
9	Ron Mercer	15.00
10	Shawn Kemp	8.00

1999-00 Hoops Name Plates

This die-cut insert features 10 players on horizontal designs that resemble license plates. A color shot of the player on the left side, while his name is across the top and the insert name is across the bottom below the player's nickname in large letters through the middle. Name Plates were numbered with an "NP" suffix and inserted 1:4 packs.

		MT
Complete Set (10):		15.00
Common Player:		.40
Inserted 1:4		
1	Shareef Abdur-Rahim	1.50
2	Allen Iverson	3.00
3	Karl Malone	.75
4	Gary Payton	.75
5	Hakeem Olajuwon	.75
6	Glenn Robinson	.40
7	Kevin Garnett	5.00
8	Anfernee Hardaway	2.50
9	David Robinson	.75
10	Shaquille O'Neal	2.50

1999-00 Hoops Pure Players

This 10-card insert displayed top players on a silver plastic stock with orange foil stamping. Pure Players were numbered with a "PP" suffix and sequentially numbered to 500 sets. Parallel versions existed that featured purple foil stamping and were numbered to 100.

		MT
Complete Set (10):		325.00
Common Player:		15.00
Production 500 Sets		
100% Pure Players:		2x
Production 100 Sets		
1	Tim Duncan	50.00
2	Keith Van Horn	15.00
3	Stephon Marbury	25.00
4	Grant Hill	50.00
5	Kobe Bryant	60.00
6	Kevin Garnett	50.00
7	Allen Iverson	50.00
8	Antoine Walker	20.00
9	Shareef Abdur-Rahim	15.00
10	Anfernee Hardaway	30.00

1999-00 Hoops Pure Players 100% Parallel

This insert paralleled Pure Players but was distinguished by purple foil stamping. Parallel versions were numbered to 100 sets.

		MT
Complete Set (10):		650.00
Common Player:		30.00
Production 100 Sets		
1	Tim Duncan	100.00
2	Keith Van Horn	30.00
3	Stephon Marbury	50.00
4	Grant Hill	100.00
5	Kobe Bryant	120.00
6	Kevin Garnett	100.00
7	Allen Iverson	75.00
8	Antoine Walker	40.00
9	Shareef Abdur-Rahim	30.00
10	Anfernee Hardaway	60.00

1999-00 Hoops Y2K Corps

This 15-card insert featured top rookies from the 1998-99 season on embossed and silver foil-stamped back cards. Y2K inserts were numbered with a "Y2K" suffix and inserted 1:16 packs.

		MT
Complete Set (10):		30.00
Common Player:		1.00
Inserted 1:16		
1	Michael Olowokandi	2.00
2	Mike Bibby	3.00
3	Jason Williams	6.00
4	Dirk Nowitzki	3.00
5	Vince Carter	10.00
6	Robert Traylor	2.00
7	Larry Hughes	3.00
8	Paul Pierce	5.00
9	Matt Harpring	1.00
10	Michael Dickerson	2.00

1999-00 Hoops Decade

Hoops Decade featured a similar design to the 1989-90 NBA Hoops product and included 180 cards, including game-action shots of the rookies. The set was paralleled twice - Hoopla (1:3 packs) and Hoopla Plus (1:30 packs). Inserts included: Up Tempo, New Style, Draft Day Dominance, Retrospective Collection, Genuine Coverage and Autographics.

		MT
Complete Set (180):		30.00
Common Player:		.10
Minor Stars:		.20
Pack (10):		1.50
Wax Box (36):		50.00
1	David Robinson	.40
2	Mookie Blaylock	.10
3	Jaren Jackson	.10
4	*Andre Miller*	1.25
5	Michael Olowokandi	.30
6	Glenn Robinson	.20
7	Steve Smith	.20
8	Eric Snow	.10
9	Antoine Walker	.30
10	Nick Anderson	.10
11	*Jonathan Bender*	2.00
12	Sean Elliott	.10
13	Danny Fortson	.10
14	Adonal Foyle	.10
15	*Richard Hamilton*	1.00
16	Shawn Kemp	.20
17	Christian Laettner	.10
18	Rashard Lewis	.40
19	Danny Manning	.10
20	Mitch Richmond	.20
21	Shawn Bradley	.10
22	Tim Duncan	1.50
23	Tim Hardaway	.30
24	Antawn Jamison	.60
25	Jeff Hornacek	.10
26	*Jumaine Jones*	.50
27	*Corey Maggette*	1.25
28	Vitaly Potapenko	.10
29	Jerry Stackhouse	.30
30	*Jason Terry*	.75
31	*Baron Davis*	1.25
32	Matt Harpring	.20
33	Glen Rice	.20
34	Vladimir Stepania	.10
35	Jayson Williams	.10
36	*Wally Szczerbiak*	1.00
37	Michael Doleac	.20
38	Hersey Hawkins	.10
39	Allan Houston	.20
40	Hakeem Olajuwon	.40
41	Damon Stoudamire	.30
42	Jelani McCoy	.20
43	*Aleksandar Radojevic*	.25
44	*Cal Bowdler*	.25
45	Tyronn Lue	.20
46	Andrae Patterson	.10
47	Karl Malone	.40
48	Alonzo Mourning	.30
49	Vince Carter	2.00
50	Darrell Armstrong	.10
51	Terrell Brandon	.20
52	*John Celestand*	.40
53	Grant Hill	1.50
54	Stephon Marbury	.50
55	Tracy McGrady	.75
56	Reggie Miller	.20
57	Clifford Robinson	.10
58	Arvydas Sabonis	.10
59	*William Avery*	.50
60	Calbert Cheaney	.10
61	Jermaine Jackson	.25
62	Allen Iverson	1.25
63	Larry Johnson	.10
64	Toni Kukoc	.30
65	Raef LaFrentz	.30
66	Isaiah Rider	.20
67	*Jeff Foster*	.25
68	Juwan Howard	.20
69	Kerry Kittles	.10
70	Brevin Knight	.10
71	Voshon Lenard	.10
72	Latrell Sprewell	.40
73	Maurice Taylor	.10
74	Chris Webber	.75
75	Jerome Williams	.10
76	*Scott Padgett*	.25
77	Vin Baker	.20
78	Chris Childs	.10
79	Erick Dampier	.10
80	Anfernee Hardaway	1.00
81	Jamal Mashburn	.20
82	Todd Fuller	.10
83	Eric Piatkowski	.10
84	Gary Trent	.10
85	Kevin Garnett	1.50
86	Chris Mullin	.10
87	Charles Oakley	.10
88	Detlef Schrempf	.10
89	*Elton Brand*	2.00
90	Patrick Ewing	.20
91	Devean George	.50
92	Brian Grant	.10
93	Larry Hughes	.40
94	Dan Majerle	.10
95	*Shawn Marion*	2.00
96	Cuttino Mobley	.20
97	Paul Pierce	.75
98	Bryant Reeves	.10
99	Keith Van Horn	.40
100	Corliss Williamson	.10
101	Tariq Abdul-Wahad	.10
102	Brent Barry	.10
103	Elden Campbell	.10
104	Mark Jackson	.10
105	Lamond Murray	.10
106	Bryon Russell	.10
107	Jason Williams	1.00
108	Ray Allen	.30
109	*Ron Artest*	.75
110	Charles Barkley	.40
111	Cedric Ceballos	.10
112	Jason Kidd	.75
113	Donyell Marshall	.10
114	John Stockton	.20
115	Mike Bibby	.30
116	Ricky Davis	.20
117	*Steve Francis*	5.00
118	Tom Gugliotta	.20
119	*Laron Profit*	.50
120	Joe Smith	.20
121	Doug Christie	.10
122	Kenny Anderson	.20
123	Michael Dickerson	.20
124	Zydrunas Ilgauskas	.10
125	Bobby Jackson	.10
126	*Quincy Lewis*	.50
127	Shandon Anderson	.10
128	Charles Outlaw	.10
129	Scottie Pippen	.75
130	Rodney Rogers	.10
131	Rik Smits	.10
132	Chauncey Billups	.10
133	Chris Crawford	.10
134	Kornel David	.10
135	Tony Delk	.10
136	Kendall Gill	.10
137	*Trajan Langdon*	.60
138	Ron Mercer	.50
139	Othella Harrington	.10
140	Gheorghe Muresan	.10
141	Isaac Austin	.10
142	*Dion Glover*	.50
143	Avery Johnson	.10
144	Antonio McDyess	.30
145	Steve Nash	.10
146	Tyrone Nesby	.20
147	Shaquille O'Neal	1.00
148	*James Posey*	.60
149	Rod Strickland	.20
150	Kobe Bryant	2.00
151	Michael Finley	.20
152	Anthony Mason	.10
153	Dikembe Mutombo	.20
154	John Starks	.10
155	*Kenny Thomas*	.60
156	Matt Geiger	.10
157	*Tim James*	.50
158	Eddie Jones	.50
159	*Lamar Odom*	3.00
160	Nick Van Exel	.20
161	Sam Cassell	.10
162	*Vonteego Cummings*	.60
163	Lindsey Hunter	.10
164	Dirk Nowitzki	.50
165	Gary Payton	.40
166	Shareef Abdur-Rahim	.50
167	Jalen Rose	.20
168	Robert Traylor	.20
169	Derek Anderson	.10
170	Corey Benjamin	.20
171	Marcus Camby	.30
172	Vlade Divac	.20
173	Mario Elie	.10
174	Felipe Lopez	.20
175	*Rafer Alston*	.50
176	Antonio Davis	.10
177	Howard Eisley	.10
178	Theo Ratliff	.10
179	Tim Thomas	.40
180	Rasheed Wallace	.20

1999-00 Hoops Decade Draft Day Dominance

This 10-card insert set focused on a top player from each draft over the last 10 years on a Hoops design from that year he was drafted. Draft Day Dominance inserts were numbered with a "DD" suffix and inserted 1:30 packs. Parallel versions exist for all 10 cards which are printed on holofoil and numbered to 1,989 sets.

		MT
Complete Set (10):		35.00
Common Player:		.50
Inserted 1:32		
Parallel versions:		2x-4x
Production 1989 Sets		
DD1	David Robinson	2.00
DD2	Gary Payton	2.00
DD3	Dikembe Mutombo	.50
DD4	Shaquille O'Neal	5.00
DD5	Anfernee Hardaway	4.00
DD6	Grant Hill	8.00
DD7	Antonio McDyess	1.00
DD8	Kobe Bryant	10.00
DD9	Keith Van Horn	2.00
DD10	Vince Carter	10.00

1999-00 Hoops Decade Draft Day Dominance

This 10-card parallel set was printed on holofoil and sequentially numbered to 1,989 sets.

	MT
Parallel versions:	2x-4x
Production 1989 Sets	

1999-00 Hoops Decade Genuine Coverage

This 10-card insert featured rookie style game-used jerseys from players who are still with the team they were playing with a decade ago. Genuine Coverage cards were inserted 1:893 packs and unnumbered.

	MT
Complete Set (12):	500.00
Common Player:	50.00
Inserted 1:893	
Shareef Abdur-Rahim	60.00
Ray Allen	75.00
Patrick Ewing	60.00
Grant Hill	125.00
Juwan Howard	25.00
Antonio McDyess	40.00
Hakeem Olajuwon	50.00
David Robinson	50.00
Keith Van Horn	25.00
Antoine Walker	30.00

1999-00 Hoops Decade Hoopla

This 180-card parallel set reprinted each card from the base set, but added foil to the arc on the front. The cards also contained the word "Hoopla" on the back below the card number and were inserted 1:3 packs.

	MT
Hoopla Stars:	2x-4x
Hoopla Rookies:	1x-2x
Inserted 1:3	

1999-00 Hoops Decade Hoopla Plus

This 180-card parallel set reprinted every card in the Hoops set, but featured an all-holofoil front. Hoopla Plus cards contained the parallel name below the card number on the back and were inserted 1:30 packs.

	MT
Common Player:	1.50
Hoopla Plus Stars:	6x-15x
Hoopla Plus Rookies:	4x-8x
Inserted 1:35	

1999-00 Hoops Decade New Style

This 15-card holofoil insert featured the top rookies from the 1999-00 season. Cards were numbered with a "NS" suffix and inserted 1:18 packs. Parallel versions were die-cut and sequentially numbered to 1,989 sets.

	MT
Complete Set (15):	25.00
Common Player:	.25
Inserted 1:18	
Parallel versions:	2x-4x
Production 1989 Sets	
NS1 Steve Francis	.25
NS2 Lamar Odom	.25
NS3 Wally Szczerbiak	.25
NS4 Elton Brand	.25
NS5 Baron Davis	.25
NS6 Corey Maggette	.25
NS7 Trajan Langdon	.25
NS8 Cal Bowdler	.25
NS9 Richard Hamilton	.25
NS10 Ron Artest	.25
NS11 Jason Terry	.25
NS12 Jonathan Bender	.25
NS13 Andre Miller	.25
NS14 hawn Marion	.25
NS15 William Avery	.25

1999-00 Hoops Decade New Style

This 15-card parallel set reprinted each New Style insert with die-cut cards numbered to 1,989 sets.

	MT
Parallel versions:	2x-4x
Production 1989 Sets	

1999-00 Hoops Decade Retrospection Collection

This 10-card insert set featured a design similar to the 1995-96 Hoops SkyView insert. Cards were numbered with a "RC" suffix and inserted 1:108 packs. Parallel versions were sequentially numbered to 89 sets.

		MT
Complete Set (10):		100.00
Common Player:		5.00
Inserted 1:108		
Parallel versions:		2x-4x
Production 89 Sets		
RC1	Kevin Garnett	20.00
RC2	Kobe Bryant	25.00
RC3	Allen Iverson	12.00
RC4	Vince Carter	25.00
RC5	Jason Williams	10.00
RC6	Ron Mercer	5.00
RC7	Tim Duncan	20.00
RC8	Anfernee Hardaway	10.00
RC9	Scottie Pippen	8.00
RC10	Shaquille O'Neal	15.00

1999-00 Hoops Decade Up Tempo

This 15-card insert set featured top players on a silver holofoil card. Up Tempo inserts were numbered with a "UT" suffix and inserted 1:9 packs. Parallel versions featured a prismatic foil front and were sequentially numbered to 1,989.

		MT
Complete Set (15):		20.00
Common Player:		.50
Inserted 1:9		
Parallel versions:		2x-4x
Production 1989 Sets		
UT1	Allen Iverson	2.50
UT2	Kevin Garnett	3.00
UT3	Shaquille O'Neal	2.00
UT4	Tim Duncan	3.00
UT5	Stephon Marbury	.75
UT6	Keith Van Horn	.60
UT7	Paul Pierce	1.00
UT8	Vince Carter	5.00
UT9	Antawn Jamison	.75
UT10	Larry Hughes	.50
UT11	Jason Williams	2.00
UT12	Antoine Walker	.40
UT13	Grant Hill	3.00
UT14	Steve Francis	3.00
UT15	Lamar Odom	3.00

1999-00 Hoops Decade Up Tempo

This 15-card parallel set reprinted Up Tempo cards on a prismatic foil stock and was sequentially numbered to 1,989 sets.

	MT
Parallel versions:	2x-4x
Production 1989 Sets	

1999-00 Hoops Sixers Sheet

		MT
Complete Sheet (6):		8.00
Common Player:		.50
P1	Larry Hughes	2.00
P2	Allen Iverson	5.00
P3	Matt Geiger	.50
P4	George Lynch	.50
P5	Eric Snow	.50
P6	Theo Ratliff	1.00
NNO	Team Card	5.00

1999 Hoops WNBA

This inaugural 110-card base set for Hoops WNBA featured 87 basic cards, seven Future Performers, eight League Leaders, six Postseason Rewind and two checklists. Cards featured a bleeding white border and arrived in 10-card packs. Inserts included: Autographs, Building Blocks, Award Winners and Talk of the Town.

		MT
Complete Set (110):		25.00
Common Player:		.05
Minor Stars:		.10
Wax Box (36):		50.00
1	Cynthia Cooper	1.00
2	Game 3 - Houston vs. Phoenix	.75
3	Game 2 - Houston vs. Phoenix	.75
4	Game 1 - Houston vs. Phoenix	.25
5	Houston vs. Charlotte	.75
6	Phoenix vs. Cleveland	.10
7	League Leaders Scoring	1.00
8	League Leaders Rebounds	.50
9	League Leaders FG Pct.	.10
10	League Leaders 3-Pt. FG Pct.	.50
11	League Leaders FT Pct.	.50
12	League Leaders Assists	.30
13	League Leaders Steals	.50
14	League Leaders Blocks	.50
15	Andrea Kuklova	.05
16	Christy Smith	.10
17	Penny Moore	.15
18	Octavia Blue	.05
19	Vickie Johnson	.15
20	Latasha Byears	.15
21	Vicky Bullett	.15
22	Franthea Price	.05
23	Tina Thompson	.40
24	Teresa Weatherspoon	.50
25	Maria Stepanova	.05
26	Merlakia Jones	.20
27	Razija Mujanovic	.05
28	Rhonda Mapp	.10
29	Kristi Harrower	.05
30	Penny Toler	.10
31	*Margo Dydek*	.50
32	Kim Perrot	.60
33	Cindy Brown	1.00
34	Eva Nemcova	.20
35	Quacy Barnes	.10
36	*Tracy Reid*	.50
37	Chantel Tremitiere	.05
38	Lady Hardmon	.05
39	Michelle Griffiths	.05
40	Sheryl Swoopes	2.00
41	*Sandy Brondello*	1.50
42	Andrea Stinson	.50
43	*Marlies Askamp*	.50
44	*Rachael Sporn*	.30
45	Nikki McCray	1.50
46	Andrea Congreaves	.05
47	Toni Foster	.10
48	Kim Williams	.05
49	*Carla Porter*	.30
50	Jamila Wideman	.20
51	Isabelle Fijalkowski	.10
52	*Korie Hlede*	.30
53	Tora Suber	.10
54	Sue Wicks	.05
55	Coquese Washington	.05
56	Sharon Manning	.05
57	Tammy Jackson	.05
58	Tangela Smith	.10
59	Suzie McConnell Serio	.25
60	Lisa Leslie	1.50
61	Wendy Palmer	.50
62	Adia Barnes	.05
63	La'Shawn Brown	.05
64	Janeth Arcain	.05
65	Ruthie Bolton-Holifield	1.00
66	Bridget Pettis	.10
67	Pamela McGee	.10
68	Rebecca Lobo	1.00
69	*Cindy Blodgett*	.50
70	Rita Williams	.30
71	Mwadi Mabika	.05
72	Sophia Witherspoon	.20
73	Janice Braxton	.10
74	Cynthia Cooper	2.00
75	Tammi Reiss	.30
76	Umeki Webb	.05
77	Kym Hampton	.15
78	*LaTonya Johnson*	.30
79	Michele Timms	.75
80	Kisha Ford	.05
81	*Monica Lamb*	.30
82	Keri Chaconas	.05
83	Elena Baranova	.50
84	Linda Burgess	.05
85	Tamecka Dixon	.15
86	Heidi Burge	.05
87	Michelle Edwards	.30
88	Yolanda Moore	.05
89	*Ticha Penicheiro*	.50
90	*Ales Santos de Oliveira*	.30
91	Rushia Brown	.05
92	Lynette Woodard	.50
93	Katrina Colleton	.05
94	Bridgette Gordon	.05
95	Jennifer Gillom	.50
96	Murriel Page	.25
97	Olympia Scott-Richardson	.05
98	*Adrienne Johnson*	.75
99	Gergana Branzova	.05
100	Allison Feaster	.05
101	*Brandy Reed*	1.00
102	*Katie Smith*	.75
103	*Natalie Williams*	2.00
104	*Jennifer Azzi*	3.00
105	*Chamique Holdsclaw*	8.00
106	*Dawn Staley*	2.00
107	*Nykesha Sales*	1.00
108	*Kristin Folkl*	.50
109	Checklist	.05
110	Checklist	.05

1999 Hoops WNBA Autographs

This 13-card insert featured autographs from top players in the WNBA. Each card featured an embossed SkyBox seal of authenticity. These were unnumbered on the back and inserted 1:144 packs.

	MT
Complete Set (13):	1000.
Common Player:	40.00
Inserted 1:144	
Cynthia Cooper	200.00
Kristin Folkl	50.00
Bridgette Gordon	50.00
Lisa Leslie	125.00
Nikki McCray	75.00
Suzie McConnell Serio	90.00
Nykesha Sales	75.00
Dawn Staley	75.00
Andrea Stinson	60.00
Sheryl Swoopes	150.00
Michele Timms	125.00
Penny Toler	60.00
Teresa Weatherspoon	100.00

1999 Hoops WNBA Award Winners

This 10-card insert set featured All-WNBA First and Second Team players on a matte silver and holographic foil-stamped card. Award Winners were numbered with an "AW" suffix and inserted 1:24 packs.

		MT
Complete Set (10):		80.00
Common Player:		4.00
Inserted 1:24		
1	Tina Thompson	5.00
2	Sheryl Swoopes	20.00
3	Jennifer Gillom	12.00
4	Cynthia Cooper	20.00
5	Suzie McConnell Serio	5.00
6	Cindy Brown	8.00
7	Eva Nemcova	4.00
8	Lisa Leslie	15.00
9	Andrea Stinson	8.00
10	Teresa Weatherspoon	8.00

1999 Hoops WNBA Building Blocks

Building Blocks featured eight top WNBA players on a matte silver foil-stamped insert with a blue background. Cards were numbered with a "BB" prefix and inserted 1:4 packs.

		MT
Complete Set (8):		12.00
Common Player:		1.00
Inserted 1:4		
1	Dawn Staley	3.00
2	Rebecca Lobo	3.00
3	Tracy Reid	2.00
4	Korie Hlede	2.00
5	Ticha Penicheiro	1.00
6	Tammi Reiss	1.00
7	Nikki McCray	3.00
8	Jennifer Gillom	3.00

1999 Hoops WNBA Talk Of The Town

Talk of the Town captured a top star from each of the 12 WNBA cities on a gold foil-stamped card. Each player was pictured against a cityscape of her team's city. Cards were numbered with a "TT" suffix and inserted 1:12 packs.

		MT
Complete Set (12):		45.00
Common Player:		2.00
Inserted 1:12		
1	Cynthia Cooper	10.00
2	Michele Timms	4.00
3	Suzie McConnell Serio	3.00
4	Lisa Leslie	8.00
5	Andrea Stinson	4.00
6	Elena Baranova	4.00
7	Cindy Brown	4.00
8	Teresa Weatherspoon	6.00
9	Nikki McCray	6.00
10	Ruthie Bolton-Holifield	4.00
11	Nykesha Sales	3.00
12	Kristin Folkl	2.00

2000-01 Hoops Hot Prospects

		MT
Complete Set (145):		800.00
Common Player:		.25
Minor Stars:		.40
Common Rookie:		10.00
Production 1,000 Sets		
Pack (5):		6.00
Box (24):		90.00
1	Vince Carter	5.00
2	Wesley Person	.25
3	Juwan Howard	.40
4	Rodney Rogers	.25
5	Tim Duncan	2.50
6	Rasheed Wallace	.50
7	Anthony Peeler	.25
8	John Amaechi	.25
9	Tim Hardaway	.50
10	Mark Jackson	.25
11	Latrell Sprewell	1.00
12	Kevin Garnett	3.00
13	Alonzo Mourning	.50
14	Jerome Williams	.25
15	Anfernee Hardaway	1.50
16	Clifford Robinson	.25
17	Mike Bibby	.50
18	Allen Iverson	2.50
19	Terrell Brandon	.40
20	Jerry Stackhouse	.40
21	Brian Grant	.25
22	Lamond Murray	.25
23	Nick Anderson	.25
24	Alan Henderson	.25
25	Bryon Russell	.25
26	Elton Brand	1.50
27	Antawn Jamison	.75
28	Mitch Richmond	.40
29	Marcus Camby	.25
30	Raef LaFrentz	.40
31	Damon Stoudamire	.40
32	Vin Baker	.25
33	Allan Houston	.40
34	Doug Christie	.25
35	Stephon Marbury	1.25
36	Tim Thomas	.50
37	Tracy McGrady	1.50
38	Shareef Abdur-Rahim	1.00
39	Eddie Jones	1.00
40	Glenn Robinson	.40
41	Sam Cassell	.40
42	Dan Majerle	.25
43	Maurice Taylor	.25
44	Anthony Mason	.25
45	Dirk Nowitzki	1.00
46	Kobe Bryant	4.00
47	Kerry Kittles	.25
48	Derrick Coleman	.40
49	Cuttino Mobley	.40
50	Nick Van Exel	.40
51	LaPhonso Ellis	.25
52	Kendall Gill	.25
53	Hakeem Olajuwon	.75
54	Rashard Lewis	.75
55	Dale Davis	.25
56	Keith Van Horn	.60
57	Michael Finley	.40
58	Othella Harrington	.25
59	Gary Payton	.75
60	Michael Dickerson	.40
61	Voshon Lenard	.25
62	Patrick Ewing	.40
63	Ron Mercer	.40
64	Kenny Anderson	.40
65	Shaquille O'Neal	2.50
66	Tariq Abdul-Wahad	.25
67	Antonio Davis	.25
68	Rick Fox	.25
69	Lamar Odom	1.50
70	Derek Anderson	.25
71	Vitaly Potapenko	.25
72	Karl Malone	.75
73	Wally Szczerbiak	.60
74	Jason Williams	.75
75	Steve Francis	3.00
76	John Starks	.25
77	Ron Artest	.50
78	Grant Hill	2.50
79	Theo Ratliff	.25
80	Antonio McDyess	.50
81	Antoine Walker	.50
82	Sean Elliott	.25
83	Ruben Patterson	.25
84	Ray Allen	.50
85	Tom Gugliotta	.40
86	Scottie Pippen	1.50
87	Jim Jackson	.25
88	Joe Smith	.25
89	Reggie Miller	.40
90	Richard Hamilton	.50
91	Paul Pierce	.60
92	Mookie Blaylock	.25
93	Glen Rice	.40
94	P.J. Brown	.25
95	Avery Johnson	.25
96	John Stockton	.40
97	Tyrone Hill	.25
98	Tracy Murray	.25
99	Darrell Armstrong	.25
100	Steve Smith	.40
101	Shawn Kemp	.40
102	Jalen Rose	.50
103	Vonteego Cummings	.25
104	Larry Hughes	1.00
105	Charles Oakley	.25
106	Rod Strickland	.40
107	Christian Laettner	.25
108	Baron Davis	.60
109	Jamal Mashburn	.40
110	Lindsey Hunter	.25
111	Toni Kukoc	.50
112	Austin Croshere	.40
113	Chris Webber	1.50
114	Vlade Divac	.25
115	Andre Miller	.60
116	Larry Johnson	.25
117	Jason Kidd	1.50
118	David Robinson	.75
119	Donyell Marshall	.25
120	Jason Terry	.25
121	*Kenyon Martin*	50.00
122	*Stromile Swift*	75.00
123	*Chris Mihm*	15.00
124	*Marcus Fizer*	30.00
125	*Courtney Alexander*	40.00
126	*Darius Miles*	200.00
127	*Jerome Moiso*	15.00
128	*Joel Przybilla*	10.00
129	*DerMarr Johnson*	30.00
130	*Mike Miller*	75.00
131	*Quentin Richardson*	40.00
132	*Morris Peterson*	60.00
133	*Craig "Speedy" Claxton*	15.00
134	*Keyon Dooling*	30.00
135	*Mark Madsen*	15.00
136	*Mateen Cleaves*	35.00
137	*Etan Thomas*	15.00
138	*Jason Collier*	10.00
139	*Erick Barkley*	15.00
140	*Desmond Mason*	40.00
141	*Mamadou N'diaye*	10.00
142	*DeShawn Stevenson*	50.00
143	*Donnell Harvey*	12.00
144	*Jamaal Magloire*	15.00
145	*Hidayet Turkoglu*	30.00

2000-01 Hoops Hot Prospects A'la Carter

		MT
Complete Set (20):		50.00
Common Player:		3.00
Inserted 1:5		
AC1	Vince Carter	6.00
AC2	Vince Carter	6.00
AC3	Vince Carter	6.00
AC4	Vince Carter	6.00
AC5	Vince Carter	6.00
AC6	Vince Carter	6.00
AC7	Vince Carter	6.00
AC8	Vince Carter	6.00
AC9	Vince Carter	6.00
AC10	Vince Carter	6.00
AC11	Vince Carter	6.00
AC12	Vince Carter	6.00
AC13	Vince Carter	6.00
AC14	Vince Carter	6.00
AC15	Vince Carter	6.00
AC16	Vince Carter	6.00
AC17	Vince Carter	6.00
AC18	Vince Carter	6.00
AC19	Vince Carter	6.00
AC20	Vince Carter	6.00

2000-01 Hoops Hot Prospects Determined

		MT
Complete Set (10):		20.00
Common Player:		1.00
Inserted 1:12		
D1	Vince Carter	6.00
D2	Lamar Odom	2.00
D3	Steve Francis	4.00
D4	Kobe Bryant	5.00
D5	Jason Williams	1.00
D6	Karl Malone	1.00
D7	Allen Iverson	3.00
D8	Elton Brand	2.00
D9	Tim Duncan	3.00
D10	Kevin Garnett	4.00

2000-01 Hoops Hot Prospects First in Flight

	MT
Warm-Up Cards:	100.00
Production 1,000 Cards	
Shooting Shirt Cards:	150.00
Production 750 Cards	
Game Jersey Cards:	300.00
Production 250 Cards	
Autographed Cards:	1500.
Production 15 Cards of each version	

2000-01 Hoops Hot Prospects Genuine Coverage

		MT
Common Player:		15.00
Inserted 1:96 Retail		
1	Lamar Odom	50.00
2	Antoine Walker	20.00
3	Shaquille O'Neal	100.00
4	Darrell Armstrong	15.00
5	Larry Hughes	50.00
6	Marcus Camby	25.00
7	Nick Van Exel	25.00
8	Michael Dickerson	20.00
9	Baron Davis	40.00
10	Vince Carter	150.00
11	Mike Bibby	25.00
12	Wally Szczerbiak	30.00
13	Jerry Stackhouse	40.00
14	Eddie Jones	40.00
15	Shawn Kemp	20.00
16	Rick Fox	15.00
17	Jamal Mashburn	25.00

2000-01 Hoops Hot Prospects Hoops Originals

		MT
Complete Set (10):		35.00
Common Player:		1.50
Inserted 1:24		
H1	Vince Carter	10.00
H2	Tim Duncan	5.00
H3	Kevin Garnett	6.00
H4	Kobe Bryant	8.00
H5	Lamar Odom	3.00
H6	Steve Francis	6.00
H7	Shaquille O'Neal	5.00
H8	David Robinson	1.50
H9	Grant Hill	5.00
H10	Allen Iverson	5.00

2000-01 Hoops Hot Prospects Rookie Headliners

		MT
Complete Set (15):		20.00
Common Player:		.60
Inserted 1:8		
RH1	Kenyon Martin	5.00
RH2	Stromile Swift	3.00
RH3	Darius Miles	6.00
RH4	Jerome Moiso	.75
RH5	Chris Mihm	1.00
RH6	Marcus Fizer	3.00
RH7	Courtney Alexander	2.00
RH8	DerMarr Johnson	2.00
RH9	Mike Miller	2.50
RH10	Quentin Richardson	2.00
RH11	Morris Peterson	2.00
RH12	Keyon Dooling	1.50
RH13	Mateen Cleaves	1.25
RH14	Etan Thomas	.60
RH15	Jamal Crawford	1.50

1992-93 Hornets Hive Five

The 11-card set consists of five player cards (2-1/2"x 5-1/8") which come with a matching player lapel pin. The final six cards (2"x 4") depict the Hornets' mascot and five cheerleaders. The set was issued by Fast Fare stores and Crown gas stations.

		MT
Complete Set (11):		18.00
Common Player:		1.00
1	Larry Johnson	4.00
2	Kendall Gill	1.50
3	Muggsy Bogues	2.50
4	Dell Curry	1.50
5	Alonzo Mourning	7.00
NNO	Hugo the Hornet (Mascot)	1.50
NNO	Kim Bailey	1.00
NNO	Paris Floyd	1.00
NNO	Michelle Lee	1.00
NNO	Angela Pooser	1.00
NNO	Tara Wood	1.00

1992-93 Hornets Standups

Issued in four sets of three each, these stand-ups were given away with a purchase at Charlotte-based Burger Kings. The stand-ups measure 4"x 8-7/8"and feature color action cut-outs on purple backgrounds with a facsimile autograph.

		MT
Complete Set (12):		12.00
Common Player:		.50
1	Tony Bennett	.50
2	Dell Curry	1.00
3	Alonzo Mourning	6.00
4	Muggsy Bogues	2.00
5	Mike Gminski	1.00
6	Johnny Newman	.50
7	Kenny Gattison	.50
8	Kendall Gill	1.00
9	David Wingate	.50
10	Sidney Green	.50
11	Larry Johnson	3.00
12	Kevin Lynch	.50

I

1972 Icee Bear

These 3"x 5"cards feature color photos on the fronts, plus the player's name, team and NBA logo. Each card back has an Icee Bear fact, plus a player biography and basketball tip. The cards are unnumbered and were given away one per every purchase of an Icee Bear Slurpee drink.

	NM
Complete Set (20):	225.00
Common Player:	3.00
Dennis Awtry	3.00
Tom Boerwinkle	3.00
Austin Carr	20.00
Wilt Chamberlain	40.00
Archie Clark	20.00
Dave DeBusschere	10.00
Walt Frazier	35.00
Connie Hawkins	15.00
John Havlicek	18.00
Kareem Abdul-Jabbar	35.00
Bob Love	4.00
Jerry Lucas	10.00
Pete Maravich	50.00
Calvin Murphy	6.00
Oscar Robertson	20.00
Jerry Sloan	7.00
Wes Unseld	7.50
Dick Van Arsdale	3.00
Jerry West	25.00
Sidney Wicks	7.50

2000 IMAX Michael Jordan Postcards

		MT
Complete Set (2):		10.00
Common Player:		5.00
1	Michael Jordan	5.00
2	Michael Jordan	5.00

J

1985 JMS

These cards, sold as single card sets or perforated sheets, were produced as part of an officially-licensed table top game called "Match Up Basketball Game." Cards were used to play the game; nine cards were issued for each of the three teams represented - the Boston Celtics, Los Angeles Lakers and Philadelphia 76ers. Each card front has a color photo, the JMS logo, the player's name, position and height, plus his 1984-85 and career statistics, all on a red background framed by a blue border. The numbered backs have additional stats. The stats on the card backs for James Worthy and Bob McAdoo are reversed.

		MT
Complete Set (27):		180.00
Common Player:		3.00
1	Maurice Cheeks	6.00
2	Moses Malone	9.00
3	Bobby Jones	6.00
4	Charles Barkley	45.00
5	Julius Erving	30.00
6	Clint Richardson	3.00
7	Andrew Toney	3.00
8	Sedale Threatt	5.00
9	Clemon Johnson	3.00
10	Bill Walton	15.00
11	Danny Ainge	10.00
12	Robert Parish	8.00
13	Kevin McHale	12.00
14	Larry Bird	50.00
15	Dennis Johnson	6.00
16	Ray Williams	3.00
17	Scott Wedman	4.00
18	Greg Kite	3.00
19	Michael Cooper	6.00
20	Kareem Abdul-Jabbar	20.00
21	Jamaal Wilkes	6.00
22	Bob McAdoo	8.00
23	James Worthy	15.00
24	Earvin (Magic) Johnson	45.00
25	Michael McGee	3.00
26	Kurt Rambis	6.00
27	Byron Scott	6.00

1988-89 Jazz Smokey

The eight-card, 8"x 10"set features color photos on the card fronts with a safety illustration on the backs, along with player statistics. The cards are unnumbered and were sponsored by the Utah Department of State Lands and Forestry and the U.S.D.A. Forest Service.

	MT
Complete Set (8):	80.00
Common Player:	2.50
Thurl Bailey	4.00
Mark Eaton	5.00
Frank Layden CO	6.00
Karl Malone	38.00
Marc Iavaroni	2.50
John Stockton	38.00
Smokey Bear	2.50
Bobby Hansen	4.00

1989 Jazz Old Home

The 1989 set was printed by Fleer and distributed in loaves of Old Home Bread. The cards measure the standard 2-1/2"x 3-1/2"and have horizontal backs. The color action photo on the card front has rounded borders and has "1989 Collector's Series" printed along the lower edge.

		MT
Complete Set (13):		65.00
Common Player:		2.50
1	Thurl Bailey	4.00
2	Mike Brown	2.50
3	Mark Eaton	4.00
4	Darrell Griffith	4.00
5	Bobby Hansen	2.50
6	Marc Iavaroni	2.50
7	Frank Layden CO	4.00
8	Eric Leckner	2.50
9	Jim Les	2.50
10	Karl Malone	30.00
11	Jose Ortiz	2.50
12	Scott Roth	2.50
13	John Stockton	30.00

1990-91 Jazz Star

The 12-card, standard-size set features purple borders and bio and stat information on the horizontal card backs.

		MT
Complete Set (12):		5.00
Common Player:		.25
1	Karl Malone	2.50
2	John Stockton	2.50
3	Mark Eaton	.50
4	Blue Edwards	.50
5	Thurl Bailey	.50
6	Mike Brown	.25
7	Jeff Malone	.50
8	Andy Toolson	.25
9	Darrell Griffith	.50
10	Delaney Rudd	.25
11	Walter Palmer	.25
12	Jerry Sloan CO	.50

1992-93 Jazz Chevron

Chevron issued this set of five cards with matching player pins during the 1992-93 season. With the pin section intact, the cards measure 2-1/2"x 5-1/4"with the Chevron logo featured on both sides.

		MT
Complete Set (5):		14.00
Common Player:		.50
1	Tyrone Corbin	.50
2	John Stockton	6.00
3	Jeff Malone	1.00
4	Tom Chambers	2.00
5	Karl Malone	6.00

1993-94 Jazz Old Home

The 11-card, standard-size set was produced by Hoops for Metz Baking Company's Old Home Bread and it was inserted into Old Home products. Twenty thousand cards of each player and coach were produced with 200,000 logo cards printed. One player card and logo card were included in each loaf package. The card design is nearly identical to the 1993-94 Hoops base set.

		MT
Complete Set (11):		18.00
Common Player:		.25
1	David Benoit	.25
2	Tom Chambers	1.00
3	Tyrone Corbin	.25
4	Mark Eaton	.50
5	Jay Humphries	.25
6	Jeff Malone	.50
7	Karl Malone	8.00
8	Jerry Sloan CO	1.00
9	Felton Spencer	.25
10	John Stockton	8.00
11	Logo Card DP	.25

1996 Jello Dream Team Tattoos

	MT
Complete Set (10):	10.00
Common Player:	.50
Anfernee Hardaway	3.00
Grant Hill	5.00
Karl Malone	2.00
Reggie Miller	1.00
Hakeem Olajuwon	1.50
Shaquille O'Neal	5.00
Scottie Pippen	3.00
David Robinson	1.50
Glenn Robinson	.75
John Stockton	2.00

1973-74 Jets Allentown CBA

The eight-card, 2-5/8"x 4-1/4"set was produced by G.S. Gallery of Allentown, Pennsylvania. The cards are printed on light-blue construction-type paper with the backs being blank.

		NM
Complete Set (8):		40.00
Common Player:		5.00
1	Tony Johnson	5.00
2	Allie McGuire	10.00
3	Frank Card	5.00
4	George Lehmann	6.00
5	Dennis Bell	5.00
6	Ken Wilburn	5.00
7	George Bruns	5.00
8	Ed Mast	6.00

K

1957 Kahn's

These cards feature black-and-white photos of members of the Cincinnati Royals. The Kahn's slogan ("The Wiener The World Awaited") and the player's facsimile autograph are also on the card front. The backs have tips on playing basketball. The cards are unnumbered and measure 3-3/16"x 3-15/16".

	NM
Complete Set (11):	2000.
Common Player:	135.00
Richard Duckett	100.00
George King	125.00
Clyde Lovelette	275.00
Tom Marshall	100.00
Jim Paxson	200.00
Dave Piontek	100.00
Richie Regan	125.00
Richard (Dick) Ricketts	125.00
Maurice Stokes	300.00
Jack Twyman	250.00
Robert Wanzer	125.00

1958 Kahn's

These cards are similar to Kahn's previous year's issue, except backs have a thought from the player about his greatest thrill in basketball. The 3-1/4"x 3-15/16"cards have black-and-white photos, a facsimile autograph and the Kahn's slogan on the front. Cards are unnumbered and feature the Cincinnati Royals.

	NM
Complete Set (10):	1000.
Common Player:	95.00
Arlen Bockhorn	95.00
Archie Dees	95.00
Sihugo Green	100.00
Vern Hatton	95.00
Tom Marshall	95.00
Jack Paar	90.00
George Palmer	95.00
Jim Palmer	90.00
David Piontek	95.00
Jack Twyman	200.00

1959 Kahn's

These cards are once again similar to Kahn's previous issues - the cards are unnumbered, 3-1/4"x 4", have the Kahn's slogan and a facsimile autograph on the front, and feature black-and- white photos. The backs, however, have a tip from the player on playing better basketball. Cincinnati Royals are featured.

	NM
Complete Set (10):	850.00
Common Player:	75.00
Arlen Bockhorn	75.00
Wayne Embry	100.00
Tom Marshall	75.00
Med Park	65.00
Dave Piontek	65.00
Hub Reed	75.00
Phil Rollins	75.00
Larry Staverman	75.00
Jack Twyman	150.00
Win Wilfong	75.00

1960 Kahn's

Kahn's included Los Angeles Lakers star Jerry West in this 12-card set devoted to the Cincinnati Royals. The cards are 3-1/4"x 3-15/16"and feature black-and-white photos, the Kahn's slogan and a facsimile autograph on the front. The unnumbered cards have a short biography and statistics on the back.

	NM
Complete Set (12):	2000.
Common Player:	50.00
Arlen Bockhorn	50.00
Bob Boozer	50.00
Ralph Davis	50.00
Wayne Embry	60.00
Mike Farmer	50.00
Phil Jordan	50.00
Hub Reed	50.00
Oscar Robertson	650.00
Larry Staverman	50.00
Jack Twyman	80.00
Jerry West	900.00
Win Wilfong	50.00

1961 Kahn's

For the first time, Kahn's also included the Cincinnati Royals' coach in its set. The 13-card unnumbered set also includes Los Angeles Lakers star Jerry West again. The cards, 3-3/16"x 4-1/16", have black-and-white photos and a facsimile autograph on the front. Backs are blank.

	NM
Complete Set (13):	1000.
Common Player:	35.00
Arlen Bockhorn	35.00
Bob Boozer	40.00
Joe Buckhalter	35.00
Wayne Embry	50.00
Bob Nordmann	35.00
Hub Reed	35.00
Oscar Robertson	275.00
Adrian Smith	35.00
Jack Twyman	65.00
Bob Wiesehahn	35.00
Jerry West	400.00
Charley Wolf	35.00
Dave Zeller	35.00

1962 Kahn's

These black-and-white cards from Kahn's feature Cincinnati Royals and their coach, plus Los Angeles Lakers star Jerry West. Cards, unnumbered, measure 3-1/4"x 4-3/16"and once again have the Kahn's slogan and a facsimile autograph on the front. Two cards, for Bob Boozer and Arlen Bockhorn, are horizontal.

	NM
Complete Set (11):	700.00
Common Player:	30.00
Arlen Bockhorn	30.00
Bob Boozer	30.00
Wayne Embry	40.00
Tom Hawkins	40.00
Bud Olsen	30.00
Hub Reed	30.00
Oscar Robertson	175.00
Adrian Smith	35.00
Jack Twyman	50.00
Jerry West	250.00
Charley Wolf (coach)	30.00

1963 Kahn's

These 3-1/4"x 4-1/4"cards from Kahn's feature Cincinnati Royals and their coach, plus Los Angeles Lakers star Jerry West. The cards can be distinguished from previous issues by the white border around the black-and-white photos on the front. The Kahn's slogan and a facsimile autograph are also on the front. The cards are unnumbered and have a comment about the player on the back. The Jerry West photo is similar to the 1962 card's photo, except it's set in smaller type. Bob Boozer's card is once again horizontal.

	NM
Complete Set (13):	625.00
Common Player:	25.00
Jay Arnette	25.00
Arlen Bockhorn	25.00
Bob Boozer	30.00
Wayne Embry	30.00
Tom Hawkins	35.00
Jerry Lucas	100.00
Jack McMahon	25.00
Bud Olsen	25.00
Oscar Robertson	125.00
Adrian Smith	25.00
Thomas P. Thacker	30.00
Jack Twyman	40.00
Jerry West	175.00

1964 Kahn's

The first three cards listed in this Kahn's set have maroon ink on the back, while the remainder use black printing. The 3"x 3-5/8"unnumbered cards feature full-bleed color photos on the front, without any writing. Backs have biographical information. There are two cards for Jerry Lucas and Oscar Robertson, plus 12 more for other Cincinnati Royals players.

	NM
Complete Set (14):	550.00
Common Player:	20.00
Happy Hairston	35.00
Jack McMahon	25.00
George "Jif" Wilson	20.00
Jay Arnette	25.00
Arlen Bockhorn	20.00
Wayne Embry	30.00
Tom Hawkins	35.00
Jerry Lucas (three windows showing)	50.00
Jerry Lucas (four windows showing)	50.00
Bud Olsen	20.00
Oscar Robertson (facing front)	125.00
Oscar Robertson (facing side)	125.00
Adrian Smith	25.00
Jack Twyman	40.00

1965 Kahn's

This is Kahn's last set devoted to the Cincinnati Royals. As did the previous issue, this set features full-bleed color photos on the card front, without any writing. The backs are in red and contain a career summary and the Kahn's slogan. Cards measure 3"x 3-9/16".

	NM
Complete Set (4):	275.00
Common Player:	35.00
Wayne Embry	35.00
Jerry Lucas	75.00
Oscar Robertson	125.00
Jack Twyman	75.00

1971 Keds KedKards

The set contains juvenile artistic renditions of top players from basketball, football, baseball and tennis who were endorsees of Keds shoes. The cards formed a panel on the shoe box. The cards vary in size and feature a facsimile autograph. The third panel, Bench and Reed, has each card at 5-1/4"x 3-1/2"while the other approximate 2-15/16"x 2-3/4".

	NM
Complete Set (3):	150.00
Common Player:	50.00

1	Dave Bing (basketball), Clark Graebner (tennis), Bubba Smith (football), Jim Maloney (baseball)	50.00
2	Willis Reed (basketball), Stan Smith (tennis), Bubba Smith (football), Johnny Bench (baseball)	50.00
3	Willis Reed (basketball), Johnny Bench (baseball)	50.00

1991-92 Kellogg's College Greats

Specially-marked boxes of Kellogg's Raisin Bran each contained one of these cards, devoted to "College Basketball Greats." The card front shows an NBA star in his collegiate uniform. The set name and Kellogg's logo also appear on the front. The horizontally-designed back has a card number, plus a summary of the player's collegiate accomplishments and his stats. Kellogg's also made the complete set available through a mail-in offer. This offer also included a special holder for the cards.

		MT
Complete Set (18):		5.00
Common Player		.25
1	Kenny Anderson	.75
2	Clyde Drexler	.50
3	Wayman Tisdale	.25
4	Horace Grant	.50
5	Kevin Johnson	.30
6	Karl Malone	.50
7	Larry Bird	1.25
8	John Stockton	.50
9	Doug Smith	.25
10	Mark Price	.30
11	Hakeem Olajuwon	1.00
12	Charles Smith	.25
13	Bernard King	.30
14	Tim Hardaway	.50
15	Spud Webb	.30
16	Mark Macon	.25
17	Scottie Pippen	.75
18	Gary Payton	.30

1992 Kellogg's Team USA Posters

The five-poster set features players from the 1992 U.S. Olympic basketball team on 6-3/4"x 9-1/2"stock and was available through two-box jumbo packs of Raisin Bran. The fronts feature the player in a posed action shot with his nickname and facsimile on the front. The backs are blank and unnumbered.

		MT
Complete Set (5):		25.00
Common Player:		2.00
(1)	Larry Legend (Larry Bird)	12.00
(2)	Mailman (Karl Malone)	6.00
(3)	Court Warrior (Chris Mullin)	3.00
(4)	Admiral (David Robinson)	6.00
(5)	Playmaker (John Stockton)	6.00

1993 Kellogg's Postercards

Star Pics produced this 10-card set for Kellogg's to randomly insert in its 20-ounce boxes of Raisin Bran starting in January 1993. About one million of the sets, subtitled "Kellogg's College Greats Postercards," were produced. The unnumbered cards measure 2-1/2"x 7"and are folded in half. One side has a color posed shot of the player in his college uniform, plus career highlights. The other side has a vertical 2-1/2"x 7"color photo of the player, with his name at the bottom. Two female collegiate stars were also included in the set.

	MT
Complete Set (10):	20.00
Common Player:	1.50
Kareem Abdul-Jabbar	3.00
Teresa Edwards	1.50
Christian Laettner	3.00
Danny Manning	1.50
Cheryl Miller	1.50
Harold Miner	5.00
Chris Mullin	2.00
Scottie Pippen	3.00
David Robinson	3.00
Isiah Thomas	2.00

1996 Kellogg's Raptors Stoudamire

		MT
Complete Set (3):		7.00
Common Player:		3.00
1	Damon Stoudamire (Damon Leads the Break)	3.00
2	Damon Stoudamire (Dish'n It Off)	3.00
3	Damon Stoudamire (Stoudamire to the Hoop)	3.00

1973-74 Kings Linnett

The nine-card, 8-1/2"x 11"set features facial drawings by artist Charles Linnett with the player's facsimile autograph appearing on the right bottom border. The backs are blank and unnumbered and the cards originally retailed for 99 cents (three-card packages).

	NM
Complete Set (9):	35.00
Common Player:	2.00
Nate Archibald	15.00
Ron Behagen	2.00
John Block	5.00
Mike D'Antoni	2.00
Ken Durrett	2.00
Sam Lacey	8.00
Larry McNeill	2.00
Jimmy Walker	8.00
Nate Williams	2.00

1985-86 Kings Smokey

The 15-card, 4"x 5-1/2"set was originally distributed as a perforated sheet at a Kings' home game. The card backs contain a fire safety cartoon with the fronts containing the Kings and Smokey the Bear logo along the bottom border.

		MT
Complete Set: (16):		25.00
Common Player:		1.50
1	Smokey Emblem	1.50
2	Phil Johnson (CO)	1.50
3	Frank Hamblen ACO, Jerry Reynolds ACO, Bill Jones TR	1.50
4	Smokey Bear	1.50
5	Michael Adams	3.00
6	Larry Drew	1.50
7	Carl Henry	1.50
8	Eddie Johnson	5.00
9	Rich Kelley	1.50
10	Joe Kleine	3.00
11	Mark Olberding	1.50
12	Reggie Theus	5.00
13	LaSalle Thompson	1.50
14	Otis Thorpe	10.00
15	Terry Tyler	1.50
16	Mike Woodson	2.00

1986-87 Kings Smokey

The 15-card, 2-3/8"x 3"set was distributed at a Kings' home game as part of a perforated sheet. The card fronts have a Smokey the Bear logo in the lower right corner while the backs have a fire safety cartoon and the player's height, weight, position and birthdate.

		MT
Complete Set (15):		25.00
Common Player:		1.50
1	Don Buse (ACO)	1.50
2	Franklin Edwards (10)	1.50
3	Eddie Johnson (8)	5.00
4	Bill Jones (TR)	1.50
5	Joe Kleine (35)	2.50
6	Mark Olberding (53)	1.50
7	Harold Pressley (21)	1.50
8	Jerry Reynolds (CO)	1.50
9	John Rogers (32)	1.50
10	Derek Smith (18)	5.00
11	Reggie Theus (24)	5.00
12	LaSalle Thompson (41)	1.50
13	Otis Thorpe (33)	8.00
14	Terry Tyler (40)	1.50
15	Othell Wilson (2)	1.50

1988-89 Kings Carl's Jr.

The 12-card, standard-size set was sponsored by Carl's Jr. fast-food restaurants and produced by Sports Marketing Inc., of Washington. The cards are unnumbered and the players are listed by uniform number.

		MT
Complete Set (12):		12.00
Common Player:		.50
2	Michael Jackson	.50
7	Danny Ainge	5.00
15	Vinny Del Negro	3.00
21	Harold Pressley	.50
22	Rodney McCray	1.00
23	Wayman Tisdale	1.50
30	Kenny Smith	3.00
34	Ricky Berry	.50
43	Jim Petersen	.50
50	Ben Gillery	.50
54	Brad Lohaus	.50
NNO	Jerry Reynolds (CO)	.50

1989-90 Kings Carl's Jr.

The 12-card, standard-size set was sponsored by Carl's Jr. and was given to Kings' fans at three different games in perforated strips of four players each. The Kings' logo appears in the lower left corner on the card front with the Carl's Jr. logo in the lower right corner. The card backs contain player bios and are unnumbered. The set is listed by the players' uniform numbers.

		MT
Complete Set (12):		10.00
Common Player:		.50
2	Michael Jackson	.50
7	Danny Ainge	3.00
15	Vinny Del Negro	1.50
21	Harold Pressley	.50
22	Rodney McCray	.75
23	Wayman Tisdale	1.00
30	Kenny Smith	1.50
32	Greg Kite	.50
40	Randy Allen	.50
42	Pervis Ellison	1.50
50	Ralph Sampson	1.00
NNO	Jerry Reynolds (CO)	.50

1990-91 Kings Safeway

The 12-card, standard-size set was sponsored by Safeway and was issued in three panels - each with four players and one coupon. The Safeway grocery store logo appears in the lower right corner with the Kings' logo printed in the lower left corner. The card backs feature stats and bio information and are unnumbered.

	MT
Complete Set (12):	9.00
Common Player:	.75
Anthony Bonner	.75
Antoine Carr	1.00
Duane Causwell	1.00
Steve Colter	.75
Bobby Hansen	.75
Eric Leckner	.75
Travis Mays	.75
Dick Motta (CO)	1.00
Lionel Simmons	1.50
Rory Sparrow	.75
Wayman Tisdale	1.50
Bill Wennington	1.00

1988-89 Knicks Frito-Lay

The 15-card, standard-size set was sponsored by Frito-Lay and was issued in two sheets. The Knicks' team logo appears in the lower left corner of the card front with the backs containing stats for career, All-Star Game and post-season action on the horizontal layout.

		MT
Complete Set (15):		40.00
Common Player:		1.00
1	Greg Butler	1.00
2	Patrick Ewing	20.00
3	Sidney Green	1.00
4	Mark Jackson	7.00
5	Pete Myers	2.00
6	Johnny Newman	2.00
7	Charles Oakley	5.00
8	Rick Pitino	6.00
9	Rod Strickland	6.00
10	Trent Tucker	1.00
11	Kiki Vandeweghe	3.00
12	Kenny Walker	2.00
13	Eddie Lee Wilkins	1.00
14	Gerald Wilkins	3.00
15	Frito Lay	1.00

1989-90 Knicks Marine Midland

The 14-card, standard-size set was sponsored by Marine Midland Bank and was issued in one sheet with three rows of five cards each. The card fronts feature a color photo with orange borders with the player's uniform number appearing in the upper left corner and the Knicks' logo in the lower right. The horizontal backs contain complete career and post-season statistics.

		MT
Complete Set (14):		35.00
Common Player:		1.25
1	Greg Butler	1.25
2	Patrick Ewing	15.00
3	Mark Jackson	4.00
4	Stu Jackson (CO)	2.00
5	Charles Oakley	4.00
6	Pete Myers	1.50
7	Johnny Newman	1.50
8	Brian Quinnett	1.25
9	Rod Strickland	3.00
10	Trent Tucker	2.00
11	Kiki Vandeweghe	2.50
12	Kenny Walker	1.50
13	Gerald Wilkins	2.00
14	Eddie Lee Wilkins	1.25

1993-94 Knicks Alamo

The five-card, 3-1/2"x 5-1/2"set was sponsored by Alamo and has a postcard-type format. The card fronts contain a color action photo.

		MT
Complete Set (5):		6.00
Common Player:		.75
1	Greg Anthony	.75
2	Anthony Mason	1.00
3	Charles Oakley	2.00
4	Pat Riley (CO)	2.00
5	John Starks	2.00

1970-71 Knicks Portraits

These 9"x 12", black-and-white illustrations are unnumbered and blank-backed. The fronts include the player's name and a facsimile autograph.

		NM
Complete Set (8):		125.00
Common Player:		10.00
1	Dick Barnett	10.00
2	Dave DeBusschere	20.00
3	Walt Frazier	30.00
4	Red Holzman	15.00
5	Willis Reed	25.00
6	Mike Riordan	10.00
7	Cazzie Russell	10.00
8	Dave Stallworth	10.00

1984-85 Knicks Getty Photos

The 11-card, 3-1/2"x 4"set was issued on 7"x 9"panels with black broken lines indicating where the cards can be separated. The card fronts feature a color borderless photo with a facsimile signature running along the left border. The card backs feature Getty's sponsorship logo under the Knicks' logo.

		MT
Complete Set (12):		50.00
Common Player:		3.00
1	James Bailey	3.00
2	Ken Bannister	3.00
3	Hubie Brown (CO)	8.00
4	Butch Carter	3.00
5	Pat Cummings	4.00
6	Ernie Grunfeld	6.00
7	Bernard King	10.00
8	Louis Orr	4.00
9	Rory Sparrow	4.00
10	Trent Tucker	4.00
11	Darrell Walker	6.00
12	Truck Robinson	8.00

L

1960-61 Lakers Bell Brand

The one card in the set measures 6"x 3-1/2"and was sponsored and distributed by Bell Brand Potato Chips. The left half of the card contains the player image while the right side has the Lakers' 1960-61 schedule. The card back has a coupon and an offer for free Lakers' game tickets.

		NM
Complete Set (1):		400.00
Common Player:		400.00
NNO	Frank Selvy	400.00

1961-62 Lakers Bell Brand

The 10-card, 6"x 3-1/2"set was sponsored and issued by Bell Brand Potato Chips - one per bag. The design is similar to the one 1960-61 card, except that the front has the player photo and Bell Brand ad for free tickets and the back has the team schedule and a description on how to get free tickets in person and by mail. Los Angeles' stars Jerry West and Elgin Baylor are the key cards in the set.

		NM
Complete Set (10):		5200.
Common Player:		250.00
1	Elgin Baylor	1200.
2	Ray Felix	250.00
3	Tom Hawkins	400.00
4	Rod Hundley	500.00
5	Howard Jolliff	250.00
6	Rudy LaRusso	400.00
7	Fred Schaus (CO)	400.00
8	Frank Selvy	275.00
9	Jerry West	2000.
10	Wayne Yates	250.00

1979-80 Lakers/Kings Alta-Dena

The eight-card, 2-3/4"x 4"set was sponsored by Alta-Dena Dairy and features four cards each of Los Angeles Lakers and Los Angeles Kings players. The complete set with the souvenir folder could be redeemed for discounts on game tickets at the Forum in Inglewood.

		NM
Complete Set (8):		20.00
Common Player:		1.00
1	Adrian Dantley	2.00
2	Don Ford	1.00
3	Kareem Abdul-Jabbar	12.00
4	Norm Nixon	2.50
5	Marcel Dionne	5.00
6	Butch Goring	1.00
7	Mike Murphy	1.00
8	Dave Taylor	3.00
xx	Souvenir Folder	5.00

1982-83 Lakers BASF

The 13-card, 5"x 7"set was produced by BASF and was distributed by Big Ben's and The Wherehouse music stores. The cards were issued on a weekly basis and the James Worthy card is the first pro card for the former North Carolina standout.

		MT
Complete Set (13):		20.00
Common Player:		.50
1	Kareem Abdul-Jabbar	5.00
2	Michael Cooper	2.00
3	Clay Johnson	.50
4	Magic Johnson	7.00
5	Eddie Jordan	.50
6	Mark Landsberger	.50
7	Bob McAdoo	2.50
8	Mike McGee	.50
9	Norm Nixon	2.00
10	*Kurt Rambis*	4.00
11	Jamaal Wilkes	1.50
12	*James Worthy*	7.00
13	Team Card (Team roster on back)	2.00

1983-84 Lakers BASF

The 14-card, 5"x 7"set was produced by BASF and is similar in design to previous BASF Lakers sets, except the BASF's video tape products are featured on the card fronts instead of the card backs. The backs are unnumbered and contain the player's facsimile autograph.

	MT
Complete Set (14):	25.00
Common Player:	.75
Kareem Abdul-Jabbar	6.00
Michael Cooper	2.00
Calvin Garrett	.75
Magic Johnson	8.00
Mitch Kupchak	.75
Bob McAdoo	2.50
Mike McGee	.75
Swen Nater	.75
Kurt Rambis	2.00
Byron Scott	3.00
Larry Spriggs	.75
Jamaal Wilkes	2.00
James Worthy	3.00
Team Photo (Team roster on back)	2.50

1984-85 Lakers BASF

The 12-card, 5"x 7"set is virtually identical to the 1983-84 set, except that the BASF logo on the card fronts does not have "Switch To" before BASF. The card backs are unnumbered and have a facsimile signature.

	MT
Complete Set (13):	35.00
Common Player:	1.00
Kareem Abdul-Jabbar	8.00
Michael Cooper	2.00
Magic Johnson	10.00
Mitch Kupchak	1.00
Ronnie Lester	1.00
Bob McAdoo	3.50
Mike McGee	1.00
Kurt Rambis	2.50
Byron Scott	2.50
Larry Spriggs	1.00
Jamaal Wilkes	3.50
James Worthy	4.00
Team Photo (Team roster on back)	4.00

1950-51 Lakers Scott's

The 13-card, 2"x 4-1/2"set was sponsored by Scott's Potato Chips on heavy cardboard stock, as it was distributed with boxes of potato chips. The fronts have a cartoon-like drawing with a facsimile autograph. The cards are unnumbered and a collector of the complete set could redeem it for tickets to Minneapolis Lakers' games. The set features George Mikan and future Minnesota Vikings coach Bud Grant.

	NM
Complete Set (13):	12000.
Common Player:	350.00
Bob Doll	350.00
Arnie Ferrin	450.00
Bud Grant	1200.
Bob Harrison	450.00
Joey Hutton	350.00
Tony Jaros	350.00
John Kundla (CO)	450.00
Slater Martin	750.00
George Mikan	6000.
Vern Mikkelsen	800.00
Kevin O'Shea	350.00
Jim Pollard	800.00
Herman Schaeffer	350.00

1985-86 Lakers Denny's Coins

The nine-coin, silver-colored set was distributed by Denny's with each coin being 1-1/2"in diameter. The coin fronts feature the player's image and jersey number with the backs having the Denny's logo.

		MT
Complete Set (9):		40.00
Common Player:		1.00
1	Kareem Abdul-Jabbar	10.00
2	Michael Cooper	3.00
3	Magic Johnson	15.00
4	Bob McAdoo	3.00
5	Mike McGee	1.00
6	Kurt Rambis	2.00
7	Byron Scott	3.00
8	Jamaal Wilkes	3.00
9	James Worthy	6.00

1992 Lakers Chevron Pins

The five-pin set was sponsored by Chevron and issued on a 2-1/2"x 5-1/8"card. The top half of the card resembles a trading card while the bottom third contains the pin and a Chevron logo. The card section has "Legend" in purple with a color shot of the player in an oval. The pin/cards are unnumbered.

	MT
Complete Set (5):	10.00
Common Player:	1.50
Elgin Baylor	4.00
Gail Goodrich	2.00
Rod Hundley	1.50
Jerry West	5.00
Jamaal Wilkes	2.00

1993 Lakers Forum

The 11-card, 2-1/2"x 5"set was sponsored by The Los Angeles Times and "Rebuild LA" and feature sports and entertainment figures who appeared at the Great Western Forum in Inglewood between 1968 and 1993. Apparently, just 25,000 sets were produced and were available at the Forum box office and through concession sales at games for $25. Each set came with a bonus card, prefixed "BC" and included five Lakers: Elgin Baylor, Wilt Chamberlain, Jerry West, Kareem Abdul-Jabbar and Magic Johnson. The card fronts are black bordered with a 25th anniversary design while the backs are horizontal and numbered.

		MT
Complete Set (11):		10.00
Common Player (1-11):		.25
Common Player (BC1-BC5):		12.00
1	Great Western Forum	.25
2	Neil Diamond	1.00
3	Chris Evert	1.00
4	John McEnroe	1.00
5	Andre Agassi	2.00
6	Muhammad Ali	4.00
7	Ken Norton	.50
8	Rogie Vachon	.50
9	Marcel Dionne	1.00
10	Wayne Gretzky	5.00
11	Title Card	.25
BC1	Elgin Baylor	12.00
BC2	Wilt Chamberlain	17.00
BC3	Jerry West	15.00
BC4	Kareem Abdul-Jabbar	15.00
BC5	Magic Johnson (HOR)	20.00

1993-94 Laker's McDonald's Magnets

This three-card magnet set was issued by McDonald's during the 1993-94 season.

		MT
Complete Set (3):		10.00
Common Player:		2.00
1	Nick Van Exel	8.00
2	Doug Christie	4.00
3	George Lynch	2.00

1998-99 Lakers 50th Anniversary Pin

This Lakers 50th Anniversary Pin was handed out at a Lakers game early in the 1998-99 season. The pin is pinned through the front of a card that features a FOX Sport West logo, KCAL9 Sports and a Toyota logo along with the 50th Anniversary logo. Six different players are featured on the card portion of the pin/card.

		MT
Complete Set (1):		15.00
	George Mikan, Jerry West, Elgin Baylor, Magic Johnson, James Worthy, Kareem Abdul-Jabbar	

1992 Lime Rock Larry Bird

The three-card, standard-size set featured hologram technology and was limited in production to 250,000 sets. Produced and distributed by Lime Rock Productions, 2,500 autographed cards were randomly inserted throughout the release. The card backs have color photos and descriptions of Bird's career.

		MT
Complete Set (3):		5.00
Common Player:		2.00
1	Larry Bird (Passing Skill developed at Indiana State)	2.00
2	Larry Bird (Legendary Shooting style at Boston)	2.00
3	Larry Bird (Posed in patriotic warm-up for Summer Olympic Games)	2.00

1991 Little Basketball Big Leaguers

The 45-card set was included in a book titled "Little Big Leaguers: Amazing Boyhood Stories of Today's Basketball Stars." The cards are located at the back of the book in nine-card perforated sheets that measure 7-1/2"x 10-1/2". When perforated, the cards measure 2-1/2"x 3-1/2"and feature black-and-white headshots of the players during childhood.

		MT
Complete Set (45):		15.00
Common Player:		.15
1	Danny Ainge	.30
2	Charles Barkley	2.00
3	Larry Bird	2.50
4	Rolando Blackman	.30
5	Tyrone Bogues	.30
6	Sam Bowie	.30
7	Brad Daugherty	.30
8	Johnny Dawkins	.30
9	James Donaldson	.15
10	Kevin Duckworth	.15
11	Chris Dudley	.15
12	A.J. English	.15
13	Harvey Grant, Horace Grant	.50
14	Jeff Hornacek	.30
15	Chris Jackson	.50
16	Mark Jackson	.30
17	Magic Johnson	2.00
18	Kevin Johnson	.50
19	Michael Jordan	6.00
20	Greg Kite	.15
21	Reggie Lewis	.50
22	Kevin McHale	.60
23	Reggie Miller	1.25
24	Johnny Newman	.15
25	Robert Parish	.50
26	John Paxson	.30
27	Chuck Person	.30
28	Terry Porter	.30
29	Mark Price	.30
30	J.R. Reid	.15
31	Glen Rice	.50
32	Doc Rivers	.15
33	Fred Roberts	.15
34	Byron Scott	.30
35	Jack Sikma	.30
36	Kenny Smith	.15
37	John Stockton	1.25
38	Wayman Tisdale	.30
39	Kiki Vandeweghe	.30
40	Spud Webb	.30
41	Dominique Wilkins	.50
42	John Williams	.15
43	David Wood	.15
44	Orlando Woolridge	.15
45	James Worthy	.50

1997 Little Sun The Pantheon Envelopes

Little Sun issued this series of commemorative envelopes to honor the first 100 years of basketball. Measuring approximately 3-5/8"x 6-1/2", the envelopes feature black-and-white photos of two players with a brief summary of their significance to the game below. They have a Centennial Olympic Games stamp and are postmarked in Trenton, N.J., on November 7, 1996 - the 100th anniversary of the first professional basketball game, which was played in Trenton. Inside the envelopes is a card that summarizes the history of that game. Each envelope is hand-numbered to 100. The only envelope that differs is the Allen-Iverson - NBA Debut. It features one black-and-white photo of Iverson, a 1996 "Yellow Rose"stamp and is postmarked in Philadelphia on November 1, 1996 - the day Iverson made his NBA debut.

		MT
Complete Set (6):		25.00
Common Player:		2.00
1	Wilt Chamberlain, Bill Russell	6.00
2	Julius Erving, Michael Jordan	10.00
3	Magic Johnson, Larry Bird	8.00
4	George Mikan, Kareem Abdul-Jabbar	3.00
5	Elgin Baylor, Bob Pettit	2.00
NNO	Elgin Baylor (NBA Debut)	2.00

1997 Little Sun Tim Duncan

		MT
Complete Set (1):		12.00
1	Tim Duncan	12.00

M

1989-90 Magic Pepsi

The eight-card, standard-size set was sponsored by Pepsi and features a color posed photo with a sweepstakes sticker on each card front. The sticker was to be peeled off and attached to an entry form for the sweepstakes. The card backs have statistics from the 1988-89 season. The fronts have "89/90 Inaugural Season" and are unnumbered. The set contains the first professional card of Nick Anderson.

		MT
Complete Set (8):		50.00
Common Player:		5.00
	Nick Anderson	20.00
	Michael Ansley	5.00
	Terry Catledge	5.00
	Dave Corzine	5.00
	Sidney Green	5.00
	Otis Smith	5.00
	Sam Vincent	5.00
	Stuff the Magic Dragon (Mascot)	6.00

2001 Magic/Topps

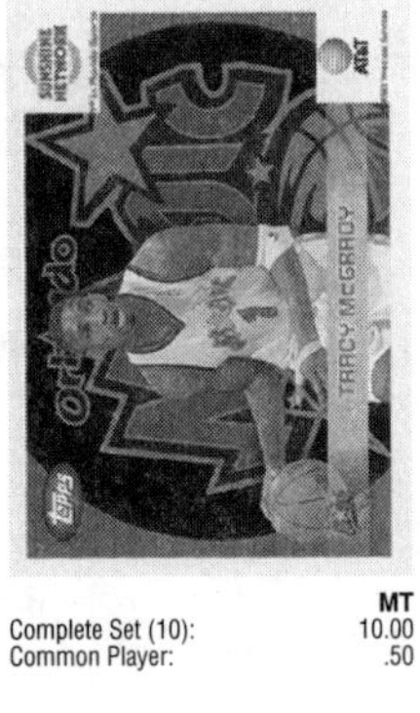

		MT
Complete Set (10):		10.00
Common Player:		.50
1	Grant Hill	3.00
2	Darrell Armstrong	1.00
3	Michael Doleac	.50
4	Pat Garrity	.75
5	Andrew DeClerq	.50
6	Mike Miller	3.00
7	Tracy McGrady	2.50
8	Bo Outlaw	.75
9	Doc Rivers CO	2.00
10	John Amaechi	.50

1989 Magnetables

This officially-licensed NBA set features blank-backed magnets depicting stars from the league on the fronts. The set, produced by Phoenix Industries, is subtitled "Pro Sports." The unnumbered magnets, each measuring 1-7/8"x 2-15/16", were sold in convenience and food stores.

		MT
Complete Set (34):		85.00
Common Player:		1.00
	Mark Aguirre	2.00
	Willie Anderson	1.50
	Charles Barkley	5.00
	Larry Bird	7.00
	Rolando Blackman	2.00
	Tom Chambers	2.00
	Clyde Drexler	5.00
	Joe Dumars	2.00
	Dale Ellis	1.50
	Alex English	2.00
	Patrick Ewing	4.00
	Roy Hinson	1.00
	Kevin Johnson	3.00
	Magic Johnson	6.00
	Vinnie Johnson	1.25
	Michael Jordan	15.00
	Bernard King	2.00
	Bill Laimbeer	1.50
	Karl Malone	6.00
	Moses Malone	4.00
	Kevin McHale	3.00
	Chris Mullin	2.00
	Ken Norman	1.50
	Akeem Olajuwon	5.00
	Chuck Person	1.50
	Mark Price	2.00
	Mitch Richmond	4.00
	Dennis Rodman	6.00
	Kenny Smith	1.25
	Jon Sundvold	1.00
	Isiah Thomas	4.00
	Kelly Tripucka	1.00
	Dominique Wilkins	4.00
	James Worthy	3.00

1971 Mattel Instant Replay

These replay records recount actual thrilling games involving the players depicted. The discs, which were 2-3/8"in diameter, were sold in two packs of four (#s 1-4 and 5-8 were sold together). Mattel produced a toy record player, which required "D" batteries, to play the records. A display box with a record for Lew Alcindor was also produced. The complete set price below does not include a Bill Russell disc, available only in a "Sports Challenges" series four-pack.

		NM
Complete Set (10):		225.00
Common Player:		12.00
1	Elgin Baylor	10.00
2	Wilt Chamberlain	10.00
3	Jerry Lucas	10.00
4	Pete Maravich	15.00
5	John Havlicek	10.00
6	Willis Reed	8.00
7	Oscar Robertson	10.00
8	Jerry West	15.00
9	Lew Alcindor	50.00
10	Bill Russell	100.00

1987-88 Mavericks Miller Lite

The five-card, 4"x 6"set was sponsored by Miller Lite and WBAP Radio 820. The card fronts feature a color action photo while the backs are blank and unnumbered. The cards are white bordered and have the player's name and jersey number below the color photo.

		MT
Complete Set (5):		10.00
Common Player:		1.00
	Mark Aguirre	3.00
	Rolando Blackman	3.00
	James Donaldson	1.00
	Derek Harper	3.00
	Sam Perkins	3.00

1988-89 Mavericks Bud Light BLC

The 14-card, standard-size set features 12 players and two coaches and was sponsored by Bud Light and produced by Big League Cards of New Jersey. The set was produced as a promotion for a Mavericks' home game, but there is some doubt as to whether the sets were actually distributed - possibly because Roy Tarpley and Mark Aguirre were included. The set is unnumbered except for the players' jersey numbers.

		MT
Complete Set (14):		20.00
Common Player:		.50
	Derek Harper	3.00
	Brad Davis	1.50
	Morlon Wiley	.50
	Rolando Blackman	3.00
	Bill Wennington	1.00
	Mark Aguirre	3.00
	Detlef Schrempf	4.00
	Uwe Blab	.50
	James Donaldson	.50
	Terry Tyler	.50
	Roy Tarpley	2.00
	Sam Perkins	3.00
	Coaching Staff (Richie Adubato ACO, Garfield Heard ACO)	.50
	John MacLeod (CO)	.50

1988-89 Mavericks Bud Light Card Night

The 13-card, standard-size set features 12 players and one coach and was sponsored by Bud Light. The set was produced for a card night at a Mavericks' home game, probably as a replacement for the above set. The cards are unnumbered, except for the uniform numbers.

		MT
Complete Set (13):		15.00
Common Player:		.50
	Adrian Dantley	3.00
	Derek Harper	3.00
	Brad Davis	1.50
	Morlon Wiley	.50
	Anthony Jones	.50
	Rolando Blackman	3.00
	Bill Wennington	1.00
	Herb Williams	1.00
	Uwe Blab	.50
	James Donaldson	.50
	Terry Tyler	.50
	Sam Perkins	3.00
	John MacLeod (CO)	.50

1989-90 Mavericks Dr. Pepper

This 13-card set was sponsored by Dr. Pepper. The fronts include a color action shot surrounded by a white border with two Dr. Pepper logos in the upper corners. The player's name and team name are at the bottom. The backs include biographical information, career highlights and an anti-drug message. The cards are not numbered.

		MT
Complete Set (13):		7.00
Common Player:		.25
1	Richie Adubato CO	.25
2	Steve Alford	.50
3	Rolando Blackman	1.00
4	Adrian Dantley	.75
5	Brad Davis	.50
6	James Donaldson	.25
7	Derek Harper	1.00
8	Anthony Jones	.25
9	Sam Perkins	1.00
10	Roy Tarpley	.25
11	Bill Wennington	.25
12	Randy White	.25
13	Herb Williams	.25

1994-95 Mavericks Bookmarks

The six-bookmark set, each one measuring 3"x 10", was given away during the 1994-95 season. Sponsored by HSE, Foot Locker and KLIF 570 AM radio, just 5,000 of each were produced. The bookmark fronts feature a color action shot with a facsimile autograph while the backs contain bio information and the "Don't foul out. Stay in school" message.

		MT
Complete Set (6):		10.00
Common Player:		1.00
1	Jim Jackson	2.00
2	Jamal Mashburn	3.00
3	Jason Kidd	5.00
4	Popeye Jones	1.50
5	Tony Dumas	1.50
6	Terry Davis	1.00

1995-96 Mavericks Taco Bell

The four-card, postcard-size set was distributed by Dallas-area Taco Bells for 99U each. The cards (3-1/2" x 5") feature artwork by comic book illustrator Larry Webber and depict each of the Triple J Mavericks (Jim Jackson, Jason Kidd and Jamal Mashburn) in caricature form on each card front. The sets were limited to a production of 83,000 with a promo ad card, distributed at a Mavericks' home game early in 1996, limited to 10,000.

		MT
Complete Set (4):		5.00
Common Player:		1.00
1	Jim Jackson	1.00
2	Jason Kidd (NBA Rookie of the Year)	2.00
3	Jason Kidd	2.00
4	Jamal Mashburn	1.00
NNO	Triple J Ad Card	5.00

2000 Mavericks Rolando Blackman Retirement Sheet

		MT
1	Rolando Blackman	2.00

1990 McDonald's Michael Jordan

Michael Jordan is featured in this eight-card set sponsored by the McDonald's Corp. The company logo is featured on the card front, along with a color action photo surrounded by a multi- colored border. The card title is given at the bottom of the card in a green panel; Jordan's facsimile autograph is in a panel at the top. Card backs give instructional advice regarding the card photo and title, plus nutritional and training tips. The set is subtitled "McDonald's Sports Tips" and was inserted into issues of Sports Illustrated for Kids. Cards 1, 2, 6, and 7 were in the October 1990 issue; the rest were in the December 1990 issue.

		MT
Complete Set (8):		10.00
Common Jordan:		1.50
1	The Lay-Up	1.50
2	The Blocked Shot	1.50
3	The Chest Pass	1.50
4	The Drive	1.50
5	The Speed Dribble	1.50
6	The Backup Dribble	1.50
7	The Jump Shot	1.50
8	The Free Throw	1.50

1994 McDonald's Nothing But Net MVPs

The six-card set was distributed by McDonalds on their large fries cardboard boxes and if cut, the cards would measure 3" x 3-7/8". The fronts feature a color action photo with a white border and the player's name is printed above the photo with the year (s) the player won the league's MVP award. The card back, which features a brief bio and stats, is printed on the back of the french fry box.

		MT
Complete Set (6):		24.00
Common Player:		2.00
1	Charles Barkley (1993 MVP)	3.00
2	Larry Bird (1984 MVP)	5.00
3	Julius Erving (1981 MVP)	4.00
4	Michael Jordan (1988, 1991, 1992 MVP)	8.00
5	Moses Malone (1979, 1982, 1983 MVP)	2.00
6	Bill Walton (1978 MVP)	3.00

1994 McDonald's USA Dream Team 2 Fry Boxes

This 11-player set was printed on the boxes of large McDonald's fries and endorsed by the NBA. Backs listed a schedule of games along with sponsor logos for TNT, TBS and NBC. The fry boxes are unnumbered and listed alphabetically.

		MT
Complete Set (11):		12.00
Common Player:		1.00
1	Derrick Coleman	1.00
2	Joe Dumars	1.50
3	Tim Hardaway	2.00
4	Larry Johnson	1.00
5	Shawn Kemp	1.50
6	Dan Majerle	1.00
7	Reggie Miller	2.00
8	Alonzo Mourning	2.00
9	Steve Smith	1.50
10	Isiah Thomas	2.00
11	Dominique Wilkins	2.00

1994 McDonald's USA Dream Team 2 Cups

This 13-cup set was sponsored by the NBA, Coke and McDonald's and features the members of the USA Dream Team 2 along with career highlights and a facsimile autograph.

		MT
Complete Set (13):		15.00
Common Player:		1.00
1	Isiah Thomas	2.00
2	Larry Johnson	1.00
3	Shawn Kemp	1.50
4	Dan Majerle	1.00
5	Dominique Wilkins	2.00
6	Derrick Coleman	1.00
7	Alonzo Mourning	2.00
8	Steve Smith	1.50
9	Joe Dumars	1.50
10	Mark Price	1.00
11	Shaquille O'Neal	5.00
12	Reggie Miller	2.00
13	Tim Hardaway	2.00

1994 McDonald's Nothing But Net MVP Cups

This six-cup set was sponsored by the NBA, Coke and McDonald's and features past MVPs. Cups are unnumbered and include dates of important games and quote from the player about the game.

		MT
Complete Set (6):		10.00
Common Player:		1.00
1	Michael Jordan	5.00
2	Julius Erving	2.00
3	Larry Bird	3.00
4	Moses Malone	1.00
5	Charles Barkley	1.50
6	Bill Walton	1.00

1995-96 Metal

Fleer issued its 1995-96 Metal set in two card series. The cards use a hand-engraved, metallized foil for the design. Each card front has a color action photo against this design background. The Fleer Metal brand logo is in the lower left corner, inside a silver metallic basketball. The player's name is stamped in silver foil along the card bottom. The back has another color photo on the left, with biographical information, 1994-95 statistics, and cummulative career stats on a plate which has been "screwed" to the card. There is also a screw in each card corner. The player's last name is spelled out along the left side of the card, above a logo of his team. A Silver Spotlight parallel set was also made; cards, seeded one per pack, have silver etched-foil backgrounds and gold foil stamping. Series I has a special Rookie Roll Call subset which spotlights 1995 rookie talent. These cards feature hand-engraved, metalized foil designs. Series II also has a 10-card subset, called Nuts and Bolts. Series II, which consists of 100 cards, includes 88 update cards, featuring veterans, traded players, free agents, rookies and 10 expansion team players. Series I inserts are: Steel Towers, Molten Metal, Maximum Metal and Slick Silver. Series II inserts are: Metal Force, Scoring Magnet, Tempered Steel and two more of the Jerry Stackhouse Scrapbook cards.

		MT
Complete Set (220):		60.00
Comp. Series 1 (120):		30.00
Comp. Series 2 (100):		30.00
Common Player:		.10
Minor Stars:		.20
Comp. Silver Spot (120):		80.00
Silver Spot Cards: 1.5x-3x		
Ser. 1 or 2 Pack (8):		1.25
Ser. 1 or 2 Wax Box (36):		40.00
1	Stacey Augmon	.10
2	Mookie Blaylock	.10
3	Grant Long	.10
4	Steve Smith	.10
5	Dee Brown	.10
6	Sherman Douglas	.10
7	Eric Montross	.10
8	Dino Radja	.10
9	Muggsy Bogues	.10
10	Scott Burrell	.10
11	Larry Johnson	.50
12	Alonzo Mourning	.50
13	Michael Jordan	6.00

14	Toni Kukoc	.10
15	Scottie Pippen	1.00
16	Terrell Brandon	.10
17	Tyrone Hill	.10
18	Mark Price	.10
19	John Williams	.10
20	Jim Jackson	.50
21	Popeye Jones	.10
22	Jason Kidd	1.50
23	Jamal Mashburn	.50
24	Mahmoud Abdul-Rauf	.20
25	Dikembe Mutombo	.30
26	Robert Pack	.10
27	Jalen Rose	.10
28	Joe Dumars	.10
29	Grant Hill	2.00
30	Lindsey Hunter	.10
31	Terry Mills	.10
32	Tim Hardaway	.20
33	Donyell Marshall	.10
34	Chris Mullin	.20
35	Clifford Rozier	.10
36	Latrell Sprewell	.30
37	Sam Cassell	.10
38	Clyde Drexler	.50
39	Robert Horry	.30
40	Hakeem Olajuwon	1.00
41	Kenny Smith	.10
42	Dale Davis	.10
43	Mark Jackson	.10
44	Derrick McKey	.10
45	Reggie Miller	.40
46	Rik Smits	.10
47	Lamond Murray	.10
48	Pooh Richardson	.10
49	Malik Sealy	.10
50	Loy Vaught	.10
51	Elden Campbell	.10
52	Cedric Ceballos	.25
53	Vlade Divac	.10
54	Eddie Jones	.50
55	Nick Van Exel	.50
56	Bimbo Coles	.10
57	Billy Owens	.10
58	Khalid Reeves	.10
59	Glen Rice	.20
60	Kevin Willis	.10
61	Vin Baker	.25
62	Todd Day	.10
63	Eric Murdock	.10
64	Glenn Robinson	.60
65	Tom Gugliotta	.10
66	Christian Laettner	.10
67	Isaiah Rider	.20
68	Kenny Anderson	.10
69	P.J. Brown	.10
70	Derrick Coleman	.10
71	Patrick Ewing	.40
72	Anthony Mason	.10
73	Charles Oakley	.10
74	John Starks	.10
75	Nick Anderson	.10
76	Horace Grant	.30
77	Anfernee Hardaway	2.00
78	Shaquille O'Neal	2.00
79	Dennis Scott	.10
80	Dana Barros	.10
81	Shawn Bradley	.10
82	Clarence Weatherspoon	.10
83	Sharone Wright	.10
84	Charles Barkley	.75
85	Kevin Johnson	.20
86	Dan Majerle	.10
87	Danny Manning	.10
88	Wesley Person	.10
89	Clifford Robinson	.10
90	Rod Strickland	.10
91	Otis Thorpe	.10
92	Buck Williams	.10
93	Brian Grant	.20
94	Olden Polynice	.10
95	Mitch Richmond	.20
96	Walt Williams	.10
97	Sean Elliott	.10
98	Avery Johnson	.10
99	David Robinson	.75
100	Dennis Rodman	2.00
101	Shawn Kemp	.75
102	Nate McMillan	.10
103	Gary Payton	.50
104	Detlef Schrempf	.10
105	B.J. Armstrong	.10
106	Oliver Miller	.10
107	John Salley	.10
108	David Benoit	.10
109	Jeff Hornacek	.10
110	Karl Malone	.50
111	John Stockton	.50
112	Greg Anthony	.10
113	Benoit Benjamin	.10
114	Byron Scott	.10
115	Calbert Cheaney	.10
116	Juwan Howard	.50
117	Gheorghe Muresan	.10
118	Chris Webber	.40
119	Checklist	.10
120	Checklist	.10
121	Stacey Augmon	.10
122	Mookie Blaylock	.10
123	*Alan Henderson*	.25
124	Andrew Lang	.10
125	Ken Norman	.10
126	Steve Smith	.10
127	Dana Barros	.10
128	Rick Fox	.10
129	*Eric Williams*	.50
130	Kendall Gill	.10
131	Khalid Reeves	.10
132	Glen Rice	.10
133	*George Zidek*	.20
134	Dennis Rodman	2.00
135	Danny Ferry	.10
136	Dan Majerle	.10
137	Chris Mills	.10
138	Bobby Phills	.10
139	*Bob Sura*	.40
140	Tony Dumas	.10
141	Dale Ellis	.10
142	Don MacLean	.10
143	*Antonio McDyess*	3.00
144	Bryant Stith	.10
145	Allan Houston	.20
146	*Theo Ratliff*	1.50
147	Otis Thorpe	.10
148	B.J. Armstrong	.10
149	Rony Seikaly	.10
150	*Joe Smith*	2.00
151	Sam Cassell	.10
152	Clyde Drexler	.50
153	Robert Horry	.10
154	Hakeem Olajuwon	1.00
155	Antonio Davis	.10
156	Ricky Pierce	.10
157	*Brent Barry*	1.00
158	Terry Dehere	.10
159	Rodney Rogers	.10
160	Brian Williams	.10
161	Magic Johnson	1.00
162	*Sasha Danilovic*	.20
163	Alonzo Mourning	.50
164	*Kurt Thomas*	.50
165	Sherman Douglas	.10
166	*Shawn Respert*	.25
167	*Kevin Garnett*	8.00
168	Terry Porter	.10
169	Shawn Bradley	.20
170	Kevin Edwards	.10
171	*Ed O'Bannon*	.20
172	Jayson Williams	.10
173	Derek Harper	.10
174	Charles Smith	.10
175	Brian Shaw	.10
176	Derrick Coleman	.10
177	Vernon Maxwell	.10
178	Trevor Ruffin	.10
179	*Jerry Stackhouse*	4.00
180	*Michael Finley*	3.00
181	A.C. Green	.10
182	John Williams	.10
183	Aaron McKie	.10
184	*Arvydas Sabonis*	1.25
185	*Gary Trent*	.25
186	*Tyus Edney*	.20
187	Sarunas Marciulionis	.10
188	Michael Smith	.10
189	*Corliss Williamson*	.40
190	Vinny Del Negro	.10
191	Hersey Hawkins	.10
192	Shawn Kemp	.50
193	Gary Payton	.20
194	Sam Perkins	.10
195	Detlef Schrempf	.10
196	Willie Anderson	.10
197	Oliver Miller	.10
198	Tracy Murray	.10
199	Alvin Robertson	.10
200	*Damon Stoudamire*	2.00
201	Chris Morris	.10
202	Greg Anthony	.10
203	Blue Edwards	.10
204	Eric Murdock	.10
205	*Bryant Reeves*	.75
206	Byron Scott	.10
207	Robert Pack	.10
208	*Rasheed Wallace*	3.00
209	Anfernee Hardaway (Nuts and Bolts)	1.25
210	Grant Hill (Nuts and Bolts)	1.00
211	Larry Johnson (Nuts and Bolts)	.10
212	Michael Jordan (Nuts and Bolts)	3.00
213	Jason Kidd (Nuts and Bolts)	.50
214	Karl Malone (Nuts and Bolts)	.10
215	Shaquille O'Neal (Nuts and Bolts)	1.25
216	Scottie Pippen (Nuts and Bolts)	.50
217	David Robinson (Nuts and Bolts)	.50
218	Glenn Robinson (Nuts and Bolts)	.30
219	Checklist	.10
220	Checklist	.10

1995-96 Metal Silver Spotlight

This 120-card parallel set was inserted one per pack and are similar to regular-issue cards except for having etched silver foil backgrounds and a gold foil basketball in the bottom left front corner.

	MT
Complete Set (120):	80.00
Common Player:	.25
Stars:	.50
Silv. Spot. Stars:	2x-3x

1995-96 Metal Maximum Metal

These insert cards highlight 10 of the NBA's impact players. The cards, seeded one per every 36 1995-96 Fleer Metal Series I packs, have a die-cut design. The card front has a color action photo against a background showing a basketball going through a net. The card is die-cut around the ball. The brand logo appears at the top of the card; the player's name and "Maximum Metal" are stamped in gold at the bottom. The card back shows the reverse of the front design, but a different color action photo is used. Cards are numbered 1 of 10, etc., at the bottom in the same color which is used for the player's name at the top of the card.

		MT
Complete Set (10):		100.00
Common Player:		2.00
1	Charles Barkley	6.00
2	Patrick Ewing	3.00
3	Grant Hill	20.00
4	Michael Jordan	40.00
5	Shawn Kemp	6.00
6	Karl Malone	3.00
7	Hakeem Olajuwon	10.00
8	Shaquille O'Neal	20.00
9	Mitch Richmond	2.00
10	David Robinson	8.00

1995-96 Metal Metal Force

This 15-card set was found exclusively in Series II retail packs at a rate of one per 54 packs. The cards arrived with a protective seal and are considered mint only when left in their original unpeeled state.

		MT
Complete Set (15):		225.00
Common Player:		4.00
1	Vin Baker	8.00
2	Charles Barkley	15.00
3	Cedric Ceballos	4.00
4	Grant Hill	50.00
5	Larry Johnson	8.00
6	Magic Johnson	25.00
7	Shawn Kemp	15.00
8	Karl Malone	8.00
9	Jamal Mashburn	6.00
10	Scottie Pippen	30.00
11	Glenn Robinson	12.00
12	Dennis Rodman	45.00
13	Joe Smith	15.00
14	Jerry Stackhouse	15.00
15	Chris Webber	15.00

1995-96 Metal Molten Metal

This 1995-96 Fleer Metal Series I insert set features 10 of the league's up-and-coming stars. They are the rarest insert set; cards are seeded one per every 72 packs. Each card has a foil-stamped laminated design.

		MT
Complete Set (10):		180.00
Common Player:		5.00
1	Anfernee Hardaway	60.00
2	Grant Hill	55.00
3	Robert Horry	5.00
4	Eddie Jones	20.00
5	Toni Kukoc	5.00
6	Jamal Mashburn	5.00
7	Alonzo Mourning	10.00
8	Glenn Robinson	15.00
9	Latrell Sprewell	10.00
10	Chris Webber	20.00

1995-96 Metal Rookie Roll Call

These cards spotlight 1995 rookie talent. Hand-engraved, metallized foil is used for the design. The cards, which also have Silver Spotlight parallel versions, show the rookies in their NBA uniforms. They have an "R" prefix for the card number, but they were a subset for 1995-96 Fleer Metal Series I. Rookie Roll Call is stamped in foil on the front.

		MT
Complete Set (10):		15.00
Common Player:		.25
Comp. Silver Spot (10):		30.00
Silver Spot Cards:		1x-2x
1	Brent Barry	1.00
2	Antonio McDyess	3.00
3	Ed O'Bannon	.25
4	Cherokee Parks	.25
5	Bryant Reeves	1.25
6	Shawn Respert	.25
7	Joe Smith	2.00
8	Jerry Stackhouse	2.00
9	Gary Trent	.25
10	Rasheed Wallace	1.50

1995-96 Metal Rookie Roll Call Silver Spotlight

Rookie Roll Call Silver Spotlight cards ran parallel to the Rookie Roll Call insert much like the Silver Spotlight parallels the entire Metal issue in 1995-96. No specific odds were given, but the cards were inserted just like regular-issue Silver Spotlight cards, at a rate of one per pack.

	MT
Complete Set (10):	30.00
Silver Spotlight Cards:	1x-2x

1995-96 Metal Scoring Magnets

Eight of the NBA's top scorers are featured on these 1995-96 Fleer Metal Series II inserts. The cards, seeded one in every 54 packs, say "Scoring Magnet" on both sides of the front.

		MT
Complete Set (8):		160.00
Common Player:		10.00
1	Anfernee Hardaway	35.00
2	Grant Hill	25.00
3	Magic Johnson	15.00
4	Michael Jordan	70.00
5	Jason Kidd	15.75
6	Hakeem Olajuwon	15.00
7	Shaquille O'Neal	25.00
8	David Robinson	10.00

1995-96 Metal Slick Silver

Ten of the NBA's premier guards are featured on these 1995-96 Fleer Metal Series I inserts. Cards, seeded one per every seven hobby packs, are clear, plastic cards which use silver foil stamping on the front for the player's name and insert set name. The front shows an action photo, with repeated ghosted images trailing behind the main photo. The back shows a ghosted, reverse image of the front, with a recap of the player's 1994-95 season inside. A card number, 1 of 10, etc., is also in the image area.

		MT
Complete Set (10):		50.00
Common Player:		1.00
1	Kenny Anderson	1.00
2	Anfernee Hardaway	14.00
3	Michael Jordan	28.00
4	Jason Kidd	5.00
5	Reggie Miller	3.00
6	Gary Payton	3.00
7	Mitch Richmond	2.00
8	Latrell Sprewell	4.00
9	John Stockton	3.00
10	Nick Van Exel	2.00

1995-96 Metal Stackhouse's Scrapbook

These two cards were part of the 10 cards devoted to chronicling Philadelphia 76ers rookie Jerry Stackhouse's rise to the NBA. Cards were inserted at a ratio of one per every 24 packs of 1995-96 Fleer Metal Series II product.

		MT
Complete Set (2):		10.00
Common Player:		5.00
1	Jerry Stackhouse	5.00
2	Jerry Stackhouse	5.00

1995-96 Metal Steel Towers

These 10 silver foil embossed cards highlight some of the league's top centers. Cards were randomly inserted in 1995-96 Fleer Metal Series I packs, in retail/magazine packs only. They were seeded one per every four packs.

		MT
Complete Set (10):		15.00
Common Player:		.50
1	Shawn Bradley	.50
2	Vlade Divac	.50
3	Patrick Ewing	1.50
4	Alonzo Mourning	2.00
5	Dikembe Mutombo	1.00
6	Hakeem Olajuwon	4.00
7	Shaquille O'Neal	7.00
8	David Robinson	3.00
9	Rik Smits	.50
10	Kevin Willis	.50

1995-96 Metal Tempered Steel

Tempered Steel is a 12-card insert set that contains the top rookies of the 1995-96 season. They were seeded one per every 12 packs of 1995-96 Fleer Metal Series II product. Card fronts say "Tempered Steel" along the left side; backs, numbered 1 of 12, etc., have a photo on the left and an assessment of the player's skills on the right.

		MT
Complete Set (12):		45.00
Common Player:		1.50
1	Sasha Danilovic	2.00
2	Tyus Edney	1.50
3	Michael Finley	5.00
4	Kevin Garnett	15.00
5	Antonio McDyess	10.00
6	Bryant Reeves	3.00
7	Arvydas Sabonis	3.00
8	Joe Smith	7.00
9	Jerry Stackhouse	7.00
10	Damon Stoudamire	8.00
11	Rasheed Wallace	4.00
12	Eric Williams	1.50

1996-97 Metal

Metal included 150 cards in Series I and 100 in Series II for 1996-97. Card fronts featured a color shot of the player cut out on a "metal" background that is made of silver foil. The player's name is embossed and runs up the right side with the Metal logo in the lower right corner. Backs are printed vertically with another shot of the player, and statistics printed horizontally on the right side. Series I includes 108 cards, 15 On the Move, 10 Metallized, five Fresh Foundations, 10 Metal Shredders and two checklists, while Series II included 73 regular cards, 10 Metal Shredders, 10 Metallized, five Fresh Foundations and two checklists. Insert sets in Series I include: Molten Metal, Power Tools, Steel Slammin', Metal Edge, Decade of Excellence, Maximum Metal and NBA Pick-Up Game. Inserts in Series II include: Cyber-Metal, Freshly Forged, Platinum Portraits, Maximum Metal, Molten Metal, Net Rageous and a 98-card parallel set (minus the two checklists) called Precious Metal.

		MT
Complete Set (250):		55.00
Complete Series 1 (150):		30.00
Complete Series 2 (100):		25.00
Common Player:		.10
Minor Stars:		.20
Pack (8):		1.25
Wax Box (24):		30.00
1	Mookie Blaylock	.10
2	Christian Laettner	.10
3	Steve Smith	.10
4	Dana Barros	.10
5	Rick Fox	.10
6	Dino Radja	.10
7	Eric Williams	.10
8	Dell Curry	.10
9	Matt Geiger	.10
10	Glen Rice	.10
11	Michael Jordan	5.00
12	Toni Kukoc	.10
13	Luc Longley	.10
14	Scottie Pippen	1.25
15	Dennis Rodman	1.75
16	Terrell Brandon	.10
17	Danny Ferry	.10
18	Chris Mills	.10
19	Bobby Phills	.10
20	Bob Sura	.10
21	Jim Jackson	.30
22	Jason Kidd	1.00
23	Jamal Mashburn	.30
24	George McCloud	.10
25	LaPhonso Ellis	.10
26	Antonio McDyess	.50
27	Bryant Stith	.10
28	Joe Dumars	.10
29	Grant Hill	2.00
30	Theo Ratliff	.10
31	Otis Thorpe	.10
32	Chris Mullin	.10
33	Joe Smith	.50
34	Latrell Sprewell	.20
35	Sam Cassell	.10
36	Clyde Drexler	.40
37	Robert Horry	.10
38	Hakeem Olajuwon	1.00
39	Antonio Davis	.10
40	Dale Davis	.10
41	Derrick McKey	.10
42	Reggie Miller	.40
43	Rik Smits	.10
44	Brent Barry	.20
45	Malik Sealy	.10
46	Loy Vaught	.10
47	Elden Campbell	.10
48	Cedric Ceballos	.20
49	Eddie Jones	.30
50	Nick Van Exel	.20
51	Sasha Danilovic	.10
52	Tim Hardaway	.10
53	Alonzo Mourning	.30
54	Kurt Thomas	.10
55	Vin Baker	.30
56	Sherman Douglas	.10
57	Glenn Robinson	.30
58	Kevin Garnett	2.00
59	Tom Gugliotta	.10
60	Doug West	.10
61	Shawn Bradley	.10
62	Ed O'Bannon	.20
63	Jayson Williams	.10
64	Patrick Ewing	.40
65	Charles Oakley	.10
66	John Starks	.10
67	Nick Anderson	.10
68	Horace Grant	.10
69	Anfernee Hardaway	2.50
70	Dennis Scott	.10
71	Brian Shaw	.10
72	Derrick Coleman	.10
73	Jerry Stackhouse	1.00
74	Clarence Weatherspoon	.10
75	Charles Barkley	.50
76	Michael Finley	.75
77	Kevin Johnson	.10
78	Wesley Person	.10
79	Aaron McKie	.10
80	Clifford Robinson	.10
81	Arvydas Sabonis	.40
82	Gary Trent	.10
83	Tyus Edney	.10
84	Brian Grant	.10
85	Billy Owens	.10
86	Olden Polynice	.10
87	Mitch Richmond	.20

88	Vinny Del Negro	.10
89	Sean Elliott	.10
90	Avery Johnson	.10
91	David Robinson	.75
92	Hersey Hawkins	.10
93	Shawn Kemp	.60
94	Gary Payton	.30
95	Sam Perkins	.10
96	Detlef Schrempf	.10
97	Doug Christie	.10
98	Damon Stoudamire	1.25
99	Sharone Wright	.10
100	Jeff Hornacek	.10
101	Karl Malone	.30
102	John Stockton	.30
103	Greg Anthony	.10
104	Blue Edwards	.10
105	Bryant Reeves	.30
106	Juwan Howard	.50
107	Gheorghe Muresan	.10
108	Chris Webber	.30
109	Kenny Anderson (On the Move)	.10
110	Stacey Augmon (On the Move)	.10
111	Chris Childs (On the Move)	.10
112	Vlade Divac (On the Move)	.10
113	Allan Houston (On the Move)	.10
114	Mark Jackson (On the Move)	.10
115	Larry Johnson (On the Move)	.10
116	Grant Long (On the Move)	.10
117	Anthony Mason (On the Move)	.10
118	Dikembe Mutombo (On the Move)	.10
119	Shaquille O'Neal (On the Move)	2.50
120	Isaiah Rider (On the Move)	.10
121	Rod Strickland (On the Move)	.10
122	Rasheed Wallace (On the Move)	.25
123	(Jalen Rose) (On the Move)	.10
124	Anfernee Hardaway (Metallized)	1.25
125	Tim Hardaway (Metallized)	.10
126	Allan Houston (Metallized)	.10
127	Eddie Jones (Metallized)	.10
128	Michael Jordan (Metallized)	2.50
129	Reggie Miller (Metallized)	.20
130	Glen Rice (Metallized)	.10
131	Mitch Richmond (Metallized)	.10
132	Steve Smith (Metallized)	.10
133	John Stockton (Metallized)	.10
134	*Stephon Marbury* (Fresh Foundations)	4.00
135	*(Shareef Abdur-Rahim)* (Fresh Foundations)	3.00
136	*Ray Allen* (Fresh Foundations)	3.00
137	*(Kobe Bryant)* (Fresh Foundations)	15.00
138	*(Steve Nash)* (Fresh Foundations)	.75
139	Grant Hill (Metal Shredders)	.75
140	Jason Kidd (Metal Shredders)	.50
141	Karl Malone (Metal Shredders)	.10
142	Hakeem Olajuwon (Metal Shredders)	.50
143	Shaquille O'Neal (Metal Shredders)	1.00
144	Gary Payton (Metal Shredders)	.10
145	Scottie Pippen (Metal Shredders)	.60
146	Jerry Stackhouse (Metal Shredders)	.50
147	Damon Stoudamire (Metal Shredders)	.60
148	Rod Strickland (Metal Shredders)	.10
149	Checklist	.10
150	Checklist	.10
151	Tyrone Corbin	.10
152	Dikembe Mutombo	.10
153	*Antoine Walker*	2.00
154	David Wesley	.10
155	Vlade Divac	.10
156	Anthony Mason	.10
157	Ron Harper	.10
158	Steve Kerr	.10
159	Robert Parish	.10
160	Tyrone Hill	.10
161	Vitaly Potapenko	.40
162	Sam Cassell	.10
163	Chris Gatling	.10
164	Samaki Walker	.40
165	Dale Ellis	.10
166	Mark Jackson	.10
167	Ervin Johnson	.10
168	Grant Hill	2.00
169	Lindsey Hunter	.10
170	Todd Fuller	.10
171	Mark Price	.10
172	Charles Barkley	.50
173	Othella Harrington	.10
174	Matt Maloney	.75
175	Kevin Willis	.10
176	Travis Best	.10
177	Erick Dampier	.50
178	Jalen Rose	.10
179	Rodney Rogers	.10
180	Lorenzen Wright	.50
181	Kobe Bryant	8.00
182	Robert Horry	.10
183	Shaquille O'Neal	2.00
184	P.J. Brown	.10
185	Dan Majerle	.10
186	Ray Allen	2.00
187	Armon Gilliam	.10
188	Andrew Lang	.10
189	Stephon Marbury	4.00
190	Stojko Vrankovic	.10
191	Kendall Gill	.10
192	*Kerry Kittles*	1.75
193	Robert Pack	.10
194	Chris Childs	.10
195	Allan Houston	.10
196	Larry Johnson	.10
197	John Wallace	.75
198	Rony Seikaly	.10
199	Gerald Wilkins	.10
200	Lucious Harris	.10
201	*Allen Iverson*	6.00
202	Cedric Ceballos	.10
203	Jason Kidd	.10
204	Danny Manning	.10
205	Steve Nash	.50
206	Kenny Anderson	.10
207	Isaiah Rider	.10
208	Rasheed Wallace	.10
209	Mahmoud Abdul-Rauf	.10
210	Corliss Williamson	.10
211	Vernon Maxwell	.10
212	Dominique Wilkins	.10
213	Craig Ehlo	.10
214	Jim McIlvaine	.10
215	*Marcus Camby*	3.00
216	Hubert Davis	.10
217	Walt Williams	.10
218	Shandon Anderson	.50
219	Bryon Russell	.10
220	Shareef Abdur-Rahim	2.50
221	Roy Rogers	.40
222	Tracy Murray	.10
223	Rod Strickland	.10
224	Kevin Garnett	1.00
225	Karl Malone	.10
226	Alonzo Mourning	.10
227	Hakeem Olajuwon	.50
228	Gary Payton	.10
229	Scottie Pippen	.75
230	David Robinson	.10
231	Dennis Rodman	1.00
232	Latrell Sprewell	.10
233	Jerry Stackhouse	.30
234	Marcus Camby	1.50
235	Todd Fuller	.10
236	Allen Iverson	2.50
237	Kerry Kittles	.75
238	Roy Rogers	.10
239	Anfernee Hardaway	1.00
240	Juwan Howard	.30
241	Michael Jordan	2.50
242	Shawn Kemp	.30
243	Gary Payton	.10
244	Mitch Richmond	.10
245	Glenn Robinson	.10
246	John Stockton	.10
247	Damon Stoudamire	.50
248	Chris Webber	.30
249	Checklist	.10
250	Checklist	.10

1996-97 Metal Precious Metal

This 98-card parallel set reprinted each card in Metal Series II, excluding the two checklists. Inserted at a rate of one per 36 hobby packs, Precious Metal cards were done with a fade in the etched foil and carried a "PM" prefix.

	MT
Complete Set (98):	1000.
Precious Stars:	15x-30x
Precious Rookies:	6x-12x

1996-97 Metal Cyber-Metal

Cyber-Metal featured 20 cards and captured a color image of a player over a fantasy-like metallized background. This insert was exclusive to Series II Metal and was seeded one per six packs. Cards are numbered with a "CM" prefix.

		MT
Complete Set (20):		45.00
Common Player:		1.00
1	Shareef Abdur-Rahim	6.00
2	Ray Allen	4.00
3	Vin Baker	2.00
4	Charles Barkley	3.00
5	Kobe Bryant	10.00
6	Patrick Ewing	2.00
7	Jason Kidd	2.00
8	Karl Malone	2.00
9	Stephon Marbury	7.50
10	Reggie Miller	2.00
11	Alonzo Mourning	1.00
12	Hakeem Olajuwon	4.00
13	Gary Payton	3.00
14	Scottie Pippen	5.00
15	Mitch Richmond	2.00
16	David Robinson	3.00
17	Joe Smith	3.00
18	Latrell Sprewell	2.00
19	John Stockton	2.00
20	Chris Webber	3.00

1996-97 Metal Decade of Excellence

These 1996-97 Fleer Metal inserts take the Decade of Excellence inserts from 1996-97 Fleer Basketball and add a metal touch to them. Cards were seeded one per every 100 packs, with 10 in Series I and 10 in Series II.

		MT
Complete Set (10):		70.00
Common Player:		3.00
1	Clyde Drexler	6.00
2	Joe Dumars	3.00
3	Derek Harper	3.00
4	Michael Jordan	50.00
5	Karl Malone	6.00
6	Chris Mullin	3.00
7	Charles Oakley	3.00
8	Sam Perkins	3.00
9	Ricky Pierce	3.00
10	Buck Williams	3.00

1996-97 Metal Freshly Forged

Freshly Forged gives attention to 15 young players on a sheet metal background, with the insert name printed across the bottom. This was inserted into every 24 packs of Series II Metal. Cards are numbered with a "FF" prefix.

		MT
Complete Set (15):		120.00
Common Player:		3.00
1	Shareef Abdur-Rahim	15.00
2	Ray Allen	10.00
3	Kobe Bryant	20.00
4	Marcus Camby	15.00
5	Kevin Garnett	20.00
6	Anfernee Hardaway	15.00
7	Grant Hill	20.00
8	Allen Iverson	20.00
9	Jason Kidd	3.00
10	Stephon Marbury	17.00
11	Glenn Robinson	3.00
12	Joe Smith	6.00
13	Jerry Stackhouse	6.00
14	Damon Stoudamire	10.00
15	Antoine Walker	7.00

1996-97 Metal Maximum Metal

Maximum Metal was a 20-card insert set that included 10 cards, in one per 180 hobby packs, the second 10 inserted in one per 120 retail packs. Although numbered consecutively, Series I cards are two layered with the foil basketball on the second layer, while Series II inserts are printed on a single layer.

	MT
Complete Set (20):	400.00
Complete Series 1 (10):	300.00
Complete Series 2 (10):	100.00
Common Player:	7.00

1	Charles Barkley	20.00
2	Anfernee Hardaway	40.00
3	Grant Hill	80.00
4	Michael Jordan	150.00
5	Jason Kidd	15.00
6	Karl Malone	15.00
7	Hakeem Olajuwon	25.00
8	Gary Payton	15.00
9	David Robinson	20.00
10	Damon Stoudamire	15.00
11	Juwan Howard	10.00
12	Shawn Kemp	10.00
13	Kerry Kittles	7.00
14	Stephon Marbury	30.00
15	Dennis Rodman	25.00
16	Joe Smith	10.00
17	Jerry Stackhouse	10.00
18	John Stockton	7.00
19	Antoine Walker	15.00
20	Chris Webber	12.00

1996-97 Metal Metal Edge

These cards highlight players who have an edge over their opponents by using their distinct aggressiveness. The 15-card set includes five rookies who signed with their NBA teams before Aug. 15, 1996. Those players are Stephon Marbury, Shareef Abdur-Rahim, Ray Allen, Antoine Walker and Kobe Bryant. Cards were seeded one per every 36 packs of 1996-97 Fleer Metal.

		MT
Complete Set (15):		80.00
Common Player:		2.00
1	Charles Barkley	6.00
2	Jamal Mashburn	2.00
3	Alonzo Mourning	4.00
4	Gary Payton	4.00
5	Scottie Pippen	10.00
6	Steve Smith	2.00
7	Latrell Sprewell	2.00
8	John Stockton	4.00
9	Nick Van Exel	2.00
10	Chris Webber	7.00
11	Stephon Marbury	20.00
12	(Shareef Abdur-Rahim)	15.00
13	(Ray Allen)	10.00
14	(Antoine Walker)	8.00
15	(Kobe Bryant)	25.00

1996-97 Metal Minted Metal

This two-card insert was available in one per 720 Series II hobby packs. The redemption cards were available in both and could be sent in for Minted Metal cards from The Highland Mint. Each player was reproduced in an all-metal 14kt. gold, gold-plated, silver and bronze cards.

		MT
Complete Set (2):		100.00
Common Player:		40.00
1	Grant Hill Bronze	75.00
2	Jerry Stackhouse Bronze	40.00

1996-97 Metal Molten Metal

Molten Metal was a 30-card insert set that had cards numbered 1-10 inserted into packs of Series I at a rate of one per 180 retail, and 11-30 inserted into packs of Series II at a rate of one per 72 hobby packs. Series I inserts were printed on a lenticular design, while Series II cards were printed on a foil background.

	MT
Complete Set (30):	550.00
Complete Series 1 (10):	200.00
Complete Series 2 (20):	375.00
Common Player:	5.00

1	Michael Finley	10.00
2	Kevin Garnett	60.00
3	Anfernee Hardaway	40.00
4	Grant Hill	60.00
5	Juwan Howard	15.00
6	Jason Kidd	10.00
7	Antonio McDyess	10.00
8	Joe Smith	15.00
9	Jerry Stackhouse	15.00
10	Damon Stoudamire	15.00
11	Shareef Abdur-Rahim	35.00
12	Ray Allen	20.00
13	Charles Barkley	15.00
14	Terrell Brandon	5.00
15	Marcus Camby	35.00
16	Tom Gugliotta	5.00
17	Allen Iverson	60.00
18	Michael Jordan	120.00
19	Kerry Kittles	20.00
20	Karl Malone	8.00
21	Hakeem Olajuwon	20.00
22	Shaquille O'Neal	40.00
23	Gary Payton	12.00
24	Scottie Pippen	30.00
25	David Robinson	12.00
26	Glenn Robinson	8.00
27	Joe Smith	12.00
28	Latrell Spewell	12.00
29	Antoine Walker	20.00
30	Chris Webber	15.00

1996-97 Metal Net Rageous

This 10-card die-cut insert features 10 top stars on a gold foil background. The word "Net" is printed in large letters down the left side, with the word "Rageous" printed horizontally on the right side. Net Rageous inserts were found every 288 packs of Metal Series II. Cards are numbered with a "NR" prefix.

		MT
Complete Set (10):		500.00
Common Player:		15.00
1	Kevin Garnett	90.00
2	Anfernee Hardaway	60.00
3	Grant Hill	90.00
4	Juwan Howard	15.00
5	Michael Jordan	200.00
6	Shawn Kemp	20.00
7	Shaquille O'Neal	60.00
8	Dennis Rodman	50.00
9	Jerry Stackhouse	20.00
10	Damon Stoudamire	20.00

1996-97 Metal Platinum Portraits

This 10-card set showcased some of the NBA's elite on a horizontal design, etched in silver foil. A close-up of the player's face was on the left side, with a large team logo. The player's name and insert name were printed across the bottom in gold foil. Platinum Portraits were available in one per 96 packs of Series II. Cards are numbered with a "PP" prefix.

		MT
Complete Set (10):		225.00
Common Player:		4.00
1	Charles Barkley	8.00
2	Kevin Garnett	40.00
3	Anfernee Hardaway	25.00
4	Grant Hill	40.00
5	Michael Jordan	80.00
6	Shawn Kemp	10.00
7	Karl Malone	4.00
8	Shaquille O'Neal	25.00
9	Hakeem Olajuwon	15.00
10	Damon Stoudamire	10.00

1996-97 Metal Power Tools

These 1996-97 Fleer Metal cards spotlight some of the NBA's top forwards on 100 percent etched foil cards. The cards were seeded one per every 18 packs in Series I.

		MT
Complete Set (10):		40.00
Common Player:		1.00
1	Vin Baker	1.00
2	Charles Barkley	4.00
3	Horace Grant	1.00
4	Juwan Howard	4.00
5	Larry Johnson	1.00
6	Shawn Kemp	4.00
7	Karl Malone	2.00
8	Antonio McDyess	5.00
9	Dennis Rodman	14.00
10	Joe Smith	6.00

1996-97 Metal Steel Slammin'

Several of the NBA's finest slam dunk artists are featured on these 1996-97 Fleer Metal embossed inserts. The cards were seeded one per every 72 packs in Series I.

		MT
Complete Set (10):		175.00
Common Player:		3.00
1	Brent Barry	3.00
2	Clyde Drexler	10.00
3	Michael Finley	8.00
4	Kevin Garnett	40.00
5	Eddie Jones	10.00
6	Michael Jordan	90.00
7	Shawn Kemp	15.00
8	Shaquille O'Neal	30.00
9	Joe Smith	12.00
10	Jerry Stackhouse	12.00

1997-98 Metal Universe Promo Sheet

This six-card perforated sheet was distributed to dealers, distributors and media members to promote the 1997-98 Metal Universe Basketball set. The sheet was geared toward the younger players, with Kobe Bryant, Tim Duncan and Kevin Garnett, and also included spokesman Grant Hill. All six cards on the sheet were base cards.

		MT
Complete Set (6):		10.00
Common Player:		1.00
9	Keith Van Horn	1.00
26	Allen Iverson	1.00
33	Grant Hill	2.00
41	Kevin Garnett	2.00
72	Tim Duncan	2.00
86	Kobe Bryant	2.00

1997-98 Metal Universe

The first series of Metal Universe contained 125 cards, including two checklists. Cards featured comic-art illustrations on 100 percent etched foil fronts. The set included some rookies, like Tim Duncan, Keith Van Horn, Tracy McGrady and Ron Mercer, and sold in eight-card packs. A Series II issue arrived later in the season, but was called Championship Series. Insert sets in Series I included: Silver Slams, Planet Metal, Titanium, Autographics, Gold Universe, Platinum Portraits and Reebok, as well as a 123-card parallel set called Precious Metal Gems.

		MT
Complete Set (125):		25.00
Common Player:		.10
Minor Stars:		.20
Pack:		3.50
Wax Box:		80.00
1	Charles Barkley	.50
2	Dell Curry	.10
3	Derek Fisher	.10
4	Derek Harper	.10
5	Avery Johnson	.10
6	Steve Smith	.10
7	Alonzo Mourning	.20
8	Rod Strickland	.10
9	Chris Mullin	.20
10	Rony Seikaly	.10
11	Vin Baker	.30
12	*Austin Croshere*	1.00
13	Vinny Del Negro	.10
14	Sherman Douglas	.10
15	Priest Lauderdale	.10
16	Cedric Ceballos	.10
17	LaPhonso Ellis	.10
18	Luc Longley	.10
19	Brian Grant	.10
20	Allen Iverson	1.50
21	Anthony Mason	.10
22	Bryant Reeves	.20
23	Michael Jordan	4.00
24	Dale Ellis	.10
25	Terrell Brandon	.20
26	Patrick Ewing	.30
27	Allan Houston	.10
28	Damon Stoudamire	.50
29	Loy Vaught	.10
30	Walt Williams	.10
31	Shareef Abdur-Rahim	.75
32	Mario Elie	.10
33	Juwan Howard	.40
34	Tom Gugliotta	.10
35	Glen Rice	.20
36	Isaiah Rider	.10
37	Arvydas Sabonis	.10
38	Derrick Coleman	.10
39	Kevin Willis	.10
40	Kendall Gill	.10
41	John Wallace	.20
42	*Tracy McGrady*	3.00
43	Travis Best	.10
44	Malik Rose	.10
45	Anfernee Hardaway	1.75
46	Roy Rogers	.10
47	Kerry Kittles	.40
48	Matt Maloney	.20
49	Antonio McDyess	.30
50	Shaquille O'Neal	1.50
51	George McCloud	.10
52	Wesley Person	.10
53	Shawn Bradley	.10
54	Antonio Davis	.10
55	P.J. Brown	.10
56	Joe Dumars	.10
57	Horace Grant	.10
58	Steve Kerr	.10
59	Hakeem Olajuwon	.75
60	Tim Hardaway	.20
61	Toni Kukoc	.20
62	*Ron Mercer*	3.00
63	Gary Payton	.40
64	Grant Hill	2.00
65	Detlef Schrempf	.10
66	*Tim Duncan*	5.00
67	Shawn Kemp	.60
68	Voshon Lenard	.10
69	Othella Harrington	.10
70	Hersey Hawkins	.10
71	Lindsey Hunter	.10
72	Antoine Walker	1.50
73	Jamal Mashburn	.20
74	Kenny Anderson	.10
75	Todd Day	.10
76	Todd Fuller	.10
77	Jermaine O'Neal	.20
78	David Robinson	.50
79	Erick Dampier	.10
80	*Keith Van Horn*	2.00
81	Kobe Bryant	3.00
82	Chris Childs	.10
83	Scottie Pippen	1.00
84	Marcus Camby	.75
85	Danny Ferry	.10
86	Jeff Hornacek	.10
87	Charles Outlaw	.10
88	Larry Johnson	.20
89	Tony Delk	.10
90	Stephon Marbury	1.25
91	Robert Pack	.10
92	Chris Webber	.75
93	Clyde Drexler	.40
94	Eddie Jones	.50
95	Jerry Stackhouse	.40
96	Tyrone Hill	.10
97	Karl Malone	.40
98	Reggie Miller	.30
99	Bryan Russell	.10
100	Dale Davis	.10
101	Steve Nash	.10
102	Vitaly Potapenko	.10
103	Nick Anderson	.10
104	Ray Allen	.40
105	Sean Elliott	.10
106	Dikembe Mutombo	.10
107	Dennis Rodman	1.00
108	Lorenzen Wright	.10
109	Kevin Garnett	2.00
110	Christian Laettner	.20
111	Mitch Richmond	.20
112	Joe Smith	.40
113	Jason Kidd	.40
114	Glenn Robinson	.30
115	Mark Price	.10
116	Mark Jackson	.10
117	Bobby Phills	.10
118	John Starks	.10
119	John Stockton	.30
120	Mookie Blaylock	.10
121	Dean Garrett	.10
122	Olden Polynice	.10
123	Latrell Sprewell	.30
124	Checklist	.10
125	Checklist	.10

1997-98 Metal Universe Precious Metal Gems

Precious Metal Gems paralleled the first 123 cards in Metal Universe, excluding the two checklists. The cards are sequentially numbered to 123 and were inserted only into hobby packs. The first 10 numbered sets are printed with green foil, while the rest are printed on red foil.

	MT
Metal Gem Stars:	75x-150x
Metal Gem Rookies:	25x-50x
Production 100 Sets	
Metal Gem Green Stars:	5x-10x
Metal Gem Green Rookies:	3x-6x
First 10 Cards Are Green	

1997-98 Metal Universe Gold Universe

Gold Universe was a 10-card insert set that was found in one per 120 retail packs of Metal Universe. Fronts featured a color shot of the player over a gold-etched, solar system background. Card backs were horizontal with a close-up of the player on the left and text on the right. Cards were numbered "of 10" and carried a "GU" suffix.

		MT
Complete Set (10):		140.00
Common Player:		10.00
1	Damon Stoudamire	30.00
2	Shawn Kemp	20.00
3	John Stockton	10.00
4	Jerry Stackhouse	20.00
5	John Wallace	10.00
6	Juwan Howard	20.00
7	David Robinson	20.00
8	Gary Payton	20.00
9	Joe Smith	20.00
10	Charles Barkley	20.00

1997-98 Metal Universe Planet Metal

Planet Metal was a 15-card insert set that was found in every 24 packs of Metal Universe. Cards feature a color shot of the player over a silver-etched background, with a basketball at his feet and a black strip across the middle containing the insert's name. Backs were horizontal and numbered "x of 15" with a "PM" suffix.

		MT
Complete Set (15):		120.00
Common Player:		3.00
1	Michael Jordan	30.00
2	Allen Iverson	15.00
3	Kobe Bryant	20.00
4	Shaquille O'Neal	10.00
5	Stephon Marbury	12.00
6	Marcus Camby	8.00
7	Anfernee Hardaway	12.00
8	Kevin Garnett	15.00
9	Shareef Abdur-Rahim	8.00
10	Dennis Rodman	10.00
11	Grant Hill	15.00
12	Hakeem Olajuwon	6.00
13	David Robinson	3.00
14	Charles Barkley	3.00
15	Gary Payton	3.00

1997-98 Metal Universe Platinum Portraits

This 15-card insert was seeded only one per 288 packs of Series I. It includes a laser-cut close-up shot of the player on a platinum card. The player's name runs up the left side along the insert's name. Backs capture the reverse shot of the player, with card numbers in the upper right with a "PP" suffix.

		MT
Complete Set (15):		700.00
Common Player:		25.00
1	Michael Jordan	180.00
2	Allen Iverson	90.00
3	Kobe Bryant	120.00
4	Shaquille O'Neal	75.00
5	Stephon Marbury	75.00
6	Marcus Camby	35.00
7	Anfernee Hardaway	75.00
8	Kevin Garnett	90.00
9	Shareef Abdur-Rahim	35.00
10	Dennis Rodman	75.00
11	Ray Allen	25.00
12	Grant Hill	90.00
13	Kerry Kittles	25.00
14	Antoine Walker	30.00
15	Scottie Pippen	35.00

1997-98 Metal Universe Reebok Value

This 15-card insert arrived in bronze, silver and gold versions and included Reebok spokesmen. The versions are virtually identical to regular-issue cards of the players, except for a Reebok logo on the back and a Web site address to Reebok's Web page.

		MT
Complete Set (15):		3.00
Common Player:		.10
Silver Cards:		1.5x
Gold Cards:		2x
5	Avery Johnson	.10
6	Steve Smith	.10
13	Vinny Del Negro	.10
16	Cedric Ceballos	.10
20	Allen Iverson	1.00
32	Mario Elie	.10
50	Shaquille O'Neal	1.00
67	Shawn Kemp	.30
68	Voshon Lenard	.10
74	Kenny Anderson	.10
91	Robert Pack	.10
93	Clyde Drexler	.25
96	Tyrone Hill	.10
114	Glenn Robinson	.20
116	Mark Jackson	.10

1997-98 Metal Universe Silver Slams

Silver Slams was a 20-card insert that was seeded one per 12 packs of Series I. The cards featured a color shot of the player over a holographic bronze/silver background depending on the angle the light is hitting. Horizontal backs include a black-and-white shot of the player on the left, with text in white letters on the right. Cards are numbered "of 20" and carry a "SS" suffix.

		MT
Complete Set (20):		45.00
Common Player:		.75
1	Ray Allen	2.50
2	Kerry Kittles	2.00
3	Antoine Walker	4.00
4	Scottie Pippen	5.00
5	Damon Stoudamire	3.00
6	Shawn Kemp	3.00
7	Jerry Stackhouse	2.00
8	John Wallace	.75
9	Juwan Howard	3.00
10	Gary Payton	2.00
11	Joe Smith	2.00
12	Terrell Brandon	.75
13	Hakeem Olajuwon	4.00
14	Tom Gugliotta	.75
15	Glen Rice	.75
16	Charles Barkley	2.50
17	David Robinson	2.50
18	Patrick Ewing	1.50
19	Christian Laettner	.75
20	Chris Webber	4.00

1997-98 Metal Universe Titanium

These die-cut plastic cards were printed on a horizontal design and included holgraphic highlights within the plastic. The set contains 20 cards and was seeded one per 72 hobby packs. Backs were numbered "x of 20" and contain a "T" suffix.

		MT
Complete Set (20):		525.00
Common Player:		6.00
1	Michael Jordan	100.00
2	Allen Iverson	50.00
3	Kobe Bryant	70.00
4	Shaquille O'Neal	40.00
5	Stephon Marbury	40.00
6	Marcus Camby	20.00
7	Anfernee Hardaway	40.00
8	Kevin Garnett	50.00
9	Shareef Abdur-Rahim	25.00
10	Dennis Rodman	40.00
11	Ray Allen	6.00
12	Grant Hill	50.00
13	Kerry Kittles	6.00
14	Antoine Walker	20.00
15	Scottie Pippen	25.00
16	Damon Stoudamire	20.00
17	Shawn Kemp	15.00
18	Hakeem Olajuwon	20.00
19	Jerry Stackhouse	15.00
20	Juwan Howard	12.00

1997-98 Metal Universe Championship

This 100-card set was essentially the Series II release for 1997-98. It included 98 regular player cards and two checklists and was oriented toward the playoffs. Each regular-issue card featured the veterans superimposed on an Earth landscape, while the rookies are featured over an intergalactic background. The full set is paralleled (minus the two checklists) in a Precious Metals insert. Other inserts include: All-Millennium Team, Future Champions, Trophy Case, Championship Galaxy, Hardware and Autographics.

		MT
Complete Set (100):		30.00
Common Player:		.10
Minor Stars:		.20
Pack (8):		2.50
Box:		50.00
1	Shaquille O'Neal	1.50
2	Chris Mills	.10
3	*Tariq Abdul-Wahad*	.50
4	*Adonal Foyle*	.75
5	Kendall Gill	.10
6	Vin Baker	.30
7	*Chauncey Billups*	2.00
8	*Bobby Jackson*	1.50
9	*Keith Van Horn*	2.00
10	Avery Johnson	.10
11	Juwan Howard	.40
12	Steve Smith	.10
13	Alonzo Mourning	.20
14	Anfernee Hardaway	1.50
15	Sean Elliott	.10
16	*Danny Fortson*	.75
17	John Stockton	.30
18	*John Thomas*	.20
19	Lorenzen Wright	.10
20	Mark Price	.10
21	Rasheed Wallace	.10
22	Ray Allen	.40
23	Michael Jordan	4.00
24	John Wallace	.10
25	Bryant Reeves	.10
26	Allen Iverson	1.50
27	Antoine Walker	1.00
28	Terrell Brandon	.20
29	Damon Stoudamire	.50
30	*Antonio Daniels*	1.50
31	Corey Beck	.10
32	Tyrone Hill	.10
33	Grant Hill	2.00
34	*Tim Thomas*	2.00
35	Clifford Robinson	.10
36	*Tracy McGrady*	2.50
37	Chris Webber	.75
38	*Austin Croshere*	.50
39	Reggie Miller	.30
40	*Derek Anderson*	1.00
41	Kevin Garnett	2.00
42	Kevin Johnson	.20
43	Antonio McDyess	.30
44	*Brevin Knight*	1.50
45	Charles Barkley	.50
46	Tom Gugliotta	.20
47	Jason Kidd	.50
48	Marcus Camby	.50
49	*God Shammgod*	.20
50	Wesley Person	.10
51	Clyde Drexler	.40
52	Paul Grant	.10
53	Rod Strickland	.10
54	Tony Delk	.10
55	Stephon Marbury	1.50
56	Detlef Schrempf	.10
57	Joe Smith	.40
58	Sam Cassell	.10
59	Gary Payton	.40
60	Chris Crawford	.10
61	Hakeem Olajuwon	.75
62	Dennis Rodman	1.25
63	Eddie Jones	.50
64	Mitch Richmond	.30
65	David Wesley	.10
66	*Tony Battie*	1.00
67	Isaac Austin	.10
68	Isaiah Rider	.10
69	*Jacque Vaughn*	.50
70	Tim Hardaway	.20
71	Darrell Armstrong	.10
72	*Tim Duncan*	5.00
73	Glen Rice	.30
74	Bubba Wells	.10
75	*Maurice Taylor*	.75
76	*Kelvin Cato*	.20
77	Shareef Abdur-Rahim	1.00
78	Shawn Kemp	.50
79	Michael Finley	.20
80	Chris Mullin	.20
81	*Ron Mercer*	3.00
82	Brian Williams	.10
83	Kerry Kittles	.30
84	David Robinson	.50
85	Scottie Pippen	1.00
86	Kobe Bryant	3.00
87	Anthony Johnson	.10
88	Karl Malone	.30
89	Mookie Blaylock	.10
90	Joe Dumars	.10
91	Patrick Ewing	.30
92	Bobby Phills	.10
93	Dennis Scott	.10
94	Rodney Rogers	.10
95	Jim Jackson	.10
96	Kenny Anderson	.10
97	Jerry Stackhouse	.40
98	Larry Johnson	.20
99	Checklist	.10
100	Checklist	.10

1997-98 Metal Universe Championship Precious Metal Gems

Precious Metal Gems paralleled 98 of the 100 cards in Metal Universe Championship, excluding the two checklists. The stated print run for this parallel is 50 sequentially numbered sets.

	MT
Metal Gem Stars:	75x-150x
Metal Gem Rookies:	40x-80x
Production 50 Sets	

1997-98 Metal Universe Championship All-Millenium Team

All-Millennium Team included 20 young stars over a gold foil etched Spalding basketball background. These cards are seeded one per six packs, while card backs are numbered with a "AM" suffix.

		MT
Complete Set (20):		40.00
Common Player:		.50
Minor Stars:		1.00
1	Stephon Marbury	6.00
2	Shareef Abdur-Rahim	3.00
3	Karl Malone	1.00
4	Scottie Pippen	3.00
5	Michael Jordan	12.00
6	Marcus Camby	.50
7	Kobe Bryant	8.00
8	Allen Iverson	6.00
9	Kerry Kittles	1.00
10	Ray Allen	1.00
11	Dennis Rodman	4.00
12	Damon Stoudamire	1.50
13	Antoine Walker	3.00
14	Anfernee Hardaway	6.00
15	Hakeem Olajuwon	2.50
16	Shawn Kemp	1.50
17	Antonio Daniels	.50
18	Juwan Howard	1.50
19	Gary Payton	1.50
20	Tim Duncan	6.00

1997-98 Metal Universe Championship Championship Galaxy

This 20-card insert highlights players who have won NBA Championships. Fronts are presented in three layers - a foil background, double-etched player image and brushed silver foil frame with embossed rivets. Cards were inserted one per 192 packs and carry a "CG" suffix.

		MT
Complete Set (15):		525.00
Common Player:		8.00
1	Michael Jordan	120.00
2	Allen Iverson	45.00
3	Kobe Bryant	80.00
4	Shaquille O'Neal	40.00
5	Stephon Marbury	45.00
6	Marcus Camby	8.00
7	Anfernee Hardaway	45.00
8	Kevin Garnett	60.00
9	Shareef Abdur-Rahim	30.00
10	Dennis Rodman	40.00
11	Grant Hill	60.00
12	Kerry Kittles	8.00
13	Antoine Walker	25.00
14	Scottie Pippen	30.00
15	Damon Stoudamire	12.00

1997-98 Metal Universe Championship Future Champions

Fifteen rookies from the 1997 NBA Draft are included in the Future Champions insert set. The cards give off a three-dimensional look with an action photo of the player encased in a copper form that appears to be hanging from the sky. Each die-cut card is inserted one per 18 packs and carries a "FC" suffix.

Complete Set (15):		85.00
Common Player:		2.00
1	Tim Duncan	20.00
2	Tony Battie	5.00
3	Keith Van Horn	10.00
4	Antonio Daniels	6.00
5	Chauncey Billups	8.00
6	Ron Mercer	12.00
7	Tracy McGrady	10.00
8	Danny Fortson	3.00
9	Brevin Knight	8.00
10	Derek Anderson	6.00
11	Bobby Jackson	6.00
12	Jacque Vaughn	2.00
13	Tim Thomas	8.00
14	Austin Croshere	2.00
15	Kelvin Cato	2.00

1997-98 Metal Universe Championship Hardware

This one-per-360-pack insert set captures 15 players who have the best shot to win top NBA awards. Fronts offer dual foil including an embossed background and a gold rainbow holographic background. Cards are inserted one per 360 packs and are numbered with a "H" suffix.

		MT
Complete Set (15):		800.00
Common Player:		15.00
1	Stephon Marbury	70.00
2	Shareef Abdur-Rahim	50.00
3	Shaquille O'Neal	60.00
4	Scottie Pippen	50.00
5	Michael Jordan	180.00
6	Marcus Camby	15.00
7	Kobe Bryant	120.00
8	Kevin Garnett	100.00
9	Kerry Kittles	15.00
10	Grant Hill	100.00
11	Dennis Rodman	60.00
12	Tim Duncan	100.00
13	Antonio Daniels	50.00
14	Anfernee Hardaway	70.00
15	Allen Iverson	70.00

1997-98 Metal Universe Championship Trophy Case

Trophy Case includes 10 players on a gold foil sculpted embossed background. The insert's name runs across the top of the card, while the player's name runs across the bottom. Cards are inserted every 96 packs and numbered with a "TC" suffix.

		MT
Complete Set (10):		120.00
Common Player:		4.00
1	Kevin Garnett	30.00
2	Grant Hill	30.00
3	Damon Stoudamire	10.00
4	Shaquille O'Neal	20.00
5	Ray Allen	4.00
6	Gary Payton	8.00
7	Shawn Kemp	8.00
8	Hakeem Olajuwon	12.00
9	John Stockton	4.00
10	Antoine Walker	15.00

1998-99 Metal Universe

Metal Universe was released in a single series, 125-card set in 1998-99 during the lockout. It contained 123 regular cards and two checklists, and was paralleled in Precious Metal Gems (numbered to 50) and Gem Masters (one of one) sets. What would have been Series II for this product was upgraded into the launch of Molten Metal. Inserts in Metal Universe include: Neophytes, Big Ups, Planet Metal, Two 4 Me, Zero 4 You, Linchpins and Autographics.

		MT
Complete Set (125):		25.00
Common Player:		.15
Minor Stars:		.30
Pack (8):		2.50
Wax Box (24):		55.00
1	Michael Jordan	5.00
2	Mario Elie	.15
3	Voshon Lenard	.15
4	John Starks	.15
5	Juwan Howard	.30
6	Michael Finley	.30
7	Bobby Jackson	.30
8	Glenn Robinson	.30
9	Antonio McDyess	.30
10	Marcus Camby	.30
11	Zydrunas Ilgauskas	.30
12	Tony Battie	.15
13	Terrell Brandon	.30
14	Kevin Johnson	.15
15	Rod Strickland	.15
16	Dennis Rodman	1.50
17	Clarence Weatherspoon	.15
18	P.J. Brown	.15
19	Anfernee Hardaway	1.50
20	Dikembe Mutombo	.30
21	Travis Best	.15
22	Patrick Ewing	.30
23	Sam Mack	.15
24	Scottie Pippen	1.25
25	Shaquille O'Neal	1.50
26	Donyell Marshall	.15
27	Bo Outlaw	.15
28	Isaiah Rider	.15
29	Detlef Schrempf	.15
30	Mark Price	.15
31	Jim Jackson	.15
32	Eddie Jones	.75
33	Allen Iverson	1.25
34	Corliss Williamson	.15
35	Tim Duncan	2.50
36	Ron Harper	.15
37	Tony Delk	.15
38	Derek Fisher	.15
39	Kendall Gill	.15
40	Theo Ratliff	.15
41	Kelvin Cato	.15
42	Antoine Walker	1.00
43	Lamond Murray	.15
44	Avery Johnson	.15
45	John Stockton	.30
46	David Wesley	.15
47	Brian Williams	.15
48	Elden Campbell	.15
49	Sam Cassell	.15
50	Grant Hill	2.50
51	Tracy McGrady	1.25
52	Glen Rice	.30
53	Kobe Bryant	3.00
54	Cherokee Parks	.15
55	John Wallace	.15
56	Bobby Phills	.15
57	Jerry Stackhouse	.30
58	Lorenzen Wright	.15
59	Stephon Marbury	1.50
60	Shandon Anderson	.15
61	Jeff Hornacek	.15
62	Joe Dumars	.15
63	Tom Gugliotta	.30
64	Johnny Newman	.15
65	Kevin Garnett	2.50
66	Clifford Robinson	.15
67	Dennis Scott	.15
68	Anthony Mason	.15
69	Rodney Rogers	.15
70	Bryon Russell	.15
71	Maurice Taylor	.30
72	Mookie Blaylock	.15
73	Shawn Bradley	.15
74	Matt Maloney	.15
75	Karl Malone	.50
76	Larry Johnson	.30
77	Calbert Cheaney	.15
78	Steve Smith	.15
79	Toni Kukoc	.15
80	Reggie Miller	.30
81	Jayson Williams	.15
82	Gary Payton	.50
83	George Lynch	.15
84	Wesley Person	.15
85	Charles Barkley	.50
86	Tim Hardaway	.30
87	Darrell Armstrong	.15
88	Rasheed Wallace	.15
89	Tariq Abdul-Wahad	.15
90	Kenny Anderson	.15
91	Chris Mullin	.15
92	Keith Van Horn	1.50
93	Hersey Hawkins	.15
94	Billy Owens	.15
95	Ron Mercer	1.50
96	Rik Smits	.15
97	David Robinson	.50
98	Derek Anderson	.50
99	Danny Fortson	.15
100	Jason Kidd	.50
101	Sean Elliott	.15
102	Chauncey Billups	.50
103	Tyrone Hill	.15
104	Alan Henderson	.15
105	Chris Anstey	.15
106	Hakeem Olajuwon	.75
107	Allan Houston	.30
108	Bryant Reeves	.15
109	Anthony Johnson	.15
110	Shawn Kemp	.60
111	Brevin Knight	.50
112	A.C. Green	.15
113	Ray Allen	.30
114	Tim Thomas	1.25
115	Walter McCarty	.15
116	Jalen Rose	.15
117	Kerry Kittles	.30
118	Vin Baker	.50
119	Shareef Abdur-Rahim	1.25
120	Alonzo Mourning	.30
121	Joe Smith	.30
122	Tracy Murray	.15
123	Damon Stoudamire	.50
124	Checklist	.15
125	Checklist	.15

1998-99 Metal Universe Precious Metal Gems

This 123-card parallel set reprinted the Metal Universe set (excluding the two checklists). Cards were sequentially numbered to 50 sets on the back.

	MT
Precious Metal Gems:	50x-100x
Production 50 Sets	

1998-99 Metal Universe Big Ups

This 15-card insert featured the player over a planet background, and was inserted 1:18 packs. Cards were numbered with a "BU" suffix.

		MT
Complete Set (15):		65.00
Common Player:		1.25
Minor Stars:		2.50
Inserted 1:18		
1	Stephon Marbury	10.00
2	Shareef Abdur-Rahim	6.00
3	Scottie Pippen	6.00
4	Marcus Camby	1.25
5	Ray Allen	1.25
6	Allen Iverson	8.00
7	Kerry Kittles	1.25
8	Dennis Rodman	10.00
9	Damon Stoudamire	2.50
10	Antoine Walker	5.00
11	Anfernee Hardaway	10.00
12	Shawn Kemp	3.00
13	Juwan Howard	2.50
14	Gary Payton	4.00
15	Tim Duncan	15.00

1998-99 Metal Universe Linchpins

Linchpins was a 10-card insert set found only 1:360 packs of Metal Universe. The cards featured a player over a blue, explosive background with small laser-cut linchpins cut out of the card. These were numbered with an "LP" suffix.

		MT
Complete Set (10):		400.00
Common Player:		20.00
Inserted 1:360		
1	Shaquille O'Neal	40.00
2	Kobe Bryant	80.00
3	Kevin Garnett	60.00
4	Grant Hill	60.00
5	Shawn Kemp	15.00
6	Keith Van Horn	30.00
7	Antoine Walker	25.00
8	Michael Jordan	120.00
9	Gary Payton	20.00
10	Tim Duncan	60.00

1998-99 Metal Universe Neophytes

Neophytes included 15 top young stars over a foil background with gold highlights. These were seeded 1:6 packs and numbered with an "NE" suffix.

		MT
Complete Set (15):		25.00
Common Player:		.50
Minor Stars:		1.00
Inserted 1:6		
1	Antonio Daniels	1.00
2	Bobby Jackson	1.00
3	Brevin Knight	2.00
4	Chauncey Billups	2.00
5	Danny Fortson	.50
6	Derek Anderson	2.00
7	Jacque Vaughn	.50
8	Keith Van Horn	4.00
9	Maurice Taylor	2.00
10	Michael Stewart	.50
11	Ron Mercer	4.00
12	Tim Thomas	4.00
13	Tim Duncan	8.00
14	Tracy McGrady	3.00
15	Zydrunas Ilgauskas	1.00

1998-99 Metal Universe Planet Metal

Planet Metal featured 15 players on a die-cut planet background. These were inserted 1:36 packs of Metal and numbered with a "PM" suffix.

		MT
Complete Set (15):		160.00
Common Player:		3.00
Minor Stars:		6.00
Inserted 1:36		
1	Michael Jordan	45.00
2	Antoine Walker	10.00
3	Scottie Pippen	12.00
4	Grant Hill	25.00
5	Dennis Rodman	15.00
6	Kobe Bryant	30.00
7	Kevin Garnett	25.00
8	Shaquille O'Neal	15.00
9	Stephon Marbury	20.00
10	Kerry Kittles	3.00
11	Anfernee Hardaway	15.00
12	Allen Iverson	15.00
13	Damon Stoudamire	6.00
14	Marcus Camby	3.00
15	Shareef Abdur-Rahim	12.00

1998-99 Metal Universe Two 4 Me

Two 4 Me, Zero 4 You was a 15-card, double-sided insert that featured the player on offense on one side and playing defense on the other. These were inserted 1:96 packs of Metal Universe and numbered with a "TZ" suffix.

Complete Set (15):		250.00
Common Player:		10.00
Inserted 1:96		
1	Kobe Bryant	40.00
2	Anfernee Hardaway	20.00
3	Allen Iverson	15.00
4	Michael Jordan	60.00
5	Stephon Marbury	20.00
6	Ron Mercer	20.00
7	Shareef Abdur-Rahim	15.00
8	Marcus Camby	10.00
9	Damon Stoudamire	10.00
10	Kevin Garnett	30.00
11	Grant Hill	30.00
12	Scottie Pippen	15.00
13	Keith Van Horn	15.00
14	Dennis Rodman	20.00
15	Shaquille O'Neal	20.00

1998-99 SkyBox Molten Metal

SkyBox Molten Metal made its debut with 150 cards in a three-tiered set. Cards 1-100 were considered the base cards and inserted four per pack. Cards 101-130 were inserted one per pack, while cards 131-150 were inserted one per two packs. The base tier contained most of the rookies, with five of the top picks included in the third tier. No rookies were found in the middle tier. Veterans were placed in tiers depending on their status in the league, with top players in the third tier and commons in the first. Inserts included every card in the set reprinted on metal in an Xplosion insert, and the second and third tiers reprinted in Fusion and Titanium Fusion parallels.

		MT
Complete Set (150):		150.00
Common Player (1-100):		.20
Minor Stars (1-100):		.40
Inserted 4:1		
Common Player (101-130):		.25
Minor Stars (101-130):		.50
Inserted 1:1		
Common Player (131-150):		1.50
Inserted 1:2		
Pack (6):		5.50
Wax Box (24):		120.00
1	Maurice Taylor	.40
2	Brian Williams	.20
3	Anthony Mason	.20
4	John Starks	.20
5	Anthony Johnson	.20
6	Calbert Cheaney	.20
7	Roshown McLeod	3.00
8	Jalen Rose	.20
9	Kelvin Cato	.40
10	Walter McCarty	.20
11	Isaac Austin	.20
12	Arvydas Sabonis	.20
13	David Wesley	.20
14	Jim Jackson	.20
15	Elden Campbell	.20
16	*Michael Doleac*	1.50
17	Chris Webber	.75
18	Mitch Richmond	.40
19	Johnny Newman	.20
20	Jayson Williams	.20
21	George Lynch	.20
22	Ron Harper	.20
23	Donyell Marshall	.20
24	Derek Fisher	.20
25	*Matt Harpring*	2.00
26	*Jason Williams*	8.00
27	Toni Kukoc	.40
28	Clarence Weatherspoon	.20
29	Eddie Jones	.75
30	Charles Outlaw	.20
31	Zydrunas Ilgauskas	.40
32	*Michael Dickerson*	3.00
33	*Tyronn Lue*	1.00
34	Theo Ratliff	.20
35	*Dirk Nowitzki*	10.00
36	*Robert Traylor*	2.00
37	Gary Trent	.20
38	Wesley Person	.20
39	*Bryce Drew*	1.00
40	P.J. Brown	.20
41	Joe Smith	.40
42	Avery Johnson	.20
43	Chris Anstey	.20
44	Mario Elie	.20
45	Voshon Lenard	.20
46	Rex Chapman	.20
47	Hersey Hawkins	.20
48	Shawn Bradley	.20
49	Matt Maloney	.20
50	Dan Majerle	.20
51	*Pat Garrity*	2.00
52	Sam Perkins	.20
53	Mookie Blaylock	.20
54	*Al Harrington*	5.00
55	Clifford Robinson	.20
56	Alan Henderson	.20
57	Chris Mullin	.20
58	Dennis Scott	.20
59	A.C. Green	.20
60	Tyrone Hill	.20
61	Chauncey Billups	.40
62	Michael Finley	.40
63	Terrell Brandon	.40
64	Detlef Schrempf	.20
65	*Bonzi Wells*	8.00
66	Larry Johnson	.40
67	Bryant Reeves	.40
68	*Raef LaFrentz*	5.00
69	Kendall Gill	.20
70	Bryon Russell	.20
71	Bobby Phills	.20
72	Tony Delk	.20
73	Lorenzen Wright	.20
74	*Keon Clark*	2.00
75	Billy Owens	.20
76	Tracy Murray	.20
77	Bobby Jackson	.20
78	Sam Cassell	.20
79	Corliss Williamson	.20
80	Jeff Hornacek	.20
81	LaPhonso Ellis	.20
82	Sam Mitchell	.20
83	Sean Elliott	.20
84	John Wallace	.40
85	Dikembe Mutombo	.40
86	Rik Smits	.20
87	Isaiah Rider	.20
88	Joe Dumars	.20
89	Allan Houston	.40
90	Sam Mack	.20
91	*Paul Pierce*	10.00
92	Lamond Murray	.20
93	Rasheed Wallace	.20
94	Danny Fortson	.20
95	Cherokee Parks	.20
96	Antonio Daniels	.20
97	Shandon Anderson	.20
98	*Ricky Davis*	3.00
99	Rodney Rogers	.20
100	Tariq Abdul-Wahad	.20
101	Glenn Robinson	.50
102	Ron Mercer	2.00
103	Alonzo Mourning	.50
104	Marcus Camby	.50
105	Steve Smith	.50
106	Tim Hardaway	.75
107	Rod Strickland	.50
108	Reggie Miller	.50
109	Juwan Howard	.50
110	Hakeem Olajuwon	1.00
111	John Stockton	.50
112	Antonio McDyess	.75
113	Charles Barkley	.75
114	Karl Malone	.75
115	Jerry Stackhouse	.50
116	Tracy McGrady	1.50
117	Brevin Knight	.50
118	Gary Payton	.50
119	Derek Anderson	.50
120	Glen Rice	.50
121	David Robinson	.75
122	Vin Baker	.75
123	Tom Gugliotta	.50
124	Patrick Ewing	.50
125	Ray Allen	.50
126	Anfernee Hardaway	2.00
127	Jason Kidd	1.25
128	Kenny Anderson	.25
129	Kerry Kittles	.50
130	Tim Thomas	1.25
131	Shareef Abdur-Rahim	2.50
132	*Mike Bibby*	6.00
133	Kobe Bryant	10.00
134	*Vince Carter*	40.00
135	Tim Duncan	8.00
136	Kevin Garnett	8.00
137	Grant Hill	8.00
138	*Larry Hughes*	10.00
139	Allen Iverson	5.00
140	*Antawn Jamison*	12.00
141	Michael Jordan	15.00
142	Shawn Kemp	1.50
143	Stephon Marbury	5.00
144	*Michael Olowokandi*	4.00
145	Shaquille O'Neal	5.00
146	Scottie Pippen	4.00
147	Dennis Rodman	4.00
148	Damon Stoudamire	1.50
149	Keith Van Horn	3.00
150	Antoine Walker	3.00

1998-99 SkyBox Molten Metal Xplosion

Xplosion reprinted all 150 cards from the base set on a metal card stock. Cards 1-100 were inserted 1:2.5 packs, 101-130 were inserted 1:18 packs and 131-150 were seeded 1:60 packs.

	MT
Veterans (1-100):	2x
Rookies (1-100):	1.5x
Inserted 1:2.5	
Veterans (101-130):	3x-6x
Inserted 1:18	
Veterans (131-150):	3x-6x
Rookies (131-150):	2x
Inserted 1:60)	

1998-99 SkyBox Molten Metal Fusion

The final 50 cards in Molten Metal (the second and third tiers) were reprinted in a Fusion parallel. Cards 1-30 in the Fusion set (101-130 of the base set) were inserted 1:16 packs, while cards 31-50 (131-150 of the base set) were numbered to 250. Due to a production error, 15 of the 20 silver-fronted Fusion cards were incorrectly labeled Titanium Fusion on the front. The players printed correctly include: Grant Hill, Allen Iverson, Michael Jordan, Shawn Kemp and Stephon Marbury. Our guide lists all silver fronted and numbered to 250 sets under Fusion, regardless of whether the front label is correct or not.

		MT
Common Player (101-130):		1.50
Inserted 1:16		
Common Player (131-150):		30.00
Numbered to 250		
Due to a production error, 15 of the Supernatural Fusion cards were labeled "Titanium Fusion." We've priced all silver and numbered to 250 versions under Fusion.		
1	Glenn Robinson	3.00
2	Ron Mercer	12.00
3	Alonzo Mourning	3.00
4	Marcus Camby	3.00
5	Steve Smith	3.00
6	Tim Hardaway	4.50
7	Rod Strickland	3.00
8	Reggie Miller	3.00
9	Juwan Howard	3.00
10	Hakeem Olajuwon	6.00
11	John Stockton	3.00
12	Antonio McDyess	4.50
13	Charles Barkley	4.50
14	Karl Malone	4.50
15	Jerry Stackhouse	3.00
16	Tracy McGrady	9.00
17	Brevin Knight	3.00
18	Gary Payton	3.00
19	Derek Anderson	3.00
20	Glen Rice	3.00
21	David Robinson	4.50
22	Vin Baker	4.50
23	Tom Gugliotta	3.00
24	Patrick Ewing	3.00
25	Ray Allen	3.00
26	Anfernee Hardaway	12.00
27	Jason Kidd	7.50
28	Kenny Anderson	1.50
29	Kerry Kittles	3.00
30	Tim Thomas	7.50
31	Shareef Abdur-Rahim	50.00
32	Mike Bibby	75.00
33	Kobe Bryant	200.00
34	Vince Carter	125.00
35	Tim Duncan	150.00
36	Kevin Garnett	150.00
37	Grant Hill	150.00
38	Larry Hughes	40.00
39	Allen Iverson	100.00
40	Antawn Jamison	60.00
41	Michael Jordan	300.00
42	Shawn Kemp	25.00
43	Stephon Marbury	100.00
44	Michael Olowokandi	60.00
45	Shaquille O'Neal	100.00
46	Scottie Pippen	75.00
47	Dennis Rodman	75.00
48	Damon Stoudamire	30.00
49	Keith Van Horn	50.00
50	Antoine Walker	50.00

1998-99 SkyBox Molten Metal Fusion Titanium Fusion

The entire Fusion insert was also available in a Titanium Fusion parallel. Cards 1-30 were inserted 1:96 packs, while 31-50 were numbered to 40 sets. As referenced in the Fusion set, 15 of the 20 cards are labeled incorrectly on the front as "Fusion." Our guide lists all Titanium colored fronts and numbered to 40 sets on the back cards under Titanium Fusion, regardless of what the front label indicates.

		MT
Common Player (101-130):		4.00
Inserted 1:96		
Common Player (131-150):		100.00
Numbered to 40		
Due to a production error, 15 of the Supernatural Titanium Fusion were labeleld "Fusion." We've priced all gold and numbered to 40 versions under Titanium Fusions, regardless of what the front says. Correct cards were Kemp, Jordan, Hill, Marbury and Iverson.		
1	Glenn Robinson	8.00
2	Ron Mercer	30.00
3	Alonzo Mourning	8.00
4	Marcus Camby	8.00
5	Steve Smith	4.00
6	Tim Hardaway	12.00
7	Rod Strickland	8.00
8	Reggie Miller	8.00
9	Juwan Howard	8.00
10	Hakeem Olajuwon	15.00
11	John Stockton	8.00
12	Antonio McDyess	12.00
13	Charles Barkley	12.00
14	Karl Malone	12.00
15	Jerry Stackhouse	8.00
16	Tracy McGrady	25.00
17	Brevin Knight	8.00
18	Gary Payton	8.00
19	Derek Anderson	8.00
20	Glen Rice	8.00
21	David Robinson	12.00
22	Vin Baker	12.00
23	Tom Gugliotta	8.00
24	Patrick Ewing	8.00
25	Ray Allen	8.00
26	Anfernee Hardaway	30.00
27	Jason Kidd	20.00
28	Kenny Anderson	4.00
29	Kerry Kittles	8.00
30	Tim Thomas	20.00
31	Shareef Abdur-Rahim	200.00
32	Mike Bibby	300.00
33	Kobe Bryant	800.00
34	Vince Carter	500.00
35	Tim Duncan	600.00
36	Kevin Garnett	600.00
37	Grant Hill	600.00
38	Larry Hughes	160.00
39	Allen Iverson	400.00
40	Antawn Jamison	240.00
41	Michael Jordan	1200.
42	Shawn Kemp	100.00
43	Stephon Marbury	400.00
44	Michael Olowokandi	240.00
45	Shaquille O'Neal	400.00
46	Scottie Pippen	300.00
47	Dennis Rodman	300.00
48	Damon Stoudamire	100.00
49	Keith Van Horn	150.00
50	Antoine Walker	200.00

1999-00 Metal

Metal consisted of 180 cards on metallic-looking designs with an etched-silver background. The set had 150 veterans and 30 rookies, which were seeded 1:2 packs. Each card was paralleled in an Emerald set, and the inserts included Rivalries, Platinum Portraits, Vince Carter Scrapbook, Scoring Magnets, Heavy Metal, Autographics and Genuine Coverage.

		MT
Complete Set (180):		50.00
Common Player:		.10
Minor Stars:		.20
Common Rookie:		.50
Inserted 1:2		
Pack (10):		2.00
Wax Box (28):		40.00
1	Vince Carter	3.00
2	Stephon Marbury	.50
3	David Robinson	.40
4	Ray Allen	.30
5	P.J. Brown	.10
6	Shawn Kemp	.20
7	Cedric Ceballos	.10
8	Dale Davis	.10
9	Rodney Rogers	.10
10	Chris Gatling	.10
11	Bryant Reeves	.10
12	Al Harrington	.30
13	Brent Barry	.10
14	Brevin Knight	.10
15	Radoslav Nesterovic	.10
16	Tom Gugliotta	.20
17	Charles Barkley	.40
18	Cuttino Mobley	.20
19	Corliss Williamson	.10
20	Hersey Hawkins	.10
21	Mike Bibby	.30
22	Pat Garrity	.20
23	Kelvin Cato	.10
24	Alan Henderson	.10
25	Alvin Williams	.10
26	Antonio McDyess	.30
27	Damon Stoudamire	.10
28	Kerry Kittles	.10
29	Michael Olowokandi	.20
30	Brent Price	.10
31	Fred Holberg	.10
32	Glenn Robinson	.20
33	Hakeem Olajuwon	.40
34	Monty Williams	.10
35	Terry Porter	.10
36	Allen Iverson	1.00
37	Juwan Howard	.20
38	Mario Elie	.10
39	Mookie Blaylock	.10
40	Sam Cassell	.20
41	Toni Kukoc	.30
42	Anthony Mason	.10
43	George Lynch	.10
44	John Starks	.10
45	Malik Rose	.10
46	Rod Strickland	.20
47	Tim Thomas	.30
48	Howard Eisley	.10
49	Kenny Anderson	.20
50	Kurt Thomas	.10
51	Lindsey Hunter	.10
52	Rick Fox	.10
53	Vlade Divac	.10
54	Avery Johnson	.10
55	Dale Ellis	.10
56	Donyell Marshall	.10
57	Elden Campbell	.10
58	Larry Hughes	.60
59	Mitch Richmond	.20
60	Chris Mills	.10
61	David Wesley	.10
62	Gary Payton	.40
63	Isaac Austin	.10
64	Robert Traylor	.20
65	Theo Ratliff	.10
66	Antawn Jamison	.60
67	Eddie Jones	.40
68	Kevin Garnett	2.00
69	Matt Geiger	.10
70	Vernon Maxwell	.10
71	Antonio Davis	.10
72	Dirk Nowitzki	.50
73	Johnny Newman	.10
74	Maurice Taylor	.20
75	Steve Smith	.20
76	Derek Anderson	.20
77	Doug Christie	.10
78	Erick Strickland	.10
79	Keith Van Horn	.40
80	Luc Longley	.10
81	Alonzo Mourning	.30
82	Christian Laettner	.10
83	Jamal Mashburn	.20
84	Jon Barry	.10
85	Patrick Ewing	.20
86	Shareef Abdur-Rahim	.50
87	Vitaly Potapenko	.10
88	Darrell Armstrong	.10
89	Eric Williams	.10
90	Jerome Williams	.10
91	Nick Anderson	.10
92	Othella Harrington	.10
93	Tim Hardaway	.30
94	Eric Piatkowski	.10
95	Isaiah Rider	.20
96	Kendall Gill	.10
97	Rasheed Wallace	.20
98	Robert Pack	.10
99	Tracy McGrady	.75
100	Allan Houston	.20
101	Brian Grant	.10
102	Dikembe Mutombo	.20
103	Karl Malone	.40
104	Nick Van Exel	.20
105	Shaquille O'Neal	1.00
106	Chris Anstey	.10
107	Michael Dickerson	.20
108	Shandon Anderson	.10
109	Tariq Abdul-Wahad	.10
110	Tim Duncan	2.00
111	Voshon Lenard	.10
112	Bimbo Coles	.10
113	Detlef Schrempf	.10
114	John Stockton	.20
115	Kobe Bryant	2.50
116	Latrell Sprewell	.40
117	Raef LaFrentz	.30
118	Antoine Walker	.30
119	Bryon Russell	.10
120	Derek Fisher	.10
121	Jason Williams	.75
122	Jerry Stackhouse	.20
123	Larry Johnson	.20
124	Clifford Robinson	.10
125	Horace Grant	.10
126	Malik Sealy	.10
127	Michael Finley	.20
128	Rik Smits	.10
129	Dell Curry	.10
130	Jim Jackson	.10
131	Ron Mercer	.40
132	Scott Burrell	.10
133	Scottie Pippen	.75
134	Troy Hudson	.10
135	Anfernee Hardaway	.75
136	Anthony Peeler	.10
137	Jalen Rose	.20
138	Lamond Murray	.10
139	Ruben Patterson	.20
140	Chris Webber	.75
141	Glen Rice	.20
142	Grant Hill	2.00
143	Jeff Hornacek	.10
144	Marcus Camby	.20
145	Paul Pierce	.75
146	Bob Sura	.10
147	Jason Kidd	.75
148	Reggie Miller	.20
149	Terrell Brandon	.20
150	Vin Baker	.20
151	*Lamar Odom*	6.00
152	*Steve Francis*	10.00
153	*Elton Brand*	4.00
154	*Wally Szczerbiak*	2.50
155	*Adrian Griffin*	.50
156	*Andre Miller*	2.50
157	*Jason Terry*	1.25
158	*Richard Hamilton*	2.00
159	*Ron Artest*	1.25
160	*Shawn Marion*	4.00
161	*James Posey*	1.00
162	*Greg Buckner*	.50
163	*Chucky Atkins*	.75
164	*Corey Maggette*	2.50
165	*Todd MacCulloch*	.50
166	*Baron Davis*	2.50
167	*Trajan Langdon*	1.00
168	*Bruno Sundov*	.50
169	*Scott Padgett*	.50
170	*Vonteego Cummings*	.75
171	*Ryan Bowen*	.50
172	*Jonathan Bender*	4.00
173	*Jermaine Jackson*	.50
174	*Devean George*	1.00
175	*Chris Herren*	.60
176	*Rodney Buford*	.60
177	*Laron Profit*	.60
178	*Mirsad Turkcan*	.50
179	*Eddie Robinson*	1.00
180	*Anthony Carter*	1.00

1999-00 Metal Emerald

This 180-card parallel set reprinted each card in the base set on an emerald-foil surface. Veterans were inserted 1:4 packs, while Rookies were seeded 1:8 packs. Emerald cards featured a black, capital "E" on the back with a circle around it.

	MT
Emerald Cards:	2x-4x
Inserted 1:4	
Emerald Rookies:	1x-2x
Inserted 1:8	

1999-00 Metal Genuine Coverage

This six-card insert set featured pieces of pre-game warm-ups from NBA players. The cards are unnumbered and listed in alphabetical order and inserted 1:288 packs.

	MT
Complete Set (6):	550.00
Common Player:	50.00
Inserted 1:288	
Vince Carter	300.00
Karl Malone	75.00
Shaquille O'Neal	150.00
Paul Pierce	60.00
John Stockton	60.00
Antoine Walker	40.00

1999-00 Metal Heavy Metal

This 10-card insert set showcases the NBA's top players on a holographic background. Cards are numbered with an "H" suffix and inserted 1:20 packs.

		MT
Complete Set (10):		20.00
Common Player:		.75
Inserted 1:20		
HM1	Kobe Bryant	6.00
HM2	Vince Carter	8.00
HM3	Lamar Odom	4.00
HM4	Kevin Garnett	5.00
HM5	Shawn Kemp	.50
HM6	Shareef Abdur-Rahim	1.50
HM7	Antonio McDyess	.75
HM8	Tim Duncan	5.00
HM9	Keith Van Horn	1.00
HM10	Shaquille O'Neal	3.00

1999-00 Metal Platinum Portraits

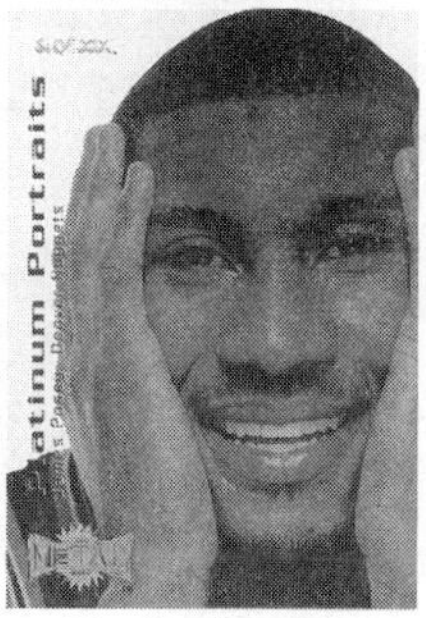

This 15-card insert features close-up facial shots from players selected in the 1999 NBA Draft. Cards have a white background, are numbered with a "PP" suffix and seeded 1:4 packs.

		MT
Complete Set (15):		15.00
Common Player:		.40
Inserted 1:4		
PP1	Elton Brand	4.00
PP2	Lamar Odom	4.00
PP3	Steve Francis	5.00
PP4	Richard Hamilton	1.00
PP5	Baron Davis	1.50
PP6	Vonteego Cummings	.75
PP7	Corey Maggette	2.00
PP8	James Posey	.75
PP9	Shawn Marion	1.50
PP10	Wally Szczerbiak	2.00
PP11	Jason Terry	.75
PP12	Andre Miller	1.50
PP13	Scott Padgett	.40
PP14	Trajan Langdon	.50
PP15	Jonathan Bender	2.00

1999-00 Metal Rivalries

This 15-card insert set highlights two players who share a similar style of play on a horizontal, split screen card with a silver foil finish. Rivalries are numbered with an "R" suffix and seeded 1:4 packs.

		MT
Complete Set (15):		15.00
Common Player:		.50
Inserted 1:4		
R1	Allen Iverson, Stephon Marbury	3.00
R2	Jason Kidd, Gary Payton	2.00
R3	Mike Bibby, Jason Williams	2.00
R4	Patrick Ewing, Alonzo Mourning	.50
R5	Tim Duncan, Kevin Garnett	4.00
R6	Anfernee Hardaway, Kobe Bryant	4.00
R7	Charles Barkley, Karl Malone	1.50
R8	Antonio McDyess, Shareef Abdur-Rahim	1.50
R9	Vince Carter, Grant Hill	5.00
R10	Antoine Walker, Keith Van Horn	.60
R11	Shawn Kemp, Elton Brand	1.50
R12	Shaquille O'Neal, David Robinson	3.00
R13	Raef LaFrentz, Dirk Nowitzki	2.00
R14	Steve Francis, John Stockton	2.50
R15	Lamar Odom, Scottie Pippen	3.00

1999-00 Metal Scoring Magnets

This 10-card die-cut insert showcases some of the game's top pure scorers. Scoring Magnets are numbered with an "SM" suffix and seeded 1:20 packs.

		MT
Complete Set (10):		15.00
Common Player:		.50
Inserted 1:20		
SM1	Grant Hill	6.00
SM2	Stephon Marbury	2.00
SM3	Allen Iverson	4.00
SM4	Ray Allen	.75
SM5	Steve Francis	5.00
SM6	Ron Mercer	1.00
SM7	Paul Pierce	2.50
SM8	Latrell Sprewell	1.50
SM9	Glenn Robinson	.50
SM10	Eddie Jones	1.50

1999-00 Metal V. Carter Scrapbook

This 10-card insert is devoted to Vince Carter, with shots of Carter on and off the court. The cards are numbered with a "VC" suffix and inserted 1:8 packs.

		MT
Complete Set (10):		25.00
Common Player:		3.00
Inserted 1:8		
VC1	Vince Carter	3.00
VC2	Vince Carter	3.00
VC3	Vince Carter	3.00
VC4	Vince Carter	3.00
VC5	Vince Carter	3.00
VC6	Vince Carter	3.00
VC7	Vince Carter	3.00
VC8	Vince Carter	3.00
VC9	Vince Carter	3.00
VC10	Vince Carter	3.00

1994 Metallic Impressions

Metallic Impressions produced this "Centers of Attention" set for Classic. Five of basketball's top centers are featured on four cards each. Only 12,500 sets were produced and each came with an individually numbered certificate of authenticity.

		MT
Complete Set (20):		50.00
Common Player:		1.50
1	Hakeem Olajuwon	4.00
2	Hakeem Olajuwon	4.00
3	Hakeem Olajuwon	4.00
4	Hakeem Olajuwon	4.00
5	Patrick Ewing	2.00
6	Patrick Ewing	2.00
7	Patrick Ewing	2.00
8	Patrick Ewing	2.00
9	Alonzo Mourning	2.00
10	Alonzo Mourning	2.00
11	Alonzo Mourning	2.00
12	Alonzo Mourning	2.00
13	Dikembe Mutombo	1.50
14	Dikembe Mutombo	1.50
15	Dikembe Mutombo	1.50
16	Dikembe Mutombo	1.50
17	Shaquille O'Neal	8.00
18	Shaquille O'Neal	8.00
19	Shaquille O'Neal	8.00
20	Shaquille O'Neal	8.00

1984-85 Miller Lite/NBA All-Star Charity Classic

This six-card set was distributed in conjunction with a half-court 3-on-3 charity game held at halftime of a

Dallas Mavericks game in 1984-85. The 5" x 7" cards feature a black-and-white action photo and logos for Spalding, Miller Lite, the Dallas Mavericks and KZEW-98. The backs are unnumbered and include information on the game.

		MT
Complete Set (6):		20.00
Common Player:		1.00
1	Connie Hawkins	4.00
2	Pete Maravich	10.00
3	Calvin Murphy	4.00
4	Nate Thurmond	4.00
5	Paul Westphal	1.00
6	Jo-Jo White	4.00

2002 Minyard/Sprite Dallas Mavericks

	MT
Complete Set (15):	10.00
Common Player:	1.00
DM-SB Shawn Bradley	1.00
DM-GB Greg Buckner	.50
DM-EE Evan Eschmeyer	.50
DM-MF Michael Finley	2.00
DM-AG Adrian Griffin	.50
DM-TH Tim Hardaway	1.00
DM-DH Donnell Harvey	.50
DM-JH Juwan Howard	1.00
DM-DRM Danny Manning	1.00
DM-EN Eduardo Najera	1.00
DM-SN Steve Nash	2.00
DM-DAN Don Nelson	1.00
DM-JN Johnny Newman	.50
DM-DN Dirk Nowitzki	3.00
DM-WZ Wang Zhizhi	3.00

N

1973-74 NBA Players Assn. 8x10

The 10-card, 8" x 10" set features color posed photos with the backs having the NBA Players Association logo. The cards are unnumbered and checklisted according to the 1973-74 order sheet.

	NM
Complete Set (10):	135.00
Common Player:	10.00
Dave DeBusschere	20.00
John Havlicek	30.00
Willis Reed	20.00
Ernie DiGregorio	10.00
Dave Cowens	20.00
Oscar Robertson	35.00
Bill Bradley	20.00
Jo-Jo White	10.00
Nate Thurmond	15.00
Gail Goodrich	15.00

1973-74 NBA Players Assn. Postcards

Measuring 3-3/8" x 5-5/8", these 40 cards have a postcard format. The fronts feature a full-bleed color photo. The backs have the player's name at the top and the NBA Player's Association logo in the center. The cards are unnumbered.

	NM
Complete Set (40):	500.00
Common Player:	3.00
Lucius Allen	3.00
Dave Bing	25.00
Bill Bradley	15.00
Fred Carter	15.00
Austin Carr	3.00
Dave Cowens	10.00
Dave De Busschere	10.00
Ernie Di Gregorio	3.00
Gail Goodrich	7.50
Hal Greer	5.00
John Havlicek	15.00
Connie Hawkins	10.00
Spencer Haywood	5.00
Lou Hudson	4.00
Bob Kauffman	3.00
Bob Lanier	7.50
Bob Love	5.00
Jack Marin	3.00
Jim McMillian	3.00
Earl Monroe	30.00
Calvin Murphy	7.50
Mike Newlin	75.00
Geoff Petrie	3.00
Willis Reed	30.00
Rich Rinaldi	3.00
Mike Riordan	15.00
Oscar Robertson	50.00
Cazzie Russell	5.00
Paul Silas	75.00
Jerry Sloan	5.00
Elmore Smith	3.00
Dick Snyder	3.00
Nate Thurmond	7.50
Rudy Tomjanovich	7.50
Wes Unseld	10.00
Dick Van Arsdale	15.00
Tom Van Arsdale	3.00
Chet Walker	15.00
Jo Jo White	5.00
Len Wilkens	10.00

1969 NBAP Members

The 18-card, 2-3/4" x 4-1/2" set features black and white photography and are blank backed. The cards were not licensed by the NBA as the logo was air-brushed off. The cards were possibly cut from Converse shoe boxes and more cards from the set may exist.

		NM
Complete Set (18):		350.00
Common Player:		8.00
1	Elgin Baylor	25.00
2	Zelmo Beaty	10.00
3	Bob Boozer	8.00
4	Bill Bradley	30.00
5	Wilt Chamberlain	45.00
6	John Havlicek	30.00
7	Don (Cochise) Kojis	8.00
8	Jerry Lucas	20.00
9	Eddie Miles	8.00
10	Jeff Mullins	10.00
11	Oscar Robertson	30.00
12	Bill Russell	70.00
13	Wes Unseld	20.00
14	Dick Van Arsdale	12.00
15	Chet Walker	15.00
16	Jerry West	35.00
17	Len Wilkens	25.00
18	NBAP Logo	8.00

1997 Nabisco/Post Penny Hardaway Posters

These four 11" x 17" posters were available in boxes of Post Honeycomb and Nabisco Frosted Shredded Wheat cereals.

		MT
Complete Set (4):		6.00
Common Poster:		2.00
1	Anfernee Hardaway	2.00
2	Anfernee Hardaway	2.00
3	Anfernee Hardaway	2.00
4	Anfernee Hardaway	2.00

1974 Nabisco Sugar Daddy

The 25-card, 1-1/16" x 2-3/4" set was included in specially marked Sugar Daddy and Sugar Mama candy bars. The first 10 cards feature football stars while 11-16 and 22 are hockey players. Cards 17-21 and 23-25 are basketball players, and include the key Kareem Abdul-Jabbar card. The cards feature a large head on a caricature body with the backs having bio and stat information.

		NM
Complete Set (25):		150.00
Common Player:		2.50
1	Roger Staubach	30.00
2	Floyd Little	5.00
3	Steve Owens	3.50
4	Roman Gabriel	3.50
5	Bobby Douglass	2.50
6	John Gilliam	2.50
7	Bob Lilly	10.00
8	John Brockington	2.50
9	Jim Plunkett	10.00
10	Greg Landry	2.50
11	Phil Esposito	8.00
12	Dennis Hull	3.50
13	Reg Fleming	2.50
14	Garry Unger	3.50
15	Derek Sanderson	5.00
16	Jerry Korab	2.50
17	Oscar Robertson	20.00
18	Spencer Haywood	5.00
19	Jo-Jo White	5.00
20	Connie Hawkins	10.00
21	Nate Thurmond	6.00
22	Mickey Redmond	3.50
23	Chet Walker	5.00
24	Calvin Murphy	6.00
25	Kareem Abdul-Jabbar	25.00

1975 Nabisco Sugar Daddy

The 25-card, 1-1/16" x 2-3/4" set featured athletes from football, basketball and hockey. The set is referred to as "Sugar Daddy All-Stars" and as with other sets, it could be placed on an 18" x 24" poster via a mail-in offer from Nabisco. The set shows the players with large heads on caricature bodies with stat and bio information on the back. The set is also referred to as a Series 2 release.

		NM
Complete Set (25):		150.00
Common Player:		2.50
1	Roger Staubach (Dallas Cowboys)	30.00
2	Floyd Little (Denver Broncos)	5.00
3	Alan Page (Minnesota Vikings)	6.00
4	Merlin Olsen (Los Angeles Rams)	10.00
5	Wally Chambers (Chicago Bears)	2.50
6	John Gilliam (Minnesota Vikings)	2.50
7	Bob Lilly (Dallas Cowboys)	10.00
8	John Brockington (Green Bay Packers)	2.50
9	Jim Plunkett (New England Patriots)	12.00
10	Willie Lanier (Kansas City Chiefs)	6.00
11	Phil Esposito (Boston Bruins)	8.00
12	Dennis Hull (Chicago Blackhawks)	3.50
13	Brad Park (New York Rangers)	6.00
14	Tom Lysiak (Atlanta Flames)	2.50
15	Bernie Parent (Philadelphia Flyers)	6.00
16	Mickey Redmond (Detroit Red Wings)	3.50
17	Jerry Sloan	7.00
18	Spencer Haywood	5.00
19	Bob Lanier	9.00
20	Connie Hawkins	10.00
21	Geoff Petrie	2.50
22	Don Awrey (St Louis Blues)	2.50
23	Chet Walker	5.00
24	Bob McAdoo	9.00
25	Kareem Abdul-Jabbar	25.00

1976 Nabisco Sugar Daddy 1

The 1976, 25-card set (1-1/16" x 2-3/4") features action scenes from a variety of sports, including basketball. Each card was issued in specially marked candy bars of Sugar Daddy and Sugar Mama. The set is referred to as "Sugar Daddy Sports World - Series 1."

		NM
Complete Set (25):		80.00
Common Player:		2.00
1	Hockey	8.00
2	High Jump	2.00
3	Tennis	2.00
4	Auto Racing	8.00
5	Hot Dog Ski	2.00
6	Football	8.00
7	Track and Field	2.00
8	Pole Vault	2.00
9	Swimming	2.00
10	Gymnastics	2.00
11	Basketball	8.00
12	Baseball (Pete Rose batting)	12.00
13	Field Hockey	2.00
14	Figure Skating	3.00
15	Tennis	2.00
16	Track and Field	2.00
17	Hurdles (Pamela Ryan)	2.00
18	Breast Stroke	2.00
19	Broad Jump	2.00
20	Slalom Ski	2.00
21	Golf	8.00
22	Diving	2.00
23	Volleyball	2.00
24	Ski Jump	2.00
25	Figure Skating	3.00

1976 Nabisco Sugar Daddy 2

The 25-card, 1-1/16" x 2-3/4" set is similar to the 1976 Series 1 set, in that it features action scenes from popular sports, including basketball. The set is referred to as "Sugar Daddy Sports World - Series 2."

		NM
Complete Set (25):		75.00
Common Player:		2.00
1	Cricket	2.00
2	Yachting	2.00
3	Diving	2.00
4	Football (Sonny Jurgensen)	8.00
5	Soccer	5.00
6	Lacrosse	2.00
7	Track and Field	2.00
8	Motorcycle	2.00
9	Hang Gliding	2.00
10	Tennis	2.00
11	Hockey	8.00
12	Shot Put	2.00
13	Basketball	8.00
14	Track and Field	2.00
15	Gymnastics	2.00
16	Power Boat Racing	2.00
17	Bike Racing	2.00
18	Golf	8.00
19	Hot Dog Ski	2.00
20	Fishing	2.00
21	Jai Alai	2.00
22	Canoeing	2.00
23	Gymnastics (Cathy Rigby)	5.00
24	Steeple Chase	2.00
25	Baseball (Bobby Murcer)	8.00

1984-85 Nets Getty

The 12-card set, with each card being 3-5/8" x 6-3/4", was produced by Getty and released in four, three-card sheets at the gas stations. The player's facsimile autograph appears below the picture with the Nets and Getty logo highlighting the backs, along with stats and bio information.

		MT
Complete Set (12):		50.00
Common Player:		3.00
1	Stan Albeck (CO)	3.00
2	Otis Birdsong	5.00
3	Darwin Cook	3.00
4	Darryl Dawkins	10.00
5	Mike Gminski	5.00
6	Albert King	4.00
7	Mike O'Koren	4.00
8	Kelvin Ransey	3.00
9	Michael Ray Richardson	5.00
10	Jeff Turner	3.00
11	Buck Williams	10.00
12	Duncan (Mascot)	3.00

1986 Nets Lifebuoy/Star

The 14-card, standard-size set features 12 player cards, one coach card and a checklist and was sponsored by Lifebuoy and produced by Star. The card front borders are royal blue with the Nets logo appearing in the lower left corner. The horizontal card backs contain career statistics.

		MT
Complete Set (14):		14.00
Common Player:		1.25
1	Dave Wohl (CO)	1.25
2	Otis Birdsong	1.25
3	Bobby Cattage	1.25
4	Darwin Cook	1.25
5	Darryl Dawkins	3.00
6	Mike Gminski	1.50
7	Mickey Johnson	1.25
8	Albert King	1.25
9	Mike O'Koren	1.25
10	Kelvin Ransey	1.25
11	Michael Ray Richardson	3.00
12	Jeff Turner	1.25
13	Buck Williams	3.00
14	Title Card (Checklist on back)	1.25

1990-91 Nets Kayo/Breyers

The 14-card, standard-size set features 12 player cards, one coach card and a schedule card. The set was sponsored by Kayo Cards and Breyers Ice Cream and features a color action photo with the Nets' logo in the lower left corner. The card backs feature bio and stat information.

		MT
Complete Set (14):		10.00
Common Player:		.50
1	Mookie Blaylock	2.50
2	Sam Bowie	1.00
3	Jud Buechler	.75
4	Derrick Coleman	2.50
5	Lester Conner	.50
6	Chris Dudley	.75
7	Tate George	.50
8	Derrick Gervin	.50
9	Jack Haley	.50
10	Kirk Lee	.50
11	Chris Morris	.75
12	Reggie Theus	1.25
13	Bill Fitch (CO)	.50
14	Nets Home Schedule	.50

2001 Nets/Topps

		MT
Complete Set (10):		10.00
Common Player:		.50
1	Stephon Marbury	1.50
2	Keith Van Horn	1.50
3	Kendall Gill	1.00
4	Jamie Feick	.50
5	Stephen Jackson	1.50
6	Byron Scott CO	2.00
7	Johnny Newman	.50
8	Aaron Williams	.75
9	Lucious Harris	.50
10	Kenyon Martin	4.00

1999 Nickelodeon Kids Choice Awards

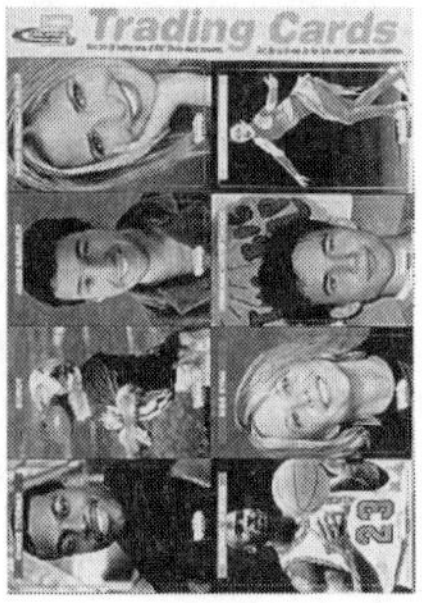

This 32-card set included those elected in an Official Viewer's Guide to the Kids Choice Awards, which was held in Los Angeles on May 1, 1999. The cards were distributed on four different eight-card sheets included in Nickelodeon Magazine. Card backs are unnumbered and contain a biography of the celebrity.

		MT
Complete Sheet (4):		10.00
(1)	Buddy the dog, Sarah Michelle Gellar, Michael Jordan, Meg Ryan, Adam Sandler, Jonathan Taylor Thomas, Chris Tucker, Kristi Yamaguchi	5.00
(2)	Tim Allen, Drew Barrymore, Dominique Moceanu (gymnast), Mary-Kate & Ashley Olsen, Shaquille O'Neal, Julia Roberts, Salem the cat, Will Smith	2.00
(3)	Babe the pig, Brandy, Drew Carey, Jim Carrey, Cynthia Cooper (WNBA), Melissa Joan Hart, Mark McGwire, Kel Mitchell	4.00
(4)	Aaliya, Jennifer Aniston, Tara Lipinski, Eddie Murphy, Spice Girls, Usher, Wishbone the dog, Tiger Woods	3.00

1985 Nike

		MT
Complete Factory Set (5):		400.00
Complete Set (5):		250.00
Common Player:		1.00
1	Dwight Gooden	3.00
2	Michael Jordan	250.00
3	James Lofton	2.00
4	John McEnroe	5.00
5	Lance Parrish	1.00

1991 Nike Michael Jordan Mars

Nike produced this six card set to commemorate memorable commercials featuring Michael Jordan. The 2-1/4" x 3-1/2" cards are in black and white, with some red used, in a poster format. The backs have a portrait of Jordan and Spike Lee, who played Mars Blackmon in the commercials. A message from the depicted commercial is also included on each card.

	MT
Complete Set (6):	5.00
Common Jordan:	1.00
Earth/Mars-1988	1.00
High Flying-1989	1.00
Do You Know-1990	1.00
Stay in School-1991	1.00
Genie-1991	1.00
Flight School-1991	1.00

1993 Nike/ Warner Brothers Michael Jordan

This set of stickers was divided into two six-sticker series; each was issued by Nike and Warner Brothers and features Michael Jordan with various Warner Brothers cartoon characters. Each sticker is unnumbered and measures 2-1/2" x 3-1/2". The first six stickers are related to an "Aerospace Jordan Trading Stickers" theme; stickers 7-12 are titled "The Scream Team." Nike has its logo on each sticker front; the backs of the stickers are white.

	MT
Complete Set (12):	10.00
Common Player:	1.00
Martian	1.00
Martian	1.00
Martian and dog	1.00
Michael Jordan	1.50
Michael Jordan	1.50
Porky Pig	1.00
Aerospace (Jordan dunking)	1.50
J-J-Just Do It	1.00
Nice Shoes Needed	1.00
The Scream Team (Bugs Bunny and Michael Jordan)	1.50
Warning	1.00
What's Up Jock	1.00

1977-78 Nugget Iron-On

This six-card set was sponsored by Pepsi-Cola and features 6-1/4-x-11-inch iron-ons of some of the Nuggets players and coaches.

		NM
Complete Set (6):		25.00
Common Player:		3.00
1	Dan Issel	8.00
2	Brian Taylor	3.00
3	Bobby Wilkerson	3.00
4	Bobby Jones	5.00
5	Larry Brown CO	5.00
6	David Thompson	10.00

1982-83 Nuggets Police

The 14-card, 2-5/8" x 4-1/8" set was sponsored by Colorado National Banks, the Nuggets and metropolitan area police Juvenile Crime Prevention Bureaus. The cards are unnumbered except for the uniform numbers.

		MT
Complete Set (14):		7.00
Common Player:		.50
	Alex English	2.00
	Billy McKinney	.50
	Rob Williams	.50
	Glen Gondrezick	.50
	T.R. Dunn	.50
	Bill Hanzlik	.50
	Dave Robisch	.50
	James Ray	.50
	Dan Issel	2.00
	Rich Kelley	.50
	Kiki Vandeweghe	1.00
NNO	Carl Scheer (Pres/GM)	.50
NNO	Doug Moe (CO)	1.00
NNO	Bill Ficke ACO, Bob Travaglini TR	.50

1983-84 Nuggets Police

The 14-card, 2-5/8" x 4-1/8" set contains safety tips on the card backs and is unnumbered, except for the jersey numbers.

		MT
Complete Set (14):		8.00
Common Player:		.50
	Alex English	2.00
	Mike Evans	.50
	Rob Williams	.50
	T.R. Dunn	.50
	Bill Hanzlik	.50
	Howard Carter	.50
	Ken Dennard	.50
	Danny Schayes	1.00
	Richard Anderson	.50
	Dan Issel	2.00
	Kiki Vandeweghe	1.00
NNO	Carl Scheer (Pres/GM)	.50
NNO	Bill Ficke (ACO)	.50
NNO	Doug Moe (CO)	1.00

1985-86 Nuggets Police/Wendy's

The 12-card, 2-1/2" x 5" set, sponsored by Wendy's, Panasonic and Continental Airlines, was distributed weekly at area Wendy's fast-food restaurants. The card fronts have blue and beige borders while the backs have bio information and a safety tip.

		MT
Complete Set (12):		8.00
Common Player:		.50
1	Alex English	2.00
2	Mike Evans	.50
3	Bill Hanzlik	.50
4	Pete Williams	.50
5	Danny Schayes	.50
6	Wayne Cooper	.50
7	Blair Rasmussen	.50
8	Elston Turner	.50
9	Lafayette (Fat) Lever	1.00
10	T.R. Dunn	.50
11	Willie White	.50
12	Calvin Natt	.75

1988-89 Nuggets Police/Pepsi

The 12-card, 2-5/8" x 4-1/8" set, sponsored by Pizza Hut, Pepsi and the Children's Hospital of Denver, feature team and sponsor logos along the bottom edge of the card front. The backs have a safety tip by the players.

		MT
Complete Set (12):		8.00
Common Player:		.50
2A	Alex English ("If someone is hurt in an accident...")	2.00
2B	Alex English ("You should never run around...")	2.00
6	Walter Davis	1.50
12A	Fat Lever ("Always wear a helmet when you're...")	.75
12B	Fat Lever ("If you're ever in danger, the most...")	.75
14	Michael Adams	1.00
20	Elston Turner	.50
24	Bill Hanzlik	.50
34	Danny Schayes	.50
35	Jerome Lane	.50
41	Blair Rasmussen	.50
42	Wayne Cooper	.50

1988-89 Nuggets Portraits

This six-poster set features some of the Nuggets on a 11-x-17-inch black-and-white poster with a facsimile signatures. The set was sponsored by 7-11 and coupons are included on the fronts.

		MT
Complete Set (6):		8.00
Common Player:		1.00
1	Wayne Cooper	1.00
2	T.R. Dunn	1.00
3	Alex English	5.00
4	Fat Lever	3.00
5	Calvin Natt	1.00
6	Elston Turner, Mike Evans, Bill Hanzlik	1.00

1989-90 Nuggets Police/Pepsi

The 12-card, 2-5/8" x 4-1/8" set was co-sponsored by Pepsi, 7-Eleven and the Children's Hospital of Denver. The cards were given away at 7-Eleven stores and with Pepsi products. The player's name appears down a stripe along the right side of the card front with a player's safety tip printed on the back.

		MT
Complete Set (12):		6.00
Common Player:		.50
1	Michael Adams	.50
2	Walter Davis	1.50
3	T.R. Dunn	.50
4	Alex English	2.00
5	Bill Hanzlik	.50
6	Ed Hughes	.50
7	Tim Kempton	.50
8	Jerome Lane	.50
9	Lafayette Lever	.75
10	Todd Lichti	.50
11	Blair Rasmussen	.50
12	Danny Schayes	.50

1994 Hakeem Olajuwon Fan Club

The two-card, standard-size set was distributed to members of the Hakeem the Dream Fan Club. The card fronts feature full-bleed photography with the Olajuwon's name running down the right side in a blue stripe. The cards are unnumbered.

		MT
Complete Set (2):		10.00
Common Player:		5.00
	Hakeem Olajuwon (Sitting on car, tossing basketball)	5.00
	Hakeem Olajuwon (Relaxing in chair outdoors)	5.00

1991-92 Outlaws Wichita GBA

The 11-card, standard-size set was produced by Rock's Dugout and printed on thick stock. The card fronts have a horizontal design with a burgundy-marble border. The card backs are also horizontally designed and feature player bio and stat information, as well as career highlights.

		MT
Complete Set (11):		10.00
Common Player:		1.00
1	Rick Shore	1.00
2	Jeff Cummings	1.00
3	Brent Dabbs	1.25
4	Melvon Foster	1.25
5	Paul Guffrovich	1.00
6	Tyrone Powell	1.00
7	Omar Roland	1.00
8	Ricky Ross	1.00
9	Robert Spellman	1.00
10	Cody Walters	1.00
NNO	Checklist Card	1.00

P

1971 Pacers Marathon Oil

The nine-card set of Marathon Oil portraits were drawn by artist Nicholas Volpe. Each card (7-1/2" x 9-7/8") features a headshot close-up over a black background with an action painting found along the side. A facsimile autograph in white is found along the bottom edge. The bottom of each card is a postcard which customers could use to apply for a Marathon credit card.

		NM
Complete Set (9):		70.00
Common Player:		5.00
1	Roger Brown	7.50
2	Mel Daniels	10.00
3	Earle Higgins	5.00
4	Billy Keller	7.50
5	Bob Leonard (CO)	7.50
6	Freddie Lewis	7.50
7	Rick Mount	10.00
8	Bob Netolicky	7.50
9	Howard Wright	5.00

1988-89 Pacers Team Issue

This 12-card set measures 5" x 7" and features black-and-white photos on paper stock. The cards are unnumbered and blank-backed.

		MT
Complete Set (12):		40.00
Common Player:		2.00
	Greg Dreiling	2.00
	Vern Fleming	1.00
	Anthony Frederick	2.00
	Stuart Gray	2.00
	John Long, Julius Erving	3.00
	Reggie Miller	10.00
	Chuck Person	5.00
	Scott Skiles	5.00
	Everette Stephens	2.00
	Steve Stipanovich	2.00
	Wayman Tisdale	5.00
	Herb Williams	2.00

1994 Pacific Prism Draft Samples

The three-card, standard-size set was issued to preview the 1994 Pacific Prism Draft Picks set. The cards were available in both silver and gold foil, with the gold values being up to two times more than the values below. The cards have "Sample" on the horizontal backs.

		MT
Complete Set (3):		12.00
Common Player:		4.00
1	Glenn Robinson - Purdue	4.00
2	Jason Kidd - California	5.00
3	Anfernee Hardaway	6.00

1994 Pacific Prisms

Pacific Prism Draft Basketball contains 72 cards and features all of the top 1994 NBA draft picks, as well as four professional players. Production was limited to 3,999 individually numbered cases, with 20 boxes per case and 36 packs per box. In addition to the normal set, which is called silver "Sonic Boom" prism cards, Pacific also has a parallel gold "Sonic Boom" set. Three Prism Draft promo cards were also produced, previewing the design for the main set. Two versions were made - silver foil and gold foil, which are two times more valuable than the silver prices listed here. The card back is numbered, but has the word "Sample" written next to it. The three cards, and silver values, are: 1) Glenn Robinson, $10; 2) Jason Kidd, $7.50; and 3) Anfernee Hardaway, $5.

		MT
Complete Set (72):		60.00
Common Player:		.50
Complete Gold Set (72):		300.00
Common Gold Player:		2.00
Unlisted Gold Stars:		2x-4x
Complete Majerle Set:		5.00
Wax Box:		36.00
1	Derrick Alston	.50
2	Adrian Autry	.50
3	Damon Bailey	.50
4	Melvin Booker	.50
5	Joey Brown	.50
6	Albert Burditt	.50
7	Robert Churchwell	.50
8	Gary Collier	.50
9	Jevon Crudup	.50
10	Bill Curley	.50
11	Yinka Dare	.75
12	Rodney Dent	.50
13	Tony Dumas	.75
14	Howard Eisley	.50
15	Travis Ford	.50
16	Lawrence Funderburke	.50
17	Anthony Goldwire	.50
18	Chuck Graham	.50
19	Brian Grant	1.00
20	Darrin Hancock	.50
21	Anfernee Hardaway	3.00
22	Carl Ray Harris	.50
23	Grant Hill	15.00
24	Askia Jones	.50
25	Eddie Jones	10.00
26	Arturas Karnishovas	.50
27	Damon Key	.50
28	Jason Kidd	6.00
29	Antonio Lang	.50
30	Donyell Marshall	1.00
31	Jamal Mashburn	1.50
32	Billy McCaffrey	.50
33	Jim McIlvaine	.50
34	Aaron McKie	.75
35	Harold Miner	.50
36	Greg Minor	.75
37	Eric Mobley	.50
38	Eric Montross	1.50
39	Dwayne Morton	.50
40	Alonzo Mourning	2.00
41	Dikembe Mutombo	1.00
42	Gaylon Nickerson	.50
43	Wesley Person	2.00
44	Derrick Phelps	.50
45	Eric Piatkowski	.50
46	Kevin Rankin	.50
47	Brian Reese	.50
48	Khalid Reeves	1.50
49	Isaiah Rider	1.00
50	Glenn Robinson	6.00
51	Carlos Rogers	1.00
52	Jalen Rose	2.00
53	Clifford Rozier	.50
54	Kevin Salvadori	.50
55	Jervaughn Scales	.50
56	Shawnelle Scott	.50
57	Dickey Simpkins	.75
58	Michael Smith	1.00
59	Shon Tarver	.50
60	Deon Thomas	.50
61	Brooks Thompson	.50
62	B.J. Tyler	.50
63	Charlie Ward	2.00
64	Jamie Watson	.50
65	Jeff Webster	.50
66	Monty Williams	.50
67	Dontonio Wingfield	.50
68	Steve Woodberry	.50
69	Anfernee Hardaway	2.50
70	Jamal Mashburn	1.00
71	Alonzo Mourning	2.00
72	Dikembe Mutombo	1.00

1994 Pacific Prism Gold

The 72-card, standard-size set was inserted twice per box and printed on 18-point, UV-coated stock. The fronts have a player cut out over a prism-foil background.

		MT
Complete Set (72):		300.00
Common Player:		2.50
Stars:		2.5x to 5x

1994 Pacific Prism Dan Majerle

The 20-card, standard-size set highlights Dan Majerle and the backs are numbered as "x of 20."

		MT
Complete Set (20):		7.00
Common Player:		.50
1	Dan Majerle (Driving for layup down left side of lane)	.50
2	Dan Majerle (Preparing to pass the ball back outside)	.50
3	Dan Majerle (Dribbling ball up court with right hand)	.50
4	Dan Majerle (Reaching back for ball)	.50
5	Dan Majerle (Rebounding)	.50
6	Dan Majerle (Dribbling ball while play develops)	.50
7	Dan Majerle (Dribbling the ball while backing in)	.50
8	Dan Majerle (Shooting layup)	.50
9	Dan Majerle (Defensive position)	.50
10	Dan Majerle (Shooting jumper)	.50
11	Dan Majerle (Dribbling with left hand)	.50
12	Dan Majerle (Shooting layup over defender)	.50
13	Dan Majerle (Shooting free throw)	.50
14	Dan Majerle (Setting up to shoot outside jumper)	.50
15	Dan Majerle (Dribbling with left hand, looking to right)	.50
16	Dan Majerle (Jump shot, just after release)	.50
17	Dan Majerle (Holding ball at shoulder height)	.50
18	Dan Majerle (Dribbling with right hand along side line)	.50
19	Dan Majerle (Playing tennis)	.50
20	Dan Majerle (Spinning basketball on finger in his sports grill)	.50

1995 Pacific Prism Draft Picks

Pacific's 1995 draft pick set includes cards for 54 players, of which 48 were drafted during the 1995 NBA Draft. Each regular card has a full-bleed color action photo on the front, with the Pacific logo in the upper left corner and the player's name in a banner in the lower right corner. The card back has a close-up shot of the player on one side, flanked on the other by his name, position, biographical information and when he was drafted. Underneath is a brief analysis of the skills the player brings to the NBA, plus a card number. The card background is a hardwood basketball court floor. There were also three parallel sets created - retail and hobby versions, used different color prism foil and were seeded three per every 37 packs. In addition, there are 40 complete sets of Presidential Gold parallel sets, which are inserted two per every 721 packs. There were four types of insert cards - Gold Crown Die-Cuts, Centers of Attention, Platinum Crown Die-Cuts (available through a wrapper mail-in offer), and Hakeem Olajuwon cards. In addition, collectors could win an autographed basketball by Hakeem Olajuwon or a Presidential Gold Prism set; winning cards were randomly packed in retail and hobby packs. There were 25 autographed basketballs available; odds of finding a winning card were one per 43,200 packs. Five Presidential Gold Prism sets were produced for those instant winners.

		MT
Complete Set (54):		35.00
Common Player:		.25
Blue/Red Cards:		4x-8x
Gold Cards:		60x-120x
1	Joe Smith	3.00
2	David Vaughn	.25
3	Anthony Pelle	.25
4	Sherrell Ford	.25
5	Corliss Williamson	.60
6	Mario Bennett	.25
7	Jason Caffey	.25
8	Rick Brunson, Erwin Claggett	.25
9	George Zidek	.75
10	Eric Snow	.25
11	Travis Best	.40
12	Theo Ratliff	.50
13	Greg Ostertag	.40
14	Lou Roe	.25
15	Eric Montross	.25
16	Hakeem Olajuwon	1.00
17	Cherokee Parks	.50
18	Glenn Robinson	1.75
19	Hakeem Olajuwon	1.00
20	Terrence Rencher	.25
21	Cory Alexander	.25
22	Tyus Edney	.25
23	Damon Stoudamire	5.00
24	Junior Burrough	.25
25	Donny Marshall	.25
26	Brent Barry	.60
27	Rasheed Wallace	1.50
28	LaZelle Durden	.25
29	Jimmy King	.25
30	Don Reid	.25
31	Loren Meyer	.40
32	Joe Smith	3.00
33	Cuonzo Martin	.25
34	Eddie Jones	3.00
35	Ed O'Bannon	1.00
36	Jason Kidd	2.50
37	Erik Meek	.25
38	Greg Ostertag	.35
39	Ed O'Bannon, Rasheed Wallace	.60
40	Eric Williams	1.00
41	Randolph Childress	.25
42	Wesley Person	.25
43	Antonio McDyess	2.00
44	Andrew DeClercq	.25
45	Constantin Popa	.25
46	Gary Trent	.60
47	Jerome Allen	.25
48	Michael Finley	2.00
49	Mark Davis	.25
50	Shawn Respert	.30
51	John Amaechi, Corey Beck	.25
52	Rashard Griffith	.35
53	Kurt Thomas	.75
54	Lawrence Moten	.25

1995 Pacific Prism Centers of Attention

These 10 crystaline cards were randomly inserted into 1995 Pacific Prism Draft Pick packs, three per every 37 packs. The cards have a clear basketball backboard at the top of the card; the player photo is die-cut on that half of the card, but is full-bleed on the bottom half. A Pacific logo is in the lower right corner; the player's name runs vertically in the lower left corner. The card back has the backboard repeated for the top half, with the ghosted image of the photo from the front in orange. The lower half of the card has a close-up photo on the left, with the player's name above. A summary of the player's skills is on the right. A card number, using a "C" prefix, is centered at the bottom.

		MT
Complete Set (10):		60.00
Common Player:		2.50
1	Jason Kidd	10.00
2	Antonio McDyess	10.00
3	Ed O'Bannon	4.00
4	Hakeem Olajuwon	8.00
5	Greg Ostertag	2.50
6	Shawn Respert	2.50
7	Glenn Robinson	8.00
8	Joe Smith	15.00
9	Damon Stoudamire	20.00
10	Rasheed Wallace	6.00

1995 Pacific Prism Gold Crown Die-Cut

Pacific's Gold Crown die-cut technology makes its first appearance in a basketball set for these 15 1995 Pacific Prism Draft Pick inserts. The cards, seeded three per every 37 packs, have a gold-foiled crown die-cut into the card at the top. The rest of the card front has a full-bleed color action photo, with the player's name stamped in gold foil along the bottom. The back has a crown at the top, with a second photo of the player, plus his name and a recap of his collegiate accomplishments. A "DC" prefix is used for the card number.

		MT
Complete Set (15):		120.00
Common Player:		2.50
1	Jason Caffey	2.50
2	Michael Finley	15.00
3	Eddie Jones	5.00
4	Jason Kidd	12.00
5	Antonio McDyess	15.00
6	Ed O'Bannon	6.00
7	Greg Ostertag	3.00
8	Cherokee Parks	3.00
9	Shawn Respert	3.00
10	Glenn Robinson	9.00
11	Joe Smith	20.00
12	Damon Stoudamire	30.00
13	Rasheed Wallace	8.00
14	Eric Williams	8.00
15	Corliss Williamson	5.00

1995 Pacific Prism Olajuwon

The cards were randomly inserted into packs with "Rockets" being air-brushed off and "Hakeem" printed on his jersey. The card backs have Olajuwon's name with "The Dream" in large block letters.

		MT
Complete Set (12):		8.00
Common Player:		1.00

1995 Pacific Prism Platinum Crown Die-Cut

These five cards were available as a set through a mail-in offer available on 1995 Pacific Prism Draft Pick Basketball wrappers. The Platinum Crown die-cuts were obtainable for 18 wrappers, plus shipping and handling charges. The cards are numbered using a "P" prefix.

		MT
Complete Set (5):		35.00
Common Player:		2.00
1	Antonio McDyess	15.00
2	Ed O'Bannon	2.00
3	Greg Ostertag	2.00
4	Joe Smith	16.00
5	Rasheed Wallace	6.00

1996 Pacific Power Prism

This 54-card set included 42 top draft picks from 1996 and 12 pro players. The cards maintained Pacific's prism look, with solid gold foil backgrounds. Fronts included the player's name in large letters up the left side, with a Pacific Crown logo in the lower right corner. Each card in the regular-issue set carried a "PP" prefix. Metallic Silver and Presidential Gold parallel sets were also produced along with four insert sets, including Gold Crown Die-Cut, Jump Ball Hoop-Cel, In the Paint and Regents of Roundball.

		MT
Complete Set (54):		20.00
Common Player:		.20
Minor Stars:		.40
Regents of Roundball:		.25x
Metalic Silver: 8x-16x		
Presidential Platinum:		75x-150x
1	Shareef Abdur-Rahim	2.00
2	Ray Allen	2.00
3	Terrell Bell	.20
4	Joseph Blair	.20
5	Marcus Brown	.20
6	Kobe Bryant	4.00
7	Marcus Camby	3.00
8	Erick Dampier	.50
9	Ben Davis	.20
10	Tony Delk	.75
11	Tyus Edney	.40
12	Brian Evans	.20
13	Michael Finley	1.00
14	Derek Fisher	.50
15	Todd Fuller	.20
16	Reggie Geary	.20
17	Steve Hamer	.20
18	Othella Harrington	.20
19	Mark Hendrickson	.20
20	Allen Iverson	4.00
21	Dontae Jones	.20
22	Jason Kidd	1.00
23	Kerry Kittles	1.50
24	Randy Livingston	.75
25	Stephon Marbury	3.00
26	Jamal Mashburn	.50
27	Walter McCarty	.20
28	Amal McCaskill	.20
29	Antonio McDyess	1.00
30	Jeff McInnis	.20
31	Russ Millard	.20
32	Ryan Minor	.20
33	Alonzo Mourning	.75
34	Dikembe Mutombo	.20
35	Steve Nash	.75
36	Moochie Norris	.20
37	Ed O'Bannon	.40
38	Jermaine O'Neal	.75
39	Mark Pope	.20
40	Vitaly Potapenko	.75
41	Ron Riley	.20
42	Darnell Robinson	.20
43	Glenn Robinson	.40
44	Roy Rogers	.20
45	Jason Sasser	.20
46	Doron Sheffer	.20
47	Joe Smith	1.00
48	Damon Stoudamire	2.00
49	Antoine Walker	.50
50	Samaki Walker	.50
51	John Wallace	1.00
52	Rasheed Wallace	.20
53	Jerome Williams	.20
54	Lorenzen Wright	.20

1996 Pacific Power Prism Metallic Silver

This 54 cardset paralleled all 54 cards in Pacfic's Power Prism Basketball, but featured silver foil instead of the regular-issue gold. These parallel versions were seeded three per 37 packs.

	MT
Complete Set (54):	300.00
Metallic Silver Cards:	8x-16x

1996 Pacific Power Prism Presidential Platinum

This set paralleled all 54 cards in Power Prism Basketball, but was printed on a blue platinum color foil. These parallel versions were seeded one per 721 packs.

	MT
Complete Set (54):	3000.
Presidential Platinum:	75x-150x

1996 Pacific Power Prism Gold Crown Die-Cut

This 15-card insert continued Pacific's Gold Crown Die- cuts that were used previously in baseball and football. Cards were inserted three per 37 packs, with card numbers carrying a "GC" prefix.

		MT
Complete Set (15):		150.00
Common Player:		3.00
1	Shareef Abdur-Rahim	15.00
2	Ray Allen	15.00
3	Kobe Bryant	20.00
4	Marcus Camby	17.00
5	Erick Dampier	3.00
6	Tony Delk	8.00
7	Allen Iverson	25.00
8	Jason Kidd	10.00
9	Stephon Marbury	17.00
10	Steve Nash	8.00
11	Jermaine O'Neal	8.00
12	Joe Smith	10.00
13	Damon Stoudamire	12.00
14	Antoine Walker	4.00
15	John Wallace	8.00

1996 Pacific Power Prism In the Paint

In the Paint highlighted 20 future stars and was seeded three per 37 packs. The cards featured an action shot of the player over a gold foil background that includes the player's name in large letters. In the Paint cards carried an "IP" prefix.

		MT
Complete Set (20):		175.00
Common Player:		3.00
1	Shareef Abdur-Rahim	17.00
2	Ray Allen	17.00
3	Kobe Bryant	25.00
4	Marcus Camby	20.00
5	Erick Dampier	3.00
6	Tyus Edney	3.00
7	Michael Finley	7.00
8	Allen Iverson	30.00
9	Dontae Jones	3.00
10	Jason Kidd	12.00
11	Stephon Marbury	20.00
12	Antonio McDyess	7.00
13	Dikembe Mutombo	3.00
14	Steve Nash	10.00
15	Ed O'Bannon	3.00
16	Jermaine O'Neal	10.00
17	Joe Smith	12.00
18	Damon Stoudamire	15.00
19	Antoine Walker	5.00
20	John Wallace	10.00

1996 Pacific Power Prism Jump Ball Hoop-Cel

This 10-card set was printed on gold foil and contained a cel in the middle resembling a basketball net. The cel featured a shot of the player, while the background included basketballs. Inserted at one per 37 packs, this insert was numbered with a "JB" prefix.

		MT
Complete Set (10):		175.00
Common Player:		4.00
1	Shareef Abdur-Rahim	20.00
2	Ray Allen	20.00
3	Kobe Bryant	35.00
4	Marcus Camby	25.00
5	Erick Dampier	4.00
6	Allen Iverson	40.00
7	Dontae Jones	4.00
8	Stephon Marbury	25.00
9	Antoine Walker	5.00
10	Lorenzen Wright	4.00

1996 Pacific Power Prism Regents of Roundball

This 55-card set pictures all the top picks and was included at a rate of two per pack. The cards contain no foil and have a brushed border with an "RR" prefix on the card number.

	MT
Complete Set (55):	5.00
Regents of Roundball:	.25x

1988-89 Panini Spanish Stickers

These 2" x 2-5/8" stickers were designed to be stored in an accompanying album which was produced. The stickers are numbered on the back; the front has a color posed photo with a white border. The album is 9" x 12". Stickers were distributed throughout Europe and were produced by Edizioni Panini S.P.A. Modena. The sticker backs say "Panini Basket NBA/89" and provide instructions on how to put the stickers in the album. Stickers 1-2 form a puzzle.

		MT
Complete Set (292):		350.00
Common Player:		1.00
1	NBA Official Licensed Product Logo	1.00
2	NBA Official Licensed Product Logo	1.00
3	Boston Celtics Logo	1.00
4	Jimmy Rodgers CO	1.00
5	Dennis Johnson	3.00
6	Brian Shaw	2.50
7	Danny Ainge	3.00
8	Larry Bird	35.00
9	Kevin McHale	8.00
10	Robert Parish	4.00
11	Robert Parish IA	3.00
12	Celtics Jersey	1.00
13	Charlotte Hornets Logo	1.00
14	Dick Harter CO	1.00
15	Rex Chapman	5.00
16	Tyrone Bogues	5.00
17	Kelly Tripucka	1.00
18	Robert Reid	1.00
19	Kurt Rambis	1.50
20	Dave Hoppen	1.00
21	Tyrone Bogues IA	3.00
22	Hornets Jersey	1.00
23	New Jersey Nets Logo	1.00
24	Willis Reed CO	2.50
25	John Bagley	1.00
26	Dennis Hopson	1.00
27	Mike McGee	1.00
28	Roy Hinson	1.00
29	Buck Williams	2.00
30	Joe Barry Carroll	1.00
31	Roy Hinson IA	1.00
32	Nets Jersey	1.00
33	New York Knicks Logo	1.00
34	Rick Pitino CO	4.00
35	Mark Jackson	5.00
36	Trent Tucker	1.00
37	Johnny Newman	1.00
38	Gerald Wilkins	1.00
39	Charles Oakley	2.00
40	Patrick Ewing	12.00
41	Gerald Wilkins IA	1.00
42	Knicks Jersey	1.00
43	Philadelphia 76ers Logo	1.00
44	Jim Lynam CO	1.00
45	Maurice Cheeks	2.50
46	Hersey Hawkins	5.00
47	Ron Anderson	1.00
48	Charles Barkley	14.00
49	Cliff Robinson	1.00
50	Mike Gminski	1.00
51	Hersey Hawkins IA	2.00
52	76ers Jersey	1.00
53	Washington Bullets Logo	1.00
54	Wes Unseld CO	2.50
55	Jeff Malone	1.00
56	Darrell Walker	1.00
57	Bernard King	2.50
58	Terry Catledge	1.00
59	John Williams	1.00
60	Dave Feitl	1.00
61	Jeff Malone IA	1.00
62	Bullets Jersey	1.00
63	Atlanta Hawks Logo	1.00
64	Mike Fratello CO	1.00
65	Glenn (Doc) Rivers	2.00
66	Spud Webb	1.50
67	Reggie Theus	1.50
68	Dominique Wilkins	6.00
69	Kevin Willis	2.50
70	Moses Malone	4.00
71	Reggie Theus IA	1.00
72	Hawks Jersey	1.00
73	Chicago Bulls Logo	1.00
74	Doug Collins CO	2.00
75	Craig Hodges	1.00
76	Michael Jordan	100.00
77	Scottie Pippen	50.00
78	Horace Grant	9.00
79	Brad Sellers	1.00
80	Bill Cartwright	1.50
81	Brad Sellers IA	1.00
82	Bulls Jersey	4.00
83	Cleveland Cavaliers Logo	1.00
84	Lenny Wilkens CO	1.50
85	Mark Price	3.00
86	Ron Harper	3.00
87	John Hot Rod Williams	1.00
88	Mike Sanders	1.00
89	Larry Nance	2.00
90	Brad Daugherty	1.50
91	Mike Sanders IA	1.00
92	Cavaliers Jersey	1.00
93	Detroit Pistons Logo	1.00
94	Chuck Daly CO	2.50
95	Isiah Thomas	7.00
96	Joe Dumars	3.00
97	Dennis Rodman	25.00
98	Adrian Dantley	2.50
99	John Sailey	1.50
100	Bill Laimbeer	1.50
101	Dennis Rodman IA	20.00
102	Pistons Jersey	1.00
103	Indiana Pacers Logo	1.00
104	Dick Versace CO	1.00
105	Vern Fleming	1.00
106	Reggie Miller	30.00
107	Chuck Person	1.50
108	Herb Williams	1.00
109	Steve Stipanovich	1.00
110	Rik Smits	5.00
111	Chuck Person IA	1.00
112	Pacers Jersey	1.00
113	Milwaukee Bucks Logo	1.00
114	Del Harris CO	1.00
115	Sidney Moncrief	2.50
116	Jay Humphries	1.00
117	Paul Pressey	1.00
118	Ricky Pierce	1.50
119	Terry Cummings	2.50
120	Jack Sikma	2.50
121	Jay Humphries IA	1.00
122	Bucks Jersey	1.00
123	Mavericks Logo	1.00
124	John MacLeod CO	1.00
125	Derek Harper	2.00
126	Rolando Blackman	2.00
127	Detlef Schrempf	4.00
128	Mark Aguirre	2.00
129	Sam Perkins	2.00
130	James Donaldson	1.00
131	Sam Perkins IA	1.50
132	Mavericks Jersey	1.00
133	Denver Nuggets Logo	1.00
134	Doug Moe CO	1.00
135	Walter Davis	2.00
136	Michael Adams	1.00
137	Lafayette Lever	1.50
138	Alex English	3.00
139	Wayne Cooper	1.00
140	Danny Schayes	1.00
141	Lafayette Lever IA	1.00
142	Nuggets Jersey	1.00
143	Houston Rockets Logo	1.00
144	Don Chaney CO	1.00
145	Eric (Sleepy) Floyd	1.00
146	Mike Woodson	1.00
147	Purvis Short	1.00
148	Buck Johnson	1.00
149	Otis Thorpe	2.50
150	Hakeem Olajuwon	17.00
151	Otis Thorpe IA	1.00
152	Rockets Jersey	1.00
153	Miami Heat Logo	1.00
154	Ron Rothstein CO	1.00
155	Jon Sundvoid	1.00
156	Kevin Edwards	1.00
157	Grant Long	1.00
158	Billy Thompson	1.00
159	Dwayne Washington	1.00
160	Rony Seikaly	3.00
161	Rony Seikaly IA	1.50
162	Heat Jersey	1.00
163	San Antonio Spurs Logo	1.00
164	Larry Brown CO	2.00
165	Johnny Dawkins	1.00
166	Alvin Robertson	1.00
167	Willie Anderson	1.00
168	Albert King	1.00
169	Greg Anderson	1.00
170	Frank Brickowski	1.00
171	Willie Anderson IA	1.00
172	Spurs Jersey	1.00
173	Utah Jazz Logo	1.00
174	Jerry Sloan CO	3.00
175	John Stockton	20.00
176	Darrell Griffith	1.50
177	Marc Iavaroni	1.00
178	Thurl Bailey	1.00
179	Karl Malone	20.00
180	Mark Eaton	1.50
181	Thurl Bailey IA	1.00
182	Jazz Jersey	1.00
183	Golden State Warriors Logo	1.00
184	Don Nelson CO	1.50
185	Mitch Richmond	18.00
186	Winston Garland	1.00
187	Larry Smith	1.00
188	Chris Mullin	4.00
189	Ralph Sampson	1.50
190	Manute Bol	1.00
191	Ralph Sampson IA	1.00
192	Warriors Jersey	1.00
193	Los Angeles Clippers Logo	1.00
194	Don Casey CO	1.00
195	Gary Grant	1.00
196	Quintin Dailey	1.00
197	Norm Nixon	2.00
198	Ken Norman	1.00
199	Danny Manning	4.00
200	Benoit Benjamin	1.00
201	Ken Norman IA	1.00
202	Clippers Jersey	1.00
203	Los Angeles Lakers Logo	1.00
204	Pat Riley CO	3.00
205	Magic Johnson	25.00
206	Byron Scott	2.50
207	James Worthy	6.00
208	A.C. Green	2.50
209	Mychal Thompson	1.50
210	Kareem Abdul-Jabbar	17.00
211	Byron Scott IA	1.50
212	Lakers Jersey	1.00
213	Phoenix Suns Logo	1.00
214	Cotton Fitzsimmons CO	1.00
215	Kevin Johnson	5.00
216	Dan Majerle	5.00
217	Eddie Johnson	1.50
218	Armon Gilliam	1.00
219	Tom Chambers	2.00
220	Mark West	1.00
221	Kevin Johnson IA	2.50
222	Suns Jersey	1.00
223	Portland Trail Blazers Logo	1.00
224	Mike Schuler CO	1.00
225	Terry Porter	2.00
226	Clyde Drexler	15.00
227	Jerome Kersey	2.00
228	Kiki Vandeweghe	2.00
229	Steve Johnson	1.00
230	Kevin Duckworth	1.00
231	Jerome Kersey IA	1.00
232	Trail Blazers Jersey	1.00
233	Sacramento Kings Logo	1.00
234	Jerry Reynolds CO	1.00
235	Kenny Smith	2.00
236	Rodney McCray	1.00
237	Derek Smith	2.00
238	Ed Pinckney	1.00
239	Jim Petersen	1.00
240	LaSalle Thompson	1.00
241	Kenny Smith IA	1.00
242	Kings Jersey	1.00
243	Seattle Supersonics Logo	1.00
244	Bernie Bickerstaff CO	1.00
245	Nate McMillan	1.50
246	Dale Ellis	1.50
247	Xavier McDaniel	1.00
248	Derrick McKey	1.00
249	Michael Cage	1.00
250	Alton Lister	1.00
251	Xavier McDaniel IA	1.00
252	Supersonics Jersey	1.00
253	AS Puzzle (Patrick Ewing, Hakeem Olajuwon)	4.00
254	AS Puzzle (Karl Malone)	4.00
255	AS Puzzle	1.00
256	AS Puzzle	1.00
257	AS Puzzle (Lafayette Lever)	1.00
258	AS Puzzle	1.00
259	Lenny Wilkens CO AS	1.50
260	Isiah Thomas AS	4.00
261	Michael Jordan AS	50.00
262	Dominique Wilkins AS	4.00
263	Charles Barkley AS	8.00
264	Moses Malone AS	2.50
265	Mark Jackson AS	2.50
266	Mark Price AS	2.00
267	Larry Nance AS	1.50
268	Terry Cummings AS	1.50
269	Kevin McHale AS	4.00
270	Brad Daugherty AS	1.00
271	Patrick Ewing AS	7.00
272	Pat Riley CO AS	2.00
273	John Stockton AS	12.00
274	Dale Ellis AS	1.00
275	Alex English AS	2.00
276	Karl Malone AS	12.00
277	Hakeem Olajuwon AS	10.00
278	Kareem Abdul-Jabbar AS	9.00
279	Clyde Drexler AS	8.00
280	Chris Mullin AS	3.00
281	James Worthy AS	4.00
282	Tom Chambers AS	1.50
283	Kevin Duckworth AS	1.00
284	Mark Eaton AS	1.00
285	Michael Jordan AW	50.00
286	Mark Jackson AW	2.00
287	Charles Barkley AW	8.00
288	Jack Sikma AW	1.00
289	Michael Cage AW	1.00
290	Mark Eaton AW	1.00
291	John Stockton AW	12.00
292	Doug Moe CO AW	1.00
293	XX Album (Dominique Wilkins, Larry Bird)	15.00

1989-90 Panini Spanish Stickers

These 2-1/8" x 3" stickers were produced by Edizioni Panini S.P.A. - Modena and were distributed throughout Europe. Each front has a color action photo of the player, with his name, team name and sticker number at the bottom. The back says "Panini Basket NBA 90" and offers directions on how to apply the sticker to a corresponding album which was produced. An NBA action photo can be formed from stickers for Ken Norman and #s 268-272.

		MT
Complete Set (272):		275.00
Common Player:		1.00
1	Boston Celtics Logo	1.00
2	Dennis Johnson	2.00
3	Reggie Lewis	2.00
4	Kevin Upshaw	1.00
5	Kevin Gamble	1.00
6	Larry Bird	25.00
7	Ed Pickney	1.00
8	Kevin McHale	6.00
9	Robert Parish	3.00
10	Miami Heat Logo	1.00
11	Jon Sundvoid	1.00
12	Rory Sparrow	1.00
13	Dwayne Washington	1.00
14	Billy Thompson	1.00
15	Grant Long	1.00
16	Kevin Edwards	1.00
17	Pat Cummings	1.00
18	Rony Seikaly	3.00
19	New Jersey Nets Logo	1.00
20	Dennis Hopson	1.00
21	Lester Conner	1.00
22	Chris Morris	1.00
23	Charles Shackleford	1.00
24	Purvis Short	1.00
25	Roy Hinson	1.00
26	Sam Bowie	1.00
27	Joe Barry Carroll	1.00
28	New York Knicks Logo	1.00
29	Mark Jackson	2.50
30	Rod Strickland	5.00
31	Gerald Wilkins	1.00
32	Trent Tucker	1.00
33	Johnny Newman	1.00
34	Kenny Walker	1.00
35	Charles Oakley	1.50
36	Patrick Ewing	9.00
37	Philadelphia 76ers Logo	1.00
38	Scott Brooks	1.00
39	Johnny Dawkins	1.00
40	Hersey Hawkins	2.00
41	Derek Smith	1.50
42	Ron Anderson	1.00
43	Charles Barkley	9.00
44	Rick Mahorn	1.00
45	Mike Gminski	1.00
46	Washington Bullets Logo	1.00
47	Steve Colter	1.00
48	Jeff Malone	1.00
49	Ledell Eackles	1.00
50	Darrell Walker	1.00
51	Bernard King	1.50
52	Charles Jones	1.00
53	Mark Alaire	1.00
54	Harvey Grant	1.50
55	Atlanta Hawks Logo	1.00
56	Anthony Webb	1.50
57	Glenn (Doc) Rivers	1.50
58	John Battle	1.00
59	Dominique Wilkins	4.00
60	Cliff Levingston	1.00
61	Jon Koncak	1.00
62	Antoine Carr	1.00
63	Moses Malone	2.00
64	Chicago Bulls Logo	2.00
65	Craig Hodges	1.00
66	John Paxson	1.00
67	Michael Jordan	75.00
68	Scottie Pippen	25.00
69	Charles Davis	1.00
70	Horace Grant	3.00
71	Will Perdue	1.00
72	Bill Cartwright	1.50
73	Cleveland Cavaliers Logo	1.00
74	Mark Price	2.00
75	Craig Ehlo	1.00
76	Chris Dudley	1.00
77	Randolph Keys	1.00
78	Larry Nance	2.00
79	John Williams	1.00
80	Paul Mokeski	1.00
81	Wayne Rollins	1.00
82	Pistons	1.00
83	Isiah Thomas	5.00
84	Vinnie Johnson	1.50
85	Joe Dumars	2.50
86	Mark Aquirre	1.50
87	Dennis Rodman	18.00
88	John Salley	1.50
89	James Edwards	1.00
90	Bill Laimbeer	1.50
91	Indiana Pacers Logo	1.00
92	Reggie Miller	12.00
93	Vern Fleming	1.00
94	Randy Wittman	1.00
95	Chuck Person	1.50
96	Mike Sanders	1.00
97	Rickey Green	1.00
98	LaSalle Thompson	1.00
99	Rik Smits	2.50
100	Milwaukee Bucks Logo	1.00
101	Jay Humphries	1.00
102	Ricky Pierce	1.50
103	Paul Pressey	1.00
104	Alvin Robertson	1.00
105	Tony Brown	1.00
106	Fred Roberts	1.00
107	Randy Breuer	1.00
108	Jack Sikma	1.50
109	Orlando Magic Logo	1.00
110	Sam Vincent	1.00
111	Reggie Theus	1.50
112	Scott Skiles	1.50
113	Otis Smith	1.00
114	Sidney Green	1.00
115	Nick Anderson	4.00
116	Terry Catledge	1.00
117	Mark Acres	1.00
118	Hornets	1.00
119	Tyrone Bogues	3.00
120	Dell Curry	1.00
121	Rex Chapman	2.50
122	Kelly Tripucka	1.00
123	Jerry Sichting	1.00
124	Brian Rowsom	1.00
125	J.R. Reid	1.00
126	Stuart Gray	1.00
127	Dallas Mavericks Logo	1.00
128	Brad Davis	1.00
129	Derek Harper	2.00
130	Rolando Blackman	2.00
131	Adrian Dantley	2.00
132	Herb Williams	1.00
133	Bill Wennington	1.00
134	Sam Perkins	1.50
135	James Donaldson	1.00
136	Denver Nuggets Logo	1.00
137	Walter Davis	2.00
138	Michael Adams	1.00
139	Lafayette Lever	1.50
140	Alex English	2.50
141	Todd Lichti	1.00
142	Jerome Lane	1.00
143	Tim Kempton	1.00
144	Blair Rasmussen	1.00
145	Houston Rockets Loop	1.00
146	Eric Floyd	1.00
147	Mike Woodson	1.00
148	Derrick Chievous	1.00
149	John Lucas	1.00
150	Buck Johnson	1.00
151	Otis Thorpe	1.00
152	Larry Smith	1.00
153	Hakeem Olajuwon	12.00
154	Minnesota T'wolves Logo	1.00
155	Pooh Richardson	1.00
156	Sidney Lowe	1.00
157	Doug West	1.00
158	Adrian Branch	1.00
159	Tony Campbell	1.00
160	David Rivers	1.00
161	Steve Johnson	1.00
162	Brad Lohaus	1.00
163	San Antonio Spurs Logo	1.00
164	Maurice Cheeks	2.00
165	Vernon Maxwell	1.00
166	Zarko Paspali	1.00
167	Sean Elliott	6.00
168	Terry Cummings	1.50
169	Frank Brickowski	1.00
170	Willie Anderson	1.00
171	David Robinson	35.00
172	Utah Jazz Logo	1.00
173	John Stockton	14.00
174	Darrell Griffith	1.00
175	Bobby Hansen	1.00
176	Karl Malone	14.00
177	Mike Brown	1.00
178	Thurl Bailey	1.00
179	Eric Leckner	1.00
180	Mark Eaton	1.00
181	Golden State Warrior Logo	1.00
182	Winston Garland	1.00
183	Mitch Richmond	9.00
184	Sarunas Marciulionis	1.00
185	Terry Teagle	1.00
186	Chris Mullin	2.50
187	Rod Higgins	1.00
188	Uwe Blab	1.00
189	Manute Bol	1.00
190	Los Angeles Clippers Logo	1.00
191	Gary Grant	1.00
192	Ron Harper	1.50
193	Ken Norman	1.00
194	Charles Smith	1.00
195	Danny Manning	2.00
196	Joe Wolf	1.00
197	Benoit Benjamin	1.00
198	Ken Bannister	1.00
199	Los Angeles Lakers Logo	1.00
200	Ervin Johnson	20.00
201	Byron Scott	2.00
202	Michael Cooper	2.00
203	Orlando Woolridge	1.50
204	James Worthy	4.00
205	A.C. Green	2.50
206	Vlade Divac	3.00
207	Mychal Thompson	1.50

208	Phoenix Suns Logo	1.00
209	Kevin Johnson	2.50
210	Jeff Hornacek	2.00
211	Greg Grant	1.00
212	Dan Majerle	2.00
213	Tim Perry	1.00
214	Eddie Johnson	1.00
215	Tom Chambers	1.50
216	Andrew Lang	1.00
217	Portland Trail Blazers Logo	1.00
218	Clyde Drexler	10.00
219	Terry Porter	1.50
220	Drazen Petrovic	2.00
221	Jerome Kersey	1.00
222	Mark Bryant	1.00
223	Danny Young	1.00
224	Wayne Cooper	1.00
225	Kevin Duckworth	1.00
226	Sacramento Kings Logo	1.00
227	Danny Ainge	2.50
228	Michael Jackson	1.00
229	Vinny Del Negro	1.00
230	Kenny Smith	1.50
231	Harold Pressley	1.00
232	Rodney McCray	1.00
233	Wayman Tisdale	1.00
234	Greg Kite	1.00
235	Seattle Supersonics Logo	1.00
236	Sedale Threatt	1.00
237	Avery Johnson	2.50
238	Nate McMillan	1.50
239	Dale Ellis	1.50
240	Xavier McDaniel	1.00
241	Derrick McKey	1.00
242	Michael Cage	1.00
243	Olden Polynice	1.00
244	Charles Barkley	6.00
245	Larry Bird	12.00
246	Tom Chambers	1.50
247	Adrian Dantley	1.00
248	Clyde Drexler	6.00
249	Joe Dumars	2.00
250	Dale Ellis	1.00
251	Patrick Ewing	5.00
252	A.C. Green	1.50
253	Ervin Johnson	10.00
254	Michael Jordan	40.00
255	Bill Laimbeer	1.50
256	Jeff Malone	1.00
257	Karl Malone	9.00
258	Moses Malone	1.50
259	Xavier McDaniel	1.00
260	Hakeem Olajuwon	5.00
261	Robert Parish	2.00
262	Mark Price	2.00
263	Jack Sikma	1.00
264	John Stockton	9.00
265	Isiah Thomas	4.00
266	Dominique Wilkins	4.00
267	James Worthy	4.00
268	NBA Logo	1.00
269	Puzzle Card	1.00
270	Puzzle Card	1.00
271	Puzzle Card	1.00
272	Puzzle Card	1.00

1990-91 Panini Stickers

These stickers each measure 1-7/8" x 2-15/16" and were produced by Panini. The stickers were issued on sheets with three rows of four, in a package which also contained an album. Each front has an action photo against a white background. The player's name and team are at the bottom. The back has an NBA licensing logo, sticker number, and Panini logo. The last 18 in the set use letters instead of numbers.

		MT
Complete Set (180):		10.00
Common Player (1-162):		.03
Common Player (A-R):		.05
1	Magic Johnson	1.00
2	Mychal Thompson	.03
3	Vlade Divac	.15
4	Byron Scott	.15
5	James Worthy	.75
6	A.C. Green	.15
7	Jerome Kersey	.05
8	Clyde Drexler	.75
9	Buck Williams	.15
10	Kevin Duckworth	.05
11	Terry Porter	.07
12	Cliff Robinson	.25
13	Tom Chambers	.07
14	Dan Majerle	.15
15	Mark West	.03
16	Kevin Johnson	.15
17	Jeff Hornacek	.20
18	Kurt Rambis	.15
19	Nate McMillan	.03
20	Shawn Kemp	.75
21	Dale Ellis	.03
22	Michael Cage	.03
23	Xavier McDaniel	.05
24	Derrick McKey	.03
25	Manute Bol	.05
26	Chris Mullin	.50
27	Terry Teagle	.03
28	Tim Hardaway	.50
29	Sarunas Marciulionis	.07
30	Mitch Richmond	.50
31	Gary Grant	.03
32	Danny Manning	.25
33	Benoit Benjamin	.03
34	Ron Harper	.15
35	Ken Norman	.05
36	Charles Smith	.05
37	Harold Pressley	.03
38	Antoine Carr	.03
39	Danny Ainge	.50
40	Wayman Tisdale	.05
41	Ralph Sampson	.25
42	Vinny Del Negro	.03
43	David Robinson	.75
44	Sean Elliott	.15
45	Terry Cummings	.10
46	Willie Anderson	.05
47	Rod Strickland	.25
48	Frank Brickowski	.03
49	Karl Malone	1.00
50	Darrell Griffith	.03
51	John Stockton	1.00
52	Blue Edwards	.05
53	Mark Eaton	.05
54	Thurl Bailey	.03
55	Rolando Blackman	.15
56	Sam Perkins	.15
57	James Donaldson	.03
58	Herb Williams	.03
59	Roy Tarpley	.05
60	Derek Harper	.15
61	Michael Adams	.05
62	Blair Rasmussen	.03
63	Jerome Lane	.03
64	Walter Davis	.25
65	Todd Lichti	.05
66	Joe Barry Carroll	.03
67	Vernon Maxwell	.05
68	Otis Thorpe	.07
69	Hakeem Olajuwon	1.00
70	Buck Johnson	.03
71	Sleepy Floyd	.03
72	Mitchell Wiggins	.03
73	Tony Campbell	.03
74	Tod Murphy	.03
75	Tyrone Corbin	.03
76	Sam Mitchell	.03
77	Randy Breuer	.03
78	Pooh Richardson	.07
79	Rex Chapman	.15
80	Dell Curry	.05
81	Tyrone Bogues	.15
82	J.R. Reid	.05
83	Armon Gilliam	.03
84	Kelly Tripucka	.03
85	Dennis Rodman	.75
86	Joe Dumars	.25
87	Isiah Thomas	.40
88	Bill Laimbeer	.05
89	Vinnie Johnson	.03
90	James Edwards	.03
91	Michael Jordan	2.00
92	Stacey King	.05
93	Scottie Pippen	1.00
94	John Paxson	.07
95	Horace Grant	.15
96	Craig Hodges	.03
97	Brad Lohaus	.03
98	Jack Sikma	.05
99	Ricky Pierce	.05
100	Greg Anderson	.03
101	Alvin Robertson	.03
102	Jay Humphries	.03
103	Mark Price	.15
104	Winston Bennett	.03
105	Brad Daugherty	.10
106	Craig Ehlo	.05
107	Larry Nance	.15
108	Hot Rod Williams	.05
109	Rik Smits	.15
110	Chuck Person	.15
111	Reggie Miller	.50
112	LaSalle Thompson	.03
113	Detlef Schrempf	.15
114	Vern Fleming	.05
115	Moses Malone	.25
116	Doc Rivers	.20
117	Dominique Wilkins	.30
118	Spud Webb	.10
119	Kevin Willis	.10
120	Kenny Smith	.15
121	Otis Smith	.03
122	Sidney Green	.03
123	Nick Anderson	.15
124	Scott Skiles	.15
125	Jerry Reynolds	.03
126	Terry Catledge	.03
127	Charles Barkley	1.00
128	Ron Anderson	.03
129	Hersey Hawkins	.15
130	Mike Gminski	.03
131	Johnny Dawkins	.03
132	Rick Mahorn	.03
133	Michael Smith	.03
134	Reggie Lewis	.15
135	Larry Bird	1.50
136	Kevin McHale	.50
137	Joe Kleine	.05
138	Robert Parish	.10
139	Maurice Cheeks	.25
140	Patrick Ewing	.75
141	Charles Oakley	.10
142	Gerald Wilkins	.05
143	Kenny Walker	.05
144	Mark Jackson	.20
145	Mark Alarie	.03
146	John Williams	.03
147	Darrell Walker	.03
148	Bernard King	.25
149	Harvey Grant	.05
150	Ledell Eackles	.03
151	Glen Rice	.50
152	Kevin Edwards	.03
153	Tellis Frank	.03
154	Rony Seikaly	.07
155	Billy Thompson	.05
156	Sherman Douglas	.05
157	Roy Hinson	.03
158	Chris Morris	.05
159	Lester Conner	.03
160	Sam Bowie	.10
161	Purvis Short	.15
162	Mookie Blaylock	.15
A	John Stockton	.75
B	Magic Johnson	1.00
C	A.C. Green	.15
D	Hakeem Olajuwon	.50
E	James Worthy	.25
F	Isiah Thomas	.25
G	Michael Jordan	2.00
H	Larry Bird	1.00
I	Patrick Ewing	.30
J	Charles Barkley	.50
K	Michael Jordan	2.00
L	Larry Bird	1.00
M	Hakeem Olajuwon	.50
N	NBA Finals	.15
O	NBA Finals	.15
P	NBA Finals	.15
Q	NBA Finals	.15
R	NBA Finals	.15
NNO	Panini Album	1.00

1990-91 Panini Spanish Stickers

This 217-card set was offered exclusively in Western Europe and were not distributed within the United States, making them much more difficult to obtain than the American Panini's of more recent years. The stickers measure 1-7/8" x 2-15/16" and are issued in sheets of three rows of four stickers each. The sheets were included with the sticker album itself and are numbered on the back.

		MT
Complete Set (217):		275.00
Common Player:		1.00
1	NBA Official Licensed Product Logo	1.00
2	Boston Celtics Logo	1.00
3	Reggie Lewis	2.00
4	Larry Bird	25.00
5	Michael Smith	1.00
6	Kevin McHale	6.00
7	Joe Kleine	1.00
8	Robert Parish	3.00
9	Miami Heat Logo	1.00
10	Sherman Douglas	2.00
11	Kevin Edwards	1.00
12	Glen Rice	5.00
13	Billy Thompson	1.00
14	Tellis Frank	1.00
15	Rony Seikaly	1.00
16	New Jersey Nets Logo	1.00
17	Mookie Blaylock	2.00
18	Lester Conner	1.00
19	Purvis Short	1.00
20	Chris Morris	1.00
21	Roy Hinson	1.00
22	Sam Bowie	1.00
23	New York Knicks Logo	1.00
24	Maurice Cheeks	2.00
25	Mark Jackson	2.50
26	Gerald Wilkins	1.00
27	Kenny Walker	1.00
28	Charles Oakley	1.50
29	Patrick Ewing	9.00
30	Philadelphia 76ers Logo	1.00
31	Johnny Dawkins	1.00
32	Hersey Hawkins	1.00
33	Ron Anderson	1.00
34	Charles Barkley	10.00
35	Rick Mahorn	1.00
36	Mike Gminski	1.00
37	Washington Bullets Logo	1.00
38	Ledell Eackles	1.00
39	Darrell Walker	1.50
40	Bernard King	2.00
41	John Williams	1.00
42	Mark Alarie	1.00
43	Harvey Grant	1.00
44	Atlanta Hawks Logo	1.00
45	Anthony Webb	1.50
46	Glenn (Doc) Rivers	2.00
47	Kenny Smith	1.50
48	Dominique Wilkins	5.00
49	Kevin Willis	1.50
50	Moses Malone	2.00
51	Charlotte Hornets Logo	1.00
52	Tyrone Bogues	2.00
53	Rex Chapman	2.00
54	Dell Curry	1.00
55	Kelly Tripucka	1.00
56	Armon Gilliam	1.00
57	J.R. Reid	2.00
58	Chicago Bulls Logo	1.00
59	Craig Hodges	1.00
60	John Paxson	2.00
61	Michael Jordan	75.00
62	Scottie Pippen	25.00
63	Horace Grant	2.00
64	Stacey King	1.00
65	Cleveland Cavaliers Logo	1.00
66	Mark Price	2.00
67	Craig Ehlo	1.00
68	Winston Bennett	1.00
69	John Williams	1.00
70	Larry Nance	2.00
71	Brad Daugherty	1.00
72	Detroit Pistons Logo	1.00
73	Isiah Thomas	3.00
74	Joe Dumars	2.50
75	Vinnie Johnson	1.50
76	Dennis Rodman	5.00
77	Bill Laimbeer	2.00
78	James Edwards	1.00
79	Indiana Pacers Logo	1.00
80	Vern Fleming	1.00
81	Reggie Miller	7.00
82	Chuck Person	1.50
83	LaSalle Thompson	1.00
84	Detlef Schrempf	2.00
85	Rik Smits	2.00
86	Milwaukee Bucks Logo	1.00
87	Alvin Robertson	1.00
88	Jay Humphries	1.00
89	Ricky Pierce	1.50
90	Brad Lohaus	1.00
91	Jack Sikma	1.50
92	Greg Anderson	1.00
93	Dallas Mavericks Logo	1.00
94	Derek Harper	2.00
95	Rolando Blackman	2.00
96	Brad Davis	1.00
97	Roy Tarpley	1.00
98	Herb Williams	1.00
99	James Donaldson	1.00
100	Denver Nuggets Logo	1.00
101	Michael Adams	1.00
102	Walter Davis	2.00
103	Todd Lichti	1.00
104	Jerome Lane	1.00
105	Blair Rasmussen	1.00
106	Joe Barry Carroll	1.00
107	Houston Rockets Logo	1.00
108	Eric Floyd	1.00
109	Mitchell Wiggins	1.00
110	Vernon Maxwell	1.00
111	Otis Thorpe	1.00
112	Buck Johnson	1.00
113	Hakeem Olajuwon	12.00
114	Minnesota Timberwolves Logo	1.00
115	Pooh Richardson	1.00
116	Tony Campbell	1.00
117	Tyrone Corbin	1.00
118	Sam Mitchell	1.00
119	Tod Murphy	1.00
120	Randy Breuer	1.00
121	Orlando Magic Logo	1.00
122	Scott Skiles	2.00
123	Otis Smith	1.00
124	Terry Catledge	1.00
125	Jerry Reynolds	1.00
126	Nick Anderson	2.00
127	Sidney Green	1.00
128	San Antonio Spurs	1.00
129	Rod Strickland	2.00
130	Willie Anderson	1.00
131	Sean Elliot	2.00
132	Terry Cummings	1.00
133	Frank Brickowski	1.00
134	David Robinson	20.00
135	Utah Jazz Logo	1.00
136	John Stockton	14.00
137	Darrell Griffith	1.00
138	Theodore Edwards	1.00
139	Karl Malone	14.00
140	Thurl Bailey	1.00
141	Mark Eaton	1.00
142	Golden State Warriors	1.00
143	Tim Hardaway	10.00
144	Mitch Richmond	5.00
145	Chris Mullin	3.00
146	Sarunas Marciulionis	1.00
147	Terry Teagle	1.00
148	Manute Bol	1.00
149	Los Angeles Clippers Logo	1.00
150	Gary Grant	1.00
151	Ron Harper	1.50
152	Ken Norman	1.00
153	Charles Smith	1.00
154	Danny Manning	2.00
155	Benoit Benjamin	1.00
156	Los Angeles Lakers Logo	1.00
157	Ervin Johnson	20.00
158	Byron Scott	2.00
159	James Worthy	4.00
160	A.C. Green	2.00
161	Vlade Divac	3.00
162	Mychal Thompson	1.00
163	Phoenix Suns Logo	1.00
164	Kevin Johnson	2.00
165	Jeff Hornacek	2.00
166	Dan Majerle	2.00
167	Tom Chambers	1.50
168	Kurt Rambis	1.00
169	Mark West	1.00
170	Portland Trail Blazers Logo	1.00
171	Terry Porter	1.50
172	Clyde Drexler	10.00
173	Jerome Kersey	1.00
174	Cliff Robinson	4.00
175	Buck Williams	1.50
176	Kevin Duckworth	1.00
177	Sacramento Kings Logo	1.00
178	Vinny Del Negro	1.00
179	Danny Ainge	2.50
180	Wayman Tisdale	1.00
181	Antoine Carr	1.00
182	Greg Kite	1.00
183	Ralph Sampson	1.50
184	Seattle Supersonics Logo	1.00
185	Nate McMillan	1.50
186	Dale Ellis	1.50
187	Xavier McDaniel	1.00
188	Shawn Kemp	7.00
189	Derrick McKey	1.00
190	Michael Cage	1.00
191	Dennis Rodman AW	3.00
192	Dennis Rodman AW	3.00
193	Darrell Walker AW	1.00
194	Darrell Walker AW	1.00
195	Ricky Pierce AW	1.00
196	Ricky Pierce AW	1.00
197	Isiah Thomas AW	3.00
198	Isiah Thomas AW	3.00
199	David Robinson AW	3.00
200	David Robinson AW	3.00
201	Ervin Johnson AW	8.00
202	Ervin Johnson AW	8.00
203	Larry Bird AW	8.00
204	Larry Bird AW	8.00
205	Michael Jordan AW	30.00
206	Michael Jordan AW	30.00
207	Hakeem Olajuwon AW	4.00
208	Hakeem Olajuwon AW	4.00
209	Puzzel Card	1.00
210	Puzzle Card	1.00
211	Puzzle Card	1.00
212	Puzzle Card	1.00
213	Puzzle Card	1.00
214	Puzzle Card	1.00
215	Puzzle Card	1.00
216	Puzzle Card	1.00
217	Puzzle Card	1.00

1991-92 Panini Stickers

These 1-3/4" x 2-11/16" stickers were sold in packs of six, with 100 packs included in each box. The front has a color action photo, with the player's name and biological information running along the left side of the sticker. The player's team name is above the photo; his 1990-91 season and career statistics are below the picture. The sticker back has a number, the Panini logo, an NBA logo and a notation that an album was made to hold the stickers.

		MT
Complete Set (192):		25.00
Common Player:		.05
1	NBA Official Licensed Product Logo	.05
2	1991 NBA Finals Logo	.05
3	Chris Mullin	.50
4	Mitch Richmond	.50
5	Alton Lister	.05
6	Tim Hardaway	.75
7	Tom Tolbert	.05
8	Rod Higgins	.05
9	Charles Smith	.07
10	Ron Harper	.15
11	Olden Polynice	.05
12	Ken Norman	.05
13	Gary Grant	.05
14	Danny Manning	.25
15	Sam Perkins	.07
16	Vlade Divac	.25
17	James Worthy	.50
18	Magic Johnson	1.50
19	A.C. Green	.15
20	Byron Scott	.15
21	Kevin Johnson	.25
22	Mark West	.05
23	Dan Majerle	.30
24	Jeff Hornacek	.20
25	Xavier McDaniel	.07
26	Tom Chambers	.15
27	Terry Porter	.07
28	Kevin Duckworth	.05
29	Clyde Drexler	.50
30	Jerome Kersey	.05
31	Buck Williams	.15
32	Danny Ainge	.50
33	Wayman Tisdale	.07
34	Antoine Carr	.05
35	Lionel Simmons	.07
36	Travis Mays	.05
37	Rory Sparrow	.05
38	Duane Causwell	.05
39	Benoit Benjamin	.05
40	Michael Cage	.05
41	Derrick McKey	.07
42	Shawn Kemp	.50
43	Gary Payton	.75
44	Ricky Pierce	.07
45	Derek Harper	.10
46	James Donaldson	.05
47	Randy White	.05
48	Rodney McCray	.05
49	Alex English	.10
50	Rolando Blackman	.10
51	Orlando Woolridge	.07
52	Todd Lichti	.05
53	Chris Jackson	.10
54	Blair Rasmussen	.05
55	Reggie Williams	.07
56	Marcus Liberty	.05
57	Hakeem Olajuwon	1.25
58	Kenny Smith	.10
59	Vernon Maxwell	.07
60	Otis Thorpe	.10
61	Buck Johnson	.05
62	Larry Smith	.05
63	Pooh Richardson	.05
64	Felton Spencer	.05
65	Tod Murphy	.05
66	Tyrone Corbin	.05
67	Tony Campbell	.05
68	Sam Mitchell	.05
69	Dennis Scott	.07
70	Nick Anderson	.20
71	Terry Catledge	.07
72	Scott Skiles	.20
73	Otis Smith	.05
74	Greg Kite	.05
75	Terry Cummings	.15
76	Rod Strickland	.20
77	David Robinson	1.50
78	Willie Anderson	.05
79	Sean Elliott	.20
80	Paul Pressey	.05
81	John Stockton	1.00
82	Jeff Malone	.07
83	Mark Eaton	.10
84	Thurl Bailey	.05
85	Karl Malone	1.00
86	Blue Edwards	.07
87	Kevin Johnson	.25
88	'91 Western Division All-Stars	.10
89	NBA All-Star Weekend Logo	.05
90	Magic Johnson	1.00
91	Karl Malone	1.00
92	David Robinson	.75
93	Chris Mullin	.25
94	Charles Barkley	.50
95	'91 Eastern Division All-Stars	.10
96	Michael Jordan	1.50
97	Isiah Thomas	.25
98	Charles Barkley	.75
99	Patrick Ewing	.50
100	Larry Bird	1.50
101	Dominique Wilkins	.40
102	Kevin Willis	.15
103	John Battle	.05
104	Doc Rivers	.15
105	Spud Webb	.15
106	Moses Malone	.25
107	J.R. Reid	.03
108	Johnny Newman	.07
109	Rex Chapman	.15
110	Muggsy Bogues	.15
111	Mike Gminski	.05
112	Kendall Gill	.25
113	Scottie Pippen	1.25
114	Bill Cartwright	.10
115	John Paxson	.07
116	Michael Jordan	5.00
117	Horace Grant	.25
118	B.J. Armstrong	.25
119	Brad Daugherty	.15
120	Larry Nance	.15
121	Hot Rod Williams	.07
122	Craig Ehlo	.07
123	Darnell Valentine	.05
124	Danny Ferry	.05
125	Isiah Thomas	.50
126	James Edwards	.05
127	Bill Laimbeer	.10
128	Vinnie Johnson	.05
129	Joe Dumars	.50
130	Dennis Rodman	1.00
131	Reggie Miller	.75
132	Detlef Schrempf	.15
133	Chuck Person	.10
134	LaSalle Thompson	.07
135	Vern Fleming	.07
136	Rik Smits	.07
137	Dale Ellis	.07
138	Frank Brickowski	.05
139	Jay Humphries	.05
140	Jack Sikma	.10
141	Fred Roberts	.05
142	Alvin Robertson	.05
143	Robert Parish	.25
144	Kevin McHale	.50
145	Kevin Gamble	.07
146	Larry Bird	2.00
147	Reggie Lewis	.25
148	Brian Shaw	.07
149	Sherman Douglas	.07
150	Rony Seikaly	.07
151	Glen Rice	.50
152	Grant Long	.07
153	Billy Thompson	.05
154	Willie Burton	.05
155	Reggie Theus	.10
156	Sam Bowie	.05
157	Derrick Coleman	.35
158	Drazen Petrovic	.25
159	Mookie Blaylock	.15
160	Chris Morris	.05
161	Gerald Wilkins	.07
162	Charles Oakley	.10
163	Patrick Ewing	.75
164	Kiki Vandeweghe	.10
165	Maurice Cheeks	.10
166	John Starks	.25
167	Hersey Hawkins	.10
168	Rick Mahorn	.07
169	Charles Barkley	1.50
170	Rickey Green	.05
171	Ron Anderson	.05
172	Armon Gilliam	.05
173	Bernard King	.25
174	Ledell Eackles	.05
175	John Williams	.05
176	Darrell Walker	.05
177	Haywoode Workman	.05
178	Harvey Grant	.07
179	Derrick Coleman (ART)	.35
180	Dee Brown (ART)	.15
181	Lionel Simmons (ART)	.10
182	Felton Spencer (ART)	.05
183	Dennis Scott (ART)	.10
184	Gary Payton (ART)	.50
185	Travis Mays (ART)	.05
186	Kendall Gill (ART)	.15
187	All-NBA First Team	.50
188	Charles Barkley (AS)	.75
189	Patrick Ewing (AS)	.50
190	Michael Jordan (AS)	1.50
191	Karl Malone (AS)	1.00
192	Magic Johnson (AS)	1.00
NNO	Panini Album	2.50

1992-93 Panini Stickers

These stickers feature full-color action photos on the front, bordered by a white frame. The player's name and team are listed at the top of the card, in a team color-coded bar. The sticker back has a number, Panini and NBA logos, and information about the corresponding album which was produced to hold the set. The stickers are 1-3/4" x 2-11/16".

		MT
Complete Set (192):		20.00
Common Player:		.05
1	Shaquille O'Neal	8.00
2	Tracy Murray	.05
3	Robert Horry	.20
4	Bryant Stith	.10
5	Randy Woods	.07
6	Adam Keefe	.07
7	Byron Houston	.07
8	Duane Cooper	.07
9	Western Playoffs (Action Scene Left)	.05
10	Western Playoffs (Action Scene Right)	.05
11	Clyde Drexler	.50
12	Michael Jordan	2.00

13 Eastern Playoffs (Action Scene Left) .05
14 Eastern Playoffs (Action Scene Right) .05
15 Chicago Bulls Logo .05
16 1992 NBA Finals (Michael Jordan) (Action Scene Upper Left) .50
17 1992 NBA Finals (Michael Jordan) (Action Scene Upper Right) .50
18 1992 NBA Finals (Michael Jordan) (Action Scene Lower Left) .50
19 1992 NBA Finals (Michael Jordan) (Action Scene Lower Right) .50
20 Michael Jordan (MVP) 2.00
21 Tim Hardaway .50
22 Chris Mullin .50
23 Billy Owens .20
24 Sarunas Marciulionis .05
25 Jeff Grayer .05
26 Tyrone Hill .07
27 Danny Manning .10
28 Ron Harper .15
29 Ken Norman .07
30 Charles Smith .07
31 Gary Grant .05
32 Doc Rivers .15
33 James Worthy .40
34 Sam Perkins .15
35 Byron Scott .15
36 Sedale Threatt .05
37 Elden Campbell .05
38 A.C. Green .15
39 Charles Barkley 1.00
40 Kevin Johnson .20
41 Tom Chambers .10
42 Dan Majerle .20
43 Mark West .05
44 Danny Ainge .50
45 Buck Williams .15
46 Clyde Drexler .50
47 Jerome Kersey .10
48 Terry Porter .10
49 Cliff Robinson .15
50 Kevin Duckworth .05
51 Mitch Richmond .50
52 Lionel Simmons .07
53 Wayman Tisdale .07
54 Spud Webb .10
55 Duane Causwell .05
56 Jim Les .05
57 Eddie Johnson .07
58 Ricky Pierce .07
59 Shawn Kemp .50
60 Benoit Benjamin .05
61 Gary Payton .75
62 Dana Barros .05
63 Herb Williams .05
64 Doug Smith .05
65 Terry Davis .05
66 Derek Harper .07
67 Mike Iuzzolino .05
68 Rodney McCray .05
69 Greg Anderson .05
70 Reggie Williams .05
71 Dikembe Mutombo .25
72 Mark Macon .05
73 Winston Garland .05
74 Chris Jackson .07
75 Otis Thorpe .10
76 Hakeem Olajuwon 1.00
77 Vernon Maxwell .07
78 Kenny Smith .10
79 Avery Johnson .20
80 Sleepy Floyd .05
81 Pooh Richardson .05
82 Tony Campbell .05
83 Thurl Bailey .05
84 Doug West .07
85 Gerald Glass .05
86 Felton Spencer .05
87 David Robinson 1.00
88 Terry Cummings .10
89 Sidney Green .05
90 Sean Elliott .15
91 Willie Anderson .05
92 Antoine Carr .05
93 Clyde Drexler (FF) .40
94 Patrick Ewing (FF) .40
95 Magic Johnson (FF) .75
96 Scottie Pippen (FF) .35
97 John Stockton (FF) .75
98 Tim Hardaway (FF) .25
99 David Robinson (FF) .75
100 Karl Malone (FF) .75
101 Chris Mullin (FF) .15
102 Michael Jordan (FF) 2.00
103 Mark Eaton .05
104 Karl Malone 1.00
105 Jeff Malone .05
106 John Stockton 1.00
107 David Benoit .05
108 Jay Humphries .05
109 Alvin Robertson .05
110 Moses Malone .20
111 Sam Vincent .05
112 Frank Brickowski .05
113 Fred Roberts .05
114 Blue Edwards .05
115 Stacey Augmon .10
116 Rumeal Robinson .05
117 Paul Graham .05
118 Dominique Wilkins .50
119 Kevin Willis .15
120 Duane Ferrell .05
121 Tyrone Bogues .15
122 Kendall Gill .15
123 Dell Curry .07
124 Larry Johnson .50
125 Johnny Newman .07
126 J.R. Reid .05
127 Scottie Pippen 1.00
128 Michael Jordan 2.50
129 Bill Cartwright .07
130 Horace Grant .15
131 John Paxson .07
132 B.J. Armstrong .15
133 Mark Price .20
134 Brad Daugherty .10
135 Larry Nance .10
136 Craig Ehlo .07
137 Hot Rod Williams .07
138 Terrell Brandon .10
139 Joe Dumars .25
140 Isiah Thomas .50
141 Dennis Rodman .75
142 Orlando Woolridge .07
143 John Salley .20
144 Bill Laimbeer .10
145 Reggie Miller .50
146 Detlef Schrempf .15
147 Chuck Person .05
148 Michael Williams .05
149 Rik Smits .15
150 Vern Fleming .05
151 Lester Conner .05
152 Nick Anderson .15
153 Scott Skiles .15
154 Terry Catledge .05
155 Jerry Reynolds .05
156 Dennis Scott .07
157 Rick Fox .07
158 Reggie Lewis .15
159 Robert Parish .25
160 Kevin Gamble .05
161 Kevin McHale .50
162 John Bagley .05
163 Steve Smith .25
164 Glen Rice .35
165 Grant Long .05
166 Rony Seikaly .07
167 Bimbo Coles .05
168 Willie Burton .05
169 Derrick Coleman .20
170 Drazen Petrovic .15
171 Sam Bowie .07
172 Chris Morris .05
173 Mookie Blaylock .10
174 Chris Dudley .05
175 Patrick Ewing .75
176 Mark Jackson .25
177 Xavier McDaniel .05
178 John Starks .25
179 Charles Oakley .10
180 Rolando Blackman .07
181 Hersey Hawkins .10
182 Johnny Dawkins .05
183 Armon Gilliam .05
184 Jeff Hornacek .15
185 Tim Perry .05
186 Andrew Lang .05
187 Pervis Ellison .07
188 Michael Adams .05
189 Harvey Grant .05
190 Ledell Eackles .05
191 A.J. English .05
192 David Wingate .05
193 Panini Album 1.50

1993-94 Panini Stickers

These stickers once again feature team color-coded backgrounds framed by a black border. A color action photo is in the center of the sticker, with the player's team name above it and the player's name at the bottom. A team logo also appears on the front. The stickers are 2-3/8" x 3-3/8" and are numbered on the back. An NBA logo, Panini logo and information about the corresponding album which was produced to hold the stickers is also given. Six stickers (A-F) at the end of the collection were part of an NBA honor roll picture which was featured in the middle of the album.

MT
Complete Set (253): 20.00
Common Player (1-247): .05
Common Player (A-F): .25
1 John Paxson (top part of photo) .07
2 John Paxson (bottom part of photo) .07
3 Charles Barkley (top part of photo) .50
4 Charles Barkley (bottom part of photo) .50
5 Victor Alexander .05
6 Chris Gatling .05
7 Tim Hardaway .50
8 Warriors Team Logo .05
9 Tyrone Hill .07
10 Sarunas Marciulionis .05
11 Chris Mullin .50
12 Billy Owens .15
13 Latrell Sprewell .35
14 Gary Grant .05
15 Ron Harper .15
16 Mark Jackson .20
17 Clippers Team Logo .05
18 Danny Manning .15
19 Ken Norman .07
20 Stanley Roberts .05
21 Loy Vaught .05
22 John Williams .05
23 Sam Bowie .07
24 Elden Campbell .05
25 Vlade Divac .15
26 Lakers Team Logo .05
27 A.C. Green .15
28 Anthony Peeler .10
29 Doug Christie .07
30 Sedale Threatt .07
31 James Worthy .25
32 Danny Ainge .50
33 Charles Barkley .75
34 Cedric Ceballos .15
35 Suns Team Logo .05
36 Tom Chambers .15
37 Richard Dumas .05
38 Kevin Johnson .25
39 Dan Majerle .25
40 Oliver Miller .07
41 Clyde Drexler .50
42 Mario Elie .07
43 Harvey Grant .05
44 Trailblazers Team Logo .05
45 Jerome Kersey .10
46 Terry Porter .10
47 Cliff Robinson .10
48 Rod Strickland .10
49 Buck Williams .15
50 Anthony Bonner .07
51 Duane Causwell .07
52 Kurt Rambis .25
53 Kings Team Logo .05
54 Mitch Richmond .25
55 Lionel Simmons .10
56 Wayman Tisdale .10
57 Spud Webb .10
58 Walt Williams .10
59 Dana Barros .15
60 Eddie Johnson .07
61 Shawn Kemp .50
62 Supersonics Team Logo .05
63 Derrick McKey .07
64 Nate McMillian .07
65 Gary Payton .75
66 Sam Perkins .10
67 Ricky Pierce .07
68 Terry Davis .07
69 Derek Harper .10
70 Donald Hodge .05
71 Mavericks Team Logo .05
72 Mike Iuzzolino .05
73 Jim Jackson .25
74 Sean Rooks .05
75 Doug Smith .07
76 Randy White .05
77 LaPhonso Ellis .25
78 Scott Hastings .05
79 Mahmoud Abdul-Rauf .10
80 Nuggets Team Logo .05
81 Marcus Liberty .05
82 Mark Macon .07
83 Dikembe Mutombo .40
84 Robert Pack .10
85 Reggie Williams .07
86 Scott Brooks .05
87 Sleepy Floyd .07
88 Carl Herrera .05
89 Rockets Team Logo .05
90 Robert Horry .25
91 Vernon Maxwell .10
92 Hakeem Olajuwon 1.00
93 Kenny Smith .10
94 Otis Thorpe .10
95 Thurl Bailey .05
96 Chris Smith .05
97 Mike Brown .05
98 Timberwolves Team Logo .05
99 Christian Laettner .25
100 Luc Longley .07
101 Chuck Person .07
102 Doug West .05
103 Michael Williams .05
104 Willie Anderson .05
105 Antoine Carr .05
106 Terry Cummings .05
107 Spurs Team Logo .05
108 Sean Elliott .15
109 Dale Ellis .10
110 Avery Johnson .15
111 J.R. Reid .07
112 David Robinson .75
113 David Benoit .05
114 Tyrone Corbin .05
115 Mark Eaton .07
116 Jazz Team Logo .05
117 Jay Humphries .05
118 Jeff Malone .07
119 Karl Malone 1.00
120 Felton Spencer .07
121 John Stockton 1.00
122 Anthony Avent .05
123 Frank Brickowski .05
124 Todd Day .10
125 Bucks Team Logo .05
126 Blue Edwards .07
127 Brad Lohaus .05
128 Moses Malone .20
129 Lee Mayberry .05
130 Eric Murdock .15
131 Stacey Augmon .25
132 Mookie Blaylock .20
133 Duane Ferrell .07
134 Hawks Team Logo .05
135 Steve Henson .05
136 Adam Keefe .07
137 Jon Koncak .05
138 Dominique Wilkins .50
139 Kevin Willis .15
140 Tyrone Bogues .15
141 Dell Curry .07
142 Kenny Gattison .05
143 Hornets Team Logo .07
144 Kendall Gill .15
145 Larry Johnson .50
146 Alonzo Mourning 2.00
147 Johnny Newman .07
148 David Wingate .05
149 B.J. Armstrong .15
150 Bill Cartwright .07
151 Horace Grant .15
152 Bulls Team Logo .05
153 Stacey King .05
154 John Paxson .07
155 Will Perdue .05
156 Scottie Pippen 1.00
157 Scott Williams .07
158 Terrell Brandon .10
159 Brad Daugherty .15
160 Craig Ehlo .10
161 Cavaliers Team Logo .05
162 Danny Ferry .07
163 Larry Nance .15
164 Mark Price .20
165 Gerald Wilkins .07
166 Hot Rod Williams .07
167 Mark Aguirre .10
168 Joe Dumars .25
169 Bill Laimbeer .10
170 Pistons Team Logo .05
171 Terry Mills .07
172 Olden Polynice .07
173 Alvin Robertson .07
174 Dennis Rodman .75
175 Isiah Thomas .75
176 Dale Davis .15
177 Vern Fleming .07
178 Reggie Miller .75
179 Pacers Team Logo .05
180 Pooh Richardson .07
181 Detlef Schrempf .15
182 Malik Sealy .10
183 Rik Smits .10
184 LaSalle Thompson .05
185 Nick Anderson .10
186 Anthony Bowie .05
187 Shaquille O'Neal 4.00
188 Magic Team Logo .05
189 Donald Royal .05
190 Dennis Scott .07
191 Scott Skiles .15
192 Tom Tolbert .05
193 Jeff Turner .05
194 Alaa Abdelnaby .05
195 Dee Brown .10
196 Sherman Douglas .10
197 Celtics Team Logo .05
198 Rick Fox .10
199 Kevin Gamble .07
200 Xavier McDaniel .10
201 Robert Parish .25
202 Lorenzo Williams .05
203 Bimbo Coles .05
204 Matt Geiger .05
205 Harold Miner .15
206 Heat Team Logo .05
207 Glen Rice .20
208 John Salley .07
209 Rony Seikaly .10
210 Brian Shaw .07
211 Steve Smith .20
212 Rafael Addison .05
213 Kenny Anderson .25
214 Benoit Benjamin .05
215 Nets Team Logo .05
216 Derrick Coleman .35
217 Chris Dudley .07
218 Rick Mahorn .07
219 Chris Morris .07
220 Rumeal Robinson .07
221 Greg Anthony .07
222 Rolando Blackman .10
223 Patrick Ewing .60
224 Knicks Team Logo .05
225 Anthony Mason .10
226 Charles Oakley .15
227 Doc Rivers .15
228 Charles Smith .07
229 John Starks .15
230 Ron Anderson .05
231 Johnny Dawkins .07
232 Armon Gilliam .07
233 76ers Team Logo .05
234 Hersey Hawkins .15
235 Jeff Hornacek .15
236 Andrew Lang .05
237 Tim Perry .07
238 Clarence Weatherspoon .25
239 Michael Adams .07
240 Rex Chapman .15
241 Kevin Duckworth .07
242 Bullets Team Logo .05
243 Pervis Ellison .10
244 Tom Gugliotta .30
245 Don MacLean .20
246 Brent Price .05
247 LaBradford Smith .07
A Charles Barkley (MVP) 1.25
B Mahmoud Abdul-Rauf (Most Improved Player) .25
C Shaquille O'Neal (ROY) 2.50
D Hakeem Olajuwon (Defensive POY) 1.25
E John Stockton (Court Vision) 1.00
F Cliff Robinson (Sixth Man Award) .25
NNO Panini Album 1.00

1994-95 Panini Stickers

The 230-card, 2-3/8" x 3-3/8" sticker set was issued in six-card packs for 49¢ each. In addition to the 220 base stickers, there are 10 1994 NBA All-Rookie stickers lettered A-J. The backs have the card number and licensing information.

MT
Complete Set (230): 30.00
Common Player (1-220/A-J): .15
1 Toronto Raptors .15
2 Toronto Raptors .15
3 Vancouver Grizzlies .15
4 Vancouver Grizzlies .15
5 Stacey Augmon .25
6 Mookie Blaylock .40
7 Craig Ehlo .15
8 Duane Ferrell .15
9 Adam Keefe .15
10 Andrew Lang .15
11 Danny Manning .50
12 Kevin Willis .50
13 Dee Brown .40
14 Sherman Douglas .15
15 Pervis Ellison .15
16 Rick Fox .50
17 Kevin Gamble .15
18 Xavier McDaniel .15
19 Dino Radja .40
20 Dominique Wilkins 1.00
21 Michael Adams .15
22 Muggsy Bogues 1.00
23 Dell Curry .15
24 Kenny Gattison .15
25 Hersey Hawkins .50
26 Larry Johnson 1.00
27 Alonzo Mourning 1.50
28 Robert Parish .75
29 B.J. Armstrong .25
30 Steve Kerr .25
31 Toni Kukoc .75
32 Luc Longley .15
33 Pete Myers .15
34 Will Perdue .15
35 Scottie Pippen 3.00
36 Bill Wennington .15
37 Terrell Brandon .75
38 Michael Cage .15
39 Brad Daugherty .25
40 Tyrone Hill .15
41 Chris Mills .50
42 Mark Price .75
43 Gerald Wilkins .15
44 John Williams .25
45 Greg Anderson .15
46 Joe Dumars .75
47 Allan Houston 1.00
48 Lindsey Hunter .15
49 Eric Leckner .15
50 Mark Macon .15
51 Terry Mills .15
52 Mark West .15
53 Antonio Davis .25
54 Dale Davis .25
55 Mark Jackson .50
56 Derrick McKey .15
57 Reggie Miller 1.50
58 Byron Scott .50
59 Rik Smits .50
60 Haywoode Workman .15
61 Vernell "Bimbo" Coles .15
62 Matt Geiger .15
63 Grant Long .15
64 Harold Miner .15
65 Glen Rice .75
66 John Salley .15
67 Rony Seikaly .15
68 Steve Smith .75
69 Vin Baker 1.25
70 Jon Barry .15
71 Anthony Cook .15
72 Todd Day .15
73 Brad Lohaus .15
74 Lee Mayberry .15
75 Eric Murdock .15
76 Ed Pinckney .15
77 Kenny Anderson .25
78 Benoit Benjamin .15
79 P.J. Brown .50
80 Derrick Coleman .25
81 Kevin Edwards .15
82 Armon Gilliam .25
83 Chris Morris .15
84 Rex Walters .15
85 Greg Anthony .15
86 Hubert Davis .15
87 Patrick Ewing 2.00
88 Derek Harper .25
89 Anthony Mason .50
90 Charles Oakley .25
91 Charles Smith .15
92 John Starks .50
93 Nick Anderson .25
94 Anthony Avent .15
95 Horace Grant .50
96 Anfernee Hardaway 3.50
97 Shaquille O'Neal 4.00
98 Donald Royal .15
99 Dennis Scott .25
100 Jeff Turner .15
101 Dana Barros .25
102 Shawn Bradley .50
103 Johnny Dawkins .15
104 Jeff Malone .25
105 Tim Perry .15
106 Clarence Weatherspoon .25
107 Scott Williams .15
108 Orlando Woolridge .15
109 Rex Chapman .25
110 Calbert Cheaney .40
111 Kevin Duckworth .15
112 Tom Gugliotta .50
113 Don MacLean .15
114 Gheorghe Muresan .50
115 Brent Price .15
116 Scott Skiles .20
117 Tony Campbell .15
118 Lucious Harris .15
119 Donald Hodge .15
120 Jim Jackson .50
121 Popeye Jones .25
122 Jamal Mashburn .50
123 Sean Rooks .15
124 Doug Smith .15
125 Mahmoud Abdul-Rauf .15
126 LaPhonso Ellis .15
127 Dikembe Mutombo .75
128 Robert Pack .15
129 Rodney Rogers .25
130 Bryant Stith .15
131 Brian Williams .15
132 Reggie Williams .15
133 Victor Alexander .15
134 Chris Gatling .15
135 Tim Hardaway 1.00
136 Keith Jennings .15
137 Chris Mullin 1.00
138 Billy Owens .25
139 Latrell Sprewell .50
140 Chris Webber 2.50
141 Sam Cassell .50
142 Mario Elie .15
143 Carl Herrera .15
144 Robert Horry .50
145 Vernon Maxwell .15
146 Hakeem Olajuwon 2.00
147 Kenny Smith .20
148 Otis Thorpe .25
149 Terry Dehere .15
150 Harold Ellis .15
151 Gary Grant .15
152 Ron Harper .50
153 Pooh Richardson .15
154 Malik Sealy .25
155 Elmore Spencer .15
156 Loy Vaught .25
157 Elden Campbell .15
158 Doug Christie .15
159 Vlade Divac .25
160 Anthony Peeler .15
161 Tony Smith .15
162 Sedale Threatt .15
163 Nick Van Exel .15
164 James Worthy 1.00
165 Thurl Bailey .15
166 Mike Brown .15
167 Stacey King .15
168 Christian Laettner .50
169 Isaiah Rider .50
170 Chris Smith .15
171 Doug West .15
172 Michael Williams .15
173 Danny Ainge .75
174 Charles Barkley 1.50
175 Cedric Ceballos .30
176 A.C. Green .75
177 Frank Johnson .15
178 Kevin Johnson .75
179 Dan Majerle .50
180 Oliver Miller .15
181 Mark Bryant .15
182 Clyde Drexler 1.50
183 Harvey Grant .15
184 Jerome Kersey .20
185 Terry Porter .20
186 Clifford Robinson .40
187 Rod Strickland .20
188 Buck Williams .50
189 Randy Brown .15
190 Olden Polynice .15
191 Mitch Richmond 1.00
192 Lionel Simmons .15
193 Andre Spencer .15
194 Wayman Tisdale .25
195 Spud Webb .50
196 Walt Williams .25
197 Willie Anderson .15
198 Vinny Del Negro .15
199 Sean Elliott .40
200 Dale Ellis .25
201 Avery Johnson .50
202 Chuck Person .25
203 David Robinson 2.00
204 Dennis Rodman 1.50
205 Kendall Gill .15
206 Ervin Johnson .15
207 Shawn Kemp 1.00
208 Sarunas Marciulionis .15
209 Nate McMillan .25
210 Gary Payton 1.50
211 Sam Perkins .25
212 Detlef Schrempf .40
213 David Benoit .15
214 Tyrone Corbin .15
215 Jeff Hornacek .40
216 Jay Humphries .15
217 Karl Malone 2.00
218 Felton Spencer .15
219 John Stockton 2.00
220 Luther Wright .15
A Chris Webber (ART) 3.00
B Anfernee Hardaway (ART) 2.50
C Vin Baker (ART) 1.00
D Jamal Mashburn (ART) .75
E Isaiah Rider (ART) .50
F Dino Radja (ART) .50
G Nick Van Exel (ART) 1.00
H Toni Kukoc (ART) .75
I Lindsey Hunter (ART) .15
J Shawn Bradley (ART) .50
NNO Panini Album 2.00

1995-96 Panini Stickers

The 288-card, 2-1/8" x 3" sticker set was to be pasted in a special album and each sticker front had the player's name printed along one border with the team logo inside a basketball icon along the bottom border. Nine sticker cards represent each of the 29 teams, with three subsets: NBA Power Players (136-144), NBA League Leaders (271-280) and NBA Rookie Sensations (281-288).

MT
Complete Set (288): 30.00
Common Player: .10
1 Dee Brown .10
2 Sherman Douglas .10
3 Pervis Ellison .10
4 Rick Fox .10
5 Greg Minor .10
6 Celtics Team Logo .10
7 Eric Montross .20
8 Dino Radja .15
9 David Wesley .15
10 Rex Chapman .15
11 Bimbo Coles .10
12 Kevin Gamble .10
13 Matt Geiger .10
14 Billy Owens .15
15 Heat Team Logo .10
16 Khalid Reeves .10
17 Glen Rice .40
18 Kevin Willis .25
19 Kenny Anderson .25
20 P.J. Brown .10
21 Chris Childs .10
22 Derrick Coleman .15
23 Kevin Edwards .10
24 Nets Team Logo .10
25 Armon Gilliam .15
26 Chris Morris .15
27 Jayson Williams .10
28 Anthony Bonner .10
29 Hubert Davis .10
30 Patrick Ewing 1.00
31 Derek Harper .25
32 Anthony Mason .25
33 Knicks Team Logo .10
34 Charles Oakley .25
35 Charles Smith .10
36 John Starks .25
37 Nick Anderson .20
38 Horace Grant .40
39 Anfernee Hardaway 2.00
40 Shaquille O'Neal 3.00
41 Donald Royal .10
42 Magic Team Logo .10
43 Dennis Scott .10

44	Brian Shaw	.10
45	Jeff Turner	.10
46	Derrick Alston	.10
47	Dana Barros	.15
48	Shawn Bradley	.25
49	Willie Burton	.10
50	Jeff Malone	.25
51	76ers Team Logo	.10
52	Clarence Weatherspoon	.25
53	Scott Williams	.10
54	Sharone Wright	.15
55	Mitchell Butler	.10
56	Calbert Cheaney	.25
57	Juwan Howard	.75
58	Don MacLean	.10
59	Gheorghe Muresan	.25
60	Bullets Team Logo	.10
61	Doug Overton	.10
62	Scott Skiles	.15
63	Chris Webber	1.50
64	Stacey Augmon	.25
65	Mookie Blaylock	.25
66	Craig Ehlo	.10
67	Andrew Lang	.10
68	Grant Long	.10
69	Hawks Team Logo	.10
70	Ken Norman	.10
71	Steve Smith	.40
72	Spud Webb	.25
73	Tony Bennett	.10
74	Muggsy Bogues	.25
75	Scott Burrell	.10
76	Dell Curry	.10
77	Kendall Gill	.10
78	Hornets Team Logo	.10
79	Larry Johnson	.50
80	Alonzo Mourning	1.00
81	Robert Parish	.40
82	Ron Harper	.25
83	Michael Jordan	5.00
84	Steve Kerr	.10
85	Toni Kukoc	.40
86	Luc Longley	.10
87	Bulls Team Logo	.10
88	Will Perdue	.10
89	Scottie Pippen	1.50
90	Bill Wennington	.10
91	Terrell Brandon	.25
92	Michael Cage	.10
93	Danny Ferry	.10
94	Tyrone Hill	.10
95	Chris Mills	.25
96	Cavaliers Team Logo	.10
97	Bobby Phills	.10
98	Mark Price	.25
99	John Williams	.15
100	Bill Curley	.10
101	Joe Dumars	.40
102	Grant Hill	2.50
103	Allan Houston	.75
104	Lindsey Hunter	.10
105	Pistons Team Logo	.10
106	Mark Macon	.10
107	Terry Mills	.10
108	Mark West	.10
109	Antonio Davis	.15
110	Dale Davis	.15
111	Duane Ferrell	.10
112	Mark Jackson	.25
113	Derrick McKey	.10
114	Pacers Team Logo	.10
115	Reggie Miller	.75
116	Rik Smits	.40
117	Haywoode Workman	.10
118	Vin Baker	.60
119	Jon Barry	.10
120	Marty Conlon	.10
121	Todd Day	.10
122	Lee Mayberry	.10
123	Bucks Team Logo	.10
124	Eric Mobley	.10
125	Eric Murdock	.10
126	Glenn Robinson	1.00
127	Willie Anderson	.10
128	B.J. Armstrong	.25
129	Acie Earl	.10
130	Jerome Kersey	.10
131	Tony Massenburg	.10
132	Raptors Team Logo	.10
133	Oliver Miller	.10
134	John Salley	.10
135	B.J. Tyler	.10
136	Larry Johnson (POW)	.50
137	Shawn Kemp (POW)	.60
138	Karl Malone (POW)	1.00
139	Jamal Mashburn (POW)	.40
140	Alonzo Mourning (POW)	.75
141	Hakeem Olajuwon (POW)	.75
142	Shaquille O'Neal (POW)	1.50
143	David Robinson (POW)	1.00
144	Chris Webber (POW)	1.25
145	Lucious Harris	.10
146	Jim Jackson	.50
147	Popeye Jones	.10
148	Jason Kidd	2.00
149	Jamal Mashburn	.75
150	Mavericks Team Logo	.10
151	George McCloud	.10
152	Roy Tarpley	.10
153	Lorenzo Williams	.10
154	Mahmoud Abdul-Rauf	.10
155	LaPhonso Ellis	.10
156	Dikembe Mutombo	.40
157	Robert Pack	.10
158	Jalen Rose	1.00
159	Nuggets Team Logo	.10
160	Bryant Stith	.10
161	Brian Williams	.10
162	Reggie Williams	.10
163	Chucky Brown	.10
164	Sam Cassell	.25
165	Clyde Drexler	1.00
166	Mario Elie	.10
167	Carl Herrera	.10
168	Rockets Team Logo	.10
169	Robert Horry	.30
170	Hakeem Olajuwon	1.50
171	Kenny Smith	.15
172	Tom Gugliotta	.25
173	Christian Laettner	.40
174	Darrick Martin	.10
175	Isaiah Rider	.30
176	Sean Rooks	.10
177	Timberwolves Team Logo	.10
178	Chris Smith	.10
179	Doug West	.10
180	Michael Williams	.10
181	Vinny Del Negro	.10
182	Sean Elliott	.40
183	Avery Johnson	.25
184	Chuck Person	.25
185	J.R. Reid	.10
186	Spurs Team Logo	.10
187	Doc Rivers	.15
188	David Robinson	1.50
189	Dennis Rodman	1.00
190	David Benoit	.10
191	Jeff Hornacek	.15
192	Adam Keefe	.10
193	Karl Malone	1.00
194	Bryon Russell	.15
195	Jazz Team Logo	.10
196	Felton Spencer	.10
197	John Stockton	1.00
198	Jamie Watson	.10
199	Greg Antony	.10
200	Benoit Benjamin	.10
201	Blue Edwards	.10
202	Doug Edwards	.10
203	Kenny Gattison	.10
204	Grizzlies Team Logo	.10
205	Antonio Harvey	.10
206	Byron Scott	.25
207	Larry Stewart	.10
208	Chris Gatling	.10
209	Tim Hardaway	.40
210	Donyell Marshall	.10
211	Chris Mullin	.40
212	Carlos Rogers	.10
213	Warriors Team Logo	.10
214	Clifford Rozier	.15
215	Rony Seikaly	.10
216	Latrell Sprewell	.50
217	Terry Dehere	.10
218	Harold Ellis	.10
219	Lamond Murray	.25
220	Charles Outlaw	.20
221	Pooh Richardson	.10
222	Clippers Team Logo	.10
223	Rodney Rogers	.25
224	Malik Sealy	.15
225	Loy Vaught	.15
226	Sam Bowie	.20
227	Elden Campbell	.10
228	Cedric Ceballos	.20
229	Vlade Divac	.25
230	Eddie Jones	1.00
231	Lakers Team Loop	.10
232	Anthony Peeler	.10
233	Sedale Threatt	.10
234	Nick Van Exel	.75
235	Charles Barkley	1.00
236	A.C. Green	.25
237	Kevin Johnson	.40
238	Dan Majerle	.25
239	Danny Manning	.40
240	Suns Team Logo	.10
241	Elliot Perry	.10
242	Wesley Person	.25
243	Wayman Tisdale	.15
244	Chris Dudley	.10
245	Harvey Grant	.10
246	Aaron McKie	.15
247	Terry Porter	.10
248	Clifford Robinson	.40
249	Trail Blazers Team Loop	.10
250	Rod Strickland	.15
251	Otis Thorpe	.15
252	Buck Williams	.25
253	Randy Brown	.10
254	Brian Grant	.50
255	Bobby Hurley	.25
256	Olden Polynice	.10
257	Mitch Richmond	.50
258	Kings Team Logo	.10
259	Lionel Simmons	.10
260	Michael Smith	.10
261	Walt Williams	.25
262	Vincent Askew	.10
263	Hersey Hawkins	.25
264	Shawn Kemp	.75
265	Sarunas Marciulionis	.10
266	Nate McMillian	.15
267	Supersonics Team Logo	.10
268	Gary Payton	.75
269	Sam Perkins	.25
270	Detlef Schrempf	.40
271	Chris Gatling (LL)	.10
272	Popeye Jones (LL)	.10
273	Steve Kerr (LL)	.10
274	Karl Malone (LL)	.75
275	Dikembe Mutombo (LL)	.30
276	Shaquille O'Neal (LL)	1.25
277	Scottie Pippen (LL)	.60
278	Dennis Rodman (LL)	.60
279	John Stockton (LL)	.75
280	Spud Webb (LL)	.10
281	Brian Grant (ROO)	.25
282	Grant Hill (ROO)	1.25
283	Juwan Howard (ROO)	.40
284	Eddie Jones (ROO)	.60
285	Jason Kidd (ROO)	1.00
286	Eric Montross (ROO)	.10
287	Wesley Person (ROO)	.10
288	Glenn Robinson (ROO)	.50
NNO	Panini Album	2.00

1977 Pepsi NBA All-Stars

These 8" x 10" cards feature color action photos of eight NBA stars. The set, sponsored by Pepsi-Cola, is unnumbered and is printed on heavy cardboard. Each card back has career stats for the pictured player, plus the set's name and checklist. Fronts have the player's name and Pepsi logo.

		NM
Complete Set (8):		295.00
Common Player:		25.00
	Kareem Abdul-Jabbar	55.00
	Rick Barry	30.00
	Dave Cowens	25.00
	Julius Erving	60.00
	Pete Maravich	70.00
	Bob McAdoo	25.00
	David Thompson	25.00
	Bill Walton	40.00

1997 Pinnacle Inside WNBA

Pinnacle Inside WNBA arrived in cans that featured a player on the outside, and when opened, yielded a pack of cards. It was the inaugural edition of WNBA cards and celebrated the first season of the new league. The set contained 81 cards and was paralleled in both Court Collection and Executive Collection sets. My Town and Team Development were the names of the two insert sets available.

		MT
Complete Set (82):		75.00
Common Player:		10.00
1	Lisa Leslie	10.00
2	Cynthia Cooper	15.00
3	Rebecca Lobo	3.00
4	Michele Timms	1.00
5	Ruthie Bolton-Holifield	2.00
6	Michelle Edwards	.75
7	Vicky Bullett	.30
8	Tammi Reiss	.75
9	Penny Toler	.10
10	Tia Jackson	.10
11	Rhonda Mapp	.10
12	Elena Baranova	1.00
13	Tina Thompson	1.00
14	Merlakia Jones	.20
15	Tora Suber	.10
16	Sophia Witherspoon	.30
17	Tajama Abraham	.10
18	Jessie Hicks	.10
19	Tina Nicholson	.10
20	Tiffany Woosley	.10
21	Chantel Tremitiere	.10
22	Daedra Charles	.10
23	Nancy Lieberman-Cline	2.00
24	Denique Graves	.10
25	Toni Foster	.10
26	Sheryl Swoopes	15.00
27	Kym Hampton	.30
28	Sharon Manning	.10
29	Janice Lawrence Braxton	.10
30	Sue Wicks	.10
31	Lady Hardmon	.10
32	Jamila Wideman	.10
33	Bridgette Gordon	.10
34	Lynette Woodard	1.00
35	Kim Perrot	.30
36	Teresa Weatherspoon	.30
37	Andrea Stinson	1.00
38	Janeth Arcain	.10
39	Pamela McGee	.10
40	Tamecka Dixon	.30
41	Wendy Palmer	1.00
42	Umeki Webb	.10
43	Isabelle Fijalkowski	.10
44	Jennifer Gillom	1.00
45	Latasha Byears	.30
46	Zheng Haixia	.10
47	Kisha Ford	.10
48	Eva Nemcova	.10
49	Penny Moore	.20
50	Mwadi Mabika	.10
51	Kim Williams	.10
52	Wanda Guyton	.10
53	Vickie Johnson	.30
54	Deborah Carter	.10
55	Bridget Pettis	.10
56	Andrea Congreaves	.10
57	Zheng Haixia (Hoop Scoops)	.10
58	Tammi Reiss (Hoop Scoops)	.30
59	Jennifer Gillom (Hoop Scoops)	.30
60	Bridgette Gordon (Hoop Scoops)	.10
61	Janice Lawrence Braxton (Hoop Scoops)	.10
62	Cynthia Cooper (Hoop Scoops)	2.00
63	Teresa Weatherspoon (Hoop Scoops)	.10
64	Elena Baranova (Hoop Scoops)	.50
65	Nancy Lieberman-Cline (Hoop Scoops)	1.00
66	Andrea Congreaves (Hoop Scoops)	.10
67	Sophia Witherspoon (Hoop Scoops)	.10
68	Vicky Bullett (Hoop Scoops)	.10
69	Ruthie Bolton-Holifield (Hoop Scoops)	1.00
70	Tina Thompson (Hoop Scoops)	.50
71	Lynette Woodard (Hoop Scoops)	.50
72	Jamila Wideman (Hoop Scoops)	.10
73	Lisa Leslie (Style & Grace)	2.00
74	Wendy Palmer (Style & Grace)	.50
75	Michele Timms (Style & Grace)	.50
76	Ruthie Bolton-Holifield (Style & Grace)	1.00
77	Andrea Stinson (Style & Grace)	.50
78	Lynette Woodard (Style & Grace)	.50
79	Cynthia Cooper (Style & Grace)	2.00
80	Rebecca Lobo (Style & Grace)	1.50
81	Checklist	.10

1997 Pinnacle Inside WNBA Court

Court Collection was an 81-card parallel set that included the insert name in foil across the bottom. These were inserted into one per seven packs.

	MT
Court Cards:	3x-6x

1997 Pinnacle Inside WNBA Executive Collection

Executive Collection was an 81-card parallel set that included a prismatic foil finish to the front of the card along with the insert name in foil letters. These were seeded one per 47 packs.

	MT
Executive Cards:	25x-50x

1997 Pinnacle Inside WNBA Cans

Pinnacle WNBA cards arrived in cans that featured a shot of a player, the WNBA logo, team logo and information about the product on the outside. When opened with a can opener, a 10-card pack of cards were inside a foil wrapper. Seventeen different cans were available.

		MT
Complete Set (17):		20.00
Common Player:		.50
1	Andrea Stinson	1.50
2	Vicky Bullett	.75
3	Lynette Woodard	1.50
4	Michelle Edwards	.75
5	Cynthia Cooper	4.00
6	Tina Thompson	1.00
7	Lisa Leslie	4.00
8	Jamila Wideman	.50
9	Teresa Weatherspoon	1.00
10	Rebecca Lobo	3.00
11	Michele Timms	1.00
12	Bridget Pettis	.50
13	Bridgette Gordon	.50
14	Ruthie Bolton-Holifield	2.00
15	Wendy Palmer	1.00
16	Elena Baranova	1.00
17	WNBA League	2.00

1997 Pinnacle Inside WNBA My Town

My Town featured eight top players on a horizontal, foil background that featured the skyline from the city she played in. These inserts were numbered "of 8" on the back and seeded one per 19 packs.

		MT
Complete Set (8):		120.00
Common Player:		5.00
1	Lisa Leslie	40.00
2	Lady Hardmon	5.00
3	Michele Timms	15.00
4	Ruthie Bolton-Holifield	25.00
5	Andrea Stinson	15.00
6	Michelle Edwards	10.00
7	Cynthia Cooper	40.00
8	Rebecca Lobo	30.00

1997 Pinnacle Inside WNBA Team Development

Team Development featured eight young stars on a silver foil background with a swoosh of the player's team color. These were numbered "of 8" on the back and inserted one per 19 packs.

		MT
Complete Set (8):		50.00
Common Player:		5.00
1	Tina Thompson	20.00
2	Pamela McGee	5.00
3	Jamila Wideman	5.00
4	Eva Nemcova	10.00
5	Tammi Reiss	15.00
6	Sue Wicks	5.00
7	Tora Suber	5.00
8	Toni Foster	5.00

1998 Pinnacle WNBA

Pinnacle WNBA returned for a second season with 85 cards, two parallel sets and three inserts. The set included 75 player cards and an eight-card Highlight subset along with two checklists. Cards featured a shot of the player with stats on the right side and the last name of the player in gold foil across the bottom. The two parallel sets were called Court Collection (1:3 packs) and Arena Collection (1:19). Insert sets in WNBA were: Coast to Coast, Number Ones and Planet Pinnacle.

		MT
Complete Set (85):		25.00
Common Player:		.10
Minor Stars:		.20
Court Cards:		2x-4x
Inserted 1:3		
Arena Collection Cards:		8x-16x
Inserted 1:19		
1	*Rhonda Blades*	.50
2	Lisa Leslie	3.50
3	Jennifer Gillom	1.00
4	Ruthie Bolton-Holifield	1.75
5	Wendy Palmer	.75
6	Sophia Witherspoon	.30
7	Eva Nemcova	.30
8	Andrea Stinson	.75
9	Heidi Burge	.10
10	Cynthia Cooper	3.50
11	Christy Smith	.20
12	Penny Moore	.20
13	Penny Toler	.20
14	Bridget Pettis	.10
15	Tora Suber	.20
16	Elena Baranova	.75
17	Rebecca Lobo	3.00
18	Isabelle Fijalkowski	.10
19	Vicky Bullett	.20
20	Tina Thompson	.75
21	Andrea Kuklova	.10
22	*Rita Williams*	.50
23	Tamecka Dixon	.20
24	Michele Timms	1.00
25	Bridgette Gordon	.10
26	Tammi Reiss	.50
27	Kym Hampton	.20
28	Janice Braxton	.10
29	Rhonda Mapp	.10
30	Janeth Arcain	.10
31	Lynette Woodard	1.00
32	Tammy Jackson	.10
33	Haixia Zheng	.10
34	Toni Foster	.20
35	Chantel Tremitiere	.10
36	Vickie Johnson	.30
37	Michelle Edwards	.50
38	Wanda Guyton	.10
39	Kim Perrot	.30
40	Sheryl Swoopes	3.00
41	Merlakia Jones	.20
42	Teresa Weatherspoon	.40
43	Kim Williams	.10
44	Lady Hardmon	.10
45	Latasha Byears	.20
46	Umeki Webb	.10
47	Pamela McGee	.20
48	*Nikki McCray*	2.50
49	Cindy Brown	.10
50	Tiffany Woosley	.10
51	Andrea Congreaves	.10
52	Jamila Wideman	.20
53	Mwadi Mabika	.10
54	*Murriel Page*	.75
55	Mikiko Hagiwara	.10
56	*Linda Burgess*	.20
57	Olympia Scott	.10
58	Dena Head	.10
59	Quacy Barnes	.10
60	*Suzie McConnell*	.50
61	Trina Trice	.10
62	Rushia Brown	.10
63	Kisha Ford	.10
64	Sharon Manning	.10
65	Tangela Smith	.10
66	Jim Lewis	.10
67	Nancy Lieberman-Cline	1.50
68	Van Chancellor	.10
69	Denise Taylor	.10
70	Heidi VanDerveer	.10
71	Marynell Meadors	.10
72	Linda Hill-MacDonald	.10
73	Nancy Darsch	.10
74	Cheryl Miller	3.00
75	Julie Rousseau	.10
76	(Rebecca Lobo) (Highlights)	1.50
77	Jennifer Gillom (Highlights)	.50
78	Janeth Arcain (Highlights)	.10
79	Rhonda Mapp (Highlights)	.10
80	Cynthia Cooper (Highlights)	1.50
81	Tina Thompson (Highlights)	.30
82	Kym Hampton (Highlights)	.10
83	Cynthia Cooper (Highlights)	1.50
84	Checklist	.10
85	Checklist	.10

1998 Pinnacle WNBA Arena Collection

Arena Collection paralleled all 85 cards in Pinnacle WNBA. The cards included a prismatic foil and an Arena Collection logo and were seeded one per 19 packs.

	MT
Arena Cards:	8x-16x

1998 Pinnacle WNBA Court

Court Collection was a parallel set of all 85 cards in Pinnacle WNBA. The cards featured a Court Collection logo and were seeded one per three packs.

	MT
Court Cards:	2x-4x

1998 Pinnacle WNBA Coast to Coast

Coast to Coast displayed 10 of the top players in the WNBA that can take the ball up and down the court. These were seeded one per nine packs.

		MT
Complete Set (10):		35.00
Common Player:		1.00
Inserted 1:9		
1	Lynette Woodard	3.00
2	Nikki McCray	6.00
3	Lisa Leslie	12.00
4	Andrea Stinson	3.00
5	Eva Nemcova	1.00
6	Cynthia Cooper	12.00
7	Teresa Weatherspoon	1.00
8	Wendy Palmer	3.00
9	Ruthie Bolton-Holifield	6.00
10	Michele Timms	3.00

1998 Pinnacle WNBA Number Ones

This nine-card insert set highlighted some of the top picks for different WNBA franchises. Number Ones were were seeded every 19 packs.

		MT
Complete Set (9):		125.00
Common Player:		5.00
Inserted 1:19		
1	Margo Dydek	30.00
2	Ticia Penicheiro	10.00
3	Murriel Page	10.00
4	Korie Hlede	20.00
5	Allison Feaster	5.00
6	Cindy Blodgett	30.00
7	Tracy Reid	25.00
8	Alicia Thompson	5.00
9	Nyree Roberts	5.00

1998 Pinnacle WNBA Planet Pinnacle

Planet Pinnacle featured 10 top stars in a swirl design that featured the insert's name and a posed shot of the player inside. These were found every nine packs.

		MT
Complete Set (10):		25.00
Common Player:		.50
Inserted 1:9		
1	Korie Hlede	3.00
2	Eva Nemcova	.50
3	Haixia Zheng	.50
4	Michele Timms	3.00

5	Ticia Penicheiro	2.00
6	Elena Baranova	2.00
7	Rebecca Lobo	10.00
8	Isabelle Fijalkowski	.50
9	Andrea Congreaves	.50
10	Sheryl Swoopes	12.00

1999 Pinnacle Kellogg's WNBA

These Kellogg's NBA and WNBA cards were distributed in 10-card packs that contained both, through a mail-in offer of two dated box tops and 95 cents for shipping and handling. Cards available in packs were silver foil, while a 56-card gold foil set was available through a mail-in offer for $9.95. The NBA cards were produced by Upper Deck, while Pinnacle produced the WNBA cards.

	MT
Complete Set (16):	15.00
Common Player:	.10
Ruthie Bolton-Holifield	1.50
Vicky Bullett	.10
Cynthia Cooper	3.00
Tamecka Dixon	.10
Michelle Edwards	.25
Bridgette Gordon	.10
Lisa Leslie	3.00
Rebecca Lobo	2.00
Eva Nevcova	.25
Wendy Palmer	.50
Bridget Pettis	.10
Tammi Reiss	.25
Andrea Stinson	.50
Sheryl Swoopes	2.00
Michele Timms	1.00
Teresa Weatherspoon	.50

1990-91 Pistons Star

The 14-card, 2-1/2" x 3-1/2" set was produced by Star and sponsored by Home Respiratory Health Care, Inc. The card fronts feature a blue border which fades to white in the middle with the Star logo along the top right border. The horizontal card backs feature bio and stat information.

		MT
Complete Set (14):		6.00
Common Player:		.25
1	Mark Aguirre	.50
2	William Bedford	.25
3	Joe Dumars	.75
4	James Edwards	.25
5	David Greenwood	.25
6	Scott Hastings	.25
7	Gerald Henderson	.25
8	Vinnie Johnson	.50
9	Bill Laimbeer	.50
10	Dennis Rodman	2.00
11	John Salley	.25
12	Isiah Thomas	1.00
13	Chuck Daly (CO)	.50
14	Maia A. Porche (PRES)	.25

1990-91 Pistons Unocal

The 16-card, standard-size set was issued by UNOCAL 76 and produced by Hoops. One card was given away each week with a fuel purchase, beginning in December of 1990. An album to store the cards in was also available for a minimal cost. The card fronts feature "Back to back ... World Champions" with the years '89 and '90. The card backs contain career statistics with bio information and are unnumbered.

	MT
Complete Set (16):	12.00
Common Player:	.50
Mark Aguirre	.75
Chuck Daly (CO)	.75
Joe Dumars	1.50
James Edwards	.50
Vinnie Johnson	.75
Vinnie Johnson (The Shot)	.75
Bill Laimbeer	.75
Lawrence O'Brien (Trophy)	.50
Dennis Rodman	4.00
John Salley	.50
Isiah Thomas	2.00
Isiah Thomas (MVP)	2.00
Celebration Card	.50
Team Photo	1.00
Two Championship Rings	.50
1990 World Champions	.50

1991-92 Pistons Unocal

The 16-card, standard-size set marked the second year that Hoops produced a Pistons set for UNOCAL 76. The production was held to under 160,000 sets and were distributed two per week with fuel purchases beginning in November of 1991. The card fronts have a blue border while the backs have bio and stat information, along with a headshot. The cards are unnumbered.

	MT
Complete Set (16):	10.00
Common Player:	.50
Mark Aguirre	.75
Dave Bing (1989 HOF Inductee)	1.00
Chuck Daly (CO)	.75
Joe Dumars	1.50
Joe Dumars (1991 Pistons MVP)	1.50
Bill Laimbeer	.75
Bill Laimbeer (All-Time Leading Rebounder)	.75
Dennis Rodman	4.00
John Salley	.50
Isiah Thomas	2.00
Isiah Thomas (All-- Time Leading Scorer)	2.00
Darrell Walker	.50
Orlando Woolridge	.50
Team Photo (1989 World Champs)	1.00
All-Stars (Mark Aguirre, Joe Dumars, Bill Laimbeer, Dennis Rodman, Dennis Thomas, Chuck Daly CO)	.75
Role Players (Brad Sellers, Bob McCann, Charles Thomas, William Bedford, Lance Blanks)	.50

1997-98 Pistons Fleer Schafer Bread

This seven-card set has the same design as the regular 1997-98 Fleer set. It features players from the Detroit Pistons. The cards were distributed in Schafer Bread products in the Michigan area. The cards in the set are not numbered.

		MT
Complete Set (7):		10.00
Common Player:		.25
1	Grant Hill	7.00
2	Lindsey Hunter	1.00
3	Grant Long	.25
4	Aaron McKie	.50
5	Terry Mills	.50
6	Theo Ratliff	2.00
7	Otis Thorpe	.25

1977-78 Post Auerbach Tips

The 12-card, 7-3/16" x 1-3/16" set was available on boxes of Post Raisin Bran and Grape Nuts. Cards 1-6 were found on 15-ounce boxes while 7-12 were on the 20-ounce products. The cards are blank-backed and feature tips from legendary Celtics coach Red Auerbach.

		NM
Complete Set (12):		75.00
Common Player:		7.00
1	The Screen	7.00
2	The Pick and Roll	7.00
3	The Give and Go	7.00
4	The Back Door Play	7.00
5	The High or Low Post	7.00
6	The Fast Break	7.00
7	Outlet Pass	7.00
8	The Defensive Switch	7.00
9	Boxing Out	7.00
10	Hitting the Open Player	7.00
11	Blocking and Charging	7.00
12	Traveling	7.00

1995 Post Honeycomb Posters

Inserted in specially marked Post Honeycomb boxes, the set of three posters measures 11" x 17" when unfolded. Patrick Ewing, Shawn Kemp and Alonzo Mourning are featured in the set which has the players first name in block letters and a facsimile signature on the bottom half.

		MT
Complete Set (3):		6.00
Common Player:		2.00
1	Patrick Ewing	2.00
2	Shawn Kemp	3.00
3	Alonzo Mourning	2.00

1995 Press Pass

Press Pass's 36-card Basketball Draft Picks set features only the top prospects from the 1995 NBA Draft, on four different versions. The regular cards have a color action photo on the front, against a checkerboard pattern which shows an action scene through it. Gold foil stamping is used for a belt at the bottom which includes the player's name and the number he was selected in the draft. The back has a basketball showing through the checkerboard design, with a color action photo in the forefront. A white box has a brief recap of the player's accomplishments in college. A card number is in the upper left corner. The player's name is in a color stripe along the bottom. Three parallel sets of the main issue were also created - Red Hot die-cuts, in hobby packs only; Cool Blue die-cuts, in retail packs only; and Holofoil cards, printed on holographic foil, which are found in both types of packs. Insert sets include the Progressive Joe Smith cards, Pandemonium NitroKrome cards, Prime Time phone cards and more than 10,000 certified autographed cards of top picks such as Joe Smith, Antonio McDyess and Rasheed Wallace.

		MT
Complete Set (36):		20.00
Common Player:		.25
Comp. Die Cut Set (36):		40.00
Common Die Cut:		.50
Die Cut Stars:		1x-2x
Comp. Foil Set (36):		250.00
Common Foil:		2.50
Foil Stars:		6x-12x
Wax Box:		70.00
1	Joe Smith	2.50
2	Antonio McDyess	1.50
3	Jerry Stackhouse	3.50
4	Rasheed Wallace	.75
5	Kevin Garnett	2.50
6	Bryant Reeves	.75
7	Damon Stoudamire	2.50
8	Shawn Respert	.50
9	Ed O'Bannon	.25
10	Kurt Thomas	.75
11	Gary Trent	.50
12	Cherokee Parks	.50
13	Corliss Williamson	.50
14	Eric Williams	.50
15	Brent Barry	.75
16	Theo Ratliff	.50
17	Randolph Childress	.50
18	Jason Caffey	.50
19	Michael Finley	1.25
20	George Zidek	.50
21	Travis Best	.50
22	David Vaughn	.25
23	Sherrell Ford	.50
24	Mario Bennett	.25
25	Lou Roe	.25
26	Frankie King	.25
27	Rashard Griffith	.25
28	Donny Marshall	.50
29	Tyus Edney	.25
30	Antonio McDyess	1.25
31	Rasheed Wallace	1.00
32	Eddie Jones	.50
33	Jason Kidd	1.25
34	Glenn Robinson	1.25
35	Jalen Rose	.25
36	Joe Smith	1.00

1995 Press Pass Die-Cuts

There were two versions of Press Pass Die-cuts available at a rate of one per pack. Red foil die-cuts were found in hobby packs, while blue foil die-cuts were exclusive to retail packs. Either version included all 36 cards with die-cutting around the top of the card.

	MT
Complete Set (36):	40.00
Die-Cut Cards:	1x-2x

1995 Press Pass Autographs

The autographed cards were randomly inserted in packs and are very similar to the base cards, except they do not have gold foil across the card front.

	MT
Complete Set (8):	250.00
Common Player:	10.00
Jimmy King	10.00
Antonio McDyess	60.00
Cherokee Parks	15.00
Joe Smith	70.00
Damon Stoudamire	80.00
David Vaughn	10.00
Rasheed Wallace	40.00
Eric Williams	20.00

1995 Press Pass Phone Cards

These phone cards, ranging in denomination from $5, $10, $20 and $1,995, were inserted at a rate beginning at one per every box of 1995 Press Pass basketball, with the higher denominations seeded at lesser rates. Cards are numbered with a "PT" prefix.

		MT
Complete Set (8):		120.00
Common Player:		8.00
Ten dollar cards:		2x-3x
Twenty dollar cards:		4x-6x
1	Kevin Garnett	13.00
2	Jason Kidd	17.00
3	Antonio McDyess	12.00
4	Ed O'Bannon	8.00
5	Glenn Robinson	10.00
6	Joe Smith	20.00
7	Jerry Stackhouse	28.00
8	Rasheed Wallace	10.00

1995 Press Pass Joe Smith

These four insert cards spotlight former Maryland star Joe Smith. Cards were randomly inserted into 1995 Press Pass basketball packs, and are progressively more difficult ratios to obtain. Card number JS 1/4 appears one in every 36 packs, while JS 2/4 is one per 72, JS 3/4 is one per 216 packs, and JS 4/4 is one per every 864 packs.

		MT
Complete Set (4):		200.00
Common Player:		10.00
Each card is printed in diff. quantities		
1	Joe Smith	10.00
2	Joe Smith	20.00
3	Joe Smith	50.00
4	Joe Smith	140.00

1995 Press Pass Pandemonium

These nine 1995 Press Pass insert cards feature Press Pass' NitroKrome embossed technology, which gives the card front a metallic shine. The player's name is at the bottom in a black panel, with "Pandemonium" written under it; both are superimposed over the player's last name. The Press Pass icon is in the lower right corner. The card back, numbered P 1/9, etc., has a full-bleed color action photo, with a black panel along the left side which contains the player's full name superimposed over his last name. The cards were seeded one per every 18 packs.

		MT
Complete Set (9):		75.00
Common Player:		5.00
P1	Antonio McDyess	12.00
P2	Ed O'Bannon	5.00
P3	Shawn Respert	5.00
P4	Joe Smith	20.00
P5	Damon Stoudamire	25.00
P6	Kurt Thomas	7.00
P7	Gary Trent	7.00
P8	Rasheed Wallace	8.00
P9	Corliss Williamson	6.00

1996 Press Pass

Press Pass' 1996 set contains 45 cards, plus seven different insert sets. Each regular card front has a full-bleed color action photo on it, with a gold-foiled banner at the bottom which includes the player's name, Press Pass logo, position and when the player was selected in the draft. The card back has a color photo, with the player's name, biographical information and a card number running down the left side. A box at the bottom of the card includes 1995-96 and career collegiate stats, plus a brief player profile. The insert sets include Net Burners, autographed cards, Jersey, Lotto, Pandemonium, Swisssh and Focused (acetate) cards. Swisssh and Net Burners cards are parallel to the main set and are each seeded one per pack. The Net Burners cards are die-cut, incorporating the net, backboard and rim of a basketball goal into the design. Swisssh cards feature a silver metallic foil in the design.

		MT
Complete Gold Set (45):		15.00
Common Gold Player:		.05
Minor Gold Stars:		.10
Comp. Silver Set (45):		30.00
Silver Cards:		2x
Comp. Net Burners (45):		30.00
Net Burners:		2x
1	Allen Iverson	2.00
2	Marcus Camby	1.50
3	Shareef Abdur-Rahim	1.00
4	Stephon Marbury	1.25
5	Ray Allen	1.00
6	Antoine Walker	.40
7	Lorenzen Wright	.40
8	Kerry Kittles	.75
9	Samaki Walker	.75
10	Erick Dampier	.30
11	Todd Fuller	.25
12	Vitaly Potapenko	.25
13	Kobe Bryant	3.00
14	Steve Nash	.40
15	Tony Delk	.50
16	Jermaine O'Neal	.50
17	John Wallace	.40
18	Walter McCarty	.50
19	Dontae Jones	.25
20	Roy Rogers	.25
21	Jerome Williams	.25
22	Brian Evans	.25
23	Travis Knight	.25
24	Othella Harrington	.25
25	Ryan Minor	.25
26	Doron Sheffer	.05
27	Jeff McInnis	.10
28	Jason Sasser	.05
29	Randy Livingston	.10
30	Malik Rose	.05
31	Jamie Feick	.05
32	Mark Pope	.05
33	Damon Stoudamire (Rookie Team)	.30
34	Jerry Stackhouse (Rookie Team)	.20
35	Joe Smith (Rookie Team)	.15
36	Michael Finley (Rookie Team)	.10
37	Rasheed Wallace (Rookie Team)	.05
38	Antonio McDyess (Rookie Team)	.10
39	Ray Allen, Travis Knight, Chad Sheffer (UConn)	.50
40	Walter McCarty, Tony Delk, Antoine Walker, Mark Pope (Kentucky)	.30
41	Jerome Williams, Allen Iverson, Othella Harrington (Georgetown)	.50
42	Erick Dampier, Dontae Jones (Miss. State)	.25
43	Stephon Marbury, Drew Barry (Georgia Tech)	.50
44	Kobe Bryant, Jermaine O'Neal (High School Sensations)	.50
45	Checklist	.05

1996 Press Pass Silver

Also referred to as Silver, Swissssh contained all 45 cards from the base set printed with a silver foil strip instead of gold foil from the regular-issue cards. These inserts were seeded one per pack.

	MT
Complete Set (45):	30.00
Silver Cards:	2x

1996 Press Pass Autographs

More than 18,000 autographed cards, covering the top players drafted, are included as inserts in 1996 Press Pass packs. Cards were seeded one per every 72 packs and include a certificate of authenticity.

	MT
Complete Set (20):	400.00
Common Player:	10.00
Ray Allen	35.00
Kobe Bryant	80.00
Marcus Camby	60.00
Tony Delk	20.00
Brian Evans	10.00
Othella Harrington	10.00
Allen Iverson	70.00
Dantae Jones	20.00
Travis Knight	10.00
Randy Livingston	20.00
Stephon Marbury	45.00
Walter McCarty	20.00
Steve Nash	20.00
Vitaly Potapenko	10.00
Roy Rogers	10.00
Jason Sasser	10.00
Antoine Walker	15.00
Samaki Walker	25.00
Jerome Williams	10.00
Lorenzen Wright	20.00

1996 Press Pass Focused

Available only in 1996 Press Pass hobby packs, these acetate cards feature nine players in action, highlighted with gold foil stamping for their names. The player's name is also repeated in the background, using different colors for the letters. A Press Pass logo also appears on the front, as does a card number F1/9 (Focused) etc. The card back shows a white reversed image of the photo from the front. Cards are numbered with a "F" prefix.

		MT
Complete Set (9):		70.00
Common Player:		3.50
1	Allen Iverson	20.00
2	Marcus Camby	16.00
3	Shareef Abdur-Rahim	12.00
4	Stephon Marbury	12.00
5	Ray Allen	10.00
6	Antoine Walker	3.00
7	Lorenzen Wright	3.50
8	Kerry Kittles	7.00
9	Samaki Walker	7.00

1996 Press Pass Jersey Cards

Jerseys of some of the NBA's top draft selections in 1996 are featured on these 1996 Press Pass inserts. Each individually-numbered jersey card includes a certificate of authenticity, an embedded piece of game-used jersey, and the likeness of the player who wore the jersey. The cards, numbered using a "J" prefix, were seeded one per every 640 hobby packs and one per every 720 retail packs.

		MT
Complete Set (4):		225.00
Common Player:		30.00
1	(Allen Iverson)	125.00
2	(Marcus Camby)	100.00
3	(Ray Allen)	65.00
4	(Shareef Abdur-Rahim)	30.00

1996 Press Pass Lotto

This six-card holofoil progressive insert set highlights the top lottery picks. The card front uses silver foil for the border, the player's name (along the right side), Lottery Pick (in the upper left corner) and the year when the player was drafted (in a basketball in the upper right corner). The Press Pass logo is also on the front. The background is the surface of a basketball, with the numbers 1-6 running throughout it. The card back, numbered L1 of 6, etc., is divided into six parts; each part shows a mug shot of one of the top six picks. A basketball is in the middle; the Press Pass logo is at the bottom. The cards were seeded as such: #1 1:720; #2 1:360; #3 1:180; #4 1:90, #5 1:45 and #6 1:36.

		MT
Complete Set (6):		190.00
Common Player:		5.00
1	Allen Iverson	100.00
2	Marcus Camby	60.00
3	Shareef Abdur-Rahim	30.00
4	Stephon Marbury	25.00
5	Ray Allen	15.00
6	Antoine Walker	2.50

1996 Press Pass Net Burners

Net Burners was a 45-card parallel set that included a die-cut basketball net and backboard with the player coming out of the rim. The insert and player's name is stamped across the bottom in gold foil. Net Burners parallel cards carry an "NB" prefix on the card number and were seeded one per pack.

	MT
Complete Set (45):	30.00
Net Burner Cards:	2x

Values quoted in this guide reflect the retail price of a card — the price a collector can expect to pay when buying a card from a dealer. The wholesale price — that which a collector can expect to receive from a dealer when selling cards — will be significantly lower, depending on desirability and condition.

1996 Press Pass Pandemonium

Twelve of the draft's strongest players are featured on these techno-advanced NitroKrome all-foil cards. The cards were seeded one per every 12 packs. The card front has a color action photo against the NitroKrome foil background. "Pandemonium" can be spelled out from the jumbled letters in the background. The player's name is in silver foil along the bottom; the Press Pass logo is in the upper right corner. The card back has a full-bleed color action photo, except for the right border. The player's name and a card number with a "PM" prefix are at the top. The Press Pass logo is in the lower right corner. A brief player profile is also given.

		MT
Complete Set (12):		65.00
Common Player:		2.00
1	Shareef Abdur-Rahim	10.00
2	Ray Allen	8.00
3	Kobe Bryant	20.00
4	Marcus Camby	12.00
5	Erick Dampier	3.00
6	Othella Harrington	2.00
7	Allen Iverson	18.00
8	Kerry Kittles	5.00
9	Stephon Marbury	10.00
10	Walter McCarty	2.00
11	Antoine Walker	2.50
12	John Wallace	2.00

1997 Press Pass

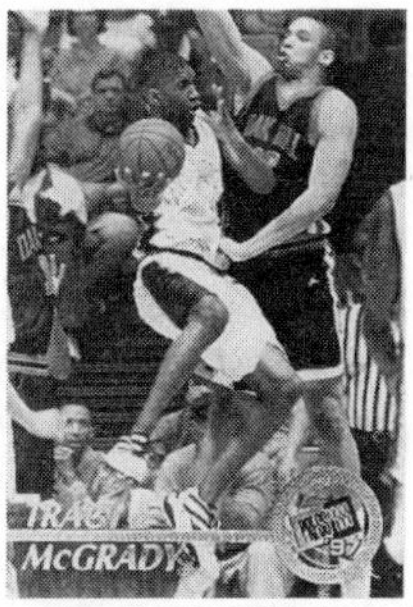

Press Pass Draft Picks included 40 players who were eligible for the 1997 NBA Draft, four multiple player cards and one checklist card. The cards featured color action shots with a gold foil strip through the bottom with the player's first name above the strip and last name under the strip, and a Press Pass logo in the lower right corner. Inserts included: Autographs, Jersey Cards, Lotto, One on One, All-American, In Your Face, Net Burners and two parallel sets - In the Zone, Torquers.

		MT
Complete Set (45):		15.00
Common Player:		.10
Minor Stars:		.20
Red Zone Cards:		2x
Wax Box:		65.00
1	Tim Duncan	3.00
2	Ron Mercer	1.00
3	Keith Van Horn	1.50
4	Tony Battie	1.25
5	Olivier Saint-Jean	.50
6	Tim Thomas	1.00
7	Adonal Foyle	.75
8	Tracy McGrady	1.75
9	Antonio Daniels	1.00
10	Kelvin Cato	.50
11	Danny Fortson	.75
12	Chauncey Billups	1.00
13	Brevin Knight	.50
14	Jacque Vaughn	.40
15	James Collins	.10
16	Johnny Taylor	.40
17	Derek Anderson	1.00
18	Austin Croshere	.75
19	Reggie Freeman	.10
20	Maurice Taylor	.10
21	Shea Seals	.10
22	Anthony Parker	.10
23	John Thomas	.40
24	Kebu Stewart	.30
25	Dedric Willoughby	.10
26	Serge Zwikker	.30
27	Paul Grant	.10
28	Victor Page	.10
29	Bubba Wells	.10
30	Ed Gray	.40
31	Charles O'Bannon	.20
32	Bobby Jackson	.40
33	Keith Booth	.20
34	Eddie Elisma	.10
35	Scot Pollard	.20
36	Harold Deane	.10
37	Jeff Capel	.20
38	Kiwane Garris	.20
39	Charles Smith	.10
40	Alvin Sims	.10
41	Serge Zwikker, Tim Duncan, Eddie Elisma	1.00
42	Austin Croshere, Tim Thomas	.10
43	Tony Battie, Jacque Vaughn, Chauncey Billups	.10
44	Ron Mercer, Derek Anderson	.10
45	Checklist (Tim Duncan)	1.00

1997 Press Pass Red Zone

Red Zone was a 45-card parallel set that was inserted one per hobby pack. These cards contain a red foil stamp across the bottom instead of the gold foil found on regular-issue cards. There is also a retail-only Torquers parallel set that features blue foil and seeded one per pack.

	MT
Complete Set (45):	30.00
Red Zone Cards:	2x

1997 Press Pass Autographs

The 29-card, standard-size set was inserted every 18 packs of Draft Pick. The card fronts contain the player's autograph while the backs inform the collectors of his/her pull. The cards are unnumbered.

	MT
Complete Set (29):	400.00
Common Player:	7.00
Tim Duncan	75.00
Chauncey Billups	25.00
Antonio Daniels	35.00
Tony Battie	25.00
Tim Thomas	25.00
Adonal Foyle	12.00
Tracy McGrady	30.00
Danny Fortson	20.00
Olivier Saint-Jean	10.00
Austin Croshere	12.00
Derek Anderson	20.00
Kelvin Cato	12.00
Brevin Knight	20.00
Johnny Taylor	7.00
Chris Anstey	7.00
Scot Pollard	7.00
Paul Grant	7.00
Anthony Parker	7.00
Bobby Jackson	20.00
John Thomas	7.00
Charles Smith	7.00
Jacque Vaughn	15.00
Serge Zwikker	7.00
Charles O'Bannon	15.00
Bubba Wells	7.00
Kebu Stewart	15.00
James Collins	7.00
Eddie Elisma	7.00

1997 Press Pass All-American

This 12-card set includes 1997 rookies printed on NitroKrome technology. The player is featured on the right half of the card, with a basketball in the lower left corner containing the insert name. These cards were included in one per 12 packs and numbered with an "A" prefix.

		MT
Complete Set (12):		80.00
Common Player:		2.00
1	Tim Duncan	20.00
2	Keith Van Horn	8.00
3	Ron Mercer	7.00
4	Tracy McGrady	12.00
5	Danny Fortson	5.00
6	Brevin Knight	3.50
7	Tony Battie	8.00
8	Jacque Vaughn	3.00
9	Chauncey Billups	7.00
10	Bobby Jackson	3.00
11	Adonal Foyle	5.00
12	Shea Seals	2.00

1997 Press Pass In Your Face

In Your Face was a hobby exclusive, nine-card set that was seeded one per 36 hobby packs. The cards were printed on clear acetate, with a shot from the sky of a player jumping off a wood basketball floor going toward the rim. The player's name is printed in a rounded shadow from the top left corner to the bottom right, with the insert name in gold foil in the lower left. These were numbered with an "IYF" prefix.

		MT
Complete Set (9):		100.00
Common Player:		7.00
1	Ron Mercer	12.00
2	Danny Fortson	9.00
3	Chauncey Billups	12.00
4	Maurice Taylor	7.00
5	Keith Van Horn	15.00
6	Bobby Jackson	7.00
7	Tony Battie	15.00
8	Tim Duncan	35.00
9	Kelvin Cato	7.00

1997 Press Pass Jersey Card

This five-card set had three cards (JC1, JC4 and a bonus Chauncey Billups card) in Press Pass Draft Picks and two additional cards in Double Threats, which was released later in the year. Fronts feature a wood basketball court frame with the player pictured in an oval and the piece of game-worn jersey included near the bottom of the oval. Seeded one per 612 packs, this insert contains a white box in the bottom left corner for individual numbering.

		MT
Complete Set (3):		300.00
Common Player:		80.00
JC1	Tim Duncan	150.00
JC4	Jacque Vaughn	80.00
Bonus	Chauncey Billups	100.00

1997 Press Pass Lotto

Lotto was a six-card progressive insert that contained the top six picks in the 1997 NBA Draft. The cards are printed on silver foil with the player's last name across the top and insert name included in the lower left corner. The back pictures all six players in the set and is numbered with an "L" prefix. Card #1 was seeded one per 720; #2 seeded one per 360; #3 seeded one per 180; #4 seeded one per 90; #5 seeded one per 45; and #6 seeded one per 36.

		MT
Complete Set (7):		250.00
Common Player:		15.00
1	Tim Duncan	125.00
2	Ron Mercer	60.00
3	Keith Van Horn	25.00
4	Tony Battie	30.00
5	Adonal Foyle	15.00
6	Tim Thomas	15.00
Bonus	Chauncey Billups	60.00

1997 Press Pass Net Burners

This 36-card parallel set featured top players from the regular-issue set on a horizontal, die-cut card. Net Burners carried an "NB" prefix on the card number and were inserted into each pack of Press Pass.

		MT
Complete Set (36):		30.00
Common Player:		.20
Minor Stars:		.40
1	Tim Duncan	6.00
2	Ron Mercer	2.00
3	Keith Van Horn	2.50
4	Tony Battie	2.50
5	Scot Pollard	.40
6	Tim Thomas	2.00
7	Adonal Foyle	1.50
8	Tracy McGrady	3.50
9	Antonio Daniels	2.00
10	Kelvin Cato	1.00
11	Danny Fortson	1.50
12	Chauncey Billups	2.00
13	Brevin Knight	1.00
14	Jacque Vaughn	.75
15	James Collins	.20
16	Alvin Sims	.20
17	Derek Anderson	2.00
18	Austin Croshere	1.50
19	Reggie Freeman	.20
20	Maurice Taylor	.20
21	Shea Seals	.20
22	Anthony Parker	.20
23	Johnny Taylor	.75
24	Kebu Stewart	.50
25	Dedric Willoughby	.20
26	Serge Zwikker	.50
27	Olivier Saint-Jean	1.00
28	Victor Page	.20
29	Bubba Wells	.20
30	Ed Gray	.75
31	Charles O'Bannon	.40
32	Bobby Jackson	.75
33	Eddie Elisma	.20
34	Kiwane Garris	.40
35	Keith Booth	.40
36	Checklist (Tim Duncan)	2.00

1997 Press Pass One on One

One on One consisted of nine cards featuring two of the year's best rookies going head to head on silver foil board. Cards are split down the middle with the words "One on One" in yellow letters, with one player on the right and one on the left. These cards carry no letter prefix and are inserted one per 18 packs.

		MT
Complete Set (9):		90.00
Common Player:		5.00
1	Tim Duncan, Tony Battie	20.00
2	Danny Fortson, Tim Duncan	20.00
3	Ron Mercer, Tracy McGrady	12.00
4	Keith Van Horn, Tim Thomas	8.00
5	Antonio Daniels, Chauncey Billups	10.00
6	Adonal Foyle, Kelvin Cato	7.00
7	Derek Anderson, Ron Mercer	10.00
8	Jacque Vaughn, Brevin Knight	5.00
9	Austin Croshere, Maurice Taylor	5.00

1997 Press Pass Double Threat

Press Pass Double Threat marked the company's second release of the year. The base set contained 45 cards that included the player's name up the left side in gold foil and the team that drafted him and the pick he was drafted with in the lower right. Double Threat added professional players like Karl Malone and David Robinson to its college star checklist. Inserts included: Certified Autographs, Double Threat Autographs, Double Thread Jersey Cards, Rookie Jersey Cards, Double Threat Nitrokrome, Light it up, Retro-active, Showdown and Lottery Club.

		MT
Complete Set (45):		15.00
Common Player:		.10
Minor Stars:		.20
Silver Cards:		1.5x
Retroactive Cards:		1.5x
Wax Box:		60.00
1	Tim Duncan	2.50
2	Keith Van Horn	1.00
3	Chauncey Billups	1.00
4	Antonio Daniels	1.00
5	Tony Battie	.75
6	Ron Mercer	1.50
7	Tim Thomas	.75
8	Adonal Foyle	.50
9	Tracy McGrady	1.50
10	Danny Fortson	.75
11	Olivier Saint-Jean	.50
12	Austin Croshere	.50
13	Derek Anderson	1.00
14	Maurice Taylor	.50
15	Kelvin Cato	.50
16	Brevin Knight	1.00
17	Johnny Taylor	.10
18	Chris Anstey	.10
19	Scot Pollard	.10
20	Paul Grant	.10
21	Anthony Parker	.10
22	Ed Gray	.50
23	Bobby Jackson	.75
24	John Thomas	.10
25	Charles Smith	.10
26	Jacque Vaughn	.50
27	Keith Booth	.10
28	Serge Zwikker	.20
29	Charles O'Bannon	.50
30	Bubba Wells	.10
31	Kebu Stewart	.25
32	James Collins	.10
33	Eddie Elisma	.10
34	Tim Duncan, David Robinson	1.25
35	Chauncey Billups, Antoine Walker	.40
36	Tony Battie, Antonio McDyess	.75
37	Ron Mercer, Antoine Walker	.40
38	Antonio Daniels, Shareef Abdur-Rahim	.75
39	Danny Fortson, Antonio McDyess	.20

40	Jacque Vaughn, Karl Malone	.20
41	Adonal Foyle, Joe Smith	.20
42	Paul Grant, Stephon Marbury	.20
43	Keith Booth, Scottie Pippen	.20
44	Charles Smith, Alonzo Mourning	.10
45	Checklist (Tim Duncan, David Robinson)	.50

1997 Press Pass Double Threat Silver

Double Threat arrived with a silver foil verions of each card in the regular-issue set. Where base cards had gold foil, these had silver, and they were seeded one per pack.

	MT
Silver Cards:	1.5x

1997 Press Pass Double Threat Autographs

Thirty players signed cards for Double Threat, with one per 18 hobby packs and one per 36 retail packs. Some of the autographs are duplicates of those inserted in Press Pass Draft Picks sets, while others were specifically created for Double Threats.

	MT
Complete Set (29):	450.00
Common Player:	7.00
Tim Duncan	100.00
Keith Van Horn	30.00
Chauncey Billups	35.00
Antonio Daniels	35.00
Tony Battie	30.00
Tim Thomas	30.00
Adonal Foyle	12.00
Tracy McGrady	40.00
Danny Fortson	20.00
Olivier Saint-Jean	20.00
Austin Croshere	20.00
Derek Anderson	25.00
Kelvin Cato	20.00
Brevin Knight	20.00
Johnny Taylor	7.00
Chris Anstey	7.00
Scot Pollard	7.00
Paul Grant	7.00
Anthony Parker	7.00
Bobby Jackson	30.00
John Thomas	7.00
Charles Smith	7.00
Jacque Vaughn	20.00
Serge Zwikker	7.00
Charles O'Bannon	15.00
Bubba Wells	7.00
Kebu Stewart	15.00
James Collins	7.00
Eddie Elisma	7.00

1997 Press Pass Double Threat Autograph Combos

This five-card insert set highlights five matchups on double-sided cards, with a rookie on one side and a veteran on the other. Both sides are autographed and all cards are individually numbered, with varying production numbers for each. Autograph Combos were inserted one per 432 packs of Double Threat.

	MT
Complete Set (5):	750.00
Common Player:	40.00
Tim Duncan, David Robinson	450.00
Jacque Vaughn, Karl Malone	125.00
Tony Battie, Antonio McDyess	40.00
Ron Mercer, Antoine Walker	100.00
Chauncey Billups, Antoine Walker	40.00

1997 Press Pass Double Threat Double-Threads

Double Threads combine a top draft pick with a veteran star from the NBA and includes a piece of game-worn jersey from each player on the card. The stated print run for each card was 325, with an insertion rate of one per 720 packs. Cards are numbered with a "DD" prefix.

		MT
Complete Set (5):		800.00
Common Player:		125.00
1	Tim Duncan, David Robinson	300.00
2	Chauncey Billups, Antoine Walker	125.00
3	Ron Mercer, Antoine Walker	125.00
4	Tony Battie, Antonio McDyess	125.00
5	Jacque Vaughn, Karl Malone	150.00

1997 Press Pass Double Threat Jersey Cards

Four rookie Jersey Cards were included in Double Threat with an insertion rate of one per 720 packs. The Mercer and Van Horn cards were numbered with a "JC" prefix, while Duncan and Battie were considered Bonus cards.

		MT
Complete Set (4):		550.00
Common Player:		100.00
JC2	Ron Mercer	150.00
JC3	Keith Van Horn	100.00
Bonus	Tony Battie	100.00
Bonus	Tim Duncan	250.00

1997 Press Pass Double Threat Light it Up

This 25-card insert was seeded one per nine packs of Double Threat and was numbered with a "LU" prefix. These inserts featured a die-cut design in the shape of a basketball hoop, with the player's image over it.

		MT
Complete Set (25):		160.00
Common Player:		4.00
1	Tim Duncan	30.00
2	Keith Van Horn	12.00
3	Chauncey Billups	12.00
4	Antonio Daniels	12.00
5	Tony Battie	12.00
6	Ron Mercer	15.00
7	Tim Thomas	10.00
8	Adonal Foyle	8.00
9	Tracy McGrady	15.00
10	Danny Fortson	10.00
11	Jacque Vaughn	8.00
12	Austin Croshere	8.00
13	Derek Anderson	10.00
14	Maurice Taylor	4.00
15	Kelvin Cato	4.00
16	Brevin Knight	12.00
17	Alonzo Mourning	4.00
18	Joe Smith	4.00
19	Shareef Abdur-Rahim	8.00
20	Scottie Pippen	4.00
21	David Robinson	4.00
22	Karl Malone	4.00
23	Stephon Marbury	10.00
24	Antonio McDyess	4.00
25	Checklist (Antoine Walker)	2.00

1997 Press Pass Double Threat Lottery Club

This eigth-card insert set was randomly inserted into packs of Double Threat, with two high draft picks - one current, one veteran - matched up by position. Card No. 1A was seeded 1:720, 1B was seeded 1:360, 2A was seeded 1:180, 2B seeded 1:90, 3A and 3B seeded 1:45 and 4A and 4B seeded 1:36. Cards are numbered with a "LC" prefix.

		MT
Complete Set (8):		200.00
Common Player:		10.00
1A	Tim Duncan	80.00
1B	David Robinson	50.00
2A	Keith Van Horn	25.00
2B	Antonio McDyess	20.00
3A	Antonio Daniels	15.00
3B	Stephon Marbury	15.00
4A	Ron Mercer	10.00
4B	Antoine Walker	5.00

1997 Press Pass Double Threat Nitrokrome

This nine-card insert featured an NBA veteran with a top draft choice that resembles that player on a foil etched card. Double Threat Nitrokrome inserts were seeded one per 18 packs and were numbered with a "DT" prefix.

		MT
Complete Set (9):		40.00
Common Player:		2.00
Minor Stars:		4.00
1	Tim Duncan, David Robinson	14.00
2	Jacque Vaughn, Karl Malone	4.00
3	Tony Battie, Antonio McDyess	6.00
4	Ron Mercer, Antoine Walker	4.00
5	Paul Grant, Stephon Marbury	4.00
6	Chauncey Billups, Antoine Walker	2.00
7	Antonio Daniels, Shareef Abdur-Rahim	6.00
8	Alonzo Mourning, Charles Smith	2.00
9	Joe Smith, Adonal Foyle	2.00

1997 Press Pass Double Threat Retroactive

Retroactive was a 36-card insert that was seeded one per pack of Double Threat. These featured top new draftees on the look of older cards that measured 2-3/8" x 2-7/8" and had a matte finish. They are numbered with a "RA" prefix.

		MT
Complete Set (36):		25.00
Common Player:		.25
1	Tim Duncan	4.00
2	Keith Van Horn	2.00
3	Chauncey Billups	2.00
4	Antonio Daniels	2.00
5	Tony Battie	1.00
6	Ron Mercer	3.00
7	Tim Thomas	2.00
8	Adonal Foyle	1.00
9	Tracy McGrady	3.00
10	Danny Fortson	1.00
11	Olivier Saint-Jean	25.00
12	Austin Croshere	.75
13	Derek Anderson	2.00
14	Maurice Taylor	1.00
15	Kelvin Cato	.75
16	Brevin Knight	1.50
17	Johnny Taylor	.25
18	Chris Anstey	.25
19	Scot Pollard	.25
20	Paul Grant	.25
21	Anthony Parker	.25
22	Ed Gray	.75
23	Bobby Jackson	1.00
24	John Thomas	.25
25	Charles Smith	.25
26	Jacque Vaughn	.75
27	Keith Booth	.25
28	Serge Zwikker	.25
29	Charles O'Bannon	.75
30	Bubba Wells	.25
31	Kebu Stewart	.75
32	James Collins	.25
33	Eddie Elisma	.25
34	Tim Duncan	3.00
35	Keith Van Horn	1.50
36	Checklist (Chauncey Billups)	1.00

1997 Press Pass Double Threat Showdown

This six-card back-to-back insert features some of the newest rivalries between veterans and rookies. Showdown inserts were seeded one per 36 hobby packs and were numbered with a "S" prefix.

		MT
Complete Set (6):		75.00
Common Player:		8.00
1	Alonzo Mourning, Tim Duncan	25.00
2	Karl Malone, Danny Fortson	8.00
3	Joe Smith, Tony Battie	12.00
4	Antonio McDyess, Keith Van Horn	10.00
5	Scottie Pippen, Ron Mercer	18.00
6	David Robinson, Adonal Foyle	8.00

1998 Press Pass

One of the first sets to portray the 1998 NBA rookies, the set numbers 45 cards, with seven levels of inserts. The set also includes, in the base set, five cards featuring teammates, and a Mike Bibby checklist card. Inserts include: Net Burners, Real Deal Rookies, Super 6, Fastbreak, In Your Face, Reflectors parallel, Solos (one-of-a-kind) parallel, Jersey Cards and Certified Autographs at a rate of two per box.

		MT
Complete Set (45):		15.00
Common Player:		.10
Minor Stars:		.20
Wax Box:		60.00
1	Mike Bibby	2.00
2	Nazr Mohammed	.75
3	Raef Lafrentz	1.50
4	Vince Carter	4.00
5	Paul Pierce	2.50
6	Michael Olowokandi	1.50
7	Larry Hughes	1.00
8	Keon Clark	.50
9	Robert Traylor	1.25
10	Michael Doleac	.75
11	Pat Garrity	.20
12	Jason Williams	1.50
13	Miles Simon	.20
14	Toby Bailey	.50
15	Bonzi Wells	.75
16	Tyrron Lue	.10
17	Matt Harpring	.10
18	J.R. Henderson	.20
19	Clayton Shields	.10
20	Michael Dickerson	.75
21	Saddi Washington	.10
22	Malcolm Johnson	.10
23	Cory Carr	.10
24	Brad Miller	.10
25	Mike Jones	.10
26	Brian Skinner	.10
27	Al Harrington	.50
28	Torraye Braggs	.10
29	Corey Louis	.10
30	DeMarco Johnson	.10
31	Anthony Carter	.10
32	Earl Boykins	.20
33	Roshown McCleod	.10
34	Casey Shaw	.10
35	Andrae Patterson	.10
36	Bryce Drew	.75
37	Jeff Sheppard	.20
38	Jahidi White	.20
39	Shammond Williams	.20
40	Ruben Patterson	.10
41	S. Williams, Carter	.75
42	Dickerson, Simon	.50
43	LaFrentz, Pierce	.75
44	Bailey, Henderson	.10
45	Checklist (Bibby)	1.00

1998 Press Pass In the Zone

This 45-card parallel set was printed with silver foil vs. the gold foil utilized on base cards. In the Zone parallels were seeded one per hobby pack.

	MT
Complete Set (45):	25.00
In The Zone cards:	2x
Inserted 1:1 Hobby	

1998 Press Pass Torquers

This 45-card parallel set was printed with blue foil vs. the gold foil utilized on base cards. Torquers were seeded one per retail pack.

	MT
Complete Set (45):	25.00
Torquers cards:	2x
Inserted 1:1 Retail	

1998 Press Pass Reflectors

This 45-card parallel set was printed on a holofoil surface and arrived with a protective film covering the card. Reflectors were inserted 1:90 packs.

	MT
Reflectors:	20x-40x
Inserted 1:90	

1998 Press Pass Autographs

The 38-card set features the top rookies from the 1998 NBA Draft. As the first autographed cards of the rookies, the fronts have an action shot with the autograph across the middle. The back has text congratulating the recipient. The cards are inserted at 1:18 hobby and 1:36 retail packs.

	MT
Common Player:	5.00
Minor Stars:	10.00
Inserted 1:18 Hobby; 1:36 Retail	
Toby Bailey	8.00
Mike Bibby	25.00
Earl Boykins	5.00
Torraye Braggs	5.00
Cory Carr	5.00
Anthony Carter	5.00
Vince Carter	75.00
Keon Clark	10.00
Michael Dickerson	15.00
Michael Doleac	10.00
Bryce Drew	10.00
Pat Garrity	10.00
Matt Harpring	12.00
Al Harrington	15.00
J.R. Henderson	5.00
Larry Hughes	25.00
DeMarco Johnson	5.00
Malcolm Johnson	5.00
Mike Jones	5.00
Raef Lafrentz	15.00
Tyrron Lue	10.00
Roshown McCleod	10.00
Brad Miller	5.00
Nazr Mohammed	10.00
Michael Olowokandi	15.00
Andrae Patterson	5.00
Paul Pierce	40.00
Casey Shaw	5.00
Jeff Sheppard	5.00
Clayton Shields	5.00
Miles Simon	5.00
Brian Skinner	5.00
Robert Traylor	15.00
Saddi Washington	5.00
Bonzi Wells	10.00
Jahidi White	5.00
Jason Williams	50.00
Shammond Williams	5.00

1998 Press Pass Fastbreak

The 12-card set highlights 12 playmakers of the 1998 NBA Draft. Inserted at 1:12, the fronts have two player images, with the athlete's last name and the word "Fastbreak" on the lower half. The back has text on his collegiate career. The cards are numbered with the prefix "FB".

		MT
Complete Set (12):		45.00
Common Player:		2.00
Inserted 1:12		
1	Raef Lafrentz	7.00
2	Toby Bailey	2.00
3	Mike Bibby	12.00
4	Vince Carter	15.00
5	Paul Pierce	5.00
6	Michael Olowokandi	12.00
7	Keon Clark	3.00
8	Robert Traylor	7.00
9	Michael Doleac	4.00
10	Larry Hughes	5.00
11	Pat Garrity	2.00
12	Miles Simon	2.00

1998 Press Pass In Your Face

This set is made up of clear acetate cards, and number nine cards in all. Hobby only cards, the fronts have a player image. This set features clear acetate cards that are hobby only. The nine-card set has a player image on the front silhouted against a clear background. The cards are inserted at 1:36, and are numbered with the prefix "IYF".

		MT
Complete Set (9):		75.00
Common Player:		2.50
Inserted 1:36 Hobby		
1	Raef Lafrentz	15.00
2	Mike Bibby	20.00
3	Michael Dickerson	7.00
4	Paul Pierce	10.00
5	Pat Garrity	2.50
6	Matt Harpring	2.50

7	Robert Traylor	12.00
8	Brad Miller	2.50
9	Vince Carter	25.00

1998 Press Pass Jerseys

The five-card pack is prefixed with a "JC" in the numbering, and highlights five draft picks from the 1998 draft. The cards contain an actual piece of game-used jersey in the card. Jersey Cards were inserted 1:720 packs and numbered to 375. Olowokandi Jersey Cards were used to fill Mike Bibby redemption cards.

		MT
Complete Set (4):		400.00
Common Player:		30.00
Inserted 1:720		
Production 375 Sets		
1	Michael Olowokandi (600)	75.00
2	Vince Carter	250.00
4	Robert Traylor	75.00
5	Toby Bailey	30.00

1998 Press Pass Net Burners

The largest of Press Pass '98 basketball insert set at 36 cards, the set has a die-cut feature, with the player portrayed in a net. The name appears in gold along the bottom. The back contains a quote on the player. The cards are inserted at 1:1.

		MT
Complete Set (36):		25.00
Common Player:		.20
Minor Stars:		.40
Inserted 1:1		
1	Mike Bibby	3.00
2	Nazr Mohammed	1.00
3	Raef Lafrentz	2.50
4	Vince Carter	4.00
5	Paul Pierce	1.75
6	Michael Olowokandi	4.00
7	Larry Hughes	2.00
8	Keon Clark	.75
9	Robert Traylor	2.00
10	Michael Doleac	1.00
11	Pat Garrity	.20
12	Saddi Washington	.20
13	Miles Simon	.20
14	Toby Bailey	.40
15	Bonzi Wells	1.00
16	Tyrron Lue	.20
17	Matt Harpring	.20
18	J.R. Henderson	.40
19	Clayton Shields	.20
20	Michael Dickerson	1.00
21	DeMarco Johnson	.20
22	Andrae Patterson	.20
23	Cory Carr	.20
24	Torraye Braggs	.20
25	Ruben Patterson	.20
26	Brian Skinner	.20
27	Bryce Drew	.75
28	Shammond Williams	.20
29	Corey Louis	.20
30	Tim Duncan	2.00
31	Keith Van Horn	1.00
32	Tim Thomas	1.00
33	Derek Anderson	.40
34	Brevin Knight	.40
35	Ron Mercer	1.25
36	Checklist (Roshown McCleod)	.20

1998 Press Pass Real Deal Rookies

The nine-card set features the top rookies from the 1997 draft. The fronts have a color player image, with a black and white image in the background. The name of the player appears in silver foil along the side. The back has text and rookie season stats. The cards are numbered with the prefix "R", and inserted at 1:18.

		MT
Complete Set (9):		40.00
Common Player:		2.00
Inserted 1:18		
1	Tim Duncan	12.00
2	Keith Van Horn	6.00
3	Tim Thomas	6.00
4	Derek Anderson	3.00
5	Brevin Knight	3.00
6	Ron Mercer	8.00
7	Tracy McGrady	6.00
8	Danny Fortson	2.00
9	Maurice Taylor	3.00

1998 Press Pass Super Six

The six-card set features the six players thought to excel right away. The set uses the holofoil inset cards, bordered in blue with the player's name in white along the left side. The back shows a color image, along with text. The cards are numbered with a prefix "S", and are inserted at 1:36.

		MT
Complete Set (6):		45.00
Common Player:		7.00
Inserted 1:36		
1	Raef Lafrentz	10.00
2	Larry Hughes	7.00
3	Mike Bibby	15.00
4	Vince Carter	18.00
5	Paul Pierce	7.00
6	Michael Olowokandi	15.00

1998-99 Press Pass BK Authentics

Press Pass' third basketball product of the 1998-99 season was hobby-only and oriented toward memorabilia. Boxes contained an average of three autographed cards and one authentic piece of memorabilia, available in the following forms: a signed 8" x 10" photo; or a redemption card valid for autographed basketballs, mini-balls or a Press Pass Game-Used Jersey Plaque. The set contained 45 cards, with each available in a holofoil-stamped parallel (one per pack). Inserts include: Lottery Club, Full Court Press, Certified Autographs and Sterlings, which were autographs limited to 10 numbered sets and inserted 1:720 packs.

		MT
Complete Set (45):		20.00
Common Player:		.25
Minor Stars:		.50
Wax Box:		
1	Michael Olowokandi	3.00
2	Mike Bibby	4.00
3	Raef LaFrentz	2.00
4	Vince Carter	6.00
5	Robert Traylor	2.00
6	Jason Williams	5.00
7	Larry Hughes	2.00
8	Paul Pierce	5.00
9	Bonzi Wells	.50
10	Michael Doleac	1.00
11	Keon Clark	1.00
12	Michael Dickerson	1.50
13	Matt Harpring	1.00
14	Bryce Drew	.50
15	Pat Garrity	.75
16	Roshown McLeod	.75
17	Brian Skinner	.25
18	Tyronn Lue	.75
19	Al Harrington	1.00
20	Sam Jacobson	.25
21	Nazr Mohammed	.25
22	Ruben Patterson	.50
23	Shammond Williams	.25
24	Casey Shaw	.25
25	DeMarco Johnson	.25
26	Miles Simon	.25
27	Jahidi White	.25
28	Sean Marks	.25
29	Toby Bailey	.25
30	Andrae Patterson	.25
31	Tyson Wheeler	.25
32	Cory Carr	.25
33	J.R. Henderson	.25
34	Torraye Braggs	.25
35	Tim Duncan	3.00
36	Keith Van Horn	1.50
37	Ron Mercer	1.50
38	Stephon Marbury	1.50
39	Ray Allen	.75
40	Glen Rice	.50
41	Brevin Knight	.75
42	Antoine Walker	.75
43	Kerry Kittles	.50
44	Derek Anderson	.50
45	Checklist (Michael Olowokandi)	1.50

1998-99 Press Pass BK Authentics Hang Time

Hang Time paralled all 45 cards from the base set, and were inserted one per pack. These cards were identical to the base set, but included prismatic silver foil on the card front.

		MT
Complete Set (45):		50.00
Hang Time Cards:		1.5x
Inserted 1:1		
1	Michael Olowokandi	6.00
2	Mike Bibby	8.00
3	Raef LaFrentz	4.00
4	Vince Carter	12.00
5	Robert Traylor	4.00
6	Jason Williams	10.00
7	Larry Hughes	4.00
8	Paul Pierce	10.00
9	Bonzi Wells	1.00
10	Michael Doleac	2.00
11	Keon Clark	2.00
12	Michael Dickerson	3.00
13	Matt Harpring	2.00
14	Bryce Drew	1.00
15	Pat Garrity	1.50
16	Roshown McLeod	1.50
17	Brian Skinner	.50
18	Tyronn Lue	1.50
19	Al Harrington	2.00
20	Sam Jacobson	.50
21	Nazr Mohammed	.50
22	Ruben Patterson	1.00
23	Shammond Williams	.50
24	Casey Shaw	.50
25	DeMarco Johnson	.50
26	Miles Simon	.50
27	Jahidi White	.50
28	Sean Marks	.50
29	Toby Bailey	.50
30	Andrae Patterson	.50
31	Tyson Wheeler	.50
32	Cory Carr	.50
33	J.R. Henderson	.50
34	Torraye Braggs	.50
35	Tim Duncan	6.00
36	Keith Van Horn	2.00
37	Ron Mercer	3.00
38	Stephon Marbury	3.00
39	Ray Allen	1.50
40	Glen Rice	1.00
41	Brevin Knight	1.50
42	Antoine Walker	1.50
43	Kerry Kittles	1.00
44	Derek Anderson	1.00
45	Checklist (Michael Olowokandi)	3.00

1998-99 Press Pass BK Authentics Autographs

Thirty different players signed Certified Autograph cards in Authentics, and they were inserted one per eight packs. These cards were identical to the base cards except the real autographed replaced the facsimile autograph and most of the foil stamping was removed from the card front. Backs included the player's name and stated "Congratulations! You are now the proud owner of a Press Pass '98 Basketball Authentics Certified Autograph. Enjoy the card and collect the entire set!"

	MT
Common Player:	5.00
Inserted 1:8	
Ray Allen	15.00
Mike Bibby	25.00
Torraye Braggs	5.00
Cory Carr	5.00
Vince Carter	100.00
Michael Doleac	10.00
Bryce Drew	7.00
Tim Duncan	80.00
Pat Garrity	10.00
Matt Harpring	12.00
Al Harrington	15.00
J.R. Henderson	5.00
Larry Hughes	25.00
Sam Jacobson	5.00
DeMarco Johnson	5.00
Kerry Kittles	10.00
Raef LaFrentz	15.00
Tyronn Lue	10.00
Stephon Marbury	35.00
Sean Marks	5.00
Roshown McLeod	7.00
Nazr Mohammed	7.00
Ruben Patterson	7.00
Paul Pierce	50.00
Casey Shaw	5.00
Brian Skinner	5.00
Robert Traylor	15.00
Antoine Walker	15.00
Tyson Wheeler	5.00
Jason Williams	60.00

1998-99 Press Pass BK Authentics Lottery Club

Lottery Club was a 12-card insert set that featured lottery picks from recent drafts on a foil card. The insert name, player's name and number pick were included on the left side. Inserted one per 12 packs, cards from this insert were numbered with an "LC" prefix.

		MT
Complete Set (12):		75.00
Common Player:		2.00
Inserted 1:12		
1	Michael Olowokandi	10.00
2	Tim Duncan	10.00
3	Mike Bibby	12.00
4	Keith Van Horn	5.00
5	Raef LaFrentz	8.00
6	Shareef Abdur-Rahim	4.00
7	Vince Carter	20.00
8	Stephon Marbury	6.00
9	Ray Allen	2.00
10	Robert Traylor	8.00
11	Antoine Walker	3.00
12	Jason Williams	15.00

1998-99 Press Pass BK Authentics Full Court Press

Full Court Press was a 12-card insert featuring top rookies and five veterans on holofoil cards. The insert name and player's name are included in white letters running up the left side. Cards are insert 1:6 packs and numbered with an "FP" prefix.

		MT
Complete Set (12):		35.00
Common Player:		.50
Inserted 1:6		
1	Paul Pierce	8.00
2	Pat Garrity	1.00
3	Nazr Mohammed	.50
4	Vince Carter	10.00
5	Tim Duncan	5.00
6	Stephon Marbury	3.00
7	Ron Mercer	3.00
8	Antoine Walker	1.50
9	Keith Van Horn	2.00
10	Michael Olowokandi	5.00
11	Mike Bibby	6.00
12	Raef LaFrentz	4.00

1998 Press Pass Double Threat

Double Threat was the second Press Pass draft picks set of 1998, and contained 45 cards. The product added some new twists, with NBA veteran autographs, Game-used Jersey cards with a veteran and rookie and double-sided autographs. Double Threat was paralleled three times in an Alley Oop, Torquers and Foil set. Inserts included: Double Thread Jerseys, Dreammates, Jackpot, Player's Club Autographs, Rookie Jerseys, Rookie Script Autographs, Retros, Two-on-One and Veteran Approved Autographs.

		MT
Complete Set (45):		15.00
Common Player:		.10
Minor Stars:		.20
Wax Box:		60.00
1	Michael Olowokandi	1.50
2	Mike Bibby	2.00
3	Raef LaFrentz	1.50
4	Vince Carter	5.00
5	Robert Traylor	1.25
6	Jason Williams	2.00
7	Larry Hughes	1.00
8	Paul Pierce	2.50
9	Bonzi Wells	.75
10	Michael Doleac	.75
11	Keon Clark	.50
12	Michael Dickerson	1.00
13	Matt Harpring	.10
14	Bryce Drew	.75
15	Pat Garrity	.20
16	Roshown McCleod	.10
17	Brian Skinner	.10
18	Tyrron Lue	.10
19	Al Harrington	.50
20	Sam Jacobson	.10
21	Nazr Mohammed	.75
22	Ruben Patterson	.10
23	Shammond Williams	.20
24	Casey Shaw	.10
25	DeMarco Johnson	.10
26	Miles Simon	.20
27	Jahidi White	.20
28	Sean Marks	.10
29	Toby Bailey	.50
30	Andrae Patterson	.10
31	Tyson Wheeler	.10
32	Cory Carr	.10
33	J.R. Henderson	.20
34	Torraye Braggs	.10
35	Tim Duncan	2.00
36	Keith Van Horn	1.00
37	Ron Mercer	1.00
38	Stephon Marbury	.75
39	Ray Allen	.20
40	Glen Rice	.10
41	Tim Thomas	.75
42	Antoine Walker	.40
43	Kerry Kittles	.10
44	Shareef Abdur-Rahim	.10
45	Checklist (Michael Olowokandi)	1.25

1998 Press Pass Double Threat Alley-Oop

This 45-card parallel set was printed with silver foil in contrast to the regular-issue set, which utilized golf foil. Alley-Oop parallel cards were inserted one per hobby pack.

	MT
Complete Set (45):	25.00
Alley-Oop Cards:	2x
Inserted 1:1 Hobby	

1998 Press Pass Double Threat Torquers

This 45-card parallel set was printed with blue foil vs. the gold foil utilized on base cards. Torquers cards were inserted one per retail pack.

	MT
Complete Set (45):	25.00
Torquers Cards:	2x
Inserted 1:1 Retail	

1998 Press Pass Double Threat Double Thread Jerseys

This three card insert was numbered DD2-DD4, with no card DD1 ever issued. The cards featured a piece of game-used jersey from a draft pick and an NBA star on the same card. These were inserted one per 720 packs of Double Threat. Cards DD2 and DD4 were inserted into packs as redemption cards.

		MT
Complete Set (3):		450.00
Common Player:		100.00
Inserted 1:720		
2	Michael Olowokandi, Tim Duncan	200.00
3	Robert Traylor, Keith Van Horn	60.00
4	Vince Carter, Glen Rice	200.00

1998 Press Pass Double Threat Dreammates

Dreammates was a nine-card insert that matched an 1998 NBA Draft pick matched up with a NBA player. The cards were numbered with a "DM" prefix and inserted every 18 packs.

		MT
Complete Set (9):		45.00
Common Player:		2.50
Inserted 1:18		
1	Mike Bibby, Tim Duncan	15.00
2	Michael Olowokandi, Stephon Marbury	8.00
3	Larry Hughes, Tim Thomas	5.00
4	Vince Carter, Glen Rice	15.00
5	Robert Traylor, Ray Allen	5.00
6	Paul Pierce, Ron Mercer	5.00
7	Raef LaFrentz, Keith Van Horn	4.00
8	Michael Dickerson, Antoine Walker	1.50
9	Jason Williams, Shareef Abdur-Rahim	2.50

1998 Press Pass Double Threat Foils

Three Foils were issued in Double Threat and were inserted one per 180 packs. The cards, featuring the top three picks in the 1998 NBA Draft, were numbered with a "F" prefix.

		MT
Complete Set (3):		90.00
Common Player:		30.00
Inserted 1:180		
1	Michael Olowokandi	30.00
2	Mike Bibby	50.00
3	Raef LaFrentz	30.00

1998 Press Pass Double Threat Jackpot

Jackpot included eight top picks in the 1998 NBA Draft on foil-etched cards. Insert odds varied depending on the which pick the player was, with the highest picks being the most difficult to find. Ratios are as follows: J1A 1:720, J1B 1:360, J2A 1:180, J2B 1:90, J3A and J3B 1:45, and J4A and J4B 1:36.

	MT
Complete Set (8):	175.00
Common Player:	8.00
Inserted 1:720 (1A), 1:360 (1B), 1:180 (2A)	
Inserted 1:90 (2B), 1:45 (3A&B), 1:36 (4A&B)	

1A	Michael Olowokandi	50.00
1B	Mike Bibby	50.00
2A	Raef LaFrentz	40.00
2B	Vince Carter	50.00
3A	Robert Traylor	8.00
3B	Jason Williams	25.00
4A	Larry Hughes	10.00
4B	Paul Pierce	15.00

1998 Press Pass Double Threat Player's Club Autographs

Player's Club Autographs were sequentially numbered to 125 sets and inserted one per 360 hobby packs of Double Threat. This 13-card set was numbered with a "PC" prefix. Cards 1, 3, 5, 6, 8, 9, 11 and 12 were inserted as redemption cards.

	MT
Complete Set (13):	800.00
Common Player:	25.00
Inserted 1:360 Hobby	
Production 125 Sets	

1	Michael Olowokandi	50.00
2	Mike Bibby	75.00
3	Raef LaFrentz	50.00
4	Vince Carter	250.00
5	Robert Traylor	50.00
6	Jason Williams	200.00
7	Larry Hughes	75.00
8	Paul Pierce	150.00
9	Bonzi Wells	25.00
10	Michael Doleac	25.00
11	Keon Clark	25.00
12	Michael Dickerson	50.00
13	Matt Harpring	35.00

1998 Press Pass Double Threat Retros

Retros displayed 36 of the players in the base set on smaller, old-fashioned looking cards. The cards were numbered with a "R" prefix and inserted one per pack.

	MT
Complete Set (36):	25.00
Common Player:	.20
Minor Stars:	.40
Inserted 1:1	

1	Michael Olowokandi	4.00
2	Mike Bibby	3.00
3	Raef LaFrentz	2.00
4	Vince Carter	2.00
5	Robert Traylor	2.00
6	Jason Williams	1.00
7	Larry Hughes	1.50
8	Paul Pierce	1.50
9	Bonzi Wells	1.00
10	Michael Doleac	.75
11	Keon Clark	.40
12	Michael Dickerson	.75
13	Matt Harpring	.20
14	Bryce Drew	.75
15	Cory Carr	.20
16	Andrae Patterson	.20
17	Pat Garrity	.40
18	Roshown McCleod	.20
19	Brian Skinner	.20
20	Tyrron Lue	.20
21	Sam Jacobson	.20
22	J.R. Henderson	.40
23	Nazr Mohammed	.75
24	Ruben Patterson	.20
25	Shammond Williams	.40
26	Toby Bailey	.40
27	DeMarco Johnson	.20
28	Miles Simon	.40
29	Jahidi White	.40
30	Tim Duncan	2.50
R31	Keith Van Horn	1.50
R32	Ron Mercer	1.50
R33	Stephon Marbury	1.00
R34	Ray Allen	.40
R35	Glen Rice	.20
R36	Checklist (Mike Bibby)	1.50

1998 Press Pass Double Threat Rookie Jerseys

Four different Rookie Jersey inserts were included in packs of Double Threat at a rate of one per 720 packs. The cards contained a piece of that player's game-used college jersey. Cards were numbered with a "JC" prefix and numbers 3 and 4 were included as redemptions.

	MT
Complete Set (4):	200.00
Common Player:	50.00
Inserted 1:720	

1	Raef LaFrentz	75.00
2	Pat Garrity	50.00
3	Paul Pierce	150.00
4	Michael Dickerson	60.00

1998 Press Pass Double Threat Rookie Script Autographs

Rookie Script Autographs were seeded one per 18 hobby packs and one per 36 retail packs. The cards are not numbered, but feature a white edge on the left side that the insert name is repeatedly printed in, with the player's signature.

	MT
Common Player:	5.00
Minor Stars:	7.00
Inserted 1:18 Hobby,1:36 Retail	

Toby Bailey	7.00
Mike Bibby	25.00
Torraye Braggs	5.00
Cory Carr	7.00
Vince Carter	100.00
Keon Clark	10.00
Michael Dickerson	15.00
Michael Doleac	10.00
Bryce Drew	10.00
Pat Garrity	10.00
Matt Harpring	12.00
Al Harrington	12.00
J.R. Henderson	7.00
Larry Hughes	25.00
Sam Jacobson	5.00
DeMarco Johnson	5.00
Raef LaFrentz	20.00
Tyrron Lue	10.00
Sean Marks	5.00
Roshown McCleod	7.00
Nazr Mohammed	7.00
Michael Olowokandi	20.00
Andrae Patterson	5.00
Ruben Patterson	7.00
Paul Pierce	50.00
Casey Shaw	5.00
Miles Simon	7.00
Brian Skinner	7.00
Robert Traylor	20.00
Bonzi Wells	7.00
Tyson Wheeler	5.00
Jahidi White	5.00
Jason Williams	60.00
Shammond Williams	7.00

1998 Press Pass Double Threat Two-On-One

This 12-card insert featured plastic die-cut cards that fit together in threes. Numbered with a "TO" prefix, The card on each end features a single player, while the middle card features both players in the panel. Two-on-One inserts were seeded one per 12 packs.

	MT
Complete Set (12):	70.00
Common Player:	4.00
Inserted 1:12	

1	Raef LaFrentz	7.00
2	Raef LaFrentz, Keith Van Horn	3.00
3	Keith Van Horn	4.00
4	Michael Olowokandi	8.00
5	Michael Olowokandi, Tim Duncan	8.00
6	Tim Duncan	7.00
7	Mike Bibby	8.00
8	Mike Bibby, Stephon Marbury	7.00
9	Stephon Marbury	4.00
10	Vince Carter	15.00
11	Vince Carter, Antoine Walker	4.00
12	Antoine Walker	2.00

1998 Press Pass Double Threat Veteran Approved Autos.

This seven-card insert contained autographs from seven NBA players and were inserted one per 360 packs. The cards are not numbered, while Ray Allen, Kerry Kittles, Ron Mercer and Glen Rice were available through redemption cards.

	MT
Complete Set (7):	450.00
Common Player:	30.00
Inserted 1:360	

Ray Allen	50.00
Tim Duncan	150.00
Kerry Kittles	30.00
Stephon Marbury	75.00
Ron Mercer	60.00
Glen Rice	50.00
Antoine Walker	30.00

1999 Press Pass

This 45-card set featured players eligible to be drafted in the 1999 NBA Draft. Press Pass signed exclusive draft pick contracts with four of the top six picks - Elton Brand, Steve Francis, Lamar Odom and Wally Szczerbiak - to produce their cards and signatures in its 1999 product. The set featured 44 different players, and repeated Brand on the 45th card, which was a checklist. While regular cards featured silver foil, there was also a Gold Zone (hobby only, gold foil) and Torquers (retail only, blue foil) parallel, as well as Reflectors and Solos. Inserts included Y2K, Autographs, Standout Signatures, Jersey Cards, Net Burners, In Your Face, Crunch Time and On Fire.

	MT
Complete Set (45):	15.00
Common Player:	.10
Minor Stars:	.20
Gold Zone Cards:	2x
Inserted 1:1 Hobby	
Torquers Cards:	2x
Inserted 1:1 Retail	
Wax Box (24):	75.00

1	Elton Brand	3.00
2	Steve Francis	3.00
3	Baron Davis	2.00
4	Lamar Odom	3.00
5	Jonathan Bender	1.50
6	Wally Szczerbiak	2.00
7	Richard Hamilton	1.50
8	Andre Miller	.75
9	Jason Terry	1.00
10	Trajan Langdon	1.00
11	William Avery	.75
12	Ron Artest	.75
13	Cal Bowdler	.20
14	James Posey	.40
15	Quincy Lewis	.40
16	Jeff Foster	.20
17	Kenny Thomas	.20
18	Devean George	.20
19	Tim James	.20
20	Vonteego Cummings	.20
21	Jumanie Jones	.20
22	Scott Padgett	.20
23	John Celestand	.10
24	Rico Hill	.10
25	Michael Ruffin	.10
26	Chris Herren	.40
27	Evan Eschmeyer	.20
28	Calvin Booth	.10
29	Obinna Ekezie	.10
30	A.J. Bramlett	.20
31	Louis Bullock	.10
32	Lee Nailon	.10
33	Tyrone Washington	.10
34	Lari Ketner	.10
35	Venson Hamilton	.10
36	Roberto Bergersen	.10
37	Rodney Buford	.10
38	Melvin Levett	.20
39	Kris Clack	.10
40	Harold Jamison	.10
41	Heshimu Evans	.10
42	Ademola Okulaja	.10
43	Jamel Thomas	.10
44	Jason Miskiri	.10
45	Elton Brand (Checklist)	1.00

1999 Press Pass Gold Zone

This 45-card set paralleled every card in the base set and was inserted one per hobby pack. Gold Zone cards used gold foil stamping vs. the silver used on base cards.

	MT
Complete Set (45):	25.00
Gold Zone Cards:	2x
Inserted 1:1 Hobby	

1999 Press Pass Torquers

This 45-card set paralled all 45 cards in the base set and was inserted one per retail pack. Torquers utilized blue foil stamping vs. the silver foil used on base cards.

	MT
Complete Set (45):	25.00
Torquers Cards:	2x
Inserted 1:1 Retail	

1999 Press Pass Reflectors

Reflectors paralleled the 45-card base set in Press Pass, but added a holofoil finish to the front, which arrived protected by a laminate and peel-off covering. Cards were numbered with an "R" prefix and inserted 1:90 packs. Reflectors cards were also sequentially numbered to 250 on the back.

	MT
Complete Set (45):	350.00
Reflectors Cards:	15x-30x
Production 250 Sets	
Inserted 1:90	

1999 Press Pass Certified Authentic

This insert featured autographed versions of player's base cards. Autographed versions featured a matte strip through the middle where the player signed. These were seeded 1:8 hobby packs and 1:36 retail packs. Redemption cards were issued for Lamar Odom, Jonathan Bender and Kenny Thomas, while John Celestand signed his on the back.

	MT
Common Player:	5.00
Minor Stars:	8.00
Inserted 1:8 Hobby, 1:36 Retail	
Standout Signature Cards:	2x
Production 100 Sets	
Inserted 1:120 Hobby	

Elton Brand	75.00
Steve Francis	75.00
Baron Davis	40.00
Lamar Odom	75.00
Jonathan Bender	40.00
Wally Szczerbiak	50.00
Richard Hamilton	30.00
Andre Miller	15.00
Jason Terry	20.00
Trajan Langdon	20.00
William Avery	15.00
Ron Artest	15.00
Cal Bowdler	8.00
James Posey	10.00
Quincy Lewis	8.00
Kenny Thomas	8.00
Devean George	8.00
Tim James	10.00
Vonteego Cummings	8.00
John Celestand	5.00
Rico Hill	5.00
Michael Ruffin	5.00
Chris Herren	8.00
Evan Eschmeyer	8.00
Calvin Booth	8.00
A.J. Bramlett	8.00
Louis Bullock	5.00
Lee Nailon	5.00
Tyrone Washington	5.00
Lari Ketner	5.00
Venson Hamilton	5.00
Roberto Bergersen	5.00
Rodney Buford	5.00
Melvin Levett	8.00
Kris Clack	5.00
Harold Jamison	5.00
Heshimu Evans	8.00
Ademola Okulaja	5.00
Jamel Thomas	5.00
Jason Miskiri	5.00

1999 Press Pass Standout Signatures

Standout Signatures paralleled the Certified Authentic Autographs, but was sequentially numbered to 100 on the back. These parallel versions also included the insert name in gold foil up the left side.

	MT
Common Player:	10.00
Standout Signature Cards:	2x
Production 100 Sets	
Inserted 1:120 Hobby	

1999 Press Pass Crunch Time

This nine-card insert featured a color shot of the player over an action foil background. Crunch Time inserts were numbered with a "CT" prefix and inserted 1:18 packs.

	MT
Complete Set (9):	40.00
Common Player:	1.00
Inserted 1:18	

1	Elton Brand	10.00
2	Steve Francis	10.00
3	Baron Davis	5.00
4	Lamar Odom	10.00
5	Wally Szczerbiak	8.00
6	Richard Hamilton	4.00
7	Andre Miller	1.00
8	Jason Terry	2.00
9	William Avery	1.00

1999 Press Pass In Your Face

This six-card insert was printed on clear acetate stock and featured above-the-rim photography. Cards were numbered with an "IYF" prefix and inserted 1:24 packs.

	MT
Complete Set (6):	35.00
Common Player:	2.00
Inserted 1:24	

1	Elton Brand	20.00
2	Baron Davis	10.00
3	Andre Miller	4.00
4	Jason Terry	6.00
5	Ron Artest	6.00
6	Kenny Thomas	2.00

1999 Press Pass Jersey Cards

This five-card insert featured a swatch of game-worn college jersey from five different players. The cards are numbered with a "JC" prefix and inserted 1:480 hobby and 1:720 retail packs.

	MT
Complete Set (5):	400.00
Common Player:	30.00
Inserted 1:480 Hobby, 1:720 Retail	

1	Elton Brand	125.00
2	Steve Francis	125.00
3	Lamar Odom	125.00
4	James Posey	50.00
5	Evan Eschmeyer	30.00

1999 Press Pass Net Burners

This 36-card set was considered a set within a set since it featured nearly all of the players in the base set and was seeded one per pack. Cards were numbered with an "NB" prefix.

	MT
Complete Set (36):	25.00
Net Burners Cards:	1x-2x
Common Player:	.20
Minor Stars:	.40

Inserted 1:1

1	Steve Francis	
2	Richard Hamilton	
3	Baron Davis	
4	Lamar Odom	
5	Elton Brand	
6	Jason Terry	
7	Andre Miller	
8	Ron Artest	
9	William Avery	
10	James Posey	
11	Tim James	
12	Evan Eschmeyer	
13	Quincy Lewis	
14	Scott Padgett	
15	Jamel Thomas	
16	Kenny Thomas	
17	Melvin Levett	
18	A.J. Bramlett	
19	Lari Ketner	
20	Kris Clack	
21	Lee Nailon	
22	Vonteego Cummings	
23	Trajan Langdon	
24	Wally Szczerbiak	
25	Obinna Ekezie	
26	Rico Hill	
27	Venson Hamilton	
28	Michael Ruffin	
29	Harold Jamison	
30	Ademola Okulaja	
31	Chris Herren	
32	Calvin Booth	
33	Jonathan Bender	
34	Rodney Buford	
35	John Celestand	
36	Steve Francis (Checklist)	

1999 Press Pass On Fire

This 12-card insert featured players on micro-etched Nitrokrome technology. Cards were numbered with an "OF" prefix on the back and inserted 1:12 packs.

	MT
Complete Set (12):	45.00
Common Player:	1.00

Inserted 1:12

1	Elton Brand	10.00
2	Steve Francis	10.00
3	Baron Davis	6.00
4	Lamar Odom	10.00
5	Wally Szczerbiak	8.00
6	Richard Hamilton	5.00
7	Andre Miller	2.00
8	Jason Terry	3.00
9	William Avery	2.00
10	Ron Artest	2.00
11	James Posey	1.50
12	Kenny Thomas	1.00

1999 Press Pass Y2K

Y2K featured eight players on a die-cut format with a basketball background. The cards were printed on foil and sequentially numbered to 2000 sets. Cards were numbered with a "Y" prefix and inserted one per 24 hobby packs.

	MT
Complete Set (8):	60.00
Common Player:	3.00

Inserted 1:24 Hobby
Production 2,000 Sets

1	Elton Brand	15.00
2	Steve Francis	15.00
3	Baron Davis	10.00
4	Lamar Odom	15.00
5	Wally Szczerbiak	10.00
6	Richard Hamilton	6.00
7	Andre Miller	3.00
8	Jason Terry	4.00

1999-00 Press Pass BK Authentics

This 45-card set included draft picks from the 1999 NBA Draft. Cards carried a Press Pass Authentics logo in the upper right corner and the word "Authentics" written in script across the bottom. While base cards were printed in silver foil, a Hang Time parallel utilized gold foil. Inserts included: Autographs, Gold Reserve Autographs, Authentic Memorabilia cards, Full Court Press, Lottery Club and Team 2000.

	MT
Complete Set (45):	15.00
Common Player:	.10
Minor Stars:	.20
Wax Box (24):	

1	Elton Brand	3.00
2	Steve Francis	3.00
3	Baron Davis	1.50
4	Lamar Odom	3.00
5	Jonathan Bender	1.00
6	Wally Szczerbiak	2.00
7	Richard Hamilton	1.00
8	Andre Miller	.60
9	Jason Terry	.60
10	Trajan Langdon	.60
11	William Avery	.60
12	Ron Artest	.60
13	Cal Bowdler	.20
14	James Posey	.50
15	Quincy Lewis	.30
16	Jeff Foster	.10
17	Kenny Thomas	.20
18	Devean George	.20
19	Tim James	.20
20	Vonteego Cummings	.20
21	Jumanie Jones	.30
22	John Celestand	.20
23	Rico Hill	.10
24	Michael Ruffin	.10
25	Chris Herren	.20
26	Evan Eschmeyer	.20
27	Calvin Booth	.20
28	Obinna Ekezie	.20
29	A.J. Bramlett	.20
30	Louis Bullock	.10
31	Lee Nailon	.10
32	Tyrone Washington	.10
33	Venson Hamilton	.10
34	Roberto Bergersen	.10
35	Rodney Buford	.10
36	Melvin Levett	.20
37	Kris Clack	.10
38	Vince Carter	2.00
39	Jason Williams	1.50
40	Paul Pierce	1.00
41	Mike Bibby	.60
42	Michael Olowokandi	.40
43	Marcus Camby	.20
44	Raef LaFrentz	.40
45	Checklist (Vince Carter)	1.00

1999-00 Press Pass BK Authentics Hang Time

This 45-card parallel set replaced the silver foil from the base cards with gold foil. Hang Time cards were inserted one per pack.

	MT
Complete Set (45):	25.00
Common Player:	.15
Hang Time Cards:	1x-2x

Inserted 1:1

1999-00 Press Pass BK Authentics Autographs

Authentic Autographs from many of the players in the set were included in this insert. Cards included no foil on the front and a "Congratulations! You are now the proud owner of a Press Pass Basketball Certified Authentic Autographed Card. Enjoy the card and collect the entire set!" message on the back. These were inserted 1:8 hobby packs and 1:36 retail. Gold versions of each existed and utilized gold color (in place of silver) on the front and were sequentially numbered to 100 on the back.

	MT
Complete Set (32):	450.00
Common Player:	3.00
Minor Stars:	5.00

Inserted 1:8

1	Elton Brand	60.00
2	Steve Francis	60.00
3	Baron Davis	40.00
4	Lamar Odom	60.00
5	Wally Szczerbiak	50.00
6	Richard Hamilton	30.00
7	Andre Miller	20.00
8	Jason Terry	203.00
9	Trajan Langdon	20.00
10	Ron Artest	20.00
11	Cal Bowdler	5.00
12	James Posey	12.00
13	Quincy Lewis	10.00
14	Jeff Foster	5.00
15	Devean George	8.00
16	Tim James	8.00
17	Vonteego Cummings	8.00
18	Jumanie Jones	8.00
19	John Celestand	5.00
20	Michael Ruffin	5.00
21	Chris Herren	8.00
22	Evan Eschmeyer	5.00
23	Calvin Booth	5.00
24	Obinna Ekezie	5.00
25	A.J. Bramlett	5.00
26	Louis Bullock	3.00
27	Lee Nailon	3.00
28	Tyrone Washington	3.00
29	Venson Hamilton	3.00
30	Roberto Bergersen	3.00
31	Melvin Levett	5.00
32	Kris Clack	3.00

1999-00 Press Pass BK Authentics Autographs Gold Reserve

This parallel version of the Autographs insert replaced the silver color on the front with gold foil and added sequential numbering to 100 on the back.

	MT
Common Player:	6.00
Minor Stars:	10.00
Gold Reserve Cards:	2x

Production 100 Sets

1999-00 Press Pass BK Authentics Full Court Press

This 12-card horizontal insert was seeded 1:12 packs and numbered with an "FC" prefix.

	MT
Complete Set (12):	35.00
Common Player:	1.00

Inserted 1:12

1	Elton Brand	8.00
2	Steve Francis	8.00
3	Baron Davis	5.00
4	Lamar Odom	8.00
5	Jonathan Bender	4.00
6	Wally Szczerbiak	6.00
7	Richard Hamilton	4.00
8	Andre Miller	2.00
9	Jason Terry	2.00
10	Trajan Langdon	2.00
11	William Avery	2.00
12	James Posey	1.00

1999-00 Press Pass BK Authentics Lottery Club

This six-card insert was numbered with an "LC" prefix and seeded 1:23 packs.

	MT
Complete Set (6):	35.00
Common Player:	5.00

Inserted 1:23

1	Elton Brand	10.00
2	Steve Francis	10.00
3	Baron Davis	6.00
4	Lamar Odom	10.00
5	Jonathan Bender	5.00
6	Wally Szczerbiak	8.00

1999-00 Press Pass BK Authentics Team 2000

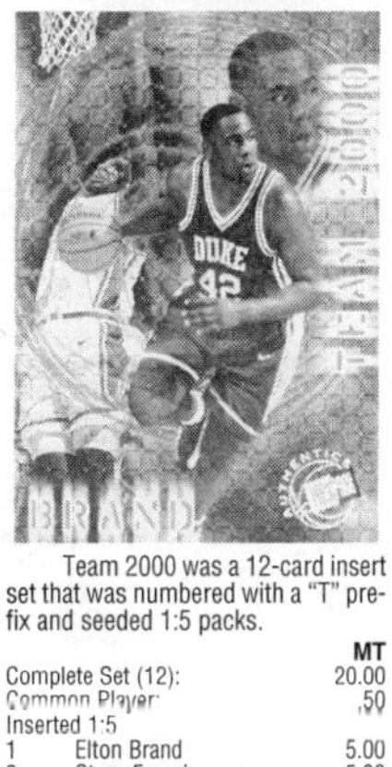

Team 2000 was a 12-card insert set that was numbered with a "T" prefix and seeded 1:5 packs.

	MT
Complete Set (12):	20.00
Common Player:	.50

Inserted 1:5

1	Elton Brand	5.00
2	Steve Francis	5.00
3	Baron Davis	3.00
4	Lamar Odom	5.00
5	Wally Szczerbiak	4.00
6	Richard Hamilton	2.00
7	Andre Miller	1.00
8	Jason Terry	1.00
9	Trajan Langdon	1.00
10	Ron Artest	1.00
11	Tim James	.50
12	William Avery	1.00

1999 Press Pass SE

Press Pass SE was a 45-card set consisting of players who were eligible for the 1999 NBA Draft. Included in the set were the four Press Pass Exclusives for that year - Elton Brand, Steve Francis, Lamar Odom and Wally Szczerbiak. The cards featured an "SE" logo in the upper right corner and a black strip across the bottom with the player's name. The set was paralleled in both an Alley-Oop (hobby) and Torquers (retail) insert. Inserts included: Autographs (three versions), In the Bonus, Instant Replay, Jersey Cards, Two on One and Old School.

	MT
Complete Set (45):	15.00
Common Player:	.10
Minor Stars:	.20
Wax Box (12):	50.00

1	Elton Brand	3.00
2	Steve Francis	4.00
3	Baron Davis	1.00
4	Lamar Odom	4.00
5	Jonathan Bender	1.50
6	Wally Szczerbiak	1.50
7	Richard Hamilton	1.00
8	Andre Miller	1.00
9	Jason Terry	.75
10	Trajan Langdon	.60
11	William Avery	.50
12	Ron Artest	1.00
13	Cal Bowdler	.10
14	James Posey	.60
15	Quincy Lewis	.40
16	Jeff Foster	.10
17	Kenny Thomas	.40
18	Devean George	.40
19	Tim James	.40
20	Vonteego Cummings	.50
21	Jumaine Jones	.30
22	John Celestand	.30
23	Rico Hill	.10
24	Michael Ruffin	.20
25	Chris Herren	.30
26	Evan Eschmeyer	.10
27	Calvin Booth	.30
28	Obinna Ekezie	.20
29	A.J. Bramlett	.10
30	Louis Bullock	.10
31	Lee Nailon	.10
32	Tyrone Washington	.10
33	Venson Hamilton	.10
34	Roberto Bergersen	.10
35	Rodney Buford	.20
36	Melvin Levett	.20
37	Kris Clack	.20
38	Galen Young	.10
39	Lari Ketner	.10
40	Eddie Lucas	.10
41	Todd MacCulloch	.20
42	Francisco Elson	.10
43	Vince Carter	1.50
44	Jason Williams	.50
45	Checklist	.10

1999 Press Pass SE Alley-Oop

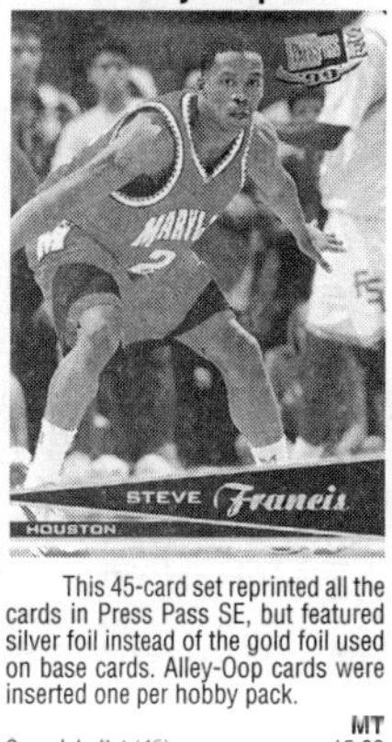

This 45-card set reprinted all the cards in Press Pass SE, but featured silver foil instead of the gold foil used on base cards. Alley-Oop cards were inserted one per hobby pack.

	MT
Complete Set (45):	15.00
Common Player:	.10
Minor Stars:	.20
Wax Box (12):	50.00

1	Elton Brand	3.00
2	Steve Francis	4.00
3	Baron Davis	1.00
4	Lamar Odom	4.00
5	Jonathan Bender	1.50
6	Wally Szczerbiak	1.50
7	Richard Hamilton	1.00
8	Andre Miller	1.00
9	Jason Terry	.75
10	Trajan Langdon	.60
11	William Avery	.50
12	Ron Artest	1.00
13	Cal Bowdler	.10
14	James Posey	.60
15	Quincy Lewis	.40
16	Jeff Foster	.10
17	Kenny Thomas	.40
18	Devean George	.40
19	Tim James	.40
20	Vonteego Cummings	.50
21	Jumaine Jones	.30
22	John Celestand	.30
23	Rico Hill	.10
24	Michael Ruffin	.20
25	Chris Herren	.30
26	Evan Eschmeyer	.10
27	Calvin Booth	.30
28	Obinna Ekezie	.20
29	A.J. Bramlett	.10
30	Louis Bullock	.10
31	Lee Nailon	.10
32	Tyrone Washington	.10
33	Venson Hamilton	.10
34	Roberto Bergersen	.10
35	Rodney Buford	.20
36	Melvin Levett	.20
37	Kris Clack	.20
38	Galen Young	.10
39	Lari Ketner	.10
40	Eddie Lucas	.10
41	Todd MacCulloch	.20
42	Francisco Elson	.10
43	Vince Carter	1.50
44	Jason Williams	.50
45	Checklist	.10

1999 Press Pass SE Torquers

This 45-card parallel set reprinted every card in Press Pass SE, but used blue foil instead of the gold foil used on base cards. Torquers were seeded one per retail pack.

	MT
Complete Set (45):	15.00
Common Player:	.10
Minor Stars:	.20
Wax Box (12):	50.00

1	Elton Brand	3.00
2	Steve Francis	4.00
3	Baron Davis	1.00
4	Lamar Odom	4.00
5	Jonathan Bender	1.50
6	Wally Szczerbiak	1.50
7	Richard Hamilton	1.00
8	Andre Miller	1.00
9	Jason Terry	.75
10	Trajan Langdon	.60
11	William Avery	.50
12	Ron Artest	1.00
13	Cal Bowdler	.10
14	James Posey	.60
15	Quincy Lewis	.40
16	Jeff Foster	.10
17	Kenny Thomas	.40
18	Devean George	.40
19	Tim James	.40
20	Vonteego Cummings	.50
21	Jumaine Jones	.30
22	John Celestand	.30
23	Rico Hill	.10
24	Michael Ruffin	.20
25	Chris Herren	.30
26	Evan Eschmeyer	.10
27	Calvin Booth	.30
28	Obinna Ekezie	.20
29	A.J. Bramlett	.10
30	Louis Bullock	.10
31	Lee Nailon	.10
32	Tyrone Washington	.10
33	Venson Hamilton	.10
34	Roberto Bergersen	.10
35	Rodney Buford	.20
36	Melvin Levett	.20
37	Kris Clack	.20
38	Galen Young	.10
39	Lari Ketner	.10
40	Eddie Lucas	.10
41	Todd MacCulloch	.20
42	Francisco Elson	.10
43	Vince Carter	1.50
44	Jason Williams	.50
45	Checklist	.10

1999 Press Pass SE Autographs

This 38-card Autograph insert was seeded one per pack of Press Pass SE. The cards are unnumbered and are checklisted in alphabetical order. They arrived in three different versions, with gold foil being the most common, blue foil versions sequentially numbered to 500 and silver holographic foil versions sequentially numbered to 100.

	MT
Common Player:	3.00
Inserted 1:1	
Blue Autographs:	1.5x
Production 500 Sets	
Silver Autographs:	2x
Production 100 Sets	
Ron Artest	12.00
William Avery	8.00
Roberto Bergersen	3.00
Mike Bibby	12.00
Calvin Booth	3.00
Cal Bowdler	3.00
A.J. Bramblett	3.00
Elton Brand	60.00
Louis Bullock	3.00
Marcus Camby	12.00
Vince Carter	125.00
John Celestand	5.00
Baron Davis	20.00
Obinna Ekezie	3.00
Francisco Elson	3.00
Evan Eschmeyer	3.00
Jeff Foster	3.00
Steve Francis	75.00
Devean George	5.00
Richard Hamilton	10.00
Venson Hamilton	3.00
Chris Herren	5.00
Jumaine Jones	5.00
Lari Ketner	3.00
Raef LaFrentz	12.00
Melvin Levett	5.00
Quincy Lewis	8.00
Eddie Lucas	3.00
Todd MacCulloch	3.00
Andre Miller	15.00
Lee Nailon	3.00
Lamar Odom	60.00
Laron Profit	3.00
Wally Szczerbiak	25.00
Jason Terry	10.00
Kenny Thomas	8.00
Tyrone Washington	3.00
Galen Young	3.00

1999 Press Pass SE Autographs Blue

This 38-card parallel set reprinted every card in Press Pass SE Autographs, but used blue foil instead of the gold foil used on the base versions. Blue foil versions were sequentially numbered to 500.

	MT
Common Player:	3.00
Inserted 1:1	
Blue Autographs:	1.5x
Production 500 Sets	

1999 Press Pass SE Autographs Silver

This 38-card parallel set reprinted every card in Press Pass SE Autographs, but used silver holographic foil instead of the gold foil used on base versions. Silver holographic Autographs were sequentially numbered to 100.

	MT
Common Player:	3.00
Inserted 1:1	
Silver Autographs:	2x
Production 100 Sets	

1999 Press Pass SE In the Bonus

This eight-card insert set featured top draft picks on a horizontal foil card. In the Bonus cards were numbered with an "IB" prefix and were inserted as follows: #1 1:144, #2-4 1:72, #5-6 1:36 and #7-8 1:24.

		MT
Complete Set (8):		40.00
Common Player:		1.00
1	Elton Brand	25.00
2	Steve Francis	15.00
3	Baron Davis	4.00
4	Lamar Odom	12.00
5	Wally Szczerbiak	5.00
6	Richard Hamilton	2.50
7	Jason Terry	1.00
8	Trajan Langdon	1.00

1999 Press Pass SE Instant Replay

This six-card insert set featured top picks from the 1999 NBA Draft. Cards were numbered with an "IR" prefix and inserted 1:6 packs.

		MT
Complete Set (6):		10.00
Common Player:		1.00
1	Elton Brand	3.00
2	Steve Francis	4.00
3	Baron Davis	1.00
4	Lamar Odom	4.00
5	Wally Szczerbiak	1.50
6	Andre Miller	1.00

1999 Press Pass SE Jersey Cards

This four-card insert set included game-used college jersey swatches from two 1999 NBA draft picks and two 1998 NBA draft picks. Jersey Cards were inserted 1:720 packs, numbered with a "JC" prefix and sequentially numbered to 300.

		MT
Complete Set (4):		250.00
Common Player:		40.00
1	Elton Brand	150.00
2	Steve Francis	150.00
3	Raef LaFrentz	40.00
4	Larry Hughes	60.00

1999 Press Pass SE Old School

This 36-card insert set included most of the players in Press Pass SE, but featured them on retro-looking cards, with no UV-coating and a white border that loosely resembled the 1972-73 Topps design. Old School cards were inserted one per pack.

		MT
Complete Set (36):		20.00
Common Player:		.15
Minor Star:		.30
1	Elton Brand	4.00
2	Steve Francis	6.00
3	Baron Davis	1.50
4	Lamar Odom	4.00
5	Jonathan Bender	2.00
6	Wally Szczerbiak	2.00
7	Richard Hamilton	1.50
8	Andre Miller	1.50
9	Jason Terry	1.25
10	Trajan Langdon	1.00
11	William Avery	.75
12	Ron Artest	1.50
13	Cal Bowdler	.15
14	James Posey	1.00
15	Quincy Lewis	.60
16	Kenny Thomas	.60
17	Tim James	.60
18	Vonteego Cummings	.75
19	Jumaine Jones	.50
20	John Celestand	.50
21	Rico Hill	.15
22	Michael Ruffin	.30
23	Chris Herren	.40
24	Evan Eschmeyer	.15
25	Calvin Booth	.40
26	Obinna Ekezie	.30
27	Kris Clack	.30
28	A.J. Bramlett	.15
29	Francisco Elson	.15
30	Louis Bullock	.15
31	Lee Nailon	.15
32	Tyrone Washington	.15
33	Galen Young	.15
34	Venson Hamilton	.15
35	Melvin Levett	.30
36	Checklist	.15

1999 Press Pass SE Two on One

Two on One was a 12-card insert set that included eight different players or four twosomes. Each player had his own card, while a third card for each twosome featured both players. All three cards for any twosome was die-cut and could fit together into a three-card panel. These inserts were numbered with a "TO" prefix and a A, B or C suffix and inserted 1:12 packs.

		MT
Complete Set (12):		40.00
Common Player:		1.00
1A	Mike Bibby	1.00
1B	Elton Brand, Mike Bibby	5.00
1C	Elton Brand	6.00
2A	Vince Carter	12.00
2B	Steve Francis, Vince Carter	15.00
2C	Steve Francis	8.00
3A	Jason Williams	4.00
3B	Wally Szczerbiak, Jason Williams	3.00
3C	Wally Szczerbiak	3.00
4A	Marcus Camby	1.00
4B	Lamar Odom, Marcus Camby	5.00
4C	Lamar Odom	6.00

2000 Press Pass

This 46-card draft pick set featured top college seniors that were eligible for the 2000 NBA Draft. The set consisted of 39 regular player cards, one checklist and six Power Pick cards that were seeded 1:14 hobby packs. Regular cards featured silver foil on a borderless design. The first 40 cards were also available in Gold Zone (1:1 hobby), Torquers (1:1 retail) and Reflectors (1:72 hobby/retail) packs. Inserts included: Autographs, Breakaway, In the Paint, In Your Face, Jersey Cards, On Fire and Power Pick Autographs.

		MT
Complete Set (46):		25.00
Common Player:		.10
Minor Stars:		.20
Pack (5):		3.50
Box (28):		75.00
1	Chris Mihm CL	.25
2	Chris Mihm	.50
3	Mike Miller	1.50
4	Chris Porter	1.00
5	Morris Peterson	1.25
6	Darius Miles	4.00
7	Jerome Moiso	.50
8	Quentin Richardson	1.00
9	Mateen Cleaves	.75
10	Etan Thomas	.50
11	Scoonie Penn	.30
12	Jason Collier	.30
13	Hanno Mottola	.20
14	Mark Madsen	.50
15	DeShawn Stevenson	1.50
16	Dan Langhi	.40
17	Jamaal Magloire	.50
18	Pepe Sanchez	.40
19	Khalid El-Amin	.50
20	Harold Arceneaux	.20
21	Mark Karcher	.20
22	Jason Hart	.20
23	Eddie House	.40
24	Gabe Muoneke	.10
25	Jake Voskuhl	.30
26	Brad Millard	.10
27	Bootsy Thornton	.20
28	Eddie Gill	.10
29	Shaheen Holloway	.20
30	Kevin Freeman	.30
31	Jarrett Stephens	.10
32	Brian Cardinal	.30
33	Brandon Kurtz	.10
34	Elton Brand	1.00
35	Steve Francis	1.50
36	Lamar Odom	1.00
37	Wally Szczerbiak	.50
38	Baron Davis	.30
39	Richard Hamilton	.30
40	Chris Carrawell	.30
41	Chris Mihm PP	1.50
42	Darius Miles PP	10.00
43	Mike Miller PP	4.00
44	Jerome Moiso PP	1.50
45	Mateen Cleaves PP	2.00
46	Morris Peterson PP	3.00

2000 Press Pass Gold Zone

This 40-card parallel set reprinted each base card, but used gold foil (instead of silver foil). Gold Zone cards were seeded one per hobby pack.

		MT
Complete Set (40):		20.00
Common Player:		.15
Inserted 1:1 Hobby		
1	Chris Mihm CL	.50
2	Chris Mihm	1.00
3	Mike Miller	2.00
4	Chris Porter	.50
5	Morris Peterson	1.00
6	Darius Miles	3.00
7	Jerome Moiso	.60
8	Quentin Richardson	1.00
9	Mateen Cleaves	1.00
10	Etan Thomas	.75
11	Scoonie Penn	.30
12	Jason Collier	.30
13	Hanno Mottola	.20
14	Mark Madsen	.30
15	DeShawn Stevenson	1.50
16	Dan Langhi	.40
17	Jamaal Magloire	.50
18	Pepe Sanchez	.40
19	Khalid El-Amin	.50
20	Harold Arceneaux	.20
21	Mark Karcher	.20
22	Jason Hart	.20
23	Eddie House	.20
24	Gabe Muoneke	.10
25	Jake Voskuhl	.30
26	Brad Millard	.10
27	Bootsy Thornton	.20
28	Eddie Gill	.10
29	Shaheen Holloway	.20
30	Kevin Freeman	.30
31	Jarrett Stephens	.10
32	Brian Cardinal	.30
33	Brandon Kurtz	.10
34	Elton Brand	1.25
35	Steve Francis	1.50
36	Lamar Odom	1.00
37	Wally Szczerbiak	.50
38	Baron Davis	.30
39	Richard Hamilton	.30
40	Chris Carrawell	.50
41	Chris Mihm PP	3.00
42	Darius Miles PP	10.00
43	Mike Miller PP	6.00
44	Jerome Moiso PP	2.00
45	Mateen Cleaves PP	3.00
46	Morris Peterson PP	3.00

2000 Press Pass Torquers

This 40-card parallel set reprinted each Press Pass card, but utilized blue foil vs. the silver foil that was used on regular-issue cards. Torquers were inserted one per retail pack.

	MT
Complete Set (40):	20.00
Common Player:	.15
Inserted 1:1 Retail	

2000 Press Pass Reflectors

This 40-card parallel set reprinted all the base cards from the set on a holofoil surface. Cards were numbered with an "R" prefix, inserted 1:72 packs and sequentially numbered to 500 sets.

	MT
Complete Set (40):	200.00
Common Player:	1.50
Reflector Cards:	7x-14x
Inserted 1:72	
Production 500 Sets	

2000 Press Pass Autographs

Many of the players in Press Pass also had Autographed cards available. These were distinguished by a matte finish and a different design than the base cards, along with a Press Pass Authentics logo and a white area for the signature. Autographed cards were unnumbered and inserted 1:9 hobby packs and 1:36 retail packs.

	MT
Complete Set (30):	450.00
Common Player:	4.00
Inserted 1:9 Hobby	
Inserted 1:36 Retail	
Elton Brand	40.00
Brian Cardinal	8.00
Mateen Cleaves	25.00
Jason Collier	8.00
Baron Davis	10.00
Keyon Dooling	15.00
Steve Francis	60.00
Eddie Gill	4.00
Jason Hart	8.00
Eddie House	8.00
Dan Langhi	8.00
Mark Madsen	8.00
Jamaal Magloire	12.00
Dan McClintock	4.00
Chris Mihm	25.00
Darius Miles	75.00
Brad Millard	4.00
Mike Miller	50.00
Jerome Moiso	15.00
Hanno Mottola	8.00
Lamar Odom	30.00
Scoonie Penn	8.00
Morris Peterson	25.00
Chris Porter	12.00
Quentin Richardson	25.00
Jarrett Stephens	4.00
DeShawn Stevenson	30.00
Wally Szczerbiak	15.00
Etan Thomas	20.00
Jake Voskuhl	8.00

2000 Press Pass BreakAway

This 36-card partial parallel set featured die-cut cards of players in the regular set, with coaches comments on the back. Breakaway cards were numbered with a "BA" prefix and seeded one per pack.

		MT
Complete Set (36):		30.00
Common Player:		.15
Breakaway Cards:		1.5x
Inserted 1:1		
1	Chris Mihm	.15
2	Mike Miller	.15
3	Chris Porter	.15
4	Morris Peterson	.15
5	Morris Peterson	.15
6	Darius Miles	.15
7	Jerome Moiso	.15
8	Quentin Richardson	.15
9	Mateen Cleaves	.15
10	Etan Thomas	.15
11	Scoonie Penn	.15
12	Jason Collier	.15
13	Hanno Mottola	.15
14	Mark Madsen	.15
15	DeShawn Stevenson	.15
16	Dan Langhi	.15
17	Jamaal Magloire	.15
18	Pepe Sanchez	.15
19	Mark Karcher	.15
20	Khalid El-Amin	.15
21	Jason Hart	.15
22	Eddie House	.15
23	Gabe Muoneke	.15
24	Jake Voskuhl	.15
25	Brad Millard	.15
26	Shaheen Holloway	.15
27	Jarrett Stephens	.15
28	Elton Brand	.15
29	Steve Francis	.15
30	Lamar Odom	.15
31	Wally Szczerbiak	.15
32	Baron Davis	.15
33	Richard Hamilton	.15
34	Bootsy Thornton	.15
35	Brian Cardinal	.15
36	Chris Carrawell	.15

2000 Press Pass In The Paint

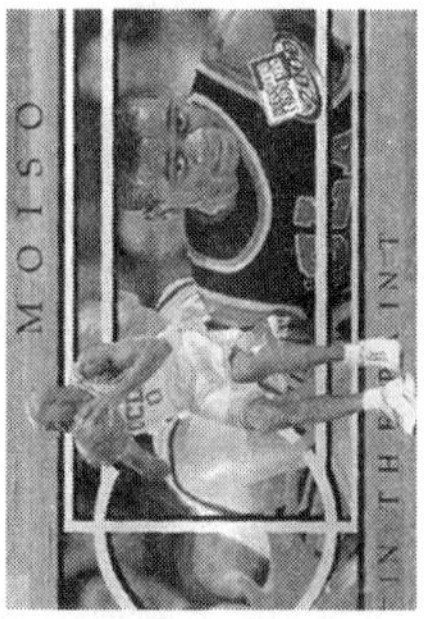

This eight-card set featured top college players on a horizontal background, with a wood colored border across the top and bottom. Cards were numbered with an "IP" prefix and inserted 1:12 packs. Die-cut versions were also available and seeded 1:24 packs.

		MT
Complete Set (8):		12.00
Common Player:		.50
Inserted 1:12		
Die-cuts:		2x
Inserted 1:24		
1	Chris Mihm	2.50
2	Mateen Cleaves	2.50
3	Morris Peterson	2.50
4	Jerome Moiso	1.50
5	Mike Miller	4.00
6	Darius Miles	6.00
7	Jason Collier	.50
8	Etan Thomas	2.00

2000 Press Pass In the Paint Die-cut

This eight-card parallel set featured die-cut versions of each In the

Paint inserts. Die-cut versions were seeded 1:24 packs.

		MT
Complete Set (8):		18.00
Common Player:		.75
Die-cuts:		1.5x
Inserted 1:24		

2000 Press Pass In Your Face

This six-card insert set featured above the rim shots on an all-foil card. Cards were numbered with an "IYF" prefix and seeded 1:28 packs.

		MT
Complete Set (6):		8.00
Common Player:		1.00
Inserted 1:28		
1	Chris Mihm	3.00
2	Mateen Cleaves	3.00
3	Morris Peterson	3.00
4	Jerome Moiso	2.00
5	Chris Porter	1.00
6	Quentin Richardson	3.00

2000 Press Pass Jersey Cards

This four-card insert set featured swatches of game-used college jerseys. Jersey Cards were numbered with a "JC" prefix and by the player's initials. Cards were seeded 1:420 hobby packs and 1:720 retail packs and sequentially numbered to 425 sets.

		MT
Complete Set (4):		300.00
Common Player:		60.00
Inserted 1:420 Hobby		
Inserted 1:720 Retail		
Production 425 Sets		
MC	Mateen Cleaves	60.00
CM	Chris Mihm	60.00
DM	Darius Miles	150.00
MM	Mike Miller	100.00

2000 Press Pass On Fire

This 11-card insert set featured players over a metal-like, foil background with a net and basketball. On Fire cards were numbered with an "OF" prefix and seeded 1:6 packs.

		MT
Complete Set (11):		12.00
Common Player:		.50
Inserted 1:6		
1	Mike Miller	4.00
2	Darius Miles	5.00
3	Chris Mihm	2.00
4	Quentin Richardson	2.00
5	Mateen Cleaves	2.00
6	Chris Porter	.75
7	Morris Peterson	2.00
8	Khalid El-Amin	.75
9	Jerome Moiso	1.00
10	Hanno Mottola	.50
11	Etan Thomas	1.50

2000 Press Pass Power Pick Autographs

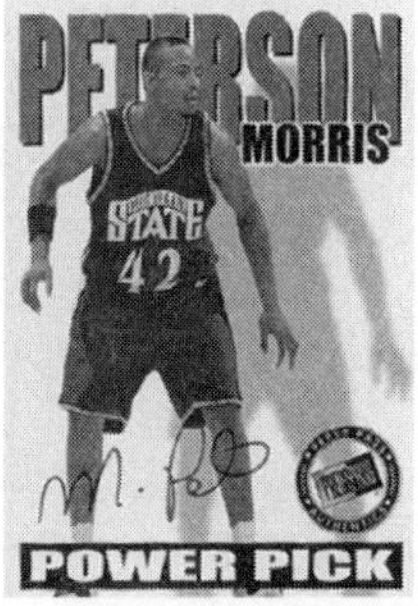

This six-card insert set added autographs to the six seeded cards from the base set. Each featured a matte finish and a Press Pass Authentics logo. Cards were hand-numbered to 250 on the back, except Morris Peterson, who was numbered to 240. Cards were unnumbered and inserted 1:269 hobby packs.

		MT
Complete Set (6):		250.00
Common Player:		25.00
Inserted 1:269 Hobby		
Production 250 Sets		
1	Chris Mihm	40.00
2	Darius Miles	100.00
3	Mike Miller	75.00
4	Jerome Moiso	25.00
5	Mateen Cleaves	40.00
6	Morris Peterson/240	40.00

2000 Press Pass SE

This 45-card set consisted of 28 player cards, one checklist, six Class of 1999 and 10 Rookie Vision cards. The base cards featured a color shot of the player in an oval-shape with a white background around the oval. Each card was reprinted in an Alley Oop parallel set. Inserts included: Autographs, Jersey Cards, Jersey Number Swatches, Lottery Club, Lottery Club Autographs, Old School, Old School Threads, Sophomore Sensation and Two On One.

		MT
Complete Set (45):		15.00
Common Player:		.10
Minor Stars:		.20
Pack (4):		10.00
Box (12):		100.00
1	Checklist (Mike Miller)	.75
2	Darius Miles	4.00
3	Mike Miller	1.50
4	Chris Mihm	.50
5	Keyon Dooling	1.00
6	Jerome Moiso	.60
7	Etan Thomas	.50
8	Mateen Cleaves	.75
9	Jason Collier	.30
10	Quentin Richardson	1.00
11	Jamaal Magloire	.50
12	Morris Peterson	1.25
13	DeShawn Stevenson	1.50
14	Mark Madsen	.30
15	A.J. Guyton	.30
16	Dan Langhi	.40
17	Jake Voskuhl	.30
18	Khalid El-Amin	.50
19	Eddie House	.40
20	Hanno Mottola	.20
21	Chris Carrawell	.30
22	Brian Cardinal	.20
23	Mark Karcher	.10
24	Jason Hart	.20
25	Dan McClintock	.10
26	Chris Porter	1.00
27	Jaquay Walls	.10
28	Scoonie Penn	.30
29	Pete Mickeal	.30
30	Elton Brand	1.00
31	Steve Francis	1.50
32	Baron Davis	.30
33	Lamar Odom	1.00
34	Wally Szczerbiak	.40
35	Richard Hamilton	.30
36	Darius Miles	2.00
37	Mike Miller	.75
38	Chris Mihm	.25
39	Keyon Dooling	.50
40	Jerome Moiso	.30
41	Etan Thomas	.25
42	Mateen Cleaves	.40
43	Jason Collier	.10
44	Quentin Richardson	.50
45	Morris Peterson	.60

2000 Press Pass SE Autographs

The Autograph lineup included 34 players, with a different design on a matte finish card. Autograph cards were unnumbered and are listed below in alphabetical order. Regular Autographs utilized gold lettering, while silver versions were machine-numbered to 500 on the back. Regular Autographs were seeded one per hobby pack and 1:18 retail packs.

		MT
Complete Set (34):		450.00
Common Player:		4.00
Inserted 1:1 Hobby		
Inserted 1:18 Retail		
1	Elton Brand	40.00
2	Brian Cardinal	4.00
3	Chris Carrawell	12.00
4	Mateen Cleaves	25.00
5	Jason Collier	8.00
6	Baron Davis	10.00
7	Keyon Dooling	15.00
8	Khalid El-Amin	8.00
9	Steve Francis	60.00
10	A.J. Guyton	6.00
11	Richard Hamilton	10.00
12	Jason Hart	8.00
13	Eddie House	8.00
14	Mark Karcher	4.00
15	Dan Langhi	8.00
16	Mark Madsen	8.00
17	Jamaal Magloire	12.00
18	Dan McClintock	4.00
19	Pete Mickeal	8.00
20	Chris Mihm	25.00
21	Darius Miles	75.00
22	Mike Miller	50.00
23	Jerome Moiso	15.00
24	Hanno Mottola	8.00
25	Scoonie Penn	8.00
26	Morris Peterson	25.00
27	Lavor Postell	8.00
28	Quentin Richardson	25.00
29	Jabari Smith	4.00
30	DeShawn Stevenson	30.00
31	Wally Szczerbiak	15.00
32	Etan Thomas	20.00
33	Jake Voskuhl	8.00
34	Jaquay Walls	4.00

2000 Press Pass SE Jersey Cards

This 12-card insert set featured jersey swatches from top college players. Jersey Cards were sequentially numbered to 200 sets on the back, numbered with a "JC" prefix and seeded 1:84 hobby packs and 1:720 retail packs.

		MT
Complete Set (12):		600.00
Common Player:		20.00
Inserted 1:84		
1	Chris Mihm	60.00
2	Mateen Cleaves	60.00
3	Darius Miles	150.00
4	Mike Miller	100.00
5	Jerome Moiso	40.00
6	Etan Thomas	50.00
7	Quentin Richardson	60.00
8	Mark Madsen	20.00
9	Morris Peterson	60.00
10	Jamaal Magloire	25.00
11	DeShawn Stevenson	100.00
12	Mark Karcher	20.00

2000 Press Pass SE Jersey Card Patch

This 12-card set featured swatches of jersey patches from top college players. These were exclusive to hobby packs, usually contained multiple colors, were numbered with a "JCP" prefix and sequentially numbered to 25 sets.

		MT
Common Player:		50.00
Production 25 Sets		
1	Chris Mihm	200.00
2	Mateen Cleaves	200.00
3	Darius Miles	400.00
4	Mike Miller	300.00
5	Jerome Moiso	100.00
6	Etan Thomas	150.00
7	Quentin Richardson	200.00
8	Mark Madsen	50.00
9	Morris Peterson	200.00
10	Jamaal Magloire	75.00
11	DeShawn Stevenson	300.00
12	Mark Karcher	50.00

2000 Press Pass SE Lottery Club

This six-card insert set was printed on holographic foil and numbered with an "LC" prefix. Cards were seeded 1:6 packs. Autographed versions also existed, but were distinguished by the matte finish used for printing.

		MT
Complete Set (6):		10.00
Common Player:		1.00
Inserted 1:6		
1	Darius Miles	5.00
2	Mike Miller	4.00
3	Chris Mihm	2.00
4	Keyon Dooling	1.00
5	Jerome Moiso	1.00
6	Etan Thomas	1.50

2000 Press Pass SE Lottery Club Autographs

This six-card insert paralleled the Lottery Club set but cards were printed on a matte finish, autographed and numbered to 100 sets.

		MT
Complete Set (6):		300.00
Common Player:		30.00
Production 100 Sets		
1	Darius Miles	125.00
2	Mike Miller	75.00
3	Chris Mihm	50.00
4	Keyon Dooling	30.00
5	Jerome Moiso	30.00
6	Etan Thomas	40.00

2000 Press Pass SE Old School

This retro-style insert contained 27 cards on a design similar to the 1986-87 Fleer set, but featured team colors around the border. These were numbered with an "OS" prefix and seeded one per pack.

		MT
Complete Set (27):		25.00
Common Player:		.15
Minor Stars:		.25
Old School Cards:		1x-2x
Inserted 1:1		
1	Darius Miles	
2	Mike Miller	
3	Chris Mihm	
4	Keyon Dooling	
5	Jerome Moiso	
6	Etan Thomas	
7	Mateen Cleaves	
8	Jason Collier	
9	Quentin Richardson	
10	Jamaal Magloire	
11	Morris Peterson	
12	DeShawn Stevenson	
13	Mark Madsen	
14	Dan Langhi	
15	Jake Voskuhl	
16	Khalid El-Amin	
17	Eddie House	
18	Hanno Mottola	
19	Chris Carrawell	
20	Brian Cardinal	
21	Mark Karcher	
22	Jason Hart	
23	Chris Porter	
24	Scoonie Penn	
25	A.J. Guyton	
26	Jabari Smith	
27	Checklist (Mateen Cleaves)	

2000 Press Pass SE Old School Threads

This two-card insert set featured jersey swatches from Elton Brand and Steve Francis. Cards were sequentially numbered to 50 sets and numbered with an "OST" prefix.

		MT
Common Player:		150.00
Production 50 Sets		
1	Elton Brand	150.00
2	Steve Francis	200.00

2000 Press Pass SE Sophomore Sensation

This six-card progressive insert featured a color shot of the player over a kaleidoscope background of team colors. Cards 1 and 2 were seeded 1:96 hobby packs and 1:192 retail; Cards 3 and 4 were seeded 1:48 hobby packs and 1:96 retail; and Cards 5 and 6 were seeded 1:24 hobby packs and 1:48 retail. Sophomore Sensation inserts were numbered with an "SS" prefix.

		MT
Complete Set (6):		25.00
Common Player:		1.00
Inserted 1:7 Hobby		
1	Elton Brand	10.00
2	Steve Francis	12.00
3	Baron Davis	5.00
4	Lamar Odom	6.00
5	Wally Szczerbiak	2.00
6	Richard Hamilton	1.00

2000 Press Pass SE Two On One

Two On One featured 12 cards that fit together into four panels of three each. Cards A and C in each panel were individual players, while Card B featured both players. Cards were numbered with a "TO" prefix and were seeded 1:12 packs.

		MT
Complete Set (12):		20.00
Common Player:		1.00
Inserted 1:12		
1A	Darius Miles	6.00
1B	Darius Miles, Quentin Richardson	4.00
1C	Quentin Richardson	2.50
2A	Mateen Cleaves	2.50
2B	Mateen Cleaves, Morris Peterson	2.50
2C	Morris Peterson	2.50
3A	Jerome Moiso	1.00
3B	Jerome Moiso, Baron Davis	1.00
3C	Baron Davis	1.00
4A	Steve Francis	4.00
4B	Steve Francis, Elton Brand	3.00
4C	Elton Brand	3.00

1980-81 Pride New Orleans WBL

The Women's Basketball League set features blue-tinted photos on the fronts with the player's uniform number and a facsimile autograph, while the backs bio information. While nine cards are checklisted, there may have been at least four more cards issued.

		NM
Complete Set (9):		75.00
Common Player:		10.00
1	Kathy Andrykowski	10.00
2	Sybil Blalock	10.00
3	Cindy Brogden	10.00
4	Vicky Chapman	10.00
5	Sharon Farrah	10.00
6	Augusta Forest	10.00
7	Bertha Hardy	10.00
8	Sue Peters	10.00
9	Heidi Wayment	10.00

1985 Prism/Jewel Stickers

The 14-card, 2-11/16" x 4" set features artist's renditions of top players on metallic, prism-like stickers. The fronts are bordered by a rounded black stripe and the backs are unnumbered.

		MT
Complete Set (14):		600.00
Common Player:		6.00
1	Kareem Abdul-Jabbar	60.00
2	Larry Bird	100.00
3	Bird vs. Worthy	75.00
4	Julius Erving	70.00
5	Patrick Ewing	65.00
6	Magic Johnson	65.00
7	Michael Jordan	350.00
8	Moses Malone	15.00
9	Malone vs. Jabbar	20.00
10	Sidney Moncrief	10.00
11	Ralph Sampson	10.00
12	Isiah Thomas	15.00
13	Kelly Tripucka	6.00
14	Buck Williams	8.00

1989-90 ProCards CBA

The 207-card, standard-size set was released in individual sealed team bags with a production limit of 2,000 sets, with a retail of $3 for each. The CBA logo appears in the upper left corner with the horizontal backs have bio and stat information. Notable cards in the set are Chris Childs, Lloyd Daniels, Mario Elie and John Starks.

		MT
Complete Set (207):		115.00
Common Player:		.30

1 Sioux Falls Checklist .50
2 Ben Wilson .40
3 Leonard Harris .40
4 Laurent Crawford .30
5 Steve Grayer .50
6 Jim Lampley .50
7 Eric Brown .30
8 Dennis Nutt .40
9 Ralph Lewis .30
10 Lashun McDaniel .40
11 Leo Parent .30
12 Ron Ekker .40
13 Terry Gould .30
14 Wichita Falls Checklist .50
15 Mark Peterson .30
16 Greg Van Soelen .30
17 Maurice Selvin .30
18 Michael Tait .40
19 Deon Hunter .50
20 Randy Henry .30
21 Kenny McClary .50
22 Earl Walker .30
23 Jeff Hodge .30
24 Martin Nessley .50
25 On Court Staff .30
26 Rapid City Checklist .50
27 Daren Queenan .30
28 Carey Scurry .40
29 Keith Smart 1.50
30 Jim Thomas .50
31 Pearl Washington .75
32 Chris Childs 9.00
33 Jarvis Basnight .50
34 Dwight Boyd .30
35 Raymond Brown .50
36 Sylvester Gray .40
37 Eric Musselman .40
38 Quad City Checklist .50
39 Kenny Gattison 2.00
40 Lafester Rhodes .50
41 Perry Young .50
42 Wiley Brown .50
43 Jose Slaughter .40
44 Gerald Greene .30
45 Lloyd Daniels 3.00
46 Bill Jones .40
47 Sean Couch .40
48 Marty Eggleston .30
49 Mauro Panaggio CO .40
50 Dan Panaggio .30
51 Pensacola Checklist .50
52 Joe Mullaney CO 1.50
53 Mark Wade .50
54 Larry Houzer .30
55 Clifford Lett .50
56 Tony Dawson .30
57 Johnathan Edwards .40
58 Jim Farmer 1.00
59 Dwayne Taylor .30
60 Bob McCann .75
61 Omaha Checklist .50
62 Silks/Rodie .30
63 Racers Front Office .30
64 Rodie-Team Mascot .30
65 Tim Price .30
66 Bobby Glanzer .30
67 Greg Wiltjer .30
68 Ron Kellogg .40
69 Tat Hunter .30
70 Reginald Turner .30
71 Jerry Adams .30
72 Roland Gray .30
73 Tim Legler 3.00
74 Corey Gaines 1.00
75 Columbus Checklist .50
76 Gary Youmans .30
77 Kelvin Ransey .75
78 Chip Engelland .50
79 Brian Martin .30
80 Ray Hall .30
81 Jay Burson .75
82 Bill Martin .75
83 Eric Mudd .30
84 Tom Schafer .40
85 Steve Harris .50
86 Eric Newsome .30
87 Rockford Checklist .50
88 Charley Rosen .30
89 Tom Hart .30
90 Team Picture .50
91 Brent Carmichael .30
92 Fred Cofield .40
93 Darren Guest .30
94 Bobby Parks .50
95 Elston Turner 1.00
96 Adrian McKinnon .30
97 Gary Massey .30
98 Tim Dillon .30
99 Herb Blunt .40
100 Greg Grissom .40
101 Albany Checklist .50
102 Leroy Witherspoon .30
103 Vincent Askew 3.00
104 Clinton Smith .30
105 Andre Patterson .30
106 Jim Ferrer .30
107 Willie Glass .75
108 Darryl Joe .50
109 Mario Elie 9.00
110 Dave Popson 1.00
111 Danny Pearson .30
112 Doc Nunnally .30
113 Gene Espeland .30
114 Gerald Oliver .30
115 Santa Barbara CL .50
116 Luther Burks .30
117 Brian Christensen .40
118 Kevin Francewar .30
119 Leon Wood 3.00
120 Derrick Gervin 1.25
121 Larry Spriggs 1.50
122 Michael Phelps .50
123 Mike Ratliff .40
124 Steffond Johnson .75
125 Mitch McMullen .30
126 Sonny Allen .50
127 Don Ford 1.00
128 Grand Rapids Checklist .50
129 Lorenzo Sutton .40
130 Willie Simmons .30
131 Kenny Fields .50
132 Winston Crite .50
133 Eric McLaughlin .30
134 Tony Brown .40
135 Ricky Wilson .40
136 Milt Newton .50
137 Albert Springs .30
138 Herbert Crook .75
139 Mike Mashak .30
140 Jim Sleeper .30
141 Tulsa Checklist .50
142 Terry Faggins .30
143 Ozell Jones .75
144 Brian Rahilly .30
145 Duane Washington .50
146 Ron Spivey .30
147 Henry Bibby CO 1.50
148 Al Gipson .40
149 Greg Jones .30
150 Andre Moore .50
151 Tracy Moore .50
152 Steve Bontranger .30
153 Bubby Breaker Team Mascot .30
154 LaCrosse Checklist .50
155 Mike Williams .30
156 Vince Hamilton .30
157 John Harris .30
158 Tony White .30
159 Todd Alexander .40
160 Richard Johnson .40
161 Leo Rautins .50
162 Dwayne McClain 1.50
163 Carlos Clark .40
164 Vada Martin .40
165 Flip Saunders 3.00
166 Topeka Checklist .50
167 Cedric Hunter .50
168 Elfrem Jackson .30
169 Glen Clem .30
170 Mike Richmond .30
171 Jim Rowinski .40
172 Craig Jackson .30
173 Tony Mack .30
174 Hubert Henderson .50
175 Kevin Nixon .30
176 Haywoode Workman 2.00
177 Porter Cutrell .30
178 Mike Riley .30
179 Cedar Rapids Checklist .50
180 Bullet Bear .30
181 George Whittaker .30
182 Tom Domako .30
183 Al Lorenzen .50
184 Darryl Johnson .50
185 Mel Braxton .30
186 Orlando Graham .30
187 Reggie Owens .40
188 John Starks 20.00
189 Kenny Drummond .30
190 Mark Plansky .40
191 Anthony Blakley .75
192 Everette Stephens 1.00
193 San Jose Checklist .50
194 Cory Russell .30
195 Jim Ellis .30
196 Butch Hays .75
197 Mike Doktorczyk .30
198 Scooter Barry 1.25
199 Monroe Douglass .40
200 Scott Fisher .75
201 David Boone .30
202 Jervis Cole .40
203 Freddie Banks .50
204 Richard Morton .30
205 Dan Williams .30
206 Mike Thibault CO .30
207 Omaha Coaches Omaha Rackers .30

1990-91 ProCards CBA

The 203-card, standard-size set features players from the CBA. The fronts have a red film-strip border with the horizontal backs featuring bio and stat information. The cards were issued in team sets, retailing for $3 each. The set is notable in that it contains the first professional card of Anthony Mason.

	MT
Complete Set (203):	95.00
Common Player:	.30

1 Jim Les 2.00
2 Ron Moore .30
3 Rod Mason .30
4 Paul Weakly .30
5 Brian Howard .75
6 Pat Bolden .30
7 Mike Thibault CO .30
8 Tim Legler 2.00
9 Cedric Hunter .50
10 Mark Peterson .30
11 Greg Wiltjer .30
12 The Idelman's .30
13 The Silks and Rodie .30
14 Basketball Staff .30
15 Front Office Staff .30
16 Omaha Checklist .50
17 Calvin Duncan .30
18 Pat Durham .50
19 Steve Grayer .50
20 Roy Marble 1.25
21 Tony Martin .50
22 Shawn McDaniel .40
23 Peter Thibeaux .40
24 Clarence Thompson .30
25 Demone Webster .30
26 A.J. Wynder .30
27 Steve Kahl .30
28 Steve Bontrager .30
29 Cedar Rapids (Checklist) .50
30 Skeeter Henry .50
31 Eugene McDowell .40
32 Bruce Wheatley .30
33 Mark Wade .50
34 Cheyenne Gibson .30
35 Clifford Lett .50
36 Larry Houzer .30
37 Tony Dawson .40
38 Richard Hollis .50
39 Ed Leonard, Joe Corona .30
40 Front Office Staff .30
41 Torry the Tornado .30
42 Fred Bryan .30
43 Jim Goodman .30
44 Pensacola Checklist .50
45 Joe Fredrick .30
46 Everette Stephens 1.00
47 Mario Donaldson .30
48 Dan Godfread .40
49 Haakon Austefjord .30
50 Gary Massey .30
51 Chris Childs 5.00
52 Gerry Wright .30
53 Marty Conlon 1.50
54 Tony Costner .30
55 Steve Hayes .50
56 Tom Hart .30
57 Paul Kulick .30
58 Rockford Team Photo .50
59 Rockford Checklist .50
60 Mike Williams .30
61 Brian Rahilly .30
62 Bill Martin .50
63 Vince Hamilton .30
64 Dwayne McClain 1.00
65 Bart Kofoed .50
66 Dominic Pressley .50
67 Herb Dixon .30
68 Todd Mitchell .50
69 Ben Mitchell .30
70 Flip Saunders 2.50
71 LaCrosse Checklist .75
72 Keith Smart 1.25
73 Stevie Thompson 1.50
74 Brian Rowsom .50
75 Tony Martin .30
76 Joe Ward .30
77 Fennis Dembo .75
78 Glenn Puddy .40
79 Lanard Copeland 1.00
80 Carl Brown .30
81 Rapid City Checklist .50
82 Dennis Nutt .40
83 Leonard Harris .50
84 Tharon Mayes .50
85 Melvin McCants .75
86 Tracy Mitchell .50
87 Ken Redfield .50
88 Frank Ross .50
89 Michael Phelps .50
90 Brian Christensen .50
91 Kevin McKenna .50
92 Steve Raab .50
93 Clay Moser .30
94 Tony Khing .30
95 Little Dude .30
96 Sioux Falls Checklist .50
97 Perry Young .50
98 Ozell Jones .50
99 Willie Simmons .30
100 Alvin Heggs .30
101 Kelsey Weems .50
102 Anthony Frederick .50
103 Royce Jeffries .30
104 Darryl McDonald .75
105 Sgt. Slammer .30
106 Charley Rosen .30
107 Oklahoma City (Checklist) .50
108 Keith Wilson .40
109 James Carter .30
110 Tracy Moore .30
111 Mark Plansky .40
112 Charles Bradley .30
113 Leroy Combs .50
114 Anthony Mason 14.00
115 Gary Voce .30
116 Jim Lampley .50
117 Henry Bibby CO 1.00
118 Tulsa Checklist .50
119 Texans Logo .30
120 Ennis Whatley 1.25
121 Mike Mitchell .75
122 Derrick Taylor .50
123 Kenny Atkinson .30
124 Jaren Jackson 1.50
125 Cedric Ball .30
126 Chris Munk .40
127 Mark Becker .30
128 Rodney Blake .30
129 Kurt Portmann .30
130 Henry James .75
131 John Treloar ACO .30
132 Dave Whitney ACO .50
133 Mike Davis ACO .30
134 Wichita Falls (Checklist) .50
135 Milt Wagner .75
136 Phil Henderson 1.00
137 Tony Harris .40
138 Steve Bardo .75
139 A.J. Wynder .50
140 Joel DeBortoli .30
141 Tim Anderson .30
142 Ron Draper .30
143 Barry Sumpter .30
144 Demone Webster .30
145 Thunderbird Dance Team .40
146 Mauro Panaggio CO .40
147 Dan Panaggio .30
148 Quad City Checklist .50
149 Albert King .75
150 Keith Smith .30
151 Mario Elie 4.50
152 Albert Springs .30
153 Jeff Fryer .40
154 Clinton Smith .30
155 Vincent Askew 2.50
156 Paul Graham 1.50
157 Ben McDonald .50
158 Willie McDuffie .30
159 George Karl CO 3.00
160 Terry Stotts .40
161 Doc Nunnally .30
162 Albany Checklist .50
163 Reggie Fox .30
164 Sedric Toney .40
165 Ron Draper .30
166 Alex Austin .30
167 Robert Brickey .75
168 Ricky Blanton .75
169 Stan Kimbrough .30
170 Ron Cavenall .40
171 Grand Rapids (Checklist) .50
172 Darren Henrie .30
173 Duane Washington .50
174 Barry Stevens .40
175 Craig Neal .30
176 Ron Spivey .40
177 Kerry Hammonds .30
178 Brian Martin .30
179 Jerome Henderson .40
180 John McIntyre .30
181 Chris Childs 5.00
182 The Jacobson's .30
183 Columbus Checklist .50
184 Luther Burks .30
185 Lee Campbell .30
186 Corey Gaines .30
187 Mike Higgins .30
188 Ron Kellogg .40
189 Bart Kofoed .50
190 Jim Rowinski .30
191 Riley Smith .30
192 Yakima Checklist .50
193 Mike Yoest .30
194 Freddie Banks .40
195 Scooter Barry .75
196 Richard Morton .40
197 Kelby Stuckey .30
198 Jervis Cole .40
199 Kenny McClary .50
200 Joe Wallace .30
201 Mark Tillmon .50
202 Greg Butler .50
203 San Jose Checklist .50

1991-92 ProCards CBA

The 206-card, standard-size set was issued in teams sets, which retailed for $3 each. The CBA logo appears in the lower left corner of the card front while the horizontal back contains bio and stat information. Seven teams had sponsors that listed their business on the card back.

	MT
Complete Set (206):	65.00
Common Player:	.30

1 Chris Childs 4.00
2 Mark Tillmon .50
3 Greg Butler .50
4 Keith Hill .30
5 Jean Derouillere .30
6 Levy Middlebrooks .30
7 Tank Collins .30
8 Sam Williams .40
9 Herman Kull CO .30
10 Don Ford ACO .40
11 Charles Charlesworth (Trainer) .30
12 Calvin Oldham .30
13 Larry Smith .50
14 Trent Jackson .30
15 Rob Rose .75
16 Walter Bond .50
17 Jeff Majerle .30
18 Brad Baldridge .30
19 Kurt Portman .30
20 Cedric Jenkins .50
21 John Treloar CO .30
22 Mike Davis ACO .30
23 Dave Whitney ACO .50
24 Wichita Falls CL .50
25 Tim Dillon .30
26 Kenny Miller .30
27 Stevie Wise .30
28 Dan Godfread .30
29 Mario Donaldson .30
30 Steve Berger .30
31 Corey Beasley .30
32 Danny Jones .30
33 Lanny Van Eman CO .30
34 Tony Morocco ACO .30
35 Rockford CL .50
36 Bobby Martin .50
37 Dwight Moody .50
38 Tim Anderson .30
39 A.J. Wynder .40
40 Keith Robinson .50
41 Steve Scheffler 1.00
42 Anthony Bowie 2.00
43 Tony Harris .30
44 Barry Mitchell .50
45 Tom Sheehey .30
46 Dan Panaggio CO .30
47 Mike Mashak ACO .30
48 Quad City CL .50
49 Bernard Thompson .75
50 Daryll Walker .40
51 Darryl Kennedy .50
52 Stevie Thompson 1.00
53 Kelsey Weems .40
54 Steve Burtt .75
55 Junie Lewis .30
56 Chris Harris .30
57 Jeff Hodge .30
58 Demone Webster .30
59 Henry Bibby CO 1.00
60 Oklahoma City CL .50
61 Jarvis Basnight .50
62 Ed Horton .50
63 Stanley Brundy .40
64 Irving Thomas .50
65 Nate Johnston .30
66 Keith Smart 1.00
67 Larry Robinson .40
68 Michael Anderson .30
69 Eric Musselman CO .40
70 Duane Ticknor ACO .30
71 Rapid City CL .50
72 Bakersfield CL .50
73 Lyndon Jones .50
74 Warren Bradley .30
75 Anthony Corbitt .30
76 Tony Karasek .30
77 Mark Peterson .30
78 Dan Palombizio .50
79 Ricky Hall .30
80 John Cooper .30
81 Carl Thomas .50
82 Travis Williams .30
83 Gerald Oliver CO .30
84 Coaching Staff (Kevin Kacer TR, Terry Stotts ACO, Dave Carrington ACO, Walter Jordan ACO) .30
85 Fort Wayne CL .50
86 Ronn McMahon .30
87 Sean Tyson .30
88 McKinley Singleton .40
89 Teo Alibegovic .30
90 Joey Johnson .30
91 Riley Smith .30
92 Alex Austin .30
93 Dennis Williams .30
94 Luther Burks .30
95 Bill Klucas CO .30
96 Jack Miller ACO .30
97 Yakima CL .50
98 Roy Fisher .50
99 Reggie Isaac .30
100 Reggie Jordan .75
101 Cedric Lewis .30
102 Jeff Martin .50
103 Dyron Nix .75
104 Walter Watts .50
105 Gary Waites .30
106 Gerald Paddio .75
107 Bruce Stewart CO .30
108 Jeff Burkhamer ACO .30
109 Grand Rapids CL .50
110 Petur Gundmundsson .40
111 Ralph Lewis .30
112 John Smith .30
113 Tony Farmer .50
114 Matt Roe .30
115 Darryl McDonald 1.00
116 Corey Gaines .50
117 Richard Rellford .50
118 Ken Redfield .50
119 Chuckie White .40
120 Kevin McKenna CO .30
121 Clay Moser ACO .30
122 Donald Royal 3.00
123 Wayne Tinkle .30
124 Jim Usevitch .30
125 Eric Dunn .30
126 Jeffty Connelly .30
127 Alan Pollard .30
128 Clifford Scales .50
129 Harold Wright .30
130 Willie Simms .40
131 Michael Holton .75
132 Terrill Hall .30
133 Calvin Duncan (Guard/Assistant CO) .30
134 Steve Hayes CO .40
135 Yakima CL .50
136 Duane Washington .40
137 Kermit Holmes .30
138 Mike Goodson .30
139 Byron Dinkins .75
140 Leonard Harris .40
141 Louis Banks .30
142 James Bradley .30
143 Jeff King .30
144 Ron Spivey .30
145 Orlando Graham .30
146 Vincent Chickerella CO .30
147 Columbus CL .50
148 Daron Hoges .30
149 Von McDade .50
150 Byron Irvin .75
151 Patrick Tompkins .30
152 Brian Rahilly .30
153 Kenny Battle 1.00
154 Jaren Jackson 1.50
155 Troy Truvillion .30
156 Mark Davis .40
157 Vince Hamilton .30
158 Don Zierden ACO, Mike McCollow ACO .30
159 LaCrosse CL .50
160 Derrick Chievous .75
161 Jeff Sanders .75
162 Marc Brown .30
163 Johnnie Hilliad .30
164 Jerry Johnson .30
165 Dave Popson .50
166 Derrick Rowland .30
167 Jose Slaughter .40
168 Steve Wright .30
169 Charley Rosen CO .30
170 Lowes Moore ACO .50
171 Albany CL .50
172 Jasper Hooks .30
173 Tracy Moore .50
174 Keith Wilson .40
175 Shawn McDaniel .40
176 Sam Johnson .30
177 Jeff Fryer .40
178 A.C. Carver .30
179 Jawann Oldham .75
180 Lefty Moore .30
181 Anthony Blakley .50
182 Steve Bontrager CO .30
183 Tulsa CL .50
184 Cedric Hunter .50
185 Ronnie Grandison .50
186 Ricky Jones .50
187 Tim Legler 1.00
188 Chip Engelland .40
189 Brian Howard .50
190 Greg Wiltjer .30
191 Rod Mason .30
192 Roland Gray .50
193 Tat Hunter .30
194 Mike Thibault CO .30
195 Omaha CL .50
196 Chris Collier .30
197 Skeeter Henry .50
198 Emmitt Smith .40
199 Anthony Houston .30
200 Michael Cutright .50
201 Michael Ansley 1.00
202 Eugene McDowell .30
203 Eric Johnson .30
204 Mo McHone CO .40
205 Birmingham CL .50
206 Sioux Falls CL .50

1994 Pro Mags Promos

This three-card set features color player cutouts superimposed on a streaked grey background.

	MT
Complete Set (3):	15.00
Common Player:	5.00

1 Shaquille O'Neal (UER name spelled O'Neil) 8.00
2 Grant Hill 8.00
3 Jason Kidd 5.00

1994 Pro Mags

Produced by Chris Martin Enterprises, Inc., the 135-magnet set was available in five-magnet packs with each blank-backed magnet measuring 2-1/8" x 3-3/8". A checklist card and a team magnet were included in each pack. The player's last name is printed vertically along the edge. The cards are grouped alphabetically by team.

	MT
Complete Set (135):	100.00
Common Player:	.75

1 Stacey Augmon 1.00
2 Mookie Blaylock 1.25
3 Doug Edwards .75
4 Adam Keefe .75
5 Danny Manning 1.00
6 Dee Brown 1.00
7 Sherman Douglas .75
8 Rick Fox 1.00
9 Xavier McDaniel .75
10 Robert Parish 2.00
11 Tyrone Bogues 2.00
12 Dell Curry .75
13 Hersey Hawkins 1.25
14 Larry Johnson 2.00
15 Alonzo Mourning 4.00
16 B.J. Armstrong .75
17 Horace Grant 1.25
18 Toni Kukoc 2.00
19 John Paxson 1.00
20 Scottie Pippen 6.00
21 Brad Daugherty .75
22 John Williams .75
23 Chris Mills .75
24 Larry Nance 1.25
25 Gerald Wilkins .75
26 Doug Smith .75
27 Jim Jackson 2.50
28 Ron Jones .75
29 Jamal Mashburn 2.00
30 Randy White .75
31 Mahmoud Abdul-Rauf .75
32 LaPhonso Ellis 1.00
33 Dikembe Mutombo 2.00
34 Reggie Williams .75
35 Rodney Rogers 1.25
36 Joe Dumars 1.50
37 Sean Elliott 1.00
38 Allan Houston 2.00
39 Lindsey Hunter .75
40 Terry Mills .75
41 Tim Hardaway 2.00
42 Chris Mullin 1.50
43 Billy Owens .75
44 Latrell Sprewell 1.00
45 Chris Webber 10.00
46 Robert Horry .75
47 Vernon Maxwell .75
48 Hakeem Olajuwon 4.00
49 Kenny Smith 1.00
50 Otis Thorpe .75
51 Dale Davis 1.00
52 Reggie Miller 3.00
53 Jerome Richardson .75
54 Rik Smits 1.00
55 LaSalle Thompson .75
56 Dominique Wilkins 2.00
57 Ron Harper 1.25
58 Mark Jackson 1.25
59 Stanley Roberts .75
60 Loy Vaught .75
61 Sam Bowie 1.00
62 Vlade Divac 1.00
63 George Lynch .75
64 Anthony Peeler .75
65 James Worthy 2.00
66 Harold Miner .75
67 Glen Rice 2.00
68 Rony Seikaly .75
69 Brian Shaw 1.00
70 Steve Smith 1.50
71 Vin Baker 4.00
72 Theodore Edwards .75
73 Todd Day .75
74 Eric Murdock .75
75 Jon Barry .75
76 Thurl Bailey .75
77 Christian Laettner 1.25
78 Chuck Person .75
79 Doug West .75
80 Micheal Williams .75
81 Derrick Coleman 1.00
82 Rick Mahorn .75
83 Johnny Newman .75
84 Kenny Anderson 1.00
85 Rex Walters .75
86 Greg Anthony 1.00
87 Rolando Blackman 1.00
88 Patrick Ewing 4.00
89 Charles Oakley 1.25
90 John Starks 1.25
91 Nick Anderson .75
92 Anfernee Hardaway 7.00
93 Donald Royal .75
94 Dennis Scott .75
95 Scott Skiles 1.00
96 Dana Barros .75
97 Shawn Bradley 1.00
98 Johnny Dawkins .75
99 Tim Perry .75
100 Clarence Weatherspoon .75
101 Charles Barkley 5.00
102 Cedric Ceballos 1.00
103 Malcolm Mackey .75
104 Dan Majerle 1.25
105 Danny Ainge 1.50
106 Clyde Drexler 4.00
107 Jerome Kersey .75
108 Rod Strickland 1.25
109 Buck Williams 1.25
110 Clifford Robinson 1.25
111 Mitch Richmond 3.00
112 Lionel Simmons .75
113 Wayman Tisdale .75
114 Walt Williams 1.00
115 Anthony Webb 1.00
116 Dale Ellis .75
117 J.R. Reid .75
118 David Robinson 5.00
119 Dennis Rodman 4.00
120 Vinny Del Negro .75
121 Kendall Gill .75
122 Ervin Johnson .75
123 Shawn Kemp 3.50
124 Gary Payton 4.50
125 Sam Perkins 1.00
126 Karl Malone 5.00
127 Tyrone Corbin .75

128	Jeff Hornacek	1.25
129	Felton Spencer	.75
130	John Stockton	5.00
131	Michael Adams	.75
132	Calbert Cheaney	.75
133	Tom Gugliotta	1.50
134	Don MacLean	.75
135	Pervis Ellison	.75

1994-95 Pro Mags Rookie Showcase

This 12-magnet set was sold in a cello-wrapped and individually numbered cardboard sleeve. The magnets measure 2-1/8" x 3-3/8" and have rounded corners. They have color player photos with "Rookie Showcase" and the number at the top. The player's name is stamped in gold foil under the picture.

		MT
Complete Set (12):		30.00
Common Player:		1.00
1	Tony Dumas	1.00
2	Brian Grant	2.50
3	Juwan Howard	4.00
4	Donyell Marshall	1.50
5	Eric Mobley	1.00
6	Eric Montross	1.00
7	Carlos Rogers	1.00
8	Jalen Rose	4.00
9	Charlie Ward	1.50
10	Grant Hill	9.00
11	Glenn Robinson	5.00
12	Jason Kidd	7.00

1995 Pro Mags

The 145-magnet set, produced by Chris Martin Enterprises, Inc., features magnets in the 2-1/4" x 3-1/2" size. Each five-magnet pack came with a checklist card. The player's name is printed in gold foil along either edge. The team logo appears in either bottom corner.

		MT
Complete Set (145):		140.00
Common Player:		.75
1	Stacey Augmon	1.00
2	Mookie Blaylock	1.25
3	Ken Norman	.75
4	Steve Smith	1.50
5	Grant Long	.75
6	Eric Williams	.75
7	Eric Montross	.75
8	Sherman Douglas	.75
9	Dee Brown	.75
10	Dino Radja	.75
11	Larry Johnson	2.00
12	Alonzo Mourning	3.50
13	Tyrone Bogues	2.00
14	Scott Burrell	.75
15	Kendall Gill	.75
16	Dennis Rodman	5.00
17	Scottie Pippen	4.00
18	Ron Harper	1.50
19	Toni Kukoc	1.50
20	Dickey Simpkins	.75
21	Danny Ferry	.75
22	Tyrone Hill	.75
23	Michael Cage	.75
24	Chris Mills	.75
25	Terrell Brandon	1.00
26	Jason Kidd	4.00
27	Jamal Mashburn	1.50
28	Tony Dumas	.75
29	Roy Tarpley	.75
30	Jim Jackson	1.50
31	Dikembe Mutombo	1.50
32	Jalen Rose	2.00
33	Robert Pack	.75
34	Antonio McDyess	5.00
35	Reggie Williams	.75
36	Grant Hill	8.00
37	Joe Dumars	1.50
38	Lindsey Hunter	.75
39	Allan Houston	2.00
40	Terry Mills	.75
41	Tim Hardaway	2.00
42	Chris Mullin	2.00
43	Joe Smith	4.00
44	Latrell Sprewell	1.00
45	Donyell Marshall	.75
46	Hakeem Olajuwon	3.50
47	Robert Horry	.75
48	Sam Cassell	1.00
49	Kenny Smith	.75
50	Clyde Drexler	3.50
51	Reggie Miller	3.00
52	Mark Jackson	1.25
53	Rik Smits	1.00
54	Dale Davis	1.25
55	Derrick McKay	.75
56	Loy Vaught	.75
57	Terry Dehere	.75
58	Lamond Murray	.75
59	Eric Piatkowski	1.00
60	Pooh Richardson	.75
61	Vlade Divac	1.25
62	Anthony Peeler	.75
63	Nick Van Exel	2.50
64	Cedric Ceballos	1.00
65	Eddie Jones	4.00
66	Sasha Danilovic	1.00
67	Glen Rice	2.00
68	Khalid Reeves	.75
69	Billy Owens	.75
70	Kevin Willis	.75
71	Glenn Robinson	2.50
72	Vin Baker	2.00
73	Todd Day	.75
74	Eric Mobley	.75
75	Jon Barry	.75
76	Isaiah Rider	.75
77	Christian Laettner	1.25
78	Kevin Garnett	15.00
79	Doug West	.75
80	Sean Rooks	.75
81	Derrick Coleman	1.00
82	Rick Mahorn	.75
83	Rex Walters	.75
84	Kenny Anderson	1.00
85	Ed O'Bannon	1.00
86	Patrick Ewing	3.00
87	John Starks	1.25
88	Charles Oakley	1.25
89	Anthony Mason	1.00
90	Derek Harper	.75
91	Anfernee Hardaway	4.00
92	Brian Shaw	.75
93	Shaquille O'Neal	8.00
94	Brooks Thompson	.75
95	Horace Grant	1.25
96	Tim Perry	.75
97	Sharone Wright	.75
98	Jerry Stackhouse	6.00
99	Clarence Weatherspoon	.75
100	Vernon Maxwell	.75
101	Charles Barkley	4.00
102	Danny Manning	.75
103	Michael Finley	6.00
104	Kevin Johnson	1.25
105	Wayman Tisdale	.75
106	Randolph Childress	.75
107	Gary Trent	.75
108	James Robinson	.75
109	Buck Williams	1.00
110	Clifford Robinson	1.25
111	Corliss Williamson	2.00
112	Bobby Hurley	1.25
113	Brian Grant	2.00
114	Mitch Richmond	2.00
115	Walt Williams	.75
116	David Robinson	4.00
117	Will Perdue	.75
118	Chuck Person	.75
119	Sean Elliot	1.00
120	Vinny Del Negro	.75
121	Ervin Johnson	.75
122	Shawn Kemp	2.50
123	Sam Perkins	1.00
124	Detlef Schrempf	1.00
125	Gary Payton	3.50
126	Karl Malone	4.00
127	John Stockton	4.00
128	Felton Spencer	.75
129	Jeff Hornacek	1.25
130	Adam Keefe	.75
131	Chris Webber	4.00
132	Juwan Howard	1.75
133	Calbert Cheaney	.75
134	Rasheed Wallace	4.00
135	Gheorghe Muresan	.75
136	Ed Pinckney	.75
137	Tony Massenburg	.75
138	Damon Stoudamire	5.00
139	Acie Earl	.75
140	Alvin Robertson	.75
141	Greg Anthony	.75
142	Benoit Benjamin	.75
143	Antonio Harvey	.75
144	Byron Scott	1.25
145	Bryant Reeves	2.00

1995-96 Pro Mags Die Cuts

These 29 magnets measure 3-1/2" x 3 1/2." The fronts have a color action shot of the player, the team logo and the player's name on a white background. The magnets are die-cut around the logo and player's name.

	MT
Complete Set (24):	70.00
Common Player:	1.50
Charles Barkley	3.00
Patrick Ewing	3.00
Anfernee Hardaway	3.00
Tim Hardaway	3.00
Grant Hill	4.00
Larry Johnson	3.00
Magic Johnson	4.00
Shawn Kemp	3.00
Jason Kidd	4.00
Karl Malone	4.00
Jamal Mashburn	2.00
Reggie Miller	3.00
Shaquille O'Neal	4.00
Hakeem Olajuwon	4.00
Mitch Richmond	3.00
Isaiah Rider	1.50
David Robinson	3.00
Glenn Robinson	2.50
Dennis Rodman	4.00
Jerry Stackhouse	3.00
John Stockton	4.00
Damon Stoudamire	3.00
Nick Van Exel	3.00
Chris Webber	3.50

1995-96 Pro Mags Lost in Space

The six-magnet set, randomly inserted in the 1995-96 set, features the player's name in gold foil with the cut-out image over a celestial background. They are numbered with a "LSI" prefix.

		MT
Complete Set (6):		15.00
Common Player:		1.00
1	Anfernee Hardaway	6.00
2	Antonio McDyess	8.00
3	Isaiah Rider	2.00
4	Ed O'Bannon	1.00
5	Latrell Sprewell	3.00
6	Robert Pack	1.00

1995-96 Pro Mags USA Basketball

This 10-magnet set features the members of the 1996 Olympic "Dream Team." They measure 2-1/4" x 3-1/2" and have rounded corners. Available in three-magnet packs, they feature a color player photo against a background that reads "USA Basketball." The player's name and facsimile autograph are printed in gold foil. Die-cut versions of these magnets were also created.

		MT
Complete Set (10):		18.00
Common Player:		1.50
1	Hakeem Olajuwon	2.50
2	Glenn Robinson	2.00
3	Karl Malone	3.00
4	Shaquille O'Neal	3.00
5	Reggie Miller	2.00
6	David Robinson	2.50
7	John Stockton	2.50
8	Anfernee Hardaway	2.50
9	Scottie Pippen	2.50
10	Grant Hill	3.00

1996 Pro Mags Team USA Die-Cuts

This 10-card magnet set featured the same players as the 1995-96 USA Basketball set, but on a larger, die-cut version.

		MT
Complete Set (10):		25.00
Common Player:		2.50
1	Hakeem Olajuwon	3.00
2	Glenn Robinson	2.50
3	Karl Malone	2.00
4	Shaquille O'Neal	3.00
5	Reggie Miller	3.00
6	David Robinson	3.00
7	John Stockton	3.00
8	Anfernee Hardaway	3.00
9	Scottie Pippen	3.00
10	Grant Hill	3.00

1998 Pro Mags Heroes of the Locker Room

		MT
Complete Set (2):		8.00
Common Player:		3.00
1	Kobe Bryant	6.00
2	Grant Hill	3.00

1991-92 Pro Set Prototypes

These five cards were manufactured by Pro Set to convince the NBA to get the company a license. Full-bleed photos highlight the card fronts, while the player's name and team were located inside color stripes at the bottom of the card. The backs featured the normal name, biography, stats and write-up. The cards, numbered "000", hold "dummy" for some information and Glenn Rice's highlights appear on the back of Michael Jordan's card. A triangle on the back contains the words "Prototype for review only."

		MT
Complete Set (5):		1400.
Common Player:		50.00
1	Tom Chambers	75.00
2	Patrick Ewing	150.00
3	Magic Johnson	350.00
4	Michael Jordan	850.00
5	Karl Malone	400.00

1996 Pro Stamps

This 12-sheet stamp set features 12 stamps per sheet and are numbered in the upper left front corner. Backs feature a checklist by team and an offer to Practice with the Pros. An album was available in retail boxes and is priced separately.

		MT
Complete Set (12):		25.00
Common Panel:		2.00
1	Brooks Thompson, Larry Johnson, Robert Pack, Mitch Richmond, Stacey Augmon, Terry Dehere, Charles Barkley, Bryant Reeves, Derek Harper, Corliss Williamson, Rex Walters, Tyrone Hill	2.00
2	Horace Grant, Derrick McKey, Antonio McDyess, Brian Grant, Mookie Blaylock, Loy Vaught, Gary Payton, Benoit Benjamin, Anthony Mason, Joe Smith, Rick Mahorn, Randolph Childress	2.00
3	Ervin Johnson, Dale Davis, Reggie Williams, Bobby Hurley, Ken Norman, Clifford Robinson, Detlef Schrempf, Antonio Harvey, Charles Oakley, Latrell Sprewell, Derrick Coleman, Gary Trent	2.00
4	Shawn Kemp, Rik Smits, Patrick Ewing, Corliss Williamson, Steve Smith, Buck Williams, Sam Perkins, Greg Anthony, John Starks, Rony Seikaly, Grant Long, James Robinson	2.00
5	Hakeem Olajuwon, Cedric Ceballos, Jason Kidd, Glen Rice, Glenn Robinson, Alvin Robertson, Toni Kukoc, David Robinson, Calbert Cheaney, Grant Hill, Isaiah Rider, Danny Ferry	4.00
6	Robert Horry, Nick Van Exel, Jamal Mashburn, Sasha Danilovic, Vin Baker, Ed Pinckney, Ron Harper, Will Perdue, Juwan Howard, Joe Dumars, Dino Radja, Sean Rooks	2.00
7	Sam Cassell, Anthony Peeler, Tony Dumas, Charles Barkley, Khalid Reeves, Damon Stoudamire, Scottie Pippen, Chuck Person, Chris Webber, Lindsey Hunter, Dee Brown, Doug West	5.00
8	Kenny Smith, Vlade Divac, Roy Tarpley, Anfernee Hardaway, Billy Owens, Tony Massenburg, Dennis Rodman, Sean Elliott, Adam Keefe, Rasheed Wallace, Sherman Douglas, Kevin Garnett	5.00
9	Clyde Drexler, Kendall Gill, Eddie Jones, Jerry Stackhouse, Kevin Willis, Acie Earl, Wayman Tisdale, Dickey Simpkins, Jeff Hornacek, Gheorghe Muresan, Eric Montross, Christian Laettner	2.00
10	Anfernee Hardaway, Scott Burrell, Jim Jackson, Sharone Wright, Todd Day, Pooh Richardson, Kevin Johnson, Vinny Del Negro, Felton Spencer, Allan Houston, Eric Williams, Tyrone Hill	3.00
11	Brian Shaw, Tyrone Bogues, Dikembe Mutombo, Tim Perry, Hakeem Olajuwon, Eric Piatkowski, Michael Finley, Reggie Miller, John Stockton, Terry Mills, Ed O'Bannon, Michael Cage	3.00
12	Dennis Scott, Alonzo Mourning, Jalen Rose, Walt Williams, Eric Murdock, Lamond Murray, Danny Manning, Mark Jackson, Karl Malone, Tim Hardaway, Kenny Anderson, Chris Mills	2.00
	Collector's Album	3.00

Q

1979 Quaker Iron-Ons

This set, officially licensed by the NBA, is sponsored by Quaker Oats and features posed photos on the fronts of the iron-on cards. The front tells how to iron the photo onto clothing; backs are blank. Cards measure 4-3/8" x 6-1/8".

	NM
Complete Set (8):	150.00
Common Player:	12.00
Kareem Abdul-Jabbar	40.00
Rick Barry	20.00
Julius Erving	40.00
George Gervin	25.00
Elvin Hayes	18.00
Maurice Lucas	12.00
David Thompson	20.00
Paul Westphal	12.00

1987 Quaker Sports Illustrated Mini Posters

		MT
Complete Set (7):		175.00
Common Player:		8.00
1	Larry Bird	40.00
2	Julius Erving	20.00
3	Magic Johnson	30.00
4	Michael Jordan	75.00
5	Hakeem Olajuwon	20.00
6	Spud Webb	8.00
7	Dominique Wilkins	12.00

R

1960 Rawlings

Rawlings Sporting Goods Co. sponsored this seven-card set which features posed color photos on the card fronts, plus the company logo and a facsimile signature of the player pictured. The 8" x 10" cards are unnumbered and have blank backs. The set is subtitled "Rawling's Advisory Staff."

	NM
Complete Set (7):	45.00
Common Player:	6.00
Cliff Hagan	8.00
Richie Guerin	6.00
Slater Martin	8.00
Bob Pettit	10.00
Frank Ramsey	6.00
Kenny Sears	6.00
Lenny Wilkens	8.00

1978 RC Cola

These 3 1/8" by 6" cards, featuring the players faces in the net of a basketball hoop, are sponsored by Royal Crown Cola and apparently licensed by the NBA Players Association. The RC logo is at the top of the card, as well as "Basketball Stars Collection." The cards are unnumbered, and were included in six-packs of the cola being sold primarily in the New England area. Each card measures 3-1/" by 6" and has a black-and-white mug shot of the player on the front, inside a basketball hoop net. Red and blue trim are used for the hoop.

	NM
Complete Set (40):	1500.
Common Player:	18.00
Kareem Abdul-Jabbar	200.00
Nate Archibald	50.00
Rick Barry	60.00
Jim Chones	18.00
Doug Collins	50.00
Dave Cowens	50.00
Adrian Dantley	45.00
Walter Davis	40.00
John Drew	20.00
Julius Erving	200.00
Walt Frazier	60.00
George Gervin	65.00
Artis Gilmore	40.00
Elvin Hayes	60.00
Dan Issel	50.00
Marques Johnson	25.00
Bernard King	45.00
Bob Lanier	45.00
Maurice Lucas	20.00
Pete Maravich	200.00
Bob McAdoo	35.00
George McGinnis	20.00
Eric Money	18.00
Earl Monroe	50.00
Calvin Murphy	30.00
Robert Parish	60.00
Billy Paultz	20.00
Jack Sikma	30.00
Rickey Sobers	18.00
David Thompson	55.00
Rudy Tomjanovich	50.00
Wes Unseld	50.00
Norm Van Lier	30.00
Bill Walton	95.00
Marvin Webster	20.00
Scott Wedman	20.00
Paul Westphal	30.00
Jo Jo White	30.00
John Williamson	20.00
Brian Winters	20.00

1992-93 Reebok Shawn Kemp

Available at Seattle-area shoe stores, the seven-card set focused on Shawn Kemp. Sponsored by Reebok and Olympic Sports, card Nos. 1-3 were available individually and Nos. 4-7 were available on four-card strips that were perforated. The green-bordered fronts showcase color photos. Kemp's name and number run along the left border. The Reebok logo is in the lower left, while the Sonics' logo is in the upper right. The backs, numbered "x of 7", have Kemp's bio and stats. The sponsors' logos are printed along the bottom of the card backs.

		MT
Complete Set (7):		45.00
Common Player:		1.00
1	Shawn Kemp #1	15.00
2	Shawn Kemp #2	15.00
3	Shawn Kemp #3	15.00
4	Cradling Rebound	1.00
5	Reverse Dunk	1.00
6	Pushing off Barkley	1.00
7	Outside Jumper	1.00

1998 Reebok Rebecca Lobo Postcard

		MT
1	Rebecca Lobo	5.00

Values quoted in this guide reflect the retail price of a card — the price a collector can expect to pay when buying a card from a dealer. The wholesale price — that which a collector can expect to receive from a dealer when selling cards — will be significantly lower, depending on desirability and condition.

1991-92 David Robinson Fan Club

Produced two straight years by TRG Inc., the cards were designed by David Robinson. The first card, issued in 1991, pictures him with a saxophone and keyboard. A signed basketball is located in the upper left, with five stars in the upper right. The bottom of the card features "Inaugural Leisure Series No. 1 '91, The Admiral." The card back has a photo of Robinson, a bio and write-up. In 1992, the second card was released that pictures Robinson with a ball on a finger. "The Admiral Leisure Series No. 2 '92" is printed at the top. The back includes a photo of Robinson golfing. It features a bio, write-up and facsimile signature. Overall, 50,000 sets were made.

		MT
	Complete Set (2):	10.00
	Common Player:	5.00
1	The Admiral No. 1 '91 (David Robinson) (Posed with saxaphone)	5.00
2	The Admiral No. 2 '92 (David Robinson) (Posed with basketball)	5.00

1968-69 Rockets Jack in the Box

Measuring 2" x 3", the 12-card set was available at participating San Diego-area Jack in the Box restaurants. The fronts have a color headshot, along with the player's name, team, Rockets' and Jack in the Box logos beneath the photo. The cards are unnumbered and blank.

	NM
Complete Set (12):	85.00
Common Player:	2.00
Common Player SP:	20.00
Rick Adelman	8.00
Harry Barnes SP	20.00
Jim Barnett	2.50
John Block	2.00
Henry Finkel SP	20.00
Elvin Hayes	15.00
Toby Kimball	2.00
Don Kojis	2.00
Stu Lantz	5.00
Pat Riley	20.00
John Q. Trapp	2.00
Art Williams	2.00

1990-91 Rockets Team Issue

Measuring 6" x 9", the five-card set is anchored by a color photo on the front bordered in white. A facsimile autograph is also included on the photo. The photos are unnumbered and blank-backed.

	MT
Complete Set (5):	10.00
Common Player:	.75
Dave Jamerson	.75
Buck Johnson	.75
Hakeem Olajuwon	8.00
Otis Thorpe	1.50
David Wood	.75

1975-76 Rockets Team Issue

		NM
	Complete Set (8):	25.00
	Common Player:	3.00
1	John Johnson	5.00
2	Kevin Kunnert	3.00
3	Mike Newlin	5.00
4	Ed Ratleff	3.00
5	Ron Riley	3.00
6	Rudy White	3.00
7	Dave Wohl	5.00
8	Tom Nissalke CO	5.00

1952 Royal Desserts

The 1952 Royal Desserts featured eight 2-5/8" x 3-1/4" horizontal cards with the card fronts divided into career highlights (right) and a blue-tinted headshot (left). A facsimile autograph appears in the headshot. "Royal Stars Of Basketball" with the card number appears along the top border. The cards formed the backs of Royal Dessert boxes. The key card in the set is that of George Mikan.

		NM
	Complete Set (8):	4000.
	Common Player:	250.00
1	Fred Schaus	300.00
2	Dick McGuire	400.00
3	Jack Nichols	250.00
4	Frank Brian	250.00
5	Joe Fulks	600.00
6	George Mikan	2000.
7	Jim Pollard	500.00
8	Harry E. Jeanette	300.00

1970-71 Royals Cincinnati Team Issue

		NM
	Complete Set (12):	75.00
	Common Player:	5.00
1	Nate Archibald	10.00
2	Bob Arnzen	5.00
3	Moe Barr	5.00
4	Bob Cousy	20.00
5	Johnny Green	6.00
6	Greg Hyder	5.00
7	Darrall Imhoff	5.00
8	Sam Lacey	6.00
9	Charlie Paulk	5.00
10	Flynn Robinson	6.00
11	Tom Van Arsdale	6.00
12	Norm Van Lier	8.00

S

1972 7-11 Cups

	NM
Complete Set (40):	400.00
Common Player:	4.00
Kareem Abdul-Jabbar	30.00
Nate Archibald	8.00
Rick Barry	10.00
Dave Bing	10.00
Austin Carr	6.00
Wilt Chamberlain	30.00
Dave DeBusschere	10.00
Walt Frazier	10.00
Gail Goodrich	10.00
Hal Greer	10.00
Happy Hairston	6.00
John Havlicek	20.00
Connie Hawkins	10.00
Elvin Hayes	10.00
Spencer Haywood	6.00
Lou Hudson	6.00
John Johnson	4.00
Don Kojis	4.00
Bob Lanier	10.00
Kevin Loughery	6.00
Jerry Lucas	10.00
Pete Maravich	45.00
Jack Marin	5.00
Jim McMillian	5.00
Jeff Mullins	6.00
Geoff Petrie	6.00
Abdul Rahman	4.00
Willis Reed	10.00
Oscar Robertson	20.00
Paul Silas	6.00
Jerry Sloan	8.00
Elmore Smith	4.00
Nate Thurmond	8.00
Wes Unseld	10.00
Dick Van Arsdale	5.00
Tom Van Arsdale	4.00
Chet Walker	6.00
John Warren	4.00
Jerry West	25.00
Jo Jo White	8.00

1998 Sage

		MT
	Complete Set (50):	20.00
	Common Player:	.20
	Minor Stars:	.30
	Pack (3):	10.00
	Wax Box (12):	110.00
1	Toby Bailey	.20
2	Corey Benjamin	.30
3	Andrew Betts	.20
4	Torraye Braggs	.20
5	Corey Brewer	.20
6	Kobe Bryant	3.00
7	Anthony Carter	.50
8	Vince Carter	8.00
9	Keon Clark	.50
10	Ricky Davis	.60
11	Michael Dickerson	1.00
12	Michael Doleac	.50
13	Bryce Drew	.50
14	Tremaine Fowlkes	.20
15	Pat Garrity	.30
16	Zendon Hamilton	.20
17	Matt Harpring	.50
18	Al Harrington	1.50
19	J.R. Henderson	.30
20	Antawn Jamison	3.00
21	DeMarco Johnson	.20
22	Charles Jones	.20
23	Rashard Lewis	1.50
24	Felipe Lopez	.75
25	Corey Louis	.20
26	Tyrron Lue	.30
27	Stephon Marbury	.75
28	Sean Marks	.20
29	Jelani McCoy	.30
30	Tracy McGrady	4.00
31	Roshown McCleod	.40
32	Brad Miller	.20
33	Cuttino Mobley	1.00
34	Nazr Mohammed	.30
35	Makhtar Ndiaye	.20
36	Radoslav Nesterovic	.30
37	Michael Olowokandi	1.00
38	Andrae Patterson	.20
39	Ruben Patterson	1.00
40	Paul Pierce	4.00
41	Jeff Sheppard	.20
42	Miles Simon	.30
43	Tim Thomas	.50
44	Robert Traylor	.75
45	Bonzi Wells	.75
46	Tyson Wheeler	.20
47	Jahidi White	.20
48	Jason Williams	5.00
49	Shammond Williams	.40
50	Korleone Young	.40

1998 Sage Red Autographs

This 52-card autographed set paralleled the base set, but featured a red background and a sequentially numbered autograph. Most players signed 999 of these, but there were as few as 99 by Corey Brewer and Tracy McGrady. Two players - Zendon Hamilton and Tim Thomas - have both a black and blue version.

		MT
	Complete Set (52):	600.00
	Common Player:	3.00
	Minor Stars:	5.00
A1	Toby Bailey/535	3.00
A2	Corey Benjamin/999	5.00
A3	Andrew Betts/475	3.00
A4	Torraye Braggs/890	3.00
A5	Corey Brewer/99	12.00
A6	Kobe Bryant/129	150.00
A7	Anthony Carter/990	12.00
A8	Vince Carter/479	100.00
A9	Keon Clark/999	5.00
A10	Ricky Davis/860	8.00
A11	Michael Dickerson/999	8.00
A12	Michael Doleac/549	5.00
A13	Bryce Drew/999	5.00
A14	Tremaine Fowlkes/999	3.00
A15	Pat Garrity/999	5.00
A16A	Zendon Hamilton (Black)/175	10.00
A16B	Zendon Hamilton (Blue)/825	3.00
A17	Matt Harpring/999	5.00
A18	Al Harrington/999	15.00
A19	J.R. Henderson/599	5.00
A20	Antawn Jamison/909	25.00
A21	DeMarco Johnson/890	3.00
A22	Charles Jones/999	3.00
A23	Rashard Lewis/999	15.00
A24	Felipe Lopez/999	8.00
A25	Corey Louis/990	3.00
A26	Tyrron Lue/999	5.00
A27	Stephon Marbury/149	40.00
A28	Sean Marks/999	3.00
A29	Jelani McCoy/125	15.00
A30	Tracy McGrady/99	100.00
A31	Roshown McLeod/970	5.00
A32	Brad Miller/879	3.00
A33	Cuttino Mobley/999	5.00
A34	Nazr Mohammed/739	5.00
A35	Makhtar Ndiaye/999	3.00
A36	Radoslav Nesterovic/999	3.00
A37	Michael Olowokandi/999	10.00
A38	Andrae Patterson/999	3.00
A39	Ruben Patterson/690	10.00
A40	Paul Pierce/199	50.00
A41	Jeff Sheppard/999	3.00
A42	Miles Simon/475	5.00
A43A	Tim Thomas (Black)/219	30.00
A43B	Tim Thomas (Blue)/819	10.00
A44	Robert Traylor/999	8.00
A45	Bonzi Wells/999	12.00
A46	Tyson Wheeler/999	3.00
A47	Jahidi White/459	3.00
A48	Jason Williams/999	30.00
A49	Shammond Williams/670	5.00
A50	Korleone Young/999	5.00

1998 Sage Bronze

This 52-card autographed set paralleled the base set, but featured a bronze background and a sequentially numbered autograph. Most players signed 650 of these, but there were as few as 65 by Corey Brewer. Two players - Zendon Hamilton and Tim Thomas - have both a black and blue version.

		MT
	Common Player:	4.00
	Bronze Autographs:	1.25x
A1	Toby Bailey/350	
A2	Corey Benjamin/650	
A3	Andrew Betts/300	
A4	Torraye Braggs/600	
A5	Corey Brewer/65	
A6	Kobe Bryant/85	
A7	Anthony Carter/625	
A8	Vince Carter/310	
A9	Keon Clark/650	
A10	Ricky Davis/600	
A11	Michael Dickerson/650	
A12	Michael Doleac/350	
A13	Bryce Drew/650	
A14	Tremaine Fowlkes/650	
A15	Pat Garrity/650	
A16A	Zendon Hamilton (Black)/120	
A16B	Zendon Hamilton (Blue)/540	
A17	Matt Harpring/650	
A18	Al Harrington/650	
A19	J.R. Henderson/385	
A20	Antawn Jamison/600	
A21	DeMarco Johnson/600	
A22	Charles Jones/650	
A23	Rashard Lewis/650	
A24	Felipe Lopez/650	
A25	Corey Louis/625	
A26	Tyrron Lue/650	
A27	Stephon Marbury/100	
A28	Sean Marks/650	
A29	Jelani McCoy/80	
A30	Tracy McGrady/70	
A31	Roshown McLeod/490	
A32	Brad Miller/570	
A33	Cuttino Mobley/650	
A34	Nazr Mohammed/490	
A35	Makhtar Ndiaye/650	
A36	Radoslav Nesterovic/650	
A37	Michael Olowokandi/650	
A38	Andrae Patterson/650	
A39	Ruben Patterson/650	
A40	Paul Pierce/130	
A41	Jeff Sheppard/650	
A42	Miles Simon/315	
A43A	Tim Thomas (Black)/150	
A43B	Tim Thomas (Blue)/530	
A44	Robert Traylor/650	
A45	Bonzi Wells/650	
A46	Tyson Wheeler/650	
A47	Jahidi White/300	
A48	Jason Williams/650	
A49	Shammond Williams/425	
A50	Korleone Young/650	

1998 Sage Gold

This 52-card autographed set paralleled the base set, but featured a gold background and a sequentially numbered autograph. Most players signed 200 of these, but there were as few as 20 by Corey Brewer. Two players - Zendon Hamilton and Tim Thomas - have both a black and blue version.

		MT
	Common Player:	10.00
	Gold Autographs:	2x-3x
A1	Toby Bailey/110	
A2	Corey Benjamin/200	
A3	Andrew Betts/95	
A4	Torraye Braggs/185	
A5	Corey Brewer/20	
A6	Kobe Bryant/30	
A7	Anthony Carter/190	
A8	Vince Carter/95	
A9	Keon Clark/200	
A10	Ricky Davis/185	
A11	Michael Dickerson/200	
A12	Michael Doleac/110	
A13	Bryce Drew/200	
A14	Tremaine Fowlkes/200	
A15	Pat Garrity/200	
A16A	Zendon Hamilton (Black)/40	
A16B	Zendon Hamilton (Blue)/165	
A17	Matt Harpring/200	
A18	Al Harrington/200	
A19	J.R. Henderson/120	
A20	Antawn Jamison/190	
A21	DeMarco Johnson/185	
A22	Charles Jones/200	
A23	Rashard Lewis/200	
A24	Felipe Lopez/200	
A25	Corey Louis/190	
A26	Tyrron Lue/200	
A27	Stephon Marbury/35	
A28	Sean Marks/200	
A29	Jelani McCoy/25	
A30	Tracy McGrady/25	
A31	Roshown McLeod/165	
A32	Brad Miller/175	
A33	Cuttino Mobley/200	
A34	Nazr Mohammed/150	
A35	Makhtar Ndiaye/200	
A36	Radoslav Nesterovic/200	
A37	Michael Olowokandi/200	
A38	Andrae Patterson/200	
A39	Ruben Patterson/140	
A40	Paul Pierce/45	
A41	Jeff Sheppard/200	
A42	Miles Simon/100	
A43A	Tim Thomas (Black)/50	
A43B	Tim Thomas (Blue)/165	
A44	Robert Traylor/200	
A45	Bonzi Wells/200	
A46	Tyson Wheeler/200	
A47	Jahidi White/90	
A48	Jason Williams/200	
A49	Shammond Williams/130	
A50	Korleone Young/200	

1998 Sage Platinum

This 52-card autographed set paralleled the base set, but featured a platinum background and a sequentially numbered autograph. Most players signed 50 of these, but there were as few as 5 by Corey Brewer, Kobe Bryant and Tracy McGrady. Two players - Zendon Hamilton and Tim Thomas - have both a black and blue version.

		MT
	Common Player:	20.00
	Platinum Autographs:	3x-6x
A1	Toby Bailey/30	
A2	Corey Benjamin/50	
A3	Andrew Betts/25	
A4	Torraye Braggs/45	
A5	Corey Brewer/5	
A6	Kobe Bryant/5	
A7	Anthony Carter/50	
A8	Vince Carter/25	
A9	Keon Clark/50	
A10	Ricky Davis/45	
A11	Michael Dickerson/50	
A12	Michael Doleac/30	
A13	Bryce Drew/50	
A14	Tremaine Fowlkes/50	
A15	Pat Garrity/50	
A16A	Zendon Hamilton (Black)/10	
A16B	Zendon Hamilton (Blue)/40	
A17	Matt Harpring/50	
A18	Al Harrington/50	
A19	J.R. Henderson/30	
A20	Antawn Jamison/50	
A21	DeMarco Johnson/45	
A22	Charles Jones/50	
A23	Rashard Lewis/50	
A24	Felipe Lopez/50	
A25	Corey Louis/50	
A26	Tyrron Lue/50	
A27	Stephon Marbury/10	
A28	Sean Marks/50	
A29	Jelani McCoy/6	
A30	Tracy McGrady/5	
A31	Roshown McLeod/45	
A32	Brad Miller/45	
A33	Cuttino Mobley/50	
A34	Nazr Mohammed/40	
A35	Makhtar Ndiaye/50	
A36	Radoslav Nesterovic/50	
A37	Michael Olowokandi/50	
A38	Andrae Patterson/50	
A39	Ruben Patterson/35	
A40	Paul Pierce/10	
A41	Jeff Sheppard/50	
A42	Miles Simon/25	
A43A	Tim Thomas (Black)/10	
A43B	Tim Thomas (Blue)/40	
A44	Robert Traylor/50	
A45	Bonzi Wells/50	
A46	Tyson Wheeler/50	
A47	Jahidi White/25	
A48	Jason Williams/50	
A49	Shammond Williams/35	
A50	Korleone Young/50	

1998 Sage Silver

This 52-card autographed set paralleled the base set, but featured a silver background and a sequentially numbered autograph. Most players signed 400 of these, but there were as few as 40 by Corey Brewer and Tracy McGrady. Two players - Zendon Hamilton and Tim Thomas - have both a black and blue version.

		MT
	Common Player:	5.00
	Silver Autographs:	1.5x
A1	Toby Bailey/215	
A2	Corey Benjamin/400	
A3	Andrew Betts/185	
A4	Torraye Braggs/375	
A5	Corey Brewer/40	
A6	Kobe Bryant/50	
A7	Anthony Carter/390	
A8	Vince Carter/190	
A9	Keon Clark/400	
A10	Ricky Davis/375	
A11	Michael Dickerson/400	
A12	Michael Doleac/220	
A13	Bryce Drew/400	
A14	Tremaine Fowlkes/400	
A15	Pat Garrity/400	
A16A	Zendon Hamilton (Black)/75	
A16B	Zendon Hamilton (Blue)/330	
A17	Matt Harpring/400	
A18	Al Harrington/400	
A19	J.R. Henderson/240	
A20	Antawn Jamison/370	
A21	DeMarco Johnson/375	
A22	Charles Jones/400	
A23	Rashard Lewis/400	
A24	Felipe Lopez/400	
A25	Corey Louis/390	
A26	Tyrron Lue/400	
A27	Stephon Marbury/65	
A28	Sean Marks/400	
A29	Jelani McCoy/50	
A30	Tracy McGrady/40	
A31	Roshown McLeod/325	
A32	Brad Miller/350	
A33	Cuttino Mobley/400	
A34	Nazr Mohammed/300	
A35	Makhtar Ndiaye/400	
A36	Radoslav Nesterovic/400	
A37	Michael Olowokandi/400	
A38	Andrae Patterson/400	
A39	Ruben Patterson/275	
A40	Paul Pierce/85	
A41	Jeff Sheppard/400	
A42	Miles Simon/200	
A43A	Tim Thomas (Black)/90	
A43B	Tim Thomas (Blue)/325	
A44	Robert Traylor/400	
A45	Bonzi Wells/400	
A46	Tyson Wheeler/400	
A47	Jahidi White/185	
A48	Jason Williams/400	
A49	Shammond Williams/265	
A50	Korleone Young/400	

1999 Sage

This 50-card set included players eligible to be drafted in the 1999 NBA Draft. Players were pictured in their college uniforms and each base card included the words "1 of 3,800" in the lower left front corner. Each base card was also available in five different autographed versions, with red being the most common, followed by bronze, silver, gold and platinum. In addition, white autographed versions of the 1998 Sage product were also found in packs.

		MT
	Complete Set (50):	15.00
	Common Player:	.15
	Minor Stars:	.30
	Pack (3):	90.00
	Wax Box (12):	
1	Ron Artest	1.00
2	William Avery	.60
3	Michael Batiste	.15
4	Jonathan Bender	2.00
5	Roberto Bergerson	.15
6	Calvin Booth	.40
7	Cal Bowdler	.15
8	A.J. Bramblett	.15
9	Kobe Bryant	3.00
10	Rodney Buford	.30
11	Vince Carter	4.00
12	John Celestand	.30
13	Kris Clack	.30
14	Lonnie Cooper	.15
15	Vonteego Cummings	.75
16	Baron Davis	1.25
17	Francisco Elson	.15
18	Evan Eshmeyer	.15
19	Jeff Foster	.15
20	Devean George	.50
21	Dion Glover	.40
22	Richard Hamilton	1.00
23	Venson Hamilton	.15
24	Rico Hill	.15
25	Tim James	.50
26	Antawn Jamison	.75
27	Jumaine Jones	.40
28	J.R. Koch	.15
29	Trajan Langdon	.75
30	Bobby Lazor	.15
31	Melvin Levett	.30
32	Quincy Lewis	.50
33	Corey Maggette	2.00
34	Shawn Marion	1.00
35	B.J. McKie	.15
36	Andre Miller	1.00
37	Lee Nailon	.40
38	Ademola Okulaja	.15
39	Scott Padgett	.40
40	Paul Pierce	1.00
41	James Posey	.75
42	Aleksandar Radojevic	.30
43	David Robinson	.60
44	Michael Ruffin	.30
45	Leon Smith	.50
46	Jason Terry	.75
47	Kenny Thomas	.60
48	Tyrone Washington	.15
49	Frederic Weis	.15
50	Alvin Young	.15

1999 Sage Red Autographs

This 48-card parallel autographed insert reprinted each base card with a red background and an autograph added to the front. Red autographs, which were the most common type of signature in Sage, were mostly limited to 999, but some players signed less, including Vince Carter and Paul Pierce who signed just 39. Two players - Rico Hill and Frederic Weis - did not sign any cards in Sage.

		MT
Common Player:		3.00
Minor Stars:		5.00
1	Ron Artest/699	25.00
2	William Avery	10.00
3	Michael Batiste	3.00
4	Jonathan Bender/369	40.00
5	Roberto Bergerson	3.00
6	Calvin Booth	3.00
7	Cal Bowdler	3.00
8	A.J. Bramblett	3.00
9	Kobe Bryant/114	120.00
10	Rodney Buford	5.00
11	Vince Carter/39	250.00
12	John Celestand	5.00
13	Kris Clack	3.00
14	Lonnie Cooper	3.00
15	Vonteego Cummings	8.00
16	Baron Davis/339	25.00
17	Francisco Elson	3.00
18	Evan Eshmeyer	3.00
19	Jeff Foster	3.00
20	Devean George	5.00
21	Dion Glover/885	5.00
22	Richard Hamilton/899	15.00
23	Venson Hamilton	3.00
25	Tim James	5.00
26	Antawn Jamison/745	20.00
27	Jumaine Jones	5.00
28	J.R. Koch	3.00
29	Trajan Langdon/699	12.00
30	Bobby Lazor	3.00
31	Melvin Levett	5.00
32	Quincy Lewis	8.00
33	Corey Maggette/464	40.00
34	Shawn Marion/789	25.00
35	B.J. McKie	3.00
36	Andre Miller	20.00
37	Lee Nailon	3.00
38	Ademola Okulaja	3.00
39	Scott Padgett	5.00
40	Paul Pierce/39	100.00
41	James Posey	10.00
42	Aleksandar Radojevic	5.00
43	David Robinson/113	60.00
44	Michael Ruffin	3.00
45	Leon Smith	10.00
46	Jason Terry	10.00
47	Kenny Thomas	8.00
48	Tyrone Washington	3.00
49	Alvin Young	3.00

1999 Sage Bronze

This 48-card autographed parallel set was the second most common autographed version in Sage. Most cards were sequentially numbered to 650 in the bronze set, but some players were more limited, with Vince Carter and Paul Pierce limited to just 29. Two players in the base set - Rico Hill and Frederic Weis - did not sign cards in any cards in Sage.

		MT
Common Player:		3.00
Bronze Autographs:		1.25x
Inserted 1:4		
1	Ron Artest/465	
2	William Avery/650	
3	Michael Batiste/650	
4	Jonathan Bender/245	
5	Roberto Bergerson/650	
6	Calvin Booth/650	
7	Cal Bowdler/650	
8	A.J. Bramblett/650	
9	Kobe Bryant/80	
10	Rodney Buford/650	
11	Vince Carter/29	
12	John Celestand/650	
13	Kris Clack/650	
14	Lonnie Cooper/650	
15	Vonteego Cummings/650	
16	Baron Davis/225	
17	Francisco Elson/650	
18	Evan Eshmeyer/650	
19	Jeff Foster/650	
20	Devean George/650	
21	Dion Glover/575	
22	Richard Hamilton/610	
23	Venson Hamilton/650	
25	Tim James/650	
26	Antawn Jamison/495	
27	Jumaine Jones/650	
28	J.R. Koch/650	
29	Trajan Langdon/450	
30	Bobby Lazor/650	
31	Melvin Levett/650	
32	Quincy Lewis/650	
33	Corey Maggette/310	
34	Shawn Marion/515	
35	B.J. McKie/650	
36	Andre Miller/650	
37	Lee Nailon/650	
38	Ademola Okulaja/650	
39	Scott Padgett/650	
40	Paul Pierce/29	
41	James Posey/650	
42	Aleksandar Radojevic/650	
43	David Robinson/80	
44	Michael Ruffin/650	
45	Leon Smith/650	
46	Jason Terry/650	
47	Kenny Thomas/650	
48	Tyrone Washington/650	
50	Alvin Young/650	

1999 Sage Gold

This 48-card parallel autographed insert reprinted each base card with a gold background and added an autograph to the front. Most gold autographs were numbered to 200, but some players were more limited, including Vince Carter and Paul Pierce, who signed just 10. Two players - Rico Hill and Frederic Weis - did not sign any cards in Sage.

		MT
Common Player:		5.00
Gold Autographs:		2x
Inserted 1:12		
1	Ron Artest/145	
2	William Avery/200	
3	Michael Batiste	
4	Jonathan Bender/75	
5	Roberto Bergerson/200	
6	Calvin Booth/200	
7	Cal Bowdler/200	
8	A.J. Bramblett/50	
9	Kobe Bryant/25	
10	Rodney Buford/200	
11	Vince Carter/10	
12	John Celestand/200	
13	Kris Clack/200	
14	Lonnie Cooper/200	
15	Vonteego Cummings/200	
16	Baron Davis/70	
17	Francisco Elson/200	
18	Evan Eshmeyer/200	
19	Jeff Foster/200	
20	Devean George/200	
21	Dion Glover/179	
22	Richard Hamilton/190	
23	Venson Hamilton/200	
25	Tim James/200	
26	Antawn Jamison/150	
27	Jumaine Jones/200	
28	J.R. Koch/200	
29	Trajan Langdon/140	
30	Bobby Lazor/200	
31	Melvin Levett/200	
32	Quincy Lewis/200	
33	Corey Maggette/100	
34	Shawn Marion/155	
35	B.J. McKie/200	
36	Andre Miller/200	
37	Lee Nailon/200	
38	Ademola Okulaja/200	
39	Scott Padgett/200	
40	Paul Pierce/10	
41	James Posey/200	
42	Aleksandar Radojevic/200	
43	David Robinson/25	
44	Michael Ruffin/200	
45	Leon Smith/200	
46	Jason Terry/200	
47	Kenny Thomas/200	
48	Tyrone Washington/200	
50	Alvin Young/200	

1999 Sage Platinum

This 48-card parallel autographed insert reprinted each base card with a platinum background and added an autograph to the front. Most platinum autographs were sequentially numbered to 50, but some players signed less, including Vince Carter and Paul Pierce who signed just three each. Two players - Rico Hill and Frederic Weis - did not sign any cards in Sage.

		MT
Common Player:		10.00
Platinum Autographs:		4x
Inserted 1:46		
1	Ron Artest/40	
2	William Avery/50	
3	Michael Batiste/50	
4	Jonathan Bender/20	
5	Roberto Bergerson/50	
6	Calvin Booth/50	
7	Cal Bowdler/50	
8	A.J. Bramblett/50	
9	Kobe Bryant/10	
10	Rodney Buford/50	
11	Vince Carter/3	
12	John Celestand/50	
13	Kris Clack/50	
14	Lonnie Cooper/50	
15	Vonteego Cummings/50	
16	Baron Davis/20	
17	Francisco Elson/50	
18	Evan Eshmeyer/50	
19	Jeff Foster/50	
20	Devean George/50	
21	Dion Glover/45	
22	Richard Hamilton/49	
23	Venson Hamilton/50	
25	Tim James/50	
26	Antawn Jamison/35	
27	Jumaine Jones/50	
28	J.R. Koch/50	
29	Trajan Langdon/35	
30	Bobby Lazor/50	
31	Melvin Levett/50	
32	Quincy Lewis/50	
33	Corey Maggette/25	
34	Shawn Marion/45	
35	B.J. McKie/50	
36	Andre Miller/50	
37	Lee Nailon/50	
38	Ademola Okulaja/50	
39	Scott Padgett/50	
40	Paul Pierce/3	
41	James Posey/50	
42	Aleksandar Radojevic/50	
43	David Robinson/10	
44	Michael Ruffin/50	
45	Leon Smith/50	
46	Jason Terry/50	
47	Kenny Thomas/50	
48	Tyrone Washington/50	
50	Alvin Young/50	

1999 Sage Silver

This 48-card parallel autographed insert reprinted each base card with a silver background and added an autograph to the front. Most silver signatures were sequentially numbered to 400, but some players signed less, including Vince Carter and Paul Pierce who signed just 18. Two players - Rico Hill and Frederic Weis - did not sign any cards in Sage.

		MT
Common Player:		4.00
Silver Autographs:		1.5x
Inserted 1:6		
1	Ron Artest/290	
2	William Avery/400	
3	Michael Batiste/400	
4	Jonathan Bender/150	
5	Roberto Bergerson/400	
6	Calvin Booth/400	
7	Cal Bowdler/400	
8	A.J. Bramblett/400	
9	Kobe Bryant/50	
10	Rodney Buford/400	
11	Vince Carter/18	
12	John Celestand/400	
13	Kris Clack/400	
14	Lonnie Cooper/400	
15	Vonteego Cummings/400	
16	Baron Davis/135	
17	Francisco Elson/400	
18	Evan Eshmeyer/400	
19	Jeff Foster/400	
20	Devean George/400	
21	Dion Glover/355	
22	Richard Hamilton/370	
23	Venson Hamilton/400	
25	Tim James/400	
26	Antawn Jamison/295	
27	Jumaine Jones/400	
28	J.R. Koch/400	
29	Trajan Langdon/275	
30	Bobby Lazor/400	
31	Melvin Levett/400	
32	Quincy Lewis/400	
33	Corey Maggette/200	
34	Shawn Marion/315	
35	B.J. McKie/400	
36	Andre Miller/400	
37	Lee Nailon/400	
38	Ademola Okulaja/400	
39	Scott Padgett/400	
40	Paul Pierce/18	
41	James Posey/400	
42	Aleksandar Radojevic/400	
43	David Robinson/50	
44	Michael Ruffin/400	
45	Leon Smith/400	
46	Jason Terry/400	
47	Kenny Thomas/400	
48	Tyrone Washington/400	
50	Alvin Young/400	

1999 Sage White Autographs

This 24-card set offered white background autographs of cards in the 1998 Sage product. Quantities varied between 10 and 100 and each card was sequentially numbered. Included in the 24 cards are two Tim Thomas (black and blue versions) autographs.

		MT
Common Player:		10.00
1	Toby Bailey/45	10.00
6	Kobe Bryant/10	10.00
9	Keon Clark/95	10.00
11	Michael Dickerson/100	20.00
12	Michael Doleac/10	10.00
13	Bryce Drew/75	10.00
15	Pat Garrity/25	40.00
17	Matt Harpring/60	15.00
18	Al Harrington/45	50.00
23	Rashard Lewis/95	25.00
24	Felipe Lopez/100	10.00
26	Tyronne Lue/65	10.00
27	Stephon Marbury/10	10.00
30	Tracy McGrady/10	10.00
31	Roshown McLeod/10	10.00
33	Cuttino Mobley/85	20.00
36	Radoslav Nesterovic/80	10.00
37	Michael Olowokandi/90	20.00
43	Tim Thomas (black)/10	100.00
43	Tim Thomas (blue)/20	50.00
44	Robert Traylor/85	15.00
45	Bonzi Wells/50	10.00
48	Jason Williams/12	10.00
50	Korleone Young/90	10.00

2000 Sage Autographed

This 50-card set pictured college players that were eligible to be drafted in the 2000 NBA Draft. The cards featured a color shot of the player, with a small border across the bottom in school colors. The bottom right corner contained the words "1 of 3,999." The big hook with SAGE was that an autographed card was inserted into each pack. Inserts included: Autographs (base red), Bronze Autographs, Silver Autographs, Gold Autographs, Platinum Autographs, Bonus White Autographs and Rookies Limited.

		MT
Complete Set (50):		10.00
Common Player:		.20
1	Dalibor Bagaric	.20
2	Vin Baker	.20
3	Jonathan Bender	.50
4	Primoz Brezec	.20
5	Brian Cardinal	.20
6	Chris Carrawell	.20
7	Eric Coley	.20
8	Jason Collier	.40
9	Ed Cota	.20
10	Schea Cotton	.20
11	Baron Davis	.40
12	Kaniel Dickens	.20
13	Keyon Dooling	1.00
14	Khalid El-Amin	.40
15	Michael Finley	.40
16	Kevin Freeman	.20
17	Gee Gervin	.20
18	Tom Gugliotta	.40
19	A.J. Guyton	.20
20	Tim Hardaway	.40
21	Jason Hart	.20
22	Johnny Hemsley	.20
23	Shaheen Holloway	.20
24	DeeAndre Hulett	.20
25	Antawn Jamison	.40
26	Marco Jaric	.20
27	Larry Johnson	.20
28	Michael Jordan	2.00
29	Dan Langhi	.20
30	Lamont Long	.20
31	Justin Love	.20
32	T.J. Lux	.20
33	Desmond Mason	2.00
34	Antonio McDyess	.40
35	Brad Millard	.20
36	Alonzo Mourning	.20
37	Gabe Muoneke	.20
38	Eduardo Najera	.75
39	Olumide Oyedji	.20
40	Scoonie Penn	.20
41	Scottie Pippen	.20
42	Rodney Rogers	.40
43	Pepe Sanchez	.20
44	Josip Sesar	.20
45	Steve Smith	.40
46	Jerry Stackhouse	.40
47	Jarrett Stephens	.20
48	Hidayet Turkoglu	1.00
49	Jaquay Walls	.20
50	Corliss Williamson	.20

2000 Sage Autographed Red Autographs

		MT
Complete Set (50):		
Common Player:		
1	Dalibor Bagaric/999	5.00
2	Vin Baker	
3	Jonathan Bender/369	20.00
4	Primoz Brezec/999	5.00
5	Brian Cardinal/999	5.00
6	Chris Carrawell/999	5.00
7	Eric Coley/999	5.00
8	Jason Collier/999	5.00
9	Ed Cota/999	5.00
10	Schea Cotton/999	5.00
11	Baron Davis/499	15.00
12	Kaniel Dickens/999	5.00
13	Keyon Dooling/999	5.00
14	Khalid El-Amin/999	5.00
15	Michael Finley/179	20.00
16	Kevin Freeman/999	5.00
17	Gee Gervin/999	5.00
18	Tom Gugliotta/299	20.00
19	A.J. Guyton/999	5.00
20	Tim Hardaway/189	10.00
21	Jason Hart/999	5.00
22	Johnny Hemsley/999	5.00
23	Shaheen Holloway/999	5.00
24	DeeAndre Hulett/999	5.00
25	Antawn Jamison/369	15.00
26	Marco Jaric	
27	Larry Johnson/299	5.00
28	Michael Jordan/999	
29	Dan Langhi/999	5.00
30	Lamont Long/999	5.00
31	Justin Love/999	5.00
32	T.J. Lux/999	5.00
33	Desmond Mason/999	15.00
34	Antonio McDyess/349	10.00
35	Brad Millard/999	5.00
36	Alonzo Mourning/189	15.00
37	Gabe Muoneke/999	5.00
38	Eduardo Najera/999	10.00
39	Olumide Oyedji/999	5.00
40	Scoonie Penn/999	5.00
41	Scottie Pippen/399	10.00
42	Rodney Rogers/149	5.00
43	Pepe Sanchez/999	5.00
44	Josip Sesar/999	5.00
45	Steve Smith/319	5.00
46	Jerry Stackhouse/369	10.00
47	Jarrett Stephens/999	5.00
48	Hidayet Turkoglu/999	10.00
49	Jaquay Walls/999	5.00
50	Corliss Williamson/169	5.00

2000 Sage Autographed Bronze Autographs

		MT
Complete Set (50):		
Common Player:		1x-2x
1	Dalibor Bagaric/650	
2	Vin Baker	
3	Jonathan Bender/245	
4	Primoz Brezec/650	
5	Brian Cardinal/650	
6	Chris Carrawell/650	
7	Eric Coley/650	
8	Jason Collier/650	
9	Ed Cota/650	
10	Schea Cotton/650	
11	Baron Davis/335	
12	Kaniel Dickens/650	
13	Keyon Dooling/650	
14	Khalid El-Amin/650	
15	Michael Finley/120	
16	Kevin Freeman/650	
17	Gee Gervin/650	
18	Tom Gugliotta/205	
19	A.J. Guyton/650	
20	Tim Hardaway/130	
21	Jason Hart/650	
22	Johnny Hemsley/650	
23	Shaheen Holloway/650	
24	DeeAndre Hulett/650	
25	Antawn Jamison/245	
26	Marco Jaric	
27	Larry Johnson/205	
28	Michael Jordan/650	
29	Dan Langhi/650	
30	Lamont Long/650	
31	Justin Love/650	
32	T.J. Lux/650	
33	Desmond Mason/650	
34	Antonio McDyess/230	
35	Brad Millard/650	
36	Alonzo Mourning/130	
37	Gabe Muoneke/650	
38	Eduardo Najera/650	
39	Olumide Oyedji/650	
40	Scoonie Penn/650	
41	Scottie Pippen/260	
42	Rodney Rogers/100	
43	Pepe Sanchez/650	
44	Josip Sesar/650	
45	Steve Smith/215	
46	Jerry Stackhouse/245	
47	Jarrett Stephens/650	
48	Hidayet Turkoglu/650	
49	Jaquay Walls/650	
50	Corliss Williamson/115	

2000 Sage Autographed Gold Autographs

		MT
Complete Set (50):		
Common Player:		2x-3x
1	Dalibor Bagaric/200	
2	Vin Baker	
3	Jonathan Bender/75	
4	Primoz Brezec/200	
5	Brian Cardinal/200	
6	Chris Carrawell/200	
7	Eric Coley/200	
8	Jason Collier/200	
9	Ed Cota/200	
10	Schea Cotton/200	
11	Baron Davis/105	
12	Kaniel Dickens/200	
13	Keyon Dooling/200	
14	Khalid El-Amin/200	
15	Michael Finley/40	
16	Kevin Freeman/200	
17	Gee Gervin/200	
18	Tom Gugliotta/65	
19	A.J. Guyton/200	
20	Tim Hardaway/40	
21	Jason Hart/200	
22	Johnny Hemsley/200	
23	Shaheen Holloway/200	
24	DeeAndre Hulett/200	
25	Antawn Jamison/75	
26	Marco Jaric	
27	Larry Johnson/65	
28	Michael Jordan/200	
29	Dan Langhi/200	
30	Lamont Long/200	
31	Justin Love/200	
32	T.J. Lux/200	
33	Desmond Mason/200	
34	Antonio McDyess/70	
35	Brad Millard/200	
36	Alonzo Mourning/40	
37	Gabe Muoneke/200	
38	Eduardo Najera/200	
39	Olumide Oyedji/200	
40	Scoonie Penn/200	
41	Scottie Pippen/80	
42	Rodney Rogers/30	
43	Pepe Sanchez/200	
44	Josip Sesar/200	
45	Steve Smith/65	
46	Jerry Stackhouse/80	
47	Jarrett Stephens/200	
48	Hidayet Turkoglu/200	
49	Jaquay Walls/200	
50	Corliss Williamson/35	

2000 Sage Autographed Platinum Autographs

		MT
Complete Set (50):		
Common Player:		3x-8x
1	Dalibor Bagaric/50	
2	Vin Baker	
3	Jonathan Bender/20	
4	Primoz Brezec/50	
5	Brian Cardinal/50	
6	Chris Carrawell/50	
7	Eric Coley/50	
8	Jason Collier/50	
9	Ed Cota/50	
10	Schea Cotton/50	
11	Baron Davis/30	
12	Kaniel Dickens/50	
13	Keyon Dooling/50	
14	Khalid El-Amin/50	
15	Michael Finley/10	
16	Kevin Freeman/50	
17	Gee Gervin/50	
18	Tom Gugliotta/20	
19	A.J. Guyton/50	
20	Tim Hardaway/10	
21	Jason Hart/50	
22	Johnny Hemsley/50	
23	Shaheen Holloway/50	
24	DeeAndre Hulett/50	
25	Antawn Jamison/20	
26	Marco Jaric	
27	Larry Johnson/20	
28	Michael Jordan/50	
29	Dan Langhi/50	
30	Lamont Long/50	
31	Justin Love/50	
32	T.J. Lux/50	
33	Desmond Mason/50	
34	Antonio McDyess/20	
35	Brad Millard/50	
36	Alonzo Mourning/10	
37	Gabe Muoneke/50	
38	Eduardo Najera/50	
39	Olumide Oyedji/50	
40	Scoonie Penn/50	
41	Scottie Pippen/20	
42	Rodney Rogers/10	
43	Pepe Sanchez/50	
44	Josip Sesar/50	
45	Steve Smith/20	
46	Jerry Stackhouse/20	
47	Jarrett Stephens/50	
48	Hidayet Turkoglu/50	
49	Jaquay Walls/50	
50	Corliss Williamson/10	

2000 Sage Autographed Silver Autographs

		MT
Complete Set (50):		
Common Player:		1x-3x
1	Dalibor Bagaric/400	
2	Vin Baker	
3	Jonathan Bender/150	
4	Primoz Brezec/400	
5	Brian Cardinal/400	
6	Chris Carrawell/400	
7	Eric Coley/400	
8	Jason Collier/400	
9	Ed Cota/400	
10	Schea Cotton/400	
11	Baron Davis/210	
12	Kaniel Dickens/400	
13	Keyon Dooling/400	
14	Khalid El-Amin/400	
15	Michael Finley/75	
16	Kevin Freeman/400	
17	Gee Gervin/400	
18	Tom Gugliotta/130	
19	A.J. Guyton/400	
20	Tim Hardaway/80	
21	Jason Hart/400	
22	Johnny Hemsley/400	
23	Shaheen Holloway/400	
24	DeeAndre Hulett/400	
25	Antawn Jamison/150	
26	Marco Jaric	
27	Larry Johnson/130	
28	Michael Jordan/400	
29	Dan Langhi/400	
30	Lamont Long/400	
31	Justin Love/400	
32	T.J. Lux/400	
33	Desmond Mason/400	
34	Antonio McDyess/140	
35	Brad Millard/400	
36	Alonzo Mourning/80	
37	Gabe Muoneke/400	
38	Eduardo Najera/400	
39	Olumide Oyedji/400	
40	Scoonie Penn/400	
41	Scottie Pippen/160	
42	Rodney Rogers/60	
43	Pepe Sanchez/400	
44	Josip Sesar/400	
45	Steve Smith/135	
46	Jerry Stackhouse/155	
47	Jarrett Stephens/400	
48	Hidayet Turkoglu/400	
49	Jaquay Walls/400	
50	Corliss Williamson/70	

2000 Sage Autographed Rookies Limited

		MT
Complete Set (25):		
Common Player:		5.00
1	Dalibor Bagaric	5.00
2	Jonathan Bender	10.00
3	Primoz Brezec	5.00
4	Brian Cardinal	5.00
5	Chris Carrawell	5.00
6	Jason Collier	5.00
7	Ed Cota	5.00
8	Baron Davis	10.00
9	Kaniel Dickens	5.00
10	Keyon Dooling	5.00
11	Khalid El-Amin	5.00
12	A.J. Guyton	5.00
13	Jason Hart	5.00
14	DeeAndre Hulett	5.00
15	Marco Jaric	5.00
16	Dan Langhi	5.00
17	Justin Love	5.00
18	Desmond Mason	10.00
19	Eduardo Najera	5.00
20	Olumide Oyedji	5.00
21	Scoonie Penn	5.00
22	Pepe Sanchez	5.00
23	Josip Sesar	5.00
24	Hidayet Turkoglu	15.00
25	Jaquay Walls	5.00

2000 Sage Autographed White Level

"Too uncommon to price."

		MT
Complete Set (24):		
Common Player:		
1	Ron Artest/40	
2	William Avery/40	
3	Jonathan Bender/20	
7	Cal Bowdler/90	
9	Kobe Bryant/10	
15	Vonteego Cummings/60	
16	Baron Davis/10	
20	Devean George/30	
21	Dion Glover/10	
22	Richard Hamilton/10	
25	Tim James/10	
26	Antawn Jamison/10	
27	Jumaine Jones/100	
29	Trajan Langdon/10	
32	Quincy Lewis/10	
33	Corey Maggette/10	
34	Shawn Marion/10	
36	Andre Miller/10	
39	Scott Padgett/10	
41	James Posey/40	
42	Aleksandar Radojevic/30	
43	David Robinson/10	
46	Jason Terry/30	
47	Kenny Thomas/40	

2000 Sage HIT

		MT
Complete Set (50):		10.00
Common Player:		.10
1	Baron Davis	.20
2	Larry Johnson	.20
3	Jerry Stackhouse	.20
4	Michael Finley	.30
5	Keyon Dooling	.50
6	Schea Cotton	.10
7	DeeAndre Hulett	.10
8	Steve Smith	.10
9	Brad Millard	.10
10	Tim Hardaway	.20
11	Eric Coley	.10
12	Scoonie Penn	.10
13	Antonio McDyess	.30
14	Pepe Sanchez	.10
15	Kevin Freeman	.10
16	Olumide Oyedji	.10
17	Dan Langhi	.10
18	Ed Cota	.10
19	Jonathan Bender	1.50
20	Lamont Long	.10
21	Eduardo Najera	1.50
22	Marco Jaric	.10
23	Michael Jordan	2.00
24	Tom Gugliotta	.20
25	A.J. Guyton	.20
26	Chris Carrawell	.10
27	Jarrett Stephens	.10
28	Hidayet Turkoglu	1.50
29	T.J. Lux	.10
30	Jaquay Walls	.10
31	Johnny Hemsley	.10
32	Alonzo Mourning	.20
33	Scottie Pippen	.20
34	Desmond Mason	.40
35	Brian Cardinal	.10
36	Shaheen Holloway	.10
37	Khalid El-Amin	.10
38	Josip Sesar	.10
39	Gabe Muoneke	.10
40	Kaniel Dickens	.30
41	Antawn Jamison	.20
42	Vin Baker	.10
43	Justin Love	.10
44	Dalibor Bagaric	.10
45	Rodney Rogers	.10
46	Jason Hart	.10
47	Gee Gervin	.10
48	Corliss Williamson	.10
49	Primoz Brezec	.10
50	Jason Collier	.20

2000 Sage HIT Diamond Autographs

		MT
Complete Set (50):		
Common Player:		
1x-2x Emerald		
1	Baron Davis/225	
2	Larry Johnson/195	
3	Jerry Stackhouse/160	
4	Michael Finley/100	
5	Keyon Dooling/385	
6	Schea Cotton/545	
7	DeeAndre Hulett/415	
8	Steve Smith/100	
9	Brad Millard/225	
10	Tim Hardaway/65	
11	Eric Coley/225	
12	Scoonie Penn/385	
13	Antonio McDyess/100	
14	Pepe Sanchez/290	
15	Kevin Freeman/225	
16	Olumide Oyedji/385	
17	Dan Langhi/385	
18	Ed Cota/225	
19	Jonathan Bender/270	
20	Lamont Long/225	
21	Eduardo Najera/385	
22	Marco Jaric	
23	Michael Jordan/225	
24	Tom Gugliotta/160	
25	A.J. Guyton/420	
26	Chris Carrawell/385	
27	Jarrett Stephens/225	
28	Hidayet Turkoglu/705	
29	T.J. Lux/100	
30	Jaquay Walls/385	
31	Johnny Hemsley/35	
32	Alonzo Mourning/50	
33	Scottie Pippen/135	
34	Desmond Mason/705	
35	Brian Cardinal/420	
36	Shaheen Holloway/225	
37	Khalid El-Amin/225	
38	Josip Sesar/385	
39	Gabe Muoneke/225	
40	Kaniel Dickens/420	
41	Antawn Jamison/160	
42	Vin Baker	
43	Justin Love/420	
44	Dalibor Bagaric/420	
45	Rodney Rogers/100	
46	Jason Hart/260	
47	Gee Gervin/225	
48	Corliss Williamson/225	
49	Primoz Brezec/705	
50	Jason Collier/385	

2000 Sage HIT Emerald Autographs

		MT
Complete Set (50):		
Common Player:		5.00
1	Baron Davis/315	5.00
2	Larry Johnson/270	10.00
3	Jerry Stackhouse/225	20.00
4	Michael Finley/135	20.00
5	Keyon Dooling/540	10.00
6	Schea Cotton/765	5.00
7	DeeAndre Hulett/585	5.00
8	Steve Smith/135	5.00
9	Brad Millard/315	5.00
10	Tim Hardaway/90	10.00
11	Eric Coley/315	5.00
12	Scoonie Penn/540	5.00
13	Antonio McDyess/135	10.00
14	Pepe Sanchez/405	5.00
15	Kevin Freeman/315	5.00
16	Olumide Oyedji/540	5.00
17	Dan Langhi/54	5.00
18	Ed Cota/315	5.00
19	Jonathan Bender/375	10.00
20	Lamont Long/315	5.00
21	Eduardo Najera/540	10.00
22	Marco Jaric	5.00
23	Michael Jordan/315	
24	Tom Gugliotta/225	10.00
25	A.J. Guyton/585	5.00
26	Chris Carrawell/540	5.00
27	Jarrett Stephens/315	5.00
28	Hidayet Turkoglu/990	15.00
29	T.J. Lux/135	5.00
30	Jaquay Walls/540	5.00
31	Johnny Hemsley/45	5.00
32	Alonzo Mourning/70	50.00
33	Scottie Pippen/190	50.00
34	Desmond Mason/990	10.00
35	Brian Cardinal/585	5.00
36	Shaheen Holloway/315	5.00
37	Khalid El-Amin/315	5.00
38	Josip Sesar/540	5.00
39	Gabe Muoneke/315	5.00
40	Kaniel Dickens/585	5.00
41	Antawn Jamison/225	10.00
42	Vin Baker	
43	Justin Love/585	5.00
44	Dalibor Bagaric/585	5.00
45	Rodney Rogers/135	5.00
46	Jason Hart/36	5.00
47	Gee Gervin/315	5.00
48	Corliss Williamson/315	5.00
49	Primoz Brezec/990	5.00
50	Jason Collier/540	5.00

2000 Sage HIT Cut Diamond Autographs

		MT
Complete Set (50):		
Common Player:		1x-3x
1	Baron Davis/45	
2	Larry Johnson/40	
3	Jerry Stackhouse/30	
4	Michael Finley/20	
5	Keyon Dooling/75	
6	Schea Cotton/105	
7	DeeAndre Hulett/80	
8	Steve Smith/20	
9	Brad Millard/45	
10	Tim Hardaway/15	
11	Eric Coley/45	
12	Scoonie Penn/75	
13	Antonio McDyess/20	
14	Pepe Sanchez/55	
15	Kevin Freeman/45	
16	Olumide Oyedji/75	
17	Dan Langhi/75	
18	Ed Cota/45	
19	Jonathan Bender/50	
20	Lamont Long/45	
21	Eduardo Najera/75	
22	Marco Jaric	
23	Michael Jordan/45	
24	Tom Gugliotta/30	
25	A.J. Guyton/80	
26	Chris Carrawell/75	
27	Jarrett Stephens/45	
28	Hidayet Turkoglu/135	
29	T.J. Lux/20	
30	Jaquay Walls/75	
31	Johnny Hemsley/10	
32	Alonzo Mourning/10	
33	Scottie Pippen/30	
34	Desmond Mason/135	
35	Brian Cardinal/80	
36	Shaheen Holloway/45	
37	Khalid El-Amin/45	
38	Josip Sesar/75	
39	Gabe Muoneke/45	
40	Kaniel Dickens/80	
41	Antawn Jamison/30	
42	Vin Baker	
43	Justin Love/80	
44	Dalibor Bagaric/80	
45	Rodney Rogers/20	
46	Jason Hart/50	
47	Gee Gervin/45	
48	Corliss Williamson/45	
49	Primoz Brezec/135	
50	Jason Collier/75	

2000 Sage HIT Cut Emerald Autographs

		MT
Complete Set (50):		
Common Player:		
		1x-2x Emerald
1	Baron Davis/120	
2	Larry Johnson/105	
3	Jerry Stackhouse/85	
4	Michael Finley/55	
5	Keyon Dooling/205	
6	Schea Cotton/290	
7	DeeAndre Hulett/225	
8	Steve Smith/55	
9	Brad Millard/120	
10	Tim Hardaway/35	
11	Eric Coley/120	
12	Scoonie Penn/205	
13	Antonio McDyess/55	
14	Pepe Sanchez/155	
15	Kevin Freeman/120	
16	Olumide Oyedji/205	
17	Dan Langhi/205	
18	Ed Cota/120	
19	Jonathan Bender/145	
20	Lamont Long/120	
21	Eduardo Najera/205	
22	Marco Jaric	
23	Michael Jordan/120	
24	Tom Gugliotta/85	
25	A.J. Guyton/225	
26	Chris Carrawell/205	
27	Jarrett Stephens/120	
28	Hidayet Turkoglu/375	
29	T.J. Lux/55	
30	Jaquay Walls/205	
31	Johnny Hemsley/20	
32	Alonzo Mourning/30	
33	Scottie Pippen/75	
34	Desmond Mason/375	
35	Brian Cardinal/225	
36	Shaheen Holloway/120	
37	Khalid El-Amin/120	
38	Josip Sesar/205	
39	Gabe Muoneke/120	
40	Kaniel Dickens/225	
41	Antawn Jamison/85	
42	Vin Baker	
43	Justin Love/225	
44	Dalibor Bagaric/225	
45	Rodney Rogers/55	
46	Jason Hart/140	
47	Gee Gervin/120	
48	Corliss Williamson/120	
49	Primoz Brezec/375	
50	Jason Collier/205	

2000 Sage HIT Draft Flashbacks

		MT
Complete Set (10):		8.00
Common Player:		1.00
1	Scottie Pippen	1.00
2	Larry Johnson	1.00
3	Steve Smith	1.00
4	Alonzo Mourning	1.00
5	Tom Gugliotta	1.00
6	Vin Baker	1.00
7	Rodney Rogers	1.00
8	Jerry Stackhouse	1.00
9	Corliss Williamson	1.00
10	Antawn Jamison	1.00

2000 Sage HIT Prospector

		MT
Complete Set (20):		
Common Player:		
1	Jonathan Bender	
2	Chris Carrawell	
3	Jason Collier	
4	Baron Davis	
5	Keyon Dooling	
6	Khalid El-Amin	
7	Michael Finley	
8	A.J. Guyton	
9	Tim Hardaway	
10	Jason Hart	
11	Larry Johnson	
12	Dan Langhi	
13	Desmond Mason	
14	Antonio McDyess	
15	Alonzo Mourning	
16	Eduardo Najera	
17	Scoonie Penn	
18	Scottie Pippen	
19	Steve Smith	
20	Jerry Stackhouse	

2001 Sage Autograph

	MT
Complete Set (36):	20.00
Common Player:	.25
Gilbert Arenas	2.00
Shane Battier	3.00
Ruben Boumtje-Boumtje	.25
Bryan Bracey	.25
Michael Bradley	.25
Jamison Brewer	.25
Damone Brown	.25
Kwame Brown	3.00
Eric Chenowith	.25
Eddy Curry	3.00
Samuel Dalembert	.50
Maurice Evans	.25
Joseph Forte	1.00
Antonis Fotsis	.25
Pau Gasol	3.00
Eddie Griffin	2.00
Trenton Hassell	.25
Brendan Haywood	.50
Steve Hunter	.25
Andre Hutson	.25
Maurice Jeffers	.25
Richard Jefferson	2.00
Ken Johnson	.25
Alvin Jones	.25
Sean Lampley	.25
Troy Murphy	1.00
Zach Randolph	.50
Jason Richardson	5.00
Jeryl Sasser	.25
Kenny Satterfield	.25
Will Solomon	.25
Jamaal Tinsley	2.00
Gerald Wallace	.25
Rodney White	.25
Loren Woods	.25
Michael Wright	.25

2001 Sage Autograph Bronze

		MT
Complete Set (36):		
Common Player:		
		1x-2x Red
A1	Gilbert Arenas/240	
A2	Shane Battier/400	
A3	Ruben Boumtje-Boumtje/500	
A4	Bryan Bracey/600	
A5	Michael Bradley/240	
A6	Jamison Brewer/600	
A7	Damone Brown/120	
A8	Kwame Brown/325	
A9	Eric Chenowith/400	
A10	Eddy Curry/325	
A11	Samuel Dalembert/240	
A12	Maurice Evans/600	
A13	Joseph Forte/240	
A14	Antonis Fotsis/600	
A15	Pau Gasol/240	
A16	Eddie Griffin/325	
A17	Trenton Hassell/400	
A18	Brendan Haywood/240	
A19	Steve Hunter/240	
A20	Andre Hutson/425	
A21	Maurice Jeffers/600	
A22	Richard Jefferson/525	
A23	Ken Johnson/120	
A24	Alvin Jones/440	
A25	Sean Lampley/650	
A26	Troy Murphy/240	
A27	Zach Randolph/240	
A28	Jason Richardson/240	
A29	Jeryl Sasser/650	
A30	Kenny Satterfield/200	
A31	Will Solomon/440	
A32	Jamaal Tinsley/240	
A33	Gerald Wallace/240	
A34	Rodney White/400	
A35	Loren Woods/525	
A36	Michael Wright/650	

2001 Sage Autograph Gold

		MT
Complete Set (36):		
Common Player:		
		2x-4x Red
A1	Gilbert Arenas/80	
A2	Shane Battier/125	
A3	Ruben Boumtje-Boumtje/160	
A4	Bryan Bracey/200	
A5	Michael Bradley/80	
A6	Jamison Brewer/200	
A7	Damone Brown/40	
A8	Kwame Brown/100	
A9	Eric Chenowith/125	
A10	Eddy Curry/100	
A11	Samuel Dalembert/80	
A12	Maurice Evans/200	
A13	Joseph Forte/80	
A14	Antonis Fotsis/200	
A15	Pau Gasol/80	
A16	Eddie Griffin/100	
A17	Trenton Hassell/125	
A18	Brendan Haywood/80	
A19	Steve Hunter/80	
A20	Andre Hutson/130	
A21	Maurice Jeffers/180	
A22	Richard Jefferson/160	
A23	Ken Johnson/40	
A24	Alvin Jones/140	
A25	Sean Lampley/200	
A26	Troy Murphy/80	
A27	Zach Randolph/80	
A28	Jason Richardson/80	
A29	Jeryl Sasser/200	
A30	Kenny Satterfield/60	
A31	Will Solomon/140	
A32	Jamaal Tinsley/80	
A33	Gerald Wallace/80	
A34	Rodney White/125	
A35	Loren Woods/160	
A36	Michael Wright/200	

2001 Sage Autograph Platinum

"Too uncommon to price."

		MT
Complete Set (36):		
Common Player:		
A1	Gilbert Arenas/20	
A2	Shane Battier/35	
A3	Ruben Boumtje-Boumtje/40	
A4	Bryan Bracey/50	
A5	Michael Bradley/20	
A6	Jamison Brewer/50	
A7	Damone Brown/10	
A8	Kwame Brown/25	
A9	Eric Chenowith/35	
A10	Eddy Curry/25	
A11	Samuel Dalembert/20	
A12	Maurice Evans/50	
A13	Joseph Forte/20	
A14	Antonis Fotsis/50	
A15	Pau Gasol/20	
A16	Eddie Griffin/25	
A17	Trenton Hassell/35	
A18	Brendan Haywood/20	
A19	Steve Hunter/20	
A20	Andre Hutson/35	
A21	Maurice Jeffers/50	
A22	Richard Jefferson/40	
A23	Ken Johnson/10	
A24	Alvin Jones/40	
A25	Sean Lampley/50	
A26	Troy Murphy/20	
A27	Zach Randolph/20	
A28	Jason Richardson/20	
A29	Jeryl Sasser/50	
A30	Kenny Satterfield/15	
A31	Will Solomon/40	
A32	Jamaal Tinsley/20	
A33	Gerald Wallace/20	
A34	Rodney White/35	
A35	Loren Woods/40	
A36	Michael Wright/50	

2001 Sage Autograph Red

		MT
Complete Set (36):		
Common Player:		5.00
A1	Gilbert Arenas/349	10.00
A2	Shane Battier/499	40.00
A3	Ruben Boumtje-Boumtje/699	5.00
A4	Bryan Bracey/849	5.00
A5	Michael Bradley/349	5.00
A6	Jamison Brewer/849	5.00
A7	Damone Brown/159	5.00
A8	Kwame Brown/500	20.00
A9	Eric Chenowith/499	5.00
A10	Eddy Curry/500	20.00
A11	Samuel Dalembert/349	5.00
A12	Maurice Evans/849	5.00
A13	Joseph Forte/349	10.00
A14	Antonis Fotsis/849	5.00
A15	Pau Gasol/349	25.00
A16	Eddie Griffin/500	15.00
A17	Trenton Hassell/499	5.00
A18	Brendan Haywood/349	5.00
A19	Steve Hunter/349	5.00
A20	Andre Hutson/549	5.00
A21	Maurice Jeffers/799	5.00
A22	Richard Jefferson/699	15.00
A23	Ken Johnson/159	5.00
A24	Alvin Jones/599	5.00
A25	Sean Lampley/999	5.00
A26	Troy Murphy/349	10.00
A27	Zach Randolph/349	5.00
A28	Jason Richardson/349	40.00
A29	Jeryl Sasser/999	5.00
A30	Kenny Satterfield/249	5.00
A31	Will Solomon/599	5.00
A32	Jamaal Tinsley/349	20.00
A33	Gerald Wallace/349	20.00
A34	Rodney White/499	5.00
A35	Loren Woods/699	5.00
A36	Michael Wright/999	5.00

2001 Sage Autograph Silver

		MT
Complete Set (36):		
Common Player:		
2x to 3x Red		
A1	Gilbert Arenas/160	
A2	Shane Battier/240	
A3	Ruben Boumtje-Boumtje/300	
A4	Bryan Bracey/400	
A5	Michael Bradley/160	
A6	Jamison Brewer/400	
A7	Damone Brown/70	
A8	Kwame Brown/200	
A9	Eric Chenowith/240	
A10	Eddy Curry/200	
A11	Samuel Dalembert/160	
A12	Maurice Evans/400	
A13	Joseph Forte/160	
A14	Antonis Fotsis/400	
A15	Pau Gasol/160	
A16	Eddie Griffin/200	
A17	Trenton Hassell/240	

A18	Brendan Haywood/160	
A19	Steve Hunter/160	
A20	Andre Hutson/260	
A21	Maurice Jeffers/370	
A22	Richard Jefferson/325	
A23	Ken Johnson/70	
A24	Alvin Jones/280	
A25	Sean Lampley/400	
A26	Troy Murphy/160	
A27	Zach Randolph/160	
A28	Jason Richardson/160	
A29	Jeryl Sasser/400	
A30	Kenny Satterfield/125	
A31	Will Solomon/280	
A32	Jamaal Tinsley/160	
A33	Gerald Wallace/160	
A34	Rodney White/240	
A35	Loren Woods/325	
A36	Michael Wright/400	

2001 Sage Autograph Jersey

		MT
Complete Set (20):		
Common Player:		10.00
J1	Gilbert Arenas	20.00
J2a	Shane Battier (blue)	40.00
J2b	Shane Battier (white)	40.00
J3	Michael Bradley	10.00
J4	Damone Brown	10.00
J5	Kwame Brown	20.00
J6	Eddy Curry	20.00
J7	Samuel Dalembert	10.00
J8	Joseph Forte	15.00
J9	Eddie Griffin	20.00
J10	Brendan Haywood	10.00
J11	Steven Hunter	10.00
J12	Richard Jefferson	15.00
J13	Troy Murphy	15.00
J14	Zach Randolph	10.00
J15	Jason Richardson	25.00
J16	Jeryl Sasser	10.00
J17	Jamaal Tinsley	15.00
J18	Gerald Wallace	10.00
J19	Rodney White	10.00
J20	Loren Woods	10.00

2001 Sage Hit

		MT
Complete Set (36):		
Common Player:		4.00
1	Kwame Brown	2.00
2	Michael Wright	.40
3	Troy Murphy	1.00
4	Eddy Curry	2.00
5	Rodney White	.40
6	Loren Woods	.40
7	Maurice Jeffers	.40
8	Eric Chenowith	.40
9	Antonis Fotsis	.40
10	Kenny Satterfield	.40
11	Jamaal Tinsley	1.00
12	Sean Lampley	.40
13	Richard Jefferson	1.00
14	Jamison Brewer	.40
15	Steven Hunter	.40
16	Pau Gasol	3.00
17	Michael Bradley	.40
18	Bryan Bracey	.40
19	Zach Randolph	.75
20	Brendan Haywood	.75
21	Joseph Forte	1.00
22	Jeryl Sasser	.75
23	Jason Richardson	5.00
24	Gerald Wallace	.75
25	Damone Brown	.40
26	Samuel Dalembert	.40
27	Will Solomon	.40
28	Maurice Evans	.40
29	Trenton Hassell	.40
30	Gilbert Arenas	2.00
31	Shane Battier	5.00
32	Ken Johnson	.40
33	Eddie Griffin	1.00
34	Andre Hutson	.40
35	Alvin Jones	.40
36	Ruben Boumtje-Boumtje	.40

2001 Sage Hit Jersey

		MT
Complete Set (20):		
Common Player:		20.00
J1	Gerald Wallace	20.00
J2	Gilbert Arenas	30.00
J3	Richard Jefferson	40.00
J4	Loren Woods	20.00
J5	Rodney White	20.00
J6	Steven Hunter	20.00
J7a	Shane Battier (blue)	60.00
J7b	Shane Battier (white)	60.00
J8	Kwame Brown	40.00
J9	Jamaal Tinsley	40.00
J10	Zach Randolph	20.00
J11	Jason Richardson	75.00
J12	Joseph Forte	30.00
J13	Brendan Haywood	20.00
J14	Troy Murphy	30.00
J15	Jeryl Sasser	20.00
J16	Samuel Dalembert	20.00
J17	Eddie Griffin	30.00
J18	Damone Brown	20.00
J19	Eddy Curry	35.00
J20	Michael Bradley	20.00

1997 Scholastic Ultimate NBA Postcards

These 30 postcards were issued in "The Ultimate NBA Postcard Book" (SRP $7.99) by Scholastic. The cards measure 5-3/4" x 6-1/3" and feature a color action shot on the front. The backs include statistics and biographical information, but the rest of the card resembles a normal postcard. The cards are not numbered and are perforated at the top where they were seperated from the book.

		MT
Complete Set (30):		15.00
Common Player:		.25
1	Greg Anthony	.25
2	Vin Baker	.50
3	Shawn Bradley	.25
4	Terrell Brandon	.50
5	Elden Campbell	.40
6	Sam Cassell	.40
7	Joe Dumars	.50
8	Patrick Ewing	.50
9	Kevin Garnett	5.00
10	Kevin Johnson	.50
11	Shawn Kemp	2.00
12	Toni Kukoc	.50
13	Karl Malone	.75
14	Jamal Mashburn	.50
15	Antonio McDyess	.75
16	Alonzo Mourning	.50
17	Dino Radja	.25
18	Glen Rice	.50
19	Mitch Richmond	.50
20	David Robinson	1.00
21	Arvydas Sabonis	.50
22	Dennis Scott	.40
23	Joe Smith	.75
24	Steve Smith	.50
25	Rik Smits	.40
26	John Starks	.40
27	Damon Stoudamire	1.25
28	Loy Vaught	.40
29	Clarence Weatherspoon	.25
30	Chris Webber	1.50

1994 Score Board Draft Day

The 13-card, standard-size set featured the top picks of the 1994 NBA Draft. Each set came with a certificate of limited edition and the production was held at 19,500. The cards are numbered with the "DD" prefix.

		MT
Complete Set (13):		20.00
Common Player:		.25
1	Milwaukee (Glenn Robinson)	3.00
2	Dallas (Glenn Robinson)	1.50
3	Detroit (Glenn Robinson)	1.50
4	Minneapolis (Jason Kidd)	2.00
5	Dallas (Jason Kidd)	4.00
6	Washington (Jason Kidd)	2.00
7	Dallas (Grant Hill)	2.50
8	Detroit (Grant Hill)	5.00
9	Boston (Eric Montross)	.50
10	Sacramento (Eric Montross)	.25
11	Washington (Juwan Howard)	2.00
12	Philadelphia (Juwan Howard)	1.00
13	Checklist	.25

1994 Score Board National Promos

The 20-card, standard-size set was distributed at the National Sports Collectors Convention and featured players from basketball, football, baseball and NASCAR. The cards are serially numbered out of 9,900 sets and have an "NC" prefix.

		MT
Complete Set (20):		40.00
Common Player:		.50
1	Glenn Robinson	3.00
2	Jason Kidd	4.00
3	Donyell Marshall	.50
4	Juwan Howard	2.00
5	Grant Hill	5.00
6	Hakeem Olajuwon	1.25
7	Patrick Ewing	.75
8	Dikembe Mutombo	.50
9	Alonzo Mourning	1.00
10	Dallas Cowboys (Troy Aikman)	3.00
11	Texas Rangers (Nolan Ryan)	3.00
12	Dallas Cowboy (Emmitt Smith)	4.00
13	Texas Heroes (Hakeem Olajuwon)	1.25
14	1979-1981 (Dale Earnhardt)	3.00
15	1982-1984 (Dale Earnhardt)	3.00
16	1985-1987 (Dale Earnhardt)	3.00
17	1988-1990 (Dale Earnhardt)	3.00
18	1991-1993 (Dale Earnhardt)	3.00
19	History of the National	.50
20A	Checklist Card (Troy Aikman)	5.00
20B	Checklist Card (Dale Earnhardt)	5.00
20C	Checklist Card (Hakeem Olajuwon)	2.50
20D	Checklist Card (Nolan Ryan)	5.00
20E	Checklist Card (Emmitt Smith)	6.00

1996-97 Score Board All Sport PPF

The set was released in two series of six-card packs. The set contains original vintage and rookie cards of top athletes of the four major sports. The set also had new cards of current players.

		MT
Complete Set (200):		30.00
Common Player:		.05
Gold:		8x
1	Shaquille O'Neal	.05
2	Scottie Pippen	.20
3	Dikembe Mutombo	.05
4	Damon Stoudamire	.40
5	Brent Barry	.05
6	Michael Finley	.15
7	Allen Iverson	1.25
8	Marcus Camby	.60
9	Stephon Marbury	1.00
10	Antonio McDyess	.20
11	Kobe Bryant	1.50
12	Ray Allen	.50
13	Antoine Walker	1.00
14	Erick Dampier	.05
15	Vitaly Potapenko	.05
16	Tony Delk	.05
17	John Wallace	.05
18	Roy Rogers	.05
19	Jerome Williams	.05
20	Travis Knight	.05
21	Ryan Minor	.05
22	Shawn Harvey	.05
23	Jason Sasser	.05
24	Doron Sheffer	.05
25	Malik Rose	.05
26	Jermaine O'Neal	.05
27	Mark Hendrickson	.05
28	Dontae Jones	.05
29	Othella Harrington	.05
30	Troy Aikman	.40
31	Kerry Collins	.40
32	Steve Young	.20
33	Kordell Stewart	.20
34	Kevin Hardy	.05
35	Joey Galloway	.20
36	Simeon Rice	.05
37	Marcus Coleman	.05
38	Eric Moulds	.05
39	Ray Farmer	.05
40	Chris Darkins	.05
41	Amani Toomer	.05
42	Daryl Gardener	.05
43	Bobby Engram	.05
44	Stepfret Williams	.05
45	Eddie George	1.50
46	Tony Brackens	.05
47	Cedric Jones	.05
48	Jason Dunn	.05
49	Mike Alstott	.25
50	Shaquille O'Neal	.20
51	Danny Kanell	.05
52	Andre Johnson	.05
53	Rickey Dudley	.05
54	Jeff Hartings	.05
55	Regan Upshaw	.05
56	Alex Molden	.05
57	Terry Glenn	1.00
58	Alex Van Dyke	.05
59	Karim Abdul-Jabbar	.75
60	Rey Ordonez	.05
61	Todd Greene	.05
62	Jermaine Dye	.05
63	Karim Garcia	.05
64	Todd Walker	.20
65	Calvin Reese	.05
66	Roger Cedeno	.05
67	Ben Davis	.05
68	Chad Hermansen	.05
69	Vladimir Guerrero	.50
70	Billy Wagner	.05
71	Ed Jovanovski	.10
72	Chris Phillips	.05
73	Alexandre Volchkov	.05
74	Adam Colagiacomo	.05
75	Jonathan Aitken	.05
76	Rico Fata	1.00
77	Andrei Zyuzin	.05
78	Josh Holden	.05
79	Boyd Devereaux	.05
80	Allen Iverson	1.25
81	Jason Kidd	.20
82	Hakeem Olajuwon	.20
83	Alonzo Mourning	.20
84	Shareef Abdur-Rahim	.75
85	Glenn Robinson	.20
86	Rasheed Wallace	.05
87	Emmitt Smith	.50
88	Drew Bledsoe	.40
89	Keyshawn Johnson	.75
90	Marshall Faulk	.20
91	Steve Young	.20
92	Lawrence Phillips	.10
93	Terry Glenn	1.00
94	Barry Bonds	.20
95	Vladimir Guerrero	.50
96	Livan Hernandez	.05
97	Bryan Berard	.20
98	Dainius Zubrus	.75
99	Radek Dvorak	.05
100	Troy Aikman (CL (51-100))	.40
101	Hakeem Olajuwon	.20
102	Alonzo Mourning	.20
103	Rasheed Wallace	.05
104	Glenn Robinson	.20
105	Tyus Edney	.05
106	Joe Smith	.20
107	Jason Kidd	.20
108	Shareef Abdur-Rahim	.75
109	Kerry Kittles	.50
110	Lorenzen Wright	.05
111	Samaki Walker	.05
112	Todd Fuller	.05
113	Steve Nash	.05
114	Jamie Feick	.05
115	Walter McCarty	.05
116	Jeff McInnis	.05
117	Derek Fisher	.05
118	Moochie Norris	.05
119	Joseph Blair	.05
120	Steve Hamer	.05
121	Randy Livingston	.05
122	Ron Riley	.05
123	Mark Pope	.05
124	Drew Barry	.05
125	Brian Evans	.05
126	Emmitt Smith	.50
127	Drew Bledsoe	.40
128	Steve McNair	.20
129	Marshall Faulk	.20
130	Keyshawn Johnson	.75
131	Lawrence Phillips	.20
132	Leeland McElroy	.05
133	Tony Banks	1.00
134	Derrick Mayes	.20
135	Jonathan Ogden	.05
136	Zach Thomas	.05
137	Tim Biakabutuka	.05
138	Ray Mickens	.05
139	Ray Lewis	.05
140	Marco Battaglia	.05
141	John Mobley	.05
142	Marvin Harrison	.75
143	Duane Clemons	.05
144	Lance Johnstone	.05
145	Eddie Kennison	.75
146	Bobby Hoying	.05
147	Brett Favre	.75
148	Reggie Brown	.05
149	Walt Harris	.05
150	Kobe Bryant (CL)	.60
151	Marcus Jones	.05
152	Je'Rod Cherry	.05
153	Brian Dawkins	.05
154	Johnny McWilliams	.05
155	Brian Roche	.05
156	Muhsin Muhammad	.05
157	Lawyer Milloy	.05
158	Jermain Mayberry	.05
159	DeRon Jenkins	.05
160	Barry Bonds	.20
161	Jay Payton	.05
162	Jose Cruz	1.00
163	Richard Hidalgo	.05
164	Bartolo Colon	.25
165	Matt Drews	.05
166	Kerry Wood	2.00
167	Ben Grieve	.60
168	Wes Helms	.50
169	Livan Hernandez	.05
170	Dainius Zubrus	.75
171	Joe Thornton	.75
172	Daniel Briere	.05
173	Radek Dvorak	.05
174	Richard Jackman	.05
175	Robert Dome	.05
176	Sergei Samsonov	.75
177	Jarome Iginla	.20
178	Daniel Cleary	.05
179	Allen Iverson	1.25
180	Antonio McDyess	.20
181	Scottie Pippen	.20
182	Dikembe Mutombo	.05
183	Damon Stoudamire	.40
184	Stephon Marbury	1.00
185	Kobe Bryant	1.50
186	Marcus Camby	.60
187	Steve Young	.20
188	Kerry Collins	.40
189	Kevin Hardy	.05
190	Kordell Stewart	.20
191	Joey Galloway	.20
192	Simeon Rice	.05
193	Eddie George	1.50
194	Brett Favre	.75
195	Emmitt Smith	.50
196	Todd Walker	.05
197	Rey Ordonez	.05
198	Todd Greene	.05
199	Andrei Zyuzin	.05
200	Eddie George (CL)	.75

1996-97 Score Board All Sport PPF Retro

These were randomly inserted in series 1 at a rate of 1:35. The 10-card set was produced on old-style card stock. The card numbers carry an "R" prefix.

		MT
Complete Set (10):		60.00
Common Player:		4.00
1	Allen Iverson	8.00
2	Keyshawn Johnson	6.00
3	Scottie Pippen	6.00
4	Emmitt Smith	6.00
5	Shaquille O'Neal	8.00
6	Marcus Camby	6.00
7	Troy Aikman	5.00
8	Damon Stoudamire	6.00
9	Lawrence Phillips	4.00
10	Rey Ordonez	4.00

1996-97 Score Board All Sport PPF Plus Rivals

Each of the ten cards in this set are printed on vintage-style stock to give the look and feel of an old-time card. The fronts have a color photo of the player on half of the card and the other half has a picture of the player in black and white. They were inserted 1:35 packs. They carry an "RV" prefix.

		MT
Complete Set (10):		60.00
Common Player:		5.00
1	Allen Iverson	10.00
2	Stephon Marbury	8.00
3	Alonzo Mourning	5.00
4	Shareef Abdur-Rahim	6.00
5	Kerry Kittles	5.00
6	Emmitt Smith	8.00
7	Keyshawn Johnson	5.00
8	Eddie George	10.00
9	Marvin Harrison	5.00
10	Barry Bonds	5.00

1996-97 Score Board Autographed BK

This 50-card set contained top rookies and veterans from basketball and was sold in six-card packs. The card fronts featured a color action shot of the player over a split background, with the right side being part of the action shot and the left side containing a brown marble look. Score Board produced 1,700 sequentially numbered cards. Inserts in this product include: Autographs, Certified Autographs, Pure Performers gold and silver, and Memorabilia Redemption cards.

		MT
Complete Set (50):		20.00
Common Player:		.15
1	Allen Iverson	4.00
2	Marcus Camby	3.00
3	Shareef Abdur-Rahim	2.25
4	Stephon Marbury	2.25
5	Ray Allen	2.00
6	Erick Dampier	.75
7	Antoine Walker	1.00
8	John Wallace	1.25
9	Kerry Kittles	2.00
10	Lorenzen Wright	.75
11	Samaki Walker	.75
12	Todd Fuller	.50
13	Malik Rose	.15
14	Roy Rogers	.50
15	Kobe Bryant	3.50
16	Walter McCarty	.50
17	Ryan Minor	.15
18	Steve Nash	.75
19	Jermaine O'Neal	1.00
20	Vitaly Potapenko	.75
21	Mark Pope	.15
22	Tony Delk	.75
23	Brian Evans	.15
24	Reggie Geary	.15
25	Dantae Jones	.15
26	Travis Knight	.30
27	Priest Lauderdale	.15
28	Moochie Norris	.15
29	Efthimis Retzias	.15
30	Jerome Williams	.15
31	Jamie Feick	.15
32	Othella Harrington	.15
33	Mark Hendrickson	.15
34	Chris Robinson	.15
35	Randy Livingston	.50
36	Marcus Mann	.15
37	Darnell Robinson	.15
38	Jason Sasser	.15
39	Doron Sheffer	.15
40	Drew Barry	.15
41	Ben Davis	.15
42	Steve Hamer	.15
43	Ronnie Henderson	.15
44	Jeff McInnis	.15
45	Scottie Pippen	.30
46	Jason Kidd	.15
47	Alonzo Mourning	.15
48	Hakeem Olajuwon	.15
49	Damon Stoudamire	.30
50	Checklist	.15

A card number in parentheses ( ) indicates the set is unnumbered.

1996-97 Score Board Autographed BK Cert. Red Autos.

Certified Red Autographs were printed in red foil and individually numbered. Every 16 packs contained a Certified Red Autograph, which featured a stamp in the lower right corner that reads "Authentic Autograph."

		MT
Complete Set (35):		500.00
Common Player:		8.00
1	Shareef Abdur-Rahim	60.00
2	Ray Allen SP	70.00
3	Drew Barry	8.00
4	Terrell Bell	8.00
5	Kobe Bryant	70.00
6	Marcus Camby	65.00
7	Erick Dampier	25.00
8	Tony Delk	25.00
9	Brian Evans	8.00
10	Jamie Feick	8.00
11	Derek Fisher	20.00
12	Steve Hamer	8.00
13	Othella Harrington	8.00
14	Shawn Harvey	8.00
15	Mark Hendrickson	8.00
16	Allen Iverson	75.00
17	Travis Knight	20.00
18	Randy Livingston	30.00
19	Stephon Marbury	60.00
20	Walter McCarty	8.00
21	Jeff McInnis	8.00
22	Ryan Minor	8.00
23	Steve Nash	25.00
24	Moochie Norris	8.00
25	Mark Pope	8.00
26	Vitaly Potapenko	25.00
27	Ron Riley	8.00
28	Chris Robinson	8.00
29	Roy Rogers	20.00
30	Malik Rose	8.00
31	Jason Sasser	8.00
32	Doron Sheffer	8.00
33	John Wallace	35.00
34	Jerome Williams	8.00
35	Lorenzen Wright	25.00

1996-97 Score Board Autographed BK Cert. Sil. Autos.

Silver Autographs were inserted into one per seven packs of Autographed Basketball. Approximately 75 different players signed for the product. There is also another, rarer version of these Autographs that is printed in red foil and individually numbered.

		MT
Complete Set (35):		600.00
Common Player:		10.00
2	Ray Allen SP	60.00
3	Drew Barry	10.00
4	Terrell Bell	10.00
5	Kobe Bryant	85.00
6	Marcus Camby	75.00
7	Erick Dampier	30.00
8	Tony Delk	30.00
9	Brian Evans	10.00
10	Jamie Feick	10.00
11	Derek Fisher	25.00
12	Steve Hamer	10.00
13	Othella Harrington	10.00
14	Shawn Harvey	10.00
15	Mark Hendrickson	10.00
17	Travis Knight	25.00
18	Randy Livingston	35.00
19	Stephon Marbury	70.00
20	Walter McCarty	10.00
21	Jeff McInnis	10.00
22	Ryan Minor	10.00
23	Steve Nash	30.00
24	Moochie Norris	10.00
25	Mark Pope	10.00
26	Vitaly Potapenko	20.00
27	Ron Riley	10.00
28	Chris Robinson	10.00
28a	Darnell Robinson	10.00

29	Roy Rogers	25.00
30	Malik Rose	10.00
31	Jason Sasser	10.00
32	Doron Sheffer	10.00
33	John Wallace	40.00
34	Jerome Williams	10.00
35	Lorenzen Wright	30.00

1996-97 Score Board Autographed BK Pure Performance

This 30-card set was inserted into Autographed Basketball at a rate of one per 10 packs. Regular versions are printed on silver foil, with a rarer version printed on gold foil (one per 50). The cards feature a cutout action shot of the player over the words "Pure Performer" running up the card. The player's name is written across the top in red foil.

		MT
Complete Set (30):		100.00
Common Player:		1.50
Gold Cards:		2x-3x
1	Allen Iverson	20.00
2	Marcus Camby	15.00
3	Shareef Abdur-Rahim	12.00
4	Stephon Marbury	12.00
5	Ray Allen	10.00
6	Erick Dampier	3.00
7	Antoine Walker	3.00
8	John Wallace	6.00
9	Kerry Kittles	10.00
10	Lorenzen Wright	3.00
11	Samaki Walker	3.00
12	Todd Fuller	1.50
13	Roy Rogers	1.50
14	Kobe Bryant	18.00
15	Walter McCarty	1.50
16	Ryan Minor	1.50
17	Steve Nash	3.00
18	Jermaine O'Neal	6.00
19	Vitaly Potapenko	3.00
20	Tony Delk	3.00
21	Brian Evans	1.50
22	Reggie Geary	1.50
23	Dontae Jones	1.50
24	Travis Knight	1.50
25	Othella Harrington	1.50
26	Alonzo Mourning	1.50
27	Scottie Pippen	1.50
28	Jason Kidd	1.50
29	Damon Stoudamire	1.50
30	Hakeem Olajuwon	1.50

1996-97 Score Board Autographed BK Pure Performers Gold

Pure Performers Gold reprints the 30 cards in Pure Performers, except that it is printed on gold foil. Gold versions are inserted every 50 packs of Autographed Basketball.

		MT
Complete Set (30):		300.00
Common Player:		4.50
1	Allen Iverson	60.00
2	Marcus Camby	45.00
3	Shareef Abdur-Rahim	36.00
4	Stephon Marbury	36.00
5	Ray Allen	30.00
6	Erick Dampier	4.50
7	Antoine Walker	10.00
8	John Wallace	18.00
9	Kerry Kittles	30.00
10	Lorenzen Wright	4.50
11	Samaki Walker	4.50
12	Todd Fuller	4.50
13	Roy Rogers	4.50
14	Kobe Bryant	25.00
15	Walter McCarty	4.50
16	Ryan Minor	4.50
17	Steve Nash	4.50
18	Jermaine O'Neal	18.00
19	Vitaly Potapenko	4.50
20	Tony Delk	4.50
21	Brian Evans	4.50
22	Reggie Geary	4.50
23	Dontae Jones	4.50
24	Travis Knight	4.50
25	Othella Harrington	4.50
26	Alonzo Mourning	4.50
27	Scottie Pippen	4.50
28	Jason Kidd	4.50
29	Damon Stoudamire	4.50
30	Hakeem Olajuwon	4.50

1996 Score Board Basketball Rookies

Score Board's 1996 100-card basketball set includes the top picks from the 1996 NBA draft. Each card front features a full-bleed color action photo, with the player's name in block letters at the top. His name, college and position are along the bottom, next to a Basketball Rookies logo in the lower left-hand corner. The card back has a ghosted image of the player, with a frame around a full-color shot of his face. Draft data runs along each side of the frame. The left side of the card has a player profile; the right side has biographical information and stats. The brand logo is in the upper right corner, opposite the card number. Subsets, each with 10 cards, include All American and Basketball Greats. Three insert sets were also created - College Jerseys, #1 Draft Picks and Vintage Rookie Cards. In all, there are 39 different, original, vintage rookie cards of top players seeded two per box of 1996 Basketball Rookies by Score Board. Among those vintage rookies found in packs are Michael Jordan and Magic Johnson (redemption cards are used for these two players), Patrick Ewing, Charles Barkley and Scottie Pippen.

		MT
Complete Set (100):		12.00
Common Player:		.05
Minor Stars:		.10
1	Allen Iverson	2.00
2	Marcus Camby	1.50
3	Stephon Marbury	1.50
4	Shareef Abdur-Rahim	1.00
5	Ray Allen	1.00
6	Erick Dampier	.25
7	Antoine Walker	.60
8	John Wallace	.30
9	Kerry Kittles	.50
10	Lorenzen Wright	.30
11	Samaki Walker	.50
12	Todd Fuller	.25
13	Jaron Boone	.05
14	Roy Rogers	.20
15	Kobe Bryant	2.00
16	Walter McCarty	.40
17	Ryan Minor	.10
18	Steve Nash	.30
19	Jermaine O'Neal	.30
20	Vitaly Potapenko	.15
21	Kwame Evans	.05
22	Tony Delk	.40
23	Brian Evans	.05
24	Dion Cross	.05
25	Dontae Jones	.10
26	Travis Knight	.10
27	Priest Lauderdale	.10
28	Moochie Norris	.05
29	Efthimis Retzias	.05
30	Jerome Williams	.05
31	Jamie Feick	.05
32	Othella Harrington	.05
33	Mark Hendrickson	.05
34	Chris Robinson	.05
35	Randy Livingston	.05
36	Marcus Mann	.05
37	Darnell Robinson	.05
38	Jason Sasser	.05
39	Doron Sheffer	.05
40	Kevin Simpson	.05
41	Joseph Blair	.05
42	Eric Gingold	.05
43	Steve Hamer	.05
44	Ronnie Henderson	.05
45	Jeff McInnis	.05
46	Dante Calabria	.05
47	Martin Muursepp	.05
48	Mark Pope	.05
49	Ron Riley	.05
50	Shandon Anderson	.05
51	Derrick Battie	.05
52	Derek Fisher	.05
53	Kevin Granger	.05
54	Shawn Harvey	.05
55	Bernard Hopkins	.05
56	Raimonds Miglinieks	.05
57	Tim Moore	.05
58	Carlos Strong	.05
59	Chucky Atkins	.05
60	Drew Barry	.05
61	Terrell Bell	.05
62	Donta Bright	.05
63	Marcus Brown	.05
64	William Cunningham	.05
65	Katu Davis	.05
66	Ben Davis	.05
67	Adrian Griffin	.05
68	Darvin Ham	.05
69	Art Long	.05
70	Jerome Lambert	.05
71	Amal McCaskill	.05
72	Mingo Johnson	.05
73	Dametri Hill	.05
74	Michael Lloyd	.05
75	Malik Rose	.05
76	Jeff Nordgaard	.05
77	Duane Simpkins	.05
78	Russ Millard	.05
79	Allen Iverson	1.00
80	Marcus Camby	.75
81	Allen Iverson	1.00
82	Marcus Camby	.75
83	Stephon Marbury	.75
84	Ray Allen	.50
85	Kerry Kittles	.25
86	Erick Dampier	.05
87	Shareef Abdur-Rahim	.50
88	John Wallace	.05
89	Lorenzen Wright	.05
90	Tony Delk	.20
91	Shaquille O'Neal	.50
92	Hakeem Olajuwon	.50
93	Joe Smith	.05
94	Brent Barry	.05
95	Jason Kidd	.05
96	Scottie Pippen	.20
97	Damon Stoudamire	.30
98	Alonzo Mourning	.05
99	Rasheed Wallace	.05
100	Glenn Robinson	.05

1996 Score Board Basketball Rookies College Jerseys

This 30-card insert set showcases top 1995-96 college stars on special embossed cards that give the look and feel of an actual uniform. The horizontal front shows a picture of the player, and his college jersey. The cards are seeded one per every 10 packs.

		MT
Complete Set (30):		75.00
Common Player:		1.00
Minor Stars:		2.00
1	Allen Iverson	15.00
2	Stephon Marbury	12.00
3	Marcus Camby	12.00
4	Ray Allen	9.00
5	Erick Dampier	3.00
6	John Wallace	3.00
7	Antoine Walker	4.00
8	Lorenzen Wright	3.00
9	Kerry Kittles	5.00
10	Todd Fuller	3.00
11	Samaki Walker	5.00
12	Roy Rogers	1.00
13	Walter McCarty	4.00
14	Dontae Jones	1.00
15	Steve Nash	3.00
16	Jerome Williams	1.00
17	Ryan Minor	1.00
18	Shareef Abdur-Rahim	9.00
19	Brian Evans	1.00
20	Travis Knight	1.00
21	Mark Hendrickson	1.00
22	Tony Delk	4.00
23	Ronnie Henderson	1.00
24	Drew Barry	1.00
25	Damon Stoudamire	1.00
26	Shaquille O'Neal	1.00
27	Joe Smith	1.00
28	Jason Kidd	1.00
29	Alonzo Mourning	1.00
30	Rasheed Wallace	1.00

1996 Score Board Basketball Rookies #1 Die-Cuts

These 1996 Score Board Basketball Rookies inserts feature the first-round picks from the 1996 draft on cards printed on duplexed metallic stock. Each card is also die-cut around a #1 on the front. The cards are seeded one per every 50 packs.

		MT
Complete Set (30):		275.00
Common Player:		2.00
Minor Stars:		4.00
1	Allen Iverson	40.00
2	Marcus Camby	30.00
3	Shareef Abdur-Rahim	20.00
4	Stephon Marbury	30.00
5	Ray Allen	20.00
6	Antoine Walker	8.00
7	Lorenzen Wright	8.00
8	Kerry Kittles	10.00
9	Samaki Walker	10.00
10	Erick Dampier	5.00
11	Todd Fuller	5.00
12	Vitaly Potapenko	2.00
13	Kobe Bryant	45.00
14	Shaquille O'Neal	25.00
15	Steve Nash	8.00
16	Tony Delk	8.00
17	Jermaine O'Neal	8.00
18	John Wallace	8.00
19	Walter McCarty	8.00
20	Jason Kidd	12.00
21	Dontae Jones	2.00
22	Roy Rogers	2.00
23	Efthimis Retzias	2.00
24	Derek Fisher	2.00
25	Martin Muursepp	2.00
26	Jerome Williams	2.00
27	Brian Evans	2.00
28	Priest Lauderdale	2.00
29	Travis Knight	2.00
30	Damon Stoudamire	20.00

1997 Autographed Collection

Autographed Collection was a 50-card set that was oriented toward autographed cards and memorabilia. The product contained memorabilia redemption cards (one per 16 packs), autgraphed cards, Certified Autographs, Game Breakers and Gold Game Breakers. Regular-issue cards featured a color shot of the player on the left side, with the same shot, but tighter, on the right. The player's name, position, team and Score Board logo were printed in silver foil across the bottom. The set included players from baseball, basketball, football and hockey.

		MT
Complete Set (50):		12.00
Common Player:		.10
Minor Stars:		.20
1	Damon Stoudamire	.30
2	Scottie Pippen	.30
3	Jason Kidd	.20
4	Hakeem Olajuwon	.30
5	Alonzo Mourning	.20
6	Antonio McDyess	.10
7	Allen Iverson	1.50
8	Rasheed Wallace	.10
9	Glenn Robinson	.20
10	Marcus Camby	.75
11	Shareef Abdur-Rahim	1.00
12	Stephon Marbury	1.25
13	Kobe Bryant	1.50
14	Ray Allen	.50
15	Antoine Walker	1.00
16	Kerry Kittles	.50
17	John Wallace	.30
18	Emmitt Smith	.50
19	Kordell Stewart	.30
20	Lawrence Phillips	.10
21	Kerry Collins	.20
22	Drew Bledsoe	.30
23	Marshall Faulk	.10
24	Steve Young	.20
25	Joey Galloway	.10
26	Keyshawn Johnson	.50
27	Eddie George	2.00
28	Karim Abdul-Jabbar	.75
29	Terry Glenn	1.50
30	Marvin Harrison	.75
31	Tim Biakabutuka	.10
32	Leeland McElroy	.10
33	Simeon Rice	.10
34	Kevin Hardy	.10
35	Rickey Dudley	.10
36	Zach Thomas	.10
37	Bobby Engram	.10
38	Barry Bonds	.10
39	Vladimir Guerrero	.50
40	Rey Ordonez	.20
41	Jermaine Dye	.10
42	Todd Walker	.20
43	Billy Wagner	.20
44	Karim Garcia	.20
45	Joe Thornton	.75
46	Daniel Cleary	.10
47	Robert Dome	.10
48	Alexandre Volchkov	.10
49	Adam Colagiacomo	.10
50	Andrei Zyuzin	.10

1997 Autographed Collection Autographs

Autographed versions of cards were inserted every seven packs of Autographed Collection. The cards were autographed on the front and contained blue foil instead of the silver used on regular-issue cards. There were also Certified Autographs, which were hand-numbered on the front and had gold foil stamping on the front.

	MT
Complete Set (49):	800.00
Common Player:	8.00
Karim Abdul-Jabbar	50.00
Shareef Abdur-Rahim	60.00
Ray Allen	40.00
Drew Barry	8.00
Marco Battaglia	8.00
Michael Cheever	8.00
Daniel Cleary	8.00
Adam Colagiacomo	8.00
Chris Darkins	8.00
Tony Delk	8.00
Robert Dome	8.00
Donnie Edwards	8.00
Ray Farmer	8.00
Karim Garcia	30.00
Vladimir Guerrero	50.00
Kevin Hardy	8.00
Othella Harrington	8.00
Jimmy Herndon	8.00
Bobby Hoying	8.00
Dietrich Jells	8.00
DeRon Jenkins	8.00
Andre Johnson	8.00
Lance Johnstone	8.00
Danny Kanell	8.00
Kerry Kittles	40.00
Travis Knight	15.00
Jeff Lewis	8.00
Stephon Marbury	80.00
Derrick Mayes	8.00
Walter McCarty	8.00
Leeland McElroy	8.00
Ray Mickens	8.00
Roman Oben	8.00
Jason Odom	8.00
Rey Ordonez	15.00
Vitaly Potapenko	8.00
Roy Rogers	15.00
Sergei Samsonov	40.00
Jermain Stephens	8.00
Matt Stevens	8.00
Joe Thornton	50.00
Billy Wagner	8.00
Antoine Walker	35.00
Todd Walker	30.00
John Wallace	15.00
Jerome Williams	8.00
Lorenzen Wright	8.00
Dainius Zubrus	8.00
Andrei Zyuzin	8.00

1997 Autographed Collection Gold Autographs

Certified Autographs featured gold foil stamping across the bottom instead of the silver foil on regular-issue cards or the blue foil used on regular autographs. Certified Autographs also contained hand-numbering on the front and a Certified Autograph seal in the lower right corner. Under 350 of each card exist and they were inserted one per 16 packs.

	MT
Complete Set (49):	1400.
Common Player:	15.00
Karim Abdul-Jabbar	100.00
Shareef Abdur-Rahim	125.00
Ray Allen	80.00
Drew Barry	15.00
Marco Battaglia	15.00
Michael Cheever	15.00
Daniel Cleary	15.00
Adam Colagiacomo	15.00
Chris Darkins	15.00
Tony Delk	15.00
Robert Dome	15.00
Donnie Edwards	15.00
Ray Farmer	15.00
Karim Garcia	60.00
Vladimir Guerrero	100.00
Kevin Hardy	15.00
Othella Harrington	15.00
Jimmy Herndon	15.00
Bobby Hoying	15.00
Dietrich Jells	15.00
DeRon Jenkins	15.00
Andre Johnson	15.00
Lance Johnstone	15.00
Danny Kanell	15.00
Kerry Kittles	75.00
Travis Knight	30.00
Jeff Lewis	15.00
Derrick Mayes	15.00
Walter McCarty	15.00
Leeland McElroy	15.00
Ray Mickens	15.00
Roman Oben	15.00
Jason Odom	15.00
Rey Ordonez	30.00
Vitaly Potapenko	30.00
Roy Rogers	30.00
Sergei Samsonov	75.00
Jermain Stephens	15.00
Matt Stevens	15.00
Zack Thomas	30.00
Joe Thornton	100.00
Billy Wagner	15.00
Antoine Walker	75.00
Todd Walker	60.00
John Wallace	30.00
Jerome Williams	15.00
Lorenzen Wright	15.00
Dainius Zubrus	15.00
Andrei Zyuzin	15.00

1997 Autographed Collection Game Breakers

This 30-card insert highlighted some of the top players in Autographed Collection. Regular Game Breakers cards were printed on silver foil and inserted one per 10 packs, while Gold versions used gold foil and were inserted one per 50 packs. The card numbers on the back include a "GB" prefix.

		MT
Complete Set (30):		200.00
Common Player:		2.50
Minor Stars:		5.00
Gold Cards:		4x
1	Damon Stoudamire	6.00
2	Scottie Pippen	6.00
3	Jason Kidd	5.00
4	Ray Allen	12.00
5	Alonzo Mourning	5.00
6	Joe Smith	5.00
7	Allen Iverson	25.00
8	Rasheed Wallace	2.50
9	Antoine Walker	15.00
10	Marcus Camby	15.00
11	Shareef Abdur-Rahim	20.00
12	Stephon Marbury	20.00
13	Kobe Bryant	30.00
14	Emmitt Smith	12.00
15	Kordell Stewart	8.00
16	Kevin Hardy	2.50
17	Kerry Collins	6.00
18	Drew Bledsoe	8.00
19	Marshall Faulk	5.00
20	Steve Young	5.00
21	Lawrence Phillips	2.50
22	Keyshawn Johnson	8.00
23	Eddie George	25.00
24	Karim Abdul-Jabbar	12.00
25	Terry Glenn	20.00
26	Marvin Harrison	10.00
27	Tim Biakabutuka	2.50
28	Rey Ordonez	2.50
29	Joe Thornton	10.00
30	Alexandre Volchkov	2.50

1997 Score Board Basketball Rookies

This 100-card set, included 60 regular cards, 10 All-Americans, 15 1996-97 All-Rookie Team and 11 Back in the Day and four checklists. The set features 1997 NBA Draft members in their college uniforms, as well as a select number of pros in a mix of college uniforms and airbrushed pro uniforms. Card fronts feature a full bleed photo with a faded, black and white background. A large black strip across the bottom contains the player's school, position and a Score Board logo in it, with the player's name above the black part in white letters. Inserts include a parallel Dean's List, Rookie #1 Die-Cuts, Varsity Club and Game Wear.

		MT
Complete Set (100):		10.00
Common Player:		.05
Minor Stars:		
Dean's List:		2x-4x
1	Tim Duncan	2.00
2	Ron Mercer	.75
3	Marc Jackson	.05
4	Tunji Awojobi	.05
5	Reggie Freeman	.05
6	John Thomas	.05
7	Scot Pollard	.10
8	Brevin Knight	.50
9	Keith Booth	.05
10	Reggie Welch	.05
11	Alvin Sims	.05
12	Victor Page	.05
13	Jason Lawson	.05
14	Paul Grant	.05
15	Kiwane Garris	.30
16	Eddie Elisma	.05
17	Antonio Daniels	.50
18	James Collins	.05
19	Kelvin Cato	.50
20	Peter Aluma	.05
21	Derek Anderson	.30
22	Lorenzo Coleman	.05
23	Austin Croshere	.50
24	Harold Deane	.05
25	Nate Erdmann	.05
26	Adonal Foyle	.50
27	Tony Gonzalez	.10
28	Ed Gray	.05
29	Quincy Lee	.05
30	Charles O'Bannon	.50
31	Shea Seals	.10
32	Keith Van Horn	1.00
33	Tony Battie	.75
34	Bobby Jackson	.30
35	Anthony Parker	.05
36	Kebu Stewart	.30
37	Chris Anstey	.05
38	Jacque Vaughn	.50
39	DeJuan Wheat	.05
40	Anthony Johnson	.05
41	Danny Fortson	.50
42	Mark Sanford	.05
43	Jerald Honeycutt	.05
44	Olivier Saint-Jean	.40
45	Chauncey Billups	.75
46	Isaac Fontaine	.05
47	Otis Hill	.05
48	Tracy McGrady	1.00
49	Johnny Taylor	.05
50	God Shammgod	.30
51	Dedric Willoughby	.05
52	Tim Thomas	.50
53	Alvin Williams	.05
54	Gordon Malone	.05
55	Serge Zwikker	.10
56	Charles Smith	.05
57	Tim Duncan	1.00
58	Ron Mercer	.30
59	Keith Van Horn	.40
60	Tim Thomas	.30
61	Checklist (Tim Duncan)	1.00
62	Tim Duncan	1.00
63	Ron Mercer	.30
64	Keith Van Horn	.40
65	Tony Battie	.30
66	Tracy McGrady	.50
67	Danny Fortson	.25
68	Brevin Knight	.25
69	DeJuan Wheat	.05
70	Adonal Foyle	.25
71	Jacque Vaughn	.25
72	Checklist (Tim Duncan)	1.00
73	Allen Iverson	.40
74	Marcus Camby	.25
75	Shareef Abdur-Rahim	.25
76	Stephon Marbury	.30
77	Ray Allen	.10
78	Antoine Walker	.20
79	Lorenzen Wright	.05
80	Kerry Kittles	.10
81	Erick Dampier	.05
82	Vitaly Potapenko	.05
83	Kobe Bryant	.40
84	Tony Delk	.05
85	John Wallace	.10
86	Walter McCarty	.05
87	Roy Rogers	.05
88	Checklist (Allen Iverson)	.40
89	Rasheed Wallace	.05
90	Damon Stoudamire	.20
91	Joe Smith	.10
92	Glenn Robinson	.05
93	Scottie Pippen	.20
94	Ed O'Bannon	.05
95	Antonio McDyess	.05
96	Alonzo Mourning	.05
97	Clyde Drexler	.10
98	Dikembe Mutombo	.05
99	Hakeem Olajuwon	.10
100	Checklist (Scottie Pippen)	.10

1997 Score Board Basketball Rookies Dean's List

This 100-card parallel set was seeded one per five packs and includes each card in the regular-issue set. Dean's List inserts are identified by a large silver foil area at the bottom of the card, with the words "Dean's List" in it. The cards carry no special prefix on the card number.

	MT
Complete Set (100):	40.00
Dean's List Cards:	2x-4x

1997 Score Board Basketball Rookies #1 Die-Cuts

Rookie #1 Die-Cuts featured 1997 lottery picks as well as established stars on silver foil board die-cut in the shape of a number one. This 20-card insert was inserted one per 36 packs. Cards are numbered with a "DC" prefix.

		MT
Complete Set (20):		250.00
Common Player:		3.00
1	Tim Duncan	35.00
2	Tony Battie	15.00
3	Ron Mercer	15.00
4	Keith Van Horn	15.00
5	Antonio Daniels	10.00
6	Tim Thomas	10.00
7	Adonal Foyle	10.00
8	Derek Anderson	3.00
9	Chauncey Billups	15.00
10	Tracy McGrady	20.00
11	Danny Fortson	10.00
12	Brevin Knight	10.00
13	Jacque Vaughn	10.00
14	Austin Croshere	10.00
15	Stephon Marbury	15.00
16	Kobe Bryant	20.00
17	Clyde Drexler	3.00
18	Scottie Pippen	8.00
19	Allen Iverson	20.00
20	Alonzo Mourning	3.00

1997 Score Board Basketball Rookies Varsity Club

Varsity Club features 20 players selected in the 1997 NBA Draft on a horizontal, basketball and wood grain background. A shot of the player is on the right side, with a large holographic, pennant design on the left side. This 20-card insert was found every 18 packs of 1997 Basketball Rookies and is numbered VC1-VC20.

		MT
Complete Set (20):		150.00
Common Player:		2.00
1	Tim Duncan	25.00
2	Ron Mercer	10.00
3	Keith Van Horn	12.00
4	Tim Thomas	7.00
5	Adonal Foyle	7.00
6	Tony Battie	10.00
7	Antonio Daniels	7.00
8	Kelvin Cato	7.00
9	Charles O'Bannon	7.00
10	Brevin Knight	7.00
11	Danny Fortson	7.00
12	Derek Anderson	2.00
13	Austin Croshere	7.00
14	Tracy McGrady	15.00
15	Jacque Vaughn	7.00
16	God Shammgod	5.00
17	DeJuan Wheat	2.00
18	Danya Abrams	2.00
19	Reggie Freeman	2.00
20	Tony Gonzalez	2.00

1997 Score Board Players Club

This 70-card set featured top draft picks from basketball, football, basketball and hockey with professional team names and logos airbrushed out. The product included insert sets #1 Die-cuts and Play Backs, but the main attraction was vintage cards and vintage wax packs. A vintage card from 1909-1979 was seeded 1:32 packs, with the highlight being a T206 Honus Wagner, while a vintage wax pack was also seeded 1:32 packs.

		MT
Complete Set (70):		15.00
Common Player:		.05
1	Brett Favre	.75
2	Duce Staley	.05
3	Barry Bonds	.25
4	Shareef Abdur-Rahim	.50
5	Karim Abdul-Jabbar	.25
6	Robert Dome	.05
7	Jose Cruz, Jr.	.75
8	Ray Allen	.50
9	Derek Anderson	.50
10	Kordell Stewart	.75
11	Mike Alstott	.25
12	Daniel Briere	.25
13	Boulware, Wilson	.25
14	Troy Davis	.25
15	Tony Battie	.40
16	Kobe Bryant	2.00
17	Matt Drews	.25
18	Marcus Camby	.50
19	Keith Van Horn	.75
20	Emmitt Smith	1.00
21	Troy Aikman	.50
22	Joe Thornton	.75
23	Chauncey Billups	.50
24	Scottie Pippen	.50
25	Warrick Dunn	1.00
26	Eddie George	1.00
27	Wes Helms	.40
28	Joey Galloway	.25
29	Jacque Vaughn	.25
30	Tim Thomas	.75
31	Clyde Drexler	.25
32	Dainius Zubrus	.25
33	Darnell Autry	.05
34	Steve Young	.50
35	Joe Smith	.05
36	Antoine Walker	.50
37	Richard Hidalgo	.50
38	Tony Gonzalez	.25
39	Jim Druckenmiller	.75
40	Hakeem Olajuwon	.25
41	Alonzo Mourning	.25
42	Sergei Samsonov	1.00
43	Stephon Marbury	1.00
44	Corey Dillon	1.00
45	Kerry Kittles	.25
46	Kerry Collins	.25
47	Byron Hanspard	.50
48	Jay Payton	.50
49	Allen Iverson	1.50
50	Rae Carruth	.05
51	Jake Plummer	1.00
52	Antonio Daniels	.25
53	Darrell Russell	.25
54	Shawn Springs	.25
55	Olivier Saint-Jean	.05
56	Bryant Westbrook	.05
57	Daniel Cleary	.05
58	Tracy McGrady	1.00
59	Orlando Pace	.25
60	Richard Jackman	.05
61	Ike Hilliard	.50
62	Johnny Taylor	.05
63	Reidel Anthony	.50
64	Austin Croshere	.05
65	Alexandre Volchkov	.05
66	Brevin Knight	.50
67	Zach Thomas	.25
68	Ron Mercer	.75
69	Kerry Wood	1.50
70	Checklist	.50

1997 Score Board Players Club Play Backs

This 15-card, multi-sport insert contains a movie reel design with the player's image superimposed over the player's jersey. Cards are numbered with a "PB" prefix.

		MT
Complete Set (15):		50.00
Common Player:		2.00
1	Brett Favre	8.00
2	Kordell Stewart	5.00
3	Emmitt Smith	8.00
4	Troy Aikman	5.00
5	Scottie Pippen	5.00
6	Steve Young	5.00
7	Allen Iverson	10.00
8	Dainius Zubrus	2.00
9	Marcus Camby	3.00
10	Joey Galloway	3.00
11	Hakeem Olajuwon	4.00
12	Zach Thomas	3.00
13	Kerry Collins	2.00
14	Joe Smith	2.00
15	Karim Abdul-Jabbar	4.00

1997 Score Board Players Club #1 Die Cuts

This 20-card, die-cut insert featured first-round picks and were die-cut in the shape of the numbered "1" with gold-foil along the left border. The were numbered with a "D" prefix.

		MT
Complete Set (20):		
Common Player:		
1	Allen Iverson	
2	Troy Aikman	
3	Darrell Russell	
4	Joe Thornton	
5	Hakeem Olajuwon	
6	Joe Smith	
7	Orlando Pace	
8	Shareef Abdur-Rahim	
9	Stephon Marbury	
10	Jose Cruz, Jr.	
11	Barry Bonds	
12	Keith Van Horn	
13	Kobe Bryant	
14	Chauncey Billups	
15	Eddie George	
16	Tim Thomas	
17	Terry Glenn	
18	Warrick Dunn	
19	Emmitt Smith	
20	Antonio Daniels	

1997 Talk N' Sports

This 50-card set featured Score Board's Frontier phone cards, with five different denominations. Regular-issue cards contain a jagged gray-black area on the bottom with the player's name. Team, position and a Talkn' Sports logo are included in a strip up the right side of the card. The product includes $1, $10, $20, $50 and $1,000 phone cards, an Essentials insert and a Honus Wagner Redemption card, redeemable for the T206 Wagner. Score Board produced 1,500 sequentially numbered cases.

		MT
Complete Set (50):		10.00
Common Player:		.10
Minor Stars:		.20
1	Brett Favre	.50
2	Marshall Faulk	.20
3	Steve Young	.20
4	Troy Aikman	.30
5	Kordell Stewart	.30
6	Kerry Collins	.30
7	Keyshawn Johnson	.20
8	Eddie George	1.00
9	Terry Glenn	.75
10	Kevin Hardy	.10
11	Emmitt Smith	.50
12	Karim Abdul-Jabbar	.20
13	Tony Banks	.20
14	Zach Thomas	.20
15	Mike Alstott	.20
16	Matt Stevens	.10
17	Troy Davis	.50
18	Warrick Dunn	1.50
19	Yatil Green	.50
20	Rae Carruth	.30
21	Darrell Russell	.10
22	Peter Boulware	.10
23	Shawn Springs	.10
24	Clyde Drexler	.30
25	Scottie Pippen	.30
26	Hakeem Olajuwon	.30
27	Alonzo Mourning	.20
28	Joe Smith	.20
29	Antonio McDyess	.10
30	Allen Iverson	.75
31	Kerry Kittles	.20
32	Stephon Marbury	.60
33	Marcus Camby	.30
34	Ray Allen	.20
35	Shareef Abdur-Rahim	.50
36	Kobe Bryant	1.00
37	Antoine Walker	.50
38	Glenn Robinson	.20
39	Dikembe Mutombo	.10
40	Barry Bonds	.20
41	Jay Payton	.20
42	Todd Walker	.20
43	Jose Cruz, Jr.	.75
44	Kerry Wood	.50
45	Wes Helms	.10
46	Dainius Zubrus	.10
47	Sergei Samsonov	.10
48	Jay McKee	.10
49	Marcus Nilsson	.10
50	Joe Thornton	.10

1997 Talk N' Sports Essentials

This 10-card set was inserted one per 20 packs and utilized cel-card technology. The cards contained a large cel "e" in the upper left corner and the word "Essentials" across the bottom. The backs were numbered with an "E" prefix.

		MT
Complete Set (10):		125.00
Common Player:		10.00
1	Brett Favre	30.00
2	Scottie Pippen	15.00
3	Barry Bonds	10.00
4	Cal Ripken Jr.	15.00
5	Clyde Drexler	10.00
6	Kobe Bryant	25.00
7	Eddie George	25.00
8	Troy Davis	10.00
9	Darrell Russell	10.00
10	Dainius Zubrus	10.00

1997 Talk N' Sports $1 Phone Cards

This 50-card phone card insert mirrors the regular-issue set checklist. Each card contains $1 of phone time, with one phone card being inserted into each pack.

		MT
Complete Set (50):		75.00
Common Player:		.75
Minor Stars:		1.50
1	Brett Favre	2.00
2	Marshall Faulk	1.50
3	Steve Young	1.50
4	Troy Aikman	1.50
5	Kordell Stewart	1.50
6	Kerry Collins	1.50
7	Keyshawn Johnson	.75
8	Eddie George	3.00
9	Terry Glenn	2.50
10	Kevin Hardy	.75
11	Emmitt Smith	2.00
12	Karim Abdul-Jabbar	2.00
13	Tony Banks	1.50
14	Zach Thomas	.75
15	Mike Alstott	1.50
16	Matt Stevens	.75
17	Troy Davis	2.00
18	Warrick Dunn	4.00
19	Yatil Green	1.50
20	Rae Carruth	1.50
21	Darrell Russell	.75
22	Peter Boulware	.75
23	Shawn Springs	.75
24	Clyde Drexler	1.50
25	Scottie Pippen	1.50
26	Hakeem Olajuwon	1.50
27	Alonzo Mourning	.75
28	Joe Smith	1.50
29	Antonio McDyess	.75
30	Allen Iverson	2.50
31	Kerry Kittles	1.50
32	Stephon Marbury	2.50
33	Marcus Camby	2.00
34	Ray Allen	1.50
35	Shareef Abdur-Rahim	2.00
36	Kobe Bryant	2.50
37	Antoine Walker	2.00
38	Glenn Robinson	.75
39	Dikembe Mutombo	.75
40	Barry Bonds	1.50
41	Jay Payton	.75
42	Todd Walker	1.50
43	Jose Cruz, Jr.	1.00
44	Kerry Wood	1.50
45	Wes Helms	.75
46	Dainius Zubrus	2.00
47	Sergei Samsonov	2.00
48	Jay McKee	.75
49	Marcus Nilsson	.75
50	Joe Thornton	2.50

1997 Talk N' Sports $10 Phone Cards

This interactive set gave collectors a chance to win autographed bats by answering trivia questions. In addition, one collector could win an autographed Babe Ruth baseball. Trivia Catch $10 phone cards were inserted into every 12th pack and sequentially numbered to 3,960. There were also 50 Instant Win cards randomly inserted.

		MT
Complete Set (10):		150.00
Common Player:		15.00
1	Brett Favre	30.00
2	Hakeem Olajuwon	15.00
3	Keyshawn Johnson	15.00
4	Steve Young	15.00
5	Kordell Stewart	20.00
6	Cal Ripken Jr.	25.00
7	Eddie George	20.00
8	Troy Aikman	15.00
9	Clyde Drexler	15.00
10	Scottie Pippen	15.00

1997 Talk N' Sports $20 Phone Cards

Ten different $20 phone cards were inserted into packs of Talkn' Sports. The cards were inserted every 36 packs and sequentially numbered to 1,440.

		MT
Complete Set (10):		220.00
Common Player:		20.00
1	Brett Favre	50.00
2	Scottie Pippen	25.00
3	Barry Bonds	20.00
4	Cal Ripken Jr.	35.00
5	Clyde Drexler	20.00
6	Kobe Bryant	40.00
7	Eddie George	40.00
8	Troy Davis	25.00
9	Darrell Russell	20.00
10	Dainius Zubrus	20.00

1997 Talk N' Sports $50 Jackie Robinson Phone Cards

This commemorative five-card phone card set celebrates the 50th anniversary of Robinson breaking baseball's color barrier. Robinson phone cards were inserted every 1,200 packs and sequentially numbered to 499.

		MT
Complete Set (5):		400.00
Common Player:		75.00
1	Jackie Robinson	75.00
2	Jackie Robinson	75.00
3	Jackie Robinson	75.00
4	Jackie Robinson	75.00
5	Jackie Robinson	75.00

1997 Talk N' Sports $1,000 Phone Cards

This five-card set gave collectors a chance to get $1,000 worth of phone time (one dollar per minute). Cards were inserted every 11,000 packs and sequentially numbered to 10.

		MT
Complete Set (5):		2500.
Common Player:		500.00
1	Cal Ripken Jr.	700.00
2	Scottie Pippen	500.00
3	Brett Favre	700.00
4	Allen Iverson	600.00
5	Eddie George	500.00

1997 Visions Signings

The 50-card set is made up of the top players from each of the four major sports. Each card has a parallel gold card that is inserted 1:2 packs. The big attraction to this product was the Autographed Memorabilia Redemption Cards that were inserted 1:16 packs. Collectors could redeem cards for autographed basketballs, baseballs, footballs, helmets, pucks, jerseys, photos, plaques or Sports Illustrated magazines. Score Board also gave away a T206 Wagner. They inserted five specially marked cards, each redeemable for an original Honus Wagner card and a chance to win the coveted T206 Wagner.

		MT
Complete Set (50):		15.00
Common Player:		.10
Minor Stars:		.20
Gold Cards:		3x
1	Barry Bonds	.20
2	Hakeem Olajuwon	.20
3	Glenn Robinson	.10
4	Steve Young	.20
5	Jose Cruz Jr.	1.50
6	Ben Grieve	1.00
7	Kerry Wood	1.00
8	Erick Dampier	.10
9	Tony Delk	.10
10	Steve Nash	.10
11	Jerry Stackhouse	.20
12	Lorenzen Wright	.10
13	Vitaly Potapenko	.10
14	Allen Iverson	1.00
15	Marcus Camby	.50
16	Shareef Abdur-Rahim	.75
17	Stephon Marbury	1.00
18	Ray Allen	.20
19	Antoine Walker	.50
20	John Wallace	.20
21	Kobe Bryant	1.25
22	Jermaine O'Neal	.10
23	Clyde Drexler	.20
24	Scottie Pippen	.20
25	Rasheed Wallace	.10
26	Joe Smith	.20
27	Antonio McDyess	.20
28	Alonzo Mourning	.20
29	Eddie George	1.25
30	Warrick Dunn	2.00
31	Darrell Russell	.10
32	Peter Boulware	.10
33	Shawn Springs	.10

34	Yatil Green	.30
35	David LaFleur	.10
36	Bryant Westbrook	.10
37	Rae Carruth	.75
38	Brett Favre	.75
39	Emmitt Smith	.75
40	Dainius Zubrus	.75
41	Joe Thornton	.75
42	Daniel Cleary	.10
43	Sergei Samsonov	.75
44	Wes Helms	.10
45	Richard Hidalgo	.10
46	Jay Payton	.10
47	Leeland McElroy	.10
48	Troy Davis	.50
49	Tony Gonzalez	.30
50	Byron Hanspard	.30

1997 Visions Signings Autographs

This 63-card set contains some of the best young stars in a variety of sports. Each of the 1997 Visions Signings pack contained either an autographed card or an insert card. One in six packs contained an autographed card.

		MT
Complete Set (63):		750.00
Common Player:		8.00
1	Shareef Abdur-Rahim	50.00
3	Ray Allen	40.00
4	Tony Banks	40.00
5	Michael Booker	8.00
6	Peter Boulware	12.00
7	Dante Calabria	8.00
8	Rae Carruth	25.00
9	Jose Cruz	50.00
10	Erick Dampier	8.00
11	Tony Delk	8.00
12	Koy Detmer	20.00
13	Corey Dillon	25.00
14	Warrick Dunn	75.00
15	Tyus Edney	8.00
16	Brian Evans	8.00
18	Derek Fisher	8.00
19	Yatil Green	20.00
20	Ben Grieve	30.00
21	Vladimir Guerrero	40.00
22	Steve Hamer	8.00
23	Byron Hanspard	20.00
24	Kevin Hardy	8.00
25	Othella Harrington	8.00
26	Wes Helms	30.00
27	Richard Hidalgo	8.00
28	Josh Holden	8.00
29	Allen Iverson	60.00
30	DeRon Jenkins	8.00
31	Andre Johnson	8.00
32	Greg Jones	8.00
33	Danny Kanell	8.00
34	Jason Kendall	12.00
35	Pete Kendall	8.00
36	Travis Knight	20.00
37	David LaFleur	15.00
38	Jeff Lewis	8.00
39	Stephon Marbury	50.00
40	Dave McCarty	8.00
41	Walter McCarty	8.00
42	Leeland McElroy	15.00
43	Ray Mickens	8.00
44	Jay Payton	12.00
45	Vitaly Potopenko	8.00
46	Trevor Pryce	8.00
47	Efthimis Retzias	8.00
48	Roy Rogers	8.00
49	Malik Rose	8.00
50	Darrell Russell	8.00
51	Sergei Samsonov	40.00
52	Antowain Smith	25.00
54	Kurt Thomas	8.00
55	Joe Thornton	30.00
56	Amani Toomer	20.00
57	Antoine Walker	40.00
58	John Wallace	8.00
59	Bryant Westbrook	8.00
60	Jerome Williams	8.00
61	Stepfret Williams	8.00
62	Paul Wilson	20.00
63	Kerry Wood	60.00
64	Lorenzen Wright	8.00
65	Dainius Zubrus	40.00
66	Andrei Zyuzin	8.00

1997 Visions Signings Artistry

The Artistry set is made up of primarily basketball and football #1 picks. Each card front has a color photo of the player along with a smaller black-and-white photo on the front. The card backs also have a color photo with a brief write-up about the player. They were inserted 1:6 packs.

		MT
Complete Set (20):		100.00
Common Player:		3.00
1	Jose Cruz Jr.	10.00
2	Allen Iverson	10.00
3	Marcus Camby	5.00
4	Shareef Abdur-Rahim	7.00
5	Stephon Marbury	8.00
6	Ray Allen	4.00
7	Antoine Walker	3.00
8	Kobe Bryant	12.00
9	Clyde Drexler	3.00
10	Scottie Pippen	4.00
11	Alonzo Mourning	3.00
12	Eddie George	10.00
13	Warrick Dunn	12.00
14	Darrell Russell	3.00
15	Peter Boulware	3.00
16	Shawn Springs	3.00
17	Yatil Green	5.00
18	Brett Favre	10.00
19	Emmitt Smith	10.00
20	Dainius Zubrus	5.00

1997 Visions Signings Artistry Autographs

The Artistry Autographs are the same as the Artistry set except for the autograph that appears on the fronts of each card. Athletes from three sports signed in this set that is inserted 1:18 packs.

	MT
Complete Set (8):	900.00
Common Player:	30.00
Peter Boulware	30.00
Jose Cruz	150.00
Warrick Dunn	150.00
Brett Favre	300.00
Stephon Marbury	125.00
Alonzo Mourning	125.00
Antoine Walker	60.00
Dainius Zubrus	60.00

1998 Autographed Collection Blue Ribbon Players

Blue Ribbon Players was inserted one per 18 packs. The card fronts feature a player photo inside a blue ribbon graphic, with the autograph in an oval frame near the bottom. The player's name is at the bottom. Each card is sequentially numbered and the number appears in the upper right corner. The backs feature a congratulatory message.

	MT
Complete Set (15):	1000.
Common Player:	10.00
Shareef Abdur-Rahim	75.00
Tony Battie	20.00
Marcus Camby	40.00
Austin Croshere	10.00
Jose Cruz Jr.	40.00
Tim Duncan	150.00
Eddie George	100.00
Danny Fortson	10.00
Kerry Kittles	15.00
Stephon Marbury	50.00
Tracy McGrady	50.00
Scottie Pippen	200.00
Emmitt Smith	200.00
Joe Thornton	25.00
Steve Young	150.00

1998 Autographed Collection

The Score Board issued this multi-sport, non-licensed product. The 50-card base set featured star players as well as rookies. The base cards feature a color player photo with the player's name at the bottom. An oval containing the player's facsimile signature and a blue background depicting a scene from the city or state he plays in is featured near the bottom. Autographed cards are inserted one per 4.5 packs, with Blue Ribbon autographs seeded 1:18. The 15-card Sports City, U.S.A. insert is found 1:9. One Autographed Memorabilia card was inserted in each box and a redemption for a T-206 Honus Wagner card was inserted in the product. Most of the redemptions were never fulfilled because The Score Board filed for bankruptcy.

		MT
Complete Set (50):		12.00
Common Player:		.05
1	Tim Duncan	2.00
2	Brett Favre	.75
3	J.D. Drew	.50
4	Joe Thornton	.50
5	Allen Iverson	.75
6	Emmitt Smith	.50
7	Scottie Pippen	.50
8	Steve Young	.25
9	Stephon Marbury	.50
10	Ike Hilliard	.50
11	Matt White	.05
12	Jay Payton	.50
13	Darrell Russell	.25
14	Keith Van Horn	.75
15	Tiki Barber	.50
16	Kobe Bryant	2.00
17	Jake Plummer	1.00
18	Tim Thomas	.75
19	Danny Wuerffel	.50
20	Hakeem Olajuwon	.50
21	Kordell Stewart	.50
22	Clyde Drexler	.25
23	Brandon Larson	.10
24	Adonal Foyle	.05
25	Alonzo Mourning	.25
26	Warrick Dunn	1.00
27	Robert Dome	.05
28	Jose Cruz Jr.	.50
29	Rae Carruth	.25
30	Joe Smith	.25
31	Troy Aikman	.50
32	Tony Battie	.25
33	Peter Boulware	.25
34	David LaFleur	.05
35	Jim Druckenmiller	.25
36	Sergei Samsonov	.50
37	Chauncey Billups	.50
38	Yatil Green	.50
39	Tracy McGrady	1.00
40	Orlando Pace	.25
41	Antoine Walker	.50
42	Byron Hanspard	.25
43	Troy Davis	.25
44	Reidel Anthony	.50
45	Ron Mercer	.75
46	Tony Banks	.50
47	Antonio Daniels	.50
48	Tony Gonzalez	.50
49	Adrian Beltre	.05
50	Kerry Kittles	.05

1998 Autographed Collection Autographs

Autographed Cards were inserted one per 4.5 packs of 1998 Autographed Collection. The fronts feature a player head-shot in a circular frame and his autograph in an oval frame at the bottom. The backs have a congratulatory message. The autograph list consists of mostly young players and rookies, but stars like Wayne Gretzky and Shaquille O'Neal were also listed.

	MT
Complete Set (23):	250.00
Common Player:	5.00
John Allred	5.00
Darnell Autry	5.00
Pat Barnes	5.00
Daniel Briere	5.00
Daniel Cleary	10.00
Tony Delk	10.00
Robert Dome	10.00
Jim Druckenmiller	25.00
Ben Grieve	50.00
Wes Helms	10.00
Richard Jackman	5.00
Brevin Knight	25.00
Dexter McCleon	5.00
Brad Otton	5.00
Anthony Parker	5.00
Jay Payton	20.00
Jake Plummer	50.00
Scot Pollard	5.00
Antowain Smith	30.00
Charles Smith	5.00
John Thomas	5.00
Reinard Wilson	5.00
Kerry Wood	75.00
Lorenzen Wright	10.00

1998 Autographed Collection Sports City USA

This 15-card insert was seeded 1:9 in 1998 Autographed Collection. Each card features two or three players from teams in the same city or state with the city's skyline or landmarks in the background.

		MT
Complete Set (15):		40.00
Common Player:		2.00
1	Adonal Foyle, Joe Smith, Steve Young	3.00
2	Matt White, Warrick Dunn, Reidel Anthony	3.00
3	Hakeem Olajuwon, Clyde Drexler, Richard Hidalgo	3.00
4	Kerry Wood, Scottie Pippen, Darnell Autry	10.00
5	Ray Allen, Brett Favre	8.00
6	Kobe Bryant, Adrian Beltre	10.00
7	Tim Thomas, Duce Staley, J.D. Drew	2.00
8	Alonzo Mourning, Yatil Green	2.00
9	Joe Thornton, Chauncey Billups	2.00
10	Emmitt Smith, Troy Aikman, Richard Jackman	4.00
11	Kordell Stewart, Robert Dome	3.00
12	Wes Helms, Byron Hanspard, Ed Gray	2.00
13	Stephon Marbury, Dwayne Rudd	3.00
14	Jay Payton, Tiki Barber, Keith Van Horn	2.00
15	Matt Drews, Bryant Westbrook, Scot Pollard	2.00

1969-70 76ers Team Issue

Each of these team-issued, black-and-white player portraits measures 5-3/4" x 7-1/4". The player's name is printed below the photo. The backs are blank and unnumbered.

		NM
Complete Set (11):		50.00
Common Player:		3.00
1	Archie Clark	5.00
2	Bill Cunningham	10.00
3	Hal Greer	6.00
4	Matt Guokas	6.00
5	Fred Hetzel	3.00
6	Darrall Imhoff	3.00
7	Luke Jackson	5.00
8	Wally Jones	5.00
9	Bud Ogden	3.00
10	Jack Ramsay CO	5.00
11	George Wilson	3.00

1975-76 76ers McDonald's Standups

Measuring about 3-3/4" x 7-1/4", the six cards have die-cut color photos on front that can be pushed out to make the player figures standup. The unnumbered cards are blank-backed. Produced by Johnny Pro Enterprises, the card fronts include the player's name and the McDonald's logo.

	NM
Complete Set (6):	30.00
Common Player:	3.00
Fred Carter	4.00
Harvey Catchings	3.00
Doug Collins	10.00
Billy Cunningham	12.00
George McGinnis	6.00
Steve Mix	4.00

1989-90 76ers Kodak

Each measuring 8" x 11", three sheets were sponsored by Jack's Cameras and Kodak. A 76ers team photo was featured on the first sheet. The second sheet had two rows of five cards each, while the third sheet had six player cards. Four cards on the third sheet were coupons for Jack's Cameras. When perforated, the cards measure 2-3/16" x 3-3/4". Anchoring the card fronts is a color action shot. The player's name, number, position, along with Jack's Cameras', 76ers' and Kodak logos were printed at the bottom of the front. The card backs have a 76ers' logo. The cards are unnumbered.

	MT
Complete Set (16):	12.00
Common Player:	.25
Ron Anderson	.25
Charles Barkley	8.00
Scott Brooks	.50
Lanard Copeland	.50
Johnny Dawkins	.50
Mike Gminski	.50
Hersey Hawkins	1.00
Rick Mahorn	.50
Kurt Nimphius	.25
Kenny Payne	.25
Derek Smith	.25
Bob Thornton	.25
Big Shot (Team Mascot)	.25
Jim Lynam CO	.25
Fred Carter ACO	.25
Buzz Braman ACO	.25

1994 Signature Rookies Gold Standard

This 100-card, multi-sport set features full-bleed photos on the card fronts. A gold seal is stamped at the top and the player's name appears in a diagonal black stripe at the bottom. The backs have a horizontal layout with a close-up photo and biographical information. Inserts include Signatures, Hall of Fame Signatures and Legends.

		MT
Complete Set (100):		8.00
Common Player:		.05
1	Derrick Alston	.05
2	Damon Bailey	.05
3	Bill Curley	.05
4	Yinka Dare	.05
5	Rodney Dent	.05
6	Brian Grant	.25
7	Juwan Howard	1.00
8	Askia Jones	.05
9	Eddie Jones	1.25
10	Donyell Marshall	.25
11	Aaron McKie	.05
12	Greg Minor	.05
13	Eric Montross	.05
14	Wesley Person	.25
15	Eric Piatkowski	.05
16	Jalen Rose	.25
17	Clifford Rozier	.05
18	Dickey Simpkins	.05
19	Deon Thomas	.05
20	Brooks Thompson	.05
21	B.J. Tyler	.05
22	Charlie Ward	.25
23	Monty Williams	.05
24	Dontonio Wingfield	.05
25	Sharone Wright	.05
26	Sam Adams	.05
27	Trev Alberts	.05
28	Derrick Alexander	.25
29	Mitch Berger	.05
30	Tim Bowens	.25
31	Jeff Burris	.05
32	Shante Carver	.05
33	Lake Dawson	.15
34	Marshall Faulk	1.00
35	Glenn Foley	.05
36	Rob Fredrickson	.25
37	Wayne Gandy	.05
38	Charles Johnson FB	.25
39	Tre Johnson	.05
40	Perry Klein	.05
41	Antonio Langham	.05
42	Eric Mahlum	.05
43	Willie McGinest	.25
44	Jamir Miller	.05
45	Byron "Bam" Morris	.25
46	Errict Rhett	.25
47	John Thierry	.05
48	DeWayne Washington	.05
49	Dan Wilkinson	.05
50	Bernard Williams	.05
51	Josh Booty	.05
52	Roger Cedeno	.05
53	Cliff Floyd	.25
54	Ben Grieve	1.50
55	Joey Hamilton	.25
56	Todd Hollandsworth	.05
57	Brian L. Hunter	.25
58	Charles Johnson BB	.25
59	Brooks Kieschnick	.25
60	Mike Kelly	.05
61	Ray McDavid	.05
62	Kurt Miller	.05
63	James Mouton	.05
64	Phil Nevin	.05
65	Alex Ochoa	.05
66	Herbert Perry	.05
67	Kirk Presley	.05
68	Bill Pulsipher	.05
69	Scott Ruffcorn	.05
70	Paul Shuey	.05
71	Michael Tucker	.25
72	Terrell Wade	.05
73	Gabe White	.05
74	Paul Wilson	.25
75	Dmitri Young	.05
76	Nolan Baumgartner	.05
77	Wade Belak	.05
78	Radek Bonk	.05
79	Brad Brown	.05
80	Dan Cloutier	.05
81	Johan Davidsson	.05
82	Yannick Dube	.05
83	Eric Fichaud	.05
84	Johann Finnstrom	.05
85	Edvin Frylen	.05
86	Patrik Juhlin	.05
87	Valeri Karpov	.05
88	Nikolai Khabibulin	.25
89	Mattias Ohlund	.25
90	Jason Podollan	.25
91	Vadim Sharifjanov	.05
92	Ryan Smyth	.25
93	Dimitri Tabarin	.05
94	Nikolai Tsulygin	.25
95	Stefan Ustorf	.05
96	Paul Vincent	.05
97	Roman Vopat	.05
98	Rhett Warrener	.05
99	Vitali Yachmenev	.25
100	Vadim Yepenchinstev	.05

1994 Signature Rookies Gold Standard Signatures

This 20-card set was inserted one per pack. The design is identical to the base set but includes "Gold Standard" stamped in gold foil and a facsimile autograph. Each card has a serial number on the back with a "GS" prefix.

		MT
Complete Set (20):		10.00
Common Signature:		.50
1	Marshall Faulk	1.50
2	Josh Booty	.50
3	Radek Bonk	.50
4	Nolan Baumgartner	.50
5	Sam Adams	.50
6	Brooks Kieschnick	.50
7	Valeri Karpov	.50
8	Charles Johnson	1.00
9	Juwan Howard	2.00
10	Cliff Floyd	.75
11	James Mouton	.50
12	Eric Montross	.50
13	Willie McGinest	.75
14	Donyell Marshall	.50
15	Perry Klein	.50
16	Sharone Wright	.50
17	Dan Wilkinson	.50
18	Ryan Smyth	.50
19	Clifford Rozier	.50
20	Jalen Rose	1.00

1994 Signature Rookies Gold Standard HOF Signatures

Inserted one per box, this 24-card set has the same basic design as the base set but the cards are signed and have "Hall of Fame" gold-foil stamped at the top. Only 2,500 of each card was produced. A redemption card randomly inserted in packs was good for unsigned versions of these cards.

		MT
Complete Set (24):		200.00
Common Signature:		8.00
1	Nate Archibald	8.00
2	Rick Barry	12.00
3	Mike Bossy	8.00
4	Bob Cousy	20.00
5	Dave Cowens	10.00
6	Dave DeBusschere	12.00
7	Tony Esposito	10.00
8	Walt Frazier	12.00
9	Otto Graham	15.00
10	Jack Ham	10.00
11	Connie Hawkins	10.00
12	Elvin Hayes	12.00
13	Paul Hornung	18.00
14	Sam Huff	10.00
15	Jim Hunter	10.00
16	Bob Lilly	12.00
17	Don Maynard	10.00
18	Ray Nitschke	12.00
19	Bob Pettit	12.00
20	Willie Stargell	12.00
21	Y.A. Tittle	12.00
22	Bill Walton	10.00
23	Paul Warfield	10.00
24	Randy White	12.00

1994 Signature Rookies Gold Standard Legends

		MT
Complete Set (5):		8.00
Common Player:		.50
L1	Larry Bird	4.00
L2	Brian Leetch	.75
L3	"Pee Wee" Reese	1.50
L4	Nolan Ryan	4.00
L5	Isiah Thomas	.75

1994 Signature Rookies Tetrad Previews

This seven-card promo set has full-bleed color photos on the fronts with the player's name and position printed in gold foil at the bottom. A stripe designed as a marble column contains the words "Promo, 1 of 10,000" printed in gold foil on the left side. The backs have a ghosted image of a Greek temple and biographical information.

		MT
Complete Set (7):		10.00
Common Player:		1.00
1	Eric Montross	1.00
2	Tim Taylor	1.00
3	Jeff Granger	1.00
4	Roger Cedeno	1.00
5	Charlie Ward	2.00
6	O.J. Simpson	5.00
---	Header Card	1.00

1994 Signature Rookies Tetrad

The cards in this 120-card set feature full-bleed photos on the front with the player's name printed in gold foil at the bottom. A vertical stripe designed as a marble column contains the words "1 of 45,000" printed in gold foil. The backs have biographical information over a ghosted image of a Greek temple.

		MT
Complete Set (120):		15.00
Common Player:		.05
1	Jay Walker	.05

2	Ricky Brady	.05
3	Paul Duckworth	.05
4	Jim Flanigan	.05
5	Brice Adams	.05
6	William Floyd	.25
7	Charlie Garner	.25
8	Pete Bercich	.05
9	Frank Harvey	.05
10	Willie Clark	.05
11	Bernie Williams	.05
12	Kurt Haws	.05
13	Dennis Collier	.05
14	Filmel Johnson	.05
15	Zane Beehn	.05
16	Johnnie Morton	.25
17	Lonnie Johnson	.05
18	Jay Kearney	.05
19	Steve Shine	.05
20	Dexter Nottage	.05
21	Ervin Collier	.05
22	Dorsey Levens	1.00
23	Kevin Knox	.05
24	Doug Nussmeier	.05
25	Bill Schroeder	.05
26	Winfred Tubbs	.05
27	Rodney Harrison	.05
28	Rob Waldrop	.05
29	Mike Davis	.05
30	John Burke	.05
31	Allen Aldridge	.05
32	Kevin Mitchell	.05
33	Greg Hill	.25
34	Ernest Jones	.05
35	Kevin Mawae	.05
36	John Covington	.05
37	Mike Wells	.05
38	Thomas Lewis	.25
39	Chad Bratzke	.05
40	Darren Studstill	.05
41	Derrick Alston	.05
42	Adrian Autry	.25
43	Damon Bailey	.05
44	Doremus Benneman	.05
45	Melvin Booker	.05
46	Jevon Crudup	.05
47	Yinka Dare	.05
48	Rodney Dent	.05
49	Tony Dumas	.05
50	Dwayne Fontana	.05
51	Travis Ford	.05
52	Lawrence Funderburke	.05
53	Anthony Goldwire	.05
54	Brian Grant	.25
55	Kenny Harris	.05
56	Juwan Howard (misspelled Juwon)	1.50
57	Askia Jones	.05
58	Eddie Jones	1.50
59	Arturas Karnishovas	.05
60	Donyell Marshall	.05
61	Billy McCaffrey	.05
62	Jim McIlvaine	.05
63	Aaron McKie	.05
64	Greg Minor	.05
65	Eric Mobley	.05
66	Eric Montross	.05
67	Gaylon Nickerson	.05
68	Wesley Person	.25
69	Eric Piatkowski	.05
70	Kevin Rankin	.05
71	Shawnelle Scott	.05
72	Melvin Simon	.05
73	Dickey Simpskins	.05
74	Michael Smith	.05
75	Stevin Smith	.05
76	Deon Thomas	.05
77	Brooks Thompson	.05
78	B.J. Tyler	.05
79	Kendrick Warren	.05
80	Jeff Webster	.05
81	Monty Williams	.05
82	Dontonio Wingfield	.05
83	Sharone Wright	.05
84	Edgardo Alfonzo	.25
85	David Bell	.05
86	Chris Carpenter	.10
87	Roger Cedeno	.05
88	Phil Geisler	.05
89	Curtis Goodwin	.05
90	Jeff Granger	.05
91	Brian L. Hunter	.25
92	Adam Hyzdu	.05
93	Scott Klingenbeck	.05
94	Derrek Lee	.75
95	Calvin Murray	.05
96	Roberto Petagine	.05
97	Bill Pulsipher	.05
98	Marquis Riley	.05
99	Frank Rodriguez	.05
100	Scott Ruffcorn	.05
101	Roger Salkeld	.05
102	Marc Valdes	.05
103	Ernie Young	.05
104	Sven Butenschon	.05
105	Dan Cloutier	.05
106	Pat Jablonski	.05
107	Valeri Karpov	.05
108	Nikolai Khabibulin	.25
109	Sergei Klimentiev	.05
110	Krzysztof Oliwa	.05
111	Dmitri Riabykin	.05
112	Ryan Risidore	.05
113	Shawn Rivers	.05
114	Vadim Sharifjanov	.05
115	Mika Stromberg	.05
116	Tim Taylor	.05
117	Vitali Yachmenev	.25
118	Wendell Young	.05
---	Checklist 1	.05
---	Checklist 2	.05

1994 Signature Rookies Tetrad Signatures

Inserted one per pack of 1994 SR Tetrad, this 117-card insert is identical in design to the base set except for the player's signature. Only 7,750 of each card were produced.

		MT
Complete Set (117):		350.00
Common Player:		2.50
1	Jay Walker	2.50
2	Ricky Brady	2.50
3	Paul Duckworth	2.50
4	Jim Flanigan	2.50
5	Brice Adams	2.50
6	William Floyd	5.00
7	Charlie Garner	5.00
8	Pete Bercich	2.50
9	Frank Harvey	2.50
10	Willie Clark	2.50
12	Kurt Haws	2.50
13	Dennis Collier	2.50
14	Filmel Johnson	2.50
15	Zane Beehn	2.50
16	Johnnie Morton	10.00
17	Lonnie Johnson	2.50
18	Jay Kearney	2.50
19	Steve Shine	2.50
20	Dexter Nottage	2.50
21	Ervin Collier	2.50
22	Dorsey Levens	25.00
23	Kevin Knox	2.50
24	Doug Nussmeier	2.50
25	Bill Schroeder	2.50
26	Winfred Tubbs	2.50
27	Rodney Harrison	2.50
28	Rob Waldrop	2.50
29	Mike Davis	2.50
30	John Burke	2.50
31	Allen Aldridge	2.50
32	Kevin Mitchell	2.50
33	Greg Hill	5.00
34	Ernest Jones	2.50
35	Kevin Mawae	2.50
36	John Covington	2.50
37	Mike Wells	2.50
38	Thomas Lewis	5.00
39	Chad Bratzke	2.50
40	Darren Studstill	2.50
41	Derrick Alston	2.50
42	Adrian Autry	5.00
43	Damon Bailey	2.50
44	Doremus Bennerman	2.50
45	Melvin Booker	2.50
46	Jevon Crudup	2.50
47	Yinka Dare	2.50
48	Rodney Dent	2.50
49	Tony Dumas	2.50
50	Dwayne Fontana	2.50
51	Travis Ford	2.50
52	Lawrence Funderburke	2.50
53	Anthony Goldwire	2.50
54	Brian Grant	10.00
55	Kenny Harris	2.50
56	Juwan Howard (misspelled Juwon)	25.00
57	Askia Jones	2.50
58	Eddie Jones	25.00
59	Arturas Karnishovas	2.50
60	Donyell Marshall	2.50
61	Billy McCaffrey	2.50
62	Jim McIlvaine	2.50
63	Aaron McKie	2.50
64	Greg Minor	2.50
65	Eric Mobley	2.50
66	Eric Montross	2.50
67	Gaylon Nickerson	2.50
68	Wesley Person	10.00
69	Eric Piatkowski	2.50
70	Kevin Rankin	2.50
71	Shawnelle Scott	2.50
72	Melvin Simon	2.50
73	Dickey Simpskins	2.50
74	Michael Smith	2.50
75	Stevin Smith	2.50
76	Deon Thomas	2.50
77	Brooks Thompson	2.50
78	B.J. Tyler	2.50
79	Kendrick Warren	2.50
80	Jeff Webster	2.50
81	Monty Williams	2.50
82	Dontonio Wingfield	2.50
83	Sharone Wright	2.50
84	Edgardo Alfonzo	5.00
85	David Bell	2.50
86	Chris Carpenter	5.00
87	Roger Cedeno	2.50
88	Phil Geisler	2.50
89	Curtis Goodwin	2.50
90	Jeff Granger	2.50
91	Brian L. Hunter	5.00
92	Adam Hyzdu	2.50
93	Scott Klingenbeck	2.50
94	Derrek Lee	15.00
95	Calvin Murray	2.50
96	Roberto Petagine	2.50
97	Bill Pulsipher	2.50
98	Marquis Riley	2.50
99	Frank Rodriguez	2.50
100	Scott Ruffcorn	2.50
101	Roger Salkeld	2.50
102	Marc Valdes	2.50
103	Ernie Young	2.50
104	Sven Butenschon	2.50
105	Dan Cloutier	2.50
106	Pat Jablonski	2.50
107	Valeri Karpov	2.50
108	Nikolai Khabibulin	8.00
109	Sergei Klimentiev	2.50
110	Krzysztof Oliwa	2.50
111	Dmitri Riabykin	2.50
112	Ryan Risidore	2.50
113	Shawn Rivers	2.50
114	Vadim Sharifjanov	2.50
115	Mika Stromberg	2.50
116	Tim Taylor	2.50
117	Vitali Yachmenev	8.00
118	Wendell Young	2.50

1994 Signature Rookies Tetrad Flip Cards

Flip cards is a five-card insert set that features players on the front and back of the card. Each player in the Flip Card set autographed 250 cards. They are numbered Flip 1 through Flip 5.

		MT
Complete Set (5):		38.00
Common Player:		5.00
1	C. Johnson/ C. Johnson	10.00
2	G Sayers/ T Dorsett	7.00
3	C. Ward/ C. Ward	5.00
4	Juwan Howard/Jalen Rose	16.00
5	Monty Williams/Glen Williams	5.00

1994 Signature Rookies Tetrad Top Prospects

This four-card set features top young players. The design of the cards are identical to the 1994 Tetrad base set. The cards are limited to 20,000, which is indicated in the column on the card fronts.

		MT
Complete Set (4):		6.00
Common Card (131-134):		1.00
131	Charlie Ward	1.50
132	Willie McGinest	1.50
133	Shante Carver	1.00
134	Paul Wilson	4.00

1994 Signature Rookies Tetrad Titans

This 12-card set was randomly inserted in packs of 1994 SR Tetrad. The design is identical to the base set except the background is blurred and the backs are numbered in Roman numerals. Only 10,000 of each card was produced.

		MT
Complete Set (12):		25.00
Common Player:		2.00
119	Bobby Allison	2.50
120	Larry Bird	8.00
121	Larry Holmes	2.50
122	Bobby Hull	4.00
123	Dan Jansen	2.50
124	Bruce Jenner	2.50
125	Tony Meola	2.00
126	Shannon Miller	2.50
127	Frank Shorter	2.00
128	Picabo Street	4.00
129	O.J. Simpson UER (misnumbered T6)	3.00
130	Isiah Thomas UER (misspelled Isaiah)	2.50

1994 Signature Rookies Tetrad Titans Signatures

This set is identical to the Tetrad Titans insert except for the player's signature on the front. Each card is numbered of 1,050 except for card #129 which is numbered of 2,500.

		MT
Complete Set (12):		700.00
Common Signatures (119-130):		25.00
Coupons Replace Some Cards:		
119	Bobby Allison	30.00
120	Larry Bird	150.00
121	Larry Holmes	60.00
122	Bobby Hull	40.00
123	Dan Jansen	30.00
124	Bruce Jenner	30.00
125	Tony Meola	30.00
126	Shannon Miller	35.00
127	Frank Shorter	25.00
128	Picabo Street	25.00
129	O.J. Simpson (2500 autographed)	175.00
130	Isiah Thomas UER (misspelled Isaiah)	60.00

1995 Signature Rookies Autobilia

The 30-card, standard-size set features a duplicate image on the card front, with the second image being shadowed. Players in the set signed 3,000 photos, 1,000 cards, 500 pennants, 400 team balls, 350 hats, 24 practice jerseys and 550 basketballs. Kevin Garnett and Jerry Stackhouse signed 250 Sports Illustrated covers.

		MT
Complete Set (30):		25.00
Common Player:		.40
Signed Cards:		15x to 30x
Signed Photos:		6x to 30x
1	Joe Smith	2.50
2	Antonio McDyess	1.50
3	Jerry Stackhouse	2.50
4	Rasheed Wallace	1.00
5	Kevin Garnett	5.00
6	Bryant Reeves	1.50
7	Damon Stoudamire	3.00
8	Shawn Respert	.40
9	Ed O'Bannon	.75
10	Kurt Thomas	.75
11	Gary Trent	.60
12	Cherokee Parks	.40
13	Corliss Williamson	.75
14	Eric Williams	.75
15	Brent Barry	1.00
16	Alan Henderson	.75
17	Bob Sura	.60
18	Theo Ratliff	.50
19	Randoilph Childress	.40
20	Jason Caffey	.40
21	Michael Finley	1.00
22	Geworge Zidek	.60
23	Travis Best	.40
24	Loren Meyer	.50
25	David Vaughn	.40
26	Sherrell Ford	.40
27	Mario Bennett	.40
28	Greg Osterlag	.40
29	Cory Alexander	.40
NNO	Checklist	.25

1995 Signature Rookies Autobilia Kevin Garnett

The five-card, standard-size set features two different player images on the card fronts with bio and stat information on the back over another color image. The cards were randomly inserted and are numbered with a "G" prefix.

		MT
Complete Set (5):		20.00
Common Player:		5.00
1	Kevin Garnett	5.00
2	Kevin Garnett	5.00
3	Kevin Garnett	5.00
4	Kevin Garnett	5.00
5	Kevin Garnett	5.00

1995 Signature Rookies Autobilia Jerry Stackhouse

The five-card, standard-size set was randomly inserted into packs with each card featuring North Carolina's Jerry Stackhouse. The fronts have two color player images with bio and stat information over another player image on the back. The cards are numbered with an "S" prefix.

		MT
Complete Set (5):		12.00
Common Player:		3.00
1	Jerry Stackhouse	3.00
2	Jerry Stackhouse	3.00
3	Jerry Stackhouse	3.00
4	Jerry Stackhouse	3.00
5	Jerry Stackhouse	3.00

1995 Signature Rookies Draft Day

The 50-card, standard-size set features borderless color action photos with the player's name and a player's silhouette printed in gold in a faded black stripe near the bottom border. The backs contain three player photos with bio and stat information. Production was limited to 38,000.

		MT
Complete Set (50):		10.00
Common Player:		.10
1	Donny Marshall	.15
2	Mario Bennett	.15
3	Dan Cross	.10
4	Devin Gray	.10
5	Dwight Stewart	.10
6	Jerome Allen	.15
7	Travis Best	.10
8	Tyus Edney	.75
9	Mark Davis	.10
10	Michael Finley	.50
11	Gary Trent	.40
12	Julius Michalik	.10
13	Clint McDaniel	.10
14	Sherell Ford	.15
15	Junior Burrough	.10
16	Bryan Collins	.10
17	Andrew DeClerq	.10
18	Glen Whisby	.10
19	Terrance Rencher	.10
20	Eric Snow	.10
21	Alan Henderson	.50
22	Bob Sura	.40
23	James Forrest	.10
24	Jimmy King	.15
25	Scotty Thurman	.10
26	Matt Maloney	.10
27	Paul O'Liney	.10
28	Lazelle Durden	.10
29	Eric Williams	.50
30	Tom Kleinschmidt	.10
31	Cory Alexander	.10
32	James Scott	.10
33	Michael McDonald	.10
34	Randy Rutherford	.10
35	Donald Williams	.10
36	Kurt Thomas	.30
37	Loren Meyer	.30
38	Donnie Boyce	.10
39	Michael Hawkins	.10
40	Lou Roe	.15
41	Larry Skyes	.10
42	Cuonzo Martin	.10
43	Jason Caffey	.15
44	Scott Highmark	.10
45	Lawrence Moten	.15
46	Anthony Pelle	.10
47	Randolph Childress	.10
48	Ray Jackson	.10
49	Corey Beck	.10
50	Fred Hoiberg	.10
KG	Kevin Garnett (AU) (260)	90.00
NNO	Checklist Card	.10

1995 Signature Rookies Draft Day Signatures

The 50-card, standard-size set was inserted in each pack of 1995 Draft Day. Each player in the 50-card set signed 7,750 cards with some of the autographed cards being represented by redemption cards.

		MT
Complete Set (50):		200.00
Common Player:		3.00
8	Tyus Edney	6.00
10	Michael Finley	10.00
11	Gary Trent	6.00
21	Alan Henderson	10.00
22	Bob Sura	8.00
29	Eric Williams	10.00
36	Kurt Thomas	8.00
37	Loren Meyer	6.00

1995 Signature Rookies Draft Day Draft Gems

The 10-card, standard-size set was inserted every 22 packs with five players having two cards each. The card fronts have two player images while the backs contain another image in a diamond-like frame. The cards are numbered with a "DG" prefix.

		MT
Complete Set (10):		40.00
Common Player:		2.00
1	Jerry Stackhouse	10.00
2	Jerry Stackhouse	10.00
3	Antonio McDyess	4.00
4	Antonio McDyess	4.00
5	Cherokee Parks	2.00
6	Cherokee Parks	2.00
7	Joe Smith	6.00
8	Joe Smith	6.00
9	Rasheed Wallace	2.50
10	Rasheed Wallace	2.50

1995 Signature Rookies Draft Day Draft Gems Signatures

Inserted every 87 packs, the cards parallel the Draft Day Draft Gems except for the players' signatures on the card fronts. Each card was limited to 525.

		MT
Complete Set (10):		475.00
Common Player:		25.00
1	Jerry Stackhouse	75.00
2	Jerry Stackhouse	75.00
3	Antonio McDyess	50.00
4	Antonio McDyess	50.00
5	Cherokee Parks	25.00
6	Cherokee Parks	25.00
7	Joe Smith	75.00
8	Joe Smith	75.00
9	Rasheed Wallace	30.00
10	Rasheed Wallace	30.00

1995 Signature Rookies Draft Day K. Abdul Jabbar

Inserted every 87 packs, the five-card set highlights different milestones in the career of Kareem Abdul-Jabbar. Abdul-Jabbar signed 105 of each card. Cards are numbered with a "K" prefix.

		MT
Complete Set (5):		15.00
Common Kareem:		4.00
Comp. Signed Set:		600.00
Common Signature:		120.00
1	Kareem Abdul-Jabbar	4.00
2	Kareem Abdul-Jabbar	4.00
3	Kareem Abdul-Jabbar	4.00
4	Kareem Abdul-Jabbar	4.00
5	Kareem Abdul-Jabbar	4.00

1995 Signature Rookies Draft Day Reflections

Inserted every 18 packs, the five standard-size cards have borderless action shots with a silhouette printed in gold in a vertical black stripe on the left. The card backs have player bio and stat information and are numbered with an "R" prefix.

		MT
Complete Set (5):		4.00
Common Player:		.50
1	Brian Grant	.75
2	Wesley Person	.75
3	Eric Montross	.50
4	Juwan Howard	1.50
5	Eddie Jones	2.00

1995 Signature Rookies Draft Day Reflections Signatures

Inserted every 346 packs, the five-card set parallels the Draft Day Reflections inserts, except for the player's autograph on the front. Cards are limited to 250 each.

		MT
Complete Set (5):		550.00
Common Player:		75.00
1	Brian Grant	75.00
2	Wesley Person	100.00
3	Eric Montross	75.00
4	Juwan Howard	200.00
5	Eddie Jones	200.00

1995 Signature Rookies Draft Day Show Stoppers

Inserted every three packs, the 25 standard-size cards depict five players on five different cards each. The card fronts are bordered by a film roll-type design while the backs have bio and stat information.

		MT
Complete Set (25):		35.00
Com. O'Bannon (E1-E5):		1.25
Com. Reeves (B1-B5):		2.00
Com. Respert (S1-S5):		1.00
Com. Stoudamire (D1-D5):		2.50
Com. Williamson (C1-C5):		1.25
B1	Bryant Reeves	2.00
B2	Bryant Reeves	2.00
B3	Bryant Reeves	2.00
B4	Bryant Reeves	2.00
B5	Bryant Reeves	2.00
C1	Corliss Williamson	1.25
C2	Corliss Williamson	1.25
C3	Corliss Williamson	1.25
C4	Corliss Williamson	1.25
C5	Corliss Williamson	1.25
D1	Damon Stoudamire	2.50
D2	Damon Stoudamire	2.50
D3	Damon Stoudamire	2.50
D4	Damon Stoudamire	2.50
D5	Damon Stoudamire	2.50
E1	Ed O'Bannon	1.25
E2	Ed O'Bannon	1.25
E3	Ed O'Bannon	1.25
E4	Ed O'Bannon	1.25
E5	Ed O'Bannon	1.25
S1	Shawn Respert	1.00
S2	Shawn Respert	1.00
S3	Shawn Respert	1.00
S4	Shawn Respert	1.00
S5	Shawn Respert	1.00

1995 Signature Rookies Draft Day Show Stoppers Signatures

Inserted every 18 packs, the cards parallel the Draft Day Show Stoppers, but with player signatures. Production was 1,050 of each card.

	MT
Complete Set (25):	450.00
Com. O'Bannon (E1-E5):	18.00
Com. Reeves (B1-B5):	25.00
Com. Respert (S1-S5):	15.00
Com. Stoudamire (D1-D5):	30.00
Com. Williamson (C1-C5):	18.00

1995 Signature Rookies Draft Day Swat Team

Inserted every three packs, the five cards highlighted top shot blockers and the card face has the "Swat Team" logo in the upper left corner. The cards are numbered with an "ST" prefix.

		MT
Complete Set (5):		3.00
Common Player:		.50
1	Tony Maroney	.50
2	Greg Ostertag	.75
3	George Zidek	1.00
4	Constantin Popa	.50
5	Theo Ratliff	1.00

1995 Signature Rookies Draft Day Swat Team Signatures

Inserted every 18 packs, the five cards parallel the base Draft Day Swat Team inserts, but with player signatures. Production was 5,000 for each. Cards are numbered with a "ST" prefix.

		MT
Complete Set (5):		35.00
Common Player:		6.00
1	Tony Maroney	6.00
2	Greg Ostertag	8.00
3	George Zidek	12.00
4	Constantin Popa	6.00
5	Theo Ratliff	10.00

1995 Signature Rookies Kro-Max Promos

		MT
Complete Set (2):		2.00
Common Player:		1.00
P1	Donyell Marshall	1.00
P2	Juwan Howard	1.50

1995 Signature Rookies Kro-Max

The 50-card, standard-size set featured a player cut out over a metallic background on the front with the Kromax emblem found on the bottom border. The backs contained a player closeup with bio and stat information, as well as career highlights. Just 1,995 eight-box cases were produced with each box containing either an autograph of a first-round pick, a Super Acrylium card or a Flash From The Past.

		MT
Complete Set (50):		20.00
Common Player:		.15
1	Donyell Marshall	.30
2	Juwan Howard	4.00
3	Sharone Wright	.75
4	Brian Grant	.75
5	Eric Montross	.75
6	Eddie Jones	4.00
7	Jalen Rose	.75
8	Yinka Dare	.30
9	Eric Piatkowski	.30
10	Clifford Rozier	.30
11	Aaron McKie	.30
12	Eric Mobley	.30
13	Tony Dumas	.30
14	B.J. Tyler	.30
15	Dickey Simpkins	.30
16	Bill Curley	.30
17	Wesley Person	.75
18	Monty Williams	.30
19	Greg Minor	.30
20	Charlie Ward	.60
21	Brooks Thompson	.30
22	Deon Thomas	.15
23	Howard Eisley	.30
24	Rodney Dent	.15
25	Jim McIlvaine	.30
26	Derrick Alston	.15
27	Gaylon Nickerson	.15
28	Michael Smith	.30
29	Andre Fetisov	.15
30	Dontonio Wingfield	.30
31	Anthony Miller	.15
32	Jeff Webster	.15
33	Shawnelle Scott	.15
34	Damon Bailey	.30
35	Jevon Crudup	.15
36	Lawrence Funderburke	.15
37	Anthony Goldwire	.30
38	Adrian Autry	.15
39	Doremus Bennerman	.15
40	Melvin Booker	.15
41	Dwayne Fontana	.15
42	Travis Ford	.15
43	Kenny Harris	.15
44	Askia Jones	.15
45	Jason Kidd	6.00
46	Bill McCaffrey	.15
47	Kevin Rankin	.15
48	Melvin Simon	.15
49	Glenn Robinson	5.00
50	Kendrick Warren	.15

1995 Signature Rookies Kro-Max Signatures

The five players signed cards that were randomly inserted into Kro-max packs. The number following the player's name is the number of cards they signed.

		MT
Complete Set (5):		75.00
Common Player:		10.00
1	Bill Curley - 2100	10.00
2	Yinka Dare - 2100	10.00
3	Eric Montross - 1050	20.00
4	Wesley Person - 1050	30.00
5	Sharone Wright - 2100	20.00

1995 Signature Rookies Kro-Max First Rounders

The 10-card, standard-size set was randomly inserted in seven-card packs and production of each card was limited to 2,500. The cards are numbered with an "FR" prefix.

		MT
Complete Set (10):		40.00
Common Player:		1.50
1	Donyell Marshall	1.50
2	Juwan Howard	15.00
3	Sharone Wright	3.00
4	Brian Grant	5.00
5	Eric Montross	3.00
6	Eddie Jones	15.00
7	Jalen Rose	4.00
8	Yinka Dare	1.50
9	B.J. Tyler	1.50
10	Charlie Ward	4.00

1995 Signature Rookies Kro-Max Flash From The Past

The 10-card, standard-size set was randomly inserted into the seven-card packs. The cards have an "FP" prefix and feature former NBA greats with air-brushed uniforms.

		MT
Complete Set (10):		25.00
Common Player:		1.50
1	Bob Cousy	3.00
2	Larry Bird	6.00
3	Walt Frazier	3.00
4	Rick Barry	3.00
5	Isiah Thomas	2.00
6	Tiny Archibald	1.50
7	Dave DeBusschere	1.50
8	Dave Cowens	2.00
9	Elvin Hayes	3.00
10	Kareem Abdul-Jabbar	3.00

1995 Signature Rookies Kro-Max Flash From The Past Sig.

The eight-card set parallels Flash From The Past inserts, but in autographed versions. Bob Cousy (No. 1) and Elvin Hayes (No. 9) did not sign cards. Each player signed 1,050 cards, except for Larry Bird (100), Isiah Thomas (100) and Kareem Abdul-Jabbar (1,550).

		MT
Complete Set (8):		1000.
Common Signature:		30.00
2	Larry Bird (100)	800.00
3	Walt Frazier (1050)	60.00
4	Rick Barry (1050)	60.00
5	Isiah Thomas (100)	275.00
6	Tiny Archibald (1050)	30.00
7	Dave DeBusschere (1050)	30.00
8	Dave Cowens (1050)	50.00
10	Kareem Abdul-Jabbar (1550)	85.00

1995 Signature Rookies Kro-Max Jumbos

The 3-1/2" x 5" set features 10 of the top picks from the 1994 NBA Draft. The player image is highlighted against a metallic background. Production of each card was listed as 3,300 and cards 11 and 12 were only available through a wrapper redemption program. Cards are numbered with a "J" prefix.

		MT
Complete Set (12):		25.00
Common Player:		1.00
1	Michigan (Juwan Howard)	8.00
2	Connecticut (Donyell Marshall)	1.00
3	Clemson (Sharone Wright)	2.00
4	Xavier (Brian Grant)	3.00
5	North Carolina (Eric Montross)	2.00
6	Temple (Eddie Jones)	8.00
7	Michigan (Jalen Rose)	2.00
8	George Washington (Yinka Dare)	1.00
9	Texas (B.J. Tyler)	1.00
10	Florida State (Charlie Ward)	2.00
11	Louisville (Clifford Rozier)	1.00
12	Auburn (Wesley Person)	4.00

1995 Signature Rookies Kro-Max Super Acrylium

The five-card, standard-size set was limited to 10,000 each. The fronts feature the player against a plain silver background with each card having an "SA" prefix.

		MT
Complete Set (5):		30.00
Common Player:		5.00
1	Scottie Pippen	10.00
2	Tim Hardaway	5.00
3	Charles Barkley	10.00
4	Dominique Wilkins	5.00
5	Patrick Ewing	8.00

1995 Signature Rookies Signature Prime

The 45-card, standard sized set arrived in five-card packs with an autographed card, an insert card, two regular-issue cards and one mail-in offer or checklist card. The card fronts feature the word "Prime" across the left border in gold foil, with career stats and bio information on the backs. The set was numbered in alphabetical order.

		MT
Complete Set (45):		25.00
Common Player:		.15
1	Cory Alexander	.15
2	Jerome Allen	.25
3	Brent Barry	1.25
4	Mario Bennett	.25
5	Travis Best	.15
6	Donnie Boyce	.15
7	Junior Burrough	.15
8	Jason Caffey	.15
9	Chris Carr	.25
10	Randolph Childress	.15
11	Mark Davis	.15
12	Andrew DeClerq	.15
13	Tyus Edney	.75
14	Michael Finley	2.00
15	Sherell Ford	.25
16	Kevin Garnett	6.00
17	Alan Henderson	1.00
18	Fred Hoiberg	.15
19	Jimmy King	.25
20	Donny Marshall	.25
21	Cuonzo Martin	.15
22	Michael McDonald	.15
23	Antonio McDyess	2.00
24	Loren Meyer	.60
25	Lawrence Moten	.15
26	Ed O'Bannon	.75
27	Greg Ostertag	.25
28	Cherokee Parks	.50
29	Anthony Pelle	.15
30	Constantin Popa	.15
31	Theo Ratliff	.60
32	Bryant Reeves	2.00
33	Don Reid	.25
34	Terrance Rencher	.15
35	Shawn Respert	.25
36	Lou Roe	.25
37	Eric Snow	.15
38	Damon Stoudamire	5.00
39	Bob Sura	.75
40	Kurt Thomas	.50
41	Gary Trent	.75
42	David Vaughn	.25
43	Corliss Williamson	.50
44	Eric Williams	1.25
45	George Zidek	.75
46	Checklist	

1995 Signature Rookies Signature Prime Signatures

The 43-card, standard-size insert set parallels the base set except that the fronts are signed by the players. Each player signed 3,000 cards, except for Ed O'Bannon and Jason Caffey who did not sign their cards.

		MT
Complete Set (43):		375.00
Common Player:		3.00
3	Brent Barry	12.00
13	Tyus Edney	10.00
14	Michael Finley	20.00
16	Kevin Garnett	40.00
17	Alan Henderson	10.00
23	Antonio McDyess	30.00
24	Loren Meyer	6.00
28	Cherokee Parks	5.00
31	Theo Ratliff	6.00
32	Bryant Reeves	15.00
39	Bob Sura	8.00
40	Kurt Thomas	6.00
41	Gary Trent	8.00
43	Corliss Williamson	6.00
44	Eric Williams	10.00
45	George Zidek	8.00

1995 Signature Rookies Signature Prime Hoopla

The five-card insert set was randomly inserted into football packs with the fronts having a color action cut out of the player on a metallic, rainbow-colored background and "Hoopla" printed along the left side. The cards are numbered with an "H" prefix.

		MT
Complete Set (5):		20.00
Common Player:		3.00
H1	Joe Smith	6.00
H2	Antonio McDyess	5.00
H3	Jerry Stackhouse	6.00
H4	Rasheed Wallace	3.00
H5	Kevin Garnett	10.00

1995 Signature Rookies Signature Prime Hoopla Signature

The five-card insert set was inserted into every 60 football packs. The cards have an "H" prefix and are limited to 500 each. The fronts have a color player cut out over a blue, red and silver foil background.

		MT
Complete Set (5):		475.00
Common Player:		50.00
1	Joe Smith	120.00
2	Antonio McDyess	80.00
3	Jerry Stackhouse	120.00
4	Rasheed Wallace	50.00
5	Kevin Garnett	175.00

1995 Signature Rookies Signature Prime Top Ten

Inserted every 30 packs, the 10-card set features some of the top draft picks from the 1995 NBA Draft first round. "Top" appears in the upper left corner with "Ten" printed in the lower right corner. The cards are numbered with the "TT" prefix.

		MT
Complete Set (10):		20.00
Common Player:		.60
1	Joe Smith	4.00
2	Antonio McDyess	3.00
3	Jerry Stackhouse	4.00
4	Rasheed Wallace	1.50
5	Kevin Garnett	7.00
6	Bryant Reeves	2.00
7	Damon Stoudamire	5.00
8	Shawn Respert	.60
9	Ed O'Bannon	1.25
10	Kurt Thomas	1.50

1995 Signature Rookies Signature Prime Top Ten Signature

Randomly inserted into packs, the 10 cards parallel the Prime Top 10 inserts in autographed versions. Each player signed 1,000 cards.

		MT
Complete Set (10):		450.00
Common Player:		12.00
1	Joe Smith	80.00
2	Antonio McDyess	60.00
3	Jerry Stackhouse	80.00
4	Rasheed Wallace	30.00
5	Kevin Garnett	125.00
6	Bryant Reeves	50.00
7	Damon Stoudamire	100.00
8	Shawn Respert	12.00
9	Ed O'Bannon	25.00
10	Kurt Thomas	20.00

1995 Signature Rookies Tetrad Previews

Inserted in SR Basketball Autobilia packs, the set contained five cards. The fronts have a borderless color action photo, with the player's name printed below. The back has another photo, with a headshot and player information also included.

		MT
Complete Set (5):		10.00
Common Player:		2.00
1	Ruben Rivera	2.00
2	Jim Carey	2.00
3	Joe Smith	2.50
4	Jerry Stackhouse	2.00
5	Ki-Jana Carter	2.00

1995 Signature Rookies Tetrad

The set contains 76 cards, with borderless fronts and a color action photo. The name of the player is in gold below the photo. The backs have a headshot, with player information as well.

		MT
Complete Set (76):		15.00
Common Player:		.10
Signatures:		20x
Erstad Set (5):		12.00
Common Erstad (B1-B5):		3.00
1	Kevin Carter	.10
2	Ruben Brown	.10
3	Kyle Brady	.10
4	Tony Boselli	.25
5	Derrick Alexander	.25
6	Mike Mamula	.10
7	Ellis Johnson	.10
8	Mark Fields	.10
9	Luther Ellis	.10
10	Hugh Douglas	.25
11	Shawn Respert	.10
12	Bryant Reeves	.50
13	Cherokee Parks	.10
14	Greg Ostertag	.25
15	Ed O'Bannon	.10
16	David Vaughn	.10
17	Gary Trent	.10
18	Kurt Thomas	.10
19	Bob Sura	.25
20	Damon Stoudamire	1.00
21	Brent Barry	.10
22	Cory Alexander	.10
23	Theo Ratliff	.25
24	Loren Meyer	.10
25	George Zidek	.10
26	Alan Henderson	.25
27	Michael Finley	.25
28	Randolph Childress	.10
29	Jason Caffey	.10
30	Mario Bennett	.10
31	Andy Yount	.10
32	Jose Cruz	3.00
33	Chad Hermanson	1.50
34	David Yocum	.10
35	Dmitri Young	.10
36	Kerry Wood (UER, Card front is Kevin)	5.00
37	Jonathan Johnson	.10
38	Shea Morenz	.10
39	Matt Morris	.10
40	Reggie Taylor	.25
41	Antone Williamson	.10
42	Derek Wallace	.10
43	Ben Grieve	1.50
44	Benji Gil	.10
45	Todd Walker	1.00
46	Jason Thompson	.10
47	Scott Stahoviak	.10
48	Chris Roberts	.10
49	Dante Powell	1.00
50	Torii Hunter	.10
51	James O. Stewart	.10
52	Rashaan Salaam	.25
53	Tyrone Poole	.10
54	Craig Newsome	.25
55	Devin Bush	.10
56	Bryan Rekar	.10
57	Jaime Jones	1.00
58	Todd Helton	3.00
59	Joe Fontenot	.10
60	Tony Clark	1.00
61	Alexei Morozov	.10
62	Radek Dvorak	.10
63	Corliss Williamson	.40
64	Eric Williams	.25
65	Sherell Ford	.10
66	Terry Ryan	.10
67	Shane Doan	.10
68	Brad Church	.10
69	Brian Boucher	.10
70	Dmitri Nabokov	.10
71	Tony McKnight	.20
72	Roy Holladay	.50
73	Mike Drumright	.10
74	Ben Davis	.50
75	Michael Barrett	.50
	NNO Checklist	.10

1995 Signature Rookies Tetrad Autobilia

Issued as one series, the set contains 100 cards. The fronts have a color cutout, with the player's name printed in a gold bar at the bottom. The backs have two more photos, with player information. Some special items include Darin Erstad-signed bats and Muhammad Ali boxing gloves, among others.

		MT
Complete Set (100):		30.00
Common Player:		.25
1	Travis Best	.50
2	Junior Burrough	.25
3	Randolph Childress	.25
4	Andrew DeClercq	.25
5	Michael Finley	1.00
6	Alan Henderson	.75
7	Ed O'Bannon	.25
8	Cherokee Parks	.25
9	Bryant Reeves	1.00
10	Shawn Respert	.25
11	Damon Stoudamire	3.00
12	Bob Sura	.50
13	Scotty Thurman	.25
14	Gary Trent	.25
15	Corliss Williamson	.75
16	Donald Williams	.25
17	Eric Williams	.75
18	Juan Acevedo	.25
19	Trey Beamon	.25
20	Tim Belk	.25
21	Mike Bovee	.25
22	Brad Clontz	.25
23	Marty Cordova	.25
24	Johnny Damon	.50
25	Jeff Darwin	.25
26	Nick Delvecchio	.25
27	Ray Durham	.75
28	Jermaine Dye	.25
29	Jimmy Haynes	.25
30	Mark Hubbard	.25
31	Russ Johnson	.25
32	Andy Larkin	.25
33	Kris Ralston	.25
34	Luis Raven	.25
35	Desi Relaford	.25
36	Jeff Suppan	.25
37	Brad Woodall	.25
38	Nolan Baumgartner	.25
39	Bryan Berard	1.50
40	Aki-Petteri Berg	.25
41	Daniel Cleary	.25
42	Radek Dvorak	.25
43	Patrik Juhlin	.25
44	Jan Labraaten	.25
45	Daymond Langkow	.25
46	Sergei Luchinkin	.25
47	Cameron Mann	.25
48	Alexei Morozov	.25
49	Oleg Tverdovsky	.50
50	Johan Ramstedt	.25
51	Wade Redden	.25
52	Sami-Ville Salomaa	.25
53	Alexei Vasilyev	.25
54	Peter Wallin	.25
55	Dave Barr	.25
56	Brandon Bennett	.25
57	Kyle Brady	.25
58	Kevin Carter	.25
59	Terrell Davis	3.00
60	Luther Ellis	.25
61	Jack Jackson	.25
62	Frank Sanders	.50
63	Ki-Jana Carter	1.00
64	Steve Stenstrom	.25
65	James A. Stewart	.25
66	James O. Stewart	.25
67	Bobby Taylor	.75
68	Michael Westbrook	.50
69	Rashaan Salaam	.50
70	Ray Zellars	.25
71	Antonio McDyess	1.00
72	Ruben Rivera	.75
73	Joe Smith	1.50
74	Jerry Stackhouse	1.00
75	J.J. Stokes	.50
76	Sherman Williams	.25
77	Kevin Garnett	5.00
78	Juwan Howard	2.00
79	Eddie Jones	1.00
80	Kerry Collins	2.00
81	Joey Galloway	1.25
82	Steve McNair	1.50
83	Errict Rhett	.25
84	Eric Zeier	.25
85	Jose Cruz	4.00
86	Darin Erstad	6.00
87	Todd Helton	4.00
88	Chad Hermanson	2.50
89	Jonathan Johnson	.25
90	Manny Ramirez	1.00
91	Kerry Wood	.25
92	Ben Davis	.25
93	Jaime Jones	2.00
94	Brian Boucher	.25
95	Martin Brodeur	1.50
96	Brad Church	.25
97	Shane Doan	.25
98	Terry Ryan	.25
99	Ryan Smyth	.25
100	Checklist 1-100	.25

1995 Signature Rookies Tetrad Mail-In

Available through the mail, the five-card set featured the top draft picks in the four major sports. The fronts have a picture of the athlete, with a fractal design. "Mail In" and "#1 pick" are printed along the top. The cards are numbered with a "P" prefix.

		MT
Complete Set (5):		5.00
Common Player:		.60
1	Joe Smith	1.00
2	Ki-Jana Carter	.60
3	Darin Erstad	3.00
4	Bryan Berard	1.00
5	#1 Picks Card (Joe Smith, Ki-Jana Carter, Darin Erstad, Bryan Berard)	1.00

1995 Signature Rookies Tetrad SR Force

The 35-card set features a white background with a color action photo on the front. Photos of one foot, the head and an arm are set out as separate photos from the main photo. "SR Force" is printed in the white border at the top. The cards are numbered with a "F" prefix, with the backs having the same picture as the front as a faded background.

		MT
Complete Set (35):		25.00
Common Player:		.25
Signatures:		20x
1	Nolan Baumgartner	.25
2	Bryan Berard	1.00
3	Aki-Petteri Berg	.25
4	Daymond Langkow	.25
5	Wade Redden	.25
6	Martin Brodeur	1.25
7	Jim Carey	.40
8	Jaromir Jagr	3.00
9	Maxim Kuznetsov	.25
10	Terry Ryan	.25
11	Manny Ramirez	1.50
12	Jaret Wright	1.50
13	Ruben Rivera	.75
14	Derek Jeter	2.50
15	Monty Farris (UER, Back reads Farris)	.25
16	Jason Isringhausen	.50
17	Marty Cordova	.25
18	Garret Anderson	.50
19	Alex Rodriquez	4.00
20	Carlton Loewer	.25
21	Joe Smith	1.50
22	Antonio McDyess	1.00
23	Jerry Stackhouse	1.50
24	Rasheed Wallace	.75
25	Kevin Garnett	5.00
26	Ki-Jana Carter	.75
27	Joey Galloway	1.50
28	Michael Westbrook	.50
29	J.J. Stokes	.50
30	Eric Zeier	.25
31	Errict Rhett	.25
32	Steve McNair	2.00
33	Kerry Collins	3.00
34	Stoney Case	.25
35	Mark Bruener	.25

1995 Signature Rookies Tetrad Titans

The five-card set has borderless fronts with action photos on a black background. The card name runs down the side in gold. The cards are numbered with a prefix "T".

		MT
Complete Set (5):		6.00
Common Player:		1.00
1	Roberto Duran	1.00
2	Dennis Rodman	2.50
3	Katarina Witt	2.00
4	Karim Abdul-Jabbar	2.50
5	Bob Griese	1.50

1990 SkyBox Promo Cards

These 10 cards preview SkyBox's 1990-91 debut basketball set. The cards are similiar in design to the company's regular set, except each one has a red diagonal banner in the upper left-hand corner which says "Prototype." The cards are numbered identical to their counterparts in the regular set and were given to dealers and members of the hobby press.

		MT
Complete Set (10):		150.00
Common Player:		5.00
Uncut Promo Sheet:		135.00
41	Michael Jordan	75.00
91	Dennis Rodman	25.00
138	Magic Johnson	25.00
151	Rony Seikaly	5.00
162	Ricky Pierce	5.00
173	Pooh Richardson	5.00
224	Kevin Johnson	5.00
233	Clyde Drexler	15.00
260	David Robinson	25.00
282	Karl Malone	25.00

1990-91 SkyBox

The 1990-91 premier issue of SkyBox was NBA Properties' attempt to get in on the basketball craze and was the first time an "official" branch of any sport became involved in the card market. Series II was issued in mid-March. Like NBA Hoops, cards were pulled from Series I to make room for updates, coaches cards and checklists.

		MT
Complete Set (423):		20.00
Complete Series 1 (300):		12.00
Complete Series 2 (123):		8.00
Common Player:		.05
Minor Stars:		.10
Series 1 Pack (15):		1.25
Series 1 Wax Box (36):		23.00
Series 2 Pack (15):		1.75
Series 2 Wax Box (36):		32.50
1	John Battle	.05
2	*Duane Ferrell* (SP)	.10
3	Jon Koncak	.05
4	Cliff Levingston (SP)	.10
5	John Long (SP)	.10
6	Moses Malone	.05
7	Glenn Rivers	.05
8	Kenny Smith (SP)	.10
9	Alexander Volkov	.05
10	Spud Webb	.05
11	Dominique Wilkins	.20
12	Kevin Willis	.05
13	John Bagley	.05
14	Larry Bird	1.00
15	Kevin Gamble	.05
16	Dennis Johnson (SP)	.10
17	Joe Kleine	.05
18	Reggie Lewis	.10
19	Kevin McHale	.10
20	Robert Parish	.10
21	Jim Paxson (SP)	.10
22	Ed Pinckney	.05
23	Brian Shaw	.10
24	Michael Smith	.05
25	Richard Anderson	.05
26	Tyrone Bogues	.05
27	Rex Chapman	.05
28	Dell Curry	.05
29	Armond Gilliam	.05
30	Michael Holton (SP)	.10
31	Dave Hoppen	.05
32	*J.R. Reid*	.10
33	Robert Reid (SP)	.10
34	Brian Rowsom (SP)	.10
35	Kelly Tripucka	.05
36	Michael Williams (SP)	.10
37	*B.J. Armstrong*	.30
38	Bill Cartwright	.05
39	Horace Grant	.20
40	Craig Hodges	.05
41	Michael Jordan	4.00
42	*Stacey King*	.10
43	Ed Nealy (SP)	.10
44	John Paxson	.05
45	Will Perdue	.05
46	Scottie Pippen	.75
47	Jeff Sanders (SP)	.10
48	Winston Bennett	.05
49	Chucky Brown	.05
50	Brad Daugherty	.05
51	Craig Ehlo	.05
52	Steve Kerr	.05
53	Paul Mokeski (SP)	.10
54	John Morton	.05
55	Larry Nance	.05
56	Mark Price	.10
57	Tree Rollins (SP)	.10
58	John Williams	.05
59	Steve Alford	.05
60	Rolando Blackman	.05
61	Adrian Dantley (SP)	.10
62	Brad Davis	.05
63	James Donaldson	.05
64	Derek Harper	.05
65	Anthony Jones (SP)	.10
66	Sam Perkins (SP)	.10
67	Roy Tarpley	.05
68	Bill Wennington (SP)	.10
69	*Randy White*	.10
70	Herb Williams	.05
71	Michael Adams	.05
72	Joe Barry Carroll (SP)	.10
73	Walter Davis	.05
74	Alex English (SP)	.10
75	Bill Hanzlik	.10
76	Tim Kempton (SP)	.10
77	Jerome Lane	.10
78	Lafayette Lever (SP)	.10
79	*Todd Lichti*	.10
80	Blair Rasmussen	.05
81	Dan Schayes (SP)	.10
82	Mark Aguirre	.05
83	*William Bedford*	.10
84	Joe Dumars	.20
85	James Edwards	.05
86	David Greenwood	.05
87	Scott Hastings	.05
88	Gerald Henderson (SP)	.10
89	Vinnie Johnson	.05
90	Bill Laimbeer	.05
91	Dennis Rodman	.75
92	John Salley	.05
93	Isiah Thomas	.20
94	Manute Bol (SP)	.10
95	*Tim Hardaway*	1.00
96	Rod Higgins	.05
97	*Sarunas Marciulionis*	.10
98	Chris Mullin	.15
99	Jim Petersen	.05
100	Mitch Richmond	.30
101	Mike Smrek	.05
102	Terry Teagle (SP)	.10
103	Tom Tolbert	.05
104	Kelvin Upshaw (SP)	.10
105	*Anthony Bowie* (SP)	.20
106	Adrian Caldwell	.05
107	Eric Floyd	.05
108	Buck Johnson	.05
109	Vernon Maxwell	.05
110	Hakeem Olajuwon	.75
111	Larry Smith	.05
112a	Otis Thorpe, Otis Thorpe (Mitchell Wiggins front)	.75
112b	Otis Thorpe (corrected)	.05
113a	Mitchell Wiggins, Mitchell Wiggins (Otis Thorpe front)	.75
113b	Mitchell Wiggins (corrected)	.05
114	Vern Fleming	.05
115	Rickey Green (SP)	.10
116	*George McCloud*	.30
117	Reggie Miller	.40
118a	Dyron Nix, Dyron Nix (Wayman Tisdale back)	2.00
118b	Dyron Nix (corrected)	.05
119	Chuck Person	.05
120	Mike Sanders	.05
121	Detlef Schrempf	.10
122	Rik Smits	.10
123	LaSalle Thompson	.05
124	Benoit Benjamin	.05
125	Winston Garland	.05
126	Tom Garrick	.05
127	Gary Grant	.05
128	Ron Harper	.05
129	Danny Manning	.25
130	Jeff Martin	.05
131	Ken Norman	.05
132	Charles Smith	.05
133	Joe Wolf (SP)	.10
134	Michael Cooper (SP)	.10
135	*Vlade Divac*	.75
136	Larry Drew	.05
137	A.C. Green	.05
138	Magic Johnson	.75
139	Mark McNamara (SP)	.10
140	Byron Scott	.05
141	Mychal Thompson	.05
142	Orlando Woolridge (SP)	.10
143	James Worthy	.10
144	Terry Davis	.05
145	*Sherman Douglas*	.20
146	Kevin Edwards	.05
147	Tellis Frank (SP)	.10
148	Scott Haffner (SP)	.10
149	Grant Long	.05
150	*Glen Rice*	1.00
151	Rony Seikaly	.10
152	Rory Sparrow (SP)	.10
153	Jon Sundvold	.05
154	Billy Thompson	.05
155	Greg Anderson	.05
156	Ben Coleman (SP)	.10
157	Jeff Grayer	.05
158	Jay Humphries	.05
159	Frank Kornet	.05
160	Larry Krystkowiak	.05
161	Brad Lohaus	.05
162	Ricky Pierce	.05
163	Paul Pressey (SP)	.10
164	Fred Roberts	.05
165	Alvin Robertson	.05
166	Jack Sikma	.05
167	Randy Breuer	.05
168	Tony Campbell	.05
169	Tyrone Corbin	.05
170	Sidney Lowe (SP)	.10
171	*Sam Mitchell*	.10
172	Tod Murphy	.05
173	*Pooh Richardson*	.20
174	*Donald Royal* (SP)	.30
175	Brad Sellers (SP)	.10
176	*Mookie Blaylock*	.50
177	Sam Bowie	.05
178	Lester Conner	.10
179	Derrick Gervin	.05
180	Jack Haley	.05
181	Roy Hinson	.05
182	Dennis Hopson (SP)	.10
183	Chris Morris	.05
184	*Pete Myers* (SP)	.20
185	Purvis Short (SP)	.10
186	Maurice Cheeks	.05
187	Patrick Ewing	.30
188	Stuart Gray	.05
189	Mark Jackson	.05
190	Johnny Newman (SP)	.10
191	Charles Oakley	.05
192	Brian Quinnett	.05
193	Trent Tucker	.05
194	Kiki Vandeweghe	.05
195	Kenny Walker	.05
196	Eddie Lee Wilkins	.05
197	Gerald Wilkins	.05
198	Mark Acres	.05
199	*Nick Anderson*	.50
200	Michael Ansley	.05
201	Terry Catledge	.05
202	Dave Corzine (SP)	.10
203	Sidney Green (SP)	.10
204	Jerry Reynolds	.05
205	Scott Skiles	.05
206	Otis Smith	.05
207	Reggie Theus (SP)	.10
208	Jeff Turner	.05
209	Sam Vincent	.05
210	Ron Anderson	.05
211	Charles Barkley	.50
212	Scott Brooks (SP)	.10
213	Lanard Copeland (SP)	.10
214	Johnny Dawkins	.05
215	Mike Gminski	.05
216	Hersey Hawkins	.10
217	Rick Mahorn	.05
218	Derek Smith (SP)	.10
219	Bob Thornton	.05
220	Tom Chambers	.05
221	*Greg Grant* (SP)	.10
222	Jeff Hornacek	.05
223	Eddie Johnson	.05
224	Kevin Johnson	.20
225	*Andrew Lang*	.10
226	Dan Majerle	.10
227	Mike McGee (SP)	.10
228	Tim Perry	.05
229	Kurt Rambis	.05
230	Mark West	.05
231	Mark Bryant	.05
232	Wayne Cooper	.05
233	Clyde Drexler	.40
234	Kevin Duckworth	.05
235	Byron Irvin (SP)	.10
236	Jerome Kersey	.05
237	*Drazen Petrovic*	.10
238	Terry Porter	.05
239	*Cliff Robinson*	.75
240	Buck Williams	.05
241	Danny Young	.05
242	Danny Ainge (SP)	.10
243	Randy Allen (SP)	.10
244a	Antoine Carr, Antoine Carr (SP) (Hawks jersey on back, Series I)	.10
244b	Antoine Carr (Wearing Kings jersey, Series II)	.10
245	Vinny Del Negro (SP)	.10
246	*Pervis Ellison* (SP)	.25
247	Greg Kite (SP)	.10
248	Rodney McCray (SP)	.10
249	Harold Pressley (SP)	.10
250	Ralph Sampson	.05
251	Wayman Tisdale	.05
252	Willie Anderson	.05
253	Uwe Blab (SP)	.10
254	Frank Brickowski (SP)	.10
255	Terry Cummings	.05
256	*Sean Elliott*	.50
257	Caldwell Jones (SP)	.10
258	Johnny Moore (SP)	.10
259	Zarko Paspali (SP)	.10
260	David Robinson	1.50
261	Rod Strickland	.05
262	David Wingate (SP)	.10
263	*Dana Barros*	.50
264	Michael Cage	.05
265	Quintin Dailey	.05
266	Dale Ellis	.05
267	Steve Johnson (SP)	.10
268	*Shawn Kemp*	1.00
269	Xavier McDaniel	.05
270	Derrick McKey	.05
271a	Nate McMillan, Nate McMillan (SP) (error Series I: head shot on back)	.10
271b	Nate McMillan (corrected Series II; jersey #10 on back)	.10
272	Olden Polynice	.05
273	Sedale Threatt	.05
274	Thurl Bailey	.05
275	Mike Brown	.05
276	Mark Eaton	.05
277	*Blue Edwards*	.10
278	Darrell Griffith	.05
279	Bobby Hansen (SP)	.10
280	Eric Johnson	.05
281	Eric Leckner (SP)	.10
282	Karl Malone	.30
283	Delaney Rudd	.05
284	John Stockton	.30
285	Mark Alaire	.05
286	Steve Colter (SP)	.10
287	Ledell Eackles (SP)	.10
288	Harvey Grant	.05
289	*Tom Hammonds*	.10
290	Charles Jones	.05
291	Bernard King	.05
292	Jeff Malone (SP)	.10
293	Darrell Walker	.05
294	John Williams	.05
295	Checklist #1 (SP)	.05
296	Checklist #2 (SP)	.05
297	Checklist #3 (SP)	.05
298	Checklist #4 (SP)	.05
299	Checklist #5 (SP)	.05
300	*Danny Ferry* (SP)	.50
301	Bob Weiss (C)	.05
302	Chris Ford (C)	.05
303	Gene Littles (C)	.05
304	Phil Jackson (C)	.05
305	Len Wilkens (C)	.05
306	Richie Adubato (C)	.05
307	Paul Westhead (C)	.05
308	Chuck Daly (C)	.05
309	Don Nelson (C)	.05
310	Don Chaney (C)	.05
311	Dick Versace (C)	.05
312	Mike Schuler (C)	.05
313	Mike Dunleavy (C)	.05
314	Ron Rothstein (C)	.05
315	Del Harris (C)	.05
316	Bill Musselman (C)	.05
317	Bill Fitch (C)	.05
318	Stu Jackson (C)	.05
319	Matt Guokas (C)	.05
320	Jim Lynam (C)	.05
321	Cotton Fitzsimmons (C)	.05
322	Rick Adelman (C)	.05
323	Dick Motta (C)	.05
324	Larry Brown (C)	.05
325	K.C. Jones (C)	.05
326	Jerry Sloan (C)	.05
327	Wes Unseld (C)	.05
328	Atlanta Hawks	.05
329	Boston Celtics	.05
330	Charlotte Hornets	.05
331	Chicago Bulls	.05
332	Cleveland Cavaliers	.05
333	Dallas Mavericks	.05
334	Denver Nuggets	.05
335	Detroit Pistons	.05
336	Golden State Warriors	.05
337	Houston Rockets	.05
338	Indiana Pacers	.05
339	L.A. Clippers	.05
340	L.A. Lakers	.05
341	Miami Heat	.05
342	Milwaukee Bucks	.05
343	Minnesota Timberwolves	.05
344	New Jersey Nets	.05
345	New York Knicks	.05
346	Orlando Magic	.05
347	Philadelphia 76ers	.05
348	Phoenix Suns	.05
349	Portland Trail Blazers	.05
350	Sacramento Kings	.05
351	San Antonio Spurs	.05
352	Seattle SuperSonics	.05
353	Utah Jazz	.05
354	Washington Bullets	.05
355	*Rumeal Robinson*	.10

356 *Kendall Gill* 1.00
357 *Mahmoud Abdul-Rauf* .50
358 *Tyrone Hill* .75
359 *Bo Kimble* .10
360 *Willie Burton* .50
361 *Felton Spencer* .10
362 *Derrick Coleman* 1.00
363 *Dennis Scott* 1.00
364 *Lionel Simmons* .10
365 *Gary Payton* 5.00
366 Tim McCormick .05
367 Sidney Moncrief .05
368 *Kenny Gattison* .10
369 Randolph Keys .05
370 Johnny Newman .05
371 Dennis Hopson .05
372 Cliff Levingston .05
373 Derrick Chievous .05
374 Danny Ferry .05
375 Alex English .05
376 Lafayette Lever .05
377 Rodney McCray .05
378 T.R. Dunn .05
379 Corey Gaines .05
380 *Avery Johnson* .75
381 Joe Wolf .05
382 Orlando Woolridge .05
383 Wayne Rollins .05
384 Steve Johnson .05
385 Kenny Smith .05
386 Mick Woodson .05
387 *Greg Dreiling* .10
388 Michael Williams .05
389 Randy Wittman .05
390 Ken Bannister .05
391 Sam Perkins .05
392 Terry Teagle .05
393 Milt Wagner .05
394 Frank Brickowski .05
395 Dan Schayes .05
396 Scott Brooks .05
397 *Doug West* .50
398 *Chris Dudley* .10
399 Reggie Theus .05
400 Greg Grant .05
401 Greg Kite .05
402 Mark McNamara .05
403 Manute Bol .05
404 Rickey Green .05
405 *Kenny Battle* .10
406 Ed Nealy .05
407 Danny Ainge .05
408 Steve Colter .05
409 Bobby Hansen .05
410 Eric Leckner .05
411 Rory Sparrow .05
412 Bill Wennington .05
413 Sidney Green .05
414 David Greenwood .05
415 Paul Pressey .05
416 Reggie Williams .05
417 Dave Corzine .05
418 Jeff Malone .05
419 Pervis Ellison .05
420 Byron Irvin .05
421 Checklist .05
422 Checklist .05
423 Checklist .05

1990-91 SkyBox Announcers

These cards were used by NBC broadcasters as business cards. The cards are standard size and follow the same format as SkyBox's regular 1990-91 set design. The card front has a color photo of the announcer against a computer-generated background, bordered in gold. The back has another photo, and biographical information about the broadcaster. The cards are unnumbered.

	MT
Complete Set (4):	200.00
Common Player:	25.00
Bob Costas	75.00
Julie Moran	25.00
Ahmad Rashad	50.00
Pat Riley	100.00

1991 SkyBox Magic Johnson Video

This card was included with the "Magic Johnson: Always Showtime" video. The front boasts a cutout photo of Johnson over a funky background with the word "Magic." The card back includes a photo of Johnson on the left, the SkyBox logo in the upper left and his career highlights on the right side. It is unnumbered.

	MT
Complete Set (1):	15.00
Common Player:	15.00
NNO Magic Johnson	15.00

1991 SkyBox Promo Cards

These cards preview the design SkyBox used for its main set in 1991-92. The standard-size cards are similar to their counterparts in the regular set, including a card number, but are identified by the black banner in the upper left corner which says "Prototype." Cards were made available to dealers and the hobby press. Chris Mullin and Dennis Rodman cards were short printed and are scarcer than the others in the set.

	MT
Complete Set (20):	100.00
Common Player:	3.00
24 Rex Chapman	3.00
86 Dennis Rodman	20.00
95 Chris Mullin	15.00
97 Mitch Richmond	6.00
114 Reggie Miller	6.00
130 Charles Smith	3.00
137 Magic Johnson	20.00
143 James Worthy	5.00
173 Pooh Richardson	3.00
189 Patrick Ewing	17.50
205 Dennis Scott	3.00
211 Charles Barkley	20.00
216 Hersey Hawkins	3.00
223 Tom Chambers	3.00
237 Clyde Drexler	5.00
238 Kevin Duckworth	3.00
240 Terry Porter	4.00
242 Buck Williams	3.00
268 Ricky Pierce	3.00
294 Bernard King	4.00

1991-92 SkyBox

These cards were in foil packs and blister packs; the blister packs had some special "chase" insert cards, also, listed at the end of the main checklist. For a limited time, boxes of Cheerios also included four cards. This set, which has several subsets, has computer-generated fronts; the card backs have stats. Subsets include SS (SkyBox Salutes), SM (Sky Masters), S (Shooting Stars), MS (Magic of SkyBox), SC (Small School Sensations), GF (Game Frame), and TW (Team Work). The original 10 members of the USA Olympic Basketball Team are also featured in a subset. Two unnumbered cards, Barcelona '92 and Clyde Drexler USA, were also produced. The 10,000 Drexler cards were available by mail. Each regular card has a color action photo on the front against a computer-generated background with different colors and geometric shapes inside. The player's name and team logo are at the bottom of the card. The card back has a casual photo of the player; he's not in action. Biographical and statistical information, plus a card number, are also given.

	MT
Complete Set (659):	50.00
Complete Series 1 (350):	20.00
Complete Series 2 (309):	30.00
Common Player:	.05
Minor Stars:	.10
Series 1 Pack (15):	.50
Series 1 Wax Box (36):	14.00
Series 2 Pack (15):	1.00
Series 2 Wax Box (36):	25.00

1 John Battle .05
2 Duane Ferrell .05
3 Jon Koncak .05
4 Moses Malone .10
5 Tim McCormick .05
6 Sidney Moncrief .05
7 Glenn Rivers .05
8 Rumeal Robinson .05
9 Anthony Webb .05
10 Dominique Wilkins .10
11 Kevin Willis .05
12 Larry Bird 1.25
13 *Dee Brown* .20
14 Kevin Gamble .05
15 Joe Kleine .05
16 Reggie Lewis .05
17 Kevin McHale .10
18 Robert Parish .10
19 Ed Pinckney .05
20 Brian Shaw .05
21 Michael Smith .05
22 Stojko Vrankovic .05
23 Tyrone Bogues .05
24 Rex Chapman .05
25 Dell Curry .05
26 Kenny Gattison .05
27 Kendall Gill .05
28 Mike Gminski .05
29 Randolph Keys .05
30 Eric Leckner .05
31 Johnny Newman .05
32 J.R. Reid .05
33 Kelly Tripucka .05
34 B.J. Armstrong .05
35 Bill Cartwright .05
36 Horace Grant .20
37 Craig Hodges .05
38 Dennis Hopson .05
39 Michael Jordan 4.00
40 Stacey King .05
41 Cliff Levingston .05
42 John Paxson .05
43 Will Perdue .05
44 Scottie Pippen 1.00
45 Winston Bennett .05
46 Chucky Brown .05
47 Brad Daugherty .05
48 Craig Ehlo .05
49 Danny Ferry .05
50 Steve Kerr .05
51 John Morton .05
52 Larry Nance .05
53 Mark Price .05
54 Darnell Valentine .05
55 John Williams .05
56 Steve Alford .05
57 Rolando Blackman .05
58 Brad Davis .05
59 James Donaldson .05
60 Derek Harper .05
61 Fat Lever .05
62 Rodney McCray .05
63 Roy Tarpley .05
64 Kelvin Upshaw .05
65 Randy White .05
66 Herb Williams .05
67 Michael Adams .05
68 Greg Anderson .05
69 Anthony Cook .05
70 Mahmoud Abdul-Rauf .10
71 Jerome Lane .05
72 Marcus Liberty .05
73 Todd Lichti .05
74 Blair Rasmussen .05
75 Reggie Williams .05
76 Joe Wolf .05
77 Orlando Woolridge .05
78 Mark Aguirre .05
79 William Bedford .05
80 Lance Blanks .05
81 Joe Dumars .10
82 James Edwards .05
83 Scott Hastings .05
84 Vinnie Johnson .05
85 Bill Laimbeer .05
86 Dennis Rodman 1.00
87 John Salley .05
88 Isiah Thomas .20
89 *Mario Elie* .30
90 Tim Hardaway .10
91 Rod Higgins .05
92 Tyrone Hill .10
93 Les Jepse .05
94 Alton Lister .05
95 Sarunas Marciulionis .05
96 Chris Mullin .10
97 Jim Petersen .05
98 Mitch Richmond .25
99 Tom Tolbert .05
100 Adrian Caldwell .05
101 Eric Floyd .05
102 Dave Jamerson .05
103 Buck Johnson .05
104 Vernon Maxwell .05
105 Hakeem Olajuwon 1.00
106 Kenny Smith .05
107 Larry Smith .05
108 Otis Thorpe .05
109 Kennard Winchester .05
110 David Wood .05
111 Greg Dreiling .05
112 Vern Fleming .05
113 George McCloud .10
114 Reggie Miller .30
115 Chuck Person .05
116 Mike Sanders .05
117 Detlef Schrempf .05
118 Rik Smits .10
119 LaSalle Thompson .05
120 Ken Williams .05
121 Michael Williams .05
122 Ken Bannister .05
123 Winston Garland .05
124 Gary Grant .05
125 Ron Harper .05
126 Bo Kimble .05
127 Danny Manning .10
128 Jeff Martin .05
129 Ken Norman .05
130 Olden Polynice .05
131 Charles Smith .05
132 Loy Vaught .05
133 Elden Campbell .05
134 Vlade Divac .05
135 Larry Drew .05
136 A.C. Green .05
137 Magic Johnson 1.00
138 Sam Perkins .05
139 Byron Scott .05
140 Tony Smith .05
141 Terry Teagle .05
142 Mychal Thompson .05
143 James Worthy .05
144 Willie Burton .05
145 Vernell Coles .05
146 Terry Davis .05
147 Sherman Douglas .05
148 Kevin Edwards .05
149 Alec Kessler .05
150 Grant Long .05
151 Glen Rice .15
152 Rony Seikaly .05
153 Jon Sundvold .05
154 Billy Thompson .05
155 Frank Brickowski .05
156 Lester Conner .05
157 Jeff Grayer .05
158 Jay Humphries .05
159 Larry Krystkowiak .05
160 Brad Lohaus .05
161 Dale Ellis .05
162 Fred Roberts .05
163 Alvin Robertson .05
164 Dan Schayes .05
165 Jack Sikma .05
166 Randy Breuer .05
167 Scott Brooks .05
168 Tony Campbell .05
169 Tyrone Corbin .05
170 Gerald Glass .05
171 Sam Mitchell .05
172 Tod Murphy .05
173 Jerome Richardson .05
174 Felton Spencer .05
175 Bob Thornton .05
176 Doug West .05
177 Mookie Blaylock .05
178 Sam Bowie .05
179 Jud Buechler .05
180 Derrick Coleman .10
181 Chris Dudley .05
182 Tate George .05
183 Jack Haley .05
184 *Terry Mills* .20
185 Chris Morris .05
186 Drazen Petrovic .05
187 Reggie Theus .05
188 Maurice Cheeks .05
189 Patrick Ewing .30
190 Mark Jackson .05
191 *Jerrod Mustaf* .10
192 Charles Oakley .05
193 Brian Quinnett .05
194 *John Starks* .50
195 Trent Tucker .05
196 Kiki Vandeweghe .05
197 Kenny Walker .05
198 Gerald Wilkins .05
199 Mark Acres .05
200 Nick Anderson .10
201 Michael Ansley .05
202 Terry Catledge .05
203 Greg Kite .05
204 Jerry Reynolds .05
205 Dennis Scott .10
206 Scott Skiles .05
207 Otis Smith .05
208 Jeff Turner .05
209 Sam Vincent .05
210 Ron Anderson .05
211 Charles Barkley .75
212 Manute Bol .05
213 Johnny Dawkins .05
214 Armon Gilliam .05
215 Rickey Green .05
216 Hersey Hawkins .05
217 Rick Mahorn .05
218 Brian Oliver .05
219 Andre Turner .05
220 Jayson Williams .05
221 Joe Barry Carroll .05
222 *Cedric Ceballos* .50
223 Tom Chambers .05
224 Jeff Hornacek .05
225 Kevin Johnson .10
226 Negele Knight .05
227 Andrew Lang .05
228 Dan Majerle .10
229 Xavier McDaniel .05
230 Kurt Rambis .05
231 Mark West .05
232 Alaa Abdelnaby .05
233 Danny Ainge .05
234 Mark Bryant .05
235 Wayne Cooper .05
236 Walter Davis .05
237 Clyde Drexler .40
238 Kevin Duckworth .05
239 Jerome Kersey .05
240 Terry Porter .05
241 Cliff Robinson .15
242 Buck Williams .05
243 Anthony Bonner .05
244 Antoine Carr .05
245 Duane Causwell .05
246 Bobby Hansen .05
247 *Jim Les* .10
248 Travis Mays .05
249 Ralph Sampson .05
250 Lionel Simmons .05
251 Rory Sparrow .05
252 Wayman Tisdale .05
253 Bill Wennington .05
254 Willie Anderson .05
255 Terry Cummings .05
256 Sean Elliott .10
257 Sidney Green .05
258 David Greenwood .05
259 Avery Johnson .05
260 Paul Pressey .05
261 David Robinson .75
262 Dwayne Schintzius .05
263 Rod Strickland .05
264 David Wingate .05
265 Dana Barros .05
266 Benoit Benjamin .05
267 Michael Cage .05
268 Quintin Dailey .05
269 Ricky Pierce .05
270 Eddie Johnson .05
271 Shawn Kemp 1.50
272 Derrick McKey .05
273 Nate McMillian .05
274 Gary Payton .50
275 Sedale Threatt .05
276 Thurl Bailey .05
277 Mike Brown .05
278 Tony Brown .05
279 Mark Eaton .05
280 Blue Edwards .05
281 Darrell Griffith .05
282 Jeff Malone .05
283 Karl Malone .40
284 Delaney Rudd .05
285 John Stockton .40
286 Andy Toolson .05
287 Mark Alarie .05
288 Ledell Eackles .05
289 Pervis Ellison .05
290 A.J. English .05
291 Harvey Grant .05
292 Tom Hammonds .05
293 Charles Jones .05
294 Bernard King .05
295 Darrell Walker .05
296 John Williams .05
297 *Haywoode Workman* .10
298 Assist-to-Turnover Ratio (Muggsy Bogues) .05
299 Steal-to-Turnover Ratio (Lester Conner) .05
300 Largest One-Year Scoring Improvement (Michael Adams) .05
301 Most Minutes per Game (Chris Mullin) .05
302 Most Consecutive Games Played (Otis Thorpe) .05
303 Highest Scoring Trio (Chris Mullin, Tim Hardaway, Mitch Richmond) .10
304 Top Rebounding Guard (Darrell Walker) .05
305 Per 48 Minutes: Rebounds (Jerome Lane) .05
306 Per 48 Minutes: Assists (John Stockton) .10
307 Per 48 Minutes: Points (Michael Jordan) 2.00
308 Michael Adams (SG) .05
309 Larry Smith, Jerome Lane (SG) .05
310 Scott Skiles (SG) .05
311 Hakeem Olajuwon, David Robinson (SG) 1.00
312 Alvin Robertson (SG) .05
313 Stay in School Jam .05
314 3-Point Shootout (Craig Hodges) .05
315 Slam Dunk Championship (Dee Brown) .05
316 All-Star Game MVP (Charles Barkley) .30
317 Behind the Scenes (Charles Barkley, Joe Dumars, Kevin McHale) .10
318 Derrick Coleman (ART) .05
319 Lionel Simmons (ART) .05
320 Dennis Scott (ART) .05
321 Kendall Gill (ART) .05
322 Dee Brown (ART) .05
323 Magic Johnson (GQ) .40
324 Hakeem Olajuwon (GQ) .40
325 Reggie Theus (GQ) .05
326 Kevin Willis, Dominique Wilkins (GQ) .05
327 Gerald Wilkins (GQ) .05
328 Centennial Logo Card .05
329 Old Fashioned Ball .05
330 Womens Basketball Players .05
331 Peach Basket .05
332 James, Dr. Naismith .05
333 Magic Johnson, Michael Jordan (Finals) 1.25
334 Michael Jordan (Finals) 2.00
335 Vlade Divac (Finals) .05
336 John Paxson (Finals) .05
337 Chicago Bulls Team (Finals) 1.00
338 English .05
339 Math .05
340 Vocational Ecucation .05
341 History .05
342 Physical Education .05
343 Art .05
344 Science .05
345 Checklist #1 .05
346 Checklist #2 .05
347 Checklist #3 .05
348 Checklist #4 .05
349 Checklist #5 .05
350 Checklist #6 .05
351 Atlanta Hawks .05
352 Boston Celtics .05
353 Charlotte Hornets .05
354 Chicago Bulls .05
356 Dallas Mavericks .05
357 Denver Nuggets .05
358 Detroit Pistons .05
359 Golden State Warriors .05
360 Houston Rockets .05
361 Indiana Pacers .05
362 Los Angeles Clippers .05
363 Los Angeles Lakers .05
364 Miami Heat .05
365 Milwaukee Bucks .05
366 Minnesota Timberwolves .05
367 New Jersey Nets .05
368 New York Knicks .05
369 Orlando Magic .05
370 Philadelphia 76ers .05
371 Phoenix Suns .05
372 Portland Trailblazers .05
373 Sacramento Kings .05
374 San Antonio Spurs .05
375 Seattle Supersonics .05
376 Utah Jazz .05
377 Washington Bullets .05
378 Bob Weiss .05
379 Chris Ford .05
380 Allan Bristow .05
381 Phil Jackson .05
382 Len Wilkens .05
383 Richie Adubato .05
384 Paul Westhead .05
385 Chuck Daly .05
386 Don Nelson .05
387 Don Chaney .05
388 Bob Hill .05
389 Mike Schuler .05
390 Mike Dunleavy .05
391 Kevin Loughery .05
392 Del Harris .05
393 Jimmy Rodgers .05
394 Bill Fitch .05
395 Pat Riley .05
396 Matt Guokas .05
397 Jim Lynam .05
398 Cotton Fitzsimmons .05
399 Rick Adelman .05
400 Dick Motta .05
401 Larry Brown .05
402 K.C. Jones .05
403 Jerry Sloan .05
404 Wes Unseld .05
405 Atlanta Hawks (Maurice Cheeks) (GF) .05
406 Boston Celtics (Dee Brown) (GF) .05
407 Charlotte Hornets (Rex Chapman) (GF) .05
408 Chicago Bulls (Michael Jordan) (GF) 2.00
409 Cleveland Cavaliers (John Williams) (GF) .05
410 Dallas Mavericks (James Donaldson) (GF) .05
411 Denver Nuggets (Dikembe Mutombo) (GF) .40
412 Detroit Pistons (Isiah Thomas) (GF) .10
413 Golden State Warriors (Tim Hardaway) (GF) .05
414 Houston Rockets (Hakeem Olajuwon) (GF) .50
415 Indiana Pacers (Detlef Schrempf) (GF) .05
416 Los Angeles Clippers (Danny Manning) (GF) .05
417 Los Angeles Lakers (Magic Johnson) (GF) .40
418 Miami Heat (Bimbo Coles) (GF) .05
419 Milwaukee Bucks (Alvin Robertson) (GF) .05
420 Minnesota Timberwolves (Sam Mitchell) (GF) .05
421 New Jersey Nets (Sam Bowie) (GF) .05
422 New York Knicks (Mark Jackson) (GF) .05
423 Orlando Magic (GF) .05
424 Philadelphia 76ers (Charles Barkley) (GF) .40
425 Phoenix Suns (Dan Majerle) (GF) .05
426 Portland Trailblazers (Robert Pack) (GF) .05
427 Sacramento Kings (Wayman Tisdale) (GF) .05
428 San Antonio Spurs (David Robinson) (GF) .40
429 Seattle Supersonics (Nate McMillan) (GF) .05
430 Utah Jazz (Karl Malone) (GF) .10
431 Washington Bullets (Michael Adams) (GF) .05
432 Duane Ferrell (6M) .05
433 Kevin McHale (6M) .10
434 Dell Curry (6M) .05
435 B.J. Armstrong (6M) .05
436 John Williams (6M) .05
437 Brad Davis (6M) .05
438 Marcus Liberty (6M) .05
439 Mark Aguirre (6M) .05
440 Rod Higgins (6M) .05
441 Eric Floyd (6M) .05
442 Detlef Schrempf (6M) .05
443 Loy Vaught (6M) .05
444 Terry Teagle (6M) .05
445 Kevin Edwards (6M) .05
446 Dale Ellis (6M) .05
447 Tod Murphy (6M) .05
448 Chris Dudley (6M) .05
449 Mark Jackson (6M) .05
450 Jerry Reynolds (6M) .05
451 Ron Anderson (6M) .05
452 Dan Majerle (6M) .05
453 Danny Ainge (6M) .05
454 Jim Les (6M) .05
455 Paul Pressey (6M) .05
456 Ricky Pierce (6M) .05
457 Mike Brown (6M) .05
458 Ledell Eackles (6M) .05
459 Atlanta Hawks (Dominique Wilkins, Kevin Willis) (TW) .10
460 Boston Celtics (Larry Bird, Robert Parish) (TW) .30
461 Charlotte Hornets (Kendall Gill, Rex Chapman) (TW) .05
462 Chicago Bulls (Michael Jordan, Scottie Pippen) (TW) 1.50
463 Cleveland Cavaliers (Craig Ehlo, Mark Price) (TW) .05
464 Dallas Mavericks (Derek Harper, Rolando Blackman) (TW) .05
465 Denver Nuggets (Reggie Williams, Chris Jackson) (TW) .05
466 Detroit Pistons (Isiah Thomas, Bill Laimbeer) (TW) .10
467 Golden State Warriors (Tim Hardaway, Chris Mullin) .10
468 Houston Rockets (Vernon Maxwell, Kenny Smith) (TW) .05
469 Indiana Pacers (Detlef Schrempf, Reggie Miller) (TW) .10
470 Los Angeles Clippers (Charles Smith, Danny Manning) (TW) .05
471 Los Angeles Lakers (Magic Johnson, James Worthy) (TW) .25
472 Miami Heat (Glen Rice, Rony Seikaly) (TW) .10
473 Milwaukee Bucks (Jay Humphries, Alvin Robertson) (TW) .05
474 Minnesota Timberwolves (Tony Campbell, Pooh Richardson) (TW) .05
475 New Jersey Nets (Derrick Coleman, Sam Bowie) (TW) .05
476 New York Knicks (Patrick Ewing, Charles Oakley) (TW) .10
477 Orlando Magic (Dennis Scott, Scott Skiles) (TW) .05
478 Philadelphia 76ers (Charles Barkley, Hersey Hawkins) (TW) .10
479 Phoenix Suns (Kevin Johnson, Tom Chambers) (TW) .05
480 Portland Trail Blazers (Terry Porter, Clyde Drexler) (TW) .10
481 Sacramento Kings (Lionel Simmons, Wayman Tisdale) (TW) .05
482 San Antonio Spurs (Terry Cummings, Sean Elliott) (TW) .05
483 Seattle Supersonics (Eddie Johnson, Ricky Pierce) (TW) .05
484 Utah Jazz (John Stockton, Karl Malone) .20
485 Washington Bullets (Harvey Grant, Bernard King) (TW) .05
486 Rumeal Robinson (RIS) .05
487 Dee Brown (RIS) .05
488 Kendall Gill (RIS) .05
489 B.J. Armstrong (RIS) .05
490 Danny Ferry (RIS) .05
491 Randy White (RIS) .05
492 Mahmoud Abdul-Rauf (RIS) .05
493 Lance Blanks (RIS) .05
494 Tim Hardaway (RIS) .10
495 Vernon Maxwell (RIS) .05
496 Michael Williams (RIS) .05
497 Charles Smith (RIS) .05
498 Vlade Divac (RIS) .05
499 Willie Burton (RIS) .05
500 Jeff Grayer (RIS) .05
501 Jerome Richardson (RIS) .05
502 Derrick Coleman (RIS) .10
503 John Starks (RIS) .10

504	Dennis Scott (RIS)	.05
505	Hersey Hawkins (RIS)	.05
506	Negele Knight (RIS)	.05
507	Cliff Robinson (RIS)	.10
508	Lionel Simmons (RIS)	.05
509	David Robinson (RIS)	.40
510	Gary Payton (RIS)	.15
511	Blue Edwards (RIS)	.05
512	Harvey Grant (RIS)	.05
513	*Larry Johnson*	2.00
514	*Kenny Anderson*	.75
515	*Billy Owens*	.50
516	*Dikembe Mutombo*	1.25
517	*Steve Smith*	.75
518	*Doug Smith*	.10
519	*Luc Longley*	.50
520	*Mark Macon*	.10
521	*Stacey Augmon*	.50
522	*Brian Williams*	.40
523	*Terrell Brandon*	1.50
524	The Ball	.05
525	The Basket	.05
526	The 24-second Shot Clock	.05
527	The Game Program	.05
528	The Championship Gift	.05
529	The Championship Trophy	.05
530	Charles Barkley (USA)	1.25
531	Larry Bird (USA)	2.50
532	Patrick Ewing (USA)	.75
533	Magic Johnson (USA)	2.00
534	Michael Jordan (USA)	10.00
535	Karl Malone (USA)	.75
536	Chris Mullin (USA)	.10
537	Scottie Pippen (USA)	2.00
538	David Robinson (USA)	1.50
539	John Stockton (USA)	.75
540	Chuck Daly (USA)	.10
541	P.J. Carlesimo (USA)	.10
542	Mike Krzyzewski (USA)	1.00
543	Lenny Wilkens (USA)	.10
544	Team USA 1	2.00
545	Team USA 2	2.00
546	Team USA 3	2.00
547	Willie Anderson	.05
548	Stacey Augmon (USA)	.10
549	Vernell "Bimbo" Coles	.05
550	Jeff Grayer	.05
551	Hersey Hawkins	.10
552	Dan Majerle (USA)	.10
553	Danny Manning (USA)	.10
554	J.R. Reid	.05
555	Mitch Richmond	.05
556	Charles Smith	.05
557	Vern Fleming	.05
558	Joe Kleine	.05
559	Jon Koncak	.05
560	Sam Perkins	.05
561	Alvin Robertson	.05
562	Wayman Tisdale	.05
563	Jeff Turner	.05
564	Tony Campbell (MS)	.05
565	Joe Dumars (MS)	.05
566	Horace Grant (MS)	.10
567	Reggie Lewis (MS)	.05
568	Hakeem Olajuwon	.40
569	Sam Perkins (MS)	.05
570	Chuck Person (MS)	.05
571	Buck Williams (MS)	.05
572	Michael Jordan (SAL)	2.00
573	Bernard King (SAL)	.05
574	Moses Malone (SAL)	.05
575	Robert Parish (SAL)	.05
576	Pat Riley (SAL)	.05
577	Dee Brown (SM)	.05
578	Rex Chapman (SM)	.05
579	Clyde Drexler (SM)	.15
580	Blue Edwards (SM)	.05
581	Ron Harper (SM)	.05
582	Kevin Johnson (SM)	.10
583	Michael Jordan (SM)	2.00
584	Shawn Kemp (SM)	.75
585	Xavier McDaniel (SM)	.05
586	Scottie Pippen (SM)	.40
587	Kenny Smith (SM)	.05
588	Dominique Wilkins (SM)	.10
589	Michael Adams (S)	.05
590	Danny Ainge (S)	.05
591	Larry Bird (S)	.75
592	Dale Ellis (S)	.05
593	Hersey Hawkins (S)	.05
594	Jeff Hornacek (S)	.05
595	Jeff Malone (S)	.05
596	Reggie Miller (S)	.10
597	Chris Mullin (S)	.05
598	John Paxson (S)	.05
599	Drazen Petrovic (S)	.05
600	Ricky Pierce (S)	.05
601	Mark Price (S)	.05
602	Dennis Scott (S)	.05
603	Manute Bol (SC)	.05
604	Jerome Kersey (SC)	.05
605	Charles Oakley (SC)	.05
606	Scottie Pippen (SC)	.40
607	Terry Porter (SC)	.05
608	Dennis Rodman (SC)	.40
609	Sedale Threatt (SC)	.05
610	Business	.05
611	Engineering	.05
612	Law	.05
613	Liberal Arts	.05
614	Medicine	.05
615	Maurice Cheeks	.05
616	Travis Mays	.05
617	Blair Rasmussen	.05
618	Alexander Volkov	.05
619	Rickey Green	.05
620	Bobby Hansen	.05
621	John Battle	.05
622	Terry Davis	.05
623	Walter Davis	.05
624	Winston Garland	.05
625	Scott Hastings	.05
626	Brad Sellers	.05
627	Darrell Walker	.05
628	Orlando Woolridge	.05
629	Tony Brown	.05
630	James Edwards	.05
631	Glenn Rivers	.05
632	Jack Haley	.05
633	Sedale Threatt	.05
634	Moses Malone	.10
635	Thurl Bailey	.05
636	*Rafael Addison*	.10
637	Tim McCormick	.05
638	Xavier McDaniel	.05
639	Charles Shackleford	.05
640	Mitchell Wiggins	.05
641	Jerrod Mustaf	.05
642	Dennis Hopson	.05
643	Les Jepsen	.05
644	Mitch Richmond	.20
645	Dwayne Schintzius	.05
646	Anthony Webb	.05
647	Jud Buechler	.05
648	Antoine Carr	.05
649	Tyrone Corbin	.05
650	Michael Adams	.05
651	Ralph Sampson	.05
652	Andre Turner	.05
653	David Wingate	.05
654	Checklist S	.05
655	Checklist K	.05
656	Checklist Y	.05
657	Checklist B	.05
658	Checklist O	.05
659	Checklist X	.05
NNO	Clyde Drexler USA	55.00
NNO	Team USA Card	10.00
NNO	Team USA	18.00
V	Magic Johnson, James Worthy	1.25
VI	Isiah Thomas, Joe Dumars	.75

1991-92 SkyBox Blister Inserts

Card Nos. 1-4 were inserted in Series I blister packs, with Nos. 5-6 randomly seeded in Series II blisters. The first four cards included logos for USA Basketball, Stay in School, Orlando All-Star Weekend and Inside Stuff. The final two cards were back-to-back cards and highlight NBA Finals MVPs from the Lakers and Pistons. The cards are numbered on the back in roman numerals inside a circle.

		MT
Complete Set (6):		2.50
Common Player (1-4):		.25
Common Player (5-6):		.50
1	USA Basketball (Numbered I)	.25
2	Stay in School - It's Your Best Move (Numbered II)	.25
3	Orlando All-Star Weekend (Numbered III)	.25
4	Inside Stuff (Numbered IV)	.25
5	Back to Back NBA Finals MVP 1987/1988 (Magic Johnson, James Worthy) (Numbered V)	1.00
6	Back to Back NBA Finals MVP 1988/1990 (Joe Dumars, Isiah Thomas) (Numbered VI)	.50

1991-92 SkyBox Mark and See Minis

This 14-card set was included on perforated sheets in two USA Basketball "Mark and See" booklets published by SkyBox and Golden Book. The first 10 2-1/4" x 2-3/4" cards were inserted in both booklets. The fronts are identical in design to the 1991-92 SkyBox Series Two set and the backs are black-and-white. The first booklet included a 7-1/4" x 3-1/2" panel that could be cut into three cards featuring multiple members of the team. The second booklet contains a 7-1/4" x 3-1/2" panel that features the entire team. It is not numbered or designed to be cut into smaller cards.

		MT
Complete Set (14):		30.00
Common Player (530-539):		1.00
Common Panel (544-546):		1.50
530	Charles Barkley	2.00
531	Larry Bird	5.00
532	Patrick Ewing	2.00
533	Magic Johnson	3.00
534	Michael Jordan	12.00
535	Karl Malone	3.00
536	Chris Mullin	1.00
537	Scottie Pippen	5.00
538	David Robinson	3.00
539	John Stockton	3.00
544	Team USA Card 1 (Chris Mullin, Charles Barkley, David Robinson)	1.50
545	Team USA Card 2 (Michael Jordan, John Stockton, Karl Malone, Magic Johnson)	3.00
546	Team USA Card 3 (Patrick Ewing, Larry Bird, Scottie Pippen)	2.00
NNO	Team Photo (7-1/4" by 3-1/2")	4.00

1991 SkyBox Mini

These cards, sponsored by Hostess/Frito-Lay, are 1-1/4" x 1-3/4" and were available, one per bag, in small bags of Hostess products sold at 75,000 locations in Canada. Except for size and numbering, they are identical to the regular 1991-92 SkyBox cards. There were 774,000 sets made, but since the cards were available only as singles, it is difficult to assemble a complete set, which has 49 players and one checklist.

		MT
Complete Set (50):		18.00
Common Player:		.25
1	Kevin Willis	.50
2	Larry Bird	2.00
3	Kevin McHale	.75
4	Robert Parish	.75
5	Kendall Gill	.50
6	J.R. Reid	.25
7	Michael Jordan	6.00
8	Scottie Pippen	2.00
9	Brad Daugherty	.50
10	Larry Nance	.25
11	Rolando Blackman	.25
12	Derek Harper	.25
13	Mahmoud Abdul-Rauf	.25
14	Jerome Lane	.25
15	Joe Dumars	.50
16	Dennis Rodman	1.50
17	Tim Hardaway	1.00
18	Chris Mullin	1.00
19	Hakeem Olajuwon	2.00
20	Otis Thorpe	.50
21	Reggie Miller	1.50
22	Detlef Schrempf	.50
23	Danny Manning	.50
24	Charles Smith	.50
25	Earvin Johnson	2.00
26	James Worthy	1.00
27	Sherman Douglas	.25
28	Rony Seikaly	.50
29	Alvin Robertson	.25
30	Tony Campbell	.25
31	Derrick Coleman	.50
32	Charles Oakley	.50
33	Dennis Scott	.25
34	Scott Skiles	.25
35	Charles Barkley	2.00
36	Hersey Hawkins	.50
37	Jeff Hornacek	.50
38	Kevin Johnson	.75
39	Clyde Drexler	1.50
40	Terry Porter	.50
41	Wayman Tisdale	.35
42	Terry Cummings	.25
43	David Robinson	2.00
44	Shawn Kemp	1.00
45	Ricky Pierce	.25
46	Karl Malone	2.50
47	John Stockton	2.50
48	Harvey Grant	.25
49	Bernard King	.35
50	Checklist	.50

1992-93 SkyBox

This set features rookies, traded players and subsets, including sets for the U.S. Olympic Men's Basketball team, Draft Picks and the David Robinson Flagship series. Four unnumbered insert cards were also made, gold and silver versions for "The Admiral Comes Prepared" and "The Magic Never Ends." Approximately 7,500 silver cards could be found in cases. Approximately 22,000 gold cards were randomly inserted in foil packs. Each regular card front has a color action photo with a screened, colored background. The player's name and team logo are also featured. The card back is numbered and includes a color photo of the player, plus stats and a brief bio note.

		MT
Complete Set (413):		45.00
Complete Series 1 (327):		25.00
Complete Series 2 (86):		20.00
Common Player:		.10
Minor Stars:		.20
Comp. D. Robinson Set (10):		5.00
Complete Series 1 (5):		2.50
Complete Series 2 (5):		2.50
Common Robinson:		.50
Series 1 Pack (12):		1.00
Series 1 Wax Box (36):		30.00
Series 2 Pack (12):		3.50
Series 2 Wax Box (36):		70.00
1	Stacey Augmon	.10
2	Maurice Cheeks	.10
3	Duane Ferrell	.10
4	Paul Graham (John Koncak)	.10
5		.10
6	Blair Rasmussen	.10
7	Rumeal Robinson	.10
8	Dominique Wilkins	.20
9	Kevin Willis	.10
10	Larry Bird	1.75
11	Dee Brown	.20
12	Sherman Douglas	.10
13	Rick Fox	.10
14	Kevin Gamble	.10
15	Reggie Lewis	.10
16	Kevin McHale	.20
17	Robert Parish	.20
18	Ed Pinckney	.10
19	Muggsy Bogues	.10
20	Dell Curry	.10
21	Kenny Gattison	.10
22	Kendall Gill	.10
23	Mike Gminski	.10
24	Tom Hammonds	.10
25	Larry Johnson	1.00
26	Johnny Newman	.10
27	J.R. Reid	.10
28	B.J. Armstrong	.10
29	Bill Cartwright	.10
30	Horace Grant	.25
31	Michael Jordan	4.50
32	Stacey King	.10
33	John Paxson	.10
34	Will Perdue	.10
35	Scottie Pippen	1.00
36	Scott Williams	.10
37	John Battle	.10
38	Terrell Brandon	.20
39	Brad Daugherty	.10
40	Craig Ehlo	.10
41	Danny Ferry	.10
42	Henry James	.10
43	Larry Nance	.10
44	Mark Price	.10
45	Mike Sanders	.10
46	John Williams	.10
47	Rolando Blackman	.10
48	Terry Davis	.10
49	Derek Harper	.10
50	Donald Hodge	.10
51	Mike Iuzzolino	.10
52	Fat Lever	.10
53	Rodney McCray	.10
54	Doug Smith	.10
55	Randy White	.10
56	Herb Williams	.10
57	Cadillac Anderson	.10
58	Walter Davis	.10
59	Winston Garland	.10
60	Mahmoud Abdul-Rauf	.25
61	Marcus Liberty	.10
62	Todd Lichti	.10
63	Mark Macon	.10
64	Dikembe Mutombo	.50
65	Reggie Williams	.10
66	Mark Aguirre	.10
67	William Bedford	.10
68	Lance Blanks	.10
69	Joe Dumars	.20
70	Bill Laimbeer	.10
71	Dennis Rodman	1.50
72	John Salley	.10
73	Isiah Thomas	.25
74	Darrell Walker	.10
75	Orlando Woolridge	.10
76	Victor Alexander	.10
77	Mario Elie	.10
78	Chris Gatling	.10
79	Tim Hardaway	.20
80	Tyrone Hill	.20
81	Alton Lister	.10
82	Sarunas Marciulionis	.10
83	Chris Mullin	.20
84	Billy Owens	.20
85	Matt Bullard	.10
86	Eric Floyd	.10
87	Avery Johnson	.20
88	Buck Johnson	.10
89	Vernon Maxwell	.10
90	Hakeem Olajuwon	1.00
91	Kenny Smith	.10
92	Larry Smith	.10
93	Otis Thorpe	.10
94	Dale Davis	.10
95	Vern Fleming	.10
96	George McCloud	.10
97	Reggie Miller	.50
98	Chuck Person	.10
99	Detlef Schrempf	.10
100	Rik Smits	.20
101	LaSalle Thompson	.10
102	Micheal Williams	.10
103	James Edwards	.10
104	Gary Grant	.10
105	Ron Harper	.10
106	Bo Kimble	.10
107	Danny Manning	.20
108	Ken Norman	.10
109	Olden Polynice	.10
110	Doc Rivers	.10
111	Charles Smith	.10
112	Loy Vaught	.10
113	Elden Campbell	.10
114	Vlade Divac	.10
115	A.C. Green	.10
116	Jack Haley	.10
117	Sam Perkins	.10
118	Byron Scott	.10
119	Tony Smith	.10
120	Sedale Threatt	.10
121	James Worthy	.10
122	Keith Askins	.10
123	Willie Burton	.10
124	Bimbo Coles	.10
125	Kevin Edwards	.10
126	Alex Kessler	.10
127	Grant Long	.10
128	Glen Rice	.20
129	Rony Seikaly	.10
130	Brian Shaw	.10
131	Steve Smith	.20
132	Frank Brickowski	.10
133	Dale Ellis	.10
134	Jeff Grayer	.10
135	Jay Humphries	.10
136	Larry Krystkowiak	.10
137	Moses Malone	.20
138	Fred Roberts	.10
139	Alvin Robertson	.10
140	Dan Schayes	.10
141	Thurl Bailey	.10
142	Scott Brooks	.10
143	Tony Campbell	.10
144	Gerald Glass	.10
145	Luc Longley	.10
146	Sam Mitchell	.10
147	Jerome "Pooh" Richardson	.10
148	Felton Spencer	.10
149	Doug West	.10
150	Rafael Addison	.10
151	Kenny Anderson	.20
152	Mookie Blaylock	.10
153	Sam Bowie	.10
154	Derrick Coleman	.20
155	Chris Dudley	.10
156	Tate George	.10
157	Terry Mills	.10
158	Chris Morris	.10
159	Drazen Petrovic	.10
160	Greg Anthony	.10
161	Patrick Ewing	.50
162	Mark Jackson	.10
163	Anthony Mason	.10
164	Tim McCormick	.10
165	Xavier McDaniel	.10
166	Charles Oakley	.10
167	John Starks	.10
168	Gerald Wilkins	.10
169	Nick Anderson	.20
170	Terry Catledge	.10
171	Jerry Reynolds	.10
172	Stanley Roberts	.10
173	Dennis Scott	.20
174	Scott Skiles	.10
175	Jeff Turner	.10
176	Sam Vincent	.10
177	Brian Williams	.10
178	Ron Anderson	.10
179	Charles Barkley	1.00
180	Manute Bol	.10
181	Johnny Dawkins	.10
182	Armon Gilliam	.10
183	Greg Grant	.10
184	Hersey Hawkins	.10
185	Brian Oliver	.10
186	Charles Shackleford	.10
187	Jayson Williamas	.10
188	Cedric Ceballos	.25
189	Tom Chambers	.10
190	Jeff Hornacek	.10
191	Kevin Johnson	.20
192	Negele Knight	.10
193	Andrew Lang	.10
194	Dan Majerle	.10
195	Jerrod Mustaf	.10
196	Tim Perry	.10
197	Mark West	.10
198	Alaa Abdelnaby	.10
199	Danny Ainge	.10
200	Mark Bryant	.10
201	Clyde Drexler	.50
202	Kevin Duckworth	.10
203	Jerome Kersey	.10
204	Robert Pack	.10
205	Terry Porter	.10
206	Cliff Robinson	.10
207	Buck Williams	.10
208	Anthony Bonner	.10
209	Randy Brown	.10
210	Duane Causwell	.10
211	Pete Chilcutt	.10
212	Dennis Hopson	.10
213	Jim Les	.10
214	Mitch Richmond	.25
215	Lionel Simmons	.10
216	Wayman Tisdale	.10
217	Spud Webb	.10
218	Willie Anderson	.10
219	Antoine Carr	.10
220	Terry Cummings	.10
221	Sean Elliott	.10
222	Sidney Green	.10
223	Vinnie Johnson	.10
224	David Robinson	1.00
225	Rod Strickland	.10
226	Greg Sutton	.10
227	Dana Barros	.10
228	Benoit Benjamin	.10
229	Michael Cage	.10
230	Eddie Johnson	.10
231	Shawn Kemp	1.00
232	Derrick McKey	.10
233	Nate McMillan	.10
234	Gary Payton	.50
235	Ricky Pierce	.10
236	David Benoit	.10
237	Mike Brown	.10
238	Tyrone Corbin	.10
239	Mark Eaton	.10
240	Blue Edwards	.10
241	Jeff Malone	.10
242	Karl Malone	.50
243	Eric Murdock	.10
244	John Stockton	.50
245	Michael Adams	.10
246	Rex Chapman	.10
247	Ledell Eackles	.10
248	Pervis Ellison	.10
249	A.J. English	.10
250	Harvey Grant	.10
251	Charles Jones	.10
252	Bernard King	.10
253	LaBradford Smith	.10
254	Larry Stewart	.10
255	Bob Weiss	.10
256	Chris Ford	.10
257	Allan Bristow	.10
258	Phil Jackson	.10
259	Lenny Wilkens	.10
260	Richie Adubato	.10
261	Dan Issel	.10
262	Ron Rothstein	.10
263	Don Nelson	.10
264	Rudy Tomjanovich	.10
265	Bob Hill	.10
266	Larry Brown	.10
267	Randy Pfund	.10
268	Kevin Loughery	.10
269	Mike Dunleavy	.10
270	Jimmy Rodgers	.10
271	Chuck Daly	.10
272	Pat Riley	.10
273	Matt Guokas	.10
274	Doug Moe	.10
275	Paul Westphal	.10
276	Rick Adelman	.10
277	Garry St. Jean	.10
278	Jerry Tarkanian	.25
279	George Karl	.10
280	Jerry Sloan	.10
281	Wes Unseld	.10
282	Dominique Wilkins (TT)	.20
283	Reggie Lewis (TT)	.10
284	Kendall Gill (TT)	.10
285	Horace Grant (TT)	.10
286	Brad Daugherty (TT)	.10
287	Derek Harper (TT)	.10
288	Mahmoud Abdul-Rauf (TT)	.10
289	Isiah Thomas (TT)	.10
290	Chris Mullin (TT)	.10
291	Kenny Smith (TT)	.10
292	Reggie Miller (TT)	.10
293	Ron Harper (TT)	.10
294	Vlade Divac (TT)	.10
295	Glen Rice (TT)	.10
296	Moses Malone (TT)	.10
297	Doug West (TT)	.10
298	Derrick Coleman (TT)	.10
299	Patrick Ewing (TT)	.20
300	Scott Skiles (TT)	.10
301	Hersey Hawkins (TT)	.10
302	Kevin Johnson (TT)	.10
303	Cliff Robinson (TT)	.10
304	Anthony Webb (TT)	.10
305	David Robinson (TT)	.40
306	Shawn Kemp (TT)	.40
307	John Stockton (TT)	.10
308	Pervis Ellison (TT)	.10
309	3-Point Shootout (Craig Hodges)	.10
310	Magic Johnson (MVP)	.50
311	Slam-Dunk Champ (Cedric Ceballos)	.15
312	West in Action	.40
313	East in Action	.10
314	Michael Jordan (MVP)	2.50
315	Clyde Drexler (Finals)	.20
316	Western Conference (Danny Ainge)	.10
317	Scottie Pippen (Finals)	.50
318	NBA Champs	.10
319	Larry Johnson (ROY)	.50
320	NBA Stay in School	.10
321	Boys & Girls Clubs	.10
322	Checklist #1	.10
323	Checklist #2	.10
324	Checklist #3	.10
325	Checklist #4	.10
326	Checklist #5	.10
327	Checklist #6	.10
328	Adam Keefe (SP)	.10
329	*Sean Rooks* (SP)	.20
330	Xavier McDaniel	.10
331	Kiki Vandeweghe	.10
332	*Alonzo Mourning* (SP)	5.00
333	Rodney McCray	.10
334	Gerald Wilkins	.10
335	*Tony Bennett* (SP)	.20
336	*Laphonso Ellis* (SP)	.25
337	*Bryant Stith* (SP)	.50
338	*Isaiah Morris* (SP)	.20
339	Olden Polynice	.10
340	Jeff Grayer	.10
341	*Byron Houston* (SP)	.20
342	*Latrell Sprewell* (SP)	4.00
343	Scott Brooks	.10
344	Frank Johnson	.10
345	*Robert Horry* (SP)	1.00
346	David Wood	.10
347	Sam Mitchell	.10
348	Pooh Richardson	.10
349	*Malik Sealy* (SP)	.30
350	Morlon Wiley	.10
351	Mark Jackson	.10
352	Stanley Roberts	.10
353	*Elmore Spencer* (SP)	.20
354	John Williams	.10
355	*Randy Woods* (SP)	.20
356	James Edwards	.10
357	Jeff Sanders	.10
358	Magic Johnson	.50
359	*Anthony Peeler* (SP)	.30
360	*Harold Miner* (SP)	.25
361	John Salley	.10
362	Alaa Abdelnaby	.10
363	*Todd Day* (SP)	.40
364	Blue Edwards	.10
365	*Lee Mayberry* (SP)	.20
366	Eric Murdock	.10
367	Mookie Blaylock	.10
368	*Anthony Avent*	.20
369	*Christian Laettner*	1.00
370	Chuck Person	.10
371	*Chris Smith* (SP)	.20
372	Michael Williams	.10
373	Rolando Blackman	.10
374	Tony Campbell	.10
375	*Hubert Davis* (SP)	.20
376	Travis Mays	.10
377	Doc Rivers	.10
378	Charles Smith	.10
379	Rumeal Robinson	.10
380	Vinny Del Negro	.10
381	Steve Kerr	.10
382	*Shaquille O'Neal*	15.00
383	Donald Royal	.10
384	Jeff Hornacek	.10
385	Andrew Lang	.10
386	Tim Perry	.10
387	*C. Weatherspoon* (SP)	1.00
388	Danny Ainge	.10
389	Charles Barkley	.50
390	Tim Kempton	.10
391	*Oliver Miller* (SP)	.40
392	*Dave Johnson* (SP)	.20
393	*Tracy Murray* (SP)	.30
394	Rod Strickland	.10
395	Marty Conlon	.10
396	*Walt Williams* (SP)	.50
397	*Lloyd Daniels*	.20
398	Dale Ellis	.10
399	Dave Hoppen	.10
400	Larry Smith	.10
401	Doug Overton	.10
402	Isaac Austin	.10
403	Jay Humphries	.10
404	Larry Krystowiak	.10
405	*Tom Gugliotta* (SP)	1.00
406	Buck Johnson	.10
407	*Don MacLean* (SP)	.20
408	*Marlon Maxey* (SP)	.20
409	*Corey Williams* (SP)	.20
410	Special Olympics	.10
411	Checklist #1	.10
412	Checklist #2	.10
413	Checklist #3	.10
NNO	Admiral Comes Prepared	7.00
NNO	Magic Never Ends	10.00
NNO	Head of the Class	35.00
AU2	Magic Auto.	275.00
NNO	Head of Class (Magic Johnson, Admiral)	15.00

1992-93 SkyBox Draft Picks

These cards feature 25 of the top 27 first-round draft picks in 1992. Cards 2, 10, 11, 15, 16 and 18 were random inserts in Series I packs. The rest were in Series II packs. There were no cards issued for #s 4 or 17, however. Odds at finding a Draft Pick card were 1 in 8. The card front has a player close-up shot, with a gold rectangle that has his name in it. The card back has player profile, statistics, his team's logo and a card number, using a "DP" prefix. An estimated 75,000 Draft Picks sets were produced.

		MT
Complete Set (25):		50.00
Complete Series 1 (6):		10.00
Complete Series 2 (19):		40.00
Common Player:		1.00
1	Shaquille O'Neal	28.00
2	Alonzo Mourning	7.00
3	Christian Laettner	3.00
5	Laphonso Ellis	2.00
6	Tom Gugliotta	4.00
7	Walt Williams	2.00
8	Todd Day	2.00
9	C. Weatherspoon	3.00
10	Adam Keefe	1.00
11	Robert Horry	3.00
12	Harold Miner	1.00
13	Bryant Stith	1.00
14	Malik Sealy	1.00
15	Anthony Peeler	1.00
16	Randy Woods	1.00
18	Tracy Murray	1.00
19	Don MacLean	1.50
20	Hubert Davis	1.00
21	Jon Barry	1.00
22	Oliver Miller	1.00
23	Lee Mayberry	1.00
24	Latrell Sprewell	5.00
25	Elmore Spencer	1.00
26	Dave Johnson	1.00
27	Byron Houston	1.00

1992-93 SkyBox Olympic Team

These cards, which feature the 12 members of the USA Olympic Men's Basketball Team, were randomly inserted in 1992-93 SkyBox Series I foil packs, one every sixth pack. Each card front features a player in his Olympic uniform and his stats from the Olympic games. The backs trace the team's success in the tournament, from their opening scrimmages to the medal ceremony. A card number, using a "USA" prefix, is also given.

		MT
Complete Set (12):		50.00
Common Player:		1.00
1	Clyde Drexler	3.00
2	Chris Mullin	1.00
3	John Stockton	2.00
4	Karl Malone	2.00
5	Scottie Pippen	6.00
6	Larry Bird	7.00
7	Charles Barkley	4.00
8	Patrick Ewing	2.00
9	Christian Laettner	3.00
10	David Robinson	4.00
11	Michael Jordan	25.00
12	Magic Johnson	4.00

1992-93 SkyBox David Robinson

This 10-card set chronicles David Robinson's rise to NBA stardom. Cards 1-5 were in 1992-93 SkyBox Series I packs; the rest were in Series II packs. There was approximately one David Robinson card in every 8th pack. The card front has a color photo of Robinson, tilted to the left. The set logo appears at the top of the card. The back also has the logo, another picture and a summary of what is pictured on the front. Card numbers use an "R" prefix.

		MT
Complete Set (10):		5.00
Common Player:		.50
1	David Robinson (Childhood)	.50
2	David Robinson (At Ease)	.50
3	David Robinson (College)	.50
4	David Robinson (College)	.50
5	David Robinson (At Ease)	.50
6	David Robinson (College)	.50
7	David Robinson (College)	.50
8	David Robinson (Awards)	.50
9	David Robinson (Awards)	.50
10	David Robinson (At Ease)	.50

1992-93 SkyBox School Ties

These 1992-93 SkyBox second series inserts, when pieced together, form puzzles of NBA players who played collegiate basketball at the same school. Two or three players are on the card; several players are featured on each team's three-card puzzle. The front shows the players in their pro uniforms, and also includes their team logos on a pennant. The card back is numbered using an "ST" prefix and has information about the players on the front, plus a checklist of players who comprise the puzzle. Each card is standard size.

		MT
Complete Set (18):		10.00
Common Player:		.25
1	Patrick Ewing, Alonzo Mourning (Georgetown)	2.00
2	Dikembe Mutombo, Eric Floyd (Georgetown)	.50
3	Reggie Williams, David Wingate (Georgetown)	.25
4	Kenny Anderson, Duane Ferrell (Georgia Tech)	.50
5	Tom Hammonds, Jon Barry, Mark Price (Georgia Tech)	.25
6	John Salley, Dennis Scott (Georgia Tech)	.25
7	Rafael Addison, Dave Johnson (Syracuse)	.25
8	Billy Owens, Rony Seikaly, Derrick Coleman (Syracuse)	.25
9	Sherman Douglas, Danny Schayes (Syracuse)	.25
10	Nick Anderson, Kendall Gill (Illinois)	.25
11	Derek Harper, Eddie Johnson (Illinois)	.25
12	Marcus Liberty, Ken Norman (Illinois)	.25
13	Stacey Augmon, Greg Anthony (UNLV)	.25
14	Armon Gilliam, Larry Johnson, Sidney Green (UNLV)	.50
15	Elmore Spencer, Gerald Paddio (UNLV)	.25
16	Michael Jordan, Sam Perkins, James Worthy (North Carolina)	8.00
17	J.R. Reid, Pete Chilcutt, Brad Daugherty, Rick Fox (North Carolina)	.25
18	Kenny Smith, Hubert Davis, Scott Williams (North Carolina)	.25

1992-93 SkyBox Thunder and Lightning

Cards from this subset were randomly inserted into 1992-93 SkyBox Series II foil packs. Each card front (Thunder) features a full-bleed action photo. The back (Lightning) does also, but of a different player. About 20,000 sets were produced. Cards are numbered 1 of 9, etc.

		MT
Complete Set (9):		45.00
Common Player:		2.00
1	Dikembe Mutombo, Mark Macon	5.00
2	Buck Williams, Clyde Drexler	5.00
3	Charles Barkley, Kevin Johnson	10.00
4	Pervis Ellison, Michael Adams	2.00
5	Larry Johnson, Muggsy Bogues	8.00
6	Brad Daugherty, Mark Price	2.00
7	Shawn Kemp, Gary Payton	8.00
8	Karl Malone, John Stockton	10.00
9	Tim Hardaway, Billy Owens	4.00

1992 SkyBox USA Basketball

This set, which pictures the USA Dream Team, was issued in conjunction with the 1992 Barcelona Olympics. There are nine cards for each of the 10 players featured; each card describes an aspect of the player's game. Fronts have full-bleed color action photos, while stats, a color photo and a topic are on the backs. The rest of the set consists of cards for the coaching staff and a nine-card "Magic On" subset devoted to Magic Johnson's thoughts on various players. Two unnumbered plastic team cards were included in every case, while wax packs could potentially contain autographed Magic Johnson or David Robinson cards.

		MT
Complete Set (110):		20.00
Common Player:		.05
Wax Box:		40.00
1	Charles Barkley (1-9/101)	.25
2	NBA Rookie (Charles Barkley)	.25
3	Game Strategy (Charles Barkley)	.25
4	NBA Best Game (Charles Barkley)	.25
5	Off the Court (Charles Barkley)	.25
6	NBA Playoffs (Charles Barkley)	.25
7	NBA All-Star Record (Charles Barkley)	.25
8	NBA Shooting (Charles Barkley)	.25
9	NBA Rebounds (Charles Barkley)	.25
10	Larry Bird (10-18/102)	.50
11	NBA Rookie (Larry Bird)	.50
12	Game Strategy (Larry Bird)	.50
13	NBA Best Game (Larry Bird)	.50
14	Off the Court (Larry Bird)	.50
15	NBA Playoffs (Larry Bird)	.50
16	NBA All-Star Record (Larry Bird)	.50
17	NBA Shooting (Larry Bird)	.50
18	NBA Rebounds (Larry Bird)	.50
19	Patrick Ewing (19-27/103)	.20
20	NBA Rookie (Patrick Ewing)	.20
21	Game Strategy (Patrick Ewing)	.20
22	NBA Best Game (Patrick Ewing)	.20
23	Off the Court (Patrick Ewing)	.20
24	NBA Playoffs (Patrick Ewing)	.20
25	NBA All-Star Record (Patrick Ewing)	.20
26	NBA Shooting (Patrick Ewing)	.20
27	NBA Rebounds (Patrick Ewing)	.20
28	Magic Johnson (28-36/104)	.50
29	NBA Rookie (Magic Johnson)	.50
30	Game Strategy (Magic Johnson)	.50
31	NBA Best Game (Magic Johnson)	.50
32	Off the Court (Magic Johnson)	.50
33	NBA Playoffs (Magic Johnson)	.50
34	NBA All-Star Record (Magic Johnson)	.50
35	NBA Shooting (Magic Johnson)	.50
36	NBA Assists (Magic Johnson)	.50
37	Michael Jordan (37-45/105)	2.00
38	NBA Rookie Game (Michael Jordan)	2.00
39	Game Strategy (Michael Jordan)	2.00
40	NBA Best Game (Michael Jordan)	2.00
41	Off the Court (Michael Mordan)	2.00
42	NBA Playoffs (Michael Jordan)	2.00
43	NBA All-Star Record (Michael Jordan)	2.00
44	NBA Shooting (Michael Jordan)	2.00
45	NBA All-Time Records (Michael Jordan)	2.00
46	Karl Malone (46-54/106)	.15
47	NBA Rookie (Karl Malone)	.15
48	Game Strategy (Karl Malone)	.15
49	NBA Best Game (Karl Malone)	.15
50	Off the Court (Karl Malone)	.15
51	NBA Playoffs (Karl Malone)	.15
52	NBA All-Star Record (Karl Malone)	.15
53	NBA Shooting (Karl Malone)	.15
54	NBA Rebounds (Karl Malone)	.15
55	Chris Mullin (55-63/107)	.05
56	NBA Rookie (Chris Mullin)	.05
57	Game Strategy (Chris Mullin)	.05
58	NBA Best Game (Chris Mullin)	.05
59	Off the Court (Chris Mullin)	.05
60	NBA Playoffs (Chris Mullin)	.05
61	NBA All-Star Record (Chris Mullin)	.05
62	NBA Shooting (Chris Mullin)	.05
63	NBA Minutes (Chris Mullin)	.05
64	Scottie Pippen (64-72/108)	.40
65	NBA Rookie Game (Scottie Pippen)	.40
66	Game Strategy (Scottie Pippen)	.40
67	NBA Best Game (Scottie Pippen)	.40
68	Off the Court (Scottie Pippen)	.40
69	NBA Playoffs (Scottie Pippen)	.40
70	NBA All-Star Record (Scottie Pippen)	.40
71	NBA Shooting (Scottie Pippen)	.40
72	NBA Steals and Blocks (Scottie Pippen)	.40
73	David Robinson (73-81/109)	.30
74	NBA Rookie (David Robinson)	.30
75	Game Strategy (David Robinson)	.30
76	NBA Best Game (David Robinson)	.30
77	Off the Court (David Robinson)	.30
78	NBA Playoffs (David Robinson)	.30
79	NBA All-Star Record (David Robinson)	.30
80	NBA Shooting (David Robinson)	.30
81	NBA All-Around (David Robinson)	.30
82	John Stockton (82-90/110)	.15
83	NBA Rookie (John Stockton)	.15
84	Game Strategy (John Stockton)	.15
85	NBA Best Game (John Stockton)	.15
86	Off the Court (John Stockton)	.15
87	NBA Playoffs (John Stockton)	.15
88	NBA All-Star Record (John Stockton)	.15
89	NBA Shooting (John Stockton)	.15
90	NBA Assists (John Stockton)	.15
91	Coach (P.J. Carlesimo)	.05
92	Coach (P.J. Carlesimo)	.05
93	Coach (Chuck Daly)	.05
94	Coach (Chuck Daly)	.05
95	Coach (Mike Krzyzewski)	.15
96	Coach (Mike Krzyzewski)	.15
97	Coach (Lenny Wilkens)	.05
98	Coach (Lenny Wilkens)	.05
99	Checklist (Lenny Wilkens)	.05
100	Checklist (Lenny Wilkens)	.05
101	Magic on Barkley	.25
102	Magic on Bird	.30
103	Magic on Ewing	.15
104	Magic on Magic	.25
105	Magic on Jordan	1.00
106	Magic on Malone	.25
107	Magic on Mullin	.15
108	Magic on Pippen	.20
109	Magic on Robinson	.25
110	Magic on Stockton	.15
NNO	Plastic team card	15.00

1992 SkyBox/Nestle

This 50-card set features cards which are identical in format to 1992-93 SkyBox Series I cards, except they are unnumbered. The standard-size cards were produced for Nestle to include in its Nestle Crunch bars, Crunch Minis, Baby Ruth, Butterfinger and Raisinets products, two cards per multi-pack. A binder was also produced for the cards and was available through a mail-in offer.

	MT
Complete Set (50):	75.00
Common Player:	.75
Michael Adams	.75
Rolando Blackman	1.00
Manute Bol	.75
Dee Brown	1.00
Tony Campbell	.75
Derrick Coleman	1.50
Brad Daugherty	1.00
Clyde Drexler	3.00
Joe Dumars	2.00
Sean Elliott	1.00
Pervis Ellison	.75
Kendall Gill	1.50
Tim Hardaway	2.50
Derek Harper	1.00
Hersey Hawkins	1.00
Chris Jackson	1.00
Mark Jackson	1.50
Kevin Johnson	1.50
Shawn Kemp	3.00
Reggie Lewis	1.50
Dan Majerle	2.00
Karl Malone	5.00
Danny Manning	2.00
Reggie Miller	3.00
Chris Mullin	2.00
Dikembe Mutombo	2.00
Charles Oakley	1.25
John Paxson	.75
Sam Perkins	.75
Drazen Petrovic	1.00
Ricky Pierce	.75
Scottie Pippen	5.00
Terry Porter	1.25
Mark Price	2.00
J.R. Reid	.75
Glen Rice	1.50
Alvin Robertson	.75
David Robinson	5.00
Dennis Rodman	2.00
Detlef Schrempf	1.50
Dennis Scott	1.00
Rony Seikaly	1.00
Scott Skiles	1.00
Charles Smith	.75
Kenny Smith	.75
John Stockton	4.00
Otis Thorpe	1.25
Wayman Tisdale	1.00
Dominique Wilkins	3.00
James Worthy	2.00

1993 SkyBox Story of a Game

Included with "The Story of a Game" video series, the three-card set showcases photos of David Robinson taken away from the court. The full-bleed photos include Robinson in a red jersey and black sweats, in a Navy uniform and at a press conference. The SkyBox logo appears in the lower left, while the video logo appears in the upper right. The card backs give a background of the videos, printed over a ghosted "Story of a Game" logo. The cards are numbered inside a circle in the lower right on the backs.

		MT
Complete Set (3):		12.00
Common Player:		4.00
1	David Robinson (in red jersey and black sweats)	4.00
2	David Robinson (in Navy uniform)	4.00
3	David Robinson (at press conference)	4.00

1993 SkyBox Promos

These cards feature the basic design for SkyBox's 1993-94 main set. Cards 1, 3 and 6 utilize the design format used for the set's regular cards; card 2 models the "All-Rookie Team" insert cards; card 4 represents the design for the "Showdown Series" inserts; card 5 models the "Center Stage" insert cards. All of these inserts were featured in Series I packs. The standard-size cards are unnumbered and are listed below alphabetically.

	MT
Complete Set (6):	25.00
Common Player:	2.00
Michael Jordan	10.00
Christian Laettner	2.00
Dan Majerle	2.00
Alonzo Mourning	4.00
Shaquille O'Neal	12.00
David Robinson	5.00

1993-94 SkyBox Premium

SkyBox's 1993-94 two-series effort features enhanced card stock, UV coating, and foil stamping. Each back has a scouting report written about the player by Hall of Fame Coach Jack Ramsay, and a candid photo of the player. Insert cards include NBA All-Rookie Team, Showdown Series, 1992 NBA Draft Picks, Center Stage, 1993 NBA Draft Picks, and Shaq Talk, devoted to Shaquille O'Neal.

		MT
Complete Set (341):		30.00
Complete Series 1 (191):		15.00
Complete Series 2 (150):		15.00
Common Player:		.05
Minor Stars:		.10
Series 1 Pack (12):		1.00
Series 1 Wax Box (36):		30.00
Series 2 Pack (12):		1.50
Series 2 Wax Box (36):		45.00
1	Checklist 1	.05
2	Checklist 2	.05
3	Checklist 3	.05
4	Larry Johnson	.10
5	Alonzo Mourning	.25
6	Hakeem Olajuwon	.50
7	Brad Daugherty	.05
8	Oliver Miller	.05
9	David Robinson	.25
10	Patrick Ewing	.10
11	Ricky Pierce	.05
12	Sam Perkins	.05
13	John Starks	.10
14	Michael Jordan	2.00
15	Dan Majerle	.05
16	Scottie Pippen	.25
17	Shawn Kemp	.20
18	Charles Barkley	.25
19	Horace Grant	.10
20	Kevin Johnson	.10
21	John Paxson	.05
22	Inside Stuff	.05
23	NBA on NBC	.05
24	Stacey Augmon	.05
25	Mookie Blaylock	.05
26	Craig Ehlo	.05
27	Adam Keefe	.05
28	Dominique Wilkins	.20
29	Kevin Willis	.05
30	Dee Brown	.05
31	Sherman Douglas	.05
32	Rick Fox	.05
33	Kevin Gamble	.05
34	Xavier McDaniel	.05
35	Robert Parish	.05
36	Muggsy Bogues	.05
37	Dell Curry	.05
38	Kendall Gill	.05
39	Larry Johnson	.25
40	Alonzo Mourning	.50
41	Johnny Newman	.05
42	B.J. Armstrong	.05
43	Bill Cartwright	.05
44	Horace Grant	.15
45	Michael Jordan	3.00
46	John Paxson	.05
47	Scottie Pippen	.75
48	Scott Williams	.05
49	Terrell Brandon	.05
50	Brad Daugherty	.05
51	Larry Nance	.05
52	Mark Price	.05
53	Gerald Wilkins	.05
54	John Williams	.05
55	Terry Davis	.05
56	Derek Harper	.05
57	Jim Jackson	.50
58	Sean Rooks	.05
59	Doug Smith	.05
60	Mahmoud Abdoul-Rauf	.05
61	LaPhonso Ellis	.05
62	Mark Macon	.05
63	Dikembe Mutombo	.20
64	Bryant Stith	.05
65	Reggie Williams	.05
66	Joe Dumars	.15
67	Bill Laimbeer	.05
68	Terry Mills	.05
69	Alvin Robertson	.05
70	Dennis Rodman	.75
71	Isiah Thomas	.15
72	Victor Alexander	.05

73 Tim Hardaway .10
74 Tyrone Hill .05
75 Sarunas Marciulionis .05
76 Chris Mullin .10
77 Billy Owens .05
78 Latrell Sprewell .50
79 Robert Horry .10
80 Vernon Maxwell .05
81 Hakeem Olajuwon .75
82 Kenny Smith .05
83 Otis Thorpe .05
84 Dale Davis .05
85 Reggie Miller .25
86 Pooh Richardson .05
87 Detlef Schrempf .05
88 Malik Sealy .05
89 Rik Smits .05
90 Ron Harper .05
91 Mark Jackson .05
92 Danny Manning .10
93 Stanley Roberts .05
94 Loy Vaught .05
95 Randy Woods .05
96 Sam Bowie .05
97 Doug Christie .05
98 Vlade Divac .05
99 Anthony Peeler .05
100 Sedale Threatt .05
101 James Worthy .05
102 Grant Long .05
103 Harold Miner .05
104 Glen Rice .10
105 John Salley .05
106 Rony Seikaly .05
107 Steve Smith .05
108 Anthony Avent .05
109 Jon Barry .05
110 Frank Brickowski .05
111 Blue Edwards .05
112 Todd Day .05
113 Lee Mayberry .05
114 Eric Murdock .05
115 Thurl Bailey .05
116 Christian Laettner .05
117 Chuck Person .05
118 Doug West .05
119 Michael Williams .05
120 Kenny Anderson .10
121 Benoit Benjamin .05
122 Derrick Coleman .10
123 Chris Morris .05
124 Rumeal Robinson .05
125 Rolando Blackman .05
126 Patrick Ewing .25
127 Anthony Mason .05
128 Charles Oakley .05
129 Doc Rivers .05
130 Charles Smith .05
131 John Starks .05
132 Nick Anderson .05
133 Shaquille O'Neal 2.00
134 Donald Royal .05
135 Dennis Scott .05
136 Scott Skiles .05
137 Brian Williams .05
138 Johnny Dawkins .05
139 Hersey Hawkins .05
140 Jeff Hornacek .05
141 Andrew Lang .05
142 Tim Perry .05
143 C. Weatherspoon .10
144 Danny Ainge .05
145 Charles Barkley .50
146 Cedric Ceballos .05
147 Kevin Johnson .10
148 Oliver Miller .05
149 Dan Majerle .05
150 Clyde Drexler .25
151 Harvey Grant .05
152 Jerome Kersey .05
153 Terry Porter .05
154 Cliff Robinson .05
155 Rod Strickland .05
156 Buck Williams .05
157 Mitch Richmond .10
158 Lionel Simmons .05
159 Wayman Tisdale .05
160 Spud Webb .05
161 Walt Williams .05
162 Antoine Carr .05
163 Lloyd Daniels .05
164 Sean Elliott .05
165 Dale Ellis .05
166 Avery Johnson .05
167 J.R. Reid .05
168 David Robinson .50
169 Shawn Kemp .50
170 Derrick McKey .05
171 Nate McMillan .05
172 Gary Payton .25
173 Sam Perkins .05
174 Ricky Pierce .05
175 Tyrone Corbin .05
176 Jay Humphries .05
177 Jeff Malone .05
178 Karl Malone .30
179 John Stockton .30
180 Michael Adams .05
181 Kevin Duckworth .05
182 Pervis Ellison .05
183 Tom Gugliotta .05
184 Don MacLean .05
185 Brent Price .05
186 *George Lynch* .10
187 *Rex Walters* .10
188 *Shawn Bradley* .40
189 *Ervin Johnson* .10
190 *Luther Wright* .10
191 *Calbert Cheaney* .50
192 Craig Ehlo .05
193 Duane Ferrell .05
194 Paul Graham .05
195 Andrew Lang .05
196 Chris Corchiani .05
197 *Acie Earl* .10
198 *Dino Radja* .30
199 Ed Pinckney .05
200 Tony Bennett .05
201 *Scott Burrell* .25
202 Kenny Gattison .05
203 Hersey Hawkins .05
204 Eddie Johnson .05
205 *Corie Blount* .15
206 Steve Kerr .05
207 *Toni Kukoc* 1.00
208 Pete Myers .05
209 Danny Ferry .05
210 Tyrone Hill .05
211 *Gerald Madkins* .10
212 *Chris Mills* .30
213 *Lucious Harris* .10
214 *Popeye Jones* .25
215 *Jamal Mashburn* 1.50
216 *Darnell Mee* .10
217 *Rodney Rodgers* .30
218 Brian Williams .05
219 Greg Anderson .05
220 Sean Elliott .05
221 *Allan Houston* 2.00
222 *Lindsey Hunter* .20
223 Chris Gatling .05
224 *Josh Grant* .10
225 Keith Jennings .05
226 Avery Johnson .05
227 *Chris Webber* 3.00
228 *Sam Cassell* 1.50
229 Mario Elie .05
230 *Richard Petruska* .10
231 *Eric Riley* .10
232 *Antonio Davis* .15
233 *Scott Haskin* .10
234 Derrick McKey .05
235 Mark Aguirre .05
236 Terry Dehere .05
237 Gary Grant .05
238 Randy Woods .05
239 Sam Bowie .05
240 Elden Campbell .05
241 *Nick Van Exel* 1.00
242 Manute Bol .05
243 Brian Shaw .05
244 *Vin Baker* 1.00
245 Brad Lohaus .05
246 Ken Norman .05
247 Derek Strong .05
248 Dan Schayes .05
249 Mike Brown .05
250 Luc Longley .05
251 *Isaiah Rider* .75
252 Kevin Edwards .05
253 Armon Gilliam .05
254 Greg Anthony .05
255 Anthony Bonner .05
256 Tony Campbell .05
257 Hubert Davis .05
258 Litterial Green .05
259 *Anfernee Hardaway* 3.00
260 Larry Krystkowiak .05
261 Todd Lichti .05
262 Dana Barros .05
263 *Greg Graham* .10
264 *Warren Kidd* .10
265 Moses Malone .05
266 A.C. Green .05
267 Joe Kleine .05
268 *Malcolm Mackey* .10
269 Mark Bryant .05
270 Chris Dudley .05
271 Harvey Grant .05
272 *James Robinson* .20
273 Duane Causwell .05
274 *Bobby Hurley* .15
275 Jim Les .05
276 Willie Anderson .05
277 Terry Cummings .05
278 Vinny Del Negro .05
279 Eric Floyd .05
280 Dennis Rodman .75
281 Vincent Askew .05
282 Kendall Gill .05
283 Steve Scheffler .05
284 Detlef Schrempf .05
285 David Benoit .05
286 Tom Chambers .05
287 Felton Spencer .05
288 Rex Chapman .05
289 Kevin Duckworth .05
290 *Gheorghe Muresan* .25
291 Kenny Walker .05
292 Atlanta (CF) .05
293 Boston (CF) .10
294 Charlotte (CF) .05
295 Chicago (CF) .10
296 Cleveland (CF) .05
297 Dallas (CF) .25
298 Denver (CF) .05
299 Detroit (CF) .05
300 Golden State (CF) .25
301 Houston (CF) .05
302 Indiana (CF) .05
303 LA Clippers (CF) .05
304 LA Lakers (CF) .25
305 Miami (CF) .05
306 Milwaukee (CF) .30
307 Minnesota (CF) .20
308 New Jersey (CF) .05
309 New York (CF) .05
310 Orlando (CF) 1.00
311 Philadelphia (CF) .05
312 Phoenix (CF) .05
313 Portland (CF) .05
314 Sacramento (CF) .05
315 San Antonio (CF) .25
316 Seattle (CF) .05
317 Utah (CF) .05
318 Washington (CF) .05
319 Karl Malone (PC) .10
320 Alonzo Mourning (PC) .25
321 Scottie Pippen (PC) .25
322 Mark Price (PC) .05
323 LaPhonso Ellis (PC) .10
324 Joe Dumars (PC) .10
325 Chris Mullin (PC) .10
326 Ron Harper (PC) .05
327 Glen Rice (PC) .05
328 Christian Laettner (PC) .10
329 Kenny Anderson (PC) .10
330 John Starks (PC) .10
331 Shaquille O'Neal (PC) 1.00
332 Charles Barkley (PC) .25
333 Clifford Robinson (PC) .05
334 Clyde Drexler (PC) .10
335 Mitch Richmond (PC) .05
336 David Robinson (PC) .25
337 Shawn Kemp (PC) .20
338 John Stockton (PC) .10
339 Checklist 4 .05
340 Checklist 5 .05
341 Checklist 6 .05
NNO Head of Class Card 35.00
DP4 Jim Jackson 3.00
DP5 Doug Christie .50

1993-94 SkyBox Premium All-Rookies

This set features the top five NBA rookies from the 1992-93 season. Cards were random inserts in Series I packs, one per every 36 packs. Fronts have a black band with the player's name and SkyBox logo in gold. The backs have a summary, mug shot and where he placed in the voting for the 1992-93 Rookie of the Year Award. Cards are numbered with an "AR" prefix.

		MT
Complete Set (5):		25.00
Common Player:		1.00
1	Shaquille O'Neal	20.00
2	Alonzo Mourning	5.00
3	Christian Laettner	1.00
4	Tom Gugliotta	1.00
5	LaPhonso Ellis	1.00

1993-94 SkyBox Premium Center Stage

Nine prominent players from 1992-93 are featured on these cards, which have a unique diffraction pattern foil process and a raised image over a black-foil background. The player's name is in silver foil. Backs, using a "CS" prefix, picture the player against a Center Stage logo. A summary describes how the player has taken the "center stage" on his team. Cards 1-5 were random inserts in Series I packs; Series II packs have cards 6-10.

		MT
Complete Set (9):		50.00
Common Player:		1.00
1	Michael Jordan	25.00
2	Shaquille O'Neal	15.00
3	Charles Barkley	4.00
4	John Starks	1.00
5	Larry Johnson	3.00
6	Hakeem Olajuwon	5.00
7	Kenny Anderson	1.00
8	Mahmoud Abdul-Rauf	1.00
9	Cliff Robinson	1.00

1993-94 SkyBox Premium Draft Picks

Nine of the top 1993 draft picks are featured in this insert set. Fronts have pictures taken of the players on draft day, and what number pick he was. Backs, numbered with a "D" prefix, include the player's collegiate stats and a summary of his accomplishments. An NBA Draft and team logo are also pictured. Cards were random inserts in Series I packs, one per every 12 packs. Series II packs were slated to have the remaining 18 first-round draft picks from 1993.

		MT
Complete Set (26):		50.00
Complete Series 1 (9):		10.00
Complete Series 2 (17):		40.00
Common Player:		.50
Number 26 Never Printed		
1	Chris Webber	15.00
2	Shawn Bradley	2.00
3	Anfernee Hardaway	15.00
4	Jamal Mashburn	6.00
5	Isaiah Rider	2.00
6	Calbert Cheaney	1.00
7	Bobby Hurley	1.00
8	Vin Baker	8.00
9	Rodney Rodgers	1.00
10	Lindsey Hunter	.50
11	Allan Houston	5.00
12	George Lynch	.50
13	Terry Dehere	.50
14	Scott Haskins	.50
15	Doug Edwards	.50
16	Rex Walters	.50
17	Greg Graham	.50
18	Luther Wright	.50
19	Acie Earl	.50
20	Scott Burrell	1.00
21	James Robinson	.50
22	Chris Mills	2.00
23	Ervin Johnson	.50
24	Sam Cassell	4.00
25	Corie Blount	1.00
27	Malcolm Mackey	.50

1993-94 SkyBox Premium Dynamic Dunks

This nine-card insert set features some of the game's top dunkers. Each front shows the player dunking the ball; backs have a second photo, with a brief comment on when the player likes to dunk. Cards, randomly inserted in SkyBox Series II packs, one every 36 packs, are numbered with a "D" prefix.

		MT
Complete Set (9):		30.00
Common Player:		.50
Minor Stars:		1.00
1	Nick Anderson	.50
2	Charles Barkley	3.00
3	Robert Horry	2.00
4	Michael Jordan	20.00
5	Shawn Kemp	3.00
6	Anthony Mason	.50
7	Alonzo Mourning	3.00
8	Hakeem Olajuwon	4.00
9	Dominique Wilkins	1.00

1993-94 SkyBox Premium Shaq Talk

These fronts feature a photo printed over a foil-stamped background. The backs have a quote from O'Neal and comments from Hall of Fame Coach Jack Ramsay. Cards, numbered with a Shaq Talk prefix, were available one per every 36 packs.

		MT
Complete Set (10):		40.00
Complete Series 1 (5):		20.00
Complete Series 2 (5):		20.00
Common Shaq:		5.00
1	Shaquille O'Neal (The Rebound)	5.00
2	(Shaquille O'Neal) (The Block)	5.00
3	(Shaquille O'Neal) (The Postup)	5.00
4	(Shaquille O'Neal) (The Dunk)	5.00
5	(Shaquille O'Neal) (Defense)	5.00
6	(Shaquille O'Neal) (Scoring)	5.00
7	(Shaquille O'Neal) (Passing)	5.00
8	(Shaquille O'Neal) (Rejections)	5.00
9	(Shaquille O'Neal) (Confidence)	5.00
10	(Shaquille O'Neal) (Legends)	5.00

1993-94 SkyBox Premium Showdown Series

These 12 cards highlight notable match-ups between some of the NBA's top stars. Cards 1-6 were random inserts, one per every 12 packs; 7-12 were in Series II packs. Each front has an action shot of both players. The backs have stats from every game the two matched up against during the 1992-93 season plus mug shots. Cards are numbered with an "SS" prefix.

		MT
Complete Set (12):		5.00
Complete Series 1 (6):		2.50
Complete Series 2 (6):		2.50
Common Player:		.50
1	Alonzo Mourning, Patrick Ewing	.75
2	Shaquille O'Neal, Patrick Ewing	1.00
3	Alonzo Mourning, Shaquille O'Neal	2.00
4	Hakeem Olajuwon, Dikembe Mutombo	.75
5	David Robinson, Hakeem Olajuwon	1.00
6	David Robinson, Dikembe Mutombo	.50
7	Shawn Kemp, Karl Malone	.30
8	Larry Johnson, Charles Barkley	.50
9	Dominique Wilkins, Scottie Pippen	.50
10	Joe Dumars, Reggie Miller	.50
11	Clyde Drexler, Michael Jordan	2.00
12	Magic Johnson, Larry Bird	1.25

1993-94 SkyBox Premium Thunder and Lightning

These insert cards, numbered with a "TL" prefix, feature two players per card and were random inserts in SkyBox Series II packs, one every 12 packs. Thunder cards feature power plays, such as dunks; Lightning cards feature quick action.

		MT
Complete Set (9):		30.00
Common Player:		.75
1	Jamal Mashburn, Jim Jackson	3.00
2	Harold Miner, Steve Smith	.75
3	Isaiah Rider, Michael Williams	1.50
4	Derrick Coleman, Kenny Anderson	.75
5	Patrick Ewing, John Starks	1.50
6	Shaquille O'Neal, Anfernee Hardaway	20.00
7	Shawn Bradley, Jeff Hornacek	.75
8	Walt Williams, Bobby Hurley	.75
9	Dennis Rodman, David Robinson	5.00

1993-94 SkyBox Premium USA Tip-Off

Collectors could pick up this 13-card set by redeeming the USA Exchange Card that was randomly inserted into SkyBox Series II packs. Posed shots are used on both the card fronts and backs. The players are pictured in their USA jerseys. The cards are numbered "x of 13."

		MT
Complete Set (14):		25.00
Common Player:		.75
1	Steve Smith, Magic Johnson	4.00
2	Larry Johnson, Charles Barkley	2.50
3	Patrick Ewing, Alonzo Mourning	3.00
4	Shawn Kemp, Karl Malone	2.00
5	Chris Mullin, Dan Majerle	.75
6	John Stockton, Mark Price	1.25
7	Christian Laettner, Derrick Coleman	.75
8	Dominique Wilkins, Clyde Drexler	1.50
9	Joe Dumars, Scottie Pippen	2.50
10	David Robinson, Shaquille O'Neal	8.00
11	Reggie Miller, Larry Bird	5.00
12	Tim Hardaway	.75
13	Isiah Thomas	1.00
NNO	Checklist	.25
NNO	Expired USA Exchange	1.50

1993-94 SkyBox Pepsi Shaq Attaq

Distributed in five-card cello packs, the five full-bleed cards include photos from Shaq's Pepsi TV commercial. "Shaq Attaq" is printed in gold lettering on the card fronts, while the Pepsi logo is located at the bottom of the card. The backs have a Shaq photo on the left side, with the Shaq logo in the upper left, a write-up printed beneath it and the SkyBox logo and card number located in the lower right.

		MT
Complete Set (5):		27.00
Common Player:		2.00
1	Shaquille O'Neal (Palming basketball)	8.00
2	Shaquille O'Neal (Bending basketball)	8.00
3	Shaquille O'Neal (Reaching for Pepsi)	8.00
4	Shaquille O'Neal (On bench with kid)	8.00
5	Cover Card	2.00

1993 SkyBox/Schick

These standard-size cards use the same basic design format as SkyBox's regular 1993-94 cards, except these cards were included three per pack with various Schick products. The cards, which are unnumbered, are listed below alphabetically.

	MT
Complete Set (50):	135.00
Common Player:	.75
Greg Anthony	1.00
Stacey Augmon	1.00
Vin Baker	7.00
Corie Blount	.75
Shawn Bradley	7.00
Terrell Brandon	2.00
P.J. Brown	1.50
Scott Burrell	.75
Sam Cassell	2.00
Calbert Cheaney	1.50
Doug Christie	1.00
Lloyd Daniels	.75
Hubert Davis	1.00
Todd Day	1.00
Terry Dehere	.75
Acie Earl	.75
LaPhonso Ellis	1.50
Tom Gugliotta	5.00
Anfernee Hardaway	14.00
Scott Haskin	.75
Robert Horry	1.50
Allan Houston	9.00
Lindsey Hunter	2.00
Bobby Hurley	2.00
Jim Jackson	4.00
Ervin Johnson	.75
Toni Kukoc	4.00
Christian Laettner	3.00
Malcolm Mackey	.75
Jamal Mashburn	7.00
Oliver Miller	1.00
Chris Mills	1.00
Harold Miner	1.00
Alonzo Mourning	14.00
Tracy Murray	.75
Shaquille O'Neal	25.00
Anthony Peeler	1.50
Dino Radja	1.50
Isaiah Rider	4.00
James Robinson	.75
Rodney Rodgers	2.50
Malik Sealy	1.50
Steve Smith	4.00
Elmore Spencer	.75
Latrell Sprewell	3.00
Rex Walters	1.00
Clarence Weatherspoon	2.50
Chris Webber	25.00
Walt Williams	2.00
Luther Wright	.75

1994 SkyBox Blue Chips Prototypes

The three-card set previewed the feature film and the upcoming movie set. Three-card packs were given away during the movie's opening weekend. Overall, 500 theaters handed out the packs. The fronts feature a full-bleed photo, with the "Blue Chips" logo in the lower left and the card's caption in the lower right. The backs have a photo on the left and a write-up on the right, along with a "prototype" stamp. The cards are unnumbered.

	MT
Complete Set (3):	4.00
Common Player:	.50
Title card (Mail-in order)	.50
Pete Pen Talk 1 (Nick Nolte and team)	1.00
A Few Tips (Nick Nolte and Shaquille O'Neal)	3.00

1994 SkyBox Blue Chips

Based on the "Blue Chips" movie, the 90-card set includes cards of Shaquille O'Neal, Anfernee Hardaway, ex-Indiana University player Matt Nover and Nick Nolte in addition to other current and former players. The fronts have full-bleed photos, with the "Blue Chips" logo in the lower left and the card caption on the lower right. The backs include a photo and a write-up, along with the card number and the "Blue Chips" logo.

		MT
Complete Set (90):		10.00
Common Player:		.05
1	Pete Pep Talk 1	.10
2	Thousands Cheer	.05
3	Stacking Hands	.05
4	Two More Points	.05
5	You're Outta Here	.05
6	Pete Punts	.05
7	Q and A	.05
8	Pete's Nemesis	.05
9	Sympathetic Ear (Bob Cousy listening to Nick Nolte)	.25
10	Pete's Dolphin Tank	.05
11	Film at 11	.05
12	Gotta Have Heart	.05
13	Pete Pep Talk 2	.05
14	Another Game, Another Loss	.05
15	Scouting at St. Joe's	.05
16	At Home With Butch (Hardaway at home with mother)	.25
17	Let's Make A Deal	.05
18	Uncle Phil's Big Score	.05
19	The First Sighting	.05
20	The First Dunk (O'Neal slam dunking)	.50
21	Hiring the Tutor (O'Neal introuced to Mary McDonnell)	.25
22	A Tutor with Class	.05
23	Hometown Parade (Matt Nover)	.05
24	Back Home in Indiana	.05
25	The Hard Sell (Nolte recruiting Nover)	.05
26	Varsity vs. Blue Chips	.05
27	Ed Smells Something Rotten	.05
28	Unfinished Business	.05
29	On Campus (O'Neal, Hardaway and Nover girl watching)	.25
30	News Crew (O'Neal with microphone in hand)	.25
31	Rick's on the Air	.05
32	Secret is Revealed	.05
33	Unhappy Seeing Happy	.05
34	Butch at Practice (Hardaway kneeling, basketball in hand)	.25
35	A Few Tips (Nolte coaching O'Neal in practice)	.25
36	More Preparation	.05
37	Two Old Friends (Nolte and Cousy)	.25
38	Pete Challenges Tony	.05
39	We Want Indiana (O'Neal in huddle)	.25
40	Taking the Lead (O'Neal shooting)	.25
41	Job Well Done (O'Neal on bench)	.25
42	On the Move (O'Neal establishing position)	.25
43	Fans Go Wild	.05
44	The Celebration (O'Neal and Hardaway celebration)	.25
45	Victory Returns	.05
46	Ed's Full-Court Press	.05
47	Happy's Last Hurrah	.05
48	No Longer the Coach	.05
49	Always the Teacher	.05
50	Coach Bell	.05
51	Pete's Assistants	.05
52	Vic Roker (Bob Cousy)	.25
53	Happy Kuykendall	.05
54	Uncle Phil	.05
55	Jenny Bell	.05
56	Butch McRae (Anfernee Hardaway)	.50
57	Neon Bodeaux (Shaquille O'Neal)	.50
58	Billy Friedkin (Movie Director)	.10
59	Tony	.05
60	The Dolphin Girl	.05
61	Team 1	.05
62	Team 2	.05
63	Lavada McRae	.05
64	Ed Axelby	.10
65	Ricky Roe (Matt Nover)	.10
66	Under the Hoop (O'Neal playing defense)	.25
67	Precision Pass (Hardaway passing)	.25
68	Up and In	.05
69	Foul	.05
70	Out of My Way (O'Neal establishing position)	.25
71	Taking a Breather (O'Neal taking breather during timeout)	.25
72	Neon at the Line (O'Neal shooting free throw)	.25
73	Give Neon the Ball (O'Neal laughing in practice)	.25
74	Mary McDonnell	.05
75	Standing Tall (O'Neal holding net)	.25
76	Nick and Rob (Nolte and Cousy conversing on campus)	.25
77	Roll Camera (O'Neal joking during filming)	.25
78	Nick and the Crew	.05
79	Pre-school with Shaq (O'Neal with pre-school kids)	.25
80	Piling On	.25
81	Mary Up in Arms (Mary McDonnell in O'Neal's arms)	.25
82	Five Blue-Chippers (Hardaway, O'Neal, Nover, Nolte and Friedkin)	.25
83	The Exorcist (O'Neal making face)	.25
84	Checking the Stats (O'Neal reading sports magazine)	.25
85	Anfernee's Tricks (Hardaway holding two basketballs)	.50
86	The Legendary	.05
87	Shaq at Practice (O'Neal holding ball over head)	.25
88	Shaq Rehearses (O'Neal posed with basketball in hand)	.25
89	Checklist A	.05
90	Checklist B	.05

1994 SkyBox Blue Chips Foil

Randomly inserted, this seven-card chase set focuses on Shaq, Hardaway and Nover. The seventh card is an SP foil card of Shaq slamming home the game-winning dunk. The SP card was only available by mail for $6.99. The card fronts feature a full-bleed photo, with the movie's logo and card caption at the bottom, while the card backs have a photo, with a write-up and the card number. SkyBox produced 12,500 of each card, which is noted on card backs.

		MT
Complete Set (7):		40.00
Common Player:		2.00
F1	Getting to Know (Butch McRae)	10.00
F2	Butch Up Close	10.00
F3	Getting to Know Neon Bodeaux	10.00
F4	Neon Takes Charge	10.00
F5	Getting to Know Ricky Roe	2.00
F6	Ricky on the Line	10.00
SP	Neon's game-winner (Mail-away)	12.00

1994 SkyBox USA Promos

These six cards preview SkyBox's 1994 set devoted to the United States Olympic team. The cards, which are not marked as prototypes, are unnumbered and feature several of the designs used for subsets in the main set. The card fronts of Joe Dumars and Shawn Kemp feature borderless, action color photos; the others show the player standing in front of an American flag. The backs for the six promo cards are all different, modeling the backs used for the subsets within the main set.

	MT
Complete Set (6):	10.00
Common Player:	1.00
Derrick Coleman	1.50
Joe Dumars	1.00
Larry Johnson	2.00
Shawn Kemp	2.00
Alonzo Mourning	4.00
Isiah Thomas	1.00

1994 SkyBox USA

SkyBox International produced these 1994 SkyBox USA Basketball cards, a 95-card set that was expanded at the last minute when Kevin Johnson was added to the United States Olympic Dream Team II in early May, replacing the injured Isiah Thomas on the squad. Thomas remained in the original set, with six cards (#43-48) in the regular issue and two insert cards. Johnson was added as cards #90 through 95, which were available only through a mail-in offer. Players are pictured in both NBA action photos and in their 1994 USA Basketball uniforms. The regular issue is highlighted by a six-card profile section for each of the 14 players, such as NBA Rookie, which recaps the player's rookie season. Other profile cards are: International Experience, Trademark Move, Best Game, NBA Update and Magic On, which offers an inside look at the team by former NBA star Magic Johnson. The final 12 regular issue cards consist of individual cards for each of the four coaches; three cards highlighting rules of international basketball, two checklists, a team card, and commemorative cards of Magic Johnson and David Robinson saluting Dream Team II. The set also features a Champion Gold insert set, with each of the 95 cards in a gold-foil, embossed version of the set; Dream Plays, with actual plays diagrammed by Hall of Fame coach Jack Ramsay and USA Basketball Portraits, an etched foil process which frames a portrait of each team member. There was also a USA Basketball Exchange Card (1 in 300) that could be redeemed for a set of game action photography of Dream Team II at the 1994 World Championship of Basketball, plus another card redeemable for a USA Basketball T-shirt (1 in 300 packs).

		MT
Complete Set (95):		10.00
Common Player:		.05
Alonzo Mourning		
1	International	.30
2	NBA Rookie	.30
3	Best Game	.30
4	NBA Update	.30
5	Trademark Move	.30
6	Magic On	.30
Larry Johnson		
7	International	.20
8	NBA Rookie	.20
9	Best Game	.20
10	NBA Update	.20
11	Trademark Move	.20
12	Magic On	.20
Shawn Kemp		
13	International	.40
14	NBA Rookie	.40
15	Best Game	.40
16	NBA Update	.40
17	Trademark Move	.40
18	Magic On	.40
Mark Price		
19	International	.05
20	NBA Rookie	.05
21	Best Game	.05
22	NBA Update	.05
23	Trademark Move	.05
24	Magic On	.05
Steve Smith		
25	International	.05
26	NBA Rookie	.05
27	Best Game	.05
28	NBA Update	.05
29	Trademark Move	.05
30	Magic On	.05
Dominique Wilkins		
31	International	.20
32	NBA Rookie	.20
33	Best Game	.20
34	NBA Update	.20
35	Trademark Move	.20
36	Magic On	.20
Derrick Coleman		
37	International	.10
38	NBA Rookie	.10
39	Best Game	.10
40	NBA Update	.10
41	Trademark Move	.10
42	Magic On	.10
Isiah Thomas		
43	International	.10
44	NBA Rookie	.10
45	Best Game	.10
46	NBA Update	.10
47	Trademark Move	.10
48	Magic On	.10
Joe Dumars		
49	International	.10
50	NBA Rookie	.10
51	Best Game	.10
52	NBA Update	.10
53	Trademark Move	.10
54	Magic On	.10
Don Majerle		
55	International	.10
56	NBA Rookie	.10
57	Best Game	.10
58	NBA Update	.10
59	Trademark Move	.10
60	Magic On	.10
Tim Hardaway		
61	International	.10
62	NBA Rookie	.10
63	Best Game	.10
64	NBA Update	.10
65	Trademark Move	.10
66	Magic On	.10
Shaquille O'Neal		
67	International	1.00
68	NBA Rookie	1.00
69	Best Game	1.00
70	NBA Update	1.00
71	Trademark Move	1.00
72	Magic On	1.00
Reggie Miller		
73	International	.15
74	NBA Rookie	.15
75	Best Game	.15
76	NBA Update	.15
77	Trademark Move	.15
78	Magic On	.15
79	International	
80	Pete Gillen	
81	Rick Majerus	
82	Don Nelson	
83	Team Card	
84	Time	
85	Court Dimensions	
86	Rules	
79	Don Chaney (coach)	.05
80	Pete Gillen (coach)	.05
81	Rick Majerus (coach)	.05
82	Don Nelson (coach)	.05
83	Team Card	.25
84	International Rules (Time)	.05
85	International Rules (Court Dimensions)	.05
86	International Rules (Rules)	.05
87	Magic Johnson	.50
88	David Robinson	.50
89	Checklist	.05
Kevin Johnson		
90	International	.15
91	NBA Rookie	.15
92	Best Game	.15
93	NBA Update	.15
94	Trademark Move	.15
95	Magic On	.15

1994 SkyBox USA Gold

This 89-card parallel of the base set was seeded one per four packs. The cards have embossed gold-foil on the fronts.

	MT
Complete Set (89):	50.00
Common Player:	.25
Stars:	2x-4x

1994 SkyBox USA Autographs

		MT
Complete Set (7):		550.00
Common Player:		50.00
11A	Larry Johnson	50.00
17A	Shawn Kemp	100.00
35A	Dominique Wilkins	125.00
47A	Isiah Thomas	125.00
53A	Joe Dumars	125.00
59A	Dan Majerle	50.00
65A	Tim Hardaway	100.00

1994 SkyBox USA Dream Play

These 14 insert cards, randomly available in packs of SkyBox's 1994 USA Basketball packs, feature actual plays diagrammed by Hall of Fame coach Jack Ramsay. Cards, numbered with a "DP" prefix, were available at a rate of 1 every 35 packs. Fronts show a dream team member; backs show a specific play drawn up for the player by Ramsay.

		MT
Complete Set (14):		125.00
Common Player:		4.00
1	Alonzo Mourning	15.00
2	Larry Johnson	7.00
3	Shawn Kemp	6.00
4	Mark Price	4.00
5	Steve Smith	4.00
6	Dominique Wilkins	10.00
7	Derrick Coleman	4.50
8	Isiah Thomas	5.00
9	Joe Dumars	4.00
10	Dan Majerle	4.00
11	Tim Hardaway	4.00
12	Shaquille O'Neal	45.00
13	Reggie Miller	6.00
14	Kevin Johnson	4.00

1994 SkyBox USA Kevin Johnson

Collectors could pick up this set by redeeming nine wrappers. Kevin Johnson's name is in silver foil on the first six cards. The other six cards have his name and the SkyBox logo in gold foil. The DP14 and PT14 cards showcase the Dream Play and Portrait chase sets, respectively. The gold cards are listed below with a "G", while the silver cards carry an "S".

		MT
Complete Set (14):		25.00
Common Player:		.50
90G	International	2.00
90S	International	.50
91G	NBA Rookie	2.00
91S	NBA Rookie	.50
92G	Best Game	2.00
92S	Best Game	.50
93G	NBA Update	2.00
93S	NBA Update	.50
94G	Trademark Move	2.00
94S	Trademark Move	.50
95G	Magic on Johnson	2.00
95S	Magic on Johnson	.50
DP14	Dream Play	3.00
PT14	Portrait	12.00

1994 SkyBox USA On The Court

Collectors could receive this 14-card set by redeeming the SkyBox USA On the Court trade card, which was randomly inserted one in every 300 SkyBox USA packs. Each member of Dream Team II is included in this series. The photos used in this set came from the World Championships in Toronto in 1994.

		MT
Complete Set (14):		30.00
Common Player:		.75
1	Isiah Thomas	2.00
2	Tim Hardaway	1.25
3	Reggie Miller	3.00
4	Steve Smith	1.25
5	Joe Dumars	1.25
6	Shawn Kemp	4.00
7	Mark Price	.75
8	Dan Majerle	1.25
9	Kevin Johnson	1.25
10	Derrick Coleman	1.25
11	Alonzo Mourning	3.00
12	Dominique Wilkins	1.25
13	Larry Johnson	2.00
14	Shaquille O'Neal	12.00
NNO	Expired - On The Court Exchange	1.00

1994 SkyBox USA Portraits

These cards, randomly inserted in SkyBox USA Basketball packs, use an etched foil process which frames a portrait of each Dream Team II member. Cards, numbered with a "PT" prefix, were available at a rate of 1 every 100 packs. Card backs have a quote from the player about his selection as a Dream Teamer.

		MT
Complete Set (14):		325.00
Common Player:		8.00
1	Alonzo Mourning	50.00
2	Larry Johnson	30.00
3	Shawn Kemp	15.00
4	Mark Price	8.00
5	Steve Smith	8.00
6	Dominique Wilins	30.00
7	Derrick Coleman	15.00
8	Isiah Thomas	10.00
9	Joe Dumars	10.00
10	Dan Majerle	8.00
11	Tim Hardaway	10.00
12	Shaquille O'Neal	125.00
13	Reggie Miller	18.00
14	Kevin Johnson	8.00

1994-95 SkyBox Promo Sheet

This 7" x 10-1/2" sheet features six cards and promotes the 1994-95 SkyBox Series Two set. The sheets are perforated so the cards can be taken apart.

		MT
Complete Set (6):		2.00
Common Player:		.25
255	Glenn Robinson	1.00
295	Scott Skiles	.25
R3	Jamal Mashburn	.50
DP12	Khalid Reeves	.25
SF14	Danny Manning	.25
SU21	Isaiah Rider	.25

1994-95 SkyBox Premium

SkyBox first series contained 200-cards, including a Dynamic Duals and NBC Playoff Highlight Reel subset. The front design resembles last year's look whereby an action photo breaks through a black bar, with the player's name highlighted within the bar. All card fronts contained the "ball swoosh" that SkyBox is known for. SkyBox Scouting Reports by Jack Ramsay, along with an up-close shot of the player, appear on the back. Insert sets include: SkyBox Head of the Class exchange card, a Hakeem Olajuwon/ David Robinson dual autographed card, Ragin' Rookies, Center Stage and Draft Picks. The exchange card was redeemable for an individually-numbered six-card set of the NBA's top rookies. An unnumbered Hakeem Olajuwon promo card was also made to preview SkyBox's main set. This card is worth $5. Series II cards began with #201, and ended with #350. Insert sets included Slammin' Universe, Draft Picks, Revolution and a Grant Hill set.

		MT
Complete Set (350):		30.00
Complete Series 1 (200):		15.00
Complete Series 2 (150):		15.00
Common Player:		.10
Minor Stars:		.20
Series 1 Pack (12):		1.50
Series 1 Wax Box (36):		50.00
Series 2 Pack (12):		1.75
Series 2 Wax Box (36):		55.00
1	Stacey Augmon	.10
2	Mookie Blaylock	.10
3	Doug Edwards	.10
4	Craig Ehlo	.10
5	Adam Keefe	.10
6	Danny Manning	.20
7	Kevin Willis	.10
8	Dee Brown	.10
9	Sherman Douglas	.10
10	Acie Earl	.10
11	Kevin Gamble	.10
12	Xavier McDaniel	.10
13	Dino Radja	.20
14	Muggsy Bogues	.10
15	Scott Burrell	.10
16	Dell Curry	.10
17	LeRon Ellis	.10
18	Hersey Hawkins	.10
19	Larry Johnson	.30
20	Alonzo Mourning	.50
21	B.J. Armstrong	.10
22	Corie Blount	.10
23	Horace Grant	.20
24	Toni Kukoc	.15
25	Luc Longley	.10
26	Scottie Pippen	.75
27	Scott Williams	.10
28	Terrell Brandon	.10
29	Brad Daugherty	.10
30	Tyrone Hill	.10
31	Chris Mills	.10
32	Bobby Phills	.10
33	Mark Price	.10
34	Gerald Wilkins	.10
35	Lucious Harris	.10
36	Jim Jackson	.50
37	Popeye Jones	.10
38	Jamal Mashburn	.40
39	Sean Rooks	.10

40	Rod Strickland, Mahmoud Abdul-Rauf	.10
41	LaPhonso Ellis	.10
42	Dikembe Motumbo	.20
43	Robert Pack	.10
44	Rodney Rodgers	.10
45	Bryant Stith	.10
46	Reggie Williams	.10
47	Joe Dumars	.20
48	Sean Elliott	.10
49	Allan Houston	.15
50	Lindsey Hunter	.10
51	Terry Mills	.10
52	Victor Alexander	.10
53	Tim Hardaway	.15
54	Chris Gatling	.10
55	Billy Owens	.10
56	Latrell Sprewell	.25
57	Chris Webber	.50
58	Sam Cassell	.20
59	Carl Herrera	.10
60	Robert Horry	.10
61	Vernon Maxwell	.10
62	Hakeem Olajuwon	1.00
63	Kenny Smith	.10
64	Otis Thorpe	.10
65	Antonio Davis	.10
66	Dale Davis	.10
67	Derrick McKey	.10
68	Reggie Miller	.30
69	Pooh Richardson	.10
70	Rik Smits	.15
71	Haywoode Workman	.10
72	Terry Dehere	.10
73	Harold Ellis	.10
74	Ron Harper	.10
75	Mark Jackson	.10
76	Loy Vaught	.10
77	Dominique Wilkins	.25
78	Elden Campbell	.10
79	Doug Christie	.10
80	Vlade Divac	.10
81	George Lynch	.10
82	Anthony Peeler	.10
83	Sedale Threatt	.10
84	Nick Van Exel	.75
85	Harold Miner	.10
86	Glen Rice	.15
87	John Salley	.10
88	Rony Seikaly	.10
89	Brian Shaw	.10
90	Steve Smith	.10
91	Vin Baker	.50
92	Jon Barry	.10
93	Todd Day	.10
94	Blue Edwards	.10
95	Lee Mayberry	.10
96	Eric Murdock	.10
97	Mike Brown	.10
98	Stacey King	.10
99	Christian Laettner	.10
100	Isaiah Rider	.30
101	Doug West	.10
102	Michael Williams	.10
103	Kenny Anderson	.15
104	P.J. Brown	.10
105	Derrick Coleman	.15
106	Kevin Edwards	.10
107	Chris Morris	.10
108	Rex Walters	.10
109	Hubert Davis	.10
110	Patrick Ewing	.50
111	Derek Harper	.10
112	Anthony Mason	.10
113	Charles Oakley	.10
114	Charles Smith	.10
115	John Starks	.10
116	Nick Anderson	.10
117	Anfernee Hardaway	2.00
118	Shaquille O'Neal	2.00
119	Donald Royal	.10
120	Dennis Scott	.10
121	Scott Skiles	.10
122	Dana Barros	.10
123	Shawn Bradley	.15
124	Johnny Dawkins	.10
125	Greg Graham	.10
126	Clarence Weatherspoon	.10
127	Danny Ainge	.10
128	Charles Barkley	.60
129	Cedric Ceballos	.10
130	A.C. Green	.10
131	Kevin Johnson	.20
132	Dan Majerle	.10
133	Oliver Miller	.10
134	Clyde Drexler	.50
135	Harvey Grant	.10
136	Tracy Murray	.10
137	Terry Porter	.10
138	Cliff Robinson	.10
139	James Robinson	.10
141	Bobby Hurley	.10
142	Olden Polynice	.10
143	Mitch Richmond	.20
144	Lionel Simmons	.10
145	Wayman Tisdale	.10
146	Spud Webb	.10
147	Walt Williams	.10
148	Willie Anderson	.10
149	Vinny Del Negro	.10
150	Dale Ellis	.10
151	J.R. Reid	.10
152	David Robinson	.60
153	Dennis Rodman	1.00
154	Kendall Gill	.10
155	Shawn Kemp	.75
156	Nate McMillan	.10
157	Gary Payton	.20
158	Sam Perkins	.10
159	Ricky Pierce	.10
160	Detlef Schrempf	.10
161	David Benoit	.10
162	Tyrone Corbin	.10
163	Jeff Hornacek	.10
164	Jay Humphries	.10
165	Karl Malone	.30
166	Bryon Russell	.10
167	Felton Spencer	.10
168	John Stockton	.30
169	Michael Adams	.10
170	Rex Chapman	.10
171	Calbert Cheaney	.10
172	Pervis Ellison	.10
173	Tom Gugliotta	.10
174	Don MacLean	.10
175	Gheorghe Muresan	.10
176	Charles Barkley	.30
177	Charles Oakley	.10
178	Hakeem Olajuwon	.10
179	Gheorghe Muresan	.10
180	Scottie Pippen	.40
181	Sam Cassell	.10
182	Karl Malone	.20
183	Reggie Miller	.15
184	Patrick Ewing	.20
185	Vernon Maxwell	.10
186	Hardaway/Smith	.30
187	Webber/O'Neal	.50
188	Mashburn/Rogers	.20
189	Kukoc/Radja	.10
190	Hunter/Anderson	.10
191	Sprewell/Jackson	.20
192	W'spoon/ Baker	.10
193	Cheaney/Mills	.10
194	Rider/Horry	.10
195	Cassell/Van Exel	.20
196	Muresan/Bradley	.10
197	Ellis/Gugliotta	.10
198	USA Basketball Team Card	.10
199	Checklist #1	.10
200	Checklist #2	.10
201	*Sergei Bazarevich*	.10
202	Tyrone Corbin	.10
203	Grant Long	.10
204	Ken Norman	.10
205	Steve Smith	.10
206	Blue Edwards	.10
207	*Greg Minor*	.20
208	*Eric Montross*	.50
209	Dominique Wilkins	.20
210	Michael Adams	.10
211	Kenny Gattison	.10
212	*Darrin Hancock*	.15
213	Robert Parish	.10
214	Ron Harper	.10
215	Steve Kerr	.10
216	Will Perdue	.10
217	*Dickey Simpkins*	.20
218	John Battle	.10
219	Michael Cage	.10
220	*Tony Dumas*	.20
221	*Jason Kidd*	2.00
222	Roy Tarpley	.10
223	Dale Ellis	.10
224	*Jalen Rose*	1.50
225	*Bill Curley*	.20
226	*Grant Hill*	4.00
227	Oliver Miller	.10
228	Mark West	.10
229	Tom Gugliotta	.10
230	Ricky Pierce	.10
231	*Carlos Rogers*	.25
232	*Clifford Rozier*	.25
233	Rony Seikaly	.10
234	*Tim Breaux*	.15
235	Duane Ferrell	.10
236	Mark Jackson	.10
237	Byron Scott	.10
238	John Williams	.10
239	*Lamond Murray*	.25
240	*Eric Piatkowski*	.25
241	Pooh Richardson	.10
242	Malik Sealy	.10
243	Cedric Ceballos	.10
244	*Eddie Jones*	2.00
245	*Anthony Miller*	.15
246	Tony Smith	.10
247	Kevin Gamble	.10
248	Brad Lohaus	.10
249	Billy Owens	.10
250	*Khalid Reeves*	.50
251	Kevin Willis	.10
252	*Eric Mobley*	.15
253	Johnny Newman	.10
254	Ed Pinckney	.10
255	*Glenn Robinson*	1.00
256	*Howard Eisley*	.15
257	*Donyell Marshall*	.25
258	*Yinka Dare*	.15
259	Sean Higgins	.10
260	Jayson Williams	.10
261	*Charlie Ward*	.20
262	*Monty Williams*	.15
263	Horace Grant	.20
264	Brian Shaw	.10
265	*Brooks Thompson*	.15
266	*Derick Alston*	.15
267	*B.J. Tyler*	.20
268	Scott Williams	.10
269	*Sharone Wright*	.25
270	*Tony Lang*	.15
271	Danny Manning	.10
272	*Wesley Person*	.50
273	*Trevor Ruffin*	.15
274	Wayman Tisdale	.10
275	Jerome Kersey	.10
276	*Aaron McKie*	.50
277	Frank Brickowski	.10
278	*Brian Grant*	.75
279	*Michael Smith*	.25
280	Terry Cummings	.10
281	Sean Elliott	.10
282	Avery Johnson	.10
283	Moses Malone	.10
284	Chuck Person	.10
285	Vincent Askew	.10
286	Bill Cartwright	.10
287	Sarunas Marciulionis	.10
288	*Dontonio Wingfield*	.15
289	Jay Humphries	.10
290	Adam Keefe	.10
291	*Jamie Watson*	.15
292	Kevin Duckworth	.10
293	*Juwan Howard*	1.00
294	*Jim McIlvaine*	.15
295	Scott Skiles	.10
296	*Anthony Tucker*	.15
297	Chris Webber	.50
298	Checklist #1	.10
299	Checklist #2	.10
300	Checklist #3	.10
301	Vin Baker	.15
302	Charles Barkley	.25
303	Derrick Coleman	.15
304	Clyde Drexler	.20
305	LaPhonso Ellis	.10
306	Larry Johnson	.20
307	Shawn Kemp	.25
308	Karl Malone	.20
309	Jamal Mashburn	.20
310	Scottie Pippen	.25
311	Dominique Wilkins	.15
312	Walt Williams	.10
313	Sharone Wright	.20
314	B.J. Armstrong	.10
315	Joe Dumars	.15
316	Tony Dumas	.10
317	Tim Hardaway	.10
318	Toni Kukoc	.10
319	Danny Manning	.10
320	Reggie Miller	.20
321	Chris Mullin	.10
322	Wesley Person	.20
323	John Starks	.10
324	John Stockton	.20
325	Charles Weatherspoon	.10
326	Shawn Bradley	.10
327	Vlade Divac	.10
328	Patrick Ewing	.15
329	Christian Laettner	.10
330	Eric Montross	.20
331	Gheorghe Muresan	.10
332	Dikembe Mutombo	.10
333	Hakeem Olajuwon	.25
334	Robert Parish	.10
335	David Robinson	.20
336	Dennis Rodman	.25
337	Rony Seikaly	.10
338	Rik Smits	.10
339	Kenny Anderson	.10
340	Dee Brown	.10
341	Bobby Hurley	.10
342	Kevin Johnson	.10
343	Jason Kidd	1.00
344	Gary Payton	.10
345	Mark Price	.10
346	Khalid Reeves	.20
347	Jalen Rose	.20
348	Latrell Sprewell	.15
349	B.J. Tyler	.10
350	Charlie Ward	.10
GHO	Grant Hill Gold	40.00
NNO	Hakeem Olajuwon Gold	25.00
NNO	Olajuwon/Robinson Auto.	200.00

1994-95 SkyBox Premium Center Stage

SkyBox Center Stage is a 9-card insert set, numbered CS1 through CS9. Cards are similar to last year in that they feature the selected player in a dark background with his name across the top in silver, sparkling letters. Backs show the player in action on the right side and a brief biography on the left side with a white background.

		MT
Complete Set (9):		80.00
Common Player:		2.00
1	Hakeem Olajuwon	12.00
2	Shaquille O'Neal	22.00
3	Anfernee Hardaway	35.00
4	Chris Webber	8.00
5	Scottie Pippen	15.00
6	David Robinson	8.00
7	Latrell Sprewell	2.00
8	Charles Barkley	7.00
9	Alonzo Mourning	6.00

1994-95 SkyBox Premium Draft Picks

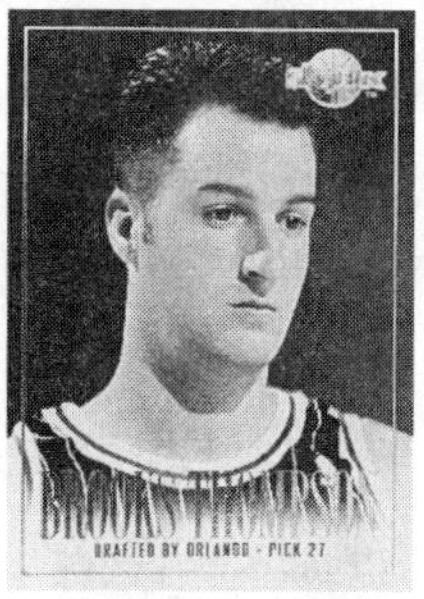

SkyBox Draft Picks contain the top picks from the 1994 draft. Cards feature a close-up of the player in non-NBA clothing, with his name printed in large gold letters across the bottom. The entire front is outlined in gold and the SkyBox logo is gold stamped in the upper right corner. Under the gold foil name is the team and position that player was drafted. The back is all black with the player name printed in team colors and white letters to describe who the Draft Pick is. Card numbers appear in the upper right corner, with the NBA Draft logo in the bottom-center. Cards 2, 4, 9, 10, 14 and 23 were Series I inserts; the remaining cards were found in Series II packs.

		MT
Complete Set (27):		100.00
Complete Series 1 (5):		30.00
Complete Series 2 (22):		70.00
Common Card:		2.00
1	Glenn Robinson	12.00
2	Jason Kidd	12.00
3	Grant Hill	35.00
4	Donyell Marshall	3.00
5	Juwan Howard	18.00
6	Sharone Wright	2.00
7	Lamond Murray	2.00
8	Brian Grant	8.00
9	Eric Montross	3.00
10	Eddie Jones	16.00
11	Carlos Rogers	2.00
12	Khalid Reeves	3.00
13	Jalen Rose	3.00
14	Yinka Dare	2.00
15	Eric Piatkowski	2.00
16	Clifford Rozier	3.00
17	Aaron McKie	3.00
18	Eric Mobley	2.00
19	Tony Dumas	2.00
20	B.J. Tyler	2.00
21	Dickey Simpkins	2.00
22	Bill Curley	2.00
23	Wesley Person	5.00
24	Monty Williams	2.00
25	Greg Minor	2.00
26	Charlie Ward	3.00
27	Brooks Thompson	3.00

1994-95 SkyBox Premium Grant Hill

This five-card set, available as inserts only in hobby packs, celebrates SkyBox's exclusive signing of Pistons' rookie star Grant Hill. One per every 36 SkyBox Series II packs contained a Hill insert. The card back is numbered using a "GH" prefix and includes a color photo, and a ghosted photo as a background. A brief player profile is also included.

		MT
Complete Set (5):		65.00
Common Player:		15.00
1	Grant Hill	15.00
2	Grant Hill	15.00
3	Grant Hill	15.00
4	Grant Hill	15.00
5	Grant Hill	15.00

1994-95 SkyBox Premium Head of the Class

Six of the top NBA rookies are featured on this 1994-95 SkyBox set, available through a Head of the Class Exchange card. The exchange cards were seeded one in every 480 packs of Series I products.

		MT
Complete Set (7):		55.00
Common Player:		1.00
1	Grant Hill	20.00
2	Juwan Howard	10.00
3	Jason Kidd	15.00
4	Donyell Marshall	1.00
5	Glenn Robinson	10.00
6	Sharone Wright	1.50
7	Checklist	1.00

1994-95 SkyBox Premium Ragin' Rookies Promos

Previewing the 1994-95 SkyBox Premium series, this seven-card set includes full-bleed color photos on the front, with a few "scratched-in" white edges. "Ragin' Rookies" is printed in white at the top of the card front, while the player's last name is in red underneath. The card backs have the player's name and write-up on the left, with a photo on the right. The cards are numbered in the upper right with an "RR" prefix. Each of the top left corners are cut off the cards to signify them as promos.

		MT
Complete Set (7):		10.00
Common Player:		1.00
8	Lindsey Hunter	1.00
10	Sam Cassell	2.00
13	Nick Van Exel	3.00
15	Vin Baker	4.00
16	Isaiah Rider	1.00
19	Shawn Bradley	2.00
23	Byron Russell	1.00

1994-95 SkyBox Premium Ragin' Rookies

Ragin' Rookies is a 24-card set of the 1993 rookies. Cards, numbered from RR1 to RR24, were randomly inserted into packs of 1994 SkyBox.

		MT
Complete Set (24):		35.00
Common Player:		.50
Minor Stars:		1.00
1	Dino Radja	1.00
2	Corie Blount	.50
3	Toni Kukoc	1.00
4	Chris Mills	.50
5	Jamal Mashburn	3.00
6	Rodney Rogers	.75
7	Allan Houston	2.00
8	Lindsey Hunter	.50
9	Chris Webber	5.00
10	Sam Cassell	1.00
11	Antonio Davis	.50
12	Terry Dehere	.50
13	Nick Van Exel	3.00
14	George Lynch	.50
15	Vin Baker	3.00
16	Isaiah Rider	3.00
17	P.J. Brown	.50
18	Anfernee Hardaway	14.00
19	Shawn Bradley	1.00
20	James Robinson	.50
21	Bobby Hurley	.50
22	Ervin Johnson	.50
23	Bryon Russell	.50
24	Calbert Cheaney	.50

1994-95 SkyBox Premium Revolution

Cards from this 10-card set could be found as random inserts in 1994-95 SkyBox Series II packs, one every 72 packs. The card front features etched foil in the design; the card back is numbered using an "R" prefix.

		MT
Complete Set (10):		75.00
Common Player:		3.00
1	Patrick Ewing	5.00
2	Grant Hill	30.00
3	Jamal Mashburn	5.00
4	Alonzo Mourning	5.00
5	Dikembe Mutombo	3.00
6	Shaquille O'Neal	25.00
7	Scottie Pippen	12.00
8	Glenn Robinson	10.00
9	Latrell Sprewell	3.00
10	Chris Webber	5.00

1994-95 SkyBox Premium SkyTech Force

These cards were random inserts in 1994-95 SkyBox Series II packs, one every two packs. Each card front has an action photo and the words "Sky Tech Force" on it. The back, numbered using an "SF" prefix, has a color photo on one half and a short player profile on the other.

		MT
Complete Set (30):		10.00
Common Player:		.25
Minor Stars:		.50
1	Kenny Anderson	.50
2	B.J. Armstrong	.25
3	Charles Barkley	1.50
4	Shawn Bradley	.25
5	LaPhonso Ellis	.25
6	Anfernee Hardaway	3.00
7	Bobby Hurley	.25
8	Kevin Johnson	.50
9	Larry Johnson	.50
10	Shawn Kemp	1.00
11	Jason Kidd	3.00
12	Christian Laettner	.25
13	Karl Malone	.75
14	Danny Manning	.50
15	Chris Mills	.25
16	Chris Mullin	.50
17	Lamond Murray	.50
18	Charles Oakley	.25
19	Hakeem Olajuwon	1.50
20	Gary Payton	.50
21	Mark Price	.25
22	Dino Radja	.25
23	Mitch Richmond	.25
24	Cliff Robinson	.25
25	David Robinson	1.00
26	Dennis Rodman	2.00
27	Dickey Simpkins	.25
28	John Starks	.25
29	John Stockton	1.00
30	Charlie Ward	.25

1994-95 SkyBox Premium Slammin' Universe

These 30 cards were random inserts in 1994-95 SkyBox Series II packs, one every two packs. The cards have a color action photo on the front against an outer space motif. The player's name, set logo and SkyBox logo are all stamped in foil on the front. The back, numbered using an "SU" prefix, has a photo on one side and a brief player profile on the other. The card format is a horizontal design.

		MT
Complete Set (30):		20.00
Common Player:		.25
Minor Stars:		.50
1	Vin Baker	1.00
2	Dee Brown	.25
3	Derrick Coleman	.50
4	Clyde Drexler	1.00
5	Joe Dumars	.50
6	Tony Dumas	.25
7	Patrick Ewing	1.00
8	Horace Grant	.50
9	Tom Gugliotta	.25
10	Grant Hill	7.50
11	Jim Jackson	1.00
12	Toni Kukoc	.50
13	Donyell Marshall	.50
14	Jamal Mashburn	.50
15	Reggie Miller	1.00
16	Eric Montross	.50
17	Alonzo Mourning	1.00
18	Dikembe Mutombo	.50
19	Shaquille O'Neal	4.00
20	Glen Rice	.50
21	Isaiah Rider	.75
22	Glenn Robinson	3.00
23	Jalen Rose	.50
24	Detlef Schrempf	.25
25	Steve Smith	.25
26	Latrell Sprewell	.75
27	Rod Strickland	.25
28	B.J. Tyler	.25
29	Nick Van Exel	1.00
30	Dominique Wilkins	.50

1995-96 SkyBox Promo Sheet Series I

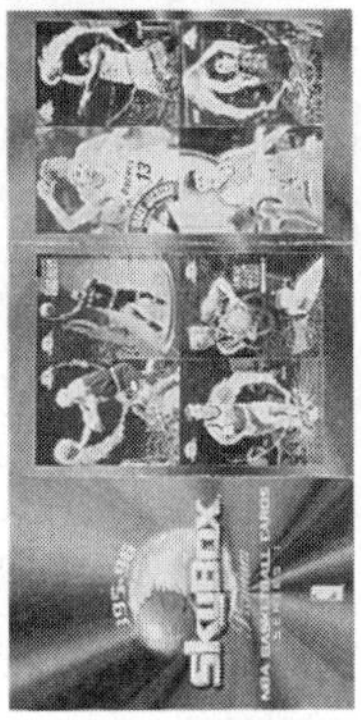

This eight-card perforated book of cards was distributed to dealers and media members to provide a sneak peak at the 1995-96 SkyBox Series I Basketball set. The book could be opened up to reveal all eight cards, which included examples of base cards, subsets and insert sets.

		MT
Complete Set (8):		5.00
Common Player:		.25
	Jason Kidd	.75
	Anfernee Hardaway (Meltdown)	2.00
	Mark Jackson (Front & Center)	.25
	Karl Malone	1.00
	Mark Price	.25
	Brian Grant (Atomic)	.25
	Gheorghe Muresan (Turning Point)	.25
	Tom Gugliotta	.50

1995-96 SkyBox Promo Sheet Series 2

Measuring 8" x 10-1/2", this promo sheet features eight cards previewing the 1995-96 SkyBox Series Two set. The cards could be removed from the perforated sheet and are identical to the cards from the regular product.

		MT
Complete Set (8):		8.00
Common Player:		.25
153	Dana Barros	.25
182	Alonzo Mourning	1.00
229	Brent Barry	.50
235	Jerry Stackhouse	1.50
255	Tim Hardaway	.75
283	Grant Hill	4.00
285	Clyde Drexler	1.00
HH13	Michael Finley	3.00

1995-96 SkyBox Premium

SkyBox released its 1995-96 Premium basketball set in two series - 150 and 151 cards. Series I includes 124 veteran players and three subsets (Expansion subset, Turning Point and Front and Center). Series I insert sets include Kinetic, Dynamic, Atomic, Standouts, Hobby Standouts, Close-Ups, Larger-Than-Life, Rookie Prevue and Exchange cards. Those who get all three draft pick exchange cards (inserted one per every 40 packs) can redeem them for a 13-card set of NBA Draft Lottery Picks who signed by Jan. 1, 1996. Series II is the first to include Magic Johnson on a regular card after his return. He's also on an insert card. The series includes 68 updated cards, 30 rookies, 28 Honor Roll cards, 22 Electrified and two checklists. Insert cards in the series include High Hopes, Hot Sparks and Meltdown.

		MT
Complete Set (301):		32.00
Complete Series 1 (150):		12.00
Complete Series 2 (151):		20.00
Common Player:		.05
Minor Stars:		.10
Ser. 1 or 2 Pack (12):		1.25
Jumbo Pack (20):		2.00
Ser. 1 or 2 Box (36):		40.00
1	Stacey Augmon	.05
2	Mookie Blaylock	.05
3	Grant Long	.05
4	Steve Smith	.05
5	Dee Brown	.05
6	Sherman Douglas	.05
7	Eric Montross	.05
8	Dino Radja	.05
9	Dominique Wilkins	.10
10	Muggsy Bogues	.05
11	Scott Burrell	.05
12	Dell Curry	.05
13	Larry Johnson	.25
14	Alonzo Mourning	.25
15	Michael Jordan	2.00
16	Steve Kerr	.05
17	Toni Kukoc	.05
18	Scottie Pippen	.75
19	Terrell Brandon	.05
20	Tyrone Hill	.05
21	Chris Mills	.05
22	Mark Price	.05
23	John Williams	.05
24	Tony Dumas	.05
25	Jim Jackson	.25
26	Popeye Jones	.05
27	Jason Kidd	1.00
28	Jamal Mashburn	.30
29	LaPhonso Ellis	.05
30	Dikembe Mutombo	.20
31	Robert Pack	.05
32	Jalen Rose	.05
33	Bryant Stith	.05
34	Joe Dumars	.05
35	Grant Hill	1.00
36	Allan Houston	.05
37	Lindsey Hunter	.05
38	Chris Gatling	.05
39	Tim Hardaway	.05
40	Donyell Marshall	.05
41	Chris Mullin	.10
42	Carlos Rogers	.05
43	Latrell Sprewell	.20
44	Sam Cassell	.10
45	Clyde Drexler	.30
46	Robert Horry	.10
47	Hakeem Olajuwon	.60
48	Kenny Smith	.05
49	Dale Davis	.05
50	Mark Jackson	.05
51	Reggie Miller	.20
52	Rik Smits	.05
53	Lamond Murray	.05
54	Eric Piatkowski	.05
55	Pooh Richardson	.05
56	Rodney Rogers	.05
57	Loy Vaught	.05
58	Elden Campbell	.05
59	Cedric Ceballos	.05
60	Vlade Divac	.05
61	Eddie Jones	.30
62	Anthony Peeler	.05
63	Nick Van Exel	.30
64	Bimbo Coles	.05
65	Billy Owens	.05
66	Khalid Reeves	.10
67	Glen Rice	.05
68	Kevin Willis	.05
69	Vin Baker	.20
70	Todd Day	.05
71	Eric Murdock	.05
72	Glenn Robinson	.60
73	Tom Gugliotta	.05
74	Christian Laettner	.05
75	Isaiah Rider	.10
76	Doug West	.05
77	Kenny Anderson	.05
78	P.J. Brown	.05
79	Derrick Coleman	.10
80	Armon Gilliam	.05
81	Patrick Ewing	.20
82	Derek Harper	.05
83	Anthony Mason	.05
84	Charles Oakley	.05
85	John Starks	.05
86	Nick Anderson	.05
87	Horace Grant	.20
88	Anfernee Hardaway	2.00
89	Shaquille O'Neal	1.50
90	Dana Barros	.05
91	Shawn Bradley	.05
92	Clarence Weatherspoon	.05
93	Sharone Wright	.05
94	Charles Barkley	.40
95	Kevin Johnson	.10
96	Dan Majerle	.05
97	Danny Manning	.05
98	Wesley Person	.05
99	Clifford Robinson	.05
100	Rod Strickland	.05
101	Otis Thorpe	.05
102	Buck Williams	.05
103	Brian Grant	.20
104	Olden Polynice	.05
105	Mitch Richmond	.10
106	Walt Williams	.05
107	Vinny Del Negro	.05
108	Sean Elliott	.05
109	Avery Johnson	.05
110	David Robinson	.40
111	Dennis Rodman	1.00
112	Shawn Kemp	.50
113	Gary Payton	.10
114	Sam Perkins	.05
115	Detlef Schrempf	.05
116	David Benoit	.05
117	Jeff Hornacek	.05
118	Karl Malone	.25
119	John Stockton	.25
120	Calbert Cheaney	.05
121	Juwan Howard	.50
122	Don MacLean	.05
123	Gheorghe Muresan	.05
124	Chris Webber	.20
125	Robert Horry (Front & Center)	.05
126	Mark Jackson (Front & Center)	.05
127	Steve Smith (Front & Center)	.05
128	Lamond Murray (Front & Center)	.05
129	Christian Laettner (Front & Center)	.05
130	Kenny Anderson (Front & Center)	.05
131	Anthony Mason (Front & Center)	.05
132	Kevin Johnson (Front & Center)	.05
133	Jeff Hornacek (Front & Center)	.05
134	Larry Johnson (Turning Point)	.10
135	Popeye Jones (Turning Point)	.05
136	Allan Houston (Turning Point)	.05
137	Chris Gatling (Turning Point)	.05
138	Sam Cassell (Turning Point)	.05
139	Anthony Peeler (Turning Point)	.05
140	Vin Baker (Turning Point)	.05
141	Dana Barros (Turning Point)	.05
142	Gheorghe Muresan (Turning Point)	.05
143	Toronto Raptors	.05
144	Vancouver Grizzlies	.05
145	Miami Charlotte	.05
146	Orlando Minnesota	.05
147	Toronto Raptors	.05
148	Vancouver Grizzlies	.05
149	Checklist #1	.05
150	Checklist #2	.05
151	Craig Ehlo	.05
152	Spud Webb	.05
153	Dana Barros	.05
154	Rick Fox	.05
155	Kendall Gill	.05
156	Khalid Reeves	.05
157	Glen Rice	.05
158	Luc Longley	.05
159	Dennis Rodman	1.75
160	Dickey Simpkins	.05
161	Danny Ferry	.05
162	Dan Majerle	.05
163	Bobby Phills	.05
164	Lucious Harris	.05
165	George McCloud	.05
166	Mahmoud Abdul-Rauf	.05
167	Don MacLean	.05
168	Reggie Williams	.05
169	Terry Mills	.05
170	Otis Thorpe	.05
171	B.J. Armstrong	.05
172	Rony Seikaly	.05
173	Chucky Brown	.05
174	Mario Elie	.05
175	Antonio Davis	.05
176	Ricky Pierce	.05
177	Terry Dehere	.05
178	Rodney Rogers	.05
179	Malik Sealy	.05
180	Brian Williams	.05
181	Sedale Threatt	.05
182	Alonzo Mourning	.25
183	Lee Mayberry	.05
184	Sean Rooks	.05
185	Shawn Bradley	.05
186	Kevin Edwards	.05
187	Hubert Davis	.05
188	Charles Smith	.05
189	Charlie Ward	.05
190	Dennis Scott	.05
191	Brian Shaw	.05
192	Derrick Coleman	.05
193	Richard Dumas	.05
194	Vernon Maxwell	.05
195	A.C. Green	.05
196	Elliot Perry	.05
197	John Williams	.05
198	Aaron McKie	.05
199	Bobby Hurley	.05
200	Michael Smith	.05
201	J.R. Reid	.05
202	Hersey Hawkins	.05
203	Willie Anderson	.05
204	Oliver Miller	.05
205	Tracy Murray	.05
206	Alvin Robertson	.05
207	Carlos Rogers	.05
208	John Salley	.05
209	Zan Tabak	.05
210	Adam Keefe	.05
211	Chris Morris	.05
212	Greg Anthony	.05
213	Blue Edwards	.05
214	Kenny Gattison	.05
215	Antonio Harvey	.05
216	Chris King	.05
217	Byron Scott	.05
218	Robert Pack	.05
219	*Alan Henderson*	.25
220	*Eric Williams*	.25
221	*George Zidek*	.20
222	*Jason Caffey*	.10
223	*Bob Sura*	.25
224	*Cherokee Parks*	.25
225	*Antonio McDyess*	2.00
226	*Theo Ratliff*	1.00
227	*Joe Smith*	1.00
228	*Travis Best*	.20
229	*Brent Barry*	.50
230	*Predrag Danilovic*	.25
231	*Kurt Thomas*	.50
232	*Shawn Respert*	.25
233	*Kevin Garnett*	6.00
234	*Ed O'Bannon*	.10
235	*Jerry Stackhouse*	2.50
236	*Michael Finley*	2.00
237	*Mario Bennett*	.20
238	*Randolph Childress*	.20
239	*Arvydas Sabonis*	.75
240	*Gary Trent*	.20
241	*Tyus Edney*	.10
242	*Corliss Williamson*	.25
243	*Cory Alexander*	.20
244	*Damon Stoudamire*	1.00
245	*Greg Ostertag*	.20
246	*Lawrence Moten*	.20
247	*Bryant Reeves*	1.00
248	*Rasheed Wallace*	2.00
249	Muggsy Bogues (Honor Roll)	.05
250	Dell Curry (Honor Roll)	.05
251	Scottie Pippen (Honor Roll)	.25
252	Danny Ferry (Honor Roll)	.05
253	Mahmoud Abdul-Rauf (Honor Roll)	.05
254	Joe Dumars (Honor Roll)	.05
255	Tim Hardaway (Honor Roll)	.10
256	Chris Mullin (Honor Roll)	.05
257	Hakeem Olajuwon (Honor Roll)	.25
258	Kenny Smith (Honor Roll)	.05
259	Reggie Miller (Honor Roll)	.15
260	Rik Smits (Honor Roll)	.05
261	Vlade Divac (Honor Roll)	.05
262	Doug West (Honor Roll)	.05
263	Patrick Ewing (Honor Roll)	.10
264	Charles Oakley (Honor Roll)	.05
265	Nick Anderson (Honor Roll)	.05
266	Dennis Scott (Honor Roll)	.05
267	Jeff Turner (Honor Roll)	.05
268	Charles Barkley (Honor Roll)	.20
269	Kevin Johnson (Honor Roll)	.05
270	Cliff Robinson (Honor Roll)	.05
271	Buck Williams (Honor Roll)	.05
272	Lionel Simmons (Honor Roll)	.05
273	David Robinson (Honor Roll)	.20
274	Gary Payton (Honor Roll)	.10
275	Karl Malone (Honor Roll)	.15
276	John Stockton (Honor Roll)	.15
277	Steve Smith (Electrified)	.05
278	Michael Jordan (Electrified)	1.50
279	Jim Jackson (Electrified)	.10
280	Jason Kidd (Electrified)	.50
281	Jamal Mashburn (Electrified)	.10
282	Dikembe Mutombo (Electrified)	.05
283	Grant Hill (Electrified)	.50
284	Tim Hardaway (Electrified)	.10
285	Clyde Drexler (Electrified)	.20
286	Cedric Ceballos (Electrified)	.10
287	Gary Payton (Electrified)	.10
288	Billy Owens (Electrified)	.05
289	Vin Baker (Electrified)	.10
290	Glenn Robinson (Electrified)	.20
291	Kenny Anderson (Electrified)	.05
292	Anfernee Hardaway (Electrified)	.75
293	Shaquille O'Neal (Electrified)	.75
294	Charles Barkley (Electrified)	.25
295	Rod Strickland (Electrified)	.05
296	Mitch Richmond (Electrified)	.05
297	Juwan Howard (Electrified)	.15
298	Chris Webber (Electrified)	.05
299	Checklist	.05
300	Checklist	.05
301	Magic Johnson	1.00
E1	Exchange Card A	12.00
E2	Exchange Card B	12.00
E3	Exchange Card C	12.00

1995-96 SkyBox Premium Atomic

These cards were random inserts in 1995-96 SkyBox Series I packs, one per every regular pack and one per every three jumbo packs. The cards, which offer high-tech graphics, feature the NBA's most powerful players. Each card front has a color action photo of a player holding a basketball which is surrounded by a molecular structure, as is the word Atomic, which is in the lower left corner. Gold foil stamping is used for the player's name, team name, position and SkyBox icon, which are in the upper corners. The back has a color action photo in the background, with a brief description of why the player is a force in the league. A small head shot also appears on the back, which is numbered using an "A" prefix.

		MT
Complete Set (15):		8.00
Common Player:		.25
1	Eric Montross	.25
2	Charles Oakley	.25
3	Rik Smits	.25
4	Vlade Divac	.25
5	Buck Williams	.25
6	Vin Baker	.50
7	Glenn Robinson	1.00
8	Isaiah Rider	.25
9	Derrick Coleman	.25
10	Clarence Weatherspoon	.25
11	Sharone Wright	.25
12	Brian Grant	.50
13	Jimmy Jackson	.50
14	Clyde Drexler	1.00
15	Anfernee Hardaway	4.00

1995-96 SkyBox Premium Close-Ups

These 1995-96 SkyBox Series I insert cards allow collectors to get up close and personal with nine NBA players. Each card front has a player profile shot dominating it, with gold foil stamping along the left side. Gold foil stamping is also used for the set logo and "Close-Up," plus the player's first name, which are all along the bottom. The player's last name is in capital letters in the lower right corner, with his first name over it. The back, numbered using a "C" prefix, has the player's name and team name in the upper left corner. Underneath is a brief player profile. A second player close-up shot dominates half of the card back. Cards were random inserts in Series I packs, one per every nine retail packs, and one per every six jumbo packs.

		MT
Complete Set (9):		18.00
Common Player:		1.00
1	Scottie Pippen	4.00
2	Grant Hill	7.00
3	Clyde Drexler	3.00
4	Nick Van Exel	2.00
5	Tom Gugliotta	1.00
6	Patrick Ewing	2.00
7	Charles Barkley	3.00
8	Karl Malone	2.00
9	Juwan Howard	3.00

1995-96 SkyBox Premium Dynamic

These 1995-96 SkyBox Series I inserts, seeded one per every four retail packs and one per every three jumbo packs, feature 12 of the NBA's most intense performers. Each card front has a color action photo, with a colored foil background. A SkyBox logo is in gold foil in the upper right corner; the player's name and "Dynamic" are written at the bottom of the card. Each card back, numbered using a "D" prefix, has a photo in the background, with a color mug shot towards the bottom, adjacent to a recap of why the player is considered an intense player.

		MT
Complete Set (12):		6.00
Common Player:		.25
1	Larry Johnson	.50
2	Alonzo Mourning	.50
3	Dikembe Mutombo	.25
4	Jalen Rose	.25
5	Grant Hill	2.50
6	Latrell Sprewell	.25
7	Reggie Miller	.75
8	John Starks	.25
9	Calbert Cheaney	.25
10	Dennis Rodman	2.00
11	Detlef Schrempf	.25
12	Chris Webber	.50

1995-96 SkyBox Premium High Hopes

The year's top rookies are featured in this 1995-96 SkyBox Series II insert set. Cards, seeded one per every 18 packs, are numbered on the back using an "HH" prefix. The card front has a color action photo, with the words "High Hopes" in fiery letters behind them. The player's team name is along the bottom of the card, with his name in gold foil letters above it. Gold foil stamping is also used for the SkyBox logo in an upper corner. The back has "High Hopes" written along the right side, with a summary of the skills the player brings to the NBA on the left side. The player's name is in the upper left corner; the card number is in the lower left corner. A small photo is also on the back.

		MT
Complete Set (20):		70.00
Common Player:		1.00
1	Alan Henderson	1.00
2	Eric Williams	1.00
3	George Zidek	1.00
4	Bob Sura	2.00
5	Cherokee Parks	1.00
6	Antonio McDyess	10.00
7	Joe Smith	7.00
8	Brent Barry	2.00
9	Shawn Respert	1.00
10	Kevin Garnett	25.00
11	Ed O'Bannon	1.00
12	Jerry Stackhouse	7.00
13	Michael Finley	5.00
14	Arvydas Sabonis	3.00
15	Gary Trent	1.00
16	Tyus Edney	1.00
17	Damon Stoudamire	10.00
18	Greg Ostertag	1.00
19	Bryant Reeves	3.00
20	Rasheed Wallace	4.00

1995-96 SkyBox Premium Hot Sparks

These cards were random inserts in 1995-96 SkyBox Series II packs, one per every 12 hobby packs. Among the players in the set is Magic Johnson. The card front has a color action photo on it, against a silvery red-tinted metallic background. Red foil stamping is used for the player's name along the right side of the card and "Hot Sparks," which is in the lower left corner. The SkyBox logo is in the upper right corner, stamped in gold foil. The card back, numbered using an "HS" prefix, has the player's name, a color photo and a brief summary of how the player can spark his team to victory.

		MT
Complete Set (11):		50.00
Common Player:		2.00

1	Mookie Blaylock	2.00
2	Jason Kidd	7.00
3	Tim Hardaway	2.00
4	Nick Van Exel	3.00
5	Kenny Anderson	2.00
6	Anfernee Hardaway	12.00
7	Rod Strickland	2.00
8	Gary Payton	3.00
9	Damon Stoudamire	15.00
10	John Stockton	4.00
11	Magic Johnson	8.00

1995-96 SkyBox Premium Kinetic

Nine of the NBA's speed demons are featured in this 1995-96 SkyBox Series I insert set. Cards were seeded one per every four retail packs and one per every three jumbo packs. Each front has a color action photo, with neon-light colored foil stamping weaved into the design. Silver foil stamping is used for the player's name, team name and "Kinetic," which are written in the lower left corner. A SkyBox logo is stamped in gold foil in the upper right corner. The card back, numbered using a "K" prefix, has a photo as the background, with a smaller mug shot and a brief description of the player's speed also included.

		MT
Complete Set (9):		2.00
Common Player:		.25
1	Mookie Blaylock	.25
2	Tim Hardaway	.25
3	Lamond Murray	.25
4	Stacey Augmon	.25
5	Nick Van Exel	.50
6	Khalid Reeves	.25
7	Kenny Anderson	.25
8	Rod Strickland	.25
9	Gary Payton	.50

1995-96 SkyBox Premium Larger Than Life

Some of the biggest accomplishments of the NBA's best are featured on these 10 1995-96 SkyBox Series I inserts. Cards were seeded one per every 48 packs or one per every 36 jumbo packs, making them the rarest of the Series I inserts. Each card front has a foiled background, with a color action photo on it. "Larger Than Life" is written along the right side of the card, with a gold-foiled SkyBox logo above it in the upper right corner. The player's name is written in the lower left corner. The card back also has a metallic foil background, plus another color photo. The player's name is in the upper right corner, with a recap of the player's accomplishments underneath. The card number, using an "L" prefix, is in the lower left corner.

		MT
Complete Set (10):		125.00
Common Player:		5.00
1	Michael Jordan	65.00
2	Jason Kidd	12.00
3	Grant Hill	25.00
4	Hakeem Olajuwon	14.00
5	Glenn Robinson	8.00
6	Patrick Ewing	5.00
7	Shaquille O'Neal	30.00
8	Charles Barkley	10.00
9	David Robinson	10.00
10	John Stockton	5.00

1995-96 SkyBox Premium Lottery Exchange

After collecting three seperate Lottery Exchange cards (inserted 1:40 Series One packs), collectors could redeem the cards for this 13-card set featuring the first 13 picks in the 1995 NBA Draft. This offer expired June 15, 1996.

		MT
Complete Set (13):		50.00
Common Player:		1.00
1	Joe Smith	4.00
2	Antonio McDyess	10.00
3	Jerry Stackhouse	12.00
4	Rasheed Wallace	10.00
5	Kevin Garnett	30.00
6	Bryant Reeves	2.50
7	Damon Stoudamire	6.00
8	Shawn Respert	1.00
9	Ed O'Bannon	1.00
10	Kurt Thomas	1.00
11	Gary Trent	1.25
12	Cherokee Parks	1.00
13	Corliss Williamson	2.00
NNO	Exchange Card 2 Expired	1.00
NNO	Exchange Card 3 Expired	1.00
NNO	Exchange Card 1 Expired	1.00

1995-96 SkyBox Premium Meltdown

The top scorers in the NBA are highlighted in this 1995-96 SkyBox Series II insert set. The cards, numbered using an "M" prefix, were random inserts one per every 54 packs. The card front has a color action photo of the player, with a lava-like meltdown occurring behind him. The player's name is in gold foil at the bottom of the card, just above his team's name. The SkyBox logo is stamped in gold foil in the upper left corner. The card back has "Meltdown" written at the top, followed by the player's name and his team name underneath. A color action photo and a description of the player's scoring skills are also included.

		MT
Complete Set (10):		125.00
Common Player:		3.00
1	Michael Jordan	50.00
2	Dan Majerle	3.00
3	Jason Kidd	6.00
4	Antonio McDyess	6.00
5	Grant Hill	25.00
6	Joe Smith	10.00
7	Hakeem Olajuwon	10.00
8	Shaquille O'Neal	20.00
9	Jerry Stackhouse	10.00
10	David Robinson	6.00

1995-96 SkyBox Premium Rookie Prevue

Twenty rookies from the 1995 NBA Draft are featured in this 1995-96 SkyBox Series I insert set. Future stars such as Joe Smith, Jerry Stackhouse and Rasheed Wallace are inserted at a ratio of one per every nine packs. Each card front has a color action photo, with the player's name stamped in gold foil in the upper left corner. "Rookie Prevue" is written in the lower left corner. The back has a color action photo on it, with a starburst design for a background. This design is also used for the front. The back also has the player's name in the upper left corner, and an assessment of the talents the player is bringing to the NBA. "Rookie Prevue" is written in the lower left corner. A card number, using an "RP" prefix, is in the upper right corner.

		MT
Complete Set (20):		90.00
Common Player:		2.00
1	Joe Smith	12.00
2	Antonio McDyess	15.00
3	Jerry Stackhouse	8.00
4	Rasheed Wallace	6.00
5	Bryant Reeves	4.00
6	Damon Stoudamire	10.00
7	Shawn Respert	2.00
8	Ed O'Bannon	2.00
9	Kurt Thomas	5.00
10	Gary Trent	2.00
11	Cherokee Parks	2.00
12	Corliss Williamson	2.00
13	Eric Williams	2.00
14	Brent Barry	3.00
15	Alan Henderson	2.00
16	Bob Sura	2.00
17	Theo Ratliff	4.00
18	Randolph Childress	2.00
19	Michael Finley	7.00
20	George Zidek	2.00

1995-96 SkyBox Premium Standouts

A dozen NBA stars who are destined for greatness are featured on these 1995-96 SkyBox Series I insert cards. The cards were seeded one per every 18 regular packs and one per every 12 jumbo packs. The card front has a color action photo against a metallic game action background. The player is under a spotlight, standing on a "SkyBox Standouts" circle. The SkyBox logo and the player's name are stamped in gold foil in the upper corners. The card back, numbered with an "S" prefix, has a color photo on it, with an explanation of why the player is a standout in the NBA, and destined for greatness.

		MT
Complete Set (12):		35.00
Common Player:		2.00
1	Alonzo Mourning	3.00
2	Scottie Pippen	10.00
3	Danny Manning	2.00
4	Jamal Mashburn	3.00
5	Latrell Sprewell	2.00
6	Reggie Miller	3.00
7	Anfernee Hardaway	18.00
8	Brian Grant	2.00
9	Shawn Kemp	5.00
10	Cliff Robinson	2.00
11	Joe Dumars	2.00
12	Chris Webber	3.00

1995-96 SkyBox Premium Standouts Hobby

These six insert cards were an added bonus to the 1995-96 SkyBox Series I hobby packs only. Cards were seeded one per every 18th hobby pack. The design is similar to that used for the Series I Standouts inserts, except the front has an all-foil background and the back has a card number which uses an "SH" prefix.

		MT
Complete Set (6):		80.00
Common Player:		5.00
1	Michael Jordan	40.00
2	Jason Kidd	5.00
3	Hakeem Olajuwon	10.00
4	Eddie Jones	12.00
5	Shaquille O'Neal	20.00
6	Grant Hill	20.00

1995-96 SkyBox Premium USA Basketball

These cards, numbered using a "U" prefix, were random inserts in 1995-96 SkyBox Series II special packs. They were also seeded one per every Series II jumbo packs.

		MT
Complete Set (10):		30.00
Common Player:		1.50
1	Anfernee Hardaway	10.00
2	Grant Hill	10.00
3	Karl Malone	1.50
4	Reggie Miller	2.50
5	Scottie Pippen	4.00
6	Hakeem Olajuwon	4.00
7	Shaquille O'Neal	8.00
8	David Robinson	3.00
9	Glenn Robinson	2.50
10	John Stockton	1.50

1996 SkyBox USA

SkyBox USA Basketball honors Dream Team III with 60 cards, including five of each player. Six subsets make up the set, including 10 Grant's Slant, 10 Brag Book, 10 Playing for Pride, 20 Contribution, five Awesome Duos, four Coaches and one checklist. Cards of four mini USAB cards-in-one can be found in the 15-card Quads inserts. These are found one per every three packs and form a parallel set. Next, each of the 10 members are showcased in Bronze (one per 12), Silver (one per 48) and Gold (one per 120). Hobby only sparkle versions were also made of these cards - Bronze are one in 18, Silver are one in 72 and Gold are one in 180 packs.

		MT
Complete Set (60):		18.00
Common Player:		.10
Wax Box:		40.00
1	Anfernee Hardaway (Grant's Slant)	1.25
2	Grant Hill (Grant's Slant)	.75
3	Karl Malone (Grant's Slant)	.10
4	Reggie Miller (Grant's Slant)	.10
5	Scottie Pippen (Grant's Slant)	.50
6	Hakeem Olajuwon (Grant's Slant)	.50
7	Shaquille O'Neal (Grant's Slant)	1.00
8	David Robinson (Grant's Slant)	.40
9	Glenn Robinson (Grant's Slant)	.25
10	John Stockton (Grant's Slant)	.10
11	Anfernee Hardaway (Brag Book)	1.25
12	Grant Hill (Brag Book)	.75
13	Karl Malone (Brag Book)	.10
14	Reggie Miller (Brag Book)	.10
15	Scottie Pippen (Brag Book)	.50
16	Hakeem Olajuwon (Brag Book)	.50
17	Shaquille O'Neal (Brag Book)	1.00
18	David Robinson (Brag Book)	.40
19	Glenn Robinson (Brag Book)	.25
20	John Stockton (Brag Book)	.10
21	Anfernee Hardaway (Playing for Pride)	1.25
22	Grant Hill (Playing for Pride)	.75
23	Karl Malone (Playing for Pride)	.10
24	Reggie Miller (Playing for Pride)	.10
25	Scottie Pippen (Playing for Pride)	.50
26	Hakeem Olajuwon (Playing for Pride)	.50
27	Shaquille O'Neal (Playing for Pride)	1.00
28	David Robinson (Playing for Pride)	.40
29	Glenn Robinson (Playing for Pride)	.25
30	John Stockton (Playing for Pride)	.10
31	Anfernee Hardaway (Contribution)	1.25
32	Grant Hill (Contribution)	.75
33	Karl Malone (Contribution)	.10
34	Reggie Miller (Contribution)	.10
35	Scottie Pippen (Contribution)	.50
36	Hakeem Olajuwon (Contribution)	.50
37	Shaquille O'Neal (Contribution)	1.00
38	David Robinson (Contribution)	.40
39	Glenn Robinson (Contribution)	.25
40	John Stockton (Contribution)	.10
41	Anfernee Hardaway (Contribution)	1.25
42	Grant Hill (Contribution)	.75
43	Karl Malone (Contribution)	.10
44	Reggie Miller (Contribution)	.10
45	Scottie Pippen (Contribution)	.50
46	Hakeem Olajuwon (Contribution)	.50
47	Shaquille O'Neal (Contribution)	1.00
48	David Robinson (Contribution)	.40
49	Glenn Robinson (Contribution)	.25
50	John Stockton (Contribution)	.10
51	Lenny Wilkens (Coaches)	.10
52	Bobby Cremins (Coaches)	.10
53	Clem Haskins (Coaches)	.10
54	Jerry Sloan (Coaches)	.10
55	Shaquille O'Neal, Anfernee Hardaway (Awesome Duos)	1.00
56	Karl Malone, John Stockton (Awesome Duos)	.25
57	David Robinson, Hakeem Olajuwon (Awesome Duos)	.25
58	Scottie Pippen, Grant Hill (Awesome Duos)	.50
59	Reggie Miller, Glenn Robinson (Awesome Duos)	.10
60	Checklist	.10
61	Charles Barkley	
62	Mitch Richmond	
63	Charles Barkley	
64	Mitch Richmond	
65	Charles Barkley	
66	Mitch Richmond	
67	Charles Barkley	
68	Mitch Richmond	
69	Charles Barkley	
70	Mitch Richmond	
71	Charles Barkley, Mitch Richmond	

1996 SkyBox USA Bronze

Two versions of these 1996 SkyBox USA insert cards were made - regular and sparkle versions. Both use a "B" prefix for the card number on the back. Each card front has a player action photo, with USA and the Olympic rings in bronze twice on the card - in larger and smaller type. The player's name, SkyBox logo and USA Basketball logo are also in bronze. The sparkle versions add a glitter effect to this foil stamping; cards are found in every 18th pack, hobby only. The regular versions are seeded one per every 12 packs. The card back has a posed shot of the player in his Olympic uniform, with the Olympic symbol in the background, plus a card number.

		MT
Complete Set (10):		25.00
Common Player:		1.00
Sparkle Bronze Cards:		2x
B1	Anfernee Hardaway	10.00
B2	Grant Hill	6.00
B3	Karl Malone	1.00
B4	Reggie Miller	1.50
B5	Scottie Pippen	4.00
B6	Hakeem Olajuwon	4.00
B7	Shaquille O'Neal	8.00
B8	David Robinson	3.00
B9	Glenn Robinson	2.00
B10	John Stockton	1.00
B11	Charles Barkley	
B12	Mitch Richmond	

1996 SkyBox USA Bronze Sparkle

Bronze Sparkle inserts paralleled the regular Bronze inserts, but featured the letters on the front printed in prismatic bronze foil. These were inserted one per 18 hobby packs and carried a "B" prefix card number.

	MT
Complete Set (10):	50.00
Sparkle Cards:	2x

1996 SkyBox USA Gold

Two versions of these 1996 SkyBox USA insert cards were made - regular and sparkle versions. Both use a "G" prefix for the card number on the back. Each card front has a player action photo, with USA and the Olympic rings in gold twice on the card - in larger and smaller type. The player's name, SkyBox logo and USA Basketball logo are also in gold. The sparkle versions add a glitter effect to this foil stamping; cards are found one per every 180 packs, hobby only. The regular versions are seeded one per every 120 packs. The card back has a posed shot of the player in his Olympic uniform, with the Olympic symbol in the background, plus a card number.

		MT
Complete Set (10):		225.00
Common Player:		10.00
Sparkle Gold Cards:		2x
G1	Anfernee Hardaway	60.00
G2	Grant Hill	60.00
G3	Karl Malone	10.00
G4	Reggie Miller	10.00
G5	Scottie Pippen	30.00
G6	Hakeem Olajuwon	25.00
G7	Shaquille O'Neal	45.00
G8	David Robinson	15.00
G9	Glenn Robinson	10.00
G10	John Stockton	10.00
G11	Charles Barkley	
G12	Mitch Richmond	

1996 SkyBox USA Gold Sparkle

Gold Sparkle inserts paralleled the regular Gold inserts, but featured prismatic gold foil lettering on the front. These were inserted one per 180 hobby packs and contained a "G" prefix on the card number.

	MT
Complete Set (10):	450.00
Sparkle Cards:	2x

1996 SkyBox USA Quads

Cards of four mini USA Basketball cards-in-one can be found in this

15-card Quads insert set. The cards show smaller versions of the player's regular cards in the 1996 SkyBox USA basketball set. They are perforated so the cards can be broken apart. Cards, numbered with a "Q" prefix, are found one per every three packs and form a parallel set to the main one.

		MT
Complete Set (15):		12.00
Common Player:		.40
Q1	Anfernee Hardaway	4.00
Q2	Grant Hill	2.00
Q3	Karl Malone	.40
Q4	Reggie Miller	.40
Q5	Scottie Pippen	1.50
Q6	Hakeem Olajuwon	1.50
Q7	Shaquille O'Neal	3.00
Q8	David Robinson	1.00
Q9	Glenn Robinson	.75
Q10	John Stockton	.40
Q11	Power Quad	1.00
Q12	Versatility Quad	1.00
Q13	Passing Quad	1.00
Q14	Defensive Quad	.50
Q15	Scorers Quad	.50
Q16	Charles Barkley	
Q17	Mitch Richmond	

1996 SkyBox USA Silver

Two versions of these SkyBox USA insert cards were made - regular and sparkle versions. Both use an "S" prefix for the card number on the back. Each card front has a player action photo, with USA and the Olympic rings in silver twice on the card - in larger and smaller type. The player's name, SkyBox logo and USA Basketball logo are also in silver. The sparkle versions add a glitter effect to this foil stamping; cards are found one per every 72 packs, hobby only. The regular versions are seeded one per every 48 packs. The card back has a posed shot of the player in his Olympic uniform, with the Olympic symbol in the background, plus a card number.

		MT
Complete Set (10):		80.00
Common Player:		4.00
Sparkle Silver Cards:		2x
S1	Anfernee Hardaway	25.00
S2	Grant Hill	25.00
S3	Karl Malone	4.00
S4	Reggie Miller	4.00
S5	Scottie Pippen	12.00
S6	Hakeem Olajuwon	10.00
S7	Shaquille O'Neal	15.00
S8	David Robinson	6.00
S9	Glenn Robinson	4.00
S10	John Stockton	4.00
S11	Charles Barkley	
S12	Mitch Richmond	

1996 SkyBox USA Silver Sparkle

Silver Sparkle inserts paralleled the regular Silver inserts, but featured prismatic silver foil printing on the front. Sparkle inserts were inserted every 72 hobby packs and carry an "S" prefix on the card number.

	MT
Complete Set (10):	160.00
Sparkle Cards:	2x

1996 SkyBox USA Texaco

This 14-card set features "Dream Team 2." Three-card packs were free with an eight-gallon gasoline purchase at participating Texaco stores or could be purchased for $0.89 per pack. The card fronts have a player action photo against a metallic gray background with the player's name at the top and USA Basketball logo at the bottom. The player's name is printed in red foil.

		MT
Complete Set (14):		5.00
Common Player:		.25
1	Charles Barkley	.50
2	Anfernee Hardaway	.75
3	Grant Hill	1.50
4	Karl Malone	.75
5	Reggie Miller	.40
6	Hakeem Olajuwon	.60
7	Shaquille O'Neal	1.50
8	Scottie Pippen	.75
9	Mitch Richmond	.25
10	David Robinson	.50
11	Glenn Robinson	.25
12	John Stockton	.50
13	Lenny Wilkens CO	.25
14	Team Card	.25

1996-97 SkyBox Premium

SkyBox Premium in 1996-97 consisted of 290 cards, with 140 in Series I and 150 in Series II. Card fronts featured a mix of posed and action shots with a full bleed design. The SkyBox Premium logo was stamped in gold foil in the top right corner with the player's name in gold foil centered on the bottom. Backs displayed another shot of the player, with biographical information to the right and statistics across the bottom. Series I had 129 regular cards, two checklists and nine Triple Threats (three more Triple Threats Bulls cards exist, but are considered inserts), while Series II had 68 player updates, 40 Rookies, 20 Point Men, 20 Double Trouble and two checklists. Inserts in Series I include: Close-Ups, Rookie Prevue, Autographics, Standouts, Larger than Life, Bonus Triple Threats and Rubies parallel cards of the first 131 cards. Series II inserts include: Intimidators, Net Set, New Edition, Autographics, Thunder & Lightning, Golden Touch, 148 Rubies and five Emeralds autograph redemption.

		MT
Complete Set (290):		40.00
Complete Series 1 (140):		20.00
Complete Series 2 (150):		20.00
Common Player:		.05
Minor Stars:		.10
Ser. 1 or 2 Pack (12):		2.50
Ser. 1 or 2 Wax Box (24):		55.00
1	Mookie Blaylock	.05
2	Alan Henderson	.05
3	Christian Laettner	.05
4	Dikembe Mutombo	.05
5	Steve Smith	.05
6	Dana Barros	.05
7	Rick Fox	.05
8	Dino Radja	.05
9	*Antoine Walker*	2.00
10	Eric Williams	.05
11	Dell Curry	.05
12	*Tony Delk*	.50
13	Matt Geiger	.05
14	Glen Rice	.05
15	Ron Harper	.05
16	Michael Jordan	4.00
17	Toni Kukoc	.05
18	Scottie Pippen	1.00
19	Dennis Rodman	1.50
20	Terrell Brandon	.05
21	Danny Ferry	.05
22	Chris Mills	.05
23	Bobby Phills	.05
24	*Vitaly Potapenko*	.25
25	Jim Jackson	.10
26	Jason Kidd	.75
27	Jamal Mashburn	.10
28	George McCloud	.05
29	*Samaki Walker*	.60
30	LaPhonso Ellis	.05
31	Antonio McDyess	.40
32	Bryant Stith	.05
33	Joe Dumars	.10
34	Grant Hill	2.00
35	Lindsey Hunter	.05
36	Theo Ratliff	.05
37	Otis Thorpe	.05
38	*Todd Fuller*	.25
39	Chris Mullin	.10
40	Joe Smith	.40
41	Latrell Sprewell	.20
42	Charles Barkley	.50
43	Clyde Drexler	.40
44	Mario Elie	.05
45	Hakeem Olajuwon	.75
46	*Erick Dampier*	.30
47	Dale Davis	.05
48	Derrick McKey	.05
49	Reggie Miller	.30
50	Rik Smits	.05
51	Brent Barry	.10
52	Rodney Rogers	.05
53	Loy Vaught	.05
54	*Lorenzen White*	.40
55	*Kobe Bryant*	12.00
56	Cedric Ceballos	.05
57	Eddie Jones	.20
58	Shaquille O'Neal	2.00
59	Nick Van Exel	.20
60	Tim Hardaway	.05
61	Alonzo Mourning	.30
62	Kurt Thomas	.05
63	*Ray Allen*	3.00
64	Vin Baker	.25
65	Shawn Respert	.05
66	Glenn Robinson	.30
67	Kevin Garnett	2.00
68	Tom Gugliotta	.05
69	*Stephon Marbury*	3.00
70	Sam Mitchell	.05
71	Shawn Bradley	.05
72	Kendall Gill	.05
73	*Kerry Kittles*	1.00
74	Ed O'Bannon	.05
75	Patrick Ewing	.05
76	Larry Johnson	.10
77	Charles Oakley	.05
78	John Starks	.05
79	*John Wallace*	.75
80	Nick Anderson	.05
81	Horace Grant	.05
82	Anfernee Hardaway	2.00
83	Dennis Scott	.05
84	Derrick Coleman	.05
85	*Allen Iverson*	6.00
86	Jerry Stackhouse	.75
87	Clarence Weatherspoon	.05
88	Michael Finley	.40
89	Robert Horry	.05
90	Kevin Johnson	.05
91	*Steve Nash*	.40
92	Wesley Person	.05
93	Aaron McKie	.05
94	*Jermaine O'Neal*	2.00
95	Clifford Robinson	.05
96	Arvydas Sabonis	.25
97	Gary Trent	.05
98	Tyus Edney	.10
99	Brian Grant	.05
100	Mitch Richmond	.20
101	Billy Owens	.05
102	Corliss Williamson	.05
103	Vinny Del Negro	.05
104	Sean Elliot	.05
105	Avery Johnson	.05
106	Chuck Person	.05
107	David Robinson	.50
108	Hersey Hawkins	.05
109	Shawn Kemp	.50
110	Gary Payton	.25
111	Sam Perkins	.05
112	Detlef Schrempf	.05
113	*Marcus Camby*	2.50
114	Carlos Rogers	.05
115	Damon Stoudamire	1.00
116	Zan Tabak	.05
117	Antoine Carr	.05
118	Jeff Hornacek	.05
119	Karl Malone	.30
120	Chris Morris	.05
121	John Stockton	.30
122	*Shareef Abdur-Rahim*	2.50
123	Greg Anthony	.05
124	Bryant Reeves	.25
125	*Roy Rogers*	.30
126	Calbert Cheaney	.05
127	Juwan Howard	.50
128	Gheorghe Muresan	.05
129	Chris Webber	.25
130	Checklist A	.05
131	Checklist B	.05
TT1	Chris Mullin (Triple Threats)	.05
TT2	Joe Smith (Triple Threats)	.10
TT3	Latrell Sprewell (Triple Threats)	.10
TT4	Avery Johnson (Triple Threats)	.05
TT5	Sean Elliot (Triple Threats)	.10
TT6	David Robinson (Triple Threats)	.10
TT7	John Stockton (Triple Threats)	.10
TT8	Karl Malone (Triple Threats)	.10
TT9	Jeff Hornacek (Triple Threats)	.05
132	Jon Barry	.05
133	Christian Laettner	.05
134	Dikembe Mutombo	.05
135	Dee Brown	.05
136	Todd Day	.05
137	David Wesley	.05
138	Vlade Divac	.05
139	Anthony Goldwire	.05
140	Anthony Mason	.05
141	Jason Caffey	.05
142	Luc Longley	.05
143	Tyrone Hill	.05
144	Antonio Lang	.05
145	Sam Cassell	.05
146	Chris Gatling	.05
147	Eric Montross	.05
148	Ervin Johnson	.05
149	Sarunas Marciulionis	.05
150	Stacey Augmon	.05
151	Grant Long	.05
152	Terry Mills	.05
153	Kenny Smith	.05
154	B.J. Armstrong	.05
155	Bimbo Coles	.05
156	Charles Barkley	.50
157	Brent Price	.05
158	Duane Ferrell	.05
159	Jalen Rose	.05
160	Terry Dehere	.05
161	Charles Outlaw	.05
162	Corie Blount	.05
163	Shaquille O'Neal	2.00
164	Rumeal Robinson	.05
165	P.J. Brown	.05
166	Ronnie Grandison	.05
167	Sherman Douglas	.05
168	Johnny Newman	.05
169	James Robinson	.05
170	Doug West	.05
171	Robert Pack	.05
172	Khalid Reeves	.05
173	Chris Childs	.05
174	Allan Houston	.05
175	Charlie Ward	.05
176	*Darrell Armstrong*	2.00
177	Gerald Wilkins	.05
178	Lucious Harris	.05
179	Robert Horry	.05
180	Danny Manning	.05
181	Kenny Anderson	.05
182	Isaiah Rider	.05
183	Rasheed Wallace	.05
184	Mahmoud Abdul-Rauf	.05
185	Cory Alexander	.05
186	Vernon Maxwell	.05
187	Dominique Wilkins	.05
188	Nate McMillan	.05
189	Larry Stewart	.05
190	Doug Christie	.05
191	Hubert Davis	.05
192	Walt Williams	.05
193	Adam Keefe	.05
194	Greg Ostertag	.05
195	John Stockton	.30
196	George Lynch	.05
197	Lee Mayberry	.05
198	Tracy Murray	.05
199	Rod Strickland	.05
200	Shareef Abdur-Rahim	2.00
201	Ray Allen	1.25
202	Shandon Anderson	.05
203	Kobe Bryant	2.00
204	Marcus Camby	2.00
205	Erick Dampier	.25
206	Emanuel Davis	.05
207	Tony Delk	.25
208	Brian Evans	.05
209	Derek Fisher	.25
210	Todd Fuller	.05
211	Dean Garrett	.40
212	Reggie Geary	.05
213	Darvin Ham	.05
214	Othella Harrington	.30
215	Shane Heal	.05
216	Allen Iverson	3.00
217	Dontae Jones	.05
218	Kerry Kittles	1.00
219	Priest Lauderdale	.05
220	Randy Livingston	.25
221	Matt Maloney	.50
222	Stephon Marbury	2.50
223	Walter McCarty	.05
224	Amal McCaskill	.05
225	Jeff McInnis	.05
226	Martin Muursepp	.05
227	Steve Nash	.25
228	Ruben Nembhard	.05
229	Jermaine O'Neal	.75
230	Vitaly Potapenko	.25
231	Virginius Praskevicius	.05
232	Roy Rogers	.25
233	Malik Rose	.05
234	Antoine Walker	1.00
235	Samaki Walker	.05
236	Ben Wallace	.05
237	John Wallace	.40
238	Jerome Williams	.05
239	Lorenzen Wright	.25
240	Sam Cassell	.05
241	Anfernee Hardaway	1.00
242	Tim Hardaway	.05
243	Grant Hill	1.00
244	Allan Houston	.05
245	Juwan Howard	.05
246	Kevin Johnson	.05
247	Michael Jordan	2.00
248	Jason Kidd	.25
249	Karl Malone	.05
250	Reggie Miller	.05
251	Gary Payton	.05
252	Wesley Person	.05
253	Glen Rice	.05
254	David Robinson	.05
255	Steve Smith	.05
256	Latrell Sprewell	.05
257	Jerry Stackhouse	.05
258	Rod Strickland	.05
259	Nick Van Exel	.05
260	Charles Barkley	.25
261	Dale Davis	.05
262	Patrick Ewing	.05
263	Michael Finley	.05
264	Chris Gatling	.05
265	Armon Gilliam	.05
266	Tyrone Hill	.05
267	Robert Horry	.05
268	Mark Jackson	.05
269	Shawn Kemp	.30
270	Jamal Mashburn	.05
271	Anthony Mason	.05
272	Alonzo Mourning	.05
273	Dikembe Mutombo	.05
274	Shaquille O'Neal	1.00
275	Isaiah Rider	.05
276	Dennis Rodman	.50
277	Damon Stoudamire	.05
278	Chris Webber	.05
279	Jayson Williams	.05
280	Checklist	.05
281	Checklist	.05

1996-97 SkyBox Premium Rubies

Rubies paralleled 279 cards from the SkyBox Series I and II set, and was inserted one per Series I and II hobby boxes. Rubies are identified by Ruby foil stamping in place of gold foil on regular-issue cards. The Ruby parallels are also twice as thick as regular-issue cards.

	MT
Complete Set (279):	2400.
Complete Series 1 (131):	1600.
Complete Series 2 (148):	800.00
Common Player:	5.00
Minor Stars:	10.00
One Per Hobby Box.	

1996-97 SkyBox Premium Autographics

Autographics were inserted into each 1996-97 SkyBox basketball product at a rate of one per 72 packs. The cards were autographed in the more common black ink and a more limited blue ink, except for Scottie Pippen and Hakeem Olajuwon, who signed all of their cards in blue ink, and Kevin Garnett who signed two-thirds of his cards in blue ink. They were inserted into Hoops I and II, SkyBox I and II, Z-Force I and II and E-X2000. The set covered 95 players with certain players being exclusive to certain products, for example Antoine Walker, Damon Stoudamire and Kerry Kittles were only in E-X2000.

	MT
Common Player:	15.00
Blue Ink:	2x-3x
All Olajuwon and Pippen cards signed in blue.	
Garnett signed two-thirds of his in blue. No John Wallace blue's exist.	
Ray Allen	80.00
Kenny Anderson	30.00
Nick Anderson	20.00
B.J. Armstrong	15.00
Vincent Askew	15.00
Dana Barros	15.00
Brent Barry	25.00
Travis Best	20.00
Muggsy Bogues	20.00
P.J. Brown	20.00
Randy Brown	20.00
Marcus Camby	100.00
Chris Childs	20.00
Dell Curry	15.00
Andrew DeClerq	15.00
Tony Delk	35.00
Sherman Douglas	15.00
Clyde Drexler	130.00
Tyus Edney	20.00
Michael Finley	45.00
Rick Fox	20.00
Kevin Garnett Black	300.00
Kevin Garnett Blue	275.00
Matt Geiger	15.00
Kendall Gill	30.00
Brian Grant	20.00
Tim Hardaway	60.00
Grant Hill	325.00
Tyrone Hill	20.00
Allan Houston	40.00
Juwan Howard	225.00
Jim Jackson	25.00
Mark Jackson	25.00
Eddie Jones	150.00
Adam Keefe	15.00
Steve Kerr	30.00
Toni Kukoc	50.00
Andrew Lang	15.00
Voshon Lenard	25.00
Grant Long	15.00
Luc Longley	30.00
George Lynch	20.00
Don MacLean	15.00
Stephon Marbury	175.00
Lee Mayberry	15.00
Walter McCarty	30.00
George McCloud	30.00
Antonio McDyess	80.00
Nate McMillan	15.00
Chris Mills	15.00
Sam Mitchell	15.00
Eric Montross	15.00
Chris Morris	15.00
Lawrence Moten	15.00
Alonzo Mourning	160.00
Gheorghe Muresan	25.00
Steve Nash	60.00
Ed O'Bannon	25.00
Charles Oakley	20.00
Hakeem Olajuwon Blue	175.00
Greg Ostertag	15.00
Billy Owens	15.00
Sam Perkins	15.00
Chuck Person	15.00
Wesley Person	20.00
Bobby Phills	15.00
Scottie Pippen Blue	325.00
Theo Ratliff	15.00
Glen Rice	75.00
Rodney Rogers	15.00
Byron Scott	15.00
Dennis Scott	20.00
Joe Smith	90.00
Kenny Smith	15.00
Rik Smits	25.00
Eric Snow	15.00
Latrell Sprewell	70.00
Jerry Stackhouse	70.00
John Starks	30.00
Bryant Stith	15.00
Damon Stoudamire	150.00
Rod Strickland	100.00
Bob Sura	25.00
Zan Tabak	15.00
Loy Vaught	15.00
Antoine Walker	60.00
Samaki Walker	30.00
John Wallace	60.00
Bill Wennington	20.00
David Wesley	20.00
Doug West	15.00
Monty Williams	15.00
Joe Wolf	15.00
Sharone Wright	15.00

1996-97 SkyBox Premium Close-Ups

Close-Ups included nine die-cut cards with the featured player cast over a large globe with the insert name on it. The team's logo is embossed in the lower right corner on the front. Inserted every 24 packs, this set is numbered CU1-CU9.

		MT
Complete Set (9):		60.00
Common Player:		3.00
1	Anfernee Hardaway	20.00
2	Grant Hill	20.00
3	Juwan Howard	7.00
4	Shawn Kemp	5.00
5	Jason Kidd	7.00
6	Alonzo Mourning	3.00
7	Hakeem Olajuwon	8.00
8	Jerry Stackhouse	6.00
9	Damon Stoudamire	8.00

1996-97 SkyBox Premium Emerald Autographs

Emeralds were inserted every 20 hobby boxes as box toppers and were numbered E1-E5. The cards were available through redemption cards and captured the base cards for five players with Emerald foil treatment.

		MT
Complete Set (5):		600.00
Common Player:		75.00
1	Ray Allen	90.00
2	Marcus Camby	130.00
3	Grant Hill	325.00
4	Kerry Kittles	90.00
5	Jerry Stackhouse	75.00

1996-97 SkyBox Premium Golden Touch

This 10-card set highlighted some of the shooters in the NBA on gold and silver foil. The words "Golden Touch" are printed in fancy letters in the background and all cards are die-cut around three sides, with the bottom side the exclusion. Golden Touch inserts were seeded one per 240 packs of Series II.

		MT
Complete Set (10):		400.00
Common Player:		10.00
1	Vin Baker	15.00
2	Terrell Brandon	10.00
3	Allan Houston	10.00
4	Allen Iverson	80.00
5	Michael Jordan	160.00
6	Shawn Kemp	20.00
7	Karl Malone	20.00
8	Stephon Marbury	70.00
9	Latrell Sprewell	25.00
10	Damon Stoudamire	35.00

1996-97 SkyBox Premium Intimidators

This 20-card insert was seeded one per eight Series II packs and captures some of the top big men in basketball. The cards are identified by featuring the players first and last name (first name runs up, last name runs down) printed in silver foil in the background.

		MT
Complete Set (20):		60.00
Common Player:		1.50
1	Shareef Abdur-Rahim	10.00
2	Charles Barkley	5.00
3	Marcus Camby	10.00
4	Elden Campbell	1.50
5	Derrick Coleman	1.50
6	Patrick Ewing	3.00
7	Michael Finley	1.50
8	Kevin Garnett	12.00
9	Jim Jackson	1.50
10	Anthony Mason	1.50
11	Antonio McDyess	1.50
12	Alonzo Mourning	3.00
13	Gheorghe Muresan	1.50
14	Dikembe Mutombo	1.50
15	Shaquille O'Neal	12.00
16	Isaiah Rider	1.50
17	Clifford Robinson	1.50
18	David Robinson	4.00
19	Dennis Rodman	12.00
20	Clarence Weatherspoon	1.50

1996-97 SkyBox Premium Larger Than Life

Larger Than Life features 18 players on a horizontal foil design. Fronts contain an action shot of the player on the left side, with a foil close-up shot on the right side and the name of the insert printed across the bottom. This insert was seeded one per 180 Series I hobby packs, and was numbered L1-L18.

		MT
Complete Set (18):		650.00
Common Player:		6.00
1	Shareef Abdur-Rahim	50.00
2	Marcus Camby	50.00
3	Kevin Garnett	60.00
4	Anfernee Hardaway	45.00
5	Grant Hill	60.00
6	Allen Iverson	80.00
7	Michael Jordan	175.00
8	Shawn Kemp	20.00
9	Stephon Marbury	60.00
10	Jamal Mashburn	6.00
11	Antonio McDyess	10.00
12	Alonzo Mourning	6.00
13	Dikembe Mutombo	6.00
14	Hakeem Olajuwon	25.00
15	Shaquille O'Neal	50.00
16	Dennis Rodman	50.00
17	Jerry Stackhouse	15.00
18	Damon Stoudamire	25.00

1996-97 SkyBox Premium Net Set

This 20-card insert was issued only in Series II hobby packs at a rate of one per 10. The fronts featured a color image of the player over the top of a gold and silver background that resembles the sun with rays reflecting down.

		MT
Complete Set (20):		250.00
Common Player:		4.00
1	Vin Baker	4.00
2	Clyde Drexler	10.00
3	Patrick Ewing	6.00
4	Anfernee Hardaway	25.00
5	Grant Hill	40.00
6	Juwan Howard	10.00
7	Allen Iverson	50.00
8	Michael Jordan	80.00
9	Shawn Kemp	10.00
10	Jason Kidd	8.00
11	Karl Malone	6.00
12	Stephon Marbury	50.00
13	Alonzo Mourning	4.00
14	Hakeem Olajuwon	20.00
15	Shaquille O'Neal	25.00
16	Scottie Pippen	20.00
17	David Robinson	12.00
18	Joe Smith	10.00
19	Damon Stoudamire	15.00
20	Chris Webber	12.00

1996-97 SkyBox Premium New Editions

This 10-card, retail only insert has a green border with the player inset on a purple etched foil area inside. New Edition inserts were seeded one per 36 packs, and contained the words "New Editions" in yellow letters across the bottom.

		MT
Complete Set (10):		75.00
Common Player:		2.00
1	Shareef Abdur-Rahim	12.00
2	Ray Allen	8.00
3	Kobe Bryant	25.00
4	Marcus Camby	12.00
5	Allen Iverson	20.00
6	Kerry Kittles	6.00
7	Matt Maloney	4.00
8	Stephon Marbury	18.00
9	Steve Nash	2.00
10	Samaki Walker	2.00

1996-97 SkyBox Premium Rookie Prevue

Rookie Prevue features the top 18 picks in the 1996 NBA Draft on a foil etched basketball background. Inserted at one per 54 packs, the insert name is stamped in gold foil across the bottom, with the player's name in the top right corner. Rookie Prevue inserts are numbered with an "R" prefix.

		MT
Complete Set (18):		250.00
Common Player:		3.00
1	Shareef Abdur-Rahim	35.00
2	Ray Allen	25.00
3	Kobe Bryant	60.00
4	Marcus Camby	35.00
5	Erick Dampier	3.00
6	Tony Delk	3.00
7	Brian Evans	3.00
8	Todd Fuller	3.00
9	Allen Iverson	55.00
10	Kerry Kittles	15.00
11	Stephon Marbury	40.00
12	Steve Nash	10.00
13	Vitaly Potapenko	3.00
14	Roy Rogers	3.00
15	Antoine Walker	20.00
16	Samaki Walker	6.00
17	John Wallace	10.00
18	Lorenzen Wright	3.00

1996-97 SkyBox Premium Standouts

Standouts was a nine-card insert that was exclusive to Series I retail packs. Inserted one per 180 packs, the insert featured a multi-colored border with a basketball net in the background. The insert name is hard to find on the front, but does appear in the lower right corner along with the player's number and a "SO" prefix.

		MT
Complete Set (9):		150.00
Common Player:		10.00
1	Grant Hill	60.00
2	Juwan Howard	15.00
3	Jason Kidd	20.00
4	Reggie Miller	10.00
5	Shaquille O'Neal	35.00
6	Gary Payton	15.00
7	Scottie Pippen	30.00
8	Mitch Richmond	10.00
9	Joe Smith	15.00

1996-97 SkyBox Premium Thunder and Lightning

Thunder and Lightning was a 10-card, two-piece insert found in one per 144 Series II packs. The card included a Thunder part that contained a glossy front and back shell. Inside it, was the Lightning part, which could be pulled out to view. The set matched a star big man and guard from the same team and was numbered "x of 10".

		MT
Complete Set (10):		250.00
Common Player:		6.00
1	Michael Jordan, Scottie Pippen	100.00
2	Kevin Johnson, Danny Manning	6.00
3	Grant Hill, Joe Dumars	50.00
4	Latrell Sprewell, Joe Smith	20.00
5	Charles Barkley, Hakeem Olajuwon	25.00
6	Vin Baker, Glenn Robinson	15.00
7	Patrick Ewing, Larry Johnson	15.00
8	Shawn Kemp, Gary Payton	15.00
9	Karl Malone, John Stockton	15.00
10	Juwan Howard, Chris Webber	20.00

1996-97 SkyBox Premium Triple Threat

This three-card set was inserted into packs of Series I at a rate of one per 240. Although these cards were inserts and called Bonus Triple Threats, they were numbered consecutively with the regular-issue subset. The regular-issue Triple Threats were numbered TT1-TT9, while the Bonus Triple Threats, which featured the Bulls, were numbered TT10-TT12.

		MT
Complete Set (3):		100.00
TT10	Dennis Rodman	25.00
TT11	Michael Jordan	75.00
TT12	Scottie Pippen	20.00

1996-97 SkyBox Z-Force

SkyBox's 1996-97 Z-Force cards combine computer graphics and NBA action on each card; each card has a silhouetted action photo of the player against a surreal background featuring colorful graphics and the player's last name in bold type. Both Series I and II consisted of 100 cards. Series I inserts included Z-Cling, Vortex, Swat Team, Autographics and Slam Cam. Series II featured Zensations, Zebut, Little Big Men, BMOC, Autographics and a Grant Hill Total Z card. Series I marked the first installment of Autographics, which would run through all 1996-97 SkyBox releases, including Z-Force Series II.

		MT
Complete Set (200):		45.00
Complete Series 1 (100):		20.00
Complete Series 2 (100):		25.00
Common Player:		.10
Minor Stars:		.20
Ser. 1 or 2 Pack (8):		1.50
Ser. 1 or 2 Wax Box (24):		35.00
1	Mookie Blaylock	.10
2	Alan Henderson	.10
3	Christian Laettner	.10
4	Steve Smith	.10
5	Rick Fox	.10
6	Dino Radja	.10
7	Eric Williams	.10
8	Tyrone Bogues	.10
9	Larry Johnson	.30
10	Glen Rice	.10
11	Michael Jordan	5.00
12	Toni Kukoc	.10
13	Scottie Pippen	1.25
14	Dennis Rodman	2.00
15	Terrell Brandon	.10
16	Bobby Phills	.10
17	Bob Sura	.10
18	Jim Jackson	.20
19	Jason Kidd	.75
20	Jamal Mashburn	.20
21	George McCloud	.10
22	Mahmoud Abdul-Rauf	.10
23	Antonio McDyess	.40
24	Dikembe Mutombo	.20
25	Joe Dumars	.10
26	Grant Hill	2.00
27	Allan Houston	.10
28	Otis Thorpe	.10
29	Chris Mullin	.10
30	Joe Smith	.50
31	Latrell Sprewell	.10
32	Sam Cassell	.10
33	Clyde Drexler	.40
34	Robert Horry	.10
35	Hakeem Olajuwon	.75
36	Travis Best	.10
37	Dale Davis	.10
38	Reggie Miller	.40
39	Rik Smits	.10
40	Brent Barry	.20
41	Loy Vaught	.10
42	Brian Williams	.10
43	Cedric Ceballos	.10
44	Eddie Jones	.20
45	Nick Van Exel	.25
46	Tim Hardaway	.10
47	Alonzo Mourning	.30
48	Kurt Thomas	.10
49	Walt Williams	.10
50	Vin Baker	.30
51	Glenn Robinson	.40
52	Kevin Garnett	2.00
53	Tom Gugliotta	.10
54	Isaiah Rider	.10
55	Shawn Bradley	.10
56	Chris Childs	.10
57	Jayson Williams	.10
58	Patrick Ewing	.30
59	Anthony Mason	.10
60	Charles Oakley	.10
61	Nick Anderson	.10
62	Horace Grant	.10
63	Anfernee Hardaway	2.50
64	Shaquille O'Neal	2.25
65	Dennis Scott	.10
66	Jerry Stackhouse	.75
67	Clarence Weatherspoon	.10
68	Charles Barkley	.50
69	Michael Finley	.50
70	Kevin Johnson	.20
71	Clifford Robinson	.10
72	Arvydas Sabonis	.30
73	Rod Strickland	.10
74	Tyus Edney	.10
75	Brian Grant	.10
76	Billy Owens	.10
77	Mitch Richmond	.20
78	Vinny Del Negro	.10
79	Sean Elliot	.10
80	Avery Johnson	.10
81	David Robinson	.75
82	Hersey Hawkins	.10
83	Shawn Kemp	.75
84	Gary Payton	.40
85	Detlef Schrempf	.10
86	Doug Christie	.10
87	Damon Stoudamire	1.00
88	Sharone Wright	.10
89	Jeff Hornacek	.10
90	Karl Malone	.30
91	John Stockton	.30
92	Greg Anthony	.10
93	Bryant Reeves	.50
94	Byron Scott	.10
95	Juwan Howard	.50
96	Gheorghe Muresan	.10
97	Rasheed Wallace	.30
98	Chris Webber	.20
99	Checklist A	.10
100	Checklist B	.10
101	Dikembe Mutombo	.10
102	Dee Brown	.10
103	Dell Curry	.10
104	Vlade Divac	.10
105	Anthony Mason	.10
106	Robert Parish	.10
107	Oliver Miller	.10
108	Eric Montross	.10
109	Ervin Johnson	.10
110	Stacey Augmon	.10
111	Charles Barkley	.50
112	Jalen Rose	.10
113	Rodney Rogers	.10
114	Shaquille O'Neal	2.50
115	Dan Majerle	.10
116	Kendall Gill	.10
117	Khalid Reeves	.10
118	Allan Houston	.10
119	Larry Johnson	.20
120	John Starks	.10
121	Rony Seikaly	.10
122	Gerald Wilkins	.10
123	Michael Cage	.10
124	Derrick Coleman	.10
125	Sam Cassell	.10
126	Danny Manning	.10
127	Robert Horry	.10
128	Kenny Anderson	.10
129	Isaiah Rider	.10
130	Rasheed Wallace	.10
131	Mahmoud Abdul-Rauf	.10
132	Vernon Maxwell	.10
133	Dominique Wilkins	.10
134	Hubert Davis	.10
135	Popeye Jones	.10
136	Anthony Peeler	.10
137	Tracy Murray	.10
138	Rod Strickland	.10
139	*Shareef Abdur-Rahim*	2.50
140	*Ray Allen*	4.00
141	*Shandon Anderson*	.10
142	*Kobe Bryant*	10.00
143	*Marcus Camby*	3.00
144	*Erick Dampier*	.40
145	*Emanuel Davis*	.10
146	*Tony Delk*	.50
147	*Todd Fuller*	.10
148	*Darvin Ham*	.20
149	*Othella Harrington*	.20
150	*Shane Heal*	.10
151	*Allen Iverson*	6.00
152	*Dontae Jones*	.10
153	*Kerry Kittles*	1.50
154	*Priest Lauderdale*	.10
155	*Matt Maloney*	.40
156	*Stephon Marbury*	4.00
157	*Walter McCarty*	.10
158	*Steve Nash*	.30
159	*Jermaine O'Neal*	2.00
160	*Ray Owes*	.10
161	*Vitaly Potapenko*	.10
162	*Roy Rogers*	.10
163	*Antoine Walker*	2.00
164	*Samaki Walker*	.30
165	*Ben Wallace*	.10
166	*John Wallace*	.50
167	*Jerome Williams*	.10
168	*Lorenzen Wright*	.40
169	Vin Baker	.20
170	Charles Barkley	.25
171	Patrick Ewing	.20
172	Michael Finley	.10
173	Kevin Garnett	1.00
174	Anfernee Hardaway	1.00
175	Grant Hill	1.00
176	Juwan Howard	.25
177	Jim Jackson	.10
178	Eddie Jones	.25
179	Michael Jordan	2.00
180	Shawn Kemp	.30
181	Jason Kidd	.25
182	Karl Malone	.10
183	Antonio McDyess	.10
184	Reggie Miller	.20
185	Alonzo Mourning	.20
186	Hakeem Olajuwon	.50
187	Shaquille O'Neal	1.00
188	Gary Payton	.20
189	Mitch Richmond	.10
190	Clifford Robinson	.10
191	David Robinson	.25
192	Glenn Robinson	.20
193	Dennis Rodman	1.00
194	Joe Smith	.25
195	Jerry Stackhouse	.30
196	John Stockton	.20
197	Damon Stoudamire	.40
198	Chris Webber	.10
199	Checklist	.10
200	Checklist	.10

1996-97 SkyBox Z-Force Z-Cling

These 100 cards form a parallel set to SkyBox's 1996-97 Z-Force Series I set. Each card front uses a design similar to that which was used for the main issue, except the Z-Cling cards have a team logo on the front. The back has the player's name and team name at the bottom, along with a card number and the NBA and SkyBox logos. If the back is peeled off, the card can cling to a wall, window or school locker. Three bonus cards were inserted into the Z-Cling insert that had no corresponding regular-issue card, and were numbered R1-R3.

		MT
Complete Set (100):		60.00
Common Player:		.20
Z-Cling Cards:		2x
#94 Never Printed		
64	Shaquille O'Neal LAK	10.00
R1	Ray Allen	7.00
R2	Stephon Marbury	12.00
R3	Shareef Abdur-Rahim	8.00

1996-97 SkyBox Z-Force Big Men on the Court

Known as its acronym, BMOC highlighted 10 top players on a die-cut format. The front included an action shot of the player over the words "Big Men on the Court" in bold letters with "big" printed in red and the rest in blue. These cards were found every 240 packs, with parallel foil versions seeded every 1,120.

		MT
Complete Set (10):		475.00
Common Player:		15.00
Inserted 1:240		
BMOC Z-Peat Cards:		3x
Inserted 1:1,120		
1	Charles Barkley	25.00
2	Anfernee Hardaway	60.00
3	Grant Hill	85.00
4	Michael Jordan	175.00
5	Shawn Kemp	15.00
6	Alonzo Mourning	15.00
7	Hakeem Olajuwon	25.00
8	Shaquille O'Neal	60.00
9	Scottie Pippen	45.00
10	David Robinson	20.00

1996-97 SkyBox Z-Force BMOC Z-Peat

BMOC Z-Peats paralleled the BMOC insert, but added a foil finish to the entire card front, and the word "Z-Peat" in gold foil on the bottom right side. This parallel version was inserted one per 1,120 packs.

		MT
Complete Set (10):		1800.
Common Player:		70.00
1	Charles Barkley	90.00
2	Anfernee Hardaway	300.00
3	Grant Hill	300.00
4	Michael Jordan	600.00
5	Shawn Kemp	75.00
6	Alonzo Mourning	70.00
7	Hakeem Olajuwon	125.00
8	Shaquille O'Neal	250.00
9	Scottie Pippen	175.00
10	David Robinson	90.00

1996-97 SkyBox Z-Force Little Big Men

Little Big Men was a 10-card retail-only insert that was seeded one per 36 packs. The fronts featured a foil-etched city skyline of large buildings, with a color shot of the player in front.

		MT
Complete Set (10):		60.00
Common Player:		2.00
1	Kenny Anderson	2.00
2	Mookie Blaylock	2.00
3	Tyrone Bogues	2.00
4	Terrell Brandon	2.00
5	Allen Iverson	25.00
6	Avery Johnson	2.00
7	Kevin Johnson	2.00
8	Stephon Marbury	20.00
9	Gary Payton	6.00
10	Nick Van Exel	2.00

1996-97 SkyBox Z-Force Slam Cam

These 1996-97 SkyBox inserts are some of the most limited ever; they are seeded one per every 240 Series I packs. Nine of the NBA's top slam dunkers are featured on the cards, which are printed in pastel tones and holographic foil, with the "Z-text" changes, resulting in the word rotating. Cards are numbered using an "SC" prefix.

		MT
Complete Set (9):		350.00
Common Player:		20.00
1	Clyde Drexler	30.00
2	Michael Finley	20.00
3	Anfernee Hardaway	60.00
4	Grant Hill	75.00
5	Michael Jordan	200.00
6	Shawn Kemp	20.00
7	Karl Malone	20.00
8	Antonio McDyess	20.00
9	Shaquille O'Neal	60.00

1996-97 SkyBox Z-Force Swat Team

These 1996-97 SkyBox Series I inserts showcase nine players who specialize in the art of rejecting shots. Each card features holographic foil, which makes the player look like he's popping off the card. Cards are numbered using an "ST" prefix and are seeded one per every 72 hobby packs only.

		MT
Complete Set (9):		100.00
Common Player:		3.00
1	Patrick Ewing	3.00
2	Kevin Garnett	35.00
3	Alonzo Mourning	3.00
4	Dikembe Mutombo	3.00
5	Hakeem Olajuwon	15.00
6	Shaquille O'Neal	30.00
7	David Robinson	10.00
8	Dennis Rodman	20.00
9	Joe Smith	10.00

1996-97 SkyBox Z-Force Vortex

These 1996-97 SkyBox Series I inserts showcase high-flying action from the likes of Anfernee Hardaway and Damon Stoudamire. They were seeded one per every 36 Series I retail packs only and are numbered using a "V" prefix.

		MT
Complete Set (15):		150.00
Common Player:		5.00
1	Charles Barkley	10.00
2	Anfernee Hardaway	20.00
3	Grant Hill	25.00
4	Juwan Howard	10.00
5	Michael Jordan	60.00
6	Jason Kidd	10.00
7	Reggie Miller	7.00
8	Gary Payton	7.00
9	Scottie Pippen	15.00
10	Mitch Richmond	5.00
11	Glenn Robinson	5.00
12	Arvydas Sabonis	5.00
13	Jerry Stackhouse	10.00
14	John Stockton	7.00
15	Damon Stoudamire	10.00

1996-97 SkyBox Z-Force Zebut

Twenty rookies were included in this insert, which was seeded one per 24 hobby packs. The fronts featured the player over a gold, silver and copper foil background, with a large "Z" emblem in back of the player. The insert name, player and team name were stamped in gold foil across the bottom. Parallel versions were also printed and featured holographic foil. These were inserted one per 240 hobby packs.

		MT
Complete Set (20):		150.00
Common Player:		2.00
Z-Peat Zebuts:		3x-6x
1	Shareef Abdur-Rahim	18.00
2	Ray Allen	12.00
3	Kobe Bryant	40.00
4	Marcus Camby	20.00
5	Erick Dampier	4.00
6	Todd Fuller	2.00
7	Othella Harrington	2.00
8	Allen Iverson	25.00
9	Kerry Kittles	8.00
10	Priest Lauderdale	2.00
11	Stephon Marbury	25.00
12	Steve Nash	4.00
13	Jermaine O'Neal	6.00
14	Ray Owes	2.00
15	Vitaly Potapenko	2.00
16	Roy Rogers	2.00
17	Antoine Walker	15.00
18	Samaki Walker	2.00
19	John Wallace	5.00
20	Lorenzen Wright	4.00

1996-97 SkyBox Z-Force Z-Peat Zebut

This insert paralleled the Zebut insert, but was printed in holographic foil and inserted one per 240 hobby packs.

	MT
Complete Set (20):	800.00
Z-Peat Cards:	3x-6x

1996-97 SkyBox Z-Force Zensations

Zensations included 20 players featured in a spotlight- like design, with the team logo included across the bottom of the card. These inserts were seeded every six packs.

		MT
Complete Set (20):		40.00
Common Player:		.75
1	Shareef Abdur-Rahim	7.00
2	Ray Allen	5.00
3	Nick Anderson	.75
4	Vin Baker	2.00
5	Mookie Blaylock	.75
6	Calbert Cheaney	.75
7	Kevin Garnett	10.00
8	Horace Grant	.75
9	Tim Hardaway	.75
10	Allen Iverson	12.00
11	Avery Johnson	.75
12	Kevin Johnson	.75
13	Danny Manning	.75
14	Stephon Marbury	10.00
15	Jamal Mashburn	.75
16	Glen Rice	.75
17	Isaiah Rider	.75
18	Latrell Sprewell	2.00
19	Rod Strickland	.75
20	Nick Van Exel	1.50

1997-98 SkyBox Premium

SkyBox Basketball in 1997-98 consisted of two, 125-card series. Series I had 123 regular cards and two checklists, while Series II had 98 veterans and rookies, a 25-card Team SkyBox insert (1:4 packs) and two checklists. Base card featured a color shot of the player on a borderless design with a colored, blurred background done with computer graphics. Star Rubies parallels ran through both series, with 246 cards (250 minus four checklists) numbered to only 50 sets. Inserts in Series I include: Next Game, Rock 'n Fire, And One..., Premium Players and Silky Smooth. Inserts in Series II include: Star Search, Jam Pack, Competitive Advantage, Thunder & Lightning and Golden Touch. Autographics cards were also inserted into both series.

		MT
Complete Set (250):		65.00
Complete Series 1 (125):		30.00
Complete Series 2 (125):		35.00
Common Player:		.10
Common Player (224-248):		.50
Minor Stars:		.20
Series 1 or 2 Pack (8):		2.75
Series 1 or 2 Wax Box (24):		60.00
1	Grant Hill	2.00
2	Matt Maloney	.20
3	Vinny Del Negro	.10
4	Bobby Phills	.10
5	Mark Jackson	.10
6	Ray Allen	.25
7	Derrick Coleman	.10
8	Isaiah Rider	.10
9	Rod Strickland	.10
10	Danny Ferry	.10
11	Antonio Davis	.10
12	Glenn Robinson	.25
13	Cedric Ceballos	.10
14	Sean Elliott	.10
15	Walt Williams	.10
16	Glen Rice	.20
17	Clyde Drexler	.30
18	Sherman Douglas	.10
19	Brian Grant	.10
20	John Stockton	.30
21	Priest Lauderdale	.10
22	Khalid Reeves	.10
23	Kobe Bryant	3.00
24	Vin Baker	.25
25	Steve Nash	.10
26	Jeff Hornacek	.10
27	Malik Rose	.10
28	Charles Barkley	.40
29	Michael Jordan	4.00
30	Latrell Sprewell	.30
31	Anfernee Hardaway	1.50
32	Steve Kerr	.10
33	Joe Smith	.30
34	Jermaine O'Neal	.20
35	*Ron Mercer*	3.00
36	Antonio McDyess	.30
37	Patrick Ewing	.25
38	Avery Johnson	.10
39	Toni Kukoc	.10
40	Chris Mullin	.10
41	Voshon Lenard	.10
42	Detlef Schrempf	.10
43	Horace Grant	.10
44	Luc Longley	.10
45	Todd Fuller	.10
46	Tim Hardaway	.20
47	Nick Anderson	.10
48	Scottie Pippen	1.00
49	Lindsey Hunter	.10
50	Shawn Kemp	.50
51	Larry Johnson	.20
52	Shawn Bradley	.10
53	Charles Outlaw	.10
54	Jamal Mashburn	.20
55	John Starks	.10
56	Rony Seikaly	.10
57	Gary Payton	.30
58	Juwan Howard	.30
59	Vitaly Potapenko	.10
60	Reggie Miller	.25
61	Alonzo Mourning	.20
62	Roy Rogers	.10
63	Antoine Walker	1.50
64	Joe Dumars	.10
65	Allan Houston	.10
66	Hersey Hawkins	.10
67	Dell Curry	.10
68	Tony Delk	.10
69	Mookie Blaylock	.10
70	Derek Harper	.10
71	Loy Vaught	.10
72	Tom Gugliotta	.20
73	Mitch Richmond	.20
74	Dikembe Mutombo	.10
75	*Tony Battie*	2.00
76	Derek Fisher	.10
77	Jason Kidd	.30
78	Shareef Abdur-Rahim	.75
79	*Tracy McGrady*	2.00
80	Anthony Mason	.10
81	Mario Elie	.10
82	Karl Malone	.30
83	Dean Garrett	.10
84	Steve Smith	.10
85	LaPhonso Ellis	.10
86	Robert Horry	.10
87	Wesley Person	.10
88	Marcus Camby	.50
89	*Antonio Daniels*	2.00
90	Eddie Jones	.50
91	Todd Day	.10
92	*Danny Fortson*	1.75
93	Chris Childs	.10
94	David Robinson	.40
95	Bryant Reeves	.10
96	Chris Webber	.40
97	P.J. Brown	.10
98	Tyrone Hill	.10
99	Dale Davis	.10
100	Allen Iverson	2.00
101	Jerry Stackhouse	.30
102	Arvydas Sabonis	.10
103	Damon Stoudamire	.40
104	*Tim Thomas*	2.00
105	Christian Laettner	.20
106	Robert Pack	.10
107	Lorenzen Wright	.10
108	Olden Polynice	.10
109	Terrell Brandon	.20
110	Erick Dampier	.10
111	Kevin Garnett	2.00
112	*Tim Duncan*	5.00
113	Bryon Russell	.10
114	*Chauncey Billups*	2.00
115	Dale Ellis	.10
116	Shaquille O'Neal	1.50
117	*Keith Van Horn*	2.00
118	Kenny Anderson	.10
119	Dennis Rodman	1.00
120	Hakeem Olajuwon	.75
121	Stephon Marbury	1.50
122	Kendall Gill	.10
123	Kerry Kittles	.30
124	Checklist	.10
125	Checklist	.10
126	Anthony Johnson	.10
127	*Chris Anstey*	.20
128	Dean Garrett	.10
129	Rik Smits	.10
130	Tracy Murray	.10
131	Charles O'Bannon	.10
132	Eldridge Recasner	.10
133	Johnny Taylor	.10
134	Priest Lauderdale	.10
135	Rod Strickland	.10
136	Alan Henderson	.10
137	*Austin Croshere*	.50
138	Buck Williams	.10
139	Clifford Robinson	.10
140	Darrell Armstrong	.10
141	Dennis Scott	.10
142	Carl Herrera	.10
143	*Maurice Taylor*	.75
144	Chris Gatling	.10
145	Alvin Williams	.10
146	Antonio McDyess	.50
147	Chauncey Billups	1.00
148	George McCloud	.10
149	George Lynch	.10
150	John Thomas	.10
151	Jayson Williams	.10
152	Otis Thorpe	.10
153	Serge Zwikker	.10
154	Chris Crawford	.10
155	Muggsy Bogues	.10
156	Mark Jackson	.10
157	Dontonio Wingfield	.10
158	*Rodrick Rhodes*	.50
159	Sam Cassell	.10
160	Hubert Davis	.10
161	Clarence Weatherspoon	.10
162	Eddie Johnson	.10
163	*Jacque Vaughn*	.30
164	Mark Price	.10
165	Terry Dehere	.10
166	Travis Knight	.10
167	Charles Smith	.10
168	David Wesley	.10
169	David Wingate	.10
170	Todd Day	.10
171	*Adonal Foyle*	.50
172	Chris Mills	.10
173	Paul Grant	.10
174	Adam Keefe	.10
175	Erick Dampier	.10
176	Ervin Johnson	.10
177	Lamond Murray	.10
178	Vlade Divac	.10
179	Bobby Phills	.10
180	Brian Williams	.10
181	Chris Dudley	.10
182	Tyrone Hill	.10
183	Donyell Marshall	.10
184	Kevin Gamble	.10
185	Scot Pollard	.10
186	Cherokee Parks	.10
187	Terry Mills	.10
188	Glen Rice	.30
189	Shawn Respert	.10
190	Terrell Brandon	.20
191	Keith Closs	.10
192	*Tariq Abdul-Wahad*	.50
193	Wesley Person	.10
194	Chuck Person	.10
195	*Derek Anderson*	1.50
196	Jon Barry	.10
197	Chris Mullin	.20
198	Ed Gray	.10
199	Charlie Ward	.10
200	*Kelvin Cato*	.20
201	Michael Finley	.20
202	Rick Fox	.10
203	Scott Burrell	.10
204	Vin Baker	.50
205	Eric Snow	.10
206	Isaac Austin	.10
207	Keith Booth	.10
208	Brian Grant	.10
209	Chris Webber	.75
210	Eric Williams	.10
211	Jim Jackson	.20
212	Anthony Parker	.10
213	*Brevin Knight*	1.00
214	Cory Alexander	.10
215	James Robinson	.10
216	*Bobby Jackson*	1.00
217	Charles Outlaw	.10
218	*God Shammgod*	.50
219	James Cotton	.10
220	Jud Buechler	.10
221	Shandon Anderson	.10
222	Kevin Johnson	.10
223	Chris Morris	.10
224	Shareef Abdur-Rahim	2.00
225	Ray Allen	.75
226	Kobe Bryant	5.00
227	Marcus Camby	.50
228	Antonio Daniels	1.50
229	Tim Duncan	4.00
230	Kevin Garnett	4.00
231	Anfernee Hardaway	3.00
232	Grant Hill	4.00
233	Allen Iverson	3.00
234	Bobby Jackson	.75
235	Michael Jordan	8.00
236	Shawn Kemp	1.00
237	Karl Malone	.50
238	Stephon Marbury	3.00
239	Hakeem Olajuwon	1.50
240	Shaquille O'Neal	3.00
241	Gary Payton	.75
242	Scottie Pippen	2.00
243	David Robinson	.75
244	Dennis Rodman	2.50
245	Jerry Stackhouse	.75
246	Damon Stoudamire	1.25
247	Keith Van Horn	1.00
248	Antoine Walker	.60
249	Grant Hill	1.25
250	Hakeem Olajuwon	.50

1997-98 SkyBox Premium Rubies

Rubies featured all 250 cards from Series I and II with red foil stamping on the front vs. the gold used on regular cards. These parallel versions were found in hobby packs only and sequentially numbered to 50 sets. In addition, the short-printed Team SkyBox subset is not short-printed in Rubies; it is numbered to 50 like the other cards.

	MT
Ruby Stars:	100x-200x
Ruby Rookies:	50x-100x

1997-98 SkyBox Premium Autographics

Autographics returned for a second season with around 150 players' signatures in all. The inserts were included in packs of Hoops I and II (1:240 packs), SkyBox I and II (1:72 packs), Z-Force I and II (1:120 packs) and E-X2001 (1:60 packs). Rarer versions of each card were also available and included prismatic foil on the front and individual, hand numbering.

	MT
Common Player:	15.00
Century Marks:	2x-3x
Shareef Abdur-Rahim	150.00
Cory Alexander	15.00
Kenny Anderson	25.00
Nick Anderson	20.00
Stacey Augmon	15.00
Isaac Austin	20.00
Vin Baker	100.00
Charles Barkley	300.00
Dana Barros	15.00
Brent Barry	25.00
Tony Battie	40.00
Travis Best	15.00
Corie Blount	15.00
P.J. Brown	20.00
Randy Brown	20.00
Jud Buechler	20.00
Marcus Camby	75.00
Elden Campbell	25.00
Antoine Carr	15.00
Chris Carr	15.00
Duane Causwell	15.00
Rex Chapman	30.00
Calbert Cheaney	20.00
Randolph Childress	15.00
Derrick Coleman	35.00
Austin Croshere	25.00
Dell Curry	15.00
Ben Davis	15.00
Mark Davis	15.00
Andrew DeClercq	20.00
Tony Delk	30.00
Vlade Divac	25.00
Clyde Drexler	120.00
Joe Dumars	50.00
Howard Eisley	15.00
Danny Ferry	15.00
Michael Finley	30.00
Derek Fisher	25.00
Danny Fortson	30.00
Todd Fuller	15.00
Chris Gatling	15.00
Matt Geiger	15.00
Brian Grant	20.00
Tom Gugliotta	70.00
Tim Hardaway	75.00
Ron Harper	25.00
Othella Harrington	15.00
Grant Hill	325.00
Tyrone Hill	15.00
Allan Houston	40.00
Juwan Howard	100.00
Lindsey Hunter	35.00
Bobby Hurley	15.00
Jimmy Jackson	25.00
Avery Johnson	15.00
Eddie Johnson	15.00
Ervin Johnson	15.00
Larry Johnson	50.00
Popeye Jones	15.00
Adam Keefe	15.00
Steve Kerr	25.00
Kerry Kittles	75.00
Brevin Knight	70.00
Travis Knight	25.00
George Lynch	15.00
Don MacLean	15.00
Stephon Marbury	175.00
Donny Marshall	20.00
Walter McCarty	30.00
Antonio McDyess	70.00
Tracy McGrady CM	325.00
Ron Mercer	175.00
Reggie Miller	200.00
Chris Mills	15.00
Sam Mitchell	15.00
Chris Morris	15.00
Alonzo Mourning	125.00
Chris Mullin	30.00
Dikembe Mutombo	50.00
Sam Perkins	20.00
Elliot Perry	15.00
Bobby Phills	15.00
Eric Piatkowski	20.00
Scottie Pippen	275.00
Vitaly Potapenko	15.00
Brent Price	15.00
Theo Ratliff	25.00
Glen Rice	60.00
Glenn Robinson	75.00
Dennis Rodman	500.00
Roy Rogers	15.00
Malik Rose	15.00
Joe Smith	75.00
Tony Smith	15.00
Eric Snow	15.00
Jerry Stackhouse Det.	75.00
Jerry Stackhouse Phi.	75.00
John Starks	25.00
Bryant Stith	15.00
Erick Strickland	20.00
Rod Strickland	45.00
Nick Van Exel	85.00
Keith Van Horn	50.00
David Vaughn	15.00
Jacque Vaughn	40.00
Antoine Walker	50.00
John Wallace	15.00
Rasheed Wallace CM	75.00
Clarence Weatherspoon	15.00
David Wesley	15.00
Dominique Wilkins	60.00
Gerald Wilkins	15.00
Erik Williams	15.00
John Williams	15.00

	Lorenzo Williams	15.00
	Monty Williams	15.00
	Scott Williams	15.00
	Walt Williams	25.00
	Lorenzen Wright	30.00

1997-98 SkyBox Premium And One

This 10-card insert features an outer layer that opens in four directions to reveal a larger photo in a diamond-shaped "poster" that is highlighted in silver and gold. In addition, there's an extra bonus card inside that is printed in silver foil. And One inserts were seeded every 96 packs of Series I and are numbered on the innermost card with an "AO" suffix.

		MT
Complete Set (10):		200.00
Common Player:		8.00
1	Shawn Kemp	8.00
2	Hakeem Olajuwon	12.00
3	Charles Barkley	8.00
4	Antoine Walker	15.00
5	Dennis Rodman	20.00
6	Tim Duncan	40.00
7	Marcus Camby	10.00
8	Keith Van Horn	15.00
9	Shareef Abdur-Rahim	15.00
10	Michael Jordan	70.00

1997-98 SkyBox Premium Competitive Advantage

This 15-card insert set highlights players between the arches of stone columns on a die-cut format. Competitive Advantage inserts were seeded one per 96 packs of Series II and numbered with a "CA" suffix.

		MT
Complete Set (15):		275.00
Common Player:		7.00
1	Allen Iverson	30.00
2	Kobe Bryant	45.00
3	Michael Jordan	70.00
4	Shaquille O'Neal	25.00
5	Stephon Marbury	35.00
6	Shareef Abdur-Rahim	25.00
7	Marcus Camby	7.00
8	Kevin Garnett	35.00
9	Dennis Rodman	20.00
10	Anfernee Hardaway	25.00
11	Ray Allen	14.00
12	Scottie Pippen	17.00
13	Shawn Kemp	10.00
14	Hakeem Olajuwon	15.00
15	John Stockton	7.00

1997-98 SkyBox Premium Golden Touch

Golden Touch is a 15-card insert set that was seeded one per 360 packs of Series II. Each card featured the color image of the player on a gold foil, die-cut card with the insert name in bold, gold letters across the top and bottom. Golden Touch inserts were numbered with a "GT" suffix.

		MT
Complete Set (15):		1000.
Common Player:		25.00
1	Michael Jordan	250.00
2	Allen Iverson	100.00
3	Kobe Bryant	150.00
4	Shaquille O'Neal	75.00
5	Stephon Marbury	125.00
6	Marcus Camby	25.00
7	Anfernee Hardaway	100.00
8	Kevin Garnett	125.00
9	Shareef Abdur-Rahim	60.00
10	Dennis Rodman	75.00
11	Grant Hill	125.00
12	Kerry Kittles	35.00
13	Antoine Walker	60.00
14	Scottie Pippen	60.00
15	Damon Stoudamire	35.00

1997-98 SkyBox Premium Jam Pack

Fifteen of the top young players in the NBA were included in the Jam Pack insert. Card fronts feature the player on a silver foil, scenery background. Jam Pack inserts were seeded one per 18 packs of Series II and numbered with a "JP" suffix.

		MT
Complete Set (15):		60.00
Common Player:		2.00
1	Ray Allen	4.00
2	Damon Stoudamire	6.00
3	Shawn Kemp	5.00
4	Hakeem Olajuwon	8.00
5	Jerry Stackhouse	4.00
6	John Wallace	2.00
7	Juwan Howard	4.00
8	David Robinson	5.00
9	Gary Payton	4.00
10	Joe Smith	4.00
11	Charles Barkley	5.00
12	Terrell Brandon	2.00
13	Vin Baker	4.00
14	Antonio McDyess	4.00
15	Tim Duncan	20.00

1997-98 SkyBox Premium Next Game

Next Game was a 15-card insert set that was seeded one per six packs of Series I. Card fronts are done with an original art background, with backs chronicling the player's college career. These inserts were numbered with a "NG" suffix.

		MT
Complete Set (15):		40.00
Common Player:		1.00
1	Derek Anderson	3.00
2	Tony Battie	3.00
3	Chauncey Billups	4.00
4	Kelvin Cato	1.00
5	Austin Croshere	1.00
6	Antonio Daniels	4.00
7	Tim Duncan	8.00
8	Danny Fortson	2.00
9	Adonal Foyle	2.00
10	Tracy McGrady	4.00
11	Ron Mercer	4.00
12	Olivier Saint-Jean	2.00
13	Maurice Taylor	1.00
14	Tim Thomas	3.00
15	Keith Van Horn	4.00

1997-98 SkyBox Premium Premium Players

Premium Players was a 15-card insert set that was seeded one per 192 packs of Series I. Fronts are done in a silver holographic rainbow foil and include a montage of action photos of that player. Backs include another shot of the player on the left, with bio information on the right and are numbered with a "PP" suffix.

		MT
Complete Set (15):		600.00
Common Player:		8.00
1	Michael Jordan	120.00
2	Allen Iverson	60.00
3	Kobe Bryant	75.00
4	Shaquille O'Neal	45.00
5	Stephon Marbury	45.00
6	Marcus Camby	15.00
7	Anfernee Hardaway	50.00
8	Kevin Garnett	60.00
9	Shareef Abdur-Rahim	30.00
10	Dennis Rodman	35.00
11	Ray Allen	8.00
12	Grant Hill	60.00
13	Kerry Kittles	8.00
14	Karl Malone	8.00
15	Scottie Pippen	25.00

1997-98 SkyBox Premium Reebok Value

This insert contained 15 cards and was included in each pack of Series I. It includes the same photos from regular-issue cards, but slightly different background photos and three color variations. Backs featured the Reebok logo and Web page address.

		MT
Complete Set (15):		4.00
Common Player:		.25
	Steve Smith	.25
	Tyrone Hill	.25
	Robert Pack	.25
	Clyde Drexler	.50
	Mario Elie	.25
	Mark Jackson	.25
	Shaquille O'Neal	1.00
	Voshon Lenard	.25
	Glenn Robinson	.40
	Allen Iverson	.50
	Cedric Ceballos	.25
	Kenny Anderson	.25
	Vinny Del Negro	.25
	Avery Johnson	.25
	Shawn Kemp	.50

1997-98 SkyBox Premium Rock'n Fire

Rock 'n Fire includes 10 rising stars with a mini-card that pulls out of a black outer frame through the top or bottom. These are inserted one per 18 packs of Series I and are numbered with a "RF" suffix.

		MT
Complete Set (10):		100.00
Common Player:		3.00
1	Allen Iverson	18.00
2	Kobe Bryant	25.00
3	Shaquille O'Neal	12.00
4	Stephon Marbury	15.00
5	Marcus Camby	8.00
6	Anfernee Hardaway	12.00
7	Kevin Garnett	18.00
8	Shareef Abdur-Rahim	10.00
9	Damon Stoudamire	3.00
10	Grant Hill	18.00

1997-98 SkyBox Premium Silky Smooth

Silky Smooth was a 10-card insert set that was seeded one per 360 packs of Series I. Each card featured a white die-cut basketball net that could be opened like a book to reveal a full-color shot of the player. Backs were primarily black, contained a portrait of the player and were numbered with a "SS" suffix.

		MT
Complete Set (10):		750.00
Common Player:		20.00
1	Michael Jordan	175.00
2	Allen Iverson	85.00
3	Kobe Bryant	140.00
4	Shaquille O'Neal	60.00
5	Stephon Marbury	75.00
6	Gary Payton	25.00
7	Anfernee Hardaway	75.00
8	Kevin Garnett	100.00
9	Scottie Pippen	45.00
10	Grant Hill	100.00

1997-98 SkyBox Premium Star Search

Star Search was a 15-card insert set that was inserted one per six packs of Series II. The front features a reddish wood grain flap with a small picture of the player near the bottom. The flap opens up to reveal a color action shot of the player,with the insert name and the player's name in the lower right corner. Card backs are numbered with a "SS" suffix.

		MT
Complete Set (15):		30.00
Common Player:		.50
1	Tim Duncan	8.00
2	Tony Battie	2.00
3	Keith Van Horn	5.00
4	Antonio Daniels	3.00
5	Chauncey Billups	4.00
6	Ron Mercer	5.00
7	Tracy McGrady	4.00
8	Danny Fortson	1.00
9	Brevin Knight	2.00
10	Derek Anderson	3.00
11	Bobby Jackson	2.00
12	Jacque Vaughn	1.00
13	Tim Thomas	3.00
14	Austin Croshere	1.00
15	Kelvin Cato	.50

1997-98 SkyBox Premium Thunder & Lightning

Thunder and Lightning captured 15 players and was included one per 192 packs of Series II. Each card had a holographic front and was numbered with a "TL" suffix.

		MT
Complete Set (15):		500.00
Common Player:		8.00
1	Stephon Marbury	40.00
2	Shareef Abdur-Rahim	25.00
3	Shaquille O'Neal	30.00
4	Scottie Pippen	25.00
5	Michael Jordan	100.00
6	Marcus Camby	8.00
7	Kobe Bryant	60.00
8	Kevin Garnett	50.00
9	Kerry Kittles	12.00
10	Grant Hill	50.00
11	Dennis Rodman	30.00
12	Damon Stoudamire	12.00
13	Antoine Walker	20.00
14	Anfernee Hardaway	40.00
15	Allen Iverson	40.00

1997-98 SkyBox Z-Force

This 110-card set included 108 player cards and two checklists in Series I, while Series II included 98 cards and two checklists. Fronts featured the player over an artsy, spiral background, with the player's name running down the right side in foil. The player's team, uniform number, position and the Z-Force logo run across the bottom. The back is white with another shot of the player, statistics and the card number in the lower right corner. Card No. 143 does not exist in the set or any of the parallels. Vin Baker and Tracy McGrady were both numbered as card No. 172. Inserts in Series I include: Boss, Super Boss, Limited Access, Rave Reviews, Total Impact, Fast Track, Autographics and the parallel Raves. Inserts in Series II included: Zensations, Star Gazing, Zebut, Slam Cam, Quick Strike, Autographics and BMOC as well as Rave and Super Rave parallels.

		MT
Complete Set (210):		30.00
Complete Series 1 (110):		15.00
Complete Series 2 (100):		15.00
Common Player:		.10
Minor Stars:		.20
Series 1 Pack:		1.50
Series 1 Box (36):		35.00
Series 2 Pack:		2.00
Series 2 Wax Box:		45.00
1	Anfernee Hardaway	1.50
2	Mitch Richmond	.20
3	Stephon Marbury	1.25
4	Charles Barkley	.40
5	Juwan Howard	.30
6	Avery Johnson	.10
7	Rex Chapman	.10
8	Antoine Walker	1.00
9	Nick Van Exel	.20
10	Tim Hardaway	.10
11	Clarence Weatherspoon	.10
12	John Stockton	.30
13	Glenn Robinson	.30
14	Anthony Mason	.10
15	Latrell Sprewell	.20
16	Kendall Gill	.10
17	Terry Mills	.10
18	Mookie Blaylock	.10
19	Michael Finley	.10
20	Gary Payton	.30
21	Kevin Garnett	1.75
22	Clyde Drexler	.30
23	Michael Jordan	3.50
24	Antonio McDyess	.30
25	Nick Anderson	.10
26	Patrick Ewing	.30
27	Anthony Peeler	.10
28	Doug Christie	.10
29	Bobby Phills	.10
30	Kerry Kittles	.40
31	Reggie Miller	.20
32	Karl Malone	.30
33	Grant Hill	1.75
34	Shaquille O'Neal	1.25
35	Loy Vaught	.10
36	Kenny Anderson	.10
37	Wesley Person	.10
38	Jamal Mashburn	.10
39	Christian Laettner	.10
40	Shawn Kemp	.50
41	Glen Rice	.20
42	Vin Baker	.30
43	David Wesley	.10
44	Derrick Coleman	.10
45	Rik Smits	.10
46	Dale Ellis	.10
47	Rod Strickland	.10
48	Mark Price	.10
49	Toni Kukoc	.10
50	David Robinson	.40
51	John Wallace	.20
52	Samaki Walker	.10
53	Shareef Abdur-Rahim	1.00
54	Rodney Rogers	.10
55	Dikembe Mutombo	.10
56	Rony Seikaly	.10
57	Matt Maloney	.20
58	Chris Webber	.50
59	Robert Horry	.10
60	Rasheed Wallace	.10
61	Jeff Hornacek	.10
62	Walt Williams	.10
63	Detlef Schrempf	.10
64	Dan Majerle	.10
65	Dell Curry	.10
66	Scottie Pippen	.75
67	Greg Anthony	.10
68	Mahmoud Abdul-Rauf	.10
69	Cedric Ceballos	.10
70	Terrell Brandon	.10
71	Arvydas Sabonis	.10
72	Dino Radja	.10
73	Jim Jackson	.10
74	Joe Dumars	.10
75	Joe Smith	.30
76	Shawn Bradley	.10
77	Gheorghe Muresan	.10
78	Dale Davis	.10
79	Bryant Stith	.10
80	Lorenzen Wright	.10
81	Chris Childs	.10
82	Bryon Russell	.10
83	Steve Smith	.10
84	Jerry Stackhouse	.30
85	Hersey Hawkins	.10
86	Ray Allen	.40
87	Dominique Wilkins	.10
88	Kobe Bryant	2.00
89	Tom Gugliotta	.10
90	Dennis Scott	.10
91	Dennis Rodman	1.00
92	Bryant Reeves	.10
93	Vlade Divac	.10
94	Jason Kidd	.20
95	Mario Elie	.10
96	Lindsey Hunter	.10
97	Olden Polynice	.10
98	Allan Houston	.10
99	Alonzo Mourning	.20
100	Allen Iverson	1.75
101	LaPhonso Ellis	.10
102	Bob Sura	.10
103	Chris Mullin	.10
104	Sam Cassell	.10
105	Eric Williams	.10
106	Antonio Davis	.10
107	Marcus Camby	.75
108	Isaiah Rider	.10
109	Checklist	.10
110	Checklist	.10
111	*Tim Duncan*	2.50
112	Joe Smith	.30
113	Shawn Kemp	.50
114	Terry Mills	.10
115	*Jacque Vaughn*	.20
116	*Ron Mercer*	1.25
117	Brian Williams	.10
118	Rik Smits	.10
119	Eric Williams	.10
120	*Tim Thomas*	.75
121	Damon Stoudamire	.40
122	*God Shammgod*	.20
123	Tyrone Hill	.10
124	Elden Campbell	.10
125	*Keith Van Horn*	1.50
126	Brian Grant	.10
127	Antonio McDyess	.30
128	Darrell Armstrong	.10
129	Sam Perkins	.10
130	Chris Mills	.10
131	Reggie Miller	.20
132	Chris Gatling	.10
133	Ed Gray	.10
134	Hakeem Olajuwon	.50
135	Chris Webber	.40
136	Kendall Gill	.10
137	Wesley Person	.10
138	Derrick Coleman	.10
139	Dana Barros	.10
140	Dennis Scott	.10
141	*Paul Grant*	.20
142	Scott Burrell	.10
143	*Tracy McGrady*	1.25
144	*Austin Croshere*	.30
145	*Maurice Taylor*	.40
146	Kevin Johnson	.10
147	*Tony Battie*	.50
148	*Tariq Abdul-Wahad*	.20
149	Johnny Taylor	.10
150	Allen Iverson	1.25
151	Terrell Brandon	.10
152	*Derek Anderson*	.50
153	Calbert Cheaney	.10
154	Jayson Williams	.10
155	Rick Fox	.10
156	John Thomas	.10
157	David Wesley	.10
158	*Bobby Jackson*	.50
159	*Kelvin Cato*	.20
160	Vinny Del Negro	.10

161	*Adonal Foyle*	.30
162	Larry Johnson	.20
163	*Brevin Knight*	.50
164	Rod Strickland	.10
165	*Rodrick Rhodes*	.30
166	*Scot Pollard*	.20
167	Sam Cassell	.10
168	Jerry Stackhouse	.30
169	Mark Jackson	.10
170	John Wallace	.20
171	Horace Grant	.10
172	Vin Baker	.30
173	Eddie Jones	.40
174	Kerry Kittles	.25
175	*Antonio Daniels*	.75
176	Alan Henderson	.10
177	Sean Elliott	.10
178	John Starks	.10
179	*Chauncey Billups*	1.00
180	Juwan Howard	.30
181	Bobby Phills	.10
182	Latrell Sprewell	.20
183	Jim Jackson	.10
184	*Danny Fortson*	.30
185	*Zydrunas Ilgauskas*	.50
186	Clifford Robinson	.10
187	Chris Mullin	.10
188	Greg Ostertag	.10
189	Antoine Walker (Zupermen)	.50
190	Michael Jordan (Zupermen)	1.50
191	Scottie Pippen (Zupermen)	.30
192	Dennis Rodman (Zupermen)	.50
193	Grant Hill (Zupermen)	.75
194	Clyde Drexler (Zupermen)	.10
195	Kobe Bryant (Zupermen)	1.00
196	Shaquille O'Neal (Zupermen)	.60
197	Alonzo Mourning (Zupermen)	.10
198	Ray Allen (Zupermen)	.10
199	Kevin Garnett (Zupermen)	.75
200	Stephon Marbury (Zupermen)	.60
201	Anfernee Hardaway (Zupermen)	.60
202	Jason Kidd (Zupermen)	.10
203	David Robinson (Zupermen)	.10
204	Gary Payton (Zupermen)	.10
205	Marcus Camby (Zupermen)	.10
206	Karl Malone (Zupermen)	.10
207	John Stockton (Zupermen)	.10
208	Shareef Abdur-Rahim (Zupermen)	.40
209	Checklist (Charles Barkley)	.10
210	Checklist (Gary Payton)	.10

1997-98 SkyBox Z-Force Raves

This 206-card parallel set (210 minus the four checklists) included prismatic silver foil on the front, and individual numbering to 399 on the back. No odds for Rave inserts were given, but it is estimated that they are seeded one per 60-80 packs. Once again, card No. 143 does not exist; both Baker and McGrady are numbered as card 172.

	MT
Rave Stars:	30x-60x
Rave Rookies:	15x-30x

1997-98 SkyBox Z-Force Super Raves

Super Raves was a second level parallel set and was numbered to only 50 sets. Super Raves featured purple prismatic foil on the front in contrast to the gold used on base cards and silver prismatic foil used on Raves. Once again, card No. 143 does not exist; both Baker and McGrady are numbered as card No. 172.

	MT
Super Rave Cards:	125x-250x
Super Rave Rookies:	60x-120x

1997-98 SkyBox Z-Force Big Men on Court

This 15-card insert was inserted into one per 288 packs of Series II. Each card is printed on a multi-dimensional thermo plastic card stock, with the NBA's elite players included in the set. Cards are numbered with a "B" prefix.

		MT
Complete Set (15):		675.00
Common Player:		25.00
1	Shareef Abdur-Rahim	40.00
2	Kobe Bryant	100.00
3	Marcus Camby	25.00
4	Tim Duncan	70.00
5	Kevin Garnett	70.00
6	Anfernee Hardaway	60.00
7	Grant Hill	70.00
8	Allen Iverson	60.00
9	Michael Jordan	140.00
10	Shawn Kemp	15.00
11	Stephon Marbury	60.00
12	Shaquille O'Neal	50.00
13	Scottie Pippen	35.00
14	Dennis Rodman	50.00
15	Antoine Walker	30.00

1997-98 SkyBox Z-Force Boss

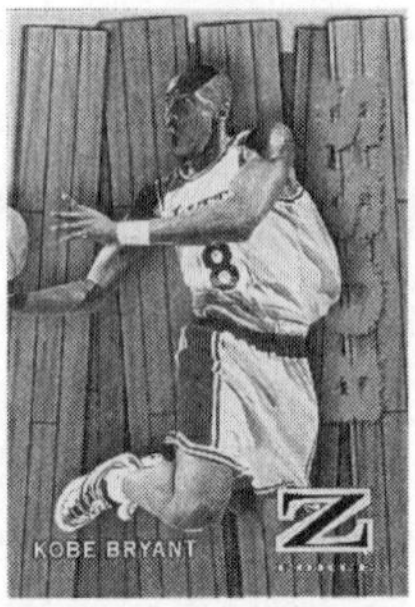

This 20-card insert was seeded one per six packs of Z-Force Series I. The cards feature an embossed player image on the front over a wood basketball floor-like background, with the insert name printed in red letters up the right side and a large "Z" in black and yellow in the lower right corner. Boss inserts were numbered "x of 20/B". There are also Super Boss parallels with a foil finish that were inserted every 36 packs and numbered "x of 20/SB".

		MT
Complete Set (20):		50.00
Common Player:		.50
Minor Stars:		1.00
Super Boss Cards:		2x-4x
1	Shareef Abdur-Rahim	4.00
2	Ray Allen	.50
3	Kobe Bryant	6.00
4	Marcus Camby	2.00
5	Kevin Garnett	6.00
6	Anfernee Hardaway	5.00
7	Grant Hill	6.00
8	Allen Iverson	6.00
9	Eddie Jones	1.50
10	Michael Jordan	12.00
11	Shawn Kemp	1.50
12	Kerry Kittles	.50
13	Stephon Marbury	5.00
14	Shaquille O'Neal	4.00
15	Hakeem Olajuwon	2.00
16	Scottie Pippen	3.00
17	Dennis Rodman	4.00
18	Joe Smith	.50
19	Damon Stoudamire	.50
20	Antoine Walker	2.00

1997-98 SkyBox Z-Force Fast Track

Fast Track highlighted 12 players who are quickly approaching superstardom. Fronts are yellow with large black felt letters "Fast" on the top and "Track" across the bottom, with the team name in a black strip across the bottom in white letters. Fast Track inserts were seeded one per 24 packs, and numbered "x of 12/FT".

		MT
Complete Set (12):		70.00
Common Player:		3.00
1	Ray Allen	3.00
2	Kobe Bryant	20.00
3	Marcus Camby	8.00
4	Juwan Howard	6.00
5	Eddie Jones	6.00
6	Kerry Kittles	3.00
7	Antonio McDyess	3.00
8	Joe Smith	6.00
9	Jerry Stackhouse	6.00
10	Damon Stoudamire	6.00
11	Antoine Walker	5.00
12	Chris Webber	8.00

1997-98 SkyBox Z-Force Limited Access

Each card takes an in-depth statistical analysis of ten players on a bi-fold card. They were available exclusively in retail packs at a rate of 1:18.

		MT
Complete Set (10):		50.00
Common Player:		2.00
1	Shareef Abdur-Rahim	6.00
2	Ray Allen	2.00
3	Charles Barkley	4.00
4	Anfernee Hardaway	10.00
5	Juwan Howard	4.00
6	Michael Jordan	20.00
7	Stephon Marbury	8.00
8	Shaquille O'Neal	8.00
9	Dennis Rodman	6.00
10	Antoine Walker	5.00

1997-98 SkyBox Z-Force Quick Strike

Quick Strike consisted of 12 cards and was seeded one per 96 packs of Series II. The cards were printed on holograpic silver plastic, with a clear oval window in the middle that included the insert name. The player's image was cast over this background. Cards were numbered with a "QS" suffix.

		MT
Complete Set (12):		200.00
Common Player:		5.00
1	Shareef Abdur-Rahim	20.00
2	Anfernee Hardaway	25.00
3	Grant Hill	35.00
4	Allen Iverson	25.00
5	Michael Jordan	70.00
6	Stephon Marbury	25.00
7	Hakeem Olajuwon	12.00
8	Scottie Pippen	18.00
9	Damon Stoudamire	5.00
10	Keith Van Horn	20.00
11	Antoine Walker	15.00
12	Chris Webber	10.00

1997-98 SkyBox Z-Force Rave Reviews

Rave Reviews showcased 12 of the top players in the NBA on gold prismatic foil with black around the edges. Inserted at a rate of one per 288 packs, these cards contained the insert name and player's name in silver foil across the middle of the card. Backs were mostly black with white lettering.

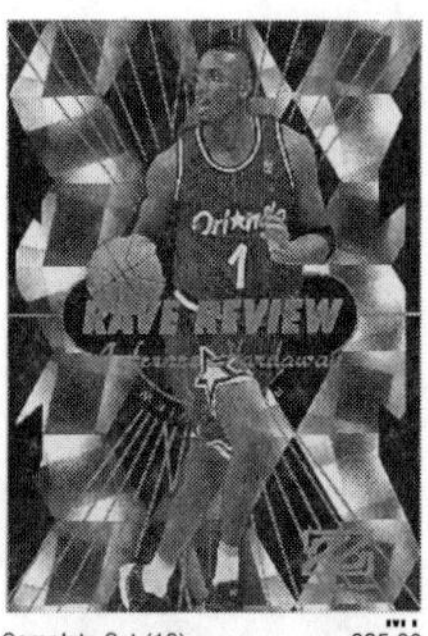

		MT
Complete Set (12):		625.00
Common Player:		25.00
1	Shareef Abdur-Rahim	50.00
2	Kevin Garnett	75.00
3	Anfernee Hardaway	60.00
4	Grant Hill	75.00
5	Allen Iverson	75.00
6	Michael Jordan	150.00
7	Shawn Kemp	20.00
8	Stephon Marbury	60.00
9	Shaquille O'Neal	50.00
10	Hakeem Olajuwon	25.00
11	Scottie Pippen	40.00
12	Dennis Rodman	40.00

1997-98 SkyBox Z-Force Star Gazing

This 15-card insert set was seeded one per 18 retail packs in Series II. Fronts captured the player over a dark, foil background with gold rings going around the basketball. Star Gazing inserts were numbered with a "SG" suffix.

		MT
Complete Set (15):		100.00
Common Player:		2.50
Inserted 1:18 Retail		
1	Shareef Abdur-Rahim	6.00
2	Kobe Bryant	15.00
3	Marcus Camby	2.50
4	Kevin Garnett	12.00
5	Anfernee Hardaway	8.00
6	Grant Hill	12.00
7	Allen Iverson	8.00
8	Stephon Marbury	10.00
9	Hakeem Olajuwon	5.00
10	Shaquille O'Neal	8.00
11	Scottie Pippen	6.00
12	Dennis Rodman	7.00
13	Damon Stoudamire	4.00
14	Keith Van Horn	5.00
15	Antoine Walker	5.00

1997-98 SkyBox Z-Force Slam Cam

Slam Cam featured 12 highlight film players on a horizontal format. Each card was made to look like a piece of film and was printed on black plastic. The player's close-up was placed on the left of the card, while a shot of him dunking and the insert's name was on the right. Slam Cam inserts were seeded one per 36 packs of Series II and numbered with a "SC" suffix.

		MT
Complete Set (12):		75.00
Common Player:		2.00
1	Kobe Bryant	18.00
2	Marcus Camby	2.00
3	Tim Duncan	18.00
4	Kevin Garnett	12.00
5	Michael Jordan	25.00
6	Shawn Kemp	3.00
7	Karl Malone	2.00
8	Antonio McDyess	4.00
9	Shaquille O'Neal	10.00
10	Joe Smith	4.00
11	Jerry Stackhouse	4.00
12	Chris Webber	5.00

1997-98 SkyBox Z-Force Total Impact

This 12-card set featured the player over a glittery background with silver highlights. The insert name runs up the left side, with the player's name in the top left corner. Inserted at a one per 48 rate, the cards were numbered "x of 12/TI".

		MT
Complete Set (12):		150.00
Common Player:		4.00
1	Kobe Bryant	30.00
2	Marcus Camby	10.00
3	Kevin Garnett	30.00
4	Grant Hill	30.00
5	Allen Iverson	30.00
6	Eddie Jones	6.00
7	Shawn Kemp	8.00
8	Kerry Kittles	4.00
9	Hakeem Olajuwon	10.00
10	Scottie Pippen	15.00
11	Joe Smith	4.00
12	Chris Webber	8.00

1997-98 SkyBox Z-Force Zebut

This 12-card insert set highlighted the top rookies from the 1997 NBA Draft and was seeded one per 24 Series II packs. Each card is printed on gold foil and die-cut around the bottom, with a large "Z" in the background and the word "Force" under it. Cards are numbered on the back with a "ZB" suffix.

		MT
Complete Set (12):		50.00
Common Player:		2.00
1	Derek Anderson	6.00
2	Tony Battie	4.00
3	Chauncey Billups	8.00
4	Austin Croshere	2.00
5	Antonio Daniels	6.00
6	Tim Duncan	15.00
7	Danny Fortson	2.00
8	Tracy McGrady	8.00
9	Ron Mercer	8.00
10	Tariq Abdul-Wahad	2.00
11	Tim Thomas	6.00
12	Keith Van Horn	8.00

1997-98 SkyBox Z-Force Zensations

Zensations consisted of 25 cards and was inserted into one per six Series II packs. Fronts contain four different blocks of wild colored patterns, with the insert's name across the top in gold foil. Zensations are numbered on the back with a "ZN" suffix.

		MT
Complete Set (25):		25.00
Common Player:		.50
Minor Stars:		1.00
1	Ray Allen	1.25
2	Vin Baker	1.00
3	Charles Barkley	1.50
4	Clyde Drexler	1.25
5	Patrick Ewing	1.00
6	Juwan Howard	1.50
7	Eddie Jones	1.75
8	Shawn Kemp	1.50
9	Jason Kidd	1.50
10	Kerry Kittles	1.00
11	Karl Malone	1.00
12	Antonio McDyess	1.00
13	Hakeem Olajuwon	2.50
14	Gary Payton	1.50
15	Glen Rice	1.00
16	Mitch Richmond	1.00
17	David Robinson	1.50
18	Dennis Rodman	4.00
19	Joe Smith	1.25
20	Latrell Sprewell	1.00
21	Jerry Stackhouse	1.25
22	John Stockton	1.00
23	Damon Stoudamire	1.75
24	Rasheed Wallace	.50
25	Chris Webber	2.00

1998 SkyBox Jam Session Knicks Sheet

This eight-card sheet was handed out at the 1998 NBA Jam Session in New York City. It contained six New York Knicks cards in SkyBox designs and was perforated.

	MT
Complete Set (1):	3.00
Patrick Ewing, Larry Johnson, John Starks, Chris Dudley, Charlie Ward, Chris Mills	3.00

1998-99 SkyBox Premium

SkyBox Premium contained 265 cards, with 125 in Series I and 140 in Series II. Series II added a 40-card Rookies subset that was seeded 1:4 packs. Card fronts had a color shot of the player over a blurred background, with the player's name, team and position, as well as his initials in script, in holographic foil. Rubies paralleled each card in the set, with the first 225 cards, called Star Rubies, numbered to 50 sets, while the final 40 cards, called Star Rookies, were numbered to 25 sets. Series II also contained a 25-card Ninety Fine subset. Inserts in Series I included Smooth, Just Cookin', Soul of the Game, Net Set, 3-D's and Intimidation Nation. Inserts in Series II included: BPO, Mod Squad, Fresh Faces, That's Jam, and Slam Funk. In addition, Autographics cards were inserted in both series, at 1:68 in Series I and 1:24 in Series II.

		MT
Complete Set (265):		200.00
Complete Series 1 (125):		25.00
Complete Series 2 (140):		175.00
Common Player:		.10
Minor Stars:		.20
Common Rookie:		1.00
Inserted 1:4		
Pack (10):		45.00
Wax Box (24):		65.00
1	Tim Duncan	2.50
2	Voshon Lenard	.10

3	John Starks	.10
4	Juwan Howard	.30
5	Michael Finley	.20
6	Bobby Jackson	.20
7	Glenn Robinson	.20
8	Antonio McDyess	.30
9	Eric Williams	.10
10	Zydrunas Ilgauskas	.20
11	Terrell Brandon	.20
12	Shandon Anderson	.10
13	Rod Strickland	.10
14	Dennis Rodman	1.50
15	Clarence Weatherspoon	.10
16	P.J. Brown	.10
17	Anfernee Hardaway	1.50
18	Dikembe Mutombo	.20
19	Patrick Ewing	.30
20	Scottie Pippen	1.25
21	Shaquille O'Neal	1.50
22	Donyell Marshall	.10
23	Michael Jordan	5.00
24	Mark Price	.10
25	Jim Jackson	.10
26	Isaiah Rider	.10
27	Eddie Jones	.75
28	Detlef Schrempf	.10
29	Corliss Williamson	.10
30	Bo Outlaw	.10
31	Allen Iverson	1.25
32	Luc Longley	.10
33	Theo Ratliff	.10
34	Antoine Walker	1.00
35	Lamond Murray	.10
36	Avery Johnson	.10
37	John Stockton	.30
38	David Wesley	.10
39	Elden Campbell	.10
40	Grant Hill	2.50
41	Sam Cassell	.10
42	Tracy McGrady	1.00
43	Glen Rice	.30
44	Kobe Bryant	3.00
45	John Wallace	.10
46	Bobby Phills	.10
47	Jerry Stackhouse	.20
48	Stephon Marbury	1.50
49	Jeff Hornacek	.10
50	Tom Gugliotta	.20
51	Joe Dumars	.10
52	Johnny Newman	.10
53	Kevin Garnett	2.50
54	Dennis Scott	.10
55	Anthony Mason	.10
56	Rodney Rogers	.10
57	Bryon Russell	.10
58	Maurice Taylor	.40
59	Mookie Blaylock	.10
60	Shawn Bradley	.10
61	Matt Maloney	.10
62	Karl Malone	.30
63	Larry Johnson	.20
64	Calbert Cheaney	.10
65	Steve Smith	.10
66	Toni Kukoc	.20
67	Reggie Miller	.30
68	Jayson Williams	.10
69	Gary Payton	.40
70	Sean Elliott	.10
71	Charles Barkley	.50
72	Tim Hardaway	.30
73	Rasheed Wallace	.10
74	Tariq Abdul-Wahad	.10
75	Kenny Anderson	.10
76	Chris Mullin	.10
77	Keith Van Horn	1.00
78	Hersey Hawkins	.10
79	Ron Mercer	1.50
80	Rik Smits	.10
81	David Robinson	.50
82	Derek Anderson	.50
83	Danny Fortson	.10
84	Jason Kidd	.75
85	Chauncey Billups	.40
86	Chris Anstey	.10
87	Hakeem Olajuwon	.75
88	Bryant Reeves	.10
89	Anthony Johnson	.10
90	Shawn Kemp	.50
91	Brevin Knight	.50
92	Ray Allen	.30
93	Tim Thomas	1.00
94	Jalen Rose	.10
95	Kerry Kittles	.20
96	Vin Baker	.50
97	Shareef Abdur-Rahim	1.00
98	Alonzo Mourning	.30
99	Joe Smith	.20
100	Damon Stoudamire	.40
101	Alan Henderson	.10
102	Walter McCarty	.10
103	Vlade Divac	.10
104	Wesley Person	.10
105	A.C. Green	.10
106	Malik Sealy	.10
107	Carl Thomas	.10
108	Brent Price	.10
109	Mark Jackson	.10
110	Lorenzen Wright	.10
111	Derek Fisher	.10
112	Michael Smith	.10
113	Tyrone Hill	.10
114	Cherokee Parks	.10
115	Kendall Gill	.10
116	Darrell Armstrong	.10
117	Derrick Coleman	.10
118	Rex Chapman	.10
119	Arvydas Sabonis	.10
120	Billy Owens	.10
121	Sam Perkins	.10
122	Gary Trent	.10
123	Sam Mack	.10
124	Tracy Murray	.10
125	Allan Houston	.10
126	Mitch Richmond	.20
127	Carl Herrera	.10
128	Ron Harper	.10
129	Gary Trent	.10
130	Chris Webber	1.00
131	Antonio Daniels	.20
132	Charles Oakley	.10
133	Marcus Camby	.40
134	Tony Battie	.20
135	Otis Thorpe	.10
136	Dale Davis	.10
137	Chuck Person	.10
138	Ervin Johnson	.10
139	Jamal Mashburn	.20
140	Brian Grant	.10
141	Chris Mills	.10
142	Doug Christie	.10
143	George McCloud	.10
144	Todd Fuller	.10
145	Jerome Williams	.10
146	Chauncey Billups	.40
147	Dean Garrett	.10
148	Robert Pack	.10
149	Clarence Weatherspoon	.10
150	Tim Legler	.10
151	Bob Sura	.10
152	B.J. Armstrong	.10
153	Charlie Ward	.10
154	Rony Seikaly	.10
155	Chris Carr	.10
156	Eldridge Recasner	.10
157	Michael Stewart	.10
158	Jim McIlvaine	.10
159	Adam Keefe	.10
160	Antonio Davis	.10
161	Lawrence Funderburke	.10
162	Greg Ostertag	.10
163	Dan Majerle	.10
164	Dale Ellis	.10
165	Greg Anthony	.10
166	Chris Whitney	.10
167	Eric Piatkowski	.10
168	Tom Gugliotta	.20
169	Luc Longley	.10
170	Antonio McDyess	.40
171	George Lynch	.10
172	Dell Curry	.10
173	Johnny Newman	.10
174	Christian Laettner	.20
175	Steve Kerr	.10
176	Popeye Jones	.10
177	Brent Barry	.10
178	Billy Owens	.10
179	Cherokee Parks	.10
180	Derek Harper	.10
181	Howard Eisley	.10
182	Matt Geiger	.10
183	Darrick Martin	.10
184	Isaac Austin	.10
185	Dennis Scott	.10
186	Derrick Coleman	.20
187	Sam Perkins	.10
188	Latrell Sprewell	.20
189	Jud Buechler	.10
190	Jason Caffey	.10
191	Vlade Divac	.20
192	Travis Best	.10
193	Loy Vaught	.10
194	Mario Elie	.10
195	Ed Gray	.10
196	Joe Smith	.40
197	John Starks	.10
198	Anthony Johnson	.10
199	Kurt Thomas	.10
200	Chris Dudley	.10
201	Shareef Abdur-Rahim	.50
202	Ray Allen	.30
203	Vin Baker	.40
204	Charles Barkley	.30
205	Kobe Bryant	1.50
206	Tim Duncan	1.25
207	Anfernee Hardaway	.75
208	Grant Hill	1.25
209	Allen Iverson	.75
210	Jason Kidd	.50
211	Shawn Kemp	.30
212	Shaquille O'Neal	.75
213	Kerry Kittles	.20
214	Karl Malone	.30
215	Stephon Marbury	.75
216	Ron Mercer	.75
217	Reggie Miller	.10
218	Kevin Garnett	1.25
219	Gary Payton	.30
220	Scottie Pippen	.60
221	David Robinson	.30
222	Hakeem Olajuwon	.40
223	Damon Stoudamire	.30
224	Keith Van Horn	.50
225	Antoine Walker	.60
226	*Cory Carr*	1.00
227	*Cuttino Mobley*	5.00
228	*Miles Simon*	1.00
229	*J.R. Henderson*	1.00
230	*Jason Williams*	10.00
231	*Felipe Lopez*	2.00
232	*Shammond Williams*	3.00
233	*Ricky Davis*	4.00
234	*Vince Carter*	40.00
235	*Antawn Jamison*	15.00
236	*Ryan Stack*	1.00
237	*Nazr Mohammed*	1.00
238	*Sam Jacobson*	1.00
239	*Larry Hughes*	12.00
240	*Ruben Patterson*	4.00
241	*Al Harrington*	5.00
242	*Ansu Sesay*	1.00
243	*Vladimir Stepania*	1.00
244	*Matt Harpring*	3.00
245	*Andrae Patterson*	1.00
246	*Pat Garrity*	3.00
247	*Bonzi Wells*	12.00
248	*Bryce Drew*	2.00
249	*Toby Bailey*	1.00
250	*Michael Doleac*	2.00
251	*Michael Dickerson*	4.00
252	*Predrag Stojakovic*	5.00
253	*Robert Traylor*	2.00
254	*Tyronn Lue*	2.00
255	*Dirk Nowitzki*	15.00
256	*Raef LaFrentz*	5.00
257	*Jelani McCoy*	2.00
258	*Michael Olowokandi*	3.00
259	*Brian Skinner*	2.00
260	*Keon Clark*	2.00
261	*Roshown McLeod*	2.00
262	*Mike Bibby*	6.00
263	*Paul Pierce*	10.00
264	*Tyson Wheeler*	1.00
265	*Corey Benjamin*	2.00

1998-99 SkyBox Premium Star Rubies

Star Rubies was a 265-card parallel set that was inserted into both Series I and II SkyBox Premium hobby packs. The cards featured ruby red foil stamping and sequentially numbered on the back, with 1-225 numbered to 50 sets and 226-265 numbered to 25 sets.

	MT
Star Ruby Cards:	75x-150x
Production 50 Sets	
Star Ruby Rookies:	10x-15x
Production 25 Sets	

1998-99 SkyBox Premium Autographics

The third season for NBA Autographics included over 120 veterans and 20 rookies. Cards were inserted into NBA Hoops I (1:144), Thunder I (1:112), Metal Universe I (1:68), SkyBox Premium I (1:68), SkyBox Premium II (1:24), Molten Metal (1:24) and E-X Century (1:18). Cards contained an embossed SkyBox seal of authenticity. Also, a parallel Century Marks version of each exists and is hand-numbered to 50.

	MT
Common Player:	10.00
Inserted 1:144 Hoops	
Inserted 1:68 Metal	
Inserted 1:68 SkyBox,	
Inserted 1:112 Thunder	
Inserted 1:24 Molten Metal	
Inserted 1:24 SkyBox II	
Blue Century Marks	4x
Production 50 sets	
Iverson signed an equal amount in blue and black.	
Tariq Abdul-Wahad	25.00
Shareef Abdur-Rahim	120.00
Cory Alexander	10.00
Ray Allen	75.00
Kenny Anderson	20.00
Nick Anderson	15.00
Chris Anstey	10.00
Isaac Austin	10.00
Vin Baker	55.00
Dana Barros	10.00
Tony Battie	20.00
Travis Best	10.00
Mike Bibby	150.00
Chauncey Billups	35.00
Corie Blount	10.00
P.J. Brown	10.00
Scott Burrell	10.00
Jason Caffey	15.00
Marcus Camby	40.00
Elden Campbell	10.00
Chris Carr	10.00
Vince Carter	350.00
Kelvin Cato	20.00
Calbert Cheaney	10.00
Keith Closs	15.00
Antonio Daniels	30.00
Dale Davis	10.00
Ricky Davis	30.00
Andrew DeClerq	10.00
Tony Delk	10.00
Michael Dickerson	75.00
Michael Doleac	30.00
Bryce Drew	30.00
Tim Duncan	300.00
Howard Eisley	10.00
Danny Ferry	10.00
Derek Fisher	15.00
Danny Fortson	15.00
Adonal Foyle	10.00
Todd Fuller	10.00
Kevin Garnett	200.00
Pat Garrity	25.00
Brian Grant	10.00
Tom Gugliotta	40.00
Tom Hammonds	10.00
Tim Hardaway	60.00
Matt Harpring	25.00
Othella Harrington	15.00
Hersey Hawkins	10.00
Cedric Henderson	20.00
Grant Hill	250.00
Tyrone Hill	10.00
Allan Houston	25.00
Juwan Howard	60.00
Larry Hughes	100.00
Zydrunas Ilgauskus	20.00
Allen Iverson	200.00
Bobby Jackson	20.00
Antawn Jamison	160.00
Anthony Johnson	10.00
Ervin Johnson	10.00
Larry Johnson	30.00
Eddie Jones	100.00
Adam Keefe	10.00
Shawn Kemp	100.00
Steve Kerr	20.00
Jason Kidd	130.00
Kerry Kittles	40.00
Brevin Knight	40.00
Raef LaFrentz	100.00
Felipe Lopez	40.00
George Lynch	10.00
Karl Malone	175.00
Danny Manning	15.00
Donyell Marshall	15.00
Tony Massenberg	10.00
Walter McCarty	10.00
Jelani McCoy	25.00
Antonio McDyess	60.00
Tracy McGrady	75.00
Ron Mercer	100.00
Sam Mitchell	10.00
Nazr Mohammed	25.00
Alonzo Mourning	75.00
Chris Mullin	20.00
Dikembe Mutombo	40.00
Hakeem Olajuwon	160.00
Michael Olowokandi	150.00
Elliot Perry	10.00
Bobby Phills	10.00
Eric Piatkowski	10.00
Paul Pierce	175.00
Scottie Pippen	200.00
Scot Pollard	20.00
Vitaly Potapenko	10.00
Brent Price	10.00
Theo Ratliff	10.00
Eldridge Recasner	10.00
Bryant Reeves	30.00
Glen Rice	50.00
Chris Robinson	10.00
David Robinson	160.00
Dennis Rodman	300.00
Bryon Russell	15.00
Danny Schayes	10.00
Detlef Schrempf	25.00
Brian Skinner	25.00
Reggie Slater	10.00
Joe Smith	45.00
Steve Smith	25.00
Rik Smits	15.00
Jerry Stackhouse	40.00
John Starks	25.00
Bryant Stith	10.00
Damon Stoudamire	100.00
Mark Strickland	10.00
Rod Strickland	35.00
Bob Sura	10.00
Tim Thomas	100.00
Robert Traylor	100.00
Gary Trent	10.00
Keith Van Horn	40.00
Jacque Vaughn	10.00
Antoine Walker	50.00
Eric Washington	10.00
Clarence Weatherspoon	15.00
David Wesley	10.00
Eric Williams	10.00
Jason Williams	175.00
Jayson Williams	25.00
Monty Williams	10.00
Walt Williams	15.00
Lorenzen Wright	10.00

1998-99 SkyBox Premium BPO

This 15-card insert was found in packs of Series II at a rate of one per six. Players were pictured over a dark background, with an orange flame trailing their body. Cards from this insert were numbered with a "BPO" suffix.

		MT
Complete Set (15):		30.00
Common Player:		.40
Minor Stars:		.75
Inserted 1:6 Series 2		
1	Ron Mercer	2.50
2	Shareef Abdur-Rahim	1.00
3	Stephon Marbury	2.50
4	Tim Thomas	2.00
5	Tim Duncan	4.00
6	Mike Bibby	3.00
7	Ray Allen	1.00
8	Shawn Kemp	.50
9	Vince Carter	5.00
10	Antoine Walker	1.00
11	Raef LaFrentz	1.00
12	Damon Stoudamire	.75
13	Keith Van Horn	1.50
14	Kerry Kittles	.40
15	Allen Iverson	2.50

1998-99 SkyBox Premium Fresh Faces

This 10-card insert featured portrait shots of top NBA rookies dressed in casual clothes. Cards added a silver rainbow holofoil finish, were seeded 1:36 packs of Series II and numbered with an "FF" suffix.

		MT
Complete Set (10):		55.00
Common Player:		2.00
Inserted 1:36 Series 2		
1	Mike Bibby	10.00
2	Vince Carter	15.00
3	Al Harrington	3.00
4	Larry Hughes	8.00
5	Antawn Jamison	8.00
6	Raef LaFrentz	6.00
7	Michael Olowokandi	6.00
8	Paul Pierce	12.00
9	Robert Traylor	6.00
10	Bonzi Wells	2.00

1998-99 SkyBox Premium Intimidation Nation

Intimidation Nation was a 10-card insert exclusive to Series I packs at a rate of one per 360. It featured close-up shots of 10 top NBA players over a blazing fire background. These inserts were numbered with an "IN" suffix.

		MT
Complete Set (10):		450.00
Common Player:		15.00
Inserted 1:360 Series 1		
1	Shaquille O'Neal	40.00
2	Kobe Bryant	80.00
3	Kevin Garnett	60.00
4	Grant Hill	60.00
5	Shawn Kemp	15.00
6	Keith Van Horn	25.00
7	Antoine Walker	20.00
8	Michael Jordan	125.00
9	Gary Payton	15.00
10	Tim Duncan	60.00

1998-99 SkyBox Premium Just Cookin'

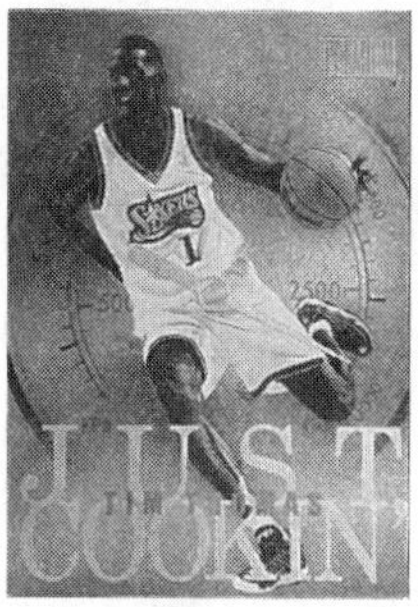

This insert featured 10 rookies from the 1997-98 season over a silver background with a temperature gauge. Just Cookin' inserts were found in 1:12 packs of Series I and numbered with a "JC" suffix.

		MT
Complete Set (10):		30.00
Common Player:		1.50
Inserted 1:12 Series 1		
1	Maurice Taylor	4.00
2	Brevin Knight	4.00
3	Tim Thomas	8.00
4	Chauncey Billups	4.00
5	Chris Anstey	1.50
6	Tracy McGrady	8.00
7	Zydrunas Ilgauskas	3.00
8	Antonio Daniels	2.00
9	Bobby Jackson	2.00
10	Derek Anderson	4.00

1998-99 SkyBox Premium Mod Squad

Mod Squad was a Series II insert that captured how 15 top players dress off the court. The players were shown over a psychedelic background, while cards were numbered with an "MS" suffix and seeded 1:18 packs.

		MT
Complete Set (16):		80.00
Common Player:		2.00
Minor Stars:		3.00
Inserted 1:18 Series 2		
1	Tim Thomas	4.00
2	Shaquille O'Neal	6.00
3	Scottie Pippen	5.00
4	Kobe Bryant	12.00
5	Kevin Garnett	10.00
6	Grant Hill	10.00
7	Anfernee Hardaway	6.00
8	Antoine Walker	3.00
9	Stephon Marbury	6.00
10	Kerry Kittles	2.00
11	Allen Iverson	6.00
12	Gary Payton	3.00
13	Damon Stoudamire	3.00
14	Marcus Camby	2.00
15	Shareef Abdur-Rahim	4.00
16	Michael Jordan	20.00

1998-99 SkyBox Premium Net Set

Net Set featured 15 top players over a silver tinted game-action shot. The insert name, along with the player's name and team were included in right and left borders that were made of black and silver. Cards were numbered with an "NS" suffix and seeded 1:36 packs of Series I.

		MT
Complete Set (15):		70.00
Common Player:		2.00
Inserted 1:36 Series 1		
1	Ron Mercer	12.00
2	Shawn Kemp	5.00
3	Brevin Knight	5.00
4	Maurice Taylor	5.00
5	Ray Allen	2.00
6	Dennis Rodman	15.00
7	Kerry Kittles	2.00
8	Tim Thomas	8.00
9	Gary Payton	4.00
10	Marcus Camby	2.00
11	Karl Malone	4.00
12	Juwan Howard	3.00
13	Zydrunas Ilgauskas	3.00
14	Scottie Pippen	12.00
15	Anfernee Hardaway	15.00

1998-99 SkyBox Premium Slam Funk

Slam Funk was a 10-card insert that featured 10 players on plastic cards with rainbow holo-lamination creating a sparkling background. These were inserted 1:360 Series II packs and numberd with an "SF" suffix.

		MT
Complete Set (10):		350.00
Common Player:		15.00
Inserted 1:360 Series 2		
1	Kobe Bryant	80.00
2	Kevin Garnett	60.00
3	Grant Hill	60.00
4	Shaquille O'Neal	35.00
5	Michael Olowokandi	20.00
6	Tim Duncan	60.00
7	Antawn Jamison	25.00
8	Keith Van Horn	20.00
9	Ron Mercer	30.00
10	Scottie Pippen	15.00

1998-99 SkyBox Premium Smooth

This 15-card insert was found in packs of Series I at a rate of 1:6. Smooth cards picture the player over a black background with the insert name printed across the bottom in large silver letters. Cards are numbered with an "SM" suffix.

		MT
Complete Set (15):		25.00
Common Player:		.75
Inserted 1:6 Series 1		
1	Stephon Marbury	4.00
2	Shareef Abdur-Rahim	2.50
3	Keith Van Horn	2.00
4	Marcus Camby	.75
5	Ray Allen	.75
6	Allen Iverson	3.00
7	Kerry Kittles	.75
8	Tim Thomas	2.00
9	Damon Stoudamire	1.50
10	Antoine Walker	2.00
11	Brevin Knight	1.50
12	Zydrunas Ilgauskas	.75
13	Ron Mercer	3.00
14	Maurice Taylor	1.50
15	Tim Duncan	6.00

1998-99 SkyBox Premium Soul of the Game

This 15-card insert featured the multi-colored words "Soul of the Game" over a white background, with the player's image over the words. These were seeded 1:18 packs of Series I and numbered with an "SG" suffix.

		MT
Complete Set (15):		75.00
Common Player:		2.00
Inserted 1:18 Series 1		
1	Michael Jordan	20.00
2	Antoine Walker	3.00
3	Scottie Pippen	5.00
4	Grant Hill	10.00
5	Dennis Rodman	6.00
6	Kobe Bryant	12.00
7	Kevin Garnett	10.00
8	Shaquille O'Neal	6.00
9	Stephon Marbury	6.00
10	Kerry Kittles	2.00
11	Anfernee Hardaway	6.00
12	Allen Iverson	5.00
13	Damon Stoudamire	3.00
14	Marcus Camby	2.00
15	Shareef Abdur-Rahim	4.00

1998-99 SkyBox Premium That's Jam!

That's Jam! included 15 players on plastic cards seeded 1:96 packs of Series II. Cards were numbered with a "TJ" suffix.

		MT
Complete Set (15):		225.00
Common Player:		5.00
Inserted 1:96 Series 2		
1	Tim Duncan	30.00
2	Stephon Marbury	15.00
3	Shareef Abdur-Rahim	12.00
4	Shaquille O'Neal	15.00
5	Ron Mercer	15.00
6	Scottie Pippen	12.00
7	Antawn Jamison	15.00
8	Anfernee Hardaway	15.00
9	Damon Stoudamire	5.00
10	Allen Iverson	15.00
11	Keith Van Horn	8.00
12	Grant Hill	30.00
13	Kevin Garnett	30.00
14	Kobe Bryant	40.00
15	Antoine Walker	8.00

1998-99 SkyBox Premium 3-D's

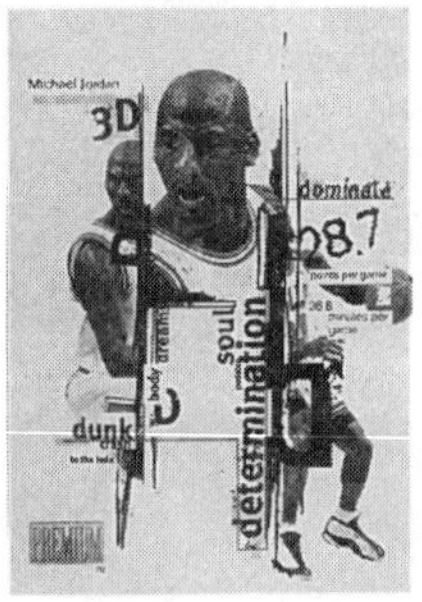

3-Ds was a 15-card insert devoted to the best at dunks, domination and determination. These were seeded 1:96 packs of Series I and numbered with a "DDD" suffix. Card fronts featured various pieces of photos of the player over a prismatic background.

		MT
Complete Set (15):		300.00
Common Player:		5.00
Inserted 1:96 Series 1		
1	Kobe Bryant	40.00
2	Anfernee Hardaway	20.00
3	Allen Iverson	15.00
4	Michael Jordan	60.00
5	Stephon Marbury	20.00
6	Ron Mercer	20.00
7	Shareef Abdur-Rahim	12.00
8	Tim Duncan	30.00
9	Damon Stoudamire	5.00
10	Kevin Garnett	30.00
11	Grant Hill	30.00
12	Scottie Pippen	20.00
13	Keith Van Horn	12.00
14	Dennis Rodman	20.00
15	Shaquille O'Neal	20.00

1999-00 SkyBox Dominion

Dominion debuted in basketball with a 220-card set that included 20 rookies. Base cards included the player's name three-quarters of the way down the front, with the Dominion logo in a bottom corner. The product also included a You Make the Call insert that gave 10 collectors a chance to participate in a live conference call with Ray Allen. Two other subsets were included: 15 World Tour and 10 3 For All. Inserts included: Game Day 2K, Game Day 2K Plus, Game Day 2K Warp Tek, Sky's the Limit, Sky's the Limit Plus, Sky's the Limit Warp Tek, 2 Point Play, 2 Point Play Plus, 2 Point Play Warp Tek, Hat's Off and Autographics.

		MT
Complete Set (220):		40.00
Common Player:		.15
Minor Stars:		.30
Pack (9):		1.89
Wax Box (36):		50.00
1	Jason Williams	2.00
2	Isaiah Rider	.30
3	Tim Hardaway	.50
4	Isaac Austin	.15
5	Joe Smith	.30
6	Mitch Richmond	.30
7	Sam Mitchell	.15
8	Terrell Brandon	.30
9	Grant Long	.15
10	Shaquille O'Neal	1.50
11	Derrick Coleman	.30
12	Rod Strickland	.30
13	J.R. Reid	.15
14	Tyrone Corbin	.15
15	Jeff Hornacek	.15
16	Malik Rose	.15
17	Terry Davis	.15
18	Theo Ratliff	.15
19	Kevin Willis	.15
20	Raef LaFrentz	.75
21	Othella Harrington	.15
22	Marcus Camby	.50
23	Keon Clark	.40
24	Robert Pack	.15
25	Sam Mack	.15
26	Shawn Kemp	.50
27	Nick Anderson	.30
28	Bill Wennington	.15
29	Steve Smith	.30
30	Kobe Bryant	3.00
31	Bobby Phills	.15
32	Cedric Ceballos	.15
33	Derek Fisher	.15
34	Doug Christie	.15
35	Danny Manning	.15
36	Eric Murdock	.15
37	Glen Rice	.30
38	Dikembe Mutombo	.30
39	Jason Kidd	1.00
40	Cedric Henderson	.15
41	Rasheed Wallace	.30
42	Tim Duncan	2.50
43	John Stockton	.30
44	Dell Curry	.15
45	Muggsy Bogues	.15
46	Danny Fortson	.15
47	Charles Oakley	.15
48	Elden Campbell	.15
49	Tony Massenburg	.15
50	Kevin Garnett	2.50
51	Cherokee Parks	.15
52	LaPhonso Ellis	.15
53	Sam Cassell	.30
54	Shawn Bradley	.15
55	David Robinson	.75
56	Juwan Howard	.30
57	Lindsey Hunter	.15
58	Mark Jackson	.15
59	Olden Polynice	.15
60	Tracy McGrady	1.00
61	Michael Finley	.40
62	Matt Geiger	.15
63	Maurice Taylor	.50
64	Rex Chapman	.15
65	Chris Mullin	.30
66	Ray Allen	.30
67	Bison Dele	.15
68	Dickey Simpkins	.15
69	Alvin Williams	.15
70	Grant Hill	2.50
71	Mark Bryant	.15
72	Adam Keefe	.15
73	Alan Henderson	.15
74	Eric Snow	.15
75	Matt Harpring	.40
76	Jalen Rose	.30
77	Derek Harper	.15
78	Kerry Kittles	.30
79	Tony Battie	.15
80	Larry Hughes	1.00
81	Arvydas Sabonis	.15
82	Allan Houston	.30
83	Tom Gugliotta	.30
84	Reggie Miller	.30
85	DeJuan Wheat	.15
86	Pat Garrity	.30
87	Karl Malone	.75
88	Sam Perkins	.15
89	Michael Olowokandi	.75
90	Anfernee Hardaway	1.50
91	Bryant Reeves	.15
92	Gary Trent	.15
93	George Lynch	.15
94	Scottie Pippen	1.00
95	Jerry Stackhouse	.30
96	Kendall Gill	.15
97	Vin Baker	.30
98	Dale Davis	.15
99	Charles Barkley	.75
100	Allen Iverson	2.00
101	Keith Van Horn	.75
102	Andrew DeClercq	.15
103	Michael Doleac	.40
104	Chauncey Billups	.15
105	Chris Mills	.15
106	Lamond Murray	.15
107	Glenn Robinson	.30
108	Brian Grant	.30
109	Christian Laettner	.30
110	Antawn Jamison	1.50
111	Erick Dampier	.15
112	Vernon Maxwell	.15
113	Kenny Anderson	.30
114	Clarence Weatherspoon	.15
115	Corliss Williamson	.15
116	Paul Pierce	1.75
117	Clifford Robinson	.15
118	Damon Stoudamire	.40
119	Dana Barros	.15
120	Stephon Marbury	1.25
121	Latrell Sprewell	.30
122	Tyronn Lue	.30
123	Walt Williams	.15
124	P.J. Brown	.15
125	Gary Payton	.75
126	Nick Van Exel	.30
127	Bryant Stith	.15
128	Eric Piatkowski	.15
129	Tyrone Nesby	.30
130	Ron Mercer	1.00
131	Hersey Hawkins	.15
132	Vlade Divac	.30
133	Darrick Martin	.15
134	Avery Johnson	.15
135	Jaren Jackson	.15
136	Brevin Knight	.15
137	Wesley Person	.15
138	Derek Anderson	.15
139	Tim Thomas	1.00
140	Antonio McDyess	.60
141	A.C. Green	.15
142	Chris Webber	1.00
143	Scott Burrell	.15
144	John Starks	.15
145	Howard Eisley	.15
146	Mike Bibby	1.00
147	Toni Kukoc	.40
148	Eddie Jones	.40
149	Otis Thorpe	.15
150	Shareef Abdur-Rahim	1.00
151	Calbert Cheaney	.15
152	Cuttino Mobley	.30
153	Michael Dickerson	.50
154	Sean Elliott	.15
155	Terry Porter	.15
156	Dean Garrett	.15
157	Charlie Ward	.15
158	Larry Johnson	.30
159	Dan Majerle	.15
160	Jayson Williams	.30
161	Anthony Peeler	.15
162	Ron Harper	.15
163	Darrell Armstrong	.30
164	Kurt Thomas	.15
165	Brent Barry	.15
166	Lawrence Funderburke	.15
167	Terry Cummings	.15
168	Jamal Mashburn	.30
169	Robert Traylor	.75
170	Greg Ostertag	.15
171	Brad Miller	.15
172	Mario Elie	.15
173	Antoine Walker	.75
174	Ricky Davis	.30
175	Vince Carter	3.00
176	Hakeem Olajuwon	.40
177	Luc Longley	.15
178	Tim Duncan	1.25
179	Rick Fox	.15
180	Zydrunas Ilgauskas	.15
181	Toni Kukoc	.15
182	Felipe Lopez	.15
183	Dikembe Mutombo	.15
184	Steve Nash	.15
185	Dirk Nowitzki	.20
186	Vitaly Potapenko	.15
187	Detlef Schrempf	.15
188	Rik Smits	.15
189	Vladimir Stepania	.15
190	Predrag Stojakovic	.15
191	Donyell Marshall	.15
192	Shareef Abdur-Rahim	.50
193	Michael Dickerson	.15
194	Damon Stoudamire	.15
195	Allen Iverson	1.00
196	Grant Hill	1.25
197	Scottie Pippen	.50
198	Bryon Russell	.15
199	Alonzo Mourning	.15
200	Patrick Ewing	.15
201	*Ron Artest*	.60
202	*William Avery*	.40
203	*Lamar Odom*	3.00
204	*Baron Davis*	1.25
205	*John Celestand*	.25
206	*Jumanie Jones*	.25
207	*Andre Miller*	1.25
208	*Elton Brand*	2.00
209	*James Posey*	.50
210	*Jason Terry*	.60
211	*Kenny Thomas*	.30
212	*Steve Francis*	5.00
213	*Wally Szczerbiak*	1.00
214	*Richard Hamilton*	1.00
215	*Jonathan Bender*	2.00
216	*Shawn Marion*	2.00
217	*Aleksandar Radojevic*	.25
218	*Tim James*	.30
219	*Trajan Langdon*	.50
220	*Corey Maggette*	1.25
NNO	You Make the Call (Ray Allen)	

1999-00 SkyBox Dominion Game Day 2K

This 20-card insert was available in three different versions - regular, Plus and Warp Tek. Game Day 2K cards featured a thick black border with the word "GAMEDAY," with the rest of the base card in silver foilboard. Regular versions were inserted 1:3 packs. Plus versions added some texture to the front and a foil "PLUS" on the back and were inserted 1:30 packs. Warp Tek cards were thicker with a prismatic, 3-D look to them and were inserted 1:300 packs. All versions of Game Day 2K cards were numbered with a "GD" suffix.

		MT
Complete Set (20):		12.00
Common Player:		.50
Inserted 1:3		
Complete Plus Set (20):		60.00
Common Plus Cards:		2.00
Plus Cards:		3x-5x
Inserted 1:30		
Common WarpTek Cards:		5.00
WarpTek Cards:		10x-20x
Inserted 1:300		
1	Vince Carter	2.00
2	Kobe Bryant	2.50
3	Dirk Nowitzki	.75
4	Cuttino Mobley	.50
5	Kevin Garnett	2.00
6	Stephon Marbury	1.25
7	Shaquille O'Neal	1.50
8	Keith Van Horn	.75
9	Paul Pierce	1.50
10	Jason Williams	1.50
11	Mike Bibby	1.00
12	Michael Dickerson	.60
13	Antawn Jamison	1.25
14	Raef LaFrentz	.75
15	Tyrone Nesby	.50
16	Ron Mercer	1.00
17	Tracy McGrady	1.00
18	Larry Hughes	1.00
19	Robert Traylor	.75
20	Michael Doleac	.50

1999-00 SkyBox Dominion Game Day 2K Plus

This 20-card insert parallel Game Day 2K, but featured a textured foil on the card front, with the word "Plus" on the back in silver foil. These were inserted 1:30 packs.

		MT
Complete Plus Set (20):		60.00
Common Plus Cards:		2.00
Plus Cards:		3x-5x
Inserted 1:30		

1999-00 SkyBox Dominion Game Day 2K Warp Tek

This 20-card insert paralleled the Game Day 2K set, but featured thicker card stock and a prismatic, three- dimensional look on the front. Warp Tek versions were inserted 1:300 packs.

		MT
Common WarpTek Cards:		5.00
WarpTek Cards:		10x-20x
Inserted 1:300		

1999-00 SkyBox Dominion Hat's Off

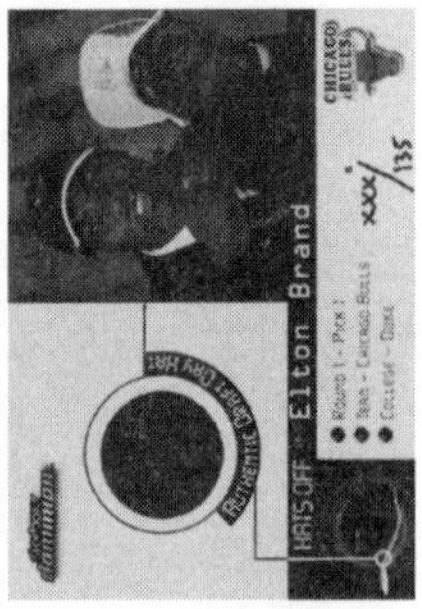

This 14-card set included swatches from the hats the players wore during the 1999 NBA Draft. The cards were horizontal in design and hand-numbered to various numbers ranging from 135 to 185. No insertion rates were given, but the cards were numbered with an "HO" suffix.

		MT
Complete Set (14):		1000.
Common Player:		50.00
1	Elton Brand	175.00
2	Steve Francis	175.00
3	Baron Davis	100.00
4	Wally Szczerbiak	150.00
5	Richard Hamilton	80.00
6	Andre Miller	100.00
7	Shawn Marion	100.00
8	Jason Terry	80.00
9	Aleksandar Radojevic	50.00
10	William Avery	70.00
11	Ron Artest	80.00
12	James Posey	70.00
13	Tim James	60.00
14	Jumanie Jones	60.00

1999-00 SkyBox Dominion Sky's the Limit

This 15-card insert set featured players on silver foilboard over a basketball, globe thing covering most of the background. Regular versions were printed on silver foilboard and inserted 1:24 packs. Plus versions added some texture to the front, the word "PLUS" to the back and were inserted 1:240 packs. Warp Tek versions were sequentially numbered to 25 sets, printed on a thicker stock and featured a prismatic, 3-D look to the front.

		MT
Complete Set (15):		100.00
Common Player:		3.00
Inserted 1:24		
Complete Plus Set (15):		300.00
Common Plus Cards:		10.00
Plus Cards:		2x-4x
Inserted 1:240		
WarpTek Cards:		10x-20x
Production 25 Sets		
1	Kevin Garnett	12.00
2	Jason Williams	10.00
3	Grant Hill	12.00
4	Keith Van Horn	2.00
5	Allen Iverson	10.00
6	Ron Mercer	3.00
7	Anfernee Hardaway	8.00
8	Kobe Bryant	15.00
9	Shareef Abdur-Rahim	3.00
10	Jason Kidd	4.00
11	Shaquille O'Neal	8.00
12	Stephon Marbury	6.00
13	Paul Pierce	8.00
14	Tim Duncan	12.00
15	Vince Carter	12.00

1999-00 SkyBox Dominion Sky's the Limit Plus

This 15-card insert paralleled the Sky's the Limit insert, but added a textured foil to the card front, with the word "Plus" insert silver foil on the back. Plus cards were inserted 1:240 packs.

		MT
Complete Plus Set (15):		300.00
Common Plus Cards:		10.00
Plus Cards:		2x-4x
Inserted 1:240		

1999-00 SkyBox Dominion Sky's the Limit Warp Tek

This 15-card insert set parallel the Sky's the Limit set, but added a prismatic, three-dimensional look to the front. WarpTek versions were sequentially numbered to 25 sets on the back.

		MT
WarpTek Cards:		10x-20x
Production 25 Sets		

1999-00 SkyBox Dominion 2 Point Play

This 10-card insert was seeded 1:9 packs of Dominion. It featured two players - one on the front and one on the back - who play the same position or play with similar styles. Plus versions contained the word "Plus" on the back, were textured on the front and inserted 1:90 packs. Warp Tek versions featured a prismatic, 3-D effect on the front and were seeded 1:900 packs. 2 Point Play inserts were numbered with a "TP" suffix on the back.

		MT
Complete Set (10):		12.00
Common Player:		.75
Inserted 1:9		
Complete Plus Set (10):		60.00
Common Plus Cards:		3.00
Plus Cards:		3x-5x
Inserted 1:90		
Common WarpTek Cards:		10.00
WarpTek Cards:		10x-20x
Inserted 1:900		
1	Keith Van Horn, Grant Hill	1.00
2	Paul Pierce, Scottie Pippen	2.00
3	Tim Duncan, Kevin Garnett	4.00
4	Kobe Bryant, Vince Carter	5.00
5	Shaquille O'Neal, Michael Olowokandi	1.00
6	Chris Webber, Shawn Kemp	.50
7	Jason Williams, Allen Iverson	3.00
8	Stephon Marbury, Anfernee Hardaway	2.00
9	Jason Kidd, Mike Bibby	1.00
10	Shareef Abdur-Rahim, Antonio McDyess	.75

1999-00 SkyBox Dominion 2 Point Play Plus

This 10-card set paralleled the 2 Point Play insert, but added a textured foil to the front and the word "Plus" on the back in silver foil. Plus versions were seeded 1:90 packs.

	MT
Complete Set (10):	12.00
Common Player:	.75
Inserted 1:9	
Complete Plus Set (10):	60.00
Common Plus Cards:	3.00
Plus Cards:	3x-5x
Inserted 1:90	
Common WarpTek Cards:	10.00
WarpTek Cards:	10x-20x
Inserted 1:900	

1999-00 SkyBox Dominion 2 Point Play Warp Tek

This 10-card insert paralleled the 2 Point Play set, but added a prismatic, three-dimensional look to the card front. Warp Tek versions were seeded 1:900 packs.

	MT
Common WarpTek Cards:	10.00
WarpTek Cards:	10x-20x
Inserted 1:900	

1998-99 SkyBox Thunder

This was the first year for the Thunder brand name, which replaced Z-Force. Series I had 125 cards, with the first 50 seeded four per pack, 51-100 seeded three per pack and 101-125 seeded one per pack. The set is paralleled in both Rave (numbered to 150) and Super Rave (numbered to 25) sets. Inserts in Series I include: Autographics, Boss, Bringin' It, Lift Off, Flight School and Noyz Boyz.

		MT
Complete Set (125):		30.00
Common Player (1-100):		.10
Minor Stars (1-100):		.20
Common Player (101-125):		.25
Minor Stars (101-125):		.50
#101-125 Inserted 1:1		
Pack (10):		1.59
Wax Box (36):		55.00
1	Kerry Kittles	.20
2	Larry Johnson	.20
3	Hakeem Olajuwon	.50
4	Glenn Robinson	.20
5	Alonzo Mourning	.20
6	Reggie Miller	.20
7	Toni Kukoc	.20
8	Corliss Williamson	.10
9	Nick Van Exel	.20
10	Mookie Blaylock	.10
11	Michael Smith	.10
12	Avery Johnson	.10
13	Brian Williams	.10
14	Doug Christie	.10
15	Danny Fortson	.10
16	Michael Stewart	.10
17	Anthony Peeler	.10
18	Cedric Henderson	.10
19	Lamond Murray	.10
20	Walt Williams	.10
21	Samaki Walker	.10
22	David Wesley	.10
23	Maurice Taylor	.30
24	Todd Fuller	.10
25	Jeff Hornacek	.10
26	Danny Manning	.10
27	Detlef Schrempf	.10
28	Nick Anderson	.10
29	Ron Harper	.10
30	Brian Shaw	.10
31	Bryant Stith	.10
32	Chris Whitney	.10
33	Patrick Ewing	.20
34	Travis Knight	.10
35	Tracy McGrady	.75
36	Dan Majerle	.10
37	Dale Davis	.10
38	Kelvin Cato	.10
39	Zydrunas Ilgauskas	.20
40	Sean Elliott	.10
41	Tony Delk	.10
42	Bobby Phills	.10
43	Clifford Robinson	.10
44	Shawn Bradley	.10
45	Aaron McKie	.10
46	Mark Jackson	.10
47	P.J. Brown	.10
48	Armon Gilliam	.10
49	Ed Gray	.10
50	Olden Polynice	.10
51	Kendall Gill	.10
52	Bryon Russell	.10
53	Dale Ellis	.10
54	Mark Price	.10
55	Donyell Marshall	.10
56	John Starks	.10
57	Jerome Williams	.10
58	Rodney Rogers	.10
59	Michael Finley	.20
60	Marcus Camby	.20
61	Chris Anstey	.10
62	Rodrick Rhodes	.10
63	Derek Anderson	.30
64	Jermaine O'Neal	.10
65	Glen Rice	.20
66	Bryant Reeves	.10
67	Jalen Rose	.10
68	Calbert Cheaney	.10
69	Steve Smith	.10
70	Shandon Anderson	.10
71	Tony Battie	.20
72	Kenny Anderson	.10
73	Tim Hardaway	.30
74	Antonio Daniels	.20
75	Charles Barkley	.30
76	Chauncey Billups	.20
77	Lindsey Hunter	.10
78	Terrell Brandon	.20
79	Anthony Mason	.10
80	Elden Campbell	.10
81	Rasheed Wallace	.10
82	Erick Dampier	.10
83	Tracy Murray	.10
84	Sam Cassell	.10
85	Bobby Jackson	.20
86	Horace Grant	.10
87	Brent Price	.10
88	Allan Houston	.20
89	Brevin Knight	.30
90	Steve Nash	.10
91	Lorenzen Wright	.10
92	Hubert Davis	.10
93	Walter McCarty	.10
94	Jamal Mashburn	.20
95	Dikembe Mutombo	.20
96	Chris Carr	.10
97	Tariq Abdul-Wahad	.10
98	Chris Mullin	.20
99	Charlie Ward	.10
100	Tim Thomas	.75
101	Tim Duncan	2.25
102	Antoine Walker	1.00
103	Stephon Marbury	1.50
104	Ray Allen	.25
105	Shawn Kemp	.50
106	Michael Jordan	4.50
107	Gary Payton	.50
108	Kobe Bryant	3.00
109	Karl Malone	.50
110	Kevin Garnett	2.25
111	Jason Kidd	.75
112	Dennis Rodman	1.50
113	Grant Hill	2.25
114	Keith Van Horn	1.00
115	Shareef Abdur-Rahim	1.00
116	Ron Mercer	1.50
117	Allen Iverson	1.00
118	Shaquille O'Neal	1.50
119	Anfernee Hardaway	1.50
120	Scottie Pippen	1.00
121	David Robinson	.50
122	Vin Baker	.75
123	John Stockton	.50
124	Eddie Jones	.75
125	Juwan Howard	.50

1998-99 SkyBox Thunder Rave

	MT
Rave Cards:	40x-80x
Production 150 Sets	

1998-99 SkyBox Thunder Super Rave

	MT
Super Rave Cards:	250x-500x
Production 25 Sets	

1998-99 SkyBox Thunder Boss

Boss was a 20-card insert that featured players on a sculpted card. These inserts were seeded one per 16 Series I packs and numbered with a "B" suffix.

		MT
Complete Set (20):		60.00
Common Player:		1.00
Inserted 1:16		
1	Shareef Abdur-Rahim	4.00
2	Vin Baker	3.00
3	Tim Duncan	8.00
4	Kevin Garnett	8.00
5	Tim Hardaway	2.00
6	Grant Hill	8.00
7	Michael Jordan	15.00
8	Shawn Kemp	2.00
9	Jason Kidd	3.00
10	Karl Malone	2.00
11	Stephon Marbury	5.00
12	Ron Mercer	5.00
13	Shaquille O'Neal	5.00
14	Gary Payton	2.00
15	Scottie Pippen	4.00
16	Glenn Robinson	1.00
17	John Stockton	2.00
18	Damon Stoudamire	2.00
19	Keith Van Horn	2.00
20	Antoine Walker	3.00

1998-99 SkyBox Thunder Bringin' It

Inserted into one per eight Series I packs, Bringin' It displays 10 top players. Cards arrived folded in half and can be opened to display a larger shot of the player over a multi-colored background.

		MT
Complete Set (10)		10.00
Common Player:		.50
Inserted 1:8		
1	Charles Barkley	.75
2	Anfernee Hardaway	2.50
3	Eddie Jones	1.25
4	Karl Malone	.75
5	Hakeem Olajuwon	1.00
6	Shaquille O'Neal	2.50
7	Scottie Pippen	1.75
8	Glen Rice	.50
9	David Robinson	.75
10	Dennis Rodman	2.50

1998-99 SkyBox Thunder Flight School

Flight School featured 12 players on cards that resembled viewfinders. Each had two magnified eyeholes that could be looked through to view a larger three-dimensional picture. This insert was seeded one per 96 packs of Series I and was numbered with a "FS" suffix.

		MT
Complete Set (12):		200.00
Common Player:		5.00
Inserted 1:96 Hobby		
1	Ray Allen	5.00
2	Kobe Bryant	35.00
3	Michael Finley	5.00
4	Kevin Garnett	25.00
5	Anfernee Hardaway	18.00
6	Grant Hill	25.00
7	Allen Iverson	18.00
8	Eddie Jones	10.00
9	Michael Jordan	50.00
10	Shawn Kemp	6.00
11	Antonio McDyess	5.00
12	Ron Mercer	18.00

1998-99 SkyBox Thunder Lift Off

Lift Off included 10 top players on a prismatic holofoil card. These were numbered with a "LO" suffix and inserted one per 56 packs of Series I.

		MT
Complete Set (10):		85.00
Common Player:		2.50
Inserted 1:56		
1	Shareef Abdur-Rahim	7.00
2	Ray Allen	2.50
3	Kobe Bryant	20.00
4	Tim Duncan	18.00
5	Allen Iverson	10.00
6	Kerry Kittles	2.50
7	Stephon Marbury	10.00
8	Ron Mercer	10.00
9	Keith Van Horn	8.00
10	Antoine Walker	5.00

1998-99 SkyBox Thunder Noyz Boyz

This 15-card insert is printed on a die-cut "Z" shape on an illusion stock with a material finish providing a 3-D effect. The cards are numbered with a "NB" suffix and inserted one per 300 packs of Series I.

		MT
Complete Set (15):		700.00
Common Player:		12.00
Inserted 1:300		
1	Shareef Abdur-Rahim	35.00
2	Ray Allen	12.00
3	Kobe Bryant	100.00
4	Tim Duncan	75.00
5	Kevin Garnett	75.00
6	Anfernee Hardaway	50.00
7	Grant Hill	75.00
8	Allen Iverson	50.00
9	Michael Jordan	150.00
10	Stephon Marbury	60.00
11	Shaquille O'Neal	50.00
12	Scottie Pippen	35.00
13	Dennis Rodman	50.00
14	Keith Van Horn	30.00
15	Antoine Walker	30.00

1999-00 SkyBox

SkyBox Premium consisted of 150 cards, including 25 Rookies. Each rookie was featured on two different cards, with a posed shot being a regular-issue card and an action shot inserted 1:8 packs. The entire set was paralleled in a Shining Star Rubies set, with the 125 regular-issue cards numbered to 45 and the 25 action-shot, seeded rookies numbered to just 25. Inserts included: Back for More, Majestic, Good Stuff, Prime Time Rookies, Prime Time Rookies Autographs, Club Vertical, Autographics and Genuine Coverage.

		MT
Complete Set (150):		125.00
Complete Set w/o SPs (125):		40.00
Common Player:		.10
Minor Stars:		.20
Common Rookie (101-125):		.50
Common SP (101-125):		1.00
SP Cards Feature Action Photo		
SP Cards Inserted 1:8		
Pack (8):		2.69
Wax Box (24):		50.00
1	Vince Carter	2.50
2	Nick Anderson	.10
3	Isaiah Rider	.20
4	Mitch Richmond	.20
5	Danny Fortson	.10
6	Kenny Anderson	.20
7	Reggie Miller	.20
8	Tracy McGrady	1.00
9	Steve Nash	.10
10	Robert Traylor	.75
11	Tom Gugliotta	.20
12	Steve Smith	.20
13	Jalen Rose	.20
14	Kerry Kittles	.10
15	Nick Van Exel	.20
16	Raef LaFrentz	.75
17	Damon Stoudamire	.30
18	Gary Trent	.10
19	Jayson Williams	.10
20	Brian Grant	.10
21	Rod Strickland	.20
22	Larry Hughes	1.00
23	Derek Anderson	.20
24	Hakeem Olajuwon	.75
25	Ray Allen	.30
26	Gary Payton	.75
27	Michael Finley	.30
28	Keith Van Horn	.75
29	Clifford Robinson	.10
30	Shawn Kemp	.50
31	Glenn Robinson	.20
32	Theo Ratliff	.10
33	Lindsey Hunter	.10
34	Chris Webber	1.00
35	Grant Hill	2.50
36	Vlade Divac	.20
37	Paul Pierce	1.50
38	Tyrone Nesby	.20
39	Larry Johnson	.20
40	Byron Russell	.10
41	Antoine Walker	.75
42	Michael Olowokandi	.75
43	John Stockton	.20
44	Elden Campbell	.10
45	Christian Laettner	.10
46	Maurice Taylor	.40
47	Shareef Abdur-Rahim	1.00
48	Ricky Davis	.20
49	Jerry Stackhouse	.30
50	Kobe Bryant	3.00
51	Jason Williams	2.00
52	Mike Bibby	1.00
53	Eddie Jones	.60
54	Antawn Jamison	1.25
55	Shaquille O'Neal	2.00
56	Tim Duncan	2.50
57	Cherokee Parks	.10
58	Antonio McDyess	.60
59	Rasheed Wallace	.20
60	Anthony Mason	.10
61	Chris Mills	.10
62	Glen Rice	.20
63	Latrell Sprewell	.30
64	Darrell Armstrong	.20
65	Sean Elliott	.10
66	Juwan Howard	.20
67	Brent Barry	.10
68	John Starks	.10
69	Tim Hardaway	.40
70	Marcus Camby	.60
71	Anfernee Hardaway	2.00
72	Avery Johnson	.10
73	Tariq Abdul-Wahad	.10
74	Charles Barkley	.75
75	Stephon Marbury	1.25
76	Jamal Mashburn	.20
77	Matt Harpring	.20
78	David Robinson	.75
79	Cedric Ceballos	.10
80	Terrell Brandon	.20
81	Jason Kidd	1.00
82	Toni Kukoc	.50
83	Michael Dickerson	.20
84	Alonzo Mourning	.40
85	Kevin Garnett	2.50
86	Matt Geiger	.10
87	Vin Baker	.20
88	Dikembe Mutombo	.20
89	Hersey Hawkins	.10
90	Joe Smith	.20
91	Charles Oakley	.10
92	Ron Mercer	1.00
93	Rik Smits	.10
94	Patrick Ewing	.20
95	Karl Malone	.75
96	Scottie Pippen	1.00
97	Zydrunas Ilgauskas	.10
98	Sam Cassell	.20
99	Detlef Schrempf	.10
100	Allen Iverson	2.00
101	*Elton Brand*	2.00
101	Elton Brand SP	8.00
102	*Steve Francis*	5.00
102	Steve Francis SP	20.00
103	*Baron Davis*	1.50
103	Baron Davis SP	6.00
104	*Lamar Odom*	3.00
104	Lamar Odom SP	12.00
105	*Jonathan Bender*	2.00
105	Jonathan Bender SP	8.00
106	*Wally Szczerbiak*	1.25
106	Wally Szczerbiak SP	5.00
107	*Richard Hamilton*	1.25
107	Richard Hamilton SP	5.00
108	*Andre Miller*	1.50
108	Andre Miller SP	6.00
109	*Shawn Marion*	2.00
109	Shawn Marion SP	8.00
110	*Jason Terry*	1.00
110	Jason Terry SP	4.00
111	*Trajan Langdon*	.75
111	Trajan Langdon SP	3.00
112	*Aleksandar Radojevic*	.30
112	Aleksandar Radojevic SP	1.00
113	*Corey Maggette*	1.50
113	Corey Maggette SP	6.00
114	*William Avery*	.60
114	William Avery SP	2.50
115	*Vonteego Cummings*	.60
115	Vonteego Cummings SP	2.50
116	*Ron Artest*	1.00
116	Ron Artest SP	4.00
117	*Cal Bowdler*	.30
117	Cal Bowdler SP	1.00
118	*James Posey*	.75
118	James Posey SP	3.00
119	*Quincy Lewis*	.50
119	Quincy Lewis SP	2.00
120	*Dion Glover*	.50
120	Dion Glover SP	2.00
121	*Jeff Foster*	.30
121	Jeff Foster SP	1.00
122	*Kenny Thomas*	.50
122	Kenny Thomas SP	2.00
123	*Devean George*	.75
123	Devean George SP	3.00
124	*Scott Padgett*	.50
124	Scott Padgett SP	2.00
125	*Tim James*	.50
125	Tim James SP	2.00

1999-00 SkyBox Shining Star Rubies

This 150-card parallel set reprinted every card in the SkyBox set, but featured prismatic foil in the background. All 125 regular-issue cards were numbered to 45, while the 25 short-printed rookies were numbered to 25.

	MT
Ruby Cards:	75x-150x.50
Ruby Young Star Cards:	40x-80x
Ruby Rookie Cards:	15x-30x
Production 45 Sets	
Ruby SP Cards:	10x-15x
SP Production 25 Sets	

1999-00 SkyBox Premium Autographics

		MT
Common Player:		6.00
Minor Stars:		8.00
1	Cory Alexander	6.00
2	Ray Allen	40.00
3	Darrell Armstrong	8.00
4	Ron Artest	12.00
5	William Avery	8.00
6	Charles Barkley	175.00
7	Dana Barros	6.00
8	Corey Benjamin	6.00
9	Travis Best	8.00
10	Mike Bibby	15.00
11	Calvin Booth	6.00
12	Cal Bowdler	6.00
13	Bruce Bowen	6.00
14	P.J. Brown	8.00
15	Jud Buechler	6.00
16	Marcus Camby	15.00
17	Elden Campbell	8.00
18	Cory Carr	6.00
19	Vince Carter	150.00
20	John Celestand	8.00
21	Dell Curry	6.00
22	Baron Davis	20.00

23	Andrew DeClercq	6.00
24	Tony Delk	8.00
25	Michael Dickerson	10.00
26	Michael Doleac	6.00
27	Bryce Drew	6.00
28	Obinna Ekezie	6.00
29	Evan Eschmeyer	6.00
30	Michael Finley	30.00
31	Greg Foster	6.00
32	Jeff Foster	6.00
33	Steve Francis	75.00
34	Todd Fuller	6.00
35	Lawrence Funderburke	6.00
36	Dean Garrett	6.00
37	Pat Garrity	8.00
38	Devean George	10.00
39	Kendall Gill	10.00
40	Dion Glover	8.00
41	Brian Grant	12.00
42	Paul Grant	6.00
43	Tom Gugliotta	12.00
44	Richard Hamilton	20.00
45	Tim Hardaway	20.00
46	Matt Harpring	8.00
47	Al Harrington	12.00
48	Othella Harrington	10.00
49	Troy Hudson	6.00
50	Larry Hughes	25.00
51	Tim James	6.00
52	Antawn Jamison	25.00
53	Anthony Johnson	6.00
54	Avery Johnson	8.00
55	Ervin Johnson	6.00
56	Eddie Jones	40.00
57	Jumaine Jones	8.00
58	Adam Keefe	6.00
59	Shawn Kemp	15.00
60	Kerry Kittles	10.00
61	Raef LaFrentz	10.00
62	Trajan Langdon	10.00
63	Quincy Lewis	8.00
64	Felipe Lopez	8.00
65	Tyronn Lue	8.00
66	George Lynch	8.00
67	Sam Mack	6.00
68	Stephon Marbury	25.00
69	Shawn Marion	40.00
70	Tony Massenburg	6.00
71	Jelani McCoy	6.00
72	Antonio McDyess	20.00
73	Tracy McGrady	50.00
74	Roshown McLeod	8.00
75	Brad Miller	8.00
76	Sam Mitchell	6.00
77	Nazr Mohammed	10.00
78	Alonzo Mourning	50.00
79	Tyrone Nesby	8.00
80	Shaquille O'Neal	200.00
81	Lamar Odom	60.00
82	Hakeem Olajuwon	40.00
83	Michael Olowokandi	10.00
84	Andrae Patterson	6.00
85	Eric Piatkowski	6.00
86	Scottie Pippen	60.00
87	Scot Pollard	6.00
88	James Posey	10.00
89	Brent Price	6.00
90	Aleksandar Radojevic	6.00
91	Theo Ratliff	10.00
92	J.R. Reid	8.00
93	David Robinson	75.00
94	Glenn Robinson	25.00
95	Jalen Rose	25.00
96	Michael Ruffin	6.00
97	Wally Szczerbiak	20.00
98	Joe Smith	15.00
99	Jerry Stackhouse	20.00
100	John Starks	12.00
101	Vladimir Stepania	6.00
102	Damon Stoudamire	15.00
103	Maurice Taylor	8.00
104	Jason Terry	15.00
105	Kenny Thomas	10.00
106	Robert Traylor	8.00
107	Gary Trent	8.00
108	Antoine Walker	25.00
109	Chris Webber	125.00
110	David Wesley	8.00
111	Aaron Williams	8.00
112	Jerome Williams	8.00
113	Haywoode Workman	6.00

1999-00 SkyBox Back For More

This 15-card insert was seeded 1:6 packs of SkyBox. Cards were numbered with a "BF" suffix on the back.

		MT
Complete Set (15):		12.00
Common Player:		.50
Inserted 1:6 Series 1		
1	Mike Bibby	1.50
2	Tyrone Nesby	.50
3	Ricky Davis	.75
4	Michael Dickerson	.75
5	Michael Doleac	.75
6	Antawn Jamison	2.00
7	Larry Hughes	1.50
8	Matt Harpring	.75
9	Predrag Stojakovic	.50
10	Raef LaFrentz	1.00
11	Michael Olowokandi	1.00
12	Robert Traylor	1.00
13	Paul Pierce	3.00
14	Kornell David	.50
15	Jason Williams	3.00

1999-00 SkyBox Club Vertical

This 10-card insert set featured top players on a die-cut embossed and red-foil stamped surface. Cards were sequentially numbered to 100 and numbered with a "CV" suffix.

		MT
Complete Set (10):		400.00
Common Player:		20.00
Production 100 Sets		
1	Vince Carter	60.00
2	Tim Duncan	60.00
3	Shaquille O'Neal	40.00
4	Paul Pierce	35.00
5	Kobe Bryant	75.00
6	Kevin Garnett	60.00
7	Keith Van Horn	15.00
8	Jason Williams	40.00
9	Grant Hill	60.00
10	Allen Iverson	40.00

1999-00 SkyBox Genuine Coverage

This six-card insert set featured swatches from player-worn game jerseys. Each card was sequentially numbered, with no insertion rates given.

	MT
Complete Set (6):	1300.
Common Player:	150.00
Kobe Bryant	350.00
Patrick Ewing	150.00
Alonzo Mourning	150.00
Vince Carter	400.00
Allen Iverson	250.00
Grant Hill	300.00

1999-90 SkyBox Good Stuff

This 10-card insert set included top veterans on fuscia- foil stamped cards with full-color overprinting 100 percent silver foil. Good Stuff inserts were numbered with a "GS" suffix and inserted 1:36 packs. A parallel version, called More Good Stuff, was also printed and sequentially numbered to 99 sets.

		MT
Complete Set (10):		50.00
Common Player:		2.00
Inserted 1:36 Series 1		
More Good Stuff Cards:		5x-10x
Production 99 Sets		
1	Kobe Bryant	10.00
2	Vince Carter	8.00
3	Jason Williams	6.00
4	Paul Pierce	5.00
5	Tim Duncan	8.00
6	Kevin Garnett	8.00
7	Grant Hill	8.00
8	Keith Van Horn	1.00
9	Allen Iverson	6.00
10	Shaquille O'Neal	6.00

1999-00 SkyBox More Good Stuff Parallel

		MT
Complete Set (10):		50.00
Common Player:		2.00
Inserted 1:36 Series 1		
More Good Stuff Cards:		5x-10x
Production 99 Sets		
1	Kobe Bryant	10.00
2	Vince Carter	8.00
3	Jason Williams	6.00
4	Paul Pierce	5.00
5	Tim Duncan	8.00
6	Kevin Garnett	8.00
7	Grant Hill	8.00
8	Keith Van Horn	1.50
9	Allen Iverson	6.00
10	Shaquille O'Neal	6.00

1999-00 SkyBox Majestic

This 15-card insert set captured top players on matte- varnished, silver-foil stamped cards printed on white pearl stock. Majestic inserts were seeded 1:12 packs and numbered with an "MJ" suffix.

		MT
Complete Set (15):		35.00
Common Player:		2.00
Inserted 1:12 Series 1		
1	Antawn Jamison	3.00
2	Jason Kidd	2.00
3	Ron Mercer	2.00
4	Shawn Kemp	1.00
5	Stephon Marbury	2.50
6	Shaquille O'Neal	4.00
7	Larry Hughes	2.00
8	Kevin Garnett	6.00
9	Antoine Walker	1.00
10	Keith Van Horn	1.00
11	Anfernee Hardaway	4.00
12	Tim Duncan	6.00
13	Scottie Pippen	2.00
14	Shareef Abdur-Rahim	2.00
15	Chris Webber	2.00

1999-00 SkyBox Prime Time Rookies

This 15-card insert set was printed on plastic with silver and clear patterned holo-foil stamping. Prime Time Rookies inserts were numbered with a "PT" suffix and inserted 1:96 packs. A parallel autographed version also existed, with 14 of the rookies (excluding Elton Brand) signing 25 of their cards.

		MT
Complete Set (15):		175.00
Common Player:		5.00
Inserted 1:96 Series 1		
1	Elton Brand	20.00
2	Steve Francis	25.00
3	Baron Davis	18.00
4	Lamar Odom	30.00
5	Jonathan Bender	15.00
6	Wally Szczerbiak	25.00
7	Richard Hamilton	12.00
8	Andre Miller	10.00
9	Shawn Marion	12.00
10	Jason Terry	8.00
11	Trajan Langdon	10.00
12	Dion Glover	5.00
13	Corey Maggette	15.00
14	William Avery	6.00
15	Tim James	5.00

1999-00 SkyBox Prime Time Rookies Autographs

This 14-card set paralleled the Prime Time Rookies insert, but the cards were limited to just 25 sets and autographed. Elton Brand did not sign in this insert due to his deal with Topps.

		MT
Complete Set (15):		175.00
Common Player:		5.00
Inserted 1:96 Series 1		
1	Elton Brand	20.00
2	Steve Francis	25.00
3	Baron Davis	18.00
4	Lamar Odom	30.00
5	Jonathan Bender	15.00
6	Wally Szczerbiak	25.00
7	Richard Hamilton	12.00
8	Andre Miller	8.00
9	Shawn Marion	12.00
10	Jason Terry	8.00
11	Trajan Langdon	10.00
12	Dion Glover	5.00
13	Corey Maggette	15.00
14	William Avery	6.00
15	Tim James	5.00

1999-00 SkyBox Apex Lamar Odom

		MT
Complete Set (1):		30.00
NNO	Lamar Odom	30.00

1999-00 SkyBox Apex

Apex debuted in 1999-00 with a 163-card set that consisted of 150 veterans and 13 rookies, which were all lottery picks and seeded 1:13 packs. The cards featured a color shot of the player surrounded by a black foil border, while the rookies were bordered with gold foil. The set was available in two parallel versions - Apex Xtra, which was numbered to 50 sets, and Apex Xtreme, which was numbered to just one set. Inserts included: Allies, Cutting Edge, First Impressions, Jam Session and Net Shredders. The Lamar Odom card was given out to dealers, is not part of the regular-issue set and is sequentially numbered to 2,000.

		MT
Complete Set (163):		100.00
Common Player:		.15
Minor Stars:		.30
Common Rookie (151-163):		1.00
Inserted 1:13		
Pack (8):		3.00
Wax Box (24):		50.00
1	Paul Pierce	1.25
2	Stephon Marbury	1.00
3	Chris Webber	1.25
4	Kobe Bryant	3.00
5	David Robinson	.60
6	Gary Payton	.60
7	Vornel David	.15
8	Glenn Robinson	.30
9	Nick Van Exel	.30
10	Jelani McCoy	.15
11	Charles Oakley	.15
12	Michael Finley	.30
13	Steve Smith	.30
14	Arvydas Sabonis	.15
15	Cuttino Mobley	.30
16	Eric Piatkowski	.15
17	Bobby Jackson	.15
18	Keith Van Horn	.75
19	Shaquille O'Neal	1.50
20	Karl Malone	.60
21	Allan Houston	.30
22	Ron Mercer	1.00
23	Vince Carter	3.00
24	Lindsey Hunter	.15
25	Scottie Pippen	1.25
26	Wesley Person	.15
27	Vitaly Potapenko	.15
28	Glen Rice	.30
29	Tyrone Nesby	.15
30	Detlef Schrempf	.15
31	Clifford Robinson	.15
32	Joe Smith	.15
33	P.J. Brown	.15
34	Christian Laettner	.15
35	Avery Johnson	.15
36	Kevin Garnett	2.50
37	Jason Kidd	1.25
38	Kenny Anderson	.30
39	Shawn Kemp	.30
40	Bison Dele	.15
41	Rodney Rogers	.15
42	Jamal Mashburn	.30
43	Grant Hill	2.50
44	Larry Johnson	.15
45	Darrell Armstrong	.30
46	Shandon Anderson	.15
47	Kendall Gill	.15
48	Jason Williams	1.50
49	Tom Gugliotta	.30
50	Ray Allen	.30
51	Sam Mitchell	.15
52	Brent Barry	.15
53	Antawn Jamison	1.00
54	Chris Mullin	.15
55	Alan Henderson	.15
56	Derek Anderson	.15
57	Tim Thomas	.60
58	Anfernee Hardaway	1.50
59	Pat Garrity	.15
60	Corliss Williamson	.15
61	Gary Trent	.15
62	Greg Ostertag	.15
63	Vin Baker	.30
64	LaPhonso Ellis	.15
65	Brevin Knight	.15
66	Rick Fox	.15
67	Bryant Reeves	.15
68	Mark Jackson	.15
69	John Starks	.15
70	Robert Traylor	.40
71	Maurice Taylor	.30
72	Hersey Hawkins	.15
73	Zydrunas Ilgauskas	.30
74	Charles Barkley	.60
75	Isaac Austin	.15
76	Mike Bibby	.75
77	Michael Olowokandi	.60
78	Brian Grant	.15
79	Felipe Lopez	.30
80	Chris Crawford	.15
81	Dee Brown	.15
82	Antoine Walker	.60
83	Vlade Divac	.15
84	Rod Strickland	.30
85	Dickey Simpkins	.15
86	Donyell Marshall	.15
87	Larry Hughes	.60
88	Rasheed Wallace	.30
89	Erick Dampier	.15
90	Kerry Kittles	.15
91	Mitch Richmond	.30
92	Isaiah Rider	.30
93	Bobby Phills	.15
94	Dirk Nowitzki	.50
95	Cedric Henderson	.15
96	Howard Eisley	.15
97	Toni Kukoc	.40
98	Jalen Rose	.30
99	Michael Doleac	.30
100	Matt Geiger	.15
101	Bryon Russell	.15
102	Alvin Williams	.15
103	Shawn Bradley	.15
104	Latrell Sprewell	.50
105	Vernon Maxwell	.15
106	Tim Hardaway	.50
107	Predrag Stojakovic	.15
108	Tracy Murray	.15
109	Theo Ratliff	.15
110	Dikembe Mutombo	.30
111	Alonzo Mourning	.40
112	Raef LaFrentz	.60
113	Marcus Camby	.30
114	Eddie Jones	.75
115	Chauncey Billups	.15
116	Jayson Williams	.15
117	Anthony Mason	.15
118	Tracy McGrady	1.25
119	John Stockton	.30
120	Matt Harpring	.30
121	Mario Elie	.15
122	Juwan Howard	.30
123	Antonio McDyess	.40
124	Ricky Davis	.30
125	Reggie Miller	.30
126	Allen Iverson	1.25
127	Terrell Brandon	.30
128	Hakeem Olajuwon	.60
129	Damon Stoudamire	.40
130	Randy Brown	.15
131	Cedric Ceballos	.15
132	Jerry Stackhouse	.30
133	Michael Dickerson	.30
134	Rik Smits	.15
135	Cherokee Parks	.15
136	Tim Duncan	2.50
137	Shareef Abdur-Rahim	1.00
138	Derek Fisher	.15
139	Charles Outlaw	.15
140	Eric Snow	.15
141	Jaren Jackson	.15
142	Tony Battie	.15
143	Derrick Coleman	.30
144	Corey Benjamin	.15
145	Steve Nash	.15
146	Mookie Blaylock	.15
147	Voshon Lenard	.15
148	Vinny Del Negro	.15
149	Jeff Hornacek	.15
150	Patrick Ewing	.30
151	*Elton Brand*	8.00
152	*Steve Francis*	20.00
153	*Baron Davis*	6.00
154	*Lamar Odom*	12.00
155	*Jonathan Bender*	8.00
156	*Wally Szczerbiak*	5.00
157	*Richard Hamilton*	5.00
158	*Andre Miller*	6.00
159	*Shawn Marion*	8.00
160	*Jason Terry*	3.00
161	*Trajan Langdon*	2.50
162	*Aleksandar Radojevic*	1.00
163	*Corey Maggette*	6.00
NNO	Lamar Odom/2000	25.00

1999-00 SkyBox Apex Xtra

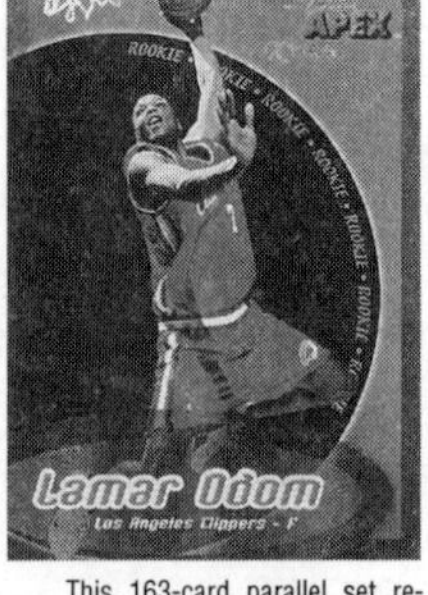

This 163-card parallel set reprinted each card from Apex, but added a holographic border. The cards were sequentially numbered to 50 sets on the back and were exclusive to hobby packs.

	MT
Xtra Veterans (1-150):	100x-150x
Xtra Rookies (151-163):	10x-15x
Production 50 Sets	

1999-00 SkyBox Apex Allies

This 15-card insert set featured two top players from the same team, with swirled team colors in the background. Allies were numbered with an "A" suffix and seeded 1:6 packs.

		MT
Complete Set (15):		20.00
Common Player:		.50
Inserted 1:6		
1	Kobe Bryant, Shaquille O'Neal	5.00
2	Keith Van Horn, Stephon Marbury	1.50
3	John Stockton, Karl Malone	1.00
4	Mike Bibby, Shareef Abdur-Rahim	1.50
5	Allen Iverson, Larry Hughes	2.00
6	Michael Olowokandi, Maurice Taylor	.50
7	Vince Carter, Tracy McGrady	4.00
8	Grant Hill, Jerry Stackhouse	3.00
9	Jason Williams, Chris Webber	2.50
10	Tim Duncan, David Robinson	3.00
11	Jason Kidd, Tom Gugliotta	1.25
12	Vin Baker, Gary Payton	1.00
13	Alonzo Mourning, Tim Hardaway	1.00
14	Shawn Kemp, Brevin Knight	.40
15	Antonio McDyess, Raef LaFrentz	.75

1999-00 SkyBox Apex Cutting Edge

This 15-card die-cut insert set featured top players over a foil, weblike background. Cutting Edge cards were numbered with a "CE" suffix and inserted 1:24 packs. Two parallel version existed; Plus versions featured textured foil and were seeded 1:240 packs, while Warp Tek versions featured a prismatic, three-dimensional look and were sequentially numbered to 25 sets.

		MT
Complete Set (15):		50.00
Common Player:		1.00
Inserted 1:24		
Plus Parallels:		2x-4x
Common Plus:		4.00
Inserted 1:240		
Warp Tek Parallels:		25x-50x
Common Warp Tek:		50.00
Production 25 Sets		
1	Allen Iverson	5.00
2	Paul Pierce	4.00
3	Vince Carter	10.00
4	Jason Williams	5.00
5	Kobe Bryant	10.00
6	Kevin Garnett	8.00
7	Stephon Marbury	3.00
8	Jason Kidd	3.00
9	Tim Duncan	8.00
10	Mike Bibby	2.00
11	Marcus Camby	1.00
12	Michael Olowokandi	1.00
13	Antawn Jamison	3.00
14	Keith Van Horn	1.50
15	Raef LaFrentz	1.50

1999-00 SkyBox Apex Cutting Edge Plus

This 15-card insert paralleled the Cutting Edge set, but was printed with a textured foil and contained the word "Plus" to the right of the player's head shot on the card back. Plus versions were seeded 1:240 packs.

	MT
Plus Parallels:	2x-4x
Common Plus:	4.00
Inserted 1:240	

1999-00 SkyBox Apex Cutting Edge Warp Tek

This 15-card insert paralleled the Cutting Edge set, but featured a prismatic, three-dimensional look on the front. Warp Tek versions were sequentially numbered to 25 sets.

	MT
Warp Tek Parallels:	25x-50x
Common Warp Tek:	50.00
Production 25 Sets	

1999-00 SkyBox Apex First Impressions

This 20-card insert set showcased the top rookies from the 1999 NBA Draft. Cards featured a holographic front, with the player's team logo in the background. First Impressions were numbered with an "FI" suffix and seeded 1:12 packs.

		MT
Complete Set (20):		45.00
Common Player:		.50
Inserted 1:12		
1	Jonathan Bender	5.00
2	Steve Francis	8.00
3	Ron Artest	2.00
4	Baron Davis	3.00
5	Shawn Marion	2.00
6	Jason Terry	2.00
7	Elton Brand	6.00
8	Kenny Thomas	1.00
9	Trajan Langdon	2.00
10	Aleksandar Radojevic	.50
11	Corey Maggette	5.00
12	Jeff Foster	.50
13	Scott Padgett	1.00
14	Lamar Odom	10.00
15	William Avery	1.50
16	Andre Miller	3.00
17	Wally Szczerbiak	5.00
18	Richard Hamilton	2.00
19	James Posey	1.50
20	Jumanie Jones	1.00

1999-00 SkyBox Apex Jam Session

Jam Session was a 10-card, die-cut plastic insert that featured some of the top dunkers in the game. The cards featured a silver prismatic foil pattern in the background. These inserts were numbered with a "JS" prefix and inserted 1:96 packs.

		MT
Complete Set (15):		150.00
Common Player:		5.00
Inserted 1:96		
1	Stephon Marbury	8.00
2	Paul Pierce	12.00
3	Kobe Bryant	30.00
4	Keith Van Horn	6.00
5	Shaquille O'Neal	15.00
6	Anfernee Hardaway	15.00
7	Grant Hill	25.00
8	Antonio McDyess	5.00
9	Kevin Garnett	25.00
10	Tracy McGrady	10.00
11	Shareef Abdur-Rahim	8.00
12	Shawn Kemp	3.00
13	Antoine Walker	4.00
14	Eddie Jones	6.00
15	Vin Baker	5.00

1999-00 SkyBox Apex Net Shredders

This 10-card set featured game-used nets from five different NBA arenas, with two players from each home team from those arenas included in the set. Net Shredders were seeded 1:216 hobby packs.

		MT
Common Player:		50.00
Inserted 1:216		
1	Vince Carter	300.00
2	Tracy McGrady	100.00
3	Allen Iverson	150.00
4	Larry Hughes	75.00
5	Glenn Robinson	50.00
6	Ray Allen	60.00
7	Jason Williams	150.00
8	Chris Webber	125.00
9	Tim Duncan	200.00
10	David Robinson	75.00

1999-00 SkyBox Impact

Impact was a base product that hit late in the basketball season, with 10 cards in each pack for only 99 cents. The set consisted of 175 veterans and 25 rookies. Impact stayed away from all the trends of seeded or numbered rookies and multiple insert sets; it offered no parallels, the rookies were not seeded and there were only three insert sets - Autographics, Rewind '99 and 29 NBA Temporary Logo Tattoos, which were offered for each team and seeded 1:4 packs. In addition, a commemorative Vince Carter card honoring his Slam Dunk Championship was available. Unautographed versions were sequentially numbered to 2,000, while autographed versions were numbered to just 15.

		MT
Complete Set (200):		30.00
Common Player:		.10
Minor Stars:		.20
Common Rookie:		.25
Pack (10):		1.00
Wax Box (36):		25.00
1	Tim Duncan	1.50
2	Doug Christie	.10
3	Mark Jackson	.10
4	Paul Pierce	.60
5	*James Posey*	.75
6	Steve Smith	.20
7	Charlie Ward	.10
8	*Elton Brand*	3.00
9	Howard Eisley	.10
10	Grant Hill	1.50
11	Christian Laettner	.10
12	*Corey Maggette*	1.25
13	Scott Pollard	.10
14	Robert Traylor	.20
15	Nick Anderson	.10
16	Pat Garrity	.20
17	Hersey Hawkins	.10
18	Troy Hudson	.10
19	Charles Oakley	.10
20	Gary Payton	.40
21	Rik Smits	.10
22	Muggsy Bogues	.10
23	Dale Davis	.10
24	Larry Johnson	.20
25	Antonio McDyess	.30
26	Alonzo Mourning	.30
27	Scottie Pippen	.75
28	Rod Strickland	.20
29	Antoine Walker	.30
30	Allen Iverson	1.00
31	Sam Cassell	.20
32	Mookie Blaylock	.10
33	Jim Jackson	.10
34	Brevin Knight	.10
35	Anthony Peeler	.10
36	Byron Russell	.10
37	Maurice Taylor	.20
38	Elden Campbell	.10
39	Austin Croshere	.10
40	Keith Van Horn	.50
41	Raef LaFrentz	.30
42	Jamal Mashburn	.20
43	Jermaine O'Neal	.20
44	Glenn Robinson	.20
45	Mitch Richmond	.20
46	Keon Clark	.20
47	Derrick Coleman	.20
48	Patrick Ewing	.20
49	Brian Grant	.10
50	Kobe Bryant	2.00
51	Dan Majerle	.10
52	Ruben Patterson	.20
53	Walt Williams	.10
54	Chris Childs	.10
55	*Baron Davis*	1.25
56	*Richard Hamilton*	1.00
57	Voshon Lenard	.10
58	Vernon Maxwell	.10
59	Hakeem Olajuwon	.40
60	Jason Williams	.75
61	Gary Trent	.10
62	Kenny Anderson	.20
63	Shawn Bradley	.10
64	*Obinna Ekezie*	.25
65	Tom Gugliotta	.20
66	Ron Harper	.10
67	Corey Benjamin	.20
68	Donyell Marshall	.10
69	David Robinson	.40
70	Stephon Marbury	.50
71	Marcus Camby	.20
72	Horace Grant	.10
73	Tim Hardaway	.30
74	Greg Foster	.10
75	Cuttino Mobley	.20
76	Rodney Buford	.40
77	Clifford Robinson	.10
78	Isaac Austin	.10
79	Robert Pack	.10
80	Eddie Jones	.60
81	*Shawn Marion*	2.00
82	Anthony Mason	.10
83	Oliver Miller	.10
84	Dirk Nowitzki	.40
85	Jayson Williams	.10
86	Brent Barry	.10
87	P.J. Brown	.10
88	Kelvin Cato	.10
89	Jim McIlvaine	.10
90	*Steve Francis*	5.00
91	Bryant Reeves	.10
92	Jerry Stackhouse	.20
93	Allan Houston	.20
94	Kevin Garnett	.50
95	Karl Malone	.40
96	David Wesley	.10
97	*Eddie Robinson*	.60
98	Ben Wallace	.10
99	Chris Webber	.75
100	*Lamar Odom*	3.00
101	Shandon Anderson	.10
102	Terrell Brandon	.20
103	Jeff Hornacek	.10
104	Terry Mills	.10
105	Tyrone Nesby	.10
106	Charles Outlaw	.10
107	Predrag Stojakovic	.20
108	*Ron Artest*	.75
109	Tony Battie	.10
110	Cedric Ceballos	.10
111	Tim Hardaway	.75
112	Othella Harrington	.10
113	Dennis Rodman	.50
114	Loy Vaught	.10
115	Malik Rose	.10
116	Vin Baker	.20
117	Charles Barkley	.40
118	Michael Finley	2.00
119	*Adrian Griffin*	.30
120	Jason Kidd	.75
121	Gheorghe Muresan	.10
122	Cherokee Parks	.10
123	Glen Rice	.20
124	Bimbo Coles	.10
125	Andrew DeClercq	.10
126	Matt Geiger	.10
127	Bobby Jackson	.10
128	Michael Olowokandi	.30
129	Greg Ostertag	.10
130	Tracy McGrady	.75
131	Rodney Rogers	.10
132	Juwan Howard	.20
133	Terry Cummings	.10
134	Mario Elie	.10
135	*Trajan Langdon*	.60
136	George Lynch	.10
137	Roshown McLeod	.10
138	Joe Smith	.10
139	John Stockton	.20
140	Ray Allen	.30
141	Vince Carter	2.50
142	Al Harrington	.30
143	Ron Mercer	.40
144	Vitaly Potapenko	.10
145	Arvydas Sabonis	.10
146	Latrell Sprewell	.40
147	Aaron Williams	.10
148	Shareef Abdur-Rahim	.50
149	*Vonteego Cummings*	.50
150	Shaquille O'Neal	1.00
151	Derek Fisher	.10
152	*Todd MacCulloch*	.25
153	*Andre Miller*	1.25
154	Dikembe Mutombo	.20
155	Ervin Johnson	.10
156	Michael Dickerson	.20
157	A.C. Green	.10
158	Kevin Willis	.10
159	Kerry Kittles	.10
160	Damon Stoudamire	.30
161	Eric Snow	.10
162	Bob Sura	.10
163	*Jason Terry*	1.00
164	Derek Anderson	.20
165	Randy Brown	.10
166	Vlade Divac	.20
167	Chris Gatling	.10
168	Lindsey Hunter	.10
169	Tim Thomas	.30
170	Antawn Jamison	.60
171	Alan Henderson	.10
172	Larry Hughes	.60
173	Shawn Kemp	.20
174	Radoslav Nesterovic	.10
175	*Scott Padgett*	.25
176	Brian Skinner	.10
177	Jerome Williams	.10
178	Corliss Williamson	.10
179	Sean Elliott	.20
180	*Wally Szczerbiak*	1.00
181	Toni Kukoc	.30
182	*Chucky Atkins*	.75
183	Jalen Rose	.20
184	Nick Van Exel	.20
185	Rasheed Wallace	.20
186	Avery Johnson	.10
187	Jamie Feick	.10
188	Adonal Foyle	.10
189	*Devean George*	.60
190	Mike Bibby	.30
191	Lamond Murray	.10
192	Billy Owens	.10
193	Isaiah Rider	.20
194	Darrell Armstrong	.10
195	Antonio Davis	.10
196	Dale Ellis	.10
197	*Tim Young*	.25
198	Roy Rogers	.10
199	Terry Porter	.10
200	Reggie Miller	.20
SD1	Vince Carter/2000	30.00
SD1	Vince Carter Auto/15	

1999-00 SkyBox Impact Rewind '99

This 40-card insert set paid tribute to the award winners during the 1998-99 season. Cards representing the 1999 NBA Champion San Antonio Spurs, NBA MVP Karl Malone, Rookie of the Year Vince Carter, the All-NBA First, Second and Third teams and the NBA All-Rookie First and Second teams were all included. Rewind '99 cards were numbered with an "RN" suffix and seeded one per pack.

		MT
Complete Set (40):		15.00
Common Player:		.10
Minor Stars:		.20
Inserted 1:1		
1	Tim Duncan	2.00
2	David Robinson	.60
3	Sean Elliott	.10
4	Mario Elie	.10
5	Avery Johnson	.10
6	Malik Rose	.10
7	Jaren Jackson	.10
8	Tim Duncan	2.00
9	Gerard King	.10
10	Jerome Kersey	.10
11	Steve Kerr	.10
12	Antonio Daniels	.10
13	Karl Malone	.60
14	Vince Carter	3.00
15	Karl Malone	.60
16	Tim Duncan	2.00
17	Alonzo Mourning	.30
18	Allen Iverson	1.50
19	Jason Kidd	1.00
20	Chris Webber	1.00
21	Grant Hill	2.00
22	Shaquille O'Neal	1.50
23	Gary Payton	.60
24	Tim Hardaway	.40
25	Kevin Garnett	2.00
26	Antonio McDyess	.40
27	Hakeem Olajuwon	.60
28	Kobe Bryant	2.50
29	John Stockton	.20
30	Vince Carter	3.00
31	Paul Pierce	.75
32	Jason Williams	1.00
33	Mike Bibby	.50
34	Matt Harpring	.20
35	Michael Dickerson	.20
36	Cuttino Mobley	.20
37	Michael Doleac	.20
38	Michael Olowokandi	.20
39	Antawn Jamison	.75
40	Vince Carter	3.00

1999-00 SkyBox Impact NBA Temporary Tattoos

NBA Temporary Tattoos included logos for all 29 NBA teams that could be applied with water. They were unnumbered and included instructions on the back. These were seeded 1:4 packs.

		MT
Complete Set (27):		8.00
Common Team:		.25
Inserted 1:4		
1	Atlanta	.25
2	Boston	.50
3	Charlotte	.25
4	Chicago	.75
5	Cleveland	.25
6	Dallas	.25
7	Denver	.25
8	Detroit	.25
9	Golden State	.25
10	Houston	.50
11	Indiana	.50
12	Los Angeles	.25
13	Los Angeles	.75
14	Miami	.50
15	Milwaukee	.25
16	Minnesota	.50
17	New Jersey	.25
18	New York	.50
19	Orlando	.25
20	Philadelphia	.50
21	Phoenix	.50
22	Portland	.50
23	Sacramento	.50
24	San Antonio	.50
25	Seattle	.50
26	Toronto	.50
27	Utah	.50
28	Vancouver	.25
29	Washington	.25

2000 SkyBox Dominion WNBA

This 156-card set included 104 player cards, 22 Expansion Draft cards and 30 Smooth Moves cards. The cards featured a white border, with a silver "2000" stamp in the upper right corner. Backs were horizontal and contained the card number in the upper right corner. The entire set was also available in a Dominion Extra parallel set, which was seeded 1:3 packs. Inserts included: The Cooper Collection, Supreme Court, All-WNBA, Girls Rock, Autographics and 500 total ticket voucher redemptions.

		MT
Complete Set (156):		25.00
Common Player:		.05
Minor Stars:		.10
Common Rookie:		.25
Pack (10):		1.50
Box (36):		45.00
1	Cynthia Cooper	3.00
2	Sue Wicks	.20
3	Clarisse Machanguana	.05
4	Adrienne Goodson	.50
5	Astou Ndiaye	.05
6	Crystal Robinson	.50
7	Tora Suber	.25
8	Lady Hardmon	.05
9	Maria Stepanova	.05
10	Mwadi Mabika	.05
11	Rebecca Lobo	1.50
12	Ticha Penicheiro	.40
13	Vicky Bullett	.30
14	Adia Barnes	.05
15	Andrea Stinson	.75
16	Sheryl Swoopes	2.50
17	Heather Owen	.05
18	Andrea Congreaves	.05
19	Brandy Reed	.05
20	Dawn Staley	.75
21	*Jennifer Rizzotti*	2.00
22	Latasha Byears	.05
23	Merlakia Jones	.30
24	Niesa Johnson	.05
25	Rushia Brown	.05
26	*Taj McWilliams*	1.00
27	Wendy Palmer	.75
28	Krystyna Lara	.05
29	Andrea Lloyd Curry	.05
30	Carla McGhee	.05
31	DeLisha Milton	.50
32	Katie Smith	1.00
33	Mery Andrade	.40
34	Nikki McCray	1.00
35	Ruthie Bolton-Holifield	1.00
36	Tamecka Dixon	.30
37	Tracy Henderson	.05
38	Yolanda Griffith	1.25
39	LaTonya Johnson	.05
40	Coquese Washington	.05
41	Chamique Holdsclaw	3.00
42	*Dominique Canty*	2.00
43	*Kendra Holland-Corn*	1.00
44	Michele Timms	1.00
45	Nykesha Sales	.75
46	Shalonda Enis	.05
47	Tamika Whitmore	.05
48	Tracy Reid	.25
49	Kate Starbird	.50
50	Amanda Wilson	.05
51	Sonia Chase	.05
52	Elaine Powell	.05
53	Michelle Edwards	.50
54	Olympia Scott-Richardson	.05
55	Shannon Johnson	.50
56	Tammy Jackson	.05
57	Ukari Figgs	.50
58	Linda Burgess	.05
59	Angie Braziel	.05
60	Tricia Bader	.05
61	Adrienne Johnson	.05
62	*Chasity Melvin*	1.00
63	Korie Hlede	.40
64	Michelle Griffiths	.05
65	Penny Moore	.30
66	Sheri Sam	.50
67	Tangela Smith	.05
68	Val Whiting	.50
69	Angie Potthoff	.05
70	Cindy Brown	.75
71	Kristin Folkl	.50
72	Lisa Leslie	2.00
73	Monica Lamb	.05
74	Teresa Weatherspoon	1.50
75	Valerie Still	.05
76	Tonya Edwards	.75
77	Heather Quella	.05
78	Cass Bauer	.05
79	Bridget Pettis	.05
80	Cindy Blodgett	.25
81	Janeth Arcain	.05
82	Kym Hampton	.25
83	Margo Dydek	.25
84	Murriel Page	.25
85	Sonja Tate	.05
86	Vickie Johnson	.25
87	Eva Nemcova	.50
88	Charlotte Smith	.50
89	*Venus Lacy*	1.00
90	Polina Tzekova	.05
91	Dalma Ivanyi	.05
92	Allison Feaster	.05
93	*Becky Hammon*	4.00
94	Amaya Valdemoro	.05
95	Jennifer Gillom	.75
96	La'Keshia Frett	.05
97	Markita Aldridge	.05
98	Natalie Williams	1.25
99	Rhonda Mapp	.05
100	Suzie McConnell Serio	.50
101	Tina Thompson	.75
102	Wanda Guyton	.05
103	Lisa Harrison	.05
104	*Andrea Nagy*	1.00
105	Edna Campbell	.05
106	Nina Bjedov	.05
107	*Sonja Henning*	1.50
108	Toni Foster	.05
109	Angela Aycock	.05
110	Charmin Smith	.05
111	Chantel Tremitiere	.05
112	Gordana Grubin	.05
113	Kara Wolters	.75
114	Rita Williams	.25
115	Stephanie McCarty	.75
116	Monica Maxwell	.05
117	Debbie Black	.05
118	Elena Baranova	.75
119	Sharon Manning	.05
120	Molly Goodenbour	1.00
121	Alisa Burras	.05
122	Mila Nikolich	.05
123	Jamila Wideman	.05
124	Michele VanGorp	.50
125	Sophia Witherspoon	.05
126	Tari Phillips	.50
127	Sheri Sam	.25
128	Mwadi Mabika	.05
129	Murriel Page	.05
130	Latasha Byears	.05
131	Dominique Canty	.75
132	Crystal Robinson	.25
133	Cynthia Cooper	1.50
134	Ruthie Bolton-Holifield	.60
135	Cindy Brown	.25
136	Kristin Folkl	.15
137	Jennifer Gillom	.40
138	Adrienne Goodson	.25
139	Vickie Johnson	.05
140	Merlakia Jones	.05
141	Rebecca Lobo	.75
142	Nikki McCray	.50
143	Suzie McConnell Serio	.25
144	DeLisha Milton	.25
145	Eva Nemcova	.25
146	Wendy Palmer	.50
147	Brandy Reed	.25
148	Nykesha Sales	.25
149	Andrea Stinson	.25
150	Michele Timms	.50
151	Valerie Still	.05
152	Andrea Nagy	.40
153	Tonya Edwards	.25
154	Taj McWilliams	.40
155	Kendra Holland-Corn	.40
156	Maria Stepanova	.40

2000 SkyBox Dominion WNBA Extra

This 156-card parallel set reprinted each card in SkyBox Dominion on a silver foilboard surface, with a black "Dominion Extra" logo in one of the upper corners on the front. Dominion Extra cards were inserted 1:3 packs.

		MT
Complete Set (100):		100.00
Common Player:		.25
Extra Cards:		2x-4x
Inserted 1:3		

2000 SkyBox Dominion WNBA Supreme Court

Supreme Court featured 20 elite players at their positions on a multi-colored background. These were numbered with an "SC" suffix and seeded 1:12 packs.

		MT
Complete Set (20):		30.00
Common Player:		1.00
Inserted 1:12		
1	Dawn Staley	3.00
2	Merlakia Jones	1.50
3	Eva Nemcova	1.50
4	Suzie McConnell Serio	2.00
5	Cynthia Cooper	10.00
6	Brandy Reed	2.00
7	Katie Smith	3.00
8	Vickie Johnson	1.00
9	Rebecca Lobo	5.00
10	Shannon Johnson	2.00
11	Nykesha Sales	2.00
12	Jennifer Gillom	3.00
13	Nikki McCray	3.00
14	Michele Timms	4.00
15	Tina Thompson	2.50
16	Ruthie Bolton-Holifield	4.00
17	Wendy Palmer	2.00
18	DeLisha Milton	1.50
19	Andrea Stinson	2.00
20	Adrienne Goodson	1.50

2000 SkyBox Dominion WNBA All-WNBA

This 10-card insert set featured the First- and Second- Team All-WNBA players. The first five have a blue prismatic background, while the second five have a red prismatic background. Cards were seeded 1:18 packs and numbered with an "AW" suffix.

		MT
Complete Set (10):		30.00
Common Player:		2.00
Inserted 1:18		
1	Sheryl Swoopes	8.00
2	Natalie Williams	4.00
3	Yolanda Griffith	4.00
4	Cynthia Cooper	10.00
5	Ticha Penicheiro	2.00
6	Chamique Holdsclaw	10.00
7	Tina Thompson	3.00
8	Lisa Leslie	6.00
9	Teresa Weatherspoon	5.00
10	Shannon Johnson	2.00

2000 SkyBox Dominion WNBA Autographics

This 12-card set featured autographs from some of the top players in the WNBA. Autographics were unnumbered and seeded 1:144 packs.

		MT
Complete Set (12):		750.00
Common Player:		30.00
Inserted 1:144		
1	Ruthie Bolten-Holifield	60.00
2	Cynthia Cooper	200.00
3	Jennifer Gillom	75.00
4	Yolanda Griffith	100.00
5	Kedra Holland-Corn	60.00
6	Lisa Leslie	125.00
7	Taj McWilliams	50.00
8	Ticha Penicheiro	60.00
9	Crystal Robinson	30.00
10	Andrea Stinson	30.00
11	Sue Wicks	60.00
12	Kate Starbird	60.00

2000 SkyBox Dominion WNBA Girls Rock!

Girls Rock! featured 10 die-cut cards with a prismatic background. The cards were die-cut around the entire left side. Cards were numbered with a "GR" suffix and seeded 1:35 packs.

		MT
Complete Set (10):		75.00
Common Player:		5.00
Inserted 1:35		
1	Sheryl Swoopes	15.00
2	Chamique Holdsclaw	15.00
3	Dawn Staley	6.00
4	Katie Smith	6.00
5	Yolanda Griffith	8.00
6	Ticha Penicheiro	5.00
7	Teresa Weatherspoon	10.00
8	Natalie Williams	8.00
9	Lisa Leslie	12.00
10	Cynthia Cooper	20.00

2000 SkyBox Dominion WNBA The Cooper Collection

This eight-card insert set was dedicated to Cynthia Cooper and was printed on a horizontal front. The cards were printed with a "CC" suffix and seeded 1:6 packs.

		MT
Complete Set (8):		12.00
Common Player:		2.00
Inserted 1:6		
1	Cynthia Cooper	2.00
2	Cynthia Cooper	2.00
3	Cynthia Cooper	2.00
4	Cynthia Cooper	2.00
5	Cynthia Cooper	2.00
6	Cynthia Cooper	2.00
7	Cynthia Cooper	2.00
8	Cynthia Cooper	2.00

1991 Smokey's Larry Johnson

The seven-card set was produced by Smokey's Sportscards, Inc. (Las Vegas) and highlights UNLV standout Larry Johnson. The set production was limited to 49,500 and a promo card was distributed at the FanFest in Toronto and the 1991 National Convention. The promo card was limited in production to 72,000. The card fronts have black borders with the backs having a black marbled design.

		MT
Complete Set (7):		5.00
Common Player:		1.00
1	Rebel Rookie	1.00
2	1989-90 Champs	1.00
3	All American	1.00
4	Undeated Season	1.00
5	Tough Loss	1.00
6	1990 NCAA Player of the Year	1.00
7	Checklist Card	1.00
PR	Larry Johnson	2.00

1994-95 SP

This set debuts Upper Deck's SP line of basketball cards. Each card in the regular set has a counterpart die-cut version, called Precision Cut, which collectively form a parallel set. Inserts within the set include Premium Collection and their die-cut counterparts (Precision Cut Premium Collection) and a special Michael Jordan card (one per box).

		MT
Complete Set (165):		40.00
Common Player:		.15
Minor Stars:		.30
Die Cut Cards:		2x
Inserted 1:1		
Pack (8):		3.00
Wax Box (32):		80.00
1	*Glenn Robinson*	4.00
2	*Jason Kidd*	10.00
3	*Grant Hill*	15.00
4	*Donyell Marshall*	.75
5	*Juwan Howard*	3.00
6	*Sharone Wright*	.25
7	*Lamond Murray*	.50
8	*Brian Grant*	2.00
9	*Eric Montross*	.25
10	*Eddie Jones*	5.00
11	*Carlos Rogers*	.25
12	*Khalid Reeves*	.25
13	*Jalen Rose*	5.00
14	*Eric Piatkowski*	.25
15	*Clifford Rozier*	.25
16	*Aaron McKie*	.50
17	*Eric Mobley*	.25
18	*Tony Dumas*	.25
19	*B.J. Tyler*	.25
20	*Dickey Simpkins*	.25
21	*Bill Curley*	.25
22	*Wesley Person*	.75
23	*Monty Williams*	.25
24	*Greg Minor*	.25
25	*Charlie Ward*	.50
26	*Brooks Thompson*	.25
27	*Trevor Ruffin*	.25
28	*Derrick Alston*	.25
29	*Michael Smith*	.25
30	*Dontonio Wingfield*	.25
31	Stacey Augmon	.15
32	Steve Smith	.30
33	Mookie Blaylock	.15
34	Grant Long	.15
35	Ken Norman	.15
36	Dominique Wilkins	.15
37	Dino Radja	.15
38	Dee Brown	.15
39	David Wesley	.15
40	Rick Fox	.15
41	Alonzo Mourning	.75
42	Larry Johnson	.30
43	Hersey Hawkins	.15
44	Scott Burrell	.15
45	Muggsy Bogues	.15
46	Scottie Pippen	2.00
47	Toni Kukoc	.50
48	B.J. Armstrong	.15
49	Will Perdue	.15
50	Ron Harper	.15
51	Mark Price	.15
52	Tyrone Hill	.15
53	Chris Mills	.15
54	John Williams	.15
55	Bobby Phills	.15
56	Jim Jackson	.30
57	Jamal Mashburn	.30
58	Popeye Jones	.15
59	Roy Tarpley	.15
60	Lorenzo Williams	.15
61	Mahmoud Abdul-Rauf	.15
62	Rodney Rogers	.15
63	Bryant Stith	.15
64	Dikembe Mutombo	.30
65	Robert Pack	.15
66	Joe Dumars	.30
67	Terry Mills	.15
68	Oliver Miller	.15
69	Lindsey Hunter	.15
70	Mark West	.15
71	Latrell Sprewell	.30
72	Tim Hardaway	.50
73	Ricky Pierce	.15
74	Rony Seikaly	.30
75	Tom Gugliotta	.50
76	Hakeem Olajuwon	1.50
77	Clyde Drexler	.75
78	Vernon Maxwell	.15
79	Robert Horry	.30
80	Sam Cassell	.15
81	Reggie Miller	.30
82	Rik Smits	.15
83	Derrick McKey	.15
84	Mark Jackson	.15
85	Dale Davis	.15
86	Loy Vaught	.15
87	Terry Dehere	.15
88	Malik Sealy	.15
89	Pooh Richardson	.15
90	Tony Massenburg	.15
91	Cedric Ceballos	.15
92	Nick Van Exel	.30
93	George Lynch	.15
94	Vlade Divac	.30
95	Elden Campbell	.15
96	Glen Rice	.50
97	Kevin Willis	.15
98	Billy Owens	.15
99	Bimbo Coles	.15
100	Harold Miner	.15
101	Vin Baker	1.25
102	Todd Day	.15
103	Marty Conlon	.15
104	Lee Mayberry	.15
105	Eric Murdock	.15
106	Isaiah Rider	.30
107	Doug West	.15
108	Christian Laettner	.30
109	Sean Rooks	.15
110	Stacey King	.15
111	Derrick Coleman	.30
112	Kenny Anderson	.30
113	Chris Morris	.15
114	Armon Gilliam	.15
115	Benoit Benjamin	.15
116	Patrick Ewing	.50
117	Charles Oakley	.15
118	John Starks	.15
119	Derek Harper	.15
120	Charles Smith	.15
121	Shaquille O'Neal	2.50
122	Anfernee Hardaway	2.50
123	Nick Anderson	.30
124	Horace Grant	.15
125	Donald Royal	.15
126	Clarence Weatherspoon	.15
127	Dana Barros	.15
128	Jeff Malone	.15
129	Willie Burton	.15
130	Shawn Bradley	.15
131	Charles Barkley	1.00
132	Kevin Johnson	.15
133	Danny Manning	.15
134	Dan Majerle	.15
135	A.C. Green	.15
136	Otis Thorpe	.15
137	Cliff Robinson	.15
138	Rod Strickland	.30
139	Buck Williams	.15
140	James Robinson	.15
141	Mitch Richmond	.50
142	Walt Williams	.15
143	Olden Polynice	.15
144	Spud Webb	.15
145	Duane Causwell	.15
146	David Robinson	1.00
147	Dennis Rodman	2.00
148	Sean Elliott	.30
149	Avery Johnson	.15
150	J.R. Reid	.15
151	Shawn Kemp	1.00
152	Gary Payton	.75
153	Detlef Schrempf	.15
154	Nate McMillan	.15
155	Kendall Gill	.15
156	Karl Malone	1.00
157	John Stockton	.50
158	Jeff Hornacek	.15
159	Felton Spencer	.15
160	David Benoit	.15
161	Chris Webber	1.25
162	Rex Chapman	.15
163	Don MacLean	.15
164	Calbert Cheaney	.15
165	Scott Skiles	.15
MJIR	Michael Jordan Red	5.00
MJIS	Michael Jordan Silver	25.00

1994-95 SP Die-Cuts

This 165-card parallel set to the base SP set was seeded one per pack. This parallel set features a silver hologram at the bottom of the card back instead of a gold hologram, which is on the regular cards. Each card is numbered with a "D" prefix.

	MT
Complete Set (165):	100.00
Common Card:	.50
Minor Stars:	1.00
Unlisted Stars:	1x-3x
Die-Cuts:	3x

1994-95 SP Holoviews

These cards were random inserts in 1994-95 Upper Deck SP packs, one per every five packs. Thirty-six top NBA stars and rookies are showcased in this Holoview set. Cards are numbered with a "PC" prefix. A parallel die-cut set, Precision Cut Premium Collection, was also produced. These cards are inserted one per every 75 packs.

		MT
Complete Set (36):		80.00
Common Player:		1.00
Minor Stars:		2.00
Inserted 1:5		
Die Cut Cards:		3x
Inserted 1:75		
1	Eric Montross	1.00
2	Dominique Wilkins	2.00
3	Larry Johnson	2.00
4	Dickey Simpkins	1.00
5	Jalen Rose	2.00
6	Latrell Sprewell	3.00
7	Carlos Rogers	1.00
8	Lamond Murray	2.00
9	Eddie Jones	10.00
10	Cedric Ceballos	1.00
11	Khalid Reeves	1.00
12	Glenn Robinson	6.00
13	Christian Laettner	2.00
14	Derrick Coleman	2.00
15	Vin Baker	6.00
16	Donyell Marshall	1.00
17	Kenny Anderson	2.00
18	Sharone Wright	1.00
19	Wesley Person	1.00
20	Brian Grant	4.00
21	Mitch Richmond	3.00
22	Shawn Kemp	4.00
23	Gary Payton	4.00
24	Juwan Howard	7.00
25	Stacey Augmon	1.00
26	Aaron McKie	1.00
27	Clifford Rozier	1.00
28	Eric Piatkowski	1.00
29	Shaquille O'Neal	12.00
30	Charlie Ward	1.00
31	Monty Williams	1.00
32	Jason Kidd	10.00
33	Bill Curley	1.00
34	Grant Hill	20.00
35	Jamal Mashburn	2.00
36	Nick Van Exel	2.00

1994-95 SP Championship

This retail exclusive SP product features a completely different card, wrapper and box design from its hobby-only counterpart. This Championship Series focuses on the NBA Playoffs, with 108 regular cards and a 27-card Road to the Finals subset. Each regular card has a full-bleed color action photo on the front, with the player's name stamped in gold foil along the left side. An SP Championship Series logo is in the upper right corner in gold foil, with a line running down the side to an oval which contains the player's team name inside. The horizontal back has the set name and logo on the left, with a square containing a recap of the playoffs next to it. Stats from the player's career and playoffs are also included. The right side of the card has a photo and the card number. A Precision Cut parallel set was also made for each card in the regular set; these cards (with a different cut than the hobby version) were seeded one per every pack. Instead of the Holoviews found in the hobby product, SP Championship Series contains two insert sets utilizing Absolute Art technology - Playoff Heroes and Future Playoff Heroes. Both of these sets also have a Precision Cut parallel set for it.

		MT
Complete Set (135):		35.00
Common Player:		.10
Minor Stars:		.20
Comp. Die Cut Set (135):		65.00
Die Cut Cards:		1x-2x
Pack (6):		2.00
Wax Box (44):		75.00
1	Mookie Blaylock	.10
2	Dominique Wilkins	.10
3	Alonzo Mourning	.25
4	Michael Jordan	7.00
5	Mark Price	.10
6	Jamal Mashburn	.30
7	Dikembe Mutombo	.20
8	Grant Hill	2.00
9	Latrell Sprewell	.20
10	Hakeem Olajuwon	.50
11	Reggie Miller	.30
12	Loy Vaught	.10
13	Nick Van Exel	.40
14	Glen Rice	.10
15	Glenn Robinson	.50
16	Isaiah Rider	.20
17	Kenny Anderson	.10
18	Patrick Ewing	.20
19	Shaquille O'Neal	1.00
20	Dana Barros	.10
21	Charles Barkley	.30
22	Cliff Robinson	.10
23	Mitch Richmond	.10
24	David Robinson	.30
25	Shawn Kemp	.30
26	Karl Malone	.20
27	Chris Webber	.20
28	Stacey Augmon	.10
29	Mookie Blaylock	.10
30	Grant Long	.10
31	Steve Smith	.10
32	Dee Brown	.10
33	*Eric Montross*	.30
34	Dino Radja	.10
35	Dominique Wilkins	.20
36	Muggsy Bogues	.10
37	Scott Burrell	.10
38	Larry Johnson	.50
39	Alonzo Mourning	.50
40	B.J. Armstrong	.10
41	Michael Jordan	7.00
42	Toni Kukoc	.20
43	Scottie Pippen	1.00
44	Tyrone Hill	.10
45	Chris Mills	.10
46	Mark Price	.10
47	John Williams	.10
48	Jim Jackson	.40
49	*Jason Kidd*	3.00
50	Jamal Mashburn	.40
51	Roy Tarpley	.10
52	Mahmoud Abdul-Rauf	.10
53	Dikembe Mutombo	.20
54	Rodney Rogers	.10
55	Bryant Stith	.10
56	Joe Dumars	.10
57	*Grant Hill*	5.00
58	Lindsey Hunter	.10
59	Terry Mills	.10
60	Tim Hardaway	.10
61	*Donyell Marshall*	.25
62	Chris Mullin	.10
63	Latrell Sprewell	.30
64	Sam Cassell	.10
65	Clyde Drexler	.50
66	Vernon Maxwell	.10
67	Hakeem Olajuwon	1.00
68	Dale Davis	.10
69	Mark Jackson	.10
70	Reggie Miller	.40
71	Rik Smits	.20
72	Terry Dehere	.10
73	*Lamond Murray*	.30
74	Pooh Richardson	.10
75	Loy Vaught	.10
76	Cedric Ceballos	.25
77	Vlade Divac	.10
78	*Eddie Jones*	3.00
79	Nick Van Exel	.60
80	Bimbo Coles	.10
81	Billy Owens	.10
82	Glen Rice	.20
83	Kevin Willis	.10
84	Vin Baker	.40
85	Marty Conlon	.10
86	Eric Murdock	.10
87	*Glenn Robinson*	3.00
88	Tom Gugliotta	.10
89	Christian Laettner	.10
90	Isaiah Rider	.20
91	Doug West	.10
92	Kenny Anderson	.10
93	Benoit Benjamin	.10
94	Derrick Coleman	.10
95	Armon Gilliam	.10
96	Patrick Ewing	.30
97	Derek Harper	.10
98	Charles Oakley	.10
99	John Starks	.10
100	Nick Anderson	.10
101	Horace Grant	.20
102	Anfernee Hardaway	3.00
103	Shaquille O'Neal	3.00
104	Dana Barros	.10
105	Shawn Bradley	.20
106	Clarence Weatherspoon	.10
107	*Sharone Wright*	.40
108	Charles Barkley	.50
109	Kevin Johnson	.10
110	Dan Majerle	.10
111	*Wesley Person*	.40
112	Terry Porter	.10
113	Cliff Robinson	.10
114	Rod Strickland	.10
115	Buck Williams	.10
116	*Brian Grant*	1.00
117	Mitch Richmond	.20
118	Spud Webb	.10
119	Walt Williams	.10
120	Vinny Del Negro	.10
121	Sean Elliott	.10
122	David Robinson	.75
123	Dennis Rodman	1.00
124	Kendall Gill	.10
125	Shawn Kemp	.50
126	Gary Payton	.25
127	Detlef Schrempf	.10
128	David Benoit	.10
129	Jeff Hornacek	.10
130	Karl Malone	.40
131	John Stockton	.40
132	Rex Chapman	.10
133	Calbert Cheaney	.10
134	*Juwan Howard*	2.00
135	Chris Webber	.40

1994-95 SP Championship Die-Cuts

Inserted one per pack, the 135-card set is a parallel to the base set. The card backs feature a silver hologram.

	MT
Complete Set (135):	100.00
Common Card:	.40
Minor Stars:	.75
Unlisted Stars:	1x-3x
Die-Cuts:	3x

1994-95 SP Championship Future Playoff Heroes

These 1994-95 Upper Deck SP Championship Series inserts feature 10 rising stars who figure to be playoff heroes in the future. The cards were seeded one per every 20 packs. Each card front has a color action photo on the left, flanked by a white panel on the right which has a brand logo, player's name and insert set logo in it. The back has a photo and brief player profile on the left, with a card number in the upper left corner (using an "F" prefix). Along the right side is a panel which includes biographical and statistical information and a recap of the player's playoff totals. A parallel Precision Cut set was also made for these cards; they were seeded one per every 300 packs.

		MT
Complete Set (10):		60.00
Common Player:		2.00
Complete Die Cut Set (10):		300.00
Die Cuts:		3x-6x
1	Brian Grant	4.00
2	Anfernee Hardaway	15.00
3	Grant Hill	15.00
4	Eddie Jones	10.00
5	Jamal Mashburn	3.00
6	Shaquille O'Neal	10.00
7	Isaiah Rider	2.00
8	Glenn Robinson	6.00
9	Latrell Sprewell	3.00
10	Chris Webber	5.00

1994-95 SP Championship Future Playoff Heroes Die-Cut

This 10-card set paralleled the Future Playoff Heroes insert in SP Championship, but featured a unique perimeter die-cut and was inserted one per 300 packs.

	MT
Die-Cut Cards:	3x-6x

1994-95 SP Championship Playoff Heroes

These 1994-95 Upper Deck SP Championship Series inserts feature 10 of the all-time greatest playoff performers. The cards were seeded one per every 15 packs. Each card front has a color action photo on the left, flanked by a white panel on the right which has a brand logo, player's name and insert set logo in it. The back has a photo and brief player profile on the left, with a card number in the upper left corner (using a "P" prefix). Along the right side of the card is a panel which includes biographical and statistical information and a recap of the player's playoff totals. A parallel Precision Cut set was also made for these cards; they were seeded one per every 225 packs.

		MT
Complete Set (10):		50.00
Common Player:		1.00
Complete Die Cut Set (10):		250.00
Die Cuts:		2x-5x
1	Charles Barkley	5.00
2	Michael Jordan	30.00
3	Shawn Kemp	4.00
4	Moses Malone	1.00
5	Reggie Miller	4.00
6	Alonzo Mourning	4.00
7	Dikembe Mutombo	1.00
8	Hakeem Olajuwon	7.00
9	Robert Parish	1.00
10	John Stockton	3.00

1994-95 SP Championship Playoff Heroes Die-Cuts

This 10-card insert paralleled the Playoff Heroes insert found in SP Championship, but featured a unique perimeter die-cut and was inserted one per 225 packs.

	MT
Die-Cut Cards:	2x-5x

1995-96 SP

Upper Deck's hobby exclusive SP basketball brand sports the new design which was also used for hockey, baseball, racing and football. The 167-card set includes 20 Premier Prospect cards and six different insert cards. Each regular card has a color action photo on it, framed by a gold foil border. A small black-and-white photo, also framed by gold, is on the right side, with the player's position underneath. The SP logo is stamped in gold in the lower left corner. The player's name is along the top of the card; his team name runs along the bottom. The metallic back has a card number in the upper left corner, with the player's name in the middle. An action photo is in the center, flanked on the left by a brief player profile. Underneath are biographical and statistical information. The six insert sets are: Holoview, Holoview Die-Cuts, NBA All-Stars (gold and silver versions), a Hakeem Olajuwon commemorative card and the continuing series of cards from the Michael Jordan Collection.

		MT
Complete Set (167):		35.00
Common Player:		.15
Minor Stars:		.30
Pack (6):		2.50
Wax Box (32):		70.00
1	Stacey Augmon	.15
2	Mookie Blaylock	.15
3	Andrew Lang	.15
4	Steve Smith	.15
5	Spud Webb	.15
6	Dana Barros	.15
7	Dee Brown	.15
8	Todd Day	.15
9	Rick Fox	.15
10	Eric Montross	.15
11	Dino Radja	.15
12	Kenny Anderson	.15
13	Scott Burrell	.15
14	Dell Curry	.15
15	Matt Geiger	.15
16	Larry Johnson	.30
17	Glen Rice	.15
18	Steve Kerr	.15
19	Toni Kukoc	.15
20	Luc Longley	.15
21	Scottie Pippen	1.00
22	Dennis Rodman	4.00
23	Michael Jordan	6.00
24	Terrell Brandon	.15
25	Michael Cage	.15
26	Danny Ferry	.15
27	Chris Mills	.15
28	Bobby Phills	.15
29	Tony Dumas	.15
30	Jim Jackson	.30
31	Popeye Jones	.15
32	Jason Kidd	1.00
33	Jamal Mashburn	.30
34	Mahmoud Abdul-Rauf	.15
35	LaPhonso Ellis	.15
36	Dikembe Mutombo	.30
37	Jalen Rose	.15
38	Bryant Stith	.15
39	Joe Dumars	.30
40	Grant Hill	1.50
41	Lindsey Hunter	.15
42	Allan Houston	.15
43	Otis Thorpe	.15
44	B.J. Armstrong	.15
45	Tim Hardaway	.15
46	Chris Mullin	.15
47	Latrell Sprewell	.30
48	Rony Seikaly	.15
49	Sam Cassell	.15
50	Clyde Drexler	.75
51	Robert Horry	.15
52	Hakeem Olajuwon	1.00
53	Kenny Smith	.15
54	Dale Davis	.15
55	Derrick McKey	.15
56	Reggie Miller	.75
57	Ricky Pierce	.15
58	Rik Smits	.15
59	Lamond Murray	.15
60	Rodney Rogers	.15
61	Malik Sealy	.15
62	Loy Vaught	.15
63	Brian Williams	.15
64	Elden Campbell	.15
65	Cedric Ceballos	.30
66	Magic Johnson	1.00
67	Eddie Jones	.30
68	Nick Van Exel	.30
69	Bimbo Coles	.15
70	Alonzo Mourning	.30
71	Billy Owens	.15
72	Kevin Willis	.15
73	Vin Baker	.30
74	Benoit Benjamin	.15
75	Sherman Douglas	.15
76	Lee Mayberry	.15
77	Glenn Robinson	.75
78	Tom Gugliotta	.15
79	Christian Laettner	.15
80	Sam Mitchell	.15
81	Terry Porter	.15
82	Isaiah Rider	.30
83	Shawn Bradley	.30
84	P.J. Brown	.15
85	Kendall Gill	.15
86	Armon Gilliam	.15
87	Jayson Williams	.15
88	Patrick Ewing	.50
89	Derek Harper	.15
90	Anthony Mason	.15
91	Charles Oakley	.15
92	John Starks	.15
93	Nick Anderson	.15
94	Horace Grant	.30
95	Anfernee Hardaway	2.50
96	Shaquille O'Neal	2.00
97	Dennis Scott	.15
98	Derrick Coleman	.15
99	Vernon Maxwell	.15
100	Trevor Ruffin	.15
101	Clarence Weatherspoon	.15
102	Sharone Wright	.15
103	Charles Barkley	.50
104	A.C. Green	.15
105	Kevin Johnson	.30
106	Wesley Person	.15
107	John Williams	.15
108	Chris Dudley	.15
109	Harvey Grant	.15
110	Aaron McKie	.15
111	Clifford Robinson	.15
112	Rod Strickland	.15
113	Brian Grant	.15
114	Sarunas Marciulionis	.15
115	Olden Polynice	.15
116	Mitch Richmond	.30
117	Walt Williams	.15
118	Vinny Del Negro	.15
119	Sean Elliott	.15
120	Avery Johnson	.15
121	Chuck Person	.15
122	David Robinson	.75
123	Hersey Hawkins	.15
124	Shawn Kemp	.50
125	Gary Payton	.40
126	Sam Perkins	.15
127	Detlef Schrempf	.15
128	Oliver Miller	.15
129	Tracy Murray	.15
130	Ed Pinckney	.15
131	Alvin Robertson	.15
132	Zan Tabak	.15
133	Jeff Hornacek	.15
134	Adam Keefe	.15
135	Karl Malone	.60
136	Chris Morris	.15
137	John Stockton	.60
138	Greg Anthony	.15
139	Blue Edwards	.15
140	Kenny Gattison	.15
141	Chris King	.15
142	Byron Scott	.15
143	Calbert Cheaney	.15
144	Juwan Howard	.75
145	Gheorghe Muresan	.15
146	Robert Pack	.15
147	Chris Webber	.30
148	*Alan Henderson*	.30
149	*Eric Williams*	.30
150	*George Zidek*	.30
151	*Bob Sura*	.30
152	*Antonio McDyess*	8.00
153	*Theo Ratliff*	1.50
154	*Joe Smith*	2.00
155	*Brent Barry*	.75
156	*Sasha Danilovic*	.30
157	*Kurt Thomas*	.30
158	*Shawn Respert*	.30
159	*Kevin Garnett*	30.00
160	*Ed O'Bannon*	.30
161	*Jerry Stackhouse*	10.00
162	*Michael Finley*	8.00
163	*Arvydas Sabonis*	1.00
164	*Cory Alexander*	.15
165	*Damon Stoudamire*	2.50
166	*Bryant Reeves*	1.00
167	*Rasheed Wallace*	8.00
C1	Hakeem Olajuwon Comm.	20.00

1995-96 SP All-Stars

These 1995-96 Upper Deck SP insert cards come in two versions - gold and silver. Each has 30 cards and features a double die-cut design printed on silver paper stock. The set consists of those athletes chosen for the 1996 NBA All-Star Game, plus six future NBA All-Stars. Silver versions are seeded one per every five packs; gold versions are seeded one per every 61 packs. The card back is numbered using an "AS" prefix. It includes a photo of the player, a brief player profile and an All-Star Game logo from San Antonio.

		MT
Complete Set (30):		75.00
Common Player:		1.00
Minor Stars:		2.00
Comp. Gold Set (30):		650.00
Gold Cards:		3x-6x
1	Anfernee Hardaway	12.00
2	Michael Jordan	25.00
3	Grant Hill	7.00
4	Scottie Pippen	5.00
5	Shaquille O'Neal	7.00
6	Vin Baker	2.00
7	Terrell Brandon	1.00
8	Patrick Ewing	2.00
9	Juwan Howard	3.00
10	Reggie Miller	2.00
11	Alonzo Mourning	2.00
12	Glen Rice	1.00
13	Clyde Drexler	2.00
14	Jason Kidd	3.00
15	Charles Barkley	3.00
16	Shawn Kemp	2.00
17	Hakeem Olajuwon	3.00
18	Sean Elliott	1.00
19	Karl Malone	2.00
20	Dikembe Mutombo	1.00
21	Gary Payton	1.50
22	Mitch Richmond	1.50
23	David Robinson	3.00
24	John Stockton	2.00
25	Jerry Stackhouse	3.00
26	Damon Stoudamire	4.00
27	Rasheed Wallace	2.00
28	Kevin Garnett	10.00
29	Antonio McDyess	5.00
30	Joe Smith	4.00

1995-96 SP All-Stars Gold

This 30-card insert parallelled the All-Stars insert found in SP, but featured gold foil stamping on the top and bottom versus silver from the regular versions. Gold versions were seeded one per 61 packs.

	MT
Gold Cards:	3x-6x

1995-96 SP Holoviews

This 40-card lineup includes at least one player from every NBA team. Each card front has a color action shot on the front, with four head shots of the player in the hologram background. The SP logo is stamped in gold at the top; the player's name and team city are stamped in gold along the bottom. The card back has an action photo toward the top, with "Premium Collection" stamped in foil in a panel along the bottom of the card. A card number is in the center in an oval with a "PC" prefix, above a brief player profile. A team logo is also on the back. Cards were seeded one per seven packs of 1995-96 Upper Deck SP Basketball.

		MT
Complete Set (40):		160.00
Common Player:		1.50
Die-Cuts:		2x-4x
1	Mookie Blaylock	1.50
2	Eric Williams	4.00
3	Larry Johnson	4.00
4	George Zidek	1.50
5	Michael Jordan	40.00
6	Bob Sura	4.00
7	Jason Kidd	5.00
8	Cherokee Parks	1.50
9	Antonio McDyess	10.00
10	Grant Hill	15.00
11	Theo Ratliff	4.00
12	Joe Smith	8.00
13	Latrell Sprewell	4.00
14	Hakeem Olajuwon	6.00
15	Travis Best	1.50
16	Brent Barry	4.00
17	Nick Van Exel	4.00
18	Kurt Thomas	1.50
19	Shawn Respert	1.50
20	Glenn Robinson	4.00
21	Christian Laettner	1.50
22	Ed O'Bannon	1.50
23	Patrick Ewing	4.00
24	Anfernee Hardaway	20.00
25	Shaquille O'Neal	14.00
26	Jerry Stackhouse	5.00
27	Mario Bennett	1.50
28	Michael Finley	6.00
29	Randolph Childress	1.50
30	Brian Grant	3.00
31	Mitch Richmond	1.50
32	Cory Alexander	1.50
33	David Robinson	6.00
34	Sherell Ford	1.50
35	Shawn Kemp	4.00
36	Damon Stoudamire	8.00
37	Greg Ostertag	1.50
38	Bryant Reeves	3.00
39	Juwan Howard	5.00
40	Rasheed Wallace	3.00

1995-96 SP Jordan Collection

Four more cards in Upper Deck's continuing series of cards in the Michael Jordan Collection are in Upper Deck's 1995-96 SP Basketball set. The cards, numbered JC17-JC20, were seeded one per every 29 packs.

		MT
Complete Set (8):		120.00
Complete SP Set (4):		60.00
Complete Champ. Set (4):		60.00
Common SP (JC17-JC20):		15.00
Com.Champ. (JC21-JC24):		15.00
JC17	Michael Jordan (1988 NBA Most Valuable Player)	15.00
JC18	Michael Jordan (1991 NBA Most Valuable Player)	15.00
JC19	Michael Jordan (1992 NBA Most Valuable Player)	15.00
JC20	Michael Jordan (The MVP Seasons)	15.00
JC21	Michael Jordan (Michael's Magic Year)	15.00
JC22	Michael Jordan (Back-to-Back NBA Championships)	15.00
JC23	Michael Jordan (Third Consecutive NBA Championship)	15.00
JC24	Michael Jordan (The Championship Seasons)	15.00

1995-96 SP Championship

Upper Deck's 1995-96 SP Championship basketball set focuses on key players for each team that was vying for a playoff spot. The product was exclusive to retail outlets. Insert sets include the Championship Shots, which come in silver and gold versions, and Champions of the Court, which come in regular and die-cut versions.

		MT
Complete Set (146):		40.00
Common Player:		.10
Minor Stars:		.20
Pack (6):		2.00
Wax Box (42):		70.00
1	Stacey Augmon	.10
2	Mookie Blaylock	.10
3	*Alan Henderson*	.40
4	Steve Smith	.10
5	Dana Barros	.10
6	Dee Brown	.10
7	Eric Montross	.10
8	Dino Radja	.10
9	*Eric Williams*	.40
10	Kenny Anderson	.10
11	Larry Johnson	.40
12	Glen Rice	.10
13	*George Zidek*	.20
14	Toni Kukoc	.10
15	Scottie Pippen	1.00
16	Dennis Rodman	2.00
17	Michael Jordan	5.00
18	Terrell Brandon	.10
19	Danny Ferry	.10
20	Chris Mills	.10
21	Bobby Phills	.10
22	Jim Jackson	.25
23	Popeye Jones	.10
24	Jason Kidd	1.00
25	Jamal Mashburn	.30
26	Mahmoud Abdul-Rauf	.10
27	Dale Ellis	.10
28	*Antonio McDyess*	3.00
29	Dikembe Mutombo	.10
30	Joe Dumars	.20
31	Grant Hill	1.50
32	Allan Houston	.10
33	Otis Thorpe	.10
34	Tim Hardaway	.10
35	Chris Mullin	.10
36	Latrell Sprewell	.20
37	*Joe Smith*	2.00
38	Sam Cassell	.10
39	Clyde Drexler	.40
40	Robert Horry	.10
41	Hakeem Olajuwon	1.00
42	Dale Davis	.10
43	Derrick McKey	.10
44	Reggie Miller	.40
45	Rik Smits	.10
46	*Brent Barry*	.75
47	Lamond Murray	.10
48	Loy Vaught	.10
49	Brian Williams	.10
50	Cedric Ceballos	.20
51	Magic Johnson	1.50
52	Eddie Jones	.30
53	Nick Van Exel	.30
54	*Sasha Danilovic*	.10
55	Alonzo Mourning	.30
56	Billy Owens	.10
57	Kevin Willis	.10
58	Vin Baker	.30
59	Sherman Douglas	.10
60	Lee Mayberry	.10
61	Glenn Robinson	.60
62	*Kevin Garnett*	12.00
63	Tom Gugliotta	.10
64	Christian Laettner	.10
65	Isaiah Rider	.10
66	Chris Childs	.20
67	Kendall Gill	.10
68	Armon Gilliam	.10
69	*Ed O'Bannon*	.20
70	Patrick Ewing	.30
71	Derek Harper	.10
72	Charles Oakley	.10
73	John Starks	.10
74	Horace Grant	.10
75	Anfernee Hardaway	2.50
76	Shaquille O'Neal	2.00
77	Dennis Scott	.10

78	Derrick Coleman	.10
79	Trevor Ruffin	.10
80	*Jerry Stackhouse*	4.00
81	Clarence Weatherspoon	.10
82	Charles Barkley	.60
83	*Michael Finley*	3.00
84	Kevin Johnson	.10
85	Danny Manning	.10
86	Randolph Childress	.10
87	Clifford Robinson	.20
88	*Arvydas Sabonis*	1.00
89	Rod Strickland	.10
90	*Tyus Edney*	.20
91	Brian Grant	.50
92	Mitch Richmond	.20
93	Walt Williams	.10
94	Sean Elliott	.10
95	Avery Johnson	.10
96	Chuck Person	.10
97	David Robinson	.75
98	Shawn Kemp	.50
99	Gary Payton	.25
100	Sam Perkins	.10
101	Detlef Schrempf	.10
102	Ed Pinckney	.10
103	Tracy Murray	.10
104	Alvin Robertson	.10
105	*Damon Stoudamire*	2.00
106	Jeff Hornacek	.10
107	Karl Malone	.30
108	Chris Morris	.10
109	John Stockton	.30
110	Greg Anthony	.10
111	Blue Edwards	.10
112	*Bryant Reeves*	.50
113	Byron Scott	.10
114	Juwan Howard	.60
115	Gheorghe Muresan	.20
116	*Rasheed Wallace*	3.00
117	Chris Webber	.25
118	Mookie Blaylock (Race for the Playoffs)	.10
119	Dana Barros (Race for the Playoffs)	.10
120	Larry Johnson (Race for the Playoffs)	.20
121	Michael Jordan RP (Race for the Playoffs)	2.00
122	Terrell Brandon (Race for the Playoffs)	.10
123	Jason Kidd RP (Race for the Playoffs)	.50
124	Mahmoud Abdul-Rauf (Race for the Playoffs)	.10
125	Grant Hill RP (Race for the Playoffs)	.75
126	Latrell Sprewell (Race for the Playoffs)	.10
127	Hakeem Olajuwon RP (Race for the Playoffs)	.50
128	Reggie Miller (Race for the Playoffs)	.20
129	Loy Vaught (Race for the Playoffs)	.10
130	Magic Johnson RP (Race for the Playoffs)	.75
131	Alonzo Mourning (Race for the Playoffs)	.10
132	Vin Baker (Race for the Playoffs)	.10
133	Tom Gugliotta (Race for the Playoffs)	.10
134	Ed O'Bannon RP (Race for the Playoffs)	.25
135	Patrick Ewing (Race for the Playoffs)	.10
136	Anfernee Hardaway RP (Race for the Playoffs)	1.25
137	Jerry Stackhouse RP (Race for the Playoffs)	1.50
138	Charles Barkley RP (Race for the Playoffs)	.30
139	Clifford Robinson (Race for the Playoffs)	.10
140	Mitch Richmond (Race for the Playoffs)	.10
141	David Robinson RP (Race for the Playoffs)	.30
142	Shawn Kemp RP (Race for the Playoffs)	.30
143	Damon Stoudamire RP (Race for the Playoffs)	2.00
144	John Stockton (Race for the Playoffs)	.10
145	Bryant Reeves RP (Race for the Playoffs)	.50
146	Juwan Howard RP (Race for the Playoffs)	.30

1995-96 SP Championship Champions of the Court

These cards showcase a top star from each NBA team, plus Michael Jordan. All 30 cards are horizontally formatted with one action photo on the left side and the same action photo in black-and-white on the right. The main feature on the card is a cell photo with a headshot and a protective film covering the cell photo on the front. Cards, printed on transparent chromium material, are seeded one per every six packs of 1995-96 Upper Deck SP Championship basketball and are numbered using a "C" prefix.

		MT
Complete Set (30):		120.00
Common Player:		1.25
Die-Cuts:		2x-4x
1	Steve Smith	1.25
2	Dino Radja	1.25
3	Glen Rice	1.25
4	Scottie Pippen	6.00
5	Terrell Brandon	1.25
6	Jason Kidd	5.00
7	Dikembe Mutombo	1.25
8	Grant Hill	12.00
9	Joe Smith	6.00
10	Hakeem Olajuwon	5.00
11	Reggie Miller	2.00
12	Loy Vaught	1.25
13	Magic Johnson	9.00
14	Alonzo Mourning	2.50
15	Vin Baker	2.50
16	Kevin Garnett	15.00
17	Ed O'Bannon	1.25
18	Patrick Ewing	2.50
19	Shaquille O'Neal	10.00
20	Jerry Stackhouse	5.00
21	Charles Barkley	4.00
22	Clifford Robinson	1.25
23	Mitch Richmond	1.25
24	David Robinson	4.00
25	Shawn Kemp	4.00
26	Damon Stoudamire	7.00
27	John Stockton	2.50
28	Bryant Reeves	3.00
29	Juwan Howard	4.00
30	Michael Jordan	30.00

1995-96 SP Championship Jordan Collection

This four-card set highlights Michael Jordan's four NBA championships at the time. Cards were inserted at a rate of one per 29 packs. Cards are numbered with a "JC" prefix.

		MT
Complete Set (4):		40.00
Common Player:		10.00
17	Michael Jordan	10.00
18	Michael Jordan	10.00
19	Michael Jordan	10.00
20	Michael Jordan	10.00

1995-96 SP Championship Shots

Championship Shots is a 20-card die-cut insert set featuring close-up shots of top NBA stars. Silver versions are seeded one per every three packs of 1995-96 Upper Deck SP Championship. Gold versions are seeded one per every 62 packs.

		MT
Complete Set (20):		40.00
Common Player:		.50
Comp. Gold Set (20):		325.00
Gold Cards:		3x-6x
1	Antonio McDyess	2.50
2	Nick Van Exel	1.00
3	Michael Finley	3.50
4	Anfernee Hardaway	6.00
5	Latrell Sprewell	.50
6	Brian Grant	.50
7	Juwan Howard	2.00
8	Ed O'Bannon	.50
9	Kevin Garnett	6.00
10	Charles Barkley	1.50
11	Joe Smith	3.00
12	Patrick Ewing	1.00
13	Brent Barry	.75
14	Dennis Rodman	5.00
15	Jerry Stackhouse	5.00
16	Michael Jordan	12.00
17	Jalen Rose	.50
18	Jamal Mashburn	.75
19	Theo Ratliff	.50
20	Shaquille O'Neal	4.50

1995-96 SP Championship Shots Gold

This insert parallelled the Championship Shots insert found in SP Championship, but featured gold foil stamping instead of silver. The 20-card insert was seeded one per 62 packs.

	MT
Gold Cards:	3x-6x

1996 SPx

Upper Deck debuted its SPx brand in basketball with this 50-card set. The regular-issue set includes 50 of the top players in the NBA along with a selection of rookies from the 1995-96 season. Each card features a perimeter die-cut design with holoviews and is printed on 32-point stock. Each card in the regular-issue set is also reprinted as part of a parallel Gold version set. These cards are seeded one per every seven packs. Only hobby locations were slated to carry SPx basketball product. Insert sets include a Michael Jordan Record Breaker card, an Anfernee Hardaway Tribute card, Holoview Heroes and Autograph Trade Cards of Jordan and Hardaway (seeded one per every 1,296 packs).

		MT
Complete Set (50):		100.00
Common Player:		1.00
Minor Stars:		2.00
Comp. Gold Set (50):		350.00
Gold Cards:		2x-4x
Pack (1):		3.00
Wax Box (36):		100.00
1	Stacey Augmon	1.00
2	Mookie Blaylock	1.00
3	Eric Montross	1.00
4	Eric Williams	2.00
5	Larry Johnson	2.00
6	George Zidek	1.00
7	Jason Caffey	1.00
8	Michael Jordan	20.00
9	Chris Mills	1.00
10	Bob Sura	1.00
11	Jason Kidd	3.00
12	Jamal Mashburn	2.00
13	Antonio McDyess	5.00
14	Jalen Rose	1.00
15	Grant Hill	10.00
16	Theo Ratliff	3.00
17	Joe Smith	4.00
18	Latrell Sprewell	2.00
19	Hakeem Olajuwon	5.00
20	Reggie Miller	2.00
21	Rik Smits	1.00
22	Brent Barry	2.00
23	Lamond Murray	1.00
24	Magic Johnson	6.00
25	Eddie Jones	3.00
26	Nick Van Exel	2.00
27	Alonzo Mourning	2.00
28	Kurt Thomas	1.00
29	Vin Baker	2.00
30	Glenn Robinson	2.00
31	Kevin Garnett	10.00
32	Ed O'Bannon	2.00
33	Patrick Ewing	2.00
34	Anfernee Hardaway	10.00
35	Shaquille O'Neal	10.00
36	Jerry Stackhouse	4.00
37	Charles Barkley	3.00
38	Michael Finley	2.00
39	Randolph Childress	1.00
40	Gary Trent	1.00
41	Brian Grant	1.00
42	Mitch Richmond	1.00
43	David Robinson	3.00
44	Shawn Kemp	3.00
45	Gary Payton	2.00
46	Damon Stoudamire	5.00
47	Karl Malone	2.00
48	John Stockton	2.00
49	Bryant Reeves	2.00
50	Rasheed Wallace	2.00

1996 SPx Gold

Gold versions of all 50 SPx cards were produced featuring the gold foil around the border instead of the silver on the base cards. One Gold card was found every seven packs.

	MT
Gold Cards:	2x-4x

1996 SPx Holoview Heroes

This insert set utilizes a special Holoview technology to showcase 10 of the top players in the NBA. The cards were seeded one per every 24 packs of 1996-97 Upper Deck SPx product. Cards are numbered with a "H" prefix.

		MT
Complete Set (10):		140.00
Common Player:		7.00
1	Michael Jordan	60.00
2	Jason Kidd	7.00
3	Grant Hill	20.00
4	Joe Smith	10.00
5	Magic Johnson	15.00
6	Antonio McDyess	7.00
7	Anfernee Hardaway	30.00
8	Jerry Stackhouse	10.00
9	Damon Stoudamire	15.00
10	Shaquille O'Neal	25.00

1996 SPx Tribute Card

This tribute card to Anfernee Hardaway was seeded one per every 24 packs of 1996-97 Upper Deck SPx product. The card is numbered using a "T" prefix.

		MT
Hardaway Autograph:		300.00
1	Anfernee Hardaway	15.00

1996 SPx Record Breaker Card

This 1996-97 Upper Deck SPx card commemorates Michael Jordan's record-tying 1995-96 season. This card, seeded one per every 75 packs numbered using an "R" prefix, honors Jordan's seven straight scoring titles (tied with Wilt Chamberlain).

		MT
Jordan Autograph:		3500.
1	Michael Jordan	25.00

1996-97 SP

The 146-card, standard-size set was released in May of 1997 in eight-card packs retailing for $3.99 each. The base set includes the 20-card Premier Prospects subset with the remaining cards consisting of an average of five players from each team. Inserts in the set are Premium Collection Holoview, Inside-Info., NBA Game Film and SPx Force (with parallel autographed versions). The basic SP card has the set logo in the upper left corner and rainbow foil in a lower quadrant. The backs feature an action shot with a headshot inset, as well as bio and stat information.

		MT
Complete Set (146):		50.00
Common Player:		.15
Minor Stars:		.30
Pack (8):		4.50
Wax Box (30):		145.00
1	Mookie Blaylock	.15
2	Christian Laettner	.30
3	Dikembe Mutombo	.30
4	Steve Smith	.30
5	Dana Barros	.15
6	Rick Fox	.15
7	Dino Radja	.15
8	Eric Williams	.15
9	Dell Curry	.15
10	Vlade Divac	.30
11	Anthony Mason	.15
12	Glen Rice	.30
13	Scottie Pippen	1.25
14	Toni Kukoc	.30
15	Luc Longley	.15
16	Michael Jordan	5.00
17	Dennis Rodman	1.50
18	Terrell Brandon	.30
19	Tyrone Hill	.15
20	Bobby Phills	.15
21	Bob Sura	.15
22	Michael Finley	.30
23	A.C. Green	.15
24	Sam Cassell	.15
25	Derek Harper	.15
26	Dale Ellis	.15
27	LaPhonso Ellis	.15
28	Ervin Johnson	.15
29	Antonio McDyess	.50
30	Bryant Stith	.15
31	Joe Dumars	.30
32	Grant Hill	2.50
33	Lindsey Hunter	.15
34	Otis Thorpe	.15
35	Chris Mullin	.30
36	Mark Price	.15
37	Joe Smith	.50
38	Latrell Sprewell	.30
39	Charles Barkley	.50
40	Clyde Drexler	.50
41	Mario Elie	.15
42	Hakeem Olajuwon	.75
43	Travis Best	.15
44	Dale Davis	.15
45	Reggie Miller	.30
46	Rik Smits	.15
47	Pooh Richardson	.15
48	Rodney Rogers	.15
49	Malik Sealy	.15
50	Loy Vaught	.15
51	Elden Campbell	.15
52	Robert Horry	.15
53	Eddie Jones	.75
54	Shaquille O'Neal	1.75
55	Nick Van Exel	.30
56	Sasha Danilovic	.15
57	Tim Hardaway	.50
58	Dan Majerle	.15
59	Alonzo Mourning	.30
60	Vin Baker	.50
61	Sherman Douglas	.15
62	Armon Gilliam	.15
63	Glenn Robinson	.30
64	Kevin Garnett	2.50
65	Tom Gugliotta	.30
66	Terry Porter	.15
67	Doug West	.15
68	Shawn Bradley	.15
69	Kendall Gill	.15
70	Robert Pack	.15
71	Jayson Williams	.15
72	Chris Childs	.15
73	Patrick Ewing	.30
74	Allan Houston	.30
75	Larry Johnson	.30
76	John Starks	.30
77	Nick Anderson	.30
78	Horace Grant	.15
79	Anfernee Hardaway	1.75
80	Dennis Scott	.15
81	Derrick Coleman	.30
82	Mark Davis	.15
83	Jerry Stackhouse	.50
84	Clarence Weatherspoon	.15
85	Cedric Ceballos	.15
86	Kevin Johnson	.15
87	Jason Kidd	1.00
88	Danny Manning	.15
89	Wesley Person	.15
90	Kenny Anderson	.15
91	Isaiah Rider	.15
92	Clifford Robinson	.15
93	Arvydas Sabonis	.15
94	Rasheed Wallace	.15
95	Mahmoud Abdul-Rauf	.15
96	Brian Grant	.15
97	Olden Polynice	.15
98	Mitch Richmond	.30
99	Corliss Williamson	.15
100	Sean Elliott	.15
101	Avery Johnson	.15
102	David Robinson	.50
103	Dominique Wilkins	.15
104	Hersey Hawkins	.15
105	Jim McIlvaine	.15
106	Shawn Kemp	.50
107	Gary Payton	.50
108	Detlef Schrempf	.15
109	Doug Christie	.15
110	Popeye Jones	.15
111	Damon Stoudamire	.75
112	Walt Williams	.15
113	Jeff Hornacek	.15
114	Karl Malone	.50
115	Greg Ostertag	.15
116	Bryon Russell	.15
117	John Stockton	.30
118	Greg Anthony	.15
119	Blue Edwards	.15
120	Anthony Peeler	.15
121	Bryant Reeves	.15
122	Calbert Cheaney	.15
123	Juwan Howard	.50
124	Gheorghe Muresan	.15
125	Rod Strickland	.30
126	Chris Webber	.75
127	*Antoine Walker* (Premier Prospects)	4.00
128	*Tony Delk* (Premier Prospects)	.50
129	*Vitaly Potapenko* (Premier Prospects)	.50
130	*Samaki Walker* (Premier Prospects)	.50
131	*Todd Fuller* (Premier Prospects)	.25
132	*Erick Dampier* (Premier Prospects)	.50
133	*Lorenzen Wright* (Premier Prospects)	.25
134	*Kobe Bryant* (Premier Prospects)	30.00
135	*Derek Fisher* (Premier Prospects)	1.00
136	*Ray Allen* (Premier Prospects)	5.00
137	*Stephon Marbury* (Premier Prospects)	7.00
138	*Kerry Kittles* (Premier Prospects)	1.50
139	*Walter McCarty* (Premier Prospects)	.25
140	*John Wallace* (Premier Prospects)	.50
141	*Allen Iverson* (Premier Prospects)	12.00
142	*Steve Nash* (Premier Prospects)	.75
143	*Jermaine O'Neal* (Premier Prospects)	3.00
144	*Marcus Camby* (Premier Prospects)	2.00
145	*Shareef Abdur-Rahim* (Premier Prospects)	4.00
146	*Roy Rogers* (Premier Prospects)	.25

1996-97 SP Game Film

The 10-card insert set features actual slide photography and video film on the die-cut cards. Inserted every 120 packs, the cards feature two slides each with "NBA Game Film" printed in a lime green along the left border. Cards are numbered with a "GF" prefix.

		MT
Complete Set (10):		375.00
Common Player:		5.00
Minor Stars:		10.00
Inserted 1:120		
1	Michael Jordan	120.00
2	Kevin Garnett	60.00
3	Charles Barkley	15.00
4	Anfernee Hardaway	45.00
5	Shaquille O'Neal	45.00
6	Jim Jackson	5.00
7	Dennis Rodman	40.00
8	Alonzo Mourning	10.00
9	Grant Hill	60.00
10	Shawn Kemp	15.00

1996-97 SP Holoviews

Inserted every 10 packs, the 40-card Holoview set features Upper Deck's Holoview technology. The cards are numbered with the "PC" prefix with a Light F/X action shot featured on the front.

		MT
Complete Set (40):		200.00
Common Player:		1.00
Minor Stars:		2.00
Inserted 1:10		
1	Mookie Blaylock	1.00
2	Antoine Walker	8.00
3	Eric Williams	1.00
4	Tony Delk	2.00
5	Michael Jordan	35.00
6	Dennis Rodman	12.00
7	Vitaly Potapenko	2.00
8	Bob Sura	1.00
9	Jamal Mashburn	2.00
10	Antonio McDyess	4.00
11	Grant Hill	12.00
12	Joe Smith	4.00
13	Latrell Sprewell	2.00
14	Charles Barkley	4.00
15	Hakeem Olajuwon	6.00
16	Erick Dampier	2.00
17	Lorenzen Wright	1.00
18	Kobe Bryant	60.00
19	Shaquille O'Neal	12.00

20 Alonzo Mourning 2.00
21 Ray Allen 7.00
22 Kevin Garnett 18.00
23 Stephon Marbury 15.00
24 Kerry Kittles 5.00
25 Walter McCarty 1.00
26 John Wallace 2.00
27 Anfernee Hardaway 12.00
28 Allen Iverson 25.00
29 Jerry Stackhouse 4.00
30 Steve Nash 2.00
31 Jermaine O'Neal 2.00
32 Brian Grant 1.00
33 Mitch Richmond 2.00
34 David Robinson 4.00
35 Shawn Kemp 4.00
36 Marcus Camby 5.00
37 Damon Stoudamire 8.00
38 John Stockton 2.00
39 Shareef Abdur-Rahim 12.00
40 Juwan Howard 4.00

1996-97 SP Inside Info

The 17-card insert set, seeded in each box, features a mini pull-out card within the standard-size card. The card fronts feature a Light F/X action shot with the mini pull-out card also having Light F/X treatment. The cards are numbered with the "IN" prefix and a gold version was inserted every 720 packs.

MT
Complete Set (17): 230.00
Common Player: 2.00
Minor Stars: 4.00
1:Box
Gold Cards: 3x
1 Charles Barkley 7.00
2 Kevin Garnett 25.00
3 Anfernee Hardaway 15.00
4 Grant Hill 25.00
5 Allen Iverson 15.00
6 Jason Kidd 8.00
7 Shawn Kemp 5.00
8 Antonio McDyess 5.00
9 Dikembe Mutombo 2.00
10 Shaquille O'Neal 15.00
11 Hakeem Olajuwon 8.00
12 Dennis Rodman 15.00
13 Jerry Stackhouse 5.00
14 John Stockton 4.00
15 Damon Stoudamire 10.00
16 Chris Webber 10.00
17 Michael Jordan 25K 60.00

1996-97 SP Rookie Jumbos

MT
Complete Set (20): 50.00
Common Player: .50
1 Antoine Walker 3.00
2 Tony Delk 1.00
3 Vitaly Potapenko .50
4 Samaki Walker 1.00
5 Todd Fuller .50
6 Erick Dampier 1.00
7 Lorenzen Wright 1.00
8 Kobe Bryant 20.00
9 Derek Fisher 2.00
10 Ray Allen 5.00
11 Stephon Marbury 5.00
12 Kerry Kittles 1.00
13 Walter McCarty 1.00
14 John Wallace 1.00
15 Allen Iverson 10.00
16 Steve Nash 2.00
17 Jermaine O'Neal 4.00
18 Marcus Camby 3.00
19 Shareef Abdur-Rahim 4.00
20 Roy Rogers .50

1996-97 SP SPx Force

Each card in this insert set features top players in four different categories: Scoring, Rebounding, Playmakers, Defenders and All Around Talents. The cards are inserted every 360 packs. The die-cut horizontal cards feature four player images within a circular holoview image with highlight text featured on the back.

MT
Complete Set (5): 325.00
Common Player: 50.00
Inserted 1:360
F1 Scorers (Latrell Sprewell, Jerry Stackhouse, Mitch Richmond, Michael Jordan) 100.00
F2 Rebounders (Shawn Kemp, Charles Barkley, Dennis Rodman, Juwan Howard) 30.00
F3 Playmakers (Mookie Blaylock, Nick Van Exel, Stephon Marbury, Damon Stoudamire) 50.00
F4 Defenders (Marcus Camby, Erick Dampier, Anfernee Hardaway, Antonio McDyess) 50.00
F5 All-around talents (Anfernee Hardaway, Michael Jordan, Shawn Kemp, Damon Stoudamire) 75.00
F5A Michael Jordan Auto. 2500.
F5B Anfernee Hardaway Auto. 500.00
F5C Shawn Kemp Auto. 250.00
F5D Damon Stoudamire Auto. 200.00

1997 SPx

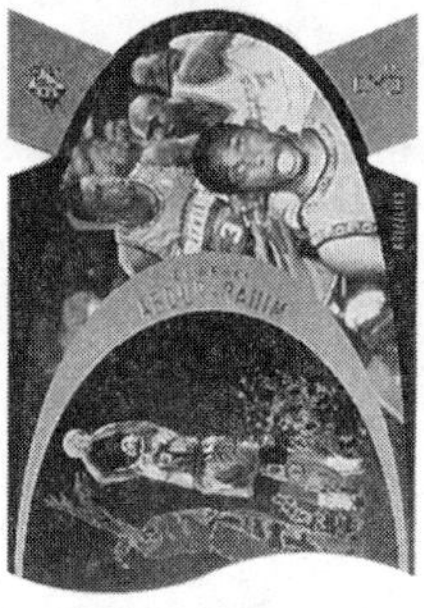

The 50-card set, released in June of 1997, features die-cut cards in the shape of an "x" along the horizontal right side. The cards have the team colors of the player featured with a holoview headshot of the player and a Light F/X action shot along the left side. The player's number and position are located in the lower right corner with the SPx logo in the upper right corner. The horizontal card backs contain a color shot in the right half with statistics and career highlights on the left. A gold parallel of each card was inserted every nine packs. Inserts to the set are Holoview Heroes, NBA PROmotion and autographed NBA PROmotion parallels.

MT
Complete Set (50): 110.00
Common Player: .75
Minor Stars: 1.50
Pack (1): 3.50
Wax Box (36): 95.00
1 Mookie Blaylock .75
2 Antoine Walker 4.00
3 Eric Williams .75
4 Tony Delk .75
5 Michael Jordan 16.00
6 Dennis Rodman 6.00
7 Vitaly Potapenko .75
8 Bob Sura .75
9 Jamal Mashburn .75
10 Samaki Walker .75
11 Antonio McDyess 1.50
12 Joe Dumars .75
13 Grant Hill 8.00
14 Joe Smith 2.50
15 Latrell Sprewell 1.50
16 Charles Barkley 2.00
17 Hakeem Olajuwon 3.00
18 Erick Dampier .75
19 Reggie Miller 1.50
20 Brent Barry .75
21 Lorenzen Wright .75
22 Kobe Bryant 20.00
23 Eddie Jones 3.00
24 Shaquille O'Neal 5.00
25 Alonzo Mourning 1.50
26 Kurt Thomas .75
27 Vin Baker 1.50
28 Glenn Robinson 1.50
29 Kevin Garnett 8.00
30 Stephon Marbury 8.00
31 Kerry Kittles 4.00
32 Patrick Ewing 1.50
33 John Wallace 2.00
34 Anfernee Hardaway 8.00
35 Allen Iverson 15.00
36 Jerry Stackhouse 2.50
37 Kevin Johnson 1.50
38 Steve Nash .75
39 Jermaine O'Neal 3.00
40 Mitch Richmond 1.50
41 David Robinson 2.00
42 Shawn Kemp 2.00
43 Gary Payton 2.00
44 Marcus Camby 6.00
45 Damon Stoudamire 4.00
46 Karl Malone 1.50
47 John Stockton 1.50
48 Shareef Abdur-Rahim 7.00
49 Bryant Reeves .75
50 Juwan Howard 1.50

1997 SPx Gold

Gold versions of all 50 cards in the SPx set were produced featuring gold foil around the border. One per nine packs contained a Gold version.

MT
Gold Cards: 2x-3x

1997 SPx Holoview Heroes

Inserted every 75 packs, the set features 20 of the top players in the league with a die-cut Holoview card. The left half of the vertical card features the Holoview action photo with the right side having a color action shot. "Holoview Heroes" is printed in a black stripe separating the two. The vertical backs have another color action shot with highlight text found on the left. The cards are numbered with the "H" prefix.

MT
Complete Set (20): 400.00
Common Player: 8.00
1 Michael Jordan 100.00
2 Grant Hill 50.00
3 Reggie Miller 8.00
4 Joe Smith 8.00
5 Kevin Garnett 50.00
6 Mitch Richmond 8.00
7 Allen Iverson 40.00
8 Patrick Ewing 8.00
9 Hakeem Olajuwon 15.00
10 David Robinson 12.00
11 Anfernee Hardaway 30.00
12 Juwan Howard 8.00
13 Gary Payton 12.00
14 Dennis Rodman 30.00
15 Shaquille O'Neal 30.00
16 Charles Barkley 12.00
17 Damon Stoudamire 15.00
18 Shawn Kemp 15.00
19 Glenn Robinson 8.00
20 John Stockton 8.00

1997 SPx ProMotion

The five-card insert set, seeded every 430 packs, features the same die-cut design as the base set with a double Holoview image of the player. The player's team name appears in the lower right corner with the player's number and position just to the left. Autographed versions of the cards were limited to 500 each.

MT
Complete Set (4): 300.00
Common Player: 20.00
1 Michael Jordan 150.00
2 Damon Stoudamire 20.00
3 Anfernee Hardaway 75.00
4 Shawn Kemp 30.00

1997 SPx ProMotion Autographs

This five-card set is a parallel of the PROmotion insert. Each of these cards was signed by the player depicted. Only 100 hand-numbered cards are available for each player.

MT
Complete Set (5): 3000.
Common Player: 100.00
Production 100 Sets
1 Michael Jordan 2500.
2 Exchange Card (Damon Stoudamire) 250.00
3 Exchange Card (Anfernee Hardaway) 425.00
4 Exchange Card (Shawn Kemp) 200.00
5 Exchange Card (Antonio McDyess) 100.00

1997-98 SP Authentic

A 176-card set that has 156 veterans and 20 cards of rising stars. Also included is six inserts, with redemption cards. The inserts include: NBA Profiles (three tiers), Sign of the Times, SP Buybacks, Premium Portraits and SP Authentics. The base cards have a color action photo on the front, with another on the back along with career statistics.

MT
Complete Set (176): 100.00
Common Player: .25
Minor Stars: .50
Pack (3): 12.00
Wax Box (18): 180.00
1 Steve Smith .25
2 Dikembe Mutombo .50
3 Christian Laettner .50
4 Mookie Blaylock .25
5 Alan Henderson .25
6 Antoine Walker 1.50
7 *Ron Mercer* 8.00
8 Walter McCarty .25
9 Kenny Anderson .25
10 Travis Knight .25
11 Dana Barros .25
12 Glen Rice .75
13 Vlade Divac .25
14 Dell Curry .25
15 David Wesley .25
16 Bobby Phills .25
17 Anthony Mason .25
18 Toni Kukoc .25
19 Dennis Rodman 2.00
20 Ron Harper .25
21 Steve Kerr .25
22 Scottie Pippen 1.50
23 Michael Jordan 6.00
24 Shawn Kemp 1.00
25 Wesley Person .25
26 *Derek Anderson* 4.00
27 Zydrunas Ilgauskas .50
28 *Brevin Knight* 4.00
29 Michael Finley .50
30 Shawn Bradley .25
31 A.C. Green .25
32 Hubert Davis .25
33 Dennis Scott .25
34 *Tony Battie* 2.00
35 *Bobby Jackson* 4.00
36 LaPhonso Ellis .25
37 Bryant Stith .25
38 Dean Garrett .25
39 *Danny Fortson* 2.00
40 Grant Hill 3.00
41 Brian Williams .25
42 Lindsey Hunter .25
43 Malik Sealy .25
44 Jerry Stackhouse .50
45 Muggsy Bogues .25
46 Joe Smith .50
47 Donyell Marshall .25
48 Erick Dampier .25
49 Bimbo Coles .25
50 Charles Barkley .75
51 Hakeem Olajuwon 1.25
52 Clyde Drexler .75
53 Kevin Willis .25
54 Mario Elie .25
55 Reggie Miller .50
56 Rik Smits .25
57 Chris Mullin .25
58 Antonio Davis .25
59 Dale Davis .25
60 Mark Jackson .25
61 Brent Barry .25
62 Loy Vaught .25
63 Rodney Rogers .25
64 Lamond Murray .25
65 *Maurice Taylor* 3.00
66 Shaquille O'Neal 2.00
67 Eddie Jones 1.00
68 Kobe Bryant 4.00
69 Nick Van Exel .50
70 Robert Horry .25
71 Tim Hardaway .50
72 Jamal Mashburn .25
73 Alonzo Mourning .50
74 Isaac Austin .25
75 P.J. Brown .25
76 Ray Allen .75
77 Glenn Robinson .25
78 Ervin Johnson .25
79 Terrell Brandon .50
80 Tyrone Hill .25
81 Stephon Marbury 2.50
82 Kevin Garnett 3.00
83 Tom Gugliotta .50
84 Chris Carr .25
85 Cherokee Parks .25
86 Sam Cassell .25
87 Chris Gatling .25
88 Kendall Gill .25
89 *Keith Van Horn* 8.00
90 Jayson Williams .25
91 Kerry Kittles .75
92 Patrick Ewing .50
93 Larry Johnson .50
94 Chris Childs .25
95 John Starks .25
96 Charles Oakley .25
97 Allan Houston .25
98 Mark Price .25
99 Anfernee Hardaway 2.00
100 Rony Seikaly .25
101 Horace Grant .25
102 Charles Outlaw .25
103 Clarence Weatherspoon .25
104 Allen Iverson 2.50
105 Jim Jackson .25
106 Theo Ratliff .25
107 *Tim Thomas* 8.00
108 Danny Manning .25
109 Jason Kidd 1.00
110 Kevin Johnson .25
111 Rex Chapman .25
112 Clifford Robinson .25
113 Antonio McDyess .50
114 Damon Stoudamire .75
115 Isaiah Rider .25
116 Arvydas Sabonis .25
117 Rasheed Wallace .25
118 Brian Grant .25
119 Gary Trent .25
120 Mitch Richmond .75
121 Corliss Williamson .25
122 *Lawrence Funderburke* .50
123 Olden Polynice .25
124 Billy Owens .25
125 Avery Johnson .25
126 Sean Elliott .25
127 David Robinson .75
128 *Tim Duncan* 50.00
129 Jaren Jackson .25
130 Detlef Schrempf .25
131 Gary Payton .75
132 Vin Baker .75
133 Hersey Hawkins .25
134 Dale Ellis .25
135 Sam Perkins .25
136 Marcus Camby .50
137 John Wallace .25
138 Doug Christie .25
139 *Chauncey Billups* 4.00
140 Walt Williams .25
141 Karl Malone .75
142 Bryon Russell .25
143 Jeff Hornacek .25
144 Greg Ostertag .25
145 John Stockton .50
146 Shandon Anderson .25
147 Shareef Abdur-Rahim 1.50
148 Bryant Reeves .25
149 *Antonio Daniels* 3.00
150 Otis Thorpe .25
151 Blue Edwards .25
152 Chris Webber 1.00
153 Juwan Howard .75
154 Rod Strickland .25
155 Calbert Cheaney .25
156 Tracy Murray .25
157 Chauncey Billups 2.00
158 *Ed Gray* .50
159 Tony Battie 1.00
160 Keith Van Horn 3.00
161 *Cedric Henderson* 1.50
162 *Kelvin Cato* .50
163 *Tariq Abdul-Wahad* .50
164 Derek Anderson 2.00
165 Tim Duncan 10.00
166 *Tracy McGrady* 70.00
167 Ron Mercer 5.00
168 Bobby Jackson 2.00
169 Antonio Daniels 1.50
170 Zydrunas Ilgauskas .25
171 Maurice Taylor 1.50
172 Tim Thomas 4.00
173 Brevin Knight 2.00
174 Lawrence Funderburke .25
175 *Jacque Vaughn* .50
176 Danny Fortson 1.00

1997-98 SP Authentic Authentics

Authentics was a redemption insert that included four different Anfernee Hardaway items, eight Michael Jordan, three Shawn Kemp and one SP uncut sheet. Collectors could send in their Authentics card for the corresponding Upper Deck Authenticated item ranging from a special card set to autographed jerseys, balls and photos. The Jordan Game Night listing includes five different cards all numbered to 100. The number of items given away for each piece is listed in parentheses. Authentics were seeded one per 288 packs.

MT
Common Player: 30.00
AH1 Anfernee Hardaway/AU Blk. Jrsy 550.00
AH2 Anfernee Hardaway/AU Blue Jrsy 450.00
AH3 Anfernee Hardaway/AU SI Cover 80.00
AH4 Anfernee Hardaway/8x10 Photo 30.00
MJ1 Michael Jordan/AU Jersey 2500.
MJ2 Michael Jordan/AU 16x20 750.00
MJ3 Michael Jordan/2-card 75.00
MJ4 Michael Jordan/8x10 75.00
MJ5 Michael Jordan/Gold Card 85.00
MJ6 Michael Jordan/Game 500.00
MJ6 Michael Jordan/Poster 100.00
MJ8 Michael Jordan/AU Game 8500.
SK1 Shawn Kemp/AU Jersey 300.00
SK2 Shawn Kemp/AU Photo 75.00
SK3 Shawn Kemp/AU Mini-ball 75.00
NNO SP Uncut Sheet 125.00

1997-98 SP Authentic BuyBack

The basketball segment of Upper Deck Authenticated involved old SP cards that were purchased and autographed through UDA, then inserted into packs. The cards were inserted at a rate of one per 309 packs and contained UDA's holographic seal with an identification number.

MT
Common Player: 60.00
1 Shareef Abdur-Rahim '96/7 100.00
2 Vin Baker '94/5 125.00
3 Vin Baker '95/6 100.00
4 Vin Baker '95/6AS 100.00
5 Clyde Drexler '94/5 100.00
6 Clyde Drexler '95/6 100.00
7 Clyde Drexler '96/7 120.00
8 Anfernee Hardaway '94/5 200.00
9 Anfernee Hardaway '95/6 180.00
10 Anfernee Hardaway '96/7 180.00
11 Tim Hardaway Exchange 75.00
14 Juwan Howard '94/5 100.00
15 Juwan Howard '95/6 75.00
16 Juwan Howard '95/6AS 100.00
17 Juwan Howard '96/7 100.00
18 Eddie Jones '94/5 125.00
19 Eddie Jones '95/6 100.00
20 Eddie Jones '96/7 100.00
21 Michael Jordan '94/5MJ1R 4000.
22 Jason Kidd Exchange 100.00
26 Kerry Kittles '96/7 75.00
27 Karl Malone '94/5 125.00
28 Karl Malone '95/6 125.00
29 Glen Rice '95/6AS 50.00
30 Glen Rice '96/7 75.00
31 Mitch Richmond '94/5 50.00
32 Mitch Richmond '95/6 50.00
33 Mitch Richmond '96/7 75.00
34 Damon Stoudamire '95/6 75.00
35 Damon Stoudamire '96/7 75.00
36 Antoine Walker '96/7 60.00

1997-98 SP Authentic Premium Portraits

The seven-card set features autographed cards of the league's stars. Inserted at 1:1,528, the cards have a color portrait of the player on the front.

MT
Complete Set (7): 1100.
Common Player: 75.00
Inserted 1:1,528
TP Tim Hardaway 200.00
EP Eddie Jones 250.00
JP Jason Kidd 300.00
KP Kerry Kittles 150.00
RP Glen Rice 150.00
DP Damon Stoudamire 185.00
MP Dikembe Mutombo 75.00

1997-98 SP Authentic Profiles

A 40-card set, it divides itself into three subsets. The front show a color photo of the athlete, bordered in red. The first subset is inserted 1:3, the second 1:12. The third is 100 sequentially-numbered die-cut cards. The cards carry a "P" prefix.

MT
Complete Set (40): 100.00
Common Player: .50
Minor Stars: 1.00
Profiles II Cards: 3x
Profiles III Cards: 20x-40x
1 Michael Jordan 16.00
2 Glen Rice 1.00
3 Brent Barry .50
4 LaPhonso Ellis .50
5 Allen Iverson 6.00
6 Dikembe Mutombo .50
7 Charles Barkley 2.00
8 Antoine Walker 3.00
9 Karl Malone 2.00
10 Jason Kidd 2.00
11 Gary Payton 2.00
12 Kevin Garnett 8.00
13 Keith Van Horn 3.00
14 Glenn Robinson 1.00
15 Michael Finley 1.00
16 Hakeem Olajuwon 3.00
17 Chris Webber 3.00
18 Mitch Richmond 1.00

19	Marcus Camby	1.00
20	Tim Hardaway	1.00
21	Shawn Kemp	2.00
22	Reggie Miller	1.00
23	Shaquille O'Neal	5.00
24	Chauncey Billups	2.00
25	Grant Hill	8.00
26	Shareef Abdur-Rahim	4.00
27	David Robinson	2.00
28	Scottie Pippen	4.00
29	Juwan Howard	1.00
30	Anfernee Hardaway	5.00
31	Jerry Stackhouse	1.00
32	Kobe Bryant	10.00
33	Patrick Ewing	.50
34	Alonzo Mourning	1.00
35	John Stockton	1.00
36	Kenny Anderson	.50
37	Tim Duncan	8.00
38	Stephon Marbury	6.00
39	Dennis Rodman	5.00
40	Joe Smith	1.00

1997-98 SP Authentic Profiles II

Profiles II was a parallel set to Profiles, but adds embossing and is marked "Profiles 2" on the front. These are inserted every 12 packs.

	MT
Profiles II Cards:	3x

1997-98 SP Authentic Profiles III

Profiles III was scarcest tier of Profiles and paralleled all 40 cards in the insert on a die-cut design that was individually numbered to 100 on the front.

	MT
Profiles III Cards:	20x-40x

1997-98 SP Authentic Sign of the Times

The 11-card set features the young and old stars of the NBA. The featured players have autographed randomly inserted cards. Insertion rate is 1:42.

		MT
Complete Set (23):		475.00
Common Player:		6.00
Minor Stars:		12.00
Inserted 1:42		
BW	Brian Williams	6.00
AH	Allan Houston	12.00
HW	Juwan Howard	40.00
KJ	Kevin Johnson	12.00
EJ	Eddie Jones	50.00
KK	Kerry Kittles	15.00
DM	Dikembe Mutombo	12.00
GR	Glen Rice	25.00
TG	Tom Gugliotta	25.00
GM	Gheorghe Muresan	6.00
MB	Mookie Blaylock	6.00
CM	Chris Mullin	6.00
SC	Sam Cassell	12.00
BB	Brent Barry	6.00
LH	Lindsey Hunter	6.00
SE	Sean Elliott	6.00
AJ	Avery Johnson	6.00
MR	Mitch Richmond	25.00
VB	Vin Baker	30.00
DS	Damon Stoudamire	30.00
TH	Tim Hardaway	40.00
TB	Terrell Brandon	25.00

A card number in parentheses ( ) indicates the set is unnumbered.

1997-98 SP Authentic Sign of the Times Stars & Rookies

		MT
Common Player:		25.00
Inserted 1:113		
TB	Tony Battie	25.00
CD	Clyde Drexler	120.00
KV	Keith Van Horn	40.00
AW	Antoine Walker	25.00
CH	Chauncey Billups	30.00
SA	Shareef Abdur-Rahim	50.00
MJ	Michael Jordan	5000.
RO	Ron Mercer	50.00
JK	Jason Kidd	100.00
KM	Karl Malone	85.00

1997-98 SPx

This hobby-only issued set contains 50 cards, with four inserts, including the last Holoview release. The cards feature three photos on the front, with the player's name across the top half. The logo "X" is at the center of the card on the front. Inserts include: Hardcourt Holoview, A Piece of History, ProMotion and five levels of Parallel Universe inserts.

		MT
Complete Set (50):		100.00
Common Player:		.50
Minor Stars:		1.00
Sky Cards:		1.5x
Bronze Cards:		2x
Silver Cards:		2x-4x
Gold Cards:		4x-8x
Pack (3):		6.00
Wax Box (18):		90.00
1	Mookie Blaylock	.50
2	Dikembe Mutombo	.50
3	Chauncey Billups	3.00
4	Antoine Walker	1.50
5	Glen Rice	1.00
6	Michael Jordan	12.00
7	Scottie Pippen	3.00
8	Dennis Rodman	4.00
9	Shawn Kemp	2.00
10	Michael Finley	1.00
11	Tony Battie	2.00
12	LaPhonso Ellis	.50
13	Grant Hill	6.00
14	Joe Dumars	.50
15	Joe Smith	1.00
16	Clyde Drexler	1.25
17	Charles Barkley	1.50
18	Hakeem Olajuwon	2.50
19	Reggie Miller	1.00
20	Brent Barry	.50
21	Kobe Bryant	8.00
22	Shaquille O'Neal	4.00
23	Alonzo Mourning	1.00
24	Glenn Robinson	1.00
25	Kevin Garnett	6.00
26	Stephon Marbury	5.00
27	Keith Van Horn	4.00
28	Patrick Ewing	1.00
29	Anfernee Hardaway	5.00
30	Allen Iverson	5.00
31	Jerry Stackhouse	1.00
32	Antonio McDyess	1.00
33	Jason Kidd	1.25
34	Kenny Anderson	.50
35	Rasheed Wallace	.50
36	Mitch Richmond	1.00
37	Tim Duncan	15.00
38	David Robinson	1.50
39	Vin Baker	1.25
40	Gary Payton	1.50
41	Marcus Camby	1.00
42	Tracy McGrady	20.00
43	Damon Stoudamire	2.00
44	Karl Malone	1.25
45	John Stockton	1.00
46	Shareef Abdur-Rahim	3.00
47	Antonio Daniels	2.00
48	Bryant Reeves	.50
49	Juwan Howard	1.00
50	Chris Webber	1.50

1997-98 SPx Grand Finale

This parallel of the 50-card base set is limited to 50 sets. Grand Finale commemorates the final series of Holoview cards in SPx with unique foil treatments.

		MT
Common Player:		25.00
Minor Stars:		50.00
1	Mookie Blaylock	25.00
2	Dikembe Mutombo	25.00
3	Chauncey Billups	90.00
4	Antoine Walker	100.00
5	Glen Rice	50.00
6	Michael Jordan	500.00
7	Scottie Pippen	140.00
8	Dennis Rodman	180.00
9	Shawn Kemp	100.00
10	Michael Finley	50.00
11	Tony Battie	60.00
12	LaPhonso Ellis	25.00
13	Grant Hill	275.00
14	Joe Dumars	25.00
15	Joe Smith	50.00
16	Clyde Drexler	60.00
17	Charles Barkley	75.00
18	Hakeem Olajuwon	120.00
19	Reggie Miller	50.00
20	Brent Barry	25.00
21	Kobe Bryant	350.00
22	Shaquille O'Neal	180.00
23	Alonzo Mourning	50.00
24	Glenn Robinson	50.00
25	Kevin Garnett	275.00
26	Stephon Marbury	225.00
27	Keith Van Horn	125.00
28	Patrick Ewing	50.00
29	Anfernee Hardaway	225.00
30	Allen Iverson	225.00
31	Jerry Stackhouse	50.00
32	Antonio McDyess	50.00
33	Jason Kidd	60.00
34	Kenny Anderson	25.00
35	Rasheed Wallace	25.00
36	Mitch Richmond	50.00
37	Tim Duncan	240.00
38	David Robinson	75.00
39	Vin Baker	60.00
40	Gary Payton	75.00
41	Marcus Camby	50.00
42	Tracy McGrady	120.00
43	Damon Stoudamire	90.00
44	Karl Malone	60.00
45	John Stockton	50.00
46	Shareef Abdur-Rahim	140.00
47	Antonio Daniels	60.00
48	Bryant Reeves	25.00
49	Juwan Howard	50.00
50	Chris Webber	75.00

1997-98 SPx Hardcourt Holoview

This 20-card set is the last of the Holoviews made by Upper Deck. Inserted at 1:54, the set has a silver decorative foil around the side. The cards are numbered with the prefix "HH".

		MT
Complete Set (20):		300.00
Common Player:		7.00
1	Michael Jordan	60.00
2	Allen Iverson	30.00
3	Antoine Walker	15.00
4	Chris Webber	15.00
5	Glenn Robinson	7.00
6	Kevin Garnett	30.00
7	Shareef Abdur-Rahim	15.00
8	Keith Van Horn	15.00
9	Kobe Bryant	50.00
10	Glen Rice	7.00
11	Damon Stoudamire	10.00
12	Hakeem Olajuwon	12.00
13	Mookie Blaylock	7.00
14	Shaquille O'Neal	20.00
15	Stephon Marbury	25.00
16	Chauncey Billups	7.00
17	Anfernee Hardaway	25.00
18	Tim Duncan	30.00
19	Mitch Richmond	7.00
20	Grant Hill	30.00

1997-98 SPx ProMotion

A 10-card set featuring the best of the NBA. The front has two color photos of a player, one as an action shot. The set is inserted at 1:252 and numbered with the prefix "PM".

		MT
Complete Set (10):		500.00
Common Player:		20.00
1	Michael Jordan	120.00
2	Shaquille O'Neal	40.00
3	Tim Duncan	60.00
4	Shareef Abdur-Rahim	30.00
5	Grant Hill	60.00
6	Karl Malone	20.00
7	Anfernee Hardaway	50.00
8	Keith Van Horn	30.00
9	Kevin Garnett	60.00
10	Damon Stoudamire	20.00

1998 SP

This 62-card set featured top college players available for the 1998 NBA Draft. The cards are printed on a foilboard stock that includes a framed picture of the player over a basketball background. The set was paralleled in a President's Edition parallel that is sequentially numbered to 10 sets. SP Top Prospects also utilizes Upper Deck's relationship with Michael Jordan to produce two Jordan-driven inserts - Phi Beta Jordan and Carolina Heroes. Others inserts include: Vital Signs autographs and Destination: Stardom.

		MT
Complete Set (62):		50.00
Common Player:		.20
Minor Stars:		.40
Wax Box:		100.00
1	Antawn Jamison	4.00
2	Vince Carter	10.00
3	Michael Olowokandi	3.00
4	Paul Pierce	2.50
5	Korleone Young	.20
6	Rashard Lewis	.75
7	Miles Simon	.40
8	Al Harrington	1.25
9	Robert Traylor	3.00
10	Ansu Sesay	.40
11	DeMarco Johnson	.20
12	Earl Boykins	.40
13	Michael Doleac	1.25
14	Felipe Lopez	.40
15	Cory Carr	.20
16	J.R. Henderson	.40
17	Michael Dickerson	1.50
18	Jason Williams	2.00
19	Bonzi Wells	1.50
20	Matt Harpring	.20
21	Pat Garrity	.20
22	Ricky Davis	.20
23	Tyrron Lue	.20
24	Corey Benjamin	.20
25	Jelani McCoy	.40
26	Shammond Williams	.20
27	Toby Bailey	.20
28	Saddi Washington	.20
29	Zendon Hamilton	.20
30	Steve Wojciechowski	.20
31	Nazr Mohammed	.20
32	Andrae Patterson	.20
33	Ryan Bowen	.20
34	Anthony Carter	.20
35	Jarod Stevenson	.20
36	Casey Shaw	.20
37	Brad Miller	.20
38	Charles Jones	.20
39	Bryce Drew	.20
40	Jeff Sheppard	.20
41	Antawn Jamison	2.00
42	Vince Carter	5.00
43	Michael Olowokandi	2.50
44	Paul Pierce	1.25
45	Rashard Lewis	.50
46	Robert Traylor	1.50
47	Michael Doleac	.50
48	Felipe Lopez	.20
49	Michael Dickerson	.75
50	Jason Williams	1.00
51	Bonzi Wells	.75
52	Matt Harpring	.20
53	Ricky Davis	.20
54	Tyrron Lue	.20
55	Corey Benjamin	.20
56	Ansu Sesay	.20
57	Pat Garrity	.20
58	Shammond Williams	.40
59	Nazr Mohammed	.20
60	Bryce Drew	.20
61	Michael Olowokandi	2.50
62	Antawn Jamison	2.00

1998 SP Carolina Heroes

This 10-card insert showcases top players that have played for North Carolina. It includes four Michael Jordan cards and two each of three other 1998 former North Carolina players drafted in 1998. Carolina Heroes are printed on etched foil, numbered with a "H" prefix and inserted one per 11 packs.

		MT
Complete Set (10):		85.00
Common Player:		2.50
Inserted 1:11		
1	Michael Jordan	20.00
2	Michael Jordan	20.00
3	Michael Jordan	20.00
4	Michael Jordan	20.00
5	Antawn Jamison	10.00
6	Antawn Jamison	10.00
7	Vince Carter	10.00
8	Vince Carter	10.00
9	Shammond Williams	2.50
10	Shammond Williams	2.50

1998 SP Destination: Stardom

Destination: Stardom featured 20 draft picks on a thick, wood-like background with a white frame. The cards were inserted one per 23 packs.

		MT
Complete Set (20):		150.00
Common Player:		5.00
Inserted 1:23		
1	Antawn Jamison	20.00
2	Vince Carter	40.00
3	Michael Olowokandi	20.00
4	Paul Pierce	25.00
5	Rashard Lewis	5.00
6	Robert Traylor	15.00
7	Michael Doleac	5.00
8	Felipe Lopez	5.00
9	Pat Garrity	5.00
10	Michael Dickerson	8.00
11	Jason Williams	20.00
12	Bonzi Wells	8.00
13	Matt Harpring	5.00
14	Ricky Davis	5.00
15	Corey Benjamin	5.00
16	Tyrron Lue	5.00
17	Al Harrington	8.00
18	Ansu Sesay	5.00
19	Nazr Mohammed	5.00
20	Bryce Drew	5.00

1998 SP Phi Beta Jordan

Phi Beta Jordan displayed 23 cards of Michael Jordan in a North Carolina uniform on foil stock. The cards are numbered with a "J" prefix and inserted every two packs.

		MT
Complete Set (23):		40.00
Common Player:		2.00
Inserted 1:2		
1	Michael Jordan	2.00
2	Michael Jordan	2.00
3	Michael Jordan	2.00
4	Michael Jordan	2.00
5	Michael Jordan	2.00
6	Michael Jordan	2.00
7	Michael Jordan	2.00
8	Michael Jordan	2.00
9	Michael Jordan	2.00
10	Michael Jordan	2.00
11	Michael Jordan	2.00
12	Michael Jordan	2.00
13	Michael Jordan	2.00
14	Michael Jordan	2.00
15	Michael Jordan	2.00
16	Michael Jordan	2.00
17	Michael Jordan	2.00
18	Michael Jordan	2.00
19	Michael Jordan	2.00
20	Michael Jordan	2.00
21	Michael Jordan	2.00
22	Michael Jordan	2.00
23	Michael Jordan	2.00

1998 SP Vital Signs

Vital Signs featured autographs from 19 top draft picks, as well as a Michael Jordan autograph numbered to 23. The cards look similar to base cards in design, but contain a closer shot of the player in the box and a white background within the photo box. These were inserted one per 12 packs.

		MT
Complete Set (20):		325.00
Common Player:		5.00
Minor Stars:		8.00
Inserted 1:12		
MJ	Michael Jordan	6000.
MO	Michael Olowokandi	20.00
AJ	Antawn Jamison	40.00
VC	Vince Carter	100.00
RT	Robert Traylor	20.00
JW	Jason Williams	60.00
PP	Paul Pierce	50.00
BW	Bonzi Wells	10.00
DO	Michael Doleac	8.00
MD	Michael Dickerson	15.00
MH	Matt Harpring	10.00
FL	Felipe Lopez	15.00
AH	Al Harrington	15.00
AS	Ansu Sesay	5.00
RL	Rashard Lewis	25.00
DJ	DeMarco Johnson	5.00
KY	Korleone Young	8.00
MS	Miles Simon	8.00
CC	Cory Carr	5.00
JR	J.R. Henderson	8.00
EB	Earl Boykins	5.00

1998-99 SP Authentic

This 120-card set consisted of 90 veterans, including 10 Michael

Jordan cards, and 30 rookies, which were sequentially numbered to 3,500 sets. The cards featured a color shot of the player over black-and-white background that faded into a white matte finish card. Inserts include: Authentics, First Class, MICHAEL, NBA 2K, and Sign of the Times (bronze, silver and gold).

		MT
Complete Set (120):		1200.
Common Player (1-90):		.25
Minor Stars:		.40
Common MJ (1-10):		3.00
Common Rookie (91-120):		8.00
Production: 3,500 sets		
Pack (5):		25.00
Wax Box (24):		500.00
1	Michael Jordan (Scoring Title #1 (86-87)	3.00
2	Michael Jordan (Scoring Title #2 (87-88)	3.00
3	Michael Jordan (Scoring Title #3 (88-89)	3.00
4	Michael Jordan (Scoring Title #4 (89-90))	3.00
5	Michael Jordan (Scoring Title #5 (90-91)	3.00
6	Michael Jordan (Scoring Title #6 (91-92)	3.00
7	Michael Jordan (Scoring Title #7 (92-93)	3.00
8	Michael Jordan (Scoring Title #8 (95-96)	3.00
9	Michael Jordan (Scoring Title #9 (96-97)	3.00
10	Michael Jordan (Scoring Title #10 (97-98)	3.00
11	Steve Smith	.40
12	Dikembe Mutombo	.25
13	Alan Henderson	.25
14	Antoine Walker	1.00
15	Ron Mercer	1.50
16	Kenny Anderson	.40
17	Derrick Coleman	.40
18	David Wesley	.25
19	Glen Rice	.40
20	Toni Kukoc	.50
21	Ron Harper	.25
22	Brent Barry	.25
23	Shawn Kemp	.75
24	Zydrunas Ilgauskas	.40
25	Brevin Knight	.50
26	Michael Finley	.50
27	Steve Nash	.40
28	Cedric Ceballos	.25
29	Antonio McDyess	.75
30	Nick Van Exel	.40
31	Grant Hill	3.00
32	Jerry Stackhouse	.40
33	Bison Dele	.25
34	John Starks	.25
35	Chris Mills	.25
36	Hakeem Olajuwon	.75
37	Charles Barkley	.75
38	Scottie Pippen	1.50
39	Reggie Miller	.40
40	Chris Mullin	.25
41	Rik Smits	.25
42	Lamond Murray	.25
43	Maurice Taylor	.50
44	Kobe Bryant	4.00
45	Dennis Rodman	1.00
46	Shaquille O'Neal	2.00
47	Alonzo Mourning	.50
48	Tim Hardaway	.60
49	Jamal Mashburn	.40
50	Ray Allen	.40
51	Glenn Robinson	.40
52	Terrell Brandon	.40
53	Kevin Garnett	3.00
54	Stephon Marbury	2.00
55	Joe Smith	.40
56	Keith Van Horn	1.25
57	Kendall Gill	.25
58	Jayson Williams	.40
59	Patrick Ewing	.40
60	Allan Houston	.40
61	Larry Johnson	.40
62	Anfernee Hardaway	1.75
63	Horace Grant	.25
64	Allen Iverson	2.50
65	Tim Thomas	1.25
66	Jason Kidd	1.50
67	Tom Gugliotta	.40
68	Rex Chapman	.25
69	Damon Stoudamire	.60
70	Isaiah Rider	.25
71	Rasheed Wallace	.40
72	Chris Webber	1.50
73	Vlade Divac	.40
74	Corliss Williamson	.25
75	Tim Duncan	3.00
76	David Robinson	.75
77	Sean Elliott	.25
78	Detlef Schrempf	.25
79	Vin Baker	.60
80	Gary Payton	.75
81	Doug Christie	.25
82	Tracy McGrady	1.50
83	Karl Malone	.75
84	John Stockton	.40
85	Jeff Hornacek	.25
86	Shareef Abdur-Rahim	1.50
87	Bryant Reeves	.40
88	Juwan Howard	.50
89	Mitch Richmond	.40
90	Rod Strickland	.40
91	*Michael Olowokandi*	15.00
92	*Mike Bibby*	60.00
93	*Raef LaFrentz*	30.00
94	*Antawn Jamison*	120.00
95	*Vince Carter*	850.00
96	*Robert Traylor*	15.00
97	*Jason Williams*	80.00
98	*Larry Hughes*	80.00
99	*Dirk Nowitzki*	150.00
100	*Paul Pierce*	150.00
101	*Bonzi Wells*	100.00
102	*Michael Doleac*	10.00
103	*Keon Clark*	40.00
104	*Michael Dickerson*	30.00
105	*Matt Harpring*	12.00
106	*Bryce Drew*	12.00
107	*Pat Garrity*	12.00
108	*Roshown McLeod*	12.00
109	*Ricky Davis*	30.00
110	*Brian Skinner*	12.00
111	*Tyronn Lue*	12.00
112	*Felipe Lopez*	15.00
113	*Al Harrington*	70.00
114	*Sam Jacobson*	8.00
115	*Cory Carr*	8.00
116	*Corey Benjamin*	15.00
117	*Nazr Mohammed*	12.00
118	*Rashard Lewis*	150.00
119	*Predrag Stojakovic*	100.00
120	*Andrae Patterson*	8.00

1998-99 SP Authentic Authentics

SP Authentics was a memorabilia redemption set that allowed collectors to redeem cards for 27 different pieces of memorabilia ranging from a Michael Jordan autographed jersey to a piece of the Great Western Forum floor. Cards were numbered with a "T" prefix and inserted 1:864 packs.

		MT
Complete Set (27):		
Common Player:		20.00
1	Larry Bird	400.00
2	Julius Erving	300.00
3	Anfernee Hardaway	25.00
4	Anfernee Hardaway	25.00
5	Tim Hardaway	25.00
6	Tim Hardaway	25.00
7	Tim Hardaway	25.00
8	Juwan Howard	25.00
9	Eddie Jones	25.00
10	Eddie Jones	25.00
11	Michael Jordan	2500.
12	Michael Jordan	2500.
13	Shawn Kemp	10.00
14	Shawn Kemp	10.00
15	Gary Payton	50.00
16	Scottie Pippen	25.00
17	Great Western Forum	100.00
18	Shaquille O'Neal	
19	Shareef Abdur-Rahim	50.00
20	Karl Malone	
21	Tim Duncan	
22	Gary Payton	
23	Antoine Walker	
24	Hakeem Olajuwon	100.00
25	Charles Barkley	
26	Allen Iverson	
27	Kevin Garnett	

1998-99 SP Authentic First Class

This 30-card insert captured some of the NBA's top stars on die-cut cards that were primarily white, with the player image over a rectangular box. SP First Class inserts were numbered with an "FC" prefix and inserted 1:7 packs.

		MT
Complete Set (30):		90.00
Common Player:		.50
Inserted 1:7		
1	Michael Jordan	15.00
2	Dikembe Mutombo	.50
3	Antoine Walker	1.50
4	Glen Rice	.75
5	Toni Kukoc	1.00
6	Shawn Kemp	1.00
7	Michael Finley	.75
8	Raef LaFrentz	2.00
9	Grant Hill	6.00
10	Antawn Jamison	6.00
11	Scottie Pippen	2.00
12	Reggie Miller	.75
13	Michael Olowokandi	2.00
14	Kobe Bryant	10.00
15	Tim Hardaway	1.50
16	Ray Allen	1.00
17	Kevin Garnett	6.00
18	Keith Van Horn	1.50
19	Allan Houston	.75
20	Anfernee Hardaway	3.00
21	Allen Iverson	4.00
22	Jason Kidd	2.00
23	Damon Stoudamire	1.00
24	Jason Williams	12.00
25	Tim Duncan	6.00
26	Gary Payton	1.00
27	Vince Carter	35.00
28	Karl Malone	1.00
29	Mike Bibby	4.00
30	Mitch Richmond	.75

1998-99 SP Authentic Michael

This 15-card insert featured Michael Jordan exclusively and utilized Ionix technology. "Michael" inserts were numbered with an "M" prefix and inserted 1:144 packs.

		MT
Complete Set (15):		500.00
Common Player:		40.00
Inserted 1:144		
1	Michael Jordan	50.00
2	Michael Jordan	50.00
3	Michael Jordan	50.00
4	Michael Jordan	50.00
5	Michael Jordan	50.00
6	Michael Jordan	50.00
7	Michael Jordan	50.00
8	Michael Jordan	50.00
9	Michael Jordan	50.00
10	Michael Jordan	50.00
11	Michael Jordan	50.00
12	Michael Jordan	50.00
13	Michael Jordan	50.00
14	Michael Jordan	50.00
15	Michael Jordan	50.00

1998-99 SP Authentic NBA 2K

NBA 2K was a 20-card insert showcasing top players that will lead the NBA into the year 2000. Cards were inserted 1:23 packs and numbered with a "2K" prefix.

		MT
Complete Set (20):		175.00
Common Player:		3.00
Inserted 1:23		
1	Michael Olowokandi	6.00
2	Mike Bibby	12.00
3	Raef LaFrentz	6.00
4	Antawn Jamison	15.00
5	Vince Carter	50.00
6	Robert Traylor	6.00
7	Jason Williams	25.00
8	Larry Hughes	12.00
9	Dirk Nowitzki	10.00
10	Paul Pierce	20.00
11	Cuttino Mobley	4.00
12	Michael Doleac	4.00
13	Corey Benjamin	3.00
14	Michael Dickerson	6.00
15	Allen Iverson	8.00
16	Kobe Bryant	15.00
17	Tim Duncan	12.00
18	Keith Van Horn	3.00
19	Kevin Garnett	12.00
20	Grant Hill	12.00

1998-99 SP Authentic Sign of the Times-Bronze

Sign of the Times - Bronze was a 45-card insert that featured autographs of NBA players. Silver and Gold Sign of the Times inserts were also available, with players signing in one of the three categories. Cards were unnumbered and identified by the player's initials (except in cases where two players had the same initials, then they would use the first two letters of the first name or some alternative identification), which appeared on the card back. Bronze level cards were inserted 1:23 packs of SP Authentic.

		MT
Common Player:		8.00
Inserted 1:23		
TQ	Tariq Abdul-Wahad	8.00
DA	Derek Anderson	12.00
KA	Kenny Anderson	12.00
NA	Nick Anderson	12.00
CB	Chauncey Billups	15.00
BL	Mookie Blaylock	8.00
TB	Terrell Brandon	12.00
PJ	P.J. Brown	8.00
CC	Chris Carr	8.00
CH	Calbert Cheaney	8.00
DC	Doug Christie	8.00
ED	Erick Dampier	8.00
BE	Blue Edwards	8.00
SE	Sean Elliott	12.00
MI	Michael Finley	15.00
DK	Derek Fisher	10.00
BG	Brian Grant	15.00
HG	Horace Grant	12.00
EG	Ed Gray	8.00
RH	Ron Harper	10.00
OH	Othella Harrington	8.00
JH	Jeff Hornacek	12.00
HW	Juwan Howard	15.00
LH	Lindsey Hunter	8.00
MK	Mark Jackson	8.00
AV	Avery Johnson	8.00
LJ	Larry Johnson	12.00
BK	Brevin Knight	12.00
TK	Toni Kukoc	25.00
DN	Danny Manning	15.00
DM	Donyell Marshall	8.00
WM	Walter McCarty	8.00
AM	Antonio McDyess	25.00
MG	Tracy McGrady	20.00
BP	Bobby Phills	8.00
TR	Theo Ratliff	12.00
RR	Rodrick Rhodes	8.00
GR	Glen Rice	25.00
JR	Jalen Rose	12.00
BR	Bryon Russell	8.00
DT	Detlef Schrempf	15.00
TY	Maurice Taylor	15.00
DV	David Wesley	8.00
JY	Jayson Williams	15.00
JW	Jerome Williams	8.00

1998-99 SP Authentic Sign of the Times-Silver

Thirteen different players autographed cards in the Silver level of Sign of the Times. These were inserted 1:115 packs and identified by the player's initials on the card back.

		MT
Common Player:		15.00
Inserted 1:115		
MB	Mike Bibby	25.00
VC	Vince Carter	400.00
PN	Anfernee Hardaway	75.00
LR	Larry Hughes	50.00
AJ	Antawn Jamison	60.00
SH	Shawn Kemp	20.00
RL	Raef LaFrentz	20.00
RM	Ron Mercer	20.00
MT	Dikembe Mutombo	15.00
HO	Hakeem Olajuwon	40.00
MO	Michael Olowokandi	20.00
DR	Dennis Rodman	100.00
RT	Robert Traylor	20.00

1998-99 SP Authentic Sign of the Times-Gold

Four different players signed Gold level cards of Sign of the Times inserts. These die-cut cards were inserted 1:1,500 packs. Cards were identified by the player's initials on the card back.

		MT
Common Player:		75.00
TH	Tim Hardaway	75.00
AI	Allen Iverson	250.00
MJ	Michael Jordan	2500.
AW	Antoine Walker	60.00

1998-99 SPx Finite

SPx Finite was a all-sequentially-numbered hobby-only set that consisted of 90 base cards (numbered to 10,000) and four different subsets. Subsets included: 60 Star Power (91-150, numbered to 5,400 sets), 30 SPx 2000 (151-180, numbered to 4,050 sets), 20 Top Flight (181-200, numbered to 3,390 sets) and 10 Finite Excellence (201-210, numbered to 1,770 sets). Upper Deck also made Rookie cards (211-240) as inserts in MJ Access later in the year, but those listings are included as an insert with that product. Each card was also paralleled in a Radiance and Spectrum level set with different sequential numbering. In addition, 23 hand-numbered Autographed Game-worn Jersey Cards of Jordan were available in this product.

		MT
Complete Set (210):		600.00
Common Player (1-90):		.50
Minor Stars (1-90):		1.00
Production 10,000 Sets		
Common Player (91-150):		1.00
Minor Stars (91-150):		2.00
Production 5,400 Sets		
Common Player (151-180):		1.50
Minor Stars (151-180):		3.00
Production 4,050 Sets		
Common Player (181-200):		1.50
Minor Stars (181-200):		3.00
Production 3,390 Sets		
Common Player (201-210):		7.00
Production 1,770 Sets		
Common Rookie (211-240):		
Production 2,500 Sets		
Cards 227 and 228 Do Not Exist		
Rookies Inserted In MJ Access		
Pack (3):		6.00
Wax Box (18):		95.00
1	Michael Jordan	16.00
2	Hakeem Olajuwon	2.50
3	Keith Van Horn	3.00
4	Rasheed Wallace	.50
5	Mookie Blaylock	.50
6	Bobby Jackson	1.00
7	Detlef Schrempf	.50
8	Antonio McDyess	1.00
9	Lamond Murray	.50
10	Chris Mullin	.50
11	Zydrunas Ilgauskas	1.00
12	Tracy Murray	.50
13	Jerry Stackhouse	1.00
14	Avery Johnson	.50
15	Larry Johnson	1.00
16	Alan Henderson	.50
17	David Wesley	.50
18	Kevin Willis	.50
19	Eddie Jones	2.50
20	Horace Grant	.50
21	Ray Allen	1.00
22	Derrick Coleman	.50
23	Derek Anderson	1.50
24	Tim Hardaway	1.00
25	Danny Fortson	.50
26	Tariq Abdul-Wahad	.50
27	Charles Barkley	2.00
28	Sam Cassell	.50
29	Kevin Garnett	8.00
30	Jeff Hornacek	.50
31	Isaac Austin	.50
32	Allan Houston	1.00
33	David Robinson	2.00
34	Tracy McGrady	4.00
35	LaPhonso Ellis	.50
36	Shawn Kemp	2.00
37	Glenn Robinson	1.00
38	Shareef Abdur-Rahim	4.00
39	Vin Baker	2.00
40	Rik Smits	.50
41	Jason Kidd	2.50
42	Erick Dampier	.50
43	Shawn Bradley	.50
44	Anfernee Hardaway	5.00
45	John Stockton	1.00
46	Calbert Cheaney	.50
47	Terrell Brandon	1.00
48	Hubert Davis	.50
49	Patrick Ewing	1.00
50	Kobe Bryant	10.00
51	Gary Payton	1.50
52	Marcus Camby	1.00
53	Bryant Reeves	.50
54	Reggie Miller	1.00
55	Antoine Walker	3.00
56	Scottie Pippen	4.00
57	Hersey Hawkins	.50
58	John Starks	.50
59	Dikembe Mutombo	1.00
60	Damon Stoudamire	1.50
61	Rodney Rogers	.50
62	Nick Anderson	.50
63	Brian Williams	.50
64	Ron Mercer	5.00
65	Donyell Marshall	.50
66	Glen Rice	1.00
67	Michael Finley	1.00
68	Tim Duncan	8.00
69	Stephon Marbury	5.00
70	Antonio Daniels	1.00
71	Chauncey Billups	1.50
72	Kerry Kittles	1.00
73	Brian Grant	.50
74	Anthony Mason	.50
75	Allen Iverson	4.00
76	Juwan Howard	1.00
77	Grant Hill	8.00
78	Tony Delk	.50
79	Olden Polynice	.50
80	Alonzo Mourning	1.00
81	Karl Malone	1.50
82	Isaiah Rider	.50
83	Shaquille O'Neal	5.00
84	Steve Smith	.50
85	Kenny Anderson	.50
86	Toni Kukoc	.50
87	Anthony Peeler	.50
88	Tim Thomas	4.00
89	Nick Van Exel	1.00
90	Jamal Mashburn	.50
91	Reggie Miller	2.00
92	Juwan Howard	2.00
93	Glen Rice	2.00
94	Grant Hill	15.00
95	Maurice Taylor	2.00
96	Vin Baker	3.00
97	Tim Thomas	6.00
98	Bobby Jackson	1.00
99	Damon Stoudamire	2.00
100	Michael Jordan	30.00
101	Eddie Jones	4.00
102	Keith Van Horn	6.00
103	Dikembe Mutombo	2.00
104	Brevin Knight	3.00
105	Shawn Bradley	1.00
106	Lamond Murray	1.00
107	Tim Duncan	15.00
108	Bryant Reeves	1.00
109	Antoine Walker	5.00
110	John Stockton	2.00
111	Nick Anderson	1.00
112	Chris Mullin	1.00
113	Glenn Robinson	2.00
114	Kevin Garnett	15.00
115	Michael Stewart	1.00
116	Antonio McDyess	2.00
117	Jim Jackson	1.00
118	Chauncey Billups	3.00
119	Sam Cassell	1.00
120	Dennis Rodman	8.00
121	Rasheed Wallace	1.00
122	Brian Williams	1.00
123	Anfernee Hardaway	8.00
124	Scottie Pippen	6.00
125	Terrell Brandon	2.00
126	Michael Finley	2.00
127	Kerry Kittles	2.00
128	Toni Kukoc	1.00
129	Hakeem Olajuwon	4.00
130	Tim Hardaway	2.00
131	Shareef Abdur-Rahim	4.00
132	Donyell Marshall	1.00
133	David Robinson	3.00
134	LaPhonso Ellis	1.00
135	Ray Allen	2.00
136	Nick Van Exel	2.00
137	Patrick Ewing	2.00
138	Anthony Mason	1.00
139	Shaquille O'Neal	8.00
140	Shawn Kemp	3.00
141	Stephon Marbury	8.00
142	Karl Malone	2.00
143	Allen Iverson	6.00
144	Kenny Anderson	1.00
145	Marcus Camby	2.00
146	Steve Smith	1.00
147	Gary Payton	3.00
148	Jason Kidd	4.00
149	Alonzo Mourning	2.00
150	Charles Barkley	3.00
151	Kobe Bryant	25.00
152	Ron Mercer	12.00
153	Maurice Taylor	3.00
154	Tim Duncan	20.00
155	Shareef Abdur-Rahim	10.00
156	Eddie Jones	8.00
157	Chauncey Billups	4.00
158	Derek Anderson	4.00
159	Bobby Jackson	3.00
160	Stephon Marbury	12.00
161	Anfernee Hardaway	12.00
162	Zydrunas Ilgauskas	3.00
163	Allen Iverson	10.00
164	Antoine Walker	6.00
165	Tracy McGrady	8.00
166	Rasheed Wallace	1.50
167	Jason Kidd	7.00
168	Kevin Garnett	20.00
169	Damon Stoudamire	4.00
170	Brevin Knight	4.00
171	Tim Thomas	10.00
172	Danny Fortson	1.50
173	Jermaine O'Neal	1.50
174	Keith Van Horn	8.00
175	Ray Allen	3.00
176	Kerry Kittles	3.00
177	Vin Baker	4.00
178	Allan Houston	3.00
179	Alan Henderson	1.50
180	Bryon Russell	1.50
181	Michael Jordan	40.00
182	Maurice Taylor	4.00
183	Isaiah Rider	1.50
184	Antonio McDyess	3.00
185	Anfernee Hardaway	15.00
186	Glenn Robinson	3.00
187	Dikembe Mutombo	3.00
188	Shawn Kemp	6.00
189	Tracy McGrady	10.00
190	Reggie Miller	4.00
191	Derek Anderson	5.00
192	Allan Houston	3.00
193	Michael Finley	3.00
194	Nick Van Exel	3.00
195	Juwan Howard	3.00
196	LaPhonso Ellis	1.50
197	Ron Mercer	15.00
198	Glen Rice	4.00
199	Joe Smith	3.00
200	Kobe Bryant	30.00
201	Michael Jordan	85.00
202	Karl Malone	10.00
203	Hakeem Olajuwon	12.00
204	David Robinson	10.00
205	Shaquille O'Neal	25.00
206	John Stockton	7.00
207	Grant Hill	40.00
208	Tim Hardaway	7.00
209	Scottie Pippen	20.00
210	Gary Payton	10.00
211	*Michael Olowokandi*	10.00
212	*Mike Bibby*	25.00
213	*Raef LaFrentz*	20.00
214	*Antawn Jamison*	60.00
215	*Vince Carter*	700.00
216	*Robert Traylor*	10.00
217	*Jason Williams*	50.00
218	*Larry Hughes*	60.00
219	*Dirk Nowitzki*	75.00
220	*Paul Pierce*	40.00
221	*Bonzi Wells*	40.00
222	*Michael Doleac*	6.00
223	*Keon Clark*	10.00
224	*Michael Dickerson*	20.00
225	*Matt Harpring*	6.00
226	*Bryce Drew*	5.00

229	*Pat Garrity*	5.00
230	*Roshown McLeod*	5.00
231	*Ricky Davis*	10.00
232	*Brian Skinner*	5.00
233	*Tyronn Lue*	5.00
234	*Felipe Lopez*	8.00
235	*Al Harrington*	30.00
236	*Ruben Patterson*	15.00
237	*Vladimir Stepania*	5.00
238	*Corey Benjamin*	8.00
239	*Nazr Mohammed*	5.00
240	*Rashard Lewis*	60.00

1998-99 SPx Finite Radiance

Each card in SPx Finite was also available in a Radiance parallel version, which featured gold foil. Regular Radiance cards (1-90) were numbered to 5,000, Star Power cards were numbered to 2,700, SPx 2000 cards were numbered to 2,025, Top Flight cards were numbered to 1,130 and Finite Excellence cards were numbered to 590. Radiance cards were labelled as such on both the front and back of the card.

	MT
Cards (1-90):	2x
Production 5,000 Sets	
Cards (91-150):	2x
Production 2,700 Sets	
Cards (151-180):	2x
Production 2,025 Sets	
Cards (181-200):	2x
Production 1,130 Sets	
Cards (201-210):	2x
Production 590 Sets	

1998-99 SPx Finite Spectrum

Each card in the SPx Finite set was also available in a Spectrum version, which featured rainbow foil. Base Spectrum cards were numbered to 350, Star Power cards were numbered to 250, SPx 2000 cards were numbered to 75, Top Flight cards were numbered to 50 and Finite Excellence cards were numbered to 25 sets. Spectrum cards were labelled as such on both the front and the back. In addition, an Extreme level of Spectrum cards was also available and numbered 1 of 1.

	MT
Cards (1-90):	8x-16x
Production 350 Sets	
Cards (91-150):	6x-12x
Production 250 Sets	
Cards (151-180):	6x-12x
Production 75 Sets	
Cards (181-200):	10x-20x
Production 50 Sets	
Cards (201-210):	15x-30x
Production 25 Sets	

1999 SP Top Prospects

This 38-card set highlighted players eligible to be drafted in the 1999 NBA Draft. The cards featured spot UV-coating on the player's image, with the action shot surrounded by a white border, then repeated the words "Top Prospects" in grey letters. The player's name and parts of the border were printed with silver foil. Cards #8, 15, 19 and 42 were not printed since Press Pass signed exclusive contracts with Brand, Francis, Odom and Szczerbiak to exclusive draft pick contracts. Inserts include: MJ Flight Mechanics 101, Vital Signs, Jordan's Scrapbook and College Legends. The entire set was also paralleled in an Upper Class parallel.

		MT
Complete Set (38):		20.00
Common Player:		.20
Minor Stars:		.40
Cards 8, 15, 19 and 42 Do Not Exist		
Wax Box (24):		90.00
1	Lee Nailon	.40
2	A.J. Bramlett	.40
3	Jason Terry	3.00
4	Kareem Reid	.20
5	Melvin Levett	.40
6	Terrell McIntyre	.20
7	Trajan Langdon	3.00
9	Chris Herren	.75
10	Shawnta Rogers	.20
11	Corey Maggette	3.00
12	Wayne Turner	.40
13	Heshimu Evans	.40
14	Bobby Lazor	.20
16	Laron Profit	.75
17	Ron Artest	2.00
18	Tim James	1.00
20	Louis Bullock	.40
21	William Avery	2.00
22	Quincy Lewis	1.00
23	Kenny Thomas	1.00
24	Evan Eschmeyer	.40
25	Adrian Peterson	.20
26	Keith Carter	.20
27	Jelani Gardner	.20
28	Baron Davis	5.00
29	Jamel Thomas	.40
30	B.J. McKie	.20
31	Arthur Lee	.40
32	Tim Young	.20
33	Richard Hamilton	3.00
34	Calvin Booth	.40
35	Andre Miller	2.00
36	Todd MacCulloch	.40
37	James Posey	1.50
38	Lenny Brown	.20
39	Scott Padgett	1.00
40	Venson Hamilton	.40
41	Geno Carlisle	.20

1999 SP Top Prospects Upper Class

Upper Class was a 38-card parallel set of SP Top Prospects. Cards from this parallel were die-cut and sequentially numbered to 50 sets.

	MT
Upper Class Cards:	15x-30x
Production 50 Sets	

1999 SP Top Prospects College Legends

This 10-card insert focused on four of the top players ever at the college level. It includes three Jordan and Bird cards and two each of Erving and Anfernee Hardaway. College Legends are numbered with an "L" prefix and inserted 1:92 packs.

		MT
Complete Set (10):		125.00
Common Player:		5.00
Inserted 1:92		
1	Michael Jordan	25.00
2	Michael Jordan	25.00
3	Michael Jordan	25.00
4	Larry Bird	15.00
5	Larry Bird	15.00
6	Larry Bird	15.00
7	Julius Erving	10.00
8	Julius Erving	10.00
9	Anfernee Hardaway	5.00
10	Anfernee Hardaway	5.00

1999 SP Top Prospects Jordan's Scrapbook

This 20-card insert highlights Michael Jordan's top moments during his collegiate career at North Carolina. Cards were numbered with a "J" prefix and inserted 1:23 packs.

		MT
Complete Set (20):		100.00
Common Player:		6.00
Inserted 1:23		
1	Michael Jordan	6.00
2	Michael Jordan	6.00
3	Michael Jordan	6.00
4	Michael Jordan	6.00
5	Michael Jordan	6.00
6	Michael Jordan	6.00
7	Michael Jordan	6.00
8	Michael Jordan	6.00
9	Michael Jordan	6.00
10	Michael Jordan	6.00
11	Michael Jordan	6.00
12	Michael Jordan	6.00
13	Michael Jordan	6.00
14	Michael Jordan	6.00
15	Michael Jordan	6.00
16	Michael Jordan	6.00
17	Michael Jordan	6.00
18	Michael Jordan	6.00
19	Michael Jordan	6.00
20	Michael Jordan	6.00

1999 SP Top Prospects MJ Flight Mechanics

This 28-card insert features players over a blue foil background and was selected by Michael Jordan. The cards were numbered with an "FM" prefix and inserted 1:4 packs. Cards 4 and 25 were never printed.

		MT
Complete Set (30):		30.00
Common Player:		.50
Minor Stars:		.75
Inserted 1:4		
1	Jason Terry	5.00
2	Geno Carlisle	.50
3	Heshimu Evans	.75
5	Keith Carter	.50
6	Trajan Langdon	5.00
7	Ron Artest	3.00
8	Kenny Thomas	1.00
9	Lenny Brown	.50
10	Kareem Reid	.50
11	Shawnta Rogers	.50
12	Quincy Lewis	1.50
13	Jamel Thomas	.75
14	James Posey	2.00
15	Lee Nailon	.75
16	Melvin Levett	.75
17	Laron Profit	.75
18	Louis Bullock	.50
19	Evan Eschmeyer	.75
20	B.J. McKie	.50
21	A.J. Bramlett	.75
22	Wayne Turner	.75
23	Jelani Gardner	.50
24	Terrell McIntyre	.50
26	Venson Hamilton	.75
27	Andre Miller	3.00
28	Chris Herren	.75
29	Adrian Peterson	.50
30	Tim James	1.50

1999 SP Top Prospects Vital Signs

Vital Signs included autographs from 39 players, including all 38 players in the base set and 23 numbered Michael Jordan autographs. The cards featured the same photograph as the base cards, but over a pure white background. In addition, the silver foil stamping was replaced by black and the grey photo border was replaced by blue. The player's signature was across the bottom of the card. Cards were numbered with a two-letter number on the back, usually involving the player's initials and inserted 1:4 packs.

		MT
Complete Set (39):		250.00
Common Player:		3.00
Minor Stars:		8.00
Inserted 1:4		
VC	Pat Bradley	3.00
AB	A.J. Bramlett	5.00
DG	Rasheed Brokenborough	5.00
LB	Lenny Brown	3.00
GC	Geno Carlisle	3.00
BD	Baron Davis	50.00
OE	Obinna Ekezie	3.00
EE	Evan Eschmeyer	5.00
HE	Heshimu Evans	5.00
DF	Damon Frierson	3.00
JG	Jelani Gardner	3.00
RH	Richard Hamilton	30.00
VH	Venson Hamilton	5.00
CH	Chris Herren	8.00
JK	Jermaine Jackson	3.00
TJ	Tim James	10.00
JA	Michael Jordan	3000.
TL	Trajan Langdon	25.00
AL	Arthur Lee	3.00
ML	Melvin Levett	5.00
QL	Quincy Lewis	8.00
GL	Gary Lumpkin	3.00
TM	Terrell McIntyre	3.00
BJ	B.J. McKie	3.00
AM	Andre Miller	20.00
LN	Lee Nailon	5.00
SP	Scott Padgett	10.00
AP	Adrian Peterson	3.00
JP	James Posey	10.00
LP	Laron Profit	8.00
KR	Kareem Reid	3.00
SR	Shawnta Rogers	5.00
TE	Jason Terry	20.00
JT	Jamel Thomas	5.00
KT	Kenny Thomas	10.00
WT	Wayne Turner	5.00
TY	Tim Young	3.00
DW	Donald Watts	3.00
OS	Kris Weems	3.00

1999-00 SP Authentic

SP Authentic featured 135 cards, with 90 veterans and 45 F/X rookies, which are numbered to 1,500. The base cards are printed on a white, matte finish, while the rookies have a black border running up the right and left side. Inserts included: SP First Class, SP Athletic, Maximum Force, Premier Powers, Sign of the Times, Sign of the Times Gold and SP Supremacy.

		MT
Complete Set (135):		1700.
Common Player:		.25
Minor Stars:		.40
Common Rookie (91-135):		10.00
Production 1,500 Sets		
Pack (5):		6.00
Wax Box (24):		140.00
1	Dikembe Mutombo	.40
2	Jim Jackson	.25
3	Alan Henderson	.25
4	Antoine Walker	.60
5	Paul Pierce	1.00
6	Kenny Anderson	.40
7	Eddie Jones	.75
8	Derrick Coleman	.25
9	Anthony Mason	.25
10	Chris Carr	.25
11	Hersey Hawkins	.25
12	B.J. Armstrong	.25
13	Shawn Kemp	.50
14	Bob Sura	.25
15	Lamond Murray	.25
16	Michael Finley	.40
17	Cedric Ceballos	.25
18	Dirk Nowitzki	1.00
19	Erick Strickland	.25
20	Antonio McDyess	.50
21	Nick Van Exel	.40
22	Grant Hill	3.00
23	Jerry Stackhouse	.40
24	Lindsey Hunter	.25
25	Christian Laettner	.25
26	Antawn Jamison	1.00
27	Chris Mills	.25
28	Larry Hughes	1.25
29	Charles Barkley	.75
30	Hakeem Olajuwon	.75
31	Cuttino Mobley	.40
32	Reggie Miller	.40
33	Jalen Rose	.40
34	Rik Smits	.25
35	Maurice Taylor	.25
36	Derek Anderson	.40
37	Tyrone Nesby	.25
38	Kobe Bryant	4.00
39	Shaquille O'Neal	2.00
40	Glen Rice	.40
41	Tim Hardaway	.60
42	Alonzo Mourning	.50
43	Jamal Mashburn	.40
44	Ray Allen	.50
45	Sam Cassell	.40
46	Glenn Robinson	.40
47	Kevin Garnett	3.00
48	Terrell Brandon	.40
49	Joe Smith	.40
50	Stephon Marbury	1.00
51	Keith Van Horn	.75
52	Jamie Feick	.25
53	Kerry Kittles	.25
54	Allan Houston	.40
55	Latrell Sprewell	.75
56	Patrick Ewing	.40
57	Darrell Armstrong	.25
58	Ron Mercer	.75
59	Michael Doleac	.25
60	Allen Iverson	2.50
61	Toni Kukoc	.50
62	Eric Snow	.25
63	Anfernee Hardaway	1.50
64	Jason Kidd	1.50
65	Tom Gugliotta	.40
66	Scottie Pippen	1.50
67	Steve Smith	.40
68	Damon Stoudamire	.40
69	Jason Williams	1.50
70	Predrag Stojakovic	.40
71	Chris Webber	1.50
72	Vlade Divac	.25
73	Tim Duncan	3.00
74	David Robinson	.75
75	Avery Johnson	.25
76	Gary Payton	.75
77	Vin Baker	.40
78	Vernon Maxwell	.25
79	Vince Carter	5.00
80	Tracy McGrady	1.50
81	Doug Christie	.25
82	Karl Malone	.75
83	John Stockton	.40
84	Jeff Hornacek	.25
85	Mike Bibby	.50
86	Shareef Abdur-Rahim	1.00
87	Othella Harrington	.25
88	Mitch Richmond	.40
89	Juwan Howard	.40
90	Rod Strickland	.40
91	*Elton Brand*	175.00
92	*Steve Francis*	400.00
93	*Baron Davis*	100.00
94	*Lamar Odom*	250.00
95	*Jonathan Bender*	125.00
96	*Wally Szczerbiak*	100.00
97	*Richard Hamilton*	100.00
98	*Andre Miller*	100.00
99	*Shawn Marion*	150.00
100	*Jason Terry*	60.00
101	*Trajan Langdon*	50.00
102	*Aleksandar Radojevic*	10.00
103	*Corey Maggette*	100.00
104	*William Avery*	25.00
105	*Ron Artest*	40.00
106	*James Posey*	40.00
107	*Quincy Lewis*	20.00
108	*Dion Glover*	20.00
109	*Kenny Thomas*	20.00
110	*Devean George*	40.00
111	*Tim James*	15.00
112	*Vonteego Cummings*	20.00
113	*Jumaine Jones*	15.00
114	*Scott Padgett*	12.00
115	*Adrian Griffin*	20.00
116	*Anthony Carter*	30.00
117	*Todd MacCulloch*	12.00
118	*Chucky Atkins*	20.00
119	*Obinna Ekezie*	10.00
120	*Eddie Robinson*	30.00
121	*Michael Ruffin*	15.00
122	*Laron Profit*	20.00
123	*Cal Bowdler*	12.00
124	*Chris Herren*	20.00
125	*Milt Palacio*	12.00
126	*Jeff Foster*	10.00
127	*Ryan Bowen*	10.00
128	*Tim Young*	10.00
129	*Derrick Dial*	10.00
130	*Greg Buckner*	10.00
131	*Rodney Buford*	20.00
132	*Evan Eschmeyer*	15.00
133	*Jermaine Jackson*	12.00
134	*John Celestand*	12.00
135	*Ryan Robertson*	10.00

1999-00 SP Authentic SP Athletic

SP Athletic was a 12-card insert that featured players on a foil card, with a small color image in the bottom right and a larger, foil image in the background. Cards were numbered with an "A" prefix and inserted 1:12 packs.

		MT
Complete Set (12):		25.00
Common Player:		.50
Inserted 1:12		
A1	Grant Hill	4.00
A2	Shareef Abdur-Rahim	1.50
A3	Jason Kidd	2.00
A4	Vince Carter	6.00
A5	Steve Francis	4.00
A6	Scottie Pippen	2.00
A7	Paul Pierce	1.50
A8	Kobe Bryant	5.00
A9	Stephon Marbury	1.50
A10	Michael Finley	.50
A11	Eddie Jones	1.00
A12	Kevin Garnett	4.00

1999-00 SP Authentic SP First Class

SP First Class was a 12-card insert featuring action shots of players inside a white frame. Cards were numbered with an "FC" prefix and seeded 1:12 packs.

		MT
Complete Set (12):		15.00
Common Player:		.50
Inserted 1:12		
FC1	Kevin Garnett	4.00
FC2	Kobe Bryant	5.00
FC3	Gary Payton	1.00
FC4	Tim Hardaway	.75
FC5	Antonio McDyess	.60
FC6	Allan Houston	.50
FC7	Jason Kidd	2.00
FC8	Reggie Miller	.50
FC9	Jason Williams	2.00
FC10	Allen Iverson	4.00
FC11	David Robinson	1.00
FC12	Shaquille O'Neal	3.00

1999-00 SP Authentic Maximum Force

This 15-card insert set was seeded 1:4 packs of SP Authentic. Cards were numbered with an "M" prefix and featured silver foil.

		MT
Complete Set (15):		10.00
Common Player:		.25
Inserted 1:4		
M1	Karl Malone	.60
M2	Antawn Jamison	.75
M3	Shareef Abdur-Rahim	.75
M4	Tim Duncan	2.00
M5	Allen Iverson	2.00
M6	Michael Finley	.25
M7	Kevin Garnett	2.00
M8	Kobe Bryant	3.00
M9	Gary Payton	.60
M10	Keith Van Horn	.60
M11	Chris Webber	1.00
M12	Glenn Robinson	.25
M13	Alonzo Mourning	.50
M14	Antoine Walker	.50
M15	Antonio McDyess	.50

1999-00 SP Authentic Premier Powers

This nine-card insert set featured the elite players in the NBA. Premier Powers were numbered with a "P" prefix and inserted 1:72 packs.

		MT
Complete Set (9):		75.00
Common Player:		8.00
Inserted 1:72		
P1	Kobe Bryant	15.00
P2	Kevin Garnett	12.00
P3	Tim Duncan	12.00
P4	Elton Brand	12.00
P5	Vince Carter	20.00
P6	Lamar Odom	8.00

P7	Grant Hill	12.00
P8	Shaquille O'Neal	8.00
P9	Allen Iverson	10.00

1999-00 SP Authentic Sign of the Times

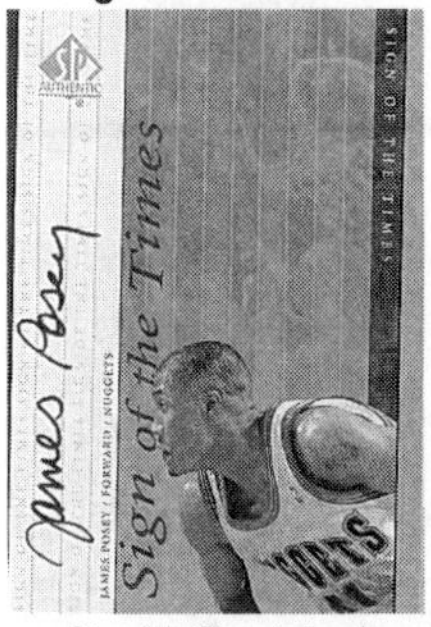

Sign of the Times featured autographs from 58 different players and were inserted 1:23 packs. The cards featured a silver background and the player's signature along a white strip on the left side. Cards were numbered with a two-letter code, usually corresponding to the player's initials. Gold versions of each card also exist and are hand-numbered to just 25 sets.

		MT
Common Player:		8.00
Inserted 1:23		
DA	Darrell Armstrong	12.00
RA	Ron Artest	25.00
CA	Chucky Atkins	12.00
WA	William Avery	10.00
JB	Jonathan Bender	35.00
MB	Mike Bibby	12.00
KB	Kobe Bryant	200.00
AC	Anthony Carter	25.00
CR	Austin Croshere	15.00
AD	Antonio Davis	8.00
BD	Baron Davis	25.00
MI	Michael Dickerson	12.00
ME	Mario Elie	8.00
SF	Steve Francis	150.00
KG	Kevin Garnett	150.00
DG	Dion Glover	10.00
BG	Brian Grant	8.00
AG	Adrian Griffin	10.00
TG	Tom Gugliotta	10.00
RH	Richard Hamilton	20.00
AN	Anfernee Hardaway	75.00
AH	Al Harrington	15.00
AL	Alan Henderson	8.00
LH	Larry Hughes	40.00
MK	Mark Jackson	10.00
AJ	Antawn Jamison	25.00
EJ	Eddie Jones	30.00
MJ	Michael Jordan	
BR	Brevin Knight	10.00
RL	Raef LaFrentz	12.00
TL	Trajan Langdon	15.00
QL	Quincy Lewis	12.00
SM	Sam Mack	8.00
CM	Corey Maggette	30.00
KM	Karl Malone	50.00
SH	Shawn Marion	25.00
MD	Antonio McDyess	15.00
TR	Tracy McGrady	40.00
AM	Andre Miller	25.00
CT	Cuttino Mobley	12.00
LM	Lamond Murray	8.00
TN	Tyrone Nesby	8.00
DN	Dirk Nowitzki	25.00
JO	Jermaine O'Neal	15.00
RP	Ruben Patterson	12.00
JP	James Posey	15.00
GR	Glen Rice	15.00
JR	Jalen Rose	20.00
JS	Jerry Stackhouse	15.00
DS	Damon Stoudamire	15.00
SU	Bob Sura	8.00
WS	Wally Szczerbiak	30.00
MT	Maurice Taylor	8.00
JT	Jason Terry	15.00
RT	Robert Traylor	8.00
AW	Antoine Walker	8.00
BW	Bonzi Wells	25.00
JY	Jayson Williams	10.00

1999-00 SP Authentic Sign of the Times Gold

This parallel version was printed with a gold background instead of the silver used on regular Sign of the Times inserts. The cards are hand-numbered to just 25 sets.

	MT
Gold	3x-5x

1999-00 SP Authentic SP Supremacy

SP Supremacy was a nine-card insert set featuring color shots of the player with the insert name and a border on the left and right side, both in holographic silver foil. Cards were numbered with an "S" prefix and seeded 1:24 packs.

		MT
Complete Set (9):		30.00
Common Player:		1.00
Inserted 1:24		
S1	Vince Carter	10.00
S2	Shaquille O'Neal	3.00
S3	Tim Duncan	5.00
S4	Kevin Garnett	5.00
S5	Jason Williams	2.00
S6	Stephon Marbury	1.50
S7	Gary Payton	1.00
S8	Kobe Bryant	8.00
S9	Grant Hill	5.00

1999-00 SPx

SPx was a 120-card set that featured 30 sequentially numbered rookies. Five rookies were signed and numbered to 500, 15 were signed and numbered to 2,500 and the remaining 10 were unsigned and numbered to 3,500. The cards featured a closer shot of the player along the left border, with an action shot taking up the remainder of the card, all on a thick, holographic finish. SPx was paralleled twice - Radiance, which has a prismatic background and numbered to 100, and Spectrum, which is numbered one of one. Inserts include: Decade of Jordan, Masters, Prolifics, SPxcitement, Spxtreme, Starscape and Winning Materials.

		MT
Complete Set (120):		2000.
Common Player:		.25
Minor Stars:		.50
Common Rookie (61-90):		8.00
Unsigned RCs numbered to 3,500		
Autographed RCs numbered to 2,500		
Cards 92/93/96/98/103 numbered to 500		
Pack (4):		10.00
Wax Box (18):		200.00
1	Dikembe Mutombo	.50
2	Alan Henderson	.25
3	Antoine Walker	.60
4	Paul Pierce	2.00
5	Kenny Anderson	.50
6	Eddie Jones	1.00
7	David Wesley	.25
8	Elden Campbell	.25
9	Toni Kukoc	.75
10	Dickey Simpkins	.25
11	Shawn Kemp	.60
12	Brevin Knight	.25
13	Michael Finley	.50
14	Cedric Ceballos	.25
15	Dirk Nowitzki	1.00
16	Antonio McDyess	.75
17	Nick Van Exel	.50
18	Chauncey Billups	.25
19	Grant Hill	4.00
20	Jerry Stackhouse	.50
21	Bison Dele	.25
22	Lindsey Hunter	.25
23	Antawn Jamison	1.50
24	Donyell Marshall	.25
25	John Starks	.25
26	Chris Mills	.25
27	Hakeem Olajuwon	1.00
28	Scottie Pippen	1.50
29	Charles Barkley	1.00
30	Reggie Miller	.50
31	Rik Smits	.25
32	Jalen Rose	.25
33	Chris Mullin	.50
34	Maurice Taylor	.75
35	Michael Olowokandi	1.00
36	Shaquille O'Neal	2.50
37	Kobe Bryant	5.00
38	Glen Rice	.50
39	Tim Hardaway	.75
40	Alonzo Mourning	.75
41	Dan Majerle	.25
42	P.J. Brown	.25
43	Glenn Robinson	.50
44	Ray Allen	.60
45	Sam Cassell	.50
46	Tim Thomas	.75
47	Kevin Garnett	4.00
48	Bobby Jackson	.25
49	Joe Smith	.50
50	Stephon Marbury	1.50
51	Keith Van Horn	1.00
52	Jayson Williams	.25
53	Patrick Ewing	.50
54	Latrell Sprewell	.50
55	Allan Houston	.50
56	Marcus Camby	.75
57	Charles Outlaw	.25
58	Darrell Armstrong	.50
59	Allen Iverson	3.00
60	Theo Ratliff	.25
61	Larry Hughes	1.00
62	Jason Kidd	1.50
63	Tom Gugliotta	.50
64	Clifford Robinson	.25
65	Brian Grant	.25
66	Jermaine O'Neal	.50
67	Rasheed Wallace	.50
68	Damon Stoudamire	.60
69	Jason Williams	2.50
70	Chris Webber	1.50
71	Vlade Divac	.25
72	Avery Johnson	.25
73	Tim Duncan	4.00
74	David Robinson	1.00
75	Sean Elliott	.25
76	Gary Payton	1.00
77	Vin Baker	.50
78	Jelani McCoy	.50
79	Charles Oakley	.25
80	Vince Carter	5.00
81	Tracy McGrady	1.50
82	Doug Christie	.25
83	Karl Malone	1.00
84	John Stockton	.50
85	Shareef Abdur-Rahim	1.25
86	Bryant Reeves	.25
87	Mike Bibby	1.00
88	Juwan Howard	.50
89	Mitch Richmond	.50
90	Rod Strickland	.50
91	*Elton Brand*	75.00
92	*Steve Francis AU500*	750.00
93	*Baron Davis AU500*	250.00
94	*Lamar Odom*	100.00
95	*Jonathan Bender*	40.00
96	*Wally Szczerbiak AU500*	150.00
97	*Richard Hamilton AU*	75.00
98	*Andre Miller AU500*	250.00
99	*Shawn Marion AU*	175.00
100	*Jason Terry AU*	60.00
101	*Trajan Langdon AU*	25.00
102	*Venson Hamilton*	8.00
103	*Corey Maggette AU500*	300.00
104	*William Avery AU*	15.00
105	*Dion Glover*	12.00
106	*Ron Artest AU*	30.00
107	*Cal Bowdler*	8.00
108	*James Posey AU*	20.00
109	*Quincy Lewis AU*	12.00
110	*Devean George AU*	30.00
111	*Tim James AU*	10.00
112	*Vonteego Cummings*	12.00
113	*Jumaine Jones AU*	15.00
114	*Scott Padgett AU*	10.00
115	*Kenny Thomas*	10.00
116	*Jeff Foster*	8.00
117	*Ryan Robertson*	8.00
118	*Chris Herren AU*	12.00
119	*Evan Eschmeyer AU*	10.00
120	*A.J. Bramlett AU*	8.00

1999-00 SPx Radiance

This 120-card parallel set reprinted every card from the base set and was sequentially numbered to 100 sets. The fronts of the cards featured a prismatic foil printing to distinguish them from the base cards.

	MT
Common Veteran (1-90):	5.00
Radiance Veterans:	15x-25x
Common Rookie (91-120):	15.00
Production 100 Sets	

1999-00 SPx Decade of Jordan

This 10-card insert featured 10 shots from Jordan's career, with one card representing each year he played. Cards were numbered with a "J" prefix and seeded 1:9 packs.

		MT
Complete Set (10):		40.00
Common Player:		5.00
Inserted 1:9		
J1	Michael Jordan	5.00
J2	Michael Jordan	5.00
J3	Michael Jordan	5.00
J4	Michael Jordan	5.00
J5	Michael Jordan	5.00
J6	Michael Jordan	5.00
J7	Michael Jordan	5.00
J8	Michael Jordan	5.00
J9	Michael Jordan	5.00
J10	Michael Jordan	5.00

1999-00 SPx SPx Masters

This 15-card insert set captured an action shot of top players over a prismatic silver background with the insert name across the top in gold foil. Masters were numbered with a "M" prefix and seeded 1:17 packs.

		MT
Complete Set (15):		65.00
Common Player:		1.00
Inserted 1:17		
M1	Michael Jordan	15.00
M2	Vince Carter	8.00
M3	Tim Duncan	5.00
M4	Allen Iverson	6.00
M5	Gary Payton	2.00
M6	Shareef Abdur-Rahim	3.00
M7	Keith Van Horn	2.00
M8	Grant Hill	8.00
M9	Kobe Bryant	10.00
M10	Kevin Garnett	8.00
M11	Karl Malone	2.00
M12	Allan Houston	1.00
M13	Jason Kidd	3.00
M14	Antoine Walker	1.50
M15	Jason Williams	5.00

1999-00 SPx Prolifics

This 15-card insert set featured top players over a red border, with the insert name across the bottom in white letters. Prolifics were numbered with a "P" prefix and inserted 1:17 packs.

		MT
Complete Set (15):		25.00
Common Player:		.75
Inseted 1:17		
P1	Michael Jordan	15.00
P2	Karl Malone	2.00
P3	Jason Kidd	3.00
P4	Reggie Miller	1.00
P5	Glen Rice	1.00
P6	Hakeem Olajuwon	2.00
P7	Mitch Richmond	.75
P8	Shawn Kemp	1.00
P9	Patrick Ewing	1.00
P10	Dikembe Mutombo	.75
P11	Scottie Pippen	3.00
P12	John Stockton	1.00
P13	David Robinson	1.50
P14	Tim Hardaway	1.50
P15	Charles Barkley	2.00

1999-00 SPx SPxcitement

This 20-card insert set features an action shot of the player over a prismatic silver-foil background. SPxcitement inserts were numbered with a "S" prefix and seeded 1:3 packs..

		MT
Complete Set (20):		10.00
Common Player:		.25
Inserted 1:3		
S1	Antoine Walker	.75
S2	Antonio McDyess	.75
S3	Antawn Jamison	1.00
S4	Vin Baker	.50
S5	Juwan Howard	.50
S6	Brian Grant	.25
S7	Brevin Knight	.25
S8	Glenn Robinson	.50
S9	Stephon Marbury	1.00
S10	Reggie Miller	.50
S11	Nick Van Exel	.50
S12	Alonzo Mourning	.60
S13	David Robinson	.75
S14	Hakeem Olajuwon	.75
S15	Toni Kukoc	.75
S16	Maurice Taylor	.75
S17	Darrell Armstrong	.50
S18	Latrell Sprewell	.50
S19	Tom Gugliotta	.50
S20	Michael Jordan	5.00

1999-00 SPx SPxtreme

This 20-card insert set featured top players with a circular pattern around the player over prismatic foil. SPxtreme inserts were numbered with a "X" prefix and inserted 1:6 packs.

		MT
Complete Set (20):		25.00
Common Player:		.50
Inserted 1:6		
X1	Michael Jordan	10.00
X2	Tim Hardaway	1.00
X3	Marcus Camby	1.00
X4	Jason Williams	3.00
X5	Shareef Abdur-Rahim	1.50
X6	Keith Van Horn	1.00
X7	Glen Rice	.50
X8	Gary Payton	1.00
X9	Grant Hill	5.00
X10	Allan Houston	.50
X11	Ray Allen	.50
X12	Michael Finley	.50
X13	Shawn Kemp	.40
X14	Shaquille O'Neal	3.00
X15	Paul Pierce	2.00
X16	Mike Bibby	1.00
X17	Michael Olowokandi	.75
X18	Damon Stoudamire	.75
X19	Mitch Richmond	.50
X20	Eddie Jones	.75

1999-00 SPx Starscape

This 10-card insert featured players over a prismatic, team colored background, with the insert name running down the right side in large, silver letters. Starscape inserts were numbered with a "ST" prefix and inserted 1:9 packs.

		MT
Complete Set (10):		15.00
Common Player:		.50
Inserted 1:9		
ST1	Michael Jordan	10.00
ST2	John Stockton	.50
ST3	Antonio McDyess	.75
ST4	Alonzo Mourning	.75
ST5	Shaquille O'Neal	3.00
ST6	Stephon Marbury	1.50
ST7	Chris Webber	1.50
ST8	Charles Barkley	1.00
ST9	Antawn Jamison	1.50
ST10	Scottie Pippen	1.50

1999-00 SPx SPx Winning Materials

This eight-card insert set featured both a piece of game-used jersey and shoe or shorts by top players. The card are horizontal and have two different areas for the game-used material to be displayed. Cards number 3 and 7 do not exist, while the rest of the set is inserted 1:252 packs. Cards are numbered with a "WM" prefix. In addition, Michael Jordan and Charles Barkley signed a limited amount of their cards, hand-numbered to the player's jersey (23 and 34, respectively).

		MT
Complete Set (8):		2500.
Common Player:		150.00
Inserted 1:252		
Cards 3 and 7 Not Issued		
WM1	Michael Jordan	1500.
WM1A	Michael Jordan	10000.
WM2	Karl Malone	100.00
WM2A	Karl Malone	750.00
WM4	Kobe Bryant	400.00
WM5	Paul Pierce	100.00
WM6	Kevin Garnett	300.00
WM8	Shaquille O'Neal	200.00
WM9	David Robinson	100.00
WM10	Charles Barkley	125.00

2000 SP Top Prospects

SP Top Prospects contained 50 cards, including 45 regular player cards and five short-printed (numbered to 3,000) Famous Firsts cards, numbered 46-50. The cards featured a color shot of the player in a brushed frame, with a large amount of white space as the border, and a SP Top Prospects logo in the bottom center. Inserts included: First Impressions, Future Glory, Game Jerseys, Honors Society and New Wave.

		MT
Complete Set (50):		75.00
Common Player:		.25
Minor Stars:		.40
Famous First (46-50):		5.00
Production 3,000 Sets		
Pack (5):		5.00
Box (15):		60.00
1	Kenyon Martin	5.00
2	Marcus Fizer	2.00
3	Michael Redd	.75
4	Desmond Mason	2.00
5	Cory Hightower	.50
6	Erick Barkley	1.00
7	A.J. Guyton	.50
8	Gabe Muoneke	.25
9	Khalid El-Amin	.75
10	Lavor Postell	.60
11	Donnell Harvey	.75
12	Terrance Roberson	.25
13	Matt Santangelo	.25
14	Jarrett Stephens	.25
15	Richie Frahm	.25
16	Pepe Sanchez	.60
17	Jason Collier	.50
18	Ed Cota	.50
19	Scoonie Penn	.40
20	Bootsy Thornton	.40
21	Eduardo Najera	.60
22	DerMarr Johnson	2.00
23	Chris Carrawell	.60
24	Craig Claxton	.75
25	Jaraan Cornell	.25
26	Gee Gervin	.25
27	Justin Love	.40
28	Joel Przybilla	.75
29	Eddie House	.50
30	Harold Arceneaux	.40
31	Johnny Hemsley	.40
32	Courtney Alexander	2.00
33	Lamont Barnes	.25
34	Pete Mickeal	.50
35	Brian Cardinal	.50
36	Kevin Freeman	.50
37	Jason Hart	.60
38	Eddie Gill	.25
39	Mamadou N'diaye	.50
40	Lamont Long	.40
41	Dan Langhi	.50
42	Shaheen Holloway	.50
43	Eric Coley	.40
44	JaRon Rush	.40
45	Stromile Swift	5.00
46	Michael Jordan FF	20.00
47	Kobe Bryant FF	15.00
48	Kevin Garnett FF	10.00
49	Anfernee Hardaway FF	5.00
50	Kenyon Martin FF	20.00

2000 SP Top Prospects New Wave

This 20-card insert set featured color action shots of players, with gold and black foil and a white border. New Wave cards are numbered with an "N" prefix and seeded 1:3 packs.

		MT
Complete Set (20):		18.00
Common Player:		.40
Inserted 1:3		
1	Kenyon Martin	5.00
2	Mamadou N'diaye	.60
3	Courtney Alexander	2.00
4	Craig Claxton	1.00
5	JaRon Rush	.40
6	Pete Mickeal	.75
7	Eduardo Najera	1.00
8	Erick Barkley	1.25
9	Scoonie Penn	.40
10	Desmond Mason	2.00
11	Chris Carrawell	1.00
12	Jason Hart	.60
13	DerMarr Johnson	2.50
14	Pepe Sanchez	.75
15	Jarrett Stephens	.40
16	Ed Cota	1.00
17	Marcus Fizer	4.00
18	A.J. Guyton	.75
19	Khalid El-Amin	1.00
20	Lavor Postell	.75

2000 SP Top Prospects First Impressions

Thirty-eight players from SP Top Prospects signed cards for inclusion in the First Impressions insert set. The cards featured a color shot of the player with the signature on the bottom of the card in the white space. The cards were numbered with a two-letter code, corresponding to the player's initials. Regular versions were seeded 1:5 packs, while Gold versions were numbered to 25 sets.

		MT
Complete Set (38):		500.00
Common Player:		4.00
Inserted 1:5		
Gold Cards:		2x-4x
Production 25 Sets		
CA	Courtney Alexander	30.00
HA	Harold Arceneaux	6.00
EB	Erick Barkley	15.00
CL	Calvin Booth	4.00
CC	Chris Carrawell	12.00
SC	Craig Claxton	15.00
JA	Jason Collier	8.00
JC	Jaraan Cornell	4.00
EC	Ed Cota	12.00
KD	Keyon Dooling	15.00
KE	Khalid El-Amin	12.00
MF	Marcus Fizer	60.00
KF	Kevin Freeman	6.00
GG	Gee Gervin	4.00
EG	Eddie Gill	4.00
AJ	A.J. Guyton	10.00
JH	Jason Hart	6.00
DH	Donnell Harvey	20.00
HE	Johnny Hemsley	4.00
CH	Cory Hightower	10.00
EH	Eddie House	6.00
DJ	DerMarr Johnson	30.00
DL	Dan Langhi	8.00
BL	Bobby Lazor	4.00
LL	Lamont Long	4.00
KM	Kenyon Martin	100.00
DM	Desmond Mason	25.00
PM	Pete Mickeal	8.00
MN	Mamadou N'diaye	8.00
EN	Eduardo Najera	12.00
SP	Scoonie Penn	6.00
LP	Lavor Postell	8.00
JP	Joel Przybilla	20.00
MR	Michael Redd	10.00
JR	JaRon Rush	8.00
PS	Pepe Sanchez	8.00
MS	Matt Santangelo	6.00
SS	Stromile Swift	60.00

2000 SP Top Prospects First Impressions Gold

This parallel set reprinted each First Impressions autographed card, but added sequential numbering to 25 sets.

	MT
Common Player:	15.00
Gold Cards:	2x-4x
Production 25 Sets	

2000 SP Top Prospects Future Glory

Future Glory consisted of 10 cards, which were numbered with an "F" prefix. The cards featured a shot of the player with the word "Future" on the left side and "Glory" on the right side, both in gold foil. These inserts were seeded 1:15 packs.

		MT
Complete Set (10):		20.00
Common Player:		.75
Inserted 1:15		
1	Scoonie Penn	.75
2	Kenyon Martin	8.00
3	Marcus Fizer	6.00
4	Chris Carrawell	1.50
5	Donnell Harvey	2.00
6	Erick Barkley	2.00
7	A.J. Guyton	1.00
8	DerMarr Johnson	3.00
9	Desmond Mason	2.50
10	Courtney Alexander	3.00

2000 SP Top Prospects Game Jersey

This nine-card insert featured swatches of game-used college jerseys on a horizontal format. A shot of the player appeared in the middle of the card, while a swatch of jersey was placed on the right. Cards were numbered with two letters, corresponding to the player's initials, and followed by "-J" suffix. Cards were inserted 1:150 packs. Two players, Kenyon Martin and Marcus Fizer, signed 25 of their cards. The signatures are numbered with "-A" suffix.

		MT
Complete Set (11):		500.00
Common Player:		25.00
Inserted 1:288		
CR	Craig Claxton	50.00
JC	Jason Collier	30.00
EC	Ed Cota	40.00
MF	Marcus Fizer	150.00
MFA	Marcus Fizer Auto/25	500.00
KF	Kevin Freeman	25.00
DL	Dan Langhi	30.00
KM	Kenyon Martin	200.00
KMA	Kenyon Martin Auto/25	1000.
PS	Pepe Sanchez	30.00
LP	Lavor Postell	30.00

2000 SP Top Prospects Honors Society

This 12-card set featured top college players on a gold tinted card, with a plain, white border. Honor Society cards were numbered with an "H" prefix and seeded 1:7 packs.

		MT
Complete Set (12):		15.00
Common Player:		.40
Inserted 1:7		
1	Kenyon Martin	5.00
2	Marcus Fizer	4.00
3	Courtney Alexander	2.00
4	Chris Carrawell	1.00
5	A.J. Guyton	.75
6	Desmond Mason	2.00
7	Erick Barkley	1.25
8	Ed Cota	1.00
9	Pepe Sanchez	.75
10	DerMarr Johnson	2.50
11	Scoonie Penn	.40
12	Stromile Swift	4.00

2000-01 SPx

		MT
Complete Set (138):		1500.
Common Player:		.25
Minor Stars:		.50
Common Rookie:		2.00
Production 4,500 Sets Unless Noted		
All Auto Cards Are Jersey Cards		
Pack (4):		7.00
Box (18):		165.00
1	Dikembe Mutombo	.25
2	Jim Jackson	.25
3	Jason Terry	.50
4	Paul Pierce	1.00
5	Kenny Anderson	.50
6	Antoine Walker	.75
7	Derrick Coleman	.50
8	Baron Davis	.75
9	David Wesley	.25
10	Elton Brand	2.00
11	Ron Artest	.50
12	Corey Benjamin	.25
13	Trajan Langdon	.25
14	Lamond Murray	.25
15	Andre Miller	.75
16	Michael Finley	.50
17	Gary Trent	.25
18	Dirk Nowitzki	1.00
19	Antonio McDyess	.75
20	Nick Van Exel	.50
21	Raef LaFrentz	.50
22	Jerry Stackhouse	.50
23	Michael Curry	.25
24	Jerome Williams	.25
25	Larry Hughes	1.50
26	Antawn Jamison	1.50
27	Mookie Blaylock	.25
28	Hakeem Olajuwon	1.00
29	Steve Francis	4.00
30	Shandon Anderson	.25
31	Reggie Miller	.50
32	Jalen Rose	.60
33	Austin Croshere	.25
34	Lamar Odom	2.00
35	Michael Olowokandi	.25
36	Tyrone Nesby	.25
37	Shaquille O'Neal	3.00
38	Kobe Bryant	5.00
39	Robert Horry	.25
40	Ron Harper	.25
41	Alonzo Mourning	.60
42	Eddie Jones	1.25
43	Tim Hardaway	.60
44	Glenn Robinson	.50
45	Sam Cassell	.50
46	Ray Allen	.60
47	Tim Thomas	.60
48	Kevin Garnett	4.00
49	Terrell Brandon	.50
50	Wally Szczerbiak	.60
51	Keith Van Horn	.75
52	Stephon Marbury	1.25
53	Jamie Feick	.25
54	Latrell Sprewell	1.50
55	Marcus Camby	.25
56	Allan Houston	.60
57	Grant Hill	3.00
58	Tracy McGrady	2.00
59	Darrell Armstrong	.25
60	Allen Iverson	3.00
61	Toni Kukoc	.60
62	Theo Ratliff	.25
63	Anfernee Hardaway	2.00
64	Jason Kidd	2.00
65	Shawn Marion	1.50
66	Steve Smith	.50
67	Rasheed Wallace	.75
68	Scottie Pippen	2.00
69	Bonzi Wells	.75
70	Jason Williams	1.00
71	Vlade Divac	.25
72	Chris Webber	2.00
73	David Robinson	1.00
74	Sean Elliott	.25
75	Tim Duncan	3.00
76	Gary Payton	1.00
77	Rashard Lewis	1.00
78	Vin Baker	.25
79	Vince Carter	6.00
80	Muggsy Bogues	.25
81	Antonio Davis	.25
82	Karl Malone	1.00
83	John Stockton	.50
84	Bryon Russell	.25
85	Shareef Abdur-Rahim	1.00
86	Michael Dickerson	.25
87	Mike Bibby	.50
88	Mitch Richmond	.50
89	Richard Hamilton	.60
90	Juwan Howard	.50
91	*Lavor Postell*	3.00
92	*Mark Madsen Auto/2500*	25.00
93	*Soumaila Samake*	2.00
94	*Michael Redd*	3.00
95	*Paul McPherson*	5.00
96	*Ruben Wolkowyski*	2.00
97	*Daniel Santiago*	3.00
98	*Pepe Sanchez*	3.00
99	*Marc Jackson/2500*	50.00
100	*Khalid El-Amin/2500*	6.00
101	*Iakovos Tsakalidis/2500*	5.00
102	*Jabari Smith/2500*	6.00
103	*Jason Hart/2500*	4.00
104	*Stephen Jackson/2500*	12.00
105	*Eduardo Najera/500*	40.00
106	*Hanno Mottola/500*	20.00
107	*Eddie House/500*	80.00
108	*Dan Langhi/500*	25.00
109	*A.J. Guyton/500*	35.00
110	*Chris Porter/500*	125.00
111	*Mike Miller Auto/2500*	125.00
112	*Keyon Dooling Auto/2500*	75.00
113	*Courtney Alexander Auto/2500*	75.00
114	*Desmond Mason Auto/2500*	75.00
115	*Jamaal Magloire Auto/2500*	30.00
116	*DeShawn Stevenson Auto/2500*	100.00
117	*DerMarr Johnson Auto/2500*	60.00
118	*Mateen Cleaves Auto/2500*	40.00
119	*Morris Peterson Auto/2500*	100.00
120	*Jerome Moiso Auto/2500*	20.00
121	*Donnell Harvey Auto/2500*	15.00
122	*Quentin Richardson Auto/2500*	75.00
123	*Jamal Crawford Auto/2500*	60.00
124	*Erick Barkley Auto/2500*	25.00
125	*Hidayet Turkoglu Auto/2500*	60.00
126	*Etan Thomas Auto/2500*	20.00
127	*Mamadou N'diaye Auto/2500*	15.00
128	*Joel Przybilla Auto/2500*	15.00
129	*Jason Collier Auto/2500*	15.00
130	*Craig "Speedy" Claxton Auto/2500*	25.00
131	*Kenyon Martin Auto/900*	150.00
132	*Stromile Swift Auto/900*	200.00
133	*Darius Miles Auto/900*	450.00
134	*Marcus Fizer Auto/900*	100.00
135	*Chris Mihm Auto/900*	50.00
136	*Jake Voskuhl Auto/2500*	12.00
137	*Pete Mickeal Auto/2500*	15.00
138	*Dalibor Bagaric*	2.00

2000-01 SPx Spectrum

	MT
Common Player:	15.00
Spectrum Veterans:	25x-50x
Production 25 Sets	
All Auto Cards Are Jersey Cards	

2000-01 SPx SPxcitement

		MT
Complete Set (20):		18.00
Common Player:		.40
Inserted 1:5		
S1	Kobe Bryant	4.00
S2	Gary Payton	.75
S3	Rasheed Wallace	.60
S4	Jason Williams	.75
S5	Ray Allen	.50
S6	Tim Duncan	2.50
S7	Stephon Marbury	1.25
S8	Allen Iverson	2.50
S9	Jerry Stackhouse	.40
S10	Kevin Garnett	3.00
S11	Antawn Jamison	1.25
S12	Paul Pierce	.75
S13	Lamar Odom	1.50
S14	Elton Brand	1.50
S15	Vince Carter	5.00
S16	Antonio McDyess	.60
S17	Michael Finley	.40
S18	Jalen Rose	.50
S19	Richard Hamilton	.50
S20	Jason Kidd	1.50

2000-01 SPx SPxtreme

		MT
Complete Set (11):		15.00
Common Player:		.75
Inserted 1:8		
X1	Kevin Garnett	3.00
X2	Steve Francis	3.00
X3	Chris Webber	1.50
X4	Elton Brand	1.50
X5	Shareef Abdur-Rahim	.75
X6	Larry Hughes	1.00
X7	Vince Carter	5.00
X8	Kobe Bryant	4.00
X9	Scottie Pippen	1.50
X10	Anfernee Hardaway	1.50
X11	Shaquille O'Neal	2.00

2000-01 SPx SPx Masters

		MT
Complete Set (11):		20.00
Common Player:		.75
Inserted 1:8		
M1	Michael Jordan	6.00
M2	Kobe Bryant	4.00
M3	Steve Francis	3.00
M4	Elton Brand	1.50
M5	Tim Duncan	2.50
M6	Jason Kidd	1.50
M7	Kevin Garnett	3.00
M8	Karl Malone	.75
M9	Shaquille O'Neal	2.50
M10	Gary Payton	.75
M11	Vince Carter	5.00

2000-01 SPx SPx Winning Materials

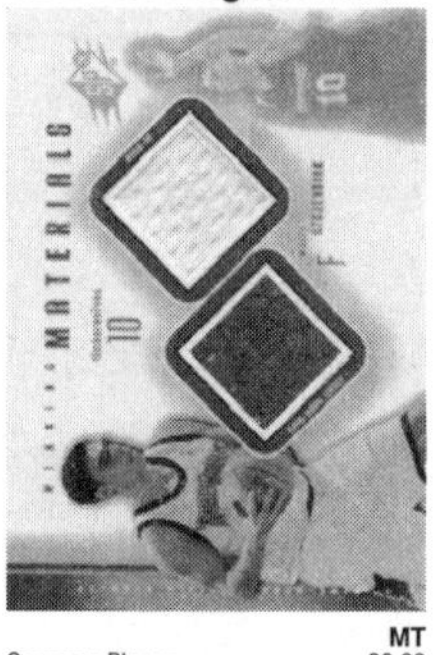

		MT
Common Player:		20.00
Regular Cards Inserted 1:72		
Autographs Inserted 1:252		
TB1	Terrell Brandon	20.00
KB1	Kobe Bryant	200.00
KB2	Kobe Bryant	200.00
KB3	Kobe Bryant	200.00
KBA1	Kobe Bryant	400.00
KBA2	Kobe Bryant	400.00
MF1	Marcus Fizer	30.00
MFA1	Marcus Fizer	50.00
KG1	Kevin Garnett	40.00
KG2	Kevin Garnett	50.00
KG3	Kevin Garnett	40.00
KGA1	Kevin Garnett	200.00
KGA2	Kevin Garnett	200.00
DM1	DerMarr Johnson	30.00
DMA1	DerMarr Johnson	40.00
MJA1	Michael Jordan	2000.
MJA2	Michael Jordan	2000.
MM1	Karl Malone	40.00
MM2	Karl Malone	
MM3	Karl Malone	50.00
KM1	Kenyon Martin	60.00
KMA1	Kenyon Martin	90.00
CM1	Chris Mihm	20.00
BR1	Bryon Russell	20.00
JS1	John Stockton	50.00
WS1	Wally Szczerbiak	25.00
WS2	Wally Szczerbiak	25.00

2000-01 SP Authentic

		MT
Complete Set (136):		1750.
Common Player:		.30
Minor Stars:		.40
Common Rookie:		8.00
Pack (5):		5.00
Box (24):		85.00
1	Jason Terry	.50
2	Alan Henderson	.30
3	Lorenzen Wright	.30
4	Paul Pierce	.75
5	Antoine Walker	.60
6	Bryant Stith	.30
7	Jamal Mashburn	.50
8	Baron Davis	.60
9	David Wesley	.30
10	Elton Brand	1.50
11	Ron Artest	.40
12	Ron Mercer	.40
13	Andre Miller	.50
14	Lamond Murray	.30
15	Jim Jackson	.30
16	Michael Finley	.50
17	Dirk Nowitzki	1.00
18	Steve Nash	.30
19	Antonio McDyess	.60
20	Nick Van Exel	.40
21	Raef LaFrentz	.30
22	Jerry Stackhouse	.40
23	Chucky Atkins	.30
24	Joe Smith	.30
25	Antawn Jamison	1.00
26	Larry Hughes	.75
27	Mookie Blaylock	.30
28	Steve Francis	3.00
29	Hakeem Olajuwon	.75
30	Cuttino Mobley	.40
31	Reggie Miller	.50
32	Jermaine O'Neal	.50
33	Jalen Rose	.50
34	Travis Best	.30
35	Lamar Odom	1.50
36	Corey Maggette	.50
37	Eric Piatkowski	.30
38	Shaquille O'Neal	2.50
39	Kobe Bryant	4.00
40	Isaiah Rider	.40
41	Horace Grant	.30
42	Eddie Jones	1.00
43	Brian Grant	.30
44	Tim Hardaway	.50
45	Ray Allen	.50
46	Glenn Robinson	.40
47	Sam Cassell	.30
48	Kevin Garnett	3.00
49	Terrell Brandon	.40
50	Chauncey Billups	.30
51	Wally Szczerbiak	.40
52	Stephon Marbury	1.00
53	Keith Van Horn	.50
54	Aaron Williams	.30
55	Latrell Sprewell	1.25
56	Allan Houston	.50
57	Glen Rice	.40
58	Tracy McGrady	1.50
59	Grant Hill	2.00
60	Darrell Armstrong	.30
61	Allen Iverson	2.50
62	Dikembe Mutombo	.30
63	Aaron McKie	.30
64	Jason Kidd	1.50
65	Clifford Robinson	.30
66	Shawn Marion	1.25
67	Damon Stoudamire	.40
68	Steve Smith	.40
69	Rasheed Wallace	.60
70	Chris Webber	2.00
71	Jason Williams	.50
72	Predrag Stojakovic	.40
73	Tim Duncan	2.50
74	David Robinson	.75
75	Derek Anderson	.40
76	Gary Payton	.75
77	Rashard Lewis	.50
78	Patrick Ewing	.40
79	Vince Carter	5.00
80	Charles Oakley	.30
81	Antonio Davis	.30
82	Karl Malone	.75
83	John Stockton	.40
84	John Starks	.30
85	Shareef Abdur-Rahim	.75
86	Mike Bibby	.40
87	Michael Dickerson	.30
88	Richard Hamilton	.50
89	Mitch Richmond	.40
90	Christian Laettner	.30
91	*Kenyon Martin Auto 500*	150.00
92	*Stromile Swift Auto 500*	150.00
93	*Darius Miles Auto 500*	500.00
94	*Marcus Fizer 1250*	35.00
95	*Mike Miller Auto 500*	200.00
96	*DerMarr Johnson Auto 500*	75.00
97	*Chris Mihm 1250*	15.00
98	*Jamal Crawford 1250*	25.00
99	*Joel Przybilla 2000*	10.00
100	*Keyon Dooling 1250*	30.00
101	*Jerome Moiso 1250*	15.00
102	*Etan Thomas 2000*	12.00
103	*Courtney Alexander 1250*	75.00
104	*Mateen Cleaves 1250*	20.00
105	*Jason Collier 2000*	10.00
106	*Hidayet Turkoglu 1250*	40.00
107	*Desmond Mason 1250*	40.00
108	*Quentin Richardson 1250*	30.00
109	*Jamaal Magloire 1250*	15.00
110	*Craig "Speedy" Claxton 2000*	12.00
111	*Morris Peterson Auto 500*	150.00
112	*Donnell Harvey 2000*	12.00
113	*DeShawn Stevenson 1250*	30.00
114	*Iakovos Tsakalidis 2000*	8.00
115	*Soumaila Samake 2000*	8.00
116	*Erick Barkley 2000*	15.00
117	*Mark Madsen 2000*	15.00
118	*A.J. Guyton 1250*	15.00
119	*Olumide Oyedji 2000*	8.00
120	*Eddie House 1250*	25.00
121	*Eduardo Najera 2000*	10.00
122	*Lavor Postell 2000*	10.00
123	*Hanno Mottola 1250*	12.00
124	*Ira Newble 2000*	8.00
125	*Chris Porter 1250*	30.00
126	*Ruben Wolkowyski 2000*	8.00
127	*Pepe Sanchez 2000*	10.00
128	*Stephen Jackson 1250*	15.00
129	*Marc Jackson 1250*	30.00
130	*Dragan Tarlac 2000*	8.00
131	*Lee Nailon 2000*	8.00
132	*Mike Penberthy 1250*	15.00
133	*Mark Blount 2000*	8.00
134	*Dan Langhi 2000*	10.00
135	*Daniel Santiago 2000*	12.00
136	*Wang Zhizhi Auto 500*	250.00

2000-01 SP Authentic Athletic

	MT
Complete Set (7):	25.00
Common Player:	1.00

Inserted 1:24
A1 Allen Iverson 4.00
A2 Elton Brand 2.00
A3 Antonio McDyess 1.00
A4 Vince Carter 10.00
A5 Kobe Bryant 8.00
A6 Grant Hill 3.00
A7 Kevin Garnett 5.00

2000-01 SP Authentic First Class

MT
Complete Set (7): 15.00
Common Player: 1.00
Inserted 1:24
FC1 Shareef Abdur-Rahim 1.25
FC2 Kevin Garnett 5.00
FC3 Baron Davis 1.00
FC4 Shaquille O'Neal 4.00
FC5 Rashard Lewis 1.00
FC6 Paul Pierce 1.25
FC7 Kobe Bryant 8.00

2000-01 SP Authentic Premier Powers

MT
Complete Set (7): 20.00
Common Player: 1.00
Inserted 1:24
P1 Chris Webber 3.00
P2 Allen Iverson 4.00
P3 Kobe Bryant 8.00
P4 Rasheed Wallace 1.00
P5 Tracy McGrady 2.50
P6 Kevin Garnett 5.00
P7 Tim Duncan 4.00

2000-01 SP Authentic Sign of the Times Double

MT
Complete Set (18):
Common Player:
CA/DH Courtney Alexander, Donnell Harvey 20.00
KB/SF Kobe Bryant, Steve Francis 300.00
KB/KG Kobe Bryant, Kevin Garnett 350.00
KB/KM Kobe Bryant, Kenyon Martin 250.00
KB/TM Kobe Bryant, Tracy McGrady 350.00
MC/MP Mateen Cleaves, Morris Peterson 30.00
JC/DS Jamal Crawford, DeShawn Stevenson 30.00
FI/JC Marcus Fizer, Jamal Crawford 30.00
KG/TM Kevin Garnett, Kenyon Martin 75.00
MJ/JB Michael Jordan, Kobe Bryant 750.00
MJ/DR Michael Jordan, Julius Erving 750.00
KM/FI Kenyon Martin, Marcus Fizer 40.00
KM/SJ Kenyon Martin, Stephen Jackson 20.00
KM/DJ Kenyon Martin, DerMarr Johnson 30.00
KM/DA Kenyon Martin, Darius Miles 50.00
KM/SS Kenyon Martin, Stromile Swift 30.00
DA/QR Darius Miles, Quentin Richardson 50.00
DA/DS Darius Miles, DeShawn Stevenson 60.00

2000-01 SP Authentic Sign of the Times-Single

MT
Common Player: 10.00
Inserted 1:23
CA Courtney Alexander 25.00
AR Darrell Armstrong 12.00
EB Erick Barkley 10.00
JB Jonathan Bender 15.00
MB Mike Bibby 12.00
KB Kobe Bryant
SC Craig "Speedy" Claxton 10.00
MC Mateen Cleaves 12.00
JC Jamal Crawford 15.00
AC Austin Croshere 12.00
MF Michael Finley 15.00
FI Marcus Fizer 15.00
SF Steve Francis 40.00
KG Kevin Garnett
RH Richard Hamilton 15.00
DH Donnell Harvey 10.00
SJ Stephen Jackson 12.00
AJ Antawn Jamison 20.00
DJ DerMarr Johnson 15.00
EJ Eddie Jones 15.00
MM Mark Madsen 12.00
MA Corey Maggette 15.00
JA Jamaal Magloire 10.00
SM Shawn Marion 25.00
KM Kenyon Martin 25.00
DE Desmond Mason 15.00
AM Antonio McDyess
TM Tracy McGrady 30.00
CM Chris Mihm 10.00
DA Darius Miles 75.00
MK Mike Miller 40.00
RM Reggie Miller 75.00
JM Jerome Moiso 10.00
MN Mamadou N'diaye 10.00
DN Dirk Nowitzki 25.00
JO Jermaine O'Neal 15.00
GP Gary Payton 15.00
MP Mike Penberthy 10.00
MP Morris Peterson 25.00
JP Joel Przybilla 10.00
QR Quentin Richardson 15.00
JR Jalen Rose 15.00
[illegible]
DS DeShawn Stevenson 15.00
SS Stromile Swift 25.00
ET Etan Thomas 10.00
TT Tim Thomas 15.00
AW Antoine Walker 15.00

2000-01 SP Authentic Sign of the Times-Single Platinum

MT
Complete Set (28):
Common Player: 2x to 4x

2000-01 SP Authentic Sign of the Times Triple

"Too uncommon to price."

MT
Complete Set (6):
Common Player:
KBKGKM Kobe Bryant, Kevin Garnett, Kenyon Martin
KMSJMJ Kenyon Martin, Stephen Jackson, Marc Jackson
DRMGLB Julius Erving, Magic Johnson, Larry Bird
KBMJKG Kobe Bryant, Michael Jordan, Kevin Garnett
KBMJMG Kobe Bryant, Michael Jordan, Magic Johnson
KMSSDA Kenyon Martin, Stromile Swift, Darius Miles

2000-01 SP Authentic Special Forces

MT
Complete Set (7): 15.00
Common Player: 1.50
Inserted 1:24
SF1 Kobe Bryant 8.00
SF2 Steve Francis 4.00
SF3 Eddie Jones 1.50
SF4 Shaquille O'Neal 4.00
SF5 Stephon Marbury 1.50
SF6 Lamar Odom 2.50
SF7 Kevin Garnett 5.00

2000-01 SP Authentic SPectacular

MT
Complete Set (7): 20.00
Common Player: 1.00
Inserted 1:24
SP1 Kobe Bryant 8.00
SP2 Chris Webber 3.00
SP3 Latrell Sprewell 2.00
SP4 Vince Carter 10.00
SP5 Rashard Lewis 1.00
SP6 Tim Duncan 4.00
SP7 Karl Malone 1.25

2000-01 SP Authentic Supremacy

MT
Complete Set (7): 25.00
Common Player: 2.50
Inserted 1:24
S1 Shaquille O'Neal 4.00
S2 Tim Duncan 4.00
S3 Kevin Garnett 5.00
S4 Allen Iverson 4.00
S5 Kobe Bryant 8.00
S6 Vince Carter 10.00
S7 Jason Kidd 2.50

2000-01 SP Game Floor

MT
Complete Set (90): 1200.
Common Player: .75
Minor Stars: 1.00
Common Rookie: 10.00
Production 300 Sets
Each Rookie Has Two Versions
Pack (3): 20.00
Box (10): 165.00
1 Jason Terry 1.25
2 Toni Kukoc 1.25
3 Antoine Walker 1.25
4 Paul Pierce 2.00
5 Jamal Mashburn 1.00
6 Baron Davis 1.50
7 Elton Brand 3.00
8 Ron Mercer 1.00
9 Andre Miller 1.50
10 Lamond Murray .75
11 Michael Finley 1.00
12 Dirk Nowitzki 2.50
13 Antonio McDyess 1.25
14 Nick Van Exel 1.00
15 Jerry Stackhouse 1.00
16 Joe Smith .75
17 Antawn Jamison 2.00
18 Larry Hughes 2.00
19 Steve Francis 6.00
20 Maurice Taylor .75
21 Jalen Rose 1.00
22 Reggie Miller 1.00
23 Lamar Odom 3.00
24 Corey Maggette 1.50
25 Kobe Bryant 8.00
26 Shaquille O'Neal 5.00
27 Horace Grant .75
28 Eddie Jones 2.00
29 Tim Hardaway 1.00
30 Glenn Robinson 1.00
31 Ray Allen 1.25
32 Kevin Garnett 6.00
33 Terrell Brandon .75
34 Wally Szczerbiak 1.00
35 Stephon Marbury 2.00
36 Keith Van Horn 1.50
37 Latrell Sprewell 2.00
38 Allan Houston 1.25
39 Tracy McGrady 3.00
40 Darrell Armstrong .75
41 Allen Iverson 5.00
42 Dikembe Mutombo .75
43 Jason Kidd 3.00
44 Shawn Marion 2.50
45 Rasheed Wallace 1.25
46 Damon Stoudamire .75
47 Chris Webber 4.00
48 Jason Williams 2.00
49 Tim Duncan 5.00
50 David Robinson 2.00
51 Gary Payton 2.00
52 Rashard Lewis 1.50
53 Vince Carter 10.00
54 Charles Oakley .75
55 Karl Malone 2.00
56 John Stockton 1.00
57 Shareef Abdur-Rahim 2.00
58 Mike Bibby 1.00
59 Richard Hamilton 1.25
60 Mitch Richmond 1.00
61 *Kenyon Martin* 50.00
62 *Marc Jackson* 40.00
63 *Darius Miles* 200.00
64 *Morris Peterson* 60.00
65 *Mike Miller* 100.00
66 *Quentin Richardson* 40.00
67 *DerMarr Johnson* 30.00
68 *Chris Mihm* 12.00
69 *Jamal Crawford* 30.00
70 *Joel Przybilla* 12.00
71 *Keyon Dooling* 30.00
72 *Jerome Moiso* 15.00
73 *Mike Penberthy* 15.00
74 *Courtney Alexander* 100.00
75 *Mateen Cleaves* 20.00
76 *Wang Zhizhi* 100.00
77 *Hidayet Turkoglu* 40.00
78 *Desmond Mason* 40.00
79 *Marcus Fizer* 30.00
80 *Jamaal Magloire* 20.00
81 *Stromile Swift* 60.00
82 *DeShawn Stevenson* 50.00
83 *Stephen Jackson* 15.00
84 *Erick Barkley* 15.00
85 *Mark Madsen* 15.00
86 *Dan Langhi* 10.00
87 *Hanno Mottola* 10.00
88 *Paul McPherson* 15.00
89 *Eddie House* 25.00
90 *Chris Porter* 30.00
91 *Jason Collier* 10.00
92 *Craig Claxton* 15.00
93 *Ruben Wolkowyski* 10.00
94 *A.J. Guyton* 15.00
95 *Donnell Harvey* 12.00
96 *Ira Newble* 10.00
97 *Lee Nailon* 10.00
98 *Pepe Sanchez* 10.00
99 *Eduardo Najera* 15.00
100 *David Vanterpool* 10.00

2000-01 SP Game Floor Authentic Fabric/ Floor Combos

MT
Common Player: 20.00
Inserted 1:10
KB-SE Kobe Bryant 100.00
KG-SE Kevin Garnett 50.00
AI-SE Allen Iverson 75.00
MA-SE Marc Jackson 20.00
JK-SE Jason Kidd 25.00
RL-SE Rashard Lewis 20.00
KA-SE Karl Malone 30.00
SM-SE Stephon Marbury 25.00
JM-SE Jamal Mashburn 20.00
MD-SE Antonio McDyess 20.00
TM-SE Tracy McGrady 40.00
DM-SE Darius Miles 75.00
SO-SE Shaquille O'Neal 60.00
PP-SE Paul Pierce 25.00

2000-01 SP Game Floor Authentic Fabric/ Floor Combos SE

MT
Complete Set (14):
Common Player:
KB-C Kobe Bryant
KG-C Kevin Garnett
AI-C Allen Iverson
MA-C Marc Jackson
JK-C Jason Kidd
RL-C Rashard Lewis
KA-C Karl Malone
SM-C Stephon Marbury
JM-C Jamal Mashburn
MD-C Antonio McDyess
TM-C Tracy McGrady
DM-C Darius Miles
SO-C Shaquille O'Neal
PP-C Paul Pierce

2000-01 SP Game Floor Authentic Floor

MT
Common Player: 10.00
Inserted 1:10
SA Shareef Abdur-Rahim 15.00
CA Courtney Alexander 25.00
RA Ray Allen 20.00
RA2 Ray Allen 20.00
KB Kobe Bryant 50.00
KB2 Kobe Bryant 50.00
MC Mateen Cleaves 15.00
BD Baron Davis 15.00
KE Khalid El-Amin 10.00
MF Michael Finley 15.00
FI Marcus Fizer 15.00
SF Steve Francis 25.00
KG Kevin Garnett 30.00
KG2 Kevin Garnett 30.00
AH Allan Houston 15.00
AH2 Allan Houston 15.00
AI Allen Iverson 30.00
MA Marc Jackson 15.00
SJ Stephen Jackson 12.00
DJ DerMarr Johnson 15.00
EJ Eddie Jones 15.00
MJ Michael Jordan 60.00
JK Jason Kidd 15.00
RL Rashard Lewis 15.00
JM Jamaal Magloire 12.00
KA Karl Malone 15.00
SM Stephon Marbury 15.00
SM2 Stephon Marbury 15.00
SH Shawn Marion 15.00
KM Kenyon Martin 20.00
DE Desmond Mason 20.00
MD Antonio McDyess 12.00
MD2 Antonio McDyess 12.00
TM Tracy McGrady 25.00
DM Darius Miles 50.00
AM Andre Miller 12.00
MM Mike Miller 30.00
MT Dikembe Mutombo 10.00
SO Shaquille O'Neal 30.00
GP Gary Payton 15.00
MP Morris Peterson 25.00
PP Paul Pierce 15.00
SP Scottie Pippen 15.00
CP Chris Porter 15.00
JP Joel Przybilla 10.00
QR Quentin Richardson 15.00
DV David Robinson 15.00
GR Glenn Robinson 12.00
LS Latrell Sprewell 15.00
LS2 Latrell Sprewell 15.00
JS Jerry Stackhouse 15.00
DS DeShawn Stevenson 20.00
PS Predrag Stojakovic 15.00
SS Stromile Swift 25.00
WS Wally Szczerbiak 12.00
JT Jason Terry 12.00
RW Rasheed Wallace 15.00
RW2 Rasheed Wallace 15.00
CW Chris Webber 20.00
JW Jason Williams 15.00

2000-01 SP Game Floor Authentic Floor Autographs

MT
Common Player: 25.00
Production 200 Sets
CA-A Courtney Alexander 75.00
KB-A Kobe Bryant/8
FI-A Marcus Fizer 50.00
SF-A Steve Francis 100.00
KG-A Kevin Garnett/21 350.00
MA-A Marc Jackson 50.00
SJ-A Stephen Jackson 30.00
DJ-A DerMarr Johnson 40.00
MJ-A Michael Jordan/23 2000.
KM-A Kenyon Martin 75.00
DM-A Darius Miles 250.00
MM-A Mike Miller 125.00
MP-A Morris Peterson 75.00
JP-A Joel Przybilla 25.00
JS-A Jerry Stackhouse 50.00
DS-A DeShawn Stevenson 60.00
SS-A Stromile Swift 100.00

2000-01 SP Game Floor Authentic Floor Combos

MT
Common Player: 15.00
Inserted 1:10
C1 Allen Iverson, Shaquille O'Neal 60.00
C2 Marc Jackson, Stephen Jackson 15.00
C3 Stephon Marbury, Steve Francis 20.00
C4 Chris Webber, Jason Williams 25.00
C5 Darius Miles, Marc Jackson 40.00
C6 Michael Jordan, Larry Bird 250.00
C7 Kenyon Martin, Chris Webber 30.00
C8 Kenyon Martin, DerMarr Johnson 20.00
C9 Kenyon Martin, Marc Jackson 20.00
C10 Kenyon Martin, Stephen Jackson 15.00
C11 Kevin Garnett, Chris Webber 40.00
C12 Kevin Garnett, Tracy McGrady 40.00
C13 Kobe Bryant, Allen Iverson 75.00
C14 Kobe Bryant, Chris Webber 50.00
C15 Kobe Bryant, Darius Miles 75.00
C16 Kobe Bryant, Jason Kidd 40.00
C17 Michael Jordan, Karl Malone
C18 Karl Malone, John Stockton
C19 Kobe Bryant, Kenyon Martin 30.00
C20 Kobe Bryant, Kevin Garnett 50.00
C21 Kobe Bryant, Kevin Garnett 50.00
C22 Kobe Bryant, Larry Bird 150.00
C23 Jason Williams, Predrag Stojakovic 25.00
C24 Kobe Bryant, Michael Jordan 200.00
C25 Kobe Bryant, Shaquille O'Neal 75.00
C26 Kobe Bryant, Steve Francis 40.00
C27 Kobe Bryant, Tracy McGrady 40.00
C28 Jason Kidd, Shawn Marion 25.00
C29 Mateen Cleaves, Morris Peterson 20.00
C30 Kevin Garnett, Rasheed Wallace 25.00

2000-01 SP Game Floor Authentic Floor Combos SE

MT
Complete Set (30):
Common Player:
C1 Allen Iverson, Shaquille O'Neal
C2 Marc Jackson, Stephen Jackson
C3 Stephon Marbury, Steve Francis
C4 Chris Webber, Jason Williams
C5 Darius Miles, Marc Jackson
C6 Michael Jordan, Larry Bird
C7 Kenyon Martin, Chris Webber
C8 Kenyon Martin, DerMarr Johnson
C9 Kenyon Martin, Marc Jackson
C10 Kenyon Martin, Stephen Jackson
C11 Kevin Garnett, Chris Webber
C12 Kevin Garnett, Tracy McGrady
C13 Kobe Bryant, Allen Iverson
C14 Kobe Bryant, Chris Webber
C15 Kobe Bryant, Darius Miles
C16 Kobe Bryant, Jason Kidd
C17 Michael Jordan, Karl Malone
C18 Karl Malone, John Stockton
C19 Kobe Bryant, Kenyon Martin
C20 Kobe Bryant, Kevin Garnett
C21 Kobe Bryant, Kevin Garnett
C22 Kobe Bryant, Larry Bird
C23 Jason Williams, Predrag Stojakovic
C24 Kobe Bryant, Michael Jordan
C25 Kobe Bryant, Shaquille O'Neal
C26 Kobe Bryant, Steve Francis
C27 Kobe Bryant, Tracy McGrady
C28 Jason Kidd, Shawn Marion
C29 Mateen Cleaves, Morris Peterson
C30 Kevin Garnett, Rasheed Wallace

2001-02 SP Authentic

MT
Complete Set (165):
Common Player: .25
#'s 91-106 #'d to 1600
#'s 107-115 #'d to 550
#'s 116-131 Autographed #'d to 1525
#'s 132-140 Autographed #'d to 700
#'s 141-159 #'d to 2000
#'s 160-165 #'d to 1000
Pack (5): 5.00
Wax Box (24): 100.00
1 Shareef Abdur-Rahim .25
2 Jason Terry .25
3 Dion Glover .25
4 Paul Pierce 1.00
5 Antoine Walker .75
6 Kenny Anderson .25
7 Baron Davis .25
8 David Wesley .25
9 Jamal Mashburn .25
10 Jalen Rose .25
11 Fred Hoiberg .25
12 Marcus Fizer .25
13 Andre Miller .50
14 Lamond Murray .25
15 Chris Mihm .25
16 Dirk Nowitzki 1.00
17 Steve Nash .50
18 Michael Finley .50
19 Nick Van Exel .25
20 Antonio McDyess .50
21 Juwan Howard .25
22 James Posey .25
23 Jerry Stackhouse .50
24 Clifford Robinson .25
25 Ben Wallace .25
26 Antawn Jamison .50
27 Larry Hughes .25
28 Danny Fortson .25
29 Steve Francis 1.00
30 Cuttino Mobley .25
31 Reggie Miller .75
32 Al Harrington .25
33 Jermaine O'Neal .50
34 Darius Miles 2.00
35 Elton Brand 1.00
36 Lamar Odom 1.00
37 Corey Maggette .25
38 Kobe Bryant 6.00
39 Shaquille O'Neal 4.00
40 Rick Fox .25
41 Lindsey Hunter .25
42 Stromile Swift .25
43 Michael Dickerson .25
44 Jason Williams .25
45 Alonzo Mourning .50
46 Eddie Jones .25
47 Anthony Carter .25
48 Ray Allen .75
49 Glenn Robinson .50
50 Sam Cassell .25
51 Kevin Garnett 1.50
52 Terrell Brandon .25
53 Wally Szczerbiak 1.00
54 Joe Smith .25
55 Jason Kidd 2.00
56 Kenyon Martin .25
57 Mark Jackson .25
58 Allan Houston .25
59 Latrell Sprewell .25
60 Marcus Camby .25
61 Tracy McGrady 1.50
62 Grant Hill 1.00
63 Mike Miller 1.00
64 Allen Iverson 4.00
65 Dikembe Mutombo .25
66 Aaron McKie .25
67 Stephon Marbury .25
68 Shawn Marion .50
69 Anfernee Hardaway .25
70 Rasheed Wallace .25
71 Bonzi Wells .25
72 Derek Anderson .25
73 Chris Webber 1.25
74 Mike Bibby 1.00
75 Peja Stojakovic .75
76 Tim Duncan 2.00
77 David Robinson 1.00
78 Antonio Daniels .25
79 Gary Payton .50
80 Rashard Lewis .25
81 Desmond Mason .25
82 Vince Carter 4.00
83 Morris Peterson .25
84 Antonio Davis .25
85 Karl Malone .50
86 John Stockton .50
87 Donyell Marshall .25
88 Richard Hamilton .50
89 Courtney Alexander .25
90 Michael Jordan 12.00
91 *Tierre Brown* 5.00
92 *Damone Brown* 5.00
93 *Michael Bradley* 8.00
94 *Kedrick Brown* 10.00
95 *Alton Ford* 5.00
96 *Jason Collins* 10.00
97 *Antonis Fotsis* 5.00
98 *Mengke Bateer* 10.00
99 *Trenton Hassell* 5.00
100 *Jamison Brewer* 5.00
101 *Bobby Simmons* 5.00
102 *Mike James* 5.00
103 *Oscar Torres* 5.00
104 *Brandon Armstrong* 5.00
105 *Willie Solomon* 5.00
106 *Vladimir Radmanovic* 10.00
107 *Kirk Haston* 8.00
108 *Gerald Wallace* 15.00
109 *Andrei Kirilenko* 15.00
110 *Joseph Forte* 20.00
111 *Brendan Haywood* 20.00
112 *Zach Randolph* 15.00
113 *DeSagana Diop* 12.00
114 *Shane Battier* 60.00
115 *Pau Gasol* 50.00
116 *Alvin Jones* 5.00
117 *Zeljko Rebraca* 20.00
118 *Kenny Satterfield* 12.00
119 *Jarron Collins* 10.00
120 *Ruben Boumtje-Boumtje* 10.00
121 *Loren Woods* 10.00
122 *Earl Watson* 10.00
123 *Jeff Trepagnier* 10.00
124 *Brian Scalabrine* 10.00
125 *Terence Morris* 10.00
126 *Gilbert Arenas* 25.00
127 *Samuel Dalembert* 10.00
128 *Jeryl Sasser* 10.00
129 *Rodney White* 10.00
130 *Eddie Griffin* 40.00
131 *Tyson Chandler* 50.00
132 *Steven Hunter* 12.00
133 *Troy Murphy* 12.00
134 *Richard Jefferson* 50.00
135 *Joe Johnson* 40.00
136 *Eddy Curry* 60.00
137 *Jason Richardson* 100.00
138 *Tony Parker* 60.00
139 *Jamaal Tinsley* 60.00
140 *Kwame Brown* 50.00
141 Paul Pierce 3.00
142 Tim Duncan 4.00
143 Stephon Marbury 2.00
144 Shareef Abdur-Rahim 1.00
145 Ray Allen 2.00
146 Bonzi Wells 1.00
147 Kenyon Martin 1.00
148 Darius Miles 5.00
149 Baron Davis 2.00
150 Dirk Nowitzki 4.00
151 Antoine Walker 3.00
152 Mike Miller 3.00
153 Shawn Marion 3.00
154 Jason Kidd 5.00
155 Elton Brand 3.00
156 Antawn Jamison 2.00
157 Rashard Lewis 1.00
158 Steve Francis 3.00
159 Tracy McGrady 4.00
160 Kobe Bryant 12.00
161 Allen Iverson 10.00
162 Vince Carter 10.00
163 Shaquille O'Neal 10.00
164 Kevin Garnett 10.00
165 Michael Jordan 50.00

2001-02 SP Authentic MJ Tributes Portrait of of Champion

MT
Complete Set (1):
Numbered to 23 too uncommon to price
PCJ3 Michael Jordan

2001-02 SP Authentic MJ Tributes MJ Milestones Autographs

MT
Complete Set (2):
Common Player:
Numbered to 30 too uncommon to price
M4 Michael Jordan
M5 Michael Jordan

2001-02 SP Authentic Rookie Authentics

MT
Complete Set (23):
Common Player: 10.00
Numbered to 1275
RA-BA Brandon Armstrong 10.00
RA-MB Michael Bradley 10.00
RA-KB Kedrick Brown 10.00
RA-KW Kwame Brown 30.00
RA-TC Tyson Chandler 40.00
RA-JA Jarron Collins 10.00
RA-JC Jason Collins 10.00
RA-EC Eddy Curry 30.00
RA-SD Samuel Dalembert 10.00
RA-JF Joseph Forte 20.00
RA-EG Eddie Griffin 25.00
RA-TH Trenton Hassell 10.00
RA-SH Steven Hunter 10.00
RA-RJ Richard Jefferson 40.00
RA-JJ Joe Johnson 40.00
RA-AK Andrei Kirilenko 40.00
RA-TM Terence Morris 20.00
RA-TP Tony Parker 60.00
RA-VR Vladimir Radmanovic 10.00
RA-JR Jason Richardson 75.00
RA-JS Jeryl Sasser 10.00
RA-GW Gerald Wallace 25.00
RA-RW Rodney White 10.00

2001-02 SP Authentic SP Dual Signatures

MT
Complete Set (6):
Common Player:
Numbered to 50
Too uncommon to price at this time
MJ/KB Michael Jordan, Kobe Bryant
MG/LB Magic Johnson, Larry Bird
KB/MG Kobe Bryant, Magic Johnson
TC/EC Tyson Chandler, Eddy Curry
MJ/DR Michael Jordan, Julius Erving
DR/LB Julius Erving, Larry Bird

2001-02 SP Authentic SP Signatures

MT
Complete Set (24):
Common Player: 10.00
Numbered to 390
GA Gilbert Arenas 30.00
KW Kwame Brown 30.00
TC Tyson Chandler 50.00
JC Jason Collins 10.00
EG Eddie Griffin 20.00
SH Steven Hunter 10.00
RJ Richard Jefferson 40.00
DJ DerMarr Johnson 10.00
JJ Joe Johnson 30.00
AJ Alvin Jones 10.00
KM Kenyon Martin 20.00
MM Mike Miller 20.00
TM Troy Murphy 15.00
TP Tony Parker 75.00
MP Morris Peterson 15.00
VR Vladimir Radmanovic 20.00
JR Jason Richardson 125.00
QR Quentin Richardson 15.00
JS Jeryl Sasser 15.00
KS Kenny Satterfield 10.00
JT Jamaal Tinsley 40.00
GW Gerald Wallace 10.00
RW Rodney White 10.00
LW Loren Woods 10.00

2001-02 SP Authentic SP Star Signatures

MT
Complete Set (6):
Common Player:
Numbered to 75
Too uncommon to price at this time
SA-S Shareef Abdur-Rahim
KB-S Kobe Bryant
KG-S Kevin Garnett
MJ-S Michael Jordan
JK-S Jason Kidd
DM-S Darius Miles

A player's name in *italic type* indicates a rookie card.

2001-02 SP Authentic SP Triple Signatures

MT
Complete Set (6):
Common Player:
Numbered to 10 too uncommon to price
MJKBKG Michael Jordan, Kobe Bryant, Kevin Garnett
MJMGKB Michael Jordan, Magic Johnson, Kobe Bryant
DRMJKB Julius Erving, Michael Jordan, Kobe Bryant
JTJRTP Jamaal Tinsley, Jason Richardson, Tony Parker
DRLBMG Julius Erving, Larry Bird, Magic Johnson
DMLOQR Darius Miles, Lamar Odom, Quentin Richardson

2001-02 SP Authentic Superstar Authentics

MT
Complete Set (7):
Common Player: 25.00
Numbered to 200
SA-KB Kobe Bryant 150.00
SA-KG Kevin Garnett 50.00
SA-AI Allen Iverson 75.00
SA-MJ Michael Jordan 300.00
SA-JK Jason Kidd 50.00
SA-TM Tracy McGrady 50.00
SA-CW Chris Webber 40.00

2001-02 SPx

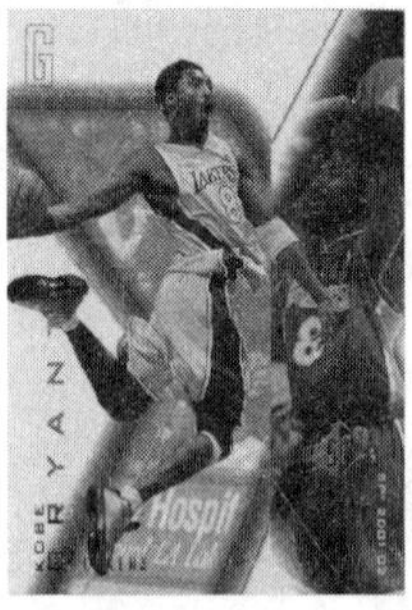

MT
Complete Set (140): 1600.
Common Player: .40
Minor Stars: .75
Common Rookie (91-105): 15.00
91-105 Production 2,400 Sets
Each #'d to 800, 3 versions
106-111 Production 750 Sets
Each #'d to 250, 3 versions
91-111 All versions have JSY & Auto
Common Rookie (121-140): 10.00
Production 1,999 Sets
Pack (4): 7.00
Box (18): 110.00
1 Jason Terry .75
2 Shareef Abdur-Rahim 1.00
3 DerMarr Johnson .75
4 Paul Pierce 1.25
5 Antoine Walker 1.00
6 Kenny Anderson .40
7 Baron Davis 1.25
8 Jamal Mashburn .75
9 David Wesley .40
10 Ron Mercer .75
11 Ron Artest .75
12 Marcus Fizer .75
13 Andre Miller 1.00
14 Lamond Murray .40
15 Chris Mihm .40
16 Michael Finley 1.00
17 Dirk Nowitzki 1.50
18 Steve Nash .75
19 Antonio McDyess 1.00
20 Nick Van Exel .75
21 Raef LaFrentz .40
22 Jerry Stackhouse 1.00
23 Chucky Atkins .40
24 Corliss Williamson .40
25 Antawn Jamison 1.50
26 Larry Hughes .40
27 Chris Porter .40
28 Steve Francis 2.50
29 Cuttino Mobley .75
30 Maurice Taylor .40
31 Reggie Miller 1.00
32 Jalen Rose 1.00
33 Jermaine O'Neal 1.25
34 Darius Miles 5.00
35 Elton Brand 1.50
36 Lamar Odom 1.50
37 Quentin Richardson 1.00
38 Kobe Bryant 6.00
39 Shaquille O'Neal 3.00
40 Rick Fox .40
41 Derek Fisher .40
42 Stromile Swift .75
43 Jason Williams .75
44 Michael Dickerson .75
45 Alonzo Mourning .75
46 Eddie Jones 1.25
47 Anthony Carter .40
48 Glenn Robinson 1.00
49 Ray Allen 1.25
50 Sam Cassell .75
51 Kevin Garnett 4.00
52 Wally Szczerbiak .75
53 Terrell Brandon .75
54 Chauncey Billups .40
55 Kenyon Martin .75
56 Keith Van Horn .75
57 Jason Kidd 2.00
58 Latrell Sprewell 1.50
59 Allan Houston 1.00
60 Marcus Camby .75
61 Tracy McGrady 3.00
62 Mike Miller 2.50
63 Grant Hill 2.00
64 Allen Iverson 4.00
65 Dikembe Mutombo .75
66 Aaron McKie .75
67 Stephon Marbury 1.25
68 Shawn Marion 1.50
69 Tom Gugliotta .40
70 Rasheed Wallace 1.00
71 Damon Stoudamire .40
72 Bonzi Wells .75
73 Chris Webber 2.50
74 Peja Stojakovic 1.25
75 Mike Bibby .75
76 Tim Duncan 2.50
77 David Robinson 1.00
78 Antonio Daniels .40
79 Gary Payton 1.25
80 Rashard Lewis 1.00
81 Desmond Mason .75
82 Vince Carter 6.00
83 Morris Peterson 1.00
84 Antonio Davis .40
85 Karl Malone 1.50
86 John Stockton 1.25
87 Donyell Marshall .40
88 Richard Hamilton 1.00
89 Courtney Alexander .75
90 Michael Jordan 15.00
91 *Tony Parker* 75.00
92 *Jamaal Tinsley* 100.00
93 *Samuel Dalembert* 15.00
94 *Gerald Wallace* 50.00
95 *Brandon Armstrong* 15.00
96 *Jeryl Sasser* 15.00
97 *Jason Collins* 15.00
98 *Michael Bradley* 20.00
99 *Steven Hunter* 15.00
100 *Troy Murphy* 40.00
101 *Richard Jefferson* 60.00
102 *Vladimir Radmanovic* 30.00
103 *Kedrick Brown* 40.00
104 *Joe Johnson* 60.00
105 *Kirk Haston* 30.00
106 *Rodney White* 75.00
107 *Eddie Griffin* 150.00
108 *Jason Richardson* 250.00
109 *Eddy Curry* 125.00
110 *Tyson Chandler* 140.00
111 *Kwame Brown* 150.00
121 *Shane Battier* 60.00
122 *Brendan Haywood* 20.00
123 *Joseph Forte* 15.00
124 *Zach Randolph* 20.00
125 *DeSagana Diop* 12.00
126 *Damone Brown* 10.00
127 *Andrei Kirilenko* 30.00
128 *Trenton Hassell* 15.00
129 *Gilbert Arenas* 10.00
130 *Earl Watson* 10.00
131 *Kenny Satterfield* 10.00
132 *Will Solomon* 10.00
133 *Bobby Simmons* 10.00
134 *Brian Scalabrine* 10.00
135 *Charlie Bell* 10.00
136 *Zeljko Rebraca* 10.00
137 *Loren Woods* 20.00
138 *Terence Morris* 10.00
139 *Jamison Brewer* 10.00
140 *Pau Gasol* 60.00

2001-02 SPx Winning Materials

MT
Common Player: 15.00
Inserted 1:18
CB Chauncey Billups 15.00
TB Terrell Brandon 15.00
KB Kobe Bryant 100.00
KG Kevin Garnett 50.00
KG2 Kevin Garnett 50.00
RH Richard Hamilton 20.00
AH Anfernee Hardaway 20.00
AI Allen Iverson 60.00
KM Karl Malone 30.00
KM2 Karl Malone 30.00
SM Shawn Marion 30.00
KE Kenyon Martin 20.00
MM Mike Miller 30.00
MO Michael Olowokandi 15.00
LP Lavor Postell 15.00
ST John Stockton 25.00
ST2 John Stockton 25.00
SS Stromile Swift 20.00
WS Wally Szczerbiak 20.00
KV Keith Van Horn 20.00

1972 Spalding

This seven-card set features black and white action and posed photos surrounded by a brown border that resembles a picture frame. The cards measure 8 1/2" x 11" and contain the words "Spalding Advisory Staff" in a gold bar under the photo.

NM
Complete Set (7): 45.00
Common Player: 4.00
(1) Rick Barry 8.00
(2) Rick Barry (Action Shot) 6.00
(3) Wilt Chamberlain (Philadelphia) 10.00
(4) Wilt Chamberlain (San Francisco) 12.00
(5) Julius Erving 8.00
(6) Gail Goodrich 5.00
(7) Luke Jackson 4.00

1978 Sports ID Patches

NM
Complete Set (6): 150.00
Common Player: 20.00
1 Darryl Dawkins 20.00
2 Julius Erving 75.00
3 Dan Issel 25.00
4 Bobby Jones 20.00
5 Nuggets Team Photo 20.00
6 David Thompson 40.00

1997 Sports Time USBL

This 50-card set was issued in two 25-card series. It includes 48 cards depicting highlights and historical moments in USBL history and two USBL logo cards.

MT
Complete Set (50): 25.00
Common Player: .25
1 Norris Coleman .25
2 Anthony Mason 3.00
3 Michael Anderson .25
4 Dallas Comegys .25
5 Anthony Pullard .25
6 Darrell Armstrong 3.00
7 Kermit Holmes .25
8 Lloyd Daniels 2.00
9 Roy Tarpley 2.00
10 Paul Graham .50
11 Nantambu Willingham .25
12 Michael Ray Richardson, Lloyd Free 2.00
13 Richard Dumas 1.00
14 International All-Star Debut .25
15 Keith Jennings .50
16 Duane Washington .50
17 Wes Matthews .50
18 Michael Adams 1.00
19 First USBL Game .75
20 Chuck Nevitt .25
21 The Awards 1.00
22 The First Game .25
23 The Beginning .25
24 Charlie Ward 1.00
25 Oliver Lee .25
26 Greg Sutton .25
27 1991 USBL Championship .25
28 Miami Tropics .25
29 New Haven SkyHawks .25
30 Back to Back Champions .25
31 Springfield Fame .25
32 Nate Johnson .25
33 Muggsy Bogues 2.00
34 Chris Collier .25
35 Sandhi Ortiz-Delvalle .25
36 Henri Abrams .25
37 Dan Cyrulik .25
38 Charles Smith .75
39 Mark Boyd .25
40 Tim Legler .75
41 Jerry Reynolds .75
42 The Road to the NBA .25
43 Series I Checklist 1.00
44 Series II Checklist 1.00
45 Atlanta Trojans-Atlantic City Seagulls .25
46 Connecticut Skyhawks-Florida Sharks .25
47 Jacksonville Barracudas-Long Island Surf .25
48 New Hampshire Thunder Loons-Philadelphia Power .25
49 Portland Wave-Raleigh Cougars .25
50 Tampa Bay Windjammers-Westchester Kings .25

1999 Sprite NBA Cans

This 10-can set was produced by Sprite, with cans available for a limited time during 1999. The cans featured a color action shot of the player on the opposite side from the Sprite logo.

MT
Complete Set (10): 8.00
Common Can: .50
Vin Baker .50
Kobe Bryant 2.00
Tim Duncan 2.00
Grant Hill 1.50
Allan Houston .50
Kerry Kittles .50
Brevin Knight .50
Alonzo Mourning .50
Mitch Richmond .50
Damon Stoudamire .50

1979-80 Spurs Police

This 15-card set was sponsored by Handy Dan and was distributed by the Express News in conjunction with the San Antonio Police. The set measures 2-5/8" x 4-1/8" and contain safey tips from the Spurs players.

NM
Complete Set (15): 6.00
Common Player: .25
1 Mike Evans .25
2 Billy Paultz .50
12 Mike Gale .25
13 James Silas .50
21 Irv Kiffin .25
30 Paul Griffin .25
31 Kevin Restani .25
35 Larry Kenon .50
44 George Gervin 4.00
53 Mark Olberding .25
54 Wiley Peck .25
NNO Bob Bass .25
NNO George Karl ACO .75
NNO Bernie LaReau .25
NNO Doug Moe CO .50

1988-89 Spurs Police/Diamond Shamrock

This eight-card set was sponsored by Diamond Shamrock, a regional convenience store chain headquartered in San Antonio. One card was given out each week with each $3 purchase or eight gallons of gas; these contain a tear-off tab. Another identical set was distributed by the San Antonio Police and doesn't contain the tear-off tab. The backs contain logos for both Diamond Shamrock and the San Antonio Police Department, with 100,000 and 50,000 sets produced, respectively.

MT
Complete Set (8): 6.00
Common Player: .50
1 Greg Anderson 33 .50
2 Willie Anderson 40 .50
3 Frank Brickowski 43 .50
4 Larry Brown CO 1.00
5 Dallas Comegys 22 .50
6 Johnny Dawkins 24 .50
7 Alvin Robertson 21 .50
8 David Robinson 50 5.00

1992-93 Stadium Club

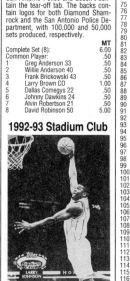

This set, which uses full-bleed photos, was issued in two 200-card series. The player's name and team are printed in gold foil at the bottom of the card, intersecting a Stadium Club logo. The backs are done horizontally and include 1991-92 and career statistics, a biography, a miniature version of the player's first Topps card, and a Sporting News Skills Rating System ranking. Subsets include Members Choice and Draft Picks cards. Beam Team cards were inserts.

MT
Complete Set (400): 60.00
Complete Series 1 (200): 20.00
Complete Series 2 (200): 40.00
Common Player: .10
Minor Stars: .20
Series 1 Pack: 1.25
Series 1 Wax Box (36): 35.00
Series 2 Pack: 4.00
Series 2 Wax Box (36): 100.00
1 Michael Jordan 7.00
2 Greg Anthony .10
3 Otis Thorpe .10
4 Jim Les .10
5 Kevin Willis .10
6 Derek Harper .10
7 Elden Campbell .10
8 A.J. English .10
9 Kenny Gattison .10
10 Drazen Petrovic .10
11 Chris Mullin .20
12 Mark Price .20
13 Karl Malone .50
14 Gerald Glass .10
15 Negele Knight .10
16 Mark Macon .10
17 Michael Cage .10
18 Kevin Edwards .10
19 Sherman Douglas .10
20 Ron Harper .10
21 Cliff Robinson .20
22 Byron Scott .10
23 Antoine Carr .10
24 Greg Dreiling .10
25 Bill Laimbeer .10
26 Hersey Hawkins .10
27 Will Perdue .10
28 Todd Lichti .10
29 Gary Grant .10
30 Sam Perkins .10
31 Jayson Williams .10
32 Magic Johnson 2.00
33 Larry Bird 1.50
34 Chris Morris .10
35 Nick Anderson .10
36 Scott Hastings .10
37 Ledell Eackles .10
38 Robert Pack .10
39 Dana Barros .10
40 Anthony Bonner .10
41 J.R. Reid .10
42 Tyrone Hill .10
43 Rik Smits .20
44 Kevin Duckworth .10
45 LaSalle Thompson .10
46 Brian Williams .10
47 Willie Anderson .10
48 Ken Norman .10
49 Mike Iuzzolino .10
50 Isiah Thomas .30
51 Alec Kessler .10
52 Johnny Dawkins .10
53 Avery Johnson .10
54 Stacey Augmon .10
55 Charles Oakley .10
56 Rex Chapman .10
57 Charles Shackleford .10
58 Jeff Ruland .10
59 Craig Ehlo .10
60 Jon Koncak .10
61 Danny Schayes .10
62 David Benoit .10
63 Robert Parish .20
64 Mookie Blaylock .10
65 Sean Elliott .10
66 Mark Aguirre .10
67 Scott Williams .10
68 Doug West .10
69 Kenny Anderson .50
70 Randy Brown .10
71 Muggsy Bogues .10
72 Spud Webb .10
73 Sedale Threatt .10
74 Chris Gatling .10
75 Derrick McKey .10
76 Sleepy Floyd .10
77 Mahmoud Abdul-Rauf .10
78 Thurl Bailey .10
79 Steve Smith .40
80 Cedric Ceballos .10
81 Anthony Bowie .10
82 John Williams .10
83 Paul Graham .10
84 Willie Burton .10
85 Vernon Maxwell .10
86 Stacey King .10
87 B.J. Armstrong .10
88 Kevin Gamble .10
89 Terry Catledge .10
90 Jeff Malone .10
91 Sam Bowie .10
92 Orlando Woolridge .10
93 Steve Kerr .10
94 Eric Leckner .10
95 Loy Vaught .10
96 Jud Buechler .10
97 Doug Smith .10
98 Sidney Green .10
99 Jerome Kersey .10
100 Patrick Ewing .50
101 Ed Nealy .10
102 Shawn Kemp 1.00
103 Luc Longley .10
104 George McCloud .25
105 Ron Anderson .10
106 Moses Malone .10
107 Tony Smith .10
108 Terry Porter .10
109 Blair Rasmussen .10
110 Bimbo Coles .10
111 Grant Long .10
112 John Battle .10
113 Brian Oliver .10
114 Tyrone Corbin .10
115 Benoit Benjamin .10
116 Rick Fox .10
117 Rafael Addison .10
118 Danny Young .10
119 Fat Lever .10
120 Terry Cummings .10
121 Felton Spencer .10
122 Joe Kleine .10
123 Johnny Newman .10

124	Gary Payton	1.00
125	Kurt Rambis	.10
126	Vlade Divac	.10
127	John Paxson	.10
128	Lionel Simmons	.10
129	Randy Wittman	.10
130	Winston Garland	.10
131	Jerry Reynolds	.10
132	Dell Curry	.10
133	Fred Roberts	.10
134	Michael Adams	.10
135	Charles Jones	.10
136	Frank Brickowski	.10
137	Alton Lister	.10
138	Horace Grant	.30
139	Greg Sutton	.10
140	John Starks	.20
141	Detlef Schrempf	.10
142	Rodney Monroe	.10
143	Pete Chilcutt	.10
144	Mike Brown	.10
145	Rony Seikaly	.10
146	Donald Hodge	.10
147	Kevin McHale	.20
148	Ricky Pierce	.10
149	Brian Shaw	.10
150	Reggie Williams	.10
151	Kendall Gill	.10
152	Tom Chambers	.10
153	Jack Haley	.10
154	Terrell Brandon	1.00
155	Dennis Scott	.10
156	Mark Randall	.10
157	Kenny Payne	.10
158	Bernard King	.10
159	Tate George	.10
160	Scott Skiles	.10
161	Pervis Ellison	.10
162	Marcus Liberty	.10
163	Rumeal Robinson	.10
164	Anthony Mason	.10
165	Les Jepsen	.10
166	Kenny Smith	.10
167	Randy White	.10
168	Dee Brown	.10
169	Chris Dudley	.10
170	Armon Gilliam	.10
171	Eddie Johnson	.10
172	A.C. Green	.10
173	Darrell Walker	.10
174	Bill Cartwright	.10
175	Mike Gminski	.10
176	Tom Tolbert	.10
177	Buck Williams	.10
178	Mark Eaton	.10
179	Danny Manning	.20
180	Glen Rice	.20
181	Sarunas Marciulionis	.10
182	Danny Ferry	.10
183	Chris Corchiani	.10
184	Dan Majerle	.10
185	Alvin Robertson	.10
186	Vern Fleming	.10
187	Kevin Lynch	.10
188	John Williams	.10
189	S.C. Checklist 1-100	.10
190	S.C. Checklist 101-200	.10
191	David Robinson (MC)	.50
192	Larry Johnson (MC)	.50
193	Derrick Coleman (MC)	.20
194	Larry Bird (MC)	1.00
195	Billy Owens (MC)	.10
196	Dikembe Mutombo (MC)	.40
197	Charles Barkley (MC)	.50
198	Scottie Pippen (MC)	1.00
199	Clyde Drexler (MC)	.30
200	John Stockton (MC)	.30
201	Shaquille O'Neal (MC)	4.00
202	Chris Mullin (MC)	.20
203	Glen Rice (MC)	.20
204	Isiah Thomas (MC)	.20
205	Karl Malone (MC)	.30
206	Christian Laettner (MC)	.30
207	Patrick Ewing (MC)	.25
208	Dominique Wilkins (MC)	.20
209	Alonzo Mourning (MC)	1.00
210	Michael Jordan (MC)	3.00
211	Tim Hardaway	.20
212	Rodney McCray	.10
213	Larry Johnson	1.00
214	Charles Smith	.10
215	Kevin Brooks	.10
216	Kevin Johnson	.25
217	*Duane Cooper*	.10
218	*Christian Laettner*	1.00
219	Tim Perry	.10
220	Hakeem Olajuwon	1.25
221	*Lee Mayberry*	.20
222	Mark Bryant	.10
223	*Robert Horry*	1.00
224	*Tracy Murray*	.20
225	Greg Grant	.10
226	Rolando Blackman	.10
227	James Edwards	.10
228	Sean Green	.10
229	Buck Johnson	.10
230	Andrew Lang	.10
231	*Tracy Moore*	.20
232	*Adam Keefe*	.25
233	Tony Campbell	.10
234	Rod Strickland	.10
235	Terry Mills	.10
236	Billy Owens	.10
237	*Bryant Stith*	.50
238	*Tony Bennett*	.20
239	David Wood	.10
240	Jay Humphries	.10
241	Doc Rivers	.10
242	Wayman Tisdale	.10
243	*Litterial Green*	.20
244	*Jon Barry*	.20
245	Brad Daugherty	.10
246	Nate McMillan	.10
247	*Shaquille O'Neal*	35.00
248	*Chris Smith*	.20
249	Duane Ferrell	.10
250	*Anthony Peeler*	.30
251	*Gundars Vetra*	.20
252	Danny Ainge	.10
253	Mitch Richmond	.30
254	*Malik Sealy*	.30
255	*Brent Price*	.20
256	Xavier McDaniel	.10
257	*Bobby Phills*	.75
258	Donald Royal	.10
259	Olden Polynice	.10
260	Dominique Wilkins	.25
261	Larry Krystkowiak	.10
262	Duane Causwell	.10
263	*Todd Day*	.50
264	Sam Mack	.10
265	John Stockton	.50
266	Eddie Lee Wilkins	.10
267	Gerald Glass	.10
268	Robert Pack	.10
269	Gerald Wilkins	.10
270	Reggie Lewis	.10
271	Scott Brooks	.10
272	*Randy Woods*	.10
273	Dikembe Mutombo	.75
274	Kiki Vandeweghe	.10
275	Rich King	.10
276	Jeff Turner	.10
277	Vinny Del Negro	.10
278	Marlon Maxey	.10
279	Elmore Spencer	.10
280	Cedric Ceballos	.50
281	*Alex Blackwell*	.10
282	Terry Davis	.10
283	Morton Wiley	.10
284	Trent Tucker	.10
285	Carl Herrera	.10
286	*Eric Anderson*	.10
287	Clyde Drexler	.50
288	*Tom Gugliotta*	1.50
289	Dale Ellis	.10
290	Lance Blanks	.10
291	Tom Hammonds	.10
292	Eric Murdock	.10
293	*Walt Williams*	.50
294	Gerald Paddio	.10
295	Brian Howard	.10
296	Ken Williams	.10
297	*Alonzo Mourning*	4.00
298	Larry Nance	.10
299	Jeff Grayer	.10
300	*Dave Johnson*	.10
301	Bob McCann	.10
302	Bart Kofoed	.10
303	Anthony Cook	.10
304	*Radisav Curcic*	.10
305	*John Crotty*	.10
306	Brad Sellers	.10
307	Marcus Webb	.10
308	Winston Garland	.10
309	Walter Palmer	.10
310	Rod Higgins	.10
311	Travis Mays	.10
312	Alex Stivrins	.10
313	Greg Kite	.10
314	Dennis Rodman	2.00
315	Mike Sanders	.10
316	Ed Pinckney	.10
317	*Harold Miner*	.30
318	Pooh Richardson	.10
319	*Oliver Miller*	.50
320	*Latrell Sprewell*	3.00
321	Anthony Pullard	.10
322	Mark Randall	.10
323	Jeff Hornacek	.10
324	Rick Mahorn	.10
325	*Sean Rooks*	.20
326	Paul Pressey	.10
327	James Worthy	.10
328	Matt Bullard	.10
329	Reggie Smith	.10
330	*Don MacLean*	.30
331	John Williams	.10
332	Frank Johnson	.10
333	*Hubert Davis*	.30
334	*Lloyd Daniels*	.20
335	*Steve Bardo*	.10
336	Jeff Sanders	.10
337	Tree Rollins	.10
338	Michael Williams	.10
339	*Lorenzo Williams*	.10
340	Harvey Grant	.10
341	Avery Johnson	.10
342	Bo Kimble	.10
343	*LaPhonso Ellis*	.25
344	Mookie Blaylock	.10
345	*Isaiah Morris*	.10
346	*C. Weatherspoon*	1.00
347	Manute Bol	.10
348	Victor Alexander	.10
349	*Corey Williams*	.10
350	*Byron Houston*	.20
351	Stanley Roberts	.10
352	*Anthony Avent*	.20
353	Vincent Askew	.10
354	Herb Williams	.10
355	J.R. Reid	.10
356	Brad Lohaus	.10
357	Reggie Miller	.50
358	Blue Edwards	.10
359	Tom Tolbert	.10
360	Charles Barkley	1.00
361	David Robinson	1.00
362	Dale Davis	.10
363	Robert Werdann	.10
364	Chuck Person	.10
365	Alaa Abdelnaby	.10
366	Dave Jamerson	.10
367	Scottie Pippen	2.00
368	Mark Jackson	.10
369	Keith Askins	.10
370	Marty Conlon	.10
371	Chucky Brown	.10
372	LaBradford Smith	.10
373	Tim Kempton	.10
374	Sam Mitchell	.10
375	John Salley	.10
376	Mario Elie	.10
377	Mark West	.10
378	David Wingate	.10
379	*Jaren Jackson*	.10
380	Rumeal Robinson	.10
381	Kennard Winchester	.10
382	*Walter Bond*	.10
383	*Isaac Austin*	.10
384	Derrick Coleman	.20
385	Larry Smith	.10
386	Joe Dumars	.30
387	*Matt Geiger*	.10
388	*Stephen Howard*	.10
389	William Bedford	.10
390	Jayson Williams	.10
391	Kurt Rambis	.10
392	*Keith Jennings*	.10
393	Steve Kerr	.10
394	Larry Stewart	.10
395	Danny Young	.10
396	Doug Overton	.10
397	Mark Acres	.10
398	John Bagley	.10
399	Checklist 201-300	.10
400	Checklist 301-400	.10

1992-93 Stadium Club Beam Team

These cards were randomly inserted into Series II Stadium Club packs, one per every 36 15-card packs. Fronts feature color action photos bordered by metallic "beams." Backs are numbered and have career highlights and a color head shot.

		MT
Complete Set (21):		260.00
Common Player:		2.00
1	Michael Jordan	90.00
2	Dominique Wilkins	5.00
3	Shawn Kemp	10.00
4	Clyde Drexler	8.00
5	Scottie Pippen	16.00
6	Chris Mullin	3.00
7	Reggie Miller	7.00
8	Glen Rice	3.00
9	Jeff Hornacek	2.00
10	Jeff Malone	2.00
11	John Stockton	7.00
12	Kevin Johnson	4.00
13	Mark Price	3.00
14	Tim Hardaway	4.00
15	Charles Barkley	13.00
16	Hakeem Olajuwon	18.00
17	Karl Malone	7.00
18	Patrick Ewing	6.00
19	Dennis Rodman	20.00
20	David Robinson	13.00
21	Shaquille O'Neal	160.00

1992-93 Stadium Club Members Only

Members Only sets were available exclusively to the Topps Members Only Club and were sold in factory sets for $199 a piece. The cards are very similar to regular-issue cards except for the gold "Members Only" stamp on the front. The set includes all 400 cards as well as the 21-card Beam Team insert. While the regular-issue cards carry a premium price, usually 2-3 times that of cards from packs, the Beam Teams go for roughly half that of their counterparts.

		MT
Complete Set (421):		350.00
Common Player:		.25
Common Beam Team (BT1-BT21):		.50
1	Michael Jordan	30.00
2	Greg Anthony	.50
3	Otis Thorpe	.50
4	Jim Les	.25
5	Kevin Willis	.50
6	Derek Harper	.50
7	Elden Campbell	.50
8	A.J. English	.25
9	Kenny Gattison	.25
10	Drazen Petrovic	.50
11	Chris Mullin	1.50
12	Mark Price	.50
13	Karl Malone	6.00
14	Gerald Glass	.25
15	Negele Knight	.25
16	Mark Macon	.25
17	Michael Cage	.25
18	Kevin Edwards	.25
19	Sherman Douglas	.25
20	Ron Harper	.50
21	Cliff Robinson	.50
22	Byron Scott	.50
23	Antoine Carr	.25
24	Greg Dreiling	.25
25	Bill Laimbeer	.50
26	Hersey Hawkins	.50
27	Will Perdue	.25
28	Todd Lichti	.25
29	Gary Grant	.25
30	Sam Perkins	.50
31	Jayson Williams	.25
32	Magic Johnson	8.00
33	Larry Bird	18.00
34	Chris Morris	.25
35	Nick Anderson	.50
36	Scott Hastings	.25
37	Ledell Eackles	.25
38	Robert Pack	.25
39	Dana Barros	.50
40	Anthony Bonner	.25
41	J.R. Reid	.25
42	Tyrone Hill	.25
43	Rik Smits	.50
44	Kevin Duckworth	.25
45	LaSalle Thompson	.25
46	Brian Williams	.25
47	Willie Anderson	.25
48	Ken Norman	.25
49	Mike Iuzzolino	.25
50	Isiah Thomas	2.50
51	Alec Kessler	.25
52	Johnny Dawkins	.50
53	Avery Johnson	.50
54	Stacey Augmon	.50
55	Charles Oakley	.50
56	Rex Chapman	.25
57	Charles Shackleford	.25
58	Jeff Ruland	.25
59	Cralg Ehlo	.25
60	Jon Koncak	.25
61	Danny Schayes	.25
62	David Benoit	.25
63	Robert Parish	1.00
64	Mookie Blaylock	.50
65	Sean Elliott	.50
66	Mark Aguirre	.50
67	Scott Williams	.25
68	Doug West	.25
69	Kenny Anderson	1.00
70	Randy Brown	.25
71	Muggsy Bogues	.50
72	Spud Webb	.50
73	Sedale Threatt	.25
74	Chris Gatling	.25
75	Derrick McKey	.25
76	Sleepy Floyd	.25
77	Mahmoud Abdul-Rauf	.50
78	Thurl Bailey	.25
79	Steve Smith	.50
80	Cedric Ceballos	.25
81	Anthony Bowie	.25
82	John Williams	.25
83	Paul Graham	.25
84	Willie Burton	.25
85	Vernon Maxwell	.25
86	Stacey King	.25
87	B.J. Armstrong	.50
88	Kevin Gamble	.25
89	Terry Catledge	.25
90	Jeff Malone	.50
91	Sam Bowie	.50
92	Orlando Woolridge	.25
93	Steve Kerr	.25
94	Eric Leckner	.25
95	Loy Vaught	.50
96	Jud Buechler	.25
97	Doug Smith	.25
98	Sidney Green	.25
99	Jerome Kersey	.25
100	Patrick Ewing	5.00
101	Ed Nealy	.25
102	Shawn Kemp	3.00
103	Luc Longley	.25
104	George McCloud	.25
105	Ron Anderson	.25
106	Moses Malone UER (Rookie Card is 1975-76, not 1976-77)	1.00
107	Tony Smith	.25
108	Terry Porter	.25
109	Blair Rasmussen	.25
110	Bimbo Coles	.25
111	Grant Long	.25
112	John Battle	.25
113	Brian Oliver	.25
114	Tyrone Corbin	.25
115	Benoit Benjamin	.25
116	Rick Fox	.25
117	Rafael Addison	.25
118	Danny Young	.25
119	Fat Lever	.25
120	Terry Cummings	.50
121	Felton Spencer	.25
122	Joe Kleine	.25
123	Johnny Newman	.25
124	Gary Payton	4.00
125	Kurt Rambis	.50
126	Vlade Divac	.50
127	John Paxson	.50
128	Lionel Simmons	.25
129	Randy Wittman	.25
130	Winston Garland	.25
131	Jerry Reynolds	.25
132	Dell Curry	.25
133	Fred Roberts	.25
134	Michael Adams	.25
135	Charles Jones	.25
136	Frank Brickowski	.25
137	Alton Lister	.25
138	Horace Grant	.50
139	Greg Sutton	.25
140	John Starks	.50
141	Detlef Schrempf	.50
142	Rodney Monroe	.25
143	Pete Chilcutt	.25
144	Mike Brown	.25
145	Rony Seikaly	.25
146	Donald Hodge	.25
147	Kevin McHale	1.50
148	Ricky Pierce	.25
149	Brian Shaw	.25
150	Reggie Williams	.25
151	Kendall Gill	.25
152	Tom Chambers	.50
153	Jack Haley	.25
154	Terrell Brandon	3.00
155	Dennis Scott	.50
156	Mark Randall	.25
157	Kenny Payne	.25
158	Bernard King	.50
159	Tate George	.25
160	Scott Skiles	.25
161	Pervis Ellison	.25
162	Marcus Liberty	.25
163	Rumeal Robinson	.25
164	Anthony Mason	.50
165	Les Jepsen	.25
166	Kenny Smith	.25
167	Randy White	.25
168	Dee Brown	.25
169	Chris Dudley	.25
170	Armon Gilliam	.50
171	Eddie Johnson	.50
172	A.C. Green	.50
173	Darrell Walker	.25
174	Bill Cartwright	.25
175	Mike Gminski	.50
176	Tom Tolbert	.25
177	Buck Williams	.50
178	Mark Eaton	.25
179	Danny Manning	.50
180	Glen Rice	2.00
181	Sarunas Marciulionis	.25
182	Danny Ferry	.25
183	Chris Corchiani	.25
184	Dan Majerle	.50
185	Alvin Robertson	.25
186	Vern Fleming	.25
187	Kevin Lynch	.25
188	John Williams	.50
189	S.C. Checklist 1-100	.25
190	S.C. Checklist 101-200	.25
191	David Robinson (MC)	3.50
192	Larry Johnson (MC)	1.00
193	Derrick Coleman (MC)	.50
194	Larry Bird (MC)	8.00
195	Billy Owens (MC)	.50
196	Dikembe Mutombo (MC)	.50
197	Charles Barkley (MC)	4.00
198	Scottie Pippen (MC)	4.00
199	Clyde Drexler (MC)	3.00
200	John Stockton (MC)	4.00
201	Shaquille O'Neal (MC)	10.00
202	Chris Mullin (MC)	1.00
203	Glen Rice (MC)	1.00
204	Isiah Thomas (MC)	1.00
205	Karl Malone (MC)	5.00
206	Christian Laettner (MC)	1.00
207	Patrick Ewing (MC)	2.00
208	Dominique Wilkins (MC)	2.00
209	Alonzo Mourning (MC)	4.00
210	Michael Jordan (MC)	14.00
211	Tim Hardaway	.50
212	Rodney McCray	.25
213	Larry Johnson	2.00
214	Charles Smith	.25
215	Kevin Brooks	.25
216	Kevin Johnson	.75
217	Duane Cooper	.25
218	Christian Laettner UER (Missing '92 Draft Pick logo)	4.00
219	Tim Perry	.25
220	Hakeem Olajuwon	5.00
221	Lee Mayberry	.50
222	Mark Bryant	.25
223	Robert Horry	3.50
224	Tracy Murray (Missing '92 Draft Pick logo)	.75
225	Greg Grant	.25
226	Rolando Blackman	.50
227	James Edwards UER (Rookie Card is 1978-79, not 1980-81)	.25
228	Sean Green	.25
229	Buck Johnson	.25
230	Andrew Lang	.25
231	Tracy Moore	.25
232	Adam Keefe UER (Missing '92 Draft Pick logo)	.50
233	Tony Campbell	.25
234	Rod Strickland	1.00
235	Terry Mills	.25
236	Billy Owens	.50
237	Bryant Stith UER (Missing '92 Draft Pick logo)	.50
238	Tony Bennett UER (Missing '92 Draft Pick logo)	.25
239	David Wood	.25
240	Jay Humphries	.25
241	Doc Rivers	.25
242	Wayman Tisdale	.50
243	Litterial Green	.25
244	Jon Barry	.25
245	Brad Daugherty	.50
246	Nate McMillan	.25
247	Shaquille O'Neal	35.00
248	Chris Smith	.25
249	Duane Ferrell	.25
250	Anthony Peeler	.75
251	Gundars Vetra	.25
252	Danny Ainge	.50
253	Mitch Richmond	2.00
254	Malik Sealy	.50
255	Brent Price	.50
256	Xavier McDaniel	.25
257	Bobby Phills	1.00
258	Donald Royal	.25
259	Olden Polynice	.25
260	Dominique Wilkins UER (Scoring 10,000th point, should be 20,000th)	.75
261	Larry Krystkowiak	.25
262	Duane Causwell	.25
263	Todd Day	1.00
264	Sam Mack	.25
265	John Stockton	3.00
266	Eddie Lee Wilkins	.25
267	Gerald Glass	.25
268	Robert Pack	.25
269	Gerald Wilkins	.25
270	Reggie Lewis	.50
271	Scott Brooks	.25
272	Randy Woods UER (Missing '92 Draft Pick logo)	.25
273	Dikembe Mutombo	1.00
274	Kiki Vandeweghe	.50
275	Rich King	.25
276	Jeff Turner	.25
277	Vinny Del Negro	.25
278	Marlon Maxey	.25
279	Elmore Spencer UER (Missing '92 Draft Pick logo)	.25
280	Cedric Ceballos	1.00
281	Alex Blackwell	.25
282	Terry Davis	.25
283	Morton Wiley	.25
284	Trent Tucker	.25
285	Carl Herrera	.25
286	Eric Anderson	.25
287	Clyde Drexler	3.00
288	Tom Gugliotta	4.00
289	Dale Ellis	.50
290	Lance Blanks	.25
291	Tom Hammonds	.25
292	Eric Murdock	.25
293	Walt Williams	2.00
294	Gerald Paddio	.25
295	Brian Howard	.25
296	Ken Williams	.25
297	Alonzo Mourning	15.00
298	Larry Nance	.50
299	Jeff Grayer	.25
300	Dave Johnson	.25
301	Bob McCann	.25
302	Bart Kofoed	.25
303	Anthony Cook	.25
304	Radisav Curcic	.25
305	John Crotty	.25
306	Brad Sellers	.25
307	Marcus Webb	.25
308	Winston Garland	.25
309	Walter Palmer	.25
310	Rod Higgins	.25
311	Travis Mays	.25
312	Alex Stivrins	.25
313	Greg Kite	.25
314	Dennis Rodman	10.00
315	Mike Sanders	.25
316	Ed Pinckney	.25
317	Harold Miner	.50
318	Pooh Richardson	.25
319	Oliver Miller	.75
320	Latrell Sprewell	6.00
321	Anthony Pullard	.25
322	Mark Randall	.25
323	Jeff Hornacek	.25
324	Rick Mahorn UER (Rookie Card is 1981-82, not 1992-93)	.25
325	Sean Rooks	.25
326	Paul Pressey	.25
327	James Worthy	1.00
328	Matt Bullard	.25
329	Reggie Smith	.25
330	Don MacLean UER (Missing '92 Draft Pick logo)	.50
331	John Williams UER (Rookie Card erroneously shows Hot Rod)	.25
332	Frank Johnson	.25
333	Hubert Davis UER (Missing '92 Draft Pick logo)	1.00
334	Lloyd Daniels	.50
335	Steve Bardo	.25
336	Jeff Sanders	.25
337	Tree Rollins	.25
338	Michael Williams	.25
339	Lorenzo Williams	.50
340	Harvey Grant	.25
341	Avery Johnson	.50
342	Bo Kimble	.25
343	LaPhonso Ellis UER (Missing '92 Draft Pick logo)	3.00
344	Mookie Blaylock	.50
345	Isaiah Morris	.25
346	Clarence Weatherspoon	1.00
347	Manute Bol	.25
348	Victor Alexander	.25
349	Corey Williams	.25
350	Byron Houston	.25
351	Stanley Roberts	.25
352	Anthony Avent	.25
353	Vincent Askew	.25
354	Herb Williams	.25
355	J.R. Reid	.25
356	Brad Lohaus	.25
357	Reggie Miller	3.00
358	Blue Edwards	.25
359	Tom Tolbert	.25
360	Charles Barkley	5.00
361	David Robinson	5.00
362	Dale Davis	.50
363	Robert Werdann UER (Missing '92 Draft Pick logo)	.25
364	Chuck Person	.50
365	Alaa Abdelnaby	.25
366	Dave Jamerson	.25
367	Scottie Pippen	10.00
368	Mark Jackson	.25
369	Keith Askins	.25
370	Marty Conlon	.25
371	Chucky Brown	.25
372	LaBradford Smith	.25
373	Tim Kempton	.25
374	Sam Mitchell	.25
375	John Salley	.25
376	Mario Elie	.25
377	Mark West	.25
378	David Wingate	.25
379	Jaren Jackson	.25
380	Rumeal Robinson	.25
381	Kennard Winchester	.25
382	Walter Bond	.25
383	Isaac Austin	.25
384	Derrick Coleman	.50
385	Larry Smith	.25
386	Joe Dumars	.75
387	Matt Geiger UER (Missing '92 Draft Pick logo)	.75
388	Stephen Howard	.25
389	William Bedford	.25
390	Jayson Williams	.25
391	Kurt Rambis	.50
392	Keith Jennings	.25
393	Steve Kerr UER (The words key stat are repeated on back)	.25
394	Larry Stewart	.25
395	Danny Young	.25
396	Doug Overton	.25
397	Mark Acres	.25
398	John Bagley	.25
399	Checklist 201-300	.25
400	Checklist 301-400	.25
BT1	Michael Jordan	50.00
BT2	Dominique Wilkins	1.00
BT3	Shawn Kemp	10.00
BT4	Clyde Drexler	5.00
BT5	Scottie Pippen	15.00
BT6	Chris Mullin	3.00
BT7	Reggie Miller	3.00
BT8	Glen Rice	3.00
BT9	Jeff Hornacek	1.00
BT10	Jeff Malone	.50
BT11	John Stockton	3.00
BT12	Kevin Johnson	1.00
BT13	Mark Price	.50
BT14	Tim Hardaway	5.00
BT15	Charles Barkley	6.00
BT16	Hakeem Olajuwon	8.00
BT17	Karl Malone	6.00
BT18	Patrick Ewing	4.00
BT19	Dennis Rodman	12.00
BT20	David Robinson	6.00
BT21	Shaquille O'Neal	30.00

1993-94 Stadium Club

Topps 1993-94 Stadium Club set has 360 cards, issued in two 180-card series. Subsets include Triple Double, High Court, and NBA Draft Picks. Inserts in Series I include Super Team cards and Beam Team cards, which were also available in Series II packs. Rim Rocker cards were also random inserts in Series II packs, as were 1st Day Issue cards. All three Series II insert types were available at a rate of one per every 24 packs. One in every six Series II packs could also include a Frequent Flyer point card featuring one of 20 different players. There are five different point cards per player; there are 100 different Frequent Flyer point cards in all. When a collector has accumulated 50 or more points of one player, he can exchange them for a limited-edition Frequent Flyer Upgrade card of the same player. Every Upgrade card uses the Topps Finest metallization process and carries the Frequent Flyer Upgrade logo.

		MT
Complete Set (360):		45.00
Complete Series 1 (180):		25.00
Complete Series 2 (180):		20.00
Common Player:		.10
Minor Stars:		.20
Series 1 Pack (12):		3.00
Series 1 Wax Box (24):		60.00
Series 2 Pack (12):		1.50
Series 2 Wax Box (24):		30.00
1	Michael Jordan (TD)	2.50
2	Kenny Anderson (TD)	.15
3	Steve Smith (TD)	.10
4	Kevin Gamble (TD)	.10
5	Detlef Schrempf (TD)	.10
6	Larry Johnson (TD)	.25
7	Brad Daugherty (TD)	.15
8	Rumeal Robinson (TD)	.10
9	Michael Williams (TD)	.10
10	David Robinson (TD)	.50
11	Sam Perkins (TD)	.10
12	Thurl Bailey	.10
13	Sherman Douglas	.10
14	Larry Stewart	.10
15	Kevin Johnson	.25
16	Bill Cartwright	.10
17	Larry Nance	.10
18	*P.J. Brown*	.15
19	Tony Bennett	.10
20	Robert Parish	.15
21	David Benoit	.10
22	Detlef Schrempf	.10
23	Hubert Davis	.10
24	Donald Hodge	.10
25	Hersey Hawkins	.10
26	Mark Jackson	.10
27	Reggie Williams	.10
28	Lionel Simmons	.10
29	Ron Harper	.10
30	*Chris Mills*	.50
31	Danny Schayes	.10
32	J.R. Reid	.10
33	Willie Burton	.10
34	Greg Anthony	.10
35	Elden Campbell	.10
36	*Ervin Johnson*	.15
37	Scott Brooks	.10
38	Johnny Newman	.10
39	Rex Chapman	.10
40	Chuck Person	.10
41	John Williams	.10
42	Anthony Bowie	.10
43	Negele Knight	.10
44	Tyrone Corbin	.10
45	Jud Buechler	.10
46	Adam Keefe	.10
47	Glen Rice	.15
48	Tracy Murray	.10
49	Rick Mahorn	.10
50	Vlade Divac	.10
51	Eric Murdock	.10
52	Isiah Morris	.10
53	*Bobby Hurley*	.25
54	Mitch Richmond	.15
55	Danny Ainge	.10
56	Dikembe Mutombo	.30
57	Jeff Hornacek	.10
58	Tony Campbell	.10
59	Vinny DelNegro	.10
60	Xavier McDaniel (HC)	.10
61	Scottie Pippen (HC)	.50
62	Larry Nance (HC)	.10
63	Dikembe Mutombo (HC)	.20
64	Hakeem Olajuwon (HC)	.60
65	Dominique Wilkins (HC)	.20
66	C. Weatherspoon (HC)	.20
67	Chris Morris (HC)	.10
68	Patrick Ewing (HC)	.30
69	Kevin Willis (HC)	.10
70	Jon Barry	.10
71	Jerry Reynolds	.10
72	Sarunas Marciulionis	.10
73	Mark West	.10
74	B.J. Armstrong	.15
75	Greg Kite	.10
76	LaSalle Thompson	.10
77	Randy White	.10
78	Alaa Abdelnaby	.10
79	Kevin Brooks	.10
80	Vern Fleming	.10
81	Doc Rivers	.10
82	*Shawn Bradley*	.50
83	Wayman Tisdale	.10
84	Olden Polynice	.10
85	Michael Cage	.10
86	Harold Miner	.10
87	Doug Smith	.10
88	Tom Gugliotta	.15
89	Hakeem Olajuwon	1.25
90	Loy Vaught	.10
91	James Worthy	.10
92	John Paxson	.10
93	Jon Koncak	.10
94	Lee Mayberry	.10
95	C. Weatherspoon	.20
96	Mark Eaton	.10
97	*Rex Walters*	.20
98	Alvin Robertson	.10
99	Dan Majerle	.10
100	Shaquille O'Neal	3.50
101	Derrick Coleman (TD)	.20
102	Hersey Hawkins (TD)	.10
103	Scottie Pippen (TD)	.50
104	Scott Skiles (TD)	.10
105	Rod Strickland (TD)	.10
106	Pooh Richardson (TD)	.10
107	Tom Gugliotta (TD)	.10
108	Mark Jackson (TD)	.10
109	Dikembe Mutombo (TD)	.20
110	Charles Barkley (TD)	.50
111	Otis Thorpe (TD)	.10
112	Malik Sealy	.10
113	Mark Macon	.10
114	Dee Brown	.10
115	Nate McMillan	.10
116	John Starks	.10
117	Clyde Drexler	.40
118	Antoine Carr	.10
119	Doug West	.10
120	Victor Alexander	.10
121	Kenny Gattison	.10
122	Spud Webb	.10
123	Rumeal Robinson	.10
124	Tim Kempton	.10
125	Karl Malone	.40
126	Randy Woods	.10
127	*Calbert Cheaney*	.50
128	Johnny Dawkins	.10
129	Dominique Wilkins	.30
130	Horace Grant	.20
131	Bill Laimbeer	.10
132	Kenny Smith	.10
133	Sedale Threatt	.10
134	Brian Shaw	.10
135	Dennis Scott	.10
136	Mark Bryant	.10
137	Xavier McDaniel	.10
138	David Wood	.10
139	*Luther Wright*	.20
140	Lloyd Daniels	.10
141	Marlon Maxey	.10
142	Pooh Richardson	.10
143	Jeff Grayer	.10
144	LaPhonso Ellis	.10
145	Gerald Wilkins	.10
146	Dell Curry	.10
147	Duane Causwell	.10
148	Tim Hardaway	.20
149	Isiah Thomas	.25
150	*Doug Edwards*	.15
151	Anthony Peeler	.10
152	Tate George	.10
153	Terry Davis	.10
154	Sam Perkins	.10
155	John Salley	.10
156	Vernon Maxwell	.10
157	Anthony Avent	.10
158	Cliff Robinson	.15
159	*Corie Blount*	.15
160	Gerald Paddio	.10
161	Blair Rasmussen	.10
162	Carl Herrera	.10
163	Chris Smith	.10
164	Pervis Ellison	.10
165	Rod Strickland	.10
166	Jeff Malone	.10
167	Danny Ferry	.10
168	Kevin Lynch	.10
169	Michael Jordan	5.00
170	Derrick Coleman (HC)	.20
171	Jerome Kersey (HC)	.10
172	David Robinson (HC)	.40
173	Shawn Kemp (HC)	.20
174	Karl Malone (HC)	.15
175	Shaquille O'Neal (HC)	1.75
176	Alonzo Mourning (HC)	.50
177	Charles Barkley (HC)	.40
178	Larry Johnson (HC)	.30
179	Checklist 1-90	.10
180	Checklist 91-180	.10
181	Michael Jordan (FF)	1.50
182	Dominique Wilkins (FF)	.20
183	Dennis Rodman (FF)	.50
184	Scottie Pippen (FF)	.50
185	Larry Johnson (FF)	.20
186	Karl Malone (FF)	.20
187	C. Weatherspoon (FF)	.20
188	Charles Barkley (FF)	.30
189	Patrick Ewing (FF)	.20
190	Derrick Coleman (FF)	.20
191	LaBradford Smith	.10
192	Derek Harper	.10
193	Ken Norman	.10
194	*Rodney Rogers*	.30
195	Chris Dudley	.10
196	Gary Payton	.20
197	Andrew Lang	.10
198	Billy Owens	.10
199	*Byron Russell*	.20
200	Patrick Ewing	.25
201	Stacey King	.10
202	Grant Long	.10
203	Sean Elliott	.10
204	Muggsy Bogues	.10
205	Kevin Edwards	.10
206	Dale Davis	.10
207	Dale Ellis	.10
208	Terrell Brandon	.10
209	Kevin Gamble	.10
210	Robert Horry	.15
211	Moses Malone	.15
212	Gary Grant	.10
213	*Bobby Hurley*	.25
214	Larry Krystkowiak	.10
215	A.C. Green	.10
216	Christian Laettner	.15
217	Orlando Woolridge	.10
218	Craig Ehlo	.10
219	Terry Porter	.10
220	*Jamal Mashburn*	1.50
221	Kevin Duckworth	.10
222	Shawn Kemp	.50
223	Frank Brickowski	.10
224	*Chris Webber*	2.00
225	Charles Oakley	.10
226	Jay Humphries	.10
227	Steve Kerr	.10
228	Tim Perry	.10
229	Sleepy Floyd	.10
230	Bimbo Coles	.10
231	Eddie Johnson	.10
232	Terry Mills	.10
233	Danny Manning	.15
234	*Isaiah Rider*	.75
235	*Darnell Mee*	.10
236	Haywood Workman	.10
237	Scott Skiles	.10
238	Otis Thorpe	.10
239	*Mike Peplowski*	.15
240	Eric Leckner	.10
241	Johnny Newman	.10
242	Benoit Benjamin	.10
243	Doug Christie	.10
244	*Acie Earl*	.20
245	Luc Longley	.10
246	Tyrone Hill	.10
247	*Allan Houston*	1.50
248	Joe Kleine	.10
249	Mookie Blaylock	.10
250	Anthony Bonner	.10
251	Luther Wright	.10
252	Todd Day	.10
253	Kendall Gill	.10
254	Mario Elie	.10
255	Pete Myers	.10
256	Jim Les	.10
257	Stanley Roberts	.10
258	Michael Adams	.10
259	Hersey Hawkins	.10
260	Shawn Bradley	.20
261	Scott Haskin	.10
262	*Corie Blount*	.15
263	Charles Smith	.10
264	Armon Gilliam	.10
265	Jamal Mashburn (NW)	.40
266	Anfernee Hardaway (NW)	2.00
267	Shawn Bradley (NW)	.20
268	Chris Webber (NW)	.50
269	Bobby Hurley (NW)	.20
270	Isaiah Rider (NW)	.25
271	Dino Radja (NW)	.20
272	Chris Mills (NW)	.10
273	Nick Van Exel (NW)	.50
274	Lindsey Hunter (NW)	.10
275	Toni Kukoc (NW)	.20
276	Popeye Jones (NW)	.10
277	Chris Mills	.10
278	Ricky Pierce	.10
279	Negele Knight	.10
280	Kenny Walker	.10
281	*Nick Van Exel*	1.00
282	Derrick Coleman	.20
283	*Popeye Jones*	.25
284	Derrick McKey	.10
285	Rick Fox	.10
286	Jerome Kersey	.10
287	Steve Smith	.10
288	Brian Williams	.10
289	Chris Mullin	.20
290	Terry Cummings	.10
291	Donald Royal	.10
292	Alonzo Mourning	.50
293	Mike Brown	.10
294	Latrell Sprewell	.50
295	Oliver Miller	.10
296	*Terry Dehere*	.10
297	Detlef Schrempf	.10
298	Sam Bowie	.10
299	Chris Morris	.10
300	Scottie Pippen	1.00
301	*Warren Kidd*	.10
302	Don MacLean	.10
303	Sean Rooks	.10
304	Matt Geiger	.10
305	Dennis Rodman	1.00
306	Reggie Miller	.30
307	*Vin Baker*	1.00
308	*Anfernee Hardaway*	5.00
309	*Lindsey Hunter*	.20
310	Stacey Augmon	.10
311	Randy Brown	.10
312	Anthony Mason	.10
313	John Stockton	.30
314	*Sam Cassell*	1.50
315	Buck Williams	.10
316	Bryant Stith	.10
317	Brad Daugherty	.10
318	*Dino Radja*	.30
319	Rony Seikaly	.10
320	Charles Barkley	.50
321	Avery Johnson	.10
322	Mahmoud Abdul-Rauf	.10
323	Larry Johnson	.30
324	Michael Williams	.10
325	Mark Aguirre	.10
326	Jim Jackson	.50
327	*Antonio Harvey*	.10
328	David Robinson	.50
329	Calbert Cheaney	.20
330	Kenny Anderson	.20
331	Walt Williams	.10
332	Kevin Willis	.10
333	Nick Anderson	.10
334	Rik Smits	.15
335	Joe Dumars	.15
336	*Toni Kukoc*	1.00
337	Harvey Grant	.10
338	Tom Chambers	.10
339	Blue Edwards	.10
340	Mark Price	.15
341	Ervin Johnson	.10
342	Rolando Blackman	.10
343	*Scott Burrell*	.25
344	*Gheorghe Muresan*	.25
345	Chris Corchiani	.10
346	*Richard Petruska*	.10
347	Dana Barros	.10
348	Hakeem Olajuwon (FF)	.50
349	Dee Brown (FF)	.10
350	John Starks (FF)	.10
351	Ron Harper (FF)	.10
352	Chris Webber (FF)	.50
353	Dan Majerle (FF)	.10
354	Clyde Drexler (FF)	.25
355	Shawn Kemp (FF)	.15
356	David Robinson (FF)	.30
357	Chris Morris (FF)	.10
358	Shaquille O'Neal (FF)	1.00
359	Checklist	.10
360	Checklist	.10

1993-94 Stadium Club Beam Team

Both series of 1993-94 Topps Stadium Club packs were to include Beam Team insert cards, which were randomly inserted about one per wax box. The cards have a refractory foil application. There were 27 different Beam Team cards - 13 in Series I, 14 in Series II.

		MT
Complete Set (27):		100.00
Complete Series 1 (13):		40.00
Complete Series 2 (14):		60.00
Common Player:		1.00
Minor Stars:		2.00
1	Shaquille O'Neal	12.00
2	Mark Price	1.00
3	Patrick Ewing	2.00
4	Michael Jordan	30.00
5	Charles Barkley	3.00
6	Reggie Miller	3.00
7	Derrick Coleman	1.00
8	Dominique Wilkins	1.00
9	Karl Malone	2.00
10	Alonzo Mourning	3.00
11	Tim Hardaway	2.00
12	Hakeem Olajuwon	4.00
13	David Robinson	4.00
14	Dan Majerle	1.00
15	Larry Johnson	2.00
16	LaPhonso Ellis	1.00
17	Nick Van Exel	7.00
18	Scottie Pippen	10.00
19	John Stockton	3.00
20	Bobby Hurley	1.00
21	Chris Webber	10.00
22	Jamal Mashburn	5.00
23	Anfernee Hardaway	45.00
24	Isaiah Rider	2.00
25	Ken Norman	1.00
26	Danny Manning	1.00
27	Calbert Cheaney	2.00

1993-94 Stadium Club Big Tips

This set of 27 cards showcased team logos and tips for the Electronic Arts NBA Showdown '94 video game. Inserted one per four packs, the card fronts have "NBA Showdown '94 Big Tip" bordered with a white line. The team name and logo appear inside a team-colored stripe at the bottom. The card backs have the game hints and a buying offer. The cards are unnumbered.

		MT
Complete Set (27):		5.00
Common Player:		.25
1	Atlanta Hawks	.25
2	Boston Celtics	.25
3	Charlotte Hornets	.25
4	Chicago Bulls	.25
5	Cleveland Cavaliers	.25
6	Dallas Mavericks	.25
7	Denver Nuggets	.25
8	Detroit Pistons	.25
9	Golden State Warriors	.25
10	Houston Rockets	.25
11	Indiana Pacers	.25
12	Los Angeles Clippers	.25
13	Los Angeles Lakers	.25
14	Miami Heat	.25
15	Milwaukee Bucks	.25
16	Minnesota Timberwolves	.25
17	New Jersey Nets	.25
18	New York Knicks	.25
19	Orlando Magic	.25
20	Philadelphia 76ers	.25
21	Phoenix Suns	.25
22	Portland Trail Blazers	.25
23	Sacramento Kings	.25
24	San Antonio Spurs	.25
25	Seattle Supersonics	.25
26	Utah Jazz	.25
27	Washington Bullets	.25

1993-94 Stadium Club First Day Cards

First Day Productions paralleled all 360 cards in Series I and II Stadium Club. Inserted one per 24 packs, the cards are identified by a silver holographic foil rectangular stamp on the card front.

		MT
Complete Set (360):		2000.
Complete Series 1 (180):		1000.
Complete Series 2 (180):		1000.
Common Player:		2.00
Minor Stars:		4.00
Unlisted Stars:		15x-40x
1	Michael Jordan (TD)	100.00
2	Kenny Anderson (TD)	4.00
3	Steve Smith (TD)	2.00
4	Kevin Gamble (TD)	2.00
5	Detlef Schrempf (TD)	2.00
6	Larry Johnson (TD)	10.00
7	Brad Daugherty (TD)	2.00
8	Rumeal Robinson (TD)	2.00
9	Michael Williams (TD)	2.00
10	David Robinson (TD)	10.00
11	Sam Perkins (TD)	2.00
12	Thurl Bailey	2.00
13	Sherman Douglas	2.00
14	Larry Stewart	2.00
15	Kevin Johnson	8.00
16	Bill Cartwright	2.00
17	Larry Nance	2.00
18	*P.J. Brown*	4.00
19	Tony Bennett	2.00
20	Robert Parish	4.00
21	David Benoit	2.00
22	Detlef Schrempf	4.00
23	Hubert Davis	2.00
24	Donald Hodge	2.00
25	Hersey Hawkins	4.00
26	Mark Jackson	4.00
27	Reggie Williams	2.00
28	Lionel Simmons	2.00
29	Ron Harper	2.00
30	*Chris Mills*	15.00
31	Danny Schayes	2.00
32	J.R. Reid	2.00
33	Willie Burton	2.00
34	Greg Anthony	2.00
35	Elden Campbell	2.00
36	*Ervin Johnson*	4.00
37	Scott Brooks	2.00
38	Johnny Newman	2.00
39	Rex Chapman	2.00
40	Chuck Person	2.00
41	John Williams	2.00
42	Anthony Bowie	2.00
43	Negele Knight	2.00
44	Tyrone Corbin	2.00
45	Jud Buechler	2.00
46	Adam Keefe	2.00
47	Glen Rice	4.00
48	Tracy Murray	2.00
49	Rick Mahorn	2.00
50	Vlade Divac	4.00
51	Eric Murdock	2.00
52	Isiah Morris	2.00
53	*Bobby Hurley*	15.00
54	Mitch Richmond	4.00
55	Danny Ainge	2.00
56	Dikembe Mutombo	15.00
57	Jeff Hornacek	2.00
58	Tony Campbell	2.00
59	Vinny DelNegro	2.00
60	Xavier McDaniel (HC)	2.00
61	Scottie Pippen (HC)	10.00
62	Larry Nance (HC)	2.00
63	Dikembe Mutombo (HC)	6.00
64	Hakeem Olajuwon (HC)	20.00
65	Dominique Wilkins (HC)	8.00
66	C. Weatherspoon (HC)	4.00
67	Chris Morris (HC)	2.00
68	Patrick Ewing (HC)	10.00
69	Kevin Willis (HC)	2.00
70	Jon Barry	2.00
71	Jerry Reynolds	2.00
72	Sarunas Marciulionis	2.00
73	Mark West	2.00
74	B.J. Armstrong	4.00
75	Greg Kite	2.00
76	LaSalle Thompson	2.00
77	Randy White	2.00
78	Alaa Abdelnaby	2.00
79	Kevin Brooks	2.00
80	Vern Fleming	2.00
81	Doc Rivers	2.00
82	*Shawn Bradley*	20.00
83	Wayman Tisdale	2.00
84	Olden Polynice	2.00
85	Michael Cage	2.00
86	Harold Miner	4.00
87	Doug Smith	2.00
88	Tom Gugliotta	4.00
89	Hakeem Olajuwon	45.00
90	Loy Vaught	2.00
91	James Worthy	4.00
92	John Paxson	2.00
93	Jon Koncak	2.00
94	Lee Mayberry	2.00
95	C. Weatherspoon	6.00
96	Mark Eaton	2.00
97	*Rex Walters*	4.00
98	Alvin Robertson	2.00
99	Dan Majerle	4.00
100	Shaquille O'Neal	130.00
101	Derrick Coleman (TD)	4.00
102	Hersey Hawkins (TD)	2.00
103	Scottie Pippen (TD)	10.00
104	Scott Skiles (TD)	2.00
105	Rod Strickland (TD)	2.00
106	Pooh Richardson (TD)	2.00
107	Tom Gugliotta (TD)	2.00
108	Mark Jackson (TD)	2.00
109	Dikembe Mutombo (TD)	6.00
110	Charles Barkley (TD)	20.00
111	Otis Thorpe (TD)	2.00
112	Malik Sealy	2.00
113	Mark Macon	2.00
114	Dee Brown	2.00
115	Nate McMillan	2.00
116	John Starks	4.00
117	Clyde Drexler	15.00
118	Antoine Carr	2.00
119	Doug West	2.00
120	Victor Alexander	2.00
121	Kenny Gattison	2.00
122	Spud Webb	2.00
123	Rumeal Robinson	2.00
124	Tim Kempton	2.00
125	Karl Malone	20.00
126	Randy Woods	2.00
127	*Calbert Cheaney*	20.00
128	Johnny Dawkins	2.00
129	Dominique Wilkins	15.00
130	Horace Grant	6.00
131	Bill Laimbeer	2.00
132	Kenny Smith	2.00
133	Sedale Threatt	2.00
134	Brian Shaw	2.00
135	Dennis Scott	4.00
136	Mark Bryant	2.00
137	Xavier McDaniel	2.00
138	David Wood	2.00
139	*Luther Wright*	4.00
140	Lloyd Daniels	2.00
141	Marlon Maxey	2.00
142	Pooh Richardson	2.00
143	Jeff Grayer	2.00
144	LaPhonso Ellis	4.00
145	Gerald Wilkins	2.00
146	Dell Curry	2.00
147	Duane Causwell	2.00
148	Tim Hardaway	8.00
149	Isiah Thomas	8.00
150	*Doug Edwards*	2.00
151	Anthony Peeler	2.00
152	Tate George	2.00
153	Terry Davis	2.00
154	Sam Perkins	2.00
155	John Salley	2.00
156	Vernon Maxwell	2.00
157	Anthony Avent	2.00
158	Cliff Robinson	4.00
159	*Corie Blount*	4.00
160	Gerald Paddio	2.00
161	Blair Rasmussen	2.00
162	Carl Herrera	2.00
163	Chris Smith	2.00
164	Pervis Ellison	2.00
165	Rod Strickland	2.00
166	Jeff Malone	2.00
167	Danny Ferry	2.00
168	Kevin Lynch	2.00
169	Michael Jordan	200.00
170	Derrick Coleman (HC)	4.00
171	Jerome Kersey (HC)	2.00
172	David Robinson (HC)	20.00
173	Shawn Kemp (HC)	10.00
174	Karl Malone (HC)	10.00
175	Shaquille O'Neal (HC)	70.00
176	Alonzo Mourning (HC)	20.00
177	Charles Barkley (HC)	20.00
178	Larry Johnson (HC)	15.00
179	Checklist 1-90	2.00
180	Checklist 91-180	2.00
181	Michael Jordan (FF)	100.00
182	Dominique Wilkins (FF)	6.00
183	Dennis Rodman (FF)	30.00
184	Scottie Pippen (FF)	10.00
185	Larry Johnson (FF)	10.00
186	Karl Malone (FF)	6.00
187	C. Weatherspoon (FF)	4.00
188	Charles Barkley (FF)	10.00
189	Patrick Ewing (FF)	8.00
190	Derrick Coleman (FF)	4.00
191	LaBradford Smith	2.00
192	Derek Harper	2.00
193	Ken Norman	2.00
194	*Rodney Rogers*	15.00
195	Chris Dudley	2.00
196	Gary Payton	8.00
197	Andrew Lang	2.00
198	Billy Owens	2.00
199	*Byron Russell*	4.00
200	Patrick Ewing	15.00
201	Stacey King	2.00
202	Grant Long	2.00
203	Sean Elliott	4.00
204	Muggsy Bogues	2.00
205	Kevin Edwards	2.00
206	Dale Davis	2.00
207	Dale Ellis	2.00
208	Terrell Brandon	2.00
209	Kevin Gamble	2.00
210	Robert Horry	4.00
211	Moses Malone	2.00
212	Gary Grant	2.00
213	*Bobby Hurley*	8.00
214	Larry Krystkowiak	2.00
215	A.C. Green	2.00
216	Christian Laettner	2.00
217	Orlando Woolridge	2.00
218	Craig Ehlo	2.00
219	Terry Porter	2.00
220	*Jamal Mashburn*	35.00
221	Kevin Duckworth	2.00
222	Shawn Kemp	25.00
223	Frank Brickowski	2.00
224	*Chris Webber*	75.00
225	Charles Oakley	2.00
226	Jay Humphries	2.00
227	Steve Kerr	2.00
228	Tim Perry	2.00
229	Sleepy Floyd	2.00
230	Bimbo Coles	2.00
231	Eddie Johnson	2.00
232	Terry Mills	2.00
233	Danny Manning	6.00
234	*Isaiah Rider*	25.00
235	*Darnell Mee*	4.00
236	Haywood Workman	2.00
237	Scott Skiles	2.00
238	Otis Thorpe	2.00
239	*Mike Peplowski*	4.00
240	Eric Leckner	2.00
241	Johnny Newman	2.00
242	Benoit Benjamin	2.00
243	Doug Christie	2.00
244	*Acie Earl*	4.00
245	Luc Longley	2.00
246	Tyrone Hill	2.00
247	*Allan Houston*	25.00
248	Joe Kleine	2.00
249	Mookie Blaylock	2.00
250	Anthony Bonner	2.00
251	Luther Wright	2.00
252	Todd Day	2.00
253	Kendall Gill	2.00
254	Mario Elie	2.00
255	Pete Myers	2.00
256	Jim Les	2.00
257	Stanley Roberts	2.00
258	Michael Adams	2.00
259	Hersey Hawkins	4.00
260	Shawn Bradley	8.00
261	Scott Haskin	2.00
262	*Corie Blount*	4.00
263	Charles Smith	2.00
264	Armon Gilliam	2.00
265	Jamal Mashburn (NW)	15.00
266	Anfernee Hardaway (NW)	80.00
267	Shawn Bradley (NW)	8.00
268	Chris Webber (NW)	20.00
269	Bobby Hurley (NW)	8.00
270	Isaiah Rider (NW)	10.00
271	Dino Radja (NW)	2.00
272	Chris Mills (NW)	2.00
273	Nick Van Exel (NW)	20.00
274	Lindsey Hunter (NW)	4.00
275	Toni Kukoc (NW)	8.00
276	Popeye Jones (NW)	2.00
277	Chris Mills	4.00
278	Ricky Pierce	2.00
279	Negele Knight	2.00
280	Kenny Walker	2.00
281	*Nick Van Exel*	50.00
282	Derrick Coleman	6.00
283	*Popeye Jones*	12.00
284	Derrick McKey	2.00
285	Rick Fox	2.00
286	Jerome Kersey	2.00
287	Steve Smith	2.00
288	Brian Williams	2.00
289	Chris Mullin	8.00
290	Terry Cummings	2.00
291	Donald Royal	2.00
292	Alonzo Mourning	25.00
293	Mike Brown	2.00
294	Latrell Sprewell	20.00
295	Oliver Miller	2.00
296	*Terry Dehere*	4.00

297 Detlef Schrempf 2.00
298 Sam Bowie 2.00
299 Chris Morris 2.00
300 Scottie Pippen 50.00
301 *Warren Kidd* 4.00
302 Don MacLean 2.00
303 Sean Rooks 2.00
304 Matt Geiger 2.00
305 Dennis Rodman 50.00
306 Reggie Miller 12.00
307 *Vin Baker* 35.00
308 *Anfernee Hardaway* 200.00
309 *Lindsey Hunter* 8.00
310 Stacey Augmon 2.00
311 Randy Brown 2.00
312 Anthony Mason 2.00
313 John Stockton 10.00
314 *Sam Cassell* 12.00
315 Buck Williams 2.00
316 Bryant Stith 2.00
317 Brad Daugherty 2.00
318 *Dino Radja* 15.00
319 Rony Seikaly 2.00
320 Charles Barkley 30.00
321 Avery Johnson 2.00
322 Mahmoud Abdul-Rauf 2.00
323 Larry Johnson 15.00
324 Michael Williams 2.00
325 Mark Aguirre 2.00
326 Jim Jackson 20.00
327 *Antonio Harvey* 4.00
328 David Robinson 35.00
329 Calbert Cheaney 4.00
330 Kenny Anderson 8.00
331 Walt Williams 4.00
332 Kevin Willis 2.00
333 Nick Anderson 4.00
334 Rik Smits 4.00
335 Joe Dumars 6.00
336 *Toni Kukoc* 25.00
337 Harvey Grant 2.00
338 Tom Chambers 2.00
339 Blue Edwards 2.00
340 Mark Price 4.00
341 Ervin Johnson 2.00
342 Rolando Blackman 2.00
343 *Scott Burrell* 8.00
344 *Gheorghe Muresan* 8.00
345 Chris Corchiani 2.00
346 *Richard Petruska* 4.00
347 Dana Barros 2.00
348 Hakeem Olajuwon (FF) 15.00
349 Dee Brown (FF) 2.00
350 John Starks (FF) 4.00
351 Ron Harper (FF) 2.00
352 Chris Webber (FF) 20.00
353 Dan Majerle (FF) 4.00
354 Clyde Drexler (FF) 8.00
355 Shawn Kemp (FF) 4.00
356 David Robinson (FF) 8.00
357 Chris Morris (FF) 2.00
358 Shaquille O'Neal (FF) 70.00
359 Checklist 2.00
360 Checklist 2.00

1993-94 Stadium Club Frequent Flyer Upgrades

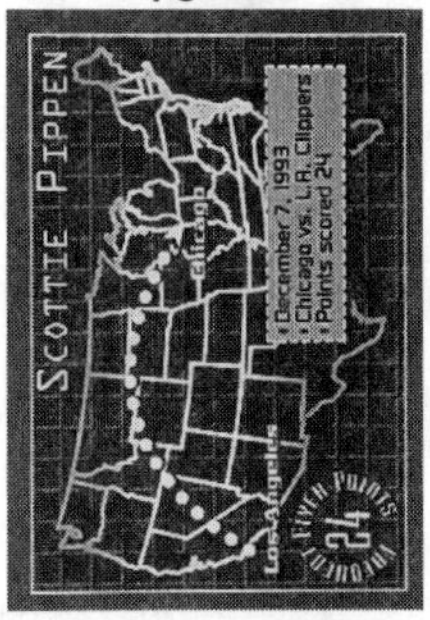

The 20-card set is based on the Frequent Flyer subsets from the base set. The card fronts are exactly the same as the base cards, except for the chrome treatment and Upgrade logo. The cards were available through a mail-in offer that was based on Frequent Flyer Point cards that were randomly seeded one per six Series II packs. The point cards did not include any player photos and do not carry any value. Collectors needed to compile 50 points or more of one player to redeem for a Frequent Flyer card.

MT
Complete Set (20): 75.00
Common Player: 1.00
182 Dominique Wilkins 2.00
183 Dennis Rodman 12.00
184 Scottie Pippen 12.00
185 Larry Johnson 3.00
186 Karl Malone 4.00
187 Clarence Weatherspoon 1.00
188 Charles Barkley 6.00
189 Patrick Ewing 4.00
190 Derrick Coleman 1.00
348 Hakeem Olajuwon 8.00
349 Dee Brown 1.00
350 John Starks 1.00
351 Ron Harper 1.00
352 Chris Webber 8.00
353 Dan Majerle 1.00
354 Clyde Drexler 5.00
355 Shawn Kemp 6.00
356 David Robinson 8.00
357 Chris Morris 1.00
358 Shaquille O'Neal 25.00
NNO Expired Point Cards .25

1993-94 Stadium Club Members Only

This 414-card parallel of the Stadium Club base set and chase sets was sold through Topps' Members Only Club. Issued in factory sets, it sold for $229 plus postage. It was the second consecutive year Topps offered such a set.

MT
Complete Set (414): 350.00
Common Player: .25
1 Michael Jordan TD 15.00
2 Kenny Anderson TD .50
3 Steve Smith TD .50
4 Kevin Gamble TD .25
5 Detlef Schrempf TD .50
6 Larry Johnson TD 1.00
7 Brad Daugherty TD .50
8 Rumeal Robinson TD .25
9 Michael Williams TD .25
10 David Robinson TD 2.50
11 Sam Perkins TD .50
12 Thurl Bailey .25
13 Sherman Douglas .25
14 Larry Stewart .25
15 Kevin Johnson 1.00
16 Bill Cartwright .25
17 Larry Nance .50
18 P.J. Brown 1.00
19 Tony Bennett .25
20 Robert Parish 1.00
21 David Benoit .25
22 Detlef Schrempf .50
23 Hubert Davis .25
24 Donald Hodge .25
25 Hersey Hawkins .50
26 Mark Jackson .25
27 Reggie Williams .25
28 Lionel Simmons .25
29 Ron Harper .50
30 Chris Mills 2.00
31 Danny Schayes .25
32 J.R. Reid .25
33 Willie Burton .25
34 Greg Anthony .25
35 Elden Campbell .50
36 Ervin Johnson .25
37 Scott Brooks .25
38 Johnny Newman .25
39 Rex Chapman .25
40 Chuck Person .50
41 John Williams .50
42 Anthony Bowie .25
43 Negele Knight .25
44 Tyrone Corbin .25
45 Jud Buechler .25
46 Adam Keefe .25
47 Glen Rice 1.00
48 Tracy Murray .25
49 Rick Mahorn .25
50 Vlade Divac .50
51 Eric Murdock .25
52 Isaiah Morris .25
53 Bobby Hurley .50
54 Mitch Richmond 2.00
55 Danny Ainge .50
56 Dikembe Mutombo 1.00
57 Jeff Hornacek .25
58 Tony Campbell .25
59 Vinny Del Negro .25
60 Xavier McDaniel HC .25
61 Scottie Pippen HC 5.00
62 Larry Nance HC .50
63 Dikembe Mutombo HC 1.00
64 Hakeem Olajuwon HC 2.00
65 Dominique Wilkins HC .50
66 Clarence Weatherspoon HC .50
67 Chris Morris HC .25
68 Patrick Ewing HC 1.00
69 Kevin Willis HC .50
70 Jon Barry .25
71 Jerry Reynolds .25
72 Sarunas Marciulionis .25
73 Mark West .25
74 B.J. Armstrong .50
75 Greg Kite .25
76 LaSalle Thompson .25
77 Randy White .25
78 Alaa Abdelnaby .25
79 Kevin Brooks .25
80 Vern Fleming .25
81 Doc Rivers .25
82 Shawn Bradley 2.00
83 Wayman Tisdale .50
84 Olden Polynice .25
85 Michael Cage .25
86 Harold Miner .25
87 Doug Smith .25
88 Tom Gugliotta 2.00
89 Hakeem Olajuwon 4.00
90 Loy Vaught .50
91 James Worthy 1.00
92 John Paxson .50
93 Jon Koncak .25
94 Lee Mayberry .25
95 Clarence Weatherspoon .75
96 Mark Eaton .25
97 Rex Walters .25
98 Alvin Robertson .25
99 Dan Majerle .50
100 Shaquille O'Neal 8.00
101 Derrick Coleman TD .50
102 Hersey Hawkins TD .50
103 Scottie Pippen TD 5.00
104 Scott Skiles TD .25
105 Rod Strickland TD .50
106 Pooh Richardson TD .25
107 Tom Gugliotta TD .50
108 Mark Jackson TD .25
109 Dikembe Mutombo TD 1.00
110 Charles Barkley TD 2.00
111 Otis Thorpe TD .50
112 Malik Sealy .25
113 Mark Macon .25
114 Dee Brown .25
115 Nate McMillan .25
116 John Starks .50
117 Clyde Drexler 2.00
118 Antoine Carr .25
119 Doug West .25
120 Victor Alexander .25
121 Kenny Gattison .25
122 Spud Webb .50
123 Rumeal Robinson .25
124 Tim Kempton .25
125 Karl Malone 4.00
126 Randy Woods .25
127 Calbert Cheaney 1.00
128 Johnny Dawkins .50
129 Dominique Wilkins .50
130 Horace Grant .50
131 Bill Laimbeer .50
132 Kenny Smith .25
133 Sedale Threatt .25
134 Brian Shaw .25
135 Dennis Scott .50
136 Mark Bryant .25
137 Xavier McDaniel .25
138 David Wood .25
139 Luther Wright .25
140 Lloyd Daniels .25
141 (Marion Maxey UER) (Name spelled Maxley on the front) .25
142 Pooh Richardson .25
143 Jeff Grayer .25
144 LaPhonso Ellis .25
145 Gerald Wilkins .25
146 Dell Curry .25
147 Duane Causwell .25
148 Tim Hardaway 2.00
149 Isiah Thomas 1.50
150 Doug Edwards .25
151 Anthony Peeler .25
152 Tate George .25
153 Terry Davis .25
154 Sam Perkins .50
155 John Salley .25
156 Vernon Maxwell .25
157 Anthony Avent .25
158 Clifford Robinson .25
159 Corie Blount .50
160 Gerald Paddio .25
161 Blair Rasmussen .25
162 Carl Herrera .25
163 Chris Smith .25
164 Pervis Ellison .25
165 Rod Strickland 1.00
166 Jeff Malone .50
167 Danny Ferry .25
168 Kevin Lynch .50
169 Michael Jordan 25.00
170 Derrick Coleman HC .50
171 Jerome Kersey HC .25
172 David Robinson HC 2.00
173 Shawn Kemp HC 2.00
174 Karl Malone HC 2.00
175 Shaquille O'Neal HC 5.00
176 Alonzo Mourning HC 2.00
177 Charles Barkley HC 2.00
178 Larry Johnson HC 1.00
179 Checklist 1-90 .25
180 Checklist 91-180 .25
181 Michael Jordan FF 15.00
182 Dominique Wilkins FF .50
183 Dennis Rodman FF 5.00
184 Scottie Pippen FF 5.00
185 Larry Johnson FF 1.00
186 Karl Malone FF 2.00
187 Clarence Weatherspoon FF .50
188 Charles Barkley FF 2.00
189 Patrick Ewing FF 1.00
190 Derrick Coleman FF .50
191 LaBradford Smith .25
192 Derek Harper .50
193 Ken Norman .25
194 Rodney Rogers 1.00
195 Chris Dudley .25
196 Gary Payton 3.00
197 Andrew Lang .25
198 Billy Owens .50
199 Bryon Russell .25
200 Patrick Ewing 2.00
201 Stacey King .25
202 Grant Long .25
203 Sean Elliott .50
204 Muggsy Bogues .50
205 Kevin Edwards .25
206 Dale Davis .25
207 Dale Ellis .50
208 Terrell Brandon 1.00
209 Kevin Gamble .25
210 Robert Horry 1.00
211 Moses Malone UER (Birthdate on back is 1993) 1.00
212 Gary Grant .25
213 Bobby Hurley .50
214 Larry Krystkowiak .25
215 A.C. Green .50
216 Christian Laettner 1.00
217 Orlando Woolridge .25
218 Craig Ehlo .25
219 Terry Porter .25
220 Jamal Mashburn 4.00
221 Kevin Duckworth .25
222 Shawn Kemp 2.50
223 Frank Brickowski .25
224 Chris Webber 10.00
225 Charles Oakley .50
226 Jay Humphries .25
227 Steve Kerr .25
228 Tim Perry .25
229 Sleepy Floyd .25
230 Bimbo Coles .25
231 Eddie Johnson .25
232 Terry Mills .25
233 Danny Manning .50
234 Isaiah Rider 2.00
235 Darnell Mee .25
236 Haywoode Workman .25
237 Scott Skiles .25
238 Otis Thorpe .50
239 Mike Peplowski .25
240 Eric Leckner .25
241 Johnny Newman .25
242 Benoit Benjamin .25
243 Doug Christie .25
244 Acie Earl .25
245 Luc Longley .25
246 Tyrone Hill .25
247 Allan Houston 3.00
248 Joe Kleine .25
249 Mookie Blaylock .50
250 Anthony Bonner .25
251 Luther Wright .25
252 Todd Day .25
253 Kendall Gill .25
254 Mario Elie .25
255 Pete Myers .25
256 Jim Les .25
257 Stanley Roberts .25
258 Michael Adams .25
259 Hersey Hawkins .50
260 Shawn Bradley 1.25
261 Scott Haskin .25
262 Corie Blount .25
263 Charles Smith .25
264 Armon Gilliam .50
265 Jamal Mashburn NW 2.00
266 Anfernee Hardaway NW 10.00
267 Shawn Bradley NW 1.00
268 Chris Webber NW 6.00
269 Bobby Hurley NW .50
270 Isaiah Rider NW 2.00
271 Dino Radja NW .50
272 Chris Mills NW 1.00
273 Nick Van Exel NW 3.00
274 Lindsey Hunter NW .50
275 Toni Kukoc NW 3.00
276 Popeye Jones NW .50
277 Chris Mills 1.50
278 Ricky Pierce .25
279 Negele Knight .25
280 Kenny Walker .25
281 Nick Van Exel 6.00
282 Derrick Coleman UER (Career stats listed under 92-93) .50
283 Popeye Jones .50
284 Derrick McKey .25
285 Rick Fox .25
286 Jerome Kersey .25
287 Steve Smith 1.00
288 Brian Williams .25
289 Chris Mullin 1.00
290 Terry Cummings .50
291 Donald Royal .25
292 Alonzo Mourning 4.00
293 Mike Brown .25
294 Latrell Sprewell 2.00
295 Oliver Miller .25
296 Terry Dehere .50
297 Detlef Schrempf .50
298 Sam Bowie UER (Last name Bowe on front) .50
299 Chris Morris .25
300 Scottie Pippen 6.00
301 Warren Kidd .25
302 Don MacLean .25
303 Sean Rooks .25
304 Matt Geiger .25
305 Dennis Rodman 6.00
306 Reggie Miller 3.00
307 Vin Baker 8.00
308 Anfernee Hardaway 20.00
309 Lindsey Hunter 1.00
310 Stacey Augmon .50
311 Randy Brown .25
312 Anthony Mason .50
313 John Stockton 2.00
314 Sam Cassell 3.00
315 Buck Williams .50
316 Bryant Stith .50
317 Brad Daugherty .50
318 Dino Radja 1.00
319 Rony Seikaly .50
320 Charles Barkley 4.00
321 Avery Johnson .50
322 Mahmoud Abdul-Rauf .50
323 Larry Johnson 2.00
324 Michael Williams .25
325 Mark Aguirre .25
326 Jim Jackson 1.00
327 Antonio Harvey .50
328 David Robinson 4.00
329 Calbert Cheaney 1.00
330 Kenny Anderson .50
331 Walt Williams 1.00
332 Kevin Willis .50
333 Nick Anderson .50
334 Rik Smits .50
335 Joe Dumars 1.00
336 Toni Kukoc 5.00
337 Harvey Grant .25
338 Tom Chambers .50
339 Blue Edwards .25
340 Mark Price .50
341 Ervin Johnson .25
342 Rolando Blackman .50
343 Scott Burrell .50
344 Gheorghe Muresan 1.00
345 Chris Corchiani .25
346 Richard Petruska .25
347 Dana Barros .50
348 Hakeem Olajuwon FF 2.50
349 Dee Brown FF .25
350 John Starks FF .50
351 Ron Harper FF .50
352 Chris Webber FF 8.00
353 Dan Majerle FF .50
354 Clyde Drexler FF 1.50
355 Shawn Kemp FF 1.50
356 David Robinson FF 2.00
357 Chris Morris FF .25
358 Shaquille O'Neal FF 5.00
359 Checklist .25
360 Checklist .25
BT1 Shaquille O'Neal 10.00
BT2 Mark Price .50
BT3 Patrick Ewing 3.00
BT4 Michael Jordan 40.00
BT5 Charles Barkley 5.00
BT6 Reggie Miller 3.00
BT7 Derrick Coleman .50
BT8 Dominique Wilkins 1.00
BT9 Karl Malone 4.00
BT10 Alonzo Mourning 4.00
BT11 Tim Hardaway 3.00
BT12 Hakeem Olajuwon 4.00
BT13 David Robinson 4.00
BT14 Dan Majerle .50
BT15 Larry Johnson 2.00
BT16 LaPhonso Ellis 1.00
BT17 Nick Van Exel 4.00
BT18 Scottie Pippen 10.00
BT19 John Stockton 3.00
BT20 Bobby Hurley .50
BT21 Chris Webber 10.00
BT22 Jamal Mashburn 5.00
BT23 Anfernee Hardaway 20.00
BT24 Isaiah Rider 1.50
BT25 Ken Norman .25
BT26 Danny Manning .50
BT27 Calbert Cheaney 1.00
ST1 Atlanta (Dominique Wilkins) .50
ST2 Boston (Robert Parish) .50
ST3 Charlotte (Larry Johnson, Alonzo Mourning) 3.00
ST4 Chicago (Horace Grant) .50
ST5 Cleveland (Brad Daugherty) .25
ST6 Dallas/Group .25
ST7 Denver (Dikembe Mutombo) .50
ST8 Detroit/Group .25
ST9 Golden State/Group .25
ST10 Houston/Group .25
ST11 Indiana/Group .25
ST12 L.A. Clippers (Danny Manning) .50
ST13 L.A. Lakers/Group .25
ST14 Miami (John Salley) .25
ST15 Milwaukee/Group .25
ST16 Minnesota (Christian Laettner) .50
ST17 New Jersey (Derrick Coleman) .25
ST18 New York (Patrick Ewing) 1.00
ST19 Orlando (Shaquille O'Neal) 4.00
ST20 Philadelphia (Clarence Weatherspoon) .50
ST21 Phoenix (Charles Barkley) 2.00
ST22 Portland (Buck Williams) .25
ST23 Sacramento (Lionel Simmons) .25
ST24 San Antonio (David Robinson) 2.00
ST25 Seattle (Shawn Kemp) 1.50
ST26 Utah/Group .25
ST27 Washington/Group .25

1993-94 Stadium Club Members Only 59

These 15 cards are a portion of the 59-card multi-sport set sent only to Stadium Club members in four different mailings. The fronts include a full-bleed photo with "Members Only" in gold foil at the bottom near the player's name. The backs, which are unnumbered, are horizontal and feature artwork of a basketball player on the right, with the player's career highlights on the left.

MT
Complete Set (15): 25.00
Common Player: .25
1 Danny Ainge .35
2 Mark Eaton .25
3 Patrick Ewing 1.00
4 Anfernee Hardaway 10.00
5 Houston Rockets (Carl Herrera) .25
6 Michael Jordan 15.00
7 Hakeem Olajuwon 2.00
8 Shaquille O'Neal 5.00
9 Cliff Robinson .50
10 David Robinson 1.50
11 Brian Shaw .25
12 John Stockton 1.00
13 Isiah Thomas .75
14 Chris Webber 6.00
15 Michael Williams .25

1993-94 Stadium Club Rim Rockers

These six chase cards were random inserts in 1993-94 Topps Stadium Club Series II packs, one per every 24 packs. The cards feature some of the game's top dunkers. The borderless card front features a color action photo. The player's first name is in white letters at the bottom of the card; his last name is stamped in gold foil. The ghosted back has a color action photo, career highlights and a card number 1 of 6, etc.

MT
Complete Set (6): 12.00
Common Player: .50
1 Shaquille O'Neal 7.00
2 Harold Miner .50
3 Charles Barkley 3.00
4 Dominique Wilkins .50
5 Shawn Kemp 1.50
6 Robert Horry 1.00

1993-94 Stadium Club Super Teams

An equal number of each of the 27 different Super Team cards were randomly inserted into 1993-94 Topps Stadium Club packs. If the team pictured on a collector's Super Team Card won a divisional title, conference championship or the NBA title, the card could be redeemed for special prizes, such as a set of all 360 Stadium Clubs with the NBA championship logo embossed in gold foil, a collection of Stadium Club Master Photos of players from that team, or a collection from that team's First Day Issue cards. If the team pictured wins more than one title, the holder may claim the corresponding prizes.

MT
Complete Set (27): 20.00
Common Team: .50
1 Atlanta Hawks .50
2 Boston Celtics .50
3 Charlotte Hornets 3.00
4 Chicago Bulls .50
5 Cleveland Cavaliers .50
6 Dallas Mavericks .50
7 Denver Nuggets .50
8 Detroit Pistons .50
9 Golden State Warriors .50
10 Houston Rockets 7.00
11 Indiana Pacers .50
12 Los Angeles Clippers .50
13 Los Angeles Lakers .50
14 Miami Heat .50
15 Milwaukee Bucks .50
16 Minnesota T'Wolves .50
17 New Jersey Nets .50
18 New York Knicks 3.00
19 Orlando Magic 7.00
20 Philadelphia 76ers .50
21 Phoenix Suns 2.00
22 Portland Trail Blazers .50
23 Sacramento Kings .50
24 San Antonio Spurs 2.00
25 Seattle Supersonics 5.00
26 Utah Jazz .50
27 Washington Bullets .50

1993-94 Stadium Club Super Teams Division Winners

Only Rockets, Sonics, Knicks or Hawks Super Team chase cards, which were randomly seeded in Series I packs, were redeemable for an 11-card Division Winners team set. The cards have the same design as the base cards, except for a gold-foil Division Winner logo on the front. For collectors' convenience we have inserted "R", "S", "K" and "H" prefixes to the card number to show which team the athlete played with during the season.

MT
Comp. Bag Hawks (11): 6.00
Comp. Bag Knicks (11): 6.00
Comp. Bag Rockets (11): 10.00
Comp. Bag Sonics (11): 10.00
Common Player: .50
H46 Adam Keefe .50
H93 Jon Koncak .50
H129 Dominique Wilkins 1.00
H150 Doug Edwards DP .50
H197 Andrew Lang .50
H218 Craig Ehlo .50
H233 Danny Manning 1.00
H249 Mookie Blaylock 1.00
H310 Stacey Augmon .50
H332 Kevin Willis .50
K23 Hubert Davis .50
K34 Greg Anthony .50
K81 Doc Rivers .50
K116 John Starks 1.00
K192 Derek Harper 1.00
K200 Patrick Ewing 3.00
K225 Charles Oakley .75
K250 Anthony Bonner .50
K263 Charles Smith .50
K312 Anthony Mason 1.00
R37 Scott Brooks .50
R89 Hakeem Olajuwon 6.00
R132 Kenny Smith .50
R156 Vernon Maxwell .50
R162 Carl Herrera .50
R210 Robert Horry 1.00
R238 Otis Thorpe .75
R254 Mario Elie .50
R314 Sam Cassell 2.00
R346 Richard Petruska .50
S85 Michael Cage .50
S115 Nate McMillan .50
S154 Sam Perkins .75
S173 Shawn Kemp HC 2.00
S196 Gary Payton 2.00
S222 Shawn Kemp 4.00
S253 Kendall Gill .50
S278 Ricky Pierce .50
S297 Detlef Schrempf .75
S341 Ervin Johnson .75
HD1 Hawks DW Super Team 1.00
KD18 Knicks DW Super Team 1.00
RD10 Rockets DW Super Team 1.00
SD25 Sonics DW Super Team 1.00

1993-94 Stadium Club Super Teams Master Photos

Only Rockets and Knicks Super Team insert cards could be redeemed for these 5" x 7" cards. The Super Team cards were inserted into Stadium Club Series I packs. The 11 cards are numbered "x of 10" in the center of the card on the card back. Prefixes of "R" and "K" have been inserted in the card numbers below to show the player's team.

MT
Comp. Bag Knicks (11): 10.00
Comp. Bag Rockets (11): 15.00
Common Player: .75
Common MP Team Card: 1.50
K1 Greg Anthony .75
K2 Anthony Bonner .75
K3 Hubert Davis .75
K4 Patrick Ewing 5.00
K5 Derek Harper 1.25

K6	Anthony Mason	1.75
K7	Charles Oakley	1.25
K8	Doc Rivers	.75
K9	Charles Smith	.75
K10	John Starks	1.25
KMP	Knicks MP Super Team	1.50
R1	Scott Brooks	.75
R2	Sam Cassell	2.00
R3	Mario Elie	.75
R4	Carl Herrera	.75
R5	Robert Horry	2.00
R6	Vernon Maxwell	.75
R7	Hakeem Olajuwon	10.00
R8	Richard Petruska	.75
R9	Kenny Smith	.75
R10	Otis Thorpe	1.00
RMP	Rockets MP Super Team	1.50

1993-94 Stadium Club Super Teams NBA Finals

This 361-card chase set parallelled the base set and was redeemable by a mail-in offer in exchange for the Rockets Super Team card, which was randomly seeded in Series I packs. A gold-foil NBA Finals logo is included on the front.

	MT
Complete Set (361):	60.00
Common Player:	.15
Semistars:	.40
Ser.1 Stars:	1.25x to 2.5x
Ser.2 Stars:	1.5x to 3x
Ser.1 Rookies:	1.25x to 2.5x
Ser.2 Rookies:	1.5x to 3x

1994-95 Stadium Club

Stadium Club's 1994-95 set includes three subsets - College Teammates (#s 100-114), Draft Picks (179-182) and Through the Glass (various numbers). The regular borderless cards feature full-bleed color action shots on the front, with the player's first name written in white letters at the bottom. His last name is stamped in gold foil. The Stadium Club logo is also stamped in gold foil, in the upper left corner. The back has a color action photo of the player, plus a black-and-white mug shot on one side; a ghosted image is on the other half, which has biographical and statistical information, plus a profile, printed over it. The player's name, team, position and card number appear at the top of the card. Insert sets include Rising Stars, Super Team cards, Clear Cut cards, Dynasty and Destiny and First Day Productions.

	MT
Complete Set (362):	45.00
Complete Series 1 (182):	25.00
Complete Series 2 (180):	20.00
Common Player:	.10
Minor Stars:	.20
Series 1 Pack (12):	2.25
Series 1 Wax Box (24):	45.00
Series 2 Pack (10):	1.75
Series 2 Wax Box (24):	35.00

1	Patrick Ewing	.50
2	Patrick Ewing	.25
3	Bimbo Coles	.10
4	Elden Campbell	.10
5	Brent Price	.10
6	Hubert Davis	.10
7	Donald Royal	.10
8	Tim Perry	.10
9	Chris Webber	.50
10	Chris Webber	.25
11	Brad Daugherty	.10
12	P.J. Brown	.10
13	Charles Barkley	.70
14	Mario Elie	.10
15	Tyrone Hill	.10
16	Anfernee Hardaway	2.00
17	Anfernee Hardaway	.75
18	Toni Kukoc	.20
19	Chris Morris	.10
20	Gerald Wilkins	.10
21	David Benoit	.10
22	Kevin Duckworth	.10
23	Derrick Coleman	.20
24	Adam Keefe	.10
25	Marion Maxey	.10
26	Vern Fleming	.10
27	Jeff Malone	.10
28	Rodney Rogers	.20
29	Terry Mills	.10
30	Doug West	.10
31	Doug West	.10
32	Shaquille O'Neal	2.00
33	Scottie Pippen	1.00
34	Lee Mayberry	.10
35	Dale Ellis	.10
36	Cedric Ceballos	.10
37	Lionel Simmons	.10
38	Kenny Gattison	.10
39	Popeye Jones	.10
40	Jerome Kersey	.10
41	Jerome Kersey	.10
42	Larry Stewart	.10
43	Rod Strickland	.10
44	Chris Mills	.10
45	Latrell Sprewell	.25
46	Haywoode Workman	.10
47	Charles Smith	.10
48	Detlef Schrempf	.10
49	Gary Grant	.10
50	Gary Grant	.10
51	Tom Chambers	.10
52	J.R. Reid	.10
53	Mookie Blaylock	.10
54	Mookie Blaylock	.10
55	Rony Seikaly	.10
56	Isaiah Rider	.30
57	Isaiah Rider	.20
58	Nick Anderson	.10
59	Victor Alexander	.10
60	Lucious Harris	.10
61	Mark Macon	.10
62	Otis Thorpe	.10
63	Randy Woods	.10
64	Clyde Drexler	.50
65	Dikembe Mutombo	.20
66	Todd Day	.10
67	Greg Anthony	.10
68	Sherman Douglas	.10
69	Chris Mullin	.20
70	Kevin Johnson	.20
71	Kendall Gill	.10
72	Dennis Rodman	1.00
73	Dennis Rodman TG	.50
74	Jeff Turner	.10
75	John Stockton	.30
76	John Stockton	.20
77	Doug Edwards	.10
78	Jim Jackson	.50
79	Hakeem Olajuwon	1.00
80	Glen Rice	.20
81	Christian Laettner	.10
82	Terry Porter	.10
83	Joe Dumars	.20
84	David Wingate	.10
85	B.J. Armstrong	.10
86	Derrick McKey	.10
87	Elmore Spencer	.10
88	Walt Williams	.10
89	Shawn Bradley	.15
90	Acie Earl	.10
91	Acie Earl	.10
92	Randy Brown	.10
93	Grant Long	.10
94	Terry Dehere	.10
95	Spud Webb	.10
96	Lindsey Hunter	.10
97	Blair Rasmussen	.10
98	Tim Hardaway	.20
99	Kevin Edwards	.10
100	(Patrick Ewing, Herb Williams)	.15
101	(Charles Barkley, Chuck Person)	.30
102	(Shaquille O'Neal, Mahmoud Abdul-Rauf)	.50
103	(Derrick Coleman, Rony Seiklay)	.10
104	(Hakeem Olajuwon, Clyde Drexler)	.50
105	(Chris Mullin, Mark Jackson)	.15
106	(Latrell Sprewell, Robert Horry)	.15
107	(Reggie Miller, Pooh Richardson)	.15
108	(Nick Anderson, Dennis Scott)	.10
109	(Ken Norman, Kendall Gill)	.10
110	(Scott Skiles, Kevin Willis)	.10
111	(Glen Rice, Terry Mills)	.10
112	(Bobby Hurley, Christian Laettner)	.10
113	(Kevin Johnson, Stacey Augmon)	.20
114	(James Worthy, Sam Perkins)	.10
115	Carl Herrera	.10
116	Sam Bowie	.10
117	Gary Payton	.20
118	Danny Ainge	.10
119	Danny Ainge	.10
120	Luc Longley	.10
121	Antonio Davis	.10
122	Terry Cummings	.10
123	Terry Cummings	.10
124	Mark Price	.10
125	Jamal Mashburn	.40
126	Mahmoud Abdul-Rauf	.10
127	Charles Oakley	.10
128	Steve Smith	.10
129	Vin Baker	.30
130	Robert Horry	.15
131	Doug Christie	.10
132	Wayman Tisdale	.10
133	Wayman Tisdale	.10
134	Muggsy Bogues	.10
135	Dino Radja	.20
136	Jeff Hornacek	.10
137	Gheorghe Muresan	.10
138	Loy Vaught	.10
139	Loy Vaught	.10
140	Benoit Benjamin	.10
141	Johnny Dawkins	.10
142	Allan Houston	.15
143	Jon Barry	.10
144	Reggie Miller	.30
145	Kevin Willis	.10
146	James Worthy	.10
147	James Worthy	.10
148	Scott Burrell	.10
149	Tom Gugliotta	.10
150	LaPhonso Ellis	.10
151	Doug Smith	.10
152	A.C. Green	.10
153	A.C. Green	.10
154	George Lynch	.10
155	Sam Perkins	.10
156	Corie Blount	.15
157	Xavier McDaniel	.10
158	Xavier McDaniel	.10
159	Eric Murdock	.10
160	David Robinson	.75
161	Karl Malone	.50
162	Karl Malone	.25
163	C. Weatherspoon	.10
164	Calbert Cheaney	.15
165	Tom Hammonds	.10
166	Tom Hammonds	.10
167	Alonzo Mourning	.50
168	Clifford Robinson	.10
169	Micheal Williams	.10
170	Ervin Johnson	.10
171	Mike Gminski	.10
172	*Jason Kidd*	7.00
173	Anthony Bonner	.10
174	Stacey King	.10
175	Rex Chapman	.10
176	Greg Graham	.10
177	Stanley Roberts	.10
178	Mitch Richmond	.15
179	*Eric Montross*	.50
180	*Eddie Jones*	3.00
181	*Grant Hill*	6.00
182	*Donyell Marshall*	.50
183	*Glenn Robinson*	2.50
184	Dominique Wilkins	.25
185	Mark Price	.15
186	Anthony Mason	.10
187	Tyrone Corbin	.10
188	Dale Davis	.10
189	Nate McMillan	.10
190	Jason Kidd	1.50
191	John Salley	.10
192	Keith Jennings	.10
193	Mark Bryant	.10
194	Sleepy Floyd	.10
195	Grant Hill	3.00
196	Joe Kleine	.10
197	Anthony Peeler	.10
198	Malik Sealy	.10
199	Kenny Walker	.10
200	Donyell Marshall	.50
201	Vlade Divac	.10
202	Dino Radja	.10
203	Carl Herrera	.10
204	Olden Polynice	.10
205	Patrick Ewing	.20
206	Willie Anderson	.10
207	Mitch Richmond	.15
208	John Crotty	.10
209	Tracy Murray	.10
210	*Juwan Howard*	1.50
211	Robert Parish	.10
212	Steve Kerr	.10
213	Anthony Bowie	.10
214	*Tim Breaux*	.10
215	*Sharone Wright*	.50
216	Brian Williams	.10
217	Rick Fox	.10
218	Harold Miner	.10
219	Duane Ferrell	.10
220	*Lamond Murray*	.50
221	Blue Edwards	.10
222	Bill Cartwright	.10
223	*Sergei Bazarevich*	.10
224	Herb Williams	.10
225	*Brian Grant*	1.50
226	Derek Harper, John Starks	.15
227	Rod Strickland, Clyde Drexler	.15
228	Kevin Johnson, Dan Majerle	.10
229	Lindsey Hunter, Joe Dumars	.10
230	Anfernee Hardaway, Latrell Sprewell	.15
231	Bill Wennington	.10
232	Brian Shaw	.10
233	*Jamie Watson*	.15
234	Chris Whitney	.10
235	Eric Montross	.30
236	Kenny Smith	.10
237	Andrew Lang	.10
238	Lorenzo Williams	.10
239	Dana Barros	.10
240	Eddie Jones	1.50
241	Harold Ellis	.10
242	James Edwards	.10
243	Don MacLean	.10
244	Ed Pinckney	.10
245	*Carlos Rogers*	.30
246	Michael Adams	.10
247	Rex Walters	.10
248	John Starks	.10
249	Terrell Brandon	.10
250	*Khalid Reeves*	.75
251	Dominique Wilkins	.15
252	Toni Kukoc	.15
253	Rick Fox	.10
254	Detlef Schrempf	.10
255	Rik Smits	.10
256	Johnny Dawkins	.10
257	Dan Majerle	.10
258	Mike Brown	.10
259	Byron Scott	.10
260	*Jalen Rose*	2.00
261	Byron Houston	.10
262	Frank Brickowski	.10
263	Vernon Maxwell	.10
264	Craig Ehlo	.10
265	*Yinka Dare*	.15
266	Dee Brown	.10
267	Felton Spencer	.10
268	Harvey Grant	.10
269	Nick Van Exel	.50
270	Bob Martin	.10
271	Hersey Hawkins	.10
272	Scott Williams	.10
273	Sarunas Marciulionis	.10
274	Kevin Gamble	.10
275	*Clifford Rozier*	.30
276	B.J. Armstrong, Ron Harper	.10
277	John Stockton, Jeff Hornacek	.15
278	Bobby Hurley, Mitch Richmond	.10
279	Anfernee Hardaway, Dennis Scott	.50
280	Jason Kidd, Jim Jackson	.75
281	Ron Harper	.10
282	Chuck Person	.10
283	John Williams	.10
284	Robert Pack	.10
285	*Aaron McKie*	.50
286	Chris Smith	.10
287	Horace Grant	.10
288	Oliver Miller	.10
289	Derek Harper	.10
290	*Eric Mobley*	.20
291	Scott Skiles	.10
292	Olden Polynice	.10
293	Mark Jackson	.10
294	Wayman Tisdale	.10
295	*Tony Dumas*	.20
296	Bryon Russell	.10
297	Vlade Divac	.10
298	David Wesley	.10
299	Askia Jones	.10
300	*B.J. Tyler*	.25
301	Hakeem Olajuwon	.40
302	Luc Longley	.10
303	Rony Seikaly	.10
304	Sarunas Marciulionis	.10
305	Dikembe Mutombo	.15
306	Ken Norman	.10
307	Dell Curry	.10
308	Danny Ferry	.10
309	Shawn Kemp	.50
310	*Dickey Simpkins*	.20
311	Johnny Newman	.10
312	Dwayne Schintzius	.10
313	Sean Elliott	.10
314	Sean Rooks	.10
315	*Bill Curley*	.20
316	Bryant Stith	.10
317	Pooh Richardson	.10
318	*Jim McIlvaine*	.10
319	Dennis Scott	.10
320	*Wesley Person*	.50
321	Bobby Hurley	.10
322	Armon Gilliam	.10
323	Rik Smits	.10
324	Tony Smith	.10
325	*Monty Williams*	.20
326	Gary Payton, Kendall Gill	.10
327	Mookie Blaylock, Stacey Augmon	.10
328	Mark Jackson, Reggie Miller	.15
329	Sam Cassell, Vernon Maxwell	.10
330	Harold Miner, Khalid Reeves	.15
331	Vinny Del Negro	.10
332	Billy Owens	.10
333	Mark West	.10
334	Matt Geiger	.10
335	*Greg Minor*	.15
336	Larry Johnson	.30
337	Donald Hodge	.10
338	Aaron Williams	.10
339	Jay Humphries	.10
340	*Charlie Ward*	.30
341	Scott Brooks	.10
342	Stacey Augmon	.10
343	Will Perdue	.10
344	Dale Ellis	.10
345	*Brooks Thompson*	.15
346	Manute Bol	.10
347	Kenny Anderson	.15
348	Willie Burton	.10
349	Michael Cage	.10
350	Danny Manning	.10
351	Ricky Pierce	.10
352	Sam Cassell	.10
353	Reggie Miller	.15
354	David Robinson	.30
355	Shaquille O'Neal	1.00
356	Scottie Pippen	.40
357	Alonzo Mourning	.25
358	Clarence Weatherspoon	.10
359	Derrick Coleman	.10
360	Charles Barkley	.30
361	Karl Malone	.25
362	Chris Webber	.25

1994-95 Stadium Club Beam Team

These cards were random inserts in Topps Stadium Club Series II packs, one per every 24 packs. The set features a premiere player from each NBA team with laser light foil at the bottom of the card. The player's name is also stamped in foil. Card backs, numbered 1 of 27, etc., have a second color photo, plus a brief player profile.

	MT
Complete Set (27):	80.00
Common Player:	1.00

1	Mookie Blaylock	1.00
2	Dominique Wilkins	2.00
3	Alonzo Mourning	6.00
4	Toni Kukoc	3.00
5	Mark Price	1.00
6	Jason Kidd	12.00
7	Jalen Rose	4.00
8	Grant Hill	20.00
9	Latrell Sprewell	3.00
10	Hakeem Olajuwon	10.00
11	Reggie Miller	6.00
12	Lamond Murray	3.00
13	George Lynch	1.00
14	Khalid Reeves	3.00
15	Glenn Robinson	7.00
16	Donyell Marshall	2.00
17	Derrick Coleman	1.00
18	Patrick Ewing	5.00
19	Shaquille O'Neal	20.00
20	Clarence Weatherspoon	1.00
21	Charles Barkley	6.00
22	Cliff Robinson	1.00
23	Bobby Hurley	1.00
24	David Robinson	6.00
25	Shawn Kemp	5.00
26	Karl Malone	5.00
27	Chris Webber	6.00

1994-95 Stadium Club Beam Team Laser Show Sheets

These 9-1/2" x 12-1/2" sheets feature nine Beam Team cards on the front. The cards have full-bleed color photos. The player's name and Stadium Club logo appear at the top of each card, with the Beam Team logo at the bottom. The back of the sheet lists the dates for the 1994-95 Topps Stadium Club Beam Team Laser Show.

	MT
Complete Set (9):	6.00
Common Player:	.25
Glenn Robinson	.50
Toni Kukoc	.50
Jason Kidd	1.00
Chris Webber	1.00
Grant Hill	2.00
Derrick Coleman	.25
Alonzo Mourning	.50
David Robinson	.75
Reggie Miller	.50

1994-95 Stadium Club Clear Cut

These 1994-95 Stadium Club inserts allow collectors to see through some of the best players in the NBA with clear Finest technology. The card front has a color action cutout photo, with the "Clearcut" logo in the lower right corner. The player's name runs along the right side, while a Stadium Club logo appears in the upper left corner. The cards are clear; you can see through them. The back has a panel which contains the player's name, team, a statistical summary and a card number.

	MT
Complete Set (27):	50.00
Common Player:	1.00
Minor Stars:	2.00

1	Stacey Augmon	1.00
2	Dino Radja	1.00
3	Alonzo Mourning	5.00
4	Scottie Pippen	10.00
5	Gerald Wilkins	1.00
6	Jamal Mashburn	4.00
7	Dikembe Mutombo	3.00
8	Lindsey Hunter	1.00
9	Chris Mullin	2.00
10	Hakeem Olajuwon	10.00
11	Reggie Miller	4.00
12	Gary Grant	1.00
13	Doug Christie	1.00
14	Steve Smith	1.00
15	Vin Baker	5.00
16	Christian Laettner	1.00
17	Derrick Coleman	2.00
18	Charles Oakley	1.00
19	Dennis Scott	1.00
20	Clarence Weatherspoon	2.00
21	Charles Barkley	6.00
22	Clifford Robinson	1.00
23	Mitch Richmond	2.00
24	David Robinson	6.00
25	Shawn Kemp	4.00
26	Karl Malone	5.00
27	Don MacLean	1.00

1994-95 Stadium Club Dynasty and Destiny

These 10 insert cards showcase 20 players with two cards (one Dynasty, one Destiny) that fit together to form 10 cards. Huge bold off-white letters reading "Dynasty" run down the left side of the card and letters reading "Destiny" run down the right side for each respective side. The cards are linked by a swoosh in the bottom corner where they connect. This side also has a full-bleed borderless photo, along with the Stadium Club logo and player's name stamped in gold foil at the top. The opposite side has a close-up shot of the player, plus statistics, a team logo, running text which fits together with the matching card, and a card number.

		MT
Complete Set (20):		10.00
Common Player:		.25
1A	Mark Price	.25
1B	Kenny Anderson	.25
2A	Karl Malone	.50
2B	Derrick Coleman	.25
3A	John Stockton	.50
3B	Anfernee Hardaway	3.00
4A	Mitch Richmond	.25
4B	Jim Jackson	.50
5A	James Worthy	.25
5B	Jamal Mashburn	.50
6A	Patrick Ewing	.50
6B	Alonzo Mourning	.75
7A	Hakeem Olajuwon	1.50
7B	Shaquille O'Neal	3.00
8A	Clyde Drexler	.75
8B	Isaiah Rider	.50
9A	Scottie Pippen	2.00
9B	Latrell Sprewell	.50
10A	Charles Barkley	1.00
10B	Chris Webber	.50

1994-95 Stadium Club First Day Cards

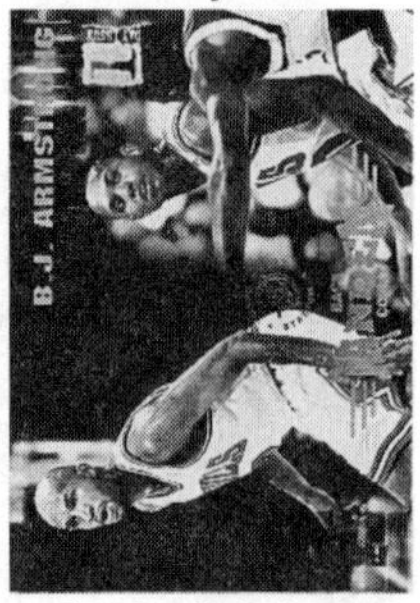

First Day Production inserts parallelled all 362 cards in the Series I and II sets, and were inserted one per 24 packs. The cards are identified by a gold foil stamp on the front instead of the holographic silver stamp used a year earlier.

	MT
Complete Set (362):	1300.
Complete Series 1 (182):	800.00
Complete Series 2 (180):	500.00
Common Player:	1.50
Minor Stars:	4.00
Unlisted Stars:	15x-30x

1	Patrick Ewing	20.00
2	Patrick Ewing	10.00
3	Bimbo Coles	1.50
4	Elden Campbell	1.50
5	Brent Price	1.50
6	Hubert Davis	1.50
7	Donald Royal	1.50
8	Tim Perry	1.50
9	Chris Webber	20.00
10	Chris Webber	10.00
11	Brad Daugherty	1.50
12	P.J. Brown	1.50
13	Charles Barkley	30.00
14	Mario Elie	1.50
15	Tyrone Hill	1.50
16	Anfernee Hardaway	75.00
17	Anfernee Hardaway	35.00
18	Toni Kukoc	4.00
19	Chris Morris	1.50
20	Gerald Wilkins	1.50
21	David Benoit	1.50
22	Kevin Duckworth	1.50
23	Derrick Coleman	6.00
24	Adam Keefe	1.50
25	Marion Maxey	1.50
26	Vern Fleming	1.50
27	Jeff Malone	1.50
28	Rodney Rogers	4.00
29	Terry Mills	1.50
30	Doug West	1.50
31	Doug West	1.50
32	Shaquille O'Neal	75.00
33	Scottie Pippen	35.00
34	Lee Mayberry	1.50
35	Dale Ellis	1.50
36	Cedric Ceballos	1.50
37	Lionel Simmons	1.50
38	Kenny Gattison	1.50
39	Popeye Jones	1.50
40	Jerome Kersey	1.50

41 Jerome Kersey 1.50
42 Larry Stewart 1.50
43 Rod Strickland 1.50
44 Chris Mills 1.50
45 Latrell Sprewell 20.00
46 Haywoode Workman 1.50
47 Charles Smith 1.50
48 Detlef Schrempf 4.00
49 Gary Grant 1.50
50 Gary Grant 1.50
51 Tom Chambers 1.50
52 J.R. Reid 1.50
53 Mookie Blaylock 1.50
54 Mookie Blaylock 1.50
55 Rony Seikaly 1.50
56 Isaiah Rider 10.00
57 Isaiah Rider 4.00
58 Nick Anderson 4.00
59 Victor Alexander 1.50
60 Lucious Harris 1.50
61 Mark Macon 1.50
62 Otis Thorpe 1.50
63 Randy Woods 1.50
64 Clyde Drexler 20.00
65 Dikembe Mutombo 10.00
66 Todd Day 4.00
67 Greg Anthony 1.50
68 Sherman Douglas 1.50
69 Chris Mullin 6.00
70 Kevin Johnson 8.00
71 Kendall Gill 4.00
72 Dennis Rodman 45.00
73 Dennis Rodman 4.00
74 Jeff Turner 1.50
75 John Stockton 15.00
76 John Stockton 6.00
77 Doug Edwards 1.50
78 Jim Jackson 20.00
79 Hakeem Olajuwon 35.00
80 Glen Rice 4.00
81 Christian Laettner 1.50
82 Terry Porter 1.50
83 Joe Dumars 4.00
84 David Wingate 1.50
85 B.J. Armstrong 4.00
86 Derrick McKey 1.50
87 Elmore Spencer 1.50
88 Walt Williams 1.50
89 Shawn Bradley 4.00
90 Acie Earl 1.50
91 Acie Earl 1.50
92 Randy Brown 1.50
93 Grant Long 1.50
94 Terry Dehere 1.50
95 Spud Webb 1.50
96 Lindsey Hunter 1.50
97 Blair Rasmussen 1.50
98 Tim Hardaway 6.00
99 Kevin Edwards 1.50
100 (Patrick Ewing, Herb Williams) 4.00
101 (Charles Barkley, Chuck Person) 4.00
102 (Shaquille O'Neal, Mahmoud Abdul-Rauf) 15.00
103 (Rony Seikaly, Derrick Coleman) 1.50
104 (Hakeem Olajuwon, Clyde Drexler) 15.00
105 (Chris Mullin, Mark Jackson) 5.00
106 (Latrell Sprewell, Robert Horry) 5.00
107 (Reggie Miller, Pooh Richardson) 5.00
108 (Nick Anderson, Dennis Scott) 5.00
109 (Ken Norman, Kendall Gill) 1.50
110 (Scott Skiles, Kevin Willis) 1.50
111 (Glen Rice, Terry Mills) 1.50
112 (Bobby Hurley, Christian Laettner) 1.50
113 (Kevin Johnson, Stacey Augmon) 4.00
114 (James Worthy, Sam Perkins) 1.50
115 Carl Herrera 1.50
116 Sam Bowie 1.50
117 Gary Payton 8.00
118 Danny Ainge 1.50
119 Danny Ainge 1.50
120 Luc Longley 1.50
121 Antonio Davis 1.50
122 Terry Cummings 1.50
123 Terry Cummings 1.50
124 Mark Price 4.00
125 Jamal Mashburn 25.00
126 Mahmoud Abdul-Rauf 1.50
127 Charles Oakley 1.50
128 Steve Smith 1.50
129 Vin Baker 15.00
130 Robert Horry 4.00
131 Doug Christie 1.50
132 Wayman Tisdale 1.50
133 Wayman Tisdale 1.50
134 Muggsy Bogues 1.50
135 Dino Radja 4.00
136 Jeff Hornacek 1.50
137 Gheorghe Muresan 1.50
138 Loy Vaught 1.50
139 Loy Vaught 1.50
140 Benoit Benjamin 1.50
141 Johnny Dawkins 1.50
142 Allan Houston 4.00
143 Jon Barry 1.50
144 Reggie Miller 15.00
145 Kevin Willis 1.50
146 James Worthy 1.50
147 James Worthy 1.50
148 Scott Burrell 1.50
149 Tom Gugliotta 1.50
150 LaPhonso Ellis 1.50
151 Doug Smith 1.50
152 A.C. Green 1.50
153 A.C. Green 1.50
154 George Lynch 1.50
155 Sam Perkins 1.50
156 Corie Blount 1.50
157 Xavier McDaniel 1.50
158 Xavier McDaniel 1.50
159 Eric Murdock 1.50
160 David Robinson 35.00
161 Karl Malone 15.00
162 Karl Malone 7.00
163 C. Weatherspoon 4.00
164 Calbert Cheaney 1.50
165 Tom Hammonds 1.50
166 Tom Hammonds 1.50
167 Alonzo Mourning 20.00
168 Clifford Robinson 1.50
169 Micheal Williams 1.50
170 Ervin Johnson 1.50
171 Mike Gminski 1.50
172 *Jason Kidd* 50.00
173 Anthony Bonner 1.50
174 Stacey King 1.50
175 Rex Chapman 1.50
176 Greg Graham 1.50
177 Stanley Roberts 1.50
178 Mitch Richmond 4.00
179 *Eric Montross* 20.00
180 *Eddie Jones* 50.00
181 *Grant Hill* 110.00
182 *Donyell Marshall* 20.00
183 *Glenn Robinson* 40.00
184 Dominique Wilkins 10.00
185 Mark Price 4.00
186 Anthony Mason 1.50
187 Tyrone Corbin 1.50
188 Dale Davis 1.50
189 Nate McMillan 1.50
190 Jason Kidd 30.00
191 John Salley 1.50
192 Keith Jennings 1.50
193 Mark Bryant 1.50
194 Sleepy Floyd 1.50
195 Grant Hill 60.00
196 Joe Kleine 1.50
197 Anthony Peeler 1.50
198 Malik Sealy 1.50
199 Kenny Walker 1.50
200 Donyell Marshall 10.00
201 Vlade Divac 1.50
202 Dino Radja 1.50
203 Carl Herrera 1.50
204 Olden Polynice 1.50
205 Patrick Ewing 10.00
206 Willie Anderson 1.50
207 Mitch Richmond 4.00
208 John Crotty 1.50
209 Tracy Murray 1.50
210 *Juwan Howard* 50.00
211 Robert Parish 1.50
212 Steve Kerr 1.50
213 Anthony Bowie 1.50
214 *Tim Breaux* 1.50
215 *Sharone Wright* 15.00
216 Brian Williams 1.50
217 Rick Fox 1.50
218 Harold Miner 1.50
219 Duane Ferrell 1.50
220 *Lamond Murray* 12.00
221 Blue Edwards 1.50
222 Bill Cartwright 1.50
223 *Sergei Bazarevich* 1.50
224 Herb Williams 1.50
225 *Brian Grant* 30.00
226 Derek Harper, John Starks 1.50
227 Rod Strickland, Clyde Drexler 4.00
228 Kevin Johnson, Dan Majerle 1.50
229 Lindsey Hunter, Joe Dumars 1.50
230 Anfernee Hardaway, Latrell Sprewell 4.00
231 Bill Wennington 1.50
232 Brian Shaw 1.50
233 *Jamie Watson* 1.50
234 Chris Whitney 1.50
235 Eric Montross 6.00
236 Kenny Smith 1.50
237 Andrew Lang 1.50
238 Lorenzo Williams 1.50
239 Dana Barros 1.50
240 Eddie Jones 20.00
241 Harold Ellis 1.50
242 James Edwards 1.50
243 Don MacLean 1.50
244 Ed Pinckney 1.50
245 *Carlos Rogers* 5.00
246 Michael Adams 1.50
247 Rex Walters 1.50
248 John Starks 1.50
249 Terrell Brandon 1.50
250 *Khalid Reeves* 12.00
251 Dominique Wilkins 4.00
252 Toni Kukoc 4.00
253 Rick Fox 1.50
254 Detlef Schrempf 1.50
255 Rik Smits 4.00
256 Johnny Dawkins 1.50
257 Dan Majerle 4.00
258 Mike Brown 1.50
259 Byron Scott 1.50
260 *Jalen Rose* 15.00
261 Byron Houston 1.50
262 Frank Brickowski 1.50
263 Vernon Maxwell 1.50
264 Craig Ehlo 1.50
265 *Yinka Dare* 1.50
266 Dee Brown 1.50
267 Felton Spencer 1.50
268 Harvey Grant 1.50
269 Nick Van Exel 30.00
270 Bob Martin 1.50
271 Hersey Hawkins 1.50
272 Scott Williams 1.50
273 Sarunas Marciulionis 1.50
274 Kevin Gamble 1.50
275 *Clifford Rozier* 5.00
276 B.J. Armstrong, Ron Harper 1.50
277 John Stockton, Jeff Hornacek 4.00
278 Bobby Hurley, Mitch Richmond 1.50
279 Anfernee Hardaway, Dennis Scott 8.00
280 Jason Kidd, Jim Jackson 20.00
281 Ron Harper 1.50
282 Chuck Person 1.50
283 John Williams 1.50
284 Robert Pack 1.50
285 *Aaron McKie* 6.00
286 Chris Smith 1.50
287 Horace Grant 4.00
288 Oliver Miller 1.50
289 Derek Harper 1.50
290 *Eric Mobley* 1.50
291 Scott Skiles 1.50
292 Olden Polynice 1.50
293 Mark Jackson 1.50
294 Wayman Tisdale 1.50
295 *Tony Dumas* 1.50
296 Bryon Russell 1.50
297 Vlade Divac 1.50
298 David Wesley 1.50
299 Askia Jones 1.50
300 *B.J. Tyler* 4.00
301 Hakeem Olajuwon 20.00
302 Luc Longley 1.50
303 Rony Seikaly 1.50
304 Sarunas Marciulionis 1.50
305 Dikembe Mutombo 1.50
306 Ken Norman 1.50
307 Dell Curry 1.50
308 Danny Ferry 1.50
309 Shawn Kemp 25.00
310 *Dickey Simpkins* 1.50
311 Johnny Newman 1.50
312 Dwayne Schintzius 1.50
313 Sean Elliott 1.50
314 Sean Rooks 1.50
315 *Bill Curley* 4.00
316 Bryant Stith 1.50
317 Pooh Richardson 1.50
318 *Jim McIlvaine* 1.50
319 Dennis Scott 1.50
320 *Wesley Person* 15.00
321 Bobby Hurley 1.50
322 Armon Gilliam 1.50
323 Rik Smits 1.50
324 Tony Smith 1.50
325 *Monty Williams* 1.50
326 Gary Payton, Kendall Gill 1.50
327 Mookie Blaylock, Stacey Augmon 1.50
328 Mark Jackson, Reggie Miller 4.00
329 Sam Cassell, Vernon Maxwell 1.50
330 Harold Miner, Khalid Reeves 1.50
331 Vinny Del Negro 1.50
332 Billy Owens 1.50
333 Mark West 1.50
334 Matt Geiger 1.50
335 *Greg Minor* 1.50
336 Larry Johnson 10.00
337 Donald Hodge 1.50
338 Aaron Williams 1.50
339 Jay Humphries 1.50
340 *Charlie Ward* 5.00
341 Scott Brooks 1.50
342 Stacey Augmon 1.50
343 Will Perdue 1.50
344 Dale Ellis 1.50
345 *Brooks Thompson* 4.00
346 Manute Bol 1.50
347 Kenny Anderson 4.00
348 Willie Burton 1.50
349 Michael Cage 1.50
350 Danny Manning 4.00
351 Ricky Pierce 1.50
352 Sam Cassell 4.00
353 Reggie Miller 4.00
354 David Robinson 15.00
355 Shaquille O'Neal 40.00
356 Scottie Pippen 6.00
357 Alonzo Mourning 6.00
358 Clarence Weatherspoon 4.00
359 Derrick Coleman 4.00
360 Charles Barkley 15.00
361 Karl Malone 8.00
362 Chris Webber 10.00

1994-95 Stadium Club Members Only

Parallelling the complete Stadium Club series, including the base and insert sets, the 509-card set was available to only those in the Members Only Club. Priced at $199 plus $10 shipping, the sets were limited to a maximum of 7,500 sets. Also included was a Members Only binder with display pages. A Member's Only logo is included on the card fronts. In addition, the Super Team cards featured different backs than the regular chase cards, making them ineligible for redemption. A Reggie Miller autographed card was also included with the set.

MT
Complete Set: (509) 350.00
Common Player: .15
1 Patrick Ewing 1.00
2 Patrick Ewing TTG .50
3 Bimbo Coles .15
4 Elden Campbell .15
5 Brent Price .15
6 Hubert Davis .15
7 Donald Royal .15
8 Tim Perry .15
9 Chris Webber 5.00
10 Chris Webber TTG 2.50
11 Brad Daugherty .30
12 P.J. Brown .15
13 Charles Barkley 2.50
14 Mario Elie .15
15 Tyrone Hill .15
16 Anfernee Hardaway 6.00
17 Anfernee Hardaway TTG 3.00
18 Toni Kukoc .50
19 Chris Morris .15
20 Gerald Wilkins .15
21 David Benoit .15
22 Kevin Duckworth .15
23 Derrick Coleman .30
24 Adam Keefe .15
25 Marion Maxey .15
26 Vern Fleming .15
27 Jeff Malone .30
28 Rodney Rogers .15
29 Terry Mills .15
30 Doug West .15
31 Doug West TTG .15
32 Shaquille O'Neal 6.00
33 Scottie Pippen 5.00
34 Lee Mayberry .15
35 Dale Ellis .30
36 Cedric Ceballos .75
37 Lionel Simmons .15
38 Kenny Gattison .15
39 Popeye Jones .15
40 Jerome Kersey .15
41 Jerome Kersey TTG .15
42 Larry Stewart .15
43 Rod Strickland .30
44 Chris Mills .50
45 Latrell Sprewell .75
46 Haywoode Workman .15
47 Charles Smith .15
48 Detlef Schrempf .50
49 Gary Grant .15
50 Gary Grant TTG .15
51 Tom Chambers .30
52 J.R. Reid .15
53 Mookie Blaylock .30
54 Mookie Blaylock TTG .30
55 Rony Seikaly .15
56 Isaiah Rider .50
57 Isaiah Rider TTG .30
58 Nick Anderson .30
59 Victor Alexander .15
60 Lucious Harris .15
61 Mark Macon .15
62 Otis Thorpe .30
63 Randy Woods .15
64 Clyde Drexler 1.50
65 Dikembe Mutombo .75
66 Todd Day .15
67 Greg Anthony .15
68 Sherman Douglas .15
69 Chris Mullin 1.00
70 Kevin Johnson .50
71 Kendall Gill .15
72 Dennis Rodman 5.00
73 Dennis Rodman TG 2.50
74 Jeff Turner .15
75 John Stockton 1.50
76 John Stockton TTG .75
77 Doug Edwards .15
78 Jim Jackson 1.00
79 Hakeem Olajuwon 2.50
80 Glen Rice 1.00
81 Christian Laettner 1.00
82 Terry Porter .15
83 Joe Dumars .50
84 David Wingate .15
85 B.J. Armstrong .30
86 Derrick McKey .15
87 Elmore Spencer .15
88 Walt Williams .30
89 Shawn Bradley .50
90 Acie Earl .15
91 Acie Earl TTG .15
92 Randy Brown .15
93 Grant Long .15
94 Terry Dehere .15
95 Spud Webb .30
96 Lindsey Hunter .15
97 Blair Rasmussen .15
98 Tim Hardaway 2.00
99 Kevin Edwards .15
100 Georgetown Hoyas (Patrick Ewing CT, Reggie Williams CT) .30
101 Auburn Tigers (Chuck Person CT, Charles Barkley CT) .50
102 LSU Tigers (Mahmoud Abdul-Rauf CT, Shaquille O'Neal CT) 1.50
103 Syracuse Orangeman (Rony Seikaly CT, Derrick Coleman CT) .15
104 Houston Cougars (Hakeem Olajuwon CT, Clyde Drexler CT) 1.50
105 St. John Red Storm (Chris Mullin CT, Mark Jackson CT) .15
106 Alabama Crimson Tide (Robert Horry CT, Latrell Sprewell CT) .30
107 UCLA Bruins (Pooh Richardson CT, Reggie Miller CT) .30
108 GA Tech Yellow Jackets (Dennis Scott CT, Kenny Anderson CT) .15
109 Illinois Fightin' Illini (Kendall Gill CT, Ken Norman CT) .15
110 Michigan State Spartans (Scott Skiles CT, Kevin Willis CT) .15
111 Michigan Wolverines (Terry Mills CT, Glen Rice CT) .15
112 Duke Blue Devils (Christian Laettner CT, Bobby Hurley CT) .30
113 UNLV Runnin' Rebels (Stacey Augmon CT, Larry Johnson CT) .30
114 North Carolina Tar Heels (Sam Perkins CT, James Worthy CT) .15
115 Carl Herrera .15
116 Sam Bowie .30
117 Gary Payton 2.50
118 Danny Ainge .30
119 Danny Ainge TTG .30
120 Luc Longley .15
121 Antonio Davis .15
122 Terry Cummings .30
123 Terry Cummings TTG .30
124 Mark Price .30
125 Jamal Mashburn 1.00
126 Mahmoud Abdul-Rauf .30
127 Charles Oakley .30
128 Steve Smith .30
129 Vin Baker 1.50
130 Robert Horry .75
131 Doug Christie .15
132 Wayman Tisdale .30
133 Wayman Tisdale TTG .30
134 Muggsy Bogues .50
135 Dino Radja .50
136 Jeff Hornacek .15
137 Gheorghe Muresan .50
138 Loy Vaught .30
139 Loy Vaught TTG .30
140 Benoit Benjamin .15
141 Johnny Dawkins .30
142 Allan Houston .50
143 Jon Barry .15
144 Reggie Miller 1.00
145 Kevin Willis .30
146 James Worthy .50
147 James Worthy TTG .30
148 Scott Burrell .15
149 Tom Gugliotta 1.00
150 LaPhonso Ellis .15
151 Doug Smith .15
152 A.C. Green .30
153 A.C. Green TTG .30
154 George Lynch .15
155 Sam Perkins .30
156 Corie Blount .15
157 Xavier McDaniel .15
158 Xavier McDaniel TTG .15
159 Eric Murdock .15
160 David Robinson 2.50
161 Karl Malone 2.50
162 Karl Malone TTG 1.25
163 Clarence Weatherspoon .30
164 Calbert Cheaney .50
165 Tom Hammonds .15
166 Tom Hammonds TTG .15
167 Alonzo Mourning 1.50
168 Clifford Robinson .50
169 Michael Williams .15
170 Ervin Johnson .15
171 Mike Giminski .30
172 Jason Kidd 15.00
173 Anthony Bonner .15
174 Stacey King .15
175 Rex Chapman .15
176 Greg Graham .15
177 Stanley Roberts .15
178 Mitch Richmond 1.00
179 Boston Celtics (Eric Montross) .75
180 Eddie Jones 10.00
181 Grant Hill 20.00
182 Donyell Marshall .50
183 Glenn Robinson 8.00
184 Dominique Wilkins .50
185 Mark Price .30
186 Anthony Mason .30
187 Tyrone Corbin .15
188 Dale Davis .15
189 Nate McMillan .15
190 Jason Kidd 7.50
191 John Salley .15
192 Keith Jennings .15
193 Mark Bryant .15
194 Sleepy Floyd .15
195 Grant Hill 10.00
196 Joe Kleine .15
197 Anthony Peeler .15
198 Malik Sealy .15
199 Kenny Walker .15
200 Donyell Marshall .30
201 Vlade Divac AI .30
202 Dino Radja AI .15
203 Carl Herrera AI .15
204 Olden Polynice AI .15
205 Patrick Ewing AI .75
206 Willie Anderson .15
207 Mitch Richmond 1.00
208 John Crotty .15
209 Tracy Murray .15
210 Juwan Howard 6.00
211 Robert Parish .50
212 Steve Kerr .15
213 Anthony Bowie .15
214 Tim Breaux .15
215 Sharone Wright .75
216 Brian Williams .15
217 Rick Fox .15
218 Harold Miner .15
219 Duane Ferrell .15
220 Lamond Murray .75
221 Blue Edwards .15
222 Bill Cartwright .15
223 Sergei Bazarevich .15
224 Herb Williams .15
225 Brian Grant 3.00
226 Derek Harper, John Starks .15
227 Rod Strickland BCT, Clyde Drexler .30
228 Kevin Johnson BCT, Dan Majerle .15
229 Lindsey Hunter BCT, Joe Dumars .15
230 Tim Hardaway BCT, Latrell Sprewell .30
231 Bill Wennington .15
232 Brian Shaw .15
233 Jamie Watson .30
234 Chris Whitney .15
235 Eric Montross .50
236 Kenny Smith .15
237 Andrew Lang .15
238 Lorenzo Williams .15
239 Dana Barros .30
240 Eddie Jones 5.00
241 Harold Ellis .15
242 James Edwards .15
243 Don MacLean .15
244 Ed Pinckney .15
245 Carlos Rogers .30
246 Michael Adams .15
247 Rex Walters .15
248 John Starks .30
249 Terrell Brandon .30
250 Khalid Reeves .30
251 Dominique Wilkins AI .30
252 Toni Kukoc AI .30
253 Rick Fox AI .15
254 Detlef Schrempf AI .30
255 Rik Smits AI .30
256 Johnny Dawkins .30
257 Dan Majerle .30
258 Mike Brown .30
259 Byron Scott .30
260 Jalen Rose .50
261 Bryon Houston .30
262 Frank Brickowski .15
263 Vernon Maxwell .15
264 Craig Ehlo .15
265 Yinka Dare .15
266 Dee Brown .15
267 Felton Spencer .15
268 Harvey Grant .15
269 Nick Van Exel 1.50
270 Bob Martin .15
271 Hersey Hawkins .30
272 Scott Williams .15
273 Sarunas Marciulionis .15
274 Kevin Gamble .15
275 Clifford Rozier .30
276 B.J. Armstrong BCT, Ron Harper .15
277 John Stockton BCT, Jeff Hornacek .30
278 Bobby Hurley BCT, Mitch Richmond .30
279 Anfernee Hardaway BCT, Dennis Scott 1.50
280 Jason Kidd BCT, Jim Jackson 1.50
281 Ron Harper .30
282 Chuck Person .30
283 John Williams .30
284 Robert Pack .15
285 Aaron McKie .50
286 Chris Smith .15
287 Horace Grant .50
288 Oliver Miller .15
289 Derek Harper .30
290 Eric Mobley .15
291 Scott Skiles .15
292 Olden Polynice .15
293 Mark Jackson .15
294 Wayman Tisdale .30
295 Tony Dumas .75
296 Bryon Russell .15
297 Vlade Divac .30
298 David Wesley .15
299 Askia Jones .15
300 B.J. Tyler .15
301 Hakeem Olajuwon AI 1.00
302 Luc Longley AI .15
303 Rony Seikaly AI .15
304 Sarunas Marciulionis AI .15
305 Dikembe Mutombo AI .50
306 Ken Norman .15
307 Dell Curry .15
308 Danny Ferry .15
309 Shawn Kemp 2.50
310 Dickey Simpkins .30
311 Johnny Newman .15
312 Dwayne Schintzius .15
313 Sean Elliot .50
314 Sean Rooks .15
315 Bill Curley .30
316 Bryant Stith .15
317 Pooh Richardson .15
318 Jim McIlvaine .15
319 Dennis Scott .30
320 Wesley Person .75
321 Bobby Hurley .30
322 Armon Gilliam .30
323 Rik Smits .50
324 Tony Smith .15
325 Monty Williams .15
326 Gary Payton BCT, Kendall Gill .15
327 Mookie Blaylock BCT, Stacey Augmon .15
328 Mark Jackson BCT, Reggie Miller .30
329 Sam Cassell BCT, Vernon Maxwell .15
330 Harold Miner BCT, Khalid Reeves .15
331 Vinny Del Negro .15
332 Billy Owens .30
333 Mark West .15
334 Matt Geiger .15
335 Greg Minor .50
336 Larry Johnson 1.00
337 Donald Hodge .15
338 Aaron Williams .15
339 Jay Humphries .15
340 Charlie Ward .50
341 Scott Brooks .15
342 Stacey Augmon .30
343 Will Perdue .15
344 Dale Ellis .30
345 Brooks Thompson .15
346 Manute Bol .15
347 Kenny Anderson .30
348 Willie Burton .15
349 Michael Cage .15
350 Danny Manning .50
351 Ricky Pierce .15
352 Sam Cassell .50
353 Reggie Miller FG .75
354 David Robinson FG 1.25
355 Shaquille O'Neal FG 2.00
356 Scottie Pippen FG 1.50
357 Alonzo Mourning FG .75
358 Clarence Weatherspoon FG .30
359 Derrick Coleman FG .30
360 Charles Barkley FG 1.25
361 Karl Malone FG 1.25
362 Chris Webber FG 3.00
BT1 Mookie Blaylock .30
BT2 Dominique Wilkins .50
BT3 Alonzo Mourning 1.00
BT4 Toni Kukoc .50
BT5 Mark Price .30
BT6 Jason Kidd 6.00
BT7 Jalen Rose 1.00
BT8 Grant Hill 10.00
BT9 Latrell Sprewell .75
BT10 Hakeem Olajuwon 2.50
BT11 Reggie Miller 1.00
BT12 Lamond Murray .75
BT13 George Lynch .15
BT14 Khalid Reeves .30
BT15 Glenn Robinson 4.00
BT16 Donyell Marshall .50
BT17 Derrick Coleman .30
BT18 Patrick Ewing 1.00
BT19 Shaquille O'Neal 4.00
BT20 Clarence Weatherspoon .30
BT21 Charles Barkley 2.00
BT22 Clifford Robinson .50
BT23 Bobby Hurley .30
BT24 David Robinson 2.00
BT25 Shawn Kemp 1.50
BT26 Karl Malone 2.00
BT27 Chris Webber 3.00
CC1 Stacey Augmon .30
CC2 Dino Radja .50
CC3 Alonzo Mourning 1.50
CC4 Scottie Pippen 3.00
CC5 Gerald Wilkins .15
CC6 Jamal Mashburn 1.00
CC7 Dikembe Mutombo .75
CC8 Lindsey Hunter .15
CC9 Chris Mullin 1.00
CC10 Hakeem Olajuwon 2.00
CC11 Reggie Miller 1.00
CC12 Gary Grant .15
CC13 Doug Christie .15
CC14 Steve Smith .30
CC15 Vin Baker 1.50
CC16 Christian Laettner .50
CC17 Derrick Coleman .30
CC18 Charles Oakley .30
CC19 Dennis Scott .30
CC20 Clarence Weatherspoon .30
CC21 Charles Barkley 2.00
CC22 Clifford Robinson .50
CC23 Mitch Richmond 1.00
CC24 David Robinson 2.00
CC25 Shawn Kemp 1.50

CC26 Karl Malone 2.00
CC27 Don MacLean .15
DD1A Mark Price .30
DD1B Kenny Anderson .30
DD2A Karl Malone .75
DD2B Derrick Coleman .30
DD3A John Stockton .75
DD3B Anfernee Hardaway 2.50
DD4A Mitch Richmond .50
DD4B Jim Jackson .50
DD5A James Worthy .30
DD5B Jamal Mashburn .75
DD6A Patrick Ewing .75
DD6B Alonzo Mourning .75
DD7A Hakeem Olajuwon 1.00
DD7B Shaquille O'Neal 2.00
DD8A Clyde Drexler .75
DD8B Isaiah Rider .30
DD9A Scottie Pippen 1.50
DD9B Latrell Sprewell .50
DD10A Charles Barkley 1.00
DD10B Chris Webber 1.50
RS1 Kenny Anderson .50
RS2 Latrell Sprewell 1.50
RS3 Jamal Mashburn 1.50
RS4 Alonzo Mourning 3.00
RS5 Shaquille O'Neal 8.00
RS6 LaPhonso Ellis .30
RS7 Chris Webber 5.00
RS8 Isaiah Rider .50
RS9 Dikembe Mutombo 1.00
RS10 Anfernee Hardaway 8.00
RS11 Antonio Davis .30
RS12 Robert Horry 1.00
SS1 Mark Price .30
SS2 Tim Hardaway .50
SS3 Keith Johnson .50
SS4 John Stockton 1.00
SS5 Mookie Blaylock .30
SS6 Reggie Miller 1.00
SS7 Jeff Hornacek .15
SS8 Latrell Sprewell .75
SS9 John Starks .30
SS10 Nate McMillian .15
SS11 Chris Mullin 1.00
SS12 Toni Kukoc .75
SS13 Anthony Mason .30
SS14 Robert Horry .75
SS15 Scottie Pippen 5.00
SS16 Charles Barkley 2.00
SS17 Dennis Rodman 4.00
SS18 Karl Malone 2.00
SS19 Chris Webber 3.00
SS20 Charles Oakley .30
SS21 Patrick Ewing 1.00
SS22 Shaquille O'Neal 5.00
SS23 Dikembe Mutombo .75
SS24 David Robinson 2.00
SS25 Hakeem Olajuwon 2.00
ST1 Atlanta Hawks/C. Ehol .15
ST2 Boston Celtics/Group .15
ST3 Charlotte Hornets/Group .15
ST4 Chicago Bulls/Group .15
ST5 Cleveland Cavaliers/Group .15
ST6 Dallas Mavericks/J.Jackson .50
ST7 Denver Nuggets/Group .15
ST8 Detroit Pistons/J.Dumars .30
ST9 Golden State Warriors/C.Webber 1.00
ST10 Houston Rockets/H. Olajuwon 1.00
ST11 Indiana Pacers/R.Smits .30
ST12 Los Angeles Clippers/Group .15
ST13 Los Angeles Lakers/N.Van Exel .75
ST14 Miami Heat/Group .15
ST15 Milwaukee Bucks/V.Baker .75
ST16 Minnesota Timberwolves/Group .15
ST17 New Jersey Nets/Group .15
ST18 New York Knicks/Group .15
ST19 Orlando Magics/S.O'Neal 2.00
ST20 Philadelphia 76ers/Group .15
ST21 Phoenix Suns/Group .15
ST22 Portland Trail Blazers/Group .15
ST23 Sacramento Kings/O.Polynice .15
ST24 San Antonio Spurs/Group .15
ST25 Seattle Supersonics/Group .15
ST26 Utah Jazz/J.Stockton .75
ST27 Washington Bullets/Group .15
TF1 Anfernee Hardaway 5.00
TF2 Latrell Sprewell .75
TF3 Grant Hill 15.00
TF4 Chris Webber 5.00
TF5 Shaquille O'Neal 5.00
TF6 Jason Kidd 10.00
TF7 Jim Jackson 1.00
TF8 Jamal Mashburn 1.00
TF9 Glenn Robinson 5.00
TF10 Alonzo Mourning 2.00
NNO Reggie Miller AU 35.00

1994-95 Stadium Club Members Only 50

This 50-card boxed set was available to Stadium Club members, who received one set of their choice and could purchase more sets for $10 each. Forty-five of the cards represent 11 of the top NBA players in each division from 1994-95, with an additional player from the Central Division. Card Nos. 46-50 showcase the top Rookie Picks cards and have a Finest-type treatment on the front. Each card front includes a Members Only gold-foil logo. The card backs have two player photos, along with the player's name and stats.

MT
Complete Set (50): 25.00
Common Player: .10
1 Shaquille O'Neal 2.00
2 Charles Oakley .15
3 Chris Webber 1.50
4 Dominique Wilkins .25
5 Kenny Anderson .15
6 Kevin Willis .15
7 Anfernee Hardaway 2.00
8 Derrick Coleman .15
9 Clarence Weatherspoon .15
10 Glen Rice .25
11 Patrick Ewing .75
12 Reggie Miller .75
13 Scottie Pippen 1.50
14 Steve Smith .15
15 Alonzo Mourning .75
16 Vin Baker .60
17 Tyrone Hill .10
18 Joe Dumars .25
19 Mookie Blaylock .15
20 Michael Jordan 10.00
21 Larry Johnson .75
22 Mark Price .15
23 Rik Smits .25
24 Hakeem Olajuwon 1.25
25 Karl Malone .75
26 Jamal Mashburn .60
27 Sean Elliott .25
28 Christian Laettner .25
29 Dikembe Mutombo .25
30 John Stockton .75
31 Clyde Drexler .75
32 Tom Gugliotta .15
33 Mahmoud Abdul-Rauf .15
34 David Robinson 1.25
35 Chris Mullin .25
36 Shawn Kemp .75
37 Mitch Richmond .50
38 Clifford Robinson .25
39 Cedric Ceballos .40
40 Charles Barkley 1.25
41 Loy Vaught .15
42 Gary Payton 1.25
43 Walt Williams .15
44 Nick Van Exel .60
45 Kevin Johnson .25
46 Glenn Robinson TRP 1.50
47 Jason Kidd TRP 3.00
48 Grant Hill TRP 5.00
49 Donyell Marshall TRP .15
50 Juwan Howard TRP 1.00

1994-95 Stadium Club Rising Stars

These insert cards mark the debut of Topps' exclusive Power Matrix technology that gives the cards a shiny, glowing appearance. Each card front shows a globe with stars rising into space. The stars are almost holographic in appearance. The featured player is shown on the bottom half of the card, next to the set's logo. His name is in the upper right corner. The card backs, numbered 1 of 12, etc., have a brief summary of the player's career, along with a color photo on a ghosted image of the same photo in a larger size. There are trimester reports on how the player performed during the 1993-94 season in minutes/rebounds/points per game during that period.

MT
Complete Set (12): 75.00
Common Player: 2.00
Minor Stars: 3.00
1 Kenny Anderson 3.00
2 Latrell Sprewell 6.00
3 Jamal Mashburn 5.00
4 Alonzo Mourning 8.00
5 Shaquille O'Neal 25.00
6 LaPhonso Ellis 2.00
7 Chris Webber 10.00
8 Isaiah Rider 5.00
9 Dikembe Mutombo 5.00
10 Anfernee Hardaway 28.00
11 Antonio Davis 2.00
12 Robert Horry 3.00

1994-95 Stadium Club Super Skills

These 25 cards were random inserts in 1994-95 Topps Stadium Club Series II packs, one every 24 packs. The set uses a new, multi-hued "rainbow" foil background for each of the top five players at each position. The card front has the set's and Stadium Club logos stamped in gold foil. The card back is numbered One of 25, etc., and gives a brief description of the player's super skills.

MT
Complete Set (25): 50.00
Common Player: 1.00
Minor Stars: 2.00
1 Mark Price 2.00
2 Tim Hardaway 2.00
3 Kevin Johnson 2.00
4 John Stockton 3.00
5 Mookie Blaylock 1.00
6 Reggie Miller 3.00
7 Jeff Hornacek 1.00
8 Latrell Sprewell 2.00
9 John Starks 1.00
10 Nate McMillan 1.00
11 Chris Mullin 2.00
12 Toni Kukoc 2.00
13 Anthony Mason 1.00
14 Robert Horry 1.00
15 Scottie Pippen 6.00
16 Charles Barkley 4.00
17 Dennis Rodman 6.00
18 Karl Malone 3.00
19 Chris Webber 3.00
20 Charles Oakley 1.00
21 Patrick Ewing 3.00
22 Shaquille O'Neal 12.00
23 Dikembe Mutombo 3.00
24 David Robinson 4.00
25 Hakeem Olajuwon 5.00

1994-95 Stadium Club Super Teams

These 27 cards were randomly inserted in 1994 Topps Stadium Club packs. The card front has the team name, set logo and brand label all stamped in silver foil. The back has game rules for the card holder to follow if he wants to cash in on the prizes being offered for those who find cards for teams which win divisional, conference or championship titles during the 1994-95 season.

MT
Complete Set (27): 40.00
Common Team: 1.00
1 Atlanta 1.00
2 Boston 1.00
3 Charlotte 2.00
4 Chicago 2.00
5 Cleveland 1.00
6 Dallas 2.00
7 Denver 1.00
8 Detroit 1.00
9 Golden State 3.00
10 Houston 15.00
11 Indiana 3.00
12 Los Angeles 1.00
13 Los Angeles 3.00
14 Miami 1.00
15 Milwaukee 3.00
16 Minnesota 1.00
17 New Jersey 1.00
18 New York 2.00
19 Orlando 15.00
20 Philadelphia 1.00
21 Phoenix 5.00
22 Portland 1.00
23 Sacramento 1.00
24 San Antonio 3.00
25 Seattle 2.00
26 Utah 2.00
27 Washington 1.00

1994-95 Stadium Club Super Teams Division Winners

Magic, Pacers, Spurs and Suns Super Team cards could be redeemed for Division Winners team sets, which each included 11 cards. Each card front design is identical to the base cards, except a gold-foil Division Winner logo is added. The Super Team cards were seeded one per 24 Series I packs. Prefixes of "M", "P", "SP" and "SU" have been inserted below in the card numbers respective to the player's team.

MT
Comp. Bag Magic (11): 12.00
Comp. Bag Pacers (11): 3.00
Comp. Bag Spurs (11): 5.00
Comp. Bag Suns (11): 6.00
Common Player: .25
Common DW Team Card: 1.00
M7 Donald Royal .25
M16 Anfernee Hardaway 6.00
M32 Shaquille O'Neal 5.00
M58 Nick Anderson .50
M74 Jeff Turner .25
M213 Anthony Bowie .25
M232 Brian Shaw .25
M287 Horace Grant .50
M319 Dennis Scott .50
M345 Brooks Thompson .25
MD19 Magic DW Super Team 1.00
P26 Vern Fleming .25
P46 Haywoode Workman .25
P86 Derrick McKey .25
P121 Antonio Davis .25
P144 Reggie Miller 1.00
P188 Dale Davis .25
P219 Duane Ferrell .25
P259 Byron Scott .35
P293 Mark Jackson .25
P323 Rik Smits .50
PD11 Pacers DW Super Team 1.00
SP52 J.R. Reid .25
SP72 Dennis Rodman 2.00
SP73 Dennis Rodman TG 1.00
SP122 Terry Cummings .25
SP160 David Robinson 2.00
SP206 Willie Anderson .25
SP282 Chuck Person .25
SP313 Sean Elliott .50
SP331 Vinny Del Negro .35
SP354 David Robinson FG 1.00
SPD24 Spurs DW Super Team 1.00
SU13 Charles Barkley 2.00
SU70 Kevin Johnson .50
SU118 Danny Ainge .50
SU152 A.C. Green .50
SU196 Joe Kleine .25
SU257 Dan Majerle .35
SU294 Wayman Tisdale .25
SU320 Wesley Person .50
SU350 Danny Manning .35
SU360 Charles Barkley FG 1.00
SUD21 Suns DW Super Team 1.00

1994-95 Stadium Club Super Teams Master Photos

Rockets and Magic Super Team cards, which were randomly seeded in Series I packs, could be redeemed for team sets of these 5" by 7" cards. The base card design is featured on the front, however, it is bordered with a funky design and includes a Master Photo logo. Card backs are numbered "of 10." "M" and "R" prefixes have been inserted below to designate which team the athlete played with during the season.

MT
Comp. Bag Magic (11): 15.00
Comp. Bag Rockets (11): 8.00
Common Player: .40
Common MP Team Card: 1.00
M1 Nick Anderson .75
M2 Anthony Bowie .40
M3 Jeff Turner .40
M4 Dennis Scott .40
M5 Horace Grant .75
M6 Shaquille O'Neal 8.00
M7 Brooks Thompson .40
M8 Anfernee Hardaway 8.00
M9 Donald Royal .40
M10 Brian Shaw .40
MM19 Magic MP Super Team 1.00
R1 Tim Breaux .40
R2 Scott Brooks .40
R3 Clyde Drexler, Hakeem Olajuwon 2.50
R4 Hakeem Olajuwon 5.00
R5 Sam Cassell .75
R6 Vernon Maxwell .40
R7 Mario Elie .40
R8 Carl Herrera .40
R9 Kenny Smith .40
R10 Robert Horry .75
MR10 Rockets MP Super Team 1.00

1994-95 Stadium Club Super Teams NBA Finals

Rockets Super Team cards could be redeemed for this 362-card set which parallels the base set. A gold-foil NBA Finals logo is what sets this apart from the base set.

MT
Complete Set (363): 60.00
Common Player: .15
Semistars: .40
Stars: 1.25x to 2.5x
Rookies: 1x to 2x

1994-95 Stadium Club Team of the Future

These cards were random inserts in 1994-95 Topps Stadium Club Series II packs, one every 24 packs. The cards utilize the Power Matrix technology which was used for Series I Rising Stars inserts. The card front has a glow and shine to it; the back, numbered 1 of 10, etc., has a photo and summary of why the player was selected as a member of the Stadium Club Team of the Future.

MT
Complete Set (10): 45.00
Common Player: 1.00
1 Anfernee Hardaway 8.00
2 Latrell Sprewell 1.50
3 Grant Hill 12.00
4 Chris Webber 4.00
5 Shaquille O'Neal 10.00
6 Jason Kidd 10.00
7 Jim Jackson 1.00
8 Jamal Mashburn 2.00
9 Glenn Robinson 5.00
10 Alonzo Mourning 3.00

1995-96 Stadium Club

Topps released its 1995-96 Stadium Club basketball set in two series, featuring 180 and 181 cards. Series I subsets include 15 players selected in the NBA Draft, on specially designed cards, plus special theme cards - Extreme Corps, Xpansion Team and Trans-Action. Two special theme cards, each foil stamped with rainbow diffraction and red foil, are in each pack. Extreme Corps cards are based on Topps' statistical composite ratings, Xpansion Team cards showcase the two new expansion teams (Toronto and Vancouver), and Trans-Action cards look at six high-impact traded players in their new roles with their new teams. A parallel version of every theme card will be inserted in rack and jumbo packs; these feature silver and blue diffraction foil. Series I inserts include Power Zone, Beam Team and Warp Speed (each continued in Series II), plus Nemeses and Wizards. Series II inserts include Reign Men, Spike Says and X-2. Series II includes 135 regular cards, 35 Draft Picks, five Trans-Action and five Xpressions cards. Seeded one per every six packs is an NBA Finals Entry card, which allows collectors the chance to win a variety of prizes. Each regular card from both series has a full-bleed color action photo on the front, with gold foil stamping used for the player's name, team name and brand logo. The back features the traditional information - stats, biographical information, a card number, and a couple of photos.

MT
Complete Set (361): 50.00
Complete Series 1 (180): 20.00
Complete Series 2 (181): 30.00
Common Player: .10
Minor Stars: .20
Ser. 1 or 2 Pack (13): 1.50
Ser. 1 or 2 Wax Box (36): 35.00
1 Michael Jordan 3.00
2 Glenn Robinson .50
3 Jason Kidd 1.50
4 Clyde Drexler .50
5 Horace Grant .25
6 Allan Houston .10
7 Xavier McDaniel .10
8 Jeff Hornacek .10
9 Vlade Divac .10
10 Juwan Howard .50
11 Keith Jennings .10
12 Grant Long .10
13 Jalen Rose .10
14 Malik Sealy .10
15 Gary Payton .20
16 Danny Ferry .10
17 Glen Rice .10
18 Randy Brown .10
19 Greg Graham .10
20 Kenny Anderson .10
21 Aaron McKie .10
22 John Salley .10
23 Darrin Hancock .10
24 Carlos Rogers .10
25 Vin Baker .25
26 Bill Wennington .10
27 Kenny Smith .10
28 Sherman Douglas .10
29 Terry Davis .10
30 Grant Hill 2.00
31 Reggie Miller .30
32 Anfernee Hardaway 2.00
33 Patrick Ewing .25
34 Charles Barkley .60
35 Eddie Jones .40
36 Kevin Duckworth .10
37 Tom Hammonds .10
38 Craig Ehlo .10
39 Micheal Williams .10
40 Alonzo Mourning .30
41 John Williams .10
42 Felton Spencer .10
43 Lamond Murray .10
44 Dontonio Wingfield .10
45 Rik Smits .10
46 Donyell Marshall .10
47 Clarence Weatherspoon .10
48 Kevin Edwards .10
49 Charlie Ward .10
50 David Robinson .60
51 James Robinson .10
52 Bill Cartwright .10
53 Bobby Hurley .10
54 Kevin Gamble .10
55 B.J. Tyler .10
56 Chris Smith .10
57 Wesley Person .10
58 Tim Breaux .10
59 Mitchell Butler .10
60 Toni Kukoc .10
61 Roy Tarpley .10
62 Todd Day .10
63 Anthony Peeler .10
64 Brian Williams .10
65 Muggsy Bogues .10
66 Jerome Kersey .10
67 Eric Piatkowski .10
68 Tim Perry .10
69 Chris Gatling .10
70 Mark Price .10
71 Terry Mills .10
72 Anthony Avent .10
73 Matt Geiger .10
74 Walt Williams .10
75 Sean Elliott .10
76 Ken Norman .10
77 Kendall Gill .10
78 Byron Houston .10
79 Rick Fox .10
80 Derek Harper .10
81 Rod Strickland .10
82 Bryon Russell .10
83 Antonio Davis .10
84 Isaiah Rider .20
85 Kevin Johnson .20
86 Derrick Coleman .20
87 Doug Overton .10
88 Hersey Hawkins .10
89 Popeye Jones .10
90 Dickey Simpkins .10
91 Rodney Rogers .10
92 Rex Chapman .10
93 Spud Webb .10
94 Lee Mayberry .10
95 Cedric Ceballos .10
96 Tyrone Hill .10
97 Bill Curley .10
98 Jeff Turner .10
99 Tyrone Corbin .10
100 John Stockton .30
101 Mookie Blaylock .10
102 Dino Radja .10
103 Alonzo Mourning .20
104 Scottie Pippen .75
105 Terrell Brandon .10
106 Jim Jackson .20
107 Mahmoud Abdul-Rauf .10
108 Grant Hill 1.00
109 Tim Hardaway .10
110 Hakeem Olajuwon .75
111 Rik Smits .10
112 Loy Vaught .10
113 Vlade Divac .10
114 Kevin Willis .10
115 Glenn Robinson .50
116 Christian Laettner .10
117 Derrick Coleman .10
118 Patrick Ewing .20
119 Shaquille O'Neal 1.50
120 Dana Barros .10
121 Charles Barkley .50
122 Rod Strickland .10
123 Brian Grant .10
124 David Robinson .50
125 Shawn Kemp .75
126 Oliver Miller .10
127 Karl Malone .20
128 Benoit Benjamin .10
129 Chris Webber .20
130 Dan Majerle .10
131 Calbert Cheaney .10
132 Mark Jackson .10
133 Greg Anthony .10
134 Scott Burrell .10
135 Detlef Schrempf .10
136 Marty Conlon .10
137 Rony Seikaly .10
138 Olden Polynice .10
139 Terry Cummings .10
140 Stacey Augmon .10
141 Bryant Stith .10
142 Sean Higgins .10
143 Antoine Carr .10
144 Blue Edwards .10
145 A.C. Green .10
146 Bobby Phills .10
147 Terry Dehere .10
148 Sharone Wright .10
149 Nick Anderson .10
150 Jim Jackson .30
151 Eric Montross .10
152 Doug West .10
153 Charles Smith .10
154 Will Perdue .10
155 Gerald Wilkins .10
156 Robert Horry .20
157 Robert Parish .10
158 Lindsey Hunter .10
159 Harvey Grant .10
160 Tim Hardaway .10
161 Sarunas Marciulionis .10
162 Khalid Reeves .10
163 Bo Outlaw .10
164 Dale Davis .10
165 Nick Van Exel .40
166 Byron Scott .10
167 Steve Smith .10

168	Brian Grant	.20
169	Avery Johnson	.10
170	Dikembe Mutombo	.20
171	Tom Gugliotta	.10
172	Armon Gilliam	.10
173	Shawn Bradley	.10
174	Herb Williams	.10
175	Dino Radja	.10
176	Billy Owens	.10
177	Kenny Gattison	.10
178	J.R. Reid	.10
179	Otis Thorpe	.10
180	Sam Cassell	.10
181	Sam Cassell	.10
182	Pooh Richardson	.10
183	Johnny Newman	.10
184	Dennis Scott	.10
185	Will Perdue	.10
186	Andrew Lang	.10
187	Karl Malone	.30
188	Buck Williams	.10
189	P.J. Brown	.10
190	Khalid Reeves	.10
191	Kevin Willis	.10
192	Robert Pack	.10
193	Joe Dumars	.10
194	Sam Perkins	.10
195	Dan Majerle	.10
196	John Hot Rod Williams	.10
197	Reggie Williams	.10
198	Greg Anthony	.10
199	Steve Kerr	.10
200	Richard Dumas	.10
201	Dee Brown	.10
202	Zan Tabak	.10
203	David Wood	.10
204	Duane Causwell	.10
205	Sedale Threatt	.10
206	Hubert Davis	.10
207	Donald Hodge	.10
208	Duane Ferrell	.10
209	Sam Mitchell	.10
210	Adam Keefe	.10
211	Clifford Robinson	.10
212	Rodney Rogers	.10
213	Jayson Williams	.10
214	Brian Shaw	.10
215	Luc Longley	.10
216	Don MacLean	.10
217	Rex Chapman	.10
218	Wayman Tisdale	.10
219	Shawn Kemp	.60
220	Chris Webber	.20
221	Antonio Harvey	.10
222	Sarunas Marciulionis	.10
223	Jeff Malone	.10
224	Chucky Brown	.10
225	Greg Minor	.10
226	Clifford Rozier	.10
227	Derrick McKey	.10
228	Tony Dumas	.20
229	Oliver Miller	.10
230	Charles Oakley	.10
231	Fred Roberts	.10
232	Glen Rice	.10
233	Terry Porter	.10
234	Mark Macon	.10
235	Michael Cage	.10
236	Eric Murdock	.10
237	Vinny Del Negro	.10
238	Spud Webb	.10
239	Mario Elie	.10
240	Blue Edwards	.10
241	Dontonio Wingfield	.10
242	Brooks Thompson	.10
243	Alonzo Mourning	.30
244	Dennis Rodman	2.00
245	Lorenzo Williams	.10
246	Haywoode Workman	.10
247	Loy Vaught	.10
248	Vernon Maxwell	.10
249	Lionel Simmons	.10
250	Chris Childs	.10
251	Mahmoud Abdul-Rauf	.10
252	Vincent Askew	.10
253	Chris Morris	.10
254	Elliot Perry	.10
255	Dell Curry	.10
256	Dana Barros	.10
257	Terrell Brandon	.10
258	Monty Williams	.10
259	Corie Blount	.10
260	B.J. Armstrong	.10
261	Jim McIlvaine	.10
262	Otis Thorpe	.10
263	Sean Rooks	.10
264	Tony Massenburg	.10
265	Steve Smith	.10
266	Ron Harper	.10
267	Dale Ellis	.10
268	Clyde Drexler	.50
269	Jamie Watson	.10
270	Doc Rivers	.10
271	Derrick Alston	.10
272	Eric Mobley	.10
273	Ricky Pierce	.10
274	David Wesley	.10
275	John Starks	.10
276	Chris Mullin	.10
277	Ervin Johnson	.10
278	Jamal Mashburn	.20
279	Joe Kleine	.10
280	Mitch Richmond	.20
281	Chris Mills	.10
282	Bimbo Coles	.10
283	Larry Johnson	.30
284	Stanley Roberts	.10
285	Rex Walters	.10
286	Donald Royal	.10
287	Benoit Benjamin	.10
288	Chris Dudley	.10
289	Elden Campbell	.10
290	Mookie Blaylock	.10
291	Hersey Hawkins	.10
292	Anthony Mason	.10
293	Latrell Sprewell	.20
294	Harold Miner	.10
295	Scott Williams	.10
296	David Benoit	.10
297	Christian Laettner	.10
298	LaPhonso Ellis	.10
299	Gheorghe Muresan	.10
300	Kendall Gill	.10
301	Eddie Johnson	.10
302	Terry Cummings	.10
303	Chuck Person	.10
304	Michael Smith	.10
305	Mark West	.10
306	Willie Anderson	.10
307	Pervis Ellison	.10
308	Brian Williams	.10
309	Danny Manning	.10
310	Hakeem Olajuwon	1.00
311	Scottie Pippen	1.00
312	Jon Koncak	.10
313	Predrag Danilovic	.10
314	Lucious Harris	.10
315	Yinka Dare	.10
316	*Eric Williams* (Draft Pick)	.40
317	*Gary Trent* (Draft Pick)	.30
318	*Theo Ratliff* (Draft Pick)	.30
319	*Lawrence Moten* (Draft Pick)	.10
320	*Jerome Allen* (Draft Pick)	.10
321	*Tyus Edney* (Draft Pick)	.20
322	*Loren Meyer* (Draft Pick)	.10
323	*Michael Finley* (Draft Pick)	2.00
324	*Alan Henderson* (Draft Pick)	.40
325	*Bob Sura* (Draft Pick)	.30
326	*Joe Smith* (Draft Pick)	1.50
327	*Damon Stoudamire* (Draft Pick)	1.50
328	*Sherell Ford* (Draft Pick)	.10
329	*Jerry Stackhouse* (Draft Pick)	3.00
330	*George Zidek* (Draft Pick)	.30
331	*Brent Barry* (Draft Pick)	.75
332	*Shawn Respert* (Draft Pick)	.30
333	*Rasheed Wallace* (Draft Pick)	2.50
334	*Antonio McDyess* (Draft Pick)	2.00
335	*David Vaughn* (Draft Pick)	.10
336	*Cory Alexander* (Draft Pick)	.10
337	*Jason Caffey* (Draft Pick)	.10
338	*Frankie King* (Draft Pick)	.10
339	*Travis Best* (Draft Pick)	.10
340	*Greg Ostertag* (Draft Pick)	.10
341	*Ed O'Bannon* (Draft Pick)	.20
342	*Kurt Thomas* (Draft Pick)	.40
343	*Kevin Garnett* (Draft Pick)	6.00
344	*Bryant Reeves* (Draft Pick)	1.00
345	*Corliss Williamson* (Draft Pick)	.30
346	*Cherokee Parks* (Draft Pick)	.30
347	*Junior Burrough* (Draft Pick)	.10
348	*Randolph Childress* (Draft Pick)	.10
349	*Lou Roe* (Draft Pick)	.10
350	*Mario Bennett* (Draft Pick)	.10
351	Dikembe Mutombo (X-pressions)	.20
352	Larry Johnson (X-pressions)	.40
353	Vlade Divac (X-pressions)	.10
354	Karl Malone (X-pressions)	.40
355	John Stockton (X-pressions)	.40
356	Alonzo Mourning (Trans-action)	.40
357	Glen Rice (Trans-action)	.10
358	Dan Majerle (Trans-action)	.10
359	John Hot Rod Williams (Trans-action)	.10
360	Mark Price (Trans-action)	.10
361	Magic Johnson	1.75

1995-96 Stadium Club Beam Team

Both series of 1995-96 Topps Stadium Club had Beam Team insert cards. Series I has cards 1-10 (seeded one per every 18 packs); Series II has cards 11-20 (seeded one per every 72 retail packs and one per every 36 hobby packs). These cards feature the words "Beam Team" and "TSC" laser cut into them. Gold foil stamping is used for the player's name and brand name, both at the top of the card. The card back, numbered using a "BT" prefix, has a color photo and biographical information towards the top, with 1994-95 stats for points per game, rebounds per game and steals per game, compared to the NBA high for the season. The cards are diffraction foil cards.

		MT
Complete Set (20):		100.00
Complete Series 1 (10):		20.00
Complete Series 2 (10):		80.00
Common Player (1-10):		2.00
Common Player (11-20):		3.00
1	David Robinson	3.00
2	Juwan Howard	3.00
3	Mitch Richmond	2.00
4	Reggie Miller	3.00
5	Glenn Robinson	3.00
6	Shaquille O'Neal	10.00
7	Shawn Kemp	2.50
8	Karl Malone	3.00
9	Jamal Mashburn	2.00
10	Alonzo Mourning	3.00
11	Charles Barkley	7.00
12	Hakeem Olajuwon	12.00
13	Kenny Anderson	3.00
14	Michael Jordan	60.00
15	Dikembe Mutombo	3.00
16	Rod Strickland	3.00
17	Patrick Ewing	6.00
18	Latrell Sprewell	4.00
19	Grant Hill	25.00
20	Cedric Ceballos	3.00

1995-96 Stadium Club Draft Picks

Fifteen players selected in the 1995 NBA Draft are featured on these 1995-96 Topps Stadium Club Series I cards. The cards, which are skip-numbered, were random inserts in Series I packs.

		MT
Complete Set (15):		15.00
Common Player:		.50
2	Antonio McDyess	3.00
3	Jerry Stackhouse	2.00
4	Rasheed Wallace	1.00
5	Kevin Garnett	5.00
6	Bryant Reeves	1.50
8	Shawn Respert	.50
9	Ed O'Bannon	.50
11	Gary Trent	.50
12	Cherokee Parks	.50
15	Brent Barry	1.00
16	Alan Henderson	.50
17	Bob Sura	.50
18	Theo Ratliff	.50
19	Randolph Childress	.50
22	George Zidek	.50

1995-96 Stadium Club Intercontinental

This 10-card insert features NBA players born outside the United States. It was inserted in 1995-96 Austrailian Stadium Club packs. The horizontal fronts feature a color player photo with a globe in the background printed in gold and silver foil. The backs are also horizontal and feature biographical information and career highlights.

		MT
Complete Set (10):		15.00
Common Player:		1.00
IC1	Hakeem Olajuwon	8.00
IC2	Dikembe Mutombo	2.00
IC3	Bill Wennington	1.00
IC4	Rick Fox	1.00
IC5	Carl Herrera	1.00
IC6	Rony Seikaly	1.00
IC7	Rik Smits	1.50
IC8	Dino Radja	1.00
IC9	Sarunas Marciulionis	1.00
IC10	Luc Longley	2.00

1995-96 Stadium Club Members Only I

This is the first time Topps divided its Members Only parallel sets into different series. Released in factory set form and sold to Members Only Club members, the 291-card set parallels the base and insert sets from Series I.

		MT
Complete Set (291):		250.00
Common Player:		.25
1	Michael Jordan	20.00
2	Glenn Robinson	1.50
3	Jason Kidd	4.00
4	Clyde Drexler	1.50
5	Horace Grant	.50
6	Allan Houston	.30
7	Xavier McDaniel	.25
8	Jeff Hornacek	.25
9	Vlade Divac	.30
10	Juwan Howard	1.00
11EB	Keith Jennings EXP Blue	.25
11ER	Keith Jennings EXP Red	.25
12	Grant Long	.25
13	Jalen Rose	.30
14	Malik Sealy	3.00
15	Gary Payton	.75
16	Danny Ferry	1.00
17	Glen Rice	.50
18	Randy Brown	.25
19	Greg Graham	.25
20	Kenny Anderson	.30
21	Aaron McKie	.25
22EB	John Salley EXP Blue	.25
22ER	John Salley EXP Red	.25
23	Darrin Hancock	1.50
24	Carlos Rogers	.25
25	Vin Baker	1.25
26	Bill Wennington	.25
27	Kenny Smith	.25
28	Sherman Douglas	10.00
29	Terry Davis	.25
30	Grant Hill	3.00
31	Reggie Miller	1.00
32	Anfernee Hardaway	5.00
33	Patrick Ewing	1.00
34	Charles Barkley	3.00
35	Eddie Jones	2.00
36	Kevin Duckworth	.25
37	Tom Hammonds	.25
38	Craig Ehlo	.25
39	Michael Williams	.25
40	Alonzo Mourning	1.50
41	John Williams	.30
42	Felton Spencer	.25
43	Lamond Murray	.25
44EB	Dontonio Wingfield EXP Blue	.25
44ER	Dontonio Wingfield EXP Red	.25
45	Rik Smits	.50
46	Donyell Marshall	.25
47	Clarence Weatherspoon	.30
48	Kevin Edwards	.25
49	Charlie Ward	.25
50	David Robinson	3.00
51	James Robinson	.25
52	Bill Cartwright	.25
53	Bobby Hurley	.30
54	Kevin Gamble	.25
55EB	B.J. Tyler EXP Blue	.25
55ER	B.J. Tyler EXP Red	.25
56	Chris Smith	.25
57	Wesley Person	.50
58	Tim Breaux	.25
59	Mitchell Butler	.25
60	Toni Kukoc	.50
61	Roy Tarpley	.25
62	Todd Day	.25
63	Anthony Peeler	.25
64	Brian Williams	.25
65	Muggsy Bogues	.50
66EB	Jerome Kersey EXP Blue	.25
66ER	Jerome Kersey EXP Red	.25
67	Eric Piatkowski	.25
68	Tim Perry	.25
69	Chris Gatling	.25
70	Mark Price	.30
71	Terry Mills	.25
72	Anthony Avent	.25
73	Matt Geiger	.25
74	Walt Williams	.30
75	Sean Elliott	.50
76	Ken Norman	.25
77TB	Kendall Gill TA Blue	.25
77TR	Kendall Gill TA Red	.25
78	Bryon Houston	.25
79	Rick Fox	.25
80	Derek Harper	.30
81	Rod Strickland	.30
82	Bryon Russell	.25
83	Antonio Davis	.25
84	Isaiah Rider	.30
85	Kevin Johnson	.50
86	Derrick Coleman	.50
87	Doug Overton	.25
88TB	Hersey Hawkins TA Blue	.30
88TR	Hersey Hawkins TA Red	.30
89	Popeye Jones	.25
90	Dickey Simpkins	.25
91TB	Rodney Rogers TA Blue	.30
91TR	Rodney Rogers TA Red	.30
92TB	Rex Chapman TA Blue	.75
92TR	Rex Chapman TA Red	.75
93TB	Spud Webb TA Blue	.25
93TR	Spud Webb TA Red	.25
94	Lee Mayberry	.25
95	Cedric Ceballos	.25
96	Tyrone Hill	.25
97	Bill Curley	.25
98	Jeff Turner	.25
99TB	Tyrone Corbin TA Blue	.25
99TR	Tyrone Corbin TA Red	.25
100	John Stockton	1.50
101B	Mookie Blaylock EC Blue	.30
101R	Mookie Blaylock EC Red	.30
102B	Dino Radja EC Blue	.30
102R	Dino Radja EC Red	.30
103B	Alonzo Mourning EC Blue	1.50
103R	Alonzo Mourning EC Red	1.50
104B	Scottie Pippen EC Blue	5.00
104R	Scottie Pippen EC Red	5.00
105B	Terrell Brandon EC Blue	1.00
105R	Terrell Brandon EC Red	1.00
106B	Jim Jackson EC Blue	.50
106R	Jim Jackson EC Red	.50
107B	Mahmoud Abdul-Rauf EC Blue	.30
107R	Mahmoud Abdul-Rauf EC Red	.30
108B	Grant Hill EC Blue	10.00
108R	Grant Hill EC Red	10.00
109B	Tim Hardaway EC Blue	2.00
109R	Tim Hardaway EC Red	2.00
110B	Hakeem Olajuwon EC Blue	3.00
110R	Hakeem Olajuwon EC Red	3.00
111B	Rik Smits EC Blue	.50
111R	Rik Smits EC Red	.50
112B	Loy Vaught EC Blue	.30
112R	Loy Vaught EC Red	.30
113B	Vlade Divac EC Blue	.30
113R	Vlade Divac EC Red	.30
114B	Kevin Willis EC Blue	.30
114R	Kevin Willis EC Red	.30
115B	Glenn Robinson EC Blue	1.50
115R	Glenn Robinson EC Red	1.50
116B	Christian Laettner EC Blue	.50
116R	Christian Laettner EC Red	.50
117B	Derrick Coleman EC Blue	.30
117R	Derrick Coleman EC Red	.30
118B	Patrick Ewing EC Blue	1.50
118R	Patrick Ewing EC Red	1.50
119B	Shaquille O'Neal EC Blue	5.00
119R	Shaquille O'Neal EC Red	5.00
120B	Dana Barros EC Blue	.30
120R	Dana Barros EC Red	.30
121B	Charles Barkley EC Blue	3.00
121R	Charles Barkley EC Red	3.00
122B	Rod Strickland EC Blue	.30
122R	Rod Strickland EC Red	.30
123B	Brian Grant EC Blue	.30
123R	Brian Grant EC Red	.30
124B	David Robinson EC Blue	3.00
124R	David Robinson EC Red	3.00
125B	Shawn Kemp EC Blue	2.50
125R	Shawn Kemp EC Red	2.50
126B	Oliver Miller EC Blue	.25
126R	Oliver Miller EC Red	.25
127B	Karl Malone EC Blue	3.00
127R	Karl Malone EC Red	3.00
128B	Benoit Benjamin EC Blue	.25
128R	Benoit Benjamin EC Red	.25
129B	Chris Webber EC Blue	5.00
129R	Chris Webber EC Red	5.00
130	Dan Majerle	.30
131	Calbert Cheaney	.30
132	Mark Jackson	.25
133EB	Greg Anthony EXP Blue	.25
133ER	Greg Anthony EXP Red	.25
134	Scott Burrell	.25
135	Detlef Schrempf	.50
136	Marty Conlon	.25
137	Rony Seikaly	.25
138	Olden Polynice	.25
139	Terry Cummings	.30
140	Stacey Augmon	.30
141	Bryant Stith	.25
142	Sean Higgins	.25
143	Antoine Carr	.25
144EB	Blue Edwards EXP Blue	.25
144ER	Blue Edwards EXP Red	.25
145	A.C. Green	.30
146	Bobby Phills	.30
147	Terry Dehere	.25
148	Sharone Wright	.25
149	Nick Anderson	.30
150	Jim Jackson	.50
151	Eric Montross	.25
152	Doug West	.25
153	Charles Smith	.25
154	Will Perdue	.25
155EB	Gerald Wilkins EXP Blue	.25
155ER	Gerald Wilkins EXP Red	.25
156	Robert Horry	.50
157	Robert Parish	.50
158	Lindsey Hunter	.25
159	Harvey Grant	.25
160	Tim Hardaway	2.00
161	Sarunas Marciulionis	.25
162	Khalid Reeves	.25
163	Bo Outlaw	.25
164	Dale Davis	.25
165	Nick Van Exel	1.25
166EB	Byron Scott EXP Blue	.30
166ER	Byron Scott EXP Red	.30
167	Steve Smith	.30
168	Brian Grant	.30
169	Avery Johnson	.30
170	Dikembe Mutombo	.50
171	Tom Gugliotta	.30
172	Armon Gilliam	.30
173	Shawn Bradley	.30
174	Herb Williams	.25
175	Dino Radja	.30
176	Billy Owens	.30
177EB	Kenny Gattison EXP Blue	.25
177ER	Kenny Gattison EXP Red	.25
178	J.R. Reid	.25
179	Otis Thorpe	.25
180	Sam Cassell	.30
BT1	David Robinson	2.00
BT2	Juwan Howard	1.00
BT3	Mitch Richmond	1.00
BT4	Reggie Miller	1.50
BT5	Vin Baker	1.25
BT6	Shaquille O'Neal	5.00
BT7	Shawn Kemp	1.50
BT8	Karl Malone	2.00
BT9	Jamal Mashburn	1.25
BT10	Alonzo Mourning	1.50
DP2	Antonio McDyess	6.00
DP3	Jerry Stackhouse	3.00
DP4	Rasheed Wallace	2.50
DP5	Kevin Garnett	10.00
DP6	Bryant Reeves	2.00
DP8	Shawn Respert	.50
DP9	Ed O'Bannon	.50
DP11	Gary Trent	1.50
DP12	Cherokee Parks	.75
DP15	Brent Barry	1.50
DP16	Alan Henderson	.75
DP17	Bob Sura	.75
DP18	Theo Ratliff	1.00
DP19	Randolph Childress	.50
DP22	George Zidek	.50
IC1	Hakeem Olajuwon	5.00
IC2	Dikembe Mutombo	1.00
IC3	Bill Wennington	.30
IC4	Rick Fox	.30
IC5	Carl Herrera	.30
IC6	Rony Seikaly	.30
IC7	Rik Smits	1.00
IC8	Dino Radja	.50
IC9	Sarunas Marciulionis	.30
IC10	Luc Longley	.30
PZ1	Shaquille O'Neal	8.00
PZ2	Charles Barkley	3.00
PZ3	Patrick Ewing	1.00
PZ4	Karl Malone	3.00
PZ5	Larry Johnson	1.00
PZ6	Derrick Coleman	1.00
WS1	Michael Jordan	40.00
WS2	Kevin Johnson	1.00
WS3	Gary Payton	3.00
WS4	Anfernee Hardaway	10.00
WS5	Mookie Blaylock	.50
WS6	Tim Hardaway	3.00
WZ1	Nick Van Exel	2.50
WZ2	Tim Hardaway	3.00
WZ3	Mookie Blaylock	.50
WZ4	Gary Payton	3.00
WZ5	Jason Kidd	5.00
WZ6	Kenny Anderson	1.00
WZ7	John Stockton	2.00
WZ8	Kevin Johnson	1.00
WZ9	Muggsy Bogues	1.00
WZ10	Anfernee Hardaway	8.00

1995-96 Stadium Club Members Only II

This set contains 233 cards and parallels the cards offered from the Stadium Club second series product.

		MT
Complete Set (233):		300.00
Common Player:		.25
181	Sam Cassell	.40
182	Pooh Richardson	.25
183	Johnny Newman	.25
184	Dennis Scott	.40
185	Will Perdue	.25
186	Andrew Lang	.25
187	Karl Malone	3.00
188	Buck Williams	.40
189	P.J. Brown	.40
190	Khalid Reeves	.25
191	Kevin Willis	.25
192	Robert Pack	.25
193	Joe Dumars	1.00
194	Sam Perkins	.40
195	Dan Majerle	.40
196	John Williams	.25
197	Reggie Williams	.25
198	Greg Anthony	.25
199	Steve Kerr	.40
200	Richard Dumas	.25
201	Dee Brown	.25
202	Zan Tabak	.25
203	David Wood	.25
204	Duane Causwell	.25
205	Sedale Threatt	.25
206	Hubert Davis	.25
207	Donald Hodge	.25
208	Duane Ferrell	.25
209	Sam Mitchell	.25
210	Adam Keefe	.25
211	Clifford Robinson	.40
212	Rodney Rogers	.25
213	Jayson Williams	.40
214	Brian Shaw	.25
215	Luc Longley	.40
216	Don MacLean	.25
217	Rex Chapman	.25
218	Wayman Tisdale	.25
219	Shawn Kemp	2.50
220	Chris Webber	5.00
221	Antonio Harvey	.25
222	Sarunas Marciulionis	.25
223	Jeff Malone	.25
224	Chucky Brown	.25
225	Greg Minor	.25
226	Clifford Rozier	.25
227	Derrick McKey	.25
228	Tony Dumas	.25
229	Oliver Miller	.25
230	Charles Oakley	.40
231	Fred Roberts	.25
232	Glen Rice	2.00
233	Terry Porter	.25
234	Mark Macon	.25
235	Michael Cage	.25
236	Eric Murdock	.25
237	Vinny Del Negro	.25
238	Spud Webb	.40
239	Mario Elie	.25
240	Blue Edwards	.25
241	Dontonio Wingfield	.25
242	Brooks Thompson	.25
243	Alonzo Mourning	2.50
244	Dennis Rodman	5.00
245	Lorenzo Williams	.25
246	Haywoode Workman	.25
247	Loy Vaught	.40
248	Vernon Maxwell	.25
249	Lionel Simmons	.25
250	Chris Childs	.25
251	Mahmoud Abdul-Rauf	.25
252	Vincent Askew	.25
253	Chris Morris	.25
254	Elliot Perry	.25
255	Dell Curry	.25
256	Dana Barros	.25
257	Terrell Brandon	1.00
258	Monty Williams	.25
259	Corie Blount	.25
260	B.J. Armstrong	.25
261	Jim McIlvaine	.25
262	Otis Thorpe	.40
263	Sean Rooks	.25
264	Tony Massenburg	.25
265	Steve Smith	1.00
266	Ron Harper	.40
267	Dale Ellis	.25
268	Clyde Drexler	2.00
269	Jamie Watson	.25
270	Doc Rivers	.40
271	Derrick Alston	.25
272	Eric Mobley	.25
273	Ricky Pierce	.25
274	David Wesley	.25
275	John Starks	.40
276	Chris Mullin	1.00
277	Ervin Johnson	.25
278	Jamal Mashburn	.60
279	Joe Kleine	.25
280	Mitch Richmond	2.00
281	Chris Mills	.25
282	Bimbo Coles	.25
283	Larry Johnson	1.00
284	Stanley Roberts	.25
285	Rex Walters	.25

286	Donald Royal	.25
287	Benoit Benjamin	.25
288	Chris Dudley	.25
289	Elden Campbell	.40
290	Mookie Blaylock	.40
291	Hersey Hawkins	.40
292	Anthony Mason	.40
293	Latrell Sprewell	1.50
294	Harold Miner	.25
295	Scott Williams	.25
296	David Benoit	.25
297	Christian Laettner	1.00
298	LaPhonso Ellis	.40
299	Gheorghe Muresan	.40
300	Kendall Gill	.40
301	Eddie Johnson	.25
302	Terry Cummings	.25
303	Chuck Person	.25
304	Michael Smith	.25
305	Mark West	.25
306	Willie Anderson	.25
307	Pervis Ellison	.25
308	Brian Williams	.25
309	Danny Manning	.40
310	Hakeem Olajuwon	3.00
311	Scottie Pippen	5.00
312	Jon Koncak	.25
313	Sasha Danilovic	.40
314	Lucious Harris	.25
315	Yinka Dare	.25
316	Eric Williams	1.00
317	Gary Trent	1.00
318	Theo Ratliff	1.00
319	Lawrence Moten	.25
320	Jerome Allen	.25
321	Tyus Edney	.40
322	Loren Meyer	.25
323	Michael Finley	5.00
324	Alan Henderson	1.00
325	Bob Sura	.50
326	Joe Smith	6.00
327	Damon Stoudamire	6.00
328	Sherell Ford	.25
329	Jerry Stackhouse	5.00
330	George Zidek	.25
331	Brent Barry	1.00
332	Shawn Respert	.25
333	Rasheed Wallace	4.00
334	Antonio McDyess	10.00
335	David Vaughn	.25
336	Cory Alexander	.25
337	Jason Caffey	.40
338	Frankie King	.25
339	Travis Best	.40
340	Greg Ostertag	.25
341	Ed O'Bannon	.40
342	Kurt Thomas	.40
343	Kevin Garnett	30.00
344	Bryant Reeves	2.00
345	Corliss Williamson	1.00
346	Cherokee Parks	.25
347	Junior Burrough	.25
348	Randolph Childress	.25
349	Lou Roe	.25
350	Mario Bennett	.25
351	Dikembe Mutombo	.50
352	Larry Johnson	1.00
353	Vlade Divac	.40
354	Karl Malone	3.00
355	John Stockton	1.00
356	Alonzo Mourning	2.00
357	Glen Rice	1.00
358	Dan Majerle	.40
359	John Williams	.25
360	Mark Price	.25
361	Magic Johnson	10.00
B11	Charles Barkley	5.00
B12	Hakeem Olajuwon	5.00
B13	Kenny Anderson	1.00
B14	Michael Jordan	50.00
B15	Dikembe Mutombo	1.00
B16	Rod Strickland	1.00
B17	Patrick Ewing	2.00
B18	Latrell Sprewell	2.00
B19	Grant Hill	20.00
B20	Cedric Ceballos	1.00
X1	Hakeem Olajuwon	4.00
X2	Shaquille O'Neal	8.00
X3	David Robinson	4.00
X4	Patrick Ewing	2.00
X5	Charles Barkley	4.00
X6	Karl Malone	4.00
X7	Derrick Coleman	1.00
X8	Shawn Kemp	3.00
X9	Vin Baker	2.00
X10	Vlade Divac	1.00
PZ7	Hakeem Olajuwon	5.00
PZ8	David Robinson	5.00
PZ9	Shawn Kemp	4.00
PZ10	Dennis Rodman	8.00
PZ11	Alonzo Mourning	2.50
PZ12	Vin Baker	2.50
RM1	Shawn Kemp	5.00
RM2	Michael Jordan	50.00
RM3	Larry Johnson	2.00
RM4	Grant Hill	20.00
RM5	Isaiah Rider	1.00
RM6	Sean Elliott	1.00
RM7	Scottie Pippen	10.00
RM8	Robert Horry	1.00
RM9	Kendall Gill	1.00
RM10	Jerry Stackhouse	5.00
SS1	Michael Jordan	15.00
SS2	Alonzo Mourning	.75
SS3	Reggie Miller	.75
SS4	Patrick Ewing	.75
SS5	Charles Barkley	2.00
SS6	Kenny Anderson	.50
SS7	Scottie Pippen	4.00
SS8	Jerry Stackhouse	2.00
SS9	Shaquille O'Neal	5.00
SS10	John Starks	.50
WS7	Scottie Pippen	8.00
WS8	Jason Kidd	8.00
WS9	Grant Hill	20.00
WS10	Nick Van Exel	2.00
WS11	Kenny Anderson	2.00
WS12	Latrell Sprewell	2.00

1995-96 Stadium Club Members Only 50

		MT
Complete Set (50):		40.00
Common Player:		.50
1	Magic Johnson	2.00
2	Steve Smith	.50
3	Scottie Pippen	2.00
4	David Robinson	1.00
5	Jason Kidd	2.00
6	Dikembe Mutombo	.25
7	Sean Elliott	.25
8	Rik Smits	.50
9	Brian Grant	.50
10	Hakeem Olajuwon	1.00
11	Greg Anthony	.50
12	Mitch Richmond	.50
13	Clyde Drexler	.50
14	Mahmoud Abdul-Rauf	.50
15	Larry Johnson	.50
16	Mookie Blaylock	.50
17	Clarence Weatherspoon	.50
18	Grant Hill	3.00
19	Vin Baker	.50
20	Patrick Ewing	.50
21	Charles Barkley	1.00
22	Glenn Robinson	.50
23	Dino Radja	.50
24	Charles Oakley	.50
25	Anfernee Hardaway	2.00
26	Jamal Mashburn	.50
27	John Stockton	1.00
28	Isaiah Rider	.50
29	Cedric Ceballos	.50
30	Shaquille O'Neal	4.00
31	Shawn Kemp	.50
32	Juwan Howard	.50
33	Alonzo Mourning	.50
34	Tom Gugliotta	.50
35	Karl Malone	1.00
36	Clifford Robinson	.50
37	Chris Webber	2.00
38	Latrell Sprewell	1.50
39	Loy Vaught	.50
40	Michael Jordan	10.00
41	Reggie Miller	1.00
42	Terrell Brandon	.50
43	Armon Gilliam	.50
44	Gary Payton	1.00
45	Glen Rice	.50
46	Jerry Stackhouse Finest	12.00
47	Michael Finley Finest	10.00
48	Joe Smith Finest	3.00
49	Damon Stoudamire Finest	5.00
50	Brent Barry Finest	2.00

1995-96 Stadium Club Nemeses

Ten Nemeses dual-etched foil cards are included in 1995-96 Topps Stadium Club Series I packs, seeded one per every 18 packs. Each card portrays a pair of arch rivals on both sides, using a metallic background and red foil. Each side has a larger picture of one player, and a smaller one of his opponent. A recap of a game where the key player bested his rival is given. Only one side has a card number, which uses an "N" prefix, and head-to-head stats from 1994-95.

		MT
Complete Set (10):		80.00
Common Player:		2.00
1	Hakeem Olajuwon, David Robinson	12.00
2	Patrick Ewing, Rik Smits	4.00
3	John Stockton, Kevin Johnson	4.00
4	Shaquille O'Neal, Alonzo Mourning	16.00
5	Charles Barkley, Karl Malone	8.00
6	Scottie Pippen, Grant Hill	18.00
7	Anfernee Hardaway, Kenny Anderson	12.00
8	Reggie Miller, John Starks	4.00
9	Toni Kukoc, Dino Radja	2.00
10	Michael Jordan, Joe Dumars	25.00

1995-96 Stadium Club Power Zone

These cards feature Topps' Power Matrix technology. Cards 1-6 were random inserts in 1995-96 Stadium Club packs, one per every 36 packs. Cards 7-12 were in every 48th Series II pack. The card front has the player's name along the left side of the card, with the brand logo underneath. "Power Zone" is written to the right of this information, below a hoop which the player is shooting at. The card back, numbered using a "PZ" prefix, has biographical information in the upper left corner, plus a "Beware" warning which summarizes the player's talents. A small player photo is given, as are a series of mathematical problems which determine the player's percentage contribution to his team in two statistical categories. This is his "Power Zone."

		MT
Complete Set (12):		80.00
Complete Series 1 (6):		35.00
Complete Series 2 (6):		45.00
Common Player:		2.00
1	Shaquille O'Neal	18.00
2	Charles Barkley	7.00
3	Patrick Ewing	5.00
4	Karl Malone	5.00
5	Larry Johnson	5.00
6	Derrick Coleman	2.00
7	Hakeem Olajuwon	12.00
8	David Robinson	10.00
9	Shawn Kemp	6.00
10	Dennis Rodman	15.00
11	Alonzo Mourning	4.00
12	Vin Baker	2.00

1995-96 Stadium Club Reign Men

These cards were random inserts in 1995-96 Topps Stadium Club Series II packs, one per every 24 retail packs or one per every 48 hobby packs. The cards, numbered using an "RM" prefix, have a color action photo on the front, with "Reign Men" written vertically along the right side of the card.

		MT
Complete Set (10):		100.00
Common Player:		3.00
1	Shawn Kemp	6.00
2	Michael Jordan	65.00
3	Larry Johnson	5.00
4	Grant Hill	20.00
5	Isaiah Rider	3.00
6	Sean Elliott	3.00
7	Scottie Pippen	12.00
8	Robert Horry	3.00
9	Kendall Gill	3.00
10	Jerry Stackhouse	12.00

1995-96 Stadium Club Spike Says

These 1995-96 Topps Stadium Club Series II inserts are chosen by movie actor/director/front row seat attendee Spike Lee, who has selected his favorite NBA players. Each card front has a color photo of the player, along with a small circle in the lower right corner with Lee's picture inside. "Spike Says" is written around the circle in foil, which is also used for the player's name, which is in the lower left corner. The brand logo is in foil in the upper right corner. The card back, numbered using an "SS" prefix, provides Lee's commentary about the player.

		MT
Complete Set (10):		30.00
Common Player:		1.00
1	Michael Jordan	25.00
2	Alonzo Mourning	3.00
3	Reggie Miller	3.00
4	Patrick Ewing	3.00
5	Charles Barkley	4.00
6	Kenny Anderson	1.00
7	Scottie Pippen	5.00
8	Jerry Stackhouse	3.00
9	Shaquille O'Neal	10.00
10	John Starks	1.00

1995-96 Stadium Club Warp Speed

Warp Speed inserts could be found in both series of Topps' 1995-96 Stadium Club basketball. Series I has cards 1-6, seeded one per every 36 packs; Series II has cards 7-12, seeded one per every 48 packs. The cards use Topps' Power Matrix technology and feature players who have the quickest first steps in the NBA. The card front has a color photo on it, with a silver metallic background that has "Warp Speed" written along the left side of the card. The player's name is in red in the lower right corner; the brand logo is in the upper left corner. The card back has "Warp Speed" written along the top; a card number, using a "WS" prefix, is below, along the left side. A jigsaw puzzle-like photo is on the left, flanked on the right by the player's name, team name, position and a description of why the player is a "Warp Speed" type of player.

		MT
Complete Set (12):		130.00
Complete Series 1 (6):		80.00
Complete Series 2 (6):		50.00
Common Player:		3.00
1	Michael Jordan	50.00
2	Kevin Johnson	3.00
3	Gary Payton	5.00
4	Anfernee Hardaway	25.00
5	Mookie Blaylock	3.00
6	Tim Hardaway	3.00
7	Scottie Pippen	14.00
8	Jason Kidd	12.00
9	Grant Hill	20.00
10	Nick Van Exel	6.00
11	Kenny Anderson	3.00
12	Latrell Sprewell	3.00

1995-96 Stadium Club Wizards

These cards were exclusive to 1995-96 Topps Stadium Club Series I hobby packs only, seeded one per every 24 packs. The cards feature 10 magicians with the ball, portrayed on shimmering etched foil. "Wizard" is written in foil along the top of the card; the player's name is stamped in gold foil along the bottom. A brand logo is stamped in gold foil in the lower left corner. A color action photo is in the center. The card back has a card number in the upper right corner, using a "W" prefix. Underneath are the player's name, team, position and a "Warning," which describes how or why the player is a "Wizard." On the left half of the card at the top is the word "Wizard," with a mug shot below. The stats which indicate the player is a magician - steals and assists divided by turnovers. His numbers are compared to the NBA average.

		MT
Complete Set (10):		40.00
Common Player:		2.00
1	Nick Van Exel	5.00
2	Tim Hardaway	2.00
3	Mookie Blaylock	2.00
4	Gary Payton	4.00
5	Jason Kidd	12.00
6	Kenny Anderson	2.00
7	John Stockton	4.00
8	Kevin Johnson	2.00
9	Muggsy Bogues	2.00
10	Anfernee Hardaway	24.00

1995-96 Stadium Club X-2

Ten NBA big men are featured on these 1995-96 Topps Stadium Club Series II inserts. The cards are seeded one per every 48 retail packs or one per every 24 hobby packs.

		MT
Complete Set (10):		40.00
Common Player:		2.00
1	Hakeem Olajuwon	10.00
2	Shaquille O'Neal	18.00
3	David Robinson	8.00
4	Patrick Ewing	4.00
5	Charles Barkley	7.00
6	Karl Malone	4.00
7	Derrick Coleman	2.00
8	Shawn Kemp	5.00
9	Vin Baker	3.00
10	Vlade Divac	2.00

1996-97 Stadium Club

Stadium Club's 1996-97 product consisted of 180 cards, which were issued in two 90-card series. The cards featured a full bleed color shot, with a silver holographic embossed strip down the right side that had the player's name. Backs included another shot of the player, stats and the card number in the bottom left corner in a red box. Inserts in Series I included: Fusion, Special Forces, Top Crop, NBA Topps Stars Finest Rookie Reprints, TSC Matrix parallels, Rookies, Shining Moments, Golden Moments and the parallel TSC Matrix. Inserts in Series II included: Mega Heroes, Fusion, Class Acts, High Risers, Rookie Showcase, Rookies, Welcome Additions and Player's Private Issue cards that weren't in Gallery.

		MT
Complete Set (180):		26.00
Complete Series 1 (90):		14.00
Complete Series 2 (90):		12.00
Common Player:		.10
Minor Stars:		.20
Dot Matrix Cards (1-90):		10x
Series 1 or 2 Pack (8):		1.50
Series 1 or 2 Wax Box (24):		35.00
1	Scottie Pippen	1.00
2	Dale Davis	.10
3	Horace Grant	.10
4	Gheorghe Muresan	.10
5	Elliot Perry	.10
6	Carlos Rogers	.10
7	Glenn Robinson	.40
8	Avery Johnson	.10
9	Dee Brown	.10
10	Grant Hill	2.50
11	Tyus Edney	.20
12	Patrick Ewing	.40
13	Jason Kidd	1.00
14	Clifford Robinson	.10
15	Robert Horry	.10
16	Dell Curry	.10
17	Terry Porter	.10
18	Shaquille O'Neal	2.00
19	Bryant Stith	.10
20	Shawn Kemp	.60
21	Kurt Thomas	.10
22	Pooh Richardson	.10
23	Bob Sura	.10
24	Olden Polynice	.10
25	Lawrence Moten	.10
26	Kendall Gill	.10
27	Cedric Ceballos	.20
28	Latrell Sprewell	.20
29	Christian Laettner	.10
30	Jamal Mashburn	.20
31	Jerry Stackhouse	.75
32	John Stockton	.40
33	Arvydas Sabonis	.30
34	Detlef Schrempf	.10
35	Toni Kukoc	.20
36	Sasha Danilovic	.10
37	Dana Barros	.10
38	Loy Vaught	.10
39	John Starks	.10
40	Marty Conlon	.10
41	Antonio McDyess	.50
42	Michael Finley	.60
43	Tom Gugliotta	.10
44	Terrell Brandon	.10
45	Derrick McKey	.10
46	Damon Stoudamire	1.25
47	Elden Campbell	.10
48	Luc Longley	.10
49	B.J. Armstrong	.10
50	Lindsey Hunter	.10
51	Glen Rice	.10
52	Shawn Respert	.10
53	Cory Alexander	.10
54	Tim Legler	.10
55	Bryant Reeves	.30
56	Anfernee Hardaway	2.50
57	Charles Barkley	.50
58	Mookie Blaylock	.10
59	Kevin Garnett	2.50
60	Hersey Hawkins	.10
61	Ed O'Bannon	.10
62	George Zidek	.10
63	Mitch Richmond	.20
64	Derrick Coleman	.10
65	Chris Webber	.75
66	Bobby Phills	.10
67	Rik Smits	.10
68	Jeff Hornacek	.10
69	Sam Cassell	.10
70	Gary Trent	.10
71	LaPhonso Ellis	.10
72	Oliver Miller	.10
73	Rex Chapman	.10
74	Jim Jackson	.20
75	Eric Williams	.10
76	Brent Barry	.20
77	Nick Anderson	.10
78	David Robinson	.75
79	Calbert Cheaney	.10
80	Joe Smith	.60
81	Steve Kerr	.10
82	Wayman Tisdale	.10
83	Steve Smith	.10
84	Clyde Drexler	.50
85	Theo Ratliff	.10
86	Charlie Ward	.10
87	Karl Malone	.40
88	Clarence Weatherspoon	.10
89	Greg Anthony	.10
90	Shawn Bradley	.10
91	Otis Thorpe	.10
92	Larry Johnson	.20
93	Sharone Wright	.10
94	Charles Barkley	.50
95	Wesley Person	.10
96	Dikembe Mutombo	.10
97	Eddie Jones	.20
98	Juwan Howard	.30
99	Grant Hill	2.50
100	Chris Carr	.10
101	Michael Jordan	4.00
102	Vincent Askew	.10
103	Gary Payton	.30
104	Chris Mills	.10
105	Reggie Miller	.30
106	Don MacLean	.10
107	John Stockton	.30
108	Mahmoud Abdul-Rauf	.10
109	P.J. Brown	.10
110	Kenny Anderson	.10
111	Mark Price	.10
112	Derek Harper	.10
113	Dino Radja	.10
114	Terry Dehere	.10
115	Mark Jackson	.10
116	Vin Baker	.25
117	Dennis Scott	.10
118	Sean Elliott	.10
119	Lee Mayberry	.10
120	Vlade Divac	.10
121	Joe Dumars	.10
122	Isaiah Rider	.10
123	Hakeem Olajuwon	.75
124	Robert Pack	.10
125	Jalen Rose	.10
126	Allan Houston	.10
127	Nate McMillan	.10
128	Rod Strickland	.10
129	Sean Rooks	.10
130	Dennis Rodman	2.00
131	Alonzo Mourning	.25
132	Danny Ferry	.10
133	Sam Cassell	.10
134	Brian Grant	.10
135	Karl Malone	.30
136	Chris Gatling	.10
137	Tom Gugliotta	.10
138	Hubert Davis	.10
139	Lucious Harris	.10
140	Rony Seikaly	.10
141	Alan Henderson	.10
142	Mario Elie	.10
143	Vinny Del Negro	.10
144	Harvey Grant	.10
145	Muggsy Bogues	.10
146	Rodney Rogers	.10
147	Kevin Johnson	.10
148	Anthony Peeler	.10
149	Jon Koncak	.10
150	Ricky Pierce	.10
151	Todd Day	.10
152	Tyrone Hill	.10
153	Nick Van Exel	.20
154	Rasheed Wallace	.10
155	Jayson Williams	.10
156	Sherman Douglas	.10
157	Bryon Russell	.10
158	Ron Harper	.10
159	Stacey Augmon	.10
160	Antonio Davis	.10
161	Tim Hardaway	.10
162	Charles Oakley	.10
163	Billy Owens	.10
164	Sam Perkins	.10
165	Chris Whitney	.10
166	Matt Geiger	.10
167	Andrew Lang	.10
168	Danny Manning	.10
169	Doug Christie	.10
170	George Lynch	.10

171	Malik Sealy	.10
172	Eric Montross	.10
173	Rick Fox	.10
174	Chris Mullin	.10
175	Ken Norman	.10
176	Sarunas Marciulionis	.10
177	Kevin Garnett	2.50
178	Brian Shaw	.10
179	Will Perdue	.10
180	Scott Williams	.10

1996-97 Stadium Club Class Acts

Class Acts was a 10-card insert that featured two stars from the same college on a double-sided Finest card. These cards were inserted every 24 packs of Series II. Refractor and Atomic Refractor versions are also available, with all three versions difficult to find on a perfectly centered card. Class Acts inserts carry a "CA" prefix.

		MT
Complete Set (10):		60.00
Common Player:		3.00
Refractors:		2x-3x
Atomic Refractors:		3x-6x
1	Michael Jordan, Jerry Stackhouse	20.00
2	Alonzo Mourning, Patrick Ewing	3.00
3	Brent Barry, Gary Payton	3.00
4	Juwan Howard, Chris Webber	6.00
5	Grant Hill, Christian Laettner	10.00
6	Jason Kidd, Shareef Abdur-Rahim	10.00
7	Clyde Drexler, Hakeem Olajuwon	6.00
8	Stephon Marbury, Kenny Anderson	10.00
9	Lorenzen Wright, Anfernee Hardaway	8.00
10	Dikembe Mutombo, Allen Iverson	10.00

1996-97 Stadium Club Class Acts Atomic Refractors

This 10-card set was inserted every 192 Series II hobby and retail packs. It paralleled the regular Class Acts insert, but featured a prismatic, streaked Refractor finish.

	MT
Atomic Refractors:	3x-6x

1996-97 Stadium Club Class Acts Refractors

Class Acts Refractors parallel the regular Class Acts insert, but featured Topps' familiar Refractor finish. These cards were found in Series II packs at a rate of one per 96 packs.

	MT
Refractors:	2x-3x

1996-97 Stadium Club Finest Reprints

This 25-card set included Finest Rookie Reprints from the NBA Topps Stars product. The set has a total of 50 cards, with 25 found in Stadium Club Series I (one per 24 hobby; one per 80 retail) and the other 25 in Topps Series II.

		MT
Complete Set (25):		125.00
Common Player:		3.00
Comp. Refractor Set (25):		500.00
Refractors:		2x-4x
2	Nate Archibald	3.00
4	Charles Barkley	10.00
5	Rick Barry	5.00
6	Elgin Baylor	5.00
7	Dave Bing	3.00
8	Larry Bird	20.00
10	Bob Cousy	8.00
12	Billy Cunningham	3.00
13	Dave DeBusschere	3.00
15	Julius Erving	8.00
17	Walt Frazier	5.00
18	George Gervin	3.00
19	Hal Greer	3.00
24	Michael Jordan	45.00
26	Karl Malone	5.00
28	Pete Maravich	5.00
29	Kevin McHale	5.00
34	Robert Parish	5.00
35	Bob Pettit	5.00
36	Scottie Pippen	10.00
41	Dolph Schayes	3.00
44	Isiah Thomas	5.00
48	Jerry West	8.00
49	Len Wilkens	5.00
50	James Worthy	3.00

1996-97 Stadium Club Finest Reprints Refractors

This insert paralleled the Finest Rookie Reprints from Stadium Club Series I, but featured Refractor technology. There were 25 cards in the set, and they were seeded every 96 hobby packs and 80 retail packs. The other 25 cards are found in Topps Series II.

	MT
Complete Set (25):	500.00
Refractors:	2x-4x

1996-97 Stadium Club Fusion

This 32-card set consisted of 16 cards from Series I and 16 cards from Series II, with both inserted one per 24 hobby packs. The card numbers carry an "F" prefix and feature two players from the same team on die-cut cards that fit together. Sixteen total matchups are captured between the two series, with eight in each. The first eight cards in each are the right side of the die-cut, while the next eight are the left side; for example, F1 and F9 match-up to form one card.

		MT
Complete Set (32):		200.00
Complete Series 1 (16):		120.00
Complete Series 2 (16):		80.00
Common Player:		1.50
1	Michael Jordan	60.00
2	Chris Webber	7.00
3	Glenn Robinson	5.00
4	Glen Rice	1.50
5	Gary Payton	5.00
6	Rik Smits	1.50
7	Grant Hill	20.00
8	Horace Grant	1.50
9	Scottie Pippen	15.00
10	Gheorghe Muresan	1.50
11	Vin Baker	1.50
12	Dell Curry	1.50
13	Shawn Kemp	8.00
14	Reggie Miller	5.00
15	Joe Dumars	1.50
16	Anfernee Hardaway	30.00
17	Charles Barkley	8.00
18	Juwan Howard	8.00
19	Patrick Ewing	6.00
20	John Stockton	6.00
21	David Robinson	8.00
22	Cedric Ceballos	1.50
23	Alonzo Mourning	6.00
24	Mookie Blaylock	1.50
25	Clyde Drexler	6.00
26	Rod Strickland	1.50
27	Larry Johnson	1.50
28	Karl Malone	6.00
29	Sean Elliott	1.50
30	Shaquille O'Neal	20.00
31	Tim Hardaway	1.50
32	Dikembe Mutombo	1.50

1996-97 Stadium Club Gallery Player's Private Issue

This 18-card insert included the first 18 Player's Private Issue cards that were accidentally never printed in 1995-96 Topps Gallery. They were found in one per 96 hobby packs of Series II Stadium Club.

		MT
Complete Set (18):		700.00
Common Player:		10.00
1	Shaquille O'Neal	70.00
2	Shawn Kemp	25.00
3	Reggie Miller	25.00
4	Mitch Richmond	20.00
5	Grant Hill	110.00
6	Magic Johnson	50.00
7	Vin Baker	20.00
8	Charles Barkley	30.00
9	Hakeem Olajuwon	50.00
10	Michael Jordan	300.00
11	Patrick Ewing	20.00
12	David Robinson	30.00
13	Alonzo Mourning	20.00
14	Karl Malone	20.00
15	Chris Webber	40.00
16	Dikembe Mutombo	10.00
17	Larry Johnson	10.00
18	Jamal Mashburn	10.00

1996-97 Stadium Club Golden/Shining Moments

This five-card set carried a "GM" prefix in the card number and was inserted into packs of Series I. The cards were considered part of the regular-issue set but were numbered as an insert. They are known in the hobby as an insert set. Fronts carry a black border on the right side with gold lettering and the date of the "golden moment" in the lower right corner.

		MT
Complete Set (20):		14.00
Common Player:		.20
Minor Stars:		.40
GM1	Robert Parish	.20
GM2	John Stockton	.40
GM3	Michael Jordan, Dennis Rodman	3.50
GM4	Dennis Scott	.20
GM5	Hakeem Olajuwon	.75
SM1	Charles Barkley	.50
SM2	Michael Jordan	4.00
SM3	Karl Malone	.40
SM4	Hakeem Olajuwon	.75
SM5	John Stockton	.40
SM6	Patrick Ewing	.40
SM7	Reggie Miller	.40
SM8	David Robinson	.75
SM9	Dennis Rodman	2.00
SM10	Damon Stoudamire	1.00
SM11	Brent Barry	.20
SM12	Tim Legler	.20
SM13	Jason Kidd	.75
SM14	Terrell Brandon	.20
SM15	Allen Iverson	4.00

1996-97 Stadium Club High Risers

High Risers captured 15 players on a bright silver background that pictures skyscrapers and the insert name in the background. Inserted one per 36 Series II retail and hobby packs, this insert is numbered with an "HR" prefix.

		MT
Complete Set (15):		175.00
Common Player:		3.00
1	Scottie Pippen	15.00
2	Anfernee Hardaway	25.00
3	Vin Baker	3.00
4	Brent Barry	3.00
5	Clyde Drexler	8.00
6	Kevin Garnett	30.00
7	Grant Hill	30.00
8	Michael Finley	3.00
9	Jerry Stackhouse	10.00
10	Isaiah Rider	3.00
11	Shaquille O'Neal	25.00
12	Antonio McDyess	3.00
13	Shawn Kemp	8.00
14	Michael Jordan	60.00
15	Juwan Howard	7.00

1996-97 Stadium Club Matrix

Matrix parallel cards were produced for each card in Stadium Club Series I and inserted one per 12 hobby and one per 10 retail packs. The cards featured Topps' Matrix technology which consisted of a flashy, foil-etched background with highlights.

	MT
Complete Set (90):	250.00
Matrix Cards:	10x-15x

1996-97 Stadium Club Mega Heroes

This nine-card insert set was found in one per 20 retail packs of Series II Stadium Club. The cards featured an NBA star on a colorful, foil-etched background with the player's nickname printed across the bottom. The cards were numbered with an "MH" prefix.

		MT
Complete Set (9):		30.00
Common Player:		1.00
1	Dennis Rodman	10.00
2	David Robinson	4.00
3	Karl Malone	2.00
4	Clyde Drexler	2.50
5	Anfernee Hardaway	15.00
6	Hakeem Olajuwon	6.00
7	Charles Oakley	1.00
8	Joe Smith	4.00
9	Glenn Robinson	2.00

1996 Stadium Club Members Only I

This set parallels the 1996-97 Stadium Club first series product and contain 173 cards.

		MT
Complete Set (173):		225.00
Common Player:		.25
1	Scottie Pippen	5.00
2	Dale Davis	.25
3	Horace Grant	.25
4	Gheorghe Muresan	.25
5	Elliott Perry	.25
6	Carlos Rogers	.25
7	Glenn Robinson	1.50
8	Avery Johnson	.25
9	Dee Brown	.25
10	Grant Hill	10.00
11	Tyus Edney	.25
12	Patrick Ewing	1.50
13	Jason Kidd	4.00
14	Clifford Robinson	.25
15	Robert Horry	.25
16	Dell Curry	.25
17	Terry Porter	.25
18	Shaquille O'Neal	6.00
19	Bryant Stith	.25
20	Shawn Kemp	2.00
21	Kurt Thomas	.25
22	Pooh Richardson	.25
23	Bob Sura	.25
24	Olden Polynice	.25
25	Lawrence Moten	.25
26	Kendall Gill	.25
27	Cedric Ceballos	.25
28	Latrell Sprewell	1.00
29	Christian Laettner	.40
30	Jamal Mashburn	.40
31	Jerry Stackhouse	1.00
32	John Stockton	1.00
33	Arvydas Sabonis	.25
34	Detlef Schrempf	.25
35	Toni Kukoc	.40
36	Sasha Danilovic	.25
37	Dana Barros	.25
38	Loy Vaught	.25
39	John Starks	.25
40	Marty Conlon	.25
41	Antonio McDyess	2.50
42	Michael Finley	1.00
43	Tom Gugliotta	.40
44	Terrell Brandon	.40
45	Derrick McKey	.25
46	Damon Stoudamire	2.00
47	Elden Campbell	.25
48	Luc Longley	.25
49	B.J. Armstrong	.25
50	Lindsey Hunter	.25
51	Glen Rice	1.00
52	Shawn Respert	.25
53	Cory Alexander	.25
54	Tim Legler	.25
55	Bryant Reeves	.25
56	Anfernee Hardaway	8.00
57	Charles Barkley	2.50
58	Mookie Blaylock	.25
59	Kevin Garnett	10.00
60	Hersey Hawkins	.25
61	Ed O'Bannon	.25
62	George Zidek	.25
63	Mitch Richmond	1.50
64	Derrick Coleman	.25
65	Chris Webber	4.00
66	Bobby Phills	.25
67	Rik Smits	.25
68	Jeff Hornacek	.25
69	Sam Cassell	.25
70	Gary Trent	.25
71	LaPhonso Ellis	.25
72	Oliver Miller	.25
73	Rex Chapman	.25
74	Jim Jackson	.25
75	Eric Williams	.25
76	Brent Barry	.25
77	Nick Anderson	.25
78	David Robinson	2.50
79	Calbert Cheaney	.25
80	Joe Smith	2.50
81	Steve Kerr	.25
82	Wayman Tisdale	.25
83	Steve Smith	.40
84	Clyde Drexler	2.00
85	Theo Ratliff	.25
86	Charlie Ward	.25
87	Karl Malone	2.50
88	Clarence Weatherspoon	.25
89	Greg Anthony	.25
90	Shawn Bradley	.25
F1	Michael Jordan	25.00
F2	Chris Webber	4.00
F3	Glenn Robinson	1.50
F4	Glen Rice	1.50
F5	Gary Payton	2.50
F6	Rik Smits	.60
F7	Grant Hill	10.00
F8	Horace Grant	.60
F9	Scottie Pippen	5.00
F10	Gheorghe Muresan	.60
F11	Vin Baker	1.50
F12	Dell Curry	.50
F13	Shawn Kemp	2.50
F14	Reggie Miller	1.50
F15	Joe Dumars	.60
F16	Anfernee Hardaway	10.00
R1	Allen Iverson	5.00
R2	Marcus Camby	1.25
R3	Shareef Abdur-Rahim	3.00
R4	Stephon Marbury	4.00
R5	Ray Allen	2.00
R6	Antoine Walker	3.00
R7	Lorenzen Wright	.30
R8	Kerry Kittles	1.00
R9	Samaki Walker	.25
R10	Erick Dampier	.30
R11	Todd Fuller	.25
R12	Kobe Bryant	10.00
R13	Steve Nash	.25
R14	Tony Delk	.30
R15	Jermaine O'Neal	1.00
R16	John Wallace	.30
R17	Walter McCarty	.25
R18	Dontae' Jones	.25
R19	Roy Rogers	.25
R20	Derek Fisher	.75
R21	Martin Muursepp	.25
R22	Jerome Williams	.25
R23	Brian Evans	.25
R24	Priest Lauderdale	.25
R25	Travis Knight	.30
GM1	Robert Parish	.25
GM2	John Stockton	.20
GM3	Chicago Bulls (Michael Jordan, Toni Kukoc, Dennis Rodman)	2.00
GM4	Dennis Scott	.25
GM5	Hakeem Olajuwon	.50
SF1	Anfernee Hardaway	5.00
SF2	Grant Hill	6.00
SF3	Shawn Kemp	1.50
SF4	Michael Jordan	15.00
SF5	Shaquille O'Neal	4.00
SF6	Scottie Pippen	3.00
SF7	Damon Stoudamire	2.00
SF8	Jerry Stackhouse	1.50
SF9	Gary Payton	1.50
SF10	Dennis Rodman	3.00
SM1	Charles Barkley	.30
SM2	Michael Jordan	5.00
SM3	Karl Malone	.25
SM4	Hakeem Olajuwon	.50
SM5	John Stockton	.20
SM6	Patrick Ewing	.20
SM7	Reggie Miller	.20
SM8	David Robinson	.30
SM9	Dennis Rodman	.75
SM10	Damon Stoudamire	.50
SM11	Brent Barry	.25
SM12	Tim Legler	.25
SM13	Jason Kidd	.25
SM14	Terrell Brandon	.25
SM15	Allen Iverson	2.50
TC1	Hakeem Olajuwon, Shaquille O'Neal	5.00
TC2	Dikembe Mutombo, Alonzo Mourning	1.25
TC3	David Robinson, Patrick Ewing	2.00
TC4	Sean Elliott, Grant Hill	5.00
TC5	Shawn Kemp, Scottie Pippen	2.50
TC6	Karl Malone, Vin Baker	2.00
TC7	Charles Barkley, Juwan Howard	2.50
TC8	Clyde Drexler, Glen Rice	2.00
TC9	Gary Payton, Michael Jordan	15.00
TC10	John Stockton, Terrell Brandon	1.25
TC11	Mitch Richmond, Reggie Miller	1.50
TC12	Jason Kidd, Anfernee Hardaway	8.00

1996-97 Stadium Club Members Only II

This set contains 210 cards and parallels the 1996-97 Stadium club second series product.

		MT
Complete Set (210):		250.00
Common Player:		.25
91	Otis Thorpe	.25
92	Larry Johnson	.40
93	Sharone Wright	.15
94	Charles Barkley	3.00
95	Wesley Person	.15
96	Dikembe Mutombo	.40
97	Eddie Jones	3.00
98	Juwan Howard	2.50
99	Grant Hill	10.00
100	Chris Carr	.25
101	Michael Jordan	25.00
102	Vincent Askew	.15
103	Gary Payton	3.00
104	Chris Mills	.15
105	Reggie Miller	1.50
106	Don MacLean	.15
107	John Stockton	1.50
108	Mahmoud Abdul-Rauf	.15
109	P.J. Brown	.25
110	Kenny Anderson	.40
111	Mark Price	.15
112	Derek Harper	.25
113	Dino Radja	.15
114	Terry Dehere	.15
115	Mark Jackson	.15
116	Vin Baker	1.50
117	Dennis Scott	.25
118	Sean Elliott	.15
119	Lee Mayberry	.15
120	Vlade Divac	.25
121	Joe Dumars	1.00
122	Isaiah Rider	.25
123	Hakeem Olajuwon	3.00
124	Robert Pack	.15
125	Jalen Rose	.15
126	Allan Houston	.25
127	Nate McMillan	.15
128	Rod Strickland	.40
129	Sean Rooks	.15
130	Dennis Rodman	5.00
131	Alonzo Mourning	1.50
132	Danny Ferry	.15
133	Sam Cassell	.25
134	Brian Grant	.50
135	Karl Malone	3.00
136	Chris Gatling	.15
137	Tom Gugliotta	1.00
138	Hubert Davis	.15
139	Lucious Harris	.15
140	Rony Seikaly	.15
141	Alan Henderson	.15
142	Mario Elie	.15
143	Vinny Del Negro	.15
144	Harvey Grant	.15
145	Muggsy Bogues	.25
146	Rodney Rogers	.15
147	Kevin Johnson	.40
148	Anthony Peeler	.15
149	Jon Koncak	.15
150	Ricky Pierce	.15
151	Todd Day	.15
152	Tyrone Hill	.15
153	Nick Van Exel	.75
154	Rasheed Wallace	.25
155	Jayson Williams	.25
156	Sherman Douglas	.15
157	Bryon Russell	.15
158	Ron Harper	.25
159	Stacey Augmon	.15
160	Antonio Davis	.15
161	Tim Hardaway	2.00
162	Charles Oakley	.25
163	Billy Owens	.15
164	Sam Perkins	.25
165	Chris Whitney	.15
166	Matt Geiger	.15
167	Andrew Lang	.15
168	Danny Manning	.25
169	Doug Christie	.15
170	George Lynch	.15
171	Malik Sealy	.15
172	Eric Montross	.15
173	Rick Fox	.15
174	Chris Mullin	1.00
175	Ken Norman	.15
176	Sarunas Marciulionis	.15
177	Kevin Garnett	12.00
178	Brian Shaw	.15
179	Will Perdue	.15
180	Scott Williams	.15
F17	Charles Barkley	2.50
F18	Juwan Howard	2.50
F19	Patrick Ewing	1.50
F20	John Stockton	1.50
F21	David Robinson	2.50
F22	Cedric Ceballos	.75
F23	Alonzo Mourning	1.50
F24	Mookie Blaylock	.75
F25	Clyde Drexler	2.00
F26	Rod Strickland	.75

F27	Larry Johnson	.75
F28	Karl Malone	2.50
F29	Sean Elliott	.75
F30	Shaquille O'Neal	6.00
F31	Tim Hardaway	2.00
F32	Dikembe Mutombo	.75
R1	Shareef Abdur-Rahim	3.00
R2	Tony Delk	.30
R3	Priest Lauderdale	.15
R4	Roy Rogers	.25
R5	Lorenzen Wright	.30
R6	Stephon Marbury	4.00
R7	Derek Fisher	.75
R8	John Wallace	.40
R9	Kobe Bryant	10.00
R10	Kerry Kittles	1.00
R11	Antoine Walker	3.00
R12	Steve Nash	.25
R13	Erick Dampier	.30
R14	Walter McCarty	.25
R15	Vitaly Potapenko	.15
R16	Allen Iverson	5.00
R17	Marcus Camby	1.25
R18	Todd Fuller	.15
R19	Ray Allen	2.00
R20	Jermaine O'Neal	1.00
CA1	Michael Jordan, Jerry Stackhouse	15.00
CA2	Patrick Ewing, Alonzo Mourning	2.00
CA3	Brent Barry, Gary Payton	2.00
CA4	Chris Webber, Juwan Howard	4.00
CA5	Christian Laettner, Grant Hill	6.00
CA6	Jason Kidd, Shareef Abdur-Rahim	5.00
CA7	Clyde Drexler, Hakeem Olajuwon	4.00
CA8	Kenny Anderson, Stephon Marbury	6.00
CA9	Anfernee Hardaway, Lorenzen Wright	5.00
CA10	Dikembe Mutombo, Allen Iverson	8.00
HR1	Scottie Pippen	5.00
HR2	Anfernee Hardaway	6.00
HR3	Vin Baker	1.50
HR4	Brent Barry	.75
HR5	Clyde Drexler	2.00
HR6	Kevin Garnett	12.00
HR7	Grant Hill	12.00
HR8	Michael Finley	2.00
HR9	Jerry Stackhouse	2.00
HR10	Isaiah Rider	.75
HR11	Shaquille O'Neal	6.00
HR12	Antonio McDyess	4.00
HR13	Shawn Kemp	2.50
HR14	Michael Jordan	25.00
HR15	Juwan Howard	2.00
MH1	Dennis Rodman	3.00
MH2	David Robinson	1.50
MH3	Karl Malone	1.50
MH4	Clyde Drexler	1.00
MH5	Anfernee Hardaway	4.00
MH6	Hakeem Olajuwon	1.50
MH7	Charles Oakley	.40
MH8	Joe Smith	1.25
MH9	Glenn Robinson	.75
RS1	Marcus Camby	4.00
RS2	Shareef Abdur-Rahim	6.00
RS3	Stephon Marbury	8.00
RS4	Ray Allen	4.00
RS5	Antoine Walker	5.00
RS6	Lorenzen Wright	1.00
RS7	Kerry Kittles	2.00
RS8	Samaki Walker	1.00
RS9	Erick Dampier	1.00
RS10	Todd Fuller	.50
RS11	Kobe Bryant	20.00
RS12	Steve Nash	1.00
RS13	Tony Delk	1.00
RS14	Jermaine O'Neal	2.00
RS15	John Wallace	1.25
RS16	Walter McCarty	1.00
RS17	Dontae' Jones	.50
RS18	Roy Rogers	.75
RS19	Derek Fisher	2.00
RS20	Martin Muursepp	.50
RS21	Jerome Williams	.50
RS22	Brian Evans	.50
RS23	Priest Lauderdale	.50
RS24	Travis Knight	1.00
RS25	Allen Iverson	15.00
WA1	Charles Barkley	.30
WA2	Armon Gilliam	.15
WA3	Larry Johnson	.25
WA4	Felton Spencer	.15
WA5	Isaiah Rider	.15
WA6	Kevin Willis	.15
WA7	Mahmoud Abdul-Rauf	.15
WA8	Chris Childs	.15
WA9	Robert Horry	.25
WA10	Dan Majerle	.25
WA11	Robert Pack	.15
WA12	Rod Strickland	.25
WA13	Tyrone Corbin	.15
WA14	Anthony Mason	.25
WA15	Derek Harper	.25
WA16	Kenny Anderson	.25
WA17	Hubert Davis	.15
WA18	Allan Houston	.25
WA19	Shaquille O'Neal	.75
WA20	Brent Price	.15
WA21	Ervin Johnson	.15
WA22	Craig Ehlo	.15
WA23	Jalen Rose	.15
WA24	Oliver Miller	.15
WA25	Mark West	.15

1996-97 Stadium Club Members Only 55

The 50 Stadium Club cards reflect the NBA's elite veteran players, showcasing at least one player from each team. The five Finest Cards represent Topps' selection of the top rookies from the 1995 NBA Draft.

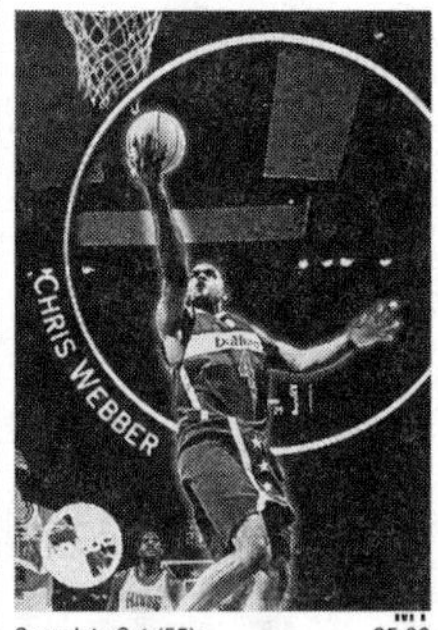

		MT
Complete Set (55):		25.00
Common Player:		.10
1	Scottie Pippen	1.25
2	Dikembe Mutombo	.25
3	Antonio McDyess	.50
4	Mark Jackson	.10
5	Vin Baker	.40
6	Kendall Gill	.20
7	Kenny Anderson	.25
8	Karl Malone	.50
9	Chris Webber	1.00
10	David Robinson	.60
11	Cedric Ceballos	.20
12	Patrick Ewing	.40
13	Alonzo Mourning	.40
14	Latrell Sprewell	.40
15	Terrell Brandon	.25
16	Anthony Mason	.20
17	Joe Dumars	.25
18	Hakeem Olajuwon	1.00
19	Brent Barry	.10
20	Shaquille O'Neal	1.50
21	Kevin Garnett	3.00
22	Anfernee Hardaway	1.50
23	Jerry Stackhouse	.60
24	Mitch Richmond	.40
25	Gary Payton	.50
26	Damon Stoudamire	.75
27	Christian Laettner	.25
28	Dino Radja	.10
29	Shawn Bradley	.10
30	John Stockton	.40
31	Sean Elliott	.10
32	Jason Kidd	.50
33	Allan Houston	.20
34	Glenn Robinson	.40
35	Tim Hardaway	.30
36	Reggie Miller	.40
37	Charles Barkley	.60
38	Joe Smith	.60
39	Grant Hill	3.00
40	LaPhonso Ellis	.20
41	Michael Jordan	8.00
42	Glen Rice	.40
43	Rony Seikaly	.10
44	Shawn Kemp	.75
45	Juwan Howard	.60
46	Tyrone Hill	.10
47	Michael Finley	.40
48	Loy Vaught	.20
49	Arvydas Sabonis	.20
50	Brian Grant	.10
51	Kerry Kittles Finest	1.00
52	Kobe Bryant Finest	15.00
53	Stephon Marbury Finest	5.00
54	Allen Iverson Finest	10.00
55	Shareef Abdur-Rahim Finest	4.00

1996-97 Stadium Club Promos

These six promo cards were issued prior to release of 1996-97 Stadium Club. The cards are identical to the regular cards except the promos have only two lines of copyright text on the backs while the regular cards have four lines.

		MT
Complete Set (6):		5.00
Common Player:		.50
1	Scottie Pippen	2.00
33	Arvydas Sabonis	.50
45	Damon Stoudamire	1.00
47	Elden Campbell	.50
77	Nick Anderson	.50
78	David Robinson	1.00

1996-97 Stadium Club Rookie Showcase

This 25-card insert set was found in Series II hobby and retail packs at a rate of one per 12 packs. The cards are printed on plastic with horizontal fronts and vertical backs. Fronts have a color picture of the player on the left third, with a holographic image taking up most of the remaining room, except for a strip on the right with basketballs containing the insert name. Backs carry an "RS" prefix on the card number.

		MT
Complete Set (25):		100.00
Common Player:		1.50
1	Marcus Camby	7.00
2	Shareef Abdur-Rahim	15.00
3	Stephon Marbury	18.00
4	Ray Allen	7.00
5	Antoine Walker	10.00
6	Lorenzen Wright	1.50
7	Kerry Kittles	8.00
8	Samaki Walker	1.50
9	Erick Dampier	1.50
10	Todd Fuller	1.50
11	Kobe Bryant	30.00
12	Steve Nash	4.00
13	Tony Delk	1.50
14	Jermaine O'Neal	5.00
15	John Wallace	1.50
16	Walter McCarty	1.50
17	Dontae Jones	1.50
18	Roy Rogers	1.50
19	Derek Fisher	1.50
20	Martin Muursepp	1.50
21	Jerome Williams	1.50
22	Brian Evans	1.50
23	Priest Lauderdale	1.50
24	Travis Knight	1.50
25	Allen Iverson	25.00

1996-97 Stadium Club Rookies 1

Rookies I cards were inserted into packs of Series I Stadium Club and numbered R1-R25. Although they were an insert, Rookies were actually considered part of the regular-issue set, which is why no odds are listed. There is also a Rookies set in Series II, however Rookies I cards are identified by the word Rookie running up the right side of the card without a border and the Stadium Club logo is in the upper right corner.

		MT
Complete Set (25):		25.00
Common Player:		.20
1	Allen Iverson	6.00
2	Marcus Camby	2.00
3	Shareef Abdur-Rahim	3.00
4	Stephon Marbury	4.00
5	Ray Allen	2.50
6	Antoine Walker	2.00
7	Lorenzen Wright	.50
8	Kerry Kittles	1.50
9	Samaki Walker	.75
10	Erick Dampier	.75
11	Todd Fuller	.40
12	Kobe Bryant	10.00
13	Steve Nash	.75
14	Tony Delk	.50
15	Jermaine O'Neal	1.00
16	John Wallace	1.00
17	Walter McCarty	.20
18	Dontae Jones	.20
19	Roy Rogers	.20
20	Derek Fisher	.50
21	Martin Muursepp	.20
22	Jerome Williams	.20
23	Brian Evans	.20
24	Priest Lauderdale	.20
25	Travis Knight	.50

1996-97 Stadium Club Rookies 2

Rookies II, like Rookies I, was considered part of the regular-issue set but is numbered as an insert, which is why no insertion ratio is given. Rookies II cards were found in Series II Stadium Club packs, numbered R1-R20 and featured a thick strip running down the left side of the card with the word "Rookie" inside it and the Stadium Club logo in the lower left corner.

		MT
Complete Set (20):		25.00
Common Player:		.20
1	Shareef Abdur-Rahim	3.00
2	Tony Delk	.20
3	Priest Lauderdale	.20
4	Roy Rogers	.20
5	Lorenzen Wright	.20
6	Stephon Marbury	4.00
7	Derek Fisher	.20
8	John Wallace	.20
9	Kobe Bryant	10.00
10	Kerry Kittles	2.00
11	Antoine Walker	2.00
12	Steve Nash	1.00
13	Erick Dampier	.20
14	Walter McCarty	.20
15	Vitaly Potapenko	.20
16	Allen Iverson	6.00
17	Marcus Camby	2.00
18	Todd Fuller	.20
19	Ray Allen	2.00
20	Jermaine O'Neal	1.00

1996-97 Stadium Club Special Forces

This 10-card insert set is numbered SF1-SF10 and was inserted one per 20 Series I retail packs. Fronts feature a foil-etched action shot with multi-colored stars in the background.

		MT
Complete Set (10):		130.00
Common Player:		5.00
1	Anfernee Hardaway	15.00
2	Grant Hill	20.00
3	Shawn Kemp	5.00
4	Michael Jordan	40.00
5	Shaquille O'Neal	20.00
6	Scottie Pippen	10.00
7	Damon Stoudamire	10.00
8	Jerry Stackhouse	8.00
9	Gary Payton	5.00
10	Dennis Rodman	10.00

1996-97 Stadium Club Top Crop

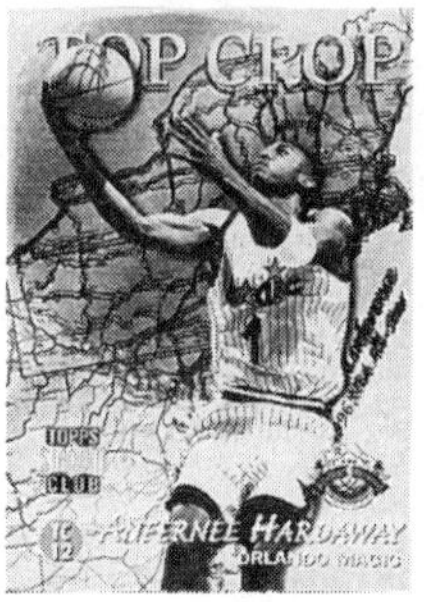

Top Crop matches two star players that play the same position on a holographic foil, double-sided card. Top Crop inserts are numbered TC1-TC10, and were inserted into Series I packs at a rate of one per 24 hobby packs and one per 20 retail packs.

		MT
Complete Set (12):		120.00
Common Player:		3.00
1	Shaquille O'Neal, Hakeem Olajuwon	20.00
2	Alonzo Mourning, Dikembe Mutombo	5.00
3	Patrick Ewing, David Robinson	7.00
4	Grant Hill, Sean Elliott	15.00
5	Scottie Pippen, Shawn Kemp	10.00
6	Vin Baker, Karl Malone	3.00
7	Juwan Howard, Charles Barkley	8.00
8	Glen Rice, Clyde Drexler	3.00
9	Michael Jordan, Gary Payton	40.00
10	Terrell Brandon, John Stockton	6.00
11	Reggie Miller, Mitch Richmond	6.00
12	Anfernee Hardaway, Jason Kidd	20.00

1996-97 Stadium Club Welcome Additions

Welcome Additions was a 25-card set that was considered part of the regular-issue set, but numbered as an insert set, which is why no insertion rate is given. Welcome Additions have a holographic purple strip down the left side with the insert name. Card numbers contain a "WA" prefix.

		MT
Complete Set (25):		5.00
Common Player:		.15
1	Charles Barkley	.75
2	Armon Gilliam	.15
3	Larry Johnson	.15
4	Felton Spencer	.15
5	Isaiah Rider	.15
6	Kevin Willis	.15
7	Mahmoud Abdul-Rauf	.15
8	Chris Childs	.15
9	Robert Horry	.15
10	Dan Majerle	.15
11	Robert Pack	.15
12	Rod Strickland	.15
13	Tyrone Corbin	.15
14	Anthony Mason	.15
15	Derek Harper	.15
16	Kenny Anderson	.15
17	Hubert Davis	.15
18	Allan Houston	.15
19	Shaquille O'Neal	2.50
20	Brent Price	.15
21	Ervin Johnson	.15
22	Craig Ehlo	.15
23	Jalen Rose	.15
24	Oliver Miller	.15
25	Mark West	.15

1997-98 Stadium Club Promos

This six-card set was a promo for the 1997-98 Stadium Club set. The card fronts feature a color player photo and a foil-embossed logo. The backs have biographical information, three-year player stats and a ranking based on those stats and the position he played.

		MT
Complete Set (6):		5.00
Common Player:		.50
21	Glen Rice	1.00
41	Reggie Miller	1.00
87	Patrick Ewing	1.00
95	Antoine Walker	2.00
115	Karl Malone	1.00
169	Kenny Anderson	.50

1997-98 Stadium Club

Stadium Club Basketball was released in two, 120-card series in 1997-98, with each series containing 100 base cards and a 20-card Rookies subset. The cards clearly focused on photography, with a full-bleed, glossy photo on each card, with a silver Stadium Club logo and a blue foil strip across the bottom that contained the player's name. Inserts in Series I included: Printing Plates, Bowman's Best Veteran Preview, Hoop Screams, Hardwood Hopefuls, Co-Signers, Triumvirates and Hardcourt Heroics, along with One of a Kind and First Day Issue parallels. Series II included: Printing Plates, Co-Signers, Bowman's Best Rookie Preview, Triumvirate, Never Compromise and Royal Court, along with One of a Kind and First Day Issue parallel sets.

		MT
Complete Set (240):		55.00
Complete Series 1 (120):		35.00
Complete Series 2 (120):		20.00
Common Player:		.10
Minor Stars:		.20
Retail Pack (6):		2.00
Retail Wax Box (24):		45.00
Ser. 1 or 2 Hobby Pack (9):		3.00
Ser. 1 or 2 Hobby Wax Box (24):		65.00
1	Scottie Pippen	1.00
2	Bryon Russell	.10
3	Muggsy Bogues	.10
4	Gary Payton	.50
5	Team of the 90's	2.00
6	(Corliss Williamson)	.10
7	Samaki Walker	.20
8	Allan Houston	.10
9	Ray Allen	.30
10	Nick Van Exel	.30
11	Chris Mullin	.20
12	Popeye Jones	.10
13	Horace Grant	.10
14	Rik Smits	.10
15	Wayman Tisdale	.10
16	Donny Marshall	.10
17	Rod Strickland	.10
18	Rod Strickland	.10
19	Greg Anthony	.10
20	Lindsey Hunter	.10
21	Glen Rice	.20
22	Anthony Goldwire	.10
23	Mahmoud Abdul-Rauf	.10
24	Sean Elliott	.10
25	Cory Alexander	.10
26	Tyrone Corbin	.10
27	Sam Perkins	.10
28	Brian Shaw	.10
29	Doug Christie	.10
30	Mark Jackson	.10
31	Christian Laettner	.20
32	Damon Stoudamire	.75
33	Eric Williams	.10
34	Glenn Robinson	.30
35	Brooks Thompson	.10
36	Derrick Coleman	.10
37	Theo Ratliff	.20
38	Ron Harper	.10
39	Hakeem Olajuwon	.75
40	Mitch Richmond	.30
41	Reggie Miller	.20
42	Reggie Miller	.20
43	Shaquille O'Neal	1.50
44	Zydrunas Ilgauskas	.10
45	Jamal Mashburn	.20
46	Isaiah Rider	.10
47	Tom Gugliotta	.20
48	Rex Chapman	.10
49	Lorenzen Wright	.10
50	Pooh Richardson	.10
51	Armon Gilliam	.10
52	Kevin Johnson	.20
53	Kerry Kittles	.40
54	Kerry Kittles	.40
55	Charles Oakley	.10
56	Dennis Rodman	1.50
57	Greg Ostertag	.10
58	Todd Fuller	.10
59	Mark Davis	.10
60	Erick Strickland	.10
61	Clifford Robinson	.10
62	Nate McMillan	.10
63	Steve Kerr	.10
64	Bob Sura	.10
65	Danny Ferry	.10
66	Loy Vaught	.10
67	A.C. Green	.10
68	John Stockton	.40
69	Terry Mills	.10
70	Voshon Lenard	.10
71	Matt Maloney	.20
72	Charlie Ward	.10
73	Brent Barry	.10
74	Chris Webber	1.00
75	Stephon Marbury	1.50
76	Bryant Stith	.10
77	Shareef Abdur-Rahim	1.00
78	Sean Rooks	.10
79	Rony Seikaly	.10
80	Brent Price	.10
81	Wesley Person	.10
82	Michael Smith	.10
83	Gary Trent	.10
84	Dan Majerle	.10
85	Rex Walters	.10
86	Clarence Weatherspoon	.10
87	Patrick Ewing	.30
88	B.J. Armstrong	.10
89	Travis Best	.10
90	Steve Smith	.10
91	Vitaly Potapenko	.10
92	Derek Strong	.10
93	Michael Finley	.20
94	Will Perdue	.10
95	Antoine Walker	1.00
96	Chuck Person	.10
97	Mookie Blaylock	.10
98	Eric Snow	.10
99	Tony Delk	.10
100	Mario Elie	.10
101	Terrell Brandon	.20
102	Shawn Bradley	.10
103	Latrell Sprewell	.20
104	Latrell Sprewell	.20
105	Tim Hardaway	.20
106	Terry Porter	.10
107	Darrell Armstrong	.10
108	Rasheed Wallace	.10
109	Vinny Del Negro	.10
110	Gheorghe Muresan	.10
111	Lawrence Moten	.10
112	Lamond Murray	.10
113	Juwan Howard	.30
114	Juwan Howard	.30
115	Karl Malone	.40
116	Kurt Thomas	.10
117	Shawn Respert	.10
118	Michael Jordan	5.00

119 Shawn Kemp .50
120 Arvydas Sabonis .10
121 Tyus Edney .10
122 Bryant Reeves .20
123 Jason Kidd .40
124 Dikembe Mutombo .20
125 Allen Iverson 2.00
126 Allen Iverson 2.00
127 Larry Johnson .20
128 Jerry Stackhouse .50
129 Kendall Gill .10
130 Kendall Gill .10
131 Vin Baker .30
132 Joe Dumars .10
133 Calbert Cheaney .10
134 Alonzo Mourning .30
135 Isaac Austin .10
136 Joe Smith .50
137 Elden Campbell .10
138 Kevin Garnett 2.50
139 Malik Sealy .10
140 John Starks .10
141 Clyde Drexler .40
142 Matt Geiger .10
143 Mark Price .10
144 Buck Williams .10
145 Grant Hill 2.50
146 Kobe Bryant 3.00
147 Dale Ellis .10
148 Jason Caffey .10
149 Toni Kukoc .10
150 Avery Johnson .10
151 Alan Henderson .10
152 Walt Williams .10
153 Greg Minor .10
154 Calbert Cheaney .10
155 Vlade Divac .10
156 Greg Foster .10
157 LaPhonso Ellis .10
158 Charles Barkley .50
159 Antonio Davis .10
160 Roy Rogers .10
161 Robert Horry .10
162 Chris Gatling .10
163 Chris Carr .10
164 Robert Pack .10
165 Sam Cassell .10
166 Rodney Rogers .10
167 Chris Childs .10
168 Shandon Anderson .10
169 Kenny Anderson .10
170 Anthony Mason .10
171 Olden Polynice .10
172 David Wingate .10
173 David Robinson .40
174 Billy Owens .10
175 Detlef Schrempf .10
176 Carlos Rogers .10
177 Marcus Camby .75
178 Dana Barros .10
179 Shandon Anderson .10
180 Jayson Williams .10
181 Eldridge Recasner .10
182 Doug West .10
183 Kevin Willis .10
184 Eddie Johnson .10
185 Derek Fisher .10
186 Eddie Jones .50
187 Sherman Douglas .10
188 Anthony Peeler .10
189 Danny Manning .10
190 Walter McCarty .10
191 Hersey Hawkins .10
192 Micheal Williams .10
193 Jeff Hornacek .10
194 Anfernee Hardaway 2.00
195 Harvey Grant .10
196 Nick Anderson .10
197 Luc Longley .10
198 Andrew Lang .10
199 P.J. Brown .10
200 Cedric Ceballos .10
201 *Tim Duncan* 5.00
202 Ervin Johnson .10
203 *Keith Van Horn* 3.00
204 David Wesley .10
205 *Chauncey Billups* 2.50
206 Jim Jackson .20
207 *Antonio Daniels* 2.50
208 Travis Knight .10
209 *Tony Battie* 2.50
210 Bobby Phills .10
211 *Bobby Jackson* 2.50
212 Otis Thorpe .10
213 *Tim Thomas* 3.00
214 Chris Mullin .20
215 *Adonal Foyle* 2.00
216 Brian Williams .10
217 *Tracy McGrady* 4.00
218 Tyus Edney .10
219 *Danny Fortson* 2.00
220 Clifford Robinson .10
221 *Olivier Saint-Jean* 2.00
222 Vin Baker .40
223 *Austin Croshere* .50
224 Brian Grant .10
225 *Derek Anderson* 3.00
226 Kelvin Cato .20
227 *Maurice Taylor* .50
228 Scot Pollard .10
229 *John Thomas* .20
230 Dean Garrett .10
231 *Brevin Knight* 3.00
232 *Ron Mercer* 2.00
233 *Johnny Taylor* .20
234 Antonio McDyess .40
235 *Ed Gray* .20
236 Terrell Brandon .20
237 *Anthony Parker* .20
238 Shawn Kemp .50
239 *Paul Grant* .20
240 Terry Mills .10

1997-98 Stadium Club First Day Issue

First Day Issue cards paralleled all 240 cards in Stadium Club Series I and II. The cards contained a First Day Issue stamp on the front and were sequentially numbered to 200 sets. They were inserted in retail packs only and seeded one per 24.

MT
F.D.I. Stars: 15x-30x
F.D.I. Rookies: 8x-16x

1997-98 Stadium Club One Of A Kind

One of a Kind was a hobby-only parallel that mirrored all 240 cards in Series I and II. Cards were printed on a foilboard stock and sequentially numbered on the back to 150. They were seeded one per 86 packs in Series I and one per 69 packs in Series II.

MT
One Of A Kind Stars: 30x-60x
One Of A Kind Rookies: 15x-30x

1997-98 Stadium Club Bowman's Best Rookie Preview

This 10-card set was inserted into packs of Stadium Club Series II packs. Regular versions were seeded one per 24 packs, Refractors were seeded one per 96 packs and Atomic Refractors every 192 packs. These were identified by a "BBP" prefix on the card number and a silver design to the Bowman's Best card on the front.

MT
Complete Set (10): 30.00
Common Player: 1.50
Refractors: 2x-3x
Atomic Refractors: 3x-6x
11 Maurice Taylor 4.00
12 Chauncey Billups 10.00
13 Paul Grant 1.50
14 Tony Battie 8.00
15 Austin Croshere 3.00
16 Brevin Knight 6.00
17 Bobby Jackson 6.00
18 Johnny Taylor 1.50
19 Scot Pollard 1.50
20 Olivier Saint-Jean 3.00

1997-98 Stadium Club Bowman's Best Veteran Preview

This 10-card set was inserted into packs of Series I, with regular versions every 24 packs, Refractor versions every 96 packs and Atomic Refractors every 192 packs. The cards are identified by a "BBP" prefix on the card number and a gold color to the Bowman's Best design on the front.

MT
Complete Set (10): 60.00
Common Player: 2.00
Refractors: 2x-3x
Atomic Refractors: 3x-6x
1 Allen Iverson 12.00
2 Gary Payton 4.00
3 Greg Hill 12.00
4 Anfernee Hardaway 10.00
5 Karl Malone 3.00
6 Glen Rice 2.00
7 Antoine Walker 4.00
8 Alonzo Mourning 2.00
9 Shareef Abdur-Rahim 6.00
10 Shaquille O'Neal 8.00

1997-98 Stadium Club Co-Signers

This 24-card insert ran through Series I and II of Stadium Club and was inserted one per 309 hobby packs. These double-sided cards featured two NBA stars, one per side, with both players autographs and were numbered with a "CO" prefix.

MT
Common Player: 75.00
1 Karl Malone, Kobe Bryant 1200.
2 Juwan Howard, Hakeem Olajuwon 325.00
3 John Starks, Joe Smith 225.00
4 Clyde Drexler, Tim Hardaway 400.00
5 Kobe Bryant, John Starks 425.00
6 Hakeem Olajuwon, Clyde Drexler 180.00
7 Tim Hardaway, Juwan Howard 125.00
8 Joe Smith, Karl Malone 125.00
9 Juwan Howard, Clyde Drexler 125.00
10 Hakeem Olajuwon, Tim Hardaway 125.00
11 Joe Smith, Kobe Bryant 225.00
12 Karl Malone, John Starks 75.00
13 Dikembe Mutombo, Chauncey Billups 175.00
14 Keith Van Horn, Chris Webber 400.00
15 Karl Malone, Kerry Kittles 275.00
16 Ron Mercer, Antoine Walker 400.00
17 Chris Webber, Karl Malone 150.00
18 Antoine Walker, Dikembe Mutombo 125.00
19 Kerry Kittles, Keith Van Horn 200.00
20 Chauncey Billups, Ron Mercer 225.00
21 Antoine Walker, Chauncey Billups 30.00
22 Dikembe Mutombo, Ron Mercer 100.00
23 Keith Van Horn, Karl Malone 75.00
24 Chris Webber, Kerry Kittles 125.00

1997-98 Stadium Club Hardcourt Heroics

This 10-card insert set was found in Series I packs at a rate of one per 12 packs. The cards were printed on a silver uniluster technology and numbered with a "H" prefix.

MT
Complete Set (10): 50.00
Common Player: 1.50
1 Michael Jordan 20.00
2 Gary Payton 3.00
3 Charles Barkley 3.00
4 Mitch Richmond 1.50
5 Shawn Kemp 2.00
6 Anfernee Hardaway 8.00
7 Vin Baker 2.00
8 Shaquille O'Neal 6.00
9 Scottie Pippen 4.00
10 Grant Hill 10.00

1997-98 Stadium Club Hardwood Hopefuls

Hardcourt Hopefuls was a 10-card insert set that was seeded one per 36 packs of Series I. The insert features 1997 NBA Draft Picks on a textured, metalized plastic card that carries a "HH" prefix.

MT
Complete Set (10): 100.00
Common Player: 3.00
1 (Brevin Knight) 8.00
2 (Adonal Foyle) 8.00
3 (Keith Van Horn) 15.00
4 (Tim Duncan) 30.00
5 (Danny Fortson) 8.00
6 (Tracy McGrady) 15.00
7 (Tony Battie) 12.00
8 (Chauncey Billups) 15.00
9 (Austin Croshere) 3.00
10 (Antonio Daniels) 15.00

1997-98 Stadium Club Hoop Screams

This 10-card set is inserted one per 12 packs of Series I. The cards capture each player on a metallized look done in blue and silver and are numbered with a "HS" prefix.

MT
Complete Set (10): 50.00
Common Player: 1.00
1 Shaquille O'Neal 6.00
2 Cedric Ceballos 1.00
3 Kevin Garnett 10.00
4 Shawn Kemp 2.00
5 Jerry Stackhouse 3.00
6 Anfernee Hardaway 10.00
7 Patrick Ewing 3.00
8 Marcus Camby 4.00
9 Kobe Bryant 12.00
10 Michael Jordan 20.00

1997-98 Stadium Club Never Compromise

This Series II exclusive included 10 veterans and 10 rookies on a glossy card featuring the insert name printed repeatedly across the background. These were found every 36 packs and numbered with a "NC" prefix.

MT
Complete Set (20): 175.00
Common Player: 2.00
Minor Stars: 4.00
1 Michael Jordan 40.00
2 Karl Malone 4.00
3 Hakeem Olajuwon 8.00
4 Kevin Garnett 20.00
5 Dikembe Mutombo 2.00
6 Gary Payton 5.00
7 Grant Hill 20.00
8 Charles Barkley 6.00
9 Shaquille O'Neal 15.00
10 Anfernee Hardaway 15.00
11 Tim Duncan 25.00
12 Keith Van Horn 15.00
13 Tracy McGrady 12.00
14 Tim Thomas 10.00
15 Austin Croshere 2.00
16 Maurice Taylor 6.00
17 Chauncey Billups 12.00
18 Adonal Foyle 2.00
19 Tony Battie 8.00
20 Bobby Jackson 6.00

1997-98 Stadium Club Royal Court

Ten rookies and 10 veterans are included in this insert that highlights each player coming out of a silver foil background. Inserted one per 12 packs of Series II, these cards are numbered with a "RC" prefix.

MT
Complete Set (20): 100.00
Common Player: 1.00
Minor Stars: 2.00
1 Scottie Pippen 5.00
2 Karl Malone 2.00
3 Gary Payton 3.00
4 Kobe Bryant 15.00
5 Antoine Walker 4.00
6 Michael Jordan 20.00
7 Shaquille O'Neal 8.00
8 Dikembe Mutombo 1.00
9 Hakeem Olajuwon 4.00
10 Grant Hill 10.00
11 Tim Duncan 15.00
12 Keith Van Horn 8.00
13 Chauncey Billups 8.00
14 Antonio Daniels 6.00
15 Tony Battie 6.00
16 Bobby Jackson 5.00
17 Tim Thomas 6.00
18 Adonal Foyle 1.00
19 Tracy McGrady 8.00
20 Danny Fortson 2.00

1997-98 Stadium Club Triumvirate

This 48-card, retail only insert was distributed in both Series I and II packs with half the set in each. Three players from eight different teams were included in each series on Finest technology cards that fit together to form a three card panel. Within each series, Triumvirates were seeded 1:48 (luminous), 1:192 (luminescent) and 1:384 (illuminator) and numbered with a "T" prefix and a "A," "B," or "C" suffix.

MT
Complete Set (48): 525.00
Complete Series 1 (24): 225.00
Complete Series 2 (24): 300.00
Common Player: 2.00
Minor Stars: 4.00
Luminescent Cards: 3x
Illuminator Cards: 3x-6x
1A Scottie Pippen 15.00
1B Michael Jordan 60.00
1C Dennis Rodman 20.00
2A Ray Allen 6.00
2B Vin Baker 8.00
2C Glenn Robinson 4.00
3A Juwan Howard 4.00
3B Chris Webber 10.00
3C Rod Strickland 2.00
4A Christian Laettner 2.00
4B Dikembe Mutombo 2.00
4C Steve Smith 2.00
5A Tom Gugliotta 2.00
5B Kevin Garnett 30.00
5C Stephon Marbury 25.00
6A Charles Barkley 8.00
6B Hakeem Olajuwon 12.00
6C Clyde Drexler 6.00
7A John Stockton 4.00
7B Karl Malone 6.00
7C Bryon Russell 2.00
8A Larry Johnson 2.00
8B Patrick Ewing 4.00
8C Allan Houston 2.00
9A Tim Hardaway 4.00
9B Michael Jordan 50.00
9C Anfernee Hardaway 20.00
10A Glen Rice 4.00
10B Scottie Pippen 12.00
10C Grant Hill 25.00
11A Dikembe Mutombo 2.00
11B Patrick Ewing 4.00
11C Alonzo Mourning 4.00
12A Ron Mercer 15.00
12B Keith Van Horn 15.00
12C Tracy McGrady 12.00
13A Gary Payton 6.00
13B John Stockton 1.00
13C Stephon Marbury 20.00
14A Karl Malone 5.00
14B Charles Barkley 6.00
14C Kevin Garnett 25.00

15A David Robinson 6.00
15B Hakeem Olajuwon 10.00
15C Shaquille O'Neal 20.00
16A Antonio Daniels 8.00
16B Tim Duncan 25.00
16C Adonal Foyle 2.00

1998-99 Stadium Club Promos

This six-card promotional set was distributed to dealers and members of the media to promote the 1998-99 Stadium Club product. The cards were identical to the regular-issue cards except they were numbered PP1-PP6 on the back.

MT
Complete Set (6): 5.00
Common Player: .25
1 Shareef Abdur-Rahim .50
2 Shaquille O'Neal 1.00
3 Keith Van Horn .75
4 Kevin Garnett 2.50
5 Tracy McGrady .50
6 Tim Hardaway .25

1998-99 Stadium Club

Stadium Club was released in two, 120-card series in 1998-99. Series I arrived during the lockout, but didn't allow that to diminish the product by including Draft Pick Redemption cards of the regular set numbered 101-120. Series I actually contains only 118 cards since cards 117 and 118 didn't exist because they were foreign players who didn't sign NBA contracts. Three parallels of Stadium Club existed - First Day Issue (numbered to 200, retail only), One of a Kind (numbered to 150, hobby only) and Printing Plates (four versions of each card, HTA packs only). While redemptions for cards 101-120 were in Series I, parallel versions of these cards were held until Series II. Inserts in Series I include: First Day Issue (200 numbered sets, retail only, 1:64), One of a Kind (150 numbered sets, hobby only, 1:56), Printing Plates (1:205 HTA), Co-Signers, Stadium Club Chrome, Triumvirates, Prime Rookies, Statliners and Never Compromise. Inserts in Series II include: First Day Issue (1:44), One of a Kind (1:55), Printing Plates (1:176), Co-Signers, Stadium Club Chrome, Triumvirate, Royal Court, Wing Men and Never Compromise Rookies.

MT
Complete Set (240): 525.00
Complete Series 1 (120): 500.00
Complete Series 2 (120): 50.00
Common Player: .15
Minor Stars: .30
Common Draft Picks: 2.00
Inserted 1:6
Pack (9): 3.50
Wax Box (24): 70.00
1 Eddie Jones 1.00
2 Matt Geiger .15
3 Ray Allen .30
4 Billy Owens .15
5 Larry Johnson .30
6 Jerry Stackhouse .30
7 Travis Best .15
8 Sam Cassell .15
9 Isaiah Rider .15
10 Walter McCarty .15
11 Hakeem Olajuwon .75
12 Detlef Schrempf .15
13 Chris Garner .15
14 Voshon Lenard .15
15 Kevin Garnett 2.50
16 Doug Christie .15
17 Dikembe Mutombo .30
18 Terrell Brandon .30

19	Brevin Knight	.15
20	Dan Majerle	.15
21	Keith Van Horn	1.00
22	Jim Jackson	.30
23	Theo Ratliff	.15
24	Anthony Peeler	.15
25	Tim Hardaway	.40
26	Charles Outlaw	.15
27	Blue Edwards	.15
28	Khalid Reeves	.15
29	David Wesley	.15
30	Toni Kukoc	.30
31	Jaren Jackson	.15
32	Mario Elie	.15
33	Nick Anderson	.15
34	Derek Anderson	.50
35	Rodney Rogers	.15
36	Jalen Rose	.15
37	Corliss Williamson	.15
38	Tyrone Corbin	.15
39	Antonio Davis	.15
40	Chris Mills	.15
41	Clarence Weatherspoon	.15
42	George Lynch	.15
43	Kelvin Cato	.15
44	Anthony Mason	.15
45	Tracy McGrady	1.00
46	Lamond Murray	.15
47	Mookie Blaylock	.15
48	Tracy Murray	.15
49	Ron Harper	.15
50	Tom Gugliotta	.30
51	Allan Houston	.30
52	Arvydas Sabonis	.15
53	Brian Williams	.15
54	Brian Shaw	.15
55	John Stockton	.30
56	Rick Fox	.15
57	Hersey Hawkins	.15
58	Danny Manning	.15
59	Chris Carr	.15
60	Lindsey Hunter	.15
61	Donyell Marshall	.15
62	Michael Jordan	5.00
63	Mark Strickland	.15
64	LaPhonso Ellis	.15
65	Rod Strickland	.30
66	David Robinson	.50
67	Cedric Ceballos	.15
68	Christian Laettner	.30
69	Anthony Goldwire	.15
70	Armon Gilliam	.15
71	Shaquille O'Neal	1.50
72	Sherman Douglas	.15
73	Kendall Gill	.15
74	Charlie Ward	.15
75	Allen Iverson	1.25
76	Shawn Kemp	.50
77	Travis Knight	.15
78	Gary Payton	.40
79	Cedric Henderson	.30
80	Matt Bullard	.15
81	Steve Kerr	.15
82	Shawn Bradley	.15
83	Antonio McDyess	.30
84	Robert Horry	.15
85	Darrick Martin	.15
86	Derek Strong	.15
87	Shandon Anderson	.15
88	Lawrence Funderburke	.15
89	Brent Price	.15
90	Reggie Miller	.30
91	Shareef Abdur-Rahim	1.00
92	Jeff Hornacek	.15
93	Antoine Carr	.15
94	Greg Anthony	.15
95	Rex Chapman	.15
96	Antoine Walker	1.00
97	Bobby Jackson	.30
98	Calbert Cheaney	.15
99	Avery Johnson	.15
100	Jason Kidd	.75
101	*Michael Olowokandi*	10.00
102	*Mike Bibby*	20.00
103	*Raef LaFrentz*	15.00
104	*Antawn Jamison*	75.00
105	*Vince Carter*	400.00
106	*Robert Traylor*	5.00
107	*Jason Williams*	40.00
108	*Larry Hughes*	50.00
109	*Dirk Nowitzki*	80.00
110	*Paul Pierce*	40.00
111	*Bonzi Wells*	40.00
112	*Michael Doleac*	4.00
113	*Keon Clark*	8.00
114	*Michael Dickerson*	15.00
115	*Matt Harpring*	6.00
116	*Bryce Drew*	2.00
117	*Pat Garrity*	5.00
118	*Roshown McLeod*	4.00
119	*Ricky Davis*	15.00
120	*Brian Skinner*	3.00
121	Dee Brown	.15
122	Hubert Davis	.15
123	Vitaly Potapenko	.15
124	Ervin Johnson	.15
125	Chris Gatling	.15
126	Darrell Armstrong	.15
127	Glen Rice	.30
128	Ben Wallace	.15
129	Sam Mitchell	.15
130	Joe Dumars	.30
131	Terry Davis	.15
132	A.C. Green	.15
133	Alan Henderson	.15
134	Ron Mercer	1.50
135	Brian Grant	.15
136	Chris Childs	.15
137	Rony Seikaly	.15
138	Pete Chilcutt	.15
139	Anfernee Hardaway	1.50
140	Bryon Russell	.15
141	Tim Thomas	1.00
142	Erick Dampier	.15
143	Charles Barkley	.50
144	Mark Jackson	.15
145	Bryant Reeves	.15
146	Tyrone Hill	.15
147	Rasheed Wallace	.15
148	Tim Duncan	2.50
149	Steve Smith	.30
150	Alonzo Mourning	.40
151	Danny Fortson	.30
152	Aaron Williams	.15
153	Andrew DeClercq	.15
154	Elden Campbell	.15
155	Don Reid	.15
156	Rik Smits	.15
157	Adonal Foyle	.15
158	Muggsy Bogues	.15
159	Chris Mullin	.15
160	Randy Brown	.15
161	Kenny Anderson	.30
162	Tariq Abdul-Wahad	.15
163	P.J. Brown	.15
164	Jayson Williams	.30
165	Grant Hill	2.50
166	Clifford Robinson	.15
167	Damon Stoudamire	.40
168	Aaron McKie	.15
169	Erick Strickland	.15
170	Kobe Bryant	4.00
171	Karl Malone	.50
172	Eric Piatkowski	.15
173	Rodrick Rhodes	.15
174	Sean Elliott	.15
175	John Wallace	.15
176	Derek Fisher	.15
177	Maurice Taylor	.40
178	Wesley Person	.15
179	Jamal Mashburn	.30
180	Patrick Ewing	.30
181	Howard Eisley	.15
182	Michael Finley	.30
183	Juwan Howard	.30
184	Matt Maloney	.15
185	Glenn Robinson	.30
186	Zydrunas Ilgauskas	.30
187	Dana Barros	.15
188	Stacey Augmon	.15
189	Bobby Phills	.15
190	Kerry Kittles	.30
191	Vin Baker	.75
192	Stephon Marbury	1.50
193	*Predrag Stojakovic*	2.00
194	Michael Olowokandi	1.00
195	Mike Bibby	1.50
196	Raef LaFrentz	1.50
197	Antawn Jamison	2.50
198	Vince Carter	12.00
199	Robert Traylor	.75
200	Jason Williams	3.00
201	Larry Hughes	2.00
202	Dirk Nowitzki	3.00
203	Paul Pierce	2.50
204	Bonzi Wells	1.50
205	Michael Doleac	.50
206	Keon Clark	.75
207	Michael Dickerson	1.00
208	Matt Harpring	.75
209	Bryce Drew	.50
210	Pat Garrity	.50
211	Roshown McLeod	.50
212	Ricky Davis	1.00
213	Brian Skinner	.50
214	*Tyronn Lue*	2.00
215	*Felipe Lopez*	3.00
216	*Al Harrington*	6.00
217	*Sam Jacobson*	1.00
218	*Vladimir Stepania*	1.00
219	*Corey Benjamin*	1.50
220	*Nazr Mohammed*	1.00
221	Tom Gugliotta	.30
222	Derrick Coleman	.15
223	Mitch Richmond	.30
224	John Starks	.15
225	Antonio McDyess	.30
226	Joe Smith	.30
227	Bobby Jackson	.30
228	Luc Longley	.15
229	Isaac Austin	.15
230	Chris Webber	.50
231	Chauncey Billups	.30
232	Sam Perkins	.15
233	Christian Laettner	.15
234	Antonio Daniels	.15
235	Brent Barry	.15
236	Latrell Sprewell	.30
237	Vlade Divac	.15
238	Marcus Camby	.30
239	Charles Oakley	.15
240	Scottie Pippen	.60

1998-99 Stadium Club First Day Issue

This 240-card parallel set reprinted every card from Series I and II, but added the words "First Day Issue" in gold foil letters across the bottom. First Day Issue cards were exclusive to retail packs, seeded 1:44 packs and sequentially numbered to 200 sets. First Day Issue versions of the 20 rookie redemptions from Series I were included in Series II packs.

	MT
First Day Issue Cards:	15x-30x
FDI Series I Rookies:	4x-8x
FDI Series II Rookies:	8x-15x

Series I Inserted 1:64 Retail
Series II Inserted 1:44 Retail
Production 200 Retail Sets

1998-99 Stadium Club One of a Kind

This 240-card parallel set reprinted all cards from Series I and II, but were printed on a plastic card stock and included the words "One of a Kind" within the Stadium Club oval on the front. Cards were hobby exclusive and sequentially numbered to 150 sets. Series I odds were 1:56 packs, while Series II odds were 1:55 packs. One of a Kind versions of the 20 rookie redemptions from Series I were included in Series II packs.

	MT
One Of A Kind Cards:	20x-40x
Series I Rookies:	5x-10x
Series II Rookies:	10x-20x

Series I Inserted 1:56 Hobby
Series II Inserted 1:55 Hobby
Production 150 Hobby Sets

1998-99 Stadium Club Chrome

Stadium Club Chrome was a 40-card insert set that was distributed with 20 cards in both Series I and II. Cards reprinted the player's Stadium Club card, but added a chromium finish. These were inserted 1:12 packs in both series and were numbered with an "SCC" prefix. Refractor versions were seeded 1:48 packs.

		MT
Complete Set (40):		150.00
Complete Series 1 (20):		60.00
Complete Series 2 (20):		90.00
Common Player:		2.00
Inserted 1:12 Series 1/2		
Refractors:		2x
Inserted 1:48 Series 1/2		
1	Alonzo Mourning	2.00
2	Scottie Pippen	5.00
3	Patrick Ewing	2.00
4	Vin Baker	2.00
5	Glenn Robinson	2.00
6	Kobe Bryant	20.00
7	Charles Barkley	3.00
8	Chris Mullin	2.00
9	Steve Smith	2.00
10	Stephon Marbury	10.00
11	Zydrunas Ilgauskas	2.00
12	Jayson Williams	2.00
13	Juwan Howard	2.00
14	Grant Hill	15.00
15	Damon Stoudamire	3.00
16	Ron Mercer	5.00
17	Tim Duncan	15.00
18	Michael Finley	2.00
19	Glen Rice	2.00
20	Karl Malone	3.00
21	Eddie Jones	3.00
22	Dikembe Mutombo	2.00
23	Keith Van Horn	6.00
24	Jason Kidd	5.00
25	Shaquille O'Neal	10.00
26	Kevin Garnett	15.00
27	Allen Iverson	10.00
28	Shawn Kemp	2.50
29	Gary Payton	3.00
30	Shareef Abdur-Rahim	5.00
31	Mike Bibby	10.00
32	Raef LaFrentz	6.00
33	Jason Williams	15.00
34	Paul Pierce	15.00
35	Michael Doleac	3.00
36	Michael Dickerson	5.00
37	Bryce Drew	2.00
38	Roshown McLeod	2.00
39	Felipe Lopez	3.00
40	Al Harrington	3.00

Post-1980 cards in Near Mint condition will generally sell for about 75% of the quoted Mint value. Excellent-condition cards bring no more than 40%.

1998-99 Stadium Club Chrome Refractor

	MT
Complete Set (40):	300.00
Refractors:	2x
Inserted 1:48 Series 1/2	

1998-99 Stadium Club Co-Signers

Co-Signers was a 24-card insert set that ran through both Series I and II, with 12 cards in each. Cards featured two players on the front, split by a white strip that included the insert name. Both players autographed the card on their respective half. These were numbered with a "CO" prefix and inserted 1:209 Series I hobby packs and 1:290 Series II hobby packs.

		MT
Common Player:		80.00
Inserted 1:209 Series 1 Hobby		
Inserted 1:290 Series 2 Hobby		
1	Tim Duncan, Kobe Bryant	900.00
2	Larry Johnson, Damon Stoudamire	200.00
3	Antoine Walker, Jason Kidd	300.00
4	Gary Payton, Shareef Abdur-Rahim	300.00
5	Kobe Bryant, Larry Johnson	400.00
6	Tim Duncan, Damon Stoudamire	275.00
7	Shareef Abdur-Rahim, Antoine Walker	125.00
8	Gary Payton, Jason Kidd	175.00
9	Damon Stoudamire, Kobe Bryant	225.00
10	Larry Johnson, Tim Duncan	150.00
11	Jason Kidd, Shareef Abdur-Rahim	80.00
12	Antoine Walker, Gary Payton	40.00
13	Tim Duncan, Eddie Jones	125.00
14	Jayson Williams, Vin Baker	100.00
15	Eddie Jones, Jayson Williams	60.00
16	Vin Baker, Tim Duncan	125.00
17	Eddie Jones, Vin Baker	40.00
18	Tim Duncan, Jayson Williams	125.00
19	Antawn Jamison, Michael Olowokandi	100.00
20	Vince Carter, Mike Bibby	250.00
21	Michael Olowokandi, Vince Carter	250.00
22	Mike Bibby, Antawn Jamison	150.00
23	Antawn Jamison, Vince Carter	500.00
24	Mike Bibby, Michael Olowokandi	80.00

1998-99 Stadium Club Never Compromise

Never Compromise was a 20-card insert with 10 cards in both Series I and II. Series I included veterans, while Series II featured rookies. Both were inserted 1:12 packs and numbered with an "NC" prefix.

		MT
Complete Set (20):		80.00
Complete Series 1 (10):		40.00
Complete Series 2 (10):		40.00
Common Series 1 (1-20):		1.00
Inserted 1:12		
Jumbo Cards:		1.5x
Inserted 1:Series 1 Hobby Box		
Jordan and Hill Do Not Exist in Jumbos		
1	Michael Jordan	15.00
2	Kobe Bryant	10.00
3	Vin Baker	2.00
4	Tim Duncan	8.00
5	Eddie Jones	2.00
6	Shawn Kemp	1.50
7	Grant Hill	8.00
8	Antoine Walker	3.00
9	Karl Malone	1.00
10	Scottie Pippen	4.00
11	Michael Olowokandi	5.00
12	Mike Bibby	6.00
13	Raef LaFrentz	4.00
14	Antawn Jamison	5.00
15	Vince Carter	10.00
16	Robert Traylor	4.00
17	Jason Williams	8.00
18	Larry Hughes	4.00
19	Paul Pierce	8.00
20	Felipe Lopez	3.00

1998-99 Stadium Club Never Compromise Jumbos

	MT
Complete Set (8):	80.00
Common Jumbo:	
Inserted 1:Series 1 Hobby Box	

1998-99 Stadium Club Prime Rookies

This 10-card set showcased the top 10 picks in the 1998 NBA Draft and was available through redemption cards inserted 1:16 packs of Series I. Cards were numbered with a "P" prefix and redemptions included the words "Prime Rookie Redemption" and the Draft Pick number over a shadowed image of a basketball player.

		MT
Complete Set (10):		100.00
Common Player:		5.00
Inserted 1:16 Series 1		
1	Michael Olowokandi	5.00
2	Mike Bibby	10.00
3	Raef LaFrentz	8.00
4	Antawn Jamison	20.00
5	Vince Carter	50.00
6	Robert Traylor	5.00
7	Jason Williams	10.00
8	Larry Hughes	15.00
9	Dirk Nowitzki	20.00
10	Paul Pierce	12.00

1998-99 Stadium Club Royal Court

Royal Court was a 15-card insert set that was exclusive to Series II packs. Cards were numbered with an "RC" prefix and inserted 1:16 packs.

		MT
Complete Set (15):		75.00
Common Player:		2.00
Inserted 1:16 Series 2		
1	Gary Payton	2.00
2	Kobe Bryant	15.00
3	Tim Duncan	10.00
4	Scottie Pippen	4.00
5	Allen Iverson	5.00
6	Shaquille O'Neal	5.00
7	Stephon Marbury	5.00
8	Antoine Walker	3.00
9	Michael Jordan	20.00
10	Keith Van Horn	3.00
11	Michael Olowokandi	3.00
12	Mike Bibby	6.00
13	Antawn Jamison	5.00
14	Robert Traylor	3.00
15	Roshown McLeod	2.00

1998-99 Stadium Club Statliners

Statliners was a 20-card insert exclusive to Series I packs. The top of each card in this die-cut set featured a jagged die-cut, with the insert name across the bottom. Cards were numbered with an "S" prefix and inserted 1:8 packs.

		MT
Complete Set (20):		60.00
Common Player:		1.00
Inserted 1:8 Series 1		
1	Karl Malone	2.00
2	Michael Jordan	15.00
3	Antoine Walker	3.00
4	Tim Duncan	8.00
5	Grant Hill	8.00
6	Allen Iverson	5.00
7	Kevin Garnett	8.00
8	Gary Payton	2.00
9	Shareef Abdur-Rahim	3.00
10	Shawn Kemp	1.50
11	Stephon Marbury	5.00
12	Vin Baker	2.00
13	Ray Allen	1.00
14	Glen Rice	1.00
15	Dikembe Mutombo	1.00
16	Shaquille O'Neal	5.00
17	Kobe Bryant	10.00
18	Scottie Pippen	3.00
19	Keith Van Horn	3.00
20	David Robinson	2.00

1998-99 Stadium Club Triumvirate Luminous

Triumvirates was a 48-card insert set that was issued in both series, with 24 cards in each. These cards featured Finest technology and included eight different three-card or player panels that had some common link and fit together with die-cut edges. Series I linked three players from the same team, while Series II linked three players that play that same position. Cards were available in three different versions, with Luminous versions seeded 1:24 packs, Luminescent versions seeded 1:96 packs and Illuminators seeded 1:192 packs. Triumvirates were a hobby exclusive insert in both Series I and II.

		MT
Complete Set (48):		250.00
Complete Series 1 (24):		100.00
Complete Series 2 (24):		150.00
Common Player:		2.00
Inserted 1:24 Series 1/2 Hobby		
Luminescent Cards:		2x
Inserted 1:96 Series 1/2 Hobby		
Illuminator Cards:		3x
Inserted 1:192 Series 1/2 Hobby		
1A	Kenny Anderson	2.00
1B	Antoine Walker	5.00
1C	Ron Mercer	8.00
2A	Kobe Bryant	20.00
2B	Shaquille O'Neal	10.00
2C	Eddie Jones	6.00
3A	Stephon Marbury	10.00
3B	Kevin Garnett	15.00
3C	Tom Gugliotta	4.00
4A	Jayson Williams	2.00
4B	Keith Van Horn	6.00
4C	Kerry Kittles	2.00
4A	Kevin Johnson	2.00
5B	Antonio McDyess	4.00
5C	Jason Kidd	6.00
6A	Avery Johnson	2.00
6B	David Robinson	6.00
6C	Tim Duncan	15.00
7A	Vin Baker	6.00
7B	Gary Payton	6.00

7C	Detlef Schrempf	2.00
8A	John Stockton	4.00
8B	Karl Malone	6.00
8C	Jeff Hornacek	2.00
9A	Shaquille O'Neal	10.00
9B	David Robinson	4.00
9C	Hakeem Olajuwon	5.00
10A	Dikembe Mutombo	2.00
10B	Alonzo Mourning	3.00
10C	Patrick Ewing	3.00
11A	Tim Duncan	15.00
11B	Kevin Garnett	15.00
11C	Shareef Abdur-Rahim	6.00
12A	Shawn Kemp	3.00
12B	Grant Hill	15.00
12C	Antoine Walker	5.00
13A	Kobe Bryant	20.00
13B	Gary Payton	4.00
13C	Stephon Marbury	10.00
14A	Ray Allen	3.00
14B	Allen Iverson	10.00
14C	Anfernee Hardaway	10.00
15A	Antawn Jamison	8.00
15B	Michael Olowokandi	8.00
15C	Raef LaFrentz	6.00
16A	Robert Traylor	6.00
16B	Larry Hughes	6.00
16C	Vince Carter	15.00

1998-99 Stadium Club Wingmen

Wingmen was a 20-card insert exclusive to Series II packs. Cards were numbered with a "W" prefix and inserted 1:8 packs.

		MT
Complete Set (20):		60.00
Common Player:		1.00
Inserted 1:8 Series 2		
1	Kobe Bryant	10.00
2	Tim Duncan	8.00
3	Michael Finley	1.00
4	Kevin Garnett	8.00
5	Shawn Kemp	1.50
6	Grant Hill	8.00
7	Eddie Jones	2.00
8	Tim Thomas	3.00
9	Vin Baker	2.00
10	Antoine Walker	3.00
11	Steve Smith	1.00
12	Glen Rice	1.00
13	Ron Mercer	5.00
14	Allen Iverson	5.00
15	Ray Allen	1.00
16	Glenn Robinson	1.00
17	Kerry Kittles	1.00
18	Vince Carter	10.00
19	Larry Hughes	4.00
20	Paul Pierce	6.00

1999-00 Stadium Club Promos

		MT
Complete Set (6):		5.00
Common Player:		.50
1	Reggie Miller	.75
2	Allan Houston	.75
3	Tim Hardaway	.75
4	Chris Webber	3.00
5	Rasheed Wallace	.75
6	John Stockton	.50

1999-00 Stadium Club

Stadium Club arrived in a single series, 201-card set that consisted of 150 veterans, 16 Transactions, nine USA Women's Basketball Team and 26 NBA Draft Picks and Rookies, which were seeded 1:3 packs. The cards featured full-color, borderless shorts, with the player's name in silver foil at the bottom inside a semi-circle basketball. Stadium Club was paralleled three times - First Day Issue (retail only), One of a Kind (hobby only) and Printing Plates (Home Team Advantage only). Inserts included: 3 X 3, Chrome Previews, Co-Signers, Lone Star Signatures, Never Compromise, Onyx Extreme, Picture Ending and Pieces of Patriotism.

		MT
Complete Set (201):		75.00
Common Player:		.15
Minor Stars:		.30
Common USA (167-175):		1.00
Common Rookie (176-201):		.50
Inserted 1:5		
Pack (6):		2.00
Wax Box (24):		40.00
1	Allen Iverson	2.00
2	Chris Crawford	.15
3	Chris Webber	1.25
4	Antawn Jamison	1.00
5	Karl Malone	.75
6	Sam Cassell	.30
7	Kerry Kittles	.15
8	Tim Thomas	.50
9	Chauncey Billups	.15
10	Shawn Bradley	.15
11	Alan Henderson	.15
12	David Wesley	.15
13	Glenn Robinson	.30
14	Mitch Richmond	.30
15	Luc Longley	.15
16	Shareef Abdur-Rahim	1.00
17	Christian Laettner	.15
18	Anthony Mason	.15
19	Randy Brown	.15
20	Charles Barkley	.75
21	Bob Sura	.15
22	Bobby Jackson	.15
23	Arvydas Sabonis	.15
24	Tracy Murray	.15
25	Matt Harpring	.30
26	Shawn Kemp	.40
27	Travis Best	.15
28	Ruben Patterson	.30
29	Mike Bibby	.75
30	Vlade Divac	.15
31	Tyrone Hill	.15
32	David Robinson	.75
33	Keith Van Horn	.75
34	Alvin Williams	.15
35	Juwan Howard	.30
36	Shaquille O'Neal	1.50
37	Dale Davis	.15
38	Alonzo Mourning	.40
39	Michael Olowokandi	.50
40	Jason Caffey	.15
41	Andrew DeClercq	.15
42	Jud Buechler	.15
43	Toni Kukoc	.50
44	Dikembe Mutombo	.15
45	Steve Nash	.15
46	Eddie Jones	.75
47	Reggie Miller	.30
48	Rick Fox	.15
49	Larry Hughes	.60
50	Tim Duncan	2.50
51	Jerome Williams	.15
52	Rod Strickland	.30
53	Anthony Peeler	.15
54	Greg Ostertag	.15
55	Patrick Ewing	.30
56	Grant Hill	2.50
57	Derrick Coleman	.15
58	Raef LaFrentz	.60
59	Mark Bryant	.15
60	Rik Smits	.15
61	Latrell Sprewell	.50
62	John Starks	.15
63	Brevin Knight	.15
64	Cuttino Mobley	.30
65	Clarence Weatherspoon	.15
66	Marcus Camby	.40
67	Stephon Marbury	1.00
68	Tom Gugliotta	.30
69	Vince Carter	3.00
70	Vladimir Stepania	.15
71	Chris Mullin	.15
72	Tyrone Nesby	.30
73	Kornel David	.15
74	Elden Campbell	.15
75	Lindsey Hunter	.15
76	Chris Childs	.15
77	Ervin Johnson	.15
78	Rasheed Wallace	.30
79	Jeff Hornacek	.15
80	Matt Geiger	.15
81	Antoine Walker	.60
82	Jason Williams	1.50
83	Robert Horry	.15
84	Jaren Jackson	.15
85	Kendall Gill	.15
86	Dan Majerle	.15
87	Bobby Phills	.15
88	Eric Piatkowski	.15
89	Robert Traylor	.30
90	Cory Carr	.15
91	P.J. Brown	.15
92	Terrell Brandon	.30
93	Corliss Williamson	.15
94	Bryant Reeves	.15
95	John Wallace	.15
96	Keith Closs	.15
97	Gary Trent	.15
98	Walter McCarty	.15
99	Wesley Person	.15
100	Chris Mills	.15
101	Glen Rice	.30
102	Predrag Stojakovic	.30
103	Jason Kidd	1.25
104	Dirk Nowitzki	.75
105	Byron Russell	.15
106	Vin Baker	.30
107	Darrell Armstrong	.15
108	Eric Snow	.15
109	Hakeem Olajuwon	.75
110	Tracy McGrady	1.25
111	Kenny Anderson	.30
112	Jalen Rose	.15
113	Greg Anthony	.15
114	Tim Hardaway	.50
115	Doug Christie	.15
116	Allan Houston	.30
117	Kobe Bryant	3.00
118	Kevin Garnett	2.50
119	Vitaly Potapenko	.15
120	Steve Kerr	.15
121	Nick Van Exel	.30
122	Jerry Stackhouse	.40
123	Derek Fisher	.15
124	Donyell Marshall	.15
125	Mark Jackson	.15
126	Ray Allen	.40
127	Avery Johnson	.15
128	Michael Doleac	.30
129	Charles Oakley	.15
130	Gary Payton	.75
131	Theo Ratliff	.15
132	Cedric Ceballos	.15
133	Paul Pierce	1.25
134	Michael Finley	.30
135	Malik Sealy	.15
136	Brian Grant	.15
137	John Stockton	.30
138	Chris Whitney	.15
139	Maurice Taylor	.30
140	Antonio McDyess	.40
141	*Adrian Griffin*	2.00
142	Vernon Maxwell	.15
143	Jamal Mashburn	.30
144	Jayson Williams	.15
145	Joe Smith	.15
146	Cliff Robinson	.15
147	Mario Elie	.15
148	Damon Stoudamire	.40
149	Felipe Lopez	.30
150	Rex Chapman	.15
151	Transactions (Antonio Davis)	.15
152	Transactions (Mookie Blaylock)	.15
153	Transactions (Ron Mercer)	.40
154	Transactions (Horace Grant)	.15
155	Transactions (Steve Smith)	.15
156	Transactions (Isaiah Rider)	.15
157	Transactions (Tariq Abdul-Wahad)	.15
158	Transactions (Michael Dickerson)	.15
159	Transactions (Nick Anderson)	.15
160	Transactions (Jim Jackson)	.15
161	Transactions (Hersey Hawkins)	.15
162	Transactions (Brent Barry)	.15
163	Transactions (Shandon Anderson)	.15
164	Transactions (Scottie Pippen)	.60
165	Transactions (Isaac Austin)	.15
166	Transactions (Anfernee Hardaway)	.75
167	(Natalie Williams (USA))	2.00
168	(Teresa Edwards (USA))	1.00
169	Yolanda Griffith (USA)	2.00
170	(Nikki McCray (USA))	2.00
171	(Katie Smith (USA))	1.00
172	(Chamique Holdsclaw (USA))	5.00
173	(Dawn Staley (USA))	2.00
174	(Ruthie Bolton-Holifield (USA))	2.50
175	(Lisa Leslie (USA))	3.00
176	*Elton Brand*	8.00
177	*Steve Francis*	8.00
178	*Baron Davis*	4.00
179	*Lamar Odom*	8.00
180	*Jonathan Bender*	3.00
181	*Wally Szczerbiak*	4.00
182	*Richard Hamilton*	4.00
183	*Andre Miller*	5.00
184	*Shawn Marion*	6.00
185	*Jason Terry*	3.00
186	*Trajan Langdon*	2.00
187	*Aleksandar Radojevic*	.50
188	*Corey Maggette*	3.00
189	*William Avery*	3.00
190	*DeMarco Johnson*	.50
191	*Ron Artest*	3.00
192	*Cal Bowdler*	.50
193	*James Posey*	2.50
194	*Quincy Lewis*	2.00
195	*Scott Padgett*	1.00
196	*Jeff Foster*	.50
197	*Kenny Thomas*	1.00
198	*Devean George*	1.50
199	*Tim James*	.75
200	*Vonteego Cummings*	1.25
201	*Jumanie Jones*	.75

1999-00 Stadium Club First Day Issue

This 201-card parallel set reprinted every Stadium Club Card, but included a First Day Issue logo above the Stadium Club logo on the front. Cards were sequentially numbered to 150 sets on the back and inserted 1:26 retail packs.

	MT
Common Player:	4.00
First Day Cards:	15x-30x
First Day Rookies:	4x-8x
Production 150 Sets	
Inserted 1:26 Retail	

1999-00 Stadium Club One of A Kind

This 201-card parallel set reprinted every card in Stadium Club, but the cards were printed on an acetate card with a One of a Kind logo underneath the Stadium Club logo. One of a Kind parallels were inserted 1:22 hobby packs (1:9 HTA) and sequentially numbered to 150 sets.

	MT
Common Player:	4.00
One of a Kind Cards:	15x-30x
One of a Kind Rookies:	4x-8x
Production 150 Sets	
Inserted 1:22 Hobby	

1999-00 Stadium Club TSC Chrome

This 20-card insert set previewed cards from Stadium Club Chrome and was inserted 1:24 packs (1:12 HTA). The cards used the same photo as regular-issue Stadium Club cards, but they were printed on chromium cards. These inserts had the word "Chrome" below the Stadium Club logo and were numbered with an "SCC" prefix. Refractor versions of each card also existed and were inserted 1:120 packs (1:60 HTA).

		MT
Complete Set (20):		75.00
Common Player:		1.00
Inserted 1:24		
Refractors:		2x
Inserted 1:120		
Jumbos:		1x
Inserted 1:box		
Jumbo Refractors:		2x
Inserted 1:12 boxes		
SCC1	Kevin Garnett	8.00
SCC2	Grant Hill	8.00
SCC3	Vince Carter	10.00
SCC4	Allen Iverson	6.00
SCC5	Shareef Abdur-Rahim	3.00
SCC6	Stephon Marbury	3.00
SCC7	Kobe Bryant	10.00
SCC8	Keith Van Horn	2.00
SCC9	Tim Duncan	8.00
SCC10	Shaquille O'Neal	5.00
SCC11	Jason Williams	5.00
SCC12	Scottie Pippen	3.00
SCC13	Gary Payton	1.00
SCC14	Karl Malone	1.00
SCC15	Elton Brand	6.00
SCC16	Steve Francis	8.00
SCC17	Baron Davis	3.00
SCC18	Lamar Odom	8.00
SCC19	Ron Artest	2.00
SCC20	Corey Maggette	4.00

1999-00 Stadium Club Co-Signers

This 26-card insert featured autographs from 13 different players matched up on dual-autographed cards. The cards were numbered with a "CS" prefix and inserted at overall odds of 1:254 hobby packs (1:102 HTA). There were four different groups of Co-Signers - Group A was inserted 1:3,294 packs (1:1332 HTA), Group B was inserted 1:2,202 packs (1:882 HTA), Group C was inserted 1:733 packs (1:294 HTA) and Group D was inserted 1:550 packs (1:220 HTA).

		MT
Common Player:		10.00
Overall Inserted 1:254 Hobby		
CS1-8 Inserted 1:3,294		
CS9-14 Inserted 1:2,202		
CS15-20 Inserted 1:733		
CS21-26 Inserted 1:550		
CS1	Tim Duncan, Tracy McGrady	200.00
CS2	Tim Duncan, Marcus Camby	125.00
CS3	Tim Duncan, Elton Brand	250.00
CS4	Tim Duncan, Steve Francis	300.00
CS5	Tim Duncan, Shawn Marion	150.00
CS6	Tim Duncan, Jonathan Bender	200.00
CS7	Tim Duncan, Wally Szczerbiak	200.00
CS8	Tim Duncan, Corey Maggette	200.00
CS9	Tracy McGrady, Steve Francis	200.00
CS10	Corey Maggette, Shawn Marion	100.00
CS11	Gary Payton, Marcus Camby	60.00
CS12	Elton Brand, Shareef Abdur-Rahim	150.00
CS13	Paul Pierce, Jonathan Bender	100.00
CS14	Tom Gugliotta, Wally Szczerbiak	60.00
CS15	Tracy McGrady, Corey Maggette	100.00
CS16	Steve Francis, Shawn Marion	125.00
CS17	Gary Payton, Jonathan Bender	60.00
CS18	Paul Pierce, Marcus Camby	50.00
CS19	Elton Brand, Tom Gugliotta	60.00
CS20	Wally Szczerbiak, Shareef Abdur-Rahim	75.00
CS21	Tracy McGrady, Shawn Marion	60.00
CS22	Steve Francis, Corey Maggette	150.00
CS23	Gary Payton, Paul Pierce	50.00
CS24	Jonathan Bender, Marcus Camby	50.00
CS25	Elton Brand, Wally Szczerbiak	125.00
CS26	Tom Gugliotta, Shareef Abdur-Rahim	40.00

1999-00 Stadium Club Lone Star Signatures

This 13-card insert set has all the players from Co-Signers, but Lone Star Signatures feature a single player with a single autograph. These inserts are numbered with an "LS" prefix and inserted 1:389 packs (1:156 HTA). There are six different groups of these autographs - LS1 was inserted 1:28,620 packs (1:12,578 HTA), LS2-5 were inserted 1:4,871 packs (1:1956 HTA), LS6-7 were inserted 1:7,269 packs (1:1:2,981 HTA), LS8-10 were inserted 1:1,024 packs (1:1:409 HTA), LS11-12 were inserted 1:1,215 (1:485 HTA) and LS13 was seeded 1:2,544 packs (1:1,010 HTA).

		MT
Common Player:		25.00
Overall Inserted 1:389		
LS1 Inserted 1:28,620		
LS2-5 Inserted 1:4871		
LS6-7 Inserted 1:7269		
LS8-10 Inserted 1:1024		
LS11-12 Inserted 1:1215		
LS13 Inserted 1:2544		
LS1	Tim Duncan	300.00
LS2	Shawn Marion	50.00
LS3	Jonathan Bender	75.00
LS4	Wally Szczerbiak	75.00
LS5	Corey Maggette	75.00
LS6	Gary Payton	75.00
LS7	Tom Gugliotta	25.00
LS8	Steve Francis	100.00
LS9	Elton Brand	75.00
LS10	Tracy McGrady	40.00
LS11	Paul Pierce	30.00
LS12	Shareef Abdur-Rahim	30.00
LS13	Marcus Camby	25.00

1999-00 Stadium Club Never Compromise

This 30-card insert set featured three groups of 10 players - Rookies, Stars and Legends. The cards were numbered with an "NC" prefix and inserted 1:12 packs. Parallel versions of each Never Compromise insert were also available. They were horizontal, included a duplicated piece of film, were sequentially numbered to 100 and available in hobby packs only.

		MT
Complete Set (30):		70.00
Common Player:		.50
Inserted 1:12		
NC1	Elton Brand	5.00
NC2	Steve Francis	8.00
NC3	Baron Davis	3.00
NC4	Lamar Odom	8.00
NC5	Jonathan Bender	4.00
NC6	Wally Szczerbiak	3.00
NC7	Richard Hamilton	2.00
NC8	Andre Miller	2.00
NC9	Corey Maggette	4.00
NC10	Jason Terry	1.00
NC11	Kevin Garnett	5.00
NC12	Grant Hill	5.00
NC13	Vince Carter	6.00
NC14	Allen Iverson	4.00
NC15	Shareef Abdur-Rahim	2.00
NC16	Stephon Marbury	2.00
NC17	Kobe Bryant	6.00
NC18	Keith Van Horn	1.50
NC19	Tim Duncan	5.00
NC20	Shaquille O'Neal	3.00
NC21	Karl Malone	1.00
NC22	Scottie Pippen	2.00
NC23	David Robinson	1.00
NC24	John Stockton	.50
NC25	Charles Barkley	1.00
NC26	Gary Payton	1.00
NC27	Shawn Kemp	.75
NC28	Alonzo Mourning	.75
NC29	Reggie Miller	.50
NC30	Mitch Richmond	.50

1999-00 Stadium Club Never Compromise Game View

This 30-card insert set paralleled the Never Compromise insert, but in a horizontal format, with the base insert card pictured on the left and a duplicate photo slide embedded in the card, which was viewable from both sides. Game View cards were numbered with an "NCG" prefix, sequentially numbered to 100 sets and inserted into hobby packs only.

		MT
Complete Set (30):		5.00
Common Player:		5.00
1	Elton Brand	50.00
2	Steve Francis	80.00
3	Baron Davis	30.00
4	Lamar Odom	80.00
5	Jonathan Bender	40.00
6	Wally Szczerbiak	30.00
7	Richard Hamilton	20.00
8	Andre Miller	20.00
9	Corey Maggette	40.00
10	Jason Terry	10.00
11	Kevin Garnett	50.00
12	Grant Hill	50.00
13	Vince Carter	60.00
14	Allen Iverson	30.00
15	Shareef Abdur-Rahim	20.00
16	Stephon Marbury	20.00
17	Kobe Bryant	60.00
18	Keith Van Horn	12.00
19	Tim Duncan	50.00
20	Shaquille O'Neal	30.00
21	Karl Malone	10.00
22	Scottie Pippen	20.00
23	David Robinson	10.00
24	John Stockton	5.00
25	Charles Barkley	10.00
26	Gary Payton	10.00
27	Shawn Kemp	8.00
28	Alonzo Mourning	7.50
29	Reggie Miller	5.00
30	Mitch Richmond	5.00

1999-00 Stadium Club Onyx Extreme

This 10-card insert pictured players on black bordered cards (except the right side). The word "Onyx" was across the top in silver and black foil, while "Extreme" ran across the bottom. Onyx Extreme cards were numbered with an "OE" prefix and seeded 1:8 packs (1:6 HTA). Die-cut versions also exist and were inserted 1:40 packs (1:30 HTA).

		MT
Complete Set (10):		10.00
Common Player:		.50
Inserted 1:8		
Die-cuts:		2x
Inserted 1:40		
OE1	Antonio McDyess	.50
OE2	Antoine Walker	.60
OE3	Jason Williams	2.50
OE4	Chris Webber	1.50
OE5	David Robinson	.75
OE6	Wally Szczerbiak	2.00
OE7	Jason Kidd	1.50
OE8	Shawn Kemp	.40
OE9	Aleksandar Radojevic	.50
OE10	Tim Duncan	4.00

1999-00 Stadium Club Onyx Extreme Die-cuts Parallel

This 10-card insert paralleled Onyx Extreme, but the top and the bottom of the card were die-cut in a jagged fashion. Die-cut versions were inserted 1:40 packs (1:30 HTA).

	MT
Complete Set (10):	10.00
Common Player:	.50
Inserted 1:8	
Die-cuts:	2x
Inserted 1:40	

1999-00 Stadium Club Picture Ending

Picture Ending was a 10-card insert that featured an action shot of a player surrounded by a blue border on all sides except the right. Cards were numbered with a "PE" prefix and inserted 1:12 packs (1:6 HTA).

		MT
Complete Set (10):		5.00
Common Player:		.25
Insered 1:12		
PE1	Allan Houston	.50
PE2	John Stockton	.50
PE3	Sean Elliott	.25
PE4	Latrell Sprewell	1.00
PE5	Darrell Armstrong	.50
PE6	Marcus Camby	1.00
PE7	Keith Van Horn	1.50
PE8	Antoine Walker	1.00
PE9	Larry Johnson	.50
PE10	Avery Johnson	.25

1999-00 Stadium Club Pieces of Patriotism

This nine-card insert set featured game-used swatches from players that participated for the US in the Qualifying Tournament of the Americas for the 2000 Summer Olympics. The cards are numbered with a "P" prefix and inserted 1:147 hobby packs (1:59 HTA).

		MT
Complete Set (9):		600.00
Common Player:		40.00
Inserted 1:147		
P1	Allan Houston	40.00
P2	Kevin Garnett	150.00
P3	Gary Payton	75.00
P4	Steve Smith	40.00
P5	Tim Hardaway	60.00
P6	Tim Duncan	150.00
P7	Jason Kidd	125.00
P8	Tom Gugliotta	40.00
P9	Vin Baker	40.00

1999-00 Stadium Club 3 x 3

This 30-card insert featured 10 groups of three players on plastic, die-cut cards. The cards fit together to form groups of three and are numbered with an A, B and C prefix. Luminous versions were inserted 1:27 packs (1:14 HTA), Luminescent versions were inserted 1:108 packs (1:54 HTA) and Illuminators were inserted 1:216 packs (1:108 HTA). The cards were labeled with one of three degrees of rarity on the back by the card number.

		MT
Complete Set (30):		175.00
Common Player:		1.00
Inserted 1:27		
Luminescent Cards:		2x
Inserted 1:108		
Illuminator Cards:		4x
Inserted 1:216		
1A	Vince Carter	20.00
1B	Shareef Abdur-Rahim	5.00
1C	Grant Hill	15.00
2A	Allen Iverson	10.00
2B	Stephon Marbury	5.00
2C	Jason Williams	10.00
3A	Kevin Garnett	15.00
3B	Antoine Walker	2.00
3C	Scottie Pippen	6.00
4A	Kobe Bryant	20.00
4B	Eddie Jones	4.00
4C	Michael Finley	2.00
5A	Tim Duncan	15.00
5B	Keith Van Horn	3.00
5C	Antonio McDyess	3.00
6A	Shaquille O'Neal	10.00
6B	Alonzo Mourning	3.00
6C	Dikembe Mutombo	1.00
7A	Karl Malone	4.00
7B	Chris Webber	6.00
7C	Shawn Kemp	2.00
8A	John Stockton	2.00
8B	Gary Payton	4.00
8C	Jason Kidd	6.00
9A	Elton Brand	8.00
9B	Lamar Odom	15.00
9C	Wally Szczerbiak	6.00
10A	Steve Francis	12.00
10B	Baron Davis	5.00
10C	Jason Terry	2.00

1999-00 Stadium Club Chrome

This 150-card set utilized the Stadium Club design and added Topps chromium technology. The set included 19 rookies, which were unseeded. The base set arrived in three parallel versions, including Refractors, First Day Issue and First Day Issue Refractors. Inserts included: Visionaries, True Colors, Clear Shots and Eyes of the Game. All four inserts were also available in Refractor versions.

		MT
Complete Set (150):		80.00
Common Player:		.20
Minor Stars:		.40
Common Rookie (132-150):		.75
Pack (4):		3.00
Wax Box (24):		50.00
1	Allen Iverson	2.50
2	Chris Webber	1.50
3	Antawn Jamison	1.00
4	Karl Malone	.75
5	Sam Cassell	.40
6	Kerry Kittles	.20
7	Tim Thomas	.50
8	Shawn Bradley	.20
9	David Wesley	.20
10	Glenn Robinson	.40
11	Mitch Richmond	.40
12	Shareef Abdur-Rahim	1.00
13	Christian Laettner	.20
14	Anthony Mason	.20
15	Randy Brown	.20
16	Charles Barkley	.75
17	Bobby Jackson	.20
18	Matt Harpring	.40
19	Shawn Kemp	.40
20	Ruben Patterson	.40
21	Mike Bibby	.60
22	Vlade Divac	.20
23	David Robinson	.75
24	Keith Van Horn	.75
25	Juwan Howard	.40
26	Shaquille O'Neal	2.00
27	Alonzo Mourning	.50
28	Michael Olowokandi	.40
29	Andrew DeClercq	.20
30	Toni Kukoc	.60
31	Dikembe Mutombo	.40
32	Steve Nash	.20
33	Eddie Jones	.75
34	Reggie Miller	.40
35	Larry Hughes	1.25
36	Tim Duncan	2.50
37	Jerome Williams	.20
38	Rod Strickland	.40
39	Patrick Ewing	.40
40	Grant Hill	2.50
41	Derrick Coleman	.40
42	Raef LaFrentz	.50
43	Rik Smits	.20
44	Latrell Sprewell	.75
45	John Starks	.20
46	Cuttino Mobley	.40
47	Marcus Camby	.40
48	Stephon Marbury	1.00
49	Tom Gugliotta	.20
50	Vince Carter	4.00
51	Chris Mullin	.20
52	Tyrone Nesby	.20
53	Elden Campbell	.20
54	Lindsey Hunter	.20
55	Rasheed Wallace	.40
56	Jeff Hornacek	.20
57	Matt Geiger	.20
58	Antoine Walker	.60
59	Jason Williams	1.50
60	Robert Horry	.20
61	Kendall Gill	.20
62	Dan Majerle	.20
63	Robert Traylor	.40
64	P.J. Brown	.20
65	Terrell Brandon	.40
66	Corliss Williamson	.20
67	Bryant Reeves	.20
68	Larry Johnson	.40
69	Keith Closs	.20
70	Walter McCarty	.20
71	Wesley Person	.20
72	Chris Mills	.20
73	Glen Rice	.40
74	Jason Kidd	1.50
75	Dirk Nowitzki	.75
76	Bryon Russell	.20
77	Vin Baker	.40
78	Darrell Armstrong	.20
79	Eric Snow	.20
80	Hakeem Olajuwon	.75
81	Tracy McGrady	1.50
82	Kenny Anderson	.40
83	Jalen Rose	.40
84	Tim Hardaway	.60
85	Doug Christie	.20
86	Allan Houston	.40
87	Kobe Bryant	3.00
88	Kevin Garnett	2.50
89	Steve Kerr	.20
90	Nick Van Exel	.40
91	Jerry Stackhouse	.40
92	Derek Fisher	.20
93	Donyell Marshall	.20
94	Mark Jackson	.20
95	Ray Allen	.50
96	Avery Johnson	.20
97	Michael Doleac	.20
98	Charles Oakley	.20
99	Gary Payton	.75
100	Theo Ratliff	.20
101	Cedric Ceballos	.20
102	Paul Pierce	1.25
103	Michael Finley	.40
104	Brian Grant	.20
105	John Stockton	.40
106	Maurice Taylor	.20
107	Antonio McDyess	.50
108	*Adrian Griffin*	1.50
109	Jamal Mashburn	.40
110	Jayson Williams	.20
111	Joe Smith	.20
112	Clifford Robinson	.20
113	Mario Elie	.20
114	Damon Stoudamire	.40
115	Felipe Lopez	.40
116	Antonio Davis	.20
117	Mookie Blaylock	.20
118	Ron Mercer	.75
119	Horace Grant	.20
120	Steve Smith	.40
121	Isaiah Rider	.40
122	Tariq Abdul-Wahad	.20
123	Michael Dickerson	.40
124	Nick Anderson	.20
125	Jim Jackson	.20
126	Hersey Hawkins	.20
127	Brent Barry	.20
128	Shandon Anderson	.20
129	Scottie Pippen	1.50
130	Isaac Austin	.20
131	Anfernee Hardaway	1.50
132	*Elton Brand*	6.00
133	*Steve Francis*	15.00
134	*Baron Davis*	5.00
135	*Lamar Odom*	10.00
136	*Jonathan Bender*	6.00
137	*Wally Szczerbiak*	4.00
138	*Richard Hamilton*	4.00
139	*Andre Miller*	5.00
140	*Shawn Marion*	6.00
141	*Jason Terry*	3.00
142	*Trajan Langdon*	2.50
143	*Aleksandar Radojevic*	.75
144	*Corey Maggette*	5.00
145	*William Avery*	2.00
146	*Ron Artest*	3.00
147	*Cal Bowdler*	.75
148	*James Posey*	2.00
149	*Quincy Lewis*	1.50
150	*Scott Padgett*	1.00

1999-00 Stadium Club Chrome First Day Issue

All 150 cards in Stadium Club Chrome were reprinted in a First Day Issue parallel set. Cards were distinguished by a "First Day Issue" stamp above the Stadium Club logo on the front and were sequentially numbered to 100 on the back. These parallel cards were seeded 1:47 packs.

	MT
First Day Issue:	15x-30x
Rookie FDI:	5x-10x
Inserted 1:47	
Production 100 Sets	

1999-00 Stadium Club Chrome First Day Issue Refractors

All 150 cards from Stadium Club Chrome were reprinted in this parallel set. Cards contain First Day Issue stamp above the Stadium Club Chrome logo and are numbered to 25 sets and feature a Refractor finish. First Day Issue Refractors were inserted 1:186 packs.

	MT
FDI Refractors:	50x-100x
FDI Rookies:	10x-20x
Inserted 1:186	
Production 25 Sets	

1999-00 Stadium Club Chrome Refractors

All 150 cards in Stadium Club Chrome were reprinted with the Refractor finish applied to the front. The word "Refractor" also appears in the number circle on the card back. These were inserted 1:12 packs.

	MT
Refractors:	5x-10x
Rookie Refractors:	3x-6x
Inserted 1:12	

1999-00 Stadium Club Chrome Clear Shots

This 10-card insert set was seeded 1:16 packs, with Refractor versions seeded 1:80 packs. Clear Shots featured 10 top rookies on a clear design with the insert name stamped all over the background. Cards showed the front view from the front, but also featured a rear view of the player on the back of the card. These were numbered with a "CS" prefix.

		MT
Complete Set (10):		20.00
Common Player:		1.00
Inserted 1:16		
Refractors:		2x
Inserted 1:80		
CS1	Lamar Odom	5.00
CS2	Elton Brand	6.00
CS3	Steve Francis	8.00
CS4	Shawn Marion	2.00
CS5	Wally Szczerbiak	3.00
CS6	Richard Hamilton	1.50
CS7	Andre Miller	2.00
CS8	Jason Terry	1.00
CS9	Baron Davis	2.00
CS10	Jonathan Bender	3.00

1999-00 Stadium Club Chrome Eyes of the Game

Eyes of the Game was a 10-card insert set featuring an action shot of the player in the foreground and a close-up shot in the background. These inserts were printed on plastic, were numberd with an "EG" prefix and inserted 1:24 packs. Refractor versions were also available and seeded 1:120 packs.

		MT
Complete Set (10):		30.00
Common Player:		1.00
Inserted 1:24		
Refractors:		2x
Inserted 1:120		
EG1	Jason Kidd	3.00
EG2	Jason Williams	3.00
EG3	Gary Payton	1.50
EG4	Kevin Garnett	8.00
EG5	Vince Carter	12.00
EG6	Kobe Bryant	10.00
EG7	Stephon Marbury	2.00
EG8	Allen Iverson	6.00
EG9	Alonzo Mourning	1.00
EG10	John Stockton	1.00

1999-00 Stadium Club Chrome True Colors

This 10-card insert was numbered with a "TC" prefix. Regular versions were seeded 1:8 packs, while Refractors were seeded 1:40 packs.

		MT
Complete Set (10):		12.00
Common Player:		.50
Inserted 1:8		
Refractors:		2x
Inserted 1:40		
TC1	Gary Payton	.75
TC2	Stephon Marbury	1.00
TC3	Karl Malone	.75
TC4	Kevin Garnett	3.00
TC5	Allen Iverson	2.50
TC6	Vince Carter	5.00
TC7	Grant Hill	3.00
TC8	Shaquille O'Neal	2.00
TC9	Reggie Miller	.50
TC10	Tim Duncan	3.00

1999-00 Stadium Club Chrome Visionaries

This 10-card insert set featured players with less than three years of experience. Visionaries were numbered with a "V" prefix and inserted 1:32 packs, while Refractor versions were seeded 1:160 packs.

		MT
Complete Set (10):		35.00
Common Player:		2.00
Inserted 1:32		
Refractors:		2x
Inserted 1:160		
V1	Vince Carter	12.00
V2	Tim Duncan	8.00
V3	Jason Williams	3.00
V4	Lamar Odom	5.00
V5	Steve Francis	8.00
V6	Paul Pierce	2.00
V7	Tracy McGrady	3.00
V8	Elton Brand	6.00
V9	Shawn Marion	2.00
V10	Antawn Jamison	2.00

2000-01 Stadium Club Promos

This six-card set was shipped to hobby dealers and members of the media to promote the upcoming Stadium Club release. Cards were numbered with a "PP" prefix and cello wrapped.

		MT
Complete Set (6):		5.00
Common Player:		.50
1	Shaquille O'Neal	3.00
2	Latrell Sprewell	1.50
3	Ray Allen	1.00
4	Clifford Robinson	.50
5	Corey Maggette	1.00
6	John Stockton	.75

2000-01 Stadium Club

		MT
Complete Set (175):		70.00
Common Player:		.10
Minor Stars:		.20
Common Rookie:		.75
Inserted 1:4		
Pack (7):		2.50
Box (24):		50.00
1	Baron Davis	.40
2	Adrian Griffin	.10
3	Dikembe Mutombo	.10
4	Andre Miller	.40
5	Kenny Anderson	.20
6	Keon Clark	.10
7	Larry Hughes	.60
8	Ruben Patterson	.10
9	Shandon Anderson	.10
10	Reggie Miller	.20
11	Lamar Odom	1.00
12	John Stockton	.20
13	Rod Strickland	.20
14	Michael Dickerson	.10
15	Quincy Lewis	.10
16	Vin Baker	.20
17	Vince Carter	3.00
18	Avery Johnson	.10
19	Michael Finley	.20
20	Eric Snow	.10
21	Kevin Garnett	2.00
22	Rodney Rogers	.10
23	Bonzi Wells	.40
24	Jason Kidd	1.00
25	Toni Kukoc	.30
26	Darrell Armstrong	.10
27	Larry Johnson	.10
28	Kendall Gill	.10
29	Wally Szczerbiak	.30
30	Tim Thomas	.30
31	Dan Majerle	.10
32	Karl Malone	.50
33	Juwan Howard	.20
34	Kobe Bryant	2.50
35	Bryant Reeves	.10
36	Cuttino Mobley	.30
37	Mookie Blaylock	.10
38	Jerome Williams	.10
39	James Posey	.10
40	Shawn Bradley	.10
41	Tim Hardaway	.30
42	Theo Ratliff	.10
43	Damon Stoudamire	.20
44	Derrick Coleman	.20
45	Ron Artest	.30
46	Antoine Walker	.30
47	Jason Terry	.30
48	Antonio McDyess	.40
49	Jonathan Bender	.60
50	Shaquille O'Neal	1.50

51	Anthony Carter	.10
52	Ray Allen	.30
53	Joe Smith	.10
54	Marcus Camby	.30
55	Keith Van Horn	.40
56	Charlie Ward	.10
57	John Amaechi	.10
58	Tom Gugliotta	.10
59	Allan Houston	.30
60	Anfernee Hardaway	1.00
61	Scottie Pippen	1.00
62	Jason Williams	.50
63	Steve Smith	.20
64	David Robinson	.50
65	Gary Payton	.50
66	Robert Horry	.10
67	Greg Ostertag	.10
68	Mike Bibby	.20
69	Tim Duncan	1.50
70	Richard Hamilton	.30
71	Bryon Russell	.10
72	Charles Oakley	.10
73	Rashard Lewis	.50
74	Chris Webber	1.50
75	Arvydas Sabonis	.10
76	Allen Iverson	2.00
77	Bo Outlaw	.10
78	Elden Campbell	.10
79	Dirk Nowitzki	.60
80	Elton Brand	1.00
81	Brevin Knight	.10
82	David Wesley	.10
83	Raef LaFrentz	.10
84	Antawn Jamison	.75
85	Hakeem Olajuwon	.50
86	Jamie Feick	.10
87	Jalen Rose	.30
88	Michael Olowokandi	.10
89	Rick Fox	.10
90	Austin Croshere	.10
91	Glenn Robinson	.20
92	Stephon Marbury	.60
93	Clifford Robinson	.10
94	Derek Fisher	.10
95	Vlade Divac	.10
96	Jim Jackson	.10
97	Paul Pierce	.50
98	Corey Benjamin	.10
99	Lamond Murray	.10
100	Steve Francis	2.00
101	Mitch Richmond	.20
102	Othella Harrington	.10
103	Nick Anderson	.10
104	Antonio Davis	.10
105	Ervin Johnson	.10
106	Rasheed Wallace	.40
107	Shawn Marion	.75
108	Latrell Sprewell	.75
109	Terrell Brandon	.20
110	Sam Cassell	.20
111	Shareef Abdur-Rahim	.50
112	Travis Best	.10
113	Tyrone Nesby	.10
114	Alan Henderson	.10
115	Vonteego Cummings	.10
116	Kelvin Cato	.10
117	Jerry Stackhouse	.20
118	Nick Van Exel	.20
119	Corliss Williamson	.10
120	Doug Christie	.10
121	Horace Grant	.10
122	Glen Rice	.20
123	Patrick Ewing	.20
124	Dale Davis	.10
125	Brian Grant	.10
126	Shawn Kemp	.25
127	Cedric Ceballos	.10
128	Christian Laettner	.10
129	Lindsey Hunter	.10
130	Donyell Marshall	.10
131	Robert Pack	.10
132	Danny Fortson	.10
133	Howard Eisley	.10
134	Andrew DeClercq	.10
135	Mark Jackson	.10
136	Grant Hill	1.50
137	Tracy McGrady	1.00
138	Maurice Taylor	.10
139	Derek Anderson	.20
140	Corey Maggette	.20
141	Jermaine O'Neal	.50
142	Ben Wallace	.10
143	Ron Mercer	.30
144	John Starks	.10
145	Erick Strickland	.10
146	Isaiah Rider	.20
147	Eddie Jones	.60
148	Anthony Mason	.10
149	P.J. Brown	.10
150	Jamal Mashburn	.10
151	*Kenyon Martin*	5.00
152	*Stromile Swift*	6.00
153	*Darius Miles*	12.00
154	*Marcus Fizer*	3.00
155	*Mike Miller*	6.00
156	*DerMarr Johnson*	3.00
157	*Chris Mihm*	1.50
158	*Jamal Crawford*	2.50
159	*Joel Przybilla*	1.00
160	*Keyon Dooling*	2.50
161	*Jerome Moiso*	1.50
162	*Etan Thomas*	1.00
163	*Courtney Alexander*	2.50
164	*Mateen Cleaves*	2.00
165	*Jason Collier*	.75
166	*Desmond Mason*	4.00
167	*Quentin Richardson*	4.00
168	*Jamaal Magloire*	1.25
169	*Craig "Speedy" Claxton*	1.00
170	*Morris Peterson*	5.00
171	*Donnell Harvey*	1.00
172	*DeShawn Stevenson*	5.00
173	*Mamadou N'diaye*	.75
174	*Erick Barkley*	1.50
175	*Mark Madsen*	1.25

2000-01 Stadium Club Beam Team

		MT
Complete Set (30):		250.00
Common Player:		3.00
Production 500 Sets		
1	Tim Duncan	20.00
2	Shaquille O'Neal	20.00
3	Kevin Garnett	25.00
4	Vince Carter	40.00
5	Kobe Bryant	35.00
6	Allen Iverson	25.00
7	Steve Francis	25.00
8	Chris Webber	15.00
9	Elton Brand	10.00
10	Larry Hughes	6.00
11	Lamar Odom	10.00
12	Shareef Abdur-Rahim	5.00
13	Jason Kidd	10.00
14	Gary Payton	5.00
15	Antonio McDyess	4.00
16	Jason Williams	5.00
17	Karl Malone	5.00
18	Eddie Jones	6.00
19	Scottie Pippen	10.00
20	Latrell Sprewell	8.00
21	Paul Pierce	5.00
22	Michael Finley	4.00
23	Jerry Stackhouse	3.00
24	Jalen Rose	4.00
25	Antoine Walker	3.00
26	Anfernee Hardaway	10.00
27	Mike Bibby	3.00
28	Kenyon Martin	25.00
29	Stromile Swift	30.00
30	Darius Miles	50.00

2000-01 Stadium Club Capture the Action

		MT
Complete Set (14):		20.00
Common Player:		.75
Inserted 1:8		
Game View Cards:		5x-10x
Production 100 Sets		
1	Shaquille O'Neal	3.00
2	Kobe Bryant	5.00
3	Vince Carter	6.00
4	Kevin Garnett	4.00
5	Allen Iverson	3.00
6	Steve Francis	4.00
7	Tracy McGrady	2.00
8	Tim Duncan	3.00
9	Elton Brand	2.00
10	Lamar Odom	2.00
11	Larry Hughes	1.25
12	Chris Webber	2.50
13	Antonio McDyess	.75
14	Gary Payton	1.00

2000-01 Stadium Club Co-Signers

		MT
Common Player:		25.00
Inserted 1:649 Hobby; 1:252 HTA		
1	Magic Johnson, Shaquille O'Neal	400.00
2	Magic Johnson, Mateen Cleaves	150.00
3	Shaquille O'Neal, Tim Duncan	
4	Tim Duncan, Elton Brand	100.00
5	Elton Brand, Ron Artest	40.00
6	Allen Iverson, Steve Francis	250.00
7	Steve Francis, Mateen Cleaves	50.00
8	Eddie Jones, Latrell Sprewell	125.00
9	Tracy McGrady, Latrell Sprewell	150.00
10	Allen Iverson, Jamal Crawford	100.00
11	Tracy McGrady, Eddie Jones	60.00
12	Ron Artest, Jamal Crawford	25.00

2000-01 Stadium Club Head to Head Jersey Relic

		MT
Common Player:		25.00
Inserted 1:96 HTA		
1	Kenyon Martin, Antoine Walker	50.00
2	Stromile Swift, Darius Miles	125.00
3	Grant Hill, Shareef Abdur-Rahim	60.00
4	Juwan Howard, Keith Van Horn	25.00
5	Keyon Dooling, Jason Kidd	60.00
6	DerMarr Johnson, Paul Pierce	40.00
7	Quentin Richardson, Shawn Marion	50.00
8	Stephon Marbury, Kenny Anderson	25.00
9	Tracy McGrady, Anfernee Hardaway	100.00
10	Jason Terry, Mike Bibby	25.00

2000-01 Stadium Club Lone Star Signatures

		MT
Common Player:		10.00
Inserted 1:237		
RA	Ron Artest	10.00
EB	Elton Brand	25.00
MC	Mateen Cleaves	15.00
JC	Jamal Crawford	20.00
TD	Tim Duncan	125.00
SF	Steve Francis	40.00
AI	Allen Iverson	75.00
MJ	Magic Johnson	150.00
EJ	Eddie Jones	20.00
TM	Tracy McGrady	40.00
SO	Shaquille O'Neal	150.00
LS	Latrell Sprewell	60.00

2000-01 Stadium Club Souvenir Game Jerseys

		MT
Common Player:		8.00
Inserted 1:20		
AH1	Dikembe Mutombo	20.00
AH2	Jason Terry	15.00
AH3	Jim Jackson	15.00
AH4	Alan Henderson	20.00
AH5	Cal Bowdler	8.00
AH6	DerMarr Johnson	20.00
AH7	Chris Crawford	8.00
AH8	Lorenzen Wright	10.00
AH9	Roshown McLeod	10.00
AH10	Dion Glover	10.00
AH11	Anthony Johnson	10.00
AH12	Hanno Mottola	10.00
BC1	Antoine Walker	25.00
BC2	Paul Pierce	35.00
BC3	Kenny Anderson	15.00
BC4	Adrian Griffin	12.00
BC5	Vitaly Potapenko	15.00
BC6	Walter McCarty	10.00
BC7	Tony Battie	12.00
NJ1	Stephon Marbury	25.00
NJ2	Keith Van Horn	20.00
NJ3	Kendall Gill	15.00
NJ4	Evan Eschmeyer	10.00
NJ5	Soumaila Samake	8.00
NJ6	Stephen Jackson	20.00
NJ7	Johnny Newman	8.00
NJ8	Jim McIlvaine	8.00
NJ9	Lucious Harris	8.00
NJ10	Sherman Douglas	12.00
NJ11	Kenyon Martin	40.00
NJ12	Aaron Williams	10.00
OM1	Grant Hill	60.00
OM2	Tracy McGrady	60.00
OM3	Darrell Armstrong	20.00
OM4	Michael Doleac	12.00
OM5	Pat Garrity	12.00
OM6	Dee Brown	10.00
OM7	Bo Outlaw	15.00
OM8	John Amaechi	12.00
OM9	Mike Miller	40.00
OM10	Monty Williams	10.00
OM11	Andrew DeClercq	8.00
OM12	Don Reid	8.00
LC1	Jeff McInnis	10.00
LC2	Michael Olowokandi	12.00
LC3	Tyrone Nesby	8.00
LC4	Derek Strong	8.00
LC5	Corey Maggette	15.00
LC6	Eric Piatkowski	12.00
LC7	Brian Skinner	10.00
LC8	Darius Miles	80.00
LC9	Keyon Dooling	20.00
LC10	Quentin Richardson	25.00
LC11	Sean Rooks	8.00
PS1	Jason Kidd	40.00
PS2	Anfernee Hardaway	50.00
PS3	Tom Gugliotta	15.00
PS4	Shawn Marion	25.00
PS5	Clifford Robinson	15.00
PS6	Rodney Rogers	15.00
PS7	Chris Dudley	8.00
PS8	Rex Chapman	20.00
PS9	Iakovos Tsakalidis	10.00
PS10	Tony Delk	15.00
PS11	Mario Elie	10.00
PS12	Corie Blount	10.00
VG1	Shareef Abdur-Rahim	25.00
VG2	Mike Bibby	15.00
VG3	Michael Dickerson	12.00
VG4	Othella Harrington	12.00
VG5	Bryant Reeves	10.00
VG6	Damon Jones	8.00
VG7	Brent Price	8.00
VG8	Stromile Swift	50.00
VG9	Grant Long	10.00
VG10	Doug West	10.00
VG11	Tony Massenburg	8.00
VG12	Isaac Austin	8.00
WW1	Mitch Richmond	20.00
WW2	Juwan Howard	25.00
WW3	Rod Strickland	20.00
WW4	Richard Hamilton	20.00
WW5	Jahidi White	15.00
WW6	Michael Smith	8.00
WW7	Chris Whitney	12.00
LL1	Shaquille O'Neal	80.00
LL2	Horace Grant	12.00
LL3	Robert Horry	10.00
LL4	Rick Fox	10.00
LL5	Brian Shaw	8.00
LL6	Ron Harper	12.00
LL7	Tyronn Lue	10.00
LL8	Isaiah Rider	15.00
LL9	Greg Foster	8.00
LL10	Mark Madsen	12.00
LL11	Devean George	12.00

2000-01 Stadium Club Striking Distance

		MT
Complete Set (20):		30.00
Common Player:		.60
Inserted 1:8		
1	Reggie Miller	.60
2	Tim Duncan	4.00
3	Allen Iverson	4.00
4	Kevin Garnett	5.00
5	Vince Carter	8.00
6	Kobe Bryant	6.00
7	Shaquille O'Neal	4.00
8	Chris Webber	3.00
9	Elton Brand	2.00
10	Steve Francis	5.00
11	Lamar Odom	2.00
12	Gary Payton	1.00
13	Karl Malone	1.00
14	Latrell Sprewell	1.50
15	Ray Allen	.60
16	Stephon Marbury	1.25
17	Rasheed Wallace	.75
18	Jason Williams	1.00
19	Scottie Pippen	2.00
20	Eddie Jones	1.25

2000-01 Stadium Club Starting Five Jersey Relic

		MT
Common Player:		50.00
Inserted 1:2,234 Hobby		
Inserted 1:858 HTA		
SF-AH	Jason Terry PG, DerMarr Johnson, Jim Jackson, Alan Henderson, Dikembe Mutombo	50.00
SF-BC	Kenny Anderson, Paul Pierce, Adrian Griffin, Antoine Walker, Vitaly Potapenko	100.00
SF-NJN	Stephon Marbury, Kendall Gill, Keith Van Horn, Kenyon Martin, Evan Eschmeyer	125.00
SF-OM	Darrell Armstrong, Tracy McGrady, Grant Hill, Bo Outlaw, John Amaechi	150.00
SF-PS	Jason Kidd, Anfernee Hardaway, Shawn Marion, Tom Gugliotta, Clifford Robinson	150.00
SF-VG	Mike Bibby, Michael Dickerson, Shareef Abdur-Rahim, Stromile Swift, Bryant Reeves	100.00
SF-WW	Rod Strickland, Mitch Richmond, Richard Hamilton, Juwan Howard, Jahidi White	75.00

2000-01 Stadium Club 11 x 14

	MT
Complete Set (12):	
Common Player:	
Ron Artest	10.00
Elton Brand	
Mateen Cleaves	15.00
Jamal Crawford	10.00
Tim Duncan	50.00
Steve Francis	25.00
Larry Hughes	25.00
Allen Iverson	50.00
Magic Johnson	100.00
Tracy McGrady	50.00
Shaquille O'Neal	100.00
Latrell Sprewell	25.00

2001-02 Stadium Club

		MT
Complete Set (134):		150.00
Common Player:		.20
Minor Stars:		.40
Common Rookie (101-133):		2.00
Inserted 1:4		
Pack (6):		3.00
Box (24):		50.00
1	Dikembe Mutombo	.40
2	Clifford Robinson	.20
3	Bonzi Wells	.40
4	Peja Stojakovic	.60
5	Gary Payton	.60
6	Morris Peterson	.50
7	Patrick Ewing	.40
8	Terrell Brandon	.40
9	Tim Thomas	.40
10	Kobe Bryant	3.00
11	Hakeem Olajuwon	.50
12	Marc Jackson	.20
13	Zhizhi Wang	1.00
14	Andre Miller	.50
15	Elton Brand	.75
16	Eddie Robinson	.40
17	Jason Terry	.40
18	Allan Houston	.40
19	Grant Hill	1.00
20	Tim Duncan	1.25
21	Kevin Garnett	2.00
22	Jahidi White	.20
23	Michael Dickerson	.20
24	Karl Malone	.75
25	Chris Webber	1.25
26	Scottie Pippen	.75
27	Latrell Sprewell	.75
28	Keith Van Horn	.40
29	Ray Allen	.60
30	Alonzo Mourning	.40
31	Lamar Odom	.75
32	Jalen Rose	40.00
33	Ben Wallace	.20
34	Shaquille O'Neal	1.50
35	Antonio McDyess	.40
36	Dirk Nowitzki	.75
37	Marcus Fizer	.40
38	Jamal Mashburn	.40
39	Paul Pierce	.60
40	DerMarr Johnson	.40
41	Steve Nash	.40
42	Jerry Stackhouse	.50
43	Larry Hughes	.40
44	Cuttino Mobley	.40
45	Horace Grant	.20
46	Eddie Jones	.40
47	Wally Szczerbiak	.40
48	Marcus Camby	.40
49	Jamal Crawford	.40
50	Vince Carter	3.00
51	Donyell Marshall	.40
52	Shareef Abdur-Rahim	.40
53	Courtney Alexander	.40
54	Kenny Anderson	.40
55	Ron Mercer	.40
56	Lamond Murray	.20
57	Michael Finley	.40
58	Raef LaFrentz	.20
59	Reggie Miller	.50
60	Steve Francis	1.50
61	Rick Fox	.20
62	Tim Hardaway	.40
63	Glenn Robinson	.40
64	LaPhonso Ellis	.20
65	Kenyon Martin	.40
66	Jason Williams	.40
67	Derek Anderson	.40
68	Eric Snow	.20
69	Darius Miles	2.50
70	Antawn Jamison	.75
71	Mateen Cleaves	.40
72	Jason Kidd	1.00
73	Rasheed Wallace	.50
74	Chris Porter	.20
75	Tracy McGrady	1.50
76	Aaron McKie	.40
77	Baron Davis	.60
78	Toni Kukoc	.40
79	Antoine Walker	.50
80	Shawn Marion	.75
81	Mike Miller	1.25
82	Stephon Marbury	.60
83	Glen Rice	.40
84	David Robinson	.50
85	Rashard Lewis	.40
86	John Stockton	.60
87	Stromile Swift	.40
88	Richard Hamilton	.40
89	Desmond Mason	.40
90	Brian Grant	.40
91	Keyon Dooling	.40
92	Jermaine O'Neal	.50
93	Nick Van Exel	.40
94	Tom Gugliotta	.20
95	Elden Campbell	.20
96	Sam Cassell	.40
97	Mike Bibby	.40
98	DeShawn Stevenson	.40
99	Antonio Davis	.20
100	Allen Iverson	2.00
101	*Kwame Brown*	8.00
102	*Tyson Chandler*	8.00
103	*Pau Gasol*	10.00
104	*Eddy Curry*	8.00
105	*Jason Richardson*	12.00
106	*Shane Battier*	12.00
107	*Eddie Griffin*	8.00
108	*DeSagana Diop*	4.00
109	*Rodney White*	5.00
110	*Joe Johnson*	8.00
111	*Kedrick Brown*	4.00
112	*Vladimir Radmanovic*	3.00
113	*Richard Jefferson*	6.00
114	*Troy Murphy*	4.00
115	*Steven Hunter*	3.00
116	*Kirk Haston*	5.00
117	*Michael Bradley*	3.00
118	*Jason Collins*	2.00
119	*Zach Randolph*	6.00
120	*Brendan Haywood*	6.00
121	*Joseph Forte*	5.00
122	*Jeryl Sasser*	2.00
123	*Brandon Armstrong*	3.00
124	*Gerald Wallace*	5.00
125	*Samuel Dalembert*	2.00
126	*Jamaal Tinsley*	10.00
127	*Tony Parker*	8.00
128	*Trenton Hassell*	5.00
129	*Gilbert Arenas*	3.00
130	*Omar Cook*	2.00
131	*Jeff Trepagnier*	2.00
132	*Loren Woods*	4.00
133	*Terence Morris*	2.00
134	*Michael Jordan*	10.00

2001-02 Stadium Club Parallel

	MT
Veterans:	6x-12x
Rookies:	2x-4x

2001-02 Stadium Club Co-Signers

"Too uncommon to price."

		MT
Complete Set (3):		
Common Player:		
CS1	Richard Hamilton, Courtney Alexander	
CS2	Shaquille O'Neal, Kareem Abdul-Jabbar	
CS3	Baron Davis, Jason Terry	

2001-02 Stadium Club Dunkus Colossus

		MT
Complete Set (15):		15.00
Common Player:		.75
Inserted 1:4		
DC1	Baron Davis	1.00
DC2	Vince Carter	5.00
DC3	Tracy McGrady	2.50
DC4	Shawn Marion	1.25
DC5	Kevin Garnett	3.00
DC6	Darius Miles	4.00
DC7	Steve Francis	2.00
DC8	Chris Webber	2.00
DC9	Alonzo Mourning	.75
DC10	Rasheed Wallace	.75
DC11	Tim Duncan	2.00
DC12	Antonio McDyess	.75
DC13	Jerry Stackhouse	1.00
DC14	Jermaine O'Neal	1.00
DC15	Shaquille O'Neal	2.50

2001-02 Stadium Club Lone-Star Signatures

		MT
Common Player:		12.00
Inserted 1:18		
LS-KAJ	Kareem Abdul-Jabbar	100.00
LS-CA	Courtney Alexander	20.00
LS-GA	Gilbert Arenas	15.00
LS-SB	Shane Battier	50.00
LS-EB	Elton Brand	25.00
LS-JF	Joseph Forte	15.00
LS-AH	Al Harrington	20.00
LS-MJ	Marc Jackson	12.00
LS-AJ	Antawn Jamison	25.00
LS-EMJ	Magic Johnson	100.00
LS-SM	Shawn Marion	30.00
LS-TM	Troy Murphy	25.00
LS-SO	Shaquille O'Neal	100.00
LS-KS	Kenny Satterfield	12.00
LS-PS	Peja Stojakovic	50.00
LS-JT	Jason Terry	12.00
LS-IT	Iakovos Tsakalidis	12.00
LS-HT	Hidayet Turkoglu	25.00

2001-02 Stadium Club Maximus Rejectus

		MT
Complete Set (10):		10.00
Common Player:		.60
Inserted 1:8		
M1	Chris Webber	2.00
M2	Shaquille O'Neal	2.50
M3	Tim Duncan	2.00
M4	Kevin Garnett	3.00
M5	Darius Miles	4.00
M6	Theo Ratliff	.60
M7	Dikembe Mutombo	.60
M8	Jermaine O'Neal	1.00
M9	Alonzo Mourning	.75
M10	Marcus Camby	.75

2001-02 Stadium Club NBA Call Signs

		MT
Complete Set (10):		25.00
Common Player:		1.50
Inserted 1:24		
C1	Steve Francis	4.00
C2	Shaquille O'Neal	5.00
C3	Allen Iverson	6.00
C4	Tracy McGrady	5.00
C5	Vince Carter	10.00
C6	Lamar Odom	2.00
C7	Gary Payton	1.50
C8	Stephon Marbury	1.50
C9	Karl Malone	2.00
C10	Glenn Robinson	1.50

2001-02 Stadium Club Stroke Of Genius

		MT
Common Player:		12.00
Inserted 1:40		
SG-BD	Baron Davis	15.00
SG-AI	Allen Iverson	50.00
SG-JK	Jason Kidd	25.00
SG-KM	Karl Malone	20.00
SG-SXM	Stephon Marbury	15.00
SG-SM	Shawn Marion	20.00
SG-DM	Darius Miles	40.00
SG-RM	Reggie Miller	20.00
SG-SO	Shaquille O'Neal	50.00
SG-GP	Gary Payton	15.00
SG-GR	Glenn Robinson	12.00
SG-JS	John Stockton	20.00
SG-RW	Rasheed Wallace	15.00
SG-CW	Chris Webber	30.00
SG-JW	Jason Williams	12.00
SGA-BD	Baron Davis Auto/1	
SGA-SM	Shawn Marion Auto/31	100.00
SGA-SO	Shaquille O'Neal Auto/34	400.00

2001-02 Stadium Club Touch Of Class

		MT
Common Player:		12.00
Inserted 1:40		
TC-RA	Ray Allen	25.00
TC-EB	Elton Brand	25.00
TC-TD	Tim Duncan	30.00
TC-MF	Michael Finley	15.00
TC-SF	Steve Francis	30.00
TC-MJ	Marc Jackson	12.00
TC-KM	Kenyon Martin	12.00
TC-AFM	Antonio McDyess	15.00
TC-TM	Tracy McGrady	30.00
TC-AM	Andre Miller	15.00
TC-MM	Mike Miller	20.00
TC-DN	Dirk Nowitzki	25.00
TC-PP	Paul Pierce	20.00
TC-JS	Jerry Stackhouse	15.00
TC-JT	Jason Terry	12.00
TCA-EB	Elton Brand Auto/24	
TCA-TD	Tim Duncan Auto/42	
TCA-AM	Andre Miller Auto/21	

2001-02 Stadium Club Traction

		MT
Common Player:		25.00
Inserted 1:844		
T-EB	Elton Brand	40.00
T-BD	Baron Davis	25.00
T-TD	Tim Duncan	60.00
T-RH	Richard Hamilton	25.00
T-AJ	Antawn Jamison	40.00
T-SM	Shawn Marion	30.00
T-SO	Shaquille O'Neal	75.00
T-PS	Peja Stojakovic	40.00
T-JT	Jason Terry	25.00

1983 Star All-Star Game

This is Star Co.'s first set; 5,000 were produced to commemorate the 1983 NBA All-Star Game in Los Angeles. The set, which has the first card of Isiah Thomas, features blue borders and "STAR 83" in the right corner. Two unnumbered cards are also included in the set.

		MT
Complete Set (32):		65.00
Common Player:		2.00
1	Julius Erving (CL)	9.00
2	Larry Bird	28.00
3	Maurice Cheeks	2.50
4	Julius Erving	12.00
5	Marques Johnson	2.50
6	Bill Laimbeer	2.50
7	Moses Malone	5.00
8	Sidney Moncrief	2.50
9	Robert Parish	5.00
10	Reggie Theus	3.00
11	Isiah Thomas	12.00
12	Andrew Toney	3.00
13	Buck Williams	8.00
14	Kareem Abdul-Jabbar	10.00
15	Alex English	4.00
16	George Gervin	6.00
17	Artis Gilmore	3.50
18	Magic Johnson	20.00
19	Maurice Lucas	2.50
20	Jim Paxson	2.00
21	Jack Sikma	2.50
22	David Thompson	5.00
23	Kiki Vandeweghe	3.00
24	Jamaal Wilkes	3.00
25	Gus Williams	2.00
26	Julius Erving (MVP)	8.00
27	One Player, Single Game Record (Theus, Malone)	2.00
28	All-Star All-Time Leaders (East Coast Line)	2.00
29	Larry Bird (Parish)	15.00
30	West Box Score (Moncrief Soars)	2.50
(1)	Gilmore and English (Back has ad)	2.00
xx	Kareem Abdul-Jabbar	8.00

1983-84 Star

The Star Co. entered the basketball card market in 1983, a year after Topps left it. Early Star Co. cards are difficult to find; print runs were so limited and only a few dealers had them. Also, Star Co. had severe problems with its trimming and cutting on several team sets and reportedly disposed of the unusable sheets. Cards were issued in the form of team sets. The toughest teams to find include Dallas (possibly only 500 sets exist), Boston (900) and Philadelphia (2,000). Cards were numbered alphabetically by player and by team according to the team's standing.

		MT
Complete Bag Set (276):		1800.
Comp. Bag 76ers (12):		125.00
Comp. Bag Lakers (13):		200.00
Comp. Bag Celtics (12):		475.00
Comp. Bag Bucks (11):		60.00
Comp. Bag Mavs (12):		450.00
Comp. Bag Knicks (12):		30.00
Comp. Bag Rockets (12):		20.00
Comp. Bag Pistons (12):		150.00
Comp. Bag Blazers (12):		225.00
Comp. Bag Suns (12):		60.00
Comp. Bag Clippers (12):		70.00
Comp. Bag Jazz (12):		25.00
Comp. Bag Nets (12):		25.00
Comp. Bag Pacers (12):		20.00
Comp. Bag Bulls (12):		25.00
Comp. Bag Nuggets (12):		30.00
Comp. Bag Sonics (11):		45.00
Comp. Bag Bullets (12):		25.00
Comp. Bag Kings (12):		25.00
Comp. Bag Cavs (13):		20.00
Comp. Bag Spurs (11):		30.00
Comp. Bag Warriors (11):		20.00
Comp. Bag Hawks (14):		225.00
Common 76ers SP:		4.00
Common Lakers SP:		4.00
Common Celtics SP:		8.00
Common Bucks SP:		4.00
Common Mavs SP:		20.00
Common Player:		2.00
Minor Stars:		4.00
1	Julius Erving	55.00
2	Maurice Cheeks	10.00
3	Franklin Edwards	4.00
4	Marc Iavaroni	4.00
5	Clemon Johnson	4.00
6	Bobby Jones	10.00
7	Moses Malone	15.00
8	Leo Rautins	4.00
9	Clint Richardson	4.00
10	*Sedale Threatt*	8.00
11	*Andrew Toney*	10.00
12	Sam Williams	4.00
13	Magic Johnson	85.00
14	Kareem Abdul-Jabbar	30.00
15	Michael Cooper	10.00
16	Calvin Garrett	4.00
17	Mitch Kupchak	5.00
18	Bob McAdoo	10.00
19	Mike McGee	4.00
20	Swen Nater	4.00
21	*Kurt Rambis*	12.00
22	*Byron Scott*	25.00
23	Larry Spriggs	4.00
24	Jamaal Wilkes	8.00
25	*James Worthy*	50.00
26	Larry Bird	290.00
27	*Danny Ainge*	50.00
28	Quinn Buckner	8.00
29	M.L. Carr	6.00
30	Carlos Clark	4.00
31	Gerald Henderson	4.00
32	Dennis Johnson	15.00
33	Cedric Maxwell	8.00
34	Kevin McHale	40.00
35	Robert Parish	35.00
36	Scott Wedman	4.00
37	*Greg Kite*	8.00
38	Sidney Moncrief	12.00
39	Nate Archibald	12.00
40	*Randy Breuer*	4.00
41	Junior Bridgeman	5.00
42	Harvey Catchings	4.00
43	Kevin Grevey	4.00
44	Marques Johnson	10.00
45	Bob Lanier	15.00
46	*Alton Lister*	4.00
47	Paul Mokeski	4.00
48	*Paul Pressey*	8.00
49	*Mark Aguirre*	40.00
50	*Rolando Blackman*	40.00
51	Pat Cummings	15.00
52	*Brad Davis*	25.00
53	*Dale Ellis*	35.00
54	Bill Garnett	20.00
55	*Derek Harper*	40.00
56	Kurt Nimphius	20.00
57	Jim Spanarkel	20.00
58	Elston Turner	20.00
59	Jay Vincent	25.00
60	*Mark West*	15.00
61	Bernard King	9.00
62	Bill Cartwright	4.00
63	Len Elmore	3.00
64	Eric Fernsten	2.50
65	Ernie Grunfeld	2.50
66	Louis Orr	2.00
67	Leonard Robinson	2.00
68	Rory Sparrow	2.00
69	*Trent Tucker*	4.00
70	*Darrell Walker*	8.00
71	Marvin Webster	2.00
72	Ray Williams	2.00
73	*Ralph Sampson*	8.00
74	James Bailey	2.00
75	Phil Ford	4.00
76	Elvin Hayes	9.00
77	Caldwell Jones	2.00
78	Major Jones	2.00
79	Allen Leavell	2.00
80	Lewis Lloyd	2.00
81	*Rodney McCray*	4.00
82	Robert Reid	2.00
83	*Terry Teagle*	4.00
84	Wally Walker	2.00
85	*Kelly Tripucka*	4.00
86	Kent Benson	2.00
87	Earl Cureton	2.00
88	Lionel Hollins	2.50
89	Vinnie Johnson	4.00
90	Bill Laimbeer	5.00
91	*Cliff Levingston*	4.00
92	John Long	2.00
93	David Thirdkill	2.00
94	*Isiah Thomas*	100.00
95	Ray Tolbert	2.00
96	Terry Tyler	2.00
97	Jim Paxson	3.00
98	Kenny Carr	2.00
99	Wayne Cooper	2.00
100	*Clyde Drexler*	175.00
101	Jeff Lamp	2.50
102	*Lafayette Lever*	6.00
103	Calvin Natt	2.50
104	Audie Norris	2.00
105	Tom Piotrowski	2.00
106	Mychal Thompson	3.00
107	Darnell Valentine	2.00
108	Pete Verhoeven	2.00
109	Walter Davis	6.00
110	Alvan Adams	3.00
111	James Edwards	3.00
112	Rod Foster	2.00
113	Maurice Lucas	4.00
114	Kyle Macy	3.00
115	*Larry Nance*	24.00
116	Charles Pittman	2.00
117	Rick Robey	3.00
118	Mike Sanders	3.00
119	Alvin Scott	2.00
120	Paul Westphal	9.00
121	Bill Walton	18.00
122	Michael Brooks	2.00
123	*Terry Cummings*	15.00
124	*James Donaldson*	2.00
125	*Craig Hodges*	5.00
126	Greg Kelser	2.00
127	Hank McDowell	2.00
128	Billy McKinney	2.00
129	Norm Nixon	4.00
130	*Ricky Pierce*	10.00
131	*Derek Smith*	6.00
132	Jerome Whitehead	2.00
133	Adrian Dantley	7.00
134	Mitch Anderson	2.00
135	*Thurl Bailey*	5.00
136	Tom Boswell	2.00
137	John Drew	2.00
138	*Mark Eaton*	6.00
139	Jerry Eaves	2.00
140	Rickey Green	3.00
141	Darrell Griffith	3.00
142	Bobby Hansen	3.00
143	Rick Kelley	2.00
144	Jeff Wilkins	2.00
145	*Buck Williams*	12.00
146	Otis Birdsong	4.00
147	Darwin Cook	2.00
148	Darryl Dawkins	6.00
149	Mike Gminski	2.00
150	Reggie Johnson	2.00
151	*Albert King*	4.00
152	Mike O'Koren	2.00
153	Kelvin Ransey	2.00
154	Michael Ray Richardson	6.00
155	Clarence Walker	2.00
156	Bill Willoughby	2.50
157	*Steve Stipanovich*	2.50
158	Butch Carter	2.00
159	Edwin Leroy Combs	2.00
160	George L. Johnson	2.00
161	*Clark Kellogg*	4.00
162	Sidney Lowe	2.00
163	Kevin McKenna	2.00
164	Jerry Sichting	3.00
165	Brook Steppe	2.00
166	Jimmy Thomas	2.00
167	Granville Waiters	2.00
168	*Herb Williams*	4.00
169	Dave Corzine	2.00
170	Wallace Bryant	2.00
171	*Quintin Dailey*	2.00
172	Sidney Green	2.00
173	David Greenwood	2.50
174	*Rod Higgins*	4.00
175	Clarence Johnson	2.00
176	Ronnie Lester	2.50
177	Jawann Oldham	2.00
178	Ennis Whatley	2.00
179	*Mitchell Wiggins*	2.00
180	*Orlando Woolridge*	8.00
181	*Kiki Vandeweghe*	7.00
182	Richard Anderson	2.00
183	Howard Carter	2.00
184	T.R. Dunn	2.00
185	Keith Edmonson	2.00
186	Alex English	10.00
187	Mike Evans	2.00
188	*Bill Hanzlik*	2.50
189	Dan Issel	12.00
190	Anthony Roberts	2.00
191	*Danny Schayes*	4.00
192	Rob Williams	2.00
193	Jack Sikma	5.00
194	Fred Brown	3.00
195	*Tom Chambers*	17.00
196	Steve Hawes	2.00
197	Steve Hayes	2.00
198	Reggie King	2.00
199	Scooter McCray	2.00
200	*Jon Sundvold*	2.00
201	Danny Vranes	2.00
202	Gus Williams	3.00
203	Al Wood	2.00
204	*Jeff Ruland*	3.00
205	Greg Ballard	2.00
206	Charles Davis	2.00
207	Daren Daye	2.00
208	Michael Gibson	2.00
209	*Frank Johnson*	3.50
210	Joe Kopicki	2.00
211	Rick Mahorn	3.00
212	*Jeff Malone*	10.00
213	Tom McMillen	3.00
214	Ricky Sobers	2.00
215	Bryan Warrick	2.00
216	Billy Knight	2.00
217	Don Buse	2.00
218	*Larry Drew*	3.00
219	*Eddie Johnson*	8.00
220	Joe Meriweather	2.00
221	Larry Micheaux	2.00
222	*Ed Nealy*	2.00
223	Mark Olderding	2.00
224	Dave Robisch	2.00
225	Reggie Theus	4.00
226	*LaSalle Thompson*	3.00
227	Mike Woodson	2.00
228	World B. Free	4.00
229	*John Bagley*	3.00
230	Jeff Cook	2.00
231	Geoff Crompton	2.00
232	John Garris	2.00
233	Stewart Granger	2.00
234	*Roy Hinson*	2.00
235	Phil Hubbard	2.00
236	Geoff Huston	2.00
237	Ben Poquette	2.00
238	Clifford Robinson	2.00
239	Lonnie Shelton	3.00
240	Paul Thompson	2.00
241	George Gervin	12.00
242	Gene Banks	3.00
243	Ron Brewer	2.00
244	Artis Gilmore	5.00
245	Edgar Jones	2.00
246	John Lucas	4.00
247a	Mike Mitchell, Mike Mitchell (error; photo is Mark McNamara)	3.00
247b	Mike Mitchell (corrected)	5.00
248a	Mark McNamara, Mark McNamara (error; photo is Mike Mitchell)	3.00
248b	Mark McNamara (corrected)	5.00
249	Johnny Moore	2.00
250	*John Paxson*	10.00
251	*Fred Roberts*	4.00
252	Joe Barry Carroll	2.00
253	Mike Bratz	2.00
254	Don Collins	2.00
255	Lester Conner	2.00
256	Chris Engler	2.00
257	*Sleepy Floyd*	8.00
258	Wallace Johnson	2.00
259	Pace Mannion	2.00
260	Purvis Short	2.50
261	Larry Smith	2.50
262	Darren Tillis	2.00
263	*Dominique Wilkins*	160.00
264	Rickey Brown	2.00
265	Johnny Davis	2.00
266	Mike Glenn	2.00
267	Scott Hastings	2.00
268	Eddie Johnson	2.00
269	Mark Landsberger	2.00
270	Billy Paultz	2.00
271	*Doc Rivers*	20.00
272	Tree Rollins	3.00
273	Dan Roundfield	2.00
274	Sly Williams	2.00
275	*Randy Wittman*	3.00

1983-84 Star All-Rookies

Members of the 1982-83 NBA All-Rookie Team are featured in this set. Cards have a "STAR 84" logo in the upper right corner even though the set was released in July 1983. The front borders are yellow; the backs have college stats. Star made 5,000 sets.

		MT
Complete Set (10):		40.00
Common Player:		1.50
1	Terry Cummings	7.00
2	Quintin Dailey	1.50
3	Roderick Higgins	1.50
4	Clark Kellogg	3.00
5	Lafayette Lever	3.00
6	Paul Pressey	2.50
7	Trent Tucker	1.50
8	Dominique Wilkins	20.00
9	Rob Williams	1.50
10	James Worthy	10.00

1983-84 Star Sixers Champs

This set commemorates the Philadelphia 76ers' championship over the Los Angeles Lakers in 1983. The red-bordered fronts have a "STAR 84" logo in the upper right even though the set was released in July of 1983. The backs have red printing. 5,000 sets were made.

		MT
Complete Set (25):		40.00
Common Player:		2.00
1	Moses Malone (CL)	3.50
2	Billy Cunningham	3.00
3	Moses Malone, Kareem Abdul-Jabbar	5.00
4	Julius Erving (IA)	6.00
5	Philly Super Sub (Clint Richardson)	2.00
6	Laker Killer (Andrew Toney)	2.00
7	Phil. 113, L.A. 107 Game 1	2.00
8	Bobby Jones (IA)	3.00
9	Maurice Cheeks (IA)	3.00
10	Julius Erving (IA)	6.00
11	Toney on the Drive (Andrew Toney)	2.00
12	Phil. 103 L.A. 93 Game 2	2.00
13	Serious Sixers (Pre-Game Line-up)	2.00
14	Moses Malone (IA)	3.00
15	Bench Strength (Clemon Johnson)	2.00
16	Maurice Cheeks (IA)	3.00
17	Phil. 111 L.A. 94 Game 3	2.00
18	Julius Erving (IA)	6.00
19	Bobby Jones	2.00
20	Moses Malone (IA)	3.00
21	World Champs Phil. 115 L.A. 108 Game 4	2.00
22	Julius Erving	6.00
23	Moses Malone	3.00
24	Julius Erving (Comm.)	5.00
25	Moses Malone (MVP)	4.00

1984 Star All-Star Game

This set features players from the 1984 All-Star Game in Denver. The East All-Stars are #'s 2-13; Westerners are 14-25. A "STAR 84" logo is on the card front, which has a white border. The backs, which have a safety tip from the player, have blue printing. Star Co. made 5,000 sets.

		MT
Complete Set (25):		75.00
Common Player:		1.50
1	Isiah Thomas (CL)	6.00
2	Larry Bird	45.00
3	Otis Birdsong	1.50
4	Julius Erving	15.00
5	Bernard King	3.00
6	Bill Laimbeer	2.00
7	Kevin McHale	8.00
8	Sidney Moncrief	3.00
9	Robert Parish	7.00
10	Jeff Ruland	1.50
11	Isiah Thomas	10.00
12	Andrew Toney	1.50
13	Kelly Tripucka	1.50
14	Kareem Abdul-Jabbar	12.00
15	Mark Aguirre	2.00
16	Adrian Dantley	3.00
17	Walter Davis	3.00
18	Alex English	4.00
19	George Gervin	6.00
20	Rickey Green	1.50
21	Magic Johnson	30.00
22	Jim Paxson	1.50
23	Ralph Sampson	1.50
24	Jack Sikma	1.50
25	Kiki Vandeweghe	2.00

1984 Star All-Star Game Denver Police

		MT
Complete Set (34):		185.00
Common Player (1-25):		2.00
Common Player (26-34):		2.00
1	Isiah Thomas (CL)	8.00
2	Larry Bird	50.00
3	Otis Birdsong	2.00
4	Julius Erving	25.00
5	Bernard King	3.00
6	Bill Laimbeer	3.00
7	Kevin McHale	12.00
8	Sidney Moncrief	3.00
9	Robert Parish	8.00
10	Jeff Ruland	2.00
11	Isiah Thomas, Magic Johnson	16.00
12	Andrew Toney	2.00
13	Kelly Tripucka	2.00
14	Kareem Abdul-Jabbar	15.00
15	Mark Aguirre	3.00
16	Adrian Dantley	3.00
17	Walter Davis	3.00
18	Alex English	3.00
19	George Gervin	6.00
20	Rickey Green	2.00
21	Magic Johnson	35.00
22	Jim Paxson	2.00
23	Ralph Sampson	3.00
24	Jack Sikma	3.00
25	Kiki Vandeweghe	2.00
26	Michael Cooper	3.00
27	Clyde Drexler	30.00
28	Julius Erving	20.00
29	Darrell Griffith	3.00
30	Edgar Jones	2.00
31	Larry Nance	6.00
32	Ralph Sampson	3.00
33	Dominique Wilkins	10.00
34	Orlando Woolridge	2.00

1984 Star Awards Banquet

These sets were distributed at the NBA Awards Banquet in 1984. Star Co., which made 1,500 sets, intended to give them to players, coaches and guests. The cards were never directly offered to the public. The fronts have blue borders and a "STAR 85" logo. The backs have blue and pink printing.

		MT
Complete Set (24):		75.00
Common Player:		1.50
1	1984 Awards Winners Checklist	1.50
2	Coach (Frank Layden)	2.00
3	R.O.Y. (Ralph Sampson)	2.00
4	Adrian Dantley (POY)	3.00
5	Kevin McHale	7.00
6	Magic Johnson (POY)	16.00
7	S. Moncrief (DEF)	3.00
8	Larry Bird (MVP)	19.00
9	Larry Nance (SD)	4.00
10	Larry Bird (LL)	9.00
11	Magic Johnson (LL)	6.00
12	Isiah Thomas (MVP)	7.00
13	Adrian Dantley (LL)	3.00
14	Artis Gilmore (LL)	3.00
15	Larry Bird (LL)	14.00
16	3pt. F.G. Pct. Leader (D. Griffith) (LL)	2.00
17	Magic Johnson (LL)	16.00
18	Steals Leader (R. Green)	2.00
19	Mark Eaton (LL)	2.00
20	Moses Malone (LL)	4.00
21	Kareem Abdul-Jabbar	12.00
22	All-Def Team	2.00
23	All Rookie Team	4.00
24	All-NBA Team	15.00

1984 Star Larry Bird

This 18-card, green-bordered set presents highlights from Larry Bird's career. 10,000 sets were produced in May 1984. The backs have green printing.

		MT
Complete Set (18):		80.00
Common Bird:		8.00
1	Checklist	5.00
2	Collegiate Stats (Larry Bird)	8.00
3	1980 R.O.Y. (Larry Bird)	8.00
4	Regular Season Stats (Larry Bird)	8.00
5	Playoff Stats (Larry Bird)	8.00
6	All-Star Stats (Larry Bird)	8.00
7	The 1979-80 Season (Larry Bird)	8.00
8	The 1980-81 Season (Larry Bird)	8.00
9	The 1981-82 Season (Larry Bird)	8.00
10	The 1982-83 Season (Larry Bird)	8.00
11	The 1983-84 Season (Larry Bird)	8.00
12	The 1984 NBA MVP (Larry Bird)	8.00
13	Member - 1984 All NBA Team (Larry Bird)	8.00
14	World Champs 1981,84 (Larry Bird)	8.00
15	1984 F.T. Pct. Leader (Larry Bird)	8.00
16	Career Data (Larry Bird)	8.00
17	Personal Data (Larry Bird)	8.00
18	The Future (Larry Bird)	12.00

1984 Star Celtics Champs

This green-bordered set honors the Boston Celtics' win over the Los Angeles Lakers in the 1984 NBA Finals. Action shots from the series are used for the fronts. The backs describe the card's photo. Star Co. produced 5,000 sets.

		MT
Complete Set (25):		250.00
Common Player:		2.00
1	Red Auerbach (CL)	10.00
2	Kareem Abdul-Jabbar	8.00
3	Kevin McHale (IA)	8.00
4	Larry Bird (IA)	35.00
5	Magic Johnson (IA)	25.00
6	Danny Ainge, K.C. Jones	6.00
7	Larry Bird (IA)	35.00
8	Kareem Abdul-Jabbar	10.00
9	James Worthy (IA)	5.00
10	Magic Johnson (IA)	25.00
11	Larry Bird (Magic IA)	65.00
12	James Worthy (IA)	4.00
13	Boston 129, L.A. 125 (OT)	2.00
14	Larry Bird (IA)	35.00
15	Pat Riley (IA)	7.00
16	Kareem Abdul-Jabbar	12.00
17	Robert Parish (IA)	5.00

18	Kareem Abdul-Jabbar	8.00
19	Dennis Johnson (IA)	5.00
20	Kareem Abdul-Jabbar	8.00
21	K.C. Jones	4.00
22	Boston 111, L.A. 102 - World Champs	2.00
23	Red Auerbach	10.00
24	Larry Bird (MVP)	40.00
25	Boston Garden	10.00

1984 Star Slam Dunk

This set features participants in the slam dunk contest during the 1984 All-Star Weekend in Denver. The white-bordered fronts say "STAR 84" in the upper right. Backs use blue printing. 5,000 sets were made.

		MT
Complete Set (11):		80.00
Common Player:		2.00
1	Group Photo (CL)	15.00
2	Michael Cooper	5.00
3	Clyde Drexler	30.00
4	Julius Erving	19.00
5	Darrell Griffith	2.00
6	Edgar Jones	2.00
7	Larry Nance	8.00
8	Ralph Sampson	2.00
9	Dominique Wilkins	20.00
10	Orlando Woolridge	5.00
11	Larry Nance (Champ)	8.00

1984-85 Star

These standard-size cards were issued in sealed-pack team sets. Two subsets are included: An Olympic set (195-200, noted in the checklist below) featuring players from the 1984 team, and a special series of NBA superstars (281-288). All sets were made in equal quantities - about 4,000 each.

		MT
Complete Bag Set (288):		5000.
Comp. Bag Celtics (12):		260.00
Comp. Bag Clippers (12):		25.00
Comp. Bag Knicks (13):		20.00
Comp. Bag Suns (14):		25.00
Comp. Bag Pacers (12):		50.00
Comp. Bag Spurs (12):		30.00
Comp. Bag Hawks (12):		85.00
Comp. Bag Nets (13):		20.00
Comp. Bag Bulls (12):		2900.
Comp. Bag Sonics (12):		25.00
Comp. Bag Bucks (12):		25.00
Comp. Bag Nuggets (12):		25.00
Comp. Bag Warriors (12):		20.00
Comp. Bag Blazers (11):		100.00
Comp. Bag Lakers (13):		170.00
Comp. Bag Bullets (10):		20.00
Comp. Bag Oly/Spec (14):		900.00
Comp. Bag 76ers (12):		250.00
Comp. Bag Cavs (12):		20.00
Comp. Bag Jazz (12):		220.00
Comp. Bag Rockets (13):		300.00
Comp. Bag Mavs (11):		50.00
Comp. Bag Pistons (9):		55.00
Comp. Bag Kings (11):		30.00
Common Pacers SP:		4.00
Common Player:		2.00
Minor Stars:		4.00
1	Larry Bird	150.00
2	Danny Ainge	15.00
3	Quinn Buckner	2.00
4	Rick Carlisle	2.00
5	M.L. Carr	2.00
6	Dennis Johnson	6.00
7	Greg Kite	2.00
8	Cedric Maxwell	3.00
9	Kevin McHale	15.00
10	Robert Parish	12.00
11	Scott Wedman	2.00
12	Larry Bird (MVP)	80.00
13	Marques Johnson	4.00
14	Junior Bridgeman	2.00
15	*Michael Cage*	5.00
16	Harvy Catchings	2.00
17	James Donaldson	2.00
18	Lancaster Gordon	2.00
19	Jay Murphy	2.00
20	Norm Nixon	3.50
21	Derek Smith	4.00
22	Bill Walton	18.00
23	Bryan Warrick	2.00
24	Rory White	2.00
25	Bernard King	6.00
26	James Bailey	2.00
27	James Bannister	2.00
28	Butch Carter	2.00
29	Bill Cartwright	4.00
30	Pat Cummings	2.00
31	Ernie Grunfield	2.50
32	Louis Orr	2.00
33	Leonard Robinson	2.00
34	Rory Sparrow	2.00
35	Trent Tucker	2.00
36	Darrell Walker	2.50
37	*Eddie Wilkins*	2.00
38	Alvan Adams	3.00
39	Walter Davis	5.00
40	James Edwards	2.00
41	Rod Foster	2.00
42	Michael Holton	2.00
43	*Jay Humphries*	5.00
44	Charles Jones	2.00
45	Maurice Lucas	4.00
46	Kyle Macy	2.50
47	Larry Nance	9.00
48	Charles Pittman	2.00
49	Rick Robey	2.50
50	Mike Sanders	2.00
51	Alvin Scott	2.00
52	Clark Kellogg	5.00
53	Tony Brown	4.00
54	Devin Durrant	4.00
55	*Vern Fleming* (SP)	8.00
56	Bill Garnett	4.00
57	Stuart Gray	4.00
58	Jerry Sichting	5.00
59	Terence Stansbury	5.00
60	Steve Stipanovich	5.00
61	Jimmy Thomas	4.00
62	Granville Waters	4.00
63	Herb Williams (SP)	5.00
64	Artis Gilmore	6.00
65	Gene Banks	2.50
66	Ron Brewer	2.00
67	George Gervin	12.00
68	Edgar Jones	2.00
69	Ozell Jones	2.00
70	Mark McNamara	2.00
71	Mike Mitchell	2.00
72	Johnny Moore	2.00
73	John Paxson	5.00
74	Fred Roberts	2.00
75	*Alvin Robertson*	5.00
76	Dominique Wilkins	60.00
77	Rickey Brown	2.00
78	*Antoine Carr*	5.00
79	Mike Glenn	2.00
80	Scott Hastings	2.00
81	Eddie Johnson	2.00
82	Cliff Levingston	2.50
83	Leo Rautins	2.00
84	Doc Rivers	5.00
85	Tree Rollins	3.00
86	Randy Wittman	3.00
87	Sly Williams	2.00
88	Darryl Dawkins	5.00
89	Otis Birdsong	2.00
90	Darwin Cook	2.00
91	Mike Gminski	2.50
92	George L. Johnson	2.00
93	Albert King	2.00
94	Mike O'Koren	2.00
95	Kelvin Ransey	2.00
96	M.R. Richardson	2.00
97	Wayne Sappleton	2.00
98	*Jeff Turner*	2.50
99	Buck Williams	5.00
100	Michael Wilson	2.00
101	*Michael Jordan*	2800.
102	Dave Corzine	2.00
103	Quintin Dailey	2.00
104	Sidney Green	2.00
105	David Greenwood	2.50
106	Rod Higgins	2.00
107	Steve Johnson	2.50
108	Caldwell Jones	2.50
109	Wes Matthews	2.00
110	Jawann Oldham	2.00
111	Ennis Whatley	2.00
112	Orlando Woolridge	4.00
113	Tom Chambers	6.00
114	Cory Blackwell	2.00
115	*Frank Brickowski*	5.00
116	Gerald Henderson	2.00
117	Reggie King	2.00
118	*Tim McCormick*	2.50
119	John Schweitz	2.00
120	Jack Sikma	4.00
121	Ricky Sobers	2.00
122	Jon Sundvold	2.00
123	Danny Vranes	2.00
124	Al Wood	2.00
125	Terry Cummings	6.00
126	Randy Breuer	2.00
127	Charles Davis	2.00
128	Mike Dunleavy	4.00
129	Kenny Fields	2.00
130	Kevin Grevey	2.00
131	Craig Hodges	2.00
132	Alton Lister	2.00
133	Larry Micheaux	2.00
134	Paul Mokeski	2.00
135	Sidney Moncrief	6.00
136	Paul Pressey	2.00
137	Alex English	9.00
138	Wayne Cooper	2.00
139	T.R. Dunn	2.00
140	Mike Evans	2.00
141	Bill Hanzlik	2.00
142	Dan Issel	10.00
143	Joe Kopicki	2.00
144	Lafayette Lever	3.00
145	Calvin Natt	3.00
146	Danny Schayes	2.00
147	Elston Turner	2.00
148	Willie White	2.00
149	Purvis Short	2.00
150	Chuck Aleksinas	2.00
151	Mike Bratz	2.00
152	Steve Burtt	2.00
153	Lester Conner	2.00
154	Sleepy Floyd	2.00
155	Mickey Johnson	2.00
156	Gary Plummer	2.00
157	Larry Smith	2.00
158	Peter Thibeaux	2.00
159	Jerome Whitehead	2.00
160	Othell Wilson	2.00
161	Kiki Vandeweghe	3.50
162	*Sam Bowie*	7.00
163	Kenny Carr	2.00
164	Steve Colter	2.00
165	Clyde Drexler	80.00
166	Audie Norris	2.00
167	Jim Paxson	3.00
168	Tom Scheffler	2.00
169	Bernard Thompson	2.00
170	Mychal Thompson	3.00
171	Darnell Valentine	2.00
172	Magic Johnson	75.00
173	Kareem Abdul-Jabbar	30.00
174	Michael Cooper	6.00
175	Earl Jones	2.00
176	Mitch Kupchak	3.00
177	Ronnie Lester	2.00
178	Bob McAdoo	7.00
179	Mike McGee	2.00
180	Kurt Rambis	5.00
181	Byron Scott	8.00
182	Larry Spriggs	2.00
183	Jamaal Wilkes	5.00
184	James Worthy	14.00
185	Gus Williams	3.00
186	Greg Ballard	2.00
187	Dudley Bradley	2.00
188	Darren Daye	2.00
189	Frank Johnson	2.50
190	Charles Jones	2.00
191	Rick Mahorn	4.00
192	Jeff Malone	4.50
193	Tom McMillen	3.00
194	Jeff Ruland	2.50
195	Michael Jordan Oly. (O)	400.00
196	Vern Fleming (OLY)	3.00
197	Sam Perkins (OLY)	8.00
198	Alvin Robertson (OLY)	2.00
199	Jeff Turner (OLY)	2.00
200	Leon Wood (OLY)	3.00
201	Moses Malone	15.00
202	*Charles Barkley*	200.00
203	Maurice Cheeks	7.00
204	Julius Erving	40.00
205	Clemon Johnson	2.00
206	George Johnson	2.00
207	Bobby Jones	6.00
208	Clint Richardson	2.00
209	Sedale Threatt	4.00
210	Andrew Toney	3.00
211	Sam Williams	2.00
212	Leon Wood	3.00
213	*Mel Turpin*	2.50
214	*Ron Anderson*	2.00
215	John Bagley	2.00
216	Johnny Davis	2.00
217	World B. Free	3.00
218	Roy Hinson	2.00
219	Phil Hubbard	2.00
220	Edgar Jones	2.00
221	Ben Poquette	2.00
222	Lonnie Shelton	3.00
223	Mark West	3.00
224	Kevin Williams	2.00
225	Mark Eaton	4.00
226	Mitchell Anderson	2.00
227	Thurl Bailey	3.00
228	Adrian Dantley	5.00
229	Rickey Green	3.00
230	Darrell Griffith	3.00
231	Rich Kelley	2.00
232	Pace Mannion	2.00
233	Billy Paultz	2.00
234	Fred Roberts	2.00
235	*John Stockton*	200.00
236	Jeff Wilkins	2.00
237	*Hakeem Olajuwon*	325.00
238	*Craig Ehlo*	15.00
239	Lionel Hollins	3.00
240	Allen Leavell	2.00
241	Lewis Lloyd	2.00
242	John Lucas	3.50
243	Rodney McCray	3.00
244	Hank McDowell	2.00
245	Larry Micheaux	2.00
246	*Jim Peterson*	2.00
247	Robert Reid	2.00
248	Ralph Sampson	4.00
249	Mitchell Wiggins	2.00
250	Mark Aguirre	6.00
251	Rolando Blackman	5.00
252	Wallace Bryant	2.00
253	Brad Davis	3.00
254	Dale Ellis	6.00
255	Derek Harper	8.00
256	Kurt Nimphius	2.00
257	*Sam Perkins*	18.00
258	Charlie Sitton	2.00
259	Tom Sluby	2.00
260	Jay Vincent	2.00
261	Isiah Thomas	40.00
262	Kent Benson	2.00
263	Earl Cureton	2.00
264	Vinnie Johnson	3.00
265	Bill Laimbeer	5.00
266	John Long	2.00
267	Dan Roundfield	2.00
268	Kelly Tripucka	2.00
269	Terry Tyler	2.00
270	Reggie Theus	4.00
271	Don Buse	2.00
272	Larry Drew	2.50
273	Eddie Johnson	5.00
274	Billy Knight	2.00
275	Joe Meriweather	2.00
276	Mark Olberding	2.00
277	LaSalle Thompson	2.00
278	*Otis Thorpe*	15.00
279	Pete Verhoeven	2.00
280	Mike Woodson	2.00
281	Julius Erving	20.00
282	Kareem Abdul-Jabbar	18.00
283	Dan Issel	6.00
284	Bernard King	4.00
285	Moses Malone	8.00
286	Mark Eaton	2.50
287	Isiah Thomas	20.00
288	Michael Jordan Spec.	400.00

1984-85 Star Arena

These team sets were sold in the arenas for the five teams depicted on the cards. Star Co. produced 3,000 sets for each team. When Milwaukee's Bob Lanier retired, his card (#6 of Bucks) was pulled from the set, making the existing ones scarce. Backs are numbered for each team.

		MT
Comp. Set w/Lanier (49):		575.00
Complete Set (48):		300.00
Complete Bag Celts (9):		100.00
1A	Larry Bird	50.00
2A	Danny Ainge	7.50
3A	Rick Carlisle	2.00
4A	Dennis Johnson	4.00
5A	Cedric Maxwell	3.00
6A	Kevin McHale	7.50
7A	Robert Parish	5.00
8A	Scott Wedman	2.00
9A	Champions	30.00
Complete Bag Mavs (11):		25.00
1B	Mark Aguirre	4.00
2B	Rolando Blackman	3.00
3B	Brad Davis	3.00
4B	Dale Ellis	4.00
5B	Bill Garnett	2.00
6B	Derek Harper	5.00
7B	Kurt Nimphius	2.00
8B	Jim Spanarkel	2.00
9B	Elston Turner	2.00
10B	Jay Vincent	2.00
11B	Mark West	3.00
Complete Bag Lakers (10):		90.00
1C	Kareem Abdul-Jabbar	20.00
2C	Michael Cooper	5.00
3C	Magic Johnson	40.00
4C	Mike McGee	2.00
5C	Swen Nater	2.00
6C	Kurt Rambis	4.00
7C	Byron Scott	4.00
8C	James Worthy	7.50
9C	Kareem Abdul-Jabbar, Magic Johnson	30.00
10C	Kareem Abdul-Jabbar	15.00
Complete Bag Bucks (8):		25.00
1D	Nate Archibald	5.00
2D	Junior Bridgeman	2.00
3D	Mike Dunleavy	3.00
4D	Kevin Grevey	2.00
5D	Marques Johnson	3.00
6D	Bob Lanier (SP)	300.00
7D	Alton Lister	2.00
8D	Sidney Moncrief	6.00
9D	Paul Pressey	2.00
Complete Bag 76ers (10):		50.00
1E	Julius Erving	25.00
2E	Maurice Cheeks	4.00
3E	Franklin Edwards	2.00
4E	Marc Iavaroni	2.00
5E	Clemon Johnson	2.00
6E	Bobby Jones	4.00
7E	Moses Malone	7.50
8E	Clint Richardson	2.00
9E	Andrew Toney	2.00
10E	Sam Williams	2.00

1984-85 Star Court Kings

This set, issued in two series, has yellow borders for the first series (1-25) and blue borders for the second (26-50). Blue and yellow printing is used for the backs of both series. 5,000 sets of each series were produced.

		MT
Complete Set (50):		450.00
Common Player:		2.00
1	Kareem Abdul-Jabbar	15.00
2	Jeff Ruland	2.00
3	Mark Aguirre	4.00
4	Julius Erving	15.00
5	Kelly Tripucka	2.00
6	Buck Williams	4.00
7	Sidney Moncrief	4.00
8	World B. Free	2.50
9	Bill Walton	8.00
10	Purvis Short	2.00
11	Rickey Green	2.00
12	Dominique Wilkins	15.00
13	Jim Paxson	2.00
14	Ralph Sampson	3.00
15	Magic Johnson	25.00
16	Reggie Theus	3.00
17	Moses Malone	6.00
18	Larry Bird	38.00
19	Larry Nance	4.00
20	Clark Kellogg	2.00
21	Jack Sikma	2.00
22	Alex English	4.00
23	Bernard King	4.00
24	Dave Corzine	2.00
25	George Gervin	4.00
26	Michael Jordan	190.00
27	Rolando Blackman	4.00
28	Dan Issel	5.00
29	Maurice Cheeks	4.00
30	Isiah Thomas	15.00
31	Robert Parish	6.00
32	Mark Eaton	3.00
33	Sam Perkins	5.00
34	Artis Gilmore	3.00
35	Andrew Toney	3.00
36	Adrian Dantley	3.00
37	Terry Cummings	4.00
38	Orlando Woolridge	3.00
39	Tom Chambers	4.00
40	Gus Williams	3.00
41	Charles Barkley	45.00
42	Kevin McHale	10.00
43	Otis Birdsong	3.00
44	Sam Bowie	4.00
45	Darrell Griffith	3.00
46	Kiki Vandeweghe	3.00
47	Akeem Olajuwon	40.00
48	Marques Johnson	3.00
49	James Worthy	9.00
50	Mel Turpin	3.00

1984-85 Star Julius Erving

This set presents highlights from Julius Erving's Hall of Fame career. The front have red borders; the backs have red printing. Star Co. produced 6,000 sets.

		MT
Complete Set (18):		75.00
Common Erving:		7.00
1	Checklist	7.00
2	NBA Regular Season Stats (Julius Erving)	7.00
3	ABA Regular Season Stats (Julius Erving)	7.00
4	NBA A.S. 8 Times (Julius Erving)	7.00
5	ABA A.S. 5 Times (Julius Erving)	7.00
6	NBA Playoff Stats (Julius Erving)	7.00
7	ABA Playoff Stats (Julius Erving)	7.00
8	NBA MVP, 1981 (Julius Erving)	7.00
9	ABA MVP, 1974,75,76 (Julius Erving)	7.00
10	Collegiate Stats (Julius Erving)	7.00
11	NBA MVP A.S. 1977,83 (Julius Erving)	7.00
12	NBA Career Highlights (Julius Erving)	7.00
13	ABA Career Highlights (Julius Erving)	7.00
14	1983 World Champs (Julius Erving)	7.00
15	ABA Champions 1974,76 (Julius Erving)	7.00
16	All-Time Scoring (Julius Erving)	7.00
17	Personal Data (Julius Erving)	7.00
18	The Future (Julius Erving)	6.00

1985 Star Kareem Abdul-Jabbar

Star Co. produced 6,000 of these sets to honor Kareem Abdul-Jabbar's career. The purple-bordered cards have a "STAR 85" logo on the front. Backs have stats and information about Abdul-Jabbar.

		MT
Complete Set (18):		50.00
Common Kareem:		4.00
1	Checklist	4.00
2	Collegiate Stats (Kareem Abdul-Jabbar)	4.00
3	Regular Season Stats (Kareem Abdul-Jabbar)	4.00
4	Playoff Stats (Kareem Abdul-Jabbar)	4.00
5	All Star Stats (Kareem Abdul-Jabbar)	4.00
6	All-Time Scoring King (Kareem Abdul-Jabbar)	4.00
7	NBA MVP 71/72/74 (Kareem Abdul-Jabbar)	4.00
8	MBA MVP 76/77/80 (Kareem Abdul-Jabbar)	4.00
9	Defensive Star (Kareem Abdul-Jabbar)	4.00
10	World Champs 71 (Kareem Abdul-Jabbar)	4.00
11	World Champs 80, 82, 85 (Kareem Abdul-Jabbar)	4.00
12	All-Time Records (Kareem Abdul-Jabbar)	4.00
13	Rookie-of-the-Year 70 (Kareem Abdul-Jabbar)	4.00
14	Playoff MVP 71/85 (Kareem Abdul-Jabbar)	4.00
15	The League Leader (Kareem Abdul-Jabbar)	4.00
16	Career Highlights (Kareem Abdul-Jabbar)	4.00
17	Personal Data (Kareem Abdul-Jabbar)	4.00
18	The Future (Kareem Abdul-Jabbar)	4.00

1985-86 Star Coaches

This unnumbered set features NBA coaches. The dark blue fronts have a "STAR 85" logo. The backs show only current coaching records. 4,000 sets were produced. The cards are listed alphabetically.

	MT
Complete Set (10):	20.00
Common Player:	1.50
John Bach	1.50
Hubie Brown	3.00
Cotton Fitzsimmons	2.00
Kevin Loughery	2.00
John MacLeod	2.00
Doug Moe	3.00
Don Nelson	3.00
Jack Ramsey	2.00
Pat Riley	5.00
Lenny Wilkens	3.00

1985 Star Crunch 'n Munch

This set features the starters in the 1985 NBA All-Star Game. Cards were distributed in sets and as singles in boxes of Crunch 'N' Munch. The fronts have a yellow/orange border. The backs show the player's all-star stats only. Star Co. produced 5,000 of these cards.

		MT
Complete Set (11):		425.00
Common Player:		2.00
1	All-Star (CL)	5.00
2	Larry Bird	95.00
3	Julius Erving	25.00
4	Michael Jordan	275.00
5	Moses Malone	10.00
6	Isiah Thomas	20.00
7	Kareem Abdul-Jabbar	60.00
8	Adrian Dantley	4.00
9	George Gervin	12.00
10	Magic Johnson	65.00
11	Ralph Sampson	3.00

1985 Star Gatorade Slam Dunk

Star Co. produced 4,000 of these sets to be given to those who attended the All-Star Weekend Banquet in Indianapolis in 1985. The green-bordered fronts have a "STAR 85" logo and a Gatorade logo. Backs have career highlights of those participants in the slam dunk contest. A card was made for Charles Barkley, but it was never issued because he withdrew from the competition. His card is listed separately at the end of the main checklist.

		MT
Complete Set (9):		250.00
Common Player:		2.50
1	Slam Dunk Checklist	4.00
2	Larry Nance	6.00
3	Terence Stansbury	2.50
4	Clyde Drexler	30.00
5	Julius Erving	25.00
6	Darrell Griffith	3.00
7	Michael Jordan	200.00
8	Dominique Wilkins	20.00
9	Orlando Woolridge	3.00
(XX)	Charles Barkley	90.00

1985 Star Last 11 R.O.Y

Star Co. produced 5,000 of these sets, which show the previous NBA rookie-of-the-year winners before 1984-85. The off-white front borders have "STAR 85" in the upper right corner, except cards #5 and #11, which say "STAR 86". The backs contain general information about the player.

		MT
Complete Set (11):		285.00
Common Player:		2.50
1	Michael Jordan	215.00
2	Ralph Sampson	3.00
3	Terry Cummings	3.50
4	Buck Williams	5.00
5	Darrell Griffith	3.00
6	Larry Bird	90.00
7	Phil Ford	2.50
8	Walter Davis	5.00
9	Adrian Dantley	5.00
10	Alvan Adams	3.00
11	Jamaal Wilkes	4.00

1985 Star Lite All-Stars

Star Co. produced 3,500 of these sets to be given to those who attended the All-Star Weekend Banquet in Indianapolis in 1985. The blue-bordered fronts have a "STAR 85" logo and a LITE beer logo. Coaches and the all-star starters are represented in this set.

		MT
Complete Set (13):		300.00
Common Player:		3.00
1	1985 NBA All-Stars Starting Line-Ups	5.00
2	Larry Bird	80.00
3	Julius Erving	25.00
4	Michael Jordan	220.00
5	Moses Malone	8.00
6	Isiah Thomas	12.00
7	K.C. Jones (Coach)	3.00
8	Kareem Abdul-Jabbar	15.00
9	Adrian Dantley	3.00
10	George Gervin	10.00
11	Magic Johnson	70.00
12	Ralph Sampson	3.00
13	Pat Riley (CO)	10.00

1985 Star Schick Legends

The participants in the Legends Classic game during the NBA's All-Star Weekend in Indianapolis in 1985 are pictured in this set, given to those who attended the All-Star Banquet. "STAR 85" and Schick logos appear on the front, which has a yellow border. The back has career highlights.

		MT
Complete Set (25):		60.00
Common Player:		1.50
1	SchickNBA Legends Checklist	1.50
2	Rick Barry	5.00
3	Zelmo Beaty	1.50
4	Walt Bellamy	2.00
5	Dave Bing	0.00
6	Roger Brown	1.50
7	Bob Cousy	10.00
8	Mel Daniels	1.50
9	Bob Davies	1.50
10	Dave DeBusschere	3.00

11	Walt Frazier	5.00
12	John Havlicek	12.00
13	Connie Hawkins	3.00
14	Tom Heinsohn	4.00
15	Red Holzman	3.00
16	Johnny Kerr	2.00
17	Bobby Leonard	1.50
18	Pete Maravich	30.00
19	Earl Monroe	4.00
20	Bob Pettit	5.00
21	Oscar Robertson	10.00
22	Nate Thurmond	2.00
23	Dick Van Arsdale	1.50
24	Tom Van Arsdale	1.50
25	George Yardley	1.50

1985 Star Slam Dunk Supers

Action shots from the NBA's 1985 slam dunk contest in Indiana are featured in this 10-card 5" x 7" set. Fronts have red borders and a "STAR 85" logo. 5,000 sets were made.

		MT
Complete Set (10):		250.00
Common Player:		2.00
1	Checklist (Group Shot)	50.00
2	Clyde Drexler	25.00
3	Julius Erving	20.00
4	Darrell Griffith	2.00
5	Michael Jordan	190.00
6	Larry Nance	5.00
7	Terence Stansbury	2.00
8	Dominique Wilkins	12.00
9	Orlando Woolridge	2.00
10	(Dominique Wilkins) (CL) (1985 Slam Dunk Champion)	12.00

1985 Star Super Teams

These 5" x 7" cards were issued in team sets and have separate numbers for each of the seven team sets. The fronts have colored borders which correspond to the pictured team's colors. 4,000 sets were made for each team.

		MT
Complete Set (40):		450.00
Common Player:		2.00
Boston Celtics		70.00
1	Larry Bird	50.00
2	Robert Parish	5.00
3	Kevin McHale	7.50
4	Dennis Johnson	4.00
5	Danny Ainge	9.00
Chicago Bulls		225.00
1	Michael Jordan	200.00
2	Orlando Woolridge	4.00
3	Quintin Dailey	2.00
4	Dave Corzine	2.00
5	Steve Johnson	2.00
Detroit Pistons		24.00
1	Isiah Thomas	14.00
2	Kelly Tripucka	2.00
3	Vinnie Johnson	3.00
4	Bill Laimbeer	3.00
5	John Long	2.00
Houston Rockets		60.00
1	Ralph Sampson	2.00
2	Akeem Olajuwon	50.00
3	Lewis Lloyd	2.00
4	Rodney McCray	3.00
5	Lionel Hollins	2.00
Los Angeles Lakers		70.00
1	Kareem Abdul-Jabbar	18.00
2	Magic Johnson	37.00
3	James Worthy	8.00
4	Byron Scott	4.00
5	Bob McAdoo	6.00
Milwaukee Bucks		14.00
1	Terry Cummings	4.00
2	Sidney Moncrief	5.00
3	Paul Pressey	3.00
4	Mike Dunleavy	4.00
5	Alton Lister	3.00
Philadelphia 76'ers		80.00
1	Julius Erving	25.00
2	Maurice Cheeks	4.00
3	Bobby Jones	5.00
4	Clemon Johnson	2.00
5	Leon Wood	4.00
6	Moses Malone	6.00
7	Andrew Toney	3.00
8	Charles Barkley	45.00
9	Clint Richardson	2.00
10	Sedale Threatt	3.00

1985-86 Star

Star's final complete set was narrowed to 172 cards and includes no subsets. Cards, again reportedly produced in equal amounts of 4,000 each, were issued in two series (1-94) and (95-172). Celtics cards have either white or green borders.

		MT
Complete Bag Set (172):		1500.
Comp. Bag 76ers (9):		100.00
Comp. Bag Pistons (8):		45.00
Comp. Bag Rockets (8):		100.00
Comp. Bag Lakers (8):		250.00
Comp. Bag Suns (8):		24.00
Comp. Bag Hawks (8):		65.00
Comp. Bag Nuggets (8):		18.00
Comp. Bag Nets (8):		18.00
Comp. Bag Sonics (8):		18.00
Comp. Bag Kings (7):		18.00
Comp. Bag Pacers (7):		18.00
Comp. Bag Clippers (7):		18.00
Comp. Bag Celtics (8):		130.00
Comp. Bag Blazers (7):		90.00
Comp. Bag Bullets (7):		18.00
Comp. Bag Bulls (7):		850.00
Comp. Bag Bucks (7):		20.00
Comp. Bag Warriors (7):		18.00
Comp. Bag Jazz (7):		95.00
Comp. Bag Spurs (7):		18.00
Comp. Bag Cavs (7):		18.00
Comp. Bag Mavs (7):		24.00
Comp. Bag Knicks (7):		185.00
Common Lakers SP:		5.00
Common Player:		2.00
Minor Stars:		4.00
1	Maurice Cheeks	4.00
2	Charles Barkley	65.00
3	Julius Erving	35.00
4	Clemon Johnson	2.00
5	Bobby Jones	4.00
6	Moses Malone	9.00
7	Sedale Threatt	2.00
8	Andrew Toney	2.00
9	Leon Wood	2.00
10	Isiah Thomas	30.00
11	Earl Cureton	2.00
12	Kent Benson	2.00
13	Vinnie Johnson	2.50
14	Bill Laimbeer	4.00
15	John Long	2.00
16	Rick Mahorn	2.00
17	Kelly Tripucka	2.00
18	Hakeem Olajuwon	80.00
19	Allen Leavell	2.00
20	Lewis Lloyd	2.00
21	John Lucas	3.00
22	Rodney McCray	2.00
23	Robert Reid	2.00
24	Ralph Sampson	4.00
25	Michael Wiggins	2.00
26	Kareem Abdul-Jabbar	40.00
27	Michael Cooper	10.00
28	Magic Johnson (SP)	120.00
29	Mitch Kupchak	5.00
30	Maurice Lucas	5.00
31	Kurt Rambis	7.00
32	Byron Scott	8.00
33	James Worthy	15.00
34	Larry Nance	9.00
35	Alvan Adams	2.50
36	Walter Davis	4.00
37	James Edwards	2.00
38	Jay Humphries	2.00
39	Charles Pittman	2.00
40	Rick Robey	2.00
41	Mike Sanders	2.00
42	Dominique Wilkins	35.00
43	Scott Hastings	2.00
44	Eddie Johnson	2.00
45	Cliff Levinston	2.00
46	Tree Rollins	2.50
47	Doc Rivers	5.00
48	*Kevin Willis*	18.00
49	Randy Wittman	2.00
50	Alex English	7.00
51	Wayne Cooper	2.00
52	T.R. Dunn	2.00
53	Mike Evans	2.00
54	Lafayette Lever	3.00
55	Calvin Natt	2.00
56	Danny Schayes	2.00
57	Elston Turner	2.00
58	Buck Williams	5.00
59	Otis Birdsong	2.00
60	Darwin Cook	2.00
61	Darryl Dawkins	4.00
62	Mike Gminski	2.00
63	Mickey Johnson	2.00
64	Mike O'Koren	2.00
65	Michael Ray Richardson	2.00
66	Tom Chambers	5.00
67	Gerald Henderson	2.00
68	Tim McCormick	2.00
69	Jack Sikma	4.00
70	Ricky Sobers	2.00
71	Danny Vranes	2.00
72	Al Wood	2.00
73	Danny Young	2.00
74	Reggie Theus	3.00
75	Larry Drew	2.00
76	Eddie Johnson	4.00
77	Mark Olberding	2.00
78	LaSalle Thompson	2.00
79	Otis Thorpe	6.00
80	Mike Woodson	2.00
81	Clark Kellogg	2.00
82	Quinn Buckner	2.00
83	Vern Fleming	2.00
84	Bill Barnett	2.00
85	Terence Stansbury	2.00
86	Steve Stipanovich	2.00
87	Herb Williams	2.00
88	Marques Johnson	3.00
89	Michael Cage	2.00
90	Franklin Edwards	2.00
91	Cedric Maxwell	2.00
92	Derek Smith	3.00
93	Rory White	2.00
94	Jamaal Wilkes	4.00
95	Larry Bird	80.00
96	Danny Ainge	12.00
97	Dennis Johnson	5.00
98	Kevin McHale	12.00
99	Robert Parish	10.00
100	Jerry Sichting	2.00
101	Bill Walton	15.00
102	Scott Wedman	2.00
103	Kiki Wandeweghe	3.00
104	Sam Bowie	3.00
105	Kenny Carr	2.00
106	Clyde Drexler	60.00
107	*Jerome Kersey*	9.00
108	Jim Paxson	3.00
109	Mychal Thompson	3.00
110	Gus Williams	2.00
111	Darren Daye	2.00
112	Jeff Malone	4.00
113	Tom McMillen	3.50
114	Cliff Robinson	2.00
115	Dan Roundfield	2.00
116	Jeff Ruland	2.00
117	Michael Jordan	800.00
119	Dave Corzine	2.00
120	Quintin Dailey	2.00
121	George Gervin	15.00
122	Jawann Oldham	2.00
123	Orlando Woolridge	4.00
124	Terry Cummings	5.00
125	Craig Hodges	2.00
127	Paul Mokeski	2.00
128	Sidney Moncrief	5.00
129	Ricky Pierce	5.00
130	Paul Pressey	2.00
131	Purvis Short	2.00
132	Joe Barry Carroll	2.00
133	Lester Conner	2.00
134	Sleepy Floyd	2.00
135	Geoff Huston	2.00
136	Larry Smith	2.00
137	Jeroeme Whitehead	2.00
138	Adrian Dantley	5.00
139	Mitchell Anderson	2.00
140	Thurl Bailey	2.00
141	Mark Eaton	3.00
142	Rickey Green	2.50
143	Darrell Griffith	3.00
144	John Stockton	85.00
145	Artis Gilmore	5.00
146	Marc Iavaroni	2.00
147	Steve Johnson	2.00
148	Mike Mitchell	2.00
149	Johnny Moore	2.00
150	Alvin Robertson	2.00
151	Jon Sundvold	2.00
152	World B. Free	3.00
153	John Bagley	2.00
154	Johnny Davis	2.00
155	Roy Hinson	2.00
156	Phil Hubbard	2.00
157	Ben Poquette	2.00
158	Mel Turpin	2.00
159	Rolando Blackman	4.00
160	Mark Aguirre	5.00
161	Brad Davis	3.00
162	Dale Ellis	3.00
163	Derek Harper	7.00
164	Sam Perkins	7.00
165	Jay Vincent	2.00
166	*Patrick Ewing*	170.00
167	Bill Cartwright	4.00
168	Pat Cummings	2.00
169	Ernie Grunfeld	2.50
170	Rory Sparrow	2.00
171	Trent Tucker	2.00
172	Darrell Walker	2.50

1985-86 Star All-Rookie Team

Star Co. produced 5,000 of these sets, which have red borders and a "STAR 85" logo on the front, except for card #11, Robertson, which says "STAR 86". The backs have the player's collegiate statistics.

		MT
Complete Set (11):		450.00
Common Player:		4.00
1	Hakeem Olajuwon	60.00
2	Michael Jordan	260.00
3	Charles Barkley	60.00
4	Sam Bowie	5.00
5	Sam Perkins	7.00
6	Vern Fleming	5.00
7	Otis Thorpe	7.00
8	John Stockton	60.00
9	Kevin Willis	7.00
10	Tim McCormick	4.00
11	Alvin Robertson	4.00

1985-86 Star Lakers Champs

This set honors the Los Angeles Lakers' 1985 championship over the Boston Celtics in the 1985 NBA Finals. Action shots from the series are featured on the fronts, which also have a "STAR 85" logo. Backs have game summaries. Star Co. produced 5,000 sets.

		MT
Complete Set (18):		100.00
Common Player:		2.00
1	Kareem Abdul-Jabbar, Buss	10.00
2	Larry Bird (IA)	28.00
3	Dennis Johnson	2.00
4	Danny Ainge (IA)	4.00
5	Byron Scott (IA)	2.00
6	Kevin McHale (IA)	6.00
7	Magic Johnson (IA)	16.00
8	Kareem Abdul-Jabbar, Robert Parish (IA)	6.00
9	Larry Bird (IA)	28.00
10	Kareem Abdul-Jabbar	8.00
11	Danny Ainge, Michael Cooper (IA)	5.00
12	Pat Riley (CO)	6.00
13	K.C. Jones	2.00
14	Magic Johnson (IA)	16.00
15	Lakers/Celtics	4.00
16	Bob McAdoo	3.00
17	Prior World Champs I (On Float)	2.00
18	Lakers with Ronald Reagan	30.00

1986 Star Best of the Best

These sets, originally scheduled to be released in 1986, were kept in storage until 1990. The set features the top players in the NBA. 1,400 sets were produced. A "STAR 86" logo appears on each card front.

		MT
Complete Set (15):		170.00
Common Player:		3.00
1	Kareem Abdul-Jabbar	7.00
2	Charles Barkley	12.00
3	Larry Bird	30.00
4	Tom Chambers	4.00
5	Terry Cummings	4.00
6	Julius Erving	10.00
7	Patrick Ewing	12.00
8	Magic Johnson	20.00
9	Michael Jordan	80.00
10	Moses Malone	4.00
11	Hakeem Olajuwon	12.00
12	John Stockton	14.00
13	Isiah Thomas	6.00
14	Dominique Wilkins	6.00
15	James Worthy	7.00

1986 Star Best of the New

Star Co. produced only 440 of these promo sets, to be given to dealers who bought the 1985-86 complete set. Dealers were given this set for every five complete sets purchased. Thus, there were 2,200 1985-86 complete sets made, as stated in the original Star Co. sales kits.

		MT
Complete Set (4):		225.00
Common Player:		7.00
1	Patrick Ewing	25.00
2	Michael Jordan	150.00
3	Hakeem Olajuwon	35.00
4	Ralph Sampson	5.00

1986 Star Best of the Old

The distribution for this set was identical to the Star Co.'s Best of the New sets. Hence, there were 440 Best of the Old sets produced.

		MT
Complete Set (4):		375.00
Common Player:		70.00
5	Abdul-Jabbar	135.00
6	Julius Erving	150.00
7	George Gervin	75.00
8	Bill Walton	75.00

1986 Star Court Kings

Star Co. made 4,000 of these sets. The fronts have a yellow border and a "STAR 86" logo. The backs provide a summary of the depicted player's career.

		MT
Complete Set (33):		275.00
Common Player:		2.00
1	Mark Aguirre	2.00
2	Kareem Abdul-Jabbar	10.00
3	Charles Barkley	25.00
4	Larry Bird	40.00
5	Rolando Blackman	3.00
6	Tom Chambers	4.00
7	Maurice Cheeks	3.00
8	Terry Cummings	3.00
9	Adrian Dantley	3.00
10	Darryl Dawkins	3.00
11	Mark Eaton	2.00
12	Alex English	3.00
13	Julius Erving	15.00
14	Patrick Ewing	15.00
15	George Gervin	6.00
16	Darrell Griffith	3.00
17	Magic Johnson	30.00
18	Michael Jordan	185.00
19	Clark Kellogg	2.00
20	Bernard King	3.00
21	Moses Malone	6.00
22	Kevin McHale	7.00
23	Sidney Moncrief	3.00
24	Larry Nance	4.00
25	Hakeem Olajuwon	35.00
26	Robert Parish	6.00
27	Ralph Sampson	3.00
28	Isiah Thomas	10.00
29	Andrew Toney	2.00
30	Kelly Tripucka	2.00
31	Kiki Vandeweghe	2.00
32	Dominique Wilkins	10.00
33	James Worthy	7.00

1986 Star Magic Johnson

This set, devoted to Magic Johnson's career, was made in 1986 but was not actually issued until 1990. The fronts say "STAR 86". There were 1,400 sets produced.

		MT
Complete Set (10):		35.00
Common Magic:		5.00
1	Checklist	5.00
2	Collegiate Stats (Magic Johnson)	5.00
3	Regular Season Stats (Magic Johnson)	5.00
4	Playoff Stats (Magic Johnson)	5.00
5	All-Star Stats (Magic Johnson)	5.00
6	Career Info #1 (Magic Johnson)	5.00
7	Career Info #2 (Magic Johnson)	5.00
8	Top Performance (Magic Johnson)	5.00
9	1980 Playoff MVP (Magic Johnson)	5.00
10	1982 Playoff MVP (Magic Johnson)	5.00

1986 Star Michael Jordan

This set highlights Michael Jordan's career. 7,500 sets were produced. Fronts have dark red borders and a "STAR 86" logo. The backs provide stats and information about Jordan, except card #1, which has the set checklist.

		MT
Complete Set (10):		725.00
Common Jordan:		80.00
1	Michael Jordan	80.00
2	Collegiate Stats (Michael Jordan)	80.00
3	1984 Olympian (Michael Jordan)	80.00
4	Pro Stats (Michael Jordan)	80.00
5	1985 All-Star (Michael Jordan)	80.00
6	1985 Rookie of the Year (Michael Jordan)	80.00
7	Career Highlights (Michael Jordan)	80.00
8	The 1986 Playoffs (Michael Jordan)	80.00
9	Personal Data (Michael Jordan)	80.00
10	The Future (Michael Jordan)	80.00

1990 Star Charles Barkley

This 11-card, red-bordered set is devoted to Charles Barkley's career. Approximately 5,000 sets were made, plus 250 glossy sets, which are worth $100 each. Star Co. contracted with Barkley to make this set, so it is not an officially-licensed NBA set. Each card back is numbered and contains information about the picture on the front.

		MT
Complete Set (11):		8.00
1	Checklist	1.00
2	Career Stats (Charles Barkley)	1.00
3	Playoff Stats (Charles Barkley)	1.00
4	1989-90 Season I (Charles Barkley)	1.00
5	1989-90 Season II (Charles Barkley)	1.00
6	Pro Info (Charles Barkley)	1.00
7	College Info (Charles Barkley)	1.00
8	Career Info (Charles Barkley)	1.00
9	Personal Info (Charles Barkley)	1.00
10	Personal Data (Charles Barkley)	1.00
11	Philadelphia 76ers (Charles Barkley)	1.00

1990 Star Dee Brown

This 11-card, green-bordered set is devoted to Dee Brown's career. Approximately 5,000 sets were produced, plus 250 glossy sets, which are worth $100 each. Star Co. contracted with Brown to produce this set, so it is not an officially-licensed NBA set. Each card back is numbered and contains information about the picture on the front.

		MT
Complete Set (11):		5.00
1	Checklist	.75
2	Collegiate Stats (Dee Brown)	.75
3	1989-90 Season (Dee Brown)	.75
4	Collegiate Info I (Dee Brown)	.75
5	Collegiate Info II (Dee Brown)	.75
6	All-SBC 2nd Team (Dee Brown)	.75
7	1991 Slam Dunk Champ (Dee Brown)	.75
8	Personal Info (Dee Brown)	.75
9	Personal Data (Dee Brown)	.75
10	Boston Celtics (Dee Brown)	.75
11	Boston Celtics (Dee Brown)	.75

1990 Star Tom Chambers

This 11-card, orange-bordered set is devoted to Tom Chambers' career. Approximately 5,000 sets were made, plus 250 glossy sets, which are worth $60 each. Star Co. contracted with Chambers to make this set, so it is not an officially-licensed set. Each card back is numbered and contains information about the picture on the front.

		MT
Complete Set (11):		5.00
1	Checklist	.75
2	Career Stats (Tom Chambers)	.75
3	Playoff Stats (Tom Chambers)	.75
4	1989-90 Season I (Tom Chambers)	.75
5	1989-90 Season II (Tom Chambers)	.75
6	Pro Info (Tom Chambers)	.75
7	Season Highs (Tom Chambers)	.75
8	Career Info (Tom Chambers)	.75
9	Personal Info (Tom Chambers)	.75
10	Personal Data (Tom Chambers)	.75
11	Seattle Supersonics (Tom Chambers)	.75

1990 Star Derrick Coleman I

This 11-card, red-bordered set is one of two devoted to Derrick Coleman's career. Approximately 5,000 sets were made, plus 250 glossy sets, which are worth $150 each. Star Co. contracted with Coleman to produce this set, so it is not an officially-licensed NBA set. Each card back is numbered and has information about the picture on the front.

		MT
Complete Set (11):		7.00
1	Checklist (Derrick Coleman)	1.00
2	Collegiate Stats (Derrick Coleman)	1.00
3	1990-91 Season (Derrick Coleman)	1.00
4	Collegiate Career (Derrick Coleman)	1.00
5	Senior Year (Derrick Coleman)	1.00
6	All-American (Derrick Coleman)	1.00
7	Personal Stats (Derrick Coleman)	1.00
8	Personal Data (Derrick Coleman)	1.00
9	New Jersey Nets (Derrick Coleman)	1.00
10	Personal Data (Derrick Coleman)	1.00
11	New Jersey Nets (Derrick Coleman)	1.00

1990 Star Derrick Coleman II

This 11-card, blue-bordered set is one of two devoted to Derrick Coleman's career. Approximately 5,000 sets were made, plus 250 glossy sets, which are worth $150 each. Star Co. contracted with Coleman to produce this set, so it is not an officially-licensed set. Each card back is numbered and contains information about the picture on the front.

		MT
Complete Set (11):		5.00
1	Checklist (Derrick Coleman)	1.00
2	Collegiate Stats (Derrick Coleman)	1.00
3	1990-91 Season (Derrick Coleman)	1.00
4	Collegiate Career (Derrick Coleman)	1.00
5	Senior Year (Derrick Coleman)	1.00
6	All-American (Derrick Coleman)	1.00
7	Personal Stats (Derrick Coleman)	1.00

8	Personal Info (Derrick Coleman)	1.00
9	New Jersey Nets (Derrick Coleman)	1.00
10	New Jersey Nets (Derrick Coleman)	1.00
11	New Jersey Nets (Derrick Coleman)	1.00

1990 Star Clyde Drexler

This 11-card, red-bordered set is devoted to Clyde Drexler's career. Approximately 5,000 sets were made, plus 250 glossy sets, which are worth $90 each. Star Co. contracted with Drexler to make this set, so it is not an officially-licensed NBA set. Each card back is numbered and has information about the picture on the front.

		MT
Complete Set (11):		8.00
1	Checklist (Clyde Drexler)	1.00
2	Career Stats (Clyde Drexler)	1.00
3	Playoff Stats (Clyde Drexler)	1.00
4	All-Star Stats (Clyde Drexler)	1.00
5	1989-90 Season I (Clyde Drexler)	1.00
6	1989-90 Season II (Clyde Drexler)	1.00
7	Pro Info (Clyde Drexler)	1.00
8	Collegiate Info (Clyde Drexler)	1.00
9	Personal Info (Clyde Drexler)	1.00
10	Personal Data (Clyde Drexler)	1.00
11	Portland Trailblazers (Clyde Drexler)	1.00

1990 Star Patrick Ewing

This 11-card, orange-bordered set is devoted to Patrick Ewing's career. Approximately 5,000 sets were produced, plus 250 glossy sets, which are worth $90 each. Star Co. contracted with Ewing to make the set, so it is not an officially-licensed set. Each card back is numbered and has information about the picture on the front.

		MT
Complete Set (11):		8.00
1	Checklist (Patrick Ewing)	1.00
2	Career Stats (Patrick Ewing)	1.00
3	Playoff Stats (Patrick Ewing)	1.00
4	All-Star Stats (Patrick Ewing)	1.00
5	Pro Info I (Patrick Ewing)	1.00
6	Pro Info II (Patrick Ewing)	1.00
7	Collegiate Info I (Patrick Ewing)	1.00
8	Collegiate Info II (Patrick Ewing)	1.00
9	Personal Info (Patrick Ewing)	1.00
10	Personal Data (Patrick Ewing)	1.00
11	New York Knicks (Patrick Ewing)	1.00

1990 Star Tim Hardaway

This 11-card, yellow-bordered set is devoted to Tim Hardaway's career. Approximately 5,000 sets were made, plus 250 glossy sets, each worth $125 each. Star Co. contracted with Hardaway to make the set, so it is not an officially-licensed NBA set. Each card back is numbered and contains information about the picture on the front.

		MT
Complete Set (11):		8.00
1	Checklist (Tim Hardaway)	1.00
2	Career Stats (Tim Hardaway)	1.00
3	Collegiate Stats (Tim Hardaway)	1.00
4	1989-90 Season I (Tim Hardaway)	1.00
5	1989-90 Season II (Tim Hardaway)	1.00
6	1989-90 Season III (Tim Hardaway)	1.00
7	Career Info (Tim Hardaway)	1.00
8	Collegiate Info I (Tim Hardaway)	1.00
9	Collegiate Info II (Tim Hardaway)	1.00
10	Personal Data (Tim Hardaway)	1.00
11	Golden State Warriors (Tim Hardaway)	1.00

1990 Star Kevin Johnson

This 11-card, orange-bordered set is devoted to Kevin Johnson's career. Approximately 5,000 sets were made, plus 250 glossy sets, which are worth $100 each. Star Co. contracted with Johnson to make this set, so it is not an officially-licensed NBA set. Each card back is numbered and contains information about the picture on the front.

		MT
Complete Set (11):		8.00
1	Checklist (Kevin Johnson)	1.00
2	Career Stats (Kevin Johnson)	1.00
3	Playoff Stats (Kevin Johnson)	1.00
4	1989-90 Season I (Kevin Johnson)	1.00
5	1989-90 Season II (Kevin Johnson)	1.00
6	Pro Info (Kevin Johnson)	1.00
7	Career Info (Kevin Johnson)	1.00
8	Season Highs (Kevin Johnson)	1.00
9	Personal Info (Kevin Johnson)	1.00
10	Personal Data (Kevin Johnson)	1.00
11	Phoenix Suns (Kevin Johnson)	1.00

1990 Star Karl Malone

This 11-card, green-bordered set is devoted to Karl Malone's career. Approximately 5,000 sets were made, plus 250 glossy sets, which are worth $90 each. Star Co. contracted with Malone to make this set, so it is not an officially-licensed NBA set. Each card back is numbered and has information about the picture on the front.

		MT
Complete Set (11):		9.00
1	Checklist (Karl Malone)	1.00
2	Career Stats (Karl Malone)	1.00
3	Playoff Stats (Karl Malone)	1.00
4	All-Star Stats (Karl Malone)	1.00
5	College Info (Karl Malone)	1.00
6	1989-90 Season I (Karl Malone)	1.00
7	1989-90 Season II (Karl Malone)	1.00
8	Career Info (Karl Malone)	1.00
9	Personal Info (Karl Malone)	1.00
10	Personal Data (Karl Malone)	1.00
11	Utah Jazz (Karl Malone)	1.00

1990 Star Hakeem Olajuwon

This 11-card, yellow-bordered set is devoted to Akeem Olajuwon's career. Approximately 5,000 sets were made, plus 250 glossy sets, which are worth $75 each. Star Co. contracted with Olajuwon to make this set, so it is not an officially-licensed NBA set. Each card back is numbered and has information about the picture on the front.

		MT
Complete Set (11):		8.00
1	Checklist (Akeem Olajuwon)	1.00
2	Career Stats (Akeem Olajuwon)	1.00
3	Playoff Stats (Akeem Olajuwon)	1.00
4	All-Star Stats (Akeem Olajuwon)	1.00
5	1989-90 Season I (Akeem Olajuwon)	1.00
6	1989-90 Season II (Akeem Olajuwon)	1.00
7	Career Info (Akeem Olajuwon)	1.00
8	College Info (Akeem Olajuwon)	1.00
9	Blocked Shots (Akeem Olajuwon)	1.00
10	Personal Info (Akeem Olajuwon)	1.00
11	Houston Rockets (Akeem Olajuwon)	1.00

1990 Star David Robinson I

This 11-card, black-bordered set is one of three devoted to David Robinson's career. There were 8,000 sets made, plus 250 glossy sets, which are worth $200 each. Star contracted with Robinson to make this set, so it is not an officially-licensed NBA set. Each card back is numbered and has information about the picture on the front.

		MT
Complete Set (11):		18.00
1	Checklist (David Robinson)	3.00
2	Career Stats (David Robinson)	3.00
3	Playoff Stats (David Robinson)	3.00
4	1989-90 Season I (David Robinson)	3.00
5	1989-90 Season II (David Robinson)	3.00
6	1989-90 Season III (David Robinson)	3.00
7	Collegiate Info (David Robinson)	3.00
8	1989-90 Top Rookie (David Robinson)	3.00
9	Personal Info (David Robinson)	3.00
10	Personal Data (David Robinson)	3.00
11	San Antonio Spurs (David Robinson)	3.00

1990 Star David Robinson II

This 11-card, purple-bordered set is one of three devoted to David Robinson's career. There were 8,000 sets made, plus 250 glossy sets, which are worth $150 each. Star Co. contracted with Robinson to make this set, so it is not an officially-licensed NBA set. Each card back is numbered and has information about the picture on the front.

		MT
Complete Set (11):		12.00
1	Checklist (David Robinson)	2.00
2	Career Stats (David Robinson)	2.00
3	Playoff Stats (David Robinson)	2.00
4	1989-90 Season I (David Robinson)	2.00
5	1989-90 Season II (David Robinson)	2.00
6	1989-90 Season III (David Robinson)	2.00
7	Collegiate Info (David Robinson)	2.00
8	1989-90 Top Rookie (David Robinson)	2.00
9	Personal Info (David Robinson)	2.00
10	Personal Data (David Robinson)	2.00
11	San Antonio Spurs (David Robinson)	2.00

1990 Star David Robinson III

This 11-card, blue-bordered set is one of three devoted to David Robinson's career. There were 8,000 sets made, plus 250 glossy sets, which are worth $150 each. Star Co. contracted with Robinson to make this set, so it is not an officially-licensed NBA set. Each card back is numbered and has information about the picture on the card front.

		MT
Complete Set (11):		8.00
1	Checklist (David Robinson)	1.00
2	Career Stats (David Robinson)	1.00
3	Playoff Stats (David Robinson)	1.00
4	1989-90 Season I (David Robinson)	1.00
5	1989-90 Season II (David Robinson)	1.00
6	1989-90 Season III (David Robinson)	1.00
7	Collegiate Info (David Robinson)	1.00
8	1989-90 Top Rookie (David Robinson)	1.00
9	Personal Info (David Robinson)	1.00
10	Personal Data (David Robinson)	1.00
11	San Antonio Spurs (David Robinson)	1.00

1990 Star John Stockton

This 11-card, purple-bordered set is devoted to John Stockton's career. Approximately 5,000 sets were made, plus 250 glossy sets, which are worth $80 each. Star Co. contracted wtih Stockton to make this set, so it is not an officially-licensed NBA set. Each card back is numbered and has information about the picture on the front.

		MT
Complete Set (11):		9.00
1	Checklist (John Stockton)	1.00
2	Career Stats (John Stockton)	1.00
3	Playoff Stats (John Stockton)	1.00
4	All-Star Stats (John Stockton)	1.00
5	College Info (John Stockton)	1.00
6	1989-90 Season (John Stockton)	1.00
7	Career Info I (John Stockton)	1.00
8	Career Info II (John Stockton)	1.00
9	Personal Info (John Stockton)	1.00
10	Personal Data (John Stockton)	1.00
11	Utah Jazz (John Stockton)	1.00

1990 Star Isiah Thomas

This 11-card, purple-bordered set is devoted to Isiah Thomas' career. Approximately 5,000 sets were made, plus with 250 glossy sets, which are worth $70 each. Star Co. contracted with Thomas to produce this set, so it is not an officially-licensed NBA set. Each card back is numbered and has information about the picture on the front.

		MT
Complete Set (11):		8.00
1	Checklist (Isiah Thomas)	1.00
2	Career Stats (Isiah Thomas)	1.00
3	Playoff Stats (Isiah Thomas)	1.00
4	All-Star Stats (Isiah Thomas)	1.00
5	1989-90 Season (Isiah Thomas)	1.00
6	Pro Info I (Isiah Thomas)	1.00
7	Pro Info II (Isiah Thomas)	1.00
8	College Info (Isiah Thomas)	1.00
9	Personal Info (Isiah Thomas)	1.00
10	Personal Data (Isiah Thomas)	1.00
11	Detroit Pistons (Isiah Thomas)	1.00

1990 Star Dominique Wilkins

This 11-card, yellow-bordered set is devoted to Dominique Wilkins' career. Approximately 5,000 sets were issued, plus 250 glossy sets, which are worth $80 each. Star Co. contracted with Wilkins to produce this set, so it is not an officially-licensed NBA set. Each card back is numbered and has information about the picture on the front. The set contains some error cards; Kevin Willis is pictured on some of the cards instead of Wilkins.

		MT
Complete Set (11):		8.00
1	Checklist (Dominique Wilkins)	1.00
2	Career Stats (Dominique Wilkins)	1.00
3	Playoff Stats (Dominique Wilkins)	1.00
4	1989-90 Season I (Dominique Wilkins)	1.00
5	1989-90 Season II (Dominique Wilkins)	1.00
6	Career Info I (Dominique Wilkins)	1.00
7	Career Info II (Dominique Wilkins)	1.00
8	Collegiate Info (Dominique Wilkins)	1.00
9	Personal Info (Dominique Wilkins)	1.00
10	Personal Data (Dominique Wilkins)	1.00
11	Atlanta Hawks (Dominique Wilkins)	1.00

1990 Star James Worthy

This 11-card, yellow-bordered set is devoted to James Worthy's career. Approximately 5,000 sets were made, plus 250 glossy sets, which are worth $70 each. Star Co. contracted with Worthy to make this set, so it is not an officially-licensed NBA set. Each card back is numbered and has information about the picture on the front.

		MT
Complete Set (11):		8.00
1	Checklist (James Worthy)	1.00
2	Career Stats (James Worthy)	1.00
3	Playoff Stats (James Worthy)	1.00
4	1989-90 Season (James Worthy)	1.00
5	Career Info I (James Worthy)	1.00
6	Career Info II (James Worthy)	1.00
7	Career Info III (James Worthy)	1.00
8	Collegiate Info (James Worthy)	1.00
9	Personal Info (James Worthy)	1.00
10	Personal Data (James Worthy)	1.00
11	Los Angles Lakers (James Worthy)	1.00

1990-91 Star Promos

		MT
Complete Set (18):		100.00
Common Player:		3.00
(1)	Charles Barkley	10.00
(2)	Dee Brown	3.00
(3)	Tom Chambers	3.00
(4)	Derrick Coleman I	3.00
(5)	Derrick Coleman II	3.00
(6)	Clyde Drexler	7.50
(7)	Patrick Ewing	7.50
(8)	Tim Hardaway	4.00
(9)	Kevin Johnson	3.00
(10)	Karl Malone	7.50
(11)	Hakeem Olajuwon	10.00
(12)	David Robinson I	15.00
(13)	David Robinson II	10.00
(14)	David Robinson III	10.00
(15)	John Stockton	7.50
(16)	Isiah Thomas	5.00
(17)	Dominique Wilkins	3.00
(18)	James Worthy	3.00

1993-94 Star

These cards, available in packs of nine, feature 17 current and former NBA stars. Each card front has a color action photo framed by team color-coded borders. The player's name is in the upper right, while the Star logo is in the upper left corner. A title appears at the bottom of the card. The back has a color action photo; this is the first time Star has had a photo on the back. A summary of the card's title is also featured on the back, along with the card number. The cards, which are standard size, have been airbrushed to exclude all NBA logos.

		MT
Complete Set (100):		15.00
Common Player:		.15
1	Career Stats 1979-1987 (Larry Bird)	1.00
2	Pro Season Stats (Chris Mullin)	.25
3	Collegiate Record (Harold Miner)	.15
4	Personal Data (Tom Gugliotta) (Misspelled Guggliotta on front and back)	.15
5	College and NBA Record (Christian Laettner)	.20
6	Collegiate Stats (Tim Hardaway)	.25
7	NBA Regular Season Stats (Shawn Kemp)	.50
8	Collegiate Record (Walt Frazier)	.20
9	Career Highlights (John Starks)	.15
10	Collegiate Stats (Charles Barkley)	1.00
11	Pro Stats 1 (Robert Parish)	.20
12	Playoff Stats (Chris Mullin)	.20
13	Collegiate Stats (Kevin McHale)	.20
14	Career Stats (Scott Burrell)	.15
15	1992/93 Season 1 (Harold Miner)	.15
16	Career Stats (Richard Dumas)	.15
17	Career Stats 1988-1992 (Larry Bird)	1.00
18	Collegiate Stars (Xavier McDaniel)	.15
19	1992-93 Season 1 (Christian Laettner)	.20
20	NBA Playoff Stats (Shawn Kemp)	.75
21	Collegiate Record (Tom Gugliotta) (Misspelled Guggliotta on front and back)	.15
22	Career Stats 1 (Walt Frazier)	.20
23	Regular Season Stats (Tim Hardaway)	.25
24	Personal Info (John Starks)	.15
25	Pro Season Stats (Charles Barkley)	1.00
26	Pro Stats 2 (Robert Parish)	.20
27	Collegiate Stats (Bill Walton)	.25
28	Regular Season Stats (Xavier McDaniel)	.15
29	All-Star Stats (Chris Mullin)	.25
30	1992/93 Season (Scott Burrell)	.15
31	1992/93 Season (Shawn Kemp)	.50
32	Career Stats (Oliver Miller)	.15
33	All-Star Stats (Larry Bird)	1.00
34	1992/93 Season (Richard Dumas)	.15
35	Pro Stats (Kevin McHale)	.20
36	Collegiate Info (Oliver Miller)	.15
37	1992/93 Season 2 (Harold Miner)	.15
38	1992/93 Season 2 (Christian Laettner)	.20
39	Pro Season Stats (Charles Barkley)	1.00
40	Career Highs (Tom Gugliotta) (Misspelled Guggliotta on front and back)	.15
41	1992/93 Season 1 (John Starks)	.15
42	Playoff/All-Star Stats (Tim Hardaway)	.25
43	All-Star Stats (Robert Parish)	.20
44	Collegiate Info 1 (Scott Burrell)	.15
45	Regular Season Stats (Bill Walton)	.25
46	Playoff Stats (Xavier McDaniel)	.15
47	Career Highs (Richard Dumas)	.15
48	Career Stats 2 (Walt Frazier)	.20
49	1992/93 Season 1 (Oliver Miller)	.15
50	All-Star Stats (Charles Barkley)	1.00
51	Playoff Stats (Larry Bird)	1.00
52	Career Best (Chris Mullin)	.25
53	Pro Info (Shawn Kemp)	.50
54	College Info (Christian Laettner)	.20
55	Playoff Stats (Robert Parish)	.20
56	1992/93 Season 2 (John Starks)	.15
57	Pro Info (Xavier McDaniel)	.15
58	Playoff/All-Star Stats (Bill Walton)	.25
59	Personal Info (Harold Miner)	.15
60	Collegeiate Info (Richard Dumas)	.15
61	1992/93 Season 2 (Oliver Miller)	.15
62	Collegiate Info (Tom Gugliotta) (Misspelled Guggliotta on front and back)	.15
63	Collegiate Info 2 (Scott Burrell)	.15
64	Pro Info 1 (Tim Hardaway)	.25
65	NBA Playoff Record (Walt Frazier)	.20
66	Career Highlights (Larry Bird)	1.00
67	Personal Info (Shawn Kemp)	.50
68	All-Star Stats (Kevin McHale)	.20
69	Personal Data (Xavier McDaniel)	.15
70	NBA Regular Season and Playoff Record (John Starks)	.15
71	Career Info 1 (Bill Walton)	.25
72	Personal Data and Collegiate Record (Christian Laettner)	.20
73	1992/93 Season (Chris Mullin)	.25
74	NBA All-Star Game Record (Walt Frazier)	.20
75	Playoff Stats (Charles Barkley)	1.00
76	Personal Info (Oliver Miller)	.15
77	Playoff Stats (Kevin McHale)	.20
78	Career Highs (Robert Parish)	.20
79	All-Time Standings (Larry Bird)	1.00
80	Collegiate Info (Harold Miner)	.15
81	Career Highs (Kevin McHale)	.20
82	Pro Info 2 (Tim Hardaway)	.25
83	Personal Data and 1992/93 Stats (Tom Gugliotta) (Misspelled Guggliotta on front and back)	.15
84	Career Info 2 (Bill Walton)	.25
85	Personal Data (Shawn Kemp)	.50
86	Personal Data (Scott Burrell)	.15
87	Personal Info (Richard Dumas)	.15
88	Pro Info (Charles Barkley)	1.00
89	Personal Info (Bill Walton)	.25
90	Personal Data (Kevin McHale)	.20
91	Personal Info (Christian Laettner)	.20
92	Personal Data (Walt Frazier)	.20

93 Collegiate and CBA Regular Season Record (John Starks) .15
94 Personal Data and NBA Regular Season Record (Harold Miner) .15
95 Personal Info (Robert Parish) .20
96 Personal Data (Tim Hardaway) .25
97 1992/93 Season (Tom Gugliotta) (Misspelled Guggliotta on front and back) .15
98 Personal Data (Larry Bird) 1.00
99 Personal Info (Chris Mullin) .25
100 Personal Info (Charles Barkley) 1.00

1990 Star Pics

Star Pics, a Michigan-based company run by a card collector, issued this first set of pre-NBA, post-college cards in August 1990. Cards were issued in a boxed set and each featured basketballs on the borders with a scouting report on each player on the back. Although the set was refused a license by the NBA (thus no NBA team affiliations), Star Pics contacted each player for permission to be included in the set. Notable about the set is the inclusion of an autograph by one of the players featured on the card in every 50th box. Also, five sets with each card autographed by the player were issued. Included here are special cards of David Robinson, 1990 NCAA champs UNLV team, 1990 NIT champs Vanderbilt, and NCAA Coach of the Year Jim Calhoun.

MT
Complete Set (70): 7.00
Medallion Set: 1.5x
Common Player: .05
Common Autograph: 15.00
Star Autographs: 40x-80x
1 Checklist .05
2 David Robinson 2.00
3 Antonio Davis .75
4 Steve Bardo .05
5 Jayson Williams .05
6 Alaa Abdelnaby .15
7 Trevor Wilson .05
8 Dee Brown .40
9 Dennis Scott .75
10 Danny Ferry .10
11 Steve Thompson .05
12 Anthony Bonner .10
13 Keith Robinson .05
14 Sean Higgins .05
15 Bo Kimble .10
16 David Jamerson .05
17 Anthony Pullard .05
18 Phil Henderson .05
19 Mike Mitchell .05
20 Vanderbilt team .05
21 Gary Payton 2.50
22 Tony Massenburg .05
23 Cedric Ceballos 1.50
24 Dwayne Schintzius .10
25 Bimbo Coles .30
26 Scott Williams .20
27 Willie Burton .30
28 Tate George .05
29 Mark Stevenson .05
30 UNLV team .50
31 Earl Wise .05
32 Alec Kessler .05
33 Les Jespen .05
34 Boo Harvey .05
35 Elden Campbell .75
36 Jud Buechler .15
37 Loy Vaught .75
38 Tyrone Hill .50
39 Toni Kukoc 2.00
40 Jim Calhoun (C) .05
41 Felton Spencer .25
42 Dan Godfread .05
43 Derrick Coleman .75
44 Terry Mills .50
45 Kendall Gill .75
46 A.J. English .05
47 Duane Causwell .05
48 Jerrod Mustaf .05
49 Alan Ogg .05
50 Pervis Ellison .25
51 Matt Bullard .05
52 Melvin Newbern .05
53 Marcus Liberty .05
54 Walter Palmer .05
55 Negele Knight .05
56 Steve Henson .05
57 Greg Foster .05
58 Brian Oliver .05
59 Travis Mays .05
60 All Rookie Team .50
61 Steve Scheffler .05
62 Mahmoud Abdul-Rauf .50
63 Derek Strong .05
64 David Butler .05
65 Kevin Pritchard .05
66 Lionel Simmons .25
67 Gerald Glass .05
68 Tony Harris .05
69 Kaplan's Top 54 .05
70 Draft Overview .05

1990 Star Pics Autographs

MT
Autos.: 15x-30x
Common Auto.: 1.50

1990 Star Pics Medallion

Star Pics produced 25,000 individually-numbered Medallion sets. The glossy card fronts use a gold metallic ink. All players who are in the regular 1990 Star Pics set are also in this set. Two special Medallion cards, #s 71 and 72, have also been included in this set.

MT
Complete Set (72): 30.00
Common Player: .10
1 Checklist .10
2 Mr. Robinson 7.00
3 Antonio Davis .12
4 Steve Bardo .20
5 Jayson Williams .35
6 Alaa Abdelnaby .25
7 Trevor Wilson .10
8 Dee Brown 5.00
9 Dennis Scott 3.00
10 Danny Ferry .50
11 Stevie Thompson .35
12 Anthony Bonner .50
13 Keith Robinson .20
14 Sean Higgins .20
15 Bo Kimble .35
16 David Jamerson .25
17 Anthony Pullard .10
18 Phil Henderson .25
19 Mike Mitchell .10
20 Vanderbilt Team .20
21 Gary Payton 7.00
22 Tony Massenburg .35
23 Cedric Ceballos 3.00
24 Dwayne Schintzuis .25
25 Bimbo Coles 1.00
26 Scott Williams 1.75
27 Willie Burton 1.50
28 Tate George .35
29 Mark Stevenson .10
30 UNLV Team 3.00
31 Earl Wise .10
32 Alec Kessler .30
33 Les Jepsen .35
34 Boo Harvey .15
35 Elden Campbell 1.75
36 Jud Buechler .25
37 Loy Vaught .90
38 Tyrone Hill 2.00
39 Toni Kukoc 4.00
40 Jim Calhoun .12
41 Felton Spencer .75
42 Dan Godfread .10
43 Derrick Coleman 5.00
44 Terry Mills 1.50
45 Kendall Gill 5.00
46 A.J. English 1.00
47 Duane Causwell .90
48 Jerrod Mustaf .75
49 Alan Ogg .30
50 Pervis Ellison 1.25
51 Matt Bullard .60
52 Melvin Newbern .25
53 Marcus Liberty 1.00
54 Walter Palmer .10
55 Negele Knight 1.00
56 Steve Henson .50
57 Greg Foster .25
58 Brian Oliver .35
59 Travis Mays .75
60 All-Star Team 1.25
61 Steve Scheffler .10
62 Mahmoud Abdul-Rauf 1.25
63 Derek Strong .25
64 David Butler .25
65 Kevin Pritchard .30
66 Lionel Simmons 2.50
67 Gerald Glass 1.50
68 Tony Harris .25
69 Lance Blanks .30
70 Kaplan-Draft .10
71 Owner Registration .10
72 Production Notes .10

1991 Star Pics

This boxed set was Star Pics' second straight set of basketball prospects. The print run was estimated at about 400,000 sets. The set has 45 of the 54 draft picks and features scouting reports by basketball authority David Kaplan. Several "flashback" cards feature current NBA pros in college uniforms. Also in the set is a tribute card to Hall of Famer Larry Fleisher. Star Pics signed exclusive contracts with Kenny Anderson, Stacey Augmon, Luc Longley, Mark Randall, Doug Smith, Steve Smith, Zan Tabak, John Turner and Shaun Vandiver. FL means flashback; SP means special cards.

MT
Complete Set (73): 5.00
Common Player: .05
Medallion Set: 3x
Common Autograph: 8.00
Star Autographs: 20x-40x
1 Draft Overview .05
2 Derrick Coleman .20
3 Treg Lee .05
4 Rich King .05
5 Kenny Anderson .50
6 John Crotty .10
7 Mark Randall .05
8 Kevin Brooks .05
9 Lamont Strothers .05
10 Tim Hardaway .10
11 Eric Murdock .20
12 Melvin Cheatum .05
13 Pete Chilcut .05
14 Zan Tabak .05
15 Greg Anthony .25
16 George Ackles .05
17 Stacey Augmon .20
18 Larry Johnson 1.25
19 Alvaro Teheran .05
20 Reggie Miller (FL) .25
21 Steve Smith .50
22 Sean Green .05
23 Johnny Pittman .05
24 Anthony Avent .10
25 Chris Gatling .15
26 Mark Macon .10
27 Joey Wright .05
28 Von McDade .05
29 Bobby Phills .40
30 Larry Fleisher (SP) .05
31 Luc Longley .30
32 Jean Derouillere .05
33 Doug Smith .20
34 Chad Gallagher .05
35 Marty Dow .05
36 Tony Farmer .05
37 John Taft .05
38 Reggie Hanson .05
39 Terrell Brandon 1.25
40 Dee Brown (FL) .15
41 Doug Overton .05
42 Joe Wylie .05
43 Myron Brown .05
44 Steve Hood .05
45 Randy Brown .15
46 Chris Corchiani .05
47 Kevin Lynch .05
48 Donald Hodge .05
49 LaBradford Smith .30
50 Shawn Kemp (FL) .30
51 Brian Shorter .05
52 Gary Waites .05
53 Mike Iuzzolino .05
54 LeRon Ellis .05
55 Perry Carter .05
56 Keith Hughes .05
57 John Turner .05
58 Marcus Kennedy .05
59 Randy Ayers (C) .05
60 All-Rookie .35
61 Jackie Jones .05
62 Shaun Vandiver .05
63 Dale Davis .25
64 Jimmy Oliver .05
65 Elliot Perry .25
66 Jerome Harmon .05
67 Darrin Chancellor .05
68 Roy Fisher .05
69 Rick Fox .20
70 Kenny Anderson (SP) .30
71 Richard Dumas .10
72 Checklist .05

1991 Star Pics Autographs

MT
Autos.: 15x-30x
Flashback Autos.: 50x-100x
Common Auto.: 1.50

1991 Star Pics Medallion

The players in this Medallion set are identical to those in the regular 1991 Star Pics set; the card fronts and numbers are the same in both sets. The only difference is that the Medallion set is glossy. Star Pics produced 15,000 sets.

MT
Complete Set (72): 40.00
Common Player: .20
1 Draft Overview .30
2 Derrick Coleman 1.25
3 Treg Lee .30
4 Rich King 1.00
5 Kenny Anderson 5.00
6 John Crotty .50
7 Mark Randall .50
8 Kevin Brooks .60
9 Lamont Strothers .35
10 Tim Hardaway 1.00
11 Eric Murdock 1.25
12 Melvin Cheatum .25
13 Pete Chilcut .50
14 Zan Tabak .20
15 Greg Anthony 1.50
16 George Ackles .35
17 Stacey Augmon 5.00
18 Larry Johnson 10.00
19 Alvaro Teheran .20
20 Reggie Miller .70
21 Steve Smith 4.00
22 Sean Green .35
23 Johnny Pittman .25
24 Anthony Avent .75
25 Chris Gatling 1.00
26 Mark Macon 1.50
27 Joey Wright .20
28 Von McDade .20
29 Bobby Phills .20
30 Larry Fleisher .20
31 Luc Longley 1.00
32 Jean Derouillere .20
33 Doug Smith 2.00
34 Chad Gallagher .35
35 Marty Dow .20
36 Tony Farmer .20
37 John Taft .20
38 Reggie Hanson .30
39 Terrell Brandon 2.50
40 Dee Brown .75
41 Doug Overton .50
42 Joe Wylie .20
43 Myron Brown .20
44 Steve Hood .20
45 Randy Brown .75
46 Chris Corchiani .30
47 Kevin Lynch .50
48 Donald Hodge 1.00
49 LaBradford Smith .75
50 Shawn Kemp 1.00
51 Brian Shorter .20
52 Gary Waites .20
53 Mike Iuzzolino .35
54 LeRon Ellis .25
55 Perry Carter .20
56 Keith Hughes .20
57 John Turner .50
58 Marcus Kennedy .20
59 Coach Randy Ayers .20
60 All Rookie Team 1.25
61 Jackie Jones .20
62 Shaun Vandiver .20
63 Dale Davis 3.00
64 Jimmy Oliver .25
65 Elliot Perry .35
66 Jerome Harmon .20
67 Darrin Chancellor .20
68 Roy Fisher .20
69 Rick Fox 1.50
70 Kenny Anderson 2.00
71 Richard Dumas .75
72 Checklist .20

1992 Star Pics

This set features pro prospects. The card fronts have color action photos and white borders. The backs have a small color head shot and list the players' strengths, weaknesses and accomplishments. FB means the card is a flashback. Kid cards show pictures of the players as children. Approximately 360,000 sets were produced.

MT
Complete Set (90): 8.00
Common Player: .05
Common Autograph: 8.00
Star Autographs: 25x-50x
1 Draft Overview .05
2 Bryant Stith .25
3 Reggie Smith .05
4 Todd Day .25
5 Bob Knight (CO) .15
6 Darren Moringstar .05
7 C. Weatherspoon .50
8 Matt Geiger .10
9 Marlon Maxey .05
10 Christian Laettner .50
11 Tony Bennett .10
12 Sean Rooks, Sean Rooks .25
13 Tom Gugliotta 1.00
14 Chris King .05
15 Mike Krzyzewski .10
16 Sam Mack .05
17 Matt Fish .05
18 Brian Davis .05
19 Oliver Miller .20
20 Daimon Sweet .05
21 Eric Anderson .05
22 Henry Williams .05
23 David Johnson .05
24 Duane Cooper .05
25 Lucius Davis .05
26 Matt Steigenga .05
27 Robert Horry .50
28 Brent Price .10
29 Chris Smith .05
30 Vlade Divac (FB) .05
31 Adam Keefe .10
32 Christian Laettner .50
33 LaPhonso Ellis (KID) .10
34 Alex Blackwell .05
35 Popeye Jones .25
36 Walt Williams .10
37 Radenko Dobras .05
38 Latrell Sprewell 2.00
39 Isaiah Morris .05
40 Horace Grant (FB) .10
41 Craig Upchurch .05
42 Alonzo Jamison .05
43 Bryant Stith .15
44 Jon Barry .10
45 Litterial Green .05
46 Malik Sealy .20
47 Anthony Peeler .15
48 Dexter Cambridge .05
49 Eric Manual .05
50 Kendall Gill (FB) .10
51 Hubert Davis .15
52 Steve Rogers .05
53 Byron Houston .15
54 Randy Woods .10
55 Elmer Bennett .05
56 Smokey McCovery .05
57 George Gilmore .05
58 Predrag Danilovic .25
59 John Pelphrey .05
60 Dan Majerle .05
61 Elmore Spencer .05
62 Calvin Talford .05
63 David Booth .05
64 Herb Jones .05
65 Benford Williams .05
66 Greg Dennis .05
67 James McCoy .05
68 Clarence Weatherspoon (Kidcards) .25
69 LaPhonso Ellis .25
70 Sarunas Marciulionis (FB) .05
71 Walt Williams .50
72 Lee Mayberry .15
73 Doug Christie .10
74 Jon Barry .10
75 Adam Keefe .10
76 Robert Werdann .05
77 P.J. Brown .05
78 Tom Gugliotta .30
79 Terrell Lowery .05
80 Tracy Murray .05
81 C. Weatherspoon .25
82 Melvin Robinson .05
83 Todd Day (KID) .10
84 Harold Miner .10
85 Tim Burroughs .05
86 Damon Patterson .05
87 Corey Williams .10
88 Harold Ellis .05
89 LaPhonso Ellis .10
90 Checklist .05

1992 Star Pics Autographs

MT
Autos.: 15x-30x
Flashback Autos.: 50x-100x
Common Auto.: 1.50

1968-69 Suns Carnation Milk

Measuring 3-1/2" x 7-1/2", the 12-card set was included on side panels of Carnation Milk cartons. The blank-backed cards showcase the Carnation and Suns logos in the upper left, while the player's name is listed in the upper right above the player photo. The player's career highlights are printed beneath the photo, with a contest printed at the bottom of the panel which states, "Win! 440 home game tickets to be given away."

NM
Complete Set (12): 950.00
Common Player: 75.00
1 Jim Fox 75.00
2 Gail Goodrich 350.00
3 Gary Gregor 75.00
4 Neil Johnson 75.00
5 John Kerr (CO) 100.00
6 Dave Lattin 80.00
7 Stan McKenzie 75.00
8 McCoy McLemore 75.00
9 Dick Snyder 75.00
10 Dick Van Arsdale 150.00
11 Bob Warlick 75.00
12 George Wilson 75.00

1969-70 Suns Carnation Milk

Measuring 3-1/2" x 7-1/2", the 10-card set was included on side panels of Carnation Milk cartons. The card fronts have white backgrounds with blue and white photos of the players. The unnumbered cards have the Carnation and Phoenix Suns' logos in the upper left, with the player's name in the upper right. The center of the card includes a drawing of the player in action and a headshot. Basketball tips are printed at the bottom of the panels in red. The player's stats are printed on the opposite side of the carton.

NM
Complete Set (10): 950.00
Common Player: 65.00
Jerry Chambers 65.00
Jim Fox 65.00
Gail Goodrich 275.00
Connie Hawkins 350.00
Stan McKenzie 65.00
Paul Silas 200.00
Dick Snyder 65.00
Dick Van Arsdale 150.00
Neal Walk 100.00
Gene Williams 65.00

1970-71 Suns A1 Premium Beer

Measuring 2-1/4" x 8-3/4", the 13 cards feature a black-and-white photo of the player and his name printed beneath the photo at the bottom of the card. The top of the card features "Phoenix Suns picture special," the A-1 Premium Beer logo and either a 95-cent price (most common), 98 cents (harder to locate) and no price printed. The player photo measures 2-1/4" x 3-3/8" and showcases the player in a posed position. The backs are blank and unnumbered.

NM
Complete Set (13): 1950.
Common Player: 85.00
A Mel Counts (95 cents) 100.00
B Mel Counts (98 cents) 125.00
Lamar Green 85.00
Clem Haskins 150.00
Connie Hawkins (98 cents) 425.00
Greg Howard 85.00
Paul Silas 200.00
Fred Taylor (CO) 85.00
A Dick Van Arsdale (ERR) (Reversed negative, no price) 200.00
B Dick Van Arsdale (COR) (No price) 150.00
A Neal Walk (95 cents) 100.00
B Neal Walk (No price) 150.00
John Wetzel (No price) 100.00

1970-71 Suns Carnation Milk

Measuring 3-1/2" x 7-1/2", the 10 cards have red or orange backgrounds. The orange background cards were from cartons containing diet milk. The unnumbered cards showcase a large photo of the player on the front, with the Carnation logo in the upper left. The Suns' logo appears in the upper right. The player's bio and highlights are printed beneath the photo. The backs are blank.

NM
Complete Set (10): 850.00
Common Player: 55.00
Mel Counts 55.00
Lamar Green 55.00
Art Harris 55.00
Clem Haskins 90.00
Connie Hawkins 275.00
Gus Johnson 125.00
Otto Moore 55.00
Paul Silas 150.00
Dick Van Arsdale 100.00
Neal Walk 90.00

1971-72 Suns Carnation Milk

Measuring 3-1/2" x 7-1/2", the five-card set was included on side panels of Carnation Milk cartons. Like the previous years' cards, the 1971-72 set is not numbered and have blank backs.

NM
Complete Set (5): 400.00
Common Player: 50.00
Connie Hawkins 250.00
Otto Moore 50.00
Fred Taylor 50.00
Neal Walk 60.00
John Wetzel 60.00

1972-73 Suns Carnation Milk

Measuring 3-1/2" x 7-1/2", the 12-card set was included on side panels of Carnation Milk cartons. The card fronts showcase the Carnation logo in the upper left and the Suns' logo in the upper right. A large player photo anchors the front, while the player's highlights are printed underneath the photo. The photo and text is printed in orange and purple. The cards are unnumbered and have blank backs.

NM
Complete Set (12): 800.00
Common Player: 50.00
Mel Counts 50.00
Lamar Green 50.00
Clem Haskins 90.00
Connie Hawkins 250.00
Gus Johnson 100.00
Dennis Layton 60.00
Otto Moore 50.00
Fred Taylor (CO) 50.00
Dick Van Arsdale 90.00
Bill Van Breda Kolff (CO) 50.00
Neal Walk 60.00
John Wetzel 60.00

1975-76 Suns

Measuring 3-1/2" by 4", the 16 cards are anchored by a full-bleed black-and-white photo. The Suns' logo is printed in the upper right, while a basketball at the bottom right includes "Western Conference Champions" and the player's name. The unnumbered cards have blank backs.

NM
Complete Set (16): 35.00
Common Player: 1.00
Alvan Adams 5.00
Dennis Awtrey 1.00
Al Bianchi (GM) 1.00
Jerry Colangelo (VP) 1.50
Keith Erickson 4.00
Nate Hawthorne 1.00
Garfield Heard 3.00
Phil Lumpkin 1.00
John MacLeod (CO) 1.50
Curtis Perry 1.50
Joe Proski (TR) 1.00
Pat Riley 12.00
Ricky Sobers 2.50
Dick Van Arsdale 4.00
Paul Westphal 7.00
John Wetzel 1.00

1976-77 Suns

Measuring 3-1/2" by 4-3/8", the 12-card set features a black-and-white circular photo inside a purple and orange Suns' logo. "Suns" is printed vertically along the left side of the horizontal cards. The player's name is located in the lower left. The card backs are blank and unnumbered.

	NM
Complete Set (12):	20.00
Common Player:	1.00
Alvan Adams	3.00
Dennis Awtrey	1.00
Keith Erickson	2.50
Butch Feher	1.00
Garfield Heard	2.50
Ron Lee	1.00
Curtis Perry	1.00
Ricky Sobers	2.50
Ira Terrell	1.50
Dick Van Arsdale	2.50
Tom Van Arsdale	2.50
Paul Westphal	6.00

1977-78 Suns Humpty Dumpty Discs

Measuring 3-1/4" in diameter, the 12-disc set features the player's photo and his name and number inside a circle in the center of the disc. "Phoenix Suns" is printed above the photo, while "Humpty Dumpty" is located in the circle beneath the photo. The borders are purple and orange. The Suns' and Humpty Dumpty logos are on the left and right, respectively. The unnumbered discs are blank on the back.

	NM
Complete Set (12):	35.00
Common Player:	1.00
Alvan Adams	4.00
Dennis Awtrey	1.00
Mike Bratz	1.00
Don Buse	1.50
Walter Davis	16.00
Bayard Forrest	1.00
Garfield Heard	2.50
Ron Lee	1.00
Curtis Perry	1.00
Alvin Scott	1.00
Ira Terrell	1.00
Paul Westphal	8.00

1977-78 Suns Team Issue

		NM
Complete Set (12):		22.00
Common Player:		1.50
1	Alvan Adams	1.50
2	Dennis Awtrey	1.50
3	Mike Bratz	1.50
4	Don Buse	1.50
5	Walter Davis	1.50
6	Bayard Forrest	1.50
7	Greg Griffin	1.50
8	Garfield Heard	1.50
9	Ron Lee	1.50
10	Curtis Perry	1.50
11	Alvin Scott	1.50
12	Paul Westphal	1.50

1980-81 Suns Pepsi

Each of the 12 cards measures the standard 2-1/2" x 3-1/2" on an advertising strip that measures 2-7/8" x 11". The cards are attached to an entry blank where Suns fans could vote for the Suns' all-time team. Each strip had two perforations. The card fronts showcase a color photo, with the player's name at the top, the Suns' logo in the lower left and a Pepsi logo in the lower right. The card backs have the player's team, position and name at the top, along with his 1979-80 stats and bio filling up the remainder of the card. The strips were included with Pepsi six- and eight-packs.

		NM
Complete Set (12):		10.00
Common Player:		.50
1	Walter Davis	3.00
2	Alvin Scott	.50
3	Johnny High	.50
4	Dennis Johnson	3.00
5	Alvan Adams	1.50
6	Rich Kelley	.50
7	Truck Robinson	1.50
8	Joel Kramer	1.00
9	Jeff Cook	.50
10	Mike Niles	.50
11	Kyle Macy	1.50
12	John MacLeod (CO)	.75

1981-82 Suns Pepsi

The 12-card set was included on strips, which measure 2-7/8" x 11". The cards are standard size. Like the 1980-81 Pepsi set, the cards were included on strips where a fan could vote for a Suns' dream team. The card fronts have a color photo of the player, with his name in the upper left, the Suns' logo in the lower left and the Pepsi logo in the lower right. The backs have the player's name, stats, career highlights and bio. The twice perforated strips were included with six- and eight-packs of Pepsi.

		MT
Complete Set (12):		45.00
Common Player:		2.00
1	Alvan Adams	4.00
2	Dudley Bradley	2.00
3	Jeff Cooke	2.00
4	Walter Davis	10.00
5	The Gorilla	5.00
6	Dennis Johnson	10.00
7	Joel Kramer	3.00
8	John MacLeod (CO)	3.00
9	Kyle Macy	4.00
10	Larry Nance	18.00
11	Truck Robinson	4.00
12	Alvin Scott	2.00

1982-83 Suns Giant Service

Measuring 3-1/4" x 4-1/2", the three-card set showcases a color full-bleed photo on the front, along with a Giant Service Stations' logo in the upper right and the Suns logo in the lower left. The player's facsimile signature is included on the photo. The backs have a player headshot, his bio, career highlights and stats. The cards were handed out at Giant Service Stations January-March and were given to fans on Giant Service Station Night at a Suns' game.

		MT
Complete Set (3):		30.00
Common Player:		8.00
1	Walter Davis (January)	12.00
2	Maurice Lucas (February)	8.00
3	Larry Nance (March)	12.00

1984-85 Suns Police

Measuring 2-5/8" x 4-1/8", the 16-card set includes a player action photo and headshot (lower right) on the front. Beneath the action photo is the player's name, jersey number and bio. The card backs feature the Suns' logo at the top, with Suns Tips included inside a box with rounded corners. The NBA, McGruff and Kiwanis logos are printed at the bottom of the card backs.

		MT
Complete Set (16):		40.00
Common Player:		2.00
4	Kyle Macy	4.00
6	Walter Davis	12.00
7	Mike Sanders	2.00
8	Rick Robey	4.00
10	Rod Foster	2.00
14	Alvin Scott	2.00
21	Maurice Lucas	4.00
22	Larry Nance	12.00
32	Charles Pittman	2.00
33	Alvan Adams	4.00
44	Paul Westphal	8.00
53	James Edwards	4.00
NNO	Suns Mascot	4.00
NNO	John MacLeod (CO)	2.00
NNO	Al Bianchi (ACO)	2.00
NNO	Joe Proski (TR)	2.00

1987-88 Suns 5x8 Wendy's

Measuring 5" x 8" inches, each of the four cards are anchored by a photo on the front. The player's name, number and position, along with the Suns' logo are listed beneath the photo. The Nance card is the only card to include the Wendy's logo on the front, while the other three cards feature "Don't foul out, say no to drugs" in the upper left. The cards are unnumbered and have blank backs.

	MT
Complete Set (4):	15.00
Common Player:	2.00
Jay Humphries	4.00
Larry Nance	8.00
Mike Sanders	2.00
Bernard Thompson	2.00

1987-88 Suns Circle K

The 15 standard-sized cards in this set were released in three, five-card strips (plus a coupon card). The card fronts include a color photo framed with white and purple borders. The player's name, number and position are printed beneath the photo. The Suns' logo and Circle K logo are located in the lower left and right, respectively. The card backs have the Suns' logo in the upper left, the player's name and bio in the upper center and the Circle K logo in the upper right. The player's stats are included in the center of the unnumbered horizontal card backs. The bottom of the card backs contain a tagline of "Produced by Sports Marketing, Seattle, WA."

	MT
Complete Set (15):	30.00
Common Player:	1.00
Alvan Adams	2.50
Hubie Brown	1.00
Jeff Cook	1.00
Winston Crite	1.00
Walter Davis	4.00
James Edwards	2.50
Armon Gilliam	8.00
Jeff Hornacek	10.00
Jay Humphries	2.50
Eddie Johnson	4.00
Larry Nance	4.00
Joe Proski (TR)	1.00
Mike Sanders	1.00
Bernard Thompson	1.00
John Wetzel (CO)	1.00

1988-89 Suns 5x8 Team Issue

Measuring 5" x 8", the seven-card set showcases a black-and-white photo of the player. His name, number and position are printed in the lower left, while the Suns' logo appears in the lower right. The unnumbered card backs are blank.

	MT
Complete Set (7):	25.00
Common Player:	2.50
Tyrone Corbin	4.00
Kenny Gattison	2.50
Armon Gilliam	4.00
Jeff Hornacek	5.00
Eddie Johnson	3.00
Kevin Johnson	15.00
Mark West	2.50

1990-91 Suns Smokey

Measuring 3" x 5", the five-card set is anchored by a large photo, which is bordered at the top and bottom in purple. The Smokey Bear logo is in the upper left, with the team name in the upper right of the stripe. The player's name and position are located in the lower left and the Suns' logo is printed in the lower right. The card backs, which are unnumbered, have the player's name and bio at the top and a fire prevention cartoon in the center. The Eddie Johnson card was pulled from the set after he was traded. It is harder to locate the Johnson card.

	MT
Complete Set (5):	25.00
Common Player:	5.00
Tom Chambers	5.00
Jeff Hornacek	5.00
Eddie Johnson (SP)	8.00
Kevin Johnson	9.00
Dan Majerle	6.00

1992-93 Suns 25th

The 26-card set honors the top players in the Suns' first 25-year history. Sponsored by The Arizona Republic and The Phoenix Gazette, the card fronts have a photo, with the Suns' 25th anniversary logo in the lower left corner. The player's first season with the Suns is printed above the photo, while his name appears below it. The front borders have a purple and beige tint. The unnumbered, horizontal card backs have the sponsors names printed at the top. The player's name and bio are printed in the center left, while the Suns' logo is in the center right. The player's first season stats round out the card backs.

	MT
Complete Set (26):	12.00
Common Player:	.25
Gail Goodrich (1968-69)	1.50
Connie Hawkins (1969-70)	2.00
Dick Van Arsdale (1970-71)	.50
Paul Silas (1971-72)	.50
Neal Walk (1972-73)	.25
Charlie Scott (1973-74)	.50
Curtis Perry (1974-75)	.25
Curtis Perry (1974-75)	.25
Alvan Adams (1975-76)	.50
Garfield Heard (1976-77)	.25
Walter Davis (1977-78)	.75
Paul Westphal (1978-79)	.75
Don Buse (1979-80)	.25
Truck Robinson (1980-81)	.50
Kyle Macy (1981-82)	.50
Dennis Johnson (1982-83)	.75
Maurice Lucas (1983-84)	.50
Larry Nance (1984-85)	.75
Walter Davis, Larry Nance (1985-86 Team Leaders)	.75
Jeff Hornacek (1986-87)	.50
Eddie Johnson (1987-88)	.50
Tyrone Corbin (1988-89)	.25
Tom Chambers (1989-90)	.50
Kevin Johnson	1.00
Dan Majerle (1991-92)	.75
Charles Barkley (1992-93)	3.00

1992-93 Suns Topps/Circle K Stickers

Benefitting Boys Club charity, these four three-sticker vertical strips were sponsored by Circle K. The 12 sticker fronts resemble the Topps cards from the same season. The Topps' logo is in the upper left, with the player's name and team printed in stripes at the bottom. Orange and white borders surround the photo. Each sticker measures 2-3/8" x 3-3/8". The peel-away backs contained entry forms for a chance to win one of 50 autographed Suns posters. The strips are numbered as Series 1-4. The players are included below with their strip number listed with an "S" prefix.

		MT
Complete Set (12):		12.00
Common Player:		.40
1	Danny Ainge (S1)	1.50
2	Charles Barkley (S3)	3.00
3	Cedric Ceballos (S3)	.75
4	Tom Chambers (S4)	.75
5	Frank Johnson (S1)	.50
6	Kevin Johnson (S1)	1.00
7	Tom Kempton (S4)	.40
8	Negele Knight (S2)	.40
9	Dan Majerle (S2)	1.00
10	Oliver Miller (S3)	.75
11	Jerrod Mustaf (S4)	.40
12	Mark West (S2)	.40

2001 Suns/Topps

		MT
Complete Set (10):		8.00
Common Player:		.50
1	Jason Kidd	2.50
2	Anfernee Hardaway	2.50
3	Tom Gugliotta	1.00
4	Shawn Marion	2.00
5	Clifford Robinson	.75
6	Rodney Rogers	.75
7	Chris Dudley	.50
8	Scott Skiles CO	1.50
9	The Gorilla	.50
10	Header Card	.50

1988 Supercampioni

The 56-sticker, 1-3/4" x 2-7/16" set was available at Fina gas stations in Italy and featured standouts from several different sports. Former Laker standout Bob McAdoo is the only American pictured in the set. The backs have the Fina logo and the sticker number while the fronts have a color photo with the player's name printed below.

		MT
Complete Set (8):		20.00
Common Player:		2.00
31	Robert Brunamonti	2.00
32	Michael D'Antoni	3.00
33	Walter Magnifico	5.00
34	Pier Luigi Marzorati	2.00
35	Bob McAdoo	8.00
36	Dino Meneghin	2.00
37	Antonello Riva	2.00
38	Renato Villalta	2.00

1994-95 Superior Pix Promos

The four-card, standard-size set was issued to preview the 1994-95 Superior Pix Draft Pix set. The promos are identical in design with the base set.

		MT
Complete Set (4):		12.00
Common Player:		2.00
1	(Glenn Robinson) (Purdue)	2.00
2	(Jason Kidd) (California)	4.00
3	(Grant Hill) (Duke)	6.00
4	(Eddie Jones) (Temple)	4.00

1995 Superior Pix

The 80-card, standard-size set, sub-licensed under Classic, was released as part of a 2,995-case production. The card fronts feature a color photo with a pebble-grain stripe along the bottom and left side. The card backs carry a small color player close-up in the upper left corner and a small black and white photo in the lower right quadrant. Bio and stat information are also included.

		MT
Complete Set (80):		10.00
Common Player:		.05
1	Glenn Robinson (Purdue)	1.50
2	Jason Kidd (California)	2.00
3	Grant Hill (Duke)	3.00
4	Donyell Marshall (Connecticut)	.15
5	Juwan Howard (Michigan)	1.75
6	Sharone Wright (Clemson)	.30
7	Brian Grant (Xavier)	.50
8	Eric Montross (North Carolina)	.25
9	Eddie Jones (Temple)	1.75
10	Carlos Rogers (Tennessee State)	.15
11	Khalid Reeves (Arizona)	.15
12	Jalen Rose (Michigan)	.30
13	Yinka Dare (George Washington)	.15
14	Eric Piatkowski (Nebraska)	.15
15	Clifford Rozier (Louisville)	.15
16	Aaron McKie (Temple)	.15
17	Eric Mobley (Pittsburgh)	.15
18	Tony Dumas (Missouri-KC)	.15
19	B.J. Tyler (Texas)	.15
20	Dickey Simpkins (Providence)	.15
21	Bill Curley (Boston College)	.05
22	Wesley Person (Auburn)	.50
23	Monty Williams (Notre Dame)	.15
24	Greg Minor (Louisville)	.15
25	Charlie Ward (Florida State)	.20
26	Brooks Thompson (Oklahoma State)	.15
27	Sam Mitchell (Cleveland State)	.05
28	Deon Thomas (Illinois)	.05
29	Antonio Lang (Duke)	.05
30	Howard Eisley (Boston College)	.05
31	Jamie Watson (South Carolina)	.05
32	Jim McIlvaine (Marquette)	.15
33	Jervaughn Scales (Southern)	.05
34	Kendrick Warren (VCU)	.05
35	Melvin Simon (New Orleans)	.05
36	Albert Burditt (Texas)	.05
37	Robert Shannon (UAB)	.05
38	Kevin Rankin (Northwestern)	.05
39	Byron Starks (SW Louisiana)	.05
40	Askia Jones (Kansas State)	.05
41	Harry Moore (St. Bonaventure)	.05
42	Abdul Fox (Rhode Island)	.05
43	Doremus Bennerman (Siena)	.05
44	Adrian Autry (Syracuse)	.05
45	Myron Walker (Robert Morris)	.05
46	Shawnelle Scott (St. John's)	.05
47	Tracy Webster (Wisconsin)	.05
48	Billy McCaffrey (Vanderbilt)	.05
49	Arturas Karnishovas (Seton Hall)	.05
50	Dwayne Morton (Louisville)	.05
51	Anthony Miller (Michigan State)	.05
52	Damon Bailey (Indiana)	.15
53	Lawrence Funderburke (Ohio State)	.05
54	Darrin Hancock (Kansas)	.05
55	Jeff Webster (Oklahoma)	.05
56	Jevon Crudup (Missouri)	.05
57	Robert Churchwell (Georgetown)	.05
58	Damon Key (Marquette)	.05
59	Chuck Graham (Florida State)	.05
60	Jamie Brandon (LSU)	.05
61	Travis Ford (Kentucky)	.05
62	Derrick Phelps (North Carolina)	.05
63	Stevin Smith (Arizona State)	.05
64	Brian Reese (North Carolina)	.05
65	Kevin Salvadori (North Carolina)	.05
66	Steve Woodberry (Kansas)	.05
67	Shon Tarver (UCLA)	.05
68	Joey Brown (Georgetown)	.05
69	Melvin Booker (Missouri)	.05
70	Carl Ray Harris (Fresno State)	.05
71	Gaylon Nickerson (NW Oklahoma)	.05
72	Trevor Ruffin (Hawaii)	.15
73	Anthony Goldwire (Houston)	.15
74	Shaquille O'Neal (LSU)	.25
75	Dikembe Mutombo (Georgetown)	.15
76	Alonzo Mourning (Georgetown)	.15
77	Jamal Mashburn (Kentucky)	.15
78	Glenn Robinson (Purdue)	1.50
79	Grant Hill (Duke)	2.50
80	Checklist	.05

1995 Superior Pix Autographs

Each box of 1995 Superior Pix contained two signed cards, with the number of cards signed by the player listed below. The cards parallel the base set except for the signature and the serial number along the bottom edge of the card front.

		MT
Complete Set (38):		1400.
Common Autograph:		6.00
1	Glenn Robinson (AU/1500)	60.00
2	Jason Kidd (AU/1500)	70.00
5	Juwan Howard (AU/2500)	70.00
6	Sharone Wright (AU/2500)	12.00
7	Brian Grant (AU/3000)	25.00
8	Eric Montross (AU/2500)	12.00
9	Eddie Jones (AU/3000)	45.00
13	Yinka Dare (AU/2000)	6.00
14	Eric Piatkowski (AU/2500)	12.00
15	Clifford Rozier (AU/2500)	8.00
16	Aaron McKie (AU/3500)	8.00
17	Eric Mobley (AU/3000)	8.00
18	Tony Dumas (AU/3000)	8.00
19	B.J. Tyler (AU/3000)	8.00
20	Dickey Simpkins (AU/2000)	8.00
21	Bill Curley (AU/3000)	8.00
22	Wesley Person (AU/3500)	20.00
23	Monty Williams (AU/2500)	8.00
24	Greg Minor (AU/2500)	8.00
25	Charlie Ward (AU/2500)	18.00
26	Brooks Thompson (AU/2000)	8.00
28	Deon Thomas (AU/2700)	15.00
30	Howard Eisley (AU/2500)	6.00
32	Jim McIlvaine (AU/2600)	8.00
40	Askia Jones (AU/3600)	8.00
41	Harry Moore (AU/3000)	6.00
44	Adrian Autry (AU/2500)	6.00
46	Shawnelle Scott (AU/4000)	6.00
52	Damon Bailey (AU/3500)	8.00
53	Darrin Hancock (AU/3000)	6.00
55	Jeff Webster (AU/1250)	6.00
57	Robert Churchwell (AU/3000)	6.00
61	Travis Ford (AU/3000)	6.00
68	Joey Brown (AU/3000)	6.00
74	Shaquille O'Neal (AU/200)	800.00
75	Dikembe Mutombo (AU/1000)	40.00
76	Alonzo Mourning (AU/1000)	100.00
77	Jamal Mashburn (AU/1000)	100.00

1995 Superior Pix Chrome

The 30-card insert set was randomly inserted into packs of Superior Pix. The checklist consists of first-round picks and a chrome gold version was inserted in each box. Basketball icons are featured prominently on the card backs and fronts.

		MT
	Complete Set (30):	20.00
	Common Player:	.15
1	Glenn Robinson (Purdue)	3.00
2	Jason Kidd (California)	4.00
3	Grant Hill (Duke)	5.00
4	Donyell Marshall (Connecticut)	.30
5	Juwan Howard (Michigan)	3.00
6	Sharone Wright (Clemson)	.60
7	Brian Grant (Xavier)	.75
8	Eric Montross (North Carolina)	.50
9	Eddie Jones (Temple)	3.00
10	Carlos Rogers (Tennessee State)	.30
11	Khalid Reeves (Arizona)	.30
12	Jalen Rose (Michigan)	.60
13	Yinka Dare (George Washington)	.30
14	Eric Piatkowski (Nebraska)	.30
15	Clifford Rozier (Louisville)	.30
16	Aaron McKie (Temple)	.30
17	Eric Mobley (Pittsburgh)	.30
18	Tony Dumas (Missouri-KC)	.30
19	B.J. Tyler (Texas)	.30
20	Dickey Simpkins (Providence)	.30
21	Bill Curley (Boston College)	.15
22	Wesley Person (Auburn)	1.00
23	Monty Williams (Notre Dame)	.30
24	Greg Minor (Louisville)	.30
25	Charlie Ward (Florida State)	.40
26	Brooks Thompson (Oklahoma State)	.30
27	Dikembe Mutombo (Georgetown)	.30
28	Alonzo Mourning (Georgetown)	.60
29	Jamal Mashburn (Kentucky)	.60
30	Shaquille O'Neal (LSU)	1.50

1995 Superior Pix Instant Impact

The 10-card insert set was found every nine packs and the fronts have a horizontal design with "Instant Impact" printed in the lower right corner. The backs feature a larger version of the color photo from the card front.

		MT
	Complete Set (10):	35.00
	Common Player:	1.50
1	Shaquille O'Neal (LSU)	8.00
2	Glenn Robinson (Purdue)	6.00
3	Jason Kidd (California)	8.00
4	Grant Hill (Duke)	10.00
5	Dikembe Mutombo (Georgetown)	1.50
6	Alonzo Mourning (Georgetown)	3.00
7	Jamal Mashburn (Kentucky)	3.00
8	Juwan Howard (Michigan)	7.00
9	Brian Grant (Xavier)	2.00
10	Wesley Person (Auburn)	2.00

1995 Superior Pix Lottery Pick

The 10-card insert set was found every 36 packs and feature a player image on clear acetate. The player's name appears in the lower left corner with the numbering (x of 10) in the upper right corner.

		MT
	Complete Set (10):	70.00
	Common Player:	1.25
1	Glenn Robinson (Purdue)	12.00
2	Jason Kidd (California)	15.00
3	Grant Hill (Duke)	18.00
4	Donyell Marshall (Connecticut)	1.25
5	Juwan Howard (Michigan)	14.00
6	Sharone Wright (Clemson)	2.00
7	Brian Grant (Xavier)	3.00
8	Eric Montross (North Carolina)	1.50
9	Eddie Jones (Temple)	14.00
10	Carlos Rogers (Tennessee State)	1.25

1969-70 Supersonics Sunbeam Bread

Measuring 2-3/4" x 2-3/4", the 11-card set was included one per specially marked packages of Sunbeam Bread. The card fronts are anchored by a color photo, with the Sonics' logo, player name and position printed on the photo. The Sunbeam Bread logo is printed at the top, while "Sonic Stars" appears along the right border of the card. The unnumbered card backs feature a player biography. In addition, a fan 16 years old or younger could exchange various cards for a free ticket to a Sonics game.

	NM
Complete Set (11):	110.00
Common Player:	10.00
Lucius Allen	20.00
Bob Boozer	12.00
Barry Clemens	10.00
Art Harris	10.00
Tom Meschery (SP)	15.00
Erwin Mueller	10.00
Dorrie Murrey	10.00
Bob Rule	10.00
John Tresvant	10.00
Len Wilkens (P/CO SP)	35.00
Seattle Coliseum (DP)	10.00

1970-71 Supersonics Sunbeam Bread

Measuring 2-3/4" x 2-3/4", the 11-card set features the same design as the 1969-70 set. The unnumbered card backs showcase a biography of the player. Each card was attached to plastic bread ties on specially marked packages of Sunbeam Bread. If a fan 16 years or younger completed a set of various players, they would receive a free ticket to a Sonics game.

	NM
Complete Set (11):	110.00
Common Player:	10.00
Tom Black	10.00
Barry Clemens	10.00
Pete Cross	10.00
Jake Ford	10.00
Garfield Heard	16.00
Don Kojis	12.00
Tom Meschery (SP)	14.00
Dick Snyder	10.00
Len Wilkens (P/CO SP)	35.00
Lee Winfield	10.00
Seattle Coliseum	10.00

1971-72 Supersonics Sunbeam Bread

Measuring 2-3/4" x 2-3/4", the 11-card set has the same design as the first two Sunbeam sets. They were issued on the plastic bread ties of loaves. The unnumbered card backs feature a player biography.

	NM
Complete Set (11):	100.00
Common Player:	10.00
Pete Cross	10.00
Jake Ford	10.00
Spencer Haywood	20.00
Garfield Heard	15.00
Don Kojis	12.00
Bob Rule	12.00
Don Smith	10.00
Dick Snyder	10.00
Len Wilkens (P/CO)	30.00
Lee Winfield	10.00
Sonics Coliseum	10.00

1973-74 Supersonics Shur-Fresh

Measuring 2-3/4" x 2-3/4", the 12 cards feature a color photo on the front, with the Sonics' logo, player name and position printed on the photo. The Shur-Fresh logo is printed at the top. "Sonic Stars" appears along the right border. The card backs, which are unnumbered, carry a player bio and instructions on how collectors could win a free ticket to a Sonics game.

	NM
Complete Set (12):	145.00
Common Player:	10.00
John Brisker	10.00
Fred Brown	20.00
Emmette Bryant (ACO)	10.00
Jim Fox	10.00
Dick Gibbs	10.00
Spencer Haywood	20.00
Bill Russell	80.00
Jim McDaniels	12.00
Kennedy McIntosh	10.00
Dick Snyder	10.00
Bud Stallworth	10.00
Lee Winfield	10.00

1974-75 Supersonics KTW-1250 Milk Cartons

Measuring 3-1/4" x 2-5/8", the two milk carton panels include a drawing in blue on a yellow background. The person's career highlights are printed beneath the portrait. "KTW 1250 Sportstalk" is printed at the bottom of the unnumbered cards.

	NM
Complete Set (2):	120.00
Common Player:	20.00
Wayne Cody (Radio broadcaster)	20.00
Bill Russell (Seattle Supersonics GM)	100.00

1978 Supersonics Team Issue

Measuring 5-7/8" x 9", the 11 photos feature color photos framed in white. A facsimile autograph is included on the blank-backed, unnumbered photos.

	NM
Complete Set (11):	25.00
Common Player:	2.00
Fred Brown	4.00
Al Fleming	2.00
Joe Hassett	2.00
Dennis Johnson	7.00
John Johnson	2.00
Jack Sikma	4.00
Paul Silas	4.00
Wally Walker	2.00
Marvin Webster	2.00
Gus Williams	4.00
Cover Photo (Smaller versions of all ten photos)	4.00

1978-79 Supersonics Police

Measuring 2-5/8" x 4-1/8", the 16 cards are anchored by a large photo. The Sonics' logo is printed inside the photo in the upper right, while the player's name and bio appear beneath the photo on the front. The unnumbered card backs include tips from the Sonics, along with logos from the Washington State Crime Prevention Association and Kiwanis Club.

	NM
Complete Set (16):	20.00
Common Player:	.75
Fred Brown	2.00
Joe Hassett	.75
Dennis Johnson	5.00
John Johnson	.75
Tom LaGarde	.75
Lonnie Shelton	1.00
Jack Sikma	2.00
Paul Silas	2.00
Dick Snyder	.75
Wally Walker	.75
Gus Williams	2.00
Len Wilkens (CO)	5.00
Les Habegger (ACO)	.75
Frank Furtado (TR)	.75
T. Wheedle, mascot	.75
Team Photo	1.50

1978-79 Supersonics Team Issue 8x10

		NM
	Complete Set (7):	22.00
	Common Player:	3.00
1	Fred Brown	3.00
2	Dennis Johnson	3.00
3	John Johnson	3.00
4	Lonnie Shelton	3.00
5	Jack Sikma	3.00
6	Wally Walker	3.00
7	Gus Williams	3.00

1979 Supersonics Portfolio

Artist Bill Vanderdasson created 11 collector prints featuring Sonics players. Measuring 11" x 14", the print showcases the player in action. The Jack Sikma print is in color, while the other prints are black-and-white on a gray background. The backs are blank and unnumbered.

	NM
Complete Set (11):	40.00
Common Player:	3.00
Dennis Awtrey	3.00
Fred Brown	6.00
Dennis Johnson	8.00
John Johnson	3.00
Tom LaGarde	3.00
Lonnie Shelton	4.00
Jack Sikma	6.00
Paul Silas	6.00
Dick Snyder	3.00
Wally Walker	3.00
Gus Williams	6.00

1979-80 Supersonics Police

Measuring 2-5/8" x 4-1/8", the 16-card set boasts a large photo on the front, with the NBA logo in the upper left and the Sonics' logo in the lower right of the photo. The player's name and bio are printed under the photo. The card backs showcase tips from the Sonics and include logos from the Washington State Crime Prevention Association, Kiwanis Club, Coca-Cola and Ranier Bank.

		NM
	Complete Set (16):	12.00
	Common Player:	.50
1	Gus Williams	1.50
2	James Bailey	.50
3	Jack Sikma	2.00
4	Tom LaGarde	.50
5	Paul Silas	2.00
6	Lonnie Shelton	.75
7	T. Wheedle (Mascot)	.50
8	Vinnie Johnson	2.00
9	Dennis Johnson	2.50
10	Wally Walker	.50
11	Les Habegger (ACO)	.50
12	Frank Furtado (TR)	.50
13	Fred Brown	1.50
14	John Johnson	.50
15	Team Photo	1.50
16	Len Wilkens (CO)	2.00

1983-84 Supersonics Police

Measuring 2-5/8" x 4-1/8", the 16-card set includes a photo on the front, with the player's name and bio listed at the bottom. A photo credit appears on the lower right of the photo. The card backs include tips from the Sonics and logos from the Washington State Crime Prevention Association, Kiwanis, Coca-Cola and Ernst Home Centers.

		MT
	Complete Set (16):	8.00
	Common Player:	.50
1	Reggie King	.50
2	Frank Furtado (TR)	.50
3	Tom Chambers	3.00
4	Dave Harshman (ACO)	.50
5	Gus Williams	1.00
6	T. Wheedle (Mascot)	.50
7	Scooter McCray	.50
8	Jack Sikma	1.00
9	Al Wood	.50
10	Bob Blackburn (ANN)	.50
11	Danny Vranes	.50
12	Charles Bradley	.50
13	Steve Hawes	.50
14	Jon Sundvoid	.50
15	Fred Brown	1.00
16	Len Wilkens (CO)	2.00

1990-91 Supersonics Kayo

Kayo Cards produced 10,000 of this 14-card set to be given away at a Sonics game. The card fronts feature a color photo, with the Kayo logo in the upper left of the photo. The Sonics' logo appears in the lower left of the card front, while the player's name and position are in the lower right of a stripe at the bottom of the card. The card backs, which are numbered inside a circle in the upper right, have the player's name and position at the top, his bio and stats are printed in the center. The Kayo logos, including the boxing kangaroo logo, are printed at the bottom of the card backs.

		MT
	Complete Set (14):	10.00
	Common Player:	.25
1	Shawn Kemp	4.00
2	Scott Meents	.25
3	Derrick McKey	.50
4	Michael Cage	.25
5	Benoit Benjamin	.25
6	Dave Corzine	.25
7	K.C. Jones (CO)	.50
8	Quintin Dailey	.25
9	Ricky Pierce	.25
10	Eddie Johnson	.50
11	Nate McMillan	.50
12	Gary Payton	5.00
13	Sedale Threatt	.25
14	Dana Barros	1.00

1990-91 Supersonics Smokey

Sponsored by the USDA Forest Service, the 16-card set was released in a sheet of four rows of four cards apiece. When perforated, the cards are standard size. The card fronts feature a color photo, with the team name at the top and the Smokey Bear logo in the lower left, the player's name in the lower center and the Sonics' logo in the lower right. The card front is bordered with team colors. The backs have the player's name and bio at the top center, with a Sonics' logo in both upper corners. A Smokey's arson tip cartoon is located in the center of the card back. The KJR radio logo is printed in the lower left.

		MT
	Complete Set (16):	20.00
	Common Player:	1.00
1	Dana Barros	2.50
2	Michael Cage	1.00
3	Dave Corzine	1.00
4	Quintin Dailey	1.00
5	Dale Ellis	1.50
6	K.C. Jones (CO)	1.50
7	Shawn Kemp	10.00
8	Bob Kloppenburg (CO)	1.00
9	Xavier McDaniel	1.00
10	Derrick McKey	1.50
11	Nate McMillan	1.50
12	Scott Meents	1.00
13	Kip Motta (CO)	1.00
14	Gary Payton	12.00
15	Olden Polynice	1.00
16	Sedale Threatt	1.00

1990-91 Supersonics Team Issue

Each card in this six-card set measures 3-3/8" x 4-3/4". The black-and-white full-bleed photos dominate the front. The card backs have the player's name in bold at the top, with his bio below it. The player's headshot and facsimile autograph appear in the lower left. The Sonics logo is printed at the lower right of the unnumbered card backs.

	MT
Complete Set (6):	30.00
Common Player:	3.00
Benoit Benjamin	3.00
Eddie Johnson	3.00
K.C. Jones (CO)	4.00
Shawn Kemp	12.00
Derrick McKey	3.00
Gary Payton	12.00

1993-94 Supersonics Taco Time

Measuring 3-1/2" x 5", the cards were produced by Alrak Enterprises for Taco Time Restaurants in Western Washington. The card fronts showcased caricatures, with the player's first name in gold-foil. The Sonics' logo is in the background of the card fronts. "Not in our house" is also printed in gold foil on the front. The backs include a headshot of the player on the right, with a photo of the Seattle skyline in the background. The card is numbered in the upper left, with his name and bio printed on a slant inside a ghosted stripe. There are two No. 5 cards, as Detlef Schrempf was traded to the Sonics during the 12-week promotion at the restaurants.

		MT
	Complete Set (9):	20.00
	Common Player:	1.00
1	Nate McMillan	2.00
2	Sam Perkins	2.00
3	Gary Payton	7.00
4	Ricky Pierce	1.00
5A	Derrick McKey	2.00
5B	Detlef Schrempf	3.00
6	Shawn Kemp	7.00
7	George Karl (CO)	1.50
8	Kendall Gill	1.00
9	Michael Cage	1.00

1976 Superstar Socks

These 5" x 6-3/4" cards were used as a promotion by Superstar Socks, which is written on the front of each card in a fancy design. The player is shown in a close-up color photo, along with his facsimile signature. "The Superstars Sock. Cushioned comfort. In thick luxurious COTTON" is also written on the front. Backs have a player biography and statistics. The unnumbered cards were used to clamp the socks together and had a hole punched through them so the socks could be hung on a display rod.

	NM
Complete Set (9):	1000.
Common Player:	100.00
Kareem Abdul-Jabbar	160.00
Lucius Allen	100.00
Nate Archibald	125.00
Rick Berry	125.00
Doug Collins	100.00
Elvin Hayes	150.00
Spencer Haywood	100.00

1958-59 Syracuse Nationals

Measuring 8" x 10", the nine glossy photos were sold for 25 cents apiece or as an entire set for $2. The photos are unnumbered.

	NM
Complete Set (9):	1200.
Common Player:	100.00
Larry Costello	150.00
Connie Dierking	125.00
Hal Greer	200.00
Bob Hopkins	100.00
John Kerr	200.00
Togo Palazzi	100.00
Dolph Schayes	300.00
Paul Seymour	100.00
Team Photo	150.00

T

1998 Taco Bell Shaquille O'Neal

		MT
1	Shaquille O'Neal	10.00

1980-81 TCMA CBA

The 45-card, standard-size set features players from the Continental Basketball Association. The sets were originally available for $5.50 each direct from the CBA. The fronts have the team name printed along the left border with the horizontal backs featuring bio and stat information.

		NM
	Complete Set (45):	50.00
	Common Player:	1.00
1	Chubby Cox	1.00
2	Sylvester Cuyler	1.00
3	Harry Davis	1.00
4	Danny Salisbury	4.00
5	Cazzie Russell	4.00
6	Al Green	1.00
7	Rick Wilson	1.00
8	Jim Brogan	1.00
9	Andre McCarter	2.00
10	Jerry Baskerville	1.00
11	James Woods	1.00
12	Geoff Crompton	1.00
13	Korky Nelson	1.00
14	George Karl CO (Montana)	6.00
15	Stan Pietkiewicz	1.00
16	Raymond Townsend	1.00
17	Lenny Horton	1.00
18	Carl Bailey	1.00
19	Ken Jones	1.00
20	Rory Sparrow	2.00
ppp	Rochester (Mauro Panaggio CO)	1.00
22	Glenn Hagan	1.00
23	Larry Fogle	1.00
24	Wayne Abrams	1.00
25	Jerry Christian	1.00
26	Edgar Jones	1.00
27	Jerry Radocha	1.00
28	Greg Jackson	1.00
29	Eddie Mast (Player/Coach, Lehigh Valley)	1.00
30	Ron Davis	1.00
31	Tico Brown	1.00
32	Freeman Blade	1.00
33	Bill Klucas CO (Anchorage)	1.00
34	Melvin Davis	1.00
35	James Hardy	1.00
36	Brad Davis	3.00
37	Andre Wakefield	1.00
38	Brett Vroman	1.00
39	Larry Knight	1.00
40	Mel Bennett	1.00
41	Stan Eckwood	1.00
42	Andrew Parker	1.00
43	Billy Ray Bates	1.00
44	Matt Teahan	1.00
45	Carlton Green	1.00

1981-82 TCMA CBA

The 90-card, standard-size set features black and white photos on the card fronts with the backs having the card number, career statistics bio information and logos.

		MT
	Complete Set (90):	115.00
	Common Player:	1.00
1	1981 CBA Champions - Rochester Zeniths (Previous champions listed on back)	5.00
2	Wayne Abrams	1.00
3	Pete Taylor	1.00
4	George Torres	1.00
5	Henry Bibby	7.00
6	Rufus Harris	1.00
7	Donnie Koonce	1.00
8	Jeff Wilkins	2.00
9	Kurt Nimphius	2.00
10	Billy Ray Bates	3.00
11	James Lee	2.50
12	Marlon Redmond	1.00
13	Gary Mazza CO (Alberta)	1.00
14	Tony Fuller	1.00
15	Brad Davis	6.00
16	Joe Cooper	1.50
17	Andra Griffin	1.00
18	Rudy White	2.50
19	Ricky Williams	1.00

20	Glenn Hagan	2.00
21	Ernie Graham	1.00
22	Kevin Graham	1.00
23	Billy Reid	1.00
24	Mauro Panaggio CO (Rochester)	1.25
25	Bo Ellis	3.00
26	Ollie Matson	2.00
27	Tony Turner	1.00
28	Leo Papile CO (Quincy)	1.00
29	Larry Holmes	1.00
30	Steve Hayes	2.00
31	Carl Bailey	1.00
32	Tico Brown	1.25
33	Percy Davis	1.00
34	Al Leslie	1.00
35	Ken Dennard	2.00
36	Larry Spriggs	3.00
37	John Smith	1.00
38	Kenny Natt	2.00
39	Harry Heineken	1.00
40	Lowes Moore	1.50
41	Curtis Berry	1.50
42	Freeman Blade CO (Anchorage)	1.00
43	Larry Lawrence	1.00
44	Purvis Miller	1.25
45	Ron Valentine	1.00
46	Charles Floyd	1.00
47	Greg Cornelius	1.00
48	Clay Johnson	2.00
49	Bill Klucas CO (Billings)	1.00
50	Cazzie Russell P/CO (Lancaster)	8.00
51	Craig Shelton	2.50
52	Dave Britton	1.00
53	Ken Green	1.00
54	Stan Pawlak CO (Atlantic City)	1.00
55	Rich Yonakor	1.50
56	Darryl Gladden	1.00
57	Norman Black	1.00
58	Pete Harris	1.00
59	Anthony Roberts	1.50
60	Jawann Oldham	3.00
61	Sam Clancy	2.50
62	Andre McCarter	2.00
63	Joe Merten	1.00
64	Eddie Moss	1.00
65	Brad Branson	1.25
66	Lenny Horton	1.00
67	Jerome Henderson	1.00
68	Terry Stotts	1.00
69	Tony Wells	1.00
70	Rickey Green	6.00
71	Don Newman	1.00
72	Randy Owens	1.00
73	Erv Giddings	1.00
74	Barry Young	1.25
75	Jim Brogan	1.00
76	Richard Johnson	1.00
77	George Karl CO (Montana)	8.00
78	U.S. Reed	2.00
79	Fran Greenberg (PR Director)	1.25
80	Ron Davis	1.00
81	Larry Fogle	1.50
82	Clarence Kea	1.00
83	Steve Craig	1.00
84	Harry Davis	1.00
85	Jacky Dorsey	1.50
86	Herb Gray	1.00
87	Randy Johnson	1.00
88	Jim Drucker COMM	1.50
89	Lynbert Johnson	1.50
90	Checklist 1-90	3.00

1981 TCMA NBA

The NBA's greatest players are showcased in this 44-card set. The fronts are dominated by a color photo, while the backs have the player's name at the top in bold. His bio, career highlights and stats round out the card backs. The card number is listed after the TCMA copyright tag line in the lower right corner.

		MT
Complete Set (44):		95.00
Common Player:		.75
1	Alex Hannum	.75
2	Larry Foust	.75
3	George Mikan	10.00
4	Mel (Hutch) Hutchins	.75
5	Bob Pettit	4.00
6	Willis Reed	3.00
7	Adolph Schayes	2.00
8	Vern Mikkelsen (SP)	10.00
9	Cazzie Russell	1.50
10	Dick Van Arsdale	.75
11	Len Wilkens	3.00
12	Ray Felix	.75
13	Ed Macauley	1.50
14	Clyde Lovellette	1.50
15	Slater (Dugie) Martin	1.50
16	Bill Russell	15.00
17	Oscar Robertson (SP)	15.00
18	Bill Bradley	6.00
19	Elgin Baylor	8.00
20	Bill Sharman	5.00
21	Thomas (Satch) Sanders	.75
22	Dave Bing	2.00
23	Carl Braun	.75
24	Frank Selvy	.75
25	George Yardley	1.50
26	Dick McGuire	1.50
27	Leroy Ellis	.75
28	Jack Twyman	1.50
29	Nate Thurmond	2.00
30	Walt Frazier	5.00
31	John (Red) Kerr	2.00
32	Jerry West	10.00
33	John J. Egan (SP)	6.00
34	Jim Loscutoff	.75
35	Bob Leonard	.75
36	Rick Barry	3.00
37	Gene Shue	.75
38	Jerry Lucas	3.00
39	Dave DeBusschere	3.00
40	John Green, Charlie Tyra, Carl Braun, Richie Guerin, John George	.75
41	Bob Cousy	8.00
42	Walt Bellamy	1.50
43	Billy Cunningham	3.00
44	Wilt Chamberlain	15.00

1982-83 TCMA CBA

The 90-card, standard-size set was issued in two 45-card series and each card front features a black and white photo bordered by red lines. The CBA logo appears in the upper left corner. The card backs form a large puzzle.

		MT
Complete Set (90):		90.00
Common Player:		1.00
1	Cazzie Russell CO (Lancaster)	6.00
2	Boot Bond	1.50
3	Ron Charles	1.25
4	Charles Pittman	2.00
5	Calvin Garrett	2.00
6	Willie Jones	1.00
7	Riley Clarida	1.00
8	Jim Johnstone	1.00
9	Bobby Potts	1.00
10	Lowes Moore	1.50
11	Dwight Anderson	6.00
12	John Coughran	1.00
13	Mike Evans	2.00
14	Alan Hardy	1.00
15	Willie Smith	1.00
16	Oliver Mack	2.00
17	Checklist 1-45	3.00
18	Picture 1 (Action under basket)	1.25
19	James Lee	2.50
20	Kenny Natt	2.00
21	Cyrus Mann	1.00
22	Bobby Cattage	1.25
23	Garry Witts	1.00
24	Bill Klucas CO (Billings)	1.00
25	Al Smith	1.25
26	B.B. Fontenet	1.00
27	Chris Giles	1.00
28	Barry Young	1.50
29	Horace Wyatt	1.00
30	Robert Smith	1.50
31	Ron Baxter	1.50
32	Charlie Jones	1.25
33	Tico Brown	1.25
34	John McCullough	1.25
35	Dan Callandrillo	2.00
36	John Leonard	1.00
37	Sam Worthen	1.50
38	Dale Wilkinson	1.00
39	Gary Johnson	1.00
40	Dean Meminger CO (Albany)	2.00
41	Lloyd Terry	1.00
42	Mike Schultz	1.00
43	Darryl Gladden	1.00
44	Clarence Kea	1.50
45	Charlie Floyd	1.00
46	Skip Dillard	1.50
47	Craig Tucker	1.00
48	Gib Hinz	1.00
49	Tom Sienkiewicz	1.50
50	Larry Spriggs	3.00
51	Perry Moss	1.00
52	Gerald Sims	1.00
53	Alan Taylor	1.00
54	James Terry	1.25
55	John Nillen CO (Ohio)	1.00
56	Steve Burks	1.00
57	Anthony Martin	1.00
58	Purvis Miller	1.50
59	Kevin Smith	1.00
60	John Neumann CO (Maine)	2.00
61	Mike Davis	1.00
62	Gary Carter	1.00
63	Checklist 46-90	2.00
64	Picture 2 (Action under basket)	1.25
65	Charles Thompson	1.00
66	John Douglas	1.50
67	John Schweitz	1.00
68	Kevin Figaro	1.00
69	John Smith	1.00
70	Joe Cooper	1.50
71	Tony Brown	1.00
72	Mike Wilson	1.25
73	Wayne Abrams	1.00
74	T.X. Martin	1.00
75	Joe Merten	1.00
76	Joe Kopicki	1.00
77	Carl Nicks	1.50
78	Wayne Kreklow	1.00
79	Tony Guy	1.50
80	Dave Harshman CO (Wisconsin)	1.25
81	Bob Davis	1.00
82	Gary Mazza CO (Detroit)	1.00
83	Randy Owens	1.00
84	David Burns	1.00
85	Erv Giddings	1.00
86	JoJo Hunter	1.50
87	Frankie Sanders	1.00
88	Dave Richardson	1.00
89	Lionel Garrett	1.00
90	Marvin Barnes	5.00

1982-83 TCMA Lancaster CBA

The 30-card, standard-size set have black and white photography with a blue border. The horizontal backs contain bio information, along with team and league logos. All cards in the set feature the Lancaster Lightning's players and coaches, as the team won the 1981-82 CBA title.

		MT
Complete Set (30):		30.00
Common Player:		1.00
1	Lightning Wins 1982 CBA Championship	3.00
2	1982-83 Lancaster Lightning Team Picture	1.50
3	Seymour Kilstein (President)	1.00
4	Cazzie Russell CO	5.00
5	Cazzie Russell CO IA	5.00
6	Ed Koback (Operations)	2.50
7	Bob Danforth (Marketing)	1.00
8	Henry Bibby (In Action)	3.00
9	Joe Cooper (Center)	2.00
10	Joe Cooper IA	1.50
11	Curtis Berry	2.00
12	Curtis Berry IA	1.50
13	James Lee	2.50
14	James Lee IA	2.50
15	Ed Sherod IA	1.50
16	Charlie Floyd	1.00
17	Charlie Floyd IA	1.00
18	Darryl Gladden	1.00
19	Gladden In Action	1.00
20	Tom Sienkiewicz	2.00
21	Tom Sienkiewicz IA	1.50
22	Stan Williams	1.00
23	Willie Redden	1.00
24	Reginald Gaines	1.00
25	Gary (Cat) Johnson	2.00
26	Cat Johnson IA	1.50
27	Keith Hilliard	1.00
28	Keith Hilliard IA	1.00
29	Donald Seals	1.00
30	Rufus Harris	2.00

1994 Ted Williams Promo

This standard-size card of Charles Barkley was issued to promote the 1995 Ted Williams basketball release. The front features the same design as the regular-issue cards, with the back containing an advertisement of the set.

		MT
Complete Set (1):		2.00
Common Player:		2.00
P1	Charles Barkley	2.00

1994 Ted Williams

This set was limited in production to 2,999 cases and features key 1994 draft picks and second-year stars. Each card has a thick black, dull-colored border on the left side, with the player's name embossed off it in black and red letters and the Ted Williams logo. The remainder of the front has a full-color action photo. The back has the player's name in a black border and college statistics and biographical information on a volcanic eruption background. Cards were sold in packs of eight, and could include one of seven inserts: Eclipse, What's Up, Sir Charles' Royal Court, Ted Williams/Classic Co-op, The Gallery, Larry's Hardwood Legends and Kareem Abdul-Jabbar.

		MT
Complete Set (90):		10.00
Common Player:		.05
1	Derrick Alston	.05
2	Adrian Autry	.05
3	Damon Bailey	.20
4	Doremus Bennerman	.05
5	Randy Blocker	.05
6	Melvin Booker	.05
7	Jamie Brandon	.05
8	Barry Brown	.05
9	Joey Brown	.05
10	Albert Burditt	.05
11	Robert Churchwell	.05
12	Gary Collier	.05
13	Jevon Crudup	.05
14	Bill Curley	.05
15	Yinka Dare	.10
16	Rodney Dent	.05
17	Tony Dumas	.10
18	Howard Eisley	.10
19	Andrei Fetisov	.05
20	Travis Ford	.10
21	Abdul Fox	.05
22	Lawrence Funderburke	.10
23	Anthony Goldwire	.05
24	Chuck Graham	.05
25	Brian Grant	.75
26	Thomas Hamilton	.05
27	Darrin Hancock	.05
28	Carl Ray Harris	.05
29	Askia Jones	.05
30	Eddie Jones	1.00
31	Arturas Karnishovas	.05
32	Damon Key	.05
33	Jason Kidd	2.00
34	Antonio Lang	.10
35	Donyell Marshall	.75
36	Billy McCaffrey	.05
37	Jim McIlvaine	.05
38	Aaron McKie	.10
39	Anthony Miller	.05
40	Greg Minor	.25
41	Eric Mobley	.10
42	Eric Montross	.75
43	Harry Moore	.05
44	Dwayne Morton	.05
45	Gaylon Nickerson	.05
46	Cornell Parker	.05
47	Wesley Person	.50
48	Derrick Phelps	.10
49	Eric Piatkowski	.25
50	Kevin Rankin	.05
51	Brian Reese	.05
52	Khalid Reeves	.50
53	Clayton Ritter	.05
54	Carlos Rogers	.25
55	Jalen Rose	.35
56	Clifford Rozier	.25
57	Kevin Salvadori	.05
58	Jervaughn Scales	.05
59	Shawnelle Scott	.05
60	Robert Shannon	.05
61	Melvin Simon	.05
62	Dickey Simpkins	.25
63	Michael Smith	.25
64	Stevin Smith	.05
65	Byron Starks	.05
66	Aaron Swinson	.05
67	Shon Tarver	.05
68	Deon Thomas	.05
69	Brooks Thompson	.10
70	B.J. Tyler	.05
71	Myron Walker	.05
72	Charlie Ward	.25
73	Kendrick Warren	.05
74	Jamie Watson	.05
75	Jeff Webster	.05
76	Tracy Webster	.05
77	Monty Williams	.25
78	Dontonio Wingfield	.10
79	Steve Woodbury	.05
80	Charles Barkley	.50
81	Larry Bird	.50
82	Anfernee Hardaway	.25
83	Jamal Mashburn	.25
84	Chris Mills	.05
85	Harold Miner	.10
86	Alonzo Mourning	.25
87	Dikembe Mutombo	.25
88	Rodney Rogers	.10
89	Checklist #1	.05
90	Checklist #2	.05

1994 Ted Williams Constellation

This nine-card set was randomly included in packs and includes cards from the main set as well as inserts, with the only difference being the numbering C1-C9 and individual numbering on the back.

		MT
Complete Set (9):		25.00
Common Player:		2.00
1	Kareem Abdul-Jabbar	3.00
2	Charles Barkley	2.50
3	Larry Bird	6.00
4	Anfernee Hardaway	2.00
5	Juwan Howard	3.00
6	Jason Kidd	5.00
7	George Mikan	2.00
8	Alonzo Mourning	2.00
9	Glenn Robinson	4.00

1994 Ted Williams Eclipse

These Ted Williams inserts feature NBA legends and could be found one per every 12 packs. The card front has an action photo, the Ted Williams logo, and the player's name and set logo at the bottom. The card back, numbered with an "EC" prefix, has a career summary of the player against a background with an eclipse motif.

		MT
Complete Set (9):		15.00
Common Player:		1.00
1	Rick Barry	2.00
2	Larry Bird	4.00
3	Bob Pettit	1.00
4	Hal Greer	1.00
5	Kareem Abdul Jabbar	3.00
6	Pete Maravich	2.00
7	George Mikan	2.00
8	Dolph Schayes	1.00
9	Checklist	1.00

1994 Ted Williams The Gallery

These nine insert cards, available one per every 16 packs, feature artistic drawings of the players. Each card front has two color sketches of the player, plus the logos for the set and card company. The artist's signature also appears. The card back, numbered using a "G" prefix, has biographical information and a career summary, along with a collection of artist's tools. A serial number also appears on the back.

		MT
Complete Set (9):		25.00
Common Player:		1.50
1	Charles Barkley	4.00
2	Larry Bird	7.00
3	Kareem Abdul Jabbar	4.00
4	Walt Frazier	2.00
5	Anfernee Hardaway	3.00
6	Jamal Mashburn	3.00
7	Alonzo Mourning	2.00
8	Dikembe Mutombo	1.50
9	Checklist	1.50

1994 Ted Williams Kareem Abdul-Jabbar

This nine-card set traces the career of Hall of Fame center Kareem Abdul-Jabbar. The cards, numbered on the back using a "KAJ" prefix, were found exclusively in mass retail packs, one per every 16 packs. The card front has a color action photo, with a marble-like panel at the bottom which contains Jabbar's name. The Ted Williams logo is also on the front. The back has a brief career summary.

		MT
Complete Set (9):		15.00
Common Player:		2.00
1	Kareem Abdul Jabbar	2.00
2	Kareem Abdul Jabbar	2.00
3	Kareem Abdul Jabbar	2.00
4	Kareem Abdul Jabbar	2.00
5	Kareem Abdul Jabbar	2.00
6	Kareem Abdul Jabbar	2.00
7	Kareem Abdul Jabbar	2.00
8	Kareem Abdul Jabbar	2.00
9	Checklist	2.00

1994 Ted Williams Larry's Hardwood Legends

These insert cards were found in hobby packs only, one every eight packs. The cards, distributed regionally, feature two legends from each of four teams - the New York Knicks, the Golden State Warriors, the Chicago Bulls and Boston Celtics. A checklist card was also included. Cards are numbered using an "HL" prefix. The front has an action photo of the player, along with the logos for the set and company. The back has biographical information, a ghosted photo and career summary.

		MT
Complete Set (9):		7.50
Common Player:		.50
1	Walt Frazier	2.00
2	Dave DeBusschere	1.00
3	Rick Barry	2.00
4	Nate Thurmond	.50
5	Artis Gilmore	.50
6	Norm Van Lier	.50
7	Bill Sharman	.50
8	Jo Jo White	.50
9	Checklist	.50

1994 Ted Williams Sir Charles' Royal Court

This nine-card set features Charles Barkley's favorite players. Cards were randomly included one per every 12th pack. The card front has a color action photo, plus logos for the set and company. The back, numbered using an "RC" prefix, has biographical information and a career summary, along with a sword, with the player's name on it, flanking the right side.

		MT
Complete Set (9):		15.00
Common Player:		.50
1	Anfernee Hardaway	2.00
2	Harold Miner	.50
3	Jason Kidd	6.00
4	Donyell Marshall	2.00
5	Jamal Mashburn	2.00
6	Juwan Howard	2.00
7	Alonzo Mourning	2.00
8	Aaron Swinson	.50
9	Checklist	.50

1994 Ted Williams TWCC/Classic Co-op

This nine-card set features current NBA superstars and rookies. Cards, random inserts in every 12th pack, are numbered on the back using a "CO" prefix. The front has an action photo of the player against a black background which has card logos for the Ted Williams and Classic card companies; Classic supplied the rights for players such as Glenn Robinson and Grant Hill to appear in the set. The back has a summary of the player's career accomplishments against a basketball court motif.

		MT
Complete Set (9):		25.00
Common Player:		1.00
1	Charles Barkley	3.00
2	Larry Bird	6.00
3	Anfernee Hardaway	2.00
4	Grant Hill	8.00
5	Jason Kidd	6.00
6	Pete Maravich	2.00
7	Alonzo Mourning	1.50
8	Glenn Robinson	6.00
9	Checklist	1.00

1994 Ted Williams What's Up?

This nine-card set showcases eight rookies who were making an impact during their NBA debut season. Each card front has a color action photo of the player, along with the set and card company logos. The back has a summary of the player's accomplishments, against a brick wall background. Cards, numbered using a "WU" prefix, were randomly included in every 12th pack.

		MT
	Complete Set (9):	15.00
	Common Player:	1.00
1	Brian Grant	2.00
2	Eric Montross	2.00
3	Jason Kidd	6.00
4	Anthony Miller	1.00
5	Khalid Reeves	1.00
6	Carlos Rogers	1.00
7	Jalen Rose	1.00
8	Charlie Ward	1.00
9	Checklist	1.00

1989-90 Timberwolves Burger King

Sponsored by Burger King to celebrate the team's first season in the NBA, the seven-card set was released with a Player Cards Collector Set that featured a schedule and places for the cards on the inside. The card fronts have the team's name, logo and "Inaugural Season" banner at the top of the photo. The player's name, position and jersey number are listed beneath the photo. The unnumbered card backs have the T-wolves' logo, team name and the player's position and number at the top. His name is included in a stripe, while his bio and stats are listed below. A tag line at the bottom explains the cards were produced by NBA Hoops.

		MT
	Complete Set (7):	5.00
	Common Player:	1.00
19	Tony Campbell	1.00
23	Tyrone Corbin	1.00
24	Pooh Richardson	2.00
35	Sidney Lowe	1.00
42	Sam Mitchell	1.00
45	Randy Breuer	1.00
54	Brad Lohaus	1.00

1957-58 Topps

Topps' first basketball set (and only basketball set until 1969) has 80 standard-size cards and lots of rookies, including Bill Sharman (only card), Easy Ed Macauley, Bob Pettit, Paul Arizin, Dolph Schayes, Harry Gallatin, Tom Gola, Clyde Lovellette, Bill Russell and Maurice Stokes, his only card. Topps double printed several cards in this set; many were the biggest stars at that time. DP means the card was double printed.

		NM
	Complete Set (80):	5500.
	Common Player:	35.00
	Common Player (DP):	25.00
1	*Nat Clifton*	250.00
2	*George Yardley*	55.00
3	*Neil Johnston* (DP)	50.00
4	Carl Braun	45.00
5	*Bill Sharman* (DP)	170.00
6	*George King*	35.00
7	*Kenny Sears* (DP)	35.00
8	*Dick Ricketts*	35.00
9	Jack Nichols	25.00
10	*Paul Arizin* (DP)	110.00
11	Chuck Noble	25.00
12	*Slater Martin*	65.00
13	*Dolph Schayes* (DP)	125.00
14	Dick Atha	25.00
15	*Frank Ramsey*	75.00
16	*Dick McGuire*	50.00
17	*Bob Cousy* (DP)	525.00
18	*Larry Foust* (DP)	35.00
19	*Tom Heinsohn*	300.00
20	Bill Thieben	25.00
21	Don Meineke (DP)	35.00
22	Tom Marshall	35.00
23	Dick Garmaker	35.00
24	*Bob Pettit* (DP)	200.00
25	Jim Krebs	35.00
26	*Gene Shue*	65.00
27	*Ed Macauley* (DP)	75.00
28	*Vern Mikkelsen*	75.00
29	*Willie Naulls*	65.00
30	*Walter Dukes*	35.00
31	Dave Piontek	25.00
32	*John Kerr*	150.00
33	*Larry Costello* (DP)	50.00
34	*Woody Sauldsberry*	35.00
35	*Ray Felix*	40.00
36	Ernie Beck	35.00
37	*Cliff Hagan*	120.00
38	Guy Sparrow	25.00
39	*Jim Loscutoff* (DP)	55.00
40	*Arnie Risen* (DP)	40.00
41	Joe Graboski	35.00
42	*Maurice Stokes* (DP)	120.00
43	*Rod Hundley*	120.00
44	*Tom Gola*	75.00
45	Med Park	40.00
46	Mel Hutchins	25.00
47	Larry Friend	25.00
48	*Lennie Rosenbluth*	55.00
49	Walt Davis	35.00
50	Richie Regan	40.00
51	*Frank Selvy* (DP)	50.00
52	Art Spoelstra	25.00
53	*Bob Hopkins* (DP)	40.00
54	*Earl Lloyd* (DP)	40.00
55	Phil Jordan	25.00
56	*Bob Houbregs*	40.00
57	Lou Tsioropoulas	25.00
58	Ed Conlin	40.00
59	*Al Bianchi*	75.00
60	*George Dempsey*	40.00
61	Chuck Share	35.00
62	*Harry Gallatan* (DP)	45.00
63	Bob Harrison	35.00
64	Bob Burrow	25.00
65	Win Wilfong	25.00
66	*Jack McMahon* (DP)	35.00
67	Jack George	35.00
68	Charlie Tyra	25.00
69	Ron Sobie	35.00
70	Jack Coleman	35.00
71	*Jack Twyman* (DP)	100.00
72	*Paul Seymour*	40.00
73	*Jim Paxson* (DP)	50.00
74	*Bob Leonard*	40.00
75	Andy Phillip	50.00
76	Joe Holup	35.00
77	*Bill Russell*	1900.
78	*Clyde Lovellette* (DP)	110.00
79	Ed Fleming	25.00
80	*Dick Schnittker*	100.00

1968-69 Topps Test

This test-issue set from Topps features posed black-and-white photos. The player's name, team and height appear at the bottom of the card. The numbered, horizontal backs are different for each player, but when pieced together form a picture of Wilt Chamberlain dunking.

		NM
	Complete Set (22):	14000.
	Common Player:	250.00
1	Wilt Chamberlain	2700.
2	Hal Greer	500.00
3	Chet Walker	250.00
4	Bill Russell	2200.
5	John Havlicek	1200.
6	Cazzie Russell	400.00
7	Willis Reed	600.00
8	Bill Bradley	800.00
9	Odie Smith	250.00
10	Dave Bing	600.00
11	Dave DeBusschere	400.00
12	Earl Monroe	600.00
13	Nate Thurmond	500.00
14	Jim King	250.00
15	Len Wilkens	600.00
16	Bill Bridges	250.00
17	Zelmo Beaty	250.00
18	Elgin Baylor	800.00
19	Jerry West	1200.
20	Jerry Sloan	375.00
21	Jerry Lucas	500.00
22	Oscar Robertson	1000.

1969-70 Topps

This 99-card set ushered in the first great era of basketball cards. Cards were oversized (approximately 2-1/2" x 4-3/4") and show a posed shot of the player in an oval with a white border containing generic basketball scenes. The showcase card in the set is the Lew Alcindor rookie, a card which was issued before he even had played a game with the Bucks (1969-70 was his first year in the NBA). The theory is Topps, knowing the NBA would receive tremendous interest when Alcindor entered the league, built a set to capitalize on that interest and thus included Lew. This marks the first and only time until the 1980s a "pre-rookie" card of any player was released by Topps. This first Topps set featured no subsets or All-Star designations.

		NM
	Complete Set (99):	1750.
	Common Player:	4.00
	Pack (10):	670.00
	Wax Box (24):	12000.
1	Wilt Chamberlain	190.00
2	*Gail Goodrich*	30.00
3	*Cazzie Russell*	15.00
4	*Darrall Imhoff*	4.00
5	Bailey Howell	5.00
6	*Lucius Allen*	10.00
7	*Tom Boerwinkle*	6.00
8	*Jimmy Walker*	6.00
9	*John Block*	5.00
10	*Nate Thurmond*	30.00
11	Gary Gregor	4.00
12	*Gus Johnson*	15.00
13	Luther Rackley	4.00
14	*Jon McGlocklin*	6.00
15	*Connie Hawkins*	45.00
16	Johnny Egan	4.00
17	Jim Washington	4.00
18	*Dick Barnett*	8.00
19	Tom Meschery	4.00
20	*John Havlicek*	175.00
21	Eddie Miles	4.00
22	Walt Wesley	4.00
23	*Rick Adelman*	10.00
24	Al Attles	4.00
25	*Kareem Abdul-Jabbar*	550.00
26	*Jack Marin*	8.00
27	*Walt Hazzard*	12.00
28	Donnie Dierking	4.00
29	*Keith Erickson*	10.00
30	*Bob Rule*	7.50
31	*Dick Van Arsdale*	9.00
32	*Archie Clark*	8.00
33	*Terry Dischinger*	6.00
34	*Henry Finkel*	5.00
35	Elgin Baylor	50.00
36	Ron Williams	4.00
37	Loy Peterson	4.00
38	Guy Rodgers	4.00
39	Toby Kimball	4.00
40	*Billy Cunningham*	50.00
41	*Joe Caldwell*	7.00
42	*Leroy Ellis*	6.00
43	*Bill Bradley*	155.00
44	Len Wilkens	35.00
45	*Jerry Lucas*	45.00
46	*Neal Walk*	5.00
47	*Emmette Bryant*	5.00
49	*Mel Counts*	5.00
50	Oscar Robertson	70.00
51	*Jim Barnett*	4.00
52	Don Smith	4.00
53	Jim Davis	4.00
54	*Wally Jones*	5.00
55	*Dave Bing*	40.00
56	*Wes Unseld*	42.00
57	Joe Ellis	4.00
58	John Tresvant	4.00
59	*Larry Siegfried*	6.00
60	*Willis Reed*	50.00
61	*Paul Silas*	20.00
62	*Bob Weiss*	10.00
63	Willie McCarter	4.00
64	*Don Kojis*	5.00
65	*Lou Hudson*	22.00
66	Jim King	4.00
67	*Luke Jackson*	5.00
68	*Len Chappell*	5.00
69	Ray Scott	4.00
70	*Jeff Mullins*	8.00
71	Howie Komives	4.00
72	*Tom Sanders*	7.00
73	Dick Snyder	4.00
74	*Dave Stallworth*	5.00
75	*Elvin Hayes*	60.00
76	Art Harris	4.00
77	Don Ohl	4.00
78	*Bob Love*	30.00
79	*Tom Van Arsdale*	10.00
80	*Earl Monroe*	45.00
81	Greg Smith	4.00
82	*Don Nelson*	35.00
83	*Happy Hairston*	10.00
84	Hal Greer	8.00
85	*Dave DeBusschere*	45.00
86	*Bill Bridges*	7.00
87	*Herm Gilliam*	5.00
88	Jim Fox	4.00
89	Bob Boozer	4.00
90	Jerry West	100.00
91	*Chet Walker*	15.00
92	*Flynn Robinson*	5.00
93	Clyde Lee	4.00
94	*Kevin Loughery*	10.00
95	Walt Bellamy	10.00
96	Art Williams	4.00
97	*Adrian Smith*	5.00
98	*Walt Frazier*	60.00
99	Checklist	300.00

1969-70 Topps Rulers

These 2-1/2" x 9-7/8" paper-like cartoon drawings were inserted in 1969-70 Topps wax packs. Ruler marks on the left side of the card tell how tall the player pictured is. The set was to be 24 cards, but card number 5 was never issued.

		NM
	Complete Set (23):	450.00
	Common Player:	5.00
1	Walt Bellamy	10.00
2	Jerry West	50.00
3	Bailey Howell	5.00
4	Elvin Hayes	20.00
5	Not Issued	
6	Bob Rule	5.00
7	Gail Goodrich	12.00
8	Jeff Mullins	6.00
9	John Havlicek	40.00
10	Lew Alcindor	120.00
11	Wilt Chamberlain	80.00
12	Nate Thurmond	12.00
13	Hal Greer	10.00
14	Lou Hudson	5.00
15	Jerry Lucas	15.00
16	Dave Bing	12.00
17	Walt Frazier	20.00
18	Gus Johnson	7.00
19	Willis Reed	18.00
20	Earl Monroe	18.00
21	Billy Cunningham	15.00
22	Wes Unseld	14.00
23	Bob Boozer	5.00
24	Oscar Robertson	40.00

1970-71 Topps

Topps' second NBA set grew to 176 cards and again continued the use of oversize (approximately 2-1/2" x 4-3/4") cards. A basketball in the lower right corner contains the player name and team. Cards again featured cut-outs of the players. For the first time, subsets were included in Topps basketball cards. These included separate All-Star cards and a game-by-game summary of the NBA championship. The second series is somewhat more difficult to find than the first. Rookies in this set include Pat Riley, Bob Dandridge, Calvin Murphy, Norm Van Lier, Pete Maravich and Jo Jo White. AS means All-Star.

		NM
	Complete Set (175):	1150.
	Common Player (1-110):	2.50
	Common Player (111-175):	3.50
	Series 1 Pack (10):	160.00
	Series 1 Wax Box (24):	2950.
	Series 2 Pack (10):	235.00
	Series 2 Wax Box (24):	4275.
1	NBA Scoring Leaders (Lew Alcindor, Jerry West, Elvin Hayes)	35.00
2	NBA Scoring (Jerry West, Lew Alcindor, Elvin Hayes) (West)	35.00
3	NBA field goal percentage leaders (Johnny Green, Darrall Imhoff, Lou Hudson)	2.50
4	NBA FT Pct. Leaders (Flynn Robinson, Chet Walker, Jeff Mullins)	9.00
5	NBA Rebound Leaders (Elvin Hayes, Wes Unseld, Lew Alcindor)	25.00
6	NBA Assist Leaders (Len Wilkens, Walt Frazier, Clem Haskins)	7.00
7	Bill Bradley	40.00
8	Ron Williams	2.50
9	Otto Moore	2.50
10	John Havlicek (SP)	70.00
11	*George Wilson*	3.50
12	John Trapp	2.50
13	*Pat Riley*	60.00
14	Jim Washington	2.50
15	Bob Rule	2.50
16	Bob Weiss	3.50
17	Neil Johnson	2.50
18	Walt Bellamy	5.00
19	McCoy McLemore	2.50
20	Earl Monroe	15.00
21	Wally Anderzunas	2.50
22	Guy Rodgers	2.50
23	Rick Roberson	2.50
24	Cl 1-110	40.00
25	Jimmy Walker	2.50
26	*Mike Riordan*	5.00
27	Henry Finkel	2.50
28	Joe Ellis	2.50
29	Mike Davis	2.50
30	Lou Hudson	5.00
31	Lucius Allen (SP)	7.00
32	Toby Kimball	2.50
33	Luke Jackson	2.50
34	Johnny Egan	2.50
35	Leroy Ellis	2.50
36	Jack Marin (SP)	7.00
37	Joe Caldwell (SP)	7.00
38	Keith Erickson	4.00
39	Don Smith	2.50
40	Flynn Robinson	2.50
41	Bob Boozer	2.50
42	Howie Komives	2.50
43	Dick Barnett	2.50
44	*Stu Lantz*	5.00
45	Dick Van Arsdale	3.50
46	Jerry Lucas	15.00
47	*Don Chaney*	9.00
48	Ray Scott	2.50
49	Dick Cunningham	2.50
50	Wilt Chamberlain	90.00
51	Kevin Loughery	6.00
52	Stan McKenzie	2.50
53	Fred Foster	2.50
54	Jim Davis	2.50
55	Walt Wesley	2.50
56	Bill Hewitt	2.50
57	Darrall Imhoff	2.50
58	John Block	2.50
59	Al Attles (SP)	5.00
60	Chet Walker	5.00
61	Luther Rackley	2.50
62	*Jerry Chambers*	7.00
63	*Bob Dandridge*	9.00
64	Dick Snyder	2.50
65	Elgin Baylor	30.00
66	Connie Dierking	2.50
67	*Steve Kuberski*	4.00
68	Tom Boerwinkle	4.00
69	Paul Silas	5.00
70	Elvin Hayes	30.00
71	Bill Bridges	3.00
72	Wes Unseld	14.00
73	Herm Gilliam	2.50
74	*Bobby Smith*	7.00
75	Lew Alcindor	110.00
76	Jeff Mullins	4.00
77	Happy Hairston	4.00
78	Dave Stallworth	2.50
79	Fred Hetzel	2.50
80	Len Wilkens	20.00
81	*Johnny Green*	4.00
82	Erwin Mueller	2.50
83	Wally Jones	2.50
84	Bob Love	8.00
85	*Dick Garrett*	3.00
86	Don Nelson (SP)	18.00
87	Neal Walk	2.50
88	Larry Siegfried	4.00
89	Gary Gregor	2.50
90	Nate Thurmond	12.00
91	John Warren	2.50
92	Gus Johnson	2.50
93	Gail Goodrich	12.00
94	Dorrie Murrey	2.50
95	Cazzie Russell (SP)	10.00
96	Terry Dischinger	2.50
97	*Norm Van Lier* (SP)	15.00
98	Jim Fox	2.50
99	Tom Meschery	2.50
100	Oscar Robertson	40.00
101	Checklist 111-175	25.00
102	Rich Johnson	2.50
103	Mel Counts	2.50
104	*Bill Hosket* (SP)	6.00
105	Archie Clark	4.00
106	Walt Frazier (AS)	14.00
107	Jerry West (AS)	28.00
108	Bill Cunningham (AS)	10.00
109	Connie Hawkins (AS)	6.00
110	Willis Reed (AS)	10.00
111	Nate Thurmond (AS)	3.00
112	John Havlicek (AS)	30.00
113	Elgin Baylor (AS)	15.00
114	Oscar Robertson (AS)	25.00
115	Lou Hudson (AS)	3.00
116	Emmette Bryant	3.00
117	Greg Howard	3.00
118	Rick Adelman	5.00
119	Barry Clemens	3.00
120	Walt Frazier	30.00
121	*Jim Barnes*	4.00
122	Bernie Williams	3.00
123	*Pete Maravich*	275.00
124	*Matt Guokas*	10.00
125	Dave Bing	14.00
126	John Tresvant	3.00
127	Shaler Halimon	3.00
128	Don Ohl	3.00
129	*Fred Carter*	7.00
130	Connie Hawkins	15.00
131	Jim King	3.00
132	*Ed Manning*	6.00
133	Adrian Smith	3.00
134	Walt Hazzard	6.00
135	Dave DeBusschere	15.00
136	Don Kojis	3.00
137	*Calvin Murphy*	40.00
138	Nate Bowman	3.00
139	Jon McGlocklin	4.00
140	Billy Cunningham	15.00
141	Willie McCarter	3.00
142	Jim Barnett	3.00
143	*Jo Jo White*	20.00
144	Clyde Lee	3.00
145	Tom Van Arsdale	5.00
146	Len Chappell	3.00
147	Lee Winfield	3.00
148	*Jerry Sloan*	20.00
149	Art Harris	3.00
150	Willis Reed	18.00
151	Art Williams	3.00
152	Don May	3.00
153	Loy Petersen	3.00
154	Dave Gambee	3.00
155	Hal Greer	5.00
156	Dave Newmark	3.00
157	Jimmy Collins	3.00
158	Bill Turner	3.00
159	Eddie Miles	3.00
160	Jerry West	55.00
161	Bob Quick	3.00
162	Fred Crawford	3.00
163	Tom Sanders	4.00
164	Dale Schlueter	3.00
165	*Clem Haskins*	8.00
166	Greg Smith	3.00
167	*Rod Thorn*	9.00
168	Playoff Game 1 (Willis Reed)	7.00
169	Playoff Game 2 (Dick Garrett)	3.00
170	Playoff Game 3 (Dave DeBusschere)	7.00
171	Playoff Game 4 (Jerry West)	15.00
172	Playoff Game 5 (Bill Bradley)	12.00
173	Playoff Game 6 (Wilt Chamberlain)	16.00
174	Playoff Game 7 (Walt Frazier)	9.00
175	Champs Knicks	22.00

1970-71 Topps Posters

One of these 24 posters was inserted into a wax pack of basketball cards. Printed on thin white paper stock, they feature an action shot of an NBA star, with his name in bold letters near the top. Since these 8x10 inch posters were folded several times to fit in the packs, it's impossible to find any in Mint condition.

		NM
	Complete Set (24):	175.00
	Common Player:	2.00
1	Walt Frazier	10.00
2	Joe Caldwell	2.00
3	Willis Reed	10.00
4	Elvin Hayes	15.00
5	Jeff Mullins	2.00
6	Oscar Robertson	20.00
7	Dave Bing	8.00
8	Jerry Sloan	4.00
9	Leroy Ellis	2.00
10	Hal Greer	3.00
11	Emmette Bryant	2.00
12	Bob Rule (Bill Russell in background of photo)	10.00
13	Lew Alcindor	50.00
14	Chet Walker	3.00
15	Jerry West	25.00
16	Billy Cunningham	5.00
17	Wilt Chamberlain	40.00
18	John Havlicek	25.00
19	Lou Hudson	4.00
20	Earl Monroe	12.00
21	Wes Unseld	8.00
22	Connie Hawkins	15.00
23	Tom Van Arsdale	3.00
24	Len Chappell	2.00

1971-72 Topps

This set not only saw an expansion in the set size from 175 to 233 cards, but a reduction in card size to the standard 2-1/2" x 3-1/2". This issue also introduced collectors to the American Basketball Association, and its stars - Dan Issel, Charlie Scott, Rick Mount, and future Hall of Famer Rick Barry. Although All-Star designations were omitted this year, subsets included a game-by-game summary of the NBA championship and NBA/ABA statistical leaders. Rookies in this set include Tiny Archibald, Rudy Tomjanovich, Bob Lanier, Larry Brown, Issel and Barry. Second-year cards included Norm Van Lier, Pete Maravich, Calvin Murphy, Bob Dandridge and Jo Jo White. This set has the final regular-issue card of Elgin Baylor.

		NM
	Complete Set (233):	800.00
	Common Player:	1.50
	Pack (10):	325.00
	Wax Box (12):	3275.
	Wax Box (24):	6000.
1	Oscar Robertson	40.00
2	Bill Bradley	25.00
3	Jim Fox	1.50
4	*John Johnson*	4.00
5	Luke Jackson	1.50
6	Don May	1.50
7	Kevin Loughery	2.50
8	Terry Dischinger	1.50
9	Neal Walk	1.50
10	Elgin Baylor	25.00
11	Rick Adelman	3.00
12	Clyde Lee	1.50
13	Jerry Chambers	1.50
14	Fred Carter	2.00
15	Tom Boerwinkle	1.50
16	John Block	1.50
17	Dick Barnett	1.50
18	Henry Finkel	1.50
19	Norm Van Lier	4.00
20	*Spencer Haywood*	9.00
21	George Johnson	1.50
22	Bobby Lewis	1.50
23	Bill Hewitt	1.50
24	Walt Hazzard	3.00
25	Happy Hairston	2.00
26	George Wilson	1.50
27	Lucius Allen	2.00
28	Jim Washington	1.50
29	*Nate Archibald*	35.00
30	Willis Reed	9.00
31	Erwin Mueller	1.50
32	Art Harris	1.50
33	Pete Cross	1.50
34	*Geoff Petrie*	5.00
35	John Havlicek	35.00
36	Larry Siegfried	1.50
37	John Tresvant	1.50
38	Ron Williams	1.50
39	Lamar Green	1.50
40	Bob Rule	1.50
41	*Jim McMillian*	3.00
42	Wally Jones	2.00
43	Bob Boozer	1.50
44	Eddie Miles	1.50
45	Bob Love	4.50
46	Claude English	1.50
47	*Dave Cowens*	50.00
48	Emmette Bryant	1.50
49	Dave Stallworth	1.50
50	Jerry West	40.00
51	Joe Ellis	1.50
52	Walt Wesley	1.50
53	Howie Komives	1.50
54	Paul Silas	3.00
55	Pete Maravich	65.00
56	Gary Gregor	1.50
57	*Sam Lacey*	2.50
58	Calvin Murphy	6.00
59	Bob Dandridge	2.50
60	Hal Greer	4.50
61	Keith Erickson	2.00
62	Joe Cooke	2.00
63	*Bob Lanier*	40.00
64	Don Kojis	1.50
65	Walt Frazier	16.00
66	Chet Walker	2.50
67	Dick Garrett	1.50
68	John Trapp	1.50
69	Jo Jo White	5.00
70	Wilt Chamberlain	50.00
71	Dave Sorenson	1.50
72	Jim King	1.50
73	Cazzie Russell	3.00
74	Jon McGlocklin	1.50
75	Tom Van Arsdale	1.50
76	Dale Schlueter	1.50
77	Gus Johnson	2.00
78	Dave Bing	7.00
79	Billy Cunningham	8.00
80	Len Wilkens	10.00
81	Jerry Lucas	7.00
82	Don Chaney	3.00
83	McCoy McLemore	1.50
84	Bob Kauffman	1.50
85	Dick Van Arsdale	1.50
86	Johnny Green	1.50
87	Jerry Sloan	4.50
88	Luther Rackley	1.50
89	Shaler Halimon	1.50
90	Jimmy Walker	1.50
91	*Rudy Tomjanovich*	25.00
92	Levi Fontaine	1.50
93	Bobby Smith	1.50
94	Bob Arnzen	1.50
95	Wes Unseld	6.00

96 Clem Haskins 2.00
97 Jim Davis 1.50
98 Steve Kuberski 2.00
99 Mike Davis 1.50
100 Kareem Abdul-Jabbar 50.00
101 Willie McCarter 1.50
102 Charlie Paulk 1.50
103 Lee Winfield 1.50
104 Jim Barnett 1.50
105 Connie Hawkins 8.00
106 Archie Clark 2.00
107 Dave DeBusschere 8.00
108 Stu Lantz 1.50
109 Don Smith 1.50
110 Lou Hudson 3.00
111 Leroy Ellis 1.50
112 Jack Marin 2.00
113 Matt Guokas 3.00
114 Don Nelson 7.00
115 Jeff Mullins 1.50
116 Walt Bellamy 4.50
117 Bob Quick 1.50
118 John Warren 1.50
119 Barry Clemens 1.50
120 Elvin Hayes 12.00
121 Gail Goodrich 8.00
122 Ed Manning 1.50
123 Herm Gilliam 1.50
124 *Dennis Awtrey* 2.50
125 John Hummer 1.50
126 Mike Riordan 1.50
127 Mel Counts 1.50
128 Bob Weiss 1.50
129 Greg Smith 1.50
130 Earl Monroe 10.00
131 Nate Thurmond 6.00
132 Bill Bridges 1.50
133 NBA Playoffs Game 1 (Lew Alcindor) 10.00
134 NBA Playoffs Game 2 (Two Straight) 1.50
135 NBA Playoffs Game 3 (Three in a Row) 1.50
136 NBA Playoffs Game 4 (Oscar Robertson) 6.00
137 NBA Champs Celebrate (Bucks/Bullets) 1.50
138 NBA Scoring Leaders (Lew Alcindor, Elvin Hayes, John Havlicek) 15.00
139 NBA Scoring Average Leaders (Lew Alcindor, John Havlicek, Elvin Hayes) 15.00
140 NBA Field Goal Percentage Leaders (Johnny Green, Lew Alcindor, Wilt Chamberlain) 12.00
141 NBA Free Throw Percentage Leaders (Chet Walker, Oscar Robertson, Ron Williams) 1.50
142 NBA Rebound Leaders (Wilt Chamberlain, Elvin Hayes, Lew Alcindor) 20.00
143 NBA Assist Leaders (Norm Van Lier, Oscar Robertson, Jerry West) 6.00
144 NBA Checklist 1-144 10.00
145 ABA Checklist 145-233 10.00
146 ABA Scoring Leaders (Dan Issel, John Brisker, Charlie Scott) 2.00
147 ABA Scoring Average Leaders (Dan Issel, Rick Barry, John Brisker) 3.00
148 ABA 2-point FG Percentage Leaders (Zelmo Beaty, Bill Paultz, Roger Brown) 1.50
149 ABA Free Throw Percentage Leaders (Rick Barry, Darrel Carrier, Billy Keller) 2.00
150 ABA Rebound Leaders (Mel Daniels, Julius Keye, Mike Lewis) 1.50
151 ABA Assist Leaders (Bill Melchionni, Mack Calvin, Charlie Scott) 1.50
152 *Larry Brown* 25.00
153 Bob Bedell 2.00
154 Merv Jackson 2.00
155 Joe Caldwell 3.00
156 *Billy Paultz* 4.00
157 Les Hunter 2.00
158 Charlie Williams 2.00
159 Stew Johnson 2.00
160 *Mack Calvin* 6.00
161 Don Sidle 2.00
162 Mike Barrett 2.00
163 Tom Workman 2.00
164 Joe Hamilton 2.00
165 *Zelmo Beaty* 7.00
166 Dan Hester 2.00
167 Bob Verga 2.00
168 Wilbert Jones 2.00
169 Skeeter Swift 2.00
170 *Rick Barry* 55.00
171 *Bill Keller* 3.00
172 Ron Franz 2.00
173 *Roland Taylor* 2.00
174 Julian Hammond 2.00
175 *Steve Jones* 5.00
176 Gerald Govan 2.00
177 *Darrell Carrier* 3.00
178 *Ron Boone* 4.00
179 George Peeples 2.00
180 John Brisker 2.00
181 *Doug Moe* 8.00
182 Ollie Taylor 2.00
183 Bob Netolicky 2.00
184 Sam Robinson 2.00
185 James Jones 2.00
186 Julius Keye 2.00
187 Wayne Hightower 2.00
188 *Warren Armstrong* 2.00
189 Mike Lewis 2.00
190 *Charlie Scott* 8.00
191 Jim Ard 2.00
192 George Lehmann 2.00
193 Ira Harge 2.00
194 *Willie Wise* 5.00
195 *Mel Daniels* 8.00
196 Larry Cannon 2.00
197 Jim Eakins 2.00
198 Rich Jones 2.00
199 *Bill Melchionni* 4.50
200 *Dan Issel* 40.00
201 George Stone 2.00
202 George Thompson 2.00
203 Craig Raymond 2.00
204 *Freddie Lewis* 3.00
205 George Carter 2.00
206 Lonnie Wright 2.00
207 Cincy Powell 2.00
208 Larry Miller 2.00
209 Sonny Dove 2.00
210 *Byron Beck* 3.00
211 John Beasley 2.00
212 Lee Davis 2.00
213 *Rick Mount* 7.50
214 Walt Simon 2.00
215 Glen Combs 2.00
216 Neil Johnson 2.00
217 Manny Leaks 2.00
218 Chuck Williams 2.00
219 Warren Davis 2.00
220 *Donnie Freeman* 4.50
221 Randy Mahaffey 2.00
222 John Barnhill 2.00
223 Al Cueto 2.00
224 *Louie Dampier* 7.00
225 *Roger Brown* 4.50
226 Joe DePre 2.00
227 Ray Scott 2.00
228 Arvesta Kelly 2.00
229 Vann Williford 2.00
230 Larry Jones 2.00
231 Gene Moore 2.00
232 *Ralph Simpson* 4.00
233 *Red Robbins* 3.00

1971-72 Topps Stickers

These stickers, which were card-size and included three players per sticker (very similar to the 1980-81 cards), showed ABA and NBA players, plus three logo stickers. Each has a black border. Because of the black borders and the flimsiness of the stickers, it's difficult to find these in Mint condition.

		NM
Complete Set (45):		500.00
Common Player:		3.00
1	Lou Hudson, Bob Rule, Calvin Murphy	5.00
1A	James Jones SP, Willie Wise, Dan Issel	25.00
4	Walt Wesley, Jo Jo White, Bob Dandridge	3.00
4A	Mack Calvin SP, Roger Brown, Bob Verga	8.00
7	Nate Thurmond, Earl Monroe, Spencer Haywood	12.00
7A	Bill Melchionni SP, Mel Daniels, Donnie Freeman	5.00
10	Dave DeBusschere, Bob Lanier, Tom Van Arsdale	12.00
10A	Joe Caldwell SP, Louie Dampier, Mike Lewis	5.00
13	Hal Greer, Johnny Green, Elvin Hayes	12.00
13A	Rick Barry SP, Larry Jones, Julius Keye	25.00
16	Jimmy Walker, Don May, Archie Clark	3.00
16A	Larry Cannon SP, Zelmo Beaty, Charlie Scott	8.00
19	Happy Hairston, Leroy Ellis, Jerry Sloan	6.00
19A	Steve Jones SP, George Carter, John Brisker	5.00
22	Pete Maravich, Bob Kauffman, John Havlicek	70.00
22A	ABA Team DP Logo Stickers	3.00
23A	ABA Team SP Logo Stickers	35.00
24A	ABA Team SP Logo Stickers	35.00
25	Walt Frazier, Dick Van Arsdale, Dave Bing	18.00
28	Bob Love, Ron Williams, Dave Cowens	15.00
31	Jerry West, Willis Reed, Chet Walker	60.00
34	Oscar Robertson, Wes Unseld, Bobby Smith	50.00
37	Connie Hawkins, Jeff Mullins, Lew Alcindor	100.00
40	Billy Cunningham, Walt Bellamy, Geoff Petrie	10.00
43	Wilt Chamberlain, Gus Johnson, Norm Van Lier	75.00
46	NBA Team logo stickers	3.00
1	Lou Hudson	7.50
2	Bob Rule	7.50
3	Calvin Murphy	7.50
4	Walt Wesley	7.50
5	Jo Jo White	7.50
6	Bob Dandridge	7.50
7	Nate Thurmond	20.00
8	Earl Monroe	20.00
9	Spencer Haywood	20.00
10	Dave DeBusschere	20.00
11	Bob Lanier	20.00
12	Tom Van Arsdale	20.00
13	Hal Greer	20.00
14	Johnny Green	20.00
15	Elvin Hayes	20.00
16	Jimmy Walker	7.50
17	Don May	7.50
18	Archie Clark	7.50
19	Happy Hairston	7.50
20	Leroy Ellis	7.50
21	Jerry Sloan	7.50
22	Pete Maravich	75.00
23	Bob Kauffman	75.00
24	John Havlicek	75.00
25	Walt Frazier	20.00
26	Dick Van Arsdale	20.00
27	Dave Bing	20.00
28	Bob Love	7.50
29	Ron Williams	7.50
30	Dave Cowens	7.50
31	Jerry West	60.00
32	Willis Reed	60.00
33	Chet Walker	60.00
34	Oscar Robertson	50.00
35	Wes Unseld	50.00
36	Bobby Smith	50.00
37	Connie Hawkins	100.00
38	Jeff Mullins	100.00
39	Lew Alcindor	100.00
40	Billy Cunningham	25.00
41	Walt Bellamy	25.00
42	Geoff Petrie	25.00
43	Wilt Chamberlain	75.00
44	Gus Johnson	75.00
45	Norm Van Lier	75.00

1972-73 Topps

The first of Topps' three straight 264-card sets began with one of the company's best designs in basketball. The set includes separate All-Star cards grouped together, statistical leaders, and a game-by-game summary of the championship series in the ABA and NBA. Cards measure 2-1/2" x 3-1/2". This set is most notable for having Julius Erving's rookie card. Other rookies include Randy Smith, Sidney Wicks, Austin Carr, Artis Gilmore and George McGinnis. Second-year cards include Dave Cowens, Rick Barry, Bob Lanier, Rudy Tomjanovich, Nate Archibald, Pat Riley and Dan Issel. The set has the final cards of Gus Johnson and Hal Greer. AS means All-Star.

		NM
Complete Set (264):		750.00
Common Player:		1.00
Pack (10):		90.00
Wax Box (24):		1500.
1	Wilt Chamberlain	40.00
2	Stan Love	1.00
3	Geoff Petrie	2.00
4	*Curtis Perry*	1.50
5	Pete Maravich	40.00
6	Gus Johnson	2.00
7	Dave Cowens	15.00
8	*Randy Smith*	4.00
9	Matt Guokas	2.00
10	Spencer Haywood	3.00
11	Jerry Sloan	3.00
12	Dave Sorenson	1.00
13	Howie Komives	1.00
14	Joe Ellis	1.00
15	Jerry Lucas	6.00
16	Stu Lantz	1.00
17	Bill Bridges	1.00
18	Leroy Ellis	1.00
19	Art Williams	1.00
20	*Sidney Wicks*	10.00
21	Wes Unseld	5.00
22	Jim Washington	1.00
23	Fred Hilton	1.00
24	*Curtis Rowe*	2.50
25	Oscar Robertson	20.00
26	*Larry Steele*	2.00
27	Charlie Davis	1.00
28	Nate Thurmond	5.00
29	Fred Carter	1.00
30	Connie Hawkins	5.00
31	Calvin Murphy	5.00
32	*Phil Jackson*	60.00
33	Lee Winfield	1.00
34	Jim Fox	1.00
35	Dave Bing	6.00
36	Gary Gregor	1.00
37	Mike Riordan	1.00
38	George Trapp	1.00
39	Mike Davis	1.00
40	Bob Rule	1.00
41	John Block	1.00
42	Bob Dandridge	1.00
43	John Johnson	1.00
44	Rick Barry	17.00
45	Jo Jo White	4.00
46	Cliff Meely	1.00
47	Charlie Scott	2.00
48	Johnny Green	1.00
49	Pete Cross	1.00
50	Gail Goodrich	3.00
51	Jim Davis	1.00
52	Dick Barnett	1.50
53	Bob Christian	1.00
54	John McGlocklin	1.00
55	Paul Silas	2.00
56	Hal Greer	3.00
57	Barry Clemens	1.00
58	Nick Jones	1.00
59	Cornell Warner	1.00
60	Walt Frazier	10.00
61	Dorrie Murray	1.00
62	Dick Cunningham	1.00
63	Sam Lacey	1.50
64	John Warren	1.00
65	Tom Boerwinkle	1.00
66	Fred Foster	1.00
67	Mel Counts	1.00
68	Toby Kimball	1.00
69	Dale Schlueter	1.00
70	Jack Marin	1.00
71	Jim Barnett	.50
72	Clem Haskins	2.50
73	Earl Monroe	7.00
74	Tom Sanders	1.00
75	Jerry West	22.00
76	Elmore Smith	2.00
77	Don Adams	1.00
78	Wally Jones	1.00
79	Tom Van Arsdale	1.00
80	Bob Lanier	12.00
81	Len Wilkens	6.00
82	Neal Walk	1.00
83	Kevin Loughery	1.00
84	Stan McKenzie	1.00
85	Jeff Mullins	1.00
86	Otto Moore	1.00
87	John Tresvant	1.00
88	*Dean Meminger*	2.00
89	Jim McMillian	1.00
90	*Austin Carr*	7.00
91	*Clifford Ray*	3.00
92	Don Nelson	6.50
93	Mahdi Abdul Rahman (Walt Hazzard)	2.00
94	Willie Norwood	1.00
95	Dick Van Arsdale	1.00
96	Don May	1.00
97	Walt Bellamy	3.00
98	*Garfield Heard*	4.00
99	Dave Wohl	1.00
100	Kareem Abdul-Jabbar	32.00
101	Ron Knight	1.00
102	*Phil Chenier*	4.00
103	Rudy Tomjanovich	9.00
104	Flynn Robinson	1.00
105	Dave DeBusschere	6.00
106	Dennis Layton	1.00
107	Bill Hewitt	1.00
108	Dick Garrett	1.00
109	Walt Wesley	1.00
110	John Havlicek	27.00
111	Norm Van Lier	2.00
112	Cazzie Russell	3.00
113	Herm Gilliam	1.00
114	Greg Smith	1.00
115	Nate Archibald	8.00
116	Don Kojis	1.00
117	Rick Adelman	2.50
118	Luke Jackson	1.00
119	Lamar Green	1.00
120	Archie Clark	1.00
121	Happy Hairston	1.50
122	Bill Bradley	20.00
123	Ron Williams	1.00
124	Jimmy Walker	1.00
125	Bob Kauffman	1.00
126	Rick Roberson	1.00
127	*Howard Porter*	3.00
128	Mike Newlin	1.00
129	Willis Reed	9.00
130	Lou Hudson	2.00
131	Don Chaney	2.00
132	Dave Stallworth	1.00
133	Charlie Yelverton	1.00
134	Ken Durrett	1.00
135	Jim King	1.00
136	Dick Snyder	1.00
137	Jim McDaniels	1.00
138	Clyde Lee	1.00
139	Dennis Awtrey	1.00
140	Keith Erickson	2.00
141	Bob Weiss	2.00
142	*Butch Beard*	3.00
143	Terry Dischinger	1.00
144	Pat Riley	14.00
145	Lucius Allen	2.00
146	*John Mengelt*	1.50
147	John Hummer	1.00
148	Bob Love	3.00
149	Bobby Smith	1.00
150	Elvin Hayes	12.00
151	Nate Williams	1.00
152	Chet Walker	3.00
153	Steve Kuberski	1.00
154	NBA Playoffs Game 1 (Earl Monroe)	3.00
155	NBA Playoffs Game 2 (Lakers Come Back)	1.25
156	NBA Playoffs Game 3 (Two in a Row)	1.25
157	NBA Playoffs Game 4	1.25
158	NBA Playoffs Game 5 (Jerry West)	7.00
159	NBA Champs - Lakers (Wilt Chamberlain)	8.00
160	Checklist 1-176	15.00
161	John Havlicek (AS)	14.00
162	Spencer Haywood (AS)	1.00
163	Kareem Abdul-Jabbar (AS)	30.00
164	Jerry West (AS)	16.00
165	Walt Frazier (AS)	4.00
166	Bob Love (AS)	1.25
167	Bill Cunningham (AS)	2.50
168	Wilt Chamberlain (AS)	20.00
169	Nate Archibald (AS)	4.00
170	Archie Clark (AS)	1.25
171	NBA Scoring Leaders (Kareem Abdul-Jabbar, John Havlicek, Nate Archibald) (Kareem)	10.00
172	NBA Scoring Average Leaders (Kareem Abdul-Jabbar, Nate Archibald, John Havlicek) (Kareem)	10.00
173	NBA FG Pct. Leaders (Wilt Chamberlain, Kareem Abdul-Jabbar, Walt Bellamy) (Bellamy)	10.00
174	NBA Free Throw Percentage Leaders (Jack Marin, Calvin Murphy, Gail Goodrich)	1.25
175	NBA Rebound Leaders (Wilt Chamberlain, Kareem Abdul-Jabbar, Wes Unseld)	12.00
176	NBA Assist Leaders (Len Wilkens, Jerry West, Nate Archibald)	6.00
177	Roland Taylor	1.00
178	Art Becker	1.00
179	Mack Calvin	2.50
180	*Artis Gilmore*	20.00
181	Collis Jones	1.00
182	*John Roche*	3.00
183	*George McGinnis*	15.00
184	Johnny Neumann	1.00
185	Willie Wise	1.00
186	Bernie Williams	1.00
187	Byron Beck	1.00
188	Larry Miller	1.00
189	Cincy Powell	1.00
190	Donnie Freeman	1.00
191	John Baum	1.00
192	Billy Keller	1.50
193	Wilbert Jones	1.00
194	Glen Combs	1.00
195	*Julius Erving*	280.00
196	Al Smith	1.00
197	George Carter	1.00
198	Louie Dampier	3.00
199	Rich Jones	1.00
200	Mel Daniels	4.00
201	Gene Moore	1.00
202	Randy Denton	1.00
203	Larry Jones	1.00
204	Jim Ligon	1.00
205	Warren Jabali	1.00
206	Joe Caldwell	1.00
207	Darrell Carrier	1.00
208	Gene Kennedy	1.00
209	Ollie Taylor	1.00
210	Roger Brown	2.00
211	George Lehmann	1.00
212	Red Robbins	1.00
213	Jim Eakins	1.00
214	Willie Long	1.00
215	Billy Cunningham	7.00
216	Steve Jones	2.00
217	Les Hunter	1.00
218	Bill Paultz	2.00
219	Freddie Lewis	2.00
220	Zelmo Beaty	1.00
221	George Thompson	1.00
222	Neil Johnson	1.00
223	*Dave Robisch*	3.00
224	Walt Simon	1.00
225	Bill Melchionni	1.00
226	*Wendell Ladner*	3.00
227	Joe Hamilton	1.00
228	Bob Netolicky	1.00
229	James Jones	1.00
230	Dan Issel	16.00
231	Charlie Williams	1.00
232	Willie Sojourner	1.00
233	Merv Jackson	1.00
234	Mike Lewis	1.00
235	Ralph Simpson	2.00
236	John Brisker	1.00
237	Rick Mount	4.50
238	Gerald Govan	1.00
239	Ron Boone	2.00
240	Tom Washington	1.00
241	Playoff Game 1	1.00
242	Playoff G2 Barry	5.00
243	Playoff G3 McGinnis	3.00
244	Playoff G4 Barry	4.00
245	Playoff Game 5	1.00
246	Playoff Game 6	1.00
247	Champs Pacers	1.00
248	ABA Checklist 177-264	14.00
249	Dan Issel (AS)	6.00
250	Rick Barry (AS)	10.00
251	Artis Gilmore (AS)	6.00
252	Donnie Freeman (AS)	1.00
253	Bill Melchionni (AS)	1.00
254	Willie Wise (AS)	1.00
255	Julius Erving (AS)	65.00
256	Zelmo Beaty (AS)	1.00
257	Ralph Simpson (AS)	1.00
258	Charlie Scott (AS)	1.00
259	ABA Scoring Average Leaders (Charlie Scott, Rick Barry, Dan Issel)	5.00
260	ABA 2pt. FG Percentage Leaders (Artis Gilmore, Tom Washington)	4.00
261	ABA 3pt FG Percentage Leaders (Glen Combs, Louie Dampier, Warren Jabali)	1.25
262	ABA Free Throw Percentage Leaders (Rick Barry, Mack Calvin, Steve Jones)	1.25
263	ABA Rebound Leaders (Artis Gilmore, Julius Erving, Mel Daniels)	20.00
264	ABA Assist Leaders (Bill Melchionni, Larry Brown, Louie Dampier)	3.00

1973-74 Topps

This was the first time an All-Star denotation appeared on the player's regular-issue card. Arguably the worst set ever produced by Topps, cards featured mostly posed shots of the players, who stood in front of brick walls, outdoors, in hallways and anywhere else (except the court) a Topps photographer could flag them down. This was the second of three straight 264-card sets. Again included were playoff and league leader subsets. Rookies in this set include Fred Brown, Henry Bibby, Paul Westphal and Bob McAdoo. Second-year issues include Sidney Wicks, Randy Smith, George McGinnis, Julius Erving and Artis Gilmore. The set held the last regular-issue cards of Willis Reed and Jerry Lucas. AS means All-Star.

		NM
Complete Set (264):		350.00
Common Player:		.70
Pack (10):		80.00
Wax Box (24):		1450.
1	Nate Archibald (AS)	8.00
2	Steve Kuberski	.70
3	John Mengelt	.70
4	Jim McMillian	.70
5	Nate Thurmond	4.00
6	Dave Wohl	.70
7	John Brisker	.70
8	Charlie Davis	.70
9	Lamar Green	.70
10	Walt Frazier (AS)	7.00
11	Bob Christian	.70
12	Cornell Warner	.70
13	Calvin Murphy	3.50
14	Dave Sorenson	.70
15	Archie Clark	.70
16	Clifford Ray	.70
17	Terry Driscoll	.70
18	Matt Guokas	.70
19	Elmore Smith	.70
20	John Havlicek (AS)	15.00
21	Pat Riley	5.00
22	George Trapp	.70
23	Ron Williams	.70
24	Jim Fox	.70
25	Dick Van Arsdale	.70
26	John Tresvant	.70
27	Rick Adelman	1.50
28	Eddie Mast	.70
29	Jim Cleamons	.70
30	Dave DeBusschere (AS)	6.00
31	Norm Van Lier	1.00
32	Stan McKenzie	.70
33	Bob Dandridge	.70
34	Leroy Ellis	.70
35	Mike Riordan	.70
36	Fred Hilton	.70
37	Toby Kimball	.70
38	Jim Price	.70
39	Willie Norwood	.70
40	Dave Cowens (AS)	6.00
41	Cazzie Russell	2.00
42	Lee Winfield	.70
43	Connie Hawkins	4.00
44	Mike Newlin	.70
45	Chet Walker	1.75
46	Walt Bellamy	1.50
47	John Johnson	.75
48	*Henry Bibby*	4.50
49	Bobby Smith	.70
50	Kareem Abdul-Jabbar (AS)	25.00
51	Mike Price	.70
52	John Hummer	.70
53	*Kevin Porter*	5.00
54	Nate Williams	.70
55	Gail Goodrich	4.00
56	Fred Foster	.70
57	Don Chaney	2.00
58	Bud Stallworth	.70
59	Clem Haskins	1.00
60	Bob Love (AS)	2.00
61	Jimmy Walker	.70
62	NBA Eastern semi-finals (Knicks/Bullets)	.70
63	NBA Eastern semi-finals (Celtics/Hawks)	.70
64	NBA Western semi-finals (Wilt Chamberlain)	6.00
65	NBA Western semi-finals (Warrior/Bucks)	.70
66	NBA Eastern finals (Willis Reed)	3.00
67	NBA Western finals (Lakers/Golden State)	.70
68	NBA Championship (Knicks champs)	3.50
69	Larry Steele	.70
70	Oscar Robertson	15.00
71	Phil Jackson	10.00
72	John Wetzel	.70
73	*Steve Patterson*	2.00
74	Manny Leaks	.70
75	Jeff Mullins	1.50
76	Stan Love	.70
77	Dick Garrett	.70
78	Don Nelson	4.00
79	*Chris Ford*	4.00
80	Wilt Chamberlain	22.00
81	Dennis Layton	.70
82	Bill Bradley	14.00
83	Jerry Sloan	2.00
84	Cliff Meely	.70
85	Sam Lacey	.70
86	Dick Snyder	.70
87	Jim Washington	.70
88	Lucius Allen	1.00
89	LaRue Martin	.70

90	Rick Barry	10.00
91	Fred Boyd	.70
92	Barry Clemens	.70
93	Dean Meminger	.70
94	Henry Finkel	.70
95	Elvin Hayes	8.00
96	Stu Lantz	.70
97	Bill Hewitt	.70
98	Neal Walk	.70
99	Garfield Heard	.70
100	Jerry West (AS)	22.00
101	Otto Moore	.70
102	Don Kojis	.70
103	*Fred Brown*	4.00
104	Dwight Davis	.70
105	Willis Reed	6.00
106	Herm Gilliam	.70
107	Mickey Davis	.70
108	Jim Barnett	.70
109	Ollie Johnson	.70
110	Bob Lanier	7.00
111	Fred Carter	.70
112	Paul Silas	2.00
113	Phil Chenier	1.50
114	Dennis Awtrey	.70
115	Austin Carr	1.50
116	Bob Kauffman	.70
117	Keith Erickson	.70
118	Walt Wesley	.70
119	Steve Bracey	.70
120	Spencer Haywood (AS)	3.00
121	Checklist 1-176	12.00
122	Jack Marin	.70
123	Jon McGlocklin	.70
124	Johnny Green	.70
125	Jerry Lucas	4.50
126	*Paul Westphal*	22.00
127	Curtis Rowe	.70
128	Mahdi Abdul Rahman	.70
129	*Lloyd Neal*	2.00
130	Pete Maravich (AS)	32.00
131	Don May	.70
132	Bob Weiss	1.50
133	Dave Stallworth	.70
134	Dick Cunningham	.70
135	*Bob McAdoo*	28.00
136	Butch Beard	.70
137	Happy Hairston	.70
138	Bob Rule	.70
139	Don Adams	.70
140	Charlie Scott	1.00
141	Ron Riley	.70
142	Earl Monroe	5.00
143	Clyde Lee	.70
144	Rick Roberson	.70
145	Rudy Tomjanovich	8.00
146	Tom Van Arsdale	.70
147	Art Williams	.70
148	Curtis Perry	.70
149	Rich Rinaldi	.70
150	Lou Hudson	1.00
151	Mel Counts	.70
152	Jim McDaniels	.70
153	NBA Scoring Leaders (Nate Archibald, Kareem Abdul-Jabbar, Spencer Haywood)	5.00
154	NBA Scoring Average Leaders (Nate Archibald, Kareem Abdul-Jabbar, Spencer Haywood)	5.00
155	NBA FG Pct. Leaders (Wilt Chamberlain, Matt Guokas, Kareem Abdul-Jabbar)	8.00
156	NBA FT Pct. Leaders (Rick Barry, Calvin Murphy, Mike Newlin)	3.00
157	NBA Rebound Leaders (Wilt Chamberlain, Nate Thurmond, Dave Cowens)	6.00
158	NBA Assist Leaders (Nate Archibald, Len Wilkens, Dave Bing)	3.00
159	Don Smith	.70
160	Sidney Wicks	2.50
161	Howie Komives	.70
162	John Gianelli	.70
163	Jeff Haliburton	.70
164	Kennedy McIntosh	.70
165	Len Wilkens	4.00
166	Corky Calhoun	.70
167	Howard Porter	.70
168	Jo Jo White	2.00
169	John Block	.70
170	Dave Bing	4.50
171	Joe Ellis	.70
172	Chuck Terry	.70
173	Randy Smith	.70
174	Bill Bridges	.70
175	Geoff Petrie	.70
176	Wes Unseld	5.00
177	Skeeter Swift	.70
178	Jim Eakins	.70
179	Steve Jones	.70
180	George McGinnis (AS)	4.00
181	Al Smith	.70
182	Tom Washington	.70
183	Louie Dampier	.70
184	Simmie Hill	.70
185	George Thompson	.70
186	Cincy Powell	.70
187	Larry Jones	.70
188	Neil Johnson	.70
189	Tom Owens	.70
190	Ralph Simpson (AS)	.70
191	George Carter	.70
192	Rick Mount	1.00
193	Red Robbins	.70
194	George Lehmann	.70
195	Mel Daniels (AS)	2.00
196	Bob Warren	.70
197	Gene Kennedy	.70
198	Mike Barr	.70
199	Dave Robisch	.70
200	Bill Cunningham (AS)	5.00
201	John Roche	.70
202	ABA Western semi-finals (Pacers/Rockets)	.70
203	ABA Western semi-finals (Stars/Conquistadors)	.70
204	ABA Eastern semi-finals (Colonels/Squires)	1.50
205	ABA Eastern semi-finals (Cougars/Nets)	.70
206	ABA Western finals (Pacers/Stars)	.70
207	ABA Eastern finals	2.00
208	ABA championship (Pacers/Colonels)	.70
209	Glen Combs	.70
210	Dan Issel (AS)	6.00
211	Randy Denton	.70
212	Freddie Lewis	.70
213	Stew Johnson	.70
214	Roland Taylor	.70
215	Rich Jones	.70
216	Billy Paultz	1.00
217	Ron Boone	.70
218	Walt Simon	.70
219	Mike Lewis	.70
220	Warren Jabali (AS)	.70
221	Wilbert Jones	.70
222	*Don Buse*	2.00
223	Gene Moore	.70
224	Joe Hamilton	.70
225	Zelmo Beaty	.70
226	*Brian Taylor*	2.00
227	Julius Keye	.70
228	*Mike Gale*	1.25
229	Warren Davis	.70
230	Mack Calvin (AS)	1.00
231	Roger Brown	.70
232	Chuck Williams	.70
233	Gerald Govan	.70
234	ABA scoring average leaders (Julius Erving, George McGinnis, Dan Issel)	7.00
235	ABA 2-pt field goal percentage leaders (Artis Gilmore, Gene Kennedy, Tom Owens)	1.50
236	ABA 3-pt field goal percentage leaders (Glen Combs, Roger Brown, Louie Dampier)	1.50
237	ABA free throw percentage leaders (Billy Keller, Ron Boone, Bob Warren)	1.50
238	ABA rebound leaders (Artis Gilmore, Mel Daniels, Billy Paultz)	1.50
239	ABA assist leaders (Bill Melchionni, Chuck Williams, Warren Jabali)	1.50
240	Julius Erving (AS)	60.00
241	Jimmy O'Brien	.70
242	ABA Checklist 177-264	10.00
243	Johnny Newmann	.70
244	Darnell Hillman	.70
245	Willie Wise	.70
246	Collis Jones	.70
247	Ted McClain	.70
248	*George Irvine*	1.25
249	Bill Melchionni	.70
250	Artis Gilmore (AS)	6.00
251	Willie Long	.70
252	Larry Miller	.70
253	Lee Davis	.70
254	Donnie Freeman	.70
255	Joe Caldwell	.70
256	Bob Netolicky	.70
257	Bernie Williams	.70
258	Byron Beck	.70
259	*Jim Chones*	2.00
260	James Jones (AS)	.70
261	Wendell Ladner	.70
262	Ollie Taylor	.70
263	Lee Hunter	.70
264	*Billy Keller*	2.25

1973-74 Topps Team Stickers

This 33-card sticker set measures 2-1/2" x 3-1/2" and captures all ABA and NBA teams. Inserted into each pack, the top portion carries a larger team logo, while the bottom includes a smaller banner with a team name in it. Since the stickers are unnumbered, they are listed below according to the top sticker for the ABA (1-10) and the NBA (11-33).

		NM
Complete Set (33):		125.00
Common ABA (1-10):		4.00
Common NBA (11-33):		3.00
1	Carolina Cougars - Stars	4.00
2	Denver Rockets - Spurs	4.00
3	Indiana Pacers - Squires	4.00
4	Kentucky Colonels - Jams	4.00
5	Memphis Tams - Cougars	4.00
6	New York Nets - Conquistadors	4.00
7	San Antonio Spurs - Nets	4.00
8	San Diego Conquistadors - Pacers	4.00
9	Utah Stars - Colonels	4.00
10	Virginia Squires - Rockets	4.00
11	Atlanta Hawks - Celtics	3.00
12	Atlanta Hawks - Supersonics	3.00
13	Boston Celtics - Braves	4.00
14	Boston Celtics - 76ers	4.00
15	Buffalo Braves - Lakers	3.00
16	Buffalo Braves - Trail Blazers	3.00
17	Capitol Bullets - Knicks	3.00
18	Chicago Bulls - Pistons	3.00
19	Cleveland Cavaliers - Hawks	3.00
20	Detroit Pistons - Warriors	3.00
21	Golden State Warriors - Bucks	3.00
22	Golden State Warriors - Kings	3.00
23	Houston Rockets - Braves	3.00
24	Kansas City Kings - Lakers	3.00
25	Los Angeles Lakers - Bullets	4.00
26	Los Angeles Lakers - Celtics	4.00
27	Milwaukee Bucks - Knicks	3.00
28	New York Knicks - Bulls	3.00
29	New York Knicks - Warriors	3.00
30	Philadelphia 76ers - Hawks	3.00
31	Phoenix Suns - Cavaliers	3.00
32	Portland Trail Blazers - Rockets	3.00
33	Seattle Supersonics - Suns	3.00

1974-75 Topps

This was Topps' third and last 264-card issue, again featuring NBA and ABA players, statistical leaders, and playoff summaries. For the first time, team leader cards were included as a subset. Most cards in this set feature a posed photo, with the background comprised of one of several tinted generic game photos. The "team-name-down-the-side" design, repeated by Topps in 1976 and 1978, was first used here. Rookies in this set include Bill Walton, Doug Collins and George Gervin. Second-year cards include Paul Westphal and Bob McAdoo. The final regular-issue cards of Walt Bellamy, Wilt Chamberlain, Oscar Robertson and Jerry West are in this set.

		NM
Complete Set (264):		340.00
Common Player:		.50
NBA Team Leaders:		1.00
ABA Team Leaders:		.75
NBA League Leaders:		1.00
ABA League Leaders:		1.25
NBA Playoffs:		1.00
ABA Playoffs:		1.25
Pack (12 - "Scratch Off"):		46.00
Wax Box (24 - "Scratch Off"):		850.00
1	Kareem Abdul-Jabbar	35.00
2	Don May	.50
3	*Bernie Fryer*	1.25
4	Don Adams	.50
5	Herm Gilliam	.50
6	Jim Chones	.50
7	Rick Adelman	1.25
8	Randy Smith	.50
9	Paul Silas	2.00
10	Pete Maravich	22.00
11	Ron Behagen	.50
12	Kevin Porter	1.00
13	Bill Bridges	.50
14	*Charles Johnson*	1.25
15	Bob Love	1.25
16	Henry Bibby	.50
17	Neal Walk	.50
18	John Brisker	.50
19	Lucius Allen	1.00
20	Tom Van Arsdale	.50
21	Larry Steele	.50
22	Curtis Rowe	1.00
23	Dean Meminger	.50
24	Steve Patterson	.50
25	Earl Monroe	5.00
26	Jack Marin	.50
27	Jo Jo White	2.00
28	Rudy Tomjanovich	6.00
29	Otto Moore	.50
30	Elvin Hayes	8.00
31	Pat Riley	7.50
32	Clyde Lee	.50
33	Bob Weiss	1.00
34	Jim Fox	.50
35	Charlie Scott	1.00
36	Cliff Meely	.50
37	Jon McGlocklin	.50
38	Jim McMillian	.50
39	*Bill Walton*	60.00
40	Dave Bing	4.00
41	Jim Washington	.50
42	Jim Cleamons	.50
43	Mel Davis	.50
44	Garfield Heard	.50
45	Jimmy Walker	.50
46	Don Nelson	3.00
47	Jim Barnett	.50
48	Manny Leaks	.50
49	Elmore Smith	1.00
50	Rick Barry	8.00
51	Jerry Sloan	1.50
52	John Hummer	.50
53	Keith Erickson	.50
54	George Johnson	.50
55	Oscar Robertson	13.00
56	*Steve Mix*	1.00
57	Rick Roberson	.50
58	John Mengelt	.50
59	*Dwight Jones*	1.00
60	Austin Carr	2.00
61	*Nick Weatherspoon*	1.25
62	Clem Haskins	1.00
63	Don Kojis	.50
64	Paul Westphal	5.00
65	Walt Bellamy	2.00
66	John Johnson	.50
67	Butch Beard	.50
68	Happy Hairston	1.00
69	Tom Boerwinkle	.50
70	Spencer Haywood	2.50
71	Gary Melchionni	.50
72	Ed Ratleff	.50
73	Mickey Davis	.50
74	Dennis Awtrey	.50
75	Fred Carter	.50
76	George Trapp	.50
77	John Wetzel	.50
78	Bobby Smith	.50
79	John Gianelli	.50
80	Bob McAdoo	7.00
81	Atlanta Hawks team (Pete Maravich, Lou Hudson, Walt Bellamy)	4.50
82	Boston Celtics team (John Havlicek, Jo Jo White, Dave Cowens)	4.00
83	Buffalo Braves team (Bob McAdoo, Ernie DiGregorio)	1.25
84	Chicago Bulls team (Bob Love, Chet Walker, Clifford Ray, Norm Van Lier)	2.00
85	Cleveland Cavaliers team (Austin Carr, Dwight Davis, Len Wilkens)	1.00
86	Detroit Pistons team (Bob Lanier, Stu Lantz, Dave Bing)	1.00
87	Golden State Warriors team (Rick Barry, Nate Thurmond)	2.00
88	Houston Rockets team (Rudy Tomjanovich, Calvin Murphy, Don Smith)	1.00
89	Kansas City/Omaha Kings team (Jimmy Walker, Sam Lacey)	1.25
90	Los Angeles Lakers team (Gail Goodrich, Happy Hairston)	1.00
91	Milwaukee Bucks team (Kareem Abdul-Jabbar, Oscar Robertson)	7.50
92	New Orleans Jazz logo	1.25
93	New York Knicks team (Walt Frazier, Bill Bradley, Dave DeBusschere)	5.00
94	Philadelphia 76ers team (Fred Carter, Tom Van Arsdale, Leroy Ellis)	1.00
95	Phoenix Suns team (Charlie Scott, Dick Van Arsdale, Neal Walk)	1.00
96	Portland Trailblazers team (Geoff Petrie, Rick Roberson, Sidney Wicks)	1.00
97	Seattle Supersonics team (Spencer Haywood, Dick Snyder, Fred Brown)	1.00
98	Washington Bullets team (Phil Chenier, Elvin Hayes, Kevin Porter)	1.00
99	Sam Lacey	.50
100	John Havlicek	10.00
101	Stu Lantz	.50
102	Mike Riordan	.50
103	Larry Jones	.50
104	Connie Hawkins	4.00
105	Nate Thurmond	3.00
106	Dick Gibbs	.50
107	Corky Calhoun	.50
108	Dave Wohl	.50
109	Cornell Warner	.50
110	Geoff Petrie	.50
111	Leroy Ellis	.50
112	Chris Ford	2.50
113	Bill Bradley	10.00
114	Clifford Ray	.50
115	Dick Snyder	.50
116	Nate Williams	.50
117	Matt Guokas	1.00
118	Henry Finkel	.50
119	Curtis Perry	.50
120	Gail Goodrich	2.00
121	Wes Unseld	4.00
122	Howard Porter	.50
123	Jeff Mullins	.75
124	Mike Bantom	.50
125	Fred Brown	1.00
126	Bob Dandridge	.50
127	Mike Newlin	.50
128	Greg Smith	.50
129	*Doug Collins*	14.00
130	Lou Hudson	.50
131	Bob Lanier	5.00
132	Phil Jackson	5.00
133	Don Chaney	1.00
134	*Jim Brewer*	1.00
135	*Ernie DiGregorio*	4.50
136	Steve Kuberski	.50
137	Jim Price	.50
138	Mike D'Antoni	.50
139	John Brown	.50
140	Norm Van Lier	1.00
141	NBA Checklist 1-176	8.00
142	*Don Watts*	2.00
143	Walt Wesley	.50
144	NBA scoring leaders (Bob McAdoo, Kareem Abdul-Jabbar, Pete Maravich)	6.00
145	NBA scoring average leaders (Bob McAdoo, Pete Maravich, Kareem Abdul-Jabbar)	5.00
146	NBA FG pct. leaders (Bob McAdoo, Kareem Abdul-Jabbar, Rudy Tomjanovich)	4.00
147	NBA free throw percentage leaders (Ernie DiGregorio, Rick Barry, Jeff Mullins)	.75
148	NBA rebound leaders (Elvin Hayes, Dave Cowens, Bob McAdoo)	3.00
149	NBA assist leaders (Ernie DiGregorio, Calvin Murphy, Len Wilkens)	.50
150	Walt Frazier	6.50
151	Cazzie Russell	2.00
152	Calvin Murphy	3.50
153	Bob Kauffman	.50
154	Fred Boyd	.50
155	Dave Cowens	7.00
156	Willie Norwood	.50
157	Lee Winfield	.50
158	Dwight Davis	.50
159	George Johnson	.50
160	Dick Van Arsdale	.50
161	NBA Eastern semi-finals (Celts/Braves Knicks/Bullets)	.75
162	NBA Western semi-finals (Bucks/Lakers Bulls/Pistons)	.75
163	NBA division finals (Celts/Knicks Bucks/Bulls)	.75
164	NBA championship (Celtics/Bucks)	.75
165	Phil Chenier	1.00
166	*Kermit Washington*	1.50
167	Dale Schlueter	.50
168	John Block	.50
169	Don Smith	.50
170	Nate Archibald	4.00
171	Chet Walker	1.00
172	Archie Clark	1.00
173	Kennedy McIntosh	.50
174	George Thompson	.50
175	Sidney Wicks	2.00
176	Jerry West	20.00
177	Dwight Lamar	.50
178	George Carter	.50
179	Wil Robinson	.50
180	Artis Gilmore	4.00
181	Brian Taylor	.50
182	Darnell Hillman	.50
183	Dave Robisch	.50
184	*Gene Littles*	1.75
185	Willie Wise	.50
186	*James Silas*	3.00
187	*Caldwell Jones*	5.00
188	Roland Taylor	.50
189	Randy Denton	.50
190	Dan Issel	5.50
191	Mike Gale	.50
192	Mel Daniels	2.00
193	Steve Jones	.50
194	Marv Roberts	.50
195	Ron Boone	.50
196	*George Gervin*	50.00
197	Flynn Robinson	.50
198	Cincy Powell	.50
199	Glen Combs	.50
200	Julius Erving	55.00
201	Billy Keller	.50
202	Willie Long	.50
203	ABA CL 177-264	8.00
204	Joe Caldwell	.50
205	*Swen Nater*	3.00
206	Rick Mount	1.50
207	ABA scoring average leaders (Julius Erving, George McGinnis, Dan Issel)	7.00
208	ABA 2-pt field goal percentage leaders (Swen Nater, James Jones, Tom Owens)	.50
209	ABA 3-pt field goal percentage leaders (Louie Dampier, Billy Keller, Roger Brown)	.50
210	ABA free throw percentage leaders (James Jones, Mack Calvin, Ron Boone)	.50
211	ABA rebound leaders (Artis Gilmore, George McGinnis, Caldwell Jones)	.50
212	ABA assist leaders (Al Smith, Chuck Williams, Louie Dampier)	.50
213	(Larry Miller)	.50
214	Stew Johnson	.50
215	*Larry Finch*	2.50
216	*Larry Kenon*	2.50
217	Joe Hamilton	.50
218	Gerald Govan	.50
219	Ralph Simpson	.50
220	George McGinnis	3.00
221	Carolina Cougars team (Billy Cunningham, Mack Calvin, Tom Owens, Joe Caldwell)	5.00
222	Denver Nuggets team (Ralph Simpson, Byron Beck, Dave Robisch, Al Smith)	1.00
223	Indiana Pacers team (George McGinnis, Billy Keller, Freddie Lewis)	1.00
224	Kentucky Colonels team (Dan Issel, Artis Gilmore)	3.00
225	Memphis Sounds team (George Thompson, Larry Finch, Randy Denton)	1.25
226	New York Nets team (Erving, John Roche, Larry Kenon)	8.00
227	San Antonio Spurs team (George Gervin, Swen Nater, James Silas)	4.00
228	San Diego Conquistadors team (Dwight Lamar, Stew Johnson, Caldwell Jones, Chuck Williams)	1.25
229	Utah Stars team (Willie Wise, James Jones, Gerald Goven)	1.25
230	Virginia Squires team (George Carter, George Irvine, Jim Eakins, Roland Taylor)	1.25
231	Bird Averitt	.50
232	John Roche	.50
233	George Irvine	.50
234	*John Williamson*	1.50
235	Billy Cunningham	4.00
236	Jimmy O'Brien	.50
237	Wilbert Jones	.50
238	Johnny Neumann	.50
239	Al Smith	.50
240	Roger Brown	.50
241	Chuck Williams	.50
242	Rich Jones	.50
243	*Dave Twardzik*	1.50
244	Wendell Ladner	.50
245	Mack Calvin	2.00
246	ABA Eastern semi-finals (Nets/Squires Colonels/Cougars)	.50
247	ABA Western semi-finals (Stars/Conquistadors Pacers/Spurs)	.50
248	ABA division finals (Nets/Colonels Stars/Pacers)	.50
249	ABA championship (Julius Erving)	7.00
250	Wilt Chamberlain	30.00
251	Ron Robinson	.50
252	Zelmo Beaty	.50
253	Donnie Freeman	.50
254	Mike Green	.50
255	Louie Dampier	.50
256	Tom Owens	.50
257	*George Karl*	5.00
258	Jim Eakins	.50
259	Travis Grant	.50
260	James Jones	.50
261	Mike Jackson	.50
262	Bill Paultz	.50
263	Fred Lewis	.50
264	Byron Beck	1.50

1975-76 Topps

The last of the great expanded Topps sets, this 330-card issue is best known for containing the Moses Malone rookie card. There are several notable "lasts" in this set - this is the last to contain ABA and NBA players (the leagues merged after the season); this is the last to have team leader cards until the goofy 1980-81 set; it's the last to have team checklists and semi-final and final cards. Rookie cards besides Malone in this include Jamaal Wilkes, John Drew, Truck Robinson, Marvin Barnes, Bobby Jones, Billy Knight, Len Elmore, and Maurice Lucas. Second-year cards include Bill Walton and George Gervin. This issue holds the final cards of Archie Clark and Rick Mount.

		NM
Complete Set (330):		475.00
Common Player:		.50
NBA Leaders:		1.00
NBA Playoffs:		1.00
ABA Leaders:		1.25
ABA Playoffs:		1.25
ABA Team Leaders:		1.25
NBA Team Leaders:		1.00
Pack (10):		39.00
Wax Box (36):		1050.
1	NBA scoring average leaders (Bob McAdoo, Rick Barry, Kareem Abdul-Jabbar)	10.00
2	NBA field goal leaders (Don Nelson, Butch Beard, Rudy Tomjanovich)	.50
3	NBA FT pct. leaders (Rick Barry, Calvin Murphy, Bill Bradley)	4.00
4	NBA rebound leaders (Wes Unseld, Dave Cowens, Sam Lacey)	1.00
5	NBA assists leaders (Kevin Porter, Dave Bing, Nate Archibald)	1.00
6	NBA steals leaders (Rick Barry, Walt Frazier, Larry Steele)	3.00
7	Tom Van Arsdale	.50
8	Paul Silas	1.00
9	Jerry Sloan	1.00
10	Bob McAdoo (AS)	5.00
11	Dwight Davis	.50
12	John Mengelt	.50
13	George Johnson	.50
14	Ed Ratleff	.50
15	Nate Archibald (AS)	4.00
16	Elmore Smith	.50
17	Bob Dandridge	.50
18	*Louis Nelson*	.50
19	Neal Walk	.50
20	Billy Cunningham	4.00
21	Gary Melchionni	.50
22	Barry Clemens	.50
23	Jimmy Jones	.50
24	*Tom Burleson*	2.00
25	Lou Hudson	1.00
26	Henry Finkel	.50
27	Jim McMillian	.50
28	Matt Guokas	1.00
29	Fred Foster	.50
30	Bob Lanier	4.50
31	Jimmy Walker	.50
32	Cliff Meely	.50
33	Butch Beard	.50
34	Cazzie Russell	1.00
35	Jon McGlocklin	.50
36	Bernie Fryer	.50
37	Bill Bradley	9.50

38	Fred Carter	.50
39	Dennis Awtrey	.50
40	Sidney Wicks	1.50
41	Fred Brown	1.50
42	Rowland Garrett	.50
43	Herm Gilliam	.50
44	Don Nelson	3.00
45	Ernie DiGregorio	.50
46	Jim Brewer	.50
47	Chris Ford	1.50
48	Nick Weatherspoon	.50
49	Zaid Abdul Aziz	.50
50	*Jamaal Wilkes*	12.00
51	Ollie Johnson	.50
52	Lucius Allen	1.00
53	Mickey Davis	.50
54	Otto Moore	.50
55	Walt Frazier (AS)	7.00
56	Steve Mix	.50
57	Nate Hawthorne	.50
58	Lloyd Neal	.50
59	Don Watts	.50
60	Elvin Hayes	7.00
61	CL 1-110	8.00
62	Mike Sojourner	.50
63	Randy Smith	.50
64	John Block	.50
65	Charlie Scott	1.00
66	Jim Chones	.50
67	Rick Adelman	1.00
68	Curtis Rowe	1.00
69	*Derrek Dickey*	.60
70	Rudy Tomjanovich	7.00
71	Pat Riley	8.00
72	Cornell Warner	.50
73	Earl Monroe	6.00
74	*Allan Bristow*	4.50
75	Pete Maravich	27.00
76	Curtis Perry	.50
77	Bill Walton	20.00
78	Leonard Gray	.50
79	Kevin Porter	.75
80	John Havlicek (AS)	10.00
81	Dwight Jones	.50
82	Jack Marin	.50
83	Dick Snyder	.50
84	George Trapp	.50
85	Nate Thurmond	2.00
86	Charles Johnson	.50
87	Ron Riley	.50
88	Stu Lantz	.50
89	*Scott Wedman*	2.00
90	Kareem Abdul-Jabbar	20.00
91	Aaron James	.50
92	Jim Barnett	.50
93	Clyde Lee	.50
94	Larry Steele	.50
95	Mike Riordan	.50
96	Archie Clark	.75
97	Mike Bantom	.50
98	Bob Kauffman	.50
99	*Kevin Stacom*	1.00
100	Rick Barry (AS)	7.00
101	Ken Charles	.50
102	Tom Boerwinkle	.50
103	Mike Newlin	.50
104	Leroy Ellis	.50
105	Austin Carr	1.00
106	Ron Behagen	.50
107	Jim Price	.50
108	Bud Stallworth	.50
109	Earl Williams	.50
110	Gail Goodrich	2.00
111	Phil Jackson	5.00
112	Rod Derline	.50
113	Keith Erickson	.50
114	Phil Lumpkin	.50
115	Wes Unseld	4.00
116	Atlanta Hawks team (John Drew, Dean Meminger, Lou Hudson)	.60
117	Boston Celtics team (Dave Cowens, Kevin Stacom, Jo Jo White, Paul Silas)	2.00
118	Buffalo Braves team (Bob McAdoo, Jack Marin, Randy Smith)	.60
119	Chicago Bulls team (Bob Love, Chet Walker, Nate Thurmond, Norm Van Lier)	2.00
120	Cleveland Cavaliers team (Bobby Smith, Dick Snyder, Jim Chones, Jim Cleamons)	.75
121	Detroit Pistons team (Bob Lanier, John Mengelt, Dave Bing)	2.00
122	Golden State Warriors team (Rick Barry, Clifford Ray)	2.00
123	Houston Rockets team (Rudy Tomjanovich, Calvin Murphy, Kevin Kunnert, Mike Newlin)	.75
124	Kansas City Kings team (Nate Archibald, Ollie Johnson, Sam Lacey)	.75
125	Los Angeles Lakers team (Gail Goodrich, Cazzie Russell, Happy Hairston)	1.00
126	Milwaukee Bucks team (Kareem Abdul-Jabbar, Mickey Davis)	5.00
127	New Orleans Jazz team (Pete Maravich, Stu Lantz, E.C. Coleman)	5.00
128	New York Knicks team (Walt Frazier, Bill Bradley, John Gianelli)	2.50
129	Philadelphia 76ers team (Fred Carter, Doug Collins, Billy Cunningham)	1.00
130	Phoenix Suns team (Charlie Scott, Keith Erickson, Curtis Perry, Dennis Awtrey)	1.00
131	Portland Trail Blazers team (Sidney Wicks, Geoff Petrie)	1.00
132	Seattle SuperSonics team (Spencer Haywood, Archie Clark, Don Watts)	1.00
133	Washington Bullets team (Elvin Hayes, Clem Haskins, Wes Unseld, Kevin Porter)	2.00
134	*John Drew*	2.00
135	Jo Jo White (AS)	2.00
136	Garfield Heard	.50
137	Jim Cleamons	.50
138	Howard Porter	.50
139	*Phil Smith*	1.00
140	Bob Love	1.50
141	John Gianelli	.50
142	Larry McNeill	.75
143	*Brian Winters*	2.00
144	George Thompson	.50
145	Kevin Kunnert	.50
146	Henry Bibby	.50
147	John Johnson	.50
148	Doug Collins	5.00
149	John Brisker	.50
150	Dick Van Arsdale	.50
151	*Leonard Robinson*	3.00
152	Dean Meminger	.50
153	Phil Hankinson	.50
154	Dale Schlueter	.50
155	Norm Van Lier	1.00
156	*Campy Russell*	3.00
157	Jeff Mullins	.75
158	Sam Lacey	.50
159	Happy Hairston	.75
160	Dave Bing	2.50
161	Kevin Restani	.75
162	Dave Wohl	.50
163	E.C. Coleman	.50
164	Jim Fox	.50
165	Geoff Petrie	1.00
166	Hawthorne Wingo	.50
167	Fred Boyd	.50
168	Willie Norwood	.50
169	Bob Wilson	.50
170	Dave Cowens	7.00
171	Tom Henderson	.50
172	Jim Washington	.50
173	Clem Haskins	.50
174	Jim Davis	.50
175	Bobby Smith	.50
176	Mike D'Antoni	.50
177	Zelmo Beaty	.50
178	*Gary Brokaw*	1.25
179	Mel Davis	.50
180	Calvin Murphy	2.50
181	Checklist 111-220	7.00
182	Nate Williams	.50
183	LaRue Martin	.50
184	George McGinnis	2.00
185	Clifford Ray	.50
186	Paul Westphal	6.00
187	Talvin Skinner	.50
188	NBA semi-finals (Warriors/Bulls Bullets/Celtics)	1.00
189	NBA finals (Warrior/Bullets)	1.00
190	Phil Chenier (AS)	.50
191	John Brown	.50
192	Lee Winfield	.50
193	Steve Patterson	.50
194	Charles Dudley	.50
195	Connie Hawkins	2.00
196	Leon Benbow	.50
197	Don Kojis	.50
198	Ron Williams	.50
199	Mel Counts	.50
200	Spencer Haywood (AS)	2.00
201	Greg Jackson	.50
202	Tom Kozelko	.50
203	Atlanta Hawks checklist	1.00
204	Boston Celtics checklist	2.00
205	Buffalo Braves checklist	1.00
206	Chicago Bulls checklist	2.00
207	Cleveland Cavaliers checklist	1.00
208	Detroit Pistons checklist	1.00
209	Golden State Warriors checklist	1.00
210	Houston Rockets checklist	1.00
211	Kansas City Kings checklist	1.00
212	Los Angeles Lakers checklist	1.00
213	Milwaukee Bucks checklist	1.00
214	New Orleans Jazz checklist	1.00
215	New York Knicks checklist	1.00
216	Philadelphia 76ers checklist	1.00
217	Phoenix Suns checklist	1.00
218	Portland Trail Blazers checklist	1.00
219	Seattle SuperSonics checklist	6.00
220	Washington Bullets checklist	1.00
221	ABA scoring average leaders (George McGinnis, Julius Erving, Ron Boone)	6.00
222	ABA 2pt. FG pct. leaders (Artis Gilmore, Bobby Jones, Moses Malone)	6.00
223	ABA 3pt. FG pct. leaders (Billy Shepherd, Louie Dampier, Al Smith)	1.50
224	ABA free throw percentage leaders (Mack Calvin, James Silas, Dave Robisch)	1.50
225	ABA rebound leaders (Swen Nater, Artis Gilmore, Marvin Barnes)	1.50
226	ABA assist leaders (Mack Calvin, Chuck Williams, George McGinnis)	1.50
227	Mack Calvin (AS)	2.00
228	*Billy Knight* (AS)	5.00
229	Bird Averitt	.50
230	George Carter	.50
231	Swen Nater (AS)	2.00
232	Steve Jones	.50
233	George Gervin	14.00
234	Lee Davis	.50
235	Ron Boone (AS)	.50
236	Mike Jackson	.50
237	*Kevin Joyce*	2.00
238	Marv Roberts	.50
239	Tom Owens	.50
240	Ralph Simpson	.50
241	Gus Gerard	.50
242	Brian Taylor (AS)	.50
243	Rich Jones	.50
244	John Roche	.50
245	Travis Grant	.50
246	Dave Twardzik	.50
247	Mike Green	.50
248	Billy Keller	.50
249	Stew Johnson	.50
250	Artis Gilmore (AS)	5.00
251	John Williamson	.50
252	*Marvin Barnes* (AS)	6.00
253	James Silas (AS)	1.50
254	*Moses Malone*	50.00
255	Willie Wise	.50
256	Dwight Lamar	.50
257	Checklist 221-330	7.00
258	Byron Beck	.50
259	*Len Elmore*	5.00
260	Dan Issel	6.00
261	Rick Mount	.50
262	Bill Paultz	.50
263	Donnie Freeman	.50
264	George Adams	.50
265	Don Chaney	1.50
266	Randy Denton	.50
267	Don Washington	.50
268	Roland Taylor	.50
269	Charlie Edge	.50
270	Louie Dampier	.50
271	Collis Jones	.50
272	*Al Skinner*	1.00
273	Coby Dietrick	.50
274	Tim Bassett	.50
275	Freddie Lewis	.50
276	Gerald Govan	.50
277	Ron Thomas	.50
278	Denver Nuggets team (Mike Green, Ralph Simpson, Mack Calvin)	1.25
279	Indiana Pacers team (George McGinnis, Bill Keller)	1.25
280	Kentucky Colonels team (Artis Gilmore, Louie Dampier)	1.25
281	Memphis Sounds team (George Carter, Larry Finch, Tom Owens, Chuck Williams)	1.25
282	New York Nets team (Julius Erving, John Williamson)	6.00
283	St. Louis Spirits team (Marvin Barnes, Freddie Lewis)	.20
284	San Antonio Spurs team (James Silas, Swen Nater, George Gervin)	3.00
285	San Diego Sails team (Travis Grant, Jim O'Brien, Caldwell Jones)	1.25
286	Utah Stars team (Ron Boone, Moses Malone, Al Smith)	5.00
287	Virginia Squires team (Willie Wise, Red Robbins, Dave Vaughn, Dave Twardzik)	1.25
288	Claude Terry	.50
289	Wilbert Jones	.50
290	Darnell Hillman	.50
291	Bill Melchionni	.50
292	Mel Daniels	3.00
293	*Fly Williams*	3.00
294	Larry Kenon	.50
295	Red Robbins	.50
296	Warren Jabali	.50
297	Jim Eakins	.50
298	*Bobby Jones*	13.00
299	Don Buse	.50
300	Julius Erving (AS)	50.00
301	Billy Shepherd	.50
302	*Maurice Lucas*	7.00
303	George Karl	2.50
304	Jim Bradley	.50
305	Caldwell Jones	3.00
306	Al Smith	.50
307	*Jan Van Breda Kolff*	1.50
308	Darrell Elston	.50
309	ABA semi-finals (Colonels/Spirits Pacers/Nuggets)	1.25
310	ABA finals (Colonels/Pacers)	1.25
311	Ted McClain	.50
312	Willie Sojourner	.50
313	Bob Warren	.50
314	Bob Netolicky	.50
315	Chuck Williams	.50
316	Gene Kennedy	.50
317	Jimmy O'Brien	.50
318	Dave Robisch	.50
319	Wali Jones	.50
320	George Irvine	.50
321	Denver Nuggets checklist	1.25
322	Indiana Pacers checklist	1.25
323	Kentucky Colonels checklist	1.25
324	Memphis Sounds checklist	1.25
325	New York Nets checklist	1.25
326	St. Louis Spirits checklist	1.25
327	San Antonio Spurs checklist	1.25
328	San Diego Sails checklist	1.25
329	Utah Stars checklist	1.25
330	Virginia Squires checklist	4.00

1975-76 Topps Team Checklists

Topps produced three nine-card panels, each featuring card checklists for ABA/NBA teams. Each checklist is printed in blue and green on white. The cards are numbered on the front, using the same numbers as their counterparts in Topps' regular set. The panels, each 7-1/2" x 10-1/2", were available as a mail-in offer and excluded one team - the ABA's Memphis Sounds.

		NM
Complete Set (27):		125.00
Common Player:		6.50
203	Atlanta Hawks	6.50
204	Boston Celtics	9.00
205	Buffalo Braves	6.50
206	Chicago Bulls	6.50
207	Cleveland Cavaliers	6.50
208	Detroit Pistons	6.50
209	Golden State Warriors	6.50
210	Houston Rockets	6.50
211	Kansas City Kings	6.50
212	Los Angeles Lakers	8.00
213	Milwaukee Bucks	6.50
214	New Orleans Jazz	6.50
215	New York Knicks	8.00
216	Philadelphia 76ers	6.50
217	Phoenix Suns	6.50
218	Portland Trail Blazers	8.00
219	Seattle Supersonics	6.50
220	Washington Bullets	6.50
321	Denver Nuggets	6.50
322	Indiana Pacers	6.50
323	Kentucky Colonels	6.50
325	New York Nets	6.50
326	Spirits of St. Louis	6.50
327	San Antonio Spurs	6.50
328	San Diego Sails	6.50
329	Utah Stars	6.50
330	Virginia Squires	6.50

1976-77 Topps

Topps' first oversize set since 1970-71 continued to showcase the improving card design and photography Topps adopted the previous year. This 144-card issue is arguably the company's best-looking basketball set, with a catchy design down the left side of the card and a good action shot to fill the front, plus an expanded statistics area on the back. The cards measure approximately 3-1/8" x 5-1/4". Key rookies in this set include Gus Williams, Alvan Adams and David Thompson. Second-year cards include Jamaal Wilkes, Moses Malone, Truck Robinson, Maurice Lucas and Bobby Jones. This set also has the final regular-issue cards of Bill Bradley, Bill Cunningham and Jerry Sloan. Because of the awkward size of the set, cards may be more difficult to find in Mint condition than other cards of this era. AS means All-Star.

		NM
Complete Set (144):		350.00
Common Player:		1.50
All-Stars (126-135):		2.00
Pack (6):		36.00
Wax Box (24):		630.00
1	Julius Erving	70.00
2	Dick Snyder	1.00
3	Paul Silas	1.75
4	Keith Erickson	1.00
5	Wes Unseld	4.00
6	Butch Beard	1.00
7	Lloyd Neal	1.00
8	Tom Henderson	1.00
9	Jim McMillan	1.00
10	Bob Lanier	4.00
11	*Junior Bridgeman*	3.00
12	Corky Calhoun	1.00
13	Billy Keller	1.00
14	*Mickey Johnson*	1.50
15	Fred Brown	2.00
16	Jamaal Wilkes	4.00
17	Louie Nelson	1.00
18	Ed Ratleff	1.00
19	Billy Paultz	1.00
20	Nate Archibald	4.00
21	Steve Mix	1.00
22	Ralph Simpson	1.00
23	Campy Russell	2.00
24	Charlie Scott	2.00
25	Artis Gilmore	6.00
26	Dick Van Arsdale	1.00
27	Phil Chenier	1.00
28	Spencer Haywood	2.00
29	Chris Ford	2.00
30	Dave Cowens	9.00
31	Sidney Wicks	2.00
32	Jim Price	1.00
33	Dwight Jones	1.00
34	Lucius Allen	2.00
35	Marvin Barnes	2.25
36	Henry Bibby	1.00
37	*Joe Meriweather*	2.00
38	Doug Collins	7.00
39	Garfield Heard	1.00
40	Randy Smith	1.00
41	Tom Burleson	1.00
42	Dave Twardzik	1.00
43	Bill Bradley	12.00
44	Calvin Murphy	2.50
45	Bob Love	2.25
46	Brian Winters	1.00
47	Glenn McDonald	1.00
48	Checklist	30.00
49	Bird Averitt	1.00
50	Rick Barry	9.00
51	Ticky Burden	1.00
52	Rich Jones	1.00
53	Austin Carr	2.00
54	Steve Kuberski	1.00
55	Paul Westphal	7.00
56	Mike Riordan	1.00
57	Bill Walton	25.00
58	*Eric Money*	2.00
59	John Drew	1.50
60	Pete Maravich	42.00
61	*John Shumate*	2.50
62	Mack Calvin	1.00
63	Bruce Seals	1.00
64	Walt Frazier	6.00
65	Elmore Smith	1.00
66	Rudy Tomjanovich	6.00
67	Sam Lacey	1.00
68	George Gervin	20.00
69	*Gus Williams*	6.00
70	George McGinnis	3.00
71	Len Elmore	2.00
72	Jack Marin	1.00
73	Brian Taylor	1.00
74	Jim Brewer	1.00
75	*Alvan Adams*	6.00
76	Dave Bing	4.00
77	Phil Jackson	12.00
78	Geoff Petrie	1.00
79	Mike Sojourner	1.00
80	James Silas	1.00
81	Bob Dandridge	1.00
82	Ernie DiGregorio	1.00
83	Cazzie Russell	1.50
84	Kevin Porter	1.00
85	Tom Boerwinkle	1.00
86	Darnell Hillman	1.00
87	Herm Gilliam	1.00
88	Nate Williams	1.00
89	Phil Smith	1.00
90	John Havlicek	15.00
91	Kevin Kunnert	1.00
92	Jimmy Walker	1.00
93	Billy Cunningham	7.00
94	Dan Issel	6.50
95	Ron Boone	1.00
96	Lou Hudson	1.75
97	Jim Chones	1.00
98	Earl Monroe	4.50
99	Tom Van Arsdale	1.00
100	Kareem Abdul-Jabbar	40.00
101	Moses Malone	25.00
102	*Ricky Sobers*	2.00
103	Swen Nater	1.00
104	Leonard Robinson	2.00
105	Don Watts	1.00
106	Otto Moore	1.00
107	Maurice Lucas	3.00
108	Norm Van Lier	1.00
109	Clifford Ray	1.00
110	*David Thompson*	40.00
111	Fred Carter	1.00
112	Caldwell Jones	1.50
113	John Williamson	1.00
114	Bobby Smith	1.00
115	Jo Jo White	1.50
116	Curtis Perry	1.00
117	John Gianelli	1.00
118	Curtis Rowe	1.00
119	*Lionel Hollins*	4.00
120	Elvin Hayes	6.00
121	Ken Charles	1.00
122	*Dave Meyers*	2.50
123	Jerry Sloan	3.00
124	Billy Knight	3.00
125	Gail Goodrich	3.00
126	Kareem Abdul-Jabbar (AS)	20.00
127	Julius Erving (AS)	25.00
128	George McGinnis (AS)	1.25
129	Nate Archibald (AS)	2.00
130	Pete Maravich (AS)	25.00
131	Dave Cowens (AS)	5.00
132	Rick Barry (AS)	5.00
133	Elvin Hayes (AS)	4.00
134	James Silas (AS)	1.25
135	Randy Smith (AS)	1.25
136	Leonard Gary	1.00
137	Charles Johnson	1.00
138	Ron Behagen	1.00
139	Mike Newlin	1.00
140	Bob McAdoo	6.00
141	Mike Gale	1.00
142	Scott Wedman	1.00
143	*Lloyd Free*	8.00
144	Bobby Jones	8.00

1977-78 Topps

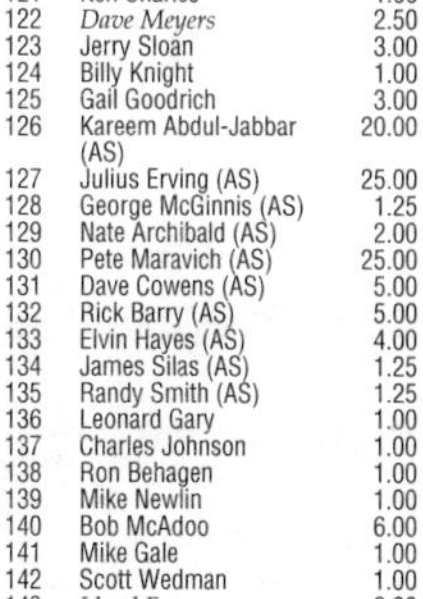

Topps' first of three 132-card runs continued to showcase a strong player selection, design and better photography. As a switch, cards were printed on white cardboard stock with green highlights on the back. Cards measure 2-1/2" x 3-1/2". Rookies in this set include Adrian Dantley, Robert Parish, and Darryl Dawkins. Second-year cards include those of David Thompson and Alvan Adams, and the last regular-issue cards of Cazzie Russell and John Havlicek are included here.

		NM
Complete Set (132):		100.00
Common Player:		.25
Pack (10):		17.50
Wax Box (36):		450.00
1	Kareem Abdul-Jabbar	18.00
2	Henry Bibby	.25
3	Curtis Rowe	.25
4	Norm Van Lier	.25
5	Darnell Hillman	.25
6	Earl Monroe	3.00
7	Leonard Gray	.25
8	Bird Averitt	.25
9	Jim Brewer	.25
10	Paul Westphal	3.00
11	*Bob Gross*	.60
12	Phil Smith	.25
13	*Dan Roundfield*	1.00
14	Brian Taylor	.25
15	Rudy Tomjanovich	2.00
16	Kevin Porter	.25
17	Scott Wedman	.25
18	Lloyd Free	.75
19	*Tom Boswell*	.50
20	Pete Maravich	12.00
21	Cliff Poindexter	.25
22	Bubbles Hawkins	.25
23	*Kevin Grevey*	1.00
24	Ken Charles	.25
25	Bob Dandridge	.25
26	*Lonnie Shelton*	.50
27	Don Chaney	.30
28	Larry Kenon	.25
29	Checklist	3.00
30	Fred Brown	.50
31	John Gianelli	.25
32	Austin Carr	.75
33	Jamaal Wilkes	1.00
34	Caldwell Jones	.25
35	Jo Jo White	1.00
36	*Scott May*	1.75
37	Mike Newlin	.25
38	Mel Davis	.25
39	Lionel Hollins	.60
40	Elvin Hayes	4.00
41	Dan Issel	3.00
42	Ricky Sobers	.25
43	Don Ford	.25
44	John Williamson	.25
45	Bob McAdoo	1.00
46	Geoff Petrie	.25
47	*M.L. Carr*	2.00
48	Brian Winters	.25
49	Sam Lacey	.25
50	George McGinnis	.75
51	Don Watts	.25
52	Sidney Wicks	.60
53	Wilbur Holland	.25
54	Tim Bassett	.25
55	Phil Chenier	.25
56	*Adrian Dantley*	8.00
57	Jim Chones	.25
58	*John Lucas*	2.50
59	Cazzie Russell	.40
60	David Thompson	2.50
61	Bob Lanier	2.00
62	Dave Twardzik	.25
63	Wilbert Jones	.25
64	Clifford Ray	.25
65	Doug Collins	1.75
66	*Tom McMillen*	2.00
67	*Rich Kelley*	.50
68	Mike Bantom	.25
69	Tom Boerwinkle	.25
70	John Havlicek	7.00
71	*Marvin Webster*	.50
72	Curtis Perry	.25
73	George Gervin	6.00
74	Leonard Robinson	.25
75	Wes Unseld	1.50
76	Dave Meyers	.50
77	Gail Goodrich	1.00
78	*Richard Washington*	1.00
79	Mike Gale	.25
80	Maurice Lucas	1.00
81	*Harvey Catchings*	.30
82	Randy Smith	.25
83	Campy Russell	.25
84	Kevin Kunnert	.25
85	Lou Hudson	.80
86	Mickey Johnson	.25
87	Lucius Allen	.25
88	Spencer Haywood	1.00
89	Gus Williams	1.00
90	Dave Cowens	3.00
91	Al Skinner	.25
92	Swen Nater	.25
93	Tom Henderson	.25
94	Don Buse	.25
95	Alvan Adams	1.00
96	Mack Calvin	.40
97	Tom Burleson	.25
98	John Drew	.25
99	Mike Green	.25
100	Julius Erving	20.00
101	John Mengelt	.25
102	Howard Porter	.25
103	Billy Paultz	.25
104	John Shumate	.70
105	Calvin Murphy	1.00
106	Elmore Smith	.25
107	Jim McMillian	.25
108	Kevin Stacom	.25
109	Jan Van Breda Kolff	.25
110	Billy Knight	.25
111	*Robert Parish*	35.00
112	Larry Wright	.25
113	Bruce Seals	.25
114	Junior Bridgeman	.50
115	Artis Gilmore	2.00
116	Steve Mix	.25
117	Ron Lee	.25
118	Bobby Jones	1.00
119	Ron Boone	.25
120	Bill Walton	10.00
121	Chris Ford	1.00
122	Earl Tatum	.25
123	E.C. Coleman	.25
124	Moses Malone	10.00
125	Charlie Scott	.25
126	Bobby Smith	.25
127	Nate Archibald	[illegible]
128	*Mitch Kupchak*	2.00
129	Walt Frazier	4.00
130	Rick Barry	3.00
131	Ernie DiGregorio	.25
132	*Darryl Dawkins*	9.00

1978-79 Topps

Topps' second of three 132-card sets featured the team name down the left side of the card, with a head shot of the player inset into the action shot. Cards are the standard 2-1/2" x 3-1/2". Rookie cards in this set include Walter Davis, Norm Nixon, Dennis Johnson, Bernard King, Jack Sikma and Marques Johnson. Notable second-year cards include those of Robert Parish and Adrian Dantley. This set contains the final cards of Dave Bing, Walt Frazier and Norm Van Lier.

		NM
Complete Set (132):		80.00
Common Player:		.25
Pack (14):		9.00
Wax Box (36):		210.00
1	Bill Walton	12.00
2	Doug Collins	1.50
3	Jamaal Wilkes	1.00
4	Wilber Holland	.25
5	Bob McAdoo	1.25
6	Lucius Allen	.25
7	Wes Unseld	2.00
8	Dave Meyers	.25
9	Austin Carr	.25
10	*Walter Davis*	5.00
11	John Williamson	.25
12	E.C. Coleman	.25
13	Calvin Murphy	1.25
14	Bobby Jones	1.00
15	Chris Ford	.75
16	Kermit Washington	.25
17	Butch Beard	.25
18	Steve Mix	.25
19	Marvin Webster	.25
20	George Gervin	4.00
21	Steve Hawes	.25
22	*Johnny Davis*	.25
23	Swen Nater	.25
24	Lou Hudson	.60
25	Elvin Hayes	2.00
26	Nate Archibald	1.25
27	*James Edwards*	3.00
28	Howard Porter	.25
29	*Quinn Buckner*	2.00
30	Leonard Robinson	.25
31	Jim Cleamons	.25
32	Campy Russell	.25
33	Phil Smith	.25
34	Darryl Dawkins	1.50
35	Don Buse	.25
36	Mickey Johnson	.25
37	Mike Gale	.25
38	Moses Malone	6.50
39	Gus Williams	.50
40	Dave Cowens	2.00
41	*Bobby Wilkerson*	.50
42	Wilbert Jones	.25
43	Charlie Scott	.25
44	John Drew	.25
45	Earl Monroe	3.00
46	John Shumate	.25
47	Earl Tatum	.25
48	Mitch Kupchak	.25
49	Ron Boone	.25
50	Maurice Lucas	1.00
51	Louie Dampier	.25
52	Aaron James	.25
53	John Mengelt	.25
54	Garfield Heard	.25
55	George Johnson	.25
56	Junior Bridgeman	.25
57	Elmore Smith	.25
58	Rudy Tomjanovich	1.00
59	Fred Brown	.60
60	Rick Barry	3.00
61	Dave Bing	1.50
62	Anthony Roberts	.25
63	*Norm Nixon*	3.00
64	*Leon Douglas*	.40
65	Henry Bibby	.25
66	Lonnie Shelton	.25
67	Checklist	2.00
68	Tom Henderson	.25
69	Dan Roundfield	.40
70	*Armond Hill*	.40
71	Larry Kenon	.25
72	Billy Knight	.25
73	Artis Gilmore	1.75
74	Lionel Hollins	.25
75	*Bernard King*	9.00
76	Brian Winters	.25
77	Alvan Adams	.75
78	*Dennis Johnson*	7.00
79	Scott Wedman	.25
80	Pete Maravich	12.00
81	Dan Issel	2.00
82	M.L. Carr	.25
83	Walt Frazier	3.00
84	Dwight Jones	.25
85	Jo Jo White	.75
86	Robert Parish	7.00
87	*Charlie Criss*	.40
88	Jim McMillian	.25
89	Chuck Williams	.25
90	George McGinnis	.50
91	Billy Paultz	.25
92	Bob Dandridge	.25
93	Ricky Sobers	.25
94	Paul Silas	.25
95	Gail Goodrich	1.00
96	Tim Bassett	.25
97	Ron Lee	.25
98	Bob Gross	.25
99	Sam Lacey	.25
100	David Thompson	2.00
101	John Gianelli	.25
102	Norm Van Lier	.25
103	Caldwell Jones	.25
104	Eric Money	.25
105	Jim Chones	.25
106	John Lucas	2.50
107	Spencer Haywood	.75
108	*Eddie Johnson*	.50
109	Sidney Wicks	.60
110	Kareem Abdul-Jabbar	10.00
111	*Sonny Parker*	.40
112	Randy Smith	.25
113	Kevin Grevey	.25
114	Rich Kelley	.25
115	Scott May	.25
116	Lloyd Free	.25
117	*Jack Sikma*	2.00
118	Kevin Porter	.25
119	Darnell Hillman	.25
120	Paul Westphal	2.00
121	Richard Washington	.25
122	Dave Twardzik	.25
123	Mike Bantom	.25
124	Mike Newlin	.25
125	Bob Lanier	1.75
126	*Marques Johnson*	3.50
127	*Foots Walker*	.50
128	*Cedric Maxwell*	2.50
129	*Ray Williams*	.60
130	Julius Erving	12.00
131	Clifford Ray	.25
132	Adrian Dantley	3.50

1979-80 Topps

Topps' final 132-card issue features a colorful design of a pennant wrapped around a basketball. Cards are once again standard size. Rookies in this set include Alex English, Mychal Thompson and Reggie Theus. Second-year cards in the set are those of Dennis Johnson, Marques Johnson, Jack Sikma, Bernard King and Walter Davis. The final cards of Spencer Haywood and Sidney Wicks are also in this set.

		NM
Complete Set (132):		75.00
Common Player:		.20
Pack (12):		6.50
Wax Box (36):		150.00
1	George Gervin	5.00
2	Mitch Kupchak	.20
3	Henry Bibby	.20
4	Bob Gross	.20
5	Dave Cowens	2.00
6	Dennis Johnson	2.00
7	Scott Wedman	.20
8	Earl Monroe	2.00
9	Mike Bantom	.20
10	Kareem Abdul-Jabbar (AS)	10.00
11	Jo Jo White	.50
12	Spencer Haywood	.40
13	Kevin Porter	.20
14	Bernard King	2.00
15	Mike Newlin	.20
16	Sidney Wicks	.50
17	Dan Issel	1.25
18	Tom Henderson	.20
19	Jim Chones	.20
20	Julius Erving	14.00
21	Brian Winters	.20
22	Billy Paultz	.20
23	Cedric Maxwell	.40
24	Eddie Johnson	.20
25	Artis Gilmore	1.00
26	Maurice Lucas	.60
27	Gus Williams	.50
28	Sam Lacey	.20
29	Toby Knight	.20
30	Paul Westphal (AS)	1.00
31	*Alex English*	10.00
32	Gail Goodrich	.75
33	Caldwell Jones	.20
34	Kevin Grevey	.20
35	Jamaal Wilkes	.50
36	Sonny Parker	.20
37	John Gianelli	.20
38	*John Long*	.75
39	George Johnson	.20
40	Lloyd Free (AS)	.20
41	Rudy Tomjanovich	1.00
42	Foots Walker	.20
43	Dan Roundfield	.20
44	*Reggie Theus*	3.00
45	Bill Walton	4.00
46	Fred Brown	.45
47	Darnell Hillman	.20
48	Ray Williams	.30
49	Larry Kenon	.20
50	David Thompson	2.00
51	Billy Knight	.20
52	Alvan Adams	.20
53	Phil Smith	.20
54	Adrian Dantley	1.50
55	John Williamson	.20
56	Campy Russell	.20
57	Armond Hill	.20
58	Bob Lanier	1.00
59	Mickey Johnson	.20
60	Pete Maravich	8.00
61	Nick Weatherspoon	.20
62	*Robert Reid*	.75
63	*Mychal Thompson*	4.00
64	Doug Collins	1.00
65	Wes Unseld	.75
66	Jack Sikma	1.25
67	Bobby Wilkerson	.20
68	Bill Robinzine	.20
69	Joe Meriweather	.20
70	Marques Johnson (AS)	1.00
71	Ricky Sobers	.20
72	Clifford Ray	.20
73	Tim Bassett	.20
74	James Silas	.20
75	Bob McAdoo	1.00
76	Austin Carr	.20
77	Don Ford	.20
78	Steve Hawes	.20
79	*Ron Brewer*	.40
80	Walter Davis	1.00
81	Calvin Murphy	.75
82	Tom Boswell	.20
83	Lonnie Shelton	.20
84	*Terry Tyler*	.40
85	Randy Smith	.20
86	Rich Kelley	.20
87	*Otis Birdsong*	.75
88	Marvin Webster	.20
89	Eric Money	.20
90	Elvin Hayes (AS)	3.00
91	Junior Bridgeman	.20
92	Johnny Davis	.20
93	Robert Parish	4.00
94	Eddie Jordan	.20
95	Leonard Robinson	.20
96	*Rick Robey*	.30
97	Norm Nixon	.50
98	Mark Olberding	.20
99	Wilbur Holland	.20
100	Moses Malone (AS)	4.00
101	Checklist	2.00
102	Tom Owens	.20
103	Phil Chenier	.20
104	John Johnson	.20
105	Darryl Dawkins	1.00
106	Charlie Scott	.20
107	M.L. Carr	.20
108	*Phil Ford*	3.00
109	Swen Nates	.20
110	Nate Archibald	1.00
111	Aaron James	.20
112	Jim Cleamons	.20
113	James Edwards	.75
114	Don Buse	.20
115	Steve Mix	.20
116	Charles Johnson	.20
117	Elmore Smith	.20
118	John Drew	.20
119	Lou Hudson	.50
120	Rick Barry	2.25
121	*Kent Benson*	.50
122	Mike Gale	.20
123	Jan Van Breda Kolff	.20
124	Chris Ford	.60
125	George McGinnis	1.00
126	Leon Douglas	.20
127	John Lucas	1.50
128	Kermit Washington	.20
129	Lionel Hollins	.20
130	Bob Dandridge (AS)	.20
131	James McElroy	.20
132	Bobby Jones	1.00

1980-81 Topps

Topps came up with a very unusual set for the 1980-81 season. The set is complete at 176 (2-1/2" x 3-1/2") perforated cards, each containing three smaller cards. The set pictures a total of 264 different players. Since the cards were printed on a pair of different sheets, there is a lot of player repetition. All the different combinations are covered in the checklist below. Subsets include all-stars (1-18), team leaders and slam dunk cards. Rookies in this set include Larry Bird, Magic Johnson, Bill Cartwright, Sidney Moncrief and Mo Cheeks. To be considered Mint, the card must be completely intact - all three parts of the perforated cards must be in the whole form. Note: print marks are very common on the Magic/Bird rookie card. Cards are arranged numerically according to the card on the far left. AS means All-Star; TL means Team Leader; SD means Slam Dunk.

		NM
Complete Set (176):		550.00
Common Player:		.25
Pack (8 Panels):		16.00
Wax Box (36):		
1	Dan Roundfield - 3 (AS), Julius Erving - 181, Ron Brewer - 258 (SD)	6.00
2	Moses Malone - 7 (AS), Steve Mix - 185, Robert Parish - 92 (TL)	1.50
3	Gus Williams - 12 (AS), Geoff Huston - 67, John Drew - 5 (AS)	.25
4	Steve Hawes - 24, Nate Archibald - 32 (TL), Elvin Hayes - 248	1.00
5	Dan Roundfield - 29, Dan Issel - 73 (TL), Brian Winters - 152	.25
6	*Larry Bird* - 34, Julius Erving - 174 (TL), *Magic Johnson* - 139	350.00
7	Dave Cowens - 36, Paul Westphal - 186 (TL), Jamaal Wilkes - 142	1.00
8	Pete Maravich - 38, Lloyd Free - 264 (SD), Dennis Johnson - 194	3.00
9	Rick Robey - 40, Adrian Dantley - 234 (TL), Eddie Johnson - 26	.25
10	Scott May - 47, K. Washington - 196 (TL), Henry Bibby - 177	.25
11	Don Ford - 55, Quinn Buckner - 145 (TL), Brad Holland - 138	.25
12	Campy Russell - 58, Kevin Grevey - 247, Dave Robisch - 52 (TL)	.25
13	Foots Walker - 60, Mick Johnson - 113 (TL), Bill Robinzine - 130	.75
14	Austin Carr - 61, Kareem Abdul-Jabbar - 8, Calvin Natt - 200	2.50
15	Jim Cleamons - 63, Robert Reid - 256 (SD), Charlie Criss - 22	.25
16	Tom LaGarde - 69, Swen Nater - 215 (TL), James Silas - 213	.25
17	Jerome Whitehead - 71, Artis Gilmore - 259 (SD), Caldwell Jones - 184	.25
18	John Roche - 74 (TL), Clifford Ray - 99, Ben Poquette - 235 (TL)	.25
19	Alex English - 75, Marques Johnson - 2 (AS), Jeff Judkins - 68	1.50
20	Terry Tyler - 82 (TL), Armond Hill - 21 (TL), M.R. Richardson - 171	.25
21	Kent Benson - 84, John Shumate - 212, Paul Westphal - 229	.25
22	Phil Hubbard - 86, Robert Parish - 93 (TL), Tom Burleson - 126	1.00
23	John Long - 88, Julius Erving - 1 (AS), Ricky Sobers - 49	2.00
24	Eric Money - 90, Dave Robisch - 57, Rick Robery - 254 (SD)	.25
25	Wayne Cooper - 95, John Johnson - 226 (TL), David Greenwood - 45	.25
26	Robert Parish - 97, Leon Robinson - 187 (TL), Dwight Jones - 46	3.00
27	Sonny Parker - 98, Dave Twardzik - 197 (TL), Cedric Maxwell - 39	.25
28	Rick Barry - 105, Otis Birdsong - 122 (TL), John Mengelt - 48	1.00
29	Allen Leavell - 106, Foots Walker - 53 (TL), Freeman Williams - 223	.25
30	Calvin Murphy - 108, Maurice Cheeks - 176 (TL), Greg Kelser - 87	.75
31	Robert Reid - 110, Wes Unseld - 243 (TL), Reggie Theus - 50	.25
32	Rudy Tomjanovich - 111, Eddie Johnson - 13 (AS), Doug Collins - 179	.25
33	Mickey Johnson - 112 (TL), Wayne Rollins - 28, M.R. Richardson - 15 (AS)	.25
34	Mike Bantom - 115, Adrian Dantley - 6 (AS), James Bailey - 227	.25
35	Dudley Bradley - 116, Eddie Jordan - 155 (TL), Allan Bristow - 239 (TL)	.25
36	James Edwards - 118, Mike Newlin - 153 (TL), Lionel Hollins - 182	.25
37	Mickey Johnson - 119, George Johnson - 154 (TL), Leonard Robinson - 193	.25
38	Billy Knight - 120, Paul Westphal - 16 (AS), Randy Smith - 59	.25
39	George McGinnis - 121, Eric Money - 83 (TL), Mike Bratz - 65	.25
40	Phil Ford - 124 (TL), Phil Smith - 101, Gus Williams - 224 (TL)	.25
41	Phil Ford - 127, John Drew - 19 (TL), Larry Kenon - 209	.25
42	Scott Wedman - 131, Bill Cartwright - 164 (TL), John Drew - 23	.25
43	Kareem Abdul-Jabbar - 132 (TL), Mike Mitchell - 56, Terry Tyler - 81 (TL)	2.00
44	Kareem Abdul-Jabbar - 135, David Thompson - 79, Brian Taylor - 216 (TL)	5.00
45	Michael Cooper - 137, Moses Malone - 103 (TL), George Johnson - 148	3.00
46	Mark Lansberger - 140, Bob Lanier - 10 (AS), Bill Walton - 222	.60
47	Norm Nixon - 141, Sam Lacey - 123 (TL), Kenny Carr - 54	.25
48	Marques Johnson - 143 (TL), Larry Bird - 30 (TL), Jack Sikma - 232	20.00
49	Junior Bridgeman - 146, Larry Bird - 31 (TL), Ron Brewer - 198	20.00
50	Quinn Buckner - 147, Kareem Abdul-Jabbar - 133 (TL), Mike Gale - 207	2.00
51	Marques Johnson - 149, Julius Erving - 262 (SD), Abdul Jeelani - 62	2.00
52	Sidney Moncrief - 151, Lonnie Shelton - 260 (SD), Paul Silas - 220	4.00
53	George Johnson - 156, Bill Cartwright - 9 (AS), Bob Gross - 199	.25
54	Maurice Lucas - 158, James Edwards - 261 (SD), Eddie Jordan - 157	.25
55	Mike Newlin - 159, Norm Nixon - 134 (TL), Darryl Dawkins - 180	.25
56	Roger Phegley - 160, James Silas - 206 (TL), Terry Tyler - 91 (UER) ((First name spelled Jams))	.25
57	Clifford Robinson - 161, Mike Mitchell - 51 (TL), Bobby Wilkerson - 80	.25
58	Jan Van Breda - 162, George Gervin - 204 (TL), Johnny Davis - 117	.25
59	Michael Ray Richardson - 165 (TL), Lloyd Free - 214 (TL), Artis Gilmore - 44	.25
60	Bill Cartwright - 166, Kevin Porter - 244 (TL), Armond Hill - 25	3.00
61	Toby Knight - 168, Lloyd Free - 14 (AS), Adrian Dantley - 240	.25
62	Joe Meriweather - 169, Lloyd Free - 218, David Greenwood - 42 (TL)	.25
63	Earl Monroe - 170, James McElroy - 27, Leon Douglas - 85	1.00
64	Marvin Webster - 172, Caldwell Jones - 175 (TL), Sam Lacey - 129	.25
65	Ray Williams - 173, John Lucas - 94 (TL), Dave Twardzik - 202	.25
66	Maurice Cheeks - 178, Magic Johnson - 18 (AS), Ron Boone - 237	20.00
67	Bobby Jones - 183, Chris Ford - 37, Joe Hassett - 66	.25
68	Alvan Adams - 189, Bill Cartwright - 163 (TL), Dan Issel - 76	.75
69	Don Buse - 190, Elvin Hayes - 242 (TL), M.L. Carr - 35	.25
70	Walter Davis - 191, George Gervin - 11 (AS), Jim Chones - 136	.20
71	Rich Kelley - 192, Moses Malone - 102 (TL), Winford Boynes - 64	1.00
72	Tom Owens - 201, Jack Sikma - 225 (TL), Purvis Short - 100	.20
73	George Gervin - 208, Dan Issel - 72 (TL), Mitch Kupchak - 249	1.00
74	Joe Bryant - 217, Bobby Jones - 263 (SD), Moses Malone - 107	2.00
75	Swen Nater - 219, Calvin Murphy - 17 (AS), Richard Washington - 70	.25
76	Brian Taylor - 221, John Shumate - 253 (SD), Larry Demic - 167	.25
77	Fred Brown - 228, Larry Kenon - 205 (TL), Kermit Washington - 203	.25
78	John Johnson - 230, Walter Davis - 4, Nate Archibald - 33	.75
79	Lonnie Shelton - 231, Allen Leavell - 104 (TL), John Lucas - 96	.25
80	Gus Williams - 233, Dan Roundfield - 20 (TL), Kevin Restani - 211	.25
81	Allan Bristow - 236 (TL), Mark Olberding - 210, James Bailey - 255 (SD)	.25
82	Tom Boswell - 238, Billy Paultz - 109, Bob Lanier - 150	.75
83	Ben Poquette - 241, Paul Westphal - 188 (TL), Charlie Scott - 77	.25
84	Greg Ballard - 245, Reggie Theus - 43 (TL), John Williamson - 252	.25
85	Bob Dandridge - 246, Reggie Theus - 41 (TL), Reggie King - 128	.25
86	Kevin Porter - 250, Johnny Davis - 114 (TL), Otis Birdsong - 125	.25
87	Wes Unseld - 251, Tom Owens - 195 (TL), John Roche - 78	.25
88	Elvin Hayes - 257 (SD), Marques Johnson - 144 (TL), Bob McAdoo - 89	.25
89	Dan Roundfield - 3, Lloyd Free - 218, David Greenwood - 42 (TL)	.25
90	Moses Malone - 7, Kevin Grevey - 247, Dave Robisch - 52 (TL)	1.00
91	Gus Williams - 12, Mark Olberding - 210, James Bailey - 255 (SD)	.25
92	Steve Hawes - 24, John Johnson - 226 (TL), David Greenwood - 45	.25
93	Dan Roundfield - 29, Mickey Johnson - 113 (TL), Bill Robinzine - 130	.25
94	Larry Bird - 34, Bill Cartwright - 164 (TL), John Drew - 23	60.00
95	Dave Cowens - 36, Paul Westphal - 16 (AS), Randy Smith - 59	1.00
96	Pete Maravich - 38, Leonard Robinson - 187 (TL), Dwight Jones - 46	1.50
97	Rick Robey - 40, Chris Ford - 37, Joe Hassett - 66	.25
98	Scott May - 47, Larry Bird - 30 (TL), Jack Sikma - 232	20.00
99	Don Ford - 55, Marques Johnson - 144 (TL), Bob McAdoo - 89	.25
100	Campy Russell - 58, Armond Hill - 21 (TL), Michael Ray Richardson - 171	.25
101	Foots Walker - 60, Otis Birdsong - 122 (TL), John Mengelt - 48	.25
102	Austin Carr - 61, Mike Mitchell - 56, Terry Tyler - 81 (TL)	.25
103	Jim Cleamons - 63, James Edwards - 261 (SD), Eddie Jordan - 157	.25
104	Tom LaGarde - 69, Billy Paultz - 109, Bob Lanier - 150	.75
105	Jerome Whitehead - 71, Calvin Murphy - 17 (AS), Richard Washington - 70	.25
106	John Roche - 74 (TL), Wayne Rollins - 28, Michael Ray Richardson - 15 (AS)	.25
107	Alex English - 75, Moses Malone - 102 (TL), Winford Bornes - 64	1.50
108	Terry Tyler - 82 (TL), David Thompson - 79, Brian Taylor - 216 (TL)	.25
109	Kent Benson - 84, Artis Gilmore - 259 (SD), Caldwell Jones - 184	.25
110	Phil Hubbard - 86, Tom Owens - 195 (TL), John Roche - 78	.25
111	John Long - 88, Magic Johnson - 18 (AS), Ron Boone - 237	15.00
112	Eric Money - 90, Swen Nater - 215 (TL), James Silas - 213	.25
113	Wayne Cooper - 95, George Johnson - 154 (TL), Leonard Robinson - 193	.25
114	Robert Parish - 97, Moses Malone - 103 (TL), George Johnson - 148	4.00
115	Sonny Parker - 98, John Lucas - 94 (TL), Dave Twardzik - 202	.25
116	Rick Barry - 105, Sam Lacey - 123 (TL), Kenny Carr - 54	1.00
117	Allen Leavell - 106, Dave Twardzik - 197 (TL), Cedric Maxwell - 39	.25
118	Calvin Murphy - 108, Mike Mitchell - 51 (TL), Bobby Wilkerson - 80	.25
119	Robert Reid - 110, Mike Newlin - 153 (TL), Lionel Hollins - 182	.25
120	Rudy Tomjanovich - 111, Dan Issel - 73 (TL), Brian Winters - 152	.25
121	Mickey Johnson - 112 (TL), Lloyd Free - 264 (SD), Dennis Johnson - 194	.50
122	Mike Bantom - 115, George Gervin - 204 (TL), Johnny Davis - 117	.25
123	Dudley Bradley - 116, Paul Westphal - 186 (TL), Jamaal Wilkes - 142	.25
124	James Edwards - 118, Nate Archibald - 32 (TL), Elvin Hayes - 248	1.00
125	Mickey Johnson - 119, Dan Issel - 72 (TL), Mitch Kupchak - 249	.25

126	Billy Knight - 120, Allen Leavell - 104 (TL), John Lucas - 96	.25
127	George McGinnis - 121, Bob Lanier - 10 (AS), Bill Walton - 222	1.00
128	Phil Ford - 124 (TL), Adrian Dantley - 234 (TL), Eddie Johnson - 26	.25
129	Phil Ford - 127, Reggie Theus - 43 (TL), John Williamson - 252	.25
130	Scott Wedman - 131, Kevin Porter - 244 (TL), Armond Hill - 25	3.00
131	Kareem Abdul-Jabbar - 132 (TL), Robert Parish - 93 (TL), Tom Burleson - 126	3.00
132	Kareem Abdul-Jabbar - 135, John Shumate - 253 (SD), Larry Demic - 167	5.00
133	Michael Cooper - 137, John Shumate - 212, Paul Westphal - 229	2.00
134	Mark Lansberger - 140, Lloyd Free - 214 (TL), Artis Gilmore - 44	.25
135	Norm Nixon - 141, Elvin Hayes - 242 (TL), M.L. Carr - 35	.25
136	Marques Johnson - 143 (TL), Dave Robisch - 57, Rick Robey - 254 (SD)	.25
137	Junior Bridgeman - 146, Julius Erving - 1 (AS), Ricky Sobers - 49	3.00
138	Quinn Buckner - 147, Marques Johnson - 2 (AS), Jeff Judkins - 68	.25
139	Marques Johnson - 149, Eric Money - 83 (TL), Mike Bratz - 65	.25
140	Sidney Moncrief - 151, Kareem Abdul-Jabbar - 133 (TL), Mike Gale - 207	6.00
141	George Johnson - 156, Caldwell Jones - 175 (TL), Sam Lacey - 129	.25
142	Maurice Lucas - 158, Julius Erving - 262 (SD), Abdul Jeelani - 62	3.00
143	Mike Newlin - 159, Wes Unseld - 243 (TL), Reggie Theus - 50	.25
144	Roger Phegley - 160, Quinn Buckner - 145 (TL), Brad Holland - 138	.25
145	Clifford Robinson - 161, Johnny Davis - 114 (TL), Otis Birdsong - 125	.25
146	Jan Van Breda Kolff - 162, Julius Erving - 174 (TL), Magic Johnson - 139	50.00
147	Michael Ray Richardson - 165 (TL), Steve Mix - 185, Robert Parish - 92 (TL)	1.00
148	Bill Cartwright - 166, Eddie Johnson - 13 (AS), Doug Collins - 179	3.00
149	Toby Knight - 168, Paul Westphal - 188 (TL), Charlie Scott - 77	.25
150	Joe Meriweather - 169, Kermit Washington - 196 (TL), Henry Bibby - 177	.25
151	Earl Monroe - 170, James Silas - 206 (TL), Terry Tyler - 91	1.00
152	Marvin Webster - 172, Eddie Jordan - 155 (TL), Allan Bristow - 239	.25
153	Ray Williams - 173, Jack Sikma - 225 (TL), Purvis Short - 100	.25
154	Maurice Cheeks - 178, George Gervin - 11 (AS), Jim Chones - 136	5.00
155	Bobby Jones, Clifford Ray, Ben Poquette	.25
156	Alvan Adams - 189, Lloyd Free - 14 (AS), Adrian Dantley - 240	.25
157	Don Buse - 190, Adrian Dantley - 6 (AS), James Bailey - 227	.25
158	Walter Davis - 191, Bill Cartwright - 9 (AS), Bob Gross - 199	.25
159	Rich Kelley - 192, Bobby Jones - 263 (SD), Moses Malone - 107	2.00
160	Tom Owens - 201, Norm Nixon - 134 (TL), Darryl Dawkins - 180	.25
161	George Gervin - 208, Foots Walker - 53 (TL), Freeman Williams - 223	1.00
162	Joe Bryant - 217, Kareem Abdul-Jabbar - 8 (AS), Calvin Natt - 200	2.00
163	Swen Nater - 219, Phil Smith - 101, Gus Williams - 224 (TL)	.25
164	Brian Taylor - 221, Robert Reid - 256 (SD), Charlie Criss - 22	.25
165	Fred Brown - 228, Larry Bird - 31 (TL), Ron Brewer - 198	20.00
166	John Johnson - 230, Bill Cartwright - 183 (TL), Dan Issel - 76	.75
167	Lonnie Shelton - 231, Larry Kenon - 205 (TL), Kermit Washington - 203	.25
168	Gus Williams - 233, Reggie Theus - 43 (TL), Reggie King - 128	.25
169	Allan Bristow - 236 (TL), Lonnie Shelton - 260 (SD), Paul Silas - 220	.25
170	Tom Boswell - 238, James McElroy - 27, Leon Douglas - 85	.25
171	Ben Poquette - 241, Maurice Cheeks - 176 (TL), Greg Kelser - 87	1.00
172	Greg Ballard - 245, Walter Davis - 4 (AS), Nate Archibald - 33	.75
173	Bob Dandridge - 246, John Drew - 19 (TL), Larry Kenon - 209	.25
174	Kevin Porter - 250, Dan Roundfield - 20 (TL), Kevin Restani - 211	.25
175	Wes Unseld - 251, Geoff Huston - 67, John Drew - 5 (AS)	.25
176	Elvin Hayes - 257 (SD), Julius Erving - 181, Ron Brewer - 258 (SD)	7.50

1980-81 Topps Posters

These posters, which measure around 5" x 7", were folded and inserted into Topps wax packs of basketball cards. Posters feature one of 16 NBA teams and feature the same design as the basketball cards. Posters are printed on thin white paper.

		NM
Complete Set (16):		15.00
Common Team:		.75
1	Atlanta Hawks	.75
2	Boston Celtics	2.50
3	Chicago Bulls	.75
4	Cleveland Cavaliers	.75
5	Detroit Pistons	.75
6	Houston Rockets	.75
7	Indiana Pacers	.75
8	Los Angeles Lakers	2.50
9	Milwaukee Bucks	1.00
10	New Jersey Nets	.75
11	New York Knicks	1.00
12	Philadelphia 76ers	2.00
13	Phoenix Suns	.75
14	Portland Trail Blazers	.75
15	Seattle Sonics	.75
16	Washington Bullets	.75

1981-82 Topps

Topps' excellent run on basketball cards bowed out with this somewhat limp issue. Cards returned to standard size with one player per card, but the design was disappointing when compared to earlier Topps sets. This set can also be described as schizophrenic. While the first 66 cards in the set were available to everyone around the country, the final 44 cards were split up into three regions for distribution: East, Midwest and West. Cards were still numbered 67-110, but have different players to suit the region. Rookies in the set include Darrell Griffith, Kevin McHale and Bill Laimbeer. The second-year cards here are those of Larry Bird, Magic Johnson, Michael Cooper, Mo Cheeks, Bill Cartwright and Sidney Moncrief. SA means super action.

		MT
Complete Set (198):		80.00
Common Player:		.15
Midwest Wax Pack (13):		8.25
Midwest Wax Box (36):		215.00
West Wax Pack (13):		8.50
West Wax Box (36):		225.00
East Wax Pack (13):		10.75
East Wax Box (36):		290.00
1	John Drew	.25
2	Dan Roundfield	.15
3	Nate Archibald	.60
4	Larry Bird	25.00
5	Cedric Maxwell	.25
6	Robert Parish	2.00
7	Artis Gilmore	.50
8	Ricky Sobers	.15
9	Mike Mitchell	.15
10	Tom LaGarde	.15
11	Dan Issel	1.00
12	David Thompson	.40
13	Lloyd Free	.15
14	Moses Malone	1.75
15	Calvin Murphy	.30
16	Johnny Davis	.15
17	Otis Birdsong	.15
18	Phil Ford	.15
19	Scott Wedman	.15
20	Kareem Abdul-Jabbar	5.00
21	Magic Johnson	15.00
22	Norm Nixon	.25
23	Jamaal Wilkes	.35
24	Marques Johnson	.40
25	Bob Lanier	.75
26	Bill Cartwright	.75
27	Michael Ray Richardson	.15
28	Ray Williams	.15
29	Darryl Dawkins	.40
30	Julius Erving	5.00
31	Lionel Hollins	.15
32	Bobby Jones	.15
33	Walter Davis	.30
34	Dennis Johnson	.50
35	Leonard Robinson	.15
36	Mychal Thompson	.30
37	George Gervin	1.00
38	Swen Nater	.15
39	Jack Sikma	.50
40	Adrian Dantley	.75
41	*Darrell Griffith*	1.50
42	Elvin Hayes	1.00
43	Fred Brown	.15
44	Atlanta Hawks team (John Drew, Dan Roundfield, Eddie Johnson)	.15
45	Boston Celtics team (Larry Bird, Nate Archibald)	2.50
46	Chicago Bulls team (Reggie Theus, Artis Gilmore)	.15
47	Cleveland Cavaliers team (Mike Mitchell, Kenny Carr, Mike Bratz)	.15
48	Dallas Mavericks team (Jim Spanarkel, Tom LaGarde, Brad Davis)	.15
49	Denver Nuggets team (David Thompson, Dan Issel, Kenny Higgs)	.15
50	Detroit Pistons team (John Long, Phil Hubbard, Ron Lee)	.15
51	Golden State Warriors team (Lloyd Free, Larry Smith, John Lucas)	.15
52	Houston Rockets team (Moses Malone, Alan Leavell)	.60
53	Indiana Pacers team (Billy Knight, James Edwards, Johnny Davis)	.15
54	Kansas City Kings team (Otis Birdsong, Reggie King, Phil Ford)	.15
55	Los Angeles Lakers team (Kareem Abdul-Jabbar, Norm Nixon)	1.50
56	Milwaukee Bucks team (Marques Johnson, Mickey Johnson, Quinn Buckner)	.15
57	New Jersey Nets team (Mike Newlin, Maurice Lucas)	.15
58	New York Knicks team (Bill Cartwright, Michael Ray Richardson)	2.00
59	Philadelphia 76ers team (Julius Erving, Caldwell Jones, Maurice Cheeks)	1.50
60	Phoenix Suns team (Truck Robinson, Alvan Adams)	.15
61	Portland Blazers team (Jim Paxson, Mychal Thompson, Kermit Washington, Kelvin Ransey)	.15
62	San Antonio Spurs team (George Gervin, Dave Corzine, Johnny Moore)	.15
63	San Diego Clippers team (Freeman Williams, Swen Nater, Brian Taylor)	.15
64	Seattle Sonics team (Jack Sikma, Vinnie Johnson)	.40
65	Utah Jazz team (Adrian Dantley, Ben Poquette, Alan Bristow)	.15
66	Washington Bullets team (Elvin Hayes, Kevin Porter)	.40
67	Charlie Criss (E)	.15
68	Eddie Johnson (E)	.15
69	Wes Matthews (E)	.15
70	Tom McMillen (E)	.30
71	Tree Rollins (E)	.25
72	M.L. Carr (E)	.15
73	Chris Ford (E)	.50
74	*Gerald Henderson* (E)	.50
75	*Kevin McHale* (E)	25.00
76	Checklist 1-110 (Rick Robey) (E)	.15
77	Darwin Cook (E)	.15
78	Mike Gminski (E)	1.00
79	Maurice Lucas (E)	.25
80	Mike Newlin (E)	.15
81	*Mike O'Koren* (E)	.40
82	Steve Hawes (E)	.15
83	Foots Walker (E)	.15
84	Campy Russell (E)	.15
85	DeWayne Scales (E)	.15
86	Randy Smith (E)	.15
87	Marvin Webster (E)	.15
88	Sly Williams (E)	.15
89	*Mike Woodson* (E)	.50
90	Maurice Cheeks (E)	1.50
91	Caldwell Jones (E)	.15
92	Steve Mix (E)	.15
93	Checklist 1-110 (E)	1.00
94	Greg Ballard (E)	.15
95	Don Collins (E)	.15
96	Kevin Grevey (E)	.15
97	Checklist 1-110 (Mitch Kupchak) (E)	.15
98	*Rick Mahorn* (E)	1.25
99	Kevin Porter (E)	.15
100	Nate Archibald (SA-E)	.40
101	Larry Bird (SA-E)	12.00
102	Bill Cartwright (SA-E)	.40
103	Darryl Dawkins (SA-E)	.15
104	Julius Erving (SA-E)	4.00
105	Kevin Porter (SA-E)	.15
106	Bobby Jones (SA-E)	.15
107	Cedric Maxwell (SA-E)	.15
108	Robert Parish (SA-E)	2.00
109	Michael Ray Richardson (SA-E)	.15
110	Dan Roundfield (SA-E)	.15
67	David Greenwood (MW)	.50
68	Dwight Jones (MW)	.15
69	Reggie Theus (MW)	.15
70	Bobby Wilkerson (MW)	.15
71	Mike Bratz (MW)	.15
72	Kenny Carr (MW)	.45
73	Geoff Huston (MW)	.15
74	*Bill Laimbeer* (MW)	3.50
75	Roger Phegley (MW)	.15
76	Checklist 1-110 (MW)	1.00
77	Abdul Jeelani (MW)	.15
78	Bill Robinzine (MW)	.15
79	Jim Spanarkel (MW)	.15
80	Kent Benson (MW)	.15
81	Keith Herron (MW)	.15
82	Phil Hubbard (MW)	.15
83	John Long (MW)	.15
84	Terry Tyler (MW)	.15
85	*Mike Dunleavy* (MW)	1.50
86	Tom Henderson (MW)	.15
87	Billy Paultz (MW)	.15
88	Robert Reid (MW)	.15
89	Mike Bantom (MW)	.15
90	James Edwards (MW)	.40
91	Billy Knight (MW)	.15
92	George McGinnis (MW)	.30
93	Louis Orr (MW)	.15
94	*Ernie Grunfeld* (MW)	.75
95	Reggie King (MW)	.15
96	Sam Lacey (MW)	.15
97	Checklist 1-110 (Junior Bridgeman) (MW)	.15
98	Mickey Johnson (MW)	.15
99	Sidney Moncrief (MW)	1.50
100	Brian Winters (MW)	.15
101	*Dave Corzine* (MW)	.30
102	Paul Griffin (MW)	.15
103	*Johnny Moore* (MW)	.50
104	Mark Olberding (MW)	.15
105	James Silas (MW)	.15
106	George Gervin (SA-MW)	.40
107	Artis Gilmore (SA-MW)	.40
108	Marques Johnson (SA-MW)	.40
109	Bob Lanier (SA-MW)	.40
110	Moses Malone (SA-MW)	1.50
67	*T.R. Dunn* (W)	.25
68	Alex English (W)	2.00
69	Billy McKinney (W)	.15
70	Dave Robisch (W)	.15
71	*Joe Barry Carroll* (W)	.75
72	Bernard King (W)	1.75
73	Sonny Parker (W)	.15
74	Purvis Short (W)	.75
75	*Larry Smith* (W)	.60
76	Jim Chones (W)	1.00
77	Michael Cooper (W)	1.50
78	Mark Landsbergers (W)	.15
79	Alvan Adams (W)	.15
80	Jeff Cook (W)	.15
81	Rich Kelley (W)	.15
82	*Kyle Macy* (W)	.50
83	Billy Ray Bates (W)	.15
84	Bob Gross (W)	.15
85	Calvin Natt (W)	.30
86	Lonnie Shelton (W)	.15
87	*Jim Paxson* (W)	1.50
88	Kelvin Ransey (W)	.15
89	Kermit Washington (W)	.15
90	Henry Bibby (W)	.15
91	Michael Brooks (W)	.15
92	Joe Bryant (W)	.15
93	Phil Smith (W)	1.00
94	Brian Taylor (W)	.15
95	Freeman Williams (W)	.15
96	James Bailey (W)	.15
97	Checklist 1-110 (W)	1.00
98	John Johnson (W)	.15
99	*Vinnie Johnson* (W)	1.50
100	Wally Walker (W)	.15
101	Paul Westphal (W)	.30
102	Allan Bristow (W)	.15
103	Wayne Cooper (W)	.15
104	Carl Nicks (W)	.15
105	Ben Poquette (W)	.15
106	Kareem Abdul-Jabbar (SA-W)	2.50
107	Dan Issel (SA-W)	.40
108	Dennis Johnson (SA-W)	.30
109	Magic Johnson (SA-W)	10.00
110	Jack Sikma (SA-W)	.40

1992-93 Topps

Topps reentered the basketball card arena in 1992-93 after a 10-year absence. The 396-card set was issued in two 198-card series. The front of the card has an action photo framed by two-color border stripes. The player's name and team are at the bottom of the card in colored bars. The backs are horizontal and have a biography, stats, a mug shot and player profile against light blue and yellow panels. Gold foil versions were also made of each card and were inserted in 15-card packs, one per pack, unless a Beam Team insert card was included. Subsets in the regular set include Highlights, All-Stars, 50 Point Club, and 20 Assist Club. Rookies in the set have a gold-foil "'92 Draft Pix" logo on the front.

		MT
Complete Set (396):		15.00
Complete Fact. Set (408):		20.00
Complete Series 1 (198):		5.00
Complete Series 2 (198):		10.00
Common Player:		.05
Complete Gold Set (396):		70.00
Comp Gold Fact Set (403):		80.00
Comp Gold Series 1 (198):		25.00
Comp Gold Series 2 (198):		45.00
Common Gold Player:		.10
Unlisted Gold Stars:		2x-4x
Series 1 Pack (15):		.50
Series 1 Wax Box (36):		18.00
Series 2 Pack (15):		1.00
Series 2 Wax Box (36):		30.00
1	Larry Bird	.50
2	Magic Johnson (RB)	.10
3	Michael Jordan (RB)	.75
4	David Robinson (RB)	.10
5	Johnny Newman	.05
6	Mike Iuzzolino	.05
7	Ken Norman	.05
8	Mahmoud Abdul-Rauf	.05
9	Duane Ferrell	.05
10	Sean Elliott	.05
11	Bernard King	.05
12	Armon Gilliam	.05
13	Reggie Williams	.05
14	Steve Kerr	.05
15	Anthony Bowie	.05
16	Alton Lister	.05
17	Dee Brown	.05
18	Tom Chambers	.05
19	Otis Thorpe	.05
20	Karl Malone	.20
21	Kenny Gattison	.05
22	Lionel Simmons	.05
23	Vern Fleming	.05
24	John Paxson	.05
25	Mitch Richmond	.10
26	Danny Schayes	.05
27	Derrick McKey	.05
28	Mark Randall	.05
29	Bill Laimbeer	.05
30	Chris Morris	.05
31	Alec Kessler	.05
32	Vlade Divac	.05
33	Rick Fox	.05
34	Charles Shackleford	.05
35	Dominique Wilkins	.15
36	Sleepy Floyd	.05
37	Doug West	.05
38	Pete Chilcutt	.05
39	Orlando Woolridge	.05
40	Eric Leckner	.05
41	Joe Kleine	.05
42	Scott Skiles	.05
43	Jerrod Mustaf	.05
44	John Starks	.05
45	Sedale Threatt	.05
46	Doug Smith	.05
47	Byron Scott	.05
48	Willie Anderson	.05
49	David Benoit	.05
50	Scott Hastings	.05
51	Terry Porter	.05
52	Sidney Green	.05
53	Danny Young	.05
54	Magic Johnson	.30
55	Brian Williams	.05
56	Randy Wittman	.05
57	Kevin McHale	.05
58	Dana Barros	.05
59	Thurl Bailey	.05
60	Kevin Duckworth	.05
61	John Williams	.05
62	Willie Burton	.05
63	Spud Webb	.05
64	Detlef Schrempf	.05
65	Sherman Douglas	.05
66	Patrick Ewing	.15
67	Michael Adams	.05
68	Vernon Maxwell	.05
69	Terrell Brandon	.05
70	Terry Catledge	.05
71	Mark Eaton	.05
72	Tony Smith	.05
73	B.J. Armstrong	.05
74	Moses Malone	.05
75	Anthony Bonner	.05
76	George McCloud	.05
77	Glen Rice	.10
78	Jon Koncak	.05
79	Michael Cage	.05
80	Ron Harper	.05
81	Tom Tolbert	.05
82	Brad Sellers	.05
83	Winston Garland	.05
84	Negele Knight	.05
85	Ricky Pierce	.05
86	Mark Aguirre	.05
87	Ron Anderson	.05
88	Loy Vaught	.05
89	Luc Longley	.05
90	Jerry Reynolds	.05
91	Terry Cummings	.05
92	Rony Seikaly	.05
93	Derek Harper	.05
94	Cliff Robinson	.10
95	Kenny Anderson	.15
96	Chris Gatling	.05
97	Stacey Augmon	.05
98	Chris Corchiani	.05
99	Pervis Ellison	.05
100	Larry Bird (AS)	.25
101	John Stockton (AS)	.10
102	Clyde Drexler (AS)	.15
103	Scottie Pippen (AS)	.15
104	Reggie Lewis (AS)	.10
105	Hakeem Olajuwon (AS)	.20
106	David Robinson (AS)	.15
107	Charles Barkley (AS)	.15
108	James Worthy (AS)	.05
109	Kevin Willis (AS)	.05
110	Dikembe Mutombo (AS)	.10
111	Joe Dumars (AS)	.05
112	Jeff Hornacek (AS)	.05
113	Mark Price (AS)	.05
114	Michael Adams (AS)	.05
115	Michael Jordan (AS)	.75
116	Brad Daugherty (AS)	.05
117	Dennis Rodman (AS)	.25
118	Isiah Thomas (AS)	.10
119	Tim Hardaway (AS)	.10
120	Chris Mullin (AS)	.10
121	Patrick Ewing (AS)	.10
122	Dan Majerle (AS)	.05
123	Karl Malone (AS)	.10
124	Otis Thorpe (AS)	.05
125	Dominique Wilkins (AS)	.10
126	Magic Johnson (AS)	.15
127	Charles Oakley	.05
128	Robert Pack	.05
129	Billy Owens	.05
130	Jeff Malone	.05
131	Danny Ferry	.05
132	Sam Bowie	.05
133	Avery Johnson	.05
134	Jayson Williams	.05
135	Fred Roberts	.05
136	Greg Sutton	.05
137	Dennis Rodman	.40
138	John Williams	.05
139	Greg Dreiling	.05
140	Rik Smits	.05
141	Michael Jordan	1.50
142	Nick Anderson	.05
143	Jerome Kersey	.05
144	Fat Lever	.05
145	Tyrone Corbin	.05
146	Robert Parish	.05
147	Steve Smith	.05
148	Chris Dudley	.05
149	Antoine Carr	.05
150	Elden Campbell	.05
151	Randy White	.05
152	Felton Spencer	.05
153	Cedric Ceballos	.05
154	Mark Macon	.05
155	Jack Haley	.05
156	Bimbo Coles	.05
157	A.J. English	.05
158	Kendall Gill	.05
159	A.C. Green	.05
160	Mark West	.05
161	Benoit Benjamin	.05
162	Tyrone Hill	.05
163	Larry Nance	.05
164	Gary Grant	.05
165	Bill Cartwright	.05
166	Greg Anthony	.05
167	Jim Les	.05
168	Johnny Dawkins	.05
169	Alvin Robertson	.05
170	Kenny Smith	.05
171	Gerald Glass	.05
172	Harvey Grant	.05
173	Paul Graham	.05
174	Sam Perkins	.05
175	Manute Bol	.05
176	Muggsy Bogues	.05
177	Mike Brown	.05
178	Donald Hodge	.05
179	Dave Jamerson	.05
180	Mookie Blaylock	.05
181	Randy Brown	.05
182	Todd Lichti	.05
183	Kevin Gamble	.05
184	Gary Payton	.10
185	Brian Shaw	.05
186	Grant Long	.05
187	Frank Brickowski	.05
188	Tim Hardaway	.10
189	Danny Manning	.10
190	Kevin Johnson	.10
191	Craig Ehlo	.05
192	Dennis Scott	.05
193	Reggie Miller	.15
194	Darrell Walker	.05
195	Anthony Mason	.05
196	Buck Williams	.05
197	Checklist 1-99	.05
198	Checklist 1-198	.05
199	Karl Malone (50P)	.10
200	Dominique Wilkins (50P)	.10
201	Tom Chambers (50P)	.05
202	Bernard King (50P)	.05
203	Kiki Vandeweghe (50P)	.05
204	Dale Ellis (50P)	.05
205	Michael Jordan (50P)	.75
206	Michael Adams (50P)	.05
207	Charles Smith (50P)	.05
208	Moses Malone (50P)	.05
209	Terry Cummings (50P)	.05
210	Vernon Maxwell (50P)	.05
211	Patrick Ewing (50P)	.10
212	Clyde Drexler (50P)	.10
213	Kevin McHale (50P)	.05
214	Hakeem Olajuwon (50P)	.25
215	Reggie Miller (50P)	.10
216	Gary Grant (20A)	.05
217	Doc Rivers (20A)	.05
218	Mark Price (20A)	.05
219	Isiah Thomas (20A)	.10
220	Nate McMillan (20A)	.05
221	Fat Lever (20A)	.05
222	Kevin Johnson (20A)	.10
223	John Stockton (20A)	.10
224	Scott Skiles (20A)	.05
225	Kevin Brooks	.05

226 *Bobby Phills* .15
227 *Oliver Miller* .15
228 John Williams .05
229 Brad Lohaus .05
230 Derrick Coleman .10
231 Ed Pinckney .05
232 Trent Tucker .05
233 Lance Blanks .05
234 Drazen Petrovic .05
235 Mark Bryant .05
236 *Lloyd Daniels* .05
237 Dale Davis .05
238 Jayson Williams .05
239 Mike Sanders .05
240 Mike Gminski .05
241 William Bedford .05
242 Dell Curry .05
243 Gerald Paddio .05
244 *Chris Smith* .05
245 Jud Buechler .05
246 Walter Palmer .05
247 Larry Krystkowiak .05
248 Marcus Liberty .05
249 Sam Mitchell .05
250 Kiki Vandeweghe .05
251 Vincent Askew .05
252 Travis Mays .05
253 Charles Smith .05
255 James Worthy .05
256 Paul Pressey .05
257 Rumeal Robinson .05
258 *Tom Gugliotta* .40
259 *Eric Anderson* .05
260 Hersey Hawkins .05
261 Terry Davis .05
262 Rex Chapman .05
263 Chucky Brown .05
264 Danny Young .05
265 Olden Polynice .05
266 Kevin Willis .05
267 Shawn Kemp .25
268 Mookie Blaylock .05
269 *Malik Sealy* .10
270 Charles Barkley .30
271 *Corey Williams* .05
272 *Stephen Howard* .10
273 Keith Askins .05
274 Matt Bullard .05
275 John Battle .05
276 Andrew Lang .05
277 David Robinson .30
278 *Harold Miner* .10
279 *Tracy Murray* .10
280 Pooh Richardson .05
281 Dikembe Mutombo .20
282 Wayman Tisdale .05
283 Larry Johnson .25
284 *Todd Day* .25
285 Stanley Roberts .05
286 *Randy Woods* .05
287 Avery Johnson .05
288 *Anthony Peeler* .10
289 Mario Elie .05
290 Doc Rivers .05
291 Blue Edwards .05
292 *Sean Rooks* .10
293 Xavier McDaniel .05
294 *C. Weatherspoon* .25
295 Morlon Wiley .05
296 LaBradford Smith .05
297 Reggie Lewis .05
298 Chris Mullin .10
299 *Litterial Green* .05
300 Elmore Spencer .05
301 John Stockton .20
302 *Walt Williams* .25
303 *Anthony Pullard* .05
304 *Gundars Vetra* .05
305 LaSalle Thompson .05
306 Nate McMillian .05
307 *Steve Bardo* .05
308 *Robert Horry* .50
309 Scott Williams .05
310 Bo Kimble .05
311 Tree Rollins .05
312 Tim Perry .05
313 *Isaac Austin* .05
314 Tate George .05
315 Kevin Lynch .05
316 Victor Alexander .05
317 Doug Overton .05
318 Tom Hammonds .05
319 *LaPhonso Ellis* .20
320 Scott Brooks .05
321 *Anthony Avent* .10
322 Matt Geiger .05
323 Duane Causwell .05
324 Horace Grant .10
325 Mark Jackson .05
326 Dan Majerle .05
327 Chuck Person .05
328 Buck Johnson .05
329 *Duane Cooper* .05
330 Rod Strickland .05
331 Isiah Thomas .10
332 Greg Kite .05
333 *Don MacLean* .20
334 *Christian Laettner* .30
335 *John Crotty* .05
336 *Tracy Moore* .05
337 Hakeem Olajuwon .40
338 *Byron Houston* .10
339 *Walter Bond* .05
340 *Brent Price* .10
341 *Bryant Stith* .15
342 Will Perdue .05
343 Jeff Hornacek .05
344 *Adam Keefe* .10
345 Rafael Addison .05
346 *Marlon Maxey* .05
347 Joe Dumars .10
348 *Jon Barry* .10
349 Marty Conlon .05
350 Alaa Abdelnaby .05
351 Micheal Williams .05
352 Brad Daugherty .05
353 *Tony Bennett* .10
354 Clyde Drexler .20
355 Rolando Blackman .05
356 Tom Tolbert .05
357 Sarunas Marciulionis .05
358 *Jaren Jackson* .05
359 Stacey King .05
360 Danny Ainge .05
361 Dale Ellis .05
362 *Shaquille O'Neal* 7.00
363 Bob McCann .05
364 *Reggie Smith* .05
365 Vinny De Negro .05
366 Robert Pack .05
367 David Wood .05
368 Rodney McCray .05
369 Terry Mills .05
370 Eric Murdock .05
371 *Alex Blackwell* .05
372 Jay Humphries .05
373 Eddie Lee Wilkins .05
374 James Edwards .05
375 Tim Edwards .05
376 J.R. Reid .05
377 Sam Mack .05
378 Donald Royal .05
379 Mark Price .05
380 Mark Acres .05
381 *Hubert Davis* .10
382 *Dave Johnson* .05
383 John Salley .05
384 Eddie Johnson .05
385 *Brian Howard* .05
386 *Isaiah Morris* .05
387 Frank Johnson .05
388 Rick Mahorn .05
389 Scottie Pippen .30
390 *Lee Mayberry* .10
391 Tony Campbell .05
392 *Latrell Sprewell* 1.00
393 *Alonzo Mourning* 1.50
394 *Robert Werdann* .05
395 Checklist 199-297 .05
396 Checklist 298-396 .05

1992-93 Topps Archives

This set fills in the gaps from 1982-92, when Topps didn't issue basketball cards, by creating cards based on the corresponding year's baseball card design. Since the cards were issued in 1992-93, they aren't considered true rookie cards, just mock rookie cards. The set includes a subset of Number 1 draft choices.

	MT
Complete Set (150):	10.00
Common Player:	.05
Minor Stars:	.10
Complete Gold Set (150):	40.00
Common Gold Player:	.10
Minor Gold Stars:	.20
Unlisted Gold Stars:	2x-4x
150 Shaq O'Neal Gold	20.00
Wax Box:	10.00

1 Mark Aguirre (FDP) .05
2 James Worthy (FDP) .05
3 Ralph Sampson (FDP) .05
4 Hakeem Olajuwon (FDP) .50
5 Patrick Ewing (FDP) .15
6 Brad Daugherty (FDP) .05
7 David Robinson (FDP) .25
8 Danny Manning (FDP) .05
9 Pervis Ellison (FDP) .05
10 Derrick Coleman (FDP) .10
11 Larry Johnson (FDP) .25
12 Mark Aguirre .05
13 Danny Ainge .05
14 Rolando Blackman .05
15 Tom Chambers .05
16 Eddie Johnson .05
17 Alton Lister .05
18 Larry Nance .05
19 Kurt Rambis .05
20 Isiah Thomas .15
21 Buck Williams .05
22 Orlando Woolridge .05
23 John Bagley .05
24 Terry Cummings .05
25 Mark Eaton .05
26 Eric Floyd .05
27 Lafayette Lever .05
28 Ricky Pierce .05
29 Trent Tucker .05
30 Dominique Wilkins .20
31 James Worthy .05
32 Thurl Bailey .05
33 Clyde Drexler .30
34 Dale Ellis .05
35 Sidney Green .05
36 Derek Harper .05
37 Jeff Malone .05
38 Rodney McCray .05
39 John Paxson .05
40 Glenn Rivers .05
41 Byron Scott .05
42 Sedale Threatt .05
43 Ron Anderson .05
44 Charles Barkley .50
45 Sam Bowie .05
46 Michael Cage .05
47 Tony Campbell .05
48 Antoine Carr .05
49 Craig Ehlo .05
50 Vern Fleming .05
51 Jay Humphries .05
52 Michael Jordan 4.00
53 Jerome Kersey .05
54 Hakeem Olajuwon .75
55 Sam Perkins .05
56 Alvin Robertson .05
57 John Stockton .30
58 Otis Thorpe .05
59 Kevin Willis .05
60 Michael Adams .05
61 Benoit Benjamin .05
62 Terry Catledge .05
63 Joe Dumars .15
64 Patrick Ewing .25
65 A.C. Green .05
66 Karl Malone .30
67 Reggie Miller .25
68 Chris Mullin .10
69 Xavier McDaniel .05
70 Charles Oakley .05
71 Terry Porter .05
72 Jerry Reynolds .05
73 Detlef Schrempf .05
74 Wayman Tisdale .05
75 Spud Webb .05
76 Gerald Wilkins .05
77 Dell Curry .05
78 Brad Daugherty .05
79 Johnny Dawkins .05
80 Armon Gilliam .05
81 Ron Harper .05
82 Jeff Hornacek .05
83 Johnny Newman .05
84 Chuck Person .05
85 Mark Price .10
86 Dennis Rodman 1.00
87 John Salley .05
88 Scott Skiles .05
89 Tyrone Bogues .05
90 Armon Gilliam .05
91 Horace Grant .20
92 Mark Jackson .05
93 Kevin Johnson .15
94 Reggie Lewis .05
95 Derrick McKey .05
96 Ken Norman .05
97 Scottie Pippen 1.00
98 Olden Polynice .05
99 Kenny Smith .05
100 John Williams .05
101 Willie Anderson .05
102 Rex Chapman .05
103 Harvey Grant .05
104 Hersey Hawkins .05
105 Dan Majerle .05
106 Danny Manning .05
107 Vernon Maxwell .05
108 Chris Morris .05
109 Mitch Richmond .10
110 Rony Seikaly .05
111 Brian Shaw .05
112 Charles Smith .05
113 Rod Strickland .05
114 Michael Williams .05
115 Nick Anderson .05
116 B.J. Armstrong .05
117 Mookie Blaylock .05
118 Vlade Divac .05
119 Sherman Douglas .05
120 Blue Edwards .05
121 Sean Elliott .05
122 Pervis Ellison .05
123 Tim Hardaway .10
124 Sarunas Marciulionis .05
125 Drazen Petrovic .05
126 J.R. Reid .05
127 Glen Rice .10
128 Pooh Richardson .05
129 Cliff Robinson .10
130 David Robinson .50
131 Dee Brown .10
132 Cedric Ceballos .10
133 Derrick Coleman .10
134 Kendall Gill .05
135 Mahmoud Abdul-Rauf .05
136 Shawn Kemp .60
137 Gary Payton .20
138 Dennis Scott .05
139 Lionel Simmons .05
140 Kenny Anderson .20
141 Greg Anthony .05
142 Stacey Augmon .05
143 Rick Fox .05
144 Larry Johnson .50
145 Luc Longley .05
146 Dikembe Mutombo .30
147 Billy Owens .05
148 Steve Smith .05
149 Checklist 1-75 .05
150 Checklist 75-150 .05

1992-93 Topps Archives Gold

There were 10,000 1992-93 Topps Archives Gold produced in factory set versions that sold in eight-set cases. The cards are identical to the regular-issue 1992-93 Archives cards but are identified by a gold foil stamp on the front. The two checklist cards, number 149 and 150, are replaced by Rumeal Robinson and Shaquille O'Neal.

	MT
Complete Set (150):	40.00
Gold Cards:	2x-4x
Common Player:	.20
Semistars:	
149G Rumeal Robinson	.50
150G Shaquille O'Neal	15.00

1992-93 Topps Archives Master Photos

Master Photo Trade cards were inserted in one per 24 packs of 1992-93 Archives and were redeemable for three full size (5" x 7") Master Photos. The Master Photos featured the 11 No. 1 draft picks from the missing years when Topps didn't produce basketball (1981-1991). The backs contain Topps and NBA trademarks and the cards are numbered by the year of the No. 1 pick. The mini- Master Photos and the 5" x 7" cards currently carry the same value.

	MT
Complete Set (12):	8.00
Common Player:	.25
1981 Mark Aguirre (1981 No.1 Draft Pick)	.25
1982 James Worthy (1982 No. 1 Draft Pick)	.50
1983 Ralph Sampson (1983 No. 1 Draft Pick)	.25
1984 Hakeem Olajuwon (1984 No. 1 Draft Pick)	3.00
1985 Patrick Ewing (1985 No. 1 Draft Pick)	1.25
1986 Brad Daugherty (1986 No. 1 Draft Pick)	.25
1987 David Robinson (1987 No. 1 Draft Pick)	2.50
1988 Danny Manning (1988 No. 1 Draft Pick)	.50
1989 Pervis Ellison (1989 No. 1 Draft Pick)	.25
1990 Derrick Coleman (1990 No. 1 Draft Pick)	.25
1991 Larry Johnson (1991 No. 1 Draft Pick)	1.00
NNO First Picks 1981-91	.50

1992-93 Topps Beam Team

These cards were randomly inserted in Topps 1992-93 basketball Series II packs, one per every 18 15-card packs. Fronts feature three players on a horizontal format and dark blue background. "Beam Team" is in green at the top. Backs have mug shots, biographies and career summaries for each player.

	MT
Complete Set (7):	7.00
Common Player:	.50
Complete Gold Set (7):	25.00
Gold Beam Teams:	2x-4x
1 Reggie Miller, Charles Barkley, Clyde Drexler	1.00
2 Patrick Ewing, Tim Hardaway, Jeff Hornacek	.50
3 Kevin Johnson, Michael Jordan, Dennis Rodman	4.00
4 Dominique Wilkins, John Stockton, Karl Malone	.75
5 Hakeem Olajuwon, Mark Price, Shawn Kemp	1.00
6 Scottie Pippen, David Robinson, Jeff Malone	.50
7 Chris Mullin, Shaquille O'Neal, Glen Rice	4.00

1992-93 Topps Gold

This 396-card parallel set featured gold foil stripes on the front instead of the team color-coded stripes. Gold cards were inserted per 15-card pack, except if the pack contained a Beam Team card, three per 45-card retail pack, two per 18-card mini-jumbo pack,five per 41-card magazine jumbo pack and 12 per factory set. In addition, complete Gold factory sets were also issued featuring all 396 cards and seven Gold Beam Team inserts. Four different players were chosen to replace the checklists, with two in each series.

	MT
Complete Set (396):	60.00
Complete Factory Set (403):	75.00
Complete Series 1 (198):	20.00
Complete Series 2 (198):	40.00
Common Player:	.10
Semistars:	.20
Stars:	2.5x to 5x
Rookies:	1.5x to 3x
197G Jeff Sanders	.50
198G Elliott Perry UER (Misspelled Elliot on front)	.75
395G David Wingate	.50
396G Carl Herrera	.50

1993-94 Topps

Topps issued its 1993 set in two series of 198 cards. Each card front has an action photo on it, framed by a team color-coded border and an outer white border. The player's name is printed in white script at the bottom of the card, while his position and team's name are in a color-coded bar. The back is horizontal and includes biographical information, statistics, a career recap and a color photo. Subsets include Highlights, 50 Point Club, All-Stars and All-Rookies. Factory sets were also made and include 14 extra cards - 10 Gold cards, three Black Gold cards and one Finest Redemption card.

	MT
Complete Set (396):	20.00
Complete Series 1 (198):	10.00
Complete Series 2 (198):	10.00
Common Player:	.05
Minor Stars:	.10
Complete Gold Set (396):	80.00
Complete Gold Series 1 (198):	35.00
Complete Gold Series 2 (198):	45.00
Common Gold Player:	.10
Minor Gold Stars:	.20
Unlisted Stars:	2x-4x
Ser. 1 or 2 Pack (12):	.50
Ser. 1 or 2 Wax Box (36:)	16.00

1 Charles Barkley (HL) .25
2 Hakeem Olajuwon (HL) .40
3 Shaquille O'Neal (HL) 1.00
4 Mahmoud Abdul-Rauf (HL) .05
5 Cliff Robinson (HL) .05
6 Donald Hodge .05
7 Victor Alexander .05
8 Chris Morris .05
9 Muggsy Bogues .05
10 Steve Smith .05
11 Dave Johnson .05
12 Tom Gugliotta .05
13 *Doug Edwards* .10
14 Vlade Divac .05
15 *Corie Blount* .15
16 Derek Harper .05
17 Matt Bullard .05
18 Terry Catledge .05
19 Mark Eaton .05
20 Mark Jackson .05
21 Terry Mills .05
22 Johnny Dawkins .05
23 Michael Jordan 2.00
24 Rick Fox .05
25 Charles Oakley .05
26 Derrick McKey .05
27 Christian Laettner .10
28 Todd Day .05
29 Danny Ferry .05
30 Kevin Johnson .10
31 Vinny Del Negro .05
32 Kevin Brooks .05
33 Pete Chilcutt .05
34 Larry Stewart .05
35 Dave Jamerson .05
36 Sidney Green .05
37 J.R. Reid .05
38 Jim Jackson .50
39 Michael Williams .05
40 *Rex Walters* .10
41 *Shawn Bradley* .25
42 Jon Koncak .05
43 Byron Houston .05
44 Brian Shaw .05
45 Bill Cartwright .05
46 Jerome Kersey .05
47 Danny Schayes .05
48 Olden Polynice .05
49 Anthony Peeler .05
50 Nick Anderson (50Pt) .10
51 David Benoit .05
52 David Robinson (50Pt) .25
53 Greg Kite .05
54 Gerald Paddio .05
55 Don MacLean .05
56 Randy Woods .05
57 Reggie Miller (50Pt) .10
58 Kevin Gamble .05
59 Sean Green .05
60 Jeff Hornacek .05
61 John Starks .05
62 Gerald Wilkins .05
63 Jim Les .05
64 Michael Jordan (50Pt) 1.00
65 Alvin Robertson .05
66 Tim Kempton .05
67 Bryant Stith .05
68 Jeff Turner .05
69 Malik Sealy .05
70 Dell Curry .05
71 Brent Price .05
72 Kevin Lynch .05
73 Bimbo Coles .05
74 Larry Nance .05
75 *Luther Wright* .10
76 Willie Anderson .05
77 Dennis Rodman .75
78 Anthony Mason .05
79 Chris Gatling .05
80 Antoine Carr .05
81 Kevin Willis .05
82 Thurl Bailey .05
83 Reggie Williams .05
84 Rod Strickland .05
85 Rolando Blackman .05
86 *Bobby Hurley* .15
87 Jeff Malone .05
88 James Worthy .05
89 Alaa Abdelnaby .05
90 Duane Ferrell .05
91 Anthony Avent .05
92 Scottie Pippen .75
93 Ricky Pierce .05
94 *P.J. Brown* .10
95 Jeff Grayer .05
96 Jerrod Mustaf .05
97 Elmore Spencer .05
98 Walt Williams .05
99 Otis Thorpe .05
100 Patrick Ewing (AS) .10
101 Michael Jordan (AS) 1.00
102 John Stockton (AS) .10
103 Dominique Wilkins (AS) .15
104 Charles Barkley (AS) .20
105 Lee Mayberry .05
106 James Edwards .05
107 Scott Brooks .05
108 John Battle .05
109 Kenny Gattison .05
110 Pooh Richardson .05
111 Rony Seikaly .05
112 Mahmoud Abdul-Rauf .05
113 Nick Anderson .05
114 Gundars Vetra .05
115 Joe Dumars (AS) .10
116 Hakeem Olajuwon (AS) .40
117 Scottie Pippen (AS) .25
118 Mark Price (AS) .10
119 Karl Malone (AS) .15
120 Michael Cage .05
121 Ed Pinckney .05
122 Jay Humphries .05
123 Dale Davis .05
124 Sean Rooks .05
125 Mookie Blaylock .05
126 Buck Williams .05
127 John Williams .05
128 Stacey King .05
129 Tim Perry .05
130 Tim Hardaway (AS) .10
131 Larry Johnson (AS) .15
132 Detlef Schrempf (AS) .05
133 Reggie Miller (AS) .10
134 Shaquille O'Neal (AS) 1.00
135 Dale Ellis .05
136 Duane Causwell .05
137 Rumeal Robinson .05
138 Billy Owens .05
139 *Malcolm Mackey* .10
140 Vernon Maxwell .05
141 LaPhonso Ellis .05
142 Robert Parish .05
143 LaBradford Smith .05
144 Charles Smith .05
145 Terry Porter .05
146 Elden Campbell .05
147 Bill Laimbeer .05
148 *Chris Mills* .25
149 Brad Lohaus .05
150 Jim Jackson .25
151 Tom Gugliotta .05
152 Shaquille O'Neal 1.00
153 Latrell Sprewell .25
154 Walt Williams .05
155 Gary Payton .15
156 Orlando Woolridge .05
157 Adam Keefe .05
158 *Calbert Cheaney* .30
159 Rick Mahorn .05
160 Robert Horry .10
161 John Salley .05
162 Sam Mitchell .05
163 Stanley Roberts .05
164 C. Weatherspoon .10
165 Anthony Bowie .05
166 Derrick Coleman .10
167 Negele Knight .05
168 Marlon Maxey .05
169 Spud Webb .05
170 Alonzo Mourning .50
171 *Ervin Johnson* .10
172 Sedale Threatt .05
173 Mark Macon .05
174 B.J. Armstrong .10
175 Harold Miner .05
176 Anthony Peeler .05
177 Alonzo Mourning .30
178 Christian Laettner .05
179 C. Weatherspoon .05
180 Dee Brown .05
181 Shaquille O'Neal 2.00
182 Loy Vaught .05
183 Terrell Brandon .05
184 Lionel Simmons .05
185 Mark Aguirre .05
186 Danny Ainge .05
187 Reggie Miller .20
188 Terry Davis .05
189 Mark Bryant .05
190 Tyrone Corbin .05
191 Chris Mullin .10
192 Johnny Newman .05
193 Doug West .05
194 Keith Askins .05
195 Bo Kimble .05
196 Sean Elliott .05
197 Checklist .05
198 Checklist .05
199 Michael Jordan 1.00
200 Patrick Ewing .10
201 John Stockton .10
202 Shawn Kemp .15
203 Mark Price .10
204 Charles Barkley .25
205 Hakeem Olajuwon .40
206 Clyde Drexler .15
207 Kevin Johnson .10
208 John Starks .05
209 Chris Mullin .10
210 Doc Rivers .05
211 Kenny Walker .05
212 Doug Christie .05
213 *James Robinson* .20
214 Larry Krystrowiak .05
215 Manute Bol .05
216 Carl Herrera .05
217 Paul Graham .05
218 Jud Buechler .05
219 Mike Brown .05
220 Tom Chambers .05
221 Kendall Gill .05
222 Kenny Anderson .05
223 Larry Johnson .25

224 *Chris Webber* 2.00
225 Randy White .05
226 Rik Smits .05
227 A.C. Green .05
228 David Robinson .40
229 Sean Elliott .05
230 Gary Grant .05
231 Dana Barros .05
232 Bobby Hurley .10
233 Blue Edwards .05
234 Tom Hammonds .05
235 Pete Myers .05
236 *Acie Earl* .10
237 Tony Smith .05
238 Bill Wennington .05
239 Andrew Lang .05
240 Ervin Johnson .05
241 Byron Scott .05
242 Eddie Johnson .05
243 Anthony Bonner .05
244 *Luther Wright* .10
245 LaSalle Thompson .05
246 Harold Miner .05
247 Chris Smith .05
248 John Williams .05
249 Clyde Drexler .25
250 Calbert Cheaney .10
251 Avery Johnson .05
252 Steve Kerr .05
253 Warren Kidd .05
254 Wayman Tisdale .05
255 Bob Martin .05
256 *Popeye Jones* .20
257 Jimmy Oliver .05
258 Kevin Edwards .05
259 Dan Majerle .05
260 Jon Barry .05
261 *Allan Houston* 1.00
262 Dikembe Mutombo .20
263 Sleepy Floyd .05
264 *George Lynch* .10
265 Stacey Augmon .05
266 Hakeem Olajuwon .60
267 Scott Skiles .05
268 Detlef Schrempf .05
269 Brian Davis .05
270 Tracy Murray .05
271 *Gheorghe Muresan* .20
272 *Terry Dehere* .10
273 Terry Cummings .05
274 Keith Jennings .05
275 Tyrone Hill .05
276 Hersey Hawkins .05
277 Grant Long .05
278 Herb Williams .05
279 Karl Malone .20
280 Mitch Richmond .10
281 Derek Strong .05
282 *Dino Radja* .25
283 Jack Haley .05
284 Derek Harper .05
285 Dwayne Schintzius .05
286 Michael Curry .05
287 *Rodney Rogers* .30
288 Horace Grant .10
289 Oliver Miller .05
290 Luc Longley .05
291 Walter Bond .05
292 Dominique Wilkins .15
293 Vern Fleming .05
294 Mark Price .05
295 Mark Aguirre .05
296 Shawn Kemp .20
297 Pervis Ellison .05
298 *Josh Grant* .10
299 *Scott Burrell* .30
300 Patrick Ewing .25
301 *Sam Cassell* 1.00
302 *Nick Van Exel* 1.00
303 Cliff Robinson .05
304 Frank Johnson .05
305 Matt Geiger .05
306 *Vin Baker* .75
307 Benoit Benjamin .05
308 Shawn Bradley .10
309 Chris Whitney .05
310 *Eric Riley* .10
311 Isiah Thomas .15
312 *Jamal Mashburn* 1.00
313 Xavier McDaniel .05
314 *Mike Peplowski* .10
315 *Darnell Mee* .10
316 *Toni Kukoc* .50
317 Felton Spencer .05
318 Sam Bowie .05
319 Mario Elie .05
320 Tim Hardaway .10
321 Ken Norman .05
322 *Isaiah Rider* .50
323 Rex Chapman .05
324 Dennis Rodman .75
325 Derrick McKey .05
326 Corie Blount .05
327 Fat Lever .05
328 Ron Harper .05
329 Eric Anderson .05
330 Armon Gilliam .05
331 *Lindsey Hunter* .15
332 Eric Leckner .05
333 Chris Corchiani .05
334 *Anfernee Hardaway* 3.00
335 Randy Brown .05
336 Sam Perkins .05
337 Glen Rice .05
338 Orlando Woolridge .05
339 Mike Gminski .05
340 Latrell Sprewell .50
341 Harvey Grant .05
342 Doug Smith .05
343 Kevin Duckworth .05
344 Cedric Ceballos .05
345 Chuck Person .05
346 Scott Haskin .05
347 Frank Brickowski .05
348 Scott Williams .05
349 Brad Daugherty .05
350 Willie Burton .05
351 Joe Dumars .15
352 Craig Ehlo .05
353 *Lucious Harris* .10
354 Danny Manning .05
355 Litterial Green .05
356 John Stockton .25
357 Nate McMillan .05
358 *Greg Graham* .10
359 Rex Walters .05
360 Lloyd Daniels .05
361 Antonio Harvey .05
362 Brian Williams .05
363 LeRon Ellis .05
364 Chris Dudley .05
365 Hubert Davis .05
366 Evers Burns .05
367 Sherman Douglas .05
368 Sarunas Marciulionis .05
369 Tom Tolbert .05
370 Robert Pack .05
371 Michael Adams .05
372 Negele Knight .05
373 Charles Barkley .40
374 Bryon Russell .05
375 Greg Anthony .05
376 Ken Williams .05
377 John Paxson .05
378 Corey Gaines .05
379 Eric Murdock .05
380 Kevin Thompson .05
381 Moses Malone .05
382 Kenny Smith .05
383 Dennis Scott .05
384 Michael Jordan 1.00
385 Hakeem Olajuwon .30
386 Shaquille O'Neal 1.00
387 David Robinson .25
388 Derrick Coleman .10
389 Karl Malone .10
390 Patrick Ewing .10
391 Scottie Pippen .25
392 Dominique Wilkins .10
393 Charles Barkley .25
394 Larry Johnson .15
395 Checklist 199-297 .05
396 Checklist 298-396 .05

1993-94 Topps Black Gold

These cards were inserts in Topps' 1993-94 basketball packs - 13 Black Gold cards in the Series I packs and 12 in Series II packs. Each Topps pack contained 11 regular cards, plus one Black Gold. Or, every fourth pack had 10 regular cards and two Black Gold cards. Each card front has a player action photo against a black background, with a gold prism effect at the top of the card, plus the set name. The player's name is in white letters in a black bar at the bottom. The card back has a player photo against a black background with a bullseye pattern in white. The player's name is foil-stamped in gold on wood-like panel, with his team name in black. Stats appear on the card in an orange background. The cards are also numbered.

MT
Complete Set (25): 30.00
Complete Series 1 (13): 5.00
Complete Series 2 (12): 25.00
Common Player: .25
Minor Stars: .50
1 Sean Elliott .25
2 Dennis Scott .25
3 Kenny Anderson .50
4 Alonzo Mourning 2.00
5 Glen Rice .50
6 Billy Owens .25
7 Jim Jackson 2.00
8 Derrick Coleman .50
9 Larry Johnson 1.00
10 Gary Payton 1.00
11 Christian Laettner .25
12 Dikembe Mutombo 1.00
13 Mahmoud Abdul-Rauf .25
14 Isaiah Rider 1.00
15 Steve Smith .25
16 LaPhonso Ellis .25
17 Danny Ferry .25
18 Shaquille O'Neal 9.00
19 Anfernee Hardaway 10.00
20 J.R. Reid .25
21 Shawn Bradley .50
22 Pervis Ellison .25
23 Chris Webber 10.00
24 Jamal Mashburn 3.00
25 Kendall Gill .25

1993-94 Topps Gold

This 396-card set paralleled the 1993-94 Topps set and is identified by gold lettering and a "Gold" logo in either top corner. One Gold card was inserted into each pack, with two Gold cards found every fourth pack. In addition, three Gold cards were inserted into rack packs and 10 in every factory set. There were four regular-issue checklists that were replaced by players in the Gold set (the final two cards of each series).

MT
Complete Set (396): 70.00
Complete Series 1 (198): 30.00
Complete Series 2 (198): 40.00
Common Player (1-396): .10
Gold Cards: 3x
197G Frank Johnson .50
198G David Wingate .50
395G Will Perdue .50
396G Mark West .50

1994-95 Topps

Topps 1994-95 regular cards feature full-color photos, with rough, white borders around them. The player's name is in gold foil along the bottom, and his team name and position are below, in team colors. The Topps logo is foil stamped in the upper right corner. Backs include statistics, a biography, a large framed close-up shot and a tiny little shot. Subsets in Series I include NBA All-Stars, presenting highlights of the league's NBA All-Star Weekend; Paint Patrol, showing players who dominate in the paint; From the Roof, which utilizes photography taken from the "eye in the sky" cameras; and Stats Ratio, which provides a look at some leaders in some unique statistical categories. Two parallel sets were also made. Special Effects cards (one in every two packs) form a 198-card set that features more colorful backgrounds than the normal cards. The Spectralight parallel set features regular cards printed again on a foil-backed, foil stamped card. They appear in every fourth pack. In every 18th pack, there's an Own the Game card, which features statistical leaders.

MT
Complete Set (396): 30.00
Complete Series 1 (198): 13.00
Complete Series 2 (198): 17.00
Common Player: .05
Minor Stars: .10
Complete Spectralight (396): 300.00
Comp. Spec. Ser. 1 (198): 130.00
Comp. Spec. Ser. 2 (198): 170.00
Common Spectra. Player: .25
Minor Spectra. Stars: .50
Unlisted Stars: 5x-10x
Series 1 Pack (12): 1.00
Series 1 Wax Box (36): 25.00
Series 2 Pack (12): 1.00
Series 2 Wax Box (36): 30.00
1 Patrick Ewing .10
2 Mookie Blaylock .05
3 Charles Oakley .05
4 Mark Price .10
5 John Starks .05
6 Dominique Wilkins .10
7 Horace Grant .10
8 Alonzo Mourning A.S. .20
9 B.J. Armstrong .05
10 Kenny Anderson .10
11 Scottie Pippen A.S. .25
12 Derrick Coleman .10
13 Shaquille O'Neal A.S. .50
14 Anfernee Hardaway A.S. .50
15 Isaiah Rider .15
16 John Williams .05
17 Todd Day .05
18 Dale Davis .05
19 Sean Rooks .05
20 George Lynch .05
21 Mitchell Butler .05
22 Stacey King .05
23 Sherman Douglas .05
24 Derrick McKey .05
25 Joe Dumars .10
26 Scott Brooks .05
27 C. Weatherspoon .05
28 Jayson Williams .05
29 Scottie Pippen .50
30 John Starks .05
31 Robert Peck .05
32 Donald Royal .05
33 Haywoode Workman .05
34 Greg Graham .05
35 Terry Cummings .05
36 Andrew Lang .05
37 *Jason Kidd* 2.00
38 Terry Mills .05
39 Alonzo Mourning .25
40 Shawn Kemp .20
41 Kevin Willis .05
42 Kevin Willis .05
43 Armon Gilliam .05
44 Bobby Hurley .05
45 Jerome Kersey .05
46 Xavier McDaniel .05
47 Chris Webber .25
48 Chris Webber .15
49 Jeff Malone .05
50 Dikembe Mutombo .10
51 Dan Majerle .05
52 Dee Brown .05
53 John Stockton .10
54 Dennis Rodman .30
55 Eric Murdock .05
56 Glen Rice .05
57 Glen Rice .05
58 Dino Radja .10
59 Billy Owens .05
60 Doc Rivers .05
61 Don MacLean .05
62 Lindsey Hunter .05
63 Sam Cassell .10
64 James Worthy .05
65 Christian Laettner .05
66 *Wesley Person* .25
67 Rich King .05
68 Jon Koncak .05
69 Muggsy Bogues .05
70 Jamal Mashburn .25
71 Gary Grant .05
72 Eric Murdock .05
73 Scott Burrell .05
74 Scott Burrell .05
75 Anfernee Hardaway 1.25
76 Anfernee Hardaway .50
77 *Yinka Dare* .10
78 Anthony Avent .05
79 Jon Barry .05
80 Rodney Rogers .05
81 Chris Mills .05
82 Antonio Davis .05
83 Steve Smith .05
84 Buck Williams .05
85 Spud Webb .05
86 Stacey Augmon .05
87 Allan Houston .10
88 Will Perdue .05
89 Chris Gatling .05
90 Danny Ainge .05
91 Rick Mahorn .05
92 Elmore Spencer .05
93 Vin Baker .20
94 Rex Chapman .05
95 Dale Ellis .05
96 Doug Smith .05
97 Tim Perry .05
98 Toni Kukoc .10
99 Terry Dehere .05
100 Shaquille O'Neal .50
101 Shawn Kemp .15
102 Hakeem Olajuwon .25
103 Derrick Coleman .10
104 Alonzo Mourning .15
105 Dikembe Mutombo .10
106 Chris Webber .15
107 Dennis Rodman .30
108 David Robinson .25
109 Charles Barkley .25
110 Brad Daugherty .05
111 Derek Harper .05
112 Detlef Schrempf .05
113 Harvey Grant .05
114 Vlade Divac .05
115 Isaiah Rider .15
116 Mitch Richmond .10
117 Tom Chambers .05
118 Kenny Gattison .05
119 Kenny Gattison .05
120 Vernon Maxwell .05
121 Reggie Williams .05
122 Chris Mullin .10
123 Harold Miner .05
124 Harold Miner .05
125 Calbert Cheaney .05
126 Randy Woods .05
127 Mike Gminski .05
128 Willie Anderson .05
129 Mark Macon .05
130 Avery Johnson .05
131 Bimbo Coles .05
132 Kenny Smith .05
133 Dennis Scott .05
134 Lionel Simmons .05
135 Nate McMillan .05
136 *Eric Montross* .30
137 Sedale Threatt .05
138 Kenny Anderson .10
139 Micheal Williams .05
140 Grant Long .05
141 Greg Anthony .05
142 Tyrone Corbin .05
143 Craig Ehlo .05
144 Gerald Wilkins .05
145 LaPhonso Ellis .05
146 Reggie Miller .20
147 Tracy Murray .05
148 Victor Alexander .05
149 Victor Alexander .05
150 Clifford Robinson .05
151 Anthony Mason .05
152 Anthony Mason .05
153 Jim Jackson .25
154 Jeff Hornacek .05
155 Nick Anderson .05
156 Mike Brown .05
157 Kevin Johnson .10
158 John Paxson .05
159 Loy Vaught .05
160 Carl Herrera .05
161 Shawn Bradley .10
162 Hubert Davis .05
163 David Benoit .05
164 Dell Curry .05
165 Dee Brown .05
166 LaSalle Thompson .05
167 *Eddie Jones* 2.00
168 Walt Williams .05
169 A.C. Green .05
170 Kendall Gill .05
171 Kendall Gill .05
172 Danny Ferry .05
173 Bryant Stith .05
174 John Salley .05
175 Cedric Ceballos .05
176 Derrick Coleman .10
177 Tony Bennett .05
178 Kevin Duckworth .05
179 Jay Humphries .05
180 Sean Elliott .05
181 Sam Perkins .05
182 Luc Longley .05
183 Mitch Richmond .10
184 Clyde Drexler .15
185 Karl Malone .10
186 Shawn Kemp .15
187 Hakeem Olajuwon .25
188 Danny Manning .05
189 Kevin Johnson .05
190 John Stockton .10
191 Latrell Sprewell .15
192 Gary Payton .05
193 Clifford Robinson .05
194 David Robinson .20
195 Charles Barkley .20
196 Mark Price .05
197 Keith Jennings .05
198 Mark Price .05
199 Patrick Ewing .20
200 Patrick Ewing .10
201 Tracy Murray .05
202 Craig Ehlo .05
203 Nick Anderson .05
204 John Starks .05
205 Rex Chapman .05
206 Hersey Hawkins .05
207 Glen Rice .10
208 Jeff Malone .05
209 Dan Majerle .05
210 Chris Mullin .10
211 *Grant Hill* 3.00
212 Bobby Phills .05
213 Dennis Rodman .50
214 Doug West .05
215 Harold Ellis .05
216 Kevin Edwards .05
217 Lorenzo Williams .05
218 Rick Fox .05
219 Mookie Blaylock .05
220 Mookie Blaylock .05
221 John Williams .05
222 Keith Jennings .05
223 Nick Van Exel .25
224 Gary Payton .10
225 John Stockton .10
226 Ron Harper .05
227 *Monty Williams* .10
228 Marty Conlon .10
229 Hersey Hawkins .05
230 Rik Smits .05
231 James Robinson .05
232 Malik Sealy .05
233 Sergei Bazarevich .05
234 Brad Lohaus .05
235 Olden Polynice .05
236 Brian Williams .05
237 Tyrone Hill .05
238 *Jim McIlvaine* .05
239 Latrell Sprewell .25
240 Latrell Sprewell .10
241 Popeye Jones .05
242 Scott Williams .05
243 Eddie Jones .50
244 Moses Malone .05
245 B.J. Armstrong .05
246 Jim Les .05
247 Greg Grant .05
248 Lee Mayberry .05
249 Mark Jackson .05
250 Larry Johnson .15
251 Terrell Brandon .05
252 Ledell Eackles .05
253 Yinka Dare .10
254 *Dontonio Wingfield* .10
255 Clyde Drexler .20
256 Andres Guibert .05
257 Gheorghe Muresan .05
258 Tom Hammonds .05
259 Charles Barkley .50
260 Charles Barkley .25
261 Acie Earl .05
262 *Lamond Murray* .40
263 Dana Barros .05
264 Greg Anthony .05
265 Dan Majerle .05
266 Zan Tabak .05
267 Ricky Pierce .05
268 Eric Leckner .05
269 Duane Ferrell .05
270 Mark Price .10
271 Anthony Peeler .05
272 Adam Keefe .05
273 Rex Walters .05
274 Scott Skiles .05
275 *Glenn Robinson* 1.00
276 *Tony Dumas* .25
277 Elliot Perry .05
278 *Charles "Bo" Outlaw* .10
279 Karl Malone .20
280 Karl Malone .10
281 Herb Williams .05
282 Vincent Askew .05
283 *Askia Jones* .05
284 Shawn Bradley .05
285 Tim Hardaway .10
286 Mark West .05
287 Chuck Person .05
288 James Edwards .05
289 *Antonio Lang* .05
290 Dominique Wilkins .15
291 *Khalid Reeves* .30
292 *Jamie Watson* .15
293 Darnell Mee .05
294 *Brian Grant* .75
295 Hakeem Olajuwon .50
296 *Dickey Simpkins* .15
297 Tyrone Corbin .05
298 David Wingate .05
299 Shaquille O'Neal 1.00
300 Shaquille O'Neal .50
301 B.J. Armstrong .05
302 Mitch Richmond .05
303 Jim Jackson .20
304 Jeff Hornacek .05
305 Mark Price .10
306 Kendall Gill .05
307 Dale Ellis .05
308 Vernon Maxwell .05
309 Joe Dumars .05
310 Reggie Miller .10
311 Geert Hammink .05
312 Charles Smith .05
313 Bill Cartwright .05
314 *Aaron McKie* .50
315 Tom Gugliotta .05
316 P.J. Brown .05
317 David Wesley .05
318 Felton Spencer .05
319 Robert Horry .05
320 Robert Horry .05
321 Larry Krystkowiak .05
322 *Eric Piatkowski* .20
323 Anthony Bonner .05
324 Keith Askins .05
325 Mahmoud Abdul-Rauf .05
326 *Darrin Hancock* .10
327 Vern Fleming .05
328 Wayman Tisdale .05
329 Sam Bowie .05
330 Billy Owens .05
331 Donald Hodge .05
332 *Derrick Alston* .10
333 Doug Edwards .05
334 Johnny Newman .05
335 Otis Thorpe .05
336 *Bill Curley* .20
337 Michael Cage .05
338 Chris Smith .05
339 Dikembe Mutombo .15
340 Dikembe Mutombo .10
341 Duane Causwell .05
342 Sean Higgins .05
343 Steve Kerr .05
344 Eric Montross .20
345 Charles Oakley .05
346 *Brooks Thompson* .15
347 Rony Seikaly .05
348 Chris Dudley .05
349 *Sharone Wright* .25
350 Sarunas Marciulionis .05
351 *Anthony Miller* .10
352 Pooh Richardson .05
353 Byron Scott .05
354 Michael Adams .05
355 Ken Norman .05
356 *Clifford Rozier* .25
357 Tim Breaux .05
358 Derek Strong .05
359 David Robinson .40
360 David Robinson .20
361 Benoit Benjamin .05
362 Terry Porter .05
363 Ervin Johnson .05
364 Alaa Abdelnaby .05
365 Robert Parish .05
366 Mario Elie .05
367 Antonio Harvey .05
368 *Charlie Ward* .15
369 Kevin Gamble .05
370 Rod Strickland .05
371 Jason Kidd 1.00
372 Oliver Miller .05
373 *Eric Mobley* .20
374 Brian Shaw .05
375 Horace Grant .10
376 Corie Blount .05
377 Sam Mitchell .05
378 *Jalen Rose* 1.50
379 Elden Campbell .05
380 Elden Campbell .05
381 *Donyell Marshall* .50
382 Frank Brickowski .05
383 *B.J. Tyler* .15
384 Bryon Russell .05
385 Danny Manning .10
386 Manute Bol .05
387 Brent Price .05
388 J.R. Reid .05
389 Byron Houston .05
390 Blue Edwards .05
391 Adrian Caldwell .05
392 Wesley Person .25
393 *Juwan Howard* 1.00
394 Chris Morris .05
395 Checklist .05
396 Checklist .05

1994-95 Topps Franchise/Futures

The current star on an NBA team and the projected star of the team are featured on the same card for this 20-card set. The cards were random inserts in 1994-95 Topps Series II packs, one every 18 packs.

MT
Complete Set (20): 70.00
Common Player: 1.00
Minor Stars: 2.00
1 Mookie Blaylock 1.00
2 Stacey Augmon 1.00
3 Dominique Wilkins 2.00
4 Eric Montross 2.00
5 Dikembe Mutombo 2.00
6 Jalen Rose 2.00
7 Joe Dumars 3.00
8 Grant Hill 20.00
9 Chris Mullin 2.00
10 Latrell Sprewell 3.00
11 Glen Rice 2.00
12 Khalid Reeves 2.00
13 Derrick Coleman 2.00
14 Yinka Dare 1.00
15 Patrick Ewing 5.00
16 Monty Williams 1.00
17 Shaquille O'Neal 15.00
18 Anfernee Hardaway 15.00
19 Charles Barkley 7.00
20 Wesley Person 2.00

1994-95 Topps Own the Game

This 50-card set features nine top players in five different statistical categories - Super Passers, Super Rebounders, Super Scorers, Super Stealers and Super Swatters - in addition to five field cards. Cards were found in packs of Series I (one per 12 regular packs, one per nine jumbos) and unnumbered. If the pictured player led the league in that respective category, it was redeemable for a 10-card Own the Game redemption set for that category. Field cards represented all other NBA players that weren't included as one of the nine in the set.

		MT
Complete Set (50):		30.00
Common Player:		.20
Minor Stars:		.40
1	Kenny Anderson PASS	.20
2	Charles Barkley SCORE	1.00
3	Mookie Blaylock PASS	.20
4	Mookie Blaylock STEAL	.20
5	Muggsy Bogues PASS	.20
6	Shawn Bradley SWAT	.20
7	Derrick Coleman REB	.20
8	Sherman Douglas PASS	.20
9	Patrick Ewing REB	.40
10	Patrick Ewing SCORE	.40
11	Patrick Ewing SWAT	.40
12	Tom Gugliotta STEAL	.40
13	Anfernee Hardaway STEAL	3.00
14	Mark Jackson PASS	.20
15	Kevin Johnson PASS	.20
16	Karl Malone REB	.75
17	Karl Malone SCORE	.75
18	Nate McMillan STEAL	.20
19	Oliver Miller SWAT	.20
20	Alonzo Mourning SWAT	.75
21	Eric Murdock STEAL	.20
22	Dikembe Mutombo REB	.20
23	Dikembe Mutombo SWAT W	.20
24	Charles Oakley REB	.20
25	Hakeem Olajuwon REB	1.50
26	Hakeem Olajuwon SCORE	1.50
27	Hakeem Olajuwon SWAT	1.50
28	Shaquille O'Neal REB	3.00
29	Shaquille O'Neal SCORE W	3.50
30	Shaquille O'Neal SWAT	3.00
31	Gary Payton STEAL	.75
32	Scottie Pippen SCORE	2.00
33	Scottie Pippen STEAL W	2.50
34	Mark Price PASS	.20
35	Mitch Richmond SCORE	.40
36	David Robinson SCORE	1.00
37	David Robinson SWAT	1.00
38	Dennis Rodman REB W	3.00
39	Latrell Sprewell STEAL	.40
40	John Stockton PASS W	.75
41	John Stockton STEAL	.40
42	Rod Strickland PASS	.20
43	Chris Webber SWAT	1.25
44	Kevin Willis REB	.20
45	Dominique Wilkins SCORE	.20
46	Passers Field Card	.20
47	Rebounders Field Card	.20
48	Scorers Field Card	.20
49	Stealers Field Card	.20
50	Swatters Field Card	.20

1994-95 Topps Own the Game Redemption

According to Topps, only 8,000 of these redemption sets were shipped to collectors. The 10-card set includes the top two players in each of five statistical categories - points, rebounds, assists, steals and blocks. The redemption program expired February 7, 1996.

		MT
Complete Set (10):		10.00
Common Player:		.15
1	Shaquille O'Neal	3.00
2	Hakeem Olajuwon	2.00
3	Dennis Rodman	3.00
4	Patrick Ewing	.75
5	John Stockton	.75
6	Kenny Anderson	.30
7	Scottie Pippen	2.50
8	Mookie Blaylock	.15
9	Dikembe Mutombo	.30
10	Shawn Bradley	.15

1994-95 Topps Spectralight

This 396-card parallel set was inserted into every fourth pack of 1994-95 Series I and II Topps. Spectralight cards feature a prismatic foil treatment on the pictures on the front. The final two cards of each series, which are checklists in the regular-issue set, were changed to feature players and are listed below.

		MT
Complete Set (396):		300.00
Complete Series 1 (198):		125.00
Complete Series 2 (198):		175.00
Common Player (1-396):		.25
Spectralight Cards:		10x
197	Keith Jennings	.50
198	Mark Price	1.00
395	Chris Webber	2.50
396	Mitch Richmond	1.00

1994-95 Topps Super Sophomore

This 10-card insert set utilizes Topps Finest technology to present the top 10 second-year players into the spotlight. The cards were random inserts in 1994-95 Topps Series II packs, one every 36 packs.

		MT
Complete Set (10):		60.00
Common Player:		2.00
1	Chris Webber	10.00
2	Anfernee Hardaway	25.00
3	Vin Baker	5.00
4	Sam Cassell	4.00
5	Jamal Mashburn	5.00
6	Isaiah Rider	3.00
7	Chris Mills	2.00
8	Antonio Davis	2.00
9	Nick Van Exel	5.00
10	Lindsey Hunter	2.00

1994-95 Topps Embossed

This set features the hobby's first double-sided embossed card. The set contains 95 regular player cards, five Houston Rockets 1994 NBA Champion cards and 20 1994 NBA Draft Picks cards, including Grant Hill, Glenn Robinson and Jason Kidd. Each regular card features an embossed player photo on the front, framed in an embossed textured border. The back also has an embossed player photo, biographical and statistical information, and a special "Did You Know" section which has information not found on any other Topps basketball card.

		MT
Complete Set (121):		30.00
Common Player:		.25
Minor Stars:		.50
Gold Cards:		1x-3x
Wax Box:		45.00
1	Stacey Augmon	.25
2	Mookie Blaylock	.25
3	Ken Norman	.25
4	Steve Smith	.25
5	Dee Brown	.25
6	Blue Edwards	.25
7	Dino Radja	.50
8	Dominique Wilkins	.50
9	Muggsy Bogues	.25
10	Dell Curry	.25
11	Larry Johnson	.75
12	Alonzo Mourning	1.00
13	B.J. Armstrong	.50
14	Ron Harper	.25
15	Toni Kukoc	.50
16	Scottie Pippen	1.50
17	Tyrone Hill	.25
18	Mark Price	.50
19	John Williams	.25
20	Jim Jackson	1.00
21	Popeye Jones	.25
22	Jamal Mashburn	.50
23	Mahmoud Abdul-Rauf	.25
24	LaPhonso Ellis	.25
25	Dikembe Mutombo	.75
26	Rodney Rogers	.25
27	Joe Dumars	.75
28	Lindsey Hunter	.25
29	Oliver Miller	.25
30	Terry Mills	.25
31	Tom Gugliotta	.50
32	Tim Hardaway	.75
33	Chris Mullin	.75
34	Latrell Sprewell	.40
35	Sam Cassell	.50
36	Robert Horry	.50
37	Vernon Maxwell	.25
38	Hakeem Olajuwon	1.00
39	Otis Thorpe	.25
40	Mark Jackson	.25
41	Reggie Miller	.75
42	Rik Smits	.50
43	Terry Dehere	.25
44	Stanley Roberts	.25
45	Loy Vaught	.25
46	Vlade Divac	.50
47	George Lynch	.25
48	Nick Van Exel	.75
49	Billy Owens	.25
50	Glen Rice	.50
51	Kevin Willis	.25
52	Vin Baker	.75
53	Todd Day	.25
54	Eric Murdock	.25
55	Christian Laettner	.25
56	Isaiah Rider	.50
57	Micheal Williams	.25
58	Kenny Anderson	.75
59	P.J. Brown	.25
60	Derrick Coleman	.75
61	Chris Morris	.25
62	Patrick Ewing	.50
63	Derek Harper	.25
64	Anthony Mason	.25
65	Charles Oakley	.25
66	John Starks	.50
67	Horace Grant	.75
68	Anfernee Hardaway	4.00
69	Shaquille O'Neal	4.00
70	Dennis Scott	.50
71	Shawn Bradley	.50
72	Jeff Malone	.25
73	Clarence Weatherspoon	.50
74	Charles Barkley	1.00
75	Kevin Johnson	.75
76	Dan Majerle	.50
77	Danny Manning	.50
78	Wayman Tisdale	.25
79	Clyde Drexler	1.00
80	Cliff Robinson	.50
81	Rod Strickland	.25
82	Bobby Hurley	.50
83	Olden Polynice	.25
84	Mitch Richmond	.75
85	Spud Webb	.25
86	Sean Elliott	.25
87	Chuck Person	.25
88	David Robinson	1.00
89	Dennis Rodman	1.50
90	Kendall Gill	.25
91	Shawn Kemp	1.00
92	Sarunas Marciulionis	.25
93	Gary Payton	.50
94	Detlef Schrempf	.50
95	Jeff Hornacek	.25
96	Karl Malone	.75
97	John Stockton	.75
98	Don MacLean	.25
99	Scott Skiles	.25
100	Chris Webber	.75
101	*Glenn Robinson*	2.50
102	*Jason Kidd*	5.00
103	*Grant Hill*	8.00
104	*Donyell Marshall*	.50
105	*Juwan Howard*	3.00
106	*Sharone Wright*	.50
107	*Lamond Murray*	.50
108	*Brian Grant*	1.00
109	*Eric Montross*	.50
110	*Eddie Jones*	4.00
111	*Carlos Rogers*	.75
112	*Khalid Reeves*	.50
113	*Jalen Rose*	.50
114	*Yinka Dare*	.50
115	*Eric Piatkowski*	.50
116	*Clifford Rozier*	.75
117	*Aaron McKie*	1.00
118	*Eric Mobley*	.50
119	*Tony Dumas*	.50
120	*B.J. Tyler*	.50
121	Michael Jordan	10.00

1994-95 Topps Embossed Golden Idols

This 121-card parallel set reprinted each card in the 1994-95 Topps Embossed set, but added a gold finish to the front of the card. One Gold parallel card was included in each pack.

	MT
Complete Set (121):	90.00
Gold Cards:	1x-3x

1995-96 Topps

Topps issued its 1995-96 basketball in two series. Series I has 181 cards, including 15 expansion team players and a 30- card Leaders subset highlighting the 1994-95 statistical leaders and career active leaders. Series II has 110 cards. Each regular card has a color photo on the front, with white borders. The player's name is in gold foil at the bottom, with the first initial of the last name not in foil. The player's team name and position are also in foil, in the lower right corner. The Topps logo is in the upper right corner in gold foil. The horizontal back has a photo on the left, with a card number, biographical information, stats and a player profile underneath. Series I inserts include: Pan for Gold, Whiz Kids, Show Stoppers and Power Boosters, which is a subset of the regular Leaders cards, except they are printed on 28-point stock. Series I also has an NBA Draft Redemption insert, which is numbered 1-29, and is redeemable for a special card of the player whose draft position corresponds with the number on the card. NBA Draft Redemption inserts are found one per every 18 packs. Series II inserts include Mystery Finest, Mystery Finest Refractors, Rattle and Roll, Sudden Impact, Spark Plugs, and All-Star Power Boosters, which parallel the 15 perennial NBA All-Stars from the regular set.

		MT
Complete Set (291):		27.00
Comp. Series 1 (181):		12.00
Comp. Series 2 (110):		15.00
Common Player:		.05
Minor Stars:		.10
Ser. 1 or 2 Pack (12):		1.00
Ser. 1 or 2 Wax Box (36):		25.00
1	Michael Jordan (Active Leaders)	1.25
2	Dennis Rodman (Active Leaders)	.25
3	John Stockton (Active Leaders)	.10
4	Michael Jordan (Active Leaders)	1.25
5	David Robinson (Active Leaders)	.20
6	Shaquille O'Neal (1994-95 Scoring Leaders)	.50
7	Hakeem Olajuwon (1994-95 Scoring Leaders)	.25
8	David Robinson (1994-95 Scoring Leaders)	.20
9	Karl Malone (1994-95 Scoring Leaders)	.10
10	Jamal Mashburn (1994-95 Scoring Leaders)	.10
11	Dennis Rodman (1994-95 Rebound Leaders)	.25
12	Dikembe Mutombo (1994-95 Rebound Leaders)	.10
13	Shaquille O'Neal (1994-95 Rebound Leaders)	.50
14	Patrick Ewing (1994-95 Rebound Leaders)	.10
15	Tyrone Hill (1994-95 Rebound Leaders)	.05
16	John Stockton (1994-95 Assist Leaders)	.10
17	Kenny Anderson (1994-95 Assist Leaders)	.05
18	Tim Hardaway (1994-95 Assist Leaders)	.05
19	Rod Strickland (1994-95 Assist Leaders)	.05
20	Muggsy Bogues (1994-95 Assist Leaders)	.05
21	Scottie Pippen (1994-95 Steal Leaders)	.25
22	Mookie Blaylock (1994-95 Steal Leaders)	.05
23	Gary Payton (1994-95 Steal Leaders)	.10
24	John Stockton (1994-95 Steal Leaders)	.10
25	Nate McMillan (1994-95 Steal Leaders)	.05
26	Dikembe Mutombo (1994-95 Block Leaders)	.10
27	Hakeem Olajuwon (1994-95 Block Leaders)	.25
28	Shawn Bradley (1994-95 Block Leaders)	.05
29	David Robinson (1994-95 Block Leaders)	.20
30	Alonzo Mourning (1994-95 Block Leaders)	.15
31	Reggie Miller	.20
32	Karl Malone	.20
33	Grant Hill	1.00
34	Charles Barkley	.40
35	Cedric Ceballos	.05
36	Gheorghe Muresan	.05
37	Doug West	.05
38	Tony Dumas	.05
39	Kenny Gattison	.05
40	Chris Mullin	.10
41	Pervis Ellison	.05
42	Vinny Del Negro	.05
43	Mario Elie	.05
44	Todd Day	.05
45	Scottie Pippen	.50
46	Buck Williams	.05
47	P.J. Brown	.05
48	Bimbo Coles	.05
49	Terrell Brandon	.05
50	Charles Oakley	.05
51	Sam Perkins	.05
52	Dale Ellis	.05
53	Andrew Lang	.05
54	Harold Ellis	.05
55	Clarence Weatherspoon	.10
56	Bill Curley	.05
57	Robert Parish	.05
58	David Benoit	.05
59	Anthony Avent	.05
60	Jamal Mashburn	.25
61	Duane Ferrell	.05
62	Elden Campbell	.05
63	Rex Chapman	.05
64	Wesley Person	.15
65	Mitch Richmond	.10
66	Micheal Williams	.05
67	Clifford Rozier	.05
68	Eric Montross	.05
69	Dennis Rodman	.50
70	Vin Baker	.15
71	Tyrone Hill	.05
72	Tyrone Corbin	.05
73	Chris Dudley	.05
74	Nate McMillan	.05
75	Kenny Anderson	.10
76	Monty Williams	.05
77	Kenny Smith	.05
78	Rodney Rogers	.05
79	Corie Blount	.05
80	Glen Rice	.10
81	Walt Williams	.05
82	Scott Williams	.05
83	Michael Adams	.05
84	Terry Mills	.05
85	Horace Grant	.10
86	Chuck Person	.05
87	Adam Keefe	.05
88	Scott Brooks	.05
89	George Lynch	.05
90	Kevin Johnson	.10
91	Armon Gilliam	.05
92	Greg Minor	.05
93	Derrick McKey	.05
94	Victor Alexander	.05
95	B.J. Armstrong	.05
96	Terry Dehere	.05
97	Christian Laettner	.05
98	Hubert Davis	.05
99	Aaron McKie	.05
100	Hakeem Olajuwon	.40
101	Michael Cage	.05
102	Grant Long	.05
103	Calbert Cheaney	.05
104	Olden Polynice	.05
105	Sharone Wright	.05
106	Lee Mayberry	.05
107	Robert Pack	.05
108	Loy Vaught	.05
109	Khalid Reeves	.05
110	Shawn Kemp	.50
111	Lindsey Hunter	.05
112	Dell Curry	.05
113	Richard Dumas	.05
114	Bryon Russell	.05
115	John Starks	.05
116	Roy Tarpley	.05
117	Dale Davis	.05
118	Nick Anderson	.05
119	Rex Walters	.05
120	Dominique Wilkins	.10
121	Sam Cassell	.05
122	Sean Elliott	.05
123	B.J. Tyler	.05
124	Eric Mobley	.05
125	Toni Kukoc	.05
126	Pooh Richardson	.05
127	Isaiah Rider	.10
128	Steve Smith	.05
129	Chris Mills	.05
130	Detlef Schrempf	.05
131	Donyell Marshall	.10
132	Eddie Jones	.20
133	Otis Thorpe	.05
134	Lionel Simmons	.05
135	Jeff Hornacek	.05
136	Jalen Rose	.10
137	Kevin Willis	.05
138	Don MacLean	.05
139	Dee Brown	.05
140	Glenn Robinson	.30
141	Joe Kleine	.05
142	Ron Harper	.05
143	Antonio Davis	.05
144	Jeff Malone	.05
145	Joe Dumars	.10
146	Jason Kidd	.75
147	J.R. Reid	.05
148	Lamond Murray	.05
149	Derrick Coleman	.05
150	Alonzo Mourning	.20
151	Clifford Robinson	.05
152	Kendall Gill	.05
153	Doug Christie	.05
154	Stacey Augmon	.05
155	Anfernee Hardaway	1.00
156	Mahmoud Abdul-Rauf	.05
157	Latrell Sprewell	.20
158	Mark Price	.05
159	Brian Grant	.20
160	Clyde Drexler	.20
161	Juwan Howard	.25
162	Tom Gugliotta	.05
163	Nick Van Exel	.25
164	Billy Owens	.05
165	Brooks Thompson	.05
166	Acie Earl	.05
167	Ed Pinckney	.05
168	Oliver Miller	.05
169	John Salley	.05
170	Jerome Kersey	.05
171	Willie Anderson	.05
172	Keith Jennings	.05
173	Doug Smith	.05
174	Gerald Wilkins	.05
175	Byron Scott	.05
176	Benoit Benjamin	.05
177	Blue Edwards	.05
178	Greg Anthony	.05
179	Trevor Ruffin	.05
180	Kenny Gattison	.05
181	Checklist	.05
182	*Cherokee Parks*	.25
183	*Kurt Thomas*	.30
184	Ervin Johnson	.05
185	Chucky Brown	.05
186	Luc Longley	.05
187	Anthony Miller	.05
188	*Ed O'Bannon*	.10
189	Bobby Hurley	.05
190	Dikembe Mutombo	.10
191	Robert Horry	.05
192	*George Zidek*	.20
193	*Rasheed Wallace*	2.00
194	Marty Conlon	.05
195	A.C. Green	.05
196	Mike Brown	.05
197	Oliver Miller	.05
198	Charles Smith	.05
199	*Eric Williams*	.20
200	Rik Smits	.05
201	Donald Royal	.05
202	*Bryant Reeves*	.50
203	Danny Ferry	.05
204	Brian Williams	.05
205	*Joe Smith*	1.00
206	*Gary Trent*	.20
207	*Greg Ostertag*	.10
208	Ken Norman	.05
209	Avery Johnson	.05
210	*Theo Ratliff*	.20
211	Corie Blount	.05
212	Hersey Hawkins	.05
213	*Loren Meyer*	.10
214	*Mario Bennett*	.10
215	Randolph Childress	.05
216	Spud Webb	.05
217	Popeye Jones	.05
218	*Shawn Respert*	.20
219	Malik Sealy	.05
220	Dino Radja	.05
221	James Robinson	.05
222	*David Vaughn*	.10
223	Michael Smith	.05
224	Jamie Watson	.05
225	LaPhonso Ellis	.05
226	Kevin Gamble	.05
227	Dennis Rodman	1.00
228	B.J. Armstrong	.05
229	*Jerry Stackhouse*	2.50
230	Muggsy Bogues	.05
231	*Lawrence Moten*	.10
232	*Cory Alexander*	.10
233	Carlos Rogers	.05
234	*Tyus Edney*	.10
235	Doc Rivers	.05
236	*Antonio Harvey*	.05
237	*Kevin Garnett*	5.00
238	Derek Harper	.05
239	Kevin Edwards	.05
240	Chris Smith	.05
241	Haywoode Workman	.05
242	Bobby Phills	.05
243	*Sherell Ford*	.10
244	*Corliss Williamson*	.20
245	Shawn Bradley	.10
246	*Jason Caffey*	.10
247	Bryant Stith	.05
248	Mark West	.05
249	Dennis Scott	.05
250	Jim Jackson	.15
251	*Travis Best*	.20
252	Sean Rooks	.05
253	Yinka Dare	.05
254	Felton Spencer	.05
255	Vlade Divac	.05
256	*Michael Finley*	2.00
257	*Damon Stoudamire*	1.00
258	Mark Bryant	.05
259	*Brent Barry*	.50
260	Rony Seikaly	.05
261	*Alan Henderson*	.20
262	Kendall Gill	.05
263	Rex Chapman	.05
264	Eric Murdock	.05
265	Rodney Rogers	.05
266	Greg Graham	.05
267	Jayson Williams	.05
268	*Antonio McDyess*	2.00
269	Sedale Threatt	.05
270	Danny Manning	.05
271	Pete Chilcutt	.05
272	*Bob Sura*	.15
273	Dana Barros	.05
274	Allan Houston	.05
275	Tracy Murray	.05
276	Anthony Mason	.05
277	Michael Jordan	1.50
278	Patrick Ewing	.15
279	Shaquille O'Neal	1.00
280	Larry Johnson	.15
281	Mark Jackson	.05

282	Chris Webber	.10
283	David Robinson	.30
284	John Stockton	.15
285	Mookie Blaylock	.05
286	Mark Price	.05
287	Tim Hardaway	.05
288	Rod Strickland	.05
289	Sherman Douglas	.05
290	Gary Payton	.10
291	Checklist	.05

1995-96 Topps Draft Redemption

These cards were random inserts in 1995-96 Topps basketball Series I packs, one per every 18 packs. Each card is numbered on the front 1 of 29, etc., and is redeemable for a special card of the player whose draft position matches the number on the card. The card back has instructions on the redemption program.

		MT
Complete Set (29):		400.00
Common Player:		2.00
1	Joe Smith	20.00
2	Antonio McDyess	50.00
3	Jerry Stackhouse	60.00
4	Rasheed Wallace	50.00
5	Kevin Garnett	300.00
6	Bryant Reeves	5.00
7	Damon Stoudamire	20.00
8	Shawn Respert	2.00
9	Ed O'Bannon	3.00
10	Kurt Thomas	4.00
11	Gary Trent	4.00
12	Cherokee Parks	2.00
13	Corliss Williamson	3.00
14	Eric Williams	2.00
15	Brent Barry	4.00
16	Alan Henderson	2.00
17	Bob Sura	2.00
18	Theo Ratliff	10.00
19	Randolph Childress	2.00
20	Jason Caffey	2.00
21	Michael Finley	50.00
22	George Zidek	2.00
23	Travis Best	10.00
24	Loren Meyer	2.00
25	David Vaughn	2.00
26	Sherell Ford	2.00
27	Mario Bennett	2.00
28	Greg Ostertag	2.00
29	Cory Alexander	2.00

1995-96 Topps Foreign Legion

This 10-card set was available only in retail packs sold in Canada and Australia, and was inserted at a rate of one per 36 six-card packs. The set features foreign players who are in the NBA on a white-bordered metallic background. The backs are identified by a close-up on a blue background with a picture of the earth. Cards are numbered with a "FL" prefix.

		MT
Complete Set (10):		20.00
Common Player:		2.00
1	Luc Longley	2.00
2	Rick Fox	2.00
3	Dikembe Mutombo	5.00
4	Gheorghe Muresan	3.00
5	Sarunas Marciulionis	2.00
6	Dino Radja	3.00
7	Detlef Schrempf	4.00
8	Rony Seikaly	3.00
9	Bill Wennington	2.00
10	Rik Smits	4.00

1995-96 Topps Mystery Finest

These cards, numbered using an "M" prefix, feature 22 of the NBA's most exciting players. The cards were random inserts in 1995-96 Topps Series II hobby and retail packs, one per every 36 packs. Mystery Finest Refractors of the same players listed here were also made; they are found one per every 36 hobby packs and one per every 216 retail packs.

		MT
Complete Set (22):		120.00
Common Player:		1.50
Comp. Refractor Set (22):		700.00
Refractors:		3x-6x
1	Michael Jordan	60.00
2	Anfernee Hardaway	25.00
3	Clyde Drexler	6.00
4	Mark Price	1.50
5	Steve Smith	1.50
6	Jimmy Jackson	3.00
7	Nick Anderson	1.50
8	Kenny Anderson	1.50
9	Mookie Blaylock	1.50
10	Jason Kidd	7.00
11	Tim Hardaway	1.50
12	Kevin Johnson	1.50
13	Gary Payton	4.00
14	John Stockton	4.00
15	Rod Strickland	1.50
16	Jamal Mashburn	3.00
17	Danny Manning	1.50
18	Billy Owens	1.50
19	Grant Hill	20.00
20	Scottie Pippen	12.00
21	Isaiah Rider	1.50
22	Latrell Sprewell	3.00

1995-96 Topps Mystery Finest Refractors

This 22-card insert was numbered M1-M22 and ran parallel to the regular Mystery Finest inserts. Inserted in one per 36 hobby and one per 216 retail Series II packs, this insert captures player against a colorful background and a blue border.

	MT
Complete Set (22):	700.00
Refractors:	3x-6x

1995-96 Topps Pan For Gold

These cards spotlight 15 players who made it big after playing at small colleges. The cards were exclusive inserts to 1995-96 Topps Series I retail packs only, one per every eight packs. Each card front has a color action photo on it, with a metallic mine shaft entrance as a background. The Topps logo, in the upper right corner, and the player's name, at the bottom, are stamped in gold foil. The player's team name is written along the top of the card. The horizontal card back has a photo on one side, with a card number, using a "PFG" prefix, in the upper right corner. The player's name, biographical information, college attended and a brief player profile are underneath.

		MT
Complete Set (15):		30.00
Common Player:		1.00
1	Vin Baker	2.00
2	John Stockton	4.00
3	Dan Majerle	1.00
4	Joe Dumars	1.00
5	Rik Smits	1.00
6	Tim Hardaway	1.00
7	Charles Oakley	1.00
8	Cedric Ceballos	1.00
9	Karl Malone	4.00
10	Scottie Pippen	10.00
11	David Robinson	7.00
12	Gary Payton	3.00
13	Mitch Richmond	1.00
14	Antonio Davis	1.00
15	Dennis Rodman	12.00

1995-96 Topps Power Boosters

These 45 cards are a parallel set to the Leaders subset cards in Topps' 1995-96 Series I and the All-Stars cards in Series II. The inserts, seeded one per every 36 packs, are printed on 28-point stock and feature the 1994-95 leaders in points, rebounding, assists, steals and blocks, as well as the career active leaders in each category. Fifteen perennial NBA All-Stars are also featured.

		MT
Complete Set (45):		350.00
Comp. Series 1 (30):		250.00
Comp. Series 2 (15):		100.00
Common Player:		2.00
1	Michael Jordan	70.00
2	Dennis Rodman	15.00
3	John Stockton	4.00
4	Michael Jordan	70.00
5	David Robinson	10.00
6	Shaquille O'Neal	18.00
7	Hakeem Olajuwon	12.00
8	David Robinson	10.00
9	Karl Malone	4.00
10	Jamal Mashburn	4.00
11	Dennis Rodman	15.00
12	Dikembe Mutombo	2.00
13	Shaquille O'Neal	18.00
14	Patrick Ewing	4.00
15	Tyrone Hill	2.00
16	John Stockton	4.00
17	Kenny Anderson	2.00
18	Tim Hardaway	2.00
19	Rod Strickland	2.00
20	Muggsy Bogues	2.00
21	Scottie Pippen	15.00
22	Mookie Blaylock	2.00
23	Gary Payton	4.00
24	John Stockton	4.00
25	Nate McMillan	2.00
26	Dikembe Mutombo	2.00
27	Hakeem Olajuwon	12.00
28	Shawn Bradley	2.00
29	David Robinson	10.00
30	Alonzo Mourning	5.00
276	Anthony Mason	2.00
277	Michael Jordan	70.00
278	Patrick Ewing	5.00
279	Shaquille O'Neal	25.00
280	Larry Johnson	6.00
281	Mark Jackson	2.00
282	Chris Webber	5.00
283	David Robinson	10.00
284	John Stockton	4.00
285	Mookie Blaylock	2.00
286	Mark Price	2.00
287	Tim Hardaway	2.00
288	Rod Strickland	2.00
289	Sherman Douglas	2.00
290	Gary Payton	4.00

1995-96 Topps Rattle and Roll

These cards were random inserts in 1995-96 Topps Series II basketball packs, one per every 12 packs. The cards, numbered using an "R" prefix, were exclusive to jumbo packs. The card front has a color action photo of the player against a metallic, swirled background. "Rattle & Roll" is written in yellow at the top; the player's name is in yellow along the bottom. The Topps logo is in the upper right corner, while the player's team logo is in the lower left corner. The back has a mug shot, with a swirled background which includes biographical information and a brief player profile. The card number is in a yellow oval at the bottom.

		MT
Complete Set (10):		35.00
Common Player:		1.00
1	Juwan Howard	3.00
2	Glenn Robinson	3.00
3	Grant Hill	10.00
4	Sharone Wright	1.00
5	Brian Grant	1.00
6	Antonio McDyess	5.00
7	Bryant Reeves	3.00
8	Gary Trent	1.00
9	Jerry Stackhouse	6.00
10	Joe Smith	7.00

1995-96 Topps Show Stoppers

These 10 cards, featuring some of the NBA's most exciting players who can single-handedly take over an NBA game, were random inserts in 1995-96 Topps Series I basketball packs. The cards, numbered using an "SS" prefix, were seeded one per every 24 hobby packs only and are all silver foil.

		MT
Complete Set (10):		80.00
Common Player:		2.00
1	Michael Jordan	30.00
2	Grant Hill	20.00
3	Glenn Robinson	5.00
4	Anfernee Hardaway	18.00
5	Charles Barkley	6.00
6	Patrick Ewing	4.00
7	Shaquille O'Neal	16.00
8	Jason Kidd	6.00
9	Glen Rice	2.00
10	Karl Malone	4.00

1995-96 Topps Spark Plugs

Ten of the NBA's catalysts are featured on these 1995-96 Topps Series II insert cards. The cards, numbered using an "SP" prefix, were seeded one per every eight packs. The card front has a color photo on it, bordered by a silver metallic frame. "Spark Plugs" is written along the left side of the cards in red foil; the player's name, Topps logo and team logo are in the lower right corner, also stamped in silver foil. A silver foil spark plug is in the background of the card. The horizontal back has a photo on the left side, with the player's name, team name, biographical information and 1994-95 team statistical trivia related to the player on the right. Spark Plugs is written just above the card number, which is in a white diamond at the bottom.

		MT
Complete Set (10):		30.00
Common Player:		1.00
1	Shaquille O'Neal	7.00
2	Michael Jordan	12.00
3	Reggie Miller	2.00
4	Anfernee Hardaway	7.00
5	John Stockton	2.00
6	David Robinson	3.00
7	Hakeem Olajuwon	4.00
8	Tim Hardaway	1.00
9	Grant Hill	7.00
10	Scottie Pippen	4.00

1995-96 Topps Sudden Impact

These cards, numbered using an "S" prefix, feature some of the NBA's most promising players who have had a sudden impact on their respective teams. The cards were seeded one per every 72 hobby packs of 1995-96 Topps Series II basketball product and use dazzling foil board.

		MT
Complete Set (10):		110.00
Common Player:		3.00
1	Damon Stoudamire	20.00
2	Cherokee Parks	4.00
3	Kurt Thomas	3.00
4	Gary Trent	3.00
5	Bryant Reeves	7.00
6	Ed O'Bannon	3.00
7	Shawn Respert	3.00
8	Antonio McDyess	25.00
9	Joe Smith	20.00
10	Jerry Stackhouse	15.00

1995-96 Topps Top Flight

The 20-card, standard-size set was inserted in retail packs of Topps Basketball. The white-bordered fronts feature the team logo in the lower right corner with a headshot on the card backs with a short biography.

		MT
Complete Set (20):		60.00
Common Player:		1.00
1	Michael Jordan	30.00
2	Isaiah Rider	1.00
3	Harold Miner	1.00
4	Dominique Wilkins	1.00
5	Clyde Drexler	4.00
6	Scottie Pippen	10.00
7	Shawn Kemp	5.00
8	Chris Webber	4.00
9	Anfernee Hardaway	18.00
10	Grant Hill	15.00
11	Kevin Johnson	2.00
12	John Starks	1.00
13	Dan Majerle	1.00
14	Latrell Sprewell	2.00
15	Dee Brown	1.00
16	Stacey Augmon	1.00
17	David Benoit	1.00
18	Sean Elliott	1.00
19	Cedric Ceballos	2.00
20	Robert Horry	1.00

1995-96 Topps Whiz Kids

Twelve top young NBA standouts are featured on these 1995-96 Topps Series I inserts. The cards are printed on Dot Matrix foil. The card front has a color photo against a silver foil background with the outline of a basketball court on it. "Whiz Kids" is written in red at the top in alphabet blocks. The Topps logo is in yellow towards the upper left corner. The player's name is in red along the bottom of the card. The card back has a basketball court design for a background. A mug shot is in the circle at the top of the key. The player's name is below, followed by biographical information, career statistics, a Whiz Quiz question and an answer to a different question. Whiz Kids is written at the top in alphabet blocks. A card number, using a "WK" prefix, is in a red circle in the upper right corner.

		MT
Complete Set (12):		60.00
Common Player:		1.00
1	Grant Hill	15.00
2	Nick Van Exel	3.00
3	Juwan Howard	4.00
4	Chris Webber	5.00
5	Brian Grant	3.00
6	Glenn Robinson	4.00
7	Donyell Marshall	1.00
8	Jason Kidd	6.00
9	Anfernee Hardaway	18.00
10	Jamal Mashburn	3.00
11	Vin Baker	3.00
12	Eddie Jones	5.00

1995-96 Topps World Class

The 10-card, standard-size insert set was inserted every 18 packs of Series II Topps Basketball Canadian and Australian packs. Cards are numbered with a "WC" prefix.

		MT
Complete Set (10):		60.00
Common Player:		3.00
1	Michael Jordan	25.00
2	Karl Malone	6.00
3	Shaquille O'Neal	10.00
4	Reggie Miller	3.00
5	Hakeem Olajuwon	5.00
6	Grant Hill	10.00
7	Anfernee Hardaway	8.00
8	Scottie Pippen	6.00
9	David Robinson	6.00
10	Clyde Drexler	5.00

1995-96 Topps Gallery

New to Topps' line of products is its Topps Gallery set, a hobby-only product that concentrates on photography. Cards are printed on 24-point stock through a high-definition printing process, and finished with a high-gloss coating and foil stamping. The regular set has 144 cards, divided into four categories. There are 90 Classics, featuring top veterans; 18 New Editions, capturing the top rookies; 18 Modernists, which showcase the top young stars; and 18 Masters, which depict franchise players. Insert sets include Expressionists; Photo Gallery; and Player's Private Issue, a parallel set marked with a special foil stamp. Some of these cards were sent to the players; the others were seeded one per every 12 packs.

		MT
Complete Set (144):		40.00
Common Player:		.10
Minor Stars:		.20
Pack (8):		2.50
Wax Box (24):		50.00
1	Shaquille O'Neal (The Masters)	2.00
2	Shawn Kemp (The Masters)	.60
3	Reggie Miller (The Masters)	.50
4	Mitch Richmond (The Masters)	.20
5	Grant Hill (The Masters)	2.00
6	Magic Johnson (The Masters)	1.50
7	Vin Baker (The Masters)	.40
8	Charles Barkley (The Masters)	.75
9	Hakeem Olajuwon (The Masters)	1.00
10	Michael Jordan (The Masters)	5.00
11	Patrick Ewing (The Masters)	.40
12	David Robinson (The Masters)	.75
13	Alonzo Mourning (The Masters)	.40
14	Karl Malone (The Masters)	.40
15	Chris Webber (The Masters)	.30
16	Dikembe Mutombo (The Masters)	.20
17	Larry Johnson (The Masters)	.40
18	Jamal Mashburn (The Masters)	.20
19	Anfernee Hardaway (The Modernists)	2.50
20	Bryant Stith (The Modernists)	.10
21	Juwan Howard (The Modernists)	.60
22	Jason Kidd (The Modernists)	1.50
23	Sharone Wright (The Modernists)	.10
24	Tom Gugliotta (The Modernists)	.10
25	Eric Montross (The Modernists)	.10
26	Allan Houston (The Modernists)	.10
27	Antonio Davis (The Modernists)	.10
28	Brian Grant (The Modernists)	.10
29	Terrell Brandon (The Modernists)	.10
30	Eddie Jones (The Modernists)	.20
31	James Robinson (The Modernists)	.10
32	Wesley Person (The Modernists)	.10
33	Glenn Robinson (The Modernists)	.60
34	Donyell Marshall (The Modernists)	.10
35	Sam Cassell (The Modernists)	.10
36	Lamond Murray (The Modernists)	.10
37	*Damon Stoudamire* (New Editions)	2.00
38	*Tyus Edney* (New Editions)	.20
39	*Jerry Stackhouse* (New Editions)	4.00
40	*Arvydas Sabonis* (New Editions)	1.00
41	*Kevin Garnett* (New Editions)	10.00
42	*Brent Barry* (New Editions)	.75
43	*Alan Henderson* (New Editions)	.40
44	*Bryant Reeves* (New Editions)	1.00

45	*Shawn Respert* (New Editions)	.25
46	*Michael Finley* (New Editions)	3.00
47	*Gary Trent* (New Editions)	.25
48	*Antonio McDyess* (New Editions)	3.00
49	*George Zidek* (New Editions)	.25
50	*Joe Smith* (New Editions)	2.00
51	*Ed O'Bannon* (New Editions)	.20
52	*Rasheed Wallace* (New Editions)	3.00
53	*Eric Williams* (New Editions)	.40
54	*Kurt Thomas* (New Editions)	.25
55	Mookie Blaylock (The Classics)	.10
56	Robert Pack (The Classics)	.10
57	Dana Barros (The Classics)	.10
58	Eric Murdock (The Classics)	.10
59	Glen Rice (The Classics)	.10
60	John Stockton (The Classics)	.40
61	Scottie Pippen (The Classics)	1.00
62	Oliver Miller (The Classics)	.10
63	Tyrone Hill (The Classics)	.10
64	Gary Payton (The Classics)	.25
65	Jim Jackson (The Classics)	.25
66	Avery Johnson (The Classics)	.10
67	Mahmoud Abdul-Rauf (The Classics)	.10
68	Olden Polynice (The Classics)	.10
69	Joe Dumars (The Classics)	.10
70	Rod Strickland (The Classics)	.10
71	Chris Mullin (The Classics)	.10
72	Kevin Johnson (The Classics)	.20
73	Derrick Coleman (The Classics)	.10
74	Clyde Drexler (The Classics)	.50
75	Dale Davis (The Classics)	.10
76	Horace Grant (The Classics)	.10
77	Loy Vaught (The Classics)	.10
78	Armon Gilliam (The Classics)	.10
79	Nick Van Exel (The Classics)	.40
80	Charles Oakley (The Classics)	.10
81	Kevin Willis (The Classics)	.10
82	Sherman Douglas (The Classics)	.10
83	Isaiah Rider (The Classics)	.10
84	Steve Smith (The Classics)	.10
85	Dee Brown (The Classics)	.10
86	Dell Curry (The Classics)	.10
87	Calbert Cheaney (The Classics)	.10
88	Greg Anthony (The Classics)	.10
89	Jeff Hornacek (The Classics)	.10
90	Dennis Rodman (The Classics)	2.00
91	Willie Anderson (The Classics)	.10
92	Chris Mills (The Classics)	.10
93	Hersey Hawkins (The Classics)	.10
94	Popeye Jones (The Classics)	.10
95	Chuck Person (The Classics)	.10
96	Reggie Williams (The Classics)	.10
97	A.C. Green (The Classics)	.10
98	Otis Thorpe (The Classics)	.10
99	Walt Williams (The Classics)	.10
100	Latrell Sprewell (The Classics)	.20
101	Buck Williams (The Classics)	.10
102	Robert Horry (The Classics)	.10
103	Clarence Weatherspoon (The Classics)	.10
104	Dennis Scott (The Classics)	.10
105	Rik Smits (The Classics)	.10
106	Jayson Williams (The Classics)	.10
107	Pooh Richardson (The Classics)	.10
108	Anthony Mason (The Classics)	.10
109	Cedric Ceballos (The Classics)	.25
110	Billy Owens (The Classics)	.10
111	Johnny Newman (The Classics)	.10
112	Christian Laettner (The Classics)	.10
113	Stacey Augmon (The Classics)	.10
114	Chris Morris (The Classics)	.10
115	Detlef Schrempf (The Classics)	.10
116	Dino Radja (The Classics)	.10
117	Sean Elliott (The Classics)	.10
118	Muggsy Bogues (The Classics)	.10
119	Toni Kukoc (The Classics)	.20
120	Clifford Robinson (The Classics)	.10
121	Bobby Hurley (The Classics)	.10
122	Lorenzo Williams (The Classics)	.10
123	Wayman Tisdale (The Classics)	.10
124	Bobby Phills (The Classics)	.10
125	Nick Anderson (The Classics)	.10
126	LaPhonso Ellis (The Classics)	.10
127	Scott Williams (The Classics)	.10
128	Mark West (The Classics)	.10
129	P.J. Brown (The Classics)	.10
130	Tim Hardaway (The Classics)	.10
131	Derek Harper (The Classics)	.10
132	Mario Elie (The Classics)	.10
133	Benoit Benjamin (The Classics)	.10
134	Terry Porter (The Classics)	.10
135	Derrick McKey (The Classics)	.10
136	Bimbo Coles (The Classics)	.10
137	John Salley (The Classics)	.10
138	Malik Sealy (The Classics)	.10
139	Byron Scott (The Classics)	.10
140	Vlade Divac (The Classics)	.10
141	Mark Price (The Classics)	.10
142	Rony Seikaly (The Classics)	.10
143	Mark Jackson (The Classics)	.10
144	John Starks (The Classics)	.10

1995-96 Topps Gallery Expressionists

These 15 insert cards were randomly seeded one per every 24 packs of 1995-96 Topps Gallery. Each card, numbered using an "EX" prefix, has a textured, brush stroke embossed on the front to emphasize the impact of each photograph. The photography is further enhanced with three foils. The etched stamped cards capture the intensity and spirit of each athlete and feature narrative on each player's emotional exploits.

		MT
Complete Set (15):		125.00
Common Player:		1.50
1	Shawn Kemp	6.00
2	Michael Jordan	50.00
3	Reggie Miller	6.00
4	Kevin Willis	1.50
5	Jason Kidd	6.00
6	Larry Johnson	3.00
7	Patrick Ewing	4.00
8	Rasheed Wallace	5.00
9	Karl Malone	4.00
10	Shaquille O'Neal	20.00
11	Joe Smith	10.00
12	Jerry Stackhouse	10.00
13	Glen Rice	1.50
14	Clyde Drexler	5.00
15	Grant Hill	17.00

1995-96 Topps Gallery Photo Gallery

This 17-card insert set chronicles some of the classic moments of some of the game's biggest stars. The cards, seeded one per every 30 packs of 1995-96 Topps Gallery, are designed so that the graphics and information supplement the photography. Multiple foils are also used on each card. Cards are numbered with a "PG" prefix.

		MT
Complete Set (17):		140.00
Common Player:		3.00
1	Vin Baker	4.00
2	Brian Grant	3.00
3	George Zidek	3.00
4	Hakeem Olajuwon	13.00
5	Stacey Augmon	3.00
6	Oliver Miller	3.00
7	Kenny Gattison	3.00
8	Dikembe Mutombo	3.00
9	Ron Seikaly	3.00
10	Tom Gugliotta	3.00
11	Scottie Pippen	13.00
12	David Robinson	10.00
13	Anfernee Hardaway	30.00
14	Dennis Rodman	25.00
15	Kevin Garnett	30.00
16	Damon Stoudamire	25.00
17	Charles Barkley	10.00

1995-96 Topps Gallery Players Private Issue

This 126-card set paralleled the Gallery regular-issue set, except for cards 1-18, which were accidentally not printed in this product but later appeared as insert in 1996-97 Stadium Club. Private Issue cards featured a silver holographic stamp on the front and were inserted one per 12 packs.

		MT
Complete Set (126):		1400.
Common Player:		5.00
Minor Stars:		10.00
Stars:		25x-50x
Rookies:		12x-25x
Cards #1-18 were produced as a 1996-97 Stadium Club insert.		
19	Anfernee Hardaway (The Modernists)	100.00
20	Bryant Stith (The Modernists)	5.00
21	Juwan Howard (The Modernists)	40.00
22	Jason Kidd (The Modernists)	40.00
23	Sharone Wright (The Modernists)	5.00
24	Tom Gugliotta (The Modernists)	20.00
25	Eric Montross (The Modernists)	5.00
26	Allan Houston (The Modernists)	20.00
27	Antonio Davis (The Modernists)	5.00
28	Brian Grant (The Modernists)	10.00
29	Terrell Brandon (The Modernists)	15.00
30	Eddie Jones (The Modernists)	50.00
31	James Robinson (The Modernists)	5.00
32	Wesley Person (The Modernists)	5.00
33	Glenn Robinson (The Modernists)	30.00
34	Donyell Marshall (The Modernists)	5.00
35	Sam Cassell (The Modernists)	5.00
36	Lamond Murray (The Modernists)	5.00
37	*Damon Stoudamire* (New Editions)	60.00
38	*Tyus Edney* (New Editions)	10.00
39	*Jerry Stackhouse* (New Editions)	45.00
40	*Arvydas Sabonis* (New Editions)	10.00
41	*Kevin Garnett* (New Editions)	150.00
42	*Brent Barry* (New Editions)	10.00
43	*Alan Henderson* (New Editions)	10.00
44	*Bryant Reeves* (New Editions)	20.00
45	*Shawn Respert* (New Editions)	5.00
46	*Michael Finley* (New Editions)	30.00
47	*Gary Trent* (New Editions)	10.00
48	*Antonio McDyess* (New Editions)	35.00
49	*George Zidek* (New Editions)	10.00
50	*Joe Smith* (New Editions)	45.00
51	*Ed O'Bannon* (New Editions)	10.00
52	*Rasheed Wallace* (New Editions)	30.00
53	*Eric Williams* (New Editions)	10.00
54	*Kurt Thomas* (New Editions)	10.00
55	Mookie Blaylock (The Classics)	10.00
56	Robert Pack (The Classics)	5.00
57	Dana Barros (The Classics)	5.00
58	Eric Murdock (The Classics)	5.00
59	Glen Rice (The Classics)	25.00
60	John Stockton (The Classics)	25.00
61	Scottie Pippen (The Classics)	85.00
62	Oliver Miller (The Classics)	5.00
63	Tyrone Hill (The Classics)	5.00
64	Gary Payton (The Classics)	30.00
65	Jim Jackson (The Classics)	10.00
66	Avery Johnson (The Classics)	5.00
67	Mahmoud Abdul-Rauf (The Classics)	5.00
68	Olden Polynice (The Classics)	5.00
69	Joe Dumars (The Classics)	10.00
70	Rod Strickland (The Classics)	5.00
71	Chris Mullin (The Classics)	10.00
72	Kevin Johnson (The Classics)	15.00
73	Derrick Coleman (The Classics)	10.00
74	Clyde Drexler (The Classics)	25.00
75	Dale Davis (The Classics)	5.00
76	Horace Grant (The Classics)	5.00
77	Loy Vaught (The Classics)	5.00
78	Armon Gilliam (The Classics)	5.00
79	Nick Van Exel (The Classics)	20.00
80	Charles Oakley (The Classics)	5.00
81	Kevin Willis (The Classics)	5.00
82	Sherman Douglas (The Classics)	5.00
83	Isaiah Rider (The Classics)	10.00
84	Steve Smith (The Classics)	10.00
85	Dee Brown (The Classics)	5.00
86	Dell Curry (The Classics)	5.00
87	Calbert Cheaney (The Classics)	5.00
88	Greg Anthony (The Classics)	5.00
89	Jeff Hornacek (The Classics)	5.00
90	Dennis Rodman (The Classics)	90.00
91	Willie Anderson (The Classics)	5.00
92	Chris Mills (The Classics)	5.00
93	Hersey Hawkins (The Classics)	5.00
94	Popeye Jones (The Classics)	5.00
95	Chuck Person (The Classics)	5.00
96	Reggie Williams (The Classics)	5.00
97	A.C. Green (The Classics)	5.00
98	Otis Thorpe (The Classics)	5.00
99	Walt Williams (The Classics)	10.00
100	Latrell Sprewell (The Classics)	30.00
101	Buck Williams (The Classics)	5.00
102	Robert Horry (The Classics)	5.00
103	Clarence Weatherspoon (The Classics)	5.00
104	Dennis Scott (The Classics)	5.00
105	Rik Smits (The Classics)	10.00
106	Jayson Williams (The Classics)	5.00
107	Pooh Richardson (The Classics)	5.00
108	Anthony Mason (The Classics)	10.00
109	Cedric Ceballos (The Classics)	5.00
110	Billy Owens (The Classics)	5.00
111	Johnny Newman (The Classics)	5.00
112	Christian Laettner (The Classics)	10.00
113	Stacey Augmon (The Classics)	5.00
114	Chris Morris (The Classics)	5.00
115	Detlef Schrempf (The Classics)	5.00
116	Dino Radja (The Classics)	5.00
117	Sean Elliott (The Classics)	5.00
118	Muggsy Bogues (The Classics)	5.00
119	Toni Kukoc (The Classics)	20.00
120	Clifford Robinson (The Classics)	5.00
121	Bobby Hurley (The Classics)	5.00
122	Lorenzo Williams (The Classics)	5.00
123	Wayman Tisdale (The Classics)	5.00
124	Bobby Phills (The Classics)	5.00
125	Nick Anderson (The Classics)	5.00
126	LaPhonso Ellis (The Classics)	10.00
127	Scott Williams (The Classics)	5.00
128	Mark West (The Classics)	5.00
129	P.J. Brown (The Classics)	10.00
130	Tim Hardaway (The Classics)	20.00
131	Derek Harper (The Classics)	5.00
132	Mario Elie (The Classics)	5.00
133	Benoit Benjamin (The Classics)	5.00
134	Terry Porter (The Classics)	5.00
135	Derrick McKey (The Classics)	5.00
136	Bimbo Coles (The Classics)	5.00
137	John Salley (The Classics)	5.00
138	Malik Sealy (The Classics)	5.00
139	Byron Scott (The Classics)	5.00
140	Vlade Divac (The Classics)	5.00
141	Mark Price (The Classics)	5.00
142	Rony Seikaly (The Classics)	5.00
143	Mark Jackson (The Classics)	5.00
144	John Starks (The Classics)	5.00

1996 Topps Kellogg's Raptors

This five-card set commemorating the Raptors inaugural season was inserted one per box of Rice Krispies in the Toronto area. The cards are similar to the Topps design of that year except the printing is done in silver foil rather than gold. The front of each card has a Raptors logo with "Inaugural Season 1995-96" printed in silver foil.

		MT
Complete Set (5):		8.00
Common Player:		1.00
1	Willie Anderson	1.00
2	Damon Stoudamire	5.00
3	Alvin Robertson	1.00
4	Tony Massenburg	1.00
5	Tracy Murray	1.00

1996 Topps USA Women's National Team

This 24-card set was sold in 10-card packs. Each of the 11 players has a regular card and a Profiles card. Cards of Head Coach Tara VanDerveer and the entire team complete the set. The regular cards feature a player photo with the American flag in the background on the front and the backs have complete biographical and statistical information. The Profiles cards have a player closeup and gold foil-stamped facsimile autograph on the fronts. The backs feature questions and answers outlining the player's personal life.

		MT
Complete Set (24):		9.00
Common Player:		.15
1	Jennifer Azzi	1.00
2	Ruthie Bolton	.50
3	Teresa Edwards	.50
4	Lisa Leslie	1.00
5	Rebecca Lobo	1.00
6	Katrina McClain	.40
7	Nikki McCray	.40
8	Carla McGhee	.20
9	Dawn Staley	.40
10	Katy Steding	.20
11	Sheryl Swoopes	1.00
12	Tara VanDerveer CO	.15
13	Jennifer Azzi PRO	.35
14	Ruthie Bolton PRO	.25
15	Teresa Edwards PRO	.25
16	Lisa Leslie PRO	.50
17	Rebecca Lobo PRO	.50
18	Katrina McClain PRO	.25
19	Nikki McCray PRO	.25
20	Carla McGhee PRO	.20
21	Dawn Staley PRO	.25
22	Katy Steding PRO	.20
23	Sheryl Swoopes PRO	.50
24	Team Photo	.75

1996-97 Topps

Topps celebrates its 50th anniversary of basketball with its 1996-97 basketball set. Both Series I and Series II contain 110 cards each. Each regular card front has a color action photo with a white border. The Topps logo is stamped in gold in the upper right corner; the player's name is in gold along the bottom. The horizontal back also has a white border, with a card number in the upper right corner. In addition to a color mug shot, the back contains biographical information, statistics and a brief player profile. Series I inserts are Holding Court, Holding Court Refractors, Pro Files, Season's Best, Hobby Masters, Super Team cards and NBA Draft Redemption (29 cards with a number corresponding to each draft position of the first round; seeded one per 18 packs). The regular set also has a parallel set which uses gold foil stamping to commemorate the NBA's 50th anniversary. These cards were seeded one per every three packs. Series II inserts include: Mystery Finest, Profiles, Youthquake, NBA Topps Stars Finest Reprints, 50th Anniversary parallels and Hobby Masters.

		MT
Complete Set (221):		25.00
Complete Series 1 (111):		10.00
Complete Series 2 (110):		15.00
Common Player:		.05
Minor Stars:		.10
Complete NBA 50 (220):		180.00
Comp. NBA 50 Ser.1 (110):		80.00
Comp. NBA 50 Ser.2 (110):		100.00
NBA 50 Cards:		4x-8x
Ser. 1 or 2 Pack (11):		1.25
Ser. 1 or 2 Wax Box (36):		40.00
1	Patrick Ewing	.20
2	Christian Laettner	.05
3	Mahmoud Abdul-Rauf	.05
4	Chris Webber	.10
5	Jason Kidd	.50
6	Clifford Rozier	.05
7	Elden Campbell	.05
8	Chuck Person	.05
9	Jeff Hornacek	.05
10	Rik Smits	.05
11	Kurt Thomas	.05
12	Rod Strickland	.05
13	Kendall Gill	.05
14	Brian Williams	.05
15	Tom Gugliotta	.05
16	Ron Harper	.05
17	Eric Williams	.05
18	A.C. Green	.05
19	Scott Williams	.05
20	Damon Stoudamire	.75
21	Bryant Reeves	.20
22	Bob Sura	.05
23	Mitch Richmond	.10
24	Larry Johnson	.20
25	Vin Baker	.15
26	Mark Bryant	.05
27	Horace Grant	.05
28	Allan Houston	.05
29	Sam Perkins	.05
30	Antonio McDyess	.25
31	Rasheed Wallace	.15
32	Malik Sealy	.05
33	Scottie Pippen	.60
34	Charles Barkley	.30
35	Hakeem Olajuwon	.40
36	John Starks	.05
37	Byron Scott	.05
38	Arvydas Sabonis	.30
39	Vlade Divac	.05
40	Joe Dumars	.05
41	Danny Ferry	.05
42	Jerry Stackhouse	.60
43	B.J. Armstrong	.05
44	Shawn Bradley	.05
45	Kevin Garnett	1.25
46	Dee Brown	.05
47	Michael Smith	.05
48	Doug Christie	.05
49	Mark Jackson	.05
50	Shawn Kemp	.30
51	Sasha Danilovic	.05
52	Nick Anderson	.05
53	Matt Geiger	.05
54	Charles Smith	.05
55	Mookie Blaylock	.05
56	Johnny Newman	.05
57	George McCloud	.05
58	Greg Ostertag	.05
59	Reggie Williams	.05
60	Brent Barry	.10
61	Doug West	.05
62	Donald Royal	.05
63	Randy Brown	.05
64	Vincent Askew	.05
65	John Stockton	.15
66	Joe Kleine	.05
67	Keith Askins	.05
68	Bobby Phills	.05
69	Chris Mullin	.10
70	Nick Van Exel	.15
71	Rick Fox	.05
72	Bulls Commemorative	1.00
73	Shawn Respert	.05
74	Hubert Davis	.05
75	Jim Jackson	.10
76	Olden Polynice	.05
77	Gheorghe Muresan	.05
78	Theo Ratliff	.05
79	Khalid Reeves	.05
80	David Robinson	.30
81	Lawrence Moten	.05
82	Sam Cassell	.05
83	George Zidek	.05
84	Sharone Wright	.05
85	Clarence Weatherspoon	.05
86	Alan Henderson	.05
87	Chris Dudley	.05
88	Ed O'Bannon	.05
89	Calbert Cheaney	.05
90	Cedric Ceballos	.05
91	Michael Cage	.05
92	Gary Trent	.05
93	Ervin Johnson	.05
94	Sherman Douglas	.05
95	Joe Smith	.40
96	Dale Davis	.05
97	Tony Dumas	.05
98	Muggsy Bogues	.05
99	Toni Kukoc	.10
100	Grant Hill	1.25
101	Michael Finley	.30
102	Isaiah Rider	.05
103	Bryant Stith	.05

104	Pooh Richardson	.05
105	Karl Malone	.15
106	Brian Grant	.05
107	Sean Elliott	.05
108	Charles Oakley	.05
109	Pervis Ellison	.05
110	Anfernee Hardaway	1.25
111	Checklist	2.00
112	Dikembe Mutombo	.10
113	Alonzo Mourning	.20
114	Hubert Davis	.05
115	Rony Seikaly	.05
116	Danny Manning	.05
117	Donyell Marshall	.05
118	Felton Spencer	.05
119	Efthimis Retzias	.05
120	Jalen Rose	.05
121	Dino Radja	.05
122	Glenn Robinson	.20
123	John Stockton	.25
124	Brent Price	.05
125	Clifford Robinson	.05
126	Steve Kerr	.05
127	Nate McMillan	.05
128	*Shareef Abdur-Rahim*	2.00
129	Loy Vaught	.05
130	Anthony Mason	.05
131	Kevin Garnett	1.25
132	Roy Rogers	.20
133	*Erick Dampier*	.25
134	Tyus Edney	.05
135	Chris Mills	.05
136	Cory Alexander	.05
137	Juwan Howard	.30
138	*Kobe Bryant*	10.00
139	Michael Jordan	2.50
140	Jayson Williams	.05
141	Rod Strickland	.05
142	*Lorenzen Wright*	.25
143	Will Perdue	.05
144	Derek Harper	.05
145	Billy Owens	.05
146	*Antoine Walker*	1.50
147	P.J. Brown	.05
148	Terrell Brandon	.05
149	Larry Johnson	.10
150	Steve Smith	.05
151	Eddie Jones	.20
152	Detlef Schrempf	.05
153	Dale Ellis	.05
154	Isaiah Rider	.05
155	*Tony Delk*	.25
156	Vincent Askew	.05
157	Jamal Mashburn	.10
158	Dennis Scott	.05
159	Dana Barros	.05
160	Martin Muursepp	.05
161	*Marcus Camby*	2.00
162	Jerome Williams	.05
163	Wesley Person	.05
164	Luc Longley	.05
165	Chris Childs	.05
166	Mark Jackson	.05
167	Derrick Coleman	.05
168	Dell Curry	.05
169	Armon Gilliam	.05
170	Vlade Divac	.05
171	*Allen Iverson*	5.00
172	Vitaly Potapenko	.20
173	Jon Koncak	.05
174	Lindsey Hunter	.05
175	Kevin Johnson	.05
176	Dennis Rodman	.75
177	*Stephon Marbury*	2.00
178	Karl Malone	.25
179	Charles Barkley	.40
180	Popeye Jones	.05
181	Samaki Walker	.25
182	*Steve Nash*	.40
183	Latrell Sprewell	.10
184	Kenny Anderson	.05
185	Tyrone Hill	.05
186	Robert Pack	.05
187	Greg Anthony	.05
188	Derrick McKey	.05
189	*John Wallace*	.40
190	Bryon Russell	.05
191	*Jermaine O'Neal*	.75
192	Clyde Drexler	.20
193	Mahmoud Abdul-Rauf	.05
194	Eric Montross	.05
195	Allan Houston	.05
196	Harvey Grant	.05
197	Rodney Rogers	.05
198	*Kerry Kittles*	1.25
199	Grant Hill	1.00
200	Lionel Simmons	.05
201	Reggie Miller	.20
202	Avery Johnson	.05
203	LaPhonso Ellis	.05
204	Brian Shaw	.05
205	Priest Lauderdale	.05
206	Jerome Kersey	.05
207	James Robinson	.05
208	Todd Fuller	.20
209	Hersey Hawkins	.05
210	Tim Legler	.05
211	Terry Dehere	.05
212	Gary Payton	.20
213	Stacey Augmon	.05
214	Don MacLean	.05
215	Greg Minor	.05
216	Tim Hardaway	.05
217	*Ray Allen*	2.00
218	Mario Elie	.05
219	Brooks Thompson	.05
220	Shaquille O'Neal	1.25
221	Checklist	.05

1996-97 Topps NBA 50th

This 220-card set paralleled the 1996-97 Topps Basketball Series I and II set and was inserted into Series I and II hobby and retail packs at a rate of one per three packs. The cards were identified by silver foil being added to the fronts, which gave the card a silver border, as well as an NBA 50th logo in the lower left corner.

	MT
NBA 50th Cards:	4x-8x

1996-97 Topps Draft Redemption

This 27-card set was available via redemption cards in Series I that carried the corresponding draft selection number. The cards were found every 18 hobby or retail packs and were redeemed through the mail with a deadline of 4/1/97.

		MT
Complete Set (27):		550.00
Common Player:		5.00
Numbers 14 and 23 were never produced.		
1	Allen Iverson	125.00
2	Marcus Camby	15.00
3	Shareef Abdur-Rahim	35.00
4	Stephon Marbury	40.00
5	Ray Allen	30.00
6	Antoine Walker	30.00
7	Lorenzen Wright	6.00
8	Kerry Kittles	6.00
9	Samaki Walker	6.00
10	Erick Dampier	6.00
11	Todd Fuller	5.00
12	Vitaly Potapenko	5.00
13	Kobe Bryant	400.00
15	Steve Nash	15.00
16	Tony Delk	6.00
17	Jermaine O'Neal	40.00
18	John Wallace	6.00
19	Walter McCarty	5.00
20	Zydrunas Ilgauskas	8.00
21	Dontae Jones	5.00
22	Roy Rogers	5.00
24	Derek Fisher	8.00
25	Martin Muursepp	5.00
26	Jerome Williams	6.00
27	Brian Evans	5.00
28	Priest Lauderdale	5.00
29	Travis Knight	5.00

1996-97 Topps Finest Reprints

This 25-card set was included in one per 36 Series II Topps packs. It included 25 of the 50 Rookie Reprints from NBA Topps Stars printed in Finest technology, with the remainder of the set found in Stadium Club I. Refractor versions were also available.

		MT
Complete Set (25):		170.00
Common Player:		5.00
Refractors:		2x-4x
1	Kareem Abdul-Jabbar	15.00
3	Paul Arizin	5.00
9	Wilt Chamberlain	15.00
11	Dave Cowens	5.00
14	Clyde Drexler	10.00
16	Patrick Ewing	10.00
20	John Havlicek	10.00
21	Elvin Hayes	5.00
22	Magic Johnson	35.00
23	Sam Jones	5.00
25	Jerry Lucas	5.00
27	Moses Malone	5.00
30	George Mikan	12.00
31	Earl Monroe	5.00
32	Shaquille O'Neal	12.00
33	Hakeem Olajuwon	15.00
37	Willis Reed	5.00
38	Oscar Robertson	10.00
39	David Robinson	10.00
40	Bill Russell	15.00
42	Bill Sharman	5.00
43	John Stockton	8.00
45	Nate Thurmond	5.00
46	Wes Unseld	5.00
47	Bill Walton	5.00

1996-97 Topps Finest Reprints Refractors

Every card in the Series II Topps Finest Rookie Reprints insert was also available in a Refractor version. This 25-card set was seeded one per 144 packs. Refractor versions were easily identifiable by the fronts, and also included the word "Refractor" just below the bottom left side of the red box on the back.

	MT
Refractors:	2x-4x

1996-97 Topps Hobby Masters

These cards, printed on 28-point full-diffraction stock, were random inserts in 1996-97 Topps Series I hobby packs only, one every 36 packs. The card front has a color action photo on it, with a close-up shot of the player dominating the background. The Topps logo is in the upper left corner; "Hobby Masters," the player's name, position and team logo are along the bottom of the card. The horizontal card back, numbered in the upper right corner using an "HM" prefix, has a small rectangle under the card number which contains a color action photo. The left side has a photo as the background, with biographical and statistical information and a recap of why collectors pursue the player's cards.

		MT
Complete Set (20):		175.00
Complete Series 1 (10):		100.00
Complete Series 2 (10):		75.00
Common Player:		4.00
11	Shaquille O'Neal	25.00
12	Jerry Stackhouse	7.00
13	Dennis Rodman	20.00
14	Joe Smith	7.00
15	Damon Stoudamire	15.00
16	Gary Payton	8.00
17	Mitch Richmond	4.00
18	Reggie Miller	6.00
19	Chris Webber	8.00
20	Vin Baker	4.00
21	Grant Hill	30.00
22	Scottie Pippen	15.00
23	Karl Malone	4.00
24	Patrick Ewing	4.00
25	Shawn Kemp	8.00
26	Anfernee Hardaway	25.00
27	Charles Barkley	7.00
28	Jason Kidd	7.00
29	Hakeem Olajuwon	10.00
30	Larry Johnson	4.00

1996-97 Topps Holding Court

These cards were inserts in 1996-97 Topps Series I packs, one per every 36 packs. The set features 15 top players on regular Finest cards which have a silver background. "Holding Court" is written along the left side of the card, with the Topps logo above and a team logo below. The player's name is written in gold along the bottom. The horizontal card back has an action shot on the left, with the player's name, team name, biographical information and a brief player profile on the right. A card number, using an "HC" prefix, is in the lower right corner. Refractor versions were also made for each card; these were seeded one per every 108 packs.

		MT
Complete Set (15):		100.00
Common Player:		1.50
Refractor Set (15):		400.00
Refractors:		2x-4x
1	Larry Johnson	3.00
2	Michael Jordan	50.00
3	Cedric Ceballos	1.50
4	Grant Hill	25.00
5	Anfernee Hardaway	25.00
6	Reggie Miller	4.00
7	Glenn Robinson	3.00
8	Patrick Ewing	3.00
9	Chris Webber	1.50
10	Shaquille O'Neal	18.00
11	John Stockton	3.00
12	Mitch Richmond	1.50
13	David Robinson	7.00
14	Gary Payton	4.00
15	Karl Malone	4.00

1996-97 Topps Holding Court Refractors

Parallel to the Holding Court Finest inserts, this 15-card set was inserted every 108 packs and featured Topps' patented Refractor finish.

	MT
Refractors:	2x-4x

1996-97 Topps Mystery Finest

This 22-card insert arrived in packs hidden behind a black opaque seal that could be removed to reveal the player. Bordered versions were the most common type, arriving one per 36 packs, while Mystery Finest inserts also came in bordered Refractor, borderless and borderless Refractor versions.

		MT
Complete Set (22):		150.00
Common Player:		2.00
Borderless Cards:		2x
Borderless Refractors:		2x-4x
Bordered Refractors:		3x-6x
M1	Scottie Pippen	12.00
M2	Jason Kidd	8.00
M3	Anfernee Hardaway	20.00
M4	Gary Payton	6.00
M5	Juwan Howard	6.00
M6	Sean Elliott	2.00
M7	Dennis Rodman	15.00
M8	Shawn Kemp	6.00
M9	David Robinson	6.00
M10	Alonzo Mourning	2.00
M11	Dikembe Mutombo	2.00
M12	Shaquille O'Neal	15.00
M13	Clyde Drexler	6.00
M14	Michael Jordan	50.00
M15	Damon Stoudamire	10.00
M16	Mitch Richmond	2.00
M17	Patrick Ewing	3.00
M18	Vin Baker	5.00
M19	Hakeem Olajuwon	10.00
M20	Joe Smith	6.00
M21	Charles Barkley	6.00
M22	Reggie Miller	3.00

1996-97 Topps Mystery Finest Bordered Refractors

This insert captured all 22 Mystery Finest inserts in a bordered version with a Refractor finish. These cards were inserted exclusively in jumbo retail packs, and played off the production mistake of 1995-96 when bordered Refractors were not supposed to exist, but did surface in small quantities.

	MT
Refractors:	3x-6x

1996-97 Topps Mystery Finest Borderless

Borderless Mystery Finest inserts - as the name indicates - are identified by their borderless design in contrast to the more common bordered cards. Borderless versions of the 22-card set are seeded one per 72 packs.

	MT
Borderless Cards: 2x	

1996-97 Topps Mystery Finest Borderless Refractors

All 22-cards in the Mystery Finest insert found in Topps Series II also arrived in Borderless Refractor versions. The cards featured Topps' familiar Refractor finish and were seeded one per 216 packs.

	MT
Refractors:	3x-6x

1996-97 Topps Pro Files

These foil board cards were seeded one per every 12 packs of 1996-97 Topps basketball. David Robinson, serving as Topps' spokesman, analyzes some of today's top stars; he wrote the backs for each card. The card front has a color action photo on it, with a ghosted image of the crowd in the background. "Pro Files" is written along the left side of the card, above a small mug shot of Robinson in the lower left corner. "By David Robinson" is written in an oval at the bottom of the card, below the action photo. The pictured player's name runs vertically in the upper right corner. The card back is numbered with a "PF" prefix and has a color mug shot on the left, with a profile which recaps some of his achievements underneath. The right side provides Robinson's analysis of the player.

		MT
Complete Set (20):		50.00
Complete Series 1 (10):		25.00
Complete Series 2 (10):		25.00
Common Player:		1.00
1	Grant Hill	5.00
2	Shawn Kemp	2.00
3	Michael Jordan	15.00
4	Vin Baker	1.00
5	Chris Webber	1.00
6	Joe Smith	2.00
7	Shaquille O'Neal	6.00
8	Patrick Ewing	1.00
9	Scottie Pippen	4.00
10	Damon Stoudamire	4.00
11	Anfernee Hardaway	6.00
12	Juwan Howard	2.00
13	Dikembe Mutombo	1.00
14	Dennis Rodman	5.00
15	Kevin Garnett	6.00
16	Jerry Stackhouse	3.00
17	Alonzo Mourning	1.00
18	Karl Malone	2.00
19	Hakeem Olajuwon	3.00
20	Gary Payton	2.00

1996-97 Topps Season's Best

Season's Best, a 1996-97 Topps Series I insert set, showcases the five leading players in five statistical categories from the previous season - points (En Fuego), rebounds (Board Members), steals (Sticky Fingers), assists (Dish Men), and blocks (Swat Team). The cards were seeded one per every eight packs. The back is horizontal and is numbered "Season's Best 1," etc., and has a hardwood floor background which includes a photo on the right. A brief player profile and NBA record are on the left; biographical information and the player's draft position are on the right. The category name runs vertically down the right side. Cards are numbered with a "SB" prefix.

		MT
Complete Set (25):		80.00
Common Player:		.75
1	Michael Jordan	25.00
2	Hakeem Olajuwon	5.00
3	Shaquille O'Neal	10.00
4	Karl Malone	2.00
5	David Robinson	3.50
6	Dennis Rodman	8.00
7	David Robinson	3.50
8	Dikembe Mutombo	.75
9	Charles Barkley	3.00
10	Shawn Kemp	4.00
11	John Stockton	2.00
12	Jason Kidd	5.00
13	Avery Johnson	.75
14	Rod Strickland	.75
15	Damon Stoudamire	7.00
16	Gary Payton	2.00
17	Mookie Blaylock	.75
18	Michael Jordan	25.00
19	Jason Kidd	5.00
20	Alvin Robertson	.75
21	Dikembe Mutombo	.75
22	Shawn Bradley	.75
23	David Robinson	3.50
24	Hakeem Olajuwon	5.00
25	Alonzo Mourning	2.00

1996-97 Topps Super Teams

These cards, seeded one per every 36 packs of 1996-97 Topps Series I packs, feature each NBA team. "Topps Super Team" is stamped in gold foil in an upper corner. The card back explains the rules for the Super Team promotion; if the team represented by the card wins a division title, conference championship or NBA Championship in 1996-97, the holder could redeem the card for prizes. The team cards, however, would not be returned. Cards are numbered with a "ST" prefix.

		MT
Complete Set (29):		100.00
Common Team:		2.00
1	Atlanta Hawks	2.00
2	Boston Celtics	2.00
3	Charlotte Hornets	2.00
4	Chicago Bulls	40.00
5	Cleveland Cavaliers	2.00
6	Dallas Mavericks	2.00
7	Denver Nuggets	2.00
8	Detroit Pistons	3.00
9	Golden State Warriors	2.00

10	Houston Rockets	4.00
11	Indiana Pacers	2.00
12	Los Angeles Clippers	2.00
13	Los Angeles Lakers	4.00
14	Miami Heat	5.00
15	Milwaukee Bucks	2.00
16	Minnesota Timberwolves	2.00
17	New Jersey Nets	2.00
18	New York Knicks	3.00
19	Orlando Magic	2.00
20	Philadelphia 76ers	2.00
21	Phoenix Suns	2.00
22	Portland Trail Blazers	2.00
23	Sacramento Kings	2.00
24	San Antonio Spurs	25.00
25	Seattle Supersonics	5.00
26	Toronto Raptors	2.00
27	Utah Jazz	10.00
28	Vancouver Grizzlies	2.00
29	Washington Bullets	2.00

1996-97 Topps Super Team Winners

		MT
Complete Atlantic (5):		8.00
Complete Central (6):		10.00
Complete Midwest (6):		8.00
Complete Pacific (5):		8.00
Complete Eastern (11):		20.00
Complete Western (11):		10.00
Common Conference/Division:		.50
Complete Finals Set (22):		200.00
NBA Finals:		4x-8x
M1	Scottie Pippen	3.00
M2	Jason Kidd	3.00
M3	Anfernee Hardaway	3.00
M4	Gary Payton	1.50
M5	Juwan Howard	.75
M6	Sean Elliott	.50
M7	Dennis Rodman	1.00
M8	Shawn Kemp	.75
M9	David Robinson	1.50
M10	Alonzo Mourning	.75
M11	Dikembe Mutombo	.50
M12	Shaquille O'Neal	5.00
M13	Clyde Drexler	.75
M14	Michael Jordan	10.00
M15	Damon Stoudamire	.75
M16	Mitch Richmond	.75
M17	Patrick Ewing	.75
M18	Vin Baker	.50
M19	Hakeem Olajuwon	1.50
M20	Joe Smith	.50
M21	Charles Barkley	1.50
M22	Reggie Miller	1.00

1996-97 Topps Youthquake

Youthquake captured 15 top young players on a wood card stock with a glossy finish on the front. Inserted into Series II retail packs at a rate of one per 36 packs, the background contains a checkered look with a wood border and the insert name printed up the left side. Cards are numbered with a "U" prefix.

		MT
Complete Set (15):		100.00
Common Player:		1.50
Minor Stars:		3.00
1	Allen Iverson	20.00
2	Samaki Walker	3.00
3	Stephon Marbury	20.00
4	Damon Stoudamire	8.00
5	John Wallace	4.00
6	Michael Finley	3.00
7	Marcus Camby	6.00
8	Kerry Kittles	6.00
9	Ray Allen	6.00
10	Jerry Stackhouse	5.00
11	Shareef Abdur-Rahim	12.00
12	Antonio McDyess	3.00
13	Joe Smith	5.00
14	Brent Barry	3.00
15	Kobe Bryant	35.00

1996-97 Topps Chrome

Topps Chrome reprinted the 220 cards from Series I and II of Topps Basketball with chromium technology. The base cards carried the identical design of Topps cards, except for this chromium upgrade. Three inserts - Profiles, Youth Quake and Season's Best - were also reprinted, along with each base card also available in a Refractor version.

		MT
Complete Set (220):		800.00
Common Player:		.25
Minor Stars:		.50
Pack (4):		33.00
Wax Box (24):		900.00
1	Patrick Ewing	1.00
2	Christian Laettner	.50
3	Mahmoud Abdul-Rauf	.25
4	Chris Webber	2.00
5	Jason Kidd	2.00
6	Clifford Rozier	.25
7	Elden Campbell	.25
8	Chuck Person	.25
9	Jeff Hornacek	.25
10	Rik Smits	.25
11	Kurt Thomas	.25
12	Rod Strickland	.50
13	Kendall Gill	.25
14	Brian Williams	.25
15	Tom Gugliotta	.50
16	Ron Harper	.25
17	Eric Williams	.25
18	A.C. Green	.25
19	Scott Williams	.25
20	Damon Stoudamire	2.00
21	Bryant Reeves	.50
22	Bob Sura	.25
23	Mitch Richmond	.75
24	Larry Johnson	.50
25	Vin Baker	1.00
26	Mark Bryant	.25
27	Horace Grant	.25
28	Allan Houston	.50
29	Sam Perkins	.25
30	Antonio McDyess	1.00
31	Rasheed Wallace	.25
32	Malik Sealy	.25
33	Scottie Pippen	2.50
34	Charles Barkley	1.50
35	Hakeem Olajuwon	2.00
36	John Starks	.25
37	Byron Scott	.25
38	Arvydas Sabonis	.25
39	Vlade Divac	.25
40	Joe Dumars	.25
41	Danny Ferry	.25
42	Jerry Stackhouse	1.00
43	B.J. Armstrong	.25
44	Shawn Bradley	.25
45	Kevin Garnett	6.00
46	Dee Brown	.25
47	Michael Smith	.25
48	Doug Christie	.25
49	Mark Jackson	.25
50	Shawn Kemp	1.25
51	Predrag Danilovic	.25
52	Nick Anderson	.25
53	Matt Geiger	.25
54	Charles Smith	.25
55	Mookie Blaylock	.25
56	Johnny Newman	.25
57	George McCloud	.25
58	Greg Ostertag	.25
59	Reggie Williams	.25
60	Brent Barry	.50
61	Doug West	.25
62	Donald Royal	.25
63	Randy Brown	.25
64	Vincent Askew	.25
65	John Stockton	1.00
66	Joe Kleine	.25
67	Keith Askins	.25
68	Bobby Phills	.25
69	Chris Mullin	.50
70	Nick Van Exel	.75
71	Rick Fox	.25
72	Chicago Bulls Commemorative	7.00
73	Shawn Respert	.25
74	Hubert Davis	.25
75	Jim Jackson	.50
76	Olden Polynice	.25
77	Gheorghe Muresan	.25
78	Theo Ratliff	.25
79	Khalid Reeves	.25
80	David Robinson	1.50
81	Lawrence Moten	.25
82	Sam Cassell	.25
83	George Zidek	.25
84	Sharone Wright	.25
85	Clarence Weatherspoon	.25
86	Alan Henderson	.25
87	Chris Dudley	.25
88	Ed O'Bannon	.25
89	Calbert Cheaney	.25
90	Cedric Ceballos	.25
91	Michael Cage	.25
92	Ervin Johnson	.25
93	Gary Trent	.25
94	Sherman Douglas	.25
95	Joe Smith	1.25
96	Dale Davis	.25
97	Tony Dumas	.25
98	Muggsy Bogues	.25
99	Toni Kukoc	.50
100	Grant Hill	6.00
101	Michael Finley	.75
102	Isaiah Rider	.25
103	Bryant Stith	.25
104	Pooh Richardson	.25
105	Karl Malone	1.00
106	Brian Grant	.25
107	Sean Elliott	.25
108	Charles Oakley	.25
109	Pervis Ellison	.25
110	Anfernee Hardaway	5.00
111	Checklist	.25
112	Dikembe Mutombo	.50
113	Alonzo Mourning	.75
114	Hubert Davis	.25
115	Rony Seikaly	.25
116	Danny Manning	.25
117	Donyell Marshall	.25
118	Gerald Wilkins	.25
119	Ervin Johnson	.25
120	Jalen Rose	.25
121	Dino Radja	.25
122	Glenn Robinson	.75
123	John Stockton	1.00
124	*Matt Maloney*	5.00
125	Clifford Robinson	.25
126	Steve Kerr	.25
127	Nate McMillan	.25
128	*Shareef Abdur-Rahim*	60.00
129	Loy Vaught	.25
130	Anthony Mason	.25
131	Kevin Garnett	6.00
132	*Roy Rogers Jr.*	3.00
133	*Erick Dampier*	10.00
134	Tyus Edney	.25
135	Chris Mills	.25
136	Cory Alexander	.25
137	Juwan Howard	1.50
138	*Kobe Bryant*	450.00
139	Michael Jordan	40.00
140	Jayson Williams	.25
141	Rod Strickland	.50
142	*Lorenzen Wright*	10.00
143	Will Perdue	.25
144	Derek Harper	.25
145	Billy Owens	.25
146	*Antoine Walker*	60.00
147	P.J. Brown	.25
148	Terrell Brandon	.50
149	Larry Johnson	.50
150	Steve Smith	.25
151	Eddie Jones	2.00
152	Detlef Schrempf	.25
153	Dale Ellis	.25
154	Isaiah Rider	.25
155	*Tony Delk*	8.00
156	Adrian Caldwell	.25
157	Jamal Mashburn	.50
158	Dennis Scott	.25
159	Dana Barros	.25
160	*Martin Muursepp*	1.00
161	*Marcus Camby*	15.00
162	*Jerome Williams*	4.00
163	Wesley Person	.25
164	Luc Longley	.25
165	Charlie Ward	.25
166	Mark Jackson	.25
167	Derrick Coleman	.50
168	Dell Curry	.25
169	Armon Gilliam	.25
170	Vlade Divac	.25
171	*Allen Iverson*	200.00
172	*Vitaly Potapenko*	3.00
173	Jon Koncak	.25
174	Lindsey Hunter	.25
175	Kevin Johnson	.50
176	Dennis Rodman	3.00
177	*Stephon Marbury*	50.00
178	Karl Malone	1.00
179	Charles Barkley	1.50
180	Popeye Jones	.25
181	*Samaki Walker*	10.00
182	*Steve Nash*	12.00
183	Latrell Sprewell	1.00
184	Kenny Anderson	.25
185	Tyrone Hill	.25
186	Robert Pack	.25
187	Greg Anthony	.25
188	Derrick McKey	.25
189	*John Wallace*	15.00
190	Bryon Russell	.25
191	*Jermaine O'Neal*	40.00
192	Clyde Drexler	1.00
193	Mahmoud Abdul-Rauf	.25
194	Eric Montross	.25
195	Allan Houston	.25
196	Harvey Grant	.25
197	Rodney Rogers	.25
198	*Kerry Kittles*	8.00
199	Grant Hill	6.00
200	Lionel Simmons	.25
201	Reggie Miller	1.00
202	Avery Johnson	.25
203	LaPhonso Ellis	.25
204	Brian Shaw	.25
205	*Priest Lauderdale*	1.00
206	*Derek Fisher*	15.00
207	Terry Porter	.25
208	*Todd Fuller*	1.00
209	Hersey Hawkins	.25
210	Tim Legler	.25
211	Terry Dehere	.25
212	Gary Payton	1.25
213	Joe Dumars	.50
214	Don MacLean	.25
215	Greg Minor	.25
216	Tim Hardaway	.50
217	*Ray Allen*	60.00
218	Mario Elie	.25
219	Brooks Thompson	.25
220	Shaquille O'Neal	4.00

1996-97 Topps Chrome Refractors

All 220 cards in the Chrome Basketball set also arrived in a parallel Refractor set. Refractors were seeded every 12 packs.

		MT
Complete Set (220):		5600.
Common Player:		10.00
Minor Stars:		20.00
1	Patrick Ewing	30.00
2	Christian Laettner	20.00
3	Mahmoud Abdul-Rauf	10.00
4	Chris Webber	50.00
5	Jason Kidd	50.00
6	Clifford Rozier	10.00
7	Elden Campbell	10.00
8	Chuck Person	10.00
9	Jeff Hornacek	10.00
10	Rik Smits	20.00
11	Kurt Thomas	10.00
12	Rod Strickland	20.00
13	Kendall Gill	10.00
14	Brian Williams	10.00
15	Tom Gugliotta	25.00
16	Ron Harper	10.00
17	Eric Williams	10.00
18	A.C. Green	10.00
19	Scott Williams	10.00
20	Damon Stoudamire	50.00
21	Bryant Reeves	10.00
22	Bob Sura	10.00
23	Mitch Richmond	30.00
24	Larry Johnson	20.00
25	Vin Baker	40.00
26	Mark Bryant	10.00
27	Horace Grant	10.00
28	Allan Houston	20.00
29	Sam Perkins	10.00
30	Antonio McDyess	30.00
31	Rasheed Wallace	10.00
32	Malik Sealy	10.00
33	Scottie Pippen	80.00
34	Charles Barkley	40.00
35	Hakeem Olajuwon	50.00
36	John Starks	10.00
37	Byron Scott	10.00
38	Arvydas Sabonis	10.00
39	Vlade Divac	10.00
40	Joe Dumars	20.00
41	Danny Ferry	10.00
42	Jerry Stackhouse	30.00
43	B.J. Armstrong	10.00
44	Shawn Bradley	20.00
45	Kevin Garnett	120.00
46	Dee Brown	10.00
47	Michael Smith	10.00
48	Doug Christie	10.00
49	Mark Jackson	10.00
50	Shawn Kemp	40.00
51	Predrag Danilovic	10.00
52	Nick Anderson	10.00
53	Matt Geiger	10.00
54	Charles Smith	10.00
55	Mookie Blaylock	20.00
56	Johnny Newman	10.00
57	George McCloud	10.00
58	Greg Ostertag	10.00
59	Reggie Williams	10.00
60	Brent Barry	20.00
61	Doug West	10.00
62	Donald Royal	10.00
63	Randy Brown	10.00
64	Vincent Askew	10.00
65	John Stockton	30.00
66	Joe Kleine	10.00
67	Keith Askins	10.00
68	Bobby Phills	10.00
69	Chris Mullin	20.00
70	Nick Van Exel	25.00
71	Rick Fox	10.00
72	Chicago Bulls Commem.	160.00
73	Shawn Respert	10.00
74	Hubert Davis	10.00
75	Jim Jackson	20.00
76	Olden Polynice	10.00
77	Gheorghe Muresan	10.00
78	Theo Ratliff	20.00
79	Khalid Reeves	10.00
80	David Robinson	40.00
81	Lawrence Moten	10.00
82	Sam Cassell	10.00
83	George Zidek	10.00
84	Sharone Wright	10.00
85	Clarence Weatherspoon	10.00
86	Alan Henderson	20.00
87	Chris Dudley	10.00
88	Ed O'Bannon	10.00
89	Calbert Cheaney	10.00
90	Cedric Ceballos	10.00
91	Michael Cage	10.00
92	Ervin Johnson	10.00
93	Gary Trent	10.00
94	Sherman Douglas	10.00
95	Joe Smith	30.00
96	Dale Davis	10.00
97	Tony Dumas	10.00
98	Muggsy Bogues	10.00
99	Toni Kukoc	25.00
100	Grant Hill	80.00
101	Michael Finley	25.00
102	Isaiah Rider	10.00
103	Bryant Stith	10.00
104	Pooh Richardson	10.00
105	Karl Malone	30.00
106	Brian Grant	10.00
107	Sean Elliott	10.00
108	Charles Oakley	10.00
109	Pervis Ellison	10.00
110	Anfernee Hardaway	100.00
111	Checklist	10.00
112	Dikembe Mutombo	20.00
113	Alonzo Mourning	25.00
114	Hubert Davis	10.00
115	Rony Seikaly	10.00
116	Danny Manning	10.00
117	Donyell Marshall	10.00
118	Gerald Wilkins	10.00
119	Ervin Johnson	10.00
120	Jalen Rose	10.00
121	Dino Radja	10.00
122	Glenn Robinson	25.00
123	John Stockton	30.00
124	Matt Maloney	30.00
125	Clifford Robinson	10.00
126	Steve Kerr	10.00
127	Nate McMillan	10.00
128	Shareef Abdur-Rahim	175.00
129	Loy Vaught	10.00
130	Anthony Mason	10.00
131	Kevin Garnett	120.00
132	Roy Rogers Jr.	20.00
133	Erick Dampier	40.00
134	Tyus Edney	10.00
135	Chris Mills	10.00
136	Cory Alexander	10.00
137	Juwan Howard	40.00
138	Kobe Bryant	2000.
139	Michael Jordan	425.00
140	Jayson Williams	10.00
141	Rod Strickland	20.00
142	Lorenzen Wright	40.00
143	Will Perdue	10.00
144	Derek Harper	10.00
145	Billy Owens	10.00
146	Antoine Walker	130.00
147	P.J. Brown	10.00
148	Terrell Brandon	25.00
149	Larry Johnson	20.00
150	Steve Smith	10.00
151	Eddie Jones	60.00
152	Detlef Schrempf	10.00
153	Dale Ellis	10.00
154	Isaiah Rider	10.00
155	Tony Delk	25.00
156	Adrian Caldwell	10.00
157	Jamal Mashburn	20.00
158	Dennis Scott	10.00
159	Dana Barros	10.00
160	Martin Muursepp	10.00
161	Marcus Camby	100.00
162	Jerome Williams	10.00
163	Wesley Person	10.00
164	Luc Longley	10.00
165	Charlie Ward	20.00
166	Mark Jackson	10.00
167	Derrick Coleman	20.00
168	Dell Curry	10.00
169	Armon Gilliam	10.00
170	Vlade Divac	10.00
171	Allen Iverson	500.00
172	Vitaly Potapenko	20.00
173	Jon Koncak	10.00
174	Lindsey Hunter	10.00
175	Kevin Johnson	20.00
176	Dennis Rodman	100.00
177	Stephon Marbury	250.00
178	Karl Malone	30.00
179	Charles Barkley	30.00
180	Popeye Jones	10.00
181	Samaki Walker	30.00
182	Steve Nash	75.00
183	Latrell Sprewell	30.00
184	Kenny Anderson	20.00
185	Tyrone Hill	10.00
186	Robert Pack	10.00
187	Greg Anthony	10.00
188	Derrick McKey	10.00
189	John Wallace	50.00
190	Bryon Russell	10.00
191	Jermaine O'Neal	160.00
192	Clyde Drexler	30.00
193	Mahmoud Abdul-Rauf	10.00
194	Eric Montross	10.00
195	Allan Houston	20.00
196	Harvey Grant	10.00
197	Rodney Rogers	20.00
198	Kerry Kittles	90.00
199	Grant Hill	80.00
200	Lionel Simmons	10.00
201	Reggie Miller	25.00
202	Avery Johnson	10.00
203	LaPhonso Ellis	10.00
204	Brian Shaw	10.00
205	Priest Lauderdale	10.00
206	Derek Fisher	35.00
207	Terry Porter	10.00
208	Todd Fuller	10.00
209	Hersey Hawkins	10.00
210	Tim Legler	10.00
211	Terry Dehere	10.00
212	Gary Payton	40.00
213	Joe Dumars	20.00
214	Don MacLean	10.00
215	Greg Minor	10.00
216	Tim Hardaway	25.00
217	Ray Allen	150.00
218	Mario Elie	10.00
219	Brooks Thompson	10.00
220	Shaquille O'Neal	120.00

1996-97 Topps Chrome Pro Files

Pro Files reprinted the 20-card insert from Topps Basketball using chromium technology. These inserts were found every eight packs of Chrome. Cards are numbered with a "PF" prefix.

		MT
Complete Set (20):		70.00
Common Player:		1.00
1	Grant Hill	10.00
2	Shawn Kemp	3.00
3	Michael Jordan	20.00
4	Vin Baker	2.00
5	Chris Webber	3.00
6	Joe Smith	3.00
7	Shaquille O'Neal	8.00
8	Patrick Ewing	1.50
9	Scottie Pippen	5.00
10	Damon Stoudamire	4.00
11	Anfernee Hardaway	10.00
12	Juwan Howard	3.00
13	Dikembe Mutombo	1.00
14	Dennis Rodman	8.00
15	Kevin Garnett	8.00
16	Jerry Stackhouse	3.00
17	Alonzo Mourning	1.50
18	Karl Malone	1.50
19	Hakeem Olajuwon	4.00
20	Gary Payton	2.00

1996-97 Topps Chrome Season's Best

This 25-card insert set reprinted the Season's Best insert from Topps Basketball with chromium technology. The cards carried an "SB" prefix and were inserted every six packs.

		MT
Complete Set (25):		70.00
Common Player:		1.00
1	Michael Jordan	20.00
2	Hakeem Olajuwon	4.00
3	Shaquille O'Neal	8.00
4	Karl Malone	1.50
5	David Robinson	2.00
6	Dennis Rodman	8.00
7	David Robinson	2.00
8	Dikembe Mutombo	1.00
9	Charles Barkley	2.00
10	Shawn Kemp	3.00
11	John Stockton	1.50
12	Jason Kidd	2.00
13	Avery Johnson	1.00
14	Rod Strickland	1.00
15	Damon Stoudamire	4.00
16	Gary Payton	2.00
17	Mookie Blaylock	1.00
18	Michael Jordan	20.00
19	Jason Kidd	2.00
20	Alvin Robertson	1.00
21	Dikembe Mutombo	1.00
22	Shawn Bradley	1.00
23	David Robinson	2.00
24	Hakeem Olajuwon	4.00
25	Alonzo Mourning	1.50

1996-97 Topps Chrome Youthquake

This 15-card insert reprinted the Youthquake insert from Topps Basketball. The cards carried a "YQ" prefix and were inserted every 15 packs.

		MT
Complete Set (15):		150.00
Common Player:		2.00
Minor Stars:		4.00
1	Allen Iverson	25.00
2	Samaki Walker	4.00
3	Stephon Marbury	15.00
4	Damon Stoudamire	5.00
5	John Wallace	4.00
6	Michael Finley	4.00
7	Marcus Camby	6.00
8	Kerry Kittles	5.00
9	Ray Allen	10.00
10	Jerry Stackhouse	6.00
11	Shareef Abdur-Rahim	10.00
12	Antonio McDyess	4.00
13	Joe Smith	5.00
14	Brent Barry	4.00
15	Kobe Bryant	100.00

1996 Topps NBA Stars

In conjunction with the NBA's 50th anniversary, Topps secured the rights to produce this NBA Topps Stars set, a 150-card set featuring the NBA's 50 greatest players of all time. Each player is featured on three different cards - a Golden Season card, which highlights his best year, and two versions of a commemorative card. One version has an all text back; the other features complete career statistics which show why the player was selected to the team. The cards each feature a different photo on the front. Each of the 150 regular cards also has three parallel versions - Finest (one per six), Finest Refractor (one per 24 retail, one per 20 hobby) and Finest Atomic Refractor (one per 96). In addition, reprints of all 50 players' original Topps, Bowman or Star Co. basketball cards are included in every six hobby packs and every nine retail packs. The final insert set is called Imagine, which pits two players from a different era against each other. Also found in packs are High Five Favorites game cards, which allow collectors to use the ballot to vote on their all-time top five players. Those players receiving the most votes will be crowned Topps' High Five Favorites. Collectors who voted for all of those players will win special prizes.

		MT
Complete Set (150):		25.00
Common Player:		.10
Finest Cards:		6x-12x
Finest Refractors:		25x-50x
Atomic Refractors:		50x-100x

Wax Box:		60.00
1	Kareem Abdul-Jabbar	.75
2	Nate Archibald	.10
3	Paul Arizin	.10
4	Charles Barkley	.60
5	Rick Barry	.30
6	Elgin Baylor	.30
7	Dave Bing	.10
8	Larry Bird	1.25
9	Wilt Chamberlain	1.00
10	Bob Cousy	.30
11	Dave Cowens	.10
12	Billy Cunningham	.10
13	Dave DeBusschere	.10
14	Clyde Drexler	.40
15	Julius Erving	.75
16	Patrick Ewing	.30
17	Walt Frazier	.20
18	George Gervin	.10
19	Hal Greer	.10
20	John Havlicek	.20
21	Elvin Hayes	.20
22	Magic Johnson	1.25
23	Sam Jones	.10
24	Michael Jordan	4.00
25	Jerry Lucas	.10
26	Karl Malone	.40
27	Moses Malone	.10
28	Pete Maravich	.50
29	Kevin McHale	.20
30	George Mikan	.50
31	Earl Monroe	.20
32	Shaquille O'Neal	1.50
33	Hakeem Olajuwon	.75
34	Robert Parish	.10
35	Bob Pettit	.20
36	Scottie Pippen	.75
37	Willis Reed	.10
38	Oscar Robertson	.50
39	David Robinson	.50
40	Bill Russell	.75
41	Dolph Schayes	.10
42	Bill Sharman	.10
43	John Stockton	.40
44	Isiah Thomas	.50
45	Nate Thurmond	.10
46	Wes Unseld	.10
47	Bill Walton	.10
48	Jerry West	.50
49	Len Wilkens	.10
50	James Worthy	.10
51	Kareem Abdul-Jabbar	.75
52	Nate Archibald	.10
53	Paul Arizin	.10
54	Charles Barkley	.60
55	Rick Barry	.30
56	Elgin Baylor	.30
57	Dave Bing	.10
58	Larry Bird	1.25
59	Wilt Chamberlain	1.00
60	Bob Cousy	.30
61	Dave Cowens	.10
62	Billy Cunningham	.10
63	Dave DeBusschere	.10
64	Clyde Drexler	.40
65	Julius Erving	.75
66	Patrick Ewing	.30
67	Walt Frazier	.20
68	George Gervin	.10
69	Hal Greer	.10
70	John Havlicek	.20
71	Elvin Hayes	.20
72	Magic Johnson	1.25
73	Sam Jones	.10
74	Michael Jordan	4.00
75	Jerry Lucas	.10
76	Karl Malone	.40
77	Moses Malone	.10
78	Pete Maravich	.50
79	Kevin McHale	.20
80	George Mikan	.50
81	Earl Monroe	.20
82	Shaquille O'Neal	1.50
83	Hakeem Olajuwon	.75
84	Robert Parish	.10
85	Bob Pettit	.20
86	Scottie Pippen	.75
87	Willis Reed	.10
88	Oscar Robertson	.50
89	David Robinson	.50
90	Bill Russell	.75
91	Dolph Schayes	.10
92	Bill Sharman	.10
93	John Stockton	.40
94	Isiah Thomas	.50
95	Nate Thurmond	.10
96	Wes Unseld	.10
97	Bill Walton	.10
98	Jerry West	.50
99	Len Wilkens	.10
100	James Worthy	.10
101	Kareem Abdul-Jabbar	.75
102	Nate Archibald	.10
103	Paul Arizin	.10
104	Charles Barkley	.60
105	Rick Barry	.30
106	Elgin Baylor	.30
107	Dave Bing	.10
108	Larry Bird	1.25
109	Wilt Chamberlain	1.00
110	Bob Cousy	.30
111	Dave Cowens	.10
112	Billy Cunningham	.10
113	Dave DeBusschere	.10
114	Clyde Drexler	.40
115	Julius Erving	.75
116	Patrick Ewing	.30
117	Walt Frazier	.20
118	George Gervin	.10
119	Hal Greer	.10
120	John Havlicek	.20
121	Elvin Hayes	.20
122	Magic Johnson	1.25
123	Sam Jones	.10
124	Michael Jordan	4.00
125	Jerry Lucas	.10
126	Karl Malone	.40
127	Moses Malone	.10
128	Pete Maravich	.50
129	Kevin McHale	.20
130	George Mikan	.50
131	Earl Monroe	.20
132	Shaquille O'Neal	1.50
133	Hakeem Olajuwon	.75
134	Robert Parish	.10
135	Bob Pettit	.20
136	Scottie Pippen	.75
137	Willis Reed	.10
138	Oscar Robertson	.50
139	David Robinson	.50
140	Bill Russell	.75
141	Dolph Schayes	.10
142	Bill Sharman	.10
143	John Stockton	.40
144	Isiah Thomas	.50
145	Nate Thurmond	.10
146	Wes Unseld	.10
147	Bill Walton	.10
148	Jerry West	.50
149	Len Wilkens	.10
150	James Worthy	.10

1996 Topps NBA Stars Finest

Each card in the 1996 NBA Topps Stars set also arrived in a Finest version. Inserted every six packs, this set utilized Finest technology for the 150-card set.

	MT
Finest Cards:	6x-12x

1996 Topps NBA Stars Refractors

Each card in the 150-card 1996 NBA Topps Stars set was also available in a Refractor version. The word Refractor appeared on the back to identify it, and they were inserted every 20 hobby packs and 24 retail packs.

	MT
Refractors:	25x-50x

1996 Topps NBA Stars Atomic Refractors

Each card in the 1996 NBA Topps Stars set also arrived in a parallel Atomic Refractor version. This 150-card set was identified by a streaked, prismatic foil on the front.

	MT
Atomic Refractors:	50x-100x

1996 Topps NBA Stars Imagine

This 25-card insert set uses computer imagery to pit two players from different eras against each other. The glossy card front has "Imagine" written across the top inside some clouds. The players' last names are stamped in gold foil at the top. The NBA/Topps Stars logo is in the lower right corner. The card back is split into two halves, each with a brief player profile alongside a photo. "Battle of Wits" is written across the middle of the card. The card number, using an "I" prefix, is in the upper right corner. Cards were seeded one per every 18 packs.

		MT
Complete Set (25):		150.00
Common Player:		3.00
1	Shaquille O'Neal, Wilt Chamberlain	20.00
2	David Robinson, Dave Cowens	7.00
3	Bill Russell, Kareem Abdul-Jabbar	10.00
4	Scottie Pippen, Patrick Ewing	15.00
5	Hakeem Olajuwon, Elvin Hayes	7.00
6	Michael Jordan, Oscar Robertson	40.00
7	Clyde Drexler, Earl Monroe	6.00
8	Magic Johnson, Jerry West	12.00
9	Larry Bird, Rick Barry	12.00
10	Kevin McHale, Dave DeBusschere	3.00
11	Moses Malone, Jerry Lucas	3.00
12	Robert Parish, Nate Thurmond	3.00
13	Pete Maravich, Sam Jones	6.00
14	John Stockton, Bob Cousy	6.00
15	Isiah Thomas, Bill Sharman	6.00
16	Karl Malone, Bob Pettit	6.00
17	Bill Walton, George Mikan	6.00
18	Patrick Ewing, Willis Reed	6.00
19	Billy Cunningham, James Worthy	3.00
20	George Gervin, Hal Greer	3.00
21	Wes Unseld, Dolph Schayes	3.00
22	Nate Archibald, Len Wilkens	3.00
23	Walt Frazier, Paul Arizin	3.00
24	Charles Barkley, Elgin Baylor	7.00
25	Dave Bing, John Havlicek	6.00

1996 Topps NBA Stars Reprints

The 50 players who were selected for Topps' set honoring the NBA's greatest players of all time are featured on this reprint set. Each of the players has his original Topps, Bowman or Star Co. card reprinted for the glossy set. Each card is identical in format to the original, except it is labeled on the back as being a reprint (1 of 50, etc.). Cards were seeded one per every six hobby packs and one per every nine retail packs.

		MT
Complete Set (50):		300.00
Common Player:		2.00
1	Kareem Abdul-Jabbar	12.00
2	Nate Archibald	2.00
3	Paul Arizin	2.00
4	Charles Barkley	10.00
5	Rick Barry	5.00
6	Elgin Baylor	5.00
7	Dave Bing	2.00
8	Larry Bird	25.00
9	Wilt Chamberlain	12.00
10	Bob Cousy	8.00
11	Dave Cowens	2.00
12	Billy Cunningham	2.00
13	Dave DeBusschere	2.00
14	Clyde Drexler	7.00
15	Julius Erving	12.00
16	Patrick Ewing	8.00
17	Walt Frazier	2.00
18	George Gervin	2.00
19	Hal Greer	2.00
20	John Havlicek	8.00
21	Elvin Hayes	2.00
22	Magic Johnson	25.00
23	Sam Jones	2.00
24	Michael Jordan	60.00
25	Jerry Lucas	2.00
26	Karl Malone	5.00
27	Moses Malone	4.00
28	Pete Maravich	8.00
29	Kevin McHale	2.00
30	George Mikan	8.00
31	Earl Monroe	4.00
32	Shaquille O'Neal	12.00
33	Hakeem Olajuwon	12.00
34	Robert Parish	2.00
35	Bob Pettit	4.00
36	Scottie Pippen	12.00
37	Willis Reed	2.00
38	Oscar Robertson	8.00
39	David Robinson	8.00
40	Bill Russell	12.00
41	Dolph Schayes	2.00
42	Bill Sharman	2.00
43	John Stockton	5.00
44	Isiah Thomas	5.00
45	Nate Thurmond	2.00
46	Wes Unseld	2.00
47	Bill Walton	2.00
48	Jerry West	10.00
49	Len Wilkens	2.00
50	James Worthy	4.00

1996 Topps NBA Stars Reprint Autographs

This 10-card set was available at a rate of one per retail box in NBA Topps Stars and one per 1996-97 Topps factory hobby set. The set consists of 10 player's rookie reprint cards from NBA Topps Stars in autographed versions with a Topps certified stamp.

		MT
Complete Set (10):		200.00
Common Player:		10.00
2	Nate Archibald	20.00
5	Rick Barry	25.00
17	Walt Frazier	20.00
18	George Gervin	25.00
21	Elvin Hayes	20.00
23	Sam Jones	10.00
30	George Mikan	80.00
31	Earl Monroe	20.00
37	Willis Reed	20.00
47	Bill Walton	25.00

1997-98 Topps Promos

This six-card promotional set was sent out with Topps sales material to promote the 1997-98 set. It arrived in a clear cello pack with cards identical to the base set.

		MT
Complete Set (6):		3.00
Common Player:		.25
1	Scottie Pippen	1.00
18	Vin Baker	.75
54	Allen Iverson	1.50
56	Mitch Richmond	.50
58	LaPhonso Ellis	.25
89	Tom Gugliotta	.50

1997-98 Topps

Topps 1997-98 consisted of 220 cards, with 110 in each Series. Card fronts featured a color shot of the player surrounded by a white border on all sides. The featured player's image was glossy, with the rest of the background slightly dulled, with two color strips up the left side and one color strip across the bottom with the player's name in gold foil stamped in it. Inserts in Series I included: Minted in Springfield parallel cards, Autographs, Rock Stars, Fantastic 15, Topps 40, Rookie Redemption, Season's Best and Bound for Glory. Inserts in Series II included: Minted in Springfield, New School, Topps 40, Generations Finest, Inside Stuff, Destiny and Clutch Time.

		MT
Complete Set (220):		32.00
Complete Series 1 (110):		12.00
Complete Series 2 (110):		20.00
Common Player:		.05
Minor Stars:		.10
Minted in Springfield: 3x-6x		
Series 1 Pack (11):		1.25
Series 1 Wax Box (36):		35.00
Series 2 Pack (11):		1.50
Series 2 Wax Box (36):		40.00
1	Scottie Pippen	.75
2	Nate McMillan	.05
3	Byron Scott	.05
4	Mark Davis	.05
5	Rod Strickland	.05
6	Brian Grant	.05
7	Damon Stoudamire	.50
8	John Stockton	.20
9	Grant Long	.05
10	Darrell Armstrong	.05
11	Anthony Mason	.05
12	Travis Best	.05
13	Stephon Marbury	.75
14	Jamal Mashburn	.10
15	Detlef Schrempf	.05
16	Terrell Brandon	.10
17	Charles Barkley	.30
18	Vin Baker	.20
19	Gary Trent	.05
20	Vinny Del Negro	.05
21	Todd Day	.05
22	Malik Sealy	.05
23	Wesley Person	.05
24	Reggie Miller	.20
25	Dan Majerle	.05
26	Todd Fuller	.05
27	Juwan Howard	.30
28	Clarence Weatherspoon	.05
29	Grant Hill	1.50
30	John Williams	.05
31	Ken Norman	.05
32	Patrick Ewing	.20
33	Bryon Russell	.05
34	Tony Smith	.05
35	Andrew Lang	.05
36	Rony Seikaly	.05
37	Billy Owens	.05
38	Dino Radja	.05
39	Chris Gatling	.05
40	Dale Davis	.05
41	Arvydas Sabonis	.05
42	Chris Mills	.05
43	A.C. Green	.05
44	Tyrone Hill	.05
45	Tracy Murray	.05
46	David Robinson	.40
47	Lee Mayberry	.05
48	Jayson Williams	.05
49	Jason Kidd	.25
50	Bryant Stith	.05
51	Latrell Sprewell	.20
52	Brent Barry	.05
53	Henry James	.05
54	Allen Iverson	1.00
55	Shandon Anderson	.05
56	Mitch Richmond	.15
57	Allan Houston	.05
58	Ron Harper	.05
59	Gheorghe Muresan	.05
60	Vincent Askew	.05
61	Ray Allen	.25
62	Kenny Anderson	.10
63	Dikembe Mutombo	.10
64	Sam Perkins	.05
65	Walt Williams	.05
66	Chris Carr	.05
67	Vlade Divac	.05
68	LaPhonso Ellis	.05
69	B.J. Armstrong	.05
70	Jim Jackson	.10
71	Clyde Drexler	.20
72	Lindsey Hunter	.05
73	Sasha Danilovic	.05
74	Elden Campbell	.05
75	Robert Pack	.05
76	Dennis Scott	.05
77	Will Perdue	.05
78	Anthony Peeler	.05
79	Steve Smith	.05
80	Steve Kerr	.05
81	Buck Williams	.05
82	Terry Mills	.05
83	Michael Smith	.05
84	Adam Keefe	.05
85	Kevin Willis	.05
86	David Wesley	.05
87	Muggsy Bogues	.05
88	Bimbo Coles	.05
89	Tom Gugliotta	.05
90	Jermaine O'Neal	.20
91	Cedric Ceballos	.10
92	Shawn Kemp	.40
93	Horace Grant	.05
94	Shareef Abdur-Rahim	.60
95	Robert Horry	.05
96	Vitaly Potapenko	.05
97	Pooh Richardson	.05
98	Doug Christie	.05
99	Voshon Lenard	.05
100	Dominique Wilkins	.10
101	Alonzo Mourning	.15
102	Sam Cassell	.05
103	Sherman Douglas	.05
104	Shawn Bradley	.05
105	Mark Jackson	.05
106	Dennis Rodman	.75
107	Charles Oakley	.05
108	Matt Maloney	.15
109	Shaquille O'Neal	1.00
110	Checklist	.05
111	Antonio McDyess	.20
112	Bob Sura	.10
113	Terrell Brandon	.10
114	*Tim Thomas*	2.00
115	*Tim Duncan*	4.00
116	*Antonio Daniels*	2.00
117	Bryant Reeves	.05
118	*Keith Van Horn*	2.00
119	Loy Vaught	.05
120	Rasheed Wallace	.05
121	*Bobby Jackson*	1.50
122	Kevin Johnson	.10
123	Michael Jordan	3.00
124	*Ron Mercer*	2.00
125	*Tracy McGrady*	3.00
126	Antoine Walker	.75
127	Carlos Rogers	.05
128	Isaac Austin	.05
129	Mookie Blaylock	.05
130	*Rodrick Rhodes*	.50
131	Dennis Scott	.05
132	Chris Mullin	.10
133	P.J. Brown	.05
134	Rex Chapman	.05
135	Sean Elliott	.05
136	Alan Henderson	.05
137	*Austin Croshere*	.50
138	Nick Van Exel	.20
139	Derek Strong	.05
140	Glenn Robinson	.25
141	Avery Johnson	.05
142	Calbert Cheaney	.05
143	Mahmoud Abdul-Rauf	.05
144	Stojko Vrankovic	.05
145	Chris Childs	.05
146	Danny Manning	.05
147	Jeff Hornacek	.05
148	Kevin Garnett	1.50
149	Joe Dumars	.10
150	*Johnny Taylor*	.20
151	Mark Price	.05
152	Toni Kukoc	.10
153	Erick Dampier	.05
154	Lorenzen Wright	.05
155	Matt Geiger	.05
156	Tim Hardaway	.20
157	Charles Smith	.05
158	Hersey Hawkins	.05
159	Michael Finley	.20
160	Tyus Edney	.05
161	Christian Laettner	.10
162	Doug West	.05
163	Jim Jackson	.20
164	Larry Johnson	.20
165	Vin Baker	.30
166	Karl Malone	.00
167	*Kelvin Cato*	.50
168	Luc Longley	.05
169	Dale Davis	.05
170	Joe Smith	.20
171	Kobe Bryant	2.00
172	Scot Pollard	.05
173	*Derek Anderson*	1.50
174	Erick Strickland	.05
175	Olden Polynice	.05
176	Chris Whitney	.05
177	Anthony Parker	.05
178	Armon Gilliam	.05
179	Gary Payton	.30
180	Glen Rice	.25
181	*Chauncey Billups*	2.00
182	Derek Fisher	.05
183	John Starks	.05
184	Mario Elie	.05
185	Chris Webber	.40
186	Shawn Kemp	.40
187	Greg Ostertag	.05
188	*Olivier Saint-Jean*	.50
189	Eric Snow	.05
190	Isaiah Rider	.05
191	*Paul Grant*	.20
192	Samaki Walker	.05
193	Cory Alexander	.05
194	Eddie Jones	.40
195	John Thomas	.05
196	Otis Thorpe	.05
197	Rod Strickland	.05
198	David Wesley	.05
199	*Jacque Vaughn*	.20
200	Rik Smits	.05
201	*Brevin Knight*	1.50
202	Clifford Robinson	.05
203	Hakeem Olajuwon	.50
204	Jerry Stackhouse	.20
205	Tyrone Hill	.05
206	Kendall Gill	.05
207	Marcus Camby	.30
208	*Tony Battie*	1.50
209	Brent Price	.05
210	*Danny Fortson*	1.00
211	Jerome Williams	.05
212	*Maurice Taylor*	.75
213	Brian Williams	.05
214	Keith Booth	.05
215	Nick Anderson	.05
216	Travis Knight	.05
217	*Adonal Foyle*	.50
218	Anfernee Hardaway	1.25
219	Kerry Kittles	.25
220	Checklist	.05

1997-98 Topps Minted in Springfield

This 220-card parallel set was gold foil stamped at the Basketball Hall of Fame in Springfield, Mass., and inserted one per six packs. Minted in Springfield inserts were identical to the base cards, except for a gold foil Basketball Hall of Fame stamp in the lower left corner. Minted in Springfield parallel cards were inserted one per nine packs.

	MT
Minted Cards: 4x-8x	

1997-98 Topps O-Pee-Chee Parallel

	MT
Complete Set (220):	300.00
Complete Series 1 (110):	100.00
Complete Series 2 (110):	200.00
Common Player:	.50
O-Pee-Chee Cards:	5x-10x
O-Pee-Chee Rookies:	6x-12x

1997-98 Topps Autographs

Eight NBA superstars, including Hakeem Olajuwon, Glenn Robinson and Juwan Howard, signed cards for hobby packs of Topps Series I. These cards can be found every 212 hobby packs.

		MT
Complete Set (8):		300.00
Common Player:		15.00
1	John Starks	20.00
2	Juwan Howard	60.00
3	Mitch Richmond	30.00
4	Hakeem Olajuwon	100.00
5	Glenn Robinson	40.00
6	Steve Smith	15.00
7	Antoine Walker	20.00
8	Clyde Drexler	60.00

1997-98 Topps Bound for Glory

Bound for Glory featured 15 top stars on a holographic foil card and inserted one per [illegible] Series I hobby packs. The card numbers carried a "BG" prefix and displayed the insert name across the top with large pillars in the background.

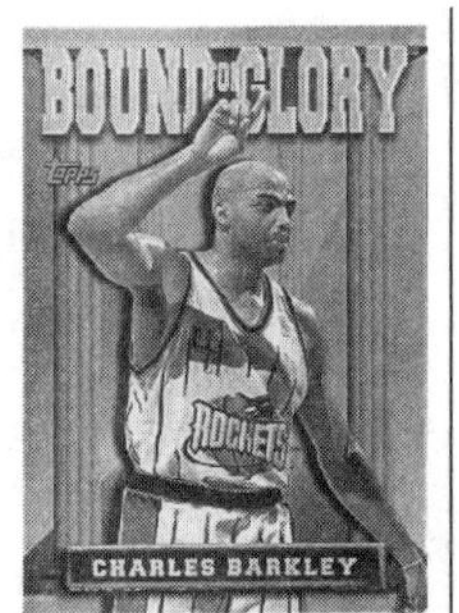

MT
Complete Set (15): 100.00
Common Player: 1.50
1 Robert Parish 1.50
2 Grant Hill 25.00
3 Chris Mullin 1.50
4 Hakeem Olajuwon 7.00
5 Dennis Rodman 15.00
6 Patrick Ewing 3.00
7 Karl Malone 3.00
8 Charles Barkley 5.00
9 David Robinson 5.00
10 Michael Jordan 40.00
11 Dominique Wilkins 1.50
12 Shaquille O'Neal 15.00
13 Clyde Drexler 4.00
14 John Stockton 3.00
15 Scottie Pippen 10.00

1997-98 Topps Clutch Time

This 20-card insert was exclusive to hobby packs and seeded at a rate of one per 36 packs. The cards have a silver dot pattern in the background and the words "Clutch Time" in gold dots across the top. The cards are numbered with a "CT" prefix.

MT
Complete Set (20): 130.00
Common Player: 2.00
Minor Stars: 4.00
1 Michael Jordan 40.00
2 Christian Laettner 2.00
3 Patrick Ewing 2.00
4 Glen Rice 4.00
5 Stephon Marbury 15.00
6 Tim Hardaway 4.00
7 Reggie Miller 4.00
8 Gary Payton 5.00
9 Charles Barkley 5.00
10 Grant Hill 20.00
11 Karl Malone 4.00
12 Dikembe Mutombo 2.00
13 Hakeem Olajuwon 8.00
14 Shawn Kemp 5.00
15 John Stockton 4.00
16 Anfernee Hardaway 15.00
17 Glenn Robinson 4.00
18 Chris Webber 8.00
19 Allen Iverson 20.00
20 Scottie Pippen 10.00

1997-98 Topps Destiny

Destiny was a 15-card insert set displaying some of the top players under the age 27. The insert name was printed in large silver foil embossed letters across the top and cards were numbered with a "D" prefix. Destiny inserts were found one per 18 retail packs of Series II.

MT
Complete Set (15): 75.00
Common Player: 2.00
1 Grant Hill 10.00
2 Kevin Garnett 10.00
3 Vin Baker 2.00
4 Antoine Walker 5.00
5 Kobe Bryant 14.00
6 Tracy McGrady 6.00
7 Keith Van Horn 6.00
8 Tim Duncan 12.00
9 Eddie Jones 3.00
10 Stephon Marbury 8.00
11 Marcus Camby 2.00
12 Antonio McDyess 2.00
13 Shareef Abdur-Rahim 6.00
14 Allen Iverson 8.00
15 Shaquille O'Neal 6.00

1997-98 Topps Draft Redemption

Topps gave collectors the chance to score the first Topps cards of the 1997 NBA Draft Picks with the inclusion of 29 Rookie Redemption cards. Every redemption card has a number corresponding to each draft position of the first round, and could be exchanged for a special card of that player taken in that draft position once he signed his NBA contract. They were seeded every 12 hobby and 18 retail packs.

MT
Complete Set (29): 275.00
Common Player: 3.00
1 Tim Duncan 100.00
2 Keith Van Horn 20.00
3 Chauncey Billups 10.00
4 Antonio Daniels 10.00
5 Tony Battie 10.00
6 Ron Mercer 15.00
7 Tim Thomas 20.00
8 Adonal Foyle 4.00
9 Tracy McGrady 200.00
10 Danny Fortson 8.00
11 Tariq Abdul-Wahad 4.00
12 Austin Croshere 15.00
13 Derek Anderson 15.00
14 Maurice Taylor 8.00
15 Kelvin Cato 5.00
16 Brevin Knight 5.00
17 Johnny Taylor 3.00
18 Chris Anstey 3.00
19 Scot Pollard 3.00
20 Paul Grant 3.00
21 Anthony Parker 3.00
22 Ed Gray 3.00
23 Bobby Jackson 5.00
24 Rodrick Rhodes 5.00
25 John Thomas 3.00
26 Charles Smith 3.00
27 Jacque Vaughn 5.00
28 Keith Booth 3.00
29 Serge Zwikker 3.00

1997-98 Topps Fantastic 15

This insert was seeded every 36 Series I retail packs and contains an "F" prefix on the card number. The insert name is printed in large letters across the top, with multi-colored holographic foil in the background.

MT
Complete Set (15): 100.00
Common Player: 2.00
1 Antoine Walker 8.00
2 Damon Stoudamire 5.00
3 Brent Barry 2.00
4 Michael Finley 2.00
5 Ray Allen 3.00
6 Allen Iverson 20.00
7 Stephon Marbury 15.00
8 Kerry Kittles 4.00
9 John Wallace 2.00
10 Kevin Garnett 20.00
11 Jerry Stackhouse 4.00
12 Kobe Bryant 25.00
13 Marcus Camby 8.00
14 Joe Smith 4.00
15 Shareef Abdur-Rahim 10.00

1997-98 Topps Generations

Generations features 30 players from three categories of draft years - 1983-1987, 1988-1992 and 1993-1997. Inserts were printed on die-cut, borderless Finest stock and insert one per 36 packs, with Refractor versions every 144 packs. Generations inserts were numbered with a "G" prefix and only inserted into Series II packs.

MT
Complete Set (30): 250.00
Common Player: 2.00
Refractors: 2x-4x
1 Clyde Drexler 4.00
2 Michael Jordan 50.00
3 Charles Barkley 5.00
4 Hakeem Olajuwon 10.00
5 John Stockton 4.00
6 Patrick Ewing 2.00
7 Karl Malone 5.00
8 Dennis Rodman 15.00
9 Scottie Pippen 12.00
10 David Robinson 5.00
11 Mitch Richmond 2.00
12 Glen Rice 2.00
13 Shawn Kemp 6.00
14 Gary Payton 4.00
15 Dikembe Mutombo 2.00
16 Steve Smith 2.00
17 Christian Laettner 2.00
18 Shaquille O'Neal 15.00
19 Alonzo Mourning 2.00
20 Tom Gugliotta 2.00
21 Anfernee Hardaway 15.00
22 Grant Hill 25.00
23 Kevin Garnett 25.00
24 Kobe Bryant 30.00
25 Stephon Marbury 20.00
26 Antoine Walker 10.00
27 Shareef Abdur-Rahim 15.00
28 Tim Duncan 25.00
29 Keith Van Horn 15.00
30 Tracy McGrady 15.00

1997-98 Topps Inside Stuff

This 10-card insert was found in one per 36 packs of Topps Series II and numbered with a "IS" prefix. The cards were printed on silver foilboard and highlighted the NBC show Inside Stuff.

MT
Complete Set (10): 60.00
Common Player: 1.50
1 Michael Jordan 25.00
2 Eddie Johnson 1.50
3 John Stockton 3.00
4 Patrick Ewing 1.50
5 Shaquille O'Neal 10.00
6 Rex Chapman 1.50
7 Shawn Kemp 3.00
8 Scottie Pippen 6.00
9 Kobe Bryant 15.00
10 Anfernee Hardaway 10.00

1997-98 Topps New School

This 15-card insert set was seeded one per 36 Series II hobby and retail packs. It featured 1997 NBA Draft picks and included a sparkling background with the insert name printed in a pennant. Card backs were numbered with a "NS" prefix.

A card number in parentheses ( ) indicates the set is unnumbered.

MT
Complete Set (15): 85.00
Common Player: 1.50
1 Austin Croshere 3.00
2 Antonio Daniels 10.00
3 Tim Thomas 10.00
4 Keith Van Horn 10.00
5 Bobby Jackson 6.00
6 Derek Anderson 10.00
7 Adonal Foyle 3.00
8 Johnny Taylor 1.50
9 Jacque Vaughn 3.00
10 Chauncey Billups 10.00
11 Brevin Knight 10.00
12 Tracy McGrady 10.00
13 Tony Battie 8.00
14 Scot Pollard 1.50
15 Tim Duncan 25.00

1997-98 Topps Rock Stars

This 20-card, die-cut and borderless insert featured 20 stars and was inserted every 36 Series I packs. The cards utilize Finest technology and are die-cut around rocks across the top of the card. The card numbers carry an "RS" prefix. There are also Refractor versions of Rock Stars inserts available.

MT
Complete Set (20): 160.00
Common Player: 2.00
Refractors: 3x
1 Michael Jordan 50.00
2 Jerry Stackhouse 4.00
3 Chris Webber 6.00
4 Charles Barkley 4.00
5 Dennis Rodman 12.00
6 Anfernee Hardaway 12.00
7 Juwan Howard 4.00
8 Tim Hardaway 2.00
9 Gary Payton 4.00
10 Dikembe Mutombo 2.00
11 Tom Gugliotta 4.00
12 Kevin Garnett 25.00
13 Shaquille O'Neal 12.00
14 Hakeem Olajuwon 8.00
15 Grant Hill 25.00
16 Karl Malone 4.00
17 Damon Stoudamire 6.00
18 Shawn Kemp 5.00
19 Alonzo Mourning 2.00
20 Scottie Pippen 10.00

1997-98 Topps Rock Stars Refractors

This insert ran parallel to the Finest Rock Stars set, but was printed using Finest technology. These parallel versions were seeded one per 144 Series I packs.

MT
Refractors: 3x

1997-98 Topps Season's Best

Season's Best is a 30-card insert that showcases 25 stars who dominated statistical categories, and five rookies. These cards were printed on borderless prismatic foilboard and inserted one per 16 Series I packs. There are six different subsets, including Key Masters, Power Core, Shooting Stars, Frontcourt Finesse, Pressure Points and Hot Shots.

MT
Complete Set (30): 100.00
Common Player: 1.50
Minor Stars: 3.00
1 Gary Payton 4.00
2 Kevin Johnson 1.50
3 Tim Hardaway 1.50
4 John Stockton 4.00
5 Damon Stoudamire 5.00
6 Michael Jordan 30.00
7 Mitch Richmond 4.00
8 Latrell Sprewell 4.00
9 Reggie Miller 4.00
10 Clyde Drexler 4.00
11 Grant Hill 20.00
12 Scottie Pippen 8.00
13 Kendall Gill 1.50
14 Glen Rice 3.00
15 LaPhonso Ellis 1.50
16 Karl Malone 4.00
17 Charles Barkley 5.00
18 Vin Baker 4.00
19 Chris Webber 5.00
20 Tom Gugliotta 1.50
21 Shaquille O'Neal 12.00
22 Patrick Ewing 4.00
23 Hakeem Olajuwon 6.00
24 Alonzo Mourning 3.00
25 Dikembe Mutombo 1.50
26 Allen Iverson 15.00
27 Antoine Walker 5.00
28 Shareef Abdur-Rahim 8.00
29 Stephon Marbury 12.00
30 Kerry Kittles 4.00

1997-98 Topps 40

This insert includes selections from NBA players, writers and coaches to come up with the top 40 players in the NBA. Series I has 20 cards, with the other 20 found in Series II, both with insertion rates of one per 12 packs and numbered "T40-x". The cards are printed on reflective, foil-stamped mirrorboard cards, with a large number 40 across the bottom.

MT
Complete Set (20): 35.00
Common Player: .50
Minor Stars: 1.00
1 Glen Rice 1.00
2 Patrick Ewing 1.50
3 Terrell Brandon .50
4 Jerry Stackhouse 2.00
5 Michael Jordan 15.00
6 Christian Laettner 1.00
7 Latrell Sprewell 1.50
8 Reggie Miller 1.50
9 Gary Payton 1.50
10 Detlef Schrempf .50
11 Kevin Garnett 8.00
12 Eddie Jones 2.50
13 Clyde Drexler 1.50
14 Anfernee Hardaway 8.00
15 Chris Webber 2.50
16 Jayson Williams .50
17 Joe Smith 2.00
18 Karl Malone 1.50
19 Tim Hardaway .50
20 Vin Baker 1.00
21 Tom Gugliotta 1.00
22 Allen Iverson 8.00
23 David Robinson 2.00
24 Dikembe Mutombo .50
25 John Stockton 1.00
26 Charles Barkley 2.00
27 Mitch Richmond 1.00
28 Damon Stoudamire 2.00
29 Anthony Mason .50
30 Shaquille O'Neal 6.00
31 Glenn Robinson 1.00
32 Juwan Howard 2.00
33 Shawn Kemp 2.00
34 Dennis Rodman 6.00
35 Grant Hill 8.00
36 Kevin Johnson .50
37 Alonzo Mourning 1.00
38 Hakeem Olajuwon 3.00
39 Joe Dumars .50
40 Scottie Pippen 4.00

1997-98 Topps Chrome

Chrome included all 220 cards from Topps Series I and II and added a chromium finish to each card. The cards identical to regular-issue Topps cards, except for the Topps Chrome logo in the upper left corner and the finish. Each card was also available in a Refractor version, while three inserts from Topps - Season's Best, Top 40 and Destiny - were also available in Refractor versions. This season's Chrome product followed up the extremely popular retail-only product of 1996-97, but was available in both retail and hobby locations.

MT
Complete Set (220): 225.00
Common Player: .25
Minor Stars: .50
Pack (4): 6.00
Wax Box (24): 140.00
1 Scottie Pippen 2.00
2 Nate McMillan .25
3 Byron Scott .25
4 Mark Davis .25
5 Rod Strickland .50
6 Brian Grant .25
7 Damon Stoudamire 1.50
8 John Stockton .75
9 Grant Long .25
10 Darrell Armstrong .25
11 Anthony Mason .25
12 Travis Best .25
13 Stephon Marbury 4.00
14 Jamal Mashburn .25
15 Detlef Schrempf .25
16 Terrell Brandon .50
17 Charles Barkley 1.00
18 Vin Baker 1.50
19 Gary Trent .25
20 Vinny Del Negro .25
21 Todd Day .25
22 Malik Sealy .25
23 Wesley Person .25
24 Reggie Miller .75
25 Dan Majerle .25
26 Todd Fuller .25
27 Juwan Howard .75
28 Clarence Weatherspoon .25
29 Grant Hill 5.00
30 John Williams .25
31 Ken Norman .25
32 Patrick Ewing .50
33 Bryon Russell .25
34 Tony Smith .25
35 Andrew Lang .25
36 Rony Seikaly .25
37 Billy Owens .25
38 Dino Radja .25
39 Chris Gatling .25
40 Dale Davis .25
41 Arvydas Sabonis .25
42 Chris Mills .25
43 A.C. Green .25
44 Tyrone Hill .25
45 Tracy Murray .25
46 David Robinson 1.00
47 Lee Mayberry .25
48 Jayson Williams .25
49 Jason Kidd 1.50
50 Bryant Stith .25
51 Bulls 4.00
52 Brent Barry .25
53 Henry James .25
54 Allen Iverson 4.00
55 Shandon Anderson .25
56 Mitch Richmond .75
57 Allan Houston .50
58 Ron Harper .25
59 Gheorghe Muresan .25
60 Vincent Askew .25
61 Ray Allen 1.25
62 Kenny Anderson .50
63 Dikembe Mutombo .50
64 Sam Perkins .25
65 Walt Williams .25
66 Chris Carr .25
67 Vlade Divac .25
68 LaPhonso Ellis .25
69 B.J. Armstrong .25
70 Jim Jackson .50
71 Clyde Drexler .75
72 Lindsey Hunter .25
73 Sasha Danilovic .25
74 Elden Campbell .25
75 Robert Pack .25
76 Dennis Scott .25
77 Will Perdue .25
78 Anthony Peeler .25
79 Steve Smith .25
80 Steve Kerr .25
81 Buck Williams .25
82 Terry Mills .25
83 Michael Smith .25
84 Adam Keefe .25
85 Kevin Willis .25
86 David Wesley .25
87 Muggsy Bogues .25
88 Bimbo Coles .25
89 Tom Gugliotta .50
90 Jermaine O'Neal .50
91 Cedric Ceballos .25
92 Shawn Kemp 1.00

93	Horace Grant	.25
94	Shareef Abdur-Rahim	2.50
95	Robert Horry	.25
96	Vitaly Potapenko	.25
97	Pooh Richardson	.25
98	Doug Christie	.25
99	Voshon Lenard	.25
100	Dominique Wilkins	.25
101	Alonzo Mourning	.50
102	Sam Cassell	.25
103	Sherman Douglas	.25
104	Shawn Bradley	.25
105	Mark Jackson	.25
106	Dennis Rodman	2.50
107	Charles Oakley	.25
108	Matt Maloney	.50
109	Shaquille O'Neal	3.00
110	Checklist	.25
111	Antonio McDyess	.50
112	Bob Sura	.25
113	Terrell Brandon	.50
114	*Tim Thomas*	10.00
115	*Tim Duncan*	70.00
116	*Antonio Daniels*	4.00
117	Bryant Reeves	.25
118	*Keith Van Horn*	12.00
119	Loy Vaught	.25
120	Rasheed Wallace	.25
121	*Bobby Jackson*	4.00
122	Kevin Johnson	.50
123	Michael Jordan	15.00
124	*Ron Mercer*	8.00
125	*Tracy McGrady*	75.00
126	Antoine Walker	1.50
127	Carlos Rogers	.25
128	Isaac Austin	.25
129	Mookie Blaylock	.25
130	*Rodrick Rhodes*	2.00
131	Dennis Scott	.25
132	Chris Mullin	.50
133	P.J. Brown	.25
134	Rex Chapman	.25
135	Sean Elliott	.25
136	Alan Henderson	.25
137	*Austin Croshere*	6.00
138	Nick Van Exel	.50
139	Derek Strong	.25
140	Glenn Robinson	.75
141	Avery Johnson	.25
142	Calbert Cheaney	.25
143	Mahmoud Abdul-Rauf	.25
144	Stojko Vrankovic	.25
145	Chris Childs	.25
146	Danny Manning	.25
147	Jeff Hornacek	.25
148	Kevin Garnett	6.00
149	Joe Dumars	.25
150	*Johnny Taylor*	2.00
151	Mark Price	.25
152	Toni Kukoc	.50
153	Erick Dampier	.25
154	Lorenzen Wright	.25
155	Matt Geiger	.25
156	Tim Hardaway	.50
157	Charles Smith	.25
158	Hersey Hawkins	.25
159	Michael Finley	.50
160	Tyus Edney	.25
161	Christian Laettner	.50
162	Doug West	.25
163	Jim Jackson	.50
164	Larry Johnson	.50
165	Vin Baker	1.50
166	Karl Malone	.75
167	*Kelvin Cato*	3.00
168	Luc Longley	.25
169	Dale Davis	.25
170	Joe Smith	.50
171	Kobe Bryant	15.00
172	Scot Pollard	.25
173	*Derek Anderson*	8.00
174	Erick Strickland	.25
175	Olden Polynice	.25
176	Chris Whitney	.25
177	*Anthony Parker*	2.00
178	Armon Gilliam	.25
179	Gary Payton	1.00
180	Glen Rice	.75
181	*Chauncey Billups*	3.00
182	Derek Fisher	.50
183	John Starks	.25
184	Mario Elie	.25
185	Chris Webber	1.25
186	Shawn Kemp	1.00
187	Greg Ostertag	.25
188	*Olivier Saint-Jean*	3.00
189	Eric Snow	.25
190	Isaiah Rider	.50
191	*Paul Grant*	2.00
192	Samaki Walker	.25
193	Cory Alexander	.25
194	Eddie Jones	1.25
195	John Thomas	.25
196	Otis Thorpe	.25
197	Rod Strickland	.50
198	David Wesley	.25
199	*Jacque Vaughn*	3.00
200	Rik Smits	.25
201	*Brevin Knight*	3.00
202	Clifford Robinson	.25
203	Hakeem Olajuwon	1.50
204	Jerry Stackhouse	.50
205	Tyrone Hill	.25
206	Kendall Gill	.25
207	Marcus Camby	1.00
208	*Tony Battie*	3.00
209	Brent Price	.25
210	*Danny Fortson*	3.00
211	Jerome Williams	.25
212	*Maurice Taylor*	6.00
213	Brian Williams	.25
214	Keith Booth	.25
215	Nick Anderson	.25
216	Travis Knight	.25
217	*Adonal Foyle*	2.00
218	Anfernee Hardaway	2.50
219	Kerry Kittles	1.00
220	Checklist	.25

1997-98 Topps Chrome Refractors

Refractors of all 220 cards in Topps Chrome were available in these parallel versions. The cards contained the word "Refractor" on the back and were inserted one per 12 packs.

	MT
Refractor Stars:	7x-14x
Refractor Rookies:	2x-4x

1997-98 Topps Chrome Destiny

Destiny featured 15 players under the age of 27 and were seeded one per 12 packs with a Refractor version every 48 packs. This insert was identical to the regular Topps version, except added the chromium finish to each card. Cards are numbered with a "D" prefix.

		MT
Complete Set (15):		120.00
Common Player:		1.50
Refractors:		3x
1	Grant Hill	15.00
2	Kevin Garnett	15.00
3	Vin Baker	4.00
4	Antoine Walker	6.00
5	Kobe Bryant	20.00
6	Tracy McGrady	10.00
7	Keith Van Horn	8.00
8	Tim Duncan	25.00
9	Eddie Jones	4.00
10	Stephon Marbury	12.00
11	Marcus Camby	1.50
12	Antonio McDyess	1.50
13	Shareef Abdur-Rahim	8.00
14	Allen Iverson	12.00
15	Shaquille O'Neal	10.00

1997-98 Topps Chrome Season's Best

All 30 Season's Best inserts from Topps were reprinted with a chromium finish and inserted into packs of Chrome. The Chrome logo appeared in either top corner, with the cards seeded one per eight packs and Refractor versions seeded every 24 packs. Cards are numbered with a "SB" prefix.

		MT
Complete Set (29):		100.00
Common Player:		1.00
Minor Stars:		2.00
Refractors:		3x
1	Gary Payton	3.00
2	Kevin Johnson	1.00
3	Tim Hardaway	2.00
4	John Stockton	2.00
5	Damon Stoudamire	3.00
6	Michael Jordan	25.00
7	Mitch Richmond	2.00
9	Reggie Miller	2.00
10	Clyde Drexler	2.00
11	Grant Hill	12.00
12	Scottie Pippen	6.00
13	Kendall Gill	1.00
14	Glen Rice	2.00
15	LaPhonso Ellis	1.00
16	Karl Malone	2.00
17	Charles Barkley	3.00
18	Vin Baker	4.00
19	Chris Webber	5.00
20	Tom Gugliotta	1.00
21	Shaquille O'Neal	8.00
22	Patrick Ewing	2.00
23	Hakeem Olajuwon	5.00
24	Alonzo Mourning	2.00
25	Dikembe Mutombo	1.00
26	Allen Iverson	10.00
27	Antoine Walker	5.00
28	Shareef Abdur-Rahim	6.00
29	Stephon Marbury	10.00
30	Kerry Kittles	2.00

1997-98 Topps Chrome Topps 40

The same 40 cards that were inserted into Topps Series I and II packs were reprinted with a chromium finish and inserted into Chrome. The logo could be found in either upper corner and regular versions and were seeded every six packs, and with Refractor versions every 18 packs. Cards are numbered with a "T40" prefix.

		MT
Complete Set (39):		110.00
Common Player:		.75
Minor Stars:		1.50
Refractors:		3x
1	Glen Rice	1.50
2	Patrick Ewing	1.50
3	Terrell Brandon	.75
4	Jerry Stackhouse	1.50
5	Michael Jordan	25.00
6	Christian Laettner	.75
8	Reggie Miller	1.50
9	Gary Payton	3.00
10	Detlef Schrempf	.75
11	Kevin Garnett	12.00
12	Eddie Jones	4.00
13	Clyde Drexler	2.00
14	Anfernee Hardaway	8.00
15	Chris Webber	4.00
16	Jayson Williams	.75
17	Joe Smith	1.50
18	Karl Malone	2.00
19	Tim Hardaway	1.50
20	Vin Baker	3.00
21	Tom Gugliotta	.75
22	Allen Iverson	10.00
23	David Robinson	3.00
24	Dikembe Mutombo	.75
25	John Stockton	1.50
26	Charles Barkley	3.00
27	Mitch Richmond	1.50
28	Damon Stoudamire	3.00
29	Anthony Mason	.75
30	Shaquille O'Neal	8.00
31	Glenn Robinson	1.50
32	Juwan Howard	2.00
33	Shawn Kemp	3.00
34	Dennis Rodman	8.00
35	Grant Hill	12.00
36	Kevin Johnson	.75
37	Alonzo Mourning	1.50
38	Hakeem Olajuwon	5.00
39	Joe Dumars	.75
40	Scottie Pippen	6.00

1998 Topps Golden Greats

Golden Greats included 18 of the greatest NBA players of all-time. The set utilized a combination of Kodamotion technology with Topps Super-Color color enhancement process to provide a finished product that allowed collectors to view three to four seconds of real game footage. Special laser-cut versions of each card were also randomly inserted one per 36 packs. Topps produced a very small quantity of Golden Greats due to limited orders. Each pack contained one card and carried a suggested retail price of $9.99.

		MT
Complete Set (18):		160.00
Common Player:		7.00
Wax Box:		130.00
1	Kareem Abdul-Jabbar	12.00
2	Elgin Baylor	7.00
3	Larry Bird	16.00
4	Wilt Chamberlain	16.00
5	Bob Cousy	10.00
6	Julius Erving	14.00
7	Walt Frazier	7.00
8	George Gervin	7.00
9	John Havlicek	10.00
10	Magic Johnson	16.00
11	Kevin McHale	7.00
12	Earl Monroe	7.00
13	Willis Reed	7.00
14	Oscar Robertson	12.00
15	Bill Russell	16.00
16	Bill Walton	10.00
17	Jerry West	14.00
18	Rick Barry	7.00

1998 Topps Golden Greats Laser Cuts

	MT
Laser Cut Cards:	2x-4x
Inserted 1:36	

1998 Topps Milk Mustache

This 8" x 10-1/2" perforated sheet features eight Topps cards and one information card from the National Fluid Milk Processor Promotion Board. The fronts of the cards feature a close-up player photo with a milk mustache added to the shot. The back of each card has a Basketball Tip and a Milk Tip.

		MT
Complete Set (9):		5.00
Common Player:		.25
1	Reggie Miller	.75
2	Jayson Williams	.25
3	Tim Hardaway	1.00
4	Brevin Knight	1.00
5	Eddie Jones	2.00
6	Kevin Johnson	.50
7	Glenn Robinson	.50
8	Dikembe Mutombo	.50
NNO	Milk ad	.50

1998-99 Topps Promos

This six-card set was distributed to dealers and members of the media to promote the 1998-99 Topps Basketball set. Cards were identical to the base cards, but were distributed in a plastic sealed wrap with sales material.

		MT
Complete Set (6):		3.00
Common Player:		.25
2	Shareef Abdur-Rahim	1.00
13	Chris Webber	1.00
39	Antoine Walker	.75
40	Patrick Ewing	.25
82	Vin Baker	.50
103	Eddie Jones	.50

1998-99 Topps

This 220-card set was released in two, 110-card series. Base cards featured the player with a gold border around the entire photo which included the team logo and player's name. Inserts in Series I include: Emmissaries, Roundball Royalty, Cornerstones, Autographs, Rookie Redemptions, Apparitions and Season's Best. Inserts in Series II include: Autographs, Kick Start, Gold Label, East/West, Legacies, Classic Collection, Topps Chrome and Coast to Coast.

		MT
Complete Set (220):		35.00
Complete Series 1 (110):		10.00
Complete Series 2 (110):		25.00
Common Player:		.10
Minor Stars:		.20
Pack (11):		1.35
Wax Box (36):		45.00
1	Scottie Pippen	.75
2	Shareef Abdur-Rahim	.75
3	Rod Strickland	.20
4	Keith Van Horn	1.00
5	Ray Allen	.30
6	Chris Mullin	.20
7	Anthony Parker	.10
8	Lindsey Hunter	.10
9	Mario Elie	.10
10	Jerry Stackhouse	.20
11	Eldridge Recasner	.10
12	Jeff Hornacek	.10
13	Chris Webber	.40
14	Lee Mayberry	.10
15	Erick Strickland	.10
16	Arvydas Sabonis	.10
17	Tim Thomas	.75
18	Luc Longley	.10
19	Detlef Schrempf	.10
20	Alonzo Mourning	.20
21	Adonal Foyle	.20
22	Tony Battie	.20
23	Robert Horry	.10
24	Derek Harper	.10
25	Jamal Mashburn	.10
26	Elliott Perry	.10
27	Jalen Rose	.10
28	Joe Smith	.20
29	Henry James	.10
30	Travis Knight	.10
31	Tom Gugliotta	.20
32	Chris Anstey	.20
33	Antonio Daniels	.20
34	Elden Campbell	.10
35	Charlie Ward	.10
36	Eddie Johnson	.10
37	John Wallace	.10
38	Antonio Davis	.10
39	Antoine Walker	.75
40	Patrick Ewing	.20
41	Doug Christie	.10
42	Andrew Lang	.10
43	Joe Dumars	.10
44	Jaren Jackson	.10
45	Loy Vaught	.10
46	Allan Houston	.20
47	Mark Jackson	.10
48	Tracy Murray	.10
49	Tim Duncan	2.00
50	Micheal Williams	.10
51	Steve Nash	.20
52	Matt Maloney	.20
53	Sam Cassell	.10
54	Voshon Lenard	.10
55	Dikembe Mutombo	.20
56	Malik Sealy	.10
57	Dell Curry	.10
58	Stephon Marbury	1.25
59	Tariq Abdul-Wahad	.20
60	Isaiah Rider	.10
61	Kelvin Cato	.20
62	LaPhonso Ellis	.10
63	Jim Jackson	.20
64	Greg Ostertag	.10
65	Glenn Robinson	.20
66	Chris Carr	.10
67	Marcus Camby	.20
68	Kobe Bryant	1.75
69	Bobby Jackson	.20
70	B.J. Armstrong	.10
71	Alan Henderson	.10
72	Terry Davis	.10
73	John Stockton	.20
74	Lamond Murray	.10
75	Mark Price	.10
76	Rex Chapman	.10
77	Michael Jordan	3.00
78	Terry Cummings	.10
79	Dan Majerle	.10
80	Charles Outlaw	.10
81	Michael Finley	.20
82	Vin Baker	.30
83	Clifford Robinson	.10
84	Greg Anthony	.10
85	Brevin Knight	.30
86	Jacque Vaughn	.20
87	Bobby Phills	.10
88	Sherman Douglas	.10
89	Kevin Johnson	.10
90	Mahmoud Abdul-Rauf	.10
91	Lorenzen Wright	.10
92	Eric Williams	.10
93	Will Perdue	.10
94	Charles Barkley	.30
95	Kendall Gill	.10
96	Wesley Person	.10
97	Buck Williams	.10
98	Erick Dampier	.10
99	Nate McMillan	.10
100	Sean Elliott	.10
101	Rasheed Wallace	.10
102	Zydrunas Ilgauskas	.20
103	Eddie Jones	.40
104	Ron Mercer	1.00
105	Horace Grant	.10
106	Corliss Williamson	.10
107	Anthony Mason	.10
108	Mookie Blaylock	.10
109	Dennis Rodman	1.00
110	Checklist	.10
111	Steve Smith	.20
112	Cedric Henderson	.10
113	*Raef Lafrentz*	1.00
114	Calbert Cheaney	.10
115	Rik Smits	.10
116	Rony Seikaly	.10
117	Lawrence Funderburke	.10
118	*Ricky Davis*	.75
119	Howard Eisley	.10
120	Kenny Anderson	.20
121	*Corey Benjamin*	.50
122	Maurice Taylor	.30
123	Eric Murdock	.10
124	Derek Fisher	.20
125	Kevin Garnett	1.50
126	Walt Williams	.10
127	*Bryce Drew*	.75
128	A.C. Green	.10
129	Ervin Johnson	.10
130	Christian Laettner	.10
131	Chauncey Billups	.10
132	Hakeem Olajuwon	.40
133	*Al Harrington*	1.00
134	Danny Manning	.10
135	*Paul Pierce*	1.50
136	Terrell Brandon	.20
137	Bob Sura	.10
138	Chris Gatling	.10
139	Donyell Marshall	.10
140	Marcus Camby	.20
141	*Brian Skinner*	.50
142	Charles Oakley	.10
143	*Antawn Jamison*	2.00
144	*Nazr Mohammed*	.50
145	Karl Malone	.30
146	Chris Mills	.10
147	Bison Dele	.10
148	Gary Payton	.30
149	Terry Porter	.10
150	Tim Hardaway	20
151	*Larry Hughes*	2.00
152	Derek Anderson	.20
153	*Jason Williams*	1.50
154	*Dirk Nowitzki*	2.00
155	Juwan Howard	.20
156	Avery Johnson	.10
157	*Matt Harpring*	.75
158	Reggie Miller	.20
159	Walter McCarty	.10
160	Allen Iverson	1.00
161	*Felipe Lopez*	.50
162	Tracy McGrady	.75
163	Damon Stoudamire	.20
164	Antonio McDyess	.20
165	Grant Hill	1.50
166	*Tyrron Lue*	.30
167	P.J. Brown	.10
168	Antonio Daniels	.10
169	Mitch Richmond	.20
170	David Robinson	.40
171	Shawn Bradley	.10
172	Shandon Anderson	.10
173	Chris Childs	.10
174	Shawn Kemp	.30
175	Shaquille O'Neal	1.00
176	John Starks	.10
177	Tyrone Hill	.10
178	Jayson Williams	.10
179	Anfernee Hardaway	1.00
180	Chris Webber	.50
181	Don Reid	.10
182	Stacey Augmon	.10
183	Hersey Hawkins	.10
184	Sam Mitchell	.10
185	Jason Kidd	.50
186	Nick Van Exel	.20
187	Larry Johnson	.20
188	Bryant Reeves	.10
189	Glen Rice	.20
190	Kerry Kittles	.20
191	Toni Kukoc	.10
192	Ron Harper	.10
193	Bryon Russell	.10
194	*Vladimir Stepania*	.30
195	*Michael Olowokandi*	.75
196	*Mike Bibby*	1.00
197	Dale Ellis	.10
198	Muggsy Bogues	.10
199	*Vince Carter*	10.00
200	*Robert Traylor*	.50
201	*Predrag Stojakovic*	1.00
202	Aaron McKie	.10
203	Hubert Davis	.10
204	Dana Barros	.10
205	*Bonzi Wells*	1.00
206	*Michael Doleac*	.75
207	*Keon Clark*	.75
208	*Michael Dickerson*	.75
209	Nick Anderson	.10
210	Brent Price	.10
211	Cherokee Parks	.10
212	*Sam Jacobson*	.50
213	*Pat Garrity*	.50
214	Tyrone Corbin	.10
215	David Wesley	.10
216	Rodney Rogers	.10
217	Dean Garrett	.10
218	*Roshown McLeod*	.50
219	Dale Davis	.10
220	Checklist 111-220	.10

1998-99 Topps O-Pee-Chee Parallel

	MT
Complete Set (220):	250.00
Complete Series 1 (110):	125.00
Complete Series 2 (110):	125.00
Common Player:	.50
O-Pee-Chee Cards:	5x-10x
O-Pee-Chee Rookies:	6x-12x

1998-99 Topps Apparitions

This 15-card insert set captured top NBA players on silver etched foil, with the insert name in large letters across the top. Cards are numbered with an "A" prefix and inserted one per 36 retail packs in Series I.

		MT
Complete Set (15):		120.00
Common Player:		1.50
Inserted 1:36 Series 1 Retail		
1	Kobe Bryant	25.00
2	Stephon Marbury	12.00
3	Brent Barry	1.50
4	Karl Malone	4.00
5	Shaquille O'Neal	10.00
6	Chris Webber	5.00
7	Shawn Kemp	4.00
8	Hakeem Olajuwon	5.00
9	Anfernee Hardaway	10.00
10	Michael Finley	1.50
11	Keith Van Horn	8.00
12	Kevin Garnett	15.00
13	Vin Baker	4.00
14	Tim Duncan	15.00
15	Michael Jordan	40.00

1998-99 Topps Autographs

This 16-card hobby exclusive insert features 18 cards each autographed and featuring the Topps "Certified Autograph Issue" stamp. Cards were numbered with an "AG" prefix, with cards 1-8 inserted 1:329 Series I packs and cards 9-18 inserted 1:378 packs of Series II.

		MT
Complete Set (18):		1150.
Complete Series 1 (8):		500.00
Complete Series 2 (10):		650.00
Common Player:		25.00
Inserted 1:329 Series 1 Hobby		
Inserted 1:378 Series 2 Hobby		
1	Joe Smith	25.00
2	Kobe Bryant	175.00
3	Stephon Marbury	80.00
4	Dikembe Mutombo	25.00
5	Shareef Abdur-Rahim	60.00
6	Eddie Jones	75.00
7	Keith Van Horn	25.00
8	Glen Rice	35.00
9	Kobe Bryant	200.00
10	Ron Mercer	60.00
11	Glen Rice	25.00
12	Stephon Marbury	60.00
13	Kerry Kittles	25.00
14	Michael Olowokandi	50.00
15	Antawn Jamison	60.00
16	Mike Bibby	80.00
17	Robert Traylor	40.00
18	Paul Pierce	125.00

1998-99 Topps Chrome Preview

This 10-card insert was found in Series II packs and previewed the upcoming release of Topps Chrome. Regular versions were seeded 1:36 packs, while Refractors were exclusive to Hobby Collector Packs at a rate of 1:40.

		MT
Complete Set (10):		75.00
Common Player:		3.00
Inserted 1:36 Series 2		
Refractor Cards:		2x-5x
Inserted 1:40 Series 2 HCP		
6	Chris Mullin	6.00
10	Jerry Stackhouse	6.00
19	Detlef Schrempf	3.00
40	Patrick Ewing	6.00
43	Joe Dumars	6.00
60	Isaiah Rider	6.00
73	John Stockton	6.00
77	Michael Jordan	50.00
81	Michael Finley	8.00
100	Sean Elliot	3.00

1998-99 Topps Chrome Preview Refractors

		MT
Complete Set (10):		300.00
Common Player:		15.00
Inserted 1:40 Series 2 HCP		
6	Chris Mullin	25.00
10	Jerry Stackhouse	25.00
19	Detlef Schrempf	15.00
40	Patrick Ewing	25.00
43	Joe Dumars	25.00
60	Isaiah Rider	25.00
73	John Stockton	25.00
77	Michael Jordan	250.00
81	Michael Finley	30.00
100	Sean Elliot	15.00

1998-99 Topps Classic Collection

This Series II insert contained 10 legends of the NBA. Cards featured the player in a framed image as well as an action shot on the front. Classic Collection cards were inserted 1:12 packs of Series II and are numbered with a "CL" prefix.

		MT
Complete Set (10):		15.00
Common Player:		.50
Minor Stars:		1.00
Inserted 1:12 Series 2		
1	Larry Bird	5.00
2	Magic Johnson	5.00
3	Kareem Abdul-Jabbar	3.00
4	Julius Erving	2.00
5	Bill Russell	3.00
6	Wilt Chamberlain	3.00
7	Oscar Robertson	1.00
8	Jerry West	1.00
9	Elgin Baylor	.50
10	Bob Cousy	.50

1998-99 Topps Coast to Coast

This 15-card insert featured 15 top players on a a silver, brushed foil front. Coast to Coast cards were inserted 1:36 Series II packs and are numbered with a "CC" prefix.

		MT
Complete Set (15):		125.00
Common Player:		1.50
Minor Stars:		3.00
Inserted 1:36 Series 1 Retail		
1	Kobe Bryant	20.00
2	Scottie Pippen	8.00
3	Eddie Jones	5.00
4	Grant Hill	15.00
5	Michael Jordan	40.00
6	Antoine Walker	6.00
7	Michael Finley	3.00
8	Kevin Garnett	15.00
9	Allen Iverson	12.00
10	Shawn Kemp	3.00
11	Glenn Robinson	3.00
12	Anfernee Hardaway	10.00
13	Tim Hardaway	3.00
14	Ron Mercer	12.00
15	Kerry Kittles	1.50

1998-99 Topps Cornerstones

This 15-card set highlights the young players NBA teams build their futures around. Players with five years or less experience in the league are used. The cards are inserted at 1:36 Series I packs and are numbered with a "C" prefix.

		MT
Complete Set (15):		100.00
Common Player:		1.50
Inserted 1:36 Series 1 Hobby		
1	Keith Van Horn	6.00
2	Kevin Garnett	15.00
3	Shareef Abdur-Rahim	8.00
4	Antoine Walker	6.00
5	Allen Iverson	12.00
6	Grant Hill	15.00
7	Marcus Camby	1.50
8	Stephon Marbury	12.00
9	Kobe Bryant	20.00
10	Bobby Jackson	1.50
11	Kerry Kittles	1.50
12	Ron Mercer	10.00
13	Eddie Jones	4.00
14	Tim Thomas	8.00
15	Tim Duncan	20.00

1998-99 Topps Draft Redemption

This 29-card insert was seeded one per 18 Series I packs. Cards featured the words "1998 NBA Draft Redemption" in large white letters, with a Draft Pick 1-29 included. The cards could be redeemed for the corresponding draft choice before the deadline of 6/1/99.

		MT
Complete Set (29):		500.00
Common Player:		5.00
Minor Stars:		8.00
Inserted 1:18 Series 1		
Cards 17 and 18 Do Not Exist		
1	Michael Olowokandi	10.00
2	Mike Bibby	25.00
3	Raef LaFrentz	15.00
4	Antawn Jamison	50.00
5	Vince Carter	250.00
6	Robert Traylor	8.00
7	Jason Williams	40.00
8	Larry Hughes	40.00
9	Dirk Nowitzki	50.00
10	Paul Pierce	30.00
11	Bonzi Wells	40.00
12	Michael Doleac	5.00
13	Keon Clark	8.00
14	Michael Dickerson	15.00
15	Matt Harpring	8.00
16	Bryce Drew	5.00
19	Pat Garrity	8.00
20	Roshown McLeod	5.00
21	Ricky Davis	15.00
22	Brian Skinner	5.00
23	Tyrron Lue	5.00
24	Felipe Lopez	8.00
25	Al Harrington	30.00
26	Sam Jacobson	5.00
27	Vladimir Stepania	5.00
28	Corey Benjamin	5.00
29	Nazr Mohammed	5.00

1998-99 Topps East/West

This 20-card, double-sided insert matched up two players - one from the Eastern Conference and one from the West - on a Finest card. Players were pictured in front of a brushed globe with the words "East" or "West" running up the side of that respective player's background. Regular versions were seeded 1:36 Series II packs, with Refractor versions seeded 1:144 packs. East/West inserts were numbered with an "EW" prefix.

		MT
Complete Set (20):		120.00
Common Player:		1.50
Minor Stars:		3.00
Inserted 1:36 Series 2		
Refractor Cards:		2x
Inserted 1:144 Series 2		
1	Antoine Walker, Shareef Abdur-Rahim	6.00
2	Alonzo Mourning, Shaquille O'Neal	10.00
3	Tim Hardaway, John Stockton	3.00
4	Scottie Pippen, Kevin Garnett	15.00
5	Michael Jordan, Kobe Bryant	35.00
6	Grant Hill, Michael Finley	12.00
7	Dikembe Mutombo, Hakeem Olajuwon	1.50
8	Keith Van Horn, Tim Duncan	10.00
9	Allen Iverson, Gary Payton	10.00
10	Patrick Ewing, David Robinson	3.00
11	Juwan Howard, Chris Webber	3.00
12	Brevin Knight, Stephon Marbury	8.00
13	Shawn Kemp, Vin Baker	3.00
14	Anthony Mason, Tom Gugliotta	1.50
15	Anfernee Hardaway, Damon Stoudamire	10.00
16	Ron Mercer, Eddie Jones	10.00
17	Rod Strickland, Jason Kidd	5.00
18	Tim Thomas, Antonio McDyess	6.00
19	Jayson Williams, Karl Malone	3.00
20	Reggie Miller, Jim Jackson	1.50

1998-99 Topps East/West Refractor

		MT
Complete Set (20):		250.00
Refractor Cards:		2x
Inserted 1:144 Series 2		

1998-99 Topps Emissaries

The Emissaries set features players who have represented their country in some form. The 20-card set has a gold map in the background on the front, with a color image of a player in the foreground. The backs contain text on their international experience. Cards are inserted at 1:24 Series I packs and numbered with an "E" prefix.

		MT
Complete Set (20):		90.00
Common Player:		1.50
Minor Stars:		3.00
Inserted 1:24 Series 1		
1	Scottie Pippen	10.00
2	Karl Malone	4.00
3	Chris Webber	6.00
4	Anfernee Hardaway	15.00
5	Detlef Schrempf	1.50
6	Mitch Richmond	3.00
7	Vlade Divac	1.50
8	Shaquille O'Neal	15.00
9	Luc Longley	1.50
10	Grant Hill	20.00
11	Christian Laettner	1.50
12	Gary Payton	4.00
13	Patrick Ewing	3.00
14	Shawn Kemp	5.00
15	Toni Kukoc	1.50
16	David Robinson	5.00
17	Hakeem Olajuwon	7.00
18	Charles Barkley	5.00
19	John Stockton	3.00
20	Arvydas Sabonis	1.50

1998-99 Topps Gold Label

This 10-card insert borrowed Topps' Gold Label brand and used it as an insert in Series II basketball. Regular versions were seeded 1:12 packs, while Black Label versions were seeded 1:96 packs and Red Label versions were numbered to 100 and inserted 1:4,967 packs. Gold Label inserts were numbered with a "GL" prefix.

		MT
Complete Set (10):		45.00
Common Player:		1.00
Inserted 1:12 Series 2		
Black Label Cards:		2x-3x
Inserted 1:96 Series 2		
Red Label Cards:		8x-16x
Production 100 Series 2 Sets		
1	Michael Jordan	15.00
2	Shaquille O'Neal	5.00
3	Kobe Bryant	10.00
4	Antoine Walker	3.00
5	Charles Barkley	1.00
6	Keith Van Horn	5.00
7	Tim Duncan	8.00
8	Stephon Marbury	5.00
9	Shareef Abdur-Rahim	3.00
10	Gary Payton	1.00

1998-99 Topps Gold Label Black Label

		MT
Complete Set (10):		100.00
Black Label Cards:		2x-3x
Inserted 1:96 Series 2		

1998-99 Topps Gold Label Red Label

		MT
Complete Set (10):		600.00
Red Label Cards:		8x-16x
Production 100 Series 2 Sets		

1998-99 Topps Kick Start

Kick Start was a 15-card insert that focused on young players, and pictured them over a silver holographic background. Cards were numbered with a "KS" prefix and inserted 1:12 packs.

		MT
Complete Set (15):		50.00
Common Player:		1.00
Minor Stars:		2.00
Inserted 1:12 Series 2		
1	Tim Duncan	6.00
2	Kobe Bryant	8.00
3	Antoine Walker	2.00
4	Stephon Marbury	4.00
5	Allen Iverson	4.00
6	Shareef Abdur-Rahim	3.00
7	Keith Van Horn	3.00
8	Ray Allen	2.00
9	Vince Carter	6.00
10	Kevin Garnett	6.00
11	Kerry Kittles	1.00
12	Tim Thomas	3.00
13	Ron Mercer	4.00
14	Antawn Jamison	4.00
15	Mike Bibby	5.00

1998-99 Topps Legacies

Legacies was a 15-card, hobby-only insert that was seeded 1:36 packs. Cards were numbered with an "L" prefix and featured the player over a silver holographic background that included a basketball and net.

		MT
Complete Set (15):		70.00
Common Player:		1.50
Minor Stars:		3.00
Inserted 1:36 Series 2		
1	Scottie Pippen	8.00
2	Grant Hill	15.00
3	Hakeem Olajuwon	4.00
4	Alonzo Mourning	3.00
5	Shaquille O'Neal	10.00
6	Shawn Kemp	3.00
7	Gary Payton	4.00
8	Karl Malone	3.00
9	Patrick Ewing	3.00
10	Tim Hardaway	3.00
11	Reggie Miller	3.00
12	Glen Rice	3.00
13	Dikembe Mutombo	1.50
14	John Stockton	3.00
15	Michael Jordan	30.00

1998-99 Topps Roundball Royalty

The 20-card set highlights 20 of the best players in the NBA. The fronts have a gray diamond background, with the player in between the words "Roundball Royalty". The back has a picture frame around another player image, with text at the bottom. The cards are inserted at 1:36 Series I packs and numbered with an "R" prefix. Refractor versions were seeded 1:144 packs.

		MT
Complete Set (20):		150.00
Common Player:		2.00
Inserted 1:36 Series 1		
Refractors:		2x
Inserted 1:144 Series 1		
1	Michael Jordan	40.00
2	Kevin Garnett	20.00
3	David Robinson	5.00
4	Allen Iverson	12.00
5	Hakeem Olajuwon	7.00
6	Anfernee Hardaway	12.00
7	Gary Payton	4.00
8	Scottie Pippen	10.00
9	Shaquille O'Neal	12.00
10	Mitch Richmond	3.00
11	John Stockton	3.00
12	Grant Hill	20.00
13	Charles Barkley	5.00
14	Dikembe Mutombo	2.00
15	Karl Malone	4.00
16	Shawn Kemp	5.00
17	Patrick Ewing	3.00
18	Kobe Bryant	25.00
19	Terrell Brandon	2.00
20	Vin Baker	4.00

1998-99 Topps Season's Best

This 30-card set included the 25 best players by position, and five of the top rookies. Six themes range in the set, from Postmen to Navigators. The cards have the theme in writing along the top, with last season's numbers on the back. Insertion rate is 1:12 Series I packs and numbered with an "SB" prefix.

		MT
Complete Set (30):		75.00
Common Player:		1.00
Minor Stars:		2.00
Inserted 1:12 Series 1		
1	Rod Strickland	2.00
2	Gary Payton	3.00
3	Tim Hardaway	2.00
4	Stephon Marbury	8.00
5	Sam Cassell	1.00
6	Michael Jordan	20.00
7	Mitch Richmond	2.00
8	Steve Smith	1.00
9	Ray Allen	2.00
10	Isaiah Rider	1.00
11	Grant Hill	10.00
12	Kevin Garnett	10.00
13	Shareef Abdur-Rahim	5.00
14	Glenn Robinson	2.00
15	Michael Finley	2.00
16	Karl Malone	3.00
17	Tim Duncan	15.00
18	Antoine Walker	4.00
19	Chris Webber	3.00
20	Vin Baker	3.00
21	Shaquille O'Neal	6.00
22	David Robinson	3.00
23	Alonzo Mourning	2.00
24	Dikembe Mutombo	1.00
25	Hakeem Olajuwon	4.00
26	Tim Duncan	15.00
27	Keith Van Horn	5.00
28	Zydrunas Ilgauskas	2.00
29	Brevin Knight	3.00
30	Bobby Jackson	2.00

1998-99 Topps Chrome

This 220-card set paralleled the regular-issue Topps Series I and II set, but added a chromium finish and a "Topps Chrome" logo to each card. Although the cards are numbered up to 235, there are only 220 cards in the set. The reason for this is that the 10

cards in a Chrome Preview insert included in Topps II are not in this set, and five players (#75 Mark Price, #89 Kevin Johnson, #90 Mahmoud Abdul-Rauf, #97 Buck Williams and #99 Nate McMillan) were not currently in the NBA and were not printed in Topps Chrome. In addition to a parallel Refractor set (1:12 packs), there are six different inserts in Topps Chrome.

		MT
Complete Set (220):		300.00
Common Player:		.25
Minor Stars:		.50
The following cards do not exist: 75/89/90/97/99		
The following cards are in Preview: 6/10/19/40/43/60/73/77/81/100		
Pack (4):		10.00
Wax Box (24):		225.00
1	Scottie Pippen	3.00
2	Shareef Abdur-Rahim	3.00
3	Rod Strickland	.50
4	Keith Van Horn	3.00
5	Ray Allen	.75
7	Anthony Parker	.25
8	Lindsey Hunter	.25
9	Mario Elie	.25
11	Eldridge Recasner	.25
12	Jeff Hornacek	.25
13	Chris Webber	3.00
14	Lee Mayberry	.25
15	Erick Strickland	.25
16	Arvydas Sabonis	.50
17	Tim Thomas	3.00
18	Luc Longley	.25
20	Alonzo Mourning	.75
21	Adonal Foyle	.25
22	Tony Battie	.50
23	Robert Horry	.25
24	Derek Harper	.25
25	Jamal Mashburn	.50
26	Elliot Perry	.25
27	Jalen Rose	.50
28	Joe Smith	.50
29	Henry James	.25
30	Travis Knight	.25
31	Tom Gugliotta	.50
32	Chris Anstey	.25
33	Antonio Daniels	.50
34	Elden Campbell	.25
35	Charlie Ward	.25
36	Eddie Johnson	.25
37	John Wallace	.25
38	Antonio Davis	.25
39	Antoine Walker	3.00
41	Doug Christie	.25
42	Andrew Lang	.25
44	Jaren Jackson	.25
45	Loy Vaught	.25
46	Allan Houston	.50
47	Mark Jackson	.25
48	Tracy Murray	.25
49	Tim Duncan	7.00
50	Micheal Williams	.25
51	Steve Nash	.50
52	Matt Maloney	.25
53	Sam Cassell	.25
54	Voshon Lenard	.25
55	Dikembe Mutombo	.50
56	Malik Sealy	.25
57	Dell Curry	.25
58	Stephon Marbury	5.00
59	Tariq Abdul-Wahad	.25
61	Kelvin Cato	.25
62	LaPhonso Ellis	.50
63	Jim Jackson	.25
64	Greg Ostertag	.25
65	Glenn Robinson	.50
66	Chris Carr	.25
67	Marcus Camby	.75
68	Kobe Bryant	10.00
69	Bobby Jackson	.25
70	B.J. Armstrong	.25
71	Alan Henderson	.25
72	Terry Davis	.25
74	Lamond Murray	.25
76	Rex Chapman	.25
78	Terry Cummings	.25
79	Dan Majerle	.25
80	Charles Outlaw	.25
82	Vin Baker	.25
83	Clifford Robinson	.25
84	Greg Anthony	.25
85	Brevin Knight	.50
86	Jacque Vaughn	.25
87	Bobby Phills	.25
88	Sherman Douglas	.25
91	Lorenzen Wright	.25
92	Eric Williams	.25
93	Will Perdue	.25
94	Charles Barkley	1.00
95	Kendall Gill	.25
96	Wesley Person	.25
98	Erick Dampier	.25
101	Rasheed Wallace	.50
102	Zydrunas Ilgauskas	.25
103	Eddie Jones	1.00
104	Ron Mercer	3.00
105	Horace Grant	.25
106	Corliss Williamson	.25
107	Anthony Mason	.25
108	Mookie Blaylock	.25
109	Dennis Rodman	3.00
110	Checklist	.25
111	Steve Smith	.50
112	Cedric Henderson	.25
113	*Raef LaFrentz*	5.00
114	Calbert Cheaney	.25
115	Rik Smits	.25
116	Rony Seikaly	.25
117	Lawrence Funderburke	.25
118	*Ricky Davis*	4.00
119	Howard Eisley	.25
120	Kenny Anderson	.50
121	*Corey Benjamin*	2.00
122	Maurice Taylor	.75
123	Eric Murdock	.25
124	Derek Fisher	.50
125	Kevin Garnett	7.00
126	Walt Williams	.25
127	*Bryce Drew*	2.00
128	A.C. Green	.25
129	Ervin Johnson	.25
130	Christian Laettner	.50
131	Chauncey Billups	.75
132	Hakeem Olajuwon	2.00
133	*Al Harrington*	8.00
134	Danny Manning	.25
135	*Paul Pierce*	12.00
136	Terrell Brandon	.50
137	Bob Sura	.25
138	Chris Gatling	.25
139	Donyell Marshall	.25
140	Marcus Camby	.75
141	*Brian Skinner*	2.00
142	Charles Oakley	.25
143	*Antawn Jamison*	20.00
144	*Nazr Mohammed*	2.00
145	Karl Malone	2.00
146	Chris Mills	.25
147	Bison Dele	.25
148	Gary Payton	2.00
149	Terry Porter	.25
150	Tim Hardaway	1.00
151	*Larry Hughes*	15.00
152	Derek Anderson	.50
153	*Jason Williams*	12.00
154	*Dirk Nowitzki*	20.00
155	Juwan Howard	.50
156	Avery Johnson	.25
157	*Matt Harpring*	3.00
158	Reggie Miller	.50
159	Walter McCarty	.25
160	Allen Iverson	5.00
161	*Felipe Lopez*	3.00
162	Tracy McGrady	3.00
163	Damon Stoudamire	1.00
164	Antonio McDyess	1.00
165	Grant Hill	7.00
166	*Tyronn Lue*	2.00
167	P.J. Brown	.25
168	Antonio Daniels	.50
169	Mitch Richmond	.50
170	David Robinson	2.00
171	Shawn Bradley	.25
172	Shandon Anderson	.25
173	Chris Childs	.25
174	Shawn Kemp	1.50
175	Shaquille O'Neal	5.00
176	John Starks	.25
177	Tyrone Hill	.25
178	Jayson Williams	.50
179	Anfernee Hardaway	5.00
180	Chris Webber	3.00
181	Don Reid	.25
182	Stacey Augmon	.25
183	Hersey Hawkins	.25
184	Sam Mitchell	.25
185	Jason Kidd	3.00
186	Nick Van Exel	.50
187	Larry Johnson	.50
188	Bryant Reeves	.25
189	Glen Rice	.50
190	Kerry Kittles	.50
191	Toni Kukoc	.50
192	Ron Harper	.25
193	Bryon Russell	.25
194	*Vladimir Stepania*	2.00
195	*Michael Olowokandi*	4.00
196	*Mike Bibby*	8.00
197	Dale Ellis	.25
198	Muggsy Bogues	.25
199	*Vince Carter*	100.00
200	*Robert Traylor*	3.00
201	*Predrag Stojakovic*	10.00
202	Aaron McKie	.25
203	Hubert Davis	.25
204	Dana Barros	.25
205	*Bonzi Wells*	12.00
206	*Michael Doleac*	3.00
207	*Keon Clark*	3.00
208	*Michael Dickerson*	6.00
209	Nick Anderson	.50
210	Brent Price	.25
211	Cherokee Parks	.25
212	*Sam Jacobson*	2.00
213	*Pat Garrity*	3.00
214	Tyrone Corbin	.25
215	David Wesley	.25
216	Rodney Rogers	.25
217	Dean Garrett	.25
218	*Roshown McLeod*	2.00
219	Dale Davis	.25
220	Checklist	.25
221	Scottie Pippen (Movin' On)	1.00
222	Antonio McDyess (Movin' On)	.50
223	Stephon Marbury (Movin' On)	2.00
224	Tom Gugliotta (Movin' On)	.25
225	Chris Webber (Movin' On)	1.00
226	Latrell Sprewell (Movin' On)	.25
227	Mitch Richmond (Movin' On)	.25
228	Joe Smith (Movin' On)	.50
229	John Starks (Movin' On)	.25
230	Charles Oakley (Movin' On)	.25
231	Dennis Rodman (Movin' On)	1.00
232	Eddie Jones (Movin' On)	.50
233	Nick Van Exel (Movin' On)	.25
234	Bobby Jackson (Movin' On)	.25
235	Glen Rice (Movin' On)	.25

1998-99 Topps Chrome Refractors

This 220-card parallel set reprinted every card from Topps Chrome in a Refractor version. These were seeded 1:12 packs and included the word "Refractor" in the white strip on the back that contained the team name.

	MT
Refractor Stars:	7x-14x
Refractor Rookies:	2x-4x
The following cards do not exist: 75/89/90/97/99	
The following cards are in Preview: 6/10/19/40/43/60/73/77/81/100	

1998-99 Topps Chrome Apparitions

Apparitions was a 14-card insert that was initially a retail-only Topps Series I insert, but was inserted 1:24 packs of Chrome. The set originally consisted of 15 players, however card #15, which was Michael Jordan, was not included in Chrome due to his retirement. Refractor versions were also printed and were sequentially numbered to 100 sets and inserted 1:1,105 packs. Cards were numbered with an "A" prefix.

		MT
Complete Set (14):		100.00
Common Player:		1.00
Inserted 1:24		
Refractors:		3x-6x
Inserted 1:1,015		
Production 100 Sets		
1	Kobe Bryant	15.00
2	Stephon Marbury	6.00
3	Brent Barry	1.00
4	Karl Malone	3.00
5	Shaquille O'Neal	8.00
6	Chris Webber	5.00
7	Shawn Kemp	2.00
8	Hakeem Olajuwon	3.00
9	Anfernee Hardaway	8.00
10	Michael Finley	2.00
11	Keith Van Horn	5.00
12	Kevin Garnett	12.00
13	Vin Baker	2.00
14	Tim Duncan	12.00

1998-99 Topps Chrome Apparitions Refractors

This 14-card parallel set reprinted each card from the Apparitions insert in a Refractor version. Cards were sequentially numbered to 100 sets and seeded 1:1,015 packs.

		MT
Refractors:		3x-6x
Inserted 1:1,015		
Production 100 Sets		
1	Kobe Bryant	90.00
2	Stephon Marbury	35.00
3	Brent Barry	5.00
4	Karl Malone	20.00
5	Shaquille O'Neal	50.00
6	Chris Webber	30.00
7	Shawn Kemp	15.00
8	Hakeem Olajuwon	20.00
9	Anfernee Hardaway	50.00
10	Michael Finley	15.00
11	Keith Van Horn	25.00
12	Kevin Garnett	75.00
13	Vin Baker	15.00
14	Tim Duncan	75.00

1998-99 Topps Chrome Back 2 Back

This seven-card insert was new for Chrome and inserted 1:12 packs. The insert name was printed in large letters across the top of the silver card, while backs were numbered with a "B" prefix.

		MT
Complete Set (7):		35.00
Common Player:		1.00
Inserted 1:12		
1	Michael Jordan	20.00
2	Scottie Pippen	5.00
3	Dennis Rodman	5.00
4	Hakeem Olajuwon	3.00
5	John Stockton	1.00
6	Dikembe Mutombo	1.00
7	Grant Hill	10.00

1998-99 Topps Chrome Championship Spirit

Championship Spirit was created specifically for Chrome and included seven players who have won championships, either on a collegiate or professional level. Cards were inserted 1:12 packs and numbered with a "CS" prefix.

		MT
Complete Set (7):		35.00
Common Player:		2.00
Inserted 1:12		
1	Michael Jordan	20.00
2	Hakeem Olajuwon	4.00
3	Ron Mercer	5.00
4	Mike Bibby	6.00
5	Michael Dickerson	5.00
6	Patrick Ewing	2.00
7	Scottie Pippen	5.00

1998-99 Topps Chrome Coast to Coast

This 15-card insert set featured players who excel on both ends of the court. Regular versions were seeded 1:24 packs, with Refractors seeded every 96 packs. Coast to Coast inserts were originally found in retail packs of Topps II, and were numbered with a "CC" prefix.

		MT
Complete Set (15):		100.00
Common Player:		1.50
Inserted 1:24		
Refractors:		3x
Inserted 1:96		
1	Kobe Bryant	20.00
2	Scottie Pippen	8.00
3	Eddie Jones	4.00
4	Grant Hill	15.00
5	Jason Kidd	8.00
6	Antoine Walker	6.00
7	Michael Finley	1.50
8	Kevin Garnett	1.50
9	Allen Iverson	1.50
10	Shawn Kemp	3.00
11	Glenn Robinson	1.50
12	Anfernee Hardaway	10.00
13	Tim Hardaway	3.00
14	Ron Mercer	8.00
15	Kerry Kittles	1.50

1998-99 Topps Chrome Instant Impact

Instant Impact was created specifically for Topps Chrome and featured 10 young players who have made a difference on their respective teams. Regular versions were seeded 1:36 packs, while Refractors were seeded 1:144 packs. Instant Impact cards were numbered with an "I" prefix.

		MT
Complete Set (10):		100.00
Common Player:		2.00
Inserted 1:36		
Refractors:		3x
Inserted 1:144		
1	Tim Duncan	20.00
2	Keith Van Horn	10.00
3	Stephon Marbury	15.00
4	Hakeem Olajuwon	2.00
5	Shaquille O'Neal	10.00
6	Michael Olowokandi	5.00
7	Raef LaFrentz	5.00
8	Vince Carter	25.00
9	Jason Williams	15.00
10	Paul Pierce	12.00

1998-99 Topps Chrome Season's Best

This 29-card set was reprinted from Topps I, and showcase five top players at each position, plus five top rookies from the 1997-98 season. The original set from Topps had 30 cards, but the Chrome version had 29 since Michael Jordan wasn't able to be used. Regular versions were seeded 1:6 packs, while Refractor versions were seeded every 24 packs. Cards were numbered with an "SB" prefix.

		MT
Complete Set (29):		85.00
Common Player:		1.00
Inserted 1:6		
Refractors:		3x
Inserted 1:24		
1	Rod Strickland	1.00
2	Gary Payton	3.00
3	Tim Hardaway	2.00
4	Stephon Marbury	8.00
5	Sam Cassell	1.00
7	Mitch Richmond	1.50
8	Steve Smith	1.50
9	Ray Allen	1.50
10	Isaiah Rider	1.00
11	Grant Hill	12.00
12	Kevin Garnett	12.00
13	Shareef Abdur-Rahim	5.00
14	Glenn Robinson	1.50
15	Michael Finley	1.50
16	Karl Malone	3.00
17	Tim Duncan	12.00
18	Antoine Walker	5.00
19	Chris Webber	5.00
20	Vin Baker	2.00
21	Shaquille O'Neal	6.00
22	David Robinson	3.00
23	Alonzo Mourning	1.50
24	Dikembe Mutombo	1.00
25	Hakeem Olajuwon	3.00
26	Tim Duncan	12.00
27	Keith Van Horn	5.00
28	Zydrunas Ilgauskas	1.50
29	Brevin Knight	1.50
30	Bobby Jackson	1.00

1999-00 Topps Promos

This six-card promotional set was distributed to dealers and members of the media to promote the 1999-2000 Topps Basketball product. The cards were identical to the regular-issue cards except they were numbered PP1-PP6 on the back.

		MT
Complete Set (6):		1.00
Common Player:		.10
1	Bryant Reeves	.10
2	Isaiah Rider	.15
3	Sean Elliot	.15
4	Mark Jackson	.10
5	Voshon Lenard	.10
6	Juwan Howard	.50

1999-00 Topps

Topps consisted of 257 cards in 1999-00, with 120 in Series I and 137 in Series II. Series I had 110 veterans with orange borders and 10 NBA Draft Picks with white borders (seeded 1:5 packs). Series II had 110 veterans with orange borders, 18 NBA Draft Picks (1:5 packs) and nine USA Basketball (1:5 packs). The first 248 cards in the set (all except the USA Basketball subset) were paralleled in a MVP Promotion parallel set. Inserts in Series I include: Autographs, Highlight Reels, Jumbos, Patriarchs, Picture Perfect, Prodigy, Record Numbers and Season's Best. Inserts in Series II include: Autographs, Impact, Team Topps, All-Matrix, 21st Century and Own the Game.

		MT
Complete Set (257):		70.00
Complete Series I (120):		35.00
Complete Series II (137):		35.00
Common Player:		.10
Minor Stars		.20
Common Rookie (111-120, 231-248):		.50
Common USA (249-257):		.50
Inserted 1:5		
Series 1 Pack (11):		1.50
Series 2 Pack (11):		1.50
Series 1 Wax Box (36):		30.00
Series 2 Wax Box (36):		30.00
1	Steve Smith	.20
2	Ron Harper	.10
3	Michael Dickerson	.30
4	LaPhonso Ellis	.20
5	Chris Webber	.75
6	Jason Caffey	.10
7	Bryon Russell	.10
8	Bison Dele	.10
9	Isaiah Rider	.20
10	Dean Garrett	.10
11	Eric Murdock	.10
12	Juwan Howard	.20
13	Latrell Sprewell	.20
14	Jalen Rose	.10
15	Larry Johnson	.20
16	Eric Williams	.10
17	Bryant Reeves	.10
18	Tony Battie	.10
19	Luc Longley	.10
20	Gary Payton	.50
21	Tariq Abdul-Wahad	.10
22	Armen Gilliam	.10
23	Shaquille O'Neal	1.00
24	Gary Trent	.20
25	John Stockton	.20
26	Mark Jackson	.10
27	Cherokee Parks	.10
28	Michael Olowokandi	.30
29	Raef LaFrentz	.30
30	Dell Curry	.10
31	Travis Best	.10
32	Shawn Kemp	.40
33	Voshon Lenard	.10
34	Brian Grant	.20
35	Alvin Williams	.10
36	Derek Fisher	.10
37	Allan Houston	.20
38	Arvydas Sabonis	.20
39	Terry Cummings	.10
40	Dale Ellis	.10
41	Maurice Taylor	.20
42	Grant Hill	1.50
43	Anthony Mason	.20
44	John Wallace	.10
45	David Wesley	.10
46	Nick Van Exel	.20
47	Cuttino Mobley	.20
48	Anfernee Hardaway	1.00
49	Terry Porter	.10
50	Brent Barry	.10
51	Derek Harper	.10
52	Antoine Walker	.75
53	Karl Malone	.50
54	Ben Wallace	.10
55	Vlade Divac	.20
56	Sam Mitchell	.10
57	Joe Smith	.20
58	Shawn Bradley	.10
59	Darrell Armstrong	.20
60	Kenny Anderson	.20
61	Jason Williams	.75
62	Alonzo Mourning	.30
63	Matt Harpring	.20
64	Antonio Davis	.10
65	Lindsey Hunter	.10
66	Allen Iverson	1.25

67	Mookie Blaylock	.10
68	Wesley Person	.10
69	Bobby Phills	.10
70	Theo Ratliff	.10
71	Antonio Daniels	.10
72	P.J. Brown	.10
73	David Robinson	.50
74	Sean Elliott	.10
75	Zydrunas Ilgauskas	.20
76	Kerry Kittles	.10
77	Otis Thorpe	.10
78	John Starks	.10
79	Jaren Jackson	.10
80	Hersey Hawkins	.10
81	Glenn Robinson	.20
82	Paul Pierce	.75
83	Glen Rice	.20
84	Charlie Ward	.10
85	Dee Brown	.10
86	Danny Fortson	.10
87	Billy Owens	.10
88	Jason Kidd	.75
89	Brent Price	.10
90	Don Reid	.10
91	Mark Bryant	.10
92	Vinny Del Negro	.10
93	Stephon Marbury	1.00
94	Donyell Marshall	.10
95	Jim Jackson	.10
96	Horace Grant	.10
97	Calbert Cheaney	.10
98	Vince Carter	2.00
99	Bobby Jackson	.10
100	Alan Henderson	.10
101	Mike Bibby	.50
102	Cedric Henderson	.10
103	Lamond Murray	.10
104	A.C. Green	.10
105	Hakeem Olajuwon	.50
106	George Lynch	.10
107	Kendall Gill	.10
108	Rex Chapman	.10
109	Eddie Jones	.50
110	Kornel David	.10
111	*Jason Terry* (Draft Picks)	1.25
112	*Corey Maggette* (Draft Picks)	2.50
113	*Ron Artest* (Draft Picks)	1.25
114	*Richard Hamilton* (Draft Picks)	2.00
115	*Elton Brand* (Draft Picks)	4.00
116	*Baron Davis* (Draft Picks)	4.00
117	*Wally Szczerbiak* (Draft Picks)	3.00
118	*Steve Francis* (Draft Picks)	10.00
119	*James Posey* (Draft Picks)	1.00
120	*Shawn Marion* (Draft Picks)	4.00
121	Tim Duncan	1.50
122	Danny Manning	.10
123	Chris Mullin	.10
124	Antawn Jamison	.60
125	Kobe Bryant	2.00
126	Matt Geiger	.10
127	Rod Strickland	.20
128	Howard Eisley	.10
129	Steve Nash	.10
130	Felipe Lopez	.20
131	Ron Mercer	.60
132	Ruben Patterson	.20
133	Dana Barros	.10
134	Dale Davis	.10
135	Charles Outlaw	.10
136	Shandon Anderson	.10
137	Mitch Richmond	.20
138	Doug Christie	.10
139	Rasheed Wallace	.20
140	Chris Childs	.10
141	Jamal Mashburn	.20
142	Terrell Brandon	.20
143	Jamie Feick	.10
144	Robert Traylor	.30
145	Rick Fox	.10
146	Charles Barkley	.40
147	Tyrone Nesby	.20
148	Jerry Stackhouse	.30
149	Cedric Ceballos	.10
150	Dikembe Mutombo	.20
151	Anthony Peeler	.10
152	Larry Hughes	.50
153	Clifford Robinson	.10
154	Corliss Williamson	.10
155	Olden Polynice	.10
156	Avery Johnson	.10
157	Tracy Murray	.10
158	Tom Gugliotta	.20
159	Tim Thomas	.40
160	Reggie Miller	.20
161	Tim Hardaway	.30
162	Dan Majerle	.10
163	Will Perdue	.10
164	Brevin Knight	.10
165	Elden Campbell	.10
166	Chris Gatling	.10
167	Walter McCarty	.10
168	Chauncey Billups	.10
169	Chris Mills	.10
170	Christian Laettner	.10
171	Robert Pack	.10
172	Rik Smits	.10
173	Tyrone Hill	.10
174	Damon Stoudamire	.30
175	Nick Anderson	.10
176	Predrag Stojakovic	.10
177	Vladimir Stepania	.10
178	Tracy McGrady	.75
179	Adam Keefe	.10
180	Shareef Abdur-Rahim	.60
181	Isaac Austin	.10
182	Mario Ellie	.10
183	Rashard Lewis	.40
184	Scott Burrell	.10
185	Othella Harrington	.10
186	Eric Piatkowski	.10
187	Bryant Stith	.10
188	Michael Finley	.20
189	Chris Crawford	.10
190	Toni Kukoc	.40
191	Danny Ferry	.10
192	Erick Dampier	.10
193	Clarence Weatherspoon	.10
194	Bob Sura	.10
195	Jayson Williams	.10
196	Kurt Thomas	.10
197	Greg Anthony	.10
198	Rodney Rogers	.10
199	Detlef Schrempf	.10
200	Keith Van Horn	.50
201	Robert Horry	.10
202	Sam Cassell	.10
203	Malik Sealy	.10
204	Kelvin Cato	.10
205	Antonio McDyess	.30
206	Andrew DeClercq	.10
207	Ricky Davis	.20
208	Vitaly Potapenko	.10
209	Loy Vaught	.10
210	Kevin Garnett	1.50
211	Eric Snow	.10
212	Anfernee Hardaway	1.00
213	Vin Baker	.20
214	Lawrence Funderburke	.10
215	Jeff Hornacek	.10
216	Doug West	.10
217	Michael Doleac	.10
218	Ray Allen	.30
219	Derek Anderson	.10
220	Jerome Williams	.10
221	Derrick Coleman	.10
222	Randy Brown	.10
223	Patrick Ewing	.20
224	Walt Williams	.10
225	Charles Oakley	.10
226	Steve Kerr	.10
227	Muggsy Bogues	.10
228	Kevin Willis	.10
229	Marcus Camby	.30
230	Scottie Pippen	.75
231	*Lamar Odom*	6.00
232	*Jonathan Bender*	4.00
233	*Andre Miller*	2.50
234	*Trajan Langdon*	1.00
235	*Aleksandar Radojevic*	.50
236	*William Avery*	1.00
237	*Cal Bowdler*	.50
238	*Quincy Lewis*	1.00
239	*Dion Glover*	.75
240	*Jeff Foster*	.50
241	*Kenny Thomas*	1.00
242	*Devean George*	1.00
243	*Tim James*	.75
244	*Vonteego Cummings*	1.00
245	*Jumanie Jones*	.75
246	*Scott Padgett*	.75
247	*Adrian Griffin*	1.00
248	*Chris Herren*	.75
249	Allan Houston	.50
250	Kevin Garnett	3.00
251	Gary Payton	1.00
252	Steve Smith	.50
253	Tim Hardaway	.75
254	Tim Duncan	3.00
255	Jason Kidd	2.00
256	Tom Gugliotta	.50
257	Vin Baker	.50

1999-00 Topps MVP Promotion

MVP Promotion cards paralleled each card in Topps Series I and II, with identical fronts except for the addition of a gold foil stamp indentifying the insert set. Backs were printed in white, unnumbered and explained the rules of the promotion. MVP Promotion cards were inserted 1:336 packs in Series I and 1:172 packs in Series II and limited to just 100 sets.

	MT
MVP Promotion Cards:	25x-50x
MVP Promotion Rookies:	3x-6x
Production 100 Sets	
Inserted 1:336 Series I Hobby	
Inserted 1:172 Series II	

1999-00 Topps MVP Promotion Exchange

		MT
Complete Set (22):		75.00
Common Player:		.50
MVP1	Allen Iverson	6.00
MVP2	Alonzo Mourning	1.00
MVP3	Anthony Mason	.50
MVP4	Chris Webber	5.00
MVP5	Eddie Jones	2.00
MVP6	Grant Hill	5.00
MVP7	Jason Kidd	3.00
MVP8	Karl Malone	1.50
MVP9	Kevin Garnett	8.00
MVP10	Kobe Bryant	12.00
MVP11	Michael Finley	1.00
MVP12	Sam Cassell	.50
MVP13	Shaquille O'Neal	6.00
MVP14	Stephon Marbury	2.00
MVP15	Terrell Brandon	.50
MVP16	Tim Duncan	6.00
MVP17	Vince Carter	15.00
MVP18	Steve Francis	8.00
MVP19	Elton Brand, Steve Francis	6.00
MVP20	Shaquille O'Neal	6.00
MVP21	Reggie Miller	1.00
MVP22	Shaquille O'Neal	6.00

1999-00 Topps All-Matrix

This 30-card insert set was seeded 1:15 packs of Series II. The insert was made up of 10 cards in three different categories - Feature Force, Instinctive Force and Future Force. All-Matrix cards featured a silver holographic background and were numbered with an "AM" prefix.

		MT
Complete Set (30):		75.00
Common Player:		.50
Inserted 1:15 Series II		
AM1	Karl Malone	1.00
AM2	Scottie Pippen	3.00
AM3	Grant Hill	8.00
AM4	Shawn Kemp	.75
AM5	Shaquille O'Neal	5.00
AM6	Anfernee Hardaway	5.00
AM7	Chris Webber	3.00
AM8	Gary Payton	1.00
AM9	Jason Kidd	3.00
AM10	John Stockton	.50
AM11	Kevin Garnett	8.00
AM12	Vince Carter	10.00
AM13	Shareef Abdur-Rahim	2.00
AM14	Antoine Walker	.75
AM15	Kobe Bryant	10.00
AM16	Tim Duncan	8.00
AM17	Keith Van Horn	1.50
AM18	Allen Iverson	6.00
AM19	Jason Williams	5.00
AM20	Stephon Marbury	2.00
AM21	Elton Brand	6.00
AM22	Jason Terry	1.00
AM23	Steve Francis	8.00
AM24	Corey Maggette	4.00
AM25	Lamar Odom	8.00
AM26	Ron Artest	2.00
AM27	Baron Davis	3.00
AM28	Andre Miller	2.00
AM29	Shawn Marion	2.00
AM30	Wally Szczerbiak	4.00

1999-00 Topps Autographs

This 21-card insert has nine cards in Series I, with Group A seeded 1:877 hobby packs and Group B seeded 1:351 packs, and 12 cards in Series II, seeded 1:196 hobby packs. Cards were numbered with a two-letter prefix, usually corresponding to the player's initials. Each Autograph card contained a Topps "Certified Autograph Issue" stamp.

		MT
Complete Set (21):		750.00
Complete Series I (9):		250.00
Complete Series II (12):		500.00
Common Player:		15.00
Inserted 1:877 (A) Hobby		
Inserted 1:351 (B) Hobby		
Inserted 1:196 (A) and (B) Hobby		
SAR	Shareef Abdur-Rahim 1B	30.00
WA	William Avery 2A	15.00
EB	Elton Brand 2B	80.00
BD	Baron Davis 2A	35.00
TD	Tim Duncan 2A	100.00
SF	Steve Francis 2B	100.00
TG	Tom Gugliotta 2B	15.00
JJ	Jumanie Jones 2A	15.00
JK	Jason Kidd 1A	60.00
CM	Corey Maggette 2A	50.00
AM	Antonio McDyess 1B	25.00
AM2	Antonio McDyess 2B	25.00
GP	Gary Payton 1B	35.00
GP2	Gary Payton 2A	35.00
PP	Paul Pierce 1B	30.00
SP	Scottie Pippen 1B	60.00
MR	Mitch Richmond 1A	15.00
SS	Steve Smith 1B	15.00
DS	Damon Stoudamire 1A	25.00
WS	Wally Szczerbiak 2A	50.00
AW	Antoine Walker 2A	15.00

1999-00 Topps Highlight Reels

Highlight Reels was a 15-card, retail exclusive insert found in packs of Topps Series I. They were numbered with an "HR" prefix and inserted 1:14 packs of Series I.

		MT
Complete Set (15):		35.00
Common Player:		.75
Inserted 1:14 Series I Retail		
1	Stephon Marbury	2.00
2	Vince Carter	6.00
3	Kevin Garnett	6.00
4	Kobe Bryant	8.00
5	Chris Webber	1.50
6	Allen Iverson	4.00
7	Grant Hill	6.00
8	Antoine Walker	1.50
9	Jason Williams	4.00
10	Tim Duncan	6.00
11	Shareef Abdur-Rahim	1.50
12	Keith Van Horn	1.50
13	Antonio McDyess	.75
14	Jason Kidd	2.00
15	Ron Mercer	1.50

1999-00 Topps Impact

This 20-card insert was seeded 1:24 packs of Series II. The cards utilized Finest technology and were numbered with an "I" prefix. Refractor versions also existed and were seeded 1:120 packs. The insert set was divided into three different categories - Initial Impact, Present Impact and Lasting Impact.

		MT
Complete Set (20):		100.00
Common Player:		1.00
Inserted 1:24 Series II		
Refractors:		2x
Inserted 1:120 Series II		
I1	Elton Brand	10.00
I2	Lamar Odom	12.00
I3	Wally Szczerbiak	6.00
I4	Jason Terry	1.00
I5	Baron Davis	5.00
I6	Ron Artest	3.00
I7	Steve Francis	12.00
I8	Andre Miller	6.00
I9	Allen Iverson	3.00
I10	Jason Williams	5.00
I11	Keith Van Horn	1.50
I12	Vince Carter	15.00
I13	Kobe Bryant	15.00
I14	Tim Duncan	12.00
I15	Scottie Pippen	3.00
I16	Kevin Garnett	12.00
I17	Shaquille O'Neal	6.00
I18	Gary Payton	1.00
I19	Karl Malone	1.00
I20	Grant Hill	12.00

1999-00 Topps Impact Refractors Parallel

This 20-card insert set paralleled the Impact insert, but utilized Refractor technology. Refractor versions were seeded 1:120 packs.

	MT
Complete Set (20):	100.00
Common Player:	1.00
Inserted 1:24 Series II	
Refractors:	2x
Inserted 1:120 Series II	

1999-00 Topps Jumbos

Eight different Jumbo cards were included in Series I and seeded one per hobby box as a box topper. The cards were identical to the regular-issue cards except they measured 3-1/4" x 4-1/2" and were numbered 1-8.

		MT
Complete Set (8):		25.00
Common Player:		1.00
Inserted 1:Box Series I Hobby		
1	Gary Payton	2.00
2	Shaquille O'Neal	4.00
3	Antoine Walker	2.00
4	Jason Williams	3.00
5	Alonzo Mourning	1.00
6	Allen Iverson	6.00
7	Stephon Marbury	4.00
8	Vince Carter	6.00

1999-00 Topps Own The Game

This 10-card insert set showcased the statistical leaders from the 1998-99 season. The cards were inserted 1:44 packs of Series II and numbered with an "OTG" prefix.

		MT
Complete Set (10):		45.00
Common Player:		1.00
Inserted 1:44 Series II		
OTG1	Allen Iverson	10.00
OTG2	Shaquille O'Neal	10.00
OTG3	Jason Kidd	5.00
OTG4	Stephon Marbury	4.00
OTG5	Dikembe Mutombo	1.00
OTG6	Tim Duncan	15.00
OTG7	Wally Szczerbiak	8.00
OTG8	Quincy Lewis	2.00
OTG9	Elton Brand	12.00
OTG10	Aleksandar Radojevic	1.00

1999-00 Topps Patriarchs

This insert featured 15 players printed with dot matrix technology. Cards were numbered with a "P" prefix and inserted 1:22 packs of Series I.

		MT
Complete Set (15):		40.00
Common Player:		1.00
Inserted 1:22 Series I		
P1	Patrick Ewing	1.00
P2	Reggie Miller	1.00
P3	Hakeem Olajuwon	3.00
P4	Scottie Pippen	5.00
P5	Grant Hill	12.00
P6	Shaquille O'Neal	8.00
P7	Mitch Richmond	1.00
P8	Glen Rice	1.00
P9	Charles Barkley	3.00
P10	Karl Malone	3.00
P11	John Stockton	1.00
P12	Gary Payton	3.00
P13	David Robinson	3.00
P14	Tim Hardaway	2.00
P15	Joe Dumars	1.00

1999-00 Topps Picture Perfect

This insert displayed 10 subjects printed with an intentional error somewhere in the picture. Backs were numbered with a "PIC" prefix and gave clues to what was wrong with the front photo. Picture Perfect cards were inserted 1:8 packs of Series I.

		MT
Complete Set (10):		10.00
Common Player:		.25
Inserted 1:8 Series I		
PIC1	Shaquille O'Neal	2.00
PIC2	Alonzo Mourning	1.00
PIC3	Shareef Abdur-Rahim	1.50
PIC4	Juwan Howard	.50
PIC5	Keith Van Horn	1.50
PIC6	Ron Mercer	1.50
PIC7	Tim Hardaway	1.00
PIC8	Kevin Garnett	3.00
PIC9	David Robinson	1.00
PIC10	Kerry Kittles	.25

1999-00 Topps Prodigy

This insert featured 20 players - 10 with less than five years of pro experience and 10 rookies - on die-cut chrome designs. Cards were numbered with a "PR" prefix and inserted 1:36 packs. Refractor versions of each card also existed and were seeded 1:144 packs of Series I.

		MT
Complete Set (20):		125.00
Common Player:		2.00
Inserted 1:36 Series I		
Refractors:		2x-3x
Inserted 1:144 Series I		
PR1	Stephon Marbury	10.00
PR2	Jason Kidd	6.00
PR3	Kevin Garnett	15.00
PR4	Kobe Bryant	20.00
PR5	Antoine Walker	6.00
PR6	Ron Mercer	6.00
PR7	Shareef Abdur-Rahim	6.00
PR8	Tim Duncan	15.00
PR9	Keith Van Horn	6.00
PR10	Ray Allen	2.00
PRr11	Michael Doleac	2.00
PR12	Jason Williams	8.00
PR13	Michael Dickerson	3.00
PR14	Mike Bibby	4.00
PR15	Paul Pierce	8.00
PR16	Michael Olowokandi	3.00
PR17	Vince Carter	12.00
PR18	Antawn Jamison	6.00
PR19	Felipe Lopez	2.00
PR20	Matt Harpring	2.00

1999-00 Topps Prodigy Refractors Parallel

All 20 cards in the Prodigy insert were also available in a parallel Refractor version. Fronts featured the Refractor finish and were seeded 1:144 packs of Series I.

Complete Set (20):		325.00
Common Player:		5.00
Refractors:		2x-3x
Inserted 1:144 Series I		
1	Stephon Marbury	10.00
2	Jason Kidd	6.00
3	Kevin Garnett	15.00
4	Kobe Bryant	20.00
5	Antoine Walker	6.00
6	Ron Mercer	6.00
7	Shareef Abdur-Rahim	6.00
8	Tim Duncan	15.00
9	Keith Van Horn	6.00
10	Ray Allen	2.00
11	Michael Doleac	2.00
12	Jason Williams	8.00
13	Michael Dickerson	3.00
14	Mike Bibby	4.00
15	Paul Pierce	8.00
16	Michael Olowokandi	3.00
17	Vince Carter	12.00
18	Antawn Jamison	6.00
19	Felipe Lopez	2.00
20	Matt Harpring	2.00

1999-00 Topps Record Numbers

This 10-card insert set featured record setting players over a blue, exploding background with a white border. Record Numbers were numbered with an "RN" prefix and inserted 1:12 packs of Series I.

		MT
Complete Set (10):		15.00
Common Player:		.50
Inserted 1:12 Series I		
RN1	Karl Malone	1.00
RN2	Kerry Kittles	.50
RN3	Reggie Miller	.75
RN4	Hakeem Olajuwon	1.00
RN5	John Stockton	.75
RN6	Dikembe Mutombo	.75
RN7	Kobe Bryant	6.00
RN8	Tim Duncan	5.00
RN9	Allen Iverson	4.00
RN10	Patrick Ewing	.75

1999-00 Topps Season's Best

Season's Best displayed 30 cards with the top five at each position and top five rookies from the 1998-99 season. Center Stage (centers), Mighty Men (power forwards), Gliders (small forwards), Shooting Stars (shooting guards), Conductors (point guards) and Fresh Foundations (rookies) were the six categories and each featured a different design. These inserts were numbered with an "SB" prefix and inserted 1:12 packs of Series I.

		MT
Complete Set (30):		65.00
Common Player:		1.00
Minor Stars:		2.00
Inserted 1:12 Series I		
SB1	David Robinson	3.00
SB2	Shaquille O'Neal	5.00
SB3	Patrick Ewing	1.00
SB4	Hakeem Olajuwon	3.00
SB5	Alonzo Mourning	2.00
SB6	Antonio McDyess	2.00
SB7	Tim Duncan	10.00
SB8	Keith Van Horn	3.00
SB9	Karl Malone	3.00
SB10	Chris Webber	4.00
SB11	Kevin Garnett	10.00
SB12	Juwan Howard	1.00
SB13	Shareef Abdur-Rahim	4.00
SB14	Glenn Robinson	1.00
SB15	Grant Hill	10.00
SB16	Michael Finley	1.00
SB17	Steve Smith	1.00
SB18	Mitch Richmond	1.00
SB19	Kobe Bryant	12.00
SB20	Ray Allen	1.00
SB21	Allen Iverson	6.00
SB22	Gary Payton	3.00
SB23	Stephon Marbury	5.00
SB24	Jason Kidd	4.00
SB25	Tim Hardaway	2.00
SB26	Jason Williams	5.00
SB27	Vince Carter	8.00
SB28	Paul Pierce	5.00
SB29	Mike Bibby	3.00
SB30	Michael Dickerson	1.00

1999-00 Topps Team Topps

This 24-card insert set featured NBA All-Stars, past and present from the Eastern and Western Conference, with 12 players from each conference. Cards were inserted 1:18 packs of Series II and numbered with a "TT" prefix.

		MT
Complete Set (24):		40.00
Common Player:		.50
Inserted 1:18 Series II		
TT1	Gary Payton	1.50
TT2	Jason Kidd	3.00
TT3	Kobe Bryant	10.00
TT4	Anfernee Hardaway	5.00
TT5	Kevin Garnett	7.00
TT6	Patrick Ewing	.75
TT7	Tim Duncan	8.00
TT8	Karl Malone	1.50
TT9	Shaquille O'Neal	5.00
TT10	Charles Barkley	1.50
TT11	John Stockton	.75
TT12	Tim Hardaway	1.00
TT13	Hakeem Olajuwon	1.50
TT14	Jayson Williams	.50
TT15	Reggie Miller	.75
TT16	David Robinson	1.50
TT17	Grant Hill	8.00
TT18	Scottie Pippen	3.00
TT19	Chris Webber	3.00
TT20	Shawn Kemp	1.00
TT21	Alonzo Mourning	1.00
TT22	Mitch Richmond	.75
TT23	Antoine Walker	1.00
TT24	Tom Gugliotta	.50

1999-00 Topps 21st Century Topps

This 16-card insert set showcased the top rookies from the 1999-00 season printed on a silver holographic background. 21st Century Topps inserts were seeded 1:27 packs of Series II and numbered with a "C" prefix.

		MT
Complete Set (16):		40.00
Common Player:		.50
Inserted 1:27 Series II		
C1	Jason Terry	2.00
C2	Baron Davis	4.00
C3	Lamar Odom	10.00
C4	Jonathan Bender	5.00
C5	Ron Artest	3.00
C6	Richard Hamilton	3.00
C7	Andre Miller	3.00
C8	Shawn Marion	3.00
C9	Steve Francis	10.00
C10	Elton Brand	8.00
C11	Wally Szczerbiak	5.00
C12	Corey Maggette	5.00
C13	James Posey	1.50
C14	Trajan Langdon	1.50
C15	Tim James	.75
C16	Cal Bowdler	.50

1999-00 Topps Chrome

Topps Chrome consisted of 257 cards, with 220 veterans, 28 NBA Draft Picks and nine USA Basketball Team cards. The cards featured the same photography from Topps I and II, but were printed on a chromium surface and included a Topps Chrome logo. Every card in the set was available in a Refractor parallel set, while inserts included Highlight Reel, All-Etch, Instant Impact, Keepers and All-Stars. All five inserts were also available in Refractor versions.

		MT
Complete Set (257):		200.00
Common Player:		.25
Minor Stars:		.40
Common Rookie:		2.00
Pack (4):		5.00
Wax Box (24):		65.00
1	Steve Smith	.40
2	Ron Harper	.25
3	Michael Dickerson	.40
4	LaPhonso Ellis	.25
5	Chris Webber	1.50
6	Jason Caffey	.25
7	Bryon Russell	.25
8	Bison Dele	.25
9	Isaiah Rider	.40
10	Dean Garrett	.25
11	Eric Murdock	.25
12	Juwan Howard	.40
13	Latrell Sprewell	.60
14	Jalen Rose	.40
15	Larry Johnson	.25
16	Eric Williams	.25
17	Bryant Reeves	.25
18	Tony Battie	.25
19	Luc Longley	.25
20	Gary Payton	.75
21	Tariq Abdul-Wahad	.25
22	Armen Gilliam	.25
23	Shaquille O'Neal	2.00
24	Gary Trent	.25
25	John Stockton	.40
26	Mark Jackson	.25
27	Cherokee Parks	.25
28	Michael Olowokandi	.40
29	Raef LaFrentz	.50
30	Dell Curry	.25
31	Travis Best	.25
32	Shawn Kemp	.40
33	Voshon Lenard	.25
34	Brian Grant	.25
35	Alvin Williams	.25
36	Derek Fisher	.25
37	Allan Houston	.40
38	Arvydas Sabonis	.25
39	Terry Cummings	.25
40	Dale Ellis	.25
41	Maurice Taylor	.25
42	Grant Hill	3.00
43	Anthony Mason	.25
44	John Wallace	.25
45	David Wesley	.25
46	Nick Van Exel	.40
47	Cuttino Mobley	.40
48	Anfernee Hardaway	1.50
49	Terry Porter	.25
50	Brent Barry	.25
51	Derek Harper	.25
52	Antoine Walker	.50
53	Karl Malone	.75
54	Ben Wallace	.25
55	Vlade Divac	.25
56	Sam Mitchell	.25
57	Joe Smith	.25
58	Shawn Bradley	.25
59	Darrell Armstrong	.25
60	Kenny Anderson	.40
61	Jason Williams	1.50
62	Alonzo Mourning	.50
63	Matt Harpring	.25
64	Antonio Davis	.25
65	Lindsey Hunter	.25
66	Allen Iverson	2.50
67	Mookie Blaylock	.25
68	Wesley Person	.25
69	Bobby Phills	.25
70	Theo Ratliff	.25
71	Antonio Daniels	.25
72	P.J. Brown	.25
73	David Robinson	.75
74	Sean Elliott	.25
75	Zydrunas Ilgauskas	.25
76	Kerry Kittles	.25
77	Otis Thorpe	.25
78	John Starks	.25
79	Jaren Jackson	.25
80	Hersey Hawkins	.25
81	Glenn Robinson	.40
82	Paul Pierce	1.25
83	Glen Rice	.40
84	Charlie Ward	.25
85	Dee Brown	.25
86	Danny Fortson	.25
87	Billy Owens	.25
88	Jason Kidd	1.50
89	Brent Price	.25
90	Don Reid	.25
91	Mark Bryant	.25
92	Vinny Del Negro	.25
93	Stephon Marbury	1.00
94	Donyell Marshall	.25
95	Jim Jackson	.25
96	Horace Grant	.25
97	Calbert Cheaney	.25
98	Vince Carter	5.00
99	Bobby Jackson	.25
100	Alan Henderson	.25
101	Mike Bibby	.50
102	Cedric Henderson	.25
103	Lamond Murray	.25
104	A.C. Green	.25
105	Hakeem Olajuwon	.75
106	George Lynch	.25
107	Kendall Gill	.25
108	Rex Chapman	.25
109	Eddie Jones	.75
110	Kornel David	.25
111	*Jason Terry*	5.00
112	*Corey Maggette*	10.00
113	*Ron Artest*	5.00
114	*Richard Hamilton*	8.00
115	*Elton Brand*	12.00
116	*Baron Davis*	10.00
117	*Wally Szczerbiak*	8.00
118	*Steve Francis*	30.00
119	*James Posey*	4.00
120	*Shawn Marion*	12.00
121	Tim Duncan	3.00
122	Danny Manning	.25
123	Chris Mullin	.25
124	Antawn Jamison	1.00
125	Kobe Bryant	4.00
126	Matt Geiger	.25
127	Rod Strickland	.40
128	Howard Eisley	.25
129	Steve Nash	.25
130	Felipe Lopez	.25
131	Ron Mercer	.75
132	Ruben Patterson	.40
133	Dana Barros	.25
134	Dale Davis	.25
135	Charles Outlaw	.25
136	Shandon Anderson	.25
137	Mitch Richmond	.40
138	Doug Christie	.25
139	Rasheed Wallace	.40
140	Chris Childs	.25
141	Jamal Mashburn	.40
142	Terrell Brandon	.40
143	Jamie Feick	.25
144	Robert Traylor	.40
145	Rick Fox	.25
146	Charles Barkley	.75
147	Tyrone Nesby	.60
148	Jerry Stackhouse	.25
149	Cedric Ceballos	.25
150	Dikembe Mutombo	.40
151	Anthony Peeler	.25
152	Larry Hughes	1.00
153	Clifford Robinson	.25
154	Corliss Williamson	.25
155	Olden Polynice	.25
156	Avery Johnson	.25
157	Tracy Murray	.25
158	Tom Gugliotta	.40
159	Tim Thomas	.60
160	Reggie Miller	.40
161	Tim Hardaway	.50
162	Dan Majerle	.25
163	Will Perdue	.25
164	Brevin Knight	.25
165	Elden Campbell	.25
166	Chris Gatling	.25
167	Walter McCarty	.25
168	Chauncey Billups	.25
169	Chris Mills	.25
170	Christian Laettner	.25
171	Robert Pack	.25
172	Rik Smits	.25
173	Tyrone Hill	.25
174	Damon Stoudamire	.50
175	Nick Anderson	.25
176	Predrag Stojakovic	.40
177	Vladimir Stepania	.25
178	Tracy McGrady	1.50
179	Adam Keefe	.25
180	Shareef Abdur-Rahim	1.00
181	Isaac Austin	.25
182	Mario Elie	.25
183	Rashard Lewis	.60
184	Scott Burrell	.25
185	Othella Harrington	.25
186	Eric Piatkowski	.25
187	Bryant Stith	.25
188	Michael Finley	.40
189	Chris Crawford	.25
190	Toni Kukoc	.50
191	Danny Ferry	.25
192	Erick Dampier	.25
193	Clarence Weatherspoon	.25
194	Bob Sura	.25
195	Jayson Williams	.25
196	Kurt Thomas	.25
197	Greg Anthony	.25
198	Rodney Rogers	.25
199	Detlef Schrempf	.25
200	Keith Van Horn	.75
201	Robert Horry	.25
202	Sam Cassell	.40
203	Malik Sealy	.25
204	Kelvin Cato	.25
205	Antonio McDyess	.50
206	Andrew DeClerq	.50
207	Ricky Davis	.40
208	Vitaly Potapenko	.25
209	Loy Vaught	.25
210	Kevin Garnett	3.00
211	Eric Snow	.25
212	Anfernee Hardaway	1.50
213	Vin Baker	.40
214	Lawrence Funderburke	.25
215	Jeff Hornacek	.25
216	Doug West	.25
217	Michael Doleac	.25
218	Ray Allen	.50
219	Derek Anderson	.40
220	Jerome Williams	.20
221	Derrick Coleman	.40
222	Randy Brown	.25
223	Patrick Ewing	.40
224	Walt Williams	.25
225	Charles Oakley	.25
226	Steve Kerr	.25
227	Muggsy Bogues	.25
228	Kevin Willis	.25
229	Marcus Camby	.40
230	Scottie Pippen	1.50
231	*Lamar Odom*	20.00
232	*Jonathan Bender*	12.00
233	*Andre Miller*	10.00
234	*Trajan Langdon*	4.00
235	*Aleksandar Radojevic*	2.00
236	*William Avery*	4.00
237	*Cal Bowdler*	2.00
238	*Quincy Lewis*	2.00
239	*Dion Glover*	2.50
240	*Jeff Foster*	2.00
241	*Kenny Thomas*	3.00
242	*Devean George*	4.00
243	*Tim James*	2.50
244	*Vonteego Cummings*	3.00
245	*Jumaine Jones*	2.50
246	*Scott Padgett*	2.00
247	*Adrian Griffin*	3.00
248	*Chris Herren*	3.00
249	Allan Houston	.40
250	Kevin Garnett	5.00
251	Gary Payton	2.00
252	Steve Smith	.40
253	Tim Hardaway	1.00
254	Tim Duncan	5.00
255	Jason Kidd	3.00
256	Tom Gugliotta	.40
257	Vin Baker	.40

1999-00 Topps Chrome Refractors

This 257-card parallel set reprinted every card in the base set with a Refractor finish. Refractors, which were also identified by the word "Refractor" on the back above the card number, were seeded 1:12 packs.

	MT
Refractor Veterans:	7x-14x
Refractor Rookies:	2x-4x
Inserted 1:12	

1999-00 Topps Chrome All-Etch

This 30-card insert set features the same shots from the All-Matrix insert in Topps II, but is printed on a chromium surface. All-Etch inserts were numbered with an "AE" prefix and inserted 1:10 packs, with Refractor versions seeded 1:100 packs.

		MT
Complete Set (30):		100.00
Common Player:		1.00
Inserted 1:10		
Refractors:		2x-4x
Inserted 1:100		
AE1	Karl Malone	1.50
AE2	Scottie Pippen	3.00
AE3	Grant Hill	8.00
AE4	Shawn Kemp	.75
AE5	Shaquille O'Neal	5.00
AE6	Anfernee Hardaway	4.00
AE7	Chris Webber	3.00
AE8	Gary Payton	1.50
AE9	Jason Kidd	3.00
AE10	John Stockton	1.00
AE11	Kevin Garnett	8.00
AE12	Vince Carter	12.00
AE13	Shareef Abdur-Rahim	2.00
AE14	Antoine Walker	1.00
AE15	Kobe Bryant	10.00
AE16	Tim Duncan	8.00
AE17	Keith Van Horn	1.50
AE18	Allen Iverson	6.00
AE19	Jason Williams	3.00
AE20	Stephon Marbury	2.00
AE21	Elton Brand	8.00
AE22	Jason Terry	1.00
AE23	Steve Francis	10.00
AE24	Corey Maggette	4.00
AE25	Lamar Odom	8.00
AE26	Ron Artest	2.00
AE27	Baron Davis	2.00
AE28	Andre Miller	2.00
AE29	Shawn Marion	2.00
AE30	Wally Szczerbiak	4.00

1999-00 Topps Chrome All-Stars

This 10-card insert set was produced exclusively for Chrome and included All-Stars who appear to be headed for the Hall of Fame. All-Stars were numbered with an "AS" prefix and inserted 1:30 packs, with Refractors 1:300 packs.

		MT
Complete Set (10):		20.00
Common Player:		1.00
Inserted 1:30		
Refractors:		2x-4x
Inserted 1:300		
AS1	Patrick Ewing	1.00
AS2	Karl Malone	2.00
AS3	Hakeem Olajuwon	2.00
AS4	Scottie Pippen	4.00
AS5	Gary Payton	2.00
AS6	John Stockton	1.00
AS7	Shaquille O'Neal	5.00
AS8	Charles Barkley	2.00
AS9	David Robinson	2.00
AS10	Grant Hill	8.00

1999-00 Topps Chrome Highlight Reels

This 15-card insert set featured the same shots as the insert from Topps I, but were printed on a chromium finish. Highlight Reels were numbered with an "HR" prefix and seeded 1:10 packs, with Refractor versions seeded 1:100 packs.

		MT
Complete Set (15):		40.00
Common Player:		.50
Inserted 1:10		
Refractors:		2x-4x
Inserted 1:100		
HR1	Stephon Marbury	1.50
HR2	Vince Carter	10.00
HR3	Kevin Garnett	6.00
HR4	Kobe Bryant	8.00
HR5	Chris Webber	2.50
HR6	Allen Iverson	4.00
HR7	Grant Hill	8.00
HR8	Antoine Walker	.75
HR9	Jason Williams	2.50
HR10	Tim Duncan	6.00
HR11	Shareef Abdur-Rahim	1.50
HR12	Keith Van Horn	1.00
HR13	Antonio McDyess	.50
HR14	Jason Kidd	2.50
HR15	Ron Mercer	1.00

1999-00 Topps Chrome Instant Impact

This 10-card insert set was produced exclusively for Chrome and included players who made a difference for their new teams during the 1999-00 season. Instant Impact cards were numbered with an "II" prefix and seeded 1:15 packs, with Refractor versions 1:150 packs.

		MT
Complete Set (10):		8.00
Common Player:		.25
Inserted 1:15		
Refractors:		2x-4x
Inserted 1:150		
II1	Scottie Pippen	3.00
II2	Nick Anderson	.50
II3	Isaiah Rider	.50
II4	Antonio Davis	.25
II5	Ron Mercer	1.50
II6	Anfernee Hardaway	3.00
II7	Isaac Austin	.25
II8	Steve Smith	.50
II9	Michael Dickerson	.50
II10	Horace Grant	.25

1999-00 Topps Chrome Keepers

This 10-card insert set was produced exclusively for Chrome and highlights the best rookies from the 1999-00 season. Keepers inserts were numbered with a "K" prefix and seeded 1:30 packs, with Refractors 1:300 packs.

		MT
Complete Set (10):		35.00
Common Player:		1.00
Inserted 1:30		
Refractors:		2x-4x
Inserted 1:300		
K1	Elton Brand	8.00
K2	Lamar Odom	8.00
K3	Steve Francis	10.00
K4	Shawn Marion	3.00
K5	Wally Szczerbiak	4.00
K6	Baron Davis	3.00
K7	Andre Miller	3.00
K8	Corey Maggette	4.00
K9	Jason Terry	1.00
K10	Richard Hamilton	2.00

1999-00 Topps Gallery Promos

		MT
Complete Set (6):		4.00
Common Player:		.50
PP1	Jason Williams	1.00
PP2	Eddie Jones	1.00
PP3	Allan Houston	.50
PP4	Alonzo Mourning	.50
PP5	Shareef Abdur-Rahim	1.00
PP6	Wally Szczerbiak	1.00

1999-00 Topps Gallery

Topps Gallery featured 150 cards in the set, each with a framed look highlighting an art theme to the set. The set has 100 regular cards, as well as 50 subset cards with 12 Masters, 12 Artisans and 26 Apprentices (rookies). Each in the set is paralleled with a silver foil insert, which is limited to 250 numbered sets. Inserts included: Autographs, Exhibits, Gallery of Heroes, Heritage, Gallery Originals and Photo Gallery.

		MT
Complete Set (150):		65.00
Common Player:		.15
Minor Stars:		.30
Common Rookie:		.50
Pack (5):		3.00
Wax Box (24):		40.00
1	Gary Payton	.60
2	Derek Anderson	.30
3	Jalen Rose	.30
4	Tim Hardaway	.50
5	Jerry Stackhouse	.30
6	Antonio McDyess	.30
7	Paul Pierce	.75
8	Reggie Miller	.30
9	Maurice Taylor	.15
10	Stephon Marbury	.75
11	Terrell Brandon	.30
12	Marcus Camby	.15
13	Michael Doleac	.15
14	Doug Christie	.15
15	Brent Barry	.15
16	John Stockton	.30
17	Rod Strickland	.30
18	Shareef Abdur-Rahim	.75
19	Vin Baker	.30
20	Jason Kidd	1.25
21	Nick Anderson	.15
22	Brian Grant	.15
23	Chris Webber	1.25
24	Tariq Abdul-Wahad	.15
25	Jason Williams	1.25
26	Joe Smith	.30
27	Ray Allen	.40
28	Glenn Robinson	.30
29	Alonzo Mourning	.40
30	Scottie Pippen	1.25
31	Mookie Blaylock	.15
32	Christian Laettner	.15
33	Mark Jackson	.15
34	Shawn Kemp	.40
35	Anfernee Hardaway	1.25
36	Chris Mullin	.15
37	Dennis Rodman	.75
38	Lamond Murray	.15
39	Jim Jackson	.15
40	Shaquille O'Neal	1.50
41	Randy Brown	.15
42	Nick Van Exel	.30
43	Robert Traylor	.15
44	Vlade Divac	.15
45	Karl Malone	.60
46	Avery Johnson	.15
47	Jayson Williams	.15
48	Darrell Armstrong	.15
49	Michael Olowokandi	.30
50	Kevin Garnett	2.50
51	Dirk Nowitzki	.60
52	Antawn Jamison	.75
53	Latrell Sprewell	.60
54	Ruben Patterson	.15
55	Vince Carter	4.00
56	Michael Dickerson	.30
57	Raef LaFrentz	.40
58	Keith Van Horn	.60
59	Tom Gugliotta	.30
60	Allen Iverson	2.00
61	Eric Snow	.15
62	Kerry Kittles	.15
63	Sam Cassell	.30
64	Rik Smits	.15
65	Isaiah Rider	.30
66	Anthony Mason	.15
67	Hersey Hawkins	.15
68	Cuttino Mobley	.30
69	Allan Houston	.30
70	Kobe Bryant	3.00
71	Damon Stoudamire	.30
72	Charles Oakley	.15
73	Mike Bibby	.40
74	David Robinson	.60
75	Eddie Jones	.60
76	Juwan Howard	.30
77	Antoine Walker	.50
78	Michael Finley	.30
79	Larry Hughes	1.00
80	Charles Barkley	.60
81	Tracy McGrady	1.25
82	Dikembe Mutombo	.30
83	Rasheed Wallace	.30
84	Jeff Hornacek	.15
85	Patrick Ewing	.30
86	P.J. Brown	.15
87	Brevin Knight	.15
88	Elden Campbell	.15
89	Kenny Anderson	.30
90	Grant Hill	2.00
91	Mitch Richmond	.30
92	Steve Smith	.30
93	Jamal Mashburn	.30
94	Toni Kukoc	.40
95	Hakeem Olajuwon	.60
96	Ron Mercer	.60
97	John Starks	.15
98	Glen Rice	.30
99	Cedric Ceballos	.15
100	Tim Duncan	2.50
101	Karl Malone	.30
102	Alonzo Mourning	.15
103	Gary Payton	.30
104	Scottie Pippen	.75
105	Shaquille O'Neal	1.00
106	Charles Barkley	.30
107	Grant Hill	1.00
108	John Stockton	.15
109	Jason Kidd	.75
110	Reggie Miller	.15
111	Shawn Kemp	.20
112	Patrick Ewing	.15
113	Kevin Garnett	1.25
114	Vince Carter	2.00
115	Kobe Bryant	1.50
116	Chris Webber	.75
117	Tracy McGrady	.75
118	Shareef Abdur-Rahim	.40
119	Paul Pierce	.40
120	Jason Williams	.75
121	Tim Duncan	1.25
122	Eddie Jones	.30
123	Allen Iverson	1.50
124	Stephon Marbury	.40
125	*Elton Brand*	4.00
126	*Lamar Odom*	6.00
127	*Steve Francis*	10.00
128	*Adrian Griffin*	.75
129	*Wally Szczerbiak*	2.00
130	*Baron Davis*	2.50
131	*Richard Hamilton*	2.50
132	*Jonathan Bender*	4.00
133	*Andre Miller*	2.50
134	*Shawn Marion*	4.00
135	*Jason Terry*	1.00
136	*Trajan Langdon*	.75
137	*Corey Maggette*	2.50
138	*William Avery*	.75
139	*Ron Artest*	1.00
140	*Cal Bowdler*	.50
141	*James Posey*	.75
142	*Quincy Lewis*	.75
143	*Kenny Thomas*	.75
144	*Vonteego Cummings*	.75
145	*Todd MacCulloch*	.50
146	*Anthony Carter*	1.00
147	*Aleksandar Radojevic*	.50
148	*Devean George*	1.00
149	*Scott Padgett*	.50
150	*Jumaine Jones*	.60

1999-00 Topps Gallery Player's Private Issue Parallel

This 150-card parallel set reprinted each card in the Gallery set with silver foil on the front and included the words "Player's Private Issue" in small silver foil letters across the top of the photo. Cards were numbered to 250 sets on the back and inserted 1:17 packs.

	MT
Common Player:	2.00
Common Rookie:	3.00
Private Issue Cards:	6x-12x
Rookies:	3x-6x
Subsets:	10x-20x
Production 250 Sets	

1999-00 Topps Gallery Autographs

This four-card insert set was included in packs of Gallery at a rate of 1:375. Maggette and Szczerbiak were seeded 1:437 packs, while Francis and Brand were seeded 1:2,637 packs. Cards were numbered with the player's initials.

		MT
Complete Set (4):		250.00
Common Player:		40.00
Inserted 1:375		
EB	Elton Brand	100.00
TD	Tim Duncan	100.00
CM	Corey Maggette	40.00
WS	Wally Szczerbiak	40.00

1999-00 Topps Gallery Exhibits

Gallery Exhibits has a 30-card insert set featuring 10 different themes, with three players in each theme. Cards were numbered with a "GE" prefix and inserted 1:24 packs.

		MT
Complete Set (30):		100.00
Common Player:		1.00
Inserted 1:24		
GE1	Shaquille O'Neal	8.00
GE2	Chris Webber	5.00
GE3	Karl Malone	2.00
GE4	Hakeem Olajuwon	2.00
GE5	Scottie Pippen	5.00
GE6	Patrick Ewing	1.50
GE7	John Stockton	1.50
GE8	Tim Duncan	10.00
GE9	Grant Hill	10.00
GE10	Dikembe Mutombo	1.00
GE11	Reggie Miller	1.50
GE12	Brian Grant	1.00
GE13	Antoine Walker	1.50
GE14	Damon Stoudamire	1.50
GE15	Tracy McGrady	5.00
GE16	Alonzo Mourning	1.50
GE17	Shawn Kemp	1.00
GE18	Isaiah Rider	1.00
GE19	Vince Carter	15.00
GE20	Antonio McDyess	1.50
GE21	Jason Kidd	5.00
GE22	Kobe Bryant	12.00
GE23	Kevin Garnett	8.00
GE24	Latrell Sprewell	2.00
GE25	Michael Finley	1.50
GE26	Nick Van Exel	1.00
GE27	Anfernee Hardaway	5.00
GE28	Elton Brand	10.00
GE29	Lamar Odom	8.00
GE30	Baron Davis	3.00

1999-00 Topps Gallery Topps Heritage

This 10-card insert set utilized the design from Topps' 1957-58 set and featured artwork of each player. Regular versions were seeded 1:12 packs, while Proof versions had more of a canvas look to them and were seeded 1:40 packs. Heritage inserts were numbered with a "TGH" prefix.

		MT
Complete Set (10):		20.00
Common Player:		1.00
Inserted 1:12		
Heritage Proofs:		2x
Inserted 1:36		
TGH1	Tim Duncan	5.00
TGH2	Elton Brand	4.00
TGH3	Shaquille O'Neal	4.00
TGH4	Stephon Marbury	2.00
TGH5	Allen Iverson	4.00
TGH6	Grant Hill	5.00
TGH7	Charles Barkley	1.50
TGH8	Jason Williams	2.00
TGH9	Scottie Pippen	2.00
TGH10	Allan Houston	1.00

1999-00 Topps Gallery Gallery of Heroes

Gallery of Heroes featured 10 players on a plastic stock with a stained-glass window look. Cards were numbered with a "GH" prefix and inserted 1:24 packs.

		MT
Complete Set (10):		30.00
Common Player:		
Inserted 1:24		
GH1	Kevin Garnett	5.00
GH2	Stephon Marbury	2.50
GH3	Kobe Bryant	8.00
GH4	Vince Carter	10.00
GH5	Tim Duncan	5.00
GH6	Gary Payton	2.00
GH7	Antoine Walker	1.00
GH8	Chris Webber	3.00
GH9	Alonzo Mourning	1.00
GH10	Karl Malone	2.00

1999-00 Topps Gallery Gallery Originals

This 10-card insert set featured rookies from the 1999-00 season on a horizontal card with a swatch of game-used jersey included. Gallery Originals were numbered with a "GO" prefix and inserted 1:87 packs.

		MT
Complete Set (10):		500.00
Common Player:		30.00
Inserted 1:87		
GO1	Elton Brand	125.00
GO2	Shawn Marion	40.00
GO3	Corey Maggette	50.00
GO4	Steve Francis	150.00
GO5	Wally Szczerbiak	50.00
GO6	Baron Davis	40.00
GO7	Jonathan Bender	50.00
GO8	Jason Terry	30.00
GO9	Richard Hamilton	35.00
GO10	Andre Miller	40.00

1999-00 Topps Gallery Photo Gallery

This 10-card insert set featured action shots of players with a thick gold foil strip across the bottom and top of the card. Photo Gallery cards were numbered with a "PG" prefix and inserted 1:12 packs.

		MT
Complete Set (10):		20.00
Common Player:		1.00
Inserted 1:12		
PG1	Tim Duncan	5.00
PG2	Allen Iverson	4.00
PG3	Gary Payton	1.50
PG4	Elton Brand	4.00
PG5	Steve Francis	5.00
PG6	Latrell Sprewell	1.00
PG7	Jason Kidd	2.00
PG8	Shawn Marion	1.50
PG9	Shareef Abdur-Rahim	1.50
PG10	Jason Williams	2.00

1999-00 Topps Gold Label

Topps Gold Label was a 100-card set that included 15 rookies and arrived in three different versions - Class 1, Class 2 and Class 3. Class 1 cards were considered the base cards, while Class 2 cards were seeded 1:2 packs and Class 3 cards were seeded 1:4 packs. All three versions were paralleled in Red and Black Label cards. Inserts included: New Standard, Prime Gold and Quest for the Gold. All inserts were also available in regular, Black and Red Label versions. In addition, each regular-card and insert was paralleled in a one-of-one set.

		MT
Complete Set (100):		65.00
Common Player:		.25
Minor Stars:		.50
Common Rookie (86-100):		.75
Class 2 Cards:		2x
Class 2 Rookies:		1x
Inserted 1:2		
Class 3 Cards:		3x
Class 3 Rooies:		1.5x
Inserted 1:4		
Pack (5):		5.00
Wax Box (24):		70.00
1	Tim Duncan	3.00
2	Steve Smith	.50
3	Jeff Hornacek	.25
4	Kevin Garnett	3.00
5	Paul Pierce	2.00
6	Doug Christie	.25
7	Charles Barkley	.75
8	Nick Van Exel	.50
9	Shareef Abdur-Rahim	1.00
10	Rod Strickland	.50
11	Keith Van Horn	.75
12	Matt Harpring	.50
13	Randy Brown	.25
14	Vin Baker	.50
15	Mark Jackson	.25
16	Latrell Sprewell	.55
17	Anthony Mason	.25
18	Brian Grant	.25
19	Brevin Knight	.25
20	Elden Campbell	.25
21	Allen Iverson	3.00
22	Kobe Bryant	4.00
23	Antawn Jamison	1.50
24	Lindsey Hunter	.25
25	Eddie Jones	.75
26	Michael Finley	.50
27	Juwan Howard	.50
28	Antonio McDyess	.60
29	David Robinson	.75
30	Karl Malone	.75
31	Jason Kidd	1.50
32	Zydrunas Ilgauskas	.50
33	Vince Carter	4.00
34	Maurice Taylor	.50
35	Alonzo Mourning	.60
36	Tim Thomas	.75
37	Dikembe Mutombo	.50
38	Grant Hill	3.00
39	Jason Williams	2.50
40	Scottie Pippen	1.50
41	Stephon Marbury	1.50
42	Reggie Miller	.50
43	Tyrone Nesby	.50
44	Ron Mercer	1.00
45	Terrell Brandon	.50
46	Darrell Armstrong	.50
47	Larry Hughes	.75
48	Alan Henderson	.25
49	Ray Allen	.50
50	Rasheed Wallace	.50
51	Toni Kukoc	.60
52	Patrick Ewing	.50
53	Tom Gugliotta	.50
54	Chris Mills	.25
55	Gary Payton	.75
56	Michael Olowokandi	.50
57	Chris Mullin	.25
58	Shawn Kemp	.40
59	Joe Smith	.50
60	Steve Nash	.25
61	Gary Trent	.25
62	Shaquille O'Neal	2.00
63	Kerry Kittles	.25
64	Tim Hardaway	.60
65	Glenn Robinson	.50
66	Damon Stoudamire	.50
67	Anfernee Hardaway	2.00
68	Vlade Divac	.25
69	John Starks	.25
70	Allan Houston	.50
71	Jerry Stackhouse	.50
72	Avery Johnson	.25
73	Glen Rice	.50
74	Felipe Lopez	.50
75	Clifford Robinson	.25
76	Jamal Mashburn	.50
77	Hakeem Olajuwon	.75
78	Matt Geiger	.25
79	John Stockton	.50
80	Chauncey Billups	.25
81	Chris Webber	1.50
82	Antoine Walker	.75
83	Mike Bibby	1.00
84	Tracy McGrady	1.50
85	Mitch Richmond	.50
86	*Elton Brand*	6.00
87	*Steve Francis*	15.00
88	*Baron Davis*	5.00
89	*Lamar Odom*	10.00
90	*Jonathan Bender*	6.00
91	*Wally Szczerbiak*	4.00
92	*Richard Hamilton*	4.00
93	*Andre Miller*	5.00
94	*Shawn Marion*	6.00
95	*Jason Terry*	3.00
96	*Trajan Langdon*	2.00
97	*Aleksandar Radojevic*	.75
98	*Corey Maggette*	5.00
99	*William Avery*	2.00
100	*Cal Bowdler*	.75

1999-00 Topps Gold Label Class 2 Parallel

Class 2 cards paralleled all 100 cards in Gold Label, but featured a Scoring pose of the player. Class 2 cards were seeded 1:2 packs, while Black Label Class 2 cards were seeded 1:16 packs and Red Label Class 2 cards were sequentially numbered to 50 sets.

	MT
Complete Set (100):	65.00
Common Player:	.25
Minor Stars:	.50
Common Rookie:	.75
Class 2 Cards:	2x
Class 2 Rookies:	1x
Inserted 1:2	
Class 3 Cards:	3x
Class 3 Rooies:	1.5x
Inserted 1:4	
Wax Box (24):	100.00

1999-00 Topps Gold Label Class 3

Class 3 cards paralleled all 100 cards in Gold Label, but featured a portrait shot of the player. Class 3 cards were inserted 1:4 packs, while Black Label Class 3 cards were seeded 1:32 packs and Red Label Class 3 were sequentially numbered to 25.

	MT
Complete Set (100):	65.00
Common Player:	.25
Minor Stars:	.50
Common Rookie:	.75
Class 2 Cards:	2x
Class 2 Rookies:	1x
Inserted 1:2	
Class 3 Cards:	3x
Class 3 Rooies:	1.5x
Inserted 1:4	
Wax Box (24):	100.00

1999-00 Topps Gold Label Black Label Parallel

Black Label was a 300-card parallel set that reprinted all Class 1, 2 and 3 cards from Gold Label. Class 1 Black Label cards were seeded 1:8 packs, Class 2 Black Label cards were seeded 1:16 packs and Class 3 Black Label cards were seeded 1:32 packs. The cards were identified on the back and distinguished on the front by the "Topps Gold Label" logo being printed in black.

	MT
Class 1 Cards:	4x
Class 1 Rookies:	1.5x
Inserted 1:8	
Class 2 Cards:	8x
Class 2 Rookies:	3x
Inserted 1:16	
Class 3 Cards:	12x
Class 3 Rookies:	5x
Inserted 1:32	

1999-00 Topps Gold Label Red Label

Red Label was a 300-card parallel set that reprinted all Class 1, 2 and 3 cards in Gold Label. Class 1 Red Label cards were sequentially numbered to 100, Class 2 Red Label cards were numbered to 50 and Class 3 Red Label cards were numbered to 25 sets.

	MT
Class 1 Cards:	10x-20x
Class 1 Rookies:	4x-8x
Inserted 1:63	
Production 100 Sets	
Class 2 Cards:	15x-30x
Class 2 Rookies:	6x-12x
Inserted 1:126	
Production 50 Sets	
Class 3 Cards:	25x-50x
Class 3 Rookies:	10x-20x
Inserted 1:253	
Production 25 Sets	

1999-00 Topps Gold Label New Standard

This 15-card insert set was numbered with an "NS" prefix and displays top young players and rookies. Regular versions were seeded 1:12 packs, Black Label cards were seeded 1:60 and Red Label cards were seeded 1:1,692 packs and numbered to 25 sets.

		MT
Complete Set (15):		75.00
Common Player:		2.00
Inserted 1:12		
Black Label Cards:		2x
Inserted 1:60		
Red Label Cards:		25x-50x
Inserted 1:692		
Production 25 Sets		
NS1	Vince Carter	10.00
NS2	Kevin Garnett	8.00
NS3	Tim Duncan	8.00
NS4	Kobe Bryant	10.00
NS5	Allen Iverson	6.00
NS6	Jason Williams	5.00
NS7	Keith Van Horn	1.50
NS8	Elton Brand	6.00
NS9	Steve Francis	8.00
NS10	Baron Davis	5.00
NS11	Lamar Odom	10.00
NS12	Jonathan Bender	5.00
NS13	Wally Szczerbiak	8.00
NS14	Jason Terry	2.00
NS15	Corey Maggette	5.00

1999-00 Topps Gold Label Prime Gold

Prime Gold featured 11 veterans that have set the standards for the NBA, and were numbered with a "PG" prefix. Regular versions were inserted 1:18 packs, Black Label versions were seeded 1:90 packs and Red Label cards were numbered to 25 sets and inserted 1:2,312 packs.

		MT
Complete Set (11):		20.00
Common Player:		1.00
Inserted 1:18		
Black Label Cards:		2x
Insereted 1:90		
Red Label Cards:		25x-50x
Inserted 1:2,312		
Production 25 Sets		
PG1	John Stockton	1.00
PG2	Hakeem Olajuwon	1.50
PG3	Charles Barkley	1.50
PG4	Shaquille O'Neal	4.00
PG5	Alonzo Mourning	1.00
PG6	Scottie Pippen	3.00
PG7	Jason Kidd	3.00
PG8	David Robinson	1.50
PG9	Gary Payton	1.50
PG10	Karl Malone	1.50
PG11	Grant Hill	8.00

1999-00 Topps Gold Label Quest For The Gold

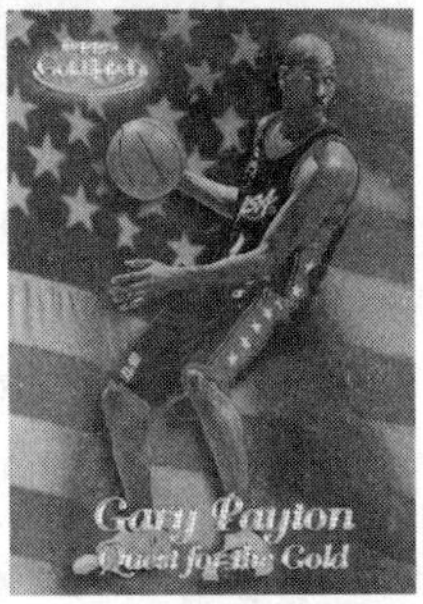

This nine-card insert features players that will be participating in the 2000 Summer Olympics for the USA. They are numbered with a "Q" prefix. Regular Quest for the Gold inserts are seeded 1:9 packs, Black Label cards are seeded 1:45 packs and Red Label cards are seeded 2,813 packs and numbered to 25 sets.

		MT
Complete Set (9):		10.00
Common Player:		.25
Inserted 1:9		
Black Label Cards:		2x
Inserted 1:45		
Red Label Cards:		50x-100x
Inserted 1:2,813		
Production 25 Sets		
Q1	Allan Houston	.25
Q2	Kevin Garnett	5.00
Q3	Gary Payton	.75
Q4	Steve Smith	.25
Q5	Tim Hardaway	.50
Q6	Tim Duncan	5.00
Q7	Jason Kidd	1.50
Q8	Tom Gugliotta	.25
Q9	Vin Baker	.25

1999-00 Topps Tipoff

This retail-exclusive product featured the first 120 cards from Topps Series I and added 12 "sneak preview" cards from Topps Series II. Cards featured the same look and design as Topps, but the rookies carried the same orange borders as the rest of the cards (in Topps Series I, the rookies were featured on white borders). The cards were distinguished by a silver foil Topps Tipoff logo. They arrived in seven-card packs for a buck and contained a Daily Double game card in each pack. The only inserts were autographed cards of Vince Carter, Tim Duncan and Allen Iverson.

		MT
Complete Set (132):		25.00
Common Player:		.10
Minor Stars		.20
Pack (7):		.99
Wax Box (36):		45.00
1	Steve Smith	.20
2	Ron Harper	.10
3	Michael Dickerson	.30
4	LaPhonso Ellis	.10
5	Chris Webber	.60
6	Jason Caffey	.10
7	Bryon Russell	.10
8	Bison Dele	.10
9	Isaiah Rider	.20
10	Dean Garrett	.10
11	Eric Murdock	.10
12	Juwan Howard	.20
13	Latrell Sprewell	.20
14	Jalen Rose	.10
15	Larry Johnson	.20
16	Eric Williams	.10
17	Bryant Reeves	.10
18	Tony Battie	.10
19	Luc Longley	.10
20	Gary Payton	.40
21	Tariq Abdul-Wahad	.10
22	Armen Gilliam	.10
23	Shaquille O'Neal	1.00
24	Gary Trent	.10
25	John Stockton	.20
26	Mark Jackson	.10
27	Cherokee Parks	.10
28	Michael Olowokandi	.40
29	Raef LaFrentz	.40
30	Dell Curry	.10
31	Travis Best	.10
32	Shawn Kemp	.30
33	Voshon Lenard	.10
34	Brian Grant	.10
35	Alvin Williams	.10
36	Derek Fisher	.10
37	Allan Houston	.20
38	Arvydas Sabonis	.10
39	Terry Cummings	.10
40	Dale Ellis	.10
41	Maurice Taylor	.30
42	Grant Hill	1.50
43	Anthony Mason	.10
44	John Wallace	.10
45	David Wesley	.10
46	Nick Van Exel	.20
47	Cuttino Mobley	.20
48	Anfernee Hardaway	1.00
49	Terry Porter	.10
50	Brent Barry	.10
51	Derek Harper	.10
52	Antoine Walker	.50
53	Karl Malone	.40
54	Ben Wallace	.10
55	Vlade Divac	.20
56	Sam Mitchell	.10
57	Joe Smith	.20
58	Shawn Bradley	.10
59	Darrell Armstrong	.20
60	Kenny Anderson	.20
61	Jason Williams	1.00
62	Alonzo Mourning	.30
63	Matt Harpring	.30
64	Antonio Davis	.10
65	Lindsey Hunter	.10
66	Allen Iverson	1.50
67	Mookie Blaylock	.10
68	Wesley Person	.10
69	Bobby Phills	.10
70	Theo Ratliff	.10
71	Antonio Daniels	.20
72	P.J. Brown	.10
73	David Robinson	.40
74	Sean Elliott	.10
75	Zydrunas Ilgauskas	.20
76	Kerry Kittles	.10
77	Otis Thorpe	.10
78	John Starks	.10
79	Jaren Jackson	.10
80	Hersey Hawkins	.10
81	Glenn Robinson	.20
82	Paul Pierce	.75
83	Glen Rice	.20
84	Charlie Ward	.10
85	Dee Brown	.10
86	Danny Fortson	.10
87	Billy Owens	.10
88	Jason Kidd	.60
89	Brent Price	.10
90	Don Reid	.10
91	Mark Bryant	.10
92	Vinny Del Negro	.10
93	Stephon Marbury	.75
94	Donyell Marshall	.10
95	Jim Jackson	.10
96	Horace Grant	.10
97	Calbert Cheaney	.10
98	Vince Carter	2.00
99	Bobby Jackson	.10
100	Alan Henderson	.10
101	Mike Bibby	.50
102	Cedric Henderson	.10
103	Lamond Murray	.10
104	A.C. Green	.10
105	Hakeem Olajuwon	.40
106	George Lynch	.10
107	Kendall Gill	.10
108	Rex Chapman	.10
109	Eddie Jones	.30
110	Kornel David	.10
111	*Jason Terry* (Draft Picks)	1.50
112	*Corey Maggette* (Draft Picks)	3.00
113	*Ron Artest* (Draft Picks)	2.00
114	*Richard Hamilton* (Draft Picks)	2.50
115	*Elton Brand* (Draft Picks)	5.00
116	*Baron Davis* (Draft Picks)	2.50
117	*Wally Szczerbiak* (Draft Picks)	3.00
118	*Steve Francis* (Draft Picks)	6.00
119	*James Posey* (Draft Picks)	1.00
120	*Shawn Marion* (Draft Picks)	2.00
121	Tim Duncan	1.50
122	Danny Manning	.10
123	Chris Mullin	.20
124	Antawn Jamison	.60
125	Kobe Bryant	2.00
126	Matt Geiger	.10
127	Rod Strickland	.20
128	Howard Eisley	.10
129	Steve Nash	.10
130	Felipe Lopez	.30
131	Ron Mercer	.60
132	Checklist	.10

1999-00 Topps Tipoff Autograph Cards

Three different players - Allen Iverson, Tim Duncan and Vince Carter - autographed cards for insertion in Topps Tipoff Basketball. Duncan autographs were inserted 1:12,910 packs, Carter was seeded 1:4,303 and Iverson was found 1:6,455 packs.

		MT
Complete Set (3):		650.00
Common Player:		200.00
AG1 Inserted 1:12,910		
AG2 Inserted 1:4,303		
AG3 Inserted 1:6,455		
AG1	Tim Duncan	300.00
AG2	Vince Carter	200.00
AG3	Allen Iverson	200.00

2000 Topps Team USA

This 96-card set featured 23 Olympians, with 12 from the Men's team and 11 from the Women's team. Each player was featured on four different cards, with one each from the following themes - Achievements, Statistics, Pro, Amatuer, International and Quotes. Each card is also available in a Gold parallel set, which was seeded one per pack. Inserts include: Autographs, National Spirit, Side by Side and USArchival.

		MT
Complete Set (96):		
Common Player:		.15
Minor Stars:		.30
Pack (8)		2.00
Wax Box (24)		40.00
1	Tim Duncan	1.50
2	Jason Kidd	.75
3	Vin Baker	.15
4	Steve Smith	.15
5	Grant Hill	1.50
6	Gary Payton	.50
7	Vince Carter	3.00
7		.15
8	Ray Allen	.30
9	Kevin Garnett	1.50
10	Tim Hardaway	.30
11	Allan Houston	.15
12	Alonzo Mourning	.30
13	Lisa Leslie	2.00
14	Dawn Staley	1.00
15	Katie Smith	1.00
16	Nikki McCray	1.00
17	Ruthie Bolton-Holifield	1.00
18	Chamique Holdsclaw	3.00
19	Yolanda Griffith	1.00
20	Teresa Edwards	.75
21	Natalie Williams	1.00
22	DeLisha Milton	.30
23	Kara Wolters	.50
24	Gary Payton	.50
25	Kevin Garnett	1.50
26	Tim Hardaway	.30
27	Steve Smith	.15
28	Ray Allen	.30
29	Alonzo Mourning	.30
30	Allan Houston	.15
31	Vince Carter	3.00
31		.15
32	Grant Hill	1.50
33	Tim Duncan	1.50
34	Jason Kidd	.75
35	Vin Baker	.15
36	Ruthie Bolton-Holifield	1.00
37	Natalie Williams	1.00
38	Lisa Leslie	2.00
39	Chamique Holdsclaw	3.00
40	Nikki McCray	1.00
41	Dawn Staley	1.00
42	Teresa Edwards	.75
43	Yolanda Griffith	1.00
44	Katie Smith	1.00
45	DeLisha Milton	.30
46	Kara Wolters	.50
47	Vin Baker	.15
48	Jason Kidd	.75
49	Allan Houston	.15
50	Ray Allen	.30
51	Alonzo Mourning	.30
52	Kevin Garnett	1.50
53	Gary Payton	.50
54	Steve Smith	.15
55	Vince Carter	3.00
55		.15
56	Grant Hill	1.00
57	Tim Duncan	1.50
58	Tim Hardaway	.30
59	Chamique Holdsclaw	3.00
60	Katie Smith	1.00
61	Yolanda Griffith	1.00
62	Nikki McCray	1.00
63	Lisa Leslie	2.00
64	Teresa Edwards	.75
65	Dawn Staley	1.00
66	Ruthie Bolton-Holifield	1.00
67	Natalie Williams	1.00
68	DeLisha Milton	.30
69	Kara Wolters	.50
70	Allan Houston	.15
71	Kevin Garnett	1.50
72	Tim Duncan	1.50
73	Tim Hardaway	.30
74	Gary Payton	.50
75	Ray Allen	.30
76	Vince Carter	3.00
76		.15
77	Grant Hill	1.50
78	Vin Baker	.15
79	Alonzo Mourning	.30
80	Steve Smith	.15
81	Jason Kidd	.75
82	Chamique Holdsclaw	3.00
83	Lisa Leslie	2.00
84	Dawn Staley	1.00
85	Natalie Williams	1.00
86	Nikki McCray	1.00
87	Katie Smith	1.00
88	Teresa Edwards	.75
89	Yolanda Griffith	1.00
90	Ruthie Bolton-Holifield	1.00
91	DeLisha Milton	.30
92	Kara Wolters	.50
93	Team USA Men's	1.00
94	Team USA Women's	1.00
95	Group Shot	1.50
96	Checklist	.15

2000 Topps Team USA Gold

This 96-card parallel set reprints each card in the set with a gold finish on the front and the words "Team Gold" below the card number on the back. USA Gold cards are seeded 1:3 packs.

	MT
Complete Set (96):	
Common Player:	.30
Gold Cards:	2x
Inserted 1:1	

2000 Topps Team USA Autograph Cards

This 10-card insert featured members of the Women's USA Basketball Team. Cards are numbered with a two-letter prefix usually corresponding with the player's initials, and the cards are seeded 1:291 packs.

		MT
Complete Set (9):		750.00
Common Player:		40.00
Inserted 1:291		
RH	Ruthie Bolton-Holifield	75.00
TE	Teresa Edwards	60.00
TG	Yolanda Griffith	75.00
CH	Chamique Holdsclaw	200.00
LL	Lisa Leslie	125.00
NM	Nikki McCray	75.00
DM	Delisha Milton	40.00
KS	Katie Smith	75.00
DS	Dawn Staley	75.00
NW	Natalie Williams	75.00

2000 Topps Team USA National Spirit

This 23-card insert set features members from both the Men's and Women's Olympic Team over a gold medal in the background. Cards are numbered with an "NS" and seeded 1:8 packs.

		MT
Complete Set (23):		45.00
Common Player:		.50
Inserted 1:8		
1	Steve Smith	.50
2	Ray Allen	.75
3	Grant Hill	5.00
4	Vince Carter	8.00
4		.50
5	Tim Hardaway	.75
6	Jason Kidd	3.00
7	Vin Baker	.50
8	Alonzo Mourning	.75
9	Tim Duncan	5.00
10	Gary Payton	1.50
11	Allan Houston	.50
12	Kevin Garnett	5.00
13	Nikki McCray	3.00
14	Dawn Staley	3.00
15	Lisa Leslie	5.00
16	Teresa Edwards	2.00
17	Yolanda Griffith	3.00
18	Chamique Holdsclaw	8.00
19	Katie Smith	3.00
20	Ruthie Bolton-Holifield	3.00
21	Natalie Williams	3.00
22	DeLisha Milton	1.00
23	Kara Wolters	1.50

2000 Topps Team USA Side by Side

This 12-card insert set matches a player from the Men's Olympic Team with a player from the Woman's Olympic Team on a horizontal card, with the insert name running down the middle. One side has a Refractor finish (random) on the base versions and those are seeded 1:12 packs, while both side Refractor versions are seeded 1:36 packs. Side by Side inserts are numbered with an "SS" prefix.

		MT
Complete Set (12):		40.00
Common Player:		2.00
Inserted 1:12		
Double Refractors:		2x
Inserted 1:36		
1	Tim Duncan, Lisa Leslie	8.00
2	Allan Houston, Ruthie Bolton-Holifield	4.00
3	Kevin Garnett, Chamique Holdsclaw	10.00
4	Jason Kidd, Katie Smith	4.00
5	Vin Baker, Natalie Williams	2.00
6	Gary Payton, Dawn Staley	4.00
7	Teresa Edwards	6.00
8	Tim Hardaway, Dawn Staley	3.00
9	Steve Smith, Kara Wolters	2.00
10	Alonzo Mourning, Yolanda Griffith	3.00
11	Ray Allen, DeLisha Milton	2.00
12	Grant Hill, Nikki McCray	5.00

2000 Topps Team USA USArchival

This nine-card insert set features a swatch of game-used jersey from the 1999 Olympic qualifying tournament in Puerto Rico. These were seeded 1:323 packs, have a stated print run of 250 sets and are numbered with a "USAR" prefix.

		MT
Complete Set (9):		450.00
Common Player:		30.00
Inserted 1:323		
1	Gary Payton	60.00
2	Jason Kidd	75.00
3	Vin Baker	30.00

4	Tim Duncan	100.00
5	Kevin Garnett	100.00
6	Allan Houston	35.00
7	Steve Smith	30.00
8	Tim Hardaway	40.00
9	Tom Gugliotta	30.00

2000-01 Topps Sean Elliot Night

		MT
Complete Set (1):		5.00
1	Sean Elliot	5.00

2000-01 Topps Dominique Wilkins Night

		MT
Complete Set (1):		5.00
1	Dominique Wilkins	5.00

2000-01 Topps Promos

This two-card set was shipped to hobby dealers and members of the media to promote the upcoming Topps set. Cards were cello wrapped and numbered with a "PP" prefix.

		MT
Complete Set (2):		3.00
Common Player:		2.00
1	Elton Brand	2.00
2	Tim Duncan	3.00

2000-01 Topps

		MT
Complete Set (265):		75.00
Complete Series I (155):		60.00
Complete Series II (140):		20.00
Common Player:		.10
Minor Stars:		.20
Common Rookie:		.50
Inserted 1:5		
Series I Pack (10):		1.50
Series I Box (36):		45.00
Series II Pack (10):		1.00
Series II Box (36):		25.00
1	Elton Brand	1.00
2	Marcus Camby	.10
3	Jalen Rose	.30
4	Jamie Feick	.10
5	Toni Kukoc	.30
6	Todd MacCulloch	.10
7	Mario Elie	.10
8	Doug Christie	.10
9	Sam Cassell	.20
10	Shaquille O'Neal	1.25
11	Larry Hughes	.60
12	Jerry Stackhouse	.20
13	Rick Fox	.10
14	Clifford Robinson	.10
15	Felipe Lopez	.10
16	Dirk Nowitzki	.50
17	Cuttino Mobley	.20
18	Latrell Sprewell	.50
19	Nick Anderson	.10
20	Kevin Garnett	1.50
21	Rik Smits	.10
22	Jerome Williams	.10
23	Chris Webber	.75
24	Jason Terry	.20
25	Elden Campbell	.10
26	Kelvin Cato	.10
27	Tyrone Nesby	.10
28	Jonathan Bender	.50
29	Otis Thorpe	.10
30	Scottie Pippen	.75
31	Radoslav Nesterovic	.10
32	P.J. Brown	.10
33	Reggie Miller	.20
34	Andre Miller	.30
35	Tariq Abdul-Wahad	.10
36	Michael Doleac	.10
37	Rashard Lewis	.40
38	Jacque Vaughn	.10
39	Larry Johnson	.20
40	Steve Francis	1.50
41	Arvydas Sabonis	.10
42	Jaren Jackson	.10
43	Howard Eisley	.10
44	Rod Strickland	.20
45	Tim Thomas	.30
46	Robert Horry	.10
47	Kenny Thomas	.20
48	Anthony Peeler	.10
49	Darrell Armstrong	.10
50	Vince Carter	2.50
51	Othella Harrington	.10
52	Derek Anderson	.20
53	Anthony Carter	.20
54	Scott Burrell	.10
55	Ray Allen	.30
56	Jason Kidd	.75
57	Sean Elliott	.10
58	Muggsy Bogues	.10
59	LaPhonso Ellis	.10
60	Tim Duncan	1.25
61	Adrian Griffin	.20
62	Wally Szczerbiak	.40
63	Austin Croshere	.20
64	Wesley Person	.10
65	James Posey	.20
66	Alan Henderson	.10
67	Ruben Patterson	.10
68	Jahidi White	.10
69	Shawn Marion	.30
70	Lamar Odom	.75
71	Lindsey Hunter	.10
72	Keon Clark	.10
73	Gary Trent	.10
74	Lamond Murray	.10
75	Paul Pierce	.40
76	Charlie Ward	.10
77	Matt Geiger	.10
78	Greg Anthony	.10
79	Horace Grant	.10
80	John Stockton	.20
81	Predrag Stojakovic	.10
82	William Avery	.20
83	Dan Majerle	.10
84	Christian Laettner	.10
85	Dana Barros	.10
86	Corey Benjamin	.10
87	Keith Van Horn	.30
88	Patrick Ewing	.20
89	Steve Smith	.20
90	Antonio Davis	.10
91	Samaki Walker	.10
92	Mitch Richmond	.20
93	Michael Olowokandi	.20
94	Baron Davis	.30
95	Dikembe Mutombo	.20
96	Andrew DeClercq	.10
97	Raef LaFrentz	.20
98	Trajan Langdon	.20
99	Ervin Johnson	.10
100	Alonzo Mourning	.30
101	Kendall Gill	.10
102	George Lynch	.10
103	Detlef Schrempf	.10
104	Donyell Marshall	.10
105	Bo Outlaw	.10
106	Kenny Anderson	.20
107	Eddie Robinson	.20
108	Jermaine O'Neal	.20
109	John Amaechi	.10
110	Glen Rice	.10
111	Vlade Divac	.10
112	Vin Baker	.20
113	Mike Bibby	.30
114	Richard Hamilton	.30
115	Mookie Blaylock	.10
116	Vitaly Potapenko	.10
117	Anthony Mason	.10
118	Robert Pack	.10
119	Vonteego Cummings	.20
120	Michael Finley	.20
121	Ron Artest	.30
122	Tyrone Hill	.10
123	Rodney Rogers	.10
124	Quincy Lewis	.20
125	*Kenyon Martin*	5.00
126	*Stromile Swift*	6.00
127	*Darius Miles*	12.00
128	*Marcus Fizer*	3.00
129	*Mike Miller*	6.00
130	*DerMarr Johnson*	3.00
131	*Chris Mihm*	2.00
132	*Jamal Crawford*	3.00
133	*Joel Przybilla*	1.50
134	*Keyon Dooling*	3.00
135	*Jerome Moiso*	1.50
136	*Etan Thomas*	1.50
137	*Courtney Alexander*	3.00
138	*Mateen Cleaves*	2.50
139	*Jason Collier*	.50
140	*Desmond Mason*	4.00
141	*Quentin Richardson*	4.00
142	*Jamaal Magloire*	1.50
143	*Craig Claxton*	1.50
144	*Morris Peterson*	5.00
145	*Donnell Harvey*	1.50
146	*DeShawn Stevenson*	5.00
147	*Mamadou N'diaye*	.75
148	*Erick Barkley*	2.00
149	*Mark Madsen*	1.50
150	Shaquille O'Neal, Allen Iverson, Grant Hill	1.25
151	Jason Kidd, Nick Van Exel, Sam Cassell	.30
152	Dikembe Mutombo, Shaquille O'Neal, Tim Duncan	.75
153	Eddie Jones, Paul Pierce, Darrell Armstrong	.30
154	Alonzo Mourning, Dikembe Mutombo, Shaquille O'Neal	.50
155	Team Championship Card	.75
156	Jason Williams	.40
157	David Robinson	.40
158	Shammond Williams	.10
159	Charles Oakley	.10
160	Greg Ostertag	.10
161	Juwan Howard	.20
162	Antoine Walker	.30
163	Alan Henderson	.10
164	Eddie Jones	.50
165	Allen Iverson	1.25
166	Grant Hill	1.25
167	Terrell Brandon	.20
168	Stephon Marbury	.50
169	Jason Caffey	.10
170	Sam Mitchell	.10
171	Jamal Mashburn	.20
172	Ron Harper	.10
173	Eric Piatkowski	.10
174	Sam Perkins	.10
175	Walt Williams	.10
176	Bob Sura	.10
177	Michael Curry	.10
178	Nick Van Exel	.20
179	Danny Ferry	.10
180	Randy Brown	.10
181	Danny Fortson	.10
182	Jim Jackson	.10
183	Brad Miller	.10
184	Shawn Bradley	.10
185	Voshon Lenard	.10
186	Erick Dampier	.10
187	Mark Jackson	.10
188	Maurice Taylor	.20
189	Kobe Bryant	2.00
190	Clarence Weatherspoon	.10
191	Bobby Jackson	.10
192	Eric Snow	.10
193	Allan Houston	.30
194	Kurt Thomas	.10
195	Chauncey Billups	.10
196	Tom Gugliotta	.20
197	Theo Ratliff	.10
198	Rasheed Wallace	.30
199	Jon Barry	.10
200	Malik Rose	.10
201	Vernon Maxwell	.10
202	Dee Brown	.10
203	Bryon Russell	.10
204	Brent Barry	.10
205	Tracy McGrady	.75
206	Bryant Reeves	.10
207	Isaac Austin	.10
208	Damon Stoudamire	.20
209	Anfernee Hardaway	.75
210	Aaron McKie	.10
211	Johnny Newman	.10
212	Scott Williams	.10
213	Brian Shaw	.10
214	Corey Maggette	.30
215	Travis Best	.10
216	Hakeem Olajuwon	.40
217	Antawn Jamison	.50
218	John Starks	.10
219	Antonio McDyess	.30
220	Cedric Ceballos	.10
221	Chris Carr	.10
222	Roshown McLeod	.10
223	Calbert Cheaney	.10
224	Gary Payton	.40
225	Karl Malone	.40
226	Michael Dickerson	.20
227	Tracy Murray	.10
228	Chris Childs	.10
229	Pat Garrity	.10
230	Rex Chapman	.10
231	Jumaine Jones	.10
232	Fred Hoiberg	.10
233	Bimbo Coles	.10
234	Shawn Kemp	.25
235	David Wesley	.10
236	Tony Battie	.10
237	Ron Mercer	.30
238	John Wallace	.10
239	Robert Traylor	.10
240	Derrick Coleman	.20
241	Steve Nash	.10
242	Ben Wallace	.10
243	Brian Skinner	.10
244	Chris Gatling	.10
245	Dale Davis	.10
246	Joe Smith	.10
247	Glenn Robinson	.20
248	Kerry Kittles	.10
249	Erick Strickland	.10
250	Sam Cassell	.20
251	Chucky Atkins	.10
252	Brian Grant	.20
253	Bonzi Wells	.30
254	Corliss Williamson	.10
255	Shareef Abdur-Rahim	.40
256	Kevin Willis	.10
257	Scott Padgett	.10
258	Terry Porter	.10
259	Tony Delk	.10
260	Avery Johnson	.10
261	Tim Hardaway	.30
262	Derek Fisher	.10
263	Isaiah Rider	.20
264	Shandon Anderson	.10
265	Adonal Foyle	.10
266	*Hidayet Turkoglu*	3.00
267	*Brian Cardinal*	.50
268	*Iakovos Tsakalidis*	.50
269	*Dalibor Bagaric*	.50
270	*Marco Jaric*	.50
271	*Dan Langhi*	1.00
272	*A.J. Guyton*	1.00
273	*Jake Voskuhl*	.75
274	*Khalid El-Amin*	1.50
275	*Mike Smith*	.50
276	*Soumaila Samake*	.50
277	*Eddie House*	1.00
278	*Eduardo Najera*	1.00
279	*Lavor Postell*	1.00
280	*Hanno Mottola*	1.00
281	*Chris Carrawell*	.75
282	*Olumide Oyedji*	.50
283	*Michael Redd*	1.00
284	*Chris Porter*	2.50
285	*Mark Karcher*	.50
286	Steve Francis, Gary Payton	1.00
287	Darius Miles, Kevin Garnett	2.00
288	Lamar Odom, Shareef Abdur-Rahim	.75
289	Tim Duncan, Alonzo Mourning	.75
290	Elton Brand, Karl Malone	.60
291	Larry Hughes, Allen Iverson	.75
292	Kobe Bryant, Reggie Miller	1.50
293	Vince Carter, Grant Hill	2.00
294	Tracy McGrady, Scottie Pippen	.75
295	Kenyon Martin, Marcus Camby	1.00

2000-01 Topps MVP Promotion

	MT
Common Player:	4.00
Minor Stars:	8.00
Common Rookie (125-149):	2.00
MVP Cards:	20x-40x
MVP Rookies:	2x-4x
Inserted 1:228 Series I	
Inserted 1:179 Series II	

2000-01 Topps Autographs

		MT
Common Player:		10.00
Inserted 1:580 Series I		
Inserted 1:465 Series II		
ROY Auto: 1:11,584 Series II		
TACA	Courtney Alexander	30.00
TARA	Ron Artest	15.00
TAEB	Elton Brand	40.00
TATB	Terrell Brandon	10.00
TAMDC	Marcus Camby	15.00
TASC	Sam Cassell	10.00
TAMC	Mateen Cleaves	25.00
TAJC	Jamal Crawford	40.00
TAKD	Keyon Dooling	30.00
TATD	Tim Duncan	100.00
TASE	Sean Elliott	10.00
TASF	Steve Francis	75.00
TAAJG	A.J. Guyton	10.00
TALH	Larry Hughes	25.00
TAAI	Allen Iverson	60.00
TAAJ	Antawn Jamison	30.00
TAMJ	Magic Johnson	150.00
TAAM	Antonio McDyess	20.00
TATM	Tracy McGrady	50.00
TASO	Shaquille O'Neal	150.00
TASP	Scoonie Penn	10.00
TAJR	Jalen Rose	25.00
TALS	Latrell Sprewell	25.00

2000-01 Topps Cards That Never Were

		MT
Complete Set (10):		40.00
Common Player:		5.00
Inserted 1:18 Series II		
MJ1	Magic Johnson	5.00
MJ2	Magic Johnson	5.00
MJ3	Magic Johnson	5.00
MJ4	Magic Johnson	5.00
MJ5	Magic Johnson	5.00
MJ6	Magic Johnson	5.00
MJ7	Magic Johnson	5.00
MJ8	Magic Johnson	5.00
MJ9	Magic Johnson	5.00
MJ10	Magic Johnson	5.00

2000-01 Topps Chrome Previews

		MT
Complete Set (20):		40.00
Common Player:		.50
Inserted 1:18 Series I		
TCP1	Shaquille O'Neal	5.00
TCP2	Kevin Garnett	6.00
TCP3	Vince Carter	10.00
TCP4	Tim Duncan	5.00
TCP5	Elton Brand	4.00
TCP6	Jason Kidd	3.00
TCP7	Lamar Odom	3.00
TCP8	Marcus Camby	.50
TCP9	Paul Pierce	1.50
TCP10	Steve Francis	6.00
TCP11	Chris Webber	3.00
TCP12	Jalen Rose	1.00
TCP13	John Stockton	1.00
TCP14	Larry Hughes	2.50
TCP15	Ray Allen	1.00
TCP16	Alonzo Mourning	1.00
TCP17	Keith Van Horn	1.50
TCP18	Scottie Pippen	3.00
TCP19	Jerry Stackhouse	.50
TCP20	Andre Miller	1.50

2000-01 Topps Combos

		MT
Complete Set (10):		20.00
Common Player:		1.00
Inserted 1:12 Series I		
Jumbos:		1x
Inserted 1:box		
TC1	California Dreamin' (Kobe Bryant, Shaquille O'Neal)	5.00
TC2	Little Giants (Stephon Marbury, Allen Iverson)	3.00
TC3	West Coast Connection (Jason Williams, Chris Webber)	3.00
TC4	Alumni Alliance (Dikembe Mutombo, Patrick Ewing, Alonzo Mourning)	1.00
TC5	All in the Family (Vince Carter, Tracy McGrady)	5.00
TC6	All NBA (Tim Duncan, Grant Hill)	4.00
TC7	Rookie Leaders (Steve Francis, Elton Brand, Lamar Odom)	5.00
TC8	Hometown Heroes (Jason Kidd, Gary Payton)	2.00
TC9	Blazing Hot (Rasheed Wallace, Steve Smith, Damon Stoudamire, Scottie Pippen)	1.00
TC10	Flash and Fundamental (Kevin Garnett, Tim Duncan)	4.00

2000-01 Topps Combos II

		MT
Complete Set (10):		12.00
Common Player:		.40
Inserted 1:12 Series II		
TC1	Hakeem Olajuwon	.75
TC2	Patrick Ewing	.40
TC3	Karl Malone	.75
TC4	Scottie Pippen	1.50
TC5	Reggie Miller	.40
TC6	Shaquille O'Neal, Magic Johnson	5.00
TC7	Marcus Fizer, Stromile Swift, Kenyon Martin	5.00
TC8	Craig "Speedy" Claxton, Keyon Dooling, Jamal Crawford	2.00
TC9	Mike Miller, DerMarr Johnson, Darius Miles	5.00
TC10	Magic Johnson, Mateen Cleaves	2.00

2000-01 Topps East Meets West Relics

		MT
Common Player:		75.00
Inserted 1:598 HTA Series II		
1	Shaquille O'Neal, Reggie Miller	200.00
2	Glen Rice, Jalen Rose	75.00

2000-01 Topps The Final Piece - Relics

		MT
Common Player:		15.00
Inserted 1:517 Series II		
FP1	Shaquille O'Neal	150.00
FP2	Glen Rice	40.00
FP3	Robert Horry	25.00
FP4	Rick Fox	25.00
FP5	Brian Shaw	25.00
FP6	Ron Harper	35.00
FP7	Derek Fisher	25.00
FP8	A.C. Green	25.00
FP9	John Salley	15.00
FP10	Travis Knight	15.00
FP11	Devean George	25.00
FP12	Reggie Miller	125.00
FP13	Jalen Rose	75.00
FP14	Dale Davis	40.00
FP15	Rik Smits	40.00
FP16	Mark Jackson	60.00
FP17	Travis Best	40.00
FP18	Austin Croshere	50.00
FP19	Derrick McKey	20.00
FP20	Sam Perkins	20.00
FP21	Chris Mullin	125.00
FP22	Jonathan Bender	40.00
FP23	Zan Tabak	15.00

2000-01 Topps Flight Club

		MT
Complete Set (20):		40.00
Common Player:		.75
Inserted 1:18 Series II		
FC1	Vince Carter	10.00
FC2	Larry Hughes	2.00
FC3	Steve Francis	6.00
FC4	Tracy McGrady	3.00
FC5	Jerry Stackhouse	.75
FC6	Kobe Bryant	8.00
FC7	Kevin Garnett	6.00
FC8	Michael Finley	.75
FC9	Latrell Sprewell	2.00
FC10	Antonio McDyess	1.00
FC11	Lamar Odom	3.00
FC12	Shareef Abdur-Rahim	1.50
FC13	Chris Webber	3.00
FC14	Eddie Jones	2.00
FC15	Scottie Pippen	3.00
FC16	Grant Hill	5.00
FC17	Paul Pierce	1.50
FC18	Shawn Marion	2.00
FC19	Rasheed Wallace	1.00
FC20	Tim Duncan	5.00

2000-01 Topps Hidden Gems

		MT
Complete Set (10):		6.00
Common Player:		.25
Inserted 1:11 Series I		
HG1	Karl Malone	1.00
HG2	Latrell Sprewell	1.50
HG3	Kobe Bryant	5.00
HG4	Michael Finley	.25
HG5	Jalen Rose	.50
HG6	Reggie Miller	.50
HG7	John Stockton	.50
HG8	Terrell Brandon	.25
HG9	Nick Van Exel	.25
HG10	Allan Houston	.50

2000-01 Topps Hobby Masters

		MT
Complete Set (10):		25.00
Common Player:		1.00
Inserted 1:5 Series I HTA		
HM1	Kevin Garnett	5.00
HM2	Jason Williams	1.00
HM3	Tim Duncan	4.00
HM4	Tracy McGrady	2.50
HM5	Kobe Bryant	6.00
HM6	Allen Iverson	4.00
HM7	Elton Brand	2.50
HM8	Steve Francis	5.00
HM9	Vince Carter	8.00
HM10	Chris Webber	2.50

2000-01 Topps Magic Johnson Reprints

		MT
Complete Set (7):		150.00
Common Player:		25.00
Inserted 1:486 Series I		
Autographs:		250.00
Inserted 1:6,792		
1	1980-81 (Magic Johnson) (On actual card back - card #18, 88)	25.00
2	1980-81 (Magic Johnson) (On actual card back - card #139)	25.00
3	1981-82 (Magic Johnson) (Card #21)	25.00
4	1981-82 (Magic Johnson) (Card #W109)	25.00
5	1992-93 (Magic Johnson) (Card #2)	25.00
6	1992-93 (Magic Johnson) (Card #54)	25.00
7	1992-93 (Magic Johnson) (Card #126)	25.00

2000-01 Topps Magic Johnson Reprints Autographs

	MT
Inserted 1:486	
Autographs:	300.00
Inserted 1:6,792	

2000-01 Topps No Limit

		MT
Complete Set (20):		25.00
Common Player:		.75
Inserted 1:6 Series II		
NL1	Kobe Bryant	4.00
NL2	Kevin Garnett	3.00
NL3	Vince Carter	5.00
NL4	Tracy McGrady	1.50
NL5	Tim Duncan	2.50
NL6	Elton Brand	1.50
NL7	Lamar Odom	1.50
NL8	Larry Hughes	1.00
NL9	Chris Webber	1.50
NL10	Shareef Abdur-Rahim	.75
NL11	Jason Kidd	1.50
NL12	Gary Payton	.75
NL13	Paul Pierce	.75
NL14	Stromile Swift	3.00
NL15	Darius Miles	4.00
NL16	Mike Miller	2.00
NL17	Jason Williams	.75
NL18	Jamal Crawford	1.50
NL19	Marcus Fizer	2.00
NL20	DerMarr Johnson	1.50

2000-01 Topps Quantum Leaps

		MT
Complete Set (10):		20.00
Common Player:		1.00
Inserted 1:22 Series I		
QL1	Chris Webber	3.00
QL2	Antonio McDyess	1.25
QL3	Stephon Marbury	2.00
QL4	Shareef Abdur-Rahim	2.00
QL5	Kobe Bryant	8.00
QL6	Jason Kidd	3.00
QL7	Elton Brand	4.00
QL8	Lamar Odom	3.00
QL9	Kevin Garnett	6.00
QL10	Jerry Stackhouse	1.00

2000-01 Topps Rise to Stardom

		MT
Complete Set (10):		25.00
Common Player:		.75
Inserted 1:36 Series II		
RS1	Elton Brand	3.00
RS2	Steve Francis	6.00
RS3	Vince Carter	10.00
RS4	Tim Duncan	5.00
RS5	Allen Iverson	5.00
RS6	Damon Stoudamire	.75
RS7	Grant Hill	5.00
RS8	Jason Kidd	3.00
RS9	Chris Webber	3.00
RS10	Shaquille O'Neal	5.00

2000-01 Topps Team Relics

		MT
Complete Set (20):		400.00
Common Player:		20.00
Inserted 1:453 Series I		
TR1	Richard Hamilton	35.00
TR2	Tracy Murray	20.00
TR3	Chris Whitney	20.00
TR4	Jahidi White	20.00
TR5	Rod Strickland	30.00
TR6	Mitch Richmond	30.00
TR7	Juwan Howard	30.00
TR8	Isaac Austin	20.00
TR9	Michael Smith	20.00
TR10	Lorenzo Williams	20.00
TR11	Tony Battie	20.00
TR12	Antoine Walker	35.00
TR13	Adrian Griffin	20.00
TR14	Vitaly Potapenko	20.00
TR15	Pervis Ellison	20.00
TR16	Paul Pierce	40.00
TR17	Eric Williams	20.00
TR18	Dana Barros	20.00
TR19	Walter McCarty	20.00
TR20	Danny Fortson	20.00

2000-01 Topps Chrome

		MT
Complete Set (200):		300.00
Common Player:		.25
Minor Stars:		.40
Common Rookie:		2.00
Production 1,999 Sets		
Pack (4):		3.00
Box (24):		70.00
1	Elton Brand	1.50
2	Marcus Camby	.40
3	Jalen Rose	.50
4	Jamie Feick	.25
5	Toni Kukoc	.50
6	Doug Christie	.25
7	Sam Cassell	.40
8	Shaquille O'Neal	2.50
9	Larry Hughes	.75
10	Jerry Stackhouse	.40
11	Rick Fox	.25
12	Clifford Robinson	.25
13	Dirk Nowitzki	1.25
14	Cuttino Mobley	.40
15	Latrell Sprewell	1.25
16	Kevin Garnett	3.00
17	Jerome Williams	.25
18	Chris Webber	2.00
19	Jason Terry	.40
20	Elden Campbell	.25
21	Jonathan Bender	.75
22	Scottie Pippen	1.50
23	Radoslav Nesterovic	.25
24	Reggie Miller	.40
25	Andre Miller	.60
26	Rashard Lewis	.60
27	Larry Johnson	.25
28	Steve Francis	3.00
29	Rod Strickland	.40
30	Tim Thomas	.50
31	Robert Horry	.25
32	Darrell Armstrong	.25
33	Vince Carter	5.00
34	Othella Harrington	.25
35	Derek Anderson	.40
36	Anthony Carter	.25
37	Ray Allen	.50
38	Jason Kidd	.75
39	Sean Elliott	.25
40	Tim Duncan	2.50
41	Adrian Griffin	.25
42	Wally Szczerbiak	.50
43	Austin Croshere	.25
44	James Posey	.40
45	Alan Henderson	.25
46	Jahidi White	.25
47	Shawn Marion	1.25
48	Lamar Odom	1.50
49	Keon Clark	.25
50	Lamond Murray	.25
51	Paul Pierce	.75
52	Charlie Ward	.25
53	Horace Grant	.25
54	John Stockton	.40
55	Predrag Stojakovic	.40
56	Christian Laettner	.25
57	Keith Van Horn	.50
58	Patrick Ewing	.40
59	Steve Smith	.40
60	Antonio Davis	.25
61	Mitch Richmond	.40
62	Michael Olowokandi	.25
63	Baron Davis	.60
64	Dikembe Mutombo	.25
65	Raef LaFrentz	.25
66	Ervin Johnson	.25
67	Alonzo Mourning	.50
68	Kendall Gill	.25
69	George Lynch	.25
70	Donyell Marshall	.25
71	Bo Outlaw	.25
72	Kenny Anderson	.25
73	John Amaechi	.25
74	Vlade Divac	.25
75	Vin Baker	.25
76	Mike Bibby	.40
77	Richard Hamilton	.50
78	Mookie Blaylock	.25
79	Vitaly Potapenko	.25
80	Anthony Mason	.25
81	Vonteego Cummings	.25
82	Michael Finley	.40
83	Ron Artest	.40
84	Rodney Rogers	.25
85	Team Championship Card	.50
86	Jason Williams	.75
87	David Robinson	.75
88	Charles Oakley	.25
89	Juwan Howard	.40
90	Antoine Walker	.50
91	Roshown McLeod	.25
92	Eddie Jones	1.00
93	Allen Iverson	2.50
94	Grant Hill	2.50
95	Terrell Brandon	.25
96	Stephon Marbury	1.00
97	Jamal Mashburn	.40
98	Ron Harper	.25
99	Jermaine O'Neal	.50
100	Nick Van Exel	.40
101	Danny Fortson	.25
102	Jim Jackson	.25
103	Brad Miller	.25
104	Shawn Bradley	.25
105	Mark Jackson	.25
106	Maurice Taylor	.25
107	Kobe Bryant	4.00
108	Clarence Weatherspoon	.25
109	Eric Snow	.25
110	Allan Houston	.40
111	Chauncey Billups	.25
112	Tom Gugliotta	.25
113	Theo Ratliff	.25
114	Rasheed Wallace	.60
115	Glen Rice	.40
116	Bryon Russell	.25
117	Tracy McGrady	1.50
118	Bryant Reeves	.25
119	Damon Stoudamire	.40
120	Anfernee Hardaway	1.50
121	Johnny Newman	.25
122	Corey Maggette	.60
123	Travis Best	.25
124	Hakeem Olajuwon	.75
125	Antawn Jamison	1.25
126	John Starks	.25
127	Antonio McDyess	.60
128	Gary Payton	.75
129	Karl Malone	.75
130	Michael Dickerson	.25
131	Shawn Kemp	.40
132	David Wesley	.25
133	P.J. Brown	.25
134	Ron Mercer	.40
135	Robert Traylor	.25
136	Derrick Coleman	.25
137	Steve Nash	.25
138	Ben Wallace	.25
139	Brian Skinner	.25
140	Chris Gatling	.25
141	Dale Davis	.25
142	Glenn Robinson	.40
143	Chucky Atkins	.25
144	Brian Grant	.25
145	Corliss Williamson	.25
146	Shareef Abdur-Rahim	.75
147	Avery Johnson	.25
148	Tim Hardaway	.50
149	Isaiah Rider	.25
150	Shandon Anderson	.25
151	*Kenyon Martin*	25.00
152	*Stromile Swift*	30.00
153	*Darius Miles*	75.00
154	*Marcus Fizer*	10.00
155	*Mike Miller*	50.00
156	*DerMarr Johnson*	10.00
157	*Chris Mihm*	6.00
158	*Jamal Crawford*	10.00
159	*Joel Przybilla*	5.00
160	*Keyon Dooling*	10.00
161	*Jerome Moiso*	6.00
162	*Etan Thomas*	5.00
163	*Courtney Alexander*	15.00
164	*Mateen Cleaves*	8.00
165	*Jason Collier*	3.00
166	*Desmond Mason*	15.00
167	*Quentin Richardson*	15.00
168	*Jamaal Magloire*	6.00
169	*Craig "Speedy" Claxton*	5.00
170	*Morris Peterson*	20.00
171	*Donnell Harvey*	5.00
172	*DeShawn Stevenson*	20.00
173	*Mamadou N'diaye*	3.00
174	*Erick Barkley*	6.00
175	*Mark Madsen*	6.00
176	*Hidayet Turkoglu*	10.00
177	*Brian Cardinal*	2.00
178	*Iakovos Tsakalidis*	2.00
179	*Dalibor Bagaric*	2.00
180	*Dragan Tarlac*	2.00
181	*Dan Langhi*	3.00
182	*A.J. Guyton*	4.00
183	*Jake Voskuhl*	2.00
184	*Khalid El-Amin*	4.00
185	*Mike Smith*	2.00
186	*Soumaila Samake*	3.00
187	*Eddie House*	8.00
188	*Eduardo Najera*	4.00
189	*Lavor Postell*	4.00
190	*Hanno Mottola*	3.00
191	*Olumide Oyedji*	3.00
192	*Michael Redd*	4.00
193	*Chris Porter*	8.00
194	*Jabari Smith*	3.00
195	*Marc Jackson*	10.00
196	*Stephen Jackson*	6.00
197	*Pepe Sanchez*	3.00
198	*Daniel Santiago*	4.00
199	*Paul McPherson*	4.00
200	*Mike Penberthy*	4.00

2000-01 Topps Chrome Refractors

	MT
Common Player:	2.00
Refractors:	4x-8x
Common Rookie:	10.00
Production 199 Sets	

2000-01 Topps Chrome Aptitude for Altitude

		MT
Complete Set (10):		10.00
Common Player:		.60
Inserted 1:20		
Refractors:		3x
Inserted 1:200		
AA1	Larry Hughes	1.00
AA2	Steve Francis	5.00
AA3	Shawn Marion	1.50
AA4	Michael Finley	.60
AA5	Allen Iverson	4.00
AA6	Jerry Stackhouse	.60
AA7	Rashard Lewis	.75
AA8	Tim Thomas	.60
AA9	Baron Davis	1.00
AA10	Darius Miles	5.00

2000-01 Topps Chrome Cards That Never Were

		MT
Complete Set (10):		30.00
Common Player:		4.00
Inserted 1:5		
Refractors:		3x
Inserted 1:50		
MJ1	Magic Johnson	4.00
MJ2	Magic Johnson	4.00
MJ3	Magic Johnson	4.00
MJ4	Magic Johnson	4.00
MJ5	Magic Johnson	4.00
MJ6	Magic Johnson	4.00
MJ7	Magic Johnson	4.00
MJ8	agic Johnson	4.00
MJ9	Magic Johnson	4.00
MJ10	Magic Johnson	4.00

2000-01 Topps Chrome Topps Combos

		MT
Complete Set (20):		35.00
Common Player:		.60
Inserted 1:30		
Refractors:		3x
Inserted 1:300		
TC1	Kobe Bryant, Shaquille O'Neal	8.00
TC2	Stephon Marbury, Allen Iverson	3.00
TC3	Jason Williams, Chris Webber	3.00
TC4	Dikembe Mutombo, Patrick Ewing, Alonzo Mourning	1.00
TC5	Vince Carter, Tracy McGrady	8.00
TC6	Tim Duncan, Grant Hill	6.00
TC7	Steve Francis, Elton Brand, Lamar Odom	6.00
TC8	Jason Kidd, Gary Payton	2.00
TC9	Rasheed Wallace, Steve Smith, Damon Stoudamire, Scottie Pippen	2.00
TC10	Kevin Garnett, Tim Duncan	6.00
TC11	Hakeem Olajuwon	1.00
TC12	Patrick Ewing	.60
TC13	Karl Malone	1.00
TC14	Scottie Pippen	1.50
TC15	Reggie Miller	.60
TC16	Shaquille O'Neal, Magic Johnson	5.00
TC17	Marcus Fizer, Stromile Swift, Kenyon Martin	3.00
TC18	Craig "Speedy" Claxton, Keyon Dooling, Jamal Crawford	1.50
TC19	Mike Miller, DerMarr Johnson, Darius Miles	6.00
TC20	Magic Johnson, Mateen Cleaves	2.00

2000-01 Topps Chrome The Final Piece Jersey Relics

		MT
Common Player:		50.00
Production 25 Sets		
Refractors:		2x-4x
Production 10 Sets		
FP1	Shaquille O'Neal	300.00
FP2	Glen Rice	100.00
FP3	Robert Horry	50.00
FP4	Rick Fox	60.00
FP5	Brian Shaw	50.00
FP6	Ron Harper	100.00
FP7	Derek Fisher	75.00
FP8	A.C. Green	60.00
FP9	John Salley	50.00
FP10	Travis Knight	50.00
FP11	Devean George	60.00
FP12	Reggie Miller	200.00
FP13	Jalen Rose	150.00
FP14	Dale Davis	60.00
FP15	Rik Smits	75.00
FP16	Mark Jackson	100.00
FP17	Travis Best	75.00
FP18	Austin Croshere	75.00
FP19	Derrick McKey	60.00
FP20	Sam Perkins	75.00
FP21	Chris Mullin	200.00
FP22	Jonathan Bender	100.00
FP23	Zan Tabak	50.00

2000-01 Topps Chrome The Final Piece Jersey Relics Refract

		MT
Common Player:		50.00
Production 25 Sets		
Refractors:		2x-4x
Production 10 Sets		
FP1	Shaquille O'Neal	300.00
FP2	Glen Rice	100.00
FP3	Robert Horry	50.00
FP4	Rick Fox	60.00
FP5	Brian Shaw	50.00
FP6	Ron Harper	100.00
FP7	Derek Fisher	75.00
FP8	A.C. Green	60.00
FP9	John Salley	50.00
FP10	Travis Knight	50.00
FP11	Devean George	60.00
FP12	Reggie Miller	200.00
FP13	Jalen Rose	150.00
FP14	Dale Davis	60.00
FP15	Rik Smits	75.00
FP16	Mark Jackson	100.00
FP17	Travis Best	75.00
FP18	Austin Croshere	75.00
FP19	Derrick McKey	60.00
FP20	Sam Perkins	75.00
FP21	Chris Mullin	200.00
FP22	Jonathan Bender	100.00
FP23	Zan Tabak	50.00

2000-01 Topps Chrome Hobby Masters

		MT
Complete Set (10):		30.00
Common Player:		1.50
Inserted 1:30		
Refractors:		3x
Inserted 1:602		
HM1	Kevin Garnett	6.00
HM2	Jason Williams	1.50
HM3	Tim Duncan	5.00
HM4	Tracy McGrady	3.00
HM5	Kobe Bryant	8.00
HM6	Allen Iverson	5.00
HM7	Elton Brand	3.00
HM8	Steve Francis	6.00
HM9	Vince Carter	10.00
HM10	Chris Webber	4.00

2000-01 Topps Chrome In the Paint

		MT
Complete Set (10):		25.00
Common Player:		1.50
Inserted 1:60		
Refractors:		3x
Inserted 1:600		
IP1	Elton Brand	6.00
IP2	Tim Duncan	10.00
IP3	Antonio McDyess	2.00
IP4	Karl Malone	3.00
IP5	Rasheed Wallace	2.00
IP6	Antoine Walker	1.50
IP7	Shareef Abdur-Rahim	3.00
IP8	Lamar Odom	6.00
IP9	Kenyon Martin	5.00
IP10	Stromile Swift	6.00

2000-01 Topps Chrome Magic Johnson Reprints

		MT
Complete Set (7):		20.00
Common Player:		4.00
Inserted 1:5		
Refractors:		3x
Inserted 1:500		
1	Magic Johnson	4.00
2	Magic Johnson	4.00
3	Magic Johnson	4.00
4	Magic Johnson	4.00
5	Magic Johnson	4.00
6	Magic Johnson	4.00
7	Magic Johnson	4.00

2000-01 Topps Chrome No Limit

		MT
Complete Set (20):		20.00
Common Player:		.75
Inserted 1:15		
Refractors:		3x
Inserted 1:150		
NL1	Kobe Bryant	4.00
NL2	Kevin Garnett	3.00
NL3	Vince Carter	5.00
NL4	Tracy McGrady	1.50
NL5	Tim Duncan	2.50
NL6	Elton Brand	1.50
NL7	Lamar Odom	1.50
NL8	Larry Hughes	.75
NL9	Chris Webber	2.00
NL10	Shareef Abdur-Rahim	.75
NL11	Jason Kidd	1.50
NL12	Gary Payton	.75
NL13	Paul Pierce	.75
NL14	Stromile Swift	1.50
NL15	Darius Miles	3.00
NL16	Mike Miller	1.50
NL17	Jason Williams	.75
NL18	Jamal Crawford	.75
NL19	Marcus Fizer	.75
NL20	DerMarr Johnson	.75

2000-01 Topps Gallery

		MT
Complete Set (150):		225.00
Common Player:		.15
Minor Stars:		.30
Common Rookie:		3.00
Production 999 Sets		
Pack (6):		3.00
Box (24):		60.00
1	Allen Iverson	2.00
2	Terrell Brandon	.30
3	Tracy McGrady	1.25
4	Shawn Marion	1.00
5	Steve Smith	.30
6	Avery Johnson	.15
7	Gary Payton	.60
8	Mark Jackson	.15
9	Mike Bibby	.30
10	Karl Malone	.60
11	Kevin Garnett	2.50
12	Tim Hardaway	.40
13	Isaiah Rider	.15
14	Corey Maggette	.40
15	Vince Carter	4.00
16	Vin Baker	.15
17	Paul Pierce	.60
18	Matt Harpring	.15
19	Ron Artest	.30
20	Kenny Anderson	.15
21	Larry Hughes	.75
22	Antonio McDyess	.40
23	Shandon Anderson	.15
24	Joe Smith	.15
25	Jermaine O'Neal	.50
26	Horace Grant	.15
27	Ray Allen	.50
28	Keith Van Horn	.50
29	Darrell Armstrong	.15
30	Shaquille O'Neal	2.00
31	Reggie Miller	.40
32	Allan Houston	.30
33	Grant Hill	2.00
34	David Robinson	.60
35	Clifford Robinson	.15
36	Theo Ratliff	.15
37	Rashard Lewis	.40
38	Predrag Stojakovic	.40
39	Jason Kidd	1.25
40	Latrell Sprewell	1.00
41	Stephon Marbury	.75
42	Sam Cassell	.15
43	Brian Grant	.15
44	Jalen Rose	.15
45	Antawn Jamison	1.00
46	Raef Lafrentz	.15
47	Dirk Nowitzki	1.00
48	Lamond Murray	.15
49	Derrick Coleman	.15
50	Steve Francis	2.50
51	Dikembe Mutombo	.15
52	Elton Brand	1.25
53	Christian Laettner	.15
54	Ben Wallace	.15
55	Jim Jackson	.15
56	Cuttino Mobley	.30
57	Jonathan Bender	.40
58	Anthony Mason	.15
59	Tim Thomas	.40
60	Lamar Odom	1.25
61	Glenn Robinson	.30
62	Kendall Gill	.15
63	Glen Rice	.30
64	Anfernee Hardaway	1.25
65	Jason Williams	.60
66	Shawn Kemp	.30
67	Derek Anderson	.30
68	Patrick Ewing	.30
69	Shareef Abdur-Rahim	.60
70	Tim Duncan	2.00
71	Rod Strickland	.30
72	Bryon Russell	.15
73	Antonio Davis	.15
74	Rasheed Wallace	.50
75	Wally Szczerbiak	.40
76	Eric Snow	.15
77	Toni Kukoc	.30
78	Michael Olowokandi	.15
79	Hakeem Olajuwon	.60
80	Kobe Bryant	3.00
81	Mookie Blaylock	.15
82	Michael Finley	.30
83	Jerry Stackhouse	.40
84	Baron Davis	.50
85	Jason Terry	.30
86	Andre Miller	.50
87	Antoine Walker	.40
88	Jamal Mashburn	.30
89	Nick Van Exel	.30
90	Eddie Jones	.75
91	Marcus Camby	.30
92	Scottie Pippen	1.25
93	John Stockton	.30
94	Richard Hamilton	.40
95	John Starks	.15
96	Juwan Howard	.30
97	Michael Dickerson	.15
98	Ron Mercer	.30
99	Chris Webber	1.50
100	Magic Johnson	2.00
101	Shaquille O'Neal	1.00
102	Tim Duncan	1.00
103	Chris Webber	.75
104	Grant Hill	1.00
105	Kevin Garnett	1.25
106	Vince Carter	2.00
107	Gary Payton	.30
108	Jason Kidd	.60
109	Kobe Bryant	1.50
110	Karl Malone	.30
111	Scottie Pippen	.60
112	Reggie Miller	.15
113	John Stockton	.15
114	Elton Brand	.60
115	Tracy McGrady	.60
116	Steve Francis	1.25
117	Lamar Odom	.60
118	Baron Davis	.30
119	Andre Miller	.15
120	Jonathan Bender	.15
121	Paul Pierce	.30
122	Jason Williams	.30
123	Rashard Lewis	.15
124	Larry Hughes	.40
125	Shawn Marion	.50
126	*Kenyon Martin*	12.00
127	*Stromile Swift*	15.00
128	*Darius Miles*	40.00
129	*Marcus Fizer*	8.00
130	*Mike Miller*	20.00
131	*DerMarr Johnson*	8.00
132	*Chris Mihm*	4.00
133	*Jamal Crawford*	8.00
134	*Joel Przybilla*	4.00
135	*Keyon Dooling*	8.00
136	*Jerome Moiso*	5.00
137	*Etan Thomas*	4.00
138	*Courtney Alexander*	10.00
139	*Mateen Cleaves*	6.00
140	*Jason Collier*	3.00
141	*Hidayet Turkoglu*	8.00
142	*Desmond Mason*	10.00
143	*Quentin Richardson*	10.00
144	*Jamaal Magloire*	5.00
145	*Craig "Speedy" Claxton*	4.00
146	*Morris Peterson*	12.00
147	*Donnell Harvey*	4.00
148	*DeShawn Stevenson*	12.00
149	*Stephen Jackson*	4.00
150	*Marc Jackson*	6.00

2000-01 Topps Gallery Charity Gallery

		MT
Complete Set (10):		6.00
Common Player:		.50
Inserted 1:12		
CG1	Eddie Jones	1.25
CG2	Ray Allen	.60
CG3	Elton Brand	2.00
CG4	Jason Kidd	2.00
CG5	Derek Anderson	.50
CG6	Karl Malone	1.00
CG7	Brian Grant	.50
CG8	Shareef Abdur-Rahim	1.00
CG9	Rasheed Wallace	.75
CG10	Marcus Camby	.50

2000-01 Topps Gallery Extremes

		MT
Complete Set (20):		40.00
Common Player:		.75
Inserted 1:18		
E1	Shaquille O'Neal	4.00
E2	Vince Carter	10.00
E3	Allen Iverson	4.00
E4	Kevin Garnett	5.00
E5	Chris Webber	3.00
E6	Larry Hughes	1.25
E7	Jason Williams	1.25
E8	Steve Francis	5.00
E9	Antonio McDyess	1.00
E10	Tim Duncan	4.00
E11	Gary Payton	1.25
E12	Lamar Odom	2.50
E13	Elton Brand	2.50
E14	Michael Finley	.75
E15	Latrell Sprewell	2.00
E16	Shareef Abdur-Rahim	1.25
E17	Jerry Stackhouse	.75
E18	Rashard Lewis	1.00
E19	Shawn Marion	2.00
E20	Darius Miles	8.00

2000-01 Topps Gallery Gallery Signatures - Autographs

		MT
Common Player:		12.00
Inserted 1:158		
Gs-EB	Elton Brand	20.00
Gs-Mc	Mateen Cleaves	12.00
Gs-Jc	Jamal Crawford	15.00
Gs-Sf	Steve Francis	30.00
Gs-MJ	Magic Johnson	125.00
Gs-Ej	Eddie Jones	25.00
Gs-Gp	Gary Payton	20.00

2000-01 Topps Gallery Gallery Originals - Jersey Relics

		MT
Common Player:		10.00
Inserted 1:209		
GO1	Kenyon Martin	20.00
GO2	Stromile Swift	25.00
GO3	Darius Miles	50.00
GO4	Marcus Fizer	15.00
GO5	Mike Miller	30.00
GO6	DerMarr Johnson	15.00
GO7	Chris Mihm	10.00
GO8	Joel Przybilla	10.00
GO9	Keyon Dooling	15.00
GO10	Jerome Moiso	10.00
GO11	Etan Thomas	10.00
GO12	Courtney Alexander	20.00
GO13	Mateen Cleaves	15.00
GO14	Jason Collier	10.00
GO15	Hidayet Turkoglu	20.00
GO16	Desmond Mason	20.00
GO17	Quentin Richardson	20.00
GO18	Jamaal Magloire	12.00
GO19	Craig "Speedy" Claxton	12.00
GO20	Morris Peterson	25.00
GO21	Donnell Harvey	10.00
GO22	DeShawn Stevenson	25.00
GO23	Mamadou N'diaye	10.00
GO24	Erick Barkley	12.00
GO25	Mark Madsen	15.00
GO26	Tracy McGrady	30.00
GO27	Shaquille O'Neal	60.00
GO28	Grant Hill	40.00
GO29	Tim Duncan	75.00
GO30	Antoine Walker	10.00
GO31	Jason Kidd	25.00

Post-1980 cards in Near Mint condition will generally sell for about 75% of the quoted Mint value. Excellent-condition cards bring no more than 40%.

2000-01 Topps Gallery Gallery of Heroes

		MT
Complete Set (10):		18.00
Common Player:		.75
Inserted 1:24		
GH1	Allen Iverson	4.00
GH2	Tim Duncan	4.00
GH3	Kobe Bryant	8.00
GH4	Elton Brand	2.50
GH5	Ray Allen	.75
GH6	Stephon Marbury	1.50
GH7	Eddie Jones	1.50
GH8	Gary Payton	1.25
GH9	Antonio McDyess	1.00
GH10	Shareef Abdur-Rahim	1.25

2000-01 Topps Gallery Heritage

		MT
Complete Set (10):		10.00
Common Player:		.60
Inserted 1:10		
Heritage Proofs:		5x
Production 150 Sets		
H1	Tim Duncan	2.50
H2	Tracy McGrady	1.50
H3	Steve Francis	3.00
H4	Elton Brand	1.50
H5	Rashard Lewis	.60
H6	Larry Hughes	1.00
H7	Shawn Marion	1.25
H8	Baron Davis	.60
H9	Antawn Jamison	1.25
H10	Keyon Dooling	1.00

2000-01 Topps Gallery Heritage Proofs

	MT
Complete Set (10):	50.00
Common Player:	3.00
Production 150 Sets	

2000-01 Topps Gallery Photo Gallery

		MT
Complete Set (10):		15.00
Common Player:		.60
Inserted 1:10		
PG1	Kevin Garnett	3.00
PG2	Grant Hill	2.50
PG3	Kobe Bryant	4.00
PG4	Vince Carter	5.00
PG5	Lamar Odom	1.50
PG6	Stephon Marbury	1.00
PG7	Baron Davis	.75
PG8	Chris Webber	2.00
PG9	Ray Allen	.60
PG10	Kenyon Martin	1.50

2000-01 Topps Gold Label

		MT
Complete Set (100):		200.00
Common Player:		.25
Minor Stars:		.40
Common Rookie:		3.00
Production 1,499 Sets		
Pack (3):		5.00
Box (24):		90.00
1	Steve Francis	3.00
2	Jalen Rose	.50
3	Allen Iverson	2.50
4	Damon Stoudamire	.40
5	David Robinson	.75
6	Bryon Russell	.25
7	Toni Kukoc	.50
8	Tracy McGrady	1.50
9	John Stockton	.40
10	Tim Duncan	2.50
11	Hakeem Olajuwon	.75
12	Antoine Walker	.50
13	Dikembe Mutombo	.25
14	Shawn Kemp	.40
15	Ron Artest	.50
16	Eddie Jones	1.00
17	Dirk Nowitzki	1.00
18	Nick Van Exel	.40
19	Grant Hill	2.50
20	Antawn Jamison	1.00
21	Cuttino Mobley	.40
22	Jonathan Bender	1.00
23	Maurice Taylor	.25
24	Kobe Bryant	4.00
25	Tim Hardaway	.50
26	Tim Thomas	.50
27	Terrell Brandon	.40
28	Marcus Camby	.25
29	Keith Van Horn	.60
30	Shawn Marion	1.00
31	Rasheed Wallace	.60
32	Corey Maggette	.60
33	Jason Kidd	1.50
34	Shaquille O'Neal	2.50
35	Rashard Lewis	.75
36	Karl Malone	.75
37	Michael Dickerson	.25
38	Richard Hamilton	.50
39	Darrell Armstrong	.25
40	Wally Szczerbiak	.50
41	Glen Rice	.40
42	Glenn Robinson	.40
43	Reggie Miller	.40
44	Alonzo Mourning	.50
45	Larry Hughes	1.00
46	Antonio McDyess	.50
47	Derrick Coleman	.40
48	Brevin Knight	.25
49	Jason Terry	.40
50	Elton Brand	1.50
51	Latrell Sprewell	1.00
52	Theo Ratliff	.25
53	Scottie Pippen	1.50
54	Jason Williams	.75
55	Gary Payton	.75
56	Mitch Richmond	.40
57	Vin Baker	.40
58	Raef LaFrentz	.25
59	Anfernee Hardaway	1.50
60	Steve Smith	.40
61	Stephon Marbury	1.00
62	Vlade Divac	.25
63	Jamal Mashburn	.40
64	Jerome Williams	.25
65	Patrick Ewing	.40
66	Lamar Odom	1.50
67	Jerry Stackhouse	.40
68	Michael Finley	.40
69	Vince Carter	5.00
70	Andre Miller	.60
71	Paul Pierce	.75
72	Baron Davis	.60
73	Derek Anderson	.40
74	Chris Webber	1.50
75	Ray Allen	.40
76	Kevin Garnett	3.00
77	Allan Houston	.50
78	Mike Bibby	.40
79	Shareef Abdur-Rahim	.75
80	Juwan Howard	.40
81	*Kenyon Martin*	15.00
82	*Stromile Swift*	25.00
83	*Darius Miles*	60.00
84	*Marcus Fizer*	10.00
85	*Mike Miller*	30.00
86	*DerMarr Johnson*	12.00
87	*Chris Mihm*	6.00
88	*Jamal Crawford*	10.00
89	*Joel Przybilla*	4.00
90	*Keyon Dooling*	10.00
91	*Jerome Moiso*	6.00
92	*Etan Thomas*	5.00
93	*Courtney Alexander*	12.00
94	*Mateen Cleaves*	10.00
95	*Jason Collier*	3.00
96	*Desmond Mason*	12.00
97	*Quentin Richardson*	15.00
98	*Jamaal Magloire*	6.00
99	*Craig "Speedy" Claxton*	5.00
100	*Morris Peterson*	15.00

2000-01 Topps Gold Label Class 2

	MT
Veterans:	1x-2x
Common Player:	.50
Inserted 1:4	
Rookies:	.5x-1x
Common Rookie:	3.00
Production 999 Sets	

2000-01 Topps Gold Lable Class 3

	MT
Veterans:	1.5x-3x
Common Player:	.75
Inserted 1:12	
Rookies:	1x-2x
Common Rookie:	6.00
Production 499 Sets	

2000-01 Topps Gold Label Premium

	MT
Veterans:	3x-6x
Common Player:	1.50
Production 1,000 Sets	
Rookies:	2x-4x
Common Rookie:	12.00
Production 100 Sets	

2000-01 Topps Gold Label Great Expectations

		MT
Complete Set (10):		20.00
Common Player:		1.50
Inserted 1:32		
GE1	Elton Brand	5.00
GE2	Shawn Marion	3.00
GE3	Jason Williams	2.00

GE4	Baron Davis	1.50
GE5	Andre Miller	1.50
GE6	Paul Pierce	2.00
GE7	Lamar Odom	5.00
GE8	Dirk Nowitzki	3.00
GE9	Kenyon Martin	5.00
GE10	Marcus Fizer	3.00

2000-01 Topps Gold Label Home Court Advantage

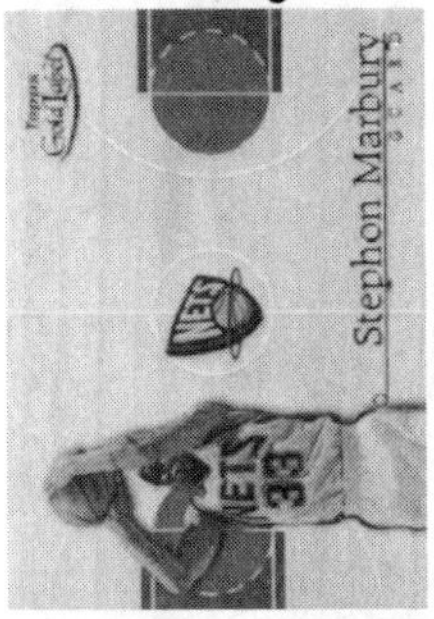

		MT
Complete Set (15):		40.00
Common Player:		1.00
Inserted 1:40		
HCA1	Tim Duncan	10.00
HCA2	Antoine Walker	2.00
HCA3	Chris Webber	6.00
HCA4	Alonzo Mourning	2.00
HCA5	Karl Malone	3.00
HCA6	Allen Iverson	10.00
HCA7	Jason Kidd	6.00
HCA8	Rasheed Wallace	2.00
HCA9	Gary Payton	3.00
HCA10	Shareef Abdur-Rahim	3.00
HCA11	Eddie Jones	4.00
HCA12	Stephon Marbury	4.00
HCA13	Scottie Pippen	6.00
HCA14	Raef LaFrentz	1.00
HCA15	Elton Brand	6.00

2000-01 Topps Gold Label Jam Artists

		MT
Complete Set (10):		15.00
Common Player:		.50
Inserted 1:8		
JA1	Vince Carter	5.00
JA2	Tracy McGrady	2.00
JA3	Steve Francis	3.00
JA4	Jerry Stackhouse	.50
JA5	Kevin Garnett	3.00
JA6	Michael Finley	.50
JA7	Stromile Swift	2.50
JA8	Kobe Bryant	4.00
JA9	Darius Miles	4.00
JA10	Larry Hughes	1.50

2000-01 Topps Gold Label NBA Finals Jersey Cards

		MT
Common Player:		15.00
Inserted 1:40		
TT1	Shaquille O'Neal	150.00
TT2	Glen Rice	40.00
TT3	Robert Horry	25.00
TT4	Rick Fox	25.00
TT5	Brian Shaw	25.00
TT6	Ron Harper	35.00
TT7	Derek Fisher	25.00
TT8	A.C. Green	25.00
TT9	John Salley	15.00
TT10	Travis Knight	15.00
TT11	Devean George	25.00
TT12	Reggie Miller	125.00
TT13	Jalen Rose	75.00
TT14	Dale Davis	40.00
TT15	Rik Smits	40.00
TT16	Mark Jackson	60.00
TT17	Travis Best	40.00
TT18	Austin Croshere	50.00
TT19	Derrick McKey	20.00
TT20	Sam Perkins	20.00
TT21	Chris Mullin	125.00
TT22	Jonathan Bender	40.00
TT23	Zan Tabak	15.00

2000-01 Topps Gold Label NBA Finals Jerseys Leather

	MT
Leather Cards:	2x
Common Player:	30.00
Inserted 1:1,039	

2000-01 Topps Gold Label NBA Playoff Autographs

		MT
Common Player:		30.00
Inserted 1:1,718		
TTA-JR	Jalen Rose	40.00
TTA-SO	Shaquille O'Neal	150.00

2000-01 Topps Heritage

		MT
Complete Set (233):		300.00
Common Player:		.15
Minor Stars:		.30
Common Rookie:		2.00
Production 1,972 Sets		
Pack (8):		4.00
Box (24):		90.00
1	Jason Kidd	1.50
2	Allen Iverson	2.50
3	Tracy McGrady	1.50
4	Tim Duncan	2.50
5	Michael Finley	.40
6	Jason Williams	.75
7	Kobe Bryant	4.00
8	Gary Payton	.75
9	Latrell Sprewell	1.25
10	Antonio McDyess	.50
11	Antoine Walker	.50
12	Steve Francis	3.00
13	Elton Brand	1.50
14	Larry Hughes	1.00
15	Shaquille O'Neal	2.50
16	Lamar Odom	1.50
17	Kevin Garnett	3.00
18	Vince Carter	5.00
19	Ray Allen	.50
20	Grant Hill	2.50
21	Chris Webber	2.00
22	Paul Pierce	.75
23	Shareef Abdur-Rahim	.75
24	Eddie Jones	1.00
25	*Kenyon Martin*	15.00
26	*Stromile Swift*	25.00
27	*Darius Miles*	40.00
28	*Marcus Fizer*	10.00
29	*Mike Miller*	20.00
30	*DerMarr Johnson*	10.00
31	*Chris Mihm*	6.00
32	*Jamal Crawford*	10.00
33	*Joel Przybilla*	4.00
34	*Keyon Dooling*	10.00
35	*Jerome Moiso*	6.00
36	*Etan Thomas*	5.00
37	*Courtney Alexander*	10.00
38	*Mateen Cleaves*	8.00
39	*Jason Collier*	3.00
40	*Hidayet Turkoglu*	10.00
41	*Desmond Mason*	12.00
42	*Quentin Richardson*	12.00
43	*Jamaal Magloire*	5.00
44	*Craig "Speedy" Claxton*	5.00
45	*Morris Peterson*	15.00
46	*Donnell Harvey*	5.00
47	*DeShawn Stevenson*	15.00
48	*Dalibor Bagaric*	2.00
49	*Iakovos Tsakalidis*	2.00
50	*Mamadou N'diaye*	2.00
51	*Erick Barkley*	6.00
52	*Mark Madsen*	5.00
53	*Dan Langhi*	3.00
54	*A.J. Guyton*	4.00
55	*Jake Voskuhl*	2.00
56	*Khalid El-Amin*	4.00
57	*Lavor Postell*	3.00
58	*Eduardo Najera*	3.00
59	*Michael Redd*	4.00
60	*Stephen Jackson*	5.00
61	Andrew DeClercq	.15
62	Darrell Armstrong	.15
63	Al Harrington	.40
64	Johnny Newman	.15
65	Baron Davis	.60
66	Adrian Griffin	.15
67	Anthony Mason	.15
68	Ron Harper	.15
69	Michael Olowokandi	.15
70	Maurice Taylor	.15
71	Travis Best	.15
72	Chucky Atkins	.15
73	Bob Sura	.15
74	Jason Terry	.40
75	Ervin Johnson	.15
76	Eric Snow	.15
77	Shawn Bradley	.15
78	Christian Laettner	.15
79	Keith Van Horn	.60
80	Damon Stoudamire	.30
81	Predrag Stojakovic	.30
82	Clifford Robinson	.15
83	Elden Campbell	.15
84	Kenny Anderson	.30
85	Patrick Ewing	.30
86	Mookie Blaylock	.15
87	Brian Skinner	.15
88	Rick Fox	.15
89	Tim Hardaway	.40
90	Brian Grant	.15
91	Joe Smith	.15
92	Kerry Kittles	.15
93	Scottie Pippen	1.50
94	Steve Smith	.30
95	Sean Elliott	.15
96	Rashard Lewis	.60
97	Michael Dickerson	.30
98	Rod Strickland	.30
99	Sam Cassell	.30
100	Lew Alcindor	2.00
101	John Amaechi	.15
102	Kendall Gill	.15
103	Terrell Brandon	.15
104	Dan Majerle	.15
105	Mark Jackson	.15
106	Hakeem Olajuwon	.75
107	Antawn Jamison	1.25
108	Cedric Ceballos	.15
109	Shandon Anderson	.15
110	Gary Trent	.15
111	Wesley Person	.15
112	James Posey	.30
113	David Wesley	.15
114	Vitaly Potapenko	.15
115	P.J. Brown	.15
116	Alan Henderson	.15
117	Terry Porter	.15
118	Lindsey Hunter	.15
119	Chauncey Billups	.15
120	Doug Christie	.15
121	Glen Rice	.30
122	Jamie Feick	.15
123	Tom Gugliotta	.15
124	Arvydas Sabonis	.15
125	Toni Kukoc	.40
126	Shawn Marion	1.25
127	Dale Davis	.15
128	Corliss Williamson	.15
129	Brent Barry	.15
130	Shammond Williams	.15
131	Nick Anderson	.15
132	Charles Oakley	.15
133	Shaquille O'Neal	1.25
134	Ron Harper	.15
135	Kobe Bryant	2.00
136	Shaquille O'Neal	1.25
137	Team Championship Card	.75
138	Vince Carter, Allen Iverson, Jerry Stackhouse	2.50
139	Allen Iverson, Grant Hill, Vince Carter	3.00
140	Dikembe Mutombo, Alonzo Mourning, Dale Davis	.30
141	Reggie Miller, Darrell Armstrong, Ray Allen	.40
142	Dikembe Mutombo, Elton Brand, Jerome Williams	.50
143	Sam Cassell, Mark Jackson, Eric Snow	.30
144	Checklist	.40
145	Checklist	.40
146	Shaquille O'Neal, Karl Malone, Gary Payton	1.50
147	Shaquille O'Neal, Karl Malone, Chris Webber	2.00
148	Shaquille O'Neal, Ruben Patterson, Rasheed Wallace	1.00
149	Jeff Hornacek, Terrell Brandon, Predrag Stojakovic	.30
150	Shaquille O'Neal, Kevin Garnett, Tim Duncan	2.50
151	Gary Payton, Nick Van Exel, John Stockton	.75
152	Chris Whitney	.15
153	Isaac Austin	.15
154	Kevin Willis	.15
155	Vin Baker	.30
156	Avery Johnson	.15
157	Rodney Rogers	.15
158	Allan Houston	.40
159	Austin Croshere	.15
160	George Lynch	.15
161	Howard Eisley	.15
162	Jerome Williams	.15
163	LaPhonso Ellis	.15
164	Ron Mercer	.40
165	Andre Miller	.60
166	Tariq Abdul-Wahad	.15
167	Donyell Marshall	.15
168	Quincy Lewis	.15
169	Mitch Richmond	.30
170	Richard Hamilton	.40
171	Bryant Reeves	.15
172	Jim Jackson	.15
173	David Robinson	.75
174	Derrick Coleman	.15
175	Anthony Peeler	.15
176	Theo Ratliff	.15
177	Roshown McLeod	.15
178	Ron Artest	.40
179	Bryon Russell	.15
180	Othella Harrington	.15
181	Juwan Howard	.30
182	Antonio Davis	.15
183	Ruben Patterson	.15
184	Shawn Kemp	.40
185	Larry Johnson	.15
186	Marcus Camby	.40
187	Eric Piatkowski	.15
188	Reggie Miller	.40
189	Anfernee Hardaway	1.50
190	Kelvin Cato	.15
191	Erick Dampier	.15
192	Keon Clark	.30
193	Dirk Nowitzki	1.25
194	Robert Traylor	.15
195	Lamond Murray	.15
196	John Wallace	.15
197	Robert Horry	.15
198	Robert Pack	.15
199	Jamal Mashburn	.30
200	Corey Benjamin	.15
201	Matt Harpring	.15
202	Nick Van Exel	.30
203	Vonteego Cummings	.15
204	Ben Wallace	.15
205	Karl Malone	.75
206	Jonathan Bender	1.00
207	Cuttino Mobley	.40
208	Isaiah Rider	.30
209	Tyrone Nesby	.15
210	Jermaine O'Neal	.75
211	Corey Maggette	.60
212	Anthony Carter	.30
213	Horace Grant	.15
214	Tim Thomas	.50
215	Wally Szczerbiak	.50
216	Stephon Marbury	1.00
217	Charlie Ward	.15
218	Bo Outlaw	.15
219	Matt Geiger	.15
220	Vlade Divac	.15
221	Rasheed Wallace	.60
222	Derek Anderson	.30
223	John Stockton	.30
224	Dikembe Mutombo	.15
225	John Starks	.15
226	Mike Bibby	.40
227	Jahidi White	.15
228	Jalen Rose	.50
229	Glenn Robinson	.30
230	Brevin Knight	.15
231	Jerry Stackhouse	.40
232	Raef LaFrentz	.15
233	Brad Miller	.15

2000-01 Topps Heritage Chrome

		MT
Common Player:		6.00
Minor Stars:		10.00
Cards 1-24 Production 272 Sets		
Cards 24-38 Production 72 Sets		
1	Jason Kidd	15.00
2	Allen Iverson	40.00
3	Tracy McGrady	15.00
4	Tim Duncan	25.00
5	Michael Finley	6.00
6	Jason Williams	10.00
7	Kobe Bryant	50.00
8	Gary Payton	10.00
9	Latrell Sprewell	15.00
10	Antonio McDyess	6.00
11	Antoine Walker	6.00
12	Steve Francis	30.00
13	Elton Brand	15.00
14	Larry Hughes	12.00
15	Shaquille O'Neal	25.00
16	Lamar Odom	15.00
17	Kevin Garnett	30.00
18	Vince Carter	60.00
19	Ray Allen	10.00
20	Grant Hill	20.00
21	Chris Webber	15.00
22	Paul Pierce	10.00
23	Shareef Abdur-Rahim	6.00
24	Eddie Jones	12.00
25	Kenyon Martin	75.00
26	Stromile Swift	75.00
27	Darius Miles	300.00
28	Marcus Fizer	40.00
29	Mike Miller	100.00
30	DerMarr Johnson	40.00
31	Chris Mihm	15.00
32	Jamal Crawford	35.00
33	Joel Przybilla	10.00
34	Keyon Dooling	35.00
35	Jerome Moiso	15.00
36	Etan Thomas	12.00
37	Courtney Alexander	40.00
38	Mateen Cleaves	25.00

2000-01 Topps Heritage Autographs

		MT
Common Player:		15.00
Inserted 1:90		
CA	Courtney Alexander	20.00
KD	Keyon Dooling	20.00
SF	Steve Francis	50.00
LH	Larry Hughes	25.00
AI	Allen Iverson	75.00
RL	Rashard Lewis	
SM	Shawn Marion	25.00
DM	Desmond Mason	25.00
TM	Tracy McGrady	50.00
SO	Shaquille O'Neal	125.00
MT	Maurice Taylor	

2000-01 Topps Heritage Authentic Arena Relics

		MT
Complete Set (7):		125.00
Common Player:		12.00
Inserted 1:87		
1	(Shaquille O'Neal)	50.00
2	Gary Payton	20.00
3	(Anfernee Hardaway)	30.00
4	Hakeem Olajuwon	20.00
5	(Toni Kukoc)	30.00
6	(Scottie Pippen)	30.00
7	(Juwan Howard)	12.00

2000-01 Topps Heritage Back to the Future Jersey Relics

		MT
Complete Set (6):		60.00
Common Player:		12.00
Inserted 1:113		
1	Joel Przybilla	12.00
2	Jerome Moiso	20.00
3	Mateen Cleaves	20.00
4	Craig "Speedy" Claxton	15.00
5	Mark Madsen	15.00
6	Jonathan Bender	20.00

2000-01 Topps Heritage Blast From the Past

		MT
Complete Set (15):		20.00
Common Player:		.60
Inserted 1:8		
1	Chris Webber	2.50
2	Kevin Garnett	3.00
3	Allen Iverson	2.00
4	Rasheed Wallace	.60
5	Elton Brand	1.50
6	Grant Hill	2.50
7	Ray Allen	.60
8	Allan Houston	.60
9	Tim Duncan	2.50
10	Eddie Jones	1.00
11	Tracy McGrady	1.50
12	Lamar Odom	1.50
13	Steve Francis	3.00
14	Jason Williams	.75
15	Vince Carter	5.00

Classic Doubles features seven pairs of NBA stars. Two figures are packaged together with a full-color collectable card for each player.

2000-01 Topps Heritage Deja Vu

		MT
Complete Set (10):		8.00
Common Player:		.50
Inserted 1:5		
1	Larry Hughes	.75
2	Elton Brand	1.25
3	Steve Francis	2.50
4	Paul Pierce	.60
5	Allen Iverson	2.00
6	Gary Payton	.60
7	Rasheed Wallace	.50
8	Jason Kidd	1.25
9	Kobe Bryant	3.00
10	Ray Allen	.50

2000-01 Topps Heritage Dynamite Duds Jersey Relics

		MT
Complete Set (17):		250.00
Common Player:		10.00
Inserted 1:97		
1	Dikembe Mutombo	10.00
2	Hanno Mottola	12.00
3	Stephon Marbury	25.00
4	Keith Van Horn	12.00
5	Anfernee Hardaway	40.00
6	Shawn Marion	30.00
7	Shareef Abdur-Rahim	25.00
8	Paul Pierce	25.00
9	Juwan Howard	10.00
10	DerMarr Johnson	20.00
11	Kenyon Martin	35.00
12	Mike Miller	30.00
13	Darius Miles	50.00
14	Keyon Dooling	20.00
15	Quentin Richardson	20.00
16	Iakovos Tsakalidis	10.00
17	Stromile Swift	

2000-01 Topps Heritage Off the Hook

		MT
Complete Set (15):		20.00
Common Player:		.75
Insered 1:8		
1	Kevin Garnett	3.00
2	Vince Carter	5.00
3	Tim Duncan	2.50
4	Allen Iverson	2.50
5	Elton Brand	1.50
6	Jason Kidd	1.50
7	Lamar Odom	1.50
8	Kobe Bryant	4.00
9	Tracy McGrady	1.50
10	Steve Francis	3.00
11	Chris Webber	2.00
12	Larry Hughes	1.00
13	Jason Williams	.75
14	Shareef Abdur-Rahim	.75
15	Darius Miles	4.00

2000-01 Topps Reserve

		MT
Complete Set (134):		500.00
Common Player:		.30
Minor Stars:		.50
Common Rookie:		3.00
Box:		100.00
1	Tim Duncan	3.00
2	Clifford Robinson	.30
3	Allen Iverson	3.00
4	Marcus Camby	.60
5	Chauncey Billups	.30
6	Anthony Mason	.30
7	Toni Kukoc	.60
8	Tim Thomas	.75
9	Corey Maggette	.75
10	Steve Francis	4.00
11	Larry Hughes	1.00
12	Jerome Williams	.30
13	Reggie Miller	.60
14	Chris Gatling	.30
15	Ron Artest	.60
16	Derrick Coleman	.30
17	Paul Pierce	1.00
18	Dikembe Mutombo	.30
19	Andre Miller	.75
20	Gary Payton	1.00
21	Kevin Garnett	4.00
22	Allan Houston	.60
23	Rasheed Wallace	.75
24	Derek Anderson	.50
25	Vin Baker	.30
26	John Stockton	.60
27	Richard Hamilton	.60
28	Mike Bibby	.50
29	Dale Davis	.30
30	Vince Carter	6.00
31	Shawn Marion	1.50
32	Karl Malone	1.00
33	Patrick Ewing	.50
34	Shaquille O'Neal	3.00
35	Jermaine O'Neal	.75
36	Danny Fortson	.30
37	Steve Nash	.30
38	Antoine Walker	.75
39	Jason Terry	.60
40	Vlade Divac	.50
41	Avery Johnson	.30
42	Elton Brand	2.00
43	Mitch Richmond	.50
44	Antonio Davis	.30
45	Shawn Kemp	.50
46	Anfernee Hardaway	2.00
47	Kendall Gill	.30
48	Glen Rice	.50
49	Tim Hardaway	.60
50	Tracy McGrady	2.00
51	Horace Grant	.30
52	Hakeem Olajuwon	1.00
53	Antawn Jamison	1.25
54	Dirk Nowitzki	1.50
55	Antonio McDyess	.75
56	Michael Dickerson	.30
57	Baron Davis	.75
58	Nick Van Exel	.50
59	Joe Smith	.30
60	Kobe Bryant	5.00
61	Ray Allen	.75
62	Keith Van Horn	.75
63	Latrell Sprewell	1.50
64	Jason Kidd	2.00
65	Chris Webber	2.50
66	David Robinson	1.00
67	Mark Jackson	.30
68	Bryon Russell	.30
69	Lamar Odom	2.00
70	Maurice Taylor	.30
71	Jonathan Bender	1.00
72	Raef LaFrentz	.30
73	Sam Cassell	.30
74	Wally Szczerbiak	.60
75	Grant Hill	3.00
76	Theo Ratliff	.30
77	Rashard Lewis	.75
78	Darrell Armstrong	.30
79	Glenn Robinson	.50
80	Stephon Marbury	1.25
81	Michael Olowokandi	.30
82	Isaiah Rider	.30
83	Jalen Rose	.60
84	Cuttino Mobley	.50
85	Jerry Stackhouse	.50
86	Jamal Mashburn	.50
87	Kenny Anderson	.30
88	Michael Finley	.60
89	Lamond Murray	.30
90	Eddie Jones	1.25
91	Eric Snow	.30
92	Terrell Brandon	.50
93	Jason Williams	1.00
94	Scottie Pippen	2.00
95	Rod Strickland	.50
96	Jim Jackson	.30
97	Ron Mercer	.50
98	Juwan Howard	.50
99	Brian Grant	.30
100	Shareef Abdur-Rahim	1.00
101	*Kenyon Martin 499*	30.00
102	*Stromile Swift 999*	20.00
103	*Darius Miles 1499*	50.00
104	*Marcus Fizer 499*	15.00
105	*Mike Miller 999*	30.00
106	*DerMarr Johnson 1499*	10.00
107	*Chris Mihm 499*	10.00
108	*Jamal Crawford 999*	12.00
109	*Joel Przybilla 1499*	4.00
110	*Keyon Dooling 499*	15.00
111	*Jerome Moiso 999*	8.00
112	*Jerome Moiso 1499*	5.00
113	*Courtney Alexander 499*	30.00
114	*Mateen Cleaves 999*	10.00
115	*Jason Collier 1499*	3.00
116	*Hidayet Turkoglu 499*	15.00
117	*Desmond Mason 999*	15.00
118	*Quentin Richardson 1499*	12.00
119	*Jamaal Magloire 499*	12.00
120	*Craig "Speedy" Claxton 999*	6.00
121	*Morris Peterson 1499*	20.00
122	*Donnell Harvey 499*	8.00
123	*DeShawn Stevenson 999*	15.00
124	*Dalibor Bagaric 1499*	3.00
125	*Iakovos Tsakalidis 499*	5.00
126	*Mamadou N'diaye 999*	4.00
127	*Erick Barkley 1499*	6.00
128	*Mark Madsen 499*	15.00
129	*A.J. Guyton 999*	6.00
130	*Khalid El-Amin 1499*	4.00
131	*Lavor Postell 499*	8.00
132	*Marc Jackson 999*	12.00
133	*Stephen Jackson 1499*	8.00
134	*Wang Zhizhi 1499*	50.00

2000-01 Topps Reserve Graded

		MT
Common MT:		6.00
Common NM/MT:		3.00
Inserted 1:Box		
101	Kenyon Martin MT	60.00
101	Kenyon Martin NM/MT	30.00
102	Stromile Swift MT	40.00
102	Stromile Swift NM/MT	20.00
103	Darius Miles MT	75.00
103	Darius Miles NM/MT	30.00
104	Marcus Fizer MT	30.00
104	Marcus Fizer NM/MT	15.00
105	Mike Miller MT	50.00
105	Mike Miller NM/MT	25.00
106	DerMarr Johnson MT	20.00
106	DerMarr Johnson NM/MT	10.00
107	Chris Mihm MT	15.00
107	Chris Mihm NM/MT	10.00
108	Jamal Crawford MT	25.00
108	Jamal Crawford NM/MT	12.00
109	Joel Przybilla MT	8.00
109	Joel Przybilla NM/MT	4.00
110	Keyon Dooling MT	30.00
110	Keyon Dooling NM/MT	15.00
111	Jerome Moiso MT	15.00
111	Jerome Moiso NM/MT	8.00
112	Etan Thomas MT	10.00
112	Etan Thomas NM/MT	5.00
113	Courtney Alexander MT	60.00
113	Courtney Alexander NM/MT	30.00
114	Mateen Cleaves MT	20.00
114	Mateen Cleaves NM/MT	10.00
115	Jason Collier Gem MT	30.00
115	Jason Collier MT	6.00
115	Jason Collier NM/MT	3.00
116	Hidayet Turkoglu MT	30.00
116	Hidayet Turkoglu NM/MT	15.00
117	Desmond Mason NM/MT	15.00
118	Quentin Richardson MT	25.00
118	Quentin Richardson NM/MT	12.00
119	Jamaal Magloire MT	25.00
119	Jamaal Magloire NM/MT	12.00
120	Craig "Speedy" Claxton MT	12.00
120	Craig "Speedy" Claxton NM/MT	6.00
121	Morris Peterson MT	40.00
121	Morris Peterson NM/MT	20.00
122	Donnell Harvey NM/MT	8.00
123	DeShawn Stevenson MT	40.00
123	DeShawn Stevenson NM/MT	15.00
124	Dalibor Bagaric MT	6.00
124	Dalibor Bagaric NM/MT	3.00
125	Iakovos Tsakalidis MT	10.00
125	Iakovos Tsakalidis NM/MT	5.00
126	Mamadou N'diaye MT	8.00
126	Mamadou N'diaye NM/MT	4.00
127	Erick Barkley MT	12.00
127	Erick Barkley NM/MT	6.00
128	Mark Madsen MT	25.00
128	Mark Madsen NM/MT	15.00
129	A.J. Guyton MT	15.00
129	A.J. Guyton NM/MT	6.00
130	Khalid El-Amin MT	8.00
130	Khalid El-Amin NM/MT	4.00
132	Mark Jackson MT	30.00
132	Mark Jackson NM/MT	12.00
133	Stephen Jackson MT	15.00
133	Stephen Jackson NM/MT	8.00
134	Wang Zhizhi MT	100.00
134	Wang Zhizhi NM/MT	50.00

2000-01 Topps Reserve Topps All-Stars - Relic Cards

		MT
Common Player:		10.00
Inserted 1:Box		
TAS1	Allen Iverson	60.00
TAS2	Grant Hill	25.00
TAS3	Alonzo Mourning	30.00
TAS4	Eddie Jones	15.00
TAS5	Allan Houston	15.00
TAS6	Dale Davis	40.00
TAS7	Reggie Miller	40.00
TAS8	Dikembe Mutombo	25.00
TAS9	Glenn Robinson	20.00
TAS10	Ray Allen	30.00
TAS11	Jerry Stackhouse	15.00
TAS12	Tim Duncan	50.00
TAS13	Shaquille O'Neal	50.00
TAS14	Jason Kidd	30.00
TAS15	Gary Payton	25.00
TAS16	John Stockton	30.00
TAS17	Karl Malone	30.00
TAS18	David Robinson	30.00
TAS19	Rasheed Wallace	25.00
TAS20	Michael Finley	25.00
TAS21	Chris Webber	30.00
TAS22	Mike Bibby	10.00
TAS23	Michael Dickerson	10.00
TAS24	Cuttino Mobley	10.00
TAS25	Raef LaFrentz	12.00
TAS26	Dirk Nowitzki	40.00
TAS27	Michael Olowokandi	10.00
TAS28	Paul Pierce	25.00
TAS29	Jason Williams	25.00
TAS30	Elton Brand	25.00
TAS31	Steve Francis	30.00
TAS32	Adrian Griffin	10.00
TAS33	Todd MacCulloch	10.00
TAS34	Andre Miller	15.00
TAS35	James Posey	10.00
TAS36	Wally Szczerbiak	15.00

2000-01 Topps Reserve Reserve Feature - Canvas

		MT
Common Player:		20.00
Inserted 1:Box		
Tr-Mb	Mike Bibby	20.00
Tr-Eb	Elton Brand	40.00
Tr-Bd	Baron Davis	30.00
Tr-Kd	Keyon Dooling	25.00
Tr-Lh	Larry Hughes	25.00
Tr-Aj	Antawn Jamison	30.00
Tr-Mj	Magic Johnson	100.00
Tr-Sm	Shawn Marion	40.00
Tr-Am	Andre Miller	25.00
Tr-Jo	Jermaine O'Neal	30.00
Tr-So	Shaquille O'Neal	150.00
Tr-Ws	Wally Szczerbiak	25.00
Tr-Mt	Maurice Taylor	20.00

2000-01 Topps Stars Promos

This six-card set was distributed to members of the media and hobby dealers to promote Topps Stars Basketball. The set arrived in a cello wrapper, with cards numbered with a "PP" prefix.

		MT
Complete Set (6):		5.00
Common Player:		.75
1	Allen Iverson	3.00
2	Jason Williams	1.50
3	Antonio McDyess	1.00
4	Alonzo Mourning	.75
5	Ray Allen	1.00
6	Larry Hughes	1.50

2000-01 Topps Stars

		MT
Complete Set (150):		60.00
Common Player:		.15
Minor Stars:		.30
Common Rookie:		.50
Pack (6):		3.00
Box (24):		60.00
1	Elton Brand	1.00
2	Paul Pierce	.40
3	Baron Davis	.50
4	Corey Benjamin	.15
5	Jason Kidd	1.00
6	Stephon Marbury	.75
7	Eric Snow	.15
8	Joe Smith	.15
9	Larry Hughes	.75
10	Tim Duncan	1.50
11	Theo Ratliff	.15
12	Dikembe Mutombo	.15
13	Tim Hardaway	.40
14	Glenn Robinson	.30
15	Grant Hill	1.50
16	Patrick Ewing	.30
17	Ron Mercer	.30
18	Ron Artest	.30
19	Tom Gugliotta	.15
20	Steve Smith	.30
21	Vlade Divac	.15
22	Rashard Lewis	.60
23	Tracy McGrady	1.50
24	Bryon Russell	.15
25	Michael Dickerson	.30
26	Juwan Howard	.30
27	Damon Stoudamire	.30
28	Hakeem Olajuwon	.60
29	Antonio McDyess	.40
30	Kobe Bryant	2.50
31	Lindsey Hunter	.15
32	Magic Johnson	1.50
33	Alonzo Mourning	.40
34	Kenny Anderson	.30
35	Allan Houston	.40
36	Keith Van Horn	.60
37	Shawn Marion	.75
38	David Robinson	.60
39	Mitch Richmond	.30
40	Shaquille O'Neal	1.50
41	Gary Payton	.60
42	Sean Elliott	.15
43	Sam Cassell	.30
44	Dale Davis	.15
45	Derek Anderson	.15
46	Jonathan Bender	.75
47	Shandon Anderson	.15
48	Raef LaFrentz	.15
49	Michael Finley	.30
50	Toni Kukoc	.40
51	Anthony Mason	.15
52	Jim Jackson	.15
53	Glen Rice	.30
54	Jalen Rose	.40
55	Keon Clark	.15
56	Anfernee Hardaway	1.00
57	Vin Baker	.30
58	Shawn Kemp	.25
59	John Stockton	.30
60	Shareef Abdur-Rahim	.60
61	Doug Christie	.15
62	Lamond Murray	.15
63	Scottie Pippen	1.00
64	Darrell Armstrong	.15
65	Marcus Camby	.30
66	Wally Szczerbiak	.40
67	Jamal Mashburn	.30
68	Antonio Davis	.15
69	Kevin Garnett	2.00
70	Cuttino Mobley	.15
71	Jerry Stackhouse	.30
72	Cedric Ceballos	.15
73	Nick Van Exel	.30
74	Latrell Sprewell	.60
75	Antoine Walker	.60
76	Allen Iverson	1.50
77	Antawn Jamison	.50
78	Derrick Coleman	.30
79	Jason Terry	.15
80	Steve Francis	2.00
81	Reggie Miller	.30
82	Rasheed Wallace	.50
83	Chris Webber	1.00
84	Donyell Marshall	.15
85	Ruben Patterson	.15
86	Terrell Brandon	.30
87	Mike Bibby	.30
88	Richard Hamilton	.40
89	Jason Williams	.60
90	Corey Maggette	.50
91	Kerry Kittles	.15
92	Karl Malone	.60
93	Rod Strickland	.30
94	Eddie Jones	.60
95	Maurice Taylor	.15
96	Dirk Nowitzki	.60
97	Andre Miller	.50
98	Lamar Odom	1.00
99	Ray Allen	.40
100	Vince Carter	3.00
101	*Chris Mihm*	1.00
102	*Kenyon Martin*	4.00
103	*Stromile Swift*	5.00
104	*Joel Przybilla*	.75
105	*Marcus Fizer*	2.50
106	*Mike Miller*	5.00
107	*Darius Miles*	10.00
108	*Mark Madsen*	.75
109	*Courtney Alexander*	2.00
110	*DeShawn Stevenson*	4.00
111	*DerMarr Johnson*	2.00
112	*Mamadou N'diaye*	.60
113	*Mateen Cleaves*	1.50
114	*Morris Peterson*	4.00
115	*Etan Thomas*	.75
116	*Erick Barkley*	1.00
117	*Quentin Richardson*	2.50
118	*Keyon Dooling*	2.00
119	*Jerome Moiso*	1.00
120	*Desmond Mason*	2.50
121	*Craig "Speedy" Claxton*	.75
122	*Jamaal Magloire*	.75
123	*Donnell Harvey*	.75
124	*Jamal Crawford*	2.00
125	*Jason Collier*	.50
126	Tim Duncan	.75
127	Shaquille O'Neal	.75
128	Vince Carter	1.50
129	Allen Iverson	.75
130	Jason Kidd	.50
131	Kevin Garnett	1.00
132	Gary Payton	.30
133	Tracy McGrady	.50
134	Jason Williams	.30
135	Kobe Bryant	1.25
136	Elton Brand	1.50
137	Ray Allen	.15
138	Grant Hill	.75
139	Chris Webber	.50
140	Latrell Sprewell	.30
141	Alonzo Mourning	.15
142	Lamar Odom	.50
143	Shareef Abdur-Rahim	.30
144	Steve Francis	1.00
145	Magic Johnson	.75
146	Darius Miles	5.00
147	Kenyon Martin	2.50
148	Marcus Fizer	1.50
149	Mateen Cleaves	.75
150	Stromile Swift	2.50

2000-01 Topps Stars Gold

		MT
Common Player:		1.50
Parallel Cards:		5x-10x
Parallel Rookies:		3x-6x
Production 299 Sets		

2000-01 Topps Stars All-Star Authority

		MT
Complete Set (15):		20.00
Common Player:		.50
Inserted 1:12		
ASA1	John Stockton	.75
ASA2	Shaquille O'Neal	4.00
ASA3	Patrick Ewing	.75
ASA4	Hakeem Olajuwon	1.50
ASA5	Karl Malone	1.50
ASA6	Grant Hill	4.00
ASA7	Alonzo Mourning	1.00
ASA8	Jason Kidd	2.00
ASA9	Gary Payton	1.50
ASA10	Scottie Pippen	2.00
ASA11	Tim Duncan	4.00
ASA12	Kevin Garnett	5.00
ASA13	Reggie Miller	.75
ASA14	David Robinson	1.50
ASA15	Dikembe Mutombo	.50

2000-01 Topps Stars Autographs

		MT
Complete Set (8):		400.00
Common Player:		20.00
Inserted 1:316		
TSCA	Courtney Alexander	40.00
TSEB	Elton Brand	40.00
TSJC	Jamal Crawford	40.00
TSTD	Tim Duncan	100.00
TSSF	Steve Francis	60.00
TSAJ	Antawn Jamison	20.00
TSMJ	Magic Johnson	150.00
TSTM	Tracy McGrady	40.00

2000-01 Topps Stars NBA Finals Game-Worn Jersey Relics

		MT
Common Player:		15.00
Lakers Home Inserted 1:646		
Lakers Away Inserted 1:117		
Pacers Home Inserted 1:359		
Inserted 1:71		
TSR1H	Shaquille O'Neal	200.00
TSR1A	Shaquille O'Neal	125.00
TSR2H	Glen Rice	75.00
TSR2A	Glen Rice	50.00
TSR3H	Robert Horry	40.00
TSR3A	Robert Horry	25.00
TSR4H	Rick Fox	40.00
TSR4A	Rick Fox	25.00
TSR5H	Brian Shaw	25.00
TSR5A	Brian Shaw	15.00
TSR6H	Ron Harper	60.00
TSR6A	Ron Harper	35.00
TSR7H	Derek Fisher	40.00
TSR7A	Derek Fisher	25.00
TSR8H	A.C. Green	40.00
TSR8A	A.C. Green	25.00
TSR9H	John Salley	25.00
TSR9A	John Salley	15.00
TSR10H	Travis Knight	30.00
TSR10A	Travis Knight	20.00
TSR11H	Devean George	40.00
TSR11A	Devean George	25.00
TSR12	Reggie Miller	125.00
TSR13	Jalen Rose	75.00
TSR14	Dale Davis	40.00
TSR15	Rik Smits	40.00
TSR16	Mark Jackson	60.00
TSR17	Travis Best	40.00
TSR18	Austin Croshere	50.00
TSR19	Derrick McKey	20.00
TSR20	Sam Perkins	20.00
TSR21	Chris Mullin	125.00
TSR22	Jonathan Bender	40.00
TSR23	Zan Tabak	15.00

2000-01 Topps Stars On The Horizon

		MT
Complete Set (10):		25.00
Common Player:		1.50
Inserted 1:36		
H1	Steve Francis	6.00
H2	Elton Brand	3.00
H3	Tracy McGrady	3.00
H4	Stephon Marbury	2.00
H5	Lamar Odom	3.00
H6	Kenyon Martin	8.00
H7	Shareef Abdur-Rahim	1.50
H8	Marcus Fizer	5.00
H9	Larry Hughes	2.00
H10	Darius Miles	10.00

2000-01 Topps Stars Progression

		MT
Complete Set (5):		12.00
Common Player:		1.00
Inserted 1:24		
P1	Patrick Ewing, Alonzo Mourning, Chris Mihm	1.00
P2	Karl Malone, Elton Brand, Kenyon Martin	6.00
P3	Scottie Pippen, Vince Carter, Darius Miles	10.00
P4	Mitch Richmond, Kobe Bryant, Courtney Alexander	4.00
P5	Magic Johnson, John Stockton, Jamal Crawford	2.00

2000-01 Topps Stars Walk of Fame

		MT
Complete Set (15):		15.00
Common Player:		.60
Inserted 1:8		
WF1	Grant Hill	2.50
WF2	Vince Carter	5.00
WF3	Kevin Garnett	3.00
WF4	Jason Kidd	1.50
WF5	Gary Payton	1.00
WF6	Tim Duncan	2.50
WF7	Allen Iverson	2.50
WF8	Kobe Bryant	4.00
WF9	Ray Allen	.75
WF10	Shareef Abdur-Rahim	1.00
WF11	Chris Webber	1.50
WF12	Karl Malone	1.00
WF13	Reggie Miller	.60
WF14	Jason Williams	1.00
WF15	Elton Brand	1.50

2000-01 Topps Tipoff

		MT
Complete Set (160):		50.00
Common Player:		.10
Minor Stars:		.20
Common Rookie:		.50
Pack (6):		1.00
Box (24):		20.00
1	Elton Brand	1.00
2	Marcus Camby	.20
3	Jalen Rose	.20
4	Jamie Feick	.10
5	Toni Kukoc	.30
6	Todd MacCulloch	.10
7	Mario Elie	.10
8	Doug Christie	.10
9	Sam Cassell	.20
10	Shaquille O'Neal	1.25
11	Larry Hughes	.60
12	Jerry Stackhouse	.20
13	Rick Fox	.10
14	Clifford Robinson	.10
15	Felipe Lopez	.10
16	Dirk Nowitzki	.50
17	Cuttino Mobley	.10
18	Latrell Sprewell	.50
19	Nick Anderson	.10
20	Kevin Garnett	1.50
21	Rik Smits	.10
22	Jerome Williams	.10
23	Chris Webber	.75
24	Jason Terry	.20
25	Elden Campbell	.10
26	Kelvin Cato	.10
27	Tyrone Nesby	.10
28	Jonathan Bender	.50
29	Otis Thorpe	.10
30	Scottie Pippen	.75
31	Radoslav Nesterovic	.10
32	P.J. Brown	.10
33	Reggie Miller	.20
34	Andre Miller	.30
35	Tariq Abdul-Wahad	.10
36	Michael Doleac	.10
37	Rashard Lewis	.60
38	Jeff Hornacek	.10
39	Larry Johnson	.10
40	Steve Francis	1.50
41	Arvydas Sabonis	.10
42	Jaren Jackson	.10
43	Howard Eisley	.10
44	Rod Strickland	.20
45	Tim Thomas	.30
46	Robert Horry	.10
47	Kenny Thomas	.10
48	Anthony Peeler	.10
49	Darrell Armstrong	.10
50	Vince Carter	2.50
51	Othella Harrington	.10
52	Derek Anderson	.20
53	Anthony Carter	.20
54	Scott Burrell	.10
55	Ray Allen	.30
56	Jason Kidd	.75
57	Sean Elliott	.10
58	Muggsy Bogues	.10
59	LaPhonso Ellis	.10
60	Tim Duncan	1.25
61	Adrian Griffin	.10
62	Wally Szczerbiak	.30
63	Austin Croshere	.10
64	Wesley Person	.10
65	James Posey	.10
66	Alan Henderson	.10
67	Ruben Patterson	.10
68	Jahidi White	.10
69	Shawn Marion	.30
70	Lamar Odom	.75
71	Lindsey Hunter	.10
72	Keon Clark	.10
73	Gary Trent	.10
74	Lamond Murray	.10
75	Paul Pierce	.40
76	Charlie Ward	.10
77	Matt Geiger	.10
78	Greg Anthony	.10
79	Horace Grant	.10
80	John Stockton	.20
81	Predrag Stojakovic	.20
82	William Avery	.10
83	Dan Majerle	.10
84	Christian Laettner	.10
85	Dana Barros	.10
86	Corey Benjamin	.10
87	Keith Van Horn	.50
88	Patrick Ewing	.20
89	Steve Smith	.20
90	Antonio Davis	.10
91	Samaki Walker	.10
92	Mitch Richmond	.20
93	Michael Olowokandi	.10
94	Baron Davis	.30
95	Dikembe Mutombo	.20
96	Andrew DeClerq	.10
97	Raef LaFrentz	.20
98	Bob Sura	.10
99	Ervin Johnson	.10
100	Alonzo Mourning	.30
101	Kendall Gill	.10
102	George Lynch	.10
103	A.C. Green	.10
104	Donyell Marshall	.10
105	Corey Maggette	.40
106	Kenny Anderson	.10
107	Eddie Robinson	.10
108	Jermaine O'Neal	.20
109	John Amaechi	.10
110	Glen Rice	.20
111	Vlade Divac	.20
112	Vin Baker	.20
113	Mike Bibby	.30
114	Richard Hamilton	.30
115	Mookie Blaylock	.10
116	Vitaly Potapenko	.10
117	Anthony Mason	.10
118	Robert Pack	.10
119	Vonteego Cummings	.20
120	Michael Finley	.30
121	Ron Artest	.30
122	Tyrone Hill	.10
123	Rodney Rogers	.10
124	Quincy Lewis	.10
125	*Kenyon Martin*	4.00
126	*Stromile Swift*	5.00
127	*Darius Miles*	10.00
128	*Marcus Fizer*	2.50
129	*Mike Miller*	5.00
130	*DerMarr Johnson*	2.00
131	*Chris Mihm*	1.00
132	*Jamal Crawford*	2.00
133	*Joel Przybilla*	.75
134	*Keyon Dooling*	2.00
135	Shaquille O'Neal, Allen Iverson, Grant Hill	1.25
136	Jason Kidd, Nick Van Exel, Sam Cassell	.50
137	Dikembe Mutombo, Shaquille O'Neal, Tim Duncan	.75
138	Eddie Jones, Paul Pierce, Darrell Armstrong	.40
139	Alonzo Mourning, Dikembe Mutombo, Shaquille O'Neal	.60
140	L.A. Lakers	.75
141	Kobe Bryant	2.00
142	Stephon Marbury	.60
143	Antoine Walker	.30
144	Jason Williams	.50
145	Shareef Abdur-Rahim	.50
146	Gary Payton	.50
147	Grant Hill	1.25
148	Allen Iverson	1.25
149	*Khalid El-Amin*	.75
150	*Chris Carrawell*	.50
151	Shaquille O'Neal	.60
152	Allen Iverson	.60
153	Kevin Garnett	.75
154	Vince Carter	1.25
155	Tim Duncan	.60
156	Karl Malone	.20
157	Chris Webber	.40
158	Latrell Sprewell	.30
159	Alonzo Mourning	.20
160	Checklist	.10

2000-01 Topps Tipoff Autographs

		MT
Common Player:		25.00
Inserted 1:1,404		
TOAEB	Elton Brand	50.00
TOASF	Steve Francis	75.00
TOAEJ	Eddie Jones	25.00
TOATM	Tracy McGrady	50.00

2001-02 Topps

		MT
Complete Set (256):		150.00
Common Player:		.15
Minor Stars		.30
Common Rookie:		1.00
Pack (10):		1.50
Box (36):		40.00
1	Shaquille O'Neal	1.50
2	Travis Best	.15
3	Allen Iverson	1.50
4	Shawn Marion	.60
5	Rasheed Wallace	.50
6	Antonio Daniels	.15
7	Rashard Lewis	.30
8	John Starks	.15
9	Stromile Swift	.30
10	Vince Carter	2.50
11	George Lynch	.15
12	Kendall Gill	.15
13	Glen Rice	.30
14	Glenn Robinson	.30
15	Wally Szczerbiak	.30
16	Rick Fox	.15
17	Darius Miles	2.00
18	Jermaine O'Neal	.50
19	Erick Dampier	.15
20	Tracy McGrady	1.25
21	Kevin Garnett	1.50
22	Tim Thomas	.30
23	Larry Hughes	.30
24	Jerry Stackhouse	.50
25	Voshon Lenard	.15
26	Howard Eisley	.15
27	Clarence Weatherspoon	.15
28	Marcus Fizer	.30
29	Elden Campbell	.15
30	Tim Duncan	1.00
31	Doug Christie	.15
32	Keon Clark	.15
33	Patrick Ewing	.30
34	Hakeem Olajuwon	.40
35	Stephen Jackson	.15
36	Larry Johnson	.15
37	Eric Snow	.15
38	Tom Gugliotta	.15
39	Scottie Pippen	.60
40	Chris Webber	1.00
41	David Robinson	.40
42	Elton Brand	.60
43	Theo Ratliff	.30
44	Paul Pierce	.50
45	Jamal Mashburn	.30
46	Eric Williams	.15
47	DerMarr Johnson	.30
48	Andre Miller	.40
49	Dirk Nowitzki	.60
50	Kobe Bryant	2.50
51	Keyon Dooling	.30
52	Brian Grant	.30
53	Ervin Johnson	.15
54	Anthony Peeler	.15
55	Dikembe Mutombo	.30
56	Steve Smith	.30
57	Hidayet Turkoglu	.30
58	Terry Porter	.15
59	Lorenzen Wright	.15
60	Jason Terry	.30
61	Vitaly Potapenko	.15
62	Derrick Coleman	.15
63	Ron Artest	.30
64	Chris Gatling	.15
65	Chris Mihm	.15
66	Reggie Miller	.50
67	Lamar Odom	.60
68	Ron Harper	.30
69	Baron Davis	.50
70	Brad Miller	.15
71	Shawn Bradley	.15
72	James Posey	.30
73	Ben Wallace	.15
74	Marc Jackson	.30
75	Maurice Taylor	.15
76	Aaron McKie	.30
77	Grant Hill	.75
78	Arvydas Sabonis	.30
79	Peja Stojakovic	.50
80	Jason Kidd	.75
81	Vin Baker	.30
82	Morris Peterson	.50
83	Bryon Russell	.15
84	Michael Dickerson	.30
85	Christian Laettner	.30
86	Jerome Williams	.15
87	Desmond Mason	.30
88	Sean Elliott	.30
89	Marcus Camby	.30
90	Stephon Marbury	.50
91	Joel Przybilla	.30
92	Alonzo Mourning	.40
93	Brian Shaw	.15
94	Austin Croshere	.15
95	Mookie Blaylock	.15
96	Mateen Cleaves	.30
97	Nick Van Exel	.40
98	Michael Finley	.50
99	Jamal Crawford	.30
100	Steve Francis	1.00
101	Tim Hardaway	.30
102	Sam Cassell	.30
103	Shammond Williams	.15
104	DeShawn Stevenson	.30
105	Bryant Reeves	.15
106	Richard Hamilton	.40
107	Antonio Davis	.15
108	Brent Barry	.30
109	Derek Anderson	.30
110	Kenny Anderson	.30
111	Brevin Knight	.15
112	Tyrone Nesby	.15
113	Erick Strickland	.15
114	Jacque Vaughn	.15
115	John Stockton	.50
116	Alvin Williams	.15
117	Craig "Speedy" Claxton	.30
118	Bo Outlaw	.15
119	Jahidi White	.15
120	Karl Malone	.60
121	Charles Oakley	.15
122	Malik Rose	.15
123	Avery Johnson	.15
124	Toni Kukoc	.30
125	Bryant Stith	.15
126	P.J. Brown	.15
127	Ron Mercer	.30
128	Lamond Murray	.15
129	Steve Nash	.30
130	Raef LaFrentz	.15
131	Corliss Williamson	.15
132	Danny Fortson	.15
133	Chris Porter	.15
134	Shandon Anderson	.15
135	Jalen Rose	.50
136	Corey Maggette	.30
137	Horace Grant	.30
138	Eddie Jones	.40
139	Chauncey Billups	.15
140	Ray Allen	.50
141	Terrell Brandon	.30
142	Keith Van Horn	.30
143	Allan Houston	.30
144	Mark Jackson	.30
145	Pat Garrity	.15
146	Anfernee Hardaway	.40
147	Iakovos Tsakalidis	.15
148	Damon Stoudamire	.15
149	Bobby Jackson	.15
150	Antawn Jamison	.60
151	Kenny Thomas	.15
152	Jonathan Bender	.40
153	Jeff McInnis	.15
154	Robert Horry	.15
155	Anthony Mason	.30
156	Lindsey Hunter	.15
157	LaPhonso Ellis	.15
158	Jamie Feick	.15
159	Kurt Thomas	.15
160	Gary Payton	.50
161	Rod Strickland	.30
162	Bonzi Wells	.30
163	Scot Pollard	.15
164	*Raja Bell*	1.50
165	Rodney Rogers	.15
166	John Amaechi	.15
167	Darrell Armstrong	.15
168	Aaron Williams	.15
169	Latrell Sprewell	.60
170	Radoslav Nesterovic	.15
171	Anthony Carter	.15
172	Quentin Richardson	.30
173	*Primoz Brezoc*	1.25
174	Michael Olowokandi	.15
175	Jason Williams	.40
176	Ruben Patterson	.15
177	Chris Childs	.15
178	Greg Ostertag	.15
179	Mike Bibby	.30
180	Mitch Richmond	.30
181	Donyell Marshall	.15
182	Dale Davis	.15
183	Tony Delk	.15
184	Mike Miller	1.00
185	Charlie Ward	.15
186	Kenyon Martin	.30
187	Walt Williams	.15
188	Al Harrington	.30
189	Chucky Atkins	.15
190	Kevin Willis	.15
191	Juwan Howard	.30
192	Jim Jackson	.15
193	Antonio McDyess	.40
194	Jamaal Magloire	.30
195	Mark Blount	.15
196	Fred Hoiberg	.15
197	Nazr Mohammed	.15
198	Antoine Walker	.50
199	Wang Zhizhi	.75
200	Shareef Abdur-Rahim	.50
201	Chris Whitney	.15
202	David Wesley	.15
203	Matt Harpring	.15
204	George McCloud	.15
205	Joe Smith	.30
206	Cuttino Mobley	.30
207	Tyrone Hill	.15
208	Clifford Robinson	.15
209	Vlade Divac	.30
210	Eddie Robinson	.30
211	Michael Curry	.15
212	Courtney Alexander	.40
213	Grant Long	.15
214	Dan Majerle	.15
215	Shaquille O'Neal, Kobe Bryant, Chris Webber, Allen Iverson, Jerry Stackhouse, Vince Carter	1.50
216	Shaquille O'Neal, Tim Duncan, Antonio McDyess, Dikembe Mutombo, Ben Wallace, Antonio Davis	.50
217	Jason Kidd, John Stockton, Nick Van Exel, Andre Miller, Mark Jackson, Sam Cassell	.50
218	Mookie Blaylock, Doug Christie, Jason Kidd, Allen Iverson, Baron Davis, Ron Artest	.30
219	Shawn Bradley, Shaquille O'Neal, Adonal Foyle, Theo Ratliff, Jermaine O'Neal, Dikembe Mutombo	.30
220	Team Championship Card	1.00
221	*Kwame Brown*	10.00
222	*Tyson Chandler*	10.00
223	*Pau Gasol*	12.00
224	*Eddy Curry*	8.00
225	*Jason Richardson*	20.00
226	*Shane Battier*	15.00
227	*Eddie Griffin*	10.00
228	*DeSagana Diop*	4.00
229	*Rodney White*	5.00
230	*Joe Johnson*	8.00
231	*Kedrick Brown*	3.00
232	*Vladimir Radmanovic*	4.00
233	*Richard Jefferson*	6.00
234	*Troy Murphy*	5.00
235	*Steven Hunter*	1.50
236	*Kirk Haston*	4.00
237	*Michael Bradley*	2.00
238	*Jason Collins*	1.50
239	*Zach Randolph*	6.00
240	*Brendan Haywood*	6.00
241	*Joseph Forte*	6.00
242	*Jeryl Sasser*	2.00
243	*Brandon Armstrong*	2.00
244	*Gerald Wallace*	5.00
245	*Samuel Dalembert*	1.00
246	*Jamaal Tinsley*	12.00
247	*Tony Parker*	10.00
248	*Trenton Hassell*	4.00
249	*Gilbert Arenas*	3.00
250	*Jeff Trepagnier*	1.50
251	*Damone Brown*	1.00
252	*Loren Woods*	5.00
253	*Ousmane Cisse*	1.00
254	*Ken Johnson*	1.00
255	*Kenny Satterfield*	2.00
256	*Alvin Jones*	2.00
257	Pre-Season Exch	40.00

2001-02 Topps Autographs

		MT
Common Player:		15.00
TA-KAJ	Kareem Abdul-Jabbar	150.00
TA-JB	Jonathan Bender	15.00
TA-RH	Richard Hamilton	20.00
TA-AJ	Antawn Jamison	20.00
TA-LJ	Larry Johnson	15.00
TA-MJ	Magic Johnson	150.00
TA-DM	Desmond Mason	20.00
TA-SO	Shaquille O'Neal	100.00
TA-JT	Jason Terry	15.00

2001-02 Topps All-Star Remnants

		MT
Common Player:		10.00
Inserted 1:160 H; 1:123 R		
TR-RA	Ray Allen	20.00
TR-MB	Mike Bibby	10.00
TR-EB	Elton Brand	20.00
TR-BD	Baron Davis	15.00
TR-TD	Tim Duncan	30.00
TR-SF	Steve Francis	25.00
TR-RH	Richard Hamilton	10.00
TR-AH	Allan Houston	10.00
TR-RL	Raef LaFrentz	10.00
TR-SM	Shawn Marion	20.00
TR-DM	Darius Miles	40.00
TR-AM	Andre Miller	10.00
TR-DN	Dirk Nowitzki	25.00
TR-LO	Lamar Odom	15.00
TR-SO	Shaquille O'Neal	40.00
TR-QR	Quentin Richardson	15.00
TR-JS	Jerry Stackhouse	20.00
TR-JT	Jason Terry	10.00
TR-RW	Rasheed Wallace	20.00
TR-CW	Chris Webber	30.00
TR-JW	Jason Williams	15.00

2001-02 Topps All-Star Remnant Autographs

		MT
Common Player:		40.00
TRA-MB	Mike Bibby/10	
TRA-EB	Elton Brand/42	75.00
TRA-BD	Baron Davis/1	
TRA-TD	Tim Duncan/21	150.00
TRA-RH	Richard Hamilton/32	50.00
TRA-RL	Raef LaFrentz/45	40.00
TRA-SM	Shawn Marion/32	75.00
TRA-AM	Andre Miller/24	50.00
TRA-SO	Shaquille O'Neal/34	
TRA-JT	Jason Terry/31	50.00

2001-02 Topps Kareem Abdul-Jabbar Reprints

		MT
Complete Set (13):		30.00
Common Player:		3.00
Inserted 1:74 H; 1:11 R		
1	Lew Alcindor	3.00
2	Lew Alcindor	3.00
3	Lew Alcindor	3.00
4	Kareem Abdul-Jabbar	3.00
5	Kareem Abdul-Jabbar	3.00
6	Kareem Abdul-Jabbar	3.00
7	Kareem Abdul-Jabbar	3.00
8	Kareem Abdul-Jabbar	3.00
9	Kareem Abdul-Jabbar	3.00
10	Kareem Abdul-Jabbar	3.00
11	Kareem Abdul-Jabbar	3.00
12	Kareem Abdul-Jabbar	3.00
13	Kareem Abdul-Jabbar	3.00

2001-02 Topps Kareem Abdul-Jabbar Reprint Autographs

		MT
Complete Set (13):		
Common Player:		
1	Lew Alcindor	
2	Lew Alcindor	
3	Lew Alcindor	
4	Kareem Abdul-Jabbar	
5	Kareem Abdul-Jabbar	
6	Kareem Abdul-Jabbar	
7	Kareem Abdul-Jabbar	
8	Kareem Abdul-Jabbar	
9	Kareem Abdul-Jabbar	
10	Kareem Abdul-Jabbar	
11	Kareem Abdul-Jabbar	
12	Kareem Abdul-Jabbar	
13	Kareem Abdul-Jabbar	

2001-02 Topps Lottery Legends

		MT
Complete Set (13):		20.00
Common Player:		.60
Inserted 1:6 H; 1:5 R		
LL1	Shaquille O'Neal	2.50
LL2	Steve Francis	2.00
LL3	Darius Miles	4.00
LL4	Stephon Marbury	1.00
LL5	Vince Carter	5.00
LL6	Antoine Walker	1.00
LL7	Jason Williams	1.00
LL8	Larry Hughes	.60
LL9	Tracy McGrady	2.50
LL10	Paul Pierce	1.00
LL11	Allan Houston	.75
LL12	Austin Croshere	.60
LL13	Kobe Bryant	5.00

2001-02 Topps Mad Game

		MT
Complete Set (10):		50.00
Common Player:		4.00
Inserted 1:38 H; 1:29 R		
MG1	Allen Iverson	6.00
MG2	Shaquille O'Neal	5.00
MG3	Tim Duncan	4.00
MG4	Vince Carter	10.00
MG5	Kevin Garnett	6.00
MG6	Kobe Bryant	10.00
MG7	Tracy McGrady	5.00
MG8	Steve Francis	4.00
MG9	Chris Webber	4.00
MG10	Darius Miles	8.00

2001-02 Topps Team Topps

		MT
Complete Set (10):		12.00
Common Player:		1.00
Inserted 1:8 H; 1:7 R		
TT1	Shaquille O'Neal	3.00
TT2	Tim Duncan	2.50
TT3	Antawn Jamison	1.50
TT4	Jason Terry	1.00
TT5	Baron Davis	1.25
TT6	Elton Brand	1.50
TT7	Peja Stojakovic	1.00
TT8	Richard Hamilton	1.00
TT9	Shawn Marion	1.50
TT10	Team Shot	2.00

2001-02 Topps Champions & Contenders

		MT
Complete Set (150):		
Common Player:		.15
Parallel		2x to 3x
Pack (6):		
Wax Box (24):		
1	Shaquille O'Neal	1.50
2	Jason Williams	.15
3	Eddie Jones	.15
4	Anthony Mason	.15
5	Joe Smith	.15
6	Kenyon Martin	.15
7	Tracy McGrady	1.00
8	Horace Grant	.15
9	Andre Miller	.75
10	Allen Iverson	2.00
11	Shawn Marion	1.00
12	Derek Anderson	.15
13	Chris Webber	1.00
14	Bruce Bowen	.15
15	Alvin Williams	.15
16	Brent Barry	.15
17	Donyell Marshall	.15
18	Richard Hamilton	.50
19	Vlade Divac	.50
20	Vince Carter	2.00
21	Kevin Garnett	.75
22	Jason Terry	.15
23	Antoine Walker	.75
24	P.J. Brown	.15
25	Baron Davis	.15
26	Eddie Robinson	.15
27	Chris Mihm	.15
28	Michael Finley	.50
29	Nick Van Exel	.50
30	Steve Francis	.75
31	Chucky Atkins	.15
32	Raef LaFrentz	.15
33	Antawn Jamison	.50
34	Jalen Rose	.15
35	Lamar Odom	.50
36	Elton Brand	.50
37	Derek Fisher	.15
38	Alonzo Mourning	.50
39	Ervin Johnson	.15
40	Tim Duncan	1.00
41	Kurt Thomas	.15
42	Latrell Sprewell	.50
43	Darrell Armstrong	.15
44	Tom Gugliotta	.15
45	Derrick Coleman	.15
46	Dale Davis	.15
47	David Robinson	.75
48	Scottie Pippen	.50
49	Hakeem Olajuwon	.50
50	Darius Miles	1.50
51	Greg Ostertag	.15
52	Karl Malone	.50

53	Morris Peterson	.15
54	Shareef Abdur-Rahim	.15
55	Dikembe Mutombo	.50
56	Elden Campbell	.15
57	Ron Mercer	.15
58	Jumaine Jones	.15
59	Wang Zhizhi	.75
60	Ray Allen	.50
61	Marcus Camby	.15
62	Jermaine O'Neal	.50
63	Kenny Thomas	.15
64	Danny Fortson	.15
65	Ben Wallace	.15
66	DeShawn Stevenson	.15
67	Antonio Davis	.15
68	Doug Christie	.15
69	Rasheed Wallace	.15
70	Stephon Marbury	.15
71	Allan Houston	.15
72	Kerry Kittles	.15
73	Todd MacCulloch	.15
74	Sam Cassell	.15
75	Kobe Bryant	4.00
76	Aaron McKie	.15
77	Terrell Brandon	.15
78	Brian Grant	.15
79	Michael Dickerson	.15
80	Jerry Stackhouse	.50
81	Antonio McDyess	.15
82	Steve Nash	.50
83	Paul Pierce	1.00
84	Jamal Mashburn	.15
85	Toni Kukoc	.15
86	James Posey	.15
87	Larry Hughes	.15
88	Cuttino Mobley	.15
89	Jeff Foster	.15
90	Jason Kidd	1.00
91	Keith Van Horn	.15
92	Mike Miller	.75
93	Anfernee Hardaway	.50
94	Bonzi Wells	.15
95	Mike Bibby	.75
96	Steve Smith	.15
97	Gary Payton	.50
98	John Stockton	.50
99	Peja Stojakovic	.50
100	Michael Jordan	10.00
101	Iakovos Tsakalidis	.15
102	Mark Jackson	.15
103	Wally Szczerbiak	.50
104	Rod Strickland	.15
105	Rick Fox	.15
106	Glenn Robinson	.40
107	Michael Olowokandi	.40
108	Reggie Miller	.40
109	Kelvin Cato	.15
110	Clifford Robinson	.15
111	Dirk Nowitzki	.75
112	Brad Miller	.15
113	David Wesley	.15
114	Kenny Anderson	.15
115	Theo Ratliff	.15
116	Rashard Lewis	.15
117	Matt Harpring	.15
118	*Eddie Griffin*	2.00
119	*Brendan Haywood*	2.00
120	*Steven Hunter*	2.00
121	*Jamaal Tinsley*	4.00
122	*Jason Richardson*	7.00
123	*Tony Parker*	6.00
124	*Pau Gasol*	5.00
125	*Shane Battier*	6.00
126	*Joe Johnson*	3.00
127	*Leon Smith*	2.00
128	*Mengke Bateer*	1.00
129	*Loren Woods*	1.00
130	*Kwame Brown*	3.00
131	*Tyson Chandler*	3.00
132	*Eddy Curry*	3.00
133	*Kedrick Brown*	1.00
134	*Joseph Forte*	2.00
135	*Troy Murphy*	2.00
136	*Richard Jefferson*	4.00
137	*DeSagana Diop*	1.00
138	*Vladimir Radmanovic*	1.00
139	*Zach Randolph*	1.50
140	*Gerald Wallace*	1.00
141	*Brandon Armstrong*	1.00
142	*Jeryl Sasser*	1.00
143	*Rodney White*	1.00
144	*Samuel Dalembert*	1.00
145	*Jason Collins*	2.00
146	*Michael Bradley*	1.00
147	*Oscar Torres*	1.00
148	*Zeljko Rebraca*	1.00
149	*Andrei Kirilenko*	2.25
150	*Trenton Hassell*	1.00

2001-02 Topps Champions & Contenders Autographs

	MT
Complete Set (27):	
Common Player:	10.00
Inserted 1:80	
CCA-GA Gilbert Arenas	20.00
CCA-SB Shane Battier	35.00
CCA-MB Mike Bibby	25.00
CCA-DB Damone Brown	10.00
CCA-KB Kedrick Brown	10.00
CCA-MD Michael Doleac	10.00
CCA-KD Keyon Dooling	10.00
CCA-JF Joseph Forte	12.00
CCA-RH Richard Hamilton	25.00
CCA-DH Donnell Harvey	10.00
CCA-BJ Bobby Jackson	10.00
CCA-JJ Joe Johnson	25.00
CCA-AJ Alvin Jones	10.00
CCA-RL Raef LaFrentz	10.00
CCA-SM Shawn Marion	15.00
CCA-DM Desmond Mason	10.00
CCA-AF M Aaron McKie	10.00
CCA-RM Roshown McLeod	10.00
CCA-AM Andre Miller	20.00
CCA-TM Troy Murphy	10.00
CCA-LP Lavor Postell	10.00
CCA-KS Kenny Satterfield	10.00
CCA-PS Peja Stojakovic	25.00
CCA-JT Jason Terry	10.00
CCA-JTR Jeff Trepagnier	10.00
CCA-HT Hidayet Turkoglu	15.00
CCA-LW Loren Woods	10.00

2001-02 Topps Champions & Contenders Challenging the Champ

	MT
Complete Set (16):	
Common Player:	10.00
Inserted 1:30	
CC-SA Shareef Abdur-Rahim	10.00
CC-EB Elton Brand	12.00
CC-BD Baron Davis	10.00
CC-TD Tim Duncan	25.00
CC-MF Michael Finley	10.00
CC-TG Tom Gugliotta	10.00
CC-AH Anfernee Hardaway	10.00
CC-TK Toni Kukoc	10.00
CC-SM Stephon Marbury	10.00
CC-SDM Shawn Marion	15.00
CC-JM Jamal Mashburn	10.00
CC-SN Steve Nash	12.00
CC-DN Dirk Nowitzki	20.00
CC-TR Theo Ratliff	10.00
CC-JT Jason Terry	10.00
CC-WZ Wang Zhizhi	20.00

2001-02 Topps Champions & Contenders Crowning Moment

		MT
Complete Set (10):		
Common Player:		1.00
Inserted 1:6		
CM1	Karl Malone	1.00
CM2	Shaquille O'Neal	2.00
CM3	Tim Duncan	1.50
CM4	Michael Jordan	8.00
CM5	Kobe Bryant	5.00
CM6	Vince Carter	4.00
CM7	Dikembe Mutombo	1.00
CM8	Elton Brand	1.00
CM9	Jason Kidd	2.00
CM10	Steve Francis	1.50

2001-02 Topps Champions & Contenders Finals Journey

	MT
Complete Set (23):	
Common Player:	10.00
Inserted 1:20	
FJ-RB Raja Bell	10.00
FJ-RAB Rodney Buford	10.00
FJ-DF Derek Fisher	10.00
FJ-GF Greg Foster	10.00
FJ-RF Rick Fox	10.00
FJ-MG Matt Geiger	10.00
FJ-DG Devean George	10.00
FJ-HG Horace Grant	10.00
FJ-RKH Ron Harper	10.00
FJ-TH Tyrone Hill	10.00
FJ-RH Robert Horry	10.00
FJ-AI Allen Iverson	40.00
FJ-JJ Jumaine Jones	10.00
FJ-TL Tyronn Lue	10.00
FJ-GL George Lynch	10.00
FJ-TM Todd MacCulloch	10.00
FJ-MM Mark Madsen	10.00
FJ-AM Aaron McKie	10.00
FJ-DM Dikembe Mutombo	15.00
FJ-KO Kevin Ollie	10.00
FJ-SO Shaquille O'Neal	40.00
FJ-BS Brian Shaw	10.00
FJ-ES Eric Snow	10.00

2001-02 Topps Champions & Contenders First Step

	MT
Complete Set (14):	
Common Player:	15.00
Inserted 1:100	
FS-SB Shane Battier	45.00
FS-EB Elton Brand	25.00
FS-KB Kwame Brown	45.00
FS-EC Eddy Curry	25.00
FS-BD Baron Davis	15.00
FS-TD Tim Duncan	45.00
FS-JF Joseph Forte	15.00
FS-RH Richard Hamilton	25.00
FS-AJ Antawn Jamison	15.00
FS-SM Shawn Marion	15.00
FS-SO Shaquille O'Neal	75.00
FS-VR Vladimir Radmanovic	15.00
FS-PS Peja Stojakovic	35.00
FS-JT Jason Terry	15.00

2001-02 Topps Champions & Contenders Heart of a Champion

		MT
Complete Set (10):		
Common Player:		2.00
Inserted 1:20		
HC1	Tim Duncan	4.00
HC2	Shaquille O'Neal	7.00
HC3	Michael Jordan	18.00
HC4	Karl Malone	2.00
HC5	Hakeem Olajuwon	2.00
HC6	David Robinson	2.00
HC7	Kobe Bryant	10.00
HC8	Scottie Pippen	2.00
HC9	Shane Battier	10.00
HC10	Jason Richardson	10.00

2001-02 Topps Champions & Contenders Heroes Honor

		MT
Complete Set (6):		
Common Player:		2.00
Inserted 1:6		
HH1	Tim Duncan	4.00
HH2	Vince Carter	6.00
HH3	Tracy McGrady	4.00
HH4	Chris Webber	4.00
HH5	Baron Davis	2.00
HH6	Allan Houston	2.00

2001-02 Topps Champions & Contenders Jump Ball

	MT
Complete Set (9):	
Common Player:	20.00
Inserted 1:500	
JB-RA Ray Allen	25.00
JB-SC Sam Cassell	20.00
JB-BD Baron Davis	20.00
JB-AI Allen Iverson	50.00
JB-SM Shawn Marion	25.00
JB-TM Tracy McGrady	35.00
JB-GR Glenn Robinson	20.00
KB-PS Peja Stojakovic	25.00
KB-CW Chris Webber	30.00

A player's name in *italic type* indicates a rookie

2001-02 Topps Champions & Contenders Setting The Stage

		MT
Complete Set (10):		
Common Player:		5.00
Inserted 1:20		
SS1	Tracy McGrady, Ray Allen	10.00
SS2	Kobe Bryant, Allen Iverson	15.00
SS3	Shaquille O'Neal, Dikembe Mutombo	10.00
SS4	Shaquille O'Neal, Tim Duncan	12.00
SS5	Patrick Ewing, Alonzo Mourning	5.00
SS6	Latrell Sprewell, Vince Carter	8.00
SS7	Shaquille O'Neal, Hakeem Olajuwon	8.00
SS8	Michael Jordan, Reggie Miller	15.00
SS9	Karl Malone, Chris Webber	8.00
SS10	John Stockton, Gary Payton	5.00

2001-02 Topps Chrome

		MT
Complete Set (165):		275.00
Common Player:		.30
Minor Stars:		.60
Common Rookie (130-165):		4.00
Pack (4):		4.00
Box (24):		80.00
1	Shaquille O'Neal	2.50
2	Steve Nash	.60
3	Allen Iverson	3.00
4	Shawn Marion	1.25
5	Rasheed Wallace	.75
6	Antonio Daniels	.30
7	Rashard Lewis	.75
8	Raef LaFrentz	.30
9	Stromile Swift	.60
10	Vince Carter	5.00
11	Danny Fortson	.30
12	Jalen Rose	.75
13	Glen Rice	.60
14	Glenn Robinson	.75
15	Wally Szczerbiak	.60
16	Rick Fox	.30
17	Darius Miles	4.00
18	Jermaine O'Neal	.75
19	Eddie Jones	1.00
20	Tracy McGrady	2.50
21	Kevin Garnett	3.00
22	Tim Thomas	.60
23	Larry Hughes	.60
24	Jerry Stackhouse	1.00
25	Ray Allen	1.00
26	Terrell Brandon	.60
27	Keith Van Horn	.60
28	Marcus Fizer	.60
29	Elden Campbell	.60
30	Tim Duncan	2.00
31	Doug Christie	.30
32	Allan Houston	.60
33	Patrick Ewing	.60
34	Hakeem Olajuwon	.75
35	Anfernee Hardaway	.75
36	Clarence Weatherspoon	.30
37	Eric Snow	.30
38	Tom Gugliotta	.30
39	Scottie Pippen	1.25
40	Chris Webber	2.00
41	David Robinson	.75
42	Elton Brand	1.25
43	Theo Ratliff	.30
44	Paul Pierce	1.00
45	Jamal Mashburn	.60
46	Damon Stoudamire	.30
47	DerMarr Johnson	.30
48	Andre Miller	.60
49	Dirk Nowitzki	1.25
50	Kobe Bryant	5.00
51	Keyon Dooling	.60
52	Brian Grant	.30
53	Antawn Jamison	1.25
54	Jonathan Bender	.60
55	Dikembe Mutombo	.60
56	Steve Smith	.60
57	Hidayet Turkoglu	.60
58	Robert Horry	.30
59	Kurt Thomas	.30
60	Jason Terry	.60
61	Vitaly Potapenko	.30
62	Gary Payton	1.00
63	Bonzi Wells	.60
64	*Raja Bell*	5.00
65	Chris Mihm	.30
66	Reggie Miller	.75
67	Lamar Odom	1.25
68	Darrell Armstrong	.30
69	Baron Davis	1.00
70	Aaron Williams	.30
71	Latrell Sprewell	1.25
72	James Posey	.60
73	Ben Wallace	.60
74	Marc Jackson	.30
75	Maurice Taylor	.30
76	Aaron McKie	.60
77	Grant Hill	1.50
78	Anthony Carter	.30
79	Peja Stojakovic	1.00
80	Jason Kidd	1.50
81	Vin Baker	.60
82	Morris Peterson	.75
83	Bryon Russell	.30
84	Michael Dickerson	.30
85	Quentin Richardson	.60
86	*Primoz Brezec*	4.00
87	Desmond Mason	.60
88	Jason Williams	.60
89	Marcus Camby	.60
90	Stephon Marbury	1.00
91	Mike Bibby	.60
92	Alonzo Mourning	.60
93	Mitch Richmond	.60
94	Donyell Marshall	.30
95	Michael Jordan	15.00
96	Mike Miller	2.00
97	Nick Van Exel	.60
98	Michael Finley	.60
99	Jamal Crawford	.60
100	Steve Francis	2.00
101	Kenyon Martin	.60
102	Sam Cassell	.60
103	Chucky Atkins	.30
104	Juwan Howard	.60
105	Bryant Reeves	.30
106	Richard Hamilton	.60
107	Antonio Davis	.60
108	Antonio McDyess	.60
109	Derek Anderson	.60
110	Kenny Anderson	.60
111	Antoine Walker	.75
112	Wang Zhizhi	1.50
113	Shareef Abdur-Rahim	.75
114	Chris Whitney	.30
115	John Stockton	1.00
116	Alvin Williams	.30
117	David Wesley	.30
118	Joe Smith	.30
119	Jahidi White	.30
120	Karl Malone	1.25
121	Cuttino Mobley	.60
122	Tyrone Hill	.30
123	Clifford Robinson	.30
124	Toni Kukoc	.30
125	Eddie Robinson	.60
126	Courtney Alexander	.60
127	Ron Mercer	.60
128	Lamond Murray	.30
129	Rodney Rogers	.30
130	*Tyson Chandler*	12.00
131	*Pau Gasol*	15.00
132	*Eddy Curry*	10.00
133	*Jason Richardson*	20.00
134	*Shane Battier*	15.00
135	*Eddie Griffin*	12.00
136	*DeSagana Diop*	5.00
137	*Rodney White*	6.00
138	*Joe Johnson*	8.00
139	*Kedrick Brown*	5.00
140	*Vladimir Radmanovic*	5.00
141	*Richard Jefferson*	8.00
142	*Troy Murphy*	6.00
143	*Steven Hunter*	4.00
144	*Kirk Haston*	5.00
145	*Michael Bradley*	5.00
146	*Jason Collins*	4.00
147	*Zach Randolph*	8.00
148	*Brendan Haywood*	6.00
149	*Joseph Forte*	6.00
150	*Jeryl Sasser*	4.00
151	*Brandon Armstrong*	5.00
152	*Gerald Wallace*	8.00
153	*Samuel Dalembert*	4.00
154	*Jamaal Tinsley*	12.00
155	*Tony Parker*	12.00
156	*Trenton Hassell*	6.00
157	*Gilbert Arenas*	8.00
158	*Jeff Trepagnier*	4.00
159	*Damone Brown*	4.00
160	*Loren Woods*	6.00
161	*Andrei Kirilenko*	10.00
162	*Zeljko Rebraca*	5.00
163	*Kenny Satterfield*	5.00
164	*Alvin Jones*	4.00
165	*Kwame Brown*	12.00

2001-02 Topps Chrome Autographs

	MT
Common Player:	15.00
Inserted 1:240	
CA-SB Shane Battier	50.00
CA-EB Elton Brand	25.00
CA-AD Antonio Daniels	15.00
CA-BD Baron Davis	25.00
CA-JF Joseph Forte	20.00
CA-ACJ Antawn Jamison	25.00
CA-JJ Joe Johnson	25.00
CA-SM Shawn Marion	25.00
CA-ZR Zach Randolph	25.00
CA-PS Peja Stojakovic	40.00

2001-02 Topps Chrome Refractors

	MT
Veterans:	4x-8x
Rookies:	3x-6x
Inserted 1:4	

2001-02 Topps Chrome Black Border Refractors

	MT
Veterans:	10x-20x
Rookies:	5x-15x
Production 50 Sets	

2001-02 Topps Chrome Fast and Furious

		MT
Complete Set (14):		45.00
Common Player:		2.00
Inserted 1:6		
Refractors:		3x
Inserted 1:30		
FF1	Steve Francis	3.00
FF2	Allen Iverson	5.00
FF3	Tracy McGrady	4.00
FF4	Vince Carter	10.00
FF5	Michael Jordan	20.00
FF6	Kobe Bryant	10.00
FF7	Kevin Garnett	5.00
FF8	Shaquille O'Neal	4.00
FF9	Ray Allen	2.00
FF10	Paul Pierce	2.00
FF11	Jerry Stackhouse	2.00
FF12	Antoine Walker	2.00
FF13	Chris Webber	3.00
FF14	Jason Richardson	10.00

2001-02 Topps Chrome Kareem Abdul-Jabbar Reprints

		MT
Common Player:		8.00
Inserted 1:20		
Common Refractor:		20.00
Inserted 1:100		
1	Lew Alcindor	
2	Lew Alcindor	
3	Lew Alcindor	
4	Kareem Abdul-Jabbar	
5	Kareem Abdul-Jabbar	
6	Kareem Abdul-Jabbar	
7	Kareem Abdul-Jabbar	
8	Kareem Abdul-Jabbar	
9	Kareem Abdul-Jabbar	
10	Kareem Abdul-Jabbar	
11	Kareem Abdul-Jabbar	
12	Kareem Abdul-Jabbar	
13	Kareem Abdul-Jabbar	

2001-02 Topps Chrome Lacing Up Relics

	MT
Common Player:	40.00
Production 50 Sets	
LU-SB Shane Battier	80.00
LU-EB Elton Brand	50.00
LU-KB Kwame Brown	60.00
LU-EC Eddy Curry	50.00
LU-BD Baron Davis	40.00
LU-TD Tim Duncan	100.00
LU-JF Joseph Forte	40.00
LU-RH Richard Hamilton	40.00
LU-AJ Antawn Jamison	40.00
LU-SM Shawn Marion	40.00
LU-SO Shaquille O'Neal	100.00
LU-VR Vladimir Radmanovic	40.00
LU-PS Peja Stojakovic	60.00
LU-JT Jason Terry	40.00

2001-02 Topps Chrome Mad Game

		MT
Complete Set (10):		50.00
Common Player:		4.00
Inserted 1:13		
Refractors:		2x-3x
Inserted 1:65		
MG1	Allen Iverson	6.00
MG2	Shaquille O'Neal	5.00
MG3	Tim Duncan	4.00
MG4	Vince Carter	10.00
MG5	Kevin Garnett	6.00
MG6	Kobe Bryant	10.00
MG7	Tracy McGrady	5.00
MG8	Steve Francis	4.00
MG9	Chris Webber	4.00
MG10	Darius Miles	8.00

2001-02 Topps Chrome Sports Illustrated Relics

		MT
Common Player:		15.00
Inserted 1:180		
Refractors:		3x-6x
Production 50 Sets		
SI-TD	Tim Duncan	40.00
SI-MF	Michael Finley	20.00
SI-DF	Derek Fisher	15.00
SI-RH	Richard Hamilton	20.00
SI-AH	Allan Houston	15.00
SI-CM	Cuttino Mobley	15.00
SI-DN	Dirk Nowitzki	40.00
SI-GP	Gary Payton	20.00
SI-WS	Wally Szczerbiak	25.00
SI-DW	David Wesley	15.00

2001-02 Topps Chrome Team Topps

		MT
Complete Set (12):		45.00
Common Player:		3.00
Inserted 1:30		
Refractors:		3x
Inserted 1:55		
TT1	Shaquille O'Neal	8.00
TT2	Tim Duncan	6.00
TT3	Antawn Jamison	4.00
TT4	Jason Terry	3.00
TT5	Baron Davis	3.00
TT6	Elton Brand	4.00
TT7	Peja Stojakovic	3.00
TT8	Richard Hamilton	3.00
TT9	Shawn Marion	4.00
TT10	Team Shot	6.00
TT11	Shane Battier	8.00
TT12	Joseph Forte	4.00

2001-02 Topps Chrome Team Topps Jersey Edition Cards

		MT
Common Player:		15.00
Inserted 1:109		
Refractors:		3x
Inserted 1:682		
TT-SB	Shane Battier	30.00
TT-EB	Elton Brand	20.00
TT-BD	Baron Davis	15.00
TT-TD	Tim Duncan	50.00
TT-JF	Joseph Forte	15.00
TT-RH	Richard Hamilton	15.00
TT-AJ	Antawn Jamison	20.00
TT-SM	Shawn Marion	20.00
TT-SO	Shaquille O'Neal	50.00
TT-PS	Peja Stojakovic	25.00
TT-JT	Jason Terry	15.00

2001-02 Topps Heritage

		MT
Complete Set (264):		300.00
Common Player:		.25
Minor Stars:		.50
Common Rookie:		3.00
Pack (8):		3.00
Box (24):		60.00
1	Shaquille O'Neal	2.50
2	Jalen Rose	.60
3	*Kwame Brown*	10.00
4	Bryon Russell	.25
5	Hakeem Olajuwon	.60
6	Shammond Williams	.25
7	Aaron McKie	.50
8	Anfernee Hardaway	.75
9	Dale Davis	.25
10	Tracy McGrady	2.50
11	Craig "Speedy" Claxton	.50
12	Kurt Thomas	.25
13	Keith Van Horn	.50
14	*Tyson Chandler*	10.00
15	Andre Miller	.60
16	Dirk Nowitzki	1.25
17	Raef LaFrentz	.50
18	Mateen Cleaves	.25
19	Danny Fortson	.25
20	Steve Francis	2.00
21	Al Harrington	.50
22	Keyon Dooling	.50
23	Rick Fox	.25
24	Michael Dickerson	.25
25	Alonzo Mourning	.60
26	Glenn Robinson	.60
27	Wally Szczerbiak	.50
28	Todd MacCulloch	.25
29	Shandon Anderson	.25
30	Kobe Bryant	5.00
31	Tyrone Hill	.25
32	Grant Hill	1.50
33	Shawn Marion	1.25
34	Derek Anderson	.50
35	Hidayet Turkoglu	.50
36	David Robinson	.75
37	Gary Payton	1.00
38	Alvin Williams	.25
39	*Pau Gasol*	12.00
40	Tim Duncan	2.00
41	Rashard Lewis	.75
42	Antonio Davis	.50
43	Donyell Marshall	.25
44	Jahidi White	.25
45	Shareef Abdur-Rahim	.75
46	Antoine Walker	.75
47	P.J. Brown	.25
48	Eddie Robinson	.50
49	Chris Mihm	.50
50	Kevin Garnett	3.00
51	Marcus Camby	.50
52	Mike Miller	2.00
53	Tony Delk	.25
54	Mike Bibby	.50
55	Dikembe Mutombo	.50
56	*Eddy Curry*	8.00
57	Shawn Bradley	.25
58	James Posey	.50
59	*Jason Richardson*	15.00
60	Jason Kidd	1.50
61	*Eddie Griffin*	10.00
62	Larry Hughes	.50
63	Ben Wallace	.25
64	Antonio McDyess	.50
65	Tim Hardaway	.50
66	Shawn Kemp	.50
67	Bobby Jackson	.25
68	Tom Gugliotta	.25
69	Antawn Jamison	1.25
70	Lamar Odom	1.25
71	*Jamaal Tinsley*	10.00
72	Moochie Norris	.25
73	Marc Jackson	.25
74	*Andrei Kirilenko*	8.00
75	Zhizhi Wang	1.50
76	Eric Snow	.50
77	Rasheed Wallace	.75
78	Antonio Daniels	.25
79	*Vladimir Radmanovic*	.25
80	Morris Peterson	.75
81	Jason Terry, Jason Terry, Dikembe Mutombo, Jason Terry	.50
82	Paul Pierce, Milt Palacio, Antoine Walker, Antoine Walker	.75
83	Jamal Mashburn, Hersey Hawkins, P.J. Brown, Baron Davis	.50
84	Elton Brand, Fred Hoiberg, Elton Brand, Fred Hoiberg	1.00
85	Andre Miller, Trajan Langdon, Clarence Weatherspoon, Andre Miller	.50
86	Dirk Nowitzki, Steve Nash, Dirk Nowitzki, Steve Nash	1.00
87	Antonio McDyess, George McCloud, Antonio McDyess, Nick Van Exel	.75
88	Jerry Stackhouse, Dana Barros, Ben Wallace, Jerry Stackhouse	.75
89	Antawn Jamison, Marc Jackson, Antawn Jamison, Mookie Blaylock	.75
90	Steve Francis, Cuttino Mobley, Steve Francis, Steve Francis	1.00
91	Jalen Rose, Reggie Miller, Jermaine O'Neal, Travis Best	1.00
92	Lamar Odom, Eric Piatkowski, Lamar Odom, Jeff McInnis	1.00
93	Shaquille O'Neal, Mike Penberthy, Shaquille O'Neal, Kobe Bryant	2.00
94	Shareef Abdur-Rahim, Shareef Abdur-Rahim, Shareef Abdur-Rahim, Mike Bibby	.75
95	Eddie Jones, Eddie Jones, Anthony Mason, Tim Hardaway	.75
96	Glenn Robinson, Ray Allen, Ervin Johnson, Sam Cassell	.75
97	Kevin Garnett, Terrell Brandon, Kevin Garnett, Terrell Brandon	1.50
98	Stephon Marbury, Johnny Newman, Aaron Williams, Stephon Marbury	.75
99	DeShawn Stevenson	.60
100	Allen Iverson	2.50
101	*Jeryl Sasser*	3.00
102	Jason Terry	.50
103	Vitaly Potapenko	.25
104	Elden Campbell	.50
105	Jamal Crawford	.50
106	Michael Finley	.60
107	*Earl Watson*	3.00
108	Clifford Robinson	.50
109	Chucky Atkins	.25
110	Glen Rice	.50
111	Jermaine O'Neal	.75
112	Jonathan Bender	.60
113	Michael Olowokandi	.50
114	Derek Fisher	.50
115	Stromile Swift	.50
116	Toni Kukoc	.50
117	*Samuel Dalembert*	3.00
118	Paul Pierce	1.00
119	Jamal Mashburn	.60
120	Ron Mercer	.50
121	Lamond Murray	.25
122	Steve Nash	.60
123	Nick Van Exel	.50
124	*DeSagana Diop*	4.00
125	Ron Artest	.50
126	Marcus Fizer	.50
127	Jumaine Jones	.25
128	Corliss Williamson	.25
129	*Rodney White*	5.00
130	Cuttino Mobley	.60
131	Reggie Miller	.75
132	Austin Croshere	.25
133	Jeff McInnis	.25
134	*Joe Johnson*	8.00
135	*Kedrick Brown*	4.00
136	Theo Ratliff	.50
137	LaPhonso Ellis	.25
138	Ervin Johnson	.25
139	Terrell Brandon	.50
140	Chauncey Billups	.25
141	Kenyon Martin	.50
142	*Richard Jefferson*	6.00
143	Howard Eisley	.25
144	Jerry Stackhouse, Allen Iverson, Shaquille O'Neal	1.50
145	Allen Iverson, Jerry Stackhouse, Shaquille O'Neal	2.00
146	Shaquille O'Neal, Bonzi Wells, Marcus Camby	1.00
147	Reggie Miller, Allan Houston, Doug Christie	.50
148	Dikembe Mutombo, Ben Wallace, Shaquille O'Neal	1.00
149	Jason Kidd, John Stockton, Nick Van Exel	1.00
150	Vince Carter	5.00
151	Calvin Booth	.25
152	Chris Whitney	.25
153	John Amaechi	.25
154	Keon Clark	.50
155	Terry Porter	.25
156	Doug Christie	.25
157	*Gerald Wallace*	6.00
158	*Zach Randolph*	6.00
159	Iakovos Tsakalidis	.25
160	*Damone Brown*	3.00
161	76ERS vs Pacers & Spurs vs. Timberwolves	2.00
162	Bucks vs Magic & Lakers vs Trail Blazers	2.00
163	Heat vs. Hornets & Kings vs. Suns	1.00
164	Knicks vs. Raptors & Jass vs. Mavericks	2.00
165	Christian Laettner	.50
166	John Starks	.25
167	Jerome Williams	.25
168	Brent Barry	.25
169	Malik Rose	.25
170	Vlade Divac	.50
171	Damon Stoudamire	.25
172	Rodney Rogers	.25
173	*Alvin Jones*	3.00
174	Darrell Armstrong	.50
175	Mark Jackson	.25
176	Kerry Kittles	.25
177	Radoslav Nesterovic	.25
178	*Brandon Armstrong*	4.00
179	Joe Smith	.50
180	Ray Allen	1.00
181	Anthony Mason	.50
182	Bryant Reeves	.25
183	Jason Williams	.50
184	*Terence Morris*	3.00
185	Travis Best	.25
186	*Troy Murphy*	5.00
187	*Gilbert Arenas*	6.00
188	Avery Johnson	.25
189	Juwan Howard	.50
190	Checklist	.25
191	Courtney Alexander	.60
192	John Stockton	1.00
193	Vin Baker	.50
194	Desmond Mason	.50
195	Steve Smith	.50
196	*Steven Hunter*	3.00
197	Stephon Marbury	1.00
198	Patrick Ewing	.50
199	Allan Houston	.50
200	Karl Malone	1.25
201	Peja Stojakovic	.75
202	Bonzi Wells	.50
203	Latrell Sprewell	1.25
204	Rafer Alston	.25
205	*Tony Parker*	10.00
206	*Michael Bradley*	3.00
207	Richard Hamilton	.60
208	*Zeljko Rebraca*	3.00
209	Joel Przybilla	.50
210	Tim Thomas	.50
211	Eddie House	.50
212	Brian Grant	.50
213	Lindsey Hunter	.25
214	Corey Maggette	.50
215	*Shane Battier*	12.00
216	*Will Solomon*	3.00
217	Mitch Richmond	.50
218	Eddie Jones	.50
219	Elton Brand	1.25
220	Quentin Richardson	.50
221	Allan Houston, Allan Houston, Marcus Camby, Charlie Ward	.50
222	Tracy McGrady, Darrell Armstrong, Bo Outlaw, Darrell Armstrong	1.00
223	Allen Iverson, Allen Iverson, Tyrone Hill, Aaron McKie	2.00
224	Shawn Marion, Jason Kidd, Shawn Marion, Jason Kidd	1.00
225	Rasheed Wallace, Steve Smith, Dale Davis, Damon Stoudamire	.75
226	Chris Webber, Doug Christie, Chris Webber, Jason Williams	1.00
227	Tim Duncan, Derek Anderson, Tim Duncan, Antonio Daniels	1.00
228	Gary Payton, Shammond Williams, Patrick Ewing, Gary Payton	.75
229	Vince Carter, Dell Curry, Antonio Davis, Mark Jackson	1.50
230	Karl Malone, John Stockton, Karl Malone, John Stockton	1.00
231	Juwan Howard, Chris Whitney, Michael Smith, Chris Whitney	.50
232	*Brendan Haywood*	5.00
233	Scottie Pippen	1.25
234	*Loren Woods*	5.00
235	Sam Cassell	.50
236	Anthony Carter	.25
237	*Raja Bell*	3.00
238	Robert Horry	.25
239	Maurice Taylor	.25
240	Zydrunas Ilgauskas	.25
241	Derrick Coleman	.50
242	Kenny Anderson	.25
243	*Joseph Forte*	6.00
244	Baron Davis	1.00
245	Nazr Mohammed	.25
246	76ERS vs. Raptors & Spurs vs. Mavericks	2.00
247	Bucks vs. Hornets & Lakers vs. Kings	2.00
248	76ERS vs. Bucks & Spurs vs. Lakers	1.00
249	Lakers vs. 76ERS	3.00
250	Darius Miles	4.00
251	Samaki Walker	.25
252	DerMarr Johnson	.50
253	David Wesley	.25
254	*Trenton Hassell*	4.00
255	*Jeff Trepagnier*	3.00
256	Jacque Vaughn	.25
257	*Kirk Haston*	4.00
258	Jamaal Magloire	.25
259	*Jason Collins*	3.00
260	Chris Webber	2.00
261	*Kenny Satterfield*	3.00
262	Horace Grant	.25
263	Jerry Stackhouse	75.00
264	Michael Jordan	10.00

2001-02 Topps Heritage Air Alert

		MT
Complete Set (12):		50.00
Common Player:		2.00
Inserted 1:8		
AIR1	Shawn Marion	2.50
AIR2	Vince Carter	8.00
AIR3	Tracy McGrady	4.00
AIR4	Steve Francis	3.00
AIR5	Kobe Bryant	8.00
AIR6	Darius Miles	6.00
AIR7	Jerry Stackhouse	2.00
AIR8	Baron Davis	2.00
AIR9	Kevin Garnett	5.00
AIR10	Michael Jordan	12.00
AIR11	Kwame Brown	5.00
AIR12	Jason Richardson	8.00

2001-02 Topps Heritage Articles of the Arena Relics

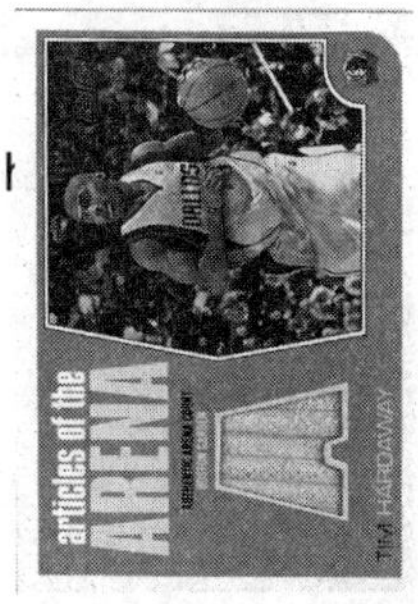

		MT
Common Player:		12.00
Inserted 1:46		
AA1	Shaquille O'Neal	30.00
AA2	Chris Webber	25.00
AA3	Jason Kidd	20.00
AA4	Latrell Sprewell	20.00
AA5	Jalen Rose	12.00
AA6	Grant Hill	20.00
AA7	Alonzo Mourning	15.00
AA8	Gary Payton	15.00
AA9	Anfernee Hardaway	15.00
AA10	Scottie Pippen	20.00
AA11	Tim Hardaway	15.00
AA12	Reggie Miller	20.00
AA13	Hakeem Olajuwon	15.00
AA14	Patrick Ewing	15.00
AA15	Karl Malone	20.00
AA16	John Stockton	20.00
AA17	Charles Oakley	12.00
AA18	Glenn Robinson	15.00
AA19	Dikembe Mutombo	12.00
AA20	Eddie Jones	15.00

2001-02 Topps Heritage Autographs

		MT
Common Player:		15.00
Inserted 1:83		
HA-EB	Erick Barkley	15.00
HA-SB	Shane Battier	40.00
HA-MB	Mike Bibby	20.00
HA-ETB	Elton Brand	25.00
HA-DB	Damone Brown	12.00
HA-AD	Antonio Daniels	12.00
HA-BD	Baron Davis	20.00
HA-JF	Joseph Forte	25.00
HA-RJ	Richard Jefferson	25.00
HA-AJ	Alvin Jones	12.00
HA-SM	Shawn Marion	25.00
HA-VR	Vladimir Radmanovic	15.00
HA-PS	Peja Stojakovic	40.00

2001-02 Topps Heritage Ball Basics Relics

		MT
Common Player:		20.00
Inserted 1:627		
BB-CA	Courtney Alexander	25.00
BB-CC	Craig "Speedy" Claxton	20.00
BB-MF	Marcus Fizer	20.00
BB-DJ	DerMarr Johnson	20.00
BB-KM	Kenyon Martin	25.00
BB-DT	Desmond Mason	25.00
BB-DM	Darius Miles	50.00
BB-MM	Mike Miller	35.00
BB-MP	Morris Peterson	30.00
BB-SS	Stromile Swift	25.00
BB-HT	Hidayet Turkoglu	30.00

2001-02 Topps Heritage Competitive Threads

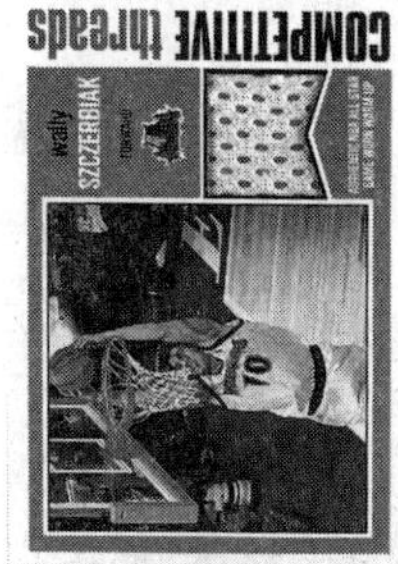

		MT
Common Player:		15.00
Inserted 1:61		
CT-RA	Ray Allen	20.00
CT-EB	Elton Brand	20.00
CT-BD	Baron Davis	15.00
CT-TD	Tim Duncan	25.00
CT-MF	Michael Finley	15.00
CT-AH	Allan Houston	10.00
CT-AI	Allen Iverson	40.00
CT-KM	Karl Malone	20.00
CT-TM	Tracy McGrady	30.00
CT-AM	Andre Miller	15.00
CT-LS	Latrell Sprewell	20.00
CT-JS	Jerry Stackhouse	15.00
CT-WS	Wally Szczerbiak	15.00
CT-RW	Rasheed Wallace	15.00
CT-CW	Chris Webber	25.00

2001-02 Topps Heritage Competitive Threads Autographs

		MT
Complete Set (5):		
Common Player:		
CTA-EB	Elton Brand	
CTA-BD	Baron Davis	
CTA-TD	Tim Duncan	
CTA-AM	Andre Miller	
CTA-WS	Wally Szczerbiak	

2001-02 Topps Heritage Crossover

		MT
Complete Set (12):		75.00
Common Player:		1.50
Inserted 1:14		
C1	Jamaal Tinsley	6.00
C2	Steve Francis	5.00
C3	Vince Carter	12.00
C4	Baron Davis	3.00
C5	Tracy McGrady	8.00
C6	Kobe Bryant	12.00
C7	Jason Terry	2.00
C8	Stephon Marbury	3.00
C9	Jason Williams	2.00
C10	Tim Hardaway	1.50
C11	Jason Richardson	12.00
C12	Michael Jordan	20.00

2001-02 Topps Heritage Out of Bounds

		MT
Complete Set (10):		18.00
Common Player:		1.00
Inserted 1:10		
001	Dirk Nowitzki	3.00
002	Peja Stojakovic	2.00
003	Zhizhi Wang	4.00
004	Dikembe Mutombo	1.00
005	Steve Nash	1.00
006	Hidayet Turkoglu	1.00
007	Hakeem Olajuwon	1.00
008	Tony Parker	4.00
009	Vladimir Radmanovic	2.00
0010	Pau Gasol	5.00

2001-02 Topps Heritage Relics

		MT
Common Player:		15.00
Inserted 1:485		
U-PB	P.J. Brown	15.00
U-EC	Elden Campbell	15.00
U-DC	Derrick Coleman	15.00
U-BD	Baron Davis	30.00
U-JDM	Jamaal Magloire	20.00
U-JM	Jamal Mashburn	30.00
U-ER	Eddie Robinson	20.00
U-DW	David Wesley	15.00

2001-02 Topps Heritage Unity Relics

		MT
Complete Set (12):		15.00
Common Player:		
U1	Jamal Mashburn	
U2	Baron Davis	
U3	Eddie Robinson	
U4	David Wesley	
U5	Elden Campbell	
U6	P.J. Brown	
U7	Derrick Coleman	
U8	Jamaal Magloire	

U9 Otis Thorpe
U10 Hersey Hawkins
U11 Scott Burrell
U12 Eldridge Recasner

2001-02 Topps High Topps

	MT
Complete Set w/o SP's (105):	50.00
Common Player:	.30
Minor Stars:	.60
Common Auto (106-113):	12.00
Production 850 Sets	
Common JSY (114-129):	12.00
Production 425 Sets	
Common RC Auto (130-140):	10.00
Production 850 Sets	
Common RC JSY (141-153):	12.00
Production 425 Sets	
Common Rookie (154-164):	5.00
Production 1,500 Sets	
Pack (4):	5.00
Box (24):	10.00

1 Shaquille O'Neal 2.50
2 Reggie Miller .75
3 Steve Francis 2.00
4 Jerry Stackhouse .75
5 Nick Van Exel .60
6 Dirk Nowitzki 1.25
7 Dikembe Mutombo .60
8 Terrell Brandon .60
9 Allan Houston .75
10 Kevin Garnett 3.00
11 Eric Snow .30
12 Stephon Marbury 1.00
13 Jalen Rose .75
14 Rick Fox .30
15 Alonzo Mourning .60
16 Tim Thomas .60
17 Keith Van Horn .60
18 Glen Rice .60
19 Mike Miller 2.00
20 Chris Webber 2.00
21 Larry Hughes .75
22 Joe Smith .60
23 Ron Mercer .60
24 Jamal Mashburn .60
25 Shareef Abdur-Rahim .75
26 P.J. Brown .30
27 Ben Wallace .30
28 Zhizhi Wang 1.50
29 Jermaine O'Neal 1.00
30 Lamar Odom 1.25
31 Stromile Swift .75
32 Theo Ratliff .60
33 Patrick Ewing .60
34 Antonio Davis .30
35 John Stockton 1.00
36 Courtney Alexander .75
37 Alvin Williams .30
38 Rashard Lewis .75
39 Mike Bibby .75
40 Scottie Pippen 1.25
41 Anfernee Hardaway 1.00
42 Marcus Camby .60
43 Glenn Robinson .75
44 Jason Williams .75
45 Horace Grant .30
46 Chris Mihm .30
47 Paul Pierce 1.00
48 DerMarr Johnson .75
49 Steve Nash .60
50 Vince Carter 5.00
51 Jahidi White 10.00
52 Donyell Marshall .30
53 Desmond Mason .60
54 Tom Gugliotta .30
55 Hidayet Turkoglu .60
56 Grant Hill 1.50
57 Kenyon Martin .75
58 Wally Szczerbiak .75
59 Eddie Jones .75
60 Kobe Bryant 5.00
61 Cuttino Mobley .60
62 Michael Dickerson .30
63 Clifford Robinson .30
64 Raef LaFrentz .30
65 Lamond Murray .30
66 Kenny Anderson .30
67 Antonio Daniels .30
68 Hakeem Olajuwon .75
69 Eddie Robinson .30
70 Karl Malone 1.25
71 Richard Hamilton .75
72 Derek Anderson .60
73 Bonzi Wells .75
74 Darrell Armstrong .30
75 Gary Payton 1.00
76 Bryon Russell .30
77 Steve Smith .60
78 Sam Cassell .60
79 Brian Grant .30
80 Antoine Walker .75
81 Marcus Fizer .60
82 Tim Duncan 2.00
83 Chris Webber 2.00
84 Shaquille O'Neal 2.50
85 Allen Iverson 3.00
86 Jason Kidd 1.50
87 Kevin Garnett 3.00
88 Vince Carter 5.00
89 Dikembe Mutombo .60
90 Kobe Bryant 5.00
91 Tracy McGrady 2.50
92 Allen Iverson 1.50
93 Dikembe Mutombo .30
94 Jason Kidd .75
95 Allen Iverson 1.50
96 Theo Ratliff .30
97 Shaquille O'Neal 1.25
98 Reggie Miller .30
99 Antoine Walker .30
100 Michael Finley .30
101 Jason Kidd .75
102 Shaquille O'Neal 1.25
103 Kobe Bryant 2.50
104 Derek Fisher .30
105 Shaquille O'Neal 1.25
106 Shawn Marion Auto 20.00
107 Antawn Jamison Auto 20.00
108 Peja Stojakovic Auto 60.00
109 Jason Terry Auto 15.00
110 Aaron McKie Auto 15.00
111 Keyon Dooling Auto 15.00
112 Al Harrington Auto 12.00
113 Chauncey Billups Auto 12.00
114 Tim Duncan JSY 30.00
115 Tracy McGrady JSY 30.00
116 Jason Kidd JSY 25.00
117 Latrell Sprewell JSY 25.00
118 David Robinson JSY 25.00
119 Baron Davis JSY 15.00
120 Allen Iverson JSY 50.00
121 Ray Allen JSY 25.00
122 Rasheed Wallace JSY 15.00
123 Morris Peterson JSY 15.00
124 Darius Miles JSY 40.00
125 Marc Jackson JSY 12.00
126 Michael Finley JSY 15.00
127 Elton Brand JSY 25.00
128 Antonio McDyess JSY 15.00
129 Andre Miller JSY 15.00
130 *Kwame Brown Auto* 40.00
131 *Eddy Curry Auto* 30.00
132 *Loren Woods Auto* 20.00
133 *Joe Johnson Auto* 50.00
134 *Richard Jefferson Auto* 25.00
135 *Zach Randolph Auto* 25.00
136 *Brendan Haywood Auto* 25.00
137 *Gilbert Arenas Auto* 30.00
138 *Damone Brown Auto* 20.00
139 *Kenny Satterfield Auto* 10.00
140 *Vladimir Radmanovic Auto* 12.00
141 *Eddie Griffin JSY* 30.00
142 *Shane Battier JSY* 60.00
143 *Michael Bradley JSY* 15.00
144 *Gerald Wallace JSY* 25.00
145 *Samuel Dalembert JSY* 12.00
146 *Tyson Chandler JSY* 30.00
147 *Pau Gasol JSY* 50.00
148 *Steven Hunter JSY* 12.00
149 *Rodney White JSY* 15.00
150 *Jeryl Sasser JSY* 12.00
151 *Brandon Armstrong JSY* 15.00
152 *Jamaal Tinsley JSY* 40.00
153 *DeSagana Diop JSY* 15.00
154 *Jason Richardson* 30.00
155 *Kirk Haston* 8.00
156 *Joseph Forte* 10.00
157 *Jason Collins* 5.00
158 *Kedrick Brown* 6.00
159 *Troy Murphy* 8.00
160 *Tony Parker* 15.00
161 *Raja Bell* 6.00
162 *Jeff Trepagnier* 5.00
163 *Terence Morris* 5.00
164 *Zeljko Rebraca* 6.00

2001-02 Topps High Topps Above & Beyond

	MT
Complete Set (7):	15.00
Common Player:	1.00
Inserted 1:10	

AB1 John Stockton 2.50
AB2 Shawn Marion 3.00
AB3 Jason Terry 1.00
AB4 Alonzo Mourning 1.00
AB5 Theo Ratliff 1.00
AB6 Marc Jackson 12.00
AB7 Marcus Camby 1.00

2001-02 Topps High Topps Dominant Figures

	MT
Complete Set (8):	40.00
Common Player:	1.00
Inserted 1:9	

DF1 Alonzo Mourning 1.00
DF2 Shaquille O'Neal 5.00
DF3 Chris Webber 4.00
DF4 Rasheed Wallace 15.00
DF5 Kevin Garnett 6.00
DF6 Tracy McGrady 5.00
DF7 Vince Carter 10.00
DF8 Dikembe Mutombo 10.00

2001-02 Topps High Topps Giant Remains

	MT
Common Player:	10.00
Inserted 1:16	

GR-AD Antonio Davis 10.00
GR-VD Vlade Divac 10.00
GR-TD Tim Duncan 25.00
GR-SF Steve Francis 25.00
GR-RH Richard Hamilton 15.00
GR-AH Allan Houston 15.00
GR-KM Karl Malone 20.00
GR-SM Stephon Marbury 20.00
GR-SD Shawn Marion 20.00
GR-KL Kenyon Martin 12.00
GR-AM Anthony Mason 10.00
GR-AK Antonio McDyess 15.00
GR-MM Mike Miller 20.00
GR-CM Cuttino Mobley 15.00
GR-SO Shaquille O'Neal 40.00
GR-GR Glenn Robinson 15.00
GR-JS Jerry Stackhouse 15.00
GR-WS Wally Szczerbiak 15.00
GR-JT Jason Terry 12.00
GR-CW Chris Webber 25.00

2001-02 Topps High Topps Lofty Lettering

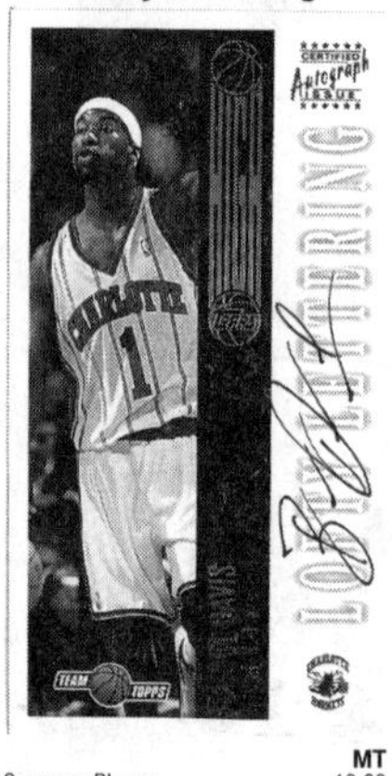

	MT
Common Player:	10.00
Inserted 1:38	

LL-SB Shane Battier 40.00
LL-MB Mike Bibby 15.00
LL-BD Baron Davis 15.00
LL-JF Joseph Forte 20.00
LL-BJ Bobby Jackson 10.00
LL-TM Troy Murphy 15.00
LL-LP Lavor Postell 10.00
LL-TT Tim Thomas 15.00
LL-HT Hidayet Turkoglu 20.00
LL-GW Gerald Wallace 25.00

2001-02 Topps High Topps Sky's The Limit

	MT
Complete Set (13):	45.00
Common Player:	2.00
Inserted 1:8	

SL1 Darius Miles 8.00
SL2 Vince Carter 10.00
SL3 Tracy McGrady 5.00
SL4 Steve Francis 4.00
SL5 Baron Davis 2.00
SL6 Tim Duncan 4.00
SL7 Shawn Marion 2.50
SL8 Paul Pierce 2.00
SL9 Rashard Lewis 2.00
SL10 Lamar Odom 2.50
SL11 Antawn Jamison 2.50
SL12 Dirk Nowitzki 2.50
SL13 Bonzi Wells 15.00

2001-02 Topps Pristine

	MT
Complete Set (50):	125.00
Common Player:	1.00
Minor Stars:	2.00
Common Rookie:	
Unc. Rookie:	1x-1.5x
Rare Rookie:	1x-2x
Pack (8):	35.00
Box (5):	160.00

1 Allen Iverson 8.00
2 Shawn Marion 3.00
3 Baron Davis 2.50
4 Peja Stojakovic 2.00
5 Dirk Nowitzki 3.00
6 Michael Jordan 20.00
7 Dikembe Mutombo 1.00
8 Antoine Walker 2.00
9 David Robinson 2.00
10 Tracy McGrady 6.00
11 Rasheed Wallace 2.00
12 Kenyon Martin 1.00
13 Glenn Robinson 2.00
14 Shareef Abdur-Rahim 2.00
15 Lamar Odom 3.00
16 Alonzo Mourning 1.00
17 Latrell Sprewell 3.00
18 Stephon Marbury 2.50
19 Chris Webber 5.00
20 Darius Miles 10.00
21 Tim Duncan 5.00
22 Antawn Jamison 3.00
23 Jason Kidd 4.00
24 John Stockton 2.50
25 Michael Finley 2.00
26 Eddie Jones 2.00
27 Jamal Mashburn 1.00
28 Paul Pierce 2.50
29 Jason Terry 1.00
30 Kobe Bryant 12.00
31 Reggie Miller 2.00
32 Elton Brand 3.00
33 Antonio McDyess 2.00
34 Ray Allen 2.50
35 Kevin Garnett 8.00
36 Allan Houston 2.00
37 Grant Hill 3.00
38 Jalen Rose 2.00
39 Gary Payton 2.50
40 Vince Carter 12.00
41 Jerry Stackhouse 2.00
42 Karl Malone 3.00
43 Zhizhi Wang 5.00
44 Marcus Fizer 1.00
45 Marcus Camby 1.00
46 Andre Miller 2.00
47 Jason Williams 1.00
48 Hakeem Olajuwon 2.00
49 Shaquille O'Neal 6.00
50 Steve Francis 5.00
51 *Eddie Griffin* 20.00
52 Eddie Griffin 1.00
53 Eddie Griffin 1.00
54 *Kwame Brown* 20.00
55 Kwame Brown 1.00
56 Kwame Brown 1.00
57 *Shane Battier* 25.00
58 Shane Battier 1.00
59 Shane Battier 1.00
60 *Eddy Curry* 15.00
61 Eddy Curry 1.00
62 Eddy Curry 1.00
63 *Tyson Chandler* 20.00
64 Tyson Chandler 1.00
65 Tyson Chandler 1.00
66 *Rodney White* 10.00
67 Rodney White 1.00
68 Rodney White 1.00
69 *Jason Richardson* 30.00
70 Jason Richardson 1.00
71 Jason Richardson 1.00
72 *Joe Johnson* 15.00
73 Joe Johnson 1.00
74 Joe Johnson 1.00
75 *Pau Gasol* 25.00
76 Pau Gasol 1.00
77 Pau Gasol 1.00
78 *DeSagana Diop* 8.00
79 DeSagana Diop 1.00
80 DeSagana Diop 1.00
81 *Vladimir Radmanovic* 8.00
82 Vladimir Radmanovic 1.00
83 Vladimir Radmanovic 1.00
84 *Troy Murphy* 10.00
85 Troy Murphy 1.00
86 Troy Murphy 1.00
87 *Zach Randolph* 12.00
88 Zach Randolph 1.00
89 Zach Randolph 1.00
90 *Brendan Haywood* 25.00
91 Brendan Haywood 1.00
92 Brendan Haywood 1.00
93 *Richard Jefferson* 15.00
94 Richard Jefferson 1.00
95 Richard Jefferson 1.00
96 *Loren Woods* 10.00
97 Loren Woods 1.00
98 Loren Woods 1.00
99 *Joseph Forte* 12.00
100 Joseph Forte 1.00
101 Joseph Forte 1.00
102 *Gerald Wallace* 12.00
103 Gerald Wallace 1.00
104 Gerald Wallace 1.00
105 *Kedrick Brown* 15.00
106 Kedrick Brown 1.00
107 Kedrick Brown 1.00
108 *Tony Parker* 25.00
109 Tony Parker 1.00
110 Tony Parker 1.00

2001-02 Topps Pristine Refractors

	MT
Stars:	10x-15x
Production 50 Sets	
Rookies:	2x-3x
Rookies/750:	2x-4x
Rookies/250:	3x-6x
All Cards Are Uncirculated	

2001-02 Topps Pristine Autographs

	MT
Common Player:	15.00
Inserted 1:4	

A-KAJ Kareem Abdul-Jabbar 175.00
A-GA Gilbert Arenas 25.00
A-SB Shane Battier 60.00
A-JB Jonathan Bender 20.00
A-MB Mike Bibby 20.00
A-CB Chauncey Billups 15.00
A-EB Elton Brand 25.00
A-DB Damone Brown 15.00
A-KBR Kedrick Brown 20.00
A-KB Kwame Brown 60.00
A-EC Eddy Curry 30.00
A-AD Antonio Daniels 15.00
A-BD Baron Davis 20.00
A-TD Tim Duncan 150.00
A-JF Joseph Forte 25.00
A-RH Richard Hamilton 20.00
A-DH Donnell Harvey 15.00
A-BH Brendan Haywood 20.00
A-BJ Bobby Jackson 15.00
A-MJ Marc Jackson 15.00
A-AJ Antawn Jamison 25.00
A-RJ Richard Jefferson 30.00
A-JJ Joe Johnson 30.00
A-RL Raef LaFrentz 15.00
A-SM Shawn Marion 20.00
A-DM Desmond Mason 15.00
A-AFM Aaron McKie 15.00
A-AM Andre Miller 15.00
A-TMU Troy Murphy 20.00
A-JO Jermaine O'Neal 25.00
A-SO Shaquille O'Neal 150.00
A-ZR Zach Randolph 20.00
A-KS Kenny Satterfield 15.00
A-PS Peja Stojakovic 40.00
A-JT Jason Terry 15.00
A-JTR Jeff Trepagnier 15.00
A-HT Hidayet Turkoglu 20.00
A-IT Iakovos Tsakalidis 15.00
A-LW Loren Woods 20.00

2001-02 Topps Pristine Oversized Relics

	MT
Common Player:	12.00
Inserted 1:Box	

BL-TD Tim Duncan 25.00
BL-RH Richard Hamilton 15.00
BL-AH Allan Houston 15.00
BL-AI Allen Iverson 30.00
BL-JK Jason Kidd 25.00
BL-KM Karl Malone 20.00
BL-CM Cuttino Mobley 12.00
BL-AM Alonzo Mourning 15.00
BL-DM Dikembe Mutombo 12.00
BL-DN Dirk Nowitzki 25.00
BL-LO Lamar Odom 20.00
BL-DR David Robinson 20.00
BL-GR Glenn Robinson 12.00
BL-LS Latrell Sprewell 20.00
BL-JS Jerry Stackhouse 15.00
BL-JHS John Stockton 20.00
BL-RW Rasheed Wallace 15.00
BL-DW David Wesley 10.00

2001-02 Topps Pristine Partners

	MT
Common Player:	10.00
Inserted 1:11	

PA-DF Derek Fisher 15.00
PA-SF Steve Francis 20.00
PA-RH Richard Hamilton 12.00
PA-GH Grant Hill 15.00
PA-AH Allan Houston 12.00
PA-TL Trajan Langdon 10.00
PA-TM Tracy McGrady 25.00
PA-CM Cuttino Mobley 12.00
PA-JW Jason Williams 15.00

2001-02 Topps Pristine Premier

	MT
Common Player:	10.00
Inserted 1:6	

PR-RA Ray Allen 15.00
PR-AD Antonio Davis 10.00
PR-DD Dale Davis 10.00
PR-VD Vlade Divac 12.00
PR-MF Michael Finley 15.00
PR-AH Allan Houston 12.00
PR-AI Allen Iverson 30.00
PR-SM Stephon Marbury 15.00
PR-AM Anthony Mason 10.00
PR-AKM Antonio McDyess 15.00
PR-TM Tracy McGrady 25.00
PR-GR Glenn Robinson 12.00
PR-JS Jerry Stackhouse 15.00
PR-RW Rasheed Wallace 15.00

2001-02 Topps Pristine Portions

	MT
Common Player:	10.00
Inserted 1:3	

PP-MB Mike Bibby 15.00
PP-MC Mateen Cleaves 10.00
PP-RD Ricky Davis 10.00
PP-MD Michael Dickerson 10.00
PP-TD Tim Duncan 30.00
PP-RH Richard Hamilton 12.00
PP-SJ Stephen Jackson 10.00
PP-EJ Eddie Jones 15.00
PP-JK Jason Kidd 25.00
PP-TCM Todd MacCulloch 10.00
PP-AM Alonzo Mourning 12.00
PP-DM Dikembe Mutombo 12.00
PP-DN Dirk Nowitzki 25.00
PP-MO Michael Olowokandi 10.00
PP-SO Shaquille O'Neal 30.00
PP-GP Gary Payton 15.00
PP-TP Terry Porter 10.00
PP-JP James Posey 10.00

2001-02 Topps Pristine Slice Of A Star

	MT
Common Player:	10.00
Inserted 1:3	

S-RA Ray Allen 15.00
S-TD Tim Duncan 30.00
S-MF Michael Finley 15.00
S-GH Grant Hill 15.00
S-LH Larry Hughes 12.00
S-AI Allen Iverson 30.00
S-EJ Eddie Jones 15.00
S-RM Reggie Miller 20.00
S-AM Alonzo Mourning 12.00
S-LO Lamar Odom 20.00
S-SO Shaquille O'Neal 30.00
S-GP Gary Payton 15.00
S-TP Terry Porter 10.00
S-DR David Robinson 20.00
S-JDS Jerry Stackhouse 15.00
S-JS John Stockton 20.00
S-BS Bob Sura 10.00
S-CW Chris Webber 20.00

2001-02 Topps Pristine Sweat and Tears

	MT
Common Player:	10.00
Inserted 1:8	

MB-RA Ray Allen 20.00
SS-DA Derek Anderson 15.00
OM-DA Darrell Armstrong 15.00
IP-JB Jonathan Bender 15.00
IP-TB Travis Best 15.00
DM-CB Calvin Booth 10.00
DM-SB Shawn Bradley 10.00
CH-PB P.J. Brown 10.00
CH-EC Elden Campbell 12.00
MB-SC Sam Cassell 15.00
CH-DC Derrick Coleman 12.00
IP-AC Austin Croshere 12.00
SS-AD Antonio Daniels 12.00
CH-BD Baron Davis 20.00
OM-AD Andrew DeClercq 10.00
PS-TD Tony Delk 15.00
SS-TD Tim Duncan 40.00
DM-HE Howard Eisley 10.00
SS-SE Sean Elliott 15.00
DM-MF Michael Finley 20.00
OM-PG Pat Garrity 12.00
PS-TG Tom Gugliotta 12.00
IP-AH Al Harrington 15.00
DM-JH Juwan Howard 12.00
SS-AJ Avery Johnson 12.00
MB-EJ Ervin Johnson 10.00
PS-JK Jason Kidd 30.00
CH-JDM Jamaal Magloire 15.00
PS-SM Shawn Marion 20.00
CH-JM Jamal Mashburn 15.00
OM-TM Tracy McGrady 30.00
OM-MM Mike Miller 20.00
IP-RM Reggie Miller 25.00
DM-SN Steve Nash 20.00
DM-DN Dirk Nowitzki 30.00
IP-JO Jermaine O'Neal 20.00
OM-BO Bo Outlaw 12.00
SS-TP Terry Porter 10.00
MB-JP Joel Przybilla 12.00
PS-CR Clifford Robinson 15.00
SS-DR David Robinson 25.00
CH-ER Eddie Robinson 15.00
MB-GR Glenn Robinson 15.00
PS-RR Rodney Rogers 12.00
IP-JR Jalen Rose 20.00
PS-DS Daniel Santiago 10.00
MB-TT Tim Thomas 15.00
PS-IT Iakovos Tsakalidis 10.00
CH-DW David Wesley 10.00
DM-WZ Wang Zhizhi 30.00

2001-02 Topps Pristine Team Topps Captain Case Loaders

	MT
Common Player:	40.00
Inserted 1:Case	

CL-TD Tim Duncan 40.00
CL-SO Shaquille O'Neal 40.00

2001-02 Topps Xpectations

		MT
Complete Set (151):		450.00
Common Player:		.25
Minor Stars:		.50
Common Rookies:		2.00
Pack (6):		5.00
Wax Box (20):		75.00
1	Baron Davis	.75
2	Jason Terry	.50
3	Paul Pierce	.75
4	Ron Mercer	.25
5	Dirk Nowitzki	1.00
6	Marc Jackson	.50
7	Cuttino Mobley	.50
8	Al Harrington	.60
9	Keyon Dooling	.50
10	Mark Madsen	.25
11	Jumaine Jones	.25
12	Shawn Marion	1.00
13	Mike Bibby	.50
14	Antonio Daniels	.25
15	Vince Carter	4.00
16	Stromile Swift	.50
17	Courtney Alexander	.60
18	Desmond Mason	.50
19	Hidayet Turkoglu	.50
20	Craig "Speedy" Claxton	.50
21	Lavor Postell	.25
22	Chauncey Billups	.25
23	Eddie House	.50
24	Maurice Taylor	.25
25	Lamar Odom	1.00
26	Antawn Jamison	1.00
27	Raef LaFrentz	.60
28	Marcus Fizer	.50
29	Chris Mihm	.25
30	Eddie Robinson	.50
31	Mark Blount	.25
32	DerMarr Johnson	.50
33	Wang Zhizhi	1.50
34	Danny Fortson	.50
35	Elton Brand	1.00
36	Anthony Carter	.25
37	Wally Szczerbiak	.75
38	Mike Miller	1.50
39	Bonzi Wells	.50
40	Tim Duncan	1.50
41	Ruben Patterson	.25
42	Keon Clark	.50
43	Jason Williams	.60
44	Richard Hamilton	.50
45	Scott Padgett	.25
46	Derek Anderson	.50
47	Keith Van Horn	.50
48	Tim Thomas	.50
49	Jonathan Bender	.50
50	Tracy McGrady	2.00
51	Tyronn Lue	.25
52	Austin Croshere	.50
53	James Posey	.50
54	Mateen Cleaves	.50
55	Matt Harpring	.50
56	Calvin Booth	.25
57	Quentin Richardson	.60
58	Joel Przybilla	.25
59	Kenyon Martin	.75
60	Iakovos Tsakalidis	.25
61	Peja Stojakovic	.75
62	Shammond Williams	.25
63	Alvin Williams	.25
64	Jahidi White	.25
65	Morris Peterson	.60
66	Larry Hughes	.50
67	Andre Miller	.75
68	Jamaal Magloire	.25
69	Steve Francis	1.50
70	Todd MacCulloch	.25
71	Rashard Lewis	.50
72	Michael Dickerson	.50
73	Nazr Mohammed	.25
74	Jamal Crawford	.50
75	Darius Miles	3.00
76	Allen Iverson	2.50
77	Shaquille O'Neal	2.00
78	Michael Finley	.60
79	Antonio McDyess	.60
80	Jerry Stackhouse	.75
81	Chris Webber	1.50
82	Eddie Jones	.60
83	Reggie Miller	.75
84	Antoine Walker	.75
85	Latrell Sprewell	.75
86	Alonzo Mourning	.60
87	Jalen Rose	.50
88	Ray Allen	.75
89	Gary Payton	.75
90	Jason Kidd	1.25
91	Stephon Marbury	.75
92	Kobe Bryant	4.00
93	Grant Hill	1.25
94	Karl Malone	1.00
95	John Stockton	.75
96	Anfernee Hardaway	.50
97	Rasheed Wallace	.60
98	Hakeem Olajuwon	.75
99	Shareef Abdur-Rahim	.60
100	Kevin Garnett	2.50
101	*Kwame Brown 250*	60.00
102	*Tyson Chandler*	8.00
103	*Pau Gasol*	12.00
104	*Eddy Curry*	8.00
105	*Jason Richardson 250*	100.00
106	*Shane Battier 250*	75.00
107	*Eddie Griffin*	8.00
108	*DeSagana Diop*	3.00
109	*Rodney White*	4.00
110	*Joe Johnson 250*	60.00
111	*Kedrick Brown*	2.00
112	*Vladimir Radmanovic*	3.00
113	*Richard Jefferson*	6.00
114	*Troy Murphy 250*	30.00
115	*Steven Hunter*	3.00
116	*Kirk Haston*	4.00
117	*Michael Bradley*	3.00
118	*Jason Collins*	2.00
119	*Zach Randolph 250*	40.00
120	*Brendan Haywood*	5.00
121	*Joseph Forte*	5.00
122	*Jeryl Sasser*	3.00
123	*Brandon Armstrong*	2.00
124	*Gerald Wallace*	4.00
125	*Samuel Dalembert*	2.00
126	*Jamaal Tinsley*	12.00
127	*Tony Parker*	10.00
128	*Trenton Hassell*	4.00
129	*Gilbert Arenas*	3.00
130	*Omar Cook*	3.00
131	*Will Solomon*	2.00
132	*Terence Morris*	2.00
133	*Brian Scalabrine*	2.00
134	*Jeff Trepagnier*	2.00
135	*Damone Brown*	2.00
136	*Michael Wright*	3.00
137	*Earl Watson*	2.00
138	*Jamison Brewer*	2.00
139	*Bobby Simmons*	2.00
140	*Eric Chenowith*	2.00
141	*Kyle Hill*	2.00
142	*Sean Lampley*	2.00
143	*Loren Woods*	5.00
144	*Ousmane Cisse*	2.00
145	*Antonis Fotsis*	2.00
146	*Ken Johnson*	2.00
147	*Ruben Boumtje-Boumtje*	2.00
148	*Andre Hutson*	2.00
149	*Kenny Satterfield*	3.00
150	*Alvin Jones*	2.00
151	Michael Jordan	8.00

2001-02 Topps Xpectations Autographs

		MT
Common Player:		10.00
Minor Stars:		15.00
TXA-CA	Courtney Alexander	15.00
TXA-GA	Gilbert Arenas	15.00
TXA-EB	Erick Barkley	10.00
TXA-SB	Shane Battier	50.00
TXA-JB	Jonathan Bender	15.00
TXA-MB	Mike Bibby	20.00
TXA-CB	Chauncey Billups	15.00
TXA-ETB	Elton Brand	25.00
TXA-DB	Damone Brown	10.00
TXA-KBR	Kedrick Brown	10.00
TXA-KB	Kwame Brown	45.00
TXA-EC	Eddy Curry	35.00
TXA-AD	Antonio Daniels	10.00
TXA-BD	Baron Davis	15.00
TXA-MD	Michael Doleac	10.00
TXA-KD	Keyon Dooling	15.00
TXA-JF	Joseph Forte	25.00
TXA-RH	Richard Hamilton	15.00
TXA-DH	Donnell Harvey	10.00
TXA-BH	Brendan Haywood	15.00
TXA-BJ	Bobby Jackson	10.00
TXA-MJ	Marc Jackson	15.00
TXA-AJ	Antawn Jamison	25.00
TXA-KJ	Ken Johnson	10.00
TXA-AJO	Alvin Jones	10.00
TXA-RL	Raef LaFrentz	15.00
TXA-SM	Shawn Marion	20.00
TXA-DTM	Desmond Mason	10.00
TXA-RM	Roshown McLeod	10.00
TXA-AM	Andre Miller	15.00
TXA-JO	Jermaine O'Neal	20.00
TXA-LP	Lavor Postell	10.00
TXA-VR	Vladimir Radmanovic	10.00
TXA-ZR	Zach Randolph	25.00
TXA-KS	Kenny Satterfield	10.00
TXA-PS	Peja Stojakovic	40.00
TXA-JT	Jason Terry	15.00
TXA-TT	Tim Thomas	15.00
TXA-JTR	Jeff Trepagnier	10.00
TXA-IT	Iakovos Tsakalidis	10.00
TXA-HT	Hidayet Turkoglu	15.00
TXA-GW	Gerald Wallace	10.00
TXA-LW	Loren Woods	25.00

2001-02 Topps Xpectations Changing of the Guard

		MT
Complete Set (10):		30.00
Common Player:		2.00
CG1	Allen Iverson	6.00
CG2	Kobe Bryant	10.00
CG3	Vince Carter	10.00
CG4	Tracy McGrady	4.00
CG5	Jason Kidd	3.00
CG6	Steve Francis	4.00
CG7	Stephon Marbury	2.00
CG8	Gary Payton	2.00
CG9	Michael Finley	2.00
CG10	Baron Davis	2.00

2001-02 Topps Xpectations Class Challenge

		MT
Common Player:		12.00
CC-MB	Mike Bibby	18.00
CC-EB	Elton Brand	25.00
CC-MC	Mateen Cleaves	15.00
CC-BD	Baron Davis	12.00
CC-MD	Michael Dickerson	12.00
CC-SF	Steve Francis	30.00
CC-AG	Adrian Griffin	12.00
CC-RH	Richard Hamilton	15.00
CC-MJ	Marc Jackson	12.00
CC-SJ	Stephen Jackson	12.00
CC-RL	Raef LaFrentz	15.00
CC-TM	Todd MacCulloch	12.00
CC-SM	Shawn Marion	25.00
CC-KM	Kenyon Martin	15.00
CC-DM	Darius Miles	40.00
CC-AM	Andre Miller	15.00
CC-MM	Mike Miller	25.00
CC-CM	Cuttino Mobley	12.00
CC-DN	Dirk Nowitzki	25.00
CC-LO	Lamar Odom	25.00
CC-MO	Michael Olowokandi	12.00
CC-MP	Morris Peterson	12.00
CC-PP	Paul Pierce	20.00
CC-JP	James Posey	12.00
CC-QR	Quentin Richardson	15.00
CC-WS	Wally Szczerbiak	15.00
CC-JT	Jason Terry	12.00
CC-JW	Jason Williams	18.00

2001-02 Topps Xpectations Class Challenge Autographs

		MT
Common Player:		45.00
CCA-EB	Elton Brand 43	85.00
CCA-RH	Richard Hamilton 32	60.00
CCA-RL	Raef LaFrentz 45	45.00
CCA-SM	Shawn Marion 31	100.00

2001-02 Topps Xpectations First Shot

		MT
Common Player:		10.00
Minor Stars:		15.00
FS1	Kwame Brown	40.00
FS2	Tyson Chandler	30.00
FS3	Pau Gasol	35.00
FS4	Eddy Curry	25.00
FS5	Jason Richardson	30.00
FS6	Shane Battier	40.00
FS7	Eddie Griffin	30.00
FS8	DeSagana Diop	10.00
FS9	Rodney White	10.00
FS10	Joe Johnson	35.00
FS11	Kedrick Brown	10.00
FS12	Vladimir Radmanovic	15.00
FS13	Richard Jefferson	15.00
FS14	Troy Murphy	20.00
FS15	Steven Hunter	15.00
FS16	Kirk Haston	10.00
FS17	Michael Bradley	10.00
FS18	Jason Collins	10.00
FS19	Zach Randolph	20.00
FS20	Brendan Haywood	20.00
FS21	Joseph Forte	25.00
FS22	Jeryl Sasser	10.00
FS23	Brandon Armstrong	10.00
FS24	Jamaal Tinsley	40.00
FS25	Tony Parker	40.00

2001-02 Topps Xpectations Forward Thinking

		MT
Complete Set (10):		20.00
Common Player:		2.00
FT1	Chris Webber	3.00
FT2	Kevin Garnett	6.00
FT3	Lamar Odom	3.00
FT4	Tim Duncan	4.00
FT5	Dirk Nowitzki	2.50
FT6	Karl Malone	2.00
FT7	Paul Pierce	2.00
FT8	Shawn Marion	2.00
FT9	Scottie Pippen	2.00
FT10	Darius Miles	7.00

2001-02 Topps Xpectations Future Features

		MT
Common Player:		10.00
FF-EB	Elton Brand	20.00
FF-SF	Steve Francis	25.00
FF-RH	Richard Hamilton	10.00
FF-SM	Shawn Marion	15.00
FF-DM	Darius Miles	25.00
FF-AM	Andre Miller	10.00
FF-DN	Dirk Nowitzki	20.00
FF-PP	Paul Pierce	10.00
FF-JT	Jason Terry	10.00
FF-RW	Rasheed Wallace	10.00

2001-02 Topps Xpectations Future Features Autographs

		MT
Common Player:		60.00
FFA-EB	Elton Brand 42	85.00
FFA-RH	Richard Hamilton 32	60.00
FFA-SM	Shawn Marion 31	100.00

2001-02 Topps Xpectations In The Center

		MT
Complete Set (6):		8.00
Common Player:		1.50
IC1	Shaquille O'Neal	6.00
IC2	Alonzo Mourning	1.50
IC3	Jermaine O'Neal	3.00
IC4	Hakeem Olajuwon	2.00
IC5	David Robinson	2.00
IC6	Dikembe Mutombo	1.50

1971-72 Trail Blazers Texaco

The 12-card, 8" x 9-5/8" set, sponsored by Texaco, featured posed photos on the fronts with career statistics on the backs.

		NM
Complete Set (12):		80.00
Common Player:		8.00
1	Rick Adelman	12.00
2	Gary Gregor	8.00
3	Ron Knight	8.00
4	Jim Marsh	8.00
5	Willie McCarter	8.00
6	Stan McKenzie	8.00
7	Geoff Petrie	15.00
8	Dale Schlueter	8.00
9	Bill Smith	8.00
10	Larry Steele	10.00
11	Sidney Wicks	20.00
12	Charlie Yelverton	8.00

1975-76 Trail Blazers Iron Ons

The seven-patch, 5" x 7-7/8" set featured black and white player portraits with the players' jerseys outlined in red. The iron-ons are unnumbered and feature a facsimile autograph in red.

	NM
Complete Set (7):	40.00
Common Player:	3.00
Dan Anderson	3.00
Barry Clemens	3.00
Bob Gross	3.00
LaRue Martin Jr.	3.00
Larry Steele	4.00
Bill Walton	20.00
Sidney Wicks	10.00

1977-78 Trail Blazers Police

The 14-card, 2-5/8" x 4-1/8" set, sponsored by Kiwanis and the Portland Police Department, featured safety tips on the unnumbered card backs.

	NM
Complete Set (14):	60.00
Common Player:	3.00
Corky Calhoun	3.00
Dave Twardzik	5.00
Lionel Hollins	5.00
Larry Steele	5.00
Johnny Davis	3.00
Maurice Lucas	10.00
T.R. Dunn	3.00
Tom Owens	3.00
Bob Gross	3.00
Bill Walton	30.00
Lloyd Neal	3.00
Jack Ramsay (CO)	5.00
Jack McKinney (ACO)	3.00
Ron Culp (TR)	3.00

1978 Trail Blazers Portfolio

The 10-card, 11" x 14" set was given to customers of Ben Franklin Federal Savings and Loan in Portland and were done by artist Michael Lundy. The prints are in black and white, except for the Maurice Lucas print. The backs are blank and unnumbered.

	NM
Complete Set (10):	40.00
Common Player:	3.00
Kim Anderson, Clemon Johnson	3.00
T.R. Dunn	3.00
Bob Gross	3.00
Lionel Hollins	6.00
Maurice Lucas	10.00
Lloyd Neal	3.00
Tom Owens	3.00
Willie Smith, Ron Brewer	3.00
Larry Steele	6.00
Dave Twardzik	6.00

1979-80 Trail Blazers Police

The 16-card, 2-5/8" x 4-1/8" set was sponsored by 7-Up, Safeway, Kiwanis, KEX-1190 AM and local law enforcement. The cards are numbered by the players' jersey numbers and the backs contain a safety tip.

		NM
Complete Set (16):		15.00
Common Player:		.75
4	Jim Paxson	2.00
9	Lionel Hollins	1.50
10	Ron Brewer	.75
11	Abdul Jeelani	.75
13	Dave Twardzik	1.50
15	Larry Steele	1.00
20	Maurice Lucas	2.00
23	T.R. Dunn	.75
25	Tom Owens	.75
30	Bob Gross	.75
42	Kermit Washington	1.00
43	Mychal Thompson	2.00
44	Kevin Kunnert	.75
XX	Jack Ramsay (CO)	1.50
XX	Bucky Buckwalter (ACO)	.75
XX	Bill Schonely (ANN)	.75

1981-82 Trail Blazers Police

The 16-card, 2-5/8" x 4-1/8" set, sponsored by Kiwanis, local law enforcement, the Trail Blazers and the NBA, features safety tips on the card backs.

		MT
Complete Set (16):		10.00
Common Player:		.75
3	Jeff Lamp	.75
4	Jim Paxson	1.00
10	Darnell Valentine	1.50
12	Billy Ray Bates	1.00
14	Kelvin Ransey	.75
30	Bob Gross	.75
31	Pete Verhoeven	.75
32	Mike Harper	.75
33	Calvin Natt	1.00
40	Petur Gudmundsson	.75
42	Kermit Washington	1.00
43	Mychal Thompson	1.50
44	Kevin Kunnert	.75
NNO	Jack Ramsay (CO)	1.50
NNO	Bucky Buckwalter (ACO)	.75
NNO	Jim Lynam (ACO)	1.00

1982-83 Trail Blazers Police

The 16-card, 2-5/8" x 4-1/8" set is virtually identical to the 1981-82 Police set with the player's facsimile autograph appearing on the card front. Safety tips are printed on the backs and the first professional card of Lafayette Lever is included.

		MT
Complete Set (16):		12.00
Common Player:		.75
2	Linton Townes	.75
3	Jeff Lamp	.75
4	Jim Paxson	1.00
12	Lafayette Lever	1.50
14	Darnell Valentine	.75
22	Jeff Judkins	.75
24	Audie Norris	.75
31	Pete Verhoeven	.75
33	Calvin Natt	1.00
34	Kenny Carr	1.00
42	Wayne Cooper	1.00
43	Mychal Thompson	1.50
NNO	Jack Ramsay (CO)	1.50
NNO	Bucky Buckwalter (ACO)	.75
NNO	Jim Lynam (ACO)	1.00

1983-84 Trail Blazers Police

The 16-card, 2-5/8" x 4-1/8" set is similar to previous Police sets, except that the facsimile signature is included on the card backs by the "Blazer Tips." The set features one of the first cards of Clyde Drexler.

		MT
Complete Set (16):		30.00
Common Player:		.75
3	Jeff Lamp	.75
4	Jim Paxson	1.00
12	Lafayette Lever	1.00
14	Darnell Valentine	.75
22	Clyde Drexler	20.00
24	Audie Norris	.75
31	Pete Verhoeven	.75
33	Calvin Natt	1.00
34	Kenny Carr	.75
42	Wayne Cooper	.75
43	Mychal Thompson	1.50
54	Tom Piotrowski	.75
NNO	Jack Ramsay (CO)	1.50
NNO	Assistant Coaches (Morris Buckwalter, Rick Adelman ACO)	1.00
NNO	Ron Culp (Trainer)	.75
NNO	Dave Twardzik ANN, Bill Schonely ANN	.75

1984-85 Trail Blazers Franz/Star

The 13-card, standard-size set is nearly identical to the Mr. Z's set above, except that the cards are 2-1/2" x 3-1/2" and the Franz logo appears in the upper right corner of the card front. The horizontal card backs feature bio and stat information.

		MT
Complete Set (13):		50.00
Common Player:		2.00
1	Jack Ramsay (CO)	4.00
2	Sam Bowie	5.00
3	Kenny Carr	2.00
4	Steve Colter	2.00
5	Clyde Drexler	35.00
6	Jerome Kersey	8.00

7	Audie Norris	2.00
8	Jim Paxson	3.00
9	Tom Scheffler	2.00
10	Bernard Thompson	2.00
11	Mychal Thompson	3.00
12	Darnell Valentine	2.00
13	Kiki Vandeweghe	4.00

1984 Trail Blazers Mr. Z's/Star

The five-card, 5" x 7" set was produced by Star and 10,000 of the cards were included with Mr. Z's frozen pizzas. The card fronts feature a Mr. Z's logo in the upper right corner with a Blazers logo appearing in the lower left corner. The horizontal backs explain to collectors about collecting "Blazer Points" for Blazers merchandise.

		MT
Complete Set (5):		175.00
Common Player:		20.00
1	Kenny Carr	20.00
2	Clyde Drexler	100.00
3	Audie Norris	20.00
4	Mychal Thompson	30.00
5	Darnell Valentine	20.00

1984-85 Trail Blazers Police

The 16-card, 2-5/8" x 4-1/8" are similar to the 1983-84 set with the "Blazer Tips" appearing on the card backs. An early professional card of Jerome Kersey is included.

		MT
Complete Set (16):		17.00
Common Player:		.50
1	Portland Team	1.00
2	Jim Paxson	.75
3	Bernard Thompson	.50
4	Darnell Valentine	.50
5	Jack Ramsay CO, Rick Adelman ACO, Bucky Buckwalter ACO	1.00
6	Steve Colter	.50
7	Clyde Drexler	8.00
8	Audie Norris	.50
9	Jerome Kersey	4.00
10	Sam Bowie	1.50
11	Kenny Carr	.50
12	Lloyd Neal	.50
13	Mychal Thompson	1.00
14	Geoff Petrie	1.00
15	Tom Scheffler	.50
16	Kiki Vandeweghe	1.50

1985-86 Trail Blazers Franz/Star

The 13-card, standard-size set features 12 player cards and one coach card and was produced by Star for Franz Bread. The horizontal backs contain bio and stat information while the fronts are labeled with "1986 Collector's Issue" in the upper left corner.

		MT
Complete Set (13):		40.00
Common Player:		2.00
1	Jack Ramsay (CO)	3.00
2	Sam Bowie	4.00
3	Kenny Carr	2.00
4	Steve Colter	2.00
5	Clyde Drexler	30.00
6	Ken Johnson	2.00
7	Caldwell Jones	2.00
8	Jerome Kersey	3.00
9	Jim Paxson	3.00
10	Terry Porter	10.00
11	Mychal Thompson	4.00
12	Darnell Valentine	2.00
13	Kiki Vandeweghe	4.00

1986-87 Trail Blazers Franz

Produced by Fleer for Franz Bread, the 13-card, standard-size set features horizontal backs with "1987 Collector's Issue" appearing in the upper left front corner.

		MT
Complete Set (13):		65.00
Common Player:		2.50
1	Walter Berry	3.00
2	Sam Bowie	5.00
3	Kenny Carr	2.50
4	Clyde Drexler	35.00
5	Michael Holton	2.50
6	Steve Johnson	2.50
7	Caldwell Jones	3.00
8	Jerome Kersey	5.00
9	Fernando Martin	2.50
10	Jim Paxson	3.00
11	Terry Porter	6.00
12	Kiki Vandeweghe	6.00
13	Mike Schuler (CO)	2.50

1987-88 Trail Blazers Franz

The 13-card, standard-size set parallels in design the 1986-87 Franz set and was produced by Fleer. One of Kevin Duckworth's first cards is included in the set.

		MT
Complete Set (13):		65.00
Common Player:		3.00
1	Clyde Drexler	35.00
2	Kevin Duckworth	4.00
3	Michael Holton	3.00
4	Steve Johnson	3.00
5	Caldwell Jones	4.00
6	Jerome Kersey	5.00
7	Maurice Lucas	6.00
8	Jim Paxson	4.00
9	Terry Porter	6.00
10	Mike Schuler (CO)	3.00
11	Kiki Vandeweghe	4.00
12	Steve Johnson	3.00
13	Kiki Vandeweghe	4.00

1988-89 Trail Blazers Franz

As with previous Franz issues, the 1988-89 set was produced by Fleer and featured horizontal card backs. The fronts feature the Franz logo in the upper left corner with "1989 Collector's Issue" appearing along the top in a red bar.

		MT
Complete Set (13):		55.00
Common Player:		2.00
1	Richard Anderson	2.00
2	Sam Bowie	4.00
3	Mark Bryant	3.00
4	Clyde Drexler	25.00
5	Kevin Duckworth	4.00
6	Rolando Ferreira	2.00
7	Steve Johnson	2.00
8	Caldwell Jones	3.00
9	Jerome Kersey	3.00
10	Terry Porter	4.00
11	Mike Schuler (CO)	2.00
12	Jerry Sichting	2.00
13	Kiki Vandeweghe	4.00

1989-90 Trail Blazers Franz

The 20-card, standard-size set honors the Blazers on their 20th anniversary and includes past and present players in the set. Produced by Fleer, the cards have horizontal backs with a 20th anniversary logo appearing on the card front's lower left margin.

		MT
Complete Set (20):		40.00
Common Player:		1.00
1	Rick Adelman (CO)	1.50
2	Mark Bryant	1.00
3	Wayne Cooper	1.00
4	Kevin Duckworth	1.50
5	Clyde Drexler	15.00
6	Byron Irvin	1.00
7	Jerome Kersey	1.50
8	Drazen Petrovic	6.00
9	Terry Porter	2.00
10	Cliff Robinson	9.00
11	Buck Williams	3.00
12	Lionel Hollins	1.50
13	Maurice Lucas	2.00
14	Calvin Natt	1.00
15	Lloyd Neal	1.00
16	Jim Paxson	1.50
17	Geoff Petrie	1.50
18	Larry Steele	1.00
19	Mychal Thompson	2.00
20	Bill Walton	8.00

1990-91 Trail Blazers British Petroleum

The six-card, 8-1/2" x 11" set was printed on high-gloss paper stock with red and white borders. The photos were taken by Bryan Drake and the card backs are blank.

		MT
Complete Set (6):		15.00
Common Player:		2.00
1	Danny Ainge	4.00
2	Clyde Drexler	8.00
3	Kevin Duckworth	2.00
4	Jerome Kersey	2.00
5	Terry Porter	2.00
6	Buck Williams	2.50

1990-91 Trail Blazers Franz

The 20-card, standard-size set was produced by Fleer for Franz Bread and was distributed in the Portland area. The cards have horizontal backs with "1991 Collector's Issue" printed along the top border on the card fronts.

		MT
Complete Set (20):		30.00
Common Player:		.75
1	Team Card	1.50
2	1989-90 Playoffs	.75
3	1989-90 Playoffs	.75
4	1989-90 Playoffs	.75
5	1989-90 Playoffs	.75
6	Bill Walton	6.00
7	Rick Adelman (CO)	1.00
8	John Schalow ACO, John Wetzel ACO	.75
9	Alaa Abdelnaby	.75
10	Danny Ainge	3.00
11	Mark Bryant	.75
12	Wayne Cooper	.75
13	Clyde Drexler	12.00
14	Kevin Duckworth	1.00
15	Jerome Kersey	1.00
16	Drazen Petrovic	3.00
17	Terry Porter	1.50
18	Cliff Robinson	6.00
19	Buck Williams	2.50
20	Danny Young	.75

1991-92 Trail Blazers Franz

The 17-card, standard-size set was produced by Hoops for Franz Bread with a production of 150,000 for each card. A card was issued each week for 17 weeks and the card fronts feature the Franz logo in the upper left corner.

		MT
Complete Set (17):		25.00
Common Player:		.75
1	Team Photo	1.50
2	Blazers All--Star Weekend	.75
3	Buck Williams (NBA All-Defensive 1st Team)	1.50
4	Rick Adelman (CO)	1.00
5	Alaa Abdelnaby	.75
6	Danny Ainge	3.50
7	Mark Bryant	.75
8	Wayne Cooper	.75
9	Walter Davis	3.00
10	Clyde Drexler	10.00
11	Kevin Duckworth	1.00
12	Jerome Kersey	1.00
13	Terry Porter	2.00
14	Cliff Robinson	5.00
15	Buck Williams	2.50
16	Danny Young	.75
17	Robert Pack	4.00

1991-92 Trail Blazers Posters

The five-poster, 7" x 18" set was produced by Line-Up Productions, Inc., as part of the "PlayMakers Collection" series. Each set was accompanied with a certificate of authenticity. The posters feature a color painting of an action pose with the backs being blank. Sponsor logos appear along the poster bottom.

		MT
Complete Set (5):		22.00
Common Player:		2.00
1	Clyde Drexler	14.00
2	Kevin Duckworth	2.00
3	Jerome Kersey	3.00
4	Terry Porter	4.00
5	Buck Williams	4.00

1992-93 Trail Blazers Franz

The 20-card, standard-size set was produced by SkyBox and distributed by Franz Bread during a 20-week promotion. Production was limited to 165,000 of each card. The backs are horizontal with the fronts featuring full-bleed color action shots with the player's name along the bottom.

		MT
Complete Set (20):		24.00
Common Player:		.50
1	Team Photo	1.50
2	Buck Williams (1991-92 NBA Playoffs)	2.00
3	Cliff Robinson (1991-92 NBA Playoffs)	1.50
4	Terry Porter (1991-92 NBA Playoffs)	1.00
5	Jerome Kersey, Clyde Drexler (1991-92 NBA Playoffs)	2.00
6	Clyde Drexler (AS)	5.00
7	Rick Adelman (CO)	.75
8	Mark Bryant	.50
9	Clyde Drexler	8.00
10	Kevin Duckworth	.75
11	Jerome Kersey (UER) (Card back has bio and stats for Tracy Murray)	.75
12	Terry Porter	1.50
13	Cliff Robinson	3.00
14	Rod Strickland	2.00
15	Buck Williams	1.50
16	Mario Elie	1.00
17	Lamont Strothers	.50
18	Dave Johnson	.50
19	Tracy Murray	1.50
20	Reggie Smith	.50

1993-94 Trail Blazers Franz

The 20-card, standard-size set was produced by SkyBox and issued by Franz during a 20-week promotion. Production of each card was 250,000. The fronts feature a color shot with a silver border with horizontal backs.

		MT
Complete Set (20):		24.00
Common Player:		.50
1	Team Photo	1.50
2	Jack Schalow, Rick Adelman CO, John Wetzel ACO (ACO)	.50
3	Harry Glickman (Trail Blazers Walk of Fame Charter Member)	.50
4	Mark Bryant	.50
5	Clyde Drexler	9.00
6	Maurice Lucas (Trail Blazers Walk of Fame Charter Member)	2.00
7	Chris Dudley	.50
8	Harvey Grant	.50
9	Geoff Petrie (Trail Blazers Walk of Fame Charter Member)	1.00
10	Reggie Smith	.50
11	Jerome Kersey (UER) (Bio, stats and career summary are Murray's)	1.00
12	Jack Ramsey (CO) (Trail Blazers Walk of Fame Charter Member)	1.50
13	Tracy Murray	1.00
14	Terry Porter	1.00
15	Bill Walton (Trail Blazers Walk of Fame Charter Member)	5.00
16	Cliff Robinson	4.00
17	James Robinson	.75
18	Larry Weinberg (Trail Blazers Walk of Fame Charter Member)	.50
19	Rod Strickland	1.50
20	Buck Williams	2.00

1994-95 Trail Blazers Franz

The 20-card, standard-size set was produced by SkyBox and honors the Blazers for their 25th anniversary. The fronts feature full-bleed color photography with the Blazers' logo appearing in the lower left corner. The backs feature the player's headshot with bio and stat information.

		MT
Complete Set (20):		20.00
Common Player:		.50
1	Team Photo	1.50
2	P.J. Carlesimo (CO)	1.50
3	Bill Walton (Glickman's, All-Time Team)	4.00
4	Mark Bryant	.50
5	Clyde Drexler	8.00
6	Chris Dudley	.50
7	Buck Williams (Glickman's, All-Time Team)	1.50
8	James Edwards	.50
9	Harvey Grant	.75
10	Jerome Kersey	.75
11	Clyde Drexler (Glickman's, All-Time Team)	4.00
12	Aaron McKie	2.00
13	Tracy Murray	.50
14	Terry Porter	.75
15	Geoff Petrie (Glickman's, All-Time Team)	.75
16	Clifford Robinson	3.00
17	James Robinson	.50
18	Rod Strickland	1.50
19	Maurice Lucas (Glickman's, All-Time Team)	1.50
20	Buck Williams	1.50

1995-96 Trail Blazers Franz

This 13-card set was produced for the Franz bread company by SkyBox. One card was inserted in each loaf of Franz and Williams bread from late 1995 to the Spring of 1996.

		MT
Complete Set (13):		15.00
Common Player:		.50
1	Clifford Robinson	1.00
2	Randolph Childress	.50
3	Chris Dudley	.50
4	Aaron McKie	.75
5	Harvey Grant	.50
6	Gary Trent	1.00
7	P.J. Carlesimo	.50
8	Dontonio Wingfield	.50
9	Arvydas Sabonis	3.00
10	James Robinson	.50
11	Rod Strickland	1.00
12	Bill Curley	.50
13	Buck Williams	1.50

1996-97 Trail Blazers Franz

SkyBox produced this seven-card set for Franz. The cards are identical to the 1996-97 SkyBox set except they are numbered from one to seven.

		MT
Complete Set (7):		9.00
Common Player:		.50
1	Jermaine O'Neal	2.00
2	Clifford Robinson	1.00
3	Gary Trent	.50
4	Gary Anderson	1.00
5	Arvydas Sabonis	1.00
6	Isaiah Rider	1.00
7	Rasheed Wallace	3.00

1999-00 Trail Blazers Franz

		MT
Complete Set (8):		7.00
Common Player:		.50
1	Scottie Pippen	3.00
2	Jermaine O'Neal	1.50
3	Steve Smith	1.00
4	Arvydas Sabonis	.50
5	Detlef Schrempf	.50
6	Brian Grant	.50
7	Rasheed Wallace	1.00
8	Damon Stoudamire	1.00

U

1992-93 Ultimate USBL Promo Sheet

The Ultimate Trading Card Company produced this 7-1/2" x 11" sheet as a promotion for the 1992-93 United States Basketball League. The sheet has nine standard-size cards featured with each card having the Ultimate logo in the upper right corner. The card backs have bio and stat information, as well as career summaries.

		MT
Complete Set (1):		5.00
Common Sheet:		5.00
NNO	USBL Promo Sheet (Norris Coleman, Dallas Comegys, Kermit Holmes, Anthony Mason, Anthony Pullard, Lloyd Daniels, Michael Anderson, Darrell Armstrong, Roy Tarpley)	5.00

1992-93 Ultra

Fleer's 1992-93 Ultra set was released in two series, both containing several insert sets. The card fronts are glossy and feature a color action photo and the set's brand logo stamped in foil. The player's name and team are at the bottom in team color-coded bars. The horizontally-designed back has two more photos and the previous year's statistics against a basketball court background. A team logo and card number also appear on the card back. Subsets in the main set include NBA Draft Picks, and NBA Jam Session. Duane Causwell, Pervis Ellison and Stacey Augmon autographed more than 2,500 cards, which were random inserts in series II packs. Insert sets include All-NBA Team, NBA Award Winners, Scottie Pippen, All-Rookies, Playmakers and Rejectors.

		MT
Complete Set (375):		30.00
Complete Series 1 (200):		15.00
Complete Series 2 (175):		15.00
Common Player:		.10
Minor Stars:		.20
Series 1 Pack (14):		1.50
Series 1 Wax Box (36):		40.00
Series 2 Pack (14):		1.75
Series 2 Wax Box (36):		50.00
1	Stacey Augmon	.10
2	Duane Ferrell	.10
3	Paul Graham	.10
4	Blair Rasmussen	.10
5	Rumeal Robinson	.10
6	Dominique Wilkins	.25
7	Kevin Willis	.10
8	John Bagley	.10
9	Dee Brown	.10
10	Rick Fox	.10
11	Kevin Gamble	.10
12	Joe Kleine	.10
13	Reggie Lewis	.10
14	Kevin McHale	.10
15	Robert Parish	.10
16	Ed Pinckney	.10
17	Muggsy Bogues	.10
18	Dell Curry	.10
19	Kenny Gattison	.10
20	Kendall Gill	.10
21	Larry Johnson	.75
22	Johnny Newman	.10
23	J.R. Reid	.10
24	B.J. Armstrong	.10
25	Bill Cartwright	.10
26	Horace Grant	.20
27	Michael Jordan	6.00
28	Stacey King	.10
29	John Paxson	.10
30	Will Perdue	.10
31	Scottie Pippen	1.50
32	Scott Williams	.10
33	John Battle	.10
34	Terrell Brandon	.10
35	Brad Daugherty	.10
36	Craig Ehlo	.10
37	Larry Nance	.10
38	Mark Price	.10
39	Mike Sanders	.10
40	John Williams	.10
41	Terry Davis	.10
42	Derek Harper	.10
43	Donald Hodge	.10
44	Mike Iuzzolino	.10
45	Fat Lever	.10
46	Doug Smith	.10
47	Randy White	.10
48	Winston Garland	.10
49	Mahmoud Abdul-Rauf	.10
50	Marcus Liberty	.10
51	Todd Lichti	.10
52	Mark Macon	.10
53	Dikembe Mutombo	.50
54	Reggie Williams	.10
55	Mark Aguirre	.10
56	Joe Dumars	.20
57	Bill Laimbeer	.10
58	Dennis Rodman	1.50
59	Isiah Thomas	.25
60	Darrell Walker	.10
61	Orlando Woolridge	.10
62	Victor Alexander	.10
63	Chris Gatling	.10
64	Tim Hardaway	.20
65	Tyrone Hill	.10
66	Sarunas Marciulionis	.10
67	Chris Mullin	.20
68	Billy Owens	.10
69	Sleepy Floyd	.10
70	Avery Johnson	.10
71	Vernon Maxwell	.10
72	Hakeem Olajuwon	1.50

73	Kenny Smith	.10
74	Otis Thorpe	.10
75	Dale Davis	.10
76	Vern Fleming	.10
77	George McCloud	.20
78	Reggie Miller	.50
79	Detlef Schrempf	.10
80	Rik Smits	.20
81	LaSalle Thompson	.10
82	Gary Grant	.10
83	Ron Harper	.10
84	Mark Jackson	.10
85	Danny Manning	.20
86	Ken Norman	.10
87	Stanley Roberts	.10
88	Loy Vaught	.10
89	Elden Campbell	.10
90	Vlade Divac	.10
91	A.C. Green	.10
92	Sam Perkins	.10
93	Byron Scott	.10
94	Tony Smith	.10
95	Sedale Threatt	.10
96	James Worthy	.10
97	Willie Burton	.10
98	Vernell Coles	.10
99	Kevin Edwards	.10
100	Grant Long	.10
101	Glen Rice	.20
102	Rony Seikaly	.10
103	Brian Shaw	.10
104	Steve Smith	.10
105	Frank Brickowski	.10
106	Moses Malone	.10
107	Fred Roberts	.10
108	Alvin Robertson	.10
109	Thurl Bailey	.10
110	Gerald Glass	.10
111	Luc Longley	.10
112	Felton Spencer	.10
113	Doug West	.10
114	Kenny Anderson	.25
115	Mookie Blaylock	.10
116	Sam Bowie	.10
117	Derrick Coleman	.25
118	Chris Dudley	.10
119	Chris Morris	.10
120	Drazen Petrovic	.10
121	Greg Anthony	.10
122	Patrick Ewing	.40
123	Anthony Mason	.10
124	Charles Oakley	.10
125	Doc Rivers	.10
126	Charles Smith	.10
127	John Starks	.20
128	Nick Anderson	.10
129	Anthony Bowie	.10
130	Terry Catledge	.10
131	Jerry Reynolds	.10
132	Dennis Scott	.10
133	Scott Skiles	.10
134	Brian Williams	.10
135	Ron Anderson	.10
136	Manute Bol	.10
137	Johnny Dawkins	.10
138	Armon Gilliam	.10
139	Hersey Hawkins	.10
140	Jeff Ruland	.10
141	Charles Shackleford	.10
142	Cedric Ceballos	.10
143	Tom Chambers	.10
144	Kevin Johnson	.25
145	Negele Knight	.10
146	Dan Majerle	.10
147	Mark West	.10
148	Mark Bryant	.10
149	Clyde Drexler	.50
150	Kevin Duckworth	.10
151	Jerome Kersey	.10
152	Robert Pack	.10
153	Terry Porter	.10
154	Cliff Robinson	.10
155	Buck Williams	.10
156	Anthony Bonner	.10
157	Duane Causwell	.10
158	Mitch Richmond	.20
159	Lionel Simmons	.10
160	Wayman Tisdale	.10
161	Spud Webb	.10
162	Willie Anderson	.10
163	Antoine Carr	.10
164	Terry Cummings	.10
165	Sean Elliott	.10
166	Sidney Green	.10
167	David Robinson	1.00
168	Dana Barros	.10
169	Benoit Benjamin	.10
170	Michael Cage	.10
171	Eddie Johnson	.10
172	Shawn Kemp	1.00
173	Derrick McKey	.10
174	Nate McMillan	.10
175	Gary Payton	.50
176	Ricky Pierce	.10
177	David Benoit	.10
178	Mike Brown	.10
179	Tyrone Corbin	.10
180	Mark Eaton	.10
181	Jeff Malone	.10
182	Karl Malone	.50
183	John Stockton	.50
184	Michael Adams	.10
185	Ledell Eackles	.10
186	Pervis Ellison	.10
187	A.J. English	.10
188	Harvey Grant	.10
189	Buck Johnson	.10
190	LaBradford Smith	.10
191	Larry Stewart	.10
192	David Wingate	.10
193	*Alonzo Mourning*	3.00
194	*Adam Keefe*	.25
195	*Robert Horry*	1.00
196	*Anthony Peeler*	.25
197	*Tracy Murray*	.20
198	*Dave Johnson*	.20
199	Checklist	.10
200	Checklist	.10
201	David Robinson (JS)	.25
202	Dikembe Mutombo (JS)	.20
203	Otis Thorpe (JS)	.10
204	Hakeem Olajuwon (JS)	.50
205	Shawn Kemp (JS)	.20
206	Charles Barkley (JS)	.25
207	Pervis Ellison (JS)	.10
208	Chris Morris (JS)	.10
209	Brad Daugherty (JS)	.10
210	Derrick Coleman (JS)	.10
211	Tim Perry (JS)	.10
212	Duane Causwell (JS)	.10
213	Scottie Pippen (JS)	.25
214	Robert Parish (JS)	.10
215	Stacey Augmon (JS)	.10
216	Michael Jordan (JS)	1.50
217	Karl Malone (JS)	.20
218	John Williams	.10
219	Horace Grant	.10
220	Orlando Woolridge	.10
221	Mookie Blaylock	.10
222	Greg Foster	.10
223	Steve Henson	.10
224	Adam Keefe	.10
225	Jon Koncak	.10
226	Travis Mays	.10
227	Alaa Abdelnaby	.10
228	Sherman Douglas	.10
229	Xavier McDaniel	.10
230	*Marcus Webb*	.10
231	*Tony Bennett*	.10
232	Mike Gminski	.10
233	Kevin Lynch	.10
234	Alonzo Mourning	1.00
235	David Wingate	.10
236	Rodney McCray	.10
237	Trent Tucker	.10
238	*Corey Williams*	.10
239	Danny Ferry	.10
240	*Jay Guidinger*	.10
241	Jerome Lane	.10
242	*Bobby Phills*	.40
243	Gerald Wilkins	.10
244	*Walter Bond*	.10
245	*Dexter Cambridge*	.10
246	*Radisav Curcic*	.10
247	*Brian Howard*	.10
248	*Tracy Moore*	.10
249	*Sean Rooks*	.20
250	Kevin Brooks	.10
251	*LaPhonso Ellis*	.25
252	Scott Hastings	.10
253	Robert Pack	.10
254	Gary Plummer	.10
255	*Bryant Stith*	.25
256	*Robert Werdann*	.10
257	Gerald Glass	.10
258	Terry Mills	.10
259	Olden Polynice	.10
260	Danny Young	.10
261	Jud Buechler	.10
262	Jeff Grayer	.10
263	*Byron Houston*	.20
264	*Keith Jennings*	.20
265	Ed Nealy	.10
266	*Latrell Sprewell*	1.50
267	Scott Brooks	.10
268	Matt Bullard	.10
269	Winston Garland	.10
270	Carl Herrera	.10
271	Robert Horry	.50
272	Tree Rollins	.10
273	Greg Dreiling	.10
274	Sean Green	.10
275	Sam Mitchell	.10
276	Pooh Richardson	.10
277	*Malik Sealy*	.20
278	Kenny Williams	.10
279	Mark Jackson	.10
280	Stanley Roberts	.10
281	Elmore Spencer	.10
282	Kiki Vandeweghe	.10
283	John Williams	.10
284	*Randy Woods*	.10
285	*Alex Blackwell*	.10
286	*Duane Cooper*	.10
287	James Edwards	.10
288	Jack Haley	.10
289	Anthony Peeler	.10
290	Keith Askins	.10
291	Matt Geiger	.10
292	Alec Kessler	.10
293	*Harold Miner*	.25
294	John Salley	.10
295	*Anthony Avent*	.10
296	*Jon Barry*	.10
297	*Todd Day*	.25
298	Blue Edwards	.10
299	Brad Lohaus	.10
300	*Lee Mayberry*	.20
301	Eric Murdock	.10
302	Dan Schayes	.10
303	Lance Blanks	.10
304	*Christian Laettner*	.50
305	*Marlon Maxey*	.10
306	Bob McCann	.10
307	Chuck Person	.10
308	Brad Sellers	.10
309	*Chris Smith*	.10
310	*Gundars Vetra*	.10
311	Michael Williams	.10
312	Rafael Addison	.10
313	Chucky Brown	.10
314	Maurice Cheeks	.10
315	Tate George	.10
316	Rick Mahorn	.10
317	Rumeal Robinson	.10
318	*Eric Anderson*	.10
319	Rolando Blackman	.10
320	Tony Campbell	.10
321	*Hubert Davis*	.20
322	Doc Rivers	.10
323	Charles Smith	.10
324	Herb Williams	.10
325	*Litterial Green*	.10
326	Steve Kerr	.10
327	Greg Kite	.10
328	*Shaquille O'Neal*	12.00
329	Tom Tolbert	.10
330	Jeff Turner	.10
331	Greg Grant	.10
332	Jeff Hornacek	.10
333	Andrew Lang	.10
334	Tim Perry	.10
335	*C. Weatherspoon*	.50
336	Danny Ainge	.10
337	Charles Barkley	.50
338	*Richard Dumas*	.10
339	Frank Johnson	.10
340	Tim Kempton	.10
341	*Oliver Miller*	.20
342	Jerrod Mustaf	.10
343	Mario Elie	.10
344	Dave Johnson	.10
345	Tracy Murray	.10
346	Rod Strickland	.10
347	Randy Brown	.10
348	Pete Chilcutt	.10
349	Marty Conlon	.10
350	Jim Les	.10
351	Kurt Rambis	.10
352	*Walt Williams*	.50
353	*Lloyd Daniels*	.15
354	Vinny Del Negro	.10
355	Dale Ellis	.10
356	Avery Johnson	.10
357	*Sam Mack*	.10
358	J.R. Reid	.10
359	*David Wood*	.10
360	Vincent Askew	.10
361	*Isaac Austin*	.10
362	*John Crotty*	.10
363	*Stephen Howard*	.10
364	Jay Humphries	.10
365	Larry Krystkowiak	.10
366	Rex Chapman	.10
367	*Tom Gugliotta*	.75
368	Buck Johnson	.10
369	Charles Jones	.10
370	*Don MacLean*	.25
371	Doug Overton	.10
372	*Brent Price*	.20
373	Checklist	.10
374	Checklist	.10
375	Checklist	.10
JS207	Pervis Ellison Auto.	15.00
JS212	Duane Causwell Auto.	15.00
JS215	Stacey Augmon Auto.	50.00
NNO	Jam Session 1-10	2.00
NNO	Jam Session 11-20	2.00

1992-93 Ultra All-NBA Team

These cards were random inserts in Fleer Ultra Series I packs. Card backs say 1 of 15, 2 of 15, etc. The fronts of this glossy set feature color action photos.

		MT
Complete Set (15):		50.00
Common Player:		.50
Minor Stars:		1.00
1	Karl Malone	3.00
2	Chris Mullin	1.00
3	David Robinson	5.00
4	Michael Jordan	25.00
5	Clyde Drexler	3.00
6	Scottie Pippen	8.00
7	Charles Barkley	5.00
8	Patrick Ewing	3.00
9	Tim Hardaway	1.00
10	John Stockton	3.00
11	Dennis Rodman	8.00
12	Kevin Willis	.50
13	Brad Daugherty	.50
14	Mark Price	1.00
15	Kevin Johnson	1.00

1992-93 Ultra All-Rookies

This insert set features 10 of the NBA's top rookies for the 1992-93 season. Cards were randomly inserted into 1992-93 Fleer Ultra Series II foil packs, one per every nine packs. The card front shows a color action photo against a background of smaller versions of the same photo. Gold foil stamping is used for the player's name and set logo, which are at the bottom of the card. The back has a player profile and color photo, plus a card number (1 of 10, etc.) and set logo.

		MT
Complete Set (10):		45.00
Common Player:		.50
1	LaPhonso Ellis	.50
2	Tom Gugliotta	2.00
3	Robert Horry	1.00
4	Christian Laettner	1.50
5	Harold Miner	.50
6	Alonzo Mourning	5.00
7	Shaquille O'Neal	30.00
8	Latrell Sprewell	3.00
9	C. Weatherspoon	1.00
10	Walt Williams	1.00

1992-93 Ultra Award Winners

These cards, honoring the previous NBA season's award winners, have color action photos; the backs give career accomplishments. Cards were inserted one per every 42 Series I packs.

		MT
Complete Set (5):		50.00
Common Player:		2.00
1	Michael Jordan	40.00
2	David Robinson	6.00
3	Larry Johnson	5.00
4	Detlef Schrempf	2.00
5	Pervis Ellison	2.00

1992-93 Ultra Jam Session Cassette Insert

This card featured five NBA players and their "dunk rank" on a grey marbleized background. The card was inserted into NBA Jam Session "Gangsta Rap" cassettes.

		MT
Complete Set:		4.00
Common Player:		4.00
1	David Robinson, Dikembe Mutombo, Otis Thorpe, Hakeem Olajuwon, Shawn Kemp	2.00

1992-93 Ultra Playmakers

This insert set features 10 of the top point guards in the NBA. Cards were randomly inserted into 1992-93 Fleer Ultra Series II foil packs, one per every 13 packs. The glossy card front has the set logo and player's name stamped in gold foil, plus a color action photo. The back has a color action photo and player profile, plus a card number 1 of 10, etc.

		MT
Complete Set (10):		5.00
Common Player:		.25
1	Kenny Anderson	1.00
2	Muggsy Bogues	.25
3	Tim Hardaway	.50
4	Mark Jackson	.25
5	Kevin Johnson	1.00
6	Mark Price	.50
7	Terry Porter	.25
8	Scott Skiles	.25
9	John Stockton	1.50
10	Isiah Thomas	1.00

1992-93 Ultra Promo Sheet

This 11" x 11-1/2" sheet features 19 of the first 20 cards from 1992-93 Ultra Series Two. Ten cards are on one side and nine on the other, so they can not be seperated. The players on the cards represent the top 20 dunkers in the NBA according to Fleer.

		MT
Complete Set (1):		5.00
Common Panel:		5.00
NNO	Ultra Panel (David Robinson, Dikembe Mutombo, Otis Thorpe, Hakeem Olajuwon, Shawn Kemp, Charles Barkley, Pervis Ellison, Chris Morris, Brad Daugherty, Derrick Coleman, Tim Perry (back), Duane Causwell (back), Scottie Pip	3.00

1992-93 Ultra Rejectors

This insert set features five of the NBA's top defensive big men. Cards were randomly inserted into 1992-93 Fleer Ultra Series II foil packs, one per every 26 packs. The glossy card front has a color action photo with a gold stripe at the bottom where the player's name and set logo are stamped in gold foil. The horizontally-designed back has a color mug shot of the player against a black background with gold borders. A card number (1 of 5, etc.) and summary of the player's defensive abilities are on the back.

		MT
Complete Set (5):		20.00
Common Player:		.50
1	Alonzo Mourning	3.00
2	Dikembe Mutombo	.50
3	Hakeem Olajuwon	2.00
4	Shaquille O'Neal	15.00
5	David Robinson	2.00

1992-93 Ultra Scottie Pippen

These glossy cards, which have a marble background for their borders, highlight Scottie Pippen's career. Backs have a career summary and a small head shot. The cards, which were inserts in Fleer Ultra foil packs, are not titled, except for the "Career Highlights" card. The rest of the set is listed by the information provided on the card backs. Two additional Pippen cards were available through a mail-in offer for 10 Fleer Ultra wrappers and $1. They are listed with this set, but the set price does not include them.

		MT
Complete Set (10):		15.00
Common Pippen:		1.50
Pippen Auto:		200.00
Mail-In Pippen (11-12):		1.50
1	Comments From Jordan (Scottie Pippen)	1.50
2	Comments From Ron Martin (Scottie Pippen)	1.50
3	From High Sch. to College (Scottie Pippen)	1.50
4	Central Arkansas (Scottie Pippen)	1.50
5	Coach Dyer's Comments (Scottie Pippen)	1.50
6	The NBA Draft (Scottie Pippen)	1.50
7	Adjustment to NBA (Scottie Pippen)	1.50
8	Early Part of NBA Career (Scottie Pippen)	1.50
9	Accolades (Scottie Pippen)	1.50
10	Winner-Pippen & the Bulls (Scottie Pippen)	1.50
11	Special Mail-In (Scottie Pippen)	1.50
12	Special Mail-In (Scottie Pippen)	1.50

1993-94 Ultra

Fleer's 1993-94 Ultra cards feature gold foil stamping and larger action photos. The backs have a portrait and action shot superimposed on a basketball court background. Cards are UV coated and color-coded by team. The set has 14 first-round draft picks; these cards have a gold foil "Draft Pick" flag. A USA Basketball 12-card team subset was also made. Insert sets include All-Rookie Team, Scoring Kings, Award Winners, All-NBA Team, All-Defensive Team, Rebound Kings, All-Rookie series, Famous Nicknames, Inside/Outside, Power in the Key, and Jam Session.

		MT
Complete Set (375):		35.00
Complete Series 1 (200):		15.00
Complete Series 2 (175):		20.00
Common Player:		.05
Minor Stars:		.10
Series 1 or 2 Pack (14):		1.50
Series 1 Wax Box (36):		42.00
Series 2 Wax Box (36):		48.00
1	Stacey Augmon	.05
2	Mookie Blaylock	.05
3	*Doug Edwards*	.10
4	Duane Ferrell	.05
5	Paul Graham	.05
6	Adam Keefe	.05
7	Dominique Wilkins	.20
8	Kevin Willis	.05
9	Alaa Abdelnaby	.05
10	Dee Brown	.05
11	Sherman Douglas	.05
12	Rick Fox	.05
13	Kevin Gamble	.05
14	Xavier McDaniel	.05
15	Robert Parish	.05
16	Muggsy Bogues	.05
17	*Scott Burrell*	.25
18	Dell Curry	.05
19	Kenny Gattison	.05
20	Hersey Hawkins	.05
21	Eddie Johnson	.05
22	Larry Johnson	.30
23	Alonzo Mourning	.50
24	Johnny Newman	.05
25	David Wingate	.05
26	B.J. Armstrong	.10
27	*Corie Blount*	.10
28	Bill Cartwright	.05
29	Horace Grant	.15
30	Michael Jordan	3.00
31	Stacey King	.05
32	John Paxson	.05
33	Will Perdue	.05
34	Scottie Pippen	1.00
35	Terrell Brandon	.05
36	Brad Daugherty	.05
37	Danny Ferry	.05
38	*Chris Mills*	.30
39	Larry Nance	.05
40	Mark Price	.10
41	Gerald Wilkins	.05
42	John Williams	.05
43	Terry Davis	.05
44	Derek Harper	.05
45	Donald Hodge	.05
46	Jim Jackson	.50
47	Sean Rooks	.05
48	Doug Smith	.05
49	Mahmoud Abdul-Rauf	.05
50	LaPhonso Ellis	.05
51	Mark Macon	.05
52	Dikembe Mutombo	.20
53	Bryant Stith	.05
54	Reggie Williams	.05
55	Mark Aguirre	.05
56	Joe Dumars	.15
57	Bill Laimbeer	.05
58	Terry Mills	.05
59	Olden Polynice	.05
60	Alvin Robertson	.05
61	Dennis Rodman	1.00
62	Isiah Thomas	.15
63	Victor Alexander	.05
64	Chris Gatling	.05
65	Tim Hardaway	.10
66	Byron Houston	.05
67	Sarunas Marciulionis	.05
68	Chris Mullin	.10
69	Billy Owens	.05
70	Latrell Sprewell	.50
71	Matt Bullard	.05
72	*Sam Cassell*	1.50
73	Carl Herrera	.05
74	Robert Horry	.10
75	Vernon Maxwell	.05
76	Hakeem Olajuwon	.75
77	Kenny Smith	.05
78	Otis Thorpe	.05
79	Dale Davis	.05
80	Vern Fleming	.05
81	Reggie Miller	.25
82	Sam Mitchell	.05

83	Pooh Richardson	.05
84	Detlef Schrempf	.05
85	Rik Smits	.05
86	Ron Harper	.05
87	Mark Jackson	.05
88	Danny Manning	.10
89	Stanley Roberts	.05
90	Loy Vaught	.05
91	John Williams	.05
92	Sam Bowie	.05
93	Doug Christie	.05
94	Vlade Divac	.05
95	*George Lynch*	.10
96	Anthony Peeler	.05
97	James Worthy	.05
98	Bimbo Coles	.05
99	Grant Long	.05
100	Harold Miner	.10
101	Glen Rice	.10
102	Rony Seikaly	.05
103	Brian Shaw	.05
104	Steve Smith	.05
105	Anthony Avent	.05
106	*Vin Baker*	1.00
107	Frank Brickowski	.05
108	Todd Day	.05
109	Blue Edwards	.05
110	Lee Mayberry	.05
111	Eric Murdock	.05
112	Orlando Woolridge	.05
113	Thurl Bailey	.05
114	Christian Laettner	.05
115	Chuck Person	.05
116	Doug West	.05
117	Michael Williams	.05
118	Kenny Anderson	.10
119	Derrick Coleman	.10
120	Rick Mahorn	.05
121	Chris Morris	.05
122	Rumeal Robinson	.05
123	*Rex Walters*	.10
124	Greg Anthony	.05
125	Rolando Blackman	.05
126	Hubert Davis	.05
127	Patrick Ewing	.25
128	Anthony Mason	.05
129	Charles Oakley	.05
130	Doc Rivers	.05
131	Charles Smith	.05
132	John Starks	.05
133	Nick Anderson	.05
134	Anthony Bowie	.05
135	Shaquille O'Neal	2.50
136	Dennis Scott	.05
137	Scott Skiles	.05
138	Jeff Turner	.05
139	*Shawn Bradley*	.50
140	Johnny Dawkins	.05
141	Jeff Hornacek	.05
142	Tim Perry	.05
143	C. Weatherspoon	.10
144	Danny Ainge	.05
145	Charles Barkley	.50
146	Cedric Ceballos	.05
147	Kevin Johnson	.15
148	Negele Knight	.05
149	*Malcolm Mackey*	.05
150	Dan Majerle	.05
151	Oliver Miller	.05
152	Mark West	.05
153	Mark Bryant	.05
154	Clyde Drexler	.25
155	Jerome Kersey	.05
156	Terry Porter	.05
157	Clifford Robinson	.05
158	Rod Strickland	.05
159	Buck Williams	.05
160	Duane Causwell	.05
161	*Bobby Hurley*	.20
162	Mitch Richmond	.10
163	Lionel Simmons	.05
164	Wayman Tisdale	.05
165	Spud Webb	.05
166	Walt Williams	.05
167	Willie Anderson	.05
168	Antoine Carr	.05
169	Lloyd Daniels	.05
170	Dennis Rodman	1.00
171	Dale Ellis	.05
172	Avery Johnson	.05
173	J.R. Reid	.05
174	David Robinson	.50
175	Michael Cage	.05
176	Kendall Gill	.05
177	*Ervin Johnson*	.10
178	Shawn Kemp	.60
179	Derrick McKey	.05
180	Nate McMillan	.05
181	Gary Payton	.15
182	Sam Perkins	.05
183	Ricky Pierce	.05
184	David Benoit	.05
185	Tyrone Corbin	.05
186	Mark Eaton	.05
187	Jay Humphries	.05
188	Jeff Malone	.05
189	Karl Malone	.30
190	John Stockton	.30
191	*Luther Wright*	.05
192	Michael Adams	.05
193	*Calbert Cheaney*	.50
194	Pervis Ellison	.05
195	Tom Gugliotta	.05
196	Buck Johnson	.05
197	LaBradford Smith	.05
198	Larry Stewart	.05
199	Checklist	.05
200	Checklist	.05
201	Doug Edwards	.05
202	Craig Ehlo	.05
203	Jon Koncak	.05
204	Andrew Lang	.05
205	Ennis Whatley	.05
206	Chris Corchiani	.05
207	*Acie Earl*	.10
208	Jimmy Oliver	.05
209	Ed Pinckney	.05
210	*Dino Radja*	.30
211	Matt Wenstrom	.05
212	Tony Bennett	.05
213	Scott Burrell	.10
214	LeRon Ellis	.05
215	Hersey Hawkins	.05
216	Eddie Johnson	.05
217	Rumeal Robinson	.05
218	Corie Blount	.10
219	Dave Johnson	.05
220	Steve Kerr	.05
221	*Toni Kukoc*	1.00
222	Pete Myers	.05
223	Bill Wennington	.05
224	Scott Williams	.05
225	John Battle	.05
226	Tyrone Hill	.05
227	*Gerald Madkins*	.05
228	*Chris Mills*	.10
229	Bobby Phills	.10
230	Greg Dreiling	.05
231	*Lucious Harris*	.05
232	*Popeye Jones*	.25
233	Tim Legler	.05
234	Fat Lever	.05
235	*Jamal Mashburn*	1.50
236	Tom Hammonds	.05
237	*Darnell Mee*	.10
238	Robert Pack	.05
239	*Rodney Rogers*	.30
240	Brian Williams	.05
241	Greg Anderson	.05
242	Sean Elliott	.05
243	*Allan Houston*	1.25
244	*Lindsey Hunter*	.20
245	Mark Macon	.05
246	David Wood	.05
247	Jud Buechler	.05
248	*Josh Grant*	.05
249	Jeff Grayer	.05
250	Keith Jennings	.05
251	Avery Johnson	.05
252	*Chris Webber*	3.00
253	Scott Brooks	.05
254	Sam Cassell	.15
255	Mario Elie	.05
256	*Richard Petruska*	.10
257	*Eric Riley*	.10
258	*Antonio Davis*	.10
259	*Scott Haskin*	.10
260	Derrick McKey	.05
261	Byron Scott	.05
262	Malik Sealy	.05
263	Kenny Williams	.05
264	Haywoode Workman	.05
265	Mark Aguirre	.05
266	*Terry Dehere*	.10
267	Harold Ellis	.05
268	Gary Grant	.05
269	Bob Martin	.05
270	Elmore Spencer	.05
271	Tom Tolbert	.05
272	Sam Bowie	.05
273	Elden Campbell	.05
274	*Antonio Harvey*	.10
275	George Lynch	.05
276	Tony Smith	.05
277	Sedale Threatt	.05
278	*Nick Van Exel*	1.50
279	Willie Burton	.05
280	Matt Geiger	.05
281	John Salley	.05
282	Vin Baker	.60
283	Jon Barry	.05
284	Brad Lohaus	.05
285	Ken Norman	.05
286	*Derek Strong*	.10
287	Mike Brown	.05
288	Brian Davis	.05
289	Tellis Frank	.05
290	Luc Longley	.05
291	Marlon Maxey	.05
292	*Isaiah Rider*	.75
293	Chris Smith	.05
294	*P.J. Brown*	.10
295	Kevin Edwards	.05
296	Armon Gilliam	.05
297	Johnny Newman	.05
298	*Rex Walters*	.10
299	*David Wesley*	.50
300	Jayson Williams	.05
301	Anthony Bonner	.05
302	Derek Harper	.05
303	Herb Williams	.05
304	Litterial Green	.05
305	*Anfernee Hardaway*	3.00
306	Greg Kite	.05
307	Larry Krystkowiak	.05
308	Keith Tower	.05
309	Dana Barros	.05
310	Shawn Bradley	.10
311	*Greg Graham*	.10
312	Sean Green	.05
313	*Warren Kidd*	.10
314	Eric Leckner	.05
315	Moses Malone	.05
316	Orlando Woolridge	.05
317	Duane Cooper	.05
318	*Joe Courtney*	.05
319	A.C. Green	.05
320	Frank Johnson	.05
321	Joe Kleine	.05
322	Chris Dudley	.05
323	Harvey Grant	.05
324	Jaren Jackson	.05
325	Tracy Murray	.05
326	*James Robinson*	.20
327	Reggie Smith	.05
328	Kevin Thompson	.05
329	Randy Brown	.05
330	*Evers Burns*	.05
331	Pete Chilcutt	.05
332	Bobby Hurley	.10
333	*Mike Peplowski*	.10
334	LaBradford Smith	.05
335	Trevor Wilson	.05
336	Terry Cummings	.05
337	Vinny Del Negro	.05
338	Sleepy Floyd	.05
339	Negele Knight	.05
340	Dennis Rodman	1.00
341	*Chris Whitney*	.10
342	Vincent Askew	.05
343	Kendall Gill	.05
344	Ervin Johnson	.05
345	Chris King	.05
346	Detlef Schrempf	.05
347	Walter Bond	.05
348	Tom Chambers	.05
349	John Crotty	.05
350	*Byron Russell*	.10
351	Felton Spencer	.05
352	*Mitchell Butler*	.10
353	Rex Chapman	.05
354	Calbert Cheaney	.10
355	Kevin Duckworth	.05
356	Don MacLean	.05
357	*Gheorghe Muresan*	.75
358	Doug Overton	.05
359	Brent Price	.05
360	Kenny Walker	.05
361	Derrick Coleman	.10
362	Joe Dumars	.10
363	Tim Hardaway	.10
364	Larry Johnson	.20
365	Shawn Kemp	.20
366	Dan Majerle	.10
367	Alonzo Mourning	.30
368	Mark Price	.10
369	Steve Smith	.10
370	Isiah Thomas	.10
371	Dominique Wilkins	.10
372	Don Nelson, Don Chaney	.10
373	Checklist	.05
374	Checklist	.05
375	Checklist	.05

1993-94 Ultra All-Defensive

These 10 cards were available as inserts only in 1993-94 Fleer Ultra Series I 19-card packs. The NBA's 1992-93 first and second team defensive players are featured. Each card front has a player photo against a ghosted image background of the same photo, along with the player's name and set logo stamped in gold foil. The back has a color photo, too, and uses a larger ghosted image of the same photo as a background. A career recap and card number (1 of 10, etc.) are also given. First team players are 1-5; second team selections are 6-10.

		MT
Complete Set (10):		140.00
Common Player:		3.00
Minor Stars:		6.00
1	Joe Dumars	6.00
2	Michael Jordan	90.00
3	Hakeem Olajuwon	15.00
4	Scottie Pippen	20.00
5	Dennis Rodman	20.00
6	Horace Grant	6.00
7	Dan Majerle	3.00
8	Larry Nance	3.00
9	David Robinson	10.00
10	John Starks	3.00

1993-94 Ultra All-NBA

Fourteen players from the NBA's 1992-93 first, second and third teams are featured on these cards, which were inserts in all types of 1993-94 Ultra I packs. Nets star Drazen Petrovic was a third-team member, but after his tragic death during the off-season, his card was omitted. The glossy card front has the set's logo foil-stamped on it, and the player's name is also stamped in gold foil. A main color action photo is flanked on the left by three smaller photos. The card back, numbered 1 of 14, etc., has three photos along the left side, plus a career summary on the right. First team players are cards 1-5; second team players are 6-10; third team selections are 11-14.

		MT
Complete Set (14):		45.00
Common Player:		1.00
1	Charles Barkley	5.00
2	Michael Jordan	25.00
3	Karl Malone	2.50
4	Hakeem Olajuwon	6.00
5	Mark Price	1.00
6	Joe Dumars	1.00
7	Patrick Ewing	2.50
8	Larry Johnson	3.00
9	John Stockton	2.50
10	Dominique Wilkins	1.50
11	Derrick Coleman	1.00
12	Tim Hardaway	1.00
13	Scottie Pippen	7.00
14	David Robinson	4.00

1993-94 Ultra All-Rookie Series

These 15 cards, random inserts in all types of 1993-94 Fleer Ultra Series II packs, feature top rookies selected in the 1993 draft. Each card front has a color action photo, with the player's name stamped in silver foil at the bottom. The set logo is also stamped on the front in the upper right corner. The back is horizontal and includes a color action shot, the set logo, a career summary and a card number (1 of 15, etc.).

		MT
Complete Set (15):		50.00
Common Player:		1.00
1	Vin Baker	6.00
2	Shawn Bradley	2.00
3	Calbert Cheaney	1.00
4	Anfernee Hardaway	15.00
5	Lindsey Hunter	1.00
6	Bobby Hurley	1.00
7	Popeye Jones	1.00
8	Toni Kukoc	3.00
9	Jamal Mashburn	5.00
10	Chris Mills	2.00
11	Dino Radja	2.00
12	Isaiah Rider	3.00
13	Rodney Rogers	2.00
14	Nick Van Exel	6.00
15	Chris Webber	15.00

1993-94 Ultra All-Rookie Team

This limited-edition set features cards randomly inserted in all types of 1993-94 Ultra Series I packs. The five hottest youngsters from the 1992-93 season are showcased. The set's logo is foil-stamped in gold at the bottom of the card front, along with the player's name. A color action photo of the player is also featured on the front, crashing out of basketball court hardwood floor design. The horizontal back is numbered 1 of 5, etc., and features a color close-up of the player and a summary of the player's career.

		MT
Complete Set (5):		15.00
Common Player:		.50
Minor Stars:		1.00
1	LaPhonso Ellis	.50
2	Tom Gugliotta	1.00
3	Christian Laettner	1.00
4	Alonzo Mourning	3.00
5	Shaquille O'Neal	10.00

1993-94 Ultra Award Winners

These insert cards, found only in 19-card 1993-94 Fleer Ultra I packs, show NBA award winners from the 1992-93 season - Rookie of the Year, MVP and Most Improved Player. Card fronts are foil-stamped with the set's logo and include a color action photo against a metallic-like background. The card back has a color or mug shot, career summary and card number 1 of 5, etc.

		MT
Complete Set (5):		30.00
Common Player:		2.00
1	Mahmoud Abdul-Rauf	2.00
2	Charles Barkley	6.00
3	Hakeem Olajuwon	8.00
4	Shaquille O'Neal	20.00
5	Cliff Robinson	2.00

1993-94 Ultra Famous Nicknames

These 15 cards, random inserts in all types of 1993-94 Fleer Ultra Series II packs, feature the player's nickname in silver foil on the front and a career summary and photo on the back. The set's logo is on the card fronts, but not foil stamped; the backs are numbered 1 of 15, etc.

		MT
Complete Set (15):		60.00
Common Player:		.50
1	Charles Barkley	3.00
2	Tyrone Bogues	.50
3	Derrick Coleman	.75
4	Clyde Drexler	2.00
5	Anfernee Hardaway	18.00
6	Larry Johnson	2.00
7	Michael Jordan	20.00
8	Toni Kukoc	1.50
9	Karl Malone	1.50
10	Harold Miner	.50
11	Alonzo Mourning	3.00
12	Hakeem Olajuwon	3.00
13	Shaquille O'Neal	10.00
14	David Robinson	3.00
15	Dominique Wilkins	.50

1993-94 Ultra Inside/Outside

These 10 cards, random inserts in all types of 1993-94 Fleer Ultra Series II packs, feature players who have developed inside and outside touches to their skills. The card front has a color action photo of the player, with a comet-like basketball scorching through the hoop. The player's name and set logo are stamped in gold foil at the bottom. This design idea is also used for the card back, which features another color photo, a career summary, set logo and card number 1 of 10, etc.

		MT
Complete Set (10):		12.00
Common Player:		.25
1	Patrick Ewing	.50
2	Jim Jackson	1.00
3	Larry Johnson	1.00
4	Michael Jordan	10.00
5	Dan Majerle	.25
6	Hakeem Olajuwon	2.00
7	Scottie Pippen	2.00
8	Latrell Sprewell	1.00
9	John Starks	.25
10	Walt Williams	.25

1993-94 Ultra Jam City

These nine cards, random inserts in 1993-94 Fleer Ultra Series II 19-card packs, feature some of the game's top dunkers. Each card front has a color action photo against a black and purple background of skyscrapers. The player's name is stamped in gold foil at the bottom. The back is numbered 1 of 9, etc., and includes a player photo on the right, with a career recap in a ghosted box on the left.

		MT
Complete Set (9):		75.00
Common Player:		1.50
1	Charles Barkley	10.00
2	Derrick Coleman	1.50
3	Clyde Drexler	7.00
4	Patrick Ewing	5.00
5	Shawn Kemp	8.00
6	Harold Miner	1.50
7	Shaquille O'Neal	30.00
8	David Robinson	10.00
9	Dominique Wilkins	1.50

1993-94 Ultra Karl Malone

These 10 cards were random inserts in all types of 1993-94 Fleer Ultra Series I packs. The featured player of the set, Karl Malone, autographed a limited number of cards, which were randomly inserted in packs. Two extra Malone cards, #s 11 and 12, were available through a mail-in offer. The card front has a color action or posed photo of Malone against a ghosted background which is tinted in purple. Malone's name is in a silver and black box at the bottom. "Career Highlights" is written in a marble panel at the bottom, too. The card back has a ghosted box with career information superimposed against a color photo.

		MT
Complete Set (10):		20.00
Common Malone:		2.00
Autograph Malone:		75.00
Mail-In Malone (11-12):		2.00
1	Karl Malone	2.00
2	Karl Malone	2.00
3	Karl Malone	2.00
4	Karl Malone	2.00
5	Karl Malone	2.00
6	Karl Malone	2.00
7	Karl Malone	2.00
8	Karl Malone	2.00
9	Karl Malone	2.00
10	Karl Malone	2.00

1993-94 Ultra Power in the Key

These cards, featuring players who use their strength in the paint, were random inserts in 1993-94 Fleer Ultra Series II 14-card packs. Each card front has a color action photo against a multi-colored metallic-like background featuring the top of the key of a basketball court. The player's name is stamped in gold foil in the lower left corner; the set logo is stamped in gold foil in the upper right corner. The back is numbered 1 of 9, etc., and is horizontal. A close-up shot of the player is on the right; a ghosted box on the left contains the player's name and a summary of his career.

		MT
Complete Set (9):		80.00
Common Player:		1.00
1	Larry Johnson	3.00
2	Michael Jordan	35.00
3	Karl Malone	3.00
4	Oliver Miller	1.00
5	Alonzo Mourning	6.00
6	Hakeem Olajuwon	8.00
7	Shaquille O'Neal	20.00
8	Otis Thorpe	1.00
9	Chris Webber	12.00

1993-94 Ultra Rebound Kings

These 10 cards, randomly inserted in all types of 1993-94 Fleer Ultra Series II packs, feature 10 of the game's top rebounders. The card front has a color action photo, plus a ghosted image at the top. The player's name is stamped in gold foil along one side; the set's logo is stamped in foil in the lower right corner. The horizontal back has a close-up shot of the player on one side against a ghosted background with career highlights. The card back is numbered 1 of 10, etc., and includes the set logo and player's name stamped in gold foil.

		MT
Complete Set (10):		10.00
Common Player:		.25
Minor Stars:		.50
1	Charles Barkley	1.25
2	Derrick Coleman	.25
3	Shawn Kemp	1.00
4	Karl Malone	.75
5	Alonzo Mourning	1.25
6	Dikembe Mutombo	.50
7	Charles Oakley	.25
8	Hakeem Olajuwon	2.00
9	Shaquille O'Neal	5.00
10	Dennis Rodman	2.00

1993-94 Ultra Scoring Kings

These cards, inserted in 14-card 1993-94 Fleer Ultra Series I packs, spotlight 10 of the NBA's top net burners. The set's logo and player's name are foil-stamped in silver on the card front. A player's action photo is also featured against a metallic background with lightning bolts running through it. The back is horizontally designed and numbered 1 of 10, etc. A close-up shot of the player is featured, along with career highlights, all against a dark background with lightning bolts streaking across it. The player's name is in silver foil, also.

		MT
Complete Set (10):		225.00
Common Player:		5.00
1	Charles Barkley	20.00
2	Joe Dumars	5.00
3	Patrick Ewing	10.00
4	Larry Johnson	12.00
5	Michael Jordan	120.00
6	Karl Malone	10.00
7	Alonzo Mourning	20.00
8	Shaquille O'Neal	70.00
9	David Robinson	20.00
10	Dominique Wilkins	5.00

1994-95 Ultra

Fleer's 1994-95 Ultra cards feature larger borderless action photos on the fronts, plus an oversized Fleer Ultra logo gold foil-stamped in the bottom corner. The player's name is printed in silver foil down the side. Backs feature a portrait and two action photos (one in duotone and one in color). Cards are color coded for each team. New to Ultra basketball are Hot Packs, which, found once every 72 packs, contain just insert cards. Each regular pack has one of several inserts: All NBA Team, NBA Award Winners, Scoring Kings, Double Trouble, Ultra Power, NBA All-Rookie Team, All-Rookie, Defensive Gems, Jam City, Inside/Outside, Rebound Kings and Power in the Key.

		MT
Complete Set (350):		40.00
Complete Series 1 (200):		20.00
Complete Series 2 (150):		20.00
Common Player:		.10
Minor Stars:		.20
Ser. 1 or 2 Pack (14):		1.75
Ser. 1 or 2 Box (36):		55.00
1	Stacey Augmon	.10
2	Mookie Blaylock	.10
3	Craig Ehlo	.10
4	Adam Keefe	.10
5	Andrew Long	.10
6	Ken Norman	.10
7	Kevin Willis	.10
8	Dee Brown	.10
9	Sherman Douglas	.10
10	Acie Earl	.10
11	Pervis Ellison	.10
12	Rick Fox	.10
13	Xavier McDaniel	.10
14	*Eric Montross*	.40
15	Dino Radja	.20
16	Dominique Wilkins	.20
17	Michael Adams	.10
18	Muggsy Bogues	.10
19	Dell Curry	.10
20	Kenny Gattison	.10
21	Hersey Hawkins	.10
22	Larry Johnson	.30
23	Alonzo Mourning	.50
24	Robert Parish	.10
25	B.J. Armstrong	.10
26	Steve Kerr	.10
27	Toni Kukoc	.20
28	Luc Longley	.10
29	Pete Myers	.10
30	Will Perdue	.10
31	Scottie Pippen	1.00
32	Terrell Brandon	.10
33	Brad Daugherty	.10
34	Tyrone Hill	.10
35	Chris Mills	.10
36	Bobby Phills	.10
37	Mark Price	.20
38	Gerald Wilkins	.10
39	John Williams	.10
40	Terry Davis	.10
41	Jim Jackson	.50
42	Popeye Jones	.10
43	*Jason Kidd*	3.00
44	Jamal Mashburn	.50
45	Sean Rooks	.10
46	Doug Smith	.10
47	Mahmoud Abdul-Rauf	.10
48	LaPhonso Ellis	.10
49	Dikembe Mutombo	.20
50	Robert Pack	.10
51	Rodney Rogers	.10
52	Bryant Stith	.10
53	Brian Williams	.10
54	Reggie Williams	.10
55	Greg Anderson	.10
56	Joe Dumars	.20
57	Allan Houston	.20
58	Lindsey Hunter	.10
59	Terry Mills	.10
60	Tim Hardaway	.20
61	Chris Mullin	.20
62	Billy Owens	.10
63	Latrell Sprewell	.25
64	Chris Webber	.50
65	Sam Cassell	.20
66	Carl Herrera	.10
67	Robert Horry	.10
68	Vernon Maxwell	.10
69	Hakeem Olajuwon	1.00
70	Kenny Smith	.10
71	Otis Thorpe	.10
72	Antonio Davis	.10
73	Dale Davis	.10
74	Mark Jackson	.10
75	Derrick McKey	.10
76	Reggie Miller	.50
77	Byron Scott	.10
78	Rik Smits	.20
79	Haywoode Workman	.10
80	Gary Grant	.10
81	Ron Harper	.10
82	Elmore Spencer	.10
83	Loy Vaught	.10
84	Elden Campbell	.10
85	Doug Christie	.10
86	Vlade Divac	.10
87	*Eddie Jones*	3.00
88	George Lynch	.10
89	Anthony Peeler	.10
90	Sedale Threatt	.10
91	Nick Van Exel	.75
92	James Worthy	.10
93	Bimbo Coles	.10
94	Matt Geiger	.10
95	Grant Long	.10
96	Harold Miner	.10
97	Glen Rice	.10
98	John Salley	.10
99	Rony Seikaly	.10
100	Brian Shaw	.10
101	Steve Smith	.10
102	Vin Baker	.50
103	Jon Barry	.10
104	Todd Day	.10
105	Lee Mayberry	.10
106	Eric Murdock	.10
107	Thurl Bailey	.10
108	Stacey King	.10
109	Christian Laettner	.10
110	Isaiah Rider	.25
111	Chris Smith	.10
112	Doug West	.10
113	Michael Williams	.10
114	Kenny Anderson	.20
115	Benoit Benjamin	.10
116	P.J. Brown	.10
117	Derrick Coleman	.20
118	*Yinka Dare*	.15
119	Kevin Edwards	.10
120	Armon Gilliam	.10
121	Chris Morris	.10
122	Greg Anthony	.10
123	Anthony Bonner	.10
124	Hubert Davis	.10
125	Patrick Ewing	.25
126	Derek Harper	.10
127	Anthony Mason	.10
128	Charles Oakley	.10
129	Doc Rivers	.10
130	John Starks	.10
131	Nick Anderson	.10
132	Anthony Avent	.10
133	Anthony Bowie	.10
134	Anfernee Hardaway	2.00
135	Shaquille O'Neal	2.00
136	Dennis Scott	.10
137	Jeff Turner	.10
138	Dana Barros	.10
139	Shawn Bradley	.20
140	Greg Graham	.10
141	Jeff Malone	.10
142	Tim Perry	.10
143	C. Weatherspoon	.10
144	Scott Williams	.10
145	Danny Ainge	.10
146	Charles Barkley	.75
147	Cedric Ceballos	.10
148	A.C. Green	.10
149	Frank Johnson	.10
150	Kevin Johnson	.20
151	Dan Majerle	.10
152	Oliver Miller	.10
153	*Wesley Person*	.50
154	Mark Bryant	.10
155	Clyde Drexler	.50
156	Harvey Grant	.10
157	Jerome Kersey	.10
158	Tracy Murray	.10
159	Terry Porter	.10
160	Cliff Robinson	.10
161	James Robinson	.10
162	Rod Strickland	.10
163	Buck Williams	.10
164	Duane Causwell	.10
165	Olden Polynice	.10
166	Mitch Richmond	.20
167	Lionel Simmons	.10
168	Walt Williams	.10
169	Willie Anderson	.10
170	Terry Cummings	.10
171	Sean Elliott	.10
172	Avery Johnson	.10
173	J.R. Reid	.10
174	David Robinson	.50
175	Dennis Rodman	1.00
176	Kendall Gill	.10
177	Shawn Kemp	.40
178	Nate McMillan	.10
179	Gary Payton	.20
180	Sam Perkins	.10
181	Detlef Schrempf	.10
182	David Benoit	.10
183	Tyrone Corbin	.10
184	Jeff Hornacek	.10
185	Jay Humphries	.10
186	Karl Malone	.50
187	Bryon Russell	.10
188	Felton Spencer	.10
189	John Stockton	.50
190	Mitchell Butler	.10
191	Rex Chapman	.10
192	Calbert Cheaney	.10
193	Kevin Duckworth	.10
194	Tom Gugliotta	.10
195	Don MacLean	.10
196	Gheorghe Muresan	.10
197	Scott Skiles	.10
198	Checklist	.10
199	Checklist	.10
200	Checklist	.10
201	Tyrone Corbin	.10
202	Doug Edwards	.10
203	Jim Les	.10
204	Grant Long	.10
205	Ken Norman	.10
206	Steve Smith	.10
207	Blue Edwards	.10
208	*Greg Minor*	.20
209	Eric Montross	.20
210	Derek Strong	.10
211	David Wesley	.10
212	Tony Bennett	.10
213	Scott Burrell	.10
214	*Darrin Hancock*	.10
215	Greg Sutton	.10
216	Corie Blount	.10
217	Jud Buechler	.10
218	Ron Harper	.10
219	Larry Krystkowiak	.10
220	*Dickey Simpkins*	.20
221	Bill Wennington	.10
222	Michael Cage	.10
223	Tony Campbell	.10
224	Steve Colter	.10
225	Greg Dreiling	.10
226	Danny Ferry	.10
227	*Tony Dumas*	.25
228	Lucious Harris	.10
229	Donald Hodge	.10
230	Jason Kidd	1.00
231	Lorenzo Williams	.10
232	Dale Ellis	.10
233	Tom Hammonds	.10
234	*Jalen Rose*	2.00
235	*Reggie Slater*	.10
236	Rafael Addison	.10
237	*Bill Curley*	.15
238	Johnny Dawkins	.10
239	*Grant Hill*	5.00
240	Eric Leckner	.10
241	Mark Macon	.10
242	Oliver Miller	.10
243	Mark West	.10
244	Victor Alexander	.10
245	Chris Gatling	.10
246	Tom Gugliotta	.10
247	Keith Jennings	.10
248	Ricky Pierce	.10
249	*Carlos Rogers*	.25
250	*Clifford Rozier*	.25
251	Rony Seikaly	.10
252	David Wood	.10
253	*Tim Breaux*	.10
254	Scott Brooks	.10
255	*Zan Tabak*	.10
256	Duane Ferrell	.10
257	Mark Jackson	.10
258	Sam Mitchell	.10
259	John Williams	.10
260	Terry Dehere	.10
261	Harold Ellis	.10
262	*Matt Fish*	.10
263	Tony Massenburg	.10
264	*Lamond Murray*	.50
265	Charles Outlaw	.10
266	*Eric Piatkowski*	.25
267	Pooh Richardson	.10
268	Malik Sealy	.10
269	Randy Woods	.10
270	Sam Bowie	.10
271	Cedric Ceballos	.10
272	Antonio Harvey	.10
273	Eddie Jones	1.50
274	*Anthony Miller*	.10
275	Tony Smith	.10
276	Ledell Eackles	.10
277	Kevin Gamble	.10
278	Brad Lohaus	.10
279	Billy Owens	.10
280	*Khalid Reeves*	.50
281	Kevin Willis	.10
282	Marty Conlon	.10
283	Alton Lister	.10
284	*Eric Mobley*	.10
285	Johnny Newman	.10
286	Ed Pinckney	.10
287	*Glenn Robinson*	2.50
288	*Howard Eisley*	.10
289	Winston Garland	.10
290	Andres Guibert	.10
291	*Donyell Marshall*	.25
292	Sean Rooks	.10
293	Yinka Dare	.10
294	Sleepy Floyd	.10
295	Sean Higgins	.10
296	Rex Walters	.10
297	Jayson Williams	.10
298	Charles Smith	.10
299	*Charlie Ward*	.25
300	Herb Williams	.10
301	*Monty Williams*	.20
302	Horace Grant	.20
303	Geert Hammink	.10
304	Tree Rollins	.10
305	Donald Royal	.10
306	Brian Shaw	.10
307	*Brooks Thompson*	.20
308	*Derrick Alston*	.10
309	Willie Burton	.10
310	Jaren Jackson	.10
311	*B.J. Tyler*	.10
312	Scott Williams	.10
313	*Sharone Wright*	.50
314	Joe Kleine	.10
315	Danny Manning	.20
316	Elliot Perry	.10
317	Wesley Person	.30
318	*Trevor Ruffin*	.20
319	Dan Schayes	.10
320	Wayman Tisdale	.10
321	Chris Dudley	.10
322	James Edwards	.10
323	Alaa Abdelnaby	.10
324	Randy Brown	.10
325	*Brian Grant*	1.00
326	Bobby Hurley	.10
327	*Michael Smith*	.30
328	Henry Turner	.10
329	Trevor Wilson	.10
330	Vinny Del Negro	.10
331	Moses Malone	.10
332	*Julius Nwosu*	.10
333	Chuck Person	.10
334	Chris Whitney	.10
335	Vincent Askew	.10
336	Bill Cartwright	.10
337	Ervin Johnson	.10
338	Sarunas Marciulionis	.10
339	Antoine Carr	.10
340	Tom Chambers	.10
341	John Crotty	.10
342	*Jamie Watson*	.15
343	*Juwan Howard*	1.50
344	*Jim McIlvaine*	.10
345	Doug Overton	.10
346	Scott Skiles	.10
347	*Anthony Tucker*	.10
348	Chris Webber	.50
349	Checklist	.10
350	Checklist	.10

1994-95 Ultra All-NBA

These 15 cards, available as random inserts in 1994-95 Fleer Ultra Series I packs, feature the players voted as the league's best in 1993-94. The team the player was selected to (first, second or third) is foil-stamped on the card front, which has reversed negative photos and a regular picture. Cards are numbered 1 of 15, etc., on the back, and also feature a reversed negative image of the player, along with a regular photo.

		MT
Complete Set (15):		18.00
Common Player:		.50
Minor Stars:		1.00
1	Karl Malone	1.00
2	Hakeem Olajuwon	2.00
3	Scottie Pippen	2.00
4	Latrell Sprewell	.50
5	John Stockton	1.00
6	Charles Barkley	2.00
7	Kevin Johnson	.75
8	Shawn Kemp	1.00
9	Mitch Richmond	.50
10	David Robinson	2.00
11	Derrick Coleman	.50
12	Shaquille O'Neal	5.00
13	Gary Payton	.75
14	Mark Price	.50
15	Dominique Wilkins	.50

1994-95 Ultra All-Rookie Team

The top 10 rookies from the NBA's 1993-94 season are depicted in this insert set. Cards, which are produced on 100 percent etched foil, were randomly inserted in 1994-95 Fleer Ultra Series I 17-card packs only. Card backs are numbered 1 of 10, etc.

		MT
Complete Set (10):		150.00
Common Player:		5.00
1	Vin Baker	20.00
2	Anfernee Hardaway	60.00
3	Jamal Mashburn	12.00
4	Isaiah Rider	10.00
5	Chris Webber	30.00
6	Shawn Bradley	7.00
7	Lindsey Hunter	5.00
8	Toni Kukoc	10.00
9	Dino Radja	7.00
10	Nick Van Exel	15.00

1994-95 Ultra All-Rookies

These 15 cards feature the top first-year players in the league. The cards, random inserts in 1994-95 Fleer Ultra Series II packs, could be found one per every five packs. Card backs are numbered 1 of 15, etc.

		MT
Complete Set (15):		30.00
Common Player:		.50
1	Brian Grant	2.00
2	Grant Hill	10.00
3	Juwan Howard	3.50
4	Eddie Jones	5.00
5	Jason Kidd	4.00
6	Donyell Marshall	1.00
7	Eric Montross	1.00
8	Lamond Murray	1.00
9	Wesley Person	1.50
10	Khalid Reeves	1.00
11	Glenn Robinson	3.00
12	Carlos Rogers	.50
13	Jalen Rose	1.50
14	B.J. Tyler	.50
15	Sharone Wright	1.00

1994-95 Ultra Award Winners

The four players who earned awards after the 1993-94 NBA season are featured in this insert set. Cards were randomly included in 1994-95 Fleer Ultra Series I packs. Cards, numbered 1 of 4, etc., feature UV coating, full-bleed photos and foil stamping.

		MT
Complete Set (4):		4.00
Common Player:		.25
1	Dell Curry	.25
2	Don MacLean	.25
3	Hakeem Olajuwon	2.00
4	Chris Webber	1.50

1994-95 Ultra Defensive Gems

These six cards feature players who excel on defense. Each front has a 100-percent etched foil design. Cards were random inserts in 1994-95 Fleer Ultra Series II packs, one every 37 packs. Each card front has a diamond-like set logo on it.

		MT
Complete Set (6):		40.00
Common Player:		3.00
1	Mookie Blaylock	3.00
2	Hakeem Olajuwon	10.00
3	Gary Payton	5.00
4	Scottie Pippen	15.00
5	David Robinson	10.00
6	Latrell Sprewell	5.00

1994-95 Ultra Double Trouble

This 10-card insert set features players who possess superior skills in two different areas of the game. The cards, random inserts in 1994-95 Fleer Ultra Series I packs, have UV coating, foil stamping and are numbered 1 of 10, etc., on the backs. Card fronts have a split screen showing two pictures of the player excelling in two different aspects of the game.

		MT
Complete Set (10):		12.00
Common Player:		.50
1	Derrick Coleman	.50
2	Patrick Ewing	1.00
3	Anfernee Hardaway	5.00
4	Jamal Mashburn	1.00
5	Reggie Miller	1.00
6	Alonzo Mourning	1.00
7	Scottie Pippen	2.00
8	David Robinson	2.00
9	Latrell Sprewell	.75
10	John Stockton	.75

1994-95 Ultra Inside/Outside

This 10-card insert set features players who can score from anywhere on the court - inside or outside. The set logo is stamped in foil on the card front; two different photos also appear on the front. Cards were random inserts in 1994-95 Fleer Ultra Series II packs, one every seventh hobby pack.

		MT
Complete Set (10):		10.00
Common Player:		.50
1	Sam Cassell	.50
2	Cedric Ceballos	.50
3	Calbert Cheaney	.50
4	Anfernee Hardaway	6.00
5	Jim Jackson	1.00
6	Dan Majerle	.50
7	Robert Pack	.50
8	Scottie Pippen	3.00
9	Mitch Richmond	.50
10	Latrell Sprewell	1.00

1994-95 Ultra Jam City

These insert cards were found in 1994-95 Fleer Ultra Series II packs, one every seventh pre-priced pack. The cards feature some of the game's best dunkers and have the player in action, dunking against a background of tall buildings.

		MT
Complete Set (10):		75.00
Common Player:		2.00
1	Vin Baker	7.00
2	Grant Hill	20.00
3	Robert Horry	2.00
4	Shawn Kemp	5.00
5	Jamal Mashburn	5.00
6	Alonzo Mourning	6.00
7	Dikembe Mutombo	4.00
8	Shaquille O'Neal	25.00
9	Glenn Robinson	8.00
10	Dominique Wilkins	2.00

1994-95 Ultra Power

This 10-card insert set features players who show raw strength and toughness in the paint. The cards, randomly inserted in 1994-95 Fleer Ultra Series I packs, have UV coating, foil stamping and full-bleed photos. Card backs are numbered 1 of 10, etc.

		MT
Complete Set (10):		10.00
Common Player:		.50
Minor Stars:		1.00
1	Charles Barkley	1.50
2	Derrick Coleman	.50
3	Larry Johnson	1.00
4	Shawn Kemp	1.00
5	Karl Malone	1.00
6	Dikembe Mutombo	1.00
7	Charles Oakley	.50
8	Shaquille O'Neal	5.00
9	Dennis Rodman	2.00
10	Chris Webber	1.00

1994-95 Ultra Power in the Key

These inserts were randomly included in 1994-95 Fleer Ultra Series II packs, exclusively one per every seven retail packs. The players featured depict the 10 most dominant players in the paint.

		MT
Complete Set (10):		25.00
Common Player:		1.00
1	Charles Barkley	3.00
2	Patrick Ewing	1.50
3	Horace Grant	1.00
4	Larry Johnson	1.50
5	Karl Malone	2.00
6	Hakeem Olajuwon	5.00
7	Shaquille O'Neal	8.00
8	David Robinson	3.00
9	Chris Webber	2.00
10	Kevin Willis	1.00

1994-95 Ultra Promo Sheet

This promo sheet was distributed at NBA Jam Session and gave collectors a look at the 1994-95 Ultra Basketball set. It has 20 cards in total, with 10 on each side.

	MT
Complete Set (10):	5.00
Common Player:	5.00
Isaiah Rider, Craig Ehlo	
Kenny Anderson, Dee Brown	
John Stockton, Alonzo Mourning	
Don MacLean, Jamal Mashburn	
David Robinson, LaPhonso Ellis	
Patrick Ewing, Tim Hardaway	
Dan Majerle, Rik Smits	
Shawn Kemp, Sam Cassell	
Anfernee Hardaway, Harold Miner	
Eric Murdock, B.J. Armstrong	

1994-95 Ultra Rebound Kings

These 10 cards feature some of the game's top rebounders. Cards were random inserts in 1994-95 Fleer Ultra Series II packs, one every two packs. The player's name is in an upper corner. Rebound King is written at the top of the card, and along the side opposite his name. An action photo dominates the front, along with a larger, closeup shot of the same picture, located in a bottom corner.

		MT
Complete Set (10):		5.00
Common Player:		.25
1	Derrick Coleman	.25
2	A.C. Green	.25
3	Alonzo Mourning	.50
4	Dikembe Mutombo	.25
5	Charles Oakley	.25
6	Hakeem Olajuwon	1.00
7	Shaquille O'Neal	2.00
8	David Robinson	.50
9	Chris Webber	.50
10	Kevin Willis	.25

1994-95 Ultra Scoring Kings

These 10 cards, which were randomly inserted in 1994-95 Fleer Ultra Series I 14-card packs only, feature players who can really light up the scoreboard. Each card is UV coated and foil-stamped. Backs are numbered 1 of 10, etc.

		MT
Complete Set (10):		100.00
Common Player:		5.00
1	Charles Barkley	14.00
2	Patrick Ewing	8.00
3	Karl Malone	8.00
4	Hakeem Olajuwon	20.00
5	Shaquille O'Neal	35.00
6	Scottie Pippen	20.00
7	Mitch Richmond	5.00
8	David Robinson	16.00
9	Latrell Sprewell	7.00
10	Dominique Wilkins	5.00

1995-96 Ultra

Fleer's 1995-96 Ultra basketball was issued in two series, loaded with insert sets. The regular cards feature the same improvements as were done for the Ultra's hockey brand, including 40-percent thicker stock and a parallel Gold Medallion set (one gold-foil embossed card per pack). Each card in the regular set has a full-bleed action photo on the front, with an Ultra logo in the upper left corner. A gold rectangle at the bottom contains the player's name, team name and position. The card back has two close-up shots of the player on the right side, next to a ghosted action shot on the left. A card number is in the upper left corner, while biographical and statistical information runs along the bottom. Series I inserts include: Ultra Power, Double Trouble, Fabulous Fifties, Rising Stars, All-NBA, and NBA All-Rookie. Series II inserts include: Jam City, All-Rookie, Scoring Kings, Spectrum, USA Basketball and Stackhouse Scrapbook.

		MT
Complete Set (350):		45.00
Comp. Series 1 (200):		20.00
Comp. Series 2 (150):		25.00
Common Player:		.10
Minor Stars:		.20
Comp. Gold Med. (200):		125.00
Common Gold Med.:		.25
Gold Med. Minor Stars:		.50
Gold Med. Stars:		3x-6x
Ser. 1 or 2 Pack (12):		1.50
Ser. 1 or 2 Wax Box (36):		40.00
Jumbo Pack:		2.00
Jumbo Wax Box		50.00
1	Stacey Augmon	.10
2	Mookie Blaylock	.10
3	Craig Ehlo	.10
4	Andrew Lang	.10
5	Grant Long	.10
6	Ken Norman	.10
7	Steve Smith	.10
8	Spud Webb	.10
9	Dee Brown	.10
10	Sherman Douglas	.10
11	Pervis Ellison	.10
12	Rick Fox	.10
13	Eric Montross	.10
14	Dino Radja	.10
15	David Wesley	.10
16	Dominique Wilkins	.20
17	Muggsy Bogues	.10
18	Scott Burrell	.10
19	Dell Curry	.10
20	Kendall Gill	.10
21	Larry Johnson	.30
22	Alonzo Mourning	.40
23	Robert Parish	.20
24	Ron Harper	.10
25	Michael Jordan	4.00
26	Toni Kukoc	.10
27	Will Perdue	.10
28	Scottie Pippen	1.00
29	Terrell Brandon	.10
30	Michael Cage	.10
31	Tyrone Hill	.10
32	Chris Mills	.10
33	Bobby Phills	.10
34	Mark Price	.20
35	John Williams	.10
36	Lucious Harris	.10
37	Jim Jackson	.40
38	Popeye Jones	.10
39	Jason Kidd	1.00
40	Jamal Mashburn	.40
41	George McCloud	.10
42	Roy Tarpley	.10
43	Lorenzo Williams	.10
44	Mahmoud Abdul-Rauf	.10
45	Dikembe Mutombo	.25
46	Robert Pack	.10
47	Jalen Rose	.20
48	Bryant Stith	.10
49	Brian Williams	.10
50	Reggie Williams	.10
51	Joe Dumars	.25
52	Grant Hill	2.00
53	Allan Houston	.20
54	Lindsey Hunter	.10
55	Terry Mills	.10
56	Mark West	.10
57	Chris Gatling	.10
58	Tim Hardaway	.20
59	Donyell Marshall	.20
60	Chris Mullin	.20
61	Carlos Rogers	.10
62	Clifford Rozier	.10
63	Rony Seikaly	.10
64	Latrell Sprewell	.30
65	Sam Cassell	.10
66	Clyde Drexler	.30
67	Mario Elie	.10
68	Carl Herrera	.10
69	Robert Horry	.20
70	Hakeem Olajuwon	.75
71	Kenny Smith	.10
72	Antonio Davis	.10
73	Dale Davis	.10
74	Mark Jackson	.10
75	Derrick McKey	.10
76	Reggie Miller	.30
77	Rik Smits	.10
78	Terry Dehere	.10
79	Lamond Murray	.10
80	Charles Outlaw	.10
81	Pooh Richardson	.10
82	Rodney Rogers	.10
83	Malik Sealy	.10
84	Loy Vaught	.10
85	Sam Bowie	.10
86	Elden Campbell	.10
87	Cedric Ceballos	.10
88	Vlade Divac	.10
89	Eddie Jones	.50
90	Anthony Peeler	.10
91	Sedale Threatt	.10
92	Nick Van Exel	.50
93	Rex Chapman	.10
94	Bimbo Coles	.10
95	Matt Geiger	.10
96	Billy Owens	.10
97	Khalid Reeves	.10
98	Glen Rice	.20
99	Kevin Willis	.10
100	Vin Baker	.25
101	Marty Conlon	.10
102	Todd Day	.10
103	Eric Murdock	.10
104	Glenn Robinson	.50
105	Winston Garland	.10
106	Tom Gugliotta	.10
107	Christian Laettner	.20
108	Isaiah Rider	.20
109	Sean Rooks	.10
110	Doug West	.10
111	Kenny Anderson	.20
112	P.J. Brown	.10
113	Derrick Coleman	.20
114	Armon Gilliam	.10
115	Chris Morris	.10
116	Anthony Bonner	.10
117	Patrick Ewing	.30
118	Derek Harper	.10
119	Anthony Mason	.10
120	Charles Oakley	.10
121	Charles Smith	.10
122	John Starks	.10
123	Nick Anderson	.10
124	Horace Grant	.25
125	Anfernee Hardaway	2.00
126	Shaquille O'Neal	2.00
127	Donald Royal	.10
128	Dennis Scott	.10
129	Brian Shaw	.10
130	Derrick Alston	.10
131	Dana Barros	.10
132	Shawn Bradley	.10
133	Willie Burton	.10
134	Jeff Malone	.10
135	Clarence Weatherspoon	.10
136	Scott Williams	.10
137	Sharone Wright	.20
138	Danny Ainge	.10
139	Charles Barkley	.50
140	A.C. Green	.10
141	Kevin Johnson	.20
142	Dan Majerle	.10
143	Danny Manning	.10
144	Elliot Perry	.10
145	Wesley Person	.20
146	Wayman Tisdale	.10
147	Chris Dudley	.10
148	Harvey Grant	.10
149	Aaron McKie	.10
150	Terry Porter	.10
151	Cliff Robinson	.10
152	Rod Strickland	.10
153	Otis Thorpe	.10
154	Buck Williams	.10
155	Brian Grant	.30
156	Bobby Hurley	.10
157	Olden Polynice	.10
158	Mitch Richmond	.20
159	Michael Smith	.10
160	Walt Williams	.10
161	Vinny Del Negro	.10
162	Sean Elliott	.10
163	Avery Johnson	.10
164	Chuck Person	.10
165	J.R. Reid	.10
166	Doc Rivers	.10
167	David Robinson	.50
168	Dennis Rodman	1.00
169	Vincent Askew	.10
170	Hersey Hawkins	.10
171	Shawn Kemp	.60
172	Sarunas Marciulionis	.10
173	Nate McMillan	.10
174	Gary Payton	.20
175	Sam Perkins	.10
176	Detlef Schrempf	.10
177	B.J. Armstrong	.10
178	Jerome Kersey	.10
179	Tony Massenburg	.10
180	Oliver Miller	.10
181	John Salley	.10
182	David Benoit	.10
183	Antoine Carr	.10
184	Jeff Hornacek	.10
185	Karl Malone	.30
186	Felton Spencer	.10
187	John Stockton	.30
188	Greg Anthony	.10
189	Benoit Benjamin	.10
190	Byron Scott	.10
191	Calbert Cheaney	.10
192	Juwan Howard	.40
193	Don MacLean	.10
194	Gheorghe Muresan	.10
195	Doug Overton	.10
196	Scott Skiles	.10
197	Chris Webber	.25
198	Checklist	.10
199	Checklist	.10
200	Checklist	.10
201	Stacey Augmon	.10
202	Mookie Blaylock	.10
203	Grant Long	.10
204	Steve Smith	.10
205	Dana Barros	.10
206	Kendall Gill	.10
207	Khalid Reeves	.10
208	Glen Rice	.10
209	Luc Longley	.10
210	Dennis Rodman	2.00
211	Dan Majerle	.10
212	Tony Dumas	.30
213	Elmore Spencer	.10
214	Otis Thorpe	.10
215	B.J. Armstrong	.10
216	Sam Cassell	.10
217	Clyde Drexler	.50
218	Robert Horry	.10
219	Hakeem Olajuwon	.75
220	Eddie Johnson	.10
221	Ricky Pierce	.10
222	Eric Piatkowski	.10
223	Rodney Rogers	.10
224	Brian Williams	.10
225	George Lynch	.10
226	Alonzo Mourning	.30
227	Benoit Benjamin	.10
228	Terry Porter	.10
229	Shawn Bradley	.20
230	Kevin Edwards	.10
231	Jayson Williams	.10
232	Charlie Ward	.10
233	Jon Koncak	.10
234	Derrick Coleman	.10
235	Richard Dumas	.10
236	Vernon Maxwell	.10
237	John Williams	.10
238	Dontonio Wingfield	.10
239	Tyrone Corbin	.10
240	Will Perdue	.10
241	Shawn Kemp	.60
242	Gary Payton	.30
243	Sam Perkins	.10
244	Detlef Schrempf	.10
245	Chris Morris	.10
246	Robert Pack	.10
247	Willie Anderson	.10
248	Oliver Miller	.10
249	Tracy Murray	.10
250	Alvin Robertson	.10
251	Carlos Rogers	.10
252	John Salley	.10
253	Damon Stoudamire	2.00
254	Zan Tabak	.10
255	Greg Anthony	.10
256	Blue Edwards	.10
257	Kenny Gattison	.10
258	Chris King	.10
259	Lawrence Moten	.10
260	Eric Murdock	.10
261	Bryant Reeves	.40
262	Byron Scott	.10
263	*Cory Alexander*	.20
264	*Brent Barry*	.75
265	*Mario Bennett*	.20
266	*Travis Best*	1.00
267	*Junior Burrough*	.20
268	*Jason Caffey*	.20
269	*Randolph Childress*	.20
270	*Sasha Danilovic*	.20
271	*Tyus Edney*	.20
272	*Michael Finley*	3.00
273	*Sherell Ford*	.20
274	*Kevin Garnett*	8.00
275	*Alan Henderson*	.30
276	*Donny Marshall*	.20
277	*Antonio McDyess*	3.00
278	*Loren Meyer*	.20
279	*Lawrence Moten*	.20
280	*Ed O'Bannon*	.20
281	*Greg Ostertag*	.20
282	*Cherokee Parks*	.40
283	*Theo Ratliff*	1.50
284	*Bryant Reeves*	1.00
285	*Shawn Respert*	.30
286	*Lou Roe*	.20
287	*Arvydas Sabonis*	1.00
288	*Joe Smith*	2.00
289	*Jerry Stackhouse*	4.00
290	*Damon Stoudamire*	2.00
291	*Bob Sura*	.25
292	*Kurt Thomas*	.50
293	*Gary Trent*	.30
294	*David Vaughn*	.20
295	*Rasheed Wallace*	3.00
296	*Eric Williams*	.40
297	*Corliss Williamson*	.40
298	*George Zidek*	.20
299	Mahmoud Abdul-Rauf	.10
300	Kenny Anderson	.10
301	Vin Baker	.20
302	Charles Barkley	.30
303	Mookie Blaylock	.10
304	Cedric Ceballos	.10
305	Vlade Divac	.10
306	Clyde Drexler	.25
307	Joe Dumars	.10
308	Sean Elliott	.10
309	Patrick Ewing	.10
310	Anfernee Hardaway	1.00
311	Tim Hardaway	.10
312	Grant Hill	.75
313	Tyrone Hill	.10
314	Robert Horry	.10
315	Juwan Howard	.25
316	Jim Jackson	.20
317	Kevin Johnson	.10
318	Larry Johnson	.25
319	Eddie Jones	.10
320	Shawn Kemp	.30
321	Jason Kidd	.50
322	Christian Laettner	.10
323	Karl Malone	.20
324	Jamal Mashburn	.20
325	Reggie Miller	.20
326	Alonzo Mourning	.20
327	Dikembe Mutombo	.10
328	Hakeem Olajuwon	.40
329	Gary Payton	.20
330	Scottie Pippen	.25
331	Dino Radja	.10
332	Glen Rice	.10
333	Mitch Richmond	.10
334	Clifford Robinson	.10
335	David Robinson	.30
336	Glenn Robinson	.30
337	Dennis Rodman	1.00
338	Carlos Rogers	.10
339	Detlef Schrempf	.10
340	Byron Scott	.10
341	Rik Smits	.10
342	Latrell Sprewell	.20
343	John Stockton	.20
344	Nick Van Exel	.20
345	Loy Vaught	.10
346	Clarence Weatherspoon	.10
347	Chris Webber	.20
348	Kevin Willis	.10
349	Checklist	.10
350	Checklist	.10

1995-96 Ultra All-NBA

These 15 cards feature the players selected for the first three All-NBA teams for 1994-95. The cards were randomly included in 1995 Fleer Ultra Series I packs, seeded one every five packs. Gold foil-stamping is used on the front for the brand name, player's name at the bottom and the insert set logo, in the bottom left corner. The back of the card, numbered 1 of 15, etc., has a panel on the left which recaps the player's achievements from the previous season. An action photo is on the left. The player's name is stamped in gold in the upper right corner.

		MT
Complete Set (15):		15.00
Common Player:		.50
Gold Medallion:		1x-3x
1	Anfernee Hardaway	5.00
2	Karl Malone	1.00
3	Scottie Pippen	3.00
4	David Robinson	1.50
5	John Stockton	1.00
6	Charles Barkley	1.50
7	Shawn Kemp	1.50
8	Shaquille O'Neal	5.00
9	Gary Payton	.50
10	Mitch Richmond	.50
11	Clyde Drexler	1.00
12	Reggie Miller	1.00
13	Hakeem Olajuwon	2.00
14	Dennis Rodman	3.00
15	Detlef Schrempf	.50

1995-96 Ultra All-NBA Gold Medallion

Ultra All-NBA Gold Medallions were reprints of the regular inserts, but included a Gold Medallion stamp on the card front. Fleer reported that less than 10 percent of the production was of the Gold Medallion variety, which would indicate odds of one per 50 Series I packs.

	MT
Complete Set (15):	45.00
Gold Medallion Cards:	1.5x-3x

1995-96 Ultra All-Rookie Team

These 10 cards, randomly inserted one per every seven pre-priced 1995-96 Fleer Ultra Series I packs, feature the first and second team selections to the 1994-95 All-Rookie team. The player is shown in action against a background of connected spheres. The team (1st or 2nd) the player was selected for and the player's name appear in gold foil along the bottom of the card. The Ultra logo is in gold foil in the upper left corner. The card back repeats the background design from the front, with a panel along the right which recaps the player's first NBA season. A color photo is on the left. The card is also numbered on the back 1 of 10, etc.

		MT
Complete Set (10):		35.00
Common Player:		2.00
Gold Medallion:		1x-3x
1	Brian Grant	2.00
2	Grant Hill	18.00
3	Eddie Jones	5.00
4	Jason Kidd	6.00
5	Glenn Robinson	5.00
6	Juwan Howard	7.00
7	Donyell Marshall, Sharone Wright	2.00
8	Eric Montross	2.00
9	Wesley Person	2.00
10	Jalen Rose	2.00

1995-96 Ultra All-Rookie Team Gold Medallion

All-Rookie Team Gold Medallion inserts were parallel to the All-Rookie Team inserts, but included a Gold Medallion stamp on the front. Production was announced to be less than 10 percent of the total production, which means the odds for these were one per 70 pre-priced Series I packs.

	MT
Complete Set (10):	100.00
Gold Medallion Cards:	1.5x-3x

1995-96 Ultra All-Rookies

These 10 cards, randomly inserted one per every 30 1995-96 Fleer Ultra Series II packs, feature top selections in the 1995 NBA draft. "All-Rookies" is written at the top of the page to distinguish these cards from the All-Rookie Team cards. The player's name and position appear in gold at the bottom of the card; the Ultra logo is in gold near the top. The card back has a spotlight effect, a design repeated from the front. A panel along the right side contains a recap of the player's collegiate accomplishments. A photo is on the left, along with a card number in the upper right corner (1 of 10, etc.).

		MT
Complete Set (10):		70.00
Common Player:		2.00
1	Tyus Edney	2.00
2	Michael Finley	6.00
3	Kevin Garnett	25.00
4	Antonio McDyess	12.00
5	Ed O'Bannon	2.00
6	Joe Smith	10.00
7	Jerry Stackhouse	10.00
8	Damon Stoudamire	10.00
9	Rasheed Wallace	6.00
10	Eric Williams	2.00

1995-96 Ultra Double Trouble

These 10 cards feature some of the NBA's top players who are exceptional in two statistical categories. The cards were seeded one per every five packs of 1995-96 Fleer Ultra Series I product. The card front has a color action photo of the player against a team color-coordinated background which repeats the set name within it, and includes a ghosted action photo. The Ultra logo is in gold foil in the upper right corner. The player's name and "Double Trouble" are spelled out in reverse gold-stamped typeface along the bottom. The card back, numbered 1 of 10, etc., has an action photo on the left, with a panel on the right which describes the player's two special categories. The background repeats the idea from the front, except there isn't a ghosted image. The player's name is stamped in gold foil at the top.

		MT
Complete Set (10):		15.00
Common Player:		.25
Gold Medallion:		1x-3x
1	Charles Barkley	1.00
2	Anfernee Hardaway	4.00
3	Michael Jordan	7.00
4	Alonzo Mourning	1.00
5	Hakeem Olajuwon	1.50
6	Shaquille O'Neal	3.00
7	Gary Payton	.25
8	Scottie Pippen	2.00
9	David Robinson	1.00
10	John Stockton	1.00

1995-96 Ultra Double Trouble Gold Medallion

Double Trouble Gold Medallion inserts were parallel to the Double Trouble inserts found in every five Series I packs, but included a Gold Medallion stamp on the front. Stated production odds were less than 10 percent of total production, meaning the odds were roughly one per 50.

	MT
Complete Set (10):	45.00
Gold Medallion Cards:	1.5x-3x

1995-96 Ultra Fabulous Fifties

These horizontally-designed 1995-96 Fleer Ultra Series I inserts depict seven players who scored more than 50 points in a game during the 1994-95 season. Card fronts have a "50's" on the left side, sandwiched between two hoops with basketballs going through them. A panel along the top says "Fabulous;" a panel along the bottom has the player's name and "Fabulous Fifties" stamped in foil. In between the panels is a hoop with a hand dunking a basketball. A color action photo is in the center of the card. Card backs have a color action photo on the left; a recap of the player's scoring outburst is on the right. The player's name and team name are at the top; a card number, 1 of 7, etc., is at the bottom. The card background is a ball going through a hoop. Cards were seeded one per every 12 Ultra Series I packs.

		MT
Complete Set (7):		20.00
Common Player:		.25
Minor Stars:		.50
Gold Medallion:		1x-3x
1	Dana Barros	.25
2	Willie Burton	.25
3	Cedric Ceballos	.50
4	Jim Jackson	1.50
5	Michael Jordan	13.00
6	Jamal Mashburn	1.00
7	Glen Rice	.50

1995-96 Ultra Fabulous Fifties Gold Medallion

This parallel Gold Medallion insert was identical to the regular Fabulous Fifties insert found in one per 12 Series I packs, but included a Gold Medallion stamp on the card front. Production was less than 10 percent of the total, which means the odds were roughly one per 120 packs.

	MT
Complete Set (7):	60.00
Gold Medallion Cards:	1.5x-3x

1995-96 Ultra Gold Medallion

Ultra Gold Medallion parallel cards were found in each pack of Series I Ultra. This 200-card parallel set pictures the same photo as regular-issue cards, but reprints the entire background in gold foil, with a large Gold Medallion logo in back of the player over much of the card. No Gold Medallion cards were issued in in Series II.

	MT
Complete Set (200):	125.00
Common Player:	.25
Semistars:	.50
Stars:	3x-6x

1995-96 Ultra Jam City

These 1995-96 Fleer Ultra Series II inserts feature 12 of the NBA's top dunkers. Cards were seeded one per every 24 retail packs, although there were also Hot Packs versions which were made. These cards were seeded one per every 72 Hot Packs, and have the Hot Packs designation on the front. The metallic front shows the player dunking. "Jam City" is written along the right side, along with the player's name. An Ultra logo, in gold foil, is in the lower left corner. The card back, which has a number (1 of 12, etc.) and the player's name at the top, has an action photo and a brief description of a situation which might occur that would lead to a dunk.

		MT
Complete Set (12):		90.00
Common Player:		2.00
Hot Packs Stamp: 33%		
1	Grant Hill	12.00
2	Robert Horry	2.00
3	Michael Jordan	30.00
4	Shawn Kemp	4.00
5	Jamal Mashburn	2.00
6	Antonio McDyess	8.00
7	Alonzo Mourning	4.00
8	Hakeem Olajuwon	8.00
9	Shaquille O'Neal	15.00
10	David Robinson	6.00
11	Joe Smith	7.00
12	Jerry Stackhouse	10.00

1995-96 Ultra Jam City Hot Packs

This 12-card insert ran parallel to the Jam City insert, but feature a red foil Hot Packs logo in the lower right corner. One per 72 retail packs of Ultra II was considered a Hot Pack and contained the full set of specially marked Jam City Hot Packs cards.

	MT
Complete Set (12):	30.00
Hot Pack Cards: 33%	

1995-96 Ultra Power

These 10 insert cards feature some of the NBA's dominating forwards and centers. Each card front has a color photo of the player, with his name and the set logo in gold foil in the bottom right corner. The brand logo is in the upper left corner. The back also uses gold foil for the player's name, which is in the upper left corner. A panel on the left has a career summary; an action photo is on the right. Cards are numbered 1 of 10, etc., and are randomly seeded one per every four packs of 1995-96 Fleer Ultra Basketball Series I.

		MT
Complete Set (10):		8.00
Common Player:		.50
Gold Medallion:		1x-3x
1	Charles Barkley	1.00
2	Patrick Ewing	.50
3	Larry Johnson	.50
4	Shawn Kemp	1.00
5	Karl Malone	.50
6	Alonzo Mourning	.75
7	Dikembe Mutombo	.50
8	Hakeem Olajuwon	1.25
9	Shaquille O'Neal	2.50
10	David Robinson	1.00

1995-96 Ultra Power Gold Medallion

Ultra Power Gold Medallion inserts were identical to the regular Ultra Power inserts found in every four packs of Ultra Series I, but included a Gold Medallion stamp on the front. The stated production of these Gold Medallion parallels was less than 10 percent of the total produced, meaning the odds were roughly one per 40.

	MT
Complete Set (10):	24.00
Gold Medallion Cards:	1.5x-3x

1995-96 Ultra Promo Sheet

This 10" x 10" sheet features six cards promoting the 1995-96 Fleer Ultra Series Two release. The cards are identical to the cards from the set and could be cut from the sheet.

		MT
Complete Set (6):		5.00
Common Player:		.25
4	Antonio McDyess	1.00
8	Damon Stoudamire	2.00
202	Mookie Blaylock	.25
310	Hakeem Olajuwon	1.00
344	Nick Van Exel	.50
S3	Jerry Stackhouse	1.00

1995-96 Ultra Rising Stars

These inserts, using a 100-percent foil-etched design, were seeded one per every 37 packs of 1995-96 Fleer Ultra Series I. The cards feature some of the top second-, third- and fourth-year players. The card front has an action photo of the player against a background of foil-etched basketballs. The player's name is incorporated into the insert set's icon, located in the lower right corner. The card back also uses basketballs in its background design and includes another action photo on the left. The right side has a brief player profile inside a white rectangle. The card is numbered 1 of 9, etc., and has the player's name stamped in gold foil above the rectangle.

		MT
Complete Set (9):		100.00
Common Player:		3.00
Gold Medallion:		1x-3x
1	Vin Baker	4.00
2	Anfernee Hardaway	30.00
3	Grant Hill	30.00
4	Jason Kidd	10.00
5	Jamal Mashburn	3.00
6	Shaquille O'Neal	25.00
7	Glenn Robinson	8.00
8	Nick Van Exel	5.00
9	Chris Webber	10.00

1995-96 Ultra Rising Stars Gold Medallion

Rising Stars Gold Medallions were identical to the regular Rising Stars seeded every 37 packs of Ultra I, but included a Gold Medallion stamp on the front. Gold Medallion production was less than 10 of the total production so the odds were roughly one per 370 packs.

	MT
Complete Set (9):	300.00
Gold Medallion Cards:	1.5x-3x

1995-96 Ultra Scoring Kings

Twelve of the top scorers in the NBA are featured on these 1995-96 Fleer Ultra Series II inserts. Cards were seeded one per every 12 hobby packs. The cards could also be found in their respective Hot Packs, which are seeded one per 72 packs.

		MT
Complete Set (12):		120.00
Common Player:		4.00
Hot Packs Stamp: 25%		
1	Patrick Ewing	4.00
2	Grant Hill	20.00
3	Jim Jackson	4.00
4	Michael Jordan	50.00
5	Karl Malone	7.00
6	Reggie Miller	7.00
7	Hakeem Olajuwon	15.00
8	Shaquille O'Neal	25.00
9	Scottie Pippen	10.00
10	David Robinson	12.00
11	Glenn Robinson	6.00
12	Jerry Stackhouse	12.00

1995-96 Ultra Scoring Kings Hot Packs

Scoring Kings Hot Packs inserts are identical to the regular Scoring Kings inserts found in every 24 Ultra I hobby packs, but are identified by a red foil Hot Packs logo on the front above the Ultra logo. Every 72 hobby packs was considered a "Hot Pack" and contained the full 12-card set of Scoring Kings Hot Packs.

	MT
Complete Set (12):	30.00
Hot Pack Cards: 25%	

1995-96 Ultra Stackhouse's Scrapbook

These two cards capture Philadelphia 76ers' rookie Jerry Stackhouse's first professional pre-season game and his regular season debut. Cards were available in 1995-96 Fleer Ultra Series II packs, one per every 24 packs.

		MT
Complete Set (2):		4.00
Common Player:		2.00
S3	Jerry Stackhouse	2.00
S4	Jerry Stackhouse	2.00

1995-96 Ultra USA Basketball

These 10 insert cards feature members of the 1996 USA Olympic men's basketball team. Cards were seeded one per every 54 packs of 1995-96 Fleer Ultra Series II product. Each card shows the player in his red, white and blue USA uniform, and is printed on two level, embossed, extra thick card stock. Spot UV coating and gold foil stamping is also used.

		MT
Complete Set (10):		175.00
Common Player:		10.00
1	Anfernee Hardaway	50.00
2	Grant Hill	50.00
3	Karl Malone	10.00
4	Reggie Miller	10.00
5	Hakeem Olajuwon	25.00
6	Shaquille O'Neal	45.00
7	Scottie Pippen	25.00
8	David Robinson	20.00
9	Glenn Robinson	10.00
10	John Stockton	10.00

1996-97 Ultra

Ultra produced a 300-card set for 1996-97 that was released in two 150-card series. Card fronts feature an action shot of the player, with the player's name and team written in foil across the bottom, and the Fleer Ultra logo in either top corner (Rookie cards are noted under the Ultra logo). Series I included On the Block (124-138), Ultra Effort (139-147), Maximum Effort (148) and Checklists (149-150) subsets, while Series II included Rookie Encore (264-278), Step it Up (279-288), Play of the Game (289-298) and Checklists (299-300). Inserts in Series I include: Ultra Decade, Full Court Trap, Rookie Flashback, Fresh Faces, Rising Stars and Court Masters. Inserts in Series II include: All Rookie, Board Game, Ultra Decade, Starring Role, Scoring Kings and Give and Take. Both Series also included Gold Medallion and Platinum Medallion parallel sets.

	MT
Complete Set (300):	60.00
Complete Series 1 (150):	40.00
Complete Series 2 (150):	20.00
Common Player:	.10
Minor Stars:	.20
Comp. Gold Set (296):	700.00
Comp. Gold Series 1 (148):	600.00
Comp. Gold Series 2 (148):	100.00
Gold Cards (1-148):	6x-12x
Inserted 1:12	
Gold Cards (151-298):	2x-3x
Inserted 1:1	
Ser. 1 or 2 Pack (10):	2.00
Ser. 1 or 2 Wax Box (24):	40.00

1	Mookie Blaylock	.10
2	Alan Henderson	.10
3	Christian Laettner	.20
4	Dikembe Mutombo	.20
5	Steve Smith	.20
6	Dana Barros	.10
7	Rick Fox	.10
8	Dino Radja	.10
9	*Antoine Walker*	2.00
10	Eric Williams	.10
11	Dell Curry	.10
12	*Tony Delk*	.50
13	Matt Geiger	.10
14	Glen Rice	.30
15	Ron Harper	.10
16	Michael Jordan	5.00
17	Toni Kukoc	.30
18	Scottie Pippen	1.00
19	Dennis Rodman	1.50
20	Terrell Brandon	.30
21	Chris Mills	.10
22	Bobby Phills	.10
23	Bob Sura	.10
24	Jim Jackson	.20
25	Jason Kidd	.75
26	Jamal Mashburn	.20
27	George McCloud	.10
28	*Samaki Walker*	.50
29	LaPhonso Ellis	.20
30	Antonio McDyess	.50
31	Bryant Stith	.10
32	Joe Dumars	.20
33	Grant Hill	2.50
34	Theo Ratliff	.20
35	Otis Thorpe	.10
36	Chris Mullin	.20
37	Joe Smith	.50
38	Latrell Sprewell	.30
39	Charles Barkley	.50
40	Clyde Drexler	.50
41	Mario Elie	.10
42	Hakeem Olajuwon	.75
43	*Erick Dampier*	.50
44	Dale Davis	.10
45	Derrick McKey	.10
46	Reggie Miller	.30
47	Rik Smits	.10
48	Brent Barry	.20
49	Malik Sealy	.10
50	Loy Vaught	.10
51	*Lorenzen Wright*	.50
52	*Kobe Bryant*	25.00
53	Cedric Ceballos	.20
54	Eddie Jones	.75
55	Shaquille O'Neal	1.75
56	Nick Van Exel	.20
57	Tim Hardaway	.50
58	Alonzo Mourning	.30
59	Kurt Thomas	.10
60	*Ray Allen*	5.00
61	Vin Baker	.50
62	Sherman Douglas	.10
63	Glenn Robinson	.30
64	Kevin Garnett	2.50
65	Tom Gugliotta	.30
66	*Stephon Marbury*	7.00
67	Doug West	.10
68	Shawn Bradley	.20
69	Kendall Gill	.10
70	*Kerry Kittles*	1.25
71	Ed O'Bannon	.10
72	Patrick Ewing	.30
73	Larry Johnson	.20
74	Charles Oakley	.10
75	John Starks	.10
76	*John Wallace*	.50
77	Nick Anderson	.20
78	Horace Grant	.20
79	Anfernee Hardaway	1.75
80	Dennis Scott	.10
81	Derrick Coleman	.20
82	*Allen Iverson*	12.00
83	Jerry Stackhouse	.50
84	Clarence Weatherspoon	.10
85	Michael Finley	.50
86	Kevin Johnson	.20
87	*Steve Nash*	.75
88	Wesley Person	.10
89	*Jermaine O'Neal*	4.00
90	Clifford Robinson	.10
91	Arvydas Sabonis	.20
92	Gary Trent	.10
93	Tyus Edney	.10
94	Brian Grant	.10
95	Olden Polynice	.10
96	Mitch Richmond	.30
97	Corliss Williamson	.10
98	Vinny Del Negro	.10
99	Sean Elliott	.20
100	Avery Johnson	.10
101	David Robinson	.50
102	Hersey Hawkins	.10
103	Shawn Kemp	.50
104	Gary Payton	.50
105	Sam Perkins	.10
106	Detlef Schrempf	.10
107	*Marcus Camby*	2.00
108	Doug Christie	.10
109	Damon Stoudamire	1.00
110	Sharone Wright	.10
111	Jeff Hornacek	.10
112	Karl Malone	.50
113	Chris Morris	.10
114	Bryon Russell	.10
115	John Stockton	.30
116	*Shareef Abdur-Rahim*	4.00
117	Greg Anthony	.10
118	Blue Edwards	.10
119	Bryant Reeves	.30
120	Calbert Cheaney	.10
121	Juwan Howard	.50
122	Gheorghe Muresan	.10
123	Chris Webber	1.00
124	Vin Baker (On the Block)	.20
125	Charles Barkley (On the Block)	.20
126	Kevin Garnett (On the Block)	1.00
127	Juwan Howard (On the Block)	.20
128	Larry Johnson (On the Block)	.10
129	Shawn Kemp (On the Block)	.30
130	Karl Malone (On the Block)	.20
131	Anthony Mason (On the Block)	.10
132	Antonio McDyess (On the Block)	.20
133	Alonzo Mourning (On the Block)	.10
134	Hakeem Olajuwon (On the Block)	.40
135	Shaquille O'Neal (On the Block)	1.00
136	David Robinson (On the Block)	.20
137	Dennis Rodman (On the Block)	.75
138	Joe Smith (On the Block)	.20
139	Mookie Blaylock (Ultra Effort)	.10
140	Terrell Brandon (Ultra Effort)	.10
141	Anfernee Hardaway (Ultra Effort)	1.00
142	Grant Hill (Ultra Effort)	1.25
143	Michael Jordan (Ultra Effort)	2.50
144	Jason Kidd (Ultra Effort)	.50
145	Gary Payton (Ultra Effort)	.20
146	Jerry Stackhouse (Ultra Effort)	.20
147	Damon Stoudamire (Ultra Effort)	.30
148	Robert Horry, Oliver Miller, Hakeem Olajuwon, David Robinson, Clarence Weatherspoon (Maximum Effort)	.30
149	Checklist	.10
150	Checklist	.10
151	Tyrone Corbin	.10
152	*Priest Lauderdale*	.20
153	Dikembe Mutombo	.20
154	Eldridge Recasner	.10
155	Todd Day	.10
156	Greg Minor	.10
157	David Wesley	.20
158	Vlade Divac	.20
159	Anthony Mason	.10
160	*Malik Rose*	.40
161	Jason Caffey	.10
162	Steve Kerr	.10
163	Luc Longley	.10
164	Danny Ferry	.10
165	Tyrone Hill	.10
166	*Vitaly Potapenko*	.40
167	Sam Cassell	.10
168	Michael Finley	.20
169	Chris Gatling	.10
170	A.C. Green	.10
171	Oliver Miller	.10
172	Eric Montross	.10
173	Dale Ellis	.10
174	Mark Jackson	.10
175	Ervin Johnson	.10
176	Sarunas Marciulionis	.10
177	Stacey Augmon	.10
178	Joe Dumars	.10
179	Grant Hill	2.50
180	Lindsey Hunter	.10
181	Grant Long	.10
182	Terry Mills	.10
183	Otis Thorpe	.10
184	*Jerome Williams*	.20
185	*Todd Fuller*	.20
186	*Ray Owes*	.20
187	Mark Price	.10
188	Felton Spencer	.10
189	Charles Barkley	.50
190	*Emanuel Davis*	.20
191	*Othella Harrington*	.75
192	*Matt Maloney*	.50
193	Brent Price	.10
194	Kevin Willis	.10
195	Travis Best	.10
196	Antonio Davis	.10
197	Jalen Rose	.20
198	Pooh Richardson	.10
199	Stanley Roberts	.10
200	Rodney Rogers	.10
201	Elden Campbell	.10
202	*Derek Fisher*	.50
203	*Travis Knight*	.40
204	Shaquille O'Neal	1.75
205	Byron Scott	.10
206	Sasha Danilovic	.10
207	Dan Majerle	.10
208	*Martin Muursepp*	.20
209	Armon Gilliam	.20
210	Andrew Lang	.10
211	Johnny Newman	.10
212	Kevin Garnett	2.50
213	Tom Gugliotta	.30
214	*Shane Heal*	.20
215	Stojko Vrankovic	.10
216	Robert Pack	.10
217	Khalid Reeves	.10
218	Jayson Williams	.10
219	Chris Childs	.10
220	Allan Houston	.20
221	Larry Johnson	.20
222	*Walter McCarty*	.25
223	Charlie Ward	.10
224	*Brian Evans*	.20
225	*Amal McCaskill*	.20
226	Rony Seikaly	.20
227	Gerald Wilkins	.10
228	Mark Davis	.10
229	Lucious Harris	.10
230	Don MacLean	.10
231	Cedric Ceballos	.10
232	Rex Chapman	.10
233	Jason Kidd	.75
234	Danny Manning	.10
235	Kenny Anderson	.10
236	Aaron McKie	.10
237	Isaiah Rider	.10
238	Rasheed Wallace	.10
239	Mahmoud Abdul-Rauf	.10
240	Billy Owens	.10
241	Michael Smith	.10
242	Vernon Maxwell	.10
243	Charles Smith	.10
244	Dominique Wilkins	.20
245	Craig Ehlo	.10
246	Jim McIlvaine	.10
247	Nate McMillan	.10
248	Hubert Davis	.10
249	Carlos Rogers	.10
250	Zan Tabak	.10
251	Walt Williams	.10
252	Jeff Hornacek	.10
253	Karl Malone	.50
254	Greg Ostertag	.10
255	Bryon Russell	.10
256	John Stockton	.25
257	George Lynch	.10
258	Lawrence Moten	.10
259	Anthony Peeler	.10
260	*Roy Rogers*	.25
261	Tracy Murray	.10
262	Rod Strickland	.20
263	*Ben Wallace*	.20
264	Shareef Abdur-Rahim (Rookie Encore)	1.50
265	Ray Allen (Rookie Encore)	1.00
266	Kobe Bryant (Rookie Encore)	4.00
267	Marcus Camby (Rookie Encore)	.50
268	Erick Dampier (Rookie Encore)	.25
269	Tony Delk (Rookie Encore)	.25
270	Allen Iverson (Rookie Encore)	2.00
271	Kerry Kittles (Rookie Encore)	.50
272	Stephon Marbury (Rookie Encore)	2.00
273	Steve Nash (Rookie Encore)	.50
274	Jermaine O'Neal (Rookie Encore)	.60
275	Antoine Walker (Rookie Encore)	1.00
276	Samaki Walker (Rookie Encore)	.20
277	John Wallace (Rookie Encore)	.25
278	Lorenzen Wright (Rookie Encore)	.20
279	Anfernee Hardaway (Step It Up)	1.00
280	Michael Jordan (Step It Up)	2.50
281	Jason Kidd (Step It Up)	.50
282	Hakeem Olajuwon (Step It Up)	.40
283	Gary Payton (Step It Up)	.25
284	Mitch Richmond (Step It Up)	.10
285	David Robinson (Step It Up)	.25
286	John Stockton (Step It Up)	.10
287	Damon Stoudamire (Step It Up)	.30
288	Chris Webber (Step It Up)	.50
289	Clyde Drexler (Play of the Game)	.20
290	Kevin Garnett (Play of the Game)	1.00
291	Grant Hill (Play of the Game)	1.00
292	Shawn Kemp (Play of the Game)	.30
293	Karl Malone (Play of the Game)	.20
294	Antonio McDyess (Play of the Game)	.20
295	Alonzo Mourning (Play of the Game)	.10
296	Shaquille O'Neal (Play of the Game)	1.00
297	Scottie Pippen (Play of the Game)	.50
298	Jerry Stackhouse (Play of the Game)	.20
299	Checklist	.10
300	Checklist	.10

1996-97 Ultra Gold

Gold Medallion was a 296-card parallel set of the entire Series I and II Ultra set, except for the four checklists. Gold Medallions featured gold foil on the front instead of the silver used in regular-issue cards and carries a "G" prefix on the back (except for the subset cards in Series I, numbers 124-148). Series I Gold Medallion inserts were seeded one per 12 packs, while Series II inserts were found one per pack. Only the Series II cards contained the words "Gold Medallion Edition" on the front.

	MT
Complete Set (296):	600.00
Complete Series 1 (148):	500.00
Complete Series 2 (148):	100.00
Gold Cards (1-148):	7x-15x
Gold Cards (151-298):	

1996-97 Ultra Platinum

This 296-card set paralleled each card in the 1996-97 Ultra set, except for the four checklist cards. Series I Platinums were inserted every 180 packs, while Series II cards were inserted every 100 packs. Series I inserts do not include the words "Platinum Medallion Edition" on the front, while Series II Platinum inserts do feature those words. In addition, cards 124-148 (subset cards from Series I) don't have a "P" prefix on the card number; all other Platinum cards contain this prefix.

	MT
Complete Set (296):	4500.
Complete Ser.1 (148):	3000.
Complete Ser.2 (148):	1500.
Common Player (1-148):	5.00
Minor Stars (1-148):	10.00
Inserted 1:180	
Common Player (151-298):	3.00
Minor Stars (151-298):	6.00
Inserted 1:100	

1	Mookie Blaylock	5.00
2	Alan Henderson	10.00
3	Christian Laettner	10.00
4	Dikembe Mutombo	10.00
5	Steve Smith	10.00
6	Dana Barros	5.00
7	Rick Fox	5.00
8	Dino Radja	5.00
9	Antoine Walker	30.00
10	Eric Williams	5.00
11	Dell Curry	5.00
12	Tony Delk	10.00
13	Matt Geiger	5.00
14	Glen Rice	15.00
15	Ron Harper	5.00
16	Michael Jordan	200.00
17	Toni Kukoc	15.00
18	Scottie Pippen	50.00
19	Dennis Rodman	60.00
20	Terrell Brandon	10.00
21	Chris Mills	5.00
22	Bobby Phills	5.00
23	Bob Sura	10.00
24	Jim Jackson	10.00
25	Jason Kidd	40.00
26	Jamal Mashburn	10.00
27	George McCloud	5.00
28	Samaki Walker	10.00
29	LaPhonso Ellis	10.00
30	Antonio McDyess	20.00
31	Bryant Stith	5.00
32	Joe Dumars	10.00
33	Grant Hill	100.00
34	Theo Ratliff	10.00
35	Otis Thorpe	5.00
36	Chris Mullin	10.00
37	Joe Smith	20.00
38	Latrell Sprewell	15.00
39	Charles Barkley	25.00
40	Clyde Drexler	20.00
41	Mario Elie	5.00
42	Hakeem Olajuwon	30.00
43	Erick Dampier	15.00
44	Dale Davis	5.00
45	Derrick McKey	5.00
46	Reggie Miller	15.00
47	Rik Smits	5.00
48	Brent Barry	10.00
49	Malik Sealy	5.00
50	Loy Vaught	5.00
51	Lorenzen Wright	10.00
52	Kobe Bryant	400.00
53	Cedric Ceballos	5.00
54	Eddie Jones	35.00
55	Shaquille O'Neal	75.00
56	Nick Van Exel	10.00
57	Tim Hardaway	20.00
58	Alonzo Mourning	15.00
59	Kurt Thomas	5.00
60	Ray Allen	30.00
61	Vin Baker	25.00
62	Sherman Douglas	5.00
63	Glenn Robinson	15.00
64	Kevin Garnett	115.00
65	Tom Gugliotta	15.00
66	Stephon Marbury	80.00
67	Doug West	5.00
68	Shawn Bradley	10.00
69	Kendall Gill	5.00
70	Kerry Kittles	20.00
71	Ed O'Bannon	5.00
72	Patrick Ewing	15.00
73	Larry Johnson	10.00
74	Charles Oakley	5.00
75	John Starks	5.00
76	John Wallace	10.00
77	Nick Anderson	10.00
78	Horace Grant	5.00
79	Anfernee Hardaway	60.00
80	Dennis Scott	5.00
81	Derrick Coleman	10.00
82	Allen Iverson	100.00
83	Jerry Stackhouse	20.00
84	Clarence Weatherspoon	5.00
85	Michael Finley	15.00
86	Kevin Johnson	10.00
87	Steve Nash	15.00
88	Wesley Person	5.00
89	Jermaine O'Neal	15.00
90	Clifford Robinson	5.00
91	Arvydas Sabonis	5.00
92	Gary Trent	5.00
93	Tyus Edney	5.00
94	Brian Grant	5.00
95	Olden Polynice	5.00
96	Mitch Richmond	10.00
97	Corliss Williamson	5.00
98	Vinny Del Negro	5.00
99	Sean Elliott	5.00
100	Avery Johnson	5.00
101	David Robinson	20.00
102	Hersey Hawkins	5.00
103	Shawn Kemp	15.00
104	Gary Payton	20.00
105	Sam Perkins	5.00
106	Detlef Schrempf	5.00
107	Marcus Camby	20.00
108	Doug Christie	5.00
109	Damon Stoudamire	30.00
110	Sharone Wright	5.00
111	Jeff Hornacek	5.00
112	Karl Malone	20.00
113	Chris Morris	5.00
114	Bryon Russell	5.00
115	John Stockton	15.00
116	Shareef Abdur-Rahim	60.00
117	Greg Anthony	5.00
118	Blue Edwards	5.00
119	Bryant Reeves	10.00
120	Calbert Cheaney	5.00
121	Juwan Howard	15.00
122	Gheorghe Muresan	5.00
123	Chris Webber	50.00
124	Vin Baker (On the Block)	10.00
125	Charles Barkley (On the Block)	10.00
126	Kevin Garnett (On the Block)	50.00
127	Juwan Howard (On the Block)	10.00
128	Larry Johnson (On the Block)	5.00
129	Shawn Kemp (On the Block)	8.00
130	Karl Malone (On the Block)	10.00
131	Anthony Mason (On the Block)	5.00
132	Antonio McDyess (On the Block)	10.00
133	Alonzo Mourning (On the Block)	5.00
134	Hakeem Olajuwon (On the Block)	15.00
135	Shaquille O'Neal (On the Block)	40.00
136	David Robinson (On the Block)	10.00
137	Dennis Rodman (On the Block)	25.00
138	Joe Smith (On the Block)	10.00
139	Mookie Blaylock (Ultra Effort)	5.00
140	Terrell Brandon (Ultra Effort)	5.00
141	Anfernee Hardaway (Ultra Effort)	30.00
142	Grant Hill (Ultra Effort)	50.00
143	Michael Jordan (Ultra Effort)	100.00
144	Jason Kidd (Ultra Effort)	20.00
145	Gary Payton (Ultra Effort)	10.00
146	Jerry Stackhouse (Ultra Effort)	10.00
147	Damon Stoudamire (Ultra Effort)	10.00
148	Robert Horry, Oliver Miller, Hakeem Olajuwon, David Robinson, Clarence Weatherspoon (Maximum Effort)	10.00
151	Tyrone Corbin	3.00
152	Priest Lauderdale	6.00
153	Dikembe Mutombo	6.00
154	Eldridge Recasner	3.00
155	Todd Day	3.00
156	Greg Minor	3.00
157	David Wesley	3.00
158	Vlade Divac	6.00
159	Anthony Mason	6.00
160	Malik Rose	8.00
161	Jason Caffey	3.00
162	Steve Kerr	3.00
163	Luc Longley	3.00
164	Danny Ferry	3.00
165	Tyrone Hill	3.00
166	Vitaly Potapenko	8.00
167	Sam Cassell	3.00
168	Michael Finley	20.00
169	Chris Gatling	3.00
170	A.C. Green	3.00
171	Oliver Miller	3.00
172	Eric Montross	3.00
173	Dale Ellis	3.00
174	Mark Jackson	3.00
175	Ervin Johnson	3.00
176	Sarunas Marciulionis	3.00
177	Stacey Augmon	3.00
178	Joe Dumars	6.00
179	Grant Hill	85.00
180	Lindsey Hunter	6.00
181	Grant Long	3.00
182	Terry Mills	3.00
183	Otis Thorpe	3.00
184	Jerome Williams	3.00
185	Todd Fuller	6.00
186	Ray Owes	6.00
187	Mark Price	3.00
188	Felton Spencer	3.00
189	Charles Barkley	20.00
190	Emanuel Davis	3.00
191	Othella Harrington	15.00
192	Matt Maloney	15.00
193	Brent Price	3.00
194	Kevin Willis	3.00
195	Travis Best	3.00
196	Antonio Davis	3.00
197	Jalen Rose	6.00
198	Pooh Richardson	3.00
199	Stanley Roberts	3.00
200	Rodney Rogers	3.00
201	Elden Campbell	3.00
202	Derek Fisher	15.00
203	Travis Knight	10.00
204	Shaquille O'Neal	50.00
205	Byron Scott	3.00
206	Sasha Danilovic	3.00
207	Dan Majerle	3.00
208	Martin Muursepp	6.00
209	Armon Gilliam	3.00
210	Andrew Lang	3.00
211	Johnny Newman	3.00
212	Kevin Garnett	85.00
213	Tom Gugliotta	8.00
214	Shane Heal	3.00
215	Stojko Vrankovic	3.00
216	Robert Pack	3.00
217	Khalid Reeves	3.00
218	Jayson Williams	3.00
219	Chris Childs	3.00
220	Allan Houston	6.00
221	Larry Johnson	6.00
222	Walter McCarty	6.00
223	Charlie Ward	3.00
224	Brian Evans	3.00
225	Amal McCaskill	3.00
226	Rony Seikaly	6.00
227	Gerald Wilkins	3.00
228	Mark Davis	3.00
229	Lucious Harris	3.00
230	Don MacLean	3.00
231	Cedric Ceballos	3.00
232	Rex Chapman	3.00
233	Jason Kidd	30.00
234	Danny Manning	3.00
235	Kenny Anderson	6.00
236	Aaron McKie	3.00
237	Isaiah Rider	3.00
238	Rasheed Wallace	3.00
239	Mahmoud Abdul-Rauf	3.00
240	Billy Owens	3.00
241	Michael Smith	3.00
242	Vernon Maxwell	3.00
243	Charles Smith	3.00
244	Dominique Wilkins	6.00
245	Craig Ehlo	3.00
246	Jim McIlvaine	3.00
247	Nate McMillan	3.00
248	Hubert Davis	3.00
249	Carlos Rogers	3.00
250	Zan Tabak	3.00
251	Walt Williams	3.00
252	Jeff Hornacek	3.00
253	Karl Malone	15.00
254	Greg Ostertag	3.00
255	Bryon Russell	3.00
256	John Stockton	6.00
257	George Lynch	3.00
258	Lawrence Moten	3.00
259	Anthony Peeler	3.00
260	Roy Rogers	6.00
261	Tracy Murray	3.00
262	Rod Strickland	6.00
263	Ben Wallace	3.00
264	Shareef Abdur-Rahim (Rookie Encore)	25.00
265	Ray Allen (Rookie Encore)	12.00
266	Kobe Bryant (Rookie Encore)	200.00
267	Marcus Camby (Rookie Encore)	8.00
268	Erick Dampier (Rookie Encore)	6.00
269	Tony Delk (Rookie Encore)	6.00
270	Allen Iverson (Rookie Encore)	40.00
271	Kerry Kittles (Rookie Encore)	8.00
272	Stephon Marbury (Rookie Encore)	35.00
273	Steve Nash (Rookie Encore)	6.00
274	Jermaine O'Neal (Rookie Encore)	6.00
275	Antoine Walker (Rookie Encore)	15.00
276	Samaki Walker (Rookie Encore)	6.00
277	John Wallace (Rookie Encore)	6.00
278	Lorenzen Wright (Rookie Encore)	6.00
279	Anfernee Hardaway (Step It Up)	30.00
280	Michael Jordan (Step It Up)	50.00
281	Jason Kidd (Step It Up)	20.00
282	Hakeem Olajuwon (Step It Up)	15.00
283	Gary Payton (Step It Up)	10.00
284	Mitch Richmond (Step It Up)	6.00
285	David Robinson (Step It Up)	10.00
286	John Stockton (Step It Up)	6.00
287	Damon Stoudamire (Step It Up)	15.00
288	Chris Webber (Step It Up)	15.00
289	Clyde Drexler (Play of the Game)	10.00
290	Kevin Garnett (Play of the Game)	60.00
291	Grant Hill (Play of the Game)	50.00
292	Shawn Kemp (Play of the Game)	10.00
293	Karl Malone (Play of the Game)	10.00

294	Antonio McDyess (Play of the Game)	10.00
295	Alonzo Mourning (Play of the Game)	6.00
296	Shaquille O'Neal (Play of the Game)	30.00
297	Scottie Pippen (Play of the Game)	20.00
298	Jerry Stackhouse (Play of the Game)	8.00

1996-97 Ultra All-Rookies

All-Rookie highlights 15 of the top rookies in the NBA during the 1996-97 season on an embossed card. The player's color photo is shown over a crystal ball, with a black background. All-Rookie inserts were inserted in every four packs of Series II.

		MT
Complete Set (15):		55.00
Common Player:		1.00
Minor Stars:		2.00
Inserted 1:4		
1	Shareef Abdur-Rahim	6.00
2	Ray Allen	3.00
3	Kobe Bryant	20.00
4	Marcus Camby	2.00
5	Tony Delk	1.00
6	Derek Fisher	2.00
7	Allen Iverson	10.00
8	Kerry Kittles	2.00
9	Matt Maloney	1.00
10	Stephon Marbury	10.00
11	Vitaly Potapenko	1.00
12	Roy Rogers	1.00
13	Antoine Walker	6.00
14	Samaki Walker	1.00
15	John Wallace	2.00

1996-97 Ultra Board Game

This 20-card insert was found in packs of Series II Ultra at a rate of one per nine. Board Game highlights the top rebounders in the NBA on a checkerboard pattern, with cards numbered on the back "x of 20."

		MT
Complete Set (20):		70.00
Common Player:		1.00
Minor Stars:		2.00
Inserted 1:9		
1	Vin Baker	2.00
2	Charles Barkley	3.00
3	Dale Davis	1.00
4	Clyde Drexler	2.00
5	Patrick Ewing	2.00
6	Grant Hill	10.00
7	Michael Jordan	20.00
8	Shawn Kemp	2.00
9	Jason Kidd	4.00
10	Karl Malone	2.00
11	Alonzo Mourning	2.00
12	Dikembe Mutombo	1.00
13	Hakeem Olajuwon	3.00
14	Shaquille O'Neal	6.00
15	Scottie Pippen	5.00
16	David Robinson	3.00
17	Dennis Rodman	6.00
18	Loy Vaught	1.00
19	Chris Webber	4.00
20	Jayson Williams	1.00

1996-97 Ultra Court Masters

Court Masters was a 15-card insert found exclusively in retail packs at a rate of one per 180. This set was printed on plastic and contains the members of the 1st, 2nd and 3rd All-NBA teams.

		MT
Complete Set (15):		500.00
Common Player:		10.00
Minor Stars:		20.00
Inserted 1:180 Retail		
1	Anfernee Hardaway	60.00
2	Michael Jordan	150.00
3	Karl Malone	20.00
4	Scottie Pippen	40.00
5	David Robinson	20.00
6	Grant Hill	80.00
7	Shawn Kemp	15.00
8	Hakeem Olajuwon	25.00
9	Gary Payton	20.00
10	John Stockton	10.00
11	Charles Barkley	20.00
12	Juwan Howard	10.00
13	Reggie Miller	10.00
14	Shaquille O'Neal	60.00
15	Mitch Richmond	10.00

1996-97 Ultra Decade of Excellence

Ultra Decade was a 20-card insert that had 10 cards inserted into both Series I and II. The set salutes 20 players that were in the 1986-87 Fleer set and were still active in 1996-97. Inserted at one per 100 packs, Ultra Decade inserts are identified by a gold foil stamp in the lower left corner that reads "Ultra Decade 1986-1996." The same 20 Decade inserts were also inserted into packs of Fleer and Metal, and are marked Ultra Decade to distinguish them from others. Cards are numbered with a "U" prefix.

		MT
Complete Set (20):		75.00
Complete Series 1 (10):		50.00
Complete Series 2 (10):		25.00
Common Player:		2.00
Minor Stars:		4.00
Inserted 1:100		
1	Clyde Drexler	4.00
2	Joe Dumars	2.00
3	Derek Harper	2.00
4	Michael Jordan	45.00
5	Karl Malone	4.00
6	Chris Mullin	2.00
7	Charles Oakley	2.00
8	Sam Perkins	2.00
9	Ricky Pierce	2.00
10	Buck Williams	2.00
11	Charles Barkley	8.00
12	Patrick Ewing	4.00
13	Eddie Johnson	2.00
14	Hakeem Olajuwon	10.00
15	Robert Parish	2.00
16	Byron Scott	2.00
17	Wayman Tisdale	2.00
18	Gerald Wilkins	2.00
19	Herb Williams	2.00
20	Kevin Willis	2.00

1996-97 Ultra Fresh Faces

Fresh Faces showcased nine top rookies from the 1996 NBA Draft, and were inserted into packs of Series I at a rate of one per 72 packs. This insert featured an action shot of the player over the top of his die-cut jersey, with the position he was drafted in, in silver foil, in the lower right corner.

		MT
Complete Set (9):		120.00
Common Player:		3.00
Minor Stars:		6.00
Inserted 1:72		
1	Shareef Abdur-Rahim	15.00
2	Ray Allen	8.00
3	Kobe Bryant	50.00
4	Marcus Camby	6.00
5	Allen Iverson	25.00
6	Kerry Kittles	6.00
7	Stephon Marbury	25.00
8	Steve Nash	6.00
9	Antoine Walker	15.00

1996-97 Ultra Full Court Trap

Full Court Trap included the 10 players who were selected on the first and second All-Defensive Team. These inserts were found in every 15 packs of Series I and contain a color shot of the player over a foil, spiral background with the player's name running up the left side and the insert name across the bottom. Parallel Gold versions of these inserts also exist with a more colorful foil background and an insertion rate of one per 180 packs.

		MT
Complete Set (10):		35.00
Common Player:		1.00
Minor Stars:		2.00
Inserted 1:15		
Gold Cards:		3x-6x
Inserted 1:180		
1	Michael Jordan	20.00
2	Gary Payton	2.00
3	Scottie Pippen	6.00
4	David Robinson	2.00
5	Dennis Rodman	7.00
6	Mookie Blaylock	1.00
7	Horace Grant	1.00
8	Derrick McKey	1.00
9	Hakeem Olajuwon	3.00
10	Bobby Phills	1.00

1996-97 Ultra Full Court Trap Gold

Full Court Trap Gold inserts reprinted the 10-card Full Court Trap set in a thicker stock, embossed gold foil card. This set was inserted into packs of Series I at a rate of one per 180 packs.

		MT
Complete Set (10):		210.00
Gold Cards:		3x-6x

1996-97 Ultra Give and Take

This 10-card insert was printed on a foil background divided into a gold and silver tone split equally from top to bottom. Give and Take inserts were found in every 18 retail packs of Ultra II, and includes players who produced assists and steals.

		MT
Complete Set (10):		60.00
Common Player:		1.50
Minor Stars:		3.00
Inserted 1:18 Retail		
1	Mookie Blaylock	1.50
2	Anfernee Hardaway	10.00
3	Tim Hardaway	3.00
4	Allen Iverson	10.00
5	Michael Jordan	30.00
6	Jason Kidd	5.00
7	Gary Payton	3.00
8	Scottie Pippen	7.00
9	John Stockton	3.00
10	Damon Stoudamire	4.00

1996-97 Ultra Rising Stars

This 10-card insert was found in hobby-only packs at a rate of one per 180. The cards feature top young stars on a canvas-like card with a rough white border surrounding it. Rising Stars inserts were exclusive to Series I.

		MT
Complete Set (10):		100.00
Common Player:		5.00
Inserted 1:180 Hobby		
1	Shareef Abdur-Rahim	12.00
2	Kobe Bryant	40.00
3	Anfernee Hardaway	15.00
4	Grant Hill	25.00
5	Juwan Howard	5.00
6	Allen Iverson	20.00
7	Jason Kidd	10.00
8	Stephon Marbury	20.00
9	Joe Smith	5.00
10	Damon Stoudamire	10.00

1996-97 Ultra Rookie Flashback

This 11-card set captures the members of the 1995-96 NBA All-Rookie Team, and was inserted every 45 packs of Series I. These inserts show a color shot of the player over a foil-etched, basketball-like background.

		MT
Complete Set (11):		45.00
Common Player:		2.00
Minor Stars:		4.00
Inserted 1:45		
1	Michael Finley (First Team)	5.00
2	Antonio McDyess (First Team)	6.00
3	Arvydas Sabonis (First Team)	2.00
4	Joe Smith (First Team)	5.00
5	Jerry Stackhouse (First Team)	5.00
6	Damon Stoudamire (First Team)	8.00
7	Brent Barry (Second Team)	4.00
8	Tyus Edney (Second Team)	2.00
9	Kevin Garnett (Second Team)	25.00
10	Bryant Reeves (Second Team)	2.00
11	Rasheed Wallace (Second Team)	2.00

1996-97 Ultra Scoring Kings

This 29-card set was found every 24 hobby packs of Series II Ultra. Fronts captured a color action shot of the player over an ornamental background and a large foil stamped "K" in the lower left corner. There was also a Scoring Kings Plus version of this insert, found every 96 hobby packs, that was printed on 100-percent foil.

		MT
Complete Set (29):		260.00
Common Player:		2.50
Minor Stars:		5.00
Inserted 1:24 Hobby		
Plus Cards:		3x
Inserted 1:96 Hobby		
1	Steve Smith	2.50
2	Dino Radja	2.50
3	Glen Rice	5.00
4	Michael Jordan	60.00
5	Terrell Brandon	5.00
6	Jim Jackson	2.50
7	Antonio McDyess	7.00
8	Grant Hill	30.00
9	Latrell Sprewell	5.00
10	Hakeem Olajuwon	10.00
11	Reggie Miller	5.00
12	Loy Vaught	2.50
13	Shaquille O'Neal	20.00
14	Alonzo Mourning	5.00
15	Vin Baker	7.00
16	Tom Gugliotta	5.00
17	Kendall Gill	2.50
18	Patrick Ewing	5.00
19	Anfernee Hardaway	20.00
20	Allen Iverson	25.00
21	Danny Manning	2.50
22	Kenny Anderson	2.50
23	Mitch Richmond	5.00
24	David Robinson	7.00
25	Shawn Kemp	6.00
26	Damon Stoudamire	10.00
27	Karl Malone	7.00
28	Shareef Abdur-Rahim	16.00
29	Chris Webber	10.00

1996-97 Ultra Scoring Kings Plus

Scoring Kings Plus reprints the 29 Scoring Kings inserts on 100-percent etched foil. This insert is seeded one per 96 hobby packs in Series II.

		MT
Complete Set (29):		900.00
Plus Cards:		1.5x-3x

1996-97 Ultra Starring Role

Starring Role inserts were found every 288 packs of Series II Ultra. The 10-card insert was printed on plastic with a color shot of the player over a darkened background with a large star and insert name running up the left side. The back contained the cut-out of the player's image with text inserted.

		MT
Complete Set (10):		325.00
Common Player:		10.00
Inserted 1:288		
1	Kevin Garnett	50.00
2	Anfernee Hardaway	35.00
3	Grant Hill	50.00
4	Michael Jordan	100.00
5	Shawn Kemp	10.00
6	Karl Malone	10.00
7	Hakeem Olajuwon	15.00
8	Shaquille O'Neal	35.00
9	David Robinson	10.00
10	Damon Stoudamire	20.00

1997-98 Ultra

Ultra Basketball was issued in two series in 1997-98, with Series I containing 150 cards and Series II including 125 cards. Series I had 123 base cards, two checklists and a 25-card Rookies insert that was seeded one per four packs. Series II had 97 base cards, three checklists and a 25-card '98 Greats subset that was seeded one per four packs. Cards featured a full-bleed glossy photo, with his name, team, position and the Ultra logo in the lower right corner. Each card in each series was paralleled three times (minus the five checklists), with Gold Medallions inserted one per pack, Platinum cards numbered to 100 and Masterpieces numbered one of one. Inserts in Series I include: Big Shots, Quick Picks, Inside/Outside, Jam City, Heir to the Throne, Ultrabilities, Ultra Stars, Diamond Ink and Million Dollar Moments. Inserts in Series II include: All Rookies, Sweet Deal, Rim Rockers, Neat Feats, View to a Thrill, Court Masters, Star Power, Diamond Ink and Million Dollar Moments.

		MT
Complete Set (275):		240.00
Complete Series 1 (150):		200.00
Complete Series 2 (125):		40.00
Common Player:		.10
Common Player (249-273):		.50
Common Rookie (124-148):		1.00
Minor Stars:		.20
Gold Cards:		x-3x
Gold Rookies (124-148):		.5x
Series 1 Pack (10):		8.00
Series 1 Wax Box (24):		160.00
Series 2 Pack (10):		3.00
Series 2 Wax Box (24):		60.00
1	Kobe Bryant	4.00
2	Charles Barkley	.50
3	Joe Dumars	.10
4	Wesley Person	.10
5	Walt Williams	.10
6	Vlade Divac	.10
7	Mookie Blaylock	.10
8	Jason Kidd	.75
9	Ron Harper	.10
10	Sherman Douglas	.10
11	Cedric Ceballos	.10
12	Karl Malone	.40
13	Antonio McDyess	.40
14	Steve Kerr	.10
15	Matt Maloney	.20
16	Glenn Robinson	.30
17	Rony Seikaly	.10
18	Derrick Coleman	.10
19	Jermaine O'Neal	.20
20	Scott Burrell	.10
21	Glen Rice	.30
22	Dale Ellis	.10
23	Michael Jordan	5.00
24	Anfernee Hardaway	2.00
25	Bryon Russell	.10
26	Toni Kukoc	.20
27	Theo Ratliff	.10
28	Tom Gugliotta	.20
29	Dennis Rodman	1.50
30	John Stockton	.40
31	Priest Lauderdale	.10
32	Luc Longley	.10
33	Grant Hill	2.50
34	Antonio Davis	.10
35	Eddie Jones	.50
36	Nick Anderson	.10
37	Shareef Abdur-Rahim	1.25
38	Stephon Marbury	2.00
39	Todd Day	.10
40	Tim Hardaway	.30
41	Larry Johnson	.20
42	Sam Perkins	.10
43	Dikembe Mutombo	.20
44	Charles Outlaw	.10
45	Mitch Richmond	.30
46	Bryant Reeves	.20
47	P.J. Brown	.10
48	Steve Smith	.10
49	Martin Muursepp	.10
50	Jamal Mashburn	.20
51	Kendall Gill	.10
52	Vinny Del Negro	.10
53	Roy Rogers	.10
54	Khalid Reeves	.10
55	Scottie Pippen	1.25
56	Joe Smith	.50
57	Mark Jackson	.10
58	Voshon Lenard	.10
59	Dan Majerle	.10
60	Alonzo Mourning	.30
61	Kerry Kittles	.30
62	Chris Childs	.10
63	Patrick Ewing	.30
64	Allan Houston	.20
65	Marcus Camby	.75
66	Christian Laettner	.20
67	Loy Vaught	.10
68	Jayson Williams	.10
69	Avery Johnson	.10
70	Damon Stoudamire	.75
71	Kevin Johnson	.20
72	Gheorghe Muresan	.10
73	Reggie Miller	.30
74	John Wallace	.30
75	Terrell Brandon	.20
76	Dale Davis	.10
77	Latrell Sprewell	.20
78	Lorenzen Wright	.10
79	Rod Strickland	.10
80	Kenny Anderson	.10
81	Anthony Mason	.10
82	Hakeem Olajuwon	1.00
83	Kevin Garnett	2.50
84	Isaiah Rider	.10
85	Mark Price	.10
86	Shawn Bradley	.20
87	Vin Baker	.40
88	Steve Nash	.20
89	Jeff Hornacek	.10
90	Tony Delk	.10
91	Horace Grant	.10
92	Othella Harrington	.20
93	Arvydas Sabonis	.10
94	Antoine Walker	1.50
95	Todd Fuller	.10
96	John Starks	.10
97	Olden Polynice	.10

98	Sean Elliott	.10
99	Travis Best	.10
100	Chris Gatling	.10
101	Derek Harper	.10
102	LaPhonso Ellis	.10
103	Dean Garrett	.10
104	Hersey Hawkins	.10
105	Jerry Stackhouse	.50
106	Ray Allen	.50
107	Allen Iverson	2.50
108	Chris Webber	.75
109	Robert Pack	.10
110	Gary Payton	.50
111	Mario Elie	.10
112	Dell Curry	.10
113	Lindsey Hunter	.10
114	Robert Horry	.10
115	David Robinson	.50
116	Kevin Willis	.10
117	Tyrone Hill	.10
118	Vitaly Potapenko	.10
119	Clyde Drexler	.40
120	Derek Fisher	.20
121	Detlef Schrempf	.10
122	Gary Trent	.10
123	Danny Ferry	.10
124	*Derek Anderson*	10.00
125	*Chris Anstey*	1.00
126	*Tony Battie*	4.00
127	*Chauncey Billups*	5.00
128	*Kelvin Cato*	2.00
129	*Austin Croshere*	2.00
130	*Antonio Daniels*	6.00
131	*Tim Duncan*	30.00
132	*Danny Fortson*	3.00
133	*Adonal Foyle*	3.00
134	*Paul Grant*	1.00
135	*Ed Gray*	2.00
136	*Bobby Jackson*	4.00
137	*Brevin Knight*	3.00
138	*Tracy McGrady*	30.00
139	*Ron Mercer*	5.00
140	*Anthony Parker*	1.00
141	*Scot Pollard*	1.00
142	*Rodrick Rhodes*	1.00
143	*Olivier Saint-Jean*	2.00
144	*Maurice Taylor*	4.00
145	*Johnny Taylor*	1.00
146	*Tim Thomas*	8.00
147	*Keith Van Horn*	8.00
148	*Jacque Vaughn*	3.00
149	Checklist	.10
150	Checklist	.10
151	Scott Burrell	.10
152	Brian Williams	.10
153	Terry Mills	.10
154	Jim Jackson	.10
155	Michael Finley	.20
156	*Jeff Nordgaard*	.20
157	Carl Herrera	.10
158	Otis Thorpe	.10
159	Wesley Person	.10
160	Tyrone Hill	.10
161	*Charles O'Bannon*	.20
162	Greg Anthony	.10
163	*Rusty LaRue*	.10
164	David Wesley	.10
165	*Chris Garner*	.10
166	George McCloud	.10
167	Mark Price	.10
168	*God Shammgod*	.20
169	Isaac Austin	.10
170	Alan Henderson	.10
171	*Eric Washington*	.10
172	Darrell Armstrong	.10
173	Calbert Cheaney	.10
174	*Cedric Henderson*	.75
175	Bryant Stith	.10
176	Sean Rooks	.10
177	Chris Mills	.10
178	Eldridge Recasner	.10
179	Priest Lauderdale	.10
180	Rick Fox	.10
181	*Keith Closs*	.10
182	Chris Dudley	.10
183	*Lawrence Funderburke*	.20
184	*Michael Stewart*	.20
185	*Alvin Williams*	.10
186	Adam Keefe	.10
187	*Chauncey Billups*	1.75
188	Jon Barry	.10
189	*Bobby Jackson*	1.25
190	Sam Cassell	.10
191	Dee Brown	.10
192	Travis Knight	.10
193	Dean Garrett	.10
194	David Benoit	.10
195	Chris Morris	.10
196	*Bubba Wells*	.10
197	James Robinson	.10
198	*Anthony Johnson*	.10
199	Dennis Scott	.10
200	*DeJuan Wheat*	.10
201	Rodney Rogers	.10
202	*Tariq Abdul-Wahad*	.10
203	Cherokee Parks	.10
204	*Jacque Vaughn*	.20
205	Cory Alexander	.10
206	*Kevin Ollie*	.10
207	George Lynch	.10
208	Lamond Murray	.10
209	Jud Buechler	.10
210	Erick Dampier	.10
211	*Malcolm Huckaby*	.10
212	Chris Webber	.75
213	*Chris Crawford*	.10
214	J.R. Reid	.10
215	Eddie Johnson	.10
216	Nick Van Exel	.25
217	Antonio McDyess	.40
218	David Wingate	.10
219	Malik Sealy	.10
220	Charles Outlaw	.10
221	*Serge Zwikker*	.20
222	Bobby Phills	.10
223	*Shea Seals*	.10
224	Clifford Robinson	.10
225	*Zydrunas Ilgauskas*	1.50
226	*John Thomas*	.10
227	Rik Smits	.10
228	Rasheed Wallace	.10
229	John Wallace	.10
230	Bob Sura	.10
231	Ervin Johnson	.10
232	*Keith Booth*	.10
233	Chuck Person	.10
234	Brian Shaw	.10
235	Todd Day	.10
236	Clarence Weatherspoon	.10
237	Charlie Ward	.10
238	Rod Strickland	.10
239	Shawn Kemp	.50
240	Terrell Brandon	.20
241	*Corey Beck*	.10
242	Vin Baker	.50
243	*Fred Hoiberg*	.40
244	Chris Mullin	.20
245	Brian Grant	.10
246	*Derek Anderson*	1.00
247	Zan Tabak	.10
248	*Charles Smith*	.10
249	Shareef Abdur-Rahim	2.50
250	Ray Allen	1.00
251	Charles Barkley	1.25
252	Kobe Bryant	6.00
253	Marcus Camby	1.00
254	Kevin Garnett	5.00
255	Anfernee Hardaway	4.00
256	Grant Hill	5.00
257	Juwan Howard	1.00
258	Allen Iverson	4.00
259	Michael Jordan	10.00
260	Shawn Kemp	1.50
261	Kerry Kittles	1.00
262	Karl Malone	.10
263	Stephon Marbury	4.00
264	Hakeem Olajuwon	2.00
265	Shaquille O'Neal	3.00
266	Gary Payton	1.50
267	Scottie Pippen	2.50
268	David Robinson	1.25
269	Dennis Rodman	3.00
270	Joe Smith	1.00
271	Jerry Stackhouse	1.00
272	Damon Stoudamire	1.50
273	Antoine Walker	2.00
274	Checklist	.10
275	Checklist	.10

1997-98 Ultra Gold

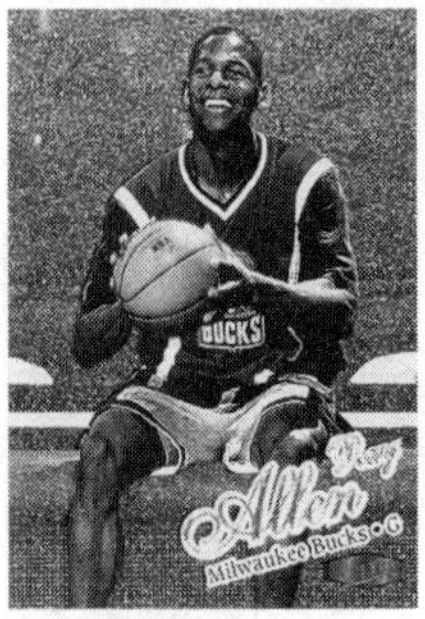

Gold Medallion versions were produced 271 of the 275 cards in Ultra Series I and II, excluding the four checklist cards. These were identified by a gold sparkling background and were inserted one per hobby pack in both series.

	MT
Gold Cards:	2x-3x
Gold Rookies: Half Price	

1997-98 Ultra Platinum

This 270-card parallel set reprinted each card in the Ultra Series I and II base set, minus the five checklists. Platinum versions were identified by a platinum colored shade added to the card front and the player shot was in black-and-white. Card backs were individually numbered up to 100 of each card.

		MT
Common Player (1-148):		15.00
Common Player (151-273):		15.00
Minor Stars (1-148):		30.00
Minor Stars (151-273):		30.00
1	Kobe Bryant	400.00
2	Charles Barkley	60.00
3	Joe Dumars	15.00
4	Wesley Person	15.00
5	Walt Williams	15.00
6	Vlade Divac	15.00
7	Mookie Blaylock	15.00
8	Jason Kidd	75.00
9	Ron Harper	15.00
10	Sherman Douglas	15.00
11	Cedric Ceballos	15.00
12	Karl Malone	50.00
13	Antonio McDyess	40.00
14	Steve Kerr	15.00
15	Matt Maloney	30.00
16	Glenn Robinson	40.00
17	Rony Seikaly	15.00
18	Derrick Coleman	15.00
19	Jermaine O'Neal	30.00
20	Scott Burrell	15.00
21	Glen Rice	40.00
22	Dale Ellis	15.00
23	Michael Jordan	625.00
24	Anfernee Hardaway	200.00
25	Bryon Russell	15.00
26	Toni Kukoc	15.00
27	Theo Ratliff	15.00
28	Tom Gugliotta	30.00
29	Dennis Rodman	150.00
30	John Stockton	40.00
31	Priest Lauderdale	15.00
32	Luc Longley	15.00
33	Grant Hill	250.00
34	Antonio Davis	15.00
35	Eddie Jones	75.00
36	Nick Anderson	15.00
37	Shareef Abdur-Rahim	130.00
38	Stephon Marbury	200.00
39	Todd Day	15.00
40	Tim Hardaway	40.00
41	Larry Johnson	30.00
42	Sam Perkins	15.00
43	Dikembe Mutombo	30.00
44	Charles Outlaw	15.00
45	Mitch Richmond	40.00
46	Bryant Reeves	15.00
47	P.J. Brown	15.00
48	Steve Smith	15.00
49	Martin Muursepp	15.00
50	Jamal Mashburn	30.00
51	Kendall Gill	15.00
52	Vinny Del Negro	15.00
53	Roy Rogers	15.00
54	Khalid Reeves	15.00
55	Scottie Pippen	125.00
56	Joe Smith	50.00
57	Mark Jackson	15.00
58	Voshon Lenard	15.00
59	Dan Majerle	15.00
60	Alonzo Mourning	40.00
61	Kerry Kittles	40.00
62	Chris Childs	15.00
63	Patrick Ewing	40.00
64	Allan Houston	30.00
65	Marcus Camby	60.00
66	Christian Laettner	30.00
67	Loy Vaught	15.00
68	Jayson Williams	15.00
69	Avery Johnson	15.00
70	Damon Stoudamire	75.00
71	Kevin Johnson	30.00
72	Gheorghe Muresan	15.00
73	Reggie Miller	40.00
74	John Wallace	30.00
75	Terrell Brandon	30.00
76	Dale Davis	15.00
77	Latrell Sprewell	30.00
78	Lorenzen Wright	15.00
79	Rod Strickland	15.00
80	Kenny Anderson	15.00
81	Anthony Mason	15.00
82	Hakeem Olajuwon	100.00
83	Kevin Garnett	250.00
84	Isaiah Rider	15.00
85	Mark Price	15.00
86	Shawn Bradley	15.00
87	Vin Baker	40.00
88	Steve Nash	30.00
89	Jeff Hornacek	15.00
90	Tony Delk	15.00
91	Horace Grant	15.00
92	Othella Harrington	15.00
93	Arvydas Sabonis	15.00
94	Antoine Walker	100.00
95	Todd Fuller	15.00
96	John Starks	15.00
97	Olden Polynice	15.00
98	Sean Elliott	15.00
99	Travis Best	15.00
100	Chris Gatling	15.00
101	Derek Harper	15.00
102	LaPhonso Ellis	15.00
103	Dean Garrett	15.00
104	Hersey Hawkins	15.00
105	Jerry Stackhouse	50.00
106	Ray Allen	50.00
107	Allen Iverson	200.00
108	Chris Webber	100.00
109	Robert Pack	15.00
110	Gary Payton	50.00
111	Mario Elie	15.00
112	Dell Curry	15.00
113	Lindsey Hunter	15.00
114	Robert Horry	15.00
115	David Robinson	60.00
116	Kevin Willis	15.00
117	Tyrone Hill	15.00
118	Vitaly Potapenko	15.00
119	Clyde Drexler	50.00
120	Derek Fisher	15.00
121	Detlef Schrempf	15.00
122	Gary Trent	15.00
123	Danny Ferry	15.00
124	Derek Anderson	60.00
125	Chris Anstey	15.00
126	Tony Battie	60.00
127	Chauncey Billups	125.00
128	Kelvin Cato	15.00
129	Austin Croshere	30.00
130	Antonio Daniels	80.00
131	Tim Duncan	275.00
132	Danny Fortson	40.00
133	Adonal Foyle	40.00
134	Paul Grant	15.00
135	Ed Gray	15.00
136	Bobby Jackson	60.00
137	Brevin Knight	60.00
138	Tracy McGrady	125.00
139	Ron Mercer	150.00
140	Anthony Parker	15.00
141	Scot Pollard	15.00
142	Rodrick Rhodes	40.00
143	Olivier Saint-Jean	30.00
144	Maurice Taylor	40.00
145	Johnny Taylor	15.00
146	Tim Thomas	100.00
147	Keith Van Horn	100.00
148	Jacque Vaughn	30.00
151	Scott Burrell	15.00
152	Brian Williams	15.00
153	Terry Mills	15.00
154	Jim Jackson	15.00
155	Michael Finley	30.00
156	*Jeff Nordgaard*	30.00
157	Carl Herrera	15.00
158	Otis Thorpe	15.00
159	Wesley Person	15.00
160	Tyrone Hill	15.00
161	*Charles O'Bannon*	30.00
162	Greg Anthony	15.00
163	*Rusty LaRue*	15.00
164	David Wesley	15.00
165	*Chris Garner*	15.00
166	George McCloud	15.00
167	Mark Price	15.00
168	*God Shammgod*	30.00
169	Isaac Austin	15.00
170	Alan Henderson	15.00
171	*Eric Washington*	15.00
172	Darrell Armstrong	15.00
173	Calbert Cheaney	15.00
174	*Cedric Henderson*	45.00
175	Bryant Stith	15.00
176	Sean Rooks	15.00
177	Chris Mills	15.00
178	Eldridge Recasner	15.00
179	Priest Lauderdale	15.00
180	Rick Fox	15.00
181	*Keith Closs*	15.00
182	Chris Dudley	15.00
183	*Lawrence Funderburke*	30.00
184	*Michael Stewart*	30.00
185	*Alvin Williams*	15.00
186	Adam Keefe	15.00
187	*Chauncey Billups*	85.00
188	Jon Barry	15.00
189	*Bobby Jackson*	50.00
190	Sam Cassell	15.00
191	Dee Brown	15.00
192	Travis Knight	15.00
193	Dean Garrett	15.00
194	David Benoit	15.00
195	Chris Morris	15.00
196	*Bubba Wells*	15.00
197	James Robinson	15.00
198	*Anthony Johnson*	15.00
199	Dennis Scott	15.00
200	*DeJuan Wheat*	15.00
201	Rodney Rogers	15.00
202	*Tariq Abdul-Wahad*	15.00
203	Cherokee Parks	15.00
204	*Jacque Vaughn*	30.00
205	Cory Alexander	15.00
206	*Kevin Ollie*	15.00
207	George Lynch	15.00
208	Lamond Murray	15.00
209	Jud Buechler	15.00
210	Erick Dampier	15.00
211	*Malcolm Huckaby*	15.00
212	Chris Webber	100.00
213	*Chris Crawford*	15.00
214	J.R. Reid	15.00
215	Eddie Johnson	15.00
216	Nick Van Exel	35.00
217	Antonio McDyess	40.00
218	David Wingate	15.00
219	Malik Sealy	15.00
220	Charles Outlaw	15.00
221	*Serge Zwikker*	30.00
222	Bobby Phills	15.00
223	*Shea Seals*	15.00
224	Clifford Robinson	15.00
225	*Zydrunas Ilgauskas*	60.00
226	*John Thomas*	15.00
227	Rik Smits	15.00
228	Rasheed Wallace	15.00
229	John Wallace	15.00
230	Bob Sura	15.00
231	Ervin Johnson	15.00
232	*Keith Booth*	15.00
233	Chuck Person	15.00
234	Brian Shaw	15.00
235	Todd Day	15.00
236	Clarence Weatherspoon	15.00
237	Charlie Ward	15.00
238	Rod Strickland	15.00
239	Shawn Kemp	60.00
240	Terrell Brandon	30.00
241	*Corey Beck*	15.00
242	Vin Baker	40.00
243	*Fred Hoiberg*	30.00
244	Chris Mullin	30.00
245	Brian Grant	15.00
246	*Derek Anderson*	50.00
247	Zan Tabak	15.00
248	*Charles Smith*	15.00
249	Shareef Abdur-Rahim	60.00
250	Ray Allen	30.00
251	Charles Barkley	30.00
252	Kobe Bryant	200.00
253	Marcus Camby	30.00
254	Kevin Garnett	125.00
255	Anfernee Hardaway	100.00
256	Grant Hill	125.00
257	Juwan Howard	15.00
258	Allen Iverson	100.00
259	Michael Jordan	300.00
260	Shawn Kemp	30.00
261	Kerry Kittles	15.00
262	Karl Malone	15.00
263	Stephon Marbury	100.00
264	Hakeem Olajuwon	50.00
265	Shaquille O'Neal	100.00
266	Gary Payton	30.00
267	Scottie Pippen	60.00
268	David Robinson	30.00
269	Dennis Rodman	75.00
270	Joe Smith	15.00
271	Jerry Stackhouse	15.00
272	Damon Stoudamire	40.00
273	Antoine Walker 2x-3x	50.00

1997-98 Ultra All-Rookies

All-Rookies was a 15-card insert set featuring the top rookies from the 1997 NBA Draft. Cards were inserted one per four packs of Series II and were numbered with an "AR" suffix.

		MT
Complete Set (15):		20.00
Common Player:		.50
1	Tim Duncan	6.00
2	Tony Battie	1.50
3	Keith Van Horn	3.00
4	Antonio Daniels	2.00
5	Chauncey Billups	2.50
6	Ron Mercer	4.00
7	Tracy McGrady	3.00
8	Danny Fortson	1.00
9	Brevin Knight	2.00
10	Derek Anderson	2.00
11	Cedric Henderson	1.50
12	Jacque Vaughn	1.00
13	Tim Thomas	2.50
14	Austin Croshere	1.00
15	Kelvin Cato	.50

1997-98 Ultra Big Shots

Big Shots was a 15-card insert featuring a wood background and an embossed red basketball rim with a net hanging from it that included the player's name. The words "Big Shots" was printed just above the bottom of the circle in silver holographic type. These inserts were seeded one per four packs of Series II and are numbered with a "BS" suffix.

		MT
Complete Set (15):		30.00
Common Player:		.50
Minor Stars:		1.00
1	Michael Jordan	10.00
2	Allen Iverson	5.00
3	Shaquille O'Neal	3.00
4	Anfernee Hardaway	4.00
5	Dennis Rodman	3.00
6	Grant Hill	5.00
7	Juwan Howard	1.50
8	David Robinson	1.50
9	Gary Payton	1.50
10	Joe Smith	1.00
11	Charles Barkley	1.50
12	Terrell Brandon	.50
13	John Stockton	1.00
14	Mitch Richmond	1.00
15	Vin Baker	1.00

1997-98 Ultra Court Masters

Court Masters is a 20-card insert set set that features two photos of each player - one his home jersey and one in his away jersey - on flip sides of the front. The holographic foil inserts are seeded one per 144 packs of Series II, and numbered with a "CM" suffix.

		MT
Complete Set (20):		600.00
Common Player:		5.00
1	Michael Jordan	100.00
2	Allen Iverson	40.00
3	Kobe Bryant	60.00
4	Shaquille O'Neal	30.00
5	Stephon Marbury	40.00
6	Shawn Kemp	15.00
7	Anfernee Hardaway	35.00
8	Kevin Garnett	50.00
9	Shareef Abdur-Rahim	25.00
10	Dennis Rodman	30.00
11	Grant Hill	50.00
12	Kerry Kittles	5.00
13	Antoine Walker	20.00
14	Scottie Pippen	25.00
15	Damon Stoudamire	12.00
16	Marcus Camby	5.00
17	Hakeem Olajuwon	20.00
18	Tim Duncan	50.00
19	Keith Van Horn	25.00
20	Chauncey Billups	25.00

1997-98 Ultra Heir to the Throne

This 15-card insert showcases the top rookies, with each sitting in a special throne of basketballs created by Fleer for the NBA rookie photo shoot. Each rookie autographed a basketball, which was then secured into a throne and given away at the 1998 SportsFest show. These inserts were seeded one per 18 packs and are numbered with a "HT" suffix.

		MT
Complete Set (15):		100.00
Common Player:		2.00
1	Derek Anderson	8.00
2	Tony Battie	8.00
3	Chauncey Billups	12.00
4	Kelvin Cato	2.00
5	Austin Croshere	2.00
6	Antonio Daniels	12.00
7	Tim Duncan	25.00
8	Danny Fortson	6.00
9	Jacque Vaughn	4.00
10	Tracy McGrady	12.00
11	Ron Mercer	12.00
12	Olivier Saint-Jean	2.00
13	Maurice Taylor	4.00
14	Tim Thomas	10.00
15	Keith Van Horn	10.00

1997-98 Ultra Inside/Outside

This 15-card insert set was seeded one per six packs of Ultra Series I. The set featured versatile players who can play under the basket or out on the perimeter. Card fronts show the player over a basketball with the insert's name printed across the bottom. Cards are numbered with a "I/O" suffix.

		MT
Complete Set (15):		12.00
Common Player:		.50
1	Shareef Abdur-Rahim	2.00
2	Juwan Howard	1.00
3	David Robinson	1.25
4	Joe Smith	1.00
5	Charles Barkley	1.25
6	Tom Gugliotta	.50
7	Glenn Robinson	.50
8	Patrick Ewing	.50
9	Chris Webber	1.50
10	Glen Rice	.50
11	Shawn Kemp	1.00
12	Antonio McDyess	.50
13	Clyde Drexler	1.00
14	Eddie Jones	1.50
15	Jason Kidd	1.25

1997-98 Ultra Jam City

Jam City was an 18-card insert set that was seeded one per eight packs of Series I. Fronts featured a color shot of the player over a black-and-white sketched city background, with the words "Jam City" across the bottom in silver foil. Cards were numbered on the back with a "JC" suffix.

		MT
Complete Set (18):		50.00
Common Player:		.75
1	Kevin Garnett	8.00
2	Antoine Walker	4.00
3	Scottie Pippen	4.00
4	Shawn Kemp	2.00
5	Hakeem Olajuwon	3.00
6	Jerry Stackhouse	2.00
7	Karl Malone	2.00
8	Shaquille O'Neal	5.00
9	John Wallace	.75
10	Marcus Camby	2.00
11	Juwan Howard	2.00
12	David Robinson	2.00
13	Gary Payton	2.00
14	Dennis Rodman	5.00
15	Joe Smith	2.00
16	Charles Barkley	2.00
17	Terrell Brandon	.75
18	Kobe Bryant	10.00

Values quoted in this guide reflect the retail price of a card — the price a collector can expect to pay when buying a card from a dealer. The wholesale price — that which a collector can expect to receive from a dealer when selling cards — will be significantly lower, depending on desirability and condition.

1997-98 Ultra Neat Feats

This 18-card insert set pictures an embossed color shot of the player over a split color background, with the left side having a blue tint and the right side having a red tint. Neat Feats were seeded one per eight packs of Series II and are numbered with a "NF" suffix.

		MT
Complete Set (18):		18.00
Common Player:		.50
1	Michael Finley	.50
2	Jason Kidd	1.75
3	Rasheed Wallace	.50
4	Shaquille O'Neal	4.00
5	Tom Gugliotta	.50
6	Marcus Camby	1.25
7	Jerry Stackhouse	1.25
8	John Wallace	.50
9	Juwan Howard	1.25
10	David Robinson	1.50
11	Gary Payton	1.50
12	Joe Smith	1.25
13	Charles Barkley	1.50
14	Terrell Brandon	.75
15	John Stockton	1.00
16	Vin Baker	1.25
17	Antonio McDyess	1.25
18	Antonio Daniels	1.50

1997-98 Ultra Quick Picks

Quick Picks featured players in front of an outdoor metal fence over a blue holographic background. This 12-card insert set was seeded one per eight packs and were numbered with a "QP" suffix.

		MT
Complete Set (12):		12.00
Common Player:		.50
Minor Stars:		1.00
1	Stephon Marbury	4.00
2	Ray Allen	1.25
3	Damon Stoudamire	2.00
4	Kerry Kittles	1.00
5	Gary Payton	1.50
6	Terrell Brandon	1.00
7	John Stockton	1.00
8	Mookie Blaylock	.50
9	Eddie Jones	3.00
10	Nick Van Exel	.50
11	Kenny Anderson	.50
12	Tim Hardaway	1.00

1997-98 Ultra Rim Rocker

This 12-card insert set was seeded one per eight packs of Series II. Each card is die-cut around the player's body and contains a holographic background. Cards are numbered with a "RR" suffix.

		MT
Complete Set (12):		10.00
Common Player:		.25
1	Ron Mercer	3.00
2	Juwan Howard	.75
3	David Robinson	1.00
4	Gary Payton	1.00
5	Joe Smith	.25
6	Charles Barkley	1.00
7	Terrell Brandon	.50
8	John Stockton	.50
9	Adonal Foyle	.25
10	Tim Thomas	2.00
11	Tony Battie	1.00
12	Antonio McDyess	.75

1997-98 Ultra Star Power

Star Power was a 20-card set that was inserted into packs of Ultra Series II. The insert arrived in three different versions, with regular versions seeded one per four packs. Star Power Plus and Star Power Supreme versions of each card also existed at more difficult odds and on a die-cut cut design. Cards are numbered with a "SP" prefix.

		MT
Complete Set (20):		40.00
Common Player:		.50
Plus Cards:		2x-4x
Supreme Cards:		15x-30x
1	Michael Jordan	8.00
2	Allen Iverson	3.00
3	Kobe Bryant	5.00
4	Shaquille O'Neal	2.50
5	Stephon Marbury	3.00
6	Shawn Kemp	1.00
7	Anfernee Hardaway	2.50
8	Kevin Garnett	4.00
9	Shareef Abdur-Rahim	2.00
10	Dennis Rodman	2.50
11	Grant Hill	4.00
12	Gary Payton	1.00
13	Antoine Walker	1.50
14	Scottie Pippen	2.00
15	Damon Stoudamire	1.00
16	Marcus Camby	.50
17	Hakeem Olajuwon	1.50
18	Tim Duncan	4.00
19	Keith Van Horn	3.00
20	Jerry Stackhouse	.75

1997-98 Ultra Stars

Ultra Stars was a 20-card insert set that was seeded one per 144 packs of Ultra Series I. Fronts were embossed and printed on holographic silver foil, with the player's color image in placed over large silver stars. Gold versions were also available, with only 10 percent of the print run including gold foil.

		MT
Complete Set (20):		700.00
Common Player:		7.00
1	Michael Jordan	120.00
2	Allen Iverson	60.00
3	Kobe Bryant	80.00
4	Shaquille O'Neal	40.00
5	Stephon Marbury	50.00
6	Marcus Camby	15.00
7	Anfernee Hardaway	50.00
8	Kevin Garnett	60.00
9	Shareef Abdur-Rahim	35.00
10	Dennis Rodman	35.00
11	Ray Allen	15.00
12	Grant Hill	60.00
13	Kerry Kittles	7.00
14	Antoine Walker	25.00
15	Scottie Pippen	30.00
16	Damon Stoudamire	20.00
17	Shawn Kemp	15.00
18	Hakeem Olajuwon	25.00
19	Jerry Stackhouse	15.00
20	John Wallace	7.00

1997-98 Ultra Sweet Deal

This 15-card insert set was seeded one per six packs of Ultra Series II. It included some of the top young players in the NBA and was numbered with a "SD" suffix.

		MT
Complete Set (12):		10.00
Common Player:		.50
1	Ray Allen	.75
2	Chauncey Billups	2.50
3	Ron Mercer	4.00
4	Hakeem Olajuwon	3.00
5	Jerry Stackhouse	.75
6	John Wallace	.50
7	Juwan Howard	.75
8	David Robinson	1.25
9	Bobby Jackson	1.75
10	Joe Smith	.75
11	Charles Barkley	1.25
12	Terrell Brandon	.50

1997-98 Ultra Ultrabilities

Ultrabilities was a 20-card insert set that was available in Ultra Series I packs. The insert was available in three different tiers - Starter (1:4 packs), All-Star (1:36) and Superstar (1:288). Starter versions had the word "Starter" running up the right side, All-Star versions had the word "All-Star" diagonal across a white background along with red and blue stars, while Superstar versions were die-cut and printed on holographic gold foil.

		MT
Complete Set (20):		50.00
Common Player:		.75
All-Star Cards:		3x-6x
Superstar Cards:		15x-30x
1	Michael Jordan	10.00
2	Allen Iverson	5.00
3	Kobe Bryant	7.00
4	Shaquille O'Neal	4.00
5	Stephon Marbury	4.00
6	Gary Payton	1.50
7	Anfernee Hardaway	4.00
8	Kevin Garnett	5.00
9	Scottie Pippen	2.50
10	Grant Hill	5.00
11	Marcus Camby	1.50
12	Ray Allen	.75
13	Kerry Kittles	.75
14	Antoine Walker	2.00
15	Shareef Abdur-Rahim	2.50
16	Damon Stoudamire	1.50
17	Shawn Kemp	1.50
18	Hakeem Olajuwon	1.50
19	Jerry Stackhouse	.75
20	Juwan Howard	.75

1997-98 Ultra View to a Thrill

This 15-card insert was seeded one per 18 packs of Ultra Series II. The card was printed on a black background, with the insert name printed across the top in yellow. The middle of the card features a film-like strip of the player in action. Cards are numbered with a "VT" suffix.

		MT
Complete Set (15):		80.00
Common Player:		1.50
1	Michael Jordan	20.00
2	Allen Iverson	10.00
3	Kobe Bryant	12.00
4	Tracy McGrady	6.00
5	Stephon Marbury	10.00
6	Shawn Kemp	3.00
7	Anfernee Hardaway	8.00
8	Kevin Garnett	10.00
9	Shareef Abdur-Rahim	5.00
10	Dennis Rodman	6.00
11	Grant Hill	10.00
12	Kerry Kittles	1.50
13	Antoine Walker	5.00
14	Scottie Pippen	5.00
15	Damon Stoudamire	3.00

1998 Ultra Jam Session Knicks Sheet

This promotional sheet featured six members of the New York Knicks on a perforated sheet. Sheets were given away by Fleer/SkyBox as part of the 1998 Jam Session show in New York City and utilize the 1997-98 Ultra design, with different photos. A similar sheet featuring SkyBox cards of the same players was also available.

		MT
Complete Set (6):		5.00
Common Player:		5.00
	Patrick Ewing	5.00
	Larry Johnson	5.00
	John Starks	5.00
	Chris Dudley	5.00
	Charlie Ward	5.00
	Chris Mills	5.00

1998-99 Ultra

Ultra arrived in a 125-card, single series set in 1998-99. The product was delayed for several months until the NBA lockout ended, and due to lack of photography, didn't include Kings rookie Jason Williams in the 25-card Rookies subset, which was seeded 1:4 packs. Cards featured a borderless, full-color shot of the player with his name, team and position written in script in the bottom center. There were three hobby-only parallel sets in Ultra: Gold Medallions were one per pack, Platinum Medallions had the first 100 cards numbered to 99 and the Rookies numbered to 66 sets and Masterpieces were numbered one-of-one. Inserts included: NBAttitude, Give and Take, World Premiere, Unstoppable, Leading Performers and Exclamation Points.

		MT
Complete Set (125):		150.00
Common Player:		.15
Minor Stars:		.30
Common Rookie:		1.00
Inserted 1:4		
Pack (10):		75.00
Wax Box (24):		
1	Keith Van Horn	1.00
2	Antonio Daniels	.15
3	Patrick Ewing	.30
4	Alonzo Mourning	.30
5	Isaac Austin	.15
6	Bryant Reeves	.15
7	Dennis Scott	.15
8	Damon Stoudamire	.50
9	Kenny Anderson	.15
10	Mookie Blaylock	.15
11	Mitch Richmond	.30
12	Jalen Rose	.15
13	Vin Baker	.75
14	Donyell Marshall	.15
15	Bryon Russell	.15
16	Rasheed Wallace	.15
17	Allan Houston	.30
18	Shawn Kemp	.50
19	Nick Van Exel	.30
20	Theo Ratliff	.15
21	Jayson Williams	.15
22	Chauncey Billups	.50
23	Brent Barry	.15
24	David Wesley	.15
25	Joe Dumars	.30
26	Marcus Camby	.30
27	Juwan Howard	.30
28	Brevin Knight	.50
29	Reggie Miller	.30
30	Ray Allen	.50
31	Michael Finley	.30
32	Tom Gugliotta	.30
33	Allen Iverson	1.25
34	Toni Kukoc	.30
35	Tim Thomas	1.00
36	Jeff Hornacek	.15
37	Bobby Jackson	.15
38	Bo Outlaw	.15
39	Steve Smith	.30
40	Terrell Brandon	.30
41	Glen Rice	.30
42	Rik Smits	.15
43	Calbert Cheaney	.15
44	Stephon Marbury	1.50
45	Glenn Robinson	.30
46	Corliss Williamson	.15
47	Larry Johnson	.30
48	Antonio McDyess	.30
49	Detlef Schrempf	.15
50	Jerry Stackhouse	.30
51	Doug Christie	.15
52	Eddie Jones	.75
53	Karl Malone	.50
54	Anthony Mason	.15
55	Tim Duncan	2.50
56	Christian Laettner	.30
57	Isaiah Rider	.15
58	Shawn Bradley	.15
59	Jim Jackson	.15
60	Mark Jackson	.15
61	Kobe Bryant	3.00
62	Zydrunas Ilgauskas	.15
63	Ron Mercer	1.50
64	Hersey Hawkins	.15
65	John Wallace	.15
66	Avery Johnson	.15
67	Dikembe Mutombo	.30
68	Hakeem Olajuwon	.75
69	Tony Battie	.15
70	Jason Kidd	1.00
71	Latrell Sprewell	.30
72	Kevin Garnett	2.50
73	Voshon Lenard	.15
74	Gary Payton	.50
75	Cherokee Parks	.15
76	Antoine Walker	1.00
77	Anthony Johnson	.15
78	Danny Fortson	.15
79	Grant Hill	2.50
80	Dennis Rodman	1.50
81	Arvydas Sabonis	.15
82	Tracy McGrady	1.00
83	David Robinson	.50
84	Tariq Abdul-Wahad	.15
85	Michael Jordan	5.00
86	Kerry Kittles	.30
87	Maurice Taylor	.50
88	Cedric Ceballos	.15
89	Anfernee Hardaway	1.50
90	John Stockton	.30
91	Shareef Abdur-Rahim	.75
92	Tim Hardaway	.50
93	Shaquille O'Neal	1.50
94	Rodney Rogers	.15
95	Derek Anderson	.50
96	Kendall Gill	.15
97	Rod Strickland	.30
98	Charles Barkley	.50
99	Chris Webber	.75
100	Scottie Pippen	1.25
101	*Raef LaFrentz*	5.00
102	*Ricky Davis*	4.00
103	*Robert Traylor*	2.00
104	*Roshown McLeod*	1.50
105	*Tyronn Lue*	1.00
106	*Vince Carter*	50.00
107	*Miles Simon*	1.00
108	*Paul Pierce*	12.00
109	*Pat Garrity*	2.00
110	*Nazr Mohammed*	1.00
111	*Mike Bibby*	8.00
112	*Michael Dickerson*	5.00
113	*Michael Doleac*	1.50
114	*Matt Harpring*	2.00
115	*Larry Hughes*	15.00
116	*Keon Clark*	3.00
117	*Felipe Lopez*	3.00
118	*Dirk Nowitzki*	15.00
119	*Corey Benjamin*	2.00
120	*Bryce Drew*	1.00
121	*Brian Skinner*	1.00
122	*Bonzi Wells*	10.00
123	*Antawn Jamison*	15.00
124	*Al Harrington*	6.00
125	*Michael Olowokandi*	4.00

Values quoted in this guide reflect the retail price of a card — the price a collector can expect to pay when buying a card from a dealer. The wholesale price — that which a collector can expect to receive from a dealer when selling cards — will be significantly lower, depending on desirability and condition.

1998-99 Ultra Gold Medallion

This 125-card parallel set reprinted each card from Fleer Ultra using a gold foil background. Cards were inserted one per pack and numbered with a "G" suffix.

	MT
Complete Set (125):	400.00
Gold Cards:	2x
Inserted 1:1	
Gold Rookies:	1.5x
Inserted 1:35	

1998-99 Ultra Platinum Medallion

Platinum Medallions were a 125-card parallel set to Ultra. They utilized the same front as the base cards, but added a platinum finish to the entire card. The first 100 cards were sequentially numbered to 99 sets, while the 25-card Rookies subset was numbered to 66 sets. Platinum Medallion cards were exclusive to hobby packs.

		MT
Common Player:		10.00
Minor Stars:		20.00
Production 99 Sets		
Common Rookie:		20.00
Production 66 Sets		
1	Keith Van Horn	75.00
2	Antonio Daniels	10.00
3	Patrick Ewing	20.00
4	Alonzo Mourning	20.00
5	Isaac Austin	10.00
6	Bryant Reeves	10.00
7	Dennis Scott	10.00
8	Damon Stoudamire	35.00
9	Kenny Anderson	10.00
10	Mookie Blaylock	10.00
11	Mitch Richmond	20.00
12	Jalen Rose	10.00
13	Vin Baker	20.00
14	Donyell Marshall	10.00
15	Bryon Russell	10.00
16	Rasheed Wallace	10.00
17	Allan Houston	20.00
18	Shawn Kemp	30.00
19	Nick Van Exel	20.00
20	Theo Ratliff	10.00
21	Jayson Williams	10.00
22	Chauncey Billups	35.00
23	Brent Barry	10.00
24	David Wesley	10.00
25	Joe Dumars	20.00
26	Marcus Camby	20.00
27	Juwan Howard	20.00
28	Brevin Knight	35.00
29	Reggie Miller	20.00
30	Ray Allen	35.00
31	Michael Finley	20.00
32	Tom Gugliotta	20.00
33	Allen Iverson	90.00
34	Toni Kukoc	30.00
35	Tim Thomas	70.00
36	Jeff Hornacek	10.00
37	Bobby Jackson	10.00
38	Bo Outlaw	10.00
39	Steve Smith	20.00
40	Terrell Brandon	20.00
41	Glen Rice	20.00
42	Rik Smits	10.00
43	Calbert Cheaney	10.00
44	Stephon Marbury	100.00
45	Glenn Robinson	20.00
46	Corliss Williamson	10.00
47	Larry Johnson	20.00
48	Antonio McDyess	40.00
49	Detlef Schrempf	10.00
50	Jerry Stackhouse	20.00
51	Doug Christie	10.00
52	Eddie Jones	50.00
53	Karl Malone	35.00
54	Anthony Mason	10.00
55	Tim Duncan	175.00
56	Christian Laettner	20.00
57	Isaiah Rider	10.00
58	Shawn Bradley	10.00
59	Jim Jackson	10.00
60	Mark Jackson	10.00
61	Kobe Bryant	200.00
62	Zydrunas Ilgauskas	10.00
63	Ron Mercer	100.00
64	Hersey Hawkins	10.00
65	John Wallace	10.00
66	Avery Johnson	10.00
67	Dikembe Mutombo	20.00
68	Hakeem Olajuwon	50.00
69	Tony Battie	10.00
70	Jason Kidd	70.00
71	Latrell Sprewell	20.00
72	Kevin Garnett	175.00
73	Voshon Lenard	10.00
74	Gary Payton	35.00
75	Cherokee Parks	10.00
76	Antoine Walker	45.00
77	Anthony Johnson	10.00

78	Danny Fortson	10.00
79	Grant Hill	175.00
80	Dennis Rodman	70.00
81	Arvydas Sabonis	10.00
82	Tracy McGrady	70.00
83	David Robinson	35.00
84	Tariq Abdul-Wahad	10.00
85	Michael Jordan	350.00
86	Kerry Kittles	20.00
87	Maurice Taylor	35.00
88	Cedric Ceballos	10.00
89	Anfernee Hardaway	100.00
90	John Stockton	20.00
91	Shareef Abdur-Rahim	50.00
92	Tim Hardaway	35.00
93	Shaquille O'Neal	100.00
94	Rodney Rogers	10.00
95	Derek Anderson	35.00
96	Kendall Gill	10.00
97	Rod Strickland	20.00
98	Charles Barkley	35.00
99	Chris Webber	70.00
100	Scottie Pippen	90.00
101	*Raef LaFrentz*	70.00
102	*Ricky Davis*	25.00
103	*Robert Traylor*	60.00
104	*Roshown McLeod*	20.00
105	*Tyronn Lue*	20.00
106	*Vince Carter*	350.00
107	*Miles Simon*	10.00
108	*Paul Pierce*	200.00
109	*Pat Garrity*	20.00
110	*Nazr Mohammed*	20.00
111	*Mike Bibby*	100.00
112	*Michael Dickerson*	40.00
113	*Michael Doleac*	35.00
114	*Matt Harpring*	35.00
115	*Larry Hughes*	90.00
116	*Keon Clark*	35.00
117	*Felipe Lopez*	40.00
118	*Dirk Nowitzki*	20.00
119	*Corey Benjamin*	20.00
120	*Bryce Drew*	20.00
121	*Brian Skinner*	20.00
122	*Bonzi Wells*	25.00
123	*Antawn Jamison*	150.00
124	*Al Harrington*	40.00
125	*Michael Olowokandi*	70.00

1998-99 Ultra Exclamation Points

Exclamation Points was a 15-card insert seeded 1:288 packs. The cards featured a hardwood look on the front and included a pull-out card inside the exterior sleeve. Cards in this insert were numbered with an "EP" suffix.

		MT
Complete Set (15):		500.00
Common Player:		12.00
Inserted 1:288		
1	Vince Carter	75.00
2	Tim Duncan	50.00
3	Shawn Kemp	15.00
4	Shaquille O'Neal	35.00
5	Mike Bibby	45.00
6	Michael Jordan	100.00
7	Michael Olowokandi	40.00
8	Larry Hughes	35.00
9	Kobe Bryant	75.00
10	Kevin Garnett	50.00
11	Keith Van Horn	20.00
12	Grant Hill	50.00
13	Gary Payton	12.00
14	Antoine Walker	15.00
15	Antawn Jamison	40.00

1998-99 Ultra Give and Take

Give and Take was a 10-card insert that was exclusive to retail packs and inserted 1:18. These double-sided cards featured the player on offense on the front and in a defensive pose on the back. Cards were numbered with a "GT" suffix.

		MT
Complete Set (10):		15.00
Common Player:		1.50
Minor Stars:		3.00
Inserted 1:18 Retail		
1	Gary Payton	3.00
2	Shawn Kemp	2.00
3	Kerry Kittles	1.50
4	Ron Mercer	7.00
5	Scottie Pippen	6.00
6	Ray Allen	3.00
7	Anfernee Hardaway	8.00
8	Maurice Taylor	3.00
9	Brevin Knight	3.00
10	Karl Malone	3.00

1998-99 Ultra Leading Performers

Leading Performers was a 15-card insert in Ultra that was seeded 1:72 packs. The cards opened up like a book to reveal two additional shots of the player. The front photo was in black and white, while the insert name appeared in large black letters in a gold box across the top. Backs were numbered with an "LP" suffix.

		MT
Complete Set (15):		275.00
Common Player:		6.00
Inserted 1:72		
1	Allen Iverson	18.00
2	Anfernee Hardaway	20.00
3	Kobe Bryant	45.00
4	Michael Jordan	60.00
5	Ron Mercer	20.00
6	Stephon Marbury	20.00
7	Tim Duncan	30.00
8	Shareef Abdur-Rahim	12.00
9	Kevin Garnett	30.00
10	Grant Hill	30.00
11	Damon Stoudamire	6.00
12	Dennis Rodman	18.00
13	Keith Van Horn	12.00
14	Scottie Pippen	15.00
15	Shaquille O'Neal	20.00

1998-99 Ultra NBAttitude

This 20-card insert was seeded 1:6 packs of Ultra. It featured the player over a blurred background with the insert name across the middle. Cards were numbered with an "NA" suffix.

		MT
Complete Set (20):		20.00
Common Player:		.75
Minor Stars:		1.50
Inserted 1:6		
1	Allen Iverson	3.00
2	Chauncey Billups	.75
3	Keith Van Horn	3.00
4	Ray Allen	1.50
5	Shareef Abdur-Rahim	2.50
6	Stephon Marbury	4.00
7	Kerry Kittles	.75
8	Tim Thomas	1.50
9	Damon Stoudamire	1.50
10	Antoine Walker	2.00
11	Brevin Knight	1.50
12	Maurice Taylor	.75
13	Ron Mercer	3.00
14	Tim Duncan	6.00
15	Zydrunas Ilgauskas	.75
16	Michael Finley	.75
17	Bobby Jackson	.75
18	Tim Hardaway	1.50
19	David Robinson	2.00
20	Vin Baker	1.50

1998-99 Ultra Unstoppable

Unstoppable was a 15-card insert seeded 1:36 packs of Ultra. Fronts featured a metallized basketball and gave the appearance of metal held in place with bolts. Cards opened up to feature a shot of the player, while backs contained another shot and were numbered with a "US" suffix.

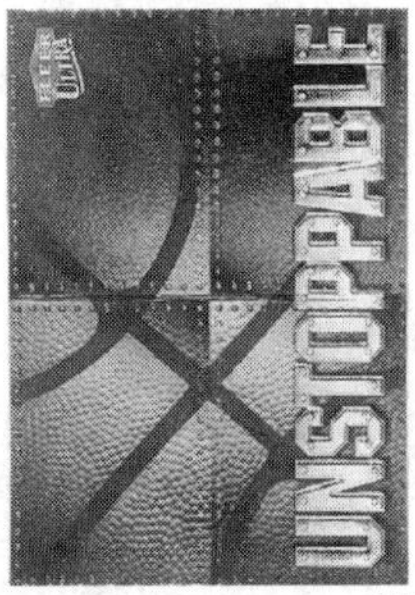

		MT
Complete Set (15):		150.00
Common Player:		4.00
Inserted 1:36		
1	Michael Jordan	40.00
2	Scottie Pippen	10.00
3	Grant Hill	20.00
4	Dennis Rodman	15.00
5	Stephon Marbury	15.00
6	Antoine Walker	8.00
7	Shareef Abdur-Rahim	8.00
8	Shaquille O'Neal	15.00
9	Damon Stoudamire	6.00
10	Kerry Kittles	4.00
11	Maurice Taylor	4.00
12	Kobe Bryant	30.00
13	Kevin Garnett	20.00
14	Anfernee Hardaway	15.00
15	Allen Iverson	12.00

1998-99 Ultra World Premiere

This 15-card insert was devoted to the top rookies from the 1998 NBA Draft and was seeded 1:20 packs. Cards featured a prismatic background with a globelike design and the embossed player image. World Premiere inserts were numbered with a "WP" suffix.

		MT
Complete Set (15):		85.00
Common Player:		2.00
Minor Stars:		4.00
Inserted 1:20		
1	Robert Traylor	3.00
2	Paul Pierce	8.00
3	Michael Olowokandi	5.00
4	Felipe Lopez	2.00
5	Raef LaFrentz	6.00
6	Antawn Jamison	8.00
7	Larry Hughes	6.00
8	Al Harrington	3.00
9	Pat Garrity	2.00
10	Bryce Drew	2.00
11	Michael Doleac	4.00
12	Michael Dickerson	3.00
13	Keon Clark	4.00
14	Vince Carter	25.00
15	Mike Bibby	5.00

1999 Ultra WNBA

Ultra marked Fleer/SkyBox's second WNBA card release of 1999. The set consisted of 125 total cards, with 90 basic player cards, 10 All-WNBA and 25 seeded rookies (1:2 packs). The cards featured a similar borderless design to other Ultra products, while the rookies had the same team color border at the bottom as ketball. The set was paralleled in Gold Medallion, Platinum Medallion and Masterpiece sets. Inserts include: WNBAttitude, World Premiere, Rock Talk and Fresh Ink.

		MT
Complete Set (125):		100.00
Common Player:		.15
Minor Stars:		.30
Common Rookie:		3.00
Inserted 1:4		
Pack (10):		3.00
Wax Box (24):		65.00
1	Sheryl Swoopes	4.00
2	Christy Smith	.15
3	Nikki McCray	2.50
4	Coquese Washington	.15
5	Vickie Johnson	.50
6	Toni Foster	.40
7	Allison Feaster	.15
8	Penny Toler	.40
9	*Brandy Reed*	2.00
10	Yolanda Moore	.30
11	Lisa Leslie	3.00
12	Kisha Ford	.15
13	Merlakia Jones	.50
14	Umeki Webb	.30
15	Tora Suber	.50
16	Octavia Blue	.15
17	Bridget Pettis	.15
18	*LaTonya Johnson*	.60
19	*Ales Santos de Oliveiro*	.60
20	Tia Paschal	.15
21	Jennifer Gillom	1.50
22	Wanda Guyton	.30
23	Franthea Price	.15
24	Andrea Kuklova	.15
25	Vicky Bullett	.50
26	Dena Head	.15
27	Isabelle Fijalkowski	.15
28	Michelle Edwards	1.00
29	Pamela McGee	.40
30	Elisabeth Cebrian	.15
31	Olympia Scott	.15
32	Murriel Page	.60
33	*Korie Hlede*	1.50
34	Andrea Stinson	1.50
35	Kristie Harrower	.15
36	Kym Hampton	.50
37	Gergana 1ranzova	.15
38	Teresa Weatherspoon	2.50
39	Rebecca Lobo	2.75
40	Michele Timms	2.50
41	Tamecka Dixon	.50
42	Tina Thompson	.50
43	Janice Braxton	.15
44	Elena Baranova	1.50
45	Adrienne Johnson	2.00
46	Adia Barnes	.15
47	Elaine Powell	.15
48	Lady Hardmon	.15
49	Kim Perrot	.75
50	*Marlies Askamp*	1.00
51	Deborah Carter	.15
52	*Sandy Brondello*	3.00
53	Heidi Burge	.15
54	Janeth Arcain	.15
55	Rushia Brown	.15
56	Suzie McConnell Serio	1.00
57	Penny Moore	.50
58	*Malgorzata Dydek*	.75
59	Angie Potthoff	.15
60	*Monica Lamb*	.40
61	Jamila Wideman	.60
62	*Ticha Penicheiro*	.75
63	Andrea Congreaves	.40
64	*Rachal Sporn*	.50
65	Chantel Tremitiere	.40
66	Carla McGhee	.15
67	Kim Williams	.30
68	Tangela Smith	.30
69	Quacy Barnes	.15
70	Sue Wicks	.50
71	*Tracy Reid*	.75
72	Linda Burgess	.15
73	Razija Brcaninovic	.15
74	Sharon Manning	.15
75	Tammy Jackson	.15
76	Rita Williams	.50
77	*Carla Porter*	.60
78	Michelle Griffiths	.30
79	Eva Nemcova	.75
80	Sophia Witherspoon	.60
81	*Sonja Tate*	.60
82	Cynthia Cooper	5.00
83	Wendy Palmer	1.50
84	Ruthie Bolton-Holifield	2.50
85	Tammi Reiss	1.00
86	Katrina Colleton	.15
87	Cindy Brown	2.00
88	Latasha Byears	.50
89	Mwadi Mabika	.15
90	Rhonda Mapp	.15
91	Tina Thompson (All-WNBA Team)	.30
92	Sheryl Swoopes (All-WNBA Team)	2.00
93	Jennifer Gillom (All-WNBA Team)	.75
94	Cynthia Cooper (All-WNBA Team)	2.50
95	Suzie McConnell Serio (All-WNBA Team)	.50
96	Cindy Brown (All-WNBA Team)	1.00
97	Eva Nemcova (All-WNBA Team)	.40
98	Lisa Leslie (All-WNBA Team)	1.50
99	Andrea Stinson (All-WNBA Team)	.75
100	Teresa Weatherspoon (All-WNBA Team)	1.25
101	*Dawn Staley*	10.00
102	*Chamique Holdsclaw*	30.00
103	*Kristin Folkl*	8.00
104	*Nykesha Sales*	8.00
105	*Natalie Williams*	10.00
106	*Yolanda Griffith*	10.00
107	*Crystal Robinson*	5.00
108	*Edna Campbell*	3.00
109	*Tari Phillips*	5.00
110	*Tonya Edwards*	3.00
111	*Debbie Black*	3.00
112	*Kate Starbird*	3.00
113	*Adrienne Goodson*	3.00
114	*Sheri Sam*	3.00
115	*DeLisha Milton*	5.00
116	*Shannon Johnson*	3.00
117	*Katie Smith*	3.00
118	*Kara Wolters*	3.00
119	*Jennifer Azzi*	10.00
120	*Michele VanGorp*	3.00
121	*Stephanie White-McCarty*	3.00
122	*Ukari Figgs*	3.00
123	*Val Whiting*	3.00
124	*Mery Andrade*	3.00
125	*Charlotte Smith*	3.00

1999 Ultra WNBA Gold Medallion

Gold Medallion cards paralleled all 125 cards in Ultra WNBA and were seeded one per pack. Card fronts featured a gold tint, while backs included the words "Gold Medallion Edition" stamped in gold and were numbered with a "G" suffix.

	MT
Complete Set (125):	175.00
Gold Cards:	2x
Gold Rookies:	1x-2x
Inserted 1:1	

1999 Ultra WNBA Platinum Medallion

Platinum Medallion cards paralleled all 125 cards in Ultra WNBA. Cards 1-100 were sequentially numbered to 99 sets on the back, while the rookies (101-125) were numbered to 66 sets. Card fronts were distinguished by a platinum tint, while backs included the words "Platinum Medallion Edition" and were numbered with a "P" suffix.

	MT
Complete Set (125):	
Platinum Cards (1-100):	15x-30x
1-100 Production 99 Sets	
Platinum Rookies (101-125):	5x-10x
101-125 Production 66 Sets	

1999 Ultra WNBA Fresh Ink

Ultra WNBA marked the first installment of Fresh Ink, an autograph program exclusive to Ultra products. The insert featured autographs from 13 WNBA players on cards numbered to 400. Each card featured a color shot of the player, with a white border across the middle for the player's signature. The cards were hand-numbered to 400 in the bottom left corner.

	MT
Common Player:	45.00
Production 400 Sets	
Elana Baranova	45.00
Cynthia Cooper	175.00
Kristen Folkl	45.00
Lisa Leslie	100.00
Suzie McConnell Serio	75.00
Nikki McCray	75.00
Nykesha Sales	75.00
Dawn Staley	75.00
Andrea Stinson	75.00
Sheryl Swoopes	150.00
Michele Timms	100.00
Penny Toler	45.00
Teresa Weatherspoon	90.00

1999 Ultra WNBA Rock Talk

Rock Talk inserts featured 10 different players over a silver holofoil pattern. Cards were numbered with an "RT" suffix and inserted 1:24 packs.

		MT
Complete Set (10):		80.00
Common Player:		5.00
Inserted 1:24		
1	Eva Nemcova	5.00
2	Cynthia Cooper	20.00
3	Ruthie Bolton-Holifield	10.00
4	Michele Timms	10.00
5	Jennifer Gillom	8.00
6	Cindy Brown	8.00
7	Lisa Leslie	15.00
8	Andrea Stinson	8.00
9	Teresa Weatherspoon	10.00
10	Rebecca Lobo	12.00

1999 Ultra WNBA WNBAttitude

This 10-card insert was seeded 1:6 packs of Ultra WNBA. Cards featured the player's image over the insert name background. Cards were numbered with a "WA" suffix.

		MT
Complete Set (10):		25.00
Common Player:		1.00
Inserted 1:6		
1	Lisa Leslie	4.00
2	Cynthia Cooper	5.00
3	Ruthie Bolton-Holifield	3.00
4	Rebecca Lobo	4.00
5	Sheryl Swoopes	4.00
6	Nikki McCray	4.00
7	Cindy Brown	3.00
8	Jennifer Gillom	2.00
9	Wendy Palmer	1.00
10	Michele Timms	3.00

1999 Ultra WNBA World Premiere

This insert featured 10 top rookies on a sculptured embossed card with a foil stamped background. World Premiere inserts were numbered with a "WP" suffix and inserted 1:12 packs.

		MT
Complete Set (10):		50.00
Common Player:		3.00
Inserted 1:12		
1	Chamique Holdsclaw	20.00
2	Dawn Staley	6.00
3	Nykesha Sales	6.00
4	Kristin Folkl	5.00
5	Natalie Williams	8.00
6	Yolanda Griffith	10.00
7	Crystal Robinson	4.00
8	Edna Campbell	4.00
9	DeLisha Milton	4.00
10	Debbie Black	3.00

1999-00 Ultra

Ultra arrived in a single-series, 150-card set that included 125 veterans and 25 rookies, which were seeded 1:4 packs. The cards were borderless in design and contained the player's name, team, position and Ultra logo across the bottom. Two parallel sets exist - Gold Medallion and Platinum Medallion, which were both die-cut around the top. Inserts included: Feel the Game, Fresh Ink, Good Looks, Heir to the Throne, Millennium Men, Parquet Players and World Premiere.

		MT
Complete Set (150):		125.00
Common Player:		.15
Minor Stars:		.25
Common Rookie (126-150):		1.00
Pack (10):		3.00
Wax Box (24):		40.00
1	Vince Carter	3.00
2	Randell Jackson	.15
3	Ray Allen	.35
4	Corliss Williamson	.15
5	Darrell Armstrong	.25
6	Charles Oakley	.15
7	Tyrone Nesby	.25
8	Eddie Jones	.60
9	Kerry Kittles	.15
10	Jason Williams	2.00
11	Elden Campbell	.15
12	Mookie Blaylock	.15
13	Brent Barry	.15
14	Mark Jackson	.15
15	Tim Hardaway	.60
16	Kendall Gill	.15
17	Larry Johnson	.15
18	Eric Snow	.15
19	Raef LaFrentz	.75
20	Allen Iverson	2.50
21	Kenny Anderson	.25
22	John Starks	.15
23	Isaiah Rider	.25
24	Tariq Abdul-Wahad	.15
25	Vitaly Potapenko	.15
26	Patrick Ewing	.25
27	Mitch Richmond	.25
28	Steve Nash	.15
29	Dickey Simpkins	.15
30	Grant Hill	2.50
31	Matt Geiger	.15
32	John Stockton	.25
33	Jayson Williams	.15
34	Reggie Miller	.25
35	Eric Piatkowski	.15
36	Jason Kidd	1.25
37	Allan Houston	.25
38	Christian Laettner	.15
39	Marcus Camby	.25
40	Shaquille O'Neal	1.50
41	Derek Anderson	.25
42	Gary Trent	.15
43	Vin Baker	.25
44	Alonzo Mourning	.40
45	Latrell Sprewell	.25
46	Rod Strickland	.25
47	Bobby Jackson	.15
48	Karl Malone	.75
49	Mario Elie	.15
50	Kobe Bryant	3.00
51	Clifford Robinson	.15
52	Jamal Mashburn	.25
53	Dirk Nowitzki	.40
54	Rik Smits	.15
55	Doug Christie	.15
56	Ricky Davis	.25
57	Jalen Rose	.15
58	Michael Olowokandi	.75
59	Cedric Ceballos	.15
60	Ron Mercer	1.00
61	Brevin Knight	.15
62	Rashard Lewis	.40
63	Detlef Schrempf	.15
64	Keith Van Horn	.60
65	Nick Anderson	.15
66	Larry Hughes	1.00
67	Antonio McDyess	.60
68	Terrell Brandon	.25
69	Felipe Lopez	.25
70	Scottie Pippen	1.25
71	Erick Dampier	.15
72	Arvydas Sabonis	.15
73	Brian Grant	.15
74	Nick Van Exel	.25
75	Bryon Russell	.15
76	Danny Fortson	.15
77	Avery Johnson	.15
78	Jerry Stackhouse	.25
79	Robert Traylor	.50
80	Tim Duncan	2.50
81	Lindsey Hunter	.15
82	Tyronn Lue	.15
83	Michael Finley	.25
84	Dikembe Mutombo	.25
85	Zydrunas Ilgauskas	.25
86	Pat Garrity	.25
87	Damon Stoudamire	.50
88	Shareef Abdur-Rahim	1.00
89	Matt Harpring	.25
90	Michael Dickerson	.25
91	Steve Smith	.25
92	Bison Dele	.15
93	Glenn Robinson	.25
94	Antawn Jamison	1.00
95	Glen Rice	.25
96	Vlade Divac	.15
97	Vladimir Stepania	.15
98	Kornel David	.15
99	Shawn Kemp	.50
100	Kevin Garnett	2.50
101	Tim Thomas	.75
102	Mike Bibby	.75
103	Maurice Taylor	.40
104	Gary Payton	.75
105	Voshon Lenard	.15
106	Theo Ratliff	.15
107	Hakeem Olajuwon	.75
108	Joe Smith	.25
109	Toni Kukoc	.50
110	Stephon Marbury	1.25
111	Anthony Mason	.15
112	Anfernee Hardaway	1.50
113	Juwan Howard	.25
114	Charles Barkley	.75
115	Antoine Walker	.50
116	Donyell Marshall	.15
117	Tom Gugliotta	.25
118	Rasheed Wallace	.25
119	Tracy McGrady	1.25
120	Paul Pierce	1.50
121	Sean Elliott	.15
122	Bryant Reeves	.15
123	Michael Doleac	.25
124	Chris Webber	1.25
125	David Robinson	.75
126	*Steve Francis*	20.00
127	*Elton Brand*	10.00
128	*Wally Szczerbiak*	5.00
129	*Richard Hamilton*	5.00
130	*Shawn Marion*	10.00
131	*Trajan Langdon*	3.00
132	*Corey Maggette*	5.00
133	*Dion Glover*	2.00
134	*James Posey*	3.00
135	*Lamar Odom*	12.00
136	*Alek Radojevic*	1.50
137	*Cal Bowdler*	1.50
138	*Scott Padgett*	2.00
139	*Jumanie Jones*	2.00
140	*Jonathan Bender*	10.00
141	*Tim James*	2.00
142	*Jason Terry*	4.00
143	*Quincy Lewis*	2.00
144	*William Avery*	2.00
145	*Galen Young*	1.50
146	*Ron Artest*	4.00
147	*Kenny Thomas*	2.50
148	*Devean George*	3.00
149	*Andre Miller*	6.00
150	*Baron Davis*	6.00

1999-00 Ultra Gold Medallion

This 150-card set paralleled each card in Ultra, but featured a gold background and a die-cut top of the card. The parallel set name was printed around the top perimeter of the card. Veterans were inserted one per pack, while rookies were seeded 1:35 packs. Gold Medallion cards were numbered with a "G" suffix.

	MT
Gold Veterans:	2x
Inserted 1:1	
Gold Rookies (126-150):	1.5x
Inserted 1:35	

1999-00 Ultra Platinum Medallion

This 150-card parallel set reprinted every card from Ultra with a platinum-foil colored background and a die-cut design across the top of the card (identical to the Gold Medallion cards). The insert name ran across the top and the cards were numbered with a "P" suffix on the back. The first 125 cards were sequentially numbered to 45, while the 25 rookies were numbered to just 25.

	MT
Common Platinum (1-125):	25.00
Production 50 Sets	
Common Platinum (126-150):	30.00
Production 25 Sets	

1999-00 Ultra Feel the Game

This 15-card insert featured player-worn swatches from the top rookies in 1999-00. The cards contained a close-up shot in the lower-right corner and a circular swatch from the jersey in the upper left. Feel the Game cards were inserted 1:168 packs. Multi-color swatches frequently sell for a premium price.

		MT
Complete Set (15):		1000.
Common Player:		25.00
Inserted 1:168		
3	Jonathan Bender	100.00
11	Cal Bowdler	25.00
4	Baron Davis	100.00
1	Steve Francis	150.00
2	Richard Hamilton	75.00
13	Tim James	25.00
15	Jumanie Jones	25.00
9	Trajan Langdon	75.00
10	Corey Maggette	100.00
7	Andre Miller	75.00
6	Lamar Odom	200.00
14	Scott Padgett	40.00
12	James Posey	50.00
5	Wally Szczerbiak	150.00
8	Jason Terry	60.00

1999-00 Ultra Fresh Ink

		MT
Common Player:		3.00
1	Ray Allen/300	40.00
2	Ron Artest/1000	10.00
3	William Avery/1000	6.00
4	Jonathan Bender/500	30.00
5	Mike Bibby/550	10.00
6	Calvin Booth/975	3.00
7	Cal Bowdler/1000	3.00
8	Bruce Bowen/1000	6.00
9	Marcus Camby/750	15.00
10	John Celestand/1000	3.00
11	Baron Davis/475	20.00
12	Michael Dickerson/975	10.00
13	Michael Doleac/1000	3.00
14	Bryce Drew/1000	3.00
15	Evan Eschmeyer/1000	3.00
16	Steve Francis/500	75.00
17	Pat Garrity/600	6.00
18	Devean George/1000	12.00
19	Dion Glover/875	6.00
20	Brian Grant/500	15.00
21	Richard Hamilton/750	12.00
22	Juwan Howard/225	25.00
23	Larry Hughes/750	20.00
24	Jumaine Jones/1000	6.00
25	Eddie Jones/250	50.00
26	Raef LaFrentz/500	10.00
27	Quincy Lewis/1000	6.00
28	Felipe Lopez/1000	6.00
29	Corey Maggette/250	30.00
30	Stephon Marbury/400	30.00
31	Shawn Marion/1000	25.00
32	Lamar Odom/350	50.00
33	Shaquille O'Neal/200	250.00
34	Scottie Pippen/130	150.00
35	James Posey/1000	10.00
36	Aleksandar Radojevic/1000	3.00
37	David Robinson/155	125.00
38	Jalen Rose/500	25.00
39	Wally Szczerbiak/500	25.00
40	Jerry Stackhouse/650	20.00
41	Maurice Taylor/400	12.00
42	Jason Terry/1000	15.00
43	Robert Traylor/1000	6.00
44	Keith Van Horn/500	15.00
45	Antoine Walker/245	30.00
46	Chris Webber/200	150.00

1999-00 Ultra Good Looks

This 15-card insert showcased top young stars and rookies and included a very close shot of the player's face printed on foil on the left half of the card, with the insert name on the right side and a player's color image near the center. Good Looks cards were numbered with a "GL" suffix and inserted 1:6 packs.

		MT
Complete Set (15):		30.00
Common Player:		.75
Inserted 1:6		
1	Grant Hill	4.00
2	Kevin Garnett	4.00
3	Richard Hamilton	1.00
4	Larry Hughes	.75
5	Shaquille O'Neal	3.00
6	Kobe Bryant	5.00
7	Antoine Walker	1.00
8	Lamar Odom	4.00
9	Allen Iverson	3.00
10	Scottie Pippen	2.00
11	Ron Mercer	2.00
12	Anfernee Hardaway	3.00
13	Chris Webber	2.00
14	Jason Williams	3.00
15	Baron Davis	1.50

1999-00 Ultra Heir to the Throne

This 10-card insert featured shots of the players with a cloud background, and a prismatic crown somewhat hidden in the background. Heir to the Throne cards were numbered with an "HT" suffix and inserted 1:24 packs.

		MT
Complete Set (10):		30.00
Common Player:		2.00
Inserted 1:24		
1	Allen Iverson	4.00
2	Keith Van Horn	1.00
3	Paul Pierce	3.00
4	Stephon Marbury	2.00
5	Vince Carter	10.00
6	Tim Duncan	8.00
7	Ron Mercer	2.00
8	Antawn Jamison	2.50
9	Shaquille O'Neal	4.00
10	Grant Hill	8.00

1999-00 Ultra Millennium Men

This rare, 15-card insert set featured players over translucent lenticular patterned plastic with silver foil stamping. Millennium Men cards were numbered with an "MM" suffix and sequentially numbered to 100 sets.

		MT
Complete Set (15):		850.00
Common Player:		25.00
Production 100 Sets		
1	Allen Iverson	60.00
2	Paul Pierce	50.00
3	Steve Francis	75.00
4	Kobe Bryant	125.00
5	Vince Carter	125.00
6	Ron Mercer	35.00
7	Jason Williams	60.00
8	Elton Brand	50.00
9	Grant Hill	100.00
10	Tim Duncan	100.00
11	Stephon Marbury	40.00
12	Keith Van Horn	20.00
13	Kevin Garnett	100.00
14	Antawn Jamison	40.00
15	Antoine Walker	15.00

1999-00 Ultra Parquet Players

This 15-card insert captures players against a debossed parquet pattern floor background with gold-foil stamping. Parquet Players cards were numbered with a "PP" suffix and inserted 1:72 packs.

		MT
Complete Set (15):		150.00
Common Player:		3.00
Inserted 1:72		
1	Kobe Bryant	25.00
2	Keith Van Horn	4.00
3	Tim Duncan	20.00
4	Shaquille O'Neal	12.00
5	Kevin Garnett	20.00
6	Jason Williams	12.00
7	Vince Carter	25.00
8	Stephon Marbury	8.00
9	Paul Pierce	10.00
10	Scottie Pippen	8.00
11	Baron Davis	6.00
12	Antoine Walker	3.00
13	Larry Hughes	3.00
14	Antawn Jamison	8.00
15	Elton Brand	10.00

1999-00 Ultra World Premiere

This 10-card insert set captures the rookies from the 1999-00 season on die-cut etched foil. World Premiere cards were numbered with a "WP" suffix and seeded 1:12 packs.

		MT
Complete Set (10):		25.00
Common Player:		1.50
Inserted 1:12		
1	Elton Brand	4.00
2	Andre Miller	1.50
3	Baron Davis	3.00
4	Steve Francis	6.00
5	Richard Hamilton	2.00
6	Jason Terry	1.50
7	Jonathan Bender	3.00
8	Trajan Langdon	2.00
9	Wally Szczerbiak	6.00
10	Lamar Odom	8.00

2000 Ultra WNBA

Ultra WNBA consisted of 125 basic cards and 25 rookies, which were seeded 1:2 packs. The cards featured a color shot of the player over a borderless design, with silver holofoil letters. Each card was reprinted in both Gold and Platinum Medallion parallels, which featured a die-cut design. Inserts included: Feminine Adrenaline, WNBAttitude, Trophy Case, Fresh Ink and Feel the Game.

		MT
Complete Set (150):		75.00
Common Player:		.10
Minor Stars:		.20
Common Rookie (126-150):		1.00
Pack (10):		3.00
Box (24):		60.00
1	Cynthia Cooper	4.00
2	Chamique Holdsclaw	4.00
3	Lisa Leslie	2.50
4	Anna DeForge	.10
5	Stephanie McCarty	.75
6	Katrina Colleton	.10
7	Clarisse Machanguana	.20
8	Adrienne Goodson	.60
9	Charlotte Smith	.75
10	DeLisha Milton	.50
11	Janeth Arcain	.10
12	Donna Harrington	.10
13	Michele Timms	1.50
14	Charmin Smith	.20
15	Tricia Bader	.10
16	Vickie Johnson	.30
17	Monica Lamb	.10
18	Dawn Staley	1.50
19	Ruthie Bolton-Holifield	1.50
20	Jennifer Azzi	1.25
21	Becky Hammon	10.00
22	Latasha Byears	.40
23	Lisa Harrison	.10
24	Jennifer Rizzotti	5.00
25	Yolanda Griffith	1.50
26	Tracy Henderson	.10
27	Sophia Witherspoon	.40
28	Sheryl Swoopes	4.00
29	Korie Hlede	.40
30	Shannon Johnson	.50
31	Chasity Melvin	2.00
32	Tamika Whitmore	.10
33	Tina Thompson	.75
34	Kendra Holland-Corn	3.00
35	Markita Aldridge	.10
36	Dalma Aldridge	.10
37	Ticha Penicheiro	.60
38	Quacy Barnes	.10
39	Ukari Figgs	.60
40	Andrea Lloyd Curry	.10
41	Tammy Jackson	.10
42	Nikki McCray	1.50
43	Kate Starbird	.75
44	Andrea Nagy	1.50
45	Bridget Pettis	.10
46	Eva Nemcova	.50
47	Tangela Smith	.20
48	Astou Ndiaye-Diatta	.10
49	Tamecka Dixon	.30
50	Taj McWilliams	2.00
51	Kristin Folkl	.50
52	Amanda Wilson	.10
53	Chantel Tremitiere	.10
54	Dominique Canty	4.00
55	Allison Feaster	.20
56	Angie Potthoff	.10
57	Nykesha Sales	.75
58	Rhonda Mapp	.10
59	Murriel Page	.30
60	Maria Stepanova	.20
61	Katie Smith	1.00
62	Michelle Edwards	.50
63	Venus Lacy	2.00
64	Adrienne Johnson	.10
65	Rita Williams	.20
66	Andrea Stinson	.75
67	La'Keshia Frett	.10
68	Jennifer Gillom	1.00
69	LaTonya Johnson	.10
70	Joy Holmes-Harris	.10
71	Rushia Brown	.10
72	Michelle Campbell	.10
73	Angie Braziel	.10
74	Crystal Robinson	.60
75	Alicia Thompson	.10
76	Suzie McConnell Serio	.60
77	Tanja Kostic	.10
78	Amaya Valdemoro	.10
79	Sue Wicks	.20
80	Sonja Tate	.10
81	Natalie Williams	1.50
82	Mery Andrade	.50
83	Tracy Reid	.30
84	Olympia Scott-Richardson	.10
85	Rebecca Lobo	1.50
86	Margo Dydek	.40
87	Sonja Henning	3.00
88	Vicky Bullett	.30
89	Mwadi Mabika	.10
90	Linda Burgess	.20
91	Merlakia Jones	.40
92	Umeki Webb	.10
93	Niesa Johnson	.10
94	Texlin Quinney	.10
95	Teresa Weatherspoon	2.00
96	Wendy Palmer	.75
97	Brandy Reed	.75
98	Oksana Zakaluzhnaya	.10
99	Sharon Manning	.10
100	Kara Wolters	.75
101	Keisha Anderson	.10
102	Edna Campbell	.60
103	DeMya Walker	.10
104	Michele VanGorp	.50
105	Coquese Washington	.10
106	Marlies Askamp	.20
107	Michelle Marciniak	1.00
108	Angela Aycock	.10
109	Tari Phillips	.75
110	Sylvia Crawley	.10
111	Tonya Edwards	.75
112	Monica Maxwell	.10
113	Beth Cunningham	.10
114	Debbie Black	.30
115	Shalonda Enis	.10
116	Naomi Mulitauaopele	.10
117	Jamila Wideman	.40
118	Shanele Stires	.10
119	Alisa Burras	.10
120	Gordana Grubin	.10
121	Elaine Powell	.10
122	Tausha Mills	.10
123	Katy Steding	.10
124	Jannon Roland	.10
125	Jessie Hicks	.10
126	*Ann Wauters*	4.00
127	*Edwina Brown*	2.00
128	*Grace Daley*	1.50
129	*Helen Darling*	1.50
130	*Summer Erb*	3.00
131	*Kamila Vodichkova*	1.50
132	*Tamicha Jackson*	1.50
133	*Betty Lennox*	10.00
134	*Maylana Martin*	2.00
135	*Lynn Pride*	1.50
136	*Paige Sauer*	1.50
137	*Madinah Slaise*	1.50
138	*Stacey Thomas*	1.00
139	*Cinthia Dos Santos*	1.50
140	*Milena Flores*	2.00
141	*Rhonda Banchero*	1.00
142	*Jameka Jones*	1.00
143	*Jessica Bibby*	1.50
144	*Adrian Williams*	1.00
145	*Olga Firsova*	3.00
146	*Usha Gilmore*	3.00
147	*Shanta Owens*	1.50
148	*Jurgita Streimikyte*	1.00
149	*Katrina Hibbert*	1.50
150	*Tonya Washington*	1.00

2000 Ultra WNBA Gold Medallion

This 150-card parallel set featured reprints of each card in the Ultra set, with a die-cut around the top and gold tint to the card front. Gold Medallion cards were seeded 1:1 for veterans and 1:24 for rookies, and were numbered with a "G" suffix.

	MT
Complete Set (150):	250.00
Common Gold (1-125):	.20
Gold Cards:	2x
Common Rookies (126-150):	4.00
Gold Rookies:	2x-4x
Cards 1-125 Inserted 1:1	
Cards 126-150 Inserted 1:24	

2000 Ultra WNBA Platinum Medallion

This 150-card parallel set featured reprints of each card in the Ultra set, with a die-cut around the top and platinum tint to the card front. Platinum Medallion cards were numbered to 50 for veterans and 25 for rookies, and numbered with a "P" suffix.

	MT
Common Platinum (1-125):	10.00
Platinum Cards:	25x-50x
Common Rookie: (126-150):	20.00
Platinum Rookies:	20x-30x
Cards 1-125 Production 50 Sets	
Cards 126-150 Production 25 Sets	

2000 Ultra WNBA Feel The Game

This 16-card set arrived unnumbered and contained a piece of player-worn jersey embedded in the card. Feel the Game inserts were seeded 1:144 packs. Two players, Cythia Cooper and Sheryl Swoopes, signed a limited amount of their Feel the Game inserts, with signed Cooper singles numbered to 14 and signed Swoopes singles numbered to 22.

		MT
	Complete Set (15):	850.00
	Common Player:	30.00
	Inserted 1:144	
1	Debbie Black	30.00
2	Ruthie Bolton-Holifield	60.00
3	Cynthia Cooper	150.00
3A	Cynthia Cooper Auto/14	600.00
4	Jennifer Gillom	50.00
5	Yolanda Griffith	50.00
6	Kendra Holland-Corn	75.00
7	Lisa Leslie	100.00
8	Suzie McConnell Serio	60.00
9	Taj McWilliams	30.00
10	DeLisha Milton	40.00
11	Ticha Penicheiro	60.00
12	Dawn Staley	50.00
13	Kate Starbird	60.00
14	Sheryl Swoopes	150.00
14A	Sheryl Swoopes Auto/22	500.00
15	Natalie Williams	50.00

2000 Ultra WNBA Feminine Adrenaline

This 10-card insert set pictured players over a streaked, holofoil background. Feminine Adrenaline cards were numbered with an "FA" suffix and seeded 1:4 packs.

		MT
	Complete Set (10):	20.00
	Common Player:	1.00
	Inserted 1:4	
1	Nikki McCray	3.00
2	Ticha Penicheiro	1.00
3	Teresa Weatherspoon	4.00
4	Jennifer Azzi	3.00
5	Lisa Leslie	5.00
6	Sheryl Swoopes	8.00
7	Tina Thompson	2.00
8	Jennifer Gillom	2.00
9	Suzie McConnell Serio	1.00
10	Dawn Staley	3.00

2000 Ultra WNBA Fresh Ink

This 18-card insert set featured autographs from top WNBA players on a horizontal format. The card backs contain a certificate of authenticity signed by a Fleer representative. Fresh Ink cards were unnumbered and seeded 1:72 packs.

		MT
	Complete Set (18):	800.00
	Common Player:	15.00
	Inserted 1:72	
	Gold Versions:	2x
	Production 50 Sets	
1	Debbie Black	15.00
2	Ruthie Bolton-Holifield	50.00
3	Cynthia Cooper	150.00
4	Tonya Edwards	30.00
5	Jennifer Gillom	50.00
6	Yolanda Griffith	75.00
7	Vickie Johnson	30.00
8	Carolyn Jones-Young	30.00
9	Lisa Leslie	75.00
10	Suzie McConnell Serio	50.00
11	DeLisha Milton	30.00
12	Eva Nemcova	30.00
13	Ticha Penicheiro	50.00
14	Nykesha Sales	30.00
15	Dawn Staley	30.00
16	Sheryl Swoopes	125.00
17	Teresa Weatherspoon	75.00
18	Natalie Williams	50.00

2000 Ultra WNBA Fresh Ink Gold

This 18-card parallel set featured each Fresh Ink autographed card in a version that was numbered to just 50 sets. The cards were machine numbered in gold foil on the end of the card that the signature appeared on.

	MT
Complete Set (18):	800.00
Common Player:	15.00
Inserted 1:72	
Gold Versions:	2x
Production 50 Sets	

2000 Ultra WNBA Trophy Case

This 10-card die-cut insert set featured the First- and Second-Team All WNBA players on a holofoil surface. Trophy Case cards were numbered with a "TC" suffix and seeded 1:12 packs.

		MT
	Complete Set (10):	50.00
	Common Player:	2.00
	Inserted 1:12	
1	Sheryl Swoopes	12.00
2	Natalie Williams	5.00
3	Yolanda Griffith	5.00
4	Cynthia Cooper	12.00
5	Ticha Penicheiro	2.00
6	Chamique Holdsclaw	12.00
7	Tina Thompson	3.00
8	Lisa Leslie	8.00
9	Teresa Weatherspoon	6.00
10	Shannon Johnson	2.00

2000 Ultra WNBA WNBAttitude

This 10-card insert featured top WNBA players on a horizontal format with holofoil background. WNBAttitude cards were numbered with a "WA" suffix and seeded 1:8 packs.

		MT
	Complete Set (10):	20.00
	Common Player:	.50
	Inserted 1:8	
1	Andrea Stinson	2.00
2	Eva Nemcova	1.00
3	Wendy Palmer	2.00
4	Shannon Johnson	2.00
5	Jennifer Gillom	2.00
6	Yolanda Griffith	4.00
7	Natalie Williams	4.00
8	Chamique Holdsclaw	8.00
9	Cynthia Cooper	8.00
10	Vickie Johnson	.50

2000-01 Ultra

		MT
	Complete Set (225):	150.00
	Common Player:	.15
	Minor Stars:	.30
	Common Rookie:	2.00
	Pack (10):	3.00
	Box (24):	40.00
1	Vince Carter	4.00
2	Antawn Jamison	.75
3	Shaquille O'Neal	2.00
4	Paul Pierce	.60
5	Antonio McDyess	.50
6	Scott Burrell	.15
7	Elton Brand	1.25
8	Lamar Odom	1.25
9	Nick Van Exel	.30
10	Kobe Bryant	3.00
11	Reggie Miller	.30
12	Sam Cassell	.30
13	Darrell Armstrong	.15
14	Rasheed Wallace	.50
15	Charles Oakley	.15
16	David Wesley	.15
17	Al Harrington	.30
18	Latrell Sprewell	.75
19	Rick Brunson	.15
20	Steve Smith	.30
21	Antonio Davis	.15
22	Michael Finley	.30
23	Shandon Anderson	.15
24	Danny Fortson	.15
25	Kerry Kittles	.15
26	Anfernee Hardaway	1.25
27	Vin Baker	.30
28	Calvin Booth	.15
29	Haywoode Workman	.15
30	Dickey Simpkins	.15
31	Jerome Williams	.15
32	Ron Artest	.40
33	Dennis Scott	.15
34	Ron Mercer	.30
35	Chris Webber	1.25
36	Bryon Russell	.15
37	Dale Davis	.15
38	Dirk Nowitzki	.75
39	Steve Francis	2.50
40	Glen Rice	.30
41	Stephon Marbury	1.00
42	Jason Kidd	1.25
43	Brent Barry	.15
44	Richard Hamilton	.40
45	Antoine Walker	.50
46	Gary Trent	.15
47	Cuttino Mobley	.15
48	P.J. Brown	.15
49	Elliot Perry	.15
50	Shawn Marion	.75
51	Horace Grant	.15
52	Juwan Howard	.30
53	Elden Campbell	.15
54	Erick Strickland	.15
55	Hakeem Olajuwon	.60
56	Anthony Carter	.15
57	Keith Van Horn	.60
58	Clifford Robinson	.15
59	Ruben Patterson	.15
60	Mitch Richmond	.30
61	Jason Terry	.30
62	Andre Miller	.50
63	Vonteego Cummings	.30
64	Joe Smith	.15
65	Toni Kukoc	.40
66	Sean Elliott	.15
67	Michael Dickerson	.30
68	Derrick Coleman	.30
69	Shawn Bradley	.15
70	Kenny Thomas	.15
71	Tim Hardaway	.40
72	Rex Chapman	.15
73	Gary Payton	.60
74	Jahidi White	.15
75	Baron Davis	.50
76	Chauncey Billups	.15
77	Moochie Norris	.15
78	Dan Majerle	.15
79	Marcus Camby	.30
80	Rodney Rogers	.15
81	Rashard Lewis	.60
82	Laron Profit	.15
83	Ricky Davis	.15
84	Keon Clark	.15
85	Anthony Miller	.15
86	Jamal Mashburn	.30
87	Chris Childs	.15
88	Brian Grant	.30
89	Muggsy Bogues	.15
90	Randy Brown	.15
91	Tariq Abdul-Wahad	.15
92	Lindsey Hunter	.15
93	Rik Smits	.15
94	Glenn Robinson	.30
95	Michael Doleac	.15
96	Quincy Lewis	.15
97	Grant Hill	2.00
98	Jalen Rose	.50
99	Ervin Johnson	.15
100	Chucky Atkins	.15
101	Jermaine O'Neal	.40
102	Howard Eisley	.15
103	Kenny Anderson	.30
104	Lamond Murray	.15
105	Adonal Foyle	.15
106	Derek Fisher	.15
107	Wally Szczerbiak	.40
108	Todd MacCulloch	.15
109	Avery Johnson	.15
110	Othella Harrington	.15
111	Tony Battie	.15
112	Bob Sura	.15
113	Larry Hughes	.75
114	Rick Fox	.15
115	Travis Best	.15
116	Theo Ratliff	.30
117	David Robinson	.60
118	Felipe Lopez	.15
119	John Amaechi	.15
120	George Lynch	.15
121	Christian Laettner	.15
122	Derek Anderson	.30
123	Tim Thomas	.50
124	Matt Harpring	.15
125	Nick Anderson	.15
126	Karl Malone	.60
127	Dion Glover	.15
128	Wesley Person	.15
129	Mikki Moore	.15
130	Michael Olowokandi	.15
131	William Avery	.15
132	Charles Outlaw	.15
133	Jason Williams	.60
134	John Stockton	.30
135	Adrian Griffin	.15
136	Hubert Davis	.15
137	Donyell Marshall	.15
138	Travis Knight	.15
139	Kendall Gill	.15
140	Tom Gugliotta	.30
141	Malik Rose	.15
142	Isaac Austin	.15
143	Alan Henderson	.15
144	Shawn Kemp	.30
145	Terry Mills	.15
146	Maurice Taylor	.15
147	Terrell Brandon	.30
148	Matt Geiger	.15
149	Corliss Williamson	.15
150	Jacque Vaughn	.15
151	Dikembe Mutombo	.30
152	Trajan Langdon	.15
153	Jason Caffey	.15
154	Tyrone Nesby	.15
155	Bobby Jackson	.15
156	Allen Iverson	2.00
157	Mario Elie	.15
158	Mike Bibby	.30
159	Robert Horry	.15
160	James Posey	.15
161	Mark Jackson	.15
162	Ray Allen	.30
163	Charlie Ward	.15
164	Damon Stoudamire	.30
165	Tracy McGrady	1.25
166	Bimbo Coles	.15
167	Chucky Brown	.15
168	Jerry Stackhouse	.30
169	Greg Ostertag	.15
170	Radoslav Nesterovic	.15
171	Corey Maggette	.50
172	Vlade Divac	.15
173	Scott Padgett	.15
174	Anthony Mason	.15
175	Raef LaFrentz	.15
176	Austin Croshere	.30
177	Mark Strickland	.15
178	Allan Houston	.40
179	Arvydas Sabonis	.15
180	Doug Christie	.15
181	Jim Jackson	.15
182	Brevin Knight	.15
183	Mookie Blaylock	.15
184	Chris Herren	.15
185	Kevin Garnett	2.50
186	Tyrone Hill	.15
187	Tim Duncan	2.00
188	Shareef Abdur-Rahim	.60
189	Eddie Jones	.75
190	Jonathan Bender	1.00
191	Alonzo Mourning	.40
192	Patrick Ewing	.30
193	Scottie Pippen	1.25
194	Scot Pollard	.15
195	Cedric Ceballos	.15
196	Clarence Weatherspoon	.15
197	Jamie Feick	.15
198	Eric Snow	.15
199	Ron Harper	.15
200	Bryant Reeves	.15
201	*Chris Mihm*	3.00
202	*Joel Przybilla*	2.50
203	*Kenyon Martin*	10.00
204	*Stromile Swift*	15.00
205	*Etan Thomas*	3.00
206	*Jason Collier*	2.00
207	*Marcus Fizer*	8.00
208	*Mateen Cleaves*	6.00
209	*Dan Langhi*	2.50
210	*Mike Miller*	15.00
211	*Jabari Smith*	2.00
212	*Hanno Mottola*	2.00
213	*Chris Porter*	6.00
214	*Desmond Mason*	10.00
215	*Erick Barkley*	3.00
216	*Donnell Harvey*	2.50
217	*DerMarr Johnson*	8.00
218	*Jerome Moiso*	3.00
219	*Quentin Richardson*	10.00
220	*Courtney Alexander*	8.00
221	*Michael Redd*	2.50
222	*Morris Peterson*	10.00
223	*Darius Miles*	25.00
224	*Jamal Crawford*	8.00
225	*Keyon Dooling*	8.00

2000-01 Ultra Gold Medallion

	MT
Complete Set (225):	150.00
Common Player:	.25
Minor Stars:	.40
Gold Veterans:	1x-1.5x
Common Rookie:	2.00
Gold Rookies:	.5x-1x

2000-01 Ultra Platinum Medallion

	MT
Common Player:	10.00
Minor Stars:	15.00
Platinum Veterans:	30x-60x
Common Rookie:	30.00
Platinum Rookies:	6x-12x

2000-01 Ultra Air Club For Men

		MT
	Complete Set (15):	20.00
	Common Player:	.75
	Inserted 1:6	
	Platinums:	10x-20x
	Production 100 Sets	
AC1	Kobe Bryant	4.00
AC2	Lamar Odom	1.50
AC3	Vince Carter	5.00
AC4	Tim Duncan	2.50
AC5	Grant Hill	2.50
AC6	Tracy McGrady	1.50
AC7	Kevin Garnett	3.00
AC8	Steve Francis	3.00
AC9	Allen Iverson	2.50
AC10	Jason Williams	.75
AC11	Shaquille O'Neal	3.00
AC12	Jason Kidd	1.50
AC13	Elton Brand	1.50
AC14	Eddie Jones	1.00
AC15	Stephon Marbury	1.00

2000-01 Ultra Air Club For Men Platinum Edition

		MT
	Complete Set (15):	400.00
	Common Player:	5.00
	Platinums:	10x-20x
	Production 100 Sets	
1	Kobe Bryant	75.00
2	Lamar Odom	30.00
3	Vince Carter	100.00
4	Tim Duncan	50.00
5	Grant Hill	50.00
6	Tracy McGrady	30.00
7	Kevin Garnett	60.00
8	Steve Francis	60.00
9	Allen Iverson	40.00
10	Jason Williams	10.00
11	Shaquille O'Neal	50.00
12	Jason Kidd	30.00
13	Elton Brand	30.00
14	Eddie Jones	15.00
15	Stephon Marbury	10.00

2000-01 Ultra Slam Show

		MT
	Complete Set (10):	35.00
	Common Player:	.50
	Inserted 1:24	
	Platinums:	6x-12x
	Platinum Vince Carter:	100.00
	Production 100 Sets	
SS1	Steve Francis	5.00
SS2	Tracy McGrady	2.50
SS3	Jerry Stackhouse	.75
SS4	Larry Hughes	2.00
SS5	Ricky Davis	.50
SS6	Vince Carter	6.00
SS7	Vince Carter	8.00
SS8	Vince Carter	10.00
SS9	Vince Carter	12.00
SS10	Vince Carter	15.00

2000-01 Ultra Slam Show Platinum Edition

		MT
	Complete Set (10):	400.00
	Common Player:	6.00
	Platinums:	6x-12x
	Platinum Vince Carter:	100.00
	Production 100 Sets	
1	Steve Francis	60.00
2	Tracy McGrady	30.00
3	Jerry Stackhouse	8.00
4	Larry Hughes	15.00
5	Ricky Davis	6.00
6	Vince Carter	100.00
7	Vince Carter	100.00
8	Vince Carter	100.00
9	Vince Carter	100.00
10	Vince Carter	100.00

2000-01 Ultra Thrillinium

		MT
	Complete Set (10):	50.00
	Common Player:	2.00
	Inserted 1:48	
	Platinums:	2x-5x
	Production 100 Sets	
T1	Vince Carter	20.00
T2	Kobe Bryant	15.00
T3	Tim Duncan	10.00
T4	Kevin Garnett	12.00
T5	Allen Iverson	10.00
T6	Jason Williams	2.00
T7	Shaquille O'Neal	10.00
T8	Lamar Odom	6.00
T9	Eddie Jones	3.00
T10	Stephon Marbury	2.00

2000-01 Ultra Thrillinium Platinum Edition

		MT
	Complete Set (10):	250.00
	Common Player:	10.00
	Platinums:	2x-5x
	Production 100 Sets	
1	Vince Carter	100.00
2	Kobe Bryant	75.00
3	Tim Duncan	50.00
4	Kevin Garnett	60.00
5	Allen Iverson	40.00

6	Jason Williams	10.00
7	Shaquille O'Neal	50.00
8	Lamar Odom	30.00
9	Eddie Jones	15.00
10	Stephon Marbury	10.00

2000-01 Ultra Two Ball

		MT
Complete Set (15):		5.00
Common Player:		.25
Inserted 1:3		
Platinums:		15x-25x
Production 100 Sets		
TB1	Lamar Odom	1.25
TB2	Elton Brand	1.25
TB3	Steve Francis	2.50
TB4	Adrian Griffin	.25
TB5	Todd MacCulloch	.25
TB6	Andre Miller	.50
TB7	James Posey	.30
TB8	Wally Szczerbiak	.40
TB9	Ron Artest	.40
TB10	Corey Maggette	.50
TB11	Shawn Marion	.75
TB12	Chucky Atkins	.25
TB13	Vonteego Cummings	.25
TB14	Kenny Thomas	.25
TB15	Richard Hamilton	.40

2000-01 Ultra Two Ball Platinum Edition

		MT
Complete Set (15):		125.00
Common Player:		5.00
Platinums:		15x-25x
Production 100 Sets		
1	Lamar Odom	30.00
2	Elton Brand	30.00
3	Steve Francis	60.00
4	Adrian Griffin	5.00
5	Todd MacCulloch	5.00
6	Andre Miller	10.00
7	James Posey	6.00
8	Wally Szczerbiak	8.00
9	Ron Artest	8.00
10	Corey Maggette	10.00
11	Shawn Marion	15.00
12	Chucky Atkins	5.00
13	Vonteego Cummings	5.00
14	Kenny Thomas	5.00
15	Richard Hamilton	8.00

2000-01 Ultra Year 3

		MT
Complete Set (10):		8.00
Common Player:		.50
Inserted 1:8		
Platinums:		8x-15x
Production 100 Sets		
YT1	Mike Bibby	.75
YT2	Michael Dickerson	.50
YT3	Larry Hughes	1.50
YT4	Raef LaFrentz	.50
YT5	Dirk Nowitzki	1.50
YT6	Michael Olowokandi	.50
YT7	Paul Pierce	1.25
YT8	Jason Williams	1.25
YT9	Vince Carter	6.00
YT10	Antawn Jamison	1.50

2000-01 Ultra Year 3 Platinum Edition

		MT
Complete Set (10):		100.00
Common Player:		5.00
Platinums:		8x-15x
Production 100 Sets		
1	Mike Bibby	8.00
2	Michael Dickerson	5.00
3	Larry Hughes	15.00
4	Raef LaFrentz	5.00
5	Dirk Nowitzki	15.00
6	Michael Olowokandi	5.00
7	Paul Pierce	10.00
8	Jason Williams	10.00
9	Vince Carter	100.00
10	Antawn Jamison	15.00

2001-02 Ultra

		MT
Complete Set (175):		250.00
Common Player:		.25
Minor Stars:		.50
Common Rookie:		3.00
Production 2,222 Sets		
Pack (10):		3.00
Wax Box (24):		60.00
1	Vince Carter	4.00
2	Allen Iverson	2.50
3	Jerry Stackhouse	.75
4	Travis Best	.25
5	Eddie Jones	.60
6	Felipe Lopez	.25
7	Antonio Daniels	.25
8	A.J. Guyton	.25
9	Quentin Richardson	.60
10	Charlie Ward	.25
11	Ron Mercer	.50
12	Shandon Anderson	.25
13	Antawn Jamison	1.00
14	Darius Miles	3.00
15	Anthony Mason	.50
16	Latrell Sprewell	1.00
17	Scottie Pippen	1.00
18	Shammond Williams	.25
19	P.J. Brown	.25
20	Dirk Nowitzki	1.00
21	Mateen Cleaves	.50
22	Tim Hardaway	.50
23	Christian Laettner	.25
24	Toni Kukoc	.50
25	Bob Sura	.25
26	Kobe Bryant	4.00
27	Wally Szczerbiak	.60
28	Darrell Armstrong	.25
29	Chris Webber	1.50
30	David Wesley	.25
31	Michael Finley	.60
32	Jermaine O'Neal	.75
33	Jason Kidd	1.25
34	Tony Delk	.25
35	Avery Johnson	.25
36	Elden Campbell	.25
37	Lamond Murray	.25
38	Ben Wallace	.25
39	Jalen Rose	.50
40	Michael Dickerson	.25
41	Shawn Marion	1.00
42	Jahidi White	.25
43	Jamal Mashburn	.50
44	Trajan Langdon	.25
45	Reggie Miller	.75
46	Stromile Swift	.50
47	Keith Van Horn	.50
48	Tom Gugliotta	.25
49	Brent Barry	.25
50	Courtney Alexander	.50
51	Antonio McDyess	.50
52	Robert Horry	.25
53	Ervin Johnson	.25
54	Speedy Claxton	.50
55	Bryon Russell	.25
56	Baron Davis	.75
57	Robert Traylor	.25
58	Chucky Atkins	.25
59	Stephon Marbury	.75
60	Desmond Mason	.50
61	Tyrone Nesby	.25
62	Brevin Knight	.25
63	Kenyon Martin	.60
64	Jumaine Jones	.25
65	Rashard Lewis	.50
66	Kenny Anderson	.25
67	Andre Miller	.75
68	Joe Smith	.50
69	Kelvin Cato	.25
70	Jason Williams	.60
71	Marcus Camby	.50
72	Eric Snow	.25
73	Gary Payton	.75
74	Robert Pack	.25
75	Brian Cardinal	.25
76	Sam Cassell	.50
77	Allan Houston	.50
78	Anfernee Hardaway	.60
79	Morris Peterson	.60
80	Chris Mihm	.25
81	Elton Brand	1.00
82	Glenn Robinson	.75
83	Damon Stoudamire	.25
84	Alvin Williams	.25
85	Paul Pierce	.75
86	James Posey	.25
87	Cuttino Mobley	.50
88	Tim Thomas	.75
89	Dikembe Mutombo	.50
90	Tim Duncan	1.50
91	John Starks	.25
92	Antoine Walker	.75
93	Moochie Norris	.25
94	Dalibor Bagaric	.25
95	Ray Allen	.75
96	David Robinson	.75
97	Shareef Abdur-Rahim	.75
98	Zhizhi Wang	1.50
99	Chris Porter	.25
100	Chauncey Billups	.25
101	Tracy McGrady	2.00
102	Michael Jordan	8.00
103	Jerome Williams	.25
104	Jason Terry	.50
105	Calvin Booth	.25
106	Shaquille O'Neal	2.00
107	Kevin Garnett	2.50
108	Doug Christie	.25
109	Karl Malone	1.00
110	Steve Nash	.50
111	Austin Croshere	.25
112	Alonzo Mourning	.60
113	Dan Majerle	.25
114	Malik Rose	.25
115	Richard Hamilton	.50
116	DerMarr Johnson	.50
117	Raef LaFrentz	.50
118	Derek Fisher	.25
119	Vlade Divac	.50
120	John Stockton	.75
121	Dion Glover	.25
122	Voshon Lenard	.25
123	Steve Francis	1.50
124	Darvin Ham	.25
125	Aaron McKie	.50
126	Predrag Stojakovic	.75
127	Ron Artest	.25
128	Keyon Dooling	.50
129	Anthony Carter	.25
130	Kurt Thomas	.25
131	Rasheed Wallace	.60
132	Theo Ratliff	.50
133	Eric Piatkowski	.25
134	Terrell Brandon	.50
135	Mike Miller	1.50
136	Mike Bibby	.50
137	Antonio Davis	.25
138	Lamar Odom	1.00
139	Eddie House	.50
140	Nick Van Exel	.75
141	Rick Fox	.25
142	Juwan Howard	.50
143	Hidayet Turkoglu	.50
144	Donyell Marshall	.25
145	Marcus Fizer	.50
146	Larry Hughes	.50
147	Steve Smith	.50
148	Brian Grant	.25
149	Grant Hill	1.25
150	Derek Anderson	.50
151	*Kwame Brown*	12.00
152	*Eddie Griffin*	12.00
153	*Eddy Curry*	10.00
154	*Jamaal Tinsley*	15.00
155	*Jason Richardson*	20.00
156	*Shane Battier*	20.00
157	*Troy Murphy*	6.00
158	*Richard Jefferson*	8.00
159	*DeSagana Diop*	5.00
160	*Tyson Chandler*	12.00
161	*Joe Johnson*	10.00
162	*Zach Randolph*	8.00
163	*Andrei Kirilenko*	10.00
164	*Loren Woods*	6.00
165	*Jason Collins*	3.00
166	*Rodney White*	6.00
167	*Jeryl Sasser*	4.00
168	*Kirk Haston*	4.00
169	*Pau Gasol*	15.00
170	*Kedrick Brown*	4.00
171	*Steven Hunter*	4.00
172	*Michael Bradley*	4.00
173	*Joseph Forte*	8.00
174	*Brandon Armstrong*	4.00
175	*Prmoz Brezec*	3.00
1U	Gerald Wallace	8.00
2U	Tony Parker	12.00
3U	Vladimir Radmanovic	5.00
4U	Trenton Hassell	6.00
5U	Zeljko Rebraca	4.00
6U	Oscar Torres	3.00

2001-02 Ultra Gold Medallion

	MT
Gold Medallion Cards:	2x
Gold Rookies:	3x-6x

2001-02 Ultra League Leaders

		MT
Complete Set (20):		45.00
Common Player:		.75
Minor Stars:		1.50
Inserted 1:20		
Game Worn:		4x-8x
Production 450 Sets		
1LL	Vince Carter	12.00
2LL	Allen Iverson	6.00
3LL	Ray Allen	2.00
4LL	Reggie Miller	1.50
5LL	Karl Malone	2.00
6LL	Jalen Rose	.75
7LL	Baron Davis	1.50
8LL	Tracy McGrady	4.00
9LL	Chris Webber	4.00
10LL	John Stockton	2.00
11LL	Dikembe Mutombo	.75
12LL	Steve Francis	4.00
13LL	Andre Miller	1.50
14LL	Kenyon Martin	1.50
15LL	Mike Miller	4.00
16LL	Antonio Davis	.75
17LL	Darius Miles	7.00
18LL	Latrell Sprewell	2.00
19LL	Cuttino Mobley	.75
20LL	Lamar Odom	3.00

2001-02 Ultra On the Road

		MT
Common Player:		12.00
Inserted 1:156		
1RG	Vince Carter	45.00
2RG	Morris Peterson	12.00
3RG	Rashard Lewis	12.00
4RG	Keith Van Horn	15.00
5RG	Cuttino Mobley	12.00
6RG	Tracy McGrady	25.00
7RG	Tom Gugliotta	12.00
8RG	Dikembe Mutombo	12.00
9RG	Stromile Swift	12.00
10RG	Mike Miller	20.00

2001-02 Ultra 02 Good

		MT
Complete Set (20):		45.00
Common Player:		.75
Minor Stars:		1.50
Inserted 1:20		
Game Worn:		4x-8x
Inserted 1:157		
1TG	Vince Carter	12.00
2TG	Allen Iverson	6.00
3TG	Shawn Marion	2.50
4TG	Jalen Rose	.75
5TG	Steve Francis	4.00
6TG	Kenyon Martin	1.50
7TG	Sam Cassell	.75
8TG	Darius Miles	7.00
9TG	Mike Miller	4.00
10TG	Jason Terry	.75
11TG	Baron Davis	1.50
12TG	Lamar Odom	2.50
13TG	Latrell Sprewell	1.50
14TG	Morris Peterson	.75
15TG	Antonio Davis	.75
16TG	Ray Allen	2.50
17TG	Rashard Lewis	1.50
18TG	Desmond Mason	.75
19TG	Antonio McDyess	1.50
20TG	Keith Van Horn	1.50

2001-02 Ultra 02 Good Signature

		MT
Complete Set (1):		
1TGS	Vince Carter	150.00

2001-02 Ultra Triple-Double Trouble

		MT
Complete Set (15):		70.00
Common Player:		5.00
Inserted 1:72		
Game Worn:		2x
Cards for Kobe, Shaq and Garnett were never released.		
Inserted 1:156		
1TD	Vince Carter	30.00
2TD	Steve Francis	12.00
3TD	Ray Allen	8.00
4TD	Chris Webber	10.00
5TD	Kobe Bryant	30.00
6TD	Kenyon Martin	7.00
7TD	Shaquille O'Neal	15.00
8TD	Kevin Garnett	18.00
9TD	Tracy McGrady	12.00
10TD	Baron Davis	5.00
11TD	Lamar Odom	7.00
12TD	Allen Iverson	18.00
13TD	Antoine Walker	6.00
14TD	Reggie Miller	6.00
15TD	Terrell Brandon	5.00

1961 Union Oil

These 4" x 5-1/2" 12-page booklets feature players and coaches providing some of the finer points of basketball. The booklets were distributed over two years at Union Oil Gas Stations in the Los Angeles area. Front covers have a drawing of the player or coach, a publication (card) number and the Union 76 logo. The eight basketball booklets were part of a multi-sport set of 44.

	NM
Complete Set (10):	200.00
Common Player:	22.00
Frank Burgess	22.00
Jeff Cohen	22.00
Lee Herman	22.00
Rick Herrscher	22.00
Lowery Kirk	22.00
Dave Mills	22.00
Max Perry	22.00
George Price	22.00
Fred Sawyer	22.00
Dale Wise	22.00

1990 Upper Deck Promos

Magic Johnson and Larry Bird are featured on these two prototype cards, created by Upper Deck when it applied for a license from the NBA to produce cards. The card numbers on the back correspond to the players' uniform numbers.

		MT
Complete Set (2):		800.00
32	Magic Johnson	350.00
33	Larry Bird	500.00

1991 Upper Deck Promos

These two promo cards, featuring Michael Jordan and David Robinson, preview the design for Upper Deck's debut basketball set in 1991. The photos are different than those used for the players in the regular set, as are the numbers.

		MT
Complete Set (2):		40.00
Common Player:		20.00
1	Michael Jordan	20.00
400	David Robinson	20.00

1991-92 Upper Deck

Upper Deck made its basketball card debut with this 500-card set. The fronts feature glossy color action photos framed by a hardwood basketball court. Backs have stats and a color action shot which takes up three-fourths of the backs. A triangular hologram is also included on the card back. Subsets include Draft Choices, Classic Confrontations, All-Rookie Team, All-Stars, team checklists, All-Star Skills and Top Prospects. Inserts in the high series of cards (#s 401-500) were cards of Hall of Famer Jerry West, who is featured in a nine-card Basketball Heroes subset. He signed 2,500 of the set's checklist cards.

		MT
Complete Set (500):		20.00
Complete Series 1 (400):		12.00
Complete Series 2 (100):		8.00
Common Player:		.05
Minor Stars:		.10
Series 1 Foil Pack (12):		.80
Series 1 Foil Wax Box (36):		15.00
Series 2 Foil Pack (12):		1.25
Series 2 Foil Wax Box (36):		23.00
1	Stacey Augmon, Rodney Monroe	.05
2	*Larry Johnson*	1.50
3	*Dikembe Mutombo*	1.25
4	*Steve Smith*	.50
5	*Stacey Augmon*	.50
6	*Terrell Brandon*	2.00
7	*Greg Anthony*	.10
8	*Rich King*	.10
9	*Chris Gatling*	.25
10	*Victor Alexander*	.15
11	John Turner	.10
12	*Eric Murdock*	.25
13	*Mark Randall*	.10
14	*Rodney Monroe*	.10
15	Myron Brown	.10
16	*Mike Iuzzolino*	.10
17	*Chris Corchiani*	.10
18	*Elliot Perry*	.25
19	*Jimmy Oliver*	.10
20	*Doug Overton*	.10
21	Steve Hood	.10
22	Michael Jordan	1.00
23	Kevin Johnson	.10
24	Kurk Lee	.05
25	Sean Higgins	.05
26	Morlon Wiley	.05
27	Derek Smith	.05
28	Kenny Payne	.05
29	Magic's Moment (Magic Johnson)	.25
30	Classic Confrontation (Larry Bird, Chuck Person)	.25
31	Classic Confrontation (Karl Malone, Charles Barkley)	.25
32	Classic Confrontation (Kevin Johnson, John Stockton)	.10
33	Classic Confrontation (Hakeem Olajuwon, Patrick Ewing)	.25
34	Classic Confrontation (Magic Johnson, Michael Jordan)	1.25
35	Derrick Coleman (ART)	.10
36	Lionel Simmons (ART)	.05
37	Dee Brown (ART)	.05
38	Dennis Scott (ART)	.05
39	Kendall Gill (ART)	.05
40	Winston Garland	.05
41	Danny Young	.05
42	Rick Mahorn	.05
43	Michael Adams	.05
44	Michael Jordan	3.00
45	Magic Johnson	.50
46	Doc Rivers	.05
47	Moses Malone	.10
48	Michael Jordan	2.00
49	James Worthy (AS)	.05
50	Tim Hardaway (AS)	.10
51	Karl Malone (AS)	.10
52	John Stockton (AS)	.10
53	Clyde Drexler (AS)	.10
54	Terry Porter (AS)	.05
55	Kevin Duckworth (AS)	.05
56	Tom Chambers (AS)	.05
57	Magic Johnson (AS)	.25
58	David Robinson (AS)	.25
59	Kevin Johnson (AS)	.10
60	Chris Mullin (AS)	.10
61	Joe Dumars (AS)	.10
62	Kevin McHale (AS)	.05
63	Brad Daugherty (AS)	.05
64	Alvin Robertson (AS)	.05
65	Bernard King (AS)	.05
66	Dominique Wilkins (AS)	.10
67	Ricky Pierce (AS)	.05
68	Patrick Ewing (AS)	.10
69	Michael Jordan (AS)	2.00
70	Charles Barkley (AS)	.25
71	Hersey Hawkins (AS)	.05
72	Robert Parish (AS)	.05
73	Bucks Team CK (Alvin Robertson)	.05
74	Bullets Team CK (Bernard King)	.05
75	Bulls Team CK (Michael Jordan)	2.00
76	Cavaliers Team CK (Brad Daugherty)	.05
77	Celtics Team CK (Larry Bird)	.40
78	Clippers Team CK (Ron Harper)	.05
79	Hawks Team CK (Dominique Wilkins)	.10
80	Heat Team CK (Rony Seikaly)	.05
81	Hornets Team CK (Rex Chapman)	.05
82	Jazz Team CK (Mark Eaton)	.05
83	Kings Team CK (Lionel Simmons)	.05
84	Knicks Team CK (Gerald Wilkins)	.05
85	Lakers Team CK (James Worthy)	.05
86	Magic Team CK (Scott Skiles)	.05
87	Mavericks Team CK (Rolando Blackman)	.05
88	Nets Team CK (Derrick Coleman)	.10
89	Nuggets Team CK (Chris Jackson)	.05
90	Pacers Team CK (Reggie Miller)	.10
91	Pistons Team CK (Isiah Thomas)	.10
92	Rockets Team CK (Hakeem Olajuwon)	.25
93	76ers Team CK (Hersey Hawkins)	.05
94	Spurs Team CK (David Robinson)	.25
95	Suns Team CK (Tom Chambers)	.05
96	Sonics Team CK (Shawn Kemp)	.40
97	Timberwolves Team CK (Pooh Richardson)	.05
98	Trail Blazers Team CK (Clyde Drexler)	.10
99	Warriors Team CK (Chris Mullin)	.10
100	Checklist	.05
101	John Shasky	.05
102	Dana Barros	.05
103	Stojko Vrankovic	.05
104	Larry Drew	.05
105	Randy White	.05
106	Dave Corzine	.05
107	Joe Kleine	.05
108	Lance Blanks	.05
109	Rodney McCray	.05
110	Sedale Threatt	.05
111	Ken Norman	.05
112	Rickey Green	.05

113	Andy Toolson	.05
114	Bo Kimble	.05
115	Mark West	.05
116	Mark Eaton	.05
117	John Paxson	.05
118	Mike Brown	.05
119	Brian Oliver	.05
120	Will Perdue	.05
121	Michael Smith	.05
122	Sherman Douglas	.05
123	Reggie Lewis	.10
124	James Donaldson	.05
125	Scottie Pippen	.50
126	Elden Campbell	.05
127	Michael Cage	.05
128	Tony Smith	.05
129	Ed Pinckney	.05
130	*Keith Askins*	.05
131	Darrell Griffith	.05
132	Vinnie Johnson	.05
133	Ron Harper	.05
134	Andre Turner	.05
135	Jeff Hornacek	.05
136	John Stockton	.25
137	Derek Harper	.05
138	Loy Vaught	.05
139	Thurl Bailey	.05
140	Olden Polynice	.05
141	Kevin Edwards	.05
142	Byron Scott	.05
143	Dee Brown	.05
144	Sam Perkins	.05
145	Rony Seikaly	.05
146	James Worthy	.05
147	Glen Rice	.10
148	Craig Hodges	.05
149	Bimbo Coles	.05
150	Mychal Thompson	.05
151	Xavier McDaniel	.05
152	Roy Tarpley	.05
153	Gary Payton	.25
154	Rolando Blackman	.05
155	Hersey Hawkins	.05
156	Ricky Pierce	.05
157	Fat Lever	.05
158	Andrew Lang	.05
159	Benoit Benjamin	.05
160	Cedric Ceballos	.50
161	Charles Smith	.05
162	Jeff Martin	.05
163	Robert Parish	.05
164	Danny Manning	.10
165	Mark Aguirre	.05
166	Jeff Malone	.05
167	Bill Laimbeer	.05
168	Willie Burton	.05
169	Dennis Hopson	.05
170	Kevin Gamble	.05
171	Terry Teagle	.05
172	Dan Majerle	.05
173	Shawn Kemp	.60
174	Tom Chambers	.05
175	Vlade Divac	.05
176	Johnny Dawkins	.05
177	A.C. Green	.05
178	Manute Bol	.05
179	Terry Davis	.05
180	Ron Anderson	.05
181	Horace Grant	.15
182	Stacey King	.05
183	William Bedford	.05
184	B.J. Armstrong	.10
185	Dennis Rodman	.75
186	Nate McMillan	.05
187	Cliff Levingston	.05
188	Quintin Dailey	.05
189	Bill Cartwright	.05
190	John Salley	.05
191	Jayson Williams	.05
192	Grant Long	.05
193	Negele Knight	.05
194	Alec Kessler	.05
195	Gary Grant	.05
196	Billy Thompson	.05
197	Delaney Rudd	.05
198	Alan Ogg	.05
199	Blue Edwards	.05
200	Checklist	.05
201	Mark Acres	.05
202	Craig Ehlo	.05
203	Anthony Cook	.05
204	Eric Leckner	.05
205	Terry Catledge	.05
206	Reggie Williams	.05
207	Greg Kite	.05
208	Steve Kerr	.05
209	Kenny Battle	.05
210	John Morton	.05
211	Kenny Williams	.05
212	Mark Jackson	.05
213	Alaa Abdelnaby	.05
214	Rod Strickland	.05
215	Michael Williams	.05
216	Kevin Duckworth	.05
217	David Wingate	.05
218	LaSalle Thompson	.05
219	*John Starks*	.50
220	Cliff Robinson	.10
221	Jeff Grayer	.05
222	Marcus Liberty	.05
223	Larry Nance	.05
224	Michael Ansley	.05
225	Kevin McHale	.05
226	Scott Skiles	.05
227	Darnell Valentine	.05
228	Nick Anderson	.10
229	Brad Davis	.05
230	Gerald Paddio	.05
231	Sam Bowie	.05
232	Sam Vincent	.05
233	George McCloud	.25
234	Gerald Wilkins	.05
235	Mookie Blaylock	.05
236	Jon Koncak	.05
237	Danny Ferry	.05
238	Vern Fleming	.05
239	Mark Price	.10
240	Sidney Moncrief	.05
241	Jay Humphries	.05
242	Muggsy Bogues	.05
243	Tim Hardaway	.10
244	Alvin Robertson	.05
245	Chris Mullin	.10
246	Pooh Richardson	.05
247	Winston Bennett	.05
248	Kevin Upshaw	.05
249	John Williams	.05
250	Steve Alford	.05
251	Spud Webb	.05
252	Sleepy Floyd	.05
253	Chuck Person	.05
254	Hakeem Olajuwon	.60
255	Dominique Wilkins	.10
256	Reggie Miller	.25
257	Dennis Scott	.05
258	Charles Oakley	.05
259	Sidney Green	.05
260	Detlef Schrempf	.05
261	Rod Higgins	.05
262	J.R. Reid	.05
263	Tyrone Hill	.05
264	Reggie Theus	.05
265	Mitch Richmond	.15
266	Dale Ellis	.05
267	Terry Cummings	.05
268	Johnny Newman	.05
269	Doug West	.05
270	Jim Peterson	.05
271	Otis Thorpe	.05
272	John Williams	.05
273	*Kennard Winchester*	.05
274	Duane Ferrell	.05
275	Vernon Maxwell	.05
276	Kenny Smith	.05
277	Jerome Kersey	.05
278	Kevin Willis	.05
279	Danny Ainge	.05
280	Larry Smith	.05
281	Maurice Cheeks	.05
282	Willie Anderson	.05
283	Tom Tolbert	.05
284	Jerrod Mustaf	.05
285	Randolph Keys	.05
286	Jerry Reynolds	.05
287	Sean Elliott	.05
288	Otis Smith	.05
289	*Terry Mills*	.30
290	Kelly Tripucka	.05
291	Jon Sundvold	.05
292	Rumeal Robinson	.05
293	Fred Roberts	.05
294	Rik Smits	.05
295	Jerome Lane	.05
296	Dave Jamerson	.05
297	Joe Wolf	.05
298	*David Wood*	.05
299	Todd Lichti	.05
300	Checklist	.05
301	Randy Bruer	.05
302	Buck Johnson	.05
303	Scott Brooks	.05
304	Jeff Turner	.05
305	Felton Spencer	.05
306	Greg Dreiling	.05
307	Gerald Glass	.05
308	Tony Brown	.05
309	Sam Mitchell	.05
310	Adrian Caldwell	.05
311	Chris Dudley	.05
312	Blair Rasmussen	.05
313	Antoine Carr	.05
314	Greg Anderson	.05
315	Drazen Petrovic	.05
316	Alton Lister	.05
317	Jack Haley	.05
318	Bobby Hansen	.05
319	Mahmoud Abdul-Rauf	.05
320	Herb Williams	.05
321	Kendall Gill	.10
322	Tyrone Corbin	.05
323	Kiki Vandeweghe	.05
324	David Robinson	.60
325	Rex Chapman	.05
326	Tony Campbell	.05
327	Dell Curry	.05
328	Charles Jones	.05
329	Kenny Gattison	.05
330	*Haywoode Workman*	.10
331	Travis Mays	.05
332	Derrick Coleman	.10
333	Isiah Thomas	.15
334	Jud Buechler	.05
335	Joe Dumars	.15
336	Tate George	.05
337	Mike Sanders	.05
338	James Edwards	.05
339	Chris Morris	.05
340	Scott Hastings	.05
341	Trent Tucker	.05
342	Harvey Grant	.05
343	Patrick Ewing	.25
344	Larry Bird	.75
345	Charles Barkley	.50
346	Brian Shaw	.05
347	Kenny Walker	.05
348	Dan Schayes	.05
349	Tom Hammonds	.05
350	Frank Brickowski	.05
351	Terry Porter	.05
352	Orlando Woolridge	.05
353	Buck Williams	.05
354	Sarunas Marciulionis	.05
355	Karl Malone	.25
356	Kevin Johnson	.15
357	Clyde Drexler	.25
358	Duane Causwell	.05
359	Paul Pressey	.05
360	*Jim Les*	.05
361	Derrick McKey	.05
362	*Scott Williams*	.10
363	Mark Alarie	.05
364	Brad Daugherty	.05
365	Bernard King	.05
366	Steve Henson	.05
367	Darrell Walker	.05
368	Larry Krystkowiak	.05
369	Henry James	.05
370	Jack Sikma	.05
371	Eddie Johnson	.05
372	Wayman Tisdale	.05
373	Joe Barry Carroll	.05
374	David Greenwood	.05
375	Lionel Simmons	.05
376	Dwayne Schintzius	.05
377	Tod Murphy	.05
378	Wayne Cooper	.05
379	Anthony Bonner	.05
380	Walter Davis	.05
381	Lester Conner	.05
382	Ledell Eackles	.05
383	Brad Lohaus	.05
384	Derrick Gervin	.05
385	Pervis Ellison	.05
386	Tim McCormick	.05
387	A.J. English	.05
388	John Battle	.05
389	Roy Hinson	.05
390	Armon Gilliam	.05
391	Kurt Rambis	.05
392	Mark Bryant	.05
393	Chucky Brown	.05
394	Avery Johnson	.05
395	Rory Sparrow	.05
396	*Mario Elie*	.25
397	Ralph Sampson	.05
398	Mike Giminski	.05
399	Bill Wennington	.05
400	Checklist	.05
401	David Wingate	.05
402	Moses Malone	.10
403	Darrell Walker	.05
404	Antoine Carr	.05
405	Charles Shackelford	.05
406	Orlando Woolridge	.05
407	*Robert Pack*	.30
408	Bobby Hansen	.05
409	*Dale Davis*	.75
410	*Vincent Askew*	.10
411	Alexander Volkov	.05
412	Dwayne Schintzius	.05
413	Tim Perry	.05
414	Tyrone Corbin	.05
415	*Pete Chilcutt*	.10
416	James Edwards	.05
417	Jerrod Mustaf	.05
418	Thurl Bailey	.05
419	Spud Webb	.05
420	Doc Rivers	.05
421	*Sean Green*	.05
422	Walter Davis	.05
423	Terry Davis	.05
424	John Battle	.05
425	Vinnie Johnson	.05
426	Sherman Douglas	.05
427	*Kevin Brooks*	.05
428	Greg Sutton	.05
429	*Rafael Addison*	.05
430	*Anthony Mason*	1.00
431	*Paul Graham*	.10
432	*Anthony Frederick*	.10
433	Dennis Hopson	.05
434	Rory Sparrow	.05
435	Michael Adams	.05
436	*Kevin Lynch*	.10
437	*Randy Brown*	.10
438	Larry Johnson, Billy Owens (CL)	.50
439	Stacey Augmon (TP)	.30
440	*Larry Stewart* (TP)	.10
441	Terrell Brandon (TP)	.10
442	*Billy Owens* (TP)	.50
443	*Rick Fox* (TP)	.10
444	*Kenny Anderson* (TP)	1.50
445	Larry Johnson (TP)	1.00
446	Dikembe Mutombo	.50
447	Steve Smith (TP)	.30
448	Greg Anthony (TP)	.10
449	East All-Star CL	.10
450	West All-Star CL	.10
451	Isiah Thomas (AS)	.20
452	Michael Jordan (AS)	3.00
453	Scottie Pippen (AS)	.40
454	Charles Barkley (AS)	.50
455	Patrick Ewing (AS)	.25
456	Michael Adams (AS)	.05
457	Dennis Rodman (AS)	.75
458	Reggie Lewis (AS)	.10
459	Joe Dumars (AS)	.10
460	Mark Price (AS)	.10
461	Brad Daugherty (AS)	.05
462	Kevin Willis (AS)	.05
463	Clyde Drexler (AS)	.25
464	Magic Johnson (AS)	.50
465	Chris Mullin (AS)	.10
466	Karl Malone (AS)	.25
467	David Robinson (AS)	.50
468	Tim Hardaway (AS)	.10
469	Jeff Hornacek (AS)	.10
470	John Stockton (AS)	.25
471	Dikembe Mutombo (AS)	.40
472	Hakeem Olajuwon (AS)	.50
473	James Worthy (AS)	.05
474	Otis Thorpe (AS)	.05
475	Dan Majerle (AS)	.05
476	Cedric Ceballos (CL)	.05
477	Nick Anderson (SD)	.05
478	Stacey Augmon (SD)	.05
479	Cedric Ceballos (SD)	.05
480	Larry Johnson (SD)	.50
481	Shawn Kemp (SD)	.60
482	John Starks (SD)	.05
483	T'Wolves (Doug West) (SK)	.05
484	Distance Shootout (Craig Hodges) (SK)	.05
485	*LaBradford Smith*	.05
486	Winston Garland	.05
487	*David Benoit*	.40
488	John Bagley	.05
489	*Mark Macon*	.05
490	Mitch Richmond	.30
491	*Luc Longley*	.50
492	Sedale Threatt	.05
493	*Doug Smith*	.10
494	Travis Mays	.05
495	Xavier McDaniel	.05
496	Brian Shaw	.05
497	*Stanley Roberts*	.10
498	Blair Rasmussen	.05
499	*Brian Williams*	.10
500	Checklist	.05

1991-92 Upper Deck Holograms

These hologram cards were randomly inserted into foil packs and Locker Series boxes of Upper Deck cards. The first six cards were in Upper Deck low series packs; the last three were in Upper Deck high packs. Statistical leaders and award winners are featured in this set. Cards are numbered with an "AW" suffix.

		MT
Complete Set (9):		30.00
Common Player:		.50
1	Michael Jordan	12.00
2	Alvin Robertson	.50
3	John Stockton	1.50
4	Michael Jordan	12.00
5	Detlef Schrempf	.50
6	David Robinson	2.50
7	Derrick Coleman	.50
8	Hakeem Olajuwon	3.00
9	Dennis Rodman	4.00

1991-92 Upper Deck Rookie Standouts

The card design is the same as Upper Deck's regular series, except the right bottom front says "Rookie Standout." Card numbers 1-40, start with the prefix "R." Cards were in the Upper Deck Locker Series boxes and Jumbo packs.

		MT
Complete Set (40):		15.00
Complete Series 1 (20):		5.00
Complete Series 2 (20):		10.00
Common Player:		.25
1	Gary Payton	2.00
2	Dennis Scott	.50
3	Kendall Gill	.50
4	Felton Spencer	.25
5	Bo Kimble	.25
6	Willie Burton	.25
7	Tyrone Hill	.50
8	Loy Vaught	1.00
9	Travis Mays	.25
10	Derrick Coleman	1.00
11	Duane Causwell	.25
12	Dee Brown	.50
13	Gerald Glass	.25
14	Jayson Williams	.25
15	Elden Campbell	.50
16	Negele Knight	.25
17	Mahmoud Abdul-Rauf	.50
18	Danny Ferry	.25
19	Tony Smith	.25
20	Cedric Ceballos	2.00
21	Victor Alexander	.25
22	Terrell Brandon	2.00
23	Rick Fox	.25
24	Stacey Augmon	1.00
25	Mark Macon	.25
26	Larry Johnson	4.00
27	Paul Graham	.25
28	Stanley Roberts	.25
29	Dikembe Mutombo	3.00
30	Robert Pack	.25
31	Doug Smith	.25
32	Steve Smith	1.00
33	Billy Owens	.50
34	David Benoit	.50
35	Brian Williams	.25
36	Kenny Anderson	2.00
37	Greg Anthony	.50
38	Dale Davis	.75
39	Larry Stewart	.25
40	Mike Iuzzolino	.25

1991-92 Upper Deck Jerry West Heroes

These cards, which recap Jerry West's career, were randomly inserted in Upper Deck Series II foil packs. Each card front recaps a significant accomplishment from West's collegiate or professional career. The front has a photo inside a jump ball circle on a basketball court. The card back (numbered 1 of 9, etc.) has a summary of the card front's photo. The Basketball Heroes logo appears on both sides of the card.

		MT
Complete Set (10):		8.00
Common West:		1.00
West Header:		1.50
Autograph West:		150.00
1	NCAA Tournament MVP (Jerry West)	1.00
2	1960 U.S. Team (Jerry West)	1.00
3	1968-69 NBA Playoff MVP (Jerry West)	1.00
4	1969-70 NBA Scoring Lead (Jerry West)	1.00
5	1972 NBA World Championship (Jerry West)	1.00
6	1973-74 25,000 Points (Jerry West)	1.00
7	1979 Basketball H.O.F. (Jerry West)	1.00
8	1982-Present, Front Office Success (Jerry West)	1.00
9	Checklist	1.00
----	Header Card	2.00

1991 Upper Deck Lakers Paris

These cards were issued at the McDonald's Open in Paris, France on Oct. 18, 1991, while the Los Angeles Lakers were representing the NBA. Fans who attended the games were given the cards, which were issued in two packs of five, plus each had a hologram card with the McDonald's logo. There were 60,000 sets produced. Card backs are in French. Cards are numbered with an "M" suffix.

		MT
Complete Set (11):		14.00
Common Player:		.75
1	Elden Campbell	1.00
2	Vlade Divac	1.50
3	A.C. Green	1.50
4	Magic Johnson	6.00
5	Sam Perkins	1.50
6	Byron Scott	1.50
7	Tony Smith	.75
8	Terry Teagle	.75
9	James Worthy	2.00
10	Checklist	.75

1991-92 Upper Deck Sheets

Upper Deck produced these 14 commemorative sheets which were given away at various events during the 1991-92 basketball season. Measuring 8-1/2" x 11", the sheets were printed on card stock and feature a collage of player's and/or coaches' images on the front. The sheets are sequentially numbered. The backs are blank and unnumbered.

		MT
Complete Set (14):		150.00
Common Sheet:		5.00
1	Number 1 Draft Choices - June 26, 1991 (Patrick Ewing, Brad Daugherty, David Robinson, Danny Manning, Pervis Ellison, Derrick Coleman) (12,000) (Number One Picks)	10.00
2	12th National Sports - June 4, 1991 (Brad Daugherty, David Robinson, Danny Manning, Pervis Ellison, Derrick Coleman, Larry Johnson) (12,000) (Collectors Convention)	5.00
3	Philadelphia Sports Heroes-Oct. 17, 1991 (Charles Barkley, Mike Schmidt, Rick Tocchet, Reggie White) (21,500)	10.00
4	McDonald's Open - Oct. 18-19, 1991 (James Worthy, Byron Scott, A.C. Green, Magic Johnson, Sam Perkins, Vlade Divac) (59,000) (Paris, France)	10.00
5	Detroit Pistons vs. - Nov. 27, 1991 (Joe Dumars, Dennis Rodman, Mark Aguirre, Bill Laimbeer, John Salley, Isiah Thomas) (38,500)	7.00
6	All-Star Weekend - Feb. 7-9, 1992 (Larry Nance, Dominique Wilkins (one-hand dunk), Spud Webb, Michael Jordan (one-hand dunk), Michael Jordan (two-hand dunk), Kenny Walker, Dominique Wilkins (two-hand dunk), Dee Brown) (22,000) (Orla	20.00
7	1971-72 World Champion - Feb. 26, 1992 (Wilt Chamberlain, Bill Sharman CO, Jerry West, Pat Riley, Jim McMillian, Gail Goodrich) (22,000) (20th Anniversary)	15.00
8	New York Knicks vs. Minn. Timberwolves Feb. 29, 1992 (Kiki Vandeweghe, Patrick Ewing, Charles Oakley, Gerald Wilkins, John Starks, Anthony Mason, Xavier McDaniel, Mark Jackson) (19,000)	7.00
9	Detroit Pistons vs. L.A. Clippers March 31, 1992 (Bill Laimbeer, John Salley, Isiah Thomas, Orlando Woolridge, Dennis Rodman, Joe Dumars) (38,500)	7.00
10	1992 NCAA Final Four - April 4-6, 1992 (John Wooden, Dean Smith, Adolph Rupp, Bob Knight) (68,000) (Championship Coaches)	15.00
11	Hoop It Up - June 6-7, 1992 (Sarunas Marciulionis, Billy Owens, Tim Hardaway, Victor Alexander, Chris Gatling, Chris Mullin) (15,000) (San Jose, California)	10.00
12	Battle of the Basketball Stars - Undated (Charles Smith, Dominique Wilkins, Pervis Ellison, Kenny Smith, Isiah Thomas, Mitch Richmond, Pooh Richardson, Tim Hardaway) (10,000) (Reportedly issued 6/20/92)	10.00
13	Upper Deck Commemorates the NBA Draft June 24, 1992 (Larry Johnson, Kenny Anderson, Billy Owens, Dikembe Mutombo, Steve Smith, Doug Smith, Luc Longley, Mark Macon) (15,000)	15.00
14	1992 USA Basketball Team - Undated (Christian Laettner, Clyde Drexler, Karl Malone, Patrick Ewing, Chris Mullin, Charles Barkley, Scottie Pippen, Larry Bird, Magic Johnson, Michael Jordan, David Robinson, John Stockton) (80	20.00

1991-92 Upper Deck Stay in School Sheets

Upper Deck produced the commemorative sheets that were given away at Orlando's 1992 All-Star Game Stay in School Jam. The sheets measure 5" x 7" and production was limited to 45,000. Nine other cities were produced and given away at Stay in School events with a production held at 3,000 each.

		MT
Complete Set (10):		50.00
Common Player:		2.00
1	Boston Celtics	6.00
2	Charlotte Hornets	6.00
3	Chicago Bulls	6.00
4	Detroit Pistons	6.00
5	Houston Rockets	6.00
6	Miami Heat	6.00
7	New Jersey Nets	6.00
8	Orlando Magic DP	2.00
9	Portland Trail Blazers	6.00
10	San Antonio Spurs	6.00

1992 Upper Deck Draft Party Sheets

The 8-1/2" x 11" sheets were given away at the 1992 Draft Dat parties hosted by the various NBA teams. The sheets are dated June 24 and numbered out of 7,000. The sheets are unnumbered and feature top draft picks from previous years: Larry Johnson, Derrick Coleman, Pervis Ellison, Danny Manning, David Robinson and Brad Daugherty.

	MT
Complete Set (20):	100.00
Common Player:	6.00
Atlanta Hawks	6.00
Charlotte Hornets	6.00
Chicago Bulls	6.00
Cleveland Cavaliers	6.00
Dallas Mavericks	6.00
Denver Nuggets	6.00
Houston Rockets	6.00
Indiana Pacers	6.00
Los Angeles Clippers	6.00
Los Angeles Lakers	6.00

	Miami Heat	6.00
	Milwaukee Bucks	6.00
	Minnesota Timberwolves	6.00
	New Jersey Nets	6.00
	New York Knicks	6.00
	Portland Trail Blazers	6.00
	Sacramento Kings	6.00
	San Antonio Spurs	6.00
	Utah Jazz	6.00
	Washington Bullets	6.00

1992 Upper Deck European

The 200-card, standard-size set has both Spanish and Italian versions. The cards parallel the U.S. 1991-92 version in design with a simulated hardwood strip along the right side. The player's highlight text is in English/Spanish, English/Italian and the Spanish cards are valued at 1.5 times values listed below.

		MT
Complete Italian Set (200):		50.00
Complete Spanish Set (200):		75.00
Common Italian (1-200):		.15
1	Checklist East All-Stars	1.00
2	Checklist West All-Stars	.50
3	Isiah Thomas AS	.40
4	Michael Jordan AS	3.00
5	Scottie Pippen AS	.75
6	Charles Barkley AS	1.00
7	Patrick Ewing AS	.50
8	Michael Adams AS	.15
9	Dennis Rodman AS	.75
10	Reggie Lewis AS	.25
11	Joe Dumars AS	.25
12	Mark Price AS	.15
13	Brad Daugherty AS	.15
14	Kevin Willis AS	.15
15	Clyde Drexler AS	.50
16	Magic Johnson AS	1.25
17	Chris Mullin AS	.25
18	Karl Malone AS	.50
19	David Robinson AS	1.00
20	Tim Hardaway AS	.25
21	Jeff Hornacek AS	.15
22	John Stockton AS	.50
23	Dikembe Mutombo AS	.50
24	Hakeem Olajuwon AS	1.00
25	James Worthy AS	.25
26	Otis Thorpe AS	.15
27	Dan Majerle AS	.15
28	Stacey Augmon	.50
29	Dominique Wilkins	.40
30	Rumeal Robinson	.15
31	Rick Fox	.40
32	Reggie Lewis	.40
33	Kevin McHale	.50
34	Robert Parish	.40
35	Muggsy Bogues	.25
36	Larry Johnson	1.25
37	Kendall Gill	.25
38	Michael Jordan	6.00
39	Scottie Pippen	2.00
40	Horace Grant	.40
41	Mark Price	.25
42	Brad Daugherty	.25
43	Doug Smith	.15
44	Derek Harper	.25
45	Dikembe Mutombo	1.00
46	Reggie Williams	.15
47	Isiah Thomas	.50
48	Joe Dumars	.40
49	Bill Laimbeer	.25
50	Dennis Rodman	2.50
51	Chris Mullin	.40
52	Tim Hardaway	.40
53	Sarunas Marciulionis	.15
54	Billy Owens	.50
55	Hakeem Olajuwon	2.00
56	Otis Thorpe	.25
57	Reggie Miller	1.00
58	Vern Fleming	.15
59	Detlef Schrempf	.40
60	Rik Smits	.40
61	Danny Manning	.40
62	Ron Harper	.25
63	James Worthy	.40
64	Vlade Divac	.40
65	Byron Scott	.25
66	Sam Perkins	.25
67	Magic Johnson	2.50
68	Rony Seikaly	.15
69	Glen Rice	.50
70	Alvin Robertson	.15
71	Moses Malone	.50
72	Doug West	.15
73	Felton Spencer	.15
74	Derrick Coleman	.40
75	Drazen Petrovic	.25
76	Patrick Ewing	1.00
77	Charles Oakley	.25
78	Scott Skiles	.15
79	Dennis Scott	.40
80	Manute Bol	.15
81	Johnny Dawkins	.25
82	Hersey Hawkins	.25
83	Tom Chambers	.25
84	Kevin Johnson	.40
85	Dan Majerle	.25
86	Clyde Drexler	1.00
87	Terry Porter	.15
88	Kevin Duckworth	.15
89	Mitch Richmond	.50
90	Spud Webb	.25
91	Terry Cummings	.25
92	David Robinson	2.00
93	Sean Elliott	.50
94	Shawn Kemp	1.50
95	Ricky Pierce	.15
96	Eddie Johnson	.25
97	Gary Payton	.75
98	Karl Malone	1.00
99	John Stockton	1.00
100	Checklist	.15
101	Jeff Malone	.25
102	Mark Eaton	.15
103	Michael Adams	.15
104	Bernard King	.15
105	Pervis Ellison	.15
106	Magic's Moment ART	1.25
107	Michael Jordan ART	3.00
108	Stacey Augmon ART	.25
109	Ferdinando Gentile INT	.25
110	Walter Magnifico INT	.40
111	Alberto Rossini INT	.25
112	Carlton Myers INT	.25
113	Riccardo Pittis INT	.25
114	Antonello Riva INT	.25
115	Ario Costa INT	.40
116	Davide Cantarello INT	.25
117	Alberto Vianini INT	.25
118	Claudio Coldebella INT	.25
119	Juan Antonio San Epifanio SNT	.40
120	Javier Fernandez SNT	.25
121	Jose A. Arcega SNT	.25
122	Juan Antonio Orenga SNT	.25
123	Jordi Villacampa SNT	.25
124	Enrique Andreu SNT	.40
125	Jose Antonio Montero SNT	.25
126	Rafael Jofresa SNT	.25
127	Jose Biriukov SNT	.25
128	Santiago Aldama SNT	.25
129	Alberto Herreros SNT	.25
130	Andres Jimenez SNT	.25
131	Hawks Logo	.15
132	Celtics Logo	.15
133	Hornets Logo	.15
134	Bulls Logo	.15
135	Cavaliers Logo	.15
136	Mavericks Logo	.15
137	Nuggets Logo	.15
138	Pistons Logo	.15
139	Warriors Logo	.15
140	Rockets Logo	.15
141	Pacers Logo	.15
142	Clippers Logo	.15
143	Lakers Logo	.15
144	Heat Logo	.15
145	Bucks Logo	.15
146	Timberwolves Logo	.15
147	Nets Logo	.15
148	Knicks Logo	.15
149	Magic Logo	.15
150	76ers Logo	.15
151	Suns Logo	.15
152	Trail Blazers Logo	.15
153	Kings Logo	.15
154	Spurs Logo	.15
155	Suprsonics Logo	.15
156	Jazz Logo	.15
157	Bullets Logo	.15
158	Michael Jordan, Rony Seikaly PO	3.00
159	Kevin McHale, Dale Davis PO	.25
160	Cavaliers/Nets PO	.15
161	Patrick Ewing, Joe Dumars PO	.40
162	Kevin Duckworth PO	.15
163	John Stockton PO	1.00
164	Tim Hardaway, Ricky Pierce PO	.25
165	Kevin Johnson, Sean Elliott PO	.40
166	Knicks/Pippen/Jordan PO	1.00
167	Brad Daugherty PO	.25
168	Terry Porter, Kevin Johnson PO	.25
169	Shawn Kemp, Kevin Malone PO	.75
170	Scottie Pippen, Larry Nance PO	.75
171	Clyde Drexler, Jeff Malone PO	.50
172	Michael Jordan FIN	6.00
173	Cliff Robinson FIN	.50
174	Clyde Drexler, Michael Jordan FIN	3.00
175	Clyde Drexler FIN	1.00
176	Michael Jordan FIN	6.00
177	Michael Jordan FIN	6.00
178	Michael Jordan COC	6.00
179	Drazen Petrovic COC	.25
180	Magic Johnson COC	2.50
181	Michael Jordan COC	6.00
182	Sarunas Marciulionis COC	.15
183	Rik Smits COC	.40
184	Rumeal Robinson WS	.15
185	Luc Longley WS	.40
186	Vlade Divac WS	.40
187	Rik Smits WS	.40
188	Drazen Petrovic WS	.25
189	Detlef Schrempf WS	.40
190	Dominique Wilkins WS	.40
191	Sarunas Marciulionis WS	.15
192	Rick Fox WS	.40
193	Patrick Ewing WS	1.00
194	Manute Bol WS	.15
195	Steve Kerr WS	.15
196	Dikembe Mutombo WS	1.00
197	Hakeem Olajuwon WS	2.00
198	Rony Seikaly WS	.15
199	Carl Herrera WS	.15
200	Checklist Card	.15

1992 Upper Deck European Award Winner Holograms

The nine-card hologram set was inserted every 10 packs of the 1992 European set. The holograms depict league leaders on the fronts with the backs blank. The cards are unnumbered and checklisted below alphabetically.

		MT
Complete Set (9):		40.00
Common Player:		1.00
(1)	Derrick Coleman	1.50
(2)	Michael Jordan MVP	17.00
(3)	Michael Jordan Scoring	17.00
(4)	Hakeem Olajuwon	6.00
(5)	Alvin Robertson	1.00
(6)	David Robinson	6.00
(7)	Dennis Rodman	8.00
(8)	Detlef Schrempf	1.50
(9)	John Stockton	4.00

1992-93 Upper Deck

These card fronts have color action photos; the backs also have a photo and stats. The Bird #32a and Johnson #33a cards were available only in first series packs. They were replaced by Jimmy Jackson (33) and Doug Christie (32) in the second series. A special Magic card (#SP1) was made and is listed at the end of the checklist. One #SP1 appeared in every 2-1/2 foil boxes. Card #1a is a special draft card for Shaquille O'Neal, available after Jan. 1, 1993. The "Trade Upper Deck" card could be returned to Upper Deck for the O'Neal card. It's listed at the end of the prices below. One subset - Scoring Threat - was made.

		MT
Complete Set (514):		55.00
Complete Series 1 (311):		20.00
Complete Series 2 (203):		35.00
Common Player:		.05
Minor Stars:		.10
Low Retail Pack (15):		1.50
Low Retail Wax Box (36):		40.00
Low Hobby Pack (15):		2.50
Low Hobby Wax Box (36):		80.00
High Retail Pack (15):		2.00
High Retail Wax Box (36):		65.00
High Hobby Pack (15):		2.50
High Hobby Wax Box (36):		100.00
1A	Draft Trade Card	.50
1A	Draft Trade Stamped	.25
1	*Shaquille O'Neal* (T)	60.00
1B	Shaquille O'Neal TRADE	12.00
2	*Alonzo Mourning*	3.00
3	*Christian Laettner*	1.50
4	*LaPhonso Ellis*	.25
5	*C. Weatherspoon*	.50
6	*Adam Keefe*	.10
7	*Robert Horry*	.50
8	*Harold Miner*	.25
9	*Bryant Stith*	.30
10	*Malik Sealy*	.20
11	*Anthony Peeler*	.15
12	*Randy Woods*	.10
13	*Tracy Murray*	.10
14	*Tom Gugliotta*	.75
15	*Hubert Davis*	.20
16	*Don MacLean*	.20
17	*Lee Mayberry*	.10
18	*Corey Williams*	.10
19	*Sean Rooks*	.10
20	*Todd Day*	.25
21	Bryant Stith, LaPhonso Ellis (CL)	.10
22	Jeff Hornacek	.05
23	Michael Jordan	3.00
24	John Sailey	.05
25	Andre Turner	.05
26	Charles Barkley	.50
27	Anthony Frederick	.05
28	Mario Elie	.05
29	Olden Polynice	.05
30	Rodney Moore	.05
31	Tim Perry	.05
32	*Doug Christie* (SP)	.50
32a	Magic Johnson (SP)	1.00
33	*Jim Jackson* (SP)	5.00
33a	Larry Bird (SP)	1.50
34	Randy White	.05
35	Bucks Checklist (Frank Brickowski)	.05
36	Bullets Checklist (Michael Adams)	.05
37	Bulls Checklist (Scottie Pippen)	.25
38	Cavaliers Checklist (Mark Price)	.05
39	Celtics Checklist (Robert Parish)	.05
40	Clippers Checklist (Danny Manning)	.05
41	Hawks Checklist (Kevin Willis)	.05
42	Heat Checklist (Glen Rice)	.05
43	Hornets Checklist (Kendall Gill)	.05
44	Jazz Checklist (Karl Malone)	.10
45	Kings Checklist (Mitch Richmond)	.05
46	Knicks Checklist (Patrick Ewing)	.10
47	Lakers Checklist (Sam Perkins)	.05
48	Magic Checklist (Dennis Scott)	.05
49	Mavericks Checklist (Derek Harper)	.05
50	Nets Checklist (Drazen Petrovic)	.05
51	Nuggets Checklist (Reggie Williams)	.05
52	Pacers Checklist (Rik Smits)	.05
53	Pistons Checklist (Joe Dumars)	.05
54	Rockets Checklist (Otis Thorpe)	.05
55	76ers Checklist (Johnny Dawkins)	.05
56	Spurs Checklist (Sean Elliott)	.05
57	Suns Checklist (Kevin Johnson)	.05
58	Supersonics Checklist (Ricky Pierce)	.05
59	Timberwolves Checklist (Doug West)	.05
60	Trail Blazers Checklist (Terry Porter)	.05
61	Warriors Checklist (Tim Hardaway)	.05
62	Michael Jordan, Scottie Pippen (ST)	1.00
63	Kendall Gill, Larry Johnson (ST)	.10
64	Tom Chambers, Kevin Johnson (ST)	.10
65	Tim Hardaway, Chris Mullin (ST)	.10
66	Karl Malone, John Stockton (ST)	.25
67	Michael Jordan (MVP)	1.50
68	Six-Million (Stacey Augmon)	.10
69	Stay in School	.10
70	Alaa Abdelnaby	.05
71	Andrew Lang	.05
72	Larry Krystkowiak	.05
73	Gerald Wilkins	.05
74	Rod Strickland	.05
75	Danny Ainge	.05
76	Chris Corchian	.05
77	Jeff Grayer	.05
78	Eric Murdock	.05
79	Rex Chapman	.05
80	LaBradford Smith	.05
81	Jay Humphries	.05
82	David Robinson	.50
83	William Bedford	.05
84	James Edwards	.05
85	Dan Schayes	.05
86	*Lloyd Daniels*	.10
87	Blue Edwards	.05
88	Dale Ellis	.05
89	Rolando Blackman	.05
90	Checklist	.05
91	Rik Smits	.10
92	Terry Davis	.05
93	Bill Cartwright	.05
94	Avery Johnson	.05
95	Michael Williams	.05
96	Spud Webb	.05
97	Benoit Benjamin	.05
98	Derek Harper	.05
99	Matt Bullard	.05
100	Tyrone Corbin	.05
101	Doc Rivers	.05
102	Tony Smith	.05
103	Doug West	.05
104	Kevin Duckworth	.05
105	Luc Longley	.05
106	Antoine Carr	.05
107	Cliff Robinson	.10
108	Grant Long	.05
109	Terry Porter	.05
110	Steve Smith	.05
111	Brian Williams	.05
112	Karl Malone	.25
113	Reggie Williams	.05
114	Tom Chambers	.05
115	Winston Garland	.05
116	John Stockton	.25
117	Mahmoud Abdul-Rauf	.05
118	Mike Brown	.05
119	Kevin Johnson	.15
120	Reggie Lewis	.05
121	Bimbo Coles	.05
122	Drazen Petrovic	.05
123	Reggie Miller	.25
124	Derrick Coleman	.10
125	Chuck Person	.05
126	Glen Rice	.10
127	Kenny Anderson	.10
128	Willie Burton	.05
129	Chris Morris	.05
130	Patrick Ewing	.25
131	Sean Elliott	.05
132	Clyde Drexler	.25
133	Scottie Pippen	1.00
134	Pooh Richardson	.05
135	Horace Grant	.15
136	Hakeem Olajuwon	.75
137	John Paxson	.05
138	Kendall Gill	.05
139	Michael Adams	.05
140	Otis Thorpe	.05
141	Dennis Scott	.10
142	Stacey Augmon	.05
143	Robert Pack	.05
144	Kevin Willis	.05
145	Jerome Kersey	.05
146	Paul Graham	.05
147	Stanley Roberts	.05
148	Dominique Wilkins	.20
149	Scott Skiles	.05
150	Rumeal Robinson	.05
151	Mookie Blaylock	.05
152	Elden Campbell	.05
153	Chris Dudley	.05
154	Sedale Threatt	.05
155	Tate George	.05
156	James Worthy	.05
157	B.J. Armstrong	.05
158	Gary Payton	.20
159	Ledell Eackles	.05
160	Sam Perkins	.05
161	Nick Anderson	.05
162	Mitch Richmond	.10
163	Buck Williams	.05
164	Blair Rasmussen	.05
165	Vern Fleming	.05
166	Duane Ferrell	.05
167	George McCloud	.05
168	Terry Cummings	.05
169	Detlef Schrempf	.05
170	Willie Anderson	.05
171	Scott Williams	.05
172	Vernon Maxwell	.05
173	Todd Lichti	.05
174	David Benoit	.05
175	Marcus Liberty	.05
176	Kenny Smith	.05
177	Dan Majerle	.05
178	Jeff Malone	.05
179	Robert Parish	.10
180	Mark Eaton	.05
181	Rony Seikaly	.05
182	Tony Campbell	.05
183	Kevin McHale	.10
184	Thurl Nailey	.05
185	Kevin Edwards	.05
186	Gerald Glass	.05
187	Hersey Hawkins	.05
188	Sam Mitchell	.05
189	Brian Shaw	.05
190	Felton Spencer	.05
191	Mark Macon	.05
192	Jerry Reynolds	.05
193	Dale Davis	.05
194	Sleepy Floyd	.05
195	A.C. Green	.05
196	Terry Catledge	.05
197	Byron Scott	.05
198	Sam Bowie	.05
199	Vlade Divac	.05
200	Checklist	.05
201	Brad Lohaus	.05
202	Johnny Newman	.05
203	Gary Grant	.05
204	Sidney Green	.05
205	Frank Brickowski	.05
206	Anthony Bowie	.05
207	Duane Causwell	.05
208	A.J. English	.05
209	Mark Aguirre	.05
210	Jon Koncak	.05
211	Kevin Gamble	.05
212	Craig Ehlo	.05
213	Herb Williams	.05
214	Cedric Ceballos	.05
215	Mark Jackson	.05
216	John Bagley	.05
217	Ron Anderson	.05
218	John Battle	.05
219	Kevin Lynch	.05
220	Donald Hodge	.05
221	Chris Gatling	.05
222	Muggsy Bogues	.05
223	Bill Laimbeer	.05
224	Anthony Bonner	.05
225	Fred Roberts	.05
226	Larry Stewart	.05
227	Darrell Walker	.05
228	Larry Smith	.05
229	Billy Owens	.05
230	Vinnie Johnson	.05
231	Johnny Dawkins	.05
232	Rick Fox	.05
233	Travis Mays	.05
234	Mark Price	.10
235	Derrick McKey	.05
236	Greg Anthony	.05
237	Doug Smith	.05
238	Alec Kessler	.05
239	Anthony Mason	.05
240	Shawn Kemp	.40
241	Jim Les	.05
242	Dennis Rodman	1.00
243	Lionel Simmons	.05
244	Pervis Ellison	.05
245	Terrell Brandon	.05
246	Mark Bryant	.05
247	Brad Daugherty	.05
248	Scott Brooks	.05
249	Sarunas Marciulionis	.05
250	Danny Ferry	.05
251	Loy Vaught	.05
252	Dee Brown	.05
253	Alvin Robertson	.05
254	Charles Smith	.05
255	Dikembe Mutombo	.30
256	Greg Kite	.05
257	Ed Pinckney	.05
258	Ron Harper	.05
259	Elliott Perry	.05
260	Rafael Addison	.05
261	Tim Hardaway	.10
262	Randy Brown	.05
263	Isiah Thomas	.15
264	Victor Alexander	.05
265	Wayman Tisdale	.05
266	Harvey Grant	.05
267	Mike Iuzzolino	.05
268	Joe Dumars	.15
269	Xavier McDaniel	.05
270	Jeff Sanders	.05
271	Danny Manning	.10
272	Jayson Williams	.05
273	Ricky Pierce	.05
274	Will Perdue	.05
275	Dana Barros	.05
276	Randy Breuer	.05
277	Manute Bol	.05
278	Negele Knight	.05
279	Rodney McCray	.05
280	Greg Sutton	.05
281	Larry Nance	.05
282	John Starks	.10
283	Pete Chilcutt	.05
284	Kenny Gattison	.05
285	Stacey King	.05
286	Bernard King	.05
287	Larry Johnson	.50
288	John Williams	.05
289	Dell Curry	.05
290	Orlando Woolridge	.05
291	Nate McMillan	.05
292	Terry Mills	.05
293	Sherman Douglas	.05
294	Charles Shackleford	.05
295	Ken Norman	.05
296	LaSalle Thompson	.05
297	Chris Mullin	.10
298	Eddie Johnson	.05
299	Armon Gilliam	.05
300	Michael Cage	.05
301	Moses Malone	.05
302	Charles Oakley	.05
303	David Wingate	.05
304	Steve Kerr	.05
305	Tyrone Hill	.05
306	Mark West	.05
307	Fat Lever	.05
308	J.R. Reid	.05
309	Ed Nealy	.05
310	Checklist	.05
311	Alaa Abdelnaby	.05
312	Stacey Augmon	.05
313	*Anthony Avent*	.10
314	*Walter Bond*	.05
315	*Byron Houston*	.10
316	Rick Mahorn	.05
317	Sam Mitchell	.05
318	Mookie Blaylock	.05
319	Lance Blanks	.05
320	John Williams	.05
321	Rolando Blackman	.05
322	Danny Ainge	.05
323	Gerald Glass	.05
324	Robert Pack	.05
325	*Oliver Miller*	.20
326	Charles Smith	.05
327	Duane Ferrell	.05
328	Pooh Richardson	.05
329	Scott Brooks	.05
330	*Walt Williams*	.50
331	Andrew Lang	.05
332	Eric Murdock	.05
333	Vinny Del Negro	.05
334	Charles Barkley	.50
335	James Edwards	.05
336	Xavier McDaniel	.05
337	Paul Graham	.05
338	David Wingate	.05
339	*Richard Dumas*	.10
340	Jay Humphries	.05
341	Mark Jackson	.05
342	John Salley	.05
343	Jon Koncak	.05
344	Rodney McCray	.05
345	Chuck Person	.05
346	Mario Elie	.05
347	Frank Johnson	.05
348	Rumeal Robinson	.05
349	Terry Mills	.05
350	Team fact card (Atlanta)	.05
351	Team fact card (Boston)	.05
352	Team fact card (Charlotte)	.05
353	Team fact card (Chicago)	.05
354	Team fact card (Cleveland)	.05
355	Team fact card (Dallas)	.05
356	Team fact card (Denver)	.05
357	Team fact card (Detroit)	.05
358	Team fact card (Golden State)	.05
359	Team fact card (Houston)	.05
360	Team fact card (Indiana)	.05
361	Team fact card (Los Angeles Clippers)	.05
362	Team fact card (Los Angeles Lakers)	.05
363	Team fact card (Miami)	.05
364	Team fact card (Milwaukee)	.05
365	Team fact card (Minnesota)	.05
366	Team fact card (New Jersey)	.05
367	Team fact card (New York)	.05
368	Team fact card (Orlando)	.05
369	Team fact card (Philadelphia)	.05
370	Team fact card (Phoenix)	.05
371	Team fact card (Portland)	.05
372	Team fact card (Sacramento)	.05
373	Team fact card (San Antonio)	.05
374	Team fact card (Seattle)	.05
375	Team fact card (Utah)	.05
376	Team fact card (Washington)	.05
377	Buck Johnson	.05
378	*Brian Howard*	.05
379	Travis May	.05
380	Jud Buechler	.05
381	*Matt Geiger*	.10
382	*Bob McCann*	.05
383	Cedric Ceballos	.05
384	Rod Strickland	.05
385	Kiki Vandeweghe	.05
386	*Latrell Sprewell*	1.50
387	Larry Krystkowiak	.05
388	Dale Ellis	.05
389	Trent Tucker	.05
390	Negele Knight	.05
391	Stanley Roberts	.05
392	Tony Campbell	.05
393	Tim Perry	.05
394	Doug Overton	.05
395	Dan Majerle	.10
396	*Duane Cooper*	.10
397	Kevin Willis	.05
398	Michael Williams	.05
399	Avery Johnson	.05
400	Dominique Wilkins	.20
401	*Chris Smith*	.10
402	Blair Rasmussen	.05
403	Jeff Hornacek	.05
404	Blue Edwards	.05
405	Olden Polynice	.05
406	Jeff Graver	.05
407	*Tony Bennett*	.10
408	Don MacLean	.10
409	Tom Chambers	.05
410	*Keith Jennings*	.10
411	Gerald Wilkins	.05
412	Kennard Winchester	.05
413	Doc Rivers	.05
414	*Brent Price*	.10
415	Mark West	.05
416	J.R. Reid	.05
417	*Jon Barry*	.10
418	Kevin Johnson	.15
419	Checklist	.05
420	Checklist	.05
421	NBA All-Star Game Checklist	.05
422	Scottie Pippen (AS)	.25
423	Larry Johnson (AS)	.20
424	Shaquille O'Neal (AS)	3.00
425	Michael Jordan (AS)	1.50
426	Isiah Thomas (AS)	.10
427	Brad Daugherty (AS)	.05
428	Joe Dumars (AS)	.10
429	Patrick Ewing (AS)	.10
430	Larry Nance (AS)	.05
431	Mark Price (AS)	.10
432	Detlef Schrempf (AS)	.05
433	Dominique Wilkins (AS)	.10
434	Karl Malone (AS)	.10
435	Charles Barkley (AS)	.30
436	David Robinson (AS)	.30
437	John Stockton (AS)	.10
438	Clyde Drexler (AS)	.15

439	Sean Elliott (AS)	.05
440	Tim Hardaway (AS)	.10
441	Shawn Kemp (AS)	.30
442	Dan Majerle (AS)	.05
443	Danny Manning (AS)	.05
444	Hakeem Olajuwon (AS)	.40
445	Terry Porter (AS)	.05
446	Harold Miner (FACE)	.10
447	David Benoit (FACE)	.05
448	Cedric Ceballos (FACE)	.05
449	Mahmoud Abdul-Rauf (FACE)	.05
450	Tim Perry (FACE)	.05
451	Kevin Smith (FACE)	.05
452	C. Weatherspoon (FACE)	.20
453a	Michael Jordan (FACE)	1.50
453b	Michael Jordan Err.	30.00
454a	Dominique Wilkins (FACE)	.20
454b	Dominique Wilkins Err.	4.00
455	Top Prospects CL	.10
456	Adam Keefe (TP)	.10
457	Alonzo Mourning (TP)	.75
458	Jim Jackson (TP)	.50
459	Sean Rooks (TP)	.10
460	LaPhonso Ellis (TP)	.10
461	Bryant Stith (TP)	.10
462	Byron Houston (TP)	.10
463	Latrell Sprewell (TP)	.30
464	Robert Horry (TP)	.25
465	Malik Sealy (TP)	.10
466	Doug Christie (TP)	.10
467	Duane Cooper (TP)	.10
468	Anthony Peeler (TP)	.10
469	Harold Miner (TP)	.10
470	Todd Day (TP)	.10
471	Lee Mayberry (TP)	.10
472	Christian Laettner (TP)	.20
473	Hubert Davis (TP)	.10
474	Shaquille O'Neal (TP)	3.00
475	C. Weatherspoon (TP)	.20
476	Richard Dumas (TP)	.10
477	Oliver Miller (TP)	.10
478	Tracy Murray (TP)	.10
479	Walt Williams (TP)	.20
480	Lloyd Daniels (TP)	.10
481	Tom Gugliotta (TP)	.10
482	Brent Price (TP)	.10
483	NBA Game Faces (Mark Aguirre)	.05
484	NBA Game Faces (Frank Brickowski)	.05
485	NBA Game Faces (Derrick Coleman)	.10
486	NBA Game Faces (Clyde Drexler)	.20
487	NBA Game Faces (Harvey Grant)	.05
488	NBA Game Faces (Michael Jordan)	1.50
489	NBA Game Faces (Karl Malone)	.15
490	NBA Game Faces (Xavier McDaniel)	.05
491	NBA Game Faces (Drazen Petrovic)	.05
492	NBA Game Faces (John Starks)	.05
493	NBA Game Faces (Robert Parish)	.05
494	NBA Game Faces (Christian Laettner)	.15
495	NBA Games Faces (Ron Harper)	.05
496	NBA Game Faces (David Robinson)	.20
497	NBA Game Faces (John Salley)	.05
498	Brad Daugherty, Mark Price (ST)	.05
499	Dikembe Mutombo, Chris Jackson (ST)	.10
500	Isiah Thomas, Joe Dumars (ST)	.10
501	Hakeem Olajuwon, Otis Thorpe (ST)	.20
502	Derrick Coleman, Drazen Petrovic (ST)	.10
503	Clyde Drexler, Terry Porter	.10
504	Lionel Simmons, Mitch Richmond (ST)	.10
505	David Robinson, Sean Elliott (ST)	.10
506	Michael Jordan (FAN)	1.50
507	Larry Bird (FAN)	.50
508	Karl Malone (FAN)	.15
509	Dikembe Mutombo (FAN)	.15
510	Larry Bird, Michael Jordan (Fan.)	1.00
SP1	Larry Bird, Ervin Johnson (Retire)	3.00
SP2	Dominique Wilkins, Michael Jordan	7.00
1SP	Magic/Bird (SP)	5.00

1992-93 Upper Deck All-Division

Cards from this 20-card set were randomly inserted in 1992-93 Upper Deck Series II jumbo packs. Each card represents one of the top five players in each of four divisions. The cards are numbered AD1-AD20 and each has a special logo representing its division, plus a full-bleed action photo and a black/team color-coded bar at the bottom. The bar, outlined with gold foil, contains the player's name and position. The backs have career highlights against a light blue background. A map of the United States shows the player's division.

		MT
	Complete Set (20):	25.00
	Common Player:	.25
1	Shaquille O'Neal	12.00
2	Derrick Coleman	.50
3	Glen Rice	.25
4	Reggie Lewis	.25
5	Kenny Anderson	.50
6	Brad Daugherty	.25
7	Dominique Wilkins	.50
8	Larry Johnson	1.00
9	Michael Jordan	8.00
10	Mark Price	.25
11	David Robinson	1.50
12	Karl Malone	1.00
13	Sean Elliott	.25
14	John Stockton	1.00
15	Derek Harper	.25
16	Kevin Duckworth	.25
17	Chris Mullin	.50
18	Charles Barkley	1.50
19	Tim Hardaway	.50
20	Clyde Drexler	1.00

1992-93 Upper Deck All-NBA

This set features NBA first team members in gold foil and second team players in silver. The cards, which were only in the Locker Series boxes, have a full-bleed design. The backs have a player biography and are numbered AN1-AN10.

		MT
	Complete Set (10):	70.00
	Common Player:	2.00
1	Michael Jordan	50.00
2	Clyde Drexler	5.00
3	David Robinson	6.00
4	Karl Malone	3.00
5	Chris Mullin	2.00
6	John Stockton	3.00
7	Tim Hardaway	2.00
8	Patrick Ewing	3.00
9	Scottie Pippen	10.00
10	Charles Barkley	6.00

1992-93 Upper Deck All-Rookies

This subset, available in Upper Deck low foil packs, features the top 10 rookies from 1991-92; both the first and second team players are represented. Fronts have an "All-Rookie Team" logo. Cards are numbered AR1-AR10.

		MT
	Complete Set (10):	10.00
	Common Player:	.50
1	Larry Johnson	5.00
2	Dikembe Mutombo	3.00
3	Billy Owens	1.00
4	Steve Smith	1.50
5	Stacey Augmon	1.00
6	Rick Fox	.50
7	Terrell Brandon	1.50
8	Larry Stewart	.50
9	Stanley Roberts	.50
10	Mark Macon	.50

1992-93 Upper Deck Holograms

This subset features hologram cards honoring NBA leaders in six categories. Cards, numbered AW1-AW6, were available in Upper Deck low foil packs; AW7-AW9 were in high series packs.

		MT
	Complete Set (9):	30.00
	Complete Series 1 (6):	15.00
	Complete Series 2 (3):	15.00
	Common Player:	.50
1	Michael Jordan	12.00
2	John Stockton	1.00
3	Dennis Rodman	3.00
4	Detlef Schrempf	.50
5	Larry Johnson	1.50
6	David Robinson	2.00
7	David Robinson	2.00
8	John Stockton	1.00
9	Michael Jordan	12.00

1992-93 Upper Deck Larry Bird Heroes

These 10 cards commemorate Larry Bird's basketball career from his collegiate days at Indiana State University to his career with the Boston Celtics. The fronts have a black border along the left side and bottom; "Basketball Heroes, Larry Bird" is inside these areas. Each back has a career summary against a background which fades from white to green. Numbering continues the Upper Deck Basketball Heroes series.

		MT
	Complete Set (10):	10.00
	Common Bird:	1.00
19	Larry Bird (1979 College Player of the Year)	1.00
20	Larry Bird (1979-80 Rookie of the Year)	1.00
21	Larry Bird (1980-92 12-Time NBA All-Star)	1.00
22	Larry Bird (1981-86 Three NBA Championships)	1.00
23	Larry Bird (1984-86 3-Time NBA MVP)	1.00
24	Larry Bird (1986-88 3-Point King)	1.00
25	Larry Bird (1990 20,000 Points)	1.00
26	Larry Bird (Larry Legend)	1.00
27	Larry Bird (Portrait by Alan Studt)	1.00
NNO	Larry Bird (Title/Header Card)	2.00

1992-93 Upper Deck Wilt Chamberlain Heroes

Wilt Chamberlain's career is recapped in this 10-card set. Cards were inserted in Upper Deck low series foil packs, jumbo packs, and Locker Series. The odds of finding a Wilt Heroes card in a foil box are 1 in 9. The cards are numbered beginning with #10 as a continuation of the Jerry West Basketball Heroes set from the year before.

		MT
	Complete Set (10):	6.00
	Common Chamberlain:	.60
	Chamberlain Header (NNO):	2.00
10	College Star 1956-58 (Wilt Chamberlain)	.60
11	Harlem Globetrotter 1958-59 (Wilt Chamberlain)	.60
12	NBA Rookie of the Year 1960 (Wilt Chamberlain)	.60
13	100-Point Game 1962 (Wilt Chamberlain)	.60
14	Four-Time NBA MVP 1960-68 (Wilt Chamberlain)	.60
15	Four-Time NBA MVP 1960-68 (Wilt Chamberlain)	.60
16	30,000 Point Plateau 1971-72 (Wilt Chamberlain)	.60
17	Basketball Hall of Fame 78' (Wilt Chamberlain)	.60
18	Checklist (Wilt Chamberlain)	.60
----	Header Card (Wilt Chamberlain)	2.00

1992-93 Upper Deck Wilt Chamberlain Box Bottom

		MT
	Complete Set (1):	1.00
	Common Player:	1.00
NNO	Wilt Chamberlain	1.00

1992-93 Upper Deck 15000-Point Club

This 20-card set features active NBA players who have scored 15,000 points in their pro careers. Cards, which are numbered 1-20 with a "PC" prefix, were randomly inserted in Series II hobby packs (1 in 9) distributed to hobby shops. The card front has team color-coded stripes which border a color action photo. "15,000 Point Club" is in the top stripe; the player's name and position are in the lower stripe. A gold set logo, providing the season the player joined the club, is also on the front. The back is numbered using a PC prefix and features a small photo at the top, next to annual scoring totals. A recap of the player's career is also given.

		MT
	Complete Set (20):	80.00
	Common Player:	2.00
1	Dominique Wilkins	3.00
2	Kevin McHale	3.00
3	Robert Parish	3.00
4	Michael Jordan	60.00
5	Isiah Thomas	4.00
6	Mark Aguirre	2.00
7	Kiki Vandeweghe	2.00
8	James Worthy	2.00
9	Rolando Blackman	2.00
10	Moses Malone	2.00
11	Charles Barkley	10.00
12	Tom Chambers	2.00
13	Clyde Drexler	6.00
14	Terry Cummings	2.00
15	Eddie Johnson	2.00
16	Karl Malone	6.00
17	Bernard King	2.00
18	Larry Nance	2.00
19	Jeff Malone	2.00
20	Hakeem Olajuwon	12.00

1992-93 Upper Deck Foreign Exchange

This 10-card subset features players born overseas who have made an impact on the NBA. Cards, which are numbered 1-10 with an "FE" prefix, were in 1992-93 Upper Deck Locker Box Series II packs. The card front incorporates the colors of the player's native country into the design and uses the set's logo, too. A full-bleed, color photo is bordered at the top by "Upper Deck" and at the bottom by the player's name, position and native country. The card back has another color photo on the top half of the card; a career summary is underneath. A flag from the player's native country appears in the lower right corner.

		MT
	Complete Set (10):	20.00
	Common Player:	1.00
	Minor Stars:	2.00
1	Manute Bol	1.00
2	Vlade Divac	1.00
3	Patrick Ewing	4.00
4	Sarunas Marciulionis	1.00
5	Dikembe Mutombo	4.00
6	Hakeem Olajuwon	10.00
7	Drazen Petrovic	1.00
8	Detlef Schrempf	1.00
9	Rik Smits	2.00
10	Dominique Wilkins	2.00

1992-93 Upper Deck Rookie Standouts

This 20-card insert set features the top rookies during the 1992-93 NBA season. Cards were randomly inserted into 1992-93 Upper Deck Series II packs and red jumbo packs (1 in 9). The card front has a full-bleed color action photo, plus the set's logo, which appears at the bottom of the card. The player's name is also at the bottom in a blue stripe. The back has another action photo, plus a career summary inside a gold box. The player's name is in a red banner at the top of the card, near the set's name and a card number, which uses an "RS" prefix.

		MT
	Complete Set (20):	30.00
	Common Player:	.50
1	Adam Keefe	.50
2	Alonzo Mourning	6.00
3	Sean Rooks	.50
4	LaPhonso Ellis	.50
5	Latrell Sprewell	3.00
6	Robert Horry	1.00
7	Malik Sealy	.50
8	Anthony Peeler	.50
9	Harold Miner	.50
10	Anthony Avent	.50
11	Todd Day	1.00
12	Lee Mayberry	.50
13	Christian Laettner	1.00
14	Hubert Davis	.50
15	Shaquille O'Neal	20.00
16	C. Weatherspoon	1.50
17	Richard Dumas	.50
18	Walt Williams	1.00
19	Lloyd Daniels	.50
20	Tom Gugliotta	2.00

1992-93 Upper Deck Team MVP's

This subset features a top player from each NBA team. Cards, numbered TM1-TM28, were produced in color and black-and-white. One "Team MVP" was inserted into each Upper Deck low series jumbo packs.

		MT
	Complete Set (28):	75.00
	Common Player:	1.00
	Minor Stars:	2.00
1	Michael Jordan (CL)	40.00
2	Dominique Wilkins	2.00
3	Reggie Lewis	1.00
4	Kendall Gill	1.00
5	Michael Jordan	40.00
6	Brad Daugherty	1.00
7	Derek Harper	1.00
8	Dikembe Mutombo	2.00
9	Isiah Thomas	2.00
10	Chris Mullin	2.00
11	Hakeem Olajuwon	8.00
12	Reggie Miller	4.00
13	Ron Harper	1.00
14	James Worthy	1.00
15	Rony Seikaly	1.00
16	Alvin Robertson	1.00
17	Pooh Richardson	1.00
18	Derrick Coleman	2.00
19	Patrick Ewing	4.00
20	Scott Skiles	1.00
21	Hersey Hawkins	1.00
22	Kevin Johnson	2.00
23	Clyde Drexler	4.00
24	Mitch Richmond	2.00
25	David Robinson	7.00
26	Ricky Pierce	1.00
27	John Stockton	4.00
28	Pervis Ellison	1.00

1992-93 Upper Deck Jerry West Selects

This set consists of Jerry West's selections of the top 10 among present and future NBA greats in several categories. The fronts are color action photos. The backs, which have West's photo, also have a player photo and West's comments about the player. Cards were inserted into foil boxes and precede the Wilt Chamberlain Heroes set. The cards have a "JW" suffix.

		MT
	Complete Set (20):	90.00
	Common Player:	1.00
	Minor Stars:	2.00
1	Michael Jordan	20.00
2	Dennis Rodman	7.00
3	David Robinson	5.00
4	Michael Jordan	20.00
5	Magic Johnson	5.00
6	Detlef Schrempf	1.00
7	Magic Johnson	5.00
8	Michael Jordan	20.00
9	Michael Jordan	20.00
10	Magic Johnson	5.00
11	Glen Rice	1.00
12	Dikembe Mutombo	2.00
13	Dikembe Mutombo	2.00
14	Stacey Augmon	1.00
15	Tim Hardaway	2.00
16	Shawn Kemp	5.00
17	Danny Manning	1.00
18	Larry Johnson	3.00
19	Reggie Lewis	1.00
20	Tim Hardaway	2.00

1992-93 Upper Deck McDonald's

The 103-card, standard-size set was issued by participating McDonald's restaurants in three-card packs - which retailed for 59¢ or were free with a purchase of an Extra Value Meal. The packs typically contained two player cards (one regional) and an instant-win card. The instant-win cards awarded collectors with various prizes, including a special jersey, a one-day NBA salary and a meeting with Michael Jordan.

		MT
	Complete Set (103):	70.00
	Complete Fact. Set (103):	70.00
	Complete Nat. Set (50):	10.00
	Complete Bost. Set (10):	8.00
	Complete Chi. Set (12):	15.00
	Complete Cle. Set (10):	8.00
	Complete LA Set (10):	8.00
	Complete Orl. Set (10):	12.00
	Common Player (P1-P50):	.05
	Common Celtics (BT1-BT10):	.50
	Common Bulls (CH1-CH12):	.50
	Common Cavs (CL1-CL-10):	.50
	Common Lakers (LA1-LA10):	.50
	Common Magic (OR1-OR10):	.50
P1	Dominique Wilkins	.10
P2	Reggie Lewis	.10
P3	Kevin McHale	.20
P4	Larry Johnson	.30
P5	Michael Jordan	3.00
P6	Horace Grant	.10
P7	Brad Daugherty	.10
P8	Mark Price	.10
P9	Derek Harper	.10
P10	Dikembe Mutombo	.20

P11	Joe Dumars	.10
P12	Isiah Thomas	.20
P13	Tim Hardaway	.15
P14	Chris Mullin	.15
P15	Hakeem Olajuwon	.50
P16	Otis Thorpe	.10
P17	Detlef Schrempf	.10
P18	Reggie Miller	.30
P19	Ron Harper	.10
P20	Danny Manning	.15
P21	James Worthy	.15
P22	Sam Perkins	.10
P23	Rony Seikaly	.05
P24	Steve Smith	.15
P25	Alvin Robertson	.05
P26	Derrick Coleman	.10
P27	Drazen Petrovic	.10
P28	Patrick Ewing	.40
P29	Scott Skiles	.05
P30	Hersey Hawkins	.10
P31	Dan Majerle	.10
P32	Kevin Johnson	.15
P33	Clyde Drexler	.40
P34	Terry Porter	.05
P35	Spud Webb	.10
P36	Antoine Carr	.05
P37	David Robinson	.60
P38	Shawn Kemp	.40
P39	Ricky Pierce	.05
P40	Karl Malone	.40
P41	John Stockton	.40
P42	Michael Adams	.05
P43	Shaquille O'Neal	2.50
P44	Alonzo Mourning	1.25
P45	Christian Laettner	.50
P46	LaPhonso Ellis	.15
P47	Walt Williams	.40
P48	Todd Day	.15
P49	Clarence Weatherspoon	.40
P50	Tom Gugliotta	.40
BT1	Dee Brown	1.00
BT2	Sherman Douglas	1.00
BT3	Rick Fox	1.00
BT4	Kevin Gamble	.50
BT5	Joe Kleine	.50
BT6	Reggie Lewis	2.00
BT7	Xavier McDaniel	.50
BT8	Kevin McHale	2.50
BT9	Robert Parish	2.00
BT10	Ed Pickney	.50
CH1	B.J. Armstrong	1.00
CH2	Bill Cartwright	.50
CH3	Horace Grant	2.00
CH4	Michael Jordan	10.00
CH5	Stacey King	.50
CH6	Rodney McCray	.50
CH7	John Paxson	1.00
CH8	Will Perdue	.50
CH9	Scottie Pippen	4.00
CH10	Trent Tucker	.50
CH11	Corey Williams	.50
CH12	Scott Williams	.50
CL1	John Battle	.50
CL2	Terrell Brandon	2.00
CL3	Brad Daugherty	1.00
CL4	Craig Ehlo	.50
CL5	Danny Ferry	1.00
CL6	Larry Nance	1.00
CL7	Mark Price	1.00
CL8	Mike Sanders	.50
CL9	Gerald Wilkins	.50
CL10	Hot Rod Williams	1.00
LA1	Elden Campbell	1.00
LA2	Duane Cooper	.50
LA3	Vlade Divac	1.00
LA4	James Edwards	.50
LA5	A.C. Green	1.00
LA6	Anthony Peeler	2.00
LA7	Sam Perkins	1.00
LA8	Byron Scott	1.00
LA9	Sedale Threatt	.50
LA10	James Worthy	2.00
OR1	Nick Anderson	1.00
OR2	Anthony Bowie	.50
OR3	Terry Catledge	.50
OR4	Greg Kite	.50
OR5	Shaquille O'Neal	8.00
OR6	Jerry Reynolds	.50
OR7	Donald Royal	.50
OR8	Dennis Scott	1.00
OR9	Scott Skiles	.50
OR10	Jeff Turner	.50
NNO	Michael Jordan (Holo)	10.00

1992-93 Upper Deck All-Star Weekend

This set features past, present, and potential NBA All-Star players. The fronts have full-bleed photos, UV coating and silver foil highlights. There are also gold foil sets included in at least every case made.

		MT
Complete Set (40):		15.00
Gold Set 1 per case:		60.00
Common Player:		.20
1	Nate Archibald	.25
2	Elgin Baylor	.35
3	Wilt Chamberlain	1.00
4	Dave Cowens	.25
5	Walt Frazier	.25
6	George Gervin	.25
7	John Havlicek	.35
8	Elvin Hayes	.25
9	Oscar Robertson	.50
10	Jerry West	.75
11	Charles Barkley	1.50
12	Brad Daugherty	.15
13	Clyde Drexler	.35
14	Patrick Ewing	1.00
15	Michael Jordan	4.00
16	Karl Malone	.75
17	Moses Malone	.25
18	Chris Mullin	.30
19	Hakeem Olajuwon	2.00
20	Robert Parish	.20
21	David Robinson	1.00
22	John Stockton	.50
23	Isiah Thomas	.35
24	Dominique Wilkins	.75
25	James Worthy	.25
26	Kenny Anderson	.35
27	Stacey Augmon	.15
28	Derrick Coleman	.50
29	Larry Johnson	1.50
30	Christian Laettner	.75
31	Harold Miner	.35
32	Alonzo Mourning	2.00
33	Dikembe Mutombo	.75
34	Shaquille O'Neal	5.00
35	Steve Smith	.25
36	Larry Nance	.15
37	Larry Bird	1.00
38	Tom Chambers	.15
39	Karl Malone, John Stockton	.50
40	Charles Barkley	1.00

1992-93 Upper Deck MVP Holograms

The 38-card, standard-size hologram set was Upper Deck's selection of an MVP from each of the 27 teams, plus nine "Future MVPs." Production was limited to 138,000 sets.

		MT
Complete Set (38):		25.00
Common Player:		.10
1	Dominique Wilkins	.40
2	Reggie Lewis	.40
3	Larry Johnson	.75
4	Michael Jordan	10.00
5	Mark Price	.20
6	Derek Harper	.20
7	Dikembe Mutombo	.60
8	Isiah Thomas	.60
9	Chris Mullin	.40
10	Hakeem Olajuwon	2.00
11	Reggie Miller	1.25
12	Danny Manning	.40
13	James Worthy	.40
14	Glen Rice	.40
15	Alvin Robertson	.10
16	Chuck Person	.20
17	Derrick Coleman	.20
18	Patrick Ewing	1.25
19	Scott Skiles	.10
20	Hersey Hawkins	.20
21	Charles Barkley	2.00
22	Clyde Drexler	1.25
23	Mitch Richmond	.75
24	David Robinson	2.00
25	Shawn Kemp	1.50
26	Karl Malone	1.25
27	Pervis Ellison	.10
28	Lloyd Daniels	.25
29	Todd Day	.40
30	Tom Gugliotta	2.00
31	Robert Horry	1.50
32	Christian Laettner	2.00
33	Harold Miner	.10
34	Alonzo Mourning	4.00
35	Shaquille O'Neal	8.00
36	Walt Williams	1.25
NNO	Checklist	.10
NNO	Album Offer Card	.10

1992-93 Upper Deck Sheets

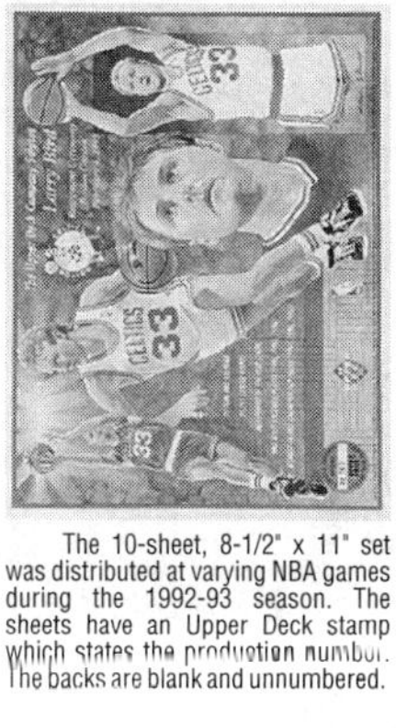

The 10-sheet, 8-1/2" x 11" set was distributed at varying NBA games during the 1992-93 season. The sheets have an Upper Deck stamp which states the production number. The backs are blank and unnumbered.

	MT
Complete Set (10):	125.00
Common Sheet:	3.00
Utah Jazz Stay in School Undated (67,000) Issued Oct. 1992 (David Benoit, Karl Malone, Mark Eaton, Jeff Malone, Mike Brown, John Stockton, Jay Humphries, Tyrone Corbin)	8.00
Cleveland Cavaliers Jan. 12 1993 (30,000, Larry Nance, Hot Rod Williams, Mark Price, Brad Daugherty, Craig Ehlo, John Battle)	6.00
Larry Bird Salute Retirement Ceremony, Boston Garden Feb. 4 1993 (25,000) Alan Studt artwork	25.00
All-Star Weekend Autograph Sheet Upper Deck Trading Card and Memorabilia Show Feb. 19-21, 1993 (75,000) Picture of Salt Lake City with mountains in background	3.00
All-Star Heroes Feb. 19-21, 1993 (10,000, Jerry West, John Havlicek, Elgin Baylor, Dave Cowens)	20.00
Milwaukee Bucks 25th Anniversary Undated (13,000) Reportedly issued 3/3/93 (Jon McGlocklin, Sidney Moncrief, Oscar Robertson, Kareem Abdul-Jabbar, Bob Lanier, Brian Winters, Junior Bridgeman)	12.00
Atlanta Hawks Undated (10,000) Reportedly issued March 25, 1993 (Stacey Augmon, Mookie Blaylock, Duane Ferrell, Adam Keefe, Dominique Wilkins, Kevin Willis)	12.00
Upper Deck Salutes April 20, 1993 (22,500, Bill Cartwright, Michael Jordan, John Paxson, Scottie Pippen, B.J. Armstrong, Horace Grant)	25.00
AT and T Long Distance Shootout Undated (22,500) Reportedly issued 6/93 (Dan Majerle, Mark Price, Terry Porter, Dana Barros, Kenny Smith, B.J. Armstrong, Reggie Miller)	12.00
Upper Deck Commemorates the NBA Draft 1992 Top Draft Choices June 30, 1993 (22,000, Shaquille O'Neal, Alonzo Mourning, Christian Laettner, Jim Jackson, LaPhonso Ellis, Tom Gugliotta, Walt Williams, Todd Day)	20.00

1993 Upper Deck Draft Party Sheets

The 27-card, 8-1/2" x 11" sets were given to 1993 Draft Day party attendees of the 27 team parties. Sheets are dated June 30 and are limited in production to 7,000. Shaquille O'Neal, Tom Gugliotta, Alonzo Mourning, Christian Laettner, Jim Jackson and LaPhonso Ellis are featured. The cards are unnumbered.

	MT
Complete Set (27):	200.00
Common Player:	8.00
Atlanta Hawks	8.00
Boston Celtics	8.00
Charlotte Hornets	8.00
Chicago Bulls	8.00
Cleveland Cavaliers	8.00
Dallas Mavericks	8.00
Denver Nuggets	8.00
Detroit Pistons	8.00
Golden State Warriors	8.00
Houston Rockets	8.00
Indiana Pacers	8.00
Los Angeles Clippers	8.00
Los Angeles Lakers	8.00
Miami Heat	8.00
Milwaukee Bucks	8.00
Minnesota Timberwolves	8.00
New Jersey Nets	8.00
New York Knicks	8.00
Orlando Magic	8.00
Philadelphia 76ers	8.00
Phoenix Suns	8.00
Portland Trail Blazers	8.00
Sacramento Kings	8.00
San Antonio Spurs	8.00
Seattle Supersonics	8.00
Utah Jazz	8.00
Washington Bullets	8.00

1993 Upper Deck European

The 255-card, standard-size set parallels in design the 1992-93 U.S. Upper Deck set except for the bilingual card text. Gold foil is featured on the card fronts with player bio and stat information printed horizontally in a ghosted NBA logo box on the back. Values below are for the Italian cards with the Spanish (1.5x) and French (2x) more valuable.

		MT
Complete French Set (255):		100.00
Complete Italian Set (255):		50.00
Complete Spanish Set (255):		75.00
Common Italian (1-255):		.15
1	Brad Daugherty CL, Mark Price, Larry Nance	.25
2	Scottie Pippen AS	.75
3	Larry Johnson AS	.50
4	Shaquille O'Neal AS	5.00
5	Michael Jordan AS	3.00
6	Isiah Thomas AS	.40
7	Brad Daugherty AS	.15
8	Joe Dumars AS	.25
9	Patrick Ewing AS	.50
10	Larry Nance AS	.15
11	Mark Price AS	.15
12	Detlef Schrempf AS	.25
13	Dominique Wilkins AS	.25
14	Karl Malone AS	.75
15	Charles Barkley AS	1.00
16	David Robinson AS	1.00
17	John Stockton AS	.75
18	Clyde Drexler AS	.50
19	Sean Elliott AS	.25
20	Tim Hardaway AS	.25
21	Shawn Kemp AS	.75
22	Dan Majerle AS	.15
23	Danny Manning AS	.25
24	Hakeem Olajuwon AS	1.00
25	Terry Porter AS	.15
26	Harold Miner FACE	.25
27	David Benoit FACE	.15
28	Cedric Ceballos FACE	.50
29	Mahmoud Abdul-Rauf FACE	.15
30	Tim Perry FACE	.15
31	Kenny Smith FACE	.15
32	Clarence Weatherspoon FACE	.50
33	Michael Jordan FACE	3.00
34	Dominique Wilkins FACE	.25
35	Shaquille O'Neal AD	6.00
36	Derrick Coleman AD	.15
37	Glen Rice AD	.25
38	Reggie Lewis AD	.25
39	Kenny Anderson AD	.25
40	Brad Daugherty AD	.15
41	Dominique Wilkins AD	.25
42	Larry Johnson AD	.50
43	Michael Jordan AD	3.00
44	Mark Price AD	.15
45	David Robinson AD	1.00
46	Karl Malone AD	.75
47	Sean Elliott AD	.25
48	John Stockton AD	.75
49	Derek Harper AD	.15
50	Kevin Duckworth AD	.15
51	Chris Mullin AD	.25
52	Charles Barkley AD	1.00
53	Tim Hardaway AD	.25
54	Clyde Drexler AD	.50
55	Adam Keefe RS	.25
56	Alonzo Mourning RS	2.50
57	Sean Rooks RS	.15
58	LaPhonso Ellis RS	.25
59	Latrell Sprewell RS	1.00
60	Robert Horry RS	1.00
61	Malik Sealy RS	.25
62	Anthony Peeler RS	.25
63	Harold Miner RS	.25
64	Anthony Avent RS	.15
65	Todd Day RS	.25
66	Lee Mayberry RS	.25
67	Christian Laettner RS	.75
68	Tom Gugliotta RS	.50
69	Shaquille O'Neal Rs	6.00
70	Clarence Weatherspoon RS	.50
71	Richard Dumas RS	.15
72	Walt Williams RS	.50
73	Lloyd Daniels RS	.25
74	Hubert Davis RS	.25
75	Manute Bol FE	.15
76	Vlade Divac FE	.15
77	Patrick Ewing FE	.50
78	Sarunas Marciulionis FE	.15
79	Dikembe Mutombo FE	.25
80	Hakeem Olajuwon FE	1.00
81	Detlef Schrempf FE	.25
82	Rony Seikaly FE	.15
83	Rik Smits FE	.25
84	Kiki Vandeweghe FE	.25
85	Dominique Wilkins FE	.25
86	Michael Jordan FAN	3.00
87	Larry Bird FAN	2.50
88	Karl Malone FAN	.75
89	Dikembe Mutombo FAN	.25
90	Michael Jordan FAN, Larry Bird	6.00
91	Stacey Augmon	.25
92	Mookie Blaylock	.25
93	Duane Ferrell	.15
94	Paul Graham	.15
95	Adam Keefe	.25
96	Jon Koncak	.15
97	Dominique Wilkins	.40
98	Kevin Willis	.25
99	Alaa Abdelnaby	.15
100	Dee Brown	.15
101	Sherman Douglas	.15
102	Rick Fox	.15
103	Reggie Lewis	.40
104	Xavier McDaniel	.15
105	Robert Parish	.40
106	Ed Pinckney	.15
107	Muggsy Bogues	.25
108	Dell Curry	.15
109	Kenny Gattison	.15
110	Kendall Gill	.15
111	Larry Johnson	1.00
112	Alonzo Mourning	5.00
113	Johnny Newman	.25
114	David Wingate	.15
115	B.J. Armstrong	.25
116	Bill Cartwright	.15
117	Horace Grant	.40
118	Michael Jordan	6.00
119	Stacey King	.15
120	John Paxson	.25
121	Scottie Pippen	2.00
122	Scott Williams	.15
123	John Battle	.15
124	Terrell Brandon	.40
125	Brad Daugherty	.25
126	Craig Ehlo	.15
127	Larry Nance	.25
128	Mark Price	.25
129	Gerald Wilkins	.15
130	Hot Rod Williams	.25
131	Walter Bond	.15
132	Terry Davis	.15
133	Derek Harper	.25
134	Donald Hodge	.15
135	Brian Howard	.15
136	Jim Jackson	4.00
137	Sean Rooks	.15
138	Doug Smith	.15
139	LaPhonso Ellis	.40
140	Mahmoud Abdul-Rauf	.25
141	Marcus Liberty	.15
142	Todd Lichti	.15
143	Mark Macon	.15
144	Dikembe Mutombo	.50
145	Robert Pack	.40
146	Reggie Williams	.15
147	Mark Aguirre	.25
148	Joe Dumars	.40
149	Gerald Glass	.15
150	Bill Laimbeer	.25
151	Terry Mills	.15
152	Olden Polynice	.15
153	Dennis Rodman	2.00
154	Isiah Thomas	.50
155	Victor Alexander	.15
156	Chris Gatling	.15
157	Tim Hardaway	.40
158	Tyrone Hill	.15
159	Sarunas Marciulionis	.15
160	Chris Mullin	.40
161	Billy Owens	.25
162	Latrell Sprewell	2.00
163	Scott Brooks	.15
164	Matt Bullard	.15
165	Sleepy Floyd	.15
166	Robert Horry	1.25
167	Vernon Maxwell	.15
168	Hakeem Olajuwon	2.00
169	Kenny Smith	.15
170	Otis Thorpe	.25
171	Dale Davis	.15
172	Vern Fleming	.15
173	Reggie Miller	1.00
174	Sam Mitchell	.15
175	Pooh Richardson	.15
176	Detlef Schrempf	.40
177	Malik Sealy	.25
178	Rik Smits	.40
179	Gary Grant	.15
180	Ron Harper	.25
181	Mark Jackson	.15
182	Danny Manning	.40
183	Ken Norman	.15
184	Stanley Roberts	.15
185	Loy Vaught	.25
186	John Williams	.15
187	Elden Campbell	.15
188	Doug Christie	.15
189	Vlade Divac	.25
190	A.C. Green	.25
191	Anthony Peeler	.40
192	Byron Scott	.25
193	Sedale Threatt	.15
194	James Worthy	.40
195	Bimbo Coles	.15
196	Kevin Edwards	.15
197	Grant Long	.15
198	Harold Miner	.25
199	Glen Rice	.40
200	John Salley	.15
201	Rony Seikaly	.15
202	Brian Shaw	.15
203	Frank Brickowski	.15
204	Todd Day	.40
205	Blue Edwards	.15
206	Eric Murdock	.15
207	Christian Laettner	1.50
208	Luc Longley	.15
209	Chuck Person	.25
210	Doug West	.15
211	Kenny Anderson	.40
212	Derrick Coleman	.25
213	Chris Morris	.15
214	Rumeal Robinson	.15
215	Patrick Ewing	1.00
216	Charles Oakley	.25
217	Doc Rivers	.30
218	John Starks	.25
219	Nick Anderson	.25
220	Shaquille O'Neal	10.00
221	Scott Skiles	.30
222	Manute Bol	.15
223	Hersey Hawkins	.25
224	Jeff Hornacek	.15
225	Danny Ainge	.25
226	Charles Barkley	2.00
227	Richard Dumas	.15
228	Kevin Johnson	.40
229	Dan Majerle	.25
230	Clyde Drexler	1.00
231	Terry Porter	.15
232	Cliff Robinson	.40
233	Buck Williams	.25
234	Mitch Richmond	.50
235	Lionel Simmons	.15
236	Spud Webb	.25
237	Walt Williams	1.00
238	Antoine Carr	.15
239	Vinny Del Negro	.15
240	Sean Elliott	.40
241	David Robinson	2.00
242	Eddie Johnson	.25
243	Shawn Kemp	1.50
244	Derrick McKey	.15
245	Ricky Pierce	.15
246	Mark Eaton	.15
247	Jeff Malone	.15
248	Karl Malone	1.25
249	John Stockton	1.25
250	Michael Adams	.15
251	Rex Chapman	.15
252	Pervis Ellison	.15
253	Tom Gugliotta	1.00
254	Michael Jordan CL	1.00
255	Michael Jordan CL	1.00

1993 Upper Deck European Award Winner Holograms

The nine-hologram set features league leaders from the previous season and each card is numbered with the "EB" prefix. The backs have a vertical player shot with award text horizontally along the right side.

		MT
Complete French Set (9):		60.00
Complete Italian Set (9):		30.00
Complete Spanish Set (9):		45.00
Common Italian (1-9):		1.00
1	Scoring (Michael Jordan)	14.00
2	Steals (John Stockton)	4.00
3	Rebounds (Dennis Rodman)	6.00
4	Sixth Man (Detlef Schrempf)	1.00
5	Rookie of the Year (Larry Johnson)	2.00
6	Blcoked Shots (David Robinson)	5.00
7	Def. Player of Year (David Robinson)	5.00
8	Assists (John Stockton)	4.00
9	Most Valuable Player (Michael Jordan)	14.00

1993 Upper Deck French McDonald's

The 40-card, standard-size set were available in three-card packs at McDonald's in France. They were free with the the purchase of a Big Mac Value Meal. The wrappers were printed in French with the card text in both French and English. Approximately 2 million packs were produced with 28,000 "Slam Dunk" insert cards which rewarded customers with a Spalding basketball.

		MT
Complete Set (40):		50.00
Common Player:		.50
1	Charles Barkley	5.00
2	Muggsy Bogues	.75
3	Derrick Coleman	.75
4	Brad Daugherty	.75
5	Vlade Divac	1.00
6	Clyde Drexler	2.50
7	Joe Dumars	1.00
8	Pervis Ellison	.50
9	Patrick Ewing	2.50
10	Horace Grant	1.00
11	Tim Hardaway	1.00
12	Derek Harper	.75
13	Hersey Hawkins	.75
14	Larry Johnson	3.00
15	Michael Jordan	15.00
16	Shawn Kemp	4.00
17	Reggie Lewis	1.00
18	Karl Malone	3.00
19	Moses Malone	1.25
20	Danny Manning	1.00
21	Sarunas Marciulionis	.50
22	Reggie Miller	2.50
23	Chris Mullin	1.00
24	Dikembe Mutombo	2.50
25	Hakeem Olajuwon	5.00
26	Robert Parish	1.00
27	Scottie Pippen	4.00
28	Mark Price	.75
29	Glen Rice	1.25
30	Mitch Richmond	1.25
31	David Robinson	5.00
32	Detlef Schrempf	1.00
33	Rony Seikaly	.50
34	Scott Skiles	.50
35	Rik Smits	1.00
36	John Stockton	3.00
37	Isiah Thomas	1.25
38	Doug West	.50
39	Dominique Wilkins	1.00
40	James Worthy	1.00

1993-94 Upper Deck

Upper Deck issued its 1993-94 cards in a Low Series/High Series format; Series II foil packs did not contain any Series I cards. Each pack has 12 UV-coated cards. Two versions of a Trade Upper Deck card - gold or silver - were random inserts, redeemable for up to 10 cards depicting the top 10 picks in the 1993 Draft who had signed NBA contracts by Dec. 3, 1993. Collectors could redeem for silver or gold foil Rookie Exchange sets, respectively. Silver cards were included one per every 72 packs; gold cards were four times as scarce. Subsets include Season Leaders, NBA Playoff Highlights, Schedules, Signature Moves, checklists, Executive Board, Breakaway Threats, Game Images, Skylights, Top Prospects, McDonald's Open and set checklists. Series I inserts include All-NBA, 3-D Triple Double, Jordan's Flight Team, Future Heroes and All-Rookie cards. Series II inserts include M.J. Mr.

June, Rookie Standouts, Team MVP, and Locker Talk cards, plus a card commemorating the Chicago Bulls' third straight NBA championship.

	MT
Complete Set (510):	40.00
Complete Series 1 (255):	20.00
Complete Series 2 (255):	20.00
Common Player:	.05
Minor Stars:	.10
Series 1 Pack (12):	1.00
Series 1 Wax Box (36):	30.00
Series 2 Retail Pack (12):	1.00
Series 2 Retail Wax Box (36):	30.00
Series 2 Hobby Pack (12):	1.50
Series 2 Hobby Wax Box (36):	40.00

1 Muggsy Bogues .05
2 Kenny Anderson .10
3 Dell Curry .05
4 Charles Smith .05
5 Chuck Person .05
6 Chucky Brown .05
7 Kevin Johnson .15
8 Winston Garland .05
9 John Salley .05
10 Dale Ellis .05
11 Otis Thorpe .05
12 John Stockton .25
13 Kendall Gill .05
14 Randy White .05
15 Mark Jackson .05
16 Vlade Divac .05
17 Scott Skiles .05
18 Xavier McDaniel .05
19 Jeff Hornacek .05
20 Stanley Roberts .05
21 Harold Miner .05
22 Terrell Brandon .05
23 Michael Jordan 3.00
24 Jim Jackson .50
25 Keith Askins .05
26 Corey Williams .05
27 David Benoit .05
28 Charles Oakley .05
29 Michael Adams .05
30 C. Weatherspoon .10
31 Jon Koncak .05
32 Gerald Wilkins .05
33 Anthony Bowie .05
34 Willie Burton .05
35 Stacey Augmon .05
36 Doc Rivers .05
37 Luc Longley .05
38 Dee Brown .05
39 Litterial Green .05
40 Dan Majerle .05
41 Doug West .05
42 Joe Dumars .15
43 Dennis Scott .05
44 Mahmoud Abdul-Rauf .05
45 Mark Eaton .05
46 Danny Ferry .05
47 Kenny Smith .05
48 Ron Harper .05
49 Adam Keefe .05
50 David Robinson .50
51 John Starks .05
52 Jeff Malone .05
53 Vern Fleming .05
54 Olden Polynice .05
55 Dikembe Mutombo .20
56 Chris Morris .05
57 Paul Graham .05
58 Richard Dumas .05
59 J.R. Reid .05
60 Brad Daugherty .05
61 Blue Edwards .05
62 Mark Macon .05
63 Latrell Sprewell .50
64 Mitch Richmond .10
65 David Wingate .05
66 LaSalle Thompson .05
67 Sedale Threatt .05
68 Larry Krystkowiak .05
69 John Paxson .05
70 Frank Brickowski .05
71 Duane Causwell .05
72 Fred Roberts .05
73 Rod Strickland .05
74 Willie Anderson .05
75 Thurl Bailey .05
76 Ricky Pierce .05
77 Todd Day .05
78 John Williams .05
79 Danny Ainge .05
80 Mark West .05
81 Marcus Liberty .05
82 Keith Jennings .05
83 Derrick Coleman .10
84 Larry Stewart .05
85 Tracy Murray .05
86 Robert Horry .10
87 Derek Harper .05
88 Scott Hastings .05
89 Sam Perkins .05
90 Clyde Drexler .25
91 Brent Price .05
92 Chris Mullin .10
93 Rafael Addison .05
94 Tyrone Corbin .05
95 Sarunas Marciulionis .05
96 Antoine Carr .05
97 Tony Bennett .05
98 Sam Mitchell .05
99 Lionel Simmons .05
100 Tim Perry .05
101 Horace Grant .10
102 Tom Hammonds .05
103 Walter Bond .05
104 Detlef Schrempf .05
105 Terry Porter .05
106 Dan Schayes .05
107 Rumeal Robinson .05
108 Gerald Glass .05
109 Mike Gminski .05
110 Terry Mills .05
111 Loy Vaught .05
112 Jim Les .05
113 Byron Houston .05
114 Randy Brown .05
115 Anthony Avent .05
116 Donald Hodge .05
117 Kevin Willis .05
118 Robert Pack .05
119 Dale Davis .05
120 Grant Long .05
121 Anthony Bonner .05
122 Chris Smith .05
123 Elden Campbell .05
124 Cliff Robinson .10
125 Sherman Douglas .05
126 Alvin Robertson .05
127 Rolando Blackman .05
128 Malik Sealy .05
129 Ed Pinckney .05
130 Anthony Peeler .05
131 Scott Brooks .05
132 Rik Smits .05
133 Derrick McKey .05
134 Alaa Abdelnaby .05
135 Rex Chapman .05
136 Tony Campbell .05
137 John Williams .05
138 Vincent Askew .05
139 LaBradford Smith .05
140 Vinny Del Negro .05
141 Darrell Walker .05
142 James Worthy .05
143 Jeff Turner .05
144 Duane Ferrell .05
145 Larry Smith .05
146 Eddie Johnson .05
147 Chris Gatling .05
148 Buck Williams .05
149 Donald Royal .05
150 *Dino Radja* .30
151 Johnny Dawkins .05
152 *Tim Legler* .05
153 Bill Laimbeer .05
154 Glen Rice .10
155 Bill Cartwright .05
156 *Luther Wright* .10
157 *Rex Walters* .10
158 *Doug Edwards* .10
159 *George Lynch* .10
160 *Chris Mills* .30
161 *Sam Cassel* 1.00
162 *Nick Van Exel* 1.00
163 *Shawn Bradley* .30
164 *Calbert Cheaney* .50
165 *Corey Blount* (Corie) .20
166 Michael Jordan (SL) 1.50
167 Dennis Rodman (SL) .40
168 John Stockton (SL) .10
169 B.J. Armstrong (SL) .05
170 Hakeem Olajuwon (SL) .50
171 Michael Jordan (SL) 1.50
172 Cedric Ceballos (SL) .05
173 Mark Price (SL) .05
174 Charles Barkley (SL) .30
175 Cliff Robertson (SL) .05
176 Hakeem Olajuwon (SL) .50
177 Shaquille O'Neal (SL) 1.00
178 New York d. Indiana 3-1 (Charles Oakley, Reggie Miller, Doc Rivers) (PH) .05
179 Charlotte d. Boston 3-1 (Rick Fox, Kenny Gattison) (PH) .05
180 Chicago d. Atlanta 3-1 (Michael Jordan, Stacey Augmon) (PH) .75
181 Cleveland d. New Jersey 3-2 (Brad Daugherty) (PH) .05
182 Phoenix d. Los Angeles 3-2 (Oliver Miller, Byron Scott) (PH) .05
183 San Antonio d. Portland 3-1 (David Robinson, Sean Elliott) (PH) .10
184 Houston d. Los Angeles Clippers (Kenny Smith, Mark Jackson) (PH) .05
185 Seattle d. Utah 3-2 (Eddie Johnson) (PH) .05
186 New York d. Charlotte 4-1 (Anthony Mason, Patrick Ewing) (PH) .05
187 Chicago d. Cleveland 4-0 (Michael Jordan, Gerald Wilkins) (PH) .75
188 Phoenix d. San Antonio 4-2 (Oliver Miller) (PH) .05
189 Seattle d. Houston 4-3 (Sam Perkins, Hakeem Olajuwon) (PH) .20
190 Chicago d. New York 4-2 (Bill Cartwright) (PH) .05
191 Phoenix d. Seattle 4-3 (Kevin Johnson) (PH) .05
192 NBA Playoff Highlights (Dan Majerle) (PH) .05
193 NBA Playoff Highlights (Michael Jordan, John Starks, Charles Oakley) (PH) 1.50
194 NBA Playoff Highlights (Larry Johnson, Muggsy Bogues) (PH) .15
195 NBA Playoff Highlights (Reggie Miller) (PH) .15
196 NBA Playoff Highlights (John Starks, Scottie Pippen) .10
197 NBA Playoff Highlights (Sedale Threatt, Vlade Divac, Charles Barkley) .10
198 Game One Finals (Michael Jordan) (FIN) 1.50
199 Game Two Finals (Scottie Pippen) (FIN) .40
200 Game Three Finals (Kevin Johnson) (FIN) .10
201 Game Four Finals (Michael Jordan) (FIN) 1.50
202 Game Five Finals (Richard Dumas) (FIN) .05
203 Game Six Finals (Horace Grant) (FIN) .10
204 1993 Finals MVP (Michael Jordan) (FIN) 1.50
205 Triple Overtime (Charles Barkley, Scottie Pippen, Tom Chambers, Scott Williams) (FIN) .10
206 Paxson Hits Three (John Paxson) (FIN) .05
207 NBA Finals Records (B.J. Armstrong) (FIN) .05
208 1992-93 Bulls .05
209 1992-93 Suns .05
210 Atlanta Hawks .05
211 Boston Celtics .05
212 Charlotte Hornets .05
213 Chicago Bulls (Michael Jordan) .75
214 Cleveland Cavaliers (Mark Price) .05
215 Dallas Mavericks (Jim Jackson, Sean Rooks) .25
216 Denver Nuggets .05
217 Detroit Pistons (Isiah Thomas) .05
218 Golden State Warriors .05
219 Houston Rockets (Hakeem Olajuwon) .10
220 Indiana Pacers (Rik Smits) .05
221 Los Angeles Clippers .05
222 Los Angeles Lakers .05
223 Miami Heat .05
224 Milwaukee Bucks .05
225 Minnesota Timberwolves .05
226 New Jersey Nets .05
227 New York Knicks .05
228 Orlando Magic (Shaquille O'Neal) .50
229 Philadelphia 76ers (Hersey Hawkins) .05
230 Phoenix Suns (Charles Barkley) .05
231 Portland Trail Blazers (Jerome Kersey, Terry Porter) .05
232 Sacramento Kings .05
233 San Antonio Spurs (David Robinson) .05
234 Seattle Supersonics .05
235 Utah Jazz .05
236 Washington Bullets (Michael Adams) .05
237 Michael Jordan (SM) 1.50
238 Clyde Drexler (SM) .10
239 Tim Hardaway (SM) .05
240 Dominique Wilkins (SM) .10
241 Brad Daugherty (SM) .05
242 Chris Mullin (SM) .10
243 Kenny Anderson (SM) .10
244 Patrick Ewing (SM) .10
245 Isiah Thomas (SM) .10
246 Dikembe Mutombo (SM) .10
247 Danny Manning (SM) .05
248 David Robinson (SM) .30
249 Karl Malone (SM) .10
250 James Worthy (SM) .05
251 Shawn Kemp (SM) .20
252 Set Checklist 1-64 .05
253 Set Checklist 65-128 .05
254 Set Checklist 129-192 .05
255 Set Checklist 193-255 .05
256 Patrick Ewing .25
257 B.J. Armstrong .05
258 Oliver Miller .05
259 Jud Buechler .05
260 Pooh Richardson .05
261 Victor Alexander .05
262 Kevin Gamble .05
263 Doug Smith .05
264 Isiah Thomas .15
265 Doug Christie .05
266 Mark Bryant .05
267 Lloyd Daniels .05
268 Michael Williams .05
269 Nick Anderson .05
270 Tom Gugliotta .05
271 Kenny Gattison .05
272 Vernon Maxwell .05
273 Terry Cummings .05
274 Karl Malone .30
275 Rick Fox .05
276 Matt Bullard .05
277 Johnny Newman .05
278 Mark Price .10
279 Mookie Blaylock .05
280 Charles Barkley .60
281 Larry Nance .05
282 Walt Williams .05
283 Brian Shaw .05
284 Robert Parish .05
285 Pervis Ellison .05
286 Spud Webb .05
287 Hakeem Olajuwon 1.00
288 Jerome Kersey .05
289 Carl Herrera .05
290 Dominique Wilkins .15
291 Billy Owens .05
292 Greg Anthony .05
293 Nate McMillan .05
294 Christian Laettner .05
295 Gary Payton .10
296 Steve Smith .05
297 Anthony Mason .05
298 Sean Rooks .05
299 *Toni Kukoc* 1.00
300 Shaquille O'Neal 2.00
301 Jay Humphries .05
302 Sleepy Floyd .05
303 Bimbo Coles .05
304 John Battle .05
305 Shawn Kemp .40
306 Scott Williams .05
307 Wayman Tisdale .05
308 Rony Seikaly .05
309 Reggie Miller .25
310 Scottie Pippen 1.00
311 *Chris Webber* 3.00
312 Trevor Wilson .05
313 *Derek Strong* .05
314 *Bobby Hurley* .15
315 Herb Williams .05
316 Rex Walters .05
317 Doug Edwards .05
318 Ken Williams .05
319 Jon Barry .05
320 *Joe Courtney* .05
321 *Ervin Johnson* .10
322 Sam Cassell .20
323 Tim Hardaway .10
324 Steve Kerr .05
325 Pete Chilcutt .05
326 Doug Overton .05
327 Reggie Williams .05
328 Avery Johnson .05
329 Stacey King .05
330 *Vin Baker* 1.00
331 Greg Kite .05
332 Michael Cage .05
333 Alonzo Mourning .60
334 *Acie Earl* .10
335 *Terry Dehere* .10
336 Negele Knight .05
337 *Gerald Madkins* .10
338 *Lindsey Hunter* .20
339 Luther Wright .10
340 *Mike Peplowski* .10
341 Dino Radja .20
342 Danny Manning .10
343 Chris Mills .05
344 Hubert Davis .05
345 Shawn Bradley .10
346 *Evers Burns* .10
347 *Rodney Rogers* .30
348 Cedric Ceballos .05
349 *Warren Kidd* .10
350 *Darnell Mee* .10
351 Matt Geiger .05
352 *Jamal Mashburn* 1.50
353 *Antonio Davis* .25
354 Calbert Cheaney .20
355 *George Lynch* .05
356 Derrick McKey .05
357 Jerry Reynolds .05
358 Don MacLean .05
359 *Scott Haskin* .05
360 *Malcolm Mackey* .10
361 *Isaiah Rider* .75
362 Detlef Schrempf .05
363 *Josh Grant* .10
364 Kurt Rambis .05
365 Larry Johnson .25
366 *Richard Petruska* .10
367 Ken Norman .05
368 Kenny Walker .05
369 *James Robinson* .25
370 Kevin Duckworth .05
371 Chris Whitney .05
372 Moses Malone .05
373 Nick Van Exel .50
374 *Scott Burrell* .25
375 Harvey Grant .05
376 Benoit Benjamin .05
377 Henry James .05
378 Peter Myers .05
379 Dwayne Schintzuis .05
380 Sean Green .05
381 Eric Murdock .05
382 *Anfernee Hardaway* 3.00
383 *Gheorghe Muresan* .25
384 Kendall Gill .05
385 David Wood .05
386 Mario Elie .05
387 Chris Corchiani .05
388 *Greg Graham* .10
389 Hersey Hawkins .05
390 Mark Aguirre .05
391 LaPhonso Ellis .10
392 Anthony Bonner .05
393 *Lucious Harris* .05
394 Andrew Lang .05
395 Chris Dudley .05
396 Dennis Rodman 1.00
397 Larry Krystkowiak .05
398 A.C. Green .05
399 Eddie Johnson .05
400 Kevin Edwards .05
401 Tyrone Hill .05
402 Greg Anderson .05
403 *P.J. Brown* .05
404 Dana Barros .05
405 *Allan Houston* 2.00
406 Mike Brown .05
407 Lee Mayberry .05
408 Fat Lever .05
409 Tony Smith .05
410 Tom Chambers .05
411 Manute Bol .05
412 Joe Kleine .05
413 Bryant Stith .05
414 Chuck Nevitt .05
415 *JoJo English* .10
416 Sean Elliott .05
417 Sam Bowie .05
418 Armon Gilliam .05
419 Brian Williams .05
420 *Popeye Jones* .25
421 Dennis Rodman .40
422 Karl Malone (Exec) .10
423 Tom Gugliotta (Exec) .05
424 Kevin Willis (Exec) .05
425 Hakeem Olajuwon (Exec) .50
426 Charles Oakley (Exec) .05
427 C. Weatherspoon (Exec) .10
428 Derrick Coleman (Exec) .10
429 Buck Williams (Exec) .05
430 Christian Laettner (Exec) .05
431 Dikembe Mutombo (Exec) .10
432 Rony Seikaly (Exec) .05
433 Brad Daugherty (Exec) .05
434 Horace Grant (Exec) .10
435 Larry Johnson (Exec) .10
436 Dee Brown (BT) .05
437 Muggsy Bogues (BT) .05
438 Michael Jordan (BT) 1.50
439 Tim Hardaway (BT) .05
440 Michael Williams (BT) .05
441 Gary Payton (BT) .10
442 Mookie Blaylock (BT) .05
443 Doc Rivers (BT) .05
444 Kenny Smith (BT) .05
445 John Stockton (BT) .10
446 Alvin Robertson (BT) .05
447 Mark Jackson (BT) .05
448 Kenny Anderson (BT) .10
449 Scottie Pippen (BT) .40
450 Isiah Thomas (BT) .10
451 Mark Price (BT) .05
452 Latrell Sprewell (BT) .25
453 Sedale Threatt (BT) .05
454 Nick Anderson (BT) .05
455 Rod Strickland (BT) .05
456 Oliver Miller (GI) .05
457 James Worthy, Vlade Divac (GI) .05
458 Robert Horry (GI) .05
459 Houston Rockets (GI) .05
460 Sean Rooks, Jimmy Jackson, Tim Legler (GI) .15
461 Mitch Richmond (GI) .10
462 Chris Morris (GI) .05
463 Mark Jackson, Gary Grant (GI) .05
464 David Robinson (GI) .20
465 Danny Ainge (GI) .05
466 Michael Jordan (SKY) 1.50
467 Dominique Wilkins (SKY) .10
468 Alonzo Mourning (SKY) .25
469 Shaquille O'Neal (SKY) 1.00
470 Tim Hardaway (SKY) .05
471 Patrick Ewing (SKY) .10
472 Kevin Johnson (SKY) .10
473 Clyde Drexler (SKY) .10
474 David Robinson (SKY) .30
475 Shawn Kemp (SKY) .20
476 Dee Brown (SKY) .05
477 Jim Jackson (SKY) .30
478 John Stockton (SKY) .10
479 Robert Horry (SKY) .05
480 Glen Rice (SKY) .05
481 Micheal Williams .05
482 George Lynch, Terry Dehere (TP) .05
483 Chris Webber (TP) .50
484 Anfernee Hardaway (TP) 1.50
485 Shawn Bradley (TP) .10
486 Jamal Mashburn (TP) .40
487 Calbert Cheaney (TP) .10
488 Isaiah Rider (TP) .25
489 Bobby Hurley (TP) .10
490 Vin Baker (TP) .30
491 Rodney Rogers (TP) .10
492 Lindsey Hunter (TP) .10
493 Allan Houston (TP) .20
494 Terry Dehere (TP) .10
495 George Lynch (TP) .10
496 Toni Kukoc (TP) .10
497 Nick Van Exel (TP) .50
498 Charles Barkley (McD) .25
499 A.C. Green (McD) .05
500 Dan Majerle (McD) .05
501 Jerrod Mustaf (McD) .05
502 Kevin Johnson (McD) .05
503 Negele Knight (McD) .05
504 Danny Ainge (McD) .05
505 Oliver Miller (McD) .05
506 Joe Courtney (McD) .05
507 McDonald's Open Checklist .05
508 Set Checklist 1 .05
509 Set Checklist 2 .05
510 Set Checklist 3 .05
SP3 Michael Jordan, Wilt Chamberlain 7.00
SP4 Chicago Bulls Third 7.00

1993-94 Upper Deck All-NBA

These 15 cards were random inserts only in 1993-94 Upper Deck Series I packs and jumbo packs. The players are NBA first, second and third team selections. The card front features a color action photo of the player, with a crowd shot as a background. The player's name is in a red stripe along the right side of the card, adjacent to a blue stripe which indicates which team he made. A set logo appears in the bottom right corner. The card back, numbered using an "AN" prefix, has another color photo on the left, with career highlights on the right. The set logo is in the upper right corner.

	MT
Complete Set (15):	20.00
Common Player:	.25
Minor Stars:	.50

1 Charles Barkley 2.00
2 Karl Malone 1.00
3 Hakeem Olajuwon 2.00
4 Michael Jordan 10.00
5 Mark Price .25
6 Dominique Wilkins .50
7 Larry Johnson 1.00
8 Patrick Ewing 1.00
9 John Stockton 1.00
10 Joe Dumars .25
11 Scottie Pippen 2.00
12 Derrick Coleman .50
13 David Robinson 2.00
14 Tim Hardaway .25
15 Michael Jordan (CL) 5.00

1993-94 Upper Deck All-Rookies

These 10 players were the top rookies in the NBA during the 1992-93 season. Cards were random inserts in 1993-94 Upper Deck Series I retail packs only and use an "AR" prefix for numbers. A full-bleed color photo is featured on the card front, which uses a red block at the top to indicate first team players, or a blue block to indicate a second team player. A corresponding stripe appears at the bottom of the card, where the player's name appears in white letters. The card back has a photo on the left, with career highlights on the right. The card number is in the upper left corner, and the "All-Rookie Team" logo is in the lower right corner.

	MT
Complete Set (10):	25.00
Common Player:	.50
Minor Stars:	1.00

1 Shaquille O'Neal 15.00
2 Alonzo Mourning 5.00
3 Christian Laettner 1.00
4 Tom Gugliotta 3.00
5 LaPhonso Ellis 1.00
6 Walt Williams 1.00
7 Robert Horry 1.00
8 Latrell Sprewell 4.00
9 C. Weatherspoon 1.00
10 Richard Dumas .50

1993-94 Upper Deck Box Bottoms

The two-card, 5" x 7" set was available through the box bottoms of Upper Deck Basketball. The backs are blank and unnumbered.

	MT
Complete Set (2):	1.25
Common Player:	.25
Bobby Hurley	.25
Michael Jordan	1.00

1993-94 Upper Deck Flight Team

These cards, inserts in 1993-94 Upper Deck Series I hobby packs only, feature Michael Jordan's 20 favorite hang-time players. Card backs have Jordan's opinions on each of the players, a card photo, and a card number, which uses an "FT" prefix. The card front has a color action photo of the player against a ghosted background which has the words "Michael Jordan's Flight Team" in it. The set logo is at the bottom of the card and includes the player's team name and his uniform number inside it. The player's name is stamped in gold foil along the bottom of the card.

	MT
Complete Set (20):	100.00
Common Player:	1.00
Minor Stars:	2.00

1 Stacey Augmon 1.00
2 Charles Barkley 12.00
3 David Benoit 1.00
4 Dee Brown 1.00
5 Cedric Ceballos 1.00
6 Derrick Coleman 2.00
7 Clyde Drexler 7.00
8 Sean Elliott 1.00
9 LaPhonso Ellis 1.00
10 Kendall Gill 1.00
11 Larry Johnson 7.00
12 Shawn Kemp 8.00
13 Karl Malone 6.00
14 Harold Miner 1.00
15 Alonzo Mourning 10.00
16 Shaquille O'Neal 45.00
17 Scottie Pippen 15.00
18 C. Weatherspoon 2.00
19 Spud Webb 1.00
20 Dominique Wilkins 2.00

1993-94 Upper Deck Future Heroes

These players are nine of the NBA's top future superstars. The cards were in 1993-94 Upper Deck Series I locker boxes, which each contain four jumbo packs (1 insert per pack). The card front has a color action photo and team color-coded panels. The panels contain the set name (along the left side) and the player's name and position (along the bottom). A silver foil basketball is in the lower left corner. The back side reverses the color-coded panels, and puts the basketball in the lower right corner between them. The card back is white and includes a career summary and card number (1 of 36, etc.).

	MT
Complete Set (10):	40.00
Common Player:	1.00
Minor Stars:	2.00
28 Derrick Coleman	2.00
29 LaPhonso Ellis	1.00
30 Jim Jackson	6.00
31 Larry Johnson	3.00
32 Shawn Kemp	5.00
33 Christian Laettner	1.00
34 Alonzo Mourning	5.00
35 Shaquille O'Neal	20.00
36 Walt Williams	1.00

1993-94 Upper Deck Locker Talk

These cards, found in Series II Locker packs only (one per pack), feature 15 of the NBA's All-Interview Team. Cards are numbered on the back with an "LT" prefix. The card front has a color action photo, with a quote about the player in the lower right corner. The player's name is along the left side in a gold stripe. The back has the same quote as the front, but this time it's in the upper right corner, adjacent to a locker door which has a smaller version of the photo from the front taped to it. A second photo and second quote also appear on the back. The card number is in the upper left corner, inside a stripe which contains the player's name.

	MT
Complete Set (15):	80.00
Common Player:	1.00
Minor Stars:	2.00
1 Michael Jordan	40.00
2 Stacey Augmon	1.00
3 Shaquille O'Neal	25.00
4 Alonzo Mourning	8.00
5 Harold Miner	1.00
6 C. Weatherspoon	2.00
7 Derrick Coleman	2.00
8 Charles Barkley	8.00
9 David Robinson	6.00
10 Chuck Person	1.00
11 Karl Malone	5.00
12 Muggsy Bogues	1.00
13 Latrell Sprewell	4.00
14 John Starks	1.00
15 Jim Jackson	6.00

1993-94 Upper Deck Mr. June

Michael Jordan is the focus of this 10-card insert set, titled "M.J. Mr. June." The cards, in Series II hobby packs only, detail Jordan's accomplishments during the previous three NBA Finals. Cards are numbered with an "MJ" prefix. The card front has a color action photo of Jordan, plus a red-and-black stripe at the bottom which includes Jordan's name, accomplishment and when it occurred. The back has a color photo in the upper right corner. Recaps of his accomplishment are below the photo and along the left side. The set's logo is on both sides of the card.

	MT
Complete Set (10):	180.00
Common Player:	18.00
1 Jordan's Stead	18.00
2 M.J.'s High Five	18.00
3 1991 NBA Finals MVP	18.00
4 35 Points in One Half	18.00
5 Three-Point King	18.00
6 Back-to-Back Finals MVP	18.00
7 55-Point Game	18.00
8 Record Scoring Average	18.00
9 Jordan's Three Peat	18.00
10 Checklist	18.00

1993-94 Upper Deck Pro View

These cards utilize a 3D effect; special glasses were also made to view the cards. The cards have a color action photo on the front, with a white border. The player's name appears along the left side in a ghosted panel. The back also has a color shot (same as on the front) on one side and a player profile on the other. The standard-size cards came in packs of five. 3D subsets include 3D Playground (#s 71-79), 3D Rookie (#s 80-88) and 3D Jams (#s 89-108).

	MT
Complete Set (110):	20.00
Common Player:	.05
Minor Stars:	.10
1 Karl Malone	.25
2 Chuck Person	.05
3 Latrell Sprewell	.50
4 Dominique Wilkins	.25
5 Reggie Miller	.25
6 Vlade Divac	.05
7 Otis Thorpe	.05
8 Patrick Ewing	.20
9 Ron Harper	.05
10 Brad Daugherty	.05
11 Robert Parish	.05
12 Glen Rice	.10
13 Kevin Johnson	.10
14 Christian Laettner	.05
15 Ricky Pierce	.05
16 Joe Dumars	.15
17 James Worthy	.05
18 John Stockton	.25
19 Robert Horry	.10
20 John Starks	.05
21 Danny Manning	.10
22 Alonzo Mourning	.50
23 Michael Jordan	3.00
24 Hakeem Olajuwon	.50
25 Scott Skiles	.05
26 Stacey Augmon	.05
27 Mitch Richmond	.10
28 Derrick Coleman	.10
29 Jeff Malone	.05
30 Larry Johnson	.30
31 Sam Perkins	.05
32 Shaquille O'Neal	2.00
33 Walt Williams	.05
34 Doug West	.05
35 Mark Price	.05
36 Rony Seikaly	.05
37 Michael Adams	.05
38 Anthony Peeler	.05
39 Larry Nance	.05
40 Shawn Kemp	.50
41 Terry Porter	.05
42 Dan Majerle	.05
43 Dennis Rodman	1.00
44 Isiah Thomas	.15
45 Spud Webb	.05
46 Pooh Richardson	.05
47 Tim Hardaway	.10
48 Derek Harper	.05
49 Pervis Ellison	.05
50 Xavier McDaniel	.05
51 Jeff Hornacek	.05
52 Ken Norman	.05
53 LaPhonso Ellis	.05
54 Charles Barkley	.40
55 Tom Gugliotta	.05
56 Cliff Robinson	.05
57 Mark Jackson	.05
58 Mahmoud Abdul-Rauf	.05
59 Todd Day	.05
60 Kenny Anderson	.10
61 Jim Jackson	.40
62 Chris Mullin	.15
63 Scottie Pippen	1.00
64 Dikembe Mutombo	.20
65 Sean Elliott	.05
66 C. Weatherspoon	.05
67 Chris Morris	.05
68 Clyde Drexler	.25
69 Dennis Scott	.05
70 David Robinson	.40
71 Larry Johnson	.20
72 Chris Webber	.40
73 Alonzo Mourning	.25
74 Lloyd Daniels	.05
75 Derrick Coleman	.10
76 Tim Hardaway	.10
77 Isiah Thomas	.10
78 Chris Mullin	.10
79 Shaquille O'Neal	1.00
80 *Shawn Bradley*	.30
81 *Chris Webber*	2.00
82 *Jamal Mashburn*	1.00
83 *Anfernee Hardaway*	4.00
84 *Calbert Cheaney*	.50
85 *Vin Baker*	1.00
86 *Isaiah Rider*	.75
87 *Lindsey Hunter*	.20
88 *Bobby Hurley*	.15
89 Dominique Wilkins	.15
90 Charles Barkley	.25
91 Michael Jordan	1.50
92 Derrick Coleman	.10
93 Scottie Pippen	.25
94 Karl Malone	.15
95 Larry Johnson	.15
96 Cedric Ceballos	.05
97 David Robinson	.25
98 Patrick Ewing	.10
99 C. Weatherspoon	.05
100 Alonzo Mourning	.25
101 Stacey Augmon	.05
102 Shaquille O'Neal	1.00
103 Clyde Drexler	.15
104 Shawn Kemp	.20
105 Harold Miner	.05
106 Chris Webber	.75
107 Dikembe Mutombo	.10
108 Doug West	.05
109 Checklist 1	.05
110 Checklist 2	.05

1993-94 Upper Deck Rookie Exchange

Collectors who obtained randomly inserted specially-marked exchange cards could mail them in for silver or gold versions of a "Rookie Exchange" card. The cards are identical, except the word "Exchange" runs along the left side in either silver or gold foil. The card front has a full-bleed color photo, with the player's name printed in white in a red stripe near the bottom. The back is gray and white and includes a color mug shot in a circle in the upper left corner, plus career highlights and statistics. The cards are numbered with an "RE" prefix. Gold cards are generally worth about two times more than the silver versions.

	MT
Complete Silver Set (10):	7.00
Common Silver Player:	.25
Gold Cards:	2x
1 Chris Webber	4.00
2 Shawn Bradley	.50
3 Anfernee Hardaway	3.00
4 Jamal Mashburn	1.00
5 Isaiah Rider	.75
6 Calbert Cheaney	.50
7 Bobby Hurley	.25
8 Vin Baker	2.00
9 Rodney Rogers	.50
10 Lindsey Hunter	.25

1993-94 Upper Deck Rookie Standouts

Twenty of the top rookies for the 1993-94 season are in this insert set. Cards, randomly included in Series II retail packs only, are numbered with an "RS" prefix. The card front has a color action photo of the player, along with the set's logo stamped in silver foil in the lower right corner. A gold foil banner attached to the set logo has the player's name printed inside. The card back has a photo of the player on the right side; the left side has a career summary. The player's name, team and card number appear in the upper left.

	MT
Complete Set (20):	60.00
Common Player:	.50
Minor Stars:	1.00
1 Chris Webber	12.00
2 Bobby Hurley	.50
3 Isaiah Rider	3.00
4 Terry Dehere	.50
5 Toni Kukoc	3.00
6 Shawn Bradley	2.00
7 Allan Houston	2.50
8 Chris Mills	2.00
9 Jamal Mashburn	7.00
10 Acie Earl	.50
11 George Lynch	.50
12 Scott Burrell	1.00
13 Calbert Cheaney	1.00
14 Lindsey Hunter	1.00
15 Nick Van Exel	6.00
16 Rex Walters	.50
17 Anfernee Hardaway	12.00
18 Sam Cassell	3.00
19 Vin Baker	6.00
20 Rodney Rogers	2.00

1993-94 Upper Deck Team MVP's

A player from each NBA team has been chosen for this 27-card set. Cards, numbered with a "TM" prefix, were included in Series II jumbo packs only. The card front has a color action photo, with the player's name printed vertically along the right side in a foil panel. "Team MVP" is at the bottom of the card. The back is horizontally designed and includes a color action photo on the left. A grey box on the right includes a career recap and a card number in the upper right corner. The player's name is in the upper left corner, above the photo.

	MT
Complete Set (27):	20.00
Common Player:	.25
Minor Stars:	.50
1 Dominique Wilkins	.50
2 Robert Parish	.25
3 Larry Johnson	.50
4 Scottie Pippen	2.00
5 Mark Price	.25
6 Jim Jackson	1.50
7 Mahmoud Abdul-Rauf	.25
8 Joe Dumars	.50
9 Chris Mullin	.50
10 Hakeem Olajuwon	2.00
11 Reggie Miller	.50
12 Danny Manning	.25
13 James Worthy	.25
14 Glen Rice	.25
15 Blue Edwards	.25
16 Christian Laettner	.25
17 Derrick Coleman	.50
18 Patrick Ewing	.50
19 Shaquille O'Neal	5.00
20 C. Weatherspoon	.25
21 Charles Barkley	1.25
22 Clyde Drexler	.75
23 Mitch Richmond	.50
24 David Robinson	1.25
25 Shawn Kemp	1.00
26 John Stockton	.50
27 Tom Gugliotta	.50

1993-94 Upper Deck Triple Double

These 10 players are top-notch players at attaining the triple-double - double figures in rebounds, points and assists. They were random inserts in all types of Upper Deck's 1993-94 basketball products and are numbered with a "TD" prefix. The card front is a horizontal hologram featuring a color photo and two hologram action shots. The three photos demonstrate the skills the player needs to attain a triple-double. "Triple Double" is written along the left side of the card; the player's name is in the right corner. The card back is also horizontal, and has an action photo of the player on the left, with a recap the player's triple-double game on the right. The player's name is in a team color-coded stripe at the bottom.

	MT
Complete Set (10):	25.00
Common Player:	.75
1 Charles Barkley	4.00
2 Michael Jordan	18.00
3 Scottie Pippen	3.00
4 Detlef Schrempf	.75
5 Mark Jackson	.75
6 Kenny Anderson	1.50
7 Larry Johnson	2.00
8 Dikembe Mutombo	1.50
9 Rumeal Robinson	.75
10 Michael Williams	.75

1993-94 Upper Deck Draft Preview Promos

The three-card, standard-size set was issued to preview an upcoming, but never released, draft-pick set. The card fronts feature a full-bleed color shot with the college name on the player's jersey air-brushed off. The backs contain bio and stat information. Cards are numbered with a "DP" prefix.

	MT
Complete Set (3):	15.00
Common Player:	4.00
1 Shawn Bradley (BYU)	8.00
2 Calbert Cheaney (Indiana)	8.00
3 Bobby Hurley (Duke)	4.00

1993-94 Upper Deck Holojams

The 36-card, standard-size set featured Upper Deck's choices for the best dunkers in the league. The box set was only available through hobby outlets as part of a set and retailed for $24.95. The checklist card had the production number listed out of 127,800. The Holojam logo appears in the lower half of the card face while the backs contain a player close-up with career highlights. Cards are numbered with a "H" prefix.

	MT
Complete Set (38):	30.00
Common Player:	.15
1 Dominique Wilkins	.30
2 Dee Brown	.15
3 Alonzo Mourning	2.00
4 Michael Jordan	12.00
5 Brad Daugherty	.25
6 Jim Jackson	.75
7 Dikembe Mutombo	.50
8 Terry Mills	.15
9 Billy Owens	.25
10 Hakeem Olajuwon	2.50
11 Reggie Miller	1.50
12 Ron Harper	.25
13 James Worthy	.30
14 Harold Miner	.15
15 Blue Edwards	.15
16 Doug West	.15
17 Derrick Coleman	.25
18 Patrick Ewing	1.50
19 Shaquille O'Neal	4.00
20 Clarence Weatherspoon	.50
21 Charles Barkley	2.50
22 Clyde Drexler	1.50
23 Walt Williams	.50
24 David Robinson	2.50
25 Shawn Kemp	1.50
26 Karl Malone	1.50
27 Tom Gugliotta	.50
28 Chris Webber	3.00
29 Shawn Bradley	1.25
30 Anfernee Hardaway	8.00
31 Jamal Mashburn	3.00
32 Isaiah Rider	.50
33 Rodney Rogers	.50
34 Lindsey Hunter	.50
35 Doug Edwards	.15
36 George Lynch	.15
NNO Checklist	.15
NNO Album mail-in card	.15

1993-94 Upper Deck Sheets

The six-sheet, 8 1/2" by 11" set was given away during the 1993-94 season at select events. The sheets have an Upper Deck stamp indicating the particular production run. The backs are blank and unnumbered.

	MT
Complete Set (6):	50.00
Common Panel:	3.00
1 1993 National Conv. - July 20-25, 1993 (Michael Jordan)	10.00
2 1993 McDonald's Open - October 21, 1993 (Danny Ainge, Dan Majerle, Oliver Miller, Charles Barkley, Kevin Johnson, Mark West, Negele Knight, Cedric Ceballos)	10.00
3 Chicago Bulls - Nov. 13, 1993 (John Paxson, B.J. Armstrong, Corie Blount, Scottie Pippen, Bill Cartwright, Horace Grant) (22,000)	15.00
4 Upper Deck Salutes - Undated NBA Standouts All-Star Weekend (Harold Miner, Patrick Ewing, Hakeem Olajuwon, Alonzo Mourning, Jim Jackson, Derrick Coleman) (30,000) (Issued Feb. 1994)	10.00
5 Upper Deck All-Star - Undated Autograph Sheet All-Star Weekend (20,000) (Issued Feb. 1994)	3.00
6 SE Preview - Undated (Shawn Bradley, Shaquille O'Neal, LaPhonso Ellis, Jamal Mashburn, Chris Webber, Calbert Cheaney) (16,000) (Issued March 1994)	12.00

1993-94 Upper Deck WalMart Jumbos

Available in blister packs at Wal-Mart, the jumbo cards (3-1/2" x 5") parallel the 1993-94 base and subsets cards.

	MT
Complete Set (28):	75.00
Common Player:	.50
32 Shawn Kemp (Future Heroes)	2.50
48 Ron Harper	.75
64 Mitch Richmond	1.50
154 Glen Rice	1.50
195 Reggie Miller	3.00
243 Kenny Anderson	.75
361 Isaiah Rider	1.50
382 Anfernee Hardaway	15.00
391 LaPhonso Ellis	.50
483 Chris Webber	6.00
485 Shawn Bradley	2.50
486 Jamal Mashburn	4.00
487 Calbert Cheaney	2.00
490 Vin Baker	6.00
492 Lindsey Hunter	1.00
497 Nick Van Exel	6.00
AN5 Mark Price	.75
AN8 Patrick Ewing	3.00
FT2 Charles Barkley	5.00
FT4 Dee Brown	.50
FT7 Clyde Drexler	3.00
FT13 Karl Malone	3.00
FT15 Alonzo Mourning	4.00
LT3 Shaquille O'Neal	8.00
TM1 Dominique Wilkins	1.00
TM4 Scottie Pippen (Chicago Bears)	5.00
TM10 Hakeem Olajuwon	4.00
TM24 David Robinson	4.00

1993-94 Upper Deck SE

Upper Deck's 1993-94 Special Edition cards feature full-bleed photos, with a black-and-white version of the card in the lower left corner. The player's name, team and Upper Deck logo are also printed on the card front in gold foil. Subsets within the regular set include Team Headlines, providing information about each NBA team; and NBA All-Star Weekend Highlights. In addition, each SE card was printed on a thicker, higher quality paper stock, in both silver foil (Electric Court, one per pack) and gold foil (Electric Gold, every 36th pack). Other insert sets are NBA All-Star cards, and redeemable Behind the Glass and USA Basketball Trade cards. Three Michael Jordan insert cards, including one in the Behind the Glass set, were also made. The Jordan cards feature his fictional alter-ego, Johnny Kilroy, from the Nike commercials Jordan was in, and a Jordan Tribute. Cards, randomly inserted into every 72nd pack, were printed using a silver-sparkle version of Upper Deck's Electric foil. The USA Basketball Trade card could be redeemed for a set of 13 cards devoted to the USA Basketball Dream Team II. Behind the Glass cards are redeemable for a 15-card set of the same name.

	MT
Complete Set (225):	15.00
Common Player:	.05
Minor Stars:	.10
Electric Court Cards:	2x
Inserted 1:1	
Electric Gold Cards:	10x-20x
Inserted 1:36	
Retail Pack (12):	1.50
Retail Wax Box (36):	35.00
East or West Pack (12):	4.00
East or West Wax Box (36):	100.00

1	Scottie Pippen	1.00
2	Todd Day	.10
3	Detlef Schrempf	.05
4	*Chris Webber*	7.00
5	Michael Adams	.05
6	Loy Vaught	.05
7	Doug West	.05
8	A.C. Green	.05
9	Anthony Mason	.05
10	Clyde Drexler	.40
11	*Popeye Jones*	.25
12	Vlade Divac	.05
13	Armon Gilliam	.05
14	Hersey Hawkins	.05
15	Dennis Scott	.05
16	Bimbo Coles	.05
17	Blue Edwards	.05
18	Negele Knight	.05
19	Dale Davis	.05
20	Isiah Thomas	.20
21	Latrell Sprewell	.25
22	Kenny Smith	.05
23	Bryant Stith	.05
24	Terry Porter	.05
25	Spud Webb	.05
26	John Battle	.05
27	Jeff Malone	.05
28	Olden Polynice	.05
29	Kevin Willis	.05
30	Robert Parish	.05
31	Kevin Johnson	.10
32	Shaquille O'Neal	2.50
33	Willie Anderson	.05
34	Micheal Williams	.05
35	Steve Smith	.05
36	Rik Smits	.10
37	Pete Myers	.05
38	Oliver Miller	.05
39	Eddie Johnson	.05
40	*Calbert Cheaney*	.30
41	Vernon Maxwell	.05
42	James Worthy	.05
43	*Dino Radja*	.40
44	Derrick Coleman	.10
45	Reggie Williams	.05
46	Dale Ellis	.05
47	Cliff Robinson	.10
48	Doug Christie	.05
49	Ricky Pierce	.05
50	Sean Elliott	.05
51	*Anfernee Hardaway*	5.00
52	Dana Barros	.05
53	Reggie Miller	.30
54	Brian Williams	.05
55	Otis Thorpe	.05
56	Jerome Kersey	.05
57	Larry Johnson	.40
58	Rex Chapman	.05
59	Kevin Edwards	.05
60	Nate McMillian	.05
61	Chris Mullin	.10
62	Bill Cartwright	.05
63	Dennis Rodman	1.00
64	Pooh Richardson	.05
65	Tyrone Hill	.05
66	Scott Brooks	.05
67	Brad Daugherty	.05
68	Joe Dumars	.10
69	*Vin Baker*	1.00
70	Rod Strickland	.10
71	Tom Chambers	.05
72	Charles Oakley	.05
73	Craig Ehlo	.05
74	LaPhonso Ellis	.05
75	Kevin Gamble	.05
76	*Shawn Bradley*	.50
77	Kendall Gill	.05
78	Hakeem Olajuwon	.75
79	Nick Anderson	.05
80	Anthony Peeler	.05
81	Wayman Tisdale	.05
82	Danny Manning	.10
83	John Starks	.10
84	Jeff Hornacek	.05
85	Victor Alexander	.05
86	Mitch Richmond	.10
87	Mookie Blaylock	.05
88	Harvey Grant	.05
89	Doug Smith	.05
90	John Stockton	.25
91	Charles Barkley	.50
92	Gerald Wilkins	.05
93	Mario Elie	.05
94	Ken Norman	.05
95	B.J. Armstrong	.05
96	John Williams	.05
97	Rony Seikaly	.05
98	Sean Rooks	.05
99	Shawn Kemp	.50
100	Danny Ainge	.05
101	Terry Mills	.05
102	Doc Rivers	.05
103	Chuck Person	.05
104	*Sam Cassell*	1.25
105	Kevin Duckworth	.05
106	Dan Majerle	.05
107	Mark Jackson	.05
108	Steve Kerr	.05
109	Sam Perkins	.05
110	C. Weatherspoon	.10
111	Felton Spencer	.05
112	Greg Anthony	.05
113	Pete Chilcutt	.05
114	Malik Sealy	.05
115	Horace Grant	.10
116	Chris Morris	.05
117	Xavier McDaniel	.05
118	Lionel Simmons	.05
119	Dell Curry	.05
120	Moses Malone	.05
121	*Lindsey Hunter*	.15
122	Buck Williams	.05
123	Mahmoud Abdul-Rauf	.05
124	Rumeal Robinson	.05
125	*Chris Mills*	.40
126	Scott Skiles	.05
127	Derrick McKey	.05
128	Avery Johnson	.05
129	Harold Miner	.05
130	Frank Brickowski	.05
131	Gary Payton	.15
132	Don MacLean	.05
133	Thurl Bailey	.05
134	*Nick Van Exel*	1.00
135	Matt Geiger	.05
136	Stacey Augmon	.05
137	Sedale Threatt	.05
138	Patrick Ewing	.25
139	Tyrone Corbin	.05
140	Jim Jackson	.40
141	Christian Laettner	.05
142	Robert Horry	.20
143	J.R. Reid	.05
144	Eric Murdock	.05
145	Alonzo Mourning	.50
146	Sherman Douglas	.05
147	Tom Gugliotta	.05
148	Glen Rice	.10
149	Mark Price	.05
150	Dikembe Mutombo	.10
151	Derek Harper	.05
152	Karl Malone	.30
153	Byron Scott	.05
154	Reggie Jordan	.05
155	Dominique Wilkins	.05
156	*Bobby Hurley*	.20
157	Ron Harper	.05
158	Byron Russell	.05
159	Frank Johnson	.05
160	*Toni Kukoc*	1.00
161	Lloyd Daniels	.05
162	Jeff Turner	.05
163	Muggsy Bogues	.05
164	Chris Gatling	.05
165	Kenny Anderson	.10
166	Elmore Spencer	.05
167	*Jamal Mashburn*	1.50
168	Tim Perry	.05
169	*Antonio Davis*	.15
170	*Isaiah Rider*	.40
171	Dee Brown	.05
172	Walt Williams	.05
173	Elden Campbell	.05
174	Benoit Benjamin	.05
175	Billy Owens	.05
176	Andrew Lang	.05
177	David Robinson	.50
178	Checklist 1	.05
179	Checklist 2	.05
180	Checklist 3	.05
181	Shawn Bradley (AS)	.10
182	Calbert Cheaney (AS)	.05
183	Toni Kukoc (AS)	.10
184	Popeye Jones (AS)	.05
185	Lindsey Hunter (AS)	.05
186	Chris Webber (AS)	.25
187	Bryon Russell (AS)	.05
188	Anfernee Hardaway	1.50
189	Nick Van Exel (AS)	.50
190	P.J. Brown (AS)	.05
191	Isaiah Rider (AS)	.15
192	Chris Mills (AS)	.05
193	Antonio Davis (AS)	.05
194	Jamal Mashburn (AS)	.30
195	Dino Radja (AS)	.05
196	Sam Cassell (AS)	.05
197	Isaiah Rider (AS)	.15
198	Mark Price-LDS (AS)	.05
199	Atlanta Hawks (Head)	.05
200	Boston Celtics (Head)	.05
201	Charlotte Hornets (Head)	.05
202	Chicago Bulls (Head)	.20
203	Cleveland Cavaliers (Head)	.05
204	Dallas (Head)	.20
205	Denver Nuggets (Head)	.05
206	Detroit Pistons (Head)	.05
207	Golden State (Head)	.50
208	Houston Rockets (Head)	.05
209	Indiana Pacers (Head)	.05
210	Los Angeles Clippers (Head)	.05
211	Los Angeles Lakers (Head)	.05
212	Miami Heat (Head)	.05
213	Milwaukee Bucks (Head)	.05
214	Minnesota (Head)	.05
215	New Jersey Nets (Head)	.05
216	New York Knicks (Head)	.05
217	Orlando Magic (Head)	1.00
218	Philadelphia 76ers (Head)	.05
219	Phoenix Suns (Head)	.05
220	Portland Trail Blazers (Head)	.05
221	Sacramento Kings (Head)	.05
222	San Antonio (Head)	.25
223	Seattle Supersonics (Head)	.05
224	Utah Jazz (Head)	.05
225	Washington Bullets (Head)	.05
JKI	Johnny Kilroy	5.00
MJRI	Michael Jordan (Retir)	10.00

1993-94 Upper Deck SE Electric Court

The 225-card, standard-size set parallels the base SE set with the only difference being the "Electric Court" logo and the cards' thicker stock. The cards were inserted one per 12-card hobby packs (East and West) and retail pack, as well as two per 10-card magazine packs.

	MT
Complete Set (225):	60.00
Common Player:	.15
Semistars:	.30
Electric Court:	2x-4x

1993-94 Upper Deck SE Electric Gold

Gold cards, randomly inserted into every 72nd pack, were printed using a silver-sparkle version of Upper Deck's Electric foil.

	MT
Complete Set (225):	700.00
Common Player:	2.00
Minor Stars:	5.00
Unlisted Stars:	10x-20x

1	Scottie Pippen	20.00
2	Todd Day	5.00
3	Detlef Schrempf	5.00
4	*Chris Webber*	50.00
5	Michael Adams	2.00
6	Loy Vaught	2.00
7	Doug West	2.00
8	A.C. Green	2.00
9	Anthony Mason	2.00
10	Clyde Drexler	15.00
11	*Popeye Jones*	8.00
12	Vlade Divac	5.00
13	Armon Gilliam	2.00
14	Hersey Hawkins	2.00
15	Dennis Scott	5.00
16	Bimbo Coles	2.00
17	Blue Edwards	2.00
18	Negele Knight	2.00
19	Dale Davis	2.00
20	Isiah Thomas	8.00
21	Latrell Sprewell	20.00
22	Kenny Smith	2.00
23	Bryant Stith	2.00
24	Terry Porter	2.00
25	Spud Webb	2.00
26	John Battle	2.00
27	Jeff Malone	2.00
28	Olden Polynice	2.00
29	Kevin Willis	2.00
30	Robert Parish	5.00
31	Kevin Johnson	7.00
32	Shaquille O'Neal	80.00
33	Willie Anderson	2.00
34	Micheal Williams	2.00
35	Steve Smith	5.00
36	Rik Smits	5.00
37	Pete Myers	2.00
38	Oliver Miller	2.00
39	Eddie Johnson	2.00
40	*Calbert Cheaney*	15.00
41	Vernon Maxwell	2.00
42	James Worthy	5.00
43	*Dino Radja*	15.00
44	Derrick Coleman	7.00
45	Reggie Williams	2.00
46	Dale Ellis	2.00
47	Cliff Robinson	5.00
48	Doug Christie	2.00
49	Ricky Pierce	2.00
50	Sean Elliott	5.00
51	*Anfernee Hardaway*	100.00
52	Dana Barros	2.00
53	Reggie Miller	15.00
54	Brian Williams	2.00
55	Otis Thorpe	2.00
56	Jerome Kersey	2.00
57	Larry Johnson	15.00
58	Rex Chapman	2.00
59	Kevin Edwards	2.00
60	Nate McMillan	2.00
61	Chris Mullin	7.00
62	Bill Cartwright	2.00
63	Dennis Rodman	25.00
64	Pooh Richardson	2.00
65	Tyrone Hill	2.00
66	Scott Brooks	2.00
67	Brad Daugherty	7.00
68	Joe Dumars	7.00
69	*Vin Baker*	30.00
70	Rod Strickland	2.00
71	Tom Chambers	2.00
72	Charles Oakley	2.00
73	Craig Ehlo	2.00
74	LaPhonso Ellis	5.00
75	Kevin Gamble	2.00
76	*Shawn Bradley*	12.00
77	Kendall Gill	5.00
78	Hakeem Olajuwon	30.00
79	Nick Anderson	5.00
80	Anthony Peeler	2.00
81	Wayman Tisdale	2.00
82	Danny Manning	7.00
83	John Starks	5.00
84	Jeff Hornacek	2.00
85	Victor Alexander	2.00
86	Mitch Richmond	5.00
87	Mookie Blaylock	2.00
88	Harvey Grant	2.00
89	Doug Smith	2.00
90	John Stockton	15.00
91	Charles Barkley	20.00
92	Gerald Wilkins	2.00
93	Mario Elie	2.00
94	Ken Norman	2.00
95	B.J. Armstrong	5.00
96	John Williams	2.00
97	Rony Seikaly	2.00
98	Sean Rooks	2.00
99	Shawn Kemp	15.00
100	Danny Ainge	2.00
101	Terry Mills	2.00
102	Doc Rivers	2.00
103	Chuck Person	2.00
104	*Sam Cassell*	15.00
105	Kevin Duckworth	2.00
106	Dan Majerle	5.00
107	Mark Jackson	2.00
108	Steve Kerr	2.00
109	Sam Perkins	2.00
110	C. Weatherspoon	5.00
111	Felton Spencer	2.00
112	Greg Anthony	2.00
113	Pete Chilcutt	2.00
114	Malik Sealy	2.00
115	Horace Grant	5.00
116	Chris Morris	2.00
117	Xavier McDaniel	2.00
118	Lionel Simmons	2.00
119	Dell Curry	2.00
120	Moses Malone	2.00
121	*Lindsey Hunter*	5.00
122	Buck Williams	2.00
123	Mahmoud Abdul-Rauf	2.00
124	Rumeal Robinson	2.00
125	*Chris Mills*	10.00
126	Scott Skiles	2.00
127	Derrick McKey	2.00
128	Avery Johnson	2.00
129	Harold Miner	5.00
130	Frank Brickowski	2.00
131	Gary Payton	8.00
132	Don MacLean	2.00
133	Thurl Bailey	2.00
134	*Nick Van Exel*	25.00
135	Matt Geiger	2.00
136	Stacey Augmon	2.00
137	Sedale Threatt	2.00
138	Patrick Ewing	15.00
139	Tyrone Corbin	2.00
140	Jim Jackson	20.00
141	Christian Laettner	5.00
142	Robert Horry	5.00
143	J.R. Reid	2.00
144	Eric Murdock	2.00
145	Alonzo Mourning	20.00
146	Sherman Douglas	2.00
147	Tom Gugliotta	5.00
148	Glen Rice	7.00
149	Mark Price	5.00
150	Dikembe Mutombo	10.00
151	Derek Harper	2.00
152	Karl Malone	15.00
153	Byron Scott	2.00
154	Reggie Jordan	2.00
155	Dominique Wilkins	15.00
156	*Bobby Hurley*	10.00
157	Ron Harper	2.00
158	Byron Russell	2.00
159	Frank Johnson	2.00
160	*Toni Kukoc*	15.00
161	Lloyd Daniels	2.00
162	Jeff Turner	2.00
163	Muggsy Bogues	2.00
164	Chris Gatling	2.00
165	Kenny Anderson	10.00
166	Elmore Spencer	2.00
167	*Jamal Mashburn*	25.00
168	Tim Perry	2.00
169	*Antonio Davis*	5.00
170	*Isaiah Rider*	20.00
171	Dee Brown	5.00
172	Walt Williams	5.00
173	Elden Cambell	2.00
174	Benoit Benjamin	2.00
175	Billy Owens	2.00
176	Andrew Lang	2.00
177	David Robinson	25.00
178	Checklist 1	2.00
179	Checklist 2	2.00
180	Checklist 3	2.00
181	Shawn Bradley (AS)	5.00
182	Calbert Cheaney (AS)	5.00
183	Toni Kukoc (AS)	5.00
184	Popeye Jones (AS)	2.00
185	Lindsey Hunter (AS)	2.00
186	Chris Webber (AS)	12.00
187	Bryon Russell (AS)	2.00
188	Anfernee Hardaway	40.00
189	Nick Van Exel (AS)	12.00
190	P.J. Brown (AS)	2.00
191	Isaiah Rider (AS)	8.00
192	Chris Mills (AS)	2.00
193	Antonio Davis (AS)	2.00
194	Jamal Mashburn (AS)	20.00
195	Dino Radja (AS)	5.00
196	Sam Cassell (AS)	5.00
197	Isaiah Rider (AS)	8.00
198	Mark Price-LDS (AS)	2.00
199	Atlanta Hawks (Head)	2.00
200	Boston Celtics (Head)	2.00
201	Charlotte Hornets (Head)	2.00
202	Chicago Bulls (Head)	5.00
203	Cleveland Cavaliers (Head)	2.00
204	Dallas (Head)	10.00
205	Denver Nuggets (Head)	2.00
206	Detroit Pistons (Head)	2.00
207	Golden State (Head)	7.00
208	Houston Rockets (Head)	2.00
209	Indiana Pacers (Head)	2.00
210	Los Angeles Clippers (Head)	2.00
211	Los Angeles Lakers (Head)	2.00
212	Miami Heat (Head)	2.00
213	Milwaukee Bucks (Head)	2.00
214	Minnesota (Head)	5.00
215	New Jersey Nets (Head)	2.00
216	New York Knicks (Head)	5.00
217	Orlando Magic (Head)	20.00
218	Philadelphia 76ers (Head)	2.00
219	Phoenix Suns (Head)	2.00
220	Portland Trail Blazers (Head)	2.00
221	Sacramento Kings (Head)	2.00
222	San Antonio (Head)	7.00
223	Seattle Supersonics (Head)	2.00
224	Utah Jazz (Head)	2.00
225	Washington Bullets (Head)	2.00

1993-94 Upper Deck SE East All Stars

These insert cards, done in Electric Court and Electric Gold versions, feature 15 All-Stars from the Eastern Conference. The cards feature a die-cut design and use either silver foil (Electric Court, one in every pack) or gold foil (Electric Gold, every 36th pack) on thicker, higher quality paper stock. These cards were distributed on a regional basis, using the NBA's conferences as a guide.

	MT
Complete Set (15):	300.00
Common Player:	3.00
Minor Stars:	6.00

1	Dominique Wilkins	6.00
2	Alonzo Mourning	16.00
3	B.J. Armstrong	3.00
4	Scottie Pippen	35.00
5	Mark Price	3.00
6	Isiah Thomas	6.00
7	Harold Miner	3.00
8	Vin Baker	35.00
9	Kenny Anderson	6.00
10	Derrick Coleman	3.00
11	Patrick Ewing	10.00
12	Anfernee Hardaway	80.00
13	Shaquille O'Neal	50.00
14	Shawn Bradley	10.00
15	Calbert Cheaney	6.00

1993-94 Upper Deck SE West All Stars

Fifteen All-Stars from the Western Conference are featured on these insert cards, done in Electric Court (silver foil, one per pack) and Electric Court (gold foil, one every 36 packs) versions. The cards, using a die-cut design, were distributed on a regional basis, using the conferences as a guideline.

	MT
Complete Set (15):	275.00
Common Player:	3.00
Minor Stars:	6.00

1	Jim Jackson	10.00
2	Jamal Mashburn	25.00
3	Dikembe Mutombo	6.00
4	Latrell Sprewell	25.00
5	Chris Webber	50.00
6	Hakeem Olajuwon	30.00
7	Danny Manning	3.00
8	Nick Van Exel	25.00
9	Isaiah Rider	3.00
10	Charles Barkley	20.00
11	Clyde Drexler	15.00
12	Mitch Richmond	10.00
13	David Robinson	20.00
14	Shawn Kemp	15.00
15	Karl Malone	15.00

1993-94 Upper Deck SE Behind the Glass

These insert cards are printed with Upper Deck's "Light F/X" printing technology. The 15-card gold set could be obtained by sending in a redeemable trade card found in Upper Deck SE packs. The trade cards were included in foil packs at retail locations only.

	MT
Complete Set (15):	60.00
Common Player:	1.00

1	Shawn Kemp	3.00
2	Patrick Ewing	3.00
3	Dikembe Mutombo	1.50
4	Charles Barkley	4.00
5	Hakeem Olajuwon	6.00
6	Larry Johnson	3.00
7	Chris Webber	8.00
8	John Starks	1.00
9	Kevin Willis	1.00
10	Scottie Pippen	5.00
11	Michael Jordan	25.00
12	Alonzo Mourning	4.00
13	Shawn Bradley	2.00
14	Shaquille O'Neal	15.00
15	Ron Harper	1.00

1993-94 Upper Deck SE USA Trade

The 24-card, standard-size set was available only to collectors through a mail-in redemption card, the USA Trade card which was inserted every 360 packs. The set depicts the 13 players selected for the Dream Team II, as well as the 11 original players from the 1992 Dream Team. The cards are numbered on the back with a "USA" prefix.

	MT
Complete Set (24):	50.00
Common Player:	.50

1	Charles Barkley	3.00
2	Larry Bird	8.00
3	Clyde Drexler	2.50
4	Patrick Ewing	2.00
5	Michael Jordan	25.00
6	Christian Laettner	1.00
7	Karl Malone	2.00
8	Chris Mullin	1.00
9	Scottie Pippen	6.00
10	David Robinson	4.00
11	John Stockton	2.00
12	Dominique Wilkins	1.00
13	Isiah Thomas	1.00
14	Dan Majerle	1.00
15	Steve Smith	1.00
16	Alonzo Mourning	3.00
17	Shawn Kemp	3.00
18	Larry Johnson	1.00
19	Tim Hardaway	1.00
20	Joe Dumars	1.00
21	Mark Price	.50
22	Derrick Coleman	.50
23	Reggie Miller	2.50
24	Shaquille O'Neal	12.00
NNO	Exp. USA Trade Card	1.50
NNO	Red. USA Trade Card	.25

1994 Upper Deck French McDonald's Team

The 27-card, standard-size set was sponsored by McDonald's and parallels in design the schedule cards from the 1993-94 Upper Deck set (210-236). The cards were available in three-card packs with six different holograms randomly inserted. The backs feature bilingual text.

	MT
Complete Set (33):	140.00
Comp. Team Card Set (27):	15.00
Comp. Hologram Set (6):	125.00
Common Player (1-27):	.25
Com. Hologram (28H-33H):	5.00

1	Atlanta/Group	.25
2	Boston/Group	.25
3	Charlotte/Group	.25
4	Chicago/M.Jordan	5.00
5	Cleveland/M.Price	.40
6	Dallas/J.Jackson	1.00
7	Denver/Group	.25
8	Detroit/I.Thomas	1.00
9	Golden State/Group	.25
10	Houston/H.Olajuwon	1.00
11	Indiana/R.Smits	.75
12	L.A.Clippers/Group	.25
13	L.A.Lakers/Group	.25
14	Miami/Group	.25
15	Milwaukee/Group	.25
16	Minnesota/Group	.25
17	New Jersey/K.Anderson	.50
18	New York/Group	.25
19	Orlando/S.O'Neal	3.00
20	Philadelphia/H.Hawkins	.50
21	Phoenix/Barkley/Ceballos	1.50

22	Portland/Group	.25
23	Sacramento/M.Richmond	1.00
24	San Antonio/D.Robinson/Elliott	1.50
25	Seattle/Payton/Kemp	1.50
26	Utah/Group	.25
27	Washington/Group	.25
28H	Hakkem Olajuwon Hologram	20.00
29H	Michael Jordan Hologram	100.00
30H	Charles Barkley Hologram	20.00
31H	Shawn Kemp Hologram	20.00
32H	Patrick Ewing Hologram	10.00
33H	Ron Harper Hologram	5.00

1994 Upper Deck European

The 195-card, standard-size set was similar in design to the U.S. 1993-94 Upper Deck set. Issued in 10-card packs, the set features the same subsets, but at tougher pull rates. Values below are for the more common Spanish versions with Italian (1.25x), French (1.5x) and German (1.75x) cards more valuable.

		MT
Complete French Set (195):		225.00
Comp. German Set (195):		275.00
Comp. Italian Set (195):		200.00
Comp. Spanish Set (195):		150.00
Common Spanish (1-195):		.15
1	Stacey Augmon	.25
2	Chris Mills	1.00
3	Joe Dumars	.40
4	Grant Long	.15
5	Robert Horry	.75
6	Rod Strickland	.25
7	Frank Brickowski	.15
8	Ricky Pierce	.15
9	Dan Majerle	.25
10	Dell Curry	.15
11	Derek Harper	.25
12	Anthony Avent	.15
13	Vern Fleming	.15
14	Dee Brown	.15
15	Kevin Johnson	.40
16	Cliff Robinson	.40
17	Doc Rivers	.25
18	Doug West	.15
19	Michael Adams	.15
20	Sherman Douglas	.15
21	Harold Miner	.15
22	John Williams	.25
23	Michael Jordan	6.00
24	Jim Jackson	1.00
25	Glen Rice	.40
26	Jeff Hornacek	.25
27	Derrick Coleman	.25
28	Sam Perkins	.25
29	Willie Anderson	.15
30	Rumeal Robinson	.15
31	Blue Edwards	.15
32	Sarunas Marciulionis	.15
33	Clyde Drexler	1.00
34	Shawn Bradley	1.00
35	Ron Harper	.25
36	Chris Morris	.15
37	Brad Daugherty	.25
38	Duane Ferrell	.15
39	Chuck Person	.25
40	Todd Day	.15
41	Sedale Threatt	.15
42	Xavier McDaniel	.15
43	Kevin Willis	.25
44	Chris Mullin	.40
45	Terrell Brandon	.25
46	Kenny Smith	.15
47	Malik Sealy	.15
48	John Starks	.25
49	Dino Radja	.75
50	David Robinson	2.00
51	John Salley	.15
52	Danny Ainge	.40
53	Sam Cassell	1.50
54	Latrell Sprewell	.75
55	Dikembe Mutombo	.40
56	Doug Edwards	.15
57	A.C. Green	.25
58	Otis Thorpe	.25
59	Antoine Carr	.15
60	Tim Legler	.15
61	Don MacLean	.15
62	Horace Grant	.40
63	John Stockton	1.00
64	Muggsy Bogues	.25
65	Rex Chapman	.15
66	Stanley Roberts	.15
67	Walt Williams	.25
68	Dominique Wilkins	.50
69	Brent Price	.15
70	Lloyd Daniels	.15
71	Mark Price	.25
72	Sean Elliott	.40
73	Scottie Pippen	2.00
74	Rodney Rogers	.40
75	Charles Barkley	2.00
76	Kevin Gamble	.15
77	Lionel Simmons	.15
78	Dennis Rodman	2.00
79	Jeff Malone	.25
80	Larry Johnson	.75
81	Armon Gilliam	.25
82	Chris Dudley	.15
83	Bryant Stith	.15
84	Mark Jackson	.50
85	Paul Graham	.15
86	Calbert Cheaney	1.00
87	Clarence Weatherspoon	.40
88	Isiah Thomas	.50
89	Scott Brooks	.15
90	Mitch Richmond	.50
91	Kendall Gill	.15
92	Robert Parish	.40
93	Karl Malone	1.50
94	Rik Smits	.40
95	Rex Walters	.15
96	Oliver Miller	.15
97	Hersey Hawkins	.25
98	Vinny Del Negro	.15
99	Spud Webb	.25
100	Chris Webber	4.00
101	Moses Malone	.50
102	Hubert Davis	.15
103	Gary Payton	.60
104	Mahmoud Abdul-Rauf	.25
105	Larry Nance	.25
106	Bobby Hurley	.40
107	David Benoit	.15
108	Danny Manning	.40
109	Pervis Ellison	.15
110	Anthony Peeler	.15
111	Tim Hardaway	.40
112	Detlef Schrempf	.40
113	Hakeem Olajuwon	2.00
114	Elden Campbell	.15
115	Charles Smith	.15
116	B.J. Armstrong	.25
117	Dennis Scott	.25
118	LaPhonso Ellis	.15
119	Isaiah Rider	1.00
120	Tim Perry	.15
121	Lindsey Hunter	.40
122	Anthony Bowie	.15
123	Micheal Williams	.15
124	Gerald Wilkins	.15
125	Tom Chambers	.25
126	Vincent Askew	.15
127	Vernon Maxwell	.15
128	Nick Van Exel	3.00
129	Buck Williams	.25
130	Alonzo Mourning	2.00
131	Lou Vaught	.25
132	Shaquille O'Neal	4.00
133	Derrick McKey	.15
134	Kenny Anderson	.25
135	Bill Cartwright	.15
136	Nick Anderson	.25
137	Billy Owens	.25
138	Anfernee Hardaway	8.00
139	Terry Mills	.15
140	John Paxson	.25
141	Charles Oakley	.25
142	Steve Smith	.40
143	Johnny Dawkins	.25
144	Thurl Bailey	.15
145	Jamal Mashburn	3.00
146	Terry Porter	.15
147	Duane Causwell	.15
148	Reggie Miller	1.00
149	Shawn Kemp	1.25
150	James Worthy	.50
151	Scott Skiles	.25
152	Donald Hodge	.15
153	Christian Laettner	.50
154	Vin Baker	2.50
155	Doug Christie	.15
156	Tyrone Corbin	.15
157	Toni Kukoc	1.50
158	Ken Norman	.15
159	Randy White	.15
160	Rony Seikaly	.15
161	Tom Gugliotta	.40
162	Vlade Divac	.25
163	Eric Murdock	.15
164	Pooh Richardson	.15
165	Patrick Ewing	1.00
166	M.Jordan/A Steal	10.00
167	M.Jordan/High Five	10.00
168	M.Jordan/Finals MVP	10.00
169	M.Jordan/35 Points	10.00
170	M.Jordan/Three-Point King	10.00
171	M.Jordan Back-To-Back	10.00
172	M.Jordan/55-Point Game	10.00
173	M.Jordan/Scoring Avg	10.00
174	M.Jordan/Third Straight MVP	10.00
175	Mr. June Checklist	10.00
176	Michael Jordan SM	10.00
177	Shawn Kemp SM	3.00
178	Karl Malone SM	3.50
179	Clyde Drexler SM	2.00
180	Tim Hardaway SM	1.00
181	Charles Barkley FT	4.00
182	Cedric Ceballos FT	1.50
183	Derrick Coleman FT	1.00
184	Clyde Drexler FT	2.00
185	Larry Johnson FT	2.00
186	Shawn Kemp FT	3.00
187	Harold Miner FT	1.00
188	Alonzo Mourning FT	4.00
189	Shaquille O'Neal FT	8.00
190	Scottie Pippen FT	3.00
191	Clarence Weatherspoon FT	1.00
192	Dominique Wilkins FT	1.00
193	Kenny Anderson CL, Xavier McDaniel CL	.25
194	Doug West CL, James Worthy CL	.25
195	Reggie Miller CL, Joe Dumars CL	.50

1994 Upper Deck European Triple Double

Inserted every five packs, the 10 insert cards parallel the 1993-94 U.S. Triple Double inserts. Values below are for the Spanish versions with the Italian (1.25x), French (1.5x) and German (1.75x) cards more valuable. Cards are numbered with a "TD" prefix.

		MT
Complete French Set (10):		40.00
Complete German Set (10):		45.00
Complete Italian Set (10):		30.00
Complete Spanish Set (10):		25.00
Common Spanish (TD1-TD10):		.50
1	Charles Barkley	5.00
2	Michael Jordan	15.00
3	Scottie Pippen	8.00
4	Micheal Williams	.50
5	Mark Jackson	1.00
6	Kenny Anderson	1.00
7	Larry Johnson	2.00
8	Dikembe Mutombo	2.00
9	Rumeal Robinson	.50
10	Detlef Schrempf	1.50

1994 Upper Deck Jordan Rare Air

The 90-card, standard-size set was sold exclusively in a factory box retailing for $19.99. The set had a serial number out of 30,000 and a gold-foil set was included in every 12-set case. The first 50 cards have pictures from Rare Air, a book by Jordan and Walter Iooss Jr., cards 51-60 are outtakes from the book while 61-90, "MJ, Decade of Dominance," highlights Jordan's career. Two black and white cards measuring 3-3/8" x 7-7/8" were also included in the set, but were not numbered.

		MT
Complete Set (90):		25.00
Common Player:		.25
1	Michael Jordan (Close-up with white robe)	1.00
2	Michael Jordan (Close-up profile)	1.00
3	Michael Jordan (Michael's shooting form)	.50
4	Michael Jordan (Close-up of his left hand)	.25
5	Michael Jordan (Entering onto court in Orlando)	.50
6	Michael Jordan (Lifting weights)	.50
7	Michael Jordan (Driving car to Chicago Stadium)	.50
8	Michael Jordan (Sitting in visitor's locker room in Miami Arena)	.50
9	Michael Jordan (Relaxing on trainer's table)	.50
10	Michael Jordan (Listening to pre-game instructions)	.50
11	Michael Jordan (Readying himself for action on the floor)	.50
12	Michael Jordan (Greeted by teammates during pre-game introductions)	.50
13	Michael Jordan (Pre-game huddle with Chicago teammates)	.25
14	Michael Jordan (Preforming final pre-game rituals)	.50
15	Michael Jordan (Close-up look at his feet)	.25
16	Michael Jordan (Stealing a pass intended for A.C. Green)	1.00
17	Michael Jordan (Guarding James Worthy)	.50
18	Michael Jordan (Greeted in mid-air by Shaquille O'Neal)	1.00
19	Michael Jordan (Slamming another one home during a game in Chicago Stadium)	.50
20	Michael Jordan (Pippen with hand on Michael's head during playoff game)	.50
21	Michael Jordan (Facing reporters in locker room after game)	.25
22	Michael Jordan (Heading to locker room after game at Chicago Stadium)	1.00
23	Michael Jordan (Listening to questions from reporters)	1.00
24	Michael Jordan (Sleeping on the bus)	.50
25	Michael Jordan (Boarding plane after bus ride to airport)	.50
26	Michael Jordan (Settling into seat on team's private airplane)	.50
27	Michael Jordan (Treating sprained ankle in hotel room)	.25
28	Michael Jordan (Getting rest and relaxation on road trip)	.50
29	Michael Jordan (Peering out of car window)	.50
30	Michael Jordan (Enjoying game of cards)	.50
31	Michael Jordan (Shooting pool)	.50
32	Michael Jordan (Caring for golf clubs)	.50
33	Michael Jordan (Preparing to drive shot onto green)	1.00
34	Michael Jordan (Sizing up a putt)	1.00
35	Michael Jordan (Calling home from golf course)	.25
36	Michael Jordan (Sitting by window, taking time out)	.50
37	Michael Jordan (Close-up view, chin resting in hand)	1.00
38	Michael Jordan (Wearing uniform, enjoying 1993 baseball All-Star Game)	1.00
39	Michael Jordan (Shaving head)	.50
40	Michael Jordan (Wearing warm-ups, standing outside locker room)	.50
41	Michael Jordan (Passing to Horace Grant in game against Atlanta)	.50
42	Michael Jordan (Preparing to shoot free throw in playoff game against Atlanta)	.50
43	Michael Jordan (Driving lane between New York's John Starks and Doc Rivers)	.50
44	Michael Jordan (Standing next to Charles Barkley during game)	.50
45	Michael Jordan (Celebrating third NBA Championship)	.50
46	Michael Jordan (Celebrating third NBA Championship, arms outstretched)	1.00
47	Michael Jordan (Celebrating with team in locker room)	.50
48	Michael Jordan (Holding up three fingers, representing three NBA titles)	1.00
49	Michael Jordan (Michael with a special friend)	.25
50	Michael Jordan (Close-up shot from back)	1.00
51	Michael Jordan (Head bowed, hand on brow)	.25
52	Michael Jordan (Palming basketball)	.25
53	Michael Jordan (Lifting weights with curl bar)	.50
54	Michael Jordan (Sitting in weight training room)	.50
55	Michael Jordan (Resting on sofa beside telephone)	.50
56	Michael Jordan (Signing sports cards)	.50
57	Michael Jordan (Boarding team bus)	.50
58	Michael Jordan (In black sports car, outside Chicago Stadium)	.50
59	Michael Jordan (In locker room, before game)	.50
60	Michael Jordan (Michael at free throw line, shot from above)	.50
61	Michael Jordan (Close-up with ball, orange background)	1.00
62	Michael Jordan (Winning NBA Slam Dunk Championship)	1.00
63	Michael Jordan (Cheering on sidelines)	1.00
64	Michael Jordan (Preparing to shoot free throw)	1.00
65	Michael Jordan (Defensive posture)	1.00
66	Michael Jordan (Efficient Scorer)	.50
67	Michael Jordan (In mid-air, preparing to dunk)	.50
68	Michael Jordan (Signing autographs for fans)	.50
69	Michael Jordan (A multi-mirror image)	.50
70	Michael Jordan (Playing wheel chair basketball with handicapped child)	.50
71	Michael Jordan (Watching a game on TV)	.50
72	Michael Jordan (Scoring over opponent)	1.00
73	Michael Jordan (Jordan defended by Mark West and Charles Barkley)	.50
74	Michael Jordan (Dunking over Patrick Ewing)	.50
75	Michael Jordan (Driving baseline)	1.00
76	Michael Jordan (Fighting for rebound position)	1.00
77	Michael Jordan (Shooting over Scott Skiles)	.50
78	Michael Jordan (Defending against Orlando Magic player)	1.00
79	Michael Jordan (Driving past Vlade Divac)	.50
80	Michael Jordan (Shooting jump shot over Orlando Magic players)	.50
81	Michael Jordan (Shooting lay up around Patrick Ewing)	.50
82	Michael Jordan (Shooting jump shot over outstretched arms)	.50
83	Michael Jordan (Driving down court)	1.00
84	Michael Jordan (In mid-air during game against Nets)	.50
85	Michael Jordan (Dribbling past New York defender)	1.00
86	Michael Jordan (Positioning for rebound in game against Phoenix)	.50
87	Michael Jordan (Shooting jump shot over Dan Majerle)	.50
88	Michael Jordan (Finger roll lay up against Phoenix)	.50
89	Michael Jordan (Shooting jump shot over Gerald Wilkins)	1.00
90	Michael Jordan (In warm-ups, shot from above)	.50
NNO	Jordan Passing Ball	1.00
NNO	Jordan Under Backboard	1.00

1994 Upper Deck Nothing But Net

The 15-card, standard-size set features scenes from McDonald's "Nothing but Net" commercials with Michael Jordan, Charles Barkely and Larry Bird. The card fronts have a special McDonald's logo in the lower left corner. Wal-Mart issued a special jumbo version of the set and each of those cards are valued at five times the prices listed below.

		MT
Complete Set (15):		12.00
Common Player:		.25
1	Larry Bird (Michael Jordan) (I've got an idea))	1.50
2	Charles Barkley (Can I play)	.50
3	Over the Grand Canyon	.25
4	Off your face (Mt. Rushmore)	.25
5	Michael Jordan (Through the window off the floor)	1.50
6	Larry Bird (Nothing but Net)	1.00
7	Michael Jordan (Larry Bird) (Watch this shot)	1.50
8	Charles Barkley (Hey, can I play)	.50
9	Michael Jordan (Larry Bird) (No)	1.50
10	Charles Barkley (The Shark)	.50
11	Charles Barkley (Please...Pretty Please)	.50
12	Larry Bird (Michael Jordan Charles Barkley) (No)	1.50
13	Michael Jordan (I'm hungry...)	1.50
14	Larry Bird (Play ya to see who buys)	1.00
15	McDonald's Logo in Outer Space	.25

1994-95 Upper Deck

Upper Deck's 1994-95 Series I cards feature full-bleed photos, gold foil stamping and UV coating. Fronts have the player's name in gold and the team name in white, both printed down the side, separated by a basketball outlined in gold. The Upper Deck logo is in gold foil in the bottom right-corner. The backs have a close-up photo of the player, with statistics and a card number. Subsets include USA Basketball Highlights and the All-Rookie and All-NBA teams. Insert sets include Basketball Heroes, which chronicles Michael Jordan's career; an NBA Draft trade card, which can be redeemed for a 10-card set featuring the top rookies from 1994-95; 90-card Special Edition sets in silver and gold foil versions; and Predictors cards, which feature nine players who have a chance to lead the league in one of four categories - scoring, assists, All-Star Game MVP and Defensive Player of the Year - plus a wild card covering all other NBA players. If the person on the card wins that category, the card holder can redeem it for a 20-card assist/scoring leader set or a 20-card All-Star Game MVP/Defensive Player of the Year set.

		MT
Complete Set (360):		45.00
Complete Series 1 (180):		25.00
Complete Series 2 (180):		20.00
Common Player:		.10
Minor Stars:		.20
Ser. 1 or 2 Pack (12):		1.50
Ser. 1 or 2 Wax Box (36):		45.00
1	Chris Webber (AR)	.25
2	Anfernee Hardaway (AR)	1.00
3	Vin Baker (AR)	.25
4	Jamal Mashburn (AR)	.20
5	Isaiah Rider (AR)	.25
6	Dino Radja (AR)	.20
7	Nick Van Exel (AR)	.20
8	Shawn Bradley (AR)	.10
9	Toni Kukoc (AR)	.10
10	Lindsey Hunter (AR)	.10
11	Scottie Pippen (AN)	.40
12	Karl Malone (AN)	.20
13	Hakeem Olajuwon (AN)	.50
14	John Stockton (AN)	.15
15	Latrell Sprewell (AN)	.30
16	Shawn Kemp (AN)	.30
17	Charles Barkley (AN)	.35
18	David Robinson (AN)	.35
19	Mitch Richmond (AN)	.15
20	Kevin Johnson (AN)	.15
21	Derrick Coleman (AN)	.15
22	Dominique Wilkins (AN)	.15
23	Shaquille O'Neal (AN)	1.00
24	Mark Price	.15
25	Gary Payton	.15
26	Dan Majerle	.10
27	Vernon Maxwell	.10
28	Matt Geiger	.10
29	Jeff Turner	.10
30	Vinny Del Negro	.10
31	B.J. Armstrong	.10
32	Chris Gatling	.10
33	Tony Smith	.10
34	Doug West	.10
35	Clyde Drexler	.35
36	Keith Jennings	.10
37	Steve Smith	.10
38	Kendall Gill	.10
39	Bob Martin	.10
40	Calbert Cheaney	.20
41	Terrell Brandon	.10
42	Pete Chilcutt	.10
43	Avery Johnson	.10
44	Tom Gugliotta	.10
45	LaBradford Smith	.10
46	Sedale Threatt	.10
47	Chris Smith	.10
48	Kevin Edwards	.10
49	Lucious Harris	.10
50	Tim Perry	.10
51	Lloyd Daniels	.10
52	Dee Brown	.10
53	Sean Elliott	.10
54	Tim Hardaway	.15
55	Christian Laettner	.10
56	Charles Outlaw	.10
57	Kevin Johnson	.20
58	Duane Ferrell	.10
59	Jo Jo English	.10
60	Stanley Roberts	.10
61	Kevin Willis	.10
62	Dana Barros	.10
63	Gheorghe Muresan	.10
64	Vern Fleming	.10
65	Anthony Peeler	.10
66	Negele Knight	.10
67	Harold Ellis	.10
68	Vincent Askew	.10
69	Ennis Whatley	.10
70	Elden Campbell	.10
71	Sherman Douglas	.10
72	Luc Longley	.10
73	Lorenzo Williams	.10
74	Jay Humphries	.10
75	Chris King	.10
76	Tyrone Corbin	.10
77	Bobby Hurley	.10
78	Dell Curry	.10
79	Dino Radja	.20
80	A.C. Green	.10
81	Craig Ehlo	.10
82	Gary Payton	.20
83	Sleepy Floyd	.10
84	Rodney Rogers	.20
85	Brian Shaw	.10
86	Kevin Gamble	.10
87	John Stockton	.25
88	Hersey Hawkins	.10
89	Johnny Newman	.10
90	Larry Johnson	.50
91	Robert Pack	.10
92	Willie Burton	.10
93	Bobby Phills	.10
94	David Benoit	.10
95	Harold Miner	.10
96	David Robinson	.50
97	Nate McMillan	.10
98	Chris Mills	.15
99	Hubert Davis	.10
100	Shaquille O'Neal	2.00
101	Loy Vaught	.10
102	Kenny Smith	.10
103	Terry Dehere	.10
104	Carl Herrera	.10
105	LaPhonso Ellis	.10
106	Armon Gilliam	.10
107	Greg Graham	.10
108	Eric Murdock	.10
109	Ron Harper	.10
110	Andrew Lang	.10
111	Johnny Dawkins	.10
112	David Wingate	.10
113	Tom Hammon	.10
114	Brad Daugherty	.10
115	Charles Smith	.10
116	Dale Ellis	.10
117	Bryant Stith	.10
118	Lindsey Hunter	.10
119	Patrick Ewing	.35
120	Kenny Anderson	.20
121	Charles Barkley	.75
122	Harvey Grant	.10
123	Anthony Bowie	.10
124	Shawn Kemp	.50
125	Lee Mayberry	.10
126	Reggie Miller	.30
127	Scottie Pippen	1.00

128	Spud Webb	.10
129	Antonio Davis	.15
130	Greg Anderson	.10
131	Jim Jackson	.40
132	Dikembe Mutombo	.20
133	Terry Porter	.10
134	Mario Elie	.10
135	Vlade Divac	.10
136	Robert Horry	.10
137	Popeye Jones	.10
138	Brad Lohaus	.10
139	Anthony Bonner	.10
140	Doug Christie	.10
141	Rony Seikaly	.10
142	Allan Houston	.15
143	Tyrone Hill	.10
144	Latrell Sprewell	.25
145	Andres Guibert	.10
146	Dominique Wilkins	.25
147	Jon Barry	.10
148	Tracy Murray	.10
149	Mike Peplowski	.10
150	Mike Brown	.10
151	Cedric Ceballos	.10
152	Stacey King	.10
153	Trevor Wilson	.10
154	Anthony Avent	.10
155	Horace Grant	.20
156	*Bill Curley*	.20
157	*Grant Hill*	6.00
158	*Charlie Ward*	.25
159	*Jalen Rose*	2.00
160	*Jason Kidd*	3.00
161	*Yinka Dare*	.25
162	*Eric Montross*	.50
163	*Donyell Marshall*	.25
164	*Tony Dumas*	.25
165	*Wesley Person*	.50
166	*Eddie Jones*	3.00
167	Tim Hardaway	.20
168	Isiah Thomas	.15
169	Joe Dumars	.15
170	Mark Price	.15
171	Derrick Coleman	.15
172	Shawn Kemp	.30
173	Steve Smith	.10
174	Dan Majerle	.10
175	Reggie Miller	.20
176	Kevin Johnson	.15
177	Dominique Wilkins	.20
178	Shaquille O'Neal	1.00
179	Alonzo Mourning	.25
180	Larry Johnson	.20
181	Brian Grant	.50
182	Darrin Hancock	.10
183	Grant Hill	2.00
184	Jalen Rose	.25
185	Lamond Murray	.25
186	Jason Kidd	1.50
187	Donyell Marhsall	.25
188	Eddie Jones	1.00
189	Eric Montross	.20
190	Khalid Reeves	.20
191	Sharone Wright	.20
192	Wesley Person	.30
193	Glenn Robinson	.75
194	Carlos Rogers	.10
195	Aaron McKie	.10
196	Juwan Howard	.75
197	Charlie Ward	.10
198	Brooks Thompson	.10
199	Tony Massenburg	.10
200	James Robinson	.10
201	Dickey Simpkins	.20
202	Johnny Dawkins	.10
203	Joe Kleine	.10
204	Bill Wennington	.10
205	Sean Higgins	.10
206	Larry Krystkowiak	.10
207	Winston Garland	.10
208	Muggsy Bogues	.10
209	Charles Oakley	.10
210	Vin Baker	.50
211	Malik Sealy	.10
212	Willie Anderson	.10
213	Dale Davis	.10
214	Grant Long	.10
215	Danny Ainge	.10
216	Toni Kukoc	.10
217	Doug Smith	.10
218	Danny Manning	.15
219	Otis Thorpe	.10
220	Mark Price	.10
221	Victor Alexander	.10
222	Brent Price	.10
223	*Howard Eisley*	.15
224	Chris Mullin	.10
225	Nick Van Exel	.50
226	Xavier McDaniel	.10
227	*Khalid Reeves*	.50
228	Anfernee Hardaway	2.00
229	*B.J. Tyler*	.15
230	Elmore Spencer	.15
231	Rick Fox	.10
232	Alonzo Mourning	.50
233	Hakeem Olajuwon	1.00
234	Blue Edwards	.10
235	P.J. Brown	.10
236	Ron Harper	.10
237	Isaiah Rider	.40
238	*Eric Mobley*	.25
239	Brian Williams	.10
240	*Eric Piatkowski*	.25
241	Karl Malone	.40
242	Wayman Tisdale	.10
243	Sarunas Marciulionis	.10
244	Sean Rooks	.10
245	Ricky Pierce	.10
246	Don MacLean	.10
247	*Aaron McKie*	.50
248	Kenny Gattison	.10
249	Derek Harper	.10
250	*Michael Smith*	.30
251	John Williams	.10
252	Pooh Richardson	.10
253	*Sergei Bazarevich*	.15
254	*Brian Grant*	1.00
255	Ed Pickney	.10
256	Ken Norman	.10
257	Marty Conlon	.10
258	Matt Fish	.10
259	*Darrin Hancock*	.15
260	Mahmoud Abdul-Rauf	.10
261	Roy Tarpley	.10
262	Chris Morris	.10
263	*Sharone Wright*	.50
264	Jamal Mashburn	.50
265	John Starks	.10
266	Rod Strickland	.15
267	Adam Keefe	.10
268	Scott Burrell	.10
269	Eric Riley	.10
270	Sam Perkins	.10
271	Stacey Augmon	.10
272	Kevin Willis	.10
273	*Lamond Murray*	.50
274	Derrick Coleman	.20
275	Scott Skiles	.10
276	Buck Williams	.10
277	Sam Cassell	.20
278	Rik Smits	.10
279	Dennis Rodman	1.00
280	Olden Polynice	.10
281	*Glenn Robinson*	2.50
282	Clarence Weatherspoon	.15
283	*Monty Williams*	.20
284	Terry Mills	.10
285	Oliver Miller	.10
286	Dennis Scott	.10
287	Michael Williams	.10
288	Moses Malone	.10
289	Donald Royal	.10
290	Mark Jackson	.10
291	Walt Williams	.15
292	Bimbo Coles	.10
293	*Derrick Alston*	.20
294	Scott Williams	.10
295	Acie Earl	.10
296	Jeff Hornacek	.10
297	Kevin Duckworth	.10
298	*Dontonio Wingfield*	.20
299	Danny Ferry	.10
300	Mark West	.10
301	Jayson Williams	.10
302	David Wesley	.10
303	*Jim McIlvaine*	.20
304	Michael Adams	.10
305	*Greg Minor*	.20
306	Jeff Malone	.10
307	Pervis Ellison	.10
308	*Clifford Rozier*	.40
309	Billy Owens	.10
310	Duane Causwell	.10
311	Rex Chapman	.10
312	Detlef Schrempf	.10
313	Mitch Richmond	.20
314	*Carlos Rogers*	.25
315	Byron Scott	.10
316	Dwayne Morton	.10
317	Bill Cartwright	.10
318	J.R. Reid	.10
319	Derrick McKey	.10
320	*Jamie Watson*	.25
321	Mookie Blaylock	.10
322	Chris Webber	.50
323	Joe Dumars	.10
324	Shawn Bradley	.10
325	Chuck Person	.10
326	Haywoode Workman	.10
327	Benoit Benjamin	.10
328	Will Perdue	.10
329	Sam Mitchell	.10
330	George Lynch	.10
331	*Juwan Howard*	2.00
332	Robert Parish	.10
333	Glen Rice	.10
334	Michael Cage	.10
335	Brooks Thompson	.10
336	Rony Seikaly	.10
337	Steve Kerr	.10
338	*Anthony Miller*	.20
339	Nick Anderson	.10
340	Cliff Robinson	.15
341	Todd Day	.10
342	Jon Koncak	.10
343	Felton Spencer	.10
344	Willie Burton	.10
345	Ledell Eackles	.10
346	Anthony Mason	.10
347	Derek Strong	.10
348	Reggie Williams	.10
349	Johnny Newman	.10
350	Terry Cummings	.10
351	*Anthony Tucker*	.20
352	Junior Bridgeman	.10
353	Jerry West	.50
354	Harvey Catchings	.10
355	John Lucas	.10
356	Bill Bradley	.20
357	Bill Walton	.20
358	Don Nelson	.10
359	Michael Jordan	2.00
360	Tom Sanders	.10

1994-95 Upper Deck Draft Trade

The set was available by redeeming the Upper Deck Draft Day card before June 30, 1995. The redemption cards were inserted every 240 Series I packs and featured the first 10 players chosen in the draft. The NBA Draft logo is in the lower left corner of the card front and each card carries a "D" prefix.

		MT
Complete Set (10):		20.00
Common Player:		.50
1	Glenn Robinson	3.00
2	Jason Kidd	4.00
3	Grant Hill	8.00
4	Donyell Marshall	.50
5	Juwan Howard	4.00
6	Sharone Wright	.50
7	Lamond Murray	1.00
8	Brian Grant	2.00
9	Eric Montross	1.00
10	Eddie Jones	5.00
NNO	Draft Title Card	1.00

1994-95 Upper Deck Jordan He's Back Reprints

The nine-card, standard-size set parallels previously released Upper Deck cards and were inserted one per Series II rack packs. The card fronts feature "He's Back" in foil.

		MT
Complete Set (9):		15.00
Common Player:		2.00
Complete Jumbo Set (3):		15.00
Common Jumbo:		5.00
23	Michael Jordan (92-93 Upper Deck)	2.00
23	Michael Jordan (93-94 Upper Deck)	2.00
41	Michael Jordan (94-95 SP Championship)	2.00
44	Michael Jordan (91-92 Upper Deck)	2.00
204	Michael Jordan (93-94 Upper Deck)	2.00
237	Michael Jordan (93-94 Upper Deck)	2.00
402	Michael Jordan (94-95 Collector's Choice)	2.00
425	Michael Jordan (92-93 Upper Deck)	2.00
453	Michael Jordan (92-93 Upper Deck)	2.00

1994-95 Upper Deck Jordan Heroes

This "Basketball Heroes" set, an insert set in Upper Deck's 1994-95 Series I packs, chronicles Michael Jordan's career, from his collegiate days through his retirement. Cards were inserted one per every 30 packs, and are numbered 28-36. An unnumbered header card was also produced. The set is a continuation of previous Upper Deck Basketball Heroes sets which have featured Jerry West, Wilt Chamberlain and Larry Bird.

		MT
Complete Set (10):		110.00
Common Jordan:		12.00
37	1985 NBA Rookie of the Year	12.00
38	1986 63-Point Game	12.00
39	1987-88 Air Raid	12.00
40	1988, 1991, 1993 UnstoppaBull	12.00
41	1985-93 9-Time NBA All-Star	12.00
42	1984, 1992 Good as Gold	12.00
43	1991-93 MJ's Highlight Zone	12.00
44	1984-93 Rare Air	12.00
45	Checklist Header Card	12.00

1994-95 Upper Deck Predictor Award Winners

These Predictor Series cards were randomly inserted in 1994-95 Upper Deck hobby packs. Two categories are represented - NBA All-Star Game MVPs and NBA Defensive Player of the Year. Each category has nine player cards and a wild card. If the player on the card wins that category, the card can be redeemed for a foil version of the 20-card hobby Predictor Series set. If the player finishes second, the card can be redeemed for a foil version of the 10-card set of that category. The wild card represents all other NBA players and is a winner if none of the nine players in the category wins. All cards are for the 1994-95 season. Fronts are foil stamped along the left side and feature a color action photo. Backs explain the mail-in offer rules and are numbered with an "H" prefix.

		MT
Complete Set (40):		130.00
Complete Series 1 (20):		50.00
Complete Series 2 (20):		80.00
Common Player:		1.00
1	Charles Barkley	5.00
2	Hakeem Olajuwon	6.00
3	Shaquille O'Neal	10.00
4	Scottie Pippen	5.00
5	David Robinson	5.00
6	Shawn Kemp	4.00
7	Alonzo Mourning	3.00
8	Larry Johnson	2.00
9	Patrick Ewing	2.00
10	Wild Card	2.00
11	Hakeem Olajuwon	6.00
12	Dikembe Mutombo	2.00
13	Nate McMillan	1.00
14	Dennis Rodman	7.00
15	Alonzo Mourning	3.00
16	Patrick Ewing	2.00
17	Charles Barkley	4.00
18	David Robinson	4.00
19	John Stockton	3.00
20	Wild Card	2.00
21	Shaquille O'Neal	15.00
22	Hakeem Olajuwon	5.00
23	David Robinson	6.00
24	Scottie Pippen	5.00
25	Alonzo Mourning	3.00
26	Shawn Kemp	3.00
27	Charles Barkley	4.00
28	Patrick Ewing	2.00
29	Larry Johnson	2.00
30	Wild Card	1.00
31	Jason Kidd	6.00
32	Grant Hill	15.00
33	Glenn Robinson	4.00
34	Eddie Jones	5.00
35	Donyell Marshall	1.00
36	Eric Montross	2.00
37	Sharone Wright	2.00
38	Juwan Howard	5.00
39	Carlos Rogers	1.00
40	Wild Card	2.00

1994-95 Upper Deck Predictor League Leaders

These Predictor Series cards were random inserts in 1994-95 Upper Deck retail packs. The cards feature two categories - scoring leaders and assist leader. Each category has nine player cards and a wild card. If the player on the card wins that category, the card can be redeemed for a foil version of the 20-card retail Predictor Series. If the player finishes second, it can be redeemed for a foil version of the 10-card set of that category. The wild card represents all other NBA players and is a winner if none of the nine players wins that category. Card backs are numbered with an "R" prefix and explain the rules. The cards, which were randomly inserted in packs at a rate of one per every 25 packs, were for the 1994-95 NBA season. The card front shows a color photo, plus the Predictor and category stamped in foil along the left side. The Upper Deck logo is also foil stamped on the card.

		MT
Complete Set (40):		100.00
Complete Series 1 (20):		50.00
Complete Series 2 (20):		50.00
Common Player:		1.00
1	David Robinson	5.00
2	Shaquille O'Neal	15.00
3	Hakeem Olajuwon	8.00
4	Scottie Pippen	5.00
5	Chris Webber	4.00
6	Karl Malone	2.00
7	Patrick Ewing	2.00
8	Mitch Richmond	2.00
9	Charles Barkley	4.00
10	Wild Card	1.00
11	John Stockton	3.00
12	Mookie Blaylock	1.00
13	Kenny Anderson	2.00
14	Kevin Johnson	2.00
15	Muggsy Bogues	1.00
16	Tim Hardaway	2.00
17	Anfernee Hardaway	12.00
18	Rod Strickland	1.00
19	Sherman Douglas	1.00
20	Wild Card	1.00
21	Shaquille O'Neal	10.00
22	Hakeem Olajuwon	6.00
23	Dennis Rodman	10.00
24	Dikembe Mutombo	2.00
25	Karl Malone	3.00
26	Kevin Willis	1.00
27	Chris Webber	4.00
28	Alonzo Mourning	3.00
29	Derrick Coleman	1.00
30	Wild Card	1.00
31	Dikembe Mutombo	2.00
32	Hakeem Olajuwon	8.00
33	David Robinson	5.00
34	Shawn Bradley	1.00
35	Shaquille O'Neal	10.00
36	Patrick Ewing	2.00
37	Alonzo Mourning	3.00
38	Shawn Kemp	3.00
39	Derrick Coleman	1.00
40	Wild Card	1.00

1994-95 Upper Deck Rookie Standouts

These cards feature the top 20 rookies for the 1994-95 NBA season. The odds of finding one of these insert cards were one in every 30 packs of 1994-95 Upper Deck Series II packs. Cards are numbered with a "RS" prefix.

		MT
Complete Set (20):		100.00
Common Player:		1.00
1	Glenn Robinson	12.00
2	Jason Kidd	12.00
3	Grant Hill	30.00
4	Donyell Marshall	2.00
5	Juwan Howard	15.00
6	Sharone Wright	2.00
7	Lamond Murray	2.00
8	Brian Grant	8.00
9	Eric Montross	2.00
10	Eddie Jones	15.00
11	Carlos Rogers	1.00
12	Khalid Reeves	2.00
13	Jalen Rose	2.00
14	Michael Smith	1.00
15	Eric Piatkowski	1.00
16	Clifford Rozier	1.00
17	Aaron McKie	1.00
18	Eric Mobley	1.00
19	Bill Curley	1.00
20	Wesley Person	3.00

1994-95 Upper Deck Slam Dunk Stars

These cards could be found one in every 30 packs of 1994-95 Upper Deck Series II packs. Upper Deck spokesman Shawn Kemp, star of the Seattle Supersonics, picks the 20 best dunkers in the league. Cards are numbered with a "S" prefix.

		MT
Complete Set (20):		130.00
Common Player:		2.00
Minor Stars:		4.00
1	Vin Baker	7.00
2	Charles Barkley	12.00
3	Derrick Coleman	4.00
4	Clyde Drexler	8.00
5	LaPhonso Ellis	2.00
6	Larry Johnson	8.00
7	Shawn Kemp	10.00
8	Donyell Marshall	4.00
9	Jamal Mashburn	7.00
10	Gheorghe Muresan	2.00
11	Alonzo Mourning	10.00
12	Shaquille O'Neal	35.00
13	Hakeem Olajuwon	20.00
14	Scottie Pippen	15.00
15	Isaiah Rider	4.00
16	David Robinson	15.00
17	Clarence Weatherspoon	2.00
18	Chris Webber	12.00
19	Dominique Wilkins	4.00
20	Rik Smits	2.00

1994-95 Upper Deck Special Edition

Upper Deck's 1994-95 Special Edition cards are printed on silver foil paper stock and are inserted one per Series I pack. A gold version was also produced, using gold ink; cards were inserted one per every 35 packs of Series I cards. Both versions have different designs and players from the regular edition.

		MT
Complete Set (180):		60.00
Complete Series 1 (90):		15.00
Complete Series 2 (90):		45.00
Common Player:		.20
Minor Stars:		.50
Complete Gold Set (180):		600.00
Complete Gold Series 1 (90):		200.00
Complete Gold Series 2 (90):		400.00
Common Gold:		1.00
Minor Gold Stars:		3.00
Gold Cards:		5x-10x
1	Stacey Augmon	.20
2	Kevin Willis	.20
3	Mookie Blaylock	.20
4	Rick Fox	.20
5	Xavier McDaniel	.20
6	Dee Brown	.20
7	Muggsy Bogues	.20
8	Kenny Gattison	.20
9	Alonzo Mourning	1.00
10	B.J. Armstrong	.20
11	Bill Cartwright	.20
12	Toni Kukoc	.50
13	Mark Price	.50
14	Gerald Wilkins	.20
15	John Williams	.20
16	Jamal Mashburn	.75
17	Sean Rooks	.20
18	Doug Smith	.20
19	Jim Jackson	1.25
20	Mahmoud Abdul-Rauf	.20
21	Rodney Rogers	.20
22	Reggie Williams	.20
23	LaPhonso Ellis	.20
24	Allan Houston	.50
25	Terry Mills	.20
26	Joe Dumars	.50
27	Chris Mullin	.50
28	Billy Owens	.20
29	Latrell Sprewell	.50
30	Chris Webber	1.00
31	Sam Cassell	.50
32	Vernon Maxwell	.20
33	Hakeem Olajuwon	2.00
34	Otis Thorpe	.20
35	Rik Smits	.50
36	Derrick McKey	.20
37	Haywood Workman	.20
38	Charles Outlaw	.20
39	Elmore Spencer	.20
40	Loy Vaught	.20
41	George Lynch	.20
42	Nick Van Exel	1.00
43	James Worthy	.20
44	Elden Campbell	.20
45	Grant Long	.20
46	Harold Miner	.20
47	Glen Rice	.50
48	Steve Smith	.20
49	Todd Day	.20
50	Eric Murdock	.20
51	Vin Baker	1.00
52	Christian Laettner	.20
53	Isaiah Rider	.50
54	Michael Williams	.20
55	Benoit Benjamin	.20
56	Derrick Coleman	.50
57	Chris Morris	.20
58	Charles Smith	.20
59	Greg Anthony	.20
60	Doc Rivers	.20
61	Derek Harper	.20
62	John Starks	.20
63	Anfernee Hardaway	5.00
64	Dennis Scott	.20
65	Nick Anderson	.20
66	Shawn Bradley	.50
67	C. Weatherspoon	.20
68	Jeff Malone	.20
69	Cedric Ceballos	.20
70	Kevin Johnson	.50
71	Oliver Miller	.20
72	Clifford Robinson	.20
73	Rod Strickland	.20
74	Buck Williams	.20
75	Mitch Richmond	.50
76	Walt Williams	.20
77	Lionel Simmons	.20
78	Willie Anderson	.20
79	Terry Cummings	.20
80	J.R. Reid	.20
81	Dennis Rodman	3.00
82	Kendall Gill	.20
83	Sam Perkins	.20
84	Detlef Schrempf	.20
85	Jeff Hornacek	.20
86	Karl Malone	1.00
87	Felton Spencer	.20
88	Calbert Cheaney	.50
89	Don MacLean	.20
90	Brent Price	.20
91	Tyrone Corbin	.20
92	Rex Chapman	.20
93	Ken Norman	.20
94	Steve Smith	.20
95	Eric Montross	.75
96	Dino Radja	.50
97	Dominique Wilkins	.50
98	Scott Burrell	.20
99	Hersey Hawkins	.20
100	Larry Johnson	.75
101	Ron Harper	.20
102	Scottie Pippen	3.00
103	Dickey Simpkins	.20
104	Tyrone Hill	.20
105	Chris Mills	.20
106	Bobby Phills	.20

107	Lorenzo Williams	.20
108	Popeye Jones	.20
109	Jason Kidd	4.00
110	Dikembe Mutombo	.50
111	Robert Pack	.20
112	Jalen Rose	.50
113	Bill Curley	.20
114	Grant Hill	10.00
115	Lindsey Hunter	.20
116	Roy Tarpley	.20
117	Tim Hardaway	.50
118	Ricky Pierce	.20
119	Carlos Rogers	.20
120	Clifford Rozier	.20
121	Rony Seikaly	.20
122	Mario Elie	.20
123	Robert Horry	.20
124	Kenny Smith	.20
125	Antonio Davis	.20
126	Dale Davis	.20
127	Reggie Miller	.75
128	Lamond Murray	.50
129	Eric Piatkowski	.20
130	Pooh Richardson	.20
131	Cedric Ceballos	.20
132	Vlade Divac	.50
133	Eddie Jones	4.00
134	Mark Jackson	.20
135	Matt Geiger	.20
136	Khalid Reeves	.50
137	Kevin Willis	.20
138	Lee Mayberry	.20
139	Eric Mobley	.20
140	Glenn Robinson	3.00
141	Doug West	.20
142	Donyell Marshall	.50
143	Chris Smith	.20
144	Kenny Anderson	.50
145	Chris Morris	.20
146	Armon Gilliam	.20
147	Dana Barros	.20
148	Patrick Ewing	.75
149	Charles Oakley	.20
150	Charlie Ward	.20
151	Horace Grant	.50
152	Shaquille O'Neal	4.00
153	Brian Shaw	.20
154	Brooks Thompson	.20
155	B.J. Tyler	.20
156	Scott Williams	.20
157	Sharone Wright	.50
158	Charles Barkley	1.50
159	Dan Majerle	.50
160	Danny Manning	.50
161	Wesley Person	.50
162	Clyde Drexler	.75
163	Harvey Grant	.20
164	Terry Porter	.20
165	Brian Grant	1.00
166	Bobby Hurley	.20
167	Olden Polynice	.20
168	Sean Elliott	.20
169	Chuck Person	.20
170	David Robinson	1.50
171	Shawn Kemp	1.50
172	Nate McMillan	.20
173	Gary Payton	.50
174	Michael Smith	.20
175	David Benoit	.20
176	Jay Humphries	.20
177	John Stockton	.75
178	Juwan Howard	3.00
179	Chris Webber	1.50
180	Scott Skiles	.20

1994-95 Upper Deck Special Edition Gold

The 180-card, standard-size set parallels the Special Edition base set, except with gold foil instead of silver foil. The cards were inserted every 35 packs.

		MT
Complete Set (180):		500.00
Complete Series 1 (90):		150.00
Complete Series 2 (90):		350.00
Common Player:		1.00
Gold Cards:		5x-10x

1994-95 Upper Deck Special Edition Jumbos

The 27-card, over-sized set was inserted into each Upper Deck Series II Special Edition hobby box. The cards parallel the basic card designs.

		MT
Complete Set (27):		50.00
Common Player:		1.00
1	Steve Smith	1.00
2	Dominique Wilkins	1.00
3	Larry Johnson	2.00
4	Scottie Pippen	8.00
5	Chris Mills	1.00
6	Jason Kidd	10.00
7	Jalen Rose	1.00
8	Lindsey Hunter	1.00
9	Tim Hardaway	1.50
10	Kenny Smith	1.00
11	Mark Jackson	1.00
12	Lamond Murray	1.00
13	Cedric Ceballos	1.00
14	Kevin Willis	1.00
15	Glenn Robinson	8.00
16	Doug West	1.00
17	Kenny Anderson	1.00
18	Patrick Ewing	3.00
19	Horace Grant	1.00
20	Sharone Wright	1.00
21	Charles Barkley	5.00
22	Clyde Drexler	4.00
23	Brian Grant	1.50
24	Sean Elliott	1.00
25	Shawn Kemp	4.00
26	John Stockton	3.00
27	Juwan Howard	6.00

1994-95 Upper Deck Sheets

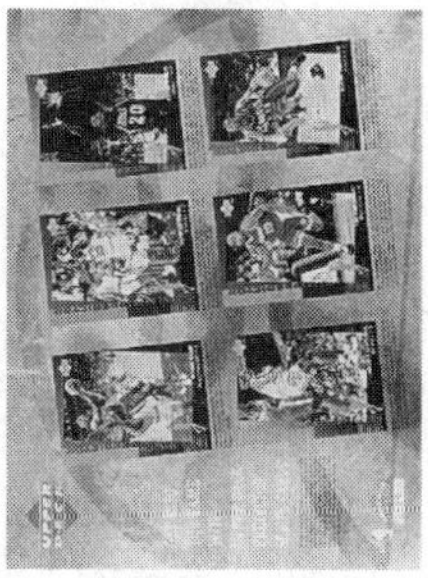

The 8-1/2" x 11" sheets were given away by Upper Deck at selected events during the 1994-95 season. The cards indicate the production total and serial number.

		MT
Complete Set (5):		40.00
Common Player:		8.00
1	Upper Deck Salutes NBA Draft Picks June 29, 1994 (25,000, Chris Webber, Shawn Bradley, Anfernee Hardaway, Jamal Mashburn, Isaiah Rider, Calbert Cheaney)	10.00
2	1994 NBA All-Rookie Team No Date (40,000, Chris Webber, Isaiah Rider, Jamal Mashburn, Vin Baker, Anfernee Hardaway)	8.00
3	Series Two NBA Basketball Cards (Promo Sheet, Shawn Kemp - Predictor, Scottie Pippen, Shaquille O'Neal, Shawn Kemp - Slam Dunk, Bobby Hurley, Jason Kidd)	4.00
4	Upper Deck Predictor Series Cards No Date (12,000, Shawn Kemp, Patrick Ewing, Kevin Willis, Mookie Blaylock, Tim Hardaway, Glenn Robinson)	5.00
4	Upper Deck Predictor Series Cards No Date (12,000, Shawn Kemp, Patrick Ewing, Kevin Willis, Mookie Blaylock, Tim Hardaway, Glenn Robinson)	5.00
5	Upper Deck Salutes Michael Jordan Jewel No Date (50,000)	8.00

1994-95 Collector's Choice

Instead of being like Mike, Upper Deck gave one lucky basketball fan the chance to be with Mike. To celebrate the debut of its new Collector's Choice line of NBA cards, Upper Deck staged an instant-win promotion similar to contests held in conjunction with other UD issues this year. More than a half-million prizes were to be awarded, including the chance to meet Jordan, plus a $10,000 shopping spree at Upper Deck Authenticated and two tickets to an NBA game. Collector's Choice Series I contains 210 regular cards, plus every card in the set will be printed with either silver or gold-foil player signature. There is one silver card in every pack, and one gold card in every box, forming two companion sets in addition to the original issue. There are also two interactive sets, called "You Crash the Game." Hobby dealer foil packs will have the 2,000-Point Club, while retail locations will have the 750 Assists Club card. There are 15 players in each series; if the player pictured on the card scores at least 2,000 (or, 750 assists, depending upon the set), the card could be redeemed for a complete , 15-card "Points" set or "Assists" set. The regular issue set includes 162 player cards plus: a Tip-Offs subset, with an inside look at each team; NBA Profiles (8); All-Star Advice, with tips from the game's top players; and Hoop-It-Up cards, with the winning teams in the national three-on-three tourney and the Upper Deck Slam Dunk Open.

		MT
Complete Set (420):		40.00
Complete Series 1 (210):		15.00
Complete Series 2 (210):		25.00
Common Player:		.05
Minor Stars:		.10
Complete Silver Set (420):		100.00
Complete Silver Series 1 (210):		40.00
Complete Silver Series 2 (210):		60.00
Common Silver:		.10
Minor Silver Stars:		.20
Unlisted Silver Stars:		2x-4x
Series 1 Wax Box:		30.00
Series 2 Wax Box:		35.00
1	Anfernee Hardaway	1.00
2	Moses Malone	.05
3	Steve Smith	.05
4	Chris Webber	.25
5	Donald Royal	.05
6	Avery Johnson	.05
7	Kevin Johnson	.10
8	Doug Christie	.05
9	Derrick McKey	.05
10	Dennis Rodman	.75
11	Johnny Dawkins	.05
12	Isiah Thomas	.15
13	Kendall Gill	.05
14	Jeff Hornacek	.05
15	Latrell Sprewell	.25
16	Lucious Harris	.05
17	Chris Mullin	.10
18	John Williams	.05
19	Tony Campbell	.05
20	LaPhonso Ellis	.05
21	Gerald Wilkins	.05
22	Clyde Drexler	.25
23	Michael Jordan	3.00
24	George Lynch	.05
25	Mark Price	.05
26	James Robinson	.05
27	Elmore Spencer	.05
28	Stacey King	.05
29	Corie Blount	.05
30	Dell Curry	.05
31	Reggie Miller	.25
32	Karl Malone	.20
33	Scottie Pippen	.75
34	Hakeem Olajuwon	.50
35	Clarence Weatherspoon	.05
36	Kevin Edwards	.05
37	Pete Myers	.05
38	Jeff Turner	.05
39	Ennis Whatley	.05
40	Calbert Cheaney	.05
41	Glen Rice	.05
42	Vin Baker	.25
43	Grant Long	.05
44	Derrick Coleman	.10
45	Rik Smits	.05
46	Chris Smith	.05
47	Carl Herrera	.05
48	Bob Martin	.05
49	Terrell Brandon	.05
50	David Robinson	.50
51	Danny Ferry	.05
52	Buck Williams	.05
53	Josh Grant	.05
54	Ed Pinckney	.05
55	Dikembe Mutombo	.20
56	Clifford Robinson	.05
57	Luther Wright	.05
58	Scott Burrell	.05
59	Stacey Augmon	.05
60	Jeff Malone	.05
61	Byron Houston	.05
62	Anthony Peeler	.05
63	Michael Adams	.05
64	Negele Knight	.05
65	Terry Cummings	.05
66	Christian Laettner	.05
67	Tracy Murray	.05
68	Sedale Threatt	.05
69	Dan Majerle	.05
70	Frank Brickowski	.05
71	Ken Norman	.05
72	Charles Smith	.05
73	Adam Keefe	.05
74	P.J. Brown	.05
75	Kevin Duckworth	.05
76	Shawn Bradley	.10
77	Darnell Mee	.05
78	Nick Anderson	.05
79	Mark West	.05
80	B.J. Armstrong	.05
81	Dennis Scott	.05
82	Lindsey Hunter	.05
83	Derek Strong	.05
84	Mike Brown	.05
85	Antonio Harvey	.05
86	Johnny Bonner	.05
87	Sam Cassell	.10
88	Harold Miner	.05
89	Spud Webb	.05
90	Mookie Blaylock	.05
91	Greg Anthony	.05
92	Richard Petruska	.05
93	Sean Rooks	.05
94	Ervin Johnson	.05
95	Randy Brown	.05
96	Orlando Woolridge	.05
97	Charles Oakley	.05
98	Craig Ehlo	.05
99	Derek Harper	.05
100	Robert Parish	.05
101	Muggsy Bogues	.05
102	Mitch Richmond	.10
103	Mahmoud Abdul-Rauf	.05
104	Joe Dumars	.15
105	Eric Riley	.05
106	Terry Mills	.05
107	Toni Kukoc	.10
108	Jon Koncak	.05
109	Haywoode Workman	.05
110	Todd Day	.05
111	Detlef Schrempf	.05
112	David Wesley	.05
113	Mark Jackson	.05
114	Doug Overton	.05
115	Vinny Del Negro	.05
116	Loy Vaught	.05
117	Mike Peplowski	.05
118	Bimbo Coles	.05
119	Rex Walter	.05
120	Sherman Douglas	.05
121	David Benoit	.05
122	John Salley	.05
123	Cedric Ceballos	.05
124	Chris Mills	.05
125	Robert Horry	.10
126	Johnny Newman	.05
127	Malcolm Mackey	.05
128	Terry Dehere	.05
129	Dino Radja	.10
130	Tree Rollins	.05
131	Xavier McDaniel	.05
132	Bobby Hurley	.05
133	Alonzo Mourning	.25
134	Isaiah Rider	.15
135	Antoine Carr	.05
136	Robert Pack	.05
137	Walt Williams	.05
138	Tyrone Corbin	.05
139	Popeye Jones	.05
140	Shawn Kemp	.30
141	Thurl Bailey	.05
142	James Worthy	.05
143	Scott Haskin	.05
144	Hubert Davis	.05
145	A.C. Green	.05
146	Dale Davis	.05
147	Nate McMillan	.05
148	Chris Morris	.05
149	Will Perdue	.05
150	Felton Spencer	.05
151	Rod Strickland	.05
152	Blue Edwards	.05
153	John Williams	.05
154	Rodney Rogers	.05
155	Acie Earl	.05
156	Hersey Hawkins	.05
157	Jamal Mashburn	.20
158	Don MacLean	.05
159	Michael Williams	.05
160	Kenny Gattison	.05
161	Rick King	.05
162	Allan Houston	.10
163	Hoop-it up	.05
164	Hoop-it up	.05
165	Hoop-it up	.05
166	Danny Manning	.05
167	Robert Parish	.05
168	Alonzo Mourning	.15
169	Scottie Pippen	.25
170	Mark Price	.05
171	Jamal Mashburn	.20
172	Dikembe Mutombo	.10
173	Joe Dumars	.10
174	Chris Webber	.15
175	Hakeem Olajuwon	.25
176	Reggie Miller	.10
177	Ron Harper	.05
178	Nick Van Exel	.10
179	Steve Smith	.05
180	Vin Baker	.10
181	Isaiah Rider	.10
182	Derrick Coleman	.05
183	Patrick Ewing	.15
184	Shaquille O'Neal	.50
185	Clarence Weatherspoon	.05
186	Charles Barkley	.20
187	Clyde Drexler	.10
188	Mitch Richmond	.05
189	David Robinson	.20
190	Shawn Kemp	.20
191	Karl Malone	.15
192	Tom Gugliotta	.05
193	Kenny Anderson	.05
194	Alonzo Mourning	.15
195	Mark Price	.05
196	John Stockton	.10
197	Shaquille O'Neal	.50
198	Latrell Sprewell	.10
199	Charles Barkley	.20
200	Chris Webber	.15
201	Larry Johnson	.10
202	Dennis Rodman	.25
203	Patrick Ewing	.15
204	Michael Jordan	1.50
205	Shaquille O'Neal	.50
206	Shawn Kemp	.15
207	Checklist 53-105 (Tim Hardaway)	.05
208	Checklist 106-157 (John Stockton)	.05
209	Checklist 158-210 (Harold Miner)	.05
210	B.J. Armstrong	.05
211	Vernon Maxwell	.05
212	John Stockton	.15
213	Luc Longley	.05
214	Sam Perkins	.05
215	Pooh Richardson	.05
216	Tyrone Corbin	.05
217	Mario Elie	.05
218	Bobby Phills	.05
219	*Grant Hill*	3.00
220	Gary Payton	.15
221	Tom Hammonds	.05
222	Danny Ainge	.05
223	Gary Grant	.05
224	Jimmy Jackson	.25
225	Chris Gatling	.05
226	Sergei Bazarevich	.05
227	*Tony Dumas*	.30
228	Andrew Lang	.05
229	*Wesley Person*	.50
230	Terry Porter	.05
231	Duane Causwell	.05
232	Shaquille O'Neal	1.00
233	Antonio Davis	.05
234	Charles Barkley	.40
235	Tony Massenberg	.05
236	Ricky Pierce	.05
237	Scott Skiles	.05
238	*Jalen Rose*	.50
239	*Charlie Ward*	.20
240	Michael Jordan	1.50
241	Elden Campbell	.05
242	Bill Cartwright	.05
243	Armon Gilliam	.05
244	Rock Fox	.05
245	Tim Breaux	.05
246	*Monty Williams*	.15
247	Dominique Wilkins	.10
248	Robert Parish	.05
249	Mark Jackson	.05
250	*Jason Kidd*	1.50
251	Andres Guibert	.05
252	Matt Geiger	.05
253	Stanley Roberts	.05
254	Jack Haley	.05
255	David Wingate	.05
256	John Crotty	.05
257	*Brian Grant*	.60
258	Otis Thorpe	.05
259	*Clifford Rozier*	.20
260	Grant Long	.05
261	*Eric Mobley*	.15
262	*Dickey Simpkins*	.20
263	J.R. Reid	.05
264	Kevin Willis	.05
265	Scott Brooks	.05
266	*Glenn Robinson*	1.00
267	Dana Barros	.05
268	Kenny Norman	.05
269	Herb Williams	.05
270	Dee Brown	.05
271	Steve Kerr	.05
272	Jon Barry	.05
273	Sean Elliott	.05
274	Elliot Perry	.05
275	Kenny Smith	.05
276	Sean Rooks	.05
277	Gheorghe Muresan	.05
278	*Juwan Howard*	1.00
279	Steve Smith	.05
280	Anthony Bowie	.05
281	Moses Malone	.05
282	Olden Polynice	.05
283	Jo Jo English	.05
284	Marty Conlon	.05
285	Sam Mitchell	.05
286	Doug West	.05
287	Cedric Ceballos	.05
288	Lorenzo Williams	.05
289	Harold Ellis	.05
290	Doc Rivers	.05
291	Keith Tower	.05
292	Mark Bryant	.05
293	Oliver Miller	.05
294	Michael Adams	.05
295	Tree Rollins	.05
296	*Eddie Jones*	.75
297	Malik Sealy	.05
298	Glue Edwards	.05
299	Brooks Thompson	.05
300	Benoit Benjamin	.05
301	Avery Johnson	.05
302	Larry Johnson	.15
303	John Starks	.05
304	Byron Scott	.05
305	Eric Murdock	.05
306	Jay Humphries	.05
307	Kenny Anderson	.10
308	Brian Williams	.05
309	Nick Van Exel	.50
310	Tim Hardaway	.10
311	Lee Mayberry	.05
312	Vlade Divac	.05
313	*Donyell Marshall*	.50
314	Anthony Mason	.05
315	Danny Manning	.10
316	Tyrone Hill	.05
317	Vincent Askew	.05
318	*Khalid Reeves*	.50
319	Ron Harper	.05
320	Brent Price	.05
321	Bryon Houston	.05
322	*Lamond Murray*	.25
323	Bryant Stith	.05
324	Tom Gugliotta	.05
325	Jerome Kersey	.05
326	*B.J. Tyler*	.15
327	*Antonio Lang*	.10
328	*Carlos Rogers*	.20
329	Waymond Tisdale	.05
330	Kevin Gamble	.05
331	*Eric Piatkowski*	.20
332	Mitchell Butler	.05
333	Patrick Ewing	.10
334	Doug Smith	.05
335	Joe Kleine	.05
336	Keith Jennings	.05
337	*Bill Curley*	.15
338	Johnny Newman	.05
339	*Howard Eisley*	.05
340	Willie Anderson	.05
341	*Aaron McKie*	.50
342	Tom Chambers	.05
343	Scott Williams	.05
344	Harvey Grant	.05
345	Billy Owens	.05
346	*Sharone Wright*	.25
347	Michael Cage	.05
348	Vern Fleming	.05
349	*Darrin Hancock*	.05
350	Matt Fish	.05
351	Rony Seikaly	.05
352	Victor Alexander	.05
353	*Anthony Miller*	.05
354	Horace Grant	.10
355	Jayson Williams	.05
356	Dale Ellis	.05
357	Sarunas Marciulionis	.05
358	Anthony Avent	.05
359	Rex Chapman	.05
360	Askia Jones	.05
361	Charles Outlaw	.05
362	Chuck Person	.05
363	Dan Scayes	.05
364	Morlon Wiley	.05
365	*Dontonio Wingfield*	.05
366	Tony Smith	.05
367	Matt Wennington	.05
368	Bryon Russell	.05
369	Geert Hammink	.05
370	*Eric Montross*	.40
371	Cliff Levingston	.05
372	Stacey Augmon	.05
373	Eric Montross	.10
374	Alonzo Mourning	.10
375	Scottie Pippen	.25
376	Mark Price	.10
377	Jason Kidd	.50
378	Jalen Rose	.20
379	Grant Hill	1.00
380	Latrell Sprewell	.10
381	Hakeem Olajuwon	.25
382	Reggie Miller	.10
383	Lamond Murray	.20
384	Eddie Jones	.25
385	Khalid Reeves	.10
386	Glenn Robinson	.50
387	Donyell Marshall	.25
388	Derrick Coleman	.10
389	Patrick Ewing	.10
390	Shaquille O'Neal	.50
391	Sharone Wright	.15
392	Charles Barkley	.20
393	Aaron McKie	.10
394	Brian Grant	.25
395	David Robinson	.20
396	Shawn Kemp	.15
397	Karl Malone	.10
398	Tom Gugliotta	.05
399	Hakeem Olajuwon	.25
400	Shaquille O'Neal	.50
401	Chris Webber	.15
402	Michael Jordan	1.50
403	David Robinson	.20
404	Shawn Kemp	.15
405	Patrick Ewing	.10
406	Derrick Coleman	.10
407	Glenn Robinson	.50
408	Jason Kidd	.50
409	Grant Hill	1.25
410	Donyell Marshall	.25
411	Sharone Wright	.15
412	Lamond Murray	.15
413	Brian Grant	.25
414	Eric Montross	.15
415	Eddie Jones	.25
416	Carlos Rogers	.10
417	Shawn Kemp	.10
418	Bobby Hurley	.05
419	Shawn Bradley	.05
420	Michael Jordan	1.00

1994-95 Collector's Choice Gold Signature

This 420-card set paralleled the base set for Collector's Choice, with 210 cards in each series. Inserted one per 35 packs, Gold Signature cards had a gold border, gold signature and a foil finish to the front.

		MT
Complete Gold Set (420):		1100.
Complete Series 1 (210):		500.00
Complete Series 2 (210):		600.00
Common Gold:		2.00
Minor Gold Stars:		4.00
Unlisted Gold Stars:		15x-30x
1	Anfernee Hardaway	60.00
2	Moses Malone	2.00
3	Steve Smith	2.00
4	Chris Webber	15.00
5	Donald Royal	2.00
6	Avery Johnson	2.00
7	Kevin Johnson	4.00
8	Doug Christie	2.00
9	Derrick McKey	2.00
10	Dennis Rodman	25.00
11	Johnny Dawkins	2.00
12	Isiah Thomas	6.00
13	Kendall Gill	2.00
14	Jeff Hornacek	2.00
15	Latrell Sprewell	15.00
16	Lucious Harris	2.00
17	Chris Mullin	4.00
18	John Williams	2.00
19	Tony Campbell	2.00
20	LaPhonso Ellis	2.00
21	Gerald Wilkins	2.00
22	Clyde Drexler	18.00
23	Michael Jordan	100.00
24	George Lynch	2.00
25	Mark Price	2.00
26	James Robinson	2.00
27	Elmore Spencer	2.00
28	Stacey King	2.00
29	Corie Blount	2.00
30	Dell Curry	2.00
31	Reggie Miller	15.00
32	Karl Malone	12.00
33	Scottie Pippen	25.00
34	Hakeem Olajuwon	30.00
35	Clarence Weatherspoon	2.00
36	Kevin Edwards	2.00
37	Pete Myers	2.00
38	Jeff Turner	2.00
39	Ennis Whatley	2.00
40	Calbert Cheaney	2.00
41	Glen Rice	2.00
42	Vin Baker	15.00
43	Grant Long	2.00
44	Derrick Coleman	4.00
45	Rik Smits	2.00
46	Chris Smith	2.00
47	Carl Herrera	2.00
48	Bob Martin	2.00
49	Terrell Brandon	2.00
50	David Robinson	20.00
51	Danny Ferry	2.00
52	Buck Williams	2.00
53	Josh Grant	2.00
54	Ed Pinckney	2.00
55	Dikembe Mutombo	10.00
56	Clifford Robinson	2.00

57	Luther Wright	2.00
58	Scott Burrell	2.00
59	Stacey Augmon	2.00
60	Jeff Malone	2.00
61	Byron Houston	2.00
62	Anthony Peeler	2.00
63	Michael Adams	2.00
64	Negele Knight	2.00
65	Terry Cummings	2.00
66	Christian Laettner	2.00
67	Tracy Murray	2.00
68	Sedale Threatt	2.00
69	Dan Majerle	2.00
70	Frank Brickowski	2.00
71	Ken Norman	2.00
72	Charles Smith	2.00
73	Adam Keefe	2.00
74	P.J. Brown	2.00
75	Kevin Duckworth	2.00
76	Shawn Bradley	4.00
77	Darnell Mee	2.00
78	Nick Anderson	2.00
79	Mark West	2.00
80	B.J. Armstrong	2.00
81	Dennis Scott	2.00
82	Lindsey Hunter	2.00
83	Derek Strong	2.00
84	Mike Brown	2.00
85	Antonio Harvey	2.00
86	Anthony Bonner	2.00
87	Sam Cassell	4.00
88	Harold Miner	2.00
89	Spud Webb	2.00
90	Mookie Blaylock	2.00
91	Greg Anthony	2.00
92	Richard Petruska	2.00
93	Sean Rooks	2.00
94	Ervin Johnson	2.00
95	Randy Brown	2.00
96	Orlando Woolridge	2.00
97	Charles Oakley	2.00
98	Craig Ehlo	2.00
99	Derek Harper	2.00
100	Robert Parish	2.00
101	Muggsy Bogues	2.00
102	Mitch Richmond	4.00
103	Mahmoud Abdul-Rauf	2.00
104	Joe Dumars	6.00
105	Eric Riley	2.00
106	Terry Mills	2.00
107	Toni Kukoc	4.00
108	Jon Koncak	2.00
109	Haywoode Workman	2.00
110	Todd Day	2.00
111	Detlef Schrempf	2.00
112	David Wesley	2.00
113	Mark Jackson	2.00
114	Doug Overton	2.00
115	Vinny Del Negro	2.00
116	Loy Vaught	2.00
117	Mike Peplowski	2.00
118	Bimbo Coles	2.00
119	Rex Walter	2.00
120	Sherman Douglas	2.00
121	David Benoit	2.00
122	John Salley	2.00
123	Cedric Ceballos	2.00
124	Chris Mills	2.00
125	Robert Horry	4.00
126	Johnny Newman	2.00
127	Malcolm Mackey	2.00
128	Terry Dehere	2.00
129	Dino Radja	4.00
130	Tree Rollins	2.00
131	Xavier McDaniel	2.00
132	Bobby Hurley	2.00
133	Alonzo Mourning	15.00
134	Isaiah Rider	6.00
135	Antoine Carr	2.00
136	Robert Pack	2.00
137	Walt Williams	2.00
138	Tyrone Corbin	2.00
139	Popeye Jones	2.00
140	Shawn Kemp	15.00
141	Thurl Bailey	2.00
142	James Worthy	2.00
143	Scott Haskin	2.00
144	Hubert Davis	2.00
145	A.C. Green	2.00
146	Dale Davis	2.00
147	Nate McMillam	2.00
148	Chris Morris	2.00
149	Will Perdue	2.00
150	Felton Spencer	2.00
151	Rod Strickland	2.00
152	Blue Edwards	2.00
153	John Williams	2.00
154	Rodney Rogers	2.00
155	Acie Earl	2.00
156	Hersey Hawkins	2.00
157	Jamal Mashburn	30.00
158	Don MacLean	2.00
159	Michael Williams	2.00
160	Kenny Gattison	2.00
161	Rick King	2.00
162	Allan Houston	4.00
163	Hoop-it up	2.00
164	Hoop-it up	2.00
165	Hoop-it up	2.00
166	Danny Manning	2.00
167	Robert Parish	2.00
168	Alonzo Mourning	6.00
169	Scottie Pippen	6.00
170	Mark Price	2.00
171	Jamal Mashburn	10.00
172	Dikembe Mutombo	4.00
173	Joe Dumars	4.00
174	Chris Webber	6.00
175	Hakeem Olajuwon	18.00
176	Reggie Miller	4.00
177	Ron Harper	2.00
178	Nick Van Exel	5.00
179	Steve Smith	2.00
180	Vin Baker	4.00
181	Isaiah Rider	4.00
182	Derrick Coleman	2.00
183	Patrick Ewing	6.00
184	Shaquille O'Neal	30.00
185	Clarence Weatherspoon	2.00
186	Charles Barkley	12.00
187	Clyde Drexler	5.00
188	Mitch Richmond	2.00
189	David Robinson	12.00
190	Shawn Kemp	8.00
191	Karl Malone	6.00
192	Tom Gugliotta	2.00
193	Kenny Anderson	4.00
194	Alonzo Mourning	6.00
195	Mark Price	2.00
196	John Stockton	4.00
197	Shaquille O'Neal	30.00
198	Latrell Sprewell	4.00
199	Charles Barkley	12.00
200	Chris Webber	6.00
201	Larry Johnson	4.00
202	Dennis Rodman	15.00
203	Patrick Ewing	6.00
204	Michael Jordan	60.00
205	Shaquille O'Neal	30.00
206	Shawn Kemp	6.00
207	Checklist 53-105 (Tim Hardaway)	2.00
208	Checklist 106-157 (John Stockton)	2.00
209	Checklist 158-210 (Harold Miner)	2.00
210	B.J. Armstrong	2.00
211	Vernon Maxwell	2.00
212	John Stockton	6.00
213	Luc Longley	2.00
214	Sam Perkins	2.00
215	Pooh Richardson	2.00
216	Tyrone Corbin	2.00
217	Mario Elie	2.00
218	Bobby Phills	2.00
219	*Grant Hill*	70.00
220	Gary Payton	6.00
221	Tom Hammonds	2.00
222	Danny Ainge	2.00
223	Gary Grant	2.00
224	Jimmy Jackson	15.00
225	Chris Gatling	2.00
226	Sergei Bazarevich	2.00
227	Tony Dumas	2.00
228	Andrew Lang	2.00
229	*Wesley Person*	25.00
230	Terry Porter	2.00
231	Duane Causwell	2.00
232	Shaquille O'Neal	50.00
233	Antonio Davis	2.00
234	Charles Barkley	15.00
235	Tony Massenberg	2.00
236	Ricky Pierce	2.00
237	Scott Skiles	2.00
238	*Jalen Rose*	15.00
239	*Charlie Ward*	8.00
240	Michael Jordan	60.00
241	Elden Campbell	2.00
242	Bill Cartwright	2.00
243	Armon Gilliam	2.00
244	Rock Fox	2.00
245	Tim Breaux	2.00
246	*Monty Williams*	6.00
247	Dominique Wilkins	4.00
248	Robert Parish	2.00
249	Mark Jackson	2.00
250	*Jason Kidd*	30.00
251	Andres Guibert	2.00
252	Matt Geiger	2.00
253	Stanley Roberts	2.00
254	Jack Haley	2.00
255	David Wingate	2.00
256	John Crotty	2.00
257	*Brian Grant*	15.00
258	Otis Thorpe	2.00
259	*Clifford Rozier*	8.00
260	Grant Long	2.00
261	*Eric Mobley*	6.00
262	*Dickey Simpkins*	8.00
263	J.R. Reid	2.00
264	Kevin Willis	2.00
265	Scott Brooks	2.00
266	*Glenn Robinson*	25.00
267	Dana Barros	2.00
268	Kenny Norman	2.00
269	Herb Williams	2.00
270	Dee Brown	2.00
271	Steve Kerr	2.00
272	Jon Barry	2.00
273	Sean Elliott	2.00
274	Elliot Perry	2.00
275	Kenny Smith	2.00
276	Sean Rooks	2.00
277	Gheorghe Muresan	2.00
278	*Juwan Howard*	30.00
279	Steve Smith	2.00
280	Anthony Bowie	2.00
281	Moses Malone	2.00
282	Olden Polynice	2.00
283	Jo Jo English	2.00
284	Marty Conlon	2.00
285	Sam Mitchell	2.00
286	Doug West	2.00
287	Cedric Ceballos	2.00
288	Lorenzo Williams	2.00
289	Harold Ellis	2.00
290	Doc Rivers	2.00
291	Keith Tower	2.00
292	Mark Bryant	2.00
293	Oliver Miller	2.00
294	Michael Adams	2.00
295	Tree Rollins	2.00
296	Eddie Jones	25.00
297	Malik Sealy	2.00
298	Glue Edwards	2.00
299	Brooks Thompson	2.00
300	Benoit Benjamin	2.00
301	Avery Johnson	2.00
302	Larry Johnson	6.00
303	John Starks	2.00
304	Byron Scott	2.00
305	Eric Murdock	2.00
306	Jay Humphries	2.00
307	Kenny Anderson	4.00
308	Brian Williams	2.00
309	Nick Van Exel	15.00
310	Tim Hardaway	4.00
311	Lee Mayberry	2.00
312	Vlade Divac	2.00
313	*Donyell Marshall*	10.00
314	Anthony Mason	2.00
315	Danny Manning	4.00
316	Tyrone Hill	2.00
317	Vincent Askew	2.00
318	*Khalid Reeves*	10.00
319	Ron Harper	2.00
320	Brent Price	2.00
321	Bryon Houston	2.00
322	*Lamond Murray*	10.00
323	Bryant Stith	2.00
324	Tom Gugliotta	2.00
325	Jerome Kersey	2.00
326	*B.J. Tyler*	6.00
327	*Antonio Lang*	4.00
328	*Carlos Rogers*	8.00
329	Waymond Tisdale	2.00
330	Kevin Gamble	2.00
331	*Eric Piatkowski*	8.00
332	Mitchell Butler	2.00
333	Patrick Ewing	4.00
334	Doug Smith	2.00
335	Joe Kleine	2.00
336	Keith Jennings	2.00
337	*Bill Curley*	6.00
338	Johnny Newman	2.00
339	*Howard Eisley*	2.00
340	Willie Anderson	2.00
341	*Aaron McKie*	10.00
342	Tom Chambers	2.00
343	Scott Williams	2.00
344	Harvey Grant	2.00
345	Billy Owens	2.00
346	*Sharone Wright*	10.00
347	Michael Cage	2.00
348	Vern Fleming	2.00
349	*Darrin Hancock*	2.00
350	Matt Fish	2.00
351	Rony Seikaly	2.00
352	Victor Alexander	2.00
353	*Anthony Miller*	2.00
354	Horace Grant	4.00
355	Jayson Williams	2.00
356	Dale Ellis	2.00
357	Sarunas Marciulionis	2.00
358	Anthony Avent	2.00
359	Rex Chapman	2.00
360	Askia Jones	2.00
361	Charles Outlaw	2.00
362	Chuck Person	2.00
363	Dan Scayes	2.00
364	Morlon Wiley	2.00
365	*Dontonio Wingfield*	2.00
366	Tony Smith	2.00
367	Matt Wennington	2.00
368	Bryon Russell	2.00
369	Geert Hammink	2.00
370	*Eric Montross*	10.00
371	Cliff Levingston	2.00
372	Stacey Augmon	2.00
373	Eric Montross	4.00
374	Alonzo Mourning	4.00
375	Scottie Pippen	4.00
376	Mark Price	4.00
377	Jason Kidd	25.00
378	Jalen Rose	10.00
379	Grant Hill	30.00
380	Latrell Sprewell	4.00
381	Hakeem Olajuwon	18.00
382	Reggie Miller	4.00
383	Lamond Murray	8.00
384	Eddie Jones	15.00
385	Khalid Reeves	4.00
386	Glenn Robinson	15.00
387	Donyell Marshall	10.00
388	Derrick Coleman	4.00
389	Patrick Ewing	4.00
390	Shaquille O'Neal	25.00
391	Sharone Wright	6.00
392	Charles Barkley	10.00
393	Aaron McKie	4.00
394	Brian Grant	10.00
395	David Robinson	15.00
396	Shawn Kemp	8.00
397	Karl Malone	4.00
398	Tom Gugliotta	2.00
399	Hakeem Olajuwon	18.00
400	Shaquille O'Neal	25.00
401	Chris Webber	8.00
402	Michael Jordan	60.00
403	David Robinson	15.00
404	Shawn Kemp	8.00
405	Patrick Ewing	4.00
406	Derrick Coleman	4.00
407	Glenn Robinson	15.00
408	Jason Kidd	15.00
409	Grant Hill	25.00
410	Donyell Marshall	15.00
411	Sharone Wright	6.00
412	Lamond Murray	6.00
413	Brian Grant	15.00
414	Eric Montross	6.00
415	Eddie Jones	15.00
416	Carlos Rogers	4.00
417	Shawn Kemp	3.00
418	Bobby Hurley	2.00
419	Shawn Bradley	2.00
420	Michael Jordan	30.00

1994-95 Collector's Choice Silver Signature

This 420-card set paralleled the regular-issue Collector's Choice issue, but featured a silver facsimile signature across the front. Silver Signature cards were seeded one per pack, with three in special jumbo packs.

	MT
Silver Cards:	2x-4x

1994-95 Collector's Choice Blow-Ups

These 5" x 7" blowups were found in 1994-95 Upper Deck Collector's Choice Series II boxes.

		MT
Complete Set (5):		10.00
Common Player:		.50
132	Bobby Hurley	.50
140	Shawn Kemp	1.00
23	Michael Jordan	7.00
76	Shawn Bradley	1.00
40	Calbert Cheaney	.50
A23	Michael Jordan AU	5000.
A40	Calbert Cheaney AU	20.00
A76	Shawn Bradley AU	25.00
A132	Bobby Hurley AU	20.00
A140	Shawn Kemp AU	75.00

1994-95 Collector's Choice Crash the Game Assists

This interactive insert set, called "You Crash the Game," features playmakers whose specialties are dishing out assists. These 750 Assists cards were randomly inserted in retail locations. If the player pictured on the card obtains 750 assists during the 1994-95 season, card holders can redeem it for a complete 15-card "Assists" set. Cards are numbered with an "A" prefix.

		MT
Complete Set (15):		20.00
Common Player:		.50
1	Michael Adams	.50
2	Kenny Anderson	1.00
3	Mookie Blaylock	.50
4	Muggsy Bogues	.50
5	Sherman Douglas	.50
6	Anfernee Hardaway	10.00
7	Tim Hardaway	1.00
8	Lindsey Hunter	.50
9	Mark Jackson	.50
10	Kevin Johnson	1.00
11	Eric Murdock	.50
12	Mark Price	1.00
13	John Stockton	4.00
14	Rod Strickland	.50
15	Michael Williams	.50

1994-95 Collector's Choice Crash the Game Rebounds

These cards, numbered using an "R" prefix, were random inserts in Upper Deck Collector's Choice Series II retail packs. The cards could be found one in every eight packs. The cards follow the "You Crash the Game" contest theme, with winners collecting prizes if the player pictured on the card gets 1,000 rebounds during the 1994-95 NBA season. The card front has a color action photo of the player, plus the contest logo; the back explains the rules and prizes.

		MT
Complete Set (15):		20.00
Common Player:		.50
1	Derrick Coleman	.75
2	Patrick Ewing	1.00
3	Horace Grant	1.00
4	Shawn Kemp	2.00
5	Karl Malone	1.00
6	Alonzo Mourning	2.00
7	Dikembe Mutombo	2.00
8	Shaquille O'Neal	8.00
9	Hakeem Olajuwon	5.00
10	Charles Oakley	.50
11	Olden Polynice	.50
12	David Robinson	4.00
13	Dennis Rodman	5.00
14	Otis Thorpe	.50
15	Kevin Willis	.50

1994-95 Collector's Choice Crash the Game Rookie Scoring

These insert cards were found only in 1994-95 Upper Deck Collector's Choice hobby packs, one every eight packs. The card back is labeled with an "H" prefix and provides details about the "You Crash The Game" contest, which awards prizes based who leads the rookies in scoring during the season.

		MT
Complete Set (15):		25.00
Common Player:		.50
1	Tony Dumas	.50
2	Brian Grant	1.00
3	Grant Hill	10.00
4	Juwan Howard	3.00
5	Eddie Jones	2.00
6	Jason Kidd	3.00
7	Donyell Marshall	1.00
8	Eric Montross	1.00
9	Lamond Murray	1.00
10	Khalid Reeves	1.25
11	Glenn Robinson	4.00
12	Jalen Rose	1.00
13	Dickey Simpkins	.50
14	Charlie Ward	.75
15	Sharone Wright	1.00

1994-95 Collector's Choice Crash the Game Scoring

These Upper Deck Collector's Choice insert cards, available in hobby dealer packs only, feature some of the NBA's top scorers. If any of the 15 players in the set scores 2,000 points during the 1994-95 NBA season, their cards can be redeemed for a complete 15-card "Points" set. Each card has the "Crash the Game" phrase on it to promote the contest. Cards are numbered with an "S" prefix.

		MT
Complete Set (15):		30.00
Common Player:		.50
1	Charles Barkley	3.00
2	Derrick Coleman	.50
3	Joe Dumars	.50
4	Patrick Ewing	1.00
5	Karl Malone	2.00
6	Reggie Miller	1.00
7	Shaquille O'Neal	10.00
8	Hakeem Olajuwon	7.00
9	Scottie Pippen	4.00
10	Glen Rice	.50
11	Mitch Richmond	.50
12	David Robinson	5.00
13	Latrell Sprewell	1.00
14	Chris Webber	1.00
15	Dominique Wilkins	.50

1994-95 Collector's Choice Draft Trade

Available by redeeming a Draft Trade card that was inserted into Series I hobby or retail packs, the 10-card set has a color photo of the player. However, the top-half of the card's background is in black-and-white. The bottom-half of the card's background is white. The NBA Draft logo is in the upper left of the front, while the card number is in the upper right in a circle. "NBA Draft Lottery Picks" is printed in the lower left. The Collector's Choice logo is in the lower right. The backs have the card number in a circle on the left, a photo of the player, along with the player's highlights.

		MT
Complete Set (10):		8.00
Common Player:		.25
1	Glenn Robinson	1.00
2	Jason Kidd	2.00
3	Grant Hill	4.00
4	Donyell Marshall	.25
5	Juwan Howard	1.00
6	Sharone Wright	.25
7	Lamond Murray	.50
8	Brian Grant	.75
9	Eric Montross	.25
10	Eddie Jones	1.50

1994 Upper Deck USA Basketball

This 90-card set features six cards of each of the 13 players on the Olympic USA Basketball Team, excluding Kevin Johnson. The card fronts feature posed and action shots of the player. His name appears at the bottom in the red, white and blue bar adjacent to the USA Basketball logo in the lower right corner. A card subtitle appears along the left side of the card; this subtitle is explained on the card back, which also includes another photo of the player against a U.S. flag background. The card number is in the upper left corner. In addition to the regular set, each of the 90 cards was produced in a gold-foil seal "Gold Medal" set; one card was inserted in every pack. Other inserts included Don Nelson Chalk Talk cards and Follow Your Dreams cards.

		MT
Complete Set (92):		10.00
Common Player:		.05
Comp. Gold Medal Set (92):		25.00
Common Gold Medal Player:		.10
Unlisted Stars:		1x-2x
1	Derrick Coleman (1-6)	.05
7	Joe Dumars (7-12)	.10
13	Tim Hardaway (13-18)	.05
19	Larry Johnson (19-24)	.20
25	Shawn Kemp (25-30)	.30
31	Dan Majerle (31-36)	.05
37	Reggie Miller (37-42)	.20
43	Alonzo Mourning (43-48)	.25
49	Shaquille O'Neal (49-54)	1.00
55	Mark Price (55-60)	.05
61	Steve Smith (61-66)	.05
67	Isiah Thomas (67-72)	.10
73	Dominique Wilkins (73-78)	.10
79	Women (79-84)	.05
85	Michael Jordan (ATG 85)	4.00
86	Larry Bird (ATG 86)	1.00
87	Jerry West (ATG 87)	.75
89	Cheryl Miller (ATG 89)	.25
CK1	Checklist 1	.50
CK2	Checklist 2	.50

1994 Upper Deck USA Gold Medal

The 90-card, regular-size set parallels the 90-card base set in a gold version, inserted in each pack.

	MT
Complete Set (90):	25.00
Gold Cards:	2x

1994 Upper Deck USA Chalk Talk

The 14-card, standard-size set was inserted every 35 packs of Upper Deck USA Basketball. The card fronts contain a hologram of Don Nelson with quotes from Nelson appearing on the card backs. Cards are numbered with a "CT" prefix.

		MT
Complete Set (14):		25.00
Common Player:		.75
1	Derrick Coleman	.75
2	Joe Dumars	1.50
3	Tim Hardaway	1.50
4	Larry Johnson	2.00
5	Shawn Kemp	4.00
6	Dan Majerle	1.00
7	Reggie Miller	4.00
8	Alonzo Mourning	4.00
9	Shaquille O'Neal	15.00
10	Mark Price	.75
11	Steve Smith	1.00
12	Isiah Thomas	2.00
13	Dominique Wilkins	1.50
14	Kevin Johnson	1.50

1994 Upper Deck USA Follow Your Dreams

The 14-card, standard-size set was inserted every 14 packs of USA Basketball. The cards are broken into three subsets: Assists, Rebounds and Scoring. The categories appear in gold foil along the side of the card front. The card backs carry the rules of the Dream Team II game. The player who led the team in assists (Kevin Johnson), rebounds (Shaquille O'Neal) and scoring (O'Neal) could be redeemed by the collector for a special 14-card set.

		MT
Complete Set (14):		20.00
Complete Rebounds Set:		20.00
Complete Scoring Set:		20.00
Common Player:		.50
1	Derrick Coleman	.50
2	Joe Dumars	.75
3	Tim Hardaway	.75
4	Kevin Johnson	.75
5	Larry Johnson	2.00
6	Shawn Kemp	2.50
7	Dan Majerle	.75
8	Reggie Miller	2.50
9	Alonzo Mourning	2.50
10	Shaquille O'Neal	10.00
11	Mark Price	.50
12	Steve Smith	.75
13	Isiah Thomas	1.25
14	Dominique Wilkins	.75

1994 Upper Deck USA Jordan's Highlights

The five-card, standard-size set features Jordan in international competition throughout his career. A facsimile autograph in gold foil appears along the bottom border of the card front. Cards are numbered with a "JH" prefix.

		MT
Complete Set (5):		40.00
Common Jordan:		10.00
1	Michael Jordan (1992 Summer Games)	10.00
2	Michael Jordan (1992 Tournament of the Americas)	10.00
3	Michael Jordan (1984 Summer Games)	10.00
4	Michael Jordan (1983 World University Games)	10.00
5	Michael Jordan (International Games)	10.00

1995 Collector's Choice Int. European

The 429-card, standard-size set was actually released in two series (210 and 219) for the French, German and Italian markets. Series I is similar in design and numbering to the U.S. 1994-95 Series I issue and all cards feature bilingual information.

		MT
Comp. French Set (429):		95.00
Comp. French Ser. 1 (219):		70.00
Comp. French Ser. 2 (210):		30.00
Comp. German Set (429):		95.00
Comp. German Ser.1 (219):		70.00
Comp. German Ser. 2 (210):		30.00
Comp. Italian Set (429):		95.00
Comp. Italian Ser. 1 (219):		70.00
Comp. Italian Ser. 2 (210):		30.00
Comp. Spanish Set (429):		95.00
Comp. Spanish Ser. 1 (219):		70.00
Comp. Spanish Ser. 2 (210):		30.00
Common Player:		.20
1	Anfernee Hardaway	3.50
2	Mark Macon	.20
3	Steve Smith	.40
4	Chris Webber	2.50
5	Donald Royal	.20
6	Avery Johnson	.40
7	Kevin Johnson	.60
8	Doug Christie	.20
9	Derrick McKey	.20
10	Dennis Rodman	2.00
11	Scott Skiles	.20
12	Johnny Dawkins	.40
13	Kendall Gill	.20
14	Jeff Hornacek	.50
15	Latrell Sprewell	.75
16	Lucious Harris	.20
17	Chris Mullin	.60
18	John Williams	.40
19	Tony Campbell	.20
20	LaPhonso Ellis	.20
21	Gerald Wilkins	.20
22	Clyde Drexler	1.75
23	Michael Jordan Baseball	7.00
24	George Lynch	.20
25	Mark Price	.75
26	James Robinson	.20
27	Elmore Spencer	.20
28	Stacey King	.20
29	Corie Blount	.20
30	Dell Curry	.20
31	Reggie Miller	1.50
32	Karl Malone	3.00
33	Scottie Pippen	2.00
34	Hakeem Olajuwon	2.00
35	Clarence Weatherspoon	.40
36	Kevin Edwards	.20
37	Pete Myers	.20
38	Jeff Turner	.20
39	Ennis Whatley	.20
40	Calbert Cheaney	.40
41	Glen Rice	.75
42	Vin Baker	1.00
43	Grant Long	.20
44	Derrick Coleman	.40
45	Rik Smits	.50
46	Chris Smith	.20
47	Carl Herrera	.20
48	Bob Martin	.20
49	Terrell Brandon	.75
50	David Robinson	2.50
51	Danny Ferry	.20
52	Buck Williams	.40
53	Josh Grant	.20
54	Ed Pinckney	.20
55	Dikembe Mutombo	.75
56	Clifford Robinson	.60
57	Luther Wright	.20
58	Scott Burrell	.20
59	Stacey Augmon	.40
60	Jeff Malone	.40
61	Byron Houston	.20
62	Anthony Peeler	.20
63	Michael Adams	.20
64	Negele Knight	.20
65	Terry Cummings	.40
66	Christian Laettner	.50
67	Tracy Murray	.20
68	Sedale Threatt	.20
69	Dan Majerle	.40
70	Frank Brickowski	.20
71	Ken Norman	.20
72	Charles Smith	.20
73	Adam Keefe	.20
74	P.J. Brown	.20
75	Kevin Duckworth	.20
76	Shawn Bradley	.60
77	Darnell Mee	.20
78	Nick Anderson	.40
79	Mark West	.20
80	B.J. Armstrong	.40
81	Dennis Scott	.40
82	Lindsey Hunter	.20
83	Derek Strong	.20
84	Mike Brown	.20
85	Antonio Harvey	.20
86	Anthony Bonner	.20
87	Sam Cassell	.60
89	Spud Webb	.40
90	Mookie Blaylock	.40
91	Greg Anthony	.20
92	Richard Petruska	.20
93	Sean Rooks	.20
94	Ervin Johnson	.20
95	Randy Brown	.20
96	Orlando Woolridge	.20
97	Charles Oakley	.40
98	Craig Ehlo	.20
99	Derek Harper	.40
100	Doug Edwards	.20
101	Muggsy Bogues	.60
102	Mitch Richmond	1.00
103	Mahmoud Abdul-Rauf	.40
104	Joe Dumars	.25
105	Eric Riley	.20
106	Terry Mills	.20
107	Toni Kukoc	.60
108	Jon Koncak	.20
109	Haywoode Workman	.20
110	Todd Day	.20
111	Detlef Schrempf	.60
112	David Wesley	.20
113	Mark Jackson	.40
114	Doug Overton	.50
115	Vinny Del Negro	.20
116	Loy Vaught	.40
117	Mike Peplowski	.20
118	Bimbo Coles	.20
119	Rex Walters	.20
120	Sherman Douglas	.20
121	David Benoit	.20
122	John Salley	.20
123	Cedric Ceballos	.60
124	Chris Mills	.40
125	Robert Horry	.75
126	Johnny Newman	.20
127	Malcolm Mackey	.20
128	Terry Dehere	.20
129	Dino Radja	.40
130	Reggie Williams	.20
131	Xavier McDaniel	.20
132	Bobby Hurley	.40
133	Alonzo Mourning	2.00
134	Isaiah Rider	.60
135	Antoine Carr	.20
136	Robert Pack	.20
137	Walt Williams	.40
138	Tyrone Corbin	.20
139	Popeye Jones	.20
140	Shawn Kemp	1.00
141	Thurl Bailey	.20
142	James Worthy	.75
143	Scott Haskin	.20
144	Hubert Davis	.20
145	A.C. Green	.50
146	Dale Davis	.20
147	Nate McMillan	.40
148	Chris Morris	.40
149	Will Perdue	.20
150	Felton Spencer	.20
151	Rod Strickland	.40
152	Blue Edwards	.20
153	John S. Williams	.20
154	Rodney Rogers	.40
155	Acie Earl	.20
156	Hersey Hawkins	.40
157	Jamal Mashburn	1.50
158	Don MacLean	.20
159	Micheal Williams	.20
160	Kenny Gattison	.20
161	Rich King	.20
162	Allan Houston	1.25
163	John Stockton	2.50
164	Kenny Anderson	.40
165	Shaquille O'Neal	6.00
166	Danny Manning TO	.40
167	Dee Brown TO	.20
168	Alonzo Mourning TO	1.50
169	Scottie Pippen TO	1.25
170	Mark Price TO	.20
171	Jamal Mashburn TO	.75
172	Dikembe Mutombo TO	.40
173	Joe Dumars TO	.40
174	Chris Webber TO	1.25
175	Hakeem Olajuwon TO	1.00
176	Reggie Miller TO	.75
177	Ron Harper TO	.20
178	Nick Van Exel TO	.75
179	Steve Smith TO	.20
180	Vin Baker TO	.60
181	Isaiah Rider TO	.40
182	Derrick Coleman TO	.20
183	Patrick Ewing TO	.75
184	Shaquille O'Neal TO	2.50
185	Clarence Weatherspoon TO	.20
186	Charles Barkley TO	1.00
187	Clyde Drexler TO	.75
188	Mitch Richmond TO	.40
189	David Robinson TO	1.50
190	Shawn Kemp TO	.50
191	Karl Malone TO	1.50
192	Tom Gugliotta TO	.20
193	Kenny Anderson ASA	.20
194	Alonzo Mourning ASA	1.00
195	Mark Price ASA	.20
196	John Stockton ASA	1.25
197	Shaquille O'Neal ASA	2.50
198	Latrell Sprewell ASA	.40
199	Charles Barkley PRO	1.00
200	Chris Webber PRO	1.00
201	Patrick Ewing PRO	.75
202	Dennis Rodman PRO	1.00
203	Shawn Kemp PRO	.50
204	Michael Jordan PRO	5.00
205	Shaquille O'Neal PRO	2.50
206	Larry Johnson PRO	.75
207	Tim Hardaway CL	.40
208	John Stockton CL	1.00
209	Harold Miner CL	.20
210	B.J. Armstrong CL	.20
211	Michael Jordan ROY	7.00
212	63-Pt. Game (Michael Jordan)	7.00
213	Slam-Dunk (Michael Jordan)	7.00
214	MVP (Michael Jordan)	7.00
215	All-Star (Michael Jordan)	7.00
216	3,000-Points (Michael Jordan)	7.00
217	Championships (M. Jordan)	7.00
218	Decade (Michael Jordan)	7.00
219	Michael Jordan CL	7.00
220	Gary Payton	1.50
221	Tom Hammonds	.20
222	Danny Ainge	1.00
223	Gary Grant	.20
224	Jim Jackson	.75
225	Chris Gatling	.20
226	Sergei Bazarevich	.20
227	Tony Dumas	.25
228	Andrew Lang	.20
229	Wesley Person	.75
230	Terry Porter	.20
231	Duane Causwell	.20
232	Shaquille O'Neal	5.00
233	Antonio Davis	.10
234	Charles Barkley	2.00
235	Tony Massenburg	.20
236	Ricky Pierce	.20
237	Scott Skiles	.40
238	*Jalen Rose*	3.00
239	Charlie Ward	.60
240	Michael Jordan COMM	5.00
241	Elden Campbell	.20
242	Bill Cartwright	.20
243	Armon Gilliam	.40
244	Rick Fox	.20
245	Tim Breaux	.20
246	Monty Williams	.20
247	Dominque Wilkins	1.00
248	Robert Parish	.60
249	Mark Jackson	.50
250	Jason Kidd	5.00
251	Andres Guibert	.20
252	Matt Geiger	.20
253	Stanley Roberts	.20
254	Jack Haley	.20
255	David Wingate	.20
256	*John Crotty*	.20
257	Brian Grant	1.50
258	Otis Thorpe	.40
259	Clifford Rozier	.40
260	Grant Long	.20
261	Eric Mobley	.20
262	Dickey Simpkins	.20
263	J.R. Reid	.20
264	Kevin Willis	.40
265	Scott Brooks	.20
266	*Glenn Robinson*	5.00
267	Dana Barros	.40
268	Ken Norman	.20
269	Herb Williams	.20
270	Dee Brown	.20
271	Steve Kerr	.20
272	Jon Barry	.20
273	Sean Elliott	.60
274	Elliott Perry	.20
275	Kenny Smith	.20
276	Sean Rooks	.20
277	Gheorghe Muresan	.40
278	*Juwan Howard*	2.50
279	Steve Smith	.40
280	Anthony Bowie	.20
281	Moses Malone	.75
282	Olden Polynice	.20
283	Jo Jo English	.20
284	Marty Conlon	.20
285	Sam Mitchell	.20
286	Doug West	.20
287	Cedric Ceballos	.40
288	Lorenzo Williams	.20
289	Harold Ellis	.20
290	Doc Rivers	.40
291	Keith Tower	.20
292	Mark Bryant	.20
293	Oliver Miller	.20
294	Michael Adams	.20
295	Tree Rollins	.20
296	Eddie Jones	5.00
297	Malik Sealy	.40
298	Blue Edwards	.20
299	Brooks Thompson	.20
300	Benoit Benjamin	.20
301	Avery Johnson	.40
302	Larry Johnson	.75
303	John Starks	.40
304	Byron Scott	.40
305	Eric Murdock	.20
306	Jay Humphries	.20
307	Kenny Anderson	.40
308	Brian Williams	.20
309	Nick Van Exel	1.00
310	Tim Hardaway	.60
311	Lee Mayberry	.20
312	Vlade Divac	.40
313	*Donyell Marshall*	.75
314	Anthony Mason	.40
315	Danny Manning	.60
316	Tyrone Hill	.20
317	Vincent Askew	.20
318	Khalid Reeves	.40
319	Ron Harper	.60
320	Brent Price	.20
321	Byron Houston	.20
322	*Lamond Murray*	.75
323	Bryant Stith	.20
324	Tom Gugliotta	.40
325	Jerome Kersey	.20
326	B.J. Tyler	.20
327	Antonio Lang	.20
328	Carlos Rogers	.40
329	Waymon Tisdale	.40
330	Kevin Gamble	.20
331	*Eric Piatkowski*	.75
332	Mitchell Butler	.20
333	Patrick Ewing	1.50
334	Doug Smith	.20
335	Joe Kleine	.20
336	Keith Jennings	.20
337	Bill Curley	.40
338	Johnny Newman	.20
339	Howard Eisley	.20
340	Willie Anderson	.20
341	*Aaron McKie*	.75
342	Tom Chambers	.40
343	Scott Williams	.20
344	Harvey Grant	.20
345	Billy Owens	.40
346	*Sharone Wright*	.50
347	Michael Cage	.20
348	Vern Fleming	.20
349	Darrin Hancock	.20
350	Matt Fish	.20
351	Rony Seikaly	.20
352	Victor Alexander	.20
353	Anthony Miller	.20
354	Horace Grant	.60
355	Jayson Williams	.20
356	Dale Ellis	.40
357	Sarunas Marciulionis	.20
358	Anthony Avent	.20
359	Rex Chapman	.40
360	Askia Jones	.20
361	*Charles Outlaw*	1.00
362	Chuck Person	.40
363	Dan Schayes	.20
364	Morlon Wiley	.20
365	Dontonio Wingfield	.40
366	Tony Smith	.20
367	Bill Wennington	.20
368	Bryon Russell	.20
369	Geert Hammink	.20
370	*Eric Montross*	.50
371	Cliff Levingston	.20
372	Stacey Augmon BP	.20
373	Eric Montross BP	.25
374	Alonzo Mourning BP	1.00
375	Scottie Pippen BP	1.00
376	Mark Price BP	.20
377	Jason Kidd BP	3.00
378	Jalen Rose BP	1.75
379	Grant Hill BP	4.00
380	Latrell Sprewell BP	.40
381	Hakeem Olajuwon BP	1.50
382	Reggie Miller BP	.75
383	Lamond Murray BP	.40
384	Eddie Jones BP	2.00
385	Khalid Reeves BP	.20
386	Glenn Robinson BP	2.00
387	Donyell Marshall BP	.40
388	Derrick Coleman BP	.20
389	Patrick Ewing BP	.75
390	Shaquille O'Neal BP	3.00
391	Sharone Wright BP	.25
392	Charles Barkley BP	1.50
393	Aaron McKie BP	.40
394	Brian Grant BP	.75
395	David Robinson BP	1.50
396	Shawn Kemp BP	.50
397	Karl Malone BP	2.00
398	Tom Gugliotta BP	.20
399	Hakeem Olajuwon TRIV	1.50
400	Shaquille O'Neal TRIV	3.00
401	Chris Webber TRIV	1.50
402	Michael Jordan TRIV	5.00
403	David Robinson TRIV	1.50
404	Shawn Kemp TRIV	.50
405	Patrick Ewing TRIV	.75
406	Charles Barkley TRIV	1.50
407	Glenn Robinson DC	2.00
408	Jason Kidd DC	3.00
409	Grant Hill DC	4.00
410	Donyell Marshall DC	.50
411	Sharone Wright DC	.25
412	Lamond Murray DC	.40
413	Brian Grant DC	1.00
414	Eric Montross DC	.40
415	Eddie Jones DC	2.00
416	Carlos Rogers DC	.20
417	Shawn Kemp CL	.40
418	Bobby Hurley CL	.20
419	Shawn Bradley CL	.40
420	Michael Jordan CL	2.00
421	Vernon Maxwell	.20
422	John Stockton	2.00
423	Luc Longley	.20
424	Sam Perkins	.40
425	Pooh Richardson	.20
426	Tyrone Corbin	.20
427	Mario Elie	.20
428	Bobby Phills	.20
429	Grant Hill	9.00

1995 Collector's Choice Int. European Gold Signature

The 72-card, skip-numbered set parallels the European base set with a gold-foil facsimile autograph on the front. The cards were inserted every 3-6 packs.

		MT
Comp. French Set (72):		350.00
Comp. French Ser. 1 (27):		100.00
Comp. French Ser. 2 (45):		275.00
Comp. German Set (72):		350.00
Comp. German Ser. 1 (27):		100.00
Comp. German Ser. 2 (45):		275.00
Comp. Italian Set (72):		350.00
Comp. Italian Ser. 1 (27):		100.00
Comp. Italian Ser. 2 (45):		250.00
Comp. Spanish Ser. 1 (27):		60.00
Common Series 1 (166-192):		2.00
Common Series 2 (372-416):		2.00
166	Danny Manning TO	3.00
167	Dee Brown TO	2.00
168	Alonzo Mourning TO	7.00
169	Scottie Pippen TO	10.00
170	Mark Price TO	3.00
171	Jamal Mashburn TO	6.00
172	Dikembe Mutombo TO	4.00
173	Joe Dumars TO	3.00
174	Chris Webber TO	9.00
175	Hakeem Olajuwon TO	12.00
177	Ron Harper TO	2.50
178	Nick Van Exel TO	6.00
179	Steve Smith TO	2.50
180	Vin Baker TO	6.00
181	Isaiah Rider TO	3.00
182	Derrick Coleman TO	2.50
183	Patrick Ewing TO	8.00
184	Shaquille O'Neal TO	15.00
185	Clarence Weatherspoon TO	2.50
187	Clyde Drexler TO	8.00
188	Mitch Richmond TO	4.00
189	David Robinson TO	10.00
190	Shawn Kemp TO	7.00
191	Karl Malone TO	10.00
192	Tom Gugliotta TO	2.50
372	Stacey Augmon BP	2.50
373	Eric Montross BP	2.50
374	Alonzo Mourning BP	7.00
375	Scottie Pippen BP	10.00
376	Mark Price BP	2.50
377	Jason Kidd BP	12.00
378	Jalen Rose BP	6.00
379	Grant Hill BP	18.00
380	Latrell Sprewell BP	4.00
381	Hakeem Olajuwon BP	15.00
382	Reggie Miller BP	8.00
383	Lamond Murray BP	3.00
384	Eddie Jones BP	10.00
385	Khalid Reeves BP	2.00
386	Glenn Robinson BP	10.00
387	Donyell Marshall BP	4.00
388	Derrick Coleman BP	2.50
389	Patrick Ewing BP	7.00
390	Shaquille O'Neal BP	15.00
391	Sharone Wright BP	2.50
392	Charles Barkley BP	10.00
393	Aaron McKie BP	3.00
394	Brian Grant BP	5.00
395	David Robinson BP	10.00
396	Shawn Kemp BP	7.00
397	Karl Malone BP	10.00
398	Tom Gugliotta BP	2.50
399	Hakeem Olajuwon TRIV	10.00
400	Shaquille O'Neal TRIV	15.00
401	Chris Webber TRIV	9.00
402	Michael Jordan TRIV	30.00
403	David Robinson TRIV	10.00
404	Shawn Kemp TRIV	7.00
405	Patrick Ewing TRIV	7.00
406	Derrick Coleman TRIV	2.50
407	Glenn Robinson DC	12.00
408	Jason Kidd DC	12.00
409	Grant Hill DC	18.00
410	Donyell Marshall DC	4.00
411	Sharone Wright DC	2.50
412	Lamond Murray DC	3.00
413	Brian Grant DC	5.00
414	Eric Montross DC	2.50
415	Eddie Jones DC	10.00
416	Carlos Rogers DC	2.00

1995-96 Collector's Choice European Stickers

This 212-card set was distributed in 100-pack boxes in Europe. The cards feature identical fronts to the 1994-95 and 95-96 Collector's Choice American stickers. The cards are slightly smaller than standard size. The backs have the card number in a large black circle and the NBA and Upper Deck/Collector's Choice logos.

		MT
Complete Set (212):		40.00
Common Player:		.15
1	Golden State Warriors Logo	.15
2	Latrell Sprewell	.75
3	Ricky Pierce	.15
4	Tim Hardaway	.75
5	Chris Mullin	.30
6	Donyell Marshall	.75
7	Clifford Rozier	.15
8	Carlos Rogers	.15
9	Rony Seikaly	.15
10	Los Angeles Clippers Logo	.15
11	Pooh Richardson	.15
12	Terry Dehere	.15
13	Eric Piatkowski	.15
14	Loy Vaught	.15
15	Malik Sealy	.15
16	Lamond Murray	.15
17	Los Angeles Lakers Logo	.15
18	Sedale Threatt	.15
19	Nick Van Exel	.75
20	Cedric Ceballos	.15
21	George Lynch	.15
22	Eddie Jones	6.00
23	Elden Campbell	.30
24	Vlade Divac	.30
25	Phoenix Suns Logo	.15
26	Kevin Johnson	.30
27	Wesley Person	.15
28	Dan Majerle	.15
29	A.C. Green	.15
30	Charles Barkley	1.00
31	Danny Manning	.15
32	Wayman Tisdale	.15
33	Portland Trail Blazers Logo	.15
34	Rod Strickland	.30
35	Terry Porter	.15
36	Aaron McKie	.15
37	Otis Thorpe	.15
38	Buck Williams	.15
39	Clifford Robinson	.30
40	Harvey Grant	.15
41	Sacramento Kings Logo	.15
42	Randy Brown	.15
43	Mitch Richmond	.75
44	Bobby Hurley	.15
45	Walt Williams	.30
46	Brian Grant	.75
47	Olden Polynice	.15
48	Duane Causwell	.15
49	Seattle Supersonics Logo	.15
50	Kendall Gill	.30
51	Gary Payton	.75
52	Sarunas Marciulionis	.15
53	Nate McMillan	.15
54	Detlef Schrempf	.15
55	Shawn Kemp	2.50
56	Sam Perkins	.15
57	Dallas Mavericks Logo	.15
58	Jim Jackson	.50
59	Jason Kidd	4.00
60	Tony Dumas	.15
61	Jamal Mashburn	.75
62	Doug Smith	.15
63	Popeye Jones	.15
64	Denver Nuggets Logo	.15
65	Robert Pack	.15
66	Bryant Stith	.15
67	Mahmoud Abdul-Rauf	.30
68	Jalen Rose	.15
69	Reggie Williams	.15
70	LaPhonso Ellis	.30
71	Dikembe Mutombo	.50
72	Houston Rockets Logo	.15
73	Sam Cassell	.30
74	Kenny Smith	.15
75	Clyde Drexler	1.00
76	Carl Herrera	.15
77	Robert Horry	.30
78	Otis Thorpe	.15
79	Hakeem Olajuwon	2.00
80	Minnesota Timberwolves Logo	.15
81	Chris Smith	.15
82	Micheal Williams	.15
83	Doug West	.15
84	Isaiah Rider	.30
85	Christian Laettner	.50
86	Tom Gugliotta	.75
87	San Antonio Spurs Logo	.15
88	Avery Johnson	.15
89	Vinny Del Negro	.15
90	Dennis Rodman	3.00
91	Sean Elliott	.30
92	Chuck Person	.15
93	J.R. Reid	.15
94	David Robinson	1.00
95	Utah Jazz Logo	.15
96	Jeff Hornacek	.15
97	John Stockton	.75
98	David Benoit	.15
99	Karl Malone	1.00
100	Tom Chambers	.15
101	Antoine Carr	.15
102	Felton Spencer	.15
103	Atlanta Hawks Logo	.15
104	Mookie Blaylock	.30

105 Craig Ehlo .15
106 Steve Smith .30
107 Stacey Augmon .15
108 Grant Long .15
109 Ken Norman .15
110 Jon Koncak .15
111 Charlotte Hornets Logo .15
112 Hersey Hawkins .15
113 Dell Curry .15
114 Muggsy Bogues .15
115 Scott Burrell .15
116 Larry Johnson .50
117 Robert Parish .30
118 Alonzo Mourning 1.00
119 Chicago Bulls Logo .30
120 Michael Jordan 12.00
121 Ron Harper .15
122 Toni Kukoc .75
123 Scottie Pippen 2.50
124 Dickey Simpkins .15
125 Will Perdue .15
126 Cleveland Cavaliers Logo .15
127 Gerald Wilkins .15
128 Mark Price .15
129 Terrell Brandon .50
130 Bobby Phills .30
131 Chris Mills .30
132 Tyrone Hill .15
133 John Williams .15
134 Detroit Pistons Logo .15
135 Lindsey Hunter .15
136 Joe Dumars .30
137 Allan Houston .50
138 Terry Mills .15
139 Grant Hill 12.00
140 Mark West .15
141 Indiana Pacers Logo .15
142 Reggie Miller .75
143 Mark Jackson .15
144 Duane Ferrell .15
145 Derrick McKey .15
146 Dale Davis .15
147 Antonio Davis .15
148 Rik Smits .15
149 Milwaukee Bucks Logo .15
150 Lee Mayberry .15
151 Todd Day .15
152 Vin Baker 1.00
153 Glenn Robinson 3.00
154 Marty Conlon .15
155 Johnny Newman .15
156 Eric Mobley .15
157 Boston Celtics Logo .15
158 Sherman Douglas .15
159 Dee Brown .15
160 Rick Fox .15
161 Dino Radja .15
162 Xavier McDaniel .15
163 Dominique Wilkins .30
164 Eric Montross .15
165 Miami Heat Logo .15
166 Bimbo Coles .15
167 Khalid Reeves .15
168 Glen Rice .75
169 Billy Owens .15
170 Kevin Willis .15
171 Matt Geiger .15
172 New Jersey Nets Logo .15
173 Kevin Edwards .15
174 Rex Walters .15
175 Kenny Anderson .30
176 Derrick Coleman .30
177 Chris Morris .15
178 Armon Gilliam .15
179 P.J. Brown .15
180 New York Knicks Logo .15
181 Derek Harper .15
182 Charlie Ward .15
183 John Starks .30
184 Charles Smith .15
185 Charles Oakley .15
186 Anthony Mason .30
187 Patrick Ewing .75
188 Orlando Magic Logo .15
189 Anthony Bowie .15
190 Anfernee Hardaway 4.00
191 Nick Anderson .30
192 Dennis Scott .30
193 Donald Royal .15
194 Horace Grant .15
195 Shaquille O'Neal 3.00
196 Philadelphia 76ers Logo .15
197 Jeff Malone .15
198 Dana Barros .15
199 Clarence Weatherspoon .15
200 Scott Williams .15
201 Sharone Wright .15
202 Shawn Bradley .30
203 Washington Bullets Logo .15
204 Scott Skiles .15
205 Mitchell Butler .15
206 Calbert Cheaney .15
207 Don MacLean .15
208 Juwan Howard 4.00
209 Kevin Duckworth .15
210 Gheorghe Muresan .30
211 Toronto Raptors Logo .15
212 Vancouver Grizzlies Logo .15

1995-96 Collector's Choice European Sticker Michael Jordan

Inserted one per every five packs of 95-96 Collector's Choice European Stickers, this nine-sticker set has a similar design to 95-96 Collector's Choice Jordan Collection and He's Back sets. They are numbered with a "MJ" prefix.

MT
Complete Set (9): 30.00
Common Player: 4.00
1 1985 NBA ROY (Michael Jordan) 4.00
2 1986-87 3,000 Points (Michael Jordan) 4.00
3 1988 NBA Defensive POY (Michael Jordan) 4.00
4 Jordan Collection (Michael Jordan) 4.00
5 He's Back (Michael Jordan) 4.00
6 He's Back (Michael Jordan) 4.00
7 He's Back (Michael Jordan) 4.00
8 He's Back (Michael Jordan) 4.00
9 He's Back (Michael Jordan) 4.00

1995 Collector's Choice Int. Japanese I

The 219-card, standard-size set was issued by Upper Deck for the Japanese card market. The cards are similar in design to the U.S. 1994-95 set and the card text is in Japanese - except for the subset cards which also have English text.

MT
Complete Set (219): 200.00
Common Player: .25
1 Anfernee Hardaway 5.00
2 Mark Macon .25
3 Steve Smith 1.00
4 Chris Webber 4.00
5 Donald Royal .25
6 Avery Johnson .50
7 Kevin Johnson .75
8 Doug Christie .25
9 Derrick McKey .25
10 Dennis Rodman 2.50
11 Scott Skiles .50
12 Johnny Dawkins .40
13 Kendall Gill .25
14 Jeff Hornacek .50
15 Latrell Sprewell 1.00
16 Lucious Harris .25
17 Chris Mullin .75
18 John Williams .40
19 Tony Campbell .25
20 LaPhonso Ellis .25
21 Gerald Wilkins .25
22 Clyde Drexler 2.00
23 Michael Jordan Baseball 10.00
24 George Lynch .25
25 Mark Price 1.00
26 James Robinson .25
27 Elmore Spencer .25
28 Stacey King .25
29 Corie Blount .25
30 Dell Curry .25
31 Reggie Miller 2.00
32 Karl Malone 4.00
33 Scottie Pippen 3.00
34 Hakeem Olajuwon 3.00
35 Clarence Weatherspoon .40
36 Kevin Edwards .25
37 Pete Myers .25
38 Jeff Turner .25
39 Ennis Whatley .25
40 Calbert Cheaney .40
41 Glen Rice .40
42 Vin Baker 1.00
43 Grant Long .25
44 Derrick Coleman .40
45 Rik Smits .60
46 Chris Smith .25
47 Carl Herrera .25
48 Bob Martin .25
49 Terrell Brandon .75
50 David Robinson 3.00
51 Danny Ferry .25
52 Buck Williams .50
53 Josh Grant .25
54 Ed Pinckney .25
55 Dikembe Mutombo 1.00
56 Clifford Robinson .75
57 Luther Wright .25
58 Scott Burrell .25
59 Stacey Augmon .40
60 Jeff Malone .40
61 Byron Houston .25
62 Anthony Peeler .25
63 Michael Adams .25
64 Negele Knight .25
65 Terry Cummings .40
66 Christian Laettner .60
67 Tracy Murray .25
68 Sedale Threatt .25
69 Dan Majerle .60
70 Frank Brickowski .25
71 Ken Norman .25
72 Charles Smith .25
73 Adam Keefe .25
74 P.J. Brown .40
75 Kevin Duckworth .25
76 Shawn Bradley .60
77 Darnell Mee .25
78 Nick Anderson .40
79 Mark West .25
80 B.J. Armstrong .40
81 Dennis Scott .25
82 Lindsey Hunter .25
83 Derek Strong .25
84 Mike Brown .25
85 Antonio Harvey .25
86 Anthony Bonner .25
87 Sam Cassell 1.00
89 Spud Webb .40
90 Mookie Blaylock .40
91 Greg Anthony .25
92 Richard Petruska .25
93 Sean Rooks .25
94 Ervin Johnson .25
95 Randy Brown .25
96 Orlando Woolridge .25
97 Charles Oakley .40
98 Craig Ehlo .25
99 Derek Harper .40
100 Doug Edwards .25
101 Muggsy Bogues .75
102 Mitch Richmond 1.25
103 Mahmoud Abdul-Rauf .40
104 Joe Dumars 1.00
105 Eric Riley .25
106 Terry Mills .25
107 Toni Kukoc .75
108 Jon Koncak .25
109 Haywoode Workman .25
110 Todd Day .25
111 Detlef Schrempf .60
112 David Wesley .25
113 Mark Jackson .25
114 Doug Overton .25
115 Vinny Del Negro .25
116 Loy Vaught .40
117 Mike Peplowski .25
118 Bimbo Coles .25
119 Rex Walters .25
120 Sherman Douglas .25
121 David Benoit .25
122 John Salley .25
123 Cedric Ceballos .50
124 Chris Mills .60
125 Robert Horry .75
126 Johnny Newman .25
127 Malcolm Mackey .25
128 Terry Dehere .25
129 Dino Radja .40
130 Reggie Williams .25
131 Xavier McDaniel .25
132 Bobby Hurley .40
133 Alonzo Mourning 2.50
134 Isaiah Rider .60
135 Antoine Carr .25
136 Robert Pack .25
137 Walt Williams .40
138 Tyrone Corbin .25
139 Popeye Jones .25
140 Shawn Kemp 2.00
141 Thurl Bailey .25
142 James Worthy .75
143 Scott Haskin .25
144 Hubert Davis .25
145 A.C. Green .75
146 Dale Davis .50
147 Nate McMillan .50
148 Chris Morris .25
149 Will Perdue .25
150 Felton Spencer .25
151 Rod Strickland .40
152 Blue Edwards .25
153 John S. Williams .25
154 Rodney Rogers .60
155 Acie Earl .25
156 Hersey Hawkins .40
157 Jamal Mashburn 1.50
158 Don MacLean .25
159 Micheal Williams .25
160 Kenny Gattison .25
161 Rich King .25
162 Allan Houston 1.50
163 John Stockton 3.00
164 Kenny Anderson .40
165 Shaquille O'Neal 6.00
166 Danny Manning TO .40
167 Dee Brown TO .25
168 Alonzo Mourning TO 1.00
169 Scottie Pippen TO 1.25
170 Mark Price TO .50
171 Jamal Mashburn TO .75
172 Dikembe Mutombo TO .75
173 Joe Dumars TO .60
174 Chris Webber TO 2.00
175 Hakeem Olajuwon TO 1.50
176 Reggie Miller TO 1.00
177 Ron Harper TO .40
178 Nick Van Exel TO .75
179 Steve Smith TO .75
180 Vin Baker TO .75
181 Isaiah Rider TO .40
182 Derrick Coleman TO .40
183 Patrick Ewing TO 1.00
184 Shaquille O'Neal TO 3.00
185 Clarence Weatherspoon TO .25
186 Charles Barkley TO 1.50
187 Clyde Drexler TO 1.25
188 Mitch Richmond TO 1.00
189 David Robinson TO 1.50
190 Shawn Kemp TO 1.00
191 Karl Malone TO 2.00
192 Tom Gugliotta TO .25
193 Kenny Anderson ASA .25
194 Alonzo Mourning ASA 1.00
195 Mark Price ASA .50
196 John Stockton ASA 2.00
197 Shaquille O'Neal ASA 3.00
198 Latrell Sprewell ASA .40
199 Charles Barkley PRO 1.50
200 Chris Webber PRO 2.00
201 Patrick Ewing PRO 1.00
202 Dennis Rodman PRO 1.00
203 Shawn Kemp PRO .75
204 Michael Jordan PRO 5.00
205 Shaquille O'Neal PRO 3.00
206 Larry Johnson PRO .75
207 Tim Hardaway CL .40
208 John Stockton CL 1.25
209 Harold Miner CL .25
210 B.J. Armstrong CL .25
211 Michael Jordan ROY 15.00
212 63-Pt. Game (Michael Jordan) 15.00
213 Slam-Dunk (Michael Jordan) 15.00
214 Michael Jordan MVP 15.00
215 All-Star (Michael Jordan) 15.00
216 3,000-Points (Michael Jordan) 15.00
217 Championships (Michael Jordan) 15.00
218 Decade (Michael Jordan) 15.00
219 Michael Jordan CL 15.00

1995 Collector's Choice Int. Japanese II

The 210-card, standard-size set was skip numbered and was similar in design to the U.S. set from 1994-95. There are no cards issued between 371 and 399. The cards have Japanese text, except for the subset cards which have English and Japanese writing.

MT
Complete Set (210): 75.00
Common Player (153-179): .25
Common Player (220-371): .25
Common Player (399-429): .25
153 Stacey Augmon BP .25
154 Eric Montross BP .60
155 Alonzo Mourning BP 1.00
156 Scottie Pippen BP 1.25
157 Mark Price BP .50
158 Jason Kidd BP 4.00
159 Jalen Rose BP 3.00
160 Grant Hill BP 6.00
161 Latrell Sprewell BP 1.00
162 Hakeem Olajuwon BP 1.50
163 Reggie Miller BP 1.00
164 Lamond Murray BP .75
165 Eddie Jones BP 3.00
166 Khalid Reeves BP .25
167 Glenn Robinson BP 3.00
168 Donyell Marshall BP 1.00
169 Derrick Coleman BP .25
170 Patrick Ewing BP 1.00
171 Shaquille O'Neal BP 4.00
172 Sharone Wright BP .40
173 Charles Barkley BP 1.50
174 Aaron McKie BP 1.00
175 Brian Grant BP 2.00
176 David Robinson BP 1.50
177 Shawn Kemp BP .75
178 Karl Malone BP 2.00
179 Tom Gugliotta BP .50
220 Gary Payton 2.00
221 Tom Hammonds .25
222 Danny Ainge 1.00
223 Gary Grant .25
224 Jim Jackson 1.25
225 Chris Gatling .25
226 Sergei Bazarevich .25
227 Tony Dumas .40
228 Andrew Lang .25
229 Wesley Person .75
230 Terry Porter .25
231 Duane Causwell .25
232 Shaquille O'Neal 6.00
233 Antonio Davis .60
234 Charles Barkley 3.00
235 Tony Massenburg .25
236 Ricky Pierce .25
237 Scott Skiles .50
238 Jalen Rose 5.00
239 Charlie Ward .75
240 Michael Jordan COMM 5.00
241 Elden Campbell .25
242 Bill Cartwright .25
243 Armon Gilliam .40
244 Rick Fox .40
245 Tim Breaux .25
246 Monty Williams .25
247 Dominique Wilkins 1.00
248 Robert Parish .75
249 Mark Jackson .75
250 Jason Kidd 7.00
251 Andres Guibert .25
252 Matt Geiger .25
253 Stanley Roberts .25
254 Jack Haley .25
255 David Wingate .25
256 John Crotty .25
257 Brian Grant 3.50
258 Otis Thorpe .40
259 Clifford Rozier .40
260 Grant Long .25
261 Eric Mobley .25
262 Dickey Simpkins .25
263 J.R. Reid .25
264 Kevin Willis .40
265 Scott Brooks .25
266 Glenn Robinson 5.00
267 Dana Barros .40
268 Ken Norman .25
269 Herb Williams .25
270 Dee Brown .25
271 Steve Kerr .25
272 Jon Barry .25
273 Sean Elliott .60
274 Elliot Perry .25
275 Kenny Smith .25
276 Sean Rooks .25
277 Gheorghe Muresan .40
278 Juwan Howard 3.00
279 Steve Smith .75
280 Anthony Bowie .25
281 Moses Malone .75
282 Olden Polynice .25
283 Jo Jo English .25
284 Marty Conlon .25
285 Sam Mitchell .25
286 Doug West .25
287 Cedric Ceballos .60
288 Lorenzo Williams .25
289 Harold Ellis .25
290 Doc Rivers .50
291 Keith Tower .25
292 Mark Bryant .25
293 Oliver Miller .25
294 Michael Adams .25
295 Tree Rollins .25
296 Eddie Jones 6.00
297 Malik Sealy .50
298 Blue Edwards .25
299 Brooks Thompson .25
300 Benoit Benjamin .25
301 Avery Johnson .50
302 Larry Johnson .75
303 John Starks .75
304 Byron Scott .40
305 Eric Murdock .25
306 Jay Humphries .25
307 Kenny Anderson .40
308 Brian Williams .25
309 Nick Van Exel 1.00
310 Tim Hardaway 1.00
311 Lee Mayberry .25
312 Vlade Divac .75
313 Donyell Marshall 2.00
314 Anthony Mason .40
315 Danny Manning .60
316 Tyrone Hill .25
317 Vincent Askew .25
318 Khalid Reeves .40
319 Ron Harper .60
320 Brent Price .25
321 Byron Houston .25
322 Lamond Murray 1.00
323 Bryant Stith .25
324 Tom Gugliotta .75
325 Jerome Kersey .25
326 B.J. Tyler .25
327 Antonio Lang .25
328 Carlos Rogers .40
329 Waymon Tisdale .40
330 Kevin Gamble .25
331 Eric Piatkowski 1.00
332 Mitchell Butler .25
333 Patrick Ewing 2.00
334 Doug Smith .25
335 Joe Kleine .25
336 Keith Jennings .25
337 Bill Curley .40
338 Johnny Newman .25
339 Howard Eisley .50
340 Willie Anderson .25
341 Aaron McKie 1.00
342 Tom Chambers .40
343 Scott Williams .25
344 Harvey Grant .25
345 Billy Owens .40
346 Sharone Wright .50
347 Michael Cage .25
348 Vern Fleming .25
349 Darrin Hancock .25
350 Matt Fish .25
351 Rony Seikaly .25
352 Victor Alexander .25
353 Anthony Miller .25
354 Horace Grant .50
355 Jayson Williams .25
356 Dale Ellis .40
357 Sarunas Marciulionis .25
358 Anthony Avent .25
359 Rex Chapman .40
360 Askia Jones .25
361 Charles Outlaw 1.25
362 Chuck Person .40
363 Dan Schayes .25
364 Morlon Wiley .25
365 Dontonio Wingfield .40
366 Tony Smith .25
367 Bill Wennington .25
368 Bryoin Russell .25
369 Geert Hammink .25
370 Eric Montross .50
371 Cliff Levingston .25
399 Hakeem Olajuwon TRIV 1.50
400 Shaquille O'Neal TRIV 4.00
401 Chris Webber TRIV 3.00
402 Michael Jordan TRIV 5.00
403 David Robinson TRIV 2.00
404 Shawn Kemp TRIV .75
405 Patrick Ewing TRIV 1.00
406 Charles Barkley TRIV 1.50
407 Glenn Robinson DC 4.00
408 Jason Kidd DC 5.00
409 Grant Hill DC 6.00
410 Donyell Marshall DC 1.00
411 Sharone Wright DC .40
412 Lamond Murray DC .75
413 Brian Grant DC 2.00
414 Eric Montross DC .60
415 Eddie Jones DC 4.00
416 Carlos Rogers DC .25
417 Shawn Kemp CL .60
418 Bobby Hurley CL .25
419 Shawn Bradley CL .40
420 Michael Jordan CL 2.00
421 Vernon Maxwell .25
422 John Stockton 3.00
423 Luc Longley .25
424 Sam Perkins .40
425 Pooh Richardson .25
426 Tyrone Corbin .25
427 Mario Elie .25
428 Bobby Phills .25
429 Grant Hill 10.00
T1 Trade (Michael Jordan) 20.00

1995 Collector's Choice Int. Japanese Gold Signature I

The 27-card, standard-size set was inserted evey 30 Series I packs and parallels the Tip-Offs subset. The cards are distinguishable by the gold-foil facsimile signature on the card front.

MT
Complete Set (27): 400.00
Common Player: 6.00
166 Danny Manning 6.00
167 Dee Brown 6.00
168 Alonzo Mourning 30.00
169 Scottie Pippen 40.00
170 Mark Price 8.00
171 Jamal Mashburn 20.00
172 Dikembe Mutombo 12.00
173 Joe Dumars 10.00
174 Chris Webber 30.00
175 Hakeem Olajuwon 45.00
177 Ron Harper 8.00
178 Nick Van Exel 20.00
179 Steve Smith 12.00
180 Vin Baker 20.00
181 Isaiah Rider 10.00
182 Derrick Coleman 8.00
183 Patrick Ewing 25.00
184 Shaquille O'Neal 60.00
185 Clarence Weatherspoon 8.00
187 Clyde Drexler 25.00
188 Mitch Richmond 15.00
189 David Robinson 45.00
190 Shawn Kemp 30.00
191 Karl Malone 35.00
192 Tom Gugliotta 10.00

1995 Collector's Choice Int. Japanese Gold Signature II

Issued every five packs of Series II, the Japanese-version cards are skip numbered and parallel the Blueprints, World of Trivia and Draft Class subsets. The fronts feature a gold-foil signature.

MT
Complete Set (45): 300.00
Common Player: 2.00
153 Stacey Augmon BP 2.00
154 Eric Montross BP 2.00
155 Alonzo Mourning BP 10.00
156 Scottie Pippen BP 12.00
157 Mark Price BP 4.00
158 Jason Kidd BP 20.00
159 Jalen Rose BP 7.00
160 Grant Hill BP 30.00
161 Latrell Sprewell BP 5.00
162 Hakeem Olajuwon BP 15.00
163 Reggie Miller BP 8.00
164 Lamond Murray BP 2.00
165 Eddie Jones BP 12.00
166 Khalid Reeves BP 2.00
167 Glenn Robinson BP 15.00
168 Donyell Marshall BP 4.00
169 Derrick Coleman BP 2.00
170 Patrick Ewing BP 8.00
171 Shaquille O'Neal BP 25.00
172 Sharone Wright BP 2.00
173 Charles Barkley BP 15.00
174 Aaron McKie BP 3.00
175 Brian Grant BP 6.00
176 David Robinson BP 15.00
177 Shawn Kemp BP 10.00
178 Karl Malone BP 15.00
179 Tom Gugliotta BP 4.00
400 Shaquille O'Neal TRIV 25.00
401 Chris Webber TRIV 15.00
402 Michael Jordan TRIV 50.00
403 David Robinson TRIV 15.00
404 Shawn Kemp TRIV 10.00
405 Patrick Ewing TRIV 8.00
406 Charles Barkley TRIV 15.00
407 Glenn Robinson DC 15.00
408 Jason Kidd DC 20.00
409 Grant Hill DC 30.00
410 Donyell Marshall DC 4.00
411 Sharone Wright DC 2.00
412 Lamond Murray DC 2.00
413 Brian Grant DC 6.00
414 Eric Montross DC 2.00
415 Eddie Jones DC 12.00
416 Carlos Rogers DC 2.00

1995 Collector's Choice Int. Japanese Silver Signature

The 27-card, standard-size insert set was issued every Collector's Choice Japanese pack and paralled Tip-Offs subset with a silver facsimile signature on the card front.

MT
Complete Set (27): 30.00
Common Player: .30
166 Danny Manning TO .75
167 Dee Brown TO .30
168 Alonzo Mourning TO 2.50
169 Scottie Pippen TO 3.00
170 Mark Price TO 1.00
171 Jamal Mashburn TO 1.50
172 Dikembe Mutombo TO 1.00
173 Joe Dumars TO 1.00
174 Chris Webber TO 4.00
175 Hakeem Olajuwon TO 4.00
177 Ron Harper TO .50
178 Nick Van Exel TO 1.50
179 Steve Smith TO 1.00
180 Vin Baker TO 1.50
181 Isaiah Rider TO .50
182 Derrick Coleman TO .50
183 Patrick Ewing TO 2.00
184 Shaquille O'Neal TO 5.00
185 Clarence Weatherspoon TO .50
187 Clyde Drexler TO 2.50
188 Mitch Richmond TO 1.75
189 David Robinson TO 4.00
190 Shawn Kemp TO 2.50
191 Karl Malone TO 5.00
192 Tom Gugliotta TO 1.50

1995 Collector's Choice Int. Decade of Dominance

The 10-card, standard-size set parallels Upper Deck's Decade of Dominance subset from the U.S. Rare Air boxed set from 1994. The cards were printed for the French, German, Italian, Spanish and Japanese versions with each pack ratio at one in five - except for the Japanese packs which are one in three. The values reflect dumping of much of the European product, while no evidence of this has occured with the Japanese product.

MT
Comp. French Set (10): 70.00
Comp. German Set (10): 70.00
Comp. Italian Set (10): 70.00
Comp. Japanese Set (10): 125.00
Comp. Spanish Set (10): 70.00
Common European Player: 8.00
Common Japanese Player:
J1 Career Stats (Michael Jordan) 8.00
J2 '84 NBA ROY (Michael Jordan) 8.00
J3 '87 Slam-Dunk Champion (Michael Jordan) 8.00
J4 NBA All-Star Game Stats (Michael Jordan) 8.00
J5 Efficient Scorer (Michael Jordan) 8.00
J6 '88 NBA Defensive POY (Michael Jordan) 8.00
J7 1991 NBA Title (Michael Jordan) 8.00
J8 Unstoppable (Michael Jordan) 8.00
J9 All-NBA First Team (Michael Jordan) 8.00
J10 Averaging over 30 ppg (Michael Jordan) 8.00

1995-96 Upper Deck

Upper Deck released its 1995-96 basketball set in two 180-card sets. Series I has 135 regular players, with 15 All-NBA Team, 11 All-Rookie Team and 19 The Rookie Years subset cards. Hobby packs included a 90-card insert set called Special Edition, which features completely different designs from the regular cards. Silver versions of Special Edition are seeded one per pack, while Gold ones are found one per every 35 hobby packs. Retail boxes also have an exclusive insert set. Electric Court cards parallel the 180-card basic set, and are found at a rate of one per pack. Gold Electric Court inserts are found one per every 35 packs. Series I insert sets include the Jordan Collection, (which continues the series of cards issued in Collector's Choice Series I, Collector's Choice Series II, Upper Deck II, SP and SP Championship); All-Star Class; Hobby Predictors; Retail Predictors; and Michael Jordan Predictors. Series II has 135 regular player cards and subsets for Major Attractions (11), USA 96! (10), Images of '95 (10) and Slams & Jams (14). There were also 90 Special Edition cards made, continued from Series I. Silver versions were seeded one per every hobby pack; Gold versions were seeded one per every 27 hobby packs. Retail packs also exclusively have Electric Court cards, which parallel the regular issue cards. They are seeded one per pack, but Electric Court Gold cards were also made and are seeded one per every 27 packs. Series II inserts include the continuation of the Michael Jordan Collection, Retail Predictors, Hobby Predictors, and Michael Jordan Predictors.

	MT
Complete Set (360):	50.00
Complete Series 1 (180):	25.00
Complete Series 2 (180):	25.00
Common Player:	.10
Minor Stars:	.20
Comp. Elec. Court Set (360):	110.00
Comp. EC Series 1 (180):	55.00
Comp. EC Series 2 (180):	55.00
Electric Court Cards:	1x-3x
Comp. EC Gold Set (360):	1100.
Comp. EC Gold Series 1 (180):	500.00
Comp. EC Gold Series 2 (180):	600.00
Elec. Court Gold Cards:	15x-30x
Ser. 1 or 2 Pack (12):	1.50
Ser. 1 or 2 Wax Box (36):	48.00

1	Eddie Jones	.30
2	Hubert Davis	.10
3	Latrell Sprewell	.30
4	Stacey Augmon	.10
5	Mario Elie	.10
6	Tyrone Hill	.10
7	Dikembe Mutombo	.20
8	Antonio Davis	.10
9	Horace Grant	.20
10	Ken Norman	.10
11	Aaron McKie	.10
12	Vinny Del Negro	.10
13	Glenn Robinson	.50
14	Allan Houston	.10
15	Bryon Russell	.10
16	Tony Dumas	.10
17	Gary Payton	.40
18	Rik Smits	.10
19	Dino Radja	.10
20	Robert Pack	.10
21	Calbert Cheaney	.10
22	Clarence Weatherspoon	.10
23	Michael Jordan	3.00
24	Felton Spencer	.10
25	J.R. Reid	.10
26	Cedric Ceballos	.10
27	Dan Majerle	.10
28	Donald Hodge	.10
29	Nate McMillan	.10
30	Bimbo Coles	.10
31	Mitch Richmond	.20
32	Scott Brooks	.10
33	Patrick Ewing	.30
34	Carl Herrera	.10
35	Rick Fox	.10
36	James Robinson	.10
37	Donald Royal	.10
38	Joe Dumars	.20
39	Rony Seikaly	.10
40	Dennis Rodman	1.00
41	Muggsy Bogues	.10
42	Gheorghe Muresan	.10
43	Ervin Johnson	.10
44	Todd Day	.10
45	Rex Walters	.10
46	Terrell Brandon	.10
47	Wesley Person	.20
48	Terry Dehere	.10
49	Steve Smith	.10
50	Brian Grant	.20
51	Eric Piatkowski	.10
52	Lindsey Hunter	.10
53	Chris Webber	.30
54	Antoine Carr	.10
55	Chris Dudley	.10
56	Clyde Drexler	.30
57	P.J. Brown	.10
58	Kevin Willis	.10
59	Jeff Turner	.10
60	Sean Elliott	.10
61	Kevin Johnson	.20
62	Scott Skiles	.10
63	Charles Smith	.10
64	Derrick McKey	.10
65	Danny Ferry	.10
66	Detlef Schrempf	.10
67	Shawn Bradley	.10
68	Isaiah Rider	.20
69	Karl Malone	.30
70	Will Perdue	.10
71	Terry Mills	.10
72	Glen Rice	.10
73	Tim Breaux	.10
74	Malik Sealy	.10
75	Walt Williams	.10
76	Bobby Phills	.10
77	Anthony Avent	.10
78	Jamal Mashburn	.40
79	Vlade Divac	.10
80	Reggie Williams	.10
81	Xavier McDaniel	.10
82	Avery Johnson	.10
83	Derek Harper	.10
84	Don MacLean	.10
85	Tom Gugliotta	.10
86	Craig Ehlo	.10
87	Robert Horry	.10
88	Kevin Edwards	.10
89	Chuck Person	.10
90	Sharone Wright	.10
91	Steve Kerr	.10
92	Marty Conlon	.10
93	Jalen Rose	.20
94	*Bryant Reeves*	.75
95	Shaquille O'Neal	1.75
96	David Wesley	.10
97	Chris Mills	.10
98	Rod Strickland	.10
99	Pooh Richardson	.10
100	Sam Perkins	.10
101	Dell Curry	.10
102	David Benoit	.10
103	Christian Laettner	.10
104	Duane Causwell	.10
105	Jason Kidd	1.00
106	Mark West	.10
107	Lee Mayberry	.10
108	Adam Keefe	.10
109	Jeff Malone	.10
110	*George Zidek*	.40
111	Kenny Smith	.10
112	George Lynch	.10
113	Toni Kukoc	.10
114	A.C. Green	.10
115	Kenny Anderson	.10
116	Robert Parish	.10
117	Chris Mullin	.10
118	Loy Vaught	.10
119	Olden Polynice	.10
120	Clifford Robinson	.10
121	Eric Mobley	.10
122	Doug West	.10
123	Sam Cassell	.10
124	Nick Anderson	.10
125	Matt Geiger	.10
126	Elden Campbell	.10
127	Alonzo Mourning	.30
128	Bryant Stith	.10
129	Mark Jackson	.10
130	*Cherokee Parks*	.25
131	*Shawn Respert*	.25
132	*Alan Henderson*	.25
133	*Jerry Stackhouse*	4.00
134	*Rasheed Wallace*	3.00
135	*Antonio McDyess*	3.00
136	Charles Barkley	.30
137	Michael Jordan	1.50
138	Hakeem Olajuwon	.40
139	Joe Dumars	.20
140	Patrick Ewing	.20
141	A.C. Green	.10
142	Karl Malone	.20
143	Detlef Schrempf	.10
144	Chuck Person	.10
145	Muggsy Bogues	.10
146	Horace Grant	.20
147	Mark Jackson	.10
148	Kevin Johnson	.20
149	Mitch Richmond	.20
150	Rik Smits	.10
151	Nick Anderson	.10
152	Tim Hardaway	.10
153	Shawn Kemp	.30
154	David Robinson	.30
155	Jason Kidd	.50
156	Grant Hill	.75
157	Glenn Robinson	.25
158	Eddie Jones	.30
159	Brian Grant	.20
160	Juwan Howard	.25
161	Eric Montross	.10
162	Wesley Person	.20
163	Jalen Rose	.20
164	Donyell Marshall	.10
165	Sharone Wright	.10
166	Karl Malone	.20
167	Scottie Pippen	.40
168	David Robinson	.30
169	John Stockton	.20
170	Anfernee Hardaway	1.00
171	Charles Barkley	.30
172	Shawn Kemp	.30
173	Shaquille O'Neal	.75
174	Gary Payton	.20
175	Mitch Richmond	.20
176	Dennis Rodman	.50
177	Detlef Schrempf	.10
178	Hakeem Olajuwon	.40
179	Reggie Miller	.20
180	Clyde Drexler	.20
181	Hakeem Olajuwon	.75
182	Vin Baker	.30
183	Jeff Hornacek	.10
184	Popeye Jones	.10
185	Sedale Threatt	.10
186	Scottie Pippen	.75
187	Terry Porter	.10
188	Dan Majerle	.10
189	Clifford Rozier	.10
190	Greg Minor	.10
191	Dennis Scott	.10
192	Hersey Hawkins	.10
193	Chris Gatling	.10
194	Charles Oakley	.10
195	Dale Davis	.10
196	Robert Pack	.10
197	Lamond Murray	.10
198	Mookie Blaylock	.10
199	Dickey Simpkins	.10
200	Kevin Gamble	.10
201	Lorenzo Williams	.10
202	Scott Burrell	.10
203	Armon Gilliam	.10
204	Doc Rivers	.10
205	Blue Edwards	.10
206	Billy Owens	.10
207	Juwan Howard	.40
208	Harvey Grant	.10
209	Richard Dumas	.10
210	Anthony Peeler	.10
211	Matt Geiger	.10
212	Lucious Harris	.10
213	Grant Long	.10
214	*Predrag Danilovic*	.20
215	Chris Morris	.10
216	Donyell Marshall	.10
217	Alonzo Mourning	.30
218	John Stockton	.30
219	Khalid Reeves	.10
220	Mahmoud Abdul-Rauf	.10
221	Sean Rooks	.10
222	Shawn Kemp	.50
223	John Williams	.10
224	Dee Brown	.10
225	Jim Jackson	.20
226	Harold Miner	.10
227	B.J. Armstrong	.10
228	Elliot Perry	.10
229	Anthony Miller	.10
230	Donny Marshall	.10
231	Tyrone Corbin	.10
232	Anthony Mason	.10
233	Grant Hill	1.50
234	Buck Williams	.10
235	Brian Shaw	.10
236	Dale Ellis	.10
237	Magic Johnson	1.00
238	Eric Montross	.10
239	Rex Chapman	.10
240	Otis Thorpe	.10
241	Tracy Murray	.10
242	Sarunas Marciulionis	.10
243	Luc Longley	.10
244	Elmore Spencer	.10
245	Terry Cummings	.10
246	Sam Mitchell	.10
247	Terrence Rencher	.10
248	Byron Houston	.10
249	Pervis Ellison	.10
250	Carlos Rogers	.10
251	Kendall Gill	.10
252	*Sherell Ford*	.10
253	*Michael Finley*	3.00
254	*Kurt Thomas*	.50
255	*Joe Smith*	2.00
256	Bobby Hurley	.10
257	Greg Anthony	.10
258	Willie Anderson	.10
259	*Theo Ratliff*	1.00
260	Duane Ferrell	.10
261	Antonio Harvey	.10
262	Gary Grant	.10
263	Brian Williams	.10
264	Danny Manning	.10
265	Micheal Williams	.10
266	Dennis Rodman	2.00
267	*Arvydas Sabonis*	1.00
268	Don MacLean	.10
269	Keith Askins	.10
270	Reggie Miller	.40
271	Ed Pinckney	.10
272	*Bob Sura*	.25
273	*Kevin Garnett*	8.00
274	Byron Scott	.10
275	Mario Bennett	.20
276	Junior Burrough	.10
277	Anfernee Hardaway	2.00
278	George McCloud	.20
279	Loren Meyer	.10
280	*Ed O'Bannon*	.20
281	Lawrence Moten	.10
282	Dana Barros	.10
283	*Damon Stoudamire*	2.00
284	*Eric Williams*	.40
285	Wayman Tisdale	.10
286	Rodney Rogers	.10
287	Sherman Douglas	.10
288	Greg Ostertag	.10
289	Alvin Robertson	.10
290	Tim Legler	.10
291	Zan Tabak	.10
292	*Gary Trent*	.25
293	Haywoode Workman	.10
294	Charles Barkley	.50
295	Derrick Coleman	.10
296	Ricky Pierce	.10
297	Benoit Benjamin	.10
298	Larry Johnson	.40
299	*Travis Best*	.75
300	*Jason Caffey*	.25
301	Cory Alexander	.10
302	Nick Van Exel	.40
303	*Corliss Williamson*	.40
304	Eric Murdock	.10
305	*Tyus Edney*	.20
306	Lou Roe	.10
307	John Salley	.10
308	Spud Webb	.10
309	*Brent Barry*	.75
310	David Robinson	.50
311	Glen Rice	.10
312	Chris King	.10
313	David Vaughn	.10
314	Kenny Gattison	.10
315	Randolph Childress	.10
316	Anfernee Hardaway (USA! '96)	1.00
317	Grant Hill (USA! '96)	.75
318	Karl Malone (USA! '96)	.25
319	Reggie Miller (USA! '96)	.25
320	Hakeem Olajuwon (USA! '96)	.50
321	Shaquille O'Neal (USA! '96)	1.00
322	Scottie Pippen (USA! '96)	.50
323	David Robinson (USA! '96)	.30
324	Glenn Robinson (USA! '96)	.30
325	John Stockton (USA! '96)	.25
326	Cedric Ceballos (Images of '95)	.10
327	Shaquille O'Neal (Images of '95)	1.00
328	Glenn Robinson (Images of '95)	.30
329	Shawn Kemp (Images of '95)	.20
330	Nick Anderson (Images of '95)	.10
331	Shawn Bradley (Images of '95)	.10
333	NBA Finals (Images of '95)	.10
334	Grizzlies/Raptors (Images of '95)	.10
335	Michael Jordan (Images of '95)	1.50
336	Nick Van Exel (Major Attractions)	.25
337	Michael Jordan (Major Attractions)	.75
338	Scottie Pippen (Major Attractions)	.25
339	Michael Jordan (Major Attractions)	.75
340	Jason Kidd (Major Attractions)	.30
341	Michael Jordan (Major Attractions)	.75
342	Charles Barkley (Major Attractions)	.30
343	Hakeem Olajuwon (Major Attractions)	.30
344	Ahmad Rashad (Major Attractions)	.10
345	Willow Bay (Major Attractions)	.10
346	Gary Payton (Major Attractions)	.10
347	Horace Grant (Slams & Jams)	.10
348	Juwan Howard (Slams & Jams)	.10
349	David Robinson (Slams & Jams)	.30
350	Reggie Miller (Slams & Jams)	.10
351	Brian Grant (Slams & Jams)	.10
352	Michael Jordan (Slams & Jams)	1.50
353	Cedric Ceballos (Slams & Jams)	.10
354	Blue Edwards (Slams & Jams)	.10
355	Acie Earl (Slams & Jams)	.10
356	Dennis Rodman (Slams & Jams)	1.00
357	Shawn Kemp (Slams & Jams)	.20
358	Jerry Stackhouse (Slams & Jams)	1.00
359	Jamal Mashburn (Slams & Jams)	.10
360	Antonio McDyess (Slams & Jams)	.50

1995-96 Upper Deck Electric Court

The 360-card, standard-size set parallels the 1995-96 base set and was inserted into each retail pack. The cards have thicker stock and special foil treatment.

	MT
Complete Set (360):	100.00
Complete Series 1 (180):	50.00
Complete Series 2 (180):	50.00
Common Player:	.15
Semistars:	.40
Stars:	1.25x to 2.5x
Rookies:	1x to 2x

1995-96 Upper Deck Electric Court Gold

The 360-card, standard-size set was inserted every 36 packs of both Series I and II retail packs. Each card features a refractive "Electric Court" logo.

	MT
Complete Set (360):	1200.
Complete Series 1 (180):	600.00
Complete Series 2 (180):	600.00
Common Player:	1.50
Semistars:	4.00
Stars:	12.5x to 25x
Rookies:	7.5x to 15x

1995-96 Upper Deck All-Star Class

These cards were random inserts in 1995-96 Upper Deck Series I packs, one per every 17 packs. The cards feature 25 of the NBA's top superstars who participated in the All-Star Game. Each card front has a color action photo of the player, against a metallic foiled background. The Upper Deck logo is stamped in the upper right corner; the player's name is in the bottom left corner, opposite the player's team name and position. The NBA All-Star Class logo is centered at the bottom of the card. The back, numbered using an "AS" prefix, has the All-Star Game logo from Phoenix, a posed shot of the player and a recap of his accomplishments in the All-Star Game.

		MT
Complete Set (25):		140.00
Common Player:		1.00
1	Anfernee Hardaway	25.00
2	Reggie Miller	6.00
3	Grant Hill	25.00
4	Scottie Pippen	12.00
5	Shaquille O'Neal	20.00
6	Larry Johnson	6.00
7	Dana Barros	1.00
8	Vin Baker	4.00
9	Alonzo Mourning	6.00
10	Joe Dumars	2.00
11	Patrick Ewing	5.00
12	Tyrone Hill	1.00
13	Latrell Sprewell	5.00
14	Dan Majerle	1.00
15	Shawn Kemp	6.00
16	Karl Malone	6.00
17	Hakeem Olajuwon	10.00
18	Gary Payton	5.00
19	Mitch Richmond	2.00
20	David Robinson	10.00
21	Detlef Schrempf	1.00
22	Cedric Ceballos	1.00
23	John Stockton	6.00
24	Dikembe Mutombo	4.00
25	Charles Barkley	10.00

1995-96 Upper Deck Jordan Collection

These eight cards were part of a continuing series of cards in Upper Deck's Michael Jordan Collection. Cards JC5-JC8 were random inserts in 1995-96 Upper Deck Series I packs, one per every 29 packs. Cards JC13-JC16 were randomly inserted one per every 23 packs of 1995-96 Upper Deck Series II product. The entire set is a chronological overview of Jordan's stellar career.

		MT
Complete Set (8):		80.00
Complete Series 1 (4):		40.00
Complete Series 2 (4):		40.00
Com. Series 1 (JC5-JC8):		10.00
Com. Series 2 (JC13-JC16):		10.00
JC5	1987 NBA Slam Dunk Champion	10.00
JC6	1988 NBA Slam Dunk Champion	10.00
JC7	Rising to the Occasion	10.00
JC8	Walking on Air	10.00
JC13	1986 Garden Party	10.00
JC14	1990 69-Point Game	10.00
JC15	1995 "He's Back"	10.00
JC16	Amazing Performances	10.00

1995-96 Upper Deck Predictor MVP

These cards were random inserts in 1995-96 Upper Deck Series II packs, one per every 24 packs. If one of the four players pictured (or a Long Shot card is found) was named the NBA's MVP, the card could be redeemed for a special version of the retail Predictor set. There were also five Michael Jordan retail predictor cards in the set. If Jordan was named the MVP, Defensive Player of the Year, or NBA Finals MVP, or is named to the All-NBA Team or NBA All-Defensive Team, the card is redeemable for a special version of the entire 10-card retail Predictor set.

		MT
Complete Set (10):		50.00
Common Player:		1.00
R1	Michael Jordan (1996 NBA MVP)	10.00
R2	Michael Jordan (1996 All-NBA Team)	10.00
R3	Michael Jordan (1996 Def. Player of the Year)	10.00
R4	Michael Jordan (1996 NBA All-Def. Team)	10.00
R5	Michael Jordan (1996 NBA Finals MVP)	10.00
R6	Hakeem Olajuwon (NBA Most Valuable Player)	4.00
R7	Charles Barkley (NBA Most Valuable Player)	3.00
R8	Karl Malone (NBA Most Valuable Player)	1.00
R9	Anfernee Hardaway (NBA Most Valuable Player)	10.00
R10	Long Shot Card (NBA Most Valuable Player)	1.00

1995-96 Upper Deck Predictor Player of the Month

If the player on these 1995-96 Upper Deck Series I inserts wins the Player of the Month Award for the 1995-96 season, the holder could redeem the card for prizes. There were four players and a Long Shot card created, along with five Michael Jordan cards. Cards were randomly included one per every 30 packs. Cards are numbered with a "R" prefix.

		MT
Complete Set (10):		50.00
Common Player:		1.00
1	Michael Jordan (Nov./Dec. 1995)	10.00
2	Michael Jordan (Jan-96)	10.00
3	Michael Jordan (Feb-96)	10.00
4	Michael Jordan (Mar-96)	10.00
5	Michael Jordan (Apr-96)	10.00
6	Jamal Mashburn (Mavericks)	1.00
7	David Robinson (Spurs)	4.00
8	Latrell Sprewell (Warriors)	1.00
9	Chris Webber (Bullets)	1.00
10	Long Shot Card (Long Shot)	1.00

1995-96 Upper Deck Predictor Player of the Week

Upper Deck's 1995-96 Series I and Series II hobby packs had Predictor insert cards randomly included in them; if the pictured player won the appropriate category, the collector could redeem the card for prizes. Series I cards, seeded one per every 30 packs, were devoted to four players, a Long Shot card and five Michael Jordan cards; they could be redeemed if the player won the Player of the Week Award. Series II, if Jordan won the scoring, assists, steals, three-point shooting percentage or scoring in the

1996 NBA Playoffs, the holder could redeem the card for a special version of the entire 10-card hobby Predictor set. Cards are numbered with a "H" prefix.

		MT
	Complete Set (10):	50.00
	Common Player:	2.00
1	Michael Jordan (Nov./Dec. 1995)	10.00
2	Michael Jordan (Jan-96)	10.00
3	Michael Jordan (Feb-96)	10.00
4	Michael Jordan (Mar-96)	10.00
5	Michael Jordan (Apr-96)	10.00
6	Anfernee Hardaway (Magic)	10.00
7	Hakeem Olajuwon (Rockets)	6.00
8	Scottie Pippen (Bulls)	6.00
9	Glenn Robinson (Bucks)	2.00
10	Long Shot Card (Long Shot)	2.00

1995-96 Upper Deck Predictor Scoring

Upper Deck 1995-96 Series II hobby packs had insert cards seeded one per every 24 packs that allowed the finder to redeem the cards for prizes if the player pictured won the NBA scoring title. There were four player cards and one Long Shot card created, plus five Michael Jordan Predictor cards. If Jordan led in scoring, assists, steals, three-point shooting or scoring during the NBA playoffs, the finder could redeem the card for a special version of the entire 10-card hobby Predictor set. Cards are numbered with a "H" prefix.

		MT
	Complete Set (10):	50.00
	Common Player:	1.00
1	Michael Jordan (Scoring Leader)	10.00
2	Michael Jordan (Assists Leader)	10.00
3	Michael Jordan (Steals Leader)	10.00
4	Michael Jordan (3 Pt. Shooting Pct. Leader)	10.00
5	Michael Jordan (NBA Playoff Scoring Leader)	10.00
6	David Robinson (Scoring Leader)	3.00
7	Scottie Pippen (Scoring Leader)	4.00
8	Jerry Stackhouse (Scoring Leader)	8.00
9	Glenn Robinson (Scoring Leader)	1.00
10	Long Shot Card (Scoring Leader)	1.00

1995-96 Upper Deck Special Edition

Hobby packs of 1995-96 Upper Deck Series I and Series II product contained these insert cards. The set features completely different designs than the regular player cards and uses an "SE" prefix for the card number. Silver versions of Special Edition cards were seeded one per pack in Series I and II. Gold Special Edition versions were seeded one per every 35 Series I hobby packs or one in every 27 Series II hobby packs.

		MT
	Complete Set (180):	85.00
	Complete Series 1 (90):	35.00
	Complete Series 2 (90):	50.00
	Common Player:	.25
	Minor Stars:	.50
	Complete Gold Set (180):	600.00
	Complete Gold Series 1 (90):	250.00
	Complete Gold Series 2 (90):	350.00
	Gold Cards:	4x-8x
1	Mookie Blaylock	.25
2	Craig Ehlo	.25
3	Grant Long	.25
4	Dee Brown	.25
5	Sherman Douglas	.25
6	Eric Montross	.25
7	Scott Burrell	.25
8	Dell Curry	.25
9	Larry Johnson	.50
10	Will Perdue	.25
11	Scottie Pippen	3.00
12	Dickey Simpkins	.25
13	Michael Cage	.25
14	Mark Price	.25
15	John Williams	.25
16	Lucious Harris	.25
17	Jim Jackson	.50
18	Popeye Jones	.25
19	Mahmoud Abdul-Rauf	.25
20	LaPhonso Ellis	.25
21	Robert Pack	.25
22	Bill Curley	.25
23	Grant Hill	8.00
24	Allan Houston	.25
25	Chris Gatling	.25
26	Tim Hardaway	.50
27	Donyell Marshall	.25
28	Clifford Rozier	.25
29	Mario Elie	.25
30	Robert Horry	.25
31	Hakeem Olajuwon	2.50
32	Kenny Smith	.25
33	Dale Davis	.25
34	Duane Ferrell	.25
35	Derrick McKey	.25
36	Reggie Miller	1.50
37	Lamond Murray	.50
38	Charles Outlaw	.25
39	Eric Piatkowski	.25
40	Anthony Peeler	.25
41	Sedale Threatt	.25
42	Nick Van Exel	1.00
43	Kevin Gamble	.25
44	Matt Geiger	.25
45	Billy Owens	.25
46	Khalid Reeves	.50
47	Vin Baker	1.00
48	Lee Mayberry	.25
49	Eric Murdock	.25
50	Christian Laettner	.25
51	Sean Rooks	.25
52	Doug West	.25
53	P.J. Brown	.25
54	Derrick Coleman	.25
55	Armon Gilliam	.25
56	Hubert Davis	.25
57	Charles Oakley	.25
58	John Starks	.25
59	Monty Williams	.25
60	Anfernee Hardaway	8.00
61	Donald Royal	.25
62	Dennis Scott	.25
63	Jeff Turner	.25
64	Clarence Weatherspoon	.25
65	Jeff Malone	.25
66	Scott Williams	.25
67	A.C. Green	.25
68	Kevin Johnson	.50
69	Elliot Perry	.25
70	Wesley Person	.50
71	Harvey Grant	.25
72	Aaron McKie	.25
73	Rod Strickland	.25
74	Buck Williams	.25
75	Randy Brown	.25
76	Bobby Hurley	.25
77	Lionel Simmons	.25
78	Terry Cummings	.25
79	Vinny Del Negro	.25
80	Avery Johnson	.25
81	David Robinson	2.00
82	Vincent Askew	.25
83	Shawn Kemp	2.00
84	Nate McMillan	.25
85	David Benoit	.25
86	Jeff Hornacek	.25
87	John Stockton	1.00
88	Juwan Howard	2.00
89	Gheorghe Muresan	.25
90	Doug Overton	.25
91	Stacey Augmon	.25
92	Alan Henderson	1.00
93	Steve Smith	.25
94	Rick Fox	.25
95	Dino Radja	.50
96	Eric Williams	1.00
97	Muggsy Bogues	.25
98	Kendall Gill	.25
99	Glen Rice	.25
100	Michael Jordan	12.00
101	Toni Kukoc	.50
102	Dennis Rodman	5.00
103	Terrell Brandon	.50
104	Tyrone Hill	.25
105	Dan Majerle	.25
106	Jason Kidd	3.00
107	Jamal Mashburn	.75
108	Cherokee Parks	.75
109	Antonio McDyess	4.00
110	Dikembe Mutombo	.50
111	Reggie Williams	.25
112	Joe Dumars	.50
113	Lindsey Hunter	.25
114	Otis Thorpe	.25
115	Chris Mullin	.50
116	Joe Smith	5.00
117	Latrell Sprewell	.50
118	Chucky Brown	.25
119	Sam Cassell	.25
120	Clyde Drexler	1.50
121	Travis Best	.50
122	Mark Jackson	.25
123	Rik Smits	.50
124	Brent Barry	2.00
125	Rodney Rogers	.25
126	Loy Vaught	.25
127	Cedric Ceballos	.50
128	Magic Johnson	4.00
129	Eddie Jones	.75
130	Alonzo Mourning	.75
131	Kurt Thomas	.50
132	Kevin Willis	.25
133	Sherman Douglas	.25
134	Shawn Respert	.75
135	Glenn Robinson	1.00
136	Kevin Garnett	10.00
137	Tom Gugliotta	.25
138	Isaiah Rider	.25
139	Kenny Anderson	.25
140	Ed O'Bannon	.50
141	Jayson Williams	.25
142	Patrick Ewing	.75
143	Derek Harper	.25
144	Charles Smith	.25
145	Nick Anderson	.25
146	Horace Grant	.50
147	Shaquille O'Neal	6.00
148	Vernon Maxwell	.25
149	Jerry Stackhouse	5.00
150	Sharone Wright	.25
151	Charles Barkley	2.00
152	Michael Finley	3.00
153	Danny Manning	.25
154	John Williams	.25
155	Clifford Robinson	.25
156	Arvydas Sabonis	3.00
157	Gary Trent	.75
158	Brian Grant	.25
159	Mitch Richmond	.50
160	Corliss Williamson	.75
161	Sean Elliott	.25
162	Will Perdue	.25
163	Doc Rivers	.25
164	Gary Payton	.50
165	Sam Perkins	.25
166	Detlef Schrempf	.25
167	Tracy Murray	.25
168	Ed Pinckney	.25
169	Carlos Rogers	.25
170	Damon Stoudamire	8.00
171	Karl Malone	1.00
172	Chris Morris	.25
173	Greg Ostertag	.25
174	Greg Anthony	.25
175	Lawrence Moten	.25
176	Bryant Reeves	2.50
177	Byron Scott	.25
178	Calbert Cheaney	.25
179	Rasheed Wallace	2.50
180	Chris Webber	.50

1995-96 Upper Deck Special Edition Gold

The 180-card, standard-size set was inserted every 35 hobby packs and featured a different design than the regular player cards.

	MT
Complete Set (180):	600.00
Complete Series 1 (90):	200.00
Complete Series 2 (90):	400.00
Common Player:	1.50
Semistars:	4.00
Stars:	4x to 8x
Rookies:	2.5x to 5x

1995-96 Upper Deck Ball Park Jordan

Collectors could obtain this five-card set by sending in two UPCs from Ball Park hot dogs and $1 for shipping. The fronts feature a color action shot within an American flag border, with the Upper Deck and Ball Park logos in the upper corners. The backs feature a flag background, the same photo and biographical information. All team and NBA logos are air-brushed out of the pictures. Cards are numbered with "BP" prefix.

		MT
	Complete Set (5):	50.00
	Common Player:	10.00
1	Michael Jordan (college uniform)	10.00
2	Michael Jordan (shooting)	10.00
3	Michael Jordan (Olympics)	10.00
4	Michael Jordan (driving)	10.00
5	Michael Jordan (defending)	10.00

1995-96 Upper Deck Chinese Basketball Alliance

The 125-card, standard-size set was issued only in Taiwan and features players of the Chinese Basketball Alliance. Four teams are featured with 18 players from each team. All of the card text is in Chinese. The set also includes subsets such as Thousand Times (71-86), 10 Thousand Score (87), Starting Five (88-107), Special Records (108-119), Team Cards (120-123) and Checklists (124-125).

		MT
	Complete Set (125):	30.00
	Common Player:	.25
1	Chu Chung-Chi	.25
2	Lin Chien-Ping	.25
3	Roderick James Hannibal	.50
4	Tau Song	.25
5	Tsi-Fu-Tsi	.25
6	Chen Hung-Zung	.25
7	Chen Cheng-Sbiun	.25
8	Kuo Tien-Lung	.25
9	Tungfang Cheieh-Teh	.25
10	Li-Yung-Kung	.25
11	Hsu Tung-Ching	.25
12	Chang Hsien-Ming	.25
13	Mark Clark	.50
14	Brenton Lloyd Moore	.50
15	Arlando F. Bennett	.50
16	Christopher Edward Knight	.50
17	Tsou Jiunn-San	.25
18	Li Chung-Shi	.25
19	Liu I-Shang	.25
20	Chio Teh-Chih	.25
21	Michael Lee Johnson	.50
22	Jeng Jyh-Long	.25
23	Lo Hsing-Liang	.25
24	Huang Chun-Hsiung	.25
25	Chang Ya-Tang	.25
26	Chu Hao-Ren	.25
27	Jye Song	.25
28	Stacey Cornilius	.50
29	Keith Smith	.50
30	Rex Harrison Manu	.50
31	Daryl Scott	.50
32	Joseph Nathenial Temple	.50
33	Laurent Crawford	.50
34	David Lewayne Cooke	.50
35	Tsou Hai-Zunkg	.25
36	Wang Li-Bin	.25
37	Bai Ming-Li	.25
38	Kofi Kyei	.25
39	Lin Chai-Hung	.25
40	Chen Chung-Chian	.25
41	Li Chi-Chian	.25
42	Sun Mao-Shen	.25
43	Tzeng Tzeng-Cho	.25
44	Cheyenne Durell Gibson	.50
45	Chen Jiunn-Chie	.25
46	Kelvin Cornell Allen	.50
47	Charng Bing-Hsiang	.25
48	Kennard Rubinson	.50
49	David Edward Davies	.50
50	Todd Alan Rowe	.50
51	Mike Sterner	.50
52	Robert Zohn Fife	.50
53	Carroll Boudreaux	.50
54	Chen Cheng-Kwei	.25
55	Hung Chang-Ching	.25
56	Yen Chao-Chyun	.25
57	Lai Kwo-Hong	.25
58	Ko Yiing-Yan	.25
59	Gerard Arcement	.50
60	Jerry Lew	.50
61	Tien Su-Chung	.25
62	Chris Collier	.50
63	Tzeng Yih-Chin	.25
64	Dwight Myvett	.25
65	Anthony Robert Block	.50
66	Lan Chih-Ming	.25
67	Lin Shin-Hwa	.25
68	Derrell Cunegin	.50
69	Harold Boudreaux	.50
70	Wu Jye-Wei	.25
71	Jerry Lew	.50
72	Tsou Jiunn-San	.25
73	Derrell Cunegin	.50
74	Huang Chun-Hsiung	.25
75	Christopher Edward Knight	.50
76	Huang Chun-Hsiung	.25
77	Joseph Nathenial Temple	.50
78	Lo Hsing-Liang	.25
79	Hung Chang-Ching	.25
80	Tsou Kiunn-San	.25
81	Christopher Edward Knight	.50
82	David Edward Davies	.50
83	Christopher Edward Knight	.50
84	Harold Boudreaux	.50
85	Arlando F. Bennett	.50
86	Arlando F. Bennett	.50
87	Tungfang Chieh-Teh	.25
88	Arlando F. Bennett	.50
89	Christopher Edward Knight	.50
90	Tungfang Chieh-Teh	.25
91	Li Yung-Kung	.25
92	Tsi-Fu-Tsi	.25
93	Tsou Jiunn-San	.25
94	Jeng Jyh-Long	.25
95	Lo Hsing-Liang	.25
96	Rex Harrison Manu	.50
97	Stacey Cornilius	.50
98	Wang Li-Bin	.25
99	Chen Chung-Chian	.25
100	Tzeng Tzeng-Cho	.25
101	Todd Alan Rowe	.50
102	Kennard Robison	.50
103	Tzeng Yih-Chin	.25
104	Jerry Lew	.25
105	Chen Cheng-Kwei	.25
106	Dwight Myvett	.25
107	Harold Boudreaux	.50
108	Dwight Myvett	.25
109	Harold Boudreaux	.50
110	Todd Alan Rowe	.50
111	Jeng Jyh-Long	.25
112	Li Chi-Chian	.25
113	Harold Boudreaux	.50
114	Dwight Myvett	.25
115	Tsou Jiunn-San	.25
116	Christopher Edward Knight	.50
117	Anthony Robert Block	.50
118	Rex Harrison Manu	.50
119	Rex Harrison Manu	.50
120	Yue Lon	.25
121	Hung Kuo	.25
122	Tera	.25
123	Luckipar	.25
124	Checklist #1	.25
125	Checklist #2	.25

1995-96 Upper Deck Chinese Alliance MVP's

Randomly inserted into packs, the nine-card set highlights the top players in the Chinese Basketball Alliance. The fronts show color photography and a granite stripe along the right edge which has the player's name. A gold-foil "MVP" appears in the upper right corner. Cards are numbered with a "M" prefix.

		MT
	Complete Set (9):	10.00
	Common Player:	1.00
1	Jeng Jyh-Long	1.00
2	Tsou Jiunn-San	1.00
3	Todd Alan Rowe	2.00
4	Tungfang Chieh-Te	1.00
5	Arlando F. Bennett	2.00
6	Roderick Nathenial Temple	2.00
7	Joseph Nathenial Temple	1.00
8	Tungfang Chieh-Te	1.00
9	CBA President	1.00

1995-96 Upper Deck Sheets

This 8-1/2" x 11" sheet was distributed at the 1996 NBA Draft. Printed on card stock, the sheet has the individual number and production run printed on it.

		MT
	Complete Set (1):	10.00
	Common Sheet:	10.00
1	1996 NBA Draft (Kevin Garnett, Antonio McDyess, Bryant Reeves, Joe Smith, Jerry Stackhouse)	10.00

1995-96 Collector's Choice

Upper Deck's 1995-96 Collector's Choice set was released in two series. Series I contains 210 cards; Series II has 200. Each series has two parallel sets: Player's Club (one per pack) and Platinum Player's Club (one per 35). Series I inserts include the continuation of the Michael Jordan Collection; NBA Draft Trade Card (one card redeemed for 10 top rookies, one in 144); and You Crash the Game (27 players; silver versions were one in five, while gold ones were one per 50). Series II inserts include more Michael Jordan Collection cards; Debut Trade Card (one card redeemed for 30 rookies, one in 30); Player's Club Debut Trade Card (one per 144); Platinum Player's Club Debut Trade Card (one per 720); and You Crash the Game (30 players; silver versions were one in five, while gold ones were one in 49).

		MT
	Complete Set (410):	35.00
	Complete Series 1 (210):	15.00
	Complete Series 2 (200):	20.00
	Common Player:	.05
	Minor Stars:	.10
	Comp. Play. Club Set (410):	60.00
	Comp. Play. Club Series 1 (210):	25.00
	Comp. Play. Club Series 2 (200):	35.00
	Player's Club Cards:	1x-3x
	Comp. Play. Club Plat. (410):	900.00
	Comp. PC Plat. Series 1 (210):	400.00
	Comp. PC Plat. Series 2 (200):	500.00
	Player's Club Plat. Cards:	15x-30x
	Series 1 or 2 Wax Box:	32.00
1	Rod Strickland	.05
2	Larry Johnson	.20
3	Mahmoud Abdul-Rauf	.05
4	Joe Dumars	.10
5	Jason Kidd	.75
6	Avery Johnson	.05
7	Dee Brown	.05
8	Brian Williams	.05
9	Nick Van Exel	.30
10	Dennis Rodman	.75
11	Rony Seikaly	.05
12	Harvey Grant	.05
13	Craig Ehlo	.05
14	Derek Harper	.05
15	Oliver Miller	.05
16	Dennis Scott	.05
17	Ed Pinckney	.05
18	Eric Piatkowski	.05
19	B.J. Armstrong	.05
20	Tyrone Hill	.05
21	Malik Sealy	.05
22	Clyde Drexler	.20
23	Aaron McKie	.05
24	Harold Miner	.05
25	Bobby Hurley	.05
26	Dell Curry	.05
27	Micheal Williams	.05
28	Adam Keefe	.05
29	Antonio Harvey	.05
30	Billy Owens	.05
31	Nate McMillan	.05
32	J.R. Reid	.05
33	Grant Hill	1.00
34	Charles Barkley	.30
35	Tyrone Corbin	.05
36	Don MacLean	.05
37	Kenny Smith	.05
38	Juwan Howard	.40
39	Charles Smith	.05
40	Shawn Kemp	.30
41	Dana Barros	.05
42	Vin Baker	.10
43	Armon Gilliam	.05
44	Spud Webb	.05
45	Michael Jordan	2.25
46	Scott Williams	.05
47	Vlade Divac	.05
48	Roy Tarpley	.05
49	Bimbo Coles	.05
50	David Robinson	.30
51	Terry Dehere	.05
52	Bobby Phills	.05
53	Sherman Douglas	.05
54	Rodney Rogers	.05
55	Detlef Schrempf	.05
56	Calbert Cheaney	.05
57	Tom Gugliotta	.05
58	Jeff Turner	.05
59	Mookie Blaylock	.05
60	Bill Curley	.05
61	Chris Dudley	.05
62	Popeye Jones	.05
63	Scott Burrell	.05
64	Dale Davis	.05
65	Mitchell Butler	.05
66	Pervis Ellison	.05
67	Todd Day	.05
68	Carl Herrera	.05
69	Jeff Hornacek	.05
70	Vincent Askew	.05
71	A.C. Green	.05
72	Kevin Gamble	.05
73	Chris Gatling	.05
74	Otis Thorpe	.05
75	Michael Cage	.05
76	Carlos Rogers	.05
77	Gheorghe Muresan	.05
78	Olden Polynice	.05
79	Grant Long	.05
80	Allan Houston	.10
81	Charles Outlaw	.05
82	Clarence Weatherspoon	.10
83	Tony Dumas	.05
84	Herb Williams	.05
85	P.J. Brown	.05
86	Robert Horry	.05
87	Byron Scott	.05
88	Horace Grant	.10
89	Dominique Wilkins	.10
90	Doug West	.05
91	Antoine Carr	.05
92	Dickey Simpkins	.05
93	Elden Campbell	.05
94	Kevin Johnson	.10
95	Rex Chapman	.05
96	John Williams	.05
97	Tim Hardaway	.10
98	Rik Smits	.05
99	Rex Walters	.05
100	Robert Parish	.05
101	Isaiah Rider	.10
102	Sarunas Marciulionis	.05
103	Andrew Lang	.05
104	Eric Mobley	.05
105	Randy Brown	.05
106	John Stockton	.20
107	Lamond Murray	.05
108	Will Perdue	.05
109	Wayman Tisdale	.05
110	John Starks	.05
111	John Salley	.05
112	Lucious Harris	.05
113	Jeff Malone	.05
114	Anthony Bowie	.05
115	Vinny Del Negro	.05
116	Michael Adams	.05
117	Chris Mullin	.10
118	Benoit Benjamin	.05
119	Byron Houston	.05
120	LaPhonso Ellis	.05
121	Doug Overton	.05
122	Jerome Kersey	.05
123	Greg Minor	.05
124	Christian Laettner	.05
125	Mark Price	.10
126	Kevin Willis	.05
127	Kenny Anderson	.10
128	Marty Conlon	.05
129	Blue Edwards	.05
130	Dan Schayes	.05
131	Duane Ferrell	.05
132	Charles Oakley	.05
133	Brian Grant	.15
134	Reggie Williams	.05
135	Steve Kerr	.05
136	Khalid Reeves	.05
137	David Benoit	.05
138	Derrick Coleman	.10
139	Anthony Peeler	.05
140	Jim Jackson	.20
141	Stacey Augmon	.05
142	Sam Cassell	.05
143	Derrick McKey	.05
144	Danny Ferry	.05
145	Anfernee Hardaway	1.25
146	Clifford Robinson	.05
147	B.J. Tyler	.05
148	Mark West	.05
149	David Wingate	.05
150	Willie Anderson	.05
151	Hersey Hawkins	.05
152	Bryant Stith	.05
153	Dan Majerle	.05
154	Chris Smith	.05
155	Donyell Marshall	.15
156	Loy Vaught	.05
157	Reggie Miller	.20
158	Hubert Davis	.05
159	Ron Harper	.05
160	Lee Mayberry	.05
161	Eddie Jones	.25
162	Shawn Bradley	.05
163	Nick Anderson	.05
164	Ervin Johnson	.05
165	Walt Williams	.05
166	Steve Smith	.05
167	Dino Radja	.10
168	Alonzo Mourning	.20
169	Michael Jordan	1.25
170	Tyrone Hill	.05
171	Jamal Mashburn	.10
172	Dikembe Mutombo	.05
173	Grant Hill	.30
174	Latrell Sprewell	.10
175	Hakeem Olajuwon	.20
176	Reggie Miller	.10
177	Pooh Richardson	.05
178	Cedric Ceballos	.05
179	Glen Rice	.05
180	Glenn Robinson	.25
181	Isaiah Rider	.10
182	Derrick Coleman	.05
183	Patrick Ewing	.10
184	Shaquille O'Neal	.40
185	Dana Barros	.05
186	Dan Majerle	.05
187	Clifford Robinson	.05
188	Mitch Richmond	.05
189	David Robinson	.15
190	Gary Payton	.10
191	Oliver Miller	.05
192	Karl Malone	.10
193	Kevin Pritchard	.05
194	Chris Webber	.10
195	Michael Jordan	1.25
196	Hakeem Olajuwon	.20
197	Vin Baker	.10
198	Grant Hill	.40
199	Clyde Drexler	.15
200	Chris Webber	.10
201	Shawn Kemp	.10
202	Shaquille O'Neal	.40
203	Stacey Augmon	.05
204	David Benoit	.05
205	Rodney Rogers	.05
206	Latrell Sprewell	.10
207	Brian Grant	.05
208	Lamond Murray	.05
209	Checklist	.10
210	Checklist	.50
211	*Cory Alexander*	.15
212	Vernon Maxwell	.05
213	George Lynch	.05
214	Terry Mills	.05

215	Scottie Pippen	.50
216	Donald Royal	.05
217	Wesley Person	.05
218	Antonio Davis	.05
219	Glenn Robinson	.50
220	*Jerry Stackhouse*	2.00
221	James Robinson	.05
222	Chris Mills	.05
223	Chuck Person	.05
224	Duane Causwell	.05
225	Gary Payton	.15
226	Eric Montross	.05
227	Felton Spencer	.05
228	Scott Skiles	.05
229	Latrell Sprewell	.15
230	Sedale Threatt	.05
231	Mark Bryant	.05
232	Buck Williams	.05
233	Brian Williams	.05
234	Sharone Wright	.05
235	Karl Malone	.20
236	Kevin Edwards	.05
237	Muggsy Bogues	.05
238	Mario Elie	.05
239	*Rasheed Wallace*	1.50
240	*George Zidek*	.20
241	Cedric Ceballos	.10
242	*Alan Henderson*	.30
243	Joe Kleine	.05
244	Patrick Ewing	.20
245	*Predrag Danilovic*	.25
246	Bill Wennington	.05
247	Steve Smith	.05
248	Bryant Stith	.05
249	Dino Radja	.05
250	Monty Williams	.05
251	*Andrew DeClercq*	.15
252	Sean Elliott	.05
253	Rick Fox	.05
254	Lionel Simmons	.05
255	Dikembe Mutombo	.15
256	Lindsey Hunter	.05
257	Terrell Brandon	.05
258	*Shawn Respert*	.25
259	Rodney Rogers	.05
260	Bryon Russell	.05
261	David Wesley	.05
262	Ken Norman	.05
263	Mitch Richmond	.15
264	Sam Perkins	.05
265	Hakeem Olajuwon	.50
266	Brian Shaw	.05
267	B.J. Armstrong	.05
268	Jalen Rose	.05
269	*Bryant Reeves*	.50
270	*Cherokee Parks*	.20
271	Dennis Rodman	1.00
272	Kendall Gill	.05
273	Elliot Perry	.05
274	Anthony Mason	.05
275	*Kevin Garnett*	4.00
276	*Damon Stoudamire*	1.00
277	*Lawrence Moten*	.15
278	*Ed O'Bannon*	.10
279	Toni Kukoc	.05
280	*Greg Ostertag*	.20
281	Tom Hammonds	.05
282	Yinka Dare	.05
283	Michael Smith	.05
284	Clifford Rozier	.05
285	*Gary Trent*	.20
286	Shaquille O'Neal	1.00
287	Luc Longley	.05
288	*Bob Sura*	.25
289	Dana Barros	.05
290	Lorenzo Williams	.05
291	Haywoode Workman	.05
292	*Randolph Childress*	.15
293	Doc Rivers	.05
294	Chris Webber	.20
295	*Kurt Thomas*	.40
296	Greg Anthony	.05
297	*Tyus Edney*	.10
298	Danny Manning	.05
299	*Brent Barry*	.50
300	*Joe Smith*	1.00
301	Pooh Richardson	.05
302	Mark Jackson	.05
303	Richard Dumas	.05
304	*Michael Finley*	1.50
305	*Theo Ratliff*	.75
306	Gary Grant	.05
307	Jamal Mashburn	.25
308	*Corliss Williamson*	.20
309	*Eric Williams*	.20
310	*Zan Tabak*	.10
311	Eric Murdock	.05
312	*Sherell Ford*	.15
313	Terry Davis	.05
314	Vern Fleming	.05
315	*Jason Caffey*	.15
316	*Mario Bennett*	.15
317	*David Vaughn*	.15
318	*Loren Meyer*	.15
319	*Travis Best*	.75
320	Byron Scott	.05
321	Mookie Blaylock	.05
322	Dee Brown	.05
323	Alonzo Mourning	.10
324	Michael Jordan	1.00
325	Terrell Brandon	.05
326	Jim Jackson	.15
327	Dikembe Mutombo	.10
328	Grant Hill	.50
329	Joe Smith	.75
330	Clyde Drexler	.15
331	Reggie Miller	.10
332	Lamond Murray	.05
333	Nick Van Exel	.15
334	Glen Rice	.10
335	Glenn Robinson	.25
336	Christian Laettner	.05
337	Kenny Anderson	.05
338	Patrick Ewing	.10
339	Shaquille O'Neal	.50
340	Jerry Stackhouse	.50
341	Charles Barkley	.20
342	Clifford Robinson	.05
343	Brian Grant	.05
344	David Robinson	.20
345	Shawn Kemp	.15
346	Damon Stoudamire	1.00
347	Karl Malone	.10
348	Bryant Reeves	.20
349	Juwan Howard	.10
350	Orlando vs. Boston	.20
351	Indiana vs. Atlanta	.05
352	New York vs. Cleveland	.05
353	Charlotte vs. Chicago	1.00
354	San Antonio vs. Denver	.20
355	Phoenix vs. Portland	.05
356	Utah vs. Houston	.15
357	Seattle vs. L.A. Lakers	.05
358	Orlando vs. Chicago	.05
359	Indiana vs. New York	.05
360	San Antonio vs. L.A. Lakers	.05
361	Phoenix vs. Houston	.15
362	Orlando vs. Indiana	.05
363	San Antonio vs. Houston	.25
364	Orlando vs. Houston	.05
365	Houston 1995 NBA Champs	.05
366	Stacey Augmon	.05
367	Sherman Douglas	.05
368	Larry Johnson	.10
369	Scottie Pippen	.10
370	Tyrone Hill	.05
371	Jamal Mashburn	.10
372	Mahmoud Abdul-Rauf	.05
373	Grant Hill	.50
374	Latrell Sprewell	.10
375	Sam Cassell	.05
376	Rik Smits	.05
377	Terry Dehere	.05
378	Eddie Jones	.10
379	Billy Owens	.05
380	Vin Baker	.05
381	Isaiah Rider	.05
382	Kenny Anderson	.05
383	John Starks	.05
384	Anfernee Hardaway	.40
385	Sharone Wright	.05
386	Charles Barkley	.20
387	Clifford Robinson	.05
388	Walt Williams	.05
389	Sean Elliott	.05
390	Gary Payton	.10
391	Carlos Rogers	.05
392	John Stockton	.10
393	Greg Anthony	.05
394	Chris Webber	.10
395	Gary Payton	.10
396	Mookie Blaylock	.05
397	Charles Barkley	.20
398	Grant Hill	.40
399	Anfernee Hardaway	.40
400	Kenny Anderson	.05
401	Mark Jackson	.05
402	Karl Malone	.10
403	Avery Johnson	.05
404	Larry Johnson	.10
405	Nick Van Exel	.15
406	Vin Baker	.05
407	Jason Kidd	.25
408	David Robinson	.20
409	Shawn Kemp (Checklist Card #1)	.10
410	Michael Jordan (Checklist Card #2)	.50
NNO	Draft Trade Card	15.00

1995-96 Collector's Choice Player's Club

One Player's Club insert was inserted into each pack of Collector's Choice. The 410-card set paralleled each card and was identified by a Player's Club silver stamp on the front.

	MT
Player's Club Cards:	1x-3x

1995-96 Collector's Choice Player's Club Platinum

Platinum Player's Club inserts paralleled each card in the 410-card Collector's Choice set. The cards were identified by a silver foil finish and a holographic Platinum Player's Club stamp. These were inserted one per 35 packs of Series I and II.

	MT
Player's Club Platinum:	15x-30x

1995-96 Collector's Choice Crash the Game Assists/Rebounds

These cards were random inserts in 1995-96 Upper Deck Collector's Choice Series II packs. Two versions were made - silver (seeded one per every five packs) and gold (seeded one per every 49 packs). The corresponding colored foil is used on the front to indicate which version the card is and which team the pictured player is trying to compile statistics against. If he accomplishes this feat, the collector can redeem the card for a prize. The card back provides the game rules. In addition to gold and silver versions, each player had three cards with three different dates for those versions. Cards are numbered with a "C" prefix.

		MT
Complete Set (90):		75.00
Common Silver:		.25
Complete Gold Set (90):		280.00
Common Gold:		2.00
Gold Cards:		2x-4x
1A	Michael Jordan (1/30 L)	8.00
1B	Michael Jordan (2/22 L)	8.00
1C	Michael Jordan (3/19 L)	8.00
2A	Tim Hardaway (2/4 L)	.25
2B	Tim Hardaway (3/12 L)	.25
2C	Tim Hardaway (4/11)	.50
3A	Juwan Howard (2/2 L)	.75
3B	Juwan Howard (2/21 L)	.75
3C	Juwan Howard (3/30 L)	.75
4A	Shawn Kemp (1/29 L)	1.00
4B	Shawn Kemp (3/15 W)	3.00
4C	Shawn Kemp (4/3)	1.00
5A	Nick Van Exel (2/4 L)	.75
5B	Nick Van Exel (2/21 L)	.75
5C	Nick Van Exel (4/14)	1.00
6A	Mookie Blaylock (2/16 L)	.25
6B	Mookie Blaylock (3/8 L)	.25
6C	Mookie Blaylock (4/20)	.50
7A	John Stockton (2/13 W)	4.00
7B	John Stockton (3/6 W)	4.00
7C	John Stockton (4/14)	.75
8A	Scottie Pippen (1/28 L)	1.00
8B	Scottie Pippen (3/15 L)	1.00
8C	Scottie Pippen (4/11)	1.25
9A	Vin Baker (2/3 L)	.50
9B	Vin Baker (3/4 W)	3.00
9C	Vin Baker (4/5)	.60
10A	Lamond Murray (2/3 L)	.25
10B	Lamond Murray (2/17 L)	.25
10C	Lamond Murray (3/30 L)	.25
11A	David Robinson (2/15 W)	4.00
11B	David Robinson (3/14 W)	4.00
11C	David Robinson (4/13)	1.50
12A	Jason Kidd (2/6 L)	1.50
12B	Jason Kidd (3/19 L)	1.50
12C	Jason Kidd (4/13)	2.00
13A	Rod Strickland (2/15 L)	.25
13B	Rod Strickland (3/8 W)	3.00
13C	Rod Strickland (4/5)	.50
14A	Glen Rice (1/29 L)	.25
14B	Glen Rice (2/28 L)	.25
14C	Glen Rice (4/2)	.50
15A	Anfernee Hardaway (2/4 W)	6.00
15B	Anfernee Hardaway (3/31 L)	3.00
15C	Anfernee Hardaway (4/21)	4.00
16A	Hakeem Olajuwon (2/15 L)	1.50
16B	Hakeem Olajuwon (3/8 L)	1.50
16C	Hakeem Olajuwon (4/15)	2.00
17A	Kenny Anderson (2/14 W)	3.00
17B	Kenny Anderson (2/29 W)	3.00
17C	Kenny Anderson (3/29 L)	.25
18A	Sharone Wright (2/14 L)	.25
18B	Sharone Wright (3/22 L)	.25
18C	Sharone Wright (4/17)	.50
19A	Dikembe Mutombo (2/16 L)	.25
19B	Dikembe Mutombo (3/2 W)	3.00
19C	Dikembe Mutombo (4/5)	.50
20A	Muggsy Bogues (2/1)	.25
20B	Muggsy Bogues (2/21 L)	.25
20C	Muggsy Bogues (3/20 L)	.25
21A	Reggie Miller	.75
21B	Reggie Miller (3/5 L)	.75
21C	Reggie Miller (4/8)	1.00
22A	Danny Manning (2/6 L)	.25
22B	Danny Manning (3/3 L)	.25
22C	Danny Manning (4/16)	.50
23A	Christian Laettner (2/5 L)	.25
23B	Christian Laettner (3/10 L)	.25
23C	Christian Laettner (3/27 W)	3.00
24A	Eric Montross (2/14 L)	.25
24B	Eric Montross (3/8 L)	.25
24C	Eric Montross (3/31 L)	.25
25A	Patrick Ewing (2/21 L)	.60
25B	Patrick Ewing (3/29 W)	3.00
25C	Patrick Ewing (4/3)	.75
26A	Damon Stoudamire (1/30 L)	4.00
26B	Damon Stoudamire (3/10 L)	4.00
26C	Damon Stoudamire (3/22 W)	6.00
27A	Bryant Reeves (2/28 L)	1.00
27B	Bryant Reeves (3/31 L)	1.00
27C	Bryant Reeves (4/9)	1.25
28A	Joe Dumars (2/15 L)	.25
28B	Joe Dumars (3/22 L)	.25
28C	Joe Dumars (4/13)	.50
29A	Tyrone Hill (2/6 L)	.25
29B	Tyrone Hill (3/10 L)	.25
29C	Tyrone Hill (4/20)	.50
30A	Brian Grant (2/13 L)	.25
30B	Brian Grant (3/20 L)	.25
30C	Brian Grant (4/21)	.50

1995-96 Collector's Choice Crash the Game Scoring

These cards were random inserts in 1995-96 Upper Deck Collector's Choice Series I packs. Two versions were made - silver (seeded one per every five packs) and gold (seeded one per every 50 packs). The corresponding colored foil is used on the front to indicate which version the card is and which team the pictured player is trying to compile stats against. If he accomplishes this feat, the collector can redeem the card for a prize. The card back provides the game rules. In addition to gold and silver versions, each player had three cards with three different dates for those versions. Cards are numbered with a "C" prefix.

		MT
Complete Silver Set (81):		75.00
Common Silver:		.25
Complete Gold Set (81):		280.00
Common Gold:		2.00
Gold Cards:		2x-4x
1A	Michael Jordan (HOU W)	12.00
1B	Michael Jordan (NY W)	12.00
1C	Michael Jordan (ORL W)	12.00
2A	Kenny Anderson (CLE)	.50
2B	Kenny Anderson (LAC L)	.25
2C	Kenny Anderson (MIA)	.50
3A	Charles Barkley (CLE L)	1.00
3B	Charles Barkley (GS W)	4.00
3C	Charles Barkley (SA W)	4.00
4A	Dana Barros (ATL L)	.25
4B	Dana Barros (BOS W)	3.00
4C	Dana Barros (LAL L)	.25
5A	Anfernee Hardaway (CHI W)	6.00
5B	Anfernee Hardaway (SA W)	6.00
5C	Anfernee Hardaway (MIL W)	6.00
6A	Mookie Blaylock (DAL L)	.25
6B	Mookie Blaylock (DET L)	.25
6C	Mookie Blaylock (TOR L)	.25
7A	Lamond Murray (ATL L)	.25
7B	Lamond Murray (MIN L)	.25
7C	Lamond Murray (VAN L)	.50
8A	Karl Malone (HOU L)	.60
8B	Karl Malone (NY L)	.60
8C	Karl Malone (POR W)	4.00
9A	Alonzo Mourning (CHI)	.75
9B	Alonzo Mourning (IND)	.75
9C	Alonzo Mourning (WASH W)	4.00
10A	Hakeem Olajuwon (LAL W)	4.00
10B	Hakeem Olajuwon (ORL W)	4.00
10C	Hakeem Olajuwon (POR W)	4.00
11A	Mark Price (CHI)	.50
11B	Mark Price (NJ L)	.25
11C	Mark Price (SEA L)	.25
12A	Isaiah Rider (BOS L)	.25
12B	Isaiah Rider (PHO L)	.25
12C	Isaiah Rider (SAC L)	.25
13A	Glen Rice (NJ W)	3.00
13B	Glen Rice (SAC W)	3.00
13C	Glen Rice (WASH W)	3.00
14A	Mitch Richmond (LAL L)	.40
14B	Mitch Richmond (MIN W)	3.00
14C	Mitch Richmond (NJ L)	.40
15A	Chris Webber (GS W)	3.00
15B	Chris Webber (IND L)	.40
15C	Chris Webber (PHI L)	.40
16A	Nick Van Exel (DAL)	1.00
16B	Nick Van Exel (MIL L)	.60
16C	Nick Van Exel (SAC L)	.60
17A	Mahmoud Abdul-Rauf (CHA L)	.25
17B	Mahmoud Abdul Rauf (PHO W)	3.00
17C	Mahmoud Abdul-Rauf (SEA)	.50
18A	Dominique Wilkins (PHI L)	.25
18B	Dominique Wilkins (POR L)	.25
18C	Dominique Wilkins (TOR L)	.25
19A	Patrick Ewing (BOS W)	4.00
19B	Patrick Ewing (CHA)	.75
19C	Patrick Ewing (PHO L)	.60
20A	David Robinson (DEN)	4.00
20B	David Robinson (SEA)	4.00
20C	David Robinson (WASH W)	4.00
21A	Shawn Kemp (DEN)	1.00
21B	Shawn Kemp (DET)	1.00
21C	Shawn Kemp (UTAH)	1.00
22A	Jason Kidd (IND W)	4.00
22B	Jason Kidd (LAC L)	1.50
22C	Jason Kidd (SA)	2.00
23A	Glenn Robinson (ATL W)	4.00
23B	Glenn Robinson (CHA)	1.25
23C	Glenn Robinson (VAN L)	1.00
24A	Reggie Miller (MIN L)	.75
24B	Reggie Miller (NY)	1.00
24C	Reggie Miller (ORL)	1.00
25A	Joe Dumars (CLE)	.50
25B	Joe Dumars (MIL)	.50
25C	Joe Dumars (UTAH L)	.25
26A	Latrell Sprewell (DAL)	.50
26B	Latrell Sprewell (HOU)	.50
26C	Latrell Sprewell (MIA)	.50
27A	Clifford Robinson (LAC)	.50
27B	Clifford Robinson (PHI L)	.25
27C	Clifford Robinson (UTAH W)	3.00

1995-96 Collector's Choice Crash The Game Gold

Each card in the 30-card You Crash the Game Scoring set arrived in both gold and silver versions. Each player had three different cards and gold versions were found every 49 packs.

	MT
Gold Cards:	2x-4x

1995-96 Collector's Choice Crash The Game II Gold

This 30-card insert ran parallel to the Silver You Crash the Game inserts and was inserted one per 49 Series II packs. Each player had three different silver or gold cards for a total of 90 different.

	MT
Gold Cards:	2x-4x

1995-96 Collector's Choice Debut Trade

This 30-card set was available through redemption of a Debut Trade card seeded one per 30 Series II packs. The redemption period expired May 8, 1996. The set carried a consistent look from the regular-issue Collector's Choice cards, but featured primarily players traded during the 1995-96 season (rookies McDyess and Sabonis were left out of the regular-issue set, but included in this set).

		MT
Complete Set (30):		4.00
Common Player:		.05
T1	Magic Johnson	1.00
T2	Arvydas Sabonis	.50
T3	Kenny Anderson	.20
T4	Antonio McDyess	1.00
T5	Sherman Douglas	.05
T6	Spud Webb	.15
T7	Glen Rice	.30
T8	Todd Day	.05
T9	John Williams	.05
T10	Chris Morris	.05
T11	Shawn Bradley	.15
T12	Dan Majerle	.15
T13	George McCloud	.05
T14	Derrick Coleman	.15
T15	Kendall Gill	.15
T16	Ricky Pierce	.05
T17	Robert Pack	.05
T18	Alonzo Mourning	.30
T19	Matt Geiger	.05
T20	Don MacLean	.05
T21	Willie Anderson	.05
T22	Oliver Miller	.05
T23	Tracy Murray	.05
T24	Ed Pinckney	.05
T25	Alvin Robertson	.05
T26	Anthony Avent	.05
T27	Blue Edwards	.05
T28	Kenny Gattison	.05
T29	Chris King	.05
T30	Eric Murdock	.05

1995-96 Collector's Choice Draft Trade

This 10-card set was available through redemption of a Draft Trade card seeded one per 144 Series I packs. The redemption period expired June 7, 1996. The set featured 10 top rookies from the 1995-96 season, with fronts showing the player's draft position and the backs numbered with a "D" prefix.

		MT
Complete Set (10):		16.00
Common Player:		.25
D1	Joe Smith	2.00
D2	Antonio McDyess	3.00
D3	Jerry Stackhouse	4.00
D4	Rasheed Wallace	3.00
D5	Kevin Garnett	8.00
D6	Bryant Reeves	1.00
D7	Damon Stoudamire	2.00
D8	Shawn Respert	.25
D9	Ed O'Bannon	.25
D10	Kurt Thomas	.25

1995-96 Collector's Choice Jordan Collection

These eight cards are a continuation of Upper Deck's series of the Michael Jordan Collection. Cards JC1-JC4 were in packs of 1995-96 Upper Deck Collector's Choice Series I packs, one per every 11 packs. Cards JC9-JC12 were seeded one per every 11 Series II packs.

		MT
Complete Set (8):		30.00
Complete Series 1 (4):		15.00
Complete Series 2 (4):		15.00
Common Ser. 1 (JC1-JC4):		4.00
Common Ser. 2 (JC9-JC12):		4.00
1	1985 NBA Rookie Of The Year	4.00
2	1986-87 3,000 Points	4.00
3	1988 NBA Defensive Player Of The Year	4.00
4	Beginnings Of A Superstar	4.00
9	Seven Consecutive Scoring Titles	4.00
10	50-Point Scoring Games	4.00
11	Career NBA Playoff Scoring Leader	4.00
12	The Scoring Records	4.00

1995-96 Collector's Choice Jordan He's Back

This five-card set was inserted one per special retail pack and commemorates the return of Michael Jordan to the NBA in the 1994-95 season. Each card highlights a particular moment, such as his first game back and his first game against the Knicks.

		MT
Complete Set (5):		6.00
Common Player:		1.50
M1	First Game Back (Michael Jordan)	1.50
M2	Buzzer beater versus Hawks (Michael Jordan)	1.50
M3	Versus Knicks (Michael Jordan)	1.50
M4	Playoffs versus Charlotte (Michael Jordan)	1.50
M5	Playoffs versus Orlando - Switch to #23 (Michael Jordan)	1.50

1996-97 Collector's Choice

Collector's Choice was issued in two, 200-card series in 1996-97. The cards feature an action shot of the player surrounded by a white border. The left side of the card has the player's name, position and team logo in a panel featuring black and the player's team's primary color. There is also a Collector's Choice logo in the upper right corner. Subsets in Series I include Anfernee Hardaway, Chicago Bulls' victory tour, 30 NBA Fundamentals and five checklists, while Series II included One on One, Assignment: Jordan, 30 NBA Playbook and five checklists. Inserts in Series I include: Mini Cards (reminiscent of the 1980-81 Topps set), Super Action Stick-Ums, You Crash the Game and an NBA Draft Trade Card. Inserts in Series II include: Super Action Stick-Ums, Mini Cards, You Crash the Game and an Update Trade Card.

MT
Complete Set (400): 30.00
Comp. Series 1 (200): 15.00
Comp. Series 2 (200): 15.00
Common Player: .05
Minor Stars: .10
Ser. 1 or 2 Pack (12): 1.00
Ser. 1 or 2 Wax Box (36): 30.00
1 Mookie Blaylock .05
2 Grant Long .05
3 Christian Laettner .05
4 Craig Ehlo .05
5 Ken Norman .05
6 Stacey Augmon .05
7 Dana Barros .05
8 Dino Radja .05
9 Rick Fox .05
10 Eric Montross .05
11 David Wesley .05
12 Eric Williams .05
13 Glen Rice .10
14 Dell Curry .05
15 Matt Geiger .05
16 Scott Burrell .05
17 George Zidek .05
18 Muggsy Bogues .05
19 Ron Harper .05
20 Steve Kerr .05
21 Toni Kukoc .05
22 Dennis Rodman 1.00
23 Michael Jordan 3.00
24 Luc Longley .05
25 (Michael Jordan, Vlade Divac) 1.00
26 (Michael Jordan Bulls) 1.00
27 Chicago Bulls .05
28 (Scottie Pippen Bulls) .25
29 (Toni Kukoc, Juwan Howard) .20
30 Terrell Brandon .05
31 Bobby Phills .05
32 Tyrone Hill .05
33 Michael Cage .05
34 Bob Sura .05
35 Tony Dumas .05
36 Jim Jackson .15
37 Loren Meyer .05
38 Cherokee Parks .05
39 Jamal Mashburn .15
40 Popeye Jones .05
41 LaPhonso Ellis .05
42 Jalen Rose .05
43 Antonio McDyess .30
44 Tom Hammonds .05
45 Mahmoud Abdul-Rauf .05
46 Dale Ellis .05
47 Joe Dumars .05
48 Theo Ratliff .05
49 Lindsey Hunter .05
50 Terry Mills .05
51 Don Reid .05
52 B.J. Armstrong .05
53 Bimbo Coles .05
54 Joe Smith .40
55 Chris Mullin .05
56 Rony Seikaly .05
57 Donyell Marshall .05
58 Hakeem Olajuwon .40
59 Robert Horry .05
60 Mario Elie .05
61 Mark Bryant .05
62 Chucky Brown .05
63 Rik Smits .05
64 Derrick McKey .05
65 Eddie Johnson .05
66 Mark Jackson .05
67 Ricky Pierce .05
68 Travis Best .05
69 Rodney Rogers .05
70 Brent Barry .10
71 Lamond Murray .05
72 Eric Piatkowski .05
73 Pooh Richardson .05
74 Cedric Ceballos .05
75 Eddie Jones .10
76 Anthony Peeler .05
77 George Lynch .05
78 Vlade Divac .05
79 Rex Chapman .05
80 Predrag Danilovic .05
81 Kurt Thomas .05
82 Keith Askins .05
83 Walt Williams .05
84 Vin Baker .15
85 Shawn Respert .05
86 Sherman Douglas .05
87 Marty Conlon .05
88 Johnny Newman .05
89 Kevin Garnett 1.00
90 Andrew Lang .05
91 Terry Porter .05
92 Sam Mitchell .05
93 Tom Gugliotta .05
94 Spud Webb .05
95 Kendall Gill .05
96 Vern Fleming .05
97 Shawn Bradley .05
98 Ed O'Bannon .10
99 Jayson Williams .05
100 Kevin Edwards .05
101 Charles Oakley .05
102 Anthony Mason .05
103 John Starks .05
104 J.R. Reid .05
105 Hubert Davis .05
106 Gary Grant .05
107 Nick Anderson .05
108 Donald Royal .05
109 Brian Shaw .05
110 Kenny Gattison .05
111 Anfernee Hardaway 1.25
112 Dennis Scott .05
113 Anfernee Hardaway .40
114 Anfernee Hardaway .40
115 Anfernee Hardaway .40
116 Anfernee Hardaway .40
117 Anfernee Hardaway .40
118 Derrick Coleman .05
119 Rex Walters .05
120 Sean Higgins .05
121 Clarence Weatherspoon .05
122 Jerry Stackhouse .50
123 Elliot Perry .05
124 Wayman Tisdale .05
125 Wesley Person .05
126 Charles Barkley .30
127 A.C. Green .05
128 Harvey Grant .05
129 Arvydas Sabonis .10
130 Aaron McKie .05
131 Gary Trent .05
132 Buck Williams .05
133 Billy Owens .05
134 Brian Grant .05
135 Corliss Williamson .05
136 Tyus Edney .10
137 Olden Polynice .05
138 Avery Johnson .05
139 Vinny Del Negro .05
140 Sean Elliott .05
141 Chuck Person .05
142 Will Perdue .05
143 Nate McMillan .05
144 Vincent Askew .05
145 Detlef Schrempf .05
146 Hersey Hawkins .05
147 Sharone Wright .05
148 Zan Tabak .05
149 Oliver Miller .05
150 Doug Christie .05
151 Damon Stoudamire .50
152 Jeff Hornacek .05
153 Chris Morris .05
154 Antoine Carr .05
155 Karl Malone .15
156 Adam Keefe .05
157 Greg Anthony .05
158 Blue Edwards .05
159 Bryant Reeves .20
160 Anthony Avent .05
161 Lawrence Moten .05
162 Calbert Cheaney .05
163 Chris Webber .10
164 Tim Legler .05
165 Gheorghe Muresan .05
166 Stacey Augmon .05
167 Dee Brown .05
168 Glen Rice .05
169 Scottie Pippen FUND .25
170 Danny Ferry .05
171 Jason Kidd FUND .50
172 Jalen Rose .05
173 Grant Hill FUND .40
174 Chris Mullin .05
175 Clyde Drexler FUND .10
176 Rik Smits .05
177 Loy Vaught .05
178 Nick Van Exel .05
179 Alonzo Mourning .05
180 Glenn Robinson .05
181 Isaiah Rider .05
182 Ed O'Bannon .05
183 Patrick Ewing .05
184 Shaquille O'Neal FUND .50
185 Derrick Coleman .05
186 Danny Manning .05
187 Clifford Robinson .05
188 Mitch Richmond .05
189 David Robinson FUND .10
190 Shawn Kemp FUND .20
191 Oliver Miller .05
192 John Stockton .05
193 Greg Anthony .05
194 Rasheed Wallace .05
195 Michael Jordan FUND 1.00
196 Checklist #1 .05
197 Checklist #2 .05
198 Checklist #3 .05
199 Checklist #4 .05
200 Checklist #5 .05
201 Alan Henderson .05
202 Steve Smith .05
203 Donnie Boyce .05
204 *Priest Lauderdale* .10
205 Dikembe Mutombo .05
206 Dee Brown .05
207 Junior Burrough .05
208 Todd Day .05
209 Pervis Ellison .05
210 Greg Minor .05
211 *Antoine Walker* 1.00
212 Rafael Addison .05
213 *Tony Delk* .25
214 Vlade Divac .05
215 Anthony Goldwire .05
216 Anthony Mason .05
217 Dickey Simpkins .05
218 Randy Brown .05
219 Jud Buechler .05
220 Jason Caffey .05
221 Scottie Pippen .50
222 Bill Wennington .05
223 Danny Ferry .05
224 Antonio Lang .05
225 Chris Mills .05
226 *Vitaly Potapenko* .15
227 Terry Davis .05
228 Chris Gatling .05
229 Jason Kidd .60
230 George McCloud .05
231 Eric Montross .05
232 *Samaki Walker* .20
233 Mark Jackson .05
234 Ervin Johnson .05
235 Sarunas Marciulionis .05
236 Eric Murdock .05
237 Ricky Pierce .05
238 Bryant Stith .05
239 Stacey Augmon .05
240 Grant Hill .75
241 Otis Thorpe .05
242 *Jerome Williams* .10
243 Andrew DeClerq .05
244 *Todd Fuller* .15
245 Mark Price .05
246 Clifford Rozier .05
247 Latrell Sprewell .10
248 Charles Barkley .25
249 Clyde Drexler .20
250 *Othella Harrington* .15
251 Sam Mack .05
252 Kevin Willis .05
253 *Erick Dampier* .15
254 Antonio Davis .05
255 Dale Davis .05
256 Duane Ferrell .05
257 Reggie Miller .20
258 Jalen Rose .05
259 Reggie Williams .05
260 Terry Dehere .05
261 Charles Outlaw .05
262 Stanley Roberts .05
263 Malik Sealy .05
264 Loy Vaught .05
265 *Lorenzen Wright* .20
266 Corie Blount .05
267 *Kobe Bryant* 3.00
268 Elden Campbell .05
269 *Derek Fisher* .25
270 Shaquille O'Neal 1.00
271 Nick Van Exel .10
272 P.J. Brown .05
273 Tim Hardaway .05
274 *Voshon Lenard* .15
275 Dan Majerle .05
276 Alonzo Mourning .10
277 *Martin Muursepp* .10
278 *Ray Allen* .75
279 Elliot Perry .05
280 Glenn Robinson .20
281 *Stephon Marbury* 1.25
282 Cherokee Parks .05
283 Doug West .05
284 Michael Williams .05
285 *Kerry Kittles* .50
286 Ed O'Bannon .05
287 Robert Pack .05
288 Khalid Reeves .05
289 David Benoit .05
290 Patrick Ewing .20
291 Allan Houston .05
292 Larry Johnson .10
293 *Dontae Jones* .10
294 *Walter McCarty* .15
295 *John Wallace* .30
296 Charlie Ward .05
297 *Brian Evans* .10
298 Horace Grant .05
299 Jon Koncak .05
300 Felton Spencer .05
301 *Allen Iverson* 2.00
302 Don MacLean .05
303 Scott Williams .05
304 Sam Cassell .05
305 Michael Finley .20
306 Robert Horry .05
307 Kevin Johnson .05
308 Joe Kleine .05
309 Danny Manning .05
310 *Steve Nash* .25
311 John Williams .05
312 Kenny Anderson .05
313 Randolph Childress .05
314 Chris Dudley .05
315 *Jermaine O'Neal* .60
316 Isaiah Rider .05
317 Clifford Robinson .05
318 Rasheed Wallace .10
319 Mahmoud Abdul-Rauf .05
320 Duane Causwell .05
321 Bobby Hurley .05
322 Mitch Richmond .10
323 Lionel Simmons .05
324 Michael Smith .05
325 Dominique Wilkins .05
326 Cory Alexander .05
327 Greg Anderson .05
328 Carl Herrera .05
329 David Robinson .30
330 Charles Smith .05
331 Craig Ehlo .05
332 Sherell Ford .05
333 Shawn Kemp .30
334 Jim McIlvaine .05
335 Gary Payton .15
336 Sam Perkins .05
337 Eric Snow .05
338 David Wingate .05
339 *Marcus Camby* 1.25
340 Acie Earl .05
341 Carlos Rogers .05
342 Greg Ostertag .05
343 Bryon Russell .05
344 John Stockton .20
345 Jamie Watson .05
346 *Shareef Abdur-Rahim* 1.25
347 Doug Edwards .05
348 George Lynch .05
349 Eric Mobley .05
350 Anthony Peeler .05
351 *Roy Rogers* .25
352 Juwan Howard .40
353 Harvey Grant .05
354 Tracy Murray .05
355 Rod Strickland .05
356 One on One 1.00
357 One on One .50
358 One on One .40
359 One on One .05
360 One on One .05
361 NBA One on One 1.00
362 Nick Anderson, Michael Jordan .50
363 Joe Dumars, Michael Jordan .50
364 John Starks, Michael Jordan .50
365 Reggie Miller, Michael Jordan .50
366 Gary Payton, Michael Jordan .50
367 Atlanta Hawks .05
368 Boston Celtics .05
369 Charlotte Hornets .05
370 Chicago Bulls .75
371 Cleveland Cavaliers .05
372 Dallas Mavericks .10
373 Denver Nuggets .10
374 Detroit Pistons .40
375 Golden State Warriors .10
376 Houston Rockets .75
377 Indiana Pacers .10
378 Los Angeles Clippers .05
379 Los Angeles Lakers .05
380 Miami Heat .05
381 Milwaukee Bucks .30
382 Minnesota Timberwolves .50
383 New Jersey Nets .05
384 New York Knicks .05
385 Orlando Magic .75
386 Philadelphia 76ers .20
387 Phoenix Suns .05
388 Portland Trail Blazers .05
389 Sacramento Kings .05
390 San Antonio Spurs .05
391 Seattle SuperSonics .30
392 Toronto Raptors .05
393 Utah Jazz .05
394 Vancouver Grizzlies .05
395 Washington Bullets .05
396 Checklist #1 .05
397 Checklist #2 .05
398 Checklist #3 .05
399 Checklist #4 .05
400 Checklist #5 .05
NNO NBA Update Trade Card 15.00
NNO NBA Draft Trade Card 15.00

1996-97 Collector's Choice Chicago Bulls Team Set

The Bulls' team set consisted of nine player cards and two Gold Mini-Cards which featured three players each. The set had a suggested retail price of $2.99 when first released.

MT
Complete Set (11): 8.00
Common Player: .05
B1 Ron Harper, Michael Jordan, Steve Kerr 2.00
B2 Toni Kukoc, Scottie Pippen, Dennis Rodman 1.50
CH1 Jason Caffey .10
CH2 Ron Harper .10
CH3 Michael Jordan 3.00
CH4 Steve Kerr .10
CH5 Toni Kukoc .15
CH6 Luc Longley .10
CH7 Scottie Pippen .75
CH8 Dennis Rodman 1.00
CH9 Bill Wennington .05

1996-97 Collector's Choice Crash the Game 1

These 1996-97 Collector's Choice inserts offer collectors more of a chance to follow their favorite stars and get their favorite stars in return. Each card front has a span of days (either a week or two) in which the player can accomplish what is designated on the front. If he does, the card can be redeemed for a special card of that player. There are two versions of each card - silver (one in five packs) and gold (one per every 49 packs). The card front has a color action photo, with the player's name, position and team name in the upper right corner. The Collector's Choice logo is in the upper left corner. The "Scorecard," which states the category the player has to fulfill, is along the right side. The "You Crash the Game" logo and the specific dates are at the bottom, in silver or gold. The card back, numbered using a "C" prefix, has the player's name, team logo and rules to the contest.

MT
Complete Set (60): 60.00
Common Player: 1.00
Minor Stars: 2.00
Gold Cards: 2x-4x
1 Mookie Blaylock 1.00
2 Dino Radja 1.00
3 Glen Rice 1.00
4 Scottie Pippen 4.00
5 Terrell Brandon 1.00
6 Jason Kidd 2.50
7 Antonio McDyess 2.00
8 Joe Dumars 1.00
9 Joe Smith 2.00
10 Hakeem Olajuwon 3.00
11 Reggie Miller 2.00
12 Loy Vaught 1.00
13 Cedric Ceballos 1.00
14 Alonzo Mourning 1.00
15 Vin Baker 1.00
16 Kevin Garnett 4.00
17 Ed O'Bannon 1.00
18 Patrick Ewing 1.00
19 Anfernee Hardaway 5.00
20 Clarence Weatherspoon 1.00
21 Kevin Johnson 1.00
22 Clifford Robinson 1.00
23 Mitch Richmond 1.00
24 Sean Elliott 1.00
25 Shawn Kemp 2.00
26 Damon Stoudamire 3.00
27 John Stockton 2.00
28 Bryant Reeves 1.00
29 Rasheed Wallace 1.00
30 Michael Jordan 10.00

1996-97 Collector's Choice Crash the Game 2

Inserted every five packs of second series Collector's Choice, the interactive cards rewarded collectors with prizes if the designated player scored over 30 points in the specified week. Gold versions were inserted every 49 packs. Cards are numbered with a "C" prefix.

MT
Complete Set (60): 60.00
Common Player: 1.00
Gold Cards: 2x-4x
1 Steve Smith 1.00
2 Dana Barros 1.00
3 Tony Delk 1.00
4 Toni Kukoc 1.00
5 Bobby Phills 1.00
6 Jamal Mashburn 1.00
7 LaPhonso Ellis 1.00
8 Jerome Williams 1.00
9 Latrell Sprewell 2.00
10 Clyde Drexler 2.00
11 Dale Davis 1.00
12 Brent Barry 1.00
13 Nick Van Exel 1.00
14 Sasha Danilovic 1.00
15 Glenn Robinson 2.00
16 Stephon Marbury 4.00
17 Shawn Bradley 1.00
18 John Wallace 1.00
19 Anfernee Hardaway 5.00
20 Jerry Stackhouse 2.00
21 Danny Manning 1.00
22 Arvydas Sabonis 1.00
23 Brian Grant 1.00
24 David Robinson 2.00
25 Gary Payton 2.00
26 Marcus Camby 3.00
27 Karl Malone 2.00
28 Shareef Abdur-Rahim 3.00
29 Juwan Howard 1.00
30 Michael Jordan 10.00

1996-97 Collector's Choice Draft Trade

The insert card, seeded every 71 packs and featuring the "DR" prefix, could be redeemed for a 30-card update set that had the latest trades, rookies and free agents. The offer ended July 1, 1997. The card front featured the Lakers' Eddie Jones in an above-the-rim action shot in the upper right corner with the NBA team nicknames listed in blue lowercase letters in a puzzle format. The back contains information on how to receive the update set.

MT
Complete Set (10): 15.00
Common Player: .50
1 Allen Iverson 6.00
2 Marcus Camby 2.00
3 Shareef Abdur-Rahim 3.00
4 Stephon Marbury 4.00
5 Ray Allen 2.00
6 Antoine Walker 2.00
7 Lorenzen Wright .50
8 Kerry Kittles 1.50
9 Samaki Walker .50
10 Erick Dampier .50
--- Draft Trade Card 1.00

1996-97 Collector's Choice Factory Blow-Ups

Upper Deck's basketball spokesmen are featured in this four-card set. One card, measuring 3-1/2" x 5", was inserted in each 1996-97 Collector's Choice Factory Set.

MT
Complete Set (4): 10.00
Common Player: 1.00
1 Michael Jordan 4.00
2 Shawn Kemp .75
3 Anfernee Hardaway 2.00
4 Michael Jordan, Anfernee Hardaway 4.00

1996-97 Collector's Choice Game Face

The 10-card insert set was inserted in each Series I retail pack. The key card in the set is of Michael Jordan, card No. 2. Each card has the "GF" prefix.

MT
Complete Set (10): 15.00
Common Player: .25
1 Anfernee Hardaway 3.00
2 Michael Jordan 7.00
3 Shawn Kemp 1.00
4 Alonzo Mourning .50
5 Cherokee Parks .25
6 Avery Johnson .25
7 LaPhonso Ellis .25
8 Rasheed Wallace .25
9 Jim Jackson .25
10 Larry Johnson .25

1996-97 Collector's Choice Houston Rockets Team Set

This set featured nine player cards and a blow up card of the Building a Winner subset from 1996-97 Upper Deck. The set had an SRP of $2.99 when first released. Cards are numbered with a "HT" prefix.

MT
Complete Set (9): 4.00
Common Player: .05
1 Charles Barkley .50
2 Matt Bullard .05
3 Clyde Drexler .50
4 Mario Elie .10
5 Othella Harrington .15
6 Sam Mack .05
7 Matt Maloney .50
8 Hakeem Olajuwon 2.00
9 Kevin Willis .05
--- Houston Rockets Blow-Up 2.00

1996 Collector's Choice Int. Jordan Collection

Inserted every 11 packs of Series II French, German, Latin, Italian, Japanese, Northern European and Portugese packs, the Jordan Collection was based on the American version, but with different numbering.

MT
Complete Set (4): 20.00
Common Player: 5.00
JC1 7 Titles (Michael Jordan) 5.00
JC2 50-point (Michael Jordan) 5.00
JC3 Playoff Scoring (Michael Jordan) 5.00
JC4 Records (Michael Jordan) 5.00

1996 Collector's Choice Int. Special Edition Hologram

Randomly inserted into Series I packs, the cards were based on the 1994-95 U.S. Special Edition inserts. The cards were randomly seeded into every five packs of French, German, Italian and Japanese versions and every 10 packs of the Latin and Spanish versions.

MT
Complete Set (9): 20.00
Common Player: 1.00
H1 Larry Johnson 1.00
H2 Scottie Pippen 3.00

H3	Grant Hill	5.00
H4	Reggie Miller	1.00
H5	Glenn Robinson	2.00
H6	Patrick Ewing	1.00
H7	Shaquille O'Neal	5.00
H8	John Stockton	1.00
H9	Chris Webber	3.00

1996 Collector's Choice International I

The 210-card, international set was distributed in France, Germany, Italy, Latin America, Northern Europe, Portugal and Spain. The cards are identical in design to the 1995-96 U.S. set except for the bilingual text for the countries. Values below are for all versions.

		MT
	Complete Set (210):	25.00
	Common Player:	.10
1	Rod Strickland	.30
2	Larry Johnson	.25
3	Mahmoud Abdul-Rauf	.10
4	Joe Dumars	.25
5	Jason Kidd	1.00
6	Avery Johnson	.25
7	Dee Brown	.10
8	Brian Williams	.10
9	Nick Van Exel	.25
10	Dennis Rodman	1.00
11	Rony Seikaly	.10
12	Harvey Grant	.10
13	Craig Ehlo	.10
14	Derek Harper	.10
15	Oliver Miller	.10
16	Dennis Scott	.10
17	Ed Pinckney	.10
18	Eric Piatkowski	.10
19	B.J. Armstrong	.10
20	Tyrone Hill	.10
21	Malik Sealy	.10
22	Clyde Drexler	.50
23	Aaron McKie	.10
24	Harold Miner	.10
25	Bobby Hurley	.10
26	Dell Curry	.10
27	Micheal Williams	.10
28	Adam Keefe	.10
29	Antonio Harvey	.10
30	Billy Owens	.10
31	Nate McMillan	.10
32	J.R. Reid	.10
33	Grant Hill	2.00
34	Charles Barkley	1.00
35	Tyrone Corbin	.10
36	Don MacLean	.10
37	Kenny Smith	.10
38	Juwan Howard	.50
39	Charles Smith	.10
40	Shawn Kemp	.75
41	Dana Barros	.10
42	Vin Baker	.50
43	Armon Gilliam	.10
44	Spud Webb	.10
45	Michael Jordan	6.00
46	Scott Williams	.10
47	Vlade Divac	.30
48	Roy Tarpley	.10
49	Bimbo Coles	.10
50	David Robinson	1.00
51	Terry Dehere	.10
52	Bobby Phills	.10
53	Sherman Douglas	.10
54	Rodney Rogers	.10
55	Detlef Schrempf	.25
56	Calbert Cheaney	.10
57	Tom Gugliotta	.30
58	Jeff Turner	.10
59	Mookie Blaylock	.10
60	Bill Curley	.10
61	Chris Dudley	.10
62	Popeye Jones	.10
63	Scott Burrell	.10
64	Dale Davis	.20
65	Mitchell Butler	.10
66	Pervis Ellison	.10
67	Todd Day	.10
68	Carl Herrera	.10
69	Jeff Hornacek	.25
70	Vincent Askew	.10
71	A.C. Green	.20
72	Kevin Gamble	.10
73	Chris Gatling	.10
74	Otis Thorpe	.10
75	Michael Cage	.10
76	Carlos Rogers	.10
77	Gheorghe Muresan	.10
78	Olden Polynice	.10
79	Grant Long	.10
80	Allan Houston	.40
81	Charles Outlaw	.10
82	Clarence Weatherspoon	.20
83	Tony Dumas	.10
84	Herb Williams	.10
85	P.J. Brown	.10
86	Robert Horry	.10
87	Byron Scott	.20
88	Horace Grant	.10
89	Dominique Wilkins	.50
90	Doug West	.10
91	Antoine Carr	.10
92	Dickey Simpkins	.10
93	Elden Campbell	.10
94	Kevin Johnson	.20
95	Rex Chapman	.10
96	John Williams	.10
97	Tim Hardaway	.50
98	Rik Smits	.10
99	Rex Walters	.10
100	Robert Parish	.50
101	Isaiah Rider	.20
102	Sarunas Marciulionis	.10
103	Andrew Lang	.10
104	Eric Mobley	.10
105	Randy Brown	.10
106	John Stockton	.50
107	Lamond Murray	.10
108	Will Perdue	.10
109	Wayman Tisdale	.10
110	John Starks	.10
111	John Salley	.10
112	Lucious Harris	.10
113	Jeff Malone	.10
114	Anthony Bowie	.10
115	Vinny Del Negro	.10
116	Michael Adams	.10
117	Chris Mullin	.50
118	Benoit Benjamin	.10
119	Byron Houston	.10
120	LaPhonso Ellis	.10
121	Doug Overton	.10
122	Jerome Kersey	.10
123	Greg Minor	.10
124	Christian Laettner	.25
125	Mark Price	.20
126	Kevin Willis	.20
127	Kenny Anderson	.20
128	Marty Conlon	.10
129	Blue Edwards	.10
130	Dan Schayes	.10
131	Duane Ferrell	.10
132	Charles Oakley	.30
133	Brian Grant	.30
134	Reggie Williams	.10
135	Steve Kerr	.10
136	Khalid Reeves	.10
137	David Benoit	.10
138	Derrick Coleman	.20
139	Anthony Peeler	.10
140	Jim Jackson	.25
141	Stacey Augmon	.30
142	Sam Cassell	.30
143	Derrick McKey	.10
144	Danny Ferry	.10
145	Anfernee Hardaway	1.00
146	Clifford Robinson	.25
147	B.J. Tyler	.10
148	Mark West	.10
149	David Wingate	.10
150	Willie Anderson	.10
151	Hersey Hawkins	.10
152	Bryant Stith	.10
153	Dan Majerle	.30
154	Chris Smith	.10
155	Donyell Marshall	.20
156	Loy Vaught	.10
157	Reggie Miller	.40
158	Hubert Davis	.10
159	Ron Harper	.20
160	Lee Mayberry	.10
161	Eddie Jones	.60
162	Shawn Bradley	.30
163	Nick Anderson	.20
164	Ervin Johnson	.10
165	Walt Williams	.20
166	Steve Smith FF	.10
167	Dino Radja FF	.10
168	Alonzo Mourning FF	.60
169	Michael Jordan FF	3.00
170	Tyrone Hill FF	.10
171	Jamal Mashburn FF	.50
172	Dikembe Mutombo FF	.30
173	Grant Hill FF w/Jordan	2.00
174	Latrell Sprewell FF	.30
175	Hakeem Olajuwon FF	.50
176	Reggie Miller FF	.20
177	Pooh Richardson FF	.10
178	Cedric Ceballos FF	.10
179	Glen Rice FF	.10
180	Glenn Robinson FF	.25
181	Isaiah Rider FF	.10
182	Derrick Coleman FF	.10
183	Patrick Ewing FF	.20
184	Shaquille O'Neal FF	1.00
185	Dana Barros FF	.10
186	Dan Majerle FF	.15
187	Clifford Robinson FF	.10
188	Mitch Richmond FF	.15
189	David Robinson FF	.50
190	Gary Payton FF	.30
191	Oliver Miller FF	.10
192	Karl Malone FF	.60
193	Kevin Pritchard FF	.10
194	Chris Webber FF	.50
195	Michael Jordan PD	3.00
196	Hakeem Olajuwon PD	.50
197	Vin Baker PD	.15
198	Grant Hill PD	1.50
199	Clyde Drexler PD	.75
200	Chris Webber PD	.75
201	Shawn Kemp PD	.40
202	Shaquille O'Neal PD	1.00
203	Stacey Augmon PD	.10
204	David Benoit PD	.10
205	Rodney Rogers PD	.10
206	Latrell Sprewell PD	.30
207	Brian Grant PD	.15
208	Lamond Murray PD	.10
209	Shawn Kemp CL	.50
210	Michael Jordan CL	1.50

1996 Collector's Choice International II

The Series II release was distributed in France, Germany, Italy, Latin America, Northern Europe, Portugal and Spain. The 200-card set paralleled the U.S. Series II version except that the cards are checklisted in alphabetical order by team. The set is numbered 1-200 and the values below refer to all language versions.

		MT
	Complete Set (200):	25.00
	Common Players:	.10
1	Alan Henderson	.25
2	Steve Smith	.30
3	Ken Norman	.10
4	Eric Montross	.10
5	Dino Radja	.10
6	Rick Fox	.10
7	David Wesley	.10
8	Dana Barros	.10
9	Eric Williams	.10
10	George Zidek	.10
11	Muggsy Bogues	.10
12	Kendall Gill	.10
13	Scottie Pippen	1.00
14	Bill Wennington	.10
15	Dennis Rodman	1.00
16	Toni Kukoc	.50
17	Luc Longley	.10
18	Jason Caffey	.10
19	Chris Mills	.10
20	Terrell Brandon	.30
21	Bob Sura	.10
22	Cherokee Parks	.10
23	Lorenzo Williams	.10
24	Jamal Mashburn	.25
25	Terry Davis	.10
26	Loren Meyer	.10
27	Bryant Stith	.10
28	Dikembe Mutombo	.25
29	Jalen Rose	.30
30	Tom Hammonds	.10
31	Terry Mills	.10
32	Lindsey Hunter	.10
33	Theo Ratliff	.60
34	Latrell Sprewell	.50
35	Andrew DeClercq	.10
36	B.J. Armstrong	.10
37	Clifford Rozier	.10
38	Joe Smith	2.00
39	Mark Bryant	.10
40	Mario Elie	.10
41	Hakeem Olajuwon	.75
42	Antonio Davis	.10
43	Haywoode Workman	.10
44	Mark Jackson	.10
45	Travis Best	.10
46	Brian Williams	.10
47	Rodney Rogers	.10
48	Brent Barry	.25
49	Pooh Richardson	.10
50	Gary Grant	.10
51	George Lynch	.10
52	Sedale Threatt	.10
53	Cedric Ceballos	.10
54	Sasha Danilovic	.10
55	Kurt Thomas	.10
56	Glenn Robinson	.50
57	Shawn Respert	.10
58	Eric Murdock	.10
59	Kevin Garnett	8.00
60	Kevin Edwards	.10
61	Ed O'Bannon	.10
62	Yinka Dare	.10
63	Vern Fleming	.10
64	Patrick Ewing	.25
65	Monty Williams	.10
66	Anthony Mason	.10
67	Donald Royal	.10
68	Brian Shaw	.10
69	Shaquille O'Neal	1.00
70	David Vaughn	.10
71	Vernon Maxwell	.10
72	Jerry Stackhouse	1.00
73	Sharone Wright	.10
74	Richard Dumas	.10
75	Wesley Person	.10
76	Joe Kleine	.10
77	Elliot Perry	.10
78	Danny Manning	.10
79	Michael Finley	1.00
80	Mario Bennett	.10
81	James Robinson	.10
82	Buck Williams	.10
83	Gary Trent	.60
84	Randolph Childress	.10
85	Duane Causwell	.10
86	Lionel Simmons	.10
87	Mitch Richmond	.25
88	Michael Smith	.10
89	Tyus Edney	.25
90	Corliss Williamson	.50
91	Cory Alexander	.25
92	Chuck Person	.10
93	Sean Elliott	.25
94	Doc Rivers	.10
95	Gary Payton	.50
96	Sam Perkins	.10
97	Sherell Ford	.10
98	Damon Stoudamire	1.50
99	Zan Tabak	.10
100	Felton Spencer	.10
101	Karl Malone	.75
102	Bryon Russell	.10
103	Greg Ostertag	.10
104	Bryant Reeves	.25
105	Lawrence Moten	.10
106	Greg Anthony	.10
107	Byron Scott	.30
108	Scott Skiles	.10
109	Rasheed Wallace	.50
110	Chris Webber	1.00
111	Mookie Blaylock SR	.10
112	Dee Brown SR	.10
113	Alonzo Mourning SR	.50
114	Michael Jordan SR	3.00
115	Terrell Brandon SR	.10
116	Jim Jackson SR	.25
117	Dikembe Mutombo SR	.10
118	Grant Hill SR	1.00
119	Joe Smith SR	1.00
120	Clyde Drexler SR	.25
121	Reggie Miller SR	.25
122	Lamond Murray SR	.10
123	Nick Van Exel SR	.25
124	Glen Rice SR	.30
125	Glenn Robinson SR	.50
126	Christian Laettner SR	.30
127	Kenny Anderson SR	.10
128	Patrick Ewing SR	.25
129	Shaquille O'Neal SR	1.00
130	Jerry Stackhouse SR	1.00
131	Charles Barkley SR	.50
132	Clifford Robinson SR	.10
133	Brian Grant SR	.10
134	David Robinson SR	.50
135	Shawn Kemp SR	.60
136	Damon Stoudamire SR	1.00
137	Karl Malone SR	.60
138	Bryant Reeves SR	.25
139	Juwan Howard SR	.50
140	Shaquille O'Neal PT, D. Brown PT	.50
141	Rik Smits PT	.10
142	H. Williams PT, T. Tolbert PT	.10
143	Michael Jordan PT	3.00
144	David Robinson PT	.50
145	T. Porter PT, K. Johnson PT	.25
146	Clyde Drexler PT	.60
147	Cedric Ceballos PT	.10
148	Horace Grant/ Group PT	.10
149	Reggie Miller PT	.10
150	Avery Johnson PT, Nick Van Exel PT	.10
151	Hakeem Olajuwon PT, Robert Horry PT	.10
152	Rik Smits PT	.10
153	David Robinson PT, Hakeem Olajuwon PT	.50
154	Robert Horry PT	.10
155	Kenny Smith PT	.10
156	Stacey Augmon LOVE	.10
157	Sherman Douglas LOVE	.10
158	Larry Johnson LOVE	.25
159	Scottie Pippen LOVE	.60
160	Tyrone Hill LOVE	.10
161	Jamal Mashburn LOVE	.10
162	Mahmoud Abdul-Rauf LOVE	.10
163	Grant Hill LOVE	1.00
164	Latrell Sprewell LOVE	.10
165	Sam Cassell LOVE	.20
166	Rik Smits LOVE	.10
167	Terry Dehere LOVE	.20
168	Eddie Jones LOVE	.25
169	Billy Owens LOVE	.10
170	Vin Baker LOVE	.50
171	Isaiah Rider LOVE	.10
172	Kenny Anderson LOVE	.10
173	John Starks LOVE	.10
174	Anfernee Hardaway LOVE	1.00
175	Sharone Wright LOVE	.10
176	Charles Barkley LOVE	.50
177	Clifford Robinson LOVE	.10
178	Walt Williams LOVE	.10
179	Sean Elliott LOVE	.10
180	Gary Payton LOVE	.30
181	Carlos Rogers LOVE	.10
182	John Stockton LOVE	.10
183	Greg Anthony LOVE	.10
184	Chris Webber LOVE	.50
185	Gary Payton PG	.30
186	Mookie Blaylock PG	.10
187	Charles Barkley PG	.50
188	Grant Hill PG	1.00
189	Anfernee Hardaway PG	1.00
190	Kenny Anderson PG	.10
191	Mark Jackson PG	.10
192	Karl Malone PG	.60
193	Avery Johnson PG	.10
194	Larry Johnson 40	.10
195	Nick Van Exel 40	.10
196	Vin Baker 40	.10
197	Jason Kidd 40	.50
198	David Robinson 40	1.25
199	Shawn Kemp CL	.50
200	Michael Jordan CL	1.50

1996 Collector's Choice International Japanese

The 410-card, two-series set was issued by Upper Deck for the Japanese market and the set was identical in design with the U.S. version except for the bilingual text.

		MT
	Complete Set (410):	125.00
	Complete Series 1 (210):	50.00
	Complete Series 2 (200):	75.00
	Common Player:	.20
1	Rod Strickland	.30
2	Larry Johnson	.75
3	Mahmoud Abdul-Rauf	.20
4	Joe Dumars	.50
5	Jason Kidd	3.00
6	Avery Johnson	.30
7	Dee Brown	.20
8	Brian Williams	.20
9	Nick Van Exel	.75
10	Dennis Rodman	2.00
11	Rony Seikaly	.20
12	Harvey Grant	.20
13	Craig Ehlo	.20
14	Derek Harper	.30
15	Drafted by the Raptors (Oliver Miller)	.20
16	Dennis Scott	.30
17	Drafted by the Raptors (Ed Pinckney)	.20
18	Eric Piatkowski	.30
19	B.J. Armstrong	.30
20	Tyrone Hill	.20
21	Malik Sealy	.20
22	Clyde Drexler	1.25
23	Aaron McKie	.20
24	Harold Miner	.20
25	Bobby Hurley	.30
26	Dell Curry	.20
27	Micheal Williams	.20
28	Adam Keefe	.20
29	Drafted by the Grizzlies (Antonio Harvey)	.20
30	Billy Owens	.30
31	Nate McMillan	.20
32	J.R. Reid	.20
33	Grant Hill	3.00
34	Charles Barkley	2.50
35	Traded to the Kings (Tyrone Corbin)	.20
36	Don MacLean	.20
37	Kenny Smith	.20
38	Juwan Howard	1.00
39	Charles Smith	.20
40	Shawn Kemp	1.50
41	Dana Barros	.20
42	Vin Baker	1.00
43	Armon Gilliam	.30
44	Traded to the Hawks (Spud Webb)	.30
45	Michael Jordan	6.00
46	Scott Williams	.20
47	Vlade Divac	.30
48	Roy Tarpley	.20
49	Bimbo Coles	.20
50	David Robinson	2.50
51	Terry Dehere	.20
52	Bobby Phills	.20
53	Sherman Douglas	.20
54	Traded to the Clippers (Rodney Rogers)	.20
55	Detlef Schrempf	.50
56	Calbert Cheaney	.30
57	Tom Gugliotta	.30
58	Jeff Turner	.20
59	Mookie Blaylock	.30
60	Bill Curley	.20
61	Chris Dudley	.20
62	Popeye Jones	.20
63	Scott Burrell	.20
64	Dale Davis	.30
65	Mitchell Butler	.20
66	Pervis Ellison	.20
67	Todd Day	.20
68	Carl Herrera	.20
69	Jeff Hornacek	.30
70	Vincent Askew	.20
71	A.C. Green	.30
72	Kevin Gamble	.20
73	Chris Gatling	.20
74	Otis Thorpe	.30
75	Michael Cage	.20
76	Carlos Rogers	.20
77	Gheorghe Muresan	.30
78	Olden Polynice	.20
79	Grant Long	.20
80	Allan Houston	.50
81	Charles Outlaw	.20
82	Clarence Weatherspoon	.30
83	Tony Dumas	.20
84	Herb Williams	.20
85	P.J. Brown	.20
86	Robert Horry	.50
87	Drafted by the Grizzlies (Byron Scott)	.30
88	Horace Grant	.50
89	Dominique Wilkins	.50
90	Doug West	.20
91	Antoine Carr	.20
92	Washington Bulls (Dickey Simpkins)	.20
93	Elden Campbell	.20
94	Kevin Johnson	.50
95	Traded to the Heat (Rex Chapman)	.20
96	John Williams	.30
97	Tim Hardaway	.50
98	Rik Smits	.50
99	Rex Walters	.20
100	Robert Parish	.20
101	Isaiah Rider	.30
102	Sarunas Marciulionis	.20
103	Andrew Lang	.20
104	Eric Mobley	.20
105	Randy Brown	.20
106	John Stockton	1.25
107	Lamond Murray	.20
108	Washington Bulls (Will Perdue)	.20
109	Wayman Tisdale	.30
110	John Starks	.30
111	John Salley	.20
112	Lucious Harris	.20
113	Jeff Malone	.30
114	Anthony Bowie	.20
115	Vinny Del Negro	.20
116	Michael Adams	.20
117	Chris Mullin	.50
118	Drafted by the Grizzlies (Benoit Benjamin)	.20
119	Byron Houston	.20
120	LaPhonso Ellis	.20
121	Doug Overton	.20
122	Drafted by the Grizzlies (Jerome Kersey)	.20
123	Greg Minor	.20
124	Christian Laettner	.50
125	Mark Price	.30
126	Kevin Willis	.30
127	Kenny Anderson	.30
128	Marty Conlon	.20
129	Drafted by the Grizzlies (Blue Edwards)	.20
130	Dan Schayes	.20
131	Duane Ferrell	.20
132	Charles Oakley	.30
133	Brian Grant	.30
134	Reggie Williams	.20
135	Steve Kerr	.20
136	Khalid Reeves	.20
137	David Benoit	.20
138	Derrick Coleman	.30
139	Anthony Peeler	.20
140	Jim Jackson	.75
141	Stacey Augmon	.30
142	Sam Cassell	.30
143	Derrick McKey	.20
144	Danny Ferry	.20
145	Anfernee Hardaway	3.00
146	Clifford Robinson	.50
147	Drafted by the Raptors (B.J. Tyler)	.20
148	Mark West	.20
149	Traded to the Sonics (David Wingate)	.20
150	Drafted by the Raptors (Willie Anderson)	.20
151	Traded to the Sonics (Hersey Hawkins)	.30
152	Bryant Stith	.20
153	Dan Majerle	.40
154	Chris Smith	.20
155	Donyell Marshall	.20
156	Loy Vaught	.30
157	Reggie Miller	1.25
158	Hubert Davis	.20
159	Ron Harper	.30
160	Lee Mayberry	.20
161	Eddie Jones	.60
162	Shawn Bradley	.30
163	Nick Anderson	.30
164	Ervin Johnson	.20
165	Walt Williams	.30
166	Steve Smith FF	.30
167	Dino Radja FF	.20
168	Alonzo Mourning FF	.60
169	Michael Jordan FF	3.00
170	Tyrone Hill FF	.20
171	Jamal Mashburn FF	.50
172	Dikembe Mutombo FF	.30
173	Grant Hill FF with Jordan	2.50
174	Latrell Sprewell FF	.30
175	Hakeem Olajuwon FF	1.25
176	Reggie Miller FF	.60
177	Pooh Richardson FF	.20
178	Cedric Ceballos FF	.30
179	Glen Rice FF	.30
180	Glenn Robinson FF	.75
181	Isaiah Rider FF	.20
182	Derrick Coleman FF	.20
183	Patrick Ewing FF	.60
184	Shaquille O'Neal FF	2.00
185	Dana Barros FF	.20
186	Dan Majerle FF	.30
187	Clifford Robinson FF	.30
188	Mitch Richmond FF	.30
189	David Robinson FF	1.25
190	Gary Payton FF	.50
191	Oliver Miller FF	.20
192	Karl Malone FF	.75
193	Kevin Pritchard FF	.20
194	Chris Webber FF	.75
195	Michael Jordan PD	3.00
196	Hakeem Olajuwon PD	1.00
197	Vin Baker PD	.50
198	Grant Hill PD	1.50
199	Clyde Drexler PD	.75
200	Chris Webber PD	.75
201	Shawn Kemp PD	.75
202	Shaquille O'Neal PD	2.00
203	Stacey Augmon PD	.20
204	David Benoit PD	.20
205	Rodney Rogers PD	.20
206	Latrell Sprewell PD	.30
207	Brian Grant PD	.30
208	Lamond Murray PD	.20
209	Shawn Kemp CL	.50
210	Michael Jordan CL	1.50
211	Cory Alexander	.50
212	Vernon Maxwell	.20
213	George Lynch	.20
214	Terry Mills	.20
215	Scottie Pippen	1.25
216	Donald Royal	.20
217	Wesley Person	.20
218	Antonio Davis	.20
219	Glenn Robinson	1.50
220	Jerry Stackhouse	6.00
221	James Robinson	.20
222	Chris Mills	.30
223	Chuck Person	.30
224	Duane Causwell	.20
225	Gary Payton	.75
226	Eric Montross	.30
227	Felton Spencer	.20
228	Scott Skiles	.30
229	Latrell Sprewell	.50
230	Sedale Threatt	.20
231	Mark Bryant	.20
232	Buck Williams	.20
233	Brian Williams	.20
234	Sharone Wright	.20
235	Karl Malone	1.25
236	Kevin Edwards	.20
237	Muggsy Bogues	.30
238	Mario Elie	.20
239	Rasheed Wallace	2.50
240	George Zidek	.50
241	Cedric Ceballos	.60
242	Alan Henderson	.60
243	Joe Kleine	.20
244	Patrick Ewing	1.25
245	Sasha Danilovic	.50
246	Bill Wennington	.20
247	Steve Smith	.30
248	Bryant Stith	.20
249	Dino Radja	.30
250	Monty Williams	.20
251	Andrew DeClercq	.20
252	Sean Elliott	.50
253	Rick Fox	.30
254	Lionel Simmons	.20
255	Dikembe Mutombo	.50
256	Lindsey Hunter	.20
257	Terrell Brandon	.30
258	Shawn Respert	.50
259	Rodney Rogers	.20
260	Bryon Russell	.20
261	David Wesley	.20
262	Ken Norman	.20
263	Mitch Richmond	.60
264	Sam Perkins	.30
265	Hakeem Olajuwon	2.00
266	Brian Shaw	.20
267	B.J. Armstrong	.30
268	Jalen Rose	.50
269	Bryant Reeves	1.50
270	Cherokee Parks	.60
271	Dennis Rodman	2.00
272	Kendall Gill	.20
273	Elliot Perry	.20
274	Anthony Mason	.30
275	Kevin Garnett	10.00
276	Damon Stoudamire	7.00
277	Lawrence Moten	.30
278	Ed O'Bannon	1.00
279	Toni Kukoc	.50
280	Greg Ostertag	.30
281	Tom Hammonds	.20
282	Yinka Dare	.20
283	Michael Smith	.20
284	Clifford Rozier	.20
285	Gary Trent	.60
286	Shaquille O'Neal	4.00
287	Luc Longley	.20
288	Bob Sura	.50
289	Dana Barros	.30
290	Lorenzo Williams	.20
291	Haywoode Workman	.20
292	Randolph Childress	.50
293	Doc Rivers	.30
294	Chris Webber	1.50
295	Kurt Thomas	.50
296	Greg Anthony	.20
297	Tyus Edney	.50
298	Danny Manning	.50
299	Brent Barry	.75
300	Joe Smith	5.00
301	Pooh Richardson	.20
302	Mark Jackson	.40
303	Richard Dumas	.20
304	Michael Finley	3.00
305	Theo Ratliff	1.00
306	Gary Grant	.20
307	Jamal Mashburn	1.00
308	Corliss Williamson	.60
309	Eric Williams	.60
310	Zan Tabak	.20
311	Eric Murdock	.20
312	Sherell Ford	.30
313	Terry Davis	.20
314	Vern Fleming	.20
315	Jason Caffey	.30
316	Mario Bennett	.50
317	David Vaughn	.30
318	Loren Meyer	.50
319	Travis Best	.30
320	Byron Scott	.30
321	Mookie Blaylock SR	.20
322	Dee Brown SR	.20
323	Alonzo Mourning SR	.60
324	Michael Jordan SR	3.00
325	Terrell Brandon SR	.20
326	Jim Jackson SR	.50
327	Dikembe Mutombo SR	.30
328	Grant Hill SR	1.50
329	Joe Smith SR	2.50
330	Clyde Drexler SR	.60
331	Reggie Miller SR	.60
332	Los Angeles Clippers (Lamond Murray SR)	.20
333	Nick Van Exel SR	.50
334	Glen Rice SR	.30
335	Glenn Robinson SR	.75
336	Christian Laettner SR	.30
337	Kenny Anderson SR	.20
338	Patrick Ewing SR	.60
339	Shaquille O'Neal SR	2.00
340	Jerry Stackhouse SR	2.50
341	Charles Barkley SR	1.25
342	Clifford Robinson SR	.30
343	Brian Grant SR	.30

344 David Robinson SR 1.25
345 Shawn Kemp SR 1.00
346 Damon Stoudamire SR 3.00
347 Karl Malone SR 1.00
348 Bryant Reeves SR .75
349 Juwan Howard SR .50
350 Orlando vs. Boston East Conf. 1st Round (Shaquille O'Neal PT, D. Brown PT) 1.25
351 Indiana vs Atlanta East Conf. 1st Round (Rik Smits PT) .30
352 New York vs Cleveland East Conf. 1st Round (H. Williams PT, T. Tolbert PT) .20
353 Chicago vs Charlotte East Conf. 1st Round (Michael Jordan PT) 3.00
354 San Antonio vs Denver West Conf. 1st Round (David Robinson PT) 1.25
355 Phoenix vs Portland West Conf. 1st Round (T. Porter PT, K. Johnson PT) .20
356 Houston vs Utah West Conf. 1st Round (Clyde Drexler PT) .60
357 L.A. Lakers vs Seattle West Conf. 1st Round (Cedric Ceballos PT) .30
358 Orlando vs Chicago East Conf. Semifinals (Horace Grant/ Group PT) .30
359 Indiana vs New York East Conf. Semifinals (Reggie Miller PT) .60
360 San Antonio vs L.A. Lakers West Conf. Semifinals (Avery Johnson PT, Nick Van Exel PT) .30
361 Houston vs Phoenix West Conf. Semifinals (Hakeem Olajuwon PT, Robert Horry PT) .60
362 Orlando vs Indiana East Conf. Finals (Rik Smits PT) .30
363 Houston vs San Antonio West Conf. Finals (David Robinson PT, Hakeem Olajuwon PT) 1.25
364 Houston vs Orlando NBA Finals (Robert Horry PT) .30
365 Houston Rockets 1995 NBA Champs (Kenny Smith PT) .20
366 Stacey Augmon LOVE .20
367 Sherman Douglas LOVE .20
368 Larry Johnson LOVE .60
369 Scottie Pippen LOVE .60
370 Tyrone Hill LOVE .20
371 Jamal Mashburn LOVE .50
372 Mahmoud Abdul-Rauf LOVE .20
373 Grant Hill LOVE 1.50
374 Latrell Sprewell LOVE .30
375 Sam Cassell LOVE .30
376 Rik Smits LOVE .30
377 Terry Dehere LOVE .20
378 Eddie Jones LOVE .30
379 Billy Owens LOVE .20
380 Vin Baker LOVE .40
381 Isaiah Rider LOVE .20
382 Kenny Anderson LOVE .20
383 John Starks LOVE .20
384 Anfernee Hardaway LOVE 1.25
385 Sharone Wright LOVE .20
386 Charles Barkley LOVE 1.25
387 Clifford Robinson LOVE .30
388 Walt Williams LOVE .20
389 Sean Elliott LOVE .30
390 Gary Payton LOVE .30
391 Carlos Rogers LOVE .20
392 John Stockton LOVE .75
393 Greg Anthony LOVE .20
394 Chris Webber LOVE .75
395 Gary Payton PG .40
396 Mookie Blaylock PG .20
397 Charles Barkley PG 1.25
398 Grant Hill PG 1.50
399 Anfernee Hardaway PG 1.25
400 Kenny Anderson PG .20
401 Mark Jackson PG .30
402 Karl Malone PG .75
403 Avery Johnson PG .20
404 Top Scorers (Larry Johnson 40) .60
405 Top Shooters (Nick Van Exel 40) .50
406 Top Rebounders (Vin Baker 40) .50
407 Top Passers (Jason Kidd 40) 1.00
408 Top Defenders (David Robinson 40) 1.25
409 Shawn Kemp CL .50
410 Michael Jordan CL 1.50

1996 Collector's Choice International NBA Extremes

The nine-card insert set was found every 10 Series II packs of French, German, Italian, Japanese, Latin, Northern European and Portuguese packs. The set is exclusive to the international set and is not based on any U.S. inserts.

MT
Complete Set (9): 5.00
Common Player: .50
E1 Muggsy Bogues .50
E2 Spud Webb .50
E3 Dana Barros .50
E4 Avery Johnson .50
E5 Vlade Divac .75
E6 Dikembe Mutombo .75
E7 Rik Smits .50
E8 Shawn Bradley .50
E9 Gheorghe Muresan .75

1996-97 Collector's Choice Jordan A Cut Above

This 10-card set was seeded one per Series I Wal-Mart pack and features some of Jordan's top career achievements. Cards feature a die-cut across the top and are numbered with a "CA" prefix.

MT
Complete Set (10): 20.00
Common Player: 2.50
CA1 1985 Rookie of the Year (Michael Jordan) 2.50
CA2 8-Time Scoring Leader (Michael Jordan) 2.50
CA3 8-Time All-NBA First Team (Michael Jordan) 2.50
CA4 Defensive POY (Michael Jordan) 2.50
CA5 10-Time All-Star (Michael Jordan) 2.50
CA6 2-Time All-Star Game MVP (Michael Jordan) 2.50
CA7 4-Time MVP (Michael Jordan) 2.50
CA8 4-Time Champion (Michael Jordan) 2.50
CA9 4-Time Finals MVP (Michael Jordan) 2.50
CA10 Continuing Excellence (Michael Jordan) 2.50

1996-97 Collector's Choice Los Angeles Lakers Team Set

This set consisted of nine player cards and two Gold Mini-Cards, each featuring three players. This set had an SRP of $2.99 when first released.

MT
Complete Set (11): 8.00
Common Player: .05
B1 Kobe Bryant, Elden Campbell, Derek Fisher 2.00
B2 Eddie Jones, Shaquille O'Neal, Nick Van Exel 1.50
LA1 Corie Blount .05
LA2 Kobe Bryant 4.00
LA3 Elden Campbell .10
LA4 Derek Fisher .50
LA5 Eddie Jones .75
LA6 Travis Knight .25
LA7 Shaquille O'Neal 2.00
LA8 Byron Scott .10
LA9 Nick Van Exel .30

1996-97 Collector's Choice Memorable Moments

This 10-card set was seeded one per Series I special retail pack and captured the top moments from the 1996 NBA season. Cards were die-cut across the top and bottom and numbered with a "MM" prefix.

MT
Complete Set (10): 15.00
Common Player: .50
1 Michael Jordan 10.00
2 Nick Van Exel .50
3 Karl Malone 1.00
4 Latrell Sprewell .75
5 Anfernee Hardaway 3.00
6 Glenn Robinson .75
7 Shaquille O'Neal 3.00
8 Damon Stoudamire 1.50
9 Clyde Drexler .75
10 Shawn Kemp 1.00

1996-97 Collector's Choice Miami Heat Team Set

This set included nine player cards and a blow up card of the Building A Winner subset from the 1996-97 Upper Deck set. The set had an SRP of $2.99 when initially released. Cards are numbered with a "M" prefix.

MT
Complete Set (9): 3.00
Common Player: .05
1 Keith Askins .05
2 P.J. Brown .10
3 Sasha Danilovic .05
4 Tim Hardaway .50
5 Voshon Lenard .10
6 Dan Majerle .10
7 Alonzo Mourning .50
8 Martin Muursepp .05
9 Kurt Thomas .05
--- Miami Heat BW Blow-Up 1.50

1996-97 Collector's Choice Mini-Cards 1

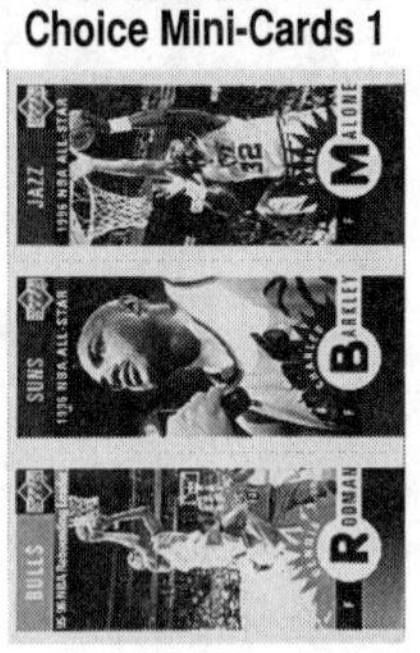

These 1996-97 Upper Deck Collector's Choice inserts offer something which hasn't been seen since the 1980-81 Topps set - three mini cards on one card. Ninety players are strategically matched up in trios, such as former UNLV players Greg Anthony, Stacy Augmon and Larry Johnson, to comprise the 30-card set. The horizontal card front is perforated, so the cards can be separated. The player's team name is in a panel at the top, which uses his team's primary color. The Upper Deck logo is also in the panel. A card title is underneath, followed by a color action photo. The player's name is at the bottom. The back has colored panels at the top, for the team names, plus a card number (using a "M" prefix). Each card also has an Upper Deck hologram on it. The middle of the card has a career summary, team logo and player's name and position. One card was inserted in each pack, but a parallel gold version was also made. These cards are seeded one per every 35 packs.

MT
Complete Set (30): 8.00
Common Player: .10
Gold Cards: 4x-8x
1 Michael Jordan, Anfernee Hardaway, Shawn Kemp 3.00
2 Stacey Augmon, Larry Johnson, Greg Anthony .25
3 Rasheed Wallace, Jerry Stackhouse, J.R. Reid .75
4 Detlef Schrempf, Toni Kukoc, Dino Radja .10
5 Matt Geiger, Dennis Scott, Travis Best .10
6 Todd Day, Oliver Miller, Andrew Lang .10
7 Sherman Douglas, Derrick Coleman, Rony Seikaly .10
8 Tyus Edney, Ed O'Bannon, George Zidek .10
9 Dennis Rodman, Charles Barkley, Karl Malone 1.50
10 Bobby Phills, Avery Johnson, Mahmoud Abdul-Rauf .10
11 Dell Curry, Bimbo Coles, Charles Oakley .10
12 Kendall Gill, Nick Anderson, Aaron McKie .10
13 Nick Van Exel, John Starks, Sam Cassell .10
14 Joe Dumars, Clyde Drexler, A.C. Green .25
15 Popeye Jones, Chris Morris, Tom Hammonds .10
16 Nate McMillan, Tom Gugliotta, Blue Edwards .10
17 Ashraf Amaya, Sharone Wright, Eric Williams .10
18 Jalen Rose, Chris Webber, Jimmy King .10
19 Randolph Childress, David Robinson, Shawn Respert .75
20 Jason Kidd, Kevin Johnson, Lamond Murray .75
21 Theo Ratliff, Shawn Bradley, Luc Longley .10
22 Chris Mullin, Jayson Williams, Terry Dehere .10
23 Cedric Ceballos, Isaiah Rider, Brent Barry .10
24 Arvydas Sabonis, Sasha Danilovic, Vlade Divac .10
25 Bobby Hurley, Christian Laettner, Grant Hill 1.25
26 Tyrone Hill, Brian Grant, Kurt Thomas .10
27 Jim Jackson, Glenn Robinson, Calbert Cheaney .25
28 Derrick McKey, Robert Horry, Keith Askins .10
29 Rex Walters, Jeff Hornacek, Mookie Blaylock .10
30 Danny Ferry, Mark Jackson, Doc Rivers .10

1996-97 Collector's Choice Mini-Cards Gold

Gold versions of all 30 Series I Mini-cards were available at a rate of one per 35 packs. The gold versions featured gold foil stamping on the front.

MT
Gold Cards: 4x-8x

1996-97 Collector's Choice Mini-Cards 2

Inserted in each pack of the second series, the 30-card insert set highlights three players on each horizontal card - identical to the first series mini cards. A gold-foil version was inserted very 35 packs.

MT
Complete Set (30): 10.00
Common Player: .10
Gold Cards: 4x-8x
1 Kevin Edwards, Doug West, Ken Norman .10
2 B.J. Armstrong, Tim Hardaway, Steve Smith .10
3 Sam Perkins, Danny Manning, Glen Rice .10
4 Dana Barros, Reggie Miller, Steve Kerr .10
5 Greg Minor, Lorenzen Wright, Samaki Walker .40
6 Clarence Weatherspoon, Kevin Willis, LaPhonso Ellis .10
7 Jason Caffey, Latrell Sprewell, Antonio McDyess .10
8 Olden Polynice, Rodney Rogers, Bob Sura .10
9 Kenny Anderson, Vinny Del Negro, Bryant Stith .10
10 Ron Harper, Eddie Jones, Lindsey Hunter .10
11 Antoine Carr, John Stockton, Otis Thorpe .20
12 Gheorghe Muresan, Hakeem Olajuwon, Rik Smits .50
13 Kevin Garnett, Jermaine O'Neal, Kobe Bryant 5.00
14 Patrick Ewing, Dikembe Mutombo, Alonzo Mourning .30
15 Scottie Pippen, Jamal Mashburn, Vin Baker .75
16 Wesley Person, Darrin Hancock, Stephon Marbury .75
17 Kerry Kittles, Marcus Camby, Allan Houston 1.50
18 Antoine Walker, Walter McCarty, John Wallace .50
19 Dale Davis, Elden Campbell, Horace Grant .10
20 Mario Elie, Tim Legler, Donald Royal .10
21 P.J. Brown, Antonio Davis, Brian Shaw .10
22 Shaquille O'Neal, Joe Smith, Allen Iverson 3.00
23 Ray Allen, Scott Burrell, Clifford Robinson .50
24 Hersey Hawkins, Will Perdue, Mitch Richmond .10
25 Sean Elliott, Terrell Brandon, Gary Payton .25
26 Tony Dumas, Johnny Newman, Doug Christie .10
27 Khalid Reeves, Chris Mills, Shareef Abdur-Rahim .50
28 Bryon Russell, Michael Smith, Lawrence Moten .10
29 Damon Stoudamire, Michael Finley, Bryant Reeves .50
30 Terry Mills, Loy Vaught, Juwan Howard .10

1996-97 Collector's Choice Mini-Cards 2 Gold

All 30 cards in the Series II Mini-Cards insert also arrived in a gold version, seeded every 35 packs. Gold versions had gold foil stamping across the front.

MT
Gold Cards: 4x-8x

1996-97 Collector's Choice Orlando Magic Team Set

This team set consists of nine player cards and two Gold Mini-Cards, each featuring three players. The set had an SRP of $2.99 when first released.

MT
Complete Set (11): 4.00
Common Player: .05
B1 Nick Anderson, Horace Grant, Anfernee Hardaway 1.00
B2 Dennis Scott, Rony Seikaly, Brian Shaw .50
OR1 Nick Anderson .10
OR2 Brian Evans .05
OR3 Horace Grant .15
OR4 Anfernee Hardaway 2.00
OR5 Derek Strong .05
OR6 Rony Seikaly .05
OR7 Dennis Scott .10
OR8 Brian Shaw .05
OR9 Gerald Wilkins .05

1996-97 Collector's Choice San Antonio Spurs Team Set

This set consists of nine player cards and a blow up card from the Building A Winner subset from the 1996-97 Upper Deck set. The set had an SRP of $2.99 when initially released. Cards are numbered with a "ST" prefix.

MT
Complete Set (9): 3.00
Common Player: .05
1 Cory Alexander .05
2 Vinny Del Negro .05
3 Sean Elliott .10
4 Carl Herrera .05
5 Avery Johnson .05
6 Will Perdue .05
7 David Robinson 1.00
8 Charles Smith .05
9 Dominique Wilkins .25
--- San Antonio Spurs Blow-Up 1.50

1996-97 Collector's Choice Seattle Supersonics Team Set

The Supersonics team set consists of nine player cards and two Gold Mini-Cards, each featuring three players. The set had an initial SRP of $2.99.

MT
Complete Set (11): 5.00
Common Player: .05
B1 Hersey Hawkins, Shawn Kemp, Nate McMillan 1.50
B2 Gary Payton, Sam Perkins, Detlef Schrempf 1.00
ST1 Craig Ehlo .05
ST2 Hersey Hawkins .10
ST3 Shawn Kemp 1.50
ST4 Jim McIlvaine .05
ST5 Nate McMillan .05
ST6 Gary Payton 1.00
ST7 Sam Perkins .10
ST8 Detlef Schrempf .10
ST9 Eric Snow .05

1996-97 Collector's Choice Stick-Ums 1

Collectors can create their own NBA action scenes with these 1996-97 Collector's Choice restickable Stick-ums inserts. The cards were seeded one per every four Series I packs. The front has an action photo of a player, plus a sticker for his name. Other stickers depict basketball terms. The back has the player's name at the top, along with a card number (which uses a "S" prefix). The player's team logo is also on the back, as is a checklist for the set.

MT
Complete Set (30): 15.00
Common Player: .25
Minor Stars: .50
1 Mookie Blaylock .25
2 Eric Montross .25
3 Larry Johnson .50
4 Dennis Rodman 2.00
5 Terrell Brandon .25
6 Jamal Mashburn .50
7 LaPhonso Ellis .25
8 Grant Hill 2.00
9 Joe Smith 1.00
10 Hakeem Olajuwon 1.00
11 Rik Smits .25
12 Brent Barry .25
13 Nick Van Exel .50
14 Predrag Danilovic .25
15 Vin Baker .50
16 Kevin Garnett 2.00
17 Shawn Bradley .25
18 Patrick Ewing .25
19 Anfernee Hardaway 2.50
20 Clarence Weatherspoon .25
21 Charles Barkley .75
22 Clifford Robinson .25
23 Mitch Richmond .25
24 David Robinson .75
25 Shawn Kemp .60
26 Damon Stoudamire 1.25
27 Karl Malone .50
28 Bryant Reeves .25
29 Gheorghe Muresan .25
30 Michael Jordan 6.00

1996-97 Collector's Choice Stick-Ums 2

The 30-card insert set, found every three packs, featured decals of top players in a similar design with the first series Stick-Ums.

MT
Complete Set (30): 10.00
Common Player: .20
Base Cards: Half Price
1 Steve Smith .20
2 Dino Radja .20
3 Glen Rice .20
4 Toni Kukoc .20
5 Bobby Phills .20
6 Jason Kidd .50
7 Antonio McDyess .40
8 Joe Dumars .20
9 Latrell Sprewell .40
10 Clyde Drexler .75
11 Reggie Miller .50
12 Loy Vaught .20
13 Eddie Jones .40
14 Alonzo Mourning .40
15 Glenn Robinson .40
16 Tom Gugliotta .20
17 Ed O'Bannon .20
18 John Starks .20
19 Anfernee Hardaway 2.00
20 Jerry Stackhouse 1.00
21 Kevin Johnson .20
22 Arvydas Sabonis .20
23 Brian Grant .20
24 Sean Elliott .20
25 Gary Payton .40
26 Zan Tabak .20
27 John Stockton .40
28 Greg Anthony .20
29 Juwan Howard .40
30 Michael Jordan 6.00

1996-97 Collector's Choice The Penny Years

MT
Complete Set (10): 15.00
Common Player: 1.50
1 Anfernee Hardaway (NBA First Round Pick) 1.50
2 Anfernee Hardaway (NBA Rookie Game MVP) 1.50
3 Anfernee Hardaway (NBA All-Rookie First Team) 1.50
4 Anfernee Hardaway (First NBA All-Star Game) 1.50
5 Anfernee Hardaway (1995 NBA Finals) 1.50
6 Anfernee Hardaway (1995 All-NBA First Team) 1.50
7 Anfernee Hardaway (Top Scoring Game) 1.50
8 Anfernee Hardaway (1996 NBA All-Star Game) 1.50
9 Anfernee Hardaway (1996 All-NBA First Team) 1.50
10 Anfernee Hardaway (Future Years) 1.50

1996-97 Upper Deck

Upper Deck was released in two, 180-card series in 1996-97. Each regular card front has a full-bleed color action photo, with a bronze and silver foil trimmed border on the left. The player's team logo is in silver in a bronze box in the lower left corner; the Upper Deck logo, also in silver, is in the upper right corner. The player's name and position are in white letters along the left side. White letters are used on the front to give a description of the game from which the photo was taken. Subsets in Series I include 29 Building a Winner and 15 The Game in Picture, while Series II has 15 Dateline: NBA and 29 Dan Patrick's From Way Downtown. There were six insert sets in Series I - Generation Excitement, Fast Break Connections, Michael Jordan Greater Heights, Predictors, Meet the Stars (one per three packs) and NBA Pickup Game (one per seven packs). There were also six inserts in Series II - four Autographs, Rookie Exclusives, Smooth Grooves, Rookie of the Year Commemorative Collection, Michael's Viewpoints and Predictors.

	MT
Complete Set (360):	50.00
Complete Series 1 (180):	30.00
Complete Series 2 (180):	20.00
Common Player:	.10
Minor Stars:	.20
Series 1 or 2 Pack (12):	2.25
Series 1 or 2 Wax Box (28):	50.00

1	Mookie Blaylock	.10
2	Alan Henderson	.10
3	Christian Laettner	.10
4	Ken Norman	.10
5	Dee Brown	.10
6	Todd Day	.10
7	Rick Fox	.10
8	Dino Radja	.10
9	Dana Barros	.10
10	Eric Williams	.10
11	Scott Burrell	.10
12	Dell Curry	.10
13	Matt Geiger	.10
14	Glen Rice	.10
15	Ron Harper	.10
16	Michael Jordan	4.00
17	Luc Longley	.10
18	Toni Kukoc	.10
19	Dennis Rodman	2.00
20	Danny Ferry	.10
21	Tyrone Hill	.10
22	Bobby Phills	.10
23	Bob Sura	.10
24	Tony Dumas	.10
25	George McCloud	.10
26	Jim Jackson	.20
27	Jamal Mashburn	.10
28	Loren Meyer	.10
29	Dale Ellis	.10
30	LaPhonso Ellis	.10
31	Tom Hammonds	.10
32	Antonio McDyess	.50
33	Joe Dumars	.10
34	Grant Hill	2.00
35	Lindsey Hunter	.10
36	Terry Mills	.10
37	Theo Ratliff	.10
38	B.J. Armstrong	.10
39	Donyell Marshall	.10
40	Chris Mullin	.10
41	Rony Seikaly	.10
42	Joe Smith	.50
43	Sam Cassell	.10
44	Clyde Drexler	.50
45	Mario Elie	.10
46	Robert Horry	.10
47	Travis Best	.10
48	Antonio Davis	.10
49	Dale Davis	.10
50	Eddie Johnson	.10
51	Derrick McKey	.10
52	Reggie Miller	.40
53	Brent Barry	.10
54	Lamond Murray	.10
55	Eric Piatkowski	.10
56	Rodney Rogers	.10
57	Loy Vaught	.10
58	*Kobe Bryant*	10.00
59	Eddie Jones	.20
60	Elden Campbell	.10
61	Shaquille O'Neal	2.00
62	Nick Van Exel	.20
63	Keith Askins	.10
64	Rex Chapman	.10
65	Sasha Danilovic	.10
66	Alonzo Mourning	.30
67	Kurt Thomas	.10
68	Tim Hardaway	.10
69	*Ray Allen*	3.00
70	Johnny Newman	.10
71	Shawn Respert	.10
72	Glenn Robinson	.40
73	Tom Gugliotta	.10
74	*Stephon Marbury*	4.00
75	Terry Porter	.10
76	Doug West	.10
77	Shawn Bradley	.10
78	Kevin Edwards	.10
79	Vern Fleming	.10
80	Ed O'Bannon	.10
83	Patrick Ewing	.40
84	Charlie Ward	.10
85	Nick Anderson	.10
86	Anfernee Hardaway	2.50
87	Jon Koncak	.10
88	Donald Royal	.10
89	Brian Shaw	.10
90	Derrick Coleman	.10
91	*Allen Iverson*	6.00
92	Jerry Stackhouse	.75
93	Clarence Weatherspoon	.20
94	Charles Barkley	.50
95	Kevin Johnson	.10
96	Danny Manning	.10
97	Elliot Perry	.10
98	Wayman Tisdale	.10
99	Randolph Childress	.10
100	Aaron McKie	.10
101	Arvydas Sabonis	.25
102	Gary Trent	.10
103	Chris Dudley	.10
104	Tyus Edney	.10
105	Brian Grant	.10
106	Bobby Hurley	.10
107	Olden Polynice	.10
108	Corliss Williamson	.10
109	Vinny Del Negro	.10
110	Avery Johnson	.10
111	Will Perdue	.10
112	David Robinson	.75
113	Hersey Hawkins	.10
114	Shawn Kemp	.50
115	Nate McMillan	.10
116	Detlef Schrempf	.10
117	Gary Payton	.20
118	*Marcus Camby*	2.50
119	Zan Tabak	.10
120	Damon Stoudamire	1.25
121	Carlos Rogers	.10
122	Sharone Wright	.10
123	Antoine Carr	.10
124	Jeff Hornacek	.10
125	Adam Keefe	.10
126	Chris Morris	.10
127	John Stockton	.40
128	Blue Edwards	.10
129	*Shareef Abdur-Rahim*	2.50
130	Bryant Reeves	.30
131	Roy Rogers	.20
132	Calbert Cheaney	.10
133	Tim Legler	.10
134	Gheorghe Muresan	.10
135	Chris Webber	.30
136	Atlanta	.10
137	Boston	.10
138	Charlotte	.10
139	Chicago	1.00
140	Cleveland	.10
141	Dallas	.25
142	Denver	.25
143	Detroit	.50
144	Golden State	.20
145	Houston	.50
146	Indiana	.20
147	Los Angeles Clippers	.10
148	Los Angeles Lakers	.75
149	Miami	.10
150	Milwaukee	.10
151	Minnesota	.40
152	New Jersey	.10
153	New York	.10
154	Orlando	.50
155	Philadelphia	.25
156	Phoenix	.10
157	Portland	.10
158	Sacramento	.10
159	San Antonio	.30
160	Seattle	.40
161	Toronto	.30
162	Utah	.30
163	Vancouver	.40
164	Washington	.25
165	(Michael Jordan)	2.00
166	(Corliss Williamson)	.10
167	(Dell Curry)	.10
168	(John Starks)	.10
169	(Clyde Drexler)	.25
170	(Chris Webber, Latrell Sprewell)	.10
171	(Cedric Ceballos)	.10
172	(Theo Ratliff)	.10
173	(Anfernee Hardaway)	1.00
174	(Grant Hill)	.75
175	(Alonzo Mourning)	.10
176	(Shawn Kemp)	.30
177	(Jason Kidd)	.75
178	(Avery Johnson)	.10
179	(Gary Payton)	.10
180	Checklist	.10
181	*Priest Lauderdale*	.10
182	Dikembe Mutombo	.10
183	Eldridge Recasner	.10
184	Steve Smith	.10
185	Pervis Ellison	.10
186	Greg Minor	.10
187	*Antoine Walker*	2.00
188	David Wesley	.10
189	Muggsy Bogues	.10
190	*Tony Delk*	.50
191	Vlade Divac	.10
192	Anthony Mason	.10
193	George Zidek	.10
194	Jason Caffey	.10
195	Steve Kerr	.10
196	Robert Parish	.10
197	Scottie Pippen	1.00
198	Terrell Brandon	.10
199	Antonio Lang	.10
200	Chris Mills	.10
201	*Vitaly Potapenko*	.10
202	Mark West	.10
203	Chris Gatling	.10
204	Derek Harper	.10
205	Jason Kidd	1.00
206	Eric Montross	.10
207	*Samaki Walker*	.40
208	Mark Jackson	.10
209	Ervin Johnson	.10
210	Sarunas Marciulionis	.10
211	Ricky Pierce	.10
212	Bryant Stith	.10
213	Stacey Augmon	.10
214	Grant Long	.10
215	Rick Mahorn	.10
216	Otis Thorpe	.10
217	*Jerome Williams*	.10
218	Bimbo Coles	.10
219	*Todd Fuller*	.20
220	Mark Price	.10
221	Felton Spencer	.10
222	Latrell Sprewell	.25
223	Charles Barkley	.50
224	*Othella Harrington*	.25
225	Hakeem Olajuwon	.75
226	*Matt Maloney*	.30
227	Kevin Willis	.10
228	*Erick Dampier*	.40
229	Duane Ferrell	.10
230	Jalen Rose	.10
231	Rik Smits	.10
232	Terry Dehere	.10
233	Charles Outlaw	.10
234	Pooh Richardson	.10
235	Malik Sealy	.10
236	*Lorenzen Wright*	.10
237	Cedric Ceballos	.10
238	*Derek Fisher*	.30
239	*Travis Knight*	.30
240	Sean Rooks	.10
241	Byron Scott	.10
242	P.J. Brown	.10
243	*Voshon Lenard*	.25
244	Dan Majerle	.10
245	*Martin Muursepp*	.10
246	Gary Grant	.10
247	Vin Baker	.30
248	Armon Gilliam	.10
249	Andrew Lang	.10
250	Elliot Perry	.10
251	Kevin Garnett	2.00
252	*Shane Heal*	.10
253	Cherokee Parks	.10
254	*Stojko Vrankovic*	.10
255	Kendall Gill	.10
256	*Kerry Kittles*	1.50
257	Xavier McDaniel	.10
258	Robert Pack	.10
259	Chris Childs	.10
260	Allan Houston	.10
261	Larry Johnson	.20
262	*Dontae Jones*	.25
263	*Walter McCarty*	.10
264	Charles Oakley	.10
265	*John Wallace*	.75
266	Buck Williams	.10
267	Brian Evans	.10
268	Horace Grant	.10
269	Dennis Scott	.10
270	Rony Seikaly	.10
271	David Vaughn	.10
272	Michael Cage	.10
273	Lucious Harris	.10
274	Don MacLean	.10
275	Mark Davis	.10
276	Sam Cassell	.10
277	Michael Finley	.25
278	A.C. Green	.10
279	Robert Horry	.10
280	*Steve Nash*	1.00
281	Wesley Person	.10
282	Kenny Anderson	.10
283	*Aleksandar Djordjevic*	.10
284	*Jermaine O'Neal*	1.50
285	Isaiah Rider	.10
286	Clifford Robinson	.10
287	Rasheed Wallace	.10
288	Mahmoud Abdul-Rauf	.10
289	Billy Owens	.10
290	Mitch Richmond	.25
291	Michael Smith	.10
292	Cory Alexander	.10
293	Sean Elliott	.10
294	Vernon Maxwell	.10
295	Dominique Wilkins	.10
296	Craig Ehlo	.10
297	Jim McIlvaine	.10
298	Sam Perkins	.10
299	Steve Scheffler	.10
300	Hubert Davis	.10
301	Popeye Jones	.10
302	Donald Whiteside	.10
303	Walt Williams	.10
304	Karl Malone	.30
305	Greg Ostertag	.10
306	Bryon Russell	.10
307	Jamie Watson	.10
308	Greg Anthony	.10
309	George Lynch	.10
310	Lawrence Moten	.10
311	Anthony Peeler	.10
312	Juwan Howard	.50
313	Tracy Murray	.10
314	Rod Strickland	.10
315	Harvey Grant	.10
316	Charles Barkley	.25
317	Clyde Drexler	.20
318	Dikembe Mutombo	.10
319	Larry Johnson	.10
320	Shaquille O'Neal	1.25
321	Mookie Blaylock	.10
322	Tim Hardaway	.10
323	Dennis Rodman	.75
324	Dan Majerle	.10
325	Stacey Augmon	.10
326	Anthony Mason	.10
327	Kenny Anderson	.10
328	Mahmoud Abdul-Rauf	.10
329	Chris Webber	.25
330	Dominique Wilkins	.10
331	Dikembe Mutombo	.10
332	Dana Barros	.10
333	Glen Rice	.10
334	Dennis Rodman	.75
335	Terrell Brandon	.10
336	Jason Kidd	.75
337	Antonio McDyess	.10
338	Grant Hill	1.00
339	Joe Smith	.25
340	Charles Barkley	.25
341	Reggie Miller	.20
342	Brent Barry	.10
343	Shaquille O'Neal	1.25
344	Alonzo Mourning	.20
345	Glenn Robinson	.10
346	Stephon Marbury	1.50
347	Kerry Kittles	.75
348	Patrick Ewing	.10
349	Anfernee Hardaway	1.00
350	Allen Iverson	2.00
351	Danny Manning	.10
352	Arvydas Sabonis	.10
353	Mitch Richmond	.10
354	David Robinson	.25
355	Shawn Kemp	.20
356	Marcus Camby	1.25
357	Karl Malone	.10
358	Shareef Abdur-Rahim	1.00
359	Gheorghe Muresan	.10
360	Checklist	.10

1996-97 Upper Deck Autographs

		MT
Complete Set (4):		550.00
Common Player:		100.00
Production 500 Sets		
A1	Anfernee Hardaway	250.00
A2	Shawn Kemp	100.00
A3	Antonio McDyess	100.00
A4	Damon Stoudamire	100.00

1996-97 Upper Deck Ball Park Jordan

This five-card set was inserted one per specially marked package of Ball Park hot dogs. Each card features a color photo with team and NBA logos airbrushed out. The same picture is featured on the card back along with biographical information. The Ball Park and Upper Deck logos are prominent on the cards. A gold version was also available by redeeming 4 UPC symbols from Ball Park products.

		MT
Complete Set (5):		50.00
Common Player:		10.00
1	Inside Offense (Michael Jordan)	10.00
2	Outside Offense (Michael Jordan)	10.00
3	Defense (Michael Jordan)	10.00
4	Competitive Desire (Michael Jordan)	10.00
5	Role Model (Michael Jordan)	10.00

1996-97 Upper Deck Fast Break Connections

Ten of the NBA's most exciting fast break triple threats are featured on these 1996-97 Upper Deck inserts. Each set of three die-cut cards, each numbered using a "FB" prefix, combines into one oversized card. This 30-card insert set is seeded one card per every four retail packs, and one per every two magazine packs.

		MT
Complete Set (30):		70.00
Common Player:		.75
1	Jim Jackson	3.00
2	Jason Kidd	4.00
3	Jamal Mashburn	3.00
4	Mario Elie	.75
5	Hakeem Olajuwon	6.00
6	Clyde Drexler	4.00
7	Cedric Ceballos	.75
8	Nick Van Exel	3.00
9	Eddie Jones	3.00
10	Danny Manning	.75
11	Michael Finley	2.00
12	Kevin Johnson	.75
13	Tyus Edney	.75
14	Brian Grant	.75
15	Mitch Richmond	.75
16	Sean Elliott	.75
17	David Robinson	5.00
18	Avery Johnson	.75
19	Shawn Kemp	4.00
20	Gary Payton	4.00
21	Detlef Schrempf	.75
22	Scottie Pippen	8.00
23	Michael Jordan	30.00
24	Toni Kukoc	.75
25	Sherman Douglas	.75
26	Glenn Robinson	3.00
27	Vin Baker	3.00
28	Jeff Hornacek	.75
29	John Stockton	3.00
30	Karl Malone	3.00

1996-97 Upper Deck Generation Excitement

Some of the game's top young stars are featured on these 1996-97 Upper Deck Series I die-cut inserts. Each card front has a color action photo of the player, with a closeup shot of him as the background. "Generation" is in the upper left corner; "Excitement" is in the lower left corner. The player's name is along the bottom. "Generation Excitement" and the Upper Deck logo are at the top. Cards, numbered using a "GE" prefix, were seeded one per every 36 packs.

		MT
Complete Set (20):		200.00
Common Player:		2.00
1	Steve Smith	2.00
2	Eric Williams	2.00
3	Jason Kidd	10.00
4	Antonio McDyess	10.00
5	Grant Hill	45.00
6	Joe Smith	14.00
7	Brent Barry	2.00
8	Eddie Jones	12.00
9	Vin Baker	6.00
10	Kevin Garnett	45.00
11	Ed O'Bannon	2.00
12	Anfernee Hardaway	30.00
13	Jerry Stackhouse	14.00
14	Michael Finley	10.00
15	Gary Trent	2.00
16	Tyus Edney	2.00
17	Sean Elliott	2.00
18	Shawn Kemp	10.00
19	Damon Stoudamire	20.00
20	Gheorghe Muresan	2.00

1996 Upper Deck German Kellogg's

This 40-card set was produced by Upper Deck and distributed three per German Kellogg's Frosties or Chocos box. The cards have identical front and back designs to the 1995-96 Upper Deck cards, except the lack of gold foil on the player's name on front.

		MT
Complete Set (40):		100.00
Common Player:		1.00
1	Jerry Stackhouse	12.00
2	Clifford Robinson	2.00
3	Glenn Robinson	4.00
4	Chris Webber	8.00
5	Dennis Rodman	6.00
6	Scottie Pippen	6.00
7	Toni Kukoc	3.00
8	Dan Majerle	1.00
9	Dino Radja	1.00
10	Loy Vaught	1.00
11	Bryant Reeves	1.00
12	Stacey Augmon	1.00
13	Kevin Willis	1.00
14	Muggsy Bogues	1.00
15	John Stockton	4.00
16	Karl Malone	6.00
17	Mitch Richmond	4.00
18	Charles Oakley	1.00
19	Nick Van Exel	2.00
20	Anfernee Hardaway	6.00
21	Horace Grant	2.00
22	Jason Kidd	6.00
23	Ed O'Bannon	2.00
24	Dikembe Mutombo	1.00
25	Dale Davis	1.00
26	Derrick McKey	1.00
27	Mark Jackson	2.00
28	Rik Smits	1.00
29	Grant Hill	12.00
30	Damon Stoudamire	6.00
31	Clyde Drexler	5.00
32	Hakeem Olajuwon	6.00
33	Detlef Schrempf	2.00
34	Gary Payton	6.00
35	Hersey Hawkins	1.00
36	Sam Perkins	1.00
37	David Robinson	6.00
38	Charles Barkley	6.00
39	Christian Laettner	2.00
40	B.J. Armstrong	1.00

1996-97 Upper Deck Italian Stickers

This 186-sticker set is similar to the 1996-97 Collector's Choice American set. The stickers measure 2" x 4". A sticker album was also produced.

		MT
Complete Set (186):		40.00
Common Player:		.10
1	NBA Logo	.10
2	Western Conference Logo	.10
3	Eastern Conference Logo	.10
4	Golden State Warriors Logo	.10
5	B.J. Armstrong	.10
6	Joe Smith	2.00
7	Donyell Marshall	.20
8	Rony Seikaly	.10
9	Chris Mullin	.20
10	Los Angeles Clippers Logo	.10
11	Rodney Rogers	.10
12	Brent Barry	.50
13	Lamond Murray	.10
14	Pooh Richardson	.10
15	Loy Vaught	.20
16	Los Angeles Lakers Logo	.10
17	Cedric Ceballos	.20
18	George Lynch	.10
19	Eddie Jones	1.00
20	Anthony Peeler	.10
21	Nick Van Exel	.40
22	Phoenix Suns Logo	.10
23	Charles Barkley	.60
24	Wayman Tisdale	.10
25	Wesley Person	.20
26	A.C. Green	.10
27	Danny Manning	.10
28	Portland Trail Blazers Logo	.10
29	Harvey Grant	.10
30	Aaron McKie	.10
31	Gary Trent	.20
32	Buck Williams	.10
33	Clifford Robinson	.10
34	Sacramento Kings Logo	.10
35	Billy Owens	.10
36	Brian Grant	.20
37	Tyus Edney	.10
38	Olden Polynice	.10
39	Mitch Richmond	.40
40	Seattle Supersonics Logo	.10
41	Nate McMillian	.10
42	Vincent Askew	.10
43	Hersey Hawkins	.10
44	Detlef Schrempf	.10
45	Shawn Kemp	.75
46	Dallas Mavericks Logo	.10
47	Tony Dumas	.10
48	Jim Jackson	.20
49	Loren Meyer	.10
50	Jamal Mashburn	.30
51	Jason Kidd	.60
52	Denver Nuggets Logo	.10
53	Mahmoud Abdul-Rauf	.10
54	Antonio McDyess	1.50
55	Tom Hammonds	.10
56	Dale Ellis	.10
57	LaPhonso Ellis	.20
58	Houston Rockets Logo	.10
59	Hakeem Olajuwon	1.00
60	Mario Elie	.10
61	Robert Horry	.10
62	Chucky Brown	.10
63	Clyde Drexler	.50
64	Minnesota Timberwolves Logo	.10
65	Kevin Garnett	5.00
66	Terry Porter	.10
67	Sam Mitchell	.10
68	Tom Gugliotta	.30
69	Isaiah Rider	.20
70	San Antonio Spurs Logo	.10
71	Avery Johnson	.10
72	Vinny Del Negro	.10
73	Sean Elliott	.20
74	Will Perdue	.10
75	David Robinson	.60
76	Utah Jazz Logo	.10
77	Jeff Hornacek	.10
78	Chris Morris	.10
79	Antoine Carr	.10
80	Karl Malone	.50
81	John Stockton	.40
82	Vancouver Grizzlies Logo	.10
83	Shareef Abdur-Rahim	5.00
84	Blue Edwards	.10
85	Bryant Reeves	1.00
86	Lawrence Moten	.10
87	Greg Anthony	.10
88	Bulls Victory Tour (Michael Jordan)	2.50
89	Bulls Victory Tour (Michael Jordan)	2.50
90	Bulls Victory Tour (Michael Jordan)	2.50
91	Bulls Victory Tour (Michael Jordan)	2.50
92	Bulls Victory Tour (Scottie Pippen)	1.00
93	Bulls Victory Tour (Luc Longley)	.10
94	Bulls Victory Tour (Luc Longley)	.10
95	Bulls Victory Tour (Toni Kukoc)	.20
96	Bulls Victory Tour (Toni Kukoc)	.20
97	Atlanta Hawks Logo	.10
98	Grant Long	.10
99	Mookie Blaylock	.20
100	Christian Laettner	.30
101	Ken Norman	.10
102	Stacey Augmon	.10
103	Charlotte Hornets Logo	.10
104	Dell Curry	.10
105	Scott Burrell	.10
106	Matt Geiger	.10
107	Muggsy Bogues	.10
108	Glen Rice	.40
109	Chicago Bulls Logo	.10
110	Steve Kerr	.10
111	Dennis Rodman	2.50
112	Scottie Pippen	1.25
113	Luc Longley	.10
114	Michael Jordan	5.00
115	Cleveland Cavaliers Logo	.10
116	Terrell Brandon	.30
117	Bobby Phills	.10
118	Tyrone Hill	.10
119	Bob Sura	.60
120	Danny Ferry	.10
121	Detroit Pistons Logo	.10
122	Joe Dumars	.20
123	Theo Ratliff	.50
124	Lindsey Hunter	.20
125	Terry Mills	.10
126	Grant Hill	2.50
127	Indiana Pacers Logo	.10
128	Derrick McKey	.10
129	Eddie Johnson	.10
130	Travis Best	.40
131	Mark Jackson	.10
132	Rik Smits	.10
133	Milwaukee Bucks Logo	.10
134	Vin Baker	.40
135	Shawn Respert	.10
136	Sherman Douglas	.10
137	Johnny Newman	.10
138	Glenn Robinson	.50
139	Toronto Raptors Logo	.10
140	Sharone Wright	.10
141	Zan Tabak	.10
142	Doug Christie	.10
143	Damon Stoudamire	3.00
144	Oliver Miller	.10
145	Boston Celtics Logo	.10
146	Dana Barros	.10
147	Rick Fox	.10
148	David Wesley	.10
149	Eric Williams	.40
150	Dee Brown	.10
151	Miami Heat Logo	.10
152	Rex Chapman	.10
153	Kurt Thomas	.40
154	Keith Askins	.10
155	Walt Williams	.10
156	Alonzo Mourning	.10
157	New Jersey Nets Logo	.10
158	Kendall Gill	.20
159	Jayson Williams	.10

160	Kevin Edwards	.10
161	Shawn Bradley	.20
162	Ed O'Bannon	.10
163	New York Knicks Logo	.10
164	Gary Grant	.10
165	J.R. Reid	.10
166	Charles Oakley	.10
167	John Starks	.20
168	Patrick Ewing	.40
169	Orlando Magic Logo	.10
170	Nick Anderson	.20
171	Brian Shaw	.10
172	Anfernee Hardaway	2.00
173	Dennis Scott	.20
174	Shaquille O'Neal	1.50
175	Philadelphia 76ers Logo	.10
176	Allen Iverson	8.00
177	Rex Walters	.10
178	Clarence Weatherspoon	.10
179	Jerry Stackhouse	2.00
180	Derrick Coleman	.20
181	Washington Bullets Logo	.10
182	Calbert Cheaney	.10
183	Chris Webber	1.00
184	Tim Legler	.10
185	Gheorghe Muresan	.20
186	Rasheed Wallace	1.00
NNO	Sticker Album	4.00

1996-97 Upper Deck Italian Stickers Eurostar

Inserted into packs of 1996-97 Upper Deck Italian stickers, this 10-sticker set features NBA players from Europe. They are similar to the regular set but feature silver borders. They are numbered with an "ES" prefix.

		MT
Complete Set (10):		4.00
Common Player:		.25
1	Sasha Danilovic	.25
2	Vlade Divac	.50
3	Toni Kukoc	1.00
4	Gheorghe Muresan	.75
5	Dino Radja	.25
6	Arvydas Sabonis	.25
7	Detlef Schrempf	.50
8	Rik Smits	.50
9	Zan Tabak	.25
10	George Zidek	.25

1996-97 Upper Deck Jordan Greater Heights

These 1996-97 Upper Deck Series I inserts focus on one of the greatest NBA players ever - Michael Jordan. Many of his spectacular drives to the hoop are featured on these cards, seeded one per every 71 packs. The card number uses a "GH" prefix.

		MT
Complete Set (10):		200.00
Common Player:		20.00
1	Michael Jordan	20.00
2	Michael Jordan	20.00
3	Michael Jordan	20.00
4	Michael Jordan	20.00
5	Michael Jordan	20.00
6	Michael Jordan	20.00
7	Michael Jordan	20.00
8	Michael Jordan	20.00
9	Michael Jordan	20.00
10	Michael Jordan	20.00

1996-97 Upper Deck Jordan's Viewpoints

The 10-card, laser-engraved set is inserted every 34 packs and features Michael Jordan's views on different game subjects such as halftime, talking with the media, shooting free throws and handling pressure. The horizontal design has two color photos on the front with a Jordan quote and a die-cut image of Jordan flying toward the hoop in the upper left corner. The backs have another Jordan quote with an action shot. A silver-foil "MVP 23" logo is on the front with the same logo in gray print also found on the back. The card number uses a "VP" prefix.

		MT
Complete Set (10):		160.00
Common Player:		16.00
		16.00
1	Michael Jordan	
2	Michael Jordan	16.00
3	Michael Jordan	16.00
4	Michael Jordan	16.00
5	Michael Jordan	16.00
6	Michael Jordan	16.00
7	Michael Jordan	16.00
8	Michael Jordan	16.00
9	Michael Jordan	16.00
10	Michael Jordan	16.00

1996 Upper Deck Nestle Slam Dunk

This 40-card set was produced by Upper Deck and distributed in Nestle Crunch bars. The design is the same as the 1996-97 Collectors Choice set but has a "Slam Dunk Series" logo at the bottom.

		MT
Complete Set (40):		60.00
Common Player:		.50
1	Grant Long	.50
2	Scott Burrell	.50
3	Ron Harper	1.00
4	Michael Jordan	20.00
5	Scottie Pippen	5.00
6	Bobby Phills	.50
7	Tyrone Hill	.50
8	Tony Dumas	.50
9	LaPhonso Ellis	.50
10	Antonio McDyess	4.00
11	Theo Ratliff	2.00
12	Joe Smith	2.00
13	Rodney Rogers	.50
14	Brent Barry	1.00
15	Cedric Ceballos	.50
16	Eddie Jones	2.00
17	Vlade Divac	.50
18	Anthony Peeler	.50
19	Kurt Thomas	.50
20	Vin Baker	1.00
21	Kevin Garnett	12.00
22	Shawn Bradley	.50
23	Ed O'Bannon	.50
24	Nick Anderson	.50
25	Clarence Weatherspoon	.50
26	Jerry Stackhouse	5.00
27	Charles Barkley	3.00
28	Gary Trent	1.00
29	Brian Grant	.50
30	Olden Polynice	.50
31	Will Perdue	.50
32	Vincent Askew	.50
33	Doug Christie	.50
34	Chris Morris	.50
35	Chris Webber	8.00
36	Grant Hill	10.00
37	Alonzo Mourning	2.00
38	Dee Brown	.50
39	Shawn Kemp	1.50
40	Rasheed Wallace	4.00

1996-97 Upper Deck Predictor Scoring 1

This interactive insert is based on the above-average game output of 30 NBA players. If the player reaches the performance goal printed on the front of the card, the card is a winner and can be redeemed for an SP-quality replacement. Cards were seeded one per every 23 Series I packs. Cards are numbered with a "P" prefix.

		MT
Complete Set (20):		50.00
Common Player:		1.00
Minor Stars:		2.00
Inserted 1:23		
TV Cel Cards:		2x
1	Mookie Blaylock	1.00
2	Dino Radja	1.00
3	Michael Jordan	30.00
4	Terrell Brandon	2.00
5	Jason Kidd	6.00
6	Joe Dumars	1.00
7	Joe Smith	3.00
8	Hakeem Olajuwon	5.00
9	Rik Smits	1.00
10	Brent Barry	1.00
11	Kurt Thomas	1.00
12	Anfernee Hardaway	10.00
13	Clarence Weatherspoon	1.00
14	Clifford Robinson	1.00
15	Mitch Richmond	2.00
16	David Robinson	4.00
17	Shawn Kemp	3.00
18	Damon Stoudamire	5.00
19	Karl Malone	3.00
20	Bryant Reeves	1.00

1996-97 Upper Deck Predictor Scoring 2

The 20-card insert set parallels in design the first series Predictor cards. Inserted every 25 packs, the player cards feature a statistic (such as 35 points) that the player had to reach during the 1996-97 season. The winning cards could then be traded in for an SP-quality card of the same player. Cards are numbered with a "P" prefix.

		MT
Complete Set (20):		80.00
Common Player:		1.00
Minor Stars:		2.00
Inserted 1:23		
TV Cel Cards:		2x
1	Glen Rice	2.00
2	Michael Jordan	30.00
3	Jamal Mashburn	1.00
4	Antonio McDyess	3.00
5	Charles Barkley	3.00
6	Reggie Miller	2.00
7	Shaquille O'Neal	10.00
8	Alonzo Mourning	2.00
9	Vin Baker	4.00
10	Kevin Garnett	15.00
11	Kerry Kittles	3.00
12	Patrick Ewing	2.00
13	Anfernee Hardaway	10.00
14	Allen Iverson	15.00
15	Robert Horry	1.00
16	Shawn Kemp	3.00
17	Marcus Camby	3.00
18	John Stockton	2.00
19	Shareef Abdur-Rahim	6.00
20	Juwan Howard	3.00

1996-97 Upper Deck Rookie of the Year Collection

The die-cut Commemorative Collection cards feature silver-foil printing with "Rookie Of The Year" printed along the left border and "Commemorative Collection" printed down the right border. The card front features a player cut-out design with the backs having rookie season highlights the player's rookie campaign. The cards are numbered with an "RC" prefix.

		MT
Complete Set (14):		300.00
Common Player:		5.00
1	Damon Stoudamire	15.00
2	Grant Hill	60.00
3	Jason Kidd	10.00
4	Chris Webber	15.00
5	Shaquille O'Neal	50.00
6	Larry Johnson	5.00
7	Derrick Coleman	5.00
8	David Robinson	15.00
9	Mitch Richmond	5.00
10	Mark Jackson	5.00
11	Chuck Person	5.00
12	Patrick Ewing	10.00
13	Michael Jordan	120.00
14	Buck Williams	5.00

1996-97 Upper Deck Rookie Exclusives

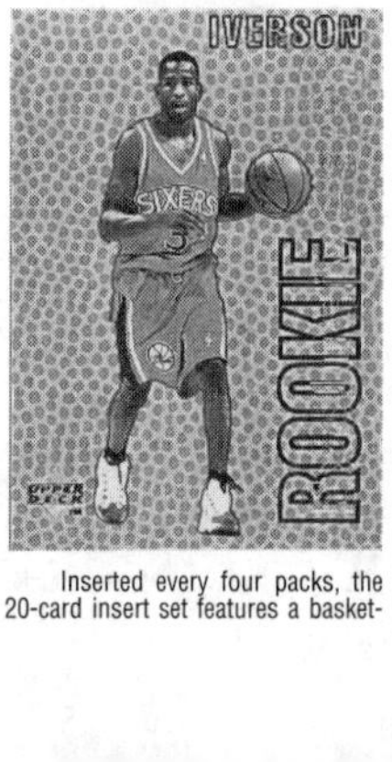

Inserted every four packs, the 20-card insert set features a basketball, leather-grain face with the player's last name featured in black in the upper right corner (the first name is in silver foil). "Exclusives 97" is printed in silver foil up the right edge. The backs feature Q & A and a player close-up and are numbered with an "R" prefix.

		MT
Complete Set (20):		60.00
Common Player:		.75
1	Allen Iverson	12.00
2	John Wallace	2.00
3	Kerry Kittles	4.00
4	Roy Rogers	1.50
5	Marcus Camby	6.00
6	Antoine Walker	6.00
7	Ray Allen	4.00
8	Samaki Walker	1.50
9	Walter McCarty	.75
10	Kobe Bryant	20.00
11	Shareef Abdur-Rahim	8.00
12	Dontae Jones	.75
13	Todd Fuller	.75
14	Lorenzen Wright	.75
15	Stephon Marbury	10.00
16	Vitaly Potapenko	.75
17	Tony Delk	1.50
18	Steve Nash	1.50
19	Jermaine O'Neal	2.50
20	Erick Dampier	1.50

1996-97 Upper Deck Smooth Grooves

The 15-card insert set, inserted every 72 packs, honors the "slick" players of the league such as Jason Kidd, Damon Stoudamire, Allen Iverson, Vin Baker, Anfernee Hardaway and Kevin Garnett. Cards are numbered with a "SG" prefix.

		MT
Complete Set (15):		300.00
Common Player:		5.00
1	Dennis Rodman	20.00
2	Jason Kidd	5.00
3	Grant Hill	40.00
4	Damon Stoudamire	10.00
5	Shaquille O'Neal	30.00
6	Clyde Drexler	10.00
7	Shareef Abdur-Rahim	25.00
8	Michael Jordan	90.00
9	Alonzo Mourning	5.00
10	Allen Iverson	40.00
11	Vin Baker	5.00
12	Kevin Garnett	40.00
13	Anfernee Hardaway	30.00
14	Jerry Stackhouse	10.00
15	Shawn Kemp	10.00

1996 Upper Deck USA

The men and women who made up the USA Olympic basketball teams are captured on this Upper Deck all die-cut set. The 72-card regular issue set has 48 Career Highlights, 12 Portraits of Power and 12 USA Woman-Shooting for Gold cards. Cards were available in hobby and retail packs. Insert sets include Michael Jordan - Made in the USA; two versions of SP Career Highlights (regular and die cut); Follow Your Dreams; and Autograph Trade cards. These rare redemption cards, seeded one per every 380 packs, are redeemable for exclusive gold-foiled autographed cards of the USA Men's Team.

		MT
Complete Set (62):		10.00
Common Player:		.10
Cards 41-48,59 and 60 are available through a USA Trade Card.		
1	Anfernee Hardaway (1994 NBA Rookie Game MVP)	1.00
2	Anfernee Hardaway (1994 All-Rookie 1st Team)	1.00
3	Anfernee Hardaway (Two-Time NBA All-Star)	1.00
4	Anfernee Hardaway (USA Basketball Record)	1.00
5	Grant Hill (1995 NBA All-Star Starter)	.50
6	Grant Hill (1995 NBA Co-Rookie of the Year)	.50
7	Grant Hill (1996 NBA All-Star)	.50
8	Grant Hill (USA Basketball Record)	.50
9	Karl Malone (1986 NBA All-Rookie Team)	.20
10	Karl Malone (Two-time NBA All-Star MVP)	.20
11	Karl Malone (20,000 Career Points)	.20
12	Karl Malone (USA Basketball Record)	.20
13	Reggie Miller (The Early Years)	.20
14	Reggie Miller (Playoff Hero)	.20
15	Reggie Miller (NBA All-Star Selections)	.20
16	Reggie Miller (USA Basketball Record)	.20
17	Shaquille O'Neal (1993 NBA Rookie of the Year)	.75
18	Shaquille O'Neal (All-NBA Selections)	.75
19	Shaquille O'Neal (NBA All-Star Selections)	.75
20	Shaquille O'Neal (USA Basketball Record)	.75
21	Hakeem Olajuwon (1985 NBA All-Rookie Team)	.30
22	Hakeem Olajuwon (NBA All-Star Selections)	.30
23	Hakeem Olajuwon (1994 NBA Most Valuable Player)	.30
24	Hakeem Olajuwon (USA Basketball Preview)	.30
25	Scottie Pippen (All-NBA Team Selections)	.25
26	Scottie Pippen (NBA Championship Seasons)	.25
27	Scottie Pippen (1994 NBA All-Star Game MVP)	.25
28	Scottie Pippen (USA Basketball Record)	.25
29	David Robinson (1990 NBA Rookie of the Year)	.25
30	David Robinson (NBA All-Star Selections)	.25
31	David Robinson (1995 NBA Most Valuable Player)	.25
32	David Robinson (USA Baketball Record)	.25
33	Glenn Robinson (1995 NBA Rookie Game)	.10
34	Glenn Robinson (1995 NBA All-Rookie First Team)	.10
35	Glenn Robinson (1995 NBA Rookie Scoring Leader)	.10
36	Glenn Robinson (USA Basketball Record)	.10
37	John Stockton (1993 NBA All-Star Co-MVP)	.20
38	John Stockton (NBA Career Assists Leader)	.20
39	John Stockton (NBA Career Steals Leader)	.20
40	John Stockton (USA Basketball Record)	.20
41	Charles Barkley (1985 NBA All-Rookie Team)	.10
42	Charles Barkley (1991 NBA All-Star Game MVP)	.10
43	Charles Barkley (1993 NBA Most Valuable Player)	.10
44	Charles Barkley (USA Basketball Record)	.10
45	Mitch Richmond (1989 NBA Rookie of the Year)	.10
46	Mitch Richmond (1995 NBA All-Star MVP)	.10
47	Mitch Richmond (All-NBA Team Selections)	.10
48	Mitch Richmond (USA Basketball Record)	.10
49	Anfernee Hardaway (Portraits of Power)	1.00
50	Grant Hill (Portraits of Power)	.50
51	Karl Malone (Portraits of Power)	.20
52	Reggie Miller (Portraits of Power)	.20
53	Shaquille O'Neal (Portraits of Power)	.75
54	Hakeem Olajuwon (Portraits of Power)	.30
55	Scottie Pippen (Portraits of Power)	.25
56	David Robinson (Portraits of Power)	.25
57	Glenn Robinson (Portraits of Power)	.10
58	John Stockton (Portraits of Power)	.20
59	Charles Barkley (Portraits of Power)	.10
60	Mitch Richmond (Portraits of Power)	.10
61	Jennifer Azzi (USA Women's Team)	.10
62	Ruthie Bolton (USA Women's Team)	.10
63	Teresa Edwards (USA Women's Team)	.10
64	Lisa Leslie (USA Women's Team)	.20
65	Rebecca Lobo (USA Women's Team)	.40
66	Katrina McClain (USA Women's Team)	.10
67	Nikki McCray (USA Women's Team)	.10
68	Carla McGhee (USA Women's Team)	.10
69	Dawn Staley (USA Women's Team)	.10
70	Katy Steding (USA Women's Team)	.10
71	Sheryl Swoopes (USA Women's Team)	.20
72	Tara VanDerveer (USA Women's Team-Coach)	.10
NNO	USA Trade Card	1.50

1996 Upper Deck USA Anfernee Hardaway

This four-card set features memorable moments from Anfernee Hardaway's career. Cards were random inserts in 1996 Upper Deck USA Basketball packs, one per every 56 packs. Cards are numbered using an "A" prefix.

		MT
Complete Set (4):		60.00
Common Player:		15.00
1	Anfernee Hardaway (Scoring)	15.00
2	Anfernee Hardaway (Defense)	15.00
3	Anfernee Hardaway (Smooth)	15.00
4	Anfernee Hardaway (Versatility)	15.00

1996 Upper Deck USA Exchange Set

This 10-card set could be attained by redeeming the USA Update Trade card (inserted 1:10). It completes the regular 1996 Upper Deck USA set by adding Charles Barkley and Mitch Richmond. The redemption program expired October 31, 1996.

		MT
Complete Set (10):		2.00
Common Player:		.20
41	Charles Barkley	.25
42	Charles Barkley	.25
43	Charles Barkley	.25
44	Charles Barkley	.25
45	Mitch Richmond	.20
46	Mitch Richmond	.20
47	Mitch Richmond	.20
48	Mitch Richmond	.20
59	Charles Barkley	.25
60	Mitch Richmond	.20

1996 Upper Deck USA Follow Your Dreams

These 12 interactive cards were random inserts in 1996 Upper Deck USA Basketball packs. Two versions were made - gold and silver. If the player featured on the card is the 1996 Olympics scoring leader, that card is redeemable for a 12-card commemorative set. Follow Your Dreams inserts are seeded one per every six packs. Cards are numbered with a "F" prefix.

		MT
Complete Set (11):		25.00
Common Player:		1.00
1	Anfernee Hardaway	5.00
2	Grant Hill	4.00
3	Karl Malone	1.00
4	Reggie Miller	3.00
5	Shaquille O'Neal	5.00
6	Hakeem Olajuwon	2.00
7	Scottie Pippen	3.00
8	David Robinson	3.00
9	Glenn Robinson	1.00
10	John Stockton	1.00
11	Eleventh & Twelfth Men	1.00

1996 Upper Deck USA Michael Jordan

This four-card insert set features memorable moments from Michael Jordan's career, including the game in which he became the USA Olympic men's basketball team's leading scorer. The cards were randomly seeded one per every 28 hobby packs of 1996 Upper Deck USA Basketball. They are numbered using an "M" prefix.

		MT
Complete Set (4):		100.00
Common Player:		25.00
1	Michael Jordan (Scoring)	25.00
2	Michael Jordan (Defense)	25.00
3	Michael Jordan (Desire)	25.00
4	Michael Jordan (Leadership)	25.00

1996 Upper Deck USA SP Career Highlights

Two versions of SP Career Highlights cards were made - regular versions, which are seeded one per pack, and die-cut versions, which are seeded one per every 27 packs. The 10-card set showcases the career highlights for each member of the USA Olympic men's basketball team. Cards are numbered with a "S" prefix.

		MT
Complete Set (10):		7.00
Common Player:		.30
Gold Cards:		5x-10x
1	Anfernee Hardaway (Career Statistics)	2.00
2	Grant Hill (Career Statistics)	1.00
3	Karl Malone (Career Statistics)	.40
4	Reggie Miller (Career Statistics)	.40
5	Shaquille O'Neal (Career Statistics)	1.50
6	Hakeem Olajuwon (Career Statistics)	.60
7	Scottie Pippen (Career Statistics)	.75
8	David Robinson (Career Statistics)	.50
9	Glenn Robinson (Career Statistics)	.30
10	John Stockton (Career Statistics)	.40

1996 Upper Deck USA SP Career Highlights Gold

Gold versions of all 10 cards in the Career Statistics insert were produced and inserted every 27 packs. The cards featured gold foil on the fronts versus the silver foil used on the regular versions.

	MT
Gold Cards:	5x-10x

1996 Upper Deck 23 Nights Jordan Experience

This set consists of 23 oversized cards (3-1/2" x 5"), a circular commemorative card and a CD with a Michael Jordan interview. The cards feature a different highlight from Jordan's career. The entire set carried an SRP of $19.99 when it was first released.

		MT
Complete Set (23) w/CD:		30.00
Complete Set (23):		25.00
Common Player:		1.50
1	Game 2, 1986 First Round (Michael Jordan)	1.50
2	Game 1, 1992 NBA Finals (Michael Jordan)	1.50
3	1985 Slam Dunk Championship (Michael Jordan)	1.50
4	Game 2, 1991 NBA Finals (Michael Jordan)	1.50
5	1996 NBA All-Star Game (Michael Jordan)	1.50
6	Game 5, 1993 Conference Finals (Michael Jordan)	1.50
7	Bulls' 70th win of the season (Michael Jordan)	1.50
8	1991 NBA Champions (Michael Jordan)	1.50
9	"The Shot" (Michael Jordan)	1.50
10	He's Back! (Michael Jordan)	1.50
11	Game 1, 1996 First Round (Michael Jordan)	1.50
12	Game 4, 1993 NBA Finals (Michael Jordan)	1.50
13	Game 4, 1996 Conference Finals (Michael Jordan)	1.50
14	Game 6, 1992 NBA Finals (Michael Jordan)	1.50
15	30th 40-point game in 1986-87 (Michael Jordan)	1.50
16	34th career 50-point game (Michael Jordan)	1.50
17	Game 3, 1992 NBA Finals (Michael Jordan)	1.50
18	NBA career-high 69 points (Michael Jordan)	1.50
19	1988 Slam Dunk Championships (Michael Jordan)	1.50
20	Michael Jordan (23,000 career points)	1.50
21	Michael Jordan (55 points at New York)	1.50
22	1993 NBA Champions (Michael Jordan)	1.50
23	1996 NBA Champions (Michael Jordan)	1.50
NNO	Compact Disc - The Jordan Interview	6.00
NNO	Cardboard Disk (Michael Jordan)	1.50

1996-97 UD3

The 60-card, standard-size set was issued in May of 1997 in three-card packs with a retail of $3.99. The inaugural edition of the retail-only release was packaged first in a foil wrapper and then in a matchbox-like cardboard container. The main set was broken into three 20-card subsets: Hardwood Prospects, NBA Star-Focus and Aerial Artists. Inserts in the set include the autographed Court Commemoratives, The Winning Edge and Super Star Spotlight.

		MT
Complete Set (60):		50.00
Common Player:		.25
Minor Stars:		.50
Pack (3):		3.00
Wax Box (24):		60.00
1	*Kerry Kittles*	1.25
2	*Stephon Marbury*	4.00
3	*Jermaine O'Neal*	2.00
4	*Shareef Abdur-Rahim*	2.50
5	*Ray Allen*	1.75
6	*Antoine Walker*	2.00
7	*Erick Dampier*	.50
8	*Walter McCarty*	.50
9	*Todd Fuller*	.25
10	*Tony Delk*	.50
11	*Marcus Camby*	1.50
12	*John Wallace*	.75
13	*Vitaly Potapenko*	.25
14	*Allen Iverson*	4.00
15	*Steve Nash*	.75
16	*Derek Fisher*	.50
17	*Samaki Walker*	.50
18	*Roy Rogers*	.25
19	*Kobe Bryant*	10.00
20	*Lorenzen Wright*	.50
21	Kevin Garnett	4.00
22	Hakeem Olajuwon	1.50
23	Michael Jordan	8.00
24	John Stockton	.25
25	Terrell Brandon	.25
26	Damon Stoudamire	1.50
27	Charles Barkley	1.00
28	Dikembe Mutombo	.25
29	Gary Payton	1.00
30	Patrick Ewing	.25
31	Dennis Rodman	3.00
32	Joe Smith	1.00
33	Grant Hill	4.00
34	Shaquille O'Neal	3.00
35	Kevin Johnson	.25
36	David Robinson	1.00
37	Juwan Howard	1.00
38	Mitch Richmond	.25
39	Alonzo Mourning	.25
40	Reggie Miller	.25
41	Shawn Kemp	1.00
42	Scottie Pippen	2.00
43	Kobe Bryant	10.00
44	Anfernee Hardaway	3.00
45	Brent Barry	.25
46	Glenn Robinson	.25
47	Karl Malone	.25
48	Chris Webber	1.00
49	Danny Manning	.25
50	Antonio McDyess	.25
51	Dominique Wilkins	.25
52	Vin Baker	.25
53	Isaiah Rider	.25
54	Eddie Jones	1.00
55	Glen Rice	.25
56	Larry Johnson	.25
57	Latrell Sprewell	.25
58	Sean Elliott	.25
59	Clyde Drexler	.25
60	Jerry Stackhouse	1.00

1996-97 UD3 Court Commemorative Autographs

The four-card inset set, seeded every 1,500 packs of UD3 Basketball, featured signed cards of Anfernee Hardaway, Shawn Kemp, Damon Stoudamire and Michael Jordan. Cards are numbered with a "C" prefix.

		MT
Complete Set (4):		2750.
Common Player:		150.00
1	Michael Jordan	2500.
2	Damon Stoudamire	150.00
3	Anfernee Hardaway	400.00
4	Shawn Kemp	200.00

1996-97 UD3 Superstar Spotlight

The 10-card insert set utilizes a special cel-chrome technology and was found every 144 packs. The set logo appears in the upper right corner with the circular cel-chrome in the middle. "Superstar" is printed in a blue stripe above the circle with "Spotlight" below in a blue stripe. Cards are numbered with a "S" prefix.

		MT
Complete Set (10):		600.00
Common Player:		15.00
1	Shaquille O'Neal	50.00
2	Alonzo Mourning	15.00
3	Anfernee Hardaway	75.00
4	Karl Malone	15.00
5	Michael Jordan	150.00
6	Hakeem Olajuwon	30.00
7	Shawn Kemp	20.00
8	Allen Iverson	75.00
9	Dennis Rodman	50.00
10	Charles Barkley	25.00

1996-97 UD3 The Winning Edge

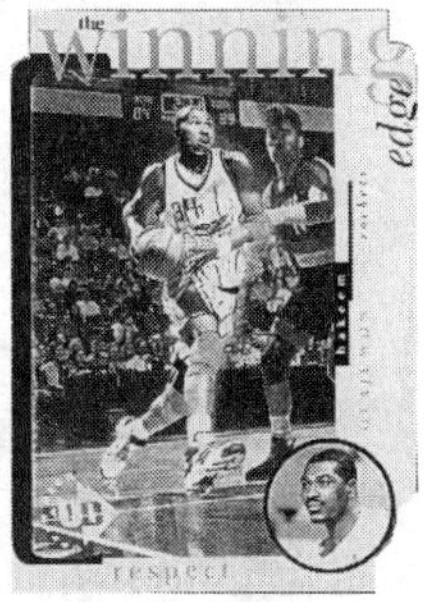

The 20-card insert set features Light F/X and highlights the characteristics that make the top players some of the best ever. "Winning" is featured prominently in red foil along the top border with a player close-up in the right corner in a small circle. The cards were inserted every 11 packs. Cards are numbered with a "W" prefix.

		MT
Complete Set (20):		120.00
Common Player:		2.00
1	Michael Jordan	40.00
2	Charles Barkley	5.00
3	Reggie Miller	2.00
4	Grant Hill	20.00
5	Larry Johnson	2.00
6	Hakeem Olajuwon	8.00
7	Anfernee Hardaway	20.00
8	Shaquille O'Neal	15.00
9	Vin Baker	2.00
10	Kevin Garnett	15.00
11	Juwan Howard	6.00
12	John Stockton	2.00
13	Mookie Blaylock	2.00
14	Shawn Kemp	5.00
15	David Robinson	5.00
16	Kevin Johnson	2.00
17	Joe Dumars	2.00
18	Marcus Camby	12.00
19	Clyde Drexler	4.00
20	Chris Webber	6.00

A player's name in *italic type* indicates a rookie

1997 Coll. Choice Int'l Italian Crash the Game Scoring

This 60-card set featured 30 players on two silver cards each. If the player on the card scored 30 points in one game during the listed week, collectors could redeem the card for a premium quality silver card. The redemption program expired June 7,1997. Cards are numbered with a "C" prefix.

		MT
Complete Set (60):		125.00
Common Player:		1.00
1A	Mookie Blaylock	1.50
1B	Mookie Blaylock	1.50
2A	Dino Radja	1.00
2B	Dino Radja	1.00
3A	Glen Rice	2.50
3B	Glen Rice	2.50
4A	Scottie Pippen	6.00
4B	Scottie Pippen	6.00
5A	Terrell Brandon	2.00
5B	Terrell Brandon	2.00
6A	Jason Kidd	3.00
6B	Jason Kidd	3.00
7A	Antonio McDyess	2.50
7B	Antonio McDyess	2.50
8A	Joe Dumars	1.50
8B	Joe Dumars	1.50
9A	Joe Smith	3.50
9B	Joe Smith	3.50
10A	Hakeem Olajuwon	6.00
10B	Hakeem Olajuwon	6.00
11A	Reggie Miller	2.50
11B	Reggie Miller	2.50
12A	Loy Vaught	1.50
12B	Loy Vaught	1.50
13A	Cedric Ceballos	1.50
13B	Cedric Ceballos	1.50
14A	Alonzo Mourning	2.50
14B	Alonzo Mourning	2.50
15A	Vin Baker	2.50
15B	Vin Baker	2.50
16A	Kevin Garnett	15.00
16B	Kevin Garnett	15.00
17A	Ed O'Bannon	1.00
17B	Ed O'Bannon	1.00
18A	Patrick Ewing	2.50
18B	Patrick Ewing	2.50
19A	Anfernee Hardaway	10.00
19B	Anfernee Hardaway	10.00
20A	Clarence Weatherspoon	1.00
20B	Clarence Weatherspoon	1.00
21A	Kevin Johnson	1.50
21B	Kevin Johnson	1.50
22A	Clifford Robinson	1.50
22B	Clifford Robinson	1.50
23A	Mitch Richmond	2.50
23B	Mitch Richmond	2.50
24A	Sean Elliott	1.50
24B	Sean Elliott	1.50
25A	Shawn Kemp	7.00
25B	Shawn Kemp	7.00
26A	Damon Stoudamire	6.00
26B	Damon Stoudamire	6.00
27A	John Stockton	2.50
27B	John Stockton	2.50
28A	Bryant Reeves	2.00
28B	Bryant Reeves	2.00
29A	Rasheed Wallace	2.00
29B	Rasheed Wallace	2.00
30A	Michael Jordan	30.00
30B	Michael Jordan	30.00

1997-98 Collector's Choice

The 400-card, standard-size set features several inserts and subsets, including five Checklist Challenge card and 30 Game Night '97 cards. Inserts in Series I set are NBA SuperAction Stick-Ums (1:3), You Crash The Game (1:5) and the tiered StarQuest (90 cards with ranging odds from 1:1 to 1:145). Series II inserts included: MJ Bullseye, StarQuest, and Mini-Standees. The base cards feature the player's name along the top edge within a team-colored stripe and his number and position in the upper right corner. Several of the cards have a horizontal design while all of the card backs have the horizontal design. Stats from the player's previous two seasons are on the back with a color photo and a brief descriptive highlight.

		MT
Complete Set (400):		30.00
Complete Series 1 (200):		15.00
Complete Series 2 (200):		15.00
Common Player:		.05
Minor Stars:		.10
MJ Dynasty Set (6):		75.00
Common MJ Dynasty:		15.00
Series 1 Wax Box:		36.00
Series 2 Wax Box:		36.00
1	Mookie Blaylock	.05
2	Dikembe Mutombo	.10
3	Eldridge Recasner	.05
4	Christian Laettner	.10
5	Tyrone Corbin	.05
6	Antoine Walker	.50
7	Eric Williams	.05
8	Dana Barros	.05
9	David Wesley	.05
10	Dino Radja	.05
11	Vlade Divac	.05
12	Dell Curry	.05
13	Muggsy Bogues	.05
14	Tony Smith	.05
15	Glen Rice	.10
16	Anthony Mason	.05
17	Dennis Rodman	.75
18	Brian Williams	.05
19	Toni Kukoc	.05
20	Jason Caffey	.05
21	Steve Kerr	.05
22	Luc Longley	.05
23	Michael Jordan	2.50
24	Chris Mills	.05
25	Tyrone Hill	.05
26	Vitaly Potapenko	.05
27	Bob Sura	.05
28	Robert Pack	.05
29	Ed O'Bannon	.05
30	Michael Finley	.05
31	Shawn Bradley	.05
32	Khalid Reeves	.05
33	Antonio McDyess	.10
34	Ervin Johnson	.05
35	Dale Ellis	.05
36	Bryant Stith	.05
37	Tom Hammonds	.05
38	Otis Thorpe	.05
39	Lindsey Hunter	.05
40	Grant Long	.05
41	Aaron McKie	.05
42	Randolph Childress	.05
43	Scott Burrell	.05
44	Bimbo Coles	.05
45	B.J. Armstrong	.05
46	Mark Price	.05
47	Latrell Sprewell	.10
48	Felton Spencer	.05
49	Charles Barkley	.25
50	Mario Elie	.05
51	Clyde Drexler	.20
52	Kevin Willis	.05
53	Antonio Davis	.05
54	Reggie Miller	.10
55	Dale Davis	.05
56	Mark Jackson	.05
57	Erick Dampier	.05
58	Pooh Richardson	.05
59	Terry Dehere	.05
60	Brent Barry	.05
61	Loy Vaught	.05
62	Lorenzen Wright	.05
63	Eddie Jones	.30
64	Kobe Bryant	1.50
65	Elden Campbell	.05
66	Corie Blount	.05
67	Shaquille O'Neal	.75
68	Dan Majerle	.05
69	P.J. Brown	.05
70	Tim Hardaway	.10
71	Isaac Austin	.05
72	Jamal Mashburn	.05
73	Ray Allen	.20
74	Glenn Robinson	.15
75	Armon Gilliam	.05
76	Johnny Newman	.05
77	Elliot Perry	.05
78	Sherman Douglas	.05
79	Doug West	.05
80	Kevin Garnett	1.25
81	Sam Mitchell	.05
82	Tom Gugliotta	.05
83	Terry Porter	.05
84	Chris Carr	.05
85	Kevin Edwards	.05
86	Jayson Williams	.05
87	Kendall Gill	.05
88	Kerry Kittles	.20
89	Chris Gatling	.05
90	John Starks	.05
91	Charlie Ward	.05
92	Larry Johnson	.10
93	Charles Oakley	.05
94	Chris Childs	.05
95	Allan Houston	.05
96	Horace Grant	.05
97	Darrell Armstrong	.05
98	Rony Seikaly	.05
99	Dennis Scott	.05
100	Anfernee Hardaway	1.00
101	Brian Shaw	.05
102	Jerry Stackhouse	.30
103	Rex Walters	.05
104	Don MacLean	.05
105	Derrick Coleman	.05
106	Lucious Harris	.05
107	Clarence Weatherspoon	.05
108	Cedric Ceballos	.05
109	Danny Manning	.05
110	Jason Kidd	.15
111	Loren Meyer	.05
112	Wesley Person	.05
113	Steve Nash	.05
114	Isaiah Rider	.05
115	Stacey Augmon	.05
116	Arvydas Sabonis	.05
117	Kenny Anderson	.05
118	Jermaine O'Neal	.15
119	Gary Trent	.05
120	Michael Smith	.05
121	Kevin Gamble	.05
122	Olden Polynice	.05
123	Billy Owens	.05
124	Corliss Williamson	.05
125	Cory Alexander	.05
126	Vinny Del Negro	.05
127	Sean Elliott	.05
128	Will Perdue	.05
129	Carl Herrera	.05
130	Shawn Kemp	.40
131	Hersey Hawkins	.05
132	Nate McMillan	.05
133	Craig Ehlo	.05
134	Detlef Schrempf	.05
135	Sam Perkins	.05
136	Sharone Wright	.05
137	Doug Christie	.05
138	Popeye Jones	.05
139	Shawn Respert	.05
140	Marcus Camby	.40
141	Adam Keefe	.05
142	Karl Malone	.20
143	John Stockton	.20
144	Greg Ostertag	.05
145	Chris Morris	.05
146	Shareef Abdur-Rahim	.50
147	Roy Rogers	.05
148	George Lynch	.05
149	Anthony Peeler	.05
150	Lee Mayberry	.05
151	Calbert Cheaney	.05
152	Harvey Grant	.05
153	Rod Strickland	.05
154	Tracy Murray	.05
155	Chris Webber	.30
156	Atlanta Hawks (Game Night '97)	.05
157	Boston Celtics (Game Night '97)	.05
158	Charlotte Hornets (Game Night '97)	.05
159	Chicago Bulls (Game Night '97)	.50
160	Cleveland Cavaliers (Game Night '97)	.05
161	Dallas Mavericks (Game Night '97)	.05
162	Denver Nuggets (Game Night '97)	.05
163	Detroit Pistons (Game Night '97)	.25
164	Golden State Warriors (Game Night '97)	.05
165	Houston Rockets (Game Night '97)	.05
166	Indiana Pacers (Game Night '97)	.05
167	Los Angeles Clippers (Game Night '97)	.05
168	Los Angeles Lakers (Game Night '97)	.05
169	Miami Heat (Game Night '97)	.05
170	Milwaukee Bucks (Game Night '97)	.05
171	Minnesota Timberwolves (Game Night '97)	.05
172	New Jersey Nets (Game Night '97)	.05
173	New York Knicks (Game Night '97)	.05
174	Orlando Magic (Game Night '97)	.05
175	Philadelphia 76ers (Game Night '97)	.05
176	Phoenix Suns (Game Night '97)	.05
177	Portland Trail Blazers (Game Night '97)	.05
178	Sacramento Kings (Game Night '97)	.05
179	San Antonio Spurs (Game Night '97)	.05
180	Seattle SuperSonics (Game Night '97)	.05
181	Toronto Raptors (Game Night '97)	.05
182	Utah Jazz (Game Night '97)	.05
183	Vancouver Grizzlies (Game Night '97)	.05
184	Washington Wizards (Game Night '97)	.05
185	1997 NBA Finals (Game Night '97)	.05
186	Michael Jordan (Catch 23)	.75
187	Michael Jordan (Catch 23)	.75
188	Michael Jordan (Catch 23)	.75
189	Michael Jordan (Catch 23)	.75
190	Michael Jordan (Catch 23)	.75
191	Michael Jordan (Catch 23)	.75
192	Michael Jordan (Catch 23)	.75
193	Michael Jordan (Catch 23)	.75
194	Michael Jordan (Catch 23)	.75
195	Michael Jordan (Catch 23)	.75
196	Checklist #1	.05
197	Checklist #2	.05
198	Checklist #3	.05
199	Checklist #4	.05
200	Checklist #5	.05
201	Steve Smith	.05
202	Chris Crawford	.05
203	Ed Gray	.05
204	Alan Henderson	.10
205	Walter McCarty	.05
206	Dee Brown	.05
207	*Chauncey Billups*	.75
208	*Ron Mercer*	1.50
209	Travis Knight	.05
210	Andrew DeClercq	.10
211	Tyus Edney	.05
212	Matt Geiger	.05
213	Tony Delk	.05
214	J.R. Reid	.05
215	Bobby Phills	.05
216	David Wesley	.05
217	Ron Harper	.05
218	Scottie Pippen	.60
219	Scott Burrell	.05
220	Keith Booth	.05
221	Bill Wennington	.05
222	Shawn Kemp	.50
223	*Zydrunas Ilgauskas*	.50
224	*Brevin Knight*	.75
225	Danny Ferry	.05
226	*Derek Anderson*	.75
227	Wesley Person	.05
228	A.C. Green	.05
229	Samaki Walker	.05
230	Hubert Davis	.05
231	Erick Strickland	.05
232	Dennis Scott	.05
233	*Tony Battie*	.50
234	LaPhonso Ellis	.05
235	Eric Williams	.05
236	*Bobby Jackson*	.50
237	Anthony Goldwire	.05
238	*Danny Fortson*	.25
239	Joe Dumars	.05

240	Grant Hill	1.25
241	Malik Sealy	.05
242	Brian Williams	.05
243	Theo Ratliff	.05
244	Scot Pollard	.05
245	Erick Dampier	.05
246	Duane Ferrell	.05
247	Joe Smith	.25
248	Todd Fuller	.05
249	*Adonal Foyle*	.25
250	Othella Harrington	.05
251	Matt Maloney	.10
252	Hakeem Olajuwon	.40
253	*Rodrick Rhodes*	.25
254	Eddie Johnson	.05
255	Brent Price	.05
256	*Austin Croshere*	.25
257	Derrick McKey	.05
258	Chris Mullin	.10
259	Rik Smits	.05
260	Jalen Rose	.05
261	Darrick Martin	.05
262	Lamond Murray	.05
263	*Maurice Taylor*	.40
264	Rodney Rogers	.05
265	James Robinson	.05
266	Rick Fox	.05
267	Nick Van Exel	.20
268	Sean Rooks	.05
269	Derek Fisher	.05
270	Jon Barry	.05
271	Robert Horry	.05
272	Terry Mills	.05
273	Charles Smith	.05
274	Alonzo Mourning	.10
275	Voshon Lenard	.05
276	Todd Day	.05
277	Ervin Johnson	.05
278	Terrell Brandon	.10
279	Michael Curry	.05
280	Andrew Lang	.05
281	Tyrone Hill	.05
282	Stephon Marbury	1.00
283	Cherokee Parks	.05
284	Stanley Roberts	.05
285	Paul Grant	.05
286	David Benoit	.05
287	Lucious Harris	.05
288	Don MacLean	.05
289	Sam Cassel	.05
290	*Keith Van Horn*	1.50
291	Patrick Ewing	.10
292	Walter McCarty	.05
293	Chris Dudley	.05
294	Chris Mills	.05
295	Buck Williams	.05
296	Nick Anderson	.05
297	Derek Strong	.05
298	Gerald Wilkins	.05
299	Johnny Taylor	.05
300	Derek Harper	.05
301	Anthony Parker	.05
302	Allen Iverson	1.00
303	Jim Jackson	.05
304	Eric Montross	.05
305	*Tim Thomas*	1.00
306	*Kebu Stewart*	.20
307	Rex Chapman	.05
308	Tom Chambers	.05
309	Kevin Johnson	.05
310	John Williams	.05
311	Clifford Robinson	.05
312	Antonio McDyess	.10
313	Rasheed Wallace	.05
314	Brian Grant	.05
315	Dontonio Wingfield	.05
316	*Kelvin Cato*	.10
317	Mahmoud Abdul-Rauf	.05
318	Lawrence Funderburke	.05
319	Mitch Richmond	.10
320	*Tariq Abdul-Wahad*	.25
321	Terry Dehere	.05
322	Michael Stewart	.05
323	*Tim Duncan*	3.50
324	Avery Johnson	.05
325	David Robinson	.30
326	Charles Smith	.05
327	Chuck Person	.05
328	Monty Williams	.05
329	Jim McIlvaine	.05
330	Gary Payton	.30
331	Eric Snow	.05
332	Dale Ellis	.05
333	Vin Baker	.20
334	Walt Williams	.05
335	*Tracy McGrady*	1.00
336	Damon Stoudamire	.30
337	Carlos Rogers	.05
338	John Wallace	.10
339	Shandon Anderson	.05
340	Jeff Hornacek	.05
341	Howard Eisley	.05
342	*Jacque Vaughn*	.25
343	Bryon Russell	.05
344	Antoine Carr	.05
345	*Antonio Daniels*	.50
346	Pete Chilcutt	.05
347	Blue Edwards	.05
348	Bryant Reeves	.05
349	*Chris Robinson*	.10
350	Otis Thorpe	.05
351	Tim Legler	.05
352	Juwan Howard	.25
353	*God Shammgod*	.10
354	Gheorghe Muresan	.05
355	Chris Whitney	.05
356	Dikembe Mutombo	.05
357	Antoine Walker	.25
358	Glen Rice	.25
359	Scottie Pippen	.30
360	Derek Anderson	.40
361	Michael Finley	.05
362	LaPhonso Ellis	.05
363	Grant Hill	.60
364	Joe Smith	.10
365	Charles Barkley	.10
366	Reggie Miller	.10
367	Loy Vaught	.05
368	Shaquille O'Neal	.40
369	Alonzo Mourning	.05
370	Glenn Robinson	.05
371	Kevin Garnett	.60
372	Kendall Gill	.05
373	Allan Houston	.05
374	Anfernee Hardaway	.50
375	Tim Thomas	.40
376	Jason Kidd	.10
377	Kenny Anderson	.05
378	Mitch Richmond	.05
379	Tim Duncan	1.25
380	Gary Payton	.10
381	Marcus Camby	.05
382	Karl Malone	.10
383	Shareef Abdur-Rahim	.25
384	Chris Webber	.20
385	Michael Jordan	1.50
386	Michael Jordan	.75
387	Michael Jordan	.75
388	Michael Jordan	.75
389	Michael Jordan	.75
390	Michael Jordan	.75
391	Michael Jordan	.75
392	Michael Jordan	.75
393	Michael Jordan	.75
394	Michael Jordan	.75
395	Michael Jordan	.75
396	Checklist #1	.05
397	Checklist #2	.05
398	Checklist #3	.05
399	Checklist #4	.05
400	Checklist #5	.05

1997 Collector's Choice Catch 23

		MT
Complete Set (10):		
Common Player:		
1	Michael Jordan	
2	Michael Jordan	
3	Michael Jordan	
4	Michael Jordan	
5	Michael Jordan	
6	Michael Jordan	
7	Michael Jordan	
8	Michael Jordan	
9	Michael Jordan	
10	Michael Jordan	

1997-98 Collector's Choice Crash the Game Scoring

This 30-card interactive insert gave collectors a chance to win if: A) either the player pictured scored 30 or more points during the week of the date shown on the front and you collected the full, 30-card set, or B) the player scored 30 or more points on the date shown on the front, or C) you redeemed 15 non-winning cards. Either scenerio could be redeemed for the 30-card redemption set. Crash the Game inserts were seeded one per five packs in Series I and the game ended 7/1/98. Cards are numbered with a "C" prefix.

		MT
Complete Set (30):		30.00
Common Player:		.50
1	Dikembe Mutombo	.50
2	Dana Barros	.50
3	Glen Rice	1.00
4	Scottie Pippen	3.00
5	Terrell Brandon	.50
6	Shawn Bradley	.50
7	Antonio McDyess	1.00
8	Lindsey Hunter	.50
9	Joe Smith	1.50
10	Hakeem Olajuwon	2.00
11	Reggie Miller	1.00
12	Rodney Rogers	.50
13	Nick Van Exel	.50
14	Tim Hardaway	.50
15	Glenn Robinson	.50
16	Kevin Garnett	5.00
17	Kerry Kittles	1.00
18	Larry Johnson	.50
19	Anfernee Hardaway	5.00
20	Allen Iverson	4.00
21	Jason Kidd	1.50
22	Arvydas Sabonis	.50
23	Mitch Richmond	1.00
24	David Robinson	2.00
25	Gary Payton	1.50
26	Marcus Camby	1.50
27	Karl Malone	1.00
28	Bryant Reeves	.50
29	Chris Webber	2.00
30	Michael Jordan	10.00

1997-98 Collector's Choice Draft Trade

		MT
Complete Factory Set (10):		300.00
Complete Set (10):		250.00
Common Player:		
1	Tim Duncan	75.00
2	Keith Van Horn	10.00
3	Chauncey Billups	4.00
4	Antonio Daniels	5.00
5	Tony Battie	2.50
6	Ron Mercer	8.00
7	Tim Thomas	10.00
8	Adonal Foyle	2.50
9	Tracy McGrady	175.00
10	Danny Fortson	7.00

1997 Collector's Choice Game Night '97 Blow-Ups

		MT
Complete Set (5):		
Common Player:		
1	Utah Jazz	
2	Los Angeles Lakers	
3	Minnesota Timberwolves	
4	Orlando Magic	
5	Chicago Bulls	

1997 Collector's Choice Int'l Italian Jordan's Journal

This six-card set was inserted in packs of 1997 Collector's Choice International Italian basketball. The backs feature a journal-type entry from Michael Jordan about his performance and the Bulls' performance during the designated month of the season. Cards are numbered with a "J" prefix.

		MT
Complete Set (6):		50.00
Common Player:		10.00
1	November (Michael Jordan)	10.00
2	December (Michael Jordan)	10.00
3	January (Michael Jordan)	10.00
4	February (Michael Jordan)	10.00
5	March (Michael Jordan)	10.00
6	April (Michael Jordan)	10.00

1997 Collector's Choice Int'l Italian Mini-Cards

This 30-card, standard size set consists of 90 Mini-Cards. Three Mini-Cards form one standard size card. The Mini-Cards are perforated so they can be seperated. Each card has its own number with a "M" prefix.

		MT
Complete Set (30):		15.00
Common Player:		.20
2	Mookie Blaylock, Jeff Hornacek, Rex Walters	.20
5	Dino Radja, Toni Kukoc, Detlef Schrempf	.40
6	Eric Williams, Sharone Wright, Ashraf Amaya	.20
10	George Zidek, Ed O'Bannon, Tyus Edney	.20
13	Luc Longley, Shawn Bradley, Theo Ratliff	.30
22	Mahmoud Abdul-Rauf, Avery Johnson, Bobby Phills	.20
23	Tom Hammonds, Chris Morris, Popeye Jones	.20
25	Grant Hill, Christian Laettner, Bobby Hurley	3.00
28	Rony Seikaly, Derrick Coleman, Sherman Douglas	.20
30	Sam Cassell, John Starks, Nick Van Exel	.40
33	Travis Best, Dennis Scott, Matt Geiger	.20
36	Brent Barry, Isaiah Rider, Cedric Ceballos	.30
37	Lamond Murray, Kevin Johnson, Jason Kidd	.50
38	Terry Dehere, Jayson Williams, Chris Mullin	.20
39	Vlade Divac, Sasha Danilovic, Arvydas Sabonis	.20
43	Kurt Thomas, Brian Grant, Tyrone Hill	.20
44	Keith Askins, Robert Horry, Derrick McKey	.20
46	Shawn Respert, David Robinson, Randolph Childress	.75
49	Andrew Lang, Oliver Miller, Todd Day	.20
56	Charles Oakley, Bimbo Coles, Dell Curry	.20
57	J.R. Reid, Jerry Stackhouse, Rasheed Wallace	.50
66	A.C. Green, Clyde Drexler, Joe Dumars	.50
67	Aaron McKie, Nick Anderson, Kendall Gill	.30
75	Doc Rivers, Mark Jackson, Danny Ferry	.20
78	Shawn Kemp, Anfernee Hardaway, Michael Jordan	10.00
79	Jimmy King, Chris Webber, Jalen Rose	1.00
83	Karl Malone, Charles Barkley, Dennis Rodman	3.00
85	Greg Anthony, Larry Johnson, Stacey Augmon	.35
86	Blue Edwards, Tom Gugliotta, Nate McMillan	.35
90	Calbert Cheaney, Glenn Robinson, Jim Jackson	.50

1997 Collector's Choice Int'l Italian Stick Ums

This 30-card set is similar to the 96-97 Collector's Choice American Stick Ums. The design is the same except the text is printed in Italian. Cards are numbered with a "S" prefix.

		MT
Complete Set (30):		25.00
Common Player:		.15
1	Mookie Blaylock	.15
2	Dana Barros	.15
3	Scott Burrell	.15
4	Dennis Rodman	3.00
5	Terrell Brandon	.50
6	Jamal Mashburn	.25
7	LaPhonso Ellis	.15
8	Grant Hill	5.00
9	Joe Smith	1.00
10	Hakeem Olajuwon	2.00
11	Rik Smits	.15
12	Brent Barry	.30
13	Nick Van Exel	.75
14	Sasha Danilovic	.15
15	Vin Baker	.75
16	Kevin Garnett	5.00
17	Shawn Bradley	.30
18	Patrick Ewing	.75
19	Anfernee Hardaway	4.00
20	Clarence Weatherspoon	.25
21	Charles Barkley	2.00
22	Clifford Robinson	.25
23	Mitch Richmond	.75
24	David Robinson	1.25
25	Shawn Kemp	2.50
26	Damon Stoudamire	2.00
27	Karl Malone	1.00
28	Bryant Reeves	.50
29	Gheorghe Muresan	.25
30	Michael Jordan	10.00

1997 Collector's Choice Int'l Italian 1

This 200-card set was distributed in Italy. The set is identical to the 96-97 Collector's Choice American set except for bilingual text and a change in card numbering.

		MT
Complete Set (200):		50.00
Common Player:		.15
1	Mookie Blaylock	.25
2	Grant Long	.15
3	Christian Laettner	.40
4	Craig Ehlo	.15
5	Ken Norman	.15
6	Stacey Augmon	.15
7	Dana Barros	.15
8	Dino Radja	.15
9	Rick Fox	.15
10	Eric Montross	.15
11	David Wesley	.15
12	Eric Williams	.15
13	Glen Rice	.50
14	Dell Curry	.15
15	Matt Geiger	.15
16	Scott Burrell	.15
17	George Zidek	.15
18	Muggsy Bogues	.15
19	Ron Harper	.15
20	Steve Kerr	.15
21	Toni Kukoc	.40
22	Dennis Rodman	2.50
23	Michael Jordan	8.00
24	Luc Longley	.15
25	Michael Jordan VT	4.00
26	Michael Jordan VT	4.00
27	Luc Longley VT	.15
28	Scottie Pippen VT	1.00
29	Toni Kukoc VT	.15
30	Terrell Brandon	.40
31	Bobby Phills	.15
32	Tyrone Hill	.15
33	Michael Cage	.15
34	Bob Sura	.25
35	Tony Dumas	.15
36	Jim Jackson	.25
37	Loren Meyer	.15
38	Cherokee Parks	.15
39	Jamal Mashburn	.25
40	Popeye Jones	.15
41	Larry Ellis	.25
42	Jalen Rose	.15
43	Antonio McDyess	.75
44	Tom Hammonds	.15
45	Mahmoud Abdul-Rauf	.15
46	Dale Ellis	.15
47	Joe Dumars	.25
48	Theo Ratliff	.25
49	Lindsey Hunter	.15
50	Terry Mills	.15
51	Don Reid	.15
52	B.J. Armstrong	.15
53	Bimbo Coles	.15
54	Joe Smith	.75
55	Chris Mullin	.25
56	Rony Seikaly	.15
57	Donyell Marshall	.15
58	Hakeem Olajuwon	1.50
59	Robert Horry	.15
60	Mario Elie	.15
61	Mark Bryant	.15
62	Chucky Brown	.15
63	Rik Smits	.15
64	Derrick McKey	.15
65	Eddie Johnson	.15
66	Mark Jackson	.15
67	Ricky Pierce	.15
68	Travis Best	.25
69	Rodney Rogers	.15
70	Brent Barry	.25
71	Lamond Murray	.15
72	Eric Piatkowski	.15
73	Pooh Richardson	.15
74	Cedric Ceballos	.25
75	Eddie Jones	1.25
76	Anthony Peeler	.15
77	George Lynch	.15
78	Vlade Divac	.25
79	Rex Chapman	.15
80	Sasha Danilovic	.25
81	Kurt Thomas	.25
82	Keith Askins	.15
83	Walt Williams	.15
84	Vin Baker	.60
85	Shawn Respert	.15
86	Sherman Douglas	.15
87	Marty Conlon	.15
88	Johnny Newman	.15
89	Kevin Garnett	4.00
90	Andrew Lang	.15
91	Terry Porter	.15
92	Sam Mitchell	.15
93	Tom Gugliotta	.40
94	Spud Webb	.15
95	Kendall Gill	.25
96	Vern Fleming	.15
97	Shawn Bradley	.25
98	Yinka Dare	.15
99	Jayson Williams	.15
100	Kevin Edwards	.15
101	Charles Oakley	.15
102	Anthony Mason	.25
103	John Starks	.15
104	J.R. Reid	.15
105	Hubert Davis	.15
106	Gary Grant	.15
107	Nick Anderson	.15
108	Donald Royal	.15
109	Brian Shaw	.15
110	Brooks Thompson	.15
111	Tim Hardaway	3.00
112	Dennis Scott	.15
113	Anfernee Hardaway	1.25
114	Anfernee Hardaway	1.25
115	Anfernee Hardaway	1.25
116	Anfernee Hardaway	1.25
117	Anfernee Hardaway	1.25
118	Derrick Coleman	.15
119	Rex Walters	.15
120	Sean Higgins	.15
121	Clarence Weatherspoon	.15
122	Jerry Stackhouse	1.00
123	Elliot Perry	.15
124	Wayman Tisdale	.15
125	Wesley Person	.15
126	Charles Barkley	1.00
127	A.C. Green	.15
128	Harvey Grant	.15
129	Arvydas Sabonis	.15
130	Aaron McKie	.15
131	Gary Trent	.25
132	Buck Williams	.15
133	Billy Owens	.15
134	Brian Grant	.25
135	Corliss Williamson	.25
136	Tyus Edney	.25
137	Olden Polynice	.15
138	Avery Johnson	.15
139	Vinny Del Negro	.15
140	Sean Elliott	.25
141	Chuck Person	.15
142	Will Perdue	.15
143	Nate McMillian	.15
144	Vincent Askew	.15
145	Detlef Schrempf	.15
146	Hersey Hawkins	.15
147	Sharone Wright	.15
148	Zan Tabak	.15
149	Oliver Miller	.15
150	Doug Christie	.15
151	Damon Stoudamire	1.00
152	Jeff Hornacek	.15
153	Chris Morris	.15
154	Antoine Carr	.15
155	Karl Malone	.75
156	Adam Keefe	.15
157	Greg Anthony	.15
158	Blue Edwards	.15
159	Bryant Reeves	.40
160	Anthony Avent	.15
161	Lawrence Moten	.15
162	Calbert Cheaney	.15
163	Chris Webber	1.00
164	Tim Legler	.15
165	Gheorghe Muresan	.25
166	Stacey Augmon FUND	.15
167	Dee Brown FUND	.15
168	Glen Rice FUND	.40
169	Scottie Pippen FUND	1.00
170	Danny Ferry FUND	.15
171	Jason Kidd FUND	.40
172	Tom Hammonds FUND	.15
173	Grant Hill FUND	2.00
174	Chris Mullin FUND	.15
175	Clyde Drexler FUND	.40
176	Rik Smits FUND	.15
177	Lamond Murray FUND	.15
178	Nick Van Exel FUND	.25
179	Alonzo Mourning FUND	.40
180	Glenn Robinson FUND	.40
181	Isaiah Rider FUND	.15
182	Ed O'Bannon FUND	.15
183	Patrick Ewing FUND	.40
184	Shaquille O'Neal FUND	1.25
185	Derrick Coleman FUND	.15
186	Danny Manning FUND	.15
187	Clifford Robinson FUND	.15
188	Mitch Richmond FUND	.40
189	David Robinson FUND	.40
190	Shawn Kemp FUND	1.00
191	Oliver Miller FUND	.15
192	John Stockton FUND	.40
193	Greg Anthony FUND	.15
194	Rasheed Wallace FUND	.25
195	Michael Jordan FUND	4.00
196	Checklist	.15
197	Checklist	.15
198	Checklist	.15
199	Checklist	.15
200	Checklist	.15

1997-98 Collector's Choice Miniatures

NBA Miniatures was a 30-card insert that was seeded one per three packs of Series II. Each card, which was called a mini-standee, featured one player from each team in a special die-cut card that could be assembled into a tiny stand-up card. Cards are numbered with a "M" prefix.

		MT
Complete Set (30):		12.00
Common Player:		.10
Minor Stars:		.20
1	Mookie Blaylock	.10
2	Chauncey Billups	.50
3	Glen Rice	.20
4	Scottie Pippen	.75
5	Bob Sura	.10
6	Erick Strickland	.10
7	Tony Battie	.30
8	Joe Dumars	.10
9	Adonal Foyle	.20
10	Charles Barkley	.30
11	Dale Davis	.10
12	Lamond Murray	.10
13	Kobe Bryant	2.00
14	Tim Hardaway	.20
15	Glenn Robinson	.20
16	Kevin Garnett	1.50
17	Keith Van Horn	1.00
18	Patrick Ewing	.20
19	Anfernee Hardaway	1.00
20	Tim Thomas	.75
21	Jason Kidd	.40
22	Isaiah Rider	.10
23	Mahmoud Abdul-Rauf	.10
24	Tim Duncan	1.75
25	Detlef Schrempf	.10
26	Damon Stoudamire	.50
27	John Stockton	.30
28	Bryant Reeves	.10
29	Juwan Howard	.30
30	Michael Jordan	3.00

1997-98 Collector's Choice MJ Bullseye

This 30-card insert was a variation of You Crash the Game, but featured Michael Jordan on each card. Collectors needed to match Jordan's point total to the numbers shown on the Bullseye targets in order to win. These inserts were found in one per five packs of Series II. Cards are numbered with a "B" prefix.

		MT
Complete Set (30):		60.00
Common Player:		2.00
1	Michael Jordan	2.00
2	Michael Jordan	2.00
3	Michael Jordan	2.00
4	Michael Jordan	2.00
5	Michael Jordan	2.00
6	Michael Jordan	2.00
7	Michael Jordan	2.00
8	Michael Jordan	2.00
9	Michael Jordan	2.00
10	Michael Jordan	2.00
11	Michael Jordan	2.00
12	Michael Jordan	2.00
13	Michael Jordan	2.00
14	Michael Jordan	2.00
15	Michael Jordan	2.00
16	Michael Jordan	2.00
17	Michael Jordan	2.00
18	Michael Jordan	2.00
19	Michael Jordan	2.00
20	Michael Jordan	2.00
21	Michael Jordan	2.00
22	Michael Jordan	2.00
23	Michael Jordan	2.00
24	Michael Jordan	2.00
25	Michael Jordan	2.00
26	Michael Jordan	2.00
27	Michael Jordan	2.00
28	Michael Jordan	2.00
29	Michael Jordan	2.00
30	Michael Jordan	2.00

1997-98 Collector's Choice Star Attractions

This 20-card set was seeded one per special Series I and II Anco packs, with cards 1-10 in Series I and 11-20 in Series II. The cards feature a die-cut across the top and bottom and are numbered with a "SA" prefix. Gold versions of these also exist and were seeded 1:20 packs.

		MT
Complete Set (20):		50.00
Complete Series 1 (10):		30.00
Complete Series 2 (10):		20.00
Common Player:		.50
Inserted 1:1 Special Retail Pack		
Gold Cards:		2x-4x
Inserted 1:20 Special Retail Pack		
1	Michael Jordan	25.00
2	Joe Smith	.50
3	Karl Malone	1.50
4	Chauncey Billups	1.50
5	Charles Barkley	1.50
6	Shaquille O'Neal	4.00
7	Jason Kidd	2.00
8	Chris Webber	2.00

9	Allen Iverson	4.00
10	Patrick Ewing	.50
11	Tim Duncan	6.00
12	Kevin Garnett	6.00
13	Tony Battie	.50
14	Gary Payton	1.00
15	Hakeem Olajuwon	2.00
16	Antonio Daniels	1.00
17	Grant Hill	6.00
18	Anfernee Hardaway	4.00
19	Scottie Pippen	3.00
20	Keith Van Horn	2.50

1997-98 Collector's Choice StarQuest

The 90-card, standard-size tiered insert set was seeded in Series I packs at varying ratios. The first 45 cards were found in each pack, while the next 20 (46-65) were inserted every 21 packs. The next 15 cards (66-80) were inserted every 71 packs with the final 10 cards (81-90) found every 145 packs. The card fronts feature the StarQuest logo in the center with the logo and name appearing in gold along the lower edge. The player's cut-out image appears over the center logo and the cards are numbered with the "SQ" prefix.

		MT
Complete Set (180):		1000.
Complete Series 1 (90):		500.00
Complete Series 2 (90):		500.00
Common Player (1-45/91-135):		.20
Common Player (46-65/136-155):		1.50
Common Player (66-80/156-170):		4.00
Common Player (81-90/171-180):		5.00
1	Dale Davis	.20
2	Jamal Mashburn	.20
3	Christian Laettner	.20
4	Billy Owens	.20
5	Vlade Divac	.20
6	Sean Elliott	.20
7	Marcus Camby	.50
8	Dana Barros	.20
9	Rod Strickland	.20
10	Jim Jackson	.20
11	Tyrone Hill	.20
12	Ervin Johnson	.20
13	Antoine Walker	1.00
14	Lorenzen Wright	.20
15	Shawn Bradley	.20
16	John Starks	.20
17	Corliss Williamson	.20
18	Steve Smith	.20
19	Chris Mills	.20
20	Vinny Del Negro	.20
21	Jayson Williams	.20
22	Anthony Mason	.20
23	Dennis Scott	.20
24	Mark Jackson	.20
25	Dino Radja	.20
26	Greg Ostertag	.20
27	Anthony Peeler	.20
28	Toni Kukoc	.20
29	Michael Finley	.20
30	Brent Barry	.20
31	Wesley Person	.20
32	Horace Grant	.20
33	Walt Williams	.20
34	Bryant Stith	.20
35	Ray Allen	.30
36	Otis Thorpe	.20
37	Rasheed Wallace	.20
38	Charles Oakley	.20
39	Robert Pack	.20
40	Kendall Gill	.20
41	Lindsey Hunter	.20
42	Cedric Ceballos	.20
43	Allan Houston	.20
44	Bryant Reeves	.20
45	Derrick Coleman	.20
46	Isaiah Rider	1.50
47	Detlef Schrempf	1.50
48	Antonio McDyess	3.00
49	Glenn Robinson	3.00
50	Damon Stoudamire	5.00
51	Terrell Brandon	1.50
52	Joe Smith	4.00
53	Tom Gugliotta	1.50
54	Loy Vaught	1.50
55	Kenny Anderson	1.50
56	Dikembe Mutombo	1.50
57	Tim Hardaway	1.50
58	Chris Webber	6.00
59	Nick Van Exel	1.50
60	Kerry Kittles	5.00
61	Chris Mullin	1.50
62	Stephon Marbury	12.00
63	Juwan Howard	5.00
64	Larry Johnson	1.50
65	Shareef Abdur-Rahim	10.00
66	Dennis Rodman	25.00
67	Vin Baker	8.00
68	Clyde Drexler	10.00
69	Eddie Jones	12.00
70	Jerry Stackhouse	8.00
71	Karl Malone	8.00
72	Mitch Richmond	4.00
73	Glen Rice	4.00
74	Jason Kidd	10.00
75	Latrell Sprewell	4.00
76	David Robinson	10.00
77	Charles Barkley	10.00
78	Gary Payton	8.00
79	Scottie Pippen	20.00
80	Reggie Miller	4.00
81	Alonzo Mourning	5.00
82	Allen Iverson	30.00
83	Michael Jordan	75.00
84	Shawn Kemp	10.00
85	Kevin Garnett	35.00
86	Grant Hill	35.00
87	Anfernee Hardaway	30.00
88	Shaquille O'Neal	25.00
89	John Stockton	5.00
90	Hakeem Olajuwon	10.00
91	Billy Owens	.20
92	Derek Anderson	.75
93	Hersey Hawkins	.20
94	Bryon Russell	.20
95	Rik Smits	.20
96	Tracy McGrady	1.00
97	Kendall Gill	.20
98	Tim Thomas	.75
99	Robert Horry	.20
100	Marcus Camby	.40
101	Rodney Rogers	.20
102	Danny Manning	.20
103	John Starks	.20
104	Mahmoud Abdul-Rauf	.20
105	Chris Childs	.20
106	Antonio Davis	.20
107	Lamond Murray	.20
108	Nick Anderson	.20
109	Antoine Walker	1.00
110	Christian Laettner	.40
111	Gary Trent	.20
112	Tony Battie	.50
113	Vlade Divac	.20
114	Kevin Johnson	.20
115	Erick Strickland	.20
116	Ray Allen	.50
117	Antonio Daniels	.75
118	Sean Elliott	.20
119	Horace Grant	.20
120	Walt Williams	.20
121	Rony Seikaly	.20
122	Allan Houston	.20
123	Michael Finley	.20
124	Rasheed Wallace	.20
125	Doug Christie	.20
126	Danny Ferry	.20
127	Arvydas Sabonis	.20
128	Shandon Anderson	.20
129	Otis Thorpe	.20
130	Adonal Foyle	.30
131	Bryant Reeves	.20
132	Theo Ratliff	.20
133	Matt Maloney	.20
134	Voshon Lenard	.20
135	Danny Fortson	.20
136	Joe Smith	4.00
137	Mookie Blaylock	1.50
138	Loy Vaught	1.50
139	Tom Gugliotta	3.00
140	Damon Stoudamire	6.00
141	Antonio McDyess	4.00
142	Kobe Bryant	20.00
143	Juwan Howard	4.00
144	Tim Hardaway	1.50
145	Ron Mercer	10.00
146	Joe Dumars	1.50
147	Clyde Drexler	4.00
148	Shareef Abdur-Rahim	10.00
149	LaPhonso Ellis	1.50
150	Dikembe Mutombo	1.50
151	Chauncey Billups	8.00
152	Chris Webber	8.00
153	Glenn Robinson	3.00
154	Patrick Ewing	1.50
155	Stephon Marbury	15.00
156	Keith Van Horn	20.00
157	Karl Malone	6.00
158	Terrell Brandon	4.00
159	Sam Cassell	4.00
160	Jerry Stackhouse	6.00
161	Vin Baker	6.00
162	Jason Kidd	8.00
163	Charles Barkley	8.00
164	Reggie Miller	6.00
165	Alonzo Mourning	4.00
166	Scottie Pippen	15.00
167	Glen Rice	4.00
168	Allen Iverson	30.00
169	David Robinson	8.00
170	Shawn Kemp	10.00
171	Michael Jordan	75.00
172	Tim Duncan	50.00
173	Anfernee Hardaway	30.00
174	Shaquille O'Neal	30.00
175	John Stockton	5.00
176	Gary Payton	10.00
177	Mitch Richmond	5.00
178	Kevin Garnett	40.00
179	Hakeem Olajuwon	12.00
180	Grant Hill	40.00

1997-98 Collector's Choice StarQuest Blow-Ups

		MT
Complete Set (5):		
Common Player:		
1	John Starks	
2	Steve Smith	
3	Toni Kukoc	
4	Rasheed Wallace	
5	Sean Elliott	

1997-98 Collector's Choice Stick-Ums

The 30-card insert set, seeded every three packs, features some of the top players in the league on a peel-off sticker card.

		MT
Complete Set (30):		10.00
Common Player:		.15
1	Steve Smith	.15
2	Antoine Walker	1.00
3	Anthony Mason	.15
4	Dennis Rodman	1.00
5	Terrell Brandon	.15
6	Michael Finley	.15
7	Antonio McDyess	.75
8	Grant Hill	2.00
9	Joe Smith	.50
10	Hakeem Olajuwon	.75
11	Reggie Miller	.30
12	Loy Vaught	.15
13	Shaquille O'Neal	1.50
14	Alonzo Mourning	.30
15	Vin Baker	.30
16	Stephon Marbury	1.50
17	Jim Jackson	.15
18	John Starks	.15
19	Anfernee Hardaway	1.50
20	Allen Iverson	2.00
21	Jason Kidd	.30
22	Kenny Anderson	.15
23	Mitch Richmond	.15
24	David Robinson	.50
25	Shawn Kemp	.75
26	Damon Stoudamire	.75
27	Karl Malone	.40
28	Bryant Reeves	.15
29	Juwan Howard	.40
30	Michael Jordan	4.00

1997-98 Collector's Choice The Jordan Dynasty

This five-card insert was found in Series I packs of Collector's Choice. All five cards featured Michael Jordan on the front and highlighted one of his five championships. The cards are sequentially numbered on the back to 23,000.

	MT
Complete Set (5):	60.00
Common Player:	12.00
Production 23,000 Sets	

1997-98 Upper Deck

Upper Deck was released in two, 180-card series in 1997- 1998. The first series had 135 base cards, 29 Jams '97 subset cards, 15 Court Perspective subset cards and one checklist. Series II had 120 current players, 29 Defining Moments subset cards, 15 Overtime subset cards and a checklist. Base cards featured an action shot of the player with a black border on the right side with silver lettering. A strip near the bottom contains the date of the photo and text about its significance. Inserts in Series I include: Game Jersey, Game-Dated, High Dimensions, Diamond Dimensions, Teammates, MJ Air Time and Ultimates. Inserts in Series II include: Jordan Power Deck, MJ Signed Jersey cards, Rookie Discovery I and II, NBA Records Collection, AIRLines, Great Eight and Jersey Cards.

		MT
Complete Set (360):		55.00
Complete Series 1 (180):		30.00
Complete Series 2 (180):		25.00
Common Player:		.10
Minor Stars:		.20
Series 1 or 2 Pack (12):		2.50
Series 1 or 2 Wax Box (24):		55.00
1	Steve Smith	.10
2	Christian Laettner	.20
3	Allan Houston	.10
4	Dikembe Mutombo	.20
5	Dana Barros	.10
6	Antoine Walker	1.00
7	Dee Brown	.10
8	Eric Williams	.10
9	Muggsy Bogues	.10
10	Dell Curry	.10
11	Vlade Divac	.10
12	Anthony Mason	.10
13	Glen Rice	.20
14	Jason Caffey	.10
15	Steve Kerr	.10
16	Toni Kukoc	.10
17	Luc Longley	.10
18	Michael Jordan	4.00
19	Terrell Brandon	.10
20	Danny Ferry	.10
21	Tyrone Hill	.10
22	*Derek Anderson*	2.00
23	Bob Sura	.10
24	Shawn Bradley	.10
25	Michael Finley	.10
26	Ed O'Bannon	.10
27	Robert Pack	.10
28	Samaki Walker	.10
29	LaPhonso Ellis	.10
30	*Tony Battie*	2.00
31	Antonio McDyess	.30
32	Bryant Stith	.10
33	Randolph Childress	.10
34	Grant Hill	2.00
35	Lindsey Hunter	.10
36	Grant Long	.10
37	Theo Ratliff	.10
38	B.J. Armstrong	.10
39	*Adonal Foyle*	1.00
40	Mark Price	.10
41	Felton Spencer	.10
42	Latrell Sprewell	.30
43	Clyde Drexler	.30
44	Mario Elie	.10
45	Hakeem Olajuwon	.75
46	Brent Price	.10
47	Kevin Willis	.10
48	Erick Dampier	.10
49	Antonio Davis	.10
50	Dale Davis	.10
51	Mark Jackson	.10
52	Rik Smits	.10
53	Brent Barry	.10
54	Lamond Murray	.10
55	Eric Piatkowski	.10
56	Loy Vaught	.10
57	Lorenzen Wright	.10
58	Kobe Bryant	3.00
59	Elden Campbell	.10
60	Derek Fisher	.10
61	Eddie Jones	.50
62	Nick Van Exel	.20
63	Keith Askins	.10
64	Isaac Austin	.10
65	P.J. Brown	.10
66	Tim Hardaway	.20
67	Alonzo Mourning	.20
68	Ray Allen	.30
69	Vin Baker	.30
70	Sherman Douglas	.10
71	Armon Gilliam	.10
72	Elliott Perry	.10
73	Chris Carr	.10
74	Tom Gugliotta	.20
75	Kevin Garnett	2.00
76	Doug West	.10
77	*Keith Van Horn*	2.00
78	Chris Gatling	.10
79	Kendall Gill	.10
80	Kerry Kittles	.40
81	Jayson Williams	.10
82	Chris Childs	.10
83	Allan Houston	.20
84	Larry Johnson	.20
85	Charles Oakley	.10
86	John Starks	.10
87	Horace Grant	.10
88	Anfernee Hardaway	1.75
89	Dennis Scott	.10
90	Rony Seikaly	.10
91	Brian Shaw	.10
92	Derrick Coleman	.10
93	Allen Iverson	1.75
94	*Tim Thomas*	2.00
95	Scott Williams	.10
96	Cedric Ceballos	.10
97	Kevin Johnson	.20
98	Loren Meyer	.10
99	Steve Nash	.10
100	Wesley Person	.10
101	Kenny Anderson	.10
102	Jermaine O'Neal	.20
103	Isaiah Rider	.10
104	Arvydas Sabonis	.10
105	Gary Trent	.10
106	Mahmoud Abdul-Rauf	.10
107	Billy Owens	.10
108	Olden Polynice	.10
109	Mitch Richmond	.20
110	Michael Smith	.10
111	Cory Alexander	.10
112	Vinny Del Negro	.10
113	Carl Herrera	.10
114	*Tim Duncan*	6.00
115	Hersey Hawkins	.10
116	Shawn Kemp	.50
117	Nate McMillan	.10
118	Sam Perkins	.10
119	Detlef Schrempf	.10
120	Doug Christie	.10
121	Popeye Jones	.10
122	Carlos Rogers	.10
123	Damon Stoudamire	.75
124	Adam Keefe	.10
125	Chris Morris	.10
126	Greg Ostertag	.10
127	John Stockton	.30
128	Shareef Abdur-Rahim	1.00
129	George Lynch	.10
130	Lee Mayberry	.10
131	Anthony Peeler	.10
132	Calbert Cheaney	.10
133	Tracy Murray	.10
134	Rod Strickland	.10
135	Chris Webber	.75
136	Christian Laettner	.10
137	Eric Williams	.10
138	Vlade Divac	.10
139	Michael Jordan	2.00
140	Tyrone Hill	.10
141	Michael Finley	.10
142	Tom Hammonds	.10
143	Theo Ratliff	.10
144	Latrell Sprewell	.10
145	Hakeem Olajuwon	.40
146	Reggie Miller	.10
147	Rodney Rogers	.10
148	Eddie Jones	.25
149	Jamal Mashburn	.10
150	Glenn Robinson	.10
151	Chris Carr	.10
152	Kendall Gill	.10
153	John Starks	.10
154	Anfernee Hardaway	.75
155	Derrick Coleman	.10
156	Cedric Ceballos	.10
157	Rasheed Wallace	.10
158	Corliss Williamson	.10
159	Sean Elliott	.10
160	Shawn Kemp	.30
161	Doug Christie	.10
162	Karl Malone	.10
163	Bryant Reeves	.10
164	Gheorghe Muresan	.10
165	Michael Jordan	2.00
166	Dikembe Mutombo	.10
167	Glen Rice	.10
168	Mitch Richmond	.10
169	Juwan Howard	.25
170	Clyde Drexler	.10
171	Terrell Brandon	.10
172	Jerry Stackhouse	.10
173	Damon Stoudamire	.10
174	Jayson Williams	.10
175	P.J. Brown	.10
176	Anfernee Hardaway	.75
177	Vin Baker	.10
178	LaPhonso Ellis	.10
179	Shawn Kemp	.30
180	Checklist	.10
181	Mookie Blaylock	.10
182	Tyrone Corbin	.10
183	Ken Norman	.10
184	*Ed Gray*	.50
185	*Chauncey Billups*	2.50
186	Tyus Edney	.10
187	Travis Knight	.10
188	*Ron Mercer*	3.00
189	Chris Mills	.10
190	Tony Delk	.10
191	Matt Geiger	.10
192	Bobby Phills	.10
193	David Wesley	.10
194	Keith Booth	.10
195	Randy Brown	.10
196	Ron Harper	.10
197	Scottie Pippen	1.25
198	Dennis Rodman	1.25
199	Zydrunas Ilgauskas	.50
200	*Brevin Knight*	1.25
201	Shawn Kemp	.60
202	Vitaly Potapenko	.10
203	Donny Marshall	.10
204	Erick Strickland	.10
205	A.C. Green	.10
206	Khalid Reeves	.10
207	Kurt Thomas	.10
208	Dennis Scott	.10
209	*Danny Fortson*	.75
210	*Bobby Jackson*	1.25
211	Eric Williams	.10
212	Dean Garrett	.10
213	Priest Lauderdale	.10
214	Joe Dumars	.10
215	Aaron McKie	.10
216	Charles O'Bannon	.10
217	Brian Williams	.10
218	Malik Sealy	.10
219	Scott Burrell	.10
220	Erick Dampier	.10
221	Todd Fuller	.10
222	Donyell Marshall	.10
223	Joe Smith	.50
224	Charles Barkley	.75
225	Matt Bullard	.10
226	Othella Harrington	.10
227	*Rodrick Rhodes*	.50
228	Eddie Johnson	.10
229	Matt Maloney	.10
230	Travis Best	.10
231	Reggie Miller	.30
232	Chris Mullin	.20
233	Fred Hoiberg	.10
234	*Austin Croshere*	.50
235	Kevin Duckworth	.10
236	Darrick Martin	.10
237	Pooh Richardson	.10
238	Rodney Rogers	.10
239	*Maurice Taylor*	1.00
240	Robert Horry	.10
241	Rick Fox	.10
242	Shaquille O'Neal	2.00
243	Corie Blount	.10
244	Duane Causwell	.10
245	Voshon Lenard	.10
246	Todd Day	.10
247	Dan Majerle	.10
248	Terry Mills	.10
249	Terrell Brandon	.20
250	Tyrone Hill	.10
251	Ervin Johnson	.10
252	Glenn Robinson	.30
253	Terry Porter	.10
254	Paul Grant	.10
255	Stephon Marbury	2.00
256	Sam Mitchell	.10
257	Cherokee Parks	.10
258	Sam Cassell	.10
259	David Benoit	.10
260	Kevin Edwards	.10
261	Don MacLean	.10
262	Patrick Ewing	.30
263	Walter McCarty	.10
264	John Starks	.10
265	John Thomas	.10
266	Chris Dudley	.10
267	Darrell Armstrong	.10
268	Nick Anderson	.10
269	Derek Harper	.10
270	Johnny Taylor	.10
271	Gerald Wilkins	.10
272	Clarence Weatherspoon	.10
273	Jerry Stackhouse	.50
274	Eric Montross	.10
275	Anthony Parker	.10
276	Antonio McDyess	.30
277	Clifford Robinson	.10
278	Jason Kidd	.50
279	Danny Manning	.10
280	Rex Chapman	.10
281	Stacey Augmon	.10
282	*Kelvin Cato*	.50
283	Brian Grant	.10
284	Rasheed Wallace	.10
285	*Lawrence Funderburke*	.30
286	Kevin Gamble	.10
287	*Tariq Abdul-Wahad*	.50
288	Corliss Williamson	.10
289	Sean Elliott	.10
290	Avery Johnson	.10
291	David Robinson	.75
292	Will Perdue	.10
293	James Cotton	.10
294	Jim McIlvaine	.10
295	Dale Ellis	.10
296	Gary Payton	.50
297	Aaron Williams	.10
298	Marcus Camby	.50
299	John Wallace	.20
300	*Tracy McGrady*	4.00
301	Walt Williams	.10
302	Shandon Anderson	.10
303	Antoine Carr	.10
304	Jeff Hornacek	.10
305	Karl Malone	.30
306	Bryon Russell	.10
307	*Jacque Vaughn*	.50
308	*Antonio Daniels*	1.50
309	Lawrence Moten	.10
310	Bryant Reeves	.10
311	Otis Thorpe	.10
312	*God Shammgod*	.30
313	Tim Legler	.10
314	Juwan Howard	.30
315	Gheorghe Muresan	.10
316	Michael Jordan	2.50
317	Allen Iverson	1.00
318	Karl Malone	.10
319	Glen Rice	.10
320	Dikembe Mutombo	.10
321	Grant Hill	1.25
322	Hakeem Olajuwon	.50
323	Stephon Marbury	1.00
324	Anfernee Hardaway	1.00
325	Shawn Kemp	.20
326	Mitch Richmond	.10
327	Kevin Johnson	.10
328	Kevin Garnett	1.25
329	Shareef Abdur-Rahim	.50
330	Damon Stoudamire	.30
331	Multiple Players	.10
332	Multiple Players	.10
333	Multiple Players	.10
334	Multiple Players	.10
335	Multiple Players	.10
336	Multiple Players	.10
337	Multiple Players	.10
338	Multiple Players	.10
339	Multiple Players	.10
340	Multiple Players	.10
341	Multiple Players	.10
342	Multiple Players	.10
343	Multiple Players	.10
344	Multiple Players	.10
345	Multiple Players	.10
346	Multiple Players	.10
347	Multiple Players	.10
348	Multiple Players	.10
349	Multiple Players	.10
350	Multiple Players	.10
351	Multiple Players	.10
352	Multiple Players	.10
353	Multiple Players	.10
354	Multiple Players	.10
355	Multiple Players	.10
356	Multiple Players	.10
357	Multiple Players	.10
358	Multiple Players	.10
359	Multiple Players	.10
360	Checklist	.10
NNO	Michael Jordan Black Audio	25.00
NNO	Michael Jordan Red Audio	12.00

1997-98 Upper Deck AIRlines

This 12-card insert set chronicles each year in Michael Jordan's NBA career. AIRLines cards were die-cut and numbered with an "AL" prefix. They were inserted one per 230 packs in both hobby and retail.

		MT
Complete Set (12):		1000.
Common Player:		100.00
1	Michael Jordan	100.00
2	Michael Jordan	100.00
3	Michael Jordan	100.00
4	Michael Jordan	100.00
5	Michael Jordan	100.00
6	Michael Jordan	100.00
7	Michael Jordan	100.00
8	Michael Jordan	100.00
9	Michael Jordan	100.00
10	Michael Jordan	100.00
11	Michael Jordan	100.00
12	Michael Jordan	100.00

1997-98 Upper Deck Diamond Dimensions

This 30-card insert paralleled the High Dimensions inserts, but was distinguished by a diamond die cut that made the shape of the card resemble an "X." Diamond Dimensions were also in Series I packs and sequentially numbered to 100 sets with a "D" prefix.

		MT
Common Player:		15.00
Minor Stars:		30.00
1	Anfernee Hardaway	225.00
2	Gary Payton	70.00
3	Marcus Camby	50.00
4	Charles Barkley	70.00
5	Jason Kidd	90.00
6	Alonzo Mourning	40.00
7	Kenny Anderson	15.00
8	Kobe Bryant	375.00
9	Dennis Rodman	175.00
10	Kerry Kittles	40.00
11	Dikembe Mutombo	15.00
12	Shaquille O'Neal	175.00
13	Glenn Robinson	30.00
14	Tony Delk	15.00
15	Larry Johnson	30.00
16	Brent Barry	15.00
17	Scottie Pippen	125.00
18	Shareef Abdur-Rahim	125.00
19	David Robinson	50.00
20	Damon Stoudamire	80.00
21	Kevin Garnett	275.00
22	Bob Sura	15.00
23	Michael Jordan	700.00
24	Joe Smith	30.00
25	Karl Malone	50.00
26	Antonio McDyess	40.00
27	Allen Iverson	250.00
28	Dale Davis	15.00
29	Antoine Walker	100.00
30	Chris Webber	100.00

1997-98 Upper Deck Game Dated Memorable Moments

Game-Dated cards paralleled 30 cards in the base set, with the addition of special foil embossing. This insert was found in one per 1,500 packs of Series I.

		MT
Complete Set (30):		1300.
Common Player:		10.00
Inserted 1:1500		
4	Dikembe Mutombo	15.00
6	Antoine Walker	50.00
13	Glen Rice	30.00
18	Michael Jordan	500.00
23	Bob Sura	10.00
25	Michael Finley	30.00
31	Antonio McDyess	50.00
34	Grant Hill	200.00
42	Latrell Sprewell	20.00
43	Clyde Drexler	50.00
45	Hakeem Olajuwon	60.00
49	Antonio Davis	10.00
56	Loy Vaught	10.00
61	Eddie Jones	60.00
66	Tim Hardaway	50.00
69	Vin Baker	50.00
75	Kevin Garnett	200.00
79	Kendall Gill	10.00
83	Allan Houston	15.00
88	Anfernee Hardaway	100.00
93	Allen Iverson	100.00
97	Kevin Johnson	15.00
103	Isaiah Rider	15.00
109	Mitch Richmond	20.00
112	Vinny Del Negro	10.00
116	Shawn Kemp	40.00
123	Damon Stoudamire	50.00
127	John Stockton	30.00
128	Shareef Abdur-Rahim	75.00
135	Chris Webber	75.00

1997-98 Upper Deck Game Jerseys

Game Jerseys was a 22-card insert set that had 12 cards in Series I and 10 more in Series II, both with an insertion rate of one per 2,500 packs. The cards were numbered with a "GJ" prefix and were horizontal in design with a swatch of the player's game-used jersey included on the card. Series II packs included 23 serial numbered autographed Jordan Game Jersey cards.

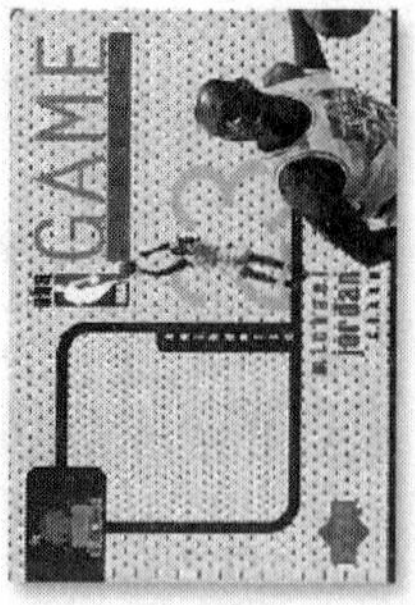

		MT
Complete Set (22):		8500.
Complete Series 1 (12):		3500.
Complete Series 2 (10):		5000.
Common Player:		200.00
1	Charles Barkley	375.00
2	Clyde Drexler	250.00
3	Kevin Garnett	600.00
4	Anfernee Hardaway	400.00
5	Grant Hill	550.00
6	Allen Iverson	450.00
7	Kerry Kittles	125.00
8	Toni Kukoc	225.00
9	Reggie Miller	225.00
10	Hakeem Olajuwon	200.00
11	Glen Rice	200.00
12	David Robinson	200.00
13	Michael Jordan	2700.
13S	Michael Jordan AUTO	15000.
14	Alonzo Mourning	250.00
15	Tim Hardaway	250.00
16	Marcus Camby	250.00
17	Antoine Walker	200.00
18	Kevin Johnson	100.00
19	Glenn Robinson	175.00
20	Patrick Ewing	275.00
21	Anfernee Hardaway	400.00
22	Grant Hill	500.00

1997-98 Upper Deck Great Eight

This eight-card insert pays tribute to the some of the top NBA veterans and was available only in Series II packs. These inserts are numbered with a "G" prefix and sequentially numbered to 800.

		MT
Complete Set (8):		275.00
Common Player:		10.00
1	Charles Barkley	25.00
2	Clyde Drexler	20.00
3	Joe Dumars	10.00
4	Patrick Ewing	15.00
5	Michael Jordan	180.00
6	Karl Malone	20.00
7	Hakeem Olajuwon	35.00
8	John Stockton	15.00

1997-98 Upper Deck High Dimensions

High Dimensions included 30 cards that were sequentially numbered to 2,000. Exclusive to Series I packs, these inserts are numbered with a "D" prefix.

		MT
Complete Set (30):		550.00
Common Player:		3.00
Minor Stars:		6.00
1	Anfernee Hardaway	45.00
2	Gary Payton	12.00
3	Marcus Camby	10.00
4	Charles Barkley	15.00
5	Jason Kidd	12.00
6	Alonzo Mourning	10.00
7	Kenny Anderson	3.00
8	Kobe Bryant	75.00
9	Dennis Rodman	30.00
10	Kerry Kittles	10.00
11	Dikembe Mutombo	3.00
12	Shaquille O'Neal	35.00
13	Glenn Robinson	8.00
14	Tony Delk	3.00
15	Larry Johnson	6.00
16	Brent Barry	3.00
17	Scottie Pippen	30.00
18	Shareef Abdur-Rahim	30.00
19	David Robinson	10.00
20	Damon Stoudamire	15.00
21	Kevin Garnett	60.00
22	Bob Sura	3.00
23	Michael Jordan	110.00
24	Joe Smith	10.00
25	Karl Malone	10.00
26	Antonio McDyess	10.00
27	Allen Iverson	60.00
28	Dale Davis	3.00
29	Antoine Walker	25.00
30	Chris Webber	25.00

1997-98 Upper Deck Jordan Air Time

		MT
Complete Set (10):		140.00
Common Jordan (1-9):		8.00
Inserted 1:12		
1	Michael Jordan	8.00
2	Michael Jordan	8.00
3	Michael Jordan	8.00
4	Michael Jordan	8.00
5	Michael Jordan	8.00
6	Michael Jordan	8.00
7	Michael Jordan	8.00
8	Michael Jordan	8.00
9	Michael Jordan	8.00
10	Michael Jordan	80.00

1997-98 Upper Deck Records Collection

This Series II insert was found in one per 23 hobby and retail packs. Cards are numbered with a "RC" prefix, and resemble a vinyl record album on the front, with a red circle center that has a shot of the player.

		MT
Complete Set (30):		130.00
Common Player:		1.00
Minor Stars:		2.00
1	Dikembe Mutombo	1.00
2	Dana Barros	1.00
3	Glen Rice	2.00
4	Dennis Rodman	12.00
5	Shawn Kemp	5.00
6	A.C. Green	1.00
7	LaPhonso Ellis	1.00
8	Grant Hill	20.00
9	Joe Smith	4.00
10	Charles Barkley	5.00
11	Reggie Miller	3.00
12	Loy Vaught	1.00
13	Shaquille O'Neal	12.00
14	Tim Hardaway	4.00
15	Glenn Robinson	4.00
16	Stephon Marbury	20.00
17	Sam Cassell	1.00
18	Patrick Ewing	3.00
19	Anfernee Hardaway	15.00
20	Allen Iverson	20.00
21	Kevin Johnson	1.00
22	Kenny Anderson	1.00
23	Mitch Richmond	3.00
24	David Robinson	5.00
25	Gary Payton	4.00
26	Damon Stoudamire	5.00
27	John Stockton	3.00
28	Bryant Reeves	1.00
29	Chris Webber	7.00
30	Michael Jordan	40.00

1997-98 Upper Deck Rookie Discovery 1

This 15-card insert showcases the top rookies from the 1997 NBA Draft. It was included in one per four packs of Series II and was numbered with a "R" prefix. Parallel versions also exist and are die-cut and numbered with a "D" prefix.

		MT
Complete Set (15):		35.00
Common Player:		.50
Minor Stars:		1.00
Inserted 1:4		
Discovery 2 Cards:		4x-8x
Inserted 1:108		
1	Tim Duncan	10.00
2	Keith Van Horn	6.00
3	Chauncey Billups	4.00
4	Antonio Daniels	3.00
5	Tony Battie	3.00
6	Ron Mercer	6.00
7	Tim Thomas	5.00
8	Adonal Foyle	1.00
9	Tracy McGrady	5.00
10	Danny Fortson	1.50
11	Olivier Saint-Jean	1.50
12	Austin Croshere	1.50
13	Derek Anderson	3.00
14	Maurice Taylor	2.00
15	Kelvin Cato	.50

1997-98 Upper Deck Teammates

Teammates was a 60-card insert that was exclusive to Series I packs and inserted at a rate of one per four packs. This insert matched up the top tandems for each team in the league, and included a special Jordan/Hardaway card, on a die-cut format that fit together. Cards are numbered with a "T" prefix.

		MT
Complete Set (60):		100.00
Common Player:		.50
Minor Stars:		1.00
1	Mookie Blaylock	.50
2	Steve Smith	.50
3	Antoine Walker	3.00
4	Eric Williams	.50
5	Anthony Mason	.50
6	Glen Rice	1.00
7	Michael Jordan	12.00
8	Scottie Pippen	3.00
9	Terrell Brandon	1.00
10	Tyrone Hill	.50
11	Shawn Bradley	.50
12	Robert Pack	.50
13	LaPhonso Ellis	.50
14	Antonio McDyess	1.50
15	Grant Hill	7.00
16	Terry Mills	.50
17	Joe Smith	1.00
18	Latrell Sprewell	1.00
19	Charles Barkley	2.00
20	Hakeem Olajuwon	2.00
21	Mark Jackson	.50
22	Reggie Miller	1.00
23	Brent Barry	.50
24	Loy Vaught	.50
25	Shaquille O'Neal	5.00
26	Nick Van Exel	.50
27	Tim Hardaway	1.00
28	Alonzo Mourning	1.00
29	Vin Baker	2.00
30	Glenn Robinson	1.00
31	Kevin Garnett	7.00
32	Stephon Marbury	6.00
33	Chris Gatling	.50
34	Kerry Kittles	1.00
35	Allan Houston	.50
36	John Starks	.50
37	Horace Grant	.50
38	Anfernee Hardaway	5.00
39	Allen Iverson	6.00
40	Jerry Stackhouse	1.00
41	Jason Kidd	1.50
42	Wesley Person	.50
43	Kenny Anderson	.50
44	Isaiah Rider	.50
45	Billy Owens	.50
46	Mitch Richmond	1.00
47	Sean Elliott	.50
48	David Robinson	2.00
49	Shawn Kemp	2.00
50	Gary Payton	1.50
51	Marcus Camby	1.00
52	Damon Stoudamire	2.00
53	Karl Malone	1.50
54	John Stockton	1.50
55	Shareef Abdur-Rahim	3.00
56	Bryant Reeves	.50
57	Juwan Howard	1.50
58	Chris Webber	2.00
59	Michael Jordan	12.00
60	Anfernee Hardaway	5.00

Values quoted in this guide reflect the retail price of a card — the price a collector can expect to pay when buying a card from a dealer. The wholesale price — that which a collector can expect to receive from a dealer when selling cards — will be significantly lower, depending on desirability and condition.

1997-98 Upper Deck Ultimates

Ultimates was a 30-card insert set found in one per 23 packs of Series I. The cards are numbered with a "U" prefix and feature statistical information over a white background.

		MT
Complete Set (30):		160.00
Common Player:		1.50
Minor Stars:		3.00
1	Michael Jordan	45.00
2	Grant Hill	20.00
3	Charles Barkley	6.00
4	Tom Gugliotta	4.00
5	Dennis Rodman	12.00
6	Reggie Miller	4.00
7	Jason Kidd	5.00
8	Loy Vaught	1.50
9	Mookie Blaylock	1.50
10	Tim Hardaway	4.00
11	Juwan Howard	4.00
12	Shawn Kemp	6.00
13	Mitch Richmond	4.00
14	Larry Johnson	4.00
15	Marcus Camby	4.00
16	Bryant Stith	1.50
17	Bryant Reeves	3.00
18	Joe Smith	4.00
19	Jerry Stackhouse	4.00
20	Arvydas Sabonis	1.50
21	John Stockton	3.00
22	Eddie Jones	6.00
23	Anfernee Hardaway	15.00
24	Ray Allen	4.00
25	Terrell Brandon	3.00
26	David Robinson	6.00
27	Anthony Mason	1.50
28	Robert Pack	1.50
29	Dana Barros	1.50
30	Kendall Gill	1.50

1997-98 Upper Deck Diamond Vision

This 29-card set includes three inserts, including an all- Jordan set. The front shows game-action footage in a hologram view, with the player's name along the bottom. The back is a white background with text on the player.

		MT
Complete Set (29):		180.00
Common Player:		2.00
Signature Moves:		2x
Wax Box:		100.00
1	Dikembe Mutombo	2.00
2	Dana Barros	2.00
3	Glen Rice	3.00
4	Michael Jordan	40.00
5	Terrell Brandon	2.00
6	Michael Finley	3.00
7	Antonio McDyess	4.00
8	Grant Hill	20.00
9	Latrell Sprewell	4.00
10	Hakeem Olajuwon	8.00
11	Reggie Miller	4.00
12	Loy Vaught	2.00
13	Shaquille O'Neal	16.00
14	Alonzo Mourning	3.00
15	Vin Baker	6.00
16	Kevin Garnett	20.00
17	Kerry Kittles	4.00
18	Patrick Ewing	4.00
19	Anfernee Hardaway	16.00
20	Allen Iverson	20.00
21	Jason Kidd	6.00
22	Isaiah Rider	2.00
23	Mitch Richmond	3.00
24	David Robinson	5.00
25	Gary Payton	5.00
26	Damon Stoudamire	6.00
27	Karl Malone	4.00
28	Shareef Abdur-Rahim	10.00
29	Chris Webber	8.00
RT1	Michael Jordan RT	200.00

1997-98 Upper Deck Diamond Vision Signature Moves

Signature Moves was a 29-card parallel set that was inserted one per five packs. They are identified by a facsimile signature of the player on the front.

	MT
Signature Move Cards:	2x

1997-98 Upper Deck Diamond Vision Dunk Vision

This six-card set features slam dunks by the superstars. Inserted at 1:40, the cards have a color action shot on the front, with the player's name in orange below the photo. The cards are numbered with the prefix "D".

		MT
Complete Set (6):		275.00
Common Player:		20.00
1	Michael Jordan	125.00
2	Anfernee Hardaway	40.00
3	Shaquille O'Neal	40.00
4	Grant Hill	60.00
5	Kevin Garnett	60.00
6	Hakeem Olajuwon	20.00

1997-98 Upper Deck Diamond Vision Reel Time

The one-card set is highlighted by Michael Jordan. The front has a photo of Jordan, with "Reel Time" along the bottom. The card is prefixed with the letter "R".

		MT
Complete Set (1):		200.00
Common Player:		200.00
1	Michael Jordan	200.00

1997 Upper Deck Holojam

One Holojam card was available in each special Wal-Mart repack in the Summer of 1997. The pack contained one Holojam card, two retail packs of 1996-97 Collector's Choice Series Two and two retail packs of 1996-97 Upper Deck Series Two for $9.97. The card fronts feature a full-bleed holographic color action photo. The backs have two photos and a player profile.

	MT
Complete Set (20):	130.00
Common Player:	2.00

1	Michael Jordan	30.00
2	Juwan Howard	4.00
3	Shaquille O'Neal	10.00
4	Kevin Garnett	15.00
5	Allen Iverson	20.00
6	Glen Rice	2.00
7	Hakeem Olajuwon	6.00
8	Patrick Ewing	2.00
9	Karl Malone	3.00
10	Reggie Miller	2.00
11	Shawn Kemp	4.00
12	Alonzo Mourning	2.00
13	Grant Hill	15.00
14	Kobe Bryant	25.00
15	Stephon Marbury	20.00
16	Vin Baker	4.00
17	Latrell Sprewell	2.00
18	Scottie Pippen	7.00
19	Shareef Abdur-Rahim	15.00
20	Anfernee Hardaway	10.00

1997 Upper Deck Michael Jordan Championship Journals

This Jordan boxed set carried an SRP of $19.99. It contained 24 oversized cards (3-1/2" x 5"), each depicting a memorable moment from one of Jordan's championship seasons. The card backs have Jordan's comments on the moment. A limited edition card (only 5,000 produced) was also included in the set. Fifty of the cards were signed by Jordan and randomly inserted in packs.

		MT
Complete Set (24):		25.00
Common Player:		1.50
1	Championship Journal 1991 (1st Round vs. New York)	1.50
2	Championship Journal 1991 (Semis vs. Philadelphia)	1.50
3	Championship Journal 1991 (Conference Finals vs. Detroit)	1.50
4	Championship Journal 1991 (NBA Finals vs. Lakers)	1.50
5	Championship Journal 1992 (1st Round vs. Miami)	1.50
6	Championship Journal 1992 (Semis vs. New York)	1.50
7	Championship Journal 1992 (Conference Finals vs. Cleveland)	1.50
8	Championship Journal 1992 (NBA Finals vs. Portland)	1.50
9	Championship Journal 1993 (1st Round vs. Atlanta)	1.50
10	Championship Journal 1993 (Semis vs. Cleveland)	1.50
11	Championship Journal 1993 (Conference Finals vs. New York)	1.50
12	Championship Journal 1993 (NBA Finals vs. Phoenix)	1.50
13	Championship Journal 1996 (1st Round vs. Miami)	1.50
14	Championship Journal 1996 (Semis vs. New York)	1.50
15	Championship Journal 1996 (Conference Finals vs. Orlando)	1.50
16	Championship Journal 1996 (NBA Finals vs. Seattle)	1.50
17	MJ's Memorable Moments (Altered Shot vs. Lakers)	1.50
18	MJ's Memorable Moments (56-point game vs. Miami)	1.50
19	MJ's Memorable Moments (Triple OT game vs. Phoenix)	1.50
20	MJ's Memorable Moments (1991 Finals celebration w/trophy)	1.50
21	MJ's Memorable Moments (Force Game 7 vs. New York)	1.50
22	MJ's Memorable Moments (Game 6 vs. Seattle)	1.50
23	MJ's Memorable Moments (1992 Finals vs. Portland)	1.50
24	MJ's Memorable Moments (1993 Finals vs. Phoenix)	1.50

1997-98 Upper Deck Nestle Crunch

		MT
Complete Set (40):		25.00
Common Player:		.25
1	Kenny Anderson	.40
2	Arvydas Sabonis	.25
3	Elliott Perry	.25
4	Chris Webber	2.00
5	Michael Jordan	10.00
6	Terrell Brandon	.40
7	Rick Fox	.25
8	Brent Barry	.25
9	Bryant Reeves	.25
10	Steve Smith	.40
11	Mookie Blaylock	.25
12	Christian Laettner	.40
13	Tim Hardaway	.50
14	Voshon Lenard	.25
15	Dan Majerle	.25
16	Glen Rice	.40
17	Dell Curry	.25
18	Karl Malone	1.00
19	John Stockton	.40
20	Mitch Richmond	.40
21	Patrick Ewing	.40
22	Kobe Bryant	6.00
23	Eddie Jones	1.00
24	Anfernee Hardaway	3.00
25	Rony Seikaly	.25
26	Chris Gatling	.25
27	Kendall Gill	.25
28	Dale Ellis	.25
29	Reggie Miller	.40
30	Terry Mills	.25
31	Damon Stoudamire	.60
32	Clyde Drexler	.40
33	Allen Iverson	5.00
34	Jerry Stackhouse	.40
35	Hersey Hawkins	.25
36	Gary Payton	1.00
37	Carl Herrera	.25
38	Rex Chapman	.25
39	Tom Gugliotta	.40
40	Latrell Sprewell	.40

1997-98 Upper Deck Slam Dunk

		MT
Complete Set (40):		25.00
Common Player:		.25
1	Chris Webber	2.00
2	Shawn Kemp	1.00
3	Dikembe Mutombo	.40
4	Alonzo Mourning	.50
5	Marcus Camby	.75
6	Otis Thorpe	.25
7	Antonio McDyess	1.00
8	Vin Baker	1.00
9	Kevin Garnett	5.00
10	Patrick Ewing	.40
11	Shareef Abdur-Rahim	2.00
12	Antoine Walker	1.50
13	Joe Smith	.40
14	Glen Rice	.40
15	Juwan Howard	.40
16	Eddie Jones	.75
17	Karl Malone	1.00
18	Bryant Reeves	.40
19	Anfernee Hardaway	4.00
20	LaPhonso Ellis	.40
21	Kerry Kittles	.40
22	Michael Jordan	10.00
23	Latrell Sprewell	.40
24	Olden Polynice	.25
25	Rik Smits	.25
26	Glenn Robinson	.75
27	Loy Vaught	.25
28	Jim Jackson	.25
29	Horace Grant	.25
30	Allen Iverson	5.00
31	Clifford Robinson	.25
32	Isaiah Rider	.40
33	Clyde Drexler	.75
34	Sean Elliott	.25
35	Eric Williams	.25
36	Larry Johnson	.40
37	Anthony Mason	.40
38	Terrell Brandon	.40
39	Reggie Miller	.40
40	Kevin Johnson	.40

1997-98 Upper Deck Slam Dunk Contestants

		MT
Complete Set (6):		75.00
Common Player:		5.00
1	Kobe Bryant (Champion)	50.00
2	Chris Carr	5.00
3	Michael Finley	10.00
4	Darvin Ham	5.00
5	Bob Sura	5.00
6	Ray Allen	15.00

1997-98 UD3

A retail-only product, UD3 consists of 60 cards, with three sets of 20-card subsets. Also included is four sets of inserts, totaling 37 cards. The three main sets - Jam Masters, Starstruck and The Big Picture - have the title on the front, with a color action photo of the player. Inserts include: Awesome Action, Rookie Portfolio, Season Ticket Autographs and MJ3 Collection.

		MT
Complete Set (60):		60.00
Common Player:		.25
Minor Stars:		.50
Pack (3):		4.00
Wax Box (24):		65.00
1	Anfernee Hardaway	2.50
2	Alonzo Mourning	.50
3	Grant Hill	3.00
4	Kerry Kittles	.75
5	Latrell Sprewell	.50
6	Rasheed Wallace	.25
7	Jerry Stackhouse	.50
8	Glen Rice	.50
9	Marcus Camby	.75
10	Scottie Pippen	1.25
11	Patrick Ewing	.50
12	Michael Finley	.50
13	Karl Malone	.75
14	Antonio McDyess	.50
15	Michael Jordan	6.00
16	Clyde Drexler	.50
17	Brent Barry	.25
18	Glenn Robinson	.50
19	Kobe Bryant	4.00
20	Reggie Miller	.50
21	John Stockton	.50
22	Gary Payton	.50
23	Michael Jordan	6.00
24	Vin Baker	.50
25	Karl Malone	.50
26	Juwan Howard	.50
27	Charles Barkley	.75
28	Jason Kidd	.75
29	Joe Dumars	.25
30	Anfernee Hardaway	2.50
31	Mitch Richmond	.50
32	Alonzo Mourning	.50
33	Grant Hill	3.00
34	Shaquille O'Neal	2.00
35	Scottie Pippen	1.25
36	Reggie Miller	.50
37	Hakeem Olajuwon	1.00
38	Tim Hardaway	.25
39	David Robinson	.75
40	Shawn Kemp	.75
41	Allen Iverson	3.50
42	Stephon Marbury	3.00
43	Dennis Rodman	2.50
44	Terrell Brandon	.25
45	Michael Jordan	8.00
46	Kerry Kittles	.75
47	Hakeem Olajuwon	1.75
48	Loy Vaught	.25
49	Antoine Walker	1.50
50	Gary Payton	1.00
51	Kevin Johnson	.25
52	Kevin Garnett	4.00
53	Shareef Abdur-Rahim	2.00
54	Larry Johnson	.50
55	Dikembe Mutombo	.25
56	Chris Webber	1.25
57	Joe Smith	.75
58	Kendall Gill	.25
59	Kenny Anderson	.25
60	Damon Stoudamire	1.00

1997-98 UD3 Awesome Action

A 20-card set, the front has a color action shot, with the featured player highlighted in a circle. The back has three sequence photos, and the numbers are prefixed with an "A". Insertion rate is 1:11.

		MT
Complete Set (20):		120.00
Common Player:		1.50
Minor Stars:		3.00
1	Michael Jordan	30.00
2	Kobe Bryant	20.00
3	Jerry Stackhouse	4.00
4	Shawn Kemp	4.00
5	Hakeem Olajuwon	6.00
6	Grant Hill	15.00
7	Scottie Pippen	8.00
8	Alonzo Mourning	1.50
9	Damon Stoudamire	5.00
10	Kevin Garnett	15.00
11	Anfernee Hardaway	10.00
12	Shareef Abdur-Rahim	8.00
13	Allen Iverson	15.00
14	Dennis Rodman	10.00
15	Shaquille O'Neal	10.00
16	Jason Kidd	3.00
17	Gary Payton	3.00
18	Dikembe Mutombo	1.50
19	Karl Malone	3.00
20	Stephon Marbury	12.00

1997-98 UD3 Michael Jordan MJ3

Just a three-card set, it's all Michael Jordan. The cards are rainbow-foiled, with red foil-stamping. The No.1 card is inserted 1:45, No.2 at 1:119 and No.3 at 1:167, prefixed "MJ".

		MT
Complete Set (3):		175.00
Common Player:		30.00
I	Michael Jordan	30.00
II	Michael Jordan	60.00
III	Michael Jordan	100.00

1997-98 UD3 Rookie Portfolio

The set features the first 10 players selected in the 1997 NBA Draft. The 10-card set has studio photos of the players on the front taken during Draft activities. The cards are inserted at 1:144. They are numbered with a "R" prefix.

		MT
Complete Set (10):		300.00
Common Player:		8.00
1	Tim Duncan	80.00
2	Keith Van Horn	35.00
3	Chauncey Billups	30.00
4	Antonio Daniels	30.00
5	Tony Battie	25.00
6	Ron Mercer	40.00
7	Tim Thomas	25.00
8	Adonal Foyle	8.00
9	Tracy McGrady	40.00
10	Danny Fortson	15.00

1997-98 UD3 Season Ticket Autographs

The four-card set is a replica of the "Season Ticket" set. The cards are simply autographed by four players and inserted at a rate of 1:1,800.

		MT
Complete Set (4):		3000.
Common Player:		100.00
MJ	Michael Jordan	2500.
AH	Anfernee Hardaway	500.00
TH	Tim Hardaway	125.00
JH	Juwan Howard	100.00

1998 UD Hardcourt

UD Hardcourt was a 90-card set that included 70 veterans and a 20-card Rookie Experience subset. The cards featured an image of the player and a circle in the background, both in etched foil. The rest of the background resembles the wood of a basketball court and also adds red stripes in a circular fashion. Hardcourt arrived with two parallels - Home Court Advantage and Home Court Advantage Plus - along with two inserts - High Court and Holding Court.

		MT
Complete Set (90):		90.00
Common Player:		.25
Minor Stars:		.50
Jordan 5x7:		7.00
Pack (4):		6.00
Wax Box (20):		110.00
1	Kobe Bryant	7.00
2	Donyell Marshall	.25
3	Bryant Reeves	.25
4	Keith Van Horn	5.00
5	David Robinson	1.00
6	Nick Anderson	.25
7	Nick Van Exel	.50
8	David Wesley	.25
9	Alonzo Mourning	.50
10	Shawn Kemp	.50
11	Maurice Taylor	3.00
12	Kenny Anderson	.25
13	Jason Kidd	1.25
14	Marcus Camby	.50
15	Tim Hardaway	.75
16	Damon Stoudamire	1.00
17	Detlef Schrempf	.25
18	Dikembe Mutombo	.50
19	Charles Barkley	1.00
20	Ray Allen	.75
21	Ron Mercer	8.00
22	Shawn Bradley	.25
23	Michael Jordan	10.00
23a	Michael Jordan	20.00
24	Antonio McDyess	.75
25	Stephon Marbury	3.50
26	Rik Smits	.25
27	Michael Stewart	.25
28	Steve Smith	.25
29	Glenn Robinson	.25
30	Chris Webber	1.50
31	Antoine Walker	2.00
32	Eddie Jones	1.50
33	Mitch Richmond	.50
34	Kevin Garnett	4.00
35	Grant Hill	4.00
36	John Stockton	.50
37	Allan Houston	.50
38	Bobby Jackson	2.00
39	Sam Cassell	.25
40	Allen Iverson	3.50
41	LaPhonso Ellis	.25
42	Lorenzen Wright	.25
43	Gary Payton	1.00
44	Patrick Ewing	.50
45	Scottie Pippen	2.00
46	Hakeem Olajuwon	1.50
47	Glen Rice	.50
48	Antonio Daniels	2.50
49	Jayson Williams	.25
50	Juwan Howard	.75
51	Reggie Miller	.50
52	Joe Smith	.50
53	Shaquille O'Neal	3.00
54	Dennis Rodman	3.00
55	Vin Baker	1.00
56	Rod Strickland	.25
57	Anfernee Hardaway	3.00
58	Zydrunas Ilgauskas	.50
59	Chris Mullin	.25
60	Rasheed Wallace	.25
61	Shareef Abdur-Rahim	2.00
62	Tom Gugliotta	.25
63	Tim Duncan	20.00
64	Michael Finley	.50
65	Jim Jackson	.50
66	Chauncey Billups	4.00
67	Jerry Stackhouse	.50
68	Jeff Hornacek	.25
69	Clyde Drexler	.75
70	Karl Malone	1.00
71	Tim Duncan	10.00
72	Keith Van Horn	3.00
73	Chauncey Billups	2.00
74	Antonio Daniels	1.25
75	Tony Battie	1.50
76	Ron Mercer	4.00
77	Tim Thomas	6.00
78	Tracy McGrady	6.00
79	Danny Fortson	2.50
80	Derek Anderson	3.00
81	Maurice Taylor	1.50
82	Kelvin Cato	1.50
83	Brevin Knight	3.00
84	Bobby Jackson	1.00
85	Rodrick Rhodes	1.00
86	Anthony Johnson	.25
87	Cedric Henderson	1.00
88	Alvin Williams	.25
89	Michael Stewart	.25
90	Zydrunas Ilgauskas	.25

1998 UD Hardcourt Home Court Advantage

	MT
Complete Set (90):	225.00
Common Player:	.75
Home Court Adv. Cards:	2x-3x
Inserted 1:4	

1998 UD Hardcourt Home Court Advantage Plus

	MT
Common Player:	4.00
HCA Plus Cards:	8x-16x
Production 500 Sets	

1998 UD Hardcourt High Court

This 30-card insert was printed on wood paper stock and included gold and silver stamping. The cards featured the insert logo in the bottom right corner, with a basketball court look over the rest of the card. Cards were sequentially numbered on the back to 3,000 sets. They are numbered with a "H" prefix.

		MT
Complete Set (30):		525.00
Common Player:		3.00
Minor Stars:		6.00
Production 1,300 Sets		
1	Dikembe Mutombo	3.00
2	Ron Mercer	30.00
3	Glen Rice	6.00
4	Scottie Pippen	25.00
5	Shawn Kemp	10.00
6	Michael Finley	6.00
7	LaPhonso Ellis	3.00
8	Grant Hill	50.00
9	Clarence Weatherspoon	3.00
10	Hakeem Olajuwon	15.00
11	Chris Mullin	3.00
12	Lamond Murray	3.00
13	Kobe Bryant	60.00
14	Tim Hardaway	6.00
15	Ray Allen	8.00
16	Stephon Marbury	30.00
17	Keith Van Horn	20.00
18	Allan Houston	3.00
19	Anfernee Hardaway	30.00
20	Allen Iverson	25.00
21	Antonio McDyess	8.00
22	Rasheed Wallace	3.00
23	Mitch Richmond	6.00
24	Tim Duncan	50.00
25	Gary Payton	10.00
26	Chauncey Billups	8.00
27	John Stockton	6.00
28	Shareef Abdur-Rahim	20.00
29	Juwan Howard	8.00
30	Michael Jordan	100.00

1998 UD Hardcourt Jordan Holding Court

Jordan Holding Court features wood on wood cards that have Jordan on one side and one of 30 stars on the other. All double-fronted cards are done on 40-point stock, foil stamped and sequentially numbered. Red foil versions are numbered to 2,300, Bronze foil to 230, Silver foil to 23 and Gold foil versions are numbered 1 of 1. Cards are numbered with a "J" prefix.

		MT
Complete Set (30):		425.00
Common Player:		2.50
Minor Stars:		5.00
Production 2,300 Sets		
Bronze Cards:		2x-4x
Production 230 Sets		
Silver Cards:		12x-24x
Production 23 Sets		
1	Steve Smith, Michael Jordan	2.50
2	Antoine Walker, Michael Jordan	15.00
3	Glen Rice, Michael Jordan	5.00

4 Scottie Pippen, Michael Jordan 20.00
5 Shawn Kemp, Michael Jordan 8.00
6 Michael Finley, Michael Jordan 5.00
7 Bobby Jackson, Michael Jordan 2.50
8 Grant Hill, Michael Jordan 40.00
9 Jim Jackson, Michael Jordan 2.50
10 Charles Barkley, Michael Jordan 10.00
11 Reggie Miller, Michael Jordan 6.00
12 Lorenzen Wright, Michael Jordan 2.50
13 Kobe Bryant, Michael Jordan 50.00
14 Tim Hardaway, Michael Jordan 8.00
15 Glenn Robinson, Michael Jordan 5.00
16 Kevin Garnett, Michael Jordan 40.00
17 Keith Van Horn, Michael Jordan 20.00
18 Patrick Ewing, Michael Jordan 5.00
19 Anfernee Hardaway, Michael Jordan 25.00
20 Allen Iverson, Michael Jordan 20.00
21 Jason Kidd, Michael Jordan 15.00
22 Damon Stoudamire, Michael Jordan 10.00
23 Mitch Richmond, Michael Jordan 5.00
24 Tim Duncan, Michael Jordan 40.00
25 Gary Payton, Michael Jordan 8.00
26 Chauncey Billups, Michael Jordan 5.00
27 Karl Malone, Michael Jordan 8.00
28 Shareef Abdur-Rahim, Michael Jordan 15.00
29 Chris Webber, Michael Jordan 15.00
30 Michael Jordan, Michael Jordan 85.00

1998 UD Hardcourt Jordan Holding Court Bronze

	MT
Common Player:	10.00
Bronze Cards:	2x-4x
Production 230 Sets	

1998 UD Hardcourt Jordan Holding Court Silver

	MT
Common Player:	60.00
Silver Cards:	12x-24x
Production 23 Sets	

1998 Upper Deck Kellogg's

These Kellogg's NBA and WNBA cards were distributed in 10-card packs that contained both, through a mail-in offer of two dated box tops and 95 cents for shipping and handling. Cards available in packs were silver foil, while a 56-card gold foil set was available through a mail-in offer for $9.95. The NBA cards were produced by Upper Deck, while Pinnacle produced the WNBA cards.

	MT
Complete Set (40):	25.00
Common Player:	.25
Shareef Abdur-Rahim	2.00
Vin Baker	.75
Brent Barry	.25
Tony Battie	.40
Chauncey Billups	.40
Mookie Blaylock	.25
Terrell Brandon	.40
Kobe Bryant	6.00
Scott Burrell	.25
Marcus Camby	.75
Sam Cassell	.40
Vlade Divac	.40
Joe Dumars	.40
Tim Duncan	4.00
Michael Finley	.15
Horace Grant	.25
Tim Hardaway	.75
Ron Harper	.25
Grant Hill	4.00
Juwan Howard	.75
Eddie Jones	.75
Jason Kidd	2.00
Luc Longley	.25
Karl Malone	1.00
Antonio McDyess	1.00
Chris Mullin	.40
Dikembe Mutombo	.40
Hakeem Olajuwon	1.00
Jermaine O'Neal	.75
Glen Rice	.40
Mitch Richmond	.40
David Robinson	1.00
Joe Smith	.40
Jerry Stackhouse	.40
John Stockton	.40
Damon Stoudamire	.75
Keith Van Horn	2.00
Antoine Walker	1.50
Samaki Walker	.25
Charlie Ward	.25

1998 UD Jordan Living Legend

This 165-card set was a retail-only Jordan set and released during the lockout. It contained 120 MJ Time Frames, along with two subsets - 15 The Elements of Style - Jordan, which took a look back at the varying styles MJ has sported over the years, and 30 The Jordan Files, which detailed his performance against each NBA franchise. Inserts include: 50 total Sign of Greatness Autographs, 23 hand-numbered Autographed Game-worn Jersey cards, 15 Jordan in Flight, 8 Cover Story and 30 Game Action.

		MT
Complete Set (165):		100.00
Common Player:		.75
Wax Box:		60.00
1	Michael Jordan	.75
2	Michael Jordan	.75
3	Michael Jordan	.75
4	Michael Jordan	.75
5	Michael Jordan	.75
6	Michael Jordan	.75
7	Michael Jordan	.75
8	Michael Jordan	.75
9	Michael Jordan	.75
10	Michael Jordan	.75
11	Michael Jordan	.75
12	Michael Jordan	.75
13	Michael Jordan	.75
14	Michael Jordan	.75
15	Michael Jordan	.75
16	Michael Jordan	.75
17	Michael Jordan	.75
18	Michael Jordan	.75
19	Michael Jordan	.75
20	Michael Jordan	.75
21	Michael Jordan	.75
22	Michael Jordan	.75
23	Michael Jordan	.75
24	Michael Jordan	.75
25	Michael Jordan	.75
26	Michael Jordan	.75
27	Michael Jordan	.75
28	Michael Jordan	.75
29	Michael Jordan	.75
30	Michael Jordan	.75
31	Michael Jordan	.75
32	Michael Jordan	.75
33	Michael Jordan	.75
34	Michael Jordan	.75
35	Michael Jordan	.75
36	Michael Jordan	.75
37	Michael Jordan	.75
38	Michael Jordan	.75
39	Michael Jordan	.75
40	Michael Jordan	.75
41	Michael Jordan	.75
42	Michael Jordan	.75
43	Michael Jordan	.75
44	Michael Jordan	.75
45	Michael Jordan	.75
46	Michael Jordan	.75
47	Michael Jordan	.75
48	Michael Jordan	.75
49	Michael Jordan	.75
50	Michael Jordan	.75
51	Michael Jordan	.75
52	Michael Jordan	.75
53	Michael Jordan	.75
54	Michael Jordan	.75
55	Michael Jordan	.75
56	Michael Jordan	.75
57	Michael Jordan	.75
58	Michael Jordan	.75
59	Michael Jordan	.75
60	Michael Jordan	.75
61	Michael Jordan	.75
62	Michael Jordan	.75
63	Michael Jordan	.75
64	Michael Jordan	.75
65	Michael Jordan	.75
66	Michael Jordan	.75
67	Michael Jordan	.75
68	Michael Jordan	.75
69	Michael Jordan	.75
70	Michael Jordan	.75
71	Michael Jordan	.75
72	Michael Jordan	.75
73	Michael Jordan	.75
74	Michael Jordan	.75
75	Michael Jordan	.75
76	Michael Jordan	.75
77	Michael Jordan	.75
78	Michael Jordan	.75
79	Michael Jordan	.75
80	Michael Jordan	.75
81	Michael Jordan	.75
82	Michael Jordan	.75
83	Michael Jordan	.75
84	Michael Jordan	.75
85	Michael Jordan	.75
86	Michael Jordan	.75
87	Michael Jordan	.75
88	Michael Jordan	.75
89	Michael Jordan	.75
90	Michael Jordan	.75
91	Michael Jordan	.75
92	Michael Jordan	.75
93	Michael Jordan	.75
94	Michael Jordan	.75
95	Michael Jordan	.75
96	Michael Jordan	.75
97	Michael Jordan	.75
98	Michael Jordan	.75
99	Michael Jordan	.75
100	Michael Jordan	.75
101	Michael Jordan	.75
102	Michael Jordan	.75
103	Michael Jordan	.75
104	Michael Jordan	.75
105	Michael Jordan	.75
106	Michael Jordan	.75
107	Michael Jordan	.75
108	Michael Jordan	.75
109	Michael Jordan	.75
110	Michael Jordan	.75
111	Michael Jordan	.75
112	Michael Jordan	.75
113	Michael Jordan	.75
114	Michael Jordan	.75
115	Michael Jordan	.75
116	Michael Jordan	.75
117	Michael Jordan	.75
118	Michael Jordan	.75
119	Michael Jordan	.75
120	Michael Jordan	.75
121	Michael Jordan	.75
122	Michael Jordan	.75
123	Michael Jordan	.75
124	Michael Jordan	.75
125	Michael Jordan	.75
126	Michael Jordan	.75
127	Michael Jordan	.75
128	Michael Jordan	.75
129	Michael Jordan	.75
130	Michael Jordan	.75
131	Michael Jordan	.75
132	Michael Jordan	.75
133	Michael Jordan	.75
134	Michael Jordan	.75
135	Michael Jordan	.75
136	Michael Jordan	.75
137	Michael Jordan	.75
138	Michael Jordan	.75
139	Michael Jordan	.75
140	Michael Jordan	.75
141	Michael Jordan	.75
142	Michael Jordan	.75
143	Michael Jordan	.75
144	Michael Jordan	.75
145	Michael Jordan	.75
146	Michael Jordan	.75
147	Michael Jordan	.75
148	Michael Jordan	.75
149	Michael Jordan	.75
150	Michael Jordan	.75
151	Michael Jordan	.75
152	Michael Jordan	.75
153	Michael Jordan	.75
154	Michael Jordan	.75
155	Michael Jordan	.75
156	Michael Jordan	.75
157	Michael Jordan	.75
158	Michael Jordan	.75
159	Michael Jordan	.75
160	Michael Jordan	.75
161	Michael Jordan	.75
162	Michael Jordan	.75
163	Michael Jordan	.75
164	Michael Jordan	.75
165	Michael Jordan	.75

1998 UD Jordan Living Legend Autograph

Michael Jordan autographed 50 hand-numbered cards for the Living Legend product. These cards were numbered "MJ1".

		MT
Complete Set (1):		5000.
Production 50 Cards		
MJ1	Michael Jordan	5000.

1998 UD Jordan Living Legend Cover Story

This eight-card insert featured magazine covers of Michael Jordan from Inside Stuff. The cards were numbered with a "C" prefix and inserted 1:14 packs.

		MT
Complete Set (8):		35.00
Common Player:		5.00
Inserted 1:14		
1	Michael Jordan	5.00
2	Michael Jordan	5.00
3	Michael Jordan	5.00
4	Michael Jordan	5.00
5	Michael Jordan	5.00
6	Michael Jordan	5.00
7	Michael Jordan	5.00
8	Michael Jordan	5.00

1998 UD Jordan Living Legend Game Action

This 30-card insert showcases some of the best action shots of Jordan, with each card containing Light F/X technology. Each card was available in three different versions, with Tier 1 sequentially numbered to 2,300 sets, Tier 2 featuring silver foil and numbered to 230 sets, and Tier 3 numbered to 23 sets.

		MT
Complete Set (30):		400.00
Common Player:		15.00
Production 2,300 Sets		
Common Silver:		125.00
Production 230 Sets		
Common Gold:		1000.
Production 23 Sets		
1	Michael Jordan	15.00
2	Michael Jordan	15.00
3	Michael Jordan	15.00
4	Michael Jordan	15.00
5	Michael Jordan	15.00
6	Michael Jordan	15.00
7	Michael Jordan	15.00
8	Michael Jordan	15.00
9	Michael Jordan	15.00
10	Michael Jordan	15.00
11	Michael Jordan	15.00
12	Michael Jordan	15.00
13	Michael Jordan	15.00
14	Michael Jordan	15.00
15	Michael Jordan	15.00
16	Michael Jordan	15.00
17	Michael Jordan	15.00
18	Michael Jordan	15.00
19	Michael Jordan	15.00
20	Michael Jordan	15.00
21	Michael Jordan	15.00
22	Michael Jordan	15.00
23	Michael Jordan	15.00
24	Michael Jordan	15.00
25	Michael Jordan	15.00
26	Michael Jordan	15.00
27	Michael Jordan	15.00
28	Michael Jordan	15.00
29	Michael Jordan	15.00
30	Michael Jordan	15.00

1998 UD Jordan Living Legend Game Action

	MT
Common Gold:	1000.
Production 23 Sets	

1998 UD Jordan Living Legend Game Action Silver

	MT
Common Silver:	125.00
Production 230 Sets	

1998 UD Jordan Living Legend In-Flight

In-Flight was a 15-card insert featuring some of MJ's top flights to the basket. Cards were numbered with an "IF" prefix and inserted 1:5 packs.

		MT
Complete Set (15):		30.00
Common Player:		2.00
Inserted 1:5		
1	Michael Jordan	2.00
2	Michael Jordan	2.00
3	Michael Jordan	2.00
4	Michael Jordan	2.00
5	Michael Jordan	2.00
6	Michael Jordan	2.00
7	Michael Jordan	2.00
8	Michael Jordan	2.00
9	Michael Jordan	2.00
10	Michael Jordan	2.00
11	Michael Jordan	2.00
12	Michael Jordan	2.00
13	Michael Jordan	2.00
14	Michael Jordan	2.00
15	Michael Jordan	2.00

1998 Upper Deck Michael Jordan Gatorade

This 12-card, postcard-sized set was available through a redemption program on the caps of Gatorade. Each card features a facsimile autograph.

		MT
Complete Set (12):		25.00
Common Player:		3.00
1	Michael Jordan	3.00
2	Michael Jordan	3.00
3	Michael Jordan	3.00
4	Michael Jordan	3.00
5	Michael Jordan	3.00
6	Michael Jordan	3.00
7	Michael Jordan	3.00
8	Michael Jordan	3.00
9	Michael Jordan	3.00
10	Michael Jordan	3.00
11	Michael Jordan	3.00
12	Michael Jordan	3.00

1998 Upper Deck Michael Jordan Career Collection

This 60-card boxed set focuses on Jordan's career from 1984-1993. The set breaks down into the following subsets - A Jordan rookie card (if they had produced cards at the time), Pictures of Excellence, Spectacular Stats and MJ Retro.

		MT
Complete Set (60):		50.00
Common Player:		1.00
1	Michael Jordan (Rookie Card)	5.00
2	Michael Jordan (Pictures of Excellence 1987)	1.00
3	Michael Jordan (Pictures of Excellence 1989)	1.00
4	Michael Jordan (Pictures of Excellence 1992)	1.00
5	Michael Jordan (Pictures of Excellence 1987)	1.00
6	Michael Jordan (Pictures of Excellence 1989)	1.00
7	Michael Jordan (Pictures of Excellence 1990)	1.00
8	Michael Jordan (Pictures of Excellence 1991)	1.00
9	Michael Jordan (Pictures of Excellence 1988)	1.00
10	Michael Jordan (Pictures of Excellence 1993)	1.00
11	Michael Jordan (Pictures of Excellence 1987)	1.00
12	Michael Jordan (Pictures of Excellence 1988)	1.00
13	Michael Jordan (Pictures of Excellence 1987)	1.00
14	Michael Jordan (Pictures of Excellence 1991)	1.00
15	Michael Jordan (Pictures of Excellence 1987)	1.00
16	Michael Jordan (Pictures of Excellence 1993)	1.00
17	Michael Jordan (Pictures of Excellence 1989)	1.00
18	Michael Jordan (Pictures of Excellence 1992)	1.00
19	Michael Jordan (Pictures of Excellence 1994)	1.00
20	Michael Jordan (Spectacular Stats 90-91)	2.00
21	Michael Jordan (Spectacular Stats 1993)	2.00
22	Michael Jordan (Spectacular Stats 92-93)	2.00
23	Michael Jordan (Spectacular Stats 89-90)	2.00
24	Michael Jordan (Spectacular Stats 1991)	2.00
25	Michael Jordan (Spectacular Stats 88-89)	2.00
26	Michael Jordan (Spectacular Stats 87-88)	2.00
27	Michael Jordan (Spectacular Stats 1988)	2.00
28	Michael Jordan (Spectacular Stats 86-87)	2.00
29	Michael Jordan (MJ Retro 91-92 UD)	1.00
30	Michael Jordan (MJ Retro 96-97 COLC ACA)	1.00
31	Michael Jordan (MJ Retro 96-97 UD ROY)	1.00
32	Michael Jordan (MJ Retro 93-94 UD)	1.00
33	Michael Jordan (MJ Retro 96-97 COLC ACA)	1.00
34	Michael Jordan (MJ Retro 97-98 Tribute)	1.00
35	Michael Jordan (MJ Retro 95-96 23 Nights)	1.00
36	Michael Jordan (MJ Retro 96-97 COLC ACA)	1.00
37	Michael Jordan (MJ Retro 95-96 23 Nights)	1.00
38	Michael Jordan (MJ Retro 92-93 UD)	1.00
39	Michael Jordan (MJ Retro 97-98 Tribute)	1.00
40	Michael Jordan (MJ Retro 93-94 UD)	1.00
41	Michael Jordan (MJ Retro 95-96 23 Nights)	1.00
42	Michael Jordan (MJ Retro 95-96 UD)	1.00
43	Michael Jordan (MJ Retro 95-96 23 Nights)	1.00
44	Michael Jordan (MJ Retro 92-93 UD AD)	1.00
45	Michael Jordan (MJ Retro 93-94 UD)	1.00
46	Michael Jordan (MJ Retro 92-93 UD West)	1.00
47	Michael Jordan (MJ Retro 97-98 Tribute)	1.00
48	Michael Jordan (MJ Retro 1997 Journals)	1.00
49	Michael Jordan (MJ Retro 93-94 UD Mr. June)	1.00
50	Michael Jordan (MJ Retro 95-96 23 Nights)	1.00
51	Michael Jordan (MJ Retro 93-94 UD Mr. June)	1.00
52	Michael Jordan (MJ Retro 93-94 UD)	1.00
53	Michael Jordan (MJ Retro 93-94 UD)	1.00
54	Michael Jordan (MJ Retro 93-94 UD Mr. June)	1.00
55	Michael Jordan (MJ Retro 1997 Journals)	1.00
56	Michael Jordan (MJ Retro 1997 Journals)	1.00
57	Michael Jordan (MJ Retro 93-94 UD)	1.00
58	Michael Jordan (MJ Retro 96-97 COLC ACA)	1.00
59	Checklist	1.00
60	Checklist	1.00

1998 Upper Deck MJx

MJx was a 135-card set featuring Michael Jordan and showcasing the future Hall of Famer's career. The product was released during the NBA lockout and capitalized on Jordan's popularity when he retired. The first 45 cards showcased his career from 1984-1990 (2:1 pack). Cards 46-55 were called "1st Quarter Highlights" and covered the years 1984-1987 (1:17). Cards 56-65 highlighted years 1988-1990 and were called "2nd Quarter Highlights" (1:12). Next, the second half lineup covered 1991-

1998 with cards 66-110 (2:1). Cards 111-120 (1:7) were called "3rd Quarter Highlights" and covered 1991-1993. The "4th Quarter Highlights" were cards 121-130 (1:1) and covered 1995-1998. Cards 131-135 formed a subset called "The Best of Times" and were inserted 1:23 packs. Inserts included: 23 hand-numbered Autographed Game-worn Jersey cards, 50 hand-numbered MJ Autographed cards, 230 Game Commemorative Game-worn Shoe cards, 230 Game Commemorative Game-worn Warm-up cards, 90 MJ Timepiece parallels and 30 MJ Live inserts numbered to 100 sets

	MT
Complete Set (135):	300.00
Common Player (1-45):	.50
Inserted 2:1	
Common Player (46-55):	15.00
Inserted 1:17	
Common Player (56-65):	10.00
Inserted 1:12	
Common Player (66-110):	.50
Inserted 1:2	
Common Player (111-120):	5.00
Inserted 1:7	
Common Player (121-130):	1.00
Inserted 1:1	
Common Player (131-135):	15.00
Inserted 1:23	
Wax Box:	130.00

1998 Upper Deck MJx Timepieces Red

This 90-card parallel set featured die-cut versions from MJ Timeline 1st Half and 2nd Half cards. MJ Timepiece Red cards were sequentially numbered to 2,300, Bronze cards were numbered to 230 and Gold versions were numbered to 23 sets.

	MT
Complete Set (90):	450.00
Common Player:	5.00
Production 2,300 Sets	
Common Bronze Player:	50.00
Production 230 Sets	
Common Gold Player:	300.00
Production 23 Sets	

1998 Upper Deck MJx Timepieces Bronze

	MT
Common Bronze Player:	50.00
Production 230 Sets	

1998 Upper Deck MJx Timepieces Gold

	MT
Common Gold Player:	300.00
Production 23 Sets	

1998 Upper Deck MJx Live

This 30-card insert features actual excerpts from interviews with MJ. Cards were sequentially numbered to 100 sets, with an "L" prefix.

	MT
Complete Set (30):	3500.
Common Player:	125.00
Production 100 Sets	

1998 Upper Deck MJx Game Commemoratives

Game Commemoratives featured two different pieces of game-worn Jordan merchandise. Next, there were 230 hand-numbered Game-Worn Shoe cards featuring a piece of shoe. Third, 230 sequentially numbered Game-worn Warm-up cards were inserted that featured an actual swatch of authentic warm-ups. Both cards were numbered with a "GC" prefix.

		MT
Complete Set (2):		2400.
Common Player:		1200.
Warm-Ups Production 230		
Shoes Production 230		
1	Michael Jordan Warm-Ups	1200.
2	Michael Jordan Shoes	1200.

1998 Upper Deck MJx Autograph

This single card was signed by Jordan and limited to 50 hand-numbered versions. No odds were given for insertion and it was numbered "A1".

		MT
Complete Set (1):		5000.
Production 50 Cards		
A1	Michael Jordan Auto.	5000.

1998-99 Upper Deck Black Diamond

Black Diamond arrived in early April of 1999 after being cancelled initially in mid-December due to the lockout. Black Diamond arrived with 120 cards, including 90 short-printed rookies and the first 13 cards in the set featuring Michael Jordan. Upper Deck added several things to the product, including five UD Authentics autographs from top rookies and two hobby-only inserts - MJ Sheer Brilliance and MJ Extreme Brilliance. There were three parallel versions to the regular set - Double Diamond cards were all-red Light F/X with the first 90 numbered to 3,000 and the 30 rookies, called Futures, numbered to 2,500; Triple Diamonds were printed on all-gold Light F/X with veterans numbered to 1,500 and Futures numbered to 1,000; and Quadruple Diamonds printed on all-emerald Light F/X with veterans numbered to 150 and Futures numbered to 50 sets. The final insert in Black Diamond was Diamond Dominance, which had two versions with regular versions numbered to 1,000 and Emerald Edition versions numbered to 100 sets.

		MT
Complete Set (120):		200.00
Common Player:		.20
Minor Stars:		.30
Common Jordan (1-13):		3.00
Common Rookie (91-120):		1.50
Inserted 1:4		
Pack (4):		4.50
Wax Box (24):		120.00
1	Michael Jordan (1984-85)	3.00
2	Michael Jordan (1985-86)	3.00
3	Michael Jordan (1986-87)	3.00
4	Michael Jordan (1987-88)	3.00
5	Michael Jordan (1988-89)	3.00
6	Michael Jordan (1989-90)	3.00
7	Michael Jordan (1990-91)	3.00
8	Michael Jordan (1991-92)	3.00
9	Michael Jordan (1992-93)	3.00
10	Michael Jordan (1994-95)	3.00
11	Michael Jordan (1995-96)	3.00
12	Michael Jordan (1996-97)	3.00
13	Michael Jordan (1997-98)	3.00
14	Dikembe Mutombo	.30
15	Steve Smith	.30
16	Mookie Blaylock	.20
17	Antoine Walker	1.00
18	Kenny Anderson	.30
19	Ron Mercer	1.50
20	Glen Rice	.30
21	Derrick Coleman	.30
22	Michael Jordan	5.00
23	Toni Kukoc	.30
24	Brent Barry	.20
25	Brevin Knight	.40
26	Derek Anderson	.40
27	Shawn Kemp	.60
28	Shawn Bradley	.20
29	Michael Finley	.40
30	Nick Van Exel	.30
31	Chauncey Billups	.40
32	Antonio McDyess	.40
33	Grant Hill	2.50
34	Jerry Stackhouse	.30
35	Bison Dele	.20
36	John Starks	.20
37	Chris Mills	.20
38	Scottie Pippen	1.25
39	Hakeem Olajuwon	.75
40	Charles Barkley	.50
41	Antonio Davis	.20
42	Reggie Miller	.30
43	Mark Jackson	.20
44	Eddie Jones	.75
45	Shaquille O'Neal	1.50
46	Kobe Bryant	4.00
47	Rodney Rogers	.20
48	Maurice Taylor	.40
49	Tim Hardaway	.40
50	Jamal Mashburn	.30
51	Alonzo Mourning	.40
52	Ray Allen	.40
53	Terrell Brandon	.30
54	Glenn Robinson	.40
55	Joe Smith	.40
56	Stephon Marbury	1.50
57	Kevin Garnett	2.50
58	Kerry Kittles	.30
59	Jayson Williams	.30
60	Keith Van Horn	1.00
61	Patrick Ewing	.40
62	Allan Houston	.30
63	Latrell Sprewell	.30
64	Anfernee Hardaway	1.50
65	Horace Grant	.20
66	Allen Iverson	1.50
67	Tim Thomas	1.00
68	Jason Kidd	1.00
69	Danny Manning	.20
70	Tom Gugliotta	.30
71	Damon Stoudamire	.40
72	Rasheed Wallace	.20
73	Isaiah Rider	.20
74	Corliss Williamson	.20
75	Chris Webber	1.00
76	Tim Duncan	2.50
77	David Robinson	.50
78	Sean Elliott	.20
79	Gary Payton	.50
80	Vin Baker	.75
81	John Wallace	.20
82	Tracy McGrady	1.00
83	Jeff Hornacek	.20
84	Karl Malone	.50
85	John Stockton	.30
86	Bryant Reeves	.20
87	Shareef Abdur-Rahim	1.00
88	Rod Strickland	.30
89	Juwan Howard	.30
90	Mitch Richmond	.30
91	*Michael Olowokandi* (Diamond Futures)	3.00
92	*Dirk Nowitzki* (Diamond Futures)	12.00
93	*Raef LaFrentz* (Diamond Futures)	4.00
94	*Mike Bibby* (Diamond Futures)	6.00
95	*Ricky Davis* (Diamond Futures)	4.00
96	*Jason Williams* (Diamond Futures)	10.00
97	*Al Harrington* (Diamond Futures)	5.00
98	*Bonzi Wells* (Diamond Futures)	10.00
99	*Keon Clark* (Diamond Futures)	4.00
100	*Rashard Lewis* (Diamond Futures)	10.00
101	*Paul Pierce* (Diamond Futures)	10.00
102	*Antawn Jamison* (Diamond Futures)	12.00
103	*Nazr Mohammed* (Diamond Futures)	1.50
104	*Brian Skinner* (Diamond Futures)	3.00
105	*Corey Benjamin* (Diamond Futures)	1.50
106	*Predrag Stojakovic* (Diamond Futures)	5.00
107	*Bryce Drew* (Diamond Futures)	3.00
108	*Matt Harpring* (Diamond Futures)	2.00
109	*Toby Bailey* (Diamond Futures)	1.50
110	*Tyronn Lue* (Diamond Futures)	3.00
111	*Michael Dickerson* (Diamond Futures)	4.00
112	*Roshown McLeod* (Diamond Futures)	3.00
113	*Felipe Lopez* (Diamond Futures)	3.00
114	*Michael Doleac* (Diamond Futures)	2.00
115	*Ruben Patterson* (Diamond Futures)	4.00
116	*Robert Traylor* (Diamond Futures)	2.00
117	*Sam Jacobson* (Diamond Futures)	1.50
118	*Larry Hughes* (Diamond Futures)	10.00
119	*Pat Garrity* (Diamond Futures)	3.00
120	*Vince Carter* (Diamond Futures)	40.00

1998-99 Upper Deck Black Diamond Double Diamond

This 120-card parallel set reprinted each card in Black Diamond, but added red foil to the card fronts. Double Diamond veterans (1-90) were sequentially numbered to 3,000 sets, while rookies (91-120) were numbered to 2,500 sets.

	MT
Complete Set (120):	300.00
Common Player:	.40
Common Rookie (91-120):	3.00
Double Diamond Cards:	2x
Production 3,000 Sets	
Double Diamond Rookies:	1.5x
Production 2,500 Sets	

1998-99 Upper Deck Black Diamond Triple Diamond

This 120-card parallel set reprinted each card in Black Diamond, but added gold foil to the card front. Triple Diamond veterans cards (1-90) were sequentially numbered to 1,500, while rookies (91-120) were numbered to 1,000 sets.

	MT
Complete Set (120):	500.00
Common Player:	.75
Common Rookie (91-120):	4.00
Triple Diamond Cards:	4x
Production 1,500 Sets	
Triple Diamond Rookies	3x
Production 1,000 Sets	

1998-99 Upper Deck Black Diamond Quadruple Diamond

This 120-card parallel set reprinted each card from Black Diamond, but added emerald foil to the card front. Quadruple Diamond veterans (1-90) were sequentially numbered to 150, while rookies (91-120) were numbered to 50 sets.

	MT
Common Player:	8.00
Common Rookie (91-120):	12.00
Quad. Diamond Cards	20x-40x
Production 150 Sets	
Quad. Diamond Rookies	4x-8x
Production 50 Sets	

1998-99 Upper Deck Black Diamond Diamond Dominance

This 30-card set featured top players printed on Light F/X technology. Cards were sequentially numbered to 1,000 sets and were numbered with a "D" prefix. Each card was also available in an Emerald Edition parallel, which was sequentially numbered to 100 sets.

		MT
Complete Set (30):		400.00
Common Player:		3.00
Production 1,000 Hobby Sets		
Emerald Cards		3x-6x
Production 100 Hobby Sets		
1	Steve Smith	3.00
2	Paul Pierce	30.00
3	Glen Rice	3.00
4	Toni Kukoc	5.00
5	Shawn Kemp	5.00
6	Michael Finley	5.00
7	Antonio McDyess	5.00
8	Grant Hill	30.00
9	Antawn Jamison	25.00
10	Scottie Pippen	15.00
11	Reggie Miller	3.00
12	Michael Olowokandi	10.00
13	Shaquille O'Neal	20.00
14	Alonzo Mourning	5.00
15	Ray Allen	5.00
16	Stephon Marbury	20.00
17	Keith Van Horn	12.00
18	Allan Houston	3.00
19	Anfernee Hardaway	20.00
20	Allen Iverson	20.00
21	Jason Kidd	15.00
22	Damon Stoudamire	5.00
23	Chris Webber	15.00
24	Tim Duncan	30.00
25	Gary Payton	8.00
26	Vince Carter	50.00
27	Karl Malone	8.00
28	Mike Bibby	15.00
29	Mitch Richmond	3.00
30	Michael Jordan	60.00

1998-99 Upper Deck Black Diamond Emerald Diamond Dominance

		MT
Common Player:		15.00
Emerald Cards		3x-6x
Production 100 Hobby Sets		
1	Steve Smith	3.00
2	Paul Pierce	30.00
3	Glen Rice	3.00
4	Toni Kukoc	5.00
5	Shawn Kemp	5.00
6	Michael Finley	5.00
7	Antonio McDyess	5.00
8	Grant Hill	30.00
9	Antawn Jamison	25.00
10	Scottie Pippen	15.00
11	Reggie Miller	3.00
12	Michael Olowokandi	10.00
13	Shaquille O'Neal	20.00
14	Alonzo Mourning	5.00
15	Ray Allen	5.00
16	Stephon Marbury	20.00
17	Keith Van Horn	10.00
18	Allan Houston	3.00
19	Anfernee Hardaway	20.00
20	Allen Iverson	20.00
21	Jason Kidd	15.00
22	Damon Stoudamire	5.00
23	Chris Webber	15.00
24	Tim Duncan	30.00
25	Gary Payton	8.00
26	Vince Carter	50.00
27	Karl Malone	8.00
28	Mike Bibby	15.00
29	Mitch Richmond	3.00
30	Michael Jordan	60.00

1998-99 Upper Deck Black Diamond MJ Sheer Brilliance

This 30-card insert exclusively featured Michael Jordan and was numbered with a "B" prefix. Regular versions were sequentially numbered to 230 sets, while a rarer Extreme Brilliance version was sequentially numbered to only 23 sets.

		MT
Complete Set (30):		2000.
Common Player:		75.00
Production 230 Hobby Sets		
Extreme Brilliance Cards:		500.00
Production 23 Hobby Sets		
1	Michael Jordan	75.00
2	Michael Jordan	75.00
3	Michael Jordan	75.00
4	Michael Jordan	75.00
5	Michael Jordan	75.00
6	Michael Jordan	75.00
7	Michael Jordan	75.00
8	Michael Jordan	75.00
9	Michael Jordan	75.00
10	Michael Jordan	75.00
11	Michael Jordan	75.00
12	Michael Jordan	75.00
13	Michael Jordan	75.00
14	Michael Jordan	75.00
15	Michael Jordan	75.00
16	Michael Jordan	75.00
17	Michael Jordan	75.00
18	Michael Jordan	75.00
19	Michael Jordan	75.00
20	Michael Jordan	75.00
21	Michael Jordan	75.00
22	Michael Jordan	75.00
23	Michael Jordan	75.00
24	Michael Jordan	75.00
25	Michael Jordan	75.00
26	Michael Jordan	75.00
27	Michael Jordan	75.00
28	Michael Jordan	75.00
29	Michael Jordan	75.00
30	Michael Jordan	75.00

1998-99 Upper Deck Black Diamond MJ Emerald Sheer Brilliance

		MT
Complete Set (30):		2000.
Common Player:		75.00
Production 200 Hobby Sets		
Extreme Brilliance Cards:		500.00
Production 23 Hobby Sets		
1	Michael Jordan	75.00
2	Michael Jordan	75.00
3	Michael Jordan	75.00
4	Michael Jordan	75.00
5	Michael Jordan	75.00
6	Michael Jordan	75.00
7	Michael Jordan	75.00
8	Michael Jordan	75.00
9	Michael Jordan	75.00
10	Michael Jordan	75.00
11	Michael Jordan	75.00
12	Michael Jordan	75.00
13	Michael Jordan	75.00
14	Michael Jordan	75.00
15	Michael Jordan	75.00
16	Michael Jordan	75.00
17	Michael Jordan	75.00
18	Michael Jordan	75.00
19	Michael Jordan	75.00
20	Michael Jordan	75.00
21	Michael Jordan	75.00
22	Michael Jordan	75.00
23	Michael Jordan	75.00
24	Michael Jordan	75.00
25	Michael Jordan	75.00
26	Michael Jordan	75.00
27	Michael Jordan	75.00
28	Michael Jordan	75.00
29	Michael Jordan	75.00
30	Michael Jordan	75.00

1998-99 Upper Deck Black Diamond UD Authentics Autographs

Five different rookies signed cards for UD Authentics. The cards were unnumbered and checklisted by the player's initials. Each player signed only 475 sequentially numbered cards.

		MT
Complete Set (5):		225.00
Common Player:		25.00
MB	Mike Bibby	60.00
LH	Larry Hughes	60.00
AJ	Antawn Jamison	80.00
RT	Robert Traylor	40.00
BW	Bonzi Wells	25.00

1998-99 UD Choice Preview

This 55-card set contained a sampling of the 1998-99 UD Choice Series I set. The cards were identified by the word "PREVIEW" stamped in gold foil at the top of the card fronts. UD Choice Preview was distributed in seven-card packs before the release of the regular set. Each pack contained one Michael Jordan NBA Finals Shots insert and six Preview cards. While regular packs retailed for 79 cents, special retail-only ANCO packs arrived in six different can variations, each featuring Jordan on the outside and a Preview pack inside. These can-packs carried a suggested retail price of $1.97.

		MT
Complete Set (55):		10.00
Common Player:		.05
Minor Stars:		.10
Wax Box:		12.00
1	Dikembe Mutombo	.10
3	Mookie Blaylock	.05
7	Ron Mercer	.75
9	Walter McCarty	.05
13	Anthony Mason	.05
14	Glen Rice	.20
18	Toni Kukoc	.10
23	Michael Jordan	2.50
26	Zydrunas Ilgauskas	.10
27	Cedric Henderson	.10
29	Michael Finley	.10
32	Hubert Davis	.05
34	Bobby Jackson	.10
37	Danny Fortson	.05

Values quoted in this guide reflect the retail price of a card — the price a collector can expect to pay when buying a card from a dealer. The wholesale price — that which a collector can expect to receive from a dealer when selling cards — will be significantly lower, depending on desirability and condition.

41	Grant Hill	1.25
43	Jerome Williams	.05
45	Erick Dampier	.05
48	Donyell Marshall	.05
50	Charles Barkley	.30
51	Hakeem Olajuwon	.40
56	Reggie Miller	.10
60	Chris Mullin	.10
64	Eric Piatkowski	.05
65	Maurice Taylor	.20
68	Shaquille O'Neal	.75
69	Kobe Bryant	1.50
74	Alonzo Mourning	.20
75	Tim Hardaway	.20
79	Ray Allen	.10
80	Terrell Brandon	.10
84	Stephon Marbury	.75
85	Kevin Garnett	1.25
89	Keith Van Horn	.60
90	Sam Cassell	.05
95	Patrick Ewing	.20
97	John Starks	.05
100	Anfernee Hardaway	.75
101	Nick Anderson	.05
105	Allen Iverson	.50
110	Jason Kidd	.30
117	Isaiah Rider	.05
118	Rasheed Wallace	.05
121	Corliss Williamson	.05
123	Billy Owens	.05
126	Tim Duncan	1.25
127	Sean Elliott	.05
131	Vin Baker	.20
135	Gary Payton	.20
137	Chauncey Billups	.20
142	John Stockton	.10
143	Karl Malone	.20
148	Bryant Reeves	.05
149	Shareef Abdur-Rahim	.50
152	Chris Webber	.20
153	Juwan Howard	.10

1998-99 UD Choice

Upper Deck changed its Collector's Choice brand name to UD Choice for 1998-99. Series I included 200 cards, with 30 NBA Flash Stats and 13 Year in Review subset cards. The set arrived with two parallel sets, including Choice Reserve and Prime Choice Reserve (100 numbered hobby sets). Inserts in Series I are: Mini Bobbing Heads, StarQuest and Draw Your Own Trading Card.

	MT
Complete Set (200):	15.00
Common Player:	.10
Minor Stars:	.20
Choice Reserve Cards:	3x-6x
PC Reserve Cards:	60x-120x
Pack (12):	1.35
Wax Box (36):	45.00

1	Dikembe Mutombo	.20
2	Alan Henderson	.10
3	Mookie Blaylock	.10
4	Ed Gray	.10
5	Eldridge Recasner	.10
6	Kenny Anderson	.10
7	Ron Mercer	.75
8	Dana Barros	.10
9	Walter McCarty	.10
10	Travis Knight	.10
11	Andrew DeClercq	.10
12	David Wesley	.10
13	Anthony Mason	.10
14	Glen Rice	.20
15	J.R. Reid	.10
16	Bobby Phills	.10
17	Dell Curry	.10
18	Toni Kukoc	.20
19	Randy Brown	.10
20	Ron Harper	.10
21	Keith Booth	.10
22	Scott Burrell	.10
23	Michael Jordan	2.50
24	Derek Anderson	.30
25	Brevin Knight	.30
26	Zydrunas Ilgauskas	.20
27	Cedric Henderson	.20
28	Vitaly Potapenko	.10
29	Michael Finley	.20
30	Erick Strickland	.10
31	Shawn Bradley	.10
32	Hubert Davis	.10
33	Khalid Reeves	.10
34	Bobby Jackson	.20
35	Tony Battie	.20
36	Bryant Stith	.10
37	Danny Fortson	.20
38	Dean Garrett	.10
39	Eric Williams	.10
40	Brian Williams	.10
41	Grant Hill	1.25
42	Lindsey Hunter	.10
43	Jerome Williams	.10
44	Eric Montross	.10
45	Erick Dampier	.10
46	Muggsy Bogues	.10
47	Tony Delk	.10
48	Donyell Marshall	.10
49	Bimbo Coles	.10
50	Charles Barkley	.30
51	Hakeem Olajuwon	.40
52	Brent Price	.10
53	Mario Elie	.10
54	Rodrick Rhodes	.10
55	Kevin Willis	.10
56	Reggie Miller	.20
57	Jalen Rose	.10
58	Mark Jackson	.10
59	Dale Davis	.10
60	Chris Mullin	.10
61	Derrick McKey	.10
62	Lorenzen Wright	.10
63	Rodney Rogers	.10
64	Eric Piatkowski	.10
65	Maurice Taylor	.30
66	Isaac Austin	.10
67	Corie Blount	.10
68	Shaquille O'Neal	.75
69	Kobe Bryant	1.50
70	Robert Horry	.10
71	Sean Rooks	.10
72	Derek Fisher	.10
73	P.J. Brown	.10
74	Alonzo Mourning	.20
75	Tim Hardaway	.20
76	Voshon Lenard	.10
77	Dan Majerle	.10
78	Ervin Johnson	.10
79	Ray Allen	.20
80	Terrell Brandon	.20
81	Tyrone Hill	.10
82	Elliot Perry	.10
83	Anthony Peeler	.10
84	Stephon Marbury	1.00
85	Kevin Garnett	1.25
86	Paul Grant	.10
87	Chris Carr	.10
88	Michael Williams	.10
89	Keith Van Horn	.75
90	Sam Cassell	.10
91	Kendall Gill	.10
92	Chris Gatling	.10
93	Kerry Kittles	.20
94	Allan Houston	.20
95	Patrick Ewing	.20
96	Charles Oakley	.10
97	John Starks	.10
98	Charlie Ward	.10
99	Chris Mills	.10
100	Anfernee Hardaway	.75
101	Nick Anderson	.10
102	Mark Price	.10
103	Horace Grant	.10
104	David Benoit	.10
105	Allen Iverson	1.00
106	Joe Smith	.20
107	Tim Thomas	.50
108	Brian Shaw	.10
109	Aaron McKie	.10
110	Jason Kidd	.40
111	Danny Manning	.10
112	Steve Nash	.20
113	Rex Chapman	.10
114	Dennis Scott	.10
115	Antonio McDyess	.20
116	Damon Stoudamire	.30
117	Isaiah Rider	.10
118	Rasheed Wallace	.10
119	Kelvin Cato	.10
120	Jermaine O'Neal	.10
121	Corliss Williamson	.10
122	Olden Polynice	.10
123	Billy Owens	.10
124	Lawrence Funderburke	.10
125	Anthony Johnson	.10
126	Tim Duncan	1.25
127	Sean Elliott	.10
128	Avery Johnson	.10
129	Vinny Del Negro	.10
130	Monty Williams	.10
131	Vin Baker	.20
132	Hersey Hawkins	.10
133	Nate McMillan	.10
134	Detlef Schrempf	.10
135	Gary Payton	.30
136	Jim McIlvaine	.10
137	Chauncey Billups	.30
138	Doug Christie	.10
139	John Wallace	.10
140	Tracy McGrady	.50
141	Dee Brown	.10
142	John Stockton	.20
143	Karl Malone	.30
144	Shandon Anderson	.10
145	Jacque Vaughn	.10
146	Bryon Russell	.10
147	Lee Mayberry	.10
148	Bryant Reeves	.10
149	Shareef Abdur-Rahim	.50
150	Michael Smith	.10
151	Pete Chilcutt	.10
152	Chris Webber	.30
153	Juwan Howard	.20
154	Calbert Cheaney	.10
155	Tracy Murray	.10
156	Dikembe Mutombo	.10
157	Antoine Walker	.40
158	Glen Rice	.10
159	Michael Jordan	1.25
160	Wesley Person	.10
161	Shawn Bradley	.10
162	Dean Garrett	.10
163	Jerry Stackhouse	.10
164	Donyell Marshall	.10
165	Hakeem Olajuwon	.20
166	Chris Mullin	.10
167	Isaac Austin	.10
168	Shaquille O'Neal	.40
169	Tim Hardaway	.10
170	Glenn Robinson	.10
171	Kevin Garnett	.50
172	Keith Van Horn	.10
173	Larry Johnson	.10
174	Horace Grant	.10
175	Derrick Coleman	.10
176	Steve Nash	.10
177	Arvydas Sabonis	.10
178	Corliss Williamson	.10
179	David Robinson	.10
180	Vin Baker	.10
181	Marcus Camby	.10
182	John Stockton	.10
183	Antonio Daniels	.10
184	Rod Strickland	.10
185	Michael Jordan	1.25
186	Kobe Bryant (All-Star debut)	.75
187	Clyde Drexler (final game 4/19)	.10
188	Gary Payton (Sea. wins 55th)	.10
189	Michael Jordan (10th scoring title)	1.25
190	Tim Duncan, David Robinson (T.T.)	.75
191	Hawks (largest crowd 62,046)	.10
192	Karl Malone (high scoring game)	.10
193	NBA Def. POY (Dikembe Mutombo)	.10
194	Nets Return to the Playoffs	.10
195	Ray Allen (hoop/movie star)	.10
196	Michael Jordan (NBA MVP)	1.25
197	Shaq and co. (Shaquille O'Neal) (Lake Show '98)	.40
198	Michael Jordan (Bulls 6th title)	1.25
199	Checklist #1	.10
200	Checklist #2	.10

1998-99 UD Choice Reserve

This 200-card parallel set reprinted each card from UD Choice, but added the words "Choice Reserve" to the card front. Backs were identical to regular-issue cards and these parallel cards were inserted 1:6 packs.

	MT
Complete Set (200):	100.00
Common Player:	.25
Choice Reserve Cards:	2x-4x
Inserted 1:6	

1998-99 UD Choice Premium Choice Reserve

This 200-card parallel set reprinted each card from UD Choice, but added the words "Premium Choice Reserve" on the card front. Premium Choice Reserve cards were sequentially numbered to 100 sets.

	MT
Common Player:	10.00
PC Reserve Cards:	60x-120x
Production 100 Sets	

1998-99 UD Choice StarQuest Blue

This 30-card insert included 30 top NBA players and arrived in four different foil versions. Numbered with a "SQ" prefix, Blue 1-Star versions were seeded one per pack, Green 2-Star versions were seeded 1:8, Red 3-Star versions were seeded 1:23 and Gold 4-Star versions were sequentially numbered to 100 sets.

	MT
Complete Set (30):	15.00
Common Player:	.25
Minor Stars:	.50
Inserted 1:1	
Green Cards:	2x-4x
Inserted 1:8	
Red Cards:	5x-10x
Inserted 1:23	
Gold Cards:	40x-80x
Production 100 Sets	

1	Steve Smith	.25
2	Kenny Anderson	.25
3	Glen Rice	.50
4	Toni Kukoc	.25
5	Shawn Kemp	.50
6	Michael Finley	.50
7	Bobby Jackson	.25
8	Grant Hill	1.50
9	Donyell Marshall	.25
10	Hakeem Olajuwon	.75
11	Reggie Miller	.50
12	Maurice Taylor	.25
13	Kobe Bryant	2.00
14	Alonzo Mourning	.50
15	Terrell Brandon	.25
16	Stephon Marbury	1.25
17	Keith Van Horn	.75
18	Patrick Ewing	.25
19	Anfernee Hardaway	1.00
20	Allen Iverson	1.00
21	Jason Kidd	.50
22	Damon Stoudamire	.25
23	Mitch Richmond	.50
24	Tim Duncan	1.50
25	Gary Payton	.50
26	Chauncey Billups	.50
27	Karl Malone	.50
28	Shareef Abdur-Rahim	.60
29	Chris Webber	.50
30	Michael Jordan	3.00

1998-99 UD Choice StarQuest Gold

This 30-card parallel set reprinted each card in the StarQuest insert, with gold foil versions being the rarest one. Cards were sequentially numbered to 100 sets.

	MT
Common Player:	10.00
Gold Cards:	40x-80x
Production 100 Sets	

1998-99 UD Choice StarQuest Green

	MT
Complete Set (30):	50.00
Common Player:	.50
Green Cards:	2x-4x
Inserted 1:8	

1998-99 UD Choice StarQuest Red

	MT
Complete Set (30):	150.00
Common Player:	1.50
Red Cards:	5x-10x
Inserted 1:23	

1998-99 UD Choice Mini Bobbing Heads

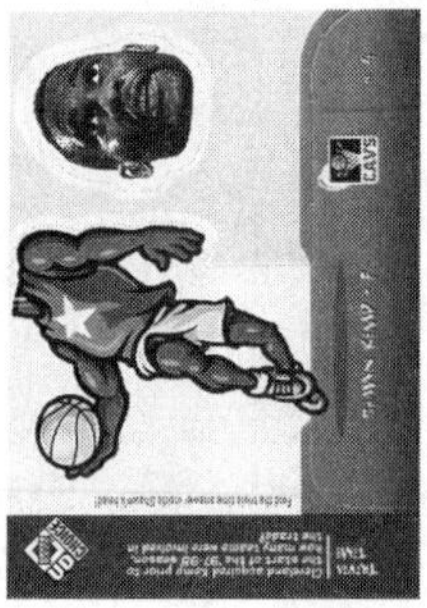

This 30-card insert set showcased miniature stand-up figures with removable bobbing heads of NBA players. These were inserted one per four packs of Series I.

	MT
Complete Set (30):	25.00
Common Player:	.50
Minor Stars:	1.00
Inserted 1:4	

1	Dikembe Mutombo	.50
2	Antoine Walker	1.00
3	Anthony Mason	.50
4	Toni Kukoc	.50
5	Shawn Kemp	1.00
6	Shawn Bradley	.50
7	Danny Fortson	.50
8	Brian Williams	.50
9	Muggsy Bogues	.50
10	Charles Barkley	1.00
11	Mark Jackson	.50
12	Rodney Rogers	.50
13	Kobe Bryant	4.00
14	Tim Hardaway	.50
15	Ray Allen	1.00
16	Kevin Garnett	3.00
17	Sam Cassell	.50
18	John Starks	.50
19	Anfernee Hardaway	2.00
20	Allen Iverson	2.00
21	Danny Manning	.50
22	Rasheed Wallace	.50
23	Mitch Richmond	.50
24	David Robinson	1.00
25	Gary Payton	1.00
26	Marcus Camby	.50
27	John Stockton	.50
28	Bryant Reeves	.50
29	Juwan Howard	1.00
30	Michael Jordan	6.00

1998-99 Upper Deck Encore

Upper Deck Encore was comprised of 90 regular player cards and three shortprinted subsets - MJ Regular Players cards 91-113 (23 cards, 1:4 packs), Rookie Watch 114-143 (30 cards, 1:4 packs) and Bonus Regular Rookie cards 144-150 (seven cards, 1:8 packs). All of the cards except the seven Bonus Regular Rookie cards were reprinted cards from Upper Deck Series I and MJ Access (UD Series II) with the addition of a holographic finish and foil enhancements. Inserts included: nine PowerDeck, one UD Authentics Michael Jordan autographed hand-numbered to 50, 30 Intensity, 14 Driving Forces, 10 Rookie Encore, 20 MJ23 and 150 Upper Deck F/X parallel cards numbered to 125 sets.

	MT
Complete Set (150):	200.00
Common Player:	.20
Minor Stars:	.40
Common Jordan (91-113):	3.00
Inserted 1:4	
Common Rookie Watch (114-143):	1.50
Inserted 1:4	
Common Rookie (144-150):	5.00
Inserted 1:8	
Pack (6):	4.50
Wax Box (24):	100.00

1	Mookie Blaylock	.20
2	Dikembe Mutombo	.40
3	Steve Smith	.40
4	Kenny Anderson	.40
5	Antoine Walker	1.00
6	Ron Mercer	1.00
7	David Wesley	.20
8	Elden Campbell	.20
9	Eddie Jones	.75
10	Ron Harper	.20
11	Toni Kukoc	.40
12	Brent Barry	.20
13	Shawn Kemp	.60
14	Brevin Knight	.40
15	Derek Anderson	.40
16	Shawn Bradley	.20
17	Robert Pack	.20
18	Michael Finley	.40
19	Antonio McDyess	.75
20	Nick Van Exel	.40
21	Danny Fortson	.20
22	Grant Hill	2.50
23	Jerry Stackhouse	.40
24	Bison Dele	.20
25	Donyell Marshall	.20
26	Tony Delk	.20
27	Erick Dampier	.20
28	John Starks	.20
29	Charles Barkley	.75
30	Hakeem Olajuwon	.75
31	Othella Harrington	.20
32	Scottie Pippen	1.25
33	Rik Smits	.20
34	Reggie Miller	.40
35	Mark Jackson	.20
36	Rodney Rogers	.20
37	Lamond Murray	.20
38	Maurice Taylor	.40
39	Kobe Bryant	4.00
40	Shaquille O'Neal	1.50
41	Derek Fisher	.20
42	Glen Rice	.40
43	Jamal Mashburn	.40
44	Alonzo Mourning	.40
45	Tim Hardaway	.60
46	Ray Allen	.40
47	Vinny Del Negro	.20
48	Glenn Robinson	.40
49	Joe Smith	.40
50	Terrell Brandon	.40
51	Kevin Garnett	2.50
52	Keith Van Horn	1.00
53	Stephon Marbury	1.50
54	Jayson Williams	.40
55	Patrick Ewing	.40
56	Allan Houston	.40
57	Latrell Sprewell	.40
58	Anfernee Hardaway	1.50
59	Horace Grant	.20
60	Nick Anderson	.40
61	Allen Iverson	1.50
62	Matt Geiger	.20
63	Theo Ratliff	.20
64	Jason Kidd	1.00
65	Rex Chapman	.20
66	Tom Gugliotta	.20
67	Rasheed Wallace	.40
68	Arvydas Sabonis	.20
69	Damon Stoudamire	.60
70	Vlade Divac	.40
71	Corliss Williamson	.20
72	Chris Webber	1.00
73	Tim Duncan	2.50
74	Sean Elliott	.20
75	David Robinson	.75
76	Vin Baker	.60
77	Gary Payton	.75
78	Detlef Schrempf	.20
79	Tracy McGrady	1.00
80	John Wallace	.20
81	Doug Christie	.20
82	Karl Malone	.75
83	John Stockton	.40
84	Jeff Hornacek	.20
85	Bryant Reeves	.40
86	Michael Smith	.20
87	Shareef Abdur-Rahim	1.00
88	Juwan Howard	.40
89	Rod Strickland	.40
90	Mitch Richmond	.40
91	Michael Jordan	3.00
92	Michael Jordan	3.00
93	Michael Jordan	3.00
94	Michael Jordan	3.00
95	Michael Jordan	3.00
96	Michael Jordan	3.00
97	Michael Jordan	3.00
98	Michael Jordan	3.00
99	Michael Jordan	3.00
100	Michael Jordan	3.00
101	Michael Jordan	3.00
102	Michael Jordan	3.00
103	Michael Jordan	3.00
104	Michael Jordan	3.00
105	Michael Jordan	3.00
106	Michael Jordan	3.00
107	Michael Jordan	3.00
108	Michael Jordan	3.00
109	Michael Jordan	3.00
110	Michael Jordan	3.00
111	Michael Jordan	3.00
112	Michael Jordan	3.00
113	Michael Jordan	3.00
114	*Michael Olowokandi*	4.00
115	*Mike Bibby*	8.00
116	*Raef LaFrentz*	5.00
117	*Antawn Jamison*	15.00
118	*Vince Carter*	50.00
119	*Robert Traylor*	3.00
120	*Jason Williams*	10.00
121	*Larry Hughes*	12.00
122	*Dirk Nowitzki*	15.00
123	*Paul Pierce*	12.00
124	*Michael Doleac*	2.00
125	*Keon Clark*	3.00
126	*Michael Dickerson*	5.00
127	*Matt Harpring*	3.00
128	*Bryce Drew*	2.00
129	*Pat Garrity*	2.00
130	*Roshown McLeod*	2.00
131	*Ricky Davis*	5.00
132	*Predrag Stojakovic*	6.00
133	*Felipe Lopez*	3.00
134	*Al Harrington*	6.00
135	*Ruben Patterson*	5.00
136	*Cuttino Mobley*	8.00
137	*Tyronn Lue*	1.50
138	*Brian Skinner*	1.50
139	*Nazr Mohammed*	1.50
140	*Toby Bailey*	1.50
141	*Casey Shaw*	1.50
142	*Corey Benjamin*	3.00
143	*Rashard Lewis*	12.00
144	(Jason Williams)	6.00
145	(Paul Pierce)	6.00
146	(Vince Carter)	25.00
147	(Antawn Jamison)	8.00
148	(Raef LaFrentz)	3.00
149	(Mike Bibby)	4.00
150	(Michael Olowokandi)	2.00
MJ	Michael Jordan Auto	3500.

1998-99 Upper Deck Encore FX

This 150-card parallel set reprints each card from Encore, but replaces the silver foil from the regular-issue card with gold foil. Cards were sequentially numbered to 125 sets.

	MT
Common Player:	5.00
Common Jordan (91-113):	60.00
Common Rookie Watch (114-143):	10.00
Common Rookie (144-150):	25.00
F/X Cards:	15x-30x
F/X Jordans:	20x
F/X Rookies:	3x-6x
Production 125 Sets	)

1998-99 Upper Deck Encore Driving Forces

Driving Forces was a 14-card insert that featured top offensive stars. The cards were numbered with an "F" prefix, and inserted 1:23 packs. A parallel version also existed and were sequentially numbered to 500 sets.

	MT
Complete Set (15):	125.00
Common Player:	2.00
Inserted 1:23	
F/X Parallel Cards:	3x
Production 500 Sets	

1	Michael Jordan	30.00
2	Kobe Bryant	20.00
3	Keith Van Horn	6.00
4	Kevin Garnett	15.00
5	Tim Duncan	15.00
6	Gary Payton	4.00
7	Antoine Walker	6.00
8	Grant Hill	15.00
9	Scottie Pippen	5.00
10	Tim Hardaway	3.00
11	Reggie Miller	2.00
12	Shareef Abdur-Rahim	5.00
13	Anfernee Hardaway	10.00
14	Allen Iverson	12.00
15	Ray Allen	3.00

1998-99 Upper Deck Encore Driving Forces F/X

	MT
Common Player:	6.00
F/X Parallel Cards:	3x
Production 500 Sets	

1998-99 Upper Deck Encore Intensity

Intensity was a 30-card insert that was reprinted from Upper Deck Series I. This insert has rainbow foil added to the front and was inserted 1:11 packs. Cards were numbered with an "I" prefix.

		MT
Complete Set (30):		60.00
Common Player:		.50
Minor Stars:		1.00
Inserted 1:11		
1	Michael Jordan	15.00
2	Mitch Richmond	1.00
3	Ron Mercer	3.00
4	Terrell Brandon	1.00
5	Brevin Knight	1.00
6	Rasheed Wallace	.50
7	Keith Van Horn	3.00
8	Antawn Jamison	5.00
9	Antonio McDyess	1.00
10	Allen Iverson	6.00
11	Anfernee Hardaway	5.00
12	Chris Webber	3.00
13	Lorenzen Wright	.50
14	Bryant Reeves	.50
15	Charles Barkley	2.00
16	Tracy McGrady	3.00
17	Larry Johnson	.50
18	Jerry Stackhouse	.50
19	Derrick Coleman	.50
20	Detlef Schrempf	.50
21	John Stockton	1.00
22	Kobe Bryant	10.00
23	Alonzo Mourning	1.00
24	Dikembe Mutombo	.50
25	Jalen Rose	.50
26	Robert Pack	.50
27	Tom Gugliotta	1.00
28	Shaquille O'Neal	5.00
29	Stephon Marbury	5.00
30	David Robinson	2.00

1998-99 Upper Deck Encore MJ23

MJ23 featured 20 cards of Michael Jordan that were first issued in Upper Deck Series I (20 of the 30 original cards were reprinted), but rainbow Light F/X foil was added. Cards were numbered with an "MJ" prefix and inserted 1:23 packs. A parallel version also existed and was sequentially numbered to 23 sets.

		MT
Complete Set (20):		150.00
Common Player:		10.00
Inserted 1:23		
Common F/X Parallel:		400.00
Production 23 Sets		
1	Michael Jordan	10.00
2	Michael Jordan	10.00
3	Michael Jordan	10.00
4	Michael Jordan	10.00
5	Michael Jordan	10.00
6	Michael Jordan	10.00
7	Michael Jordan	10.00
8	Michael Jordan	10.00
9	Michael Jordan	10.00
10	Michael Jordan	10.00
11	Michael Jordan	10.00
12	Michael Jordan	10.00
13	Michael Jordan	10.00
14	Michael Jordan	10.00
15	Michael Jordan	10.00
16	Michael Jordan	10.00
17	Michael Jordan	10.00
18	Michael Jordan	10.00
19	Michael Jordan	10.00
20	Michael Jordan	10.00

1998-99 Upper Deck Encore MJ23 F/X

	MT
Common F/X Parallel:	400.00
Production 23 Sets	

1998-99 Upper Deck Encore PowerDeck

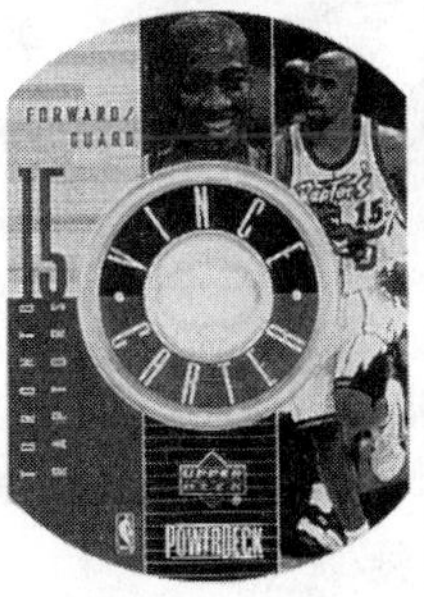

PowerDeck was a nine-card interactive insert that featured CD-Roms of top players with game-action footage, sound, photos and career highlights. These were numbered with a "PD" prefix and arrived in a protective sleeve out of the pack. PowerDeck cards were inserted 1:47 packs of Encore.

		MT
Complete Set (9):		225.00
Common Player:		10.00
Inserted 1:47		
1	Michael Jordan	65.00
2	Kobe Bryant	30.00
3	Charles Barkley	10.00
4	Shaquille O'Neal	15.00
5	Kevin Garnett	30.00
6	Jason Williams	30.00
7	Paul Pierce	20.00
8	Vince Carter	35.00
9	Julius Erving	15.00

1998-99 Upper Deck Encore Rookie Encore

This 10-card insert featured top players from the 1998 NBA Draft and was inserted 1:23 packs. Rookie Encore cards were numbered with an "RE" prefix. A parallel, gold foil version also existed and was sequentially numbered to 1,000 sets.

		MT
Complete Set (10):		100.00
Common Player:		2.00
Inserted 1:23		
F/X Parallel Cards:		2x
Production 1,000 Sets		
1	Jason Williams	20.00
2	Michael Olowokandi	6.00
3	Paul Pierce	15.00
4	Robert Traylor	6.00
5	Raef LaFrentz	6.00
6	Mike Bibby	10.00
7	Dirk Nowitzki	10.00
8	Antawn Jamison	12.00
9	Larry Hughes	10.00
10	Vince Carter	35.00

1998-99 Upper Deck Encore Rookie Encore F/X

	MT
Complete Set (10):	200.00
Common Player:	4.00
F/X Parallel Cards:	[illegible]
Production 1,000 Sets	

1998-99 Upper Deck Ionix

This 80-card set featured 53 veterans, seven Michael Jordan cards and 20 seeded rookies in an Electrix subset (1:4 packs). Each card was printed on a double-laminated, metalized stock. Inserts included: 23 hand-numbered Michael Jordan autographed cards, five UD Authentics, 60 Ionix Reciprocals (numbered to 750 sets), 20 Electrix Reciprocals (numbered to 100 sets), 20 Kinetix, 10 Area 23, 25 Skyonix, 15 Warp Zone and 10 MJ HoloGrFX.

		MT
Complete Set (80):		100.00
Common Player (1-60):		.20
Minor Stars:		.40
Common Jordan (1-6):		2.00
Common Electrix Rookie (61-80):		2.00
Inserted 1:4		
Pack (4):		5.00
Wax Box (20):		90.00
1	1991 NBA Championship Year (Michael Jordan)	2.00
2	1992 NBA Championship Year (Michael Jordan)	2.00
3	1993 NBA Championship Year (Michael Jordan)	2.00
4	1996 NBA Championship Year (Michael Jordan)	2.00
5	1997 NBA Championship Year (Michael Jordan)	2.00
6	1998 NBA Championship Year (Michael Jordan)	2.00
7	Steve Smith	.40
8	Dikembe Mutombo	.20
9	Ron Mercer	1.50
10	Antoine Walker	1.00
11	Derrick Coleman	.40
12	Glen Rice	.40
13	Michael Jordan	5.00
14	Toni Kukoc	.40
15	Derek Anderson	.40
16	Shawn Kemp	.60
17	Michael Finley	.40
18	Steve Nash	.20
19	Antonio McDyess	1.00
20	Nick Van Exel	.40
21	Grant Hill	2.50
22	Jerry Stackhouse	.20
23	Donyell Marshall	.20
24	John Starks	.20
25	Charles Barkley	1.00
26	Hakeem Olajuwon	1.00
27	Scottie Pippen	1.50
28	Reggie Miller	.40
29	Rik Smits	.20
30	Maurice Taylor	.50
31	Kobe Bryant	4.00
32	Shaquille O'Neal	2.00
33	Tim Hardaway	.60
34	Alonzo Mourning	.40
35	Ray Allen	.40
36	Glenn Robinson	.40
37	Stephon Marbury	2.00
38	Kevin Garnett	2.50
39	Jayson Williams	.40
40	Keith Van Horn	1.00
41	Patrick Ewing	.40
42	Allan Houston	.40
43	Anfernee Hardaway	2.00
44	Isaac Austin	.20
45	Tim Thomas	1.50
46	Allen Iverson	2.00
47	Tom Gugliotta	.40
48	Jason Kidd	1.50
49	Damon Stoudamire	.50
50	Chris Webber	1.50
51	Tim Duncan	2.50
52	David Robinson	1.00
53	Gary Payton	1.00
54	Vin Baker	.40
55	Tracy McGrady	1.50
56	John Stockton	.40
57	Karl Malone	1.00
58	Shareef Abdur-Rahim	1.50
59	Juwan Howard	.40
60	Mitch Richmond	.40
61	*Michael Olowokandi* (Electrix)	3.00
62	*Mike Bibby* (Electrix)	5.00
63	*Raef LaFrentz* (Electrix)	4.00
64	*Antawn Jamison* (Electrix)	10.00
65	*Vince Carter* (Electrix)	40.00
66	*Robert Traylor* (Electrix)	2.00
67	*Jason Williams* (Electrix)	8.00
68	*Larry Hughes* (Electrix)	10.00
69	*Dirk Nowitzki* (Electrix)	10.00
70	*Paul Pierce* (Electrix)	10.00
71	*Cuttino Mobley* (Electrix)	[illegible]
72	*Corey Benjamin* (Electrix)	2.00
73	*Predrag Stojakovic* (Electrix)	4.00
74	*Michael Dickerson* (Electrix)	3.00
75	*Matt Harpring* (Electrix)	2.00
76	*Rashard Lewis* (Electrix)	10.00
77	*Pat Garrity* (Electrix)	2.00
78	*Roshown McLeod* (Electrix)	2.00
79	*Ricky Davis* (Electrix)	4.00
80	*Felipe Lopez* (Electrix)	3.00
J1A	Michael Jordan Auto	6000.

1998-99 Upper Deck Ionix Reciprocal

This 80-card parallel set reprinted each Ionix card, with the regular-issue front becoming the Reciprocal back and the regular-issue back becoming the Reciprocal front. Reciprocal versions of cards 1-60 (Veterans) were numbered to 750, while Reciprocal versions of cards 61-80 (Rookies) were sequentially numbered to 100 sets.

	MT
Common Player (1-60):	2.00
Common Electrix Rookie (61-80):	30.00
Reciprocals (1-60):	6x-10x
Production 750 sets	
Reciprocals (61-80):	8x-12x
Production 100 sets	

1998-99 Upper Deck Ionix Area 23

This 10-card set featured only Michael Jordan on cards enhanced with rainbow Ionix technology. The cards were numbered with an "A" prefix and inserted 1:18 packs.

		MT
Complete Set (10):		100.00
Common Player:		12.00
Inserted 1:18		
1	Michael Jordan	12.00
2	Michael Jordan	12.00
3	Michael Jordan	12.00
4	Michael Jordan	12.00
5	Michael Jordan	12.00
6	Michael Jordan	12.00
7	Michael Jordan	12.00
8	Michael Jordan	12.00
9	Michael Jordan	12.00
10	Michael Jordan	12.00

1998-99 Upper Deck Ionix Kinetix

Kinetix displayed 20 top young stars on a rainbow foil enhanced card. Each card was numbered with a "K" prefix and inserted 1:9 packs.

		MT
Complete Set (20):		125.00
Common Player:		2.00
Inserted 1:8		
1	Michael Jordan	20.00
2	Michael Olowokandi	5.00
3	Keith Van Horn	3.00
4	Grant Hill	10.00
5	Stephon Marbury	5.00
6	Larry Hughes	8.00
7	Vince Carter	20.00
8	Jason Kidd	3.00
9	Robert Traylor	5.00
10	Ron Mercer	3.00
11	Dirk Nowitzki	5.00
12	Antawn Jamison	10.00
13	Kobe Bryant	12.00
14	Jason Williams	12.00
15	Raef LaFrentz	4.00
16	Gary Payton	2.00
17	Tim Duncan	10.00
18	Paul Pierce	12.00
19	Mike Bibby	8.00
20	Scottie Pippen	3.00

1998-99 Upper Deck Ionix MJ HoloGrFX

Michael Jordan was featured on all 10 cards in this MJ HoloGrFx insert. Cards were numbered with an "MJ" prefix and inserted 1:1,500 packs.

		MT
Complete Set (10):		2500.
Common Player:		300.00
Inserted 1:1,500		
1	Michael Jordan	300.00
2	Michael Jordan	300.00
3	Michael Jordan	300.00
4	Michael Jordan	300.00
5	Michael Jordan	300.00
6	Michael Jordan	300.00
7	Michael Jordan	300.00
8	Michael Jordan	300.00
9	Michael Jordan	300.00
10	Michael Jordan	300.00

1998-99 Upper Deck Ionix Skyonix

Skyonix displayed 25 players who are known for flying through the air. Cards were numbered with an "S" prefix and inserted 1:53 packs.

		MT
Complete Set (25):		325.00
Common Player:		3.00
Inserted 1:53		
1	Michael Jordan	100.00
2	Scottie Pippen	15.00
3	Derek Anderson	3.00
4	Jason Kidd	15.00
5	Damon Stoudamire	5.00
6	Antoine Walker	8.00
7	Shaquille O'Neal	20.00
8	Tim Thomas	12.00
9	Reggie Miller	3.00
10	Allen Iverson	25.00
11	Antonio McDyess	8.00
12	Michael Finley	5.00
13	Charles Barkley	8.00
14	Shareef Abdur-Rahim	12.00
15	Gary Payton	8.00
16	David Robinson	8.00
17	Anfernee Hardaway	20.00
18	Ray Allen	5.00
19	Ron Mercer	15.00
20	Tim Hardaway	6.00
21	Chris Webber	15.00
22	Kevin Garnett	40.00
23	Juwan Howard	3.00
24	Karl Malone	8.00
25	Keith Van Horn	10.00

1998-99 Upper Deck Ionix Warp Zone

This 15-card insert set featured 15 top players with rainbow technology. Warp Zone inserts were numbered with a "Z" prefix and inserted 1:216 packs.

		MT
Complete Set (15):		800.00
Common Player:		6.00
Inserted 1:216		
1	Michael Jordan	200.00
2	Tim Duncan	100.00
3	Robert Traylor	20.00
4	Michael Olowokandi	20.00
5	Vince Carter	150.00
6	Dirk Nowitzki	25.00
7	Antawn Jamison	40.00
8	Jason Williams	60.00
9	Larry Hughes	30.00
10	Raef LaFrentz	20.00
11	Allen Iverson	50.00
12	Kobe Bryant	125.00
13	Grant Hill	100.00
14	Mike Bibby	30.00
15	Paul Pierce	50.00

1998-99 Upper Deck Ionix UD Authentics

Five different rookies signed cards for UD Authentics. The second installment of this insert was in Ionix, while the first appeared in Black Diamond. The cards were unnumbered and identified by the initials of the player, except in the case of Michael Doleac who was "numbered" "DO". Each player signed 475 sequentially numbered cards.

		MT
Complete Set (5):		250.00
Common Player:		30.00
Production 475 sets		
CB	Corey Benjamin	30.00
DO	Michael Doleac	35.00
RL	Raef LaFrentz	50.00
RM	Roshown McLeod	30.00
JW	Jason Williams	125.00

1998-99 Upper Deck Ovation

Ovation arrived during the NBA lockout and included 80 cards in the base set, with the last 10 being redemption cards for the top 10 picks in the 1998 NBA Draft. The short-printed redemption cards were seeded 1:9 packs and numbered with a "T" suffix. Ovation featured cards printed on a basketball card stock, with Light F/X technology used in the background of the circular shot of the player. Inserts included: 23 hand-numbered Autographed Game-worn Jersey cards of Jordan, 90 Game-used Basketball cards of Jordan, 80 Gold Parallel cards, 15 Jordan Rules, 20 Superstars of the Court and 20 Future Forces.

		MT
Complete Set (80):		120.00
Common Player:		.20
Minor Stars:		.40
Jordan Basketball Numbered to 90		
Pack (4):		3.00
Wax Box (24):		60.00
1	Steve Smith	.20
2	Dikembe Mutombo	.40
3	Antoine Walker	1.50
4	Ron Mercer	3.00
5	Glen Rice	.50
6	Bobby Phills	.20
7	Michael Jordan	10.00
8	Toni Kukoc	.40
9	Dennis Rodman	2.50
10	Scottie Pippen	2.00
11	Shawn Kemp	.75
12	Derek Anderson	.75
13	Brevin Knight	.75
14	Michael Finley	.50
15	Shawn Bradley	.20
16	LaPhonso Ellis	.20
17	Bobby Jackson	.40
18	Grant Hill	5.00
19	Jerry Stackhouse	.40
20	Donyell Marshall	.20
21	Erick Dampier	.20
22	Hakeem Olajuwon	1.25
23	Charles Barkley	1.00
24	Reggie Miller	.50
25	Chris Mullin	.20
26	Rik Smits	.20
27	Maurice Taylor	.75
28	Lorenzen Wright	.20
29	Kobe Bryant	6.00
30	Eddie Jones	1.50
31	Shaquille O'Neal	2.50
32	Alonzo Mourning	.50
33	Tim Hardaway	.50
34	Jamal Mashburn	.20
35	Ray Allen	.50
36	Terrell Brandon	.20
37	Glenn Robinson	.50
38	Kevin Garnett	5.00

39	Tom Gugliotta	.40
40	Stephon Marbury	3.00
41	Keith Van Horn	2.00
42	Kerry Kittles	.40
43	Jayson Williams	.20
44	Patrick Ewing	.40
45	Allan Houston	.40
46	Larry Johnson	.40
47	Anfernee Hardaway	2.50
48	Nick Anderson	.20
49	Allen Iverson	2.00
50	Joe Smith	.40
51	Tim Thomas	2.00
52	Jason Kidd	1.50
53	Antonio McDyess	.50
54	Damon Stoudamire	.75
55	Isaiah Rider	.20
56	Rasheed Wallace	.20
57	Tariq Abdul-Wahad	.20
58	Corliss Williamson	.20
59	Tim Duncan	5.00
60	David Robinson	1.00
61	Vin Baker	1.00
62	Gary Payton	.75
63	Chauncey Billups	.50
64	Tracy McGrady	1.75
65	Karl Malone	1.00
66	John Stockton	.75
67	Shareef Abdur-Rahim	1.50
68	Bryant Reeves	.20
69	Juwan Howard	.50
70	Rod Strickland	.20
71T	*Michael Olowokandi*	5.00
72T	*Mike Bibby*	10.00
73T	*Raef LaFrentz*	6.00
74T	*Antawn Jamison*	20.00
75T	*Vince Carter*	70.00
76T	*Robert Traylor*	3.00
77T	*Jason Williams*	15.00
78T	*Larry Hughes*	15.00
79T	*Dirk Nowitzki*	20.00
80T	*Paul Pierce*	15.00
NNO	Jordan Basketball	2000.

1998-99 Upper Deck Ovation Gold

This 80-card parallel set reprinted each card from Ovation, but replaced the silver foil on the front with gold foil. Gold foil versions were sequentially numbered to 1,000 sets.

	MT
Common Gold Cards:	2.00
Gold Cards:	5x-10x
Production 1,000 Sets	

1998-99 Upper Deck Ovation Future Forces

Future Forces was a 20-card insert that featured top young players on foil cards with a silver border on the right and left side. These were numbered with an "F" prefix and inserted 1:29 packs.

		MT
Complete Set (20):		175.00
Common Player:		2.50
Inserted 1:29		
1	Tim Duncan	25.00
2	Keith Van Horn	10.00
3	Kobe Bryant	30.00
4	Tracy McGrady	12.00
5	Maurice Taylor	5.00
6	Shareef Abdur-Rahim	10.00
7	Kevin Garnett	25.00
8	Brevin Knight	5.00
9	Ron Mercer	15.00
10	Tim Thomas	12.00
11	Antoine Walker	8.00
12	Michael Finley	2.50
13	Grant Hill	25.00
14	Jerry Stackhouse	2.50
15	Erick Dampier	2.50
16	Lorenzen Wright	2.50
17	Ray Allen	2.50
18	Stephon Marbury	15.00
19	Allen Iverson	12.00
20	Damon Stoudamire	5.00

1998-99 Upper Deck Ovation Jordan Rules

This 15-card insert featured only Michael Jordan on three different levels. Cards 1-5 were bronze in color and inserted 1:23 packs, cards 6-10 were silver in color and inserted 1:45 packs and cards 11-15 were die-cut and gold in color and inserted 1:99 packs. Cards were numbered with a "J" prefix.

		MT
Complete Set (15):		400.00
Common Player (J1-J5):		15.00
Inserted 1:23		
Common Player (J6-J10):		25.00
Inserted 1:45		
Common Player (J11-J15):		50.00
Inserted 1:99		
1	Michael Jordan	15.00
2	Michael Jordan	15.00
3	Michael Jordan	15.00
4	Michael Jordan	15.00
5	Michael Jordan	15.00
6	Michael Jordan	25.00
7	Michael Jordan	25.00
8	Michael Jordan	25.00
9	Michael Jordan	25.00
10	Michael Jordan	25.00
11	Michael Jordan	50.00
12	Michael Jordan	50.00
13	Michael Jordan	50.00
14	Michael Jordan	50.00
15	Michael Jordan	50.00

1998-99 Upper Deck Ovation Superstars of the Court

Superstars of the Court was a 20-card insert that featured top players on a holographic foil card. Cards were numbered with a "C" prefix and inserted 1:2 packs.

		MT
Complete Set (20):		75.00
Common Player:		1.00
Inserted 1:2		
1	Michael Jordan	15.00
2	Tim Duncan	8.00
3	Grant Hill	8.00
4	Karl Malone	2.00
5	Dennis Rodman	4.00
6	Hakeem Olajuwon	3.00
7	Keith Van Horn	3.00
8	Kobe Bryant	10.00
9	Jason Kidd	3.00
10	Stephon Marbury	5.00
11	Reggie Miller	1.00
12	Damon Stoudamire	2.00
13	Tracy McGrady	3.00
14	Scottie Pippen	4.00
15	Vin Baker	2.00
16	Shaquille O'Neal	5.00
17	Anfernee Hardaway	5.00
18	Charles Barkley	2.00
19	Kevin Garnett	8.00
20	Antoine Walker	3.00

1998-99 Upper Deck

Upper Deck Series I consisted of 175 cards, including 133 regular player cards, 30 Heart and Soul, 10 To the Net and two checklists. Later in the year, Upper Deck produced a Series II product called MJ Access, but that is listed separately. The entire 175-card set was paralleled in UD Exclusives, which were hobby-only and numbered to 100 sets, and a 1-of-1 version of UD Exclusives. Inserts included: Game Jerseys, Hobby Exclusive Game Jerseys, one MJ Autographed Game Jersey card, AeroDynamics, Intensity and Forces.

		MT
Complete Set (175):		75.00
Common Player:		.15
Minor Stars:		.30
Common Heart & Soul:		.50
Inserted 1:4		
Common To The Net:		.50
Inserted 1:9		
Bronze Cards:		35x-70x
Bronze Heart & Soul:		10x-20x
Bronze To The Net:		10x-20x
Production 100 Sets		
Series 1 Pack (10):		3.00
Series 1 Wax Box (24):		60.00
Series 2 Pack (10):		8.00
Series 2 Wax Box (24):		300.00
1	Mookie Blaylock	.15
2	Ed Gray	.15
3	Dikembe Mutombo	.30
4	Steve Smith	.15
5	Dikembe Mutombo, Steve Smith	.50
6	Kenny Anderson	.15
7	Dana Barros	.15
8	Travis Knight	.15
9	Walter McCarty	.15
10	Ron Mercer	1.50
11	Greg Minor	.15
12	Antoine Walker, Ron Mercer	2.00
13	B.J. Armstrong	.15
14	David Wesley	.15
15	Anthony Mason	.30
16	Glen Rice	.40
17	J.R. Reid	.15
18	Bobby Phills	.15
19	Glen Rice, Anthony Mason	1.00
20	Ron Harper	.15
21	Toni Kukoc	.30
22	Scottie Pippen	1.25
23	Michael Jordan	5.00
24	Dennis Rodman	1.50
25	Michael Jordan, Scottie Pippen	10.00
26	Michael Jordan, Michael Jordan	12.00
27	Shawn Kemp	.60
28	Zydrunas Ilgauskas	.30
29	Cedric Henderson	.30
30	Vitaly Potapenko	.15
31	Derek Anderson	.50
32	Shawn Kemp, Zydrunas Ilgauskas	1.00
33	Shawn Bradley	.15
34	Khalid Reeves	.15
35	Robert Pack	.15
36	Michael Finley	.30
37	Erick Strickland	.15
38	Michael Finley, Shawn Bradley	1.00
39	Bryant Stith	.15
40	Dean Garrett	.15
41	Eric Williams	.15
42	Bobby Jackson	.30
43	Danny Fortson	.15
44	LaPhonso Ellis, Bryant Stith	.50
45	Grant Hill	2.50
46	Lindsey Hunter	.15
47	Brian Williams	.15
48	Scot Pollard	.15
49	Grant Hill, Brian Williams	5.00
50	Donyell Marshall	.15
51	Tony Delk	.15
52	Erick Dampier	.15
53	Felton Spencer	.15
54	Bimbo Coles	.15
55	Muggsy Bogues	.15
56	Donyell Marshall, Muggsy Bogues	.50
57	Charles Barkley	.50
58	Brent Price	.15
59	Hakeem Olajuwon	.75
60	Rodrick Rhodes	.15
61	Charles Barkley, Hakeem Olajuwon	1.50
62	Dale Davis	.15
63	Antonio Davis	.15
64	Chris Mullin	.15
65	Jalen Rose	.15
66	Reggie Miller	.30
67	Mark Jackson	.15
68	Reggie Miller, Mark Jackson	1.00
69	Rodney Rogers	.15
70	Lamond Murray	.15
71	Eric Piatkowski	.15
72	Lorenzen Wright	.15
73	Maurice Taylor	.50
74	Maurice Taylor, Lamond Murray	.50
75	Kobe Bryant	3.00
76	Shaquille O'Neal	1.50
77	Derek Fisher	.15
78	Elden Campbell	.15
79	Corie Blount	.15
80	Shaquille O'Neal, Kobe Bryant	7.00
81	Jamal Mashburn	.30
82	Alonzo Mourning	.30
83	Tim Hardaway	.40
84	Voshon Lenard	.15
85	Alonzo Mourning, Tim Hardaway	1.00
86	Ray Allen	.30
87	Terrell Brandon	.30
88	Elliot Perry	.15
89	Ervin Johnson	.15
90	Ray Allen, Glenn Robinson	1.00
91	Micheal Williams	.15
92	Anthony Peeler	.15
93	Chris Carr	.15
94	Kevin Garnett	2.50
95	Kevin Garnett, Stephon Marbury	5.00
96	Keith Van Horn	1.00
97	Kerry Kittles	.30
98	Kendall Gill	.15
99	Sam Cassell	.15
100	Chris Gatling	.15
101	Keith Van Horn, Sam Cassell	2.00
102	Patrick Ewing	.30
103	John Starks	.15
104	Allan Houston	.30
105	Chris Mills	.15
106	Chris Childs	.15
107	Charlie Ward	.15
108	Patrick Ewing, John Starks	1.00
109	Anfernee Hardaway	1.50
110	Horace Grant	.15
111	Nick Anderson	.15
112	Johnny Taylor	.15
113	Anfernee Hardaway, Horace Grant	3.50
114	Allen Iverson	1.25
115	Scott Williams	.15
116	Tim Thomas	1.25
117	Brian Shaw	.15
118	Anthony Parker	.15
119	Allen Iverson, Tim Thomas	2.50
120	Jason Kidd	.75
121	Rex Chapman	.15
122	Danny Manning	.15
123	Jason Kidd, Danny Manning	1.50
124	Rasheed Wallace	.15
125	Walt Williams	.15
126	Kelvin Cato	.15
127	Arvydas Sabonis	.15
128	Brian Grant	.15
129	Rasheed Wallace, Isaiah Rider	.50
130	Tariq Abdul-Wahad	.15
131	Corliss Williamson	.15
132	Olden Polynice	.15
133	Chris Robinson	.15
134	Tariq Abdul-Wahad, Olden Polynice	.50
135	Tim Duncan	2.50
136	Avery Johnson	.15
137	David Robinson	.50
138	Monty Williams	.15
139	Tim Duncan, David Robinson	5.00
140	Vin Baker	.50
141	Hersey Hawkins	.15
142	Detlef Schrempf	.15
143	Jim McIlvaine	.15
144	Gary Payton, Vin Baker	1.50
145	Chauncey Billups	.50
146	Tracy McGrady	1.00
147	John Wallace	.15
148	Doug Christie	.15
149	Dee Brown	.15
150	Tracy McGrady, Chauncey Billups	2.00
151	Karl Malone	.50
152	John Stockton	.30
153	Adam Keefe	.15
154	Howard Eisley	.15
155	Karl Malone, John Stockton	1.50
156	Bryant Reeves	.15
157	Lee Mayberry	.15
158	Michael Smith	.15
159	Shareef Abdur-Rahim, Bryant Reeves	2.00
160	Juwan Howard	.30
161	Calbert Cheaney	.15
162	Tracy Murray	.15
163	Juwan Howard, Calbert Cheaney	1.00
164	Shaquille O'Neal	3.50
165	Maurice Taylor	.50
166	Stephon Marbury	3.50
167	Tracy McGrady	2.00
168	Antoine Walker	2.00
169	Michael Jordan	10.00
170	Keith Van Horn	1.50
171	Shareef Abdur-Rahim	2.00
172	Kobe Bryant	7.00
173	Gary Payton	1.00
174	Checklist #1 (Michael Jordan)	2.00
175	Checklist #2 (Michael Jordan)	2.00
176	Kevin Johnson	.30
177	Glenn Robinson	.30
178	Antoine Walker	1.00
179	Jerry Stackhouse	.30
180	Mark Price	.15
181	Stephon Marbury	1.50
182	Shareef Abdur-Rahim	.75
183	Wesley Person	.15
184	Keith Booth	.15
185	Sean Elliott	.15
186	Alan Henderson	.15
187	Bryon Russell	.15
188	Jermaine O'Neal	.30
189	Steve Nash	.30
190	Eldridge Recasner	.15
191	Damon Stoudamire	.50
192	Dell Curry	.15
193	Michael Stewart	.15
194	Bruce Bowen	.15
195	Steve Kerr	.15
196	Dale Ellis	.15
197	Shandon Anderson	.15
198	Larry Johnson	.30
199	Chris Webber	.75
200	Matt Geiger	.15
201	Chris Anstey	.15
202	Loy Vaught	.15
203	Aaron McKie	.15
204	A.C. Green	.15
205	Bo Outlaw	.15
206	Antonio McDyess	.50
207	Priest Lauderdale	.15
208	Greg Ostertag	.15
209	Dan Majerle	.15
210	Johnny Newman	.15
211	Tyrone Corbin	.15
212	Pervis Ellison	.15
213	Shawnelle Scott	.15
214	Travis Best	.15
215	Stacey Augmon	.15
216	Brevin Knight	.50
217	Jerome Williams	.15
218	Terry Mills	.15
219	Matt Maloney	.30
220	Dennis Scott	.15
221	John Thomas	.15
222	Nick Van Exel	.30
223	Duane Ferrell	.15
224	Chris Whitney	.15
225	Luc Longley	.15
226	Robert Horry	.15
227	Clifford Robinson	.15
228	Samaki Walker	.15
229	Derrick McKey	.15
230a	Michael Jordan	4.00
230b	Michael Jordan	4.00
230c	Michael Jordan	4.00
230d	Michael Jordan	4.00
230e	Michael Jordan	4.00
230f	Michael Jordan	4.00
230g	Michael Jordan	4.00
230h	Michael Jordan	4.00
230i	Michael Jordan	4.00
230j	Michael Jordan	4.00
230k	Michael Jordan	4.00
230l	Michael Jordan	4.00
230m	Michael Jordan	4.00
230n	Michael Jordan	4.00
230o	Michael Jordan	4.00
230p	Michael Jordan	4.00
230q	Michael Jordan	4.00
230r	Michael Jordan	4.00
230s	Michael Jordan	4.00
230t	Michael Jordan	4.00
230u	Michael Jordan	4.00
230v	Michael Jordan	4.00
230w	Michael Jordan	4.00
231	Armon Gilliam	.15
232	Andrew DeClercq	.15
233	Stojko Vrankovic	.15
234	Jayson Williams	.15
235	Vinny Del Negro	.15
236	Theo Ratliff	.30
237	Othella Harrington	.15
238	Mitch Richmond	.30
239	Vlade Divac	.30
240	Duane Causwell	.15
241	Todd Fuller	.15
242	Tom Gugliotta	.30
243	LaPhonso Ellis	.30
244	Brian Evans	.15
245	Jason Caffey	.15
246	Pooh Richardson	.15
247	George Lynch	.15
248	Bill Wennington	.15
249	Rik Smits	.15
250	Kevin Willis	.15
251	Mario Elie	.15
252	Austin Croshere	.15
253	Sharone Wright	.15
254	Danny Ferry	.15
255	Jacque Vaughn	.15
256	Adonal Foyle	.15
257	Billy Owens	.15
258	Randy Brown	.15
259	Joe Smith	.30
260	Joe Dumars	.30
261	Sean Rooks	.15
262	Eric Montross	.15
263	Hubert Davis	.15
264	Gary Payton	.50
265	Tyrone Hill	.15
266	John Crotty	.15
267	P.J. Brown	.15
268	Michael Cage	.15
269	Scott Burrell	.15
270	Marcus Camby	.30
271	Rod Strickland	.30
272	Jim Jackson	.15
273	Corey Beck	.15
274	James Robinson	.15
275	Cedric Ceballos	.15
276	Charles Oakley	.15
277	Anthony Johnson	.15
278	Bob Sura	.15
279	Isaiah Rider	.15
280	Jeff Hornacek	.15
281	Rony Seikaly	.15
282	Charles Smith	.15
283	Eddie Jones	.75
284	Lucious Harris	.15
285	Andrew Lang	.15
286	Terry Cummings	.15
287	Keith Closs	.15
288	Chris Anstey	.15
289	Clarence Weatherspoon	.15
290	Michael Jordan	2.50
291	Shawn Kemp	.40
292	Tracy McGrady	.30
293	Glen Rice	.15
294	David Robinson	.30
295	Antonio McDyess	.30
296	Vin Baker	.30
297	Juwan Howard	.15
298	Ron Mercer	.75
299	Michael Finley	.15
300	Scottie Pippen	.50
301	Tim Thomas	.30
302	Rasheed Wallace	.15
303	Alonzo Mourning	.15
304	Dikembe Mutombo	.15
305	Derek Anderson	.30
306	Ray Allen	.30
307	Patrick Ewing	.30
308	Sean Elliott	.15
309	Shaquille O'Neal	.75
310	(Michael Jordan CL)	1.50
311	(Michael Jordan CL)	1.50
312	*Michael Olowokandi*	4.00
313	*Mike Bibby*	8.00
314	*Raef LaFrentz*	5.00
315	*Antawn Jamison*	15.00
316	*Vince Carter*	50.00
317	*Robert Traylor*	3.00
318	*Jason Williams*	12.00
319	*Larry Hughes*	15.00
320	*Dirk Nowitzki*	15.00
321	*Paul Pierce*	12.00
322	*Bonzi Wells*	12.00
323	*Michael Doleac*	2.00
324	*Keon Clark*	3.00
325	*Michael Dickerson*	5.00
326	*Matt Harpring*	3.00
327	*Bryce Drew*	2.00
328	*Pat Garrity*	2.00
329	*Roshown McLeod*	2.00
330	*Ricky Davis*	5.00
331	*Predrag Stojakovic*	6.00
332	*Felipe Lopez*	4.00
333	*Al Harrington*	6.00
UDX1	Michael Jordan Extra	2.00

1998-99 Upper Deck AeroDynamics

This 30-card, multi-tiered insert is numbered with an "A" prefix. Regular versions are inserted 1:6 packs, while Tier 1 are numbered to 2,000, Tier 2 are numbered to 100 and Tier 3 are numbered to 25 sets.

		MT
Complete Set (30):		70.00
Common Player:		.75
Minor Stars:		1.50
Inserted 1:6		
Bronze Cards:		2x
Production 2,000 Sets		
Silver Cards:		10x-20x
Production 100 Sets		
Gold Cards:		20x-40x
Production 25 Sets		
1	Michael Jordan	15.00
2	Shawn Kemp	2.00
3	Anfernee Hardaway	5.00
4	Tracy McGrady	3.00
5	Glen Rice	1.50
6	Maurice Taylor	1.50
7	Kevin Garnett	7.50
8	Jason Kidd	2.50
9	Grant Hill	7.50
10	Kendall Gill	.75
11	Hakeem Olajuwon	2.50
12	Mookie Blaylock	.75
13	Toni Kukoc	1.50
14	Kobe Bryant	10.00
15	Corliss Williamson	.75
16	Ray Allen	1.50
17	Vin Baker	2.00
18	Reggie Miller	1.50
19	Allan Houston	.75
20	Shareef Abdur-Rahim	3.00
21	Tim Duncan	7.50
22	Michael Finley	1.50
23	Damon Stoudamire	1.50
24	Juwan Howard	1.50
25	Antoine Walker	3.00
26	Donyell Marshall	.75
27	Allen Iverson	3.50
28	Karl Malone	2.00
29	Bobby Jackson	.75
30	Tim Hardaway	1.50

1998-99 Upper Deck Forces

This 30-card, multi-tiered insert is numbered with an "F" prefix. Regular versions are inserted 1:24, while Tier 1 are numbered to 1,000, Tier 2 are numbered to 50 and Tier 3 are numbered to 25 sets.

		MT
Complete Set (30):		175.00
Common Player:		2.00
Minor Stars:		4.00
Inserted 1:24		
Bronze Cards:		2x
Production 1,000 Sets		
Silver Cards:		15x-30x
Production 50 Sets		
Gold Cards:		20x-40x
Production 25 Sets		
1	Michael Jordan	40.00
2	Shareef Abdur-Rahim	8.00
3	Shaquille O'Neal	12.00
4	Gary Payton	5.00
5	Allen Iverson	10.00
6	Allan Houston	2.00
7	LaPhonso Ellis	2.00
8	Kevin Garnett	20.00
9	Chauncey Billups	5.00
10	Tim Hardaway	4.00
11	Reggie Miller	4.00
12	Glen Rice	4.00
13	Damon Stoudamire	5.00
14	Lamond Murray	2.00
15	Shawn Kemp	4.00
16	Steve Smith	2.00
17	Tim Duncan	20.00
18	Hakeem Olajuwon	6.00
19	Karl Malone	5.00
20	Donyell Marshall	2.00
21	Anfernee Hardaway	12.00
22	Grant Hill	20.00
23	Antoine Walker	8.00
24	Toni Kukoc	4.00
25	Corliss Williamson	2.00
26	Glenn Robinson	4.00
27	Keith Van Horn	8.00
28	Jason Kidd	6.00
29	Juwan Howard	4.00
30	Michael Finley	4.00

1998-99 Upper Deck Game Jerseys

This 10-card insert featured a swatch of Game-Used Jersey from 10 different players on cards numbered GJ1-GJ10. These were inserted across both hobby and retail packs at a rate of 1:2,500.

		MT
Complete Set (49):		13000.
Common Player:		60.00
Cards 1-10; 21-30; 41-50 Inserted 1:2500		
Cards 11-20; 31-40 Inserted 1:288 Hobby		
GJ38 Does Not Exist		
1	Glen Rice	200.00
2	Shawn Kemp	200.00
3	Reggie Miller	200.00
4	Shaquille O'Neal	400.00
5	Ray Allen	250.00
6	Keith Van Horn	200.00
7	Allen Iverson	350.00
8	David Robinson	250.00
9	Karl Malone	250.00
10	Shareef Abdur-Rahim	300.00
11	Grant Hill	250.00
12	Hakeem Olajuwon	150.00
13	Kevin Garnett	250.00
14	Jayson Williams	80.00
15	Tim Duncan	250.00
16	Gary Payton	100.00
17	John Stockton	100.00
18	Bryant Reeves	80.00
19	Kobe Bryant	650.00
20	Michael Jordan	1700.
21	Kobe Bryant	1000.
22	Grant Hill	450.00
23	Anfernee Hardaway	400.00
24	Tim Thomas	150.00
25	Hakeem Olajuwon	175.00
26	Damon Stoudamire	175.00
27	Gary Payton	200.00
28	Jason Kidd	300.00
29	Reggie Miller	225.00
30	Kevin Garnett	450.00
31	Tim Duncan	250.00
32	Keith Van Horn	75.00
33	Stephon Marbury	175.00
34	Shaquille O'Neal	200.00
35	Allen Iverson	225.00
36	Antoine Walker	75.00
37	Karl Malone	175.00
39	Shareef Abdur-Rahim	150.00
40	David Robinson	100.00
41	Corey Benjamin	100.00
42	Mike Bibby	250.00
43	Vince Carter	1800.
44	Michael Doleac	125.00
45	Larry Hughes	250.00
46	Antawn Jamison	300.00
47	Raef LaFrentz	150.00
48	Robert Traylor	150.00
49	Bonzi Wells	100.00
50	Jason Williams	425.00

1998-99 Upper Deck Intensity

This 30-card, multi-tiered insert is numbered with an "I" prefix. Regular versions are inserted 1:12, while Tier 1 are numbered to 1,500, Tier 2 are numbered to 75 and Tier 3 are numbered to 25 sets.

		MT
Complete Set (30):		60.00
Common Player:		1.50
Minor Stars:		3.00
Inserted 1:12		
Bronze Cards:		2x
Production 1,500 Sets		
Silver Cards:		10x-20x
Production 75 Sets		
Gold Cards:		20x-40x
Production 25 Sets		
1	Michael Jordan	25.00
2	Tracy Murray	1.50
3	Ron Mercer	8.00
4	Terrell Brandon	3.00
5	Brevin Knight	3.00
6	Rasheed Wallace	1.50
7	Sam Cassell	1.50
8	Erick Dampier	1.50
9	LaPhonso Ellis	1.50
10	Tim Thomas	6.00
11	Anfernee Hardaway	8.00
12	Tariq Abdul-Wahad	1.50
13	Lorenzen Wright	1.50
14	Bryant Reeves	1.50
15	Charles Barkley	4.00
16	Chauncey Billups	3.00
17	John Starks	1.50
18	Jerry Stackhouse	3.00
19	Vlade Divac	1.50
20	Detlef Schrempf	1.50
21	John Stockton	3.00
22	Nick Anderson	1.50
23	Alonzo Mourning	3.00
24	Dikembe Mutombo	1.50
25	Jalen Rose	1.50
26	Robert Pack	1.50
27	Antonio McDyess	[illegible]
28	Eddie Jones	5.00
29	Stephon Marbury	8.00
30	David Robinson	4.00

1998-99 Upper Deck MJ23

This 23-card set was devoted to Michael Jordan and was inserted 1:23 packs of MJ Access. Cards were numbered with an "MJ" prefix. Quantum parallel versions of each card were also available, with Bronze level cards numbered to 2,300 sets, Silver level cards were numbered to 23 sets and Gold level cards were numbered to one set.

		MT
Complete Set (30):		300.00
Common Player:		10.00
Inserted 1:23		
Bronze Cards:		2x
Production 2,300 Sets		
Silver Cards:		50x
Production 23 Sets		
1	Michael Jordan	10.00
2	Michael Jordan	10.00
3	Michael Jordan	10.00
4	Michael Jordan	10.00
5	Michael Jordan	10.00
6	Michael Jordan	10.00
7	Michael Jordan	10.00
8	Michael Jordan	10.00
9	Michael Jordan	10.00
10	Michael Jordan	10.00
11	Michael Jordan	10.00
12	Michael Jordan	10.00
13	Michael Jordan	10.00
14	Michael Jordan	10.00
15	Michael Jordan	10.00
16	Michael Jordan	10.00
17	Michael Jordan	10.00
18	Michael Jordan	10.00
19	Michael Jordan	10.00
20	Michael Jordan	10.00
21	Michael Jordan	10.00
22	Michael Jordan	10.00
23	Michael Jordan	10.00
24	Michael Jordan	10.00
25	Michael Jordan	10.00
26	Michael Jordan	10.00
27	Michael Jordan	10.00
28	Michael Jordan	10.00
29	Michael Jordan	10.00
30	Michael Jordan	10.00

1998-99 Upper Deck Next Wave

Next Wave displayed 30 top young stars and was seeded 1:11 packs of MJ Access. Cards were numbered with an "NW" prefix. Quantum levels of this insert were also available, with Bronze level cards numbered to 1,500 sets, Silver levels numbered to 200 sets and Gold levels numbered to 75 sets.

		MT
Complete Set (30):		55.00
Common Player:		.50
Minor Stars:		1.00
Inserted 1:11		
Bronze Cards:		3x
Production 1,500 Sets		
Silver Cards:		5x-10x
Production 200 Sets		
Gold Cards:		8x-16x
Production 75 Sets		
1	Kobe Bryant	15.00
2	John Wallace	.50
3	Kerry Kittles	1.00
4	Tim Thomas	5.00
5	Maurice Taylor	2.00
6	Antonio McDyess	1.50
7	Jermaine O'Neal	1.00
8	Zydrunas Ilgauskas	1.00
9	Danny Fortson	.50
10	Tim Duncan	10.00
11	Derek Anderson	2.00
12	Ron Mercer	6.00
13	Joe Smith	1.50
14	Eddie Jones	4.00
15	Rodrick Rhodes	.50
16	Kevin Garnett	10.00
17	Ed Gray	.50
18	Bobby Jackson	1.00
19	Allan Houston	1.00
20	Chauncey Billups	2.00
21	Keith Booth	.50
22	Brevin Knight	2.00
23	Othella Harrington	.50
24	Keith Van Horn	5.00
25	Michael Finley	1.00
26	Tracy McGrady	5.00
27	Derek Fisher	.50
28	Ray Allen	1.50
29	Anthony Johnson	.50
30	Vin Baker	2.00

1998-99 Upper Deck Super Powers

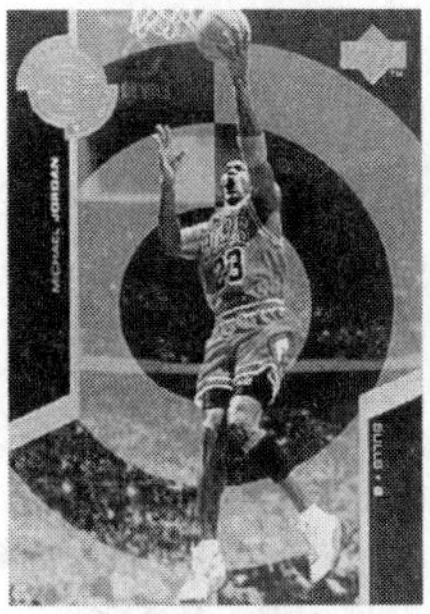

Super Powers was a 30-card insert that was seeded 1:5 packs of MJ Access. Cards were numbered with an "S" prefix. There were also Quantum parallel versions of Super Powers, with Bronze level cards numbered to 1,000, Silver levels numbered to 100 and Gold levels numbered to 50 sets.

		MT
Complete Set (30):		75.00
Common Player:		.50
Minor Stars:		1.00
Inserted 1:5		
Bronze Cards:		3x-6x
Production 1,000 Sets		
Silver Cards:		8x-16x
Production 100 Sets		
Gold Cards:		15x-30x
Production 50 Sets		
1	Dikembe Mutombo	.50
2	Ron Mercer	5.00
3	Glen Rice	1.00
4	Scottie Pippen	3.00
5	Shawn Kemp	1.50
6	Michael Finley	1.00
7	Bobby Jackson	.50
8	Grant Hill	8.00
9	Jim Jackson	.50
10	Hakeem Olajuwon	2.50
11	Reggie Miller	1.00
12	Maurice Taylor	1.50
13	Kobe Bryant	10.00
14	Tim Hardaway	1.50
15	Ray Allen	1.00
16	Stephon Marbury	5.00
17	Keith Van Horn	4.00
18	Allan Houston	.50
19	Anfernee Hardaway	5.00
20	Allen Iverson	4.00
21	Jason Kidd	3.00
22	Damon Stoudamire	2.00
23	Corliss Williamson	.50
24	Tim Duncan	8.00
25	Gary Payton	2.00
26	Tracy McGrady	4.00
27	Karl Malone	2.00
28	Shareef Abdur-Rahim	3.00
29	Juwan Howard	1.00
30	Michael Jordan	15.00

1999 Upper Deck Employee Game Jersey

This card was given out to Upper Deck employees as a "thank you" for the 1999 year. Each card was sequentially numbered to 275 and featured a swatch of game-worn jersey from Jordan.

		MT
NNO	Michael Jordan	1500.

1999 Upper Deck Kevin Garnett Santa Game Jersey

This postcard sized card of Garnett was issued as a Christmas card to various dealers and media outlets. It includes a swatch of a red felt Christmas hat worn by Garnett, while the back has a message from Upper Deck president and CEO Richard McWilliam and carries a "HH" prefix.

		MT
HH2	Kevin Garnett	75.00

1999 Upper Deck PowerDeck Athletes of the Century

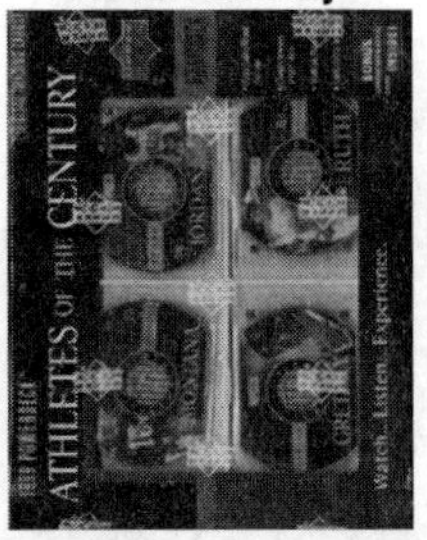

		MT
Complete Boxed Set (4):		25.00
Common Player:		5.00
1	Babe Ruth	10.00
2	Michael Jordan	10.00
3	Joe Montana	5.00
4	Wayne Gretzky	8.00

1999 UD Century Legends

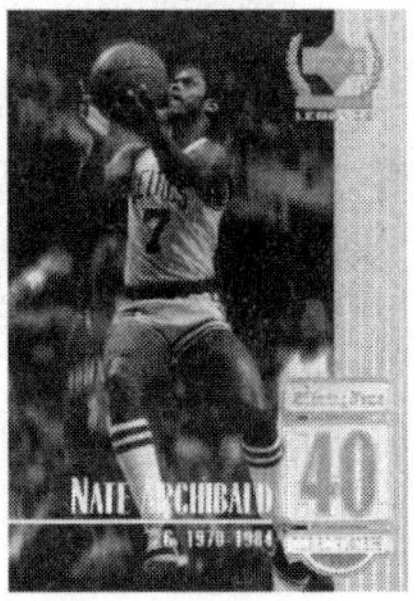

Upper Deck released this 90-card set during the off-season of 1999. The first 50 cards highlight players selected on the Sporting News' list of Basketball's 100 Greatest Players, with each card bearing a Sporting News photo of the featured player and his ranking in silver and copper foil. The next 30 cards in the set feature Upper Deck's 21st Century Phenoms, while the final 10 cards profile Michael Jordan's career and are called Jordan - Player of the Century. The 90-card set is paralleled in Century Collection with sequential numbering to 100. Inserts include: Jerseys of the Century, Epic Signatures, Century Epic Signatures, All-Century Team, MJ's Most Memorable Shots, Epic Milestones and Generations.

		MT
Complete Set (90):		45.00
Common Player:		.10
Minor Stars:		.20
Common Jordan (81-90):		2.00
Card #6 Does Not Exist		
Pack (6):		4.50
Wax Box (24):		100.00
1	Michael Jordan	5.00
2	Bill Russell	1.50
3	Wilt Chamberlain	1.50
4	George Mikan	1.00
5	Oscar Robertson	1.25
7	Larry Bird	3.00
8	Karl Malone	.40
9	Elgin Baylor	.40
10	Kareem Abdul-Jabbar	1.50
11	Jerry West	.60
12	Bob Cousy	.50
13	Julius Erving	1.50
14	Hakeem Olajuwon	.40
15	John Havlicek	.75
16	John Stockton	.20
17	Rick Barry	.10
18	Moses Malone	.25
19	Nate Thurmond	.10
20	Bob Pettit	.20
21	Pete Maravich	.75
22	Willis Reed	.20
23	Isiah Thomas	.30
24	Dolph Schayes	.10
25	Walt Frazier	.25
26	Wes Unseld	.20
27	Bill Sharman	.10
28	George Gervin	.30
29	Hal Greer	.10
30	Dave DeBusschere	.20
31	Earl Monroe	.25
32	Kevin McHale	.30
33	Charles Barkley	.40
34	Elvin Hayes	.20
35	Scottie Pippen	.75
36	Jerry Lucas	.10
37	Dave Bing	.10
38	Lenny Wilkens	.25
39	Paul Arizin	.10
40	Nate Archibald	.25
41	James Worthy	.30
42	Patrick Ewing	.20
43	Billy Cunningham	.20
44	Sam Jones	.10
45	Dave Cowens	.20
46	Robert Parish	.30
47	Bill Walton	.30
48	Shaquille O'Neal	1.50
49	David Robinson	.40
50	Dominique Wilkins	.20
51	Kobe Bryant	3.00
52	Vince Carter	3.00
53	Paul Pierce	1.25
54	Allen Iverson	2.00
55	Stephon Marbury	1.50
56	Mike Bibby	.50
57	Jason Williams	1.50
58	Kevin Garnett	2.50
59	Tim Duncan	2.50
60	Antawn Jamison	.75
61	Antoine Walker	.75
62	Shareef Abdur-Rahim	.60
63	Michael Olowokandi	.40
64	Robert Traylor	.40
65	Keith Van Horn	.75
66	Shaquille O'Neal	1.50
67	Ray Allen	.20
68	Gary Payton	.40
69	Raef LaFrentz	.40
70	Grant Hill	2.50
71	Anfernee Hardaway	1.50
72	Maurice Taylor	.30
73	Ron Mercer	.60
74	Michael Finley	.20
75	Jason Kidd	.75
76	Allan Houston	.20
77	Damon Stoudamire	.30
78	Antonio McDyess	.40
79	Eddie Jones	.30
80	Michael Dickerson	.30
81	Michael Jordan	2.00
82	Michael Jordan	2.00
83	Michael Jordan	2.00
84	Michael Jordan	2.00
85	Michael Jordan	2.00
86	Michael Jordan	2.00
87	Michael Jordan	2.00
88	Michael Jordan	2.00
89	Michael Jordan	2.00
90	Michael Jordan	2.00

1999 UD Century Legends Century Collection Parallel

Century Collection parallels all 90 cards of the base set, but adds a die-cut border on the left side and some holographic foil. Cards are also sequentially numbered to 100 on the front right.

	MT
Common Player:	5.00
Century Collection Cards:	25x-50x
Common Jordan Century Collection:	100.00
Production 100 Sets	

1999 UD Century Legends All-Century Team

This 12-card insert highlights Upper Deck's All-Time All-Star Team. The player's image is in black and white over a foil background. All-Century Team cards are numbered with an "A" prefix and seeded 1:11 packs.

		MT
Complete Set (12):		35.00
Common Player:		1.00
Inserted 1:11		
1	Michael Jordan	15.00
2	Oscar Robertson	3.00
3	Wilt Chamberlain	5.00
4	Larry Bird	8.00
5	Julius Erving	5.00
6	Jerry West	2.00
7	Charles Barkley	[illegible]
8	John Stockton	1.00
9	Hakeem Olajuwon	2.00
10	Karl Malone	2.00
11	Scottie Pippen	3.00
12	David Robinson	2.00

1999 UD Century Legends Epic Milestones

This 12-card insert showcases some of the most impressive milestones ever established in the NBA. Cards feature a black-and-white photo of the player over a foil background. Epic Milestones are numbered with an "EM" prefix and inserted 1:11 packs.

		MT
Cpmplete Set (12):		30.00
Common Player:		1.00
Inserted 1:11		
1	Michael Jordan	15.00
2	Jerry West	2.00
3	John Stockton	1.00
4	Wilt Chamberlain	5.00
5	Julius Erving	5.00
6	Reggie Miller	1.00
7	Hakeem Olajuwon	2.00
8	Robert Parish	1.00
9	Kobe Bryant	10.00
10	Rick Barry	1.00
11	Patrick Ewing	1.00
12	Charles Barkley	2.00

1999 UD Century Legends Epic Signatures

Epic Signatures was a collection of 33 autographed cards from current and retired players. The cards feature a photo of the player inside a television shape on the top half of the card, with the bottom featuring the player's signature over a white background. Cards were seeded 1:23 packs and numbered with two letters, usually corresponding to the player's initials.

		MT
Common Player:		20.00
Inserted 1:23		
Century Cards:		2x
Production 100 Sets		
KA	Kareem Abdul-Jabbar	150.00
NA	Nate Archibald	25.00
EB	Elgin Baylor	40.00
MB	Mike Bibby	30.00
LB	Larry Bird	400.00
WC	Wilt Chamberlain	250.00
BC	Bob Cousy	40.00
DC	Dave Cowens	25.00
CD	Clyde Drexler	40.00
AE	Alex English	20.00
DR	Julius Erving	250.00
WF	Walt Frazier	40.00
GG	George Gervin	30.00
TH	Tim Hardaway	40.00
JH	John Havlicek	40.00
EH	Elvin Hayes	25.00
AI	Allen Iverson	125.00
MJ	Michael Jordan	2500.
BL	Bob Lanier	20.00
JL	Jerry Lucas	20.00
MM	Moses Malone	25.00
EM	Earl Monroe	40.00
HK	Hakeem Olajuwon	75.00
MO	Michael Olowokandi	25.00
BP	Bob Pettit	25.00
WR	Willis Reed	25.00
OR	Oscar Robertson	75.00
BR	Bill Russell	400.00
BS	Bill Sharman	20.00
DT	David Thompson	25.00
WU	Wes Unseld	[illegible]
BW	Bill Walton	25.00
JW	Jerry West	60.00

1999 UD Century Legends Epic Signatures Century

Epic Signatures Century Collection was a parallel of Epic Signatures, but was limited and sequentially numbered to 100 sets. Players that do not have 100 of these include: Bill Russell (6), Julius Erving (6), Larry Bird (33) and Michael Jordan (23).

		MT
Common Player:		40.00
Century Signatures:		2x
Production 100 Sets		
KA	Kareem Abdul-Jabbar	
NA	Nate Archibald	
EB	Elgin Baylor	
MB	Mike Bibby	
LB	Larry Bird (33)	
WC	Wilt Chamberlain	
BC	Bob Cousy	
DC	Dave Cowens	
CD	Clyde Drexler	
AE	Alex English	
DR	Julius Erving (6)	
WF	Walt Frazier	
GG	George Gervin	
TH	Tim Hardaway	
JH	John Havlicek	
EH	Elvin Hayes	
AI	Allen Iverson	
MJ	Michael Jordan (23)	
BL	Bob Lanier	
JL	Jerry Lucas	
MM	Moses Malone	
EM	Earl Monroe	
HK	Hakeem Olajuwon	
MO	Michael Olowokandi	
BP	Bob Pettit	
WR	Willis Reed	
OR	Oscar Robertson	
BR	Bill Russell (6)	
BS	Bill Sharman	
DT	David Thompson	
WU	Wes Unseld	
BW	Bill Walton	
JW	Jerry West	

1999 UD Century Legends Generations

This 12-card, double-sided insert featured a modern-day NBA star on the front printed on foil, with an NBA legend with comparable skills on the back printed in color. Generations were numbered with a "G" prefix and inserted 1:4 packs.

		MT
Complete Set (12):		25.00
Common Player:		1.00
Inserted 1:4		
1	Michael Jordan, Julius Erving	8.00
2	Kobe Bryant, Michael Jordan	8.00
3	Shaquille O'Neal, Wilt Chamberlain	4.00
4	Jason Williams, Pete Maravich	3.00
5	Stephon Marbury, Nate Archibald	1.00
6	Antoine Walker, Karl Malone	.75
7	Grant Hill, George Gervin	2.00
8	Gary Payton, Isiah Thomas	2.00
9	Kevin Garnett, Dominique Wilkins	1.00
10	Hakeem Olajuwon, Moses Malone	1.00
11	Keith Van Horn, Larry Bird	2.00
12	Vince Carter, Oscar Robertson	3.00

1999 UD Century Legends Jerseys of the Century

Jerseys of the Century was an eight-card insert that featured a swatch of game-worn jersey from top current and retired players. These were inserted 1:475 packs and numbered with two letters corresponding to the player's initials except Erving's card is numbered "DR". In addition, Erving and Abdul-Jabbar autographed a limited amount of their cards, which are hand-numbered to the player's jersey number (6 and 33, respectively).

		MT
Complete Set (8):		3000.
Common Player:		150.00
Inserted 1:475		
KA	Kareem Abdul-Jabbar	250.00
KA-A	Kareem Abdul-Jabbar Auto (33)	1000.
LB	Larry Bird	400.00
CD	Clyde Drexler	150.00
DR	Julius Erving	300.00
DR-A	Julius Erving Auto (6)	3000.
MJ	Michael Jordan	2000.
KM	Karl Malone	150.00
SO	Shaquille O'Neal	150.00
JS	John Stockton	150.00

1999 UD Century Legends MJ's Most Memorable Shots

This six-card insert focuses on some of the most memorable shots made by Michael Jordan during his 13-year NBA career. MJ's Most Memorable Shots were numbered with an "MJ" prefix and inserted 1:23 packs.

		MT
Complete Set (6):		80.00
Common Player:		15.00
Inserted 1:23		
1	Michael Jordan	15.00
2	Michael Jordan	15.00
3	Michael Jordan	15.00
4	Michael Jordan	15.00
5	Michael Jordan	15.00
6	Michael Jordan	15.00

1999 UD Jordan Athlete of the Century The Jordan Era

	MT
Complete Set (16):	50.00
Common Player:	3.00
Inserted 1:11	

1999 UD Jordan Athlete of the Century Total Dominance

	MT
Complete Set (20):	150.00
Common Player:	8.00
Inserted 1:23	

1999 UD Jordan Athlete of the Century UD Remembers

	MT
Complete Set (16):	50.00
Common Player:	6.00
Inserted 1:11	

1999 Upper Deck Michael Jordan Retirement

		MT
Complete Set (23):		15.00
Common Player:		1.00
1	Michael Jordan	1.00
2	Michael Jordan	1.00
3	Michael Jordan	1.00
4	Michael Jordan	1.00
5	Michael Jordan	1.00
6	Michael Jordan	1.00
7	Michael Jordan	1.00
8	Michael Jordan	1.00
9	Michael Jordan	1.00
10	Michael Jordan	1.00
11	Michael Jordan	1.00
12	Michael Jordan	1.00
13	Michael Jordan	1.00
14	Michael Jordan	1.00
15	Michael Jordan	1.00
16	Michael Jordan	1.00
17	Michael Jordan	1.00
18	Michael Jordan	1.00
19	Michael Jordan	1.00
20	Michael Jordan	1.00
21	Michael Jordan	1.00
22	Michael Jordan	1.00
23	Michael Jordan	1.00

1999 Upper Deck Michael Jordan Career

This 60-card boxed set highlighted Michael Jordan's career, from the early years all the way through retirement. Each set also contained one of six different blow-up cards, which are checklisted at the end of the set and are numbered with a "CC" prefix.

		MT
Complete Set (66):		40.00
Common Player:		1.00
1	Michael Jordan	1.00
2	Michael Jordan	1.00
3	Michael Jordan	1.00
4	Michael Jordan	1.00
5	Michael Jordan	1.00
6	Michael Jordan	1.00
7	Michael Jordan	1.00
8	Michael Jordan	1.00
9	Michael Jordan	1.00
10	Michael Jordan	1.00
11	Michael Jordan	1.00
12	Michael Jordan	1.00
13	Michael Jordan	1.00
14	Michael Jordan	1.00
15	Michael Jordan	1.00
16	Michael Jordan	1.00
17	Michael Jordan	1.00
18	Michael Jordan	1.00
19	Michael Jordan	1.00
20	Michael Jordan	1.00
21	Michael Jordan	1.00
22	Michael Jordan	1.00
23	Michael Jordan	1.00
24	Michael Jordan	1.00
25	Michael Jordan	1.00
26	Michael Jordan	1.00
27	Michael Jordan	1.00
28	Michael Jordan	1.00
29	Michael Jordan	1.00
30	Michael Jordan	1.00
31	Michael Jordan	1.00
32	Michael Jordan	1.00
33	Michael Jordan	1.00
34	Michael Jordan	1.00
35	Michael Jordan	1.00
36	Michael Jordan	1.00
37	Michael Jordan	1.00
38	Michael Jordan	1.00
39	Michael Jordan	1.00
40	Michael Jordan	1.00
41	Michael Jordan	1.00
42	Michael Jordan	1.00
43	Michael Jordan	1.00
44	Michael Jordan	1.00
45	Michael Jordan	1.00
46	Michael Jordan	1.00
47	Michael Jordan	1.00
48	Michael Jordan	1.00
49	Michael Jordan	1.00
50	Michael Jordan	1.00
51	Michael Jordan	1.00
52	Michael Jordan	1.00
53	Michael Jordan	1.00
54	Michael Jordan	1.00
55	Michael Jordan	1.00
56	Michael Jordan	1.00
57	Michael Jordan	1.00
58	Michael Jordan	1.00
59	Michael Jordan	1.00
60	Michael Jordan	1.00
CC1	Michael Jordan	1.00
CC2	Michael Jordan	1.00
CC3	Michael Jordan	1.00
CC4	Michael Jordan	1.00
CC5	Michael Jordan	1.00
CC6	Michael Jordan	1.00

1999 Upper Deck Michael Jordan 22 Kt. Gold

This five-card set was issued by Upper Deck Authenticated and Upper Deck and commemorated Jordan's retirement. Cards were not numbered individually, but were sequentially numbered to 9,923 on the back.

		MT
Complete Set (5):		100.00
Common Player:		25.00
1	Michael Jordan (Retires)	25.00
2	Michael Jordan (91/92 UD)	25.00
3	Michael Jordan (84/85 Reprint)	25.00
4	Michael Jordan (Championship)	25.00
5	Michael Jordan (Final Shot)	25.00

1999 Upper Deck Tribute to Michael Jordan

This 30-card set featured highlights of Jordan's career and was issued in a lunch box.

		MT
Complete Set (30):		25.00
Common Player:		1.00
1	Michael Jordan	1.00
2	Michael Jordan	1.00
3	Michael Jordan	1.00
4	Michael Jordan	1.00
5	Michael Jordan	1.00
6	Michael Jordan	1.00
7	Michael Jordan	1.00
8	Michael Jordan	1.00
9	Michael Jordan	1.00
10	Michael Jordan	1.00
11	Michael Jordan	1.00
12	Michael Jordan	1.00
13	Michael Jordan	1.00
14	Michael Jordan	1.00
15	Michael Jordan	1.00
16	Michael Jordan	1.00
17	Michael Jordan	1.00
18	Michael Jordan	1.00
19	Michael Jordan	1.00
20	Michael Jordan	1.00
21	Michael Jordan	1.00
22	Michael Jordan	1.00
23	Michael Jordan	1.00
24	Michael Jordan	1.00
25	Michael Jordan	1.00
26	Michael Jordan	1.00
27	Michael Jordan	1.00
28	Michael Jordan	1.00
29	Michael Jordan	1.00
30	Michael Jordan	1.00

1999-00 Upper Deck

This 360-card set was released in two series of 180 cards each. Series I contained a 20-card Air of Greatness subset (134-153) and 25 Rookie Class cards (156-180), with both seeded 1:4 packs. Series II included 133 base cards and 45 short-printed Rookie Action cards (1:4 packs) along with two checklists. The second series was known as Game Jersey Edition. Series I inserts included: Now Showing, Future Charge, Jamboree, History Class, Basketball Heroes Dr. J, MJ - A Higher Power, Exclusives parallel (all 180 cards), PowerDeck, MJ PowerDeck, Game Jerseys and Game-used Jersey Patches. Series II inserts included: BioGraphics, Rookies Illustrated, High Definition, Star Surge, Wild!, Cool Air, Exclusives (of all 180 cards), PowerDeck, PowerDeck Extreme, Game Jerseys, Game Jersey Patches and MJ Final Floor.

		MT
Complete Set (360):		200.00
Complete Series I (180):		125.00
Complete Series II (180):		75.00
Common Player:		.10
Minor Stars:		.20
Common Air of Greatness (134-153):		3.00
Inserted 1:4		
Common Rookie (156-180/316-360):		1.00
Inserted 1:4		
Series 1 Pack (10):		3.00
Series 2 Pack (10):		3.00
Series 1 Box (24):		65.00
Series 2 Box (24):		65.00
1	Roshown McLeod	.20
2	Dikembe Mutombo	.20
3	Alan Henderson	.10
4	LaPhonso Ellis	.10
5	Chris Crawford	.10
6	Kenny Anderson	.20
7	Antoine Walker	.75
8	Paul Pierce	1.50
9	Vitaly Potapenko	.10
10	Dana Barros	.10
11	Elden Campbell	.10
12	Eddie Jones	.60
13	David Wesley	.10
14	Derrick Coleman	.20
15	Ricky Davis	.20
16	Corey Benjamin	.20
17	Randy Brown	.10
18	Kornel David	.20
19	Toni Kukoc	.50
20	Keith Booth	.10
21	Shawn Kemp	.60
22	Wesley Person	.10
23	Brevin Knight	.10
24	Bob Sura	.10
25	Zydrunas Ilgauskas	.20
26	Michael Finley	.30
27	Shawn Bradley	.10
28	Dirk Nowitzki	.50
29	Steve Nash	.10
30	Antonio McDyess	.60
31	Nick Van Exel	.20
32	Chauncey Billups	.10
33	Bryant Stith	.10
34	Raef LaFrentz	.75
35	Grant Hill	2.50
36	Lindsey Hunter	.10
37	Bison Dele	.10
38	Jerry Stackhouse	.30
39	John Starks	.10
40	Antawn Jamison	1.25
41	Erick Dampier	.10
42	Jason Caffey	.10
43	Hakeem Olajuwon	.75
44	Scottie Pippen	1.00
45	Cuttino Mobley	.20
46	Charles Barkley	.75
47	Bryce Drew	.20
48	Reggie Miller	.20
49	Jalen Rose	.20
50	Mark Jackson	.10
51	Dale Davis	.10
52	Chris Mullin	.10
53	Maurice Taylor	.40
54	Tyrone Nesby	.20
55	Michael Olowokandi	.75
56	Eric Piatkowski	.10
57	Troy Hudson	.10
58	Kobe Bryant	3.00
59	Shaquille O'Neal	2.00
60	Glen Rice	.20
61	Robert Horry	.10
62	Tim Hardaway	.40
63	Alonzo Mourning	.40
64	P.J. Brown	.10
65	Dan Majerle	.10
66	Ray Allen	.30
67	Glenn Robinson	.20
68	Sam Cassell	.20
69	Robert Traylor	.75
70	Kevin Garnett	2.50
71	Sam Mitchell	.10
72	Dean Garrett	.10
73	Bobby Jackson	.10
74	Radoslav Nesterovic	.20
75	Keith Van Horn	.75
76	Stephon Marbury	1.25
77	Kendall Gill	.10
78	Scott Burrell	.10
79	Patrick Ewing	.20
80	Allan Houston	.20
81	Latrell Sprewell	.20
82	Larry Johnson	.10
83	Marcus Camby	.60
84	Darrell Armstrong	.20
85	Derek Strong	.10
86	Matt Harpring	.20
87	Michael Doleac	.20
88	Charles Outlaw	.10
89	Allen Iverson	2.50
90	Theo Ratliff	.10
91	Larry Hughes	1.00
92	Eric Snow	.10
93	Jason Kidd	1.00
94	Clifford Robinson	.10
95	Tom Gugliotta	.20
96	Luc Longley	.10
97	Rasheed Wallace	.10
98	Arvydas Sabonis	.10
99	Damon Stoudamire	.30
100	Brian Grant	.10
101	Jason Williams	2.00
102	Vlade Divac	.10
103	Predrag Stojakovic	.20
104	Lawrence Funderburke	.10
105	Tim Duncan	2.50
106	Sean Elliott	.10
107	David Robinson	.75
108	Mario Elie	.10
109	Avery Johnson	.10
110	Gary Payton	.75
111	Vin Baker	.20
112	Rashard Lewis	.40
113	Jelani McCoy	.20
114	Vladimir Stepania	.10
115	Vince Carter	3.00
116	Doug Christie	.10
117	Kevin Willis	.10
118	Dee Brown	.10
119	John Thomas	.10
120	Karl Malone	.75
121	John Stockton	.20
122	Howard Eisley	.10
123	Bryon Russell	.10
124	Greg Ostertag	.10
125	Shareef Abdur-Rahim	1.00
126	Mike Bibby	1.00
127	Felipe Lopez	.30
128	Cherokee Parks	.10
129	Juwan Howard	.20
130	Rod Strickland	.20
131	Chris Whitney	.10
132	Tracy Murray	.10
133	Jahidi White	.10
134	Michael Jordan	3.00
135	Michael Jordan	3.00
136	Michael Jordan	3.00
137	Michael Jordan	3.00
138	Michael Jordan	3.00
139	Michael Jordan	3.00
140	Michael Jordan	3.00
141	Michael Jordan	3.00
142	Michael Jordan	3.00
143	Michael Jordan	3.00
144	Michael Jordan	3.00
145	Michael Jordan	3.00
146	Michael Jordan	3.00
147	Michael Jordan	3.00
148	Michael Jordan	3.00
149	Michael Jordan	3.00
150	Michael Jordan	3.00
151	Michael Jordan	3.00
152	Michael Jordan	3.00
153	Michael Jordan	3.00
154	Michael Jordan	1.50
155	Michael Jordan	1.50
156	*Elton Brand*	8.00
157	*Steve Francis*	20.00
158	*Baron Davis*	6.00
159	*Lamar Odom*	12.00
160	*Jonathan Bender*	8.00
161	*Wally Szczerbiak*	5.00
162	*Richard Hamilton*	5.00
163	*Andre Miller*	6.00
164	*Shawn Marion*	8.00
165	*Jason Terry*	4.00
166	*Trajan Langdon*	3.00
167	*Kenny Thomas*	2.50
168	*Corey Maggette*	6.00
169	*William Avery*	2.00
170	*Jumanie Jones*	2.50
171	*Ron Artest*	3.00
172	*Cal Bowdler*	1.00
173	*James Posey*	2.00
174	*Quincy Lewis*	2.00
175	*Vonteego Cummings*	2.00
176	*Jeff Foster*	1.00
177	*Dion Glover*	2.00
178	*Devean George*	2.50
179	*Evan Eschmeyer*	1.00
180	*Tim James*	2.00
181	Jim Jackson	.10
182	Isaiah Rider	.10
183	Lorenzen Wright	.10
184	Bimbo Coles	.10
185	Anthony Johnson	.10
186	Calbert Cheaney	.10
187	Pervis Ellison	.10
188	Walter McCarty	.10
189	Eric Williams	.10
190	Tony Battie	.10
191	Anthony Mason	.10
192	Bobby Phills	.10
193	Todd Fuller	.10
194	Brad Miller	.10
195	Eldridge Recasner	.10
196	Chris Anstey	.10
197	Fred Hoiberg	.10
198	Hersey Hawkins	.10
199	Will Perdue	.10
200	Mark Bryant	.10
201	Lamond Murray	.10
202	Cedric Henderson	.10
203	Andrew DeClerq	.10
204	Danny Ferry	.10
205	Erick Strickland	.10
206	Cedric Ceballos	.10
207	Hubert Davis	.10
208	Robert Pack	.10
209	Gary Trent	.10
210	Ron Mercer	.75
211	George McCloud	.10
212	Roy Rogers	.10
213	Keon Clark	.20
214	Terry Mills	.10
215	Michael Curry	.10
216	Christian Laettner	.10
217	Jerome Williams	.10
218	Loy Vaught	.10
219	Jud Buechler	.10
220	Mookie Blaylock	.10
221	Terry Cummings	.10
222	Donyell Marshall	.10
223	Chris Mills	.10
224	Adonal Foyle	.10
225	Shandon Anderson	.10
226	Kelvin Cato	.10
227	Walt Williams	.10
228	Al Harrington	.50
229	Rik Smits	.10
230	Derrick McKey	.10
231	Sam Perkins	.10
232	Austin Croshere	.10
233	Derek Anderson	.10
234	Keith Closs	.10
235	Eric Murdock	.10
236	Brian Skinner	.20
237	Charles Jones	.10
238	Ron Harper	.10
239	Derek Fisher	.10
240	Rick Fox	.10
241	A.C. Green	.10
242	Jamal Mashburn	.20
243	Mark Strickland	.10
244	Rex Walters	.10
245	Clarence Weatherspoon	.10
246	Ervin Johnson	.10
247	J.R. Reid	.10
248	Dale Ellis	.10
249	Danny Manning	.10
250	Tim Thomas	.50
251	Terrell Brandon	.20
252	Malik Sealy	.10
253	Joe Smith	.10
254	Anthony Peeler	.10
255	Jayson Williams	.10
256	Jamie Feick	.10
257	Kerry Kittles	.10
258	Johnny Newman	.10
259	Chris Childs	.10
260	Kurt Thomas	.10
261	Charlie Ward	.10
262	Chris Dudley	.10
263	John Wallace	.10
264	Tariq Abdul-Wahad	.10
265	John Amaechi	.10

266	Chris Gatling	.10
267	Monty Williams	.10
268	Ben Wallace	.10
269	George Lynch	.10
270	Tyrone Hill	.10
271	Billy Owens	.10
272	Anfernee Hardaway	1.50
273	Rex Chapman	.10
274	Oliver Miller	.10
275	Rodney Rogers	.10
276	Randy Livingston	.10
277	Scottie Pippen	1.25
278	Detlef Schrempf	.10
279	Steve Smith	.20
280	Jermaine O'Neal	.20
281	Bonzi Wells	.30
282	Chris Webber	1.25
283	Nick Anderson	.10
284	Darrick Martin	.10
285	Corliss Williamson	.10
286	Samaki Walker	.10
287	Terry Porter	.10
288	Malik Rose	.10
289	Jaren Jackson	.10
290	Antonio Daniels	.10
291	Steve Kerr	.10
292	Brent Barry	.10
293	Horace Grant	.10
294	Vernon Maxwell	.10
295	Ruben Patterson	.20
296	Shammond Williams	.10
297	Antonio Davis	.10
298	Tracy McGrady	1.25
299	Dell Curry	.10
300	Charles Oakley	.10
301	Muggsy Bogues	.10
302	Jeff Hornacek	.10
303	Adam Keefe	.10
304	Olden Polynice	.10
305	Doug West	.10
306	Michael Dickerson	.30
307	Othella Harrington	.10
308	Bryant Reeves	.10
309	Brent Price	.10
310	Mitch Richmond	.20
311	Aaron Williams	.10
312	Isaac Austin	.10
313	Michael Smith	.10
314	Michael Jordan	1.00
315	Kevin Garnett	.50
316	Elton Brand	6.00
317	Steve Francis	10.00
318	Baron Davis	3.00
319	Lamar Odom	6.00
320	Jonathan Bender	4.00
321	Wally Szczerbiak	3.00
322	Richard Hamilton	2.50
323	Andre Miller	3.00
324	Shawn Marion	4.00
325	Jason Terry	2.00
326	Trajan Langdon	2.00
327	*Aleksandar Radojevic*	1.00
328	Corey Maggette	3.00
329	William Avery	1.50
330	Ron Artest	2.00
331	Cal Bowdler	.50
332	James Posey	1.50
333	Quincy Lewis	1.25
334	Dion Glover	.75
335	Jeff Foster	.50
336	Kenny Thomas	1.00
337	Devean George	1.00
338	Tim James	.75
339	Vonteego Cummings	1.50
340	Jumaine Jones	.75
341	*Scott Padgett*	1.50
342	*John Celestand*	2.00
343	*Adrian Griffin*	2.00
344	*Michael Ruffin*	1.50
345	*Chris Herren*	2.00
346	Evan Eschmeyer	.50
347	*Eddie Robinson*	3.00
348	*Obinna Ekezie*	1.00
349	*Laron Profit*	2.00
350	*Jermaine Jackson*	1.00
351	*Lazaro Borrell*	1.00
352	*Chucky Atkins*	2.50
353	*Ryan Robertson*	1.00
354	*Todd MacCulloch*	2.00
355	*Rafer Alston*	2.00
356	*Mirsad Turkcan*	1.00
357	*Anthony Carter*	3.00
358	*Ryan Bowen*	1.50
359	*Rodney Buford*	1.50
360	*Tim Young*	1.00

1999-00 Upper Deck Exclusives

Exclusives or Bronze cards paralleled every card in the 360-card Series I and II sets. Cards featured bronze foil on the front and were sequentially numbered to 100 sets also on the front. The cards also contained the words "UD Exclusives" on the back in white letters. There was also a Gold, one-of-one version inserted into packs.

	MT
Common Player:	5.00
Minor Stars:	10.00
Exclusive Cards:	25x-50x
Common Air of Greatness (134-153):	50.00
[illegible]	[illegible]
Rookie Class Cards:	3x-6x

1999-00 Upper Deck Basketball Heroes-Dr. J

This 10-card, Series I insert set featured Julius Erving. The cards were numbered H46-H55 and regular versions were inserted 1:23 packs. There were also two parallel versions - Quantum Level I (hobby exclusive, numbered to 100) and Quantum Level II (hobby exclusive, numbered to 1).

		MT
Complete Set (10):		40.00
Common Player:		5.00
Inserted 1:23		
Quantum Level I Cards:		5x-10x
Production 100 Hobby Sets		
Quantum Level II Cards:		
Production 1 Hobby Set		
H46	Julius Erving	5.00
H47	Julius Erving	5.00
H48	Julius Erving	5.00
H49	Julius Erving	5.00
H50	Julius Erving	5.00
H51	Julius Erving	5.00
H52	Julius Erving	5.00
H53	Julius Erving	5.00
H54	Julius Erving	5.00
H55	Julius Erving	5.00

1999-00 Upper Deck BioGraphics

This 30-card, Game Jersey Edition insert set was inserted 1:4 packs. Biographics were numbered with a "B" prefix and featured horizontal backs.

		MT
Complete Set (30):		30.00
Common Player:		.50
Inserted 1:4 Series II		
Quantum Level I Cards:		10x-20x
Production 100 Sets		
Quantum Leve II Cards:		40x-80x
Production 25 Sets		
B1	Antawn Jamison	2.00
B2	Mike Bibby	.75
B3	Antoine Walker	.75
B4	Ray Allen	.75
B5	Anfernee Hardaway	3.00
B6	Hakeem Olajuwon	1.00
B7	Jason Williams	3.00
B8	Keith Van Horn	1.50
B9	Jason Kidd	2.50
B10	Reggie Miller	.50
B11	Eddie Jones	1.00
B12	Jim Jackson	.50
B13	Jerry Stackhouse	.75
B14	Tim Duncan	5.00
B15	Kevin Garnett	5.00
B16	Mitch Richmond	.50
B17	Steve Smith	.50
B18	Charles Barkley	1.00
B19	Glen Rice	.50
B20	Paul Pierce	2.00
B21	Alonzo Mourning	.75
B22	Karl Malone	1.00
B23	Stephon Marbury	2.00
B24	Chris Webber	2.50
B25	Michael Finley	.50
B26	Shawn Kemp	.50
B27	John Stockton	.50
B28	Ron Mercer	1.50
B29	Tim Hardaway	.75
B30	Allan Houston	.50

1999-00 Upper Deck Cool Air

This eight-card, Game Jersey Edition insert set featured Michael Jordan. Cards were inserted 1:72 packs and numbered with a "MJ" prefix. Two parallel versions were also produced - Quantum Silver (hobby exclusive, numbered to 100) and Quantum Gold (hobby exclusive, numbered to 25).

		MT
Complete Set (8):		75.00
Common Player:		10.00
Inserted 1:23 Series II		
Quantum Level I Cards:		5x-10x
Production 100 Hobby Sets		
MJ1	Michael Jordan	10.00
MJ2	Michael Jordan	10.00
MJ3	Michael Jordan	10.00
MJ4	Michael Jordan	10.00
MJ5	Michael Jordan	10.00
MJ6	Michael Jordan	10.00
MJ7	Michael Jordan	10.00
MJ8	Michael Jordan	10.00

1999-00 Upper Deck Future Charge

This 15-card, Series I insert set was seeded 1:8 packs and numbered with an "FC" prefix. Two parallel versions were also printed - Quantum Level I (numbered to 100) and Quantum Level II (numbered to 25).

		MT
Complete Set (15):		30.00
Common Player:		1.00
Inserted 1:8		
Quantum Level I Cards:		5x-10x
Production 100 Sets		
Quantum Level II Cards:		10x-20x
Production 25 Sets		
FC1	Antawn Jamison	3.00
FC2	Mike Bibby	2.00
FC3	Antoine Walker	1.50
FC4	Baron Davis	5.00
FC5	Jason Terry	2.00
FC6	Andre Miller	2.00
FC7	Ray Allen	1.00
FC8	Wally Szczerbiak	8.00
FC9	Raef LaFrentz	1.50
FC10	William Avery	2.00
FC11	Jason Williams	4.00
FC12	Michael Olowokandi	1.50
FC13	Stephon Marbury	3.00
FC14	Quincy Lewis	1.00
FC15	Shawn Marion	3.00

1999-00 Upper Deck Game Jersey

This 65-card set had 20 cards in Series I and 45 cards in Game Jersey Edition. They were numbered with a "GJ" prefix. Cards 1-10 were inserted 1:2,500 hobby/retail packs; 11-20 were inserted 1:287 hobby packs; 21-42 were inserted 1:2,500 hobby/retail packs; and 43-65 were inserted 1:288 hobby packs. The cards were horizontal in design and featured a swatch of game-worn jersey embedded in the card.

		MT
Common Player:		50.00
Cards 1-10 Inserted 1:2,500		
Cards 11-20 Inserted 1:287 Hobby		
Cards 21-42 Inserted 1:288H/1:2500R		
Cards 43-64 Inserted 1:288 Hobby		
Century Club Cards:		1.5x
Cent. Club Production 100 Sets		
GJ1	Jason Kidd	200.00
GJ2	Shaquille O'Neal	250.00
GJ3	Tim Duncan	250.00
GJ4	Charles Barkley	200.00
GJ4A	Charles Barkley Auto/4	
GJ5	Kevin Garnett	250.00
GJ5A	Kevin Garnett Auto/21	1200.
GJ6	John Stockton	150.00
GJ7	Keith Van Horn	75.00
GJ8	Hakeem Olajuwon	75.00
GJ9	Paul Pierce	100.00
GJ10	Michael Jordan	1500.
GJ10A	Michael Jordan Auto/23	10000.
GJ11	Kobe Bryant	350.00
GJ12	Scottie Pippen	175.00
GJ13	Grant Hill	150.00
GJ14	Gary Payton	125.00
GJ15	Vince Carter	500.00
GJ16	Reggie Miller	125.00
GJ17	Allen Iverson	175.00
GJ18	David Robinson	100.00
GJ19	Antoine Walker	60.00
GJ20	Karl Malone	75.00
GJ20A	Karl Malone Auto/32	600.00
GJ21	Kobe Bryant	350.00
GJ21A	Kobe Bryant Auto/8	
GJ22	Wally Szczerbiak	125.00
GJ23	Richard Hamilton	75.00
GJ24	Shawn Marion	150.00
GJ25	Trajan Langdon	60.00
GJ26	Alek Radojevic	50.00
GJ27	Corey Maggette	125.00
GJ28	William Avery	60.00
GJ29	Quincy Lewis	60.00
GJ30	Dion Glover	60.00
GJ31	Jeff Foster	50.00
GJ32	Devean George	75.00
GJ33	Shareef Abdur-Rahim	125.00
GJ34	John Stockton	125.00
GJ35	Allen Iverson	175.00
GJ36	Kevin Garnett	250.00
GJ36A	Kevin Garnett Auto/23	1200.
GJ37	Grant Hill	125.00
GJ38	Vin Baker	50.00
GJ39	Keith Van Horn	75.00
GJ40	Reggie Miller	125.00
GJ41	Tim Hardaway	60.00
GJ42	Hakeem Olajuwon	75.00
GJ43	Steve Francis	400.00
GJ44	Jonathan Bender	175.00
GJ45	Andre Miller	100.00
GJ46	Jason Terry	60.00
GJ47	Alonzo Mourning	100.00
GJ48	Cal Bowdler	50.00
GJ49	James Posey	60.00
GJ50	Kenny Thomas	50.00
GJ51	Tim James	50.00
GJ52	Vonteego Cummings	60.00
GJ53	Jumaine Jones	50.00
GJ54	Scott Padgett	50.00
GJ55	Baron Davis	100.00
GJ55A	Baron Davis Auto/1	
GJ56	Karl Malone	75.00
GJ56A	Karl Malone Auto/32	
GJ57	Gary Payton	125.00
GJ58	Michael Finley	100.00
GJ59	Bryon Russell	60.00
GJ60	Antoine Walker	60.00
GJ61	Shaquille O'Neal	200.00
GJ62	Jason Kidd	150.00
GJ63	Jason Williams	125.00
GJ64	Antonio McDyess	75.00

1999-00 Upper Deck Game Jersey Patch

This 30-card insert was available with 20 cards in Series I and 10 cards in Series II. Cards were numbered with a "GP" prefix and inserted 1:7,500 packs. Game Jersey Patch cards featured a swatch from the names, numbers and team patches from a game-worn jersey. Super versions of each were also available and sequentially numbered to 25.

		MT
Common Player:		300.00
Inserted 1:7,500		
1	Jason Kidd	550.00
2	Shaquille O'Neal	600.00
3	Tim Duncan	750.00
4	Charles Barkley	500.00
5	Kevin Garnett	1000.
6	John Stockton	500.00
7	Keith Van Horn	300.00
8	Hakeem Olajuwon	350.00
9	Paul Pierce	400.00
10	Michael Jordan	3000.
11	Kobe Bryant	1200.
12	Scottie Pippen	500.00
13	Grant Hill	1000.
14	Gary Payton	400.00
15	Vince Carter	1500.
16	Reggie Miller	400.00
17	Allen Iverson	800.00
18	David Robinson	400.00
19	Antoine Walker	300.00
20	Karl Malone	450.00
21	Baron Davis	400.00
22	Shaquille O'Neal	600.00
23	Grant Hill	1000.
24	Allen Iverson	800.00
25	Steve Francis	1000.
26	Jonathan Bender	500.00
27	Kobe Bryant	1200.
28	Kevin Garnett	1000.
29	Jason Williams	700.00
30	Jason Kidd	550.00

1999-00 Upper Deck High Definition

This 20-card, Game Jersey Edition insert was seeded 1:11 packs and numbered with a "HD" prefix. Two parallel versions were also available - Quantum Silver (numbered to 100) and Quantum Gold (numbered to 25).

		MT
Complete Set (20):		50.00
Common Player:		.75
Inserted 1:11 Series II		
Quantum Level I Cards:		5x-10x
Production 100 Sets		
Quantum Level II Cards:		25x-50x
Production 25 Sets		
HD1	Antonio McDyess	1.00
HD2	Kevin Garnett	8.00
HD3	Vince Carter	10.00
HD4	Shareef Abdur-Rahim	2.50
HD5	Patrick Ewing	.75
HD6	Gary Payton	2.00
HD7	Glenn Robinson	.75
HD8	Kobe Bryant	10.00
HD9	Antawn Jamison	2.50
HD10	Chris Webber	3.00
HD11	Corey Maggette	2.50
HD12	Shawn Kemp	.75
HD13	Derek Anderson	.75
HD14	Michael Finley	.75
HD15	Allan Houston	.75
HD16	Anfernee Hardaway	4.00
HD17	Grant Hill	8.00
HD18	Shaquille O'Neal	5.00
HD19	Paul Pierce	3.00
HD20	Scottie Pippen	3.00

1999-00 Upper Deck History Class

This 20-card, Series I insert was seeded 1:11 packs and numbered with a "HC" prefix. Two parallel versions were also available - Quantum Level I (hobby exclusive, numbered to 100) and Quantum Level II (hobby exclusive, numbered to 25).

		MT
Complete Set (20):		30.00
Common Player:		1.00
Inserted 1:11		
Quantum Level I Cards:		5x-10x
Production 100 Hobby Sets		
Quantum Level II Cards:		10x-20x
Production 25 Hobby Sets		
HC1	Michael Jordan	15.00
HC2	Julius Erving	5.00
HC3	Jamaal Wilkes	1.00
HC4	John Havlicek	3.00
HC5	Moses Malone	1.50
HC6	Nate Archibald	1.50
HC7	Jerry West	2.00
HC8	Dave DeBusschere	1.50
HC9	Bob Cousy	1.75
HC10	Kevin McHale	1.50
HC11	Dave Bing	1.00
HC12	Walt Frazier	1.50
HC13	Bob Lanier	1.50
HC14	George Gervin	1.50
HC15	Hal Greer	1.00
HC16	Earl Monroe	1.50
HC17	David Thompson	1.50
HC18	Wes Unseld	1.00
HC19	Bill Walton	1.50
HC20	Larry Bird	8.00

1999-00 Upper Deck Jamboree

This 15-card, Series I insert was seeded 1:11 packs and numbered with a "J" prefix. Two parallel versions were also available - Quantum Level I (numbered to 100) and Quantum Level II (numbered to 25).

		MT
Complete Set (15):		50.00
Common Player:		1.00
Inserted 1:11		
Quantum Level I Cards:		5x-10x
Production 100 Sets		
Quantum Level II Cards:		10x-20x
Production 25 Sets		
J1	Michael Jordan	15.00
J2	Karl Malone	3.00
J3	Kevin Garnett	10.00
J4	Antonio McDyess	2.00
J5	Shareef Abdur-Rahim	[illegible]
J6	David Robinson	3.00
J7	Marcus Camby	2.00
J8	Kobe Bryant	12.00
J9	Jason Kidd	5.00
J10	Scottie Pippen	5.00
J11	Keith Van Horn	3.00
J12	Glenn Robinson	1.00
J13	Grant Hill	10.00
J14	Michael Finley	2.00
J15	Alonzo Mourning	2.00

1999-00 Upper Deck MJ-A Higher Power

This 12-card, Series I insert was seeded 1:23 packs and numbered with a "MJ" prefix. Two parallel versions were also available - Quantum Level I (hobby exclusive, numbered to 100) and Quantum Level II (hobby exclusive, numbered to 1).

		MT
Complete Set (12):		100.00
Common Player:		10.00
Inserted 1:23		
Quantum Level I Cards:		5x-10x
Production 100 Hobby Sets		
Quantum Level II Cards:		
Production 1 Hobby Set		
MJ1	Michael Jordan	10.00
MJ2	Michael Jordan	10.00
MJ3	Michael Jordan	10.00
MJ4	Michael Jordan	10.00
MJ5	Michael Jordan	10.00
MJ6	Michael Jordan	10.00
MJ7	Michael Jordan	10.00
MJ8	Michael Jordan	10.00
MJ9	Michael Jordan	10.00
MJ10	Michael Jordan	10.00
MJ11	Michael Jordan	10.00
MJ12	Michael Jordan	10.00

1999-00 Upper Deck Now Showing

This 30-card, Series I insert was seeded 1:4 packs and was numbered with an "NS" prefix. Two parallel versions were also available - Quantum Level I (numbered to 100 sets) and Quantum Level II (numbered to 25 sets).

		MT
Complete Set (30):		50.00
Common Player:		.50
Inserted 1:4		
Quantum Level I Cards:		5x-10x
Production 100 Retail Sets		
Quantum Level II Cards:		10x-20x
Production 25 Retail Sets		
NS1	Dikembe Mutombo	.50
NS2	Antoine Walker	1.50
NS3	Eddie Jones	1.00
NS4	Toni Kukoc	.75
NS5	Shawn Kemp	1.00
NS6	Michael Finley	.75
NS7	Antonio McDyess	1.00
NS8	Grant Hill	5.00
NS9	Antawn Jamison	2.00
NS10	Scottie Pippen	2.00
NS11	Reggie Miller	.50
NS12	Maurice Taylor	1.00
NS13	Shaquille O'Neal	3.00
NS14	Tim Hardaway	1.00
NS15	Ray Allen	.75
NS16	Kevin Garnett	5.00
NS17	Stephon Marbury	2.50
NS18	Marcus Camby	1.00
NS19	Darrell Armstrong	.50
NS20	Allen Iverson	4.00
NS21	Jason Kidd	2.00
NS22	Damon Stoudamire	1.00
NS23	Jason Williams	3.00
NS24	Tim Duncan	5.00
NS25	Gary Payton	1.25
NS26	Vince Carter	5.00
NS27	Karl Malone	1.25
NS28	Shareef Abdur-Rahim	2.00
NS29	Juwan Howard	.50
NS30	Michael Jordan	8.00

1999-00 Upper Deck Power Deck

This 14-card set included seven cards from each series. Cards were numbered with a "PD" prefix and distributed in a thick plastic top loader. The "cards" were actually CD-Rom highlights of the player with stats, etc. Power Deck cards were seeded 1:23 hobby packs in Series I and 1:72 hobby packs in Series II.

		MT
Complete Set (14):		150.00
Complete Set (7):		60.00
Complete Set (7):		90.00
Common Player:		8.00
Cards 1-7 Inserted 1:23 Hobby		
Cards 8-14 Inserted 1:72 Hobby		
PD1	Michael Jordan	25.00
PD2	Kobe Bryant	20.00
PD3	Tim Duncan	15.00
PD4	Allen Iverson	12.00

PD5	Vince Carter	15.00
PD6	Jason Kidd	8.00
PD7	Scottie Pippen	8.00
PD8	Elton Brand	20.00
PD9	Steve Francis	25.00
PD10	Baron Davis	12.00
PD11	Lamar Odom	25.00
PD12	Wally Szczerbiak	15.00
PD13	Richard Hamilton	10.00
PD14	Shawn Marion	10.00

1999-00 Upper Deck MJ PowerDeck

This two-card, hobby-only set focuses on Michael Jordan's six championships, with three on each cd-card. MJ PowerDeck cards were inserted 1:288 packs.

		MT
Complete Set (2):		60.00
Common Player:		30.00
Inserted 1:288 Hobby		
MJPD1	Michael Jordan - Titles 1,2,3	30.00
MJPD2	Michael Jordan - Titles 4,5,6	30.00

1999-00 Upper Deck Power Deck Extreme

This two CD-Rom set was distributed in packs of Game Jersey Edition, or Series II. Michael Jordan and Kevin Garnett were both included and seeded 1:2,500 hobby packs.

		MT
Complete Set (2):		200.00
Inserted 1:2,500 Series II		75.00
PDX1	Michael Jordan	125.00
PDX2	Kevin Garnett	75.00

1999-00 Upper Deck Rookies Illustrated

This 10-card set highlighted the season's top rookies on a foil background with gold foil lettering. Cards were numbered with an "RI" prefix and inserted 1:11 packs of Game Jersey Edition, or Series II. Two parallel sets existed - Level I was numbered to 100, while Level II cards were numbered to 25.

		MT
Complete Set (10):		15.00
Common Player:		1.00
Inserted 1:11 Series II		
Quantum Level I Cards:		5x-10x
Production 100 Retail Sets		
Quantum Level II Cards:		25x-50x
Production 25 Retail Sets		
RI1	Elton Brand	4.00
RI2	Shawn Marion	1.50
RI3	Trajan Langdon	1.00
RI4	Adrian Griffin	1.00
RI5	Baron Davis	2.00
RI6	Richard Hamilton	1.50
RI7	Lamar Odom	5.00
RI8	Corey Maggette	2.50
RI9	Steve Francis	5.00
RI10	Wally Szczerbiak	2.50

1999-00 Upper Deck Star Surge

This 15-card insert set was found in packs of Game Jersey Edition, or Upper Deck Series II. Cards were inserted 1:23 packs and numbered with an "S" prefix. Two hobby-only parallel sets also exist for this insert - Level I cards are numbered to 100 sets, while Level II cards are numbered to 25.

		MT
Complete Set (15):		75.00
Common Player:		1.00
Inserted 1:23 Series II		
Quantum Level I Cards:		5x-10x
Production 100 Hobby Sets		
Quantum Level II Cards:		20x-40x
Production 25 Hobby Sets		
S1	Michael Jordan	20.00
S2	Kevin Garnett	10.00
S3	Allen Iverson	6.00
S4	Vince Carter	12.00
S5	Karl Malone	2.00
S6	Tim Duncan	10.00
S7	Grant Hill	10.00
S8	Scottie Pippen	4.00
S9	Shaquille O'Neal	6.00
S10	Antoine Walker	1.50
S11	Shareef Abdur-Rahim	3.00
S12	Keith Van Horn	1.50
S13	Gary Payton	2.00
S14	John Stockton	1.00
S15	Stephon Marbury	3.00

1999-00 Upper Deck Wild!

This 19-card insert set was found in Series II, or Game Jersey Edition. Cards were numbered with a "W" prefix and seeded 1:23 packs. Two hobby-only parallels also exist for this insert - Level I cards are numbered to 100 sets, while Level II cards are numbered to 25.

		MT
Complete Set (19):		100.00
Common Player:		1.50
Inserted 1:23 Series II		
Quantum Level I Cards:		5x-10x
Production 100 Hobby Sets		
Quantum Level II Cards:		20x-40x
Production 25 Hobby Sets		
W1	Kobe Bryant	12.00
W2	Kevin Garnett	10.00
W3	Shareef Abdur-Rahim	3.00
W4	Tim Hardaway	1.50
W5	Jason Williams	5.00
W6	Grant Hill	10.00
W7	Vince Carter	12.00
W8	Ron Mercer	3.00
W9	Charles Barkley	2.00
W10	Eddie Jones	2.00
W11	Tim Duncan	10.00
W12	Antonio McDyess	1.50
W13	Allen Iverson	6.00
W14	Anfernee Hardaway	5.00
W15	Michael Jordan	20.00
W16	Stephon Marbury	3.00
W17	Paul Pierce	3.00
W18	Elton Brand	6.00
W19	Jason Terry	1.50

1999-00 UD Black Diamond

This 120-card set consisted of 90 veterans and 30 Diamond Debut rookies seeded 1:3 packs. Cards featured all foil fronts with the player's color image over a diamond design background. Two parallel sets existed - Diamond Cut and Final Cut. Inserts include: A Piece of History, Diamonation, Jordan Diamond Gallery, Might, Myriad and Diamond Skills, along with MJ's Final Floor.

		MT
Complete Set (120):		75.00
Common Player:		.15
Minor Stars:		.30
Common Rookie (91-120):		.75
Inserted 1:3		
Pack (6):		4.00
Wax Box (24):		40.00
1	Dikembe Mutombo	.30
2	Alan Henderson	.15
3	Roshown McLeod	.15
4	Kenny Anderson	.30
5	Paul Pierce	1.25
6	Antoine Walker	.60
7	Eddie Jones	.75
8	Elden Campbell	.15
9	David Wesley	.15
10	Toni Kukoc	.50
11	Randy Brown	.15
12	Dickey Simpkins	.15
13	Shawn Kemp	.40
14	Zydrunas Ilgauskas	.15
15	Brevin Knight	.15
16	Michael Finley	.30
17	Dirk Nowitzki	.60
18	Robert Pack	.15
19	Antonio McDyess	.40
20	Nick Van Exel	.30
21	Ron Mercer	.75
22	Grant Hill	2.50
23	Lindsey Hunter	.15
24	Jerry Stackhouse	.40
25	Antawn Jamison	1.00
26	John Starks	.15
27	Donyell Marshall	.15
28	Hakeem Olajuwon	.60
29	Charles Barkley	.60
30	Cuttino Mobley	.30
31	Reggie Miller	.30
32	Rik Smits	.15
33	Jalen Rose	.30
34	Maurice Taylor	.30
35	Tyrone Nesby	.30
36	Michael Olowokandi	.40
37	Shaquille O'Neal	1.50
38	Kobe Bryant	3.00
39	Glen Rice	.30
40	P.J. Brown	.15
41	Tim Hardaway	.50
42	Alonzo Mourning	.40
43	Jamal Mashburn	.30
44	Glenn Robinson	.30
45	Ray Allen	.40
46	Tim Thomas	.60
47	Kevin Garnett	2.50
48	Joe Smith	.15
49	Terrell Brandon	.30
50	Stephon Marbury	1.00
51	Jayson Williams	.15
52	Keith Van Horn	.75
53	Latrell Sprewell	.50
54	Allan Houston	.30
55	Patrick Ewing	.30
56	Marcus Camby	.40
57	Darrell Armstrong	.30
58	Charles Outlaw	.15
59	Michael Doleac	.30
60	Allen Iverson	2.00
61	Theo Ratliff	.15
62	Larry Hughes	.60
63	Anfernee Hardaway	1.50
64	Jason Kidd	1.25
65	Tom Gugliotta	.30
66	Brian Grant	.15
67	Damon Stoudamire	.30
68	Rasheed Wallace	.30
69	Jason Williams	1.50
70	Chris Webber	1.25
71	Vlade Divac	.15
72	Tim Duncan	2.50
73	David Robinson	.60
74	Avery Johnson	.15
75	Sean Elliott	.15
76	Gary Payton	.60
77	Vin Baker	.30
78	Brent Barry	.15
79	Vince Carter	3.00
80	Tracy McGrady	1.25
81	Doug Christie	.15
82	Karl Malone	.60
83	John Stockton	.30
84	Bryon Russell	.15
85	Shareef Abdur-Rahim	1.00
86	Mike Bibby	.60
87	Felipe Lopez	.30
88	Juwan Howard	.30
89	Rod Strickland	.30
90	Mitch Richmond	.30
91	*Elton Brand*	6.00
92	*Steve Francis*	15.00
93	*Baron Davis*	5.00
94	*Lamar Odom*	10.00
95	*Jonathan Bender*	6.00
96	*Wally Szczerbiak*	4.00
97	*Richard Hamilton*	4.00
98	*Andre Miller*	5.00
99	*Shawn Marion*	6.00
100	*Jason Terry*	3.00
101	*Trajan Langdon*	3.00
102	*Aleksandar Radojevic*	1.00
103	*Corey Maggette*	5.00
104	*William Avery*	2.50
105	*Ron Artest*	3.00
106	*Adrian Griffin*	2.00
107	*James Posey*	3.00
108	*Quincy Lewis*	2.00
109	*Dion Glover*	1.00
110	*Jeff Foster*	.75
111	*Kenny Thomas*	1.50
112	*Devean George*	2.50
113	*Tim James*	1.00
114	*Vonteego Cummings*	2.00
115	*Jumanie Jones*	1.00
116	*Scott Padgett*	1.00
117	*Obinna Ekezie*	.75
118	*Ryan Robertson*	.75
119	*Chucky Atkins*	1.50
120	*A.J. Bramlett*	.75

1999-00 UD Black Diamond Diamond Cut

Diamond Cut was a 120-card parallel set that reprinted each card in the base set with a die-cut, foil card that included a silver Light F/X treatment. The first 90 cards (veterans) were seeded 1:6 packs, while the Diamond Debut rookies were seeded 1:12 packs.

		MT
Complete Set (120):		175.00
Common Player:		.30
Diamond Cut (1-90):		2x
Inserted 1:12		
Common Rookie (91-120):		.75
Diamond Cut Rookies:		1.5x
Inserted 1:24		

1999-00 UD Black Diamond Final Cut

This 120-card parallel set reprinted every card from Black Dimond on die-cut foil, with gold Light F/X treatment. The first 90 cards (veterans) were sequentially numbered to 100 sets, while the 30 Diamond Debut cards were numbered to 50.

		MT
Common Player:		6.00
Diamond Cut (1-90):		20x-40x
Production 100 Sets		
Common Rookie (91-120):		15.00
Diamond Cut Rookies:		10x-20x
Production 50 Sets		

1999-00 UD Black Diamond A Piece of History-Common

This 12-card insert was inserted into both hobby and retail boxes, and contained a diamond-shaped piece of a game-used basketball. Cards were numbered with two-letters on the back, usually corresponding to the player's initials. Three versions existed - Single Diamond cards were inserted 1:336, Double Diamond cards were inserted 1:1,008 and Triple Diamond cards were sequentially numbered to 25.

		MT
Complete Set (12):		450.00
Common Player:		25.00
Singles inserted 1:336		
Double Piece:		2x
Doubles inserted 1:1008		
Triple Piece:		4x
Triples numbered to 25		
SA	Shareef Abdur-Rahim	40.00
CB	Charles Barkley	50.00
MF	Michael Finley	30.00
AH	Allan Houston	25.00
CM	Corey Maggette	50.00
SO	Shaquille O'Neal	60.00
PP	Paul Pierce	40.00
DR	David Robinson	50.00
JS	John Stockton	40.00
WS	Wally Szczerbiak	40.00
JT	Jason Terry	30.00
KT	Kenny Thomas	25.00

1999-00 UD Black Diamond A Piece of History-Hobby

This 13-card insert was inserted into hobby boxes only, and contained a diamond-shaped piece of a game-used basketball. Cards were numbered with two-letters on the back, usually corresponding to the player's initials. Three versions existed - Single Diamond cards were inserted 1:144 packs, Double Diamond cards were inserted 1:864.and Triple Diamond cards were sequentially numbered to 25.

		MT
Complete Set (13):		550.00
Common Player:		25.00
Singles inserted 1:144		
Double Piece:		2x
Doubles inserted 1:864		
Triple Piece:		4x
Triples numbered to 25		
JB	Jonathan Bender	50.00
TB	Terrell Brandon	25.00
BD	Baron Davis	40.00
SF	Steve Francis	75.00
KG	Kevin Garnett	75.00
DG	Devean George	25.00
KM	Karl Malone	50.00
RM	Reggie Miller	40.00
HO	Hakeem Olajuwon	50.00
GP	Gary Payton	50.00
AW	Antoine Walker	25.00
CW	Chris Webber	60.00
JW	Jason Williams	50.00

1999-00 UD Black Diamond Diamond Might

Diamond Might was a 20-card insert that capture players over a foil, rectangular background. Cards were numbered with a "DM" prefix and inserted 1:3 packs.

		MT
Complete Set (20):		10.00
Common Player:		.25
Inserted 1:3		
DM1	Shaquille O'Neal	2.50
DM2	Allan Houston	.25
DM3	Keith Van Horn	.75
DM4	Antoine Walker	.60
DM5	Latrell Sprewell	.60
DM6	Hakeem Olajuwon	.75
DM7	David Robinson	.75
DM8	Antonio McDyess	.50
DM9	Shawn Kemp	.40
DM10	Ray Allen	.50
DM11	Karl Malone	.75
DM12	Tim Hardaway	.60
DM13	Mike Bibby	.75
DM14	Antawn Jamison	1.00
DM15	Dikembe Mutombo	.25
DM16	Michael Finley	.40
DM17	Juwan Howard	.25
DM18	Maurice Taylor	.25
DM19	Gary Payton	.75
DM20	Shareef Abdur-Rahim	1.00

1999-00 UD Black Diamond Diamond Skills

Diamond Skills was a 10-card insert featuring players over a foil background, with the word "Diamond" in large gold letters across the bottom and the word "Skills" in small gold letters under it. Cards were numbered with a "DS" prefix and inserted 1:24 packs.

		MT
Complete Set (10):		15.00
Common Player:		1.00
Inserted 1:24		
DS1	Stephon Marbury	2.00
DS2	Grant Hill	8.00
DS3	Reggie Miller	1.00
DS4	Jason Kidd	2.50
DS5	Mike Bibby	1.50
DS6	John Stockton	1.00
DS7	Jason Williams	5.00
DS8	Shaquille O'Neal	5.00
DS9	Antonio McDyess	1.25
DS10	Hakeem Olajuwon	1.50

1999-00 UD Black Diamond Diamonation

Diamonation was a 10-card insert set that featured the player over a silver foil background with the insert name across the bottom in gold foil. Cards were numbered with a "D" prefix and seeded 1:8 packs.

		MT
Complete Set (10):		15.00
Common Player:		.50
Inserted 1:8		
D1	Vince Carter	5.00
D2	Tim Duncan	4.00
D3	Kobe Bryant	5.00
D4	Stephon Marbury	1.00
D5	Ron Mercer	1.00
D6	Allen Iverson	3.00
D7	Shareef Abdur-Rahim	1.00
D8	Kevin Garnett	4.00
D9	Jason Kidd	1.50
D10	Allan Houston	.50

1999-00 UD Black Diamond Jordan Diamond Gallery

This 10-card insert set was devoted to Michael Jordan and featured 10 shots from his glorius career. Cards were numbered with a "DG" prefix and inserted 1:12 packs. A Gold version of each card also existed and was numbered one of one.

		MT
Complete Set (10):		40.00
Common Player:		5.00
Inserted 1:12		
DG1	Michael Jordan	5.00
DG2	Michael Jordan	5.00
DG3	Michael Jordan	5.00
DG4	Michael Jordan	5.00
DG5	Michael Jordan	5.00
DG6	Michael Jordan	5.00
DG7	Michael Jordan	5.00
DG8	Michael Jordan	5.00
DG9	Michael Jordan	5.00
DG10	Michael Jordan	5.00

1999-00 UD Black Diamond Myriad

This 10-card insert set displayed top NBA stars over a foil background. Cards were numbered with an "M" prefix and inserted 1:24 packs.

		MT
Complete Set (10):		50.00
Common Player:		2.00
Inserted 1:24		
M1	Kobe Bryant	10.00
M2	Tim Duncan	8.00
M3	Kevin Garnett	8.00
M4	Keith Van Horn	2.00
M5	Vince Carter	10.00

M6	Grant Hill	8.00
M7	Anfernee Hardaway	5.00
M8	Karl Malone	2.00
M9	Allen Iverson	5.00
M10	Jason Williams	5.00

1999-00 Upper Deck Encore

Encore was a 120-card set that featured selected cards from Upper Deck Series I and II, which were reprinted with a holographic finish. The set contained 90 veterans and 30 rookies, which were sequentially numbered to 1,999 sets. Inserts included: Electric Currents, Future Charge, Game Jerseys, High Definition, Jamboree, MJ - A Higher Power and Upper Realm.

		MT
Complete Set (120):		300.00
Common Player:		.15
Minor Stars:		.30
Common Rookie (91-120):		3.00
Production 1,999 Sets		
Pack (6):		4.50
Wax Box (15):		40.00
1	Dikembe Mutombo	.30
2	Alan Henderson	.15
3	Isaiah Rider	.30
4	Kenny Anderson	.30
5	Antoine Walker	.50
6	Paul Pierce	1.00
7	Elden Campbell	.15
8	Eddie Jones	.60
9	David Wesley	.15
10	Hersey Hawkins	.15
11	Randy Brown	.15
12	Toni Kukoc	.50
13	Shawn Kemp	.40
14	Bob Sura	.15
15	Michael Finley	.30
16	Dirk Nowitzki	.75
17	Gary Trent	.15
18	Antonio McDyess	.40
19	Nick Van Exel	.30
20	Raef LaFrentz	.50
21	Christian Laettner	.15
22	Grant Hill	2.50
23	Lindsey Hunter	.15
24	Jerry Stackhouse	.40
25	John Starks	.15
26	Antawn Jamison	.75
27	Tony Farmer	.15
28	Hakeem Olajuwon	.60
29	Cuttino Mobley	.30
30	Charles Barkley	.60
31	Reggie Miller	.30
32	Jalen Rose	.30
33	Mark Jackson	.15
34	Maurice Taylor	.15
35	Derek Anderson	.30
36	Michael Olowokandi	.40
37	Kobe Bryant	3.00
38	Shaquille O'Neal	1.50
39	Glen Rice	.30
40	Tim Hardaway	.50
41	Alonzo Mourning	.40
42	Ray Allen	.40
43	Glenn Robinson	.30
44	Sam Cassell	.30
45	Tim Thomas	.50
46	Kevin Garnett	2.50
47	Terrell Brandon	.30
48	Keith Van Horn	.60
49	Stephon Marbury	1.00
50	Kendall Gill	.15
51	Patrick Ewing	.30
52	Allan Houston	.30
53	Latrell Sprewell	.60
54	Darrell Armstrong	.15
55	John Amaechi	.15
56	Michael Doleac	.15
57	Allen Iverson	2.00
58	Theo Ratliff	.15
59	Larry Hughes	.75
60	Jason Kidd	1.25
61	Tom Gugliotta	.30
62	Anfernee Hardaway	1.50
63	Rasheed Wallace	.30
64	Steve Smith	.30
65	Damon Stoudamire	.40
66	Scottie Pippen	1.25
67	Corliss Williamson	.15
68	Jason Williams	1.25
69	Vlade Divac	.15
70	Chris Webber	1.25
71	Tim Duncan	2.50
72	David Robinson	.60
73	Avery Johnson	.15
74	Mario Elie	.15
75	Gary Payton	.60
76	Vin Baker	.30
77	Ruben Patterson	.30
78	Brent Barry	.15
79	Vince Carter	4.00
80	Antonio Davis	.15
81	Tracy McGrady	1.25
82	Karl Malone	.60
83	John Stockton	.30
84	Bryon Russell	.15
85	Shareef Abdur-Rahim	1.00
86	Mike Bibby	.15
87	Othella Harrington	.15
88	Juwan Howard	.30
89	Rod Strickland	.30
90	Mitch Richmond	.30
91	*Elton Brand*	20.00
92	*Steve Francis*	60.00
93	*Baron Davis*	20.00
94	*Lamar Odom*	40.00
95	*Jonathan Bender*	30.00
96	*Wally Szczerbiak*	15.00
97	*Richard Hamilton*	15.00
98	*Andre Miller*	20.00
99	*Shawn Marion*	35.00
100	*Jason Terry*	12.00
101	*Trajan Langdon*	10.00
102	*Kenny Thomas*	6.00
103	*Corey Maggette*	20.00
104	*William Avery*	8.00
105	*Ron Artest*	10.00
106	*Aleksandar Radojevic*	3.00
107	*James Posey*	8.00
108	*Quincy Lewis*	6.00
109	*Vonteego Cummings*	6.00
110	*Jeff Foster*	3.00
111	*Dion Glover*	5.00
112	*Devean George*	8.00
113	*Evan Eschmeyer*	5.00
114	*Tim James*	5.00
115	*Adrian Griffin*	6.00
116	*Anthony Carter*	8.00
117	*Obinna Ekezie*	3.00
118	*Todd MacCulloch*	5.00
119	*Chucky Atkins*	8.00
120	*Lazaro Borrell*	3.00

1999-00 Upper Deck Encore Future Charge

This 15-card insert was the same used in Upper Deck I, but added a holographic foil finish, with a spherical background. Future Charge inserts were numbered with an "FC" prefix and seeded 1:6 packs.

		MT
Complete Set (15):		12.00
Common Player:		.50
Inserted 1:15		
FC1	Antawn Jamison	2.00
FC2	Mike Bibby	1.00
FC3	Antoine Walker	.75
FC4	Baron Davis	1.50
5	Jason Terry	.75
6	Andre Miller	1.50
7	Ray Allen	.75
8	Wally Szczerbiak	2.00
9	Raef LaFrentz	.75
10	William Avery	.50
11	Jason Williams	3.00
12	Michael Olowokandi	.50
13	Stephon Marbury	1.50
14	Quincy Lewis	.50
15	Shawn Marion	1.50

1999-00 Upper Deck Encore Electric Currents

This 20-card insert set featured players over a lightning background. Electric Currents were numbered with an "EC" prefix and inserted 1:3 packs. F/X versions also existed and were sequentially numbered to 150 sets. This insert was produced exclusively for Encore.

		MT
Complete Set (20):		25.00
Common Player:		.25
Inserted 1:3		
F/X Parallel Cards:		2x-4x
Production 150 Sets		
EC1	Kevin Garnett	4.00
EC2	Anfernee Hardaway	2.00
EC3	Shareef Abdur-Rahim	1.25
EC4	Allan Houston	.25
EC5	Michael Finley	.40
EC6	Tim Duncan	4.00
EC7	Gary Payton	1.00
EC8	Kobe Bryant	5.00
EC9	Derek Anderson	.40
EC10	Reggie Miller	.40
EC11	Keith Van Horn	.75
EC12	Jason Kidd	1.50
EC13	Ray Allen	.60
EC14	Tim Hardaway	.75
EC15	Darrell Armstrong	.25
EC16	Antonio McDyess	.50
EC17	Eddie Jones	1.00
EC18	Paul Pierce	1.25
EC19	Stephon Marbury	1.25
EC20	Chris Webber	1.50

1999-00 Upper Deck Encore Electric Currents F/X

This 15-card parallel set reprinted each card in the Electric Currents insert set, but was sequentially numbered to 150 sets.

	MT
Complete Set (20):	25.00
Common Player:	.25
Inserted 1:3	
F/X Parallel Cards:	2x-4x
Production 150 Sets	

1999-00 Upper Deck Encore UD Game Jersey F/X

This 17-card insert featured swatches of game-used jerseys and were printed with a holographic foil. Game Jerseys were numbered with a two-letter code, usually corresponding to the player's initials, followed by a "J". Game Jerseys were inserted 1:300 packs. Autographed versions of Michael Jordan, Kevin Garnett and Kobe Bryant cards were also available and are numbered with the player's initials followed by an "A". Autographed versions are not included in the set price.

		MT
Common Player:		75.00
Inserted 1:300		
JB	Jonathan Bender	150.00
BD	Baron Davis	100.00
KB	Kobe Bryant	300.00
SF	Steve Francis	300.00
KG	Kevin Garnett	200.00
RH	Richard Hamilton	90.00
GH	Grant Hill	150.00
AI	Allen Iverson	150.00
JK	Jason Kidd	150.00
TL	Trajan Langdon	75.00
SM	Shawn Marion	100.00
MC	Antonio McDyess	75.00
AM	Andre Miller	100.00
SO	Shaquille O'Neal	150.00
WS	Wally Szczerbiak	150.00
JT	Jason Terry	75.00
JW	Jason Williams	150.00

1999-00 Upper Deck Encore High Definition

This 20-card insert set was the same used in Upper Deck Series II, but cards featured a holographic finish. High Definition inserts were numbered with an "HD" prefix and seeded 1:15 packs.

		MT
Complete Set (20):		60.00
Common Player:		.75
Inserted 1:15		
HD1	Antonio McDyess	1.00
HD2	Kevin Garnett	8.00
HD3	Vince Carter	12.00
HD4	Shareef Abdur-Rahim	3.00
5	Stephon Marbury	3.00
6	Gary Payton	2.00
7	Glenn Robinson	.75
8	Kobe Bryant	10.00
9	Antawn Jamison	3.00
10	Chris Webber	4.00
11	Corey Maggette	4.00
12	Shawn Kemp	1.00
13	Derek Anderson	1.00
14	Michael Finley	1.00
15	Allan Houston	.75
16	Anfernee Hardaway	4.00
17	Grant Hill	8.00
18	Shaquille O'Neal	5.00
19	Paul Pierce	3.00
20	Scottie Pippen	4.00

1999-00 Upper Deck Encore Jamboree

This 15-card insert was the same that was inserted into Upper Deck Series I, but was printed on holographic foil. Jamboree cards were numbered with a "J" prefix and seeded 1:6 packs.

		MT
Complete Set (15):		35.00
Common Player:		
Inserted 1:6		
J1	Michael Jordan	10.00
J2	Karl Malone	1.50
J3	Kevin Garnett	5.00
J4	Antonio McDyess	1.00
5	Shareef Abdur-Rahim	2.00
6	David Robinson	1.25
7	Marcus Camby	1.00
8	Kobe Bryant	6.00
9	Jason Kidd	3.00
10	Tim Duncan	5.00
11	Keith Van Horn	1.00
12	Glenn Robinson	.50
13	Grant Hill	5.00
14	Michael Finley	.50
15	Vince Carter	8.00

1999-00 Upper Deck Encore MJ - A Higher Power

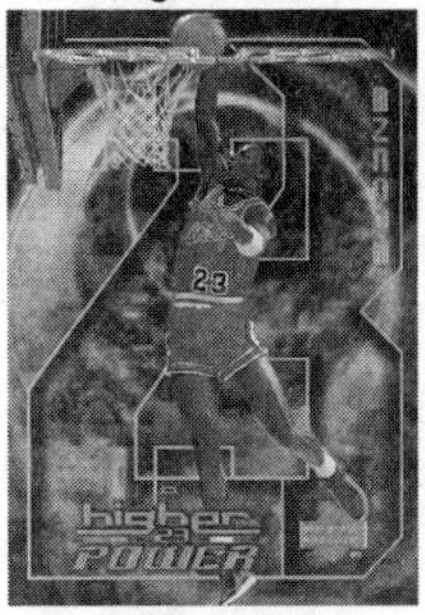

This 10-card Michael Jordan insert was identical to the one inserted into Upper Deck Series I packs, but was printed on holographic foil. MJ - A Higher Power cards were numbered with an "MJ" prefix and seeded 1:90 packs.

		MT
Complete Set (10):		100.00
Common Player:		12.00
Inserted 1:90		
MJ1	Michael Jordan	12.00
MJ2	Michael Jordan	12.00
MJ3	Michael Jordan	12.00
MJ4	Michael Jordan	12.00
5	Michael Jordan	12.00
6	Michael Jordan	12.00
7	Michael Jordan	12.00
8	Michael Jordan	12.00
9	Michael Jordan	12.00
10	Michael Jordan	12.00

1999-00 Upper Deck Encore Upper Realm

This 10-card insert was produced exclusively for Encore and included the NBA's elite. Upper Realm cards were numbered with a "UR" prefix and seeded 1:6 packs. F/X parallel versions of each card also existed and they were sequentially numbered to 150 sets.

		MT
Complete Set (10):		15.00
Common Player:		.75
Inserted 1:6		
F/X Parallel Cards:		2x-4x
Production 150 Sets		
UR1	Kevin Garnett	3.00
UR2	Kobe Bryant	4.00
UR3	Tim Duncan	3.00
UR4	Vince Carter	5.00
UR5	Gary Payton	.75
UR6	Allen Iverson	2.50
UR7	Karl Malone	.75
UR8	Jason Williams	1.50
UR9	Scottie Pippen	1.50
UR10	Shaquille O'Neal	2.00

1999-00 Upper Deck Encore Upper Realm F/X

This 10-card parallel set reprinted each Upper Realm insert, but added sequential numbering to 150 sets.

	MT
Complete Set (10):	15.00
Common Player:	.75
Inserted 1:6	
F/X Parallel Cards:	2x-4x
Production 150 Sets	

1999-00 Upper Deck Gold Reserve

Gold Reserve was a 270-card set that was distributed exclusively through 7-Eleven stores, with a small amount going to hobby dealers. The cards were identical to those included in Upper Deck I and II, but added a gold foil finish. The set included 240 veterans and 30 rookies, which were sequentially numbered to 3,500 sets. Three inserts were included with this product - Gold Mine, Gold Strike and UD Authentics.

		MT
Complete Set (270):		150.00
Common Player:		.15
Minor Stars:		.30
Common Rookie:		2.00
Production 3,500 Sets		
Pack (10):		3.00
Wax Box (24):		40.00
1	Roshown McLeod	.15
2	Dikembe Mutombo	.30
3	Alan Henderson	.15
4	Chris Crawford	.15
5	Jim Jackson	.15
6	Isaiah Rider	.30
7	Lorenzen Wright	.15
8	Bimbo Coles	.15
9	Kenny Anderson	.30
10	Antoine Walker	.50
11	Paul Pierce	.75
12	Vitaly Potapenko	.15
13	Dana Barros	.15
14	Calbert Cheaney	.15
15	Pervis Ellison	.15
16	Eric Williams	.15
17	Tony Battie	.15
18	Elden Campbell	.15
19	Eddie Jones	.60
20	David Wesley	.15
21	Derrick Coleman	.30
22	Ricky Davis	.30
23	Anthony Mason	.15
24	Todd Fuller	.15
25	Brad Miller	.15
26	Corey Benjamin	.30
27	Randy Brown	.15
28	Dickey Simpkins	.15
29	Toni Kukoc	.50
30	Fred Hoiberg	.15
31	Hersey Hawkins	.15
32	Will Perdue	.15
33	Chris Anstey	.15
34	Shawn Kemp	.50
35	Wesley Person	.15
36	Brevin Knight	.15
37	Bob Sura	.15
38	Danny Ferry	.15
39	Lamond Murray	.15
40	Cedric Henderson	.15
41	Andrew DeClerq	.15
42	Michael Finley	.30
43	Shawn Bradley	.15
44	Dirk Nowitzki	.75
45	Erick Strickland	.15
46	Cedric Ceballos	.15
47	Hubert Davis	.15
48	Robert Pack	.15
49	Gary Trent	.15
50	Antonio McDyess	.50
51	Nick Van Exel	.30
52	Chauncey Billups	.30
53	Bryant Stith	.15
54	Raef LaFrentz	.40
55	Ron Mercer	.60
56	George McCloud	.15
57	Roy Rogers	.15
58	Keon Clark	.30
59	Grant Hill	2.50
60	Lindsey Hunter	.15
61	Jerry Stackhouse	.40
62	Terry Mills	.15
63	Michael Curry	.15
64	Christian Laettner	.15
65	Jerome Williams	.15
66	Loy Vaught	.15
67	John Starks	.15
68	Antawn Jamison	.75
69	Erick Dampier	.15
70	Jason Caffey	.15
71	Terry Cummings	.15
72	Donyell Marshall	.15
73	Chris Mills	.15
74	Tony Farmer	.15
75	Adonal Foyle	.15
76	Hakeem Olajuwon	.60
77	Cuttino Mobley	.30
78	Charles Barkley	.60
79	Bryce Drew	.15
80	Shandon Anderson	.15
81	Kelvin Cato	.15
82	Walt Williams	.15
83	Carlos Rogers	.15
84	Reggie Miller	.30
85	Jalen Rose	.30
86	Mark Jackson	.15
87	Dale Davis	.15
88	Chris Mullin	.15
89	Al Harrington	.40
90	Rik Smits	.15
91	Sam Perkins	.15
92	Austin Croshere	.15
93	Maurice Taylor	.30
94	Tyrone Nesby	.15
95	Michael Olowokandi	.40
96	Eric Piatkowski	.15
97	Troy Hudson	.15
98	Derek Anderson	.30
99	Eric Murdock	.15
100	Brian Skinner	.15
101	Kobe Bryant	3.00
102	Shaquille O'Neal	1.50
103	Glen Rice	.30
104	Robert Horry	.15
105	Ron Harper	.15
106	Derek Fisher	.15
107	Rick Fox	.15
108	A.C. Green	.15
109	Tim Hardaway	.50
110	Alonzo Mourning	.40
111	P.J. Brown	.15
112	Dan Majerle	.15
113	Jamal Mashburn	.30
114	Voshon Lenard	.15
115	Clarence Weatherspoon	.15
116	Rex Walters	.15
117	Ray Allen	.40
118	Glenn Robinson	.30
119	Sam Cassell	.30
120	Robert Traylor	.30
121	J.R. Reid	.15
122	Ervin Johnson	.15
123	Danny Manning	.15
124	Tim Thomas	.50
125	Kevin Garnett	2.50
126	Sam Mitchell	.15
127	Dean Garrett	.15
128	Bobby Jackson	.15
129	Radoslav Nesterovic	.15
130	Terrell Brandon	.30
131	Joe Smith	.30
132	Anthony Peeler	.15
133	Keith Van Horn	.60
134	Stephon Marbury	.75
135	Kendall Gill	.15
136	Scott Burrell	.15
137	Jayson Williams	.15
138	Jamie Feick	.15
139	Kerry Kittles	.15
140	Johnny Newman	.15
141	Patrick Ewing	.30
142	Allan Houston	.30
143	Latrell Sprewell	.50
144	Larry Johnson	.15
145	Marcus Camby	.30
146	Chris Childs	.15
147	Kurt Thomas	.15
148	Charlie Ward	.15
149	Darrell Armstrong	.15
150	Matt Harpring	.30
151	Michael Doleac	.30
152	Charles Outlaw	.15
153	Tariq Abdul-Wahad	.15
154	John Amaechi	.15
155	Ben Wallace	.15
156	Monty Williams	.15
157	Allen Iverson	2.00
158	Theo Ratliff	.15
159	Larry Hughes	.75
160	Eric Snow	.15
161	George Lynch	.15
162	Tyrone Hill	.15
163	Billy Owens	.15
164	Aaron McKie	.15
165	Jason Kidd	1.00
166	Clifford Robinson	.15
167	Tom Gugliotta	.30
168	Luc Longley	.15
169	Anfernee Hardaway	1.00
170	Rex Chapman	.15
171	Oliver Miller	.15
172	Rodney Rogers	.15
173	Rasheed Wallace	.30
174	Arvydas Sabonis	.15
175	Damon Stoudamire	.40
176	Brian Grant	.15
177	Scottie Pippen	1.00
178	Detlef Schrempf	.15
179	Steve Smith	.30
180	Jermaine O'Neal	.15
181	Bonzi Wells	.40
182	Jason Williams	1.00
183	Vlade Divac	.15
184	Predrag Stojakovic	.30
185	Lawrence Funderburke	.15
186	Chris Webber	1.00
187	Nick Anderson	.15
188	Darrick Martin	.15
189	Corliss Williamson	.15
190	Tim Duncan	2.50
191	Sean Elliott	.15
192	David Robinson	.60
193	Mario Elie	.15
194	Avery Johnson	.15
195	Terry Porter	.15
196	Malik Rose	.15
197	Jaren Jackson	.15
198	Gary Payton	.60
199	Vin Baker	.30
200	Rashard Lewis	.50
201	Jelani McCoy	.15
202	Brent Barry	.15
203	Horace Grant	.15
204	Vernon Maxwell	.15
205	Ruben Patterson	.30
206	Vince Carter	4.00
207	Doug Christie	.15
208	Kevin Willis	.15
209	Dee Brown	.15
210	Antonio Davis	.15
211	Tracy McGrady	1.00
212	Dell Curry	.15
213	Charles Oakley	.15
214	Karl Malone	.60
215	John Stockton	.30
216	Howard Eisley	.15
217	Bryon Russell	.15
218	Greg Ostertag	.15
219	Jeff Hornacek	.15
220	Olden Polynice	.15
221	Adam Keefe	.15
222	Shareef Abdur-Rahim	.75
223	Mike Bibby	.50
224	Felipe Lopez	.30
225	Cherokee Parks	.15
226	Michael Dickerson	.40
227	Othella Harrington	.15
228	Bryant Reeves	.15
229	Brent Price	.15
230	Michael Smith	.15
231	Juwan Howard	.30
232	Rod Strickland	.30

233	Chris Whitney	.15
234	Tracy Murray	.15
235	Mitch Richmond	.30
236	Aaron Williams	.15
237	Isaac Austin	.15
238	Kobe Bryant	.75
239	Michael Jordan	1.00
240	Kevin Garnett	.50
241	*Elton Brand*	15.00
242	*Steve Francis*	40.00
243	*Baron Davis*	12.00
244	*Lamar Odom*	25.00
245	*Jonathan Bender*	15.00
246	*Wally Szczerbiak*	10.00
247	*Richard Hamilton*	10.00
248	*Andre Miller*	12.00
249	*Shawn Marion*	15.00
250	*Jason Terry*	6.00
251	*Trajan Langdon*	5.00
252	*Aleksandar Radojevic*	2.00
253	*Corey Maggette*	12.00
254	*William Avery*	4.00
255	*Ron Artest*	6.00
256	*Cal Bowdler*	2.00
257	*James Posey*	5.00
258	*Quincy Lewis*	4.00
259	*Dion Glover*	4.00
260	*Jeff Foster*	2.00
261	*Kenny Thomas*	3.00
262	*Devean George*	5.00
263	*Tim James*	3.00
264	*Vonteego Cummings*	4.00
265	*Jumaine Jones*	3.00
266	*Scott Padgett*	3.00
267	*Rodney Buford*	3.00
268	*Adrian Griffin*	3.00
269	*Anthony Carter*	5.00
270	*Eddie Robinson*	6.00

1999-00 Upper Deck Gold Reserve Gold Mine

This 15-card insert featured top players over an action background with the word "Gold" outlined near the bottom and the word "Mine" in large, bold, gold letters across the bottom. Gold Mine cards were numbered with an "R" prefix and seeded 1:11 packs.

		MT
Complete Set (15):		40.00
Common Player:		.75
Inserted 1:11		
R1	Kobe Bryant	8.00
R2	Vince Carter	10.00
R3	Steve Francis	6.00
R4	Kevin Garnett	5.00
R5	Elton Brand	5.00
R6	Gary Payton	1.00
R7	Lamar Odom	5.00
R8	Grant Hill	5.00
R9	Jason Williams	2.00
R10	Shareef Abdur-Rahim	1.50
R11	Tim Duncan	5.00
R12	Keith Van Horn	1.00
R13	Tim Hardaway	.75
R14	Karl Malone	1.00
R15	Shaquille O'Neal	3.00

1999-00 Upper Deck Gold Reserve Gold Strike

This 15-card insert set featured a mix of rookies and young stars, and included a gold border on three sides, with only the right side being borderless. Gold Strike inserts were numbered with a "GS" prefix and seeded 1:4 packs.

		MT
Complete Set (15):		20.00
Common Player:		.50
Inserted 1:4		
GS1	Kevin Garnett	3.00
GS2	Kobe Bryant	4.00
GS3	Tim Duncan	3.00
GS4	Adrian Griffin	1.00
GS5	Lamar Odom	3.00
GS6	Jason Kidd	1.50
GS7	Wally Szczerbiak	2.00
GS8	Stephon Marbury	1.00
GS9	Shaquille O'Neal	2.00
GS10	Elton Brand	3.00
GS11	Allen Iverson	2.50
GS12	Shawn Marion	1.50
GS13	Jason Williams	1.50
GS14	Antonio McDyess	.50
GS15	Vince Carter	5.00

1999-00 Upper Deck Gold Reserve UD Authentics

This 10-card insert featured autographs of top players and was numbered with a two-letter code corresponding to the player's initials. UD Authentics cards were seeded 1:480 packs.

		MT
Complete Set (10):		700.00
Common Player:		15.00
Inserted 1:480		
JB	Jonathan Bender	60.00
KB	Kobe Bryant	200.00
BD	Baron Davis	40.00
SF	Steve Francis	125.00
KG	Kevin Garnett	125.00
RH	Richard Hamilton	25.00
AH	Anfernee Hardaway	100.00
WS	Wally Szczerbiak	60.00
JT	Jason Terry	20.00
AW	Antoine Walker	12.00

1999-00 Upper Deck Hardcourt

This 90-card set consisted of 60 veterans and 30 rookies, which were seeded 1:4 packs. Hardcourt cards were printed on thick stock that had the look and feel of a basketball floor. Base cards featured a primarily red back, while the two parallels - Baseline Grooves Rainbow and Baseline Grooves Silver - had different color backs to distinguish them from base cards. Inserts included: Court Authority, Court Forces, Legends of the Hardcourt, MJ Records Almanac, New Court Order, Power in the Paint and Game Floor cards of Jordan and Chamberlain.

		MT
Complete Set (90):		100.00
Common Player:		.25
Minor Stars:		.50
Common Rookie (61-90):		1.00
Inserted 1:4		
GF1 Numbered to 50		
GF6 Numbered to 100		
Pack (5):		5.00
Wax Box (24):		50.00
1	Dikembe Mutombo	.50
2	Alan Henderson	.25
3	Antoine Walker	.60
4	Paul Pierce	2.00
5	Eddie Jones	1.00
6	Elden Campbell	.25
7	Toni Kukoc	.75
8	Randy Brown	.25
9	Shawn Kemp	.60
10	Brevin Knight	.25
11	Michael Finley	.75
12	Dirk Nowitzki	1.00
13	Antonio McDyess	.75
14	Nick Van Exel	.50
15	Grant Hill	4.00
16	Jerry Stackhouse	.50
17	Antawn Jamison	1.50
18	John Starks	.25
19	Hakeem Olajuwon	1.00
20	Scottie Pippen	1.50
21	Reggie Miller	.50
22	Jalen Rose	.25
23	Maurice Taylor	.75
24	Michael Olowokandi	1.00
25	Shaquille O'Neal	2.00
26	Kobe Bryant	5.00
27	Tim Hardaway	.75
28	Alonzo Mourning	.75
29	Glenn Robinson	.50
30	Ray Allen	.50
31	Kevin Garnett	4.00
32	Terrell Brandon	.50
33	Stephon Marbury	1.50
34	Keith Van Horn	1.00
35	Latrell Sprewell	.50
36	Allan Houston	.50
37	Patrick Ewing	.50
38	Darrell Armstrong	.50
39	Charles Outlaw	.25
40	Allen Iverson	3.00
41	Larry Hughes	1.00
42	Jason Kidd	1.50
43	Tom Gugliotta	.50
44	Brian Grant	.25
45	Damon Stoudamire	.75
46	Jason Williams	2.50
47	Vlade Divac	.25
48	Tim Duncan	4.00
49	David Robinson	1.00
50	Avery Johnson	.25
51	Gary Payton	1.00
52	Vin Baker	.50
53	Vince Carter	5.00
54	Tracy McGrady	1.50
55	Karl Malone	1.00
56	John Stockton	.50
57	Shareef Abdur-Rahim	1.50
58	Mike Bibby	1.25
59	Juwan Howard	.50
60	Mitch Richmond	.50
61	*Elton Brand*	12.00
62	*Jason Terry*	3.00
63	*Kenny Thomas*	2.00
64	*Jonathan Bender*	8.00
65	*Aleksandar Radojevic*	1.00
66	*Galen Young*	1.00
67	*Baron Davis*	5.00
68	*Corey Maggette*	5.00
69	*Dion Glover*	2.00
70	*Scott Padgett*	1.00
71	*Steve Francis*	20.00
72	*Richard Hamilton*	5.00
73	*James Posey*	4.00
74	*Jumanie Jones*	2.00
75	*Chris Herren*	2.00
76	*Andre Miller*	6.00
77	*Lamar Odom*	12.00
78	*Wally Szczerbiak*	5.00
79	*William Avery*	3.00
80	*Devean George*	3.00
81	*Trajan Langdon*	3.00
82	*Cal Bowdler*	1.00
83	*Kris Clack*	1.00
84	*Tim James*	2.00
85	*Shawn Marion*	8.00
86	*Ryan Robertson*	1.00
87	*Quincy Lewis*	2.00
88	*Vonteego Cummings*	3.00
89	*Obinna Ekezie*	1.00
90	*Jeff Foster*	1.00
GF1	Michael Jordan/50	1200.
GF6	Wilt Chamberlain/100	250.00

1999-00 Upper Deck Hardcourt Baseline Grooves

This 90-card parallel reprinted every card in Hardcourt, but featured holographic printing on the front, including the words "Baseline Grooves" written in script across the middle of the cards. Both the front and back featured blue coloring instead of red (in the base cards). These were sequentially numbered to 500 sets.

	MT
Veterans (1-60):	5x-10x
Rookies (61-90):	2x-4x
Production 500 Sets	

1999-00 Upper Deck Hardcourt Baseline Grooves Silver

This 90-card parallel set reprinted all 90 cards in Hardcourt, but contained green and silver on the front and back. Baseline Grooves Silver cards were sequentially numbered to 50 sets.

	MT
Veterans (1-60):	20x-40x
Rookies (61-90):	5x-10x
Production 50 Sets	

1999-00 Upper Deck Hardcourt Court Authority

This 10-card insert features top players in the NBA, with two shots of the player divided by a wood textured strip. Cards are numbered with an "A" prefix and inserted 1:99 packs.

		MT
Complete Set (10):		175.00
Common Player:		.50
Inserted 1:99		
A1	Tim Duncan	25.00
A2	Vince Carter	35.00
A3	Allen Iverson	15.00
A4	Jason Williams	15.00
A5	Kevin Garnett	25.00
A6	Keith Van Horn	5.00
A7	Jason Kidd	12.00
A8	Grant Hill	25.00
A9	Antoine Walker	4.00
A10	Michael Jordan	50.00

1999-00 Upper Deck Hardcourt Court Forces

This 10-card insert features an action shot over the hardwood background on the left 2/3 of the card, with a closer shot printed on foil on the right side. Cards are numbered with a "CF" prefix and inserted 1:8 packs.

		MT
Complete Set (10):		8.00
Common Player:		.50
Inserted 1:8		
CF1	Shareef Abdur-Rahim	1.50
CF2	Scottie Pippen	2.00
CF3	Latrell Sprewell	.50
CF4	Tim Hardaway	1.00
CF5	Shaquille O'Neal	3.00
CF6	Mike Bibby	1.00
CF7	Allen Iverson	4.00
CF8	John Stockton	.50
CF9	Michael Finley	.75
CF10	Reggie Miller	.50

1999-00 Upper Deck Hardcourt Legends of the Hardcourt

Legends of the Hardcourt showcases 10 NBA legends, with a colored strip down the right side containing the insert name. Cards were numbered with an "L" prefix and inserted 1:19 packs.

		MT
Complete Set (10):		40.00
Common Player:		1.00
Inserted 1:19		
L1	Michael Jordan	25.00
L2	Elgin Baylor	2.00
L3	Kevin McHale	1.00
L4	Julius Erving	6.00
L5	Larry Bird	12.00
L6	George Gervin	1.00
L7	Bob Cousy	2.00
L8	John Havlicek	3.00
L9	Jerry West	2.00
L10	Walt Frazier	1.00

1999-00 Upper Deck Hardcourt MJ Records Almanac

MJ Records Almanac features 10 cards of Jordan with an action shot on the right half and a closer shot printed on foil on the left half. These inserts were seeded 1:19 packs and numbered with a "J" prefix.

		MT
Complete Set (10):		40.00
Common Player:		5.00
Inserted 1:19		
J1	Michael Jordan	5.00
J2	Michael Jordan	5.00
J3	Michael Jordan	5.00
J4	Michael Jordan	5.00
J5	Michael Jordan	5.00
J6	Michael Jordan	5.00
J7	Michael Jordan	5.00
J8	Michael Jordan	5.00
J9	Michael Jordan	5.00
J10	Michael Jordan	5.00

1999-00 Upper Deck Hardcourt New Court Order

This 20-card insert featured top young stars of the NBA. New Court Order cards were numbered with a "NC" prefix and inserted 1:3 packs.

		MT
Complete Set (20):		15.00
Common Player:		.25
Inserted 1:3		
NC1	Vince Carter	4.00
NC2	Allan Houston	.50
NC3	Paul Pierce	2.00
NC4	Eddie Jones	.75
NC5	Antawn Jamison	1.50
NC6	Mike Bibby	1.00
NC7	Tim Duncan	3.00
NC8	Kobe Bryant	4.00
NC9	Maurice Taylor	.75
NC10	Darrell Armstrong	.50
NC11	Stephon Marbury	1.50
NC12	Gary Payton	1.00
NC13	Brian Grant	.25
NC14	Jason Williams	2.50
NC15	Shareef Abdur-Rahim	1.50
NC16	Damon Stoudamire	.75
NC17	Keith Van Horn	1.00
NC18	Tom Gugliotta	.50
NC19	Antonio McDyess	.75
NC20	Ray Allen	.50

1999-00 Upper Deck Hardcourt Power in the Paint

Power in the Paint displayed 12 top low post performers over a basketball court lane background. Cards were numbered with a "P" prefix and inserted 1:6 packs.

		MT
Complete Set (12):		5.00
Common Player:		.25
Inserted 1:6		
P1	Antoine Walker	.75
P2	Karl Malone	.75
P3	Hakeem Olajuwon	.75
P4	David Robinson	.75
P5	Antonio McDyess	.50
P6	Shawn Kemp	.60
P7	Glenn Robinson	.25
P8	Juwan Howard	.25
P9	Patrick Ewing	.25
P10	Alonzo Mourning	.50
P11	Antawn Jamison	1.50
P12	Dikembe Mutombo	.25

1999-00 Upper Deck HoloGrFX

HoloGrFX was a 90-card set that consisted of 60 veterans and 30 rookies, which were seeded 1:2 packs. The cards picture the player over a prismatic background with two colors - usually team colors - splitting the background. The set was paralleled with an AUsome set, which utilized gold foil in the background instead of team colors and was marked with a gold foil AUsome logo. Inserts included: HoloFame, Maximum Jordan, NBA 24.7, NBA Shoetime and UD Authentics.

		MT
Complete Set (90):		60.00
Common Player:		.15
Minor Stars:		.25
Common Rookie (61-90):		.50
Inserted 1:2		
Pack (3):		2.00
Wax Box (36):		30.00
1	Dikembe Mutombo	.25
2	Alan Henderson	.15
3	Antoine Walker	.60
4	Paul Pierce	1.50
5	Eddie Jones	.75
6	David Wesley	.15
7	Dickey Simpkins	.15
8	Toni Kukoc	.60
9	Shawn Kemp	.60
10	Zydrunas Ilgauskas	.25
11	Michael Finley	.50
12	Cedric Ceballos	.15
13	Antonio McDyess	.60
14	Nick Van Exel	.25
15	Grant Hill	2.50
16	Bison Dele	.15
17	Jerry Stackhouse	.50
18	Antawn Jamison	1.00
19	John Starks	.15
20	Scottie Pippen	1.00
21	Charles Barkley	.75
22	Hakeem Olajuwon	.75
23	Reggie Miller	.25
24	Rik Smits	.15
25	Michael Olowokandi	.75
26	Maurice Taylor	.60
27	Shaquille O'Neal	1.50
28	Kobe Bryant	3.00
29	Tim Hardaway	.60
30	Alonzo Mourning	.50
31	Ray Allen	.40
32	Glenn Robinson	.25
33	Kevin Garnett	2.50
34	Terrell Brandon	.25
35	Stephon Marbury	1.25
36	Keith Van Horn	.75
37	Allan Houston	.25
38	Latrell Sprewell	.25
39	Charles Outlaw	.15
40	Darrell Armstrong	.25
41	Allen Iverson	2.50
42	Larry Hughes	.75
43	Jason Kidd	1.25
44	Tom Gugliotta	.25
45	Damon Stoudamire	.40
46	Rasheed Wallace	.25
47	Jason Williams	2.00
48	Chris Webber	1.25
49	Tim Duncan	2.50
50	David Robinson	.75
51	Gary Payton	.75
52	Vin Baker	.25
53	Vince Carter	3.00
54	Tracy McGrady	1.25
55	John Stockton	.25
56	Karl Malone	.75
57	Mike Bibby	1.00
58	Shareef Abdur-Rahim	1.00
59	Juwan Howard	.25
60	Mitch Richmond	.25
61	*Elton Brand*	6.00
62	*Lamar Odom*	10.00
63	*Kenny Thomas*	1.25
64	*Scott Padgett*	1.25
65	*Trajan Langdon*	2.00
66	*James Posey*	2.00
67	*Shawn Marion*	6.00
68	*Chris Herren*	1.00
69	*Tim James*	1.00
70	*Evan Eschmeyer*	.50
71	*Corey Maggette*	5.00
72	*Richard Hamilton*	4.00
73	*Baron Davis*	5.00
74	*Galen Young*	.50
75	*Dion Glover*	1.00
76	*Jumanie Jones*	1.00
77	*Wally Szczerbiak*	4.00
78	*Andre Miller*	5.00
79	*Devean George*	2.00
80	*Obinna Ekezie*	.50
81	*Steve Francis*	15.00
82	*Jason Terry*	3.00
83	*Quincy Lewis*	1.50
84	*Ryan Robertson*	.50
85	*William Avery*	2.00
86	*Aleksandar Radojevic*	.50
87	*Jonathan Bender*	8.00
88	*Cal Bowdler*	.50
89	*Vonteego Cummings*	1.50
90	*Jeff Foster*	.50

1999-00 Upper Deck HoloGrFX AU

This 90-card parallel set replaced the team colors used on the base cards with gold coloring, and included a gold foil AUsome logo in the lower right corner. AUsome parallel cards were inserted 1:12 packs.

	MT
Complete Set (90):	150.00
Commmon Veteran (1-60):	2x-4x
Common Rookie (61-90):	2x
Inserted 1:12	

1999-00 Upper Deck HoloGrFX HoloFame

This nine-card insert featured top players on a prismatic, framed card, with the insert name in silver foil across the bottom. HoloFame cards were numbered with a "HF" prefix and inserted 1:17 packs. Gold versions of these also existed and featured gold foil on the front with an AUsome logo. Gold versions were inserted 1:210 packs.

		MT
Complete Set (9):		50.00
Common Player:		1.00
Inserted 1:17		
AU Cards:		3x-6x
Inserted 1:210		
HF1	Michael Jordan	15.00
HF2	Julius Erving	4.00
HF3	Larry Bird	10.00
HF4	George Gervin	1.00
HF5	Tim Duncan	8.00
HF6	Kevin Garnett	8.00
HF7	Kobe Bryant	10.00
HF8	Jason Williams	6.00
HF9	Vince Carter	10.00

1999-00 Upper Deck HoloGrFX HoloFame AU

HoloFame AU parallel cards reprinted all nine HoloFame inserts with gold foil and an AUsome logo on the front. These were inserted 1:210 packs.

	MT
Complete Set (9):	300.00
AU Cards:	3x-6x

1999-00 Upper Deck HoloGrFX Maximum Jordan

This six-card insert was devoted to Michael Jordan and pictured him over a red and black background with a silver frame. Maximum Jordan cards were numberd with a "MJ" prefix and inserted 1:34 packs. Gold versions also existed and were printed on gold foil and featured an AUsome logo on the front. Gold versions were inserted 1:431 packs.

		MT
Complete Set (6):		25.00
Common Player:		5.00
Inserted 1:34		
Common AU:		30.00
Inserted 1:431		
MJ1	Michael Jordan	5.00
MJ2	Michael Jordan	5.00
MJ3	Michael Jordan	5.00
MJ4	Michael Jordan	5.00
MJ5	Michael Jordan	5.00
MJ6	Michael Jordan	5.00

1999-00 Upper Deck HoloGrFX NBA Shoetime

This 19-card insert incorporated pieces of game-used shoes from some of the top players in the league. The cards were numbered with a two-letter prefix followed by an "-S". The letters usually corresponded to the player's initials, for example, Allen Iverson is numbered AI-S. NBA Shoetime inserts were seeded 1:431 packs. Karl Malone and Michael Jordan signed a limited number of their NBA Shoetime inserts hand-numbered to the player's jersey number (32 and 23, respectively).

		MT
Common Player:		40.00
Inserted 1:431		
CB	Charles Barkley	125.00
KB	Kobe Bryant	275.00
PE	Patrick Ewing	100.00
TH	Tim Hardaway	75.00
GH	Grant Hill	150.00
AI	Allen Iverson	200.00
MJ	Michael Jordan	900.00
JK	Jason Kidd	150.00
KM	Karl Malone	125.00
SM	Stephon Marbury	100.00
JM	Jamal Mashburn	50.00
DM	Dikembe Mutombo	40.00
SO	Shaquille O'Neal	150.00
GP	Gary Payton	100.00
SP	Scottie Pippen	125.00
DR	David Robinson	100.00
BR	Bryon Russell	40.00
JS	John Stockton	100.00
CW	Chris Webber	150.00

1999-00 Upper Deck HoloGrFX NBA 24.7

This 15-card insert featured players over a huge "NBA" in silver letters in the background. Cards were numbered with an "N" prefix and inserted 1:3 packs. Gold versions also existed, and featured gold foil instead of the silver used on regular versions. These were inserted 1:105 packs.

		MT
Complete Set (15):		15.00
Common Player:		.50
Inserted 1:3		
AU Cards:		3x-6x
Inserted 1:105		
N1	Tim Duncan	2.50
N2	Allen Iverson	2.50
N3	Vince Carter	3.00
N4	Kevin Garnett	2.50
N5	Shaquille O'Neal	2.00
N6	Shareef Abdur-Rahim	1.00
N7	Jason Williams	2.00
N8	Kobe Bryant	3.00
N9	Grant Hill	2.50
N10	Antoine Walker	.50
N11	Stephon Marbury	1.00
N12	Antonio McDyess	.50
N13	Jason Kidd	1.00
N14	Keith Van Horn	.75
N15	Karl Malone	.50

1999-00 Upper Deck HoloGrFX NBA 24.7 AU

Gold versions of all 15 NBA 24.7 inserts existed and featured gold foil on the front vs. the silver used on regular cards and also included a gold AUsome logo. These were inserted 1:105 packs.

	MT
Complete Set (15):	100.00
AU Cards:	3x-6x

1999-00 Upper Deck HoloGrFX UD Authentics

This 21-card insert featured autographs from a host of players on a horizontally designed card. UD Authentics were numbered with two letters usually corresonding to the player's initials. Those autographed inserts were seeded 1:431 packs.

		MT
Common Player:		8.00
Inserted 1:431		
DA	Darrell Armstrong	15.00
MB	Mike Bibby	20.00
BD	Baron Davis	30.00
MF	Michael Finley	25.00
SF	Steve Francis	100.00
BG	Brian Grant	10.00
TG	Tom Gugliotta	12.00
RD	Richard Hamilton	15.00
LH	Larry Hughes	25.00
MK	Mark Jackson	12.00
AJ	Antawn Jamison	50.00
JO	Michael Jordan	3500.
RL	Raef LaFrentz	20.00
SM	Sam Mack	8.00
WA	Corey Maggette	40.00
ShM	Shawn Marion	30.00
RH	Wally Szczerbiak	75.00
JS	Jerry Stackhouse	25.00
MT	Maurice Taylor	10.00
JT	Jason Terry	12.00
RT	Robert Traylor	10.00

1999-00 Upper Deck Ionix

This 90-card set consisted of 60 veterans and 30 Futuristic Rookies, which were sequentially numbered to 3,500. Each card in the base set is also available in a Reciprocal parallel version. Inserts include: Awesome Powers, BIOrhythm, Pyrotechnics, UD Authentics, Warp Zone and MJ Final Floor.

		MT
Complete Set (90):		150.00
Common Player:		.15
Minor Stars:		.30
Common Rookie (61-90):		2.00
Production 3,500 Sets		
Pack (5):		4.00
Wax Box (24):		40.00
1	Dikembe Mutombo	.30
2	Isaiah Rider	.30
3	Antoine Walker	.50
4	Paul Pierce	1.00
5	Eddie Jones	.60
6	Anthony Mason	.15
7	Toni Kukoc	.50
8	Hersey Hawkins	.15
9	Shawn Kemp	.30
10	Lamond Murray	.15
11	Michael Finley	.30
12	Cedric Ceballos	.15
13	Antonio McDyess	.40
14	Ron Mercer	.60
15	Grant Hill	2.50
16	Jerry Stackhouse	.40
17	Antawn Jamison	.75
18	Mookie Blaylock	.15
19	Charles Barkley	.60
20	Hakeem Olajuwon	.60
21	Reggie Miller	.30
22	Rik Smits	.15
23	Maurice Taylor	.15
24	Derek Anderson	.30
25	Kobe Bryant	3.00
26	Shaquille O'Neal	1.50
27	Tim Hardaway	.50
28	Alonzo Mourning	.40
29	Ray Allen	.40
30	Glenn Robinson	.30
31	Kevin Garnett	2.50
32	Terrell Brandon	.30
33	Stephon Marbury	1.00
34	Keith Van Horn	.60
35	Allan Houston	.30
36	Latrell Sprewell	.60
37	Darrell Armstrong	.15
38	Tariq Abdul-Wahad	.15
39	Allen Iverson	2.00
40	Larry Hughes	.75
41	Anfernee Hardaway	1.50
42	Jason Kidd	1.25
43	Tom Gugliotta	.30
44	Scottie Pippen	1.25
45	Damon Stoudamire	.40
46	Rasheed Wallace	.30
47	Jason Williams	1.25
48	Chris Webber	1.25
49	Tim Duncan	2.50
50	David Robinson	.60
51	Gary Payton	.60
52	Vin Baker	.30
53	Vince Carter	4.00
54	Tracy McGrady	1.25
55	Karl Malone	.60
56	John Stockton	.30
57	Mike Bibby	.50
58	Shareef Abdur-Rahim	1.00
59	Mitch Richmond	.30
60	Juwan Howard	.30
61	*Elton Brand*	15.00
62	*Steve Francis*	40.00
63	*Baron Davis*	12.00
64	*Lamar Odom*	25.00
65	*Jonathan Bender*	15.00
66	*Wally Szczerbiak*	10.00
67	*Richard Hamilton*	10.00
68	*Andre Miller*	12.00
69	*Shawn Marion*	15.00
70	*Jason Terry*	6.00
71	*Trajan Langdon*	5.00
72	*Aleksandar Radojevic*	2.00
73	*Corey Maggette*	12.00
74	*William Avery*	3.00
75	*Ron Artest*	6.00
76	*Cal Bowdler*	2.00
77	*James Posey*	5.00
78	*Quincy Lewis*	3.00
79	*Dion Glover*	3.00
80	*Jeff Foster*	2.00
81	*Kenny Thomas*	3.00
82	*Devean George*	5.00
83	*Tim James*	3.00
84	*Vonteego Cummings*	4.00
85	*Jumaine Jones*	3.00
86	*Scott Padgett*	2.00
87	*Chucky Atkins*	4.00
88	*Adrian Griffin*	3.00
89	*Todd MacCulloch*	3.00
90	*A.J. Bramlett*	2.00

1999-00 Upper Deck Ionix Reciprocal

This 90-card parallel set reprinted each base card, swapping the back and front from regular versions. Veterans were inserted 1:4 packs, while Futuristic Rookies were sequentially numbered to 100. Reciprocal cards were numbered with an "R" prefix.

	MT
Reciprocal Cards (1-60):	2x-4x
Inserted 1:6	
Rookie Reciprocal (61-90):	1.5x
Production 100 Sets	

1999-00 Upper Deck Ionix Awesome Powers

This 15-card insert set featured young stars of the NBA. Cards pictured the player over a multi-colored, retro look, with a close-up shot in the top right corner. Awesome Powers were numbered with an "AP" prefix and seeded 1:23 packs.

		MT
Complete Set (15):		50.00
Common Player:		1.00
Inserted 1:23		
AP1	Elton Brand	8.00
AP2	Corey Maggette	5.00
AP3	Wally Szczerbiak	5.00
AP4	Charles Barkley	3.00
AP5	Shawn Marion	4.00
AP6	Jason Terry	2.00
AP7	Keith Van Horn	2.00
AP8	Steve Francis	10.00
AP9	Trajan Langdon	1.00
AP10	Reggie Miller	1.00
AP11	Richard Hamilton	3.00
AP12	Jonathan Bender	5.00
AP13	Baron Davis	4.00
AP14	Paul Pierce	4.00
AP15	Andre Miller	4.00

1999-00 Upper Deck Ionix BIOrhythm

This 15-card insert set featured players over a multi- colored background made up of tiny squares. BIOrhythm cards were numbered with a "B" prefix and inserted 1:7 packs.

		MT
Complete Set (15):		20.00
Common Player:		.50
Inserted 1:7		
B1	Grant Hill	5.00
B2	Antawn Jamison	2.00
B3	Shaquille O'Neal	3.00
B4	Stephon Marbury	2.00
B5	Michael Finley	.50
B6	Hakeem Olajuwon	1.50
B7	Ron Mercer	1.50
B8	Tim Hardaway	1.00
B9	Jason Kidd	2.50
B10	Allan Houston	.50
B11	Ray Allen	.75
B12	Shawn Kemp	.50
B13	Alonzo Mourning	.75
B14	Tim Duncan	5.00
B15	Eddie Jones	1.50

1999-00 Upper Deck Ionix Pyrotechnics

This 15-card insert set featured players over a design with protons and electrons in the background. Pyrotechnics cards were numbered with a "P" prefix and inserted 1:72 packs.

		MT
Complete Set (15):		150.00
Common Player:		3.00
Inserted 1:72		
P1	Kevin Garnett	20.00
P2	Shareef Abdur-Rahim	8.00
P3	Jason Kidd	10.00
P4	Antonio McDyess	3.00
P5	Karl Malone	5.00
P6	Eddie Jones	5.00
P7	Antoine Walker	3.00
P8	Kobe Bryant	25.00
P9	Anfernee Hardaway	12.00
P10	Antawn Jamison	8.00
P11	Keith Van Horn	5.00
P12	Grant Hill	20.00
P13	Gary Payton	5.00
P14	Allen Iverson	15.00
P15	Vince Carter	30.00

1999-00 Upper Deck Ionix UD Authentics

This 22-card insert set featured autographs from various NBA players. Cards were numbered with a two-letter system, usually corresponding to the player's initials. UD Authentics were inserted 1:144 packs.

		MT
Common Player:		5.00
Inserted 1:144		
RA	Ron Artest	25.00
AW	William Avery	10.00
JB	Jonathan Bender	40.00
KB	Kobe Bryant	200.00
BD	Baron Davis	25.00
SF	Steve Francis	100.00
KG	Kevin Garnett	125.00
BG	Brian Grant	10.00
TG	Tom Gugliotta	8.00
RH	Richard Hamilton	20.00
AH	Anfernee Hardaway	100.00
AJ	Antawn Jamison	35.00
MJ	Michael Jordan	
TL	Trajan Langdon	12.00
CM	Corey Maggette	40.00
SM	Shawn Marion	25.00
AM	Andre Miller	25.00
JP	James Posey	15.00
WS	Wally Szczerbiak	10.00
JT	Jason Terry	15.00
RT	Robert Traylor	5.00

1999-00 Upper Deck Ionix Warp Zone

This 15-card insert captured the top players on an Ionix rainbow foil design. Warp Zone cards were numbered with a "WZ" prefix and inserted 1:144 packs.

		MT
Complete Set (15):		500.00
Common Player:		15.00
Inserted 1:144		
WZ1	Kobe Bryant	50.00
WZ2	Kevin Garnett	50.00
WZ3	Tim Duncan	30.00
WZ4	Elton Brand	20.00
WZ5	Wally Szczerbiak	20.00
WZ6	Stephon Marbury	15.00
WZ7	Allen Iverson	30.00
WZ8	Anfernee Hardaway	25.00
WZ9	Shaquille O'Neal	30.00
WZ10	Baron Davis	15.00
WZ11	Scottie Pippen	20.00
WZ12	Jason Williams	20.00
WZ13	Steve Francis	50.00
WZ14	Vince Carter	75.00
WZ15	Lamar Odom	40.00

1999-00 Upper Deck MVP

Upper Deck MVP consisted of 220 cards, including 178 regular-player cards, 30 MJ Exclusives, 10 rookies and two checklists. The cards featured a color photo with a white border and some silver foil stamping. The first 218 cards (two checklists not included) were paralleled three times - Silver Script (1:2 packs), Gold Script (hobby-only, numbered to 100) and Super Script (hobby-only, numbered to 25). Insert sets include: Game-Used Souvenirs, ProSign, Draw Your Own Trading Card Winners, Jam Time, MVP Theatre, 21st Century NBA, Dynamics, Jordan's MVP Moments and Electrifying.

		MT
Complete Set (220):		45.00
Common Player:		.10
Minor Stars		.20
Common MJ Exclusives (179-208):		1.00
Pack (10):		2.00
Wax Box (28):		45.00
1	Dikembe Mutombo	.20
2	Steve Smith	.20
3	Mookie Blaylock	.10
4	Alan Henderson	.10
5	LaPhonso Ellis	.20
6	Grant Long	.10
7	Kenny Anderson	.20
8	Antoine Walker	.60
9	Ron Mercer	.50
10	Paul Pierce	.75
11	Vitaly Potapenko	.10
12	Dana Barros	.10
13	Elden Campbell	.10
14	Eddie Jones	.40
15	David Wesley	.10
16	Bobby Phills	.10
17	Derrick Coleman	.20
18	Ricky Davis	.20
19	Toni Kukoc	.30
20	Brent Barry	.10
21	Ron Harper	.10
22	Kornel David	.10
23	Mark Bryant	.10
24	Dickey Simpkins	.10
25	Shawn Kemp	.30
26	Derek Anderson	.30
27	Brevin Knight	.20
28	Andrew DeClercq	.10
29	Zydrunas Ilgauskas	.20
30	Cedric Henderson	.10
31	Shawn Bradley	.10
32	A.C. Green	.10
33	Gary Trent	.20
34	Michael Finley	.25
35	Dirk Nowitzki	.30
36	Steve Nash	.10
37	Antonio McDyess	.40
38	Nick Van Exel	.20
39	Chauncey Billups	.20
40	Danny Fortson	.10
41	Eric Washington	.10
42	Raef LaFrentz	.40
43	Grant Hill	1.50
44	Bison Dele	.10
45	Lindsey Hunter	.10
46	Jerry Stackhouse	.20
47	Don Reid	.10
48	Christian Laettner	.10
49	John Starks	.10
50	Antawn Jamison	.60
51	Erick Dampier	.10
52	Donyell Marshall	.10
53	Chris Mills	.10
54	Bimbo Coles	.10
55	Charles Barkley	.40
56	Hakeem Olajuwon	.40
57	Scottie Pippen	.50
58	Othella Harrington	.10

59	Bryce Drew	.10
60	Michael Dickerson	.20
61	Rik Smits	.10
62	Reggie Miller	.20
63	Mark Jackson	.10
64	Antonio Davis	.10
65	Jalen Rose	.20
66	Dale Davis	.10
67	Chris Mullin	.20
68	Maurice Taylor	.30
69	Lamond Murray	.10
70	Rodney Rogers	.10
71	Darrick Martin	.10
72	Michael Olowokandi	.40
73	Tyrone Nesby	.10
74	Kobe Bryant	2.00
75	Shaquille O'Neal	1.00
76	Robert Horry	.10
77	Glen Rice	.20
78	J.R. Reid	.10
79	Rick Fox	.10
80	Derek Fisher	.10
81	Tim Hardaway	.40
82	Alonzo Mourning	.30
83	Jamal Mashburn	.20
84	P.J. Brown	.10
85	Terry Porter	.10
86	Dan Majerle	.10
87	Ray Allen	.20
88	Vinny Del Negro	.10
89	Glenn Robinson	.20
90	Dell Curry	.10
91	Sam Cassell	.20
92	Robert Traylor	.40
93	Kevin Garnett	1.50
94	Terrell Brandon	.20
95	Joe Smith	.20
96	Sam Mitchell	.10
97	Anthony Peeler	.10
98	Bobby Jackson	.10
99	Keith Van Horn	.60
100	Stephon Marbury	.75
101	Jayson Williams	.20
102	Kendall Gill	.10
103	Kerry Kittles	.10
104	Scott Burrell	.10
105	Patrick Ewing	.20
106	Allan Houston	.20
107	Latrell Sprewell	.20
108	Larry Johnson	.20
109	Marcus Camby	.20
110	Charlie Ward	.10
111	Anfernee Hardaway	1.00
112	Darrell Armstrong	.20
113	Nick Anderson	.20
114	Horace Grant	.10
115	Isaac Austin	.10
116	Matt Harpring	.20
117	Michael Doleac	.20
118	Allen Iverson	1.50
119	Theo Ratliff	.20
120	Matt Geiger	.10
121	Larry Hughes	.40
122	Tyrone Hill	.10
123	George Lynch	.10
124	Jason Kidd	.60
125	Tom Gugliotta	.20
126	Rex Chapman	.10
127	Clifford Robinson	.10
128	Luc Longley	.10
129	Danny Manning	.20
130	Rasheed Wallace	.20
131	Arvydas Sabonis	.10
132	Damon Stoudamire	.30
133	Brian Grant	.20
134	Isaiah Rider	.20
135	Walt Williams	.10
136	Jim Jackson	.10
137	Jason Williams	1.00
138	Vlade Divac	.20
139	Chris Webber	.60
140	Corliss Williamson	.10
141	Predrag Stojakovic	.10
142	Tariq Abdul-Wahad	.10
143	Tim Duncan	1.50
144	Sean Elliott	.10
145	David Robinson	.40
146	Mario Elie	.10
147	Avery Johnson	.10
148	Steve Kerr	.10
149	Gary Payton	.40
150	Vin Baker	.20
151	Detlef Schrempf	.20
152	Hersey Hawkins	.10
153	Dale Ellis	.10
154	Olden Polynice	.10
155	Vince Carter	2.00
156	John Wallace	.10
157	Doug Christie	.10
158	Tracy McGrady	.60
159	Kevin Willis	.10
160	Charles Oakley	.10
161	Karl Malone	.40
162	John Stockton	.20
163	Jeff Hornacek	.10
164	Bryon Russell	.10
165	Howard Eisley	.10
166	Shandon Anderson	.10
167	Shareef Abdur-Rahim	.50
168	Mike Bibby	.50
169	Bryant Reeves	.20
170	Felipe Lopez	.30
171	Cherokee Parks	.10
172	Michael Smith	.10
173	Juwan Howard	.20
174	Rod Strickland	.20
175	Mitch Richmond	.20
176	Otis Thorpe	.10
177	Calbert Cheaney	.10
178	Tracy Murray	.10
179	Michael Jordan (MJ Exclusives)	1.00
180	Michael Jordan (MJ Exclusives)	1.00
181	Michael Jordan (MJ Exclusives)	1.00
182	Michael Jordan (MJ Exclusives)	1.00
183	Michael Jordan (MJ Exclusives)	1.00
184	Michael Jordan (MJ Exclusives)	1.00
185	Michael Jordan (MJ Exclusives)	1.00
186	Michael Jordan (MJ Exclusives)	1.00
187	Michael Jordan (MJ Exclusives)	1.00
188	Michael Jordan (MJ Exclusives)	1.00
189	Michael Jordan (MJ Exclusives)	1.00
190	Michael Jordan (MJ Exclusives)	1.00
191	Michael Jordan (MJ Exclusives)	1.00
192	Michael Jordan (MJ Exclusives)	1.00
193	Michael Jordan (MJ Exclusives)	1.00
194	Michael Jordan (MJ Exclusives)	1.00
195	Michael Jordan (MJ Exclusives)	1.00
196	Michael Jordan (MJ Exclusives)	1.00
197	Michael Jordan (MJ Exclusives)	1.00
198	Michael Jordan (MJ Exclusives)	1.00
199	Michael Jordan (MJ Exclusives)	1.00
200	Michael Jordan (MJ Exclusives)	1.00
201	Michael Jordan (MJ Exclusives)	1.00
202	Michael Jordan (MJ Exclusives)	1.00
203	Michael Jordan (MJ Exclusives)	1.00
204	Michael Jordan (MJ Exclusives)	1.00
205	Michael Jordan (MJ Exclusives)	1.00
206	Michael Jordan (MJ Exclusives)	1.00
207	Michael Jordan (MJ Exclusives)	1.00
208	Michael Jordan (MJ Exclusives)	1.00
209	*Elton Brand*	3.00
210	*Steve Francis*	5.00
211	*Baron Davis*	1.25
212	*Wally Szczerbiak*	1.00
213	*Richard Hamilton*	1.00
214	*Andre Miller*	1.25
215	*Jason Terry*	.75
216	*Corey Maggette*	1.25
217	*Shawn Marion*	2.00
218	*Lamar Odom*	3.00
219	Checklist	.10
220	Checklist	.10

1999-00 Upper Deck MVP Gold Script

This 218-card parallel set reprinted each card from MVP (except for the two checklists), but added a gold foil facsimile signature on the front. Gold Script cards were hobby exclusives and sequentially numbered to 100 sets.

	MT
Gold Script Cards:	30x-60x
Gold Script Rookies:	10x-20x
Gold MJ Exclusive (179-208):	50.00
Production 100 Sets	

1999-00 Upper Deck MVP Silver Script

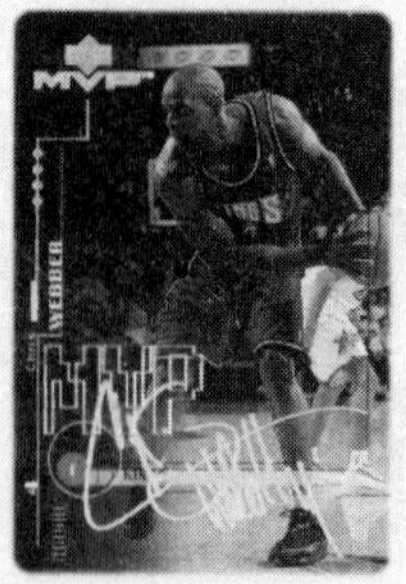

This 218-card parallel set reprinted each card from MVP (except for the two checklists), but added a silver foil facsimile signature on the front. Silver Script cards were inserted 1:2 packs.

	MT
Complete Set (220):	150.00
Silver Script Cards:	2x-4x
Silver Script Rookies:	1x-2x
Silver MJ Exlusive (179-208):	4.00
Inserted 1:2	

1999-00 Upper Deck MVP Super Script

This 218-card parallel set reprinted each card from MVP (except for the two checklists), but added a holographic foil facsimile signature on the front. Super Script cards were hobby exclusives and sequentially numbered to 25 sets.

	MT
Super Script Cards:	75x-150x
Super Script Rookies:	20x-40x
Super Script MJ Exclusive (179-208): 150.00	
Production 25 Sets	

1999-00 Upper Deck MVP Draw Your Own Trading Card

This 26-card insert featured winners to Upper Deck's Draw Your Own Trading Card promotion. Cards 1-8 were ages 5-8, cards 9-18 were ages 9-14 and cards 20-30 were ages 15 and up. Cards 11, 15, 19 and 27 were not printed. Cards from this insert are numbered with a "W" prefix and inserted 1:6 packs.

		MT
Complete Set (26):		18.00
Common Player:		.10
Inserted 1:6		
1	Michael Jordan	2.00
2	Grant Hill	1.00
3	Kobe Bryant	1.25
4	Michael Jordan	2.00
5	Glen Rice	.10
6	Michael Jordan	2.00
7	David Robinson	.20
8	Grant Hill	1.00
9	Stephon Marbury	.50
10	Michael Jordan	2.00
12	Charles Barkley	.20
13	Antoine Walker	.30
14	Shaquille O'Neal	.50
16	Michael Jordan	2.00
17	Stephon Marbury	.50
18	Michael Jordan	2.00
20	Allen Iverson	1.00
21	Michael Jordan	2.00
22	Shareef Abdur-Rahim	.30
23	Reggie Miller	.10
24	Karl Malone	.20
25	Christian Laettner	.10
26	John Stockton	.10
28	Michael Jordan	2.00
29	Michael Jordan	2.00
30	Michael Jordan	2.00

1999-00 Upper Deck MVP Dynamics

This six-card insert highlights players over a silver foil background and hardwood design. Cards were numbered with a "D" prefix and inserted 1:27 packs.

		MT
Complete Set (6):		35.00
Common Player:		2.00
Inserted 1:6		
1	Michael Jordan	15.00
2	Kobe Bryant	10.00
3	Grant Hill	8.00
4	Shareef Abdur-Rahim	2.00
5	Kevin Garnett	8.00
6	Vince Carter	6.00

1999-00 Upper Deck MVP Electrifying

This 15-card insert featured some of the most exciting players in the NBA on a foil background. Cards are numbered with an "E" prefix and inserted 1:9 packs.

		MT
Complete Set (15):		12.00
Common Player:		.50
Inserted 1:9		
1	Shaquille O'Neal	3.00
2	Steve Smith	.50
3	Toni Kukoc	.75
4	Ron Mercer	1.50
5	Damon Stoudamire	.75
6	Tim Hardaway	.75
7	Paul Pierce	2.50
8	Jason Kidd	1.50
9	Stephon Marbury	2.00
10	Terrell Brandon	.50
11	Reggie Miller	.50
12	Ray Allen	.50
13	Maurice Taylor	.75
14	Chris Webber	1.50
15	Charles Barkley	1.00

1999-00 Upper Deck MVP Game-used Souvenirs

This 15-card, hobby-only insert included a piece of a game-used basketball from some of the top players. Game-used Souvenirs were inserted 1:131 packs and cards were numbered with two letters followed by "-S," with the two letters corresponding to the player's initials in most cases. In addition, Anfernee Hardaway and Karl Malone autographed a number of their cards, which are hand-numbered to the player's jersey numbers. This means that Hardaway signed just one card and Malone signed 32. The autographed versions are numbered with the player's initials followed by "-A."

		MT
Complete Set (15):		750.00
Common Player:		25.00
Inserted 1:131 Hobby		
MB	Mike Bibby	30.00
KB	Kobe Bryant	100.00
TD	Tim Duncan	75.00
MF	Michael Finley	25.00
KG	Kevin Garnett	75.00
AH	Anfernee Hardaway	60.00
AH-A	Anfernee Hardaway Auto (1)	
AJ	Antawn Jamison	50.00
JK	Jason Kidd	60.00
KM	Karl Malone	50.00
KM-A	Karl Malone Auto (32)	600.00
AM	Antonio McDyess	30.00
MO	Michael Olowokandi	25.00
SO	Shaquille O'Neal	60.00
GP	Gary Payton	40.00
SP	Scottie Pippen	50.00
JW	Jason Williams	75.00

1999-00 Upper Deck MVP Jam Time

This 12-card insert highlighted some of the best leapers in the NBA. Cards were printed on foil, with the left third displaying the insert name in silver foil over a black background and the rest showing the player. Jam Time inserts are numbered with a "JT" prefix and inserted 1:6 packs.

		MT
Complete Set (14):		10.00
Common Player:		.50
Inserted 1:6		
1	Michael Jordan	5.00
2	Alonzo Mourning	.50
3	Shawn Kemp	.50
4	Juwan Howard	.50
5	Chris Webber	1.00
6	Tim Duncan	2.50
7	Keith Van Horn	1.00
8	Eddie Jones	.50
9	Michael Finley	.50
10	Anfernee Hardaway	1.50
11	Antonio McDyess	.75
12	Charles Barkley	.75
13	Latrell Sprewell	.50
14	Hakeem Olajuwon	.75

1999-00 Upper Deck MVP Jordan-MVP Moments

This 14-card insert set highlights all of MJ's MVP awards from his regular season awards to his All-Star game and post-season honors. Jordan's MVP Moments were numbered with an "MJ" prefix and inserted 1:27 packs.

		MT
Complete Set (14):		125.00
Common Player:		10.00
Inserted 1:27		
1	Michael Jordan (1988 MVP)	10.00
2	Michael Jordan (1991 MVP)	10.00
3	Michael Jordan (1992 MVP)	10.00
4	Michael Jordan (1996 MVP)	10.00
5	Michael Jordan (1998 MVP)	10.00
6	Michael Jordan (1988 All-Star MVP)	10.00
7	Michael Jordan (1996 All-Star MVP)	10.00
8	Michael Jordan (1998 All-Star MVP)	10.00
9	Michael Jordan (1991 Final MVP)	10.00
10	Michael Jordan (1992 Final MVP)	10.00
11	Michael Jordan (1993 Final MVP)	10.00
12	Michael Jordan (1996 Final MVP)	10.00
13	Michael Jordan (1997 Final MVP)	10.00
14	Michael Jordan (1998 Final MVP)	10.00

1999-00 Upper Deck MVP MVP Theatre

This 15-card, foil insert displays those players who have the best shot at winning the MVP. MVP Theatre inserts are numbered with an "M" prefix and seeded 1:9 packs.

		MT
Complete Set (15):		
Common Player:		.50
Inserted 1:9		
1	Karl Malone	1.00
2	Tom Gugliotta	.50
3	Shaquille O'Neal	2.50
4	Mitch Richmond	.50
5	David Robinson	1.00
6	Gary Payton	1.00
7	Allen Iverson	4.00
8	Glenn Robinson	.50
9	Antoine Walker	1.50
10	Hakeem Olajuwon	1.00
11	Patrick Ewing	.50
12	Antonio McDyess	1.00
13	Tim Hardaway	.75
14	Scottie Pippen	1.50
15	Anfernee Hardaway	3.00

1999-00 Upper Deck MVP ProSign

This 16-card, retail-only insert from MVP featured autographs from NBA players. Cards were numbered with two letters, usually corresponding to the player's initials, and inserted 1:144 packs.

		MT
Common Player:		6.00
Inserted 1:144 Retail		
DA	Darrell Armstrong	30.00
SA	Stacey Augmon	8.00
IA	Isaac Austin	6.00
VC	Vince Carter	300.00
TC	Terry Cummings	8.00
MD	Michael Dickerson	15.00
DF	Derek Fisher	12.00
JK	Jaren Jackson	8.00
JJ	Jim Jackson	10.00
MJ	Michael Jordan	
TR	Theo Ratliff	8.00
JR	Jalen Rose	15.00
RT	Robert Traylor	12.00
NV	Nick Van Exel	20.00
CH	Charlie Ward	10.00
CW	Clarence Weatherspoon	8.00

1999-00 Upper Deck MVP 21st Century NBA

This 10-card insert featured the best young players in the NBA over a motion, foil background. 21st Century MVP cards were numbered with an "N" prefix and inserted 1:13 packs.

		MT
Complete Set (10):		25.00
Common Player:		2.00
Inserted 1:13		
1	Jason Williams	2.50
2	Paul Pierce	2.50
3	Antoine Walker	1.50
4	Keith Van Horn	1.50
5	Allen Iverson	5.00
6	Antawn Jamison	2.00

Values quoted in this guide reflect the retail price of a card — the price a collector can expect to pay when buying a card from a dealer. The wholesale price — that which a collector can expect to receive from a dealer when selling cards — will be significantly lower, depending on desirability and condition.

7	Kobe Bryant	8.00
8	Shareef Abdur-Rahim	2.00
9	Stephon Marbury	3.00
10	Grant Hill	6.00

1999-00 Upper Deck Ovation

Ovation consisted of 90 cards, with 60 veterans and 30 rookies seeded 1:4 packs. The cards are thick with a framed action shot of the player over a Spalding NBA basketball background. The set is paralleled once by Standing Ovation, which replaces the gold foil of the base cards with a rainbow foil. Inserts include: A Piece of History, Curtain Calls, Lead Performers, Center Stage, Premier Performers, Spotlight and Superstar Theatre. Ovation also contained a special Michael Jordan signature card, which was hand-numbered to 23.

		MT
Complete Set (90):		130.00
Common Player:		.25
Minor Stars:		.40
Common Rookie (61-90):		1.50
Inserted 1:4		
Pack (5):		4.00
Wax Box (24):		40.00
1	Dikembe Mutombo	.40
2	Alan Henderson	.25
3	Antoine Walker	.60
4	Paul Pierce	1.50
5	David Wesley	.25
6	Eddie Jones	.75
7	Toni Kukoc	.60
8	Randy Brown	.25
9	Shawn Kemp	.50
10	Zydrunas Ilgauskas	.40
11	Michael Finley	.40
12	Dirk Nowitzki	.75
13	Nick Van Exel	.40
14	Antonio McDyess	.60
15	Grant Hill	3.00
16	Jerry Stackhouse	.40
17	Antawn Jamison	1.25
18	John Starks	.25
19	Hakeem Olajuwon	.75
20	Charles Barkley	.75
21	Cuttino Mobley	.40
22	Reggie Miller	.40
23	Rik Smits	.25
24	Maurice Taylor	.40
25	Michael Olowokandi	.75
26	Kobe Bryant	4.00
27	Shaquille O'Neal	1.50
28	Tim Hardaway	.60
29	Alonzo Mourning	.50
30	Glenn Robinson	.40
31	Ray Allen	.40
32	Kevin Garnett	3.00
33	Joe Smith	.25
34	Stephon Marbury	1.25
35	Keith Van Horn	.75
36	Patrick Ewing	.40
37	Latrell Sprewell	.40
38	Darrell Armstrong	.40
39	Charles Outlaw	.25
40	Allen Iverson	2.50
41	Larry Hughes	1.00
42	Jason Kidd	1.25
43	Anfernee Hardaway	2.00
44	Brian Grant	.25
45	Damon Stoudamire	.50
46	Jason Williams	2.00
47	Chris Webber	1.25
48	Tim Duncan	3.00
49	David Robinson	.75
50	Sean Elliott	.25
51	Gary Payton	.75
52	Vin Baker	.40
53	Vince Carter	4.00
54	Tracy McGrady	1.25
55	Karl Malone	.75
56	John Stockton	.40
57	Shareef Abdur-Rahim	1.00
58	Mike Bibby	1.00
59	Juwan Howard	.40
60	Mitch Richmond	.40
61	*Elton Brand*	20.00
62	*Steve Francis*	25.00
63	*Baron Davis*	8.00
64	*Lamar Odom*	15.00
65	*Jonathan Bender*	10.00
66	*Wally Szczerbiak*	6.00
67	*Richard Hamilton*	6.00
68	*Andre Miller*	8.00
69	*Shawn Marion*	10.00
70	*Jason Terry*	5.00
71	*Trajan Langdon*	3.00
72	*Aleksandar Radojevic*	1.50
73	*Corey Maggette*	8.00
74	*William Avery*	4.00
75	*Galen Young*	1.50
76	*Chris Herren*	2.00
77	*Cal Bowdler*	1.50
78	*James Posey*	4.00
79	*Quincy Lewis*	2.00
80	*Dion Glover*	2.00
81	*Jeff Foster*	1.50
82	*Kenny Thomas*	2.50
83	*Devean George*	1.00
84	*Tim James*	2.00
85	*Vonteego Cummings*	3.00
86	*Jumanie Jones*	2.00
87	*Scott Padgett*	2.00
88	*Obinna Ekezie*	1.50
89	*Ryan Robertson*	1.50
90	*Evan Eschmeyer*	2.00

1999-00 Upper Deck Ovation Standing Ovation

Standing Ovation consisted of parallel cards of all 90 cards in Ovation. The cards featured rainbow foil in contrast to the golf foil on the base cards. These parallel cards were sequentially numbered to 50 sets.

		MT
Common Player (1-60):		20.00
Standing Ovation Cards:		50x-100x
Common Rookie (61-90):		15.00
Standing Ovation Rookies:		10x-15x
Production 50 Sets		
1	Dikembe Mutombo	25.00
2	Alan Henderson	25.00
3	Antoine Walker	60.00
4	Paul Pierce	150.00
5	David Wesley	25.00
6	Eddie Jones	100.00
7	Toni Kukoc	75.00
8	Randy Brown	25.00
9	Shawn Kemp	40.00
10	Zydrunas Ilgauskas	25.00
11	Michael Finley	40.00
12	Dirk Nowitzki	125.00
13	Nick Van Exel	35.00
14	Antonio McDyess	50.00
15	Grant Hill	300.00
16	Jerry Stackhouse	50.00
17	Antawn Jamison	125.00
18	John Starks	25.00
19	Hakeem Olajuwon	75.00
20	Charles Barkley	75.00
21	Cuttino Mobley	40.00
22	Reggie Miller	40.00
23	Rik Smits	25.00
24	Maurice Taylor	35.00
25	Michael Olowokandi	40.00
26	Kobe Bryant	400.00
27	Shaquille O'Neal	200.00
28	Tim Hardaway	60.00
29	Alonzo Mourning	50.00
30	Glenn Robinson	50.00
31	Ray Allen	50.00
32	Kevin Garnett	300.00
33	Joe Smith	35.00
34	Stephon Marbury	100.00
35	Keith Van Horn	60.00
36	Patrick Ewing	50.00
37	Latrell Sprewell	75.00
38	Darrell Armstrong	35.00
39	Charles Outlaw	25.00
40	Allen Iverson	200.00
41	Larry Hughes	100.00
42	Jason Kidd	150.00
43	Anfernee Hardaway	150.00
44	Brian Grant	30.00
45	Damon Stoudamire	40.00
46	Jason Williams	150.00
47	Chris Webber	150.00
48	Tim Duncan	300.00
49	David Robinson	75.00
50	Sean Elliott	25.00
51	Gary Payton	75.00
52	Vin Baker	35.00
53	Vince Carter	400.00
54	Tracy McGrady	150.00
55	Karl Malone	75.00
56	John Stockton	50.00
57	Shareef Abdur-Rahim	100.00
58	Mike Bibby	60.00
59	Juwan Howard	40.00
60	Mitch Richmond	40.00
61	*Elton Brand*	250.00
62	*Steve Francis*	300.00
63	*Baron Davis*	75.00
64	*Lamar Odom*	200.00
65	*Jonathan Bender*	125.00
66	*Wally Szczerbiak*	125.00
67	*Richard Hamilton*	75.00
68	*Andre Miller*	75.00
69	*Shawn Marion*	75.00
70	*Jason Terry*	40.00
71	*Trajan Langdon*	40.00
72	*Aleksandar Radojevic*	20.00
73	*Corey Maggette*	125.00
74	*William Avery*	40.00
75	*Galen Young*	20.00
76	*Chris Herren*	30.00
77	*Cal Bowdler*	20.00
78	*James Posey*	50.00
79	*Quincy Lewis*	40.00
80	*Dion Glover*	30.00
81	*Jeff Foster*	20.00
82	*Kenny Thomas*	40.00
83	*Devean George*	30.00
84	*Tim James*	20.00
85	*Vonteego Cummings*	50.00
86	*Jumanie Jones*	20.00
87	*Scott Padgett*	20.00
88	*Obinna Ekezie*	20.00
89	*Ryan Robertson*	20.00
90	*Evan Eschmeyer*	20.00

1999-00 Upper Deck Ovation A Piece of History

This 14-card insert featured a circular piece of game-used basketball on a horizontal design. The cards were numbered with two letters, usually corresponding to the player's initials and inserted 1:352 packs. There was a total of 4,560 A Piece of History cards produced. In addition, Kevin Garnett, Karl Malone, Richard Hamilton, Steve Francis, Shawn Marion and Wally Szczerbiak signed a limited amount of cards, each hand-numbered to that player's jersey number.

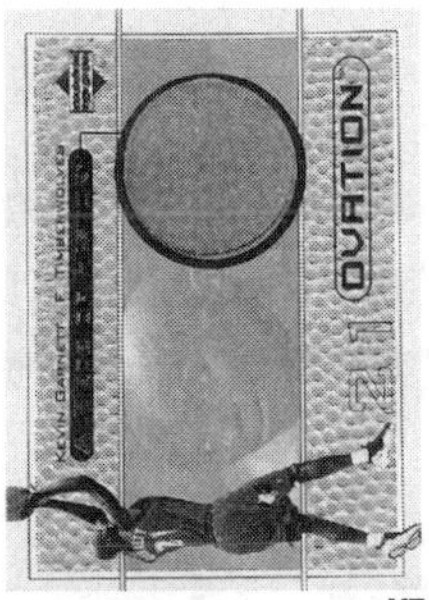

		MT
Common Player:		40.00
Inserted 1:352		
JB	Jonathan Bender	100.00
KB	Kobe Bryant	150.00
BD	Baron Davis	75.00
SF	Steve Francis	125.00
SF-A	Steve Francis	
KG	Kevin Garnett	100.00
KG-A	Kevin Garnett	
RH	Richard Hamilton	50.00
RH-A	Richard Hamilton	
KM	Karl Malone	75.00
KM-A	Karl Malone	
SM	Shawn Marion	50.00
SM-A	Shawn Marion	
AM	Andre Miller	50.00
RM	Reggie Miller	60.00
HO	Hakeem Olajuwon	60.00
WS	Wally Szczerbiak	100.00
WS-A	Wally Szczerbiak	
JS	John Stockton	60.00
JW	Jason Williams	90.00

1999-00 Upper Deck Ovation Curtain Calls

This 10-card insert focused on the accomplishments of certain players during the 1998-99 season. Cards were numbered with a "CC" prefix and inserted 1:9 packs.

		MT
Complete Set (10):		10.00
Common Player:		.50
Inserted 1:9		
CC1	Hakeem Olajuwon	1.00
CC2	Karl Malone	1.00
CC3	Latrell Sprewell	.50
CC4	Allen Iverson	4.00
CC5	Tim Hardaway	.75
CC6	Shaquille O'Neal	3.00
CC7	Jason Kidd	2.00
CC8	Charles Barkley	1.00
CC9	Antonio McDyess	.75
CC10	Gary Payton	1.00

1999-00 Upper Deck Ovation Lead Performers

Lead Performers featured 10 top players who are leaders on the court. The cards were numbered with an "LP" prefix and inserted 1:9 packs.

		MT
Complete Set (10):		20.00
Common Player:		1.50
Inserted 1:9		
LP1	Tim Duncan	4.00
LP2	Kevin Garnett	4.00
LP3	Keith Van Horn	1.00
LP4	Shareef Abdur-Rahim	1.50
LP5	Antoine Walker	1.00
LP6	Shaquille O'Neal	2.50
LP7	Grant Hill	4.00
LP8	Kobe Bryant	5.00
LP9	Allen Iverson	3.00
LP10	Jason Williams	2.50

1999-00 Upper Deck Ovation M.J. Center Stage

MJ Center Stage was devoted to Michael Jordan and included 15 cards, with three tiers of five cards each. The first five cards were silver and seeded 1:9. The second five cards were gold and seeded 1:39. The third five cards (11-15) were rainbow and seeded 1:99 packs. These inserts were numbered with a "CS" prefix.

		MT
Complete Set (15):		175.00
Common Silver (1-5):		4.00
Silver Inserted 1:9		
Common Gold (6-10):		10.00
Gold Inserted 1:39		
Common Rainbow (11-15):		25.00
Rainbow Inserted 1:99		
CS1	Michael Jordan	4.00
CS2	Michael Jordan	4.00
CS3	Michael Jordan	4.00
CS4	Michael Jordan	4.00
CS5	Michael Jordan	4.00
CS6	Michael Jordan	10.00
CS7	Michael Jordan	10.00
CS8	Michael Jordan	10.00
CS9	Michael Jordan	10.00
CS10	Michael Jordan	10.00
CS11	Michael Jordan	25.00
CS12	Michael Jordan	25.00
CS13	Michael Jordan	25.00
CS14	Michael Jordan	25.00
CS15	Michael Jordan	25.00

1999-00 Upper Deck Ovation Premiere Performers

This 10-card insert showcased the top rookies of the season. Premiere Performers were numbered with a "PP" prefix and inserted 1:19 packs.

		MT
Complete Set (10):		40.00
Common Player:		2.00
Inserted 1:19		
PP1	Elton Brand	6.00
PP2	Steve Francis	8.00
PP3	Baron Davis	5.00
PP4	Lamar Odom	10.00
PP5	Jonathan Bender	5.00
PP6	Wally Szczerbiak	8.00
PP7	Richard Hamilton	4.00
PP8	Andre Miller	2.00
PP9	Shawn Marion	4.00
PP10	Jason Terry	2.00

1999-00 Upper Deck Ovation Spotlight

This 10-card insert focused on young players and was inserted 1:3 packs. Ovation Spotlight inserts were numbered with an "OS" prefix.

		MT
Complete Set (10):		12.00
Common Player:		1.00
Inserted 1:3		
OS1	Kevin Garnett	2.50
OS2	Antawn Jamison	1.00
OS3	Kobe Bryant	3.00
OS4	Shareef Abdur-Rahim	1.00
OS5	Keith Van Horn	.75
OS6	Vince Carter	3.00
OS7	Stephon Marbury	1.00
OS8	Paul Pierce	1.25
OS9	Tim Duncan	2.50
OS10	Jason Williams	1.50

1999-00 Upper Deck Ovation Superstar Theatre

This 20-card insert featured many of the top players in the game. Cards were inserted 1:19 packs and numbered with an "ST" prefix.

		MT
Complete Set (20):		125.00
Common Player:		2.00
Inserted 1:19		
ST1	Michael Jordan	30.00
ST2	Vince Carter	15.00
ST3	Kevin Garnett	12.00
ST4	Paul Pierce	8.00
ST5	Jason Williams	10.00
ST6	Tim Duncan	12.00
ST7	Allen Iverson	10.00
ST8	Antawn Jamison	4.00
ST9	Kobe Bryant	15.00
ST10	Grant Hill	12.00
ST11	Antoine Walker	2.00
ST12	Tracy McGrady	4.00
ST13	Shareef Abdur-Rahim	4.00
ST14	Stephon Marbury	4.00
ST15	Jason Kidd	4.00
ST16	Shaquille O'Neal	8.00
ST17	Tim Hardaway	2.00
ST18	Keith Van Horn	2.50
ST19	Gary Payton	2.00
ST20	Karl Malone	2.00

1999-00 UD Retro

This 110-card set was created by Upper Deck and featured a mix of NBA legends, current stars and rookies. Cards were printed with a retro look on a white matte finish and card backs included full statistics. Retro arrived in six-card packs with 24 packs included in a collectible lunch box that featured Michael Jordan, Larry Bird and Julius Erving in 11 different combinations. The set was paralleled in Gold (numbered to 250) and Platinum (numbered to 1) parallel sets and included the following inserts: Epic Jordan, NBA Old School/New School, Distant Replay, NBA Fast Forward and Inkredible.

		MT
Complete Set (110):		50.00
Common Player:		.10
Minor Stars:		.20
Pack (6):		5.00
Wax Box (24):		85.00
1	Michael Jordan	5.00
2	John Havlicek	1.00
3	Antawn Jamison	1.00
4	Chris Webber	1.00
5	Maurice Taylor	.30
6	Kevin Garnett	3.00
7	Walter Davis	.20
8	Kobe Bryant	4.00
9	Tim Duncan	3.00
10	Karl Malone	.60
11	Larry Bird	3.00
12	Juwan Howard	.20
13	Bill Walton	.30
14	Bob Cousy	.75
15	Dave DeBusschere	.30
16	Toni Kukoc	.30
17	Allan Houston	.20
18	Grant Hill	3.00
19	Rik Smits	.10
20	Glenn Robinson	.20
21	Dave Cowens	.20
22	Isaac Austin	.10
23	Derek Anderson	.20
24	Tracy McGrady	1.00
25	Nate Thurmond	.20
26	Dikembe Mutombo	.20
27	Oscar Robertson	1.00
28	Antonio McDyess	.50
29	Jamaal Wilkes	.10
30	Eddie Jones	.40
31	Nick Van Exel	.20
32	Reggie Miller	.20
33	David Thompson	.20
34	Ray Allen	.20
35	Anfernee Hardaway	1.50
36	Brian Grant	.20
37	Allen Iverson	2.50
38	Vince Carter	4.00
39	Mitch Richmond	.20
40	Kareem Abdul-Jabbar	1.50
41	Alonzo Mourning	.40
42	*Jonathan Bender*	3.00
43	Scottie Pippen	1.00
44	George Gervin	.40
45	Shawn Kemp	.40
46	Dave Bing	.10
47	John Starks	.10
48	Earl Monroe	.30
49	Stephon Marbury	1.00
50	Cedric Maxwell	.10
51	Tom Gugliotta	.20
52	David Robinson	.60
53	Shareef Abdur-Rahim	1.00
54	Elvin Hayes	.30
55	Wilt Chamberlain	1.50
56	Willis Reed	.20
57	Kevin McHale	.20
58	Elden Campbell	.10
59	Steve Smith	.20
60	Brent Barry	.10
61	Jerry Stackhouse	.20
62	Otis Birdsong	.10
63	Michael Olowokandi	.50
64	Joe Smith	.20
65	Tim Thomas	.60
66	Rick Barry	.20
67	Jason Williams	2.00
68	Julius Erving	1.50
69	John Stockton	.20
70	*Cal Bowdler*	.30
71	Nate Archibald	.30
72	Elgin Baylor	.75
73	Ron Mercer	.75
74	Damon Stoudamire	.30
75	Jerry West	1.00
76	Michael Finley	.20
77	Charles Barkley	.60
78	Shaquille O'Neal	1.50
79	Paul Pierce	1.50
80	Keith Van Horn	.75
81	Jason Kidd	1.00
82	Gary Payton	.60
83	James Worthy	.30
84	Mike Bibby	.60
85	Bill Russell	1.50
86	Wes Unseld	.20
87	Robert Parish	.30
88	Walt Frazier	.30
89	Antoine Walker	.60
90	Steve Nash	.10
91	Moses Malone	.30
92	Hakeem Olajuwon	.60
93	Tim Hardaway	.30
94	Patrick Ewing	.20
95	Vin Baker	.20
96	*Trajan Langdon*	1.00
97	*Ron Artest*	1.50
98	*James Posey*	1.25
99	*Shawn Marion*	3.00
100	*Jumanie Jones*	.50
101	*William Avery*	.75
102	*Corey Maggette*	2.50
103	*Andre Miller*	2.50
104	*Jason Terry*	1.50
105	*Wally Szczerbiak*	2.00
106	*Richard Hamilton*	2.00
107	*Elton Brand*	3.00
108	*Baron Davis*	2.50
109	*Steve Francis*	6.00
110	*Lamar Odom*	5.00

1999-00 UD Retro Gold

This 110-card parallel set added gold foil to the logo and player's name, and also arrived sequentially numbered to 250 sets.

	MT
Common Player:	3.00
Gold Stars:	15x-30x
Gold Rookies:	10x-20x
Production 250 Sets	

1999-00 UD Retro Distant Replay

This 15-card insert set features retired stars from the NBA. Cards contained a framed action shot, with a head shot in the lower right corner. Cards were inserted 1:11 packs and numbered with a "D" prefix. Parallel versions also existed and were numbered to 100 sets.

		MT
Complete Set (10):		25.00
Common Player:		.50
Inserted 1:11		
Complete Parallel Set (10):		150.00
Common Parallel:		3.00
Parallels:		3x-6x
Production 100 Sets		
D1	Michael Jordan	10.00
D2	Kareem Abdul-Jabbar	3.00
D3	Bill Russell	3.00
D4	Julius Erving	3.00
D5	George Gervin	.50
D6	Moses Malone	.50
D7	Larry Bird	6.00
D8	Jerry West	1.50
D9	Oscar Robertson	2.00
D10	Elgin Baylor	1.00

1999-00 UD Retro Epic Jordan

Epic Jordan was a 10-card insert featuring Michael Jordan. Cards featured the word "Epic" running down the left side in a red box, while "Jordan" ran across the bottom in a black box. These were inserted 1:23 packs and numbered with a "J" prefix. Parallel versions also existed and were sequentially numbered to 50 sets.

		MT
Complete Set (10):		90.00
Common Player:		10.00
Inserted 1:23		
Common Parallel:		100.00
Parallels:		10x
Production 50 Sets		
J1	Michael Jordan	10.00
J2	Michael Jordan	10.00
J3	Michael Jordan	10.00
J4	Michael Jordan	10.00
J5	Michael Jordan	10.00
J6	Michael Jordan	10.00
J7	Michael Jordan	10.00
J8	Michael Jordan	10.00
J9	Michael Jordan	10.00
J10	Michael Jordan	10.00

1999-00 UD Retro Fast Forward

This 15-card set featured the only "new wave" looking insert of Retro, and the player selection included young stars. Fast Forward cards were inserted 1:23 packs and were numbered with an "F" prefix.

		MT
Complete Set (15):		50.00
Common Player:		1.00
Inserted 1:23		
F1	Kevin Garnett	8.00
F2	Kobe Bryant	10.00
F3	Keith Van Horn	2.00
F4	Allen Iverson	6.00
F5	Vince Carter	8.00
F6	Paul Pierce	5.00
F7	Shareef Abdur-Rahim	2.00
F8	Jason Williams	6.00
F9	Tim Duncan	8.00
F10	Shaquille O'Neal	5.00
F11	Scottie Pippen	3.00
F12	Anfernee Hardaway	5.00
F13	Antawn Jamison	3.00
F14	Antonio McDyess	1.00
F15	Stephon Marbury	4.00

1999-00 UD Retro Inkredible

This autographed insert out of Retro contained 24 players and was inserted 1:23 packs. The cards featured the insert name across the top and a large "Retro" logo space in which the autograph appeared. Cards were numbered on the back with two letters, usually corresponding to the player's initials. A parallel version existed in which cards were hand-numbered to the player's jersey number.

		MT
Common Player:		5.00
Inserted 1:23		
CA	Cory Alexander	5.00
NA	Nate Archibald	15.00
DA	Darrell Armstrong	20.00
MB	Mookie Blaylock	5.00
VC	Vince Carter	200.00
WC	Wilt Chamberlain	350.00
BC	Bob Cousy	35.00
WF	Walt Frazier	30.00
GG	George Gervin	20.00
BG	Brian Grant	12.00
AH	Anfernee Hardaway	100.00
JH	John Havlicek	35.00
EH	Elvin Hayes	15.00
MJ	Mark Jackson	8.00
AJ	Antawn Jamison	35.00
TK	Toni Kukoc	25.00
RL	Raef LaFrentz	20.00
GR	Glen Rice	20.00
JR	Jalen Rose	12.00
BR	Bill Russell	300.00
ES	Eric Snow	8.00
MT	Maurice Taylor	12.00
RT	Robert Traylor	15.00
JW	Jerry West	50.00

1999-00 UD Retro Inkredible II

This parallel version of Inkredible featured a gold-tinted card and was hand-numbered to the player's jersey number.

		MT
Complete Set (26):		
Common Player:		
CA	Cory Alexander (7)	
NA	Nate Archibald (7)	
DA	Darrell Armstrong (10)	
MB	Mookie Blaylock (10)	
VC	Vince Carter (15)	
WC	Wilt Chamberlain (13)	
BC	Bob Cousy (14)	
JE	Julius Erving (6)	
WF	Walt Frazier (10)	
GG	George Gervin (44)	
BG	Brian Grant (44)	
AH	Anfernee Hardaway (1)	
JH	John Havlicek (17)	
EH	Elvin Hayes (11)	
MJ	Mark Jackson (13)	
AJ	Antawn Jamison (7)	
MJ	Michael Jordan (23)	
TK	Toni Kukoc (7)	
RL	Raef LaFrentz (45)	
GR	Glen Rice (41)	
JR	Jalen Rose (5)	
BR	Bill Russell (6)	
ES	Eric Snow (20)	
MT	Maurice Taylor (23)	
RT	Robert Traylor (54)	
JW	Jerry West (44)	

1999-00 UD Retro Lunch Boxes

Instead of the traditional cardboard boxes, Retro arrived in 11 different collectible lunch boxes featuring Michael Jordan, Larry Bird and Julius Erving.

	MT
Complete Set (11):	90.00
Common Player:	8.00
Michael Jordan #1	10.00
Michael Jordan #2	10.00
Michael Jordan #3	10.00
Julius Erving	8.00
Larry Bird	12.00
Michael Jordan #1, Julius Erving	12.00
Michael Jordan #2, Larry Bird	15.00
Julius Erving, Larry Bird	10.00
Michael Jordan #1, Michael Jordan #2	10.00
Michael Jordan #1, Michael Jordan #3	10.00
Michael Jordan #2, Michael Jordan #3	10.00

1999-00 UD Retro Old School/New School

Old School/New School was 30-card insert, with cards 1-15 featuring retired stars ("NBA Old School") and cards 16-30 featuring current stars ("NBA New School"). These were numbered with an "S" prefix and inserted 1:3 packs. A parallel version also existed and was sequentially numbered to 500 sets.

		MT
Complete Set (30):		45.00
Common Player:		.25
Inserted 1:3		
Common Parallel:		2.50
Parallels:		5x-10x
Production 500 Sets		
S1	Michael Jordan	8.00
S2	Wilt Chamberlain	2.00
S3	Oscar Robertson	1.50
S4	Julius Erving	2.00
S5	George Gervin	.50
S6	John Havlicek	1.00
S7	Elgin Baylor	.75
S8	Earl Monroe	.50
S9	Jerry West	.75
S10	Larry Bird	4.00
S11	Elvin Hayes	.50
S12	Moses Malone	.40
S13	Bill Walton	.40
S14	Kareem Abdul-Jabbar	1.50
S15	Bill Russell	1.50
S16	Kobe Bryant	5.00
S17	Allen Iverson	2.50
S18	Stephon Marbury	1.00
S19	Shaquille O'Neal	1.50
S20	Kevin Garnett	3.00
S21	Keith Van Horn	.75
S22	Jason Williams	2.00
S23	Paul Pierce	1.50
S24	Vince Carter	3.00
S25	Tim Duncan	3.00
S26	Antoine Walker	.60
S27	Shareef Abdur-Rahim	.75
S28	Ray Allen	.25
S29	Anfernee Hardaway	1.50
S30	Grant Hill	3.00

1999-00 Upper Deck Ultimate Victory

Ultimate Victory consisted of 90 veterans, 30 MJ Greatest Hits, which were seeded 1:2 packs, and 30 Ultimate Rookies, which were seeded 1:4 packs. The first 120 cards were reprints from Victory Basketball, with a chromium finish, while the Ultimate Rookies were designed specifically for this product. Two parallel sets existed - Victory Collection and Ultimate Collection. Inserts include: Court Impact, Dr. J. Glory Days, Got Skills?, MJ's World Famous, Scorin' Legion, Surface to Air and Ultimate Fabrics.

		MT
Complete Set (150):		200.00
Common Player:		.25
Minor Stars:		.40
Jordan GH (91-120)		2.00
Common Rookie (121-150):		2.00
Inserted 1:4		
Pack (5):		5.00
Wax Box (24):		60.00
1	Dikembe Mutombo	.40
2	Alan Henderson	.25
3	LaPhonso Ellis	.25
4	Kenny Anderson	.40
5	Antoine Walker	.60
6	Paul Pierce	1.50
7	Elden Campbell	.25
8	Eddie Jones	.75
9	David Wesley	.25
10	Michael Jordan	8.00
11	Kornel David	.25
12	Toni Kukoc	.60
13	Shawn Kemp	.40
14	Brevin Knight	.25
15	Zydrunas Ilgauskas	.25
16	Michael Finley	.40
17	Shawn Bradley	.25
18	Dirk Nowitzki	1.00
19	Antonio McDyess	.60
20	Nick Van Exel	.40
21	Ron Mercer	.75
22	Grant Hill	4.00
23	Lindsey Hunter	.25
24	Jerry Stackhouse	.50
25	John Starks	.25
26	Antawn Jamison	1.00
27	Mookie Blaylock	.25
28	Hakeem Olajuwon	.75
29	Cuttino Mobley	.40
30	Charles Barkley	.75
31	Reggie Miller	.40
32	Rik Smits	.25
33	Jalen Rose	.40
34	Maurice Taylor	.40
35	Tyrone Nesby	.40
36	Michael Olowokandi	.60
37	Kobe Bryant	5.00
38	Shaquille O'Neal	2.50
39	Glen Rice	.40
40	Robert Horry	.25
41	Tim Hardaway	.60
42	Alonzo Mourning	.50
43	Jamal Mashburn	.40
44	Ray Allen	.50
45	Glenn Robinson	.40
46	Robert Traylor	.40
47	Kevin Garnett	4.00
48	Joe Smith	.25
49	Bobby Jackson	.25
50	Keith Van Horn	.75
51	Stephon Marbury	.25
52	Jayson Williams	.25
53	Patrick Ewing	.40
54	Allan Houston	.40
55	Latrell Sprewell	.60
56	Marcus Camby	.50
57	Darrell Armstrong	.40
58	Matt Harpring	.40
59	Charles Outlaw	.25
60	Allen Iverson	3.00
61	Theo Ratliff	.25
62	Larry Hughes	.75
63	Jason Kidd	1.50
64	Tom Gugliotta	.40
65	Anfernee Hardaway	2.50
66	Scottie Pippen	1.50
67	Damon Stoudamire	.50
68	Brian Grant	.25
69	Jason Williams	2.50
70	Vlade Divac	.25
71	Chris Webber	1.50
72	Tim Duncan	4.00
73	Sean Elliott	.25
74	David Robinson	.75
75	Avery Johnson	.25
76	Gary Payton	.75
77	Vin Baker	.40
78	Brent Barry	.25
79	Vince Carter	5.00
80	Doug Christie	.25
81	Tracy McGrady	1.50
82	Karl Malone	.75
83	John Stockton	.40
84	Bryon Russell	.25
85	Shareef Abdur-Rahim	1.00
86	Mike Bibby	.75
87	Felipe Lopez	.40
88	Juwan Howard	.40
89	Rod Strickland	.40
90	Mitch Richmond	.40
91	Michael Jordan	2.00
92	Michael Jordan	2.00
93	Michael Jordan	2.00
94	Michael Jordan	2.00
95	Michael Jordan	2.00
96	Michael Jordan	2.00
97	Michael Jordan	2.00
98	Michael Jordan	2.00
99	Michael Jordan	2.00
100	Michael Jordan	2.00
101	Michael Jordan	2.00
102	Michael Jordan	2.00
103	Michael Jordan	2.00
104	Michael Jordan	2.00
105	Michael Jordan	2.00
106	Michael Jordan	2.00
107	Michael Jordan	2.00
108	Michael Jordan	2.00
109	Michael Jordan	2.00
110	Michael Jordan	2.00
111	Michael Jordan	2.00
112	Michael Jordan	2.00
113	Michael Jordan	2.00
114	Michael Jordan	2.00
115	Michael Jordan	2.00
116	Michael Jordan	2.00
117	Michael Jordan	2.00
118	Michael Jordan	2.00
119	Michael Jordan	2.00
120	Michael Jordan	2.00
121	*Elton Brand*	15.00
122	*Steve Francis*	40.00
123	*Baron Davis*	12.00
124	*Lamar Odom*	25.00
125	*Jonathan Bender*	15.00
126	*Wally Szczerbiak*	10.00
127	*Richard Hamilton*	10.00
128	*Andre Miller*	12.00
129	*Shawn Marion*	15.00
130	*Jason Terry*	6.00
131	*Trajan Langdon*	5.00
132	*Aleksandar Radojevic*	2.00
133	*Corey Maggette*	12.00
134	*William Avery*	4.00
135	*Ron Artest*	6.00
136	*Cal Bowdler*	2.00
137	*James Posey*	5.00
138	*Quincy Lewis*	3.00
139	*Dion Glover*	2.50
140	*Jeff Foster*	2.00
141	*Kenny Thomas*	3.00
142	*Devean George*	5.00
143	*Tim James*	2.50
144	*Vonteego Cummings*	4.00
145	*Jumaine Jones*	2.50
146	*Scott Padgett*	2.00
147	*John Celestand*	2.50
148	*Adrian Griffin*	3.00
149	*Chris Herren*	2.50
150	*Anthony Carter*	4.00

1999-00 Upper Deck Ultimate Victory Ultimate Collection

This 150-card parallel set reprinted every card with a prismatic foil pattern in the background. Cards were sequentially numbered to 100 on the front in silver foil.

	MT
Common Player:	6.00
Ultimate Cards:	15x-25x
Ultimate Rookies:	3x-6x
Production 100 Sets	

1999-00 Upper Deck Ultimate Victory Collection

Victory Collection paralled all 150 cards in the base set with a foil-highlighted background. The first 120 cards were inserted 1:12 packs, while Victory Collection rookies were seeded 1:24 packs.

	MT
Common Collection:	1.50
Collection Cards:	3x-6x
Inserted 1:12	
Collection Rookies:	1.5x
Inserted 1:24	

1999-00 Upper Deck Ultimate Victory Court Impact

This 10-card insert featured stars over a holographic background with the free throw circle in the background. Court Impact cards were numbered with a "C" prefix and inserted 1:24 packs.

		MT
Complete Set (10):		50.00
Common Player:		1.00
Inserted 1:24		
C1	Michael Jordan	15.00
C2	Vince Carter	10.00
C3	Kobe Bryant	10.00
C4	Kevin Garnett	8.00
C5	Tim Duncan	8.00
C6	Jason Williams	5.00
C7	Grant Hill	8.00
C8	Keith Van Horn	1.50
C9	Allen Iverson	6.00
C10	Karl Malone	1.00

1999-00 Upper Deck Ultimate Victory Dr. J-Glory Days

This eight-card insert set was devoted to Julius Erving and featured a retro look with Dr. J over a silver, holographic background. Cards were inserted 1:24 packs and numbered with a "DR" prefix.

		MT
Complete Set (8):		30.00
Common Player:		5.00
Inserted 1:24		
DR1	Julius Erving	5.00
DR2	Julius Erving	5.00
DR3	Julius Erving	5.00
DR4	Julius Erving	5.00
DR5	Julius Erving	5.00
DR6	Julius Erving	5.00
DR7	Julius Erving	5.00
DR8	Julius Erving	5.00

1999-00 Upper Deck Ultimate Victory Got Skills?

Got Skills? was an eight-card insert set that featured some of the top guards in the league. Cards were numbered with a "GS" prefix and inserted 1:24 packs.

		MT
Complete Set (8):		15.00
Common Player:		.50
Inserted 1:24		
GS1	Kevin Garnett	8.00
GS2	Tim Hardaway	.75
GS3	Mike Bibby	1.00
GS4	Stephon Marbury	2.00
GS5	Reggie Miller	.50
GS6	Jason Williams	5.00
GS7	Antoine Walker	.75
GS8	Jason Kidd	3.00

1999-00 Upper Deck Ultimate Victory MJ's World Famous

MJ's World Famous was a 12-card insert devoted entirely to Michael Jordan. Cards were numbered with an "MJ" prefix and inserted 1:24 packs.

		MT
Complete Set (12):		100.00
Common Player:		10.00
Inserted 1:24		
MJ1	Michael Jordan	10.00
MJ2	Michael Jordan	10.00
MJ3	Michael Jordan	10.00
MJ4	Michael Jordan	10.00
MJ5	Michael Jordan	10.00
MJ6	Michael Jordan	10.00
MJ7	Michael Jordan	10.00
MJ8	Michael Jordan	10.00
MJ9	Michael Jordan	10.00
MJ10	Michael Jordan	10.00
MJ11	Michael Jordan	10.00
MJ12	Michael Jordan	10.00

1999-00 Upper Deck Ultimate Victory Scorin' Legion

This 10-card insert showcased some of the most potent scorers around the league. Cards were numbered with an "SL" prefix and inserted 1:12 packs.

		MT
Complete Set (10):		20.00
Common Player:		.50
Inserted 1:12		
SL1	Tim Duncan	6.00
SL2	Karl Malone	1.00
SL3	Stephon Marbury	2.00
SL4	Shaquille O'Neal	4.00
SL5	Antonio McDyess	.50
SL6	Gary Payton	1.00
SL7	Allen Iverson	5.00
SL8	Keith Van Horn	1.50
SL9	Shareef Abdur-Rahim	2.00
SL10	Grant Hill	6.00

1999-00 Upper Deck Ultimate Victory Surface to Air

This 12-card insert captured some of the top leapers in the game. Cards were numbered with an "SA" prefix and inserted 1:6 packs.

		MT
Complete Set (12):		15.00
Common Player:		.50
Inserted 1:6		
SA1	Vince Carter	5.00
SA2	Antawn Jamison	1.00
SA3	Eddie Jones	1.00
SA4	Anfernee Hardaway	2.50
SA5	Latrell Sprewell	.75
SA6	Antonio McDyess	.50
SA7	Michael Finley	.50
SA8	Kobe Bryant	5.00
SA9	Chris Webber	1.50
SA10	Shawn Kemp	.40
SA11	Ray Allen	.75
SA12	Shaquille O'Neal	2.50

1999-00 Upper Deck Ultimate Victory Ultimate Fabrics

This three-card insert featured game-used jerseys from Julius Erving, Wilt Chamberlain and one with Erving and Kobe Bryant. The cards were numbered with a "UF" prefix and sequentially numbered, with Chamberlain numbered to 100, Erving numbered to 300 and the Erving/Bryant card numbered to 25. In addition, Erving signed six (his jersey number) of his Ultimate Fabrics cards.

		MT
Common Player:		250.00
UF1	Julius Erving/300	250.00
UF1A	Julius Erving Auto/6	
UF2	Wilt Chamberlain/100	500.00
UF3	Julius Erving, Kobe Bryant/25	1200.

1999-00 Upper Deck Victory

This 440-card release from Upper Deck was distributed exclusively in retail locations and arrived in 12-card packs for 99 cents. The cards featured a traditional white border, while the set was made up of eight different subsets, including: 33 Check It Out, 20 Rookie Flashback, 30 Dynamite Dunks, 15 Court Catalysts, 15 Power Corps, 15 Scoring Circle, 50 Jordan's Greatest Hits and 10 1999 Rookies. No inserts were available in this product, with the exception of a web promo card inserted into each pack.

		MT
Complete Set (440):		75.00
Common Player:		.10
Minor Stars:		.20
Common Jordan (381-430):		.50
Pack (11):		.99
Wax Box (36):		20.00
1	Hawks Check It Out!	.10
2	Steve Smith	.20
3	Dikembe Mutombo	.20
4	Ed Gray	.10
5	Alan Henderson	.10
6	LaPhonso Ellis	.20
7	Roshown McLeod	.20
8	Bimbo Coles	.10
9	Chris Crawford	.10
10	Anthony Johnson	.10
11	Celtics Check It Out!	.10
12	Kenny Anderson	.20
13	Antoine Walker	.75
14	Greg Minor	.10
15	Tony Battie	.10
16	Ron Mercer	.75
17	Paul Pierce	1.50
18	Vitaly Potapenko	.10
19	Dana Barros	.10
20	Walter McCarty	.10
21	Hornets Check It Out!	.10
22	Elden Campbell	.10
23	Eddie Jones	.30
24	David Wesley	.10
25	Bobby Phills	.10
26	Derrick Coleman	.20
27	Anthony Mason	.20
28	Brad Miller	.20
29	Eldridge Recasner	.10
30	Ricky Davis	.30
31	Bulls Check It Out!	.20
32	Michael Jordan	5.00
33	Brent Barry	.10
34	Randy Brown	.10
35	Keith Booth	.10
36	Kornel David	.10
37	Mark Bryant	.10
38	Toni Kukoc	.30
39	Rusty LaRue	.10
40	Cavaliers Check It Out!	.10
41	Shawn Kemp	.50
42	Wesley Person	.10
43	Johnny Newman	.10
44	Derek Anderson	.20
45	Brevin Knight	.10
46	Bob Sura	.10
47	Andrew DeClercq	.10
48	Zydrunas Ilgauskas	.20
49	Danny Ferry	.10
50	Mavericks Check It Out!	.10
51	Michael Finley	.25
52	Robert Pack	.10
53	Shawn Bradley	.10
54	John Williams	.10
55	Hubert Davis	.10
56	Dirk Nowitzki	.30
57	Steve Nash	.10
58	Chris Anstey	.10
59	Erick Strickland	.10
60	Nuggets Check It Out!	.10
61	Antonio McDyess	.40
62	Nick Van Exel	.20
63	Bryant Stith	.10
64	Chauncey Billups	.20
65	Danny Fortson	.10
66	Eric Williams	.10
67	Eric Washington	.10
68	Raef LaFrentz	.40
69	Johnny Taylor	.20
70	Pistons Check It Out!	.10
71	Grant Hill	2.00
72	Lindsey Hunter	.10
73	Bison Dele	.10
74	Loy Vaught	.10
75	Jerome Williams	.10
76	Jerry Stackhouse	.20
77	Christian Laettner	.20
78	Jud Buechler	.10
79	Don Reid	.10
80	Warriors Check It Out!	.40
81	John Starks	.10
82	Antawn Jamison	.75
83	Adonal Foyle	.10
84	Jason Caffey	.10
85	Donyell Marshall	.10
86	Chris Mills	.10
87	Tony Delk	.10
88	Mookie Blaylock	.10
89	Rockets Check It Out!	.20
90	Hakeem Olajuwon	.50
91	Scottie Pippen	.75
92	Charles Barkley	.40
93	Bryce Drew	.20
94	Cuttino Mobley	.20
95	Othella Harrington	.10
96	Matt Maloney	.10
97	Michael Dickerson	.30
98	Matt Bullard	.10
99	Pacers Check It Out!	.10
100	Reggie Miller	.20
101	Rik Smits	.10
102	Jalen Rose	.20
103	Antonio Davis	.10
104	Mark Jackson	.10
105	Sam Perkins	.10
106	Travis Best	.10
107	Dale Davis	.10
108	Chris Mullin	.20
109	Clippers Check It Out!	.20
110	Maurice Taylor	.30
111	Tyrone Nesby	.20
112	Lamond Murray	.10
113	Darrick Martin	.10
114	Michael Olowokandi	.40
115	Rodney Rogers	.10
116	Eric Piatkowski	.10
117	Lorenzen Wright	.10
118	Brian Skinner	.20
119	Lakers Check It Out!	1.25
120	Kobe Bryant	2.50
121	Shaquille O'Neal	1.50
122	Derek Fisher	.10
123	Tyronn Lue	.25
124	Travis Knight	.10
125	Glen Rice	.20
126	Derek Harper	.10
127	Robert Horry	.10
128	Rick Fox	.10
129	Heat Check It Out!	.20
130	Tim Hardaway	.30
131	Alonzo Mourning	.30
132	Keith Askins	.10
133	Jamal Mashburn	.20
134	P.J. Brown	.10
135	Clarence Weatherspoon	.10
136	Terry Porter	.10
137	Dan Majerle	.10
138	Voshon Lenard	.10
139	Bucks Check It Out!	.10
140	Ray Allen	.30
141	Vinny Del Negro	.10
142	Glenn Robinson	.20
143	Dell Curry	.10
144	Sam Cassell	.20
145	Haywoode Workman	.10
146	Armen Gilliam	.10
147	Robert Traylor	.40
148	Chris Gatling	.10
149	T-Wolves Check It Out!	1.00
150	Kevin Garnett	2.00
151	Malik Sealy	.10
152	Radoslav Nesterovic	.20
153	Joe Smith	.20
154	Sam Mitchell	.10
155	Dean Garrett	.10
156	Anthony Peeler	.10
157	Tom Hammonds	.10
158	Bobby Jackson	.10
159	Nets Check It Out!	.10
160	Keith Van Horn	.75
161	Stephon Marbury	1.25
162	Jayson Williams	.20
163	Kendall Gill	.10
164	Kerry Kittles	.20
165	Jamie Feick	.10
166	Scott Burrell	.10
167	Lucious Harris	.10
168	Knicks Check It Out!	.20
169	Patrick Ewing	.20
170	Allan Houston	.20
171	Latrell Sprewell	.20
172	Kurt Thomas	.10
173	Larry Johnson	.10
174	Chris Childs	.10
175	Marcus Camby	.30
176	Charlie Ward	.10
177	Chris Dudley	.10
178	Magic Check It Out!	.10
179	Anfernee Hardaway	1.50
180	Darrell Armstrong	.20
181	Nick Anderson	.20
182	Horace Grant	.10
183	Isaac Austin	.10
184	Matt Harpring	.25
185	Michael Doleac	.25
186	Charles Outlaw	.10
187	76ers Check It Out!	.75
188	Allen Iverson	2.00
189	Theo Ratliff	.20
190	Matt Geiger	.10
191	Larry Hughes	.50
192	Tyrone Hill	.10
193	George Lynch	.10
194	Eric Snow	.10
195	Aaron McKie	.10
196	Harvey Grant	.10
197	Suns Check It Out!	.40
198	Jason Kidd	.75
199	Tom Gugliotta	.20
200	Rex Chapman	.10
201	Clifford Robinson	.10
202	Luc Longley	.10
203	Danny Manning	.10
204	Pat Garrity	.20
205	George McCloud	.10
206	Toby Bailey	.20
207	Trail Blazers Check It Out!	.10
208	Rasheed Wallace	.20
209	Arvydas Sabonis	.10
210	Damon Stoudamire	.25
211	Brian Grant	.20
212	Isaiah Rider	.20
213	Walt Williams	.10
214	Jim Jackson	.10
215	Greg Anthony	.10
216	Stacey Augmon	.10
217	Kings Check It Out!	.10
218	Jason Williams	1.50
219	Vlade Divac	.20
220	Chris Webber	.75
221	Nick Anderson	.10
222	Predrag Stojakovic	.20
223	Tariq Abdul-Wahad	.10
224	Vernon Maxwell	.10
225	Lawrence Funderburke	.10
226	Jon Barry	.10
227	Spurs Check It Out!	.20
228	Tim Duncan	2.00
229	Sean Elliott	.10
230	David Robinson	.40
231	Mario Elie	.10
232	Avery Johnson	.10
233	Steve Kerr	.10
234	Malik Rose	.10
235	Jaren Jackson	.10
236	SuperSonics Check It Out!	.10
237	Gary Payton	.40
238	Vin Baker	.25
239	Detlef Schrempf	.20
240	Hersey Hawkins	.10
241	Dale Ellis	.10
242	Rashard Lewis	.40
243	Billy Owens	.10
244	Aaron Williams	.10
245	Raptors Check It Out!	1.00
246	Vince Carter	2.50
247	John Wallace	.10
248	Doug Christie	.10
249	Tracy McGrady	.75
250	Kevin Willis	.10
251	Michael Stewart	.10
252	Dee Brown	.10
253	John Thomas	.10
254	Alvin Williams	.10
255	Jazz Check It Out!	.20
256	Karl Malone	.40
257	John Stockton	.20
258	Jacque Vaughn	.10
259	Bryon Russell	.10
260	Howard Eisley	.10
261	Greg Ostertag	.10
262	Adam Keefe	.10
263	Todd Fuller	.10
264	Grizzlies Check It Out!	.40
265	Shareef Abdur-Rahim	.75
266	Mike Bibby	.60
267	Bryant Reeves	.10
268	Felipe Lopez	.30
269	Cherokee Parks	.10
270	Michael Smith	.10
271	Tony Massenburg	.10
272	Rodrick Rhodes	.10
273	Wizards Check It Out!	.10
274	Juwan Howard	.20
275	Rod Strickland	.20
276	Mitch Richmond	.20
277	Otis Thorpe	.10
278	Calbert Cheaney	.10
279	Tracy Murray	.10
280	Ben Wallace	.10
281	Terry Davis	.10
282	Michael Jordan	2.00
283	Reggie Miller	.10
284	Dikembe Mutombo	.10
285	Patrick Ewing	.10
286	Allan Houston	.10
287	Danny Manning	.10
288	Jalen Rose	.10
289	Rasheed Wallace	.10
290	Jerry Stackhouse	.10
291	Damon Stoudamire	.10
292	Kenny Anderson	.10
293	Shawn Kemp	.20
294	Vlade Divac	.10
295	Larry Johnson	.10
296	Jamal Mashburn	.10
297	Ron Harper	.10
298	Steve Smith	.10
299	Kendall Gill	.10
300	Chris Mullin	.10
301	Robert Horry	.10
302	Dikembe Mutombo	.10
303	Ron Mercer	.40
304	Eddie Jones	.20
305	Toni Kukoc	.20
306	Derek Anderson	.10
307	Shawn Bradley	.10
308	Danny Fortson	.10
309	Bison Dele	.10
310	Antawn Jamison	.40
311	Scottie Pippen	.40
312	Reggie Miller	.10
313	Maurice Taylor	.20
314	Glen Rice	.10
315	Alonzo Mourning	.20
316	Glenn Robinson	.10
317	Anthony Peeler	.10
318	Kerry Kittles	.10
319	Latrell Sprewell	.10
320	Darrell Armstrong	.10
321	Larry Hughes	.25
322	Tom Gugliotta	.10
323	Brian Grant	.10
324	Chris Webber	.40
325	David Robinson	.20
326	Vin Baker	.10
327	Vince Carter	1.00
328	Bryon Russell	.10
329	Felipe Lopez	.20
330	Juwan Howard	.10
331	Michael Jordan	2.00
332	Jason Kidd	.40
333	Rod Strickland	.10
334	Stephon Marbury	.50
335	Gary Payton	.20
336	Mark Jackson	.10
337	John Stockton	.10
338	Brevin Knight	.10
339	Bobby Jackson	.10
340	Nick Van Exel	.10
341	Tim Hardaway	.10
342	Darrell Armstrong	.10
343	Avery Johnson	.10
344	Mike Bibby	.30
345	Damon Stoudamire	.10
346	Jason Williams	.75
347	Allen Iverson	1.00
348	Kobe Bryant	1.50
349	Karl Malone	.20
350	Keith Van Horn	.30
351	Kevin Garnett	1.00
352	Antoine Walker	.40
353	Tim Duncan	1.00
354	Scottie Pippen	.40
355	Paul Pierce	.75
356	Michael Finley	.20
357	Shaquille O'Neal	.75
358	Grant Hill	1.00
359	Jason Williams	.75
360	Antonio McDyess	.20
361	Shareef Abdur-Rahim	.40
362	Allen Iverson	1.00
363	Shaquille O'Neal	.75
364	Karl Malone	.20
365	Shareef Abdur-Rahim	.40
366	Keith Van Horn	.30
367	Tim Duncan	1.00
368	Gary Payton	.20
369	Stephon Marbury	.40
370	Antonio McDyess	.20
371	Grant Hill	1.00
372	Kevin Garnett	1.00
373	Shawn Kemp	.20
374	Kobe Bryant	1.50
375	Michael Finley	.20
376	Vince Carter	1.00
377	Checklist 1-110	.10
378	Checklist 111-220	.10
379	Checklist 221-330	.10
380	Checklist 331-440	.10
381	Jordan's Greatest Hits	.50
382	Jordan's Greatest Hits	.50
383	Jordan's Greatest Hits	.50
384	Jordan's Greatest Hits	.50
385	Jordan's Greatest Hits	.50
386	Jordan's Greatest Hits	.50
387	Jordan's Greatest Hits	.50
388	Jordan's Greatest Hits	.50
389	Jordan's Greatest Hits	.50
390	Jordan's Greatest Hits	.50
391	Jordan's Greatest Hits	.50
392	Jordan's Greatest Hits	.50
393	Jordan's Greatest Hits	.50
394	Jordan's Greatest Hits	.50
395	Jordan's Greatest Hits	.50
396	Jordan's Greatest Hits	.50
397	Jordan's Greatest Hits	.50
398	Jordan's Greatest Hits	.50
399	Jordan's Greatest Hits	.50
400	Jordan's Greatest Hits	.50
401	Jordan's Greatest Hits	.50
402	Jordan's Greatest Hits	.50
403	Jordan's Greatest Hits	.50
404	Jordan's Greatest Hits	.50
405	Jordan's Greatest Hits	.50
406	Jordan's Greatest Hits	.50
407	Jordan's Greatest Hits	.50
408	Jordan's Greatest Hits	.50
409	Jordan's Greatest Hits	.50
410	Jordan's Greatest Hits	.50
411	Jordan's Greatest Hits	.50
412	Jordan's Greatest Hits	.50
413	Jordan's Greatest Hits	.50
414	Jordan's Greatest Hits	.50
415	Jordan's Greatest Hits	.50
416	Jordan's Greatest Hits	.50
417	Jordan's Greatest Hits	.50
418	Jordan's Greatest Hits	.50
419	Jordan's Greatest Hits	.50
420	Jordan's Greatest Hits	.50
421	Jordan's Greatest Hits	.50
422	Jordan's Greatest Hits	.50
423	Jordan's Greatest Hits	.50
424	Jordan's Greatest Hits	.50
425	Jordan's Greatest Hits	.50
426	Jordan's Greatest Hits	.50
427	Jordan's Greatest Hits	.50
428	Jordan's Greatest Hits	.50
429	Jordan's Greatest Hits	.50
430	Jordan's Greatest Hits	.50
431	*Elton Brand*	6.00
432	*Steve Francis*	10.00
433	*Baron Davis*	4.00
434	*Lamar Odom*	8.00
435	*Wally Szczerbiak*	3.00
436	*Richard Hamilton*	3.00
437	*Andre Miller*	4.00
438	*Shawn Marion*	6.00
439	*Jason Terry*	2.50
440	*Corey Maggette*	4.00

2000 Upper Deck Employee Game Jersey

This postcard sized card was given out to Upper Deck employees and media outlets as a "thank you" gift. The card featured a piece of a santa suit worn by Kobe Bryant. The cards were unnumbered on the back. There were 25 hand-numbered autographed versions also.

		MT
NNO	Kobe Bryant	100.00
NNO	Kobe Bryant Auto/25	750.00

2000 Upper Deck Lakers Championship Jumbos

This 10-card set was released soon after the Lakers won the NBA Championship and was issued in four-card packs, which carried a SRP of $20. Cards in the set were postcard sized and two inserts were included - a Kobe Bryant jersey card, which was numbered to 100, and an autographed jersey card of Bryant, which was numbered to 8.

		MT
Complete Set (11):		25.00
Common Player:		1.00
1	Shaquille O'Neal	5.00
2	Kobe Bryant	10.00
3	Glen Rice	2.00
4	A.C. Green	1.00
5	Ron Harper	2.00
6	Robert Horry	1.00
7	Derek Fisher	1.00
8	Rick Fox	1.00
9	Kobe Bryant	10.00
10	Team Photo	5.00
11	Kobe Bryant Jersey/100	1000.

2000 Upper Deck National Kobe Bryant

This 10-card set was distributed at the 2000 National Convention in Anaheim, Calif., in July 2000. Cards arrived in packs and were numbered with a "KB" prefix.

		MT
Complete Set (10):		15.00
Common Player:		2.00
1	Kobe Bryant	2.00
2	Kobe Bryant	2.00
3	Kobe Bryant	2.00
4	Kobe Bryant	2.00
5	Kobe Bryant	2.00
6	Kobe Bryant	2.00
7	Kobe Bryant	2.00
8	Kobe Bryant	2.00
9	Kobe Bryant	2.00
10	Kobe Bryant	2.00

2000 UD Lakers Master Collection

The Lakers Master Collection was sold as a complete set around July 2000 and carried a suggested retail price of $3,000. It featured a 25-card base set, one mystery pack, ten game-used jersey cards, one Forum floor card and one Wilt Chamberlain warm-up card. Only 300 Master Collections were produced and the set arrived in a wooden box.

		MT
Complete Set (25):		400.00
Common Player:		10.00
Production 300 sets		
1	Magic Johnson	60.00
2	Wilt Chamberlain	50.00
3	Kareem Abdul-Jabbar	40.00
4	Jerry West	30.00
5	Elgin Baylor	25.00
6	James Worthy	20.00
7	Byron Scott	15.00
8	Kurt Rambis	10.00
9	Michael Cooper	10.00
10	Norm Nixon	10.00
11	Gail Goodrich	10.00
12	Jamaal Wilkes	10.00
13	A.C. Green	10.00
14	Kobe Bryant	100.00
15	Shaquille O'Neal	75.00
16	Glen Rice	12.00
17	Derek Fisher	10.00
18	Robert Horry	10.00
19	Rick Fox	10.00
20	Ron Harper	10.00
21	Chick Hearn	15.00
22	Phil Jackson	15.00
23	Pat Riley	20.00
24	Mitch Kupchak	10.00
25	L.A. Forum	10.00

2000 UD Lakers Master Coll. Fabulous Forum Floor Cards

This six-card set was from UD Lakers Master Collection and featured pieces of the Forum floor. The cards are sequentially numbered to 50 sets and are numbered with the player's initials. One Forum floor card was inserted into each Master Collection box.

		MT
Complete Set (6):		1200.
Common Player:		100.00
Production 50 sets		
KA-FO	Kareem Abdul-Jabbar	100.00
EB-JO	Elgin Baylor	400.00
WC-FO	Wilt Chamberlain	150.00
EJ-FO	Magic Johnson	300.00
JW-FO	Jerry West	400.00
WO-JO	James Worthy	100.00

2000 UD Lakers Master Collection Game Jerseys

This 10-card set was inserted into each Lakers Master Collection set. All 10 cards were included and were each numbered to 300 sets.

		MT
Complete Set (10):		1500.
Common Player:		50.00
Production 300 sets		
KA	Kareem Abdul-Jabbar	50.00
KB	Kobe Bryant	75.00
MC	Michael Cooper	400.00
AG	A.C. Green	150.00
RH	Robert Horry	200.00
EJ	Magic Johnson	400.00
SO	Shaquille O'Neal	50.00
BS	Byron Scott	50.00
JW	Jerry West	350.00
WO	James Worthy	100.00

2000 UD Lakers Master Collection Mystery Pack Inserts

One Mystery pack was included in each UD Lakers Master Collection set. The pack included a game-used card from one of six different Lakers greats and cards were hand-numbered the player's jersey number. Cards were numbered with the player's initials.

		MT
Common Player:		150.00
All items are autographed.		
KAAFO	Kareem Abdul-Jabbar FF/33	400.00
KAAJO	Kareem Abdul-Jabbar GJ/33	500.00
EBAFO	Elgin Baylor FF/22	250.00
B1	Kobe Bryant SS/1	
K1	Kobe Bryant SS/1	
KB-SO	Kobe Bryant SS/8	
KBAJO	Kobe Bryant GJ/8	
EJAFO	Magic Johnson FF/32	750.00
EJAJO	Magic Johnson GJ/32	1000.
JWAFO	Jerry West FF/44	400.00
JWAJO	Jerry West GJ/44	500.00
WOAJO	James Worthy GJ/42	150.00

2000 UD Lakers Master Collection Warm-Ups

This card featured a swatch of Chamberlain's game-used warm-ups. One of these memorabilia cards was inserted into each Lakers Master Collection and were numbered with Chamberlain's initials.

		MT
Common Player:		250.00
Production 300 sets		
WC	Wilt Chamberlain	250.00

2000 Upper Deck NBA Legends

NBA Legends consisted of 90 cards, with 50 regular player cards, 20 History of the Dunk, 10 All-Upper Deck Team and 10 Jordan - The Best cards. Each subset carried a distinctly different card design, with base cards featuring all-foil fronts, and History of the Dunk cards containing basketball texture on the right half. The set was paralleled twice - UD Commemorative Collection (numbered to 50 sets) and UD Commemorative Collection Gold (numbered to one set). Inserts included: Players of the Century, History's Heroes, Legendary Jerseys, Legendary Signatures, MJ Final Floor Jumbos, NBA Originals and Recollections.

		MT
Complete Set (90):		30.00
Common Player:		.10
Minor Stars:		.15
Common Jordan (66-71, 81-90):		2.00
Pack (5):		5.00
Box (24):		100.00
1	Michael Jordan	5.00
2	Michael Jordan	2.00
3	Larry Bird	3.00
4	Bob Cousy	.50
5	Bill Russell	1.00
6	Julius Erving	1.00
7	Nate Archibald	.40
8	Oscar Robertson	1.00
9	Elgin Baylor	.50
10	Jo Jo White	.10
11	Hal Greer	.15
12	Clyde Drexler	.30
13	Wilt Chamberlain	1.00
14	Walt Bellamy	.10
15	Walt Frazier	.40
16	Earl Monroe	.40
17	John Havlicek	.75
18	George Mikan	1.00
19	George Karl	.10
20	Tom Heinsohn	.10
21	Kareem Abdul-Jabbar	1.00
22	Bill Sharman	.10
23	Elvin Hayes	.15
24	Rick Barry	.30
25	Paul Silas	.10
26	Mitch Kupchak	.10
27	Dave Cowens	.15
28	Nate Thurmond	.10
29	Dave DeBusschere	.10
30	Jerry Lucas	.10
31	Bill Walton	.10
32	Jerry West	.50
33	David Thompson	.30
34	Spencer Haywood	.10
35	Moses Malone	.40
36	Alex English	.15
37	Willis Reed	.15
38	George Gervin	.30
39	Dolph Schayes	.15
40	Wes Unseld	.10
41	Bob Lanier	.10
42	James Worthy	.30
43	Maurice Lucas	.10
44	Pete Maravich	.75
45	Isiah Thomas	.40
46	Robert Parish	.30
47	Dominique Wilkins	.30
48	Walter Davis	.10
49	Bob Pettit	.10
50	Kevin McHale	.30
51	Julius Erving	.50
52	Dominique Wilkins	.15

53	George Gervin	.15
54	Kareem Abdul-Jabbar	.50
55	Clyde Drexler	.15
56	David Thompson	.15
57	Walter Davis	.10
58	James Worthy	.10
59	Moses Malone	.10
60	Bob Lanier	.10
61	Robert Parish	.10
62	Maurice Lucas	.10
63	Wes Unseld	.10
64	Ron Boone	.10
65	Larry Nance	.10
66	Michael Jordan	2.00
67	Michael Jordan	2.00
68	Michael Jordan	2.00
69	Michael Jordan	2.00
70	Michael Jordan	2.00
71	Michael Jordan	2.00
72	Wilt Chamberlain	.50
73	Magic Johnson	1.00
74	Julius Erving	.50
75	Larry Bird	1.50
76	Bill Russell	.50
77	Jerry West	.25
78	Oscar Robertson	.50
79	John Havlicek	.40
80	Elgin Baylor	.15
81	Michael Jordan	2.00
82	Michael Jordan	2.00
83	Michael Jordan	2.00
84	Michael Jordan	2.00
85	Michael Jordan	2.00
86	Michael Jordan	2.00
87	Michael Jordan	2.00
88	Michael Jordan	2.00
89	Michael Jordan	2.00
90	Michael Jordan	2.00

2000 Upper Deck NBA Legends Commemorative Collection

This 90-card parallel set reprints all cards from the base set, but cards are sequentially numbered to 50 sets.

		MT
Common Player:		5.00
Common MJ (66-71, 81-90):		100.00
Collection Cards:		25x-50x
Production 50 Sets		
1	Michael Jordan	5.00
2	Michael Jordan	2.00
3	Larry Bird	3.00
4	Bob Cousy	.50
5	Bill Russell	1.00
6	Julius Erving	1.00
7	Nate Archibald	.40
8	Oscar Robertson	1.00
9	Elgin Baylor	.50
10	Jo Jo White	.10
11	Hal Greer	.15
12	Clyde Drexler	.30
13	Wilt Chamberlain	1.00
14	Walt Bellamy	.10
15	Walt Frazier	.40
16	Earl Monroe	.40
17	John Havlicek	.75
18	George Mikan	1.00
19	George Karl	.10
20	Tom Heinsohn	.10
21	Kareem Abdul-Jabbar	1.00
22	Bill Sharman	.10
23	Elvin Hayes	.15
24	Rick Barry	.30
25	Paul Silas	.10
26	Mitch Kupchak	.10
27	Dave Cowens	.15
28	Nate Thurmond	.10
29	Dave DeBusschere	.10
30	Jerry Lucas	.10
31	Bill Walton	.30
32	Jerry West	.50
33	David Thompson	.30
34	Spencer Haywood	.10
35	Moses Malone	.40
36	Alex English	.15
37	Willis Reed	.15
38	George Gervin	.30
39	Dolph Schayes	.15
40	Wes Unseld	.10
41	Bob Lanier	.10
42	James Worthy	.30
43	Maurice Lucas	.10
44	Pete Maravich	.75
45	Isiah Thomas	.40
46	Robert Parish	.30
47	Dominique Wilkins	.30
48	Walter Davis	.10
49	Bob Pettit	.10
50	Kevin McHale	.30
51	Julius Erving	.50
52	Dominique Wilkins	.15
53	George Gervin	.15
54	Kareem Abdul-Jabbar	.50
55	Clyde Drexler	.15
56	David Thompson	.15
57	Walter Davis	.10
58	James Worthy	.10
59	Moses Malone	.10
60	Bob Lanier	.10
61	Robert Parish	.10
62	Maurice Lucas	.10
63	Wes Unseld	.10
64	Ron Boone	.10
65	Larry Nance	.10
66	Michael Jordan	2.00
67	Michael Jordan	2.00
68	Michael Jordan	2.00
69	Michael Jordan	2.00
70	Michael Jordan	2.00
71	Michael Jordan	2.00
72	Wilt Chamberlain	.50
73	Magic Johnson	1.00
74	Julius Erving	.50
75	Larry Bird	1.50
76	Bill Russell	.50
77	Jerry West	.25
78	Oscar Robertson	.50
79	John Havlicek	.40
80	Elgin Baylor	.15
81	Michael Jordan	2.00
82	Michael Jordan	2.00
83	Michael Jordan	2.00
84	Michael Jordan	2.00
85	Michael Jordan	2.00
86	Michael Jordan	2.00
87	Michael Jordan	2.00
88	Michael Jordan	2.00
89	Michael Jordan	2.00
90	Michael Jordan	2.00

2000 Upper Deck NBA Legends History's Heroes

This nine-card insert set features the player on a colored-foil background, with the insert name printed "History's" across the top and "Heroes" across the bottom in gold foil. History's Heroes cards are numbered with an "HH" prefix and seeded 1:12 packs.

		MT
Complete Set (9):		20.00
Common Player:		1.00
Inserted 1:12		
1	Michael Jordan	12.00
2	Julius Erving	3.00
3	Larry Bird	6.00
4	Clyde Drexler	1.50
5	Elgin Baylor	1.50
6	George Gervin	1.50
7	Oscar Robertson	3.00
8	Jerry West	2.00
9	Alex English	1.00

2000 Upper Deck NBA Legends Legendary Jerseys

This 10-card insert set features jersey swatches from retired NBA greats on a horizontal card. Cards are numbered with a two letter code, usually corresponding to the players initials, followed by a "-J" indicating jersey card. These are inserted 1:288 packs. Two players, Larry Bird and Michael Jordan, signed a limited amount of their jersey cards, which are hand-numbered to the player's jersey number (33 for Bird, 23 for Jordan). The autographs are numbered with "-A" suffix.

		MT
Complete Set (12):		1500.
Common Player:		50.00
Inserted 1:288		
KA	Kareem Abdul-Jabbar	175.00
LB	Larry Bird	250.00
LBA	Larry Bird	2500.
WC	Wilt Chamberlain	250.00
BC	Bob Cousy	100.00
CD	Clyde Drexler	75.00
DR	Julius Erving	200.00
MJ	Michael Jordan	750.00
MJA	Michael Jordan Auto (23)	7500.
MM	Moses Malone	50.00
IT	Isiah Thomas	125.00
DW	Dominique Wilkins	60.00

2000 Upper Deck Century Legends Legendary Jerseys Gold

	MT
Common Player:	150.00
Production 25 Sets	
KA-GO Kareem Abdul-Jabbar	300.00
LB-GO Larry Bird	750.00
WC-GOWilt Chamberlain	300.00
DR-GO Julius Erving	300.00
MJ-GO Michael Jordan	2500.
IT-GO Isiah Thomas	150.00

2000 Upper Deck NBA Legends Legendary Signatures

Legendary Signatures features autographs from 42 retired NBA greats on a horizontal format. The cards feature a shot of the player on the right half of the card, with the signature on the left side. Michael Jordan is available in the gold version only. The cards are numbered with a two-letter code, usually corresponding to the player's initials, and were inserted 1:24 packs. Gold versions are numbered to 25 sets.

		MT
Common Player:		10.00
Inserted 1:24		
KA	Kareem Abdul-Jabbar	125.00
NA	Nate Archibald	20.00
PA	Paul Arizin	10.00
RB	Rick Barry	30.00
EB	Elgin Baylor	30.00
WB	Walt Bellamy	10.00
LB	Larry Bird	600.00
BC	Bob Cousy	30.00
DC	Dave Cowens	10.00
DD	Dave DeBusschere	10.00
CD	Clyde Drexler	30.00
AE	Alex English	10.00
DR	Julius Erving	300.00
WF	Walt Frazier	30.00
GG	George Gervin	20.00
GA	Gail Goodrich	10.00
HG	Hal Greer	10.00
JH	John Havlicek	50.00
EH	Elvin Hayes	20.00
SH	Spencer Haywood	10.00
MG	Magic Johnson	400.00
BL	Bob Lanier	10.00
JL	Jerry Lucas	10.00
MM	Moses Malone	20.00
EM	Earl Monroe	30.00
BP	Bob Pettit	20.00
WR	Willis Reed	20.00
OR	Oscar Robertson	50.00
BR	Bill Russell	400.00
DS	Dolph Schayes	10.00
BS	Bill Sharman	10.00
PS	Paul Silas	10.00
IT	Isiah Thomas	75.00
DT	David Thompson	20.00
NT	Nate Thurmond	10.00
WU	Wes Unseld	10.00
BW	Bill Walton	25.00
JW	Jerry West	50.00
JJ	Jo Jo White	10.00
JA	Jamaal Wilkes	10.00
DW	Dominique Wilkins	25.00

2000 Upper Deck NBA Legends M.J.'s Final Floor Blow-Up

This 12-card insert was issued as a box topper, with one per box. The cards measure 3-x-5 inches and parallel the Jordan Final Floor insert set. Cards are numbered with an "FF" prefix.

		MT
Complete Set (12):		500.00
Common Player:		50.00
Inserted one per box		
1	Michael Jordan	50.00
2	Michael Jordan	50.00
3	Michael Jordan	50.00
4	Michael Jordan	50.00
5	Michael Jordan	50.00
6	Michael Jordan	50.00
7	Michael Jordan	50.00
8	Michael Jordan	50.00
9	Michael Jordan	50.00
10	Michael Jordan	50.00
11	Michael Jordan	50.00
12	Michael Jordan	50.00

2000 Upper Deck NBA Legends NBA Originals

This six-card insert set featured a player over a foil background with a brushed white border on all four sides. NBA Originals were numbered with an "O" prefix and seeded 1:12 packs.

		MT
Complete Set (6):		15.00
Common Player:		
Inserted 1:12		
1	Magic Johnson	
2	Julius Erving	
3	Michael Jordan	
4	David Thompson	
5	Kareem Abdul-Jabbar	
6	Clyde Drexler	

2000 Upper Deck NBA Legends Players of the Century

This 20-card insert set pictured players over a colored marble border, with a gold and silver foil logo centered across the bottom of the card. Players of the Century cards were numbered with a "P" prefix and seeded 1:4 packs.

		MT
Complete Set (20):		25.00
Common Player:		.50
Inserted 1:4		
1	Michael Jordan	10.00
2	Wilt Chamberlain	3.00
3	Magic Johnson	5.00
4	Larry Bird	6.00
5	Bill Russell	3.00
6	Jerry West	1.50
7	Oscar Robertson	3.00
8	John Havlicek	2.00
9	Kareem Abdul-Jabbar	3.00
10	Pete Maravich	2.00
11	Willis Reed	.50
12	Bob Lanier	.50
13	George Gervin	1.00
14	Bill Walton	1.00
15	Elvin Hayes	.50
16	Julius Erving	3.00
17	Rick Barry	1.00
18	Walt Frazier	1.00
19	Nate Thurmond	.50
20	Moses Malone	1.00

2000 Upper Deck NBA Legends Recollections

This seven-card insert set features NBA greats on the right two-thirds of the card, with the insert name in team colors on the left third. Recollections were numbered with an "R" prefix and seeded 1:24 packs.

		MT
Complete Set (7):		25.00
Common Player:		2.00
Inserted 1:24		
1	Michael Jordan	15.00
2	Isaac Thomas	2.00
3	Julius Erving	5.00
4	Wilt Chamberlain	5.00
5	Clyde Drexler	2.00
6	Bill Walton	2.00
7	Dominique Wilkins	2.00

2000 UDA Michael Jordan Final Shot

This 3-1/2-x-5-inch card was issued by UDA and sold through its direct marketing channel. Cards contained a piece of the game floor from the Delta Center, where Jordan made his last shot. There were a total of 1,000 cards produced, with the first 100 being signed (SRP $3,995) and the final 900 unsigned (SRP $395).

		MT
Complete Set (2):		4400.
1A	Michael Jordan/100	4000.
1B	Michael Jordan/900	4000.

2000 UDA 22kt Gold Michael Jordan Final Shot

This 2-1/2-x-3-1/2-inch card features a solid gold card with a piece of Delta Center floor, which Jordan took his final shot. The card was issued by UDA and sold through its direct marketing channels. The card carried a SRP of $79.99.

		MT
Complete Set (1):		80.00
1	Michael Jordan	80.00

2000 UDA The Jordan Experience Printer's Proofs

This 12-proof set highlights Jordan's career and features 22kt gold on the cards. The set was released by UDA and sold directly through UDA's direct marketing channel. Each set is sequentially numbered to 23,000 and was available for an SRP of $29.95.

		MT
Complete Set (12):		30.00
Common Player:		3.00
1	Michael Jordan	3.00
2	Michael Jordan	3.00
3	Michael Jordan	3.00
4	Michael Jordan	3.00
5	Michael Jordan	3.00
6	Michael Jordan	3.00
7	Michael Jordan	3.00
8	Michael Jordan	3.00
9	Michael Jordan	3.00
10	Michael Jordan	3.00
11	Michael Jordan	3.00
12	Michael Jordan	3.00

2000-01 Upper Deck

		MT
Complete Set (445):		200.00
Complete Series I (245):		125.00
Complete Series II (200):		75.00
Common Player:		.15
Minor Stars:		.30
Common Rookie (201-245):		.75
Inserted 1:4		
Common Kobe (186-190):		1.00
Common Garnett (191-195):		.75
Common Martin (196-200):		2.00
Common Kobe (431-445):		1.00
Series I Pack (10):		3.00
Series II Pack (10):		3.00
Series I Box (24):		40.00
Series II Box (24):		60.00
1	Dikembe Mutombo	.30
2	Jim Jackson	.15
3	Alan Henderson	.15
4	Jason Terry	.30
5	Roshown McLeod	.15
6	Lorenzen Wright	.15
7	Paul Pierce	.50
8	Antoine Walker	.50
9	Vitaly Potapenko	.15
10	Kenny Anderson	.15
11	Tony Battie	.15
12	Adrian Griffin	.15
13	Eric Williams	.15
14	Derrick Coleman	.30
15	David Wesley	.15
16	Baron Davis	.50
17	Elden Campbell	.15
18	Jamal Mashburn	.30
19	Eddie Robinson	.30
20	Elton Brand	1.25
21	Chris Carr	.15
22	Ron Artest	.40
23	Michael Ruffin	.15
24	Fred Hoiberg	.15
25	Corey Benjamin	.15
26	Shawn Kemp	.40
27	Lamond Murray	.15
28	Andre Miller	.50
29	Cedric Henderson	.15
30	Wesley Person	.15
31	Brevin Knight	.15
32	Mark Bryant	.15
33	Michael Finley	.30
34	Cedric Ceballos	.15
35	Dirk Nowitzki	.75
36	Hubert Davis	.15
37	Steve Nash	.15
38	Gary Trent	.15
39	Antonio McDyess	.40
40	James Posey	.30
41	Nick Van Exel	.30
42	Raef LaFrentz	.15
43	George McCloud	.15
44	Keon Clark	.15
45	Jerry Stackhouse	.30
46	Christian Laettner	.15
47	Loy Vaught	.15
48	Jerome Williams	.15
49	Michael Curry	.15
50	Lindsey Hunter	.15
51	Antawn Jamison	.50
52	Larry Hughes	.75
53	Chris Mills	.15
54	Donyell Marshall	.15
55	Mookie Blaylock	.15
56	Vonteego Cummings	.30
57	Erick Dampier	.15
58	Steve Francis	2.50
59	Shandon Anderson	.15
60	Hakeem Olajuwon	.60
61	Walt Williams	.15
62	Kenny Thomas	.30
63	Kelvin Cato	.15
64	Cuttino Mobley	.30
65	Reggie Miller	.30
66	Jalen Rose	.40
67	Austin Croshere	.30
68	Dale Davis	.15
69	Travis Best	.15
70	Jonathan Bender	1.00
71	Al Harrington	.30
72	Lamar Odom	1.25
73	Tyrone Nesby	.15
74	Michael Olowokandi	.15
75	Brian Skinner	.15
76	Eric Piatkowski	.15
77	Keith Closs	.15
78	Shaquille O'Neal	2.00
79	Ron Harper	.15
80	Kobe Bryant	3.00
81	Rick Fox	.15
82	Robert Horry	.15
83	Derek Fisher	.15
84	Devean George	.15
85	Alonzo Mourning	.40
86	Eddie Jones	.75
87	Anthony Carter	.30
88	Bruce Bowen	.15
89	Clarence Weatherspoon	.15
90	Tim Hardaway	.40
91	Ray Allen	.40
92	Tim Thomas	.40
93	Glenn Robinson	.30
94	Scott Williams	.15
95	Sam Cassell	.30
96	Ervin Johnson	.15
97	Darvin Ham	.15
98	Kevin Garnett	2.50
99	Wally Szczerbiak	.40
100	Terrell Brandon	.30
101	Joe Smith	.15
102	Radoslav Nesterovic	.15
103	William Avery	.15
104	Stephon Marbury	1.00
105	Kerry Kittles	.15
106	Keith Van Horn	.60
107	Lucious Harris	.15
108	Jamie Feick	.15
109	Johnny Newman	.15
110	Patrick Ewing	.30
111	Latrell Sprewell	.75
112	Marcus Camby	.30
113	Larry Johnson	.30
114	Charlie Ward	.15
115	Allan Houston	.40
116	Chris Childs	.15
117	Grant Hill	2.00
118	John Amaechi	.15
119	Tracy McGrady	1.25
120	Michael Doleac	.15
121	Darrell Armstrong	.15
122	Bo Outlaw	.15
123	Allen Iverson	2.00
124	Theo Ratliff	.15
125	Matt Geiger	.15
126	Tyrone Hill	.15
127	George Lynch	.15
128	Toni Kukoc	.50
129	Jason Kidd	1.25
130	Rodney Rogers	.15
131	Anfernee Hardaway	1.25
132	Clifford Robinson	.15
133	Tom Gugliotta	.30
134	Shawn Marion	.75
135	Luc Longley	.15
136	Rasheed Wallace	.50
137	Scottie Pippen	1.25
138	Arvydas Sabonis	.15
139	Steve Smith	.30
140	Damon Stoudamire	.30
141	Bonzi Wells	.30
142	Jermaine O'Neal	.30
143	Chris Webber	1.25
144	Jason Williams	.60
145	Nick Anderson	.15
146	Vlade Divac	.15
147	Predrag Stojakovic	.15
148	Jon Barry	.15
149	Corliss Williamson	.15
150	Tim Duncan	2.00
151	David Robinson	.60
152	Terry Porter	.15
153	Malik Rose	.15
154	Steve Kerr	.15
155	Avery Johnson	.15
156	Gary Payton	.60
157	Brent Barry	.15
158	Vin Baker	.30
159	Rashard Lewis	.60
160	Ruben Patterson	.15
161	Shammond Williams	.15
162	Vince Carter	4.00
163	Dell Curry	.15
164	Doug Christie	.15
165	Antonio Davis	.15
166	Kevin Willis	.15
167	Charles Oakley	.15
168	Karl Malone	.60
169	John Stockton	.30
170	Bryon Russell	.15
171	Olden Polynice	.15
172	Quincy Lewis	.30
173	Scott Padgett	.15
174	Shareef Abdur-Rahim	.60
175	Mike Bibby	.40
176	Michael Dickerson	.15
177	Bryant Reeves	.15
178	Othella Harrington	.15
179	Grant Long	.15
180	Mitch Richmond	.30
181	Richard Hamilton	.40
182	Juwan Howard	.30
183	Rod Strickland	.30
184	Tracy Murray	.15
185	Chris Whitney	.15
186	Kobe Bryant	1.00
187	Kobe Bryant	1.00
188	Kobe Bryant	1.00
189	Kobe Bryant	1.00
190	Kobe Bryant	1.00
191	Kevin Garnett	.75
192	Kevin Garnett	.75
193	Kevin Garnett	.75
194	Kevin Garnett	.75
195	Kevin Garnett	.75
196	Kenyon Martin	2.00
197	Kenyon Martin	2.00
198	Kenyon Martin	2.00
199	Kenyon Martin	2.00
200	Kenyon Martin	2.00
201	Kenyon Martin	6.00
202	*Stromile Swift*	10.00
203	*Chris Mihm*	2.50
204	*Marcus Fizer*	4.00
205	*Darius Miles*	15.00
206	*Joel Przybilla*	2.00
207	*Mike Miller*	10.00
208	*Courtney Alexander*	4.00
209	*DerMarr Johnson*	4.00
210	*Iakovos Tsakalidis*	.75

211	*Jerome Moiso*	2.50
212	*Keyon Dooling*	4.00
213	*Erick Barkley*	2.50
214	*Jason Collier*	1.00
215	*Jamaal Magloire*	2.00
216	*DeShawn Stevenson*	6.00
217	*Hidayet Turkoglu*	4.00
218	*Morris Peterson*	6.00
219	*Jamal Crawford*	4.00
220	*Etan Thomas*	2.00
221	*Quentin Richardson*	5.00
222	*Mateen Cleaves*	2.50
223	*Chris Carrawell*	1.00
224	*Cory Hightower*	1.25
225	*Donnell Harvey*	2.00
226	*Mark Madsen*	2.00
227	*Jake Voskuhl*	.75
228	*Soumaila Samake*	.75
229	*Mamadou N'diaye*	1.25
230	*Dan Langhi*	1.00
231	*Hanno Mottola*	1.00
232	*Olumide Oyedji*	.75
233	*Jason Hart*	.75
234	*Mike Smith*	.75
235	*Chris Porter*	2.50
236	*Jabari Smith*	1.00
237	*Desmond Mason*	5.00
238	*Eddie House*	1.00
239	*A.J. Guyton*	1.00
240	*Craig Claxton*	2.00
241	*Lavor Postell*	1.50
242	*Khalid El-Amin*	2.00
243	*Pepe Sanchez*	1.00
244	*Eduardo Najera*	1.50
245	*Michael Redd*	1.50
246	DerMarr Johnson	2.50
247	Hanno Mottola	.50
248	Dion Glover	.15
249	Matt Maloney	.15
250	Jason Terry	.40
251	Jerome Moiso	1.25
252	Bryant Stith	.15
253	Randy Brown	.15
254	Mark Blount	.15
255	Chris Herren	.15
256	Jamal Mashburn	.30
257	P.J. Brown	.15
258	Lee Nailon	.15
259	Jamaal Magloire	1.00
260	Otis Thorpe	.15
261	Ron Mercer	.30
262	Marcus Fizer	3.00
263	Jamal Crawford	2.50
264	A.J. Guyton	.50
265	*Dalibor Bagaric*	.75
266	Chris Mihm	1.25
267	Robert Traylor	.15
268	Matt Harpring	.15
269	Clarence Weatherspoon	.15
270	Bimbo Coles	.15
271	Etan Thomas	1.00
272	Courtney Alexander	2.50
273	Donnell Harvey	1.00
274	Eduardo Najera	.75
275	Christian Laettner	.15
276	Mamadou N'diaye	.50
277	Tariq Abdul-Wahad	.15
278	Voshon Lenard	.15
279	Robert Pack	.15
280	Tracy Murray	.15
281	Mateen Cleaves	1.50
282	Ben Wallace	.15
283	Chucky Atkins	.15
284	Billy Owens	.15
285	Brian Cardinal	.30
286	Chris Porter	2.00
287	Bob Sura	.15
288	Vinny Del Negro	.15
289	*Marc Jackson*	5.00
290	Danny Fortson	.15
291	Jason Collier	.15
292	Maurice Taylor	.15
293	Dan Langhi	.30
294	Carlos Rogers	.15
295	Moochie Norris	.15
296	Jermaine O'Neal	.50
297	Derrick McKey	.15
298	Sam Perkins	.15
299	Zan Tabak	.15
300	Jeff Foster	.15
301	Corey Maggette	.50
302	Darius Miles	8.00
303	Keyon Dooling	2.50
304	Quentin Richardson	2.50
305	Jeff McInnis	.15
306	Isaiah Rider	.15
307	Mark Madsen	1.00
308	*Mike Penberthy*	1.50
309	Brian Shaw	.15
310	Horace Grant	.15
311	Eddie Jones	.75
312	Brian Grant	.15
313	Anthony Mason	.15
314	Duane Causwell	.15
315	Eddie House	1.00
316	Lindsey Hunter	.15
317	Jason Caffey	.15
318	Joel Przybilla	.50
319	Michael Redd	.30
320	Rafer Alston	.15
321	Chauncey Billups	.15
322	LaPhonso Ellis	.15
323	Sam Mitchell	.15
324	Dean Garrett	.15
325	Tom Hammonds	.15
326	Kenyon Martin	3.00
327	Soumaila Samake	.30
328	Aaron Williams	.15
329	Kendall Gill	.15
330	*Stephen Jackson*	2.00
331	Lavor Postell	.75
332	*Pete Mickeal*	1.00
333	Kurt Thomas	.15
334	Erick Strickland	.15
335	Glen Rice	.30
336	Grant Hill	2.00
337	Tracy McGrady	1.25
338	Pat Garrity	.15
339	Troy Hudson	.15
340	Mike Miller	5.00
341	Craig "Speedy" Claxton	1.00
342	Eric Snow	.15
343	Pepe Sanchez	.30
344	Aaron McKie	.15
345	Nazr Mohammed	.15
346	*Ruben Garces*	.75
347	*Daniel Santiago*	1.50
348	Tony Delk	.15
349	*Paul McPherson*	2.00
350	Iakovos Tsakalidis	.15
351	Dale Davis	.15
352	Shawn Kemp	.40
353	Erick Barkley	1.25
354	Greg Anthony	.15
355	Stacey Augmon	.15
356	Bobby Jackson	.15
357	Hidayet Turkoglu	1.50
358	Jabari Smith	.30
359	Doug Christie	.15
360	Darrick Martin	.15
361	Sean Elliott	.15
362	Jaren Jackson	.15
363	Samaki Walker	.15
364	Derek Anderson	.30
365	Antonio Daniels	.15
366	Patrick Ewing	.30
367	Desmond Mason	2.50
368	Jelani McCoy	.15
369	*Ruben Wolkowyski*	1.00
370	Emanuel Davis	.15
371	Mark Jackson	.15
372	Morris Peterson	3.00
373	Muggsy Bogues	.15
374	Alvin Williams	.15
375	Corliss Williamson	.15
376	John Starks	.15
377	Danny Manning	.15
378	DeShawn Stevenson	3.00
379	Donyell Marshall	.15
380	David Benoit	.15
381	Isaac Austin	.15
382	Mahmoud Abdul-Rauf	.15
383	Stromile Swift	4.00
384	Kevin Edwards	.15
385	Brent Price	.15
386	Popeye Jones	.15
387	*Mike Smith*	1.00
388	Jahidi White	.15
389	Laron Profit	.15
390	Felipe Lopez	.15
391	Dikembe Mutombo	.15
392	Paul Pierce	.30
393	Derrick Coleman	.15
394	Elton Brand	.60
395	Andre Miller	.30
396	Michael Finley	.15
397	Antonio McDyess	.15
398	Jerry Stackhouse	.15
399	Larry Hughes	.40
400	Steve Francis	1.25
401	Reggie Miller	.15
402	Lamar Odom	.60
403	Shaquille O'Neal	1.00
404	Tim Hardaway	.15
405	Ray Allen	.15
406	Kevin Garnett	1.25
407	Stephon Marbury	.40
408	Allan Houston	.15
409	Grant Hill	1.00
410	Allen Iverson	1.50
411	Jason Kidd	.60
412	Rasheed Wallace	.15
413	Chris Webber	.60
414	Tim Duncan	1.00
415	Gary Payton	.30
416	Vince Carter	2.00
417	Karl Malone	.30
418	Shareef Abdur-Rahim	.30
419	Mitch Richmond	.15
420	Kobe Bryant	1.50
421	Mateen Cleaves	.75
422	Craig "Speedy" Claxton	.50
423	Courtney Alexander	1.00
424	Desmond Mason	1.00
425	Mike Miller	1.00
426	DerMarr Johnson	1.00
427	Chris Mihm	.50
428	Jamal Crawford	1.00
429	Joel Przybilla	.30
430	Keyon Dooling	1.00
431	Kobe Bryant	1.00
432	Kobe Bryant	1.00
433	Kobe Bryant	1.00
434	Kobe Bryant	1.00
435	Kobe Bryant	1.00
436	Kobe Bryant	1.00
437	Kobe Bryant	1.00
438	Kobe Bryant	1.00
439	Kobe Bryant	1.00
440	Kobe Bryant	1.00
441	Kobe Bryant	1.00
442	Kobe Bryant	1.00
443	Kobe Bryant	1.00
444	Kobe Bryant	1.00
445	Kobe Bryant	1.00
CL1	Checklist #1	.15
CL2	Checklist #2	.15
CL3	Checklist #3	.15

2000-01 Upper Deck Gold Exclusives

	MT
Silver Cards:	15x-25x
Common Player:	3.00
Minor Stars:	4.00
Production 100 Hobby Sets	
Silver Rookies:	10x-20x
Production 25 Hobby Sets	
Common Kobe (186-190):	50.00
Common Garnett (191-195):	25.00
Common Martin (196-200):	50.00

2000-01 Upper Deck Silver Exclusives

	MT
Silver Cards:	3x-6x
Common Player:	1.00
Minor Stars:	1.50
Production 500 Hobby Sets	
Silver Rookies:	3x-6x
Production 100 Hobby Sets	
Common Kobe (186-190):	20.00
Common Garnett (191-195):	10.00
Common Martin (196-200):	25.00

2000-01 Upper Deck All-Star Class

		MT
Complete Set (10):		30.00
Common Player:		1.00
Inserted 1:23 Series II		
1	Tim Duncan	5.00
2	Shaquille O'Neal	5.00
3	Chris Webber	4.00
4	Allan Houston	1.00
5	Kobe Bryant	8.00
6	Ray Allen	1.00
7	Karl Malone	1.50
8	Rasheed Wallace	1.00
9	Kevin Garnett	6.00
10	Vince Carter	10.00

2000-01 Upper Deck Combo Materials Cards

		MT
Common Player:		25.00
Inserted 1:144 Series II		
MC	Mateen Cleaves	25.00
JK	Jason Kidd	40.00
SM	Shawn Marion	40.00
DM	Darius Miles	125.00
AM	Andre Miller	25.00
QR	Quentin Richardson	30.00
JS	Jerry Stackhouse	30.00

2000-01 Upper Deck E-Cards 1

		MT
Complete Set (6):		8.00
Common Player:		.75
Inserted 1:12		
EC1	Kobe Bryant	6.00
EC2	Kevin Garnett	5.00
EC3	Anfernee Hardaway	2.50
EC4	Shareef Abdur-Rahim	1.50
EC5	Reggie Miller	.75
EC6	Karl Malone	1.50

2000-01 Upper Deck E-Cards 2

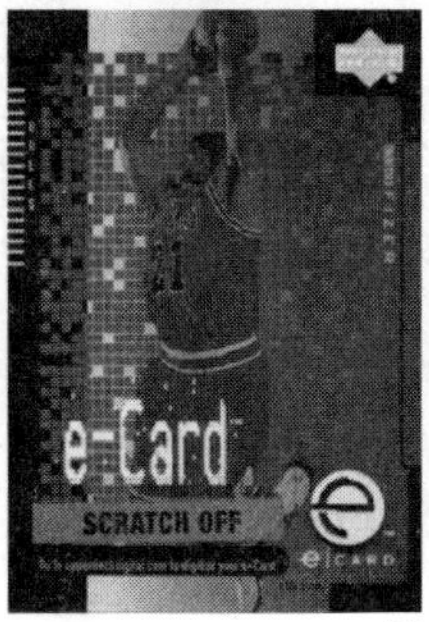

		MT
Complete Set (6):		15.00
Common Player:		2.00
Inserted 1:12 Series II		
1	Kobe Bryant	6.00
2	Kevin Garnett	5.00
3	Kenyon Martin	4.00
4	Stromile Swift	4.00
5	Darius Miles	8.00
6	Marcus Fizer	2.00

2000-01 Upper Deck Game Jersey - Common 1

		MT
Common Player:		15.00
Inserted 1:287		
Auto versions numbered to player jersey		
SA	Shareef Abdur-Rahim	30.00
SA-A	Shareef Abdur-Rahim Auto/3	
VB	Vin Baker	15.00
VB-A	Vin Baker Auto/32	75.00
KB	Kobe Bryant	150.00
KB-A	Kobe Bryant Auto/8	
KG	Kevin Garnett	75.00
KG-A	Kevin Garnett Auto/21	750.00
AI	Allen Iverson	60.00
JK	Jason Kidd	50.00
SM	Stephon Marbury	30.00
RM	Reggie Miller	50.00
RM-A	Reggie Miller Auto/31	
AM	Alonzo Mourning	40.00
SO	Shaquille O'Neal	60.00
GP	Gary Payton	40.00
GP-A	Gary Payton Auto/20	
DR	David Robinson	40.00
JS	Joe Smith	15.00
ST	John Stockton	40.00
KV	Keith Van Horn	20.00
AW	Antoine Walker	20.00
AW-A	Antoine Walker Auto/8	

2000-01 Upper Deck Game Jersey - Hobby 1

		MT
Common Player:		20.00
Inserted 1:287 Hobby		
WA	William Avery	20.00
MB	Mike Bibby	40.00
TB	Terrell Brandon	25.00
KB	Kobe Bryant	300.00
BD	Baron Davis	60.00
KG	Kevin Garnett	200.00
AG	Adrian Griffin	20.00
AH	Anfernee Hardaway	100.00
EJ	Eddie Jones	75.00
PP	Paul Pierce	60.00
GR	Glenn Robinson	40.00
WS	Wally Szczerbiak	40.00

2000-01 Upper Deck Game Jersey - Common 2

		MT
Common Player:		12.00
Inserted 1:287 Hobby		
DB-C	Dalibor Bagaric	12.00
KB-A	Kobe Bryant Auto/8	
KB-C	Kobe Bryant	125.00
MC-C	Mateen Cleaves	20.00
KD-C	Keyon Dooling	25.00
MF-C	Marcus Fizer	25.00
KG-A	Kevin Garnett Auto/21	
KG-C	Kevin Garnett	75.00
TG-C	Tom Gugliotta	12.00
AH-C	Allan Houston	25.00
JK-C	Jason Kidd	50.00
SM-C	Shawn Marion	40.00
KM-A	Kenyon Martin Auto/6	
KM-C	Kenyon Martin	50.00
AM-C	Andre Miller	25.00
QR-C	Quentin Richardson	25.00
LS-C	Latrell Sprewell	50.00
JS-C	Jerry Stackhouse	30.00

2000-01 Upper Deck Game Jersey - Hobby 2

		MT
Common Player:		15.00
Inserted 1:72 Hobby		
DA-H	Darrell Armstrong	15.00
A-KB	Kobe Bryant	400.00
KB-H	Kobe Bryant	125.00
MA-H	Marcus Camby	20.00
A-JC	Jamal Crawford	50.00
JC-H	Jamal Crawford	25.00
KD-H	Keyon Dooling	25.00
A-KG	Kevin Garnett	200.00
KG-H	Kevin Garnett	75.00
A-AG	Adrian Griffin	15.00
A-AH	Anfernee Hardaway	100.00
AH-H	Anfernee Hardaway	50.00
GH-H	Grant Hill	50.00
JK-H	Jason Kidd	50.00
A-JM	Jamaal Magloire	25.00
JM-H	Jamaal Magloire	15.00
SM-H	Shawn Marion	40.00
TM-H	Tracy McGrady	50.00
A-CM	Chris Mihm	25.00
CM-H	Chris Mihm	15.00
A-DM	Darius Miles	400.00
DM-H	Darius Miles	125.00
LS-H	Latrell Sprewell	50.00
A-SS	Stromile Swift	150.00
SS-H	Stromile Swift	50.00

2000-01 Upper Deck Game Jersey Combos 1

		MT
Common Player:		400.00
Production 50 Sets		
KB/KG	Kobe Bryant, Kevin Garnett	400.00
KB/SO	Kobe Bryant, Shaquille O'Neal	600.00
KB/DR	Kobe Bryant, Julius Erving	400.00
MJ/LB	Magic Johnson, Larry Bird	600.00
DR/LB	Julius Erving, Larry Bird	500.00
KM/JS	Karl Malone, John Stockton	400.00
JK/AH	Jason Kidd, Anfernee Hardaway	400.00
WC/BR	Wilt Chamberlain, Bill Russell	600.00
KB/KG-A	Kobe Bryant, Kevin Garnett	
DR/LB-A	Julius Erving, Larry Bird	

2000-01 Upper Deck Game Jersey Combos 2

		MT
Common Player:		250.00
Production 50 Sets		
Auto Production 10 Sets		
KB/KG	Kobe Bryant, Kevin Garnett	400.00
KB/SO	Kobe Bryant, Shaquille O'Neal	600.00
KB/KM	Kobe Bryant, Kenyon Martin	400.00
KB/DM	Kobe Bryant, Darius Miles	600.00
AH/LS	Allan Houston, Latrell Sprewell	250.00
SA/SS	Shareef Abdur-Rahim, Stromile Swift	250.00
MJ/KB	Michael Jordan, Kobe Bryant	1000.
KB/KG-A	Kobe Bryant, Kevin Garnett	
KB/KM-A	Kobe Bryant, Kenyon Martin	
KB/DM-A	Kobe Bryant, Darius Miles	
SA/SS-A	Shareef Abdur-Rahim, Stromile Swift	
MJ/KB-A	Michael Jordan, Kobe Bryant	

2000-01 Upper Deck Game Jersey Patch 1

		MT
Common Player:		200.00
Inserted 1:7,500		
SA	Shareef Abdur-Rahim	200.00
KB	Kobe Bryant	1000.
KBPA	Kobe Bryant Auto/8	
KG	Kevin Garnett	500.00
KGPA	Kevin Garnett Auto/21	750.00
AH	Anfernee Hardaway	350.00
AHPA	Anfernee Hardaway Auto/1	
AI	Allen Iverson	400.00
MJ	Michael Jordan	1200.
MJPA	Michael Jordan Auto/23	4000.
JK	Jason Kidd	300.00
SM	Stephon Marbury	250.00
RM	Reggie Miller	300.00
SO	Shaquille O'Neal	400.00
SO-P	Shaquille O'Neal	
GP	Gary Payton	200.00
GPPA	Gary Payton Auto/20	
ST	John Stockton	350.00
SS-P	Stromile Swift	

2000-01 Upper Deck Game Jersey Patch Gold 1

		MT
Complete Set (10):		
Common Player:		
SA	Shareef Abdur-Rahim	
KB	Kobe Bryant	
KB-G	Kobe Bryant	
MF-G	Marcus Fizer	
KG	Kevin Garnett	
KG-G	Kevin Garnett	
TH	Tim Hardaway	
GH	Grant Hill	
AI	Allen Iverson	
AI-G	Allen Iverson	
MJ	Michael Jordan	
MJ-G	Michael Jordan	
JK	Jason Kidd	
KM-G	Kenyon Martin	
DM-G	Darius Miles	
MM-G	Mike Miller	
SO	Shaquille O'Neal	
SO-G	Shaquille O'Neal	
GP	Gary Payton	
SS-G	Stromile Swift	

2000-01 Upper Deck Game Jersey Patch 2

		MT
Common Player:		150.00
Inserted 1:6,000		
KB-A	Kobe Bryant Auto/8	
KB	Kobe Bryant	1000.
JC	Jamal Crawford	150.00
KD	Keyon Dooling	150.00
MF	Marcus Fizer	150.00
KG-A	Kevin Garnett Auto/21	
KG	Kevin Garnett	500.00
AI	Allen Iverson	400.00
DJ	DerMarr Johnson	150.00
MJ-A	Michael Jordan Auto/23	
MJ	Michael Jordan	1200.
KM-A	Kenyon Martin Auto/6	
KM	Kenyon Martin	200.00
DM-A	Darius Miles Auto/21	
DM	Darius Miles	600.00
MM	Mike Miller	200.00
SO	Shaquille O'Neal	400.00
SS	Stromile Swift	250.00

2000-01 Upper Deck Graphic Jam

		MT
Complete Set (12):		20.00
Common Player:		.75
Inserted 1:14		
G1	Kobe Bryant	6.00
G2	Kevin Garnett	5.00
G3	Chris Webber	2.50
G4	Larry Hughes	2.00
G5	Tim Duncan	4.00
G6	Latrell Sprewell	1.50
G7	Vince Carter	8.00
G8	Shareef Abdur-Rahim	1.00
G9	Elton Brand	2.50
G10	Antonio McDyess	.75
G11	Lamar Odom	2.50
G12	Rasheed Wallace	.75

2000-01 Upper Deck Highlight Zone

		MT
Complete Set (10):		25.00
Common Player:		1.50
Inserted 1:23 Series II		
1	Kobe Bryant	10.00
2	Eddie Jones	2.00
3	Lamar Odom	3.00
4	Steve Francis	6.00
5	Stephon Marbury	2.00
6	Scottie Pippen	3.00
7	Kevin Garnett	6.00
8	Chris Webber	4.00
9	Anfernee Hardaway	3.00
10	Shareef Abdur-Rahim	1.50

2000-01 Upper Deck Lightning Strikes

		MT
Complete Set (15):		20.00
Common Player:		.75
Inserted 1:12		
LS1	Allen Iverson	4.00
LS2	Stephon Marbury	2.00
LS3	Ray Allen	.75
LS4	Allan Houston	.75
LS5	Kevin Garnett	5.00
LS6	Gary Payton	1.50
LS7	Shawn Marion	2.00
LS8	Kobe Bryant	6.00

LS9	Tim Duncan	4.00
LS10	Scottie Pippen	2.50
LS11	Andre Miller	1.00
LS12	Steve Francis	5.00
LS13	Jalen Rose	.75
LS14	Jason Williams	1.50
LS15	Larry Hughes	2.00

2000-01 Upper Deck Live Action

		MT
Complete Set (8):		8.00
Common Player:		.50
Inserted 1:12 Series II		
1	Kevin Garnett	3.00
2	Lamar Odom	1.50
3	Jalen Rose	.50
4	Larry Hughes	1.00
5	Tim Thomas	.50
6	Kobe Bryant	5.00
7	Wally Szczerbiak	.50
8	Anfernee Hardaway	1.50

2000-01 Upper Deck Masters of Arts

		MT
Complete Set (10):		8.00
Common Player:		.40
Inserted 1:6		
MA1	Vince Carter	3.00
MA2	Ray Allen	.40
MA3	Larry Hughes	.75
MA4	Kevin Garnett	2.00
MA5	Antonio McDyess	.40
MA6	Steve Francis	2.00
MA7	Stephon Marbury	.75
MA8	Kobe Bryant	2.50
MA9	Paul Pierce	.60
MA10	Reggie Miller	.40

2000-01 Upper Deck MJ Materials

		MT
Common Player:		100.00
MJ1-MJ3 Inserted 1:288		
MJ4 Numbered to 250		
MJ5-MJ6 Numbered to 100		
MJ1	Michael Jordan/Suit	100.00
MJ2	Michael Jordan/Jersey	300.00
MJ3	Michael Jordan/Shoe	200.00
MJ4	Michael Jordan Suit/Jersey	350.00
MJ5	Michael Jordan Shorts/Shoe	500.00
MJ6	Michael Jordan Jersey/Shorts	500.00
MJ7	Michael Jordan Suit/Jersey/Shorts/Patch	

2000-01 Upper Deck Pure Basketball

		MT
Complete Set (8):		6.00
Common Player:		.40

Inserted 1:12 Series II		
1	Elton Brand	1.50
2	Andre Miller	.75
3	Mitch Richmond	.40
4	Kobe Bryant	5.00
5	John Stockton	.40
6	Antawn Jamison	1.00
7	Kevin Garnett	3.00
8	Reggie Miller	.40

2000-01 Upper Deck Rookie Focus

		MT
Complete Set (9):		15.00
Common Player:		1.00
Inserted 1:10 Series II		
1	Kenyon Martin	4.00
2	Jamal Crawford	2.00
3	Keyon Dooling	2.00
4	Mike Miller	3.00
5	Morris Peterson	3.00
6	DerMarr Johnson	2.00
7	Marcus Fizer	3.00
8	DeShawn Stevenson	3.00
9	Chris Mihm	1.00

2000-01 Upper Deck Super Powers

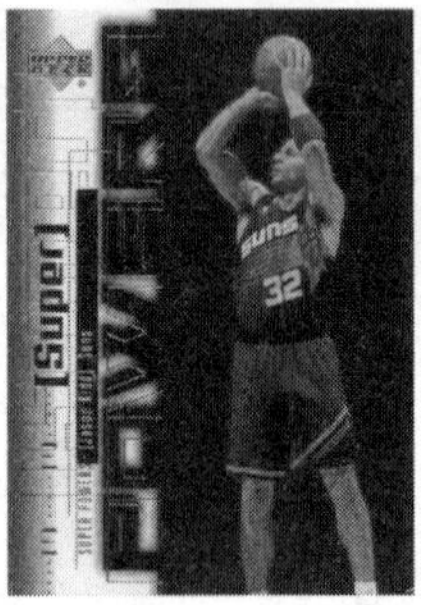

		MT
Complete Set (10):		60.00
Common Player:		3.00
Inserted 1:72 Series II		
1	Kobe Bryant	20.00
2	Vince Carter	25.00
3	Tim Duncan	10.00
4	Steve Francis	12.00
5	Gary Payton	3.00
6	Chris Webber	8.00
7	Kevin Garnett	12.00
8	Allen Iverson	10.00
9	Jason Kidd	6.00
10	Elton Brand	6.00

2000-01 Upper Deck Total Dominance

		MT
Complete Set (15):		30.00
Common Player:		.75
Inserted 1:12		
TD1	Shaquille O'Neal	4.00
TD2	Gary Payton	1.50
TD3	Kevin Garnett	5.00
TD4	Elton Brand	2.50
TD5	Jalen Rose	.75
TD6	Allen Iverson	4.00
TD7	Vince Carter	8.00
TD8	Kobe Bryant	6.00
TD9	Lamar Odom	2.50
TD10	Jason Kidd	2.50
TD11	Rasheed Wallace	.75
TD12	Chris Webber	2.50
TD13	Ray Allen	.75
TD14	Alonzo Mourning	.75
TD15	Tim Duncan	4.00

2000-01 Upper Deck Touch the Sky

		MT
Complete Set (9):		8.00
Common Player:		.50
Inserted 1:10 Series II		
1	Kobe Bryant	5.00
2	Kevin Garnett	3.00
3	Michael Finley	.50
4	Anfernee Hardaway	1.50
5	Scottie Pippen	1.50
6	Antonio McDyess	.75
7	Larry Hughes	1.00
8	Latrell Sprewell	1.00
9	Rashard Lewis	.75

2000-01 Upper Deck True Talents

		MT
Complete Set (20):		10.00
Common Player:		.25
Inserted 1:3		
TT1	Kobe Bryant	3.00
TT2	Jalen Rose	.40
TT3	Chris Webber	1.50
TT4	Alonzo Mourning	.50
TT5	Paul Pierce	.75
TT6	Allan Houston	.50
TT7	Keith Van Horn	.60
TT8	Andre Miller	.75
TT9	Dirk Nowitzki	1.00
TT10	Richard Hamilton	.40
TT11	Jason Williams	.75
TT12	Antonio McDyess	.40
TT13	Antoine Walker	.40
TT14	Antawn Jamison	.75
TT15	Glenn Robinson	.25
TT16	Lamar Odom	1.50
TT17	Scottie Pippen	1.50
TT18	Mike Bibby	.40
TT19	Elton Brand	1.50
TT20	Kevin Garnett	2.50

2000-01 Upper Deck Unleashed!

		MT
Complete Set (8):		12.00
Common Player:		1.00
Inserted 1:12 Series II		
1	Vince Carter	6.00
2	Lamar Odom	1.50
3	Jason Williams	1.00
4	Kevin Garnett	3.00
5	Paul Pierce	1.00
6	Shareef Abdur-Rahim	1.00
7	Elton Brand	1.50
8	Kobe Bryant	5.00

A card number in parentheses ( ) indicates the set is unnumbered.

2000-01 Upper Deck Black Diamond

		MT
Complete Set (132):		400.00
Common Player:		.15
Minor Stars:		.30
Common Rookie:		2.00
Cards 91-100 Production 2,000 Sets		
Cards 101-110 Production 1,000 Sets		
Cards 111-120 Production 750 Sets		
Cards 121-126 Production 1,750 Sets		
Cards 127-132 Production 900 Sets		
Pack (5):		4.00
Box (24):		45.00
1	Dikembe Mutombo	.15
2	Alan Henderson	.15
3	Jason Terry	.30
4	Paul Pierce	.60
5	Antoine Walker	.50
6	Kenny Anderson	.15
7	Jamal Mashburn	.30
8	Derrick Coleman	.15
9	Baron Davis	.50
10	Elton Brand	1.25
11	Ron Artest	.30
12	Ron Mercer	.30
13	Lamond Murray	.15
14	Andre Miller	.50
15	Matt Harpring	.15
16	Michael Finley	.30
17	Dirk Nowitzki	1.00
18	Steve Nash	.15
19	Antonio McDyess	.50
20	Nick Van Exel	.30
21	Raef LaFrentz	.15
22	Jerry Stackhouse	.30
23	Joe Smith	.15
24	Chucky Atkins	.15
25	Antawn Jamison	1.00
26	Larry Hughes	.60
27	Chris Mills	.15
28	Steve Francis	2.50
29	Hakeem Olajuwon	.60
30	Cuttino Mobley	.40
31	Reggie Miller	.40
32	Jalen Rose	.40
33	Jermaine O'Neal	.60
34	Austin Croshere	.15
35	Lamar Odom	1.25
36	Corey Maggette	.50
37	Jeff McInnis	.15
38	Kobe Bryant	3.00
39	Shaquille O'Neal	2.00
40	Ron Harper	.15
41	Isaiah Rider	.30
42	Eddie Jones	.75
43	Tim Hardaway	.40
44	Brian Grant	.15
45	Glenn Robinson	.30
46	Sam Cassell	.30
47	Ray Allen	.40
48	Kevin Garnett	2.50
49	Terrell Brandon	.30
50	Wally Szczerbiak	.40
51	Stephon Marbury	.75
52	Keith Van Horn	.50
53	Kendall Gill	.15
54	Latrell Sprewell	1.00
55	Allan Houston	.40
56	Marcus Camby	.40
57	Grant Hill	2.00
58	Tracy McGrady	1.25
59	Darrell Armstrong	.15
60	Allen Iverson	2.00
61	Toni Kukoc	.40
62	Theo Ratliff	.15
63	Jason Kidd	1.25
64	Shawn Marion	1.00
65	Anfernee Hardaway	1.25
66	Scottie Pippen	1.25
67	Rasheed Wallace	.50
68	Damon Stoudamire	.30
69	Steve Smith	.30
70	Chris Webber	1.50
71	Jason Williams	.60
72	Predrag Stojakovic	.30
73	Tim Duncan	2.00
74	David Robinson	.60
75	Derek Anderson	.30
76	Gary Payton	.60
77	Patrick Ewing	.30
78	Rashard Lewis	.50
79	Vince Carter	4.00
80	Mark Jackson	.15
81	Antonio Davis	.15
82	Karl Malone	.60
83	John Stockton	.30
84	Bryon Russell	.15
85	Shareef Abdur-Rahim	.60
86	Michael Dickerson	.15
87	Mike Bibby	.40
88	Mitch Richmond	.30
89	Richard Hamilton	.40
90	Juwan Howard	.30
91	*Eduardo Najera/2000*	3.00
92	*Eddie House/2000*	4.00
93	*Michael Redd/2000*	3.00
94	*Ruben Wolkowyski/2000*	2.00
95	*Dan Langhi/2000*	2.00
96	*Mark Madsen/2000*	4.00
97	*Craig "Speedy" Claxton/2000*	4.00
98	*Iakovos Tsakalidis/2000*	2.00
99	*Dragan Tarlac/2000*	2.00
100	*Donnell Harvey/2000*	4.00
101	*Etan Thomas/1000*	6.00
102	*Hidayet Turkoglu/1000*	10.00
103	*Mike Penberthy/1000*	4.00
104	*Paul McPherson/1000*	4.00
105	*Jason Collier/1000*	3.00
106	*Hanno Mottola/1000*	3.00
107	*A.J. Guyton/1000*	4.00
108	*Daniel Santiago/1000*	3.00
109	*Lavor Postell/1000*	4.00
110	*Erick Barkley/1000*	6.00
111	*Chris Porter/750*	10.00
112	*Mateen Cleaves/750*	12.00
113	*Marc Jackson/750*	15.00
114	*Joel Przybilla/750*	8.00
115	*Courtney Alexander/750*	20.00
116	*Khalid El-Amin/750*	8.00
117	*Keyon Dooling/750*	15.00
118	*Desmond Mason/750*	20.00
119	*Stephen Jackson/750*	8.00
120	*Morris Peterson/750*	30.00
121	*Jerome Moiso/GJ 1750*	12.00
122	*Jamal Crawford/GJ 1750*	25.00
123	*DeShawn Stevenson/GJ 1750*	30.00
124	*Quentin Richardson/GJ 1750*	25.00
125	*Marcus Fizer/GJ 1750*	25.00
126	*Mike Miller/GJ 1750*	40.00
127	*Jamaal Magloire/GJ 900*	15.00
128	*Chris Mihm/GJ 900*	15.00
129	*DerMarr Johnson/GJ 900*	25.00
130	*Stromile Swift/GJ 900*	50.00
131	*Darius Miles/GJ 900*	125.00
132	*Kenyon Martin/GJ 900*	40.00

2000-01 Upper Deck Black Diamond Gold

	MT
Common Player (1-90):	.60
Gold Parallels:	2x-4x
Production 500 Sets	
Common Rookie (91-120):	6.00
Gold Rookies (91-120):	2x-3x
Production 250 Sets	
Common Rookie (121-132):	15.00
Production 100 Sets	

2000-01 Upper Deck Black Diamond Gold Jersey Autographs

		MT
Common Player:		25.00
Inserted 1:280		
121A	Jerome Moiso/150	25.00
122A	Jamal Crawford/200	50.00
123A	DeShawn Stevenson/200	75.00
124A	Quentin Richardson/150	60.00
125A	Marcus Fizer/150	50.00
126A	Mike Miller/150	150.00
127A	Jamaal Magloire EX	40.00
128A	Chris Mihm/100	30.00
129A	DerMarr Johnson/200	50.00
130A	Stromile Swift/100	150.00
131A	Darius Miles/100	400.00
132A	Kenyon Martin EX	125.00

2000-01 Upper Deck Black Diamond Diamonation

		MT
Complete Set (14):		25.00
Common Player:		.60
Inserted 1:7		
1	Kobe Bryant	5.00
2	Steve Francis	4.00
3	Allen Iverson	3.00
4	Kevin Garnett	4.00
5	Tracy McGrady	2.00
6	Michael Finley	.60
7	Paul Pierce	1.00
8	Shaquille O'Neal	3.00
9	Vince Carter	6.00
10	Larry Hughes	1.00
11	Grant Hill	3.00
12	Latrell Sprewell	1.50
13	Jerry Stackhouse	.60
14	Tim Duncan	3.00

2000-01 Upper Deck Black Diamond Diamond Gallery

		MT
Complete Set (6):		25.00
Common Player:		5.00
Inserted 1:18		
1	Kobe Bryant	8.00
2	Vince Carter	10.00
3	Kevin Garnett	6.00
4	Shaquille O'Neal	5.00
5	Tim Duncan	5.00
6	Steve Francis	6.00

2000-01 Upper Deck Black Diamond Diamond Might

		MT
Complete Set (11):		18.00
Common Player:		.75
Inserted 1:8		
1	Shaquille O'Neal	3.00
2	Allen Iverson	3.00
3	Vince Carter	6.00
4	Chris Webber	2.50
5	Elton Brand	2.00
6	Karl Malone	1.00
7	Rasheed Wallace	.75
8	Antawn Jamison	1.50
9	Kevin Garnett	4.00
10	Antonio McDyess	.75
11	Kobe Bryant	5.00

2000-01 Upper Deck Black Diamond Diamond Skills

		MT
Complete Set (11):		15.00
Common Player:		.60
Inserted 1:8		
1	Kevin Garnett	4.00
2	Jason Kidd	2.00
3	Allen Iverson	3.00
4	Gary Payton	1.00
5	Tim Duncan	3.00
6	Eddie Jones	1.25
7	Grant Hill	3.00
8	Andre Miller	.75
9	Jason Williams	1.00
10	Kobe Bryant	5.00
11	Ray Allen	.60

2000-01 Upper Deck Black Diamond Game Gear

		MT
Common Player:		10.00
Inserted 1:20		
RA	Ron Artest	10.00
TB	Terrell Brandon	10.00

KB Kobe Bryant 100.00
MC Marcus Camby 12.00
BD Baron Davis 15.00
KE Khalid El-Amin 10.00
MF Michael Finley 15.00
KG1 Kevin Garnett 50.00
KG2 Kevin Garnett 50.00
TG Tom Gugliotta 10.00
AH Anfernee Hardaway 30.00
GH Grant Hill 30.00
LH Larry Hughes 15.00
KM Karl Malone 20.00
SM Stephon Marbury 20.00
JM Jamal Mashburn 12.00
TM Tracy McGrady 30.00
MM Mike Miller 30.00
DM Dikembe Mutombo 10.00
DN Dirk Nowitzki 25.00
PP Paul Pierce 20.00
CP Chris Porter 15.00
GR Glen Rice 12.00
IR Isaiah Rider 12.00
LS Latrell Sprewell 25.00
DS DeShawn Stevenson 25.00
WS Wally Szczerbiak 12.00
AW Antoine Walker 12.00

2000-01 Upper Deck Encore

MT
Complete Set (165): 175.00
Common Player: .15
Minor Stars: .30
Common Rookie: 2.00
Production 1600 Sets
Pack (5): 5.00
Box (16): 60.00
1 Brevin Knight .15
2 Lorenzen Wright .15
3 Alan Henderson .15
4 Jason Terry .30
5 Paul Pierce .60
6 Antoine Walker .40
7 Kenny Anderson .15
8 Tony Battie .15
9 Adrian Griffin .15
10 Derrick Coleman .15
11 David Wesley .15
12 Baron Davis .50
13 Elden Campbell .15
14 Jamal Mashburn .30
15 Elton Brand 1.25
16 Ron Mercer .30
17 Ron Artest .30
18 Michael Ruffin .15
19 Lamond Murray .15
20 Andre Miller .50
21 Matt Harpring .15
22 Jim Jackson .15
23 Michael Finley .30
24 Dirk Nowitzki 1.00
25 Steve Nash .15
26 Howard Eisley .15
27 Antonio McDyess .40
28 James Posey .30
29 Nick Van Exel .30
30 Raef LaFrentz .15
31 Voshon Lenard .15
32 Jerry Stackhouse .40
33 Ben Wallace .15
34 Michael Curry .15
35 Joe Smith .15
36 Chucky Atkins .15
37 Antawn Jamison 1.00
38 Larry Hughes .60
39 Chris Mills .15
40 Mookie Blaylock .15
41 Vonteego Cummings .15
42 Steve Francis 2.50
43 Maurice Taylor .15
44 Hakeem Olajuwon .60
45 Walt Williams .15
46 Cuttino Mobley .30
47 Reggie Miller .30
48 Jalen Rose .30
49 Austin Croshere .15
50 Travis Best .15
51 Jermaine O'Neal .50
52 Lamar Odom 1.25
53 Jeff McInnis .15
54 Michael Olowokandi .15
55 Brian Skinner .15
56 Corey Maggette .40
57 Shaquille O'Neal 2.00
58 Ron Harper .15
59 Kobe Bryant 3.00
60 Robert Horry .15
61 Isaiah Rider .15
62 Eddie Jones .75
63 Anthony Carter .30
64 Tim Hardaway .40
65 Brian Grant .15
66 Anthony Mason .15
67 Ray Allen .40
68 Tim Thomas .40
69 Glenn Robinson .30
70 Sam Cassell .15
71 Lindsey Hunter .15
72 Kevin Garnett 2.50
73 Wally Szczerbiak .40
74 Terrell Brandon .30
75 Chauncey Billups .15
76 Stephon Marbury .75
77 Keith Van Horn .50
78 Lucious Harris .15
79 Kendall Gill .15
80 Latrell Sprewell 1.00
81 Marcus Camby .15
82 Larry Johnson .15
83 Allan Houston .30
84 Glen Rice .30
85 Grant Hill 2.00
86 Tracy McGrady 1.25
87 John Amaechi .15
88 Darrell Armstrong .15
89 Allen Iverson 2.00
90 Dikembe Mutombo .15
91 George Lynch .15
92 Aaron McKie .15
93 Eric Snow .15
94 Jason Kidd 1.25
95 Tony Delk .15
96 Clifford Robinson .15
97 Tom Gugliotta .15
98 Shawn Marion 1.00
99 Rasheed Wallace .50
100 Scottie Pippen 1.25
101 Steve Smith .30
102 Damon Stoudamire .30
103 Bonzi Wells .40
104 Chris Webber 1.50
105 Jason Williams .60
106 Predrag Stojakovic .40
107 Vlade Divac .15
108 Doug Christie .15
109 Tim Duncan 2.00
110 David Robinson .60
111 Derek Anderson .30
112 Antonio Daniels .15
113 Sean Elliott .15
114 Gary Payton .60
115 Patrick Ewing .30
116 Vin Baker .15
117 Rashard Lewis .50
118 Vince Carter 4.00
119 Alvin Williams .15
120 Antonio Davis .15
121 Charles Oakley .15
122 Karl Malone .60
123 John Stockton .30
124 Bryon Russell .15
125 John Starks .15
126 Shareef Abdur-Rahim .60
127 Mike Bibby .30
128 Michael Dickerson .15
129 Grant Long .15
130 Mitch Richmond .30
131 Richard Hamilton .40
132 Chris Whitney .15
133 Jahidi White .15
134 Checklist #1 (Kobe Bryant) 1.00
135 Checklist #2 (Kevin Garnett) .50
136 *Kenyon Martin* 10.00
137 *Stromile Swift* 12.00
138 *Chris Mihm* 3.00
139 *Marcus Fizer* 8.00
140 *Darius Miles* 30.00
141 *Joel Przybilla* 3.00
142 *Mike Miller* 12.00
143 *Courtney Alexander* 8.00
144 *DerMarr Johnson* 8.00
145 *Stephen Jackson* 4.00
146 *Jerome Moiso* 4.00
147 *Keyon Dooling* 8.00
148 *Erick Barkley* 4.00
149 *Jason Collier* 2.50
150 *Jamaal Magloire* 4.00
151 *DeShawn Stevenson* 10.00
152 *Hidayet Turkoglu* 8.00
153 *Morris Peterson* 10.00
154 *Jamal Crawford* 8.00
155 *Etan Thomas* 3.00
156 *Quentin Richardson* 8.00
157 *Mateen Cleaves* 5.00
158 *Donnell Harvey* 3.00
159 *Mark Madsen* 4.00
160 *Desmond Mason* 8.00
161 *Craig "Speedy" Claxton* 3.00
162 *Hanno Mottola* 2.00
163 *Mamadou N'diaye* 2.00
164 *Eduardo Najera* 2.50
165 *Khalid El-Amin* 2.50

2000-01 Upper Deck Encore High Definition

MT
Complete Set (6): 12.00
Common Player: 1.25
Inserted 1:16
HD1 Stephon Marbury 1.25
HD2 Steve Francis 4.00
HD3 Shaquille O'Neal 3.00
HD4 Kevin Garnett 4.00
HD5 Kobe Bryant 5.00
HD6 Tracy McGrady 2.00

Post-1980 cards in Near Mint condition will generally sell for about 75% of the quoted Mint value. Excellent-condition cards bring no more than 40%.

2000-01 Upper Deck Encore NBA Warm-ups

MT
Common Player: 10.00
Inserted 1:8 Hobby
Autographs Numbered to 50 Sets
CA-A Courtney Alexander Auto
CA-W Courtney Alexander 15.00
KB-A Kobe Bryant Auto
KB-W Kobe Bryant 50.00
JC-A Jamal Crawford Auto
JC-W Jamal Crawford 15.00
BD-W Baron Davis 12.00
KD-W Keyon Dooling 15.00
KE-A Khalid El-Amin Auto
KE-W Khalid El-Amin 10.00
MF-A Marcus Fizer Auto
MF-W Marcus Fizer 15.00
KG-A Kevin Garnett Auto
KG-W Kevin Garnett 25.00
DJ-A DerMarr Johnson Auto
DJ-W DerMarr Johnson 15.00
MA-W Corey Maggette 12.00
KM-A Kenyon Martin Auto
KM-W Kenyon Martin 15.00
TM-A Tracy McGrady Auto
TM-W Tracy McGrady 25.00
CM-A Chris Mihm Auto
CM-W Chris Mihm 10.00
DM-A Darius Miles Auto
DM-W Darius Miles 40.00
AM-A Andre Miller Auto
AM-W Andre Miller 12.00
MM-A Mike Miller Auto
MM-W Mike Miller 20.00
JM-W Jerome Moiso 10.00
HM-W Hanno Mottola 10.00
JS-A Jerry Stackhouse Auto
JS-W Jerry Stackhouse 15.00
DS-A DeShawn Stevenson Auto
DS-W DeShawn Stevenson 15.00
WS-W Wally Szczerbiak 12.00

2000-01 Upper Deck Encore Performers

MT
Complete Set (12): 12.00
Common Player: .50
Inserted 1:8
EP1 Jason Kidd 1.50
EP2 Stephon Marbury 1.00
EP3 Gary Payton .75
EP4 Kevin Garnett 3.00
EP5 Antonio McDyess .60
EP6 Shareef Abdur-Rahim .75
EP7 Tim Duncan 2.50
EP8 Allan Houston .50
EP9 Kobe Bryant 4.00
EP10 Andre Miller .60
EP11 Vince Carter 5.00
EP12 Ray Allen .60

2000-01 Upper Deck Encore Powerful Stuff

MT
Complete Set (12): 15.00
Common Player: .75
Inserted 1:8

PS1 Kobe Bryant 4.00
PS2 Tim Duncan 2.50
PS3 Allen Iverson 2.50
PS4 Karl Malone .75
PS5 Tracy McGrady 1.50
PS6 Shaquille O'Neal 2.50
PS7 Vince Carter 5.00
PS8 Chris Webber 2.00
PS9 Eddie Jones 1.00
PS10 Kevin Garnett 3.00
PS11 Elton Brand 1.50
PS12 Paul Pierce .75

2000-01 Upper Deck Encore Star Signatures

MT
Common Player: 10.00
Inserted 1:47 Hobby
CA Courtney Alexander 30.00
EB Erick Barkley 12.00
KB Kobe Bryant 150.00
SC Craig "Speedy" Claxton 12.00
MC Mateen Cleaves 15.00
CR Jamal Crawford 15.00
KE Khalid El-Amin 10.00
MF Marcus Fizer
SF Steve Francis
RH Richard Hamilton 15.00
TH Tim Hardaway 15.00
DH Donnell Harvey 12.00
LH Larry Hughes 15.00
DJ DerMarr Johnson 15.00
EJ Eddie Jones 25.00
MK Mark Madsen 15.00
CO Corey Maggette 15.00
JA Jamaal Magloire 12.00
SM Shawn Marion 25.00
KM Kenyon Martin 25.00
CM Chris Mihm 12.00
DM Darius Miles 100.00
MM Mike Miller 60.00
RM Reggie Miller 100.00
JM Jerome Moiso 10.00
HM Hanno Mottola 10.00
MN Mamadou N'diaye 10.00
JO Jermaine O'Neal 20.00
GP Gary Payton 25.00
MP Morris Peterson 30.00
JP Joel Przybilla 12.00
QR Quentin Richardson 20.00
JS Jerry Stackhouse 20.00
DS DeShawn Stevenson 30.00
SS Stromile Swift 40.00
WS Wally Szczerbiak 15.00
ET Etan Thomas 10.00

2000-01 Upper Deck Encore Upper Realm

MT
Complete Set (6): 12.00
Common Player: 2.50
Inserted 1:16
UR1 Shaquille O'Neal 3.00
UR2 Allen Iverson 3.00
UR3 Tim Duncan 3.00
UR4 Kobe Bryant 5.00
UR5 Chris Webber 2.50
UR6 Kevin Garnett 4.00

2000-01 Upper Deck Encore Vertical Forces

MT
Complete Set (6): 15.00
Common Player: 1.00
Inserted 1:16
VF1 Kobe Bryant 5.00
VF2 Vince Carter 6.00
VF3 Rashard Lewis 1.00
VF4 Chris Webber 2.50
VF5 Steve Francis 4.00
VF6 Kevin Garnett 4.00

2000-01 Upper Deck Hardcourt

MT
Complete Set (102): 800.00
Common Player: .15
Minor Stars: .30
Common Rookie (61-102): 3.00
Pack (5): 5.00
Box (15): 65.00
1 Dikembe Mutombo .15
2 Jason Terry .30
3 Antoine Walker .50
4 Paul Pierce .50
5 Eddie Jones .75
6 Baron Davis .50
7 Elton Brand 1.50
8 Ron Artest .50
9 Andre Miller .50
10 Shawn Kemp .50
11 Dirk Nowitzki .60
12 Michael Finley .30
13 Antonio McDyess .40
14 Nick Van Exel .15
15 Grant Hill 2.00
16 Jerry Stackhouse .15
17 Antawn Jamison .75
18 Larry Hughes 1.00
19 Steve Francis 3.00
20 Hakeem Olajuwon .60
21 Reggie Miller .30
22 Jalen Rose .40
23 Lamar Odom 1.25
24 Eric Piatkowski .15
25 Shaquille O'Neal 2.00
26 Kobe Bryant 4.00
27 Alonzo Mourning .40
28 Jamal Mashburn .15
29 Ray Allen .30
30 Glenn Robinson .15
31 Kevin Garnett 3.00
32 Wally Szczerbiak .60
33 Keith Van Horn .60
34 Stephon Marbury .75
35 Allan Houston .30
36 Latrell Sprewell .75
37 Darrell Armstrong .15
38 Ron Mercer .30
39 Allen Iverson 2.00
40 Toni Kukoc .40
41 Jason Kidd 1.25
42 Anfernee Hardaway 1.25
43 Shawn Marion .50
44 Scottie Pippen 1.25
45 Damon Stoudamire .30
46 Chris Webber 1.25
47 Jason Williams .75
48 Tim Duncan 2.00
49 David Robinson .60
50 Gary Payton .60
51 Vin Baker .15
52 Rashard Lewis .50
53 Tracy McGrady 1.25
54 Vince Carter 5.00
55 Karl Malone .60
56 John Stockton .30
57 Shareef Abdur-Rahim .75
58 Mike Bibby .40
59 Mitch Richmond .30
60 Richard Hamilton .40
61 *Kenyon Martin* 40.00
62 *Marcus Fizer* 15.00
63 *Chris Mihm* 10.00
64 *Chris Porter* 20.00
65 *Stromile Swift* 40.00
66 *Morris Peterson* 30.00
67 *Quentin Richardson* 20.00
68 *Courtney Alexander* 25.00
69 *Scoonie Penn* 3.00
70 *Mateen Cleaves* 12.00
71 *Erick Barkley* 10.00
72 *A.J. Guyton* 8.00
73 *Darius Miles* 125.00
74 *DerMarr Johnson* 15.00
75 *Hidayet Turkoglu* 20.00
76 *Hanno Mottola* 6.00
77 *Mike Miller* 40.00
78 *Desmond Mason* 25.00
79 *Mark Madsen* 10.00
80 *Eduardo Najera* 6.00
81 *Craig Claxton* 8.00
82 *Joel Przybilla* 5.00
83 *Brian Cardinal* 3.00
84 *Khalid El-Amin* 6.00
85 *Etan Thomas* 8.00
86 *Cory Hightower* 3.00
87 *Dan Langhi* 4.00
88 *Michael Redd* 6.00
89 *Pete Mickeal* 5.00
90 *Mamadou N'diaye* 4.00
91 *Jerome Moiso* 10.00
92 *Chris Carrawell* 3.00
93 *Jason Collier* 3.00
94 *Keyon Dooling* 15.00
95 *Mark Karcher* 3.00
96 *Jamaal Magloire* 10.00
97 *Jason Hart* 3.00
98 *Jabari Smith* 3.00
99 *Donnell Harvey* 8.00
100 *Lavor Postell* 6.00
101 *Eddie House* 12.00
102 *Dan McClintock* 3.00

2000-01 Upper Deck Hardcourt Court Authority

MT
Complete Set (15): 45.00
Common Player: 1.00
Inserted 1:15
CA1 Kobe Bryant 8.00
CA2 Allen Iverson 4.00
CA3 Gary Payton 1.50
CA4 Tim Duncan 5.00
CA5 Kevin Garnett 6.00
CA6 Steve Francis 6.00
CA7 Vince Carter 10.00
CA8 Shaquille O'Neal 5.00
CA9 Jason Kidd 3.00
CA10 Karl Malone 1.50
CA11 Shareef Abdur-Rahim 2.00
CA12 Grant Hill 5.00
CA13 Reggie Miller 1.00
CA14 Keith Van Horn 1.50
CA15 John Stockton 1.00

2000-01 Upper Deck Hardcourt Court Forces

MT
Complete Set (11): 10.00
Common Player: .50
Inserted 1:12
C1 Elton Brand 2.00
C2 Steve Francis 3.00
C3 Allan Houston .60
C4 Lamar Odom 1.50
C5 Andre Miller .75
C6 Jason Williams 1.25
C7 Ron Mercer .60
C8 Kobe Bryant 4.00
C9 Kevin Garnett 3.00
C10 Jerry Stackhouse .50
C11 Latrell Sprewell 1.25

2000-01 Upper Deck Hardcourt Floor Leaders

MT
Complete Set (20): 15.00
Common Player: .30
Inserted 1:7
FL1 Kobe Bryant 5.00
FL2 Eddie Jones 1.25
FL3 Kevin Garnett 4.00
FL4 Andre Miller 1.00
FL5 Keith Van Horn 1.00
FL6 Allan Houston .50
FL7 Larry Hughes 1.25
FL8 Jason Williams 1.00
FL9 Tracy McGrady 2.00
FL10 Shawn Kemp .60
FL11 Stephon Marbury 1.00
FL12 Glenn Robinson .30
FL13 Mike Bibby .50
FL14 Baron Davis .75
FL15 Scottie Pippen 2.00
FL16 David Robinson .75
FL17 Paul Pierce 1.00
FL18 Wally Szczerbiak 1.00
FL19 Jalen Rose .60
FL20 Lamar Odom 2.00

A player's name in *italic type* indicates a rookie card.

2000-01 Upper Deck Hardcourt Game Floor

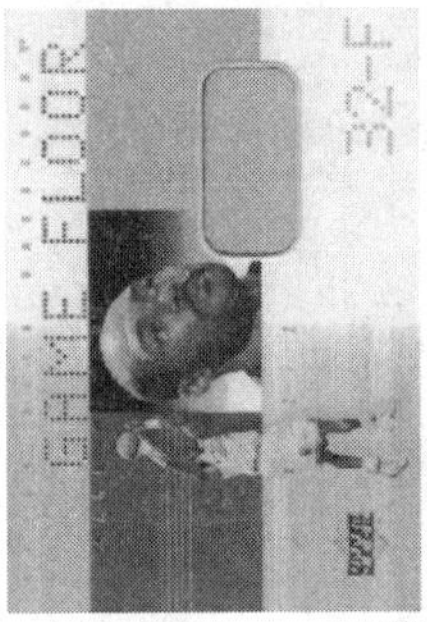

		MT
Complete Set (29):		425.00
Common Player:		15.00
Inserted 1:15		
SA-F	Shareef Abdur-Rahim	20.00
RA-F	Ray Allen	20.00
KB-F	Kobe Bryant	50.00
KB-A	Kobe Bryant	
MF-F	Michael Finley	15.00
KG-F	Kevin Garnett	40.00
KG-A	Kevin Garnett	600.00
AH-F	Anfernee Hardaway	25.00
TH-F	Tim Hardaway	15.00
GH-F	Grant Hill	30.00
AL-F	Allan Houston	15.00
AI-F	Allen Iverson	30.00
EJ-F	Eddie Jones	20.00
MJ-A	Michael Jordan	
JK-F	Jason Kidd	25.00
KM-F	Karl Malone	20.00
KM-A	Karl Malone	250.00
SM-F	Stephon Marbury	20.00
MC-F	Antonio McDyess	15.00
RM-F	Ron Mercer	15.00
RG-F	Reggie Miller	20.00
AM-F	Alonzo Mourning	20.00
SO-F	Shaquille O'Neal	40.00
GP-F	Gary Payton	25.00
SP-F	Scottie Pippen	25.00
DR-F	David Robinson	20.00
AW-F	Antoine Walker	15.00
RW-F	Rasheed Wallace	15.00
CW-F	Chris Webber	25.00

2000-01 Upper Deck Hardcourt Night Court

		MT
Complete Set (15):		30.00
Common Player:		1.00
Inserted 1:15		
NC1	Kevin Garnett	6.00
NC2	Tim Duncan	5.00
NC3	Larry Hughes	2.00
NC4	Elton Brand	4.00
NC5	Kobe Bryant	8.00
NC6	Anfernee Hardaway	3.00
NC7	Tracy McGrady	3.00
NC8	Antonio McDyess	1.00
NC9	Paul Pierce	1.50
NC10	Lamar Odom	3.00
NC11	Chris Webber	3.00
NC12	Ray Allen	1.00
NC13	Allan Houston	1.00
NC14	Wally Szczerbiak	1.50
NC15	Alonzo Mourning	1.00

2000-01 Upper Deck Hardcourt Thriller Instinct

		MT
Complete Set (11):		12.00
Common Player:		.50
Inserted 1:12		
TI1	Kevin Garnett	3.00
TI2	Vince Carter	5.00
TI3	Shawn Marion	.75
TI4	Stephon Marbury	1.00
TI5	Antawn Jamison	1.00
TI6	Jason Williams	1.00
TI7	Michael Finley	.50
TI8	Kobe Bryant	4.00
TI9	Richard Hamilton	.60
TI10	Reggie Miller	.50
TI11	Elton Brand	2.00

2000-01 Upper Deck Hardcourt UD Authentics

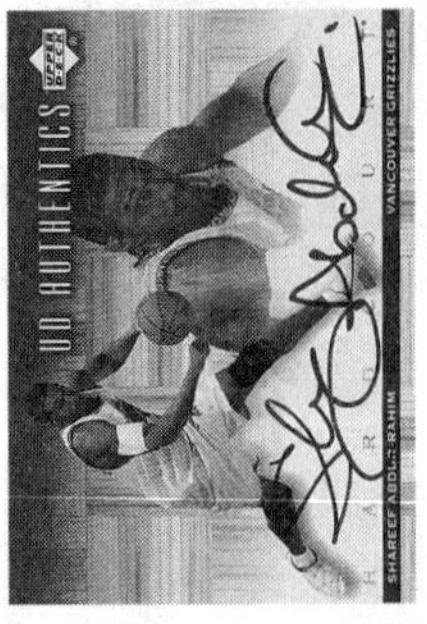

		MT
Complete Set (20):		700.00
Common Player:		10.00
Inserted 1:100		
SA	Shareef Abdur-Rahim	25.00
RA	Ray Allen	25.00
KB	Kobe Bryant	200.00
BD	Baron Davis	20.00
MF	Michael Finley	15.00
SF	Steve Francis	60.00
KG	Kevin Garnett	125.00
AH	Anfernee Hardaway	75.00
TH	Tim Hardaway	15.00
LH	Larry Hughes	30.00
AI	Allen Iverson	60.00
KM	Karl Malone	50.00
MC	Antonio McDyess	15.00
AM	Andre Miller	20.00
GP	Gary Payton	30.00
PP	Paul Pierce	20.00
JR	Jalen Rose	25.00
JS	Jerry Stackhouse	10.00
DS	Damon Stoudamire	20.00
WS	Wally Szczerbiak	20.00

2000-01 Upper Deck Hardcourt Rookie Exclusive Signatures

		MT
Complete Set (4):		250.00
Common Player:		40.00
MF	Marcus Fizer	75.00
DM	Darius Miles	125.00
JM	Jerome Moiso	40.00
QR	Quentin Richardson	50.00

2000-01 Upper Deck MVP

		MT
Complete Set (220):		45.00
Common Player:		.10
Minor Stars:		.20
Common Rookie (191-220):		.50
Pack (10):		1.50
Box (28):		35.00
1	Dikembe Mutombo	.10
2	Jason Terry	.20
3	Jim Jackson	.10
4	Alan Henderson	.10
5	Roshown McLeod	.10
6	Bimbo Coles	.10
7	Lorenzen Wright	.10
8	Antoine Walker	.30
9	Paul Pierce	.40
10	Kenny Anderson	.20
11	Adrian Griffin	.20
12	Vitaly Potapenko	.10
13	Dana Barros	.10
14	Eric Williams	.10
15	Eddie Jones	.50
16	Eddie Robinson	.20
17	Ricky Davis	.10
18	Elden Campbell	.10
19	Derrick Coleman	.10
20	David Wesley	.10
21	Baron Davis	.30
22	Elton Brand	1.00
23	Ron Artest	.30
24	Hersey Hawkins	.10
25	Chris Carr	.10
26	Corey Benjamin	.10
27	Will Perdue	.10
28	Andre Miller	.30
29	Shawn Kemp	.30
30	Wesley Person	.10
31	Lamond Murray	.10
32	Bob Sura	.10
33	Andrew DeClercq	.10
34	Dirk Nowitzki	.50
35	Michael Finley	.20
36	Cedric Ceballos	.10
37	Shawn Bradley	.10
38	Erick Strickland	.10
39	Hubert Davis	.10
40	Antonio McDyess	.30
41	Raef LaFrentz	.20
42	Keon Clark	.10
43	Nick Van Exel	.20
44	James Posey	.20
45	Chris Gatling	.10
46	George McCloud	.10
47	Grant Hill	1.25
48	Jerry Stackhouse	.20
49	Lindsey Hunter	.10
50	Christian Laettner	.10
51	Jerome Williams	.10
52	Terry Mills	.10
53	Antawn Jamison	.40
54	Donyell Marshall	.10
55	Chris Mills	.10
56	Larry Hughes	.50
57	Mookie Blaylock	.10
58	Vonteego Cummings	.20
59	Steve Francis	1.50
60	Shandon Anderson	.10
61	Cuttino Mobley	.10
62	Hakeem Olajuwon	.40
63	Walt Williams	.10
64	Kelvin Cato	.10
65	Reggie Miller	.20
66	Austin Croshere	.20
67	Rik Smits	.10
68	Jalen Rose	.30
69	Dale Davis	.10
70	Jonathan Bender	.50
71	Michael Olowokandi	.10
72	Lamar Odom	.75
73	Tyrone Nesby	.10
74	Etdrick Bohannon	.10
75	Eric Piatkowski	.10
76	Shaquille O'Neal	1.25
77	Kobe Bryant	2.00
78	Robert Horry	.10
79	Ron Harper	.10
80	Rick Fox	.10
81	Derek Fisher	.10
82	Devean George	.10
83	Alonzo Mourning	.30
84	Clarence Weatherspoon	.10
85	Anthony Carter	.20
86	P.J. Brown	.10
87	Tim Hardaway	.30
88	Jamal Mashburn	.20
89	Voshon Lenard	.10
90	Ray Allen	.30
91	Glenn Robinson	.20
92	Tim Thomas	.30
93	Sam Cassell	.20
94	Robert Traylor	.10
95	Ervin Johnson	.10
96	Danny Manning	.10
97	Kevin Garnett	1.50
98	Wally Szczerbiak	.40
99	Terrell Brandon	.20
100	William Avery	.20
101	Anthony Peeler	.10
102	Radoslav Nesterovic	.10
103	Dean Garrett	.10
104	Keith Van Horn	.30
105	Kerry Kittles	.10
106	Stephon Marbury	.40
107	Evan Eschmeyer	.10
108	Jim McIlvaine	.10
109	Lucious Harris	.10
110	Jamie Feick	.10
111	Allan Houston	.20
112	Latrell Sprewell	.50
113	Patrick Ewing	.20
114	Chris Childs	.10
115	Marcus Camby	.10
116	Charlie Ward	.10
117	Larry Johnson	.10
118	Darrell Armstrong	.10
119	Corey Maggette	.40
120	Ron Mercer	.30
121	Pat Garrity	.10
122	Chucky Atkins	.10
123	Ben Wallace	.10
124	Michael Doleac	.10
125	Allen Iverson	1.25
126	Matt Geiger	.10
127	Eric Snow	.10
128	Toni Kukoc	.30
129	Theo Ratliff	.10
130	George Lynch	.10
131	Jason Kidd	.75
132	Tom Gugliotta	.10
133	Rodney Rogers	.10
134	Shawn Marion	.30
135	Clifford Robinson	.10
136	Kevin Johnson	.10
137	Anfernee Hardaway	.75
138	Scottie Pippen	.75
139	Damon Stoudamire	.20
140	Arvydas Sabonis	.10
141	Jermaine O'Neal	.20
142	Bonzi Wells	.30
143	Rasheed Wallace	.30
144	Detlef Schrempf	.10
145	Chris Webber	.75
146	Vlade Divac	.20
147	Predrag Stojakovic	.10
148	Jason Williams	.50
149	Corliss Williamson	.10
150	Nick Anderson	.10
151	Jon Barry	.10
152	Tim Duncan	1.25
153	David Robinson	.40
154	Avery Johnson	.10
155	Terry Porter	.10
156	Mario Elie	.10
157	Jaren Jackson	.10
158	Steve Kerr	.10
159	Gary Payton	.40
160	Vin Baker	.10
161	Brent Barry	.10
162	Horace Grant	.10
163	Ruben Patterson	.10
164	Rashard Lewis	.30
165	Tracy McGrady	.75
166	Charles Oakley	.10
167	Doug Christie	.10
168	Antonio Davis	.10
169	Vince Carter	2.50
170	Kevin Willis	.10
171	Karl Malone	.40
172	John Stockton	.20
173	Bryon Russell	.10
174	Quincy Lewis	.20
175	Olden Polynice	.10
176	Jacque Vaughn	.10
177	Shareef Abdur-Rahim	.40
178	Michael Dickerson	.10
179	Bryant Reeves	.10
180	Mike Bibby	.30
181	Othella Harrington	.10
182	Felipe Lopez	.10
183	Mitch Richmond	.20
184	Richard Hamilton	.30
185	Jahidi White	.10
186	Aaron Williams	.10
187	Juwan Howard	.20
188	Rod Strickland	.20
189	Kobe Bryant	1.00
190	Kevin Garnett	.75
191	*Kenyon Martin*	2.00
192	*Marcus Fizer*	1.50
193	*Chris Mihm*	1.00
194	*Stromile Swift*	3.00
195	*Morris Peterson*	2.00
196	*Quentin Richardson*	1.50
197	*Courtney Alexander*	1.50
198	*Scoonie Penn*	.50
199	*Mateen Cleaves*	1.25
200	*Erick Barkley*	1.00
201	*A.J. Guyton*	.75
202	*Darius Miles*	5.00
203	*DerMarr Johnson*	1.50
204	*Jerome Moiso*	1.00
205	*Jamaal Magloire*	1.00
206	*Hanno Mottola*	.50
207	*Mike Miller*	3.00
208	*Desmond Mason*	1.50
209	*Chris Carrawell*	.75
210	*Eduardo Najera*	.75
211	*Craig Claxton*	1.00
212	*Joel Przybilla*	1.00
213	*Mark Madsen*	.60
214	*Khalid El-Amin*	.75
215	*Etan Thomas*	1.00
216	*Jason Collier*	.60
217	*Jason Hart*	.50
218	*Michael Redd*	.60
219	*Keyon Dooling*	1.50
220	*Mamadou N'diaye*	.60

2000-01 Upper Deck MVP Silver Script

	MT
Complete Set (220):	100.00
Silver Cards:	2x
Common Player:	.20
Minor Stars:	.40
Common Rookie (191-220):	1.00
Inserted 1:2	

2000-01 Upper Deck MVP Super Script

	MT
Common Player:	15.00
Super Script Cards:	75x-150x
Super Script Rookies:	30x-60x
Production 25 Sets	

2000-01 Upper Deck MVP Gold Script

	MT
Common Player:	3.00
Gold Cards:	15x-30x
Gold Rookies:	10x-20x
Production 100 Sets	

2000-01 Upper Deck MVP Dynamics

		MT
Complete Set (20):		50.00
Common Player:		1.00
Inserted 1:28		
D1	Shaquille O'Neal	5.00
D2	Allen Iverson	4.00
D3	Paul Pierce	2.00
D4	Scottie Pippen	3.00
D5	Lamar Odom	3.00
D6	Kobe Bryant	8.00
D7	Gary Payton	2.00
D8	Antonio McDyess	1.25
D9	Stephon Marbury	2.50
D10	Alonzo Mourning	1.25
D11	Vince Carter	10.00
D12	Jason Kidd	3.00
D13	Michael Finley	1.00
D14	Chris Webber	3.00
D15	Anfernee Hardaway	3.00
D16	Kevin Garnett	6.00
D17	Jason Williams	2.00
D18	Allan Houston	1.00
D19	Elton Brand	4.00
D20	Karl Malone	2.00

2000-01 Upper Deck MVP Electrifying

		MT
Complete Set (10):		5.00
Common Player:		.30
Inserted 1:9		
E1	Kevin Garnett	2.50
E2	Stephon Marbury	.75
E3	Damon Stoudamire	.30
E4	Jalen Rose	.30
E5	Eddie Jones	.75
E6	Elton Brand	1.50
E7	Wally Szczerbiak	.60
E8	Kobe Bryant	3.00
E9	Shawn Marion	.50
E10	Mike Bibby	.30

2000-01 Upper Deck MVP Game-Used Souvenirs

		MT
Common Player:		20.00
Inserted 1:130 Hobby		
RY	Ray Allen	30.00
RA	Ron Artest	20.00
MB	Mike Bibby	20.00
KB	Kobe Bryant	100.00
MF	Michael Finley	20.00
SF	Steve Francis	75.00
KG	Kevin Garnett	75.00
RH	Richard Hamilton	20.00
AN	Anfernee Hardaway	40.00
AH	Allan Houston	20.00
LH	Larry Hughes	40.00
AI	Allen Iverson	50.00
AJ	Antawn Jamison	30.00
EJ	Eddie Jones	30.00
JK	Jason Kidd	40.00
KM	Karl Malone	30.00
SM	Stephon Marbury	30.00
MC	Antonio McDyess	20.00
TM	Tracy McGrady	40.00
AM	Andre Miller	30.00
RM	Reggie Miller	20.00
SO	Shaquille O'Neal	60.00
GP	Gary Payton	30.00
PP	Paul Pierce	20.00
SP	Scottie Pippen	40.00
WS	Wally Szczerbiak	30.00
RW	Rasheed Wallace	30.00
JW	Jason Williams	30.00

2000-01 Upper Deck MVP MVP Theatre

		MT
Complete Set (10):		10.00
Common Player:		.50
Inserted 1:14		
M1	Kobe Bryant	4.00
M2	Alonzo Mourning	.60
M3	Reggie Miller	.50
M4	Chris Webber	1.50
M5	John Stockton	.50
M6	Vince Carter	5.00
M7	Richard Hamilton	.60
M8	Hakeem Olajuwon	1.00
M9	Kevin Garnett	3.00
M10	David Robinson	1.00

2000-01 Upper Deck MVP MVPerformers

		MT
Complete Set (11):		15.00
Common Player:		1.00
Inserted 1:28		
P1	Kobe Bryant	8.00
P2	Antawn Jamison	2.00
P3	John Stockton	1.00
P4	Andre Miller	1.50
P5	Latrell Sprewell	2.00
P6	Jason Williams	2.00
P7	Kevin Garnett	6.00
P8	Lamar Odom	3.00
P9	Allan Houston	1.00
P10	Keith Van Horn	1.00
P11	Antoine Walker	1.00

2000-01 Upper Deck MVP ProSign

		MT
Common Player:		10.00
Inserted 1:216 Retail		
SA	Shareef Abdur-Rahim	25.00
RA	Ray Allen	30.00
DA	Darrell Armstrong	15.00
MB	Mike Bibby	20.00
CB	Calvin Booth	10.00
KB	Kobe Bryant	10.00
SF	Steve Francis	75.00
KG	Kevin Garnett	125.00
AH	Anfernee Hardaway	75.00
LH	Larry Hughes	40.00
MJ	Michael Jordan	10.00
KA	Karl Malone	50.00
MD	Antonio McDyess	25.00
GP	Gary Payton	50.00
PP	Paul Pierce	25.00
VP	Vitaly Potapenko	10.00
JR	Jalen Rose	25.00
DS	Damon Stoudamire	15.00
WS	Wally Szczerbiak	25.00

2000-01 Upper Deck MVP World Jam

		MT
Complete Set (20):		18.00
Common Player:		.25
Inserted 1:5		
WJ1	Kobe Bryant	4.00
WJ2	Vince Carter	5.00
WJ3	Steve Francis	3.00
WJ4	Keith Van Horn	.40
WJ5	Rasheed Wallace	.40
WJ6	Corey Maggette	.75
WJ7	Kevin Garnett	3.00
WJ8	Larry Hughes	.75
WJ9	Tim Duncan	2.50
WJ10	Alonzo Mourning	.40
WJ11	Chris Webber	2.00
WJ12	Shareef Abdur-Rahim	.60
WJ13	Lamar Odom	2.00
WJ14	Ron Mercer	.40
WJ15	Rashard Lewis	.75
WJ16	Michael Dickerson	.25
WJ17	Jerry Stackhouse	.25
WJ18	Latrell Sprewell	.75
WJ19	Shawn Kemp	.40
WJ20	Elton Brand	2.50

2000-01 Upper Deck Ovation

		MT
Complete Set (90):		200.00
Common Player:		.25
Minor Stars:		.40
Common Rookie:		2.50
Production 2,000 Sets		
Pack (5):		4.00
Box (20):		45.00
1	Dikembe Mutombo	.25
2	Jim Jackson	.25
3	Paul Pierce	.75
4	Antoine Walker	.60
5	Derrick Coleman	.40
6	Baron Davis	.60
7	Elton Brand	1.25
8	Ron Artest	.50
9	Lamond Murray	.25
10	Andre Miller	.60
11	Michael Finley	.40
12	Dirk Nowitzki	.75
13	Antonio McDyess	.60
14	Nick Van Exel	.40
15	Jerry Stackhouse	.40
16	Jerome Williams	.25
17	Larry Hughes	1.00
18	Antawn Jamison	1.00
19	Steve Francis	2.50
20	Hakeem Olajuwon	.75
21	Reggie Miller	.40
22	Jalen Rose	.50
23	Lamar Odom	1.25
24	Michael Olowokandi	.25
25	Shaquille O'Neal	2.00
26	Kobe Bryant	3.00
27	Alonzo Mourning	.50
28	Anthony Carter	.40
29	Ray Allen	.40
30	Tim Thomas	.50
31	Kevin Garnett	2.50
32	Wally Szczerbiak	.50
33	Stephon Marbury	1.00
34	Keith Van Horn	.60
35	Allan Houston	.50
36	Latrell Sprewell	1.00
37	Grant Hill	2.00
38	Tracy McGrady	1.25
39	Allen Iverson	2.00
40	Toni Kukoc	.50
41	Jason Kidd	1.25
42	Anfernee Hardaway	1.25
43	Rasheed Wallace	.50
44	Scottie Pippen	1.25
45	Damon Stoudamire	.40
46	Chris Webber	1.25
47	Jason Williams	.75
48	Tim Duncan	2.00
49	David Robinson	.75
50	Gary Payton	.75
51	Brent Barry	.25
52	Rashard Lewis	.75
53	Vince Carter	4.00
54	Antonio Davis	.25
55	Karl Malone	.75
56	John Stockton	.40
57	Shareef Abdur-Rahim	.75
58	Mike Bibby	.40
59	Mitch Richmond	.40
60	Richard Hamilton	.50
61	*Kenyon Martin*	15.00
62	*Stromile Swift*	20.00
63	*Darius Miles*	40.00
64	*Marcus Fizer*	10.00
65	*Mike Miller*	20.00
66	*DerMarr Johnson*	10.00
67	*Chris Mihm*	5.00
68	*Jamal Crawford*	10.00
69	*Joel Przybilla*	4.00
70	*Keyon Dooling*	10.00
71	*Jerome Moiso*	5.00
72	*Etan Thomas*	4.00
73	*Courtney Alexander*	10.00
74	*Mateen Cleaves*	6.00
75	*Jason Collier*	2.50
76	*Hidayet Turkoglu*	10.00
77	*Desmond Mason*	12.00
78	*Quentin Richardson*	12.00
79	*Jamaal Magloire*	4.00
80	*Craig "Speedy" Claxton*	4.00
81	*Morris Peterson*	15.00
82	*Donnell Harvey*	4.00
83	*DeShawn Stevenson*	15.00
84	*Mamadou N'diaye*	2.50
85	*Erick Barkley*	5.00
86	*Mark Madsen*	3.00
87	*A.J. Guyton*	3.00
88	*Khalid El-Amin*	4.00
89	*Eddie House*	2.50
90	*Chris Porter*	8.00

A player's name in *italic type* indicates a rookie card.

2000-01 Upper Deck Ovation Standing Ovation

		MT
Common Player:		10.00
Standing Ovation Cards:		20x-40x
Common Rookie:		20.00
Standing Ovation Rookies:		4x-8x
Production 2,000 Sets		
1	Dikembe Mutombo	.25
2	Jim Jackson	.25
3	Paul Pierce	.75
4	Antoine Walker	.60
5	Derrick Coleman	.40
6	Baron Davis	.60
7	Elton Brand	1.25
8	Ron Artest	.50
9	Lamond Murray	.25
10	Andre Miller	.60
11	Michael Finley	.40
12	Dirk Nowitzki	.75
13	Antonio McDyess	.60
14	Nick Van Exel	.40
15	Jerry Stackhouse	.40
16	Jerome Williams	.25
17	Larry Hughes	1.00
18	Antawn Jamison	1.00
19	Steve Francis	2.50
20	Hakeem Olajuwon	.75
21	Reggie Miller	.40
22	Jalen Rose	.50
23	Lamar Odom	1.25
24	Michael Olowokandi	.25
25	Shaquille O'Neal	2.00
26	Kobe Bryant	3.00
27	Alonzo Mourning	.50
28	Anthony Carter	.40
29	Ray Allen	.40
30	Tim Thomas	.50
31	Kevin Garnett	2.50
32	Wally Szczerbiak	.50
33	Stephon Marbury	1.00
34	Keith Van Horn	.60
35	Allan Houston	.50
36	Latrell Sprewell	1.00
37	Grant Hill	2.00
38	Tracy McGrady	1.25
39	Allen Iverson	2.00
40	Toni Kukoc	.50
41	Jason Kidd	1.25
42	Anfernee Hardaway	1.25
43	Rasheed Wallace	.50
44	Scottie Pippen	1.25
45	Damon Stoudamire	.40
46	Chris Webber	1.25
47	Jason Williams	.75
48	Tim Duncan	2.00
49	David Robinson	.75
50	Gary Payton	.75
51	Brent Barry	.25
52	Rashard Lewis	.75
53	Vince Carter	4.00
54	Antonio Davis	.25
55	Karl Malone	.75
56	John Stockton	.40
57	Shareef Abdur-Rahim	.75
58	Mike Bibby	.40
59	Mitch Richmond	.40
60	Richard Hamilton	.50
61	*Kenyon Martin*	30.00
62	*Stromile Swift*	25.00
63	*Darius Miles*	40.00
64	*Marcus Fizer*	15.00
65	*Mike Miller*	15.00
66	*DerMarr Johnson*	10.00
67	*Chris Mihm*	5.00
68	*Jamal Crawford*	10.00
69	*Joel Przybilla*	4.00
70	*Keyon Dooling*	8.00
71	*Jerome Moiso*	5.00
72	*Etan Thomas*	4.00
73	*Courtney Alexander*	10.00
74	*Mateen Cleaves*	6.00
75	*Jason Collier*	2.50
76	*Hidayet Turkoglu*	8.00
77	*Desmond Mason*	10.00
78	*Quentin Richardson*	10.00
79	*Jamaal Magloire*	4.00
80	*Craig "Speedy" Claxton*	4.00
81	*Morris Peterson*	12.00
82	*Donnell Harvey*	4.00
83	*DeShawn Stevenson*	12.00
84	*Mamadou N'diaye*	2.50
85	*Erick Barkley*	5.00
86	*Mark Madsen*	3.00
87	*A.J. Guyton*	3.00
88	*Khalid El-Amin*	4.00
89	*Eddie House*	2.50
90	*Chris Porter*	6.00

2000-01 Upper Deck Ovation A Piece of History

		MT
Common Player:		20.00
Inserted 1:120		
SA-B	Shareef Abdur-Rahim	20.00
RA-B	Ray Allen	20.00
KB-A	Kobe Bryant Auto/8	
KB-B	Kobe Bryant	75.00
KB-C	Kobe Bryant Combo/25	
KB-S	Kobe Bryant	100.00
BD-B	Baron Davis	20.00
MF-B	Michael Finley	20.00
KG-A	Kevin Garnett Auto/21	600.00
KG-B	Kevin Garnett	50.00
KG-C	Kevin Garnett Combo/25	
KG-S	Kevin Garnett	75.00
AH-B	Anfernee Hardaway	40.00
LH-B	Larry Hughes	25.00
AI-B	Allen Iverson	40.00
MJ-A	Michael Jordan Auto/23	2500.
MJ-S	Michael Jordan	200.00
KM-S	Karl Malone	50.00
AM-B	Andre Miller	20.00
AL-B	Alonzo Mourning	20.00
SO-S	Shaquille O'Neal	75.00
GP-B	Gary Payton	25.00
PP-B	Paul Pierce	20.00
SP-B	Scottie Pippen	30.00
JS-B	Jerry Stackhouse	20.00
WS-B	Wally Szczerbiak	20.00
CW-S	Chris Webber	
JW-B	Jason Williams	25.00

2000-01 Upper Deck Ovation Center Stage

		MT
Complete Set (10):		25.00
Common Player:		1.00
Inserted 1:19		
Silver versions:		2x
Production 200 Sets		
Gold versions:		5x-10x
Production 25 Sets		
CS1	Kevin Garnett	6.00
CS2	Tim Duncan	5.00
CS3	Lamar Odom	3.00
CS4	Jason Kidd	3.00
CS5	Vince Carter	10.00
CS6	Alonzo Mourning	1.00
CS7	Elton Brand	3.00
CS8	Chris Webber	3.00
CS9	Anfernee Hardaway	3.00
CS10	Kobe Bryant	8.00

2000-01 Upper Deck Ovation Lead Performers

		MT
Complete Set (11):		20.00
Common Player:		1.00
Inserted 1:12		
LP1	Shaquille O'Neal	3.00
LP2	Vince Carter	6.00
LP3	Kevin Garnett	4.00
LP4	Allen Iverson	3.00
LP5	Jason Kidd	2.00
LP6	Elton Brand	2.00
LP7	Gary Payton	1.00
LP8	Kobe Bryant	5.00
LP9	Steve Francis	4.00
LP10	Stephon Marbury	1.00
LP11	Tim Duncan	3.00

2000-01 Upper Deck Ovation Ovation Spotlight

		MT
Complete Set (20):		20.00
Common Player:		.50
Inserted 1:7		
OS1	Kobe Bryant	5.00
OS2	Larry Hughes	1.50
OS3	Andre Miller	.75
OS4	Michael Finley	.50
OS5	Ray Allen	.50
OS6	Latrell Sprewell	1.50
OS7	Jalen Rose	.60
OS8	Antonio McDyess	.75
OS9	Karl Malone	1.00
OS10	Paul Pierce	1.00
OS11	Shareef Abdur-Rahim	1.00
OS12	Chris Webber	2.00
OS13	Stephon Marbury	1.25
OS14	Scottie Pippen	2.00
OS15	Lamar Odom	2.00
OS16	Alonzo Mourning	.60
OS17	Kevin Garnett	4.00
OS18	Anfernee Hardaway	2.00
OS19	Jason Williams	1.00
OS20	Rasheed Wallace	.60

2000-01 Upper Deck Ovation Ovation Signatures

		MT
Common Player:		10.00
Inserted 1:200		
Gold level numbered to player's jersey		
SA	Shareef Abdur-Rahim	25.00
CA	Courtney Alexander	20.00
DA	Darrell Armstrong	10.00
KB	Kobe Bryant	200.00
MF	Marcus Fizer	30.00
KG	Kevin Garnett	125.00
AH	Anfernee Hardaway	75.00
LH	Larry Hughes	25.00
DM	DerMarr Johnson	20.00
SM	Shawn Marion	25.00
KY	Kenyon Martin	50.00
CM	Chris Mihm	15.00
JP	Joel Przybilla	10.00
SS	Stromile Swift	40.00

2000-01 Upper Deck Ovation Superstar Theatre

		MT
Complete Set (11):		20.00
Common Player:		.50
Inserted 1:12		
S1	Kobe Bryant	5.00
S2	Vince Carter	6.00
S3	Jason Kidd	2.00
S4	Steve Francis	4.00
S5	Reggie Miller	.50
S6	Tim Duncan	3.00
S7	Kevin Garnett	4.00
S8	Gary Payton	1.00
S9	Elton Brand	2.00
S10	Allen Iverson	3.00
S11	Shaquille O'Neal	3.00

2000-01 UD Pros & Prospects

		MT
Complete Set (120):		800.00
Common Player:		.15
Minor Stars:		.30
Common Rookie (91-120):		5.00
Production 999 Sets		
Pack (5):		5.00
Box (24):		65.00
1	Dikembe Mutombo	.30
2	Alan Henderson	.15
3	Jim Jackson	.15
4	Paul Pierce	.60
5	Kenny Anderson	.30
6	Antoine Walker	.40
7	Baron Davis	.40
8	Derrick Coleman	.30
9	David Wesley	.15
10	Elton Brand	1.50
11	Ron Artest	.30
12	Hersey Hawkins	.15
13	Andre Miller	.30
14	Lamond Murray	.15
15	Shawn Kemp	.30
16	Michael Finley	.30
17	Dirk Nowitzki	.60
18	Cedric Ceballos	.15
19	Antonio McDyess	.40
20	Nick Van Exel	.30
21	Raef LaFrentz	.30
22	Christian Laettner	.15
23	Jerry Stackhouse	.30
24	Lindsey Hunter	.15
25	Antawn Jamison	.60
26	Larry Hughes	.75
27	Chris Mills	.15
28	Steve Francis	2.50
29	Hakeem Olajuwon	.60
30	Shandon Anderson	.15
31	Reggie Miller	.30
32	Jonathan Bender	.60
33	Jalen Rose	.40
34	Lamar Odom	1.00
35	Michael Olowokandi	.15
36	Tyrone Nesby	.15
37	Kobe Bryant	4.00
38	Shaquille O'Neal	2.00
39	Ron Harper	.15
40	Robert Horry	.15
41	Alonzo Mourning	.50
42	P.J. Brown	.15
43	Jamal Mashburn	.30
44	Ray Allen	.40
45	Glenn Robinson	.30
46	Sam Cassell	.30
47	Kevin Garnett	2.50
48	Wally Szczerbiak	.40
49	Terrell Brandon	.30
50	William Avery	.15
51	Stephon Marbury	.75
52	Keith Van Horn	.60
53	Kerry Kittles	.15
54	Latrell Sprewell	.60
55	Allan Houston	.40
56	Patrick Ewing	.30
57	Darrell Armstrong	.15
58	Pat Garrity	.15
59	Michael Doleac	.15
60	Allen Iverson	2.00
61	Theo Ratliff	.15
62	Tyrone Hill	.15
63	Jason Kidd	1.00
64	Anfernee Hardaway	1.00
65	Shawn Marion	.40
66	Scottie Pippen	1.00
67	Rasheed Wallace	.40
68	Damon Stoudamire	.30
69	Bonzi Wells	.30
70	Chris Webber	1.00
71	Predrag Stojakovic	.30
72	Jason Williams	.75
73	Tim Duncan	2.00
74	David Robinson	.60
75	Terry Porter	.15
76	Gary Payton	.60
77	Rashard Lewis	.75
78	Vin Baker	.30
79	Vince Carter	5.00
80	Doug Christie	.15
81	Antonio Davis	.15
82	Karl Malone	.60
83	John Stockton	.30
84	Bryon Russell	.15
85	Shareef Abdur-Rahim	.60
86	Mike Bibby	.40
87	Michael Dickerson	.15
88	Mitch Richmond	.30
89	Richard Hamilton	.40
90	Juwan Howard	.30
91	*Kenyon Martin/Jersey*	60.00
92	*Stromile Swift*	50.00
93	*Darius Miles*	120.00
94	*Marcus Fizer/Jersey*	25.00
95	*Mike Miller*	50.00
96	*DerMarr Johnson*	20.00
97	*Chris Mihm*	10.00
98	*Chris Porter*	25.00
99	*Joel Przybilla*	8.00
100	*Keyon Dooling*	20.00
101	*Jerome Moiso*	10.00
102	*Etan Thomas*	8.00
103	*Courtney Alexander*	30.00
104	*Mateen Cleaves*	15.00
105	*Jason Collier*	6.00
106	*Dan Langhi*	6.00
107	*Desmond Mason*	30.00
108	*Quentin Richardson*	25.00
109	*Jamaal Magloire*	10.00
110	*Craig Claxton*	8.00
111	*Morris Peterson*	35.00
112	*Donnell Harvey*	8.00
113	*Hanno Mottola*	5.00
114	*Mamadou N'diaye*	6.00
115	*Erick Barkley*	10.00
116	*Mark Madsen*	10.00
117	*A.J. Guyton*	8.00
118	*Khalid El-Amin*	6.00
119	*Lavor Postell*	6.00
120	*Eddie House*	12.00

2000-01 UD Pros & Prospects ProActive

		MT
Complete Set (10):		10.00
Common Player:		.50
Inserted 1:6		
PA1	Kobe Bryant	3.00
PA2	Kevin Garnett	2.50
PA3	Vince Carter	4.00
PA4	Jason Kidd	1.00
PA5	Steve Francis	2.50
PA6	Chris Webber	1.00
PA7	Shaquille O'Neal	2.00
PA8	Larry Hughes	.75
PA9	Gary Payton	.50
PA10	Allen Iverson	2.00

2000-01 UD Pros & Prospects ProMotion

		MT
Complete Set (10):		12.00
Common Player:		.75
Inserted 1:6		
PM1	Darius Miles	5.00
PM2	Stromile Swift	2.50
PM3	Marcus Fizer	2.50
PM4	Kenyon Martin	4.00
PM5	Courtney Alexander	1.25
PM6	Keyon Dooling	1.00
PM7	DerMarr Johnson	1.50
PM8	Chris Mihm	1.00
PM9	Chris Porter	.75
PM10	Mike Miller	2.00

2000-01 UD Pros & Prospects Signature Jerseys I

		MT
Common Player:		25.00
Inserted 1:96		
SA	Shareef Abdur-Rahim	75.00
WA	William Avery	25.00
VB	Vin Baker	25.00
MB	Mike Bibby	60.00
TB	Terrell Brandon	25.00
KB	Kobe Bryant	400.00
BD	Baron Davis	50.00
MF	Michael Finley	50.00
KG	Kevin Garnett	300.00
AH	Anfernee Hardaway	150.00
CM	Corey Maggette	75.00
KM	Karl Malone	100.00
GP	Gary Payton	100.00
PP	Paul Pierce	60.00
GR	Glenn Robinson	40.00
DS	Damon Stoudamire	40.00
WS	Wally Szczerbiak	50.00
AW	Antoine Walker	50.00

2000-01 UD Pros & Prospects Signature Jerseys II

		MT
Complete Set (10):		
Common Player:		
KB	Kobe Bryant/8	
KG	Kevin Garnett/21	
KM	Karl Malone/32	
AH	Anfernee Hardaway/1	
MF	Michael Finley	
CM	Corey Maggette	
SA	Shareef Abdur-Rahim	
WS	Wally Szczerbiak	
BD	Baron Davis/1	
MJ	Michael Jordan/23	

2000-01 UD Pros & Prospects Star Command

		MT
Complete Set (12):		25.00
Common Player:		1.00
Inserted 1:12		
SC1	Kobe Bryant	6.00
SC2	Vince Carter	8.00
SC3	Allen Iverson	4.00
SC4	Shaquille O'Neal	4.00
SC5	Chris Webber	2.00
SC6	Karl Malone	1.00
SC7	Lamar Odom	2.00
SC8	Jason Kidd	2.00
SC9	Steve Francis	5.00

SC10 Kevin Garnett 5.00
SC11 Larry Hughes 1.50
SC12 Gary Payton 1.00

2000-01 UD Pros & Prospects Star Future

MT
Complete Set (10): 30.00
Common Player: 1.00
Inserted 1:12
SF1 Kenyon Martin 8.00
SF2 Keyon Dooling 1.50
SF3 Chris Porter 1.00
SF4 Courtney Alexander 2.50
SF5 Darius Miles 10.00
SF6 Mike Miller 4.00
SF7 Mateen Cleaves 2.50
SF8 Stromile Swift 5.00
SF9 Marcus Fizer 5.00
SF10 DerMarr Johnson 3.00

2000-01 UD Pros & Prospects UD Exclusives

MT
Common Player: 20.00
Production 200 Sets
CM Chris Mihm 25.00
JP Joel Przybilla 20.00

2000-01 Upper Deck Reserve

MT
Complete Set (120): 60.00
Common Player: .15
Minor Stars: .30
Common Rookie: 1.00
Inserted 1:2
Pack (5): 3.00
Box (24): 50.00
1 Dikembe Mutombo .15
2 Jason Terry .30
3 Alan Henderson .15
4 Paul Pierce .60
5 Antoine Walker .50
6 Kenny Anderson .15
7 Derrick Coleman .15
8 Baron Davis .50
9 Jamal Mashburn .30
10 Elton Brand 1.25
11 Ron Mercer .30
12 Ron Artest .30
13 Lamond Murray .15
14 Andre Miller .50
15 Matt Harpring .15
16 Michael Finley .30
17 Dirk Nowitzki 1.00
18 Steve Nash .15
19 Antonio McDyess .50
20 James Posey .15
21 Nick Van Exel .30
22 Jerry Stackhouse .30
23 Jerome Williams .15
24 Chucky Atkins .15
25 Antawn Jamison 1.00
26 Larry Hughes .60
27 Chris Mills .15
28 Steve Francis 2.50
29 Hakeem Olajuwon .60
30 Cuttino Mobley .40
31 Reggie Miller .40
32 Jalen Rose .40
33 Austin Croshere .15
34 Lamar Odom 1.25
35 Jeff McInnis .15
36 Corey Maggette .50
37 Shaquille O'Neal 2.00
38 Kobe Bryant 3.00
39 Isaiah Rider .30
40 Horace Grant .15
41 Eddie Jones .75
42 Tim Hardaway .40
43 Brian Grant .15
44 Ray Allen .40
45 Tim Thomas .40
46 Glenn Robinson .30
47 Sam Cassell .30
48 Kevin Garnett 2.50
49 Wally Szczerbiak .40
50 Terrell Brandon .30
51 Chauncey Billups .15
52 Stephon Marbury .75
53 Keith Van Horn .50
54 Kendall Gill .15
55 Latrell Sprewell 1.00
56 Marcus Camby .40
57 Allan Houston .40
58 Grant Hill 2.00
59 Tracy McGrady 1.25
60 Darrell Armstrong .15
61 Allen Iverson 2.00
62 Theo Ratliff .15
63 Toni Kukoc .40
64 Jason Kidd 1.25
65 Clifford Robinson .15
66 Shawn Marion 1.00
67 Rasheed Wallace .50
68 Scottie Pippen 1.25
69 Damon Stoudamire .30
70 Chris Webber 1.50
71 Jason Williams .60
72 Vlade Divac .15
73 Tim Duncan 2.00
74 David Robinson .60
75 Derek Anderson .30
76 Gary Payton .60
77 Patrick Ewing .30
78 Rashard Lewis .40
79 Vince Carter 4.00
80 Mark Jackson .15
81 Antonio Davis .15
82 Karl Malone .60
83 John Stockton .30
84 John Starks .15
85 Shareef Abdur-Rahim .60
86 Mike Bibby .40
87 Michael Dickerson .15
88 Mitch Richmond .30
89 Richard Hamilton .40
90 Juwan Howard .30
91 *Kenyon Martin* 4.00
92 *Stromile Swift* 5.00
93 *Darius Miles* 10.00
94 *Marcus Fizer* 3.00
95 *Mike Miller* 5.00
96 *DerMarr Johnson* 2.50
97 *Chris Mihm* 1.25
98 *Jamal Crawford* 2.50
99 *Joel Przybilla* 1.00
100 *Keyon Dooling* 2.50
101 *Jerome Moiso* 1.25
102 *Etan Thomas* 1.25
103 *Courtney Alexander* 3.00
104 *Mateen Cleaves* 1.50
105 *Hidayet Turkoglu* 2.50
106 *Desmond Mason* 3.00
107 *Quentin Richardson* 3.00
108 *Jamaal Magloire* 1.25
109 *Craig "Speedy" Claxton* 1.25
110 *Morris Peterson* 4.00
111 *Donnell Harvey* 1.00
112 *DeShawn Stevenson* 4.00
113 *Mamadou N'diaye* .75
114 *Erick Barkley* 1.25
115 *Mark Madsen* 1.25
116 *Eduardo Najera* 1.00
117 *Lavor Postell* 1.00
118 *Hanno Mottola* 1.00
119 *Stephen Jackson* 1.25
120 *Marc Jackson* 2.50

2000-01 Upper Deck Reserve Bank Shots

MT
Complete Set (10): 8.00
Common Player: .50
Inserted 1:14
BK1 Kevin Garnett 3.00
BK2 Lamar Odom 1.50
BK3 Grant Hill 2.50
BK4 Rashard Lewis .75
BK5 Reggie Miller .50
BK6 Ray Allen .50
BK7 Eddie Jones 1.00
BK8 Kobe Bryant .50
BK9 Michael Finley .50
BK10 Jerry Stackhouse .50

2000-01 Upper Deck Reserve Fast Company

MT
Complete Set (10): 10.00
Common Player: .75
Inserted 1:14
FC1 Steve Francis 3.00
FC2 Kobe Bryant 5.00
FC3 Allen Iverson 2.50
FC4 Jason Kidd 1.50
FC5 Larry Hughes .75
FC6 Stephon Marbury 1.00
FC7 Jason Williams .75
FC8 Andre Miller .75
FC9 Gary Payton .75
FC10 Paul Pierce .75

2000-01 Upper Deck Reserve NBA Start-ups

MT
Common Player: 20.00
Inserted 1:120
Common Autograph: 40.00
Autographs Inserted 1:479
KB Kobe Bryant 60.00
KB-A Kobe Bryant Auto
MC Mateen Cleaves 20.00
JC Jamal Crawford 30.00
JC-A Jamal Crawford Auto 50.00
MF Marcus Fizer 30.00
MF-A Marcus Fizer Auto 75.00
KG Kevin Garnett 40.00
KG-A Kevin Garnett Auto
DJ DerMarr Johnson 25.00
DJ-A DerMarr Johnson Auto 40.00
KM Kenyon Martin 35.00
KM-A Kenyon Martin Auto 60.00
DA Darius Miles 60.00
DA-A Darius Miles Auto 200.00
QR Quentin Richardson 30.00
QR-A Quentin Richardson Auto 50.00

2000-01 Upper Deck Reserve Power Portfolios

MT
Complete Set (6): 12.00
Common Player: 2.00
Inserted 1:23
PW1 Tim Duncan 3.00
PW2 Chris Webber 2.50
PW3 Grant Hill 3.00
PW4 Elton Brand 2.00
PW5 Kevin Garnett 4.00
PW6 Kobe Bryant 6.00

2000-01 Upper Deck Reserve Principal Powers

MT
Complete Set (10): 15.00
Common Player: .60
Inserted 1:14
PP1 Shaquille O'Neal 2.50
PP2 Tim Duncan 2.50
PP3 Vince Carter 6.00
PP4 Elton Brand 1.50
PP5 Kevin Garnett 3.00
PP6 Tracy McGrady 1.50
PP7 Karl Malone .75
PP8 Kobe Bryant 5.00
PP9 Shareef Abdur-Rahim .75
PP10 Antonio McDyess .60

2000-01 Upper Deck Reserve Setting the Standard

MT
Complete Set (6): 15.00
Common Player: 3.00
Inserted 1:23
SS1 Steve Francis 4.00
SS2 Vince Carter 8.00
SS3 Kobe Bryant 6.00
SS4 Kevin Garnett 4.00
SS5 Allen Iverson 3.00
SS6 Shaquille O'Neal 3.00

2000-01 Upper Deck Slam

MT
Complete Set (100):250.00
Common Player:.15
Minor Stars:.30
Common Rookie:2.00
Production 2,500 Sets
Pack (4):4.00
Box (18):55.00
1Dikembe Mutombo .15
2Jim Jackson .15
3Paul Pierce .60
4Antoine Walker .50
5Eddie Jones .75
6Baron Davis .50
7Derrick Coleman .15
8Elton Brand 1.25
9Ron Artest .40
10Andre Miller .50
11Shawn Kemp .40
12Michael Finley .40
13Dirk Nowitzki .60
14Antonio McDyess .40
15James Posey .30
16Jerry Stackhouse .30
17Jerome Williams .15
18Larry Hughes .75
19Antawn Jamison .60
20Steve Francis 2.50
21Hakeem Olajuwon .60
22Reggie Miller .30
23Jalen Rose .40
24Lamar Odom 1.25
25Michael Olowokandi .15
26Shaquille O'Neal 2.00
27Kobe Bryant 4.00
28Alonzo Mourning .40
29Jamal Mashburn .30
30Ray Allen .40
31Glenn Robinson .30
32Kevin Garnett 2.50
33Wally Szczerbiak .50
34Stephon Marbury .75
35Keith Van Horn .50
36Latrell Sprewell .75
37Allan Houston .40
38Darrell Armstrong .15
39Ron Mercer .40
40Allen Iverson 2.00
41Toni Kukoc .40
42Jason Kidd 1.25
43Anfernee Hardaway 1.50
44Shawn Marion 1.00
45Scottie Pippen 1.25
46Rasheed Wallace .50
47Chris Webber 1.25
48Vlade Divac .15
49Tim Duncan 2.00
50David Robinson .60
51Gary Payton .60
52Rashard Lewis .75
53Vince Carter 5.00
54Doug Christie .15
55Karl Malone .60
56Bryon Russell .15
57Shareef Abdur-Rahim .75
58Michael Dickerson .15
59Juwan Howard .30
60Richard Hamilton .40
61*Jerome Moiso* 4.00
62*Etan Thomas* 3.00
63*Courtney Alexander* 8.00
64*Mateen Cleaves* 5.00
65*Jason Collier* 3.00
66*Hidayet Turkoglu/900* 25.00
67*Desmond Mason* 10.00
68*Quentin Richardson* 10.00
69*Jamaal Magloire* 4.00
70*Craig Claxton* 3.00
71*Morris Peterson* 12.00
72*Donnell Harvey* 3.00
73*Ira Newble* 1.50
74*Mamadou N'diaye* 1.50
75*Erick Barkley* 4.00
76*Mark Madsen* 4.00
77*Dan Langhi* 2.50
78*A.J. Guyton* 3.00
79*Olumide Oyedji/900* 5.00
80*Eddie House/900* 12.00
81*Eduardo Najera/900* 10.00
82*Lavor Postell/900* 8.00
83*Hanno Mottola/900* 6.00
84*Chris Carrawell* 2.00
85*Michael Redd/900* 8.00
86*Jabari Smith/900* 6.00
87*Jason Hart/900* 5.00
88*Cory Hightower* 1.50
89*Chris Porter* 8.00
90*Justin Love/900* 4.00
91*Kenyon Martin* 12.00
92*Stromile Swift* 15.00
93*Darius Miles* 30.00
94*Marcus Fizer* 10.00
95*Mike Miller* 15.00
96*DerMarr Johnson* 10.00
97*Chris Mihm* 4.00
98*Jamal Crawford* 10.00
99*Joel Przybilla* 3.00
100*Keyon Dooling* 10.00

2000-01 Upper Deck Slam Extra Strength I

MT
Common Player: 1.00
Minor Stars: 1.50
Extra Strength Cards: 3x-6x
Extra Strength Rookies/2500: 1x
Extra Strength Rookies/900: .5x
Production 500 Sets

2000-01 Upper Deck Slam Extra Strength II

MT
Common Player: 10.00
Minor Stars: 15.00
Extra Strength Cards: 30x-60x
Extra Strength Rookies/2500: 3x-6x
Extra Strength Rookies/900: 1x-2x
Production 2,500 Sets

2000-01 Upper Deck Slam Air Styles

MT
Complete Set (9): 15.00
Common Player: 1.00
Inserted 1:9
AS1 Kevin Garnett 4.00
AS2 Vince Carter 6.00
AS3 Gary Payton 1.00
AS4 Steve Francis 4.00
AS5 Shareef Abdur-Rahim 1.50
AS6 Allen Iverson 3.00
AS7 Elton Brand 2.00
AS8 Kobe Bryant 5.00
AS9 Scottie Pippen 2.00

2000-01 Upper Deck Slam Air Supremacy

MT
Complete Set (6): 20.00
Common Player: 3.00
Inserted 1:18
S1 Kobe Bryant 8.00
S2 Vince Carter 10.00
S3 Shaquille O'Neal 4.00
S4 Allen Iverson 4.00
S5 Steve Francis 5.00
S6 Kevin Garnett 5.00

2000-01 Upper Deck Slam UD Flight Gear

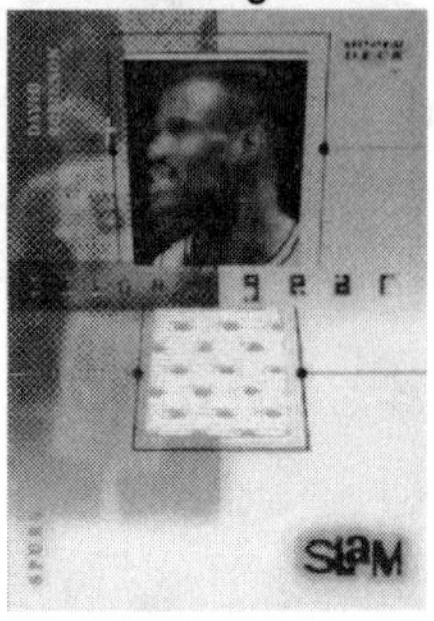

MT
Complete Set (20):
Common Player: 20.00
Inserted 1:45
SA Shareef Abdur-Rahim 25.00
KB Kobe Bryant 150.00
KB2 Kobe Bryant 150.00
KB-A Kobe Bryant
KG Kevin Garnett 75.00
KG2 Kevin Garnett 75.00
KG-A Kevin Garnett 700.00
TH Tim Hardaway 20.00
AI Allen Iverson 75.00
MJ Michael Jordan 1000.
KM Karl Malone 25.00
AM Alonzo Mourning 20.00
SO Shaquille O'Neal 75.00
GP Gary Payton 35.00
DR David Robinson 35.00
WS Wally Szczerbiak 25.00

2000-01 Upper Deck Slam Power Windows

MT
Complete Set (6): 15.00
Common Player: 1.00
Inserted 1:18
PW1 Shaquille O'Neal 4.00
PW2 Kevin Garnett 5.00
PW3 Karl Malone 1.00
PW4 Kobe Bryant 8.00
PW5 Elton Brand 2.50
PW6 Vince Carter 10.00

2000-01 Upper Deck Slam Signature Slams

MT
Common Player: 10.00
Inserted 1:108
RA Ray Allen 15.00
KB Kobe Bryant 150.00
BD Baron Davis 15.00
KG Kevin Garnett 100.00
AH Anfernee Hardaway 50.00
AJ Antawn Jamison 20.00
TM Tracy McGrady 40.00
AM Andre Miller 15.00
WS Wally Szczerbiak 20.00

2000-01 Upper Deck Slam Slam Exam

MT
Complete Set (9): 10.00

Common Player: .50
Inserted 1:6
SE1 Kobe Bryant 5.00
SE2 Kevin Garnett 4.00
SE3 Anfernee Hardaway 1.50
SE4 Lamar Odom 1.50
SE5 Michael Finley .50
SE6 Latrell Sprewell 1.00
SE7 Larry Hughes 1.00
SE8 Chris Webber 1.50
SE9 Antonio McDyess .50

2000-01 UD Ultimate Collection

MT
Complete Set (60): 300.00
Common Player: 1.00
Minor Stars: 1.50
Pack: 200.00
Box (4): 650.00
1 Dikembe Mutombo 1.00
2 Hanno Mottola 10.00
3 Paul Pierce 4.00
4 Antoine Walker 3.00
5 Derrick Coleman 1.00
6 Baron Davis 3.00
7 Elton Brand 8.00
8 Michael Jordan 40.00
9 Andre Miller 3.00
10 Chris Mihm 15.00
11 Michael Finley 1.50
12 Donnell Harvey 15.00
13 Antonio McDyess 2.00
14 Nick Van Exel 1.50
15 Jerry Stackhouse 1.50
16 Jerome Williams 1.00
17 Larry Hughes 5.00
18 Antawn Jamison 5.00
19 Steve Francis 15.00
20 Hakeem Olajuwon 4.00
21 Reggie Miller 2.00
22 Jalen Rose 2.00
23 Lamar Odom 8.00
24 Michael Olowokandi 1.00
25 Shaquille O'Neal 12.00
26 Kobe Bryant 20.00
27 Ron Harper 1.00
28 Alonzo Mourning 2.00
29 Eddie House 25.00
30 Glenn Robinson 1.50
31 Ray Allen 1.50
32 Kevin Garnett 15.00
33 Wally Szczerbiak 2.00
34 Terrell Brandon 1.00
35 Stephon Marbury 5.00
36 Keith Van Horn 3.00
37 Allan Houston 2.00
38 Latrell Sprewell 6.00
39 Grant Hill 12.00
40 Tracy McGrady 8.00
41 Allen Iverson 12.00
42 Toni Kukoc 2.00
43 Jason Kidd 8.00
44 Anfernee Hardaway 8.00
45 Scottie Pippen 8.00
46 Rasheed Wallace 3.00
47 Chris Webber 10.00
48 Jason Williams 3.00
49 Tim Duncan 12.00
50 David Robinson 4.00
51 Gary Payton 4.00
52 Rashard Lewis 4.00
53 Vince Carter 25.00
54 Morris Peterson 50.00
55 Karl Malone 4.00
56 John Stockton 2.00
57 Shareef Abdur-Rahim 4.00
58 Mike Bibby 2.00
59 Mike Smith 10.00
60 Richard Hamilton 2.00

2000-01 UD Ultimate Collection Rookies Graded

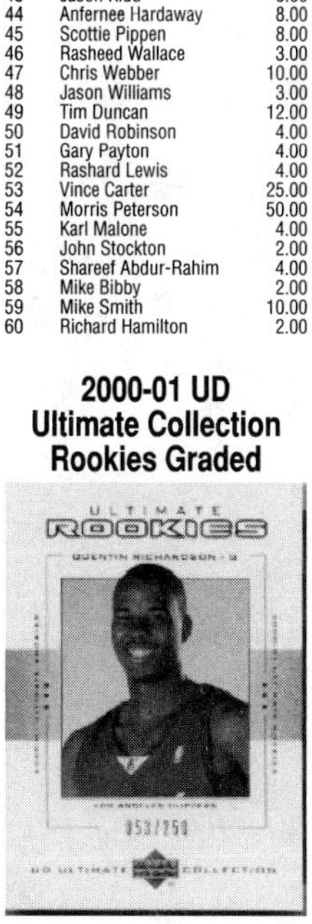

MT
Common Gem Mint:
Common Mint: 25.00
Common NM/M: 15.00
Production 250 Sets
Population Report Listed in
61 *Mamadou N'diaye GEM (4)*
61 *Mamadou N'diaye MT (199)* 40.00
61 *Mamadou N'diaye NM/MT (47)* 20.00
62 *Erick Barkley GEM (4)*
62 *Erick Barkley MT (146)* 50.00
62 *Erick Barkley NM/MT (100)* 30.00
63 *Desmond Mason GEM (50)* 300.00
63 *Desmond Mason MT (162)* 150.00
63 *Desmond Mason NM/MT (38)* 75.00
64 *Speedy Claxton GEM (12)*
64 *Speedy Claxton MT (201)* 50.00
64 *Speedy Claxton NM/MT (37)* 30.00
65 *Jamaal Magloire GEM (13)* 100.00
65 *Jamaal Magloire MT (185)* 50.00
65 *Jamaal Magloire NM/MT (52)* 30.00
66 *DeShawn Stevenson GEM (12)*
66 *DeShawn Stevenson MT (226)* 200.00
66 *DeShawn Stevenson NM/MT (12)* 100.00
67 *Etan Thomas GEM (18)* 100.00
67 *Etan Thomas MT (184)* 40.00
67 *Etan Thomas NM/MT (48)* 25.00
68 *Jamal Crawford GEM (20)* 200.00
68 *Jamal Crawford MT (218)* 60.00
68 *Jamal Crawford NM/MT (12)* 35.00
69 *Joel Przybilla GEM (8)*
69 *Joel Pryzbilla MT (198)* 45.00
69 *Joel Pryzbilla NM/MT (44)* 25.00
70 *Keyon Dooling GEM (40)* 225.00
70 *Keyon Dooling MT (197)* 75.00
70 *Keyon Dooling NM/MT (13)* 40.00
71 *Jerome Moiso GEM (26)* 100.00
71 *Jerome Moiso MT (189)* 50.00
71 *Jerome Moiso NM/MT (35)* 30.00
72 *Quentin Richardson GEM (10)*
72 *Quentin Richardson MT (180)* 125.00
72 *Quentin Richardson NM/MT (60)* 75.00
73 *Courtney Alexander GEM (16)* 300.00
73 *Courtney Alexander MT (175)* 100.00
73 *Courtney Alexander NM/MT (59)* 50.00
74 *Mateen Cleaves GEM (18)*
74 *Mateen Cleaves MT (172)* 60.00
74 *Mateen Cleaves NM/MT (60)* 35.00
75 *Mike Miller Auto GEM (4)*
75 *Mike Miller MT (80)* 200.00
75 *Mike Miller Auto NM/MT (162)* 100.00
76 *DerMarr Johnson Auto MT (58)* 150.00
76 *DerMarr Johnson Auto NM/MT (183)* 75.00
77 *Darius Miles Auto MT (98)* 1000.
77 *Darius Miles Auto NM/MT (151)* 600.00
78 *Marcus Fizer Auto MT (74)* 150.00
78 *Marcus Fizer Auto NM/MT (175)* 75.00
79 *Kenyon Martin Auto GEM (6)*
79 *Kenyon Martin Auto MT (121)* 300.00
79 *Kenyon Martin Auto NM/MT (123)* 150.00
80 *Stromile Swift Auto GEM (1)*
80 *Stromile Swift Auto MT (123)* 400.00
80 *Stromile Swift Auto NM/MT (126)* 225.00

2000-01 UD Ultimate Collection Game Jerseys Bronze

MT
Common Player: 15.00
Inserted 1:3
KB Kobe Bryant 125.00
MF Marcus Fizer 25.00
KG Kevin Garnett 50.00
MJ Michael Jordan 200.00
JK Jason Kidd 30.00
KM Kenyon Martin 40.00
JS John Stockton 30.00
DS Damon Stoudamire 15.00
WS Wally Szczerbiak 15.00

2000-01 UD Ultimate Collection Game Jerseys Bronze Graded

MT
Common Player MT: 25.00
Common Player NM/MT: 15.00
KB Kobe Bryant MT 175.00
KB Kobe Bryant NM/MT 125.00
MF Marcus Fizer MT 50.00
MF Marcus Fizer NM/MT 25.00
KG Kevin Garnett MT 75.00
KG Kevin Garnett NM/MT 50.00
MJ Michael Jordan MT 300.00
MJ Michael Jordan NM/MT 200.00
JK Jason Kidd MT 50.00
JK Jason Kidd NM/MT 30.00
KM Kenyon Martin MT 60.00
KM Kenyon Martin NM/MT 40.00
JS John Stockton MT 50.00
JS John Stockton NM/MT 30.00
DS Damon Stoudamire MT 25.00
DS Damon Stoudamire NM/MT 15.00
WS Wally Szczerbiak MT 25.00
WS Wally Szczerbiak NM/MT 15.00

2000-01 UD Ultimate Collection Game Jerseys Silver

MT
Common Player: 20.00
Inserted 1:6
KB Kobe Bryant 150.00
MF Marcus Fizer 30.00
KG Kevin Garnett 60.00
MJ Michael Jordan 250.00
JK Jason Kidd 40.00
KM Kenyon Martin 50.00
JS John Stockton 40.00
DS Damon Stoudamire 20.00
WS Wally Szczerbiak 20.00

2000-01 UD Ultimate Collection Game Jerseys Gold Graded

MT
Common Player MT: 50.00
Common Player NM/MT: 30.00
KB Kobe Bryant MT 300.00
KB Kobe Bryant NM/MT 200.00
MF Marcus Fizer MT 60.00
MF Marcus Fizer NM/MT 40.00
KG Kevin Garnett MT 150.00
KG Kevin Garnett NM/MT 100.00
SF Steve Francis MT 150.00
SF Steve Francis NM/MT 100.00
MJ Michael Jordan MT 500.00
MJ Michael Jordan NM/MT 400.00
JK Jason Kidd MT 100.00
JK Jason Kidd NM/MT 60.00
KM Kenyon Martin MT 125.00
KM Kenyon Martin NM/MT 75.00
JS John Stockton MT 100.00
JS John Stockton NM/MT 60.00
DS Damon Stoudamire MT 50.00
DS Damon Stoudamire NM/MT 30.00
WS Wally Szczerbiak MT 50.00
WS Wally Szczerbiak NM/MT 30.00

2000-01 UD Ultimate Collection Game Jerseys Gold

MT
Common Player: 25.00
Inserted 1:17
KB Kobe Bryant 200.00
MF Marcus Fizer 40.00
SF Steve Francis 100.00
KG Kevin Garnett 100.00
MJ Michael Jordan 400.00
JK Jason Kidd 60.00
KM Kenyon Martin 75.00
JS John Stockton 60.00
DS Damon Stoudamire 30.00
WS Wally Szczerbiak 30.00

2000-01 UD Ultimate Collection Game Jerseys Silver Graded

MT
Common Player MT: 30.00
Common Player NM/MT: 20.00
KB Kobe Bryant MT 200.00
KB Kobe Bryant NM/MT 150.00
MF Marcus Fizer MT 50.00
MF Marcus Fizer NM/MT 30.00
KG Kevin Garnett MT 90.00
KG Kevin Garnett NM/MT 60.00
MJ Michael Jordan MT 350.00
MJ Michael Jordan NM/MT 250.00
JK Jason Kidd MT 60.00
JK Jason Kidd NM/MT 40.00
KM Kenyon Martin MT 75.00
KM Kenyon Martin NM/MT 50.00
JS John Stockton MT 60.00
JS John Stockton NM/MT 40.00
DS Damon Stoudamire MT 30.00
DS Damon Stoudamire NM/MT 20.00
WS Wally Szczerbiak MT 30.00
WS Wally Szczerbiak NM/MT 20.00

2000-01 UD Ultimate Collection Game Jersey Patch

MT
Common Player: 100.00
Inserted 1:11
SA Shareef Abdur-Rahim/100 100.00
RA Ray Allen/100 150.00
KB Kobe Bryant/8
KB Kobe Bryant Auto/8
MF Michael Finley/75 100.00
KG Kevin Garnett/21 400.00
KG Kevin Garnett Auto/21 600.00
AH Anfernee Hardaway/75 250.00
AI Allen Iverson/75 400.00
MJ Michael Jordan Auto/23 2500.
JK Jason Kidd/75 150.00
KM Karl Malone/100 125.00
SM Stephon Marbury/75 150.00
SH Shawn Marion/25 300.00
RM Reggie Miller/100 200.00
AM Alonzo Mourning/100 125.00
SO Shaquille O'Neal/75 250.00
GP Gary Payton/100 100.00
PP Paul Pierce/50 100.00
DR David Robinson/100 150.00
JS John Stockton/100 150.00
DS Damon Stoudamire/75 100.00
WS Wally Szczerbiak/100 100.00
KV Keith Van Horn/100 100.00
JW Jason Williams/25 350.00

2000-01 UD Ultimate Collection Signatures Bronze

MT
Common Player: 20.00
Production 200 Sets
SA Shareef Abdur-Rahim 20.00
CA Courtney Alexander 30.00
KB Kobe Bryant 150.00
MF Marcus Fizer 35.00
KG Kevin Garnett 75.00
AH Anfernee Hardaway 50.00
LH Larry Hughes 30.00
AJ Antawn Jamison 30.00
DJ DerMarr Johnson 25.00
SM Shawn Marion 40.00
TM Tracy McGrady 50.00
AM Andre Miller 25.00
JM Jerome Moiso 20.00
QR Quentin Richardson 35.00
JR Jalen Rose 25.00

2000-01 UD Ultimate Collection Signatures Bronze Graded

MT
Common Player MT: 25.00
Common Player NM/MT: 20.00
SA Shareef Abdur-Rahim MT 25.00
SA Shareef Abdur-Rahim NM/MT 20.00
CA Courtney Alexander MT 40.00
CA Courtney Alexander NM/MT 30.00
KB Kobe Bryant MT 200.00
KB Kobe Bryant NM/MT 150.00
MF Marcus Fizer MT 45.00
MF Marcus Fizer NM/MT 35.00
KG Kevin Garnett NM/MT 75.00
AH Anfernee Hardaway MT 60.00
AH Anfernee Hardaway NM/MT 50.00
LH Larry Hughes MT 40.00
LH Larry Hughes NM/MT 30.00
AJ Antawn Jamison MT 40.00
AJ Antawn Jamison NM/MT 30.00
DJ DerMarr Johnson MT 35.00
DJ DerMarr Johnson NM/MT 25.00
SM Shawn Marion MT 50.00
SM Shawn Marion NM/MT 40.00
TM Tracy McGrady MT 60.00
TM Tracy McGrady NM/MT 50.00
AM Andre Miller MT 35.00
AM Andre Miller NM/MT 25.00
JM Jerome Moiso MT 30.00
JM Jerome Moiso NM/MT 20.00
QR Quentin Richardson MT 45.00
QR Quentin Richardson NM/MT 35.00
JR Jalen Rose MT 35.00
JR Jalen Rose NM/MT 25.00

2000-01 UD Ultimate Collection Signatures Silver

MT
Common Player: 30.00
Production 75 Sets
KB Kobe Bryant 250.00
MC Mateen Cleaves 40.00
JC Jamal Crawford 40.00
SF Steve Francis 75.00
KG Kevin Garnett 100.00
AH Anfernee Hardaway 75.00
TH Tim Hardaway 40.00
SM Shawn Marion 60.00
AM Antonio McDyess 30.00
MM Mike Miller 75.00
GP Gary Payton 40.00
MP Morris Peterson 100.00
PP Paul Pierce 40.00
DS DeShawn Stevenson 75.00

2000-01 UD Ultimate Collection Signatures Silver Graded

MT
Common Player MT: 40.00
Common Player NM/MT: 30.00
KB Kobe Bryant MT 300.00
KB Kobe Bryant NM/MT 250.00
MC Mateen Cleaves NM/MT 40.00
JC Jamal Crawford MT 50.00
JC Jamal Crawford NM/MT 40.00
SF Steve Francis MT 100.00
SF Steve Francis NM/MT 75.00
KG Kevin Garnett NM/MT 100.00
AH Anfernee Hardaway MT 100.00
AH Anfernee Hardaway NM/MT 75.00
TH Tim Hardaway MT 50.00
TH Tim Hardaway NM/MT 40.00
SM Shawn Marion NM/MT 60.00
AM Antonio McDyess MT 40.00
AM Antonio McDyess NM/MT 30.00
MM Mike Miller MT 100.00
MM Mike Miller NM/MT 75.00
GP Gary Payton MT 50.00
GP Gary Payton NM/MT 40.00
MP Morris Peterson MT 150.00
MP Morris Peterson NM/MT 100.00
PP Paul Pierce MT 50.00
PP Paul Pierce NM/MT 40.00
DS DeShawn Stevenson MT 100.00
DS DeShawn Stevenson NM/MT 75.00

2000-01 UD Ultimate Victory

MT
Complete Set (120): 300.00
Common Player: .25
Minor Stars: .40
Common Rookie: 4.00
Production 1,500 Sets
Common Kobe (61-75): 4.00
Common KG (76-90): 2.00
Pack (5): 3.00
Box (24): 50.00
1 Dikembe Mutombo .25
2 Jim Jackson .25
3 Paul Pierce .75
4 Antoine Walker .60
5 Jamal Mashburn .40
6 Baron Davis .60
7 Elton Brand 1.50
8 Ron Artest .50
9 Lamond Murray .25
10 Andre Miller .60
11 Michael Finley .40
12 Dirk Nowitzki 1.25
13 Antonio McDyess .60
14 Nick Van Exel .40
15 Jerry Stackhouse .40
16 Chucky Atkins .25
17 Antawn Jamison 1.25
18 Larry Hughes 1.00
19 Steve Francis 3.00
20 Hakeem Olajuwon .75
21 Reggie Miller .40
22 Jalen Rose .50
23 Lamar Odom 1.50
24 Corey Maggette .60
25 Shaquille O'Neal 2.50
26 Kobe Bryant 4.00
27 Ron Harper .25
28 Tim Hardaway .50
29 Eddie Jones 1.00
30 Ray Allen .50
31 Tim Thomas .50
32 Kevin Garnett 3.00
33 Wally Szczerbiak .50
34 Terrell Brandon .25
35 Stephon Marbury 1.00
36 Keith Van Horn .60
37 Allan Houston .50
38 Latrell Sprewell 1.25
39 Grant Hill 2.50
40 Tracy McGrady 1.25
41 Allen Iverson 2.00
42 Toni Kukoc .50
43 Jason Kidd 1.50
44 Anfernee Hardaway 1.50
45 Scottie Pippen 1.50
46 Rasheed Wallace .60
47 Jason Williams .75
48 Chris Webber 1.50
49 Tim Duncan 2.50
50 David Robinson .75
51 Gary Payton .75
52 Rashard Lewis .75
53 Vince Carter 5.00
54 Mark Jackson .25
55 Karl Malone .75
56 John Stockton .40
57 Shareef Abdur-Rahim .75
58 Mike Bibby .40
59 Mitch Richmond .40
60 Richard Hamilton .50
61 Kobe Bryant 4.00
62 Kobe Bryant 4.00
63 Kobe Bryant 4.00
64 Kobe Bryant 4.00
65 Kobe Bryant 4.00
66 Kobe Bryant 4.00
67 Kobe Bryant 4.00
68 Kobe Bryant 4.00
69 Kobe Bryant 4.00
70 Kobe Bryant 4.00
71 Kobe Bryant 4.00
72 Kobe Bryant 4.00
73 Kobe Bryant 4.00
74 Kobe Bryant 4.00
75 Kobe Bryant 4.00
76 Kevin Garnett 2.00
77 Kevin Garnett 2.00
78 Kevin Garnett 2.00
79 Kevin Garnett 2.00
80 Kevin Garnett 2.00
81 Kevin Garnett 2.00
82 Kevin Garnett 2.00
83 Kevin Garnett 2.00
84 Kevin Garnett 2.00
85 Kevin Garnett 2.00
86 Kevin Garnett 2.00
87 Kevin Garnett 2.00
88 Kevin Garnett 2.00
89 Kevin Garnett 2.00
90 Kevin Garnett 2.00
91 *Kenyon Martin* 15.00
92 *Stromile Swift* 25.00
93 *Darius Miles* 50.00
94 *Marcus Fizer* 10.00
95 *Mike Miller* 25.00
96 *DerMarr Johnson* 10.00
97 *Chris Mihm* 5.00
98 *Jamal Crawford* 10.00
99 *Joel Przybilla* 4.00
100 *Keyon Dooling* 10.00
101 *Jerome Moiso* 5.00
102 *Etan Thomas* 4.00
103 *Courtney Alexander* 10.00
104 *Mateen Cleaves* 8.00
105 *Jason Collier* 3.00
106 *Hidayet Turkoglu* 10.00
107 *Desmond Mason* 12.00
108 *Quentin Richardson* 12.00
109 *Jamaal Magloire* 5.00
110 *Craig "Speedy" Claxton* 4.00
111 *Morris Peterson* 15.00
112 *Donnell Harvey* 4.00
113 *DeShawn Stevenson* 15.00
114 *Mamadou N'diaye* 3.00
115 *Erick Barkley* 5.00
116 *Mike Smith* 3.00
117 *Eddie House* 6.00
118 *Eduardo Najera* 3.00
119 *Jason Hart* 3.00
120 *Chris Porter* 8.00

2000-01 UD Ultimate Victory Victory Collection

MT
Common Player: 2.00
Veterans: 4x-8x
Common Rookie: 4.00
Rookies: .5x-1x
Common Kobe (61-75): 20.00
Common KG (76-90): 10.00
Production 350 Sets

2000-01 UD Ultimate Victory Ultimate Collection

MT
Common Player: 5.00
Veterans: 10x-20x
Common Rookie: 8.00
Rookies: 1x-2x
Common Kobe (61-75): 20.00
Common KG (76-90): 10.00
Production 100 Sets

2000-01 UD Ultimate Victory Ultimate Victory

MT
Common Player: 15.00
Veterans: 30x-60x
Common Rookie: 20.00
Rookies: 3x-5x
Common Kobe (61-75): 100.00
Common KG (76-90): 50.00
Production 25 Sets

2000-01 UD Ultimate Victory Championship Fabrics

MT
Common Player: 50.00
Inserted 1:480
CF1 Kobe Bryant 125.00
CF2 Shaquille O'Neal 75.00
CF3 Michael Jordan 400.00
CF4 Julius Erving 150.00
CF5 Larry Bird 200.00
CF6 Isiah Thomas 50.00
CFA1 Kobe Bryant Auto/15
CFC1 Kobe Bryant, Larry Bird Auto/25

2000-01 UD Ultimate Victory Starstruck

		MT
Complete Set (10):		15.00
Common Player:		1.00
Inserted 1:11		
S1	Kobe Bryant	5.00
S2	Gary Payton	1.00
S3	Chris Webber	2.00
S4	Kevin Garnett	4.00
S5	Stephon Marbury	1.25
S6	Shareef Abdur-Rahim	1.00
S7	Steve Francis	4.00
S8	Tim Duncan	3.00
S9	Anfernee Hardaway	2.00
S10	Vince Carter	6.00

2000-01 UD Ultimate Victory The Reel World

		MT
Complete Set (10):		15.00
Common Player:		1.00
Inserted 1:11		
RW1	Kobe Bryant	5.00
RW2	Vince Carter	6.00
RW3	Tim Duncan	3.00
RW4	Allen Iverson	2.50
RW5	Elton Brand	2.00
RW6	Jason Kidd	2.00
RW7	Kevin Garnett	4.00
RW8	Lamar Odom	2.00
RW9	Scottie Pippen	2.00
RW10	Karl Malone	1.00

2000-01 UD Ultimate Victory Ultimate Fabrics Combo

		MT
Common Player:		50.00
Inserted 1:240		
UFC1	Kenyon Martin, Stromile Swift	100.00
UFC2	Kenyon Martin, Darius Miles	150.00
UFC3	Kenyon Martin, DerMarr Johnson	50.00
UFC4	Kenyon Martin, Marcus Fizer	50.00
UFCA1	Kenyon Martin, Stromile Swift Auto/25	

2000-01 UD Ultimate Victory Ultimate Powers

		MT
Complete Set (10):		30.00
Common Player:		1.50
Inserted 1:23		
U1	Shaquille O'Neal	5.00
U2	Grant Hill	5.00
U3	Vince Carter	10.00
U4	Allen Iverson	4.00
U5	Kevin Garnett	6.00
U6	Tim Duncan	5.00
U7	Gary Payton	1.50
U8	Kobe Bryant	8.00
U9	Steve Francis	6.00
U10	Elton Brand	3.00

2000-01 Upper Deck Victory

		MT
Complete Set (330):		50.00
Common Player:		.05
Minor Stars:		.10
Common Rookie (261-280):		.50
Common Kobe (281-305):		.50
Common Garnett (305-330):		.40
Pack (12):		1.00
Box (36):		30.00
1	Dikembe Mutombo	.10
2	Jim Jackson	.05
3	Jason Terry	.10
4	Roshown McLeod	.05
5	Alan Henderson	.05
6	Bimbo Coles	.05
7	Dion Glover	.10
8	Lorenzen Wright	.05
9	Paul Pierce	.30
10	Kenny Anderson	.10
11	Antoine Walker	.30
12	Adrian Griffin	.10
13	Vitaly Potapenko	.05
14	Dana Barros	.05
15	Eric Williams	.05
16	Calbert Cheaney	.05
17	Derrick Coleman	.10
18	Eddie Jones	.40
19	Anthony Mason	.05
20	Elden Campbell	.05
21	Eddie Robinson	.10
22	David Wesley	.05
23	Baron Davis	.30
24	Ricky Davis	.10
25	Elton Brand	.75
26	Ron Artest	.25
27	Chris Carr	.05
28	Fred Hoiberg	.05
29	Hersey Hawkins	.05
30	Dickey Simpkins	.05
31	Corey Benjamin	.05
32	Matt Maloney	.05
33	Shawn Kemp	.30
34	Lamond Murray	.05
35	Wesley Person	.05
36	Andre Miller	.30
37	Bob Sura	.05
38	Andrew DeClercq	.05
39	Brevin Knight	.05
40	Earl Boykins	.05
41	Michael Finley	.20
42	Dirk Nowitzki	.40
43	Cedric Ceballos	.05
44	Robert Pack	.05
45	Erick Strickland	.05
46	Sean Rooks	.05
47	Shawn Bradley	.05
48	Steve Nash	.05
49	Antonio McDyess	.20
50	Nick Van Exel	.10
51	Keon Clark	.10
52	Raef LaFrentz	.20
53	James Posey	.20
54	Chris Gatling	.05
55	George McCloud	.05
56	Bryant Stith	.05
57	Jerry Stackhouse	.10
58	Lindsey Hunter	.05
59	Christian Laettner	.05
60	Jerome Williams	.05
61	Michael Curry	.05
62	Loy Vaught	.05
63	Eric Montross	.05
64	Grant Hill	1.00
65	Antawn Jamison	.30
66	Chris Mills	.05
67	Vonteego Cummings	.10
68	Larry Hughes	.50
69	Donyell Marshall	.05
70	Mookie Blaylock	.05
71	Erick Dampier	.05
72	Jason Caffey	.05
73	Steve Francis	1.25
74	Shandon Anderson	.05
75	Hakeem Olajuwon	.40
76	Walt Williams	.05
77	Kenny Thomas	.10
78	Carlos Rogers	.05
79	Bryce Drew	.05
80	Kelvin Cato	.05
81	Reggie Miller	.10
82	Austin Croshere	.10
83	Rik Smits	.05
84	Jalen Rose	.20
85	Dale Davis	.05
86	Jonathan Bender	.40
87	Travis Best	.05
88	Chris Mullin	.05
89	Lamar Odom	.60
90	Tyrone Nesby	.05
91	Michael Olowokandi	.10
92	Eric Piatkowski	.05
93	Jeff McInnis	.05
94	Brian Skinner	.05
95	Pete Chilcutt	.05
96	Eric Murdock	.05
97	Shaquille O'Neal	1.00
98	Kobe Bryant	1.50
99	Ron Harper	.05
100	Robert Horry	.05
101	Rick Fox	.05
102	Derek Fisher	.05
103	Tyronn Lue	.05
104	Devean George	.20
105	Alonzo Mourning	.30
106	Jamal Mashburn	.10
107	Anthony Carter	.10
108	P.J. Brown	.05
109	Clarence Weatherspoon	.05
110	Otis Thorpe	.05
111	Voshon Lenard	.05
112	Tim Hardaway	.20
113	Ray Allen	.20
114	Glenn Robinson	.10
115	Sam Cassell	.10
116	Robert Traylor	.05
117	Ervin Johnson	.05
118	Scott Williams	.05
119	Tim Thomas	.30
120	Vinny Del Negro	.05
121	Kevin Garnett	1.25
122	Wally Szczerbiak	.30
123	Terrell Brandon	.10
124	Dean Garrett	.05
125	William Avery	.10
126	Sam Mitchell	.05
127	Radoslav Nesterovic	.05
128	Anthony Peeler	.05
129	Stephon Marbury	.50
130	Keith Van Horn	.40
131	Kerry Kittles	.05
132	Lucious Harris	.05
133	Evan Eschmeyer	.05
134	Jamie Feick	.05
135	Jim McIlvaine	.05
136	Kendall Gill	.05
137	Allan Houston	.20
138	Marcus Camby	.10
139	Latrell Sprewell	.40
140	Patrick Ewing	.10
141	Larry Johnson	.05
142	Charlie Ward	.05
143	Chris Childs	.05
144	John Wallace	.05
145	Darrell Armstrong	.05
146	Corey Maggette	.30
147	Pat Garrity	.05
148	John Amaechi	.05
149	Matt Harpring	.05
150	Michael Doleac	.05
151	Ron Mercer	.20
152	Chucky Atkins	.05
153	Allen Iverson	1.00
154	Matt Geiger	.05
155	Eric Snow	.05
156	Tyrone Hill	.05
157	Theo Ratliff	.05
158	George Lynch	.05
159	Kevin Ollie	.05
160	Toni Kukoc	.20
161	Jason Kidd	.60
162	Anfernee Hardaway	.60
163	Rodney Rogers	.05
164	Shawn Marion	.30
165	Clifford Robinson	.05
166	Tom Gugliotta	.05
167	Luc Longley	.05
168	Randy Livingston	.05
169	Scottie Pippen	.60
170	Steve Smith	.10
171	Damon Stoudamire	.10
172	Bonzi Wells	.20
173	Jermaine O'Neal	.20
174	Arvydas Sabonis	.05
175	Rasheed Wallace	.20
176	Detlef Schrempf	.05
177	Jason Williams	.40
178	Chris Webber	.60
179	Predrag Stojakovic	.10
180	Vlade Divac	.10
181	Lawrence Funderburke	.05
182	Tony Delk	.05
183	Jon Barry	.05
184	Tim Duncan	1.00
185	Sean Elliott	.05
186	Terry Porter	.05
187	David Robinson	.40
188	Samaki Walker	.05
189	Malik Rose	.05
190	Jaren Jackson	.05
191	Steve Kerr	.05
192	Gary Payton	.40
193	Brent Barry	.05
194	Vin Baker	.10
195	Horace Grant	.05
196	Ruben Patterson	.05
197	Vernon Maxwell	.05
198	Shammond Williams	.05
199	Rashard Lewis	.50
200	Tracy McGrady	.60
201	Charles Oakley	.05
202	Doug Christie	.05
203	Antonio Davis	.05
204	Vince Carter	2.00
205	Kevin Willis	.05
206	Dell Curry	.05
207	Dee Brown	.05
208	Karl Malone	.40
209	John Stockton	.10
210	Bryon Russell	.05
211	Olden Polynice	.05
212	Jacque Vaughn	.05
213	Greg Ostertag	.05
214	Quincy Lewis	.10
215	Armen Gilliam	.05
216	Shareef Abdur-Rahim	.40
217	Michael Dickerson	.10
218	Mike Bibby	.20
219	Bryant Reeves	.05
220	Othella Harrington	.05
221	Grant Long	.05
222	Felipe Lopez	.05
223	Obinna Ekezie	.05
224	Mitch Richmond	.10
225	Richard Hamilton	.20
226	Tracy Murray	.05
227	Jahidi White	.05
228	Aaron Williams	.05
229	Juwan Howard	.10
230	Rod Strickland	.10
231	Isaac Austin	.05
232	Dikembe Mutombo	.05
233	Antoine Walker	.15
234	Derrick Coleman	.15
235	Elton Brand	.40
236	Shawn Kemp	.15
237	Michael Finley	.10
238	Antonio McDyess	.15
239	Grant Hill	.50
240	Antawn Jamison	.20
241	Steve Francis	.60
242	Jalen Rose	.10
243	Lamar Odom	.30
244	Shaquille O'Neal	.50
245	Alonzo Mourning	.15
246	Ray Allen	.10
247	Kevin Garnett	.60
248	Stephon Marbury	.25
249	Allan Houston	.10
250	Darrell Armstrong	.05
251	Allen Iverson	.50
252	Jason Kidd	.30
253	Rasheed Wallace	.10
254	Chris Webber	.30
255	Tim Duncan	.50
256	Gary Payton	.20
257	Vince Carter	2.00
258	Karl Malone	.20
259	Shareef Abdur-Rahim	.20
260	Mitch Richmond	.05
261	*Kenyon Martin*	4.00
262	*Marcus Fizer*	3.00
263	*Chris Mihm*	1.50
264	*Stromile Swift*	5.00
265	*Keyon Dooling*	3.00
266	*Morris Peterson*	4.00
267	*Quentin Richardson*	3.00
268	*Courtney Alexander*	3.00
269	*Desmond Mason*	3.00
270	*Mateen Cleaves*	2.00
271	*Erick Barkley*	1.50
272	*A.J. Guyton*	.75
273	*Darius Miles*	10.00
274	*DerMarr Johnson*	3.00
275	*Joel Przybilla*	1.00
276	*Hanno Mottola*	.50
277	*Mike Miller*	5.00
278	*Donnell Harvey*	1.00
279	*Craig "Speedy" Claxton*	1.00
280	*Khalid El-Amin*	1.00
281	Kobe Bryant	.50
282	Kobe Bryant	.50
283	Kobe Bryant	.50
284	Kobe Bryant	.50
285	Kobe Bryant	.50
286	Kobe Bryant	.50
287	Kobe Bryant	.50
288	Kobe Bryant	.50
289	Kobe Bryant	.50
290	Kobe Bryant	.50
291	Kobe Bryant	.50
292	Kobe Bryant	.50
293	Kobe Bryant	.50
294	Kobe Bryant	.50
295	Kobe Bryant	.50
296	Kobe Bryant	.50
297	Kobe Bryant	.50
298	Kobe Bryant	.50
299	Kobe Bryant	.50
300	Kobe Bryant	.50
301	Kobe Bryant	.50
302	Kobe Bryant	.50
303	Kobe Bryant	.50
304	Kobe Bryant	.50
305	Kobe Bryant	.50
306	Kevin Garnett	.40
307	Kevin Garnett	.40
308	Kevin Garnett	.40
309	Kevin Garnett	.40
310	Kevin Garnett	.40
311	Kevin Garnett	.40
312	Kevin Garnett	.40
313	Kevin Garnett	.40
314	Kevin Garnett	.40
315	Kevin Garnett	.40
316	Kevin Garnett	.40
317	Kevin Garnett	.40
318	Kevin Garnett	.40
319	Kevin Garnett	.40
320	Kevin Garnett	.40
321	Kevin Garnett	.40
322	Kevin Garnett	.40
323	Kevin Garnett	.40
324	Kevin Garnett	.40
325	Kevin Garnett	.40
326	Kevin Garnett	.40
327	Kevin Garnett	.40
328	Kevin Garnett	.40
329	Kevin Garnett	.40
330	Kevin Garnett	.40

2001 Upper Deck Legends

		MT
Complete Set (90):		25.00
Common Player:		.25
Minor Stars:		.50
Common Rookie:		
91-110 Production 3,250 Sets		
111-125 Production 1,999 Sets		
126-132 Production 500 Sets		
Pack ( ):		
Box ( ):		
1	Michael Jordan	4.00
2	Wilt Chamberlain	1.00
3	Karl Malone	1.00
4	Steve Francis	1.50
5	George McGinnis	.50
6	Julius Erving	1.00
7	Alonzo Mourning	.50
8	Kobe Bryant	3.00
9	Glen Rice	.50
10	Mitch Kupchak	.25
11	Isiah Thomas	.75
12	Rick Barry	.50
13	Moses Malone	.50
14	Larry Bird	2.50
15	Vince Carter	3.00
16	Jamaal Wilkes	.50
17	John Havlicek	.75
18	Elgin Baylor	.75
19	Dave Bing	.50
20	Steve Smith	.50
21	Kevin Garnett	2.50
22	Hakeem Olajuwon	.75
23	Walt Bellamy	.25
24	Kevin McHale	.75
25	Kareem Abdul-Jabbar	1.00
26	Chris Webber	1.50
27	Tom Heinsohn	.25
28	Walt Frazier	.75
29	Ron Boone	.25
30	Gary Payton	.75
31	Wes Unseld	.25
32	Magic Johnson	2.00
33	David Thompson	.50
34	Maurice Lucas	.25
35	Paul Pierce	.75
36	Dikembe Mutombo	.50
37	Gail Goodrich	.50
38	Bob Lanier	.25
39	Chris Mullin	.50
40	Allen Iverson	2.50
41	Sam Jones	.25
42	James Worthy	.75
43	Cedric Maxwell	.25
44	George Gervin	.75
45	Earl Monroe	.75
46	Lenny Wilkens	.50
47	Tracy McGrady	2.00
48	Walter Davis	.25
49	Stephon Marbury	.75
50	Bob Cousy	.75
51	Spencer Haywood	.25
52	Dave Cowens	.25
53	Scottie Pippen	1.00
54	Hal Greer	.25
55	Kiki Vandeweghe	.25
56	Paul Silas	.50
57	Elton Brand	1.00
58	John Stockton	.75
59	Shareef Abdur-Rahim	.75
60	Reggie Miller	.75
61	Nate Thurmond	.25
62	Billy Cunningham	.25
63	Patrick Ewing	.50
64	Nate Archibald	.75
65	Tim Duncan	1.50
66	Lafayette Lever	.25
67	Willis Reed	.50
68	Ray Allen	.75
69	Jo Jo White	.25
70	Pete Maravich	.75
71	Grant Hill	1.25
72	Jerry West	.75
73	George Karl	.50
74	Bill Sharman	.25
75	Dave DeBusschere	.25
76	Tim Hardaway	.50
77	Bill Walton	.75
78	Jerry Lucas	.25
79	Antonio McDyess	.75
80	Robert Parish	.75
81	Shaquille O'Neal	2.00
82	Bill Russell	1.00
83	Clyde Drexler	.75
84	Dolph Schayes	.50
85	K.C. Jones	.25
86	Bob Pettit	.50
87	Jason Kidd	1.25
88	Mitch Richmond	.50
89	Oscar Robertson	.75
90	David Robinson	.75
91	*Bobby Simmons*	5.00
92	*Jamison Brewer*	5.00
93	*Earl Watson*	5.00
94	*Kenny Satterfield*	6.00
95	*Zeljko Rebraca*	8.00
96	*Damone Brown*	5.00
97	*Ruben Boumtje-Boumtje*	5.00
98	*Brian Scalabrine*	6.00
99	*Terence Morris*	5.00
100	*Willie Solomon*	6.00
101	*Primoz Brezec*	5.00
102	*Gilbert Arenas*	12.00
103	*Trenton Hassell*	8.00
104	*Loren Woods*	10.00
105	*Tony Parker*	20.00
106	*Jamaal Tinsley*	20.00
107	*Samuel Dalembert*	5.00
108	*Gerald Wallace*	12.00
109	*Andrei Kirilenko*	12.00
110	*Brandon Armstrong*	8.00
111	*Jeryl Sasser*	8.00
112	*Joseph Forte*	12.00
113	*Brendan Haywood*	12.00
114	*Zach Randolph*	15.00
115	*Jason Collins*	8.00
116	*Michael Bradley*	8.00
117	*Kirk Haston*	12.00
118	*Steven Hunter*	8.00
119	*Troy Murphy*	12.00
120	*Richard Jefferson*	15.00
121	*Vladimir Radmanovic*	10.00
122	*Kedrick Brown*	10.00
123	*Joe Johnson*	30.00
124	*Rodney White*	12.00
125	*DeSagana Diop*	10.00
126	*Eddie Griffin*	40.00
127	*Shane Battier*	100.00
128	*Jason Richardson*	100.00
129	*Eddy Curry*	40.00
130	*Pau Gasol*	80.00
131	*Tyson Chandler*	50.00
132	*Kwame Brown*	50.00

2001 Upper Deck Legends Autographed Legendary Floor

		MT
Common Player:		75.00
Production 100 Sets		
KA-AF	Kareem Abdul-Jabbar	200.00
LB-AF	Larry Bird	300.00
KB-AF	Kobe Bryant	400.00
DR-AF	Julius Erving	200.00
SF-AF	Steve Francis	75.00
KG-AF	Kevin Garnett	150.00
JH-AF	John Havlicek	100.00
MA-AF	Magic Johnson	250.00
MJ-AF	Michael Jordan	
MM-AF	Moses Malone	100.00

A card number in parentheses ( ) indicates the set is unnumbered.

2001 Upper Deck Legends Generations

		MT
Complete Set (9):		
Common Player:		5.00
Inserted 1:24		
G1	Michael Jordan, Kobe Bryant	15.00
G2	Oscar Robertson, Jason Kidd	6.00
G3	Walt Frazier, Ray Allen	5.00
G4	Elvin Hayes, Kevin Garnett	8.00
G5	Moses Malone, Tim Duncan	8.00
G6	Bob Lanier, David Robinson	5.00
G7	George Gervin, Tracy McGrady	6.00
G8	Nate Archibald, Steve Francis	6.00
G9	Michael Jordan, Vince Carter	15.00

2001 Upper Deck Legends Record Producers

		MT
Complete Set (9):		
Common Player:		3.00
Inserted 1:24		
RP1	Michael Jordan	15.00
RP2	John Stockton	3.00
RP3	Reggie Miller	3.00
RP4	Oscar Robertson	3.00
RP5	Hakeem Olajuwon	3.00
RP6	Elgin Baylor	3.00
RP7	Karl Malone	3.00
RP8	Kobe Bryant	10.00
RP9	Jerry West	3.00

2001 Upper Deck Legends The Fiorentino Collection

		MT
Complete Set (15):		
Common Player:		2.00
Inserted 1:15		
F1	Michael Jordan	12.00
F2	Larry Bird	8.00
F3	Magic Johnson	6.00
F4	Julius Erving	4.00
F5	Bill Russell	4.00
F6	Jerry West	3.00
F7	Oscar Robertson	3.00
F8	Wilt Chamberlain	4.00
F9	Kareem Abdul-Jabbar	4.00

F10	Isiah Thomas	2.00
F11	George Gervin	2.00
F12	Elgin Baylor	3.00
F13	Bob Cousy	3.00
F14	Pete Maravich	3.00
F15	John Havlicek	3.00

2001 Upper Deck Legends Upper Deck Yearbook

		MT
Complete Set (9):		
Common Player:		3.00
Inserted 1:24		
Y1	Michael Jordan	15.00
Y2	Kobe Bryant	10.00
Y3	Walt Frazier	3.00
Y4	Pete Maravich	3.00
Y5	Clyde Drexler	3.00
Y6	Bob Lanier	3.00
Y7	Bill Russell	4.00
Y8	Bill Walton	3.00
Y9	Kevin Garnett	6.00

2001 Upper Deck Legends Legendary Floor

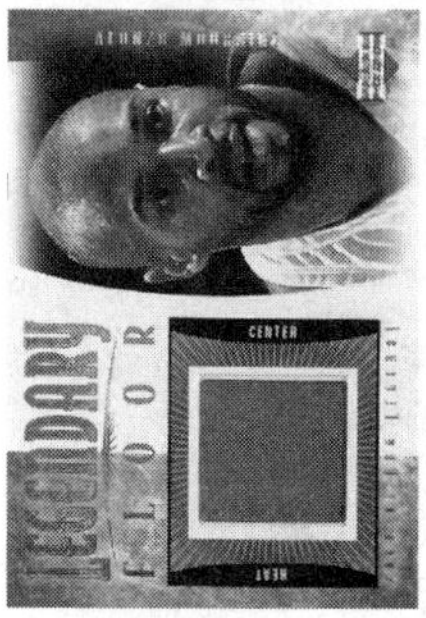

		MT
Common Player:		12.00
Inserted 1:23		
KA-F	Kareem Abdul-Jabbar	50.00
LB-F	Larry Bird	60.00
KB-F	Kobe Bryant	50.00
WC-F	Wilt Chamberlain	50.00
DR-F	Julius Erving	40.00
PE-F	Patrick Ewing	12.00
SF-F	Steve Francis	20.00
KG-F	Kevin Garnett	30.00
TH-F	Tim Hardaway	12.00
JH-F	John Havlicek	25.00
GH-F	Grant Hill	15.00
AI-F	Allen Iverson	30.00
MA-F	Magic Johnson	50.00
MJ-F	Michael Jordan	60.00
JK-F	Jason Kidd	20.00
KM-F	Karl Malone	20.00
MM-F	Moses Malone	20.00
PM-F	Pete Maravich	50.00
SM-F	Stephon Marbury	15.00
TM-F	Tracy McGrady	20.00
RM-F	Reggie Miller	15.00
AM-F	Alonzo Mourning	12.00
HO-F	Hakeem Olajuwon	15.00
SP-F	Scottie Pippen	20.00
DA-F	David Robinson	15.00
JS-F	John Stockton	20.00
IT-F	Isiah Thomas	25.00
CW-F	Chris Webber	20.00
JW-F	James Worthy	30.00

2001 Upper Deck Legends Legendary Jersey

		MT
Common Player:		20.00
KB-J	Kobe Bryant	60.00
DD-J	Dave DeBusschere	20.00
CD-J	Clyde Drexler	40.00
PE-J	Patrick Ewing	20.00
KG-J	Kevin Garnett	40.00
GH-J	Grant Hill	20.00
AI-J	Allen Iverson	40.00
MJ/KB-J	Michael Jordan, Kobe Bryant	500.00
MJ/DR-J	Michael Jordan, Julius Erving	400.00
MJ-LB/J	Michael Jordan, Larry Bird	500.00
KM-J	Karl Malone	25.00
MC-J	Kevin McHale	25.00
EM-J	Earl Monroe	30.00
RP-J	Robert Parish	20.00
SP-J	Scottie Pippen	25.00
DA-J	David Robinson	20.00
JS-J	John Stockton	40.00
BW-J	Bill Walton	25.00

2001 Upper Deck Legends Leg. Jersey (Fiorentino)

		MT
Common Player:		20.00
Inserted 1:23		
KA-J	Kareem Abdul-Jabbar	60.00
LB-J	Larry Bird	125.00
DR-J	Julius Erving	75.00
GG-J	George Gervin	25.00
JH-J	John Havlicek	40.00
MA-J	Magic Johnson	100.00
MJ-J	Michael Jordan	300.00
BR-J	Bill Russell	100.00
IT-J	Isiah Thomas	40.00
JW-J	Jerry West	40.00

2001 Upper Deck Legends Legendary Signatures

		MT
Common Player:		15.00
Inserted 1:71		
KA	Kareem Abdul-Jabbar	75.00
NA	Nate Archibald	15.00
EB	Elgin Baylor	25.00
LB	Larry Bird	500.00
KB	Kobe Bryant	400.00
DR	Julius Erving	300.00
SF	Steve Francis	60.00
KG	Kevin Garnett	100.00
GG	George Gervin	15.00
MM	Moses Malone	20.00
EM	Earl Monroe	20.00
WR	Willis Reed	15.00
OR	Oscar Robertson	40.00
BR	Bill Russell	400.00
BS	Bill Sharman	15.00
DT	David Thompson	15.00
KV	Kiki Vandeweghe	15.00
JW	Jerry West	40.00

2001-02 Upper Deck

		MT
Complete Set (450):		275.00
Complete Series I Set (225):		200.00
Complete Series II Set (225):		75.00
Common Player:		.25
Minor Stars:		.50
Common Rookie:		1.50
Inserted 1:4		
Pack Series I (8):		3.00
Pack Series II (8):		
Wax Box Series I (24):		60.00
Wax Box Series II (24):		
1	Jason Terry	.50
2	Toni Kukoc	.25
3	Alan Henderson	.25
4	Theo Ratliff	.25
5	Shareef Abdur-Rahim	.75
6	DerMarr Johnson	.25
7	Paul Pierce	.75
8	Antoine Walker	.75
9	Kenny Anderson	.25
10	Vitaly Potapenko	.25
11	Eric Williams	.25
12	Jamal Mashburn	.50
13	Baron Davis	.75
14	David Wesley	.25
15	P.J. Brown	.25
16	Elden Campbell	.25
17	Jamaal Magloire	.25
18	Lee Nailon	.25
19	A.J. Guyton	.25
20	Ron Mercer	.50
21	Jamal Crawford	.50
22	Fred Hoiberg	.25
23	Marcus Fizer	.50
24	Ron Artest	.25
25	Lamond Murray	.25
26	Andre Miller	.75
27	Jim Jackson	.50
28	Chris Mihm	.25
29	Trajan Langdon	.25
30	Chris Gatling	.25
31	Michael Finley	.75
32	Dirk Nowitzki	.75
33	Steve Nash	.50
34	Juwan Howard	.50
35	Zhizhi Wang	1.25
36	Eduardo Najera	.75
37	Shawn Bradley	.25
38	Antonio McDyess	.50
39	Nick Van Exel	.50
40	Raef LaFrentz	.50
41	James Posey	.25
42	Voshon Lenard	.25
43	Ben Wallace	.25
44	Jerry Stackhouse	.75
45	Corliss Williamson	.25
46	Chucky Atkins	.25
47	Michael Curry	.25
48	Dana Barros	.25
49	Antawn Jamison	.75
50	Larry Hughes	.50
51	Bob Sura	.25
52	Marc Jackson	.50
53	Chris Porter	.25
54	Vonteego Cummings	.25
55	Steve Francis	1.50
56	Cuttino Mobley	.50
57	Maurice Taylor	.50
58	Kenny Thomas	.50
59	Moochie Norris	.25
60	Walt Williams	.25
61	Reggie Miller	.75
62	Jalen Rose	.50
63	Jermaine O'Neal	.75
64	Austin Croshere	.25
65	Travis Best	.25
66	Jonathan Bender	.50
67	Eric Piatkowski	.25
68	Darius Miles	2.50
69	Lamar Odom	1.00
70	Quentin Richardson	.75
71	Corey Maggette	.50
72	Elton Brand	1.00
73	Jeff McInnis	.25
74	Kobe Bryant	4.00
75	Shaquille O'Neal	2.00
76	Derek Fisher	.50
77	Rick Fox	.50
78	Mitch Richmond	.50
79	Ron Harper	.25
80	Brian Shaw	.25
81	Stromile Swift	.50
82	Michael Dickerson	.25
83	Jason Williams	.50
84	Grant Long	.25
85	Bryant Reeves	.25
86	Alonzo Mourning	.50
87	Eddie Jones	.75
88	Brian Grant	.25
89	Anthony Mason	.50
90	LaPhonso Ellis	.25
91	Anthony Carter	.25
92	Jason Caffey	.25
93	Ray Allen	.75
94	Glenn Robinson	.75
95	Sam Cassell	.50
96	Tim Thomas	.50
97	Ervin Johnson	.25
98	Joel Przybilla	.25
99	Kevin Garnett	2.50
100	Terrell Brandon	.50
101	Wally Szczerbiak	.50
102	Felipe Lopez	.25
103	Chauncey Billups	.25
104	Anthony Peeler	.25
105	Kenyon Martin	.75
106	Keith Van Horn	.75
107	Jamie Feick	.25
108	Aaron Williams	.25
109	Lucious Harris	.25
110	Jason Kidd	1.00
111	Latrell Sprewell	.50
112	Allan Houston	.50
113	Marcus Camby	.50
114	Mark Jackson	.50
115	Othella Harrington	.25
116	Kurt Thomas	.25
117	Tracy McGrady	2.00
118	Mike Miller	1.50
119	Darrell Armstrong	.25
120	Grant Hill	1.25
121	Pat Garrity	.25
122	Bo Outlaw	.25
123	Allen Iverson	2.50
124	Dikembe Mutombo	.50
125	Aaron McKie	.25
126	Matt Geiger	.25
127	Eric Snow	.25
128	George Lynch	.25
129	*Raja Bell*	1.50
130	Shawn Marion	1.00
131	Tom Gugliotta	.50
132	Rodney Rogers	.50
133	Anfernee Hardaway	.50
134	Tony Delk	.25
135	Stephon Marbury	.75
136	Rasheed Wallace	.50
137	Damon Stoudamire	.25
138	Rod Strickland	.50
139	Dale Davis	.25
140	Scottie Pippen	1.00
141	Bonzi Wells	.50
142	Predrag Stojakovic	.75
143	Chris Webber	1.50
144	Doug Christie	.25
145	Mike Bibby	.75
146	Hidayet Turkoglu	.50
147	Scot Pollard	.25
148	Vlade Divac	.50
149	Tim Duncan	1.50
150	David Robinson	.75
151	Antonio Daniels	.25
152	Danny Ferry	.25
153	Malik Rose	.25
154	Terry Porter	.25
155	Rashard Lewis	.75
156	Gary Payton	.75
157	Brent Barry	.25
158	Vin Baker	.50
159	Desmond Mason	.50
160	Shammond Williams	.25
161	Vince Carter	4.00
162	Antonio Davis	.25
163	Morris Peterson	.50
164	Keon Clark	.25
165	Chris Childs	.25
166	Alvin Williams	.25
167	Karl Malone	1.00
168	John Stockton	.75
169	Donyell Marshall	.25
170	John Starks	.25
171	Bryon Russell	.25
172	David Benoit	.25
173	DeShawn Stevenson	.75
174	Richard Hamilton	.50
175	Jahidi White	.25
176	Courtney Alexander	.50
177	Chris Whitney	.25
178	Michael Jordan	6.00
179	Kobe Bryant	.75
180	Kevin Garnett	.50
181	*Sean Lampley*	1.50
182	*Andrei Kirilenko*	8.00
183	*Brandon Armstrong*	2.00
184	*Gerald Wallace*	6.00
185	*Tony Parker*	10.00
186	*Jeryl Sasser*	2.00
187	*Alton Ford*	1.50
188	*Kenny Satterfield*	3.00
189	*Will Solomon*	1.50
190	*Earl Watson*	1.50
191	*Michael Wright*	1.50
192	*Samuel Dalembert*	1.50
193	*Ousmane Cisse*	1.50
194	*Ruben Boumtje-Boumtje*	1.50
195	*Damone Brown*	1.50
196	*Jarron Collins*	1.50
197	*Terence Morris*	1.50
198	*Pau Gasol*	12.00
199	*Trenton Hassell*	3.00
200	*Kirk Haston*	3.00
201	*Brian Scalabrine*	1.50
202	*Gilbert Arenas*	4.00
203	*Jeff Trepagnier*	2.00
204	*Joseph Forte*	6.00
205	*Steven Hunter*	4.00
206	*Omar Cook*	3.00
207	*Jason Collins*	3.00
208	*Kedrick Brown*	3.00
209	*Michael Bradley*	3.00
210	*Zach Randolph*	6.00
211	*Richard Jefferson*	6.00
212	*Jamaal Tinsley*	12.00
213	*Vladimir Radmanovic*	4.00
214	*Brendan Haywood*	6.00
215	*Troy Murphy*	5.00
216	*DeSagana Diop*	3.00
217	*Jason Richardson*	15.00
218	*Joe Johnson*	8.00
219	*Rodney White*	5.00
220	*Loren Woods*	5.00
221	*Tyson Chandler*	10.00
222	*Eddy Curry*	10.00
223	*Shane Battier*	15.00
224	*Eddie Griffin*	10.00
225	*Kwame Brown*	10.00
226	Shareef Abdur-Rahim	.75
227	Nazr Mohammed	.25
228	Hanno Mottola	.25
229	Emmanual Davis	.25
230	Dion Glover	.25
231	Chris Crawford	.25
232	Mark Blount	.25
233	Joe Johnson	3.00
234	Milt Palacio	.25
235	Kedrick Brown	.25
236	Tony Battie	.25
237	Erick Strickland	.25
238	Kirk Haston	.25
239	Stacey Augmon	.25
240	Matt Bullard	.25
241	Bryce Drew	.25
242	Jerome Moiso	.25
243	Robert Traylor	.25
244	Tyson Chandler	5.00
245	Eddy Curry	4.00
246	Charles Oakley	.25
247	Brad Miller	.25
248	Kevin Ollie	.25
249	Trenton Hassell	2.00
250	Ricky Davis	.25
251	Jumaine Jones	.25
252	DeSagana Diop	2.00
253	Bryant Stith	.25
254	Jeff Trepagnier	.25
255	Michael Doleac	.25
256	Tim Hardaway	.25
257	Danny Manning	.25
258	Johnny Newman	.25
259	Adrian Griffin	.25
260	Greg Buckner	.25
261	Donnell Harvey	.25
262	Evan Eschmeyer	.25
263	Avery Johnson	.25
264	Kenny Satterfield	.25
265	Scott Williams	.25
266	Tariq Abdul-Wahad	.25
267	George McCloud	.25
268	Clifford Robinson	.25
269	Jon Barry	.25
270	Brian Cardinal	.25
271	Rodney White	2.00
272	Mikki Moore	.25
273	Victor Alexander	.25
274	Jason Richardson	8.00
275	Adonal Foyle	.25
276	Troy Murphy	.25
277	Chris Mills	.25
278	Gilbert Arenas	3.00
279	Erick Dampier	.25
280	Glen Rice	.25
281	Eddie Griffin	5.00
282	Kevin Willis	.25
283	Terence Morris	.25
284	Kelvin Cato	.25
285	Dan Langhi	.25
286	Jason Collier	2.00
287	Jamaal Tinsley	5.00
288	Carlos Rogers	.25
289	Jeff Foster	.25
290	Al Harrington	.50
291	Bruno Sundov	.25
292	Elton Brand	1.00
293	Keyon Dooling	.50
294	Michael Olowokandi	.25
295	Obinna Ekezie	.25
296	Earl Boykins	.25
297	Harold Jamison	.25
298	Sean Rooks	.25
299	Lindsey Hunter	.25
300	Samaki Walker	.25
301	Mitch Richmond	.50
302	Stanislav Medvedenko	.25
303	Devean George	.25
304	Robert Horry	.25
305	Jelani McCoy	.25
306	Pau Gasol	6.00
307	Shane Battier	6.00
308	Jason Williams	.50
309	Isaac Austin	.25
310	Will Solomon	.25
311	Lorenzen Wright	.25
312	Kendall Gill	.25
313	LaPhonso Ellis	.25
314	Sean Marks	.25
315	Rod Strickland	.50
316	Jim Jackson	.25
317	Eddie House	.50
318	Jason Caffey	.25
319	Rafer Alston	.25
320	Anthony Mason	.50
321	Mark Pope	.25
322	Michael Redd	.25
323	Darvin Ham	.25
324	Joe Smith	.50
325	William Avery	.25
326	Sam Mitchell	.25
327	Loren Woods	2.00
328	Dean Garrett	.25
329	Gary Trent	.25
330	Jason Kidd	1.25
331	Todd MacCulloch	.25
332	Richard Jefferson	3.00
333	Brandon Armstrong	.25
334	Jason Collins	.25
335	Kerry Kittles	.25
336	Shandon Anderson	.25
337	Howard Eisley	.25
338	Charlie Ward	.25
339	Lavor Postell	.25
340	Clarence Weatherspoon	.25
341	Travis Knight	.25
342	Horace Grant	.25
343	Steven Hunter	.25
344	Patrick Ewing	.50
345	Jeryl Sasser	.25
346	Don Reid	.25
347	Troy Hudson	.25
348	Craig "Speedy" Claxton	.50
349	Derrick Coleman	.50
350	Damone Brown	.25
351	Samuel Dalembert	.25
352	Vonteego Cummings	.25
353	Matt Harpring	.25
354	Corie Blount	.25
355	Stephon Marbury	.75
356	Dan Majerle	.25
357	Jake Voskuhl	.25
358	Alton Ford	.25
359	Iakovos Tsakalidis	.25
360	John Wallace	.25
361	Derek Anderson	.25
362	Erick Barkley	.25
363	Ruben Boumtje-Boumtje	.25
364	Zach Randolph	3.00
365	Steve Kerr	.25
366	Shawn Kemp	.50
367	Mateen Cleaves	.25
368	Bobby Jackson	.25
369	Mike Bibby	.50
370	Gerald Wallace	3.00
371	Jabari Smith	.25
372	Lawrence Funderburke	.25
373	Brent Price	.25
374	Bruce Bowen	.25
375	Stephen Jackson	.25
376	Tony Parker	5.00
377	Steve Smith	.50
378	Cherokee Parks	.25
379	Mark Bryant	.25
380	Jerome James	.25
381	Earl Watson	.25
382	Vladimir Radmanovic	.25
383	Art Long	.25
384	Calvin Booth	.25
385	Olumide Oyedji	.25
386	Jerome Williams	.25
387	Hakeem Olajuwon	.50
388	Dell Curry	.25
389	Michael Bradley	.25
390	Tracy Murray	.25
391	Eric Montross	.25
392	John Amaechi	.25
393	John Crotty	.25
394	Scott Padgett	.25
395	Andrei Kirilenko	3.00
396	Jarron Collins	.25
397	Quincy Lewis	.25
398	Kwame Brown	5.00
399	Christian Laettner	.25
400	Tyrone Nesby	.25
401	Brendan Haywood	.25
402	Tyronn Lue	.25
403	Michael Jordan	8.00
404	Kobe Bryant	1.50
405	Michael Jordan	3.00
406	*Zeljko Rebraca*	3.00
407	*Jamison Brewer*	2.00
408	Shawn Marion	2.00
409	*Primoz Brezec*	2.00
410	*Antonis Fotsis*	2.00
411	*Bobby Simmons*	2.00
412	*Malik Allen*	2.00
413	*Ratko Varda*	2.00
414	*Tierre Brown*	2.00
415	*Norm Richardson*	2.00
416	*Oscar Torres*	2.00
417	*Chris Anderson*	2.00
418	*Predrag Drobnjak*	2.00
419	Dirk Nowitzki	2.00
420	Shareef Abdur-Rahim	1.50
421	Kenny Anderson	1.00
422	Jamal Mashburn	1.00
423	Charles Oakley	1.00
424	Andre Miller	1.00
425	Michael Finley	1.50
426	Tim Hardaway	1.00
427	Nick Van Exel	1.50
428	Jerry Stackhouse	1.50
429	Mookie Blaylock	1.00
430	Glen Rice	1.00
431	Reggie Miller	1.50
432	Elton Brand	2.00
433	Kobe Bryant	8.00
434	Jason Williams	1.00
435	Eddie Jones	1.50
436	Alonzo Mourning	1.50
437	Glenn Robinson	1.00
438	Kevin Garnett	5.00
439	Jason Kidd	2.50
440	Latrell Sprewell	2.00
441	Grant Hill	2.00
442	Dikembe Mutombo	1.00
443	Anfernee Hardaway	1.00
444	Scottie Pippen	2.00
445	Mike Bibby	1.00
446	David Robinson	1.50
447	Gary Payton	1.50
448	Vince Carter	0.00
448	John Stockton	1.50
450	Michael Jordan	15.00

2001-02 Upper Deck UDX

	MT
UDX Cards:	12x-24x
UDX Rookies:	3x-6x

2001-02 Upper Deck 10th Power Game Jersey

		MT
Common Player:		15.00
Inserted 1:144		
RA-X	Ray Allen	35.00
KB-X	Kobe Bryant	175.00
KG-X	Kevin Garnett	60.00
RH-X	Richard Hamilton	15.00
MJ-X	Michael Jordan	350.00
MT-X	Dikembe Mutombo	15.00
DR-X	David Robinson	30.00
WS-X	Wally Szczerbiak	15.00
NV-X	Nick Van Exel	15.00
KV-X	Keith Van Horn	15.00

2001-02 Upper Deck 15,000 Point Club Jersey

		MT
Common Player:		20.00
Inserted 1:120		
LB-15K	Larry Bird	125.00
PE-15K	Patrick Ewing	20.00
JH-15K	John Havlicek	40.00
MJ-15K	Michael Jordan	750.00
KM-15K	Karl Malone	30.00
MM-15K	Moses Malone	20.00
GR-15K	Glen Rice	20.00
IT-15K	Isiah Thomas	40.00
JW-15K	Jerry West	50.00

2001-02 Upper Deck All-Star Authentics

		MT
Complete Set (5):		
Common Player:		10.00
BD-AS	Baron Davis	15.00
RL-AS	Rashard Lewis	15.00
DM-AS	Desmond Mason	10.00
PS-AS	Predrag Stojakovic	20.00
SS-AS	Stromile Swift	15.00

2001-02 Upper Deck Breakout Performers

		MT
Complete Set (15):		25.00
Common Player:		1.00
Inserted 1:12		
BP1	Kenyon Martin	1.00
BP2	Steve Francis	2.50
BP3	Stromile Swift	1.00
BP4	Baron Davis	1.50
BP5	Rashard Lewis	1.00
BP6	Vince Carter	6.00
BP7	Richard Hamilton	1.00
BP8	Kobe Bryant	6.00
BP9	DerMarr Johnson	1.00
BP10	Andre Miller	1.00
BP11	Kevin Garnett	4.00
BP12	Morris Peterson	1.00
BP13	Dirk Nowitzki	2.00
BP14	Mike Miller	3.00
BP15	Shawn Marion	2.00

2001-02 Upper Deck Class

		MT
Complete Set (7):		25.00
Common Player:		2.50
Inserted 1:24		
C1	Michael Jordan	15.00
C2	Shaquille O'Neal	6.00
C3	Alonzo Mourning	2.50

C4 Steve Francis 5.00
C5 Kobe Bryant 10.00
C6 Tim Duncan 5.00
C7 Kevin Garnett 6.00

2001-02 Upper Deck Cool Cats Jersey

MT
Common Player: 20.00
Inserted 1:288
BR-C Michael Bradley 20.00
TD-C Tony Delk 20.00
RJ-J Richard Jefferson 25.00
DJ-C DerMarr Johnson 25.00
KM-C Kenyon Martin 25.00
JM-C Jamal Mashburn 25.00
RM-C Ron Mercer 20.00
AW-C Antoine Walker 30.00

2001-02 Upper Deck Game Jersey Autographs

MT
Common Player: 25.00
Production 100 Sets
KB-A Kobe Bryant 400.00
MA-A Marcus Fizer 30.00
KG-A Kevin Garnett 125.00
LH-A Larry Hughes 40.00
DJ-A DerMarr Johnson 25.00
CM-A Corey Maggette 25.00
KM-A Kenyon Martin 50.00
CH-A Chris Mihm 25.00
MM-A Mike Miller 50.00
MP-A Morris Peterson 40.00
WZ-A Wang Zhizhi 100.00

2001-02 Upper Deck Game Jersey

MT
Common Player: 15.00
Inserted 1:144
RA Ron Artest 15.00
KB Kobe Bryant 175.00
KG Kevin Garnett 60.00
MC Marc Jackson 15.00
KM Karl Malone 30.00
CM Cuttino Mobley 15.00
GP Gary Payton 20.00
BR Bryon Russell 15.00
JS Joe Smith 15.00
JT Jason Terry 15.00

2001-02 Upper Deck Game Jersey Combos

MT
Common Player: 12.00
Inserted 1:144
JM/BD Jamal Mashburn, Baron Davis 12.00
DM/CM Darius Miles, Corey Maggette 50.00
AM/LM Andre Miller, Lamond Murray 12.00
JC/RM Jamal Crawford, Ron Mercer 12.00
KB/KG Kobe Bryant, Kevin Garnett 125.00
JT/TK Jason Terry, Toni Kukoc 12.00
MF/DN Michael Finley, Dirk Nowitzki 50.00
AJ/LH Antawn Jamison, Larry Hughes 18.00
DM/QR Darius Miles, Quentin Richardson 50.00
KM/JS Karl Malone, John Stockton 40.00

2001-02 Upper Deck Higher Ground

MT
Complete Set (10): 25.00
Common Player: 2.00
Inserted 1:18
HG1 Vince Carter 12.00
HG2 Kevin Garnett 7.00
HG3 Paul Pierce 2.00
HG4 Mike Miller 5.00
HG5 Jamal Mashburn 2.00
HG6 Steve Francis 5.00
HG7 Jerry Stackhouse 2.00
HG8 Kobe Bryant 12.00
HG9 Eddie Jones 2.00
HG10 Shawn Marion 3.00

2001-02 Upper Deck Motion Pictures

MT
Complete Set (10): 40.00
Common Player: 2.00
Inserted 1:18
MP1 Kobe Bryant 8.00
MP2 Tim Duncan 4.00
MP3 Michael Jordan 12.00
MP4 Elton Brand 3.00
MP5 Vince Carter 8.00
MP6 Eddie Jones 2.00
MP7 Kevin Garnett 2.00
MP8 Michael Finley 2.00
MP9 Paul Pierce 2.00
MP10 Shaquille O'Neal 5.00

2001-02 Upper Deck NBA Finals Fabrics

MT
Common Player: 15.00
Inserted 1:120
RJ-F Raja Bell 15.00
KB-F Kobe Bryant 200.00
RB-F Rodney Buford 15.00
DF-F Derek Fisher 25.00
GF-F Greg Foster 15.00
RF-F Rick Fox 15.00
DG-F Devean George 15.00
HG-F Horace Grant 15.00
TH-F Tyrone Hill 15.00
RO-F Robert Horry 25.00
AI-F Allen Iverson 75.00
JJ-F Jumaine Jones 15.00
TL-F Tyronn Lue 15.00
TM-F Todd MacCulloch 15.00
MM-F Mark Madsen 15.00
AM-F Aaron McKie 20.00
DM-F Dikembe Mutombo 25.00
KO-F Kevin Ollie 15.00
BS-F Brian Shaw 15.00
ES-F Eric Snow 20.00

2001-02 Upper Deck Sky High

MT
Complete Set (7): 40.00
Common Player: 5.00
Inserted 1:24
SH1 Kobe Bryant 10.00
SH2 Kevin Garnett 6.00
SH3 Darius Miles 8.00
SH4 Tracy McGrady 5.00
SH5 Kwame Brown 8.00
SH6 Eddy Curry 6.00
SH7 Tyson Chandler 8.00

2001-02 Upper Deck SlamCenter

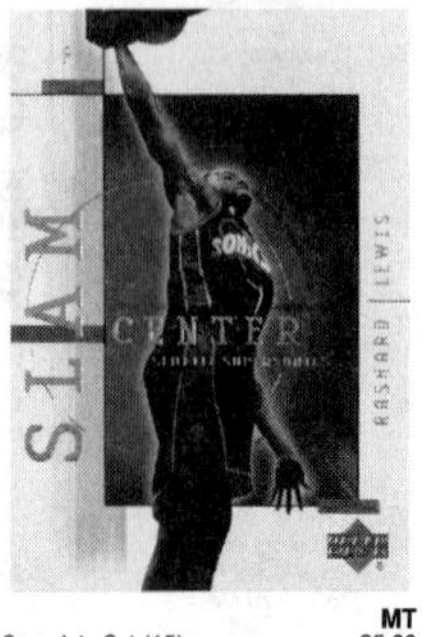

MT
Complete Set (15): 25.00
Common Player: 1.50
Inserted 1:12
SC1 Kobe Bryant 10.00
SC2 Desmond Mason 1.50
SC3 Vince Carter 10.00
SC4 Antonio McDyess 1.50
SC5 Lamar Odom 2.00
SC6 Rashard Lewis 1.50
SC7 Chris Webber 3.00
SC8 Latrell Sprewell 1.50
SC9 Antoine Walker 1.50
SC10 Stromile Swift 1.50
SC11 Glenn Robinson 1.50
SC12 Kevin Garnett 6.00
SC13 Antawn Jamison 1.50
SC14 Jerry Stackhouse 1.50
SC15 Shaquille O'Neal 5.00

2001-02 Upper Deck Superstar Summit

MT
Complete Set (10): 30.00
Common Player: 2.00
Inserted 1:12
SS1 Kobe Bryant 6.00
SS2 Vince Carter 6.00
SS3 Kevin Garnett 4.00
SS4 Chris Webber 2.50
SS5 Shaquille O'Neal 3.00
SS6 Tim Duncan 2.50
SS7 Allen Iverson 4.00
SS8 Ray Allen 2.00
SS9 Steve Francis 2.50
SS10 Michael Jordan 10.00

2001-02 Upper Deck Upper Decade Team

MT
Complete Set (10): 30.00
Common Player: 2.00
Inserted 1:18
UD1 Michael Jordan 12.00
UD2 Kobe Bryant 10.00
UD3 Vince Carter 10.00
UD4 Kevin Garnett 6.00
UD5 Shaquille O'Neal 5.00
UD6 Tim Hardaway 2.00
UD7 Gary Payton 2.00
UD8 Scottie Pippen 2.00
UD9 Tim Duncan 4.00
UD10 David Robinson 2.00

2001-02 Upper Deck UD Game Jersey Patch

"Too uncommon to price."

MT
Complete Set (17):
Common Player:
RA-P Ray Allen
KB-P Kobe Bryant
MF-P Michael Finley
KG-P Kevin Garnett
AI-P Allen Iverson
MA-P Marc Jackson
SM-P Shawn Marion
KM-P Kenyon Martin
JM-P Jamal Mashburn
TM-P Tracy McGrady
AM-P Andre Miller
MM-P Mike Miller
PP-P Paul Pierce
QR-P Quentin Richardson
JT-P Jason Terry
RW-P Rasheed Wallace
CW-P Chris Webber

2001-02 Upper Deck UD Originals - The New School

MT
Common Player: 15.00
Inserted 1:120
RA-O Ray Allen 25.00
KB-O Kobe Bryant 200.00
BD-O Baron Davis 20.00
KG-O Kevin Garnett 40.00
SM-O Stephon Marbury 20.00
SH-O Shawn Marion 20.00
DM-O Darius Miles 40.00
MM-O Mike Miller 30.00
SS-O Stromile Swift 15.00
CW-O Chris Webber 30.00

2001-02 Upper Deck Winning Touch Game Jersey

MT
Common Player: 15.00
Inserted 1:144
SE-WT Sean Elliott 15.00
PE-WT Patrick Ewing 25.00
RF-WT Rick Fox 15.00
AI-WT Allen Iverson 85.00
SK-WT Steve Kerr 15.00
KM-WT Karl Malone 30.00
DR-WT David Robinson 30.00
JS-WT John Stockton 30.00

2001-02 Upper Deck World Piece Game Jersey

MT
Common Player: 15.00
Inserted 1:288
DB-WP Dalibor Bagaric 15.00
VL-WP Vlade Divac 15.00
TK-WP Toni Kukoc 25.00
FL-WP Felipe Lopez 15.00
HM-WP Hanno Mottola 15.00
MT-WP Dikembe Mutombo 15.00
SN-WP Steve Nash 25.00
DN-WP Dirk Nowitzki 50.00
MO-WP Michael Olowokandi 15.00
ZW-WP Wang Zhizhi 40.00

2001-02 Upper Deck MJ Jersey Collection

MT
Complete Set (10):
Common Player: 500.00
MJC1 Michael Jordan 500.00
MJC2 Michael Jordan 500.00
MJC3 Michael Jordan 500.00
MJC4 Michael Jordan 500.00
MJC5 Michael Jordan 500.00
MJC6 Michael Jordan 500.00
MJC7 Michael Jordan 500.00
MJC8 Michael Jordan 500.00
MJC9 Michael Jordan 500.00
MJC10 Michael Jordan 500.00

2001-02 Upper Deck Flight Team

MT
Complete Set (140):
Common Player: .15
Card numbers 91-140 have three versions
Versions: Action, Portrait, Performance
#'s 90-120 numbered to 500
#'s 121-134 numbered to 375
#'s 135-140 numbered to 250
Pack (4): 7.00
Copper parallel numbered to 250
Gold parallel numbered to 100
Copper stars 8X to 20X Rookies 1X to 3X
Gold stars 10X to 30X Rookies 2X to 5X
1 Michael Jordan 10.00
2 Dirk Nowitzki 1.00
3 Antawn Jamison .75
4 Latrell Sprewell .75
5 Peja Stojakovic 1.00
6 Dikembe Mutombo .50
7 Jason Williams .15
8 Kobe Bryant 5.00
9 Baron Davis .15
10 Wally Szczerbiak 1.00
11 Reggie Miller .75
12 Marcus Fizer .15
13 Desmond Mason .15
14 Glenn Robinson .15
15 Vince Carter 4.00
16 James Posey .15
17 Darius Miles 1.00
18 Jason Kidd 1.00
19 Anfernee Hardaway .15
20 Karl Malone .75
21 Kevin Garnett 1.00
22 Shareef Abdur-Rahim .15
23 Steve Francis .50
24 Paul Pierce .75
25 Mike Miller .75
26 Tim Duncan 1.00
27 Derek Anderson .15
28 Eddie Jones .15
29 Keith Van Horn .15
30 Chris Mihm .15
31 Clifford Robinson .15
32 Gary Payton .50
33 Courtney Alexander 1.00
34 Shaquille O'Neal 3.00
35 Tim Thomas .15
36 Raef LaFrentz .15
37 Stromile Swift .15
38 Stephon Marbury .50
39 Morris Peterson .15
40 Donyell Marshall .15
41 Kenny Thomas .15
42 Juwan Howard .15
43 Tracy McGrady 1.00
44 Kenny Anderson .15
45 Larry Hughes .15
46 Allan Houston .15
47 Chris Webber 1.00
48 Andre Miller .50
49 Corey Maggette .15
50 Sam Cassell .15
51 Steve Smith .15
52 Jamal Mashburn .15
53 Al Harrington .15
54 Brian Grant .15
55 Rasheed Wallace .15
56 Rick Fox .15
57 Jason Terry .15
58 Rashard Lewis .15
59 Joe Smith .15
60 Michael Dickerson .15
61 Michael Finley .50
62 Danny Fortson .15
63 Allen Iverson 3.00
64 Richard Hamilton 1.00
65 Antonio McDyess .15
66 David Wesley .15
67 Ben Wallace .15
68 Mike Bibby 1.00
69 Antonio Davis .15
70 Cuttino Mobley .15
71 Lamond Murray .15
72 Antoine Walker .75
73 Jermaine O'Neal .75
74 Alonzo Mourning .50
75 Shawn Marion .50
76 John Stockton .50
77 Marcus Camby .15
78 Derek Fisher .15
79 DerMarr Johnson .15
80 Aaron McKie .15
81 David Robinson .50
82 Steve Nash .50
83 Ray Allen .50
84 Elton Brand .15
85 Kenyon Martin .50
86 Bonzi Wells .15
87 Grant Hill .50
88 Terrell Brandon .15
89 Toni Kukoc .15
90 Jerry Stackhouse .50
91 *Tierre Brown* 3.00
92 *Jamison Brewer* 3.00
93 *Antonis Fotsis* 3.00
94 *Mike James* 3.00
95 *Primoz Brezec* 3.00
96 *Jeryl Sasser* 3.00
97 *DeSagana Diop* 4.00
98 *Mengke Bateer* 6.00
99 *Gerald Wallace* 4.00
100 *Kenny Satterfield* 3.00
101 *Ruben Boumtje-Boumtje* 3.00
102 *Brian Scalabrine* 3.00
103 *Oscar Torres* 3.00
104 *Jarron Collins* 4.00
105 *Jeff Trepagnier* 3.00
106 *Brendan Haywood* 6.00
107 *Vladimir Radmanovic* 5.00
108 *Loren Woods* 4.00
109 *Terence Morris* 3.00
110 *Kirk Haston* 4.00
111 *Earl Watson* 3.00
112 *Brandon Armstrong* 3.00
113 *Zach Randolph* 5.00
114 *Bobby Simmons* 3.00
115 *Alton Ford* 3.00
116 *Predrag Drobnjak* 3.00
117 *Michael Bradley* 4.00
118 *Samuel Dalembert* 3.00
119 *Gilbert Arenas* 10.00
120 *Kedrick Brown* 5.00
121 *Trenton Hassell* 3.00
122 *Zeljko Rebraca* 6.00
123 *Jason Collins* 5.00
124 *Willie Solomon* 3.00
125 *Joseph Forte* 10.00
126 *Steven Hunter* 5.00
127 *Eddy Curry* 15.00
128 *Troy Murphy* 6.00
129 *Shane Battier* 40.00
130 *Tyson Chandler* 30.00
131 *Joe Johnson* 20.00
132 *Richard Jefferson* 25.00
133 *Eddie Griffin* 25.00
134 *Rodney White* 10.00
135 *Andrei Kirilenko* 20.00
136 *Tony Parker* 40.00
137 *Jamaal Tinsley* 35.00
138 *Pau Gasol* 50.00
139 *Jason Richardson* 60.00
140 *Kwame Brown* 25.00

2001-02 UD Flight Team MJ Tributes Portrait of a Champion

MT
Complete Set (1):
Numbered to 23 too uncommon to price
PCJ4 Michael Jordan

2001-02 UD Flight Team MJ Tributes MJ Milestones Autograph

MT
Complete Set (2):
Common Player:
Numbered to 30 too uncommon to price
M6 Michael Jordan
M7 Michael Jordan

2001-02 Upper Deck Flight Team Flight Patterns

MT
Complete Set (24):
Common Player: 10.00
Inserted 1:15
KE Kedrick Brown 10.00
KW Kwame Brown 20.00
BD Baron Davis 12.00
MF Marcus Fizer 10.00
DG Devean George 10.00
AH Anfernee Hardaway 10.00
AL Al Harrington 10.00
GH Grant Hill 15.00
AJ Antawn Jamison 12.00
JK Jason Kidd 25.00
CM Corey Maggette 10.00
SH Shawn Marion 15.00
JM Jamal Mashburn 10.00
DM Desmond Mason 10.00
AM Andre Miller 12.00
LO Lamar Odom 15.00
MP Morris Peterson 12.00
QR Quentin Richardson 10.00
BR Bryon Russell 10.00
JS Jerry Stackhouse 12.00
DS DeShawn Stevenson 10.00
WS Wally Szczerbiak 20.00
JT Jason Terry 15.00
KV Keith Van Horn 12.00

2001-02 Upper Deck Flight Team Flight Patterns Gold

MT
Complete Set (24):
Common Player:
Numbered to 125
2X to 4X base Flight Patterns
KE Kedrick Brown
KW Kwame Brown
BD Baron Davis
MF Marcus Fizer
DG Devean George
AH Anfernee Hardaway
AL Al Harrington
GH Grant Hill
AJ Antawn Jamison
JK Jason Kidd
CM Corey Maggette
SH Shawn Marion
JM Jamal Mashburn
DM Desmond Mason
AM Andre Miller
LO Lamar Odom
MP Morris Peterson
QR Quentin Richardson
BR Bryon Russell
JS Jerry Stackhouse
DS DeShawn Stevenson
WS Wally Szczerbiak
JT Jason Terry
KV Keith Van Horn

2001-02 Upper Deck Flight Team Key Signatures

MT
Complete Set (15):
Common Player:
Numbered to 100 (Jordan to 23)
Too uncommon to price at this time
BA-S Brandon Armstrong
KW-S Kwame Brown
KB-S Kobe Bryant
TC-S Tyson Chandler
EC-S Eddy Curry
SD-S Samuel Dalembert
KG-S Kevin Garnett
RJ-S Richard Jefferson
MJ-S Michael Jordan
JK-S Jason Kidd
CW-S Kenyon Martin
TM-S Troy Murphy
TP-S Tony Parker
JR-S Jason Richardson
JT-S Jamaal Tinsley

2001-02 Upper Deck Flight Team 2 the Air Gold

MT
Complete Set (6):
Common Player:
Numbered to 10 too uncommon to price
2-KB Kobe Bryant
2-KG Kevin Garnett
2-AI Allen Iverson
2-MJ Michael Jordan
2-MC Tracy McGrady
2-CW Chris Webber

2001-02 Upper Deck Flight Team 2 the Air

MT
Complete Set (6):
Common Player: 75.00
Numbered to 100
2-KB Kobe Bryant 250.00
2-KG Kevin Garnett 75.00
2-AI Allen Iverson 75.00
2-MJ Michael Jordan 450.00
2-MC Tracy McGrady 75.00
2-CW Chris Webber 75.00

2001-02 UD Flight Team Superstar Flight Patterns Gold

MT
Complete Set (6):
Common Player:
Numbered to 25 too uncommon to price
KB Kobe Bryant
KG Kevin Garnett
AI Allen Iverson
MJ Michael Jordan
MC Tracy McGrady
Chris Webber

2001-02 Upper Deck Flight Team Superstar Flight Patterns

MT
Complete Set (6):
Common Player:
Numbered to 100
Gold version numbered to 25
Gold too uncommon to price
KB Kobe Bryant
KG Kevin Garnett
AI Allen Iverson
MJ Michael Jordan
MC Tracy McGrady
Chris Webber

2001-02 Upper Deck Flight Team UD Jersey Jams Gold

MT
Complete Set (24):
Common Player:
Numbered to 50
2X to 4X (except for Jordan)
SA-J Shareef Abdur-Rahim
KB-J Kobe Bryant
TC-J Tyson Chandler
EC-J Eddy Curry
BD-J Baron Davis
SF-J Steve Francis
KG-J Kevin Garnett
EG-J Eddie Griffin
SH-J Steven Hunter
RJ-J Richard Jefferson
MJ-J Michael Jordan
JK-J Jason Kidd
RL-J Rashard Lewis
KM-J Karl Malone
SM-J Stephon Marbury
DM-J Darius Miles
TM-J Troy Murphy
LO-J Lamar Odom
PP-J Paul Pierce
JR-J Jason Richardson
GR-J Glenn Robinson
JS-J Jeryl Sasser
WS-J Wally Szczerbiak
AW-J Antoine Walker

2001-02 Upper Deck Flight Team UD Jersey Jams

MT
Complete Set (24):
Common Player: 15.00

Inserted 1:19
Pierce, Richardson & Bryant are SP
SA-J Shareef Abdur-Rahim 15.00
KB-J Kobe Bryant 100.00
TC-J Tyson Chandler 40.00
EC-J Eddy Curry 30.00
BD-J Baron Davis 15.00
SF-J Steve Francis 15.00
KG-J Kevin Garnett 20.00
EG-J Eddie Griffin 15.00
SH-J Steven Hunter 15.00
RJ-J Richard Jefferson 25.00
MJ-J Michael Jordan
JK-J Jason Kidd 50.00
RL-J Rashard Lewis 15.00
KM-J Karl Malone 20.00
SM-J Stephon Marbury 15.00
DM-J Darius Miles 30.00
TM-J Troy Murphy 15.00
LO-J Lamar Odom 15.00
PP-J Paul Pierce 40.00
JR-J Jason Richardson 40.00
GR-J Glenn Robinson 15.00
JS-J Jeryl Sasser 15.00
WS-J Wally Szczerbiak 25.00
AW-J Antoine Walker 20.00

2001-02 Upper Deck Hardcourt

MT
Complete Set (121): 500.00
Common Player: .30
Minor Stars: .60
Common Rookie (91-100): 5.00
Production 3,000 Sets
Common Rookie (101-110): 8.00
Production 1,800 Sets
Common Rookie (110-120): 15.00
Production 900 Sets
Pack (5): 5.00
Box (15): 75.00
1 Jason Terry .60
2 DerMarr Johnson .60
3 Toni Kukoc .60
4 Antoine Walker .75
5 Paul Pierce 1.00
6 Kenny Anderson .60
7 Jamal Mashburn .60
8 Baron Davis 1.00
9 David Wesley .30
10 Ron Artest .30
11 Jamal Crawford .60
12 Ron Mercer .60
13 Andre Miller .75
14 Lamond Murray .30
15 Matt Harpring .30
16 Michael Finley .75
17 Dirk Nowitzki 1.25
18 Steve Nash .60
19 Antonio McDyess .75
20 Nick Van Exel .75
21 James Posey .60
22 Jerry Stackhouse .75
23 Chucky Atkins .30
24 Mateen Cleaves .60
25 Antawn Jamison 1.25
26 Larry Hughes .60
27 Marc Jackson .60
28 Steve Francis 2.00
29 Maurice Taylor .30
30 Cuttino Mobley .60
31 Reggie Miller .75
32 Jalen Rose .60
33 Jermaine O'Neal .75
34 Darius Miles 4.00
35 Lamar Odom 1.25
36 Elton Brand 1.25
37 Kobe Bryant 5.00
38 Shaquille O'Neal 2.50
39 Derek Fisher .60
40 Robert Horry .60
41 Alonzo Mourning .60
42 Eddie Jones .75
43 Brian Grant .60
44 Anthony Mason .60
45 Ray Allen 1.00
46 Glenn Robinson .75
47 Tim Thomas .60
48 Kevin Garnett 3.00
49 Wally Szczerbiak .60
50 Terrell Brandon .60
51 Anthony Peeler .30
52 Jason Kidd 1.50
53 Kenyon Martin .60
54 Stephen Jackson .30
55 Latrell Sprewell 1.25
56 Allan Houston .60
57 Glen Rice .60
58 Tracy McGrady 2.50
59 Darrell Armstrong .60
60 Mike Miller 1.50
61 Allen Iverson 3.00
62 Dikembe Mutombo .60
63 Aaron McKie .60
64 Stephon Marbury 1.00
65 Shawn Marion 1.25
66 Tom Gugliotta .30
67 Rasheed Wallace .75
68 Scottie Pippen 1.25
69 Damon Stoudamire .30
70 Chris Webber 2.00
71 Mike Bibby .60
72 Peja Stojakovic .75
73 Tim Duncan 2.00
74 David Robinson .75
75 Derek Anderson .60
76 Gary Payton 1.00
77 Rashard Lewis .60
78 Desmond Mason .60
79 Vince Carter 5.00
80 Morris Peterson .75
81 Antonio Davis .60
82 Karl Malone 1.25
83 John Stockton 1.00
84 Donyell Marshall .30
85 Bryant Reeves .30
86 Jason Williams .60
87 Stromile Swift .60
88 Richard Hamilton .60
89 Courtney Alexander .60
90 Chris Whitney .30
91 *Kenny Satterfield* 5.00
92 *Jeff Trepagnier* 6.00
93 *Michael Wright* 5.00
94 *Terence Morris* 5.00
95 *Omar Cook* 5.00
96 *Gilbert Arenas* 8.00
97 *Joseph Forte* 10.00
98 *Jamaal Tinsley* 25.00
99 *Samuel Dalembert* 5.00
100 *Gerald Wallace* 10.00
101 *Brendan Haywood* 15.00
102 *Richard Jefferson* 20.00
103 *Michael Bradley* 12.00
104 *Loren Woods* 15.00
105 *Jeryl Sasser* 10.00
106 *Jason Collins* 8.00
107 *Kirk Haston* 12.00
108 *Steven Hunter* 8.00
109 *Troy Murphy* 15.00
110 *Vladimir Radmanovic* 15.00
111 *Rodney White* 15.00
112 *Kedrick Brown* 15.00
113 *Joe Johnson* 30.00
114 *Eddie Griffin* 40.00
115 *Shane Battier* 60.00
116 *Eddy Curry* 30.00
117 *Jason Richardson* 75.00
118 *DeSagana Diop* 15.00
119 *Tyson Chandler* 30.00
120 *Kwame Brown* 40.00
121 *Michael Jordan* .30

2001-02 Upper Deck Hardcourt Exclusives

MT
Veterans: 30x-60x
Rookies: 2x
Production 25 Sets
Rookies have three versions
1 Jason Terry .60
2 DerMarr Johnson .60
3 Toni Kukoc .60
4 Antoine Walker .75
5 Paul Pierce 1.00
6 Kenny Anderson .60
7 Jamal Mashburn .60
8 Baron Davis 1.00
9 David Wesley .30
10 Ron Artest .30
11 Jamal Crawford .60
12 Ron Mercer .60
13 Andre Miller .75
14 Lamond Murray .30
15 Matt Harpring .30
16 Michael Finley .75
17 Dirk Nowitzki 1.25
18 Steve Nash .60
19 Antonio McDyess .75
20 Nick Van Exel .75
21 James Posey .60
22 Jerry Stackhouse .75
23 Chucky Atkins .30
24 Mateen Cleaves .60
25 Antawn Jamison 1.25
26 Larry Hughes .60
27 Marc Jackson .60
28 Steve Francis 2.00
29 Maurice Taylor .30
30 Cuttino Mobley .60
31 Reggie Miller .75
32 Jalen Rose .60
33 Jermaine O'Neal .75
34 Darius Miles 4.00
35 Lamar Odom 1.25
36 Elton Brand 1.25
37 Kobe Bryant 5.00
38 Shaquille O'Neal 2.50
39 Derek Fisher .60
40 Robert Horry .60
41 Alonzo Mourning .60
42 Eddie Jones .75
43 Brian Grant .60
44 Anthony Mason .60
45 Ray Allen 1.00
46 Glenn Robinson .75
47 Tim Thomas .60
48 Kevin Garnett 3.00
49 Wally Szczerbiak .60
50 Terrell Brandon .60
51 Anthony Peeler .30
52 Jason Kidd 1.50
53 Kenyon Martin .60
54 Stephen Jackson .30
55 Latrell Sprewell 1.25
56 Allan Houston .60
57 Glen Rice .60
58 Tracy McGrady 2.50
59 Darrell Armstrong .60
60 Mike Miller 1.50
61 Allen Iverson 3.00
62 Dikembe Mutombo .60
63 Aaron McKie .60
64 Stephon Marbury 1.00
65 Shawn Marion 1.25
66 Tom Gugliotta .30
67 Rasheed Wallace .75
68 Scottie Pippen 1.25
69 Damon Stoudamire .30
70 Chris Webber 2.00
71 Mike Bibby .60
72 Peja Stojakovic .75
73 Tim Duncan 2.00
74 David Robinson .75
75 Derek Anderson .60
76 Gary Payton 1.00
77 Rashard Lewis .60
78 Desmond Mason .60
79 Vince Carter 5.00
80 Morris Peterson .75
81 Antonio Davis .60
82 Karl Malone 1.25
83 John Stockton 1.00
84 Donyell Marshall .30
85 Bryant Reeves .30
86 Jason Williams .60
87 Stromile Swift .60
88 Richard Hamilton .60
89 Courtney Alexander .60
90 Chris Whitney .30
91 *Kenny Satterfield* 5.00
92 *Jeff Trepagnier* 6.00
93 *Michael Wright* 5.00
94 *Terence Morris* 5.00
95 *Omar Cook* 5.00
96 *Gilbert Arenas* 8.00
97 *Joseph Forte* 10.00
98 *Jamaal Tinsley* 25.00
99 *Samuel Dalembert* 5.00
100 *Gerald Wallace* 10.00
101 *Brendan Haywood* 15.00
102 *Richard Jefferson* 20.00
103 *Michael Bradley* 12.00
104 *Loren Woods* 15.00
105 *Jeryl Sasser* 10.00
106 *Jason Collins* 8.00
107 *Kirk Haston* 12.00
108 *Steven Hunter* 8.00
109 *Troy Murphy* 15.00
110 *Vladimir Radmanovic* 10.00
111 *Rodney White* 15.00
112 *Kedrick Brown* 15.00
113 *Joe Johnson* 30.00
114 *Eddie Griffin* 40.00
115 *Shane Battier* 60.00
116 *Eddy Curry* 30.00
117 *Jason Richardson* 75.00
118 *DeSagana Diop* 15.00
119 *Tyson Chandler* 30.00
120 *Kwame Brown* 40.00
121 *Michael Jordan* .30

2001-02 Upper Deck Hardcourt Fantastic Floor

MT
Common Player: 30.00
Production 100 Sets
RA/GR Ray Allen, Glenn Robinson 40.00
KB/SF Kobe Bryant, Steve Francis 60.00
KB/KG Kobe Bryant, Kevin Garnett 75.00
KB/AI Kobe Bryant, Allen Iverson 100.00
KB/RL Kobe Bryant, Rashard Lewis 50.00
KB/DM Kobe Bryant, Darius Miles 75.00
MFDNSN Michael Finley, Dirk Nowitzki, Steve Nash 50.00
KGTBWS Kevin Garnett, Terrell Brandon, Wally Szczerbiak 75.00
AH/LS Allan Houston, Latrell Sprewell 30.00
EJ/TH Eddie Jones, Tim Hardaway 30.00
MJKBKG Michael Jordan, Kobe Bryant, Kevin Garnett 600.00
KM/JS Karl Malone, John Stockton 50.00
JM/BD Jamal Mashburn, Baron Davis 30.00
MC/NV Antonio McDyess, Nick Van Exel 30.00
TM/MM Tracy McGrady, Mike Miller 40.00
RMJOJB Reggie Miller, Jermaine O'Neal, Jonathan Bender 40.00
GPRLDM Gary Payton, Rashard Lewis, Desmond Mason 40.00
PP/AW Paul Pierce, Antoine Walker 30.00
JS/MC Jerry Stackhouse, Mateen Cleaves 30.00
RWSPDS Rasheed Wallace, Scottie Pippen, Damon Stoudamire 40.00
CW/PS Chris Webber, Peja Stojakovic 50.00

2001-02 Upper Deck Hardcourt Game Floor

MT
Common Player: 10.00
Inserted 1:15
RA Ray Allen 15.00
KB Kobe Bryant 30.00
BD Baron Davis 12.00
MF Michael Finley 12.00
SF Steve Francis 20.00
KG Kevin Garnett 25.00
AI Allen Iverson 25.00
SJ Stephen Jackson 10.00
EJ Eddie Jones 10.00
KM Karl Malone 15.00
MA Shawn Marion 15.00
KE Kenyon Martin 10.00
JM Jamal Mashburn 10.00
DM Desmond Mason 10.00
MC Antonio McDyess 12.00
TM Tracy McGrady 20.00
DA Darius Miles 20.00
MM Mike Miller 15.00
RM Reggie Miller 15.00
MP Morris Peterson 12.00
PP Paul Pierce 12.00
DR David Robinson 15.00
LS Latrell Sprewell 15.00
JS Jerry Stackhouse 10.00
PS Peja Stojakovic 15.00
JT Jason Terry 10.00
CW Chris Webber 15.00

2001-02 Upper Deck Hardcourt Game Floor Autographs

MT
Common Player:
Inserted 1:150
RA-A Ray Allen 50.00
KB-A Kobe Bryant 250.00
KG-A Kevin Garnett 100.00
KE-A Kenyon Martin 50.00
JM-A Jamal Mashburn 40.00
DM-A Desmond Mason 40.00
MC-A Antonio McDyess 40.00
DA-A Darius Miles 75.00
MM-A Mike Miller 50.00
MP-A Morris Peterson 40.00
PP-A Paul Pierce 75.00
JS-A Jerry Stackhouse 40.00

2001-02 Upper Deck Hardcourt Game Floor/Game Film

MT
Common Player: 12.00
Inserted 1:15
RA-F Ray Allen 20.00
KB-F Kobe Bryant 50.00
BD-F Baron Davis 15.00
MF-F Michael Finley 15.00
SF-F Steve Francis 25.00
KG-F Kevin Garnett 40.00
AI-F Allen Iverson 40.00
SJ-F Stephen Jackson 12.00
EJ-F Eddie Jones 15.00
KM-F Karl Malone 20.00
MA-F Shawn Marion 20.00
KE-F Kenyon Martin 12.00
JM-F Jamal Mashburn 12.00
DM-F Desmond Mason 12.00
MC-F Antonio McDyess 15.00
TM-F Tracy McGrady 25.00
DA-F Darius Miles 30.00
MM-F Mike Miller 20.00
RM-F Reggie Miller 20.00
MP-F Morris Peterson 15.00
PP-F Paul Pierce 15.00
DR-F David Robinson 20.00
LS-F Latrell Sprewell 20.00
JS-F Jerry Stackhouse 15.00
PS-F Peja Stojakovic 20.00
JT-F Jason Terry 12.00
CW-F Chris Webber 25.00

2001-02 UD Honor Roll

MT
Complete Set (90): 175.00
Common Player: .25
Minor Stars: .40
Common Rookie (91-120): 3.00
91-120 Production 2,499 Sets
121-130 Production 1,000 Sets
Pack (5): 3.00
Box (24): 60.00
1 Shareef Abdur-Rahim .60
2 Jason Terry .50
3 Dion Glover .25
4 Paul Pierce .75
5 Antoine Walker .60
6 Kenny Anderson .50
7 Baron Davis .75
8 Jamal Mashburn .50
9 David Wesley .25
10 Ron Mercer .50
11 Brad Miller .25
12 Andre Miller .50
13 Lamond Murray .25
14 Chris Mihm .25
15 Michael Finley .50
16 Dirk Nowitzki 1.00
17 Steve Nash .50
18 Juwan Howard .50
19 Nick Van Exel .60
20 Raef LaFrentz .50
21 Antonio McDyess .60
22 James Posey .25
23 Jerry Stackhouse .60
24 Clifford Robinson .25
25 Ben Wallace .50
26 Antawn Jamison 1.00
27 Larry Hughes .50
28 Steve Francis 1.50
29 Cuttino Mobley .50
30 Glen Rice .50
31 Reggie Miller .75
32 Jalen Rose .50
33 Jermaine O'Neal .75
34 Darius Miles 3.00
35 Elton Brand 1.00
36 Lamar Odom 1.00
37 Corey Maggette .50
38 Kobe Bryant 4.00
39 Shaquille O'Neal 2.00
40 Rick Fox .50
41 Lindsey Hunter .25
42 Stromile Swift .50
43 Jason Williams .50
44 Alonzo Mourning .50
45 Eddie Jones .60
46 Anthony Carter .25
47 Brian Grant .50
48 Ray Allen .75
49 Glenn Robinson .60
50 Sam Cassell .50
51 Kevin Garnett 2.50
52 Terrell Brandon .50
53 Wally Szczerbiak .50
54 Joe Smith .25
55 Jason Kidd 1.25
56 Kenyon Martin .50
57 Allan Houston .50
58 Latrell Sprewell 1.00
59 Marcus Camby .50
60 Mark Jackson .25
61 Tracy McGrady 2.00
62 Grant Hill 1.25
63 Mike Miller 1.50
64 Allen Iverson 2.50
65 Dikembe Mutombo .50
66 Aaron McKie .50
67 Stephon Marbury .75
68 Shawn Marion 1.00
69 Anfernee Hardaway .50
70 Tom Gugliotta .25
71 Rasheed Wallace .60
72 Damon Stoudamire .25
73 Derek Anderson .50
74 Chris Webber 1.50
75 Mike Bibby .50
76 Peja Stojakovic .60
77 Tim Duncan 1.50
78 David Robinson .60
79 Steve Smith .50
80 Gary Payton .75
81 Rashard Lewis .50
82 Desmond Mason .25
83 Vince Carter 4.00
84 Morris Peterson .60
85 Antonio Davis .50
86 Karl Malone 1.00
87 John Stockton .75
88 Donyell Marshall .25
89 Richard Hamilton .50
90 Michael Jordan 10.00
91 *Andrei Kirilenko* 10.00
92 *Gilbert Arenas* 8.00
93 *Earl Watson* 3.00
94 *Terence Morris* 3.00
95 *Kedrick Brown* 5.00
96 *Zach Randolph* 8.00
97 *Joe Johnson* 10.00
98 *Brandon Armstrong* 5.00
99 *DeSagana Diop* 5.00
100 *Joseph Forte* 8.00
101 *Brendan Haywood* 6.00
102 *Samuel Dalembert* 3.00
103 *Jason Collins* 4.00
104 *Michael Bradley* 4.00
105 *Gerald Wallace* 8.00
106 *Tierre Brown* 3.00
107 *Troy Murphy* 6.00
108 *Alton Ford* 3.00
109 *Vladimir Radmanovic* 4.00
110 *Ruben Boumtje-Boumtje* 3.00
111 *Bobby Simmons* 3.00
112 *Oscar Torres* 3.00
113 *Jeryl Sasser* 4.00
114 *Loren Woods* 6.00
115 *Shane Battier* 20.00
116 *Jamison Brewer* 3.00
117 *Richard Jefferson* 10.00
118 *Pau Gasol* 15.00
119 *Damone Brown* 3.00
120 *Rodney White* 6.00
121JSY *Kwame Brown*, Kevin Garnett 40.00
122JSY *Tyson Chandler*, Darius Miles 40.00
123JSY *Eddy Curry*, Karl Malone 30.00
124JSY *Jason Richardson*, Kobe Bryant 100.00
125JSY *Tony Parker*, Jason Kidd 50.00
126JSY *Eddie Griffin*, Anfernee Hardaway 30.00
127JSY *Kirk Haston*, Jamal Mashburn 12.00
128JSY *Jamaal Tinsley*, Andre Miller 30.00
129JSY *Trenton Hassell*, Marcus Fizer 12.00
130JSY *Steven Hunter*, Tracy McGrady 25.00

2001-02 UD Honor Roll All-NBA Authentics Jersey

MT
Common Player: 12.00
Inserted 1:88
SA Shareef Abdur-Rahim 12.00
RA Ray Allen 15.00
KB Kobe Bryant 100.00
BD Baron Davis 15.00
MF Marcus Fizer 12.00
KG Kevin Garnett 50.00
AI Allen Iverson 50.00
JK Jason Kidd 25.00
TK Toni Kukoc 12.00
KM Karl Malone 20.00
SM Stephon Marbury 15.00
TM Tracy McGrady 30.00
RM Ron Mercer 12.00
DM Darius Miles 30.00
AM Andre Miller 12.00
MM Mike Miller 20.00
MT Dikembe Mutombo 12.00
LO Lamar Odom 20.00
JS John Stockton 20.00

2001-02 UD Honor Roll All-NBA Authentic Jersey Combos

MT
Common Player: 20.00
Inserted 1:240
KB/KG Kobe Bryant, Kevin Garnett 150.00
KB/AI Kobe Bryant, Allen Iverson 150.00
BD/AM Baron Davis, Andre Miller 25.00
JK/KM Jason Kidd, Kenyon Martin 40.00
KM/JS Karl Malone, John Stockton 50.00
EB/KG Elton Brand, Kevin Garnett 50.00
GH/MM Grant Hill, Mike Miller 30.00
SM/SM Stephon Marbury, Shawn Marion 25.00
SA/JT Shareef Abdur-Rahim, Jason Terry 20.00

2001-02 UD Honor Roll Fab Five All-Stars

MT
Complete Set (10):
Common Player: 2.50
Inserted 1:24
F5-AS1 Tim Duncan 4.00
F5-AS2 Chris Webber 4.00
F5-AS3 Kevin Garnett 6.00
F5-AS4 Kobe Bryant 10.00
F5-AS5 Shaquille O'Neal 5.00
F5-AS6 Vince Carter 10.00
F5-AS7 Allen Iverson 6.00
F5-AS8 Tracy McGrady 5.00
F5-AS9 Latrell Sprewell 2.50
F5-AS10 Michael Jordan 12.00

2001-02 UD Honor Roll Fab Floor Autographs

MT
Common Player: 40.00
Inserted 1:480
KB-A Kobe Bryant 350.00
KG-A Kevin Garnett 150.00
MJ-A Michael Jordan 1200.
JK-A Jason Kidd 75.00
DM-A Darius Miles 75.00
AM-A Andre Miller 40.00
WS-A Wally Szczerbiak 40.00
AW-A Antoine Walker 50.00

2001-02 UD Honor Roll Fab Floor Duos

MT
Common Player: 15.00
Inserted 1:96
KB/MJ-F Kobe Bryant, Michael Jordan 150.00
KB/KG-F Kobe Bryant, Kevin Garnett 50.00
AM/SM-F Antonio McDyess, Shawn Marion 15.00
JT/DJ-F Jason Terry, DerMarr Johnson 15.00
KG/RL-F Kevin Garnett, Rashard Lewis 25.00
KG/TB-F Kevin Garnett, Terrell Brandon 25.00
KG/DM-F Kevin Garnett, Darius Miles 30.00
SM/SM-F Stephon Marbury, Shawn Marion 15.00
MF/DN-F Michael Finley, Dirk Nowitzki 20.00
AW/PP-F Antoine Walker, Paul Pierce 20.00
RW/DA-F Rasheed Wallace, Derek Anderson 15.00
RA/GR-F Ray Allen, Glenn Robinson 15.00
JS/RW-F Jerry Stackhouse, Rasheed Wallace 15.00
LS/AH-F Latrell Sprewell, Allan Houston 15.00
DR/DM-F David Robinson, Dikembe Mutombo 15.00
BD/JM-F Baron Davis, Jamal Mashburn 15.00
GP/DM-F Gary Payton, Desmond Mason 15.00

2001-02 UD Honor Roll Fab Floor Triples

MT
Common Player:
Inserted 1:240
KBKGMJ Kobe Bryant, Kevin Garnett, Michael Jordan 250.00
KBKGKM Kobe Bryant, Kevin Garnett, Kenyon Martin 60.00
KGWSTB Kevin Garnett, Wally Szczerbiak, Terrell Brandon 40.00
GRRATT Glenn Robinson, Ray Allen, Tim Thomas 25.00
RMJOJB Reggie Miller, Jermaine O'Neal, Jonathan Bender 25.00

2001-02 UD Honor Roll Fab Five Rookies

MT
Complete Set (10):
Common Player: 5.00
Inserted 1:24
F5-R1 Tony Parker 8.00
F5-R2 Jamaal Tinsley 8.00
F5-R3 Pau Gasol 10.00
F5-R4 Jason Richardson 12.00
F5-R5 Kwame Brown 8.00
F5-R6 Shane Battier 10.00
F5-R7 Eddie Griffin 8.00
F5-R8 Eddy Curry 6.00
F5-R9 Andrei Kirilenko 5.00
F5-R10 Joe Johnson 5.00

2001-02 UD Honor Roll Fab Five Scorers

MT
Complete Set (10):
Common Player: 1.50
Inserted 1:24
F5-S1 Michael Jordan 12.00
F5-S2 Kobe Bryant 10.00
F5-S3 Vince Carter 10.00
F5-S4 Shaquille O'Neal 6.00
F5-S5 Dirk Nowitzki 2.50
F5-S6 Tim Duncan 4.00
F5-S7 Kevin Garnett 6.00
F5-S8 Paul Pierce 2.00
F5-S9 Shareef Abdur-Rahim 1.50
F5-S10 Jerry Stackhouse 1.50

2001-02 Upper Deck Inspirations

		MT
	Complete Set (182):	
	Common Player:	.20
	Minor star	.40
	Common rookie	5.00
	Pack (5):	4.99
	Wax Box (24):	100.00
	Rookie Inspirations #'d to 2249	
	Signed Rookie Inspirations #'d to 275	
	Dual signed Rookie Inspirations to 1149	
	Jersey Rookie Inspirations #'d to 1500	
	Dual Jersey Rookie to 1100 and 275	
1	Shareef Abdur-Rahim	.20
2	Jason Terry	.20
3	Dion Glover	.20
4	Antoine Walker	.50
5	Paul Pierce	.50
6	Larry Bird	.50
7	Baron Davis	.20
8	Jamal Mashburn	.20
9	David Wesley	.20
10	Elden Campbell	.20
11	Jalen Rose	.20
12	Marcus Fizer	.20
13	Andre Miller	.20
14	Lamond Murray	.20
15	Chris Mihm	.20
16	Dirk Nowitzki	.50
17	Steve Nash	.50
18	Michael Finley	.40
19	Nick Van Exel	.20
20	Raef LaFrentz	.20
21	Antonio McDyess	.20
22	Juwan Howard	.20
23	Tim Hardaway	.20
24	James Posey	.20
25	Jerry Stackhouse	.20
26	Ben Wallace	.20
27	Isiah Thomas	.50
28	Antawn Jamison	.20
29	Larry Hughes	.20
30	Steve Francis	.50
31	Moses Malone	.50
32	Reggie Miller	.50
33	Jermaine O'Neal	.20
34	Elton Brand	.50
35	Darius Miles	.50
36	Lamar Odom	.20
37	Quentin Richardson	.20
38	Kobe Bryant	2.00
39	Shaquille O'Neal	2.00
40	Derek Fisher	.20
41	Devean George	.20
42	Stromile Swift	.20
43	Jason Williams	.20
44	Alonzo Mourning	.50
45	Eddie Jones	.20
46	Anthony Carter	.20
47	Ray Allen	.50
48	Sam Cassell	.20
49	Glenn Robinson	.20
50	Tim Thomas	.20
51	Oscar Robertson	.50
52	Kevin Garnett	.50
53	Wally Szczerbiak	.50
54	Terrell Brandon	.20
55	Chauncey Billups	.20
56	Jason Kidd	1.00
57	Kenyon Martin	.20
58	Latrell Sprewell	.20
59	Allan Houston	.20
60	Marcus Camby	.20
61	Kurt Thomas	.20
62	Grant Hill	.75
63	Mike Miller	.50
64	Tracy McGrady	1.00
65	Allen Iverson	2.00
66	Julius Erving	1.00
67	Bobby Jones	.20
68	Stephon Marbury	.20
69	Shawn Marion	.20
70	Anfernee Hardaway	.20
71	Rasheed Wallace	.20
72	Bill Walton	1.00
73	Chris Webber	.75
74	Peja Stojakovic	.20
75	Mike Bibby	.50
76	Tim Duncan	1.00
77	David Robinson	.50
78	George Gervin	.50
79	Gary Payton	.50
80	Rashard Lewis	.20
81	Desmond Mason	.20
82	Vince Carter	2.00
83	Morris Peterson	.20
84	Antonio Davis	.20
85	Hakeem Olajuwon	.20
86	Karl Malone	.40
87	John Stockton	.40
88	Donyell Marshall	.20
89	Richard Hamilton	.40
90	Michael Jordan	6.00
91	Zeljko Rebraca, Shaquille O'Neal/2249	5.00
92	Oscar Robertson, Oscar Torres/2249	3.00
93	Jamison Brewer, Reggie Miller/2249	3.00
94	Peja Stojakovic, Predrag Drobnjak/2249	3.00
95	Mengke Bateer, Wang Zhi-Zhi/2249	4.00
96	Jerry West, Willie Solomon/2249	3.00
97	Tim Duncan, Malik Allen/2249	4.00
98	Walt Frazier, Damone Brown/2249	3.00
99	Shawn Marion, Alton Ford/2249	3.00
100	Toni Kukoc, Antonis Fotsis/2249	3.00
101	Bill Walton, Zach Randolph/2249	3.00
102	Stephon Marbury, Joseph Crispin/2249	3.00
103	Wes Unseld, Bobby Simmons/2249	2.00
104	Jason Kidd, Jamaal Tinsley/275	40.00
105	Kevin Garnett, Pau Gasol/275	40.00
106	Kobe Bryant, Shane Battier/275	60.00
107	Vince Carter, Jeff Trepagnier/275	15.00
108	Julius Erving, Kwame Brown/275	20.00
109	Tim Duncan, Eddy Curry/275	25.00
110	Lamar Odom, Eddie Griffin/1149	25.00
111	Courtney Alexander, Earl Watson/1149	10.00
112	Morris Peterson, Gilbert Arenas/1149	20.00
113	Kenyon Martin, Brian Scalabrine/1149	10.00
114	Tyson Chandler, Marcus Fizer/1149	10.00
115	Corey Maggette, Ruben Boumtje-Boumtje/1149	10.00
116	Jarron Collins, Mark Madsen/1149	10.00
117	Vince Carter, Joseph Forte/1500	12.00
118	Antawn Jamison, Troy Murphy/525	12.00
119	Kenyon Martin, Brandon Armstrong/1500	5.00
120	Steve Francis, Terence Morris/1500	5.00
121	Grant Hill, Steven Hunter/1500	10.00
122	Alonzo Mourning, Vladimir Radmanovic/1500	10.00
123	Brendan Haywood, Shaquille O'Neal/1500	15.00
124	Samuel Dalembert, Moses Malone/1500	5.00
125	Wally Szczerbiak, Primoz Brezec/1100	5.00
126	Peja Stojakovic, Michael Bradley/1100	5.00
127	Anfernee Hardaway, Joe Johnson/1100	5.00
128	Loren Woods, Theo Ratliff/1100	5.00
129	Chris Webber, Gerald Wallace/1100	15.00
130	Antoine Walker, Kedrick Brown/1100	5.00
131	Baron Davis, Jamison Brewer/1100	5.00
132	Dirk Nowitzki, Andrei Kirilenko/1100	15.00
133	Joe Smith, Alton Ford/1100	5.00
134	John Stockton, Joseph Crispin/1100	5.00
135	Karl Malone, Rodney White/275	25.00
136	Tracy McGrady, Jeryl Sasser/275	40.00
137	Elton Brand, Jason Collins/275	50.00
138	Kobe Bryant, Richard Jefferson/275	125.00
139	Allen Iverson, Tony Parker/275	75.00
140	Michael Jordan, Jason Richardson/275	300.00
141	Rookie Trade card	5.00
142	Rookie Trade card	5.00
143	Rookie Trade card	5.00
144	Rookie Trade card	5.00
145	Rookie Trade card	5.00
146	Rookie Trade card	5.00
147	Rookie Trade card	5.00
148	Rookie Trade card	8.00
149	Rookie Trade card	5.00
150	Rookie Trade card	5.00
151	Rookie Trade card	5.00
152	Rookie Trade card	5.00
153	Rookie Trade card	5.00
154	Rookie Trade card	10.00
155	Rookie Trade card	5.00
156	Rookie Trade card	5.00
157	Rookie Trade card	5.00
158	Rookie Trade card	5.00
159	Rookie Trade card	10.00
160	Rookie Trade card	10.00
161	Rookie Trade card	10.00
162	Rookie Trade card	5.00
163	Rookie Trade card	20.00
164	Rookie Trade card	5.00
165	Rookie Trade card	5.00
166	Rookie Trade card	40.00
167	Rookie Trade card	10.00
168	Rookie Trade card	10.00
169	Rookie Trade card	10.00
170	Rookie Trade card	10.00
171	Rookie Trade card	10.00
172	Rookie Trade card	30.00
173	Rookie Trade card	40.00
174	Rookie Trade card	10.00
175	Rookie Trade card	30.00
176	Rookie Trade card	20.00
177	Rookie Trade card	50.00
178	Rookie Trade card	40.00
179	Rookie Trade card	75.00
180	Rookie Trade card	125.00
181	Rookie Trade card	200.00
182	Rookie Trade card	200.00

2001-02 Upper Deck Inspirations - Hardwood Imagery

		MT
	Common Player:	8.00
	Inserted 1:47	
SA	Shareef Abdur-Rahim	8.00
RA	Ray Allen	15.00
KB	Kobe Bryant	50.00
MF	Michael Finley	15.00
SF	Steve Francis	15.00
KG	Kevin Garnett	30.00
AI	Allen Iverson	30.00
MJ	Michael Jordan	125.00
JK	Jason Kidd	15.00
SM	Stephon Marbury	8.00
SH	Shawn Marion	8.00
KM	Kenyon Martin	25.00
TM	Tracy McGrady	40.00
DM	Darius Miles	25.00
AM	Andre Miller	15.00
MM	Mike Miller	15.00
DN	Dirk Nowitzki	30.00
MP	Morris Peterson	8.00
PP	Paul Pierce	40.00
JS	Jerry Stackhouse	10.00
CW	Chris Webber	15.00

2001-02 Upper Deck Inspirations - Hardwood Imagery Combo

		MT
	Common Player:	10.00
	Inserted 1:47	
SA/DJ	Shareef Abdur-Rahim, DerMarr Johnson	10.00
RA/GR	Ray Allen, Glenn Robinson	10.00
KB/KG	Kobe Bryant, Kevin Garnett	20.00
KB/JK	Kobe Bryant, Jason Kidd	30.00
KB/JS	Kobe Bryant, Jerry Stackhouse	15.00
MF/DN	Michael Finley, Dirk Nowitzki	10.00
AI/SF	Steve Francis, Allen Iverson	20.00
KG/CW	Kevin Garnett, Chris Webber	15.00
EJ/BG	Eddie Jones, Brian Grant	10.00
MJ/KB	Michael Jordan, Kobe Bryant	150.00
JK/KM	Jason Kidd, Kenyon Martin	20.00
KM/JS	Karl Malone, John Stockton	10.00
SM/SM	Stephon Marbury, Shawn Marion	10.00
BD/JM	Jamal Mashburn, Baron Davis	10.00
TM/DM	Tracy McGrady, Darius Miles	25.00
RM/JO	Reggie Miller, Jermaine O'Neal	10.00
LO/QR	Lamar Odom, Quentin Richardson	10.00
RW/SP	Scottie Pippen, Rasheed Wallace	10.00
AH/LS	Latrell Sprewell, Allan Houston	10.00
KG/WS	Wally Szczerbiak, Kevin Garnett	20.00
PP/AW	Antoine Walker, Paul Pierce	15.00

2001-02 Upper Deck Inspirations Like Mike Autograph Cards

		MT
	Complete Set (1):	
	Numbered to 100	
LBW	Lil' Bow Wow	125.00

2001-02 UD Insp. Like Mike Dual Jersey Rookie Inspirations

		MT
	Complete Set (4):	200.00
	Common Player:	40.00
	Inserted 1:576	
LBW-CW	Lil' Bow Wow, Chris Webber	40.00
LBW-AI	Lil' Bow Wow, Allen Houston	100.00
LBW-GP	Lil' Bow Wow, Gary Payton	40.00
LBW-JK	Lil' Bow Wow, Jason Kidd	75.00

2001-02 Upper Deck MVP

		MT
	Complete Set (220):	
	Common Player:	.15
	Minor Stars:	.30
	Pack (8):	2.00
	Box (24):	40.00
1	Jason Terry	.30
2	Alan Henderson	.15
3	Toni Kukoc	.30
4	Hanno Mottola	.15
5	Theo Ratliff	.30
6	DerMarr Johnson	.30
7	Paul Pierce	.50
8	Antoine Walker	.50
9	Bryant Stith	.15
10	Kenny Anderson	.30
11	Vitaly Potapenko	.15
12	Eric Williams	.15
13	Jamal Mashburn	.30
14	David Wesley	.15
15	Baron Davis	.50
16	Elden Campbell	.15
17	P.J. Brown	.15
18	Jamaal Magloire	.30
19	Eddie Robinson	.30
20	Elton Brand	.60
21	Ron Mercer	.30
22	Fred Hoiberg	.15
23	Jamal Crawford	.30
24	Ron Artest	.30
25	Marcus Fizer	.30
26	Andre Miller	.40
27	Lamond Murray	.15
28	Jim Jackson	.15
29	Chris Mihm	.15
30	Matt Harpring	.15
31	Chris Gatling	.15
32	Michael Finley	.40
33	Steve Nash	.30
34	Dirk Nowitzki	.60
35	Juwan Howard	.30
36	Howard Eisley	.15
37	Eduardo Najera	.15
38	Wang Zhizhi	.75
39	Antonio McDyess	.40
40	Nick Van Exel	.30
41	Raef LaFrentz	.30
42	James Posey	.30
43	George McCloud	.15
44	Voshon Lenard	.15
45	Jerry Stackhouse	.50
46	Chucky Atkins	.15
47	Corliss Williamson	.15
48	Joe Smith	.30
49	Mateen Cleaves	.30
50	Ben Wallace	.15
51	Antawn Jamison	.60
52	Marc Jackson	.15
53	Larry Hughes	.30
54	Bob Sura	.15
55	Chris Porter	.15
56	Vonteego Cummings	.15
57	Steve Francis	1.00
58	Hakeem Olajuwon	.50
59	Cuttino Mobley	.30
60	Maurice Taylor	.15
61	Shandon Anderson	.15
62	Walt Williams	.15
63	Moochie Norris	.15
64	Reggie Miller	.50
65	Jalen Rose	.40
66	Jermaine O'Neal	.50
67	Austin Croshere	.15
68	Travis Best	.15
69	Al Harrington	.30
70	Jonathan Bender	.30
71	Darius Miles	2.00
72	Corey Maggette	.30
73	Lamar Odom	.60
74	Quentin Richardson	.30
75	Keyon Dooling	.30
76	Jeff McInnis	.15
77	Eric Piatkowski	.15
78	Kobe Bryant	2.50
79	Shaquille O'Neal	1.25
80	Rick Fox	.15
81	Derek Fisher	.30
82	Robert Horry	.15
83	Ron Harper	.30
84	Brian Shaw	.15
85	Alonzo Mourning	.30
86	Eddie Jones	.40
87	Tim Hardaway	.30
88	Anthony Mason	.30
89	Brian Grant	.30
90	Anthony Carter	.15
91	Bruce Bowen	.15
92	Ray Allen	.50
93	Glenn Robinson	.50
94	Sam Cassell	.30
95	Tim Thomas	.30
96	Ervin Johnson	.15
97	Joel Przybilla	.30
98	Kevin Garnett	1.50
99	Terrell Brandon	.30
100	Wally Szczerbiak	.30
101	Chauncey Billups	.15
102	LaPhonso Ellis	.15
103	Anthony Peeler	.15
104	Stephon Marbury	.50
105	Keith Van Horn	.50
106	Kenyon Martin	.30
107	Kendall Gill	.15
108	Lucious Harris	.15
109	Stephen Jackson	.15
110	Latrell Sprewell	.60
111	Allan Houston	.30
112	Marcus Camby	.30
113	Mark Jackson	.30
114	Glen Rice	.30
115	Kurt Thomas	.15
116	Tracy McGrady	1.25
117	Darrell Armstrong	.15
118	Mike Miller	1.00
119	Grant Hill	.75
120	Pat Garrity	.15
121	John Amaechi	.15
122	Allen Iverson	1.50
123	Dikembe Mutombo	.30
124	Aaron McKie	.30
125	Tyrone Hill	.15
126	George Lynch	.15
127	Eric Snow	.15
128	Matt Geiger	.15
129	Jason Kidd	.75
130	Shawn Marion	60.00
131	Tony Delk	.15
132	Rodney Rogers	.15
133	Tom Gugliotta	.15
134	Anfernee Hardaway	.30
135	Rasheed Wallace	.50
136	Damon Stoudamire	.15
137	Arvydas Sabonis	.30
138	Scottie Pippen	.60
139	Steve Smith	.30
140	Stacey Augmon	.15
141	Bonzi Wells	.30
142	Jason Williams	.30
143	Chris Webber	1.00
144	Peja Stojakovic	50.00
145	Doug Christie	.15
146	Scot Pollard	.15
147	Hidayet Turkoglu	.30
148	Vlade Divac	.30
149	Tim Duncan	1.00
150	David Robinson	.50
151	Antonio Daniels	.15
152	Sean Elliott	.30
153	Derek Anderson	.30
154	Avery Johnson	.15
155	Malik Rose	.15
156	Gary Payton	.50
157	Rashard Lewis	.30
158	Patrick Ewing	.30
159	Vin Baker	.30
160	Emanuel Davis	.15
161	Desmond Mason	.30
162	Vince Carter	2.50
163	Morris Peterson	.40
164	Antonio Davis	.15
165	Keon Clark	.15
166	Chris Childs	.15
167	Charles Oakley	.15
168	Alvin Williams	.15
169	Dell Curry	.15
170	Karl Malone	.60
171	John Stockton	.50
172	Donyell Marshall	.15
173	John Starks	.15
174	Bryon Russell	.15
175	David Benoit	.15
176	Jacque Vaughn	.15
177	Shareef Abdur-Rahim	.40
178	Mike Bibby	.30
179	Michael Dickerson	.30
180	Bryant Reeves	.15
181	Grant Long	.15
182	Stromile Swift	.30
183	Richard Hamilton	.30
184	Tyrone Nesby	.15
185	Jahidi White	.15
186	Chris Whitney	.15
187	Courtney Alexander	.40
188	Christian Laettner	.30
189	Kobe Bryant	1.00
190	Kevin Garnett	.50
191	*Vladimir Radmanovic*	1.00
192	*Alvin Jones*	1.00
193	*Tyson Chandler*	4.00
194	*Omar Cook*	1.00
195	*Kedrick Brown*	1.50
196	*DeSagana Diop*	1.50
197	*Eddie Griffin*	4.00
198	*Zach Randolph*	2.00
199	*Eddy Curry*	4.00
200	*Jeryl Sasser*	1.25
201	*Gerald Wallace*	2.00
202	*Jamaal Tinsley*	5.00
203	*Kirk Haston*	1.25
204	*Terence Morris*	.75
205	*Jarron Collins*	.75
206	*Joseph Forte*	2.00
207	*Kenny Satterfield*	1.25
208	*Michael Wright*	.75
209	*Jason Richardson*	6.00
210	*Michael Bradley*	1.00
211	*Gilbert Arenas*	1.50
212	*Jeff Trepagnier*	1.00
213	*Samuel Dalembert*	1.00
214	*Troy Murphy*	1.50
215	*Rodney White*	1.50
216	*Joe Johnson*	3.00
217	*Richard Jefferson*	2.00
218	*Kwame Brown*	4.00
219	*Jason Collins*	1.00
220	*Steven Hunter*	1.00

2001-02 Upper Deck MVP Airborne

		MT
	Complete Set (7):	25.00
	Common Player:	1.00
	Inserted 1:24	
A1	Kobe Bryant	10.00
A2	Vince Carter	10.00
A3	Baron Davis	2.00
A4	Kevin Garnett	1.00
A5	Tracy McGrady	5.00
A6	Shaquille O'Neal	5.00
A7	Desmond Mason	1.00

2001-02 Upper Deck MVP Authentic Kobe

		MT
	Complete Set:	
	Common Player:	
KBA1	Kobe Bryant	150.00
KBA2	Kobe Bryant	150.00
KBW	Kobe Bryant	50.00
KBSS	Kobe Bryant	50.00
KBF1	Kobe Bryant	40.00
KBF2	Kobe Bryant	40.00
KBF3	Kobe Bryant	40.00
KBF4	Kobe Bryant	40.00
KBF5	Kobe Bryant	40.00
KBF6	Kobe Bryant	40.00
KBF7	Kobe Bryant	40.00
KBF8	Kobe Bryant	40.00
KBFA1	Kobe Bryant	
KBFA2	Kobe Bryant	
KBFA3	Kobe Bryant	
KBFA4	Kobe Bryant	
KBFA5	Kobe Bryant	
KBFA6	Kobe Bryant	
KBFA7	Kobe Bryant	
KBFA8	Kobe Bryant	
KBGA1	Kobe Bryant	
KBGA2	Kobe Bryant	

2001-02 Upper Deck MVP Basketball Diary

		MT
	Complete Set (14):	20.00
	Common Player:	1.00
	Inserted 1:12	
BD1	Alonzo Mourning	1.00
BD2	Wang Zhizhi	2.00
BD3	Chris Webber	2.50
BD4	Paul Pierce	1.50
BD5	Kevin Garnett	5.00
BD6	Dirk Nowitzki	2.00
BD7	Marc Jackson	1.00
BD8	Kobe Bryant	8.00
BD9	Ray Allen	1.50
BD10	Tracy McGrady	4.00
BD11	Jerry Stackhouse	1.50
BD12	Kenyon Martin	1.00
BD13	Rasheed Wallace	1.50
BD14	Steve Francis	2.50
		1.00

2001-02 Upper Deck MVP Game Night Gear

		MT
	Common Player:	8.00
	Inserted 1:96 H; 1:120 R	
JA-G	John Amaechi	8.00
DA-G	Darrell Armstrong	10.00
KB-G	Kobe Bryant	50.00
MA-G	Marcus Camby	10.00
BC-G	Brian Cardinal	8.00
KG-G	Kevin Garnett	25.00
DG-G	Dean Garrett	8.00
AJ-G	A.J. Guyton	8.00
DH-G	Donnell Harvey	8.00
AI-G	Allen Iverson	40.00
JK-G	Jason Kidd	15.00
CO-G	Corey Maggette	10.00
MC-G	Antonio McDyess	12.00
RM-G	Ron Mercer	8.00
CM-G	Chris Mihm	8.00
LM-G	Lamond Murray	8.00
IR-G	Isaiah Rider	8.00
JS-G	Jerry Stackhouse	12.00
WS-G	Wally Szczerbiak	12.00
KV-G	Keith Van Horn	10.00

2001-02 Upper Deck MVP Game Night Gear, Signed

		MT
	Common Player:	15.00
	Production 100 Sets	
DA-A	Darrell Armstrong	20.00
KB-A	Kobe Bryant	200.00
KG-A	Kevin Garnett	75.00
DH-A	Donnell Harvey	15.00
CO-A	Corey Maggette	20.00
MC-A	Antonio McDyess	40.00
CM-A	Chris Mihm	15.00
LM-A	Lamond Murray	15.00
JS-A	Jerry Stackhouse	40.00
WS-A	Wally Szczerbiak	40.00

2001-02 Upper Deck MVP MVP Watch

		MT
	Complete Set (7):	30.00
	Common Player:	2.00
	Inserted 1:24	
M1	Shaquille O'Neal	5.00
M2	Vince Carter	10.00
M3	Chris Webber	4.00
M4	Karl Malone	2.00
M5	Kevin Garnett	6.00
M6	Kobe Bryant	10.00
M7	Tim Duncan	4.00

2001-02 Upper Deck MVP Respect the Game

MT
Complete Set (14): 35.00
Common Player: 1.00
Inserted 1:12
RG1 Kobe Bryant 8.00
RG2 Gary Payton 1.50
RG3 Tim Duncan 2.50
RG4 Lamar Odom 2.00
RG5 Vince Carter 8.00
RG6 Eddie Jones 1.50
RG7 Kevin Garnett 5.00
RG8 Jamal Mashburn 1.00
RG9 Michael Finley 1.00
RG10 Shaquille O'Neal 4.00
RG11 Latrell Sprewell 1.50
RG12 Steve Francis 3.00
RG13 Reggie Miller 1.50
RG14 Ray Allen 1.50

2001-02 Upper Deck MVP Souvenirs

MT
Common Player: 10.00
Inserted 1:96 Hobby
Gold Versions: 3x
Production 50 Sets
TB Terrell Brandon 10.00
KB Kobe Bryant 50.00
MF Michael Finley 12.00
SF Steve Francis 25.00
KG Kevin Garnett 30.00
RH Richard Hamilton 12.00
AJ Antawn Jamison 15.00
JK Jason Kidd 15.00
KM Karl Malone 15.00
SM Stephon Marbury 12.00
SH Shawn Marion 15.00
MC Antonio McDyess 10.00
RM Ron Mercer 10.00
DM Darius Miles 40.00
AM Andre Miller 12.00
DR David Robinson 12.00
JS Jerry Stackhouse 15.00
JT Jason Terry 12.00
CW Chris Webber 25.00

2001-02 Upper Deck MVP Souvenirs, Combo

MT
Common Player: 25.00
Inserted 1:288
Gold Versions: 2x
Production 50 Sets
AW/PP Antoine Walker, Paul Pierce 40.00
BD/JM Baron Davis, Jamal Mashburn 25.00
DMQRCM Darius Miles, Quentin Richardson, Corey Maggette 60.00
DR/DA David Robinson, Derek Anderson 25.00
JK/SM Jason Kidd, Shawn Marion 50.00
KM/JS Karl Malone, John Stockton 75.00
KB/DM Kobe Bryant, Darius Miles 100.00
KB/KG Kobe Bryant, Kevin Garnett 100.00
SMKMKV Stephon Marbury, Kenyon Martin, Keith Van Horn 50.00

2001-02 Upper Deck Ovation

MT
Complete Set (90): 45.00
Common Player: .25
Minor Stars: .50
Common Rookie (91-110): 4.00
Three versions numbered to 625 each
Common Rookie (111-120): 10.00
Three versions numbered to 250 each
Pack (5): 4.00
Wax Box (20): 90.00
1 Jason Terry .50
2 DerMarr Johnson .50
3 Shareef Abdur-Rahim .60
4 Paul Pierce .75
5 Antoine Walker .75
6 Kenny Anderson .50
7 Jamal Mashburn .50
8 David Wesley .25
9 Baron Davis .75
10 Ron Mercer .50
11 Marcus Fizer .50
12 Ron Artest .25
13 Andre Miller .75
14 Lamond Murray .25
15 Chris Mihm .25
16 Michael Finley .60
17 Steve Nash .50
18 Dirk Nowitzki 1.00
19 Antonio McDyess .50
20 Nick Van Exel .60
21 Raef LaFrentz .50
22 Jerry Stackhouse .75
23 Chucky Atkins .25
24 Corliss Williamson .25
25 Antawn Jamison 1.00
26 Chris Porter .25
27 Larry Hughes .50
28 Steve Francis 1.50
29 Cuttino Mobley .50
30 Maurice Taylor .25
31 Reggie Miller .75
32 Jalen Rose .50
33 Jermaine O'Neal .75
34 Darius Miles 3.00
35 Corey Maggette .50
36 Lamar Odom 1.00
37 Elton Brand 1.00
38 Kobe Bryant 4.00
39 Shaquille O'Neal 2.00
40 Rick Fox .25
41 Derek Fisher .50
42 Stromile Swift .50
43 Michael Dickerson .25
44 Jason Williams .60
45 Alonzo Mourning .60
46 Eddie Jones .60
47 Anthony Carter .25
48 Ray Allen .75
49 Glenn Robinson .75
50 Sam Cassell .50
51 Kevin Garnett 2.50
52 Terrell Brandon .50
53 Wally Szczerbiak .50
54 Joe Smith .50
55 Kenyon Martin .60
56 Keith Van Horn .50
57 Jason Kidd 1.25
58 Latrell Sprewell .75
59 Allan Houston .50
60 Marcus Camby .60
61 Tracy McGrady 2.00
62 Mike Miller 1.50
63 Grant Hill 1.25
64 Allen Iverson 2.50
65 Dikembe Mutombo .50
66 Aaron McKie .50
67 Stephon Marbury .75
68 Shawn Marion 1.00
69 Tom Gugliotta .25
70 Rasheed Wallace .50
71 Damon Stoudamire .25
72 Bonzi Wells .50
73 Chris Webber 1.50
74 Peja Stojakovic .50
75 Mike Bibby .50
76 Tim Duncan 1.50
77 David Robinson .75
78 Antonio Daniels .25
79 Gary Payton .75
80 Rashard Lewis .50
81 Desmond Mason .50
82 Vince Carter 4.00
83 Morris Peterson .75
84 Antonio Davis .50
85 Karl Malone 1.00
86 John Stockton .75
87 Donyell Marshall .25
88 Richard Hamilton .50
89 Courtney Alexander .50
90 Michael Jordan 10.00
91 *Jeff Trepagnier* 4.00
92 *Pau Gasol* 25.00
93 *Will Solomon* 4.00
94 *Gilbert Arenas* 6.00
95 *Andrei Kirilenko* 15.00
96 *Jamaal Tinsley* 25.00
97 *Samuel Dalembert* 5.00
98 *Gerald Wallace* 10.00
99 *Brandon Armstrong* 5.00
100 *Jeryl Sasser* 5.00
101 *Joseph Forte* 12.00
102 *Brendan Haywood* 12.00
103 *Zach Randolph* 12.00
104 *Jason Collins* 6.00
105 *Michael Bradley* 6.00
106 *Kirk Haston* 8.00
107 *Steven Hunter* 4.00
108 *Troy Murphy* 10.00
109 *Richard Jefferson* 12.00
110 *Vladimir Radmanovic* 8.00
111 *Kedrick Brown* 10.00
112 *Joe Johnson* 30.00
113 *Rodney White* 15.00
114 *DeSagana Diop* 10.00
115 *Eddie Griffin* 30.00
116 *Shane Battier* 50.00
117 *Jason Richardson* 60.00
118 *Eddy Curry* 25.00
119 *Tyson Chandler* 30.00
120 *Kwame Brown* 30.00

2001-02 Upper Deck Ovation Superstar Warm-Up

MT
Common Player: 10.00
Minor Stars: 15.00
Inserted 1:10
DA Darrell Armstrong 10.00
TB Terrell Brandon 10.00
KB Kobe Bryant 70.00
BD Baron Davis 15.00
KD Keyon Dooling 10.00
MF Michael Finley 15.00
KG Kevin Garnett 35.00
RH Richard Hamilton 10.00
GH Grant Hill 25.00
DJ DerMarr Johnson 10.00
CM Corey Maggette 15.00
JA Jamaal Magloire 10.00
KM Karl Malone 15.00
SM Shawn Marion 20.00
JM Jamal Mashburn 10.00
MC Antonio McDyess 15.00
RM Ron Mercer 10.00
DM Darius Miles 30.00
AM Andre Miller 15.00
HM Hanno Mottola 10.00
DN Dirk Nowitzki 20.00
MO Michael Olowokandi 10.00
MP Morris Peterson 10.00
PP Paul Pierce 15.00
QR Quentin Richardson 15.00
JS Joe Smith 10.00
ST John Stockton 15.00
WS Wally Szczerbiak 15.00
AW Antoine Walker 15.00

2001-02 Upper Deck Ovation Superstar Warm-Up Autographs

MT
Common Player: 25.00
Inserted 1:240
DA-S Darrell Armstrong 25.00
KB-S Kobe Bryant 275.00
KG-S Kevin Garnett 125.00
JM-S Jamal Mashburn 25.00
DM-S Darius Miles 75.00
HM-S Hanno Mottola 25.00
MP-S Morris Peterson 25.00
QR-S Quentin Richardson 30.00

2001-02 Upper Deck Ovation Tremendous Trios

MT
Common Player: 40.00
Inserted 1:240
BDJMDW Baron Davis, Jamal Mashburn, David Wesley 40.00
MJKBKG Michael Jordan, Kobe Bryant, Kevin Garnett 400.00
RMRAJC Ron Mercer, Ron Artest, Marcus Fizer 40.00
KGTBWS Kevin Garnett, Terrell Brandon, Wally Szczerbiak 70.00
AJLHMA Antawn Jamison, Larry Hughes, Marc Jackson 40.00
TMGHMM Tracy McGrady, Grant Hill, Mike Miller 80.00

2001-02 UD Playmakers

MT
Complete Set (100): 325.00
Common Player: .25
Minor Stars: .50
Common Rookie (101-130): 3.00
Production 1,999 Sets
Common Rookie (131-145): 8.00
Production 999 Sets
Pack (5): 3.00
Box (24): 70.00
1 Shareef Abdur-Rahim .60
2 Dion Glover .25
3 Jason Terry .50
4 Toni Kukoc .50
5 Theo Ratliff .50
6 Paul Pierce .75
7 Antoine Walker .60
8 Baron Davis .75
9 Jamal Mashburn .50
10 Ron Mercer .50
11 Brad Miller .25
12 Marcus Fizer .50
13 Andre Miller .50
14 Chris Mihm .25
15 Lamond Murray .25
16 Michael Finley .60
17 Dirk Nowitzki 1.00
18 Steve Nash .50
19 Tim Hardaway .50
20 Antonio McDyess .60
21 Nick Van Exel .60
22 Raef LaFrentz .50
23 Jerry Stackhouse .75
24 Clifford Robinson .50
25 Ben Wallace .50
26 Antawn Jamison 1.00
27 Larry Hughes .50
28 Danny Fortson .25
29 Steve Francis 1.50
30 Cuttino Mobley .50
31 Kenny Thomas .25
32 Jalen Rose .50
33 Reggie Miller .75
34 Jermaine O'Neal .60
35 Darius Miles 3.00
36 Elton Brand 1.00
37 Corey Maggette .50
38 Quentin Richardson .50
39 Kobe Bryant 4.00
40 Shaquille O'Neal 2.00
41 Mitch Richmond .50
42 Derek Fisher .50
43 Lindsey Hunter .25
44 Stromile Swift .50
45 Jason Williams .50
46 Michael Dickerson .25
47 Eddie Jones .60
48 Alonzo Mourning .50
49 Anthony Carter .25
50 Brian Grant .50
51 Glenn Robinson .60
52 Ray Allen .75
53 Sam Cassell .50
54 Tim Thomas .50
55 Anthony Mason .50
56 Kevin Garnett 2.50
57 Wally Szczerbiak .50
58 Terrell Brandon .50
59 Joe Smith .50
60 Jason Kidd 1.25
61 Kenyon Martin .50
62 Allan Houston .60
63 Latrell Sprewell 1.00
64 Marcus Camby .50
65 Mark Jackson .25
66 Kurt Thomas .25
67 Tracy McGrady 2.00
68 Grant Hill 1.25
69 Mike Miller 1.50
70 Allen Iverson 2.50
71 Dikembe Mutombo .50
72 Aaron McKie .50
73 Stephon Marbury .75
74 Shawn Marion 1.00
75 Anfernee Hardaway .50
76 Tom Gugliotta .25
77 Rasheed Wallace .60
78 Derek Anderson .50
79 Bonzi Wells .50
80 Chris Webber 1.50
81 Peja Stojakovic .60
82 Mike Bibby .50
83 Doug Christie .25
84 Tim Duncan 1.50
85 David Robinson .60
86 Antonio Daniels .25
87 Steve Smith .50
88 Gary Payton .75
89 Rashard Lewis .60
90 Desmond Mason .25
91 Vince Carter 4.00
92 Morris Peterson .60
93 Antonio Davis .50
94 Hakeem Olajuwon .60
95 Karl Malone 1.00
96 John Stockton .75
97 Donyell Marshall .25
98 Michael Jordan 10.00
99 Courtney Alexander .50
100 Richard Hamilton .50
101 *Jeryl Sasser* 4.00
102 *DeSagana Diop* 5.00
103 *Alvin Jones* 4.00
104 *Gerald Wallace* 8.00
105 *Kenny Satterfield* 4.00
106 *Ruben Boumtje-Boumtje* 3.00
107 *Brian Scalabrine* 4.00
108 *Oscar Torres* 3.00
109 *Jarron Collins* 4.00
110 *Jeff Trepagnier* 4.00
111 *Brendan Haywood* 6.00
112 *Vladimir Radmanovic* 4.00
113 *Loren Woods* 6.00
114 *Terence Morris* 3.00
115 *Kirk Haston* 6.00
116 *Earl Watson* 3.00
117 *Brandon Armstrong* 4.00
118 *Zach Randolph* 8.00
119 *Bobby Simmons* 3.00
120 *Alton Ford* 3.00
121 *Trenton Hassell* 6.00
122 *Damone Brown* 3.00
123 *Michael Bradley* 4.00
124 *Zeljko Rebraca* 5.00
125 *Jason Collins* 4.00
126 *Samuel Dalembert* 3.00
127 *Gilbert Arenas* 8.00
128 *Willie Solomon* 3.00
129 *Joseph Forte* 8.00
130 *Steven Hunter* 3.00
131 *Andrei Kirilenko* 12.00
132 *Eddy Curry* 15.00
133 *Tony Parker* 20.00
134 *Troy Murphy* 10.00
135 *Shane Battier* 25.00
136 *Kedrick Brown* 8.00
137 *Tyson Chandler* 15.00
138 *Jamaal Tinsley* 20.00
139 *Pau Gasol* 20.00
140 *Joe Johnson* 12.00
141 *Jason Richardson* 30.00
142 *Richard Jefferson* 12.00
143 *Eddie Griffin* 15.00
144 *Rodney White* 10.00
145 *Kwame Brown* 15.00

Values quoted in this guide reflect the retail price of a card — the price a collector can expect to pay when buying a card from a dealer. The wholesale price — that which a collector can expect to receive from a dealer when selling cards — will be significantly lower, depending on desirability and condition.

2001-02 UD Playmakers Bobbleheads

MT
Common Player: 20.00
Inserted 1:Box
APM-KB Kwame Brown 25.00
PM-KoB Kobe Bryant 40.00
APM-TC Tyson Chandler 25.00
APM-EC Eddy Curry 20.00
APM-JE Julius Erving 40.00
APM-KG Kevin Garnett 30.00
APM-EG Eddie Griffin 25.00
APM-AI Allen Iverson 30.00
APM-JJ Joe Johnson 20.00
PM-KM Kenyon Martin 20.00
APM-TM Tracy McGrady 30.00
APM-JR Jason Richardson 40.00
PM-LS Latrell Sprewell 25.00

2001-02 UD Playmakers Triple Overtime

"Too uncommon to price."

MT
Common Player:
Production 50 Sets
SA-OT Shareef Abdur-Rahim
TB-OT Terrell Brandon
KW-OT Kwame Brown
KB-OT Kobe Bryant
TC-OT Tyson Chandler
EC-OT Eddy Curry
KG-OT Kevin Garnett
EG-OT Eddie Griffin
AH-OT Anfernee Hardaway
JK-OT Jason Kidd
CM-OT Corey Maggette
KM-OT Karl Malone
SM-OT Stephon Marbury
DM-OT Darius Miles
MM-OT Mike Miller
NA-OT Steve Nash
JS-OT Joe Smith
SS-OT Stromile Swift
WS-OT Wally Szczerbiak
JA-OT Jason Terry
GW-OT Gerald Wallace

2001-02 UD Playmakers Player's Club Game Jersey

MT
Common Player: 15.00
Production 350 Sets
KE-J Kedrick Brown 15.00
KW-J Kwame Brown 25.00
KB-J Kobe Bryant 80.00
EC-J Eddy Curry 25.00
BD-J Baron Davis 15.00
KG-J Kevin Garnett 30.00
EG-J Eddie Griffin 25.00
SH-J Steven Hunter 15.00
AI-J Allen Iverson 40.00
AJ-J Antawn Jamison 15.00
JJ-J Joe Johnson 20.00
JK-J Jason Kidd 25.00
KM-J Karl Malone 20.00
SM-J Stephon Marbury 15.00
MA-J Kenyon Martin 15.00
DE-J Desmond Mason 15.00
TM-J Tracy McGrady 30.00
DM-J Darius Miles 30.00
MM-J Mike Miller 25.00
DN-J Dirk Nowitzki 25.00
LO-J Lamar Odom 20.00
PP-J Paul Pierce 20.00
JR-J Jason Richardson 40.00
JS-J John Stockton 20.00
JT-J Jamaal Tinsley 25.00
GW-J Gerald Wallace 20.00
CW-J Chris Webber 25.00

2001-02 UD Playmakers Player's Club Game Jerseys Gold

MT
Gold: 2x
Production 100 Sets
KW-GJ Kwame Brown
KB-GJ Kobe Bryant
EC-GJ Eddy Curry
KG-GJ Kevin Garnett
EG-GJ Eddie Griffin
AI-GJ Allen Iverson
JJ-GJ Joe Johnson
KM-GJ Kenyon Martin
TM-GJ Tracy McGrady
DM-GJ Darius Miles
LO-GJ Lamar Odom
JR-GJ Jason Richardson
JT-GJ Jamaal Tinsley
CW-GJ Chris Webber

2001-02 UD Playmakers Player's Club Game Jerseys Autos

"Too uncommon to price."

MT
Production 10 Sets
KE-AJ Kedrick Brown
KW-AJ Kwame Brown
KB-AJ Kobe Bryant
EC-AJ Eddy Curry
KG-AJ Kevin Garnett
EG-AJ Eddie Griffin
SH-AJ Steven Hunter
RJ-AJ Richard Jefferson
JJ-AJ Joe Johnson
MA-AJ Kenyon Martin
DE-AJ Desmond Mason
LO-AJ Lamar Odom
JR-AJ Jason Richardson

2001-02 UD Playmakers Player's Club Shooting Shirt

MT
Common Player: 12.00
Production 350 Sets
VB-S Vin Baker 12.00
SB-S Shane Battier 30.00
TB-S Terrell Brandon 12.00
KW-S Kwame Brown 25.00
KB-S Kobe Bryant 60.00
TC-S Tyson Chandler 25.00
KD-S Keyon Dooling 15.00
MF-S Michael Finley 15.00
KG-S Kevin Garnett 30.00
PG-S Pau Gasol 30.00
EG-S Eddie Griffin 25.00
AI-S Allen Iverson 30.00
AK-S Andrei Kirilenko 20.00
JA-S Jamaal Magloire 12.00
KM-S Karl Malone 20.00
DM-S Desmond Mason 15.00
TM-S Tracy McGrady 30.00
MO-S Michael Olowokandi 12.00
ZR-S Zach Randolph 15.00
JS-S Joe Smith 12.00
JE-S Jerry Stackhouse 20.00
SS-S Stromile Swift 15.00
WS-S Wally Szczerbiak 15.00
JT-S Jason Terry 12.00
TI-S Jamaal Tinsley 25.00
NV-S Nick Van Exel 15.00

2001-02 UD Playmakers Player's Club Shooting Shirt Gold

MT
Gold: 1.5x
Production 150 Sets
KW-GS Kwame Brown
KB-GS Kobe Bryant
TC-GS Tyson Chandler
MF-GS Michael Finley
KG-GS Kevin Garnett
PG-GS Pau Gasol
EG-GS Eddie Griffin
AI-GS Allen Iverson
AK-GS Andrei Kirilenko
KM-GS Karl Malone
DM-GS Desmond Mason
TM-GS Tracy McGrady
JE-GS Jerry Stackhouse
SS-GS Stromile Swift
WS-GS Wally Szczerbiak
TI-GS Jamaal Tinsley

2001-02 UD Playmakers Player's Club Shooting Shirt Autos

"Too uncommon to price."

MT
Production 25 Sets
KW-AS Kwame Brown
KB-AS Kobe Bryant
TC-AS Tyson Chandler
KG-AS Kevin Garnett
EG-AS Eddie Griffin
MJ-AS Michael Jordan
JM-AS Jamaal Magloire
JE-AS Jerry Stackhouse
WS-AS Wally Szczerbiak
TI-AS Jamaal Tinsley

2001-02 UD Playmakers Player's Club Warm-Up

MT
Common Player: 12.00
Production 350 Sets
RY-W Ray Allen 15.00
JB-W Jonathan Bender 12.00
TB-W Terrell Brandon 12.00
KB-W Kobe Bryant 60.00
TC-W Tyson Chandler 25.00
EC-W Eddy Curry 20.00
MF-W Michael Finley 15.00
KG-W Kevin Garnett 30.00

AL-W Al Harrington 15.00
GH-W Grant Hill 15.00
AH-W Allan Houston 15.00
CM-W Corey Maggette 12.00
JA-W Jamaal Magloire 12.00
KM-W Kenyon Martin 12.00
JM-W Jamal Mashburn 12.00
MC-W Antonio McDyess 12.00
TM-W Tracy McGrady 25.00
AM-W Andre Miller 15.00
DN-W Dirk Nowitzki 25.00
GP-W Gary Payton 15.00
MP-W Morris Peterson 15.00
PP-W Paul Pierce 20.00
DR-W David Robinson 15.00
JS-W Joe Smith 12.00
LS-W Latrell Sprewell 20.00
ST-W John Stockton 20.00
WS-W Wally Szczerbiak 15.00
AW-W Antoine Walker 15.00

2001-02 UD Playmakers Player's Club Warm-Up Gold

MT
Gold: 1.5x
Production 250 Sets
RY-GW Ray Allen
KB-GW Kobe Bryant
TC-GW Tyson Chandler
EC-GW Eddy Curry
MF-GW Michael Finley
KG-GW Kevin Garnett
AL-GW Al Harrington
AH-GW Allan Houston
JA-GW Jamaal Magloire
TM-GW Tracy McGrady
AM-GW Andre Miller
DN-GW Dirk Nowitzki
GP-GW Gary Payton
PP-GW Paul Pierce
DR-GW David Robinson
JS-GW Joe Smith
LS-GW Latrell Sprewell
ST-GW John Stockton
WS-GW Wally Szczerbiak
AW-GW Antoine Walker

2001-02 UD Playmakers Player's Club Warm-Up Autos

MT
Common Player: 30.00
Production 50 Sets
TB-AW Terrell Brandon 30.00
KB-AW Kobe Bryant 500.00
KG-AW Kevin Garnett 200.00
CM-AW Corey Maggette 30.00
JA-AW Jamaal Magloire 30.00
KM-AW Kenyon Martin 30.00
AM-AW Andre Miller 40.00
MP-AW Morris Peterson 50.00
PP-AW Paul Pierce 100.00
WS-AW Wally Szczerbiak 60.00

2001-02 Upper Deck Pros & Prospects

MT
Complete Set (131): 750.00
Common Player: .25
Minor Stars: .50
Common Rookie (91-131): 6.00
91-125 Production 1,000 Sets
126-131 Production 350 Sets
Pack (5): 5.00
Box (24): 100.00
1 Jason Terry .50
2 Toni Kukoc .50
3 DerMarr Johnson .50
4 Paul Pierce .75
5 Antoine Walker .60
6 Kenny Anderson .50
7 Jamal Mashburn .50
8 Baron Davis .75
9 David Wesley .25
10 Elton Brand 1.00
11 Ron Mercer .50
12 Jamal Crawford .50
13 Andre Miller .60
14 Lamond Murray .25
15 Chris Mihm .25
16 Michael Finley .50
17 Wang Zhizhi 1.50
18 Dirk Nowitzki 1.00
19 Antonio McDyess .50
20 Nick Van Exel .50
21 Raef LaFrentz .50
22 Jerry Stackhouse .60
23 Joe Smith .50
24 Mateen Cleaves .50
25 Antawn Jamison 1.00
26 Marc Jackson .50
27 Larry Hughes .50
28 Steve Francis 1.50
29 Maurice Taylor .25
30 Hakeem Olajuwon .60
31 Reggie Miller .60
32 Jermaine O'Neal .75
33 Jalen Rose .50
34 Lamar Odom 1.00
35 Darius Miles 3.00
36 Quentin Richardson .50
37 Kobe Bryant 4.00
38 Shaquille O'Neal 2.00
39 Derek Fisher .50
40 Rick Fox .25
41 Alonzo Mourning .50
42 Eddie Jones .60
43 Tim Hardaway .50
44 Brian Grant .50
45 Ray Allen .75
46 Glenn Robinson .60
47 Tim Thomas .50
48 Kevin Garnett 2.50
49 Terrell Brandon .50
50 Wally Szczerbiak .50
51 Chauncey Billups .25
52 Stephon Marbury .75
53 Kenyon Martin .50
54 Keith Van Horn .50
55 Allan Houston .50
56 Latrell Sprewell 1.00
57 Glen Rice .50
58 Tracy McGrady 2.00
59 Mike Miller 1.50
60 Darrell Armstrong .50
61 Allen Iverson 3.00
62 Dikembe Mutombo .50
63 Aaron McKie .50
64 Jason Kidd 1.25
65 Shawn Marion 1.00
66 Tom Gugliotta .25
67 Rasheed Wallace .60
68 Damon Stoudamire .25
69 Scottie Pippen 1.00
70 Peja Stojakovic .75
71 Jason Williams .50
72 Chris Webber 1.50
73 Tim Duncan 1.50
74 Derek Anderson .50
75 David Robinson .60
76 Gary Payton .60
77 Rashard Lewis .50
78 Desmond Mason .50
79 Vince Carter 4.00
80 Morris Peterson .60
81 Antonio Davis .50
82 Karl Malone 1.00
83 John Stockton .75
84 Donyell Marshall .25
85 Shareef Abdur-Rahim .50
86 Mike Bibby .50
87 Stromile Swift .50
88 Richard Hamilton .50
89 Courtney Alexander .50
90 Chris Whitney .25
91 *Ruben Boumtje-Boumtje* 6.00
92 *Sean Lampley* 6.00
93 *Ken Johnson* 6.00
94 *Earl Watson* 8.00
95 *Jamaal Tinsley* 50.00
96 *Damone Brown* 6.00
97 *Michael Wright* 8.00
98 *Alvin Jones* 8.00
99 *Omar Cook* 8.00
100 *Jarron Collins* 8.00
101 *Brian Scalabrine* 8.00
102 *Jeryl Sasser* 12.00
103 *Samuel Dalembert* 8.00
104 *Terence Morris* 8.00
105 *Will Solomon* 8.00
106 *Kirk Haston* 15.00
107 *Richard Jefferson* 40.00
108 *Jason Collins* 12.00
109 *Troy Murphy* 20.00
110 *Gerald Wallace* 20.00
111 *Shane Battier* 60.00
112 *Jeff Trepagnier* 12.00
113 *Brandon Armstrong* 10.00
114 *Loren Woods* 20.00
115 *Joseph Forte* 20.00
116 *Michael Bradley* 15.00
117 *Joe Johnson* 40.00
118 *Gilbert Arenas* 30.00
119 *Ousmane Cisse* 8.00
120 *Kenny Satterfield* 8.00
121 *Vladimir Radmanovic* 12.00
122 *DeSagana Diop* 15.00
123 *Kedrick Brown* 20.00
124 *Trenton Hassell* 20.00
125 *Steve Hunter* 10.00
126 *Rodney White* 40.00
126a *Rodney White* 40.00
127 *Eddy Curry* 60.00
127a *Eddy Curry* 60.00
128 *Jason Richardson* 100.00
128a *Jason Richardson* 100.00
129 *Tyson Chandler* 60.00
129a *Tyson Chandler* 60.00
130 *Eddie Griffin* 60.00
130a *Eddie Griffin* 60.00
131 *Kwame Brown* 60.00
131a *Kwame Brown* 60.00

2001-02 Upper Deck Pros & Prospects All-Star Team-Ups

MT
Common Player: 25.00
Inserted 1:192
Gold Versions: 2x-4x
Production 25 Sets
AI/KB Allen Iverson, Kobe Bryant 150.00
AD/DM Antonio Davis, Dikembe Mutombo 25.00
TM/SM Tracy McGrady, Stephon Marbury 50.00
DR/KG David Robinson, Kevin Garnett 50.00
CW/AM Chris Webber, Antonio McDyess 40.00
KM/MF Karl Malone, Michael Finley 40.00
JK/GP Jason Kidd, Gary Payton 40.00
RA/GR Ray Allen, Glenn Robinson 30.00
JS/RW Jerry Stackhouse, Rasheed Wallace 30.00
AH/LS Allan Houston, Latrell Sprewell 40.00

2001-02 Upper Deck Pros & Prospects Alley-oop Team-Ups

MT
Common Player: 30.00
Production 100 Sets
Gold Versions: 2x-4x
Production 25 Sets
KG-KB Kevin Garnett, Kobe Bryant 150.00
PP-AW Paul Pierce, Antoine Walker 50.00
NV-AM Nick Van Exel, Antonio McDyess 30.00
JS-KM John Stockton, Karl Malone 75.00
TB-KG Terrell Brandon, Kevin Garnett 50.00
DA-TM Darrell Armstrong, Tracy McGrady 50.00
QR-DM Quentin Richardson, Darius Miles 60.00
CP-AJ Chris Porter, Antawn Jamison 30.00
BD-JM Baron Davis, Jamal Mashburn 50.00
GP-RL Gary Payton, Rashard Lewis 40.00

2001-02 Upper Deck Pros & Prospects Game Jerseys

MT
Common Player: 10.00
Inserted 1:24
Gold Versions: 2x
Production 75 Sets
KA Kenny Anderson 10.00
DA Darrell Armstrong 10.00
WA William Avery 10.00
TB Terrell Brandon 10.00
KB Kobe Bryant 75.00
DC Derrick Coleman 10.00
JC Jamal Crawford 10.00
KG Kevin Garnett 30.00
AI Allen Iverson 50.00
AJ Antawn Jamison 20.00
RL Raef LaFrentz 10.00
CO Corey Maggette 15.00
MA Desmond Mason 12.00
RM Ron Mercer 12.00
CM Chris Mihm 10.00
DM Darius Miles 30.00
JM Jerome Moiso 10.00
HM Hanno Mottola 10.00
LM Lamond Murray 10.00
MO Michael Olowokandi 10.00
MP Morris Peterson 15.00
GR Glen Rice 10.00
JS John Stockton 20.00
SS Stromile Swift 12.00
KV Keith Van Horn 15.00
AW Antoine Walker 15.00

2001-02 Upper Deck Pros & Prospects Game Jersey Autos

MT
Common Player: 20.00
Inserted 1:192
Gold Versions: 1.5x
Production 50 Sets
DA-A Darrell Armstrong 25.00
TB-A Terrell Brandon 20.00
KB-A Kobe Bryant 350.00
KG-A Kevin Garnett 125.00
CO-A Corey Maggette 40.00
CM-A Chris Mihm 20.00
DM-A Darius Miles 125.00
LM-A Lamond Murray 20.00
MP-A Morris Peterson 50.00
SS-A Stromile Swift 40.00
AW-A Antoine Walker 50.00

2001-02 Upper Deck Pros & Prospects ProActive

MT
Complete Set (10): 30.00
Common Player: 1.50
Inserted 1:23
PA1 Kobe Bryant 10.00
PA2 Vince Carter 10.00
PA3 Tim Duncan 4.00
PA4 Ray Allen 2.00
PA5 Michael Finley 1.50
PA6 Paul Pierce 2.00
PA7 Latrell Sprewell 2.50
PA8 Steve Francis 4.00
PA9 Kevin Garnett 6.00
PA10 Eddie Jones 1.50

2001-02 Upper Deck Pros & Prospects ProMotion

MT
Complete Set (12): 25.00
Common Player: 1.00
Inserted 1:18
PM1 Kevin Garnett 5.00
PM2 Chris Webber 3.00
PM3 Michael Finley 1.00
PM4 Tim Duncan 3.00
PM5 Ray Allen 1.50
PM6 Jamal Mashburn 1.00
PM7 Antonio McDyess 1.00
PM8 Kobe Bryant 8.00
PM9 Latrell Sprewell 2.00
PM10 Vince Carter 8.00
PM11 Shaquille O'Neal 4.00
PM12 Karl Malone 2.00

2001-02 Upper Deck Pros & Prospects Star Command

MT
Complete Set (10): 40.00
Common Player: 4.00
Inserted 1:23
SC1 Allen Iverson 6.00
SC2 Steve Francis 4.00
SC3 Kevin Garnett 6.00
SC4 Vince Carter 10.00
SC5 Kobe Bryant 10.00
SC6 Tim Duncan 4.00
SC7 Chris Webber 4.00
SC8 Tracy McGrady 5.00
SC9 Darius Miles 8.00
SC10 Shaquille O'Neal 5.00

2001-02 Upper Deck Pros & Prospects Star Futures

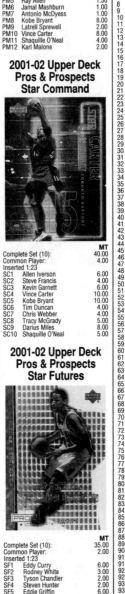

MT
Complete Set (10): 35.00
Common Player: 2.00
Inserted 1:23
SF1 Eddy Curry 6.00
SF2 Rodney White 3.00
SF3 Tyson Chandler 2.00
SF4 Steven Hunter 2.00
SF5 Eddie Griffin 6.00
SF6 Kwame Brown 6.00
SF7 DeSagana Diop 2.00
SF8 Troy Murphy 3.00
SF9 Joe Johnson 6.00
SF10 Jason Richardson 10.00

2001-02 Upper Deck Sweet Shot

MT
Complete Set (120): 450.00
Common Player: .25
Minor Stars: .50
Common Rookie (91-110): 5.00
Common Rookie JSY (91-110): 10.00
Production 1,200 Sets
Common Rookie (111-120): 10.00
Common Rookie JSY (111-120): 12.00
Production 600 Sets
Pack (4): 10.00
Box (18): 169.00
1 Jason Terry .50
2 Shareef Abdur-Rahim .75
3 Toni Kukoc .25
4 Paul Pierce .75
5 Antoine Walker .75
6 Kenny Anderson .25
7 Baron Davis .75
8 Jamal Mashburn .50
9 David Wesley .25
10 Ron Mercer .25
11 Ron Artest .25
12 A.J. Guyton .25
13 Andre Miller .60
14 Lamond Murray .25
15 Chris Mihm .25
16 Michael Finley .75
17 Dirk Nowitzki 1.00
18 Steve Nash .50
19 Antonio McDyess .75
20 Nick Van Exel .50
21 Raef LaFrentz .25
22 Jerry Stackhouse .75
23 Chucky Atkins .25
24 Corliss Williamson .25
25 Antawn Jamison 1.00
26 Marc Jackson .50
27 Larry Hughes .50
28 Steve Francis 1.50
29 Cuttino Mobley .50
30 Maurice Taylor .25
31 Reggie Miller .75
32 Jalen Rose .50
33 Jermaine O'Neal .75
34 Darius Miles 3.00
35 Elton Brand 1.00
36 Corey Maggette .50
37 Quentin Richardson .50
38 Kobe Bryant 4.00
39 Shaquille O'Neal 2.00
40 Rick Fox .25
41 Derek Fisher .50
42 Stromile Swift .50
43 Jason Williams .50
44 Michael Dickerson .25
45 Alonzo Mourning .50
46 Eddie Jones .75
47 Anthony Carter .25
48 Glenn Robinson .50
49 Ray Allen .75
50 Sam Cassell .50
51 Kevin Garnett 2.50
52 Chauncey Billups .25
53 Terrell Brandon .50
54 Joe Smith .50
55 Kenyon Martin .60
56 Keith Van Horn .50
57 Jason Kidd 1.25
58 Latrell Sprewell 1.00
59 Allan Houston .50
60 Marcus Camby .50
61 Tracy McGrady 2.00
62 Mike Miller 1.50
63 Grant Hill 1.25
64 Allen Iverson 2.50
65 Dikembe Mutombo .50
66 Aaron McKie .50
67 Stephon Marbury .75
68 Shawn Marion 1.00
69 Tom Gugliotta .25
70 Rasheed Wallace .75
71 Damon Stoudamire .25
72 Bonzi Wells .50
73 Chris Webber 1.50
74 Peja Stojakovic .75
75 Mike Bibby .50
76 Tim Duncan 1.50
77 David Robinson .75
78 Antonio Daniels .25
79 Gary Payton .75
80 Rashard Lewis .50
81 Desmond Mason .50
82 Vince Carter 4.00
83 Morris Peterson .75
84 Antonio Davis .25
85 Karl Malone 1.00
86 John Stockton .75
87 Donyell Marshall .25
88 Richard Hamilton .50
89 Courtney Alexander .50
90 Michael Jordan 10.00
91 *Zach Randolph* 12.00
91 Zach Randolph JSY 20.00
92 *Troy Murphy* 10.00
92 Troy Murphy JSY 12.00
93 *Michael Bradley* 6.00
93 Michael Bradley JSY 10.00
94 *Vladimir Radmanovic* 8.00
94 Vladimir Radmanovic JSY 10.00
95 *Kirk Haston* 8.00
95 Kirk Haston JSY 12.00
96 *Joseph Forte* 12.00
96 Joseph Forte JSY 20.00
97 *Jamaal Tinsley* 25.00
97 Jamaal Tinsley JSY 40.00
98 *Jason Collins* 6.00
98 Jason Collins JSY 10.00
99 *Brendan Haywood* 12.00
99 Brendan Haywood JSY 15.00
100 *Richard Jefferson* 12.00
100 Richard Jefferson JSY 15.00
101 *Gerald Wallace* 10.00
101 Gerald Wallace JSY 12.00
102 *Jeryl Sasser* 5.00
102 Jeryl Sasser JSY 10.00
103 *Samuel Dalembert* 5.00
104 *Tony Parker* 25.00
104 Tony Parker JSY 40.00
105 *Kedrick Brown* 6.00
106 *Brandon Armstrong* 5.00
106 Brandon Armstrong JSY 10.00
107 *Steven Hunter* 6.00
107 Steven Hunter JSY 10.00
108 *Andrei Kirilenko* 25.00
108 Andrei Kirilenko JSY 40.00
109 *Primoz Brezec* 5.00
109 Primoz Brezec JSY 10.00
110 *Terence Morris* 5.00
110 Terence Morris JSY 10.00
111 *Eddie Griffin* 30.00
111 Eddie Griffin JSY 50.00
112 *DeSagana Diop* 10.00
112 DeSagana Diop JSY 12.00
113 *Tyson Chandler* 30.00
113 Tyson Chandler JSY 50.00
114 *Joe Johnson* 25.00
114 Joe Johnson JSY 50.00
115 *Rodney White* 15.00
115 Rodney White JSY 15.00
116 *Eddy Curry* 30.00
116 Eddy Curry JSY 40.00
117 *Shane Battier* 50.00
117 Shane Battier JSY 75.00
118 *Jason Richardson* 50.00
118 Jason Richardson JSY 75.00
119 *Kwame Brown* 30.00
119 Kwame Brown JSY 50.00
120 *Pau Gasol* 40.00
120 Pau Gasol JSY 60.00

2001-02 Upper Deck Sweet Shot Game Jerseys

MT
Common Player: 10.00
Inserted 1:18
TB Terrell Brandon 10.00
KB Kobe Bryant 80.00
BD Baron Davis 12.00
MF Marcus Fizer 10.00
KG Kevin Garnett 30.00
LH Larry Hughes 10.00
AI Allen Iverson 50.00
AJ Antawn Jamison 15.00
DJ DerMarr Johnson 10.00
TK Toni Kukoc 10.00
CM Corey Maggette 15.00
KM Karl Malone 20.00
SM Shawn Marion 15.00
KE Kenyon Martin 12.00
JM Jamal Mashburn 10.00
TM Tracy McGrady 25.00
RM Ron Mercer 10.00
DM Darius Miles 30.00
MM Mike Miller 15.00
ST John Stockton 20.00
WS Wally Szczerbiak 12.00
JT Jason Terry 10.00
KV Keith Van Horn 12.00
AW Antoine Walker 15.00
CW Chris Webber 25.00

2001-02 Upper Deck Sweet Shot Hot Spot Floor

MT
Common Player: 10.00
Inserted 1:18
RA-F Ray Allen 15.00
KB-F Kobe Bryant 50.00
SF-F Steve Francis 20.00
KG-F Kevin Garnett 25.00
RH-F Richard Hamilton 12.00
AH-F Allan Houston 10.00
MA-F Marc Jackson 10.00
EJ-F Eddie Jones 12.00
MJ-F Michael Jordan
JK-F Jason Kidd 20.00
RL-F Rashard Lewis 12.00
SM-F Stephon Marbury 15.00
SH-F Shawn Marion 15.00
JM-F Jamal Mashburn 10.00
DE-F Desmond Mason 10.00
TM-F Tracy McGrady 20.00
AM-F Andre Miller 10.00
RM-F Reggie Miller 15.00
JO-F Jermaine O'Neal 15.00

SP-F Scottie Pippen 20.00
QR-F Quentin Richardson 12.00
DV-F David Robinson 15.00
LS-F Latrell Sprewell 20.00
JS-F Jerry Stackhouse 15.00
WS-F Wally Szczerbiak 12.00
JT-F Jason Terry 12.00
RW-F Rasheed Wallace 15.00
BW-F Bonzi Wells 10.00

2001-02 Upper Deck Sweet Shot Network Executives

MT
Common Player: 15.00
Inserted 1:108
AG-N A.J. Guyton 15.00
RH-N Richard Hamilton 25.00
AJ-N Antawn Jamison 30.00
DJ-N DerMarr Johnson 20.00
RM-N Ron Mercer 20.00
DM-N Darius Miles 50.00
QR-N Quentin Richardson 25.00
JA-N Jason Terry 20.00

2001-02 Upper Deck Sweet Shot Signature Shots

MT
Common Player: 15.00
Inserted 1:8
DA-S Darrell Armstrong 20.00
KW-S Kwame Brown 50.00
KB-S Kobe Bryant
TC-S Tyson Chandler 40.00
EC-S Eddy Curry 40.00
KG-S Kevin Garnett 100.00
EG-S Eddie Griffin 40.00
LH-S Larry Hughes 20.00
HU-S Steven Hunter 20.00
RJ-S Richard Jefferson 30.00
DJ-S DerMarr Johnson 20.00
JJ-S Joe Johnson 40.00
MJ-S Michael Jordan
KE-S Kenyon Martin 25.00
JM-S Jamal Mashburn 20.00
DE-S Desmond Mason 20.00
TM-S Troy Murphy 30.00
PP-S Paul Pierce 40.00
JP-S Joel Przybilla 15.00
JR-S Jason Richardson 100.00
JS-S Jerry Stackhouse 30.00
SS-S Stromile Swift 25.00
WS-S Wally Szczerbiak 40.00
AW-S Antoine Walker 25.00

2001-02 Upper Deck Sweet Shot Three-point Shots

"Too uncommon to price."

MT
Complete Set (15):
Common Player:
DA-T Darrell Armstrong
KB-T Kobe Bryant
KG-T Kevin Garnett
DJ-T DerMarr Johnson
MJ-T Michael Jordan
KE-T Kenyon Martin
JM-T Jamal Mashburn
DE-T Desmond Mason
DM-T Darius Miles
MM-T Mike Miller
PP-T Paul Pierce
JS-T Jerry Stackhouse
SS-T Stromile Swift
WS-T Wally Szczerbiak
AW-T Antoine Walker

2001-02 UD Ultimate Collection

MT
Complete Set (90): 550.00
Common Player: 3.00
Minor Stars: 5.00
61-70 Production 750 Sets
71-84 Production 250 Sets
85-90 Production 250 Sets
Pack (4): 150.00
Box (4): 600.00
1 Jason Terry 5.00
2 Shareef Abdur-Rahim 5.00
3 Paul Pierce 8.00
4 Antoine Walker 8.00
5 Baron Davis 8.00
6 Jamal Mashburn 3.00
7 Ron Mercer 3.00
8 Marcus Fizer 3.00
9 Andre Miller 5.00
10 Lamond Murray 3.00
11 Dirk Nowitzki 10.00
12 Michael Finley 8.00
13 Antonio McDyess 8.00
14 Nick Van Exel 5.00
15 Jerry Stackhouse 8.00
16 Zeljko Rebraca 3.00
17 Antawn Jamison 10.00
18 Larry Hughes 5.00
19 Steve Francis 15.00
20 Cuttino Mobley 5.00
21 Reggie Miller 8.00
22 Jalen Rose 5.00
23 Darius Miles 30.00
24 Quentin Richardson 5.00
25 Kobe Bryant 40.00
26 Shaquille O'Neal 20.00
27 Mitch Richmond 3.00
28 Stromile Swift 5.00
29 Jason Williams 5.00
30 Alonzo Mourning 5.00
31 Eddie Jones 5.00
32 Ray Allen 8.00
33 Glenn Robinson 5.00
34 Kevin Garnett 25.00
35 Terrell Brandon 3.00
36 Wally Szczerbiak 8.00
37 Jason Kidd 12.00
38 Kenyon Martin 5.00
39 Latrell Sprewell 10.00
40 Allan Houston 5.00
41 Tracy McGrady 20.00
42 Grant Hill 12.00
43 Allen Iverson 25.00
44 Dikembe Mutombo 3.00
45 Stephon Marbury 8.00
46 Anfernee Hardaway 8.00
47 Rasheed Wallace 8.00
48 Derek Anderson 5.00
49 Chris Webber 12.00
50 Peja Stojakovic 8.00
51 Tim Duncan 15.00
52 David Robinson 8.00
53 Rashard Lewis 5.00
54 Desmond Mason 5.00
55 Vince Carter 40.00
56 Morris Peterson 8.00
57 Karl Malone 10.00
58 John Stockton 8.00
59 Richard Hamilton 5.00
60 Michael Jordan 75.00
61 Andrei Kirilenko 40.00
62 Gilbert Arenas 40.00
63 Trenton Hassell 20.00
64 Tony Parker 50.00
65 Jamaal Tinsley 50.00
66 Samuel Dalembert 15.00
67 Gerald Wallace 40.00
68 Brandon Armstrong 15.00
69 Jeryl Sasser 15.00
70 Joseph Forte 25.00
71 Pau Gasol 200.00
72 Brendan Haywood 40.00
73 Zach Randolph 40.00
74 Jason Collins 25.00
75 Michael Bradley 25.00
76 Kirk Haston 25.00
77 Steven Hunter 25.00
78 Troy Murphy 40.00
79 Richard Jefferson 60.00
80 Vladimir Radmanovic 25.00
81 Kedrick Brown 30.00
82 Joe Johnson 60.00
83 DeSagana Diop 30.00
84 Shane Battier 150.00
85 Rodney White 80.00
86 Eddie Griffin 200.00
87 Jason Richardson 450.00
88 Eddy Curry 150.00
89 Tyson Chandler 200.00
90 Kwame Brown 200.00

2001-02 UD Ultimate Collection Game Jerseys

MT
Common Player: 30.00
Production 250 Sets
RA Ray Allen 50.00
BR Kedrick Brown 30.00
KW Kwame Brown 50.00
KB Kobe Bryant 150.00
KB2 Kobe Bryant 150.00
TC Tyson Chandler 50.00
EC Eddy Curry 40.00
MF Michael Finley 40.00
SF Steve Francis 40.00
KG Kevin Garnett 50.00
KG2 Kevin Garnett 50.00
EG Eddie Griffin 50.00
AI Allen Iverson 60.00
RJ Richard Jefferson 40.00
JJ Joe Johnson 40.00
MJ Michael Jordan 300.00
MJ2 Michael Jordan 300.00
KM Karl Malone 50.00
KE Kenyon Martin 30.00
TM Tracy McGrady 50.00
DM Darius Miles 50.00
MM Mike Miller 40.00
NO Dirk Nowitzki 50.00
TP Tony Parker 50.00
PP Paul Pierce 40.00
JR Jason Richardson 75.00
JS John Stockton 50.00
JT Jamaal Tinsley 50.00
CW Chris Webber 50.00
RW Rodney White 30.00

2001-02 UD Ultimate Collection Game Jersey Gold

MT
Common Player: 75.00
Production 50 Sets
KW Kwame Brown 100.00
KB Kobe Bryant 300.00
TC Tyson Chandler 100.00
EC Eddy Curry 75.00
SF Steve Francis 75.00
KG Kevin Garnett 100.00
EG Eddie Griffin 100.00
AI Allen Iverson 125.00
MJ Michael Jordan 600.00
TM Tracy McGrady 100.00
DM Darius Miles 100.00
MM Mike Miller 75.00
JR Jason Richardson 200.00
JT Jamaal Tinsley 100.00
CW Chris Webber 100.00

2001-02 UD Ultimate Collection Game Jersey Silver

MT
Common Player: 50.00
Production 125 Sets
KW Kwame Brown 60.00
KB Kobe Bryant 200.00
TC Tyson Chandler 60.00
EC Eddy Curry 50.00
SF Steve Francis 50.00
KG Kevin Garnett 60.00
EG Eddie Griffin 60.00
AI Allen Iverson 75.00
MJ Michael Jordan 400.00
TM Tracy McGrady 60.00
DM Darius Miles 60.00
MM Mike Miller 50.00
JR Jason Richardson 125.00
JT Jamaal Tinsley 50.00
CW Chris Webber 60.00

2001-02 UD Ultimate Collection Game Jersey Patch

MT
Complete Set (30):
Common Player:
BRP Kedrick Brown 60.00
KWP Kwame Brown 100.00
KBP Kobe Bryant 400.00
KB2P Kobe Bryant 400.00
TCP Tyson Chandler 100.00
ECP Eddy Curry 100.00
BDP Baron Davis 80.00
MFP Michael Finley 80.00
SFP Steve Francis 125.00
KGP Kevin Garnett 200.00
KG2P Kevin Garnett 200.00
EGP Eddie Griffin 100.00
AIP Allen Iverson 250.00
JJP Joe Johnson 80.00
MJP Michael Jordan 1000.
MJ2P Michael Jordan 1000.
KMP Karl Malone 100.00
KEP Kenyon Martin 80.00
TMP Tracy McGrady 175.00
DMP Darius Miles 175.00
MMP Mike Miller 80.00
NOP Dirk Nowitzki 200.00
TPP Tony Parker 100.00
PPP Paul Pierce 80.00
JRP Jason Richardson 200.00
JSP John Stockton 100.00
JTP Jason Terry 60.00
JTP Jamaal Tinsley 150.00
CWP Chris Webber 175.00
RWP Rodney White 60.00

2001-02 UD Ultimate Collection Game Jersey Patch Gold

"Too uncommon to price."

MT
Complete Set (15):
Common Player:
KWP Kwame Brown
KBP Kobe Bryant
TCP Tyson Chandler
ECP Eddy Curry
SFP Steve Francis
KGP Kevin Garnett
EGP Eddie Griffin
AIP Allen Iverson
MJP Michael Jordan
TMP Tracy McGrady
DMP Darius Miles
MMP Mike Miller
JRP Jason Richardson
JTP Jamaal Tinsley
CWP Chris Webber

2001-02 UD Ultimate Collection Game Jersey Patch Silver

"Too uncommon to price."

MT
Complete Set (15):
Common Player:
KWP Kwame Brown
KBP Kobe Bryant
TCP Tyson Chandler
ECP Eddy Curry
SFP Steve Francis
KGP Kevin Garnett
EGP Eddie Griffin
AIP Allen Iverson
MJP Michael Jordan
TMP Tracy McGrady
DMP Darius Miles
MMP Mike Miller
JRP Jason Richardson
JTP Jamaal Tinsley
CWP Chris Webber

2001-02 UD Ultimate Collection Signatures Gold

"Too uncommon to price."

MT
Complete Set (15):
Common Player:
LB-A Larry Bird
KW-A Kwame Brown
KB-A Kobe Bryant
TC-A Tyson Chandler
EC-A Eddy Curry
DR-A Julius Erving
KG-A Kevin Garnett
EG-A Eddie Griffin
JJ-A Joe Johnson
MG-A Magic Johnson
MJ-A Michael Jordan
JK-A Jason Kidd
DM-A Darius Miles
JR-A Jason Richardson
RW-A Rodney White

2001-02 UD Ultimate Collection Ultimate Buybacks

"Too uncommon to price."

MT
Complete Set (14):
Common Player:
Courtney Alexander
Larry Bird
Kobe Bryant
Julius Erving
Kevin Garnett
Larry Hughes
Magic Johnson
Michael Jordan
Jason Kidd
Kenyon Martin
Lamar Odom
Paul Pierce
Wally Szczerbiak
Antoine Walker

2001-02 UD Ultimate Collection Ultimate Signatures

MT
Common Player: 30.00
Inserted 1:4
LB-A Larry Bird 300.00
KW-A Kwame Brown 60.00
KB-A Kobe Bryant 250.00
TC-A Tyson Chandler 50.00
EC-A Eddy Curry 50.00
DR-A Julius Erving 200.00
KG-A Kevin Garnett 100.00
EG-A Eddie Griffin 60.00
JJ-A Joe Johnson 40.00
MG-A Magic Johnson 150.00
MJ-A Michael Jordan 1000.
JK-A Jason Kidd 60.00
DM-A Darius Miles 80.00
JR-A Jason Richardson 100.00
RW-A Rodney White 30.00

2002 Upper Deck Collectors Club

MT
Complete Set (20): 25.00
Common Player: 1.00
NBA1 Kobe Bryant 3.00
NBA2 Allen Iverson 2.00
NBA3 Vince Carter 2.00
NBA4 Jason Kidd 1.00
NBA5 Tracy McGrady 1.00
NBA6 Pau Gasol 1.00
NBA7 Kevin Garnett 1.00
NBA8 Steve Francis 1.00
NBA9 Chris Webber 1.00
NBA10 Ray Allen 1.00
NBA11 Kwame Brown 1.00
NBA12 Paul Pierce 1.00
NBA13 Stephon Marbury 1.00
NBA14 Tim Duncan 1.00
NBA15 Shaquille O'Neal 2.00
NBA16 Jerry Stackhouse 1.00
NBA17 Rashard Lewis 1.00
NBA18 Darius Miles 1.00
NBA19 Jamaal Tinsley 1.00
NBA20 Michael Jordan 5.00

1971-72 Warriors Team Issue

The 13-card, 10" x 8-1/8" set features black and white posed player photos on the right side of the card with a headshot portrait in the upper left quadrant. The Warriors logo appears in the lower left corner. The backs are blank and unnumbered.

NM
Complete Set (13): 45.00
Complete Player: 4.00
Odis Allison 4.00
Al Attles 8.00
Jim Barnett 5.00
Vic Bartolome 4.00
Joe Ellis 5.00
Nick Jones 4.00
Clyde Lee 5.00
Jeff Mullins 8.00
Bob Portman 4.00
Cazzie Russell 10.00
Nate Thurmond 12.00
Bill Turner 4.00
Ron (Fritz) Williams 5.00

1988-89 Warriors Smokey

The four-card, 5" x 8" set features color action photos on the card fronts with a safety cartoon on the back. The cards are unnumbered and were sponsored by the California Department of Forestry and Fire Protection and the Bureau of Land Management.

MT
Complete Set (4): 50.00
Common Player: 3.00
1 Winston Garland 4.00
2 Chris Mullin 35.00
3 Ralph Sampson 10.00
4 Larry Smith 5.00

1993-94 Warriors Topps/Safeway

The 16-card, standard-size set was produced by Topps and issued by Safeway grocery stores in the Bay Area in four perforated five-card strips - the fifth card being a coupon card. The cards are numbered with the "GS" prefix and parallel, in design, the 1993-94 Topps Basketball release.

MT
Complete Set (16): 10.00
Common Player: .25
1 Chris Mullin 1.00
2 Byron Houston .25
3 Chris Gatling .25
4 Don Nelson CO .40
5 Nate Thurmond LEGEND 1.00
6 Chris Webber 6.00
7 Latrell Sprewell 2.00
8 Jeff Grayer .25
9 Al Attles LEGEND .40
10 Tim Hardaway 1.50
11 Jud Buechler .25
12 Victor Alexander .25
13 Keith Jennings .25
14 Sarunas Marciulionis .25
15 Billy Owens .40
16 Avery Johnson .75

1994-95 Warriors Topps/Safeway

Topps produced this 12-card set which came in five card strips measuring 12-1/2" x 3-1/2". The perforated strips had four cards and a coupon for either Kellogg's Pop-Tarts Minis or Safeway film developing. The cards have the same design as the 1994-95 Topps set. The sheets were distributed at California Safeway stores in 1995. Cards are numbered with a "GS" prefix.

MT
Complete Set (12): 6.00
Common Player: .25
1 Tim Hardaway 1.00
2 Victor Alexander .25
3 Latrell Sprewell (numbered GS13 on back) 1.00
4 Rod Higgins (numbered GS16 on back) .25
5 Chris Mullin 1.00
6 Clifford Rozier .25
7 Chris Gatling .40
8 Keith Jennings .25
9 Rony Seikaly .25
10 Carlos Rogers .40
11 Ricky Pierce (numbered 267 on back) .25
12 Bob Lanier CO 1.00

1995-96 Warriors Topps/Safeway

Topps produced this 12-card set in three 12-1/2" x 3-1/2" perforated sheets. Each sheet had four player cards and one of three Kellogg or Kodak advertising cards. The card design is identical to the 1995-96 Topps set. The sheets were distributed at California Safeway stores in 1996. Cards are numbered with a "GS" prefix.

MT
Complete Set (15): 6.00
Common Player: .25
1 Chris Gatling .50
2 Donyell Marshall 1.00
3 Tim Hardaway 1.00
4 Rick Adelman CO .50
5 B.J. Armstrong .50
6 Jon Barry .50
7 Latrell Sprewell 1.00
8 Joe Smith 2.00
9 Jerome Kersey .50
10 Rony Seikaly .75
11 Chris Mullin 1.00
12 Clifford Rozier .25
NNO Kellogg's Ad Card 2 .25
NNO Kellogg's Ad Card 1 .25
NNO Kodak Ad Card .25

1997 Wheels Rookie Thunder

The 45-card set features picks from the 1997 NBA Draft. The fronts have a silhouetted image, with a multi-colored background and the player's name in silver underneath. The backs have a partial photo with statistical data and text. The set was paralleled twice in Rising Storm (hobby) and Storm Front (retail) parallels. Insert sets include: Game Ball, Boomers, Lights Out, Double Trouble, Shooting Stars along with Stroke Autographs.

MT
Complete Set (45): 15.00
Common Player: .10
Rising Storms: 4x-8x
Storm Fronts: 4x-8x
1 Tim Duncan 2.50
2 Keith Van Horn 1.00
3 Chauncey Billups .75
4 Antonio Daniels .75
5 Tony Battie .75
6 Ron Mercer 1.50
7 Tim Thomas .50
8 Adonal Foyle .20
9 Tracy McGrady 1.00
10 Danny Fortson .40
11 Olivier Saint-Jean .10
12 Austin Croshere .25
13 Derek Anderson 1.00
14 Maurice Taylor .50
15 Kelvin Cato .50
16 Brevin Knight .75
17 Johnny Taylor .10
18 Chris Anstey .10
19 Scot Pollard .10
20 Paul Grant .10
21 Anthony Parker .10
22 Ed Gray .10
23 Bobby Jackson .50
24 John Thomas .10
25 Charles Smith .10
26 Jacque Vaughn .40
27 Keith Booth .10
28 Serge Zwikker .10
29 Charles O'Bannon .10
30 Bubba Wells .10
31 Kebu Stewart .10
32 James Collins .10
33 Eddie Elisma .10
34 Ron Mercer (Take Two) .40
35 Derek Anderson (Take Two) .25
36 Scot Pollard (Take Two) .10
37 Jacque Vaughn (Take Two) .25
38 Bobby Jackson (Take Two) .40
39 John Thomas (Take Two) .10
40 Chauncey Billups (Young Guns) .10
41 Ron Mercer (Young Guns) .25
42 Tim Thomas (Young Guns) .20
43 Tracy McGrady (Young Guns) .20
44 Maurice Taylor (Young Guns) .20
45 Checklist .10

1997 Wheels Rookie Thunder Rising Storm/Storm Front

Rising Storm was the hobby parallel, while Storm Front was the retail parallel to Wheels Rookie Thunder. Each set contained all 45 cards in the base set and was seeded one per 12 packs.

MT
Rising Storm Cards: 4x-8x
Inserted 1:12 Hobby
Storm Front Cards: 4x-8x
Inserted 1:12 Retail

1997 Wheels Rookie Thunder Boomers

A 10-card set that highlights 10 draft picks from 1997. Inserted at 1:28, the background on the front is a red flame with a player image in the foreground. The backs have another image, and are numbered with the prefix "TB".

MT
Complete Set (10): 75.00
Common Player: 4.00
1 Tim Duncan 25.00

2	Tony Battie	8.00
3	Tracy McGrady	10.00
4	Danny Fortson	8.00
5	Maurice Taylor	8.00
6	Serge Zwikker	4.00
7	Scot Pollard	4.00
8	Charles O'Bannon	4.00
9	Adonal Foyle	4.00
10	Keith Van Horn	10.00

1997 Wheels Rookie Thunder Double Trouble

A six-card set, the cards feature rookies from the 1997 draft. The cards are two-sided featuring embossed player images, with silver foil and micro-etching. The cards are inserted at 1:42, and numbered with the prefix "DT".

		MT
Complete Set (6):		60.00
Common Player:		6.00
1	Tim Duncan, Keith Van Horn	12.00
2	Chauncey Billups, Jacque Vaughn	8.00
3	Tracy McGrady, Ron Mercer	15.00
4	Bobby Jackson, Brevin Knight	8.00
5	Tim Duncan, Tony Battie	18.00
6	Danny Fortson, Tim Thomas	6.00

1997 Wheels Rookie Thunder Game Ball

The highlight of this six-card set is the official basketball leather embedded in the background of a player image. The rest of the front is bordered in red. The backs have text on the player, and are numbered with the prefix "T". Insertion rate is 1:216.

		MT
Complete Set (10):		500.00
Common Player:		20.00
1	Tim Duncan	120.00
2	Keith Van Horn	60.00
3	Chauncey Billups	50.00
4	Antonio Daniels	40.00
5	Tony Battie	50.00
6	Ron Mercer	70.00
7	Tim Thomas	40.00
8	Adonal Foyle	20.00
9	Tracy McGrady	50.00
10	Danny Fortson	40.00

1997 Wheels Rookie Thunder Lights Out

This five-card set of rookies uses black light ink to glow in the dark. The fronts have two player images, with one in color. The cards were inserted at 1:96, and are numbered with the prefix "L".

		MT
Complete Set (5):		100.00
Common Player:		12.00
1	Chauncey Billups	18.00
2	Keith Van Horn	15.00
3	Tim Duncan	40.00
4	Ron Mercer	20.00
5	Antonio Daniels	12.00

1997 Wheels Rookie Thunder Shooting Stars

A 10-card set that highlights the rookies from the 1997-98 season. Numbered with the prefix "SS", the set was inserted at a rate of 1:11. The fronts have a color action shot, with a space background. The back says "Shooting Stars" across the top, followed by text.

		MT
Complete Set (9):		50.00
Common Player:		2.50
1	Chauncey Billups	5.00
2	Tracy McGrady	6.00
3	Brevin Knight	5.00
4	Austin Croshere	2.50
5	Derek Anderson	5.00
6	Jacque Vaughn	4.00
7	Bobby Jackson	5.00
8	Tim Duncan	15.00
9	Keith Van Horn	6.00
10	Ron Mercer	10.00

1991 Wild Card Promos

These two cards were produced to preview Wild Card's 1991-92 basketball set. Each color action photo on the front is framed in black, with the various denominations in the border. The back is numbered with a "P" prefix, and includes a close-up shot of the player, plus statistics and biographical information. Two versions of each card were made - a random insert in Wild Card football packs, or a 1991 San Francisco Sports Card Expo version. The card show version has a San Francisco Sports Expo logo on the front; the insert card does not. The inserts are scarcer than the show cards.

		MT
Complete Set (2):		10.00
Common Player:		3.00
1	Larry Johnson (UNLV)	6.00
2	Kenny Anderson (Georgia Tech)	3.00

1991 Wild Card

This set features the top selections in the 1991 NBA draft. Subtitled "Wild Card Collegiate Premier Edition," the set is an officially-licensed Collegiate product; that logo is on the front of the cards. The backs have a color photo and the player's career accomplishments. The Wild Card concept involves the six denominations (5, 10, 20, 50, 100 or 1,000) which may appear on any one card. Collectors could send to the Wild Card Center any combination of the denominations and trade for cards of equal value. Approximately one Wild Card was inserted into every seven foil packs. Five Surprise cards were also produced and could be sent to Wild card for two cards - the Surprise card and a bonus card from the 1992 draft. Five prototype Surprise cards (Ellis, Keefe, Horry, Stith and Laettner) were also produced.

		MT
Complete Set (120):		7.00
Common Player:		.05
5/10/20/50/100 Stripes:		.20x-.40x
1000 Stripes: .10x-.30x		
1	Larry Johnson	.50
2	LeRon Ellis	.05
3	Alvaro Teheran	.05
4	Eric Murdock	.25
5a	Surprise Card #1	.25
5b	(Dikembe Mutombo)	.75
6	Anthony Avent	.10
7	Isiah Thomas	.20
8	Abdul Shamsid-Deen	.05
9	Linton Townes	.05
10	Joe Wylie	.05
11	Cozell McQueen	.05
12	David Benoit	.25
13	Chris Mullin	.15
14	Dale Davis	.35
15	Patrick Ewing	.25
16	Greg Anthony	.15
17	Robert Pack	.35
18	Phil Zevenbergen	.05
19	Rick Fox	.15
20	Chris Corchiani	.05
21	Elliott Perry	.30
22	Kevin Brooks	.05
23	Mark Macon	.10
24	Larry Johnson	1.50
25	George Ackles	.05
26a	Surprise Card #5	.25
26b	(Christian Laettner)	.25
27	Andy Fields	.05
28	Kevin Lynch	.05
29	Graylin Warner	.05
30	James Bullock	.05
31	Steve Bucknall	.05
32	Carl Thomas	.05
33	Doug Overton	.05
34	Brian Shorter	.05
35	Chad Gallagher	.05
36	Antonio Davis	.10
37	Sean Green	.05
38	Randy Brown	.05
39	Richard Dumas	.10
40	Terrell Brandon	.20
41	Marty Embry	.05
42	Ronald Coleman	.05
43	King Rice	.05
44	Perry Carter	.05
45	Andrew Gaze	.05
46a	Surprise Card #2	.25
46b	(Billy Owens)	.50
47a	Surprise Card #3	.25
47b	(Stacey Augmon)	.40
48	Jimmy Oliver	.05
49	Treg Lee	.05
50	Ricky Winslow	.05
51	Danny Vranes	.05
52	Jay Murphy	.05
53	Adrian Dantley	.05
54	Joe Arlauckas	.05
55	Moses Scurry	.05
56	Andy Toolson	.05
57	Ramon Rivas	.05
58	Charles Davis	.05
59	Butch Wade	.05
60	John Pinone	.05
61	Bill Wennington	.05
62	Walter Berry	.05
63	Terry Dozier	.05
64	Mitchell Anderson	.05
65	Pace Mannion	.05
66	Pete Myers	.05
67	Eddie Lee Wilkins	.05
68	Mark Hughes	.05
69	Darryl Dawkins	.10
70	Jay Vincent	.05
71	Douglas Lee	.05
72	Russ Schoene	.05
73	Tim Kempton	.05
74	Earl Cureton	.05
75	Terence Stansbury	.05
76	Frank Kornet	.05
77	Robert McAdoo	.05
78	Haywoode Workman	.05
79	Vinny Del Negro	.05
80	Harold Pressley	.05
81	Robert Smith	.05
82	Adrian Caldwell	.05
83	Scottie Pippen	.25
84	John Stockton	.20
85	Elwayne Campbell	.05
86	Chris Gatling	.20
87	Cedric Henderson	.05
88	Mike Iuzzolino	.05
89	Fennis Dembo	.05
90	Darnell Valentine	.05
91	Mike Brooks	.05
92	Marty Conlon	.05
93	Lamont Strothers	.05
94	Donald Hodge	.05
95	Pete Chilcutt	.05
96	Kenny Anderson	.75
97	Ian Lockhart	.05
98a	Surprise Card #4	.25
98b	(Steve Smith)	.50
99	Larry Lawrence	.05
100	Jerome Mincy	.05
101	Ben Coleman	.05
102	Tom Copa	.05
103	Demetrius Calip	.05
104	Myron Brown	.05
105	Derrick Pope	.05
106	Kelvin Upshaw	.05
107	Andrew Moten	.05
108	Terry Tyler	.05
109	Kevin Magee	.05
110	Tharon Mayes	.05
111	Perry McDonald	.05
112	Jose Ortiz	.05
113	Rick Mahorn	.05
114	David Butler	.05
115	Carl Herrera	.05
116	Darrell Mickens	.05
117	Stephen Bardo	.05
118	Checklist #1	.05
119	Checklist #2	.05
120	Checklist #3	.05
1P	LaPhonso Ellis	1.00
2P	Adam Keefe	.25
3P	Robert Horry	.40
4P	Bryant Stith	.25
5P	Christian Laettner (#5)	3.00
6P	Malik Seal	.20
5	Dikembe Mutombo (#1)	1.00
46	Billy Owens (#2)	1.00
47	Stacey Augmon (#3)	.50
98	Steve Smith (#4)	.75

1991 Wild Card Red Hot Rookies

These special glossy subset cards were random inserts in foil packs. The fronts have color photos with a black border and a "Red Hot Rookies" logo in the corner. Card backs also have a photo and the player's career stats.

		MT
Complete Set (10):		30.00
Common Player:		.50
5/10/20/50/100 Stripes: .20x-.40x		
1000 Stripes: .10x-.30x		
1	Dikembe Mutombo	5.00
2	Larry Johnson	10.00
3	Steve Smith	2.00
4	Billy Owens	2.00
5	Mark Macon	.50
6	Stacey Augmon	3.00
7	Victor Alexander	.50
8	Mike Iuzzolino	.50
9	Rick Fox	1.00
10	Terrell Brandon	1.00

1991 Wild Card Redemption Promos

These cards, numbered on the back with a "P" prefix, feature a color action photo on the front, framed by a white border. The denomination numbers are included within the upper and right borders of the card. The player's name is at the bottom, while his collegiate school's nickname appears in the left border. His school's team logo is also on the front. The card back has a mug shot of the player, along with biographical and statistical information. These cards were available as a mail-in offer from Wild Card; a mail-in card, good for two of these prototype redemption cards and a replacement card, was included with the 1991-92 Wild Card set.

		MT
Complete Set (6):		2.00
Common Player:		.10
1	LaPhonso Ellis (Notre Dame)	.75
2	Adam Keefe (Stanford)	.10
3	Robert Horry (Alabama)	.75
4	Bryant Stith (Virginia)	.25
5	Christian Laettner (Duke)	1.00
6	Malik Sealy (St. John's)	.10

1997-98 Mexico Wonder Snacks

	MT
Complete Set (40):	75.00
Common Player:	1.00
Dikembe Mutombo	1.00
Mookie Blaylock	1.00
Dino Radja	1.00
Glen Rice	2.00
Toni Kukoc	2.00
Luc Longley	1.00
Terrell Brandon	1.00
A.C. Green	1.00
Antonio McDyess	3.00
Otis Thorpe	1.00
Joe Dumars	2.00
Chris Mullin	2.00
Hakeem Olajuwon	3.00
Charles Barkley	3.00
Rik Smits	1.00
Brent Barry	1.00
Eddie Jones	4.00
Elden Campbell	1.00
Alonzo Mourning	2.00
Tim Hardaway	2.00
Vin Baker	1.00
Tom Gugliotta	1.00
Kevin Garnett	10.00
Jayson Williams	1.00
Allan Houston	1.00
Anfernee Hardaway	5.00
Jerry Stackhouse	2.00
Allen Iverson	8.00
Cedric Ceballos	1.00
Arvydas Sabonis	1.00
Mitch Richmond	2.00
David Robinson	3.00
Avery Johnson	1.00
Gary Payton	3.00
Shawn Kemp	3.00
Damon Stoudamire	2.00
Marcus Camby	2.00
Karl Malone	3.00
Shareef Abdur-Rahim	4.00
Chris Webber	5.00

COLLEGE

1992 ACC Tournament Champs

This 40-card set features 36 ACC Championship teams from 1954 to 1989 and was limited to 10,000 sets. It arrived in a box with the set number indicated on a sequentially numbered gold card of authenticity. Each set also included a bonus card, which was a parallel of the regular-issue cards but carried a gold foil ACC seal. The card fronts picture a team photo during the season and the backs include a synopsis of the championship game, box score and listing of the players and coaches as well as the team's MVP.

		MT
Complete Set (40):		23.00
Common Player:		.25
1	'54 NC State Wolfpack	.50
2	'55 NC State Wolfpack	.25
3	'56 NC State Wolfpack	.25
4	'57 UNC Tar Heels	.25
5	'58 Maryland Terrapins	.25
6	'59 NC State Wolfpack	.25
7	'60 Duke Blue Devils	.25
8	'61 Wake Forest Demon Deacons (Bill Packer)	.50
9	'62 Wake Forest Demon Deacons (Bill Packer)	.50
10	'63 Duke Blue Devils	.25
11	'64 Duke Blue Devils	.25
12	'65 NC State Wolfpack	.25
13	'66 Duke Blue Devils	.25
14	'67 UNC Tar Heels	.25
15	'68 UNC Tar Heels	.25
16	'69 UNC Tar Heels	.25
17	'70 NC State Wolfpack	.25
18	'71 SC Gamecocks	.25
19	'72 UNC Tar Heels	.25
20	'73 NC State Wolfpack	.50
21	'74 NC State Wolfpack	1.00
22	'75 UNC Tar Heels	.25
23	'76 Virginia Cavaliers	.25
24	'77 UNC Tar Heels	.25
25	'78 Duke Blue Devils	.25
26	'79 UNC Tar Heels	.25
27	'80 Duke Blue Devils	.25
28	'81 UNC Tar Heels	.50
29	'82 UNC Tar Heels (Michael Jordan)	12.00
30	'83 NC State Wolfpack (Jim Valvano)	1.00
31	'84 Maryland Terrapins (Len Bias)	4.00
32	'85 Georgia Tech Yellow Jackets (Mark Price)	1.00
33	'86 Duke Blue Devils	1.00
34	'87 NC State Wolfpack	.25
35	'88 Duke Blue Devils	1.00
36	'89 UNC Tar Heels	.50
xx	'91 FSU Joins ACC	.25
xx	Original ACC Seal	.25
xx	Revised ACC Seal (With Florida State)	.25
xx	Certificate of Authenticity	.25

1994-95 Air Force

This standard sized, 16-card set was issued on a large perforated sheet and was sponsored by the USDA Forest Service and Colorado State Forest Service. The fronts contain the player's photo surrounded by a gray border, while the backs have a fire prevention cartoon starring Smokey.

		MT
Complete Set (16):		10.00
Common Player:		.50
1	The Air Force Falcon (Performing Mascot)	.50
2	The Bird (Mascot)	.50
3	The Chapel	.50
4	The Color Guard	.50
5	Commander-in-Chief's Trophy	.50
6	Football (Fisher DeBerry CO)	1.00
7	Doolittle Hall	.50
8	Football (Dee Dowis)	1.00
9	Basketball (Ray Dudley)	.75
10	Falcon Stadium	.50
11	Graduation	.50
12	Football (Chad Hennings)	2.00
14	Basketball (Reggie Minton CO)	.75
15	The Parachute Team	.50
16	Tennis (Laura Simmons)	.75

1992-93 Alabama-Birmingham

This 16-card set was issued on two eight-card perforated sheets. The fronts feature a color shot of the player or coach with a black border and the team name running up the left side in yellow. Backs have a black and white photo with biographical information below it and a card number "of 16" across the bottom.

		MT
Complete Set (16):		10.00
Common Player:		.50
1	Reginald Allen	.50
2	Jeremy Bearden	.50
3	Carlos Browning	.50
4	Willie Chapman	.50
5	Patrick Craft	.50
6	Travis Harper	.50
7	Frank Haywood	.50
8	Nigel Hodges	.50
9	Corey Jackson	.50
10	Stanley Jackson	2.00
11	Carter Long	.50
12	Robert Shannon	1.00
13	Clarence Thrash	.50
14	George Wilkerson	.50
15	Gene Bartow CO	2.00
16	Blazer Seniors (Willie Chapman, Stanley Jackson, George Wilkerson)	1.00

1993-94 Alabama-Birmingham

The white-bordered set contains 14 standard sized cards with color action shots and some posed player photos. The team name is printed across the top in yellow and green lettering, with the white backs including the player's number, biographical information and the card number in the upper right corner.

		MT
Complete Set (14):		7.00
Common Player:		.50
1	Gene Bartow CO	2.00
2	Frank Haywood	.50
3	Reginald Allen	.50
4	Carlos Browning	.50
5	George Wilkerson	.50
6	Clarence Thrash	.50
7	Robert Shannon	1.00
8	Carter Long	.50
9	Corey Jackson	.50
10	Jeremy Bearden	.50
11	Chad Jones	.50
12	Travis Harper	.50
13	Blazer Seniors (Reginald Allen, Frank Haywood, Carter Long, Robert Shannon, Clarence Thrash, George Wilkerson)	.75
14	Checklist	.50

1980-81 Arizona

This standard-sized set was sponsored by Golden Eagle Distributors and the Tucson Police Department. The 19-card set has color fronts with posed photos. Three sides of the cards are full bleed with the bottom containing a white border with the player's name. The backs have biographical information, a tip on basketball and a safety message. Cards of Greg Cook and David Mosebar were pulled before distribution and are very hard to find.

		NM
Complete Set (19):		150.00
Common Player:		3.00
1	John Belobraydic	3.00
2	Russell Brown	3.00
3	Jeff Collins	3.00
4	Greg Cook SP	80.00
5	Ron Davis	3.00
6	Robbie Dosty	3.00
7	Mike Frink ACO	3.00
8	Len Gordy ACO	4.00
9	Mike Green ACO	3.00
10	Jack Magno	3.00
11	Donald Mellon	3.00
12	Charles Miller	3.00
13	David Mosebar SP	60.00
14	Frank Smith	3.00
15	John Smith	3.00
16	Fred Snowden CO	4.00
17	Harvey Thompson	3.00
18	Ernie Valenzuela	3.00
19	Ricky Walker	4.00

1981-82 Arizona

This 20-card set features players from the Arizona basketball team on cards measuring 2-5/8" x 3-5/8". The fronts are in color with a posed photo of the player and a thin white strip across the bottom that includes the player's name and number. The card backs give bio information, discusses a basketball tip and gives a safety tip. These cards are unnumbered and therefore appear in alphabetical order.

		MT
Complete Sets (20):		40.00
Commons Player:		2.50
1	Ken Atkins CO	2.50
2	John Belobraydic - 55	2.50
3	Brock Brunkhorst - 10	2.50
4	Jeff Collins - 24	2.50
5	Greg Cook - 22	4.00
6	Len Gordy CO	3.00
7	Gary Heintz CO	2.50
8	Keith Jackson - 21	2.50
9	Mark Jung - 33	2.50
10	Jack Magno - 41	2.50
11	Donald Mellow - 35	2.50
12	Charles Miller - 52	2.50
13	Pete Murphy - 15	2.50
14	Kevin Roundfield - 44 (Misspelled Ronndfield)	2.50
15	Frank Smith - 31	2.50
16	Fred Snowden CO	3.00
17	Ernest Taylor-Harris - 32	2.50
18	Harvey Thompson - 34	2.50
19	John Vlahogeorge - 14	2.50
20	Ricky Walker - 12	3.00

1983-84 Arizona

This 18-card set measures 2-1/4" x 3-3/4" and was sponsored by the Tucson Police and Golden Eagle Distributors. The fronts feature full bleed color photos on three sides with the bottom containing the player's name and number in a white strip. The cards are unnumbered and listed below in alphabetical order. In addition, the Beard and Haskin cards feature the 1983-84 basketball schedule on the front, which is different from the rest of the set.

		MT
Complete Set (18):		28.00
Common Player:		1.50
1	Van Beard - 54	1.50
2	Ricky Byrdsong ACO	3.50
3	Brock Brunkhorst - 10	1.50
4	Ken Burmeister ACO	1.50
5	Troy Cooke - 20	1.50
6	Ken Ensor - 22	1.50
7	David Haskin - 24	1.50
8	Keith Jackson - 21	1.50
9	Steve Kerr - 25	10.00
10	Lute Olson CO	9.00
11	Eddie Smith - 14	1.50
12	Michael Tait - 11	1.50
13	Greg Taylor - 52	1.50
14	Harvey Thompson - 34	1.50
15	Scott Thompson ACO	1.50
16	Pete Williams - 32	2.00
17	Andy Woodtli - 44	1.50
18	The Brain Trust (Scott Thompson ACO, Lute Olson CO, Ricky Byrdsong ACO, Ken Burmeister ACO)	4.00

1984-85 Arizona

The Tucson Police and Golden Eagle Distributors sponsored this 16-card set that measures 2-1/4" x 3-3/4". The fronts feature a full bleed photo on three sides, with a white strip across the bottom containing the player's name and uniform number. The backs are black and white with bio information, rules of the game and a safety tip.

		MT
Complete Set (16):		20.00
Common Player:		1.25
1	Brock Brunkhorst - 10	1.25
2	Ken Burmeister ACO	1.25
3	Ricky Byrdsong ACO	3.00
4	John Edgar - 50	1.25
5	Bruce Fraser - 22	1.25
6	David Haskin - 24	1.25
7	Keith Jackson - 21	1.25
8	Rolf Jacobs - 13	1.25
9	Steve Kerr - 25	6.00
10	Craig McMillan - 20	1.25
11	Lute Olson CO	6.00
12	Eddie Smith - 14	1.25
13	Morgan Taylor - 34	1.25
14	Scott Thompson CO	1.25
15	Joe Turner - 33	1.25
16	Pete Williams - 32	1.25

1985-86 Arizona

This 14-card set was sponsored by the Tucson Police and Golden Eagle Distributors. The cards measure 2-1/4" x 3-3/4" and contain a full bleed photo on three sides with a white strip across the bottom containing the player's name and number. The set is highlighted by its inclusion of Sean Elliot as well as baseball star Kenny Lofton.

LUTE OLSON—HEAD COACH

		MT
Complete Set (14):		50.00
Common Player:		1.00
1	Anthony Cook - 00	2.00
2	Eric Cooper - 21	1.00
3	Brian David - 34	1.00
4	John Edgar - 50	1.00
5	Sean Elliott - 32	20.00
6	Bruce Fraser - 22	1.00
7	David Haskin - 24	1.00
8	Rolf Jacobs - 13	1.00
9	Steve Kerr - 25	4.00
10	Kenny Lofton - 11	30.00
11	Craig McMillan - 20	1.00
12	Lute Olson CO	4.00
13	Joe Turner - 33	1.00
14	Bruce Wheatley - 45	1.00

1986-87 Arizona

This 12-card set measures 2-1/4" x 3-3/4" and was sponsored by the Tucson Police and Golden Eagle Distributors. The fronts contain a full bleed photos for three sides with a white strip across the bottom containing the player's name, number and a Pac 10 logo (this was the first year the logo appeared on these cards). The backs featured an anti-crime or public service message in addition to bio information. This set also includes Sean Elliot and baseball star Kenny Lofton.

		MT
Complete Set (12):		40.00
Common Player:		1.00
1	Jud Buechler - 33	5.00
2	Anthony Cook - 00	1.50
3	Brian David - 34	1.00
4	Sean Elliott - 32	14.00
5	Bruce Fraser - 22	1.00
6	Steve Kerr - 25	4.00
7	Kenny Lofton - 11	20.00
8	Harvey Mason - 44	1.00
9	Craig McMillan - 20	1.00
10	Lute Olson CO	4.00
11	Tom Tolbert - 31	4.00
12	Joe Turner - 33	1.00

1987-88 Arizona

This 14-card set features 14 cards and measures 2-1/4" x 3-3/4". It was sponsored by the Tucson Police and Golden Eagle Distributors. Card fronts feature a posed photo of the player and a white strip across the bottom with the player's name and number. The set includes NBA players Jud Buechler, Sean Elliot, Steve Kerr and Sean Rooks as well as baseball star Kenny Lofton.

		MT
Complete Set (14):		30.00
Common Player:		1.00
1	Jud Buechler - 35	3.00
2	Anthony Cook - 00	1.50
3	Brian David - 34	1.00
4	Sean Elliott - 32	10.00
5	Mark Georgeson - 34	1.00
6	Steve Kerr - 25	3.50
7	Kenny Lofton - 11	16.00
8	Harvey Mason - 44	1.00
9	Craig McMillan - 20	1.00
10	Matt Muehlebach - 44	1.50
11	Lute Olson CO	5.00
12	Sean Rooks - 23	4.00
13	Tom Tolbert - 23	3.00
14	Joe Turner - 33	1.00

1988-89 Arizona

Although this 13-card set was sponsored by the Tucson Police and Golden Eagle Distributors, some sets have been found without the Golden Eagle logo on the back. The cards feature a full bleed posed photo on the front for three sides with a white strip across the bottom containing the player's name and number. The set includes NBA players Jud Buechler, Sean Elliott (misspelled Elliot), and Sean Rooks as well as baseball star Kenny Lofton.

		MT
Complete Set (13):		25.00
Commons Player:		1.00
1	Jud Buechler - 35	2.50
2	Anthony Cook - 00	1.50
3	Ron Curry - 33	1.00
4	Brian David - 34	1.00
5	Sean Elliott - 32 UER (Misspelled Elliot)	8.00
6	Mark Georgeson - 45	1.00
7	Kenny Lofton - 11	10.00
8	Harvey Mason - 44	1.00
9	Matt Muehlebach - 24	1.50
10	Lute Olson CO	4.00
11	Matt Othick - 12	1.50
12	Sean Rooks - 42	2.50
13	Wayne Womack - 30	1.50

1989-90 Arizona

This 14-card set was cosponsored by the Tucson Police and Golden Eagle Distributors and measures 2-1/4" x 3-3/4". Card fronts feature a full bleed design on three sides with the bottom containing a white border that includes the player's name and uniform number. The cards are unnumbered and checklisted in alphabetical order. Key cards include NBA players Chris Mills, Sean Rooks and Brian Williams.

	MT
Complete Set (14):	25.00
Common Player:	1.00
Jud Buechler - 35	2.50
Brian David - 34	1.00
Kevin Flanagan - 51	1.00
Deron Johnson - 23	1.00
Harvey Mason - 44	1.00
Chris Mills - 42	9.00
Matt Muehlebach - 24	1.50
Lute Olson CO	4.00
Matt Othick - 12	1.50
Sean Rooks - 45	2.50
Casey Schmidt - 11	1.00
Ed Stokes - 41	1.50
Brian Williams - 21	8.00
Wayne Womack - 30	1.50

1990-91 Arizona

This 13-card set measures 2-1/4" x 3-5/8" and was sponsored by the Tucson Police and Golden Eagle Distributors. The fronts feature borderless posed photos that are full bleed on three sides with a white strip across the bottom containing the player's name and uniform number. The cards are unnumbered and listed in alphabetical order. Key cards include Chris Mills, Sean Rooks and Brian Williams.

	MT
Complete Set (13):	28.00
Common Player:	1.00
Tony Clark	1.00
Kevin Flanagan	1.00
Deron Johnson	1.00
Chris Mills	8.00
Matt Muehlebach	1.25
Lute Olson CO	2.00
Matt Othick	1.00
Khalid Reeves	5.00
Sean Rooks	2.00
Casey Schmidt	1.00
Ed Stokes	1.25
Brian Williams	5.00
Wayne Womack	1.25

1990-91 Arizona Collegiate Collection

The set, produced by the Collegiate Collection, contains 125 cards. The fronts have black-and-white and color photos of the player, while the back has statistical and biographical information.

		MT
Complete Set (125):		14.00
Common Player:		.05
1	Steve Kerr	.50
2	Sean Elliott	.75
3	Vance Johnson	.25
4	Lute Olson CO	.50
5	Chris Singleton	.25
6	Robert Gamez	.75
7	Ricky Hunley	.15
8	Terry Francona	.10
9	Chuck Cecil	.30
10	Craig Lefferts	.15
11	Warren Rustand	.05
12	Tommy Tunnicliffe	.05
13	Steve Strong	.05
14	T. Bell	.10
15	Jerry Kindall CO	.10
16	Kevin Long	.05
17	Fred Snowden CO	.05
18	Anthony Smith	.30
19	Laurie Brunet	.05
20	Wes Clements	.05
21	Larry Demic	.10
22	Peter Evans	.05
23	Gilbert Heredia	.10
24	Chuck Cecil	.30
25	Todd Trafton	.10
26	Alan Durden	.05
27	Eric Meeks	.05
28	Steve Kerr	.50
29	Rosie Wegrich	.05
30	Danny Lockett	.10
31	Dana Wells	.05
32	Katrena Johnson	.05
33	Anthony Cook	.10
34	Anita Moss	.05
35	David Adams	.05
36	Eddie Leon	.10
37	Vance Johnson	.25
38	Sean Elliott	1.00
39	Alan Zinter	.15
40	Russell Brown	.05
41	Joe Magrane	.25
42	Derek Hill	.15
43	Hubie Oliver	.10
44	Scott Geyer	.05
45	Bill Wright	.05
46	Max Zendejas	.10
47	Jim Young CO	.10
48	Mark Arneson	.10
49	Doug Pfaff	.05
50	George DiCarlo	.05
51	Brad Henke	.05
52	Bruce Hill	.15
53	Ron Hassey	.15
54	Jim Gault	.05
55	Byron Evans	.25
56	Hoan Hansen	.05
57	Pete Williams	.05
58	Frank Busch	.05
59	David Wood	.10
60	Dave Murray	.05
61	Carla Garrett	.05
62	Ivan Lesnik	.05
63	J.T. Snow	.50
64	Al Fleming	.05
65	Don Lee	.05
66	Dave Towne	.05
67	Brad Anderson	.05
68	Chuck Cecil	.30
69	Mike Dawson	.10
70	Ed Vosberg	.10
71	Joe Tofflemire	.10
72	Rick LaRose	.05
73	Larry Silveria	.05
74	Lamonte Hunley	.05
75	June Olkowski	.05
76	Dave Stegman	.10
77	Melissa McLinden	.05
78	Chris Johnson	.05
79	Kenny Lofton	3.00
80	Ken Erickson	.05
81	Martina Koch	.05
82	Joel Estes	.05
83	Diane Johnson	.05
84	Jon Abbott	.05
85	Sean Elliott	.75
86	Thom Hunt	.05
87	Jeff Kiewel	.05
88	Morris Udall	.30
89	Becky Bell	.05
90	Ruben Rodriguez	.10
91	Randy Robbins	.05
92	Eddie Smith	.05
93	Steve Kerr	.50
94	Dwight Taylor	.05
95	Mike Candrea	.05
96	Vance Johnson	.25
97	Bob Elliott	.05
98	Glenn Parker	.15
99	Joe Nehls	.05
100	Director Card 1-99	.05
101	Derek Huff	.05
102	Mark Roby	.05
103	Lute Olson CO	.50
104	Art Luppino	.05
105	Kevin Long	.05
106	Bob Elliott	.05
107	George Young	.05
108	Don Pooley	.05
109	Bryon Evans	.40
110	Sean Elliott	1.00
111	Kim Haddow	.05
112	David Adams	.05
113	Bobby Thompson	.10
114	Brad Anderson	.05
115	Eddie Wilson	.05
116	Dan Pohl	.30
117	Joe Hernandez	.05
118	J.F. (Pop) McKale	.05
119	Gayle Hopkins	.10
120	Carl Cooper	.05
121	Kenny Lofton	3.00
122	Robert Lee Thompson	.10
123	Robert Ruman	.05
124	Meg Ritchie	.05
125	John Byrd Salmon	.10

1987-88 Arizona State

The 22-card set was sponsored by the Valley of the Sun Kiwanis Club and "Our Quest: Their Best", and produced by Sports Marketing Inc. The cards feature Arizona State athletes from various sports, with a color action photo on the front and player profiles on the back. Various sports represented include: basketball, baseball, swimming and tennis, among others.

		MT
Complete Set (22):		20.00
Common Player:		1.00
1	Mark Becker	1.00
2	Peter Boden	1.00
3	Jim Brock CO	2.00
4	Mark Carlino	1.00
5	John Cooper	3.00
6	Aaron Cox	2.00
7	Mike Davies	1.00
8	Bob Dombrowski	1.00
9	Karen Fifield	1.00
10	Darryl Harris	1.00
11	Linty Ingram	1.00
12	Gea Johnson	1.00

13 Paul Linne 1.00
14 Randall McDaniel 3.00
15 Shamona Mosley 1.00
16 Anthony Parker 2.00
17 Shawn Patterson 1.00
18 Steve Patterson CO 2.00
19 Doug Sachs 1.00
20 Regina Stahl 1.00
21 Arthur Thomas 1.00
22 Channing Williams 1.00

1982-83 Arkansas

This 16-card set was sponsored by Tom Kamerling's Sports Magazine and measures the standard size. Card fronts feature a black and white posed photo with a red border and Razorbacks logo centered above the photo. The card backs have a 1982-83 schedule, but are unnumbered and listed alphabetically. Key cards include NBA players Joe Kleine, Alvin Robertson and Darrell Walker.

MT
Complete Set (16): 65.00
Common Player: 3.00
Charles Balentine 4.00
Darryl Bedford 3.00
Robert Brannon 3.00
Willie Cutts 3.00
Keenan DeBose 3.00
Casey Kelly 3.00
Robert Kitchen 3.00
Joe Kleine 15.00
Ricky Norton 4.00
Eric Poerschke 3.00
Mike Ratliff 3.00
Alvin Robertson 18.00
John Snively 3.00
Eddie Sutton CO 10.00
Leroy Sutton 3.00
Darrell Walker 15.00

1989-90 Arkansas

This 24-card, standard size set was produced to commemorate the 1989-90 Razorbacks' appearance in the Final Four. The fronts feature the player's name in a diagonal bar in the lower right, with the words "1990 Final Four" in the upper left. The cards are unnumbered and checklisted below in alphabetical order. Key cards include multiple cards of Lee Mayberry and Todd Day.

MT
Complete Set (24): 50.00
Common Player: 1.50
Nolen Richardson CO 5.00
Clyde Fletcher 1.50
Larry Marks 1.50
Mario Credit 1.50
Warren Linn 1.50
Ernie Murry 1.50
Darrell Hawkins 1.50
Cannon Whitby 1.50
Ron Huery 1.50
Lenzie Howell 1.50
Lee Mayberry 5.00
Todd Day 8.00
Arlyn Bowers 1.50
Shawn Davis 1.50
Lee Mayberry 5.00
Lenzie Howell 1.50
Lee Mayberry 5.00
Todd Day 8.00
Nolen Richardson CO 5.00
SWC Classic Champs 1.50
Barnhill Arena 1.50
Todd Day 8.00
Oliver Miller 8.00
Edgar ACO, Nolen Richardson, Anderson ACO 3.00

1991-92 Arkansas Collegiate Collection

This 25-card, standard sized set was produced by Collegiate Collection. The fronts feature either action or posed shots with a black strip across the bottom containing the player's name and a black border. The backs are printed horizontally and printed over a grey Razorback. Cards are generally in numerical order, with the key cards being Todd Day and Lee Mayberry.

MT
Complete Set (25): 30.00
Common Player: 1.00
1 Nolen Richardson CO 5.00
2 Ray Biggers 1.00
3 Ken Biley 1.00
4 Shawn Davis 1.00
5 Todd Day 5.00
6 Clyde Fletcher 1.00
7 Darrell Hawkins 1.50
8 Warren Linn 1.00
9 Elmer Martin 1.00
10 Lee Mayberry 4.00
11 Clint McDaniel 3.00
12 Oliver Miller 5.00
13 Isaiah Morris 2.00
14 Davor Rimac 1.00
15 Robert Shepherd 1.00
16 Roosevelt Wallace 1.50
17 Alfred Warren 1.00
18 Barnhill Arena 1.00
19 Mike Anderson ACO 1.00
20 Brad Dunn ACO 1.00
21 Wayne Stehlik ACO 1.00
22 Volunteer Assistant CO (Nolan Richardson III) 1.50
23 Graduate Assistant CO (Ernie Murry) 1.00
24 Team Photo 2.00
25 Director Card Checklist 1.00

1992-93 Arkansas

This 15-card, standard size set features color action shots bordered on the left or right by a grey strip that has the words "Razorbacks" running down it. The backs are printed on a horizontal format with a head shot of the player, stats and bio information. The cards are numbered on the back, with the key card in the set being the first of Corliss Williamson.

MT
Complete Set (15): 15.00
Common Player: .75
1 Nolen Richardson CO 3.00
2 Dwight Stewart 2.00
3 Ken Biley 1.00
4 Craig Tyson .75
5 Corey Beck 2.50
6 Darrell Hawkins 1.00
7 Scotty Thurman 3.00
8 Warren Linn .75
9 Davor Rimac .75
10 Robert Shepherd .75
11 Roger Crawford .75
12 Corliss Williamson 7.00
13 Elmer Martin .75
14 Clint McDaniel 1.50
15 Ray Biggers .75

1993-94 Arkansas

This 18-card set showcases action shots of the 1993-94 Razorbacks and commemorates the inaugural season of Walton Arena. The photo are surrounded by a red border with the words "Walton Arena Inaugural Season" on the top and "Razorbacks" across the bottom. The back contains another shot of the player and a card number. There was a second printing of this issue, which is identified by the words "1994 NCAA Champs." Key cards include Corliss Williamson and Darnell Robinson.

MT
Complete Arena Set (18): 20.00
Complete Champs Set (18): 15.00
Common Player: .50
1 Corey Beck 2.50
2 Ray Biggers .50
3 Ken Biley .50
4 Roger Crawford .50
5 Alex Dillard .75
6 Elmer Martin .50
7 Clint McDaniel 1.00
8 Nolen Richardson CO 3.00
9 Davor Rimac .50
10 Darnell Robinson 3.00
11 Dwight Stewart 1.00
12 Scotty Thurman 3.00
13 Corliss Williamson 5.00
14 Lee Wilson 1.00
15 Assistant Coaches (Mike Anderson, Brad Dunn, Wayne Stehlik, Nolen Richardson) .50
16 Team Card .75
17 Walton Arena .75
18 Title Card .50

1994-95 Arkansas Tickets

This 18-card ticket set features the 1994-95 Razorbacks and measures 1-1/2" x 5". The ticket is divided into a top portion and perforated tab. The top portion contains a color photo with a 1994 National Champions banner across the picture, as well as the opponent at the bottom of the picture. The back consists of a Coca-Cola and Subway advertisement. The tickets are numbered according to the event, with No. 1 picturing President Bill Clinton congratulating coach Nolen Richardson.

MT
Complete Set (18): 12.00
Common Ticket: .50
1 Nolen Richardson CO (Bill Clinton - Pres.) 3.00
2 John Engskov .50
3 Reggie Merritt .50
4 Nat'l Championship Trophy .50
5 Kareem Reed 3.00
6 Lee Wilson .75
7 Elmer Martin .50
8 Landis Williams .50
9 Nolen Richardson CO 2.00
10 Davor Rimac .50
11 Darnell Robinson 1.00
12 Corey Beck 1.00
13 Corliss Williamson 4.00
14 Scotty Thurman 1.00
15 Dwight Stewart .75
16 Clint McDaniel .75
17 Reggie Garrett .50
18 Alex Dillard .75

1955 Ashland/Aetna Oil

This 96-card set was printed on thin card stock and measures 2-5/8" x 3-3/4". The cards were passed out one at a time at Ashland Oil (Kentucky and West Virginia) and Aetna Oil (Ohio), and arrive in two different versions - with an Ashland or Aetna ad on the back - depending on where they were passed out. The set includes 12 players each from eight different schools, with the Aetna versions appearing more limited as well as lower production of smaller schools. The cards are unnumbered and checklisted below accordingly: Eastern Kentucky 1-12, Kentucky 13-24, Louisville 25-36, Marshall 37-48, Morehead 49-60, Murray St. 61-72, Western Kentucky 73-84 and West Virginia 85-96.

NM
Complete Set (96): 6000.
Common Player (1-36/73-84): 45.00
Common Player (37-60): 60.00
Common Player (61-72): 75.00
Common Player (85-96): 90.00
1 Jack Adams 45.00
2 William Baxter 45.00
3 Jeffrey Brock 45.00
4 Paul Collins 45.00
5 Richard Culbertson 45.00
6 James Floyd 45.00
7 Harold Fraler 45.00
8 George Francis Jr 45.00
9 Paul McBrayer CO 90.00
10 James Mitchell 45.00
11 Ronald Pellegrinon 45.00
12 Guy Strong 45.00
13 Earl Adkins 50.00
14 William Bibb 50.00
15 Jerry Bird 60.00
16 John Brewer 50.00
17 Robert Burrow 60.00
18 Gerry Calvert 50.00
19 William Evans 75.00
20 Phillip Grawemeyer 50.00
21 Ray Mills 50.00
22 Linville Puckett 60.00
23 Gayle Rose 80.00
24 Adolph Rupp CO 475.00
25 William Darrah 45.00
26 Vladimir Gastevich 45.00
27 Allan Glaza 45.00
28 Herbert Harrah 45.00
29 Bernard Hickman CO 100.00
30 Richard Keffer 45.00
31 Gerald Moreman 45.00
32 James Morgan 45.00
33 John Prudhoe 45.00
34 Phillip Rollins 45.00
35 Roscoe Shackelford 45.00
36 Charles Tyra 100.00
37 Robert Ashley 60.00
38 Lewis Burns 60.00
39 Francis Crum 60.00
40 Raymond Frazier 60.00
41 Cam Henderson CO 100.00
42 Joseph Hunnicutt 60.00
43 Clarence Parkins 60.00
44 Jerry Pierson 60.00
45 David Robinson 60.00
46 Paul Underwood 60.00
47 Cebert Price 60.00
48 Charles Slack 60.00
49 David Breeze 60.00
50 Leonard Carpenter 60.00
51 Omar Fannin 60.00
52 Donnie Gaunce 60.00
53 Steve Hamilton 120.00
54 Bobby Laughlin CO 60.00
55 Jesse Mayabb 60.00
56 Jerry Riddle 60.00
57 Howard Shumate 60.00
58 Dan Swartz 60.00
59 Harlan Tolle 60.00
60 Donald Whitehouse 60.00
61 Rex Alexander CO 75.00
62 Jorgen Anderson 75.00
63 Jack Clutter 75.00
64 Howard Crittenden 75.00
65 James Gainey 75.00
66 Richard Kinder 75.00
67 Theo. Koenigsmark 75.00
68 Joseph Mikez 75.00
69 John Powless 100.00
70 Dolph Regelsky 75.00
71 Reinhard Tauck 75.00
72 Francis Watrous 75.00
73 Forrest Able 45.00
74 Tom Benbrook 45.00
75 Ronald Clark 45.00
76 Lynn Cole 45.00
77 Robert Daniels 45.00
78 Ed Diddle CO 250.00
79 Victor Harned 45.00
80 Dencil Miller 45.00
81 Ferrel Miller 45.00
82 George Orr 45.00
83 Jerry Weber 45.00
84 Jerry Whitsell 45.00
85 William Bergines 90.00
86 James Brennan 90.00
87 Marc Constantine 90.00
88 Michael Holt 90.00
89 Hot Rod Hundley 450.00
90 Clayce Kishbaugh 90.00
91 Ronald LaNeve 90.00
92 Gary Mullins 90.00
93 Fred Schaus CO 250.00
94 Frank Spadafore 90.00
95 Peter White 90.00
96 Paul Witting 90.00

1987-88 Auburn

The 16-card set issued by Auburn University has members from all different sports. With a reported production total of 5,000 sets made by McDag Productions, they were then issued by the Opelika, Ala. police department. The key card in the set is a Frank Thomas card. The set also includes Tiger greats Bo Jackson, Chuck Person and Rowdy Gaines.

MT
Complete Set (16): 125.00
Common Player: 1.00
1 Pat Dye CO 2.00
2 Frank Thomas 100.00
3 Jeff Burger 1.50
4 Sonny Smith CO 1.50
5 Kurt Crain 1.00
6 Joe Ciampi 1.50
7 Aubie (Mascot) 1.00
8 Tiger (Mascot) 1.00
9 Jeff Moore 1.50
10 Vickie Orr 1.50
11 Tracy Rocker 1.50
12 Brian Shulman 1.00
13 Lawyer Tillman 2.00
14 Chuck Person 12.00
15 Rowdy Gaines 3.50
16A Bo Jackson (playing baseball) 20.00
16B Bo Jackson (playing football) 30.00

1992-93 Auburn

This 14-card, standard size set was produced by Collegiate Products. The fronts feature color action or posed shots, with a dark blue strip running down the left side displaying the school's name. The backs are printed in a horizontal format with a head shot, statistics and biographical information. The key card is the first of Wesley Person.

MT
Complete Set (14): 10.00
Common Player: .50
1 Tommy Joe Eagles CO 1.00
2 Aubrey Wiley .75
3 Wesley Person 7.00
4 Aaron Swinson 1.00
5 Ronnie Battle .75
6 Cameron Boozer .50
7 Reggie Gallon .50
8 Leonard Smith .50
9 Rod Joyce .50
10 Bryon Bell .50
11 Pat Burke .50
12 Mark Hutton .50
13 Shawn Stuart .50
14 Lance Weems .75

1987-88 Baylor

The set sponsored by the Hillcrest Baptist Medical Center, among others, totaled 17 cards, with four sports being represented. The fronts have a color action shot, while the backs have instructional sports information.

MT
Complete Set (17): 25.00
Common Player: 1.00
1 Nate Jones 1.00
2 Pat Combs 2.00
3 Mickey Sullivan 1.00
4 Micheal Williams 7.00
5 Darryl Middleton 2.00
6 Gene Iba CO 2.00
7 Victor Valen 1.00
8 Raymond Pierre 1.00
9 Darnell Chase 1.00
10 Clyde Hart CO 1.00
11 Ray Crockett 3.00
12 Joel Porter 1.00
13 James Francis 7.00
14 Russell Sheffield 1.00
15 Matt Clark 1.00
16 Eugene Hall 1.00
17 Grant Teaff CO 3.00

1989-90 Baylor

This 15-card set was sponsored by the Waco Tribune-Herald, and contains the first card of David Wesley. The fronts feature a posed color shot against a yellow background, with white and green borders. The horizontal backs are unnumbered and checklisted below alphabetically.

MT
Complete Set (15): 14.00
Common Player: 1.00
(1) Kelvin Chalmers 1.00
(2) Toby Christian 1.00
(3) Julius Denton 1.00
(4) Joey Fatta 1.00
(5) Mitch Fogle 1.00
(6) Michael Hobbs 1.00
(7) Alex Holcombe 1.00
(8) Melvin Hunt 1.00
(9) Gene Iba CO 3.00
(10) Ivan Jones 1.00
(11) Dennis Lindsey 1.00
(12) Tim Schumacher 1.00
(13) David Wesley 6.00
(14) Brian Zvonocek 1.00
(15) Team photo 1.00

1990-91 Baylor

The Waco Tribune-Herald sponsored this 16-card set featuring the Baylor men's basketball team. The fronts have a close-up player photo inside a green border with the Baylor University logo and player's name, position and number at the bottom. The backs have a horizontal layout and include biographical and statistical information. The cards are unnumbered.

MT
Complete Set (17): 12.00
Common Player: 1.00
Ulises Asprilla 1.00
Herb Baker 1.00
Kelvin Chalmers 1.00
Toby Christian 1.00
Joey Fatta 1.00
David Hamilton 1.00
Alex Holcombe 1.00
Melvin Hunt 1.00
Gene Iba CO 1.50
Anthony Lewis 1.00
Dennis Lindsey 1.00
Tim Schumacher 1.00
Willie Sublett 1.00
Joe Tanksley 1.00
David Wesley 5.00
Brian Zvonocek 1.00
Baylor Bear CL 1.00

1985-86 Bradley

This 56-card, playing card deck features black and white photos with a white border containing the card number and suit in opposite corners. The back has the Bradley Braves name and logo on a pink surface with red and bordered in white. The cards are listed below according to suits and then numbers within each suit.

MT
Complete Set (56): 45.00
Common Player: 1.00
C1 Chet Walker 5.00
C2 Al Smith 1.50
C3 Mike Owens 1.00
C4 Tom Les 1.00
C5 195-51 Team Photo 1.50
C6 WMBD Radio (Jack Brickhouse, Mark Holz, Tom Kelly, Vince Lloyd, Dave Snell, Bob Starr) (Broadcasters) 6.00
C7 Levern Tart 1.50
C8 Chuck Orsborn CO 1.00
C9 Willie Scott 1.00
C10 1956-57 Team Photo 1.50
C11 Forddy Anderson CO 1.00
C12 1963-64 Team Photo 1.50
C13 1981-82 Team Photo 1.50
D1 Gene Morse 1.00
D2 Joe Stowell CO 1.00
D3 Steve Kuberski 2.50
D4 L. C. Bowen 1.00
D5 Bobby Humbles 1.00
D6 Assistant Coaches (Joe Allen, Tony Barone, Chuck Buescher, Mark Dohner, Ron Harris, Rudy Keeling) 1.50
D7 Journal Star Writers (Gary Childs, Kenneth Jones, Paul King, Dick Lien, Max Siebel, Phil Theobald, Lefty Tyler) 1.00
D8 Harry Wilcoxen 1.00
D9 Joe Billy McDade 1.00
D10 Ron Ferguson CO 1.00
D11 Mitchell Anderson 2.50
D12 1978-80 Team Photo 1.50
D13 Joe Allen 1.50
H1 Paul Unruh 2.00
H2 Voise Winters 1.00
H3 PA Announcers (Frank Busone, Paul Herzog, Bob Loy) 1.00
H4 Radio and TV Broadcasters (Ken Brown, Lorne Brown, Frank Busone, Mort Cantor) 1.00
H5 1965-66 Team Photo 1.50
H6 Joe Strawder 1.00
H7 Chiefs Club Presidents (Grant Bush, Mort Cantor, Ed Erhgott, Henry Holling, Keith Holloway, Grant Mathey, Paul Unruh) 1.00
H8 Marcel DeSouza 1.00
H9 1959-60 Team Photo 1.50
H9 1959-60 Team Photo 1.50
H10 Shellie McMillon 1.50
H11 Gene Melchiorre 1.50
H12 Bradley's Famous Five 1.50
H13 A.J. Robertson CO 1.00
S1 Bob Carney 1.00
S2 Ray Ramsey 1.00
S3 Barney Cable 1.50
S4 Dutch Meinen CO 1.00
S5 All-Stars Who Toured Brazil (Jim Caruthers, Mike Davis, Mark Dohner, Tom Les, Seymour Reed) 2.00
S6 Bradley Area Automobile Sponsors (Joe McCarthy, Dick Miller, Neil Norton, John Pearl, Mickey Smith, Bill and Ken Schaffnit) 1.00
S7 Club Presidents (Ron Baurer, Larry Cowling, Jack Heintzman, Glen McCullough, Bill Ridgely, William Robertson, Carl Traficana) 1.00
S8 Bobby Joe Mason 2.50
S9 Dick Versace CO 2.50
S10 Stan Albeck 2.00
S11 Roger Phegley 2.50
S12 Jack Brickhouse (HOF broadcaster) 2.50
S13 1949-50 Team Photo 1.50
JK 1985-86 Schedule 1.00
NNO Joker (Peoria Civic Center) 1.00
NNO Schedule card 1.00

1990-91 Bradley

This 25-card set was issued in five five-card sheets and was sponsored by Kodacolor and Peoria Camera Shop, with one strip being given away at each of five home games. The set is mostly in color, with the exception of a Braves from the Past subset. The backs are plain white with stats, biograpical information and no card numbers.

MT
Complete Set (25): 25.00
Common Player: 1.00
Stan Albeck CO 2.00
James Bailey 1.00
Mark Bailey 1.00
Andy Bastock 1.00
Scott Behrends 1.00
Duane Broussard 1.00
Kwame Brown 1.00
Adam Carl 1.00
Mark Dietrich 1.00
Marty Gillespie CO 1.00
James Hamilton 1.00
Hersey Hawkins 8.00
Xanthus Houston 1.50
Paul Lee 1.00
Jim Les 2.00
Mo McHone ACO 1.00
Roger Phegley 1.50
Sean Smith 1.00
Maurice Stovall 1.00
Curtis Stuckey 1.50
Paul Unruh 1.50
Chet Walker 3.00
Charles White 1.00
Tom Wilson 1.00
Tony Wysinger 1.00

1993-94 Bradley

This 18-card set was sponsored by the Peoria Downtown Kiwanis Club. The fronts feature color photos with white borders, while the horizontal backs have another player shot along with a short biography. The cards are unnumbered and listed below alphabetically.

MT
Complete Set (18): 10.00
Common Player: .50

	Checklist	.50
	Duane Broussard	.50
	Jim Molinari	.75
	Duane Broussard ACO, Duane Broussard ACO, Rob Judson ACO	.50
	Marcus Pollard	.50
	Roger Suchy	.50
	David Winslow	.50
	Dwayne Funches	.50
	Rick Harris	.50
	Deon Jackson	.75
	Chad Kleine	.50
	Billy Wright	.75
	James Baptist	.50
	Kerry Burrell	.50
	Anthony Parker	.75
	Aaron Zobrist	.50
	Jim Les, Hersey Hawkins (Bradley Alumni in the NBA)	3.00
	WMBD Broadcast Team (Dave Snell, Joe Stowell, Jim Watson)	.50

1994-95 Bradley

This 18-card set features color shots of the 1994-95 Bradley Braves over a simulated wood background. The set was sponsored by Peoria Downtown Kiwanis Club, and has horizontal backs with a smaller shot of the player on the left side and text filling the rest.

		MT
	Complete Set (18):	10.00
	Common Player:	.50
1	Checklist (Bob Carney, Joe Allen)	.50
2	Jim Molinari CO	.75
3	Duane Broussard ACO, Pat Donahue ACO, Rob Judson ACO	.50
4	David Winslow	.50
5	Aaron Zobrist	.50
6	Billy Wright	.75
7	Marcus Samuels	.50
8	Anthony Parker	.75
9	Kerry Burrell	.50
10	Chad Kleine	.50
11	Dwayne Funches	.50
12	Deon Jackson	.75
13	Mbaukwu Nwaogwugwu	.50
14	James Baptist	.50
15	Adebayo Akinkunle	.50
16	Ben Coupet	.50
17	Dave Snell ANN, Jim Stowell ANN, Jim Watson ANN	.50
18	Marcus Pollard	.50

1995-96 Bradley

The Peoria Downtown Kiwanis Club sponsored this 18-card set featuring the Bradley men's basketball team. The fronts feature a color action photo with a red border and the player's name and position at the bottom. The backs have a horizontal layout with another color photo, player biography and statistics and a list of sponsors.

		MT
	Complete Set (18):	15.00
	Common Player:	.50
1	Checklist - Banquet/Hall of Fame (Gene Gathers, Chet Walker)	1.50
2	Jim Molinari CO	.75
3	Assistant Coaches (Duane Broussard, Pat Donahue, Rob Judson)	.50
4	Deon Jackson	.75
5	Chad Kleine	.50
6	Billy Wright	.75
7	Dwayne Funches	.50
8	Mbaukwu Nwaogwugwu	.50
9	Anthony Parker	2.00
10	Ben Coupet	.50
11	Kerry Burrell	.50
12	Aaron Zobrist	.50
13	James Baptist	.50
14	Adebayo Akinkunle	.50
15	Marcus Samuels	.50
16	Gavin Schairer	.50
17	WMBD Broadcast Team (Jim Watson, Dave Snell, Joe Stowell)	.50
18	Kiwanis Builder Award (Billy Wright)	.50

1972-73 Bradley Schedules

Five schedules measuring 2-1/2" x 3-3/4" printed on thick cardboard stock make up this set. The fronts show a black and white photo and the backs contain the 1972-73 basketball schedule.

		NM
	Complete Set (5):	100.00
	Common Player:	15.00
1	Sam Allen	25.00
2	Mark Dohner	15.00
3	Dave Klobucher	20.00
4	Seymour Reed	30.00
5	Doug Shank	15.00

1987-88 BYU

This 25-card set was individually numbered from 1 to 20,000 on the back of each set and was issued by Brigham Young University. The cards feature a color shot on the front with a blue border. The backs are horizontal with statistics and biographical information.

		MT
	Complete Set (25):	12.50
	Common Player:	.50
1	Michael Smith	2.00
2	BYU Header Card	1.00
3	Jim Usevitch	.50
4	Nathan Call	.50
5	Brian Taylor	.50
6	Ladell Anderson CO	1.00
7	Roger Reid	.75
8	Carl Ingersoll	.50
9	Jeff Chatman	.75
10	Team Photo	1.50
11	Mike Herring	.50
12	Chris Lynch	.50
13	Steve Schreiner	.50
14	Gary Trost	.75
15	David Lynch	.50
16	Brian Taylor	.75
17	Andy Toolson	1.50
18	Jim Usevitch	.50
19	Vince Bryan	.50
20	Mark Clausen	.50
21	Alan Astle	.50
22	Nathan Call	.50
23	Jeff Chatman	.75
24	Marty Haws	.75
25	Michael Smith	2.00

1988-89 BYU

This 25-card set was limited to 5,000 and arrived in a clear plastic bag with the set serial number printed on a cardboard tag attached. The fronts feature a color photo with a light blue strip under the photo, all surrounded by a white border. The backs are horizontal, with numbers 1-17 containing statistics and 18-24 information listed below.

		MT
	Complete Set (25):	10.00
	Common Player:	.50
1	Team Photo	1.50
2	Michael Smith	1.50
3	Alan Framton	.50
4	Alan Astle	.50
5	Mike Herring	.50
6	Mark Heslop	.50
7	Steve Andrus	.50
8	Steve Schreiner	.50
9	Andy Toolson UER (Misspelled Toolsen)	1.00
10	Vince Bryan	.50
11	Marty Haws	.75
12	Kevin Santiago	.50
13	David Wolfe	.50
14	John Fish	.50
15	Carl Ingersoll ACO	.50
16	Roger Reid ACO	.75
17	Ladell Anderson	1.00
18	Alan Astle (Seven Wonders on back)	.50
19	Marty Haws (UPI Top 20 on back)	.75
20	Michael Smith (Coaching records on back)	1.25
21	Michael Smith (Team schedule on back)	1.25
22	Marty Haws (1988-89 outlook on back)	.75
23	Andy Toolson UER (BYU basketball statistics on back; misspelled Toolsen)	1.00
24	Marty Haws (BYU No. 1 scorer and No. 1 rebounder, statistics on back)	.75
25	Title Card	.75

1989-90 California

This 16-card set was sponsored by USDA Forest Service, California Dept. of Forestry and Fire Protection and USDI Bureau of Land Management. The posed and action color shots are surrounded by a white border. The backs contain biographical information and a fire prevention cartoon starring Smokey the Bear. The cards are unnumbered and listed below alphabetically.

		MT
	Complete Set (16):	20.00
	Common Player:	1.50
(1)	Rich Branham	1.50
(2)	Andrew Brigham	1.50
(3)	DeShon Brown	1.50
(4)	Lou Campanelli CO	2.00
(5)	John Carty	1.50
(6)	Gary Colson	2.00
(7)	Ryan Drew	1.50
(8)	Bill Elleby	1.50
(9)	Roy Fisher	2.00
(10)	Sean Harrell	1.50
(11)	Brian Hendrick	2.00
(12)	Eric McDonough	1.50
(13)	Andre Reyes	1.50
(14)	Keith Smith	1.50
(15)	Bryant Walton	1.50
(16)	Jeff Wulburn ACO	1.50

1994-95 California

Power Bar sponsored this 16-card set of the California men's basketball team. The fronts have full-bleed color photos with the player's name written vertically on the side. The backs have biographical information and the Power Bar logo inside a blue border. The cards are unnumbered.

		MT
	Complete Set (16):	12.00
	Common Player:	.50
1	Monty Buckley	.50
2	Randy Duck	1.50
3	Tremaine Fowlkes	2.00
4	Jelani Gardner	2.00
5	Tony Gonzalez	5.00
6	Alfred Grigsby	.75
7	Ryan Jamison	.50
8	Sean Marks	.50
9	Anwar McQueen	.50
10	K.J. Roberts	.50
11	Michael Stewart	5.00
12	Todd Bozeman CO	1.00
13	Assistant Coaches (Billy Kennedy, Kurtis Townsend, Charles Payne)	.50
14	Oski (Mascot)	.50
15	Team Photo	.75
16	Team Photo	.75

1996-97 California

This 10-card set was sponsored by California Highway Patrol. Card backs are numbered and contain a police/ safety message on the back.

		MT
	Complete Set (10):	12.00
	Common Player:	.50
1	Randy Duck	1.50
2	Tony Gonzalez	.50
3	Ed Gray	2.50
4	Alfred Grigsby	.50
5	Sean Jackson	.50
6	Kenyon Jones	.50
7	Sean Marks	.50
8	Prentice McGruder	.50
9	Anwar McQueen	.50
10	Michael Stewart	5.00

1996-97 California (Woman's)

This 10-card set was sponsored by the California Highway Patrol and features two players on each card. The cards are numbered on the back and contain a police/safety message.

		MT
	Complete Set (10):	8.00
	Common Player:	.50
1	Patrycja Czepiec, Tatiana Dmitrieva	1.00
2	Elke Snijder, Lexy Tamony	1.00
3	Sherrise Smith, Kobie Kennon	1.00
4	Geneva McDaniel, Paige Bowie	1.00
5	Mary Scotty, Liz Rizzo	1.00
6	Jamilla Churchill, Jennie Leander	1.00
7	Marie Folsom, Angie Wong	1.00
8	Coaching Staff (Marianne Stanley, Barbara Thaxton, Marie Christian)	2.00
9	Team Card (dress clothes)	1.00
10	Team Card (basketball uniforms)	1.00

1994-95 Cassville HS

The 28-card, standard-size set features the high school boys' and girls' teams, including Sam Okey, who would go on to sign with the University of Wisconsin. The horizontal backs features the the high school athletes' favorite activities.

		MT
	Complete Set (28):	20.00
	Common Player:	1.00
111	Scott Uppena	1.00
112	Chris Koopman, John Koopman	1.00
113	John Koopman	1.00
114	Chris Koopman	1.00
115	Tim Ackerman, Todd Ackerman	1.00
116	Tim Ackerman	1.00
117	Todd Ackerman	1.00
118	Marty Riedl	1.00
119	Katie Koopman	1.00
120	Maureen White	1.00
121	Jaime Hochhausen	1.00
122	Annie Klein	1.00
123	Sara Wunderlin	1.00
124	Laura Uppena	1.00
125	Jessica Kartman	1.00
126	Carolyn Hughes	1.00
127	Jane Tennessen	1.50
128	Jason Schulting CO	1.00
129	Jeff Adrian	1.00
130	Tom Tennessen	1.00
131	T.J. Whyte	1.00
132	Kris Willis	1.00
133	Dennis Uppena CO	1.50
134	Adam Plossl	1.00
135	Sam Okey	3.00
147	Sam Okey	3.00
148	Sam Okey	3.00
149	Sam Okey	3.00

1992-93 Cincinnati

This 14-card set captures the 1992-93 Cincinnati Bearcats on full-bleed color photos. The card fronts feature a diagonal gray stripe across one of the top corners with the school's name. The horizontal back features another shot of the player and biographical information. The set is unnumbered and listed alphabetically, with the key cards being Nick Van Exel and Corie Blount.

		MT
	Complete Set (14):	12.00
	Common Player:	.50
	Corie Blount	3.00
	Curtis Bostic	1.00
	LaZelle Durden	1.00
	David Evans	.50
	Darrick Ford	.50
	Tarrnce Gibson	.50
	Keith Gregor	.75
	Mike Harris	.50
	Bob Huggins CO	2.50
	Allen Jackson	.50
	John Jacobs	.50
	Erick Martin	.75
	Terry Nelson	.75
	Nick Van Exel	7.00

1993-94 Cincinnati

This 18-card set features color player cutouts on a maroon background with a red border around the card. The words "Cincinnati Bearcats" appear in large lettering across the card top. Backs are horizontal with another shot of the player and a red border. The cards are unnumbered, with key singles of Nick Van Exel, Corie Blount and Dontonio Wingfield.

		MT
	Complete Set (18):	12.00
	Common Player:	.50
	Corie Blount, Nick Van Exel (Bearcats in the Pros)	4.00
	Curtis Bostic	1.00
	Darren Burton	1.00
	LaZelle Durden	1.00
	David Evans	.50
	Damon Flint	2.00
	Keith Gregor	.50
	Mike Harris	.50
	Larry Harrison ACO, Steve Moeller ACO, John Loyer ACO	.50
	Bob Huggins CO	2.00
	John Jacobs	.50
	Jackson Julson	.50
	Dontonio Wingfield	2.50
	Brian Wolf	.50
	Marko Wright	.50
	The Shoemaker Center	.50
	Cincinnati in the NCAA Tournament	.50
	Title Card	.50

1988-89 Clemson

This 15-card set was sponsored by Carolina Pride and features color shots of the players on a white card, with the Carolina Pride logo in the top right corner. The cards are unnumbered and listed below alphabetically, with key singles of Elden Campbell and Dale Davis.

		MT
	Complete Set (15):	30.00
	Common Player:	1.00
	Colby Brown	1.00
	Donnell Bruce	1.00
	Elden Campbell	14.00
	Marion Cash	1.00
	Dale Davis	14.00
	Cliff Ellis CO	2.50
	Derrick Forrest	1.00
	Len Gordy ACO	1.00
	Eugene Harris ACO	1.00
	Kirland Howling	1.00
	Ricky Jones	1.00
	Tim Kincaid	1.00
	Rod Mitchell	1.00
	Jerry Pryor	1.00
	David Young	1.00

1989-90 Clemson

This 16-card set was sponsored by Carolina Pride and arrived in an unperforated sheet with four rows of four cards. The fronts feature a color head shot, with the team name above it and the player's name below. The backs contain "Tips from the Tigers" and are unnumbered. Key singles include Elden Campbell and Dale Davis.

		MT
	Complete Set (16):	25.00
	Common Player:	1.00
	Colby Brown - 44	1.00
	Donnell Bruce - 14	1.00
	Wayne Buckingham - 42	1.00
	Elden Campbell - 41	12.00
	Marion Cash - 12	1.00
	Dale Davis - 34	12.00
	Cliff Ellis CO	2.00
	Derrick Forrest - 13	1.00
	Len Gordy CO	1.00
	Eugene Harris CO	1.00
	Kirland Howling - 4	1.00
	Ricky Jones - 25	1.00
	Zlatko Josic - 32	1.00
	Shawn Lastinger - 15	1.00
	Sean Tyson - 22	1.00
	David Young - 11	1.00

1990-91 Clemson

This 16-card set has orange color fronts with a color action shot of the player and the words "Clemson" (left) and "Tigers" (right) running down the sides. The cards were unnumbered and are listed alphabetically below, with the key single being Dale Davis.

		MT
	Complete Set (16):	17.00
	Common Player:	1.00
	Andre Bovain - 31	1.00
	Colby Brown - 44	1.00
	Donnell Bruce - 14	1.00
	Eric Burks - 24	1.00
	Dale Davis - 34	7.00
	Cliff Ellis CO	1.50
	Len Gordy ACO	1.00
	Eugene Harris ACO	1.00
	Steve Harris - 13	1.00
	Ricky Jones - 25	1.00
	Shawn Lastinger - 15	1.00
	Jimmy Mason - 10	1.00
	Tyrone Paul - 32	1.00
	Sean Tyson - 22	1.00
	Joey Watts - 20	1.00
	David Young - 11	1.00

1990-91 Clemson Women

This standard sized, 16-card set was sponsored by Carolina Pride and features color action photos inside of a thick orange border. The backs contain "Tips from the Lady Tigers" and biographical information. The cards are unnumbered and listed below alphabetical order.

		MT
	Complete Set (16):	7.00
	Common Player:	.50
1	Kerry Boyatt	.50
2	Shandy Bryan	.50
3	Jim Davis CO	.75
4	Jackie Farmer	.50
5	Donna Forrest	.50
6	Shanna Howard	.50
7	Courtney Johnson	.50
8	Jackie Mattress	.50
9	Melissa Miller	.50
10	Angie Peters	.50
11	Dana Puckett	.50
12	Peggy Sells	.50
13	Kim Stephens	.50
14	Cheron Wells	.50
15	Imani Wilson	.50
16	Title Card (The Davis Era)	.50

1990-91 Clemson Collegiate Collection

Produced by Collegiate Collection, the set numbers a total of 200 cards. The front has a picture of the athlete, and the back has biographical and statistical information placed in a horizontal format with a white background.

		MT
	Complete Set (200):	15.00
	Common Player:	.05
1	William Perry	.40
2	Kevin Mack	.30
3	Wayne (Tree) Rollins	.30
4	Donald Igwebuike	.10
5	Michael Dean Perry	.40
6	Larry Nance	.50
7	Steve Fuller	.15
8	Horace Grant	1.00
9	Frank Howard CO	.40
10	Orange Bowl Champs '82	.15
11	Brian Barnes	.15
12	Bobby Joe Conrad	.15
13	John Phillips	.05
14	Kevin Johnson	.05
15	Terry Allen	.75
16	Chris Morocco	.05
17	Elden Campbell	.50
18	Jimmy Key	.50
19	Tracy Johnson	.10
20	Bill Spiers	.10
21	Lawson Duncan	.05
22	Eric Eichmann	.05
23	Tim Teufel	.15
24	Vincent Hamilton	.05
25	Mike Eppley	.10
26	Hans Koeleman	.05
27	Tennis Facilities	.05
28	Marvin Sim	.05
29	Tigers Win Classic	.05
30	Jim Riggs	.10
31	Adubarie Otorubio	.05
32	Mike Milchin	.10
33	Bruce Murray	.25
34	Banks McFadden	.05
35	Murray Jaman	.05
36	The Kick 1986	.10
37	Gary Conner	.05
38	Jason Griffith	.05
39	Terrance Flagler	.15
40	Grayson Marshall	.10
41	David Treadwell	.30
42	Perry Tuttle	.15
43	Billy Williams	.05
44	Homer Jordan	.10
45	Dale Hatcher	.15
46	Steve Reese	.05
47	Ray Williams	.10
48	Obed Ariri	.10
49	Soccer Team Wins '87	.05
50	Miquel Nido	.05
51	Cliff Austin	.10
52	Chris Sherman	.05
53	Jeff Nunamacher	.05
54	Steve Berlin	.05
55	Jess Neely	.10
56	Rick Rudeen	.05
57	Jeff Bryant	.15
58	Jerry Butler	.15
59	Randy Mazey	.05
60	Bob Pauling	.05
61	Matuszewski and Walters	.05
62	James Farr	.05
63	Bob Boettner	.05
64	Chuck McSwain	.10
65	Jim Stuckey	.10
66	Neil Simons	.05
67	Rodney Williams	.10
68	Butch Zatezalo	.05
69	Dr. I.M. Ibrahim	.05
70	Richard Matuszewski	.05
71	Dwight Clark	.50
72	Chuck Baldwin	.05
73	Kenny Flowers	.10
74	Michael Tait	.10
75	John Lee	.05
76	Horace Wyatt	.05
77	Terrence Herrington	.05
78	Gary Cooper	.10
79	Bert Hefferman	.10
80	Tigers with ACC Title	.10
81	Fred Cone	.05
82	Clarence Rose	.30
83	Jean Desdunes	.05
84	Donnell Woolford	.30
85	Ric Aronberg	.05
86	Mike Brown	.05
87	Howard Hall of Fame	.05
88	Swimming Pool	.05
89	Terry Kinard	.15
90	Chris Patton	.15
91	Baseball Stadium	.05
92	Cliff Ellis CO	.15
93	1989 Senior Football	.10
94	The Clemson Tiger	.10
95	Howard's Rock	.10
96	Jeff Davis	.10
97	Derrick Forrest	.10
98	Mack Dickson	.05
00	Clemson Wins Nebraska	.10
100	Director Card 1-99	.05

101 Hill shot from field .05
102 Ray Williams .10
103 Jim McCollom .05
104 Charlie Waters .50
105 Soccer and Tennis Area .05
106 Bill Wilhelm .05
107 Bubba Brown .05
108 Ken Hatfield is hired .15
109 Lester Brown .05
110 James Robinson .05
111 Michael Dean Perry, William Perry .30
112 Nuamoi Nwokocha .05
113 Frank Howard CO .40
114 Bill Foster CO .15
115 Wesley McFadden .05
116 Clemson 35, Penn State 10 .10
117 Jay Berger .30
118 Andy Headen .15
119 Hall of Famers .10
120 Hill shot from board .05
121 Harry Olszewski .05
122 CU clinches season .10
123 Super Bowl rings .10
124 Otis Moore .05
125 Kirk Howling .05
126 Defensive Rankings .05
127 Jeff Bostic, Joe Bostic .25
128 Bob Pollock .05
129 Randy Scott .05
130 Noel Loban .05
131 Clemson and Stanford .05
132 All-Americans .10
133 Danny Ford record .10
134 Larry Penley .05
135 Littlejohn Coliseum .05
136 Clyde Browne .05
137 Clemson 13, Oklahoma 6 .10
138 Clemson vs. West Virginia .05
139 Clemson and Notre Dame .10
140 George Bush (in jacket) 1.00
141 Fuller and Butler .25
142 Safety Celebration .05
143 Oswald Drawdy .05
144 Phillips .05
145 Chuck Kriese .05
146 Balloon Launch .05
147 Perry with poster .25
148 Jim Davis .10
149 Jim Brennan .05
150 Death Valley .15
151 Tina Krebs .05
152 Andy Johnston .05
153 Wayne Coffman .05
154 Andy Tribble .05
155 Mitzi Kremer .05
156 Rusty Adkins .05
157 Choppy Patterson .05
158 Jill Bakehorn .05
159 Baker vs. Tanner .20
160 Jerry Butler .15
161 Championship Rings .10
162 Shawn Weatherly .40
163 Homecoming .05
164 Barbara Kennedy .05
165 Sports Facilities .05
166 Tommy Mahaffey .25
167 Dillard Pruitt .25
168 Bill Yarborough .05
169 Billy O'Dell .15
170 Joe Blalock .05
171 Ute Jamrozy .05
172 Jerry Pryor .05
173 Susan Hill .05
174 Eddie Griffin .05
175 Jane Forman .05
176 Obed Ariri .10
177 Richie Mahaffey .05
178 Bobby Gage .05
179 John Heisman CO .25
180 Joe Landrum .05
181 Soccer and Tennis .05
182 Clemson vs. USC .05
183 Linda White .05
184 Denise Murphy .05
185 Mary Ann Cubelic .05
186 Pam Hayden .05
187 Coy Cobb .05
188 Randy Mahaffey .05
189 Lou Cordileone .05
190 1949 Gator Bowl .10
191 Karen Ann Jenkins .05
192 Bobbie Mims .05
193 Janet Knight .05
194 Ray Matthews .10
195 Gigi Fernandez .50
196 Joey McKenna .05
197 Denny Walling .10
198 Janet Ellison .05
199 Donnie Mahaffey .05
200 Director Card 101-200 .05

1990-91 Connecticut

This 16-card set was issued in four strips of four cards each and was sponsored by Petro Pantry Foods, WTIC 1080 radio and Citgo. The fronts feature a color action photo on a dark blue background and the team name in white lettering across the top. The back has biographical information and "Husky Rap." The cards are unnumbered and listed below in alphabetical order, with key singles of Scott Burrell and Chris Smith.

MT
Complete Set (16): 15.00
Common Player: .75
Scott Burrell - 24 4.00
Jim Calhoun CO 3.00
Dan Cyrulik - 55 1.00
Lyman DePriest - 23 1.00
Shawn Ellison .75
John Gwynn - 15 .75
Gilad Katz - 10 1.25
Oliver Macklin - 11 .75
Steve Pikiell - 21 .75
Tim Pikiell - 31 .75
Rod Sellers - 22 1.00
Chris Smith - 13 2.50
Marc Suhr - 30 .75
Toraino Walker - 42 1.00
Murray Williams - 20 .75
Jonathan (Mascot) .75

1991-92 Connecticut

This 16-card set was sponsored by Petro Pantry Food Stores and Citgo. The fronts feature an action shot of the player with dark blue and white around the border. The backs contain biographical information and "Husky Rap" in a dark blue strip across the middle. The cards are unnumbered and listed in alphabetical order. Key cards include Donyell Marshall and Scott Burrell.

MT
Complete Set (16): 15.00
Common Player: .50
Rich Ashmeade .50
Scott Burrell 3.00
Jeff Calhoun .75
Dan Cyrulik .75
Brian Fair 1.00
Rudy Johnson .50
Gilad Katz 1.00
Oliver Macklin .75
Donny Marshall 3.00
Donyell Marshall 5.00
Kevin Ollie .75
Tim Pikiell .50
Rod Sellers .75
Chris Smith 2.00
Toraino Walker .75
Nantambu Willingham .50

1991-92 Connecticut Legends

This 16-card set was issued in four strips of four cards each and was sponsored by Petro Pantry Food Stores and WTIC-1080. The set features top players and coaches for the University of Connecticut. Fronts feature a mix of black and white and color photos, with a white border on each side and the top containing the words "Connecticut Basketball Legends." Backs contain biographical information and a "Husky Rap." The cards are unnumbered and listed below in alphabetical order, with the key card from the set being Clifford Robinson.

MT
Complete Set (16): 12.00
Common Player: .50
(1) Wes Bialosuknia .50
(2) Jim Calhoun CO 2.00
(3) Walt Dropo 1.50
(4) Phil Gamble .50
(5) Tate George 1.00
(6) Hugh Greer .50
(7) Tony Hanson .50
(8) Nadav Henefeld 1.50
(9) Toby Kimball .50
(10) Mike McKay .50
(11) Cliff Robinson 6.00
(12) Dee Rowe CO .50
(13) John Thomas .50
(14) Corny Thompson 1.00
(15) Art Quimby .50
(16) UCONN Field House .50

1992-93 Connecticut

This 16-card set was issued in one perforated sheet and features a color action shot of the player with a blue border on the top and left. The white backs include a head shot of the player, statistics and biographical information. The cards are unnumbered and listed below in alphabetical order, with key singles of Scott Burrell, Travis Knight and Donyell Marshall.

MT
Complete Set (16): 30.00
Common Player: 1.00
Scott Burrell 4.00
Jeff Calhoun 1.00
Jim Calhoun CO 3.00
Covington Cormier 1.00
Steve Emt 1.00
Brian Fair 1.50
Eric Hayward 1.00
Rudy Johnson 1.00
Travis Knight 6.00
Oliver Macklin 1.00
Donny Marshall 3.50
Donyell Marshall 4.00
Kevin Ollie 1.50
Nantambu Willingham 1.00
Assistant Coaches (Howie Dickenman, Dave Leitao, Glen Miller) 1.00
Cheerleaders 1.00

1993-94 Connecticut

This 16-card set was issue in a perforated sheet and features color player action shots that contain a blue border on the top and right. The horizontal backs feature a black and white head shot and biographical information. The cards are unnumbered and listed below in alphabetical order, with the key single being the first card of Ray Allen.

MT
Complete Set (16): 35.00
Common Player: .75
Ray Allen 20.00
Jeff Calhoun .75
Jim Calhoun CO 3.00
Brian Fair 1.00
Eric Hayward .75
Ruslan Inyatkin .75
Rudy Johnson .75
Kirk King 2.00
Travis Knight 4.00
Donny Marshall 2.50
Donyell Marshall 4.00
Kevin Ollie .75
Doron Sheffer 3.00
Marcus Thomas .75
Nantambu Willingham .75
Assistant Coaches (Howie Dickenman, Dave Leitao, Glen Miller) .75

1993-94 Connecticut Women

This 16-card set was issued in one perforated sheet featuring color action shots containing a blue border on the top and right side. The word "Connecticut" runs down the left side, with the horizontal card backs featuring another head shot of the player and biographical information. The cards are unnumbered and listed below in alphabetical order, with key cards of Rebecca Lobo, Jennifer Rizzotti and Kara Wolters.

MT
Complete Set (16): 35.00
Common Player: 1.00
Geno Auriemma CO 4.00
Carla Berube .75
Kim Better 1.00
Tonya Boone 1.00
The Connecticut Fans 1.00
Jamelle Elliott 1.00
Colleen Healy 1.00
Jonathan the Husky Dog (Mascot) 1.00
Rebecca Lobo 14.00
Shea Matlock 1.00
Sue Mayo 1.00
Jennifer Rizzotti 8.00
Missy Rose 1.00
Pam Webber .75
Kara Wolters 6.00
Assistant Coaches (Chris Dailey, Meghan Pattyson, Wendy Davis) 1.00

1994-95 Connecticut

This 16-card set was issued in a single perforated sheet that was sponsored by First Fidelity. The fronts feature color action player photos superimposed over a dark blue stripe that include the school and year. The horizontal backs show a black and white closeup, biography and player profile. The cards are unnumbered and listed below alphabetically, with key singles being Ray Allen and Travis Knight.

MT
Complete Set (16): 30.00
Common Player: .50
Ray Allen 14.00
Jim Calhoun CO 4.00
Uri Cohen-Mintz .50
Brian Fair .75
Eric Hayward .50
Ruslan Inyatkin .50
Rudy Johnson .75
Kirk King 1.50
Travis Knight 3.00
Donny Marshall 2.00
Kevin Ollie .75
Doron Sheffer 2.00
Justin Srb .50
Marcus Thomas .50
Nantambu Willingham .50
Greg Yeomens .50

1995-96 Connecticut

First Union Bank sponsored this perforated sheet of 16 standard-size cards. The fronts have a color action photo inside a blue border. The backs have a black-and-white head shot and biographical information. The cards are unnumbered. The sheets were distributed at UConn home games during the 1995-96 season.

MT
Complete Set (16): 20.00
Common Player: .50
1 Ray Allen 10.00
2 Jim Calhoun CO 1.50
3 Dion Carson .50
4 Kyle Chapman .50
5 Eric Hayward .50
6 Ruslan Inyatkin .50
7 Rudy Johnson .50
8 Rashamel Jones 2.00
9 Pete Kane .50
10 Kirk King .75
11 Antric Klaiber .50
12 Travis Knight 3.00
13 Predrag Materic .50
14 Rickey Moore 2.00
15 Doron Sheffer 1.00
16 Justin Srb .50

1996-97 Connecticut

This 16-card set was sponsored by First Union. The cards are unnumbered and featured biographical information and statistics on the back.

MT
Complete Set (16): 20.00
Common Player: .50
Coach Jim Calhoun 2.00
Dion Carson .50
Kyle Chapman .50
Kevin Freeman 2.00
Sam Funches .50
Richard Hamilton 10.00
Monquencio Hardnett .50
Ruslan Inyatkin .50
Rashamel Jones 2.00
Kirk King .50
Antric Klaiber .50
Michael LeBlanc .50
Pete McCann .50
Ricky Moore 1.50
Mike Smith .50
Jake Voskuhl 2.00

1997-98 Connecticut

This 16-card set was sponsored by First Union. Cards are unnumbered and feature biographical information and statistics on the back.

MT
Complete Set (16): 20.00
Common Player: .50
Jeff Cybart .50
Khalid El-Amin 3.00
Kevin Freeman 2.00
Richard Hamilton 7.50
Monquencio Hardnett .50
E.J. Harrison .50
Rashamel Jones 2.00
Antric Klaiber .50
Ricky Moore 1.50
Albert Mourning .50
Jake Voskuhl 1.50
Souleymane Wane .50
Coach Jim Calhoun 2.00
Coach Karl Hobbs .50
Asst. Coach Dave Leitao .50
Asst. Coach Tom Moore .50

1997-98 Connecticut (Women's)

This 16-card set was sponsored by First Union. Cards are unnumbered and featured biographical information and statistics on the back.

MT
Complete Set (16): 20.00
Common Player: .50
Coach Geno Auriemma 2.50
Tihana Abrlic .50
Svetlana Abrosimova .50
Jean Clark .50
Amy Duran 1.00
Courtney Gaine .50
Marci Glenney .50
Stacy Hansmeyer .50
Kelley Hunt .50
Shea Ralph .50
Nykesha Sales 8.00
Paige Sauer .50
Kelly Schumacher .50
Rita Williams 2.50
Asst. Coach Chris Dailey .50
Asst. Coaches (Tonya Cartloza, Jamelle Elliott) .50

1998-99 Connecticut

The 20-card set was sponsored by First Union and features the NCAA Championship team. Cards are unnumbered and included biographical information and statistics on the back.

MT
Complete Set (20): 20.00
Common Player: .50
Beau Archibald .50
Justin Brown .50
Ajou Ajou Deng .50
Khalid El-Amin 2.00
Kevin Freeman 2.00
Richard Hamilton 7.00
Rashamel Jones 1.75
Antric Klaiber .50
Ricky Moore 1.50
Albert Mourning .50
Edmund Saunders .50
Jake Voskuhl 1.50
Coach Jim Calhoun 2.00
Asst. Coach Karl Hobbs .50
Asst. Coach Dave Leitao .50
Asst. Coach Tom Moore .50
Harry A. Gampel Pavillion .50
Hartford Civic Center .50

1998-99 Connecticut (Women's)

This 19-card set was sponsored by First Union. Cards are unnumbered and included biographical information and statistics on the back.

MT
Complete Set (19): 20.00
Common Player: .50
Coach Geno Auriemma 2.50
Tihana Abrlic .50
Svetlana Abrosimova .50
Sue Bird .50
Swintayla Cash .50
Marci Czel .50
Amy Duran 1.00
Courtney Gaine .50
Marci Glenney .50
Stacy Hansmeyer .50
Asjha Jones .50
Shea Ralph .50
Kelly Schumacher .50
Keirsten Walters 2.00
Tamika Williams 2.00
Asst. Head Coach Chris Dailey .50
Asst. Coach Tonya Cardoza .50
Asst. Coach Jamelle Elliott .50
Student Asst. Coach Rita Williams .50

1991-92 David Lipscomb

This 30-card set features players and coaches from David Lipscomb University Bison basketball team. The fronts have color action shots superimposed on a geometric background that fades between pink and purple and is surrounded by a black border. The backs are numbered with a black and white head shot of the player.

MT
Complete Set (30): 12.00
Common Player: .50
1 Chuck Ross .50
2 Shannon Terry .50
3 Rob Browne .50
4 Greg Eubanks .50
5 Greg Thompson .50
6 Brian Ayers .50
7 Lyndell Goldston .50
8 Jerry Meyer .50
9 Mark Campbell .50
10 Michael Green .50
11 John Pierce .50
12 Daniel Dennison .50
13 Malcolm Montgomery .50
14 Kevin Dixon .50
15 Andy McQueen .50
16 Lee Anderson .50
17 Aaron Pierce .50
18 Thomas Lanier .50
19 Paul Rogers ACO .50
20 Gene Barnett ACO .50
21 Robert Sain ACO .50
22 Jon Fouss ACO .50
23 Greg Brown ACO .50
24 Todd Fouss ACO .50
25 Robert Butler ACO .50
26 Chris Snoddy TR .50
27 Jonathan Seamon ADM .50
28 Mike Roller ACO .50
29 Ralph Turner ACO .50
30 Don Meyer CO .50

1992-93 David Lipscomb

The black-bordered 30-card set showcased color photos of the players placed over a funky background of pink and purple. The player's name and team name are included in a purple bar at the bottom of the card front. Included on the card backs are the card number, black-and-white headshot, bio, stats and a player profile.

MT
Complete Set (30): 10.00
Common Player: .50
1 Chuck Ross .50
2 Shannon Terry .50
3 Rob Browne .50
4 Greg Eubanks .50
5 Greg Thompson .50
6 Brian Ayers .50
7 Lyndell Goldston .50
8 Jerry Meyer .50
9 Mark Campbell .50
10 Michael Green .50
11 John Pierce .50
12 Daniel Dennison .50
13 Malcolm Montgomery .50
14 Kevin Dixon .50
15 Andy McQueen .50
16 Lee Anderson .50
17 Adam Pierce .50
18 Thomas Lanier .50
19 Paul Rogers ACO .50
20 Gene Barnett ACO .50
21 Robert Sain ACO .50
22 Jon Fouss ACO .50
23 Greg Brown ACO .50
24 Todd Fouss ACO .50
25 Robert Butler ACO .50
26 Chris Snoddy TR .50
27 Jonathan Seamon ADM .50
28 Mike Roller ACO .50
29 Ralph Turner ACO .50
30 Don Meyer CO .50

1983-84 Dayton

Blue-tinted photos anchor the fronts of this 20-card set. The player's name is printed at the top, with "Flyers" located beneath the photo. The horizontal card backs have the player's name, bio and stats at the top, with his career highs listed beneath. The Blue Cross and Blue Shield and TV-7 logos appear at the bottom of the card backs.

MT
Complete Set (20): 18.00
Common Player: 1.00
1 Jack Butler ACO, Dan Hipsher ACO 1.00
2 Roosevelt Chapman 3.00
3 Dan Christie 1.00
4 Dave Colbert 1.00
5 Rory Dahlinghaus 1.00
6 Don Donoher CO 2.00
7 Damon Goodwin 1.00
8 Anthony Grant 1.00
9 Ted Harris 1.00
10 Mike Hartsock 1.00
11 Paul Hawkins 1.00
12 Mick Hubert 1.00
13 Don Hughes 1.00
14 Larry Schellenberg 1.00
15 Jim Shields 1.00
16 Sedric Toney 3.00
17 Jeff Tressler 1.00
18 Ed Young 1.00
19 Jeff Zern 1.00
20 Flyer Fan Card 1.00

1986-87 DePaul Playing Cards

The 54-card set featured a black-and-white player photo on the back, with the card number and suit listed in both the upper left and lower right. The player's name and year are printed beneath the photo. The card fronts are bordered in white with the Blue Demons' logo, the school's name, Ray Meyers' name and "42 Memorable Years" printed over a turquoise background. A headshot of Ray Meyer is printed inside a heart at the bottom center. The cards are listed below with prefixes respective to their suits: clubs (C), diamonds (D), hearts (H) and spades (S). The joker cards did not feature a picture of a player.

MT
Complete Set (54): 45.00
Common Player: .75
C1 Coach of the Year 1944 1.00
C2 Frank Blum, Jim Lamkin .75
C3 Bill Robinzine, Ron Sobieszcyk 1.25
C4 Howie Carl 1.00
C5 McKinley Cowsen .75
C6 M.C. Thompson .75
C7 Emmette Bryant 1.00
C8 NIT Tournament 1963 1.00
C9 Tom Meyer .75
C10 Starting Five 1965-66 1.00
C11 Dave Mills .75
C12 400th Victory Celebration 1.00
C13 Joey Meyer 1.25
D1 Basketball Hall of Fame 1.00
D2 Jim Mitchem .75
D3 Mark Aquirre 2.50
D4 Gary Garland 1.00
D5 Final Four NCAA 1978-79 1.00
D6 Curtis Watkins .75
D7 Joe Ponsetto .75
D8 Ray and Digger Phelps 1.50
D9 Ron Norwood .75
D10 Dave Corzine 1.25
D11 Ray and Al McGuire 2.00
D12 Bill Robinzine Jr 1.25
D13 500th Victory 1.00
H1 Ray Meyer 2.50
H2 1st Team (1942) 1.00
H3 Dick Triptow .75
H4 1st NIT Championship 1945 3.00
H5 George Mikan 8.00
H6 NIT Starting Five 1945 3.00
H7 Ed Mikan, Whitey Kachan 2.00
H8 Early Great Team 1.50
H9 George Mikan, Bill Donato 5.00
H10 Bato Govedarica .75
H11 1947 Team 1.00
H12 Ray, Marge and Family 1.00
H13 Dick Heise .75
S1 700th Victory 1.00
S2 Jerry McMillan 1.00
S3 Last Home Game .75
S4 Rosemont Horizon .75
S5 Ray and Joey 1.00
S6 Terry Cummings turns Pro 2.00
S7 Terry Cummings 2.50
S8 No. 1 Basketball Family 1.00
S9 Last Game at Alumni Hall 1.00
S10 Mark Aquirre, Clyde Bradshaw 1.50
S11 Mark Aguirre, Terry Cummings 2.50
S12 1979-80 Team 1.00
S13 1979-80 Team Clowning 1.00
xx Joker Card (Year by year record) .75
xx Joker Card (Milestones) .75

1987-88 Duke

The fronts of the 13-card set feature color photos on the front, with "Adolescent Care Unit" and "Glaxo" printed at the top. "Blue Devils" is printed directly above the photo. At the bottom center of the card front is the player's name, number and position. The Duke logo is printed in the bottom left and right. The backs have the years printed in the upper corners, with the player's name and bio printed in the upper center. His career highlights and tips from the Blue Devils round out the card backs. The sponsors' names and logos are printed at the bottom of the card backs.

		MT
Complete Set (13):		45.00
Common Player:		2.00
13	Joe Cook	2.00
14	Quin Snyder	3.00
21	Robert Brickey	3.00
22	Greg Koubek	3.00
30	Alaa Abdelnaby	5.00
31	Kevin Strickland	3.00
33	John Smith	2.00
35	Danny Ferry	10.00
42	George Burgin	2.00
44	Phil Henderson	4.00
45	Clay Buckley	2.00
55	Billy King	3.00
xx	Mike Krzyzewski CO	20.00

1988-89 Duke

Bordered in blue, the card fronts have a color player photo in the center. The set's sponsors are listed at the top, while "Blue Devils" is printed directly above the photo. The player's name, number and his year are printed beneath the photo, with the Duke logo in the lower left. The card backs have the years, along with the player's name and bio, listed at the top. His career highlights, tips from the Blue Devils and sponsors are printed at the bottom of the card backs. The 13-card set is unnumbered and nearly impossible to find in mint condition.

		MT
Complete Set (13):		90.00
Common Player:		2.00
1	Alaa Abdelnaby	5.00
2	Robert Brickey	3.00
3	Clay Buckley	2.00
4	George Burgin	2.00
5	Brian Davis	5.00
6	Danny Ferry	10.00
7	Phil Henderson	4.00
8	Greg Koubek	3.00
9	Mike Krzyzewski CO	20.00
10	Christian Laettner	60.00
11	Crawford Palmer	2.00
12	John Smith	2.00
13	Quin Snyder	5.00

1988-89 East Carolina

The six-card set is sponsored by Pizza Hut. Color photos are bordered by team colors, while a purple border at the bottom of the card front includes the player's name. The player's name and bio are included on the back, along with tips from the Pirates. The card backs are numbered.

		MT
Complete Set (6):		16.00
Common Player:		2.00
1	Gus Hill	2.00
2	Kenny Murphy	2.00
3	Jeff Kelly	2.00
4	Mike Steele CO	2.00
5	Reed Lose	2.00
6	Blue Edwards	10.00

1989-90 East Tennessee State

The 12-card set is anchored by a color photo on the front, with the school and its nickname printed above the photo. The player's name, number and position are located in the bottom center. The Shoney's logo appears in the lower left. The card backs have the years in the upper corners, with the team's nickname, player name and bio in the upper center. The player's career highlights are located in the center. A safety message from the player is boxed at the bottom of the card back. The Shoney's logo and ETSU logos are printed in the lower left and right, respectively.

		MT
Complete Set (12):		14.00
Common Player:		.75
1	Greg Dennis	2.00
2	Major Geer	2.00
3	Keith (Mister) Jennings	5.00
4	Chad Keller	.75
5	Avery Marshall	.75
6	Jerry Pelphrey, Robert Spears, James Jacobs, Darell Jones	1.50
7	Les Robinson CO	2.50
8	Marty Story	1.00
9	Calvin Talford	2.00
10	Alvin West	.75
11	Michael Woods	.75
12	East Tennessee State Team Card	2.00

1990-91 East Tennessee State

The 14-card set includes a color photo on the front, with the years in the upper corners. "ETSU Buccaneers" are included inside a diamond at the top. The player's name, number and position are listed beneath the photo. Shoney's logo is printed in the lower left. The backs have the player's name inside a stripe at the top and his bio is listed beneath it. His stats and safety quote round out the back. Shoney's and ETSU logos are located in the lower left and right on the card backs, respectively.

		MT
Complete Set (14):		10.00
Common Player:		.75
1	Buccaneers Assistants (Jeff Lebo ACO, Grafton Young ACO, John Shulman ACO, Ed Howat ACO)	1.00
2	Buccaneer Trio (Eric Palmer, Trazel Silvers, Moe Hayes)	1.00
3	Greg Dennis	1.50
4	Rodney English	1.50
5	Major Geer	1.50
6	Keith (Mister) Jennings	4.00
7	Darell Jones	.75
8	Alan LeForce CO	1.50
9	Jerry Pelphrey	1.00
10	Robert Spears	.75
11	Marty Story	1.00
12	Calvin Talford	1.50
13	Alvin West	.75
14	Michael Woods	.75

1991-92 East Tennessee State

The 15-card set is anchored by a color photo in the center, with the years and "ETSU Buccaneers" printed at the top. The player's name, number and position are located at the bottom center. The unnumbered card backs have the player's name inside a stripe at the top, with his bio, stats and safety message printed below. The Shoney's and ETSU logos are printed on the left and right, respectively.

	MT
Complete Set (15):	10.00
Common Player:	.75
Buccaneer Assistants (Grafton Young ACO, Ed Howat ACO, John Shulman ACO, Jeff Lebo ACO)	1.00
Greg Dennis	1.25
Rodney English	1.25
Moe Hayes, Loren Riddick	.75
Damien Hodge, Justin McClellan, Reece Dudley, Leslie Brunn	.75
Darell Jones	.75
Alan LeForce CO	1.50
Jason Niblett	1.00
Eric Palmer	.75
Jerry Pelphrey	1.00
Trazel Silvers	.75
Southern Conference (Trophy and Ball)	1.00
Robert Spears	.75
Marty Story	1.00
Calvin Talford	1.25

1992-93 East Tennessee State

The 14-card set was totally redesigned with a photo bordered by jagged lines. The years and "ETSU Buccaneers" are printed at the top. The player's name, position and number are printed at the bottom of the card. The card fronts are bordered in blue. The backs, which are unnumbered, have the player's name inside a stripe at the top, with his bio, stats and safety message rounding out the back. Shoney's and ETSU logos are printed on the lower left and right, respectively, of the card back.

	MT
Complete Set (14):	12.00
Common Player:	.75
Leslie Brunn	.75
Robert Doggett, Geoff Herman, Tony Patterson	1.00
Darell Jones	.75
Alan LeForce CO	1.50
Alan LeForce CO ((Cutting down net))	1.50
Justin McClellan	.75
Jason Niblett	1.00
Jay Nidiffer ACO, John Shulman, Grafton Young	.75
Eric Palmer	.75
Jerry Pelphrey	1.00
Andy Pennington, Phil Powe	.75
Trazel Silvers	.75
Robert Spears	.75
Team Photo	1.00

1993-94 East Tennessee State

The 15-card set includes a color photo on the front, with "Hooked on the Bucs '94" printed in the upper left. "ETSU" appears vertically along the left border, while the Shoney's logo, the player's name, position and jersey number are printed in the lower right. The card backs, which are unnumbered, have the player's name printed inside a stripe at the top. His bio, stats and safety message follow. The Shoney's and ETSU logos are located in the lower left and right, respectively.

	MT
Complete Set (15):	8.00
Common Player:	.75
Leslie Brunn	.75
Robert Doggett	1.00
Junior Floyd	.75
Geoff Herman	.75
Corrie Johnson, Mike Biggs	.75
Darell Jones	.75
Alan LeForce CO	1.50
Justin McClellan	.75
Tony Patterson	.75
Andy Pennington	.75
Shahid Perkins	.75
Phil Powe	.75
Trazel Silvers	.75
Steve Snell ACO, John Shulman, Jay Nidiffer, Jerry Pelphrey	.75
Chris Timmerman, James Abrams	.75

1992-93 Eastern Illinois

This 12-card set features a color photo on the front, with "Big League Cards" printed in the upper left. The player's name, number, year and position are located in the bottom left, while the EIU logo and the years are printed in the lower right. The card backs have a safety message printed in a box at the top, while the player's name, number, year and position are printed beneath it. His bio, Little Caesars and The Bank logos are printed at the bottom of the card.

		MT
Complete Set (12):		10.00
Common Player:		1.00
1	Rick Samuels CO (and Assistants)	1.00
2	Team Photo	1.50
3	Michael Slaughter, Johnny Hernandez	1.50
4	Steve Weemer, Steven Nichols	1.00
5	Andre Rodriquez, Louis Jordan	1.50
6	Kurt Comer, Walter Graham	1.00
7	Troy Collier, Derrick Landrus	1.50
8	C.J. Williams, Darrell Young	1.00
9	Eric West	1.50
10	Curtis Leib	1.50
11	Derek Kelley	1.50
12	Billy Panther (Mascot)	1.00

1986-87 Emporia State

Issued as an uncut unperforated sheet, the nine-card set has a photo of the player in the center of the card front. "Hornets" is printed at the top, while the player's name is located beneath the photo. The card backs, which are unnumbered, have the player's name, position and bio printed inside a stripe at the top. His stats and career highlights round out the card back. Each card on the sheet is standard size at 2-1/2" x 3-1/2". The cards are sponsored by B and K Nostalgia.

		MT
Complete Set (9):		20.00
Common Player:		3.00
1	Eric Anderson, Bill Pitko	3.00
2	Cardell Armstrong	3.00
3	Johnny Craven	3.00
4	Dennis Fort	3.00
5	Derrick Howse	3.00
6	John Hughes	3.00
7	Ron Slaymaker CO (Hornets Logo)	3.00
8	Chris Sparks	3.00
9	Ryan Sprecker	3.00

1993-94 Evansville

A color action shot anchors the fronts of this 16-card set. "UE" and "'93-94" are printed inside a basketball in the upper left corner. The player's name and school are printed inside two stripes at the bottom of the card front. The backs have the player's headshot in the upper left, with his career highlights at the upper right. His bio and stats are located inside boxes at the bottom of the backs.

		MT
Complete Set (16):		7.00
Common Player:		.50
1	Jermaine Ball	.50
2	Todd Cochenour	.50
3	Jim Crews CO	1.00
4	Andy Elkins	1.50
5	Mark Hisle	.75
6	Reed Jackson	.50
7	Brent Kell	.50
8	Jeff Layden	.50
9	Toby Madison	.50
10	Arad McCutchan CO	.50
11	Chris Quinn	.50
12	Carl Reeder	.50
13	Scott Sparks	.50
14	Ace Purple (Mascot)	.50
15	Ace-Ettes	.50
16	Cheerleaders	.50

1982-83 Fairfield

The card fronts on this 18-card set has a color photo on the front, with "Big League Cards" printed in the upper left. The player's name and school are located in the lower left. A basketball and the years are printed in the lower right. The card backs have a cartoon and a player's hobby inside a box at the top. His name, position and bio are included in the center. The player's profile is featured inside a box at the bottom of the card back.

		MT
Complete Set (18):		12.00
Common Player:		1.00
1	Jay Byrne	1.00
2	Vin Cazzetta	1.50
3	Pete DeBisschop	1.00
4	Joe DeSantis CO	1.50
5	Tony George	1.00
6	Craig Golden	1.00
7	Bobby Hurt	1.50
8	Ed Janka CO	1.00
9	Jerry Johnson	1.00
10	John Leonard	1.00
11	Terry O'Connor	1.50
12	Tim O'Toole	1.00
13	Brendan Potter	1.50
14	Ron Ross CO	1.50
15	Greg Schwartz	1.00
16	Don Wilson	1.00
17	Pat Yerina	1.00
18	Fairfield Stags	1.50

1988-89 Florida

The set compiles 14 cards sponsored by Burger King and the University Athletic Association. The standard-sized cards have an action shot of an athlete engaging in a particular sport, with the two sponsor's logos on the front as well.

		MT
Complete Set (14):		15.00
Common Player:		.75
1	Men's Swimming	.75
2	Baseball	1.00
3	Men's Basketball	6.00
4	Women's Tennis	.75
5	Women's Track and Field	.75
6	Gymnastics	.75
7	Cross Country	.75
8	Women's Volleyball	.75
9	Women's Swimming	.75
10	Women's Basketball	4.00
11	Men's Track and Field	.75
12	Men's Tennis	.75
13	Women's Golf	1.00
14	Men's Golf	2.00

1990-91 Florida State Collegiate Collection

A 200-card set, the FSU Collegiate Collection is the standard size, with an action color photo on the front along with the FSU logo. The back has biographical information. Past and current players are featured.

		MT
Complete Set (200):		15.00
Common Player:		.05
1	Dick Howser	.30
2	Edwin Alicea	.10
3	Randy White	.05
4	Steve Gabbard	.05
5	Pat Tomberlin	.10
6	Herb Gainer	.05
7	Bobby Jackson	.10
8	Redus Coggin	.05
9	Pat Carter	.15
10	Kevin Grant	.05
11	Peter Tom Willis	.25
12	Phil Carollo	.05
13	Derek Schmidt	.05
14	Rick Stockstill	.05
15	Mike Martin	.05
16	Terry Anthony	.05
17	Darrin Holloman	.05
18	John McLean	.05
19	Rudy Maloy	.05
20	Gary Huff	.15
21	Jamey Shouppe	.05
22	Isaac Williams	.05
23	Weegie Thompson	.15
24	Jose Marzan	.05
25	Gerald Nichols	.05
26	John Brown	.05
27	Danny McManus	.15
28	Parrish Barwick	.05
29	Paul McGowan	.05
30	Keith Jones	.05
31	Alphonso Williams	.05
32	Luis Alicea	.15
33	Tony Yeomans	.05
34	Michael Tanks	.05
35	Stan Shiver	.05
36	Willie Jones	.05
37	Wally Woodham	.05
38	Chip Ferguson	.05
39	Sam Childers	.05
40	Paul Piurowski	.05
41	Joey Ionata	.05
42	John Hadley	.05
43	Tanner Holloman	.05
44	Fred Jones	.05
45	Terry Warren	.05
46	John Merna	.05
47	Jimmy Jordan	.05
48	Dave Capellen	.05
49	Martin Mayhew	.15
50	Barry Barco	.05
51	Ronald Lewis	.05
52	Tom O'Malley	.10
53	Rick Tuten	.10
54	Ed Fulton	.05
55	Marc Ronan	.05
56	Bobby Bowden	.50
57	Bobby Bowden	.50
58	Bobby Bowden	.50
59	Bobby Bowden	.50
60	Bobby Bowden	.50
61	John Grubb	.10
62	Joe Wessel	.05
63	Alphonso Carreker	.15
64	Shelton Thompson	.05
65	Tracy Sanders	.05
66	Bobby Bowden	.50
67	Bobby Bowden	.50
68	Bobby Bowden	.50
69	Bobby Bowden	.50
70	Bobby Bowden	.50
71	David Palmer	.10
72	Jason Kuipers	.05
73	Dayne Williams	.05
74	Mark Salva	.05
75	Bobby Butler	.10
76	Bobby Bowden	.50
77	Bobby Bowden	.50
78	Bobby Bowden	.50
79	Bobby Bowden	.50
80	Bobby Bowden	.50
81	Mike Loynd	.10
82	Dexter Carter	.30
83	Dedrick Dodge	.05
84	Greg Allen	.05
85	Barry Blackwell	.05
86	Bobby Bowden	.50
87	Bobby Bowden	.50
88	Bobby Bowden	.50
89	Bobby Bowden	.50
90	Bobby Bowden	.50
91	Bill Capece	.05
92	Eric Hayes	.05
93	Garth Jax	.15
94	Odell Haggins	.05
95	LeRoy Butler	.40
96	Monk Bonasorte	.05
97	Richie Lewis	.25
98	Terry Kennedy	.15
99	Hubert Green	.30
100	Director Card	.05
101	Doc Hermann	.05
102	Gary Futch	.05
103	Tony Romeo	.05
104	Lee Corso	.40
105	Steve Bratton	.05
106	Barry Rice	.05
107	Jeff Hogan	.05
108	John Wachtel	.05
109	Dick Artmeier	.05
110	Vic Szezepanik	.05
111	Danny Litwhiler	.10
112	Jack Fenwick	.05
113	Nolan Henke	.05
114	Mark Meseroll	.05
115	Jimmy Everett	.05
116	Gary Schull	.05
117	Les Murdock	.05
118	Ron Schomburger	.05
119	Scott Warren	.05
120	Eric Williams	.05
121	Buddy Strauss	.05
122	Juan Bonilla	.10
123	Rowland Garrett	.10
124	Kenny Knox	.05
125	Bill Cappleman	.05
126	Bill Kimber	.05
127	Mike Fuentes	.10
128	Bill Proctor	.05
129	Kurt Unglaub	.05
130	Woody Woodward	.25
131	Dave Cowens	.75
132	Lee Nelson	.05
133	Robert Ulrich	.50
134	Ron Fraser	.15
135	Randy Coffield	.05
136	Jimmy Lee Taylor	.05
137	Max Wettstein	.05
138	Brian Williams	.10
139	T.K. Wetherell	.05
140	Dale McCullers	.05
141	Peter Tom Willis	.25
142	Doug Little	.05
143	J.T. Thomas	.15
144	Hassan Jones	.15
145	Deion Sanders	2.00
146	Barry Smith	.05
147	Hugh Durham	.15
148	Bill Moremen	.05
149	Gary Henry	.05
150	John Madden	1.00
151	J.T. Thomas	.15
152	Tony Avitable	.05
153	Keith Kinderman	.05
154	Bill Dawson	.05
155	Mike Good	.05
156	Kim Hammond	.05
157	Buddy Blankenship	.05
158	Jimmy Black	.05
159	Vic Prinzi	.05
160	Bobby Renn	.05
161	Mark Macek	.10
162	Wayne McDuffie	.05
163	Joe Avezzano	.30
164	Hector Gray	.10
165	Grant Guthrie	.05
166	Tom Bailey	.05
167	Ron Sellers	.05
168	Dick Hermann	.05
169	Bob Harbison	.05
170	Winfred Bailey	.05
171	James Harris	.05
172	Jerry Jacobs	.05
173	Mike Kincaid	.05
174	Jimmy Heggins	.05
175	Steve Kalenich	.05
176	Del Williams	.10
177	Fred Pickard	.05
178	Walt Sumner	.10
179	Bud Whitehead	.05
180	Bobby Anderson	.05
181	Paul Azinger	1.00
182	Burt Reynolds	1.00
183	Ron King	.05
184	H. Donald Loucks	.05
185	Jim Lyttle	.10
186	Richard Amman	.05
187	Bobby Crenshaw	.05
188	Bill Dawkins	.05
189	Ken Burnett	.05
190	Duane Carrell	.10
191	Gene McDowell	.05
192	Paul Wernke	.05
193	Beryl Rice	.05
194	Dave Fedor	.05
195	Brian Schmidt	.05
196	Rhett Dawson	.05
197	Greg Futch	.05
198	Joe Majors	.05
199	Stan Dobosz	.05
200	Director Card	.05

1992-93 Florida State

The set measures 80 cards and features "Seminole Superstars" from various FSU teams. The fronts have posed photos, with the players name at the bottom. The backs contain personal information.

		MT
Complete Set (80):		30.00
Common Player:		.10
1	Ernest Lanford CO	.10
2	Bobby Cochran	.10
3	Debbie Dillman CO	.10
4	Marie-Jose E. Rouleau	.10
5	David Barron CO	.10
6	Ken McKenzie	.10
7	Alice Reen CO	.10
8	Audra Brannon	.10
9	Terry Maul CO	.10
10	Gary Cole CO	.10
11	Robert Caicedo	.10
12	Missy Connolly	.10
13	Brad Hoffman	.10
14	Kiki Steinberg	.10
15	Terry Long CO	.10
16	Sue Addison CO	.10
17	Jeff Bray	.10
18	Sheryl Covington	.10
19	Kevin Crist	.10
20	Trinette Johnson	.10
21	Patrice Verdun	.10
22	Joanne Graf CO	.10
23	Leslie Barton	.10
24	Susan Buttery	.10
25	Toni Gutierrez	.10
26	Marynell Meadors CO	.10
27	Allison Peercy	.13
28	Ursula Woods	.13
29	Cecile Reynaud CO	.10
30	Adria Ciraco	.10
31	Jennifer McCall	.10
32	Mike Martin CO	.13
33	Bryan Harris	.13
34	Link Jarrett	.13
35	Paul Wilson	5.00
36	Kevin McCray	.13
37	Ty Mueller	.13
38	Colby Weaver	.13
39	Pat Kennedy CO	.25
40	Sam Cassell	7.00
41	Rodney Dobard	.13
42	Chuck Graham	.13
43	Charlie Ward	6.00
44	Bobby Bowden CO	5.00
45	Clifton Abraham	.13
46	Ken Alexander	.13
47	Robbie Baker	.13
48	Shannon Baker	.25
49	Derrick Brooks	2.00
50	Lavon Brown	.13
51	Deondri Clark	.13
52	Richard Coes	.13
53	Chris Cowart	.13
54	John Davis	.13
55	Marvin Ferrell	.13
56	William Floyd	5.00
57	Dan Footman	.25
58	Leon Fowler	.13
59	Reggie Freeman	.13
60	Matt Frier	.13
61	Corey Fuller	.13
62	Felix Harris	.13
63	Tommy Henry	.13
64	Lonnie Johnson	.25
65	Marvin Jones	3.00
66	Toddrick McIntosh	.25
67	Tiger McMillion	.13
68	Patrick McNeil	.13
69	Sterling Palmer	.25
70	Troy Sanders	.13

71	Corey Sawyer	1.00
72	Carl Simpson	.50
73	Robert Stevenson	.25
74	Charlie Ward	6.00
75	Seminole Coaches	.25
76	Ad Card Motion Sports	.10
---	Front Card	.10
---	Back Card	.10
---	Checklist 1-38	.10
---	Checklist 39-76	.10

1985-86 Fort Hays State

Sponsored by K-Bob's Steakhouse, this 18-card set is anchored by a black-and-white head shot of the player on the front, with his name listed below inside a yellow stripe. "FHSU" is printed inside a yellow stripe in the upper right corner of the front. The years are also included in the upper right. The card backs, which are unnumbered, showcase a tiger paw print in the upper left corner, while the player's name, year and position are listed to the right of the paw. His bio, career stats and career highlights round out the card back. The K-Bob's logo is located in the lower right.

	MT
Complete Set (18):	7.00
Common Player:	1.00
Tyree Allen	1.00
Joe Anderson	1.00
Troy Applegate (Student Coach)	1.00
Kale Barton	1.00
Bruce Brawner	1.00
Fred Campbell	1.50
Craig Cox CO	1.00
Thomas Hardnett	1.00
Archie Johnson	1.00
David Lackey	1.00
Greg Lackey CO	1.00
Raymond Lee	1.00
Mike Miller	1.00
Bill Morse CO	1.00
Ron Morse	1.00
Cedric Williams	1.00
Team Photo	1.25
Title Card	1.25

1989-90 Fresno State

Sponsored by the USDA Forest Service, the 16-card set showcases a color photo, with "Fresno State Bulldogs" printed above the photo. The Smokey Bear logo is in the lower left of the card front, while the player's name, position and number are at the bottom center. A Grandy's logo is also printed on the front, in the lower right. The unnumbered card backs have the player's name and bio at the top center, with "Bulldogs" in the upper left and the Grandy's logo in the upper right. A Smokey's Arson Tips cartoon rounds out the card backs.

	MT
Complete Set (16):	12.00
Common Player:	1.00
Ron Adams CO	1.00
Bijou Baly - 15	1.00
Dave Barnett - 12	1.00
Tod Bernard - 33	1.25
Chris Henderson - 25	1.00
Wilbert Hooker - 30	1.25
Pasi Lahtinen - 3	1.00
Dimitri Lambrecht - 32	1.00
Sammie Lindsey - 50	1.00
Joey Paglierani - 00	1.00
Todd Peebles - 23	1.00
Pat Riddlesprigger - 34	1.00
Sammy Taylor - 22	1.00
Carlo Williams - 44	1.00
Rey Young - 54	1.00
Greg Zuffelato - 24	1.00

1990-91 Fresno State

Sponsored by Grandy's and the USDA Forest Service, the 16-card set showcases a color photo on the front of the blue-bordered cards. "Fresno State Bulldogs" is printed above the photo, while the Smokey Bear logo, player's name, position and years at the school and a Grandy's logo are featured at the bottom from left to right, respectively. The card backs feature the Bulldogs' logo in the upper left, with the player's name and bio in the upper center and the Grandy's logo in the upper right. A Smokey Bear tip and cartoon round out the unnumbered card backs.

	MT
Complete Set (16):	10.00
Common Player:	.75
Ron Anderson	2.50
Dave Barnett - 12	.75
Tod Bernard - 33	1.00
Tyrone Bradley	.75
Gary Colson CO	1.25
Carl Ray Harris - 11	1.25
Doug Harris - 20	.75
Wilbert Hooker - 30	1.00
Dimitri Lambrecht - 32	.75
Sammie Lindsey - 50	.75
Michael Pearson - 3	.75
Pat Riddlesprigger - 34	.75
Sammy Taylor - 22	.75
Rey Young - 54	.75
Fresno State Mascot	.75
Selland Arena	.75

1981-82 Georgetown

Sponsored by Safeway and the District of Columbia police, the 20-card set measures 2-5/8" x 4-1/8". The player's photo is framed in white on the blue-bordered fronts. "Hoya Motion" is located in the lower right. The card backs have a Kids and Cops tip at the top with a cartoon. In addition, a policeman drawing appears in the lower right. The bottom of the card backs have the Safeway logo. The cards are numbered by the tip number. This set contains Patrick Ewing's first card.

		MT
Complete Set (20):		115.00
Common Player:		2.00
1	Jack the Bulldog (Mascot)	2.00
2	Elvado Smith	2.00
3	Eric Smith	3.00
4	Patrick Ewing	95.00
5	Anthony Jones	3.00
6	Bill Martin	2.50
7	Bill Stein ACO	2.00
8	Norman Washington (Grad. Asst. Coach)	2.00
9	Ed Spriggs	2.50
10	Eric (Sleepy) Floyd	10.00
11	Gene Smith	2.50
12	Fred Brown	4.00
13	Mike Hancock	2.00
14	Kurt Kaull	2.00
15	Ed Meyers	2.00
16	Ron Blaylock	2.00
17	David Blue	2.00
18	John Thompson CO	15.00
19	Ralph Dalton	2.50
20	Hoyas Team 1981-1982	7.50

1982-83 Georgetown

Measuring 2-5/8" x 4-1/8", the 15-card set is anchored on the front by a player photo framed in white. The blue-bordered card fronts have the player's name, number and bio on the bottom left of the card, with "Hoya Motion" printed in the lower right. The card backs have a Kids and Cops tip and drawings on the back. The bottom of the card backs have the Games Production Inc. logo. The cards are numbered by the tip number.

		MT
Complete Set (15):		45.00
Common Player:		1.50
1	John Thompson CO	8.00
2	Patrick Ewing	35.00
3	David Dunn	1.50
4	Ralph Dalton	2.00
5	Fred Brown	3.00
6	Horance Broadnax	2.00
7	David Blue	1.50
8	Michael Jackson (listed as Center on card front)	3.00
9	David Wingate	6.00
10	Vadi Smith	1.50
11	Gene Smith	2.00
12	Victor Morris	1.50
13	Bill Martin	2.00
14	Kurt Kaull	1.50
15	Anthony Jones	2.00

1983-84 Georgetown

Measuring 2-5/8" x 4-1/8", the 15-card set is anchored by a photo on the front. The year and team nickname are printed above the photo, while the player's name, position and bio are printed in the lower left. The card backs, which are numbered by the tip number, have a Kids and Cops tip, along with two cartoons. The "Coke is it!" slogan is printed at the bottom of the card backs.

		MT
Complete Set (15):		40.00
Common Player:		1.50
1	John Thompson CO	5.00
2	Hoya 1983-84 Team	5.00
3	Michael Jackson	3.00
4	Bill Martin	2.00
5	Jack the Bulldog (Hoya Mascot)	1.50
6	Gene Smith	2.00
7	Fred Brown	2.50
8	Horance Broadnax	2.00
9	Victor Morris	1.50
10	Patrick Ewing	25.00
11	Ralph Dalton	2.00
12	Michael Graham	2.00
13	Clifton Dairsow	1.50
14	David Wingate	5.00
15	Reggie Williams	8.00

1984-85 Georgetown

Measuring 2-5/8" x 4-1/8", this 14-card set is anchored on the front by a player photo. The year and "Hoyas" are printed above the photo, while "1984 National Champions Men's Basketball," along with the player's name, bio and facsimile autograph are printed beneath the photo. The card backs, which are numbered by the tip number, feature a Kids and Cops tip. The bottom of the card backs feature the "Coke is it!" slogan. Patrick Ewing is included in this set.

		MT
Complet Set (14):		40.00
Common Player:		1.50
1	John Thompson CO	5.00
2	Horance Broadnax	2.00
3	Ralph Dalton	2.00
4	Patrick Ewing	25.00
5	Kevin Floyd	1.50
6	Ron Highsmith	2.00
7	Michael Jackson	2.00
8	Bill Martin	2.00
9	Grady Mateen	1.50
10	Perry McDonald	2.00
11	Reggie Williams	6.00
12	David Wingate	3.00
13	NCAA Championship Trophy	1.50
14	Team Photo	5.00

1985-86 Georgetown

Measuring 2-1/2" x 4", the 16-card set is anchored by a large photo on the front. "1985-86 Hoyas" is printed at the top, while the player's name, bio and facsimile signature are located beneath the photo. The card backs feature a Kids and Cops tip. The bottom of the card backs have a Coca-Cola and Prince George's County Police logos.

		MT
Complete Set (16):		9.00
Common Player:		.50
1	1985-86 Hoyas Team Photo	1.00
2	Gene Thompson CO	4.00
3	Horance Broadnax	.75
4	Ralph Dalton	.75
5	Johnathan Edwards	.75
6	Hoyas Mascot	.50
7	Ronnie Highsmith	.50
8	Jaren Jackson	1.00
9	Michael Jackson	1.00
10	Grady Mateen	.50
11	Perry McDonald	.75
12	Victor Morris	.50
13	Charles Smith	1.50
14	Reggie Williams	2.50
15	David Wingate	2.00
16	Bobby Winston	.50

1986-87 Georgetown

Measuring 2-1/2" x 4", the 14-card set includes 12 player cards, one coach card and one team picture card. The card fronts are anchored by a photo, with "1986-87 Hoyas" printed at the top. The player's name and bio are printed in the lower left corner. The card backs have a Kids and Cops tip. Coca-Cola and police logos are included at the bottom of the card backs.

		MT
Complete Set (14):		9.00
Common Player:		.50
1	1986-87 Hoyas	1.00
2	John Thompson CO	2.00
3	Anthony Allen	.50
4	Dwayne Bryant	.50
5	Johnathan Edwards	.75
6	Ben Gillery	.50
7	Ronnie Highsmith	.50
8	Jaren Jackson	2.00
9	Sam Jefferson	.50
10	Perry McDonald	.75
11	Charles Smith	1.00
12	Mark Tillmon	.75
13	Reggie Williams	2.00
14	Bobby Winston	.50

1987-88 Georgetown

Measuring 2-1/2" x 4", the 17-card set is anchored by a photo on the front, with "1987-88 Hoyas" printed above the photo. The player's name and bio are listed beneath the photo. The card backs include a Kids and Cops tip and Coca-Cola and District of Columbia police logos.

		MT
Complete Set (16):		9.00
Common Player:		.50
1	1987-88 Hoyas	1.00
2	John Thompson CO	2.00
3	Anthony Allen	.50
4	Dwayne Bryant	.50
5	Johnathan Edwards	.75
6	Ben Gillery	.50
7	Ronnie Highsmith	.50
8	Jaren Jackson	2.00
9	Sam Jefferson	.50
10	Johnny Jones	.50
11	Tom Lang	.50
12	Perry McDonald	.75
13	Charles Smith	1.00
14	Mark Tillmon	.75
15	Anthony Tucker	.50
16	Bobby Winston	.50

1988-89 Georgetown

Spotlighting cards of Alonzo Mourning and Dikembe Mutombo, this 17-card set measures 2-1/2" x 4". The card fronts are anchored by a large photo, with "1988-89 Hoyas" printed above the photo. The player's name and bio are printed beneath the photo. The card backs feature a Kids and Cops tip, along with McGruff the Crime Dog and Coca-Cola logos.

		MT
Complete Set (17):		55.00
Common Player:		.50
1	1988-89 Hoyas	5.00
2	John Thompson CO	2.00
3	Anthony Allen	.50
4	Dwayne Bryant	.50
5	Johnathan Edwards	.75
6	Ronnie Thompson	.50
7	Milton Bell	.50
8	Jaren Jackson	1.25
9	Sam Jefferson	.50
10	Johnny Jones	.50
11	Alonzo Mourning	30.00
12	John Turner	1.00
13	Charles Smith	.75
14	Mark Tillmon	.75
15	Dikembe Mutombo	20.00
16	Bobby Winston	.50
17	McGruff The Crime Dog and Jack The Bulldog	.50

1989-90 Georgetown

Showcasing cards of Alonzo Mourning and Dikembe Mutombo, the 17-card set measures 2-1/2" x 4". The card fronts are anchored by a large photo, with "1989-90 Hoyas" printed above the photo. The player's name and bio are listed beneath the photo. The card backs feature a Kids and Cops tip, along with The Washington Post, Coca-Cola and McGruff the Crime Dog logos.

		MT
Complete Set (17):		8.00
Common Player:		.25
1	1989-90 Hoyas	1.00
2	John Thompson CO	.75
3	Anthony Allen	.25
4	Dwayne Bryant	.25
5	David Edwards	.25
6	Ronny Thompson	.25
7	Milton Bell	.25
8	Kayode Vann	.25
9	Sam Jefferson	.25
10	Johnny Jones	.25
11	Alonzo Mourning	4.50
12	Mike Sabol	.25
13	Michael Tate	.50
14	Mark Tillmon	.50
15	Dikembe Mutombo	3.00
16	Antoine Stoudamire	.25
17	McGruff The Crime Dog and Jack the Bulldog	.25

1990-91 Georgetown

Showcasing cards of Alonzo Mourning and Dikembe Mutombo, the 15-card set measures 2-1/2" x 4". The front is anchored by a large photo, with "1990-91 Hoyas" printed above the photo and the player's name and bio listed at the bottom. The card backs have Kids and Cops tips, along with Coca-Cola and McGruff the Crime Dog logos.

		MT
Complete Set (15):		8.00
Common Player:		.25
1	1990-91 Hoyas Team Photo	1.00
2	Kayode Vann	.25
3	Mike Sabol	.25
4	Antoine Stoudamire	.25
5	Alonzo Mourning	3.50
6	Ronny Thompson	.25
7	Dikembe Mutombo	2.50
8	Charles Harrison	.25
9	Brian Kelly	.25
10	Robert Churchwell	.75
11	Joey Brown	.50
12	Vladimir Bosanac	.25
13	Lamont Morgan	.25
14	John Thompson CO	.75
15	McGruff The Crime Dog and Jack The Bulldog	.25

1991-92 Georgetown

Spotlighting a card of Alonzo Mourning, the 18-card set measures 2-1/2" x 4". The fronts are anchored by a large photo, with "1991-92 Hoyas" printed above the photo. The player's name and bio are printed inside a stripe beneath the photo. The card backs feature a Kids and Cops tip, along with McGruff the Crime Dog and Coca-Cola logos.

		MT
Complete Set (18):		6.00
Common Player:		.25
1	Team Photo	.75
2	Robert Churchwell	.50
3	Charles Harrison	.25
4	Joey Brown	.50
5	Alonzo Mourning	3.50
6	Ronny Thompson	.25
7	Vladimir Bosanac	.25
8	Pascal Fleury	.25
9	Brian Kelly	.25
10	Lamont Morgan	.25
11	Kevin Millen	.25
12	Don Reid	2.00
13	Derrick Patterson	.25
14	Lonnie Harrell	.25
15	Irvin Church	.50
16	John Jacques	.25
17	McGruff The Crime Dog and Jack The Bulldog	.25
18	John Thompson CO	.75

1991 Georgetown Collegiate Collection

Collegiate Collection issued the 100-card set with color photos on the card fronts. Above the photo, from left, are the Georgetown Bulldogs logo, the school's name and Collegiate Collection logo. The player's name is printed inside a stripe beneath the photo. The horizontal card backs feature the player's name and bio in the upper left and the card number on the upper right. His career highlights round out the rest of the card back. The Collegiate Collection copyright of 1991 is printed at the bottom.

		MT
Complete Set (100):		15.00
Common Player:		.05
1	John Thompson CO	.50
2	Patrick Ewing	1.00
3	Eric (Sleepy) Floyd	.30
4	Reggie Williams	.40
5	John Duren	.10
6	Craig Shelton	.25
7	Charles Smith	.20
8	Michael Jackson	.15
9	Jaren Jackson	.25
10	David Wingate	.30
11	Mark Tillmon	.15
12	Fred Brown	.15
13	Kurt Kaull	.05
14	Ron Highsmith	.05
15	Dwayne Bryant	.05
16	Michael Jackson	.15
17	Al Dutch	.05
18	Jim Barry	.05
19	Ralph Dalton	.10
20	1984 NCAA Champs	.40
21	Craig Esherick	.05
22	Bobby Winston	.05
23	Bill Martin	.10
24	Horance Broadnax	.10
25	John Thompson CO	.50
26	Dwayne Bryant	.05
27	Tom Lang	.05
28	Perry McDonald	.10
29	Reggie Williams	.40
30	Patrick Ewing	1.00
31	Patrick Ewing	1.00
32	Perry McDonald	.10
33	Sam Jefferson	.10
34	Michael Jackson	.15
35	Anthony Allen	.05
36	Mike Riley	.05
37	John Duren	.10
38	Mark Tillmon	.15
39	Mike Frazier	.05
40	Eric Smith	.10
41	Ed Spriggs	.10
42	Johnathan Edwards	.10
43	Derrick Jackson	.05
44	Mike Hancock	.05
45	Tom Scales	.05
46	David Blue	.05
47	Charles Smith	.20
48	John Thompson CO	.50
49	Patrick Ewing	1.00
50	Al Dutch	.05
51	Eric (Sleepy) Floyd	.30
52	Craig Shelton	.25
53	Reggie Williams	.40
53	Tom Lang	.05
54	Michael Jackson	.15
55	Patrick Ewing	1.00
56	Bill Thomas	.05
57	Ed Hopkins	.05
58	John Thompson CO	.50
59	Jon Smith	.05
60	Merlin Wilson	.05
61	Gene Smith	.10
62	Johnny Jones	.05
63	Senior Night	.05
64	Eric (Sleepy) Floyd	.30
65	Reggie Williams	.40
66	Steve Martin	.05
67	Mark Gallagher	.05
68	Mike McDermont	.05
69	Greg Brooks	.05
70	Larry Long	.05
71	Felix Yeoman	.05
72	Lonnie Duren	.05
73	Terry Fenlon	.05
74	Steve Martin	.05
75	Fred Brown	.15
76	Bill Lynn	.05
77	Patrick Ewing	1.00
78	Mike Laska	.05
79	Paul Tagliabue	1.00
80	Don Weber	.05
81	Jaren Jackson	.25
82	1982 NCAA Finalists	.25
83	1985 NCAA Finalists	.20
84	Jim Brown	.05
85	Jim Christy	.05
86	Tim Mercier	.05
87	Joe Missett	.05
88	Charlie Adrian	.05
89	John Thompson CO	.50
90	Craig Esherick	.05
91	Dennis Cesar	.05
92	Ken Pichette	.05
93	Charlie Adrian	.05
94	Mike Laughna	.05
95	Tommy O'Keefe	.05
96	Merlin Wilson	.05
97	Craig Shelton	.25
98	Derrick Jackson	.05
99	Mike Riley	.05
100	Director Card	.05

1992-93 Georgetown

Measuring 2 1/2" x 4", the 16-card set is anchored by a large photo on the front. "1992-93 Hoyas" is printed above the photo, while the player's name and bio are located inside a stripe beneath the photo. The card backs have a Kids and cops tip, along with McGruff the Crime Dog and Coca-Cola logos.

		MT
Complete Set (16):		5.00
Common Player:		.25
1	Team Photo	.75
2	John Thompson CO	.75
3	Duane Spencer	.25
4	Derrick Patterson	.25
5	Vladimir Bosanac	.25
6	Don Reid	1.00
7	Othella Harrington	3.00
8	John Jacques	.25
9	Irvin Church	.50
10	Joey Brown	.50
11	Robert Churchwell	.50
12	Lonnie Harrell	.25
13	Eric Micoud	.25
14	Lamont Morgan	.25
15	Kevin Millen	.25
16	Jack The Bulldog (Mascot McGruff the Crime Dog)	.25

1993-94 Georgetown

Measuring 2-1/2" x 4", the 16-card set is anchored by a large photo on the front, with "1993-94 Hoyas" located at the top. The player's name and bio are printed inside a stripe beneath the photo. The card backs have a Kids and Cops tip, along with McGruff the Crime Dog and Coca-Cola logos.

		MT
Complete Set (16):		5.00
Common Player:		.25
1	Team Photo	.75
2	John Thompson CO	.75
3	Joey Brown	.50
4	John Jacques	.25
5	Vladimir Bosanac	.25
6	Robert Churchwell	.50
7	Eric Micoud	.25
8	Lamont Morgan	.25
9	Kevin Millen	.25
10	George Butler	.50
11	Othella Harrington	2.50
12	Cheikh Dia	.25
13	Duane Spencer	.25
14	Don Reid	1.00
15	Irvin Church	.50
16	McGruff Crime Dog and Jack the Bulldog	.25

1994-95 Georgetown

Measuring 2-1/2" x 4", this 16-card set features Allen Iverson's first card. The card fronts are anchored by a large photo, with "1994-95 Hoyas" at the top. The player's name and bio are printed inside a stripe beneath the photo. The card backs feature a Kids and Cops tip, along with McGruff the Crime Dog, Nissan and Coca-Cola logos.

		MT
Complete Set (16):		55.00
Common Player:		.25
1	Team Photo	1.00
2	John Thompson CO	.75
3	John Jacques	.25
4	Boubacar Aw	.75
5	Allen Iverson	50.00
6	Irvin Church	.50
7	Kevin Millen	.25
8	George Butler	.25
9	Jerry Nichols	.75
10	Othella Harrington	1.50
11	Cheikh Dia	.50
12	Jerome Williams	2.50
13	Eric Myles	.25
14	Jahidi White	1.50
15	Don Reid	.75
16	McGruff the Crime Dog and Jack The Bulldog	.25

1996-97 Georgetown

This 18-card set was sponsored by the National Crime Prevention Council, Nissan and Coca-Cola, among others. The cards measure 2-1/2" x 4" and feature a player photo with his name, position and year in school underneath. The backs are printed in blue and red. They feature sponsor logos and a Kids & Cops safety tip.

		MT
Complete Set (18):		12.00
Common Player:		.50
1	Team Photo	1.00
2	Joseph Touomou	.50
3	Daymond Jackson	.50
4	Dean Berry	.50
5	Brendan Gaughan	.50
6	Cheikh Ya-Ya Dia	.75
7	Shernard Long	.50
8	Boubacar Aw	.75
9	Rhese Gibson	.50
10	Jerry Nichols	.50
11	Ed Sheffey	.50
12	Godwin Owinje	.50
13	Jahidi White	.75
14	Jameel Watkins	.50
15	Victor Page	3.00
16	Shamel Jones	.75
17	John Thompson CO	1.00
18	Law Enforcement Agencies Group Photo	.50

1989-90 Georgia

Sponsored by the USDA Forest Service, the card fronts feature color photos. "Georgia" is printed at the top in red, while the team name and player's name are printed in white on a black bar below the photo. The Smokey Bear logo is located in the lower left. The unnumbered card backs include the player's name and bio, along with a Smokey safety tip cartoon.

		MT
Complete Set (12):		20.00
Common Player:		1.00
	Neville Austin	1.00
	Arlando Bennett	1.00
	Rod Cole	1.00
	Hugh Durham CO	2.50
	Lillerial Green	5.00
	Pat Hamilton	1.00
	Mike Harron	1.00
	Lemuel Howard	1.00
	Alec Kessler	4.00
	Jody Patton	1.00
	Elmore Spencer	4.00
	Marshall Wilson	1.00

1990-91 Georgia

Sponsored by the USDA Forest Service, the 16-card set is anchored by a photo, which is bordered in red. "University of Georgia" is printed at the top in a white stripe, while the Smokey Bear logo is in the lower left and the player's name and bio is in the lower right. The unnumbered card backs have the Georgia basketball logos in the upper left and right, while the player's name is in the top center. His stats are printed beneath his name. A Smokey fire tip and cartoon round out the card backs.

		MT
Complete Set (16):		14.00
Common Player:		1.00
	Arlando Bennett - 32	1.00
	Charles Claxton - 33	2.50
	Rod Cole - 22	1.00
	Bernard Davis - 23	1.00
	Hugh Durham CO	2.50
	Shaun Golden - 10	1.00
	Lillerial Green - 11	4.00
	Antonio Harvey - 34	3.00
	Neville Austin - 35	1.00
	Lem Howard - 25	1.00
	Marcel Kon - 51	1.00
	Jody Patton - 12	1.00
	Kendall Rhine - 15	1.00
	Reggie Tinch - 24	1.00
	Marshall Wilson - 44	1.00
	1990-91 Bulldogs Team Photo	2.50

1992-93 Georgia

The 16-card set, sponsored by the USDA Forest Service, was available as a perforated sheet in four rows of four cards apiece. The red-bordered card fronts have a color photo in the center, with "Georgia Bulldogs Basketball" printed above the photo. The Smokey Bear logo is in the lower left, while the player's name, number and position are listed at the bottom right. The unnumbered card backs have the Georgia basketball logo in the upper left and right. Sandwiched between the logos are the player's name and bio. A Smokey fire tip and cartoon rounds out the card back.

		MT
Complete Set (16):		15.00
Common Player:		.75
	Shandon Anderson	8.00
	Terrell Bell	2.00
	Arlando Bennett	.75
	Dathon Brown	.75
	Charles Claxton	2.00
	Bernard Davis	.75
	Shaun Golden	.75
	Cleveland Jackson	.75
	Steve Jones	.75
	Kris Nordholz	.75
	Brian Peterson	.75
	Kendall Rhine	1.00
	Pertha Robinson	1.00
	Carlos Strong	4.00
	Chris Tiger	.75
	Ty Wilson	.75

1993-94 Georgia

The 16-card set was released in a perforated sheet that had four rows of four cards apiece. The red-bordered card fronts have a large color photo in the center, with "University of Georgia" printed at the top and the Georgia basketball logo printed inside a diamond in the upper center. Smokey Bear's 50th anniversary logo is included inside a diamond at the bottom of the card front, while the player's name and bio are printed on either side of the diamond at the bottom. The unnumbered card backs feature the Georgia basketball logo in both upper corners, while the player's name and bio are sandwiched in the top center. A Smokey tip and cartoon round out the card backs.

		MT
Complete Set (16):		12.00
Common Player:		.75
	Shandon Anderson	5.00
	Terrell Bell	1.50
	Dathon Brown	.75
	Charles Claxton	1.50
	Bernard Davis	.75
	Melvin Drake	.75
	Hugh Durham CO	1.50
	Cleveland Jackson	.75
	Steve Jones	.75
	Kris Nordholz	.75
	Brian Peterson	.75
	Pertha Robinson	1.00
	Carlos Strong	2.50
	Chris Tiger	.75
	Ty Wilson	.75
	Team Photo	1.00

1988-89 Georgia Tech

Sponsored by Nike, the 12-card sets were handed out to fans at various home games during the season. Color photos anchor the fronts, while "88-89" and "Yellow Jackets" are printed in the upper left corner. The Nike logo is located in the upper right. The Georgia Tech logo appears in the lower left. The player's name, number and position are printed inside a stripe beneath the photo. The card backs have the player's name and bio sandwiched between two Yellow Jacket logos at the top. The player's career highlights and tips from the Yellow Jackets round out the card backs. The Nike Logo appears in the lower right corner.

		MT
Complete Set (12):		25.00
Common Player:		1.00
1	Maurice Brittain - 52	1.00
2	Karl Brown - 5	1.50
3	Bobby Cremins CO	6.00
4	Brian Domalik - 12	1.00
5	Tom Hammonds - 20	5.00
6	Johnny McNeil - 44	1.50
7	James Munlyn - 24	1.00
8	Brian Oliver - 13	2.50
9	Willie Reese - 31	1.00
10	Dennis Scott - 4	8.00
11	Anthony Sherrod - 42	1.50
12	David Whitmore - 23	1.00

1989-90 Georgia Tech

Reportedly 10,000 sets were distributed by the Atlanta Police Athletic League. The 20-card set is anchored on the front by a photo. The years are printed in the upper left and the Coca-Cola logo appears in the upper right. "Yellow Jackets" appears beneath the logos and above the photos. The player's name, number, year and position are printed beneath the photo. The card backs include the player's name and bio, Georgia Tech logos and tips from the Yellow Jackets. The Coke logo is in the lower right. Three Kenny Andersons and two Dennis Scott cards are included in the set.

		MT
Complete Set (20):		15.00
Common Player:		.50
1	Kenny Anderson - 12 (Portrait)	3.00
2	Kenny Anderson - 12 (Free Throw)	3.00
3	Kenny Anderson - 12 (Jump Shot)	3.00
4	Rod Balanis - 34	.50
5	Darryl Barnes - 15	.50
6	Brian Black - 23	.50
7	Karl Brown - 5	.75
8	Bobby Cremins CO	1.50
9	Brian Domalik - 3	.50
10	Matt Geiger - 52	3.00
11	Malcolm Mackey - 32	1.00
12	Johnny McNeil - 44	.75
13	James Munlyn - 24	.50
14	Ivano Newbill - 33	.75
15	Brian Oliver - 13	1.00
16	Dennis Scott - 4 (Free Throw)	2.00
17	Dennis Scott - 4 (Shooting)	2.00
18	Greg White - 14	.50
19	Team Photo	1.00
20	Lethal Weapon 3 (Brian Oliver, Dennis Scott and, Kenny Anderson)	2.00

1990-91 Georgia Tech

Coca-Cola and the Atlanta City Police Department sponsored this 20-card standard-sized set. Overall, 10,000 sets were printed, with 5,000 going to the housing projects and children in the Atlanta Police Athletic Program. The white-bordered cards feature a color photo on the front, with the years and Coca-Cola logo in the upper left and right corners, respectively. "Yellow Jackets" is printed above the photo, but underneath the year and the Coke logo. The player's name, number, year and position are printed beneath the photo. The unnumbered backs have the player's name, bio and Georgia Tech logos at the top. Tips from the Yellow Jackets and a Coke logo also appear.

		MT
Complete Set (20):		15.00
Common Player:		.50
	Kenny Anderson - 12 (Shooting lay-up)	2.50
	Kenny Anderson - 12 (Driving past defender)	2.50
	Kenny Anderson - 12 (Dribbling)	2.50
	Rod Balanis - 34	.50
	Darryl Barnes - 15	.50
	Jon Barry - 14	2.50
	Brian Black - 23	.50
	Bobby Cremins CO	1.50
	Brian Domalik - 3	.50
	James Gaddy - 10	.50
	Todd Harlicka - 30	.50
	Bryan Hill - 11	.75
	Matt Geiger - 52	2.50
	Brian Gemberling - 41	.50
	Malcolm Mackey - 32	1.00
	Malcolm Mackey - 32	1.00
	James Munlyn - 24	.50
	Ivano Newbill - 33	.75
	Greg White - 31	.50
	Team Photo	1.00

1991-92 Georgia Tech

Sponsored by Coca-Cola and the Atlanta Police Athletic League, the 15-card set is anchored by a gold border and a color photo on the front. The years are printed in the upper left, the Coca-Cola logo is in the top center and the player's jersey number is in the upper right. "Yellow Jackets" is printed directly above the photo. The player's name, number, year and position are at the bottom. The unnumbered card backs have the player's name, bio and Georgia Tech logos at the top, along with tips from the Yellow Jackets. The Coke logo is at the bottom center.

		MT
Complete Set (15):		15.00
Common Player:		.50
	Rod Balanis	.50
	Darryl Barnes	.50
	Drew Barry	3.50
	Jon Barry	2.50
	Travis Best	6.00
	Bobby Cremins CO	1.50
	James Forrest	2.50
	James Gaddy	.50
	Matt Geiger	2.50
	Todd Harlicka	.50
	Bryan Hill	.75
	Malcolm Mackey	.75
	Ivano Newbill	1.00
	Fred Vinson	.75
	Greg White	.50

1992-93 Georgia Tech

The 15-card set was totally redesigned for this season, as a gold border on the left side includes the school's name vertically along the border. The player's name is housed inside a stripe at the bottom. The card backs, which are horizontal, showcase a head shot on the left, and the Georgia Tech logo, player's name and bio on the right side. The card number appears below the school's logo. The player's stats are listed in the center, with the bottom of the card featuring his career highlights.

		MT
Complete Set (15):		10.00
Common Player:		.50
1	Bobby Cremins CO	1.50
2	Bryan Hill	.75
3	James Gaddy	.50
4	Ivano Newbill	.75
5	Malcolm Mackey	.75
6	Rod Balanis	.50
7	Travis Best	3.50
8	Fred Vinson	.75
9	Darryl Barnes	.50
10	James Forrest	1.50
11	Todd Harlicka	.50
12	Drew Barry	2.00
13	Keith Kenney	.50
14	John Kelly	.50
15	Martice Moore	2.00

1991-92 Hawaii-Hilo

Measuring 2-1/4" x 3-1/2", the 15-card set is sponsored by Mauna Loa. The blue-bordered card fronts are anchored with a large photo, with the player's name and position printed in the upper right of the photo. The school's logo and year are located in the lower left of the photo. The sponsor's name is printed at the bottom center of the card front. The horizontal card backs are unnumbered. The player's name, position and jersey number appear in a stripe at the top, with his bio, career highlights and stats rounding out the rest of the card. The Mauna Loa logo is printed at the bottom of the card back.

		MT
Complete Set (15):		10.00
Common Player:		1.00
	Steve Armstrong	1.00
	Darren Buchanan	1.00
	Jason Cabral	1.00
	Chris Dane	1.00
	Jeff Garner	1.00
	Russ Harper	1.00
	Warren Harrell	1.00
	Mike Helm	1.00
	Paul Lee	1.00
	Jim Malinchak	1.00
	Cris Murphy	1.00
	Brett Nesland	1.00
	Mike Pollock	1.00
	Dwayne Sarver	1.00
	Booker Waugh	1.00

1992-93 Hawaii-Hilo

The red-bordered, 15-card set features a photo on the front with the player's name and jersey number at the bottom and the school's name and years listed vertically along the right side. The vertical card backs, which are unnumbered, have a headshot in the upper left and the player's name, number and bio on the right. The player's career highlights and stats round out the card back. The KTA logo also appears on the back.

		MT
Complete Set (15):		10.00
Common Player:		1.00
	Dan Androff	1.00
	Tyro Banks	1.00
	Fred Crawford	1.00
	Jerome Facione	1.00
	Jeff Garner	1.00
	Eddie Hayward	1.00
	Paul Lee	1.00
	Tim Lovejoy ACO	1.00
	Brett Nesland	1.00
	Mike Redwood	1.00
	Dwayne Sarver	1.00
	Mike Seawright	1.00
	Mike Van Staveren	1.00
	Bob Wilson CO	1.00
	Syrus Yarbrough	1.00

1992-93 Houston

Produced by Motion Sports Inc., the 28-card set includes color photos on the front inside black borders. The player's name and school name are printed inside red stripes on the card front. The numbered card backs include the standard bio and career highlights, along with an action photo of the player.

		MT
Complete Set (29):		25.00
Common Player:		.25
1	Pat Foster CO (Close-up)	.50
2	Bo Outlaw	6.00
3	Jessie Drain	.25
4	Derrick Smith	.25
5	Craig Lillie	.50
6	Tyrone Evans	.25
7	Rafael Carrasco	.25
8	Brandon Rollins	.25
9	David Diaz	.25
10	Jermaine Johnson	.25
11	Darrell Grayson	.25
12	Anthony Goldwire	1.50
13	Lloyd Wiles	.25
14	Pat Foster CO (Standing)	.50
15	Tommy Jones ACO	.25
16	Alvin Brooks ACO	.25
17	Team Photo	.50
18	Game of Century Houston vs. UCLA	1.00
19	Otis Birdsong	.50
20	Elvin Hayes	4.00
21	Hakeem Olajuwon	7.00
22	Clyde Drexler	6.00
23	Guy V. Lewis (Former CO)	1.00
24	1968 UPI and AP National Champs	.50
25	Cougar Pride (Trophies)	.25
26	Ad Card Motion Sports	.25
NNO	Front Card	.25
NNO	Back Card	.25
NNO	Checklist	.25

1994-95 IHSA Boys A State Tournament

The 215-card, standard-size set features players that participated in the Illinois High School Tournament. Cards vary with color and black and white photos and the horizontal backs feature player bio information over a basketball icon. "March Madness" is printed on the both sides. Just 1,000 sets were produced and the set numbering is not in order and there are frequent duplications.

		MT
Complete Set (215):		40.00
Common Player:		.25
1	Neal Cotts	.25
2	Richard Douglas	.25
3	John Flick	.25
4	Chad Kerksick	.25
5	Jason Kunz	.25
6	Duane Roth	.25
7	Parnell Roulds	.25
8	Adam Schieppe	.25
9	Eric Schwehr	.25
10	Justin Tarver	.50
11	Steve Walraven	.25
12	DeMarcus Walter	.25
13	Mike Schaefer	.25
14	Steve St. Jules	.25
15	Jim Ward	.25
16	Matt Becker	.25
17	Brad Bryan	.25
18	Duane Goebel	.25
19	Scott Huegen	.25
20	Kurt Kalmer	.25
21	Jeff Kehrer	.25
22	Nathan Kreke	.25
23	Glenn Lammers	.25
24	Troy Pingsterhaus	.25
25	Brett Schulte	.25
26	Bob Tebbe	.25
27	Luke Woltering	.25
28	Adam Zieren	.25
29	Clayton Arnett	.25
30	Tyson Bottom	.25
31	Andy Brannan	.25
32	Brian Clough	.25
33	Blake Cunningham	.25
34	Derek Freand	.25
35	Ben Goetten	.25
36	Ryan Graner	.25
37	Brian Hires	.25
38	Matt Hoots	.25
39	Adam Price	.25
40	Matt Ruyle	.25
41	Daryl Schnelten	.25
42	Mark Tepen	.25
43	Dan Walker	.25
44	Josh Allen	.25
45	Eric Glass	.25
46	Kyle Herring	.25
47	Charlie Holland	.25
48	Damon Lampley	.25
49	Robert Neal	.25
50	Martin Nicholes	.25
51	Dale Overstreet UER (Card misnumbered as 581)	.25
52	C.R. Rath	.25
53	Brandon Reynolds	.25
54	Jared Sperling	.25
55	Brad Vineyard	.25
56	Daniel Wenzel	.25
57	Brock Billings	.25
59	Peter Craig	.25
61	Heath Hall	.25
62	Jimmy Harris	.25
63	Marty Hull	.25
65	Rusty Lynch	.25
67	Kirk Mosley	.25
68	Ryan Pulliam	.25
70	Jason Stotts	.25
71	Joe Wilson	.25
72	Neil Banwart	.25
73	Brandon Branson	.25
74	Kevin Dyer	.25
75	Derric Eisenmann	.25
76	Chris Fowler	.25
77	Ryan Hivley	.25
78	Jeff Howard	.25

79	Ryan Martin	.25
80	Matt Mougey	.25
81	Jeff Peterson	.25
82	Cory Richmond	.25
83	Tim Sinclair	.25
84	Dustin Sullivan	.25
85	Kendell Welch	.25
86	Matt Wills	.25
87	Jonah Batambuze	.25
88	Jason Graf	.25
89	D.J. Hubbard	.25
90	Nathan Hubbard	.25
91	Kevin Jones	.25
92	Andy Matthews	.25
93	Matt McClintock	.25
94	Jason Naffziger	.25
95	Kurt Olson	.25
96	Eric Schlipf	.25
97	Nitai Spiro	.25
98	Jeremy Stanton	.25
99	Darrin York	.25
100	Bryan Butt	.25
101	Mark Churchill	.25
102	Nathlan DeBaillie	.25
103	Mark Gannon	.25
104	Jamie Hixson	.25
105	Chris John	.25
106	Ryan Jones	.25
107	Aaron Kunert	.25
108	Jason Larson	.25
109	Tim Shields	.25
110	Josh Talley	.25
111	Brandon Welborn	.25
112	Justin Welborn	.25
113	Ryan Westlund	.25
114	Jarred Wilson	.25
115	Scott Cornelis	.25
116	Dan Coyne-Logan	.25
117	Mike Coyne-Logan	.25
118	Tim Dinneen	.25
119	Matt Gripp	.25
120	Shawn Keeven	.25
121	Ryan Kelly	.25
122	Charles Manis	.25
123	Brian Moran	.25
124	Steve Sottos	.25
125	Tony Stock	.25
126	Brian Trapkus	.25
127	Pat Voss	.25
128	Chris Watson	.25
129	Pat Watson	.25
130	Josh Anderson	.25
131	Marc Carlson	.25
132	Tyson Erdelac	.25
133	Scott Frank	.25
134	Erik Frykholm	.25
135	Sam Glomp	.25
136	Andre Green	.25
137	Anthony Harris	.25
138	John Harris	.25
139	Bret Holmertz	.25
140	Dan Jameson	.25
141	Neil Kessman	.25
142	Bob Lindwall	.25
143	Shannon Tripplett	.25
144	Rich Beyers	.25
145	Jim Brix	.25
149	Kevin Herdes	.25
150	Roger Jones	.25
151	Harlan Kennell	.25
152	Alex Miller	.25
153	Aaron Rohdemann	.25
154	Ryan Shambo	.25
155	Ben Short	.25
156	Mike Steers	.25
157	Todd Wilderman	.25
158	Derek Williams	.25
159	Eric Roley	.25
160	Ryan Cox	.25
161	Brock Friese	.25
162	Mark Giertz	.25
163	Phil Manhart	.25
164	Scott Meers	.50
165	Christian Merriman	.25
166	Patrick Merriman	.25
167	Ryan Moomaw	.25
168	Craig Ogle	.25
170	Brock Vonderheide	.25
171	Ben Commare	.25
172	Peter Doetschman	.25
173	Brian Duffy	.25
174	Jake Engler	.25
175	Trevor Gartner	.25
176	Scott Gengler	.25
177	Greg Johnson	.25
178	Pat Keller	.25
179	Peter Knaub	.25
180	Matt Lowry	.25
181	Jake Nauman	.25
182	Matt Pavesich	.25
183	Gary Anderson	.25
184A	Ricky Brown	.25
184B	Brian Cardinal	.25
185A	Kendall Caples	.25
185B	C.J. Franks	.25
186	Sterling Chears	.25
187A	Vincent Dawkins	.25
187B	Jacques LeFaivre	.25
188A	Roosevelt Deanes	.25
188B	Lyndon Mumm	.25
189A	Ephraim Eaddy	.25
189B	Brad Siuts	.25
190A	Hiawatha Griffin	.25
190B	Eric Stevens	.25
191A	Philip Johnson	.25
191B	Eric Tempel	.25
192A	Craig Jones	.25
192B	Zach Trimble	.25
193A	John Jones	.25
193B	Brady Allison	.25
193C	Matt VanNote	.25
194A	Reginald Jones	.25
194B	Ryan Rich	.25
195A	Jamell McLaurin	.25
195B	John Hausman	.25
196	Thaddeus Bates	.25
321	Derrick York	.25
323	Dustin Rothrock	.25
341	Adam Law	.25
342	PJ McKinney	.25
343	Jed Cryder	.25
344	Jabari Harrell	.25
345	Brad Punke	.25
346	Zeno Weems	.25
347	Matt Scott	.25
348	Joe Mann	.25
349	Steve Becker	.25
350	Aaron Sovern	.25
351	Nathan Thompson	.25
352	Josh Wayne	.25
353	Julian Harrell	.25
354	Mark Allen	.25

1994-95 IHSA Boys A Slam Dunk

The 65-card set was produced to honor the participants of the slam dunk competition. Just 500 sets were issued. "Slam Dunk" is printed above the front photo and along the right side. The card backs are similar to the base set.

		MT
Complete Set (65):		10.00
Common Player:		.25
1	Charles Adams	.25
2	Ricky Brown	.25
3	Jeff Averkamp	.25
4	Tim Cavinder	.25
5	Phil Durkin	.25
6	Robert Hahn	.25
7	Mike Hawks	.25
8	Jason Peake	.25
9	Damiano Scalera	.25
10	James Gast	.25
11	Bryan Zotz	.25
12	Mike Tyler	.25
13	Tim West	.25
14	Jim Vance	.25
15	Tom Pshak	.25
16	Tommy Sawyer	.25
17	Derek Crabill	.25
18	Rick Lawson	.25
19	Brian Shaw	.25
20	Joel Hubbard	.25
21	Josh Born	.25
22	Jamie Reel	.25
23	Shawn Lade	.25
24	Jeff Peterson	.25
25	Josh Pistole	.25
26	Josh Jones	.25
27	A.J. Strum	.25
28	Kale Sellers	.25
29	Andy Ellet	.25
30	Chad Brecunier	.25
31	Eric Esker	.25
32	Marty Hull	.25
33	Matt Alepra	.25
34	Mark Rasmussen	.25
35	Robert Clark	.25
36	Damon Lampley	.25
37	Trevor Hiel	.25
38	Greg McDanel	.25
39	Todd Stewart	.25
40	William Newton	.25
41	Cory Eshleman	.25
42	Jackson Jones	.25
43	Tim Volpert	.25
44	Tony Zook	.25
45	Thomas Robinson	.25
46	Matt Gunier	.25
47	Ronnie Kammes	.25
48	Ryan Ashley	.25
49	Michael Glover	.25
50	Chris Prather	.25
51	Brandon Merchalnt	.25
52	Duane Roth	.25
53	Dusty Johnson	.25
54	Jason Ogorzaly	.25
55	Jeremy Browne	.25
56	Derrick DeWilde	.25
57	Brian Miller	.25
58	Alan Loy	.25
59	Kris Stoneking	.25
60	Michael Klinger	.25
61	Shea Banning	.25
62	James Gast	.25
63	David Cerven	.25
64	Alvin Valentine	.25
65	Andre Williams	.25

1994-95 IHSA Boys A 3-Point Showdown

The 52-card set depicts the participants of the three-point competition at the state tournament. The cards measure the standard size and production was limited to 500. "Three- Point" is printed along the left front border with "Showdown" featured along the top border.

		MT
Complete Set (52):		10.00
Common Player:		.25
1	Mike Abner	.25
2	Rob Buckley	.25
3	Mike Cox	.25
4	Corey Fox	.25
5	Ryan Fritch	.25
6	Drazen Jozic	.25
7	Muamer Karamovic	.25
9	Josh Komnick	.25
10	Steven Lester	.25
11	Mike Martin	.25
13	Patrick Presser	.25
14	Willie Reinburg	.25
15	Torey Rein	.25
16	Douglas Scott	.25
17	Michael Sommer	.25
18	Tom Stirnaman	.25
19	Brian Tackitt	.25
20	Josh Williams	.25
21	Joe Whitmore	.25
22	Andy Murray	.25
23	Luke Williams	.25
24	Michael Torman	.25
25	Michael Siegfried	.25
26	Aaron Sovern	.25
27	Scot Kent	.25
31	Guy Kuhn	.25
32	Dru McCulley	.25
33	Tony Merlie	.25
35	Eric Sherrier	.25
36	Bill Heisler	.25
37	Tony Hartman	.25
38	Ryan Hammer	.25
39	Chad Hammond	.25
40	David Griffiths	.25
41	Brent Fowler	.25
42	Chad Fulton	.25
43	Adam Crenshaw	.25
44	Ryan Clark	.25
45	Jason Clark	.25
46	Brian Ball	.25
47	Brent Baker	.25
48	Michael Arroyo	.25
52	Jeremy Lansaw	.25
53	John Harris	.25
54	Jacob Mundell	.25
55	Josh Menser	.25
56	Nick Pestka	.25
66	Troy Kemmerling	.25
67	Matt Morris	.25
302	J.C. Murray	.25
NNO	Ryan Knuppel	.25

1994-95 IHSA Boys AA State Tournament

The 328-card, standard-size set features players from the final 16 AA teams at the Illinois High School State Tournament with just 1,000 sets produced. The first card of NBA standout Kevin Garnett is included in the set (No. 226). The card design is virtually identical to the A team set with the horizontal backs having player bio information over a basketball icon.

		MT
Complete Set (328):		110.00
Common Player:		.25
1	Mike Becker	.25
1	Josh Veith	.25
2	Brad Bowsher	.25
3	Rob Brynjelsen	.25
4	Todd Dahlstrom	.25
5	Robert Davis	.25
6	Tom Honeycutt	.25
7	Chris Jacobs	.25
8	Steve Koliopoulos	.25
9	Dan Korvas	.25
10	Zach Maddox	.25
11	Jason McKinney	.25
12	Steve Nelson	.25
13	Chris Nowinski	.25
14	Joe Potocnic	.25
15	Brent Prorok	.25
16	Michael White	.25
17	Paul Wolf	.25
18	John Wotal	.25
19	Hector Barnes	.25
20	Durius Cunningham	.25
21	Corey Dagley	.25
22	Chuck Garrett	.25
23	Rick Garrett	.25
24	Mark Hamilton	.25
25	Tyrone Jones	.25
26	Justin Knolhoff	.25
27	Andre Marshall	.25
28	Ivan McPhail	.25
29	Ewin Meeks	.25
30	Ty Moss	.25
31	Chad Schnitker	.25
32	Luke Sharp	.25
33	Brett Skort	.25
34	Kimonie Evans	.50
35	Jerry Harris	.25
36	Kevin Thornton	.25
37	Jason Price	.25
38	Nick Irvin	.25
39	John Smith	.25
40	Marcel O'Neal	.25
41	Jason Garcia	.25
42	Keith Coley	.25
43	Chris Worrell	.25
44	Rodderick Thompson	.25
45	Artis James	.25
46	Alvin Robinson	.25
47	Darius Hampton	.25
48	Matt Horner	.25
49	Mark Wiggins	.25
50	Mike Valentine	.25
51	Andrew LeCrone	.25
52	Eric Norberg	.25
53	Milo Moreland	.25
54	Harry Beck	.25
55	Ed Precht	.25
56	Antwan Cuble	.25
57	Marty Mulcrone	.25
58	Matt Koch	.25
59	Doug Meyers	.25
60	Steve Rogala	.25
61	Andy Mitchell	.25
62	Erasmus Baffour	.25
63	Mark Allaria	.25
64	Antonio Brown	.25
65	Derek Cowan	.25
66	Jim Dougherty	.25
67	Maurice Douglas	.25
68	Eric Ess	.25
69	Jon Harris	.25
70	Tom Hofeditz	.25
71	Anthony Jumper	.25
72	Steffan Nicholson	.25
73	Joe Semith	.25
74	Mark Thomas	.25
75	Stacy Vaughn	.25
76	Dwight Woods	.25
77	Chris Wright	.25
78	Joe Bongratz	.25
79	Eric Bradley	.25
80	Joel Dangel	.25
81	Damion Forrest	.25
82	Maurice Foster	.25
83	Chris Hayes	.25
85	Brian Jaworski	.25
86	Ryan Kelver	.25
87	Ted Makela	.25
88	Joe Merrick	.25
89	David Moo	.25
90	Luke Moo	.25
92	Darnell Smith	.25
93	Carlton DeBose	.25
94	Denard Eaves	.25
95	Melvin Ely	.25
96	Corey Harris	.25
97	Napoleon Harris	.25
98	Erik Herring	.25
99	James Johnson	.25
100	Chauncey Jones	.25
101A	Richard King (Running down court)	.25
101B	Richard King (In action against other team)	.25
102	Nick Love	.25
103	Antwaan Randle El	.25
104	Curtis Randle El	.25
105	Maurice Scott	.25
106A	Tai Streets (Crashing the boards)	.35
106B	Tai Streets (different shot)	.35
107	Chip Bates	.25
108	Gary Bell	.35
109	Eric Breuer	.25
110	Dwayne Edmon	.25
111	Adrice Edwards	.25
112	John Ford	.25
113	Paul Forsythe	.25
114	Joel House	.25
115	Michael Mines	.25
116	Blowery Moody	.25
117	Rory O'Connell	.25
118	Eric Patnoudes	.25
119	Paul Purcell	.25
120	Kevin Raub	.25
121	Oku Satcher	.25
122	Erik Walton	.25
123	Tim Barrett	.25
125	Peter Carroll	.25
127	James Dombkiewicz	.25
128	Bill Donlon	.25
129	Michael Downes	.25
130	Sean Eggert	.25
131	Gabe Frank	.25
132	Joe Hein	.25
133	Stu Katz	.25
134	Jon Moeller	.25
135	Doug Rosen	.25
136	Adam Schimel	.25
138	Tim Caldwell	.25
139	Willie Coleman	.35
140	Kahil Gayton	.25
141	Marcus Griffin	.25
142	Darrell Ivory	.25
143	Dewayne Johnson	.25
144	Sergio McClain	.25
145	Charles Russell	.25
146	Willie Simmons	.25
148	Sean Walls	.25
149	Jeff Walraven	.25
150	Ivan Watson	.25
151	Frank Williams	.25
152	Willie Williams	.25
168	L.T. Boyd	.25
169	Josh Elston	.25
170	Heith Gadient	.25
171	Cory Jenkins	.25
172	Monte Jenkins	.35
173	Mike King	.25
174	Pete Mickeal	.25
175	Andy Milton	.25
176	Matt Quinones	.25
177	Larry Stevens	.25
178	Tymon Vesey	.25
179	Marlon White	.25
180	Brad Wilson	.25
181	Luke Woods	.25
183	Ricky Boone	.25
184	Dexter Gipson	.25
185	Pat Hand	.25
187	Walter Hill	.25
188	Craig Hopson	.25
189	Jon Luchetti	.25
190	Ryan Melling	.25
192	Charlie Newman	.25
193	Ryan Peterson	.25
195	Jeremy Warner	.25
196	Ali Azim	.25
197	Steve Ball	.25
198	Garrett Beatty	.25
199	Schaun Catey	.25
200	Kevin DePiazza	.25
201	Cameron Deppe	.25
202	Casey Dodson	.25
203	Mike Gullickson	.25
204	Daryl Kowalski	.25
205	Phillip Krahenbuhl	.25
206	Chris Levandowski	.25
207	Ryan Lindgren	.25
208	Lynwood Schambach	.25
209	Matt Wisinger	.25
210	Chris Wright	.25
211	Marcus Betts	.25
212	Ron Blanchard	.25
213	Gregory Bryant	.25
214	Danny Cassell	.25
215	Rubin Conway	.25
216	Marcus Crump	.25
217	Ian Dent	.25
218	Jim Devereux	.25
219	Mike Gadomski	.25
220	Richard James	.25
221	Aaron McIntosh	.25
222	Derrick Mims	.25
223	Ted Moore	.25
224	Justin Papuga	.35
225	Rob Walls	.25
226	Kevin Garnett	80.00
227	Ronnie Fields	4.00
228	Michael Wright	.25
229	Jonathon Washington	.25
230	Charles Johnson	.25
231	Maurice Woodfork	.25
233	Jerome McBride	.25
234	Daniel Sierra	.25
235	Miguel Estrada	.25
236	Jamal Rome (Misnumbered 237)	.25
237	Frank Smith (Identical to 238)	.25
238	Frank Smith (Identical to 237)	.25
342	Tory Hickman	.25
343	Brandon Douglas	.25
344	Brian Trowbridge	.25
345	Jim Flynn	.25
346	Loren Wallace CO, Tim Wallace ACO, Jeff Wallace ACO	.25
347	Brett Douglas	.25
348	Kendall Davis	.25
349	Mike Reddington	.25
350	Cory VonderHaar	.25
351	Adam Requet	.25
352	Ryan Stanton	.25
353	Kyle Cartmill	.25
354	Everette Abbey	.25

1994-95 IHSA Boys AA State Tournament Garnett Special Ed.

This two-card set features Kevin Garnett during his high school career in Chicago.

		MT
Complete Set (2):		120.00
Common Player:		60.00
239	Kevin Garnett	65.00
240	Kevin Garnett	60.00

1994-95 IHSA Boys AA 3-Point Showdown

The 60-card set features the players who participated in the three-point competition and the set mirrors the A set 3-Point Showdown in design. Production of the set was limited to 500.

		MT
Complete Set (60):		10.00
Common Player:		.25
1	Marcus Blossom	.25
2	Durwood McCoy	.25
3	Brad Mann	.25
4	Brett Nishibayashi	.25
5	Micah Ogburn	.25
6	Matt Wasinger	.25
7	Ray Hooks	.25
8	Charlie McKenna	.25
9	Steve Dahl	.25
11	Nick Sanchez	.25
12	Greg Gilberg	.25
13	Brian Sims	.25
14	Steven Wennstrom	.25
15	Tony Alvarado	.25
16	Josh Suter	.50
17	Dave Zell	.25
18	Ali Ali	.25
19	Ryan Naughton	.25
20	Frederick Smith	.25
21	Greg Moog	.25
22	Dominic Catalano	.25
23	Brad Fuller	.25
24	David Mikes	.25
25	Jon Heider	.25
26	Korey Coon	.25
27	Michael Mines	.25
28	Mark Richardson	.25
29	Kyle Breden	.25
30	Danny Nicholas	.25
31	Todd Meggos	.25
32	Chris Johnston	.25
33	Jasper Mallory	.25
34	Cordell Henry	.25
35	Adam Riva	.25
36	Alfonzo Lewis	.25
37	Luke Windy	.25
38	Bob Castelli	.25
39	Jeff Peterson	.25
40	Arthur Stapleton	.25
41	Darius Wesley	.25
42	Matt Boudeman	.25
43	Kevin Casey	.25
44	John Lackaff	.25
45	Tom Schmidt	.25
46	Mike Pryor	.25
47	Mike Geurin	.25
48	Bob Tolone	.25
49	Jonathan Daniels	.25
50	John Mackinson	.25
51	Tarise Bryson	.25
52	Jeremy Lansaw	.25
53	John Harris	.25
54	Jacob Mundell	.25
55	Josh Menser	.25
56	Nick Pestka	.25
57	Brandon Frerichs	.25
58	Donya Jackson	.25
61	Adrian Diaz	.25
64	Danyell Cresswell	.25
NNO	Chris Berezniak	.25

1994-95 IHSA Girls A State Tournament

Roox Limited Corporation produced this set featuring the 16 teams in the Illinois Girls A state tournament. Some photos are color, some are black-and-white and some cards have no photos. All the cards have a gold border across the top with the player's name and "March Madness '95" printed inside. The backs have basic information on the players. Numbering on this set is confusing because some cards are numbered out of sequence and other numbers are skipped entirely. Only 1,000 sets were produced.

		MT
Complete Set (195):		50.00
Common Player:		.40
29	Michelle Donahoo	.40
30	Leslie Dumstorff	.40
31	Sara Evans	.40
32	Heather Fruend	.40
33	Danielle Funderburk	.40
34	Kristin Hustedde	.40
35	Tara Kell	.40
36	Erin Knuf	.40
37	Racheal Nelson	.40
38	Shannon Pollmann	.40
39	Courtney Smith	.40
40	Amy Allison	.40
43	Lindsay Fecht	.40
45	Cassie Kinnamon	.40
46	Andrea Livingston	.40
47	Alisha Nagel	.40
52	Koula Toubekis	.40
53	Sabrina Bannister	.40
54	Ladonna Barton	.40
55	Lawanda Burras	.40
56	Christina Evans	.40
57	Sabrina Minter	.40
58	Latrice Payne	.40
59	Latrice Ray	.40
60	Whitney Wells	.40
61	Quinlora Smith	.40
62	Tondalaya Wilson	.40
115	Lindsey Armstrong	.40
116	Heather Cassady	.40
117	Jacey Cook	.40
118	Melissa Cotter	.40
119	Jessi Davis	.40
120	Stephanie Donovan	.40
121	Tracie Gramkow	.40
122	Sara Harlan	.40
123	Stephanie Marino	.40
124	Lisa Nicoll	.40
125	Kari Singer	.40
126	Jaima Stowell	.40
128	Sara Urban	.40
172	Corrie Allan	.40
173	Randi Anderson	.40
174	Theresa Bertolino	.40
175	Kami Derganc	.40
176	Margo Girardi	.40
177	Kara Joyce	.40
178	Celia Jubelt	.40
179	Laura Mansholt	.40
180	Jodi Ottersburg	.40
181	Kristine Polo	.40
182	Deneisch Reiniesch	.40
183	Alisha Saracco	.40
184	Angie Thompson	.40
185	Wendy Wolff	.40
186	Anna Banks	.40
187	Kelly Cartwright	.40
188	Rachyl Clayton	.40
189	Jaylyn Crabb	.40
190	Ricki DeAmon	.40
191	Amanda Duggins	.40
192	Dawn Halverson	.40
193	Alisha Logan	.40
194	Chrystal Milligan	.40
195	Amy Molinarolo	.40
196	Audrey Murphy	.40
197	Traci Richerson	.40
198	Jessica Stafford	.40
199	Tory Teckenbrock	.40
200	Erin Watson	.40
230	Monica Blyenberg	.40
231	Kristen Bruinsma	.40
232	Linda DeJong	.40
233	Suzanne DeJong	.40
234	Kim DeYoung	.40
235	Karri Hamstra	.40
237	Jennifer Huizenga	.40
238	Jennifer Kreykes	.40
239	Jill Scott	.40
240	Nicole Terpstra	.40
241	Becky Vugleveen	.40
286	Julie Abell	.40
287	Kim Beer	.40
288	Shanda Cushing	.40
289	Laura Dwyer	.40
290	Jenelle Halm	.40
291	Hilary Hamer	.40
292	Lisa Hendrickson	.40
293	Meredith Jackson	.40
294	Courtney Jones	.40
295	Nikki McCleary	.40
296	Erin Micheletti	.40
297	Christine O'Connor	.40
327	Nicki Bradford	.40
328	Cali Broege	.40
329	Stacy Ditzler	.40
330	Stephanie Fransen	.40
331	Kara Hillmer	.40
332	Kendra Hillmer	.40
333	Kelley Hofmaster	.40
334	Jody Knoup	.40
335	Kim Koehn	.40
336	Cari Pacey	.40
337	Elaine Smielewski	.40
338	Jocelyn Stiefel	.40
339	Sara Thompson	.40
340	Tiffany Gallamore	.40
341	Shannon Hoyt	.40
342	Julie Knuffman	.40
344	Susan Laws	.40
345	Julie Ludwig	.40
346	Robyn Martin	.40
347	Dana Schutte	.40
348	Deanna Schutte	.40
349	Becky Smith	.40
350	Michelle Sulewski	.40
351	Deanna Venvertloh	.40
352	Abby Williams	.40
353	Angie Zanger	.40
354	Amy Hope	.40
355	Jennie Baird	.40
356	Cindy Cheney	.40
357	Jill Cheney	.40
358	Karen Davis	.40
359	Brandi Heleine	.40
360	Kasi High	.40
361	Lisa Hillary	.40
363	Laine Kistler	.40
364	Angela Pryle	.40
365	Billy Reagan	.40
366	Amy Thompson	.40
367	Jamie Todd	.40
368	Lisa Holley	.40
369	Amy Johnson	.40
370	Trish Kazak	.40
371	Lisa Kuppler	.40
372	Stephanie Morphey	.40
373	Jacqui Powers	.40
374	Amy Reiss	.40
375	Cori Stahl	.40
376	Leanne Stinson	.40
377	LeAnne Stout	.40
379	Haylie Behmer	.40
380	Brianne Bennett	.40
381	Michelle Fager	.40
382	Jennifer Harms	.40
383	Lea Horii	.40
384	Mandey Johnson	.40
385	Shelley Johnson	.40
386	Angie Patzner	.40
387	Jill Schwitters	.40
388	Elizabeth Stout	.40
389	Jill Tyler	.40
390	Katie Tyler	.40
391	Erin York	.40
392	Gina Bloemer	.40
393	Karla Campbell	.40
394	Sara Gebben	.40
395	Karen Kroeger	.40
396	Marcia Meyer	.40
397	Amy Niebrugge	.40
398	Maria Niebrugge	.40
399	Sarah Niebrugge	.40

400 Elizabeth Ordner .40
401 Emily Probst .40
402 Kari Probst .40
403 Christina Sehy .40
404 Monica Tegeler .40
405 Kim Walk .40
406 Crystal Worman .40
407 Stormy Young .40
408 Sherry Austin .40
409 Jennifer Bales .40
410 Alicia Brown .40
411 Carissa Brown .40
412 Kristy Duncan .40
413 Katie Edgecombe .40
414 Julie Farr .40
415 Amy Friend .40
416 Stacey Garner .40
417 Leslie Harris .40
418 Chrissy Kunz .40
419 Amanda Park .40
420 Carrie Wickline .40
423 Amy Anderson .40
424 Hilary Anderson .40
425 Lynette Carlson .40
427 Laura Curry .40
428 Kindel McLaughlin .40
429 Shanna Metzler .40
430 Tara Miller .40
431 Jodie Peterson .40
432 Rachel Peterson .40
433 April Schultz .40
436 Laura Bearrows .40
443 Corrie Allan .40

1994-95 IHSA Girls A 3-Point Showdown

This 64-card set features the participants in the Three-Point Showdown at the Illinois Girls A state tournaments. The photos are color on some cards and black-and-white on others. On the card fronts, "Three-Point Showdown" is printed on the left and top, with the player's name and "The Happening '95" below the photo. The backs have basic player information. Only 500 sets were produced.

MT
Complete Set (64): 15.00
Common Player: .40
1 Missy Barrett .40
2 Ami Beck .40
3 Kristi Bosman .40
4 Nicole Brinker .40
5 Trudy Brooks .40
6 Amanda Colgan .40
7 Patty Conover .40
8 Kami Dergane .40
9 Heather Downing .40
10 Bethany Ellis .40
11 Jill Gomric .40
12 Alicia Granger .40
13 Liza Gualandi .40
14 Stacie Hall .40
15 Erin Henderson .40
16 Heather Holsapple .40
17 Shannon Huff .40
18 Kim Jones .40
19 Ning Kongrut .40
20 Kari Koonce .40
21 Megan Linke .40
22 Traci Lloyd .40
23 Kimberly Lowe .40
24 Ashley Mathias .40
25 Paula Meeker .40
26 Kendra Meyer .40
27 Crystal Miller .40
28 Bridget Monahan .40
29 Dobee Oros .40
30 Heidi Ott .40
31 Cari Pacey .40
32 Jenny Pansa .40
33 Melissa Piper .40
34 Michelle Plack .40
35 Stephanie Rolf .40
36 Maggie Ross .40
37 Kelli Ryan .40
38 Mary Saline .40
39 Kimberly Shafer .40
40 Kelly Slaughter .40
41 Mandy Snell .40
42 Shavon Ellen Sork .40
43 Kimberly Stephenson .40
44 Laura Stucker .40
45 Jody Turrell .40
46 Jesse Weber .40
47 Cathy Wells .40
48 Laurie Zawila .40
49 Lisa Dolan .40
50 Amber Grubbs .40
51 Jessica Kittel .40
52 Amanda White .40
53 Sarah Hunt .40
54 Valerie Lepper .40
55 Gina Fisher .40
56 Brooke Moyer .40
57 Addie Ahlemeyer .40
58 Kris Slavin .40
59 Melanie Mueller .40
60 Melissa Signa .40
61 Alisha Logan .40
62 Teara Backens .40
63 Erin Murphy .40
64 Meredith Jackson .40

1994-95 IHSA Girls AA State Tournament

Roox Limited Corporation produced this set featuring the 16 teams that participated in the Illinois Girls AA state tournament. Some of the photos in this set are color, some are black-and-white and some cards have no photos at all. All the cards have a gold border at the top with the player's name and "March Madness '95" printed in it. The backs have basic player information. Only 1,000 sets were produced.

MT
Complete Set (227): 50.00
Common Player: .40
1 Kathy Fioresi .40
2 Dana Hellgren .40
3 Julie Janota .40
4 Anna Johnson .40
5 Mary Beth Johnson .40
6 Kathy Kirkpatrick .40
7 Melissa Parker .40
8 Kim Pompa .40
9 Cathy Ptasnik .40
10 Leslie Schock .40
11 Suzy Smith .40
12 Karisa Turek .40
13 Rachel Voss .40
14 Tina Wenckaitis .40
15 Nykisha Barefield .40
16 Samantha Cartwright .40
17 Shelia Ahern .40
18 Tanisha Brewer .40
19 Cherise Compobasso .40
20 Kate Harker .40
21 Lisa Holman .40
22 Christina Jost .40
23 Stacy Kondziolka .40
24 Kelly Ludy .40
25 Kelly Murman .40
26 Anne Sudlow .40
27 Diana Wendell .40
28 Karen Zygowicz .40
63 Cheri Buchanan .40
64 Jill Fagan .40
65 Andrea Gunnell .40
66 Valerie Kobel .40
67 Jenny Linane .40
68 Katie McAlinden .40
69 Annie McDonald .40
70 Mary Moravek .40
71 Katie Morrissey .40
72 Jeanene Novick .40
73 Katie Schumacher .40
75 Karen Siska .40
76 Karen Valentas .40
77 Trish Watson .40
78 Latasha Love .40
79 Lakendra Moffett .40
80 Kilah Moore .40
81 Michelle Roberts .40
82 Virginia Sellers .40
83 Lori Shelby .40
84 Janelle Tabor .40
85 Stephanie Wallace .40
86 Jenny Accardo .40
87 Amy Anderson .40
88 Tara Babich .40
89 Ann Brophy .40
90 Melissa Collins .40
91 Michelle Foley .40
92 Beth Gawlinski .40
93 Jackie Geraci .40
94 Julie Johnson .40
95 Lauren Manczko .40
96 Mary Ellen O'Grady .40
97 Kristen Rezny .40
98 Sara Shrader .40
99 Erin Stafford .40
100 Krista Thomas .40
101 Marcella Barry .40
102 Dominique Canty .40
103 Shereena Clarke .40
104 Deon Cooper .40
105 Clarissa Flores .40
106 Yolanda Howard .40
107 Jaqui Jones 1.00
108 Terica Keaton .40
109 Lawanda McCants .40
110 Kimberly Moore .40
111 Danielle Pinkston .40
112 Natasha Pointer .40
113 Danielle Scott 1.00
129 Sandi Andersen .40
130 Stefanie Boerema .40
131 Kristi Bosman .40
132 Beth Boven .40
133 Anna Christen .40
134 Laurie Decker .40
135 Cheryl Koolma .40
136 Marisa Kottke .40
137 Becky Lanenga .40
138 Heidi Rimpila .40
139 Sira Rimpila .40
140 Lora Vandenberg .40
141 Stephanie Webber .40
142 Nicole Wieringa .40
143 Katie Zeilstra .40
144 Kristine Abramowski .40
145 Kim Brock .40
146 Betsy Byers .40
147 Tracy Clay .40
148 Amy Coleman .40
149 Jenny Crouse .40
150 Emily Dale .40
151 Tanya Deutscher .40
152 Heather Dittmar .40
153 Melissa Meyers .40
154 Emily Stadel .40
155 Colleen Stebbins .40
156 Lindsay Wentz .40
157 Bonny Apsey .40
158 Jennifer Bulkeley .40
160 Angie Galyean .40
161 Heidi Gengenbacher .40
162 Jenny Crimotich .40
162 Kathy Kelley .40
163 Steph Latham .40
164 Julie Lofing .40
165 Gina Miller .40
167 Ami Pendry .40
168 Stefanie Mitchell .40
168 Mandy Rinker .40
169 Molly Watson .40
170 Sara Wood .40
171 Jen Wright .40
201 Beth Bear .40
202 Lori Breitweiser .40
203 Julie Carroll .40
204 Brieanna Coffman .40
205 Becky Cox .40
206 Paula Hawkins .40
207 Jara Hellrung .40
208 Michelle Jarman .40
209 Karla Krueger .40
210 Amy Mortensen .40
211 Katie Mortensen .40
212 Kristen Norton .40
213 Jana Shortal .40
214 Amanda Vaughn .40
216 Jennifer Buell .40
217 Kelly Byrne .40
218 Lashonda Clay .40
219 Jamie Hankins .40
220 Katie Maley .40
221 Kelly Maley .40
222 Alicia Mesi .40
223 Amanda Miller .40
224 Kim Nischik .40
225 Ellen Sauser .40
226 Aubrey Sekal .40
227 Jamie Selip .40
228 Beth Walse .40
229 Kate Walse .40
242 Aarin Bartelt .40
243 Ashley Campbell .40
244 Kimberly Carter .40
245 Tamika Catchings 1.00
246 Tauja Catchings .40
247 Amy Chaness .40
248 Kelly Cole .40
249 Katie Coleman .40
250 Tricia DeClark .40
251 Rebekah Ford .40
252 Noelle Mendenwaldt .40
253 Christy Miller .40
254 Felice Rosenzwig .40
255 Carolyn Roth .40
256 Jamie Smith .40
257 Jennifer Warkins .40
258 Laura Boyer .40
259 Amanda Ely .40
260 Kristie Hamman .40
261 Jessica Jackson .40
262 Jennifer Klein .40
263 Kari Kuefler .40
264 Jenny Leigh .40
265 Liz Luthman .40
266 Jamila Minnicks .40
267 Heather Ory .40
268 Suzie Rizek .40
269 Alicia Stewart .40
270 Tjunia (T.J.) Williams .40
271 Sara Eggleston .40
272 Jaime Gray .40
273 Samantha Hardwick .40
274 Missi Keeley .40
275 Jackie Kopp .40
276 Abby Lewis .40
277 Katy McCain .40
278 Jill McDaniel .40
279 Kelly Moore .40
280 Sara Mozingo .40
281 Jenny Reeves .40
282 Jenny Schmidt .40
283 Kristy Schutz .40
284 Sparkle Thornton .40
298 Kim Bugel .40
299 Laura Castelloni .40
300 Maureen Enright .40
301 Becky Gorecki .40
302 Nora Hogueisson .40
303 Tina LaCombe .40
304 Meggan MacFarlane .40
305 Jenny Malone .40
306 Trisha Monahan .40
307 Jean Nagler .40
308 Amy Novak .40
309 Julie Ricci .40
310 Jenny Sosnowski .40
311 Jill Turner .40
312 Jodi Williams .40
313 Kim Anderson .40
314 Dixie Brazelton .40
315 Missi Clark .40
316 Katie Cutright .40
317 Angi Dewitt .40
318 Bessie Fulk .40
319 Erin Hutchinson .40
320 Randi Johnson .40
321 Adrienne Kraemer .40
322 Erin McNary .40
323 Danette Pine .40
324 Denise Pine .40
325 Shelby Strow .40
326 Emily Stuck .40
436 Tammy Cartwright .40
437 Vanessa Harris .40
438 Danyell Humphries .40
439 Quatoya Johnson .40
445 Laurie Schumacher .40

1994-95 IHSA Girls AA 3-Point Showdown

This 56-card set features the participants in the Three-Point Showdown at the Illinois Girls AA state tournament. The photos are color on some cards and black-and-white on others. On the card fronts, "Three-Point Showdown" is printed on the left and top, with the player's name and "The Happening '95" below the photo. The backs have basic player information. Only 500 sets were produced.

MT
Complete Set (56): 15.00
Common Player: .40
65 Stacy Albrecht .40
66 Michelle Allured .40
67 Tamika Coleman .40
68 Latavia Davis .50
69 Manali Doshi .40
70 Bessie Jo Fulk .40
71 Mackenzie Goebel .40
72 Danielle Green .40
73 Andrea Gunnell .40
74 K.C. Hammond .40
75 Esther Henigan .40
76 Keesha Humphrey .40
77 Holly Johnson .40
78 Jaime Johnson .40
79 Yulonda Jones .40
80 GeGe King .40
81 Tammie Krysh .40
82 Maggie Lamb .40
83 Roz Leeck .40
84 Jenny Lindemann .40
85 Karen Niebrugge .40
86 Denise Pavichevich .40
87 Lisa Perales .40
88 Stacey Pohar .40
89 Holly Palombi .40
90 Tania Price .40
91 Michelle Roof .40
92 Daryl Schaffeld .40
93 Jennifer Sciortino .40
94 Anne Sudlow .40
95 Amanda Vaughn .40
96 Beth Walse .40
97 Jodi Williams .40
98 Carly Zilligen .40
99 Karneelah Morgan .40
100 Anne Mucci .40
101 Denise McMillan .40
102 Jaime Maurer .40
103 Anne McDonald .40
104 Jaime Lynn Burandt .40
105 Shannon O'Neill .40
106 Jenny Schmidt .40
107 Jaime Gray .40
108 Amanda Cavitt .40
109 Jill Carpenter .40
110 Trish Ackerman .40
111 Crystal Tarr .40
112 Danielle Moles .40
113 Laura Valente .40
114 Kelly Gilbert .40
115 Monique Daniel .40
116 Erin Backman .40
117 Nicole LaBuhn .40
118 Wakeelah Ross .40
119 Vanessa Johnson .40
120 Melissa Frawley .40

1994-95 IHSA Historic Record Holders

The 30-card set features standout players from past Illinois state high school tournaments. The set was limited to a production of 500 and contains players who went on to play in the NBA such as Dave Robisch and LaPhonso Ellis.

MT
Complete Set (30): 10.00
Common Player: .50
62 Fernando Bunch .50
63 Sandy Braun .50
64 Brent Carmichael .50
65 Walter Downing .50
66 Mike Duff .50
67 Jim Edmondson .50
68 LaPhonso Ellis 3.00
69 Jo Jo Johnson .50
70 Dale Kelley .50
71 Jim Lazenby .50
72 Nora Lewis .50
73 Matt Maton .50
74 Chris Payne .50
75 Courtney Porter .50
76 Dave Robisch 1.00
77 Johnny Selvie .75
78 Jay Shidler .75
79 Cathy Shoup .50
80 Marty Simmons .50
81 Gary Tidwell .50
82 Tammy Van Oppen .50
83 Kevin Washington .50
84 Connie Erickson .50
85 Lori Fitzjarrald .50
86 Dee Dee Franklin .50
87 Shannon Hickenbottom .50
88 Cammy Hudson .50
89 Tina Hutchinson .50
90 Cindy Kaufmann .50
91 Jamie Brandon .75

1980-81 Illinois

Cards of Derek Harper and Eddie Johnson are included in this 15-card set sponsored by Arby's. The card fronts feature a color photo at the top, with the player's facsimile autograph and an Arby's advertisement printed below the photo. The horizontal card backs feature the player's name, number and bio at the top, while his career highlights and stats are printed in the center of the card. "The '80s belong to the Illini" is printed in the lower left, while an Arby's ad is printed in the lower right.

MT
Complete Set (15): 25.00
Common Player: 1.00
1 Kevin Bontemps 1.00
2 James Griffin 1.00
3 Derek Harper 12.00
4 Lou Henson CO 4.00
5 Derek Holcomb 1.50
6 Eddie Johnson 12.00
7 Bryan Leonard 1.00
8 Dick Nagy ACO 1.00
9 Perry Range 1.00
10 Quinn Richardson 1.00
11 Mark Smith 1.00
12 Neale Stoner 1.00
13 Craig Tucker 1.00
14 Tony Yates ACO 1.50
15 Team Photo 5.00
1.00

1981-82 Illinois

A Derek Harper card is featured in this 16-card set sponsored by Arby's. The card fronts are anchored by a photo at the top, with his facsimile signature and an Arby's ad are printed beneath it. The horizontal card backs have the player's name, number and bio at the top, with his career stats and highlights printed below. "The '80s belong to the Illini" appears in the lower left, with an Arby's logo in the lower right.

MT
Complete Set (16): 20.00
Common Player: 1.00
1 Kevin Bontemps 1.00
2 Jay Daniels 1.00
3 James Griffin 1.00
4 Derek Harper 10.00
5 Lou Henson CO UER (Misspelled Hensen on card back) 3.00
6 Dan Klier 1.00
7 Bryan Leonard 1.00
8 Dee Maras 1.00
9 George Montgomery 1.00
10 Dick Nagy ACO 1.00
11 Perry Range 1.00
12 Quinn Richardson 1.00
13 Craig Tucker 1.00
14 Anthony Welch 1.50
15 Tony Yates ACO 1.50
16 Team Photo 2.00

1992-93 Illinois

This 32-card set features both male (1-15) and female (17-32) members of the Illinois basketball teams. The set was sponsored by Pepsi and produced by Flying Color Graphics, Inc. It features color fronts with an orange border running up the left side of the card containing the school name. Backs, which are different for males and females, contain biographical information, the sponsor logo and a public service message.

MT
Complete Set (32): 18.00
Common Player: .25
1 Robert Bennett .25
2 Rennie Clemons 2.00
3 Jimmy Collins ACO .50
4 Mark Coomes ACO .25
5 Marc Davidson .25
6 Chris Gandy .25
7 Lou Henson CO 2.00
8 Chief Illiniwek (Mascot) .25
9 Andy Kaufmann 1.50
10 Richard Keene .50
11 Tom Michael .50
12 Dick Nagy ACO .25
13 Brooks Taylor .25
14 Deon Thomas 2.00
15 T.J. Wheeler .50
16 Assembly Hall .50
17 Tonya Booker .25
18 Anita Clinton .25
19 Mandy Cunningham .25
20 Merimartha Cunningham .25
21 Cindy Dilger .25
22 Kris Dupps .25
23 Jill Estey .25
24 Keila Flagg .25
25 Cindi Hanna .25
26 Jackie Hemann .25
27 Bridget Inman .25
28 Vicki Klingler .25
29 Kathy Lindsey CO .25
30 Lolita Platt .25
31 Robbyn Preacely .25
32 Connie Ruholl .25

1986-87 Indiana Greats I

Sponsored by Bank One, this 42-card set is the first in a series. The fronts are anchored by a large color or black-and-white photo. Beneath the photo, from left, are the Indiana University logo, the player's name and Bank One logo. The horizontal card backs have the player's name, bio, stats and career highlights. The card number is in the upper right inside a basketball.

MT
Complete Set (42): 19.00
Common Player: .50
1 Bobby Knight CO 4.00
2 Walt Bellamy 2.00
3 Pete Obremskey .50
4 Jim Wisman .50
5 Frank Radovich .50
6 Ted Kitchel .50
7 Don Schlundt 1.00
8 Uwe Blab 1.00
9 Lou Watson .50
10 Bobby Masters .50
11 Steve Redenbaugh .50
12 Bob Wilkerson .75
13 Kent Benson 1.50
14 Everett Dean 1.00
15 Rick Ford .50
16 Hallie Bryant .50
17 Dan Dakich .75
18 Sam Gee .50
19 George McGinnis 2.00
20 John Ritter .50
21 Jon McGlocklin 1.00
22 Landon Turner 1.50
23 Gary Long .50
24 Jim Crews 1.00
25 Steve Downing 1.00
26 Vern Huffman .50
27 Ernie Andres .50
28 Charles Hodson .50
29 Jerry Thompson .50
30 Tom Abernethy .75
31 Tom Bolyard .50
32 Jimmy Rayl 1.00
33 John Laskowski .75
34 Archie Dees .75
35 Joby Wright 1.00
36 Gary Greiger .50
37 Randy Wittman 1.00
38 Steve Green .50
39 Erv Inniger .50
40 Steve Risley .50
41 Bill DeHeer .50
42 Checklist Card .75

1987-88 Indiana Greats II

Series II features 18 cards and has the same basic design of the first series. The front is anchored by a large photo, with the Indiana University logo on the left, the player's name in the center and Bank One logo on the right. The backs, which are horizontal, have the player's name, career highlights and stats. The card's number is printed inside a basketball in the upper right.

MT
Complete Set (42): 24.00
Common Player: .50
1 Steve Alford's Farewell 1.50
2 Bob Dro .50
3 Butch Joyner .50
4 Bobby Leonard .75
5 Branch McCracken 1.00
6 Ray Tolbert 1.50
7 Wayne Radford .75
8 Earl Schneider .50
9 Jim Strickland .50
10 Al Harden .50
11 Bob Menke .50
12 Steve Alford 2.00
13 Mike Woodson 1.50
14 Tom Van Arsdale, Dick Van Arsdale 2.00
15 Wally Choice .50
16 Charlie Hall .50
17 Indiana Coach Legend 1.00
18 Stew Robinson .75
19 Dynamic Duo 1.00
20 Steve Alford 2.00
21 Quinn Buckner 1.50
22 Indiana Coach Legends 1.00
23 Winston Morgan .50
24 1975-76 Seniors 1.00
25 Jim Thomas .75
26 Vern Payne .50
27 Scott May 1.50
28 Dave Porter .50
29 Dick Farley .50
30 Isiah Thomas 6.00
31 Butch Carter .75
32 Burke Scott .50
33 Jack Johnson .50
34 Charley Kraak .50
35 Marv Huffman .50
36 Steve Bouchie .50
37 Bobby Knight's Record 1.50
38 Bill Garrett .50
39 Jerry Bass .50
40 Jay McCreary .50
41 Ken Johnson .50
42 Checklist Card (Send-in offer on back) .75

1991-92 Indiana Magazine Insert

These 12 cards were included with the first issue of Hoosier College Basketball (November 1991). Nine of the cards were on an unperforated sheet, while three other cards were included on a strip. Overall, 5,000 sets were printed. The cards would measure standard size if cut from the sheet. The fronts showcase a color photo inside a gold-foil and black border. The backs have the player's name at the top, with his career highlights in the center and his bio at the bottom. His jersey number appears in a circle in the lower right. In addition, a red-bordered version of the set was produced (100 sets). These cards sell for three to four times more than the black cards.

MT
Complete Set (12): 50.00
Common Player: 1.50
1 Eric Anderson 3.00
2 Damon Bailey 8.00
3 Calbert Cheaney 12.00
4 Brian Evans 8.00
5 Greg Graham 6.00
6 Pat Graham 3.00
7 Alan Henderson 10.00
8 Bobby Knight CO 12.00
9 Pat Knight 1.50
10 Jamal Meeks 1.50
11 Matt Nover 4.00
12 Chris Reynolds 1.50

1992-93 Indiana

Phipps Sports Marketing Inc. printed this 18-card set. The red bordered cards have a color photo over a background of a basketball. The player's name and number run vertically along the left border. The years, Indiana logo and "Hoosiers" are all included inside a circle in the lower right corner. The horizontal card backs are unnumbered. They have a head shot in the upper left, with his name in the upper right. His bio, career highlights and stats are all printed inside a box which is placed over a basketball background.

MT
Complete Set (18): 12.00
Common Player: .50
Damon Bailey 2.00
Calbert Cheaney 4.00
Brian Evans 2.00
Greg Graham 1.50
Pat Graham .75
Alan Henderson 4.00
Bob Knight CO 3.00
Pat Knight .50
Todd Leary .50
Todd Lindeman .75
Matt Nover 1.00
Chris Reynolds .50
Malcolm Sims .50
Assemby Hall .75
Coaching Staff (Dan Dakich ACO, Norm Ellenberger ACO, Ron Felling ACO) .50
Team Photo 1.00
The Knight Era (Trophies) .75
Title Card .50

1993-94 Indiana

This 18-card set was also printed by Phipps Sports Marketing Inc. The card fronts feature a red border around a color photo. Inside the photo is "Indiana" along the left side of the photo and the player's name in the upper right. "1993-94 Indiana Hoosiers Basketball" is printed beneath the photo. The vertical card backs have a head shot in the upper left, with the player's career highlights on the right. His stats are in the center. The player's name, number and bio are printed at the bottom.

		MT
	Complete Set (18):	12.00
	Common Player:	.50
1	Damon Bailey	1.50
2	Robbie Eggers	.50
3	Brian Evans	1.50
4	Robert Foster	.50
5	Pat Graham	.75
6	Steve Hart	.50
7	Alan Henderson	2.00
8	Bob Knight CO	2.00
9	Pat Knight	.50
10	Todd Leary	.50
11	Todd Lindeman	.75
12	Richard Mandeville	.50
13	Sherron Wilkerson	.75
14	Team Photo	.75
15	Dan Dakich ACO, Ron Felling ACO, Norm Ellenberger ACO, Tim Garl ACO	.50
16	Assembly Hall	.75
17	Chris Reynolds, Matt Nover, Greg Graham, Calbert Cheaney (The Class of 1993)	1.00
18	Title Card	.50

1994-95 Indiana

The Indiana Hoosiers are featured in this 14-card set. The fronts have a color player photo against a wood background and inside a red border. The team name is printed vertically on one of the sides and basic player info is located under the photo. The cards are blankbacked and unnumbered. This is a questionable issue since the cards were released as a poster and may have been cut into cards by dealers.

		MT
	Complete Set (14):	15.00
	Common Player:	.50
1	Bob Knight CO, Brian Evans	3.00
2	Robbie Eggers	.50
3	Brian Evans	1.50
4	Steve Hart	.50
5	Alan Henderson	2.50
6	Michael Hermon	.50
7	Rob Hodgson	.50
8	Pat Knight	.50
9	Todd Lindeman	1.00
10	Richard Mandeville	.50
11	Charlie Miller	.50
12	Andre Patterson	3.00
13	Neil Reed	.50
14	Sherron Wilkerson	1.00

1982-83 Indiana State

The 16-card set features Olympic participants Kurt Thomas and Bruce Baumgarter, and NBA legend Larry Bird. The front has a drawing of the mascot and the words "Sycamore Rampage. The backs feature safety tips and biographical information.

		MT
	Complete Set (16):	130.00
	Common Player:	2.00
1	Bruce Baumgartner (wrestling)	15.00
2	Larry Bird	90.00
3	Terry Braun	2.00
4	Myron Christian	2.00
5	Al Cole	2.00
6	Rick Fields	2.00
7	Mark Golden	2.00
8	Jeff McComb	2.00
9	Scott Mugg	2.00
10	Dave Schellhase CO	2.00
11	Craig Shaffer (football)	2.00
12	James Smith	2.00
13	Kurt Thomas (gymnastics)	10.00
14	Chief Ouibachi and the Indian Princess	2.00
15	Cheerleaders	2.00
16	John Sherm. Williams	25.00

1987-88 Iowa

Sponsored by Nike, the 15-card set has "Hawkeyes '87-88" in the upper left, with the Nike logo in the upper right. The Hawkeyes' logo is in the lower left. The player photo is featured in the center, while the player's name, number, year and position are printed inside a stripe beneath the photo. The card backs have the player's name and bio sandwiched between two Iowa logos at the top. His career highlights and tips from the Hawkeyes round out the card backs. The Nike logo appears in the lower right.

		MT
	Complete Set (15):	30.00
	Commond Player	1.00
1	B.J. Armstrong	15.00
2	Curtis Cuthbert	1.00
3	Rodell Davis	1.50
4	Brian Garner	1.00
5	Kent Hill	1.00
6	Ed Horton	1.50
7	Les Jepsen	3.00
8	Mark Jewell	1.00
9	Bill Jones	1.00
10	Al Lorenzen	1.00
11	Roy Marble	3.00
12	Jeff Moe	1.00
13	Michael Morgan	1.00
14	Mike Reaves	1.00
15	Brig Tubbs	1.00

1990-91 Iowa

The 14-card set features a black border, with a photo of the player anchoring the card front. The player's name, number, position and team are printed inside a stripe at the bottom to the right of a basketball, which is in the lower left. The unnumbered card backs feature the 1990-91 basketball schedule. The KCRG 1600 radio logo is in the upper right.

	MT
Complete Set (14):	20.00
Common Player:	1.00
Val Barnes	2.50
Jim Bartels	1.00
Philip Chime	1.00
Rodell Davis	1.50
Acie Earl	7.00
Wade Lookingbill	1.00
Paul Lusk	1.00
James Moses	1.50
Troy Skinner	1.00
Kevin Smith	1.00
Chris Street	8.00
Brig Tubbs	1.00
Jay Webb	1.00
James Winters	1.00

1991-92 Iowa

The 15-card set showcases a player photo framed inside a parquet floor border. The Hawkeyes' logo is housed inside a basketball in the lower left. The player's name, number, position and team are printed in the lower right. The card backs, which are unnumbered and horizontal, have a head shot in the upper left, with the player's name and bio to the right. His career highlights and career bests are printed below his name. The Iowa logo is in the lower left.

	MT
Complete Set (15):	20.00
Common Player:	.75
Val Barnes	1.50
Jim Bartels	.75
Phil Chime	.75
Rodell Davis	1.00
Acie Earl	7.00
Wade Lookingbill	.75
Paul Lusk	.75
Russ Millard	2.50
James Moses	1.00
Troy Skinner	.75
Kevin Smith	.75
Chris Street	7.00
Brig Tubbs	.75
Jay Webb	.75
James Winters	.75

1992-93 Iowa

The fronts of this 13-card set include a photo in the upper left, with his name and number included inside two stripes beneath the photo. "Hawkeyes" is located along the right border, while the player's year and "University of Iowa basketball" appears in the lower left. The Hawkeyes' logo is in the lower right. The unnumbered horizontal card backs have the player's head shot in the upper left, with his name, bio, career highlights and career best on the right. The Iowa logo is in the lower left.

	MT
Complete Set (13):	12.00
Common Player:	.50
Val Barnes	1.25
Jim Bartles	.50
Fred Brown Jr.	.50
Acie Earl	3.00
Mon'ter Glasper	1.00
Wade Lookingbill	.50
Russ Millard	1.50
Kenyon Murray	2.00
Kevin Skillett	.50
Kevin Smith	.50
Chris Street	4.00
Jay Webb	.50
James Winters	.50

1992-93 Iowa Women

The 13-card set features the player's name and team at the top above the photo on a slant. The photo also is tilted. The Wendy's logo is printed inside a square in the lower left, while the player's number is inside a basketball in the lower right. The horizontal and unnumbered card backs feature the player's name, bio and career highlights.

	MT
Complete Set (13):	9.00
Common Player:	.60
Laurie Aaron	.60
Karen Clayton	.60
Virgie Dillingham	.60
Toni Foster	.60
Andrea Harmon	.60
Tia Jackson	.60
Antonia Macklin	.60
Cathy Marx	.60
Jenny Noll	.60
Vivian Stringer CO	3.00
Molly Tideback	.60
Necole Tunsil	.60
Arneda Yarbrough	.60

1993-94 Iowa

The 11-card set features "Hawkeyes" printed at the top, while a photo is slanted on the left side of the front. The player's name and number are printed under the photo. The entire front is bordered with a parquet floor. The unnumbered card backs have the players's name, bio, career highlights and best, along with his head shot.

	MT
Complete Set (11):	9.00
Common Player:	.50
Jim Bartels	.50
John Carter	.50
Mon'ter Glasper	.75
Chris Kingsbury	2.00
Russ Millard	1.50
Kenyon Murray	1.50
Jess Settles	3.00
Kevin Skillett	.50
Chris Street MEM	2.50
James Winters	.50
Andre Woolridge	1.50

1993-94 Iowa Women

The 13-card set has "Iowa Hawkeyes" and "93-94" printed in the upper left. A slanted photo is on the right of the card front. Wendy's logo is in the lower left, with the player's name in the lower center and the player's number printed inside a basketball on the lower right. The unnumbered card backs have the player's name and number at the top, with her bio in the center and career highlights at the bottom.

	MT
Complete Set (13):	8.00
Common Player:	.50
Karen Clayton	.50
Virgie Dillingham	.50
Simone Edwards	.50
Andrea Harmon	.50
Tia Jackson	.50
Susan Koering	.50
Antonia Macklin	.50
Cathy Marx	.50
Jenny Noll	.50
Erinn Reed	.50
Vivian Stringer CO	3.00
Necole Tunsil	.50
Arneda Yarbrough	.50

1994-95 Iowa

The 13-card set, bordered in white, features a player action photo on the front, with his name and number, year and team printed in two team-color coded stripes at the bottom. The Iowa logo is in the lower right inside a circle. The unnumbered horizontal card backs have the player's head shot in the upper left, his name, bio, career highlights and stats. The sponsors' logos are printed at the bottom of the backs.

	MT
Complete Set (13):	10.00
Common Player:	.50
Jim Bartels	.50
Ryan Bowen	1.00
John Carter	.50
Mon'ter Glasper	.75
Herky (Mascot)	.50
Chris Kingsbury	1.00
Kent McCausland	.50
Kenyon Murray	1.00
Jess Settles	2.50
Kevin Skillett	.50
Andre Woolridge	1.00
Black and Gold Blowout	.50
Carver-Hawkeye Arena	.75

1995-96 Iowa

This 15-card was sponsored by Partners In Excellence (Northwest Banks, Coca-Cola). The cards were unnumbered and included biographical information and statistics on the back.

	MT
Complete Set (15):	10.00
Common Player:	.50
Ryan Bowen	.75
Trey Bullet	.50
Monter Glasper	.50
Greg Helmers	.50
Chris Kingsbury	.50
J.R. Koch	2.00
Kent McCausland	.50
Russ Millard	.50
Kenyon Murray	1.00
Alvin Robinson	.50
Guy Rucker	.50
Jess Settles	2.00
Andre Woolridge	1.00
Herky (mascot)	.50

1996-97 Iowa

This 13-card was sponsored by Partners In Excellence (Northwest Banks, Coca-Cola). The cards were unnumbered and included biographical information and statistics on the back.

	MT
Complete Set (13):	10.00
Common Player:	.50
Ryan Bowen	1.00
Marcelo Gomes	.50
Greg Helmers	.50
J.R. Koch	2.00
Ryan Luehrsmann	.50
Kent McCausland	.50
Alvin Robinson	.50
Guy Rucker	.50
Jess Settles	2.00
Vernon Simmons	.50
Andre Woolridge	1.00
Herky (mascot)	.50
Hawkeye Sports.com	.50

1997-98 Iowa

This 13-card was sponsored by Partners In Excellence (Northwest Banks, Coca-Cola). The cards were unnumbered and included biographical information and statistics on the back.

	MT
Complete Set (13):	13.00
Common Player:	.50
Jason Bauer	.50
Ryan Bowen	1.00
Ricky Davis	6.00
Marcelo Gomes	.50
Greg Helmers	.50
J.R. Koch	2.00
Ryan Luehrsmann	.50
Kent McCausland	.50
Daryl Moore	.50
Dean Oliver	1.00
Guy Rucker	.50
Jess Settles	2.00
Vernon Simmons	.50

1988-89 Jacksonville

Measuring 2-1/2" x 4-1/2", the card fronts have "Blue Cross and Blue Shield of Florida" at the top, with "Jacksonville University" printed above the photo. Beneath the photo is the team nickname, player name and bio on the left and the Jacksonville logo in the lower right. The card backs have the player's name and bio at the top, with his career highlights and safety tip printed below. The sponsors are listed at the bottom of the card backs. Each card also included a one-inch coupon tab which was good for a child's free admission to a home game.

		MT
	Complete Set (15):	25.00
	Common Player:	1.50
1	Ken Aldrich	1.50
2	Tyrone Boykin	1.50
3	Dee Brown	10.00
4	Sean Byrd	1.50
5	Jim Cavanaugh	1.50
6	Steve Gilbert	1.50
7	Rich Haddad	1.50
8	Willie Ivey	1.50
9	Pat Laguerre	1.50
10	Reggie Law	1.50
11	Adrian Simmons	1.50
12	Chris Slocum	1.50
13	Curtis Taylor	1.50
14	JU-D2 (Mascot)	1.50
15	Team Photo	2.50

1989-90 Jacksonville

Sponsored by Blue Cross and Blue Shield of Florida, the 13-card set features "Jacksonville University Dolphins" printed at the top of the card front. Below the photo are the university's logo, player's name, position and year. The sponsor is listed at the bottom of the card front. The backs have the player's name, bio, career highlights, saftey tip and sponsors' logos. The cards are unnumbered. A tab at the bottom of the card is good for one free child's admission to any home game. The back of the tab has the season's schedule.

	MT
Complete Set (13):	25.00
Common Player:	1.50
Tyrone Boykin	1.50
Dee Brown	10.00
Sean Byrd	1.50
Chris Capers	2.00
Steve Gilbert	1.50
Rich Haddad	1.50
Tabarris Hamilton, Alonzo Harris	1.50
Willie Ivey	1.50
Reggie Law	1.50
Jerome McDuffie, Danny Tirado	1.50
Al Powell, Kent Shafer	1.50
Curtis Taylor	1.50
Team Photo	2.50

1989-90 Jacksonville Classic

This eight-card set focuses on the 1969-70 team which was the runner-up in the NCAA title game. The card fronts have a sepia-toned photo bordered with a gold frame and a green outer border. "Jacksonville University Dolphins" is printed at the top. In the top left of the photo a gold diagonal stripe states, "Classic Card." The university's logo, player's name and "1969-70 NCAA runner-up" are printed inside a stripe beneath the photo. The bottom of the card front lists "Blue Cross and Blue Shield of Florida." The unnumbered card backs have the player's name, career highlights and bio. The sponsors' logos are included at the bottom of the card back.

	MT
Complete Set (8):	18.00
Common Player:	2.00
Mike Blevins	2.00
Pembrook Burrows	2.00
Chip Dublin	2.00
Artis Gilmore	8.00
Rob McIntyre	2.00
Rex Morgan	2.00
Greg Nelson	2.00
Vaughn Wedeking	2.00

1991-92 James Madison

Sponsored by the USDA Forest Service, the 12-card set features a color photo in the center of the front. A stripe at the top of the card includes the university and nickname, while a square on the left side of the stripe includes the Smokey Bear logo. A stripe at the bottom of the card includes the player's name. A box in the lower right of the photo includes the school's logo. The unnumbered card backs feature the player's name and bio, along with two team logos. A Smokey Bear tip and cartoon round out the card back.

	MT
Complete Set (12):	10.00
Common Player:	1.00
Troy Bostic	1.00
Paul Carter	1.00
Jeff Chambers	1.00
Vladimir Cuk	1.00
Kent Culuko	1.50
William Davis	1.00
Lefty Driesell CO	4.00
Bryan Edwards	1.50
Gerry Lancaster	1.00
Keith Peoples	1.00
Clayton Ritter	1.00
Michael Venson	1.50

1992-93 James Madison

The design of this 12-card set is identical to the previous year's set. The unnumbered card backs carry the team logo and player bio, along with a Smokey Bear tip and cartoon.

	MT
Complete Set (12):	10.00
Common Player:	.75
Paul Carter	.75
Jeff Chambers	.75
Vladimir Cuk	.75
Kent Culuko	1.25
William Davis	.75
Duke Dog (Mascot)	.75
Lefty Driesell CO	3.00
Bryan Edwards	1.50
Channing McGuffin	.75
Clayton Ritter	.75
Michael Venson	1.25
Travis Wells	.75

1993-94 James Madison

The 13-card set features the university's name and nickname at the top, with a photo framed in the middle and a Smokey Bear 50th anniversary logo in the bottom center in a diamond. The player's name and position are in the lower left, while "Celebrating 50 years of prevention" is printed in the lower right. The card backs have the player's name and bio sandwiched between two JMU logos at the top. A Smokey Bear safety tip and cartoon round out the card back. The cards are unnumbered.

	MT
Complete Set (13):	8.00
Common Player:	.50
Vladimir Cuk	.50
Ryan Culicerto	.50
Kent Culuko	.75
Lefty Driesell CO	5.00
Dennis Leonard	.50
Charles Lott	.50
Darren McLinton	.50
Clayton Ritter	.50
Kareem Robinson	.50
Louis Rowe	.50
Michael Venson	.75
Emeka Wilson	.50
Duke Dog (Mascot)	.50

1994-95 James Madison

Released as a 10" x 14" perforated sheet, the 16-card set has four rows of four cards. When separated, the cards are standard size. The purple-bordered cards have the team nickname at the top, with the university name printed vertically along the left side of the card. The photo is in the center right of the card. The player's name, position and Smokey Bear logo are located beneath the photo. The card backs are unnumbered and feature the player's name and bio sandwiched between two JMU logos at the top. A Smokey Bear safety tip and cartoon round out the card back.

	MT
Complete Set (16):	8.00
Common Player:	.50
Lamont Boozer	.50
Eric Carpenter	.50
Cheerleaders	.50
James Colemano	.50
Ryan Culicerto	.50
Kent Culuko	.75
Charles Driesell CO (Lefty)	4.00
Duke Dog (Mascot)	.50
Duke Dog (Mascot) Smokey Bear	.50
Dennis Leonard	.50
Charles Lott	.50
Darren McLinton	.50
James Pelham	.50
Kareem Robinson	.50
Louis Rowe	.50
Heath Smith	.50

1987-88 Kansas

The 16-card set was released as an unperforated sheet. It includes "Jayhawks" and "87-88" in the upper left, with the Nike logo in the upper right. The player photo is in the middle, with his name, number, year and position printed beneath it. The lower left features the Jayhawks' logo. The unnumbered card backs feature the player's name and bio sandwiched between two KU logos at the top. The player's career highlights and tips from the Jayhawks round out the card back. The Nike logo is in the lower right corner of the card back.

	MT
Complete Set (16):	40.00
Common Player:	1.00
Sean Alvarado - 52	1.00
Scooter Barry - 10	3.00
Marvin Branch - 54	1.00
Larry Brown CO	8.00
Jeff Gueldner - 33	1.00
Keith Harris - 45	1.00
Otis Livingston - 12	1.00
Mike Maddox - 32	1.00
Danny Manning - 25	20.00

Archie Marshall - 23 1.00
Mike Masucci - 44 1.00
Lincoln Minor - 11 1.00
Milt Newton - 21 3.00
Chris Piper - 24 2.00
Kevin Pritchard - 14 4.00
Mark Randall - 42 4.00

1989-90 Kansas

The 16-card set showcased a color photo on the front, framed in white and black. The card is bordered in blue. The player's name in printed in the lower left, with the Jayhawks' logo inside a basketball in the lower right. The Leesley logo is in the lower left of the photo. The backs have the player's number and name at the top, with his bio and career highlights printed inside a box.

		MT
	Complete Set (16):	20.00
	Common Player:	.75
41	Frequent Flyers Poster Card	1.50
42	Jeff Gueldner	.75
43	Freeman West	.75
44	Rick Calloway	1.00
45	Mark Randall	2.50
46	Mike Maddox	1.00
47	Alonzo Jamison	1.50
48	Kevin Pritchard	2.50
49	Terry Brown	.75
50	Kirk Wagner	.75
51	Pekka Markkanen	.75
52	Sean Tunstall	.75
53	Malcolm Nash	.75
54	Todd Alexander	.75
55	Adonis Jordan	5.00
56	Roy Williams CO	5.00
NNO	Title Card	.75

1991-92 Kansas

Color action photos are framed by red and blue borders on the front of this 18-card set. The years are printed in the upper left of the photo, the player's position appears in a vertical stripe on the right and his name is in a stripe at the bottom beneath the photo. The horizontal backs have a head shot in the upper left, with his name, bio and KU logo to the right of the photo. Also included are his career highlights and stats. The cards are unnumbered.

	MT
Complete Set (18):	18.00
Common Player:	.75
Lane Czaplinski	.75
Ben Davis	2.00
Greg Gurley	.75
Alonzo Jamison	1.50
David Johanning	.75
Adonis Jordan	2.00
Malcolm Nash	.75
Greg Ostertag	3.00
Eric Pauley	1.00
Sean Pearson	1.00
Calvin Rayford	.75
Patrick Richey	.75
Richard Scott	1.00
Rex Walters	3.00
Roy Williams CO	3.00
Steve Woodberry	2.50
The O-Zone (Alonzo Jamison)	1.50
Team Photo/Checklist	1.00

1992-93 Kansas

Color player photos are bordered in red and blue on the front of this 16-card set. The years are printed in the upper left of the photo, while the player's position is located inside a vertical stripe along the right side. His name appears in a stripe beneath the photo. The unnumbered card back has a headshot in the left corner, with his name, bio and KU logo to the right of it. His career stats and highlights are printed below.

	MT
Complete Set (16):	12.00
Common Player:	.50
Matt Doherty ACO, Steve Robinson ACO, Kevin Stallings ACO	.50
Greg Gurley	.50
Darrin Hancock	2.00
Adonis Jordan	1.50
Danny Manning Art	3.00
Greg Ostertag	2.00
Eric Pauley	.75
Sean Pearson	.75
Calvin Rayford	.75
Patrick Richey	.50
Richard Scott	.75
Rex Walters	2.00
Rex Walters, Eric Pauley, Adonis Jordan	1.50
Roy Williams CO	3.00
Steve Woodberry	1.25
Team Photo	.75

1993-94 Kansas

The photo on the card front is borderless, except at the bottom, on this 15-card set. The player's name and position are printed beneath the photo, along with the Jayhawks' logo. The card back has the player's head shot in the upper left, with his name, bio and facsimile signature in the center. The Jayhawks' logo is in the upper right. The player's career highlights fill out the rest of the back.

		MT
	Complete Set (15):	15.00
	Common Player:	.50
1	Greg Gurley	.50
2	Greg Ostertag	2.00
3	Sean Pearson	.75
4	Scot Pollard	3.00
5	Nick Proud	.50
6	Calvin Rayford	.50
7	Patrick Richey	.50
8	Richard Scott	.75
9	Jacque Vaughn	5.00
10	Blake Weichbrodt	.50
11	T.J. Whatley	.50
12	B.J. Williams	.75
13	Roy Williams CO	2.00
14	Steve Woodberry	1.00
15	Assistant Coaches (Matt Doherty, Joe Holladay, Steve Robinson)	.50

1987-88 Kansas State

Saint Mary Hospital sponsored this 13-card set featuring the Kansas State men's basketball team. The front has a player photo and the backs feature biographical information and an anti-drug message. The cards are unnumbered.

		MT
	Complete Set (13):	80.00
	Common Player:	3.00
1	Charles Bledsoe	3.00
2	Carlos Diggins	3.00
3	Mark Dobbins	3.00
4	Buster Glover	3.00
5	Steve Henson	3.00
6	Lon Kruger CO	3.00
7	Fred McCoy	3.00
8	Ron Meyer	3.00
9	Mark Nelson	3.00
10	John Rettiger	3.00
11	Mitch Richmond	50.00
12	William Scott	3.00
13	Willie the Wildcat Mascot	3.00

1997-98 Kansas State Legends

This 20-card set was sponsored by Blind Tiger Brewery and Restaurant. With the exception of the 1997-98 team card, the set includes all-time greats from Kansas State.

		MT
	Complete Set (20):	18.00
	Common Player:	.50
1	Ernie Barrett	.50
2	Rolando Blackman	2.00
3	Bob Boozer	1.00
4	Mike Evans	.75
5	Steve Henson	.75
6	Lon Kruger	.75
7	Dick Knostman	.50
8	Ed Nealy	.75
9	Mitch Richmond	3.50
10	Howard Shannon	.50
11	Willie Murrell	.50
12	Jack Gardner	.50
13	Jack Hartman	.50
14	Tex Winter	1.00
15	Elliot Hatcher	.50
16	Askia Jones	.75
17	Eddie Elder	.50
18	Jack Parr	.75
19	Rick Harman	.50
20	1997-98 Team Card	.75

1998-99 Kansas State

This 16-card set resembles the 1997-98 set in design, but no sponsor is noted on the card. Cards are unnumbered and include biographical information and statistics on the back.

	MT
Complete Set (16):	15.00
Common Player:	.50
Team Card	.50
Willie the Wildcat (mascot)	.50
Tom Asbury (coach)	1.00
Manny Dies	.50
Chris Griffin	.50
Cortez Groves	.50
Jay Heidrick	.50
Josh Kimm	.50
Tony Kitt	.50
Joe Leonard	.50
Ayome "Paco" May	.50
Josh Reid	.50
Travis Reynolds	.50
Shawn Rhodes	.50
David Ries	.50
Ty Sims	.50

1976-77 Kentucky Schedules

Measuring 2-1/4" x 3-3/4", the fronts have a full-bleed photo which has a blue-toned photo. A white stripe beneath the photo includes the player's name and bio. The backs are unnumbered and carry the season's schedules.

	NM
Complete Set (12):	70.00
Common Player:	4.00
Dwane Casey	10.00
Truman Claytor	8.00
Jack Givens	10.00
Merion Haskins	4.00
Larry Johnson	6.00
James Lee	8.00
Kyle Macy	10.00
Rick Robey	10.00
Mike Phillips	8.00
Jay Shidler	8.00
Tim Stephens	6.00
LaVon Williams	6.00

1977-78 Kentucky Schedules

Measuring 2-1/4" x 3-3/4", the 19-card set showcase blue-toned photos. The player's bio is included in a white area beneath the photo on the card front. The backs are unnumbered and carry the season's schedule.

	NM
Complete Set (19):	75.00
Common Player:	4.00
Chuck Aleksinas	6.00
Dwane Casey	8.00
Truman Claytor	6.00
Scott Courts	4.00
Fred Cowan	6.00
Joe Dean ACO	4.00
Joe B. Hall CO (Blue tint photo)	6.00
Joe B. Hall CO (Color photo)	6.00
Leonard Hamilton ACO	4.00
Chris Gettelfinger	4.00
Jack Givens	10.00
James Lee	8.00
Kyle Macy	8.00
Dick Parsons ACO	4.00
Mike Phillips	6.00
Rick Robey	8.00
Jay Shidler	6.00
Tim Stephens	4.00
LaVon Williams	4.00

1977-78 Kentucky

Measuring 2-1/2" x 3-3/4", the 22-card set showcases black and white photos on the front. The Wildcats' logo is printed in the upper left, with the years in the top center and the card number in a basketball on the right. The player's name, year and position are located in the lower right. The backs have the player's bio in the upper left, with his head shot in the upper right. His career highlights and stats round out the card back.

		NM
	Complete Set (22):	40.00
	Common Player:	1.00
1	The Fabulous Five (Ralph Beard, Kenny Rollins, Wah Wah Jones, Alex Groza, Cliff Barker, Adolph Rupp CO)	5.00
2	Joe Hall's First UK Team (Team Photo)	2.00
3	1975 NCAA Runnrs-Up (Team photo in plaid blazers)	1.50
4	1977-78 Wildcats	2.00
5	Leonard Hamilton CO	1.50
6	Joe Dean CO	1.00
7	Joe B. Hall CO	3.00
8	Dick Parsons CO	1.50
9	Scott Courts	1.00
10	Chuck Aleksinas	1.00
11	LaVon Williams	1.50
12	Chris Gettelfinger	1.00
13	Dwane Casey	3.00
14	Fred Cowan	1.50
15	Kyle Macy	7.00
16	Tim Stephens	1.00
17	James Lee	3.00
18	Jay Shidler	3.00
19	Rick Robey	4.00
20	Truman Claytor	2.00
21	Jack Givens	7.00
22	Mike Phillips	2.00

1978-79 Kentucky

Measuring 2-1/2" x 3-3/4", the 22-card set showcases the Wildcats' logo in the upper left, the years running vertically down the center of the left border and the card number inside a basketball in the lower left. The card caption appears beneath the photo. The card backs have the player's bio at the top, with his career highlights in the center. The Foodtown logo is in the lower right.

		NM
	Complete Set (22):	15.00
	Common Player:	.75
1	Homeward Bound (Joe B. Hall and wife)	1.00
2	Celebratin' Seniors (Jack Givens, Mike Phillips, Rick Robey, James Lee)	1.50
3	Moment of Glory (Jack Givens)	2.00
4	(Cliff) Hagan's Hall of Fame Induction	1.50
5	1978-79 Wildcats Team Photo	1.25
6	1978 NCAA Champions Team Photo	1.50
7	Dwight Anderson	2.00
8	Clarence Tillman	.75
9	Chuck Verderber	1.00
10	Dwane Casey	2.00
11	Truman Claytor	1.50
12	Tim Stephens	.75
13	Kyle Macy	4.00
14	LaVon Williams	1.25
15	Jay Shidler	1.50
16	Freddie Cowan	1.25
17	Chuck Aleksinas	.75
18	Chris Gettelfinger	.75
19	Joe B. Hall CO	1.50
20	Dick Parsons ACO	1.00
21	Leonard Hamilton ACO	1.00
22	Joe Dean ACO	.75

1978-79 Kentucky Schedules

Measuring 2-1/4" x 3-3/4", the 16-card set features blue-toned photos on the front. The player's bio appears in a white area beneath the photo. The season's schedule appears on the unnumbered back.

	NM
Complete Set (16):	70.00
Common Player:	4.00
Chuck Aleksinas	4.00
Dwight Anderson	8.00
Dwane Casey	8.00
Truman Claytor	6.00
Fred Cowan	4.00
Joe Dean ACO	4.00
Chris Gettelfinger	4.00
Joe B. Hall CO	6.00
Leonard Hamilton ACO	4.00
Kyle Macy	8.00
Dick Parsons ACO	4.00
Jay Shidler	6.00
Tim Stephens	4.00
Clarence Tillman	4.00
Chuck Verderber	6.00
LaVon Williams	4.00

1979-80 Kentucky

Measuring 2-1/2" x 3-3/4", the 22-card set features a black and white photo on the left of the card. The player's name runs vertically from the upper right. The card number is inside a basketball in the lower left, while the years are printed in the lower center and the Wildcats' logo is located on the lower right. The player's bio is in the upper left, while his headshot is in the upper right. His highlights fill out the center of the card. The Foodtown logo is in the lower right on the card back.

		NM
	Complete Set (22):	19.00
	Common Player:	.75
1	1979-1980 Wildcats Team Photo	1.25
2	Kyle Macy	3.00
3	Jay Shidler	1.00
4	LaVon Williams	1.00
5	Chris Gettelfinger	.75
6	Fred Cowan	1.00
7	Dwight Anderson	1.50
8	Bo Lanter	.75
9	Chuck Verderber	.75
10	Dirk Minniefield	2.50
11	Sam Bowie	6.00
12	Charles Hurt	2.00
13	Derrick Hord	1.50
14	Tom Heitz	.75
15	Joe Dean CO	.75
16	Leonard Hamilton CO	1.00
17	Dick Parsons CO	1.00
18	Joe B. Hall CO	1.50
19	Rupp Arena	.75
20	Pan Am Gold Medalist (Kyle Macy) (Schedule on back)	2.00
21	The Freshman Five (Sam Bowie, Tom Heitz, Derrick Hord, Charles Hurt, Dirk Minniefield)	2.00
22	The Seniors (Kyle Macy, LaVon Williams, Jay Shidler)	1.50

1979-80 Kentucky Schedules

Measuring 2-1/4" x 3-3/4", the 17-card set showcases blue-toned photos on the front. A white area at the bottom of the card has the player's bio. The card backs are unnumbered and feature the season's schedule.

	NM
Complete Set (17):	45.00
Common Player:	3.00
Dwight Anderson	5.00
Sam Bowie	10.00
Fred Cowan	3.00
Joe Dean ACO	3.00
Chris Gettelfinger	3.00
Joe B. Hall CO	4.00
Leonard Hamilton ACO	3.00
Tom Heitz	3.00
Derrick Hord	5.00
Charles Hurt	5.00
Bo Lanter	3.00
Kyle Macy	5.00
Dirk Minniefield	6.00
Dick Parsons ACO	3.00
Jay Shidler	4.00
Chuck Verderber	3.00
LaVon Williams	3.00

1980-81 Kentucky Schedules

Measuring 2-1/4" x 3-3/4", the 16-card set features blue-toned photos of the players on the front. Their bio appears in a white area beneath the photo. The unnumbered card backs showcase that season's schedule.

	NM
Complete Set (16):	22.00
Common Player:	2.25
Dickey Beal	2.25
Bret Bearup	2.25
Sam Bowie	2.25
Fred Cowan	2.25
Joe Dean ACO	2.25
Chris Gettelfinger	2.25
Joe B. Hall CO	2.25
Leonard Hamilton ACO	2.25
Tom Heitz	2.25
Derrick Hord	2.25
Charles Hurt	2.25
Bo Lanter	2.25
Jim Master	2.25
Dirk Minniefield	2.25
Melvin Turpin	2.25
Chuck Verderber	2.25

1981-82 Kentucky Schedules

Measuring 2-1/4" x 3-3/4", the 17-card set features a black-and-white player photo on the front. The white area beneath the photo includes the player's bio. The unnumbered card backs feature that season's schedule.

	MT
Complete Set (17):	40.00
Common Player:	3.00
Mike Ballenger	3.00
Dickey Beal	3.00
Butch Bearup	3.00
Sam Bowie	6.00
Bob Chambers ACO	3.00
Joe Dean ACO	3.00
Joe B. Hall CO	4.00
Leonard Hamilton ACO	3.00
Tom Heitz	3.00
Derrick Hord	4.00
Charles Hurt	4.00
Bo Lanter	3.00
Jim Master	3.00
Troy McKinley	3.00
Dirk Minniefield	6.00
Melvin Turpin	6.00
Chuck Verderber	3.00

1982-83 Kentucky Schedules

Measuring 2-1/4" x 3-1/4", the 17-card set showcases a blue-toned player photo on the front. The white area beneath the photo includes the player's bio. The unnumbered card back features that season's schedule.

	MT
Complete Set (17):	45.00
Common Player:	3.00
Dickey Beal	3.00
Bret Bearup	3.00
Sam Bowie	8.00
Bob Chambers ACO	3.00
Joe Dean ACO	3.00
Joe B. Hall CO	4.00
Leonard Hamilton ACO	3.00
Roger Harden	3.00
Tom Heitz	3.00
Derrick Hord	4.00
Charles Hurt	4.00
Todd May	3.00
Jim Master	4.00
Troy McKinley	3.00
Dirk Minniefield	6.00
Melvin Turpin	6.00
Kenny Walker	8.00

1983-84 Kentucky Schedules

Measuring 2-1/4" x 3-3/4", the 16-card set showcases a blue-toned photo on the front. The player's bio appears in a white area beneath the photo. The unnumbered card backs feature that season's schedule.

	MT
Complete Set (17):	40.00
Common Player:	3.00
Paul Andrews	3.00
Dicky Beal	3.00
Bret Bearup	3.00
Winston Bennett	6.00
James Blackmon	4.00
Sam Bowie	6.00
Joe B. Hall CO	4.00
Leonard Hamilton ACO	3.00
Hatfield	3.00
Tom Heitz	3.00
John Kelly	3.00
Jim Master	4.00
Todd May	3.00
Troy McKinley	3.00
Melvin Turpin	6.00
Kenny Walker	6.00
Todd Ziegler	3.00

1984-85 Kentucky Schedules

Measuring 2-1/4" x 3-3/4", the 16-card set showcases a blue-toned player photo at the top, with his bio in a white area at the bottom. The unnumbered card backs feature that season's schedule.

	MT
Complete Set (16):	40.00
Common Player:	3.00
Joe B. Hall CO	4.00
Leonard Hamilton ACO	3.00
John Kelly ACO	3.00
Hatfield	3.00
Troy McKinley	3.00
Leroy Byrd	3.00
Todd Ziegler	3.00
Rob Lock	3.00
James Blackmon	3.00
Cedric Jenkins	4.00
Richard Madison	3.00
Butch Bearup	3.00
Kenny Walker	6.00
Ed Davender	3.00
Roger Harden	3.00
Paul Andrews	3.00

1988-89 Kentucky Big Blue

Oscar Combs' Big Blue Basketball magazine included this 18-card set in its Summer 1989 Volume 3, No. 2 issue. The cards were printed in two perforated panels, with each card being standard size. The card fronts, which are bordered in blue and black, have a color photo. The award the player earned is printed in white at the top, with his name in the lower left inside a white rectangle. The card backs have a head shot of the player in the upper left, with his name inside a stripe on the right. His bio and card number appear directly below his name. Past award winners are listed inside a blue box on the bottom of the card.

		MT
	Complete Set (18):	20.00
	Common Player:	.75
1	Leadership (Sean Sutton)	1.00
2	Chris Mills	5.00
3	Mike Scott	.75
4	Best Free Throw Percentage (Richie Farmer)	2.00
5	Fewest Turnovers (Derrick Miller)	1.00
6	Freshman Leadership (Chris Mills)	5.00
7	Scholastic (Mike Scott)	.75
8	Most Assists (Sean Sutton)	1.00
9	Most Rebounds (Chris Mills)	5.00
10	Leading Scorer (LeRon Ellis)	1.50
11	Best Defender (Reggie Hanson)	1.50
12	110 Percent Award (Deron Feldhaus)	1.50
13	Sacrifice Award (Sean Sutton, LeRon Ellis)	1.00
14	Best Field Gold Percentage (LeRon Ellis)	1.50
15	Best Three-pt. Field Goal Percentage (Sean Sutton)	1.00
16	Most Steals (Reggie Hanson)	1.50
17	Eddie Sutton CO	1.50
18	Checklist Card UER (Misspelled sacrifice as sacrafice)	.75

1987 Kentucky Champions Against Drugs

Sponsored by Coca-Cola and Valvoline, the 24-card set showcased a color photo framed in white with a blue and white outer border. The player's name is printed beneath the photo. The Coca-Cola logo is printed in the lower left, while the Valvoline logo is in the lower right. The card backs have the player's name and bio at the top, with the card number in a circle in the upper right. A safety quote is printed in the center of the back. The local sheriffs departments and highway patrol handed out one card per week. If a fan collected each of the cards, they could be redeemed for prizes. Overall, 350 sets were distributed. Many sports are represented in the set.

		MT
Complete Set (24):		70.00
Common Player:		.50
1	Martha Layne Collins (Governor of Kentucky)	.50
2	Kenny Walker	1.25
3	Dr. William DeVries	.50
4	Dan Issel	4.00
5	Doug Flynn	.75
6	Melinda Cumberledge	.50
7	Melvin Turpin, Sam Bowie	2.00
8	Darrell Griffith	1.50
9	Winston Bennett	1.00
10	Ricky Skaggs	2.50
11	Wildcat Mascot	.50
12	Cardinal Mascot	.50
13	"Pee Wee" Reese	3.00
14	Mary T. Meagher	.75
15	Jim Master	.75
16	Kyle Macy	1.50
17	Pervis Ellison	3.00
18	Dale Baldwin	.50
19	Frank Minniefield	1.00
20	Mark Higgs	1.25
21	Rex Chapman	5.00
22	A.B. (Happy) Chandler	1.50
SC	Billy Packer SP	8.00
SC	David Robinson SP	50.00

1988-89 Kentucky Collegiate Collection

The 269-card set showcases the university's best basketball players. The card fronts, which are bordered in blue, showcase "Kentucky's Finest" in the upper left, with the Kentucky logo in the upper right. The photo is in the center, with the UK logo in the lower left, the player's name in the bottom center and the Collegiate Collection logo in the lower right. The horizontal card backs have the player's name and bio in the upper left, with the card number in the upper right. The player's career highlights are printed in the center over a ghosted University of Kentucky logo. A Collegiate Collection copyright tag line appears at the bottom of the backs.

		MT
Complete Set (269):		25.00
Common Player:		.07
1	Adolph Rupp CO	.75
2	Cliff Hagan	.50
3	Frank Ramsey	.40
4	Ralph Beard	.40
5	Alex Groza	.40
6	Wallace Jones	.10
7	Dan Issel	.75
8	Cotton Nash	.25
9	Kevin Grevey	.15
10	Kyle Macy	.30
11	Kenny Walker	.20
12	Louie Dampier	.15
13	Vernon Hatton	.07
14	Johnny Cox	.07
15	Jack Givens	.25
16	Bill Spivey	.10
17	Pat Riley	.75
18	Ellis Johnson	.07
19	Forest Sale	.07
20	Kenny Rollins	.10
21	Sam Bowie	.30
22	John DeMoisey	.07
23	Leroy Edwards	.07
24	Lee Huber	.07
25	Rick Robey	.15
26	Bob Burrow	.07
27	Cliff Barker	.10
28	Bernie Opper	.07
29	Ralph Carlisle	.07
30	Joe B. Hall CO	.25
31	Bob Brannum	.10
32	Jack Parkinson	.07
33	Jack Tingle	.07
34	Joe Holland	.07
35	Jim Line	.07
36	Bobby Watson	.07
37	Bill Evans	.07
38	Bill Lickert	.07
39	Larry Conley	.30
40	Eddie Sutton	.30
41	Larry Steele	.10
42	Tom Parker	.07
43	Shelby Linville	.07
44	Lou Tsioropoulos	.10
45	Gayle Rose	.10
46	Jim Andrews	.07
47	Ed Davender	.10
48	Winston Bennett	.15
49	Willie Rouse	.07
50	Mike Pratt	.10
51	Harry C. Lancaster	.10
52	Dirk Minniefield	.15
53	Russell Rice	.07
54	Carey Spicer	.07
55	Paul McBrayer	.07
56	Burgess Carey	.07
57	Ermal Allen	.10
58	Dale Barnstable	.07
59	Kenton Campbell	.07
60	Guy Strong	.07
61	Lucian Whitaker	.07
62	Bennie Coffman	.07
63	C.M. Newton	.30
64	Walt Hirsch	.07
65	John Brewer	.10
66	Phil Grawemeyer	.07
67	John Crigler	.07
68	Gerry Calvert	.07
69	Ed Beck	.07
70	Jerry Bird	.07
71	Harold Ross	.07
72	Adrian Smith	.10
73	Don Mills	.07
74	Ned Jennings	.07
75	Sid Cohen	.07
76	Dickie Parsons	.07
77	Larry Pursiful	.07
78	Herky Rupp	.10
79	Charles Ishmael	.07
80	Jim McDonald	.07
81	Terry Mobley	.07
82	Tommy Kron	.10
83	Randy Embry	.07
84	Steve Clevenger	.07
85	Jim LeMaster	.07
86	Basil Hayden	.07
87	Cliff Berger	.07
88	Jim Dinwiddie	.07
89	Randy Pool	.07
90	Terry Mills	.07
91	Bob McCowan	.07
92	Mike Casey	.10
93	Kent Hollenbeck	.07
94	Scotty Baesler	.07
95	Phil Argento	.07
96	John R. Adams	.07
97	Larry Stamper	.07
98	Ray Edelman	.07
99	Ronnie Lyons	.07
100	G.J. Smith	.07
101	Jerry Hale	.07
102	Bob Guyette	.07
103	Mike Flynn	.10
104	Jimmy Dan Connor	.10
105	Larry Johnson	.10
106	Joey Holland	.07
107	Reggie Warford	.07
108	Merion Haskins	.07
109	James Lee	.10
110	Dwane Casey	.25
111	Truman Claytor	.10
112	LaVon Williams	.10
113	Jay Shidler	.10
114	Fred Cowan	.10
115	Dwight Anderson	.25
116	Chuck Verderber	.10
117	Bo Lanter	.07
118	Charles Hurt	.10
119	Derrick Hord	.10
120	Tom Heitz	.07
121	Dicky Beal	.10
122	Bret Bearup	.10
123	Melvin Turpin	.20
124	Jim Master	.10
125	Troy McKinley	.07
126	Roger Harden	.10
127	James Blackmon	.10
128	Leroy Byrd	.10
129	Cedric Jenkins	.10
130	Rob Lock	.10
131	Richard Madison	.10
132	Cawood Ledford	.15
133	'47-'48 Team	.15
134	'48-'49 Team	.15
135	'50-'51 Team	.15
136	'57-'58 Team	.15
137	'77-'78 Team	.15
138	Stan Key	.07
139	Mike Phillips	.10
140	Joe B. Hall CO	.25
141	Mike Flynn	.10
142	Thad Jaracz	.10
143	Larry Conley	.30
144	Rex Chapman	.50
145	Pat Riley	.75
146	Melvin Turpin	.20
147	Kenny Walker	.20
148	Wallace Jones	.10
149	Alex Groza	.40
150	Mike Pratt	.10
151	Cliff Barker	.10
152	Jim Andrews	.07
153	Kenny Walker	.20
154	Kevin Grevey	.15
155	Kyle Macy	.30
156	Jim Line	.07
157	Pat Riley	.75
158	Larry Steele	.10
159	Jack Givens	.25
160	Ed Davender	.10
161	Ralph Beard	.40
162	Vernon Hatton	.07
163	Frank Ramsey	.40
164	Bob Burrow	.07
165	Sam Bowie	.30
166	Dan Issel	.75
167	Rick Robey	.15
168	Winston Bennett	.15
169	Louie Dampier	.15
170	Gayle Rose	.10
171	Cliff Hagan	.50
172	Cotton Nash	.25
173	Mike Pratt	.10
174	Richard Madison	.10
175	Kyle Macy	.30
176	Rob Lock	.10
177	Larry Johnson	.10
178	Cedric Jenkins	.10
179	Dan Issel	.75
180	Charles Hurt	.10
181	Cliff Hagan	.50
182	Wallace Jones	.10
183	Roger Harden	.10
184	Bob Guyette	.07
185	Kevin Grevey	.15
186	Jack Givens	.25
187	Ed Davender	.10
188	Jimmy Dan Connor	.10
189	Fred Cowan	.10
190	Larry Conley	.30
191	Leroy Byrd	.10
192	Sam Bowie	.30
193	James Blackmon	.10
194	Winston Bennett	.15
195	Dicky Beal	.10
196	Jim Andrews	.07
197	Kenny Walker	.20
198	Pat Riley	.75
199	Frank Ramsey	.40
200	Truman Claytor	.10
201	Dwane Casey	.25
202	Rex Chapman	.50
203	Jim Master	.10
204	Mike Phillips	.10
205	Dirk Minniefield	.50
206	Jimmy Dan Connor	.10
207	Bill Lickert	.07
208	Leroy Byrd	.10
209	Mike Pratt	.10
210	Rob Lock	.10
211	Dickie Parsons	.07
212	Frank Ramsey	.40
213	Adolph Rupp CO	.75
214	G.J. Smith	.07
215	Rick Robey	.15
216	James Blackmon	.10
217	Mike Casey	.10
218	LaVon Williams	.10
219	Larry Pursiful	.07
220	Terry Mobley	.07
221	Kyle Macy	.30
222	Larry Conley	.30
223	Dirk Minniefield	.15
224	Jim Master	.10
225	Jerry Bird	.07
226	Dan Issel	.75
227	Larry Johnson	.10
228	Bret Bearup	.10
229	Ronnie Lyons	.07
230	James Lee	.10
231	Don Mills	.07
232	Truman Claytor	.10
233	Rex Chapman	.50
234	Fred Cowan	.10
235	Truman Claytor	.10
236	Dicky Beal	.10
237	Larry Johnson	.10
238	John R. Adams	.07
239	Sam Bowie	.30
240	Thad Jaracz	.10
241	Phil Argento	.07
242	Cedric Jenkins	.10
243	Charles Hurt	.10
244	Charles Hurt	.10
245	Cliff Hagan	.50
246	Kent Hollenbeck	.07
247	Wallace Jones	.10
248	Roger Harden	.10
249	Bob Guyette	.07
250	Richard Madison	.10
251	Kevin Grevey	.15
252	Jack Givens	.25
253	Tommy Kron	.10
254	Derrick Hord	.10
255	Tom Heitz	.07
256	Cliff Hagan	.50
257	Louie Dampier	.15
258	Jimmy Dan Connor	.10
259	Dwane Casey	.25
260	Cliff Hagan	.50
261	Walt Hirsch	.07
262	Merion Haskins	.07
263	Roger Harden	.10
264	Bob Guyette	.07
265	Phil Grawemeyer	.07
266	Jay Shidler	.10
267	Jim Dinwiddie	.07
268	Fred Cowan	.10
269	Leroy Byrd	.10

1988 Kentucky Soviet Program Insert

Inserted into the game program for the U.S. AAU All-Stars vs. Soviet Junior Nationals game, which was played in Lexington, Ky., this 18-card set was produced in two perforated panels. When perforated, each of the cards measured approximately standard size. The card fronts are anchored by a black-and-white photo, bordered in blue. The AAU's 100th anniversary logo is included in the upper left corner of the photo. Beneath the photo on the left is the player's name and bio, while the AAU/Soviet Tour logo is pictured in the lower right. The card backs feature the player's head shot in the upper left, with his bio, highlights and stats also showcased.

		MT
Complete Set (18):		150.00
Common Player:		1.50
1	Checklist	2.50
2	Scott Davenport CO	1.50
3	Keith Adkins	1.50
4	Mike Allen	1.50
5	Damon Bailey	12.00
6	Scott Boley	1.50
7	David DeMarcus	1.50
8	Richie Farmer	4.00
9	Travis Ford	8.00
10	Pat Graham	4.00
11	Robbie Graham	1.50
12	Allan Houston	55.00
13	Shawn Kemp	75.00
14	Don MacLean	15.00
15	Kenneth Martin	1.50
16	Chris Mills	20.00
17	Derek Miller	2.00
18	Sean Woods	5.00

1989-90 Kentucky Big Blue

Inserted into the Winter 1990 issue of Oscar Combs' Big Blue Basketball magazine (Volume 3, No. 4), the 18-card set was released in two perforated panels of standard sized cards. The blue- and black-bordered cards have a basketball printed in the upper left, with his name inside a gray rectangle above the card photo on the right. The player's achievement is located in an orange stripe along the left border of the card. The card backs have the player's head shot in the upper left, with his name on the right inside a stripe. His bio and the card number are printed beneath his name. Past award winners are printed inside a blue box at the bottom of the card.

		MT
Complete Set (18):		20.00
Common Player:		.75
19	Checklist Card	1.00
20	Best FT Shooter (Richie Farmer)	1.50
21	Most Rebounds (Reggie Hanson)	1.25
22	Fewest Turnovers (Deron Feldhaus)	1.25
23	UK Assistants Best Defense (Billy Donovan, Herb Sendek, Tubby Smith, Ralph Willard)	.75
24	Mr. Hustle Award (Deron Feldhaus)	1.25
25	Leadership (Reggie Hanson)	1.25
26	Student Athlete (John Pelphrey)	1.50
27	Outstanding Senior (Derrick Miller)	1.00
28	Most Improved (Deron Feldhaus)	1.25
29	Fan of the Year (Happy Chandler)	2.50
30	Best Playmaker (John Pelphrey)	1.50
31	Mr. Deflection (Hanson/Pelphrey)	1.25
32	Most Valuable (Reggie Hanson)	1.25
33	Best FG Shooter (Deron Feldhaus)	1.25
34	Most Assists (Sean Woods)	1.00
35	Leading Scorer (Derrick Miller)	1.00
36	Coach of the Year (Rick Pitino)	6.00

1989-90 Kentucky Big Blue Team of the 80's

Inserted into Oscar Combs' Big Blue Basketball magazine's Spring 1990 Volume 4, No. 1 edition, this 18-card set was produced in two perforated panels. The set focuses on the best Wildcat players of the 1980s. A color photo anchors the card fronts, with his name printed in the upper left corner inside a light-blue border. The card backs, which are numbered inside a square in the upper right, have the player's name inside a stripe in the upper left, with his bio, head shot and post-UK career info following underneath. The player's career UK stats are printed inside a box at the bottom of the card. A 1990 Wildcat News Co. copyright is on the bottom center.

		MT
Complete Set (18):		20.00
Common Player:		.75
37	Checklist Card	1.00
38	Kyle Macy	2.00
39	Rex Chapman	3.00
40	Kenny Walker	1.50
41	Winston Bennett	1.25
42	Melvin Turpin	1.25
43	Sam Bowie	2.50
44	Dicky Beal	.75
45	Dirk Minniefield	1.00
46	Jim Master	1.00
47	Rob Lock	.75
48	Chris Mills	4.00
49	Roger Harden	.75
50	Jay Shidler	1.00
51	LeRon Ellis	1.00
52	Fred Cowan	.75
53	Derrick Hord	1.00
54	Coaches (Joe Hall, Eddie Sutton, Rick Pitino)	2.00

1989-90 Kentucky Collegiate Collection

The 300 standard-sized card set features former and current players of the time, with the past players highlighted in black and white photos and the current players in color photos. The top reads "Kentucky's Finest", with career summaries on the back.

		MT
Complete Set (300):		24.00
Common Player:		.05
1	C.M. Newton	.30
2	Dan Issel	.75
3	Alex Groza	.40
4	Jack Givens	.25
5	Kenny Walker	.20
6	Cliff Hagan	.50
7	Ralph Beard	.40
8	Dirk Minniefield	.15
9	Louie Dampier	.15
10	Dicky Beal	.10
11	Larry Pursiful	.05
12	Rex Chapman	.25
13	Rick Pitino CO	1.00
14	Marvin Akers	.05
15	Allen Fieldhaus	.10
16	Carroll Burchett	.05
17	Sam Potter	.05
18	Ted Deeken	.05
19	Dwight Anderson	.25
20	Charles Schrader	.05
21	Bill Trott	.05
22	Henry Besuden	.05
23	Edwin Knadler	.05
24	Vince Del Negro	.10
25	James Durham	.05
26	Mickey Gibson	.05
27	John Mauer	.05
28	John McIntosh	.05
29	Van Buren Ropke	.05
30	B.G. Marsh	.05
31	Tom Zerfoss	.05
32	George Zerfoss	.05
33	Harry Denham	.05
34	Mike Scott	.05
35	Adolph Rupp CO	.75
36	Jack Parkinson	.05
37	1953-54 Team	.15
38	Pat Riley	1.00
39	Joe B. Hall	.25
40	Memorial Coliseum	.05
41	Sam Bowie	.30
42	Bob Burrow	.05
43	Melvin Turpin	.20
44	Frank Ramsey	.40
45	Pat Riley	1.00
46	Mascot	.05
47	Charles Hurt	.10
48	Cliff Barker	.10
49	Kevin Grevey	.15
50	Bill Spivey	.10
51	Delmar C. Buchheit	.05
52	Ray Mills	.05
53	Irving Thomas	.10
54	Chuck Aleksinas	.10
55	Paul Andrews	.05
56	Brad Bounds	.05
57	Clyde Parker	.05
58	Bill Busey	.05
59	Billy Ray Cassady	.05
60	George Critz	.05
61	Paul Noel	.05
62	Pat Doyle	.05
63	Rick Drewitz	.05
64	Fred Curtis	.05
65	Darrell Darby	.05
66	Humzey Yessin	.05
67	Chris Gettelfinger	.05
68	Sam Harper	.05
69	Bill Davis	.05
70	Lincoln Collinsworth	.05
71	Keith Farnsley	.05
72	Foster Helm	.05
73	Dick Howe	.05
74	Phil Johnson	.05
75	Roger Layne	.05
76	Art Laib	.05
77	Dave Lawrence	.05
78	Larry Lentz	.05
79	Steve Lochmueller	.05
80	Louis McGinnis	.05
81	Doug Pendygraft	.05
82	Tommy Porter	.05
83	Linville Puckett	.10
84	Don Rolfes	.05
85	Mark Soderberg	.05
86	Tim Stephens	.05
87	Gene Stewart	.05
88	George Yates	.05
89	Randy Noll	.05
90	Earl Adkins	.05
91	Truett Demoisey	.05
92	Todd Ziegler	.05
93	Clint Wheeler	.05
94	Patrick Campbell	.05
95	Charles Alberts	.05
96	Brinkley Barnett	.05
97	Cecil Bell	.05
98	Mel Brewer	.05
99	Jake Bronston	.05
100	Albert Cummins	.05
101	Jerry D. Claiborne	.20
102	Bill Leskovar	.05
103	Sam Ball	.10
104	Sonny Collins	.15
105	Bob Hardy	.05
106	Mike Siganos	.05
107	Al Bruno	.05
108	Rick Norton	.10
109	Ray Correll	.05
110	Irvin Goode	.05
111	Bob Gain	.10
112	Paul "Bear" Bryant	.75
113	Rick Kestner	.05
114	Larry Seiple	.20
115	George Blanda	.50
116	Calvin Bird	.05
117	Don Phelps	.05
118	Herschel Turner	.05
119	Harry Jones	.05
120	Larry Jones	.05
121	Doug Moseley	.05
122	Rodger Bird	.10
123	Howard Schnellenberger	.40
124	Vito "Babe" Parilli	.30
125	Jim Kovach	.15
126	Randy Jenkins	.05
127	Emery Clark	.05
128	David Hardt	.05
129	Andy Molls	.05
130	Tom Dornbrook	.05
131	George Adams	.10
132	Lou Michaels	.10
133	Paul Calhoun	.05
134	Joey Worley	.05
135	Doug Kotar	.15
136	Dicky Lyons	.10
137	Art Still	.25
138	Warren Bryant	.10
139	Joe Federspiel	.10
140	Mark Higgs	.25
141	Steve Meilinger	.10
142	Wilbur Hackett	.05
143	Marc Logan	.25
144	Rick Nuzum	.05
145	Wilbur Jamerson	.05
146	Felix Wilson	.05
147	Rod Stewart	.10
148	Tom Hutchinson	.05
149	Greg Long	.05
150	Mike Fanuzzi	.05
151	Richard S. Webb Jr.	.10
152	John S. Kelly	.05
153	Eger V. Murphree	.05
154	Ernal Allen	.10
155	John G. Heber	.05
156	Howard Kinne	.05
157	Albert D. Kirwan	.05
158	Price McLean	.05
159	Curtis M. Sanders	.05
160	Bob Davis	.05
161	Bert Johnson	.05
162	Ralph Kercheval	.10
163	Charles Hughes	.05
164	Clyde Johnson	.05
165	Blanton Collier	.10
166	Charlie Bradshaw	.10
167	Johnny Ray	.05
168	Fran Curci	.10
169	James Park	.05
170	Ivy Joe Hunter	.10
171	Chris Chenault	.05
172	Jeff Van Note	.25
173	Dick Barbee	.05
174	Darryl Bishop	.05
175	Jay Rhodemyre	.10
176	William Rodes	.05
177	Noah Mullins	.05
178	Gene Myers	.05
179	Darrell Cox	.05
180	Jerry Eisaman	.05
181	Ben Zaranka	.05
182	Wash Serini	.05
183	Dallas Owens	.05
184	Bernie Scruggs	.05
185	Wallace Jones	.15
186	Walt Yowarsky	.10
187	Clarkie Mayfield	.05
188	John Grimsley	.10
189	Jerry Woolum	.05
190	John Tatterson	.05
191	Delmar Hughes	.05
192	Lowell Hughes	.05
193	Frank Lemaster	.10
194	Bill Ransdell	.05
195	Tony Mayes	.05
196	Dominic Fucci	.05
197	David Roller	.05
198	Bernie A. Shively	.05
199	William Tuttle	.10
200	Jerry Claiborne	.20
201	Warfield Donohue	.05
202	Russell Ellington	.05
203	Kenny England	.05
204	J.C. Everett	.05
205	Jake Gaiser	.05
206	Elmer Gilb	.05
207	Jim Goforth	.05
208	James Goodman	.05
209	George Gumbert	.05
210	Joseph Hagan	.05
211	W.C. Harrison	.05
212	D.W. Hart	.05
213	Elmo Head	.05
214	Walter Hodge	.05
215	Charles T. Hughes	.05
216	Lowell Hughes	.05
217	R.Y. Ireland	.05
218	Irvine Jeffries	.05
219	Jim King	.05
220	Bill Kleiser	.05
221	Gary Gamble	.05
222	Lawrence McGinnis	.05
223	Ralph Morgan	.05
224	Hays Owens	.05
225	James Park	.05
226	Buddy Parker	.10
227	Sam Ridgeway	.05
228	R.C. Preston	.05
229	Roy Roberts	.05
230	Wilber Schu	.05
231	Evan Settle	.05
232	Bobby Slusher	.05
233	Bill Smith	.05
234	Vince Splane	.05
235	Carl Staker	.05
236	John Stough	.05
237	Milt Ticco	.05
238	Homer Thompson	.05
239	Clarence Tillman	.05

240	Garland Townes	.05
241	Charles Worthington	.05
242	Rudy Yessin	.05
243	Kark Zerfoss	.05
244	Bob Lavin	.05
245	J.A. Dishman	.05
246	Jim Server	.05
247	Fred Fest	.05
248	Ralph Boren	.05
249	James McFarland	.05
250	A.T. Rice	.05
251	Walter White	.05
252	Tom Moseley	.05
253	Paul Jenkins	.05
254	Lovell Underwood	.05
255	William Tuttle	.10
256	Bob Tallent	.05
257	Jack Tucker	.05
258	Roger Newman	.05
259	Stanley Milward	.05
260	Bill Sturgill	.05
261	Gayle Mohney	.05
262	Will Milward	.05
263	Ercel Little	.05
264	Garland Lewis	.05
265	Ron Kennett	.05
266	Howard Kreuter	.05
267	William King	.05
268	Walter Johnson	.10
269	Jim Jordan	.05
270	Mulford Davis	.05
271	Berkley Davis	.05
272	Cecil Combs	.05
273	Carl Combs	.05
274	Milerd Anderson	.05
275	George Vulich	.05
276	Paul Adkins	.05
277	Hugh Coy	.05
278	J. Rice Walker	.05
279	Adrian Back	.05
280	Charley Combs	.05
281	Harry Hurd	.05
282	Tom Harper	.05
283	Dan Hall	.05
284	Ed Lander	.05
285	Bill Barlow	.05
286	James Sharp	.05
287	Al Robinson	.05
288	Frank Phipps	.05
289	Bob Fowler	.05
290	George Skinner	.05
291	Harry Bliss	.05
292	Bill Bibb	.05
293	Herschel Scott	.05
294	Clair Dees	.05
295	Lawrence Burnham	.05
296	Lloyd Ramsey	.05
297	Bruce Davis	.05
298	Bob Taylor	.05
299	Alonzo Nelson	.05
300	Herbert Jerome	.10

1990-91 Kentucky Big Blue 18

Inserted into an issue of Oscar Combs' Big Blue Basketball magazine, the 18-card set was printed on a perforated sheet. The cards measure 2-5/8" x 3-5/8". The white-bordered card fronts have a color photo at the bottom, with the player's name printed inside a stripe above the photo and to the right of a basketball. The backs are horizontal and feature a head shot in the upper left. The player's name, card number, bio and fun fact are printed in boxes to the right of the head shot. The rest of the back is filled up with a "Coach Pitino Sez" quote.

		MT
Complete Set (18):		20.00
Common Player:		.60
1	Johnathon Davis	1.00
2	Reggie Hanson	1.00
3	Richie Farmer	1.50
4	Deron Feldhaus	1.00
5	John Pelphrey	1.25
6	Sean Woods	.75
7	Todd Bearup	.60
8	Junior Braddy	.60
9	Jeff Brassow	.75
10	Gimel Martinez	.75
11	Jamal Mashburn	9.00
12	Henry Thomas	.60
13	Carlos Toomer	.60
14	Travis Ford	2.50
15	Rick Pitino CO	2.50
16	UK Cracks Top 10	.60
17	UK 93, U of L 85	.60
18	Checklist Card	1.00

1990-91 Kentucky Big Blue Dream Team/Award Winners

Inserted into Oscar Comb's Big Blue Basketball magazine in the Spring 1991 Volume 5, No. 1, issue, the 18-card set was printed in two perforated panels. When separated, the cards measure 2-9/16" x 3-5/8". A color photo anchors the white-bordered fronts. "Big Blue Basketball Award Winner" is printed inside a box in the upper left corner, while a cup award with "Cats" printed at the bottom of it appears in the lower left. The player's name is located inside a stripe in the lower right. The player's head shot appears in the upper left, with his name, bio, "Big Blue Basketball" and the card number printed in the upper right. A newspaper layout includes the player's highlights.

		MT
Complete Set (18):		100.00
Common Player:		.75
19	LSU (Shaquille O'Neal)	70.00
20	Tennessee (Allan Houston)	20.00
21	Indiana (Calbert Cheaney)	7.50
22	North Carolina (Rick Fox)	3.00
23	Georgia (Litterial Green)	1.50
24	Indiana (Bobby Knight CO)	3.00
25	North Carolina (Dean Smith)	5.00
26	Freedom Hall	.75
27	Checklist	1.00
28	Richie Farmer	1.25
29	Jamal Mashburn	12.00
30	Jeff Brassow	.75
31	Todd Bearup	.75
32	Sean Woods	1.00
33	Deron Feldhaus	1.00
34	John Pelphrey	1.50
35	Reggie Hanson	1.00
36	Rick Pitino CO	3.00

1990 Kentucky Program Insert

Inserted into the Kentucky All "A" Classic official game program at the state tournament, the 18-card set was printed on two perforated sheets. Each card measures standard size. Black and white photos anchor the front, with a gray stripe beneath the photo featuring the player's region number on the left and his name on the right. The All "A" Classic logo is in the lower left, with the player's bio and team listed in the lower right. The card backs have the player's head shot in the upper left and his name inside a stripe on the upper right. The player's bio is printed beneath his name on the right. His highlights and stats round out the card backs.

		MT
Complete Set (18):		10.00
Common Player:		.75
1	Checklist Card	1.00
2	Scott Baesler	1.00
3	Eugene Alexander	.75
4	Sergio Luyk	1.25
5	Chris Knight	.75
6	Chris Huffman	1.00
7	Shannon Phillips	.75
8	Glen Wathen	.75
9	Jason Hagan	.75
10	Bryan Milburn	1.00
11	Andre McClendon	.75
12	Chris Harrison	1.00
13	Daniel Swintosky	1.00
14	Jamie Cromer	.75
15	Mo Hollingsworth	.75
16	Jeff Moore	1.00
17	Jody Thompson	.75
18	Mike Helton	.75

1990 Kentucky Soviet Program Insert

Inserted into the AAU/Soviet Tour game program, the 18-card set was printed in two perforated panels. The cards, which measure standard size, focus on members of the Kentucky AAU All-Stars. The card fronts are anchored by a black-and-white photo, with "KY. AAU All-Stars" printed inside a white rectangle in the upper left. The player's name is printed inside a white stripe beneath the photo. The card backs, which are numbered inside a square in the upper right corner, showcase a head shot in the upper left. His name appears inside a stripe to the right of the photo. His bio is printed beneath his name. The player's career highlights and stats round out the backs.

		MT
Complete Set (18):		30.00
Common Player:		.75
1	Checklist Card	1.00
2	Kentucky/USSR rosters	1.00
3	Jim Lankster	.75
4	Paul Bingham	.75
5	James Crutcher	.75
6	Jason Eitutis	.75
7	Greg Glass	.75
8	Arlando Johnson	.75
9	Gimel Martinez	1.00
10	Jamal Mashburn	20.00
11	Jeff Moore	.75
12	Dwayne Morton	3.00
13	Keith Peel	.75
14	Andy Penick	.75
15	Daniel Swintosky	.75
16	Jody Thompson	.75
17	Carlos Toomer	.75
18	Kelly Wells	.75

1990-91 Kentucky Women Schedules

Measuring 2-1/4" x 3-3/4", the 16-card set showcases blue-toned player head shots at the top, with the player's name, number, bio and team inside a white area at bottom of the card fronts. The card backs are unnumbered and include the 1990-91 Lady Kats' schedule.

	MT
Complete Set (16):	10.00
Common Player:	.75
Kayla Campbell	.75
Kristi Cushenberry	.75
Mia Daniel	.75
Tracye Davis	.75
Tedra Eberhart	.75
Jennifer Gray	.75
Sharon Fanning CO	.75
Jamie Hobgood	.75
Christe Jordan	.75
Karen Killen	.75
Pattresa Leonard	.75
Tiundra Love	.75
Stacy McIntyre	.75
Jocelyn Mills	.75
Cathy Proctor	.75
Rebekah Reasor	.75

1991-92 Kentucky Big Blue 20

Inserted in Oscar Combs' Big Blue Basketball magazine's Summer 1991 Volume 5, No. 2, issue, this 20-card set was included with an 8-1/2" x 11" photo. When separated, the cards measure 2-9/16" x 3-5/8". The horizontal fronts have a color head shot on the left, with his name inside a red stripe in the lower right. The year and team name are printed inside a blue stripe at the top. The Kentucky logo is printed in the right center of the front. The backs include a full-bleed, black and white photo, with the card number at the top left and "Big Blue Basketball" printed at the top center. A white "Not for sale - 1991 Wildcat News Co." stripe is at the bottom.

		MT
Complete Set (20):		20.00
Common Player:		.60
1	John Pelphrey	1.25
2	Deron Feldhaus	1.00
3	Richie Farmer	1.50
4	Jeff Brassow	.75
5	Junior Braddy	.60
6	Sean Woods	.75
7	Gimel Martinez	.75
8	Travis Ford	2.00
9	Dale Brown	.75
10	Chris Harrison	.60
11	Carlos Toomer	.60
12	Jamal Mashburn	9.00
13	Rick Pitino CO	2.50
14	Aminu Timberlake	.60
15	Andre Riddick	2.00
16	Bernadette Locke-Mattox (Asst. Co)	1.50
17	Billy Donovan ACO	1.00
18	Herb Sendek ACO	.75
NNO	Wildcat Seniors 1991-92 (Volume 5, Number 2)	3.00
NNO	Team Photo (Volume 5, Number 3)	5.00

1993-94 Kentucky

The blue-borderd, standard-sized 18-card set showcases "Cats" at the top of the card front. The player's name is written in blue and white script in the lower left corner of the photo, while "1993-94 University of Kentucky Wildcats" is printed inside the blue border at the bottom of the card. The horizontal card backs, which are numbered in the lower right corner, have a player photo on the left side, with the player's highlights, stats, name, bio and Kentucky logo all located to the right of the photo. The sets were available by mail through the university's bookstore for $9.25 plus shipping.

		MT
Complete Set (18):		15.00
Common Player:		.50
1	Jeff Brassow	.50
2	Tony Delk	4.00
3	Rodney Dent	1.50
4	Anthony Epps	1.00
5	Travis Ford	2.00
6	Chris Harrison	.50
7	Bill Keightley	.50
8	Gimel Martinez	.50
9	Walter McCarty	4.00
10	Rick Pitino CO	2.00
11	Jared Prickett	.75
12	Rodrick Rhodes	2.00
13	Andre Riddick	1.50
14	Jeff Sheppard	.75
15	Assistant Coaches (Delray Brooks, Shaun Brown, Billy Donovan, Bernadette Locke-Mattox)	1.00
16	1993 SEC Champions	1.00
17	Team Photo Card	1.00
18	Title Card	.50

1998-99 Kentucky Schedules

		MT
Complete Set (3):		10.00
Common Player:		3.00
1	Heshimu Evans	3.00
2	Scott Padgett	6.00
3	Wayne Turner	3.00

1999 Kentucky Basketball Greats

	MT
Complete Set (36):	20.00
Common Player:	.25
Cliff Barker	.25
Ralph Beard	.25
Jerry Bird	.25
Rex Chapman	1.00
Johnny Cox	.25
Louie Dampier	.25
John DeMoisey	.25
Billy Evans	.25
Richie Farmer	.25
Jack Givens	.25
Phil Grawemeyer	.25
Kevin Grevey	.25
Alex Groza	.25
Cliff Hagan	.25
Joe B. Hall	1.00
Vernon Hatton	.25
Basil Hayden	.25
Dan Issel	2.00
Wallace Jones	.25
Kyle Macy	.50
Jamal Mashburn	3.00
Cotton Nash	.25
Frank Ramsey	.25
Pat Riley	5.00
Kenny Rollins	.25
Gayle Rose	.25
Layton Rouse	.25
Adolph Rupp	5.00
Forest Sale	.25
Jeff Sheppard	.25
Orlando Smith	.25
Carey Spicer	.25
Lou Tsioropoulos	.25
Antoine Walker	3.00
Rupp Arena	1.00
0 Univ. of Kentucky logo/checklist card	.25

1985-86 LSU

Sponsored by Baton Rouge General Medical Center, LSU, various law enforcement agencies and the Chemical Dependency Unit of Baton Rouge, the 16-card set showcases a color photo in the center of the card front. Two sponsor logos are printed in the upper left and right corners of the front, with "Tigers" printed in the top center. Beneath the photo, from left, are the LSU Tigers' logos, player name and bio and the Tigers logo. The unnumbered card backs have the LSU Tigers' logo in the upper left and right, while the player's name and bio appear in the top center. The player's highlights, tips from the Tigers and sponsor logos round out the card backs. The set, produced by McDag Productions, features players from both basketball and baseball. Joey (Albert) Belle, Mark Guthrie and Jeff Reboulet each are included in the set. A "B" suffix represents baseball and "BK" stands for basketball after the players' names.

		MT
Complete Set (16):		20.00
Common Player:		.50
1	Joey (Albert) Belle B	14.00
2	Skip Bertman B CO	1.00
3	Ricky Blanton BK	1.00
4	Dale Brown BK CO	3.00
5	Ollie Brown BK	.50
6	Mark Guthrie B	1.00
7	Rob Leary B	.50
8	Stan Loewer B	.50
9	Greg Patterson B	.50
10	Jeff Reboulet B	1.00
11	Don Redden BK	.50
12	Derrick Taylor BK	.50
13	Jose Vargas BK	.50
14	John Williams BK	2.00
15	Nikita Wilson BK	1.00
16	Anthony Wilson BK	.50

1986-87 LSU

This 16-card set featured eight basketball and eight baseball players from LSU. It was sponsored by "local" law enforcement agencies, LSU, Baton Rouge General Medical Center and Chemical Dependency Unit of Baton Rouge. It was produced by McDag Productions and the cards were unnumbered.

	MT
Complete Set (16):	18.00
Common Player:	.50
Ricky Blanton BK	1.50
Dennis Brown BK	.50
Oliver Brown BK	.50
Zoran Jovanovich BK	.50
Jose Vargas BK	1.00
Anthony Wilson BK	.50
Nikita Wilson BK	1.00
Bernard Woodside BK	1.00
Joey Belle BB	10.00
Craig Faulkner BB	.50
Mark Guthrie BB	1.50
Dan Kite BB	.50
Stan Loewer BB	.50
Barry Manuel BB	.50
Mike Papajohn BB	.50
Gregg Patterson BB	1.00

1987-88 LSU

Sponsored by Baton Rouge General Medical Center, LSU, various law enforcement agencies and the Chemical Dependency Unit of Baton Rouge, the standard-sized, 16-card set was produced by McDag. The card fronts have "LSU" in the upper left, the player's name, position and year in the upper right of the card front and sponsor logos in the corners beneath the photo. The card backs have "Tigers" located in the upper left, player's name and bio in the top center and card number in the top right. The player's highlights, tips from the Tigers and sponsor logos round out the card backs.

		MT
Complete Set (16):		35.00
Common Player:		1.00
1	Dale Brown BK CO	3.00
2	Ricky Blanton BK	1.50
3	Jose Vargas BK	1.00
4	Fess Irvin BK	1.50
5	Darryl Joe BK	1.00
6	Bernard Woodside BK	1.00
7	Neboisha Bukumirovich BK	1.00
8	Parker Griffin B	1.00
9	Skip Bertman B CO	1.50
10	Dan Kite B	1.00
11	Russ Springer B	1.50
12	Ben McDonald B	4.00
13	Richie Vasquez B	1.00
14	Andy Galy B	1.00
15	Pete Bush B	1.00
16	Pete Maravich BK MEM	25.00

1988-89 LSU All-Americas

Sponsored by Baton Rouge General Medical Center, LSU, various law enforcement agencies and Chemical Dependency Unit of Baton Rouge, the standard-sized, 16-card set has the Tigers' logo in the upper left, with the name of the set in the upper right. A color photo anchors the card front. Sponsor logos appear in the bottom corners, with the player's name, year and sport in the bottom center. The card backs have the player's name, sport, position and hometown in the top center, with the card number inside a pennant in the upper right. The player's highlights, tips from the Tiger All-Americas and sponsor logos round out the card backs.

		MT
Complete Set (16):		14.00
Common Player:		.50
1	Chris Jackson	2.00
2	Durand Macklin	1.00
3	Ben McDonald	3.00
4	Wes Grisham	.50
5	Barry Manuel	.50
6	Dawn Sowell	.50
7	Wendy Stammer	.50
8	Nacho Albergamo	.50
9	Wendell Davis	1.25
10	Michael Brooks	1.50
11	Lance Smith	1.00
12	Eric Martin	1.50
13	James Britt	.50
14	Albert Richardson	.50
15	Greg Jackson	1.00
16	Rob McNamara	.50

1988-89 LSU

Sponsored by Baton Rouge General Medical Center, LSU, law enforcement agencies and Chemical Dependency Unit of Baton Rouge, the standard-sized, 16-card set has "LSU Tigers" and the years printed at the top of the card front. The color photo anchors the center, with sponsor logos printed in the bottom corners and the player's name and position located at the bottom center. The card backs have "LSU" in the upper left, the player's name and bio are in the top center and the card number is in the upper right inside a circle. The player's highlights, tips from the Tigers and sponsor logos round out the card back.

		MT
Complete Set (16):		14.00
Common Player:		.50
1	Ricky Blanton	1.00
2	Dale Brown CO	2.00
3	Wayne Simms	.50
4	Chris Jackson	3.50
5	Kyle McKenzie	.50
6	Lyle Mouton	1.50
7	Vernel Singleton	1.00
8	Russell Grant	.50
9	Skip Bertman	1.00
10	Ben McDonald	3.00
11	Pete Bush	.50
12	Mike Bianco	.50
13	Craig Cala	.50
14	Matt Gruver	.50
15	Keith Osik	.50
16	Russell Springer	1.00

1990 LSU Collegiate Collection

The 200-card set is mostly black and white photos bordered by purple and gold. The front has the player's name on the at the bottom and the school's name at the top. The back highlights the player's career.

		MT
Complete Set (200):		15.00
Common Player:		.05
1	Pete Maravich	1.50
2	Chris Jackson	.50
3	Y.A. Tittle	.75
4	Ricky Blanton	.20
5	Charles Alexander	.05
6	Joe Dean	.15
7	Billy Cannon	.25
8	Dalton Hilliard	.25
9	Bert Jones	.40
10	Tommy Hodson	.25
11	Dale Brown CO	.40
12	Mike Archer	.15
13	Jimmy Taylor	.40
14	John Williams	.20
15	Brian Kinchen	.25
16	Chris Carrier	.05
17	Jess Fatheree	.05
18	Chris Jackson	.50
19	Orlando McDaniel	.05
20	Billy Hendrix	.05
21	Eddie Ray	.05
22	Glenn Hansen	.05
23	Bo Strange	.05
24	Eric Hill	.25
25	Leonard Mitchell	.05
26	Larry Shipp	.05
27	Malcolm Scott	.05
28	A.J. Duhe	.20
29	George Brancato	.05
30	Jim Roshso	.05
31	Karl Wilson	.20
32	Ethan Martin	.05
33	Julie Gross	.05
34	Lyman White	.05

35	Eddie Palubinskas	.05
36	Michael Brooks	.30
37	Frank Brian	.05
38	Gaynell Tinsley	.05
39	Mike Anderson	.05
40	Howard Carter	.15
41	Jerry Stovall	.25
42	Nikita Wilson	.20
43	Bill Fortier	.05
44	Mike V	.10
45	Richard Granier	.05
46	DeWayne Scales	.10
47	Pinky Rohm	.05
48	Bernie Moore Stadium	.05
49	Toby Caston	.20
50	Durand Macklin	.15
51	John Ed Bradley	.05
52	Mark Lumpkin	.05
53	Joyce Walker	.05
54	Bobby Lowther	.05
55	Al Sanders	.05
56	Curt Gore	.05
57	Eric Martin	.30
58	George Nattin	.05
59	Roland Barray	.05
60	Craig Duhe	.05
61	Maree Jackson	.05
62	Sparky Wade	.05
63	Karl Dunbar	.10
64	Mike Williams	.05
65	Al Green	.05
66	Lew Sibley	.05
67	John Sage	.05
68	Craig Burns	.05
69	Schwoonda Williams	.05
70	Wendell Davis	.25
71	Dick Maile	.05
72	Kenny Bordelon	.05
73	Rusty Jackson	.05
74	Pete Maravich	1.50
75	Garry James	.20
76	Lance Smith	.10
77	Willie Teal	.05
78	John Wood	.05
79	Mike Robichaux	.05
80	Earl Leggett	.10
81	Alex Box Stadium	.05
82	Steve Cassidy	.05
83	Kenny Konz	.10
84	Wendell Harris	.15
85	Alan Risher	.05
86	Gerald Keigley	.05
87	Robert Dugas	.05
88	Chris Williams	.05
89	John DeMarie	.05
90	Eddie Fuller	.05
91	Chris Jackson	.50
92	Bo Harris	.10
93	Mel Lyle	.05
94	Greg Jackson	.25
95	Liffort Hobley	.15
96	Shawn Burks	.05
97	David Browndyke	.10
98	Jerry Reynolds	.25
99	Eric Andolsek	.25
100	Director Card 1-99	.05
101	Jon Streete	.05
102	Barry Wilson	.05
103	Remi Prudhomme	.10
104	Abe Mickal	.05
105	Henry Thomas	.40
106	George Tarasovic	.05
107	Tiger Stadium	.15
108	Benjy Thibodeaux	.05
109	Jeffery Dale	.05
110	Sid Fournet	.05
111	John Adams	.05
112	Dennis Gaubatz	.10
113	Ben McDonald	.40
114	Joe Tuminello	.05
115	Billy Truax	.15
116	Warren Rabb	.10
117	Albert Richardson	.05
118	Jay Whitey	.05
119	Clinton Burrell	.10
120	Mike Miley	.15
121	Tommy Casanova	.30
122	George Bevan	.05
123	Binks Miciotto	.05
124	Joe Michaelson	.05
125	Mickey Mangham	.05
126	Ronnie Estay	.05
127	John Hazard	.05
128	Darrell Phillips	.05
129	Nacho Albergamo	.05
130	John Garlington	.15
131	Arthur Cantrelle	.05
132	Monk Guillot	.05
133	Gene Knight	.05
134	Gerry Kent	.05
135	Ron Sancho	.05
136	Kenny Higgs	.10
137	Rip Collins	.05
138	Bob Pettit	.75
139	Mike Vincent	.05
140	Tyler LaFauci	.05
141	Richard Brooks	.05
142	Billy Booth	.05
143	Brad Davis	.05
144	Roy Winston	.10
145	Andy Hamilton	.10
146	Rene Bourgeois	.05
147	Terry Robiskie	.15
148	Godfrey Zaunbrecher	.05
149	George Atiyeh	.05
150	Billy Hardin	.05
151	Jeff Wickersham	.15
152	Charlie McClendon	.15
153	Hokie Gajan	.10
154	Pete Maravich Center	.15
155	Bill Arnsparger	.15
156	Max Fuglar	.25
157	Greg Lafleur	.05
158	George Rice	.05
159	Dave McCormick	.05
160	Fred Miller	.05
161	Steve Van Buren	.40
162	Sid Bowman	.05
163	Wes Grisham	.05
164	Jeff Torrance	.05
165	Buddy Blair	.05
166	Doug Moreau	.10
167	Mike DeMarie	.05
168	James Britt	.05
169	Matt DeFrank	.05
170	Al Moreau	.05
171	Joe Bill Padcock	.05
172	Pat Screen	.05
173	Ralph Norwood	.10
174	Marcus Quinn	.10
175	Johnny Robinson	.25
176	Tony Moss	.05
177	Dan Alexander	.05
178	Norman Jefferson	.05
179	Bert Jones	.40
180	Joe LaBruzzo	.05
181	Jimmy Field	.05
182	David Woodley	.15
183	Paul Dietzel	.15
184	Abner Wimbley	.05
185	Steve Ensminger	.05
186	Carlos Carson	.20
187	Ken Kanauna Sr.	.05
188	Paul Ziegler	.05
189	Chris Jackson	.50
190	Chris Jackson	.50
191	W.T. Robinson Tennis	.05
192	Donnie Leaycraft	.05
193	Fernando Perez	.05
194	Steve Faulk	.05
195	Warren Capone	.05
196	Howard Carter	.15
197	Glenn Hansen	.05
198	Durand Macklin	.15
199	Sam Grezaffi	.10
200	Director Card	.05

1993-94 LSU

Produced by McDag Inc., the standard-sized, 16-card set showcases a color photo on the front, with "LSU Tigers" in the upper left and years in the upper right. Beneath the photo in the lower left is a basketball, with the player's name, position and number in the lower right. The unnumbered backs have "LSU Tigers" in the upper left, while the player's name and bio are in the top center. The player's jersey number is printed inside a basketball in the upper right. The player's highlights and Collegiate Licensed Product logo rounds out the card backs.

		MT
Complete Set (16):		8.00
Common Player:		.50
	Doug Annison	.50
	David Bosley	.50
	Dale Brown CO	1.50
	Jamie Brandon	.75
	Lenear Burns	.50
	Clarence Ceasar	.75
	Sean Gipson	.50
	Ronnie Henderson	1.50
	Glover Jackson	.50
	Randy Livingston	2.00
	Andre Owens	.75
	Roman Roubtchenko	.50
	Brandon Titus	.50
	Mike the Tiger (The Tiger)	.50
	Mike the Tiger (The Mascot)	.50
	Cheerleaders	.50

1989-90 Louisiana Tech

The standard-sized, 16-card set showcases members of the men's (card Nos. 1-8) and women's (Nos. 9-16) basketball teams. The card fronts are anchored by a large photo, framed in red and white. A gray box above the photo contains the school's name and year, while a blue box featuring the player's name, number and position appears below the photo. The unnumbered card backs feature the usual player information and a fire safety message and cartoon.

		MT
Complete Set (16):		12.00
Common Player:		.50
	Eldon Bowman	.50
	P.J. Brown	7.00
	Dickie Crawford	.50
	Anthony Dade	1.50
	Reggie Gibbs	.50
	Jo Jo Goldsmith	.50
	Brett Guillory	.50
	Roosevelt Powell	.50
	Barbara Bolden	.50
	Sheila Ethridge	.50
	Cara Gullion	.50
	Shantel Hardison	.50
	Venus Lacy	3.50
	Annie Lockett	.50
	Sebrena Smith	.50
	Pam Wells	1.00

1981-82 Louisville

Sponsored by Pepsi, Greater Louisville Police Departments, and the Chamber of Commerce, the 31-card set measures 2-5/8" by 4-1/8". Black and white photos are framed by a red border. The player's name, number and bio are located in the lower left, with "Cardinal Spirit!" printed in the lower right on a slant. The backs, which are numbered according to the tip number, have a kids and kops tip at the top and a safety tip. The Pepsi Challenge and Pepsi-Cola logos round out the card backs.

		MT
Complete Set (31):		60.00
Common Player:		1.50
1	Charles Jones	2.50
2	Rodin's The Thinker	1.50
3	1981-82 Schedule	1.50
4	Bill Olsen ATH DIR and family	1.50
5	Coaching Staff	2.50
6	Lancaster Gordon	5.00
7	Donald C. Swain PRES	1.50
8	Scooter McCray	4.00
9	Cheerleaders	1.50
10	Marty Pulliam	1.50
11	Derek Smith	5.00
12	Jack Tennant ANN, Van Vance ANN	1.50
13	Jerry Eaves	2.50
14	Greg Deuser	1.50
15	Manuel Forrest	2.50
16	Danny Mitchell	1.50
17	Team Photo Men's Team	4.00
18	Dir. Sports Medicine (Jerry May TR, Rudy Ellis)	1.50
19	Poncho Wright	2.50
20	James Jeter	1.50
21	Cardinal Bird Mascot	1.50
22	Milt Wagner	5.00
23	1981-82 Freshman (Denny Crum CO)	5.00
24	Team Photo Women's Team	1.50
25	Willie Brown	2.50
26	Kent Jones	1.50
27	Returning Starters (Denny Crum CO)	5.00
28	U of L Professional Basketball Players (Darrell Griffith)	8.00
29	Denny Crum CO	8.00
30	Rodney McCray	6.00
NNO	Logo Card SP	40.00

1983-84 Louisville

Measuring 4" x 5", the 20-card set showcase a borderless photo on the left, with the player's head shot, team name, player's name and number and Louisville logo in a red area on the right side of the card front. The card backs, which are unnumbered, have the player's name and career highlights on the left side of the card, while his stats appear in the upper right. The entire card back is done in a two-column format.

		MT
Complete Set (20):		60.00
Common Player:		2.50
(1)	Denny Crum CO	5.00
(2)	Manuel Forrest	2.50
(3)	Lancaster Gordon	5.00
(4)	Darrell Griffith	2.50
(5)	Jeff Hall	2.50
(6)	James Jeter	2.50
(7)	Charles Jones	3.00
(8)	Kent Jones	3.00
(9)	Mark McSwain	3.00
(10)	Danny Mitchell	7.00
(11)	Will Olliges	3.00
(12)	Barry Sumpter	4.00
(13)	Billy Thompson	2.50
(14)	Robbie Valentine	5.00
(15)	Milt Wagner	7.00
(16)	Chris West	3.00
(17)	Assistant Coaches (Bobby Dotson, Wade Houston, Jerry Jones)	2.50
(18)	Cheerleaders	2.50
(19)	Pep Band	2.50
(20)	Freedom Hall Home of the Cardinals	4.00

1988-89 Louisville Collegiate Collection

The standard-sized, 194-card set showcases a red and white border on the front, with "Louisville's Finest" in the upper left and the Cardinals' logo in the upper right. Beneath the photo, are "U of L" in the lower left, the player's name in the center and the sponsor's logo in the lower right. The horizontal backs have the player's name and bio in the upper left, with the card number in the upper right. "Did you know", WHAS radio logo and Collegiate Collection 1988 tag line round out the card back.

		MT
Complete Set (194):		17.00
Common Player:		.05
1	Denny Crum CO	.40
2	Wes Unseld	.50
3	Darrell Griffith	.30
4	John Dromo	.10
5	Bernard (Peck) Hickman	.10
6	Butch Beard	.30
7	Herbert Crook	.15
8	Milt Wagner	.20
9	Lancaster Gordon	.20
10	Billy Thompson	.20
11	Rod McCray	.25
12	Scooter McCray	.15
13	Wade Houston	.15
14	Jerry Jones	.05
15	Derek Smith	.15
16	Tony Branch	.10
17	Wesley Cox	.10
18	Manuel Forrest	.10
19	Jerry Eaves	.10
20	1980 NCAA Champs	.25
21	Junior Bridgeman	.15
22	Jeff Hall	.10
23	Charles Jones	.10
24	Rick Wilson	.05
25	The Cardinal Bird	.05
26	Wiley Brown	.10
27	Charles Tyra	.10
28	Phil Rollins	.05
29	James Jeter	.05
30	Poncho Wright	.05
31	Vladimir Gastevich	.05
32	Terry Howard	.05
33	Mark McSwain	.10
34	Ricky Gallon	.05
35	1975 NCAA Final Four	.10
36	1972 NCAA Final Four	.10
37	Mike Lawhon	.05
38	Bill Bunton	.10
39	Roger Burkman	.05
40	Henry Bacon	.05
41	Larry Williams	.05
42	Phil Bond	.05
43	Bobby Brown	.05
44	Charles Jones	.10
45	Mike Grosso	.05
46	Freedom Hall	.15
47	Fred Holden	.05
48	1948 NAIB Champs	.10
49	Glen Combs	.10
50	Jadie Frazier	.05
51	Marty Pulliam	.05
52	Eddie Whitehead	.05
53	Bobby Turner	.05
54	Will Olliges	.05
55	Eddie Creamer	.05
56	Corky Cox	.05
57	Bob Lochmueller	.05
58	Jeff Hall	.10
59	Al Vilcheck	.05
60	Jim Morgan	.05
61	Jim Price	.10
62	Ron Thomas	.10
63	Bobby Dotson	.05
64	Jerry Eaves	.10
65	1956 NIT Champs	.10
66	John Reuther	.05
67	Ron Hawley	.05
68	Kent Jones	.05
69	1983 NCAA Final Four	.15
70	1982 NCAA Final Four	.15
71	1959 Louisville Cardinals	.10
72	Fred Sawyer	.05
73	Kenny Reeves	.05
74	Chris West	.05
75	Dick Peloff	.05
76	Allen Murphy	.05
77	John Prudhoe	.05
78	Mike Abram	.05
79	Bud Olsen	.05
80	Ron Rubenstein	.05
81	Gerald Moreman	.05
82	Chuck Noble	.05
83	Bill Darragh	.05
84	Jerry Dupont	.05
85	Danny Mitchell	.05
86	John Turner	.05
87	Daryl Cleveland	.05
88	Greg Deuser	.05
89	Don Goldstein	.05
90	Marv Selvy	.05
91	Dave Gilbert	.05
92	Tommy Finnegan	.05
93	Joe Liedtke	.05
94	Jack Coleman	.05
95	Dennis Clifford	.05
96	Robbie Valentine	.05
97	Ron Rooks	.05
98	The Coaching Staff	.15
99	Denny Crum CO	.40
100	Manuel Forrest	.10
101	Darrell Griffith	.30
102	Wesley Cox	.10
103	Wes Unseld	.50
104	John Dromo	.10
105	Peck Hickman	.10
106	Butch Beard	.30
107	Herbert Crook	.15
108	Milt Wagner	.20
109	Lancaster Gordon	.20
110	Billy Thompson	.20
111	Rodney McCray	.25
112	Scooter McCray	.15
113	Derek Smith	.15
114	Tony Branch	.10
115	Manuel Forrest	.10
116	Jerry Eaves	.10
117	Jeff Hall	.10
118	Charles Jones	.10
119	Rick Wilson	.05
120	Wiley Brown	.10
121	Charlie Tyra	.10
122	Phil Rollins	.05
123	Poncho Wright	.05
124	Terry Howard	.05
125	Mark McSwain	.10
126	Ricky Gallon	.05
127	Mike Lawhon	.05
128	Roger Burkman	.05
129	Henry Bacon	.05
130	Larry Williams	.05
131	Phil Bond	.05
132	Stanley Bunton	.05
133	Fred Holden	.05
134	Marty Pulliam	.05
135	Bobby Turner	.05
136	Will Olliges	.05
137	Al Vilcheck	.05
138	Jim Price	.10
139	Chris West	.05
140	Allen Murphy	.05
141	Mike Abram	.05
142	Danny Mitchell	.05
143	John Turner	.05
144	Daryl Cleveland	.05
145	Don Goldstein	.05
146	Marv Selvy	.05
147	Dave Gilbert	.05
148	Joe Liedtke	.05
149	Robbie Valentine	.05
150	Tony Branch	.10
151	Manuel Forrest	.10
152	Jerry Eaves	.10
153	Rick Wilson	.05
154	Jeff Hall	.10
155	Charles Jones	.10
156	Derek Smith	.15
157	Scooter McCray	.15
158	Robbie Valentine	.05
159	Mike Abram	.05
160	Rodney McCray	.25
161	Roger Burkman	.05
162	Henry Bacon	.05
163	Mike Lawhon	.05
164	Ricky Gallon	.05
165	Billy Thompson	.20
166	Milt Wagner	.20
167	Lancaster Gordon	.20
168	Butch Beard	.30
169	Herbert Crook	.15
170	Wes Unseld	.50
171	Wesley Cox	.10
172	Darrell Griffith	.30
173	Denny Crum CO	.40
174	Mark McSwain	.10
175	Wiley Brown	.10
176	Will Olliges	.05
177	Phil Bond	.05
178	Phil Bond	.05
179	Wiley Brown	.10
180	Mark McSwain	.10
181	Denny Crum CO	.40
182	Darrell Griffith	.30
183	Wesley Cox	.10
184	Peck Hickman	.10
185	Lancaster Gordon	.20
186	Billy Thompson	.20
187	Rodney McCray	.25
188	Stanley Bunton	.05
189	Henry Bacon	.05
190	Scooter McCray	.15
191	Derek Smith	.15
192	Jerry King	.05
193	Van Vance, Jock Sutherland	.05
194	Bill Olsen	.05

1989-90 Louisville Collegiate Collection

The standard-sized set contains 300 cards with a mixture of black and white photos and color photos for the former and current players. The photos are superimposed over a red and white-striped card face. The backs have biographical information with the card numbers there as well.

		MT
Complete Set (300):		20.00
Common Player:		.05
1	Denny Crum CO	.40
2	Darrell Griffith	.30
3	Wes Unseld	.50
4	Pervis Ellison	.40
5	Charlie Tyra	.10
6	Phil Bond	.05
7	Butch Beard	.25
8	Jim Price	.10
9	Jerry Eaves	.10
10	Manuel Forrest	.10
11	Butch Beard	.25
12	Herbert Crook	.15
13	John Turner	.05
14	Wes Unseld	.50
15	Fred Holden	.05
16	Bill Bunton	.10
17	Milt Wagner	.20
18	Ricky Gallon	.05
19	Jerry King	.05
20	Don Goldstein	.05
21	Rick Wilson	.05
22	John Reuther	.05
23	Charles Jones	.10
24	Bobby Turner	.05
25	Darrell Griffith	.30
26	Scooter McCray	.15
27	George Hauptfuhrer	.05
28	Frank Epley	.05
29	Ed Kupper	.05
30	Don Kinker	.05
31	Roger Burkman	.05
32	Jerry Eaves	.10
33	Derek Smith	.15
34	Jeff Hall	.10
35	Billy Thompson	.20
36	Mike Abram	.05
37	Mark McSwain	.10
38	Herbert Crook	.15
39	Kenny Payne	.10
40	Johnny Knopf	.05
41	Pervis Ellison	.40
42	Deward Compton	.05
43	Poncho Wright	.05
44	Scooter McCray	.15
45	Rodney McCray	.25
46	Milt Wagner	.20
47	Lancaster Gordon	.20
48	Manuel Forrest	.10
49	Charles Jones	.10
50	Cal Johnson	.05
51	Forrest Able	.05
52	Bob Peterson	.05
53	Clyde (Ace) Parker	.10
54	Roy Rubin	.05
55	Al Russak	.05
56	Roy Combs	.05
57	Robert Davis	.05
58	Randall Ford	.05
59	Clyde Bryant	.05
60	Frank Lentz	.05
61	Bob Dunbar	.05
62	William Powell	.05
63	Bob Manion	.05
64	Al Glaza	.05
65	Harold Andrews	.05
66	Wade Houston	.15
67	Joe Reuther	.05
68	Judd Rothman	.05
69	Tony Kinnaird	.05
70	Danny Brown	.05
71	Ike Whitefield	.05
72	Billy Harmon	.05
73	Joe Meiman	.05
74	Ed Linonis	.05
75	Larry Carter	.05
76	Ken Bradley	.05
77	Ken Butters	.05
78	John Studer	.05
79	Dennis Deeken	.05
80	Bob Gorius	.05
81	Paul Pry	.05
82	Ron Stallings	.05
83	John Varoscak	.05
84	Bob Naber	.05
85	Howard Stacey	.05
86	Buddy Leathers	.05
87	Joe Kitchen	.05
88	Alex Mantel	.05
89	Rodger Tieman	.05
90	Dick Keffer	.05
91	Dick Robison	.05
92	Barry Sumpter	.05
93	Herb Harrah	.05
94	Bill Sullivan	.05
95	Chet Beam	.05
96	Roscoe Shackelford	.05
97	David Smith	.05
98	Jerry Armstrong	.05
99	James "Lum" Edwards	.05
100	Jesse "Oz" Johnson	.05
101	Howard Schnellenberger	.25
102	Johnny Unitas	1.00
103	Lenny Lyles	.15
104	Ken Porco	.05
105	Jay Gruden	.05
106	Tom Lucia	.05
107	Ken Kortas	.10
108	Howard Stevens	.10
109	Doug Buffone	.15
110	Lenny Lyles	.15
111	Wilbur Summers	.05
112	Dean May	.05
113	Deon Booker	.05
114	Walter Peacock	.05
115	Ernest Givins	.40
116	Otis Wilson	.25
117	Mark Clayton	.40
118	Dwayne Woodruff	.15
119	Frank Minnifield	.25
120	Ernie Green	.15
121	Wally Oyler	.05
122	Nathan Poole	.05
123	Ron Davenport	.10
124	Tom Laframboise	.05
125	Ed Rubbert	.05
126	Jon Cade	.05
127	Howard Schnellenberger	.25
128	Rick Lantz	.05
129	Brad Bradford	.05
130	Danny Hope	.05
131	Bob Maddox	.05
132	Gary Nord	.05
133	Ty Smith	.05
134	Christ Vagotis	.05
135	Trent Walters	.05
136	Jeff Morrow	.05
137	Vince Gibson	.05
138	Lee Corso	.40
139	Frank Camp	.05
140	Benny Russell	.05
141	Paul Mattingly	.05
142	Joe Jacoby	.25
143	Jay Gruden	.05
144	Chris Thieneman	.05
145	Matt Battaglia	.05
146	Eddie Johnson	.05
147	Stu Stramm	.05
148	Donald Craft	.05
149	Pete Compise	.05
150	Jim Zamberlan	.05
151	Marc Mitchell	.05
152	Tom Abood	.05
153	Lee Calland	.05
154	Larry Ball	.10
155	Phil Ellis	.05
156	Greg Pianko	.05
157	Bruce Armstrong	.15
158	Calvin Prince	.05
159	Marty Smith	.05
160	Joe Trabue	.05
161	Gene Sartini	.05
162	Rodney Knighton	.05
163	George Cain	.05
164	Stu Gibson	.05
165	Larry Compton	.05
166	Charlie Mudd	.05
167	Al MacFarlane	.05
168	Willie Shelby	.05
169	Herbie Phelps	.05
170	Dale Orem	.05
171	Lee Bouggess	.10
172	John Neidert	.05
173	Amos Martin	.05
174	Norman Heard	.05
175	Charlie Johnson	.10
176	Len Depaola	.05
177	Dave Nuss	.05
178	Tom Lucia	.05
179	Bill Gatti	.05
180	Greg Hickman	.05

181 Wayne Patrick .05
182 Otto Knop Sr. .05
183 John Giles .05
184 Doug Hockensmith .05
185 A.J. Jacobs .05
186 Pat Patterson .05
187 David Hatfield .05
188 Eric Vaughn .05
189 Brian Miller .05
190 Leon Williams .05
191 Kenny Robinson .05
192 John Madeya .05
193 Zarko Ellis .05
194 Cookie Brinkman .05
195 Kevin Miller .05
196 Ricky Skiles .05
197 John Adams .05
198 Dave Betz .05
199 Jeff Henry .05
200 Tom Jackson .40
201 Louisville Cardinals .05
202 Louisville Cardinals .05
203 Louisville Cardinals .05
204 Louisville Cardinals .05
205 Louisville Cardinals .05
206 Pervis Ellison .40
207 Wes Unseld .50
208 Charlie Tyra .10
209 Darrell Griffith .30
210 Steve Clark .05
211 Ellis Bryant .05
212 Gil Waggoner .05
213 Bob Borah .05
214 Bill Akridge .05
215 Cliff York .05
216 Harry Hinton .05
217 Ray Potts .05
218 Bob Wellman .05
219 Truett Demoisey .05
220 John Prudhoe .05
221 Dale Hall .05
222 Phil Rollins .05
223 Ron Thomas .10
224 John Turner .05
225 Charles Tyra .10
226 Henry Bacon .05
227 Butch Beard .25
228 Phillip Bond .05
229 Junior Bridgeman .15
230 Jim Price .10
231 Jack Coleman .05
232 Wesley Cox .10
233 Jerry Eaves .10
234 Lancaster Gordon .20
235 Milt Wagner .20
236 Mike Grosso .05
237 Rick Wilson .05
238 Wes Unseld .50
239 Scooter McCray .15
240 Allen Murphy .05
241 Chuck Noble .05
242 Bud Olsen .15
243 Roger Burkman .05
244 Henry Bacon .05
245 Jim Price .10
246 Al Vilcheck .05
247 Ron Thomas .10
248 Mike Lawhon .05
249 Don Goldstein .05
250 John Turner .05
251 Fred Sawyer .05
252 Wiley Brown .10
253 Pervis Ellison .40
254 Herbert Crook .15
255 Mark McSwain .10
256 Jeff Hall .10
257 Billy Thompson .20
258 Milt Wagner .20
259 Charles Jones .10
260 Lancaster Gordon .20
261 Poncho Wright .05
262 Jerry Eaves .10
263 Scooter McCray .15
264 Rodney McCray .25
265 Derek Smith .15
266 Darrell Griffith .30
267 Roger Burkman .05
268 Kevin Walls .10
269 Allen Murphy .05
270 Junior Bridgeman .15
271 Wesley Cox .10
272 Bill Bunton .10
273 Phillip Bond .05
274 Ricky Gallon .05
275 Manuel Forrest .10
276 Jerry Jones .05
277 Scooter McCray .15
278 Larry Williams .05
279 Peck Hickman .10
280 John Dromo .10
281 Darrell Griffith .30
282 Derek Smith .15
283 Paul Pry .05
284 Henry Bacon .05
285 Charles Jones .10
286 Butch Beard .25
287 Herbert Crook .15
288 Denny Crum CO .40
289 Mike Abram .05
290 Pervis Ellison .40
291 Billy Thompson .20
292 Rodney McCray .25
293 Terry Howard .05
294 Mike Grosso .10
295 Kenny Payne .10
296 Chris West .05
297 Darrell Griffith .30
298 Denny Crum CO .40
299 Jeff Hall .10
300 Billy Thompson .20

1992-93 Louisville

The standard-sized, 31-card set showcases a black border around the edge of the card, while a red "L" shaped border runs along the left and bottom. "U of L" and "University of Louisville" are printed beneath the photo. An upside down "L" shape runs along the right and top of the photo. The player's name and number are printed inside the white stripe above the photo. The backs have the Cardinals' logo in the upper left, with the player's name and bio in the upper right. The card number, bio and career highlights round out the card backs. The cards were issued by Motion Sports. Uncut sheets were available for $20 plus shipping.

MT
Complete Set (31): 15.00
Common Player: .25
1 Denny Crum CO 3.00
2 NCAA Championship (Trophies) .50
3 Brian Hopgood (Portrait) .25
4 Clifford Rozier 2.00
5 Keith LeGree (Portait) .50
6 Tick Rogers (Portrait) .50
7 Jimmy King (Portrait) .25
8 Brian Kiser (Portrait) .25
9 Doug Calhoun (Portrait) .25
10 Mike Case (Portrait) .25
11 James Brewer (Portrait) .25
12 Dwayne Morton (Portrait) 1.50
13 Greg Minor (Portrait) 3.00
14 Troy Smith (Portrait) .25
15 Robby Wine (Portrait) .25
16 Derwin Webb (Portrait) .25
17 Brian Hopgood (Action shot) .25
18 Keith LeGree (Action shot) .50
19 Mike Case (Action shot) .25
20 James Brewer (Action shot) .25
21 Dwayne Morton (Action shot) 1.00
22 Greg Minor (Action shot) 3.00
23 Troy Smith (Action shot) .25
24 Derwin Webb (Action shot) .25
25 Seniors (Mike Case, Troy Smith, Derwin Webb, James Brewer) .25
26 Cardinal Mascot .25
27 500th Career Victory (Denny Crum CO) 3.00
28 Ad Card Motion Sports .25
NNO Title Card .25
NNO Back Card .25
NNO Card Directory Checklist .25

1992-93 Louisville Schedules

Measuring 4-1/2" x 3-1/2", the five-card set showcases a Storer Cable Communications ad on the left side of the card fronts, with a full-bleed color photo on the right. The unnumbered card backs include that season's schedule.

MT
Complete Set (5): 4.00
Common Player: 1.00
1 James (Boo) Brewer 1.00
2 Mike Case 1.00
3 Neil Knox 1.00
4 Troy Smith 1.00
5 Derwin Webb 1.00

1993-94 Louisville

The standard-sized, 20-card set showcases a white border on the card fronts, with the player's name printed inside a red stripe beneath the photo. The Cardinals' logo is printed inside a circle to the right of the player's name. A black stripe at the bottom carries the player's position. The horizontal card backs have the player's name, number and position at the top, with his stats directly underneath. The player's highlights appear in a vertical stripe along the right. The Metro conference logo appears next to the state box. The cards are unnumbered.

MT
Complete Set (20): 15.00
Common Player: .50
(1) Doug Calhoun .50
(2) Denny Crum CO 2.00
(3) Jimmy King .50
(4) Brian Kiser .75
(5) Greg Minor 3.00
(6) Dwayne Morton 1.50
(7) Jason Osborne .50
(8) Tick Rogers 1.00
(9) Clifford Rozier 2.00
(10) Matt Simons .50
(11) Alvin Sims 1.00
(12) Beau Zach Smith .50
(13) DeJuan Wheat 3.00
(14) Robby Wine .50
(15) Assistant Coaches (Larry Gay ACO, Jerry Jones ACO, Scooter McCray ACO) .50
(16) Seniors (Greg Minor, Doug Calhoun, Dwayne Morton) 1.50
(17) Seniors and Mascot (Greg Minor, Doug Calhoun, Dwayne Morton) 1.50
(18) Team Photo .75
(19) Freedom Hall .75
(20) Title Card .50

1986-87 Maine

This 14-card set, part of a "Kids and Kops" promotion, was printed one card at a time in the Saturday issue of the Bangor Daily News. The cards measure 2 1/2" x 4" and feature posed player photos on the front. Player information is given below the picture in the lower left hand corner with a facsimile autograph in the lower right corner.

MT
Complete Set (14): 15.00
Common Player: 1.00
1 Bananas 1.00
2 Jack Capuano 1.00
3 Amadou Coco Barry 1.00
4 Doug Dorsey 1.00
5 Dan Kane 1.00
6 Michelle Duprey 1.00
7 Tina Ouellette 1.00
8 Jeff Plympton 1.00
9 Jim Boylen 1.00
10 Bob Wilder 1.00
11 Eric Weinrich 4.00
12 Lynn Hearty 1.00
13 Matt Rossignoi 1.00
--- Kids and Kops Rules 1.00

1987-88 Maine

This 14-card set was part of a "Kids and Kops" promotion and was printed every Saturday in the Bangor Daily News. The cards were to be collected from any participating police officer and could be turned in upon set completion to register for a grand-prize drawing and a free T shirt.

MT
Complete Set (14): 15.00
Common Player: 1.00
1 Bananas (Mascot, K.C. Jones) 6.00
2 Mike McHugh 2.00
3 Matt Rossignoi 1.00
4 Cindy Sprague 1.00
5 Gary LaPierre 1.00
6 Dana Billington 1.00
7 Scott Atherley 1.00
8 Elke Brutsaert 1.00
9 Elizabeth (Liz) Coffin 1.00
10 David Ingalls 1.00
11 Wendy J. Nadeau 1.00
12 Stacy Caron 1.00
13 Amadou Coco Barry 1.00
--- Kids and Kops Rules 1.00

1982-83 Marquette

The standard-sized, 16-card set showcases a black and white photo inside an arrowhead on the front of the yellow-bordered cards. The player's name is printed in the upper right, while his height and position are in the lower left. "Warriors" is printed in bold letters across the bottom of the front. The backs have the player's name and bio at the top center, while his stats and career highs are printed directly below. Marquette's 1981-82 overall record and a player highlight are printed at the bottom center. The Lite Beer logo is in the lower left, while the WTMJ-TV 4 logo is printed in the lower right.

MT
Complete Set (16): 17.00
Common Player: .75
1 Ric Cobb ACO 1.00
2 Dwayne (DJ) Johnson .75
3 Mandy Johnson .75
4 Vic Lazzaretti .75
5 Rick Majerus ACO 6.00
6 Marc Marotta .75
7 Lloyd Moore .75
8 Paul Newman .75
9 Tom Pipines .75
10 Hank Raymonds CO 1.25
11 Terry Reason .75
12 Glenn (Doc) Rivers 10.00
13 Terrell Schlundt 1.25
14 Don Smolinski .75
15 Kerry Trotter .75
xx Title Card 1.25

1991-92 Marquette

The standard-sized, 12-card set are perforated. The white-bordered cards have the player's name in the top left, his number in the upper right and years and team above the photo. The 75th anniversary of Marquette basketball logo is printed in the lower left. The player's height and year are located at the bottom center. The horizontal card backs feature the player's name and bio in the upper left. His highlights and stats follow in the center. The Warriors' logo is in the lower left, years and team name in the bottom center and "Cyganiak Planning Inc." printed in the lower right.

MT
Complete Set (12): 12.00
Common Player: .75
1 Craig Aamot .75
2 Ron Curry 1.00
3 William Gates 4.00
4 Robb Logterman 1.00
5 Jim McIlvaine 2.50
6 Tony Miller .75
7 Kevin O'Neill CO 2.00
8 Ben Peavy .75
9 Shannon Smith .75
10 Team Photo 1.50
11 Building on a Great Tradition (Team photo at construction site) 1.00
12 Bradley Center .75

1992-93 Marquette

Released on four perforated strips, the 20-card set is standard size when separated. Sponsored by Cyganiak Planning Inc., the white-bordered fronts are anchored by a color photo. The player's name is printed at the top center. The Warriors' logo is in the lower left. The years, player's position and number are printed in the bottom center, while the sponsor's logo and name are in the lower right. The card backs, which are unnumbered, have the player's name and bio in the upper left, while his highlights and stats follow. The Warriors' logo is the lower left, years and team name in the bottom center and sponsor's logo and name in the bottom right.

MT
Complete Set (20): 14.00
Common Player: .50
Craig Aamot .75
Ron Curry .50
Roney Eford 1.50
William Gates 3.00
Damon Key 1.00
Robb Logterman .75
Amal McCaskill 2.00
Jim McIlvaine 2.00
Tony Miller .75
Kevin O'Neill CO 2.00
Ben Peavy .50
Adam Schabes .50
Shannon Smith .50
Dwaine Streater .50
Jay Zulauf .75
Team Photo Roster .50
Sponsor Card .50
Sponsor Card .50
Sponsor Card .50
Sponsor Card .50

1994-95 Marquette

Released in four perforated strips, the 20-card set measures standard size when separated. The gold-bordered card fronts have the player's name at the top, with the Golden Eagles' logo in the lower left. The Cyganiak Planning Inc. logo and name are in the bottom right. The unnumbered card backs have the player's number in large print in the upper left, with his name and bio inside a stripe to the right of the number. The player's highlights and stats are printed directly below his name. The year, school and nickname are printed in the lower left, while the sponsor's name and logo are in the lower right. "Hoop Dreams" star William Gates is featured in this set.

MT
Complete Set (20): 14.00
Common Player: .50
Faisal Abraham 1.00
Chris Crawford 1.25
Mike Deane CO .75
Roney Eford 1.25
William Gates 2.50
Aaron Hutchins 2.00
Abel Joseph .75
Shane Littles .75
Zack McCall .75
Amal McCaskill 2.00
Tony Miller .75
Anthony Pieper 1.00
Richard Shaw 1.25
Dwaine Streater .75
1969-70 Team Photo 1.00
Team Photo 1994-95 Roster 1.00
Sponsor Card .50
Sponsor Card .50
Sponsor Card .50
Sponsor Card .50

1984 Marshall Playing Cards

Released in association with an old-timers game, the 54-card set is a playing card deck housed in a box. Printed by Triangle Productions Inc., the cards measure 2-1/4" x 3-1/2" and were sold at the university's bookstore. Black and white photos are included on the fronts, with his name, number and position beneath the photo. The card number and suit are featured in the upper left and lower right. The back have the Marshall logo printed in green on a white background. "All Time Greats" is printed at the bottom center. In the list below, Clubs are represented by "C", Diamonds with a "D", Hearts with an "H" and Spades with an "S". Aces are listed below by No. 1, while Jacks are No. 11, Queens are No. 12 and Kings are No. 13. The jokers are unnumbered.

MT
Complete Set (54): 25.00
Common Player: .25
C1 Stewart Way CO .25
C2 Jim Davidson .25
C3 Tom Langfitt .25
C4 Bill Hall .25
C5 Bill Toothman .25
C6 Gene James .25
C7 Bob Koontz .25
C8 Andy Tonkovich .25
C9 Danny D'Antoni .25
C10 Paul Underwood .25
C11 Walt Walowac .25
C12 Cebe Price .25
C13 John Milhoan .25
D1 Ellis Johnson CO .25
D2 Walt Walowac .25
D3 George Stone .40
D4 Charlie Slack .25
D5 Mike D'Antoni .75
D6 Jules Rivlin .25
D7 Danny D'Antoni .25
D8 Greg White .25
D9 Ken Labanowski .25
D10 Bob Burgess .25
D11 Bob Allen .25
D12 Leo Byrd .25
D13 Hal Greer 4.00
H1 Stu Aberden CO .25
H2 Stu Aberden CO (Same picture as H1) .25
H3 Bob Daniels CO .25
H4 Bunny Gibson .40
H5 Cebe Price .25
H6 Carl Tacy CO .40
H7 Stewart Way CO .25
H8 Ellis Johnson CO .25
H9 Cam Henderson CO .75
H10 Mike D'Antoni .75
H11 Bob Daniels CO .25
H12 Jules Rivlin .25
H13 Russell Lee .50
S1 Cam Henderson CO .75
S2 Ken Labanowski .25
S3 Greg White .25
S4 Randy Noll .25
S5 Bob Redd .25
S6 George Stone .40
S7 Bunny Gibson .40
S8 Bob Wright .25
S9 Charlie Slack .25
S10 Russell Lee .50
S11 Carl Tacy CO .40
S12 Leo Byrd .25
S13 Hal Greer 8.00
NNO Joker Marshall University .25
NNO Joker .25

1988 Marshall Women

This standard-sized set was originally a 20-card set. However, the sets were later offered by the university for a $20 donation to the program. Two years later a 21st card was added featuring coach Judy Southard. The full-bleed photos on the front have a white frame inside the photo. The years are printed at the upper right, while the Lady Herd logo is in the lower left. The card backs, which are unnumbered, have the player's name, position, years and hometown at the top, while her career highlights are printed below. The back is printed in green. The sponsor logos printed at the bottom of the backs, from left, are Super America, Ashland Oil and Valvoline.

MT
Complete Set (21): 10.00
Common Player: .50
1907 Team Picture .75
The Head Coaches .75
1969-70 (Donna Lawson CO, Judy Southard CO)
1970-71 (Beverly Duckwyler) .50
1971-72 Team .50
1972-73 (Jody Lambert) .50
1973-74 (Brenda Dennis) .50
1974-75 (Agnes Wheeler) .50
Gullickson Hall Action .50
1975-76
1976-77 (Mary Lopez) .50
1977-78 Season (Stephanie Austin, Agnes Wheeler, Mary Lopez, Kim Williams, Kathy Baker, Donna Lawson CO) .75
1978-79 (Tammie Green) 2.50
National Prominence .75
1979-80 (Saundra Fullen, Thea Garland, Becky Williamson, Paula Hatten, Deanna Carter)
1980-81 (Lisa Prunner) .50
1981-82 (Barb McConnell) .50
The Class of '86 1982-83 (Tywands Abercrombie, Karla May, Karen Pelphrey, Debbie Van Liew) .50
1983-84 (Karen Pelphrey) .50
1984-85 (Tammy Wiggins) .50
1985-86 (Chris Laslo) .50
The Challenge 1986-87 .50
1987-88 (Kim Lewis) .50
1989-90 (Judy Southard CO) 1.00

1988-89 Maryland

The standard-sized, 12-card set features "Terrapins" and "88-89" in the upper left corner, with "Group Health Association" in the upper right of the card front. A color photo anchors the front. The player's name, number, year and position are printed in a red stripe beneath the photo. A Terrapins' logo is in the lower left. The card backs, which are unnumbered, have the player's name and bio at the top center, sandwiched between two Terps' logos. The player's highlights and tips from the Terrapins round out the card backs. The Group Health Insurance logo appears at the bottom center.

MT
Complete Set (12): 18.00
Common Player: .75
Vincent Broadnax .75
Dave Dickerson .75
John Johnson SP 3.00
Matt Kaluzienski .75
Mitch Kasoff .75
Cedric Lewis 1.00
Jesse Martin .75
Tony Massenburg 4.00
Jerrod Mustaf 2.00
Greg Nared SP 3.00
Bob Wade CO 1.00
Walt Williams 8.00

1992-93 Memphis State

Measuring standard size, the 15-card set features "Memphis State" in a blue stripe on the left border of the card front. The player's name is printed in blue inside a white rectangle at the bottom of the color photo. The horizontal backs have a player head shot in the upper left, with the MSU logo, card number, player's name, bio and stats printed to the right of the photo. The player's highlights round out the card backs. The school produced less than 10,000 sets.

MT
Complete Set (15) 18.00
Common Player: .50
1 Larry Finch CO 1.50
2 Kelvin Allen .50
3 Anthony Douglas .50
4 Anfernee Hardaway 12.00
5 Chris Haynes .50

#	Player	MT
6	Leon Mitchell	.50
7	Marcus Nolan	.50
8	Billy Smith	.50
9	David Vaughn	3.00
10	Sidney Coles	.50
11	Jerrel Horne	.50
12	Rodney Newsom	1.00
13	Team Photo	2.00
14	The Pyramid	.50
15	Tom II (Mascot)	.50

1993-94 Memphis State

Measuring standard size, the 16-card set is bordered on the front in gray. A color photo anchors the front with the MSU logo in the lower left. The player's name and position are listed in the lower right. The unnumbered card backs have a player head shot in the upper left with the MSU logo, player's name and bio to the right of the photo. The player's number is listed in the upper right. The player's highlights round out the card backs.

	MT
Complete Set (16):	10.00
Common Player:	.50
Larry Finch CO	1.50
David Vaughn	2.00
Jerrel Horne	.50
Leon Mitchell	.50
Sidney Coles	.50
Rob Forrest	.50
Jason Fox	.50
Rodney Newsom	1.00
Marcus Nolan	.50
Chris Garner	1.50
Deuce Ford	.50
Cedric Henderson	1.50
Johnny Miller	.50
Michael Simmons	.50
Jason Smith	.50
Justin Wimmer	.50

1994-95 Memphis

Measuring standard size, the 17-card set showcases a full-bleed color photo on the front, with the player's name and number printed vertically in blue inside a white rectangle on the left. The Memphis logo appears in the lower left. The horizontal card backs, which are unnumbered, have the player's bio and highlights, along with the Memphis logo inside a box on the left side. The player's head shot is on the right, with the player's name printed vertically in white along the right border. The set was released by Seventh Inning. Memphis is formerly Memphis State.

	MT
Complete Set (16):	12.00
Common Player:	.50
Larry Finch CO	1.50
Deuce Ford	.50
Rob Forrest	.50
Jason Fox	.50
Chris Garner	1.00
Cedric Henderson	1.00
Mingo Johnson	1.50
Leon Mitchell	.50
Rodney Newsom	.75
Marcus Nolan	.50
Jason Smith	.50
David Vaughn	2.00
Michael Wilson	1.00
Justin Wimmer	.50
Lorenzen Wright	6.00
Team Photo	.50

1993-94 Miami

Measuring 2-1/2" x 3-5/8", the cards were released in four-card perforated sheets. The 20-card set showcases black and green borders on the front. Five basketballs and the University of Miami logo are printed in the upper left. The player's name is printed in the upper right. Bumble Bee's logo appears in the lower left, while the player's position, number and basketball appear in the lower right. The card backs have the player's name, number and bio at the top. His highlights are printed directly underneath in both English and Spanish. The Bumble Bee logo is printed at the bottom center of the unnumbered backs.

	MT
Complete Set (20):	10.00
Common Player:	.25
William Davis	.50
Adam Dusewicz, Chris Parker, Anthony Rosa	.50
Steven Edwards	1.00
Alex Fraser	.50
Steve Frazier	1.00
Michael Gardner	.50
Leonard Hamilton CO	1.00
Tshombe High	.50
Jamal Johnson	.50
Pat Lawrence	.50
Torey McCormick	.50
Lorenzo Pearson	.50
Constantin Popa	1.50
Steve Rich	1.00
Brad Timpf	.50
Assistant Coaches (Thad Fitzpatrick, Scott Howard, Mike Jaskulski)	.50
Free Ticket Offer	.25
Free Ticket Offer	.25
Free Ticket Offer	.25
Checklist	.25

1994-95 Miami

Released in an unperforated sheet that measures 10-1/2" x 18", the five rows of four cards are sponsored by Bumble Bee. The first three cards in each row are player cards. The last card includes a ticket offer. One strip of cards were given away at five different University of Miami games. The 20-card set showcases black and orange borders. The player's name and number are printed at the top in a stencil font. His position is in the lower left of the photo. The Bumble Bee logo is in the lower left of the front, while the U of M logo is in the lower right. The unnumbered backs have the player's name, bio and highlights at the top, with a basketball tip and Bumble Bee logo printed at the bottom. The university's logo is ghosted in the background of the center of the card back.

	MT
Complete Set (20):	9.00
Common Player:	.25
Chuck Barker, David Isles, Jaime Waggoner	.50
Will Davis	.50
Mitchell Dunn	.50
Steven Edwards	.75
Alex Fraser	.50
Steve Frazier	.75
Leonard Hamilton CO	1.00
Scott Howard ACO, Mike Jaskulski ACO, Silas McKinnie ACO	.50
Torey McCormick	.75
Kevin Norris	.75
Lorenzo Pearson	.75
Constantin Popa	1.00
Steve Rich	.75
Anthony Rosa	.50
Brad Timpf	.50
Team Photo	.75
Free Ticket Offer CL	.25
Free Ticket Offer	.25
Free Ticket Offer	.25
Free Ticket Offer	.25

1988-89 Michigan

Handed out to fans at University of Michigan games, the standard-sized, 16-card set features "Wolverines" and "88-89" printed in the upper left, while the Nike logo is printed in the upper right of the card fronts. The color photo is bordered on the left in yellow and on the right in purple. The player's name, number, year and position are listed beneath the photo. The Michigan logo appears in the lower left. The unnumbered backs have the player's name and bio in the top center, sandwiched between two Michigan logos. The player's highlights, tips from the Wolverines and the Nike logo round out the card backs.

	MT
Complete Set (16):	65.00
Common Player:	2.00
Demetrius Calip	3.00
Bill Frieder CO	5.00
Mike Griffin	2.00
Sean Higgins	5.00
Mark Hughes	2.00
Marc Koenig	2.00
Terry Mills	12.00
J.P. Oosterbaan	2.00
Rob Pelinka	3.00
Glen Rice	35.00
Eric Riley	5.00
Rumeal Robinson	8.00
Chris Seter	2.00
Kirk Taylor	2.00
Loy Vaught	15.00
James Voskuil	3.00

1989 Michigan Champs

Measuring 2-3/8" x 4", the 17-card set pictures the members of the 1989 NCAA Tournament champions. A color photo anchors the card front, with the team name and nickname printed at the top center. The Michigan logo is located in the lower left and the player's name appears in the lower right. The card backs have the player's name and bio at the top, with his highlights following. The bottom of the card backs feature the Michigan logo in the lower left and the card number "of 17" in the lower right.

#	Player	MT
	Complete Set (17):	25.00
	Common Player:	.75
1	Steve Fisher CO	4.00
2	Brian Dutcher	.75
3	Kirk Taylor	.75
4	Chris Seter	.75
5	Glen Rice	12.00
6	Rob Pelinka	1.50
7	Rumeal Robinson	3.00
8	Terry Mills	4.00
9	Demetrius Calip	1.50
10	James Voskuil	1.50
11	Loy Vaught	5.00
12	J.P. Oosterbaan	.75
13	Sean Higgins	2.00
14	Marc Koenig	.75
15	Mark Hughes	.75
16	Eric Riley	2.00
17	Mike Griffin	.75

1991 Michigan

This 56-card multi-sport set, offered by College Classics,

#	Player	MT
	Complete Set (56):	17.00
	Common Player:	.20
1	Jim Abbott	1.00
2	Moby Benedict	.20
3	Red Berenson	.30
4	John Blum	.20
5	Marty Bodnar	.20
6	Dave Brown	.20
7	M.C. Burton	.20
8	Andy Cannavino	.20
9	Anthony Carter	.50
10	Gil Chapman	.20
11	Bob Chappuis	.20
12	Casey Close	.20
13	Evan Cooper	.20
14	Tom Curtis	.20
15	Diane Dietz	.20
16	Dean Dingman	.30
17	Mark Donahue	.20
18	Donald Dufek	.30
19	Bump Elliott	.30
20	Greg Everson	.20
21	Gerald Ford	2.50
22	Wally Grant	.20
23	Curtis Greer	.30
24	Ali Haji-Sheikh	.30
25	Elroy Hirsch	1.00
26	Stefan Humphries	.30
27	Phil Hubbard	.50
28	Ron Johnson	.50
29	Brad Jones	.20
30	Eric Kattus	.20
31	Ron Kramer	.30
32	Barry Larkin	3.00
33	Michael Leach	.20
34	Jim Mandich	.50
35	Wilf Martin	.20
36	Tim McCormick	.30
37	Hal Morris	.50
38	Jeff Norton	.20
39	Frank Nunley	.30
40	Calvin O'Neal	.20
41	Steve Ontiveros	.30
42	Bennie Oosterbaan	.30
43	Richard Rellford	.20
44	Steve Richmond	.20
45	Cazzie Russell	.75
46	Chris Sabo	.50
47	Alicia Seegert	.20
48	Warren Sharples	.20
49	Ted Sizemore	.30
50	Lary Sorensen	.30
51	Bob Timberlake	.30
52	Rudy Tomjanovich	1.50
53	John Wangler	.20
54	Gary Wayne	.20
55	Tripp Welborne	.30
56	Wistert Brothers (Gerald Ford)	.20
	Gerald Ford Auto	300.00

1992-93 Michigan

The 15-card standard-sized set showcases a color photo on the front, with "Michigan" printed vertically inside a blue stripe on the left border. The player's name is printed in yellow inside a white rectangle at the bottom center of the photo. The card backs have a photo in the upper left, with the Michigan logo, player's name and bio to the right of it. The player's stats and highlights round out the backs. The sets were priced at $7 and available at the M Den at Yost and Crisler Arena. The card number is printed beneath the Michigan logo.

#	Player	MT
	Complete Set (15):	18.00
	Common Player:	.50
1	Steve Fisher CO	1.50
2	Jason Bossard	.50
3	Juwan Howard	4.00
4	Eric Riley	.75
5	Jalen Rose	5.00
6	Michael Talley	.75
7	James Voskuil	.75
8	Chris Webber	10.00
9	Ray Jackson	1.00
10	Jimmy King	1.50
11	Rob Pelinka	.75
12	Leon Derricks	.50
13	Dugan Fife	.75
14	Checklist	.50
15	Sean Dobbins	.50

1990-91 Michigan State Collegiate Collection 20

Released by Collegiate Collection, the standard-sized, 20-card set is bordered in green on the front. The school's name is centered at the top above the photo. The school's logo is housed inside a circle in the upper left, while the Collegiate Collection is printed in the upper right. The player's name is printed in the center beneath the photo. The green-bordered backs have the player's name and bio in the upper left, with the card number in the upper right. The player's stats and highlights, along with the Collegiate Collection copyright line round out the card back.

#	Player	MT
	Complete Set (20):	25.00
	Common Player:	.75
1	Jud Heathcote CO	6.00
2	Matt Hofkamp	.75
3	Parish Hickman	1.50
4	Matt Steigenga	2.50
5	Dwayne Stephens	.75
6	Jon Zulauf	.75
7	Shawn Respert	5.00
8	Jeff Casler	.75
9	Steve Smith	15.00
10	Andy Penick	.75
11	Mark Montgomery	1.50
12	Kris Weshinskey	.75
13	Jack Breslin Center	.75
14	Spartan Captains (Steve Smith, Matt Steigenga)	6.00
15	Brian Gregory CO	.75
16	Jim Boylen CO	.75
17	Stan Joplin CO	.75
18	Tom Izzo	5.00
19	Mike Peplowski	2.50
20	Team Photo	3.00

1990-91 Michigan State Collegiate Collection 200

This set of standard-sized cards includes black and white photos of earlier players and color photos of more recent ones. The back of the cards in the 200-card set feature biography text laid out in a horizontal manner. The cards are numbered on the back.

#	Player	MT
	Complete Set (200):	15.00
	Common Player:	.05
1	Ray Stachowicz	.05
2	Larry Fowler	.05
3	Allen Brenner	.05
4	Greg Montgomery	.15
5	Ron Goovert	.05
6	Ed Bagdon	.05
7	Carl (Buck) Nystrom	.05
8	Earl Lattimer	.05
9	Bob Kula	.05
10	James Ellis	.05
11	Brad Van Pelt	.25
12	Andre Rison	.40
13	Sherman Lewis	.10
14	Eric Allen	.05
15	Robert Apisa	.15
16	Earl Morrall	.30
17	Danny Litwhiler	.10
18	Harold Lucas	.05
19	Lorenzo White	.30
20	Dorne Dibble	.05
21	Ronald Saul	.10
22	Ed Budde	.10
23	Gene Washington	.25
24	John S. Pingel	.05
25	Morten Andersen	.40
26	Lynn Chandnois	.25
27	Don Coleman	.05
28	Dave Behrman	.05
29	Bill Simpson	.05
30	LeRoy Bolden	.05
31	Lorenzo White	.30
32	Sidney P. Wagner	.05
33	Ellis Duckett	.05
34	Dick Tamburo	.05
35	Gerald Planutis	.05
36	Steve Juday	.05
37	Everett Grandelius	.05
38	Spartans All-American	.15
39	Ray Stachowicz	.05
40	Mark Brammer	.05
41	James Burroughs	.05
42	Harlon Barnett	.15
43	Charles (Bubba) Smith	.50
44	Percy Snow	.10
45	Norman Masters	.05
46	Jerry West	.05
47	Williams and Daugherty	.10
48	Tom Yewcic	.10
49	Kirk Gibson	.25
50	Clinton Jones	.25
51	Frank E. Pellerin	.05
52	Don (Zippy) Thompson	.05
53	Kirk Gibson	.25
54	Edward Erickson	.05
55	Doug Roberts	.05
56	Percy Snow	.10
57	Dick Idzkowski	.05
58	Robert W. (Bob) Carey	.05
59	Clarence Munn	.05
60	Dan Currie	.10
61	Al Dorow	.10
62	Amo Bessone	.05
63	Joe DeLamielleure	.20
64	Tom Ross	.05
65	Steve Preston	.05
66	Kirk Gibson, Steve Garvey	.30
67	Eric Allen	.05
68	George Smith	.05
69	John Chandik	.05
70	Cordell Ross	.05
71	George Saimes	.15
72	Walt Kowalczyk	.05
73	Billy Joe Dupree	.30
74	Phil Fulton	.05
75	Weldon Olson	.05
76	Kirk Gibson	.25
77	Andre Rison	.50
78	Dean Look	.05
79	Hugh (Duffy) Daugherty	.25
80	Don McAuliffe	.10
81	Ronald Curl	.05
82	Percy Snow	.10
83	Carl Banks	.30
84	Joe Selinger	.05
85	Mel Behney	.05
86	Lorenzo White	.30
87	Ron Pruitt	.05
88	George Webster	.25
89	Tony Mandarich	.10
90	Ray Stachowicz	.05
91	Blake Miller	.05
92	Billy Joe DuPree, Brad Van Pelt, Duffy Daugherty CO	.25
93	Morten Andersen	.40
94	Kevin Dalson	.05
95	Norm Barnes	.05
96	Andre Rison	.40
97	Craig Simpson	.15
98	Kirk Gibson	.25
99	Ralf Mojsiejenko	.10
100	Director Card 1-99	.05
101	Michael Robinson	.05
102	Jack Quiggle	.05
103	Robert Anderegg	.05
104	Rick Miller	.05
105	Steve Garvey	.30
106	John Herman Kobs	.05
107	Steve Garvey	.30
108	Vernon Carr	.05
109	Albert R. Ferrari	.05
110	Lance Olson	.05
111	Lee Lafayette	.05
112	Gregory Kelser	.15
113	Stan Washington	.05
114	Ron Perranoski	.25
115	Doug Volmar	.05
116	Robert Clancy	.05
117	Bob Boyd	.05
118	Lindsay Hairston	.05
119	Kevin Willis	.40
120	Bill Rapchak	.05
121	Marcus Sanders	.05
122	Mike Brkovich	.05
123	Jay Vincent	.10
124	Ron Scott	.05
125	Craig Simpson	.05
126	Mike Davidson	.05
127	Jim Watt	.05
128	Johnny Green	.15
129	Robert Chapman	.05
130	Pete Gent	.25
131	Magic Johnson	1.00
132	Gregory Kelser	.15
133	Magic Johnson	1.00
134	Bobby Reynolds	.05
135	Joe Murphy	.30
136	Mike Donnelly	.05
137	Bob Essensa	.30
138	Kevin Smith	.05
139	Kirk Manns	.05
140	Scott Skiles	.25
141	Matthew Aitch	.05
142	Rudy Benjamin	.05
143	Michael Robinson	.05
144	Kip Miller	.15
145	Kelly Miller	.25
146	Ron Mason CO	.05
147	Dan McFall	.05
148	Sam Vincent	.10
149	Carlton Valentine	.05
150	Ron Charles	.05
151	John Bennington	.05
152	Scott Skiles	.25
153	William Kilgore	.05
154	Dick Holmes	.05
155	Steven Colp	.05
156	Robert Ellis	.05
157	Brian Wolcott	.05
158	Ken Redfield	.05
159	Jud Heathcote CO	.25
160	Dave Fahs	.05
161	Pete Newell	.25
162	Larry Polec	.05
163	Kevin Willis	.40
164	Gaye Cooley	.05
165	Richard Vary	.05
166	Al Weston	.05
167	Scott Makarewicz	.05
168	Darryl Johnson	.05
169	Derek Perry	.05
170	Ralph Simpson	.15
171	Terry Furlow	.10
172	Forrest Anderson	.05
173	Ted Williams	.05
174	Dan Masteller	.10
175	Brad Lamont Jr.	.05
176	Steve Garvey	.30
177	Mike Eddington	.05
178	Jud Heathcote CO	.30
179	Kevin Willis	.40
180	Ben Van Alstyne	.05
181	Chet Aubuchon	.05
182	Magic Johnson	1.00
183	Larry Hedden	.05
184	Larry Ike	.05
185	Frank Kush	.10
186	Magic Johnson	1.00
187	Mitch Messier	.05
188	Julius McCoy	.05
189	Magic Johnson	1.00
190	Forrest Anderson	.05
191	Gus Ganakas	.05
192	Jay Vincent	.10
193	Horace Walker	.05
194	Magic Johnson	1.00
195	Tom Smith	.05
196	Don McSween	.05
197	Rod Brind'Amour	.50
198	Sam Vincent	.10
199	Terry Donnelly	.10
200	Director Card 101-199	.05

1998 Michigan State Basketball Greats

	MT
Complete Set (36):	25.00
Common Player:	.25
Michigan State 100 Seasons logo card	.25
Bob Anderegg	.25
Chet Aubuchon	.25
Rickey Ayala	.25
Bob Chapman	.25
Bill Curtis	.25
Al Ferrari	.25
Terry Furlow	.25
Pete Gent	.25
Johnny Green	.25
Lindsay Hairston	.25
Larry Izzo (coach)	2.00
Darryl Johnson	.25
Earvin Johnson	8.00
Gregory Kelser	2.00
Bill Kilgore	.25
Lee Lafayette	.25
Julius McCoy	.25
Mark Montgomery	.25
Lance Olson	.25
Mike Peplowski	.25
Jack Quiggle	.25
Shawn Respert	1.00
Mike Robinson	.25
Ralph Simpson	.50
Scott Skiles	2.00
Steve Smith	2.00
Eric Snow	1.00
Matt Steigenga	.50
Jay Vincent	.75
Sam Vincent	.50
Horace Walker	.25
Stan Washington	.25
Breslin Center	.25
Jenison Fieldhouse	.25
Michigan State logo/Checklist card	.25

1991-92 Minnesota

The standard-sized, 17-card set features an orange-yellow border. The player's first name is printed horizontally in the upper left, while his last name runs vertically down the left border of the card. The player's photo is printed to the right. The Gophers' logo is in the lower left, with the Hardee's logo appearing in the lower right. The player's jersey number is printed in the upper left, while his name is in the upper right. His bio and highlights are housed inside an orange-yellow box, rounding out the back. Voshon Lenard is featured in this set.

		MT
Complete Set (17):		12.00
Common Player:		.50
1	Randy Carter	.75
2	Chris Clark	.50
3	David Grim	.75
4	Clem Haskins CO	2.00
5	Dana Jackson	.50
6	Chad Kolander	.75
7	Jon Laster	.50
8	Voshon Lenard	8.00
9	Bob Martin	.50
10	Arriel McDonald	.75
11	Josh Nichols	.50
12	Ernest Nzigamasabo	.50
13	Townsend Orr	.75
14	Robert Roe	.50
15	Nate Tubbs	.50
16	Jayson Walton	.75
17	Ryan Wolf	.50

1992-93 Minnesota

The 17-card set, which measures standard size, has the school's name printed in a gray stripe at the top of the front. A yellow rectangle at the bottom houses the player's name, which is printed in red. The horizontal backs have a head shot in the upper left, with the Minnesota logo, card number, player name and bio to the right of it. The player's stats round out the back.

		MT
Complete Set (17):		10.00
Common Player:		.50
1	Clem Haskins CO	2.00
2	Milton Barnes ACO, Dan Kosmoski ACO, Dave Thorson ACO	.50
3	Kevin Baker	.50
4	Randy Carter	.75
5	David Grim	.75
6	Dana Jackson	.50
7	Chad Kolander	.75
8	Voshon Lenard	5.00
9	Arriel McDonald	.75
10	Ernest Nzigamasabo	.50
11	Townsend Orr	.75
12	Robert Roe	.50
13	Nate Tubbs	.50
14	Jayson Walton	.75
15	David Washington	.50
16	Trevor Winter	.50
17	Ryan Wolf	.50

1993-94 Minnesota

The 18 standard-sized cards showcase team-colored borders on the front, with "Golden Gophers" printed vertically along the left border. The player's name is printed inside the photo. The horizontal card backs, which are unnumbered, have "Gophers" printed vertically along the left border. The player's head shot is printed in the upper left, with his name and jersey number to the right of it. Boxed in the lower part of the back are the player's bio, stats and highlights over a ghosted image of the gopher mascot.

	MT
Complete Set (18):	10.00
Common Player:	.50
Kevin Baker	.50
Randy Carter	.75
Hosea Crittenden	.50
David Grim	.75
Clem Haskins CO	2.00
Chad Kolander	.75
Voshon Lenard	3.00
Arriel McDonald	.75
Ernest Nzigamasabo	.50
Townsend Orr	.75
John Thomas	2.00
Jayson Walton	.75
David Washington	.50
Sean Whitlock	.50
Trevor Winter	.50
Ryan Wolf	.50
1993 NIT Champions (Milton Barnes ACO, Dan Kosmoski ACO, Dave Thorson ACO)	.75
Title Card	.50

1994-95 Minnesota

The 17 standard sized cards showcase red borders on the front, with the Minnesota logo in the upper left inside a circle. "Golden Gophers", the player's name and position are printed vertically along the left. A color photo is printed on the right side of the card. The backs, which are unnumbered, have the player's name, number and position printed vertically along the left, with his stats printed inside a box with rounded corners beneath his name. The Big Ten logo is inside a circle in the upper left. The player's highlights and Minnesota logo are in a box on the right side of the card. A box in the lower right corner features the Hardee's logo.

	MT
Complete Set (17):	12.00
Common Player:	.50
Hosea Crittenden	.50
David Grim	.75
Eric Harris	.50
Clem Haskins CO	1.50
Sam Jacobson	2.00
Chad Kolander	.75
Voshon Lenard	3.00
Townsend Orr	.75
John Thomas	1.50
Jayson Walton	.75
Micah Watkins	.50
Darrell Whaley	.50
Trevor Winter	.50
Ryan Wolf	.50
Williams Arena (The Barn)	.50
Coaching Staff (Milton Barnes ACO, Larry Davis ACO, Bill Brown ACO)	.50
Title Card	.50

1996-97 Minnesota

Collect-A-Sport produced this 17-card set of the Minnesota Gophers, sponsored by Coca-Cola. The fronts have a color photo with a maroon and white border. The Coca-Cola and University of Minnesota logos also appear on the front. The backs have a biography and statistics as well as the Minnesota and Big Ten Conference logos. The cards are not numbered.

	MT
Complete Set (17):	12.00
Common Player:	.50
Russ Archambault	.50
Eric Harris	.50
Bobby Jackson	3.00
Sam Jacobson	3.00
Courtney James	.75
Quincy Lewis	1.50
Kevin Lodge	.50
Kyle Sanden	.50
Aaron Stauber	.50
Jason Stanford	.50
Jermaine Stanford	.50
Miles Tarver	.50
Charles Thomas	.75
John Thomas	1.00
Trevor Winter	.50
Coaching Staff (Bill Brown CO)	.50

1988-89 Missouri

The 16 standard-sized cards showcase "Missouri Fighting Tigers" at the top of the card. Beneath the photo are the Missouri logo in the lower left and player's name in the lower right. The unnumbered backs have "Mizzou '88-89" printed at the top center. The player's name and bio is sandwiched between two Missouri logos. The player's highlights, tips for better sports pictures and sponsor logos of Kodak KMIZ-17 TV and Columbia Photo to round out the card backs.

	MT
Complete Set (16):	45.00
Common Player:	2.00
Nathan Buntin	2.00
Derrick Chievous PRO	2.00
Greg Church	2.00
Jamal Coleman	2.00
Jim Horton	2.00
Byron Irvin	3.00
Gary Leonard	2.00
John McIntyre	2.00
Anthony Peeler	20.00
Mike Sandbothe	2.00
Doug Smith	6.00
Norm Stewart CO	3.00
Steve Stipanovich	3.00
Jon Sundvold PRO	3.00
Bradd Sutton	2.00
Mike Wawrzyniak	2.00

1989-90 Missouri

Released on three four-card sheets, the 16-card set measures standard size when perforated. The school-colored borders frame the front, with the school and nickname printed at the top center. The Missouri logo is in the lower left, with the player's name, year and position in the bottom center. The player's number appears inside a basketball in the lower right of the photo. The unnumbered card backs have "Mizzou '89-90" printed at the top. The player's name and bio are sandwiched between two Missouri logos. The player's highlights, tips for better sports pictures and sponsor logos of Kodak, KFRU 1400 Radio, Columbia Photo and Video round out the backs.

	MT
Complete Set (16):	35.00
Common Player:	1.50
Nathan Buntin - 22	1.50
John Burns - 33	1.50
Jamal Coleman - 32	1.50
Lee Coward - 4	1.50
Larry Drew	2.50
Travis Ford - 5	4.00
Chris Heller - 41	1.50
Jim Horton - 13	1.50
John McIntyre - 23	1.50
Anthony Peeler - 44	10.00
Todd Satalowich - 54	1.50
Doug Smith - 34	4.00
Norm Stewart CO	3.00
Steve Stipanovich	2.00
Bradd Sutton - 35	1.50
Jeff Warren - 45	1.50

1990-91 Missouri

Released in four four-card strips, the 16-card set measures standard size when perforated. The school-colored borders frame the photo on the front. The school's name and nickname appear at the top center, while the Missouri logo is in the lower left. The player's name, year and position is at the bottom center. The player's number is printed inside a basketball at the bottom right of the photo. The unnumbered card backs have "Mizzou '90-91" at the top center. The player's name and bio are sandwiched between two Missouri logos. The player's highlights, Missouri basketball fun fact and sponsor logos of O'Reilly Automotive, K102 radio and Diet Pepsi round out the backs.

	MT
Complete Set (16):	25.00
Common Player:	.75
Melvin Booker	4.00
John Brown (Tiger of the Past)	1.25
John Burns	.75
Jamal Coleman	.75
Jevon Crudup	3.00
Derek Dunham	.75
Lamont Frazier	.75
Jed Frost	.75
Chris Heller	.75
Jim Horton	.75
Anthony Peeler	7.00
Doug Smith	3.00
Reggie Smith	.75
Willie Smith (Tiger of the Past)	1.25
Norm Stewart	3.00
Jeff Warren	.75

1991-92 Missouri

The 16-card set was handed out in two eight-card sheets. When perforated the card measure standard size. The black-bordered fronts have "Mizzou Tigers" printed at the top. Beneath the photo is the player's name in the lower left. The player's jersey number is printed inside a basketball in the lower right of the photo. The unnumbered card backs have the years printed in the upper left and right corners. The Mizzou logo is in the top center. The player's name and bio, along with player's highlights, tips for better sports pictures and sponsor logos of Coca-Cola, Farm Bureau Insurance and Columbia Photo to round out the backs. 9,000 sets were printed.

	MT
Complete Set (16):	20.00
Common Player:	.75
Tiger of the Past (Kim Anderson)	1.00
Melvin Booker	3.00
John Burns	.75
Jamal Coleman	.75
Jevon Crudup	2.00
Derek Dunham	.75
Lamont Frazier	.75
Tiger of the Past (Ricky Frazier)	1.00
Jed Frost	.75
Chris Heller	.75
Steve Horton	.75
Anthony Peeler	5.00
Chris Smith	.75
Reggie Smith	.75
Norm Stewart CO	3.00
Jeff Warren	.75

1992-93 Missouri

The 16-card set was released in four four-card strips. When perforated, the cards measure standard size. The black bordered card fronts have "Mizzou Tigers" at the top center. The player's name is in the lower left, while the player's number is inside a basketball in the lower right of the photo. The unnumbered card backs have the years in the upper left and right corners. The player's name, bio, highlights, tips for better sports pictures and sponsor logos of Coca-Cola, Hearnes Center KOMU-TV and Columbia photo round out the backs.

	MT
Complete Set (16):	16.00
Common Player:	.75
Mark Atkins	.75
Melvin Booker	2.50
John Burns	.75
Jevon Crudup	1.50
Derek Dunham	.75
Marlo Finner	.75
Lamont Frazier	.75
Jed Frost	.75
Chris Heller	.75
Steve Horton	.75
Derrick Johnson	.75
Reggie Smith	.75
Norm Stewart CO	3.00
Jon Sundvold	1.00
Chip Walther	.75
Jeff Warren	.75

1993-94 Missouri

This 16-card set was issued in two perforated eight-card strips. The fronts have a color photo with "Mizzou Tigers" above and the player's name and number below. The photos are bordered in black, white and yellow. The backs have a player profile and the logos of Missouri University, Ford and Modern Business Systems, Inc. The cards are unnumbered.

	MT
Complete Set (16):	15.00
Common Player:	.75
Mark Atkins	.75
Melvin Booker	2.00
Jevon Crudup	1.50
Marlo Finner	.75
Lamont Frazier	.75
Jed Frost	.75
Derek Grimm	.75
Chris Heller	.75
Derrick Johnson	.75
Paul O'Liney	.75
Reggie Smith	.75
Norm Stewart CO	1.50
Jason Sutherland	.75
Kelly Thames	1.50
Chip Walther	.75
Julian Winfield	1.50

1995-96 Missouri

The 16-card set is framed by a black border on the front. "Mizzou Tigers" is printed at the top, while the player's name is listed in the lower left. The player's jersey number appears inside a basketball in the lower right corner of the photo. The unnumbered card fronts feature the years in the upper left and right corners. The Mizzou logo is in the top center, while the player's bio, highlights, did you know?, Missouri paw print logo and sponsor logos of KCMQ 96.7 radio, Pizza Hut and Subway round out the card backs.

	MT
Complete Set (16):	10.00
Common Player:	.50
Danny Allouche	.50
Scott Combs	.50
Desmond Ferguson	.50
Derek Grimm	.50
Sammie Haley	1.50
Simeon Haley	1.00
Monte Hardge	.50
Kenderick Moore	.50
L. Dee Murdock	.50
Dustin Reeve	.50
Norm Stewart CO	2.00
Jason Sutherland	.50
Corey Tate	.50
Kelly Thames	1.00
Chip Walther	.50
Julian Winfield	1.00

1989 McNeese State

Measuring standard size, the 16-card set showcases the school's logo in the upper left, with the player's name and bio in the upper right. The Behavioral Health Unit of Lake Charles Memorial Hospital logo is at the bottom center of the card front. The card back has the player's name and bio at the top center, with the card's number in the upper right. The player's highlights and tips from the Cowboys round out the card back. The sponsor's logo appears at the bottom center of the card back. Basketball players are pictured on card Nos. 1-6 and 9-12. Other sports featured in the set are softball, golf and baseball.

		MT
Complete Set (16):		8.00
Common Player:		.50
1	Kevin Williams	.75
2	Terry Griggley	.50
3	Tab Harris	.50
4	Chandra Davis	1.00
5	Tom McGrath	.50
6	Angie Perry	1.00
7	Christine Lee	.50
8	Lawrence David	.50
9	Michael Cutright	1.00
10	Anthony Pullard	1.50
11	Mark Thompson	.50
12	Kim Turner	.50
13	Steve Boulet	.50
14	Charlie Phillips	.50
15	Mark Bowling	.50
16	Team Physician (David J. Drez)	.50

1989-90 Montana Smokey

Smokey the Bear is featured on the backs of cards in this set of 12 multi-sport pieces featuring the 1989-1990 Montana Grizzlies. The cards are unnumbered and standard size.

	MT
Complete Set (12):	15.00
Common Player:	1.00
Cheryl Brandell (women's basketball)	2.00
Jay Fagan (men's football)	1.00
Dwayne Hans (men's football)	1.00
Tim Hauck (men's football)	1.00
K.C. McGowan (men's basketball)	2.00
Lisa McLeod (women's basketball)	2.00
Jean McNulty (women's basketball)	2.00
Mike Rankin (men's football)	1.00
John Reckard (men's basketball)	2.00
Tony Reed (men's basketball)	2.00
Kirk Scrafford (men's football)	1.00
Wayne Tinkle (men's basketball)	2.00

1990-91 Montana State

Measuring 2-1/2" x 3-7/16", the 16-card set has the school's name printed above the photo on the card front. The player's name is listed beneath the photo. The unnumbered card backs have the player's name, bio, highlights and fire safety message and cartoon. The set includes players from both the men's and women's teams. The set is sponsored by the USDA Forest Service.

	MT
Complete Set (16):	16.00
Common Player (1-8):	1.50
Common Player (9-16):	1.00
Willard Dean	2.00
Todd Dickson	1.50
Chris Herriford	1.50
Allen Lightfoot	1.50
Johnny Mack	2.00
Dave Moritz	1.50
Johnny Perkins	2.00
Greg Powell	1.50
Alaina Bauer	1.00
Debbie Cober	1.00
Sarah Flock	1.00
Sandy Neiss, Susan Neiss	1.50
Terri Ross	1.00
Judy Spoelstra CO	1.50
Karen Weeter	1.00
Anna Wheery	1.00

1992-93 Montana

The 20 standard-sized cards feature the school's name and nickname at the top of the fronts, while the player's name and position are printed in the lower left. The Taco Bell logo appears in the lower right. The unnumbered backs have the player's name, jersey number and bio at the top left inside the black box. Inside a white box in the center of the card are his bio and highlights. Taco Bell locations are printed inside the black box at the bottom of the backs.

	MT
Complete Set (20):	10.00
Common Player:	.50
Guy Bonner	.50
Nate Covill	.50
Brandon Dade	.50
Travis DeCuire	.50
Israel Evans	.50
Don Hedge	.50
Don Holst CO	.50
Gary Kane	.50
Matt Kempfert	1.00
Josh Lacheur	.50
Jeremy Lake	.75
Kevin McLeod ACO	.50
Paul Perkins	.50
Shawn Samuelson	1.00
Chris Spoja	.75
Blaine Taylor CO	.50
Scott Tharp	.50
Kirk Walker	.50
Leroy Washington ACO	.50
Title Card	.50

1990-91 Murray State

Measuring 2-1/2" x 3-1/4", the 16-card set showcases yellow borders on the front. "Murray State Basketball" is printed at the top above the photo, while the player's name is listed beneath the photo. The Pro Image's logo appears at the bottom of the card front. The horizontal backs have the player's name, number and bio in the upper left, with card number in the upper right. The player's stats and highlights round out the back.

		MT
Complete Set (16):		12.00
Common Player:		.40
1	Paul King	.40
2	Doug Gold	.40
3	Donald Overstreet	.40
4	Greg Coble	.40
5	John Jackson	.40
6	Popeye Jones	6.00
7	Donnie Langhi	.40
8	Terry Birdsong	.40
9	Scott Adams	.40
10	Frank Allen	.40
11	Scott Sivills	.40
12	Cedric Gumm	.60
13	Jerry Wilson	.40
14	Jason Karem	.40
15	Coaching Staff (Steve Newton CO, Craig Morris ACO, James Holland ACO)	.60
16	Team Photo	1.00

1991-92 Murray State

The standard-sized 17 card set is bordered on the front in white. A black-and-white photo is at the top, with "Racers" printed on a slant in a blue stripe. To the right of the nickname is the player's jersey number printed inside a basketball. The Pro Image's logo is in the lower left, while the player's name is in the lower right. The vertical card backs have the player's number, name and bio at the top left, with his stats, highlights and card number "of 17". Overall, 1,500 of the sets were printed, with 1,000 sets handed out and the remaining cards were given away as singles.

		MT
Complete Set (17):		10.00
Common Player:		.40
1	Scott Adams	.40
2	Popeye Jones	4.00
3	Frank Allen	.60
4	Maurice Cannon	.60
5	Jamal Evans	.40
6	Darren Hill	.40
7	Michael Hunt	.40
8	Rafeal Peterson	.40
9	Scott Sivills	.40
10	Bo Walden	.40
11	Craig Gray	.40
12	Cedric Gumm	.60
13	Jerry Wilson	.40
14	Scott Edgar CO	.40
15	Ken Roth ACO	.40
16	Eddie Fields ACO	.40
17	Team Photo	1.00

1992-93 Murray State

The 17-card standard-sized set features an orange-yellow stripe on the left side of the fronts that includes "Racers" in the upper left corner and "Murray State" and the player's name printed vertically in the lower left corner. The player photo is printed on the right. The Pro Image's logo is at the bottom center of the front. The card backs have the player's number, name and bio in a yellow area at the top, with his highlights printed below.

		MT
Complete Set (17):		7.50
Common Player:		.40
1	Frank Allen	.60
2	Tony Bailey	.40
3	Marcus Brown	2.50
4	Lawrence Bussell	.40
5	Maurice Cannon	.60
6	Scott Edgar CO	.60
7	Cedric Gumm	.60
8	Antwan Hoard	.40
9	Michael Hunt	.40
10	Michael James	.40
11	Jeremy Park	.40
12	Scott Sivills	.40
13	Kenneth Taylor	.40
14	Antonie Teague	.40
15	Bo Walden	.40
16	Jerry Wilson	.40
17	Team Photo	1.00

1984-85 Nebraska

Distributed by the Lincoln police department, this 31-card multi-sport set featured cards measuring approximately 2-1/4" x 3-5/8". The cards, printed on thin stock, feature color player photos enclosed in a red border. The usual player information is included, and a "Husker Tip" is presented on the back.

		MT
Complete Set (31):		40.00
Common Player:		1.00
1	Mark Traynowicz	2.00
2	Tom Osborne CO	15.00
3	Jeff Smith	4.00
4	Scott Strasburger	2.00
5	Craig Sundberg	1.00
6	Bill Weber	1.00
7	Shane Swanson	1.00
8	Neil Harris	1.00
9	Mark Behning	2.00
10	Dave Burke	1.00
11	Mary Buysee	1.00
12	Cathy Noth	1.00
13	Terri Furman	1.00
14	Char Hagamann	1.00
15	Wes Suter	1.00
16	Dave Hoppen	4.00
17	Debra Powell	1.00
18	Ronnie Smith	2.00
19	Angie Miller	1.00
20	Bill McGuire	1.00
21	Paul Meyers	1.00
22	Jeff Carter	2.00
23	Kurt Eubanks	1.00
24	Mori Emmons	1.00

25	Glen Cunningham	1.00
26	Denise Eckert	1.00
27	Angela Thacker	1.00
28	Ann Schroeder	1.00
29	Darren Burton	1.00
30	Lori Sippel	1.00
31	Rhonda Blanford	1.00

1985-86 Nebraska

Color action and posed shots appear on these cards, measuring 2-1/2" x 4". Player information including jersey number, name and additional info., appears beneath the picture. The backs have "Husker Tips," offering sports advice as well as a crime prevention tip.

		MT
	Complete Set (37):	40.00
	Common Player:	1.00
1	Title Card	2.00
2	Doug DuBose	2.00
3	Marc Munford	1.00
4	Travis Turner	1.00
5	Mike Knox	1.00
6	Todd Frain	1.00
7	Danny Noonan	3.00
8	Tom Rathman	6.00
9	Jim Skow	3.00
10	Stan Parker	1.00
11	Bill Lewis	2.00
12	Michelle Smith	1.00
13	Wes Suter	1.00
14	Karen Dahlgren	1.00
15	Renee Gould	1.00
16	Neil Palmer	1.00
17	Racine Smith	1.00
18	Gerald O'Callaghan	1.00
19	Moe Iba CO	3.00
20	Angela Thacker	1.00
21	Stacy Imming	1.00
22	Ernie Duran	1.00
23	Dave Hoppen	3.00
24	Emily Ricketts	1.00
25	Maurice Ivy	1.00
26	Brian Carr	1.00
27	Ed Jowdy	1.00
28	Erin Hurley	1.00
29	Von Sheppard	1.00
30	Laura Wight	1.00
31	Lori Sippel	1.00
32	Paul Meyers	1.00
33	Donna Deardorff	1.00
34	Larry Mimms	1.00
35	Lori Richins	1.00
36	Rich King	3.00
37	Amy Love	1.00

1986-87 Nebraska

Black and white photos appear against a red card face in this 30-card multi-sport set, distributed by the Lincoln Police Department. The "Husker Tips" on this version of the Nebraska cards feature comments about the players combined with crime prevention tips.

		MT
	Complete Set (30):	35.00
	Common Player:	1.50
1	McGruff the Crime Dog (Bob Devaney)	2.00
2	Doug DuBose	2.00
3	Marc Munford	1.50
4	Von Sheppard	1.50
5	Dale Klein	1.50
6	Robb Schnitzler	1.50
7	Chris Spachman	1.50
8	Brian Davis	1.50
9	Ken Kaelin	1.50
10	Karen Dahlgren	1.50
11	Tisha Delaney	1.50
12	Brian Carr	1.50
13	Angie Miller	1.50
14	Bill Jackman	1.50
15	Maurice Ivy	1.50
16	Anthony Bailous	1.50
17	Jeaneane Smith	1.50
18	Neil Palmer	1.50
19	Crystal Savage	1.50
20	Tom Schlesinger	1.50
21	John Hastings	1.50
22	Jill Noel	1.50
23	Regis Humphrey	1.50
24	Tammy Thurman	1.50
25	Lori Richins	1.50
26	Todd Bunge	1.50
27	Rhonda Gorraiz	1.50
28	Jeff Taylor	1.50
29	Marlys Handley	1.50
30	Bruce Wobken	1.50

1987-88 Nebraska

A 26-card multi-sport set, these cards were distributed by the Lincoln police department. The cards, printed on a thin cardboard stock, feature black and white player photos. In black lettering, "87-88 Huskers" appears over the player's photo.

		MT
	Complete Set (26):	40.00
	Common Player:	1.50
1	Keith Jones	1.50
2	Broderick Thomas	5.00
3	Dana Brinson	1.50
4	John McCormick	1.50
5	Steve Taylor	1.50
6	Lee Jones	1.50
7	Rod Smith	1.50
8	Neil Smith	10.00
9	Kathi Deboer	1.50
10	Virginia Stahr	1.50
11	Henry T. Buchanan	1.50
12	Maurice Ivy	1.50
13	Derrick Vick	1.50
14	Stephanie Bolli	1.50
15	Jeff Rekeweg	1.50
16	Amy Stephens	1.50
17	Beth Webster	1.50
18	Regis Humphrey	1.50
19	Linetta Wilson	1.50
20	Terry Goods	1.50
21	Ken Ramos	1.50
22	Lori Sippel	1.50
23	John Lepley	1.50
24	Leeanna Miles	1.50
25	Rocky Johnson	1.50
26	Jane Kremer	1.50

1988-89 Nebraska

This 33-card multi-sport set features cards printed on thin stock and measuring roughly 2-1/2" x 4". While black and white player photos comprise the card fronts, "Husker Tips" and sponsor logos round out the back.

		MT
	Complete Set (33):	35.00
	Common Player:	1.00
1	Steve Taylor	1.00
2	Broderick Thomas	3.00
3	LaRoy Etienne	1.00
4	Tyreese Knox	1.00
5	Mark Blazek	1.00
6	Charles Fryar	1.00
7	Tim Jackson	1.00
8	Andy Keeler	1.00
9	John Kroeker	1.00
10	Lori Endicott	4.00
11	Virginia Stahr	1.00
12	Mike Epperson	1.00
13	Crystal Savage	1.00
14	Patrick Kirksey	1.00
15	Jeaneane Smith	1.00
16	Eric Johnson	1.00
17	Amy Stephens	1.00
18	Pete Manning	1.00
19	Kim Harris	1.00
20	Richard Van Poelgeest	1.00
21	Amy Bullock	1.00
22	James Morris	1.00
23	Toyia Barnes	1.00
24	Frank Graham	1.00
25	Linetta Wilson	1.00
26	Ken Sirak	1.00
27	Jane Kremer	1.00
28	Pat Leinen	1.00
29	Ruth Chatwin	1.00
30	Bruce Wobken	1.00
31	Janelle Frese	1.00
32	Bobby Benjamin	1.00
33	Mary (Katy) Wolda	1.00

1989-90 Nebraska

A 33-card multi-sport offering, this set is marked by player action photographs on the front, along with pertinent information. The card backs include "Husker Tips" and sponsor logos. "89-90 Huskers" appears over the front player photo.

		MT
	Complete Set (33):	30.00
	Common Player:	1.00
1	Ken Clark	1.00
2	Reggie Cooper	1.00
3	Gerry Gdowski	1.00
4	Monte Kratzenstein	1.00
5	Gregg Barrios	1.00
6	Morgan Gregory	1.00
7	Jeff Mills	1.00
8	Richard Bell	1.00
9	Jake Young	1.00
10	Mike Croel	4.00
11	Bryan Carpenter	1.00
12	Kent Wells	1.00
13	Sam Schmidt	1.00
14	Virginia Stahr	1.00
15	Carla Baker	1.00
16	Patrick Kirksey	1.00
17	Tami Bair	1.00
18	Bob Stelter	1.00
19	Michele Bryant	1.00
20	Ray Richardson	1.00
21	Ann Halsne	1.00
22	Clifford Scales	1.50
23	Kelly Hubert	1.00
24	Richard Van Poelgeest	1.00
25	Kim Yancey	1.00
26	Unknown	1.00
27	Jill Rishel	1.00
28	Dale Kistaitis	1.00
29	Marie Bowie	1.00
30	Unknown	1.00
31	Lori Cook	1.00
32	Mike Zajeski	1.00
33	Joy Rishel	1.00

1990-91 Nebraska

This 28-card set, sponsored by the National Bank o Commerce, University of Nebraska and Lincoln police department, includes 2 1/2" x 4" cards printed on thin stock. Player information appears on the front of the card, while "Husker Tips" and "Crime Prevention Tips" appear on the back.

		MT
	Complete Set (28):	30.00
	Common Player:	1.00
1	Bob Devaney CO	4.00
2	Reggie Cooper	1.00
3	Terry Rodgers	1.00
4	Kenny Walker	2.00
5	Gregg Barrios	1.00
6	Mike Croel	3.00
7	Tom Punt	1.00
8	Mike Grant	1.00
9	Joe Sims	1.50
10	Mickey Joseph	1.50
11	Lance Lewis	1.00
12	Bruce Pickens	2.00
13	Nate Turner	1.50
14	Linda Barsness	1.00
15	Becky Bolli	1.00
16	Jason Kelber	1.00
17	Brad Bryan	1.00
18	Ted Dimas	1.00
19	Nita Lichtenstein	1.00
20	Lisa McCrady	1.00
21	Clifford Scales	1.50
22	Ann Halsne	1.00
23	Carl Hayes	1.50
24	Kelly Hubert	1.00
25	Deanna Mays	1.00
26	Shawn Buchanan	1.00
27	Michelle Cuddeford	1.00
28	Eddie Anderson	2.00

1991-92 Nebraska

This 22-card multi-sport set features athletes and coaches from the University of Nebraska. Four men's basketball cards (#13-14, 16, 18) and three women's (15, 17, 19) are included. The cards feature a color photo with a thick red border. The top reads "91-92 Huskers" and the bottom has the player's name and basic information. The backs have a "Husker Tip" and a "Crime Prevention Tip." The set was sponsored by the National Bank of Commerce, the University of Nebraska and the Lincoln Police Department.

		MT
	Complete Set (22):	25.00
	Common Player:	.75
1	Mickey Joseph	1.50
2	Pat Engelbert	.75
3	Jon Bostick	.75
4	Scott Baldwin	1.50
5	Tim Johnk	.75
6	Tom Haase	.75
7	Erik Wiegert	.75
8	Chris Garrett	.75
9	John Buxton	.75
10	Chris Nelson	.75
11	Janet Kruse	.75
12	Chris Hall	.75
13	Danny Lee CO	1.50
14	Carl Hayes	1.50
15	Carol Russell	.75
16	Eric Piatkowski	7.00
17	Karen Jennings	.75
18	DaPreis Owens	.75
19	Sue Hesch	.75
20	Ann Halsne	.75
21	Misty Guenther	.75
22	Kris Vucurevic	.75

1992-93 Nebraska

This Nebraska set features player photos that are ghosted except for an oval ring that encompasses the player in action. The multi-sport set contains 27 cards which measure approximately 2-5/8" x 3-1/2". "Husker Tips," "Crime Prevention Tips," and sponsor logos are featured on the backs.

		MT
	Complete Set (27):	25.00
	Common Player:	.75
1	Will Shields	1.50
2	Tyrone Hughes	3.00
3	Kenny Wilhite	.75
4	William Washington	.75
5	Mike Stigge	.75
6	Tyrone Byrd	.75
7	Travis Hill	1.50
8	John Parrella	1.50
9	Jim Scott	.75
10	Eileen Shannon	.75
11	Stephanie Thater	.75
12	Derrick Chandler	1.50
13	Karen Jennings	.75
14	Jamar Johnson	.75
15	Kristi Anderson	.75
16	Eric Piatkowski	5.00
17	Rissa Taylor	.75
18	Martha Jenkins	.75
19	Dennis Harrison	.75
20	Lori Phillips	.75
21	Fran Ten Bensel	.75
22	Kevin Coleman	.75
23	Steve Boyd	.75
24	Kris Vucurevic	.75
25	Darin Petersen	.75
26	Denise McMillan	.75
27	Jed Dalton	.75

1993-94 Nebraska

The University of Nebraska sponsored this set along with the National Bank of Commerce and the Lincoln P.D. Featured sports include wrestling, gymnastics, football, basketball and baseball. Player photos are featured on the card front and "Husker Tips" on the back.

		MT
	Complete Set (25):	25.00
	Common Player:	.75
1	Trev Alberts	2.50
2	Mike Anderson	.75
3	Ernie Beler	.75
4	Byron Bennett	.75
5	Corey Dixon	1.50
6	Troy Dumas	.75
7	Calvin Jones	3.00
8	Bruce Moore	.75
9	David Noonan	1.50
10	Jamar Johnson	.75
11	Eric Piatkowski	4.00
12	NaFeesha Brown	.75
13	Meggan Yedsena	.75
14	Sumner Darling	.75
15	Nicole Duval	.75
16	Dennis Harrison	.75
17	Lori Phillips	.75
18	Troy Bromawn	.75
19	Jed Dalton	.75
20	Amy Erlenbusch	.75
21	Denise McMillen	.75
22	Laura Luther	.75
23	Nikki Stricker	.75
24	Mike Eierman	.75
25	Frank Velazquez	.75

1994-95 Nebraska

These extra wide cards are printed on thin stock and feature athletes from various sports. The set was sponsored by the Union Bank, the Lincoln police and the University. 21 cards are featured in this set.

		MT
	Complete Set (21):	25.00
	Common Player:	.75
1	Jed Dalton	.75
2	Darin Peterson	.75
3	Jaron Boone	1.50
4	Erick Strickland	5.00
5	Emily Thompson	.75
6	Tanya Upthegrove	.75
7	Terry Connealy	.75
8	Troy Dumas	.75
9	Donta Jones	1.50
10	Barron Miles	1.50
11	Cory Schlesinger	2.00
12	Ed Stewart	.75
13	Zach Wiegert	1.50
14	Rob Zatechka	1.50
15	Richard Grace	.75
16	Rick Kieffer	.75
17	Nicole Duval	.75
18	Joy Taylor	.75
19	Cody Dusenberry	.75
20	Kelly Aspegren	.75
21	Billie Winsett	.75

1995-96 Nebraska

These unnumbered color cards frame their photos in red borders. The set, which consists of 21 multi-sport cards, was sponsored by the Lincoln P.D., the National Bank and the University of Nebraska. The cards are printed on thin stock and are a bit wider than normal.

	MT
Complete Set (21):	30.00
Common Player:	.75
Jaron Boone	1.50
Erick Strickland	4.00
Tom Wald	.75
Pyra Aarden	.75
Anna DeForge	.75
Kate Galligan	.75
Brook Berringer	9.00
Doug Colman	.75
Tommie Frazier	5.00
Aaron Graham	1.50
Chester Johnson	.75
Jeff Makovicka	.75
Tony Veland	.75
Jason Christie	.75
Tanya Franck	.75
Penny Heyns	.75
Allison Weston	.75
Christy Johnson	.75
Lisa Reitsma	.75
Billie Winsett	.75
Tolly Thompson	.75

1996-97 Nebraska

This 21-card, multi-sport set was sponsored by the Lincoln Police Dept. and the National Bank of Commerce. The cards featured top Nebraska student-athletes from various sports, including football, men's basketball, women's basketball, wrestling, track and field, volleyball, softball, soccer and gymnastics.

	MT
Complete Set (21):	24.00
Common Player:	.50
Matt Turman (football)	.50
Damon Benning (football)	1.00
Mike Minter (football)	2.00
Jon Hesse (football)	.50
Jared Tomich (football)	.50
Michael Booker (football)	1.00
Brendan Holbein (football)	.50
Chris Dishman (football)	2.00
Jeff Ogard (football)	.50
Scott Saltsman (football)	.50
Bernard Garner (men's basketball)	.50
Mikki Moore (men's basketball)	1.00
Anna DeForge (women's basketball)	.50
LaToya Doage (women's basketball)	.50
Tolly Thompson (wrestling)	.50
Angee Henry (track & field)	.50
Kate Crnich (volleyball)	.50
Sarah Sinclair (softball)	.50
Kari Uppinghouse (soccer)	.50
Kim Dehaan (gymnastics)	.50
Ryan McEwen (gymnastics)	.50

1997-98 Nebraska

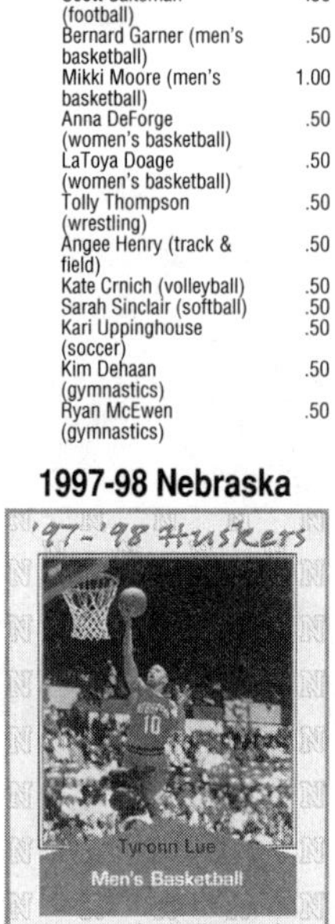

This 21-card, multi-sport set was sponsored by the Lincoln Police Dept. and the National Bank of Commerce. The set included Nebraska student-athletes from the following sports - football, men's basketball, women's basketball, baseball, track and field, volleyball, softball, gymnastics and swimming.

	MT
Complete Set (21):	20.00
Common Player:	.50
Matt Hoskinson (football)	.50
Aaron Taylor (football)	2.00
Eric Anderson (football)	1.00
Jon Zatechka (football)	.50
Eric Warfield (football)	1.00
Fred Pollack (football)	.50
Grant Wistrom (football)	2.00
Scott Frost (football)	3.00
Jason Peter (football)	1.00
Vershan Jackson (football)	.50
Tyronn Lue (basketball)	2.00
Venson Hamilton (basketball)	1.00
Anna DeForge (women's basketball)	.50
Ken Harvey (baseball)	.50
Chris Wright (track & field)	.50
Tressa Thompson (track & field)	.50
Lisa Reitsma (volleyball)	.50
Fiona Nepo (volleyball)	.50
Ali Viola (softball)	.50
Misty Oxford (gymnastics)	.50
Mark Bennett (swimming)	.50

1998-99 Nebraska

		MT
	Complete Set (21):	18.00
	Common Player:	.50
1	Kris Brown, FB	3.00
2	Monte Christo, FB	.50
3	Jose DeAnda, Wrestling	.50
4	Keith Ebbert, Swimming	.50
5	Jay Foreman, FB	.50
6	Venson Hamilton, BK	2.00
7	Josh Heskew, FB	1.00
8	Sheldon Jackson, FB	1.00
9	Brian Johnson, BB	1.00
10	Chad Kelsay, FB	.50
11	Bill Lafleur, FB	.50
12	Shane Lavy, Track and Field	.50
13	Joel Makovicka, FB	3.00
14	Andy Markowski, BK	.50
15	Cori McDill, Women's BK	.50
16	Laurie McLaughlin, Women's Gymnastics	.50
17	Fiona Nepo, Women's Volleyball	.50
18	Kelly Pinkepank, Women's Softball	.50
19	Mike Rucker, FB	1.00
20	Shevin Wiggins, FB	1.00
21	Monet Williams, Women's BK	.50

1999-00 Nebraska

		MT
	Complete Set (19):	20.00
	Common Player:	.50
1	Mike Brown, FB	4.00
2	Ralph Brown, FB	2.00
3	T.J. DeBates, FB	1.00
4	Lindsay Eddleman, Soccer	.50
5	Paul Gomez, Wrestling	.50
6	Dalhia Ingram, Track and Field	.50
7	Julius Jackson, FB	1.00
8	Nicole Kubik, Women's Bk	1.00
9	Jennifer Lizama, Women's Softball	.50
10	Mandy Monson, Women's Volleyball	.50
11	Sharolta Nonen, Soccer	.50
12	Tony Ortiz, FB	1.00
13	David Riggert, Track and Field	.50
14	Charlie Rogers, Men's Bk	2.00
15	Brian Shaw, FB	1.00
16	James Sherman, FB	1.00
17	Jamal Strong, BB	1.00
18	Jenny Voss, Women's Softball	.50
19	Steve Warren, FB	1.00

2000-01 Nebraska

		MT
	Complete Set (20):	17.00
	Common Player:	.50
1	Dan Alexander FB	4.00
2	Matt Davison FB	.50
3	Russ Hochstein FB	.50
4	Bobby Newcombe FB	2.00
5	Carlos Polk FB	2.00
6	Cookie Belcher BK	.50
7	Amanda Went BK	.50
8	Brad Vering Wrestling	2.00
9	Seth Porter Golf	.50
10	Amy Roux Golf	.50
11	Shaun Kologinczak Track and Field	.50
12	Melissa Price Track and Field	.50
13	Jason Hardabura Gymnastics	.50
14	Amy Ringo Gymnastics	.50
15	Karina LeBlanc Soccer	.50
16	Jamie Fuente Softball	.50
17	Peter Fry Swimming	.50
18	Beth Karaica Swimming	.50
19	Kai Reike Tennis	.50
20	Kim Behrends Volleyball	.50

1988-89 New Mexico

The standard-sized 18-card set features white borders on the front. The KGGM-TV 13 logo is in the upper left corner, while the Drug Emporium logo is in the upper right. "Lobos 88-89" is printed in bold letters directly above the player photo. The New Mexico logo is in the lower left, the player's name, number, year and position is printed at the bottom center. A basketball appears in the lower right. The unnumbered card backs have the player's name and bio sandwiched between two New Mexico logos. His highlights, tips from the Lobos, KGGM-TV and Drug Emporium logos round out the backs.

	MT
Complete Set (18):	30.00
Common Player:	1.50
Doug Ash ACO	1.50
Willie Banks	2.00
Dave Bliss CO	3.00
Scott Duncan ACO	1.50
Rob Loeffel	1.50
Luc Longley	15.00
Marvin McBurrows	1.50
John McCullough ACO	2.00
Darrell McGee	1.50
Kurt Miller	1.50
Chriss O'Gorman	1.50
Rob Robbins	2.00
Tony Steffen	1.50
Charlie Thomas	2.00
Chris Tower	1.50
Donnie Walker	1.50
Mike Winters (Graduate Assistant)	1.50
The Pit (Univeristy Arena)	2.00

1989-90 New Mexico

The 18-card set measures standard size. It features the KGGM-TV 13 logo in the upper left and Drug Emporium logo in the upper right. "Lobos 89-90" is printed in bold letters directly above the photo. The New Mexico logo is in the lower left of the card front. The player's name, year and position appear at the bottom center, while a basketball is printed in the lower right. The player's name and bio appears at the top center of the unnumbered card backs, sandwiched between two New Mexico logos. The player's highlights, stats, tips from the Lobos, KGGM-TV and Drug Emporium logos round out the backs.

	MT
Common Set (18):	25.00
Common Player:	1.25
Doug Ash ACO	1.25
Willie Banks	2.00
Dave Bliss CO	3.00
Scott Duncan ACO	1.25
J.J. Griego	1.25
Samie Liberatore	1.25
Luc Longley	10.00
Marvin McBurrows	1.25
John McCullough ACO	1.25
Andre McGee	1.25
Darrell McGee	1.25
Kurt Miller	1.25
Rob Newton	1.25
Rob Robbins	2.00
Omar Sierra	1.25
Tony Steffen	1.25
Donnie Walker	1.25
Mike Winters	1.25

1990-91 New Mexico

The 17-card set measures standard size. The fronts have the KGGM-TV 13 logo in the upper left, the Arby's restaurants logo in the top center and Guynes logo in the upper right. "Lobos 90-91" is boldly printed directly above the photo. The New Mexico logo is in the lower left, with the player's name, year and position appearing in the bottom center. A basketball is in the lower right. The unnumbered card backs feature the player's name and bio in the top center, sandwiched between two New Mexico logos. The player's highlights, stats and sponsor logos round out the backs.

	MT
Complete Set (17):	22.00
Common Player:	.75
Doug Ash ACO	.75
Willie Banks	1.00
Dave Bliss CO	2.00

Paul Graham ACO	.75
Khari Jaxon	1.50
Luc Longley	8.00
Marvin McBurrows	.75
Vladimir McCrary	.75
John McCullough ACO	.75
Lance Milford	.75
Kurt Miller	.75
Rob Newton	.75
George Powdrill SP	12.00
Rob Robbins	1.50
Jimmy Taylor	.75
Ike Williams	1.00
The Pit (Univeristy Arena)	1.00

1991-92 New Mexico

The three sponsors' logos appear at the top of the card fronts of this 18-card set, which measures standard size. "Lobos 91-92" is boldly printed above the photo. In the lower left of the front is the New Mexico logo, while the player's name, year and position are printed at the bottom center. A basketball is printed in the lower right. The unnumbered card backs have the player's name and bio sandwiched between two New Mexico logos at the top. Rounding out the card backs are the player's highlights, stats, did you know? and three sponsor logos.

	MT
Complete Set (18):	8.00
Common Player:	.50
Doug Ash ACO	.50
Willie Banks	1.00
Dave Bliss CO	1.50
Paul Graham ACO	.50
J.J. Griego	.50
Brian Hayden	.50
Trent Heffner	.50
Khari Jaxon	1.00
Lewis Lamar	.50
Steve Logan	1.00
Vladimir McCrary	.50
John McCullough ACO	.50
Andre McGee	.50
Lance Milford	.50
Scott Pritchett	.50
Will Scott	.50
Eric Thomas	.50
Ike Williams	1.00

1992-93 New Mexico

Released in two eight-card perforated strips, the 16-card set showcases "UNM Lobo Basketball" inside a red banner at the top of the card front. The years are printed beneath the banner. The player's name is printed inside a basketball in the lower right. The bottom of the front has the First National Bank of Albuquerque and KRQE logos are printed inside a green rectangle. The card backs have the player's name and number at the top. His bio, highlights and major are printed in the center of the backs, while the sponsors are listed at the bottom of the backs. Reportedly, 15,000 sets were distributed.

		MT
Complete Set (16):		7.00
Common Player:		.50
1	Dave Bliss CO	1.50
2	Greg Brown	.50
3	J.J. Griego	.50
4	Brian Hayden	.50
5	Trent Heffner	.50
6	Khari Jaxon	1.00
7	Corey Jenkins	.50
8	Lewis LaMar	.50
9	Lobo Lucy and Louie (Mascots)	.50
10	Steve Logan	.50
11	Lance Milford	.50
12	Canonchet Neves	.50
13	Mike Powers (Sports Director)	.50
14	Eric Thomas	.50
15	Ike Williams	.75
16	Frank Willis	.50

1988 New Mexico State

Multi-sports are included in this 12-card set, which measures 2-5/8" x 4". The black and white photo anchors the front, with his name, position and years beneath the photo. "First series" is printed at the bottom center. A red line borders the photo and the player's name. The unnumbered card backs have the player's name and bio at the top left. A cartoon of Chum the mascot is at left center, with a "Chum Says" safety message on the right. The Charter Hospital of Santa Teresa logo is printed at the bottom of the card back.

	MT
Complete Set (12):	17.00
Common Player:	1.50
Presley Askew CO	1.50
Tom Byrum	1.50
Jimmy Collins	2.00
Steve Colter	2.00
Ron (Po) James	2.00
Charley Johnson	3.00
Sam Lacey	3.00
Roadrunner Golf (Paul Brilliant CO)	1.50
Greg Trammell	1.50
Kris Veatch	1.50
Fredd Young	2.00
Warren Woodson CO	1.50

1992-93 New Mexico State

The standard-sized 17-card set has the school's name printed vertically inside a gray stripe along the left border of the card. The photo is on the right, with the player's name prined in maroon inside a white rectangle at the bottom of the photo. The horizontal card backs have a player head shot at the top left, with the New Mexico State logo, player's name, bio and card number to the right of the photo. His stats and highlights, along with the sponsors' logos round out the card backs.

		MT
Complete Set (13):		8.00
Common Player:		.50
1	Neil McCarthy CO	2.00
2	Ron Putzi	.50
3	Eric Traylor	1.00
4	Tracey Ware	.75
5	Marc Thompson	.75
6	David Lofton	.75
7	D.J. Jackson	.75
8	Corey Rogers	.75
9	Cliff Reed	.50
10	Ron Coleman	.50
11	Juriad Hughes	.50
12	James Dockery	1.00
13	Sam Crawford	2.00

1993-94 New Mexico State

The standard-sized 18-card set features a full-bleed photo on the front, with "Aggies" in a red rectangle at the bottom corner. The player's name is printed inside a black stripe, which is directly to the right of the team rectangle. The horizontal backs have the player's head shot in the upper left, with the NMS logo, player name, bio, stats and card number printed to the right of it. His highlights are printed in the lower left, with the sponsors' names printed in the lower right.

		MT
Complete Set (18):		8.00
Common Player:		.50
1	Ron Coleman	.50
2	James Dockery	.75
3	D.J. Jackson	.50
4	Corey Rogers	.75
5	Chris Lopez	.50
6	Mike Schutz	.50
7	Dwain Bradberry	.50
8	William Howze	.50
9	Lance Jackson	.50
10	Paul Jarrett	.50
11	Keith Johnson	.50
12	Skip McCoy	.50
13	Johnny Selvie	.75
14	Rodney Walker	.75
15	Thomas Wyatt	.75
16	Pistol Pete (Mascot)	.50
17	Dr. James Halligan PR	.50
18	Neil McCarthy CO	2.00

1996-97 New Mexico State

This 14-card set was sponsored by White Sands Federal Credit Union. The cards are numbered on the back and contain biographical information and statistics.

		MT
Complete Set (14):		8.00
Common Player:		.50
1	Charles Gosa	2.00
2	Antoine Hubbard	.50
3	Chris Lopez	.50
4	Louis Richardson	.50
5	Carl Laws	.50
6	Maurice Lawson	.50
7	Aaron Brodt	.50
8	Denmark Reid	.50
9	Joaquin Chavez	.50
10	Bostjan Leban	.50
11	Rhoate Davis	.50
12	Dominic Ellison	.50
13	Neil McCarthy (coach)	2.00
14	Team Card	.50

1973-74 North Carolina Playing Cards

This deck of 54 playing cards features a black-and-white photo of the player on the front with the number and the suit in the upper left and lower right. The player's name and hometown are printed beneath the photo. The backs are blue and white and have the UNC Tarheels' logo. In the list below Hearts are listed with an "H", Diamonds with a "D", Clubs with a "C" and Spades with an "S". In addition, aces are labeled with a No. 1, Jacks 11, Queens 12 and Kings 13.

		NM
Complete Set (54):		120.00
Common Player:		1.00
1C	1956-57 National Champs	1.00
1D	Bobby Jones	8.00
1H	Homer Rice DIR	2.00
1S	Dean Smith CO	20.00
2C	Bob Lewis	1.00
2D	Dave Hanners	1.00
2H	Jerry Vayda	1.00
2S	James Smith	1.00
3C	Dennis Wuycik	1.00
3D	Billy Cunningham	1.00
3H	Steve Previs	1.00
3S	Bruce Buckley	1.00
4C	Billy Cunningham	10.00
4D	Mickey Bell	1.00
4H	Dick Grubar	1.00
4S	Tommy LaGarde	2.00
5C	Lee Shaffer	1.00
5D	Charles Waddell	1.00
5H	Rusty Clark	1.00
5S	John Kuester	1.00
6C	Hook Dillon	1.00
6D	Brad Hoffman	1.00
6H	Joe Quigg	1.00
6S	Tony Shaver	1.00
7C	York Larese	1.00
7D	Ray White	1.00
7H	Tommy Kearns	1.00
7S	Eddie Fogler	4.00
8C	Jim Jorden	1.00
8D	Walter Davis	8.00
8H	Bill Bunting	1.00
8S	Bill Guthridge	2.00
9C	Doug Moe	4.00
9D	Ed Stahl	1.00
9H	Larry Brown	8.00
9S	1971-72 Third Nationally	1.50
10C	Pete Brennan	1.00
10D	Mitch Kupchak	4.00
10H	Bill Chamberlain	1.00
10S	1970-71 NIT Champs	1.50
11C	Charlie Scott	8.00
11D	John O'Donnell	1.00
11H	Robert McAdoo	10.00
11S	1968-69 ACC Champs	2.00
12C	Larry Miller	4.00
12D	Ray Harrison	1.00
12H	Lailee McNair	1.00
12S	1967-68 Second Nationally	1.50
13C	Lennie Rosenbluth	4.00
13D	Darrell Elston	1.00
13H	George Karl	4.00
13S	1966-67 ACC Champs	2.00
JK	Bell Tower	1.00
JK	Old Well	1.00

1986-87 North Carolina

The standard-sized 13-card set has the Adolescent Care Unit logo in the upper left of the front, while "North Carolina 1986-87" are printed in the upper right. A color photo anchors the center of the front, with "Tar Heels" listed in the lower left and right. The player's name and number appear at the bottom center. The card backs, which are unnumbered, have the player's name and bio at the top, with his career highlights, tips from the Tar Heels and Adolescent Care Unit logos rounding out the back.

	MT
Complete Set (13):	20.00
Common Player:	1.00
Jeff Denny	1.00
Jeff Lebo	2.00
Steve Bucknall	1.50
Michael Norwood	1.00
Joe Wolf	3.00
Kenny Smith	8.00
Pete Chilcutt	3.00
Ranzino Smith	1.50
J.R. Reid	4.00
Dave Popson	1.50
Scott Williams	3.00
Curtis Hunter	1.50
Marty Hensley	1.00

1987-88 North Carolina

Measuring 2-1/2" x 3-1/2", the 12-card set showcases the Adolescent Care Unit logo in the upper left of the front. The Blue Cross and Blue Shield logos appear in the upper right. "Tar Heels" is printed above the photo in blue. Sandwiched between two basketballs are the player's name, number and year in the bottom center. The unnumbered card backs have the years in the upper left and right corners. The player's name and bio is printed at the top center. Rounding out the back are the player's highlights, tips from the Tar Heels and logos of Adolescent Care Unit and Blue Cross and Blue Shield.

	MT
Complete Set (12):	22.00
Common Player:	1.00
Jeff Denny	1.00
Rodney Hyatt	1.00
Jeff Lebo	1.50
Steve Bucknall	1.00
King Rice	1.50
Kevin Madden	1.00
Pete Chilcutt	2.00
Ranzino Smith	1.00
J.R. Reid	3.00
Scott Williams	2.00
Rick Fox	10.00
Marty Hensley	1.00

1988-89 North Carolina

Measuring 2-1/2" x 3-1/2", the 15-card set features a blue border, with a black frame around the photo and logos on the card fronts. The Adolescent Care Unit and Blue Cross Blue Shield logos appear in the upper left and right, respectively. "Tar Heels" is printed in white directly above the photo. The North Carolina logo is printed in the lower left, while the player's name and number are listed in the lower right. The unnumbered card backs have the years printed in the upper corners. The player's name and bio are sandwiched between two NC logos at the top center. Rounding out the backs are player highlights, tips from the Tar Heels and sponsors' logos.

	MT
Complete Set (15):	24.00
Common Player:	.75
Jeff Denny	.75
Jeff Lebo	1.25
Steve Bucknall	.75
King Rice	1.25
Kevin Madden	.75
Pete Chilcutt	2.50
J.R. Reid	4.00
Scott Williams	2.50
Rick Fox	6.00
Marty Hensley	.75
Dean Smith	7.00
Teamwork	.75
Defense (Scott Williams and Jeff Lebo defending)	2.00
The Fast Break (King Rice dribbling)	1.25
A Fun Game (bench scene with Rick Fox and Scott Williams)	4.00

1989-90 North Carolina Collegiate Collection

Released by Collegiate Collection, the 200-card set is bordered in blue on the front. The photos which anchor the center are either black-and-white or color. The Coca-Cola logo is printed in the lower left, with the player's name in the lower right beneath the photo. The horizontal backs have the player's name and bio in the upper left, with the card's number in the upper right. The player's Tar Heel career highlights are printed in the center of the back. The Collegiate Collection copyright tag line is printed at the bottom center.

		MT
Complete Set (200):		24.00
Common Player:		.05
1	Dean Smith	.50
2	Dean Smith	.50
3	Dean Smith	.50
4	Dean Smith	.50
5	Dean Smith	.50
6	Dean Smith	.50
7	Phil Ford	.20
8	Phil Ford	.20
9	Phil Ford	.20
10	Phil Ford	.20
11	Phil Ford	.20
12	Phil Ford	.20
13	Michael Jordan	3.00
14	Michael Jordan	3.00
15	Michael Jordan	3.00
16	Michael Jordan	3.00
17	Michael Jordan	3.00
18	Michael Jordan	3.00
19	James Worthy	.25
20	James Worthy	.25
21	James Worthy	.25
22	James Worthy	.25
23	James Worthy	.25
24	Larry Miller	.10
25	Larry Miller	.10
26	Larry Miller	.10
27	Larry Miller	.10
28	Charlie Scott	.25
29	Charlie Scott	.25
30	Charlie Scott	.25
31	Charlie Scott	.25
32	Sam Perkins	.25
33	Sam Perkins	.25
34	Sam Perkins	.25
35	Sam Perkins	.25
36	Sam Perkins	.25
37	Billy Cunningham	.25
38	Billy Cunningham	.25
39	Billy Cunningham	.25
40	Billy Cunningham	.25
41	Lennie Rosenbluth	.25
42	Lennie Rosenbluth	.25
43	Lennie Rosenbluth	.25
44	Bobby Jones	.25
45	Bobby Jones	.25
46	Bobby Jones	.25
47	Mitch Kupchak	.10
48	Mitch Kupchak	.10
49	Mitch Kupchak	.10
50	1980-81 Tar Heels	.10
51	Walter Davis	.25
52	Walt Davis	.25
53	Walter Davis	.25
54	Walter Davis	.25
55	Mike O'Koren	.10
56	Mike O'Koren	.10
57	Mike O'Koren	.10
58	Mike O'Koren	.10
59	The Huddle	.05
60	Larry Brown	.25
61	Billy Cunningham	.25
62	Matt Doherty	.10
63	Phil Ford	.20
64	Doug Moe	.20
65	Michael Jordan	3.00
66	Kenny Smith	.20
67	Kenny Smith	.20
68	Kenny Smith	.20
69	Bob Lewis	.05
70	Bob Lewis	.05
71	Bob Lewis	.05
72	Charlie Scott	.25
73	Sam Perkins	.25
74	Doug Moe	.20
75	Doug Moe	.20
76	Bob McAdoo	.25
77	Bob McAdoo	.25
78A	Pete Brennan ERR (No trademark on back)	.05
78B	Pete Brennan COR	.05
79	Pete Brennan	.05
80	J.R. Reid	.20
81	J.R. Reid	.20
82	J.R. Reid	.20
83	Tommy Kearns	.10
84	Tommy Kearns	.10
85	John Dillon	.05
86	The Smith Center	.10
87	Dick Grubar	.05
88	Dick Grubar	.05
89	Rusty Clark	.05
90	Rusty Clark	.05
91	Bill Bunting	.05
92	Bill Bunting	.05
93	Jimmy Black	.10
94	Jimmy Black	.10
95	Five Tournament Titles	.10
96	UNC Cheerleaders	.05
97	Bobby Jones	.25
98	J.R. Reid	.20
99	Frank McGuire	.25
100	1957 NCAA Champions	.10
101	Bill Guthridge	.05
102	York Larese	.10
103	York Larese	.10
104	Frank McGuire	.25
105	Bones McKinney	.25
106	Larry Miller	.10
107	Kenny Smith	.20
108	Steve Previs	.05
109	Steve Previs	.05
110	Larry Brown	.25
111	Larry Brown	.25
112	Eddie Fogler	.25
113	Eddie Fogler	.25
114	James Worthy	.25
115	Bob McAdoo	.25
116	UNC Basketball	.05
117	UNC Baskeball	.05
118	Cartwright Carmichael	.05
119	Steve Hale	.05
120	Steve Hale	.05
121	Joe Quigg	.10
122	Joe Quigg	.10
123	Bob Cunningham	.05
124	Bob Cunningham	.05
125	Jim Delany	.05
126	Bones McKinney	.25
127	Jerry Vayda	.05
128	Matt Doherty	.10
129	Matt Doherty	.10
130	Bob Paxton	.05
131	Dave Chadwick	.05
132	Dave Hanners	.05
133	Jim Jordan	.05
134	Jeff Lebo	.10
135	Jeff Lebo	.10
136	Lee Shaffer	.10
137	Lee Shaffer	.10
138	Joe Wolf	.10
139	Joe Wolf	.10
140	Warren Martin	.05
141	Warren Martin	.05
142	Carmichael Auditorium	.10
143	Jim Hudock	.05
144	Darrell Elston	.05
145	Brad Hoffman	.05
146	Harvey Salz	.05
147	Dave Colescott	.05
148	Ed Stahl	.05
149	Joe Brown	.05
150	Gerald Tuttle	.05
151	Richard Tuttle	.05
152	Tony Radovich	.05
153	Dave Popson	.10
154	Donnie Walsh	.05
155	Rich Yonakor	.05
156	Jeff Wolf	.05
157	Pete Budko	.05
158	Randy Wiel	.05
159	Tom Gauntlett	.05
160	Mike Pepper	.05
161	Jim Braddock	.05
162	Yogi Poteet	.05
163	Charlie Shaffer	.05
164	Lee Dedmon	.05
165	Bob Bennett	.05
166	Ray Hite	.05
167	Tom Zaliagiris UER (Tim on front)	.05
168	Kim Huband	.05
169	Ranzino Smith	.05
170	Donn Johnston	.05
171	Dale Gipple	.05
172	Curtis Hunter	.05
173	John Yokley	.05
174	Bryan McSweeney	.05
175	John O'Donnell	.05
176	Hugh Donahue	.05
177	1968-69 Tar Heels	.10
178	Bruce Buckley	.05
179	Ray Respess	.05
180	Buzz Peterson	.05
181	Mike Cooke	.05
182	Mickey Bell	.05
183	John Virgil	.05
184	Charles Waddell	.05
185	Mark Mirken	.05
186	Ralph Fletcher	.05
187	1971-72 ACC Champs	.10
188	Ged Doughton	.05
189	Bill Chambers	.05
190	Bill Chambers	.05
191	James Daye	.05
192	Jeb Barlow	.05
193	Chris Brust	.05
194	Eric Kenny	.05
195	1970-71 NIT Champs	.10
196	Don Eggleston	.05
197	Ricky Webb	.05
198	Jim Frye	.05
199	Timo Makkonen	.05
200	1982 NCAA Champions	1.00

1990-91 North Carolina Collegiate Collection

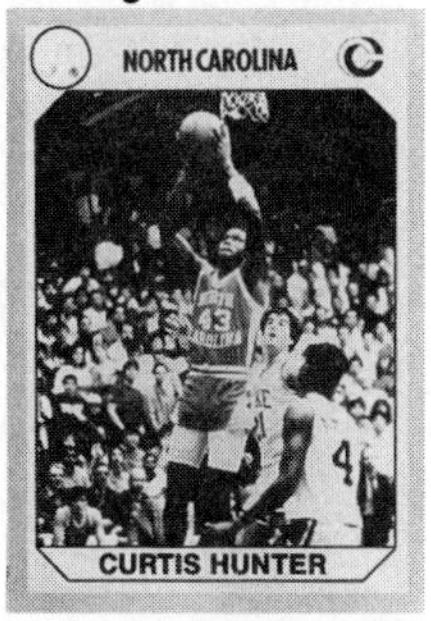

Dean Smith and Michael Jordan make appearances in this 200-card set which highlights NC stars from various sports. Black and white and color photos are featured on these cards, while the corners of the photos appear clipped. The card backs feature career information and biographical data.

		MT
Complete Set (200):		18.00
Common Player:		.05
1	Dean Smith CO	.50
2	John Swofford	.05
3	Michael Jordan	2.00
4	Lawrence Taylor	.60
5	James Worthy	.30
6	Kelvin Bryant	.15
7	Phil Ford	.20
8	Chris Hanburger	.15
9	Walter Davis	.25
10	Ethan Horton	.15
11	J.R. Reid	.20
12	Rod Elkins	.05
13	Buzz Peterson	.05
14	Darrell Nicholson	.05
15	Mark Maye	.05
16	Kenny Smith	.20
17	Matt Kupec	.05
18	Dave Popson	.10
19	Matt Doherty	.10
20	Buddy Curry	.05
21	Donnell Thompson	.05
22	Sam Perkins	.25
23	Mack Brown	.20
24	Ranzino Smith	.05
25	Curtis Hunter	.05
26	Doug Paschal	.05
27	Dean Smith	.25
28	Steve Streater	.05
29	David Drechsler	.05
30	Jimmy Black	.10
31	Kelvin Bryant	.15
32	Steve Hale	.05
33	Kenny Smith	.20
34	Tim Goad	.10
35	Harris Barton	.25
36	Jeff Lebo	.10
37	Rick Donnalley	.05
38	Don McCauley	.20
39	Sam Perkins	.25
40	Bill Paschall	.05
41	Scott Stankavage	.05
42	Joe Wolf	.10
43	Rueben Davis	.05
44	Michael Jordan	2.00
45	Jeff Garnica	.05
46	Kevin Anthony	.05
47	Eddie Fogler CO	.25
48	Warren Martin	.05
49	Buddy Curry	.05
50	Jim Braddock	.05
51	Matt Kupec	.05
52	Dean Smith CO	.50
53	Danny Talbott	.05
54	Sam Perkins	.25
55	Randy Wiel	.05
56	Mike Chatham	.05
57	Jimmy Black	.10
58	Harris Barton	.25
59	Dave Popson	.10
60	Tom Biddle	.05
61	Michael Jordan	2.00
62	Ron Wooten	.05
63	J.R. Reid	.20
64	Lawrence Taylor	.60
65	Matt Doherty	.10
66	Alan Caldwell	.05
67	Warren Martin	.05
68	Tyrone Anthony	.05
69	Brook Barwick	.05
70	Steve Hale	.05
71	Mike Salzano	.05
72	Kelvin Bryant	.15
73	Ken Willard	.25
74	Jeff Lebo	.10
75	Kenny Smith	.20
76	Ramses (Mascot)	.05
77	Mike Voight	.05
78	James Worthy	.30
79	Joe Wolf	.10
80	Ethan Horton	.15
81	Ricky Barden	.05
82	Steve Hale	.05
83	Joe Wolf	.10
84	Bob Loomis	.05
85	Kenan Stadium	.05

86	Lawrence Taylor	.60
87	Sam Perkins	.25
88	Ron Wooten	.05
89	Michael Jordan	2.00
90	Tom Gauntlett	.05
91	Tyrone Anthony	.05
92	Mark Maye	.05
93	Michael Jordan	2.00
94	Kenny Smith	.20
95	David Drechsler	.05
96	York Larese	.10
97	Joe Quigg	.10
98	Lennie Rosenbluth	.25
99	Pete Brennan	.05
100	Director Card 1-99	.05
101	Chris Kupec	.05
102	Moyer Smith	.05
103	Brad Hoffman	.05
104	James Worthy	.30
105	Hosea Rodgers	.05
106	Johnny Swofford	.05
107	Charlie Justice	.25
108	Mitch Kupchak	.10
109	Steve Previs	.05
110	Jimmy DeRatt	.05
111	Phil Ford	.20
112	Chris Kupec	.05
113	Lou Angelo	.05
114	John Bunting	.05
115	Dick Grubar	.05
116	Gerald Tuttle	.05
117	Bill Guthridge CO	.05
118	Junior Edge	.05
119	Art Weiner	.05
120	Dave Hanners CO	.05
121	George Barclay	.05
122	Joe Brown	.05
123	Mitch Kupchak	.10
124	Ken Powell	.05
125	Larry Miller	.10
126	Jerry Sain	.05
127	Don McCauley	.20
128	Bobby Jones	.25
129	Jimmy Jerome	.05
130	Larry Miller	.10
131	Ronny Johnson	.05
132	Ron Rusnak	.05
133	Charlie Scott	.25
134	Pete Budko	.05
135	Robert Pratt	.05
136	Bill Bunting	.05
137	Al Goldstein	.05
138	Charlie Carr	.05
139	Charlie Scott	.25
140	Ken Huff	.05
141	Don McCauley	.20
142	Dave Colescott	.05
143	Charlie Justice	.25
144	Ernie Williamson	.05
145	Dave Chadwick	.05
146	Rich Yonakor	.05
147	George Karl	.25
148	Ken Willard	.25
149	Phil Blazer	.05
150	Dean Smith CO	.50
151	Carl Snavely	.05
152	James Worthy	.30
153	Ron Rusnak	.05
154	Mike O'Koren	.10
155	Lewis and Miller	.20
156	Gene Brown	.05
157	Ed Stahl	.05
158	Rusty Clark	.05
159	Joe Robinson	.05
160	Gayle Bomar	.05
161	Bob Lewis	.05
162	Jim Delaney	.05
163	Paul Hoolahan	.05
164	Rod Broadway	.05
165	Darrell Elston	.05
166	Mickey Bell	.05
167	Ray Farris	.05
168	Charlie Justice	.25
169	Buddy Payne	.05
170	Lee Shaffer	.10
171	Mike Voight	.05
172	Kim Huband	.05
173	Dean Smith CO	.50
174	Charlie Justice	.25
175	George Karl	.25
176	Ed Sutton	.05
177	Ken Craven	.05
178	Jeff Wolf	.05
179	Tom Zaliagiris	.05
180	Charles Waddell	.05
181	Lee Dedmon	.05
182	Irv Holdash	.05
183	Jack Cummings	.05
184	Bob Lewis	.05
185	Phil Ford	.20
186	Bobby Lacey	.05
187	Larry Brown	.25
188	Larry Voight	.05
189	Mike O'Koren	.10
190	Crowell Little	.05
191	Paul Miller	.05
192	Tommy Kearns	.10
193	Frank McGuire CO	.25
194	Sammy Johnson	.05
195	Carmichael Auditorium	.10
196	Nick Vidnovic	.05
197	Paul Severin	.05
198	Don Walsh	.05
199	Smith Center	.10
200	Director Card 101-199	.05

1973-74 North Carolina State Playing Cards

The deck of 54 playing cards have a black-and-white player photo on the front, with the number and suit listed in the upper left and lower right. The player's name and his hometown are printed beneath the photo. The card backs have "Pack Power!" at the top, with the Wolfpack logo in the center. "N.C. State U." is printed beneath the logo. "Wolfpack Country!" is listed at the bottom of the card back. A red frame boxes in all of the graphic on the back. In the list below, Clubs are listed with a "C", Diamonds with a "D", Spades with an "S" and Hearts with an "H". Aces are numbered 1, Jacks 11, Queens 12 and Kings with a 13. The jokers are unnumbered.

		NM
Complete Set (54):		80.00
Common Player:		1.00
C1	Willis Casey AD	1.00
C2	Ken Gehring	1.00
C3	Steve Smith	2.00
C4	Dwight Johnson	1.00
C5	Jerry Hunt	1.00
C6	Tommy Burleson	5.00
C7	John Richter	1.00
C8	Lou Pucillo	1.00
C9	Vic Molodet	1.00
C10	Ronnie Shavlik	1.00
C11	Bob Speight	1.00
C12	Sammy Ranzino	1.00
C13	Dick Dickey	1.00
D1	Everett Case CO	2.00
D2	1965 ACC Champs	2.00
D3	1959 ACC Champs	2.00
D4	1956 ACC Champs	2.00
D5	1955 ACC Champs	2.00
D6	1954 ACC Champs	2.00
D7	1953 Dixie Classic Champs	2.00
D8	1952 S.C. Champs	2.00
D9	1951 S.C. Champs	2.00
D10	1950 S.C. Champs	2.00
D11	1949 S.C. Champs	2.00
D12	1948 S.C. Champs	2.00
D13	1947 S.C. Champs	2.00
H1	Tommy Burleson	5.00
H2	Bruce Dayhuff	1.00
H3	Bill Lake	1.00
H4	Mike Buurma	1.00
H5	Greg Hawkins	1.00
H6	Greg Kuszmaul	1.00
H7	Mark Moeller	1.00
H8	Phil Spence	1.00
H9	Steve Nuce	2.00
H10	Moe Rivers	2.00
H11	Tim Stoddard	2.00
H12	Monte Towe	3.00
H13	David Thompson	16.00
S1	Norm Sloan CO	3.00
S2	Vann Williford	2.00
S3	Jo Ann Sloan	1.00
S4	Everett Case CO (The Old Gray Fox Does It Again)	2.00
S5	Tommy Burleson, Monte Towe	3.00
S6	Three All-Americans 1973 (Tommy Burleson, Monte Towe, David Thompson)	8.00
S7	David Thompson	20.00
S8	David Thompson	20.00
S9	1970 ACC Champs	2.00
S10	1973 ACC Champs	3.00
S11	Sam Esposito ACO	2.00
S12	Art Musselman ACO	1.00
S13	Eddie Biedenbach ACO	1.00
JK	Pack Power	2.00
JK	Reynolds Coliseum	2.00

1987-88 North Carolina State

Measuring standard size, the 15-card set showcases the Adolescent Care Unit logo in the upper left and the IBM logo in the upper right of the card front. "N.C. State ACC Champions" is listed directly above the photos. A red shadow box outlines the lower corner of the photo. The Wolfpack's logo is in the lower left, with the player's name and year listed inside the red stripe beneath the photo. The unnumbered card backs have the years in the upper corners, with the player's name and bio in the top center. Rounding out the backs are the player's highlights, tips from the Wolfpack and logos of sponsors Adolescent Care Unit and IBM. The cards were handed out at an N.C. State game. Many fans received a 14-card set because Sean Green transferred after the cards were printed. His cards were pulled from the set, however, some of his cards did make it into the public's hands.

	MT
Complete Set (15):	25.00
Common Player:	.75
Chucky Brown	4.00
Chris Corchiani	2.00
Brian D'Amico	.75
Vinny Del Negro	6.00
Sean Green SP	6.00
Brian Howard	1.25
Quentin Jackson	.75
Avie Lester	1.25
Rodney Monroe	2.00
Kenny Poston	.75
Charles Shackleford	1.25
Byron Tucker	.75
Jim Valvano CO	8.00
Kelsey Weems	.75
Team Photo	2.00

1988-89 North Carolina State

Measuring standard size, the 16-card set features the Adolescent Care Unit logo in the upper left and the IBM logo in the upper right of the card fronts. "N.C. State Wolfpack" is printed directly above the photo. The photo includes a red shadow box in the lower right. The Wolfpack logo appears in the lower left, while the player's name, number, year and position are printed inside the red stripe beneath the photo. The unnumbered card backs have the player's name and bio sandwiched between two Wolfpack logos. Rounding out the card backs are his highlights, tips from the Wolfpack and sponsor logos.

	MT
Complete Set (16):	30.00
Common Player:	.75
Chucky Brown - 52	3.00
Chris Corchiani - 13	2.00
Brian D'Amico - 54	.75
Tom Gugliotta - 24	20.00
Mickey Hinnant - 3	.75
Brian Howard - 22	1.25
James Knox - 23	.75
David Lee - 25	.75
Avie Lester - 32	.75
Rodney Monroe	1.25
Kenny Poston - 30	1.25
Jim Valvano CO	6.00
Kelsey Weems - 11	1.25
Mr. and Mrs. Wuf (Mascots)	.75
Kay Yow CO (Women's Basketball)	2.00
Women's Team	1.25
Basketball Schedule	

1989 North Carolina State Collegiate Collection

Released by Collegiate Collection, the 200-card set showcased red borders on the front. Black-and-white and color photos anchor the fronts, with "N.C. State's Finest" printed in the upper left and the Wolfpack logo in the top right. The Coca-Cola logo is in the lower left and the player's name is in the lower right. Two diagonal red stripes also run across the card fronts. The card backs have the player's name and bio in the upper left and the card number in the upper right. His career stats, highlights and a 1989 Collegiate Collection copyright tag line round out the backs.

		MT
Complete Set (200):		25.00
Common Player:		.07
1	Rick Anheuser	.07
2	Rick Anheuser	.07
3	Rick Anheuser	.07
4	Pete Auksel	.07
5	Pete Auksel	.07
6	Pete Auksel	.07
7	Clyde Austin	.10
8	Clyde Austin	.10
9	Clyde Austin	.10
10	Thurl Bailey	.25
11	Thurl Bailey	.25
12	Thurl Bailey	.25
13	Eddie Bartels	.07
14	Eddie Bartels	.07
15	Eddie Bartels	.07
16	Alvin Battle	.07
17	Alvin Battle	.07
18	Alvin Battle	.07
19	William Bell	.07
20	William Bell	.07
21	Eddie Bierderbach	.07
22	Eddie Bierderbach	.07
23	Eddie Bierderbach	.07
24	Dick Braucher	.07
25	Dick Braucher	.07
26	Dick Braucher	.07
27	Chucky Brown	.15
28	Chucky Brown	.15
29	Chucky Brown	.15
30	Vic Bubas	.15
31	Vic Bubas	.15
32	Tom Burleson	.25
33	Tom Burleson	.25
34	Tom Burleson	.25
35	Charles Shackleford	.10
36	Charles Shackleford	.10
37	Charles Shackleford	.10
38	Terry Shackleford	.07
39	Ronnie Shavlik	.07
40	Ronnie Shavlik	.07
41	Ronnie Shavlik	.07
42	Jon Garwood Speaks	.07
43	Jon Garwood Speaks	.07
44	Jon Garwood Speaks	.07
45	Craig Watts	.07
46	Phil Spence	.07
47	Phil Spence	.07
48	Phil Spence	.07
49	Tim Stoddard	.10
50	Tim Stoddard	.10
51	Tim Stoddard	.10
52	Glenn Joseph Sudhop	.07
53	Glenn Joseph Sudhop	.07
54	Glenn Joseph Sudhop	.07
55	Joe Cafferky	.07
56	Joe Cafferky	.07
57	Larry Wosley	.07
58	Kenny Carr	.15
59	Kenny Carr	.15
60	Kenny Carr	.15
61	Horace McKinney	.25
62	John Richter	.07
63	Warren Cartier	.07
64	Paul Coder	.07
65	Paul Coder	.07
66	Paul Coder	.07
67	Bill Kretzer	.07
68	Darnell Adell	.07
69	Gary Stokan	.07
70	Pete Coker	.07
71	Derek Whittenburg	.15
72	Pete Coker	.07
73	Craig Davis	.07
74	Smedes York	.07
75	Craig Davis	.07
76	Dick Dickey	.07
77	Dick Dickey	.07
78	Dick Dickey	.07
79	Tommy Dinardo	.07
80	Tommy Dinardo	.07
81	Vann Williford	.07
82	Bob Distefano	.07
83	Dan Englehardt	.07
84	Dan Englehardt	.07
85	Gary Stokan	.07
86	Smedes York	.07
87	Vann Williford	.07
88	Vinny Del Negro	.25
89	Vinny Del Negro	.25
90	Vinny Del Negro	.25
91	Larry Larkins	.07
92	Larry Larkins	.07
93	Larry Larkins	.07
94	Larry Larkins	.07
95	Sidney Lowe	.15
96	Sidney Lowe	.15
97	Ernest Myers	.07
98	Ernest Myers	.07
99	Ernest Myers	.07
100	Checklist 1-100	.07
101	Hal Blondeau	.07
102	Les Robinson	.25
103	Nate McMillan	.35
104	Nate McMillan	.35
105	Nate McMillan	.35
106	Charles G. Nevitt	.15
107	Charles G. Nevitt	.15
108	Charles G. Nevitt	.15
109	Quinton Leonard	.07
110	Bruce Hoadley	.07
111	Les Robinson	.25
112	Bruce Hoadley	.07
113	Emmett Lay	.07
114	Emmett Lay	.07
115	Larry Worsley	.07
116	Harold Thompson	.07
117	Harold Thompson	.07
118	Harold Thompson	.07
119	Howard Turner	.07
120	Mike O'Neal Warren	.07
121	Mike O'Neal Warren	.07
122	Kenny Matthews	.07
123	Anthony Warren	.07
124	Anthony Warren	.07
125	Vann Williford	.07
126	Raymond Walters	.07
127	Raymond Walters	.07
128	Raymond Walters	.07
129	Craig Watts	.07
130	Larry Worsley	.07
131	Craig Watts	.07
132	Spud Webb	.50
133	Spud Webb	.50
134	Spud Webb	.50
135	Ray Hodgdon	.07
136	Herb Applebaum	.07
137	Bill Kretzer	.07
138	Charles Whitney	.10
139	Charles Whitney	.10
140	Charles Whitney	.10
141	Derek Whittenburg	.15
142	Derek Whittenburg	.15
143	Tom Mattocks	.07
144	Tom Mattocks	.07
145	Tom Mattocks	.07
146	Mark Moeller	.07
147	Mark Moeller	.07
148	Mark Moeller	.07
149	Cheerleader/Mascot	.07
150	Quentin Jackson	.07
151	Quentin Jackson	.07
152	Steve Nuce	.07
153	Steve Nuce	.07
154	Steve Nuce	.07
155	Scott Parzych	.07
156	Scott Parzych	.07
157	Scott Parzych	.07
158	Dan Wherry	.07
159	Hal Blondeau	.07
160	Dan Wherry	.07
161	Mascots	.07
162	Max Perry	.07
163	Max Perry	.07
164	David Thompson	.75
165	David Thompson	.75
166	David Thompson	.75
167	Monte Towe	.15
168	Monte Towe	.15
169	Monte Towe	.15
170	Press Maravich	.25
171	Terry Gannon	.15
172	Nick Pond	.07
173	Lou Pucillo	.07
174	Ray Hodgdon	.07
175	Darnell Adell	.07
176	Herb Applebaum	.07
177	Max Perry	.07
178	John Richter	.07
179	Kenny Poston	.10
180	Terry Gannon	.15
181	Pete Coker	.07
182	Quentin Jackson	.07
183	Jim Rezinger	.07
184	Kenny Poston	.10
185	Rick Hoot	.07
186	Everett Case	.15
187	Everett Case	.15
188	Everett Case	.15
189	Kenny Matthews	.07
190	Reynolds Stadium	.10
191	Jim Valvano CO	.50
192	Jim Valvano CO	.50
193	Jim Valvano CO	.50
194	Cheerleaders	.07
195	Ray Hodgdon	.07
196	Lou Pucillo	.07
197	Kenny Poston	.10
198	Everett Case	.15
199	Reynolds Coliseum	.10
200	Checklist 101-200	.07

1989-90 North Carolina State

Measuring standard size, the 16-card set lists the Hardee's, WPTF 680 AM radio and IBM logos on the top of the fronts, from left to right. A color action photo is bordered at the top, right and bottom in red. "N.C. State" is printed at the top inside the border, while the player's name, position and number are printed in the border on the bottom right of the photo. The years are printed on the lower left of the photo. The unnumbered card backs have "Wolfpack 1989-90" at the top, with the player's name and bio sandwiched between two Wolfpack logos. The player's highlights, tips from the Wolfpack and sponsor logos round out the backs.

	MT
Complete Set (16):	24.00
Common Player:	.75
Chris Corchiani - 13	1.25
Brian D'Amico - 54	.75
Bryant Feggins - 34	1.25
Tom Gugliotta - 24	14.00
Mickey Hinnant - 3	.75
Brian Howard - 22	1.25
Jamie Knox - 23	.75
David Lee - 25	.75
Avie Lester - 32	.75
Rodney Monroe - 21	1.25
Andrea Stinson - 32	1.25
Kevin Thompson - 42	1.25
Jim Valvano CO	6.00
Roland Whitley - 15	.75
Wuf (Mascot)	.75
Kay Yow (Women's Coach)	2.00

1990-91 North Carolina State

Measuring standard size, the 16-card set features a photo on the front, bordered in red. "N.C. State" is printed above the photo, while the player's name, position and number are printed directly beneath the photo on the left. The Wolfpack logo is housed inside a circle in the lower right. The IBM and Nabisco Brands logos are in the lower left and center, respectively. The unnumbered backs have the Wolfpack logo in the upper left, with "1990-91 Wolfpack" and the player's bio to the right of it. The player's highlights, anti-drug message and sponsor logos round out the backs.

	MT
Complete Set (16):	20.00
Common Player:	.75
Migjen Bakalli	.75
Chris Corchiani	1.25
Bryant Feggins	.75
Adam Fletcher	.75
Tom Gugliotta	10.00
Jamie Knox	.75
David Lee	.75
Marc Lewis	.75
Rodney Monroe	1.25
Anthony Robinson	.75
Les Robinson CO	1.25
Andrea Stinson	1.25
Kevin Thompson	1.25
Kay Yow CO (Women's Basketball)	2.00
Celebrating a Victory (Paul Campion, Chris Ritter, Tim Thompson)	.75
Mr. Wuf (Mascot)	.75

1991-92 North Carolina State

Measuring standard size, the 16-card set is bordered in red on the front. A color photo anchors the front, with "Wolfpack" printed in white at the top of the photo. The player's name is printed beneath the photo, with the Wolfpack logo in the lower right. The IBM and Nabisco Brands logos are printed in the lower left and center of a white stripe at the bottom of the front. The unnumbered backs have a head shot in the upper left, with "1991-92 Wolfpack" at the upper right. The player's number and name are listed inside a stripe above his bio and career highlights on the right. An anti-drug message is inside a black rectangle beneath the head shot.

	MT
Complete Set (16):	18.00
Common Player:	.75
Migjen Bakalli	.75
Mark Davis	.75
Bryant Feggins	.75
Adam Fletcher	.75
Tom Gugliotta	9.00
Jamie Knox	.75
Marc Lewis	.75
Curtis Marshall	.75
Lakista McCuller	.75
Victor Newman	.75
Anthony Robinson	.75
Les Robinson CO	1.25
Donnie Seale	.75
Kevin Thompson	1.25
Mr. Wuf (Mascot)	.75
Reynolds Coliseum	1.25

1993-94 North Carolina State

Measuring standard size, the 16-card set showcases a color photo on the front, framed in team-colored borders. The unnumbered backs have a player head shot, with the player's bio and highlights rounding out the back.

	MT
Complete Set (16):	9.00
Common Player:	.75
Greg Clucas	.75
Ricky Daniels	.75
Mark Davis	.75
Bryant Feggins	.75
Todd Fuller	2.00
Jeremy Hyatt	.75
Bill Kretzer	.75
Marc Lewis	.75
Lakista McCuller	.75
Curtis Marshall	.75
Les Robinson CO	1.50
Lewis Sims	.75
Jason Sutton	.75
Marcus Wilson	.75
Mr. Wuf (Mascot)	.75
Coaching Staff	.75

1994-95 North Carolina State

Measuring standard size, the 16-card set showcases a color photo on the front, framed with team-color borders. The unnumbered backs have a player head shot on the left, with a player bio and highlights rounding out the back.

	MT
Complete Set (16):	8.00
Common Player:	.75
Ishua Benjamin	2.00
Ricky Daniels	.75
Mark Davis	.75
Bryant Feggins	.75
Todd Fuller	2.00
Clint "C.C." Harrison	.75
Jeremy Hyatt	.75
Bill Kretzer	.75
Lakista McCuller	.75
Curtis Marshall	.75
Al Pinkins	.75
Geoff Richards	.75
Les Robinson CO	1.50
Jason Sutton	.75
Marcus Wilson	.75
Coaching Staff	.75

1997-98 North Carolina State

Action Graphics produced this 17-card set, sponsored by Sears Roebuck and the National Association of Basketball Coaches. The front has a color photo bordered in black. "Wolfpack Basketball" is printed above the photo and the Action Graphics logo is at the bottom. The backs have a black-and-white player photo, biographical and statistical information and a public service message.

		MT
Complete Set (17):		10.00
Common Player:		.50
1	Team Photo CL	1.00
2	Herb Sendek CO	.50
3	John Groce ACO, Larry Harris ACO, Sean Miller ACO	.50
4	Ishua Benjamin	1.50
5	Luke Buffum	.50
6	Justin Gainey	.50
7	Clint "C.C." Harrison	.50
8	Jeremy Hyatt	1.00
9	Andre McCullum	1.50
10	Steve Norton	.50
11	Al Pinkins	.50
12	Danny Strong	1.00
13	Jason Sutton	.50
14	Damon Thornton	1.00
15	Tim Wells	.50
16	Mr. Wuf (Mascot)	.50
NNO	Sears Coaches vs. Cancer Cover Card	.50

1992-93 North Carolina State

Measuring standard size, the 16-card set showcases a color photo on the front, framed in team colors. The unnumbered backs have a player head shot and a player bio and highlights.

	MT
Complete Set (16):	12.00
Common Player:	.75
Migjen Bakalli	.75
Mark Davis	.75
Todd Fuller	3.00
Jamie Knox	.75
Chuck Kornegay	1.50
Bill Kretzer	.75
Marc Lewis	.75
Curtis Marshall	.75
Lakista McCuller	.75
Victor Newman	.75
Les Robinson CO	1.50

	Donnie Seale	.75
	Kevin Thompson	.75
	Marcus Wilson	.75
	Mr. Wuf (Mascot)	.75
	Coaching Staff	.75

1998-99 Northwestern Women

		MT
Complete Set (16):		5.00
Common Player:		.50
1	Leah Berki	.50
2	Megan Chawansky	.50
3	Kristina Divjak	.50
4	Becky Fisher	.50
5	Clarissa Flores	.50
6	Anne Giblin	.50
7	Chala Holland	.50
8	Sara Jurek	.50
9	Dana Leonard	.50
10	Shannon McGarrigle	.50
11	Billee Russell	.50
12	Leslie Schock	.50
13	Tami Sears	.50
15	Don Perrelli CO	1.00
16	Assistants (Robin Garrett, Amy Backus, Jennifer Kiefer)	.50

1990-91 Notre Dame

Measuring standard size, the 58-card set chronicles the stars who played at Notre Dame through the years. The white-bordered cards on the front are anchored by either a color or black and white photo. "Notre Dame" is spelled out at the top center of the front, while the school's logo is printed in the upper right of the photo. The player's name is printed beneath the photo in the bottom center. The backs have the player's name and position at the top center, with his years played, hometown and highlights following. "Notre Dame" is listed in the lower left, while the card number "of 58" is in the lower right. The Cap Anson card is not numbered and is not part of the factory-wrapped set.

		MT
Complete Set (58):		16.00
Common Player:		.25
1	Richard (Digger) Phelps	.75
2	Collis Jones	.25
3	Dick Rosenthal	.25
4	Tim Singleton	.25
5	Austin Carr	1.00
6	Kevin O'Shea	.25
7	Keith Tower	.50
8	Tom Hawkins	.50
9	Leo Barnhorst	.25
10	John Shumate	.75
11	Donald Royal	.75
12	Edward (Moose) Krause	.25
13	Bill Laimbeer	2.00
14	Adrian Dantley	2.00
15	Keith Robinson	.50
16	Edward (Monk) Malloy	.25
17	Leo Klier	.25
18	Rich Branning	.25
19	Don (Duck) Williams	.25
20	Kevin Ellery	.25
21	Eddie Smith	.25
22	Ken Barlow	.50
23	LaPhonso Ellis	5.00
24	John Nyikos	.25
25	Daimon Sweet	.50
26	Jack Stephens	.25
27	Orlando Woolridge	1.50
28	Noble Kizer	.25
29	John Smyth	.25
30	John Paxson	2.00
31	Paul Nowak	.25
32	Elmer Bennett	.50
33	Toby Knight	.25
34	Dave Batton	.25
35	Bob Whitmore	.25
36	David Rivers	1.00
37	Gary Brokaw	1.00
38	Gary Novak	.25
39	Lloyd Aubrey	.25
40	Robert Faught	.25
41	Raymond Scanlan	.25
42	Bill Hanzlik	.75
43	Vince Boryla	.50
44	Eddie Riska	.25
45	Dwight Clay	.25
46	Bruce Flowers	.25
47	Ray Meyer	.75
48	Monty Williams	2.00
49	John Moir	.25
50	Bill Hassett	.25
51	Bob Arnzen	.50
52	Robert Rensberger	.25
53	Larry Sheffield	.25
54	Kelly Tripucka	1.00
55	Ron Reed	.75
56	George Ireland	.25
57	Tracy Jackson	.75
58	Walt Sahm	.25
NNO	Andrian (Cap) Anson	1.50

1991-92 Ohio State

Measuring standard size, the 15-card set is bordered in red and gray on the front. The photo anchors the front, with the Ohio State logo in the upper right. His position runs vertically down the right border and his name is printed inside a gray stripe beneath the photo. The backs, which are horizontal and unnumbered, include a head shot in the upper left. To the right of the photo are the Ohio State logo, the player's bio and highlights. The stats round out the back, along with a College Classics of Columbus, Ohio tag line at the bottom. The cards were originally sold in the university's bookstore. More than 10,000 sets were sold.

	MT
Common Set (15):	16.00
Common Player:	.50
Randy Ayers CO	1.50
Mark Baker	1.00
Tom Brandewie	.50
Jamaal Brown	.50
Alex Davis	.50
Rickey Dudley	2.00
Doug Etzler	.50
Lawrence Funderburke	3.50
Steve Hall	.50
Jim Jackson	12.00
Chris Jent	2.00
Jimmy Ratliff	.50
Joe Reid	.50
Bill Robinson	.50
Jamie Skelton	1.00

1992-93 Ohio State

Measuring standard size, the 15-card set features a full-bleed photo on the front, with the exception of a gray stripe that includes the school's name on the right border. The player's name is printed in red inside a gray rectangle at the bottom of the photo. The card backs, which are horizontal, include a head shot in the upper left. To the right of the photo are the Ohio State logo, card number, player name and bio and stats. The career highlights round out the back.

		MT
Complete Set (15):		14.00
Common Player:		.50
1	Randy Ayers CO	1.50
2	Derek Anderson	8.00
3	Tom Brandewie	.50
4	Alex Davis	.50
5	Rickey Dudley	2.00
6	Gerald Eaker	.50
7	Doug Etzler	.50
8	Lawrence Funderburke	2.00
9	Charles Macon	.50
10	Jimmy Ratliff	.50
11	Greg Simpson	1.00
12	Jamie Skelton	1.00
13	Antonio Watson	.50
14	Nate Wilbourne	.50
15	Otis Winston	.50

1992-93 Ohio State Women

Measuring standard size, the 16-card set has a color photo on the front, while the backs include a player bio and stats. The cards are unnumbered.

	MT
Complete Set (16):	8.00
Common Player:	.50
Alysiah Bond	.50
Audrey Burcy	.50
Nancy Darsch CO	.50
Kelly Fergus	.50
Stacie Howard	.50
Erin Ingwersen	.50
Gigi Jackson	.50
Adrienne Johnson	.50
Nikki Keyton	.50
Lisa Negri	.50
Averrill Roberts	.50
Lisa Sebastian	.50
Katie Smith	3.00
Lavona Turner	.50
Big Bear (Sponsor card)	.50
820 WOSU-AM (Sponsor card)	.50

1993-94 Ohio State

Measuring standard size, the 12-card set showcases a color photo on the front, with the player's name at the top center. Basketballs (eight in all) are "bouncing" from the lower left corner to the lower right corner. The player's jersey number and his position are listed in the lower left. The card backs have a head shot in the upper left, with the player's name, bio, Ohio State logo and card number printed to the right of the photo. The player's highlights round out the back. Card No. 2 was never released with the set.

		MT
Complete Set (12):		12.00
Common Player:		.50
1	Randy Ayers CO	1.50
3	Jamie Skelton	.75
4	Jimmy Ratliff	.50
5	Derek Anderson	6.00
6	Doug Etzler	.50
7	Charles Macon	.50
8	Greg Simpson	.75
9	Antonio Watson	.50
10	Rickey Dudley	1.25
11	Gerald Eaker	.50
12	Nate Wilbourne	.50
13	Otis Winston	.50

1993-94 Ohio State Women

Measuring standard size, the 16-card set includes a color photo on the front, while the backs feature a player bio and stats. The cards are unnumbered.

	MT
Complete Set (16):	6.00
Common Player:	.50
Marcie Alberts	.50
Alysiah Bond	.50
Nancy Darsch CO	.50
Kelly Fergus	.50
Stacie Howard	.50
Erin Ingwersen	.50
Gigi Jackson	.50
Adrienne Johnson	.50
Lisa Negri	.50
Katie Smith	2.00
Marlene Stollings	.50
Amy Turner	.50
Lavona Turner	.50
Team Photo	.75
Big Bear (Sponsor card)	.50
1460 WBNS-AM (Sponsor card)	.50

1994-95 Ohio State Women

Measuring standard size, the 16-card set includes color photos on the front of the white-bordered cards. The player's name is showcased inside a rectangle on a basketball floor design. The unnumbered card backs showcase a player highlight and bio printed over a ghosted image of the Buckeyes' logo.

	MT
Complete Set (16):	5.00
Common Player:	.50
Marcie Alberts	.50
Alysiah Bond	.50
Peggy Evans	.50
Kelly Fergus	.50
Tiffany Glosson	.50
Erin Ingwersen	.50
Gigi Jackson	.50
Adrienne Johnson	.50
Lisa Negri	.50
Katie Smith	1.50
Marlene Stollings	.50
Amy Turner	.50
OSU Coaching Staff (Melissa McFerrin ACO, Nancy Darsch CO, Nikita Lowry ACO)	.50
1994-95 OSu Buckeyes (Go Bucks!)	.50
Big Bear (Sponsor card)	.50
1460 WBNS-AM Radio (Sponsor card)	.50

1992-93 Ohio Valley Conference ATG

The 1993 Ohio Valley Conference Basketball Tournament program included two perforated sheets which featured this 18-card set. When perforated, the card measures 2-5/8" x 3-1/2". The white-bordered cards showcase a black-and-white photo. The Ohio Valley Conference logo is printed in the upper left corner. The player's name is listed in a white area below the photo, while the school he attends is printed in a green stripe below his name. The player's bio, stats and highlights are included in the unnumbered card backs.

	MT
Complete Set (18):	15.00
Common Player:	1.00
John (Sonny) Allen	1.50
Jim Baechtold	1.00
Jerry Beck	1.00
Tom Chilton	1.00
Howie Crittenden	1.00
Jimmy Hagan	1.00
Steve Hamilton	1.50
Clem Haskins	3.00
Joe Jakubick	1.00
Ronald (Popeye) Jones	2.00
Tom Marshall	1.00
Jeff Martin	1.00
Anthony Mason	3.00
Jim McDaniels	1.50
Brett Roberts	1.00
Kenny Sidwell	1.00
James (Fly) Williams	2.00

	Stars of the Past	1.50
	Checklist Card (OVC Dream Team)	

1991-92 Oklahoma State

Two sets were available to fans. The university-issued set included 57 cards and was produced in an edition of 5,000. Another set available was an 8" x 10" photo set that was signed by each of the players and coaches. This set was housed in a leather binder and sold for $99.95. The regular cards are standard sized. The 57-card set is broken up into three subset designs. Card Nos. 1 - 25 include a head shot of the player, framed in red and bordered in black. The player's name is inside a red and gray bar at the top of the photo, while the team name and Johnsons' logo is in a stripe at the bottom of the card. Card Nos. 28-32 include a color action shot of the team's seniors. Card Nos. 37-54 are almost identical to the SkyBox design with player photos placed over a computer-generated background. The card backs have the OSU logo in the upper left, while the player's name and bio are in a stripe in the upper left. His highlights are included in a box rounding out the back. All of the information is printed over a background of a ghosted action photo. The Motion Sports logo is printed in the bottom right of the backs.

		MT
Complete Set (57):		25.00
Common Player:		.25
1	Earl Jones	.25
2	Corey Williams	.50
3	Jason Turk	.25
4	Binky Triplett	.25
5	Sean Sutton	.50
6	Darwyn Alexander	.25
7	Sean Walker	.25
8	Terry Collins	.25
9	Byron Houston	1.50
10	Randy Davis	.25
11	Scott Sutton	.25
12	Brooks Thompson	2.00
13	Mike Philpott	.25
14	Cornell Hatcher	.25
15	Milton Brown	.25
16	Sean Pell	.25
17	Von Bennett	.25
18	Bryant Reeves	6.00
19	Steve Anthis ACO	.25
20	Scott Streller ACO	.25
21	Russ Pennell ACO	.25
22	Eddie Sutton CO	2.00
23	Rob Evans ACO	.25
24	Bill Self ACO	.25
25	Pistol Pete (Mascot)	.25
26	Eddie Sutton CO	2.00
27	Trophies	.25
28	Cornell Hatcher	.25
29	Byron Houston	1.50
30	Corey Williams	.50
31	Sean Sutton	.50
32	Darwyn Alexander	.25
33	Eddie Sutton CO, Henry Iba CO	1.50
34	Team Photo	1.50
35	Mike Johnson, John Johnson (Basketball Sponsors)	.25
36	Scott Sutton, Sean Sutton, Eddie Sutton CO	1.50
37	Milton Brown	.25
38	Earl Jones	.25
39	Terry Collins	.25
40	Von Bennett	.25
41	Byron Houston	1.50
42	Darwyn Alexander	.25
43	Mike Philpott	.25
44	Sean Pell	.25
45	Bryant Reeves	6.00
46	Randy Davis	.25
47	Cornell Hatcher	.25
48	Jason Turk	.25
49	Sean Sutton	.50
50	Sean Walker	.25
51	Sean Walker	.25
52	Binky Triplett	.25
53	Corey Williams	.25
54	Brooks Thompson	1.50
NNO	Ad Card Motion Sports	.25
NNO	Card Directory CL	.25
NNO	Title Card	.25

1991 Oklahoma State Collegiate Collection

This set numbers 100 cards and portrays multiple sports. The front has black and white photos, along with color ones, with orange borders. The back is in horizontal format with biographical and statistical information.

		MT
Complete Set (100):		14.00
Common Player:		.05
1	Henry Iba	.30
2	Barry Sanders	1.00
3	Thurman Thomas	.75
4	Robin Ventura	.50
5	Bob Kurland	.40
6	Athletic Tradition	.05
7	1959 NCAA Baseball Champions	.05
8	1945 NCAA Basketball Champions	.10
9	Bob Tway	.75
10	Allie Reynolds	.30
11	Rodney Harling	.05
12	Ed Gallagher	.05
13	Walt Garrison	.40
14	Terry Miller	.15
15	Bob Fenimore	.05
16	Gerald Hudson	.05
17	Hart Lee Dykes	.15
18	1976 Big 8 Conference	.05
19	Jimmy Johnson	.75
20	Terry Brown	.05
21	Derrel Gofourth	.05
22	Paul Blair	.25
23	John Little	.05
24	1983 Bluebonnet Bowl	.05
25	John Smith	.05
26	1976 Tangerine Bowl	.05
27	Gary Cutsinger	.10
28	Rusty Hilger	.10
29	Ron Baker	.05
30	Pat Jones	.15
31	Phillip Dokes	.05
32	Neil Armstrong	.05
33	Joel Horlen	.15
34	Jon Kolb	.10
35	1958 NCAA Wrestling Champs	.05
36	Doug Tewell	.05
37	1984 Gator Bowl Catch	.05
38	Scott Verplank	.40
39	1946 Sugar Bowl	.05
40	John Starks	.50
41	Liz Brown	.05
42	1984 Gator Bowl	.05
43	Yojiro Uetake	.05
44	1988 Holiday Bowl	.05
45	Ernest Anderson	.05
46	Leslie O'Neal	.25
47	Ken Monday	.05
48	Leonard Thompson	.10
49	Jess (Cob) Rennick	.05
50	Mike Gundy	.10
51	Mark Moore	.05
52	Clinette Jordan	.05
53	O.A. (Bum) Phillips	.50
54	John Ward	.05
55	Larry Roach	.05
56	Jerry Sherk	.10
57	Matt Monger	.05
58	Dick Soergel	.05
59	Ricky Young	.10
60	1963 NCAA Championship Team (Labron Harris)	.05
61	Barry Sanders	1.00
62	Gary Green	.10
63	Henry Iba	.30
64	David Edwards	.05
65	Tom Chesbro	.05
66	Chris Rockins	.05
67	Buddy Ryan	.25
68	Thurman Thomas	.75
69	Frank Lewis	.05
70	Doug Dascenzo	.10
71	Pete Incaviglia	.25
72	Willie Wood	.30
73	James Butler	.05
74	Lori McNeil	.40
75	Monty Farris	.10
76	Barry Sanders	1.00
77	Mickey Tettleton	.25
78	Barry Sanders, Thurman Thomas	.75
80	Gale McArthur	.05
81	Thurman Thomas	.75
82	Danny Edwards	.05
83	Barry Sanders	1.00
84	Mike Sheets	.05
85	Jerry Adair	.15
86	Thurman Thomas	.75
87	Garth Brooks	3.00
88	John Farrell	.05
89	1987 NCAA Championship Team (Mike Holder)	.05
90	Jim Traber	.10
91	Lindy Miller	.05
92	Mike Henneman	.30
93	Thurman Thomas	.75
94	John Washington	.05
95	Michael Daniel	.05
96	Ralph Higgins	.05
97	1987 Sun Bowl	.05
98	Garrett Limbrick	.05
99	Eddie Sutton	.25
100	Director Card	.05

1996-97 Oregon Women

The University of Oregon women's basketball team is featured in this 12-card set sponsored by Pepsi. The set was distributed as a perforated sheet. The fronts have a color photo with "Oregon" above and the player's name and position below. The backs have biographical information and career highlights as well as the Oregon and Pepsi logos. The cards are unnumbered.

	MT
Complete Set (12):	8.00
Common Player:	.75
Mendy Benson	.75
Betty Ann Boeving	.75
Lisa Bowyer	.75
Adrianne Boyer	1.00
Sonja Curtis	.75
Cinde Edamura	.75
Sandie Edwards	.75
Renae Fegent	1.00
Kirsten McKnight	.75
Jenny Mowe	.75
Elsa Oliveira	.75
Jody Runge CO	.75

1989-90 Oregon State

Measuring 3" x 4-1/16", the 16 cards were released as one sheet. A black and white photo anchors the upper part of the card fronts. The player's number is printed inside a basketball in the upper left corner. A black slanted stripe fills the bottom of the card front and includes "Beavers" at the bottom, with his name, year and position printed in white above the team's nickname. The unnumbered card backs have "Orange Express" printed at the top. The player's name and bio are in the upper left, with the OSU logo and the player's head shot printed to the right. The player's "file" fills out the rest of the back, including his highlights and stats.

	MT
Complete Set (16):	30.00
Common Player:	1.00
Teo Alibegovic - 12	1.00
Karl Anderson - 22	1.50
Jim Anderson CO	1.50
Will Brantley - 25	1.50
Bob Cavell - 4	1.00
Allan Celestine - 40	1.00
Kevin Grant - 11	1.00
Kevin Harris - 14	1.00
Scott Haskin - 44	2.50
Earl Martin - 24	1.00
Lamont McIntosh - 33	1.00
Charles McKinney - 23	1.50
Gary Payton - 20	24.00
Chris Ruepell - 21	1.00
Travis Stel - 13	1.00
Jim Anderson CO	1.50

1990-91 Oregon State

Released as a perforated sheet, with three rows of six cards each, the 18 cards measured 2-1/2" x 3-1/2". Overall, 2,000 sets were issued. A black and white photo is housed inside an oval on the front and framed in orange. The player's name, position and year is printed beneath the photo. The unnumbered card backs have the player's jersey number in the upper left, with his name and bio to the right. His highlights are listed in the "file", with his headshot in an oval to the right of his highlights in the right center of the card. The bottom of the card includes the player's stats.

	MT
Complete Set (18):	15.00
Common Player:	.75
Teo Alibegovic	.75
Jim Anderson CO	1.00
Karl Anderson	.75
Brent Barry	6.00
Will Brantley	.75
Bob Cavell	.75
Allan Celestine	.75
Canaan Chatman	.75
Kevin Harris	.75
Scott Haskin	1.50
Mario Jackson	.75
Charles McKinney	.75
Henrik Ringmar	.75
Tony Ross	.75
Chris Ruepell	.75
Chad Scott	1.00
Travis Stel	.75
Assistant Coaches (Fred Boyd, Andy McClouskey, Jim Shaw, Brent Wilder)	.75

1991-92 Oregon State

Released as a perforated sheet with three rows of six cards, the 18 cards measured 2-1/2" x 3-1/2". The white-bordered fronts include a black and white photo, framed in black and orange. "Oregon State 1991-92" is printed inside a white box in the upper right of the photo. The player's name is listed at the bottom center under the photo. The unnumbered backs have the player's bio at the top, with his career highlights printed inside a shadow box with rounded corners. Overall, 2,000 sets were released. Earnest Killum passed away two days before the sets were finished.

	MT
Complete Set (18):	12.00
Common Player:	.75
Jim Anderson CO	1.00
Kareem Anderson	1.25
Karl Anderson	.75
Brent Barry	4.00
Freddie Boyd ACO	.75
David Brown	.75
Canaan Chatman	.75
Kevin Harris	.75
Scott Haskin	1.25
Mario Jackson	.75
Earnest Killum	1.50
David Lawson	.75
Andy McClouskey ACO	.75
Charles McKinney	.75
Ray Ross	.75
Chad Scott	1.00
Pat Strickland	.75
Brent Wilder ACO	.75

1992-93 Oregon State

Released in a perforated sheet with three rows of six cards, the 18 cards measure 2-1/2" x 3-1/2". The black-bordered cards have "Oregon State 1992-93" printed vertically along the left border. The photo is on the right of the card front, with the player's name printed at the bottom center. The unnumbered card backs have a player head shot in the upper left, with his name, bio and highlights to the right. His stats are listed at the bottom of the back.

	MT
Complete Set (18):	12.00
Common Player:	.75
Jim Anderson CO	1.00
Kareem Anderson	1.00
Brent Barry	3.50
David Brown	.75
Jerohn Brown	1.00
Kevin Harris (Dribbling ball)	.75
Kevin Harris (Lay up)	.75

Scott Haskin (Blocking shot)	1.00
Scott Haskin (Shooting hook shot)	1.00
Mustapha Hoff	.75
David Lawson	.75
Charles McKinney (Looking down court)	.75
Charles McKinney (Looking at ball while dribbling)	.75
Brandon Peterson	.75
Chad Scott	1.00
Pat Strickland	.75
Ibou Thioune	.75
J.D. Vetter	.75

1993-94 Oregon State

Released as a perforated sheet with four rows of three cards each, the 12 cards measure 3" x 4". The white-bordered cards have "Oregon State Beavers" printed at the top above the photo, while the Beavers' logo is in the lower left. The player's name is in the bottom center, while his jersey number is in the bottom right. The unnumbered card backs have the player's name and bio at the top center with his highlights and a safety message and cartoon printed below.

	MT
Complete Set (12):	10.00
Common Player:	.75
Kareem Anderson	1.00
Brent Barry	3.00
Sonny Benjamin	1.00
Jelani Boline	.75
David Brown	.75
Jerohn Brown	.75
Stephane Brown	1.00
David Drakeford	.75
Dwayne Franklin	.75
Mustapha Hoff	1.00
Brandon Peterson	.75
J.D. Vetter	.75

1991 Penn State

This 16-card set was sponsored by The Jostens Foundation and the The Second Mile. Cards are unnumbered and contain biographical information and a Nittany Lion Tips by each player.

		MT
Complete Set (16):		15.00
Common Player:		1.00
1	Freddie Barnes	3.00
2	Jim Barnes	1.00
3	Allison Barber	1.00
4	Paula Bright	1.00
5	Monroe Brown	1.00
6	Wayne Cowden	1.00
7	Jamie Downer	1.00
8	Chad Dubin	1.00
9	Tanya Garner	1.00
10	Kathy Phillips	1.00
11	Susan Robinson	1.00
12	Janice Rogers	1.00
13	Mark Sohn	1.00
14	Jason Suter	1.00
15	Tim Wittman	1.00
16	The Nittany Lion	1.00

1992 Penn State

The 1992 set contains 16 cards and features numerous sports. The color photos on the front are superimposed on the background, and tilted slightly to the left. The back has a career summary and player safety tip quotes.

		MT
Complete Set (16):		15.00
Common Player:		1.00
1	Freddie Barnes	3.00
2	Monroe Brown	1.00
3	Adam Carton	1.00
4	Wayne Cowden	1.00
5	Dave Degitz	1.00
6	Lynn Dougherty	1.00
7	Dana Eikenberg	1.00
8	Jada Hiltabrand	1.00
9	Kathy Phillips	1.00
10	Jeff Prescott	1.00
11	Mike Reichenbach	1.00
12	Susan Robinson	1.00
13	Janice Rogers	1.00
14	Laurie Russo	1.00
15	Troy Sunderland	1.00
16	Tim Wittman	1.00

1993 Penn State

Printed on card stock, the set contains 25 cards and is sponsored by the Second Mile and The Caritas Foundation, along with Penn State Intercollegiate Athletics. The backs contain Nittany Lion tips in the form of player quotes.

		MT
Complete Set (25):		12.00
Common Player:		.50
1	Sanshiro Abe	.50
2	John Amaechi	2.00
3	Greg Bartram	.50
4	Karen Cimochowski	.50
5	Carla Coleman	.50
6	Mark Cooper	.50
7	Jim Delaney	.50
8	Jackie Donovan	.50
9	Bridget Foley	.50
10	Matt Gaudio	.50
11	Helen Holloway	.50
12	Michael Jennings	.50
13	Cary Kolat	.50
14	Katina Mack	.50
15	Michelle Manzolillo	.50
16	Missy Masley	.50
17	Kerry McCoy	.50
18	Shawn Nelson	.50
19	Joel Neuwirth	.50
20	Tony Pansy	.50
21	Dave Riordan	.50
22	Josh Robbins	.50
23	Kerry Slattery	.50
24	Dana Toscano	.50
25	Steve Wydman	.50

1994 Penn State

The 25-card set features a red border with the player's photo featured in the middle of the card. The back contains career summaries and player quotes as Nittany Lion quotes.

		MT
Complete Set (25):		12.00
Common Player:		.50
1	Sanshiro Abe	.50
2	Liz Agnew	.50
3	John Amaechi	1.50
4	Greg Bartram	.50
5	Tony Bobulinski	.50
6	Leigh Cappello	.50
7	Carla Coleman	.50
8	Mark Cooper	.50
9	John Hughes	.50
10	Michael Joseph	.50
11	Joanna Knox	.50
12	Katina Mack	.50
13	Nicole Malinak	.50
14	Missy Masley	.50
15	Kerry McCoy	.50
16	Tina Nicholson	.50
17	Tony Pansy	.50
18	Lee Ricketts	.50
19	Dave Riordan	.50
20	Glenn Sekunda	1.00
21	Bea Selz	.50
22	Shelby Thayer	.50
23	Donovan Williams	.50
24	Brandy Wood	.50
25	Nittany Lion (Mascot)	.50

1996 Penn State

This 25-card set features two men's and women's sports: basketball and gymnastics, and men's wrestling. Each sport was given five cards printed on thin non-coated stock.

		MT
Complete Set (25):		15.00
Common Player:		.75
1	Sanshiro Abe	.75
2	Tyson Bryant	.75
3	Heather Bundy	.75
4	Kim Calhoun	.75
5	Lauren Cutshaw	.75
6	Dan Earl	2.00
7	Tom Ellefson	.75
8	Matt Gaudio	.75
9	Matt Hardy	.75
10	Rachael Hills	.75
11	Carey Hoyt	.75
12	Christi Huch	.75
13	John Hughes	.75
14	Pete Lisickey, Calvin Booth	1.50
15	Tiffany Longworth	.75
16	Katina Mack	.75
17	Kerry McCoy	.75
18	J.M. Michel	.75
19	Frank Morici	.75
20	Tina Nicholson	.75
21	Angie Potthoff	.75
22	Joe Roemer	.75
23	Glenn Sekunda	1.50
24	Phil Williams	.75
25	Brandy Wood	.75

1989-90 Pittsburgh

The 12-card set features orange and blue borders on the fronts, with a color photo anchoring the center of the card. "Panthers" is printed in orange at the top, while his name, jersey number, year and position are printed directly above the photo. The unnumbered backs have the years in the upper corners, with the player's name and bio sandwiched between two Pitt logos. His highlights, tips from the Panthers and the Foodland logo round out the card backs.

	MT
Complete Set (12):	6.00
Common Player:	.50
Rod Brookin	1.00
Pat Cavanaugh	.50
Paul Evans CO	.75
Gilbert Johnson	.75
Bobby Martin	.75
Jason Matthews	.50
Sean Miller	1.50
Darren Morningstar	1.00
Pitt Panther (team mascot)	.75
Darelle Porter	.50
Brian Shorter	.75
Travis Ziegler	.50

1990-91 Pittsburgh

The 12-card set has "Panthers" printed at the top of the card front. The player photo anchors the center of the card, while the Pitt logo is in the bottom left. Two stripes at the bottom of the card front include the player's name and number and Foodland logo, respectively. The unnumbered backs have the player's name and bio at the top, with his highlights, tips from the Panthers and Foodland logo rounding out the backs.

	MT
Complete Set (12):	6.00
Common Player:	.50
Antoine Jones - 21	.50
Gandhi Jordan - 4	.50
Bobby Martin - 55	.50
Jason Matthews - 22	.50
Chris McNeal - 24	.50
Jermaine Morgan - 42	.50
Sean Miller - 3	1.00
Darren Moringstar - 33	1.25
Omo Moses - 44	.50
Darelle Porter - 20	.50
Ahmad Shareef - 13	.50
Brian Shorter - 00	1.00

1991-92 Providence

Measuring standard size, the 24-card set showcases the legends of Providence basketball. Produced by Ballpark Cards, the sets were sold by the school for $7. The white-bordered fronts have the Providence Friars logo at the top, with the player's photo below. These are framed in orange. The horizontal backs have the player's name, bio, stats, and highlights, along with the card number (in a circle in the lower right), all printed inside a gray-shaded box. The Ballpark Cards tag line is in the lower left of the back.

		MT
Complete Set (24):		12.00
Common Player:		.50
1	Joseph Mullaney CO (1955-1969, 1981-1985)	.75
2	Dave Gavitt CO (1969-1979)	.75
3	Rick Pitino CO (1985-1987)	2.00
4	Rick Barnes CO (1988-Present)	1.00
5	Team Photo (1973 Friars)	.50
6	Team Photo (1987 Friars)	.50
7	Lenny Wilkens	4.00
8	John Egan	.50
9	Jim Hadnot	.75
10	Vinny Ernst	.50
11	Ray Flynn	.75
12	John Thompson	2.00
13	Mike Riordan	.75
14	Jimmy Walker	.75
15	Jim Larranaga	.50
16	Ernie DiGregorio	1.50
17	Marvin Barnes	2.00
18	Kevin Stacom	.75
19	Joe Hassett	.50
20	Bruce Campbell	.50
21	Otis Thorpe	2.00
22	Billy Donovan	.75
23	Eric Murdock	2.00
24	Checklist Card	.50

1992-93 Purdue

Measuring standard size, the 18-card set showcases a color photo on the front, framed in gold and black. The player's name and number are printed in the lower right of the photo, with "1992-93 Purdue Boilermakers" printed at the bottom. The unnumbered card backs have a head shot in the upper left, with his name, bio and Purdue logo all to the right of it. The highlights and stats round out the back.

	MT
Complete Set (18):	20.00
Common Player:	.50
Brandon Brantley	.75
Linc Darner	.75
Herb Dove	1.00
Todd Foster	.75
Justin Jennings	.75
Gene Keady CO	3.00
Cuonzo Martin	2.50
Cornelius McNary	.50
Matt Painter	.50
Porter Roberts	1.00
Glenn Robinson	15.00
Tim Spiker	.50
Ian Stanback	.50
Matt Waddell	1.00
Bruce Weber ACO, Frank Kendrick ACO, Gene Keady CO, Gary Johnson TR, Tom Reiter ACO	.50
Kenny Williams	.50
Mackey Arena	.75
Title Card (Checklist)	.50

1993-94 Purdue

Measuring standard size, the 18-card set showcases "1993-94 Purdue University Men's Basketball" printed at the top. A color player photo is on the left, with "Purdue" printed at the bottom in a metallic font. The player's name is printed vertically in script along the right border. The unnumbered card backs have a head shot in the upper left, with the player's name, number and bio to the right of it. His highlights are listed below.

	MT
Complete Set (18):	18.00
Common Player:	.50
Brandon Brantley	1.00
Matt ten Dam	.50
Linc Darner	.75
Herb Dove	1.00
Tim Ervin	.50
Todd Foster	.75
Paul Gilvydis	.50
Justin Jennings	.75
Gene Keady CO	2.50
Cuonzo Martin	2.00
Cornelius McNary	.50
Porter Roberts	1.00
Glenn Robinson	12.00
Ian Stanback	.50
Matt Waddell	1.50
Kenny Williams	.50
Purdue CO Staff (Larry Leverenz, Jay Price, Gene Keady, Frank Kendrick, Bruce Weber)	.50
Title Card	.50

1993-94 Purdue Women

The 18-card set showcases "1993-94 Purdue University Women's Basketball" printed at the top, with the photo on the left, framed in gold. Purdue is printed at the bottom of the photo in a metallic font. The player's name is printed vertically in a script font along the right border. The unnumbered backs have a player head shot in the upper left, with the player's name, number and bio to the right of it. Her stats round out the backs.

	MT
Complete Set (17):	12.00
Common Player:	.50
Melina Griffin	.50
Andrea Hildebrand	.50
Jennifer Jacoby	.75
Leslie Johnson	2.00
Tonya Kirk	.50
Cindy Lamping	.75
Shannon Lindsey	.50
Stacey Lovelace	.75
Danielle McCulley	.50
Jannon Roland	.75
Nicki Taggart	.50
Lin Dunn CO	1.00
Student Managers (Tracy Brown, Tammi Hoffman, Angie Brown)	.50
Assistant Coaches (Sarah Sharp, Dallas Boychuk, MaCelle Joseph)	.50
1993-94 Boiler Makers	.50
Mackey Arena	.50
Title card	.50

1998 Purdue Basketball Greats

	MT
Complete Set (36):	15.00
Common Player:	.50
Logo card	.50
(Mark Atkinson)	1.00
(Chad Austin)	1.00
(Joe Barry Carroll)	.50
(Russell Cross)	.50
(Terry Dischinger)	.50
(Keith Edmonson)	.50
(Bob Ford)	.50
(Mel Garland)	.50
(John Garrett)	.50
(Herman Gilliam)	1.00
(Paul Hoffman)	.50
(Walter Jordan)	.50
Gene Keady	2.00
Billy Keller	.50
Frank Kendrick	.50
Troy Lewis	1.00
Mackey Arena	.50
(Cuonzo Martin)	1.00
(Willie Merriweather)	.50
(Brad Miller)	.50
(Rick Mount)	1.00
Charles "Stretch" Murphy	1.00
Eugene Parker	.50
Bruce Parkinson	.50
Glenn Robinson	3.00
Jim Rowinski	.50
Steven Scheffler	.50
Dave Schellhase	.50
Joe Sexson	.50
Jerry Sichting	.50
Everette Stephens	.50
Matt Waddell	.50
Brian Walker	.50
John Wooden	3.00
Jewell Young	.50

1999 Purdue Women's Best of the Best

This 36-card set honored female legends in all Boilermaker sports. The set was sponsored by American Marketing Association and contains student-athletes in tennis, swimming, golf, track and field, volleyball, softball and basketball. Two players, Ukari Figgs and Stephanie White-McCarty, are featured on both individual cards and together on the set's cover card.

	MT
Complete Set (36):	
Common Player:	
Best of the Best cover card	.50
Erica Adams	.50
Carol Emanuel	.50
Kim Fritsch	.50
Ukari Figgs	.50
Donna Gill	.50
Joy Holmes	.50
Jennifer Jacoby	.50
Lisa Jahner	.50
Machelle Joseph	.50
Christa LaCroix	.50
Kristin Lindstrom	.50
Stacey Lovelace	.50
Mary Beth Maggart	.50
Andrea Marek	.50
Debbie McDonald	.50
Molly McGrath	.50
Jamie McNeair	.50
Jane Neff	.50
Yvonne Netterville	.50
Peach Payne	.50
Sybil Perry	.50
Heidi Reynolds	.50
Jannon Roland	.50
Amy Ruley	.50
Sheryl Scheve	.50
Jenny Schoen	.50
Marianne Smith	.50
Cathey Tyree	.50
Sharon Versyp	.50
Darlene Warta	.50
Brooke White	.50
Stephanie White-McCarty	.50
Jeanne Wilson	.50
Corissa Yasen	.50
Purdue logo/checklist card	.50

1990-91 San Jose State

The nine-card set showcases "San Jose State University" printed at the top above the photo on the front. The Smokey logo is in the lower left, while the player's name, number and year are printed in the lower right. The unnumbered backs have the player's name and bio sandwiched between two San Jose State logos. A safety message and cartoon round out the backs.

	MT
Complete Set (9):	6.00
Common Player:	1.00
Troy Batiste	1.00
Terry Cannon	1.00
Robert Dunlap	1.00
Kevin Logan	1.00
Stan Morrison CO	1.50
Daryl Scott	1.00
Charles Terrell	1.50
Event Center	1.00
Smokey Bear	1.00

1987-88 Southern

Ther 16-card, standard-size set was sponsored by McDonald's, Southern University and local law enforcement agencies. The McDonald's logo appears on the front in the lower left corner and on the card back. A Jaguar icon appears on the front's lower right corner. Notable in the set is Avery Johnson.

		MT
Complete Set (16):		14.00
Common Player:		.50
1	Marino Casem CO	.50
2	Gerald Perry	3.00
3	Michael Ball, Toren Robinson	.50
4	Ben Jobe CO	1.50
5	Daryl Battles	.50
6	Patrick Garner	.50
7	Avery Johnson	9.00
8	Rodney Washington	.50
9	Kevin Florent	.50
10	Dervynn Johnson	.50
11	Claudene Stovall	.50
12	Michelle Currie	.50
13	Gibbie Phillips	.50
14	Allan Ratliff	.50
15	Eric Foxworth	.50
16	Jeff Swain	.50

1990-91 Southern Cal

Sponsored by the USDA Forest Service, among others, this 20- card set features the first cards of running back Ricky Ervins and NBA guard Robert Pack. Three cards are basketball cards, numbers 1,2 and 12, with the rest being football cards.

		MT
Complete Set (20):		25.00
Common Player:		.50
1	Calvin Banks BKB	4.00
2	Ronnie Coleman BKB	4.00
3	Ricky Ervins 34	4.00
4	Shane Foley 10	.50
5	Gene Fruge 91	.50
6	Don Gibson 92	.50
7	Frank Griffin 87	.50
8	Pat Harlow 77	2.00
9	Craig Hartsuyker 40	.50
10	Marcus Hopkins 2	.50
11	Pat O'Hara 4	.50
12	Robert Pack BKB	10.00
13	Marc Preston 22	.50
14	Quin Rodriguez 11	.50
15	Scott Ross 35	.50
16	Grant Runnerstrum 23	.50
17	Mark Tucker 75	.50
18	Brian Tuliau 56	.50
19	Gary Wellman 83	2.00
20	Checklist Card - Smokey Bear	.50

1991 Southern Cal

This 100-card set contains cards of former Trojan athletes of various sports, with the majority being football. The set also contain autographs by numerous individuals like Tom Seaver and Fred Lynn, inserted throughout 1,000 of the sets.

		MT
Complete Set (100):		20.00
Common Player:		.10
1	Charles White	.50
2	Anthony Davis	.50
3	Clay Matthews	.50
4	Hoby Brenner	.10
5	Mike Garrett	.50
6	Bill Sharman (basketball)	1.00
7	Bob Seagren (track)	.10
8	Mike McKeever	.10
9	Celso Kalache (volleyball)	.10
10	John Williams CO (water polo)	.10
11	John Naber (swimming)	.25
12	Brad Budde	.10
13	Tim Tyan	.10
14	Mark Tucker	.10
15	Rodney Peete	.75
16	Art Mazmanian (baseball)	.10
17	Red Badgro (baseball)	.10
18	Sue Habernigg (women's swimming)	.10
19	Craig Fertig	.10
20	John Block (basketball)	.50
21	Jen-Kai Liu (volleyball)	.10
22	Kim Ruddins (women's volleyball)	.10
23	Al Cowlings	.50
24	Ronnie Lott	1.50
25	Adam Johnson (volleyball)	.50
26	Fred Lynn (baseball)	.50
27	Rick Leach (tennis)	.10
28	Tim Rossovich	.25
29	Marvin Powell	.25
30	Ron Yary	.50
31	Ken Ruettgers	.50
32	Bob Yoder CO (men's volleyball)	.10
33	Megan McCallister (women's volleyball)	.10
34	Dave Cadigan	.25
35	Jeff Bregel	.10
36	Michael Wayman (tennis)	.10
37	Sippy Woodhead-Kantzer (women's swimming)	.10
38	Tim Hovland (volleyball)	.50
39	Steve Busby (baseball)	.25
40	Tom Seaver (baseball)	2.00
41	Anthony Colorito	.10
42	Wayne Carlander (basketball)	.25
43	Erik Affholter	.25
44	Jim Obradovich	.10
45	Duane Bickett	.50
46	Leslie Daland (women's swimming)	.10
47	Ole Oleson (track)	.10
48	Ed Putnam (baseball)	.10
49	Stan Smith (tennis)	.75
50	Jeff Hart (golf)	.10
51	Jack Del Rio	.50
52	Bob Boyd CO (basketball)	.25
53	Pat Haden	1.00
54	John Lambert (basketball)	.25
55	Pete Beathard	.50
56	Anna-Maria Fernandez (women's tennis)	.10
57	Marta Figueras-Dotti (women's golf)	.10
58	Don Mosebar	.25
59	Don Doll	.10
60	Dave Stockton (golf)	.75
61	Trisha Laux (women's tennis)	.10
62	Roy Foster	.25
63	Bruce Matthews	.50
64	Steve Sogge	.10
65	Tracy Nakamura (women's golf)	.25
66	Marv Montgomery	.10
67	Jack Tingley (swimming)	.10
68	Larry Stevens	.10
69	Harry Smith	.10
70	Bill Bain	.10
71	Mark McGwire (baseball)	3.00
72	Brad Brink (baseball)	.10
73	Richard Wood	.10
74	Rod Dedeaux CO (baseball)	.50
75	Paul Westphal (basketball)	1.00
76	Al Krueger	.10
77	James McConica (swimming)	.10
78	Rod Martin	.25
79	Bill Yardley (volleyball)	.10
80	Bill Stetson (volleyball)	.10
81	Ray Looze (swimming)	.10
82	Dan Jorgensen (swimming)	.10
83	Anna-Lucia Fernandez (women's tennis)	.10
84	Terri O'Loughlin (women's swimming)	.10
85	John Grant	.10
86	Chris Lewis (tennis)	.10
87	Steve Timmons (volleyball)	.75
88	Dr. Dallas Long (track)	.10
89	John McKay CO	.25
90	Joe Bottom (swimming)	.10
91	John Jackson	.10
92	Paul McDonald	.10
93	Jimmy Gunn	.10
94	Rod Sherman	.10
95	Cecilia Fernandez (women's tennis)	.10
96	Doug Adler (tennis)	.10
97	Ron Orr (swimming)	.10
98	Debbie Landreth Brown (women's volleyball)	.10
99	Debbie Green (women's volleyball)	.10
100	Pat Harrison (baseball)	.10

1987-88 Southern Mississippi

The 14-card, 2-3/8" x 3-1/2" set was co-sponsored by Deposit Guaranty National Bank and Coca-Cola. The card fronts have a team logo in the upper right corner with company sponsors appearing along the bottom white border. The backs have bio and stat information.

		MT
Complete Set (14):		12.00
Common Player:		1.00
1	The Freshmen	1.00
2	The Coaches	1.00
3	Casey Fisher	1.00
4	Derrek Hamilton	1.00
5	Randolph Keys	3.00
6	John White	1.00
7	D.J. and Allen (D.J. Bowe, Allen Chapman)	1.00
8	The Browns (John Brown, Willie Brown)	1.00
9	Jurado Hinton	1.00
10	Jay Ladner	1.00
11	Randy Pettus	1.00
12	Jimmy Smith	2.00
13	Roger Boyd	1.00
14	The Team	2.00

1994-95 Southwest Missouri State University

This 11-card set was sponsored by Citizen's National Bank, RE/MAX and Midwest Sports Medicine Center. The cards are unnumbered and contain biographical information and statistics on the back.

	MT
Complete Set (11):	9.00
Common Player:	.50
Team Card	.50
Joe Blasingim	.50
Anthony Edwards	1.00
Johnny Epps	.50
Chris Hayes	.50
Ben Kandlbinder	.50
Shawn Latimer	.50
Monte Marsh	1.00
Johnny Murdock	.50
Clint Thomas	.50
Robert Wilkerson	.50

1994-95 Southwest Missouri St. Women

This 14-card set was sponsored by the Springfield News-Leader and the Southwest Missouri State Athletic Program. Card fronts feature a color photo within a red border. The player's name, position and jersey number are listed below the picture. The backs have biographical info, career highlights and statistics and the sponsors' logos. The cards are unnumbered.

	MT
Complete Set (14):	12.00
Common Player:	1.00
Marsha Burton	1.00
Lisa Davies	1.00
Latanya Davis	1.00
Shannon Gage	1.00
Kindra Garst	1.00
Marla Harrison	1.00
Julie Howard	1.00
Charitee Longstreth	1.00
Lisa Moore	1.00
Courtney Murdock	1.00
Donease Smith	1.00
Stephanie Thurman	1.00
Richelle Winn	1.00
Team Photo	1.00

1996-97 Southwest Missouri State University

This 14-card set was sponsored by Coldwell Banker. The cards are unnumbered and contain biographical information and statistics on the back.

	MT
Complete Set (14):	10.00
Common Player:	.50
Team Card	.50
Steve Alford (coach)	3.00
Kevin Aull	.50
Ryan Bettenhausen	.50
Coleco Buie	.50
JoJo Dabbs	.50
Tony Davis	.50
William Fontleroy	.50
Josh Hotz	.50
Ben Kandlbinder	.50
Omar Lincoln	.50
Monte Marsh	1.00
Omar Lincoln	.50

1986-87 Southwestern Louisiana

The 16-card set was only produced 3,500 times. The front has color action photos, with a colorless border. Four sports are represented in the set.

		MT
Complete Set (16):		10.00
Common Player:		.75
1	Stephen Beene	.75
2	Eddie Citronnelli	.75
3	Hollis Conway	1.50
4	Teena Cooper	.75
5	Herb Erhardt	.75
6	Bret Garnett	.75
7	Allison Gray	.75
8	Bobby Hobbs	.75
9	Brian Jolivette	.75
10	Dianne Lowings	.75
11	Rodney McNeil	.75
12	Cathy O'Donovan	.75
13	Ashley Rhoney	.75
14	Alisa Smith	.75
15	Randal Smith	.75
16	Merv Waukau	.75

1987-88 Southwestern Louisiana

The color action photos on a white card face come in 16-card sets. The front also has the team's logo and player information below the photo. Included in the set is Olympic high jumper Hollis Conway.

		MT
Complete Set (16):		9.00
Common Player:		.75
1	Randal Smith	.75
2	Earl Watkins	.75
3	Kevin Brooks	2.00
4	Stephen Beene	.75
5	Kim Perrot	1.50
6	Teena Cooper	.75
7	Bret Garnett	.75
8	Ashley Rhoney	.75
9	Terry Fitzpatrick	.75
10	Joe Turk	.75
11	Brad Hebets	.75
12	Ron Vincent	.75
13	Hollis Conway	1.25
14	Marria Blackwell	.75
15	Stefni Whitton	.75
16	Janine Johnson	.75

1979-80 St. Bonaventure

The 18-card, standard-size set features sepia-tone images on the card front with "Bonnies" appearing along the bottom border. The horizontal back has bio and stat information.

		NM
Complete Set (18):		50.00
Common Player:		3.00
1	Earl Belcher - 25	4.00
2	Dan Burns - 41	3.00
3	Bruno DeGiglio - 24	3.00
4	Jim Elenz - 10	3.00
5	Lacey Fulmer - 20	3.00
6	Delmar Harrod - 52	3.00
7	Alfonza Jones - 12	3.00
8	Mark Jones - 11	4.00
9	Bill Kalbaugh CO	3.00
10	Lloyd Praedel - 44	3.00
11	Pat Rodgers - 35	3.00
12	Bob Sassone CO	3.00
13	Jim Satalin CO	3.00
14	Mark Spencer - 15	3.00
15	Eric Stover - 40	3.00
16	Shawn Waterman - 33	3.00
17	Brian West - 30	3.00
18	Title Card	5.00

1996-97 Stanford

High Step Trading Cards produced this 16-card set. The fronts have a color action photo with Stanford above and the player's name below. The backs have the player's biography and statistics. The cards are not numbered.

	MT
Complete Set (16):	17.00
Common Player:	.50
Rich Jackson	.50
Brevin Knight (charging)	5.00
Brevin Knight (passing)	5.00
Arthur Lee	2.00
Mark Madsen	2.50
Ryan Mendez	.50
Mike Montgomery CO	1.50
David Moseley	.50
Peter Sauer	1.00
Mark Seaton	1.00
Mark Thompson	.50
Kamba Tshionyi	.50
Peter Van Elswyk	.50
Kris Weems	1.00
Karl Wente	.50
Tim Young	2.00

1998-99 Stanford

This 16-card set was produced by High Step Trading Cards. The set is unnumbered and listed in alphabetical order and is sponsored by Pepsi.

	MT
Complete Set (16):	17.00
Common Player:	.50
Mike Montgomery (coach)	.75
Jarron Collins	2.50
Jason Collins	2.50
Alex Gelbard	.50
Tony Giovacchini	.50
Arthur Lee	3.00
Kyle Logan	.50
Mark Madsen	2.50
Michael McDonald	.50
Ryan Mendez	.50
David Moseley	.50
Peter Sauer	.50
Mark Seaton	.50
Kris Weems	.50
Tim Young	3.00
The Stanford Tree	.50

1999-00 Stanford

This 17-card set from High Step Trading Cards was sponsored by Pepsi. The cards are unnumbered and listed below alphabetically. Card backs contain biographical information and stats.

	MT
Complete Set (17):	15.00
Common Player:	.50
Julius Barnes	.50
Tyler Besecker	.50
Curtis Borchardt	.50
Jarron Collins	2.00
Jason Collins	2.00
Justin Davis	.50
Alex Gelbard	.50
Tony Giovacchini	.50
Casey Jacobsen	2.00
Joe Kirchofer	.50
Kyle Logan	.50
Mark Madsen	2.00
Michael McDonald	.50
Ryan Mendez	.50
Mike Montgomery, CO	1.50
David Moseley	.50
6th Man Club	.50

2000-01 Stanford

		MT
Complete Set (16):		15.00
Common Player:		.50
1	Julius Barnes	.50
2	Tyler Besecker	.50
3	Curtis Borchardt	.50
4	Jarron Collins	3.00
5	Jason Collins	3.00
6	Justin Davis	.50
7	Tony Giovacchini	.50
8	Casey Jacobsen	5.00
9	Teyo Johnson	.50
10	Joe Kirchofer	.50
11	Kyle Logan	.50
12	Matt Lottich	.50
13	Mike McDonald	1.00
14	Ryan Mendez	1.00
15	Mike Montgomery Coach	2.50
16	Nick Robinson	.50

1988-89 Syracuse

The 12-card, standard-size set was sponsored by Louis Rich and each front has "Basketball" prominently featured over the player photograph. The backs have stat and bio information, as well as career highlights, and the Louis Rich logo appears along the bottom border.

		MT
Complete Set (12):		55.00
Common Player:		2.00
1	Jim Boeheim CO	10.00
2	Derrick Coleman	25.00
3	Sherman Douglas	15.00
4	Herman Harried	2.00
5	Dave Johnson	4.00
6	Rich Manning	2.00
7	Billy Owens	15.00
8	Matt Roe	3.00
9	Erik Rogers	2.00
10	Anthony Scott	2.00
11	Dave Slock	2.00
12	Stephen Thompson	4.00

1989-90 Syracuse

The 15-card, 2-5/8" x 3-1/2" set was sponsored by Pepsi, Y94 FM and Burger King. Below the color photo is the player's name and "Syracuse University 1989-90" in an orange box. The backs contain stat and bio information, as well as company logos.

		MT
Complete Set (15):		10.00
Common Player:		.50
1	Derrick Coleman - 44	3.00
2	LeRon Ellis - 25	.75
3	Rich Manning - 34	.50
4	Stephen Thompson - 32	.75
5	Michael Edwards - 5	.50
6	Dave Johnson - 23	.75
7	Billy Owens - 30	2.00
8	Conrad McRae - 13	.50
9	Jim Boeheim CO	1.50
10	Stephen Thompson - 32	.75
11	Mike Hopkins - 33	.50
12	Tony Scott - 40	.50
13	Billy Owens - 30	2.00
14	Erik Rogers - 41	.50
15	Derrick Coleman - 44	3.00

1988-89 Tennessee

The 12-card, standard-size set features a color action photo on the front and a Smokey The Bear logo. The backs have bio information and a fire safety cartoon.

		MT
Complete Set (12):		20.00
Common Player:		1.50
11	Clarence Swearengen	2.50
23	Greg Bell	2.50
24	Rickey Clark	1.50
25	Travis Henry	1.50
31	Dyron Nix	4.00
33	Mark Griffin	1.50
34	Ronnie Reese	1.50
50	Doug Roth	1.50
51	Ian Lockhart	2.50
xx	Don Devoe CO	2.50
xx	Somkey The Hound (Mascot)	1.50
xx	Thompson-Boling Arena	2.50

1990-91 Tennessee Women

The 16-card, standard-size set was sponsored by the USDA Forest Service and features a Smokey The Bear headshot in the lower left corner. The backs have a fire safety cartoon.

		MT
Complete Set (16):		20.00
Common Player:		1.00
1	Jody Adams	1.00
2	Nikki Caldwell	1.00
3	Tamara Carver	1.00
4	Kelli Casteel	1.00
5	Daedra Charles	3.00
6	Regina Clark	1.00
7	Mickie DeMoss ACO	1.00
8	Peggy Evans	1.00
9	Lisa Harrison	1.00
10	Debbie Hawhee	1.00
11	Dena Head	2.00
12	Marlene Jeter	1.00
13	Pat Summitt CO	6.00
14	Holly Warlick ACO	1.00
15	Thompson-Boling Arena	1.00
16	Smokey (Mascot)	1.00

1992-93 Tennessee Women

The 16-card, standard-size set is similar to the 1990-91 set in that each card front has a Smokey The Bear headshot in the lower left corner. The backs are highlighted by fire safety cartoons.

		MT
Complete Set (16):		14.00
Common Player:		.75
1	Jody Adams	.75
2	Nikki Caldwell	.75
3	Latina Davis	2.00
4	Mickie DeMoss ACO	.75
5	Rachone Dilligard	.75
6	Peggy Evans	.75
7	Lisa Harrison	.75
8	Dana Johnson	.75
9	Michelle Johnson	.75
10	Nikki McCray	5.00
11	Pat Summitt CO	4.00
12	Pam Tanner ACO	.75
13	Vonda Ward	.75
14	Holly Warlick ACO	.75
15	Tiffany Woosley	1.50
16	Chearleaders	.75

1993-94 Tennessee Women

The 16-card, standard-size set features a 50th anniversary logo centered along the card front's bottom border. The backs have a fire safety cartoon.

		MT
Complete Set (16):		12.00
Common Player:		.50
1	Nikki Caldwell	.50
2	Abby Conklin	1.50
3	Latina Davis	1.50
4	Mickie DeMoss ACO	.50
5	Rachone Dilligard	.50
6	Dana Johnson	.50
7	Michelle Marciniak	2.00
8	Nikki McCray	4.00
9	Carolyn Peck ACO	.50
10	Tanika Smith	.50
11	Pat Summitt CO	4.00
12	Pashen Thompson	1.50
13	Vonda Ward	.50
14	Holly Warlick ACO	.50
15	Tiffany Woosley	1.25
16	The Cheerleaders	.50

1994-95 Tennessee Women

The 16-card set was issued on a 10" x 14" perforated sheet. When perforated, the cards measure the standard size. The set is sponsored by the USDA Forest Servive and each back has a fire safety cartoon.

		MT
Complete Set (16):		12.00
Common Player:		.75
1	Abby Conklin	1.25
2	Latina Davis	1.25
3	Mickie DeMoss ACO	.75
4	Dana Johnson	.75
5	Tiffani Johnson	1.25
6	Brynae Laxton	.75
7	Michelle Marciniak	1.50
8	Nikki McCray	3.00
9	Laurie Milligan	.75
10	Carolyn Peck ACO	.75
11	Tanika Smith	.75
12	Pat Summitt CO	3.00
13	Pashen Thompson	1.00
14	Vonda Ward	.75
15	Holly Warlick	.75
16	Tiffany Woosley	1.00

1995-96 Tennessee Women

This 16-card set was sponsored by the US Forest Service. The cards were issued as a perforated sheet. A color photo appears on the front surrounded by an orange border. Basic player information and the Smokey the Bear logo are at the bottom. The backs have the player info at the top with a Smokey cartoon and fire safety tip. The cards are not numbered.

	MT
Complete Set (16):	12.00
Common Player:	.50
Abby Conklin	1.00
Latina Davis	1.00
Mickie DeMoss ACO	.50
Dana Johnson	.50
Tiffani Johnson	1.00
Brynae Laxton	.50
Michelle Marciniak	1.00
Nikki McCray	3.00
Laurie Milligan	.50
Carolyn Peck ACO	.50
Tanika Smith	.50
Pat Summitt CO	3.00
Pashen Thompson	1.00
Vonda Ward	.50
Holly Warlick ACO	.50
Tiffany Woosley	1.00

1998-99 Tennessee

		MT
Complete Set (16):		15.00
Common Player:		.50
1	Krystal Title Card	.50
2	Team Photo	1.00
3	Del Baker	.50
4	C.J. Black	3.00
5	Vegas Davis	.50
6	Aaron Green	.50
7	Jerry Green CO	1.00
8	Tony Harris	3.00
9	Torrey Harris	1.00
10	Charles Hathaway	.50
11	Rashard Lee	.50
12	Isiah Victor	3.00
13	John Ward	.50
14	Brandon Wharton	.50
15	Vincent Yarbrough	5.00
16	The 6th Man	.50

1991-92 Tennessee Tech

The 16-card, standard-size set was sponsored by Little Caesar Pizza. The fronts feature posed shots while the backs have player bio and stat information and the player's uniform number in a large purple circle.

		MT
Complete Set (16):		8.00
Common Player:		.75
1	John Best	.75
2	Mitch Cupples	.75
3	Damon Davis	.75
4	John Dykstra	.75
5	Charles Edmonson	.75
6	Frank Harrell CO	.75
7	Clyde Hopkins	.75
8	Maurice Houston	.75
9	P.J. Mays	.75
10	Eric Mitchell	.75
11	Jesse Nayadley	.75
12	Donnie Paulk	.75
13	Ronnie Robinson	.75
14	Van Usher	1.00
15	Rob West	.75
16	Wade Wester	.75

1992-93 Tennessee Tech

The 18-card, standard-size set was also sponsored by Little Caesar Pizza and each card front features a posed photo. The cards are unnumbered and the player's number appears prominently in a circle on the back.

	MT
Complete Set (18):	9.00
Common Player:	.75
John Best	.75
Greg Bibb	1.25
Carlos Carter	.75
Chad Crouch	.75
Mitch Cupples	.75
Charley Dean	.75
John Dykstra	.75
Carlos Floyd	1.25
Maurice Houston	.75
David Ingram	.75
Trent McCracken	.75
Eric Mitchell	.75
Jesse Nayadley	.75

	Brian Riggins	.75
	Earl Smith	.75
	Rob West	.75
	Wade Wester	.75
	Team Leaders (Angelo Volpe PRES, Frank Harrell CO)	.75

1993-94 Tennessee Tech

The 18-card, standard-size set was sponsored by Little Caesar Pizza with the fronts featuring posed photos. The card backs feature bio and stat information along with career highlights.

		MT
	Complete Set (18):	9.00
	Common Player:	.75
1	Greg Bibb	1.00
2	Dennis Buckley	.75
3	Marc Burnett ('93 Inductee HOF)	1.00
4	Carlos Carter	.75
5	Lorenzo Coleman	1.50
6	Chad Crouch	.75
7	Charley Dean	.75
8	Carlos Floyd	1.00
9	Maurice Houston	.75
10	David Ingram	.75
11	Reggie Mayo	.75
12	Eric Mitchell	.75
13	Jesse Nayadley	.75
14	Earl Smith	.75
15	Chris Turner	.75
16	Steve Taylor (Distinguished Career)	.75
17	Rob West	.75
18	Eblen Center (Arena)	.75

1994-95 Tennessee Tech

The 18-card, standard-size set features posed photography on the card front with the horizontal backs having bio and stat information. The player's jersey number appears prominently on the card backs along the right side.

		MT
	Complete Set (18):	8.00
	Common Player:	.75
1	Greg Bibb	1.00
2	Carlos Carter	.75
3	Lorenzo Coleman	1.00
4	Romain Coleman	.75
5	Chad Crouch	.75
6	Theron Curry	.75
7	Carlos Floyd	1.00
8	Marc Glanton	.75
9	Eric Mitchell	.75
10	Jesse Nayadley	.75
11	Ricky Norris	.75
12	Lance Parr	.75
13	Kenneth Smith	.75
14	Chris Turner	.75
15	Coaching Staff (Frank Harrell CO, Kevin Bray ACO, Bob Eskew ACO, Jason Craighead MG, Susan Fitzpatrick SECY)	.75
16	Loyal Fans (Johnny Donnelly)	.75
17	Radio Legend (Gene Davidson ANN, Eldon Burgess ANN)	.75
18	Team Managers (Chad Smith MG, Timmy Rogers MG, Phil Dennis MG)	.75

1990 Texas

The 32-card set features multiple sports printed on thin card stock. The front has color action shots with a black frame. Eight different sports are spotlighted.

		MT
	Complete Set (32):	20.00
	Common Player:	.75
1	Brad Agee	1.50
2	Susan Anderson	.75
3	Ellen Bayer	.75
4	Lance Blanks	1.00
5	Patrik Boden	.75
6	Angie Bradburn	.75
7	Steve Bryan	.75
8	Jody Conradt CO	2.00
9	Brian Dare	.75
10	Kirk Dressendorfer	1.00
11	Leigh Ann Fetters	.75
12	Annette Garza	.75
13	Doug Gjertsen	.75
14	Janine Gremmel	.75
15	Carlette Guidry	1.00
16	Cliff Gustafson CO	2.00
17	Ken Hackenmack	.75
18	Quandalyn Harrell	.75
19	Michiko Hattori	1.50
20	Andrea Hayes	.75
21	Kelly Jenkins	.75
22	Tony Jones	1.00
23	Erin Keogh	.75
24	Bobby Lilljedahl	.75
25	Travis Mays	1.50
26	Lyssa McBride	1.00
27	David McWilliams CO	1.00
28	Diane Merrett	.75
29	George Muller	.75
30	Tom Penders CO	3.00
31	Dagmara Szyszczak	.75
32	David Tollison	.75

1994-95 Texas A and M

The 20-card, multi-sport set was sponsored by Star Tel Long Distance Telephone Service and was issued in 12-1/2" x 3-1/2" unperforated strips. When cut the cards measure the standard size. The set contains baseball (1-5), men's basketball (6-10), women's basketball (11-15) and women's volleyball (16-20). The cards are unnumbered.

	MT
Complete Set (20):	8.00
Common Player:	.50
Chad Alexander	.50
Stephen Claybrook, Mark Johnson CO	.50
John Codrington	.50
Robert Harris	.50
Sponsor Card	.50
Coaches (Tony Barone CO, Peter Moser ACO, Mitch Buonaguro ACO, Frank Haith ACO)	1.00
1994-95 Recruits (Kyle Kessel, Waseem Ali, Quinton James, Chris Oney, John Stevens, Dario Quesada, Sean Clarke, Chris LeBlanc)	1.00
Underclassmen (Jimmy Smith, Chris Pulliams, John Stevens, Chris LeBlanc) (1994-95 Schedule)	.50
Seniors (Roy Wills, Damon Johnson, Tony McGinnis, Corey Henderson, Joe Wilbert, John Jungers) (1994 Basketball Roster)	1.00
Sponsor Card	.50
Freshmen (Carey Owens, Sutton Helvey, Kim Linder)	.50
Sophomores (Christy Lake, Shanae Ford, Marianne Miller, Lana Tucker) (1994-95 Schedule)	.50
Junior and Seniors (Angel Spinks, Martha McClelland, Kelly Cerny, Debbie Biermann, Donyale Canada, Bambi Ferguson, Lisa Branch) (1994 Basketball Roster)	.50
Coaches (Angela Taylor ACO, Kristy Sims ACO, Candi Harvey CO, Lisa Jordon ACO)	.50
Sponsor Card	.50
Freshman (Farah Mensik, Cindy VanderWoude, Kristie Smedsrud, Jennifer Wells)	.50
Sophomores (Jan Schudder, Brooke Polak, Page White, Bonni Chaffe) (1994 Volleyball Schedule)	.50
Juniors and Seniors (Suzy Wente, Andrea Williams, Anna Klasing, Jennifer Bronner, Joni Keister, Dana Santleben, Renee Kukla) (1994 Volleyball Roster)	.50
Coaches (Genny Wood ACO, John Corbelli ACO, Laurie Corbelli ACO, Jennifer Smith ACO)	.50
Sponsor Card	.50

1992-93 Texas Tech Women

The 19-card, standard-size set was sponsored by the Lubbock Avalanche-Journal and various local businesses. The card fronts have the player's jersey in the upper right corner with sponsor logos and company logos on the back. Notable in the set is Sheryl Swoopes.

		MT
	Complete Set (19):	15.00
	Common Player:	.50
1	Michi Atkins	1.50
2	Cynthia Clinger	.50
3	Nikki Heath	.50
4	Noel Johnson	.50
5	Diana Kersey	.50
6	Krista Kirkland	.50
7	Kim Pruitt	.50
8	Raider Red (Mascot)	.50
9	Roger Reding ACO	.50
10	Stephanie Scott	.50
11	Marsha Sharp CO	2.00
12	Sheryl Swoopes	10.00
13	Michelle Thomas	.50
14	Linden Weese ACO	.50
15	Terri Weldon (Graduate Assistant)	.50
16	Melinda White	.50
17	Checklist	.50
18	Sponsor Card	.50
19	Texas Tech Sign	.50

1992-93 Texas Tech Women NCAA Champs

The 25-card, standard-size set was sponsored by United Supermarket and honors the Lady Raiders for their NCAA title. The card backs contain a headshot in the upper left corner with bio, stat and career highlights. Sheryl Swoopes is featured in the set on five cards.

		MT
	Complete Set (25):	20.00
	Common Player:	.50
1	Trophy Card	.75
2	Diana Kersey	.50
3	Nikki Heath	.50
4	Stephanie Scott	.50
5	Krista Kirkland	.50
6	Sheryl Swoopes	6.00
7	Noel Johnson	.50
8	Janice Farris	.50
9	Kim Pruitt	.50
10	Cynthia Clinger	.50
11	Michelle Thomas	.50
12	Melinda White	.50
13	Michi Atkins	1.50
14	Marsha Sharp CO	2.00
15	Linden Weese ACO	.50
16	Roger Reding ACO	.50
17	Terri Weldon (Graduate Assistant)	.50
18	Jeannine McHaney DIR	.50
19	SWC Championship	.75
20	National Semifinals (Michi Atkins)	.75
21	National Finals (Sheryl Swoopes)	3.00
22	Emotional Finish (Sheryl Swoopes, Krista Kirkland)	3.00
23	1992-93 Season Record (Krista Kirkland, Sheryl Swoopes, Cynthia Clinger)	.50
24	Sheryl Swoopes (Player of the Year - Records and Accolades)	3.00
25	Team Photo CL	.75

1990-91 UCLA

The 40-card, standard-size set features basketball players from the UCLA men's and women's teams. The horizontal backs feature bio and stat information. The Keith Owens card actually features Destah Owens and a coupon was included in the set for a free replacement card.

		MT
	Complete Set (40):	17.00
	Common Player:	.25
1	Team Photo	1.50
2	Tracy Murray	3.00
3	Ed O'Bannon	6.00
4	Darrick Martin	1.75
5	Mitchell Butler	2.00
6	Mike Lanier	.25
7	Chris Kenny	.25
8A	Keith Owens ERR (Photo actually Destah Owens)	2.50
8B	Keith Owens COR	1.00
9	Dave Paulsell	.25
10	Shon Tarver	1.50
11	Rodney Zimmerman	.25
12	Zan Mason	.25
13	Gerald Madkins	1.50
14	Don MacLean	3.00
15	Lou Richie	.25
16	Billie Moore CO	.25
17	Rehema Stephens	.25
18	Nicole Anderson	.25
19	Amy Jalewalia	.25
20	Pam Walker ACO	.25
21	Lynn Kamrath	.25
22	Detra Lockhart	.25
23	Stacie Gravely	.25
24	Laura Collins	.25
25	Genevieve Vanoostveen	.25
26	Dede Mosman	.25
27	Nicole Young	.25
28	Dawn Baker	.25
29	Melissa Gische	.25
30	Rachelle Roulier	.25
31	Marcy Tarabochia	.25
32	Natalie Williams	2.50
33	Kathy Olivier ACO	.25
34	Mary Hegarty ACO	.25
35	Jim Harrick CO	1.50
36	Brad Holland ACO	.75
37	Tony Fuller ACO	.25
38	Ken Barone ACO	.25
39	Mark Gottfried ACO	.25
40	Checklist Card	.25

1991-92 UCLA

The 21-card, standard-size set was produced by Collegiate Collection and is similar in design to the UCLA team set from the previous year. The horizontal backs have player stat and bio information.

		MT
	Complete Set (21):	15.00
	Common Player:	.50
1	Mike Lanier	.50
2	Don MacLean	3.00
3	Rodney Zimmerman	.50
4	Pauley Pavilion	1.00
5	Tyus Edney	3.00
6	Jiri (George) Zidek	2.00
7	Brad Holland CO	.50
8	Ed O'Bannon	4.00
9	Richard Petruska	1.00
10	Darrick Martin	1.50
11	Tony Fuller CO	.50
12	Tracy Murray	2.00
13	Gerald Madkins	1.00
14	Mitchell Butler	1.00
15	Mark Gottfried	.50
16	Jim Harrick CO	1.50
17	Jonah Naulls	.50
18	Steve Lavin CO	1.50
19	Steve Elkind	.50
20	Shon Tarver	1.00
21	Checklist Card	.50

1991 UCLA Collegiate Collection

The 144-card, standard-size set features cards in color and black and white with royal blue borders. The players featured include past and present standouts. The horizontal backs include career highlights.

		MT
	Complete Set (144):	15.00
	Common Player:	.05
1	John Wooden CO	.75
2	Kareem Abdul-Jabbar	.75
3	Bill Walton	.50
4	Larry Farmer	.15
5	Marques Johnson	.30
6	Walt Hazzard	.25
7	Henry Bibby	.15
8	Gail Goodrich	.30
9	Jim Harrick	.40
10	Kareem Abdul-Jabbar	.75
11	Mike Warren	.25
12	Gary Maloncon	.05
13	James Wilkes	.15
14	Kiki Vandeweghe	.25
15	1969 NCAA Champs	.15
16	Sidney Wicks	.30
17	Andre McCarter	.05
18	Michael Holton	.10
19	Greg Lee	.05
20	John Wooden CO	.75
21	Gene Bartow CO	.15
22	Richard Washington	.10
23	Brad Wright	.05
24	Pooh Richardson	.20
25	Terry Schofield	.05
26	Gig Sims	.05
27	Darren Daye	.10
28	Dave Immel	.05
29	Tommy Curtis	.05
30	Bill Walton	.50
31	Larry Brown CO	.40
32	Kevin Walker	.05
33	Kareem Abdul-Jabbar	.75
34	Kenny Heitz	.10
35	Gary Cunningham	.05
36	Lynn Shackelford	.10
37	Keith Wilkes	.25
38	1975 NCAA Champs	.15
39	Raymond Townsend	.05
40	Pete Trgovich	.05
41	Kelvin Butler	.05
42	Ed Sheldrake	.05
43	Larry Hollyfield	.10
44	Montel Hatcher	.05
45	Denise Curry	.25
46	Curtis Rowe	.25
47	David Meyers	.20
48	Lucius Allen	.25
49	Kenny Fields	.10
50	John Vallely	.10
51	John Wooden, Nell Wooden	.50
52	Sidney Wicks	.30
53	1973 NCAA Champs	.15
54	Jack Haley	.10
55	Ralph Drollinger	.10
56	Don Johnson	.05
57	Bill Ellis	.05
58	Willie Naulls	.15
59	Ron Livingston	.05
60	Bill Putnam	.05
61	Rod Foster	.10
62	Bill Walton	.50
63	Roy Hamilton	.05
64	Jim Spillane	.05
65	Ralph Jackson	.05
66	Morris Taft	.05
67	Dick Ridgeway	.05
68	Dave Minor	.05
69	1965 Champs	.15
70	Karl Kraushaar	.05
71	Craig Jackson	.05
72	Kenny Washington	.15
73	Keith Wilkes	.25
74	Stuart Gray	.10
75	John Green	.05
76	Doug McIntosh	.05
77	Walt Hazzard	.25
78	Frank Lubin	.05
79	Don Piper	.05
80	1967 Champs	.15
81	Kenny Booker	.05
82	Marques Johnson	.30
83	Bill Walton	.50
84	1972 Champs	.15
85	Steve Patterson	.05
86	1964 NCAA Champs	.15
87	Alan Sawyer	.05
88	Walt Torrence	.05
89	Gail Goodrich	.30
90	Ralph Bunche	.50
91	Swen Nater	.25
92	Larry Farmer	.15
93	Kareem Abdul-Jabbar	.75
94	Mike Sanders	.15
95	Niguel Miguel	.05
96	Jackie Robinson	1.25
97	Dick West	.05
98	Rafer Johnson	.40
99	John Berberich	.05
100	Director Card	.05
101	Richard Linthicum	.05
102	Chuck Clustka	.05
103	John Wooden CO, Denny Crum CO, Gary Cunningham CO	.50
104	Jerry Norman	.05
105	John Moore	.05
106	Trevor Wilson	.25
107	David Greenwood	.15
108	John Wooden CO, J.D. Morgan AD	.50
109	Kareem Abdul-Jabbar	.75
110	Ann Meyers	.50
111	Denny Crum	.30
112	Pierce Works	.05
113	Carl Cozens	.05
114	George Stanich	.05
115	Don Ashen	.05
116	David Greenwood	.15
117	1971 Team Photo	.15
118	Johns Barksdale	.05
119	1978 Champion	.10
120	John Stanich	.05
121	Don Barksdale	.15
122	1968 Champs	.15
123	Carl Knowles	.05
124	Don Bragg	.10
125	Ducky Drake	.10
126	John Ball	.05
127	Pauley Pavilion	.25
128	Sam Balter	.05
129	A Caddy Works Team	.05
130	John Wooden CO	.75
131	Fred Goss	.05
132	Keith Erickson	.25
133	Pete Blackman	.05
134	Gail Goodrich	.30
135	Kent Miller	.05
136	Jack Ketchum	.05
137	1970 Team Photo	.15
138	Jim Milhorn	.05
139	Bill Rankin	.05
140	Kenny Heitz	.10
141	Bob (Ace) Calkins	.05
142	J.D. Morgan AD	.05
143	Fred Slaughter	.10
144	Director Card	.05

1988-89 UNLV

The 12-card, standard-size set was produced by Hall of Fame Cards, Inc., and just 10,000 sets were produced. "Runnin' Rebels" appears in red above the photo on the card front with an anti-drug message on the back.

		MT
	Complete Set (12):	19.00
	Common Player:	1.00
1	Stacey Augmon	8.00
2	Greg Anthony	8.00
3	Anderson Hunt	2.00
4	George Ackles	2.00
5	David Butler	2.00
6	Clint Rossum	1.00
7	Moses Scurry	2.00
8	Barry Young	1.00
9	James Jones	1.00
10	Stacey Cvijanovich	1.00
11	Chris Jeter	1.00
12	Bryan Emerzian	1.00

1989-90 UNLV 7-Eleven

The 14-card set, sponsored by 7-Eleven, 98.5 KLUC-FM and Nationwide Communications, Inc., measure the standard size and just 25,000 sets were produced. The set had the first cards of Larry Johnson and Jerry Tarkanian.

		MT
	Complete Set (14):	18.00
	Common Player:	.75
1	Greg Anthony	2.50
2	Stacey Augmon	3.00
3	Travis Bice	1.00
4	David Butler	1.00
5	Stacey Cvijanovich	.75
6	Bryan Emerzian	.75
7	Anderson Hunt	1.00
8	Chris Jeter	.75
9	Larry Johnson	8.00
10	James Jones	.75
11	David Rice	.75
12	Moses Scurry	1.00
13	Barry Young	.75
14	Jerry Tarkanian CO	5.00

1989-90 UNLV HOF

The 14-card, standard-size set was limited in production by Hall of Fame Cards, Inc., to just 5,000 sets. After UNLV won the title, 3,000 more sets were produced. The horizontal backs contain anti-drug messages.

		MT
	Complete Set (14):	18.00
	Common Player:	.75
1	Stacey Augmon	3.00
2	Greg Anthony	2.50
3	Larry Johnson	9.00
4	George Ackles	1.00
5	Moses Scurry	1.00
6	Anderson Hunt (Hank Gathers visible in background)	2.00
7	Travis Bice	1.00
8	David Butler	1.00
9	Stacey Cvijanovich	.75
10	Chris Jeter	.75
11	Bryan Emerzian	.75
12	James Jones (Hank Gathers visible in background)	2.00
13	Barry Young	.75
14	Dave Rice	.75

1990-91 UNLV HOF

The 15-card set was limited in production to 15,000 sets (individually numbered on card No. 4). The fronts have a stripe in the lower right corner designating UNLV the 1990 National Champions. The horizontal backs have an anti-drug message.

		MT
	Complete Set (15):	14.00
	Common Player:	.75
1	Larry Johnson	6.00
2	Stacey Augmon	2.00
3	Greg Anthony	2.00
4	Anderson Hunt	1.00
5	Travis Bice	.75
6	George Ackles	1.00
7	Bryan Emerzian	.75
8	Dave Rice	.75
9	Chris Jeter	.75
10	Anderson Hunt	1.00
11	Evric Gray	1.00
12	Bobby Joyce	.75
13	H. Waldman	1.00
14	Larry Johnson	6.00
15	Runnin' Rebels (Card lists records broken by UNLV)	1.00

1990-91 UNLV Season to Remember

The 15-card set features UNLV after its runnerup outing at the 1991 NCAA Championship. The standard-size cards have red borders with the bottom front having "A Season To Remember."

MT
Complete Set (15): 9.00
Common Player: .25
1 Larry Johnson 3.00
2 Stacey Augmon 1.50
3 Greg Anthony 1.50
4 Anderson Hunt .50
5 Travis Bice .25
6 George Ackles .50
7 Bryan Emerzian .25
8 Dave Rice .25
9 Chris Jeter .25
10 Elmore Spencer .50
11 Evric Gray .50
12 Bobby Joyce .25
13 H. Waldman .50
14 Melvin Love .25
15 Rebel All-Americans (Hunt, Anthony, Ackles, Johnson and Augmon) 1.50

1990-91 UNLV Smokey

The 15-card set was sponsored by the USDA Forest Service and the standard-size cards were issued as either single cards or as a sheet. The card fronts are predominantly red with a Smokey The Bear illustration on the back.

MT
Complete Set (15): 12.00
Common Player: .75
1 George Ackles - 44 1.00
2 Greg Anthony - 50 2.50
3 Stacey Augmon - 32 2.00
4 Travis Bice - 3 .75
5 Bryan Emerzian - 15 .75
6 Evric Gray - 23 1.00
7 Anderson Hunt - 12 1.00
8 Chris Jeter - 53 .75
9 Larry Johnson - 4 6.00
10 Bobby Joyce - 42 .75
11 Melvin Love - 40 .75
12 Dave Rice - 30 .75
13 Elmore Spencer - 24 1.00
14 Jerry Tarkanian CO 3.00
15 H. Waldman - 31 1.00

1992-93 UNLV

The 16-card, standard-size set was sponsored by KVBC Channel 3 (Las Vegas) and Centel First Source phone books. The set includes an early card of J.R. (Isaiah) Ryder.

MT
Complete Set (16): 23.00
Common Player: .75
1 Derrick Alesevich .75
2 Dexter Boney 1.50
3 Jason Brooks .75
4 Clint Clausen .75
5 Ken Gibson .75
6 Evric Gray 1.50
7 Fred Haygood .75
8 Sean Loughran .75
9 Reggie Manuel .75
10 Rollie Massimino CO 3.00
11 Isaiah (J.R.) Rider 10.00
12 Damian Smith .75
13 Dedan Thomas 1.00
14 Lawrence Thomas .75
15 Sponsor Card (KVBC Channel 3) .75
16 Sponsor Card (Centel First Source) .75

1989-90 UTEP

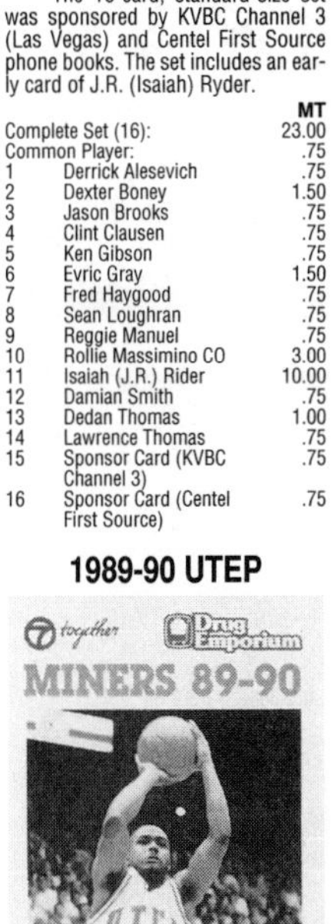

The 24-card set was sponsored by 7-Together and Drug Emporium and "Star Miners" is featured along the top border on the card front. Former UTEP standouts from the past and present are featured.

MT
Complete Set (24): 25.00
Common Player: .50
1 Nate Archibald 4.00
2 Jim Barnes 1.00
3 Rus Bradburd .50
4 Dallas David .50
5 Antonio Davis 6.00
6 Ralph Davis .75
7 Norm Ellenberger CO .75
8 Francis Ezenwa .50
9 Greg Foster 1.00
10 Joe Griffin .50
11 Henry Hall .75
12 Tim Hardaway 9.00
13 Don Haskins CO 3.00
14 Merle Heimer .50
15 Bobby Joe Hill .75
16 Greg Lackey .50
17 David Lattin 1.00
18 Marlon Maxey 1.00
19 Mark McCall .50
20 Chris Perez .50
21 Nolen Richardson 2.50
22 Arlandis Rush .50
23 Alprentice Stewart .50
24 David Van Dyke .50

1992-93 UTEP

The 14-card set, sponsored by Whataburger, 95.5 KLAQ and Major Players, measure the standard size. The horizontal backs contain a headshot and bio and stat information.

MT
Complete Set (14): 8.00
Common Player: .50
1 Don Haskins CO 2.50
2 Gym Bice .50
3 Jeff Deal .50
4 Roy Howard .50
5 Johnny Melvin 1.00
6 John Portis .50
7 Daryl Christopher .50
8 Eddie Rivera .75
9 Ralph Davis .75
10 Bryan Barnes .50
11 Antoine Gillespie .75
12 Hector Gonzalez .50
13 Phil Crocker .50
14 G. Ray Johnson ACO, Gary Brewster ACO, Gilbert Miranda (Restricted Earnings CO) .50

1987-88 Vanderbilt

The 14-card set was sponsored by Vanderbilt University Police and Security. The cards, measuring 2-1/2" x 4", have bio and stat information on the backs with emergency phone numbers. Will Perdue is included in the set and Chip Rupp's card, No. 5, is limited because he transfered and his card was pulled. Most sets found have just 13 cards, missing Rupp's card.

MT
Complete Set (14): 75.00
Common Player: 1.50
1 Team Photo 4.00
2 C.M. Newton CO 4.00
3 Fred Benjamin 1.50
4 Barry Booker 1.50
5 Chip Rupp SP 50.00
6 Scott Laughinghouse 1.50
7 Eric Reid 1.50
8 Steve Grant 1.50
9 Derrick Wilcox 1.50
10 Will Perdue 10.00
11 Frank Kornet 3.00
12 Charles Mayes 1.50
13 Barry Goheen 3.00
14 Scott Draud 2.00

1982-83 Victoria

The 15-card, 2-1/8" x 4" set was sponsored by Honda City, Weathergard Shop, Factory Sound, CJVI 900 Radio and the Saanich Police. The backs feature a player quote and a safety slogan and the cards are unnumbered.

MT
Complete Set (15): 15.00
Common Player: 1.25
Dave Bakken 1.25
Dan Brosseuk 1.25
Ryan Burles 1.25
Kelly Dukeshire 1.25
Quinn Groenheyde 1.25
Gerald Kazanowski 1.25
Gregg Kazanowski 1.25
Tom Narbeshuber 1.25
Phil Ohl 1.25
Eli Pasquale 1.25
Vito Pasquale 1.25
David Sheehan 1.25
Ken Shields CO 1.25
Billy Turney-Loos ACO 1.25
Craig Higgins ACO 1.25

1983-84 Victoria

The 15-card, 2-5/8" x 4" set features posed action shots on a white card front. The backs contain company sponsor logos of Sprite, CJVI 900 Radio, Sanyo and other local businesses.

MT
Complete Set (15): 12.00
Common Player: 1.00
1 Cord Clemens 1.00
2 Quinn Groenhyde 1.00
3 Ian Hyde-Lay ACO 1.00
4 Sean Kalinovich 1.00
5 Ken Larson 1.00
6 John Munro 1.00
7 Jamie Newman 1.00
8 Phil Ohl 1.00
9 Eli Pasquale 1.00
10 Dave Sheehan 1.00
11 Ken Shields CO 1.00
12 Randy Steel 1.00
13 Graham Taylor 1.00
14 Greg Wiltjer 1.00
15 Logo Card (Saanich Police) 1.50

1984-85 Victoria

The 16-card, 2-5/8" x 4" set is virtually identical to previous team issues with white card fronts and sponsor logos on the back.

MT
Complete Set (16): 12.00
Common Player: 1.00
1 Cord Clemens 1.00
2 Jerry Divoky 1.00
3 Quinn Groenhyde ACO 1.00
4 Shawn Kalinovich 1.00
5 Robert Kreke 1.00
6 Wade Loukes 1.00
7 James Newman 1.00
8 Phil Ohl 1.00
9 Vito Pasquale 1.00
10 Lloyd Scrubb UER (Name misspelled Llyod on front) 1.00
11 David Sheehan 1.00
12 Ken Shields CO 1.00
13 Randy Steel 1.00
14 Graham Taylor 1.00
15 Ellis Whalen 1.00
16 Logo Card 1.50

1985-86 Victoria

The 1985-86 set is virtually identical with previous team sets with the size kept at 2-5/8" x 4". As with past issues, a facsimile autograph appears on the card back with the sponsor logos.

MT
Complete Set (17): 12.00
Common Player: 1.00
1 Maurice Basso 1.00
2 Clint Hamilton 1.00
3 Fraser Jefferson 1.00
4 Tom Johnson 1.00
5 Jim Knox 1.00
6 David Lescheid 1.00
7 Vesa Linnamo 1.00
8 David McIntosh 1.00
9 Geoff McKay 1.00
10 Spencer McKay 1.00
11 Rick Mesich 1.00
12 Kevin Ottewell 1.00
13 Roger Rai 1.00
14 Chris Schriek 1.00
15 Scott Stinson ACO 1.00
16 Guy Vetrie CO 1.00
17 Logo Card 1.50

1986-87 Victoria

The 16-card set (2-5/8" x 4") features the same design as previous issues, including the white card front and the players' facsimile autograph on the card backs.

MT
Complete Set (16): 12.00
Common Player: 1.00
1 Jerry Divoky 1.00
2 Shawn Kalinovich 1.00
3 Jay Kenyon 1.00
4 Rob Kreke 1.00
5 Brian Kruger 1.00
6 Wade Loukes 1.00
7 Geoff McKay 1.00
8 Spencer McKay 1.00
9 Steve Mitton 1.00
10 Vito Pasquale 1.00
11 Alan Phillips 1.00
12 Rob Poole 1.00
13 Tom Johnson 1.00
14 Lloyd Scrubb 1.00
15 Ken Shields CO 1.00
16 Mark Simpson ACO 1.00

1988-89 Victoria

The 16-card set parallels previous team sets in design. The fronts feature a posed action photo with the "Vikes" logo in the lower left corner. The backs contain player quotes, a facsimile autograph and sponsor logos.

MT
Complete Set (16): 10.00
Common Player: .75
1 Maurice Basso .75
2 Colin Brousson .75
3 Jerry Divoky .75
4 Kevin Harrington .75
5 Tom Johnson .75
6 Daryn Lansdell .75
7 Wade Loukes .75
8 Geoff McKay .75
9 Spencer McKay .75
10 Rick Mesich .75
11 Dale Olson .75
12 Ken Olynyk ACO .75
13 Kevin Ottewell .75
14 Tug Rados .75
15 Ken Shields CO .75
16 Guy Vetrie ACO .75

1988-89 Virginia

The 16-card set was sponsored by Hardee's fast food restaurants and measured the standard 2-1/2" x 3-1/2". The color photo on the card face is bordered by blue and orange with the Hardee's logo appearing in the upper left corner. The backs feature the player's career highlights. Notable cards are Bryant Stith, John Crotty and Matt Blundin, who was drafted by the Kansas City Chiefs of the NFL as a quarterback.

MT
Complete Set (16): 50.00
Common Player: 2.50
1 Brent Bair 2.50
2 Matt Blundin 8.00
3 Mark Cooke 2.50
4 John Crotty 8.00
5 Brent Dabbs 2.50
6 Jeff Daniel 2.50
7 Terry Holland CO 6.00
8 Dirk Katstra 2.50
9 Richard Morgan 2.50
10 Anthony Oliver 2.50
11 Bryant Stith 18.00
12 Kenny Turner 2.50
13 Curtis Williams 2.50
14 Cheerleaders 2.50
15 Coaching Staff 2.50
16 Title Card 2.50

1991-92 Virginia

The 16-card, standard-size set was sponsored by Capitol Sports Network and arrived on a perforated sheet. The front photos have the players in posed shots with white and purple borders. The backs have bio information, career highlights and the player's quote.

MT
Complete Set (16): 27.00
Common Player: 1.00
1 Chris Alexander 1.00
2 Cory Alexander 5.00
3 Yuri Barnes 1.50
4 Junior Burrough 4.00
5 Chris Havlicek 2.00
6 Ted Jeffries 1.50
7 Derrick Johnson 1.00
8 Jeff Jones CO 3.00
9 Terry Kirby 7.00
10 Anthony Oliver 1.50
11 Cornel Parker 1.50
12 Doug Smith 1.00
13 Corey Stewart 1.00
14 Bryant Stith 9.00
15 Jason Williford 1.50
16 Shawn Wilson 1.00

1991-92 Virginia Women

The 16-card, standard-size set was sponsored by McDonald's and includes a card of standout Dawn Staley. "Food, Folks & Fun" appears along the top border. Player bio information is printed on the back, which also features a McDonald's logo.

MT
Complete Set (16): 20.00
Common Player: .50
1 Charleata Beale .50
2 Heather Burge 2.50
3 Heidi Burge 2.50
4 Dena Evans 1.00
5 Chris Lesoravage .50
6 Amy Lofstedt .50
7 Allison Moore .50
8 Tammi Reiss 2.00
9 Debbie Ryan CO 2.00
10 Felicia Santelli .50
11 Audra Smith .50
12 Dawn Staley 9.00
13 Wendy Toussaint 1.00
14 Melanee Wagener .50
15 NCAA Midwest Regional Tournament Champions March 17-21, 1991 .50
16 Virginia vs. NC State February 23, 1991 .50

1992-93 Virginia

The 16-card, 2-1/2" x 3-1/2" set was sponsored by Coca-Cola and was issued as a perforated sheet with four rows of four cards each. "Virginia" is featured prominently along the front top border with a small Coca-Cola logo along the bottom edge. The backs contain player bio information with career highlights and another Coca-Cola logo along the lower border.

MT
Complete Set (16): 14.00
Common Player: .50
1 Chris Alexander .50
2 Cory Alexander 3.00
3 Yuri Barnes .75
4 Junior Burrough 2.00
5 Chris Havlicek 1.00
6 Ted Jeffries .75
7 Cornel Parker .75
8 Doug Smith .50
9 Jason Williford .75
10 Shawn Wilson .50
11 Jeff Jones CO 1.50
12 Brian Ellerbe ACO, Dennis Wolff ACO, Tom Perrin ACO .50
13 1980 NIT Champions .75
14 1981 NCAA East Regional Tournament Champions .75
15 1984 NCAA East Regional Tournament Champions .75
16 1992 NIT Champions .75

1992-93 Virginia Women

The 16-card, standard-size set was identical to the 1992-93 men's set in design, including delivery by perforated sheets. The set, as with the men's, was sponsored by Coca-Cola.

MT
Complete Set (16): 14.00
Common Player: .50
1 Charleata Beale .50
2 Jenny Boucek .50
3 Heather Burge 1.50
4 Heidi Burge 1.50
5 Dena Evans .75
6 Jeffra Gausepohl .50
7 Chris Lesoravage .50
8 Amy Lofstedt .50
9 Allison Moore .50
10 Wendy Palmer 2.00
11 Debbie Ryan CO 2.00
12 Kristen Somogyi .50
13 Cheryl Taylor .50
14 Wendy Toussaint .75
15 1992 Atlantic Coast Conference Tournament Champions .50
16 1992 East Regional Tournament Champions .50

1993-94 Virginia

The 16-card, standard-size set was originally produced as part of a perforated sheet. The blue-bordered fronts have "Virginia" in large letters and the player's photo in an oval. The backs contain bio and career highlights. The set was sponsored by Coca-Cola and its logos appear on both sides.

MT
Complete Set (16): 12.00
Common Player: .50
1 Chris Alexander .50
2 Cory Alexander 2.50
3 Yuri Barnes .75
4 Mark Bogosh .50
5 Junior Burrough 2.50
6 Harold Deane 2.50
7 Bobby Graves .50
8 Chris Havlicek .75
9 Cornel Parker .75
10 Mike Powell .50
11 Jamal Robinson .75
12 Maurice Watkins .50
13 Jason Williford .75
14 Shawn Wilson .50
15 Jeff Jones CO 1.50
16 Assistant Coaches (Brian Ellerbe, Dennis Wolff, Tom Perrin) .50

1993-94 Virginia Women

The 16-card, standard-size set after perforation identically paralleled the 1993-94 men's set in design, except that the women's set was sponsored by Cavalier Inn, not Coca-Cola.

MT
Complete Set (16): 14.00
Common Player: .50
1 Charleata Beale .50
2 Jenny Boucek .50
3 Konecka Drakeford .50
4 Tammy Gardner .50
5 Jeffra Gausepohl .50
6 Jackie Glessner .50
7 Chris Lesoravage .50
8 Amy Lofstedt .50
9 Wendy Palmer 1.25
10 Debbie Ryan CO 2.00
11 Tora Suber 1.50
12 Cheryl Taylor .50
13 Wendy Toussaint .75
14 Dawn Staley's Number Retired 4.00
15 NCAA East Regional Tournament Champions .50
16 Mascot Day .50

1999-00 Virginia

MT
Complete Set (15): 6.00
Common Player: .50
1 William Dersch .75
2 Stephane Dondon .50
3 Jason Dowling .50
4 Colin Ducharme .50
5 Keith Friel .50
6 Pete Gillen 1.00
7 Adam Hall .50
8 Donald Hand .50
9 Josh Hare .50
10 Cade Lemcke .50
11 Majestic Mapp 1.00
12 Roger Mason 1.00
13 Jason Rogers .50
14 Travis Watson .50
15 Chris Williams .50

1999-00 Virginia Women

MT
Complete Set (13): 5.00
Common Player: .50
1 Anna Crosswhite .50
2 Marcie Dickson .50
3 Lisa Hosac .50
4 Elena Kravchenko .50
5 Schuye Larue .50
6 Chalois Lias .50
7 Dean'na Mitchelson .50
8 Telisha Quarles .50
9 Renee Robinson .50
10 Debbie Ryan CO 1.00
11 Lauren Swierczek .50
12 Katie Tracy .50
13 Svetlana Volnaya .50

1992-93 Virginia Tech

The 12-card set is full of color action photos, with the player's name and position on the bottom. The back has a public service message, along with biographical information. Five different sports are listed.

MT
Complete Set (12): 12.00
Common Player: .50
1 HokieBird (Mascot) .50
2 Will Furrer 2.00
3 Phyllis Tonkin, Dayna Sonovick, Tisa Brown .50
4 David Dallas .50
5 Eugene Chung 1.00
6 Eric McClellan .50
7 Thomas Elliott, Jay Purcell .50
8 Dell Curry 5.00
9 Lisa Pikalek .50
10 Tony Kennedy .50
11 Vaughn Hebron 2.00
12 Logo Card .50

1988-89 Wake Forest

The 16-card, standard-size set was sponsored by Adolescent Care Unit of Almanac Health Services, local law enforcement agencies and Wake Forest University. The card fronts have black and yellow borders with the Demon Deacons logo in the lower left corner. The backs feature career highlights and safety tips.

MT
Complete Set (16): 20.00
Common Player: 1.50
1 Tony Black 1.50
2 Cal Boyd 1.50
3 David Carlyle 1.50
4 Darryl Cheeley 1.50
5 Sam Ivy 2.00
6 Antonio Johnson 1.50
7 Daric Keys 1.50
8 Chris King 3.00
9 Ralph Kitley 1.50
10 Derrick McQueen 1.50
11 Phil Medlin 1.50
12 Steve Ray 1.50
13 Todd Sanders 1.50
14 Robert Siler 1.50
15 Bob Staak CO 1.50
16 Tom Wise 1.50

1991 Washington

The 17-card, standard-size set was sponsored by Prime Sports Northwest and TCI Cablevision of Washington. The set contains cards of players from both the men's and women's teams. The cards are unnumbered and are listed below in alphabetical order within sex.

MT
Complete Set (17): 10.00
Common Player: .75
Dion Brown .75
Tim Caviezel .75
James French .75
Mike Hayward .75
Todd Lautenbach .75
Doug Meekins 1.00
Brent Merritt .75
Lynn Nance CO 1.00
Quentin Youngblood .75
Tara Davis .75
Karen Deden .75
Chris Gobrecht CO .75
Erika Hardwick .75
Jocelyn McIntire .75
Laurie Merlino .75
Diana Moore .75
Dianne Williams .75

1991-92 Washington State

The 12-card, standard-size set was sponsored by Prime Sports Northwest and Cablevision. The set arrived as part of a perforated sheet with three rows of four cards each. The set features players from both the men's and women's teams and the cards are unnumbered.

		MT
Complete Set (12):		8.00
Common Player:		.75
	Rob Corkrum	1.00
	Ken Critton	1.00
	Eddie Hill	1.00
	Tyrone Maxey	1.00
	Sean Tresvant	1.00
	Joey Warmenhoven	1.00
	Janel Benton, Erika Wheeler	.75
	Lori Lollis	.75
	Heather Norman	.75
	Camille Thompson, Kathy Weber	.75
	Darla Williamson	.75
	Team Photo Women's Basketball	1.00

1996-97 Weber State

This 13-card set features a color photo on the card front with a white border. A basketball logo that says "Weber Fever" is located on the front, as is the team and player's name. The back has a player profile and the logos of Weber State and Matrix Marketing at the bottom.

		MT
Complete Set (13):		6.00
Common Player:		.50
1	Damien Baskerville	.50
2	Ryan Cuff	.50
3	Jimmy DeGraffenried	.50
4	Bryan Emery	.50
5	Joey Haws	.50
6	Squirt Hicks	.50
7	Eric Ketcham	.50
8	Bart McIntire	.50
9	Justyn Nielsen	.50
10	Andy Smith	.50
11	Justin Tebbs	.50
12	Women's Basketball Team	.50
13	WSU Cheerleaders	.50

1977-78 West Virginia Schedules

The set of four schedules measure 2-1/2" x 3-1/2" feature a player front with a schedule back. The player photo on the front is in black and white.

		NM
Complete Set (4):		8.00
Common Player:		2.00
1	Sid Bostick	2.00
2	Dennis Hosey	2.00
3	Tommy Roberts	2.00
4	Maurice Robinson	4.00

1978-79 West Virginia Schedules

The 15-card, 2-5/16" x 3-1/2" schedule set featured player headshots on the front with the team schedule on the back. The schedule cards are unnumbered and checklisted in alphabetical order.

		NM
Complete Set (15):		18.00
Common Player:		1.50
	Gale Catlett CO	3.00
	John Goots	1.50
	Vic Herbert	1.50
	Dennis Hosey	1.50
	Junius Lewis	1.50
	Steve McCune	1.50
	Lowes Moore	3.00
	Noah Moore	1.50
	Greg Nance	1.50
	Dana Perno	1.50
	Mike Richardson	1.50
	Jeff Szczepanski	1.50
	Lanny Van Eman ACO	3.00
	Coaching Staff	1.50
	Eastern Eight Logo	1.50

1980-81 Wichita State

The 15-card, standard-size set was sponsored by Service Auto Glass and the Wichita Police Department. The fronts feature a player closeup with "Love Ya Shockers" along the top right edge. The backs feature "If you see a crime, CALL 911" prominently.

		NM
Complete Set (15):		75.00
Common Player:		3.00
1	Antoine Carr	40.00
2	Mike Denny	3.00
3	Zarko Djuricic	3.00
4	James Gibbs	3.00
5	Jay Jackson	3.00
6	Mike Jones	3.00
7	Ozell Jones	6.00
8	Eric Kuhn	3.00
9	Cliff Levingston	25.00
10	Tony Martin	3.00
11	Karl Papke	3.00
12	Zoran Rdovic	3.00
13	Gene Smithson CO	3.00
14	Randy Smithson	3.00
15	Team Photo	5.00

1987-88 Wichita State

The 12-card, standard-size set was sponsored by Scholfield Honda, KNSS Nes Radio (1240 AM) and Riverside Hospital. Sponsor logos appear above the color player photos on the fronts with "Tips From The Shockers" highlighting the backs.

		MT
Complete Set (12):		35.00
Common Player:		2.00
1	John Cooper	2.00
2	Aaron Davis	2.00
3	John Felton	2.00
4	Eddie Fogler CO	8.00
5	Steve Grayer	2.00
6	Joe Griffin	2.00
7	Paul Guffrovich	2.00
8	Tom Kosich	2.00
9	Dwayne Praylow	2.00
10	Dwight Praylow	2.00
11	Sasha Radunovich	8.00
12	Team Photo	6.00

1988-89 Wichita State

The 11-card, standard-size set was sponsored by KWCH TV, KNSS Radio and Schofield Auto Dealership. The fronts feature posed photos with anti-drug messages on the unnumbered backs.

		MT
Complete Set (11):		20.00
Common Player:		2.00
	Keith Bonds	2.00
	John Cooper	2.00
	Aaron Davis	2.00
	Darin Dugger	2.00
	John Felter	2.00
	Steve Graver	2.00
	Paul Guffrovich	2.00
	Phil Mendelson	2.00
	Dwayne Praylow	2.00
	Dwight Praylow	2.00
	Sasha Radunovich	5.00

1989-90 Wisconsin

The 14-card set sponsored by the USDA Forest Service, was issued on an unperforated sheet and after cutting, each card measured the standard 2-1/2" x 3-1/2". The card fronts feature "Wisconsin" prominently along the top border with a Smokey The Bear headshot in the lower left corner. The backs have a forestry illustration.

		MT
Complete Set (14):		10.00
Common Player:		1.00
1	Bobby Douglass	1.00
2	John Ellenson	1.00
3	Brian Good	1.00
4	Damon Harrell	1.00
5	Larry Hisle Jr.	1.25
6	Danny Jones	1.00
7	Jason Johnsen	1.00
8	Grant Johnson	1.00
9	Tim Locum	1.00
10	Carlton McGee	1.00
11	Kurt Portmann	1.00
12	Willie Simms	1.25
13	Patrick Tompkins	1.00
14	Steve Yoder CO	2.00

1991 Wooden Award Winners

This set features 14 winners of the John R. Wooden Award, college basketball's most prestigious award. Each player is featured on the card front wearing his collegiate uniform. Most of the fronts have color photos, except for some black-and-white photos on cards devoted to Wooden. The sets were produced by Little Sun, of Monrovia, Calif., as indicated on the front by its logo in the upper left corner. The left side of the is a grey panel, interrupted at the bottom by a lavender bar which gives the card's title. The card back is numbered and, if it is a player card, provides a color photo of the player and biographical information. If it is a Wooden card, it details his career highlights. There were 28,000 numbered sets produced; this number is indicated on an accompanying certificate. A card album was also produced for the set.

		MT
Complete Set (21):		15.00
Common Player:		.50
1	John Wooden (1991)	1.00
2	Wooden Trophy	.50
3	John Wooden (Purdue)	.50
4	John Wooden (UCLA)	.50
5	Wooden Summer Camp	.50
6	Duke Llewellyn	.60
7	Marques Johnson	.75
8	Phil Ford	.60
9	Larry Bird	3.00
10	Darrell Griffith	.60
11	Danny Ainge	1.00
12	Ralph Sampson	.50
13	Michael Jordan	8.00
14	Chris Mullin	1.00
15	Walter Berry	.50
16	David Robinson	2.00
17	Danny Manning	.75
18	Sean Elliott	.75
19	Lionel Simmons	.75
20	Larry Johnson	1.00
21	Press Conference 1991	.50

1991-92 Wright State

The 18-card, standard-size set was sponsored by Synergy Building Systems, Inc. The fronts feature color action shots with black, green and lime geometric shapes in a yellow background. The horizontal backs contain stat and bio information.

		MT
Complete Set (18):		12.00
Common Player:		1.00
1	Scott Blair	1.00
2	Lincoln Bramlage	1.00
3	Bill Edwards	2.00
4	Mike Haley II	1.00
5	Sean Hammonds	1.25
6	Rob Haucke	1.00
7	Delme Herriman	1.25
8	Andy Holderman	1.25
9	Chris McGuire	1.00
10	Marcus Mumphrey	1.00
11	Mike Nahar	1.25
12	Renaldo O'Neal	1.00
13	Jon Ramey	1.00
14	Dan Skeoch	1.00
15	Ralph Underhill CO	1.50
16	Jeff Unverferth	1.00
17	Eric Wills	1.00
18	Coaching Staff (Ralph Underhill, Jim Brown, Jack Butler, Jim Ehler)	1.00

1993-94 Wright State

The 17-card, standard-size set features green and yellow borders with the horizontal backs having stat and bio information. The cards are unnumbered and checklisted below in alphabetical order.

		MT
Complete Set (17):		10.00
Common Player:		.75
	Scott Blair	.75
	Sterling Collins	.75
	Sean Hammonds	1.00
	Delme Herriman	1.00
	Andy Holderman	1.00
	Rick Martinez	1.25
	Mike Nahar	1.00
	Jon Ramey	.75
	Dan Skeoch	.75
	Jason Smith	.75
	Ralph Underhill CO	1.00
	Rob Welch	1.25
	Eric Wills	.75
	Daryl Woods	1.00
	Assistant Coaches (Jim Brown, Jack Butler, Jim Ehler)	.75
	Mid-Continent Champs	1.00
	Student Assistants (Brad Hess, Brian Kelly, Tom Rhoades, Matt Brown)	.75

1994-95 Wright State

The 21-card, standard-size set was sponsored by Cap 'n Bogey's Family Entertainment Center and Fairborn Camera and Video and the card front features the player's name and uniform number vertically along the left side. The horizontal backs have a posed shot with player career highlights.

		MT
Complete Set (21):		10.00
Common Player:		.75
1	Ralph Underhill CO	1.00
2	Quincy Brann	.75
3	Jon Ramey	.75
4	Eric Wills	.75
5	Daryl Woods	.75
6	Delme Herriman	1.00
7	Jason Smith	.75
8	Bilaal Neal	.75
9	Keith Blankenship	.75
10	Mike Conner	.75
11	Rick Martinez	1.00
12	Vitaly Potapenko	.75
13	Rob Welch	1.00
14	Thad Burton	.75
15	Antuan Johnson	.75
16	Derek Watkins	.75
17	Jim Brown ACO, Jack Brown ACO, Jim Ehler ACO	.75
18	Student Assistants (Matt Brown, Skip Carter, Joe Dick, Brad Hess, Dela Angela Mayho)	.75
19	Rowdy Raider (Mascot)	.75
20	Cap'n Bogey	.75
NNO	Team Photo	1.00

1994-95 Wyoming

The 16-card set was issued on perforated sheets that measured 10" x 14" and when separated, the cards measure the standard size. Sponsored by the USDA Forest Service, the card fronts have a posed color shot with a Smokey The Bear headshot centered along the lower bottom border. The backs have a fire prevention illustration.

		MT
Complete Set (16):		18.00
Common Player:		.75
1	Jeff Allen	.75
2	H.L. Coleman	.75
3	Chris Haslam	.75
4	Billy Hessel	.75
5	Savalious (Sly) Johnson	.75
6	Pat Kelsey	.75
7	Theo Ratliff	10.00
8	Jeron Roberts	.75
9	Gregg Sawyer	.75
10	Aaron Smith	.75
11	Bobby Traylor	1.00
12	LaDrell Whitehead	.75
13	Alma Mater	.75
14	Cowboy Joe Song	.75
15	Team Logo	.75
16	Team Logo	.75

1994-95 Wyoming Women

The 16-card set was issued on a 10" x 14" perforated sheet with four rows of four cards. When the cards are separated, they measure the standard size. The set is sponsored by the USDA Forest Service and is virtually identical in design with the men's set of the same year. A fire prevention illustration highlights the back.

		MT
Complete Set (16):		7.00
Common Player:		.50
1	Lauren Andrade	.50
2	Amy Burnett	.50
3	Jesseca Cross	.50
4	Casey Crouch	.50
5	Heather McAdams	.50
6	Laura Peisa	.50
7	Jennifer Rider	.50
8	Nichole Rider	.50
9	Jennifer Russell	.50
10	Courtney Stapp	.50
11	Jessica Thompson	.50
12	Rebecca Tomlin	.50
13	Alma Mater	.50
14	Cowboy Joe Song	.50
15	Team Logo	.50
16	Team Logo	.50

BASKETBALL HALL OF FAME AUTOGRAPH GUIDE

Kareem Abdul-Jabbar (Lew Alcindor) (1947-) 1995
Basketball . . . .$100-$150
Cut signature $15
3x5 index card $25
8x10 photograph . . . .$40-$50
Signed as Lew Alcindor
Basketball $800
8x10 photograph . . . .$200-$400

Nate Archibald (1948-) 1991
Basketball . . . .$90-$110
Cut signature $6
3x5 index card $10
8x10 photograph . . . .$15-$20

Paul Arizin (1928-) 1977
Basketball $100
Cut signature $5
3x5 index card $10
8x10 photograph . . . .$20-$30

Red Auerbach (1917-) 1968
Basketball . . . .$150-$175
Cut signature . . . .$15-$25
3x5 index card . . . .$20-$30
8x10 photograph . . . .$40-$50

Thomas Barlow (1896-1983) 1980
Basketball . . . . .Unknown
Cut signature . . . .$10-$15
3x5 index card . . . .$15-$20
8x10 photograph . . . .$30-$40

Rick Barry (1944-) 1987
Basketball . . . .$100-$125
Cut signature . . . .$5-$8
3x5 index card . . . .$5-$10
8x10 photograph . . . .$20-$25

Elgin Baylor (1934-) 1976
Basketball . . . .$100-$125
Cut signature . . . .$5-$10
3x5 index card . . . .$8-$10
8x10 photograph . . . .$30-$40

John Beckman (1895-1968) 1972
Basketball . . . . .Unknown
Cut signature . . . .$20-$25
3x5 index card . . . .$25-$30
8x10 photograph . . . .$40-$50

Clair Bee (1896-1983) 1967
Basketball . . . . .Unknown
Cut signature . . . .$25-$30
3x5 index card . . . .$40-$50
8x10 photograph . . . .$75-$100

Walt Bellamy (1939-) 1992
Basketball . . . .$75-$100
Cut signature $5
3x5 index card $10
8x10 photograph . . . .$15-$20

Danny Biasone (1909-1992) 2000
Basketball $100
Cut signature . . . .$10-$15
3x5 index card . . . .$10-$15
8x10 photograph . . . .$25-$40

Sergei Belov (1944-) 1992
Basketball . . . .$75-$100
Cut signature $5
3x5 index card . . . .$6-$8
8x10 photograph . . . .$15-$17

Dave Bing (1943-) 1990
Basketball . . . .$100-$110
Cut signature . . . .$4-$5
3x5 index card $10
8x10 photograph . . . .$15-$18

Larry Bird (1956-) 1998
Basketball $200
Cut Signature . . . .$25-$30
3x5 index card . . . .$30-$40
8x10 photograph . . . .$70-$80

Carol Blazejowski (1956-) 1994
Basketball . . . .$75-$100
Cut signature $5
3x5 index card . . . .$6-$7
8x10 photograph . . . .$15-$17

Ernest Blood (1872-1955) 1960
Basketball . . . . .Unknown
Cut signature . . . .$40-$50
3x5 index card . . . .$40-$50
8x10 photograph . . . .$100-$150

Bennie Borgmann (1899-1978) 1961
Basketball . . . . .Unknown
Cut signature . . . .$10-$15
3x5 index card . . . .$15-$20
8x10 photograph . . . .$40-$50

Bill Bradley (1943-) 1982
Basketball . . . .$125-$150
Cut signature . . . .$8-$12
3x5 index card $15
8x10 photograph . . . .$60-$75

Joseph Brennan (1900-1989) 1974
Basketball . . . . .Unknown
Cut signature . . . .$8-$10
3x5 index card . . . .$10-$15
8x10 photograph . . . .$30-$40

Lou Carnesseca (1925-) 1991
Basketball $100
Cut signature $7
3x5 index card $10
8x10 photograph . . . .$12-$16

Alfred Cervi (1917-) 1984
Basketball $100
Cut signature . . . .$4-$6
3x5 index card $10
8x10 photograph . . . .$12-$14

Wilt Chamberlain (1936-1999) 1978
Basketball $400
Cut signature . . . .$40-$50
3x5 index card . . . .$80-$90
8x10 photograph $200

John Chaney 2001
Basketball $100
Cut signature $5
3x5 index card $7
8x10 photograph $20

Jody Conradt (1941-) 1998
Basketball . . . .$75-$100
Cut signature $5
3x5 index card $7
8x10 photograph . . . .$12-$15

Charles Cooper (1926-1984) 1976
Basketball . . . . .Unknown
Cut signature . . . .$10-$15
3x5 index card . . . .$15-$20
8x10 photograph . . . .$35-$40

Bob Cousy (1928-) 1970
Basketball . . . .$125-$150
Cut signature . . . .$10-$15
3x5 index card . . . .$10-$20
8x10 photograph . . . .$25-$30

Dave Cowens (1948-) 1991
Basketball . . . .$100-$125
Cut signature . . . .$6-$7
3x5 index card $7
8x10 photograph $30

Denny Crum (1937-) 1994
Basketball . . . .$100-$125
Cut signature . . . .$6-$7
3x5 index card $7
8x10 photograph . . . .$20-$30

Billy Cunningham (1943-) 1986
Basketball $110
Cut signature . . . .$6-$7

3x5 index card $9
8x10 photograph .... $15-$17

Chuck Daly (1930-) 1994
Basketball .... $85-$100
Cut signature $5
3x5 index card $7
8x10 photograph .... $15-$18

Robert Davies (1920-1990) 1969
Basketball .... $100-$125
Cut signature $20
3x5 index card $25
8x10 photograph .... $40-$50

Forrest DeBernardi (1899-1970) 1961
Basketball .... Unknown
Cut signature .... $15-$20
3x5 index card .... $20-$30
8x10 photograph .... $40-$60

Dave DeBusschere (1940-) 1982
Basketball .... $125-$150
Cut signature .... $5-$6
3x5 index card $8
8x10 photograph .... $15-$20

Henry Dehnert (1898-1979) 1968
Basketball .... Unknown
Cut signature .... $10-$15
3x5 index card .... $15-$20
8x10 photograph .... $30-$50

Antonio Diaz-Miguel (1933-2000) 1997
Basketball $100
Cut signature .... $5-$10
3x5 index card .... $8-$10
8x10 photograph .... $15-$25

Anne Donovan (1961-) 1995
Basketball $75-100
Cut signature .... $5-$6
3x5 index card $8
8x10 photograph .... $15-$20

Wayne Embry (1937-) 1999
Basketball .... $80-$100
Cut signature $6
3x5 index card $10
8x10 photograph .... $15-$18

Paul Endacott (1902-1977) 1971
Basketball .... Unknown
Cut signature .... $10-$20
3x5 index card .... $15-$25
8x10 photograph .... $30-$50

Alex English (1954-) 1997
Basketball .... $100-$125
Cut signature .... $8-$10
3x5 index card .... $10-$12
8x10 photo .... $20-$30

Julius Erving (1950-) 1992
Basketball .... $175-$225
Cut signature .... $15-$20
3x5 index card .... $25-$35
8x10 photograph .... $30-$50
Authenticated Jersey $700

Bud Foster (1906-1996) 1964
Basketball $125
Cut signature .... $20-$30
3x5 index card .... $25-$35
8x10 photograph .... $40-$50

Walt Frazier (1945-) 1987
Basketball .... $100-$125
Cut signature $15
3x5 index card $20
8x10 photograph $20

Max "Marty" Friedman (1889-1986) 1971
Basketball .... Unknown
Cut signature .... $10-$15
3x5 index card .... $10-$20
8x10 photograph .... $30-$40

Joe Fulks (1921-1976) 1977
Basketball .... Unknown
Cut signature .... $15-$20
3x5 index card .... $25-$35
8x10 photograph .... $40-$60

Clarence Gaines (1923-) 1981
Basketball $100
Cut signature .... $7-$9
3x5 index card .... $8-$10
8x10 photograph .... $15-$20

Laddie Gale (1917-1996) 1976
Basketball $100
Cut signature .... $7-$10
3x5 index card .... $10-$15
8x10 photograph .... $20-$25

Harry Gallatin (1927-) 1990
Basketball .... $100-$110
Cut signature .... $6-$8
3x5 index card $15
8x10 photograph .... $15-$18

William "Pop" Gates (1917-1999) 1988
Basketball $125
Cut signature .... $8-$10
3x5 index card .... $12-$15
8x10 photograph .... $20-$25

George Gervin (1952-) 1996
Basketball .... $110-$120
Cut signature $6
3x5 index card $10
8x10 photograph .... $20-$25

Tom Gola (1933-) 1975
Basketball .... $90-$100
Cut signature $5
3x5 index card $8
8x10 photograph .... $15-$18

Alexsandr Gomelsky (1928-) 1995
Basketball .... $75-$100
Cut signature $5
3x5 index card $7
8x10 photograph .... $15-$17

Gail Goodrich (1943-) 1996
Basketball .... $100-$110
Cut signature .... $6-$8
3x5 index card $10
8x10 photograph .... $15-$20

Edward Gottlieb (1898-1979) 1972
Basketball .... Unknown
Cut signature .... $10-$15
3x5 index card .... $15-$20
8x10 photograph .... $30-$50

Hal Greer (1936-) 1981
Basketball $100
Cut signature $4
3x5 index card .... $3-$6
8x10 photograph .... $15-$20

Robert Gruenig (1913-1958) 1963
Basketball .... Unknown
Cut signature .... $20-$30
3x5 index card .... $30-$50
8x10 photograph .... $100-$150

Cliff Hagan (1931-) 1977
Basketball $125
Cut signature .... $4-$7
3x5 index card $6
8x10 photograph $20

Alex Hannum (1923-) 1998
Basketball .... $75-$100
Cut signature $5
3x5 index card $6
8x10 photograph .... $15-$17

Victor Hanson (1903-1982) 1960
Basketball .... Unknown
Cut signature .... $10-$15
3x5 index card .... $15-$25
8x10 photograph .... $40-$60

Lusia Harris-Stewart (1955-) 1992
Basketball .... $75-$100
Cut signature $5
3x5 index card .... $6-$7
8x10 photograph .... $15-$17

Marv Harshman (1917-) 1985
Basketball .... $75-$100
Cut signature .... $5-$6
3x5 index card .... $7-$8
8x10 photograph .... $15-$17

Don Haskins (1930-) 1997
Basketball .... $75-$100
Cut signature $5
3x5 index card .... $6-$7
8x10 photograph .... $15-$17

John Havlicek (1940-) 1983

Basketball . . . . $150-$160
Cut signature . . . . $10-$15
3x5 index card . . . . $15-$20
8x10 photograph . . . . $25-$40

Connie Hawkins (1942-) 1991
Basketball $125
Cut signature $8
3x5 index card $10
8x10 photograph . . . . $20-$25

Elvin Hayes (1945-) 1990
Basketball . . . . $100-$125
Cut signature . . . . $5-$8
3x5 index card . . . . $8-$10
8x10 photograph . . . . $15-$20

Marques Haynes (1926-) 1998
Basketball . . . . $100-$120
Cut signature $7
3x5 index card $10
8x10 photograph $20

Tommy Heinsohn (1934-) 1985
Basketball . . . . $100-$125
Cut signature $6
3x5 index card $8
8x10 photograph . . . . $30-$40

Nat Holman (1896-1995) 1964
Basketball $150
Cut signature . . . . $10-$15
3x5 index card . . . . $15-$20
8x10 photograph . . . . $75-$100

Red Holzman (1920-1998) 1985
Basketball . . . . $125-$150
Cut signature . . . . $12-$15
3x5 index card . . . . $15-$25
8x10 photograph . . . . $55-$65

Robert Houbregs (1932-) 1986
Basketball $110
Cut signature . . . . $5-$7
3x5 index card $10
8x10 photograph $15

Bailey Howell (1937-) 1997
Basketball $100
Cut signature` . . . . $6-$8
3x5 index card $10
8x10 photo . . . . $15-$20

Chuck Hyatt (1908-1978) 1959
Basketball . . . . Unknown
Cut signature . . . . $10-$20
3x5 index card . . . . $15-$25
8x10 photograph . . . . $40-$60

Henry Iba (1904-1993) 1968
Basketball $150
Cut signature . . . . $10-$20
3x5 index card . . . . $15-$25
8x10 photograph . . . . $30-$50

Edward "Ned" Irish (1905-1982) 1964

Basketball . . . . Unknown
Cut signature . . . . $10-$20
3x5 index card . . . . $15-$25
8x10 photograph . . . . $40-$60

Dan Issel (1948-) 1992
Basketball . . . . $100-$115
Cut signature $7
3x5 index card $12
8x10 photograph $15

Buddy Jeannette (1917-1998) 1994
Basketball $120
Cut signature . . . . $4-$7
3x5 index card $9
8x10 photograph . . . . $20-$30

William Johnson (1911-1980) 1976
Basketball . . . . Unknown
Cut signature . . . . $10-$15
3x5 index card . . . . $15-$25
8x10 photograph . . . . $40-$60

Neil Johnston (1929-1978) 1989
Basketball . . . . Unknown
Cut signature . . . . $10-$20
3x5 index card . . . . $15-$25
8x10 photograph . . . . $40-$60

K.C. Jones (1932-) 1988
Basketball $100
Cut signature $6
3x5 index card $8
8x10 photograph $20

Sam Jones (1933-) 1983
Basketball . . . . $100-$120
Cut signature . . . . $6-$8
3x5 index card $10
8x10 photograph . . . . $20-$30

Bobby Knight (1931-) 1990
Basketball . . . . $100-$125
Cut signature . . . . $10-$15
3x5 index card . . . . $15-$20
8x10 photograph . . . . $25-$35

Edward Krause (1913-1942) 1975
Basketball . . . . Unknown
Cut signature . . . . $50-$75
3x5 index card . . . . $75-$100
8x10 photograph . . . . $150-$200

Mike Krzyzewski 2001
Basketball . . . . $100-$125
Cut signature . . . . $8-$10
3x5 index card . . . . $10-$15
8x10 photograph . . . . $20-$30

John Kundla (1916-) 1995
Basketball . . . . $75-$100
Cut signature $5
3x5 index card . . . . $6-$7
8x10 photograph . . . . $15-$17

Bob Kurland (1924-) 1961

Basketball $110
Cut signature $5
3x5 index card $10
8x10 photograph . . . . $15-$20

Bob Lanier (1948-) 1992
Basketball $100
Cut signature $7
3x5 index card $10
8x10 photograph $15

Joe Lapchick (1900-1970) 1966
Basketball . . . . Unknown
Cut signature . . . . $20-$30
3x5 index card . . . . $25-$35
8x10 photograph . . . . $75-$100

Nancy Lieberman-Cline (1958-) 1996
Basketball . . . . $75-$100
Cut signature $5
3x5 index card . . . . $7-$8
8x10 photograph . . . . $15-$17

Clyde Lovellette (1929-) 1987
Basketball $110
Cut signature . . . . $4-$7
3x5 index card $9
8x10 photograph . . . . $15-$17

Jerry Lucas (1940-) 1979
Basketball $125
Cut signature $5
3x5 index card $10
8x10 photograph . . . . $15-$20

Hank Luisetti (1916-) 1959
Basketball $125
Cut signature $7
3x5 index card $12
8x10 photograph . . . . $15-$25

Ed Macauley (1928-) 1960
Basketball . . . . $100-$125
Cut signature . . . . $5-$10
3x5 index card . . . . $8-$10
8x10 photograph . . . . $20-$25

Moses Malone 2001
Basketball . . . . $100-$125
Cut signature . . . . $6-$7
3x5 index card $7
8x10 photograph . . . . $25-$30

Pete Maravich (1947-1988) 1987
Basketball $1,000
Cut signature . . . . $50-$75
3x5 index card . . . . $60-$80
8x10 photograph . . . . $250-$300

Slater Martin (1925-) 1981
Basketball . . . . $100-$125
Cut signature . . . . $4-$6
3x5 index card $9
8x10 photograph . . . . $15-$20

Bob McAdoo (1961-) 2000

Basketball . . . .$100-$110
Cut signature . . . .$6-$8
3x5 index card $9
8x10 photograph . . . .$20-$25

Branch McCracken (1908-1970) 1960
Basketball . . . . .Unknown
Cut signature . . . .$10-$15
3x5 index card . . . .$15-$25
8x10 photograph . . . .$40-$60

Jack McCracken (1911-1958) 1962
Basketball . . . . .Unknown
Cut signature . . . .$20-$30
3x5 index card . . . .$30-$50
8x10 photograph . . . .$150-$200

Bobby McDermott (1914-) 1987
Basketball $110
Cut signature . . . .$6-$7
3x5 index card $14
8x10 photograph . . . .$15-$20

Al McGuire (1928-2001) 1991
Basketball . . . .$100-$150
Cut signature . . . .$7-$10
3x5 index card . . . .$10-$15
8x10 photograph . . . .$35-$45

Dick McGuire (1926-) 1992
Basketball . . . .$75-$100
Cut signature $5
3x5 index card $10
8x10 photograph . . . .$15-$20

Frank McGuire (1916-1994) 1976
Basketball . . . .$150-$200
Cut signature . . . .$10-$20
3x5 index card . . . .$15-$25
8x10 photograph . . . .$50-$75

Kevin McHale (1957-) 1999
Basketball $110
Cut signature $8
3x5 index card $10
8x10 photograph . . . .$18-$20

John McLendon (1915-1999) 1979
Basketball $100
Cut signature . . . .$6-$7
3x5 index card . . . .$8-$9
8x10 photograph . . . .$17-$20

Walter Meanwell (1884-1953) 1959
Basketball . . . . .Unknown
Cut signature . . . .$20-$30
3x5 index card . . . .$30-$50
8x10 photograph . . . .$150-$200

Ray Meyer (1913-) 1978
Basketball . . . .$100-$125
Cut signature $15
3x5 index card $20
8x10 photograph . . . .$20-$30

Ann Meyers (1955-) 1993

Basketball . . . .$90-$100
Cut signature $5
3x5 index card $6
8x10 photograph . . . .$15-$20

George Mikan (1924-) 1959
Basketball . . . .$125-$150
Cut signature . . . .$10-$20
3x5 index card . . . .$15-$25
8x10 photograph . . . .$40-$50

Vern Mikkelsen (1928-) 1995
Basketball $110
Cut signature $6
3x5 index card $9
8x10 photograph $20

Cheryl Miller (1964-) 1995
Basketball $100
Cut signature $6
3x5 index card $8
8x10 photograph . . . .$20-$25

William Mokray (1907-1974) 1965
Basketball . . . . .Unknown
Cut signature . . . .$15-$20
3x5 index card . . . .$25-$30
8x10 photograph . . . .$50-$75

Billie Moore (1943-) 1999
Basketball . . . .$75-$100
Cut signature $5
3x5 index card . . . .$6-$7
8x10 photograph . . . .$15-$17

Earl Monroe (1944-) 1989
Basketball . . . .$100-$125
Cut signature . . . .$8-$10
3x5 index card $12
8x10 photograph . . . .$20-$25

Calvin Murphy (1948-) 1992
Basketball $100
Cut signature $6
3x5 index card $8
8x10 photograph $15

Charles Murphy (1907-1992) 1960
Basketball . . . .$150-$200
Cut signature . . . .$10-$15
3x5 index card . . . .$15-$20
8x10 photograph . . . .$30-$40

James Naismith (1861-1939) 1959
Basketball $1,000
Cut signature $200
3x5 index card $300
8x10 photograph $500

C. M. Newton (1931-) 2000
Basketball $100
Cut signature $6
3x5 index card $8
8x10 photograph . . . .$15-$17

Aleksandar Nikolic (1924-2000) 1998

Basketball $100
Cut signature $8
3x5 index card $10
8x10 photograph . . . .$20-$25

Larry O'Brien (1917-1990) 1990
Basketball . . . .$150-$200
Cut signature . . . .$25-$30
3x5 index card . . . .$30-$40
8x10 photograph . . . .$50-$75

Harlan Page (1887-1965) 1962
Basketball . . . . .Unknown
Cut signature . . . .$15-$20
3x5 index card . . . .$25-$30
8x10 photograph . . . .$75-$100

Bob Pettit (1932-) 1970
Basketball . . . .$125-$150
Cut signature . . . .$5-$10
3x5 index card . . . .$10-$15
8x10 photograph . . . .$20-$25

Andy Phillip (1922-) 1961
Basketball $100
Cut signature . . . .$5-$7
3x5 index card $7
8x10 photograph . . . .$15-$25

Maurice Podoloff (1890-1985) 1973
Basketball . . . .$150-$200
Cut signature . . . .$10-$15
3x5 index card . . . .$15-$20
8x10 photograph . . . .$30-$50

Jim Pollard (1922-1993) 1977
Basketball . . . .$100-$150
Cut signature . . . .$5-$10
3x5 index card . . . .$10-$15
8x10 photograph . . . .$30-$40

Frank Ramsey (1931-) 1981
Basketball $100
Cut signature . . . .$6-$7
3x5 index card $10
8x10 photograph $15

Jack Ramsey (1925-) 1991
Basketball . . . .$100-$125
Cut signature $7
3x5 index card $10
8x10 photograph $20

Willis Reed (1942-) 1981
Basketball . . . .$100-$125
Cut signature $9
3x5 index card $12
8x10 photograph . . . .$20-$25

Arnie Risen (1924-) 1998
Basketball $110
Cut Signature $10
3x5 index card $12
8x10 photograph . . . .$20-$25

Oscar Robertson (1938-) 1979

Basketball $125
Cut signature $8
3x5 index card $10
8x10 photograph ....$25-$35

John Roosma (1900-1983) 1961
Basketball ....Unknown
Cut signature ....$10-$15
3x5 index card ....$15-$20
8x10 photograph ....$40-$60

Adolph Rupp (1901-1977) 1968
Basketball................$200-$300
Cut signature ....$20-$30
3x5 index card ....$30-$50
8x10 photograph ....$75-$100

Bill Russell (1934-) 1974
Basketball $350
Cut signature ....$25-$50
3x5 index card ....$30-$50
8x10 photograph...........$125-$150

John Russell (1902-1973) 1974
Basketball ....Unknown
Cut signature ....$15-$20
3x5 index card ....$20-$25
8x10 photograph ....$40-$60

Abe Saperstein (1901-1966) 1970
Basketball................$200-$300
Cut signature ....$25-$35
3x5 index card ....$40-$60
8x10 photograph...........$100-$150

Dolph Schayes (1928-) 1972
Basketball................$100-$125
Cut signature $10
3x5 index card $15
8x10 photograph ....$15-$20

Ernest Schmidt (1911-1986) 1973
Basketball................$110-$150
Cut signature ....$10-$15
3x5 index card ....$10-$20
8x10 photograph ....$40-$60

John Schommer (1884-1960) 1959
Basketball ....Unknown
Cut signature ....$25-$40
3x5 index card ....$30-$50
8x10 photograph ....$75-$100

Barney Sedran (1891-1964) 1962
Basketball ....Unknown
Cut signature ....$25-$40
3x5 index card ....$30-$50
8x10 photograph ....$75-$100

Bill Sharman (1926-) 1975
Basketball $100
Cut signature $5
3x5 index card $7
8x10 photograph $20

Dean Smith (1931-) 1982

TRI-STAR PRODUCTIONS

Basketball $150
Cut signature ....$30-$40
3x5 index card $40
8x10 photograph ....$45-$55

Amos Alonzo Stagg (1862-1965) 1959
Basketball ....Unknown
Cut signature ....$20-$30
3x5 index card ....$25-$50
8x10 photograph..........$150-$200

Christian Steinmetz (1887-1963) 1961
Basketball ....Unknown
Cut signature ....$15-$20
3x5 index card ....$25-$30
8x10 photograph ....$75-$100

Earl Strom (1927-1994) 1995
Basketball................$150-$200
Cut signature ....$10-$15
3x5 index card ....$15-$20
8x10 photograph ....$30-$50

Pat Summitt (1952-) 2000
Basketball ....$75-$100
Cut signature ....$5-$6
3x5 index card ....$7-$8
8x10 photograph ....$15-$17

Isiah Thomas (1961-) 2000
Basketball $125
Cut signature $10
3x5 index card $12
8x10 photograph ....$25-$30

David Thompson (1954-) 1996
Basketball $110
Cut signature ....$5-$8
3x5 index card $7
8x10 photograph ....$20-$25

John Thompson (1906-1990) 1962
Basketball................$150-$200
Cut signature ....$10-$15
3x5 index card ....$15-$25
8x10 photograph ....$40-$60

John R. Thompson (1941-) 1999
Basketball $100
Cut signature $7

3x5 index card $9
8x10 photograph ....$20-$25
Nate Thurmond (1941-) 1984
Basketball $115
Cut signature ....$6-$8
3x5 index card $12
8x10 photograph ....$15-$20

Arthur Trester (1878-1944) 1995
Basketball ....Unknown
Cut signature ....$100-$150
3x5 index card ....$100-$150
8x10 photograph...........$200-$300

Jack Twyman (1934-) 1982
Basketball................$100-$125
Cut signature ....$6-$9
3x5 index card ....$9-$10
8x10 photograph ....$15-$18

Wes Unseld (1946-) 1987
Basketball................$100-$110
Cut signature ....$6-$10
3x5 index card $9
8x10 photograph ....$15-$20

Robert Vandivier (1903-1993) 1974
Basketball................$100-$150
Cut signature ....$10-$15
3x5 index card ....$15-$20
8x10 photograph ....$30-$40

Edward Wachter (1883-1966) 1961
Basketball ....Unknown
Cut signature ....$15-$25
3x5 index card ....$20-$40
8x10 photograph ....$75-$100

Margaret Wade (1912-1995) 1985
Basketball................$150-$200
Cut signature ....$10-$15
3x5 index card ....$15-$25
8x10 photograph ....$40-$60

Bill Walton (1952-) 1992
Basketball $135
Cut signature $6
3x5 index card $10
8x10 photograph ....$20-$25

David Walsh (1889-1975) 1961
Basketball................$150-$175
Cut signature ....$10-$15
3x5 index card ....$15-$20
8x10 photograph ....$40-$60

Robert Wanzer (1921-) 1986
Basketball................$100-$125
Cut signature ....$5-$6
3x5 index card $10
8x10 photograph ....$16-$17

Stanley Watts (1911-2000) 1986
Basketball ....$100-$125
Cut signature ....$5-$6
3x5 index card ....$7-$8

8x10 photograph . . . .$15-$20

Clifford Wells (1896-1977) 1972
Basketball . . . . .Unknown
Cut signature . . . .$10-$15
3x5 index card . . . .$15-$20
8x10 photograph . . . .$40-$60

Jerry West (1938-) 1979
Basketball $150
Cut signature $7
3x5 index card $10
8x10 photograph . . . .$30-$40

Lenny Wilkens (1937-) 1988 and 1998
Basketball $100
Cut signature . . . .$6-$10
3x5 index card $20
8x10 photograph . . . .$12-$15

John Wooden (1910-) 1961, 1972
Basketball . . . .$115-$125
Cut signature . . . .$8-$10
3x5 index card $15
8x10 photograph . . . .$20-$30

Morgan Wootten (1931-) 2000
Basketball $100
Cut signature $6
3x5 index card . . . .$7-$8
8x10 photograph . . . .$15-$17

George Yardley (1928-) 1996
Basketball $110
Cut signature $10
3x5 signature $15
8x10 photograph . . . .$20-$25

Fred Zollner (1901-1982) 1999
Basketball $250
Cut signature . . . .$40-$50
3x5 signature . . . .$50-$60
8x10 photograph . . . .$75-$100a

BASKETBALL RETIRED-PLAYER AUTOGRAPH GUIDE

"Signed Photo" and "Signed Ball" pricing refers to an 8-by-10 signed photograph or signed basketball without an authentication system. "Auth. Photo" and "Auth. Ball" refers to a photo or basketball that has been signed and authenticated via a sticker or hologram placed on the item at the time of signing. Remember that Certificates of Authenticity are only as valuable as the reputation of the company issuing them.

	Signed 8x10	Auth.8x10	Sig'd Ball	Auth.Ball
Aguirre, Mark	15		75	
Ainge, Danny	20		90	
Barkley, Charles	45		180	320
Cartwright, Bill	15		90	
Chambers, Tom	15		75	
Cheeks, Maurice	15		90	
Cooper, Michael	15		90	
Dantley, Adrian	12		85	
Daugherty, Brad	12		90	
Dawkins, Darryl	12	25	90	
Drexler, Clyde	20		125	
Dumars, Joe	20		100	
Elliott, Sean	15		85	
Floyd, Sleepy	12		90	
Free, Lloyd "World B"	12		90	
Green, A.C.	15		85	
Harper, Derek	15		85	
Johnson, Dennis	12	20	90	
Johnson, Larry	30	85	90	
Johnson, Magic	75	115	250	350
Johnson, Marques	12		90	
Jones, Bobby	12		85	
King, Bernard	12	20	85	
Laimbeer, Bill	15		90	
Lever, Fat	12		85	
Lewis, Reggie*	60		350	
Love, Bob	12		85	
Lucas, Maurice	12		85	
Moncrief, Sidney	15		90	
Mullin, Chris	20		85	
Nance, Larry	12		85	
Parish, Robert	18		100	
Paxson, John	12		90	
Rambis, Kurt	12		85	
Robertson, Alvin	12		90	
Rodman, Dennis	30	90	125	200
Sabonis, Arvydas	15		90	
Salley, John	12		90	
Sampson, Ralph	15		75	
Seikaly, Rony	15		75	
Sikma, Jack	15		90	
Smith, Kenny	12		90	
Theus, Reggie	12		85	
Thorpe, Otis	15		75	
Webb, Spud	15		75	
Wilkins, Dominique	20		125	
Williams, Jayson	18		100	
Woolridge, Orlando	12		85	
Worthy, James	25	30	100	

Coaches

	Signed 8x10	Auth.8x10	Sig'd Ball	Auth.Ball
Brown, Larry	15		90	
Collins, Doug	20		85	
Dunleavy, Mike	18		90	
Floyd, Tim	15		90	
Jackson, Phil	75		150	
Karl, George	15		90	
Hamilton, Leonard	15		75	
Nelson, Don	15		90	
Pitino, Rick	25		120	
Popovich, Gregg	18		100	
Riley, Pat	40		125	
Rivers, Doc	15		95	
Saunders, Flip	15		85	
Scott, Byron	15		85	
Skiles, Scott	12		90	
Sloan, Jerry	18		100	
Smith, Tubby	15		90	
Summitt, Pat	15		90	
Tomjanovich, Rudy	15		90	
Van Gundy, Jeff	12		85	

***Asterisk denotes deceased player**

BASKETBALL ACTIVE-PLAYER AUTOGRAPH GUIDE

TRI-STAR PRODUCTIONS

"Signed Photo" and "Signed Ball" pricing refers to an 8-by-10 signed photograph or signed basketball without an authentication system. "Auth. Photo" and "Auth. Ball" refers to a photo or basketball that has been signed and authenticated via a sticker or hologram placed on the item at the time of signing. Remember that Certificates of Authenticity are only as valuable as the reputation of the company issuing them.

	Signed 8x10	Auth.8x10	Sig'd Ball	Auth.Ball
Abdur-Rahim, Shareef	15		90	
Allen, Ray	35		90	
Anderson, Derek	15		85	
Anderson, Kenny	13		95	
Armstrong, Darrell	15		90	
Artest, Ron	20		75	
Baker, Vin	15		95	
Barry, Brent	15		75	
Battie, Tony	15		75	
Best, Travis	15		75	
Bibby, Mike	30		90	
Billups, Chauncey	15		85	
Blaylock, Mookie	18		90	
Brand, Elton	35	75	100	100
Brandon, Terrell	15		100	
Bryant, Kobe	75	220	175	500
Camby, Marcus	20		100	130
Carter, Vince	75	140	175	250
Cassell, Sam	15		85	
Clark, Keon	15	30	75	
Cleeves, Mateen	12		80	
Coleman, Derrick	15		90	
Croshere, Austin	15		75	
Daniels, Antonio	15		75	
Davis, Antonio	15		75	
Davis, Baron	30		75	
Dickerson, Michael	15		90	
Divac, Vlade	25		85	
Doleac, Michael	15		85	
Duncan, Tim	40		150	
Ewing, Patrick	100		175	
Finley, Michael	30		100	
Fisher, Derek	20		75	
Fortson, Danny	15		75	
Francis, Steve	30		110	180
Garnett, Kevin	40		150	350
Gill, Kendall	15		85	
Gugliotta, Tom	15		90	
Hamilton, Richard	20		100	
Hardaway, Anfernee	25	60	125	
Hardaway, Tim	20	45	150	
Harrington, Al	15		75	
Hill, Grant	35		135	
Hill, Tyrone	15		75	
Horry, Robert	25	50	80	
Houston, Allan	25		80	
Howard, Juwan	20		100	
Hughes, Larry	18		100	
Hunter, Lindsey	12		70	
Iverson, Allen	60	90	160	
Jackson, Jimmy	15		75	
Jackson, Marc	15		75	
Jackson, Mark	18		85	
Jackson, Stephen	15		75	
Jamison, Antawn	20		100	
Johnson, Avery	18		85	
Johnson, DerMarr	15		75	
Jones, Eddie	20		100	
Jordan, Michael	125	550	500	1500
Kemp, Shawn	20		100	
Kidd, Jason	50	100	125	200
Kittles, Kerry	15		90	
Knight, Brevin	15	20	100	
Kukoc, Tony	15		75	
Laettner, Christian	20		100	
LaFrentz, Raef	15		85	
Lopez, Felipe	12		75	
Maggette, Corey	15		90	
Majerle, Dan	15		85	

	Signed 8x10	Auth.8x10	Sig'd Ball	Auth.Ball
Malone, Karl	50	130	175	300
Manning, Danny	18		90	135
Marbury, Stephon	25		125	
Marion, Shawn	20		100	
Marshall, Donyell	15		85	
Martin, Kenyon	20		75	
Mashburn, Jamal	15		100	
Mason, Anthony	15		80	
Mason, Desmond	15		75	
McDyess, Antonio	20	40	100	145
McGrady, Tracy	50	90	120	200
McKie, Aaron	15		75	
Mercer, Ron	20		100	
Miles, Darius	25		75	
Miller, Andre	15		85	
Miller, Mike	15		75	
Miller, Reggie	50		125	200
Mourning, Alonzo	30	60	110	190
Mutombo, Dikembe	20		100	
Nowitzki, Dirk	35		100	
Nash, Steve	20		75	
O'Neal, Jermaine	25	50	90	140
O'Neal, Shaquille	75	225	175	400
Oakley, Charles	15		85	
Odom, Lamar	25		110	
Olajuwon, Hakeem	30		150	
Olowokandi, Michael	15		90	
Outlaw, Bo	15		75	
Payton, Gary	30		100	
Penicheiro, Ticha	15		75	
Perkins, Sam	15		85	
Person, Wesley	15		75	
Peterson, Morris	15		75	
Pierce, Paul	40	80	90	140
Pippen, Scottie	50		150	
Ratliff, Theo	18		85	
Reeves, Bryant	15		80	
Rice, Glen	20		120	
Richardson, Quentin	25		75	
Richmond, Mitch	15		100	
Rider, Isiah	15		70	
Robinson, Cliff	18		90	
Robinson, David	30		150	
Robinson, Glenn	20		180	
Rose, Jalen	20		100	
Smith, Joe	15		90	
Smith, Steve	15		90	
Snow, Eric	15		75	
Sprewell, Latrell	25		90	
Stackhouse, Jerry	20		90	
Stevenson, DeShawn	15		70	
Stockton, John	40		175	
Stojakovic, Predrag	30		85	
Stoudamire, Damon	20		110	
Strickland, Rod	18		100	
Swift, Stromile	15		75	
Szczerbiak, Wally	20		110	
Terry, Jason	15		90	
Thomas, Tim	15		75	
Traylor, Robert	15		85	
Turkoglu, Hidayet	15		75	
Van Exel, Nick	20	40	100	
Van Horn, Keith	25		125	145
Walker, Antoine	25	30	100	
Wallace, John	15		75	
Wallace, Rasheed	25		100	
Ward, Charlie	25	80	75	
Webber, Chris	45		150	
Wells, Bonzi	15		75	
Wesley, David	15		75	
Williams, Jason	20		90	
Williams, Walt	15		75	
Zhizhi, Wang	15		85	

BASKETBALL FIGURES PRICE GUIDE

…PS

…ALL

…	$5,500.00
…ox	60.00
…d w/o box	40.00

Player	Mint
Abdul-Jabbar, Kareem	50.00
Adams, Michael	55.00
Aguirre, Mark	85.00
Ainge, Danny	80.00
Bailey, Thurl	275.00
Barkley, Charles	75.00
Berry, Walter	45.00
Bird, Larry	70.00
Blackman, Rolando	95.00
Cage, Michael	50.00
Carroll, Joe Barry	50.00
Chambers, Tom	40.00
Cheeks, Maurice	50.00
Cooper, Michael	65.00
Cummings, Terry	60.00
Dantley, Adrian	105.00
Daugherty, Brad	50.00
Dawkins, Johnny	40.00
Drexler, Clyde	100.00
Eaton, Mark	325.00
Ellis, Dale	60.00
English, Alex	80.00
Ewing, Patrick	45.00
Floyd, Eric "Sleepy"	65.00
Garland, Winston	50.00
Gilliam, Armon	45.00
Gminski, Mike	45.00
Greenwood, David	55.00
Harper, Derek	75.00
Harper, Ron	60.00
Higgins, Rod	60.00
Hopson, Dennis	65.00
Hornacek, Jeff	60.00
Jackson, Mark	50.00
Johnson, Dennis	80.00
Johnson, Eddie	40.00
Johnson, Magic	70.00
Johnson, Steve	50.00
Johnson, Vinnie	150.00
Jordan, Michael	110.00
King, Bernard	45.00
Laimbeer, Bill	130.00
Lever, Lafayette	50.00
Malone, Jeff	40.00
Malone, Karl	800.00
Malone, Moses	130.00
Manning, Danny	40.00
McCray, Rodney	100.00
McDaniel, Xavier	60.00
McHale, Kevin	55.00
McKey, Derrick	50.00
Miller, Reggie	250.00
Moncrief, Sidney	60.00
Mullin, Chris	50.00
Olajuwon, Hakeem	70.00
Parish, Robert	60.00
Paxson, John	75.00
Perkins, Sam	120.00
Person, Chuck	75.00
Pippen, Scottie	125.00
Porter, Terry	50.00
Pressey, Paul	60.00
Price, Mark	125.00
Rivers, Doc	55.00
Robertson, Alvin	60.00
Robinson, Cliff	40.00
Sampson, Ralph	55.00
Schayes, Danny	90.00
Sikma, Jack	75.00
Smith, Kenny	65.00
Stipanovich, Steve	80.00
Stockton, John	550.00
Thomas, Isiah	55.00
Thompson, Lasalle	55.00
Thorpe, Otis	60.00
Tisdale, Wayman	60.00
Vandeweghe, Kiki	65.00
Webb, Spud	45.00
Wilkins, Dominique	50.00
Wilkins, Gerald	40.00
Williams, Buck	40.00
Williams, John	50.00
Williams, Reggie	55.00
Willis, Kevin	55.00
Worthy, James	60.00

1989 BASKETBALL

Complete Set (5) $125.00

Player	Mint
Chapman, Rex (R)	35.00
Curry, Dell (R)	30.00
Harper, Ron	35.00
Nance, Larry (R)	35.00
Tripucka, Kelly (R)	30.00

1990 BASKETBALL

Complete Set (17) $550.00

Player	Mint
Barkley, Charles	70.00
Bird, Larry	80.00
Chambers, Tom	15.00
Drexler, Clyde	50.00
Dumars, Joe (R)	24.00
Ewing, Patrick	25.00
Johnson, Magic	40.00
Jordan, Michael	110.00
Malone, Karl	75.00
Mullin, Chris	20.00
Robinson, David (R)	45.00
Scott, Byron (R)	50.00
Stockton, John	60.00
Thomas, Isiah	25.00
Webb, Spud	14.00
Wilkins, Dominique	30.00
Worthy, James	15.00

1990 BASKETBALL SLAM DUNK

Red Box Set (6) $700.00
White Box Set (6) $400.00

RED BOX

Bird, Larry	200.00
Ewing, Patrick	100.00
Johnson, Magic	150.00
Jordan, Michael	320.00
Thomas, Isiah	80.00
Wilkins, Dominique	80.00

WHITE BOX

Bird, Larry	100.00
Ewing, Patrick	60.00
Johnson, Magic	100.00
Jordan, Michael	200.00
Thomas, Isiah	60.00
Wilkins, Dominique	50.00

1991 BASKETBALL

Complete Set (16) $500.00

Player	Mint
Barkley, Charles	80.00
Bird, Larry	70.00
Coleman, Derrick (R)	25.00
Drexler, Clyde	30.00
Dumars, Joe	14.00
Ewing, Patrick	25.00
Johnson, Kevin (R)	24.00
Johnson, Magic	30.00
Jordan, Michael	
(jumping)	120.00
(regular)	120.00
Lewis, Reggie (R)	25.00
Robinson, David	15.00
Rodman, Dennis (R)	55.00
Thomas, Isiah	15.00
Webb, Spud	15.00
Wilkins, Dominique	25.00

1992 BASKETBALL

Complete Set (30) $1,000.00

Player	Mint
Barkley, Charles	45.00
Bird, Larry	60.00
Bol, Manute (R)	10.00
Brown, Dee (R)	12.00
Coleman, Derrick	10.00
Divac, Vlade (R)	18.00
Drexler, Clyde	25.00
Dumars, Joe	12.00
Ewing, Patrick	20.00
Hardaway, Tim (R)	20.00
Johnson, Kevin	12.00
Johnson, Larry (R)	30.00
Johnson, Magic	
(purple)	60.00
(yellow)	275.00
Jordan, Michael	
(regular)	140.00
(warm up)	150.00
Majerle, Dan (R)	15.00
Malone, Karl	25.00
Miller, Reggie	45.00
Mullin, Chris	20.00
Mutombo, Dikembe (R)	22.00
Olajuwon, Hakeem	30.00
Paxson, John	20.00
Pippen, Scottie	30.00
Price, Mark	15.00
Robinson, David	
(regular)	18.00
(warm up)	24.00
Rodman, Dennis	40.00
Stockton, John	30.00
Thomas, Isiah	10.00

1992 HEADLINE BASKETBALL

Complete Set (8) $400.00

Player	Mint
Barkley, Charles	85.00
Bird, Larry	85.00
Ewing, Patrick	45.00
Johnson, Magic	75.00
Jordan, Michael	150.00
Mutombo, Dikembe	25.00
Pippen, Scottie	60.00
Robinson, David	40.00

1993 BASKETBALL

Complete Set (29) $600.00

Player	Mint
Anderson, Kenny (R)	15.00
Augmon, Stacey (R)	12.00
Barkley, Charles	27.00
Daugherty, Brad	12.00
Day, Todd (R)	10.00
Drexler, Clyde	20.00
Elliott, Sean (R)	16.00
Ewing, Patrick	22.00
Grant, Horace (R)	25.00
Gugliotta, Tom (R)	25.00
Hardaway, Tim	20.00
Johnson, Larry	15.00
Jordan, Michael	200.00
Kemp, Shawn (R)	15.00
Laettner, Christian (R)	25.00
Majerle, Dan	10.00
Malone, Karl	18.00
Mourning, Alonzo (R)	30.00
Mutombo, Dikembe	15.00
O'Neal, Shaquille (R)	80.00
Pippen, Scottie	35.00
Porter, Terry	10.00
Price, Mark	12.00
Rice, Glen (R)	20.00
Richmond, Mitch (R)	25.00
Robinson, David	24.00
Schrempf, Detlef (R)	12.00
Stockton, John	20.00
Wilkins, Dominique	12.00

1994 BASKETBALL

Complete Set (26) $450.00

Player	Mint
Armstrong, B.J. (R)	10.00
Augmon, Stacey	10.00
Barkley, Charles	20.00
Bradley, Shawn (R)	10.00
Cheaney, Calbert (R)	10.00
Coleman, Derrick	10.00
Elliott, Sean	10.00
Ellis, Laphonso (R)	12.00
Ewing, Patrick	12.00
Hardaway, Anfernee (R)	35.00
Jackson, Jim (R)	15.00
Johnson, Larry	10.00
Kemp, Shawn	10.00
Malone, Karl	15.00
Mashburn, Jamal (R)	25.00
Miner, Harold (R)	12.00
Mourning, Alonzo	15.00
Mullin, Chris	12.00
Olajuwon, Hakeem	15.00
O'Neal, Shaquille	30.00
Pippen, Scottie	25.00
Robinson, David	18.00
Rodman, Dennis	
(white)	50.00
(red)	100.00
Sprewell, Latrell (R)	25.00
Webber, Chris (R)	40.00
Wilkins, Dominique	10.00

1995 BASKETBALL

Complete Set (31) $450.00

Player	Mint
Barkley, Charles	15.00
Bogues, Tyrone (R)	14.00
Ewing, Patrick	15.00
Grant, Horace	
(blue goggles)	10.00
(black goggles)	20.00
Hardaway, Anfernee	15.00
Hill, Grant (R)	
(regular)	20.00
(Kmart)	20.00
Hornacek, Jeff	8.00
Jackson, Jimmy	10.00
Kemp, Shawn	10.00
Kidd, Jason (R)	55.00
Kukoc, Toni (R)	15.00
Majerle, Dan	8.00
Malone, Karl	16.00
Miller, Reggie	20.00
Montross, Eric (R)	10.00
Mourning, Alonzo	12.00
Olajuwon, Hakeem	12.00
O'Neal, Shaquille	35.00
Pack, Robert (R)	10.00
Pippen, Scottie	25.00
Price, Mark	10.00
Robinson, Cliff (R)	17.00
Robinson, David	15.00
Robinson, Glenn (R)	30.00
Smith, Steve (R)	16.00
Sprewell, Latrell	15.00
Starks, John (R)	10.00
Van Exel, Nick (R)	25.00
Weatherspoon, Clarence (R)	10.00
Webber, Chris	20.00
Wilkins, Dominique	10.00

1996 BASKETBALL

Complete Set (37) $500.00

Player	Mint
Baker, Vin (R)	15.00
Barkley, Charles	15.00
Drexler, Clyde	16.00
Elliott, Sean	8.00
Ewing, Patrick	10.00
Garnett, Kevin (R)	50.00
Hardaway, Anfernee	10.00
Hill, Grant	
(dribbling)	15.00
(Pistons)	20.00
Hill, Tyrone (R)	15.00
Howard, Juwan (R)	18.00
Johnson, Larry	10.00
Jones, Eddie (R)	30.00
Kidd, Jason	20.00
Malone, Karl	15.00
Mashburn, Jamal	12.00
McDyess, Antonio (R)	20.00
Miller, Reggie	12.00
Mourning, Alonzo	10.00
Olajuwon, Hakeem	15.00
O'Neal, Shaquille	20.00
Payton, Gary (R)	35.00
Pippen, Scottie	15.00

Player	Mint
Radja, Dino (R)	10.00
Reeves, Bryant (R)	10.00
Richardson, Pooh (R)	10.00
Richmond, Mitch	12.00
Robinson, Cliff	10.00
Robinson, David	14.00
Robinson, Glenn	14.00
Rodman, Dennis	
(green hair)	30.00
(orange hair)	30.00
(yellow hair)	30.00
Smith, Joe (R)	16.00
Smits, Rick (R)	10.00
Stackhouse, Jerry (R)	35.00
Stoudamire, Damon (R)	17.00

EXTENDED

Complete Set (8) $225.00

Player	Mint
Barkley, Charles	16.00
Bryant, Kobe (R)	105.00
Hill, Grant	20.00
Iverson, Allen (R)	70.00
Johnson, Larry	12.00
Mutombo, Dikembe	12.00
O'Neal, Shaquille	30.00
Stoudamire, Damon	14.00

1996 FAR EAST BASKETBALL

Complete Set (14) $500.00

Player	Mint
Barkley, Charles	18.00
Elliott, Sean	10.00
Hardaway, Penny	25.00
Hill, Grant	15.00
Johnson, Larry	10.00
Johnson, Magic	250.00
Jones, Eddie	30.00
Miller, Reggie	12.00
Olajuwon, Hakeem	15.00
O'Neal, Shaquille	25.00
Pippen, Scottie	12.00
Rodman, Dennis	
(green hair)	40.00
(orange hair)	40.00
(yellow hair)	40.00

1997 BASKETBALL

Complete Set (46) $450.00

Player	Mint
Abdur-Rahim, Shareef (R)	20.00
Allen, Ray (R)	
(SLU card)	32.00
(Upper Deck card)	25.00
Anderson, Kenny	10.00
Baker, Vin	12.00
Barkley, Charles	10.00
Brandon, Terrell (R)	15.00
Camby, Marcus (R)	20.00
Divac, Vlade	10.00
Ewing, Patrick	10.00
Finley, Michael (R)	25.00
Garnett, Kevin	
(SLU card)	18.00
(Upper Deck card)	18.00
Grant, Horace	10.00
Hardaway, Tim	12.00
Hill, Grant	12.00
Houston, Allan (R)	15.00
Howard, Juwan	10.00
Iverson, Allen	
(SLU card)	30.00
(Upper Deck card)	25.00
Jackson, Mark	10.00
Kemp, Shawn	10.00
Kidd, Jason	15.00
Kittles, Kerry (R)	15.00
Marbury, Stephon (R)	
(SLU card)	25.00
(Upper Deck card)	25.00
Miller, Reggie	14.00
Mourning, Alonzo	10.00
Olajuwon, Hakeem	10.00
O'Neal, Shaquille	15.00
Payton, Gary	
(SLU card)	10.00
(Upper Deck card)	12.00
Pippen, Scottie	
(SLU card)	12.00
(Upper Deck card)	15.00
Richmond, Mitch	12.00
Robinson, David	14.00
Rodman, Dennis	20.00
Smith, Steve	10.00
Sprewell, Latrell	12.00
Stockton, John	
(SLU card)	10.00
(Upper Deck card)	12.00
Stoudamire, Damon	
(SLU card)	10.00
(Upper Deck card)	12.00
Van Exel, Nick	12.00
Vaught, Loy (R)	12.00
Walker, Antoine (R)	32.00
Webber, Chris	15.00

EXTENDED

Complete Set (8) $150.00

Player	Mint
Drexler, Clyde	12.00
Duncan, Tim (R)	70.00
Hardaway, Anfernee	12.00
Jones, Eddie	18.00
Longley, Luc (R)	10.00
Mason, Anthony (R)	15.00
McDyess, Antonio	10.00
Van Horn, Keith (R)	22.00

1997 BASKETBALL CLASSIC DOUBLES

Complete Set (7) $150.00

Player	Mint
Bird, L./McHale, K.	30.00
Chamberlain, W./Russell, B.	33.00
Ewing, P./Reed, W.	20.00
Hill, G./Dumars, J.	25.00
Malone, K./Stockton, J.	28.00
Olajuwon, H./Russell, B.	20.00
O'Neal, S./Abdul-Jabbar, K.	34.00

1997 BASKETBALL BACKBOARD KINGS

Complete Set (6) $100.00

Player	Mint
Barkley, Charles	20.00
Hill, Grant	25.00
Malone, Karl	20.00
O'Neal, Shaquille	28.00
Pippen, Scottie	24.00
Stoudamire, Damon	20.00

1997 BASKETBALL 14" FIGURES

Complete Set (5) $175.00

Player	Mint
Barkley, Charles	30.00
Hill, Grant	28.00
Kemp, Shawn	18.00
O'Neal, Shaquille	35.00
Rodman, Dennis	40.00

1998 BASKETBALL

Complete Set (16) $150.00

Player	Mint
Baker, Vin	8.00
Brandon, Terrell	8.00
Bryant, Kobe	35.00
Ewing, Patrick	10.00
Garnett, Kevin	15.00
Hill, Grant	10.00
Iverson, Allen	25.00
Johnson, Magic	15.00
Kemp, Shawn	8.00
Kidd, Jason	14.00
Malone, Karl	12.00
Marbury, Stephon	15.00
Mourning, Alonzo	10.00
O'Neal, Shaquille	20.00
Rodman, Dennis	12.00
Smits, Rik	8.00

1998 BASKETBALL 12" FIGURES

Complete Set (5) $80.00

Player	Mint
Duncan, Tim	25.00
Garnett, Kevin	25.00
Howard, Juwan	15.00
Iverson, Allen	30.00
Rice, Glen	15.00

1998 COLLEGIATE BASKETBALL

Complete Set (9) $120.00

Player	Mint
Abdul-Jabbar, Kareem	10.00
Bird, Larry	15.00
Ewing, Patrick	10.00
Howard, Juwan	10.00
Iverson, Allen	25.00
Johnson, Magic	12.00
Kidd, Jason	90.00
Russell, Bill	10.00
Swoopes, Sheryl	12.00

2000 BASKETBALL NCAA MARCH MADNESS

Complete Set (6) $35.00

Player	Mint
Robinson, David	8.00
Stackhouse, Jerry	8.00
Swoopes, Sheryl	8.00
Thomas, Isiah	8.00
Walton, Bill	8.00
Worthy, James	8.00

MATTEL

1998-99 BASKETBALL SUPERSTARS

Complete Set (24) $275.00

Player	Mint
Allen, Ray	16.00
Baker, Vin	10.00
Barkley, Charles	10.00
Bryant, Kobe	22.00
Duncan, Tim	25.00
Garnett, Kevin	12.00
Hardaway, Anfernee	10.00
Hill, Grant	10.00
Houston, Allan	8.00
Howard, Juwan	8.00
Iverson, Allen	18.00
Jordan, Michael (#1)	36.00
Jordan, Michael (#2)	36.00
Kemp, Shawn	8.00
Kidd, Jason	8.00
Miller, Reggie	10.00
Mourning, Alonzo	10.00
Mutombo, Dikembe	10.00
Pippen, Scottie	10.00
Rice, Glen	10.00
Rodman, Dennis	12.00
Stockton, John	10.00
Van Horn, Keith	12.00
Walker, Antoine	12.00

1999 BASKETBALL ONE-ON-ONE

Complete Set (6) $60.00

Player	Mint
Bryant, K./Hill, G.	10.00
Hardaway, A./Hardaway, T.	10.00
Jordan, M./Robinson, D.	14.00
Kidd, J./Stockton, J.	12.00
Miller, R./Rice, G.	10.00
Rodman, D./Malone, K.	10.00

1999-00 BASKETBALL SUPERSTARS

Player	Mint
Baker, Vin	8.00
Bibby, Mike (R)	20.00
Bird, Larry	25.00
Bradley, Shawn	8.00
Bryant, Kobe	20.00
Carter, Vince (R)	35.00
Duncan, Tim	15.00
Hardaway, Anfernee	10.00
Hardaway, Tim	12.00
Hill, Grant	12.00
Howard, Juwan	10.00
Iverson, Allen	18.00
Jamison, Antawn (R)	22.00
Kemp, Shawn	10.00
LaFrentz, Raef (R)	17.00
Miller, Reggie	10.00
O'Neal, Shaquille	20.00
Pippen, Scottie	10.00
Rice, Glen	8.00
Walker, Antoine	10.00
Williams, Jayson	8.00

1999-00 COLLEGE & PRO SERIES

Player	Mint
Carter, Vince	35.00
Rice, Glen	10.00
Van Horn, Keith	10.00
Walker, Antoine	15.00

1999-00 NBA MAXIMUM AIR

Complete Set (10) $180.00

Player	Mint
Jordan Sil. Edition 3.5"	25.00
Jordan College POY	30.00
Jordan NBA ROY	30.00
Jordan Playoff Sensation	20.00
Jordan Champ '91	20.00
Jordan Champ '92	20.00
Jordan Champ '93	20.00
Jordan AS MVP '88	20.00
Jordan AS MVP '96	20.00
Jordan ASMVP '98	20.00

1999-00 NBA 13" FIGURES

Complete Set (4) $75.00

Player	Mint
Bryant, Kobe	30.00
Duncan, Tim	25.00
Hill, Grant	18.00
Pippen, Scottie	18.00

2000 OLYMPIC FIGURES

Complete Set (12) $160.00

Player	Mint
Allen, Ray	14.00
Baker, Vin	10.00
Carter, Vince	25.00
Duncan, Tim	20.00
Garnett, Kevin	18.00
Hardaway, Tim	12.00
Hill, Grant	12.00
Houston, Allan	12.00
Kidd, Jason	20.00
Mourning, Alonzo	18.00
Payton, Gary	15.00
Smith, Steve	10.00
Team Set (Target Exclusive)	45.00
Carter/Kidd/Houston/Duncan /Garnett	

CONVENTION/ SHOW PIECES

Player	Mint
Rice, Glen National Conv.	20.00
Bryant, Kobe 2000 NBA AS.	70.00
Carter, Vince 2000 NBA AS	100.00
Francis, Steve 2000 NBA AS	50.00

MCFARLANE

2002 BASKETBALL SERIES 1

Complete Set (6) $60.00

Player	Mint
Bryant, Kobe (yellow jersey)	18.00
Bryant, Kobe (purple jersey)	65.00
Carter, Vince (white jersey)	15.00
Carter, Vince (purple jersey)	30.00
Duncan, Tim (black jersey)	15.00
Duncan, Tim (white jersey)	35.00
Garnett, Kevin (white jersey)	12.00
Garnett, Kevin (blue jersey)	30.00
Iverson, Allen (white jersey)	18.00
Iverson, Allen (black jersey)	
Open Mouth	50.00
Closed Mouth	35.00
Kidd, Jason (blue jersey)	12.00
Kidd, Jason (white jersey)	28.00

CHRONOLOGICAL INDEX